EDWARD GREENFIELD, until his retirement in 1993, was for forty years on the staff of the *Guardian*, succeeding Neville Cardus as Music Critic in 1975. He still contributes regularly to the record column, which he founded in 1954. At the end of 1960 he joined the reviewing panel of *Gramophone* specializing in operatic and orchestral issues. He is a regular broadcaster on music and records for the BBC, not just on Radios 3 and 4 but also on the BBC World Service, latterly with his weekly programme, *The Greenfield Collection*. In 1958 he published a monograph on the operas of Puccini. More recently he has written studies on the recorded work of Joan Sutherland and André Previn. He has been a regular juror on International Record awards and has appeared with such artists as Dame Elisabeth Schwarzkopf, Dame Joan Sutherland and Sir Georg Solti in public interviews. In October 1993 he was given a *Gramophone* Award for Special Achievement and in June 1994 he received the OBE for services to music and journalism.

ROBERT LAYTON studied at Oxford with Edmund Rubbra for composition and with Egon Wellesz for the history of music. He spent two years in Sweden at the universities of Uppsala and Stockholm. He joined the BBC Music Division in 1959 and was responsible for Music Talks, including such programmes as *Interpretations on Record*. He contributed 'A Quarterly Retrospect' to *Gramophone* magazine for thirty-four years and writes for the *BBC Music Magazine, International Record Review* and other journals. His books include studies of the Swedish composer Berwald and of Sibelius, as well as a monograph on the Dvořák symphonies and concertos for the *BBC Music Guides*, of which he was General Editor for many years. His prize-winning translation of Erik Tawaststjerna's definitive five-volume study of Sibelius was completed in 1998. In 1987 he was awarded the Sibelius Medal and in the following year he was made a Knight of the Order of the White Rose of Finland for his services to Finnish music. His other books include *Grieg: An Illustrated Life*, and he has edited the *Guide to the Symphony* and the *Guide to the Concerto* (OUP). In 2001, at a ceremony to mark the Swedish presidency of the European Union, he was made a Knight of the Royal Order of the Polar Star.

IVAN MARCH is a former professional musician. He studied at Trinity College of Music, London, and at the Royal Manchester College. After service in the Central Band of the RAF, he played the horn professionally for the BBC and travelled with the Carl Rosa and D'Oyly Carte opera companies. He is a well-known lecturer, journalist and personality in the world of recorded music and acts as a consultant to Squires Gate Music Ltd, a UK mail order source for classical CDs (www.lprl.demon.co.uk). As a journalist he has contributed to a number of record-reviewing magazines, but now reviews solely for *Gramophone*.

THE PENGUIN GUIDE TO COMPACT DISCS AND DVDs YEARBOOK 2006/7

Completely revised and updated

IVAN MARCH,
EDWARD GREENFIELD and
ROBERT LAYTON

Edited by Ivan March

Assistant Editor: Paul Czajkowski

PENGUIN BOOKS

PENGUIN BOOKS

Published by the Penguin Group
Penguin Books Ltd, 80 Strand, London WC2R ORL, England
Penguin Group (USA) Inc., 375 Hudson Street, New York, New York 10014, USA
Penguin Group (Canada), 90 Eglinton Avenue East, Suite 700, Toronto, Ontario, Canada M4P 2Y3
(a division of Pearson Penguin Canada Inc.)
Penguin Ireland, 25 St Stephen's Green, Dublin 2, Ireland (a division of Penguin Books Ltd)
Penguin Group (Australia), 250 Camberwell Road, Camberwell, Victoria 3124, Australia
(a division of Pearson Australia Group Pty Ltd)
Penguin Books India Pvt Ltd, 11 Community Centre, Panchsheel Park, New Delhi – 110 017, India
Penguin Group (NZ), 67 Apollo Drive, Mairangi Bay, Auckland 1310, New Zealand
(a division of Pearson New Zealand Ltd)
Penguin Books (South Africa) (Pty) Ltd, 24 Sturdee Avenue, Rosebank, Johannesburg 2196, South Africa

Penguin Books Ltd, Registered Offices: 80 Strand, London WC2R ORL, England

www.penguin.com

This edition first published 2006
1

Set in Minion and ScalaSans
Typeset by Letterpart Ltd, Reigate, Surrey
Printed in England by Clays Ltd, St Ives plc

ISBN-13: 978-0-141-02723-4
ISBN-10: 0-141-02723-1

THE *PENGUIN GUIDE*:
CD, SACD, SURROUND SOUND AND DVD

The CD remains the basis on which the coverage of classical music currently rests, but the undoubted success of SACD has added a new dimension to older recordings as well as new. The early stereo RCA Fritz Reiner/Chicago and Munch/Boston recordings from the late 1950s and early 1960s are continuing to be re-issued as compatible SACDs, using the original three-channel masters to achieve enhanced sound on normal CD equipment.

However, we talked in Boston recently to the sound engineer John Newton, who is remastering these RCA SACDs, and he is of the view that the future of sound recording must lie with developing the surround-sound SACD system, with its use of back and front speakers to give the listener the feeling of actually being in the concert hall.

The available repertoire in surround sound is already expanding, and these SACDs are virtually all compatible, so they are impressive enough when heard through just two speakers. Yet when the back speakers subtly add their extra dimension, the sound image becomes uncannily present and tangible. Even so, there still appears to be consumer resistance to the SACD system.

The arrival of DVD is another matter. It is a profound advance. Now at last we can watch and be involved in the performance itself, almost like being in the theatre, concert hall or opera house, as well as listening to the music in very good sound; and if we prefer to dispense with the visual image, this can be managed at the touch of a button. And all this is possible with just the purchase of a DVD player (now very inexpensive) and setting up one's stereo speakers on either side of a reasonably large TV screen.

While this advantage is obvious in the world of ballet and opera (where optional surtitles are available), DVD can and does add immediacy to the musical experience in the concert hall. It catches the magnetism between the conductor and orchestra, between soloist and accompanist, the communication within a small group of chamber musicians and, above all, it can convey to a remarkable degree the projection of tension from performers to their audience. We just sit in a comfortable chair and enjoy the performance alongside those in the concert hall, opera house or theatre.

However, what complicates the situation still further is that some recent DVDs are provided with an optional Dolby 5.1 surround soundtrack which is not compatible with SACD, and needs five (!) speakers: the normal four, plus a so-called 'woofer'. This appears to be of interest to those using DVD for viewing films, and provides domestically the special effects one experiences in the cinema. With a conventional DVD or SACD player all you get is the stereo sound from the two front speakers. However, using a Dolby 5.1 DVD player, plus any necessary other equipment, the reproduction can be very impressive indeed, and add greatly to the visual image with concert, ballet and operatic DVDs.

CONTENTS

EDITOR'S NOTE:
THE KEY RECORDINGS AND
THE REISSUE LOGOS

Because of the huge number of recordings now covered by our main *CD Guide* and this *Yearbook*, we have thought it essential to continue to offer our readers a selection of 'Key' recordings which may be used as a basis for a personal collection. We have also sometimes included more than one choice where there are attractive alternative couplings of music available, and also where there are highly recommendable versions on both CD and DVD. In this *Yearbook*, some of these are reissues of recordings already chosen and which, in most cases, are made even more attractive by being less expensive.

The major manufacturers now see these reissues as a very important way of remarketing their back catalogues. One of the pioneering methods of achieving this was DG's mid-priced series of 'Originals', described as 'Legendary Recordings', perceptively chosen, properly documented and neatly repackaged. The 'Originals' have now been extended – in considerable quantity – to cover the Decca and Philips labels also, bringing back mostly deleted CDs, again at medium price, with full booklet notes, libretti and translations.

Most of them are first class, but we wonder if this is going to replace quality with quantity by including recordings which are less than 'legendary'. Universal (which sponsors all three of the above labels) also has 'Penguin Rosette' and 'Critics' Choice' Collections, and 'Gramophone Award' winners. EMI, too, have their own 'Great Recordings of the Century' and 'Great Artists of the Century', and RCA/Sony a 'Classic Library' series. There are budget labels too. DG has an Entrée logo (aimed at novice collectors), EMI have the Encore and HMV series (the latter available only from HMV shops or from hmv.com) and, more important, the Gemini super-bargain double CDs, which are often very good value indeed. Warner Classics, similarly, has the Apex series (also sometimes paired), which includes some really outstanding bargains.

Naxos, whose entry into the marketplace has had a profound effect on classical record production and pricing worldwide, continue to issue recordings of the highest quality at the lowest possible cost, all properly documented and, ironically, Naxos have also taken on the expert remastering and reissue of recordings actually derived from their major competitors – recordings which are now out of copyright.

IVAN MARCH

FOREWORD

I. THE MAINLINE REPERTOIRE

We are now entering the fourth decade of the *Penguin Guide* and we continue to be astonished, as the years go by, at the sheer profusion of today's recorded repertoire, not only the expansion of available music by composers we already know, but the appearance of new, recently discovered names. The Rome-born Giulio Caccini, (*c.* 1545–1601), for instance, who was one of the first composers to write chordally accompanied song (i.e. without polyphony); Elisabeth Jacquet de la Guerre (1665-1729), a child prodigy at the Court of Louis XIV, whose remarkable harpsichord music has been surveyed by Elizabeth Farr (for Naxos); or the Dutchman Jakob van Eyck (1590–1657), and his *Der Fluyten Lust-hof*, which is supposedly the largest existing collection of music for a single unaccompanied wind instrument, here the recorder – 143 pieces in all. You can sample them on BIS, while the Flemish composer, Philippe de Monte (1521–1603), who wrote around 250 motets, also, amazingly, corresponded with William Byrd in England, and they were the first pair of musicians living in different countries who arranged to exchange their settings of the same liturgical texts without apparently meeting personally!

Friedrich August Kummer (1797–1879) composed a series of *Duets* for a pair of cellos, which are unexpectedly entertaining, and they are now recorded.

Alice Mary Smith (1839–84) was the first British woman to have written a symphony and had it performed. In fact, she wrote two, and they are all but worthy of Mendelssohn, and are available on Chandos. Ernest Walker, director of Music at Balliol College, Oxford, between 1901 and 1925, wrote a fine *Cello Sonata* and it has been issued on CD by the British Music Society.

But there are many more recordings of familiar names within these pages and it seemed to us useful, instead of making a short list of, say, 100 outstanding records, to offer a concise survey of the more important issues and reissues and to direct the reader's attention to some of the most interesting and rewarding repertoire.

The centenary of the birth of the English composer William Alwyn came in 2005 and brought a group of new recordings to add to the extensive coverage already available on Chandos. Richard Addinsell's multitude of memorable film scores (including the famous *Warsaw Concerto*) is also now adequately covered, and, on an even lighter note, the brilliant Eastman Rochester collections of Leroy Anderson's orchestral lollipops has returned to the catalogue as one of Mercury's brilliant, remastered 'Living Presence' reissues.

However, there is also plenty of new mainline repertoire – led by a superb, new, period-instrument recording of the Bach *Brandenburg Concertos* from the Concerto Italiano under Alessandrini (on Naïve), Angela Hewitt's recording of the seven Bach *Clavier Concertos* (on Hyperion), and a truly inspired new account of the *Well-Tempered Clavier* from Vladimir Ashkenazy on Decca, which gives the listener the impression of hearing Bach's masterly exploration for the very first time. On SACD, Pearlman's Boston Baroque provides an exciting surround-sound coupling of Bach's *Magnificat* with Vivaldi's *Gloria*.

Turning to Beethoven, there is a Penguin Rosette reissue of Wilhelm Kempff's refreshing DG mono cycle of the five *Piano Concertos* (with Paul van Kempen), a Testament set of the *Third*, *Fourth* and *Fifth Concertos* by Arrau with the Philharmonia Orchestra under Klemperer, and, as an EMI 'Great Recording of the Century', an unforgettable coupling of the *Fourth* and *Fifth Concertos* by Gilels and the Berlin Philharmonic Orchestra under Leopold Ludwig.

The bargain coupling of the *Triple Concerto* on Arte Nova (with Bronfman, Shaham and Mørk) and the *Septet* is unique in linking this concerto to his chamber music. Zinman and his soloists treat it that way, and the *Septet* is played with similar blitheness, and light, clear textures.

Alongside his LP recordings, Karajan also filmed a cycle of the nine Beethoven symphonies for DG, and this makes a riveting DVD experience. The six EMI DVDs of the complete *String Quartets* from the Alban Berg Quartet is more controversial. It is undoubtedly very compelling, but readers are advised to read our extended review below before deciding whether to invest in what is not the least expensive way of acquiring this great instrumental collection.

On CD, Barenboim conducting his West-Eastern Divan Orchestra of Arab and Jewish musicians provides an electrifying performance of the *Fifth Symphony*, while on Orfeo Carlos Kleiber gives us an unforgettably thrilling account of the *Seventh*, one of the finest ever put on disc. Then, for bargain-hunters come a pair of EMI Gemini doubles, covering the complete *Piano Trios*, played with striking freshness by Barenboim, Du Pré and Zukerman. But if you want the very finest complete performances and recordings of these works on CD, you must turn to the Florestan Trio on Hyperion, led by the excellent Susan Tomes.

Three of their four discs are discussed in our main volume (CDA 62427, 67369 and 67393) and the final disc of the set is praised below.

Boccherini's music, always underrated, is of quality, and Capriccio's *Boccherini Edition* of 10 CDs would make a fine investment for any collector who wants to explore this composer's always listener-friendly output. Turning to Brahms, Ivan Moravec (on Supraphon), with richly supportive accompaniments from the Czech PO under Bělohlávek, provides the first modern coupling of the two Brahms *Piano Concertos* to match the famous Gilels and Jochum partnership; alternatively an excellent four-disc coverage from Kovacevich on Philips brings together all his recordings of Brahms's piano music for Philips, from the late 1960s through to the early 1980s (including the *Piano Concertos*).

Recorded at the Proms in the Royal Albert Hall in 1989, Sir Georg Solti's brilliant Arthaus DVD of Berlioz's *Damnation de Faust* with Chicago forces is excellent in every way, wonderfully dramatic; while Sir Colin Davis's companion Arthaus DVD of the *Grande Messe des Morts* from the Bavarian Radio Chorus and Orchestra was recorded and filmed in the spectacular setting of Regensburg Cathedral, which adds greatly to the impact of this inspired performance.

Another EMI reissue not to be missed is Karajan's (perhaps unlikely) 1953 Philharmonia mono coupling of Britten's *Variations on a Theme of Frank Bridge* and the Vaughan Williams *Tallis Fantasia*, truly inspired performances, marvellously played and given sound of such richness and realism that we originally wrote: 'if all stereo issues sounded like Karajan's mono recording of Britten's *Variations* there would be no need for a *Penguin Guide*'.

Jochum was one of the finest of all Brucknerians, and EMI have just issued a DVD of his beautifully prepared and subtly executed reading of the *Seventh Symphony* with the Orchestre National de France which is quite magnificent. It beggars belief that Busoni's wonderful *Violin Concerto* has taken so long to reach the CD catalogue but, played as eloquently as it is by Zimmermann on Sony, it has been worth waiting for.

DG have been exploring their early LP catalogue for outstanding Chopin recordings, and they have uncovered collections of excellence from Stefan Askenase (mono, but DG made very realistic mono recordings of the piano) and his stereo successor, Tamás Vásáry. To bring us right up to date on Decca, the Korean pianist Kun-Woo Paik provides outstanding new recordings of all Chopins's concertante music for piano and orchestra; while for good measure the Chinese pianist, Yundi Li, a recent Chopin prizewinner, offers the *First, E Minor Concerto* and *Four Scherzi*, coupled with the Liszt *Sonata*, another memorable disc.

Clementi is best known for his keyboard music, but on a budget Warner Apex reissue Claudio Scimone and the Philharmonia Orchestra have

rescued six of his 20 symphonies, and very attractive they are.

Dutton, famous for superb transfers of early recordings, now has an ongoing English composers series of new recordings, including compilations of the chamber music of Coleridge-Taylor and, even more intriguingly, Anthony Collins's short orchestral works, featuring his *Vanity Fair*, which (he once said on the radio) he valued more than his famous Decca mono Sibelius cycle (available again on Beulah), as it would still be listened to with pleasure after he had left us.

At Hyperion, Angela Hewitt has moved on from recording Bach's keyboard music to François Couperin and, more recently, Chabrier, with equal success, while the keyboard music of Giles Farnaby (who is new to our pages and was an exact contemporary of Dowland) is brilliantly played by Glen Wilson. This is part of the continuing exploration by Naxos of early music in which Tonus Peregrinus, directed by Arthur Pitts, has gone back as far as the aurally fascinating twelfth-century *Organa* of Leonin and Perotinus, the earliest written-down music, and also provides an admirable survey of the vocal polyphony of the celebrated fifteenth-century composer John Dunstable, including his isorhythmic motet *Veni sancti spiritus*, as famous in its day as Tallis's *Spem in Alium* a century later.

At this point we must not forget Antoine Brumel (c. 1460–1520), one of the very first composers to write a *Requiem*, unelaborate but very beautiful, dramatic too in the *Dies irae*; and Edward Wickham's performance with the Clerks' Group on ASV Gaudeamus is masterly.

Returning to our own century, the symphonies of Henry Cowell are among the works reissued by an enterprising new label called First Edition, which has picked up a series of pioneering recordings of twentieth-century music by the Louisville Orchestra (usually conducted by Robert Whitney), made in the USA in the 1950s and 1960s, including Hindemith, Malipiero, Milhaud, and the *Violin Concerto* and *Fifth Symphony* of Roy Harris.

Two new names stand out among the new Debussy piano CDs: Noriko Ogawa (on BIS), who offers a distinguished miscellaneous recital, including *La Boîte à joujoux*, rarely heard in its piano version; while Melvyn Tan moves from fortepiano to a modern Steinway to record a splendid set of both books of *Préludes* (Deux-Elles).

On a compatible RCA SACD, the vintage RCA Reiner/Chicago Symphony recording of Debussy's *La Mer* is spectacularly paired with Respighi's *Fountains* and *Pines of Rome*.

Harnoncourt has recently recorded a successful Dvořák series with the Concertgebouw Orchestra for Warner Classics, and these have reappeared at mid-price. The highlight is a very recommendable coupling of the *Piano Concerto* (with Pierre-Laurent Aimard) and *The Golden Spinning Wheel*.

Turning to Elgar, Richard Hickox on Chandos provides an exciting new pairing of the *Second Symphony* and *In the South* in opulent surround sound, with the BBC Symphony Orchestra of Wales, and there are fascinating new versions of the *Cello Concerto* (from Raphael Wallfisch on Nimbus) and the *Violin Concerto* (from Philippe Graffin with Vernon Handley, on Avie), in both cases returning to the original scores. The textural differences are small, but both performances give an inspirationally fresh look at familiar and much-loved works.

El-Khoury is Lebanese-born, but lives in Paris, a contemporary composer whose recordings have been enterprisingly taken up by Naxos. His orchestral music is avant garde but vividly tonal, and he is one of the first composers to have written a short but moving valedictory work about 9/11.

A more familiar French name, Fauré, is the latest to appear in Graham Johnson's ongoing Hyperion songbook. Surveying his mélodies, Johnson draws on a hand-picked group of mostly English singers, and the first two volumes are very successful indeed.

On Warner it is good to see Oramo and the CBSO taking an interest in John Foulds, a composer who inhabits a world between Elgar's England and modern composers such as Tippett and Britten, while (acccording to R.L.) Josef Foerster's *Fourth Symphony (Easter Eve)* was 'the best kept secret of Czech music', until recently discovered and recorded by Naxos.

Another new name to us is Hans Gál, the son of a Viennese doctor who was driven from Austria to Britain by the *Anschluss* in 1938. An enterprising Avie three-CD set surveys his piano music, which deserves – and receives – dedicated advocacy from Leon McCawley.

More Dutton issues cover Edward German's *Symphony* and his Shakespearean incidental music, and a rewarding collection by the Lake District composer Humphrey Proctor-Gregg includes his *Westmorland Sketches* for piano, as well as his three *Sonatas*, for *Clarinet*, *Horn* and *Violin*.

Johann Goldberg, a pupil of Johann Sebastian Bach, was supposedly (at the age of 14) the first performer of the *Goldberg Variations*, by so doing giving them his name. But he has also left us a pair of amiable *Harpsichord Concertos* of his own, played with engaging freshness by Jacques Ogg on the Verso label.

One of the very finest Grieg records ever is the BIS surround-sound compilation of all his richly atmospheric string music, beautifully played by the Bergen Philharmonic Orchestra, conducted by Ole Christian Ruud. The SACD offers ravishing string textures, yet provides a supreme example where adding the back speakers enhances the realism and sonic beauty even further.

For us, Handel's set of *Concerti grossi*, Op. 6, is at the high-water mark of baroque orchestral music, and the return of Iona Brown's modern-instrument recording with the ASMF is most welcome. But the supreme Handel bargain is Ton Koopman's recording, with the Amsterdam Baroque Orchestra, of the complete *Organ Concertos* from Opus 4 and Opus 7 on a pair of Warner Apex CDs.

A delightful new Virgin set of *Aci, Galatea e Polifemo* with Sandrine Piau and Sara Mingardo and dominated by Laurent Naouri, a superbly resonant bass, as the one-eyed giant Polifemo, tends to upstage earlier versions; and there are three new performances of *Messiah*. Harnoncourt's Warner Vienna Concentus Musicus account with the Arnold Schoenberg Choir is endearingly full of eccentricities, yet he is never dull, and it is beautifully sung and gloriously recorded in spectacular surround sound. Mackerras on Signum, choosing the fully scored Mozart edition (plus the original *Trumpet shall sound*), is fully traditional, freshly spontaneous, and again he uses top-class soloists, plus the Huddersfield Choral Society and the RPO. But top choice rests with Hogwood's 1982 smaller-scale Warner DVD version of the 1754 score, very realistically recorded and beautifully filmed in Westminster Abbey with the Abbey Choir, the Academy of Ancient Music, and Emma Kirkby and Judith Nelson leading the soloists – a totally engulfing experience, both musically and visually.

From Mercury comes a set of four CDs of classic Mercury recordings of the symphonies and orchestral music of Howard Hanson, played by Eastman Rochester groups and directed by the composer. This is supplemented by a modern Telarc recording of the *Second Symphony*, plus the engaging *Merry Mount Suite*, gloriously recorded in Cincinnati under Kunzel.

If you enjoy eighteenth-century music on a fortepiano, Andreas Staier is your man. On Harmonia Mundi he gives memorably fresh accounts of the three principal Haydn *Clavier Concertos*, and Gottfried von der Gölz's accompaniments with the Freiburg Baroque Orchestra are a joy in themselves. The Lindsays are close to completing their series of Haydn's *Quartets* for ASV; their two most recent issues, including Opus 74, Opus 77 and Opus 103, are well up to standard, while Naxos follow up their very successful version of *The Creation* with an equally lively account of Haydn's *The Seasons*, recorded in Leipzig.

Elizabethan repertoire flourishes in the form of Anthony Holborne's *Pavans, Galliards* and *Almains* in the hands of Paul O'Dette (lute) and the Kings Noyse on Harmonia Mundi and the *Consort Music* of John Jenkins from Phantasm on Avie, while the keyboard music of Peter Philips is covered by Hyperion, and the sacred music by ASV Gaudeamus and Naxos.

Roy Harris's *Third* and *Fourth Symphonies* from Marin Alsop and the Colorado Symphony arrive opportunely from Naxos, with the promise of a complete cycle to come, while the five Honegger *Symphonies* plus *Pacific 231* and *Rugby* return, equally inexpensively, on Warner Apex in first-class performances from the Bavarian Radio Orchestra under Charles Dutoit. There is also a bargain Dutton CD offering a group of Honegger's own orchestral recordings, some of which go back as far as 1930.

The most important Ives collection is from Sony:

orchestral music played by the New York Philharmonic under Bernstein and Ozawa, including the *Second Symphony*, *Central Park in the Dark* and his supreme masterpiece *The Unanswered Question*. But there are also three new competing versions of the *Concord Piano Sonata* and the *Four Violin Sonatas* (Curt Thompson, Rodney Waters) which are new to the catalogue. But the highlight of the Naxos series is an often outrageously experimental collection of instrumental pieces from Continuum, of which the most fascinating is a descriptive piece called *The Gong on the Hook and Ladder* – a picture of a hand-held fire appliance going downhill! – and there is also a two-disc Etcetera collection from Roberta Alexander and Tan Crone containing 54 of Ives's published songs.

One of the surprises of the year is the new Warner recording of Khachaturian's *Piano Concerto*, given a thrillingly Russian but highly imaginative performance by Berezovsky with the Ural Philharmonic Orchestra, conducted by Dimitri Liss. This surpasses every previous version by a clear margin and almost makes one value the work alongside the same composer's *Violin Concerto*, even though its invention is much less distinguished.

The Malaysian Philharmonic Orchestra, conducted by Kees Bakel, proves to be one that can be compared with the finest European ensembles, and they provide a useful account of Lalo's *Symphony in G minor* and the *Cello Concerto* with Torleif Thedéen a very sensitive soloist. (They have also recorded for BIS a pair of outstanding CDs of the music of Rimsky-Korsakov.)

Bo Linde is little known outside Sweden, but he was a composer of great talent, and is one of our major *Yearbook* discoveries. His *Cello* and *Violin Concertos* offer music of real nobility and a natural eloquence, and the Naxos performances, by Maria Kliegel and Karen Gomyo respectively, are fully worthy.

Leading the Liszt discography is a Gemini budget reissue of Beecham's stereo recordings of the *Faust Symphony* and *Orpheus*, never since surpassed; but there are also two major sets, an EMI seven-disc vintage collection of the complete orchestral works and concertos (with Béroff) from Leipzig, directed with distinction by Kurt Masur, and a modern coverage of just the major concertante works on three mid-priced Chandos discs by Louis Lortie and the Hague Residentie Orchestra, under Pehlivanian.

From Chandos also comes James MacMillan's *The Confession of Isobel Gowdie*, the work which at the Proms in 1990 brought its composer instant success, and he directs the performance by the BBC Philharmonic Orchestra alongside his *Third Symphony*.

DG has reassembled Bernstein's complete DG Mahler CD cycle with the Vienna Philharmonic on five discs, with substantial vocal couplings; but in addition on DVD we are offered the *Ten Symphonies* plus *Das Lied von der Erde* with the VPO, LSO or Israel PO in three DVD triple boxes (with Dame Janet Baker among the soloists), recorded for video in the early 1970s, which represent a rather more reflective Bernstein. Arguably, this is the finest of his three

cycles, and certainly the addition of video adds another layer of intensity.

Otherwise, the new CDs of Mahler *Symphonies* which stand out are Ormandy's reissued RCA recording of the early version of Mahler's *First Symphony*, which contained the *Blumine* movement, Sir Simon Rattle's reading of Mahler's *Second Symphony*, among his very finest records, and his DVD of the *Fifth*, recorded in November 2002 at his inaugural concert as music director of the Berlin Philharmonic. The CBSO recording of *No. 8* satisfyingly caps his Mahler cycle, and Abbado's transcendental account of *No. 9* is equally fine.

But the pair of DVDs of Haitink's live Berlin Philharmonic recordings of the first three symphonies is another of those examples where watching the conductor adds enormously to the thrilling compulsion of the performances, and the sound in the *Resurrection Symphony* is in the demonstration class.

There are plenty of attractive new Mendelssohn CDs, including a delightful, mid-priced RCA coupling of the *Scottish* and *Italian Symphonies*, conducted by Claus Peter Flor, a natural Mendelssohnian. But it is in the field of chamber music that he is especially well represented, with the Nash Ensemble's live Wigmore Hall recording of the *String Octet* and dazzling accounts of the *Piano Trios* from the Florestan Trio on Hyperion.

Sir Simon Rattle's outstanding version of Messiaen's *Turangalíla Symphony* is coupled with a distinguished performance of another inspired chamber work, the *Quatuor pour la fin du temps*, and this EMI Gemini set is very good value indeed.

The coverage of the Monteverdi *Madrigals* continues apace, and Rinaldo Alessandrini and the Concerto Italiano come completely into their own with their outstanding Naïve recording of Book VI. We also now have a Naxos set of Monteverdi's *Canzonette*, which he wrote in 1586, delightful fledgling works for three voices. The title-page makes the point that their composer was just 17 at the time he wrote them!

Robert King and his King's Consort offer three more volumes of their invaluable and comprehensive series of Monteverdi's sacred music and crown this enterprise for Hyperion with an equally fine new version of the *Vespers*, including not only the usual text, but the other two works that appeared in the same 1610 publication: the six-part *Magnificat* and the *Missa illo tempore*. Another well-planned Monteverdi issue from Hyperion, and one of Emma Kirkby's finest records, contrasting the two settings of *Lamento d'Olympia* by Monteverdi and his younger contemporary, Sigismondo d'India.

Not surprisingly, there is a huge Mozart CD coverage for the composer's 250th anniversary year, and standing out is a complete bargain coverage, on modern instruments, of all the symphonies by the ECO under Jeffery Tate, perhaps his finest achievement on record. Barenboim's much earlier EMI series, made between 1966 and 1971, is also very recommendable, offering *Symphonies 29* through to *41* on a pair of

Gemini doubles; and there are remarkable Pentatone SACD transfers of the earliest symphonies from Marriner and the ASMF. Among the most recent issues, Minkowski's period-instrument coupling with Les Musiciens du Louvre of the last two Mozart symphonies is also truly memorable.

On CD, the Virgin pairing of *Piano Concertos 17 in G*, K.453, and *20 in D min.*, K.466, by Piotr Anderszewski with the Scottish Chamber Orchestra is one of the finest Mozart discs of the year, while Mitsuko Uchida's complete cycle of the Mozart piano concertos with Tate will surely entice her admirers in a Philips bargain box.

But no fewer than 10 concertos (*Nos. 5, 6, 8, 9, 12, 17, 19, 20, 26* and *27*) have arrived from EuroArts on DVD (usually three allotted to each disc) in a stimulating series of live Mozart piano concerto recordings, using different soloists (of the calibre of Ashkenazy, Malcolm Frager and Radu Lupu), conductors (such as Bělohlávek, Previn and Zinman), fine orchestras and acoustically attractive venues, with consistently stimulating results.

A companion pair of DVDs from DG presents Gidon Kremer, with the Vienna Philhamonic Orchestra vividly conducted by Harnoncourt, playing all five of the violin concertos, with Kim Kashkashian joining the group inspirationally on the viola in the *Sinfonia Concertante*, K.364, to make a most successful set overall.

However, we have said before that it is the chamber music repertoire that would prove to be the most revelatory when reproduced in a DVD visual format. And so it proves, with another treasurable EuroArts DVD of 'Famous String Quartets' from the Leipzig Gewandhaus Quartet (who have been playing together since 1993). Their performances, within a most attractive setting, of two of Mozart's 'Haydn' string quartets, *Nos. 14 in G*, K. 387, and *19 in C (Dissonance)*, plus *21 in D (Prussian 1)*, K.575, and *Eine kleine Nachtmusik*, helped by a beautifully balanced recording and perceptive video direction, are very rewarding indeed.

Another outstanding SACD from Alia Vox which should not be missed comes from Jordi Savall and his Concert des Nations, presenting the first really convincing recorded performance of the *Notturno for Four Orchestras*, scored by Mozart for four separate groups, uncannily separated here within a four-dimensional acoustic. Together with the *Serenata Notturna*, *Eine kleine Nachtmusik* and a wittily plangent *Musical Joke*, this is one of the most imaginatively devised of the new SACDs to reach us during the anniversary year.

In the field of solo piano music, there are more really distinctive issues, led by Ronald Brautigam's absolutely complete mid-priced coverage (ten discs offered for the price of four), supplemented by an EMI double from Lars Vogt, a single treasurable CD from Wilhelm Kempff, and another outstanding recital from Andreas Staier on the fortepiano, as in Haydn, where he has again surpassed himself.

In the field of CD opera it is René Jacobs who appears to lead the new Mozart releases, with refreshing new versions of *La Clemenza di Tito* and *Le Nozze di Figaro*, both cast from strength. The latter won the *Gramophone* 'Record of the Year' award in 2004, so it is quite something to suggest that Abbado's DG *Zauberflöte* (the first he has ever recorded) is even more recommendable – easily the finest performance of this delightful opera to appear on CD, while Erika Miklós's Queen of the Night's second aria, *Die Holle Rache*, can be spoken of in the same breath as Rita Streich's famous mono version.

Conlon Nancarrow's *Third String Quartet* was the formidable opening item of a daring concert of avant-garde string quartets played by the Arditti group, recorded live at the Wigmore Hall in April 2005, also including works by Dutilleux and Ligeti. The concentration of the playing throughout is amazing, and without question this – by no means easy music – communicates compellingly. A complete set of the six Nielsen *Symphonies* is provided by a pair of Dacapo DVDs by Michael Schønwandt and the Danish National Radio Symphony Orchestra. These are the same performances as those discussed in our main volume, but this time with vision attached!

Martinon's celebrated and unique Decca mono LP collection of Offenbach *Overtures* with the LPO has been out of the catalogue for far too long. But now, at last, it has made it to CD, if only on an Australian Decca reissue, which may not be easy to obtain. On a pair of Apex discs, Jean Martinon also conducts the French Radio Orchestra in unsurpassed versions of four key works by Roussel, *Aeneas*, the *Bacchus et Ariane Suites 1* and *2*, *Le Festin de l'araignée* and the *Second Symphony*.

From Gergiev and the LSO comes a new, complete CD set of the Prokofiev *Symphonies*, recorded at the Barbican in May 2005, which now becomes the clear primary recommendation we have needed for some time; while Prokofiev's *Love of Three Oranges*, an Australian Opera recording conducted by Hickox, and Smetana's *Bartered Bride*, conducted by Mackerras, are two Chandos opera recordings, sung in English, that are a major success on all counts.

Turning to Purcell, EMI offers Cleobury's illuminating new King's College, Cambridge, collection, gathering together the *Odes* and *Funeral Music* written by Purcell for Queen Mary, superbly sung. A companion CD features John Rutter, another English composer, but of our own time, again conducting the King's College Choir, but with the CBSO, in full orchestral arrangements of his *Gloria*, *Magnificat* and *Psalm 150*.

Rachmaninov's reissued 10-disc RCA collection covers all the mono recordings he made from 1919 until 1942, the year before his death. It includes all four of his *Piano Concertos*, the *Paganini Rhapsody*, *Third Symphony* and *The Isle of the Dead*, plus all his solo piano records of his own and other composers' music, and it is self-recommending, while EMI have also reissued Gilels's superb 1955 (stereo) recording of the *Third Concerto*, which is coupled with an equally dazzling performance of Saint-Saëns's *Second*.

Trevor Pinnock returns to the recording studio for Avie with an 80-minute collection of Rameau's *Pièces de clavecin*, played on a particularly attractive two-manual instrument, built in Paris in 1764; while on Warner, Sharon Isbin with the NYPO under Serebrier provides a remarkably imaginative new recording of Rodrigo's *Concierto de Aranjuez*, coupling it with freshly captivating accounts of the *Guitar Concertos* of Ponce and Villa-Lobos.

For the Quartz label, the talented young British cellist Jamie Walton plays a grouping of Saint-Saëns's two *Cello Concertos*, plus the *Cello Sonata* and *Le Cygne* that is near ideal, while on Hyperion the Florestan Trio returns with captivating performances of the two Saint-Saëns *Piano Trios*.

The Schubert listing has many highlights. There are arresting new recordings of the *(Great) C major Symphony* from Rattle in romantic/dramatic mood on EMI, and the finest-ever version of the *Octet* on Onyx by a first-class ensemble, led by Viktoria Mullova, while the two *Piano Trios* are beautifully played by the Vienna Piano Trio on MDG. But most valuable of all is the Testament DVD of the *Trout Quintet*, filmed and recorded in Aldeburgh by John Culshaw in 1977, an unalloyed pleasure, with Clifford Cuzon leading the Amadeus Quartet.

Evgeny Kissin and James Levine, heard live in Carnegie Hall, offer the piano duet repertoire with winning spontaneity on Sony/RCA, and there is an outstanding Decca collection of the major *Piano Sonatas* from Radu Lupu, while the *Impromptus* and *Moments musicaux* come from DG and Wilhelm Kempff, who includes a a truly Elysian performance of the greatest *Sonata* of all, *21 in B flat*.

But what stand out most proudly are the two handsome boxed sets of Graham Johnson's complete Lieder Edition (on 40 CDs with 60 soloists), and DG's earlier coverage from Fischer-Dieskau and Gerald Moore, including the three song-cycles and no fewer that 405 songs.

Regis, too, have done sterling work in rescuing the famous old Saga recording of Schumann's *Frauenliebe und Leben* by a young Janet Baker with Martin Isepp – a vintage recording if ever there was one; while on another of EMI's Gemini doubles Sawallisch, Klee and Frühbeck de Burgos in turn conduct Dusseldorf forces in Schumann's *Mass*, Op. 147, the *Requiem*, Op. 148, and *Requiem für Mignon*, plus the cantata *Der Rose Pilgerfahrt*, rare repertoire and altogether a remarkable bargain.

Decca has celebrated the centenary of Shostakovich's birth lavishly, sub-dividing the repertoire into four boxes, the first three being Concertos and Orchestral Music, Chamber Symphonies and Chamber Music, but without a complete set of the *String Quartets*. This gap is filled on the Fuga Libera label by the Danel Quartet, whose survey, recorded by Bavarian Radio over the period 2001–5, is of the highest quality, thoughtful and inward. Decca's fourth box is of Vocal Music, including the opera, *Lady Macbeth*

of Mtsensk District. While the Decca set of the symphonies is still waiting in the wings, Dmitri Kitajenko and the Gürzenich Orchestra of Cologne on Capriccio offer a complete survey of all 15, excellently recorded and with performances that rarely fall short of distinction. There are, of course, some fine individual recordings, notably Previn's and Bernstein's accounts of the *Fifth*, and Karajan's of *No. 10*.

On a pair of BIS CDs the Lahti Symphony Orchestra conducted by Osmo Vänskä offers a fairly comprehensive collection of Sibelius's shorter orchestral works, from the *Andante Festivo* and *The Bard* to *Tapiola* and *The Wood-Nymph*. *Karelia* comes with a sung version of the *Ballade* by Raimo Laukka, and Kavakos is the soloist in the *Violin Concerto*. Vänskä and his fine orchestra are thoroughly at home in this repertoire, and the recording is first class.

One of the first recordings made on the Royal Concertgebouw Orchestra's own mid-priced label, has Mariss Jansons's version of Sibelius's *Second Symphony* in a splendidly fresh reading so that at times you feel you are listening to this familiar music for the first time. Similarly, the LSO and Sir Colin Davis offer two bargain recordings on that orchestra's own label: Sibelius's *Kullervo* (now the top recommendation) and Smetana's *Má Vlast*, in every way recommendable.

On Chandos comes a long-awaited Hickox SACD of Stanford's *Songs of the Sea* and *Songs of the Fleet*, with Gerald Finley and the BBC National Chorus of Wales, while Naxos have gone to Germany to record (magnificently) Strauss's *Alpine Symphony* with the superb Weimar Staatskapelle, conducted by Anthony Wit. This, like Rattle's Berlin Philharmonic *Ein Heldenleben* (plus *Le Bourgeois gentilhomme*) is part of a new generation of Strauss recordings, while an EMI 'Great Recordings of the Century' reissue by the Dresden State Orchestra and Rudolf Kempe of *Don Juan*, *Metamorphosen*, the *Rosenkavalier Waltzes* and *Till Eulenspiegel* represents the previous era. So does Jessye Norman's vintage Philips collection of Strauss Lieder with Geoffrey Parsons, plus the *Four Last Songs* with Masur and the Leipzig Gewandhaus Orchestra.

Among the Stravinsky recordings is a Pentatone SACD by the Russian National Orchestra, conducted by Jurowski, of the *Divertimento*, *Le Baiser de la fée* (which draws on Tchaikovsky's music), aptly coupled with Tchaikovsky's own *Third Orchestral Suite* with its inspired *Theme and Variations* finale. A first-class Harmonia Mundi CD equally aptly combines Stravinsky's *Cantata on Old English Texts*, the *Mass* and *Les Noces*, superbly sung, with Carolyn Sampson standing out among the excellent soloists. The performances here are directed with great vitality by Daniel Reuss and they confirm these works as among the composer's supreme masterpieces.

It is good to have more music of Tanyev. His *Piano Quintet* is a particularly enjoyable work and the *Piano Trio* is nearly as impressive, especially when Pletnev and a group of his colleagues are such persuasive advocates. Alexander Tcherepnin is another Russian composer worth exploring, and Regis offer three of his *Piano Concertos* at budget price on a single disc (*Nos. 2, 4* and *6*) with brilliant playing throughout from Murray McLachlan.

It is Naxos again who are exploring the less familiar music of Tchaikovsky, and a fascinating collection comes from Kuchar and the Ukraine National Symphony Orchestra, including the melodramatic early symphonic poem *Fatum* of 1868, but also a rewarding selection of entr'actes and dances from the little-known operas.

Vladimir Jurowski, the LPO's brilliant young music director, directs a powerful performance of *Manfred* on the orchestra's own label; it presses the music hard, but generates plenty of adrenalin; while Daniele Gatti's interpretation of the *Fourth Symphony* with the RPO also favours tempi which propel the music on more swiftly than usual, but grippingly so, matching his performance of the *Pathétique* in conveying the white heat of Tchaikovsky's inspiration.

A representative collection of Telemann at his best – concertos, suites and chamber music – comes in another Capriccio Box (with the five CDs in a slip case), which is hard to better. He was immensely prolific and his new recordings should suit all tastes, with its balance of period- and modern-instrument performances. One of the more unusual collections, from La Stagione of Frankfurt, offers the *Six Partitas* from *Die Kleine Kammermusik*, but transformed by the composer into *Orchestral Suites*, scored for oboes, strings and continuo.

Like Hans Gál, Ernst Toch escaped from Germany just before Hitler came to power, settling in the United States. His seven symphonies are a major discovery, rather like the piano music of his compatriot.

Vaughan Williams composed his score for Aristophanes' satirical comedy *The Wasps* for a production of the play in Greek at Cambridge University as long ago as 1909, and the *Overture and Suite* are justly well known, but it is only now that all the music has been recorded, set around a complete narrated version of the play, on the Hallé Orchestra's own label, conducted by Mark Elder.

Verdi recordings on CD are now almost completely dominated by reissues, with the interesting new versions all on DVD, and these are listed below. But, as with Telemann, there are plenty of excellent new collections of the concertos of Vivaldi. On EMI, Emmanuel Pahud is dazzling in the *Flute Concertos* of Opus 10, while Nigel Kennedy returns to the recording studio with the Berlin Philharmonic in a collection of solo and double *Violin Concertos*. Alessandrini and the Concerto Italiano predictably provide vibrant accounts of the *Concertos for Strings*, and a Naxos disc creates a diverting collection of chamber concertos for recorder with other solo woodwind and string instruments. But the most attractive disc of all comes from Andrew Manze and the English Concert, who (on Harmonia Mundi) bring together six of his best violin concertos which Vivaldi presented to the Holy Roman Emperor Charles VI in 1728, hoping he might be offered a position at the court. (He wasn't!)

The new CD recordings of Wagner are dominated by Thielemann's new DG set of *Parsifal*, with Domingo outstanding in the title-role; but there are also two reissued sets from Testament, from the 1955 Bayreuth *Ring* cycle, conducted by Keilberth, of great distinction. Both *Siegfried* and *Die Walküre* were the first Bayreuth recordings made in stereo, with *Siegfried* technically the finer of the two. As remastered for the present reissues, the sound is quite remarkably vivid and full-bodied.

On ASV, Helen Callus, with sumptuous viola tone and flawless intonation, gives the most beautiful account of the Walton *Viola Concerto* in the catalogue. Coupled with works by York Bowen and Vaughan Williams, this is a very desirable disc indeed, while Sir Colin Davis's live recording (again on the LSO's own label) of the Walton *First Symphony* is pretty impressive too.

It is good to have Kubelik's DG recording of Weber's opera *Oberon* back in the catalogue, for all the failings of its libretto, while on CPO the quality and sweep of the symphonies of Egon Wellesz confirm him as another major symphonic writer. Perhaps one cannot say that of the *Organ Symphonies* of Widor but, although uneven, they certainly have their moments when played as well are they are by Marie-Claire Alain on Warner Classics and by Jeremy Fisell on ASV.

II. DVDs OF BALLET AND OPERA

Ballet DVDs

In the field of ballet there are outstanding new DVDs of Adam's *Giselle* (a filmed version, with the camera able to move out beyond the stage set) and a fascinating Basle *La Fille mal gardée* (from Heinz Spoerli) which returns in part to the original score and scenario of 1789, but still retains most of the features which make Frederick Ashton's version so enjoyable.

It is best to stay well away from John Neumeier's new realization of Delibes's *Sylvia* (he considers the original 'outmoded') from the Ballet of the Opéra National de Paris. In this instance only the music – very well played – would be recognized by the composer. But there are excellent traditional productions, particularly from Russian sources, of other ballets which welcome the original choreography and staging.

The elegant Kirov version of Tchaikovsky's *Nutcracker*, and the Bolshoi's *Sleeping Beauty* (with breathtaking dancing) are splendid, both visually and musically, although Khachaturian's epic, spectacular (and overlong) Bolshoi *Spartacus* will not be to all tastes. But most fascinating of all is a DVD called 'The Return of the Firebird', which re-creates Fokine's original choreography and, as far as possible, restores the original Diaghilev Ballets Russes sets and costumes to Stravinsky's *Firebird* and *Petrushka*. This DVD also includes a highly erotic *Scheherazade* (using only part of Rimsky's score), which caused something of a scandal in its day.

But our favourite among new DVDs of modern ballets is the Birmingham City Ballet's 1990 production (on Arthaus) of David Bintley's *Hobson's Choice*, a wonderfully authentic, Lancashire-styled realization of the Harold Brighouse play and book. The score, composed by the late Paul Reade and brilliantly orchestrated by Lawrence Ashmore, is endlessly tuneful, the choreography never puts a foot (or clog) wrong, the acting is superb, and the ballet itself, gently humorous and touching, is a joy from beginning to end, and very repeatable.

Opera DVDs

The swift expansion of opera on DVD is phenomenal. Over the last few decades a hitherto unsuspected number of key productions have been filmed and recorded to a high standard in many venues, not least Glyndebourne, Verona and La Scala, Milan. Many famous singers who took part while their voices were at their freshest, and many stars who have now retired or left us, are preserved on video to be enjoyed anew.

The DVD collector can pick and choose, unlike the current opera-goer, who too often has to accept a highly indulgent production from a self-regarding producer who has no desire whatsover to re-create the composer's vision, preferring to project his own ideas, however unsuitable.

What the DVD viewer of opera needs is obvious. No dustbins in the Gorbals, no T-shirts or pairs of holed jeans in sight, but a faithful attempt to match what the composer might have expected to see on stage: a performance and production that will be well sung, stimulating to watch and repeatable.

Fortunately, many of the vintage opera DVDs discussed in our pages are traditional performances in which the composer's intentions and values are respected; and among those we especially recommend the 1979 Glyndebourne production (on Arthaus) of Beethoven's *Fidelio*, superbly conducted by Haitink, with Elisabeth Söderström as Leonora.

John Eliot Gardiner's *Les Troyens* (on Opus Arte) comes from the Théâtre du Châtelet in Paris. It is magnificently sung and at least has the virtue of simplicity, although Act III is unevocatively bare, and there is a certain idiosyncrasy in the presentation of the last Act.

But it is the La Scala, Milan, productions that are the most reliably straightforward and which are usually rewarding on all counts. These include Cilea's *Adriana Lecouvreur*, which gives great visual pleasure from the extravagance of the ultra-realistic sets and costumes; whereas the Glyndebourne *Pelléas et Mélisande* is virtually unwatchable, with its plush, glittering set quite out of keeping with Debussy's subtle score.

The TDK version of Donizetti's *L'Elisir d'amore* is acceptable but nothing more; the companion set of *Lucia di Lammermoor*, sung in French (if you want

that), is traditional but with eccentric camera angles. David Pountney's English National Opera *Rusalka* (in English) is set in an Edwardian nursery, full of toys, with the Watergnome as Rusalka's grandfather in a wheelchair and Rusalka herself first seen on a swing with her feet bound together! One wonders how repeatable this would be to watch, although musically it is impressive.

In the Opus Arte 2005 Glyndebourne *Giulio Cesare* (recorded live) William Christie conducts a fine, splendidly sung performance with the music in authentic period style while, ironically, the action is updated, with the Roman army presented in the uniforms of the Britsh army of the nineteenth century! However, we do have a very soft spot for the richly opulent Ramond Leppard/Glyndebourne productions of Monteverdi's *L'Incoronazione di Poppea* (on Warner) and *Il ritorno d'Ulisse in patria* (from Arthaus) which are far removed from today's scrupulously authentic versions; and the settings are visually sumptuous, to match Leppard's luxuriant conceptions, vividly directed by Peter Hall.

But it is Peter Hall who, in his 1977 Glyndebourne *Don Giovanni* (on Arthaus), updates the action to the Regency period, providing a deliberately gloomy backcloth of a dark and rainy Seville, to some extent mitigated by the camera's concentration on frequent close-ups.

Mehta's *Die Entführung aus dem Serail* from Florence (on TDK) is in every way successful, and for once the direction is staightforward, the sets are visually most appealing, and the result is highly enjoyable to listen to and to watch. Even finer is Stephen Medcalf's 1994 Glyndebourne production of *Nozze di Figaro* on NVC, with Gerald Finley as Figaro opposite the charming Susanna of Alison Hagley and Renée Fleming as the Countess, using John Gunter's sets plus traditional costumes, which work perfectly.

So does Jean-Pierre Ponnelle's 1982 Vienna State Opera production of *Die Zauberflöte*, conducted by Levine, with evocative sets and costumes. This has been revived more often than any other production in the history of the Salzburg Festival and can be recommended on every count.

John Cox's alternative lively (1978) Glyndebourne *Magic Flute* effectively uses the sets and designs of David Hockney, and the images are striking, with stylized scenery and landscapes in false perspective – a rare example of a new look succeeding because the imagination of the designer is not misguided.

The Bolshoi *Boris Godunov*, conducted by Alexander Lazarev on Warner, with Nesterenko as Boris, uses the Rimsky-Korsakov score grippingly, and satisfyingly seeks to create the imperial Russian backcloth the composer intended.

An up-to-date *La Bohème* from Australia with mixed modern sets and a young, contemporary cast makes a good deal of Puccini's opera in contemporary terms; but would one want to return to it very often?

We needed an *Il Trittico* on DVD, and the Warner/La Scala set brings a fairly straightforward and dramatic approach to the stage presentation (*Il tabarro* is especially vivid) which is very acceptable, as the casting does not disappoint either. But David Pountney's lavish TDK production of *Turandot*, for the 2002 Salzburg Festival, creates an unpleasantly ruthless visual background of death and torture for the opera which has nothing to do with Puccini's narrative.

Just now and then, everything is perfect. The DVD of the 2004 Glyndebourne production of Rachmaninov's *The Miserly Knight*, filmed live, is visually sumptuous; musically it is superlative, and Sergei Leiferkus dominates the stage as he should.

Recorded in 1990 at the Deutsche Opera in Berlin, the Warner DVD of Richard Strauss's *Salome* offers a powerfully expressive performance under Giuseppe Sinopoli. If viscerally unpleasant at its climax, it is well directed, if with the singers shown against stylized white sets like great blocks of concrete.

Both the Warner DVDs of Stravinsky's *The Rake's Progress* and *Le Rossignol* offer, not regular stagings but filmed versions. In the latter, Christian Chaudet is inventive – perhaps too inventive, as he draws attention away from the music. But both productions are effective enough.

On the whole, Tchaikovsky fares better. Graham Vick's Glyndebourne production of *Eugene Onegin* from 1994 (on Warner) is an outstanding example in which both production and cast are completely convincing, with no intrusive camera detail. In the Bolshoi *Maid of Orleans* (also on Warner) the staging is somewhat stiffly traditional, and this is an opera that needs all the help it can get. But the Maryinsky *Mazeppa* is the opposite, sumptuous to look at, and full of period atmosphere.

Turning to Verdi, the Opus Arte 1991 production of *Attila* from La Scala, with Riccardo Muti taut and incisive, is outstandingly dramatic, in a production (with traditional costumes) which uses minimal but atmospheric sets; and it is again Muti who ensures that the live La Scala, Milan, production of *Ernani* is so gripping. Once again the La Scala staging is traditional, thank goodness, though not unimaginative. The *I vespri sicilani* production is similarly straightforward, with no crazy impositions from a self-conscious stage director, and Muti again keeps the adrenalin flowing throughout. The ballet is included, but it is effectively presented and well danced.

Muti's *Falstaff* was recorded at the Teatro Verdi, Busseto, in 2001, to commemorate the centenary of the composer's death, acted out against a re-creation of the same sets used in 1913 by Toscanini, who believed that Verdi should sound and look like Verdi.

But the production of *Macbeth*, staged in the Liceu in Barcelona, offers a production set on a bare stage, with stylized geometric squares taking the place of scenery. It works reasonably well in the theatre, with the opening large chorus of witches exotically dressed in black with vermilion turbans. Otherwise, costumes are relatively conventional.

Recorded at the Vienna State Opera in 2001, the TDK *Nabucco* offers a spectacular production which makes full use of the very large stage. But the biblical story is updated to the 1940s, bringing out the parallels with the plight of the Jewish people in Europe at that time. The costumes are drab and dark with the men in trilbies and bowler hats. Vocally it is often thrilling; but who would want to watch it very often?

Back to La Scala (with TDK) for *Otello*. With an imaginative set and traditional costumes, this production is very recommendable, with Domingo and Frittoli always singing and acting movingly to create real-life situations.

How lucky we are that, when Karajan returned to direct a great performance of *Il trovatore* at the Vienna State Opera, the cameras were there and the staging was without eccentricity, with nothing to mar an evening of glorious singing.

James Levine has already given us an outstanding traditional *Ring* cycle, and he matches it with an expansive and warm-hearted *Meistersinger*. The production is again traditional, which is what his New York audience wants. The singers are all outstanding, led by James Morris's warmly genial Sachs, matched vocally by René Pape's Pogner and by Ben Heppner, who is an equally convincing Walther. Karita Mattila sings beautifully as Eva, to make this a strong recommendation. The alternatve Zurich performance, conducted by Welser-Möst, is also vocally satisfying, but the production has some irritating features. In the second scene of Act III, for instance, the chorus are placed in rows as if in choir stalls, and they wear modern dress, while the main characters have Victorian costumes, with the Masters emerging in black robes and tall, stove-pipe hats. Why?

At a fairly recent live staging of Wagner's *Siegfried* at Covent Garden, as the curtain began to rise the audience could see a baby's pram on the left and what appeared be an operating table with instruments on the right. As the curtain rose fully, a crashed aircraft came into view in Mime's cave; and later, when the Wanderer makes his entrance, he emerges from the plane itself. What followed concerning the gestation of Siegfried's sword, using a small child, is too mind-boggling to describe. We can only hope that the potential sales for DVD will have some restraining influence on such arrogantly planned stage business which has nothing to do with Wagner, for surely no one would want to own a video of a production of this kind.

III. OPERETTA AND MUSICAL PLAYS

In the months before we went to press, EMI made a major release (on the Classics for Pleasure label) of a remarkably wide-ranging series of excerpts from the light operettas and musical plays which dominated the musical theatre in the early decades of the last century. They were recorded, mainly in the 1950s and early 1960s, by excellent casts who were familiar with the musical styles needed for period authenticity.

Peter Gammond, an expert in this field, has said

that a musical play of this genre eventually stands or falls by its book rather than its music. Many of these productions have a stream of memorable and catchy tunes, but their plots are too dated to survive. *The Arcadians* is a prime example, with a wonderfully tuneful score and a fine overture that is still played. But the show would have to be rewritten before it could be staged.

There are many others, including *The Bohemian Girl*, *Chu Chin Chow*, *The Desert Song*, *The Geisha*, *Lilly of Killarney*, *The Maid of the Mountains*, *The New Moon*, *The White Horse Inn*, and so on. Even Noël Coward's masterly *Bitter Sweet*, which does have a fine book and is still occasionally seen, seems incapable of commercial revival, and only Jerome Kern's *Show Boat* continues to hold the stage. But the tunes are all still there, often unforgettable, ready to be enjoyed and hummed. Many of these inexpensive CDs will give very great pleasure, and all of them are well documented.

IV. CONCERTS AND RECITALS

One of the main features of our Concerts section is the now remarkably comprehensive coverage of the work of the 'Great Conductors', always illuminating, and offering younger readers an introduction to the interpretative skills of artists from a past era, as well as those of our own time. Additional compilations in the present volume cover Antal Dorati, Rafael Kubelik and Sir Charles Mackerras. Of course, in many cases a conductor's anthology may appear later under the orchestra with which his name is indelibly associated.

The expansion of recordings in the area of British light orchestral music has been something of a record industry phenomenon in recent years, and our listings include many highly attractive miscellaneous anthologies from the New London Orchestra under Ronald Corp, the Royal Ballet Sinfonia conducted by Gavin Sutherland and, for Scottish repertoire, John Wilson. This music occupies a musical world all its own, and a very British one. Unpretentious, well crafted, tuneful, engagingly and often seductively orchestrated, it is repertoire that may not ever seek profundity but does not wear out its welcome either.

Ballet music, too, is well covered, not only by the anthologies compiled and conducted by Richard Bonynge, but by newer collections from Barry Wordsworth and the Royal Ballet Sinfonia. But there are countless other compilations from many different sources, covering short works of every kind, often important, but which now seldom find their way into the programmes of live concerts, which almost never open with an overture these days.

The range of instrumental and vocal recitals is equally wide. From the former we would especially draw readers' attention to the recordings of the master guitarist, Manuel Barrueco – not as familiar a name as Julian Bream and Segovia (who are both well represented) but equally important. The Decca boxes of the recordings of Clifford Curzon should not be passed

by, and Horowitz has a DVD to himself, recorded in Moscow, to add to his generous CD coverage. Julius Katchen's Decca records are available either as domestic issues or on Decca's asscociated Australian label.

Kempff is well represented in our composer section, but he too has a DVD to himself, much of it in black and white, but still treasurable. EMI's star violinist, Itzhak Perlman, is much in evidence, and the discography of the great Russian pianist Sviatoslav Richter has greatly expanded in recent years. There are plenty of organ recitals too under many different names (but the instrument seems to be of equal importance to the performer).

Among the historical vocal recitals, the comprehensive Naxos Caruso Edition is a quite remarkable achievement – as well documented as it is technically impressive – and it has still a long way to go. Among singers of our own time, Dame Janet Baker proves to have an exceptionally wide-ranging discography, led by a five-disc collection of Philips and Decca recordings, made in the 1970s, in which she explored a remarkably wide repertoire in five separate recitals.

The art of Cecilia Bartoli, too, is notably well covered; but many other Decca artists are featured in a new mid-priced 'Classic Recitals' series, each packaged in a flimsy cardboard case, but notable for including the artwork from both the front and back of the original LP sleeve. The drawback is the documentation, which comes in a disgracefully reduced, minuscule typeface which is sometimes all but impossible to read without a magnifying glass.

There is a new series of Wigmore Hall live vocal recitals which has appeared on Wigmore's own label. They are very well documented but are proving to be of rather mixed success, except for the recital by Sir Thomas Allen, which is very winning indeed.

EMI seem to be reissuing every possible Callas recording, not always flattering to her voice but never, never dull. But if you want to sample the most beautiful of all recitals of lyric soprano arias on disc, you must turn to Maria Chiara's ravishing début Decca recordings from 1972 which at last have been been reissued – over three decades later. She went on to make an impressive reputation in Italy and can also be seen on DVD at Verona in her most famous role of *Aida* in a recording praised in our main volume.

Angela Gheorghiu too, together with her husband and partner, Roberto Alagna, confirms that glorious, lyrical singing is still with us.

Other artists now well covered by comprehensive new anthologies include Gundula Janowitz, Emma Kirkby, Jessye Norman (exceptionally generous), Birgit Nilsson, Pavarotti, Rita Streich, Joan Sutherland, Tebaldi and, not least, the golden-voiced Fritz Wunderlich. Even Mario del Monaco is given a five-disc box to himself, while Decca's Kathleen Ferrier Edition has been afforded a facelift, and DG's Fischer-Dieskau Lieder Edition now runs to 46 CDs!

One of the joys of the choral repertoire is the Collegium series by the Cambridge Singers, conducted by John Rutter who, such is his transatlantic reputation, had the honour of being invited with his choir to America to perform at a special commemoration service at a church near the site of 9/11. But do not miss the reissued Decca disc that made Rutter's original reputation, a joyous seasonal collection called *Christmas from Clare*, with the Clare College Choir, including his own irresistible *Donkey carol* and *Mary's Lullaby*, which I.M. has played every Christmas since it first appeared on an Argo LP, decades ago. Other Christmas anthologies are generously provided by the Choir of King's College, Cambridge, and much else besides, while on Regis the Magdalen College Choir of Oxford, under Dr John Harper, sing a distinguished four-disc English Anthem collection.

David Munrow's Early Music Consort should not be forgotten, for they often made early music performances fun, as well as conjecturally authentic, while Christopher Page's Gothic Voices have continued the further exploration of such repertoire over 17 CDs for Hyperion, now reissued on the bargain Helios label.

The World of English Song is unbelievably well covered by a two-disc EMI bargain set, the finest and most comprehensive recital of this repertoire ever put on record; and there is also a companion double-CD collection of English orchestral songs. Kenneth McKellar's similar pair of Decca anthologies of Scottish songs, including a group from the Hebrides, are unsurpassed. All in all, an extraordinarily diverse collection, and many of these CDs are very reasonably priced.

V. THE GARDINER BACH ODYSSEY

When DG decided they could no longer sustain John Eliot Gardiner's ongoing pilgrimage to record all the Bach *Cantatas* in various venues throughout the liturgical calendar of the church year, he bravely decided to set up his own label and underwrite the cost himself. So far, eight volumes have been issued, but they were not received by us in time to review for the present volume. They are beautifully packaged, each with a finely reproduced portrait on the cover, discerningly chosen by Mrs Gardiner and, of course, each has full documentation, including texts and translations.

Our sampling suggests that these performances are of a high standard, especially with regard to the soloists; and, above all, they are both refined and dedicated, fully worthy of Johann Sebastian, and while (obviously) ensemble is not always as immaculate as it would be in the studio, the extra vividness of live communication more than compensates. We hope to discuss the series in greater depth in our next main volume. The recordings already on the DG label are expected to reappear on SDG in the course of time. Meanwhile, we append the details of the issues already available on this new Soli Deo Gloria label:

Volume 1: SGD 101: *Cantatas for the Feast of St John the Baptist & 1st Sunday after Trinity* (with Lunn, Agnew, Te Brummelstroete, Herschel, Keith)

Volume 8: SGD 104: *Cantatas for 15th Sunday after Trinity* (with Keith, Hartelius, Towers, Gilchrist, Harvey); *16th Sunday after Trinity* (with Fuge, Tyson, Padmore, Guthrie)

Volume 10: SGD 110: *Cantatas for 19th Sunday after Trinity & Feast of the Reformation* (with Lunn, Towers, Gilchrist, Harvey)

Volume 14: SGD 113: *Cantatas for Christmas Day & 2nd Day after Christmas* (with Fugue, Lunn, Tyson, Gilchrist, Harvey)

Volume 19: SGD 115: *Cantatas for the 2nd Sunday after Epiphany & 4th Sunday after Epiphany* (with Lunn, Wyn Roberts, Podger, Finley, Fuge, Towers, Agnew, Harvey)

Volume 21: SGD 118: *Cantatas for Quinquagesima & for the Annunciation (Palm Sunday)* (with Holton, Schubert, Oxley, Harvey, Hartelius, Stutzmann, Gilchrist)

Volume 24: SGD 107 *Cantatas for the 3rd & 4th Sundays after Easter* (with Geller, Towers, Padmore, Clarkson, Tyson, Gilchrist, Varcoe)

Volume 26: SGD 121: *Cantatas for Whit Sunday & Whit Monday* (with Larsson, Stutzmann, Lee Ragin, Geriz, Genz, Iconomou)

INTRODUCTION

As in previous editions, the object of *The Penguin Guide Yearbook* is to give the serious collector a continuing survey of the finest recordings of permanent music on CD, irrespective of price, but also evaluating the quality of SACDs, particularly those offering surround sound, and DVDs. As most recordings are issued almost simultaneously on both sides of the Atlantic and use identical international catalogue numbers, this *Guide* should be found to be equally useful in the UK and the USA, as it will be in Australia, Canada, India, New Zealand and South Africa. The internationalization of repertoire and numbers now applies to almost all CDs issued by the major international companies and also by the smaller ones. Many European labels are imported in their original formats, into both Britain and the USA. Those CDs that are only available in England can be easily obtained by overseas collectors via the Web address given on page xxix.

We feel that it is a strength of our basic style to let our own conveyed pleasure and admiration (or otherwise) for the merits of an individual recording come over directly to the reader, even if this produces a certain ambivalence in the matter of such a final choice. Where there is disagreement between us (and this rarely happens), readers will find an indication of our different reactions in the text.

We have considered (and rejected) the use of initials against individual reviews, since this is essentially a team project. The occasions for disagreement generally concern matters of aesthetics – in the manner of recording balance for instance, where a contrived effect may trouble some ears more than others, or in the matter of style, where the difference between robustness and refinement of approach appeals differently to listening sensibilities rather than involving a question of artistic integrity. But over the years our views seem to have grown closer together rather than having diverged; perhaps we are getting mellower, but we are seldom ready to offer strong disagreement following the enthusiastic reception by one of the team of a controversial recording, providing the results are creatively stimulating.

As period-instrument playing standards have advanced and mellowed, our perceptions of the advantages and disadvantages of performances of early music on original (as against modern) instruments seem almost irrelevant. It is the quality of the performance itself which counts, and so expert is the performer's control of period instruments today, while modern-instrument performances have often been so influenced by period-instrument styles, that sometimes one is hardly aware of the difference, especially in orchestral music.

EVALUATION

Most major recordings issued today are of a high technical standard and offer performances of a quality at least as high as is experienced in the concert hall. In adopting a star system for the evaluation of records, we have decided to make use of from one to three stars. Brackets around one or more of the stars indicate some reservations about a recording's rating, and readers are advised to refer to the text. Brackets around all the stars usually indicate a basic qualification: for instance, a mono recording of a performance of artistic interest, where some allowances may have to be made for the sound quality, even though the recording may have been digitally remastered.

For the present volume we have introduced a fourth star, a re-evaluation which we intend to continue in the future. However, there are only five four-star recordings selected in these pages, one of which is a DVD. We hope readers will be intrigued to discover which they are.

Our evaluation system may be summarized as follows:

- ⌐ Key recording – suitable as a basis for a collection
- **** A really exceptional issue on every count
- *** An outstanding performance and recording in every way
- ** A good performance and recording of today's normal high standard
- * A fair or somewhat routine performance, reasonably well performed or recorded

Our evaluation is normally applied to the record as a whole, unless there are two main works or groups of works, and by different composers. In this case, each is dealt with separately in its appropriate place.

ROSETTES

To certain special records we have awarded a Rosette: ❀.

Unlike our general evaluations, in which we have tried to be consistent, a Rosette is a quite arbitrary compliment by a member of the reviewing team to a recorded performance which, he finds, shows special illumination, magic, a spiritual quality, or even outstanding production values, that place it in a very special class. Occasionally a Rosette has been awarded for an issue that seems to us to offer extraordinary value for money, but that presupposes that the performance or performances are outstanding too. The choice is essentially a personal one (although often it represents a shared view) and in some cases it is applied to an issue where certain reservations must also be mentioned in the text of the review. The Rosette symbol is placed before the usual evaluation and the record number. It is quite small – we do not mean to imply an 'Academy Award' but a personal token of appreciation for something uniquely valuable. We hope that, once the reader has discovered and perhaps acquired a ❂ CD, its special qualities will soon become apparent. There are, of course, more of them now, for our survey has become a distillation of the excellence of CDs issued and reissued over a considerable time span.

DIGITAL RECORDINGS

Nearly all new compact discs are recorded digitally, but an increasingly large number of digitally remastered, reissued analogue recordings are now appearing, and we think it important to include a clear indication of the difference.

All listed CDs are digital *unless* the inclusion of (ADD) in the titling indicates Analogue-to-Digital remastering, while of course the term mono is self-explanatory. The indication ADD/DDD or DDD/ADD applies to a compilation where recordings come from mixed sources.

LISTINGS AND PRICE RANGES

Our listing of each recording assumes that it is in the premium-price category, unless it indicates otherwise, as follows:

(M)   Medium-priced label
(B)   Bargain-priced label
(BB) Super-bargain label

See below for differences in price structures in the UK and the USA.

LAYOUT OF TEXT

We have aimed to make our style as simple as possible. So, immediately after the evaluation and before the catalogue number, the record make is given, sometimes in abbreviated form. In the case of a set of two or more CDs, the number of units involved is given in brackets after the catalogue number.

AMERICAN CATALOGUE NUMBERS

The numbers which follow in square brackets are US catalogue numbers if they are different from UK catalogue numbers (and this applies in particular to EMI's 'Great Recordings of the Century', which have a different number on each side of the Atlantic). Some

EMI Encore CDs are also differently numbered, so it is always advisable to check.

EMI and Virgin have now abandoned the use of alphabetical prefixes, and it is no longer possible to determine the price range from the catalogue listing itself, although budget Encore CDs are clearly marked, as are the two-for-the-price-of-one *double forte* Gemini and Virgin reissues.

We have taken care to check catalogue information as far as is possible, but as all the editorial work has been done in England there is always the possibility of error; American readers are therefore invited, when ordering records locally, to take the precaution of giving their dealer the fullest information about the music and recordings they want.

The indications (M), (B) and (BB) immediately before the starring of a disc refer primarily to the British CD, as pricing systems are not always identical on both sides of the Atlantic. When CDs are imported by specialist distributors into the USA, this again usually involves a price difference. When mid-priced CDs on the smaller labels are imported into the USA, they often move up to the premium-price range. American readers are advised to consult their local record store.

ABBREVIATIONS

To save space we have adopted a number of standard abbreviations in listing record companies, orchestras and performing groups (a list is provided below), and the titles of works are often shortened, especially where they are listed several times. Artists' forenames are often omitted if they are not absolutely necessary for identification purposes. Also we have not usually listed the contents of operatic highlights and collections.

We have followed common practice in the use of the original language for titles where it seems sensible. In most cases, English is used for orchestral and instrumental music, and the original language for vocal music and opera. There are exceptions, however; for instance, the Johann Strauss discography uses the German language in the interests of consistency.

ORDER OF MUSIC

The order of music under each composer's name broadly follows the following system: orchestral music, including concertos and symphonies; chamber music; solo instrumental music (in some cases with keyboard and organ music separated); vocal and choral music; opera; vocal collections; miscellaneous collections. Within each group, our listing follows an alphabetical sequence, and couplings within a single composer's output are *usually* discussed together instead of separately with cross-references. Occasionally (and inevitably because of this alphabetical approach), different recordings of a given work can become separated when a record is listed and discussed under the first work of its alphabetical sequence. The editor feels that alphabetical consistency is essential if the reader is to learn to find his or her way about.

CATALOGUE NUMBERS

Enormous care has gone into the checking of CD catalogue numbers and contents to ensure that all details are correct, but the editor and publishers cannot be held responsible for any mistakes that may have crept in despite all our zealous checking. When ordering CDs, readers are urged to provide their record dealer with full details of the music and performers, as well as the catalogue number.

DELETIONS

Compact discs regularly succumb to the deletions axe, and many are likely to disappear during the lifetime of this book. Sometimes copies may still be found in specialist shops, and there remains the compensatory fact that most really important and desirable recordings are eventually reissued, often costing less!

COVERAGE

As the output of major and minor labels continues to expand, it is obviously impossible for us to mention every CD that is available within the covers of a single book; this is recognized as a practical limitation if we are to update our survey regularly. Indeed, we have now to be very selective in choosing the discs to be included, and some good recordings inevitably fall by the wayside. There is generally a reason for omissions, and usually it is connected with the lack of ready availability. However, we do welcome suggestions from readers about such omissions if they seem to be of special interest, although we cannot guarantee to include them in a future survey!

ACKNOWLEDGEMENTS

Our thanks are due as usual to Paul Czajkowski, Assistant Editor, who was responsible for most of the titling; he helped with retrieval of earlier reviews (connected with reissues); and he also contributed many specialist reviews, especially in the areas of film and ballet music, light music and operetta. Our Penguin copy-editor, Roger Wells, continued to be indispensable, as were Penguin's in-house editorial staff, Ellie Smith, and her colleague Emma Brown.

Alan Livesey and Kathleen March have once again helped with checking the final copy for factual and musical errors, and our team of Penguin proofreaders have also proved themselves invaluable. Grateful thanks also go to all those readers who write to us to point out factual errors and to remind us of important recordings which have escaped our notice.

THE AMERICAN SCENE

CDs are much less expensive in the USA than they are in Great Britain and because of this (so we are told) many bargain recordings available in England are not brought into the USA by their manufacturers, so that they have to be imported by the major US record stores and mail order outlets. What this means is that while almost any recording mentioned in these pages will be available in the USA, sometimes it will cost more than the buyer might reasonably expect.

Duos and Doubles, where available, remain at two-discs-for-the-cost-of-one-premium-priced CD in both countries, and here US collectors can have a price advantage. However, many excellent lower-priced discs are not issued in the USA. Where a recording is of extra special interest, American collectors can obtain it readily by mail order from England, through the website address given; however, this will inevitably cost more than it would domestically.

PRICE DIFFERENCES IN THE UK AND USA

Retail prices are not fixed in either country, and various stores may offer even better deals at times, so our price structure must be taken as a guideline only. This particularly applies to the line between Bargain and Super-bargain CDs. Premium-priced CDs cost on average approximately the same number of dollars in the USA as they do pounds in the UK.

Duos, Doubles and Dyads are two-for-the-cost-of-one-premium-priced disc the world over. Classics for Pleasure, EMI Gemini and the Virgin Classics 2x1 Doubles are two-for-the-price-of-one-mid-priced-CD.

OTHER COMPARABLE PRICES IN THE UK AND USA

Here are comparative details of the other price-ranges (note that sets are multiples of the prices quoted):

MID-PRICED SERIES (as indicated by (M) in text)
   UK: £10.99; often £9–£10
   USA: Under $13; usually under $12
BARGAIN-PRICED SERIES (as indicated by (B) in text)
   UK: £5.50–£7
   USA: Under $7
SUPER-BARGAIN BUDGET SERIES (as indicated by (BB) in text)
   UK: £5.50
   USA: $5–$6

THE AUSTRALIAN SCENE

We have been fortunate in obtaining for review a considerable number of recordings from the Australian branch of Universal Classics (responsible for the three key labels, Decca, DG and Philips), who have been making a series of local issues of Decca, DG and Philips repertoire of considerable interest, mostly not otherwise available. These are bargain issues in Australia but, because of import costs, are more expensive in the UK and USA. All these Universal Australia CDs can be purchased via the Australian website:

www.buywell.com

Residents in the UK should be able to obtain them to special order from the international mail-order source given below.

AN INTERNATIONAL MAIL-ORDER SOURCE FOR RECORDINGS IN THE UK

Readers are urged to support a local dealer if he is prepared and able to give a proper service, and to remember that obtaining many CDs involves expertise and perseverance. However, in recent years many specialist sources have disappeared; for that reason, if any difficulty is experienced in obtaining the CDs you want, we suggest the following mail-order alternative, which offers competitive discounts in the UK but also operates world-wide. Through this service, advice on choice of recordings from the Editor of the *Penguin Guide* is always readily available to mail-order customers.

Squires Gate Music Centre Ltd (PG Dept)
615 Lytham Road
Squires Gate
Blackpool
Lancashire FY4 1RG
UK
Tel./Fax: (+44) (0)1253 405599
Website address: www.lprl.demon.co.uk
Email address: sales@lprl.demon.co.uk

This organization can supply any recording available in Britain and patiently extends compact disc orders until they finally come to hand. A full guarantee of safe delivery is made on any order undertaken. Please write or fax for further details, or make a trial credit-card order, by fax, email or telephone.

❀ **The Rosette Service**
Squires Gate also offers a try-before-you-buy weekly loan service (within the UK only) so that customers can try out rosetted recordings at home, plus a hand-picked group of recommended key-repertoire CDs, for a small charge, without any obligation to purchase. A short list of recommended DVDs is also available. If a recording is subsequently purchased, it will be discounted and the trial charge waived. Full details sent on request.

Squires Gate Music Centre also offers a simple three-monthly mailing service, listing a hand-picked selection of current new and reissued CDs, chosen by the Editor of the *Penguin Guide* Ivan March. Customers of Squires Gate Music Centre Ltd, both domestic and overseas, receive the bulletin as available, and it is sent automatically with their purchases.

ABBREVIATIONS

AAM	Academy of Ancient Music	LCO	London Chamber Orchestra
Ac.	Academy, Academic	LCP	London Classical Players
Amb.	S. Ambrosian Singers	LMP	London Mozart Players
Ara.	Arabesque	LOP	Lamoureux Orchestra of Paris
arr.	arranged, arrangement	LPO	London Philharmonic Orchestra
ASMF	Academy of St Martin-in-the-Fields	LSO	London Symphony Orchestra
(B)	bargain-price CD	(M)	mid-price CD
(BB)	super-bargain-price CD	Mer.	Meridian
Bar.	Baroque	Met.	Metropolitan
Bav.	Bavarian	min.	minor
BBC	British Broadcasting Corporation	MoC	Ministry of Culture
BPO	Berlin Philharmonic Orchestra	movt	movement
BRT	Belgian Radio & Television (Brussels)	N.	North, Northern
		nar.	narrated
Cal.	Calliope	Nat.	National
Cap.	Cappriccio	Nim.	Nimbus
CBSO	City of Birmingham Symphony Orchestra	NY	New York
		O	Orchestra, Orchestre
CfP	Classics for Pleasure	OAE	Orchestra of the Age of Enlightenment
Ch.	Choir; Chorale; Chorus		
Chan.	Chandos	O-L	Oiseau-Lyre
CO	Chamber Orchestra	Op.	Opera (in performance listings); opus (in music titles)
COE	Chamber Orchestra of Europe		
Col. Mus. Ant.	Musica Antiqua, Cologne	orch.	orchestrated
Coll.	Collegium	ORR	Orchestre Révolutionnaire et Romantique
Coll. Aur.	Collegium Aureum		
Coll. Voc.	Collegium Vocale	ORTF	L'Orchestre de la radio et télévision française
Concg. O	Royal Concertgebouw Orchestra of Amsterdam		
		Ph.	Philips
cond.	conductor, conducted	Phd.	Philadelphia
Cons.	Consort	Philh.	Philharmonia
DG	Deutsche Grammophon	PO	Philharmonic Orchestra
DHM	Deutsche Harmonia Mundi	Qt	Quartet
E.	England, English	R.	Radio
E. Bar. Sol.	English Baroque Soloists	Ref.	Références
ECCO	European Community Chamber Orchestra	RLPO	Royal Liverpool Philharmonic Orchestra
ECO	English Chamber Orchestra	ROHCG	Royal Opera House, Covent Garden
ENO	English National Opera Company	RPO	Royal Philharmonic Orchestra
Ens.	Ensemble	RSNO	Royal Scottish National Orchestra
ESO	English Symphony Orchestra	RSO	Radio Symphony Orchestra
Fr.	French	RTE	Radio Television Eireann
GO	Gewandhaus Orchestra	S.	South, Southern
Häns.	Hänssler	SCO	Scottish Chamber Orchestra
HM	Harmonia Mundi	Sinf.	Sinfonietta
Hung.	Hungaroton	SIS	Special Import Service (EMI – UK only)
Hyp.	Hyperion		
IMS	Import Music Service (Polygram – UK only)	SNO	Scottish National Orchestra
		SO	Symphony Orchestra
☙	key recordings	Soc.	Society
L.	London	Sol. Ven.	I Solisti Veneti
LA	Los Angeles	SRO	Suisse Romande Orchestra

Sup.	Supraphon	VCM	Vienna Concentus Musicus
trans.	transcription, transcribed	VPO	Vienna Philharmonic Orchestra
V.	Vienna	VSO	Vienna Symphony Orchestra
V/D	Video Director	W.	West
Van.	Vanguard	WNO	Welsh National Opera Company

ABEL, Carl Friedrich (1723–87)

6 Symphonies, Op. 7
**(*) Chan. 8648. Cantilena, Shepherd

The six *Symphonies* of Op. 7 speak much the same language as J. C. Bach or early Mozart. The performances are not the last word in elegance but they are lively and enjoyable and well recorded.

ABRIL, Anton Garcia (born 1933)

Concierto Mudéjar
*** Analekta FL 2 3049. Boucher, Amati Ens., Dessaints –
TORROBA: *Sonatina*, etc. ***

The *Concerto* by the Aragonese composer Anton Abril is attractively idiomatic, and the haunting central *Andante* clearly draws on slow movements by predecessors Castelnuovo-Tedesco and Rodrigo. The dancing zapateado finale is also highly individual. The performance is superb in all respects. The recording too is truthful, warm and pleasing.

ADAM, Adolphe (1803–56)

Giselle (ballet; complete) (Film by Hugo Niebling; Choreography: David Blair, after Jules Perrot & Jean Coralli)
*** DG **DVD** 073 4069. Fracci, Bruhn, Marks, Lander, American Ballet Theatre, Deutsche Op. O, Berlin, Lanchbery (Director: David Blair)

This very enjoyable film, based on the American Ballet Theatre production by Lucia Chase and Oliver Smith, has certain advantages and disadvantages. The basic set is spacious and realistic and, in Act I, pleasingly rustic, complete with an active waterwheel. The opening of Act II is very evocative and the shots of the ensemble dance of the Willis as they enter are magically lit. For the most part the camera follows the story simply and gives the chance of close-ups in the dramatic moments.

This brings an extra dimension, for Carla Fracci not only dances Giselle superbly but she is also a touchingly fine actress, and the close of Act I is very moving. Her partnership with Albrecht – Erik Bruhn, handsome, very aristocratic in demeanour, and also a splendid dancer – is celebrated, and justifiably so. Myrthe, Queen of the Willis (Toni Lander), is coolly malignant and her famous Act II entry on points is exquisite. Bruce Marks is a suitably robust and angry Hilarion, and the *Peasant Pas de deux* in the first act is given a virtuoso performance by Eleanor D'Antuono and Ted Kivitt. They are introduced to entertain the ducal hunting party, who arrive spectacularly on horseback, riding through the forest to Adam's lively hunting music – one advantage of a film version, which can temporarily extend beyond the basic set. It also provides an opportunity for fades, dissolves and, less pleasingly, a deliberate loss of focus, and other camera tricks. During the memorable corps de ballet's hopping dance in Act II (a choreographic highlight) the visual image all but evaporates into an unnecessary special effect for a few seconds, and the arrival of the Shade of Giselle from her grave could also have been managed less awkwardly. But on the whole the camera is where one needs it to be (although the repeated shots of the dancers' feet seem overdone), and one can enjoy the colourful costumes, and follow the story and

the truly wonderful American Ballet Theatre dancers with great pleasure. Of course, in this great classical ballet there is more dancing than story, but who minds, when it is visually as captivating as this. The Deutsche Opera Orchestra too plays very beautifully indeed under the experienced John Lanchbery, and they are warmly and spaciously recorded, with the option of 5.1 DTS surround sound, if you have the necessary equipment. This would make a great present for any ballet-lover.

Giselle (ballet: older, European Score)
(M) **(*) Decca (ADD) 475 7507. VPO, Karajan

Karajan's Vienna recording returns to the catalogue, admirably remastered, for Universal's extended series of Originals, which now covers both the Decca and Philips labels, as well as DG. Adam's delectable score is lovingly played, with the suave blandishments of the Karajan baton guiding the famous orchestra to produce a reading of beauty and elegance. The glowing Decca recording is first rate, and as the legend of the Willis (the ghosts of dead girls jilted by their lovers) on which *Giselle* is based is a German one, to have a distinct impression of Austrian peasantry and hunting music will seem to many very appropriate.

But Bonynge's complete recording with the Royal Opera House, Covent Garden, Orchestra on a Double Decca is more idiomatic, and the bright recording very appropriate. This costs very little more (453 185-2).

ADAMS, John (born 1947)

Shaker Loops
(M) *** Ph. 475 7551. San Francisco SO, Edo de Waart –
REICH: *Variations for Winds* ***

Shaker Loops is one of the most appealing of John Adams's early (1978) minimalist works. He adapted the piece from an even earlier string sextet when he became composer in residence to the San Francisco Symphony Orchestra. The inspiration was from the Shakers, the religious sect whose devotions regularly led to shaking and trembling. (The shaking was a substitute for sex, which they didn't believe in – so perhaps it is not surprising that the Shakers are no longer numerous.) Adams reproduces the shaking in prolonged ostinatos and trills and, whatever the limitations, there is a genuine poetic imagination at work here. Both performance and recording are outstanding, but the (appropriate) Reich coupling is not very generous, and the work is also available in a bountiful all-Adams anthology, superbly played by the Bournemouth Symphony Orchestra under Marin Alsop on Naxos 8.559031 (see our main volume).

I was looking at the ceiling and I saw the sky (Song Play)
⦿ (BB) *** Naxos 8.669003/4. Mühlpointer, Trotman, Neisser, Friedrich, De Haas, Gardell, Jonas Holst, Freiburg Young Op. Co., Band of Holst Sinf., Simon

This new Naxos recording of John Adams's 'song play', set to a remarkably imaginative libretto by June Jordan, is a complete revelation, showing it to be an undoubted masterpiece, an intriguing amalgam of opera and musical, drawing on all kinds of sources, but in the main extending the style of musical pioneered by Bernstein. It is a true crossover work, and its basic parlando style, laced with set pieces, is all Adams's own.

There is no linking dialogue; the numbers themselves carry the action forward – which is a strength, not a drawback –

making the piece musically concise. (Dialogue can too often be a problem in the opera house.) Rarely among twentieth-century composers, Adams writes for the voice absolutely naturally so that every number is vocally rewarding for the singers. The work is inspired by the 1994 Californian earthquake, which alters the lives of all the principal characters, and we first meet them against a background of persistent ostinatos in Adams's early minimalist style, but here always aurally imaginative. Adams then launches into melodic lines, echoing jazz and pop of all kinds, but transmuted into music of quality, and rhythmically intriguing.

The piece centres on seven everyday characters, all young people from Los Angeles, of varying social and ethnic backgrounds. The key couples are Consuelo and Dewain, David who courts Leila (who is to perish in the earthquake), Mike (who is gay) and Tiffany, who loves him but who finally pairs with Rick, a Vietnamese-born lawyer. Consuelo is an illegal immigrant, and Dewain is a black gang-leader, in prison for a minor crime. These two, although mutually attracted, go their separate ways at the end of the story. This diversity of character gives the work its kernel, and Adams's set numbers bring outstanding lyrical inspirations. In Act I these include Consuelo's tender *Donde Estias*, in which she worries about her young son, her later, gently rapturous dream of a normal life with Dewain, and Leila's idyll of loneliness. The Act closes with a catchy ensemble *About the Sweet Majority Population of the World*.

Act II brings Mike and Tiffany's long duet as they recognize their mutual attraction, the key dramatic scene in the whole work, and Dewain's *Song of Liberation* (a yearning piano ballad) sung when he is freed, since the earthquake has brought down the walls of his prison. But the work is capped by the passionate duet (worthy of Bernstein) between Consuelo and Dewain as they realize they must part, *One last look at the angel in your eyes*. It then ends with a retrospective finale, a wonderful passacaglia, over which Adams recalls his main themes, leading to a return of the opening title song.

One can only say that this complete performance under Klaus Simon's vivid direction is most colloquially and persuasively sung and played, and excellently recorded. It all but eclipses the composer's own recording on Nonesuch, which of course has its own insights to offer but which is incomplete. The Naxos presentation includes a full number-by-number synopsis; and you can hear all the words. The enterprise alone deserves a ✹, but so does the exhilarating and heart-warming result. This is going to be a repertoire piece of the future.

ADDINSELL, Richard (1904–77)

Film music: *The Admirable Crichton: Polka; Galop; Waltz sequence. The Black Rose: Suite. Blithe Spirit: Prelude; Waltz.* (i) *Goodbye Mr Chips: Suite. Love on the Dole: Suite. Tom Brown's Schooldays: Overture* (all arr. or reconstructed Philip Lane). (ii) *Dangerous Moonlight: Warsaw Concerto* (arr. Roy Douglas). *Out of the Clouds: Flame Tango* (arr. Robert Sharples). *Scrooge: Suite* (arr. Stephen Bernstein)

*** Chan. 10046. BBC PO, Gamba; with (i) Chetham's Chamber Ch. & Manchester Cathedral Ch.; (ii) Roscoe

This fine Chandos collection tends to all but trump the opposition, although Kenneth Alwyn's two selections with the Royal Ballet Sinfonia are also highly desirable, offering only a small amount of duplication, besides having a price advantage. But the Chandos recording is well up to the high standards of the house, and the strings of the BBC Philharmonic sound ravishing, especially in the gentler music. The excellent choral singing in the tuneful school song from *Goodbye Mr Chips* is a highlight (and here the gentler string writing brings sentimental memories of a truly memorable film for which Robert Donat won an Oscar).

But there are tunes galore here, not least in the romantic title-theme for *Love on the Dole* and the jolly, spirited 'Blackpool' sequence, the lyrical *Black Rose Theme*, the engaging 'Waltz' sequence from *The Admirable Crichton* and the luscious *Flame Tango* from *Out of the Clouds*, vividly scored by Robert Sharples. The *Scrooge Suite* understandably draws heavily on Christmas carols but brings with it (as part of the excellent documentation) an unforgettable portrait of Alastair Sim in the title-role, a glorious performance, never approached, let alone equalled, in any of the subsequent remakes. All in all, this is music to lift the spirits.

(i) Film music: *Blithe Spirit (Waltz Theme)*. (ii) *The Day Will Dawn (Tea-time Music). Greengage Summer: Suite.* (ii) *Highly Dangerous: Theme. The Lion Has Wings: Cavalry of the Clouds (March). Out of the Clouds: Theme. The Passionate Friends: Lover's Moon. Sea Devils (Prologue). Under Capricorn: Theme. Radio themes: Britain to America: March of the United Nations.* (ii) *Journey into Romance: Invocation for Piano & Orchestra.* (i) *Warsaw Concerto*

☀–⚊ (M) *** ASV CDWHL 2108. Royal Ballet Sinfonia, Alwyn; with (i) M. Jones; (ii) Lawson

Roy Douglas here receives belated recognition for his work in fashioning Addinsell's musical ideas and cleverly scoring them as a Rachmaninov pastiche for the justly famous *Warsaw Concerto*. But there are many other good things here, and Philip Lane's cleverly fashioned suite from the film *The Greengage Summer* brims over with delightful ideas. Douglas Gamley assisted the composer in this instance, and other credits include Leonard Isaac and Ron Goodwin (who scored the *Cavalry of the Clouds* march). When trifles like the *Tea-time Music* from *The Day Will Dawn* and the delicious *Waltz* from *Blithe Spirit* are played with such affection and polish under the understanding Kenneth Alwyn, their gentle spirit is life-enhancing. The *Warsaw Concerto* is treated as a miniature masterpiece and given a performance that is as dramatic as it is heart-warming. Martin Jones is the splendid soloist, and Peter Lawson contributes equally sensitively to the several other concertante numbers. The recording is first class in every way. Not to be missed.

Film Music: *Blithe Spirit: Prelude & Waltz. Encore: Miniature Overture. Fire Over England: Suite. Parisienne – 1885. The Passionate Friends: Suite. Scrooge: Suite. Southern Rhapsody; South Riding: Prelude. Waltz of the Toreadors: March & Waltz. WRNS March* (arr. Douglas)

(M) **(*) ASV CDWHL 2115. Royal Ballet O, Alwyn

Richard Addinsell's distinct melodic gift is heard at its best here in his early score for *Fire Over England* (1937) and, more especially, in the suite of music from *Scrooge*. As the *Waltz* for *Blithe Spirit* and the brief *March* for *Waltz of the Toreadors* show, there are some deft inventions elsewhere, but their composer needed help from others to realize them orchestrally. All this music is slight, but it is very well played by the Royal Ballet Orchestra, affectionately and stylishly conducted by Kenneth Alwyn and very well recorded.

Film and theatre music: *Fire Over England: Suite. Goodbye Mr Chips: Theme. Journey to Romance: Invocation. The*

Prince and the Showgirl: selection. *Ring round the Moon: Invitation Waltz.* (i) *A Tale of Two Cities: Theme. Tom Brown's Schooldays: Overture.* (ii) *Trespass: Festival* (beguine). *The Isle of Apples;* (ii) *Smokey Mountain Concerto;* (i) *Tune in G*

**(*) Marco 8.223732. BBC Concert O, Alwyn, with (i) Elms;
(ii) Martin

Kenneth Alwyn has pieced a good deal of the material together here where original scores are lost, notably in the 'Overture' from the film music for *Tom Brown's Schooldays* and the charming introductory sequence for *Goodbye Mr Chips.* The *Invitation Waltz* for Christopher Fry's translation, *Ring round the Moon,* of Jean Anouilh's *L'Invitation au château* is quite haunting, as is the gentle idyll *The Isle of Apples* and the simple *Tune in G* with its piano embroidery. These pieces, like the *Smokey Mountain Concerto,* were independent compositions. Alwyn and the BBC Concert Orchestra are thoroughly at home in this repertoire, and they present it all freshly, the recording bright but with rather a brash sonority.

ADÈS, Thomas (born 1971)

Asyla (complete)

*** EMI DVD 4 90325-9 (2). BPO, Rattle (V/D: Bob Coles) –
MAHLER: *Symphony 5* ***

Thomas Adès's brilliant orchestral piece, with its exotic use of a vast range of percussion instruments, was Simon Rattle's choice of work to complete his inaugural programme as the new music director of the Berlin Philharmonic in November 2002. The main work at that historic concert was Mahler's *Fifth Symphony,* a recording of which appeared promptly on CD. On DVD, by contrast, there is room for the complete concert to be included on a single disc, which brings every advantage. The package also includes a second disc, containing an extended interview with Rattle by his biographer and former Controller of Music at the BBC, Nicholas Kenyon.

ADORNO, Theodor (1903–69)

String Quartet; 2 Pieces for String Quartet, Op. 2; 6 Studies for String Quartet

(BB) *** CPO 999 341-2. Leipzig Qt – EISLER: *Prelude & Fugue on B-A-C-H,* etc. ***

Adorno's *Six Studies* show an awareness of Schoenberg's musical language. There are many imaginative touches, both here and in the *String Quartet* of the following year. Neither is negligible, even if neither possesses a significantly personal voice. Berg exerted some influence on the *Two Pieces for String Quartet, Op. 2.* The performances and recordings qualify for a three-star rating – though the music itself is another matter! But at its new budget price this is worth trying.

AGRICOLA, Alexander (c. 1446–1506)

Songs: *Adieu m'amour* (3 versions); *A la mignonne de fortune; Allez, regretz; Ay je rien fet; Cecus non in dicat de coloribus; De tous bien plaine* (3 versions); *Et qui la dira; Fortuna desperata; Guarde vostre visage* (3 versions); *J'ay beau huer; S'il vous plaist; Soit loing ou pres; Sonnes muses melodieusement*

(BB) *** Naxos 8.553840. Unicorn Ens., Posch

Agricola's music is expressive, but its structure and polyphony are quite complex, his polyphonic style nearer to Ockeghem than to Josquin, while his musical personality is less individual than either. Nevertheless, these secular love songs (sung in medieval French) are full of interest, the more so as they are often presented with a mixed consort of voices and instruments sharing the polyphony, with close blending of the whole ensemble. The piece that gives the disc its title, the sombre *Fortuna desperata,* makes a powerfully sonorous conclusion. The presentation is scholarly, direct and appealing, the recording excellent, and the documentation could hardly be bettered, with full translations included.

AKSES, Necil Kâzim (1908–99)

Violin Concerto.

*** CPO 999 799-2. Askin, NDR RO, Hannover, Gökman

Necil Akses is a key figure among the first generation of twentieth-century Turkish composers who turned to the West for their musical training. As an accomplished violinist – he was a pupil of Suk – it is not surprising that his 1969 *Concerto* provides an impressively diverse, predominantly melodic solo role. It opens with a powerfully rumbustious toccata-like tutti (laced with tam tam and percussion) which all but submerges the soloist. But the movement's lyricism soon predominates, even through bold rhythmic orchestral interruptions, and leads to a long cadenza, which in turn moves without a break into the hauntingly doleful slow movement. The wild Scherzo is almost a tarantella; then the melting Adagio theme returns nostalgically, to take the listener to a second, even more movingly ruminative cadenza, before being interrupted by the rumbustious return of the introductory tutti.

This live performance is passionately committed, and if Cihat Askin's timbre is small, his technique is fully up to the work's musical and technical demands.

ALBÉNIZ, Isaac (1860–1909)

Iberia (complete)

(BB) ** EMI Gemini (ADD) 4 76906-2 (2). Ciccolini –
GRANADOS: *Goyescas* *(*)

Aldo Ciccolini's complete recording of *Iberia* comes in harness with *Goyescas* of Granados and on the face of it offers good value in EMI's Gemini series. Book I, comprising *Evocación, El Puerto* and *Fête-Dieu à Séville,* comes after the Granados on the first CD, the remaining three Books being accommodated on the second disc. The recordings were made in the Salle Wagram and date from 1966. The performances are idiomatic – *Evocación* is immediately beguiling – and overall very acceptable, but unfortunately the sound is unappealing, a bit shallow in timbre and sometimes clattery.

GUITAR MUSIC

Suite española 1, Op. 47,excerpts: Granada; Sevilla; Astorias

(BB) *** HMV 5 86758-2. Byzantine (with GRANADOS: *Andaluza (Playera), Op. 37/5;* TÁRREGA: *Memories of the Alhambra (Ghiglia);* MYERS: *The Deer Hunter: Cavatina;* (Manuel Barrueco & Steve Morse) – RODRIGO: *Concierto de Aranjuez* etc. ***

These pieces make a fine bonus for the excellent Romero/Previn Rodrigo concertante couplings. Julian Byzantine plays magnetically in the three evocations of famous Spanish cities, and he is especially seductive in his sultry portrayal of *Granada*. Oscar Ghiglia is rather less enticing in the famous Tárrega *Recuerdos*, but he plays it with remarkably precise figuration, and the programme ends with a 'pop' favourite, Stanley Myers's hauntingly memorable film theme, here (perfectly reasonably) electronically enhanced.

ALBERT, Eugen d' (1864–1932)

Piano Concertos 1 in B min., Op. 2; 2 in E, Op. 12
*** Hyp. CDA 66747. Lane, BBC Scottish SO, Francis

The *Piano Concerto 1 in B minor* (1884) is the more ambitious of the two works, written in a style halfway between Liszt and Rachmaninov, with a rather extraordinary fugal outburst towards the end of the work. Piers Lane plays with delicacy and virtuosity and is well supported by the BBC Scottish Symphony Orchestra. The *Piano Concerto 2 in E major* is a one-movement piece, though in four sections, following the style of Liszt's concertos. The recording is expertly balanced by Tony Kime.

Overture: Esther, Op. 8
*** Hyp. CDA 67387. BBC Scottish SO, Brabbins – LAMOND: *Symphony in A*, etc. ***

This colourful, generously inventive overture of Eugen d'Albert makes an apt coupling for the orchestral works of Frederic Lamond, when each was born in the Glasgow area of Scotland in the 1860s (d'Albert of a French father and a Scottish mother) and each gravitated to Germany, both becoming famous as piano virtuosos. Like Lamond, d'Albert had an easy mastery of orchestration, with dramatic writing for brass punctuating the piece, beautifully played by the BBC Scottish Symphony Orchestra under Martyn Brabbins and very well recorded by the BBC engineers.

Piano Sonata in F sharp min., Op. 10; 8 Klavierstücke, Op. 5; Klavierstücke, Op. 16/2–3; 5 schliche Klavierstücke (Capriolen), Op. 32; Serenata
*** Hyp. CDA 66945. Lane

Eugen d'Albert's solo keyboard music inhabits the worlds of Brahms and Liszt, but there is much that can lay claim to a quiet individuality. Piers Lane plays it with total commitment. No want of virtuosity and dedication here, and very good recorded sound.

Die toten Augen (complete)
*** CPO 999 692-2 (2). Schellenberger, Gjevang, Walker, Orth, Chalker, Odinius, Bär, Dresden PO Ch. & O, Weikert

Die toten Augen ('The Dead Eyes') is a luscious piece set at the time of Christ. The central action is framed by a Prelude and Postlude in which a shepherd (beautifully sung here by the tenor Lothar Odinius), meets another symbolic character, the Reaper (the celebrated Olaf Bär), and goes off in search of a lost sheep. The central action, much more realistic, is then compressed into a single Act, telling of a Roman official, Arcesius, whose wife, Myrtocle, is blind. She is cured by the intervention (offstage) of Christ but, as predicted by Christ, the gift of sight proves a curse, bringing the disruption of her marriage and the murder of the handsome Galba, whom she initially mistakes for her husband. In her love for Arcesius she opts to be blind again, with her 'dead eyes'.

The evocative pastoral sweetness of the Prelude and Postlude is set against the ripe German *verismo* style of the central action. It could easily be a sickly story, but d'Albert with rich orchestration and surging melody carries it off impressively. This live recording of a concert performance, well recorded, offers a persuasive account of the piece, with Dagmar Schellenberger powerful as Myrtocle, well matched by the fine mezzo, Anne Gjevang, as Mary of Magdala. A rarity to recommend to those with a sweet tooth.

ALBICASTRO, Henricus (1661–c. 1730)

Concerti à 4, Op. 7/2 & 12; Violin Sonata with Continuo (La follia), Op. 9/12; Trio Sonatas, Op. 8/9 & 11; (i) Motet: Coelestes angelici chori
(B) *** HM HMA 1905208. Ens. 415, Banchini; (i) with De Mey

Swiss-born Henricus Albicastro's *La follia* variations are a shade conventional but, like the *Trio Sonatas*, are pleasingly assured and easily inventive. The two *Concerti* are even more striking in character, the *Allegros* vivacious and neatly imitative and the *Grave* slow movements rather fine. But the best work here is the cantata, which has both melodic appeal and genuine emotional eloquence. It is quite beautifully sung by Guy de Mey (and a translation is provided). Chiara Banchini and Ensemble 415 are on excellent form throughout, and the whole concert is very well recorded.

ALBINONI, Tomaso (1671–1751)

12 Concerti a cinque, Op. 7; Sonatas for Strings a 5: in D & G min., Op. 2/5–6
(M) *** Ph. 475 7757 (2). Holliger, Bourgue, I Musici

Albinoni's Opus 7 consists of four each of solo oboe concertos, double oboe concertos, and concertos for strings with continuo. This recording by Heinz Holliger and Maurice Bourgue with I Musici, which Philips have chosen as one of their Originals, is comparatively robust in using modern instruments, but it is eminently stylish, the effect sunny and lively by turns, with the many fine solo movements all warmly relished. The digital recording is fresh and naturally balanced. The two *String Sonatas* from Opus 2 are particularly attractive works, and here the recording is slightly closer.

CHAMBER MUSIC

6 Sonate da chiesa, Op. 4; Trattenimenti armonici per camera, Op. 6
(B) *** Hyp. 2x1 Dyad CDD 22048 (2). Locatelli Trio

Albinoni's lyrically appealing 'Church' *Sonatas* are here contrasted with the plainer and more secular (but no less rewarding) *Trattenimenti*, which translates as 'Entertainments'. The performances on original instruments are of high quality, as is the recording, and this set is even more attractive at its new lower price.

ALFANO, Franco (1875–1954)

Cyrano de Bergerac (opera; complete)
*** DG **DVD** 476 739-6. Alagna, Manfrino, Troxell, Rivenq, Barrard, O Nat. de Montpellier, Guidarini (Producers: David and Frédérico Alagna)

Alfano, best known for completing Puccini's unfinished

opera, *Turandot*, was also a successful opera composer in his own right, and this adaptation of Edmond Rostand's play about the legendary Cyrano de Bergerac with his inordinately long nose demonstrates his gifts in creating what by any standards is a well-made opera. Henri Cain was the author who adapted the play, keeping the overall shape in five distinct scenes, here presented by the Opéra National de Montpellier in a lavish, realistic production by David and Frédérico Alagna, with sets designed by themselves. With Roberto Alagna impressively taking the title-role, acting convincingly, the performance under Marco Guidarini works well. Natalie Manfrino is a bright-toned Roxane, casually dismissing the love-lorn Christian when he proves an incoherent rather than a poetic lover. The handsome Richard Troxell is well cast in that second tenor role, lighter and well contrasted with Alagna; and the others make an excellent team. The one notable shortcoming is that Alfano, unlike Puccini, is not a natural melodist, and in such a romantic piece one craves the sort of impact that Puccini was able to achieve by launching a great melody.

Cyrano de Bergerac (opera; complete) (CD version)
*** CPO 999 909-2 (2). Sadnik, Uhl, McNamara, Newerla, Klein, Kiel Op. O & Ch., Frank

The opening prelude demonstrates the richness and refinement of Alfano's orchestral palette, rather like an Italian updating of *Petrushka*, with offstage choral effects adding to the atmospheric beauty at various points. On CD Markus Frank, the young music director of the Kiel Opera Company, draws a warm and colourful performance from his singers and players, with the tenor, Roman Sadnik, commanding in the very taxing title-role. His weighty, almost baritonal tenor is well contrasted with the light lyrical tenor of Paul McNamara, in the role of Christian, while Manuela Uhl, despite a rather throaty production, sings powerfully and movingly as Roxane. The recording, taken from two live performances in May 2002, is warmly atmospheric, with the voices well balanced.

ALLEGRI, Gregorio (1582–1652)

Miserere
🎵 (M) *** Gimell (ADD) GISME 401. Tallis Scholars, Phillips – MUNDY: *Vox patris caelestis*; PALESTRINA: *Missa Papae Marcelli* ***

Mozart was so impressed by Allegri's *Miserere* when he heard it in the Sistine Chapel (which originally claimed exclusive rights to its performance) he wrote the music out from memory so that it could be performed elsewhere. With its soaring treble solo celestially sung by Alison Stamp, this performance by the Tallis Scholars holds its place at the top of the list and is now most welcome as a mid-priced celebration of the group's 25th anniversary.

ALMEIDA, Francisco António de
(*c.* 1702–55)

La Giuditta (oratorio)
(B) *** HM HMA 901411/12. Lootens, Congiu, Hill, Köhler, Concerto Köln, Jacobs

Here is a superb oratorio (based on the story from the Apocrypha of Judith's deception of Holofernes) by a virtually unknown Portuguese composer. His music keeps reminding one of Handel at his finest. Almeida is surely lucky that René Jacobs has assembled such a fine cast, with Lena Lootens singing freshly and appealingly as Giuditta, Martyn Hill a generally fine Holofernes (though perhaps not an entirely convincing seducer) and Alex Köhler most impressive of all as Ozia, Commander of Bethulia. The work is brimful of melody. The orchestral writing, using flutes, oboes, horns (which come through spectacularly) and strings, shows a true feeling for the orchestral palette and the way it can be used to sharpen and colour the narrative. Jacobs directs a performance that springs vividly to life, and everything about this production, including the recording, is first class. With excellent documentation this is very highly recommended.

ALWYN, William (1905–85)

(i) *Autumn Legend* (for cor anglais); (ii) *Lyra Angelica* (concerto for harp); (iii) *Pastoral Fantasia* (for viola); *Tragic Interlude*
*** Chan. 9065. (i) Daniel; (ii) Masters; (iii) Tees; City of L. Sinfonia, Hickox

Autumn Legend (1954) is a highly atmospheric tone-poem, very Sibelian in feeling. So too is the *Pastoral Fantasia*, yet the piece has its own developing individuality. A fine performance, with Stephen Tees highly sympathetic to the music's fluid poetic line. The *Tragic Interlude* is a powerful lament for the dead of wars past. But the highlight of the disc is the *Lyra Angelica*, a radiantly beautiful, extended piece (just over half an hour in length) inspired by the metaphysical poet Giles Fletcher's '*Christ's victorie and triumph*'. The performance here is very moving, and the recording has great richness of string-tone and a delicately balanced harp texture. Rachel Masters's contribution is distinguished.

Concerti Grossi 1 in B flat for Chamber Orchestra; 2 in G for String Orchestra; 3 for Woodwind, Brass & Strings; (i) Oboe Concerto
*** Chan. 8866. (i) Daniel; City of L. Sinfonia, Hickox

The improvisatory feeling and the changing moods of the *Oboe Concerto* are beautifully caught by Nicholas Daniel, with Hickox and the Sinfonia players providing admirable support. They then turn to the more extrovert and strongly contrasted *Concerti Grossi*, the first a miniature concerto for orchestra, the second in the ripest tradition of English string-writing. The third is a fine *in memoriam* for Sir Henry Wood. Excellent Chandos sound.

(i) *Piano Concerto 1. Symphony 1*
*** Chan. 9155. (i) Shelley; LSO, Hickox

Hickox's performance of the *First Symphony* is most compelling. The *First Piano Concerto* is also a flamboyant piece, in a single movement. Howard Shelley is a splendid soloist, fully up to the rhetoric and touching the listener when the passion subsides, creating a haunting stillness at the very end. Again splendid recording.

(i) *Piano Concerto 2. Sinfonietta for Strings; Symphony 5 (Hydriotaphia)*
*** Chan. 9196. (i) Shelley; LSO, Hickox

The *Piano Concerto 2* opens boldly and expansively and is romantically rhetorical, with sweeping use of the strings. The imaginative *Andante* is its highlight, but the jazzy 'fuoco' finale with its calm central section is overlong (13 minutes). Howard Shelley plays with brilliance and much sensitivity, and Alwyn admirers will be glad to have the work available on record, even if it is flawed. The cogent *Fifth Symphony* has its dense argument distilled into one movement with four sub-sections, and the work is dedicated to the memory of physician/philosopher Sir Thomas Browne (1605–82), whose writings were always on the composer's bedside table. The string writing of the *Sinfonietta for Strings* is very much in the English tradition and is hauntingly atmospheric. Hickox is consistently sympathetic, with the structure of the *Symphony* held in a strong grip.

(i) *Piano Concertos 1–2. Elizabethan Dances; Overture to a Masque.*
*** Chan. 9935. (i) Shelley; LSO, Hickox

The two piano concertos also now come coupled together with the *Elizabethan Dances* and *Overture to a Masque* to fill out the disc generously.

(i) *Violin Concerto. Symphony 3*
*** Chan. 9187. (i) Mordkovitch; LSO, Hickox

The *Violin Concerto* – so sympathetically played here by Lydia Mordkovitch – is discursive but has moments of intense beauty, especially at the rapt closing section of the first movement, where Mordkovitch plays exquisitely. Hickox's reading of the *Third Symphony* is very convincing, while the LSO again respond to a symphony that is strongly conceived, powerfully argued, consistently inventive and impressively laid out. The expansive Chandos recording suits both works admirably.

Film scores: *The Fallen Idol; The History of Mr Polly; Odd Man Out; The Rake's Progress: Calypso* (all restored and arr. Palmer)
*** Chan. 9243. LSO, Hickox

Unfortunately, all Alwyn's major film-scores were inadvertently destroyed at Pinewood Studios, and Christopher Palmer has had to return to the composer's sketches for these recordings. The result is impressive. *Odd Man Out* (about the IRA) has the most compellingly poignant music, but the lightweight *History of Mr Polly* is charming and *The Fallen Idol* sophisticated in its delineation of action and character. The orchestral playing is both warmly committed and polished, and the recording is out of Chandos's top drawer.

Film Scores, Vol. 2: *The Card: Suite. The Crimson Pirate; Desert Victory: Prologue & excerpts. Green Girdle; In Search of the Castaways: Rhumba; Waltz. State Secret: Main titles & excerpts.* (i) *Svengali: Libera me. Take My Life. The Winslow Boy: Suite*
*** Chan. 9959. BBC PO, Gamba; (i) with Bullock, Canzonetta

Alwyn worked in the British film industry when directors wanted quality writing for their background music. Alwyn's gifts made him an ideal source, and with the scores no longer in existence, Philip Lane's reconstructions from the original soundtracks are most welcome. In *Take My Life* Alwyn composed a pastiche aria for the operatic heroine and wrote a second for *Svengali*, both impressively sung by Susan Bullock. But the highlight here is the delightful suite compiled from the film of Arnold Bennett's *The Card*, with Alec Guinness as the whimsical hero. Both *In Search of the Castaways* and (especially) *Desert Victory* inspired Alwyn to some of his most atmospheric writing, all splendidly played here by the BBC Philharmonic under Rumon Gamba and given top-quality Chandos sound.

Film Scores: Vol. 3: *The Cure for Love: Waltz. Geordie: Suite. The Magic Box: Suite. The Million Poumd Note: Waltz. The Penn of Pennsylvania: Suite. The Rocking Horse Winner: The Ride. The Running Man: Suite. The Swiss Family Robinson: Suite. The True Glory: March. The Way Ahead: March*
*** Chan. 10349. BBC PO, Gamba

Volume Three of Chandos's Alwyn film music series brings more varied selections from the composer's many film scores. There is some particularly delicate writing (and playing) in *The Magic Box*, and the jolly and robust numbers, such as the *March* from *The Way Ahead*, or the *Waltz* from *The Cure for Love*, come off well too. The sinister *Last Ride* from *The Rocking Horse Winner* is a good reminder of a terrifying film. There is plenty of colour and variety on this CD, with the music from *The Penn of Pennsylvania* and *The Running Man* forming entertaining suites, and if the quality of invention isn't always of the composer's best, admirers of this composer, and film music buffs, will not be disappointed. Excellent sound and performances.

(i) *Lyra Angelica* (Harp Concerto). *Symphonies 2; 5 (Hydriotaphia)*
(BB) *** Naxos 8.557647. RLPO, Lloyd-Jones; (i) with Suzanne Willison

It is good to see that, with his centenary, William Alwyn is again enjoying new exposure on CD. The *Lyra Angelica* is a haunting and lyrical piece to which collectors will want to return. The symphonies have been recorded by Richard Hickox on Chandos, and now David Lloyd-Jones is bringing them within the more modest budgets of bargain-label collectors. Like his contemporary, Benjamin Frankel, Alwyn learned from writing for the cinema over a long period, which enabled him to gain both fluency and expertise in orchestration. His sound-world is individual within the post-Sibelian tradition and his music exerts a strong appeal. The *Second Symphony* (1953) is in two movements and is a well-argued piece with a real sense of the symphonic. The powerful single-movement *Fifth* (1973) takes its inspiration from Sir Thomas Browne's 'Urn Burial' or *Hydriotaphia – a Discourse of the Sepulchral Urns lately found in Norfolk!* Each section of the piece is prefaced by a quotation from the book. A strong piece, which is well served by David Lloyd-Jones and his orchestra, as well as by the Naxos recording team. This is a good record to start with for those beginning to explore the music of this highly rewarding composer.

Symphonies 1 & 2
(M) (***) Dutton mono CDSJB 1029. BBC SO, Barbirolli

The *First Symphony* was premièred by Barbirolli and the Hallé Orchestra at the 1950 Cheltenham Festival, but it was nearly three years before Barbirolli gave it in London with the LSO. Shortly before that, Sir John conducted a studio performance with the BBC Symphony Orchestra in Maida Vale Studio 1. In those days the Third Programme used to broadcast important concerts twice, and the present recording, taken from the first, conveys the freshness and commitment that these artists brought to this fine score. Sir John and the Hallé also gave the première of the *Second*, in Manchester in 1953, and the BBC, which in the 1950s used to invite major non-house orchestras for special repertoire, brought it into the Maida Vale Studios a few days later. Even if you have Alwyn's own recordings on Lyrita or either of the modern versions, this disc is an invaluable and authoritative document, and Dutton Laboratories get very good sound, considering the opaque quality normally associated with this venue.

Symphonies 1–4, 5 (Hydriotaphia); Sinfonietta for Strings
*** Chan. 9429 (3). LSO, Hickox

William Alwyn's five symphonies plus the expansive *Sinfonietta for Strings* are given outstanding performances from the LSO under Hickox to match the composer's own in natural understanding. The Chandos recordings are consistently up to the high standard of the house, and this set can be commended without reservation.

Symphony 2; Derby Day Overture; Fanfare for a Joyful Occasion; The Magic Island; Overture to a Masque
*** Chan. 9093. LSO, Hickox

Hickox's account of the Sibelian *Second Symphony* is very fine, and the Chandos digital recording provides full and expansive sound for brass and strings and a natural concert-hall balance. *The Magic Island* is a fine piece, inspired by *The Tempest*, and Hickox's account is beautifully played. The pithy *Derby Day Overture* has plenty of energy here, but the *Overture to a Masque* with its 'pipe and tabor' Elizabethan flavour is comparatively slight. The brilliant *Fanfare* ends the concert spectacularly.

Symphony 4; Elizabethan Dances; Festival March
*** Chan. 8902. LSO, Hickox

Richard Hickox's conception of the *Fourth* is marginally more spacious than the composer's own – as the timings of the outer movements demonstrate. Yet he has a masterly grip on the score. The *Elizabethan Suite* doesn't bridge the opposing styles of the times of the queens Elizabeth I and II too convincingly, but there is a graceful waltz, an engaging mock-morris dance and a pleasing pavane.

Symphony 4; Sinfonietta for strings
(BB) *** Naxos 8.557649. RLPO, Lloyd-Jones

In every way a worthy addition to David Lloyd-Jones's survey of the Alwyn symphonies, and those who have collected the companion issues need not hesitate. The *Sinfonietta* is a particularly fine work.

CHAMBER MUSIC

Concerto for Flute & 8 Wind Instruments; Music for 3 Players; Naiades Fantasy (Sonata for Flute & Harp); Suite for Oboe & Harp; Trio for Flute, Cello & Piano
*** Chan. 9152. Haffner Wind Ens. of L., Daniel, with Jones, Drake

Alwyn's *Concerto for Flute and Eight Wind Instruments* is richly textured, yet the consistent inner movement fascinates the ear. The charmingly pastoral *Suite for Oboe and Harp* is most delectably played by Nicholas Daniel (oboe) and Ieuan Jones (harp). The *Naiades Fantasy for Flute and Harp* is a chimerical piece in six movements. The final work is an equally attractive two-movement *Trio*. The Haffner Wind Ensemble are very impressive, both individually as solo personalities and as a team. The recording is admirably balanced and very realistic.

Crépuscule for Solo Harp; Divertimento for Solo Flute; Clarinet Sonata; Flute Sonata; Oboe Sonata; Sonata Impromptu for Violin & Viola
*** Chan. 9197. Haffner Wind Ens. of L. (members), Daniel; Drake

The *Oboe Sonata* is an inspired work; it is beautifully played here by Nicholas Daniel and Julius Drake. The *Clarinet Sonata* is a fantasy piece in which Joy Farrall combines extrovert freedom with a more thoughtful reserve, yet with wild excursions into the upper tessitura. By contrast the solo *Divertimento* for flute (the responsive Kate Hill) is neo-classical. The *Crépuscule* for solo harp (Ieuan Jones) is a quiet evocation of a cold, clear and frosty Christmas Eve. The *Sonata for Flute and Piano* and the *Sonata Impromptu for Violin and Viola* are no less striking. Overall, this programme is consistently rewarding and the recording is very real and immediate.

(i) Rhapsody for Piano Quartet. String Quartet 3; String Trio
*** Chan. 8440. (i) Willison; Qt of London

The *Third Quartet* is the most important work on this record; like its two predecessors, it is a concentrated and thoughtful piece of very considerable substance, elegiac in feeling. The playing of the Quartet of London throughout (and of David Willison in the *Rhapsody*) is both committed and persuasive. The recording brings the musicians vividly into one's living-room.

String Quartets 1 in D min.; 2 (Spring Waters)
**(*) Chan. 9219. Qt of London

Both *Quartets* are works of substance. The *First* has a probing, deeply felt first movement, a dancing, gossamer Scherzo and a profound, yearning *Andante*. Its companion comes 20 years later and derives its subtitle, *Spring Waters*, from Turgenev. Both works are well played and the performances are obviously felt and thoroughly committed. The digital recording sounds admirably natural, but the playing time is too short for a full-priced record (45 minutes).

PIANO MUSIC

Fantasy-Waltzes; Green Hills; Movements; Night Thoughts; Sonata alla toccata
*** Chan. 9825. Milford

Julian Milford plays the engaging *Fantasy-Waltzes* quite as persuasively as John Ogdon, his rubato particularly felicitous. He is given state-of-the-art recording. The *Sonata alla toccata*, too, is a most attractive work, with a single theme permeating all three movements. The vivacious finale is further enlivened by touches of syncopation, but ends with a very positive statement of the dominating chorale. The more turbulent *Movements* might be regarded as another sonata. It was the composer's first key work for the piano after a nervous breakdown, and it is dedicated to his wife, Mary. The second movement uses a 'tone row' but remains thoroughly accessible, while the *Devil's Reel* of the finale is in essence another formidable toccata laced with angular syncopations. After this the nostalgic *Night Thoughts* and the memorably tranquil *Green Hills* come as balm.

Fantasy-Waltzes; 12 Preludes
**(*) Chan. 8399. Ogdon

The *Fantasy-Waltzes* are highly attractive and are excellently played by John Ogdon, who is also responsible for a perceptive insert-note. The *Twelve Preludes* are equally fluent and inventive pieces that ought to be better known and well repay investigation. However, this reissue is expensive.

VOCAL MUSIC

(i) *Invocations;* (ii) *A Leave-Taking* (song-cycles)
*** Chan. 9220. (i) Gomez, Constable; (ii) Rolfe Johnson, Johnson

Alwyn shows a keen ear for matching word-movement in music with a free *arioso* style. Notable in the tenor cycle, *A Leave-Taking*, is *The Ocean Wood*, subtly evocative in its marine inspirations. The soprano cycle is almost equally distinguished, leading to a beautiful *Invocation to the Queen of Moonlight* which suits Jill Gomez's sensuous high soprano perfectly. Excellent performances, not least from the accompanists, and first-rate recording.

ANDERSON, Leroy (1908–75)

Belle of the Ball; The Bluebells of Scotland; Blue Tango; Chicken Reel; China Doll; Fiddle-Faddle; The First Day of Spring; The Girl in Satin; Horse and Buggy; Jazz Legato; Jazz Pizzicato; Phantom Regiment; Plink Plank Plunk!; Promenade; Saraband; Serenata; Sleigh Ride; Song of the Bells; Song of Jupiter; The Syncopated Clock; Summer Skies; The Typewriter; The Waltzing Cat
(M) *** Mercury **SACD** (ADD) 475 6942. Eastman-Rochester Pops O, Fennell

The bulk of these classic recordings were made in two sessions, in 1958 and 1964 respectively, with a couple of items dating from 1956, yet the sound is full and vivid throughout. The performances are superb, with a witty precision which is very attractive and, of course, an endless succession of rollickingly good tunes. In every way this CD is thoroughly recommendable.

Belle of the Ball; Blue Tango; Bugler's Holiday; Fiddle-Faddle; Forgotten Dreams; The Girl in Satin; Jazz Legato; Jazz Pizzicato; March of the Two Left Feet; The Penny Whistle Song; The Phantom Regiment; Plink, Plank, Plunk!; Promenade; Sandpaper Ballet; Saraband; Serenata; Sleigh Ride; The Syncopated Clock; Trumpeter's Lullaby; The Typewriter; The Waltzing Cat
(BB) ** Naxos 8.559125. O, Hayman

The Naxos disc is acceptable enough, but not distinctive. Richard Hayman's performances are good, but the recording lacks the presence and bite of the classic versions by Fennell and the Eastman-Rochester Pops Orchestra.

ANERIO, Felix (c. 1560–1614)

Motets: Ad te levavi; Christe redemptor omnium; Christus factus est; Magnificat quinti toni; Salve Regina III; Vidi speciosam
●→ (B) *** Hyp. CDH 55213. Westminster Cathedral Ch., O'Donnell – Giovanni ANERIO: *Requiem* ***

This disc is a real find, for it introduces music by two little-known brothers, born into a Roman musical family in the 1560s. Felix Anerio, the elder of the two, served as a choirboy at St Peter's under Palestrina, whom he eventually succeeded as composer to the Papal Chapel. His music is very much of its period, and richly communicative. The most famous piece here is *Christus factus est*, which is regularly found in anthologies (often not clearly attributed). It is a beautiful, homophonic piece, with its harmonic progression of appealing simplicity. The other motets here offer more elaborate part-writing, with effective interchanges for double choir. *Vidi speciosam* (a text from the Song of Songs with strikingly evocative imagery) and the four-voice Christmas hymn, *Christe redemptor omnium*, are immediately appealing examples. The more restrained and touching *Salve Regina* contrasts a high choir with a low one most distinctively, and the closing *Magnificat* shows Felix at his most ardently joyful. The performances and recording could hardly be bettered, and this disc is a marvellous bargain.

ANERIO, Giovanni Francesco
(c. 1567–1630)

Requiem (Missa Pro defunctis)
●→ (B) *** Hyp. CDH 55213. Westminster Cathedral Ch., O'Donnell – Felix ANERIO: *Motets* ***

Giovanni's career was less grand than that of his brother, for after singing in Rome he left for Poland in 1624, where he served King Sigismund until he died on a journey back to his homeland. Yet his *Requiem* setting (published in 1624) brings the same lyrical richness and flowing lines that are part of Palestrina's vocabulary. Yet it has its own individuality in treating the *Dies Irae* as its expressive centrepiece, alternating plainsong and polyphony. Then, after a poignant setting of the three-part *Agnus Dei* and a deeply felt *Libera me*, he very unusually ends the work with a brief but movingly serene *Kyrie in absolutione*. The performance is wonderfully responsive and, like the music of his brother, beautifully recorded in Westminster Cathedral.

ARÁMBARRI, Jesús (1902–60)

Fantasía española; 4 Impromptus; In memoriam (Elegy); Ofrenda; Preludio Gabon-zar sorgiñak (Witches on New Year's Eve); Viento sur (South Wind); (i) *8 Basque Songs*
(BB) ** Naxos 8.557275. Bilbao SO, Mena; (i) with Itxaro Mntxaka

Jesús Arámbarri is a Basque composer who studied composition in Paris with Dukas and conducting with Vladimir Golschmann and then with Felix Weingartner. On his return to Bilbao, Arámbarri spent the greater part of his time as a conductor; the majority of the pieces on this disc come from his early years, apart from *Elegía* (1939) and the *Ofrenda*, composed in 1946 on the death of Falla. Don't be put off by the rather crude *Preludio Gabon-zar sorgiñak* that begins the CD, as many of the other pieces are scored with great transparency and skill. There are reminders of Ravel and Falla, and some of the quicker, dance-like pieces sound like the work of a Basque Malcolm Arnold. Very slight but often attractive music here, and decent rather than distinguished performances and acceptable sound.

ARBÓS, Enrique Fernández (1863–1939)

(i) *Pieza de concurso* (for Cello & Piano); (ii) *3 Piezas originales en estilo español, Op. 1* (for Piano Trio); (iii)

Tango, Op. 2; (iv) 4 canciones para la marquesa de Bolaños, Op. 4; 6 rimas de Gustavo Adolfo Bécquer, Op. 3

*(*) Verso VRS 2017. (i) Ramos, Chavaldas; (ii) Trio Bellas Artes; (iii) Malikian, Kradjian; (iv) Sánchez, Turina

This collection serves to introduce a name more familiar as that of an arranger/orchestrator (notably of the *Iberia Suite* of Albéniz) who was also, for 35 years, a celebrated conductor of the Madrid Symphony Orchestra. This disc is described as Arbós's 'complete chamber works', but in fact it includes two sets of songs which are more distinctive. These are full of local colour, and Emilio Sánchez (very well accompanied by Fernando Turina) sings them with much Latin temperament, vividly and idiomatically. But in his fervour he forces his voice at *fortissimos*, and not everyone will take to this (we didn't). The *Three Original Pieces* for piano trio (*Bolero, Habanera* and *Seguidillas gitanas*) are little more than salon music, flashily colourful but not very substantial, although they are well played. The piece for cello and piano sounds rather wan on the bow of Rafael Ramos. Easily the most memorable item here is the well-known *Tango*, a catchy display piece, appropriately dedicated to Sarasate, and that comes off well. The recording is serviceable but not flattering (except to the piano).

ARENSKY, Anton (1861–1906)

Suites: 1 in G min., Op. 7; 2 (Silhouettes), Op. 23; 3 (Variations in C), Op. 33

(BB) **(*) Naxos 8.553768. Moscow SO, Yablonsky.

What a good idea to put Arensky's attractive orchestral *Suites* on a single CD. *Suite No. 1 in G minor* opens with a Russian theme with variations, and the Russian feel continues in the ensuing three dance numbers, with a bright Scherzo in the middle. *Suite No. 2, Silhouettes*, the best known, is a suite of character studies: *The Scholar, The Coquette, The Buffoon*, etc.; each has generous invention (there's an especially beautiful number for *The Dreamer*), and the finale is a lively portrait of *The Dancer. Suite No. 3* is a set of variations (mainly dance forms), brightly coloured, the *Andante* theme itself beginning in a romantic, chorale style and ending as a lively *Polonaise*. The performances are good and enthusiastic, if not always refined, and while it all emerges quite vividly the (1995) sound lacks the richness and depth of the best recordings. A highly enjoyable disc, nevertheless.

ARMSTRONG, Thomas (1898–1994)

Sinfonietta; Fantasy Quintet; Vocal music: (i, ii) Friends Departed; (ii) Never Weather-beaten Sail; O Mortal Folk; (ii, iii) A Passer-by; (ii) She Is Not Fair to Outward View; Sweet Day; With Margerain Gentle.

*** Chan. 9657. LPO, Daniel; with (i) Watson; (ii) LPO Ch.; (iii) Varcoe

As a distinguished academic Sir Thomas Armstrong was a key figure in British musical life. In their echoes of English choral music from Parry to Vaughan Williams, and Holst by way of Delius, both *A Passer-by* (with baritone soloist) and *Friends Departed* (with soprano) have an immediate impact, passionate, not academic. The *Fantasy Quintet* and the *Sinfonietta* are even more sensuous yet amiable pieces, and the six part-songs are beautifully written too. Paul Daniel is a most

persuasive advocate in the big pieces, and the recording is warm and atmospheric.

ARNELL, Richard (born 1917)

Symphony 3. The New Age: Overture

(M) *** Dutton CDLX 7161. RSNO, Martin Yates

This is good news. The neglect of the symphonies of Richard Arnell has been nothing short of scandalous. The *Fourth* was championed at the Cheltenham Festival in 1950 or thereabouts, and Beecham made a classic recording of his elegant and often touching ballet, *Punch and the Fool*. The *Third Symphony* was written during the war in New York and is a powerfully conceived and inventive score, albeit at 60 minutes a bit overlong. We understand that plans are afoot to record all the Arnell symphonies on Toccata Records, and they should begin to appear during the lifetime of this volume and before the composer's ninetieth birthday in 2007. Very good recording and an impressive performance.

ARRIAGA, Juan (1806–26)

String Quartets 1 in D min.; 2 in A; 3 in E flat

(BB) *** Naxos 8.557628. Camerata Boccherini

Despite their musical quality, the three quartets of Arriaga ('the Spanish Mozart') are seldom heard in the recital room. Arriaga died when he was only nineteen, and these pieces were composed after he moved to Paris in 1821 to be a pupil (and soon teaching assistant) to Fétis. They were published when he was 17 and have an astonishing assurance and miraculous purity of invention. They are within the tradition of the Mozart quartets and Beethoven's Op. 18, but they also have a Schubertian feel to them.

The Camerata Boccherini are thoroughly in sympathy with these delightful quartets and they play them on original instruments with vivacity, but never losing their elegance or expressive warmth. Indeed, the use of period instruments brings only a greater delicacy of texture, as at the opening of the *Pastorale* second movement of the *Third Quartet*. The mood then darkens, but lifts in the light-hearted finale. The performance of the *A major Quartet* is also particuarly engaging. Hitherto our first choice has rested with the Cuerteto Casals (HMI 1987038), but this new version is thoroughly recommendable in its own right, especially at Naxos price. The recording is admirably balanced and truthful.

ATTERBERG, Kurt (1887–1974)

Ballade and Passacaglia, Op. 38; (i) Piano Concerto in B flat min., Op. 37; Rhapsody for Piano & Orchestra, Op. 1.

*** CPO 999732-2. (i) Derwinger; N. German R. PO, Hanover, Rasilainen

The Finnish conductor Ari Rasilainen gives a very good account of the attractive *Ballade and Passacaglia*. The *Piano Concerto* is pure kitsch, the Rich Man's 'Warsaw Concerto'. The solo piano writing is unremitting and relentless, with hardly a minute's rest, and the work is overscored. Dan Franklin Smith recorded it for the ever-enterprising Sterling label, but this is the more subtle of the two performances. Even so, not even the artistry of Love Derwinger and the ardour of Rasilainen and the NordDeutscher Rundfunk Orchestra, Hanover, can save the day. Atterberg struggled for eight long years before finishing the *Piano Concerto*, but it remains one of his feeblest efforts. The *Rhapsody*, Op. 1, comes from 1908, the year after he began his studies in electrical engineering, and before he decided to opt for a musical career. It is an accomplished piece, Lisztian in character but very well crafted. The three stars are for the performers and the very acceptable recorded sound – not for the music.

Symphonies 1 in B min., Op. 3; 4 in G min. (Sinfonia piccola), Op. 14
*** CPO 999639-2. Frankfurt RSO, Rasilainen

Atterberg's *First Symphony* is naturally derivative, but none the worse for that. The *Fourth (Sinfonia piccola)* of 1918 is distinctly folksy but enjoyable, particularly in this committed performance. Anyone coming to these symphonies for the first time will find these performances well played and with the advantage of superior recorded sound.

Symphonies 2 in F, Op. 6; 5 in D min., Op. 20 (Sinfonia funèbre)
*** CPO 999565-2. Frankfurt RSO, Rasilainen

Ari Rasilainen's survey has maintained a generally high standard. The *Second Symphony* may be flawed (the composer was persuaded to add a finale to the original three movements) but there are many good things in it. The *Fifth Symphony* dates from 1922, the same year as Nielsen's *Fifth*, and though it is not to be mentioned (or even thought of) in the same breath, it is far from negligible. The finale does not wholly convince but, in spite of this, there is some deeply felt writing and the symphony as a whole must be numbered among the most successful of the canon. Good playing and recording.

Symphonies 3 in D (Västkustsbilder), Op. 10; 6 in C, Op. 31
*** CPO 999640-2. Hanover RSO, Rasilainen

The *Third (West Coast Pictures)* and the *Sixth* (the so-called *Dollar Symphony*, since it won the composer $10,000 in the 1928 Schubert Centenary Competition) are representative of the best in Atterberg's symphonic output. This issue maintains the high artistic and technical standards that Ari Rasilainen set in his earlier CPO recording of Nos. 1 and 4.

Symphony 6; Ballad without Words, Op. 56; A Värmland Rhapsody, Op. 36
** BIS CD 553. Norrköping SO, Hirokami

Atterberg's *Sixth Symphony* is a colourful and inventive score that deserves wide popularity. *A Värmland Rhapsody* is, appropriately enough, strongly folkloric. The *Ballad without Words* has many imaginative touches. The Norrköping orchestra includes many sensitive players, but the string-tone lacks weight and opulence. The recording is very clean.

Symphonies 7 (Sinfonia romantica), Op. 45; 8, Op. 48
*** CPO 999641-2 SW RSO, Stuttgart, Rasilainen
** Sterling CDS 1026-2. Malmö SO, Jurowski

No. 7 is the more impressive of the two symphonies. It draws on (or, in this instance, rescues) material from an earlier opera. It is romantic in feeling, a protest against the modernity of the times. The *Eighth* is less successful, even if the slow movement has some characteristically beautiful ideas. The finale is insufferably folksy. Ari Rasilainen and the Sudwestfunk Orchestra of Stuttgart give a very good account of both symphonies, more persuasive than Jurowski – though there is

not a great deal in it. The CPO recording is excellent.

Good playing from the Malmö orchestra and well-detailed recording, but this is very much second best.

(i) Symphony 9 (Sinfonia visionaria). Alven (The River), Op. 33
*** CPO 999913-2. NDR. PO, Rasilainen, with (i) Vihavainen, Suovanen, NDR. Ch., Prague Chamber Ch.

The *Ninth Symphony (Sinfonia visionaria)* is scored for two solo singers, chorus and orchestra, and is a setting of verses from the *Edda*. First performed in Helsinki in 1957 (Atterberg was very much a back number in 1950s and '60s Sweden) it did not receive a performance in his homeland until 1975, a year after his death, when it was given in Gothenburg. It is undoubtedly derivative (and a bit overblown) with lots of Strauss – and Wagner too, as one might expect from a work inspired by Norse mythology. But to be fair it is by no means as inflated as its immediate predecessors and, though there are naive touches (and one would welcome greater rhythmic variety), there are some imaginative – indeed, highly imaginative – passages. The level of inspiration is higher than in the *Seventh* and *Eighth Symphonies*, and both soloists and the fine NDR orchestra under their Finnish conductor give a dedicated performance.

The *River* is much earlier and was commissioned by the Gothenburg orchestra just after Atterberg scored a notable success with the *Sixth Symphony*. Comparisons have been made with Smetana's *Vltava* (doubtless because of the subject-matter and also perhaps because Smetana had been conductor in Gothenburg in the late 1850s), though they are very much in Smetana's favour. Be that as it may, this is an effective (if distinctly overlong) piece of post-romantic tone-painting – and it is very expertly laid out for the orchestra. Good recording and excellent notes.

AUBERT, Jacques (1689–1753)

Concerts de Simphonies for Violins, Flutes & Oboes: Suites: 2 in D; 5 in F; Concertos for 4 Violins, Cello & Bass Continuo: in D & G min., Op. 17/1 & 6; in E min. (Le Carillon), Op. 26/4
*** Chan. 0577. Coll. Mus. 90, Standage

Aubert was a contemporary of Rameau and Leclair; he possessed much of the former's melodic flair and feeling for orchestral colour and he shared the latter's interest in extending violin technique. The leader (here the inestimable Simon Standage) has most of the bravura; the other violin soloists are subservient, and sometimes the cello joins the solo team. The orchestral concertos are neatly scored and full of attractive ideas. The performances here are polished, refreshingly alive and invigorating, and the recording is first class. Well worth investigating.

AUERBACH, Lera (born 1937)

Lonely Suite (Ballet for a Lonely Violinist), Op. 70; Violin Sonata 2 (in one movt)
*** BIS CD 1592. Glutzman, Yoffe – SHOSTAKOVICH: *Violin Sonata; Jazz Suite 1* ***

The Russian-born composer and pianist Lera Auerbach emigrated to the United States after a concert tour in 1991. Her intriguingly titled *Lonely Suite* is dedicated to Vadim Glutzman, who does it full justice here. It is a highly theatrical series of miniatures: *Dancing with Oneself, Boredom, No Escape*, and so on, each strongly characterized and inventive.

She began writing the *Second Sonata* on 12 September 2001, a searching, obsessive work in a single movement, dominated by a striking main theme. It opens violently and is at times very angry, before it progresses to an improvisatory solo cadenza, leading into a highly atmospheric central *Adagio* lament and haunting funeral procession with bell-like parallel sevenths. The passionate protest returns and the rapt closing section is again based on the main theme. Glutzman plays it with great passion and feeling, well partnered by the excellent pianist, Angela Yoffe.

AUFSCHNAITER, Benedikt Anton (1665–1742)

Concors Discordia: Serenades 1–6
*** CPO 999457-2. L'Orféo Bar. O, Gaigg

These six *Serenades* are in essence elegant orchestral suites in the French style. Originally scored for strings alone, the composer commended the use of oboes or shawms, and bassoons, if 'among your musicians a few do a fine job of playing them'. So Michi Gaigg has taken him at his word and also included a recorder, to double up the string parts. They are given vigorous, polished performances. Although the somewhat edgy attack that the Orféo violins bring to allegros seems a shade over-enthusiastic, the ear soon adjusts when the contrasting dance movements are so graceful and amiable, and the wind playing is excellent. The recording too is warm and the acoustic unconfined.

AVALON, Robert (born 1955)

(i) *Piano Concerto, Op. 10;* (ii) *Flute & Harp Concerto, Op. 31*
**(*) Centaur CRC 2482. (i) composer; (ii) Meisenbach, Golden; Houston Foundation for Modern Music O, composer

The *Piano Concerto* of the Texan composer, Robert Avalon, is a large-scale, accessible work with an essentially lyrical core. The first movement is effectively written and scored, but at 20 minutes 26 seconds is a shade too long, although its invention does not really falter. The Scherzo is busy and light-hearted; the delicately atmospheric *Andante* is the work's highlight and is quite haunting; the finale sums up what has gone before and ends positively. The *Concerto for Flute and Harp*, written to be played either with string quartet or with string orchestra as here, is texturally attractive, but less tangible in melodic content. However, both works are very well played, with the composer a confident soloist in the *Piano Concerto*. The recording is first class, but it is a pity that the notes offer a 'press-type' interview with the composer, instead of offering his analysis of the music.

(i) *Flute Sonata, Op. 26;* (ii) *Violin Sonata;* (iii) *Sextet to Julia de Burgos, Op. 21*
☞ *** Centaur CRC 2430. (i) Meisenbach; (ii) Lewis; (iii) Lattimore, Ens.; composer

This is an outstanding CD in every respect. Both the *Violin* and *Flute Sonatas* are inspired works, profoundly lyrical, showing Avalon writing in a highly communicative and appealingly melodic style, yet with his own individual voice.

The Adagio of the *Violin Sonata* has real depth of feeling, and the brief *moto perpetuo* finale ends the piece with infectious brilliance. The *Flute Sonata* is also haunting from the first bar and has a memorably imaginative closing climax to cap the first movement, before the gentle melancholy of the flowing *Adagio*. With the composer at the piano, both performances are outstanding, conveying a natural spontaneity, as at a live performance. The *Sextet*, for soprano, string trio, flute and piano, was inspired by Casals, whom the composer greatly admires. A passionate setting of three extraordinarily intense poems by the Puerto Rican poet Julia de Burgos, it is remarkably colloquial in its Mediterranean style and atmosphere, with the instrumental writing just as ear-catching as the solo line, passionately declaimed here by Jonita Lattimore. The recordings are of great vividness and this collection is highly recommended.

BABADZHANIAN, Arno Harutyuni (1921–83)

Heroic Ballade; Nocturne
*** ASV CDDCA 984. Babakhanian, Armenian PO, Tjeknavorian – TJEKNAVORIAN: *Piano Concerto* ***

Babadzhanian won a Stalin Prize for the *Heroic Ballade* but, after a flamboyant opening, it turns out to be a rather engaging set of concertante variations. The writing is eclectic (mixing Armenian influences with Rachmaninov and water), returning to populist flamboyance at the close, but not before giving the soloist a chance to be poetically expressive. The performance is excellent, the recording vivid.

(i–iii) *Piano Trio in F sharp min.;* (ii, iii) *Violin Sonata in B flat min.* (Piano) (i) *Impromptu.*
*** Marco 8.225030. (i) Kuyumjian; (ii) Kavafian; (iii) Bagratuni

Both major works here show a strong lyrical impulse, plenty of ideas, recognizably Armenian in colouring, and an ability to create a cogent whole out of a loosely structured form. The volatile *Violin Sonata* (1959) has plenty of energy, but even the vibrant, syncopated finale gives way to a hauntingly nostalgic closing section – reminiscent of Shostakovich. The *Piano Trio* opens with a grave, sustained *Largo* (whose theme is to dominate the work) and it develops a passionate impetus of a very Russian kind. The catchy, syncopated finale has the energetic rhythmic drive we recognize in Khachaturian's better music, balanced by a warmly flowing secondary theme on the cello. The engaging *Impromptu* for piano acts as a cantabile encore. The performances here are fiercely passionate, but the players relax naturally into tenderness whenever needed. The recording is bright, full and well balanced.

BABBITT, Milton (born 1916)

Around the Horn; Beaten Paths; Homily; Melismata; None but the Lonely Flute; Play it again, Sam; Soli e Duettini; Whirled Series
(BB) *** Naxos 8.559259. Group for Contemporary Music

It is surprising to find a composer like Milton Babbitt, famed for his uncompromising intellectualism, offering a series of musical squibs that brim with energy and fun. Each of the items, all but three of them short, involves just one or two instruments, but teasingly Babbitt consistently uses the widest range available to each instrument, regularly in sudden switches from one register to another. At times it seems as though he is seeking to convey the impression that more than one instrument is involved, as in the two-movement piece, *Around the Horn* (for horn) or, even more strikingly, *None but the Lonely Flute*, with regularly alternating registers for the flute, the most flexible of instruments. *Beaten Paths* involves the marimba, and *Homily* a snare drum on its own. *Whirled Series* introduces a piano and saxophone, and *Soli e Duettini* flute and guitar, each seeming to ignore the other. A surprisingly attractive collection, superbly played and recorded.

BACEWICZ, Grażyna (1909–69)

String Quartet 4
*** Avie 2092. Szymanowski Qt – DVOŘÁK: *Quartet 14;* HAYDN: *Quartet 58* ***

Grażyna Bacewicz was born in Poland of a musical family (her two brothers were also composers). She studied both violin and composition at the Warsaw Conservatoire and came under the influence of Szymanowski, which is undoubtedly felt here. But he ensured that she went on to Paris, where she worked with Nadia Boulanger. She has written four symphonies and even more violin concertos and, on the evidence of this superb little quartet, they should be explored further.

It is the fourth quartet of seven, ambivalent in mood, moving from moments of introspection and mysticism to stimulating rhythmic pungency, and is often quite luscious in texture. But the invention is continually appealing and its *giocoso* finale, based on a Polish folk dance, is infectious, and has a subtle touch of humour. In short, it is a remarkably individual and rewarding piece, and it is played superbly here. The recording too is first class.

Violin Sonatas 2; 4 & 5; Capriccio; Oberek 1; Partita; Polish Capriccio
*** Chan. 10250. Kurkowicz, Chien

Grażyna Bacewicz was a prolific composer and a highly accomplished musician. She was good enough to be the soloist in both her violin and piano concertos, and her writing for both is highly idiomatic. (She competed in the 1935 Wieniawski Competition and was surpassed only by Ginette Neveu and David Oistrakh.) After studies in Warsaw as a pupil of Kazimierz Sikorski, at the same time reading philosophy in the university, she went to Paris, where she became a pupil of Nadia Boulanger. Her idiom remained 'conservative' and her writing purposeful, with some elements of Bartók or Martinů. The *Fourth Violin Sonata*, written in 1949, has touches of Prokofiev and Shostakovich. Not all the ideas of the *Fifth* or the other works on this disc are equally characterful or memorable, but there is enough here to make this issue worth investigating.

BACH, Carl Philipp Emanuel (1714–88)

Keyboard Concertos: in A min., Wq.26; E flat, Wq.40; Sonatina in C, Wq.101
** BIS CD 1487. Spányi (tangent piano), Opus X Ens., Mattson

Carl Philipp Emanuel was certainly resourceful, for the *A minor Concerto*, written in 1750, also exists in versions for flute and cello, and the *E flat major* work is an arrangement of

an oboe concerto. The *A minor Concerto* is notable for a lyrical *Andante*, whose course is interrupted by accented spurts from the strings; and its finale, in quick-march style, is very rhythmic too. The *E flat* work is more conventional, yet it is the *Sonatina* which catches the ear, with its scoring for flutes and horns, while the piano plays obbligato-like pasages, but has more of a dialogue in the *Polacca* finale. Miklós Spányi makes his usual spirited contribution, and the period-instrument performances are characteristically robust, very gruff in the *Sonatina*, where one feels that the ensemble tuttis might with advantage have been more refined, even less loud!

Sinfonia in G, Wq.182/1
(M) *** EuroArts Invitation **DVD** 2050746. Il Giardino Armonica, Antonini (V/D: Karina Fibich) – J. S. BACH: *Double & Triple Keyboard Concertos;* VIVALDI: *Violin Concerto in D* ***

Il Giardino Armonico, recorded live in the Vienna Grosse Musikvereinsaal, are on top form here, giving a first-rate and stimulatingly authentic account of one of C. P. E. Bach's finest *Hamburg Sinfonias*. The poised account of the *Poco Adagio* is particularly diverting. The *Sinfonia* is used as a centrepiece between the concertos. Straightforward camerawork and good recording; the couplings are good, too.

KEYBOARD MUSIC

Alla Polaccas: in C & D, Wq.116/4 & 6; Menuets I & II in E flat, D & C, Wq.116/1, 3 & 15; Polonaise in E flat, Wq.116/2; Sonatas: in A & B flat, Wq.65/37–39
** BIS CD 1329. Spányi (clavichord)

These dance movements are agreeable but not distinctive, although the pair of *Minuets in D* is rather attractive. Spányi plays them with commendable directness, but he tends to over-accentuate, specially in the *Polaccas*. He does the same thing in the opening movement of the *A major Sonata*, but the finale is pleasingly fluent, as is the equally appealing last movement of the *B flat major* work, and the contrastingly brilliant opening movement of the *E flat Sonata*. The sonatas all date from 1763. Good recording, but close.

Keyboard Sonatas: in D min., Wq.51/4; in F sharp min., Wq.52/4; in A, Wq.55/3; in E, Wq.65/29; in C, Wq.65/47; Rondos: in D min., Wq.61/4; in B flat, Wq.85/5
(BB) *** Naxos 8.557450. Hinterhuber (piano)

Christopher Hinterhuber has the full measure of Carl Philipp Emanuel's quirky keyboard style, with its sudden changes of mood and pace, and spurts of emotional intensity. The *D minor Sonata* opens the collection well, with its bravura outer movements and gently poised central *Largo sostenuto*, but it is the first movement of *F sharp minor* work that is the most striking example of C. P. E.'s 'Sturm und Drang'. Its swirling bravado passages alternate with more lyrically measured phrases, and after the graceful *Poco andante* comes an unpredictable finale. The other works are full of variety and character. The two *Rondos* are lively and engaging, the *B flat major* work particularly friendly, and Hinterhuber closes with a delightful *Cantabile* encore. Hinterhuber plays a modern piano with clear, pellucid tone, modest colouring, and an attractive control of light and shade. The Naxos recording is real and vivid, and this can be recommended alongside – but not in prefernce to – Pletnev's outstanding collection, which duplicates only one work (the stormy *F minor*, Wq.52/4) and was given a Rosette in our main volume (DG 459 614-2).

BACH, Johann Christian (1735–82)

Sinfonias concertantes: in B flat for Oboe, Violin, Cello, Fortepiano & Orchestra; in C for Flute, Oboe, Violin, Cello & Orchestra; in G for Fortepiano, 2 Violins, Cello & Orchestra; Cadenza in C for Oboe, Violin, Viola & Orchestra.
Fortepiano Concerto in G
**(*) CPO 999 845-2. Soloists, Hanover Band, Halstead

Of these two *Sinfonias concertantes*, the B flat major work is a mature piece from around 1780, using the soloists felicitously, but the invention is comparatively routine and the music springs completely into focus only in the vivacious Rondo finale, led by the solo piano. The *C major* work, from a few years earlier, is altogether different, with a really strong first movement and an equally inventive *Larghetto*, with the solo instruments all taking their colourful solos in turn. The swinging finale is delightful. The *Cadenza* is a most attractive miniature; but it was a pity that it was not used within the *Sinfonia concertante*, even though it was not designed for it. The 'Fortepiano Concerto' (really a fortepiano quartet) is also attractive, with a delicate central *Andante* and an elegant *Allegretto* finale, with a neat dialogue between piano and strings. Good performances, as ever, from this fine period-instrument ensemble and a well-balanced recording.

Sinfonia concertante in C for Flute, Oboe, Violin & Cello; Sinfonias: in G min., Op. 6/6; in E flat (for Double Orchestra); in D, Op. 18/1 & 4; Overture: Adriano in Siria
(M) **(*) Chan. 0713X. AAM, Standage

This is a mid-priced reissue of a collection discussed in our main *Guide*. The *G minor Sinfonia* is the key work here, showing J. C. Bach's imagination at full stretch. The other works are well played but less memorable.

Sinfonias concertantes: in A for Violin, Cello & Orchestra; in E flat for 2 Clarinets, Bassoon & Orchestra; in E flat for 2 Violins, 2 Violas, Cello & Orchestra; in G for 2 Violins, Cello & Orchestra
(BB) *** ASV Resonance CD RSN 3059. L. Festival O, Pople

The four *Sinfonias concertantes* recorded here are delightfully fresh and inventive. The performances are eminently vital and enthusiastic – this band is obviously composed of excellent players, and the recording is very bright and present. This is an invigorating disc that can be strongly recommended, especially at its modest price.

6 Symphonies for Wind Sextet (1782)
*** MDG 301 0434-2. Consortium Classicum

There is already a recommended recording of these *Symphonies for Wind Sextet*, by the London Wind Soloists under Jack Brymer, mentioned in our main volume. But good though that is, this new set from the Consortium Classicum, equally well played and beautifully recorded, has more warmth and charm, and a certain bucolic flavour from the horns, that make it even more enjoyable. A clear first choice, though not to be played all the way through at a single sitting.

BACH, Johann Sebastian (1685–1750)

The Art of Fugue, BWV 1080
(B) ** DHM/BMG 82876 70047-2 (2). Coll. Aur.

(B) (**) Divine Art mono 27804 (Arr. Roy Harris and Mary Norton, with conjectural completion composed by Sir Donald Tovey). Roth Qt & Tovey (piano)

The Collegium Aureum helped to pioneer the return to authentic textures with 'original instruments', but they sugared the pill a little by the use of a widely reverberant acoustic which serves to mellow Bach's fugal writing, although *Contrapunctus XIII* is performed on a pair of harpsichords (Fritz Neumeyer and Lilly Berger), and *Contrapuncti XIV–XVII* on a single instrument; the full group returning for *Contrapunctus XVIII*. The consistency of tempo throughout is an asset to this set, as the playing has plenty of warmth.

The great interest of the 1934/5 historic recording by the Roth Quartet (arranged by the American composer Roy Harris and Mary Norton) is its inclusion of the imposing conjectural ending composed and played here by Sir Donald Tovey on the piano. The performance sets off at a very similar tempo to that chosen by the Collegium Aureum and proceeds in a very relaxed fashion to *Contrapunctus XIV*, when Tovey continues to take this last fugue to a resoundingly positive close. The recording is a bit wan, with the upper range reduced owing to the filtering of backgound noise; if not absolutely secure it is acceptable enough, while the piano is real and vivid.

Brandenburg Concertos 1–6, BWV 1046–51 (DVD versions)
▶—●(M) *** EuroArts Invitation 2050916. Freiburg Bar. O, Von der Göltz
**(*) DG 073 4147 (5x1 DTS Surround Sound). Munich Bach O, Richter

The superb Freiburg set of the *Brandenburgs* (recorded in 2000) is highly praised in our main edition, and it is still an out-and-out first choice for these works on period instruments. It now arrives on EuroArts' mid-priced Invitation label and becomes even more recommendable. Recorded at Cöthen, where Bach composed the concertos, this set is musically and visually totally compelling.

We are astonished to find that Karl Richter's early set of *Brandenburgs* was recorded and filmed by DG 30 years earlier, in another visually attractive and appropriate venue (the Munich Schloss Schleißheim). Morover, the visual communication, as with so many concert DVDs, adds a completely new dimension to the listening experience. The video director, Arne Arnbom, is clearly a first-class musician, for he has arranged for his cameras to follow the players as they share the part-writing, which is remarkably illuminating. This is immediately obvious in the fully scored *First Concerto*, but is particularly striking in the *Sixth*, which is limited to a pair of violas in the concertino, while the ripieno group has just two gambas, double bass and harpsichord (Richter himself). In the rest of the works, where Bach used an orchestra of 18 players in Cöthen in 1719, Richter 'saw no reason to limit himself to these numbers' and used a full-scaled modern string group, at the same time adopting quite lively tempi, imbuing slow movements with warmth but without sentimentality. He draws superb playing from his orchestra, and the brightly lit recording is remarkably vivid and clear, with the various excellent soloists well focused in separate groups. Rhythmically, Richter is not as flexible as one would expect in more recent authentic versions, but the playing is always alert and vivacious, and in slow movements he allows a greater degree of expressive relaxation. The string-playing in the *Third Concerto* is glorious, and Richter, directing from the harpsichord, provides a brief link between the two outer movements, which have plenty of energy. But in the *Fifth Concerto*, with the spotlight on him, one is well aware that his solo contributon, although brilliant, is too heavy-handed. Nevertheless, the excellence and communication of the playing light up Bach's music in every bar, in what is now a historic approach to this music.

Brandenburg Concertos 1–6, BWV 1046–51

*** Naïve OP 30412 (2). Concerto Italiano, Alessandrini (with *Sinfonia* from *Cantata*, BWV 174, and DVD by Phillippe Béziat on the making of the recording)

(B) ** DHM 82876 70043-2 (2). Coll. Aur., Maier; Leonhardt (continuo).

Alessandrini and his Concerto Italiano seldom disappoint, and his new recording of the *Brandenburgs* goes to the top of the list. Tempi throughout seem unerringly right and the solo playing on period instruments is rich in baroque colour. The strings are bright and resilient without abrasiveness and the recording, made in March 2005 in the Rome Palazzo Farnese, has a most attractive ambience. It followed a concert tour during which the players got this music into their very beings, and their spontaneity here shows that they had in no way become stale or over-familiar with the repertoire. The set includes the cantata sinfonia in which Bach scored the opening movement of the *Third Brandenburg Concerto* for strings and also oboes and horns. A DVD on the making of the recording is included as a bonus, including interesting information about the music and the early instruments involved. This set can be recommended alongside Il Giardino Armonico, Pinnock, and Goodman, but our first choice remains with the superb DVD by the Freiburg Baroque Orchestra (EuroArts 2050916) – see above.

By the side of Pinnock, the approach of the Collegium Aureum, also using original instruments, is endearingly oldfashioned in its *espressivo*; the famous *Air*, for example, is restrained but exudes underlying warmth and feeling. Tempi are often similar to modern practice, although the slow introductions are measured. The woodwind instruments make some delightful baroque sounds, especially in Nos. 1 and 4. With the early trumpets, however, one has to accept moments of poor intonation in the upper register, something not banished from period performances in the mid-1960s, when this set was made. Just the same, the performances are enjoyable in their relaxed way.

(i) Brandenburg Concertos 1–6; (ii; iii) Harpsichord Concerto 7 in G min., BWV 1058; (ii; iv) Violin Concerto 2 in E, BWV 1042; (ii) Sinfonia from Cantata 42

(BB) (***) Dutton mono 2CDBP 9759 (2). (i) Boyd Neel String O, Neel; (ii) LCO, Bernard; with (iii) Malcolm (harpsichord); (iv) Da Vito (violin)

The Boyd Neel Orchestra made its concert début in 1933; the London Chamber Orchestra is a decade older, being founded in 1921. Both were to achieve standards in repertoire ('unsuitable for symphony orchestras', as Anthony Bernard put it) that had never been achieved in Britain before. There had been pioneering recordings of the *Brandenburgs* in Paris directed by Alfred Cortot, and later the 1935 78-set by the Busch Chamber Players set the standard for a decade. But when the Boyd Neel Orchestra made this recording for Decca between 1945 and 1947 *The Record Guide* declared it 'on the whole the best'. Certainly the Decca recording was of astonishingly natural quality. (In Mike Dutton's transfer it sounds most realistic through modern stereo equipment even today.)

The orchestral soloists, too, were of the very top rank – Frederick Grinke (lead violin), Léon Goossens and Evelyn Rothwell (oboe), Dennis Brain and Norman Del Mar (horn), Arthur Cleghorn and Gareth Morris (flute), George Eskdale (trumpet), Archie Camden (bassoon), while Kathleen Long played the solo keyboard part of No. 5 on the piano.

When one sits down to listen to the first concerto, one has an aural double-take at the very relaxed speed of the opening movement. But the ear adjusts almost immediately, and the sheer quality of the playing throughout, particularly of the soloists, and the feeling of 'live music-making' pervades the set, even though it was made in the studio. The string ripieno too is first class, and the performance of the *Third Concerto* is particularly spirited and joyous. (No link was provided between the two movements, as Decca were anxious to release the work complete on a single 78 disc.)

The recordings by Bernard and the London Chamber Orchestra (from 1949/50) are no less pleasurable, with George Malcolm the inimitable soloist in the *Harpsichord Concerto*, and Gioconda da Vito ravishing in the slow movement of the *E major Violin Concerto*. The recording is again of remarkably high quality, and overall this is a historic set to cherish.

(i) Brandenburg Concertos 2 & 4, BWV 1047 & 1050; (ii) Orchestral Suite 2 in B min., BWV 1067; (i; iii) Cantata 202 (Wedding Cantata)

(M) ** RCA (ADD) 82876 76222-2. (i) Levine & Ens.; (ii) Galway, Württemberg CO, Heilbronn, Faerber; (iii) Battle

A curious but rather engaging anthology. James Levine is obviously enjoying himself playing the harpsichord (especially in the bravura solo part of No. 5) in these spirited and fresh accounts of the pair of *Brandenburgs*. James Galway, too, is an excellent soloist in the *B minor Suite* but he is rather weighed down by the accompanying chamber orchestra, offering full-bodied modern-instrument string textures. Kathleen Battle then gives an unashamedly romantic performance of the cantata – but why not, when it was probably designed for a local wedding? Good recording.

(i) Brandenburg Concertos 1–3; (ii) Orchestral Suite 2 in B min.

(BB) **(*) HMV 5 86661-2. (i) OAE; (ii) Krueger, Boston Early Music Festival O, Parrott

(i) Brandenburg Concertos 4–6; (ii) Orchestral Suite 3 in D

(BB) **(*) HMV 5 86662-2. (i) OAE; (ii) Boston Early Music Festival O, Parrott

With the direction shared among four violinists (Monica Huggett (Nos. 2, 4 and 6), Catherine Mackintosh (No. 1), Alison Bury (No. 3) and Elizabeth Wallfisch (No. 5)), the Orchestra of the Age of Enlightenment presents an amiable period-instrument set of the *Brandenburgs*. These performances bring all the advantages of light, clear textures and no sense of haste, even when a movement is taken faster than has become traditional. With generally excellent recording this is certainly very good value, even if ensemble is not always absolutely crisp. The additional performances of the two favourite *Suites* from Parrott and his Boston players, with one instrument to a part, are similarly transparent in texture and rhythmically well sprung, with the balance again very well judged. The flautist Christopher Krueger is an outstanding soloist in No. 2, and this is a stimulating new look at much-recorded repertoire.

Brandenburg Concerto 5 in D, BWV 1050; (i) *Double Harpsichord Concerto 1 in C, BWV 1061;* (ii) *Orchestral Suite 2 in B min., BWV 1067*

(**) Cap. **SACD** Compatible Surround Sound 71 048. Berlin Academie für Alte Musik; with (i) Schornsheim & Alpermann; (ii) Ernst-Burghard Hilse

This was presumably intended by Capriccio to be a demonstration of three popular and contrasted Bach orchestral works in suround sound, but it doesn't come off on several counts. While the playing is first class, the performances themselves are eccentric. The first movement of the *Fifth Brandenburg* is breathlessly fast (and there is a slight edge on the violin timbre), yet the finale is delightfully nimble. By contrast, the tempi in the *B minor Orchestral Suite* are very relaxed, and the Overture sounds bass-heavy. The later dance movements, the *Bourrée, Polonaise* and *Menuet*, are beautifully played, yet are stylized (agreeably so), but the final *Badinerie* is surely too slow. In the *Double Harpsichord Concerto* (always difficult to get right) the harpsichord imagery is too puny against the resonant orchestral tutti and does not aurally separate into a pair of keyboards, because of the backward balance and the hall resonance.

Harpsichord Concertos: 1 in D min.; 2 in E; 3 in D, BWV 1052–4

**(*) CPO 999 989-2. Mortensen, Concerto Copenhagen

Lars Ulrik Mortensen is obviously going to provide an enjoyable (if not absolutely distinctive) new set of the solo concertos, for he is given spirited, expressive accompaniments by the Concerto Copenhagen. Among period-instrument performances this will be attractive for those who like a fairly robust though not heavy sound and style in outer movements, and a nimble soloist who is pleasingly thoughtful in slow movements. The *Siciliano* centrepiece of the *E major Concerto* is played with appealing simplicity. The recording is truthful and well balanced, with the harpsichord not too forward.

Clavier Concertos 1–7; Brandenburg Concerto 5; (i) *Triple Concerto in A min., BWV 1044*

*** Hyp. CDA 67307 (*Concertos 1 & 7; Brandenburg & Triple Concerto*); CDA 67308 (*Concertos 2–6*). Hewitt (piano), Australian CO, Tognetti; (i) with A. Mitchell

Angela Hewitt always has something new (and sometimes something surprising) to contribute to Bach's keyboard music, and the concertos are no exception. Using a small chamber orchestra, led and conducted by the admirable Richard Tognetti, she provides refreshingly lightweight performances, both texturally and in their style. Her playing is nimble, crisply articulated and small-scale, and she is perfectly balanced with the accompanying group. Yet first movements have striking energy (No. 1 attractively robust) and momentum, slow movements are expressive, but without any romantic emphasis. They are often quite delicate (as in the delightfully played *Siciliano* of the *E major*, No. 2), while the famous *Adagio* of the *F minor* could not be more poised in its cool beauty. No. 6 is, of course, another version of the *Fourth Brandenburg* and the opening movement swings along with strong rhythmic accents. No. 7 is better known as the *A minor Violin Concerto*, but in Hewitt's hands it works very well on the piano, if sounding more forthright.

It was appropriate to include also the *Fifth Brandenburg Concerto*, and here the *affettuoso* marking for the slow movement is also applied to the spirited *Gigue* finale (without loss of sparkle or pace), underpinned with some brilliant virtuosity from the keyboard. By contrast, the central *Adagio* of the *Triple Concerto* (marked *dolce*) brings a precise delicacy of articulation which is just as engaging. Throughout, the recording is most natural, wonderfully clear and transparent, and this set is very well worth exploring.

(i) *Harpsichord Concerto 1 in D min., BWV 1052;* (ii; iii) *Double Concerto for Oboe & Violin, BWV 1060;* (iii; iv) *Triple Concerto in A min. for Flute, Violin & Harpsichord, BWV 1044*

(B) ** DHM/BMG (ADD) 82876 70044-2. (i) Leonhardt; (ii) Hucke; (iii) Maier; (iv) Berthold Kuijken, Van Asperen; Coll. Aur.

With agreeably resonant recordings dating from 1965 (BWV 1052) and 1976, this collection might suit those who want the *Double* and *Triple Concertos* together on an inexpensive disc, for both are authentically played by expert soloists with notably sensitive accounts of each slow movement. The solo *Harpsichord Concerto* with Leonhardt comes off quite well too, but seems isolated here.

Double Clavier Concerto 2 in C, BWV 1061; (i) *Triple Clavier Concerto in D min., BWV 1063*

(M) **(*) EuroArts Invitation **DVD** 2050746. Katia & Marielle Labèque (fortepianos), (i) with Dantone; Il Giardino Armonico, Antonini (V/D: Karina Fibich) – c. p. e. BACH: *Sinfonia in G, Wq.182/1;* VIVALDI: *Violin Concerto in D ***

Katia and Marielle Labèque play very well in the *Double Concerto* but, disappointingly, the two fortepianos are placed closely together on the stage of the Musikvereinsaal and so there is no possibility of any antiphonal keyboard interplay. However, when they are joined by the excellent Ottavio Dantone, who plays brilliantly on the third instrument, the flow of music between the three soloists is most winningly displayed, and this performance of BWV 1063 is one of the most successful and enjoyable on record (provided you don't object to the gently audible vocalise from one of the pianists).

Oboe Concertos: in F (after BWV 1053); *in C* (after BWV 1055); *in G min.* (after BWV 1056 & BWV 156)

(BB) *** EMI Gemini (ADD) 3 50905-2 (2). De Vries, I Solisti di Zagreb – TELEMANN; VIVALDI: *Oboe Concertos ****

As can be seen in the listing, these are all transcriptions, but no harm in that when they sound so well on the oboe (a modern instrument). All three of Bach's memorable slow movements are played very beautifully by Han de Vries; indeed, the *Siciliano* of BWV 1053 is exquisite, and is made to sound as if written for the oboe. I Solisti di Zagreb provide most stylish accompaniments, and the recording is excellent (with the soloist fairly well forward). Altogther a delectable bargain anthology.

Concertante Oboe works: (i) *Sinfonias from Cantatas 12 & 156; Easter Oratorio: Sinfonia; Partita in G min.* (transcribed from *Partita in A min.* for unaccompanied Flute, BWV 1013); (ii) *Oboe Sonata in G min., BWV 1030b*

**(*) Crystal CD 726. Lucarelli, with (i) String Ens. & B. Brookshire; (ii) Stevens (harpsichord)

Humbert Lucarelli has found some additional concertante music for the oboe, and he filled in gaps with transcribed flute repertoire – the unaccompanied *Partita*, which he plays very flexibly, and the *Sonata*, with Dolores Stevens, both of which suit the oboe rather well – the *Largo e dolce* of the *Sonata* especially so. The *Sinfonias* are much prized in the cantatas from which they come, and the ravishing excerpt from the *Easter Oratorio*, the performance highlight of the disc, is most treasured of all. Altogether this is a pleasing anthology, sensitively presented, with subtle use of vibrato. The oboe image is very real and vivid, out front in the *Sinfonias*, where the string group accompanies responsively, but well integrated with the harpsichord in the *Sonata*. A useful collection, if not essential, except for oboe enthusiasts.

(i) *Violin Concertos 1 in A min.; 2 in E, BWV 1041–2; in G min.* (from *BWV 1056*); (i; ii) *Double Concerto for Violin and Oboe, BWV 1060.* (Unaccompanied) *Violin Partitas 1–3, BWV 1002, 1004 & 1006*
(B) ** Ph. 2 CD 475 7451 (2). Mullova, with (i) Mullova Ens.; (ii) Leleux

Viktoria Mullova's performances use modern instruments, but the transparent string-textures, with one instrument to a part, are very agreeable, and there is light, chimerical solo playing in allegros, with attractive buoyancy in the accompaniments. She phrases the famous cantabile melody in the *Largo* of BWV 1056 (an arrangement of the *F minor Harpsichord Concerto*) simply and pleasingly, although in the *Adagio* of the work for violin and oboe, in which she is joined by François Leleux, the line is rather less imaginatively flexible. The three solo *Partitas* are undeniably impressive, but anyone wanting these will surely want the *Sonatas* too. The recording is of good quality.

Violin Concertos 1–2;(i) Double Violin Concerto, BWV 1041–3;(ii) Double Concerto for Violin and Oboe, BWV 1060
**(*) DG 474 199-2. Hahn, with (i) Batjer; (ii) Vogel; LACO, Kahane
(BB) ** HMV 5 86663-2. Perlman, Israel PO, with (i) Zukerman; (ii) Ray Still

Athletically dynamic allegros and warmly expressive slow movements are Hilary Hahn's hallmarks in these stimulating period-instrument performances, most striking in the the two *Double Concertos*, where she is joined by Margaret Batjer and oboist Allan Vogel respectively. Jeffrey Kahane follows her style vividly (or does he set the swift pacing?) and the Los Angeles Chamber Orchestra articulates brilliantly. But some may feel the playing could ideally be a little more relaxed, although it is certainly vibrant and committed.

These Israel recordings, dry and close, are far less acceptable than Perlman's earlier versions of the concertos with the ECO under Barenboim (EMI Encore 5 74720-2 – see our main volume). Though he plays with imagination, and is heavier this time. The other concerto, the violin version of the *F minor Harpsichord Concerto*, is even heavier in the first two movements, with the *Largo* almost coming to a halt.

Orchestral Suites 1–4, BMW 1066–9
*** BIS **SACD** 1431 (Surround Sound/Compatible) (2). Japan Bach Coll., Suzuki

Like Pearlman in Boston before him, Suzuki alters the order of the *Suites*, only he elects to begin with the favourite *Third Suite in D*, followed by the *First in C* and then the *B minor Suite* (with Lilio Maeda the splendid solo flautist). These all fit on the first CD, and the second (included at no extra cost) is reserved for the *Fourth Suite*. Above all, these are exhilarating performances, for some of Suzuki's tempi are very fast, especially in the allegros of the *Overtures*. But by no means all: the famous *Air* of the *Third Suite* could not be more restrained and noble in feeling. The recording is spectacularly

realistic, especially in surround sound, which adds attractively to the ambient effect and gives a remarkable feeling of presence. So this BIS set can be recommended alongside Pearlman and the Boston Baroque on Telarc (CD 80619), whose tempi are less controversial.

Orchestral Suites 1–3, BWV 1066–8
(BB) **(*) Virgin Virgo 4 82118-2. ECO, Ledger

Philip Ledger directs fresh and stylish performances of the first three *Suites*, very well recorded, with his own harpsichord continuo placed rather more prominently than in most rival versions. However, Marriner on Decca offers all four *Suites* on a single CD (Decca 430 379-2) and this will obviously be a preferable bargain choice, except for those wanting a digital recording.

CHAMBER & INSTRUMENTAL MUSIC

(Unaccompanied) *Cello Suites 1–6, BWV 1007–12*
*** Virgin 5 45650-2. Truls Mørk
(BB) **(*) HMV (ADD) 5 86664-2 (1–3); 5 86665-2 (4–6). Paul Tortelier

Not only does the Norwegian cellist Truls Mørk possess a fine sense of line and a wonderfully rich and expressive tone, but he has imagination too, and a feeling for character. In short, fine fingers at the service of a fine mind. Readers will find these as musically satisfying as any rival accounts now before the public, and we are inclined to rank this newcomer second to none. Rostropovich on EMI is magnificent, of course, and both Fournier and Gendron are distinguished by aristocratic finesse and profound musicianship, but this truthfully recorded set belongs among the very best of recent versions.

The HMV reissue brings Tortelier's first stereo set of the Bach *Suites*, made at the beginning of the 1960s. His rhythmic grip is strong, his technique masterly and his intonation true. Yet at the same time there are touches of reticence – one is tempted to say inhibition: it is as if he is consciously resisting the temptation to give full rein to his musical and lyrical instinct. Comparing his *Sarabande* from the *D minor Suite* (No. 2) with Casals leaves no doubts as to the greater freedom, range and inwardness of the latter; Tortelier sounds very reserved by comparison. Nevertheless the faster movements are splendidly played and the *Prelude* to the *E flat major Suite* finds him at his most imposing. While his later (1982) set undoubtedly has a stronger profile (EMI 5 62878-2 [5 62879] – see our main volume), the present reissue is good value, and the recording is truthful, more sharply focused than the later, digital version.

(Unaccompanied) *Cello Suites 1–3, BWV 1007–9* (trans. for theorbo by Pascal Monteilhet)
(BB) *** Virgin 2x1 4 82094-2 (2). Monteilhet – VISÉE: *Suites de dances* (for theorbo) ***

These transcriptions are an unexpected success. Pascal Monteilhet's performances are consistently thoughtful and musical, and the intimacy of the music-making is very beguiling, throwing a whole new light on these remarkable works. The recording is wholly natural, in a most persuasive acoustic. A highly recommendable disc, with a fascinating mystery at the end of the *Third Suite*, where there is a six-minute silence following the final *Gigue* and then a brief cadential passage. This is explained in the note as follows: 'At the request of

Pascal Monteilhet, track 18 contains a "lost track of six minutes".

Viola da gamba Sonatas 1–3, BWV 1027–9
(B) **(*) DHM/BMG 82876 70045-2. Koch (viola da gamba), Leonhardt (harpsichord)
(B) **(*) HM Musique d'Abord. HMA 1951712. Quintana (viola da gamba), Frisch (harpsichord) (with *Sonata in G, BWV 1019*)

There is not a great deal to choose between the two new bargain sets of the three *Viola da gamba Sonatas*, although the Harmonia Mundi offer the more modern recording, and a bonus of a transcription of the *Violin and Harpsichord Sonata, BWV 1019*. The playing on both discs is pleasingly musical, but we are inclined marginally to prefer the Deutsche Harmonia Mundi/BMG performances, as Johannes Koch's timbre is that bit more firmly focused, and Gustav Leonhardt's harpsichord playing too is distinguished, very firm and clear.

(Unaccompanied) Violin Sonatas 1–3, BWV 1001, 1003 & 1005; Violin Partitas 1–3, BWV 1002, 1004 & 1006
⚹ ⊶ (M) *** EMI 4 76808-2 [4 76811-2] (2). Perlman
(M) *** Ph. (ADD) 475 7552 (2). Grumiaux
**(*) ECM 476 7291 (2). Kremer

Perlman's inspired survey, dating from 1986/7, has long been a top recommendation for the solo *Sonatas* and *Partitas*. Here he triumphantly demonstrates his insight in bringing out the deepest qualities of these six searching masterpieces, and this reissue is fully worthy of being included among EMI's 'Great Recordings of the Century'.

Arthur Grumiaux's fine performances were recorded in Berlin in 1960/61. Now they return, rightly assigned to Philips's new series of Originals and with the recording remastered. The venue offers a pleasingly warm background ambience against which the violin is forward, recorded in strong profile with complete realism, and with no microphonic exaggeration of the upper partials. He strikes just the right balance between expressive feeling and purity of style. Some may prefer a rhythmically faster, more charismatic approach, as with Perlman and Milstein for instance, but Grumiaux's simplicity of manner, without exaggerated temperament, lets the music unfold naturally, and his readings of all six works are the product of superlative technique and a refined musical intellect.

Gidon Kremer's approach is very different from Grumiaux's, with comparatively little ruminative inner feling. This is a bold, extrovert approach, gripping in its virtuosity, as in the dazzling *Presto* of the *First Sonata*. It is often gutsy, with the rasp of bow on string – witness the *Allemanda* of the *B minor Partita* – yet not without its reflective moments, as in the *Double* of the same work, while the bouncing *Corrente* of the *D minor Partita* is followed by a freely rhapsodical *Sarabande* and a light-hearted, beautifully pointed *Giga*. Kremer's sense of dramatic contrast is at its most effective in the famous *Chaconne*, where with free rubato and constantly varying tempo and dynamic (moments even of gentle pianissimo) he proceeds, with an unrelenting impulse, grippingly to the climax. The recording is superbly realistic and present, and in its way the set makes a compelling experience, for this is truly superb fiddling, full of spontaneous intensity. But it is not the whole story, and some may not respond to its emotional excesses.

(Unaccompanied) Violin Partita 2 in D min., BWV 1004
*** Sony SK 92938. Skride – BARTÓK: *Solo Violin Sonata*; YSAŸE: *Sonata 1* ***

Baiba Skride is a Latvian violinist now in her mid-twenties; she won the *Prix Concours* at the Queen Elisabeth Competition in Brussels in 2001 when she was nineteen. She has a flawless technique and makes a wonderful sound, and it is evident from all these pieces that she is a musician first and a virtuoso second: in short, an artist first and foremost. In the Bach *Partita* she brings great concentration and intelligence, and rather greater warmth than her compatriot, Gidon Kremer.

(Unaccompanied) Violin Sonata 3 in C, BWV 1005
(BB) (***) Naxos mono 8.111127. Y. Menuhin – ENESCU: *Violin Sonata 3*; PIZETTI: *Violin Sonata 1* (***)

Recorded in London in 1929 when Menuhin was a boy of 13, this serves as a reminder of just how remarkable a player he was in his youth. His celebrated LP set from the mid-1950s offers greater wisdom perhaps, but this is still pretty breathtaking. A Ward Marston transfer, which is a byword for the highest quality.

KEYBOARD MUSIC

The Art of Fugue, BWV 1080; Canons 1–4. Chromatic Fantasia and Fugue, BWV 903; Fantasia in A min., BWV 922; arr. of music for unaccompanied violin: Adagio in G min., BWV 968; Partita in E, BWV 1006a
*** Lyrichord LEMS 8048 (2). Troeger (clavichord)

There is no reason why *The Art of Fugue* should not be played on the clavichord, and Richard Troeger here offers its début on this relatively intimate instrument. It works well, and he provides enough variety of tempi and colour to keep the listener's attention. Moreover, he has decided to complete the final fugue himself, very simply and logically, in a passage of 40 bars, which is pehaps better than being left hanging in mid-air!

He adds the four *Canons* at the beginning of the second disc and follows with brilliant performances of the *Chromatic Fantasia and Fugue* and *A minor Fantasia*, used to frame his transcription of the *Violin Partita*, all of which sound very different from harpsichord or piano performances, and engagingly so. The recording is truthful and the discs come with excellent documentation.

Capriccio on the Departure of a Beloved Brother, BWV 992; Concerto in D after Vivaldi, Op. 3/9; Fantasias in C min., BWV 906 & 919; Goldberg Variations, BWV 988; 2-Part Inventions, BWV 772–86; 3-Part Inventions, BWV 787–801; Partita 2 in C min., BWV 826; Prelude, Fugue & Allegro in E flat, BWV 998; The Well-Tempered Clavier, Books I & II, BWV 846–93
(B) (***) RCA 82876 67891-2 (7) Wanda Landowska (harpsichord)

Wanda Landowska (in 1933) not only discovered and reintroducd Bach's complete *Goldberg Variations* to the European musical public, but soon afterwards she made its first recording. These are later recordings, made between 1945 and 1959. She favours a large, two-manual Pleyel harpsichord built especially for her, and at times she gives it a grand presence, but for the most part her playing is quite contained and is often expressive. At other times her virtuosity is very compelling. One must remember that she had to choose her own tempi, for when she was pioneering this music there was no precedent. She is not only convincing but she leads the ear forward most spontaneously. *The Well-Tempered Clavier* was recorded over a period (between 1949 and 1954) and still sounds marvellous. Her playing has a colour, vitality, authority and grandeur that make it difficult for one to stop listening. Styles in Bach playing have changed over the intervening 50 years – it would be strange if they had not – but this playing still carries all before it, and the CD transfers are very well managed.

Chromatic Fantasia and Fugue in D min., BWV 903; Chorale Preludes: Ich ruf zu dir, BWV 639; Nun komm' der Heiden Heiland, BWV 659 (both arr. Busoni); Fantasia in A min., BWV 922; Fantasia & Fugue in A min., BWV 922; Italian Concerto in F, BWV 971

(M) *** Ph. (ADD) 475 7760. Brendel (piano)

Brendel's fine Bach recital originally appeared in 1978. The performances are of the old school, with no attempt made to strive after harpsichord effects and with every piece creating a sound-world of its own. The *Italian Concerto* is particularly imposing, with a finely sustained sense of line and beautifully articulated rhythm. The original analogue recording was in every way truthful, and it sounds admirably present in this new CD remastering for Universal's extended series of Originals.

Chromatic Fantasia & Fugue, BWV 903; 4 Duets, BWV 802–5; Italian Concerto, BWV 970; Goldberg Variations; Partitas 1–6, BWV 825–30; in B min., BWV 831

✪ ☞ (B) Decca 475 7079 (4). Rousset (harpsichord)

Christophe Rousset's playing combines the selfless authority and scholarly dedication of such artists as Leonhardt and Gilbert with the flair of younger players. He plays a 1751 Hemsch, which is superbly recorded within a generous but not too resonant acoustic, so that the harpsichord is very real and apparent. On their original issue we placed the *Goldberg Variations* and the *Partitas* at the top of the list. In the former Rousset opens with an appealingly thoughtful account of the *Aria*, and the variations which follow are strong in character and consistently thoughtful. A playing time of 77 minutes ensures that repeats can be fully observed, and the playing has great freshness and spontaneity. The *Partitas*, too, have complete naturalness and are obviously, like the *Goldberg*, the product of a vital imagination.

(i) French Suites 1–6, BWV 812–17; (ii) English Suite 3, BWV 808; Italian Concerto, BWV 971

(BB) *** EMI Gemini 4 76933-2 (2). (i) Gavrilov; (ii) Bunin (piano)

Gavrilov's *French Suites* are full of interesting things, and there is some sophisticated – not to say masterly – pianism. In his hands the part-writing is keenly alive and the playing is full of subtle touches. He draws a wide range of tone and colour from the keyboard and employs a wider dynamic range than might be expected. There is an element of the self-conscious here, and a measure of exaggeration in some of the *Gigues*, but there is also much that is felicitous. The recording is excellent. Stanislav Bunin's two encores are also played with character; his style is bolder, less subtle in allegros, emphasized by more forward recording, but there is plenty of contrast in slow movements.

Goldberg Variations, BWV 988

(M) *** Decca 475 7508. A. Schiff (piano)

(BB) *(**) Warner Apex 0927 49979-2. Crossland (piano)

(BB) ** HMV 5 8 6666-2. Maria Tipo (piano)

Goldberg Variation, BWV 988; Goldberg Canons 1–12, 13, 14; BWV 1087

**(*) HMU 907 425.26 (2) Richard Egarr (harpsichord)

Goldberg Variations, BWV 988; Italian Concerto, BWV 971

(M) *** DG (ADD) 477 5902. Pinnock (harpsichord)

For the *Goldberg Variations* (in 1980) Trevor Pinnock used a Rückers dating from 1646, modified over a century later by Taskin, and restored most recently in 1968 by Hubert Bédard; and for the *Italian Concerto*, a year earlier, he chose a copy of a two-manual Dulcken. In the *Goldberg Variations* he retains repeats in more than half the variations – which seemed a good compromise in that variety is maintained, yet it meant that there was no necessity at the time of the recording for an additional LP. The playing is eminently vital and intelligent, with alert, finely articulated rhythm. If tempi are generally brisk in the *Goldberg*, there are few with which listeners are likely to quarrel, and Pinnock shows himself flexible and imaginative in the inward-looking variations, such as No. 25. The recording is very truthful and vivid.

It is good to see András Schiff's earlier, Decca piano recording returning in the same Universal series of Originals. It can receive enthusiatic advocacy, and in some respects is preferable to his later, premium-priced version on ECM, for the Decca digital recording is excellent in every way, clean and realistic, so that the part-writing emerges with splendid definition and subtlety. Schiff does not play as if he is performing a holy ritual, but with a keen sense of enjoyment of the piano's colour and sonority.

Jill Crossland's performance is characteristcally free and volatile. She takes the opening *Aria* very slowly (6' 17" with repeat) and is similarly lingering at its final reprise. Yet with the first variation she is off with the wind, and then articulates delicately in Variation 2, while Variation 5 is bold and robust. So it is throughout the work; after the delicacy of Variation 13, there is a complete contrast in the brilliant account of Variation 14. The famous *Adagio* of Variation 26 brings the slowest tempo of all (9' 43"), giving the music a sense of static, absorbed, peaceful reflection, while in her direct manner in the closing three variations she clearly has her sights on the contrast of the final reprise of the *Aria*, in which she is again completely absorbed. So this is an intensely personal reading, idiosyncratic and wayward, with which some listeners may not identify, but her integrity is in no doubt. The recording is very truthful.

In the note accompanying his recording, Richard Egarr tells us that his concern was 'to let this music sing and to keep free from rigidity'. In this he succeeds admirably, but the result is to give an almost improvisatory feel to the variations, and in this flexibility some of their individual sharpness of character is lost. In its softer focus, we found this account less convincing than Pinnock's, although the modern Dutch Latzman harpsichord (a copy of a Rückers) is beautifully recorded. As all repeats are played, a second disc was needed, so Egarr includes the recently discovered *Goldberg Canons*, which are simple and unexpectedly enjoyable. He multitracks the works that need more than a single pair of hands, and plays in duet with himself. The Harmonia Mundi presentation is most handsome, and the notes are exemplary.

Maria Tipo's recording was made in the Salle Wagram,

Paris. Her approach is freely romantic in spirit, with far from unpleasing variety and subtlety of tonal shading. She observes first repeats only (even so the CD runs to 64 minutes) and generally speaking the playing is free from expressive idiosyncrasy, with rubati not overdone, though variations 22 and 26 are an exception. The recording is fresh and immediate; but with Schiff's Decca account reissued at mid-price, this could hardly be a first recommendation, even for those who favour an uncompromisingly pianistic approach to this masterpiece.

Partitas 4 in D, BWV 828; 6 in E min., BWV 830
*** BIS CD 1330. Kempf

Poised, elegant playing from this young player, who is still in his twenties and is as much an artist as he is a pianist. Freddy Kempf is a stylist and the recording, made some four years ago at Nybrokajen 11, the old Musical Academy in Stockholm, is fresh and lifelike.

The Well-Tempered Clavier (48 Preludes & Fugues), BWV 846–93 (complete)
➡ *** Decca 475 6832 (3). Ashkenazy (piano)
(M) ((**(*)) DG mono 463 305-2 (4). Tureck (piano)

Having been fully occupied in his role as orchestral conductor, Ashkenazy has not recorded anything of substance on the piano for some years. But he returned to the studio (or, rather, to Potton Hall, Suffolk) on two occasions in 2004 and once in 2005, to record Bach's *Well-Tempered Clavier*. The result is an extraordinary *tour de force* in the variety of its pianism. Ashkenazy obviously prepared well and he thought deeply about every prelude and every fugue as an individual entity, and he also considered the way each pair links and brings a potential for contrast. While the consistent spontaneity of his playing often brings an improvisatory feeling in the *Preludes*, he is very economical in the matter of ornamentation, obviously preferring to leave well alone, rather than to over-embellish.

Obviously the keys in which the music is written mean something personal to him, and they influence the character of the performances. While the recording was made in chronological order, Ashkenazy characterizes each *Prelude* and *Fugue* individually, and the result is like an extended suite of keyboard pieces, of which every other one is fugal. The very opening *C major Prelude* is overwhelmingly expressive, but the following *Fugue* is simplicity itelf, yet with growing tension as it proceeds. The *C minor Prelude* is then dazzling in its bravura, a free fantasia, with accelerando as it reaches its climax and then pulling back, while the *Fugue* is then delectably clear and pointed. The *C sharp minor Prelude* is quite different, gently reflective, and its *Fugue* poignant and emotionally withdrawn, while the brilliantly nimble *moto perpetuo* of the *D major Prelude* sounds almost like Scarlatti, again contrasting with its bolder *Fugue*.

It has been suggested that Book II is less expressively distinct than Book I, yet if one samples Ashkenazy's approach to a select group, one still finds the same diversity. In the *F major* and *F minor* pairings, the *Preludes* are fluid, the *Fugues* bold and pointed; yet both *Prelude* and *Fugue in F sharp minor* flow peacefully; with the *G major* pairing, both the *Prelude* and *Fugue* bring bravura and strong articulation. Ashkenazy closes the final *B minor Fugue* positively; one feels he is suggesting that this is just one more piece in an endlessly fascinating cycle. He is very truthfully recorded, and his set has the added advantage of economy, in being complete on three CDs.

Rosalyn Tureck's classic mono recording, magnetic and concentrated, was made in New York in the early 1950s. The dry mono sound and limited dynamic range tend to exaggerate the muscularity of the playing, but the tonal contrasts are still brought out strongly, at times echoing in sharp staccato a harpsichord sound. Tureck's Bach is always special; even so, it is disconcerting to find her adopting such idiosyncratically slow speeds for some of the most formidable fugues of Book II. It has now been reissued by DG in their 'Critics' Choice' series. But this is more idiosyncratic than her later recordings, and the dry, mono sound and limited dynamic range reduce the appeal of this set (see our main volume).

The Well-Tempered Clavier, Book I, Preludes & Fugues 1–24, BWV 846–69
(BB) *** Virgin 2x1 3 49963-2 (2). Van Asperen (harpsichord)

Bob van Asperen was a pupil of Gustav Leonhardt, and his account of the 'Forty-eight' enshrines many of the finest of his master's qualities and outshines most of his rivals on CD. His playing is marked by consistent vitality, elegance and concentration; he plays every note as if he means it and he is refreshingly unmetronomic without being too free. He plays a 1728 harpsichord by Christian Zell from the Hamburg Museum, which the engiers capture vividly. The acoustic is modestly resonant, which is an advantage, and this set is strongly recommendable at its new bargain-basement price. No doubt Book II is to follow.

The Well-Tempered Clavier, Book II: Preludes and Fugues 25–48, BWV 870–93
*** Warner 2564 61940-2 (3). Barenboim (piano)

Barenboim has already given us Book I and this is discussed in our main *Guide* (Warner 2564 61553-2). For some reason his Book II is issued on three discs, but these are offered for the price of two. His performance is quite different from Ashkenazy in that the *Preludes and Fugues* are played not so much as individual movements as an ongoing personal discourse, full of drama and expressive feeling. His insights are undoubted, and the playing itself is very communicative and involving. As we said in discussing Book I, this is satisfying in its way, but is thoroughly self-absorbed. Barenboim is very well recorded, but Ashkenazy is concerned solely with Bach, and must be a clear first choice.

ORGAN MUSIC

Aria in F (from CORELLI: Trio Sonata), BWV 587; Chorale Preludes, Herzlich tut mich verlangen, BWV 727; Liebster Jesu, wir sind hier, BWV 731; O Mensch, bewein' dein' Sunde gross, BWV 622; Concerto in D min. (after VIVALDI, Op. 3/11); Fugue à la Gigue in G, BWV 577; Toccata, Adagio & Fugue in C, BWV 64; Toccata & Fugue in D min., BWV 565; Trio Sonata 5 in C, BWV 529
(BB) *** HMV 5 86667-2. Peter Hurford (organs of Martinkerk, Gröningen, Holland, or Ludgenkirche, Norden, Germany)

This excellent and inexpensive disc offers the same programme as is included in the two-disc set CfP 585 6302 discussed in our main volume.

VOCAL MUSIC

Volume VIII: *Cantatas 40; 46; 60; 64–5; 77; 81; 83; 89;*
Appendix 89a; 90; 109; 167
(M) *** Chall. CC 72208 (3). Röschmann, Von Magnus,
Bartosz, Dürmüller, Mertens

The eighth volume in Ton Koopman's admirable series (now
reissued on Challege Classics – see our main volume) brings
12 cantatas as well as the appendix to No. 89, *Was soll ich aus
dir machen, Ephraim?*. Like its two immediate predecessors
and Volume IX, below, it is devoted to the first annual cycle of
Leipzig cantatas from 1723–4, during a period of intense and
concentrated creativity. Koopman still sticks to solo voices in
the chorus of *Ich glaube, lieber Herr, hilf meinem* (BWV 109)
but, for the most part, the cantatas have the positive elements
of earlier sets (light accents and well-ventilated textures)
without too many of the negative ones (indifferent singing
and all-too-brisk tempi). Of the soloists, Dorothea
Röschmann has a radiant and glorious quality that enhances
the music's claims (try her in *Du sollst Gott, deinen Herren,
lieben,* BWV 77). The recorded sound is of pleasing clarity.

Volume IX: *Cantatas 37; 48; 66; 70; 86; 138; 153; 154; 166; 173a
(Durchlauchtster Leopold); 194*
(M) *** Chall. CC 72209 (3). Rubens, Stam, Larsson,
Landauer, Prégardien, Mertens

The Leipzig cycle continues here, the exception being *Durch-
lauchster Leopold,* BWV 173a, a secular cantata written in
Cöthen. It was reworked as a sacred cantata as *Erhötes Fleisch
und Blut,* BWV 173, and as such it is included in Volume VII
of the Koopman series (see our main survey). No. 66, *Erfreut
euch, ihr Herzen,* also originates from the composer's time in
Cöthen. Koopman's cycle continues to go from strength (or
near strength) to strength. The performances unfold effortlessly and with great naturalness; they were recorded in
Amsterdam in 1998 and have exemplary clarity and warmth,
and this could be applied equally to the interpretations. The
odd blemish – some suspect intonation from Sibylla Rubens
and the occasionally less-than-beautiful tone from the
counter-tenor Bernhard Landauer – does not detract from
the overall artistic excellence and depth that Koopman
achieves. His version of *Warum betrübst du dich,* BWV 138, is
among the most eloquent and searching readings he has
given us so far. This is an enjoyable and satisfying set,
enhanced by excellent, authoritative notes from Christoph
Wolff.

Volume XVIII: *Cantatas 36; 45; 47; 52; 55; 98; 137; 151; 157;
164; 187*
(M) *** Chall. CC 72218 (3). Piau, Rubens, Zomer, Bartosz,
Prégardien, Gilchrist, Mertens

Volume 18 is devoted exclusively to works from Bach's third
yearly Leipzig cycle, written in 1725–6. They often feature
lavish instrumental sections. No. 52, for instance, brings the
listener an aural double take by opening with the first movement of the *First Brandenburg Concerto!*; and there is much
memorable instrumental obbligato writing for the woodwind
throughout. Both *Lobe den Herren,* BWV 137, and *Ihr, die ihr
euch von Christo nennet,* BWV 164, feature a solo trumpet,
and in Cantata 47, *Wer sich selbst erhöhet,* which Sandrine
Piau and Klaus Mertens share so impressively, there is a
virtuoso concertante organ obbligato which Koopman himself plays very nimbly. There is also delightful writing for flute
and oboe in the *Cantata for the Feast of the Purification* (No.

157), which opens with a beautiful tenor/bass duet, *Ich lasse
dich nicht.* Indeed, the solo singing is excellent throughout.
Johannette Zomer sings the opening soprano aria in No. 151
quite delightfully. The spirited Klaus Mertens has a bravura
bass arioso, *Es werden viele zu mir sagen* in No. 45, and the
closing *Schwingt freudig euch empor,* BWV 36, brings some
fine singing from the chorus, but it also has a lovely soprano/
alto duet based on the chorale, *Nun komm, der Heiden
Heiland,* in which Sandrine Piau again participates engagingly alongside Bogna Bartosz. The recording is excellent
throughout.

*Cantata 51: Jauchzet Gott in allen Landen!; Cantata 210:
Aria: Spielt, ihr besellen Lieder. Aria: Alles mit Gott und
nichts ohn' ihn, BWV 1127*
*** BIS SACD 1471 (Surround Sound compatible). Sampson,
Bach Collegium, Japan, Masaaki Suzuki

On this latest disc in Suzuki's cantata series, apart from a
beautiful performance of the familiar solo cantata, *Jauchzet
Gott in allen Landen!,* Carolyn Sampson gives a ravishing
première of a newly discovered Bach aria which is undoubtedly authentic. More than that, it is Bach's only known
'strophic' aria. The text is by Burgermeister Johann Anthon
Mylius, praising Wilhelm Ernst, Duke of Saxony (his and
Bach's employer), on the occasion of his birthday in 1713. It
has 12 verses, all linked by the repeated opening phrase '*Alles
mit Gott und nichts ohn' ihn einher*', for which Bach provided
a catchy, melodic hook. The 12 stanzas make up a work of 48
minutes in length, a truly remarkable discovery, even though
it is repetitive, and the whole piece was probably not performed in its entirety on the occasion for which it was
originally written. Nevertheless, Carolyn Sampson, accompanied by Suzuki and his excellent players, does it full justice.
The recording is of the highest quality, and if you have a
surround sound SACD facility, you will be doubly impressed.

Cantatas 1, 22–3, 54, 127, 129 & 182
(M) *** Soli Deo Gloria SGD 118 (2). Holton, Hartelius,
Schubert, Stutzman, Gilchrist, Oxley, Harvey, Monteverdi
Ch., Trinity College, Cambridge, Ch., E. Bar. Sol., Gardiner

When DG decided they could no longer sustain John Eliot
Gardiner's ongoing pilgrimage to record all of Bach's cantatas
in various venues, he bravely decided to set up his own label
and underwrite the project himself. On the evidence of the
present collection, recorded live in King's College Chapel,
Cambridge, and Walpole St Peter in March 2000, the project
has proved successful on all counts. The cantatas here are
connected with the Annunciation and pre-Easter period of
Lent, including Palm Sunday, with *Wie schön leuchtet der
Morgenstern* the undoubted highlight. Performances are of a
high standard, especially with regard to the soloists, and while
ensemble cannot be as immaculate as it would be in the
studios, the extra vividness of 'live communication' more
than compensates.

Cantatas 63; 91; 121 & 133. Magnificat in E flat, BWV 243a
*** HM **SACD**: HMC 80 1781/2 (CD: 90 1781/2). Mields,
Sampson, Danz, Padmore, Kooy, Noack, Ghent Coll. Voc.,
Herreweghe

A splendid compilation of Christmas cantatas from 1723/4,
plus the glorious original version of the *Magnificat,* which
was also intended for Christmas Day. *Cantata 63, Christen,
äztet diesen Tag,* is equally jubilant and celebratory, richly
scored for brass; and the other cantatas offer considerable
variety of mood, reflecting Bach's remarkably varied musical

response to this special time in the Christian calendar. Apart from fine choral singing, the soloists are memorable, especially Carolyn Sampson, surely an ideal Bach soprano, Ingeborg Danz and Mark Padmore. Spectacular recording, especially on SACD, confirms this as a major issue in its field.

Cantatas (i) 80; 140; (ii) 147; 227

(BB) **(*) EMI Gemini (ADD) 4 76936-2 (2). (i) Ameling, J. Baker, Altmeyer, Sotin, S. German Madrigal Ch., Instrumental Consortium, Gönnenwein; (ii) Sutherland, Watts, Brown, Hemsley, Geraint Jones Singers & O, Jones

Two cantata LPs coupled together here; the one recorded earlier (with Geraint Jones) was a classic LP of *Cantatas 147* and *227* which dates from 1957, yet the sound is astonishingly good. Joan Sutherland is not associated with Bach (or with EMI!) but here she displays an unfamiliar facet of her vocal agility, making of Bach's tricky and tortuous melodic lines a memorably beautiful impression, rich in ornament and variety of texture. The other soloists sing with heart as well as voice, and their German is excellent. Thomas Hemsley deserves special praise in this respect, and he is almost matched by the impeccable clarity of Wilfred Brown's diction. The singers and orchestra give firm and buoyant support in the style of the day, and it is impossible not to respond to the vividness of the music-making. The second CD dates from 1967 and sounds acceptable in this transfer. Gönnenwein gives a reliable account of *Cantata No. 80*, using trumpets, believed to be added after Bach's death. The singing is sensitive, with the possible exception of the bass, whose tone is not wholly pleasing. *Cantata No. 140* makes an attractive coupling, with Janet Baker providing a small but distinguished contribution. The singing throughout is admirable and Gönnenwein secures good results on the whole, but he misses that touch of inspiration which the earlier Jones CD possesses; this performance plods along a bit, whereas the earlier account sounds fresher.

Cantatas 82 & 199

*** None. 7559 79692-2. Hunt Lieberson, O of Emmanuel Music, Craig Smith

The American mezzo, Lorraine Hunt Lieberson, with her rich, firmly focused timbre, enters the lists of the many distinguishd singers who have recorded *Ich habe genug*, and she emerges with flying colours. She is hardly less memorable in *Mein Herz schwimmt in Blut*. Deeply felt, these are performances of distinction, the vocal line movingly enhanced by infinite subtlety of colour and dynamic in both these masterly settings. Craig Smith and his Boston instrumental group are equally persuasive in support, as is the fine obbligato oboe d'amore soloist. Excellent recording ensures a most rewarding coupling.

Cantatas 202 (Wedding); 209: Non sa che sia dolore; 211 (Coffee Cantata); 212 (Peasant Cantata)

(B) ** DHM 82876 70046-2 (2). Ameling, Nimsgern, English, Coll. Aur., Peters

A potentially very attractive grouping is let down by uneven performances. Elly Ameling sings very well throughout, but she is at her radiant best in the *Wedding Cantata*, with a fine contribution from the oboist Helmut Hucke, and in *Non sa che sia dolore*, where Hans-Martin Linde's flute obbligato is another asset. Reinhard Peters directs these two works sensitively and with plenty of life, whereas his approach is plain-spun in the *Coffee* and *Peasant Cantatas*. Siegmund

Nimsgern's histrionic approach to the father's role in the *Coffee Cantata* is less appealing. The recording, from the mid- to late 1960s, is very acceptable.

Magnificat in D, BWV 243

☛ *** Telarc **SACD** 60651. Tamara Matthews, Deanne Meek, Mary Phillips, Boston Baroque, Pearlman – VIVALDI: *Gloria* ***

The opening of the new Telarc (Surround Sound) SACD from Martin Pearlman's Boston Baroque is immediately arresting. They use period instruments pleasingly and stylishly, with gleaming trumpets, and the result is most stimulating and enjoyable. If one gets the balance of the back speakers just right, the sense of presence in the warm hall acoustic is very real. All the soloists are excellent, and they blend beautifully when they sing together in the *Et misericordia* and *Suscepit Israel*. The fine oboe d'amore obbligato in the touching soprano solo, *Quia respexit*, is matched by the delightful contribution of the flutes in the alto aria, *Esurientes*. The choral singing is committedly expressive and, if not always precise in the runs, this is partly the effect of the warm acoustic which prevents absolute sharpness of focus. But the overall impression is wholly natural and Pearlman's tempi are aptly vivacious, while he draws the music together impressively for the closing *Gloria Patri* and *Sicut erat in principio*. The Vivaldi coupling is comparably successful.

(i–iv) Magnificat in D, BWV 243. Cantata Chorales: (v) Jesu, Joy of Man's desiring, from BWV 147; (i; vi) Sheep may safely graze, from BWV 208; (vii) Zion hört die Wächter singen, from BWV 140. (viii; ix) Ave Maria (arr. Gounod); (viii; iv) Bist du bei mir, BWV 508 (attrib. to Bach, but by H. STÖLZEL)

(BB) *** HMV (DDD/ADD) 5 86784-2. (i) Hendricks; (ii) Murray (iii) Rigby, Heilmann, Hynninen; ASMF Ch.; (iv) ASMF, Marriner; (v) King's College Ch., ASMF, Willcocks; (vi) C. P. E. Bach CO, Schreier; (vii) South German Madrigal Ch., Consortium Musicum, Gonnenwein; (viii) J. Baker; (ix) Ledger (organ) – VIVALDI: *Gloria in D, RV 589* ***

Marriner's recording, also coupled with Vivaldi's *Gloria* (praised in our main volume), now comes at budget price with some attractive encores. Though perhaps not a first choice, the performance can be recommended with confidence on all counts; the added chorales are all successfully sung and presented (the King's version of *Jesu, joy* the highlight), and many will be glad to have Dame Janet Baker's beautiful performance of *Ave Maria* in Gounod's romantic adaptation, plus the familiar *Bist du bei mir*, which turns out not to be by Bach at all.

Mass in B min., BWV 232 (DVD version)

** DG **DVD** 073 4148. (Compatible Surround Sound 5.1). Janowitz, Töpper, Laubenthal, Prey, Munich Bach Ch. & O, Karl Richter (V/D: Arn Arnbom)

Karl Richter's DVD recording dates from 1969 and is seen and heard against the beautiful baroque backcloth of the Klosterkirchein Diessen am Ammersee. The soloists are good (Herta Töpper is the least impressive) but not really outstanding, and the choral contribution is a little uneven – there is some poor intonation in *Qui tollis peccata mundi*, shown up by the obbligato flutes. But the orchestral playing is first rate, as is the recording; taken as a whole, this still has a lot going for it. The camera makes it very involving.

Mass in B min., BWV 232 (CD version)

(M) ** EMI (ADD) 4 76814-2 (2) [4 76817-2]. Giebel, J. Baker, Gedda, Prey, Crass, BBC Ch., New Philh. O, Klemperer

Although the CD remastering of the 1967 recording is impressively full and clear, Klemperer's performance is disappointing. Leaving aside any questions of authenticity of scale, the sobriety of his reading, with plodding tempi and a dogged observance of the *Neue Bach-Ausgabe* (Bärenreiter) utterly unornamented, was no doubt predictable. Only when the drama of the Mass takes over in the *Crucifixus* and *Et resurrexit* does the majesty of Klemperer's conception become apparent. Dame Janet Baker stands out among the soloists, with superb accounts of the *Qui sedes* and *Agnus Dei*. Whatever the initial shortcomings, however, the *Sanctus* (faster than usual) has wonderful momentum, the *Osanna* is genuinely joyful and the concluding sections of this sublime work come vividly to life. However, only Klemperer aficionados will feel this set worthy of being included among EMI's 'Great Recordings of the Century'.

Motets: *Singet dem Herrn ein Neues Lied; Der Geist hilft unsrer Schwachheit; Jesu, meine Freude; Der Gerechte Kommt um Fürchte dich nicht; Komm, Jesu, Komm; Lobet den Herrn; Sei Lob und Preis mit Ehren, BWV 225–31*

(BB) **(*) Virgin 2x1 4 82100-2 (2). Trebles of Hannover Boys' Ch., Hilliard Ens., L. Bar., Hillier – SCHÜTZ: *Der Schwanengesang ****

(BB) ** EMI Encore 3 41410-2. Eric Ericson Chamber Ch., Drottningholm Bar. Ens., Ericson

These works were for generations regarded as Bach's 'unaccompanied motets', though providing accompaniments is now regarded as the authentic course. Hillier opts for simple continuo instrumentation of cello, violone, organ and lute. That goes with small choral forces to match the intimate approach. The results are fresh, light and alert, thoughtful too; but the element of grandeur in the elaborate *Singet dem Herrn* is undermined. Very good, atmospheric sound.

The Ericson performances were recorded in St Thomas Church, Stockholm, and the sound is resonant and lacks a sharp focus. The well-blended performances are lively, rhythmically almost jaunty at times, although *Jesu, meine Freude* and *Komm, Jesu komm* have considerable expressive feeling, and *Fürchte dich nicht* flows pleasingly. But this is not a top choice when the sound is comparatively opaque.

St John Passion, BWV 245 (DVD versions)

🔊 (M) *** EuroArts Invitation **DVD** 2050396. Türk, Midori Suzuki, Blaze, Urano, MacLeod, Japan Bach Coll., Masaaki Suzuki (includes interview with conductor)

(*) DG **DVD (Compatible Surround Sound 5.1) 073 4112. Schreier, Schramm, Nimsgern, Donath, Hamari, Laubenthal, Engen, Munich Bach Ch. & O, Karl Richter (Video Producer: Harald Gericke)

There is a very distinct difference between Bach's two major Passion settings, with the St John's narrative compelling, above all, for its drama. The events begin to unfold from the very opening of the work, and the pace of the action is hardly held up by the chorales and arias. So a great deal depends on the Evangelist, who must keep the unfolding events moving forward spontaneously, at the same time conveying the full tragedy of the final outcome. This Gerd Türk does movingly in the superb set from Suzuki's Japanese Collegium, which now comes on EuroArt's Invitation label at a reduced cost.

Recorded in Suntory Hall, Tokyo, on 28 July 2000 – the day marking the 250th anniversary of Bach's death – this is an outstanding version on DVD, a tribute to the work of Masaaki Suzuki in Japan. In a brief interview which comes as a supplement he comments on the intensive training in period performance he undertook in Holland, and this performance consistently demonstrates the vigour and sensitivity of his approach to Bach. The interpretation remains very similar to Suzuki's earlier CD account on BIS, with fresh, light textures and generally brisk speeds which yet allow for depth of feeling, and the sense of occasion is irresistible. Only Gerd Türk as the Evangelist is presented as a soloist in front of the choir, giving an achingly beautiful performance, with his profound involvement all the more evident when seen as well as heard. Türk also sings the tenor arias, and the other soloists, all first rate, also have double roles, singing in the sixteen-strong choir (4-4-4-4) before stepping forward when needed as soloists: Stephan MacLeod singing Christus as well as the bass arias, Chiyuki Urano singing Pilate and other incidental solos, Robin Blaze a superb alto soloist and the ravishing Midori Suzuki in the two soprano arias. The leaflet offers minimal information and no text, though on DVD one can opt for subtitles in either the original German or the English translation, but not both together.

Karl Richter's performance on DG was recorded and filmed as long ago as 1969, but there is no sense of the recording being dated. Indeed, Arne Arnbom's camerawork is first class, vividly directing the eye as well as the ears. Richter uses large-scale forces of course, but the result, to unprejudiced ears, restores an all-but-lost tradition of Bach performance which has its own appeal, when the Evangelist, Horst Laubenthal, has a fine voice and is clear and direct in his narrative. Among the soloists, Helen Donath, in fine voice stands out, and Keith Engen is impressive too. However, Julia Hamari, good though she is, is no match for Robin Blaze in the alto solos. The video production is simple, with the placing of the chorus for the chorales especially effective. At the same time, a manuscript giving the German word appears on the screen; so if you have elected also to have the English subtitles, you have the best of both worlds. Altogether this is very involving, even if its competitor remains a clear first choice.

St Matthew Passion, BWV 244 (DVD version)

(*) DG **DVD 073 4149 (2). Schreier, Schramm, Nimsgern, Donath, Hamari, Laubenthal, Berry, Munich Bach Ch. & O, Karl Richter (V/D: Hugo Käch)

Richter used to be thought of as a somewhat dry, even prosaic interpreter of Bach, but this fine, moving and always stylish reading tells of warmth and affection. There is no attempt to create an antiphonal effect in the great opening chorus, and some may object to the use of a such a large body of strings. Yet their phrasing is flexible, the sound itself is glorious, and this performance has the feeling of a real spiritual experience, with outstanding contributions from the soloists, choir and orchestra. Peter Schreier makes a strong and sensitive Evangelist, narrating vividly; Ernst Schramm is a committed Jesus and Sigmund Nimsgern a striking Judas and Pilate. The dialogues between the principal characters are very well done, and the soprano and contralto arias, so important in this work, are movingly sung by Helen Donath and Julia Hamari. The recording was made over a period of nine days in May 1971, and the sets are plainly but effectively designed, with the chorales more intimately presented than the major choruses. The female chorus are attired plainly but strikingly, and the choristers sing without their music books, which adds to the feeling of dedication. The camerawork is

...dmirably managed, and the Video Director is to be con-...ratulated for the overall presentation, with its horizontal ...verhead symbol of the cross, which is surely in keeping with ...e spirit of Bach's masterpiece.

...: *Matthew Passion, BWV 244*
...) **(*) Ph. 475 7761 (3). Schreier, Adam, Popp, Lipovšek,
  Holl, Dresden Children's Ch., Leipzig R. Ch., Dresden State
  O, Schreier

...was an astonishing achievement of Peter Schreier to con-...uct this most exacting of choral works as well as taking the ...ading role of the Evangelist. His aim in Bach interpretation ...to bring new lightness without following the full dictates of ...uthentic performance, and in this he succeeds superbly, for ...s fondness for quick speeds is here kept in check. Such ...editative arias as the contralto's *Erbarme dich* or the ...prano's *Aus liebe* bring a natural gravity and depth of ...xpression, though Marjana Lipovšek has a tendency to sit on ...e flat side of the note, and Lucia Popp's silvery soprano is ...ot always caught at its sweetest. The end result is a refresh-...g and cohesive performance, since the recording is first rate, ...ith the choral forces well separated. The set has been out of ...e catalogue for some time but now returns, honoured with ...place among Universal's 'Originals', and it is certainly that.

...uitar Arrangements

horale Preludes: Jesu, joy of man's desiring: Wachet auf,
Schübler), BWV 645; Lute Suite 4 (from BWV 1006a);
artita (for unaccompanied Violin) 2, BWV 1004; Prelude,
ugue & Allegro, BWV 998
** Telarc CD 80584. David Russell (guitar)

...avid Russell has already given us a splendid disc of Spanish ...uitar music (see below, in Instrumental Recitals). Now he ...rns his attention to the stand-by of all guitarists, Bach ...anscriptions. We know he has that special gift of bringing ...usic spontaneously to life in the recording studio, and he ...ain displays it here so that the works for violin are almost ...ade to sound is if originally written for his instrument. The ...ance movements in the two (violin) *Partitas* come off with ...reat freshness, the *Sarabandes* engagingly flexible, but it is ...e famous *Chaconne* which catches the ear as Russell builds ...is climax unerringly. His final famous encore (*Jesu, joy of ...an's desiring*) matches the best-known *Schübler Chorale* in ...e way the *cantus firmus* is brought out clearly and firmly. ...ith excellent, truthful recording, the guitar not balanced ...o closely, this is a fine disc for the late evening, with a glass ...f wine to hand.

...iano Transcriptions

...omplete Bach Piano Transcriptions by Walter Rummel:
...rias from: *Cantatas 49, 68, 78 (Duet), 92, 94, 122, 126, 127,*
...1, 173a (London Serenata) & Magnificat. Chorales from
...antatas 4, 22, 26, 29 (Finale), 94 (Overture) & 129 (Finale).
horale Prelude from Christmas Oratorio. Chorus from
...antata 99. Obbligato for Harpsichord from Cantata 203;
vertures from Cantatas 26, 146 & 130 (Michaelis). Organ
reludes, BWV 614, BWV 731 & BWV 760. Sinfonia from
antata 12
...*(*) Hyp. CDA 67481/2. Jonathan Plowright (piano)

...Ve can compare Bach's chorales and arias to the rose win-...ows of cathedrals, in which reflections continually change ...om brilliant major to sombre minor. They constitute the ...manic element of his immense output and they speak to ...s like no other romanticism.' This was the credo of Walter

Rummel (1887–1953), whose transcriptions (published between 1922 and 1938) were among the first of their kind in devoting themselves almost entirely to Bach's vocal music.

Rummel was a truly fascinating figure, born and raised in Berlin of a musical family. He studied there until 1901 when, after his father's death, his mother moved to Washington, DC. But Rummel then returned to Berlin for five years, and studied the piano with Godowsky. In 1907 he became an American citizen, yet he made his début as composer back in Berlin, and his early songs were championed by such lumi-naries as Schumann-Heink, Maggie Teyte and John McCor-mack. In 1909, moving on to Paris, he soon became a friend of Debussy; he then married another pianist, and they became celebrities as a piano duo. It was then that his first transcriptions appeared, and as he expanded his solo career they became an important part of his wide repertoire. He was soon a much-celebrated soloist throughout Europe; he also visited London, where his Bach playing was critically acclaimed.

In some ways he was the Stokowski of his day, although his instrument was the piano, rather than the orchestra. But the inherent problem in his arrangements was the need to con-dense the complicated linear writing of the original works. He did this skilfully enough, and even if most of them still sound very prolix (if not quite in the flamboyant manner of Busoni and Liszt), he usually managed to bring out the *cantus firmus* impressively, and never better than in *Gelobet sei mein Gott*, the impressive chorale finale from Bach's *Cantata 130*. In the light-hearted *Mein gläubliches Herze, frohlocke, sing, scherze* he sounds almost like Percy Grainger, and the tran-scription of the charming *Serenata* from *Cantata 173* and the delicate version of *Esurientes implevit bonis* from the *Magnifi-cat* are very diverting.

The gentle, very romantic arrangement of *Die Seele ruht in Jesu Händen* from *Cantata 127* is another very extended example. *Vom Himmel hoch* (from the *Christmas Oratorio*) is similar (but shorter), and all these pieces (many of which were probably used by their arranger as encores) bring some lovely quiet playing from Jonathan Plowright, who is just as confident and convincing in the more prolix examples. He is very well recorded.

BACH, P. D. Q. (1807–1742?)

The Abduction of Figaro (opera; ed. Peter Schickele)
*** VAI **DVD** VAIDVD 4251. Kruger, Brustadt, Lloyd, Burt,
  Roy, Ferrante, Walsh, Lehr, Kaemmer, Ford, Minnesota Op.
  Ch., Corpse de Ballet & O, Peter Schickele (includes
  excerpts from *Concerto for Diverse Flutes* and 1972 TV
  Interview: Schickele in conversation with Gordon Hunt)

In the words of Peter Schickele, his amanuensis and creator (?), 'P. D. Q. Bach is the last and least of Johann Sebastian Bach's twenty-one children, a pimple on the face of music', with the unlikely dates (1807–1742). It is P. D. Q.'s 'master-piece', *The Abduction of Figaro*, which is recorded here in a 1984 live performance. Mr Schickele conducts it vivaciously himself in an undoubtedly first-class live performance by members of the Minnesota Opera.

After the cleverly contrived Overture, the opening scene mirrors that in *Gianni Schicchi*, with the key characters gathered round Figaro's bedside (the doctor dubious as to his survival) singing a preposterous opening ensemble, 'Found a peanut'. But this is immediately contrasted with Susanna's quite touching aria to her husband, 'Stay with me'. This establishes the basic style: Mozartian pastiche, drawing primarily on the five key operas, but also with a dash of *The Pirates of Penzance*, when Captain Kadd arrives and sails off with Figaro, still in his bed.

The sub-plot centres on Donald Giovanni's determination to elude the matrimonial ambitions of the no longer chaste Donna Anna, balanced by the pair of real lovers, the intendingly faithful but thwarted Pecadillo and the worldly-wise Blondie. In the extended final scene of Act II she tells the angrily thwarted Donna Anna, 'You show me a man who is faithful and I'll show you a man that's impotent'. Then she sings her spectacular coloratura aria, *Macho macho*, which begins very like Mozart's *Batti batti* and ends with the abrupt admonition, 'I kid you not'!

Act III, set in *A Magic Forest*, opens with a mock ballet sequence, made the more amusing because, despite various mishaps, it is danced so gracefully by the Minnesota *corpse de ballet*. By now all the principal characters have arrived on Pasha Shaboom's island, and Opec, the amiable male alto equivalent of Osmin, sings an aria that takes us straight into the Pasha's Seraglio, echoed even more recognizably by the Mozartian chorus that follows. Papa Geno and Mama Geno arrive to sing a mock Country-and-Western duet. But it is Schlepporello who stops the show by stealing the pirate treasure and demanding his chance to sing an aria, '*Why oh why?*', before he restores it for the grand finale.

The composer has a remarkable affinity with Mozartian vocal ensemble and part-writing, and this provides charming musical substance to offset the various extravagances and vulgarities of the text. Indeed, much of the P. D. Q. Bach music is memorable. The closing Quartet from Scene 1, *Love is gone*, Pedrillo's charming aria, *Behold Fair Maiden*, in Scene 2, the sparkling Scene 3 Sextet, *What a downer*, are all most enjoyable, while the famous Trio from *Così fan tutte* is obviously the derivation for the delightful quintet and ensemble that ends Act I. The duet, shared by Pecadillo and Donald Giovanni as they survive their shipwreck, *God be praised*, which opens Act II, is no less attractive.

The soloists are all excellent, with Marilyn Brustadt a formidable Donna Anna, and the elusive but warm-voiced Donald Giovanni (Michael Burt) making a splendid duo. Lisbeth Lloyd confidently reaches up into the coloratura stratosphere as the cynical Blondie, and the heady tenor of Bruce Edwin Ford as Peccadillo is a pleasure throughout.

When the curtain falls, we hear what became of all the characters after the story ended, including the surviving Figaro, who 'ended up in Paris where he founded a newspaper'. It is all nonsense – but very enjoyable nonsense, especially if one enters fully into the spirit of Peter Schickele's skilful parody. At the opening of the DVD he introduces, using his characteristic deadpan manner (which we encounter again in the Bonus Interview), his special creation/discovery (?) of the composer's music. However, the weaker humour of the bonus excerpts from the *Gross Concerto for Diverse Flutes*, all of which Schickele plays himself, just about raises a smile, though his instrumental expertise is remarkable.

BACH, Wilhelm Friedemann (1710–84)

Flute Sonatas: in E min. & F; 2 Sonatas for 2 Flutes in D; Fragment in A min., F.48–50; Trio Sonata in B flat for 2 Violins (all with bass continuo)
*** CPO 777 087-2. Camerata Köln

These agreeable works for a pair of flutes and continuo chortle along, with the finale of the *D major* work irrepressibly gay. The solo sonatas are also attractive, with the *E minor* especially inventive. The string *Trio Sonata* is not quite so striking but it provides central contrast, although the listing on the leaflet puts it in the wrong place. Fine performance and recording.

The BACH FAMILY, including Johann Sebastian

Johann Christoph (1642–1703)
Georg Christoph (1642–97)
Johann Michael (1648–94)
Johann Ludwig (1677–1731)
Johann Sebastian (1685–1750)
Wilhelm Friedemann (1710–84)
Carl Philipp Emanuel (1714–88)
Johann Ernst (1722–77)
Johann Christoph Friedrich (1732–95)
Johann Christian (1735–82)

'*Sacred Music of the Bach Family*': (i) Disc 1: J. S. BACH: Motets, BWV 225, 227, 228, 229, 230, 315, 356, 361, 434; *Magnificat, BWV 243*: Choruses: *Vom Himmel Hoch; Freut euch und jubiliert; Gloria in excelsis Deo*

Disc 2: (ii) C. P. E. BACH: *Gott hat den Herrn auferwecket*, Wq.244; *Easter Cantata*, Wq.217; *Wer ist so würdig als du*, Wq.222; *Anbetung dem Erbarmer*, Wq.243

Disc 3: (ii) Johann Christian Friedrich BACH: Motet: *Wachet auf;* Chorale; *Die Kindheit Jesu*. Johann Ernst BACH: Motet: *Meine Seele erhebt den Herrn; Das Vertrauen der Christen auf Gott*

Disc 4: (ii; iii) Johann Ludwig BACH: Motet: *Gedenke meiner, mein Gott; Trauermusik:* Final Chorus. Johann Christian BACH: *Tantum ergo*. Wilhelm Friedemann BACH: *Cantata for Easter Sunday: Erzitert und fallet*

Disc 5: (iv) Cantatas from the Alten Archive: (i) Georg Christoph BACH: *Siehe, wie fin und lieblich ist*. Johann Christoph BACH: *Mein Freudin, du bist schön*. Johann Michael BACH: *Ach bleib bei uns, Herr Jesu Christ; Ach wie sehnlich wart*.

(B) **(*) Cap. 49432 (5). (i) Rostock Motet Ch., Leipzig, or Capella Fidicinia, Eschenberg; (ii) Soloists, Rheinische Kantorei, Das Kleine Konzert, Max; (iii) Dresden Chamber Ch., La Stagione Frankfurt, Schneider; (iv) Leipzig Capella Fidicinia, Grüss

This Capriccio set provides what is described as 'Sacred music of the Bach family' but, unlike other compilations of its kind discussed in our main volume which concentrate on the unknown and little-known Bach relatives, here two of the five discs are devoted to Johann Sebastian himself, and his number one son, Carl Philipp Emanuel. On Disc 1, the collection of familiar Bach *Chorales* and *Motets* is framed by the *Singet dem Herrn* and *Jesu meine Freude*. They are sung by two different choirs, and it is not clear who sings what. But because of the resonance, the recording generally is less sharply focused than in the rest of the collection, although the ambience is pleasing.

The second disc offers three outstanding cantatas by Carl Philipp Emanuel, including an inspired *Easter Cantata* which has many good things to offer, not least the lovely extended soprano aria, with its delightful fluting, delectably sung here by Martina Lins. The work then closes with a noble performance of the chorale, *O süsser Herre Jesu Christ*. This is followed by *Helig* ('Holy') an intensely devotional work for contralto soloist (Hilke Helling), two choirs and two orchestras. The soloist opens the work freshly, and then the chorus creates a powerfully atmospheric sonority before setting off into the exhilaratingly fugal *Helig ist Gott* with the cantus firmus ringing out clearly. *Anbetung dem Erbarmer* was another work written for Easter, again devotional in feeling, and powerfully expressive from the opening chorus onwards. This closes exultantly, then each of the four soloists is featured in turn. The soprano's brilliant *Sei gegrüsset* then prepares the way for the vigorous closing chorus and chorale.

The fourth disc is outstanding in every way and deserves a separate reissue. Alas, our copy had the wrong documentation (duplicating details of the J. S. Bach motets on disc 1). The music, however, is all of the very highest quality, including two remarkably fine works by Bach's distant cousin, Johann Ludwig. The first is an ambitious eight-voiced motet for double choir, with male and female voices answering each other movingly, and with a particularly fine close. His spectacular *Trauermusik* is even more impressive, the orchestration brilliantly laced with trumpets and leading to a strophic presentation of the memorable chorale on which it is based.

J. C. Bach's *Tantum ergo* is in two parts, the first an eloquent soprano aria, beautifully sung by Barbara Schlick, with an engaging flute obbligato and effective use of the horns, leading to a fully scored, exultant second section for four soloists, choir and orchestra. Wilhelm Friedemann's Easter Sunday cantata is most ambitious of all. In seven sections, framed by writing for joyous celebratory trumpets, it includes an ardently sung tenor aria (Wilfried Jochens) with recorders, and an even finer soprano/tenor duet with an oboe obbligato.

The works on the third disc have famous chorales as their basis, and are most effectively written and persuasively performed, yet none stands out. Johann Ernst's German *Magnificat, Meine Seele erhebt den Herren*, has two (well-sung) solo movements for soprano, and a duet with the contralto (Silke Weisheit), but is most notable for the richness of the choral writing, with the opening five-part chorus especially commanding. *Das Vertrauen der Christen* is a freely poetic adaptation of Psalm 77 and has a very striking finale. The motet by Johann Christoph Friedrich is similarly well wrought, but less imposing than the final chorus of *Die Kindheit Jesu*, which closes the disc.

The cantatas on the fifth disc all come from Johann Sebastian's own family archive. Georg Christoph's *Siehe, wie fin und lieblich ist* is a pleasing little dialogue cantata for two tenors and a bass, a cheerful, good-natured work, only seven minutes long. Of the two cantatas by Johann Michael the first is an ensemble cantata, appealing but not distinctive, but the following *Ach wie sehnlich wart'ich der Zeit* is a delightful solo cantata, with a repeated 'refrain' which Gisela Burkhardt sings with pure, sweet tone. However, the key work here is Johann Christoph's *Wedding Cantata*. Johann Sebastian must have thought highly of it, as the manuscript has a cover written in his own hand. The text draws on the vivid word-imagery of Solomon's Song of Songs and tells of a prospective bride wandering alone in the garden, discovered by two of the male guests. They offer to go with her to look for her beloved, and the final meeting leads to a joyous outcome, with the mood of the music changing from dolorous exchanges (with Gisela Burkhardt again dominating the

expressive writing) to a sparklingly happy final quartet.

Altogether this is a very worthwhile set, with the one great drawback that the documentation is disgracefully poor, with no texts or translations and little detail as to what the various cantatas are all about!

BAGUER, Carlos (1768–1808)

Symphonies 12 in E flat; 13 in E flat; 16 in G; 18 in B flat
*** Chan. 9456. LMP, Bamert

The Catalan composer Carlos Baguer was born in Barcelona and spent his musical life there. The orchestra of the Barcelona Opera gave evening concerts, to which symphonies were introduced in the 1780s, and those of Haydn were to dominate the musical scene from 1782 onwards. Baguer soon adopted the four-movement Haydn pattern, and these symphonies date from a decade later. The craftsmanship is sound but conventional, as is the scoring, although there is some pleasingly assured invention. Although there is a certain warm graciousness to the writing, it is perhaps surprising that there is no local colour and no gypsy influences, not even in the finales. The performances here are nicely turned and beautifully recorded in the best Chandos manner.

BAINES, William (1899–1922)

The Chimes; Coloured Leaves; Etude in F sharp min.; Idyll;
The Naiad; Paradise Gardens; 7 Preludes; Silverpoints; Tides;
Twilight Pieces
*** Priory PRCD 550. Parkin

William Baines spent his whole life in Yorkshire. It is his piano music for which he is renowned, and this collection explains why. His rhapsodic melodic style is undoubtedly individual and his use of irregular rhythms is so smoothly employed that they seem imperceptible. The majority of these pieces are pictorial and the harmonic progressions are often quite strikingly effective; but Baines was at his finest when writing reflectively, and the three *Twilight Pieces* are delightful, while the brief *Etude in F sharp minor*, which ends the recital somewhat abruptly, is melodically quite haunting. Eric Parkin proves an ideal advocate of this rewarding music, and he is very naturally recorded.

BAINTON, Edgar (1880–1956)

Edgar Bainton was born in London and studied with Stanford at the Royal College of Music. In 1901 he was appointed to teach piano and composition at the Newcastle-upon-Tyne Conservatoire, becoming its Principal some years later. A keen Wagnerian, in the summer of 1914 he was arrested on his way to Bayreuth and was interned in Ruhleben, in company with Benjamin Dale, Carl Fuchs and other musicians. In 1934 he was offered the directorship of the Sydney Conservatoire, where he spent the remainder of his days.

Epithalamion; (i) An English Idyll
*** Chan. 10019. (i) Whelan; BBC PO, Brabbins – CLIFFORD:
A Kentish Suite, etc. ***

This follows up the excellent Chandos disc coupling symphonies by Edgar Bainton and Hubert Clifford (see below), the one English-born with a distinguished academic career in Australia, the other an Australian who made his home in

England. The rhapsody, *Epithalamion*, is a brilliant fantasy Scherzo dazzlingly orchestrated, which carries you exhilaratingly along with its elaborate cross-rhythms. The *English Idyll* sets words by the critic Neville Cardus, who at the time, 1946, was also an English exile in Sydney. Atmospheric and sensuous, it vividly catches a mood of nostalgia for England, not just the countryside but central London and a West Country cathedral. Martyn Brabbins draws dedicated performances from the BBC Philharmonic, with Paul Whelan a sensitive baritone soloist. An excellent coupling for the attractive pieces by Hubert Clifford.

Symphony 2 in D min.
*** Chan. 9757. BBC PO, Handley – CLIFFORD: *Symphony*; GOUGH: *Serenade* ***

Symphony 2 is exactly contemporaneous with the Hubert Clifford work with which it is coupled. It is in one movement but falls into a dozen or so short sections, all played without a break. Its outlook is overtly romantic, but whereas Clifford's music has a stronger affinity with, say, Bliss or Walton, Bainton is closer to Arnold Bax. He certainly knows how to score and, although this symphony is uneven in quality of ideas, there is a lot of it that is both inventive and rewarding. A worthwhile and enterprising issue, with first-rate playing from the BBC Philharmonic under Handley, and excellent recording.

String Quartet in A
(M) *** Dutton Epoch CDLX 7163. Locrian Ens. – CLIFFORD: *String Quartet* ***

Bainton's *Quartet* was written and first performed while he was interned, but it was revised for its London première after the war. It is far from negligible; it is pastoral in feeling and lyrical in content, with some touches of Ravelian influence. It is well served by the Locrian Ensemble and the recording is exemplary.

BALADA, Leonardo (born 1933)

Leonardo Balada is a native of Barcelona; he studied at the Conservatorio del Liceu and later at the Juilliard School in New York, where his composition professors included Aaron Copland and Vincent Persichetti. Since 1970 he has been professor of composition at Pittsburgh. Many of his works, including *Torquemada* and the *Concerto for Piano, Winds and Percussion*, have been recorded, mainly on the New World label. His early works blended avant-garde styles with ethnic elements.

(i) *Cello Concerto 2 (New Orleans)*; (ii) *Concerto for 4 Guitars and Orchestra. Celebració; Passacaglia*
(BB) *** Naxos 8.557049. (i) Sanderling; (ii) Versailles Guitar Qt; Barcelona SO & Catalonia Nat. O, Pearce

Cello Concerto 2 (New Orleans), superbly played here by its dedicatee, Michael Sanderling, and the *Passacaglia for Orchestra* are recent works, both dating from 2002. The *Concerto for Four Guitars and Orchestra* of 1976 represents the avant-garde side of his personality, while the *Celebració* from 1992, commissioned to mark the millennium of Catalonia, embraces Catalan folk melodies. Those of an exploratory cast of mind should investigate this interesting figure.

(i) *Piano Concerto 3*; (ii) *Concierto mágico for Guitar & Orchestra*; (iii) *Music for Flute & Orchestra*
✪ (BB) *** Naxos 8.555039. (i)Torres-Pardo; (ii) Fisk; (iii) Martinez; Barcelona SO & Catalonia Nat. O, Serebrier

There is no better entry into Balada's very Spanish soundworld than with the *Third Piano Concerto*. Audaciously popular in style, the rumbustious first movement is based on the infectious rhythm of a paso doble, as used at a bull fight. The bizarre orchestral effects are dazzling, while the pianist responds with infectious roulades. The second movement is hardly less exotic in its mysterious evocation of a medieval Andalusian scenario, with the piano creating an effect of dripping water; and the finale opens by continuing that primitive evocation, before the piano wittily interrupts with a *Jota*, with the orchestra soon joining in exuberantly. The *Concierto mágico* draws on Andalusian gypsy music, and the influence of Rodrigo is apparent. The toccata-like first movement pulses with intense flamenco rhythms, while the nocturnal central *Luna* is rhapsodic and improvisatory in feeling and the *zapateado* finale is in the form of a sparkling *moto perpetuo*.

The *Music for Flute and Orchestra* draws on Catalan folk melodies against a background of flashing orchestral colours. All three works are superbly played and Serebrier's accompaniments combine atmosphere with infectious gusto. The Naxos recording is enormously vivid, and for sheer joyful exuberance this Naxos triptych is hard to beat.

Violin Concerto 1; Fantasías sonoras; Folk Dreams; Sardana
(BB) *** Naxos 8.554708. (i) Cárdenes; Barcelona SO, Aeschbacher

Balada's *First Violin Concerto* is again strongly influenced by Catalan folk idioms and the first movement ends with an engagingly simple Minuet. This leads into an ecstatic and yet meditative *Adagio* (beautifully played by Andrés Cárdenes) and on to a deliciously folksy, toccata-like finale, full of sparkling bravura from soloist and orchestra alike. The intensely atmospheric three-movement *Folk Dreams* is Dali-influenced in its pictorial surrealism, the three movements drawing in turn on Latvian, Catalonian and (in the delectably jiggy finale) very recognizable Irish folk themes. *Sardana* is the national dance of Catalonia, and Balada's 'symphonic movement' is a brilliantly scored popular kaleidoscope of rhythm and colour. *Fantasías sonoras* is minimalist, based on an ear-tickling variation of a simple melodic cell. All in all, a highly rewarding collection, splendidly played and recorded.

BALAKIREV, Mily (1837–1910)

(i) *Piano Concerto 1. In Bohemia; King Lear Overture; Symphonies 1–2; Tamara*
(M) *** Chan. 2 for 1 CHAN 241-20. (i) Shelley; BBC PO, Sinaisky

Howard Shelley is a powerful soloist in the *Piano Concerto* and, although the *Second Symphony* cannot compare with the *First* in scale or memorability, Vassily Sinaisky makes a most persuasive case for it. The other works are also successful, and this makes an attractive two-for-one reissue. The performances are discussed more fully in our main volume.

Islamey (Oriental Fantasy)

(BB) *** EMI Encore 5 86881-2. Gavrilov – PROKOFIEV: *Piano Concerto 1* etc.; TCHAIKOVSKY: *Piano Concerto 1*, etc. ***

(M) *(*) Sony (ADD) S2K 94737 (2). Graffman – TCHAIKOVSKY: *Piano Concertos 1–3*; MUSSORGSKY: *Pictures at an Exhibition* **

Gavrilov's dazzling account of Balakirev's fantasy is outstandingly charismatic; it is well recorded too. It comes in harness with an equally dazzling account of Prokofiev's *First Piano Concerto* and a performance of the Tchaikovsky *B flat minor Concerto* which is rather less convincing. At Encore price, however, this is a remarkable bargain.

Graffman's account too is brilliantly played, but the recording is unsympathetic and the music's sensuous middle section fails to make its mark.

BALFE, Michael (1808–70)

The Bohemian Girl (complete)

(M) ** Decca 473 077-2 (2). Thomas, Power, Summers, Cullen, De Carlo, RTE Philharmonic Ch., Nat. SO of Ireland, Bonynge

Michael Balfe's lyrical facility comes out at its most charming in *The Bohemian Girl*, with the heroine's aria, '*I dreamt I dwelt in marble halls*', justly still popular as a separate number. While Richard Bonynge is the ideal conductor for this opera, he is not particularly well served by either the Irish orchestra or the principal singers. Patrick Power, as the hero, Thaddeus, has a light, lyrical tenor which sounds well enough until it is stressed, when it acquires a throaty bleating tone on top. Nova Thomas as the heroine, Arline, is at once throaty-sounding and fluttery, yet bright on top, not helped by her curious vowel sounds. Jonathan Summers is the strongest in the cast, as Count Arnhem, but even he has sounded better focused on disc; while the bass tones of John de Carlo as Devilshoof, King of the Gypsies, are marred by his unashamedly aspirated style in florid passages. A separate cast of actors is lined up for the spoken dialogue. The recording too, being slightly recessed, is not up to the usual standards Decca gives to Bonynge, but it remains the only way to sample this engaging work.

The Bohemian Girl: Highlights

(B) ** CfP (ADD) 3 35948-2. Hinds, Dunne, Dean, O'Callaghan, O, Nelson (with Irish Love Songs: *Danny Boy; If I had a-knew; Kitty Magee; Lovely Jimmy; Open the door softly; Shaun O'Neill; She moved thro' the fair; The Star of the County Down; The Stuttering Lovers; Trottin' to the Fair*. Dunn, Hinds, Nelson, (piano)) – BENEDICT: *The Lily of Killarney*; WALLACE: *Maritana* **(*)

This 1968 CD collects together music from the three operas which some have cynically christened 'the Irish Ring'. *The Bohemian Girl* is the most famous of the three and gets the largest selection, with the conductor putting plenty of life into it: the *Overture*, *Waltz* and *Galop* are very successful indeed. The singing is variable: Eric Hinds makes a suitably dolorous Count, Veronica Dunne is better in the second verse of *I dreamt I dwelt* than she is in the first (which she over-sings), and the tenor is lyrically minded, if somewhat weak. The recordings, made in Dublin, are good enough (Eric Hind's diction is superb) and with the interesting couplings, including a highly enjoyable collection of Irish love songs, this disc is good value.

BANCHIERI, Adriano (1568–1634)

Festino nella sera del giovedi grasso avanti cena, Op. 18; Il Zabaione musicale

(BB) *** Naxos 8.553785. R. Svizzara (Lugano) Ch., Sonatori de la Gioiosa Marca, Treviso, Fasolis

Banchieri here presents a pair of musical entertainments built on varied sequences of madrigals. *Il Zabaione musicale* consists of an introduction and three Acts, made up of 17 very brief madrigals. The *Festino* – an 'Entertainment for the Eve of Carnival Thursday before Dinner' – is a sequence of 21 very light-hearted madrigals, some of them involving animal and bird noises, as for example the memorable quartet for owl, cuckoo, cat and dog. Diego Fasolis draws superb singing from his Lugano choir, with incisively crisp ensemble, colourfully enhanced by brass and timpani. Excellent recording, made in the studios of Radio Lugano. A splendid example of Naxos enterprise. Full texts and an English translation are provided.

BANKS, Tony (born 1950)

Seven (suite)

(BB) **(*) Naxos 8.5547466. LPO, Dixon

Tony Banks's celebrity is as keyboard player and composer for a celebrated rock group. He has also written several successful film scores, composing from the piano, with the orchestration provided by others. But for the genesis of his first major 'classical' composition, he worked painstakingly alongside arranger Simon Hale to create his suite directly in orchestral terms. The resulting seven movements remain in the style of film music, but show a genuine melodic gift, even if his themes are short-breathed. The snag is the repetition and inflation of the simple basic material, especially in the opening and closing numbers. The first, *Spring Tide*, introduces a kind of sinuous chorale, out of which grows the catchy six-note motive that dominates the movement and that is built to a big climax, then gently subsiding. *Black Dawn*, which follows ('influenced by the music of Vaughan Williams'), opens darkly on lower strings but flowers expressively as the music moves up to the violins and ends nostalgically.

The Gateway begins with a gentle flute solo, and is divertingly scored throughout. *The Ram* then makes a robust contrast, 'more rhythmic and up-tempo', exuberantly repetitive but bringing occasional crudeness in the scoring, as in the combination of strings and trombones. *Earthlight* creates a Romantic pastoral mood and is in the form of simple variations, while *Neap Tide* is more sustained and evocative, characteristically repetitive, but rather affecting.

The final *Spirit of Gravity* is the most extended movement of all, 'travelling through a number of different musical ideas', notably another expanding chorale-like figure, 'only to end up finally where it began'. It is a curiously abrupt close for such an extended movement, but the composer obviously needed to stop. Overall this is an ambitious début, yet one that is, in the main, successful. The LPO under Mike Dixon play the whole work committedly, bringing out any individuality of colouring. The recording is good, not outstanding but acceptably spacious, and it seems likely that such listener-friendly music has every chance of success with the composer's many admirers.

BANTOCK, Granville (1868–1946)

Overture to a Greek Tragedy; Pierrot of the Minute; (i)
*Christ in the Wilderness: The Wilderness and the Solitary
Place.* (i; ii) *Song of Songs: 3 Scenes*
*** Hyp. CDA 67395. RPO, Handley; with (i) Connell; (ii)
Begley

Pierrot of the Minute is familiar from a much earlier,
Chandos recording from Norman del Mar, but Handley's
performance has an even lighter touch, and he changes gear
readily for the more opulent and dramatic *Greek Overture*,
which is equally enjoyable in its more majestic manner.
Elizabeth Connell then sings a rather engaging aria from
the all but forgotten *Wilderness* oratorio; but it is the group
of scenes from the *Song of Songs* that are the most sensuously appealing, including a love duet (Connell and Kim
Begley rising to the romantic occasion) and a luscious
orchestral sequence for the Third Day. Altogether outstanding performances, and superb, demonstration-worthy
recording.

BARATI, George (1913–96)

(i) *Symphony 1 (Alpine);* (ii) *Chant of Darkness;* (i) *Chant of
Light*
(BB) **(*) Naxos 8.559063. (i) Budapest SO, Kováks; (ii)
Czech RSO, Válek

Barati's *Alpine Symphony* was written in 1963, and although
serialism is inherent in its structure, it is far from being an
inaccessible work. For most listeners, it will be the colourful
orchestration, with a huge battery of percussion instruments
and bold orchestral effects (some of which are very loud
indeed), that make the most impression. The work certainly
makes an impact, though its coherence is not immediately
apparent. The two orchestral pieces are late works; the *Chant
of Darkness* was written as an expression of mourning for the
composer's daughter, who had died of cancer in 1992. It is
interspersed with dramatic passages, and its 16 minutes are
unremittingly bleak. The *Chant of Light* occupies a similar
sound-world but is not quite so desolate. First-rate performances and recordings from both sets of orchestras and conductors, but this is not a collection to recommend
unreservedly.

BARBER, Samuel (1910–81)

(i) *Adagio for Strings;* (ii) *Cello Concerto, Op. 22;* (iii; iv)
Violin Concerto, Op. 14; (iv) *Essay 1, Op. 121;* (v) *Agnus Dei*
(BB) *** HMV 5 86669-2. (i) LSO, Previn; (ii) Kirschbaum,
SCO, Saraste; (iii) Oliveira; (iv) Saint Louis SO, Slatkin; (v)
Winchester Cathdral Ch., Hill

An excellent anthology in every respect. The *Adagio for
Strings* and the *First Essay for Orchestra* were the works by
which Barber was first introduced to the public and which
gained him the advocacy of Toscanini and Ormandy. Anyone
who enjoys the *Adagio* must also respond to the *Violin
Concerto*. It is genuinely beautiful and has consistent warmth,
freshness and humanity. Elmer Oliveira's version responds to
the nostalgia of the *Andante* with a vein of bitter-sweet
yearning that is most affecting. It is a fine performance
overall, with a brilliantly played finale, and is warmly and
realistically recorded, with Slatkin directing an entirely sympathetic accompaniment, with rich, atmospheric sound. He is

equally sympathetic in the *Essay*. The *Cello Concerto* makes a
good foil for the work with violin, for it is darker and spikier
in Kirschbaum's hands than those of his direct rivals, more
urgent in the opening movement; yet it is just as beautifully
played, with splendid support from Saraste and the Scottish
Chamber Orchestra. The *Agnus Dei* is none other than our
old friend the *Adagio*, arranged for voices by the composer in
1967. It is admirably sung in Winchester under David Hill.

(i; ii) *Adagio for Strings;* (iii) *Toccata festiva, Op. 36;* (iv; ii)
Vanessa: Intermezzo, Act II; (v) *String Quartet, Op. 11;* (vi)
Summer Music; (vii) *4 Excursions, Op. 20;* (viii) *Dover
Beach*
(M) **(*) Sony (ADD) SK 94739. (i) NYPO; (ii) Schippers;
(iii) E. Power Biggs, Phd. O, Ormandy; (iv) Columbia SO;
(v) Beaux Arts Qt; (vi) Phd. Woodwind Quintet; (vii) Previn
(piano); (viii) Fischer-Dieskau, Juilliard Qt

This valuable Sony collection gathers together recordings
from the early to mid-1906s, and the remastering brings
considerable improvement in the body of the sound, with
plenty of bloom on the strings, though of course the consistently forward balance remains intractable. The famous *Adagio* is given a richly expansive rather than an intense
performance, followed later by a boldly passionate account of
the *String Quartet* of which the *Adagio* was the centrepiece.
The Philadelpia Wind Quintet play the engaging *Summer
Music* with finesse and just a touch of nostalgia. *Dover Beach*,
Barber's coolly atmospheric yet haunting setting of Matthew
Arnold (with Fischer-Dieskau immaculate in his English,
rightly treating the piece like Lieder) is another highlight, but
Previn's vivacious and witty account of the piano *Excursions*
is also endearing. The *Toccata* makes a spectacular finale; it
was written for the Philadelphia Orchestra (to celebrate the
arrival of a new organ) and they are very much at home in
the lyrical music as well as the spectacle, and Biggs is a
suitably flamboyant soloist, managing the famous cadenza
for pedals with aplomb.

Violin Concerto, Op. 14
(M) *** Decca 475 7710 – Bell, Baltmore SO, Zinman –
BLOCH: *Baal Shem;* WALTON: *Violin Concerto* ***

Joshua Bell's passionate playing in the Barber, full of tender
poetry, is well matched by the excellent orchestra, ripely and
brilliantly recorded, with the soloist well forward, but not
aggressively so. This now takes pride of place among available
versions. It won the 1998 *Gramophone* Concerto Award and
has now become one of Decca's Originals.

BARTÓK, Béla (1881–1945)

*Concerto for Orchestra; Dance Suite; The Miraculous
Mandarin: Suite*
(M) *** Decca 475 7711. Chicago SO, Solti

Decca have now reissued this Solti triptych as one of their
mid-priced Orignals. It has previously been available on a
Double Decca (470 516-2 – see our main volume) but this
single-disc reissue is worth considering, for, while his Chicago performances may not have quite the degree of intensity
of his earlier, LSO accounts (still available on Decca 467
686-2), there is extra warmth in Chicago, and of course
modern, digital recording too.

Concerto for Orchestra; Music for Strings, Percussion &
Celesta
(B) *** EMI (ADD) 4 76897-2. BPO, Karajan

Comparison between Karajan's 1974 EMI performance of the *Concerto for Orchestra* and the earlier, DG version, dating from 1966, shows how little this conductor's view of the score changed. The advantage of the newer disc comes mainly in the recording, more opulent and atmospheric. This suits Karajan's approach, with the Berlin Philharmonic in superb form on both discs. He draws a performance that is rich, romantic and smooth – for some ears, perhaps excessively so. Karajan is right in treating Bartók emotionally, but comparison with Solti points the contrast between Berlin romanticism and earthy, red-blooded Hungarian passion. Both conductors allow themselves a fair degree of rubato, but Solti's is linked with the Hungarian folk-song idiom whereas Karajan's moulding of phrases is essentially from the German tradition. Yet, with such excellent recording, the work's atmosphere comes over impressively and there is rather more sparkle than in the earlier, DG version.

The recording of the *Music for Strings, Percussion and Celesta* is much earlier (1957), and here the later, DG version is sonically superior, with more body and colour. Yet the effect on EMI is still tellingly atmospheric, and the performance is in some ways fresher and more spontaneous than the later version.

(i) *Concerto for Orchestra;* (ii) *Sonata for 2 Pianos &*
Percussion; (iii) *Improvisation on Hungarian Peasant Songs*
(M) **(*) Sony SK 94726. (i) Phd. O, Ormandy; (ii) Robert,
  Gaby & Jean-Claude Casadesus, Drouet; (iii) Rosen

These recordings all come from 1963, but the choice of couplings will not suit all tastes. The *Concerto for Orchestra* is superbly played and there is plenty of panache in Ormandy's reading. The recording has been splendidly remastered and the Philadelphia strings now sound rich and full-blooded, while orchestral detail combines bloom with clarity. The *Sonata for Two Pianos and Percussion* is also impressive, with the central *Lento* full of tension; however, the Paris recording is less flattering. Charles Rosen gives a bravura account of the *Hungarian Improvisation*, but again the studio recording, although basically truthful, is rather hard and close.

Piano Concertos (i) *1;* (ii) *2;* (iii) *3*
⊖→ *** DG 477 5330. (i) Zimerman, Chicago SO; (ii)
  Andsnes, BPO; (iii) Grimaud, LSO; all cond. Boulez

There are several versions of all three Bartók piano concertos with one pianist (Anda, Schiff, Kocsis, Kovacevich and Ashkenazy) but this magnificent newcomer is unusual in collecting three orchestras and three soloists but one conductor. Krystian Zimerman gives an aristocratic and searching account of the *First* with the Chicago orchestra, made in 2001. Leif Ove Andsnes with the Berlin Philharmonic give a thrilling reading of the *Second*, arguably the most visionary of the three, which many readers will recall from BBC broadcasts. Hélène Grimaud's performance of the *Third* with the LSO is the most recent and can hold its own with any of the current competition. Masterly performances and clean, meticulously conducted support from all three orchestras, plus eminently fine DG recording. Arguably the most recommendable set of the concertos now before the public.

Piano Concerto 2 in G
(BB) *(*) EMI Gemini (2) (ADD) 3 50849-2. S. Richter, O de
  Paris, Maazel – PROKOFIEV: *Piano Concerto 5* *(*);
  TCHAIKOVSKY: *Piano Concertos 1–3* **

This budget collection from the early 1970s, featuring both Richter and Gilels (in Tchaikovsky), looks attractive on paper and undoubtedly has interest, but it turns out to be a curious mixed bag. Richter plays here with less than his usual incisiveness and he is much less convincing than Anda, for instance, who made his recording at the same time; although the EMI recording quality is full-bodied, this remains disappointing.

Violin Concerto 2 in B min.
(B) ** Ph. 2-CD 475 7547 (2). Mullova, LAPO, Salonen –
  PROKOFIEV: *Violin Concerto 2* **; SHOSTAKOVICH:
  Violin Concerto 1 *(*); STRAVINSKY: *Violin Concerto* ***

Viktoria Mullova gives a brilliant enough account of Bartók's marvellous concerto and she is well supported by the Los Angeles orchestra under Esa-Pekka Salonen. But there is all too little of the warmth and humanity that others, from Menuhin onwards, have found in this powerful score. Good recorded sound and enterprising couplings. Our first choice for a modern recording of this concerto (if you don't want Korcia's collection, below) rests with Shaham, coupled with the two *Rhapsodies* for violin and orchestra (DG 459 639-2), or Tetzlaff with Janáček and Weill (Virgin 5 620632); but György Pauk on Naxos is also very recommendable, and he offers the *First Violin Concerto* as well (8.554321).

(i) *Violin Concerto 2;* (ii) *Contrasts for Clarinet, Violin &*
Piano; (iii) *Violin Sonata 1. Sonata for Solo Violin*
*** Naïve V4991 (2). Korcia, with (i) CBSO, Oramo; (ii)
  Portal; (ii; iii) Bavouzet

Laurent Korcia is a protégé of Pierre Barbizet who has won much acclaim and many international prizes. This two-CD Bartók set shows his virtuosity and musicianship to excellent effect. The *Concerto* was recorded in 2004 in Symphony Hall, Birmingham, and the *Contrasts* the following year in Brussels. The *Solo Sonata* and the *First Violin Sonata* are earlier (Marseilles, 1997) but are no less accomplished and persuasive. This concerto version must rank alongside the Tetzlaff and Shaham recordings, and moreover it has the advantage of the additional pieces.

CHAMBER MUSIC

(i) *Contrasts for Clarinet, Violin & Piano;* (ii) *Violin Sonata*
1 (finale)
(***) EMI **DVD** mono 4 904519. Y. Menuhin, with (i) Thea
  King; Jeremy Menuhin; (ii) Hephzibah Menuhin (with
  MENDELSSOHN: *Variations sérieuses, Op. 54*) – ENESCU:
  Violin Sonata 3; SCHUBERT: *Piano Trio in B flat;* FRANCK:
  Violin Sonata in A (***)

Both *Contrasts* and the finale of the *First Violin Sonata* were recorded in the ORTF Studios in Paris in 1972. A valuable memento of Thea King's artistry as well as of Menuhin père et fils.

String Quartets 1–6
(BB) *** Warner Apex 2564 62686-2. Keller Qt

The Keller are a Hungarian group who have attracted international attention. They made their recordings of the Bartók cycle in 1993/4, and enjoyed the imprimatur of no less an authority than Sándor Végh. Indeed, these recordings were made in the Salle de Musique de la Chaux-de-Fonds, where the Végh recorded their second cycle. The performances are totally idiomatic, intense yet natural, and at their new and highly competitive price are among the best you can find.

Solo Violin Sonata

*** Sony SK 92938. Baiba Skride – BACH: *Partita 2;* YSAŸE: *Sonata 1 in G min.* ***

Baiba Skride has superb technique and a comparable tone. In the Bartók *Sonata* she has great concentration and intelligence, and this is part of a thoroughly recommendable triptych.

PIANO MUSIC

For Children (Books 1–4)

➐ (BB) *** Warner Apex 2564 62188-2. Ránki

Dezsö Ránki gives outstanding performances of all four Books of Bartók's *For Children*, using the composer's original edition of 1908/9. He is very well recorded, and this Apex reissue is a truly remarkable bargain.

For Children (Books 1 & 2)

(BB) **(*) Naxos 8.555998. Jandó.

Jenö Jandó's style is rather plain, but his intergrity is in no doubt and his characterization is strong. He is well recorded, but he offers only half as much music as Ránki for the same cost.

For Children, Volumes I & II (revised version); 10 Easy Pieces; 15 Hungarian Peasant Songs. Mikrokosmos, Vol. VI: 6 Bulgarian Dances; 6 Romanian Folk Dances; Sonata; Sonatina

(BB) *** EMI Gemini (ADD) 3 50869-2 (2). Béroff

Bartók's pieces for children are a collection of Hungarian (Book I) and Slovak (Book II) folksongs which possess a beguiling simplicity and (when taken in small doses) unfailing musical interest. Choice between Michel Béroff and Dezsö Ránki on Warner Apex is simplified by the fact that Béroff records the revised score and Ránki gives us the original edition of 1908/9. Moreover, Béroff offers a number of Bartók's other major piano works. Béroff's playing has an unaffected eloquence that is touching, and the recording, made in the Salle Wagram, Paris, is very good.

BAX, Arnold (1883–1953)

The Garden of Fand; In the Faery Hills; November Woods; Sinfonietta

➐ *** Chan. 10362. BBC PO, Handley

Vernon Handley's triumphant cycle of the Bax symphonies for Chandos scored a great critical success and, more importantly, an enthusiastic public response at the end of 2003. He now turns to the tone-poems and gives equally strong accounts of them. The pioneering post-war 78s of *Fand* by Sir Thomas Beecham and fine subsequent accounts from Barbirolli and Sir Adrian Boult have served this magical score well. But Handley has the benefit of finely detailed recorded sound, with an excellent and truthful balance. The rarity here is the *Sinfonietta*, written between the *Fourth* and *Fifth Symphonies*, a richly inventive score in the finest Bax tradition.

The Garden of Fand; The Happy Forest; November Woods; The Tale the Pine Trees Knew; Tintagel

(BB) **(*) Naxos 8.557599. RSNO, Lloyd-Jones

A truly attractive collection of symphonic poems, which originally accompanied David Lloyd-Jones's recordings of the symphonies. The performances are warm and flexible and very well played. The slight reservation concerns the recording, which is not always as expansive in the middle frequencies as it might be, though the gentler passages in *The Garden of Fand*, *Happy Forest* and *November Woods* have attractive atmospheric lustre.

PIANO MUSIC

A Hill Tune; Lullaby; The Maiden and the Daffodil; Mediterranean; A Mountain Mood; Pæan; The Princess's Rose Garden; 2 Russian Tone Poems; Sleepy-Head; What the Minstrel Told Us

(BB) *** Naxos 8.557769. Wass

The four sonatas which Ashley Wass has already recorded (see our main volume) lie at the centre of Bax's keyboard music, but there are also a number of evocative miniatures (and not-so-miniatures). The earliest here are the *Two Russian Tone Poems*, the *Nocturne – May Night in the Ukraine* and *Gopak*, written in 1912, two years after his visit to the Ukraine in pursuit of Natalia Skarginska. They are inventive and atmospheric works, as are most of the pieces here. The annotations by Bax's biographer, Lewis Foreman, are very helpful and highly interesting. What a fine pianist this young artist is!

VOCAL MUSIC

(i) Enchanted Summer; (ii) Fatherland; (iii) Walsingham

(M) *** Chan. 10366X. Brighton Festival Ch., RPO, Handley; with (i) Williams-King; (i; ii) McWhirter; (ii; iii) Hill

Three richly romantic choral works of Bax, with *Enchanted Summer* especially sumptuous, the evocative colouring of the orchestration at times anticipating *Tintagel*. Each work was linked with a turbulent affair in the composer's personal life, which perhaps accounts for the unrestrained moments of passion. *Enchanted Summer*, an ambitious score of almost half an hour, was first given in 1912 but, after a bare handful of performances, remained unplayed until 1970. It is the finest of the three works here, an imaginatively ambitious setting of the text of Act II of Shelley's *Prometheus Unbound*, using three soloists. The earliest is the quite brief *Fatherland* (from 1907, but revised in 1934); it was Bax's very first choral piece, a setting of the Swedish-language Finnish poet, Runeberg. It envisaged a strolling ballad singer (here the eloquent Martyn Hill in good voice). But its patriotic feeling was originally directed to Scandinavia. *Walsingham* (1926) sets a poem by Sir Walter Raleigh and was composed after Bax had finished scoring the *Second Symphony*. Again, it was long neglected and is every bit as much of a revelation as *Enchanted Summer*, showing Bax at his most fluently mature. But all three works here are given dedicatedly intense performances, with Handley at his finest, and chorus and orchestra responding to his spontaneous fervour. The Chandos recording too is magnificently full-blooded.

The Morning Watch; (i) *Nocturnes; St Patrick's Breastplate;*
(i) *To the Name above every Name*
*** Chan. 10164. (i) Bunning; Huddersfield Choral Soc., BBC
PO, Brabbins

More virtually unknown Bax. *The Morning Watch* (a setting
of Henry Vaughan) is the most impressive work here, commissioned, like *To the Name above every Name*, for the
Worcester Three Choirs Festival. The two *Nocturnes,* for
soprano soloist, use German texts, but Christine Bunning
makes less than the most of their distinct appeal because of
her intrusive vibrato. *St Patrick's Breastplate* features an
eighth-century Gaelic text by its namesake, and it is certainly
full of Baxian passion. With a strong response from the
Huddersfield choir and obviously sympathetic conducting
from Martyn Brabbins, this is an enterprising triptych, but
more for the dedicated Baxian than for the general collector.
It almost goes without saying that it is all superbly recorded.

BAYER, Josef (1852–1913)

Die Puppenfee; Sonne und Erde (complete ballets)
(BB) ** Naxos 8.557098. Slovak RSO, Mogrelia

Joseph Bayer was head of the Vienna Ballet from 1885 to 1898,
when he retired. He composed some 22 ballets, as well as
many other dance pieces and divertissements, but *Die Puppenfee* (*The Fairy Doll,* 1888) was his greatest success. Its
(mostly) short numbers are eminently tuneful, and quite
prettily scored. What it lacks is the genius of a Delibes or
Adam to make it memorable. The same applies to the shorter
Sonne und Erde, a ballet based on the four seasons. The
orchestra plays sympathetically for Mogrelia and the recording is adequate.

BEAMISH, Sally (born 1956)

The Caledonian Road; The Day Dawn; (i) *No, I'm Not
Afraid;* (ii) *The Imagined Sound of Sun on Stone*
*** BIS CD 1161. Swedish CO, Rudner; with (i) Beamish; (ii)
Harle

Sally Beamish began her career as a violist in the London
Sinfonietta before turning to full-time composition when she
was in her thirties. Her musical speech is direct and often
powerful, and she has a genuine feeling for nature. *The
Imagined Sound of Sun on Stone,* a concerto for soprano
saxophone and chamber orchestra, is most resourceful in its
handling of the instrument and imaginative in its musical
content, and it is played brilliantly here by John Harle and the
Swedish Chamber Orchestra. All four pieces are inventive and
well worth getting to know, and the BIS recording is state of
the art.

(i) *Cello Concerto (River);* (ii) *Viola Concerto;* (iii) *Tam Lin*
(for oboe and orchestra)
*** BIS CD 971. (i) Cohen; (ii) Dukes; (iii) Hunt; Swedish CO,
Rudner

Tam Lin is a scena for oboe and small orchestra including
harp and percussion but no violins. It is based on a Scottish
ballad in which the elfin knight, Tam Lin, is saved from
damnation by the love of a girl, Janet. The composer calls the
Viola Concerto 'a personal response to the story of the Apostle
Peter's denial of Christ' and casts the solo viola as Peter's
voice, the horn being associated with Jesus. The three denials
are punctuated by illustrations of Christ's trial in film-like

contrasts. The *Cello Concerto* illustrates poems from Ted
Hughes's 'River' collection, with orchestral colourings suggested by the words. The music is consistently imaginative,
with clean, luminous textures. The writing is eventful and
holds the listener in its spell. Robert Cohen and Philip Dukes,
the dedicatees who commissioned the cello and viola works
respectively, give committed performances, as does the oboist, Gordon Hunt, with distinctive plangent tone. Excellent
support from the Swedish players, very well recorded.

BECK, Franz Ignaz (1734–1809)

*Sinfonias: in D, F, and B flat, Op. 3/1, 2 & 6; Overture: La
mort d'Orphée*
*** CPO 777 034-2. La Stagione Frankfurt, Schneider

Under Schneider, the opening *D major Symphony* explodes
into life, boldly driven, but enjoyably so. Indeed, these symphonies (in three and four movements), with their *Sturm und
Drang* tendencies, are highly compelling. La Stagione are
consistently invigorating, making the most of the dramatic
qualities of the music, with their rasping horns and vivid
woodwind, and allowing all the detail to emerge sharply
focused. The string playing is neatly turned and, while Schneider goes for out-and-out excitement, the music's elegant
qualities are not overlooked, such as the witty exchange
between the woodwind and strings in the finale of Op. 3/6
and in the *Prestissimo* of Op. 3/2. The composer's gift for
drama, as well as creating imaginative orchestral effects, is
also well highlighted in the overture, *La mort d'Orphée.* The
sound is full and brilliant, and these CPO recordings are now
top choice for this repertoire.

Sinfonias: in B flat; D; G, Op. 3/1–3; in D, Op. 10/2; in E
(BB) *** Naxos 8.553790. N. CO, Ward
Sinfonias: in G min.; E flat; D min., Op. 3/3–5
(BB) *** CPO 999 390-2. La Stagione, Frankfurt, Schneider

Franz Ignaz Beck's three-movement *Sinfonias* are concise and
sharply characterized, even if they are little more than Italian
overtures. The *D major Sinfonia* is the exception, with a
Haydnesque pattern of four movements. Ideas are fresh,
scoring simple but felicitous. The graceful *Largo* of the *B flat
major* work, with its string cantilena floating over a pizzicato
bass, is worthy of Boccherini, and the *E major,* Op. 13/1, is a
winning little work with a diverting finale. The performances
on Naxos are very persuasive, warmly elegant and full of
vitality. The recording, too, is first class.

The CPO disc offers mature later works (especially the *G
minor,* with the themes interrelated), which are very much in
the Haydn *Sturm und Drang* style. The *D minor Sinfonia* is for
strings alone, but the *E flat major,* which has a remarkably
searching *Adagio,* uses the horns most effectively as soloists in
the *Minuet* and *Trio* and in the closing section of the finale.
The period performances here are aggressively full of gusto
and vitality, creating a sound-world very different from that
on the Naxos collection.

BEECKE, Ignaz von (1733–1803)

String Quartets 9 in G; 11 in G; 16 in B flat, M.9, 11 & 16
*** CPO 999 509-2. Arioso Qt

Ignaz von Beecke is not to be confused with Franz Ignaz
Beck, above (although he was an almost exact contemporary). Beecke's string quartets were less well known in his

own time than his symphonies. They are finely crafted, cultivated works, which Haydn would surely not have been ashamed to own. The disarming warmth of the opening of the *G major*, M.11 (which is first on the disc), leads to a fine opening movement with two striking themes; the Minuet comes second and is equally personable, and after the elegant *Adagio* the finale is as spirited as you could wish. The *B flat Quartet* is in three movements and is hardly less pleasing, with a songful *Adagio* marked *sotto voce*. The companion *G major* work brings a striking minor-key slow movement, opening with a grave slow fugue; the Minuet lightens the mood and prepares for a most engaging finale. All three works are thoroughly diverting when played with such warmth, vitality and finesse, and this excellent quartet is very naturally recorded.

BEETHOVEN, Ludwig van (1770–1827)

Piano Concertos 1–5
✪ (M) *** DG (ADD) 476 5299 (3). Kempff, BPO, Van Kempen

Even more than in his later stereo cycle, this mono recording from 1953 finds Kempff at his most individual, turning phrases and pointing ornamentation with a sparkle. The articulation is uniquely crisp and clear, the lightness of touch so extraordinary that Kempff barely seems to brush the keys in such passages as the opening of the finale of no. 4. The slow movements, flowing easily and lyrically, yet convey a depth of meditation rarely equalled and Kempff's bright, muscular attack in the first movement of the *Emperor* gives it considerable power, combined with clarity. In the first four concertos Kempff plays his own cadenzas, making them sound like spontaneous improvisations. A classic recording guaranteed to give refreshment, which has been transferred to CD in full, immediate, well-detailed sound.

Piano Concertos 1–2
(B) ** EMI (ADD) 4 76884-2. Weissenberg, BPO, Karajan

Piano Concertos 3; 5 (Emperor)
(B) ** EMI (ADD) 4 76885-2. Weissenberg, BPO, Karajan

(i) Piano Concerto 4;(ii) Triple Concerto for Violin, Cello and Piano, Op. 56
(B) ** EMI (ADD) 4 76886-2. (i) Weissenberg; (ii) D. Oistrakh, Rostropovich, S. Richter; BPO, Karajan

Alexis Weissenberg's playing in these piano concertos, reissued as part of the Karajan Edition, is rather run-of-the-mill, although there are individual felicities. Karajan and the Berlin Philharmonic create a strong impression in the beautifully played accompaniments. There are no complaints on sonic grounds: the recordings from the mid- to late 1970s are full and well balanced. The *Triple Concerto* is treated with apt opulence by the star soloists, with Beethoven's priorities among them well preserved in the extra dominance of Rostropovich over his colleagues. This is warm, expansive music-making, and if the 1969 recording is rather too reverberant the sound here is better focused than it was on LP, and the balance between the soloists and the orchestra is well managed.

(i) Piano Concertos 1–5. (ii) Piano & Wind Quintet in E flat, Op. 16. 2 Rondos, Op. 51; Piano Sonatas 8 (Pathétique); 14 (Moonlight); 21 (Waldstein); 32 Variations in C min., WoO 80
(B) **(*) Decca (DDD/ADD) 475 7065 (4). Lupu, with (i) Israel PO, Mehta; (ii) De Vries, Pieterson, Zarzo, Pollard.

Radu Lupu's Beethoven survey began very successfully with the *C minor Variations* in 1970, and then he recorded the concertos between 1978 and 1981, Nos. 1, 2, 3 and 5 in the Kingsway Hall and No. 4 (with the *Rondos*) in Tel Aviv, with almost equally impressive results. Nos. 1 and 2 were particularly successful and were highly praised by us at the time. The readings favour fast, resilient speeds, slow movements are treated with lightness too, and throughout it is the pianist who dominates. Lupu's playing has both sparkle and sensitivity, and its poetry is ever apparent. He never tries to invest detail with undue expressive intensity, nor does he view early Beethoven through the eyes of his maturity. These are marvellously articulated readings and, if the playing of the Israel Philhamonic at times lacks the last degree of refinement, it is full of character and always sympathetic. The *Third Concerto* is forthright and dramatic, yet again Lupu is attentive to every detail of colour and dynamic nuance. He is unfailingly perceptive and, though unsmiling at those moments when a gentle poetry surfaces, this is in every sense a powerfully conceived reading. If it is slightly let down by the orchestral support – the first desks of the Israel strings are not always heard to flattering effect and the woodwind, though not insensitive, is not distinctive – it is still stimulating. The quality of the orchestral response is again a disadvantage in the *Fourth Concerto*. Lupu brings rare eloquence, inner serenity and repose to this magical work. But the orchestral opening of the slow movement is distinctly coarse, and at no time does one feel that Mehta's sensibility is a match for his soloist. Lupu's *Emperor* completes the cycle characteristically, a performance which, without lacking strength, brings thoughtfulness and poetry even to the magnificence of the first movement, with classical proportions made clear. The slow movement has delicacy and fantasy, the finale easy exhilaration, though neither conductor nor orchestra matches the soloist's distinction. Throughout the cycle the digital recording is outstandingly successful; the balance is excellently judged and the overall effect is vividly realistic.

Lupu went on in 1986 to record a glorious account of the *Piano and Wind Quintet*. His playing has sparkle and freshness, and the first movement has real eloquence and – when required – wit. The wind offer beautifully blended and cultured playing, the spacious acoustic of the Kleine Zaal of the Amsterdam Concertgebouw adding to the success of the recording; and the balance achieved by the Decca engineers is very natural and true to life. The unusual triptych of Beethoven named sonatas is available separately (Decca 476 7218), with the *Waldstein* standing out. Lupu's deliberation at the opening of the *Moonlight* and in the famous slow movement of the *Pathétique* will disturb some listeners, but overall his playing is individual and carries conviction. The two *Rondos* are immaculately played, and again the Decca recording is first rate.

Piano Concerto 2
✪ (BB) (***) Naxos mono 8.110767. Kapell, NBC SO, Golschmann – SCHUBERT: *Waltzes*, etc.; RACHMANINOV: *Cello Sonata* (***)

We have written with enthusiasm about the Kapell Beethoven

B flat Concerto in earlier editions, and its commanding authority is evident from the outset. Even if you possess the earlier transfer on RCA (see our main volume) or Dutton's exemplary transcription, coupled with the Khachaturian and three of the Shostakovich Op. 34 *Preludes*, this newcomer is worth investigating for the sake of the Rachmaninov *Sonata*.

Piano Concertos 3 in C min., Op. 37; 4 in G, Op. 58

(BB) *** Arte Nova 82876 64010-2. Bronfman, Tonhalle O, Zurich, Zinman

Following the example of Zinman and the Tonhalle Orchestra in their Beethoven symphony interpretations, Yefim Bronfman plays very stylishly, with exceptionally clean attack and clarity of articulation. This does not result at all in small-scale readings for, quite apart from the weight of orchestral sound, Bronfman's range of expression is formidable, and rightly he opts to play the longest and most demanding of Beethoven's cadenzas for No. 3. The slow movement of No. 3 also brings high contrasts, as does the dialogue in the slow movement of No. 4. The sparkle of the finale in No. 3 is matched by the rippling wit of the playing in the finale of No. 4, while poetry marks the whole performance. A splendid coupling, the more attractive at super-bargain price, with excellent sound.

(i) *Piano concertos 3–5 (Emperor). Piano Sonatas 24, Op. 78; 31, Op. 110*

❂ (***) Testament mono SBT2 1351 (2). Arrau; (i) with Philh. O, Klemperer

These 1957 Festival Hall performances sound as magnificent and magisterial on CD as they did in the concert hall, all those years ago. (R.L. remembers hearing Nos. 4 & 5 as well as the Brahms concertos a year or so later, when Arrau paired them in the one concert.) The *Fourth* is particularly fine and the *Emperor* is masterful. (The notes quote one review speaking of the latter: 'every detail was carefully calculated in dynamics, touch and phrasing, yet it was the overall conception that left the listener thinking that Mr Arrau was possessed of some superhuman power over and above his superb technique, his generous emotion and penetrating intellect'). The two sonatas were recorded at about the same time for Walter Legge's EMI Columbia blue label and are, as one might expect, performances of some stature: poised, considered, cultivated. Paul Baily's transfers give a truthful and vivid sound-picture and enhance the musical experience these artists offer. Not to be missed.

Piano Concertos 3 in C min., Op. 37; 5 (Emperor) in E flat, Op. 73

**(*) DG DVD 073 4097 (2). Pollini, VPO, Boehm – MOZART: *Piano Concertos 19 & 23*; BRAHMS: *Piano Concerto 2* **(*)

Pollini's magisterial account of the *C minor Concerto* comes from November 1977 and the *Emperor* from April 1978, both being recorded at the Musikvereinssaal. They occupy the first DVD in this package, the two Mozart concertos and the Brahms *B flat Concerto* being accommodated on its companion. Both Beethoven concertos exhibit the cool and dedicated classicism, shorn of expressive exaggeration, characteristic of this partnership. There is considerable poetic feeling in both slow movements, but the overall impression is of majestic prose resounding, rather than the poetic vision and power one finds in, say, the Perahia set with Haitink and the Concertgebouw on CD. Pollini is faithful and sober in much the same way that Backhaus was in the 1950s. In the *C minor*,

Christopher Nupen's camera is always where one wants it to be and the production is straightforward and unfussy, with no attempt at eye-catching visual tricks. In the *Emperor*, Franz Kebelka's direction is similarly unobtrusive and the sound-balance from the legendary Günther Hermanns is clean but full-bodied.

Piano Concertos 4; 5 in E flat (Emperor)

❂— ❂ (M) *** EMI (ADD) 4 76828-2 [4 76829-2]. Gilels, Philh. O, Ludwig

(BB) **(*) HMV 5 86674-2. Kovacevich, Australian CO

Fascinatingly, EMI have chosen Gilels's earlier (1957) Philharmonia performances with Leopold Ludwig rather than the later, Cleveland versions partnered by Szell, to be included among their 'Great Recordings of the Century'. Both these remarkable performances were reviewed in our very first *Stereo Record Guide* in 1960, but they have been out of the catalogue for some years. About the magisterial *G major Concerto* there can be no reservations whatsoever. It is a masterly reading of striking authority and eloquence, strong and poetic, yet warm-hearted. The poetry of the dialogue in the slow movement is of the purest kind, tone control such as we rarely hear these days is finely realized, and there is a rare combination of strength and sparkle in the finale. The early stereo recording is remarkably good and is splendidly remastered.

In the *Emperor* Gilels is nothing if not totally compelling, and his imperial account of this masterpiece is outstanding in every way, not just in the passages of grandeur but also in the magical moments of gentle *pianissimo* articulation which recur in the first movement. Ludwig is a sympathetic accompanist in both concertos, alert to every move Gilels makes. Ludwig can also bring a magnificent feeling of drive to tuttis, such as at the grandiose opening of the first movement of the *Emperor*. For power and excitement this is remarkable, but he also shapes the opening of the slow movement with the deepest feeling, to receive a comparable and totally spontaneous response from Gilels. The recording is amazingly good, vivid and full-blooded, and very well balanced with a warmly resonant bass, especially telling in the Adagio. On the original LP the piano timbre had a slightly metallic ring in its highest register; this remains but is not really a problem, and while the orchestral sound lacks the last degree of refinement it lacks nothing in impact, and this disc is one that should be in every collection.

Controversially, in his Australian performance Kovacevich arpeggiates the first chord of No. 4, but that might be thought to enhance his characteristically searching manner. Later on, that movement loses some of the brightness and point that are typical of this pianist, though the slow movement is poised and dedicated and the finale relaxed. About the *Emperor*, sharper and tauter than his earlier, Philips account, there are no reservations, and this is also available coupled on Classics for Pleasure – less appropriately – with the *Grosse Füge* (CfP 585 6162).

Piano Concerto 5 in E flat (Emperor), Op. 73

(BB) (***) Naxos mono 8.110787. Horowitz, RCA Victor SO, Reiner – RACHMANINOV: *Piano Concerto 3* (***)

Both the *Emperor* and its companion come from the early 1950s and are among the classics of the gramophone. Horowitz was underrated as a Beethoven interpreter: his *Emperor* is wonderfully authoritative and completely devoid of ostentation or display. It is among the most classical of readings and Reiner is a totally like-minded partner. Good new transfers.

(i; ii) *Violin Concerto; (ii) Coriolan Overture; (i; iii)*
Romances 1 & 2, Opp. 40 & 50
🎵 (BB) *** HMV (ADD) 5 86675-2. (i) Suk; (ii) New Philh.
O, Boult; (iii) ASMF, Marriner

(i) *Violin Concerto; (ii) Romances 1 in G, Op. 40; 2 in F,*
Op. 50
(BB) *** Arte Nova 82876 76994-2. Tetzlaff, Tonhalle O,
Zinman

David Zinman has followed up his outstandingly successful
set of the Beethoven symphonies for Arte Nova – taking due
note of aspects of period performance – with a series of
concerto recordings, of which this excellent version of the
Violin Concerto is a prime example. Christian Tetzlaff proves
an ideal soloist in this context, his clean attack and pure tone
combining with extreme clarity of articulation in even the
most elaborate passagework. Just how wide a range of expression he has comes out in his account of the first-movement
cadenza – one which, following Beethoven's own cadenza for
the piano version of the concerto, uses the timpani – with the
slow movement marked by big contrasts of poetic tenderness
and romantic warmth. The finale is fast, light and clear, with
rippling passagework. The two *Romances* are equally compelling, and the sound is well suited to bringing out the transparency of the performances. An outstanding bargain.

Suk's performance was widely praised when it first
appeared at the beginning of the 1970s. It is very well
recorded, but the first movement is controversial: it is taken
at an unusually slow tempo and some may feel that the
playing lacks the final degree of concentration to sustain its
conception. Yet, for R.L., Suk's playing is both noble and
spacious. The performance is classical in style, although Suk,
like Kreisler, pulls back at the G minor section in the development of the first movement. But it is the breadth and
grandeur of design that emerge, and the eloquence of the
slow movement and the lightness and sparkle of the finale are
in no doubt. Boult's superbly played account of *Coriolan* is a
real bonus, and the two *Romances* suit the soloist's combination of romantic warmth and stylish classicism perfectly.

(i) *Triple Concerto for Violin, Cello & Piano. Symphony 7*
(B) *** LSO Live LSO 0078.(i) Nikolitch, Hugh, Vogt; LSO,
Haitink

An appealingly spontaneous account of the *Triple Concerto*
(recorded live in the Barbican in November 2005), successfully combining a tonally lightweight trio of soloists, with
Haitink's full-bodied orchestral backing. The balance has
been deftly managed so that the solo group is never dwarfed,
and Haitink's bold tuttis are like a weighty ripieno backing a
chimerical solo concertino. The slow movement brings a
moving cantilena from cellist Tim Hugh, and in the ebullient
finale Lars Vogt leads the high spirits with scintillating piano
roulades.

The coupling is even more impressive. Haitink is not
thought of primarily as a Beethoven symphonist, yet he has
the full measure of the *Seventh Symphony*, and the weight of
his reading gives it strength and gravitas, while still preserving the spirit of the dance. The LSO play superbly for him,
and the gradation of the climax of the slow movement is
magnetically achieved, while the Scherzo really takes off in its
vivacity. The finale too, swiftly but not hectically paced,
builds to an exciting finish, obviously urged on by the presence of the audience. Good, full-bodied sound, but the
Barbican acoustic is slightly damped by the close microphones. But not the performance.

(i) *Triple Concerto for Violin, Cello & Piano; (ii) Septet*
(BB) *** Arte Nova 82876 64015-2. Shaham, Mørk; with (i)
Bronfman, Tonhalle O, Zinman; (ii) Rouilly, Dangel, Reid,
Jenny, Helfti

The coupling of the *Triple Concerto* and the *Septet* is unique,
making a significant point that the *Triple Concerto*, far more
than Beethoven's other concertos, is related to his chamber
music. Zinman and his soloists treat it that way, with light,
clear textures and wonderfully clean articulation from all
three soloists. The slow movement with its soaring cello
melody is played by Truls Mørk with total dedication and
not a hint of sentimentality. The finale is lightly pointed
and, like the rest, is marked by extreme clarity, not least in
the rapid triplets that grace much of the passagework. The
Septet is played with similar blitheness, with allegros often
challengingly fast, yet never rushed, and the wit of the
fifth-movement Scherzo, with its galumphing horn, beautifully brought out. Fine soloists from the orchestra join
Shaham and Mørk in joyful music-making, with the clarinettist exceptionally imaginative. First-rate, cleanly focused
sound.

SYMPHONIES (DVD VERSIONS)

Symphonies 1–3 (Eroica)
🎵 *** DG **DVD** 073 4101 (5.1 Surround Sound). BPO,
Karajan (V/D: No. 1: Arne Arnbohm; No. 2: Hans Joachim
Schulz; No. 3: Karajan)

During the analogue LP era, Karajan recorded the Beethoven
symphonies in stereo, both in 1961/2 and again in 1977, and
undoubtedly the later set was the more successful of the two.
But Karajan also planned a video cycle, and this has now been
issued on DVD. Nos. 1–7 were filmed in 1971; No. 5 was made
a year later; but the joyous *Pastoral* dates from 1967.

The DVD accounts of the earlier symphonies are interpretatively closer to the second cycle. No. 1 is elegant enough, but
the finale is already giving way to genuine Beethovenian
strength and urgency, and this maturity is even more noticeable in No. 2, where the slow movment is richly and beautifully played, and the finale full of characteristic energy and
impulse. The *Eroica* is splendid: the first movement presses
forward strongly but does not sound rushed (especially today
when we are more used to brisk pacing), and the hushed
opening of the *Funeral March* brings an account which is
both deeply felt and intense.

The ever-reliable Arne Arnbohm was the Video Director
for the *First Symphony*, where the cameras follow the music
vividly, moving around freely, catching the powerful response
of the players, but often centring on Karajan, conveying his
personal involvement, eyes closed throughout. Hans Joachim
Schulz directs the cameras in the same vein in No. 2, but
Karajan himself apparently takes over for the *Eroica*, where
the orchestra is re-positioned, now laid out in three triangu-
lar groups, with wind and brass placed in the central triangle.
The camera close-ups continue to involve the listener in the
intensity of the music-making.

Symphonies 4–6 (Pastoral)
🎵 **(*) DG **DVD** 073 4102 (5.1 Surround Sound). BPO,
Karajan (V/D: Nos. 4 & 5: Karajan; 6: conceived and
directed by Hugo Niebling)

The *Fourth* and *Fifth Symphonies* are live performances and
have all the added communicative intensity that this brings.
Karajan is now credited as having taken over the video

direction himself, and the very opening of the *Fourth* is arresting, both visually and musically. The camera often places one very close to the orchestra, seeing the players almost from the conductor's own viewpoint. The *Fifth* (with exposition repeat included) is superb, with all the adrenalin and warmth for which Karajan is famous, and a thrilling finale. Alas, the *Pastoral*, beautifully played though it is, is the one blot on the set. Hugo Niebling, the Director, lays out the orchestra in serried ranks, as if on the barrack square, and there are exaggerated lighting effects, fades, disconcertingly quick changes of camera shots and angles, curious close-ups (as at the start of the *Andante*), losses of focus, and so on. It is all very eccentric and self-aware, and one is often tempted to close one's eyes – which is a pity, for the music-making is glorious and deserves better.

Symphonies 7–9 (Choral)

🔁 *** DG **DVD** 073 4103 (5.1 Surround Sound). Janowitz, Ludwig, Thomas, Berry. Deutsche Opera, Berlin, Ch. in No. 9; BPO, Karajan (V/D: No. 8: Hans Joachim Scholz; Nos. 7 & 9: Karajan)

The *Seventh Symphony* returns the orchestral layout to the triple triangle, but the cameras again frequently take us among the players, which is very stimulating. The performance of the *Seventh* is excitingly hard-driven and rhythmically vibrant, but it mellows in the beautifully played *Allegretto*. The visual layout for the *Eighth* is more conventional, but not the performance. For Karajan it is no 'little' symphony. He takes the first-movement exposition repeat, and drives forward strongly. The central movements bring lighter, refined contrast, but the finale again has powerful thrust and an exciting coda.

The *Choral Symphony*, which dates from 1968, brings four superb soloists, both individually and singing splendidly as a team. Karajan opens his eyes at last, to communicate with the chorus. The performance caps the cycle thrillingly and exudes all the vitality of live music-making, even though recorded in the studio. The layout, with a huge chorus who sing with great involvement and zest, is visually gripping. The sound throughout is excellent, brilliant, wide-ranging and full-bodied, and the chorus has plenty of bite. Karajan's final *accelerando* and the burst of adrenalin at the close of the finale is unforgettable. Altogether this set reminds us what a great Beethoven conductor Karajan was, and the calibre of the Berlin Philharmonic's playing establishes standards which are difficult for rivals to surpass. Even with the flawed production of the *Pastoral Symphony* this set is wonderfully stimulating.

SYMPHONIES (CD VERSIONS)

Symphonies 1–9; Overtures Egmont & Leonora 3

(B) **(*) Ph. 475 6883 (6). Dresden State O, C. Davis (with Sweet, Rappé, Frey, Grundheber & State Op. Ch. in No. 9).

In opulent sound, Sir Colin Davis takes a spacious view of the Beethoven symphonies, drawing beautiful playing from the Dresden State Orchestra. At broad speeds he gives each symphony a concentrated strength, though the grinding dissonances at the heart of the development section of the *Eroica* are warm rather than violent. Reflecting the mature response of a conductor in his late sixties, this is comfortable Beethoven. Anyone wanting a mellow view will be well pleased, but this is not a top choice.

Symphony 3 (Eroica); Overtures: Egmont; Leonora 3; The Ruins of Athens

(BB) *** HMV 5 86670-2. RLPO, Mackerras

Mackerras's powerful *Eroica* is also available on Classics for Pleasure (CfP 575 9842 – see our main volume), where it is coupled with a crisp, alert account of the *First Symphony*. Those preferring these three overtures (which here serve to introduce the symphony) will find Daniel Harding's strongly characterized and beautifully played performances excellent in every way.

Symphony 5

🔁 *** Warner 2564 621791-2. West-Eastern Divan O, Barenboim (with ELGAR: *Nimrod*) – MOZART: *Sinfonia Concertante, K.297b* ***

Recorded in Ramallah in August 2005, Barenboim conducts an electrifying performance of Beethoven's *Fifth* with his brilliantly talented young musicians, Arab and Israeli. Characteristically, he takes an emphatic view of the opening 'Fate knocking on the door' motif, but then launches into the first movement at exhilaratingly high speed. The mystery of the Scherzo (in which the strings play with wonderfully clean articulation in the Trio) leads then to the bold and thrustful account of the finale. Barenboim makes a moving speech afterwards (in English) and rounds the concert off with Elgar's *Nimrod*, an account joyful rather than valedictory in its nobility at a steady speed, wonderfully warm. That such magnetic, finely detailed performances have stemmed from a single live event makes them all the more remarkable.

Symphonies 5; 6

**(*) Sony 82876 74726-2. Tafelmusik, Weil

(M) **(*) RCA (ADD) 82876 67898-2. Boston SO, Munch

Bruno Weil is certainly a powerful Beethovenian, and his Tafelmusik respond to his fast and strongly driven account of the opening movement of the *Fifth* and the firmly motivated *Andante* which, beautifully played, has a balancing warm lyricism. The bold Scherzo makes an admirable foil, and its closing section is subtly managed, as is the preparation for the finale, which storms in, Toscanini fashion, and holds the tension through to the exciting coda.

The opening movement of the *Pastoral Symphony* is brisk (especially when compared with Bruno Walter) with light, resilient playing, is certainly fresh, and the *Scene by the brook* flows beguilingly. The Scherzo has exhilarating rhythmic energy, and the *Storm* bursts in with a real thunderclap, with ferocious timpani rolls sustaining the impact. The finale then moves along at a comparatively relaxed gait, with accent on the swinging duple time, yet the climaxes blossom, and overall this is certainly enjoyable, if not a first choice. Both first-movement exposition repeats are included here, and the recording is first class. One is hardly aware that these are period-instrument performances (apart from the penetrating timpani), so polished and pleasing are the string textures, and this stands quite high among 'authentic' versions of this coupling.

Charles Munch, in this remarkable reissue from 1955, with sound which is unbelievably warm and full for its date, offers an absolutely individual reading, full of energy; his clipped manner and drive remind one very much of the authentic approach, but with a style in the Gallic tradition, with clarity very much a key feature. The first movement of the *Fifth* is propelled with the right sort of nervous tension, but Munch relaxes enough in the slow movement, without ever lingering.

The finale, although at quite a steady tempo, builds up to a blaze of excitement, especially in the brass.

The *Pastoral* gets off to a bracing start and, with its natural phrasing and sprung rhythm, is definitely a spring walk in the countryside. If the *Scene by the brook* does not relax as much as it might, there is a rustically earthy Scherzo, where one enjoys crisp articulation from both the strings and woodwind. The *Thunderstorm* is again impressive with its rhythmic bite, and if in the Finale Munch does not relax as many have done, his fresh approach brings its own rewards. However, Abbado remains first choice for this coupling (DG 471 489-2), and Karajan offers *Symphonies 5, 6* and a truly great recording of the *Choral Symphony* on a DG two-CD set (474 260-2).

Symphonies 5; 7
(BB) *** HMV 5 86671-2. RLPO, Mackerras

Mackerras's revelatory performances are also available on Classics for Pleasure (CfP 572 8492 – see our main volume) and as such are more widely available than this slightly cheaper HMV issue.

(i) Symphony 6 (Pastoral); Overtures:Creatures of Prometheus; (ii) Coriolan; (iii) Fidelio; (i) Leonora No. 3
(BB) (***) Naxos mono 8. 111032. (i) VPO; (ii) British SO; (iii) LSO; Walter

Symphony 6; Overture: Leonora 3
(BB) ** EMI Encore 3 41416-2. Phd. O, Muti

Bruno Walter's readings of the *Pastoral Symphony*, mellow and full of human warmth, have always been special, and his pre-war recording with the Vienna Philharmonic, made in the Musikvereinsaal in 1936, was most special of all. The musical phrasing has a uniquely spontaneous and natural flow, with the *Scene by the brook* eddying peacefully, yet moving forward in an Elysian calm. The finale too has a glorious sense of lyrical apotheosis, with the players creating a radiant climax without forcefulness. The snag is the recording which, in Mark Obert-Thorn's clear, clean transfer, retains the hall's ambient bloom so far as the woodwind is concerned, but produces an unattractively thin texture for the upper strings which is at odds with the music. Obviously this is a recording which needs the alchemy of Mike Dutton. The *Overtures* sound better, even the exciting *Leonora No. 3*, recorded with the same orchestra in the same venue.

With the first two movements youthfully urgent, Muti's is an exhilarating performance, fresh and direct. It is a strong, symphonic view, rather than a programmatic one. The recording is robustly rich and wide-ranging, though the high violins do not always live up to the 'Philadelphia sound'.

Symphony 7 in A, Op. 92 (see also under Missa solemnis, below)
●→ ● (M) *** Orfeo SACD (Surround Sound Compatible) C 700 051B . Bav. State Op. O, Carlos Kleiber

This is the real thing! Carlos Kleiber's DG recording of the *Fifth Symphony* (DG 471 630-2) has long been celebrated as among the finest ever; but his companion account of the *Seventh* never reached quite the same heights. Now Orfeo have released a (1982) live recording of the *Seventh*, made in Munich with the Bavarian State Orchestra, that is if anything even more electrifying than his *Fifth*. The Bavarian orchestra play as if their very lives depended on it: the first movement is riveting enough, with a thrilling coda. But the tension is maintained through the finely graduated and ideally paced *Allegretto*, with richly expressive string-playing. The Scherzo

is dazzling, but the finale, taken *Allegro molto* (rather than *con brio*), carries all before it, generating enormous energy and thrust, and the coda is built to a height of tension not even matched by Toscanini. Yet overall this is a performance that, for all its excitement, has an underlying depth of feeling. The sound has a superbly resonant hall acoustic, and the orchestra is naturally balanced within that ambience; on SACD playback, with the back speakers properly balanced, the feeling of sitting in the hall is uncanny.

Symphony 9 in D min. (Choral), Op. 125
(BB) *** HMV 5 86673-2. Rodgers, Della Jones, Bronder, Terfel, RLPO Ch., RLPO, Mackerras

Symphony 9 (Choral); Overture Egmont
(M) **(*) Sony SK 94745. Obrazsova, Popp, Vickers, Talvela, Cleveland O & Ch., Maazel

Like other performances in his Liverpool cycle, Mackerras's inspired account of the *Choral Symphony* is also available on Classics for Pleasure (CfP 575 9882); it is highly praised in our main volume.

The monumental grandeur of the *Ninth* stands up well to Maazel's urgent and often aggressive Beethoven style. His is a strong performance, but one which misses warmer feelings. The solo quartet is a fine one – Vickers characterful if miscast – and the choral singing is energetic. The recording matches the reading in its clarity and forwardness, with the finale clear and excitingly projected. But this is far from a first choice.

CHAMBER MUSIC

Piano Trios: 1–3, Op. 1/1–3; 7 (Archduke); 9 (Allegretto in E flat), WoO39; 10 (Variations in E flat), Op. 44; 12 (Allegretto in E flat), Hess 48
(BB) *** EMI (ADD) Gemini 3 50798-2 (2). Barenboim, Zukerman, Du Pré

(i) Piano Trios: 4 in D (Ghost); 5 in E flat, Op. 70/1–2; 8 in E flat, WoO38; 11 (Variations on 'Ich bin der Schneider Kakadu'), Op. 121a; (ii) Cello Sonatas 3 in A, Op. 69; 5 in D, Op. 102/2
(BB) *** EMI (ADD) Gemini 3 50807-2 (2). (i) Barenboim, Zukerman, Du Pré; (ii) Du Pré, Kovacevich

The 1970 Barenboim/Zukerman/du Pré set is economically fitted here on to a pair of super-bargain Gemini Doubles, together with the two *Cello Sonatas* Barenboim and du Pré recorded earlier, in 1966. In the *Piano Trios*, even more than usual, the individual takes involved long spans of music, often complete movements, sometimes even a complete work. The result is music-making of rare concentration, spontaneity and warmth. Any tendency to self-indulgence – and this aspect of the playing may seem intrusive to some ears – plus a certain leaning towards romantic expressiveness, is counterbalanced by their urgency and intensity. Speeds tend to be extreme in both directions, and the *Innigkeit* of some of the slow movments, especially in the *Ghost Trio*, Opus 70, No. 1, has the depth of really mature artistry, extraordinary in the work of musicians so young at the time of the recordings, borne out by the photograph of Barenboim and du Pré taken at the time, included in the first box. The excellent analogue recording has been newly remastered on CD, and the players are given a natural presence, with plenty of depth to the sound and a convincing hall ambience.

The recordings of the *Cello Sonatas* come from the year after Jacqueline had made her definitive recording of the

Elgar *Cello Concerto*. The very opening of the *D major Sonata* underlines an unbuttoned quality in Beethoven's writing and when, after the hushed intensity of the slow introduction of Opus 69, the music launches into the allegro, both artists soar away fearlessly. More remarkable still is the range of expressiveness in the slow movement of Opus 102, No. 2. Du Pré's tone ranges from full-blooded *fortissimo* to the mere whisper of a half-tone, and these artists allow the most free range of expressive rubato. With excellent recording, well transferred, these performances make a welcome return to the catalogue, sounding crisp and present on CD, without loss of body and warmth.

Piano Trios: 3, Op. 1/3; 4 in B flat, Op. 11; 10 (Variations in E flat), Op. 44. Theme & Variations on 'Pria ch'io l'impegno' from Weigl's 'L'amor marinaro'
🔴 *** Hyp. CDA 67466. Florestan Trio

This admirable disc completes the Florestan survey of the piano trios, led by the excellent Susan Tomes. The rare set of variations makes a neat encore. The other discs (CDA 62327, 67369 and 67393) are highly praised in our main volume, and the set as a whole can be strongly recommended as a key recommendation in this repertoire.

Piano Trios: 3 in C min., Op. 1/3; 5 (Ghost) in D, Op. 70/1; 11 in G, Op. 121a; 12 (Allegretto in E flat), Hess 48
(M) (**(*)) Pristine mono 2803. Trio Santoliquido

These performances originate from the mid-1950s DG label, where they appeared in the then customary austere presentation of a simple yellow banner title, flanked by white borders. They are particularly strong accounts, tautly held together, sensitive and intelligent and, as far as we know, they have never been reissued before. The *Geistertrio* is even better than we remembered it. All three are wonderful players, and in particular the aristocratic cellist, Massimo Amfitreathof. The pianist Ornello Puliti Santoliquido is vital and imaginative, as is their violinist, Arrigo Pelliccia. Distinguished playing which it is good to have after half a century's absence from the catalogue.

Septet in E flat, Op. 20; Octet for Wind in E flat, Op. 103
(BB) *** EMI Gemini (ADD) 3 50864-2 (2). Melos Ens. of London – MENDELSSOHN: *Octet* **; SCHUBERT: *Octet* ***

With Gervase de Peyer often a dominating personality in a distinguished group (partly because the tone of the leader, Emanuel Hurwitz, is just a little thin as recorded) the Melos Ensemble gives a reading of the *Septet* that brims with life and energy, wonderfully idiomatic and spontaneous-sounding. The recording, from the late 1960s, also still sounds pretty good, and much the same comments apply to the companion work for wind instruments.

STRING QUARTETS (DVD VERSIONS)

String Quartets: 1, 3 & 4, Op. 18/1, 3 & 4; 10 (Harp), Op. 74; 13, Op. 130; 14, Op. 131
*** EMI DVD DVB 3 38567-9 (2). Alban Berg Qt
String Quartets: 2, Op. 18/2; 7 (Rasumovsky), Op. 59/1; 11, Op. 95; 12, Op. 127; 15, Op. 132
*** EMI DVD DVB 3 38580-9 (2). Alban Berg Qt

String Quartets: 5–6, Op. 18/5–6; 8–9 (Rasumovsky), Op. 59/2–3; 16, Op. 135; Grosse Fuge, Op. 133
*** EMI DVD DVB 3 38592-9 (2). Alban Berg Qt

While we are all agreed that the Alban Berg's set of the Beethoven *Quartets* is a very special DVD début, there are some differences of response about the performances themselves that are well expressed by the two following summaries.

E.G. writes: Anyone who has ever felt that the Alban Berg Quartet's performances of Beethoven are too rigid or lack warmth should watch these fascinating DVDs. Austrian Radio recorded this complete cycle in the Konzerthaus in Vienna in 1989 and, quite apart from the smiling portraits of the players on the cover, these are performances that bring out the many varied aspects of Beethoven, the joy of the early quartets and the power of the middle-period works, as well as the depth and weight of the last-period works. Where too often on disc this quartet has seemed to slide over the profundities, here they give rapt, dedicated performances, with hushed intensity a necessary element, and fine shading of dynamic as evident as the brilliance and precision of the ensemble. The order of their play may seem unexpected, with most of the late works included in the middle of concerts rather than at the end, but the rightness of their choice is always evident over the six separate recitals contained on the six separate discs. Only the *B flat Quartet*, Op. 130, and the *A minor Quartet*, Op. 132, come at the ends of concerts, respectively the second and fourth; but each recital represents a satisfying summary of the greatness of these works. The camerawork is rather fussy, with shots of the organ in the Konzerthaus regularly shown hazily behind images of the players themselves.

R.L. agrees that the Alban Berg's cycle as the only DVD set of the Beethoven is obviously welcome, and he continues: They possess a wonderfully burnished tone, superbly blended ensemble and unanimity of attack, as well as flawless intonation. Some may find their dynamics exaggerated and the *pianissimos* do occasionally strike one as a little self-conscious. But there is far more to admire than to cavil at, and the cycle offers much musical satisfaction. Other ensembles, such as the Végh and the Quartetto Italiano, are more deeply in tune with Beethoven's humanity and wisdom, but for technical address and sheer intensity few surpass the Alban Berg. As distinguished a Beethoven authority as the composer Robert Simpson found 'a tendency towards glossiness' in this ensemble and, writing in the late 1970s, he hoped that the Alban Berg would not 'degenerate into highly efficient beautifiers of the classics'. Watching and listening to them, one's thoughts occasionally returned to these words; but for the most part this is music-making on such a high level of accomplishment that criticism is muted. Visually, the direction is impeccable, completely unobtrusive and musical. However, there were occasions when one could wish the tuning between movements could have been a little shortened. (Between the slow movement and Scherzo of Op. 18, No. 6, it is almost 90 seconds long, with an inevitable loss of tension.)

STRING QUARTETS (CD VERSIONS)

String Quartets 1–6, Op. 18/1–6
(B) **(*) Cal. CAL 3633.4 (2). Talich Qt

The Talich have great directness of approach and a simplicity of manner which is disarming. They are recorded clearly, if somewhat dryly. It has to be said that this set won a Grand Prix du Disque and a Diapason D'Or. Excellent value, but we would prefer to stay with the Takács Quartet on Decca (470 848-2).

String Quartets 1–6, Op. 18/1–6
*** Chan. 10381 (3). Borodin Qt

String Quartets 11, Op. 95; 14, Op. 131, Grosse Fuge, Op. 133
*** Chan. 10268. Borodin Qt

Although the Borodins included Op. 95 in one of their first concerts, they have never essayed a complete Beethoven cycle before now. Theirs is as deeply felt as any; their survey, which will be complete within the lifetime of this volume, can be recommended alongside the very finest of recent years, such as the Takács. Recorded in the Grand Hall of the Moscow Conservatory, the sound is satisfyingly warm and present. Most distinguished performances.

String Quartets 1 in F, Op. 18/1; 11 in F min., Op. 95; 16 in F, Op. 135; Satz (Allegretto) in B min., WoO
*** Warner 2564 62161-2. Endellion Qt

String Quartets 3 in D, Op. 18/3; 15 in A min., Op. 132
*** Warner 2564 62196-2. Endellion Qt

The Endellion Quartet is the latest ensemble to embark on a complete cycle, based on the new Henle edition. It is some four decades since the last edition (based on a reprint of the first edition parts) was published. This newcomer, as Jonathan Del Mar observes in a note, embodies some newer discoveries, based on the original first edition parts and a set of the parts in manuscript which came to light in the 1980s with some corrections in Beethoven's hand. The autograph manuscript of Opus 132 survives in the Staatsbibliothk zu Berlin, and the 2002 edition includes a number of corrections, two actually affecting the melodic line. The Endellions are, as always, selfless interpreters, unconcerned with anything other than presenting the music as expertly and imaginatively as possible. They are recorded in the excellent acoustic of Potton Hall, Ipswich, and are truthfully balanced by Tony Faulkner. Recommended.

String Quartets 1 in F, Op. 18/1; 11 in F min., Op. 95; 16 in F, Op. 135
✿ (BB) (***) Dutton mono CDBP 9765. Busch Qt

The Busch recordings come from 1932–3 and were made at the then new Abbey Road Studios. To say that they have never been equalled – let alone surpassed – is no exaggeration. These great musicians penetrated to the core of the Beethoven *Quartets* in much the same way as Schnabel did the *Sonatas*. Of course, there have been many great cycles since (the Busch did not record them all): from the Budapest, the Quartetto Italiano, Végh, and others, but no serious collector of these great works should be without the Busch. Dutton makes them sound better than ever.

String Quartets 3 in D, Op. 18/3; 11 in F min., Op. 95
(BB) (***) Dutton mono CDBP 9752. Griller Qt

String Quartet 15 in A min., Op. 132
(BB) (***) Dutton mono CDBP 9753. Griller Qt

Writing in 1955, when 20 or so different Beethoven quartets were listed in *The Record Guide*, including those above by the Griller Quartet, Desmond Shawe-Taylor and Edward Sackville West could say, 'there is not one single performance of a Beethoven string quartet that can be recommended'. The

Budapest set – in mono, of course – had not then appeared in Europe, and the only complete cycle, by the Pascal Quartet on the short-lived Nixa label, was pretty scruffy.

The Griller's version of the *A minor*, Op. 132, received short shrift: 'there is little to choose between the Griller and the Pascal; as in Op. 95 the Griller quartet is weak in grasp'. Of course the authors were measuring the performances by the standards of the Busch and the pre-war Budapest Quartets. True, the Grillers did not match the former in terms of depth, but there is much to admire in their fluent, well-thought-out and finely balanced readings, which Decca recorded with admirable fidelity and which the Dutton transfers reveal afresh to striking effect.

String Quartets 12–16; Grosse Fuge, Op. 133
(M) *** EMI 4 76820-2 (3) [4 76824-2]. Alban Berg Qt

String Quartets 14–15
(B) **(*) EMI 5 86981-2. Alban Berg Qt

The Alban Berg's second digital set of the late quartets, recorded at public concerts in the Mozartsaal Konzerthaus in 1989 has rightly been chosen for repesentation in EMI's 'Great Recordings of the Century'. On balance, these performances, seeking to ensure the greater intensity and spontaneity generated by the presence of an audience, are freer and more vital than those on the earlier set, but the differences are small. Though the very perfection and sheer beauty of sound are not always helpful in this repertoire, these performances are genuinely felt and not superficial or slick

The separate bargain coupling of Opp. 131 and 132 is drawn from the earlier digital set of 1983, and these recordings do full justice to the magnificently burnished tone they command and the perfection of blend they so consistently achieve.

String Quartets 12 in E flat, Op. 127; 15 in A min., Op. 132
**(*) DG 477 5705. Hagen Qt

The Hagens bring wonderful control and unanimity of ensemble to these great works. There are rival groups who bring greater depth to them and, although they are by no means glib or superficial – indeed, there is much that is deeply musical and carefully considered – they would not be a first choice in either *Quartet*.

String Quartet 16, Op. 135 (arr for strings, van Prooijen)
*** Channel Classics CCSSA 23005. Amsterdam Sinf. –
WALTON: *Sonata for Strings* ***

Beethoven's last quartet comes here in an arrangement by Marijn van Prooijen, an adaptation of the original that in no way inflates it. In this the players seek to follow their maxim of conceiving the orchestra in terms of a string quintet, remaining small in size 'for the exact purpose of preserving the intimate character of works such as these'. In this they contrast the Sinfonietta's approach with that of Leonard Bernstein in his recording of Beethoven's Opus 135 with the Vienna Philharmonic, in which he uses a full body of strings. With the individual Amsterdam players treating their music-making with the give-and-take, ebb-and-flow normal between members of small chamber groups, the result amply bears out that aim, achieving both a rare refinement and natural warmth. The bite and precision are most impressive, with the rhythmic lift of the Scherzo and of the finale after the ominous opening bringing a joyful lightness. Yet it is in the sublime *Lento* slow movement that the performance achieves its greatest heights in playing of hushed dedication, conveying an inner tension such as one finds in a great performance of the original string quartet.

Violin Sonatas 1–10
(B) *** DG 477 5502 (3). Schneiderhan, Seeman

Schneiderhan's stereo set with Carl Seeman was excellently recorded in the Brahms-Saal of the Vienna Musikverein in 1959, and the performances are beautifully played, with understanding from both artists and a characteristically pure and classical line from Schneiderhan. The performances are full of character and joy in the music, and totally spontaneous; and Seeman makes an admirable partner for Schneiderhan. Scheiderhan's earlier (1953) mono set with Kempff still remains highly competitive on all counts. The mono recording (DG 463 605-2) obviously does not separate violin and piano as clearly as this later stereo set, but the internal balance could hardly be bettered. Nevertheless, the later performances have a pleasing stereo ambience and are most enjoyable in their own right.

Violin Sonatas 1–3, Op. 12/1–3; 4, Op. 23; 5 (Spring); 6, Op. 30/1
(BB) **(*) EMI Gemini (ADD) 3 50854-2 (2). Zukerman, Barenboim

Zukerman and Barenboim, friends and colleagues, are both strong and positive artists, and in their collaborations on record thy have consistently struck sparks of imagination off each other. They do so in this set, recorded in 1972 and 1973. But there is a hint that they may have been conscious of earlier criticism that their collaborations were too idiosyncratic. These are much more central performances than those of the cycle of Beethoven Trios with du Pré. Nevertheless, this is a safe recommendation, if not as imaginatively volatile as the series by Perlman and Ashkenazy. The rest of the sonatas will almost certainly follow.

Violin Sonatas (i) 5 (Spring); (ii) 9 (Kreutzer)
(M) *** Decca 475 7509. Perlman, Ashkenazy
(BB) **(*) EMI Encore 5 87001-2. Yehudi & Jeremy Menuhin

On Decca, an obvious candidate for the new Originals label. The dynamism is there but never becomes too extrovert, and the music unfolds naturally and spontaneously. The recording quality is excellent: the disc has been remastered for this reissue.

In 1986 Yehudi Menuhin re-recorded these works, this time with his son. Jeremy plays remarkably well, if not quite matching Hephzibah in the slow movement of the Kreutzer. Menuhin's timbre may be less rounded than formerly and his technique less refined, but the nobility of line is still apparent, and the spontaneity and family chemistry are as potent as ever. The Kreutzer finale is joyfully spirited. Excellent recording in a resonant acoustic.

PIANO MUSIC

Piano Sonatas 1–32 (complete)
(BB) *** Warner 2564 62767-2 (10). Pommier
(B) **(*) Decca (ADD; No. 29 is mono) 475 7198 (8). Backhaus

Jean-Bernard Pommier's Beethoven sonata cycle was recorded in the Fontfroide Abbey in Narbonne between 1990 and 1997, and it was generally well received. As is also evident from the interview included in the booklet, he is a thoughtful

and intelligent artist, and this shows throughout. No one acquiring this bargain set is likely to be disappointed and the sound is eminently satisfactory. In the competitive world of 2006 it does not displace Stephen Kovacevich's set, which is still readily available, or those of Kempff and Richard Goode. However, this is still of three-star quality, both artistically and technically.

Backhaus recorded his survey over a decade, from 1958 to 1969 (with the exception of the Hammerklavier, which came much earlier, in 1953, and is mono). As it happens, this last represents the peak of the cycle, offering playing of great power and concentration. When the other records appeared individually as LPs, they received a mixed press, and our own welcome for them was not always enthusiastic. Now a reassessment is due, for Backhaus's direct, sometimes brusque manner does not derive from any lack of feeling, rather from a determination to present Beethoven's thoughts adorned with no idiosyncratic excrescences.

At his best, as in the Waldstein and Appassionata Sonatas, the performances present a characteristic mixture of rugged spontaneity and wilfulness, which can be remarkably compelling. But there are many other examples of his positive, alert and imaginative response which balance the apparently uncompromising wilfulness of manner. He was less suited to the more lightweight works, such as the sprightly little G major Sonata of Opus 14 (No. 10), and the literal manner also robs the G minor of Opus 49 (No. 19) of charm. Yet even here he plainly enjoyed himself in his own way, so that his responses are conveyed to the listener.

Generally – as with the Hammerklavier – the bigger the challenge for him, the more impressive his performance. Yet he could relax, and his account of No. 18 in E flat, Op. 31/3, is an almost ideal interpretation, full of grace and poise in the first movement, and never lacking brio in the finale. His account of the A major, Op. 26 (No. 12), also shows him at his finest; his way of handling violent irregularities of the Scherzo and his undeniably heroic approach to the Marcia funèbre are matched by the variety of touch in the variations, and at the minor section of the finale.

His massive, rather gruff style naturally suits the later rather than the earliest sonatas, but even in Opus 101, where the challenge is greatest, the uningratiating manner will not suit all tastes, and the very powerful accounts of Opus 109 and Opus 111 do not always leave the music quite enough space to breathe. But overall the set is a formidable achievement, and a reminder of a keyboard giant from the past. The recording is remarkably faithful; the only real drawback is that the close balance brings a comparative lack of dynamic range. For I.M., with a Backhaus performance, at times he imagines a visual image of Beethoven himself sitting at the keyboard. We do not know how he played his own music, but it was surely uncompromisingly direct, and maybe the great German pianist captures something of its character.

Piano Sonatas 3 in C, Op. 2/3; 32 in C min., Op. 111
*** Opus Arte DVD OA 0939D. Michelangeli – GALUPPI; SCARLATTI: Sonatas ***

These magisterial performances come from the Archives of RAI (Italian Radio-TV) and derive from a 1962 recital given in Turin. The playing is of the utmost elegance and refinement, and there is a cool poise that is totally appropriate to the early C major Sonata but less so to Op. 111. We found his Decca LP recording of Op. 111 (SXL 6181) from the 1960s cool and marmoreal, though a rather close balance did not help matters. Perhaps the presence of an audience makes him less unyielding, though he still holds the rhythm on a very tight rein. Marvellous pianism in terms of range and colour, and something to wonder at rather than to be involved by. His demeanour is, as always, aloof as if he was not expecting an audience and is not quite sure that he welcomes it. Unobtrusive camerawork. Though the black-and-white image is not always sharp in focus, Michelangeli is totally compelling.

Piano Sonatas 7 in D, Op. 10/3; 14 (Moonlight); 22 in F, Op. 54; 23 (Appassionata), Op. 57
*** Warner 2564 62300-2. Lugansky

Nikolai Lugansky is emerging as a pianist of stature and an artist to his fingertips. These are immaculate performances and among the finest Beethoven sonata discs to have come our way recently – and there have been no lack of them. One tends to associate great Beethoven playing with artists from mittel-Europa: Schnabel, Kempff, Backhaus, Brendel and so on. But with Lugansky one's thoughts turn to his great compatriot, Gilels. Truthful recorded sound.

Piano Sonatas 8 (Pathétique); 13 in E flat, Op. 27/1; 14 (Moonlight), Op. 27/2; 23 (Appassionata)
(BB) *** HMV (ADD) 5 86676-2. Barenboim

Barenboim's 1966 disc of Beethoven's three most famous named sonatas has stood the test of time, the performances volatile, even wilful at times, but convincingly spontaneous. For this inexpensive reissue the second of the two Opus 27 Sonatas has been added, no less impulsive but equally compelling. The recording is remarkably realistic.

Piano Sonatas 8 (Pathétique); 14 (Moonlight); 23 (Appassionata)
(M) *** Telarc CD 80118. O'Connor

John O'Connor's performances are far from barnstorming, but their thoughtful seriousness makes them distinctly individual. He opens the *Pathétique* gravely, just as Beethoven indicated, and finds a link with the similarly sustained central *Adagio*. He begins the *Appassionata* with similar gravity, again creating an affinity with the central variations, which are most beautifully played. The *Moonlight* opens *sotto voce*, but has no lack of concentration, and its natural pacing is again magnetic in its simplicity. Yet while the *Allegretto* then makes a delightfully light-fingered contrast, in the central section one might have liked stronger accenting. But once the allegros are under way, in any of these three works, the playing has an impetuous spontaneity which is very communicative and O'Connor's keyboard control is commanding. The 1985 recording (not unexpectedly from Telarc) is in the demonstration bracket and is beautifully balanced. But both Brendel and Rubinstein offer an extra sonata for a similar cost.

Piano Sonatas 8 (Pathétique); 14 (Moonlight); 23 (Appassionata); 26 (Les Adieux)
🏻➔ ⏺(M) *** RCA (ADD) **SACD** 82876 71619-2. Rubinstein
(M) *** Ph. 475 7555. Brendel

Artur Rubinstein had never recorded the *Moonlight* previously, and he brings to it a combination of freshness and maturity to make it stand out even among many fine recorded versions, with an improvisatory feel to the opening movement which is unforgettable and which also extends to the performance of *Les Adieux*, which is hardly less magical. The *Pathétique* has a youthful urgency in the outer movements, and the simplicity of the *Adagio cantabile* brings a

wonderfully sustained sense of spiritual peace, while the impulsive surge of feeling in the *Appassionata* is equally compelling. The recordings, made in the Manhattan Center in New York City in 1962 and 1963, have been superbly remastered by John Newton from the original three-track source, and this compatible SACD brings a remarkable sense of realism and presence, and is firmer in the bass than on LP.

Brendel's, too, are undeniably impressive performances, and for this reissue as one of Philips's Originals, *Les Adieux* is now added to the original favourite triptych. He is given really first-rate sound but, good though this disc is, the performances must yield to Rubinstein's for incandescent spontaneity.

Piano Sonatas 13 in E flat; 14 (Moonlight), Op. 27/1–2; 23 (Appassionata)
(BB) ** EMI Encore 5 86085-2 [5 86086-2]. Watts

André Watts uses a Yamaha which has a warm, full-bodied timbre and articulates as clearly as one could wish. However, it was a strange choice to have the *E flat Sonata* instead of one of the other popular named works in a collection like this. Yet in the event it is the most successful performance here, for the *Appassionata* is let down by the direct, comparatively unimaginative account of the central variations, and the *Moonlight* too lacks the aura of the very finest peformances on disc.

Piano Sonatas 17 in D (Tempest), Op. 31/2; 31 in A flat, Op. 110
(*) EuroArts Callico Classics CCCR 101 Jill Crossland – MOZART: *Sonata in F* *

Jill Crossland is a new name to be reckoned with. Yorkshire-born, she studied at the Royal Northern College of Music and while a student performed the complete cycle of Bach's *Well-Tempered Klavier*. She went on to Vienna to work with Paul Badura-Skoda. A highly individual player, thoughtful yet compelling, she has the gift of spontaneity in the recording studio to carry the personal insights of her interpretations, as at a live performance. Her account of the *Adagio* of the '*Tempest*' *Sonata* is wonderfully lyrical, and the delicacy of the finale equally persuasive. The following performance of Opus 110 is undoubtedly very wayward, but her strength of commitment is always convincing, and in the *Adagio* and *Fugue* she is at her most magnetic, with the tension sustained and increased to the powerful close of the sonata. She is very well recorded.

Piano Sonata 29 (Hammerklavier); Bagatelles, Op. 126/2 & 3
*** EMI **DVD** 4 901229. Alfred Brendel (with SCHUBERT: *Wanderer Fantasy*; Julius Katchen)

Brendel has made several commercial recordings of the *Hammerklavier*, most notably a commanding account on the old Vox-Turnabout label from the 1960s, as well as a studio recording for Philips in the 1970s. His 1982 recording, made at a Queen Elizabeth Hall recital, has also won much acclaim. The present DVD, in black and white, was made in Paris in February 1970 and offers a rare opportunity to see as well as hear him. He puts the listener immediately under his spell and proves (as ever) a dedicated and faithful guide.

In Solomon Volkov's *Testimony*, we are told that the great Russian pianist Sofronitzky, when a student at St Petersburg, was summoned to the exalted office of the director, Glazunov. He was naturally apprehensive as to what was so urgent. Glazunov merely asked him what he thought of the *Hammerklavier*, and the pianist stammered his admiration. Glazunov nodded his head in consternation and muttered that he 'couldn't stand the piece!' Well, had he heard this (or the wonderful accounts by Gilels, Solomon or Kovacevich) he might, perhaps, have seen the light. The bonus is a rare tele-recording from ORTF of Julius Katchen playing the *Wanderer Fantasy* in the last months before his death.

Piano Sonatas 30 in E flat, Op. 109; 31 in A flat, Op. 110; 32 in C min., Op. 111
**(*) Ph. 475 6935. Uchida

Mitsuko Uchida receives (and of course deserves) a state-of-the-art recording. As piano sound it would be difficult to better. As piano playing too it is quite superlative, but as Beethoven playing it is more problematic. The first movement of Opus 110 has great beauty, but she exaggerates *pianissimos* and tends to beautify detail. There are not really enough rough edges in the *Allegro molto*. Many will find it difficult to resist this as piano playing, but compared with, say, Stephen Kovacevich (to name one of the more recent Beethoven interpreters who spring to mind) she offers beauty, while he gives us truth first and beauty second.

Piano Sonatas 29 (Hammerklavier); 32 in C min., Op. 111
(B) (*(**)) EMI mono 4 76865-2. Solomon

Readers not collecting the Testament series of Solomon's mono recordings might have been be pleased to have this well chosen re-coupling of the *Hammerklavier* and Op. 111, now reissued in EMI's 'Great Artists of the Century' series. But, alas, in the transfer of the *Hammerklavier Sonata* the *fortissimos* are very clattery and shallow.

Piano Sonatas 31, Op. 110; 32, Op. 111; Bagatelles, Op. 126/5 & 6
*** EMI **DVD** 3 149090-2. Stephen Kovacevich

Beethoven's last two piano sonatas have inspired Stephen Kovacevich for many years to some of the most dedicated pianism imaginable. Here, in a DVD recorded in August 2004 at La Roque d'Antheron, one can visually witness the depth of his concentration, adding to the intensity of the experience. These are not just thoughtful readings but powerful ones, notably in the first movement of Opus 111. Some may find the camerawork distracting when, quite frequently, the pianist's hands are made to fill the whole screen, but that is a minor distraction.

Bagatelles, Op. 126; Rondo à Capriccio, Op. 129; 33 Variations on a Waltz by Diabelli
◉ (BB) (***) Naxos mono 8.110765. Schnabel

Schnabel's account of the *Diabelli Variations* was made in the 1930s. It has never been surpassed, although there have been readings which have come some of the way close to approaching it (Horszowski, Kovacevich, Brendel and, more recently, Piotr Anderszewski). But there is a special authority and wisdom here, and this set should be in every collector's library.

33 Variations on a Waltz by Diabelli, Op. 120
(M) *** Ph. (ADD) 474 7556. Kovacevich

33 Variations on a Waltz by Diabelli; Piano Sonata 24 in F sharp, Op. 78
(BB) * ASV Resonance GLD 4017. Demidenko

Stephen Kovacevich here gives one of his most deeply satisfying performances ever recorded. But this has previously been available as a bargain disc. Now, with its elevation to Philips's Originals label, although it has been remastered, it comes at

medium price. We have to say that it is worth it, though Anderszewski's more recent Virgin recording is even finer, the most outstanding, most thoughtful set of the *Diabelli Variations* to have appeared for many years (5 45468-2).

Nikolai Demidenko was one of the runners-up at the 1978 Moscow Tchaikovsky Competition, when Pletnev won First Prize. Demidenko has fashioned a considerable international reputation for himself over the years and has made some impressive records. Never is his virtuosity in doubt. However, this *Diabelli* is impossible. Demidenko wilfully disregards many of Beethoven's markings – in variation 8, for example, the left hand is marked *sempre legato*, but in Demidenko's reading it is staccato. And this is only one of so many instances in which he distorts or ignores the composer's intentions. Nor does the *Sonata* escape his ego. Demidenko, not Beethoven, is what you get here; and if it is the latter that you want, there are plenty of fine alternatives from the likes of (in alphabetical order) Anderszewski, Brendel, Kovacevich and, above all, Schnabel listed above.

32 Variations on a Waltz by Diabelli, Op. 120; 32 Variations on an Orginal Theme in C min., WoO 80
(BB) *** ASV Resonance CD RSN 3058. Frith

Benjamin Frith brings out both the rhythmic urgency and power of the *Diabelli Variations*, playing with a consistent sense of spontaneity, persuasively leading on from one variation to the next and bringing magnetic intensity to the meditative variations. He then takes the great fugue just before the end of the work at a sensible speed that allows him to spring the rhythms and shape it effectively, rounding off the work with a crisply pointed account of the final Minuet which keeps in mind its dance origin. He follows with a masterly account of the 32 *Variations in C minor*, in which flamboyant virtuosity and poetry are well contrasted. Good, bright piano-sound, set in a helpfully warm acoustic.

VOCAL MUSIC

(i) Mass in C, Op. 86; Meeresstille und glückliche Fahrt (Calm Sea and a Prosperous Voyage), Op. 112
(BB) * Warner Apex 2564 62081-2. Audrey Michael, Bizimeche-Eisinger, Schaeffer, Brodard, Gulbenkian Ch. & O, Corboz

Corboz is usually a reliable conductor and he has made many fine recordings. But this is not one of them, disapppointingly let down by the resonant acoustic of the Egreria de Jesus, Lisbon, where the definition of the chorus, who sing well, is not sharp enough in focus to make a real impact. But Corboz's direction, too, could be more dramatic (especially in *Calm Sea and Proeperous Voyage*, which needs the strongest advocacy) and he could have chosen a more characterful team of soloists. Not recommended – the Hickox/Chandos coupling is the one to have (Chan. 0703 – see our main volume).

Missa solemnis in D, Op. 123
🔊 *** DG 435 770-2 (2). Studer, Norman, Domingo, Moll, Leipzig R. Ch., Swedish R. Ch., VPO, Levine

(i) Missa solemnis in D; (ii) Choral Fantasia in C, Op. 80
(M) *(*) RCA 82876 76223-2 (2). (i) Orgonasova, Rappé, Heilmann, Rootering; (ii) Oppitz; Bav. R. Ch. & O, C. Davis

The 1991 Salzburg Festival honoured its late music director, Herbert von Karajan, in this performance of Beethoven's

Missa solemnis, conducted by James Levine. With a starry quartet of soloists, the live recording has an incandescence that conveys the atmosphere of a great occasion, and the DG engineers have obtained rich, weighty sound. For such an intense visionary experience, defying the conventional view of Levine, this is a version not to be missed.

During his years as music director of the Bavarian Radio Orchestra, Sir Colin Davis's view of Beethoven, always direct, had grown broader, not just in speeds but in manner. So in the *Missa solemnis* both the *Kyrie* and the opening of the *Credo* are so measured, with rhythms evenly stressed, that they do not avoid stodginess. That the chorus is balanced rather distantly also mutes the impact, and the soloists do not make a perfect match, with the tenor, Uwe Heilmann, sounding fluttery. Having the *Choral Fantasia* as makeweight, with a fine piano contribution from Gerhard Oppitz, is some compensation, but hardly justifies a strong recommendation, when there is already an outstanding recording directed by Levine (which is now chosen by DG for their 'Critics' Choice series) and, at budget price, Zinman (Arte Nova 74321 87074-2), praised in our main volume.

OPERA

Fidelio (complete; DVD versions)

*** Arthaus DVD 101 099. Söderström, De Ridder, Gale, Appelgren, Allman, Glyndebourne Festival Ch, LPO, Haitink (Director: Peter Hall; V/D: Dave Heather)

It is good to have as consummate an actress as Elisabeth Söderström as Leonore in this vintage Glyndebourne account of *Fidelio*, recorded in 1979. That was well before the new opera house was built there; in the old, small auditorium there is no question of Söderström's pure soprano being overwhelmed, even if the dry acoustic is not a help. Bernard Haitink conducts a powerful performance, with Kurt Appelgren a superb Rocco, Elizabeth Gale a sweet Marzelline, and Anton de Ridder an unstrained Florestan. Though Robert Allman is a rather gritty-toned Pizarro, that goes well with the character. John Busy's sets for Peter Hall's production vividly capture the atmosphere of the Napoleonic period, including the domestic scenes at the start. A clear first choice on DVD.

Fidelio (complete; CD versions)

(M) ** Warner 3984 25249-2 (2). Meier, Domingo, Pape, Struckmann, Isokoski, Güra, Deutsche State Op., Berlin, Ch. & O, Barenboim (with *Overtures Leonora 1–3*)

(M) * EMI 3 52430-2 (2). Denoke, Vickers, Held, Polgár, Banse, Trost, Quastoff, Arnold Schoenberg Ch., BPO, Rattle

In Barenboim's version the links are provided in the cued synopsis, and the recording simply omits dialogue, except in passages of accompanied melodrama. The other oddity is that Barenboim prefers the magnificent *Leonora No. 2 Overture* as a prelude to the opera and holds back the usual one for *Fidelio* as an appendix, following performances of *Leonora Nos. 1* and *3* at the end of the opera. He also reverses the order of the first two numbers, with Marzelline's little aria coming first. Barenboim is a dedicated Beethoven interpreter, but this is not one of his most inspired recordings. It is worth hearing for the sake of Plácido Domingo's heroic account of the role of Florestan, clean and incisive, if strained at times. Waltraud Meier becomes shrill under pressure, and Soile Isokoski with her marked vibrato is a matronly Marzelline. René Pape is an excellent, firm Rocco, but Falk Struckmann is wobbly and strained as Pizarro, and Kwangchul Youn is a lightweight Fernando.

Rattle's Berlin version was made at a concert performance in the Philharmonie, soon after he had conducted stage performances at the Salzburg Easter Festival in 2003. As his performances at Glyndebourne demonstrated, his approach to the opera is brisk and incisive, with one or two unexpectedly slow speeds for contrast. Yet with all that preparation, the serious disappointment of this set is that it offers a comfortable run-through rather than a genuinely dramatic experience. Even the Canon Quartet in Act I lacks tension, with none of the rapt mystery it should have. Only at the end of Act II does the performance acquire something of the bite one expects, and even then the opening of the finale is brisk to the point of sounding perfunctory. The cast too is seriously flawed: Angela Denoke with her big, fruity voice is far too approximate in her tuning to be a convincing Leonore, sometimes squally and too often sounding cautious. As Florestan, Jon Vickers is a tenor gritty with vibrato, and Alan Held as Pizarro similarly sings between the cracks, with pitch ill-determined. Laszló Polgár is a lightweight Rocco, making the gaoler a *buffo* character, and Juliane Banse is too mezzo-ish to make a convincing Marzelline. Only Rainer Trost as Jaquino and Thomas Quasthoff come near to matching those in rival casts; and the Arnold Schoenberg Choir sounds surprisingly uninvolved, with ensemble far less crisp than usual.

Fidelio (sung in English; CD Version)

(M) *** Chan. 3123 (2). Brewer, Lloyd, Evans, Hunka, Purves, Margison, Philh. Ch. & O, Parry

It is a measure of David Parry's achievement as an opera conductor (not least in Peter Moores' Opera in English series) that, facing the challenge of directing Beethoven's *Fidelio*, he offers so strong and cohesive a reading. His speeds for the Overture and most of the opening domestic scenes are brisk but never breathless, yet when he is faced with such a sublime number as the Canon Quartet he allows full expansiveness, as he does in so many of the transcendent moments, such as the '*Komm Hoffnung*' section of Leonore's *Abscheulicher*, the Prisoners' Chorus and the radiant climax of the Act II finale. Parry is helped not only by outstandingly vivid recording, among the finest ever to come from Chandos, but an exceptionally consistent cast, with no weak link in it. It is good to have so distinguished a soprano as Christine Brewer as Leonore, at once heroic but intensely human and warm, brilliant in the demanding *Abscheulicher*. She is well matched by the Florestan of Richard Margison, who sings his long opening aria in Act II with unusual subtlety, starting on the gentlest *pianissimo*, always vocalizing lyrically and never barking in Heldentenor style, suggesting a fresh, youthful hero. Rebecca Evans, sweet and radiant, is outstanding as Marzelline, opposite the light, clear Jaquino of Peter Wedd, with the veteran, Robert Lloyd, as a characterful Rocco. Like the Florestan, the Pizarro of Pavlo Hunka sounds relatively youthful, again a singer who vocalizes well instead of barking, and Christopher Purves too as the governor, Don Fernando, sounds youthfully firm. A fresh, convincing reading that offers well-produced dialogue in English.

BELLINI, Vincenzo (1801–35)

Norma (complete; DVD version)

** TDK DVD DV-OPNOR. Anderson, Barcellona, Shin Young Hoon, Abdrakov, Melani, Verdi Festival Ch., Europa Galante, Biondi (V/D: Carlo Battistoni)

The TDK *Norma* was filmed at the Teatro Regio, Parma, in 2001.

June Anderson sings freshly enough in the title-role but is no match for Sutherland or Caballé on the two competing sets. Daniela Barcellona is an impressive Adalgisa, and the cast overall is sound, as is the conducting of Fabio Biondi and the stylized traditional production. But there is nothing special here, and the photography of the singers is at times garish. The alternative versions from Sydney (Arthaus 100 180), with modern, digital sound, or the dramatic Turin version with Josephine Veasey as Adalgisa making a superb foil for Caballé, are the DVDs to go for – although, alas, the Hardy set offers restricted mono recording (Hardy HCD 4003) – see our main volume.

BENATZKY, Ralph (1884–1957)
Stolz, Robert (1880–1975)

L'Auberge du cheval blanc (The White Horse Inn (operetta; complete)
(B) ** EMI (ADD) 5 74070-2 (2). Bourvil, Forli, Dens, Ervil, Germain, René Duclos Ch., Paris Conservatoire O, Nuvolone

The Czech composer Ralph Benatzky had quite a distinguished career in the field of light music and operetta during the first half of the twentieth century and is chiefly remembered for his Johann Strauss pastiche *Casanova* (1928) and, especially, for *The White Horse Inn* (1930). The present operetta enjoyed some success in the 1930s, both in Paris and on Broadway. Its mixture of the styles of operetta and early musical is attractive: there are waltzes alongside the dance rhythms of the day. Highlights include a fully fledged *Tyrolienne* in Act II, along with a drunken version, complete with hiccups, in the same Act. There is also a lively tango duet and some melting waltzes, some with off-stage choruses. Alas, there are absolutely no texts – nor even notes in English. The performance is quite a good one, with voices suited to this style of music and with lively characterizations. The 1962 recording is vivid, although some voices are very closely miked.

The White Horse Inn: highlights (in English)
(B) *** CfP (ADD) 3 35952-2. Grimaldi, Croft, Weir, Leigh, Sammes, Hawk, Mike Sammes Singers, 20th Century O, Douglas – STOLZ: *Wild Violets* **; YOUMANS: *No, No, Nanette* **(*)

This lively performance of *White Horse Inn* captures many of the best numbers from this delightfully sentimental operetta, first performed in 1930 (the show contained various interpolated numbers, with two by Robert Stolz). Not all the singing is first rate, but it is all in the right style and the diction is excellent. The lovely *You Too* is wonderfully nostalgic and one of the work's many highlights. The 1961 recording is very upfront, more in the manner of a film soundtrack, and, the odd bit of distortion aside, is certainly vivid, if just a little unyielding after a while. Interesting and enjoyable couplings, too.

BENDA, František (1709–86)

Violin Concertos: in D; D min.
(BB) *** Naxos 8.553902. Suk or Pfister, Suk CO, Christian Benda – JAN JIRI BENDA: *Concerto in G* ***

Of these two concertos, the *D minor* is certainly the finer, for it has a memorably gentle slow movement and a buoyantly lively finale, which Christian Benda and his chamber orchestra relish for its sparkling vitality. Both soloists play most elegantly, and if these works are not highly individual they are both enjoyable when so sympathetically presented. The recording too cannot be faulted.

BENDA, Jan Jiří (1713–52)

Violin Concerto in G
(BB) *** Naxos 8.553902. Suk, Suk CO, Christian Benda – FRANTISEK BENDA: *Concertos in D; D min.* ***

Jan Jiří Benda was a member of a celebrated Bohemian family of musicians, and his *G major Concerto* sparkles with vitality in the outer movements (with a faint flavour of Bach) and has a rather fine solo cantilena as its centrepiece. Josef Suk is highly sympathetic and dazzles the ear in the sharply pointed rhythms of the finale. Excellent, polished accompaniments and full, natural recording. This disc is well worth its modest cost.

BENDA, Jiří Antonín (1722–95)

Sinfonias 1 in D; 2 in G; 3 in C; 4 in F; 5 in G; 6 in E flat
(BB) **(*) Naxos 8.553408. Prague CO, Christian Benda
Sinfonias 7 in D; 8 in D; 9 in A; 10 in G; 11 in F; 12 in A
(BB) **(*) Naxos 8.553409. Prague CO, Christian Benda

The Bohemian Benda family was something of a musical dynasty in Europe over a period of some 300 years. Jiří's twelve three-movement symphonies are conventional but are kept alive by the rhythmic vigour of the allegros and the graceful but uneventful *Andantes*. Occasionally he features a solo flute or (as in the *Larghetto* of No. 7) a pair of flutes, in No. 9 a songful oboe, and in No. 6, one of the finest of the series, a solo violin takes a concertante role; the scoring for woodwind and horns in the finale is very effective. But the orchestration is seldom a striking feature, and these sinfonias are best approached singly, rather than in a group. Christian Benda is a more recent member of the family clan, and he directs the excellent Prague Chamber Orchestra with vigour and spirit, shaping slow movements with affection. The Naxos recording is admirably fresh and truthful, and the ambience is most pleasing.

BENEDICT, Julius (1804–85)

The Lily of Killarney: Highlights
(B) ** CfP (ADD) 3 35948-2. Hinds, Dunne, Dean, O'Callaghan, O, Nelson (with Irish Love Songs) – BALFE: *The Bohemian Girl* **; WALLACE: *Maritana* **(*)

Benedict's music has a soft Irish lilt and also a strong rhythmic flavour of Sullivan. Its pastel shades make a pleasing contrast with the primary colours of Wallace's *Maritana* selection. *The Moon hath raised* is typical, but the other three numbers here are equally pleasant, and they bring out the best in the soloists, who do not attempt to over-sing them. Especially charming is Veronica Dunne's performance of *I'm alone*. The opera (first performed at Covent Garden in 1862), which has a rustic plot with mistaken accusations of murder, has a happy ending, just in case you were worried. Bright sound.

BENJAMIN, Arthur (1893–1960)

Symphony 1; Ballad for String Orchestra
**(*) Marco Polo 8.223764. Queensland SO, Lyndon-Gee

The composer had served in each World War, and when his symphony was written, in 1944–5, he was surely reflecting his personal experience in both conflicts. The opening of the first movement with its violent drum-beats immediately creates a darkness of mood which is seldom to lift throughout the work. The *Ballad* is hardly less disconsolate in feeling, again expressing its melancholy through an ongoing string cantilena. Here the Queensland strings are especially impressive, and Christopher Lyndon-Gee always responds convincingly to the emotional intensity which all this music carries. The recording is spacious if a little two-dimensional.

(i) *Cello Sonatina*; (ii) *Viola Sonata*; (iii) *Violin Sonatina; 3 Pieces for Violin & Piano; Jamaican Rumba*; (iv) *Le Tombeau de Ravel* (for clarinet and piano)
*** Tall Poppies TP 134. Tall Poppies Ensemble: Munro, with (i) Pereira; (ii) Van Stralen; (iii) Harding; (iv) Jenkin

Although opening with a lilting account of the *Jamaican Rumba* in the 1944 arrangement for violin and piano, dedicated to and played by Heifetz, the earliest music here is also for violin and piano, a set of *Three Pieces*. A lively *Humoresque* and *Carnavalesque* (with a curious tolling-bell introduction) frame a ghostly *Arabesque*. The *Violin Sonatina* followed in 1924, with its opening movement, *Tranquilly flowing*, becoming increasingly passionate, followed by a perky *Scherzo* and a charming closing *Rondo*.

The *Cello Sonatina* of 1938 is perhaps the most warmly lyrical of Benjamin's string duos, easily melodic but with a highly rhythmic closing *March*. The *Viola Sonata*, written in 1942 for William Primrose, is a particularly fine work, combining a haunting *Elegy* with a nostalgic *Waltz*, and ending with a boldly virtuosic *Toccata*. But especially beguiling is the *Tombeau de Ravel*, written for Gervase de Peyer, which exploited that artist's melting cantabile timbre and his virtuosity in six quixotic central waltz interludes, framed by an introduction and finale. All the performances here are of high quality and show a composer of great resource who always captures and holds the listener's ear. The recording is excellent.

Pastoral Fantasy (for string quartet); *5 Spirituals* (for cello & piano); *Viola Sonata; 3 Violin Pieces; A Tune & Variations for Little People; Violin Sonatina.*
(M) *** Dutton Epoch CDLX 7110. Locrian Ens.

This excellent Dutton collection duplicates the *Viola Sonata* and *Violin Sonatina*, and the *Three Pieces* also offered on the Tall Poppies disc above, with the performances here if anything more persuasive, no less passionate and often with appealing touches of fantasy. The *Three Violin Pieces* are more intimate in style and are presented in a different order. These artists are completely inside all this music and have the advantage of the warm acoustic of The Maltings, Snape. The *Five Spirituals* are delightful vignettes which ought to be in the regular cello repertoire, while the *Pastoral Fantasy* is in the best tradition of English pastoralism. The composer avoids quoting actual folksongs, yet introduces a seductive pastiche *Musette* within the Scherzo, which is marked *Andante molto languido*. The *Tune* on which he bases his *Variations for Little People* is also very beguiling. This disc has

a price advantage over its equally admirable Tall Poppies competitor, but both collections are well worth investigating.

PIANO MUSIC

Brumas Tunes; Chinoiserie; Elegiac Mazurka; Fantasies I–II; Haunted House; Jamaican Rumba; Let's Go Hiking; 3 New Fantasies; Odds and Ends I–II; Pastorale, Arioso & Finale; Romance-impromptu; Saxophone Blues; Scherzino; Siciliana; Suite
*** Tall Poppies TP 105. Munro

Australian born, Arthur Benjamin's *Jamaican Rumba* was the result of a professional examination visit to England in 1938, and it soon became a worldwide hit. He did not repeat that success, yet his other genre pieces here are full of attractive ideas and comparably catchy rhythmic invention, at times cool in the jazz sense of the word (*Saxophone Blues*), at others (the *Odds and Ends* or the *Fantasies*, for instance) offering writing of charming but indelible simplicity. Throughout Ian Munro plays with great style and elegance and with obvious affection. This is a wholly delightful recital, with never a dull moment throughout its 78 minutes. The recording is admirably natural. (If you find it difficult to obtain this CD, you can order it direct from Tall Poppies, PO Box 373, Glebe, NSW 2037, Australia.)

BENJAMIN, George (born 1960)

(i) *Ringed by the Flat Horizon*; (ii) *At First Light; A Mind of Winter*
*** Nim. NI 5075. (i) BBC SO, Elder; (ii) Walmsley-Clark, L. Sinf., composer

Ringed by the Flat Horizon is a 20-minute orchestral piece, with the big climax masterfully built. *A Mind of Winter* is a nine-minute setting of *The Snowman* by Wallace Stevens, beautifully sung by the soprano Penelope Walmsley-Clark. *At First Light* makes up a stimulating group of works. Sound of great warmth and refinement to match the music makes this a collection well worth exploring.

Piano Sonata
** Nim. Single NI 1415. composer

George Benjamin's *Piano Sonata* dates from 1978, when he was still a student at the Paris Conservatoire. The influences are predominantly Gallic, and in particular the music of Messiaen. Benjamin is also a very good pianist; but the recording, made in 1980, sounds rather synthetic. A 'single', this runs to 22 minutes 26 seconds.

BENNETT, Richard Rodney (born 1936)

(i) *Piano Concerto 1*; (ii) *(Saxophone) Concerto for Stan Getz*; (iii) *Dream Sequence*. Film music from: (iv) *Four Weddings and a Funeral; Murder on the Orient Express: Waltz*
(M) *** Decca (ADD/DDD) 470 371-2. (i) Kovacevich, BBC SO, Gibson; (ii) Harle, BBC Concert O, Wordsworth; (iii) Lloyd Webber, composer; (iv) Hollywood Bowl O, Mauceri

Richard Rodney Bennett wrote his *Piano Concerto*, a work involving complex, endlessly fluttering figuration, especially with Stephen Bishop (Kovacevich) in mind. It is one of his most thoughtful works, music that repays the detailed study possible on CD, particularly in a performance as dedicated as this, and the 1971 (Philips) sound emerges especially vividly in this transfer. The *Concerto for Stan Getz* (1990) is an unashamedly cross-over piece, an enjoyable mixture of jazz and film music styles, melodic and colourful, offering the soloist plenty of opportunity to explore the instrument's colour. The famous *Waltz* from *Murder on the Orient Express* receives a most winning performance here (complete with a whoosh of steam to get it going!). The haunting piece from *Four Weddings and a Funeral* and the gentle *Dream Sequence* provide contrast. This is an excellent CD, and the sound is bright and vivid.

Film music: (i) *Enchanted April; Far from the Madding Crowd; Four Weddings and a Funeral: Love theme;* **(ii)** *Lady Caroline Lamb (Elegy for Viola & Orchestra); Murder on the Orient Express; Tender is the Night: Nicola's Theme*
*** Chan. 9867. (i) Miller; (ii) Dukes; BBC PO, Gamba

Richard Rodney Bennett ranks alongside Malcolm Arnold as an outstanding English composer of film scores of quality that can stand up in their own right, away from the cinema screen. Bennett's music displays a ready flow of memorable melody, more lushly romantic, less whimsical than Arnold's, but equally ready to move across to sophisticated popular rhythms. His orchestral palette is equally rich, and *Murder on the Orient Express*, in which the train theme is in lilting waltz-time, is a splendid example of his musical diversity, also including a catchy tango. The lovely, evocative opening of *Far from the Madding Crowd*, with a solitary flute answered by a solo oboe, and then taken up by the strings, is romantic English pastoralism at its most elegiacally haunting. Later the score brings in folksy dance-rhythms, then the opening sequence returns more romantically, but with a closing passage that could well have been written by Vaughan Williams. *Lady Caroline Lamb* inspired a two-movement concertante work for viola (here Philip Dukes) and orchestra, and introduces one of the composer's most delectable melodies which is rapturously expanded at the climax. *Nicola's Theme* is more modern in outline but hardly less indelible, but the atmospheric writing for *Enchanted April*, with its solo ondes martenot, is (at 19 minutes) perhaps a little over-extended. The romantic theme from *Four Weddings and a Funeral* stood out from an otherwise pop-music backcloth. Rumon Gamba and the BBC Philharmonic are splendidly eloquent advocates of all this music, and they are sumptuously recorded.

Film music: (i) *Lady Caroline Lamb (including the Elegy for Viola & Orchestra); (ii) Murder on the Orient Express*
(B) *** EMI (ADD) 5 86188-2. Composer, with (i) Mark, New Philh. O; (ii) ROHCG

On this CD are offered the original soundtracks from two of Richard Rodney Bennett's most entertaining and tuneful film scores. The *Lady Caroline Lamb* score (1972) features a simple but memorable theme which runs throughout the score like a leitmotiv (once heard, it is difficult to get out of your head) and this is developed in a 16-minute *Elegy for Viola and Orchestra*, also included on this CD. The use of harpsichord adds a nice touch of piquancy, and the orchestration is always felicitous. The main theme from *Murder on the Orient Express* (1974) is an irresistible, exhilarating waltz. If not all the music matches this, there is plenty to enjoy, especially in the period (1930s) numbers, such as in the

catchy *Entr'acte* (with piano), and the 11-minute *Orient Express* track. The sweeping grand finale is another highlight. Good (but not outstanding) sound, and helpful notes by the composer.

5 Carols; (i) *A Farewell to Arms; Goodnight; Lullay mine Liking; Missa brevis; Puer nobis; Sea Change* **(Song-Cycle);** *Verses; What sweeter Music*
*** Coll. **SACD** CSACD 901. Cambridge Singers, Rutter, (i) with Wall, Evans

As we know from his film scores, Richard Rodney Bennett is a composer with a genuine melodic gift; in John Rutter's words, he is 'quintessentially English', and in his concert music he seeks direct communication with his listeners. All the choral works here show this, and also his willingness to be retrospective – drawing on influences from English music of the past, as in *A Farewell to Arms*, a dual setting of two poems, one Elizabethan, one Jacobean. They are introduced by a warmly romantic solo cello (beautifully played here by Sue Dorey) which returns to add an obbligato to the choral writing. The cycle, *Sea Change*, summoned by tubular bells, is more challenging, demanding startling virtuosity from the singers, especially in the vividly swirling *The waves come rolling*. The five settings draw on texts from Shakespeare, Andrew Marvell and Spenser, which make a characteristically successful amalgam.

The Mines of Sulphur (complete opera)
*** Chan. **SACD** 5036 (2). Irmiter, Clayton, Jovanovich, Maddalena, Byrne, Anderson, Glimmerglass Op. O, Robertson

When Richard Rodney Bennett's first full-length opera, *The Mines of Sulphur*, was such a success at its first production at Sadler's Wells in 1965, prompting performances all over Europe and a completely new production at La Scala, Milan, by John Huston, it is surprising that it took until 2004 for it to have a modern revival. That was thanks to the enterprise of the Glimmerglass Festival in upper New York State, from which this live recording was taken. It is an exceptionally well-made piece, owing in part to the beautifully crafted libretto of Beverley Cross, but above all to the eerily atmospheric music that Bennett writes for this ghostly horror story. In that he was helped by his experience as a highly successful film-composer, making the atonal Bergian idiom that he favoured at that time very approachable.

Though a live recording inevitably brings intrusive stage noises, and the balance between voices and orchestra is not ideal, clarity is what matters, and the performance under Stewart Robertson effectively creates the weird atmosphere of a country house invaded by a deserter and a tramp, which is then visited by a troupe of travelling players from a different age. There is a play within a play, *Hamlet*-style, but it is only at the end of Act III that the true horror is revealed, that these players are ghosts who have brought with them the plague, leaving the deserter, the tramp and their companion, the gypsy, Rosalind, fearfully murmuring '*Lord have mercy on us.*'

The cast is uniformly good, with Brandon Jovanovich as Boconnion, the deserter, and James Maddalena as Tovey, the tramp, outstanding in every way. Beth Clayton as Rosalind develops a heavy vibrato under pressure; but generally it is a most acceptable, powerful revival, even though it might have been even more effective, had the main scenes of Boconnion, Tovey and Rosalind not been updated.

BENNETT, Robert Russell (1894–1981)

Abraham Lincoln (A Likeness in Symphonic Form); Sights and Sounds (An Orchestral Entertainment)

(BB) ** Naxos 8.5509004. Moscow SO, Stromberg

Robert Russell Bennett, the orchestrator of many famous musicals, is best known on record for his Gershwin score, the *Symphonic Picture of Porgy and Bess*. The present works show his great orchestral skill, but the quality of the invention does not match the vividly imaginative orchestral sounds. There are longueurs in the four-movement *Lincoln Portrait*, and the various American *Sights and Sounds* are little more than clever orchestral effects. Only the evocation of a *Night Club*, with its saxophone riff, has anything approaching a memorable idea. The orchestral playing and the commitment of the conductor cannot be faulted, nor can the recording. But the result does not encourage repeated listenings.

BENTZON, Jørgen (1897–1951)

Divertimento for Violin, Viola & Cello, Op. 2; Intermezzo for Violin & Clarinet, Op. 24; Sonatina for Flute, Clarinet & Bassoon, Op. 7; Variazioni interrotti for Clarinet, Bassoon, Violin, Viola & Cello, Op. 12; (i) Mikrofoni 1, for Baritone, Flute, Violin, Cello & Piano, Op. 44

**(*) dacapo 8.224129. Danish Chamber Players; (i) with Bertelsen

Jørgen Bentzon's music has a clean, fresh, diatonic feel to it, though some of it sounds a bit manufactured. By far the best piece here is the *Mikrofoni*, Op. 44, though it is let down by the solo baritone, and by far the wittiest is the *Variazioni interrotti*.

BENTZON, Niels Viggo (born 1919)

Piano Sonatas 2, Op. 42; 4, Op. 57; 7, Op. 121

*** dacapo 8.226030. Bjørkøe

The *Second Sonata* comes from 1946 and continues the kind of writing that distinguished the *Partita* for piano. The *Fourth Sonata* (1949) is a big-boned and impressive work that comes immediately after the inspired *Fourth Symphony (Metamorphoses)*. This was a vintage period in Bentzon's development, and the shorter and concentrated *Seventh* (1959) is hardly less compelling. The Bentzon sonatas are masterly and will reward repeated hearings. Christina Bjørkøe is a capable player and the recording is better than the earlier issue in this series (*Sonatas 3, 5* and *9*), discussed in our main volume.

BERG, Alban (1885–1935)

Lyric Suite (String Quartet version)

*** Testament SBT 1374 Juilliard Qt – CARTER: *Quartet 2;* SCHUMAN: *Quartet 3* ***

Recorded in 1959, this is as fine an account of the *Lyric Suite* as you can ever hope to hear; indeed, a first recommendation. The Juilliard took the piece into their repertoire at an early stage and play it with consistent fervour and deep understanding. Excellent recorded sound, too.

Lulu (in English)

(M) **(*) Chan. 3130 (3). Saffer, Parry, Kale, Hayward, Graham-Hall, Howell, ENO Ch. & O, Daniel

Based directly on the highly successful Richard Jones production for English National Opera, this *Lulu* in English was recorded at studio sessions immediately following performances in the 2005 revival. Paul Daniel (using his own English translation) conducts an exceptionally persuasive account, more than is usual bringing out the work's lyricism alongside the lilt of the many dance-passages. The element of cabaret and circus is after all behind much of Berg's writing, but this is also a performance which underlines the stylized structure that Berg ingeniously developed – sonata, variations, rondo, etc. In the title-role Lisa Saffer with her bright, fresh soprano is most convincing through all the sinister developments in this often repellent story, well supported by a strong team of incidental characters, of whom the most striking are Gwynne Howell as Schigolch and Susan Parry as Geschwitz. Saffer sings strongly and movingly, even though this is a role which has prompted even more characterful readings from others.

Wozzeck (complete)

(M) *** Decca 417 348-2 (2). Waechter, Silja, Laubenthal, Jahn, Malta, Sramek, VPO, Dohnányi – SCHOENBERG: *Erwartung* ***

Dohnányi, with refined textures and superb playing from the Vienna Philharmonic, presents an account of *Wozzeck* that not only is more accurate than almost any other on record, but also more beautiful. It is now reissued at mid-price, with full documentation, as part of Universal's 'Critic's Choice' series.

BERIO, Luciano (1925–2003)

Orchestral Transcriptions: BACH: *Art of Fugue: Contrapunctus XIX.* BOCCHERINI: *Riterata notturna di Madrid.* BRAHMS: *Clarinet Sonata 1 in F min., Op. 20/1.* MOZART: *Variations on Papageno's Aria: Ein Mädchen oder Weibchen.* PURCELL: *The modification of a famous Hornpipe as a merry and sincere homage to Uncle Alfred.* SCHUBERT: *Rendering for Orchestra*

*** Decca 476 2830. Giuseppi Verdi O of Milan, Chailly

A fascinating disc, which starts with the deliciously piquant arrangement of Purcell's Hornpipe from *The Fairy Queen*, transcribed as a present to Alfred Kalmus, the founder of the London division of Universal Edition – the title is rather longer than the piece! Berio, while very much of the post-war avant-garde school, is totally fascinated with the music of the past, and here his distinctive style has blended perfectly into producing some striking textures. Most impressive is the *Contrapunctus XIX*, the finale of *The Art of Fugue*, in which Berio's orchestral palette is exquisitely etched, and he hauntingly ends with a 'piercing sense of failing strength' (the sleeve-note writer's words), with the music fading on the notes B-A-C-H; it really is very memorable. Berio's sound-world gives a new twist to the well-known items, notably Boccherini's *Ritirata notturna di Madrid*, where Berio has superimposed four different versions of the work on top of one another, which build up to a mightily impressive, startling climax. The Mozart transcription is the most avant-garde piece here; interesting, but it will not be to everyone's taste. Berio's *Rendering for Orchestra*, based on an unfinished symphony in D major by Schubert, is as curious as it is enjoyable: the Schubertian fragments are held together by pure Berio, who fills in the missing gaps with often rather mysterious and ethereal music: it is initially disconcerting, but enjoyably so and surprisingly effective (in the opening of the finale, for example, Berio's sound-world quickly melts into Schubert's, to striking effect, with each style highlighting the other). The transcription of the *Clarinet Sonata* remains faithful to the spirit of the work, very much using Brahms's orchestral colours, Berio adding only a few extra bars by way of introduction in the first two movements. The slow movement is especially beautifully done, but there is great warmth throughout this performance. One almost forgets that this is not Brahms's own orchestration. Excellent recording and performances, and well worth exploring.

BERIOT, Charles-Auguste de (1802–70)

Violin Concertos 1 (Military), Op. 16; 8 in D, Op. 99; 9 in A min., Op. 104

(BB) *** Naxos 8.555104. Nishizaki, RTBF SO, Brussels, Walter

The original Marco Polo CD of these attractive concertos was missed by us when it first appeared in 1990, and the reissue is quite a find. Beriot was a Belgian virtuoso fiddler who had a similar compositional talent to his Italian contemporary, Paganini. Although he did not essay quite such a fiendish range of solo histrionics, his concertos are technically very demanding, balanced by an appealing lyricism. Catchy themes came readily to him, and he handled the orchestra with confidence. The jaunty rhythmic style of his opening movements also reminds the listener of Hummel. Takako Nishizaki is obviously completely at home in this repertoire, fully up to its technical demands and relishing the lyrical, operatic lines. She plays the gentle *Andantino* of the *D major Concerto* beautifully, and phrases the *Adagio* of the *A minor Concerto* exquisitely, then dances away vivaciously with the infectious Rondo finale. Her small, perfectly formed timbre is beautifully caught by the recording, and she is well balanced with the excellent accompaniments from Alfred Walter and the Belgian Radio Orchestra. A most enjoyable and highly recommendable disc in all respects.

BERKELEY, Lennox (1903–89)

Mont Juic – see under Britten (joint composer)

String Quartet 2

*** Chan. 10364. Chilingirian Qt – Michael BERKELEY: *Abstract Mirror; Magnetic Field* ***

Written in wartime, in 1941, Lennox Berkeley's *Second Quartet* is a typically thoughtful, refined piece in three movements. A powerful first movement leads on from emphatic chordal writing, followed by a rapt slow movement which builds to an impressive climax, rounded off in an energetic finale, the most immediately approachable movement of the three. Coupled with much grittier string works by the composer's son Michael, this certainly a challenging triptych. Superb playing by the Chilingirians, ideal interpreters.

BERKELEY, Michael (born 1948)

(i) *Abstract Mirror. Magnetic Field*

*** Chan. 10364. Chilingirian Qt; (i) with Thomas Carroll – Lennox BERKELEY: *String Quartet 2* ***

Abstract Mirror for string quintet and *Magnetic Field* for quartet represent Michael Berkeley's music at its most uncompromising. Almost all of the first half of *Abstract*

BERLIOZ, Hector (1803–69)

(i) *Grande symphonie funèbre et triomphale;* (ii) *Overtures: Benvenuto Cellini; Le Carnaval romain; Le Corsaire; Les Francs-juges;* (iii) *Les Troyens: Royal Hunt and Storm; Ballet Music; Trojan March;* (iv) *La Mort de Cléopâtre*

(BB) *** Warner Apex 2564 6183-2 (2). (i) Chorale Populaire de Paris, Musiques des Gardiens de la Paix, Dondeyne; (ii) Strasbourg PO, Lombard; (iii) & (iv) Nouvel PO de Strasbourg, Amy; (iv) with Denize

Désiré Dondeyne's 1958 performance of the *Grande symphonie funèbre et triomphale*, spaciously recorded in Notre Dame, is exciting and convincing in a specially French way. The wind and brass group (with a convincing solo trombone) has an authentic tang, with the chorus at the end producing an exhilaratingly robust fervour. The sound has plenty of spectacle and bite. Nadine Denize is equally at home in *La Mort de Cléopâtre*, which combines dramatic flair with a moving closing section. The four key overtures, recorded digitally two decades later, are also very well played, and the programme ends with excerpts from *Les Troyens*, the *Royal Hunt and Storm*, without chorus but still impressive. Excellent recording throughout, but the documentation is totally inadequate, with no texts.

Symphonie fantastique, Op. 14

(M) *** Ph. 475 7557. Concg. O, C. Davis

(i) *Symphonie fantastique;* (ii) *Overture: Le Carnaval romain*

(BB) *** HMV (ADD/DDD) 5 86677-2. (i) French Nat. R. O, Bernstein; (ii) Concg. O, Jansons – DUKAS: *Sorcerer's Apprentice* ***

Symphonie fantasique; Overtures: Le carnaval romain; Le Corsaire

(BB) **(*) ASV Resonance CDRSN 3045. RPO, Bátiz

Symphonie fantastique; Overtures: Le carnaval romain; Le Corsaire. La damnation de Faust: Marche hongroise. Les Troyens: Trojan March

(M) **(*) RCA (ADD) **SACD** 82876 67899-2. Boston SO, Munch

Sir Colin Davis's 1974 Concertgebouw account, surpassed only by Beecham's classic version with the Orchestre National de France (EMI 567971-2 [5 67972-2]), now arrives back in the catalogue, remastered, as one of Philips's Originals, a performance which has superb life and colour.

Bernstein directs a brilliant and understanding performance which captures more than most the wild, volatile quality of Berlioz's inspiratiom. Sir Colin Davis may give a clearer idea of the structure of the piece, but Bernstein (unlike Davis, omitting the exposition repeat) has great urgency, and his reading culminates in superb accounts of the 'March to the Scaffold' and the 'Witches' Sabbath', full of rhythmic swagger and natural flair. The newly remastered, late-1970s analogue

cellent, with the upper range now much
before, and the warm resonance retaining the
the orchestral sound. Jansons's lively account of
val romain, if not quite as volatile as Bernstein, is
with much finesse and given first-rate digital sound to
ch the coupled Dukas showpiece.

Bátiz's ASV Resonance reissue (from 1987) remains fully
competitive in the super-bargain range, with excellent digital
recording. He brings the score vividly to life, with the RPO's
playing consistently warm, intensely persuasive. One has the
feeling of live music-making, and the two overtures are
equally strong and persuasive.

On Mercury comes another vintage reissue, and again one
marvels that a stereo recording from as early as 1958/9 should
remain so impressive today, with only an occasional thinness
in the violins to betray its age (though they sound fuller when
played through an SACD set-up). Paray's excitingly hard-
pressed reading is full of passionate, mercurial neurosis. The
first movement immediately spurts away, and it is only the
conductor's firm grip which prevents the movement from
getting out of hand as it almost does with Munch. The *Waltz*,
too, is fast, though not inelegant, and the *Adagio*, even
though it has moments of pastoral repose, never drags its
feet. The final two movements have great verve, and there are
few performances that combine such a high level of tension
with a true understanding of the music's inner pulse. Fine
playing, of course, and the encores are similarly exciting and
vivid.

Munch's 1954 *Symphonie fantastique* was one of the very
first stereo recordings RCA made in the superb acoustics of
Boston's Symphony Hall, and it still sounds pretty remarkable even today, in John Newton's SACD remastering of the
original three-track recording. The performance has always
been controversial because of Munch's extremely erratic
tempi in the first movement. Yet for those who find his
approach mercurial rather than eccentric, the slow movement is gloriously played, and Munch achieves quite
piquantly grotesque colouring in the *March to the Scaffold*,
while the finale lacks nothing in spectacle. The romanticism
of the Love Music from *Roméo et Juliette* again shows the
depth of Munch's sympathy, and the ardour and incandescence of the Boston playing is another plus point.

La Damnation de Faust (complete; DVD version)

*** Arthaus DVD 102 023. Von Otter, Lewis, Van Dam, Rose,
Chicago SO Ch. & O, Solti

Recorded at the Proms at the Royal Albert Hall in 1989, with
Chicago forces imported *en masse*, Sir Georg Solti's brilliant
version is excellent in every way. The performance is not as
fierce as this conductor could be in this music, but it is
wonderfully dramatic, with the Prom audience cheering the
visitors on. Margaret Hillis's Chicago Symphony Chorus
matches the orchestra in brilliance and responsiveness, and
the trio of soloists makes an ideal team. Keith Lewis as Faust
is fresh and unstrained, while José van Dam is a superb
Mephistopheles, tender and seductive as well as flamboyant,
and Anne Sofie von Otter, handsome in royal blue, sings
flawlessly as Marguerite, at her most tender in the *Roi de
Thule* aria. Rodney Greenberg's video direction effectively
brings out the atmospheric qualities of the Royal Albert Hall.

Les Nuits d'été (song-cycle)

⊕→ (M) *** Decca 475 7712. Crespin, SRO, Ansermet (with
Recital of French Songs ***)) – RAVEL: *Shéhérazade* *** ⊙

With Crespin's richness of tone, and with Ansermet at his

finest, accompanying brilliantly, this glowing performance is
truly legendary and fully worthy of a place among Universal's
'Originals'. Moreover, the Ravel coupling is even more
inspired, and the superb new transfers enhance the listener's
pleasure further. The disc is discussed more fully below, in
our Vocal Recitals section.

Requiem (Grande Messe des Morts, Op. 5; DVD version)

*** Arthaus Musik DVD 102 027. Keith Lewis, Bav. R.
Symphony Ch. and O, C. Davis (V/D: Klaus Lindemann)

The spectacular setting of Regensburg Cathedral adds greatly
to the impact of Sir Colin Davis's inspired performance of the
Berlioz *Requiem*. The nave is exceptionally high and relatively
narrow, and that works surprisingly well, both for the sound,
which focuses far better than in many other reverberant
cathedrals, and visually too. With orchestra and chorus set at
the far end, like an elaborate altar-piece, there is less spread of
sound than in a broader church or concert hall, but the
clarity of detail is remarkable, no doubt a tribute to the
engineers as well. Davis as ever gives a dedicated performance, rising brilliantly to the relatively few moments of Ber-
liozian drama, as in the *Tuba mirum*, with its array of brass
and timpani, but bringing out the fundamentally devotional
quality of the work. That stamp of dedication is sealed when,
at the very end of the final *Agnus Dei*, Davis remains standing
impassively, and one hears the distant boom of the bells from
outside. Chorus and orchestra are superb, at once warm and
incisive, responding to Davis's every gesture, as he leads them
through a work they are unlikely to know well. Unison
passages for whichever section emerge with exceptional
purity. In the *Sanctus* Keith Lewis, at his peak, gives an ideal
performance as soloist, totally unstrained. The DVD gives
one the option of having the Latin text on the screen as
though on a gauze over the main picture.

(i) Requiem Mass; (ii) Te Deum

(M) **(*) Ph. (ADD) 475 7765 (2). (i) Dowd; (ii) Tagliavini;
Wandsworth School Boy' Ch. L. Symphony Ch., LSO, C.
Davis

Sir Colin Davis's earlier CD recording of the *Requiem* was
made in Westminster Cathedral, which means that the microphones had to be placed unnaturally close. However, both the
large-scale brass sound and the choral *fortissimos* (effectively
remastered) are formidably caught. In the *Te Deum*, Davis
conveys the massiveness without pomposity, the drama without unwanted excesses of emotion; and once again his massed
forces respond superbly. However, Tagliavini's singing is not
really in style with the others, or, for that matter, with Berlioz,
so this set is a doubtful candidate for Universal's Originals.

Roméo et Juliette, Op. 17 (DVD version)

*** Arthaus DVD 102 017. Schwarz, Langridge, Meven, Bav.
R. Ch. & SO, C. Davis (V/D: Klaus Lindemann)

Sir Colin Davis is without peer as a Berlioz interpreter and it is
good to have this fine (and often inspired) account of the
master's dramatic symphony on DVD. Recorded fairly early in
his days in Munich with the Bayerischer Rundfunk Orchestra,
it has great fire and dramatic intensity – as well as the sensibility and poetic feeling we associate with him. Quite apart from
the virtuosity of this wonderful orchestra, listeners will be
riveted by the singing of the three soloists: Hanna Schwarz,
whom we associate mainly with Wagner, the impeccable
Philip Langridge and the splendid, dark-toned Peter Meven,
who, alas, died three years ago. The video direction of Klaus
Lindemann could hardly be bettered. A thrilling performance.

Les Troyens (complete DVD version)

*** Opus Arte OA 0900D (3). Graham, Antonacci, Pokupic, Kunde, Tezier, Monteverdi Ch., ORR, Gardiner (Director: Yannis Kokkos; V/D: Peter Maniura)

In October 2003 John Eliot Gardiner with his Monteverdi Choir and the Orchestre Révolutionnaire et Romantique had a great success when they visited Paris to give Berlioz's epic opera, a work which, surprisingly, the French have seriously neglected. The venue was the relatively intimate Théâtre du Châtelet but, as the video shows, the stage production by Yannis Kokkos neatly achieves clarity and directness in the complex plot with an economical but effective staging. The first two Acts, covering the fall of Troy, have the darkest of settings, with costumes of unrelieved black, with an angled mirror giving one views from above as well as laterally.

The performance gains from the fine singing in the central role of Cassandra of Anna Caterina Antonacci, then coming to the fore as a star of the future. Ludovic Tezier is also excellent as her lover, Chorebus, and the final chorus of Trojan women, led by Cassandra, brings a thrilling climax.

In Act III, 'The Trojans in Carthage', the sets brings a complete contrast, light and airy and with bright colours. Again simplicity is the keynote, with spaciousness rather than crowded scenes; and again, surprisingly, it works well, with the story clarified. What is slightly disappointing is that the great love duet between Aeneas and Dido uses a set without any hint of foliage or any atmospheric background; but the singing of Susan Graham as well as of Gregory Kunde as Aeneas is first rate. What is remarkable in an age of wobblers is that Gardiner has gathered a whole team of singers, most of them native French-speakers, with exceptionally well-focused voices. The final Act, of Aeneas's departure and Dido's death, brings a return of the angled mirror, with Aeneas's feet represented by model ships floating in the air. Fine as Graham's singing is, it does not have quite the weight of emotions of a Janet Baker, yet it still makes a moving impact. Altogether a preferable video presentation, with its period instruments and excellent cast, to the Salzburg Festival DVD of the opera, good as that is.

BERNERS, Lord (1883–1950)

Luna Park; March; (i) A Wedding Bouquet

** Marco 8.223716. (i) RTE Chamber Ch.; RTE Sinf., Alwyn

Stravinsky spoke of Lord Berners as 'droll and delightful'. Apart from Constant Lambert, he was the only English composer taken up by Diaghilev. *Luna Park* (1930) was written for a C. B. Cochran revue, with choreography by Balanchine. *A Wedding Bouquet* was choreographed by Frederick Ashton and mounted at Sadler's Wells in 1937, with décor and costumes, as well as music, by Berners. This is good light music. Performances are decent, as are the recordings, but the acoustic does not permit tuttis to open out.

Les Sirènes (ballet; complete); **Caprice péruvien; Cupid and Psyche** (ballet suite)

** Marco 8.223780. Blennerhassett, RTE Sinf., Lloyd-Jones

Les Sirènes was not a great success, and the music, despite some bright moments, does not sustain a high level of invention. The *Caprice péruvien* was put together expertly by Constant Lambert with Berners's help. The ballet *Cupid and Psyche* was another Ashton work, mounted in 1939. Good performances, but not well polished. Again the recordings are wanting in bloom.

Piano music: *Le Poisson d'or; Dispute entre le papillon et le crapaud; The Expulsion from Paradise; Fragments psychologiques; March; 3 Petites marches funèbres; Polka; Valse.* (i) **Songs:** *A long time ago; Come on Algernon; The Rio Grande; Theodore or The Pirate King; 3 Chansons; 3 English Songs; Lieder Album (3 Songs in the German Manner); Red roses and red noses*

**(*) Marco 8.225159. (i) Partridge; Vorster

Lord Berners was a diplomat as well as a musician and was essentially self-taught, but he was the only English composer who was admired by both Diaghilev and Beecham. Both responded to Berners's witty eccentricity and hints of Gallic wit, within a musical style that often retained an underlying Englishness – demonstrated subtly here in the opening *Polka*. Berners was a painter and poet too; the minuscule, lovelorn *Le Poisson d'or* was based on his own poem and has a certain Debussian atmosphere, while the *Trois petites marches* and *Fragments psychologiques* are Satiesque, and not just in their titles. The longest of the piano pieces is the engagingly nostalgic *Valse*.

Berners's pastiche of German *Lieder* has the piano opening gruffly to contrast a lyrical vocal line, romantically addressing a white pig. The French *chansons*, however, are not parodies but readily idiomatic, with *La Fiancée du timbalier* engagingly spirited. Of the English songs, *Tom Filuter's dialogue* is brilliantly chimerical, and the 1920 set is most winning, especially the opening *Lullaby*. The three later songs of 1921 are a charming rediscovery of the English folk idiom, while the sentimental *Red roses and red noses* has a flowing lyrical line. It is followed by the irrepressible *Come on Algernon*, about the insatiable Daisy, who always 'asked for more!' – a perfect music-hall number, written for the film *Champagne Charlie*, it makes a delightful pay-off to end the recital. Ian Partridge obviously relishes the many stylistic changes like a vocal chameleon, and his words are clear too. Len Vorster backs him up splendidly and is completely at home in the solo piano music. The recording is truthful, and this makes a fine introduction to an underrated composer who has a distinctive voice of his own.

BERNSTEIN, Leonard (1918–90)

Divertimento for Orchestra; Facsimile: Choreographic Essay for Orchestra; (i) Serenade for Solo Violin, Strings, Harp & Percussion

(BB) ****(*)** Naxos 8.559245. Bournemouth SO, Alsop; (ii) Quint, Bournemouth SO (members)

The *Serenade* for solo violin and strings is one of the deepest, most ambitious works that Bernstein ever wrote, which makes it a pity that he gave this half-hour work the title 'Serenade', suggesting lightness, rather than calling it a full violin concerto. Despite the name, it has increasingly been recognized at its true worth; here the violinist, Philippe Quint, gives a thoughtful, refined reading of a work inspired by the idea of mirroring Plato's *Symposium*. He is well supported by Marin Alsop and the Bournemouth orchestra. Technically, he has every quality required, with double-stopping that is immaculate, and a fine range of dynamic shading. The other two works represent Bernstein in less inspired form. *Facsimile* is a ballet score on the theme of post-war life and the vain attempt to fill a spiritual vacuum, which results in a grim score with little evidence of Bernstein's lyrical gifts; it is most effective in the fast music, which distantly echoes *West Side Story*. The *Divertimento*, written for the Boston Symphony Orchestra, is an occasional piece that has its moments of fun, but which fails to make its full mark in this performance, refined as it is. Excellent sound.

(i) *Facsimile;* (ii) *On the Town;* (iii) *Jeremiah Symphony*
(BB) (***) Dutton mono CDBP 9758. (i) RCA Victor SO; (ii) On the Town O; (iii) Merriman, St Louis SO; composer – RAVEL: *Piano Concerto in G* (***)

Bernstein made brilliant stereo recordings of these three pieces, but these accounts from the 1940s have enormous zest and freshness, and they are every bit as treasurable as the later, LP versions he made. Dutton draws very lively and lifelike sounds from the 78-r.p.m. grooves. The disc also brings Bernstein's 1946 recording of the Ravel *G major Concerto* with the then newly formed Philharmonia Orchestra.

BERWALD, Franz (1796–1868)

(i) *Konzertstück for Bassoon & Orchestra. Drottningen av Golconda: Overture; Reminiscences of the Norwegian Mountains (Erinnerung an die norwegischen Alpen); Play of the Elves; Racing (Wettlauf); Serious and Joyful Fancies (Ernst und heitere Grillen)*
(BB) *** Naxos 8.555370. Gävle SO, Sakari; (i) with Håkansson

Like the symphonies, most of the tone-poems come from the early 1840s, and Castegren even thought it likely that the *Overture* to *Drottningen av Golconda* ('The Queen of Golconda') of 1868 was the *Humoristisches Capriccio* of 1841, the score of which could not be found among Berwald's effects. Be that as it may, it is one of the Swedish master's most delightful and engaging pieces and deserves the widest currency. All the tone-poems come from 1841–2, a very productive period, and are of the highest quality. The performances under Petri Sakari are eminently lively and musical, though the Gävle strings do not command the weight of sonority of the Danish orchestra. Those who do not know these pieces will find them rewarding, full of imagination and invention – *Wettlauf* and *Play of the Elves* are particularly enjoyable. Least original is the *Konzertstück for Bassoon* (excellently played though it is by Patrik Håkansson), which is much indebted to Spohr. A pity that time could not be found to include *Bayaderen-Fest* ('The Festival of the Bayadères'), composed at the same time; but there is nothing to preclude a strong recommendation.

Duo in D for Violin & Piano; Grand Septet in B flat; Piano Quintet 1 in C min.; Piano & Wind Quintet in E flat; Piano Trios 2 in F min.; 4 in C
(M) **(*) Hyp. Dyad CDD 22063 (2). Tomes, Gaudier Ens.

Hyperion have put together their two separate discs of Berwald's chamber music as a Dyad. The performances, which are nearly all first class, are discussed in our main edition. If the recording balance is not always ideal, the *Piano Quintet* (1853) comes off marvellously and, with Susan Tomes participating, there is much elsewhere to delight the ear, even if in the *Duo* Marieke Blankestijn's violin timbre sounds too pale and reticent.

BIBER, Heinrich (1644–1704)

Violin Sonatas: in C min.; E; Ciacona in D. attrib.: Sonatas in B flat, D & G min. (all for violin & continuo)
*** CPO 777 124-2. Steck, Rieger, Santana, Perl (with MUFFAT: *Violin Sonata in D*)

The bravura *C minor Sonata*, which opens this programme, comes from the 1681 published collection of which we already have recordings reviewed in our main volume, and it includes an impressive central passacaglia, a form at which Biber was adept. The *E major work* is impressively unusual in including three sets of variations one after the other. But this collection centres on manuscripts found in the Archive of Kremsier in Moravia, in which the works have survived anonymously but are stylistically very close to Biber and demand equal virtuosity of the soloist. Anton Steck is a first-rate fiddler, and the excellent continuo is varied from harpsichord or organ (Christian Rieger), viola da gamba (Hille Perl) to archlute (Lee Santana). The famous *Ciacona* is given a particularly attractive performance, rhythmically bouncy; then follows the fine *D major Sonata* of Biber's contemporary, Georg Muffat, dating from 1677, which has a rich, lyrical vein to offset the bravura writing. Excellent recording, most convincingly balanced, with the violin forward but not excessively so.

Missa Christi Resurgens
*** Kleos **SACD** Compatible Surround Sound KL 5135.
Soloists, NY Coll., Parrott

Andrew Parrott and his excellent New York Collegium here première on CD the lyrically exultant *Missa Christi Resurgens* from around 1673. It is written for the usual double choir, groups of soloists, cornets, sackbuts and strings, and two trumpets stationed across the transept from the other musicians. The performance places the Mass in the context of contemporary Salzburg performance, interspersing appropriate chant and instrumental interludes, mainly string pieces, taken from Biber's own works. It opens, however, with a setting of the Easter introit, *Resurrexi*, by Johann Stadlmayr, a normal procedure for the time. Then follows a brief festive instrumental *Sonata*, before the *Kyrie* and *Gloria*, which is a series of duets exploiting all the available forces. The *Sanctus* interchanges voices and brass and the *Benedictus* brings a duet between alto soloist and principal violin. Organ voluntaries (by Alessandro Poglietti) frame the beautiful *Agnus Dei*, and the performance ends with an evocation of the Resurrection by using one of Biber's own *Mystery Sonatas*. In this way the New York performance imaginatively and authentically brings together a great variety of music, and the playing and singing could hardly be more persuasive. The outstanding recording combines spectacle with intimacy quite admirably, and the acoustic offers an ideal ambience without loss of clarity. Full texts are included, and the presentation is very handsome.

Missa Salisburgensis
(M) ** DHM/BMG 82876 70810-2. Escolania de Montserrat, Tölz Boys' Ch., Coll. Aur., Segarra

This appears to be the first – or certainly one of the first – recordings of the *Missa Salisburgensis*, made in 1974, at a time when it was still not ascertained that the work was almost certainly by Biber. It is a considerable account, with fine choral singing; but the balance is unsatisfactory, with the soloists recessed and the (otherwise attractive) resonance preventing an overall sharpness of focus. It is quite outclassed by Paul McCreesh's SACD version on DG (457 611-2 – see our main volume).

BILLINGS, William (1746–1800)

Anthems and fuging tunes: Africa; As the hart panteth; Brookfield; Creation; David's Lamentation; Emmaus;

Euroclydon; Hear my Pray'r; I am the Rose of Sharon; Is any afflicted?; Jordan; The Lord is ris'n indeed; O Praise the Lord of Heaven; Rutland; Samuel the Priest (Funeral Anthem); Shiloh

✪ (B) *** HM HCX 3957048. His Majesties's Clerkes, Hillier

William Billings was a Boston tanner and singing-master who flourished in New England in the years of the emergence of the new American nation, and his anthems and what he engagingly called 'fuging tunes' are wonderfully fresh and appealing. Although usually they are simply structured, they are written in an idiom that has broken away from the sober Lutheran tradition. The opening anthem here, *O Praise the Lord of Heaven*, has a joyous, spirited vigour in its part-writing, and the repeated phrase, 'singing and making melody' which enlivens *Is any afflicted?* avoids any possible hint of sanctimoniousness. Indeed the exuberant sailors' anthem, *Euroclydon*, sounds for all the world like a sea-shanty. Yet *Africa* has a simple, touching melancholy, which reminds one a little of the *Coventry Carol*.

Billings's funeral anthem, *Samuel the Priest*, is similarly touching, but his very characteristic text 'merrily they sing' restores the cheerfulness to *Shiloh*, while the Easter anthem, *The Lord is ris'n indeed*, with its joyful 'Allelujas', is wonderfully direct and exultant. Two of the 'hits' in his own time were the plain one-stanza *Brookfield* and the magnetic, hymn-like *Jordan*; but *Rutland*, often touchingly expressive, brings an almost madrigalesque flavour to the linear interplay. The spirit of this music brings to mind the visually striking white churches of New England rather than the devotional atmosphere of a cathedral. To quote the *Chicago Tribune*, the music is sung with 'impeccable musicianship, full-throated tone, warmth and security of blend and expressive intelligence', and, one might add, with great vitality by His Majestie's Clerkes under Paul Hillier. It is beautifully recorded in a not too reverberant acoustic; the words are clear, but a website address is given from which full texts can be obtained.

BINGE, Ronald (1910–79)

(i) *Elizabethan Serenade*; (ii; iii) *Saxophone Concerto*; (iii) *Saturday Symphony*; (iv) *At the End of the Day; Autumn Dream; Butterflies; Candles on the Table; Farewell Waltz; Fugal Fun; Give Me a Ring; Homeward; Inamorata; I Like Your Smile; I Sent You Roses; The Last of the Clan; The Look in Your Eyes; Man in a Hurry; Miss Melanie; The Moon Looks Down; Morning Light; Perhaps I'm Young; Sailing By; A Scottish Rhapsody; The Sound of Music is Everywhere; A Star is Born; Tango Corto; There's a Light in Your Eyes; Under the Sun; Waiting for Moonlight; The Watermill; What Do You Know?; When You are Young*

(M) *** ASV (ADD) CDWLZ 245 (2). (i) Nat. PO, Gerhardt; O, Heller; (ii) Voss; (iii) S German R. O, composer; (iv) Walter Heller & his O; O Raphael, Hotter; or Dreamland O

Ronald Binge's three most famous pieces must be the *Elizabethan Serenade* (which rightly opens disc 1), *Sailing By*, which has been played at the closing of BBC Radio 4, accompanying the Shipping Forecast, since 1973, or the delightful watercolour portrait of *The Water Mill*. As this CD shows, his fund of melody was unquenchable and, with his deftness of orchestration, it resulted in some first-class light classical music of the type that blossomed in the 1950s and

1960s. The *Saxophone Concerto* and *Saturday Symphony* (conducted here by the composer) are much longer than his usual short character-pieces, though they are just as enjoyable. The recordings (mainly from the 1960s) are taken from a variety of sources but mostly feature Walter Heller and his Orchestra. Recommended to all lovers of good tunes. The recordings range from very good to thoroughly acceptable, and it is fascinating to note that the performers of four of the pieces are unknown.

BISHOP, Henry Rowley (1786–1855)

Shakespearean song settings: *Come live with me; Come, thou monarch of the vine; Flower of the purple dye; Hark, hark, each Spartan hound; It was a lover and his lass; Lo! Hear the gentle lark; Lo! Oh! Never say that I was false of heart; Now the hungry lions roar; Orpheus with his lute; Should he upbraid; Sing willow; Spirits advance; Take, Oh! Take those lips away; That time of year; Under the greenwood tree; Welcome to this place; When that I was a tiny little boy; Who is Sylvia, what is she?* (2 versions)

(M) *** Decca 470 381-2. Musicians of the Globe, Pickett

There is an abundance of delightful songs here, matching the charm of the most famous number, *Lo! Hear the gentle lark*. The rustic feeling runs through all these pieces, typified in such numbers as *It was a lover and his lass*, with its hint of Scottish colour, or the hunting horns of the *Hark, hark, each Spartan hound*, and the gently lilting *Welcome to this place*. Some are more robust and substantial, such as the six-minute *Spirits advance*, with the ghost of Weber not too far away; *When that I was a tiny little boy* has the simple charm of a folk-song; *Now the hungry lions roar* starts in appropriately leonine style yet ends with great delicacy and is another highlight. These essentially simple songs/arias are performed in imaginative orchestrations, with over a dozen singers (in solo, duets and ensembles) adding to the colour and variety of the programme. The sound is full and perfectly balanced, and this CD is strongly recommended.

BIZET, Georges (1838–75)

Symphony in C

(BB) **(*) Virgin 2x1 4 82103-2. City of L. Sinf., Hickox (with FAURÉ: *Pavane*) – IBERT: *Divertissement*; RAVEL: *Tombeau de Couperin*; TCHAIKOVSKY: *Serenade for Strings; Souvenir de Florence* **(*)

Hickox's account of this engaging symphony is part of an attractive bargain package, perhaps lacking the last degree of distinction, but bringing vivacious playing throughout, and especially sparkling in the outer movements. Nicholas Daniel is a sensitive oboe soloist in the *Adagio* and the recording, though resonant, is very good.

OPERA

Carmen (complete DVD version)

**(*) EuroArts DVD 2054529. Krasteva, Antonenko, Holecek, Elmgren, Ch. & O of Nat. Theatre, Brno, Märzendorfer (Stage Director: Gianfranco de Bosio; V/Directors: Rudi Dolezai & Hannes Rossacher)

Although it has its drawbacks, the EuroArts DVD of *Carmen*, filmed live in the open air at the 2005 St Margarethen Festival in one continuous sequence, still has a lot going for it. It is a spectacular production on a huge set which, like the costumes, is very colourful (and often vividly lit). The snag is that Act II, which is set at Lillas Pastia's Inn, is obviously the same place as in the first Act, and when Lieutenant Zuniga turns up, one wonders why he doesn't have Carmen re-arrested! Equally, in Act III, which is supposed to be in a ravine outside the gates of Seville (the journey there simulated by abseiling at the side of the stage), the same magnificent backcloth rather spoils the illusion of an uncomfortable sojourn in the mountains.

However, the four principals are all in fine voice, and Nadia Krasteva, the gypsy Carmen, is beautiful in a dark-haired, Spanish way and, if not sultry, she is both convincingly seductive and impetuously fiery. Aleksandr Antonenko is an ingenuously gullible Don José in Act I, and he sings his famous *Flower Song* with ardent if unrefined romantic passion in Act II. By the opera's dramatic closing scene he has convincingly turned into a clumsy, desperately jealous murderer. Sebastian Holecek's Escamillo has just the right self-confident ebullience, and his vigorous *Toreador Song* lights up the opera at his first entry; later, the famous gypsy Quintet also sparkles. Åsa Elmgren's Micaëla is very sympathetic, not in the least wilting, in her glorious aria in Act III. The orchestra plays splendidly throughout under the vibrant direction of Ernst Märzendorfer; and Oscar Hammerstein's admiring comment, that in *Carmen* every number is a hit, is certainly realized here. If only the stage direction had been comparable, this would have been a top recommendation. But, alas, the stage movements of a large cast are very poorly co-ordinated; the moment when Carmen pushes over Don José in order to escape is unconvincing and, most surprisngly, the dancing of the Ballet Español de Valencia, to indifferent choreography by Marieta Romero, is sadly lacking in sparkle. Even so, the interaction between the principal characters gathers pace, and one is increasingly caught up in the story as the opera proceeds. The Act III duel between José and Escamillo is managed dramatically and, overall, with excellent recording (5.1 surround sound available) and not too fussy camerawork, this is easy to enjoy. But Karajan's Salzburg production, with Grace Bumbry as Carmen (DG 073 4032) is markedly superior, and Mario Rossi's Tristar film, with Julia Migenes the most characterful Carmen and Plácido Domingo at his finest as Don José, is much more imaginatively produced (Columbia CDR 10530).

Carmen (highlights)
(BB) *** HMV (ADD) 5 86678-2 (from complete recording with De los Angeles, Gedda, Blanc, Micheau, French R. Ch. & O, Beecham).

Beecham's *Carmen* dates from the earliest days of stereo (1958/9) and, as is shown in this remastered selection, still sounds remarkably vivid and atmospheric. De los Angeles's *Carmen* is utterly delightful, and Gedda, Micheau and Ernest Blanc are all on excellent form. But it is the Beecham touch which makes this generous selection (77 minutes) so enjoyable. A real bargain.

Carmen: Suite
(M) (**(*)) DG mono 477 5908. Berlin RIAS Chamber Ch., Berlin RSO, Fricsay – ROSSINI: *Overtures* (***)

The 1956 sound may be bit lacking in body and richness (but not in clarity), but there's nothing wrong with this lively performance: a good bonus to the excellent set of Rossini overtures which is the main feature of this CD.

BLACHER, Boris (1903–75)

Concertante Musik; (i) *Concerto for Clarinet & Chamber Orchestra. Fürstin Tarakanowa: Suite, Op. 19a; 2 Inventionen, Op. 46; Music for Cleveland, Op. 53.*
*** Ondine ODE-912-2. (i) Dimitri Ashkenazy; Deutsches SO, Berlin, Vladimir Ashkenazy

The *Concertante Musik* of 1937 was the first Blacher work to find its way on to record. Incidentally, it was conducted by Carl Schuricht (not Johannes Schüler as the label said, as Schuricht was blacklisted) and its relaxed air and clever syncopations found no favour with the Nazi authorities. It is strongly diatonic and possesses a dry wit that is quite captivating. Its economy and lightness of touch are also to be found in the *Suite* from the opera *Fürstin Tarakanowa* and, for that matter, the *Zwei Inventionen* of 1954. Those who know Blacher's dazzling *Variations on a Theme of Paganini* will know what to expect: a resourceful and inventive musical mind and expert orchestration – in short, civilized musical discourse. The *Concerto for Clarinet and Chamber Orchestra,* written for the clarinettist of the Deutsches Symphonie-Orchester, Berlin, is highly entertaining and Dimitri Ashkenazy gives a good account of it. His father directs lithe and vital performances and is recorded with exemplary clarity. Strongly recommended.

Der Grossinquisitor (oratorio; complete)
*** Berlin Classics 0093782 BC. Nimsgern, Leipzig R. Ch., Dresden PO, Kegel

The Grand Inquisitor strikes a serious note; Blacher's oratorio draws for its inspiration on Dostoevsky's *The Brothers Karamazov*. The musical idiom remains strongly neo-classical, with Stravinsky and Hindemith closely in view. There is some powerful writing here, and the composer is well served by the distinguished soloist and the fine Dresden orchestra under Herbert Kegel. Very good, well-balanced recorded sound with fine definition and no lack of warmth.

BLAKE, Howard (born 1938)

Clarinet Concerto
(BB) *** Hyp. Helios CDH 55068. King, ECO, composer (with LUTOSLAWSKI: *Dance Preludes*; SEIBER: *Concertino* ***)

Howard Blake provides a comparatively slight but endearing *Clarinet Concerto*, which is played here with great sympathy by Thea King, who commissioned the work. At budget price this is even more attractive.

(i) *Violin Concerto (Leeds). A Month in the Country* (film incidental music): *Suite; Sinfonietta for Brass*
*** ASV CDDCA 905. (i) Edlinger; E. N. Philh., Daniel

It was the success of his music for *The Snowman* that gave Howard Blake the encouragement and the artistic breathing-space to write his beautiful and stimulating *Violin Concerto*. Christiane Edlinger is the soloist in what proves to be an inspired performance, caught 'on the wing'. The only snag is the excessively wide dynamic range of the recording. Blake's suite of string music written for the film *A Month in the Country* brings moments of comparable bitter-sweet, elegiac feeling. It is played most sensitively, as is the brass *Sinfonietta*, sonorous and jolly by turns. In terms of overall concert-hall realism, the recording is impressive and this record is strongly recommended.

PIANO MUSIC

Ballad in G min.; Berceuse in C; Chaconne in D min.; Impromptu in E min; Jump in A flat; Mazurka in A min.; Nocturne in B; 2 Preludes: Andantino in B min.; Allegro risoluto in F min. Rag in G; Romanza in B flat min.; Scherzo in D; Study in C min.; Toccatina in E; Walking Song in A. Transcriptions: Eva (Ballet): Dance of the Hunters; Dance of the Sun and Moon. The Changeling: The Music Box. Grandpa: Make-believe. Isabella in E flat. The Land of Counterpane: Night and Day. Mamako: Serioso – come una marcia lenta in A flat min. A Midsummer Night's Dream: Oberon. The Snowman: Walking in the Air
*** ABC Classics 476 118-4. Chen

Howard Blake has a natural, easy-going melodic gift, which makes this series of unassuming piano miniatures very beguiling when they are so sympathetically played by William Chen and very well recorded in the Eugene Goossens Hall of the Australian Broadcasting Company. The simple, tuneful items like the *Ballad, Impromptu, Berceuse, Walking Song* and the film theme, *The Music Box*, may lack contemporary harmonic astringencies, yet they contrast well with the dancing staccato of the *Toccatino*, while the gentle portrait of Isabelle, written for a wedding, makes a foil for the vigorous ballet number, *Dance of the Hunters*, and the catchily syncopated *Rag* and *Jump*. Blake's famous *Snowman* tune is predictably included; perhaps the final item, *Make-Believe*, written for the animated film *Grandpa* will become a similar hit.

BLANCAFORT, Manuel (1897–1987)

Piano Music: 12 Cançons; Cançons de muntanya (Mountain Songs); Notes d'antany (Notes from years gone by); 7 Peces de joventut (Youthful Pieces)
(BB) *** Naxos 8.557332. Villalba

Cants intims I (Intimate Songs I); Jocs i danses al camp (Country Games & Dances); 6 Peces breus; 8 Peces per a piano
(BB) *** Naxos 8.557333. Villalba

Two CDs that pay tribute to the little-known Catalan, Manuel Blancafort, a contemporary and friend of Mompou. He was four years younger and died within a few months of him. These pieces were all composed in Blancafort's youth and, although pianistically less advanced even than those of his friend, they have a certain melancholy that is just as haunting. Blancafort is not included in the *Everyman Encylopaedia* or Michael Kennedy's *Oxford Dictionary* but the *Grove 6* entry describes him as being influenced by Les Six and Stravinsky. These piano pieces are indebted a little to Ravel and Debussy, but they have a charm and individuality all their own. Miquel Villalba is a sympathetic advocate and is very well served by the engineers.

BLISS, Arthur (1891–1975)

(i; iii) *Adam Zero* (Ballet Suite); (iii; iv) *Christopher Columbus* (Film Score: Suite); (v) *Cello Concerto*; (iii; vi) *Concerto for 2 Pianos*; (vii) *A Colour Symphony*; (ii; iii) *Discourse for Orchestra*; (vii) *Things to Come* (Music from the film)

(B) *** EMI 5 86589-2 (2). (i) RLPO; (ii) Handley; (iii) CBSO; (iv) Marcus Dods; (v) Noras, Bournemouth SO, Berglund; (vi) Smith & Sellick; cond. Arnold; (vii) RPO, Groves

A fascinating cross-section of Bliss's orchestral and concertante music. *Adam Zero* for the most part shows his muse at its most fertile; if it is at times rather overblown, there are many good things in it, and Vernon Handley makes a good case for the 34 minutes (out of 42) of its music included here, securing playing of great spirit from the Liverpool orchestra.

The *Cello Concerto*, which Bliss originally called a concertino, was written for Rostropovich, who first played it at at the 1970 Aldeburgh Festival, and it was Britten who persuaded the composer to change the diminutive title. With a passionate opening of Brahmsian eloquence, the first movement is one of the most inspired that Bliss ever wrote. The slow movement, with its rhapsodic style and elegiac atmosphere, is not sharply memorable, but the finale has splendid vigour and momentum. Arto Noras is the superbly eloquent soloist, and Berglund's accompaniment, pulsing with life, is little short of inspired.

The *Two-Piano Concerto* started life as a Concerto for piano, tenor, strings and percussion in 1921, being turned into a *Double Piano Concerto* three years later. Bliss then worked with Clifford Phillips to arrange the work for three hands for Cyril Smith and Phyllis Sellick to play. The vigour of early Bliss makes for attractive results, with echoes of *Petrushka* and Debussy nicely worked in. If you think Bliss cribbed from the Ravel *Piano Concerto* in the finale, you are wrong; Bliss wrote his concerto well before the Ravel appeared. Superbly played and richly recorded, it makes a delightful companion for the piano work.

A Colour Symphony dates from 1922, and this was its first recording since the composer's own, made in the mid-1950s. Inspired by a chance encounter with a book on heraldry, Bliss conceived this series of mood pictures on the theme of the symbolic meanings associated with primary colours. The work is too episodic to be truly symphonic, but it is nevertheless highly effective and is expertly scored. It comes into its own in Groves's sympathetic performance.

The *Discourse* was a commission from the Louisville Orchestra in 1957 which Bliss subsequently revised for larger orchestra in the mid-1960s. It shows the composer in extrovert but by no means unappealing mood; only the brash ending slightly lets it down.

Of the two examples of Bliss's film music, the score of *Christopher Columbus* was written for the 1949 Gainsborough biopic. Marcus Dods's miniature suite opens with a jolly *Polacca*, continues with an atmospherically romantic interlude and ends with a characteristic swaggering *Alla marcia* which accompanied Columbus's triumphant return home. But it is the *March* from *Things to Come* which offers what is perhaps the single most memorable idea to come from its composer's pen. Here the excerpts were assembled by Christopher Palmer in the mid-1970s, who also scored the opening *Prelude*, since the full score did not survive. The invention shows Bliss at his finest, and once again Groves and the RPO are splendid advocates and the HMV engineers rise to the occasion. Indeed, throughout this fine collection, the recordings, mostly from the mid- and late 1970s, come up splendidly on CD.

BLOMDAHL, Karl-Birger (1916–68)

Symphonies 1–2; 3 (Facetter)
*** BIS CD 611. Swedish RSO, Segerstam

Karl-Birger Blomdahl's *First Symphony* is not particularly individual. At the same time, a strong symphonic impulse runs through it. The *Third* is a dark and powerful piece; though it is, as one critic put it, 'deficient in thematic vitality', there is a powerful atmosphere. Good performances by the Swedish Radio Orchestra under Segerstam, and excellent BIS recording.

BLOW, John (1649–1708)

John Blow was one of the key musical figures of the Restoration. After first serving as a treble in the choir from 1660 onwards, he entered the Chapel Royal fully as an adult in 1674, and two years later he was appointed Organist of the Chapel in succession to Gibbons. He was a celebrated teacher too, and among his students were the Purcells, Henry and Daniel, Croft and Jeremiah Clarke. Blow became organist at Westminster Abbey in 1668, and he went on to take the same post at St Paul's Cathedral a decade later. He wrote much music, both secular and for the restored church, but his major contribution was over 100 anthems.

Anthems: *Blessed is the man that hath not walked; Cry aloud and spare not; God is our hope and strength; God spake sometime in visions; How doth the city sit solitary; I behold, and lo! a great multitude; I said in the cutting off of my days; Lift up your heads, O ye gates; Lord, who shall dwell in thy tabernacle; O give thanks unto the Lord for he is gracious; O Lord, I have sinned; Oh Lord, thou hast searched me out and known me; The Lord is my Shepherd; Turn thee unto me, O Lord*
(M) *** Hyp. Dyad CDD 22055 (2). Winchester Cathedral Ch., Parley of Instruments, Hill

Blow's anthems are of diverse kinds. The opening *God spake sometimes in visions* is a glorious example of the grandest style of all; it was written for the Coronation of James II in 1685. Then there is the 'full and contrapuntal' anthem, of which *God is our help and strength* is a sonorous illustration. Many listeners will also be delighted to encounter a new and memorable setting of *The Lord is my Shepherd*, in which the layout is in sections, with limited polyphony and a warmly lyrical style. Other anthems are less ambitious, yet musically poignant. *O Lord I have sinned* (written for a funeral) is particularly beautiful, using a solo group intimately, with organ accompaniment. *Lord, who shall dwell in thy tabernacle?* has three obbligato recorders and combines soloists with a full chorus, like a vocal concerto grosso.

The closing *I said in the cutting off of my days* is permeated with melancholy, but the central 'Alleluias' from the full choir immediately lift the spirits, as does the last sentence, 'But the living, they shall praise thee, as I do', and Blow resourcefully brings back the 'Alleluias' at the end. In short, there is great variety here, and enough contrast to ensure that both discs offer the possibility of listening right through; alternatively, the listener can choose individual anthems. The soloists from the choir sing most pleasingly individually, and (of course) beautifully together; the full choir is stirring, and the accompaniments are warm and refined. Altogether a remarkably valuable anthology. Full texts are included.

BLUMER, Theodor (1881–1964)

Theodor Blumer studied and worked in Dresden in the early years of his career, moving to Leipzig as conductor of the Radio Orchestra in 1931, then in 1952 on to Berlin until his death. He created a reputation for *Hausmusik* like the present works, which are really intended for professional performance.

Kinderspielzeug (Children's Toys); Schweizer (Swiss) Quintet; (i) Sextet for Piano & Winds (Chamber Symphony), Op. 92
✪ *** Crystal CD 755. Moran Woodwind Quintet; (i) with Paul Barnes

This collection is a real find. Theodor Blumer writes for woodwind with disarming facility, and with a voicing of parts all but worthy of Mozart, but also with an almost Gallic lightness of touch. The *Swiss Quintet* is a little masterpiece, opening with a *Prelude*, followed by a charming *Gavotte*, a delicate *Arietta* for flute and clarinet, and then a wistful *Lied* for oboe solo. But then comes a set of seven variations on a Swiss folksong, '*Es blühen die Rosen im Tale*' with a richly scored introduction, before the perky little theme, introduced by the horn, receives a series of witty variants of great charm using various woodwind combinations, ending with a delicious little fugue in which everyone takes part. The *Children's Toys* suite is equally felicitous, with mainly tranquil evocations, including dolls on parade and a musical clock, and it ends with a sleigh ride.

Although it also opens daintily, the four-movement *Sextet* with piano, is rather more ambitious, with a chattering *Scherzo*, a gentle *Andante sostenuto*, featuring the solo piano and ending with a dancing *Molto vivace* Rondo. The Moran Quintet play all this music with the lightest touch and elegantly polished ensemble, catching equally its moments of mock humour and gentle lyricism. They are recorded most realistically, and this very engaging collection is worth seeking out: (www.crystalrecords.com).

BOCCHERINI, Luigi (1743–1805)

Capriccio Boccherini Edition

Symphonies 13 in C, 15 in D min.; 16 in A, Op. 37/1, 3 & 4, G.515–8
Cap. 10457. New Berlin CO, Erxleben

Symphonies 17 in C min., Op. 41; 18 in D, Op. 42; 19 in D, Op. 43; 20 in D min., Op. 45, G.519–22
Cap. 10458. New Berlin CO, Erxleben

Divertimenti 1–4, Op. 16/1–4, G.461 & G.464–6
Cap. 10456. Haupt, Lee, Walch, Poppem, Quandt, Teutsch, Laine

Guitar Quintets 1–6
Cap. 49472 (1–3); 49473 (4–6). Jumez, Dimov Qt

Titled Works: Notturno (Duet) 7 in E flat (La bona notte), G.62; String Quartet 65 in G (La Tiranna), Op. 44/4, G.223; String Quintets: 60 in C (La Musica Notturna della strade di Madrid), Op. 30/6, G.324; 72 in F (Quintetto dello Scacciapensiero), Op. 36/6, G.336
Cap. 10453. Seiler, Walch, Poppen, Lester, Penny

Oboe Quintets: 13–18, Op. 55/1–6, G.431–6

Cap. 10454. Lencsés, Parish Qt

String Quartets: 19 in D, Op. 15/1; 36 in G min., Op. 24/6; 55 in A, Op. 39; 90 in F, Op. 64/1, G.177, G.194, G.213 & G.248

Cap. 10451. Petersen Qt

String Quintets: 15 in A, Op. 60/3, G.393; 16 in D min., Op. 13/4, G.280; 23 in D, Op. 62/5, G.401; 62 in D, Op. 31/2, G.326

Cap. 10452. Augmented Petersen Qt

String Sextets: in E flat; E; F min.; F, Op. 23/1, 3–4 & 6

Cap. 10450. Seiler, Juda, Poppen, Dickel, Lester, Penny

Boccherini Edition Complete
B) *** Cap. 49463 (10) As above (CDs not available separately)

Boccherini's music is of real quality and Capriccio's Boccherini Edition of ten CDs would make a fine investment for any collector who wants to explore this composer's always listener-friendly output, leaving aside the concertos. The three surviving *Symphonies* from Op. 37 (No. 2 is lost), written in 1786/7, are among his most stimulating works, and the three mature works in the second collection, from 1788, are comparably inventive, with the two minor-key symphonies among his most imaginative, especially the *D minor*, with both outer movements opening with an *Adagio* and an unusual, flowing *Andante*. This was his last orchestral work, except for an arrangement from an early string quintet.

The four Opus 16 *Divertimenti* of 1770 (for flute, viola, two violins, two cellos and bass) are certainly diverting, and unpredictably so. Unlike the comparable works of Mozart, they are each in four movments, and the *First* opens elegantly and characteristically with an *Andantino grazioso*. But No. 5 brings a touching opening *Adagio*, followed by a bouncing second-movement *Allegro*, and it has one of Boccherini's most vivacious *moto perpetuo* finales, matched later by the *Prestissimo* finale of No. 6.

The six *Oboe Quintets* are equally felicitous. They were originally sextets, but Boccherini decided that the ad lib. double bass could be dispensed with. They are charmingly inconsequential, all in two movements, usually a vivaciously perky *Andantino* or *Allegretto*, followed by a Minuet of which Haydn would have approved; the exception is No. 5, in which a pair of all-but-identical slow movements frame the Minuet.

The four string works with titles all have some kind of programmatic background. The *Musica Notturna* evokes the music heard at night on the streets of Madrid and opens with guitar-like strumming. Also included is a mandolin imitation, and the work ends with the familiar *Retreat*. The closing *Presto* of the *Notturno* (*Duet*), for a pair of violins (which opens with a charming *Amoroso*), closes with a brief two-chord 'goodnight', while the F major '*Jews Harp*' *String Quintet* brings harmonic and *sul ponticello* effects which readily evoke that strange instrument.

The *String Quartets* and *String Quintets* are the part of Boccherini's output (alongside the *Guitar Quintets*) with which we are most familiar on disc. The four *Quartets* chosen here are all immdiately engaging, with amiable opening movements, and with slow movements in which the composer's expressive dolour is gently touching; the *Grave* of Op. 55 is a wistful example. But the *String Quintets* are even finer, and the work in D, Op. 6/5, has one of Boccherini's most

memorable *Adagio cantabile* slow movements, followed by a predictably busy closing *Allegro assai*. The G major, after a friendly first movement, has a most affecting *Andante*. The earliest work here, *16 in D minor*, brings one of the composer's rare fugue finales, and a neatly crafted example it is, too.

Apart from a wrongly attributed work, the six *String Sextets* of Op. 23 (1776) are Boccherini's only contribution to this form. Yet they brought out the very best in him, and again in all four works there is a delicacy of feeling, a gentle pathos that is the hallmark of his best, most expressive music, and it is very difficult to evaluate any particular one here as the finest.

The *Guitar Quintets* are special to Boccherini and are much recorded, and justly so. They are consistently inventive, vivid in colour and often original. Only one of the two most famous is included here, G.448 with its *Fandango* finale, but the quality of invention throughout is so consistently pleasing that it is difficult to pick and choose; although No. 5 in D (G.449) is notable for a fine set of variations as its finale.

These ten CDs are packaged in individual jewel cases with excellent documentation, and they come together in a slipcase. The standard of performance throughout is very high indeed: each chamber group seems absolutely in sympathy with the composer's muse, and they are beautifully balanced and recorded. The symphonies too are admirably played by the spiritedly expressive New Berlin Chamber Orchestra under Michael Erxleben and they are among the best available performances of this repertoire.

Symphonies: in A, Op. 35/3, G.511; in D min. (Grande), Op. 37/3, G.517; Guitar Quintet 4 in D (Fandango), G.448; String Quintet 9 in C (La Musica Notturna delle Strada di Madrid), Op. 30/6, G.324
*** Alia Vox SACD AVSA 9815. Lislevand, Concert des Nations (members), Savall

Anyone wanting a single Boccherini disc as a sampler, in authentic, period-instrument costume, could hardly do better than this. The performances are exceptionally vivid. Rolf Lislevand is an excellent guitarist, and José de Udaeta's castanets glitter appropriately in the famous *Fandango*, while in the *C major Quintet* the patrol sequence is admirably managed. The outer movements of the two symphonies are played with abrasive period-instrument vigour and gusto, but the inner movements are engagingly refined. Jordi Savall keeps the pot on the boil throughout, and altogether this is very stimulating, while the SACD recording has both depth and striking presence.

BOISMORTIER, Joseph Bodin de
(1689–1755)

Ballets de village: 1–4, Op. 52; Gentilesse 5, Op. 45; Sérénade 1, Op. 39
(BB) *** Naxos 8.554295. Le Concert Spirituel, Niquet

Boismortier's four *Ballets de village* are colourful sets of pastoral dances which make vivid use of rustic instruments – the musette and hurdy-gurdy – with an underlying drone, in concert with wind and string instruments, in continuous lively three-part writing. The three-movement *Gentillesse* is rather more refined. However, the *Sérénade*, Op. 39, with its 18 sections is much more ambitious. Here the texture is based on flutes, violins and oboes. There is an opening *Ouverture* and an extended closing *Chaconne*. In between come more dances, *Gavottes*, a *Gigue*, a *Sarabande*, a fast and piquantly vivacious *Villageoise* introduced by the treble recorder, as well as an *Entrée rustique*, an elegant *Air gracieux*, a charming *Air modéré* and even a *Chœur imaginaire*. Boismortier's invention is unflagging, the instrumental colouring ear-catching, and when played with such authenticity and sparkle this is very attractive, if not to be taken in a continuous sequence. The recording is excellent.

(i) *Bassoon Concerto*; (ii) *Musette (Zampogna) Concerto*. *Fragments mélodiques* (French dance suite); *Sérénade or Symphonie française 2*. Stage works: *Daphnis et Chloé: Chaconne; Les Voyages de l'amour: Entrées des génies élémentaires*

(BB) *** Naxos 8.554456. (i) Le Chenadec; (ii) Maillard; Le Concert Spirituel, Niquet

Naxos at last are filling out a fuller picture of Joseph Bodin de Boismortier, tax collector (for the French Royal Tobacco Company) as well as musician. As this collection shows, he composed with easy facility so that a contemporary writer portrayed him in verse: 'Happy is he, Boismortier, whose fertile quill, / Each month, without pain, conceives a new air at will.'

The *Bassoon Concerto* shows this facility most agreeably, as does the equally engaging work for musette (Boismortier chose the Italian name to describe the instrument) with its underlying drone. His orchestral palette is shown even more colourfully in the two collections of dances, felicitously and lightly scored for flutes, oboes, hurdy-gurdy, musette and strings. One of his specialities was to write inventive chaconnes in duple instead of triple time. Both the *Fragments mélodiques* and *Sérénade* end with a typical example. But his finale for *Daphnis et Chloé* (which is used to open the concert) is even more individual and deserves to be better known. Most remarkable of all is the *Entrées des génies élémentaires*, a bubbling kaleidoscope of contrasting character dances. Hervé Niquet directs his excellent ensemble with animation and finesse, and both his soloists are in good form. A first-class disc in every way, well worth exploring.

6 *Concertos for 5 Flutes*, Op. 15/1–6

(BB) ** Naxos 8.553639. Soloists of Le Concert Spirituel

Although Boismortier's invention holds up well throughout, his predilection for block chords in slow movements means that the music has relatively little variety of colour. These excellent players blend and match their timbres expertly, often presenting a very homogeneous sound, the effect emphasized by the close balance. A disc to recommend primarily to amateur flautists.

6 *Flute Sonatas*, Op. 91

*** Analekta FL2 3008. Guimond, Beauséjour

Boismortier's Op. 91 is elegant and well crafted, and these sonatas nicely blend French and Italian influences. All except the first, which has an opening *Sicilienne*, are in the fast–slow–fast Italian tradition. They are played beautifully and stylishly by this excellent French-Canadian duo: Claire Guimond on the baroque flute and Luc Beauséjour. They play with an appealing delicacy to charm the ear, yet there is an underlying robustness that makes the music seem far from merely trivial. The recording (as one expects from this Canadian label) is expertly balanced and altogether natural.

(i) *Suites for Solo Flute 3, 5 & 6*; (ii) *Harpsichord Suites 1–4* (1731)

(B) *** HM Cal. (ADD) CAL 6865. (i) Urbain; (ii) Lagacé

(i) *Suites for Solo Flute 4; 3 & 6* (with continuo); (ii) *Harpsichord Suites 1–4*

(BB) *** Naxos 8.554457. (i) Savignat, Plubeau; (ii) Martin

These four *Harpsichord Suites* were Boismortier's only works for harpsichord. They are very much in the style of the *Pièces de clavecin* of Rameau, and Boismortier follows his practice in giving each movement a colourful sobriquet. *La Cavernesque*, which begins the *First Suite*, is aptly titled. The invention is attractive, if perhaps not as individual as with Rameau, although the finale of the last suite shows Boismortier writing a very characterful set of variations. Mireille Lagacé is an excellent advocate and she uses a restored Hemsch, which is truthfully recorded and suits the repertoire admirably. The *First Suite* is also played expertly by Lagacé, and the recording is realistic, provided you turn down the volume. Interleaved with the harpsichord works are three suites for unaccompanied flute. Again the playing is highly responsive, to make this a rewarding concert.

The harpsichord that Béatrice Martin uses on the Naxos disc is not named, but if anything it is an even more attractive instrument than that used by Mireille Lagacé, warmly resonant yet well focused. Anne Savignat plays the charming *Fourth Flute Suite* as a solo work, but in Nos. 3 and 6 she is partnered by Christine Plubeau, who plays a simple bass line on the viola da gamba. Certainly these performances are every bit the equal of those on their Calliope competitor and again make one reflect that the works for harpsichord ought to be far better known.

Harpsichord Suites: excerpts: *La Caverneuse; La Décharnée; La Marguillière; La Transalpine; La Valétudinaire*

(BB) *** Warner Apex 2564 60372-2. Boulay (harpsichord) – DUPHLY: *Pièces de clavecin* ***

Boismortier was born in Thionville but he eventually found his way to Paris, where he earned his living as an orchestral conductor. He wrote a good deal of music but only four suites of harpsichord pieces, which were published in 1736. They are striking and attractive, as these elegantly played excerpts readily show. All are subtitled according to the French style of the period, but the titles are not usually descriptive. Here *La Transalpine* and *La Décharnée* are particularly winning. They will surely tempt collectors to explore the suites themselves, of which there are alternative performancs listed in our main volume.

BOMTEMPO, João Domingos
(1771–1842)

Symphonies 1, Op. 11; 2

(BB) (*) Naxos 8.557163. Algarve O, Cassuto

It is good to hear these symphonies by the Portuguese pianist/composer, João Bomtempo, whose contribution to musical life in Europe and London during his lifetime was far from uninfluential. The early *First Symphony* is an appealing work in the classical tradition, with some nice turns of phrase and ideas, Haydn and Mozart being the obvious models. The *Second Symphony* is bigger in scope, with its long serious introduction, more obviously a work of the romantic era. Alas, the quality of playing of the Algarve Orchestra is not really good enough to give an unreserved recommendation, though undoubtedly they are committed. Moreover, the recording is subfusc, lacking sparkle and clarity.

BORODIN, Alexander (1833–87)

*Symphony 2 in B min.; In the Steppes of Central Asia; Prince
Igor: Overture; Polovtsian March; Polovtsian Dances*
🔊 (BB) *** Regis RRC 1215. RPO, Schmidt

Too long neglected on disc, Ole Schmidt with the RPO offers
an outstanding bargain version of Borodin's *Second Symphony*, beautifully played and recorded in vivid, open sound,
one of the finest at any price. In the first movement Schmidt
evades the pitfall of adopting too slow a speed, thus avoiding
any ponderousness while giving the music an idiomatically
earthy spring. So, the flurries at the opening have a fiercely
Slavonic bite, heightened by the way that Schmidt slightly
exaggerates the pauses between them; from then on, rhythms
are delectably sprung. After that brisk first movement,
Schmidt takes a relatively relaxed view of the *Prestissimo*
Scherzo, again beautifully sprung. At a nicely flowing tempo
the great horn solo of the slow movement is gloriously
played by the RPO's long-time principal, Jeffrey Bryant.
Beautifully shaded, with perfectly controlled rubato, his
radiant playing matches and even outshines the finest of the
past. The crisp finale is full of panache. The *Prince Igor
Overture* again brings masterly horn-playing, while the
Polovtsian Dances and *March* show off the brilliance of the
RPO wind soloists.

Prince Igor (complete CD version)
(BB) (***) Naxos mono 8.111071/73. Ivanov, Smolenskaya,
 Lemershev, Pirogov, Reizen, Bolshoi Opera Ch. & O,
 Melik-Pashayev

Although there were 78-r.p.m. discs of various arias from
Nina Koshetz, Chaliapin and Kipnis (and Decca issued a
four-sides set with Baturin, Mikhailev and Jerzinskaya) this
1951 recording was first issued on 32 78-r.p.m. sides, and only
then on LP. Apart from the distinction of the singing and, of
course, the conducting of Alexander Melik-Pashayev, the
sheer magnificence of the voices of Sergei Lemershev and
Andrei Ivanov (Igor and his son respectively) are a source of
wonder and put an altogether different pespective on more
modern recordings. Alexander Pirogov's Prince Galitzky and
Mark Reizen's Khan Konchak are hardly less thrilling. Older
readers will recall the coarse climaxes and rough timbres of
Soviet recordings of this period, and they can be assured as to
the quality of the sound restoration. Ward Marston has
worked wonders when compared with the originals, though
there is naturally a limit to what even he can do. The sound
inevitably remains two-dimensional. As was normal practice
at the time, Act III is omitted. There is an appendix on the
third CD which offers classic recordings of arias by
Chaliapin, Koshetz, Nadezhda Oboukhova and Charles Fri-
ant. Lovers of Russian music and of great singing should not
fail to investigate this set.

Prince Igor: Polovtsian Dances
(BB) *** HMV (ADD) 5 86757-2. Beecham Choral Soc., RPO,
 Beecham – KHACHATURIAN: *Ballet music;*
 RIMSKY-KORSAKOV: *Scheherazade; Flight of the
 Bumble-Bee* ***

Beecham's justly famous and unsurpassed choral recording of
the *Polovtsian Dances* is also available as a 'Great Recording of
the Century', coupled with his own unsurpassed account of
Scheherazade (EMI 5 66983-2 [5 669982]). But Yuasa's LPO
Scheherazade is also highly recommendable, especially at

budget price, and the Khachaturian ballet excerpts are well
worth having too.

BØRRESEN, Hakon (1876–1954)

At Uranienborg or Tycho Brahe's Dream (ballet); (i)
Romance for Cello & Orchestra. The Royal Guest: Prelude
**(*) dacapo 8.224105. Aalborg SO, Hughes; (i) with
 Brendstrup

The Royal Guest, a one-act opera from 1919, was Børresen's
greatest success, and its *Prelude* whets the appetite. The 12
numbers that constitute the ballet *At Uranienborg or Tycho
Brahe's Dream* are given a committed performance, as is the
Romance, played by Henrik Brendstrup and written in 1908 at
the time of the *Second Symphony*. Owain Arwel Hughes and
his Aalborg musicians sound as if they are enjoying themselves. But the acoustic of the Aalborg hall is not ideal: the
sound is tubby in climaxes and lacks transparency.

Symphonies 2 in A (The Sea), Op. 7; 3 in C, Op. 21
*** CPO 999 353-2. Frankfurt RSO, Schmidt

Both symphonies have a lot going for them. The delightful
Scherzo of No. 1 is as transparent in its orchestration as
Mendelssohn, and the first movement has a Dvořákian sense
of openness and space. Attractive works, not the last word in
originality, but presented very persuasively by Ole Schmidt
and the Frankfurt Radio Orchestra, and well recorded.

BORTNYANSKY, Dmitri (1751–1825)

Sacred Concertos 1–35.
*** Chan. 9729 *1–9*; 9783 *10–16*; 9840 *17–23*; 9878 *24–29*;
 9956 *30–35* Russian State Symphonic Cappella, Polyansky

Bortnyansky became Kapellmeister of the Court Cappella in
1779, where he remained for the rest of his life. These choral
concertos are more indebted to the Italian motet than to
Byzantine traditions of chant, but Bortnyansky wrote for
voices with consummate expertise and no mean artistry. The
performances by the Russian State Symphonic Cappella
under Valeri Polyansky have great eloquence, and though
there is a long period of reverberation in the acoustic of both
the Dormition Cathedral, Smolensk, and St Sophia's Cathedral, Polotsk (where the recordings were made in 1989–90),
the sound is beautifully focused.
 The fifth collection (Nos. 30–35) represents Bortnyansky's
crowning achievement in the genre as is well borne out here,
and the second disc might be a good place to start exploring
the series, for Tchaikovsky himself declared that *Concerto No.
32* (*Lord, let me Know mine End*) with its ethereal opening is
the finest of the set. But the other works are also very
beautiful. Performances and recording are of the very highest
standard.

Sacred Concertos for Double Choir 1–10
*** Chan. 9922. Russian State Symphonic Cappella,
 Polyansky

The hardly less beautiful works for double choir are mainly
Psalm settings, and they have a radiant simplicity. But
throughout, Polyansky and his singers make rich use of the
composer's antiphonal interplay, and, although these settings
are often more peaceful, less expressively extrovert than many
of the works for single choir, their effect is hardly less potent.
First class recording.

BÖRTZ, Daniel (born 1943)

Trumpet Concerto (Songs & Dances)

*** BIS CD 1021. Hardenberger, Malmö SO, Varga (with
RABE: *Sardine Sarcophagus*; SANDSTROM: *Trumpet
Concerto 2* ***)

Börtz's *Trumpet Concerto* is highly imaginative and has a
compelling quality, thanks to his feeling for sound and colour, whether or not you respond to the idiom. It is subtitled
Songs and Dances and is one of four concertos with related
titles. Hardenberger is quite stunning, as is the BIS recording.

Sinfonias 1; 7; Parados; Strindberg Suite

*** Chan. 9473. Stockholm PO, Rozhdestvensky

Daniel Börtz is never boring, though his limited range of
expressive devices makes it hard to listen to all these pieces
straight off, despite the refined sense of orchestral colour. The
music is too static, with extensive use of chord-clusters and
strong dynamic contrasts, but both the *First* and *Seventh
Symphonies* are powerfully atmospheric. The playing of the
Stockholm orchestra is superb and the Chandos recording is
of demonstration standard: marvellously present, well balanced and realistic.

BOTTESINI, Giovanni (1821–89)

(i; ii) *Double Bass Cello Concertos 1 in F sharp min.* (orch.
Gaydos); *2 in B min.*; (i; iii) *Gran Duo Passione Amorosa*
(for two double basses and orchestra, orch. Furtok)

*** CPO 999 665-2. Furtok, with (i) Frankfurt RSO; (ii)
Tetzlaff; (iii) Stähle (double bass); Edelmann (cond.)

Apart from being a composer and virtuoso double-bass
player (once dubbed the 'Paganini of the Double Bass'),
Bottesini was also an important conductor and life-long
friend of Verdi, conducting the premiere of *Aida* in Cairo in
1871. He also scored some success at writing operas and a
body of solo, chamber and orchestral music (much of it for
his chosen instrument). These undoubtedly attractive concertos clearly stretch the double bass beyond its usual standard
range, exploring its possibilities and emotional range to a
surprising degree. They are full of pleasing ideas, very much
in the early romantic tradition (there is a hint of Schumann
in both the first and slow movements), while the jolly finales
display a light-hearted brilliance rarely associated with this
instrument. In the *Gran Duo Passione Amorosa*, the brilliance
and repartee between the two soloists make for highly engaging results. The performances are excellent, and if the soloists'
intonation is not always spot on, they surmount the bravura
with admirable aplomb. The sound is warm and well balanced.

(i) *Double-Bass Concertino in C min.*; (i-ii) *Duo concertante
on Themes from Bellini's 'I Puritani' for Cello, Double-Bass
& Orchestra*; (i) *Elégie in D*; (i; iii) *Passioni amorose* (for 2
double-basses); *Ali Baba Overture*; *Il diavolo della notte*; *Ero
e Leandro: Prelude*

*** ASV CDDCA 907. (i) Martin; (ii) Welsh; (iii) Petracchi;
LSO, Petracchi or (iii) Gibson

A contemporary said of Bottesini's virtuoso playing, 'Under
his bow the double-bass sighed, cooed, sang, quivered,' and it
does all those things here on the flamboyant bow of Thomas
Martin, himself a musician of the strongest personality. For
the *Passioni amorose* the conductor, Francesco Petracchi,

exchanges his baton for another bow to join his colleague,
establishing a close, decisive partnership. Further contrast is
provided in the *Duo concertante* on melodies of Bellini. The
programme is interspersed with colourful orchestral miniatures. The *Sinfonia*, *Il diavolo della notte*, turns naturally
from warm lyricism to galloping liveliness, and the brief *Ali
Baba Overture* brings a spirited whiff of Rossini. The recording engineers have worked marvels to balance everything so
convincingly, and this programme is surprisingly rewarding
and entertaining.

*Gran duo concertante for Violin, Double-Bass & Orchestra;
Gran concerto in F sharp min. for Double-Bass; Andante
sostenuto for Strings; Duetto for Clarinet & Double-Bass*

**(*) ASV CDDCA 563. Garcia, Martin, Johnson, ECO, Litton

The ASV recording combines the *Gran duo concertante* with
another *Duetto for Clarinet and Double-Bass*, which Emma
Johnson ensures has plenty of personality, though none of
this amiable music is very distinctive. The recording is excellent, well balanced and truthful.

*Capriccio di bravura; Elegia in Re; Fantasia on 'Beatrice di
Tenda'; Fantasia on 'Lucia di Lammermoor'; Grand allegro
di concerto; Introduzione e bolero; Romanza drammatica; (i)
Romanza: Une bouche aimée*

**(*) ASV CDDCA 626. Martin, Halstead; (i) with Fugelle

Thomas Martin is a superb virtuoso of the double-bass and
he obviously relishes these display pieces, but some of the
high tessitura is inevitably uncomfortable. The recording is
most realistic.

BOURGAULT-DUCOUDRAY, Louis-Albert (1840–1910)

Rhapsodie cambodgienne

**(*) Marco Polo 8.225234. Slovak RSO, Adriano – FANELLI:
Tableaux symphoniques d'après 'Le Roman de la Momie'.
**(*)

The impressively named French composer Louis-Albert
Bourgault-Ducoudray is hardly well known today. He was
appointed professor of music history at the Paris Conservatoire in 1878, and wrote music throughout his life. His taste
for exotic colours and folk tunes is well in evidence in his
tone-poem *Rhapsodie cambodgienne* of 1882 (its subtitle is
The Feast of Water). With colourful orchestration and the use
of some genuine Cambodian folk tunes – the second part, the
Fête des Eaux, is especially enjoyable – it makes an enjoyable
seventeen-minute companion to Fanelli's impressive *Tableaux symphoniques*. The recording is good and Adriano is
obviously a sympathetic exponent; while the orchestra enter
into the spirit, they are not always immaculate in execution,
with the strings sounding taxed under pressure. Still, a must
for all those with an interest in the byways of French music.

BOWEN, York (1884–1961)

Cello Sonata

*** British Music Soc. BMS 423CD. Cole, Talbot – FOULDS:
WALKER: *Cello Sonatas* ***

Jo Cole does not produce a big tone, but she is highly
sensitive to York Bowen's very English lyricism and brings out

the gentle romanticism of the first movement's secondary theme very persuasively, especially on its reprise. But she is at her finest in the elegiac main theme of the slow movement and in catching its passionate, rhapsodic feeling. The finale is a brilliant rondo, which brings back the principal themes from all three movements to make a powerful close, and it invites and receives a passionate response from both artists. The recording is essentially well balanced, but the piano often dominates, as much as anything because of the bold character of the piano writing.

BOYCE, William (1711–79)

Symphonies 1–8, Op. 2
(BB) * Naxos 8.557278. Arcadia Ens., Mallon

Mallon's performances are reasonably well played, but no more than that. There is an element of blandness here, and the music-making rarely sparks to life. Better to pay more for Hogwood on Decca (473 081-2), a top choice among period-instrument recordings; or, if you prefer modern instruments, the Bournemouth Sinfonietta will serve you well at mid-price (CRD 3356).

BRÆIN, Edvard Fliflet (1924–76)

Anne Pedersdotter (opera): complete
*** Simax PSC3121 (2). Ekeberg, Handssen, Carlsen, Sandve, Thorsen, Norwegian Nat. Op. Ch. & O, Andersson

Edvard Fliflet Bræin was a highly talented Norwegian composer who died in his early fifties. His opera, *Anne Pedersdotter* (1971), is based on the most famous witchcraft trial in Norway: the burning of Anne Pedersdotter in Bergen in 1590. Fliflet Bræin called it 'a symphonic opera' and, like Schoeck's *Venus*, its invention unfolds in an effortlessly organic fashion; in other words, his is the art that conceals art. It is effective music-theatre and many of its ideas, as so often with this composer, are memorable. It gets a fine performance here, with good singing from Kjersti Ekeberg as the eponymous heroine, Svein Carlsen as her husband, Absolon Pedersøn-Beyer, and Kjell Magnus Sandve as his son by his first marriage. The Norwegian Opera troops under the baton of Per Ake Andersson are excellent, and the recording, produced by Michael Woolcock, is very good indeed. Strongly recommended.

BRAHMS, Johannes (1833–97)

Academic Festival Overture; Variations on a Theme of Haydn; (i) Alto Rhapsody
** Pentatone PTC5 186045. Netherlands RSO, Vonk; (i) with Naef, Netherlands R. Ch.

Hans Vonk was already in a wheelchair when, in August 2003, not long before his untimely death, he came to the Hilversum studio of Dutch Radio to record these Brahms items. They were originally intended as the fill-ups for Pentatone's projected cycle of the Brahms symphonies, but sadly Vonk's illness took him more quickly than expected, and the project remained unfinished. The performances, beautifully played and vividly recorded, are marked by Vonk's characteristic qualities of fine balancing of sound, with clear textures and a firm control of structure. Yet the speeds incline to be very measured, with a rhythmic squareness tending to undermine

the positive qualities, except in the bursts of fast music. The *Alto Rhapsody*, with Yvonne Naef a rich, firm mezzo soloist, fares best, not the most perceptive or characterful version, but very beautiful, with clear, fresh backing from the male chorus.

Piano Concertos. 1 in D min., Op. 15; 2 in B flat, Op. 83
⊕ (M) *** Sup. SU 3865-2 (2). Ivan Moravec, Czech PO, Bělohlávek

(i) *Piano Concertos 1–2;* (ii) *Academic Festival Overture; Tragic Overture; Variations on a Theme of Haydn, Op. 56a*
⊕━ (BB) *** EMI (ADD) Gemini 4 76939-2 (2). (i) Barenboim, New Philh. O; (ii) VPO; (i; ii) Barbirolli

This is the first coupling of the two Brahms *Piano Concertos* to match the famous Gilels and Jochum partnership (DG 447 446-2), with electrifying playing from Ivan Moravec, matched by Bělohlávek's wonderfully understanding accompaniments. Moreover, this newer set also has the advantage of first-class digital recording and a natural orchestral balance, with the piano forward and dramatically present, within the warm acoustic of the Dvořák Hall of the Rudolfinum in Prague. The recordings were made in 1988 and 1989 respectively, and so gripping and spontaneous is the playing throughout that it is difficult to believe that the music-making did not take place in front of a live audience.

The orchestral balance means that the opening of the *First Concerto* has not quite the bite in the strings for which the Curzon/Szell version is famous, but there is weight instead, and in all other respects the performance is every bit as compelling. The gentle arrival of the second subject is a frisson-creating moment, and the *Adagio* has an intensity of concentration comparable with the Barenboim/Barbirolli version. The finale then releases the tension in rollicking high spirits.

The *Second Concerto* is no less commanding, the poetic opening horn solo recognizable as being by a Czech player. The first movement is boldly paced, and the music unfolds with magisterial depth and powerful momentum. The *Allegro appassionato* is both weighty and brilliant, but the underlying lyricism remains, and the middle section makes an arresting contrast. Framed by two superbly played cello solos, the *Andante* unfolds with a natural eloquence and much warmth, and the close of the movement (as in the *First Concerto*) is raptly sustained to the last bar. The finale ripples away with sparkling delicacy, yet never loses its depth of lyrical feeling. Altogether this is a very remarkable reissue of a pair of recordings which, as far as we can ascertain, have not been available before in the UK, and they are not to be missed.

Barenboim's performances with Barbirolli of the two *Piano Concertos* from the late 1960s (and especially the *First* with the New Philharmonia) are among the most inspired ever committed to disc, and the orchestral works also show Barbirolli at his finest. Excellent recording makes this budget Gemini reissue very desirable indeed.

(i) *Piano Concertos 1–2. 4 Ballades, Op. 10; 7 Fantasias, Op. 116; 3 Intermezzi, Op. 117; 8 Pieces, Op. 76; 6 Pieces, Op. 118; 4 Pieces, Op. 119; 2 Rhapsodies, Op. 79; Scherzo, Op. 4; Variations & Fugue on a Theme by Handel, Op. 24; 16 Waltzes, Op. 39*
(B) *** Ph. (DDD/ADD) 475 7160 (4). Kovacevich; (i) LSO, C. Davis

An excellent coverage from Kovacevich which brings together all his Brahms recordings for Philips from the late 1960s through to the early 1980s. In the *D minor Concerto* he plays with great tenderness and lyrical feeling. Similarly No. 2, the favourite of the soloist's concerto recordings from this period, combines poetic feeling and intellectual strength, and reflects an unforced naturalness that consistently commands admiration. Colin Davis provides admirable support with the LSO: the beautifully played opening horn solo of the *B flat Concerto* is immediately magnetic. The 1979 recordings are splendidly transferred and still sound full and fresh.

The solo piano music can also receive the fullest recommendation. Kovacevich's performances of the *Ballades* and the Op. 76 *Pieces* have both fire and tenderness, and he finds the fullest range of emotional contrast in the Op. 116 *Fantasias*, but he is at his finest in the Op. 117 *Intermezzi* and the *Four Pieces*, Op. 119, which contain some of Brahms's most beautiful and lyrical inspirations for the piano. The other works bring interpretations of comparable distinction. The playing is not only thoughtful but full of the sharpest contrasts. Even the gentle inspiration of the much-loved set of *Waltzes* has him using the fullest range of dynamic and expression, and the result is most compelling, both here and in the later, more demanding pieces. The *Allegro risoluto* of the final *Rhapsody* of Op. 119, which ends the third disc, has splendid flair and presence. The recordings too, whether analogue or digital, are very realistic and the CD transfers first class.

Piano Concerto 1 in D min., Op. 15
*** DG 477 6021. Zimerman, BPO, Rattle

(i) *Piano Concerto 1. Variations & Fugue on a Theme of Handel, Op. 24*
(BB) ** HMV (ADD) 5 86867-2. Gelber; (i) Munich PO, Decker

Krystian Zimerman, Simon Rattle and the Berlin Philharmonic took their masterly account of the *D minor Concerto* into the studio the day after a concert performance. Of the latter, the *Frankfurter Allgemeine Zeitung* is quoted as saying, 'Zimerman infused his piano part with that spark of individual genius which separates a merely committed and faithful interpretation from the revelation of absolute truth.' There is no doubt that this is a distinguished performance, and it is very well recorded, save for the fact that Ulrich Vette's balance gives the soloist an artifical prominence. However, this is a disc that must be heard, even if the Gilels–Jochum account must still take precedence.

The Buenos Aires pianist Bruno Leonardo Gelber's performance of the *D minor Concerto*, while still a considerable achievement, is not as successful as his account of the *B flat* work. Franz Decker proves a less than inspired accompanist, and the first movement tends to hang fire, not helped by the rather poor focus of the Munich recording. The warmly sensitive slow movement and the bold, lilting finale, in both of which the soloist dominates, show him in a much better light, and his outstanding and commandingly imaginative account of the *Handel Variations*, very well recorded, shows him at his very finest – very much a three-star performance.

(i) *Piano Concerto 1. 3 Intermezzi, Op. 117; 6 Pieces, Op. 118; 4 Pieces, Op. 119; Piano Sonata 3 in F min., Op. 5; 2 Rhapsodies, Op. 79; Theme & Variations in D min.from String Sextet in B flat (arr. composer)*
(B) *** Decca (ADD/DDD) 475 7070 (3). Lupu, (i) with LPO, De Waart

In the *D minor Concerto* Radu Lupu characteristically eschews *Sturm und Drang*. His is not a reading that compares readily with the dramatic account Szell and Curzon made so famous. Lupu approaches the work through the eyes of a decade when the piano was not the leonine monster it was to become later in the century. His is a deeply reflective and intelligent performance, certainly not without power and tension, and full of masterly touches and an affecting poetry that falls short of the thrusting combative power that we expect from a Serkin or Curzon. Edo de Waart provides sensitive accompaniment and matches Lupu's approach admirably. The reading is a valuable corrective to the accepted modern view of this masterpiece, deeply Brahmsian and warmly enjoyable in its own right. Moreover, Decca's 1974 Kingsway Hall recording is in every way excellent. The truthful analogue sound has transferred faithfully to CD. The acoustic is warm, yet fresh and open, every detail registers and the relationship of piano and orchestra is ideal.

Noble, dignified and spacious are the adjectives that spring to mind when listening to Lupu's account of the *F minor Sonata*. He brings to the music qualities of the mind and spirit that ensure the listener's attention. He does not have the sheer ardour of a Katchen and at times in the first movement one feels the need for a greater sense of forward movement: Lupu's approach is inward, ruminative and always beautifully rounded. The recording is again most realistic, the piano set slightly back, the timbre fully coloured and the focus natural. About the collection of late Brahms *Pieces* and *Intermezzi* there can be no reservations whatsoever; the individual collection survived in the catalogue from 1978 until quite recently. Lupu's performances have great intensity and inwardness when these qualities are required, and a keyboard mastery that is second to none. The quality of the recorded sound is wide in range and splendidly immediate, and Lupu's delicacy of colouring is most truthfully conveyed.

Piano Concerto 2 in B flat, Op. 83
(*) DG **DVD 073 4097. Pollini, VPO, Abbado –
BEETHOVEN: *Piano Concertos 3 & 5*; MOZART: *Piano Concertos 19 & 23* **(*)
(M) **(*) DG (ADD) 474 838-2. Anda, PO, Karajan – GRIEG: *Piano Concerto* **

(i) *Piano Concerto 2 in B flat. Rhapsody in G min., Op. 79/2; 16 Waltzes, Op. 39*
(BB) **(*) HMV (ADD) 5 86869-2. Gelber; (i) RPO, Kempe

Pollini is commanding and majestic in the *B flat concerto*, recorded in May 1976 at the Musikvereinssaal, Vienna, and Böhm and the Vienna Philharmonic give sympathetic support. By the side of the Gilels–Jochum performances that held sway in the early 1970s (and which we all thought swept the board) this does not seem as warm or involving. Of course it offers some superb pianism and eloquent orchestral playing but, as with the Beethoven, it exhibits cool and dedicated classicism, shorn of expressive exaggeration, characteristic of this partnership. Exemplary visual direction and predictably fine sound from Klaus Hiemann and Rainer Brock.

EMI's full-bodied sound-picture presents Bruno Leonardo Gelber's performance of the *B flat Concerto* with Kempe in the most persuasive light, and it is a performance of note, lyrically wayward but with striking spontaneity of feeling. The first movement is especially fine, spacious yet powerful, the tension held consistently. The *Andante* is comparably eloquent; the finale has a rippling lightness at the opening which is highly engaging, but it develops a degree of lyrical fervour to match the earlier movements without ever losing its *grazioso* feeling. Gelber's boldly passionate account of the famous *G minor Rhapsody* is hardly less compelling. Both recordings were made at Abbey Road in the early 1970s, but the *Waltzes*, also perceptively and attractively characterized, were made in the Paris Salle Wagram in 1976, and the sound (typical of that venue) is comparatively shallow, as is obvious at the very opening work in B major.

The 1968 partnership of Geza Anda and the BPO provides much fine playing from soloist and orchestra alike. The performance opens slowly and is rhapsodically free; it has plenty of impulse, and if Anda is wayward at times, he is always commanding. There is poetry here and undoubted power. The slow movement is often richly eloquent, and the finale has a persuasive, lyrical charm. There is much to enjoy, not least in the glorious orchestral response. The recording is appropriately bold and full, and the balance good, sounding better than ever in this new Originals transfer.

Violin Concerto in D, Op. 77

(M) (***) EMI mono 4 76830-2 [4 76831-2]. Neveu, Philh. O, Susskind – SIBELIUS: Violin Concerto (***)

(i) *Violin Concerto in D; (ii) Academic Festival Overture; Variations on a Theme by Haydn; (iii) Hungarian Dances 1 & 5;(iv) Wiegenlied*

(BB) *** HMV 5 86716-2. (i) Little, RLPO, Handley; (ii) LPO, Boult; (iii) RPO, Kubelik; (iv) De los Angeles, L. Sinf., Frühbeck de Burgos

(i) *Violin Concerto; (ii) Piano Trio 1 in B, Op. 8; (iii) Violin Sonatas 1–3*

(M) **(*) Ph. 2-CD 475 7464 (2). Mullova, with (i) BPO, Abbado; (ii) Previn & Schiff; (iii) Anderszewski

Tasmin Little gives a warmly satisfying account, at once brilliant and deeply felt. The rapt poetry she finds in the first two movements has rarely been matched, with powerful bravura set against yearning *pianissimos*. She also brings an element of fun to the Hungarian dance finale, seldom caught so winningly. Even more than in her earlier recordings, there is a dramatic thrust and intensity that mirrors live communication, strongly matched by the RLPO under Handley. Some might feel it a pity that the original coupling of the Sibelius *Concerto* was abandoned for this reissue. But the Boult and Kubelik orchestral bonuses are enjoyable too, and many will welcome Victoria de los Angeles's ravishing account of the famous *Lullaby*. In Boult's hands the *Academic Festival Overture* is nobly expansive as well as lively. The *Variations* too are vividly presented and strongly characterized, while Kubelik's pair of *Hungarian Dances* have plenty of impetus and warmth; all these works are given a full Brahmsian sound by the EMI recording team.

Ginette Neveu's magnificent performance now becomes one of EMI's 'Great Recordings of the Century' in its coupling with a magnetic account of the Sibelius *Concerto*. We are inclined to prefer the Dutton transfer of the Brahms (CDBP 9710), but that comes with music by Ravel, Suk and others, and the EMI transfer from the original 78s is very acceptable, clear and not lacking body.

Mullova's is a commanding performance of the *Violin Concerto*, recorded at a concert the Berlin Philharmonic gave in Suntory Hall, Tokyo, in 1992. She plays with breathtaking assurance, pure and true throughout, made the more compelling by the spontaneous expressiveness that goes with live performance, for, apart from over-prominent timpani, the recording is first rate, and Abbado and the Berlin Philharmonic here match their Brahmsian achievement in the DG symphony cycle. With the solo instrument not spotlit, the wide dynamic range of Mullova's playing is the more telling, with the many reflective passages in the first movement, as well as the central *Adagio*, given a rapt intensity at a true *pianissimo*.

The *Piano Trio* is also a distinct success – not surprisingly, with Previn at the piano, and Heinrich Schiff also on top form, and the three artists very much a dedicated Brahmsian team. Alas, the *Violin Sonatas* are not quite so appealing. Mullova's playing has elegance and sweetness of tone, though by comparison with such partnerships as Osostowicz and Tomes (on Hyperion Helios CDH 55087) there is a certain coolness. But her admirers will find this two-CD set fair value, for the concerto is outstanding.

(i) Double Concerto for Violin and Cello: Tragic Overture

(M) *** EMI (ADD) 3 45758-2 [3 45765-2]. (i) D. Oistrakh, Fournier; Philh. O, Galliera – BRUCH: *Violin Concerto 1* (***)

The reissue as a 'Great Recording of the Century' of David Oistrakh's first (1959) stereo recording of the *Double Concerto* with Fournier has claims to be considered the most desirable of all versions, and it is joined by a splendid account of the *Tragic Overture* which opens the CD compellingly. It has been remastered and the recording is remarkably rich, yet with plenty of detail. This is perhaps the most powerful recorded performance since the days of Heifetz and Feuermann, with a glorious slow movement, although we must include alongside it the later DVD by Oistrakh and Rostropovich, recorded in 1964, and which also shows both artists at their most intense yet profoundly disciplined (EMI 4 90449-9 – see our main volume).

Symphonies 1–4; Academic Festival Overture; Tragic Overture; Variations on a theme of Haydn; (i; ii) German Requiem; (i) Schicksalslied (Song of Destiny)

(B) *(*) Warner 2564 62768-2 (5). NYPO, Masur; with (i) Westminster Symphonic Ch.; (ii) McNair, Hagegård

A very disappointing set, the more so as the symphonies are live performances (recorded between 1991 and 1995) and one would have expected a tauter grip. In the event, Kurt Masur is surprisingly slack in the *First Symphony*, with fast movements lacking in dramatic tension. Only the beautifully moulded slow movement reveals his usual mastery, and even that is not as hushed as it might be (probably because of the comparatively close microphone placing to minimize audience noises). Masur is obviously better attuned to the lyrical *Second Symphony*, but despite some first-rate playing from the New York orchestra, the result still sounds too easy, lacking in tension until the finale. He is more sympathetic in the *Third*, but it is still a reading which lacks the fullest detail and some of the bite that is really needed. A more appropriately broad view of the *Fourth* nevertheless brings comparable problems, with the performance again lacking a really firm grip and, as in the *Third*, detail is often smoothed over.

The *Requiem* and *Schicksalslied* (which is spacious and strong) are more successful, if hardly among the finest available. The *Requiem* has a rather subdued opening but then springs into life, and the famous *Denn alls Fleisch* certainly doesn't languish, while *Der Gerechten* has a strikingly energetic pulse. Both soloists are responsive and, if neither is really memorable, the choral singing is excellent.

Symphonies 1 in C min., 2 in D, Op. 73
*** Arthaus **DVD** 101243. West German RSO, Cologne, Bychkov (V/D: Hans Hadulla)

Here is something for the serious collector. The performances are very fine – indeed, they are of stature. Bychkov never tries to make points or indulge in any interpretative idiosyncrasies. He gives us both symphonies pure and simple, shaping detail sensitively and keeping a firm grip on the flow of the music. Camerawork is unfussy and clearly directed, both in the fine and warm studio acoustic and in the intelligent documentary about the conductor that comes as a bonus.

Symphony 2 in D, Op. 73 (Rehearsal only)
** TDK **DVD** DV DOCBW. Vancouver International Festival O, Walter

We see Bruno Walter rehearsing, with his usual mixture of courtesy and firmness, Brahms's *Second Symphony*, interspersed with a conversation he recorded towards the end of his life which ranges widely and which was televised in the early 1960s. He leaves us in no doubt as to his distaste for Schoenberg and his school. A strong and sympathetic personality emerges. It is a pity that the complete performance does not survive (or, if it does exist, was not included).

Symphonies 3–4
(BB) **(*) HMV (ADD) 5 86679-2. LSO or LPO, Boult.

Admirers of Sir Adrian's Brahms will surely want this inexpensive reissue of his recordings from the early 1970s, even if the two performances are uneven. In his hands the *Third Symphony* has great dignity and spaciousness. It is essentially a mellow performance, and he captures the autumnal feeling of the slow movement with great success, yet the LSO respond with enthusiasm and fire in the outer movements. In the finale Boult indulges in his only eccentricity, a sudden spurt at bar 70 and at the corresponding passage later in the movement. The *Fourth Symphony* comes off less well. The LPO is very well recorded, but Boult's reading is rather sober. If it lacks the fire and eloquence of the *Third*, it has an underlying strength and impulse characteristic of the conductor.

CHAMBER MUSIC

Cello Sonatas 1 in E min., Op. 38; 2 in F, Op. 99; 7 Lieder (arr. for cello & piano by Mørk)
(B) ** Virgin 2-CD 3 49933-2 (2). Mørk, Lagerspetz – GRIEG: *Cello Sonata; Intermezzo;* SIBELIUS: *Malinconia* etc. **

Truls Mørk seems completely at home in Brahms, and in Juhani Lagerspetz he has a good (if not quite an equal) partner. Their style is warm and rhapsodic, and both performances are compelling, if not the finest available. The Lieder transcriptions are played affectionately, but are hardly essential listening and, as in the couplings, the balance favours the piano which all but overwhelms the cello at times.

Clarinet Sonatas 1 in F min.; 2 in E flat, Op. 120/1–2
(BB) *** CfP 5 87023-2. Gervase de Peyer, Barenboim – SCHUMANN: *Fantasiestücke; Märchenerzählungen* ***

Whatever reservations one may have about various details (for these are individual accounts), these are eminently satisfying performances of these late sonatas which stand up quite well against the competition, especially at bargain price. The recordings are particularly good so far as piano-tone is concerned.

Clarinet Sonatas 1–2; (i) Clarinet Trio in A min. Op. 114
*** BIS CD/**SACD** 1353. Fröst, Pöntinen, (i) with Torleif Thedéen.

The Op. 114 *Trio*, relatively neglected on disc, usually comes coupled with the *Clarinet Quintet* almost as though it were a poor relation. Here BIS have had the excellent idea of coupling this equal masterpiece with the two other clarinet works of Brahms's mellow last period, the *Sonatas*, Op. 120, each on a scale closer to that of the *Trio*, and very successful it is. The young Swedish clarinettist Martin Fröst has already established himself as a leading soloist, inspiring works from a number of composers, including Krzysztof Penderecki. Here in the *Trio* he tends to favour speeds on the fast side so that the dramatic bite and purposeful thrust of the outer movements are enhanced, with the coda of the first movement fading away mysteriously on a ghostly scale passage. Though the cellist Torleif Thedéen matches the impressive tonal range of Fröst in equally imaginative playing, the pianist Roland Pöntinen is more recessive, largely a question of the recording balance. The backward balance for the piano is even more noticeable in the two sonatas, but Fröst's dedicated playing makes the performances magnetic. There are a number of distinguished accounts in the catalogue which we have said it would be difficult to surpass. This certainly matches them and, as far as the recorded sound is concerned, the BIS is wonderfully lifelike and natural.

Clarinet Sonatas 1 & 2 (arr. Khaner for flute)
*** Avie AV 2075. Khaner, Abramovic – (with SCHUMANN: *3 Romances;* CLARA SCHUMANN: *3 Romances* (all arr. Khaner)) ***

Jeffrey Khaner, the distinguished principal flute of the Philadelphia Orchestra, has made transcriptions for flute of the two Brahms *Clarinet Sonatas*. His alterations to the solo parts are discreet, involving occasional octave transpositions, mainly upwards, to make the result more effective on the lighter instrument. Where these late chamber works have an autumnal quality in their clarinet versions, or in the viola alternatives which the composer himself suggested, the freshness of flute-tone brings more of a spring-like feeling. Though few will prefer them to the originals, they make a splendid showpiece for an outstanding flautist, helped by warmly understanding accompaniment from Charles Abramovic. The apt coupling offers more Khaner transcriptions of *Romances* by Robert and Clara Schumann.

Piano Quintet in F min., Op. 34
(M) **(*) DG (ADD) 474 839-2. Pollini, Italian Qt

There is some electrifying and commanding playing from Pollini, and the Italian Quartet is eloquent too. The balance, however, is in the pianist's favour, though the effect in this new Originals transfer seems a touch better than on the original 1980 LP release. There are some minor agogic exaggerations but none that should put off prospective purchasers, though the playing time of under 44 minutes for this disc might. Even so, one is hardly short-changed on quality.

Violin Sonatas 1 in G, Op. 78; 2 in A, Op. 100; 3 in D min., Op. 108
** Sterling CDA 1651-2 Ringborg, Kilström

The Swedish Sterling label is so identified with exploring the byways of the nineteenth century that one is surprised to find such core repertory in its purview. Tobias Ringborg and Anders Kilström are among the most gifted native artists of their generation, and they give persuasive and musical accounts of these masterpieces. They are let down by a close balance in a claustrophobic acoustic, with no air round the aural image. This inhibits the strong recommendation which their playing in itself would deserve.

PIANO MUSIC

Ballades, Op. 10; Fantasias, Op. 116; Intermezzi, Op. 117; Pieces. Opp. 76, 118–119; 2 Rhapsodies, Op. 79; Scherzo, Op. 4; Sonatas 1–3, Opp. 1, 2 & 5; Variations & Fugue on a Theme of Handel, Op. 24; Variations: on a Hungarian Song; on an Original Theme, Op. 21/1–2; on a Theme of Paganini, Op. 35; on a Theme of Schumann, Op. 9; Waltzes, Op. 39
(B) ✹✹ RCA 82875 67887-2 (5). Oppitz

Gerhard Oppitz is much admired in Germany; he was a pupil of Kempff, whose mantle he appears to have inherited. It is obvious from his five-disc Brahms set that he is a dedicated and intelligent Brahmsian, though he is not always subtle in the use of colour and dynamics and, in that respect, cannot match his mentor. He has a commanding technique and is thoroughly inside the composer's mind. His accounts of the F minor Sonata and the sets of Variations are very impressive, but in the gentler pieces one would have liked a more beguiling warmth. When one returns to Kovacevich and Lupu in the late piano Pieces and Intermezzi, one enters a far more beguiling sound-world. Oppitz plays a Bösendorfer Imperial, which might have sounded better in a more appropriate acoustic. As it is, it is dryish, even clattery in certain registers, and the closely balanced recording does not give his pianissimo playing space to register fully.

4 Ballades, Op. 10; 2 Rhapsodies, Op. 79; Variations on a theme of Paganini, Op. 35
✹✹✹ Virgin 3 32628-2. Nicholas Angelich

Nicholas Angelich is American by birth but is active in France (this recording was made in the Maison de la Culture, Grenoble) and he is a natural Brahmsian. He seems completely attuned to this world and, whether in the virtuosity of the Paganini Variations or the poetic sensibility of the Ballades, he plays with rare authority and conviction. He has received plaudits in both the British and French press, and he deserves them. One of the most impressive Brahms recitals of recent times, and the piano-sound is very well captured by the Virgin Classics engineer.

VOCAL MUSIC

7 Alpendlieder: Der Abend; Abendlied; Abendständchen; Nächtens; O schöne Nacht; Rote Abendwolken; Waldesnacht. Liebeslieder Waltzes, Op. 52; New Liebeslieder Waltzes, Op. 65
(M) ✹✹ Telarc CD 80326. Robert Shaw Festival Singers, Shaw, Mackenzie & Wustman

Robert Shaw's Festival Singers, accompanied by the piano duo, Norman Mackenzie and John Wustman, sing this repertoire with richly blended tone and no lack of subtlety in the matter of light and shade. They are also very well recorded. But they have the same problems with the Liebeslieder Waltzes as John Eliot Gardiner and his Monteverdi Choir (see below),

for the effect is simply not intimate enough in songs designed for a small group of solo voices. There are fine alternatives which show just how delightful these songs can be, notably a BBC recording with a stellar team including Heather Harper, Dame Janet Baker, and Peter Pears (BBCB 8001-2).

Lieder: Botschaft; (i) 2 Songs with Viola, Op. 91. Immer leiser wird mein Schlummer; Meine Liebe ist grün; O komme, holde Sommernacht; Die Mainacht; Ständchen; Therese; Der Tod, das ist die kühle Nacht; Von ewiger Liebe; Wie Melodien zieht es mir
(B) ✹✹(✹) Ph. ADD 475 6374 (2). Norman, Parsons, (i) with Von Wrochem – SCHUMANN: Frauenliebe und leben, etc.
✹✹

The scale and tonal range of Jessye Norman's voice are ideal for many of these songs, but in some of them there is a studied quality which makes the result a little too static. This is particularly so in the most ambitious of the songs, Von ewiger Liebe, which mistakenly is put first. Nevertheless, there is distinguished playing from Geoffrey Parsons and the recital was superbly recorded (in 1980).

(i) Gesang, Op. 17; Gesänge, Opp. 42 & 104; (ii) Liebeslieder Waltzes, Op. 52; (iii) Quartets, Op. 92
(M) ✹✹ Ph. 475 7558. Shaw, Salmon, Monteverdi Ch.; with (i) Wynne (harp), Halstead, Rutherford (horns); (ii) Perry (piano), (ii–iiii) Levin (piano); cond. Gardiner

Even though it contains rare repertoire, this was a curious choice for reissue among Philips Originals. Certainly the members of the Monteverdi Choir under Gardiner give beautifully moulded, finely sprung performances. But unfortunately the reverberant acoustic of St Giles, Cripplegate, combined with rather backward placing of the choir, is totally unsuited to the intimate charms of the first book of Liebeslieder Waltzes. It does not help that both here and in the Opus 92 Quartets, an 1860 Riedl fortepiano is used. The music loses its smiling quality, the sense of domestic music-making that Brahms has in mind. The other pieces work much better in such a setting, with the accompaniment for women's voices of two horns and harp for Op. 17 sounding magical. It is fascinating to deduce the influence of polyphonic and baroque composers on Brahms, a great scholar, in the superb six-part a cappella pieces of Op. 42.

BRANDL, Johann Evangelist (1760–1837)

Bassoon Quintets: Op. 14; B flat, Op. 51/1; F min., Op. 52/2
✹✹✹ MDG 603 1133-2. Calamus Ens.

Brandl's 77-year life had been almost entirely forgotten until this enterprising MDG recording resurrected his name. These delightful Bassoon Quintets are amiable and charming works, full of good tunes and humour, offset with occasional short, passing moments of greater seriousness. They were written in 1798 (Op. 14) and 1824 (Op. 52), and offer an hour of unpretentious music-making, with enough incident to keep the listener entertained – the atmospheric opening to the F minor Quintet, with some portentous string-writing, is one such example. The Calamus Ensemble, with Rainer Schottstädt a fine soloist, plays these works beautifully, fully understanding the style of the music, with the instruments excellently balanced and defined, captured in a natural acoustic. As usual with MDG, the sleeve-notes are excellent. Most diverting.

BRÉVILLE, Pierre de (1861–1949)

Violin Sonata 1 in C sharp min .
*** Hyp. CDA 67427. Graffin, Devoyon – CANTELOUBE:
Dans le montagne ***

Pierre de Bréville was born in the Ornain valley of Lorraine, studied with Franck for two years, and all his music acknowledged the influence of his master. So if you enjoy the Franck *Violin Sonata*, you will surely be delighted to discover this fine work by his individually gifted pupil. The profoundly lyrical first movement has a haunting second subject and, as Philippe Graffin and Pascal Devoyon demonstrate superbly, it has a strong, passionate impetus (with bravura writing for both instruments). The second-movement Scherzo ('*gais mais pas trop vite*') makes an engaging interlude, but the powerfully expressive *Lamento* opens darkly and sadly, and is based on the composer's First World War song, *Héros, je vous aime*, a very touching melody. The extended finale maintains the ardent, Franckian world of both the opening and slow movements, yet produces another more light-hearted secondary theme. It is altogether a rewarding piece, and it could hardly be played and recorded more persuasively than here. Moreover, the coupling is equally worth exploring.

BRIAN, Havergal (1876–1972)

(i) *Violin Concerto. The Jolly Miller (Comedy Overture);*
Symphony 18
(BB) ** Naxos 8.557775. (i) Bisengaliev; BBC Scottish SO,
Friend

Havergal Brian wrote the first draft of his *Violin Concerto* in the spring of 1934, then left the manuscript on the train. It was never recovered and he had to start all over again. The result is a work on the most ambitious scale, obviously with an eye on the Elgar *Concerto* in the use of a large orchestra as a backcloth. While its melodic inspiration does not match Elgar's masterpiece, it has attractive and readily identifiable folksong-like ideas, notably the second subject of the first movement and the lyrical theme on which the slow movement's 15 chimerical variations are based. The finale has an important cadenza in which the orchestra finally joins, and it is the orchestra which, unusually, finishes the concerto without the soloist, in a last grandiloquent treatment of a march theme which, when it first appeared, was on a much smaller scale, even nonchalant in mood. It is an impressive work, and it is played with much feeling by Marat Bisengaliev, who is given powerful support by the BBC Scottish Orchestra under Lionel Friend. The snag is the close-miked recording, which at times brings an edge to the solo violin-timbre and makes the many passionate orchestral tuttis sound thin and over-bright, instead of opulent in an Elgarian way. The *Concerto* is prefaced by a jolly little overture introducing the folksong, *The Miller of Dee*, and is followed by a rather good, small-scale symphony, with its three movements all based on march-like themes, ranging over a whole gamut of emotions and ending forcefully. There is very good back-up documentation and, helpfully, its full analysis of the *Concerto*'s structure is matched by cues within each of the three movements to identify salient points of interest.

Symphony 1 (Gothic)
(BB) *** Naxos 8.557418/9. Jenisová, Pecková, Dolžal,
Mikuláš, Slovak Op. Ch., Slovak Folk Ens. Ch., Lúčnica Ch.,
Bratislava City Ch. & Children's Ch., Youth Echo Ch.,
Slovak RSO & PO & Ch., Lénard

The first of the Havergal Brian symphonies here receives a passionately committed performance from Slovak forces. Despite a few incidental flaws, it conveys surging excitement from first to last, helped by a rich recording, which gives a thrilling impression of massed forces. The final *Te Deum*, alone lasting 72 minutes, brings fervent choral writing of formidable complexity, with the challenge taken up superbly by the Czech musicians. Originally on Marco Polo, this is now a very real bargain in its Naxos reissue.

Symphony 3 in C sharp min.
(BB) **(*) Hyp. Helios CDH 55029. Ball, Jacobson, BBC SO,
Friend

The *Third Symphony* began life as a concerto for piano; this perhaps explains the prominent role given to two pianos in the score. The work is full of extraordinarily imaginative and original touches, but the overall lack of rhythmic variety is a handicap. The playing of the BBC Symphony Orchestra under Lionel Friend is well prepared and dedicated, but the recording does not open out sufficiently in climaxes. Even so, this is well worth considering at Helios price.

(i) *Symphonies 7 in C; (ii) 8 in B flat min.; 9 in A min.; (i)*
31; The Tinker's Wedding: Comedy Overture
(B) *** EMI 5 75782-2 (2). RLPO, with (i) Mackerrras or (ii)
Groves

Undoubtedly, this reissue is the best starting point for exploring the symphonies of this extraordinary figure. The *Eighth Symphony*, composed in 1949, is one of the richest, most wide-ranging in character and most rewarding of his scores. Its inspiration was Goethe's ballad *Die Braut von Corinth*, though Brian was at pains to disclaim any programmatic intent. The *Ninth* (1951) is hardly less fine and, though not as immediately approachable, is every bit as rewarding. Both were recorded in the late 1970s and are impressive in both range and colour. The *Seventh* was recorded in 1987, very well too, by Charles Mackerras and the Liverpool orchestra. Written in 1948, it also reflects Brian's preoccupation with Goethe and with the Gothic splendour of Strasbourg Cathedral. Although not as consistently rewarding as Nos. 8 or 9, it contains some arresting ideas alongside some relatively routine ones. The *Thirty-first Symphony* is a one-movement piece of under a quarter of an hour, but it is a remarkable work to come from the pen of a 92-year-old. One critic summed it up as 'a survivor from a different age, yet curiously of its time'. Again the recording quality is first class – as are the performances – and readers intrigued by this enigmatic figure should start here.

BRICCIALDI, Giulio (1818–81)

Wind Quintet in D, Op. 124
(BB) *** Naxos 8.553410. Avalon Wind Quintet – CAMBINI:
Wind Quintets 1–3 ***

Giulio Briccialdi was an Italian flautist of considerable fame during his lifetime. His *Wind Quintet in D major* is carefree, empty, lightweight – and utterly charming. It is played expertly by these young German musicians, and the recording is as delightfully natural as the playing. Well worth its three stars.

BRIDGE, Frank (1879–1941)

Oration: Concerto elegiaco (for cello & orchestra)
*** Nim. NI 5763. Wallfisch, RLPO, Dickins – ELGAR: *Cello Concerto*; HOLST: *Invocation* ***

Bridge's masterly *Oration* was written in 1929/30: its ethos is a passionate outcry against the human slaughter of the First World War, which haunted the composer. The work is written in a single movement like an arch, with seven diverse episodes, and the solo cello dominating hauntingly throughout. The luminously introspective opening is interrupted by a burst of angst, and a bleak, frenetic allegro leads to a slow marching rhythm which is to return very positively at the end before the poignant *Epilogue*, in which sadness is subtly underpinned by hope. The work is superbly played by Raphael Wallfisch, movingly accompanied by the RLPO, sensitively directed by Richard Dickins. The recording is beautifully balanced, and of the highest quality. The coupled Elgar and Holst performances are no less distinctive.

PIANO MUSIC

Fairy Tale Suite; The Hour Glass; In Autumn; 3 Lyrics; Miniature Pastorals, Set I; 3 Pieces; 3 Poems
(BB) *** Naxos 8.557842. Wass

Ashley Wass, who has already given us a distinguished Bax collection, now turns his attention to another very appealing English composer of piano music, whose output is worthy to be ranked alongside that of John Ireland. Yet Bridge's writing has a pensive simplicity, an almost ingenuous quality which is all his own. The *Three Pieces* are from 1912, and the first, *Columbine*, is a deliciously inconsequential portrait in waltz-time, and the third, a *Romance*, is charmingly and delicately understated. The other early works, *A Fairy Tale*, *The Hour Glass* and the *Miniature Pastorals*, all written between 1917 and 1920, are delightfully impressionistic miniatures, often nocturnal in feeling, and of immediate appeal, while the later pair of pieces called *In Autumn* (1924) marks a distinct step forward and are more adventurous, even visionary.

Solitude and *Sunset*, two of the *Three Poems* of 1914/15, with which Wass chooses to end the recital, are linked to similarly evocative orchestral works; but the most concentrated in feeling is the central *Ecstasy*, gently simmering. Wass's performances are totally sympathetic throughout, he is beautifully recorded, and this programme will give much pleasure.

BRITTEN, Benjamin (1913–76)

Canadian Carnival, Op. 19; (i) *Violin Concerto, Op. 15.* (with Lennox BERKELEY) *Mont Juic, Op. 12*
(BB) *** Naxos 8.557198 (i) McAslan; ECO, Bedford

Britten's *Violin Concerto* grows in stature with each hearing, and Lorraine McAslan and the ECO under Steuart Bedford give a particularly intense and sensitive account. She is brilliant in the second movement, and in the *Passacaglia* underlines the tragic overtones (the Spanish Civil War) of the work. It is a most moving account, in some ways even more searching than Mark Lubotsky's with the composer himself

(i) *Vio...*
Op. 31...
(B) ***...
Prit...
***

This is a ... issue, which now has a new and preferable performance of the Tippett as its coupling. Rodney Friend proves a masterful soloist in the *Violin Concerto*, magnificently incisive and expressive. As for Ian Partridge, one of the most consistently stylish of recording tenors, he gives a reading, often strikingly new in its illumination, more tenderly beautiful than Peter Pears's classic reading, culminating in a heavenly performance of the final Keats sonnet setting. Excellent recording in both works and a fine Tippett coupling, giving an overall playing time of 79 minutes.

The Prince of the Pagodas (Complete Ballet; choreography Kenneth Macmillan)
*** Warner DVD 9031-738262. Darcey Bussell, Jonathan Cope, Artists of The Royal Ballet, ROHCGO, Ashley Lawrence (V/D: Derek Bailey). Includes *Out of Line* (feature on Kenneth MacMillan by Derek Bailey)

This 1990 performance of Britten's only full-length ballet has long been available on videotape and LaserDisc, and now makes a long-awaited appearance on DVD, in which the image is much more sharply defined. *The Prince of the Pagodas* is a masterly score that repays much repetition, and both the outer Acts are wonderfully inventive. The performances of Darcey Bussell as Princess Rose and Jonathan Cope as the Prince are every bit as impressive as we remembered them, and MacMillan's choreography is, as always, distinguished by imagination and his great musicality. The DVD also includes the feature on MacMillan by Derek Bailey which is full of interest and includes excerpts from some of his other ballets, most notably *The Burrow* to Frank Martin's *Concerto for Seven Wind Instruments*, *Manon*, and Poulenc's *Gloria*. Oliver Knussen's splendid Virgin CDs are a key audio recommendation, but seeing MacMillan's choreography greatly enhances the musical experience. As young reviewers say these days, 'a must have'.

(i) *The Prince of the Pagodas* (complete ballet: CD version); (ii) *Gloriana (Symphonic Suite, Op. 53a)*
(B) *** EMI 3 52274-2 (2). (i) L. Sinf., Knussen; (ii) Bournemouth SO, Segal

The multicoloured instrumentation of *The Prince of the Pagodas* – much influenced by Britten's visit to Bali – is caught with glorious richness in Oliver Knussen's complete version of the full-length ballet, and his own performance is no less dramatic and persuasive. But in addition he scores significantly in opening out more than 40 cuts, most of them small, which Britten only sanctioned for the original Decca recording in order to fit the three Acts on to four LP sides. So Knussen includes four whole numbers omitted before, as well

...e-eights' which, as Knus-
...musical argument. The track-
... – but, alas, there is no cued
... The ballet is paired with a suite of
...hich, by concentrating on the pageant
...ion was made and prepared by the com-
...a misleading idea of what is in reality a deep
...work. However, it remains enjoyable in its own
... the performance is warmly understanding and
...recorded, even if the playing of the Bournemouth
...estra is not quite as crisp in ensemble as in some of its
...nest records.

Sinfonia da Requiem Op. 20

(BB) *** EMI Encore 5 86871-2. CBSO, Rattle –
SHOSTAKOVICH: *Symphony 10* **

Rattle's passionate view of the *Sinfonia da Requiem* is unashamedly extrovert, yet it finds subtle detail too. The EMI
recording is admirably vivid and clear. It now comes, recoupled with Shostakovich, at budget price.

Variations on a Theme of Frank Bridge, Op. 10

☛ ✪ (B) (***) EMI mono 4 76880-2. Philh. O, Karajan (with
HANDEL (arr. Harty): *Water Music Suite*) – VAUGHAN
WILLIAMS: *Fantasia on a Theme by Thomas Tallis* *** ✪

As we commented in our original review of this marvellous
disc, 'If all stereo issues sounded like Karajan's 1953 mono
recording of Britten's *Variations* there would be little need for
a *Penguin Guide*!' The sound is astonishingly fresh and vivid,
and the playing of the Philharmonia strings is of the highest
order of distinction. They produce beautifully blended tone,
rich and full-bodied yet marvellously delicate at the *pianissimo* end of the spectrum, and their finesse in the *Romance* is
matched by their dazzling virtuosity in the *Aria italiana*.
Karajan's reading is unaffected yet impassioned, quite electrifying in the *Funeral March*. The effect is amazingly real, and
one can hardly believe that this is not real stereo. The *Water
Music* in Harty's arrangement makes an enjoyable if hardly
apt bonus. It is very well played, but Karajan's tempo for the
closing *Allegro deciso* is too measured.

Cello Sonata in C, Op. 65

(M) *** Decca (ADD) 452 895-2. Rostropovich, composer –
DEBUSSY: *Sonata*; SCHUMANN: *5 Stücke in Volkston* ***
*** Berlin Classics 0017832BC. Bohorquez, Groh – DEBUSSY;
PROKOFIEV: *Cello Sonatas* **

The reissue in the Decca 'Critics' Choice' series restores the
original couplings. The strange, five-movement *Cello Sonata*
was written especially for Rostropovich's appearance in 1961
at the Aldeburgh Festival, and the recording was made soon
after the first performance. The idiom itself is unexpected,
sometimes recalling Soviet models, as in the spiky *March*,
perhaps out of tribute to the dedicatee. Although technically
it demands fantastic feats of the cellist, it is hardly a display
piece. It is an excellent work to wrestle with on a record,
particularly when the performance is never likely to be outshone. The recording is superb in every way.

Under the title 'Modern Milestones', Claudio Bohorquez,
with a fine fellow artist as pianist, brings together three
twentieth-century cello sonatas that may have little relation
one with another but which work well as a nicely contrasted
programme on disc. Of Peruvian and Uruguayan parentage,
Bohorquez was born and raised in Germany, and is currently
based in Berlin; he is a young cellist with the gift of drawing
out the emotional undertow in these works which regularly

break away from the conventions of the cello sonata.

As in the Prokofiev, Rostropovich was the inspirer of
Britten's *Cello Sonata* of 1961, the first of a whole sequence
of works he composed for that great cellist. The opening,
with its seemingly hesitant repetitions of a simple two-note
motif, seems to convey the composer's own hesitation at
launching into his project, and Bohorquez, like Rostropovich himself in his classic recording with the composer at
the piano, makes it seem like an improvisation, music
conceived at that moment.

As in the Debussy, he relishes the wit in the pizzicato
writing of the second movement and, in the *Elegia* slow
movement which follows, the hushed tension is even more
intense than with Rostropovich at a rather broader tempo.
After the brief jangling March movement the finale is just as
thrilling in its brilliance, with well-balanced digital sound
adding to the impact. An unusual mix of works, but a
rewarding one.

String Quartet 2 in C, Op. 36

*** Testament **DVD** SBDVD1001. Amadeus Qt – SCHUBERT:
Piano Quintet in A (Trout); Quartettsatz ***

The Amadeus made the first recording of the Britten Op. 36
Quartet on seven 78-r.p.m. plum label sides, not long after its
composition and their own formation. This performance was
tele-recorded in Aldeburgh in September 1977, a year after
Britten's death, by a team that included John Culshaw, previously of Decca but by then Head of Music at BBC Television.
It is superbly and simply directed with totally unobtrusive
camerawork and expertly balanced sound, with the legendary
Jimmy Burnett in charge. The performance is every bit as
authoritative as the Decca audio recording discussed in our
main volume and made at much the same time.

String Quartet 3, Op. 94

*** Testament **DVD** SBDVD1002. Amadeus Qt – SCHUBERT:
String Quintet in C ***

The *Third Quartet* was composed for the Amadeus, dedicated
to Hans Keller, and first performed by them only a week after
Britten's death. This performance came from the week
devoted to Britten and Schubert at a special autumn festival
in 1977 and, like its companion issue, was recorded by the
same team: John Culshaw and Jimmy Burnett. The performance is every bit as authoritative as (and even more moving
than) the Decca sound recording discussed in our main
volume and made at much the same time.

VOCAL MUSIC

(i) *Cantata Academica;* (ii) *Ceremony of Carols; The Golden
Vanity;* (i) *Hymn to St Cecilia;* (ii) *The Little Sweep (Let's
Make an Opera);* (iii) *Noye's Fludde;* (ii) *3 Parables for Church
Performance (The Burning Fiery Furnace; Curlew River; The
Prodigal Son); Psalm 150; Rejoice in the lamb; Saint Nicholas;
Songs from Friday Afternoons; Spring Symphony; War
Requiem (with Rehearsal);* (iv) *Gemini Variations*

(B) *** Decca (ADD; *Ceremony of Carols* mono) 475 6040
(10). Pears, Watts, Vyvyan, Brannigan, and soloists,
Copenhagen Boys' Ch. (with Edith Simon, harp), E. Op.
Group, Wandsworth School Boys' Ch., Bach Ch., L.
Symphony Ch., LSO, (i) Malcolm; (ii) composer; (iii) Del
Mar. (iv) G. & Z. Jeney

A self-recommending set, tracing Britten's vocal recordings
over nearly two decades, for the most part directed by the

composer and including the famous first recording (1953) of the *Ceremony of Carols* in Copenhagen, still one of his most memorable works. Del Mar directs *Noye's Fludde*, which is also memorable for Owen Brannigan's portrait of Noah. Few of the performances have been equalled and none surpassed, and the composer's touch is inimitable. Room has also been found for the *Gemini Variations* which Britten wrote for Gabriel and Zoltán Jeney, who between them play violin and flute as well as piano duet.

(i; ii) *Nocturne, Op. 60;* **(iii; iv)** *Les Illuminations, Op. 18;* **(i; iv; v)** *Serenade for Tenor, Horn and Strings, Op. 32*
(B) *** EMI (DDD/ADD) 3 52286-2. (i) Tear; (ii) ECO, Tate; (iii) Harper; (iv) N. Sinfonia, Marriner; (v) with Civil

Les Illuminations, originally written by Britten with the soprano Sophie Weiss in mind, is more headily beautiful with glorious tone from Heather Harper. The couplings both feature Robert Tear, a singer very much in the Aldeburgh tradition created by Peter Pears. Tear yet gives a new and positive slant to each of the lovely songs in the *Serenade*, with the Jonson *Hymne to Diana* given extra jollity, thanks partly to the brilliant galumphing of Alan Civil on the horn. In the *Nocturne*, Britten's wide-ranging cycle on the subject of night and sleep, full of memorable moments, each song has a different obbligato instrument (with the ensemble unified for the final Shakespeare song), and each instrument gives the song it is associated with its own individual character. Here again Tear proves a true successor to Pears, and the intricate instrumental parts are splendidly managed by members of the ECO under the ever-versatile Jeffrey Tate.

(i) *Les Illuminations, Op. 18; Nocturne, Op. 60;* **(ii)** *Serenade for Tenor, Horn and Strings, Op. 31;* **(iii)** *Noyes Fludde, Op. 59*
(BB) **(*) Virgin 2x1 3 49923-2 (2). Hill, (i) City of L. Sinfonia, (ii) with Lloyd; (iii) Maxwell, Ormiston, Pasco, Salisbury & Chester Schools Ch. & O, Coull Qt, Alley & Watson (piano duet), Harwood (organ), Endymion Ens. (members); all cond. Hickox

From his student days on, Martyn Hill has been an outstanding interpreter of Britten's song-cycles, and here he gives heartfelt performances of three great orchestral cycles, rewarding alternatives to the classic recordings by their inspirer, Peter Pears. With Richard Hickox a warmly sympathetic interpreter, relishing delicate textures, Hill produces ravishing half-tones in such delicate songs as the opening Cotton item in the *Serenade*. He is able to give heroic weight when necessary, though the recording balance does not help him; placed among the orchestra, rather than in front of it, he is not able to bite through heavy textures, though it is very satisfying to have such a weighty orchestral climax in the deeply moving final Shakespearean setting of the *Nocturne*. Most remarkable of all in some ways is the dashingly fast account of *Queen and Huntress* in the *Serenade*, with the horn soloist, Frank Lloyd, extraordinarily agile in playing the fast triplets. It is a pity that he is barely audible in his offstage solo at the end, yet the atmospheric beauty of the digital recording presents a powerful case for the Virgin recording, even next to the Pears.

For the reissue *Noyes Fludde* has been added, in which the instrumental forces, including a schools orchestra as well as professional soloists, are relatively recessed. Compare the storm sequence here with the Decca account (436 397-2), and the distancing undermines any feeling of threat, so that the entry of the hymn, *Eternal Father*, instantly submerges the

orchestral sound ins...
Donald Maxwell as Noah, ...
ries of the incomparable Owe...

War Requiem, Op. 66
(M) *** Decca (ADD) 475 7511 (2). Vishnev...
Fischer-Dieskau, Bach Ch., L. Symphoy Ch., LS...

Britten's own 1963 recording of the *War Requiem* co...
to the ideal and it has been splendidly remastered for this ...
reissue at mid-price, to take an honoured place among Universal's new series of Originals (which now include Decca and Philips recordings alongside the present DG list). Full documentation is included.

OPERA

(i) *Death in Venice;* **(ii)** *Gloriana;* **(iii)** *A Midsummer Night's Dream;* **(iv)** *Phaedra (Dramatic Cantata);* **(v)** *The Rape of Lucretia;* **(vi)** *The Turn of the Screw*
(B) *** Decca (ADD/DDD) 475 6029 (10). (i) Shirley-Quirk, Bowman; (i; v; vi) Pears; (ii) Barstow, Langridge, Della Jones, Opie, Van Allan; (iii) Deller, Harwood, Terry, Shirley-Quirk, Brannigan; (iv) J. Baker; (v) Harper, Shirley-Quirk, Luxon; (vi) Vyvyan, Hemmings, Dyer, Cross; (i; iv) ECO, Bedford; (ii) Welsh Nat. Op. O, Mackerras; (iii) LSO, composer; (v–vi) ECO, composer

Decca's second bargain box of Britten's operas perhaps may not be of such universal appeal as the first (see our main volume), but the set remains an essential bargain investment for collectors drawn to this repertoire: *A Midsummer Night's Dream* and *The Turn of the Screw* are key works (as indeed is Dame Janet Baker's *Phaedra*, an imaginative inclusion). As before, the documentation includes cued synopses.

A Midsummer Night's Dream (DVD version)
** Virgin DVD 3 39202 9 (2). Daniels, Sala, Wolk, Gietz, Meek, Dazeley. Hahn, Rose, Gillett, SO of Gran Teatre del Liceu, Barcelona, Escolania de Montserrat, Bicket (Director: Robert Carsen)

With a largely English-speaking cast and Harry Bicket conducting, the production from the Liceu in Barcelona was originally seen at the Aix-en-Provence Festival. The big point in favour is the singing of the counter-tenor, David Daniels, as Oberon, strong and imaginative. Opposite him, Ofelia Sala is a fruity-toned Titania, but the quartet of lovers is consistently fine, and the Rude Mechanicals are also a strong team, well led by the characterful Bottom of Peter Rose; it is hardly their fault that the humour in the Pyramus and Thisbe scene is too broad. Curiously, the speaking role of Puck is taken not by a youth but by a balding man, who is lively enough but hardly suits the part. What is disappointing is the visual impact of Robert Carsen's production, with designs by Michael Levine that can only be described as coarse, with bright blue and grass-green the predominant colours. So the fairies, sung (as is required) by boy-trebles, have green tailcoats and blue trousers with puce gloves. Worse still, they wear green moustaches, which undermines the magic of the fairy choruses. Extravagantly, the set comes on two discs.

Peter Grimes (CD version)
(M) *** Decca (ADD) 475 7712 (2). Pears, C. Watson, Pease, Nilsson, Brannigan, Evans, ROHCG Ch. & O, composer

...d-
...one
...sal's
...uding

...llan, Opie,
...iend

(Director...

The English Natio... ...y from Arthaus, recorded in 1987, offers an... ...ation of an imaginative if rather bald production... ...n dress by Michael Simpson. So at the start, Kathryn Ha... ...s and Anthony Rolfe Johnson as the Female and Male Choruses, both singing strongly, appear in severe grey costumes, and the set for the main action might have been devised for *Madam Butterfly* with its sliding translucent panels like Japanese shosees. At least the visual side of the production does not distract from the excellence of the singing and acting, led by Jean Rigby, steady as a rock as Lucretia, darkening her tone for her response to Tarquinius's assault with a powerful chest register. Opposite her as Bianca, Anne-Marie Owens makes a splendid foil, while the male cast is well led by the Tarquinius of Russell Smythe, with Richard van Allan equally positive as Collatinus. One of the few oddities is that Rolfe Johnson's narration for the actual rape is whispered, not spoken, making it less characterful.

The Turn of the Screw (DVD version)

*** Opus Arte **DVD** OA 0907D. Milne, Padmore, Wyn Davies, Montague, Kirby Johnson, Wise, City of L. Sinfonia, Hickox (TV Director: Katie Mitchell)

What Katie Mitchell has devised is a highly evocative film to go with a performance of *The Turn of the Screw*. The result is very different from a conventional staging, with the singers, for much of the time, acting out their roles without being seen singing. This allows for great flexibility in the presentation of detail, as when Miles is seen roller-skating about the house before the Governess arrives; and many of the outdoor scenes, most of them very atmospheric, have the singers just acting and not singing. The flexibility also encourages artistic shots of the house from all angles, and the presence of Peter Quint's ghost is made clear long before his official arrival, with simple shots of his feet. The performance itself is excellent, with Richard Hickox drawing taut playing from the City of London Sinfonia in support of a first-rate cast. Lisa Milne (as the Governess) and Diana Montague make an impressive duo, vocally outstanding, though the small, buxom Milne and the tall, statuesque Montague are visually the wrong way round. Mark Padmore is superb as Peter Quint and as the Prologue, establishing himself as the most mellifluous of Britten tenors, while Catrin Wyn Davies sings with a rich mezzo as Miss Jessel. The children both sing and act beautifully, very well cast, genuinely youthfully exuberant. A distinctive version with many great qualities, most of all in presenting the full horror of the story, set against an eerie background.

BROSSARD, Sébastien de (1655–1730)

Elevations et motets (for 1, 2, or 3 voices): Festis laeta sonent; O Domine quia refugium; Oratorio seu Dialogus poenitentis animae cum Deo; Psallite superi; Qui non diliget te; Salve Rex Christe; Templa nunc fumet

(B) **(*) Opus 111 OP 10002. Rime, Fouchécourt, Honeyman, Delétré, Parlement de Musique, Gester

Sébastien de Brossard came from Normandy to take a position as Chapel Master at Strasbourg Cathedral. These motets are mainly dialogue cantatas. *O Domine quia refugium* is a fine example, although the expressive and touching *Qui non diliget te* (for which the composer wrote the text) is a solo work, and very beautifully sung by Noémi Rime. The *Dialogue of the repentant soul with God* is shared by soprano and tenor: it is not especially dramatic, but the pace quickens as forgiveness is given. The final work, *Festis laeta sonent cantibus organa* ('May the organ ring out with solemn songs'), is very well sung by the tenor Jean-Paul Fouchécourt; but Brossard's weakness lies in the lack of a more robust spirit to many of these interchanges – surprising from a musician who was an advocate of the introduction of Italian styles into French music. Excellent recording and full texts.

BROUWER, Margaret (born 1940)

(i) *Aurolucent Circles (Concerto for Percussion & Orchestra). Mandala; Pulse; Remembrances; Sizzle*

(BB) *** Naxos 8.559250. (i) Glennie; RLPO, Schwarz

Margaret Brouwer is in charge of the composition department at the Cleveland Institute of Music in the USA, and she is nothing if not versatile. Her touching threnody, *Remembrances*, a tribute to another musician/composer and loved one, is genuinely beautiful, and it shows she can write real lyrical music of quality, create a believably passionate climax, and return to an elegiac mood for the close.

Aurolucent Circles 'was inspired by the sparkling and lucent sounds of so many of the percussion instruments used in the orchestra' (melodic and otherwise). The three sections, *Floating in Dark Space*, the weird *Stardance* and the swirling energy of *Cycles and Currents*, invite Evelyn Glennie to provide one of her most spectacular displays, exploiting the widest range of dynamic, colour and rhythmic bangs, although this is a piece you really need to see acted out rather than just hear.

Mandala is influenced by the culture of Tibetan monks but springs from a chant, introduced on the trombone, which is based on a Christian Psalm from a Dutch songbook. *Pulse* is a venture into Reich/Adams minimalist territory, amd *Sizzle*, at frying pan heat, spectacularly 'suggests twentieth-century life, fast-paced, energized, and filled with emphatic and mesmerising rhythms'. The performances throughout are full of effervescent vitality and are vividly recorded, but Schwarz keeps a strong hand on the proceedings, while the Liverpool players all enthusiastically enter into the fray.

BRUCH, Max (1838–1920)

Violin Concerto 1 in G min., Op. 26

🎵 *** Telarc CD 80507. McDuffie, SCO, Swensen –
MENDELSSOHN: *Violin Concerto* ***

(M) (***) EMI mono 3 45758-2 [3 45765-2]. D. Oistrakh, Fournier, Philh. O, Galliera – BRAHMS: *Double Concerto; Tragic Overture* (***)

The American violinist Robert McDuffie has made an international name pioneering twentieth-century violin concertos by Adams, Barber, Glass and Rozsa. Here – with Joseph Swensen and the Scottish Chamber Orchestra – he turns his attention to a pair of key romantic works, and there are few concerto recordings in which the partnership between soloist and accompanying group is so complementary.

McDuffie opens the work gently and tenderly, with bewitching phrasing and the most beautiful tone, never pressing too hard. The big orchestral tutti storms in passionately and Swensen prepares the way for the ravishing re-entry of the violin, still playing gently on a half-tone. The hushed opening of the beautiful *Adagio* again finds a tenderness that gives a magical frisson. Throughout the concerto, the interchanges between soloist and orchestra have the natural flowing spontaneity of live music-making and the closing pages of the slow movement bring a rapt intensity, elegiac yet ardent, before the finale bounces off spiritedly, with the bold orchestral tuttis in a stimulating balance with the dancing soloist. The Telarc recording, full-blooded and with a believable perspective, is well up to the high standards of the house, and the Mendelssohn coupling is also outstandingly fine.

David Oistrakh's mono recording was made at Abbey Road in 1954, but the sound and balance are excellent. The performance is full of simmering intensity and is marvellously played, and it makes a very suitable coupling for a truly unforgettable and unsurpassed account of the Brahms *Double Concerto* in which Oistrakh is joined by Pierre Fournier at his very finest.

Violin Concerto 1 in G min., Op. 26; Scottish Fantasy, Op. 46
(M) *** RCA **SACD** 82876 71622-2. Heifetz, New SO of London, Sargent – VIEUXTEMPS: *Violin Concerto 5* ***

Heifetz plays with supreme assurance, and the slow movement shows this fine artist in masterly form. Heifetz's panache and the subtlety of his bowing and colour also bring a striking freshness to Bruch's charming Scottish whimsy. Sargent accompanies sympathetically and, though the soloist is balanced much too closely, there is never any doubt that he can produce a true *pianissimo*. The new SACD transfer adds body to the sound, and certainly the violin is vividly real. But the more natural balance of the Telarc CD above is much preferable.

(i; ii) *Violin Concerto 1 in G min.; (i; iii) Scottish Fantasy, Op. 46; (iv) Kol Nidrei, Op. 47*
(BB) *** HMV 5 86717-2. (i) Little; (ii) RLPO; (iii) RSNO; both cond. Handley; (iv) Han-Na Chang, LSO, Rostropovich

This is a most attractive bargain triptych. Tasmin Little is on top form in both the violin works. The movement in the *G minor Concerto* where her individuality comes out most clearly is the central *Adagio*, raptly done with a deceptive simplicity of phrasing, totally unselfconscious, that matches the purity of her sound. Her speeds in the outer movements are broader than some rivals, but she remains completely convincing. In the *Scottish Fantasy*, recorded seven years later, she takes a ripe, robust and passionate view. In this she is greatly helped by the fine, polished playing of the Scottish orchestra under Vernon Handley, a most sympathetic partner. The recording is superb, with brass in particular vividly caught. Little plays the Guerriero finale absolutely complete. But what makes this disc unmissable is the inclusion of Han-Na Chang's lovely performance of *Kol Nidrei*, wonderfully fresh and sympathetic and most understandingly accompanied by her mentor, Rostropovich.

BRUCKNER, Anton (1824–96)

Symphony 3 in D min. (original, 1873 version)
(BB) ** Virgin 2x1 4 82091-2 (2). LCP, Norrington –
  WAGNER: *Siegfried idyll; Preludes* ** (*)

There are in all three versions of the *Third Symphony*, and Norrington follows Inbal and Tintner in choosing the first. From Ur-text the next step is Ur-instrumentation, and this is the first reading to use period instruments. The balance of the texture is, of course, much altered, as is much else besides. Bracing tempi tend to rob the symphony of its atmosphere and breadth. It is all very well to 'humanize' the score and divest it of being a 'religious tract', as Norrington puts it in his stimulating notes; but many would argue that religious feeling and Bruckner are indivisible. It goes without saying that there are many points to make you think, but tempi are far too brisk to make this an unqualified recommendation. Inbal does not dawdle, but Norrington takes some eight minutes less overall. (His first movement alone is five minutes faster.) Splendid playing from the London Classical Players and no lack of thought from the conductor, but the wrong kind of feeling. The Tintner version on Naxos is the one to go for, and it is very economically priced (8.553454).

Symphony 4 in E flat (Romantic)
(B) ** (*) EMI (ADD) 4 76887-2. BPO, Karajan.

Karajan's earlier (1970) recording for EMI has undoubted electricity and it combines simplicity and strength. The playing of the Berlin Philharmonic is very fine. The remastering is successful, but the touch of harshness on the considerable *fortissimos* remains; the sound is full if a little dry.

Symphony 6 in A
** (*) TDK **DVD** DV-COWAND2. NDR SO, Wand (V/D: Andreas Missler-Morell) – HAYDN: *Symphony 76 in E flat* ***

In the 1980s Günter Wand enjoyed something like cult status in both Germany and London; he was frequently invited to conduct Bruckner symphonies with the BBC Symphony Orchestra. Most of these performances were very fine and left listeners feeling, as we do here, that Wand was much more than a provincial Kapellmeister but less perhaps than a great conductor. This is a fine performance – though put alongside the likes of Karajan or Jochum, less than a great one. The camerawork is unobtrusive and the sound very well balanced. Wand is a conscientious and sympathetic guide in this glorious symphony and gives much musical satisfaction.

Symphony 7 in E (DVD version)
*** EMI **DVD** 3 101909 O Nat. de France, Jochum (with WAGNER: *Tristan and Isolde: Prelude and Liebestod*. MOZART: *Le Nozze di Figaro: Overture* ***)

Jochum was one of the finest Brucknerians of his day and this beautifully prepared and subtly executed reading of the *Seventh Symphony* is magnificent. The Orchestre National de France is in responsive form and play with great sensitivity and feeling. Recorded in the Théâtre des Champs-Elysées, Paris, in 1980, along with the *Tristan Prelude and Liebestod*. As a bonus we have a black-and-white *Figaro Overture* with the French Radio Orchestra, well played, though not the lightest in touch. But this is easily the best Bruckner we have had yet on DVD. Unobtrusive and intelligent camerawork, and it is very compelling.

Symphony 7 in E (CD version)

(B) *** EMI 4 76888-2. BPO, Karajan

Karajan's outstanding early EMI version, recorded in the Jesus Christus Kirche in 1971, remains among the very finest. The reading shows a special feeling for the work's architecture, and the playing of the Berlin Philharmonic is gorgeous. The sound has striking resonance and amplitude. This EMI reading, generally preferable to his later, digital recording for DG, has a special sense of mystery.

Symphony 8 in C min. (DVD versions)

*** TDK **DVD** DV-COWAND3. NDR SO, Wand (V/D: Barrie Gavin)

(*) EuroArts **DVD 2012756. VPO, Boulez (V/D: Brian Large)

Günter Wand recorded the *Eighth Symphony* with his Nord-Deutscher Rundfunk Orchestra on LP in the 1980s and, more recently, with the Berlin Philharmonic. Wand has great musical integrity and is a totally dedicated Brucknerian and, as we said above, he was much more than a provincial Kapellmeister. He conveys a genuine sense of mystery, though ultimately he does not surpass the finest CD versions. The performance is very fine, however, and Barrie Gavin's camerawork places the viewer at the best vantage point. The orchestral sound is very well balanced.

We have discussed Boulez's account of the *Eighth Symphony* in our main volume, saying that 'the great slow movement proceeds majestically, in Boulez's hands a powerful symphonic structure rather than a visionary statement'. In this televised version, which is managed with exemplary taste and skill, one can follow Boulez's masterly direction, even if one looks in vain for a real sense of mystery. He maps out the topography of the terrain without bringing its landscape before our eyes. Neither he nor Günter Wand challenges Karajan on CD – either with the Berlin Philharmonic or the later Vienna version – in this score.

Symphony 8 in C min. (CD version)

(B) *** EMI (ADD) 4 76901-2. BPO, Karajan (with Overtures: WEBER *Der Freischütz.* MENDELSSOHN: *Fingal's Cave.* WAGNER: *Der fliegende Holländer.* NICOLAI: *The Merry Wives of Windsor* ***)

The new transfer of Karajan's early (1957) Berlin Philharmonic recording is remarkably successful. The EMI sound is spacious and, if the sonorities are not quite as sumptuous as we would expect today, the strings have substance and the brass makes a thrilling impact. The performance has much in common with Karajan's later (mid-price) version for DG, and has compelling power. The slow movement is very fine indeed, conveying dark and tragic feelings, and the finale makes a real apotheosis. While Karajan's last VPO version remains special (DG 476 1654), this is very worthwhile and the Overtures are all splendidly played and recorded, with *Der fliegende Holländer* standing out.

Symphony 9 in D min. (DVD version)

*** TDK **DVD** DV-COWAND4. N. German RSO, Wand – SCHUBERT: *Symphony 8 (Unfinished)* ***

Günter Wand recorded this coupling of two unfinished symphonies at the 2001 Schleswig-Holstein Festival in Lübeck at the Musik-und-Kongreßhalle when he was 89. He had recorded the *Ninth Symphony* with his NordDeutscher Rundfunk Orchestra, Cologne, on LP in 1979, then again in Lübeck Cathedral (1980), Hamburg (1993) and Berlin with the Berlin Philharmonic (1998). The present account with the NDR

Orchestra has great majesty and a magnificent string sonority; the wind players are very fine, as indeed are the brass. Hugo Käch's camera direction is exemplary and never draws attention to itself. In all, a satisfying reading and, as always with Wand, selfless and free from idiosyncrasy.

Symphony 9 in D min. (CD version)

*** Profil-Medien PH 4058. Stuttgart RSO, Wand

Günter Wand's fame was beginning to resonate outside Germany at about the time when he first recorded the *Ninth Symphony* with his Cologne forces. The Stuttgart account with the SüdWestfunk Orchestra was made only two weeks later. It is a live performance in the opulent acoustic of the Benedictine Monastery of Ottobeuren, which the Stuttgart engineers manage with real mastery; it offers a glorious, satisfying sound, rich and sonorus. This ranks high among Bruckner *Nines* both interpretatively and as sound.

BRUHNS, Nicolaus (1665–97)

2 Preludes in E min.; Preludes: in G ; G min.; (i) Fantasia on 'Nun komm der Heiden Heiland'

*** Chan. 0539. Kee (organ of Roskilde Cathedral, Denmark), (i) with Rehling – BUXTEHUDE: *Chorale Preludes* ***

Just five Bruhns organ works survive (all included in this recital). Though he uses the term 'Praeludium', each consists of an introduction and one or two fugues, written with an eager flair that recalls the early organ works of the young Bach, who certainly knew of this music. The *Fantasia on 'Nun komm der Heiden Heiland'* has its *cantus firmus* introduced by a soprano voice, and she returns to repeat the chorale (undecorated) at a central point, after three variants. Piet Kee presents all this music with splendid life and colour, and his Danish organ, recently restored, brings vivid registration which is a pleasure to the ear. The recording is in the demonstration bracket.

BRÜLL, Ignaz (1846–1907)

Piano Concertos 1 in F, Op. 10; 2 in C, Op. 24; Andante & Allegro, Op. 88

*** Hyp. CDA 67069. Roscoe, BBC Scottish SO, Brabbins

Like so many issues in Hyperion's admirable 'Romantic Piano Concerto' series, this brings real revelation about a composer who till now has seemed a shadowy figure, one of a Viennese group associated with Brahms. Both the concertos are early works, the *Second* built on rather more distinguished material than the *First*, and their innocent flamboyance is superbly caught in these brilliant performances, with Martin Roscoe excelling himself in his dazzling virtuosity. The *Andante & Allegro*, a much later work, provides a warmly expressive makeweight. Full, well-balanced sound of best Hyperion quality.

BRUMEL, Antoine (c. 1460–c. 1520)

Requiem

☛ *** ASV Gaudeamus CDGAU 352. Clerks' Group, Wickham – DE LA RUE: *Requiem* ***

Brumel was one of the very first composers to write a *Requiem*, and uniquely beautiful it is. Most of the music is not much more than rich, simple harmonization of the traditional Gregorian chants of the Office of the Dead. But in Brumel's hands the plainchant becomes far from plain and the languorous poise of the melodic lines is hypnotic. Then comes a masterstroke, for Brumel dramatizes the *Dies Irae* with polyphony (probably the first example of this practice to have survived), and Wickham and his singers increase the tension by quickening the pace, gradually pulling back at the *Recordare Jesu pie*, the request for forgiveness and absolution. Brumel then reverts to his rich, dark, chordal sonorities. The *Sanctus* is brief but radiant, and the supplication of the *Agnus Dei* even more moving. The setting closes with the Communion, *Lux aeterna, luceat eis*, with the eternal light shining out of the music, and the work ends with the luminously peaceful *Cum Sanctus*. Wickham's direction is masterly, and the Clerks' Group have never sung with more refined feeling. The recording too is outstanding in its combination of clarity and ambient warmth.

BULL, John (c. 1562–1628)

Clavichord Pieces: *Dr Bulles Pavin chromatik & Galliard in D min.;The Duchess of Brunswicks Toye in A min.; The Duke of Brunswick's Alman in A min.; Fantasia in D min.; Fantasia on Ut, re, mi, fa, sol, la in G; A Gigge, Doctor Bulls my selfe in G.* **Harpsichord Pieces:** *My Juell in C; Pavane & Galliard of my Lord Lumley in G; In Nomine in D min.; Praeludium in C.* **Organ Pieces:** *Christe Redemptor in A; Een Kindeken is ons geboren, Versions I & II; Fantasia op de fuge van magister Jan pietersson (Sweelinck) in A min.; God save the Kinge in C; In nomine in A min.; Praeludium in A min.; Walsingham in A min.* **Virginal Pieces:** *Praeludium in G; St Thomas Wake in C; My Griefe in G*
*** MDG 3141 1258-2. Rampe (clavichord, harpsichord, organ, virginals)

An aurally fascinating disc. Siegbert Rampe plays two different clavichords (very different in sound, one quite tinkly), a pair of organs (again with contrasting colours), harpsichord and virginals, each a period instrument or copy. All the music is characterful and lively, and Bull's divisions are complex, especially in the showpiece, *Walsingham*, which lasts a quarter of an hour and gives the disc its title. But the closing *In Nomine* is also a busy piece, and there is much bravura elsewhere, especially in the opening organ *Praeludium*, which sounds like a peal of bells. All most entertaining and splendidly recorded.

BURGMÜLLER, Norbert (1810–36)

String Quartets 1 in D min., Op. 4; 3 in A flat, Op. 9.
*** MDG 336 0994-2. Mannheim Qt

String Quartets 2 in D min., Op. 7; 4 in A min., Op. 14
*** MDG 336 0993-2. Mannheim Qt

Though dying at the early age of twenty-six, the German composer Norbert Burgmüller was much admired by Mendelssohn and Schumann, and his music has also been likened to Schubert's. That is easy to understand, and in the *D minor Quartet* (No. 1) – the composer's first surviving work, dating from 1825 – an appealing melancholic vein runs through the music, and while the influences of Spohr and Weber are evident, it is hard to believe that this is a work of a fifteen-year-old. The *A flat Quartet* (No. 3, 1826) is more relaxed, with many pleasing ideas, basking in a warm summer glow. The *D minor Quartet* has plenty of romantic charm, while in

the last, *A minor, Quartet*, the nickname 'the Schubert of the Rhine', as Burgmüller was once dubbed, can be clearly understood. Here there is a charmingly rustic-sounding Scherzo. The performances are appealingly sympathetic and are recorded with MDG's usual warm, well-balanced sound.

BUSONI, Ferruccio (1866–1924)

(i) *Violin Concerto in D;* (ii) *Violin Sonata 2, Op. 36a*
*** Sony SK 94497. Zimmermann; (i) Italian Nat. RSO, Turin, Storgårds; (ii) Pace

It beggars belief that Busoni's wonderful concerto has taken so long to reach the CD catalogue. Szigeti's pioneering recording from the turn of the 1940s–50s has long been out of circulation and, to the best of our knowledge, the concerto has languished in neglect ever since. Its première in Berlin in 1897 served to establish Busoni's reputation as a serious composer and not just a great piano virtuoso and conductor. Its opening is magical, and the work proceeds effortlessly yet purposefully and is relaxed. All credit then to Frank Peter Zimmermann for his championing of the score and for his impressive account of the *Second Sonata* of 1900, a key work in Busoni's creative development. Strongly recommended.

BUTTERWORTH, Arthur (born 1923)

Piano Trios 1, Op. 73; 2, Op. 121; Viola Sonata, Op. 78
(M) *** Dutton CDLX 7164. Terroni Piano Trio (members)

Arthur Butterworth is best known for his orchestral works with their Sibelian reflection of the atmosphere of the North Yorkshire Moors, but his chamber music has its own distinct character too. The fully mature *First Piano Trio*, written for the 1983 Cheltenham Festival, has associations with Sibelius's *Sixth Symphony* and is fully mature. It is the highlight of the disc; its confident opening movement, surging forward lyrically, and the lighter, engaging *Allegretto* finale are used to frame a hauntingly atmospheric central *Adagio*, translucent in texture, which the composer tells us recalls a radiant summer evening crossing the Baltic. The *Second Trio*, much more recent (2004), again has a nostalgic *Adagio* as its lyrical kernel, and an energetically driven finale suggestive of a 'cor de chasse'. The viola is a solo instrument much loved by English composers, and Butterworth acknowledges his early debt to Vaughan Williams. However, his *Viola Sonata*, written in the early 1980s, brings 'a faint whiff of the Celtic twilight of Bax'. It is a comparatively robust and lively work in which the piano takes a major role: the passionate first movement is followed by a Scherzo, and it is the finale, marked *Lento penserosiamente*, which is more characteristic of the viola's usual darker, nostalgic role. Performances here are strong and spontaneous, persuasive in their expressive eloquence, and the recordings are first class and most realistically balanced.

BUXTEHUDE, Dietrich (c. 1637–1707)

CHAMBER MUSIC

7 Trio Sonatas, Op. 2, BuxWV 259–65
(BB) *** Naxos 8.557249. Holloway, Mortensen, Ter Linden

These works are attractively varied; the performances on period instruments, led by John Holloway, are fresh and alive.

They are discussed in detail in our main volume : the present disc is a bargain reissue of dacapo 8.224004. Opus 1 is already available on Naxos 8.557248.

Complete Organ Music, Volume 1: *Ciaconas: in C; E min.,* BuxWV 159–60; *Chorales,* BuxWV 182, 189–90, 197–200, 202, 208–9, 211, 217; *Passacaglia in D min.,* BuxWV 161; *Preludes: in C; G min.,* BuxWV 137, 148–9
*** dacapo 8.226002. Bryndorf (Elsinore Chapel organ)

Complete Organ Music, Volume 2: *Chorales,* BuxWV 178; 180; 206; 214–15; 220–24; *Praeludia,* BuxWV 136; 142; 151–3
**(*) dacapo 8.226008. Bryndorf (organ of St Mary's Church, Elsinore)

Complete Organ Music, Volume 3: *Canzonettas: in G; G min.; A min.,* BuxWV 172–3, 225; *Chorales,* BuxWV 183–7, 191–3, 201, 219; *Preambulum in A min.,* BuxWV 158; *Preludes in G min.; C,* BuxWV 138, 150, 163; *Toccatas: in F; G,* BuxWV 156 & 164
*** dacapo 8.226023. Bryndorf (organ of St Mary's Church, Helsingborg)

Complete Organ Music, Volume 4: *Canzonettas: in C; D min.; G,* BuxWV 167–8, 171; *Chorales,* BWV 188, 196, 210, 212, 223; *Magnificat I Tobi,* BuxWV 204; *Preludes: in F; G,* BuxWV 144, 147; *Toccatas: in D min.: F,* BuxWV 155, 157
*** dacapo 6.220514. Bryndorf (organ of German Church, Stockholm)

A collaboration between Danish Radio and dacapo, these two issues are Volumes 1, 3 and 4 of a complete survey of the organ works, using different organs but with 8.226002 recorded splendidly on the famous Elsinore organ, 8.226023 on another equally fine organ in Helsingborg, and 6.220514, as recently as 2005, in Stockholm. The discs are authoritatively annotated with details of registration, and with music-type illustrations for the choral harmonization. Bine Bryndorf studied in Vienna, Boston and Paris, and collected various prizes in Bruges and Innsbruck. Since 1996 she has been at Vartov Church, Copenhagen, and an Artist in Residence with Danish Radio. Listening to these vividly recorded and expertly balanced programmes leaves no doubt as to her artistry and intelligence, and the discs provide an admirable start to the series. Bach walked 300 miles to listen to Buxtehude and remained in Lübeck for three months, obviously impressed, not only by his playing but also by his music. These discs reaffirm the quality of Buxtehude's musical invention (which had a profound influence on Bach) and imagination. And these days we need not travel on foot (or at all) to experience Buxtehude's music ourselves.

Cantatas: *An filius non est Dei,* BuxWV 6; *Dixit Dominus Domino meo,* BuxWV 17; *Herr, nun läßt du deinen Deiner,* BuxWV 37; *Jesu dolcis memoria,* BuxWV 57; *Jesu, komm, mein Trost und Lachen,* BuxWV 58; *Lobe den Herrn, meine Seele,* BuxWV 71; *Das neugebor'ne Kindelein,* BuxWV 13; *Nichts soll uns scheiden von der Liebe Gottes,* BuxWV 77; *Quemadmodum desiderat cervus,* BuxWV 92
*** Chan. 0723. Kirkby, Chance, Daniels, Harvey, Augmented Purcell Qt

This further selection of Buxtehude's cantatas follows on naturally from the first, with its star-studded cast, individual voices which yet blend beautifully togther, stylish accompaniments and a recording which is again attractively warm and intimate.

Membra Jesu nostri, BuxWV 75; Fried- und Freudenreich Hinfahrth, BuxWV 76
*** Channel Classics SACD CCS SA 4006. Grimm, Zomer, De Groot, Tortise, Ramselaar, Netherlands Bach. Soc., Van Veldhoven

The *Membra Jesu nostri* is a cycle of seven cantatas, each addressed to a different part of the body of the crucified Christ, all of a simple and dignified expressive power that movingly makes the strongest impression. Yet although each cantata is prefaced by a Bible motto, the cycle was not intended for liturgical use. The layout of each work is: Instrumental Sonata, Concerto (Vocal tutti), Aria with instrumental ritornelli, and Concerto da capo. The Netherlands performances under Jos van Veldhoven are very beautifully sung within an ideal acoustic, warmly resonant, yet with everything clearly detailed. The accompanying instrumental group which provides the sonatas and interludes is just as impressive. At the opening of the *Third Sonata,* 'To His Hands', the strings set the scene dramatically before the vocal group asks, 'What are the wounds in thy hands?' and Buxtehude's setting here brings extraordinarily powerful dissonances. But there is much variety among the seven cantatas, and in the penultimate work, *Ad Cor* ('To His Heart'), the Bible motto quotes from the Song of Songs and the violins and cellos are replaced by a consort of five violas da gamba, while the final work has a closing *Amen.* The disc is rounded off with another solo cantata, *Fried- und Freudenreiche Hinfahrth,* in which the closing *Lamentation* is beautifully sung by Johannette Zomer. This is a very successful collection indeed, which can hardly be praised too highly.

BYSTRÖM, Oscar (1821–1909)

Symphony in D min.; Andantino; Concert Waltzes 1 & 3; Overture in D; Overture to Herman Vimpel
** Sterling CDS 1025-2. Gävle SO, Spierer

Oscar Byström is an interesting figure. He was an accomplished pianist and conductor who, like his fellow Swede Berwald, pursued a career outside music alongside his work as a composer. His *Symphony in D minor* is clearly influenced by Berwald. The second group of the first movement is delightful and the work as a whole has much to commend it. The overtures all come from much the same period and are pleasing, though no one would make great claims for them. They are well served on this CD.

CABEZÓN, Antonio de (1510–66)

Collection of *Diferencias, Hymns, Pavanas, Tientos* and other pieces
(BB) *** Naxos 8. 554836. Ens. Accentus, Wimmer

In another of their well-conceived single-disc surveys, Naxos offer us a well-chosen and varied programme of instrumental pieces by this blind Spanish composer played by a varied ensemble, including recorders, viols, double harp, harpsichord and organ. The presentation by this excellent Ensemble Accentus has plenty of life and expressive feeling, and many of the pieces represent intriguing early examples of simple variations of form. The engaging opening *Diferencias sobre la gallarda milanesa* could hardly be more different from the variations on the chorale-like *La dama le demanda,* and the sombre hymn *Ave maris stella,* played on viols, contrasts well with the engaging *Pavana con su glosa,* which uses recorder and double harp with continuo. Also included among the music for viols is a set of expressive but melancholy variations on a Castilian song, *Pues a mi desconsolado* by Antonio's brother Juan, and a *Glosado* by Hernando de Cabezón on a chanson by Lassus, *Susanna un jur*. The recording is of good quality, and this makes a good introduction to a little-known figure of the Spanish Renaissance.

'Music for the Spanish Kings': *Keyboard Tablatures* (excerpts, arr. Savall) inc. Cabezón's arrangements of music by CRECQUILLON and WILLAERT

(BB) *** Virgin 2×1 5 61875 (2). Hespèrion XX, Savall (with fifteenth- and sixteenth-century music from the Spanish Courts of Alphonso I, Ferdinand I and Charles V ***)

Cabezón was Philip II of Spain's favourite court musician and he accompanied his king on journeys to Italy, Germany and the Netherlands – and to London. He was one of the greatest contrapuntalists of his age, and his output is preserved in the form of keyboard tablatures, intended for keyboard, harp or vihuela. Jordi Savall's group of vihuela players produce some glorious sounds here, as do the highly accomplished brass players. In addition to the music of Cabezón himself there are his arrangements of music by Crecquillon and Willaert.

The companion CD includes earlier music from the Spanish court, offered in conjectural instrumentation, using brass and simple percussion liberally, although Hayne van Ghizeghem's melancholy piece for viols, *De tous biens plaine*, makes a striking contrast. Throughout the disc Montserrat Figuerras makes a major contribution in the various canciós and dance songs. Also included on the second disc is an extra instrumental piece by Cabezón, the memorable *Diferencias sobre el cano del caballero*. The closing *Galliarda Napolitana* of Antonio Valente and the *Villanesca all napolitana*, *Vecchie letrose*, by Adrian Willaert both have potential hit status. Again excellent recording.

CACCINI, Giulio (c. 1545–1618)

La Nove Musiche (Florence, 1601): *Amarilla mia bella; Amor, io parto; Belle rose porporine; Dolcissimo sospiro; Movetevi à pietà; Queste lagrimé amare; Vedrò'l mio sol. Nuove Musiche e Nuove Maniera de scriverle* (Florence, 1614): *Alme luci beate; Amor ch'attendi; Con le luci d'un bel ciglio; Dalla porta d'oriente; Torna, deh torna; Tu ch'hai le penne; Tutto 'l dì piango*

(M) *** DHM/BMG 82876 70038-2. Figueras, Smith, Clancy, Schindler, Savall

Giulio Caccini, born in Rome, joined the court of the Medicis in his youth and was to become an outstanding singer and, on the evidence of this CD, a very fine composer too. He was among several writer/musicians of his time who began to use chordally accompanied song (i.e. without polyphony). His vocal line was also forward-looking in the use of poignant dissonances or leaps above the chord and, most importantly of all, he indicated the required (often complicated) ornamentation rather than leaving it to the performer. This has proved an important source for later singers, providing authentic ornamentation for other music of the period.

He published his first group of 'New' songs in 1601 (pre-dated to 1601) and the second in 1614, four years before he died. The present collection draws on some of the finest examples from both sets which between them offer a variety of madrigal-styled compositions, arias and freer virtuoso songs. The writing is often poignantly compelling. The most

famous is the exquisite *Amarilla mia bella* (1601) but *Movetevi à pietà* is hardly less affecting and *Tutto 'l dì piango* (1614) might almost be by Monteverdi. Other items are light-hearted, like *Dalla porta d'oriente* or the closing *Con le luci d'un bel ciglio*, both of which have striking cross-rhythmic accompaniments. But much of this music is deeply expressive. It could not be more beautifully or authentically sung than by Montserrat Figueras, or more sensitively accompanied than it is here by lute, or combinations of baroque guitar, harp and Jordi Savall's viola da gamba. This is an enchanting disc and one can only regret that no texts or translations are included, although the documentation is otherwise good.

CAMBINI, Giuseppe Maria (1746–1825)

Wind Quintets 1 in B; 2 in D min.; 3 in F

(BB) *** Naxos 8.553410. Avalon Wind Quintet –
BRICCIALDI: *Wind Quintet in D ***

These *Wind Quintets* are doubtless inconsequential, but they are charming, particularly when played so superbly and elegantly by these fine young German musicians. The recording is expertly balanced and very natural. Slight music, but so well served that it will give much pleasure.

CAMPION, Thomas (1567–1620)

Lute Songs: *Are you not what your fair looks express?; Author of light; Awake thou spring of speaking grace; Beauty is but a painted hell; Beauty, since you so much desire; Come you pretty false-eyed wanton; The Cypress curtain of the night; Fair, if you expect admiring; Fire, fire; I care not for these ladies; It fell upon a summer's day; Kind are her answers; Love me or not; Never love unless you can; Never weather-beaten sail; O never to be moved; Pined I am, and like to die; See where she flies; Shall I come, sweet love to thee?; So tired are all my thoughts; Sweet exclude me not; Your fair looks*

(B) **(*) HM HCX 3957023. Minter, O'Dette

Thomas Campion was an almost exact contemporary of Dowland but his lute songs are much less well known – undeservedly so, for their lyrical melancholy is often comparably affecting, as *Love me or not* and *The Cypress curtain of the night*, *Never weather-beaten sail* and the lovely *Author of light* readily demonstrate. Most touching of all is the plaintive *Shall I come, sweet love to thee?*, while the livelier and lighter-hearted *I care not for these ladies* is quite catchy. Drew Minter has an appealing alto voice and forms a sensitive vocal line, and (not surprisingly) Paul O'Dette's accompaniments are highly supportive. The balance is excellent and this disc is very good value, but the recital would have been even more attractive if several different singers had been employed, affording greater variety of timbre.

Lute songs: *Author of light; Beauty, since you so much desire; Come let us sound with melody; Come you pretty false-ey'ed wanton; The Cypress curtain of the night; Fair, if you expect admiring; Fire, fire, fire, fire!; Her rosie cheeks; I care not for these ladies; It fell on a sommers daie; Jacke and Jone they think no ill; Most sweet and pleasing are thy ways; Never weather-beaten sail; Shall I come, sweet love to thee?; Sweet exclude me not; There is a garden in her face; There is none, O none but you; Though you are yoong and I am olde; Thou joy'st, fond boy; To musicke bent; Tune thy musicke to thy hart; Turn all thy thoughts to eyes; What is it that all men possess?; When to her lute Corrina sings; Vaile, love mine eyes* (with ROSSETER: *My sweetest Lesbia; When then is love but mourning?;* ANON.: *Miserere my maker*)

(B) **(*) Naxos 8.553380. Rickards, Linell

Thomas Campion's song output included lighter settings too. *I care not for these ladies* could hardly have naughtier implications in its repeated pay-off line: 'She never will say no.' Steven Rickards, a young American counter-tenor, has a pleasing voice and delivery. At times one listens in vain for more variety of colour, but his presentation is appealingly simple, as are the lute accompaniments of Dorothy Linell, who attempts no elaborations or embellishments. They are well recorded in a pleasing acoustic and, with full texts included, this is yet another enterprising Naxos disc well worth its modest cost.

CAMPO, Conrado del (1878–1953)

La divina comedia; Evocacion y nostalgia de los molinos de viento; Ofrenda; 6 Little Compositions

*** ASV CDDCA 1100. Gran Canaria PO, Leaper

Conrado del Campo, unlike his close contemporary, Manuel de Falla, has never been appreciated outside Spain, maybe because his music has few nationalistic flavours, echoing instead such composers as Richard Strauss and Liszt. Adrian Leaper with the Gran Canaria Philharmonic, of which he is principal conductor, here offers an attractive collection, well played, representing the full span of Del Campo's career from *La divina comedia* of 1908, an evocation of Dante's *Inferno* with a warmly lyrical interlude representing Paolo and Francesca, to his last major piece, a 'poetic overture' inspired by the composer's love of windmills, *Molinos de viento.* Completed in 1952, the year before he died, it leads to a passionate climax, while *Ofrenda,* dating from 1934, is equally sensuous, with exotic echoes of Respighi, suggesting that Del Campo could have made his fortune as a Hollywood composer.

CANNABICH, Johann Christian (1731–98)

Christian Cannabich was born and made his career in Mannheim, where in 1774 he became conductor of what at that time was the most celebrated orchestra in Europe. Cannabich was to be described by Mozart as the finest conductor he had ever encountered, but he was also a prolific and accomplished, if not always individual, symphonist.

Symphonies 47 in G; 48 in B flat; 49 in F; 50 in D min.; 51 in D; 52 in E, Op. 10/1-6

(BB) *** Naxos 8.554340. Nicolaus Esterházy Sinf., Grodd

Symphonies 59 in D; 63 in D; 64 in F; 67 in G; 68 in B flat

(BB) *** Naxos 8.553960. Lukas Cons., Lukas

Cannabich's six works published in 1772 as Op. 10 are each in three movements and are effectively scored for flutes (or oboes) and horns. Opening movements are conventional, but the expressively gracious slow movements and lively finales more than compensate, and very soon we encounter the famous Mannheim 'crescendo' (the opening movement of No. 51 provides a very striking example). There are even hints of Mozart. The performances are lively, stylish and well recorded.

The second group of symphonies (though still in three movements) mark a considerable step forward. The scoring of No. 59 uses the oboes more freely as soloists, and its *Andante* is strikingly gracious. But when we reach the dramatic opening of No. 63 the scoring is much more ambitious, using trumpets and timpani, as well as full woodwind, including clarinets. All the celebrated Mannheim effects are here, with an emphatic unison in the introduction, plus the carefully regulated, almost Rossinian crescendos. The lilting oboe melody of the slow movement contrasts with the strong, Mozartian finale.

No. 64 brings more crescendo sequences, and the *Andante* is again very fetching, to be followed by another bold finale, featuring the horns, which are again used most effectively in Nos. 67 and 68. No. 68 begins amiably but energetically, and the solo horns are given the full limelight with the principal theme of the *Andante.* The lighthearted second subject of the finale again demonstrates the variety of Cannabich's invention, and the whole movement displays his deft use of orchestral colour. Viktor Lukas and his Consort give admirable performances, full of life and with the necessary light and shade. They are again very well recorded and this pair of inexpensive discs provides a most stimulating introduction to a composer/conductor justly renowned in his own time.

Flute Quintets, Op. 7/3-6

*** CPO 999 544-2. Camerata Köln

Cannabich's *Flute Quintets* are for one (or usually two) flutes, violin, viola and cello, and sometimes have optional keyboard parts. The music is elegant, well crafted and charming, if very lightweight, with the 'concertante' flute parts always dominant. Excellent performances here, and natural recording within a pleasing ambience.

CANTELOUBE, Marie-Joseph (1879–1957)

Chants d'Auvergne: Baïlèro; 3 Bourrées; Brezairola; Chut, chut; La Delaïssado; Hé beyla-z-y dau fé (Bourrée); Lo Fiolaire; Lou coucut; Malurous qu'o uno fenno (Bourrée); Oi ayai; Passo pel prat; Pastorale; Uno jionto postouro (Regret)

(BB) *** HMV (ADD) 5 86718-2. De los Angeles, LAP, Jacquillat – VILLA-LOBOS: *Bachianas brasileiras 1, 2 & 5,* etc. ***

A more extensive selection of Victoria de los Angeles's delightful and alluring *Songs of the Auvergne* is available at mid-price as one of EMI's 'Great Recordings of the Century' (5 66978-2 [66993-2]), which also includes texts. However, the present compilation offers many favourites, including the famous *Baïlèro,* so if the Villa-Lobos coupling is attractive this is excellent value, even without the translations.

CAPLET, André (1878–1925)

(i) *Conte fantastique: La Masque de la mort rouge. Divertissement; Les Prières; Septet; 2 Sonnets*

(B) *** HM Musique d'abord HMA 1951497. Coste, Piau, Deguy, Ens. Musique Oblique; (i) with Laurence Cabel (harp)

A welcome reissue of a 1992 disc which was awarded a Diapason d'Or. André Caplet is not well represented on CD. Although his idiom is strongly Debussian, he possessed fastidious craftsmanship and a refined sensibility of distinctive quality. His best-known work is the *Conte fantastique* for harp and strings, based on Edgar Allan Poe's *Masque of the Red Death*, a work strong on evocative menace. The present Harmonia Mundi version offers the more intimate chamber version of the score and makes a strong challenge to previous versions, for the accompanying programme is well chosen and serves to flesh out a portrait of Caplet himself. It is very well played and balanced, and is well worth its modest cost.

CARDOSO, Frei Manuel (c. 1566–1650)

Requiem (Missa pro defunctis)
(B) *** Gimell CDGIM 205 (2). Tallis Scholars, Philips – Duarte LOBO: *Requiem;* Alonso LOBO: *Motets;* VICTORIA: *Requiem,* etc. ***

Cardoso's *Requiem* is in every way original and rewarding, and the Tallis Scholars' performance (also available with a collection of Motets – see our main volume) is outstanding in every way. The new bargain-priced Double links it to music by Lobo and Victoria which is equally desirable.

CARISSIMI, Giacomo (1605–74)

Damnation lamentatio; Felicitas batorum; Historia di Jephte
*** Opus 111 Naïve OP 30296. Franzetti, Hernandez, Halimi, Van Dyck, Dordolo, Imboden, Le Parlement de Musique, Gester (with Lelio COLISTA: *Sinfonia in D min.*) – FRESCOBALDI: *Motets & Partita* ***

A first-class programme which attempts to re-create a sacred concert in Rome in the middle of the seventeenth century. Carissimi's *Jephte* is comparatively well known, and it is beautifully and dramatically sung here. The two shorter Lenten works might be described as motet/oratorios for, although they have no characters, they combine solos and ensembles, and are poignantly linked by their dialogue format, and their concern with the desperation of the damned and the joy of those who are saved.

The two brief minor-key *Sinfonias* by Lelio Colista (1629–80), celebrated in his day for such works, serve as expressive interludes between the vocal works and capture their sombre mood, as does the coupled music of Frescobaldi. Excellent documentation and full texts and translations make this a very attractive compilation.

CARMINA BURANA (c. 1300)

Carmina Burana – Songs from the Original Manuscript
(BB) *** Naxos 8. 554837. Unicorn Ens., Posch; Oni Wytars Ens., Ambrosini

This was the collection on which Carl Orff drew for his popular cantata. The original manuscript comprises more than 200 pieces from many countries, dating from the late eleventh to the thirteenth century, organized according to subject-matter: love songs, moralizing and satirical songs, eating, drinking, gambling and religious texts.

The selection gathered on Naxos, using two different ensembles, is both lively and stimulating, offering an imaginatively wide variation of conjectural scoring, sometimes gentle and atmospheric. Individual instrumentations are given in the excellent documentation. Vocal contributions too are distinguished. The repeated melody of *Tempus transit gelidum* (scored for recorder, fiddles and hurdy-gurdy) is

quite haunting, as are the two counter-tenor melismas, the accompanied *Procurans odium* ('Producing hatred') and unaccompanied *Celum, non animum.* The recording is excellent. Most rewarding.

CARPENTER, John Alden (1876–1951)

Adventures in a Perambulator; Symphonies 1–2
(BB) *** Naxos 8.558065. Nat. SO of Ukraine, McLaughlin Williams

John Alden Carpenter came from a wealthy Illinois family, and in spite of receiving every encouragement to develop his musical talent (which showed itself when he was still quite young) he put the family business first, eventually becoming Vice-President. His musical training included study under Elgar and this shows in his confident handling of the orchestra. *Adventures in a Perambulator* (which includes encounters with *Dogs, Dreams, The Lake, The Hurdy-Gurdy* and *The Policeman*) is charmingly scored and pleasantly tuneful. The *First Symphony*, a well-planned single-movement work, divided into five linked sections, is hardly more ambitious. But again its invention is warmly attractive and its nostalgic atmosphere holds the listener in its undemanding spell.

The *Second* opens more dramatically, but similarly it does not probe any depths, seeking mainly to divert, especially the jolly, boisterous finale. The Ukraine orchestra obviously enjoy this music and play it very well indeed. The Naxos recording is first class and the documentation includes the composer's own notes for *Adventures in a Perambulator.*

String Quartet; (i) Piano Quintet; (i; ii) Violin Sonata
(BB) *** Naxos 8.559103 Vega Qt; (i) Posnik; (ii) Chen

These three immediately attractive chamber works are a splendid way of experiencing and enjoying the calibre of Carpenter's music. The early *Violin Sonata* (1912) is a delightfully spontaneous piece, sweetly lyrical but by no means slight, with striking ideas throughout all four traditional movements. The *String Quartet* of 1927 is altogether more nostalgic and chromatically searching; the Adagio is poignantly expressive, the finale, with its off-beat rhythm, more folksy, but still comparatively restrained in feeling. The *Piano Quintet* of a decade later is more extrovert, the first movement cheerfully animated, but with a tranquil underlay, the Adagio much more ruminatively intense, the finale syncopated and characterfully energetic. First-class performances and fine recording make this a very enjoyable programme indeed – and one to return to.

CARTELLIERI, Casimir Anton (1772–1807)

Clarinet Concertos 1 in B flat; 2: Adagio pastorale; 3 in E flat
*** MDG 301 0527-2. Klöcker, Prague CO

Hardly a household name, Casimir Anton Cartellieri was born in Danzig and eventually found his way to Vienna. His three *Clarinet Concertos* (only the slow movement of the second survives) are expertly laid out for the instrument. While they are not searching or profound, they are astonishingly inventive and full of both charm and wit. Dieter Klöcker and the Prague Chamber Orchestra give thoroughly committed accounts of these delightful pieces, and the MDG recording is immaculate.

(i)*Double Concerto for 2 Clarinets in B flat*; (ii) *Flute Concerto in G*; (i) *Movement for Clarinet & Orchestra in B flat*
*** MDG 301 0960-2. (i) Klöcker, Arnold; (ii) Brandkamp; Prague CO

The *Concerto for Two Clarinets* reaffirms the strong impression made by its companions above. It bubbles over with high spirits and has a strikingly original opening. Klöcker and his pupil, Sandra Arnold, give a masterly account of the piece, and Kornelia Brandkamp is hardly less expert in the diverting and delightful *Flute Concerto*. As always with the Dabringhaus & Grimm label, the recordings are beautifully balanced and very natural. Not great music, perhaps, but very rewarding all the same.

Clarinet Quartets 1 in D; 2 in E flat; 4 in E flat
*** MDG 301 1097-2. Klöcker, Consortium Classicum

Those readers who have already discovered Cartellieri's *Clarinet Concertos* will not need persuading to explore these even more delightful companion chamber works. Their style brings an occasional whiff of Mozart but is more *galant* than the music of that master, and there are also touches of the kind of wit one finds in Rossini's *String Sonatas*. Dieter Klöcker plays beguilingly and he is given splendid support from the Consortium Classicum, elegant and fresh, and they are beautifully recorded.

CARVER, Robert *(c. 1484–c. 1568)*

Mass: Cantate Domino for 6 Voices
*** Gaudeamus CDGAU 136. (i) Lovett; Hamilton, Cappella Nova, Tavener (with ANGUS: *All my Belief*; (i) *The Song of Simeon*. ANON.: *Descendi in hortum meum*. BLACK: *Ane lesson upone the feiftie psalme*; *Lytill Blak*; PEEBLES: *Psalms 107; 124; Si quis diligit me*) ***

Most of the pieces, by David Peebles (who flourished 1530–76), John Black (*c.* 1520–87) and John Angus (fl. 1562–90), come from *Musica Britannica* Vol. XV ('Music of Scotland, 1500–1700') and appear on record for the first time. Though the authorship of the *Mass: Cantate Domino* is not definitely established, it is related to the five-part *Fera pessima* by Robert Carver and is almost certainly a re-working, possibly by Carver himself, of the earlier, five-part piece for six voices. In any event, this is a record of much interest, well sung and recorded.

5 Masses; 2 Motets (as listed below)
(M) *** Gaudeamus CD GAX 319 (3). Cappella Nova, Tavener

Mass Dum sacrum mysterium in 10 parts; Motets: *Gaude flore Virginali; O bone Jesu*
*** Gaudeamus CDGAU 124. Cappella Nova, Tavener

The motet *O bone Jesu* is in 19 parts and is of exceptional luminosity and richness. The 10-part *Mass, Dum sacrum mysterium*, is undoubtedly the grandest in scope, the most extended in development and the richest in detail. The motet *Gaude flore Virginali* for five voices, though less sumptuous, has some adventurous modulations. The Cappella Nova under Alan Tavener give a thoroughly dedicated account of all three pieces, though the pitch drops very slightly in the *Gaude flore Virginali*. The recording is very good indeed.

Masses: Fera pessima for 5 voices; Pater creator omnium for 4 voices
*** Gaudeamus CDGAU 127. Cappella Nova, Tavener
Missa: L'Homme armé for 4 Voices; Mass for 6 Voices
*** Gaudeamus CDGAU 126. Cappella Nova, Tavener

These two CDs, together with his ten-part *Missa Dum sacrum mysterium* (and probably the *Cantate Domino* listed above), represent the complete sacred music of the early-sixteenth-century Scottish composer, Robert Carver. The six-part *Mass* of 1515 is cyclic (each Mass section opens with similar music), and the presence of other common material suggests that it is a parody Mass, possibly based, it is thought, on an earlier Carver motet.

Like *L'Homme armé*, the *Fera pessima* is another *cantus firmus* Mass and dates from 1525; its companion, the four-part *Pater creator omnium*, comes from 1546 and reflects the changing style of the period. It survives only in incomplete form; the two missing parts in the *Kyrie* and *Gloria* have been added by Kenneth Elliott. Committed singing from the Cappella Nova and Alan Tavener, and very well recorded too.

As can be seen the 3 discs above are also available in a mid-priced box.

CARWITHEN, Doreen *(1922–2003)*

(i) *Concerto for Piano & Strings. Overtures: ODTAA ('One damn thing after another'); Bishop Rock; Suffolk Suite*
(M) *** Chan. 10365X. (i) Shelley; LSO, Hickox

Doreen Carwithen here emerges as a warmly communicative composer in her own right, owing rather more to Walton's style than to that of her husband (William Alwyn). The two overtures in their vigour and atmospheric colour relate readily to her film music, the one inspired by John Masefield's novel, *ODTAA*, the other inspired by the rock in the Atlantic that marks the last contact with the British Isles, stormy in places, gently sinister in others. The charming *Suffolk Suite* uses melodies originally written for a film on East Anglia. Much the most ambitious work is the *Concerto for Piano and Strings*, with powerful virtuoso writing for the piano set against rich-textured strings. A deeply melancholy slow movement – in which the piano is joined by solo violin – leads to a strong finale which in places echoes the Ireland *Piano Concerto*. Howard Shelley is the persuasive soloist, with Richard Hickox and the LSO equally convincing in their advocacy of all four works. Warm, atmospheric sound.

(i) *Violin Sonata*; (ii) *String Quartets 1 & 2*
*** Chan. 9596. (i) Mordkovitch, Milford; (ii) Sorrel Qt

The *First Quartet*, written in 1948 when she was still a student, firmly establishes Doreen Carwithen's personal idiom, tautly constructed in three movements. The result, identifiably English, yet points forward, though it is only in the *Second Quartet* of 1952, in two extended movements, that one detects a hint that she may have been studying the quartets of Bartók; it comes with warmly expressive performances from the well-matched Sorrel Quartet. The *Violin Sonata*, written later, brings high dramatic contrasts, most strikingly in the central *Vivace*, a *moto perpetuo* in 9/8 rhythm. Lydia Mordkovitch, as ever, proves a passionate advocate, finding a depth and poignancy in the lyrical writing that may reflect her Russian roots. Julian Milford makes an ideal partner, though the piano is rather backwardly balanced. Otherwise the recording is first rate.

CASADESUS, Robert (1899-1972)

Symphonies 1 in D, Op. 19; 5 (sur le nom de Haydn), Op. 60;
(i) 7 (Israël), Op. 68
** Chan. 10263. N. Sinfonia, Howard Shelley; (i) with Gibson, Mark, Druiett, Gateshead Children's Ch., N. Sinfonia Ch.

The great French pianist was a prolific composer, many of whose works were recorded in the last days of LP. Anyone who remembers his Mozart concertos with Szell or his Ravel will know what a wonderful musician he was. His *First Symphony*, composed in 1934–5 when he was in his mid-thirties, is an attractive piece which bears some resemblance to Poulenc and Les Six; but its two companions are less satisfying. The idiom is what one might call general-purpose Gallic, and although the music is always well crafted and intelligently laid out, the musical substance is not consistently compelling. The string-tone is a little wanting in body, but the performances under Howard Shelley are well prepared. However, the choral singing in the *Seventh*, composed in the wake of the six-day Arab-Israeli war of 1967, is less than first class. For those with an exploratory turn of mind the *First Symphony* is well worth hearing, and Howard Shelley gets generally good results from the orchestra. As usual from this source, good recorded sound.

CAURROY, Eustache du (1549–1609)

Missa pro defunctis; Motets: Ave Maria; Ave virgo gloriosa;
Benedicamus Domino; Christe qui lux es; Salve Regina; Veni
sancte spiritus; Victimae Pascali
(M) *** CRD 3518. New College, Oxford, Ch., Higginbottom

Eustache du Caurroy was yet another master of the French Renaissance whose name is virtually unknown to us, mainly because – as Edward Higginbottom tells us in his excellent note – of the lack of accessible and reliable editions. Du Caurroy first entered the French Court as a singer in about 1570 and eventually became Vice-Maître of the Chapelle Royal and Surintendant de la Musique, serving under the successive reigns of three kings, Charles IX, Henri III and Henri IV. To quote a contemporary opinion, 'he reigned supreme for the great harmoniousness of his composition', and that is immediately displayed in his gloriously rich setting of *Veni sancte spiritus*, which opens this programme. His *Missa pro defunctis* (1606) was first performed at the funeral of Henri IV. It lacks the *Dies irae*, and instead Du Caurroy sets two verses from Psalm 123. The first six Mass sections are consistently slow and solemn, and then in the *Agnus Dei* the mood lifts and there is a sense of acceptance in the *Lux aeterna*. The following motet, *Benedicamus Domino*, lifts the spirits even higher, proceeding with joyous vigour, and ending with a rousing *Alleluia*. Of the other works, *Salve Regina* is particularly eloquent, alternating between separate four- and five-part choruses. *Christe qui lux es* is more sober, a three-section motet in four, three and six parts respectively; the concert closes with the deeply expressive *Victimae Paschali* for double choir. Altogether this is a splendid reminder of a little-known sixteenth-century master, and these Oxford performances are fully worthy of him – as is the beautiful sound of the choir, which Mike Hatch has balanced so successfully in the warm ambience of the Abbaye de Valoires in the Somme.

CERHA, Friedrich (born 1926)

String Quartets 1–3; (i) 8 Movements after Hölderlin
Fragments for String Sextet
*** CPO 999 646-2. Arditti Qt; (i) with Kakuska, Erben

Friedrich Cerha is best known as a champion of the Second Viennese School and as the scholar-composer who completed the third act of Alban Berg's *Lulu*. The three quartets recorded here come from the period 1989–92: the *First Quartet* is subtitled *Maqam*, inspired by Arab music. It makes liberal use of microtones, as does, though to a lesser extent, the minimalist *Second*, inspired by his contact with the Papuan peoples at Sepik in New Guinea. The *Hölderlin Fragments* (1995) are settings for string sextet without voice, though the poems that inspired them are reproduced in the excellent and detailed booklet. The Arditti Quartet play with great expertise and attention to detail, and are vividly recorded. Recommended for those with a special interest in contemporary Austrian music.

CHABRIER, Emmanuel (1841–94)

Aubade; Ballabile; Bourrée fantasque; Caprice; Feuillet
d'album; Habanera; Impromptu; 10 pièces pittoresques;
Ronde champêtre
⊙— *** Hyp. CDA 67515. Hewitt

What enchanting music this is – and, for that matter, enchanting playing! Poulenc thought the *Pièces pittoresques* were 'as important for French music as the *Préludes* of Debussy', and they deserve as honoured a place in the repertoire as Debussy, Fauré, Satie and Poulenc himself. Angela Hewitt may have built her reputation on playing Bach, but she demonstrates here that she can bring just as much life and imagination to interpreting French piano music. This is a model collection of pieces by one of the most engaging of all nineteenth-century French composers, showing what sparkling inventiveness she brings to any idea. The 18 pieces here range delightfully from the slinky rhythms of the *Habanera* and the extrovert energy of the *Bourrée fantasque* to the haunting beauty of the *Aubade*, all beautifully realized by Hewitt, with exquisite control of the widest tonal range and ever-persuasive control of rubato. Beautifully recorded.

CHAMINADE, Cécile (1857–1944)

Piano Trios 1 in G min., Op. 11; 2 in A min., Op. 34; Pastorale
enfantine, Op. 12; Ritournelle; Sérénade, Op. 29 (all 3 arr.
Marcus); *Serenade espagnole* (arr. Kreisler)
*** ASV CDDCA 965. Tzigane Piano Trio

In these two *Piano Trios* Chaminade confidently controls larger forms, building on a fund of melody. The two central movements of the *Piano Trio No. 1* are charming, a passionately lyrical *Andante* and a sparkling, Mendelssohnian Scherzo. The *Piano Trio No. 2*, in three movements, without a Scherzo, is weightier, almost Brahmsian, with themes rather more positive. Three of the four miniatures that come as fill-ups have been arranged for trio by the Tzigane's pianist, Elizabeth Marcus.

PIANO MUSIC

Air à danser, Op. 164; Air de ballet, Op. 30; Automne;
Autrefois; Contes bleus 2, Op. 122; Danse créole, Op. 94;
Guitare, Op. 32; Lisonjera, Op. 50; Lolita, Op. 54; Minuetto,
Op. 23; Pas des écharpes, Op. 37; Pas des sylphes: Intermezzo;
Pierette, Op. 41; 3 Romances sans paroles, Op. 76/1, 3 & 6;
Sérénade, Op. 29; Sous le masque, Op. 116; Toccata, Op. 39;
Valse arabesque

*** Chan. 8888. Parkin

Album des enfants, Op. 123/4, 5, 9 & 10; Op. 126/1, 2, 9 & 10;
Arabesque, Op. 61; Cortège, Op. 143; Inquiétude, Op. 87/3; Le
Passé; Prelude in D min., Op. 84/3; Rigaudon, Op. 55/6;
Sérénade espagnole; Sonata in C min., Op. 21; Les Sylvains,
Op. 60; Valse-ballet, Op. 112; Valse brillante 3, Op. 80; Valse
4, Op. 91

(BB) *** Hyp. Helios CDH 55199. Jacobs

Callirhoë (Air de Ballet); Chaconne, Op. 8; Etudes de
concert: Automne; Scherzo in C, Op. 35/1–2; Etude mélodique
in G flat, Op. 18; Etude pathétique in B min., Op. 124; Etude
scholastique, Op. 129; La Lisonjera; L'Ondine, Op. 101; Pièces
humoristiques: Autrefois, Op. 87/4; Poèmes provençales:
Pêcheurs de nuit; Solitude, Op. 127/2 & 4; Romance in D,
Op. 137; Romances sans paroles: Elévation in E, Souvenance,
Op. 76/1–2; Sérénade in D, Op. 29; Thème varié in A, Op. 89;
Valse 2, Op. 77; Valse romantique

(BB) *** Hyp. Helios CDH 55197. Peter Jacobs

Artistically these pieces are rather stronger than one had
suspected and, although they are by no means the equal of
Grieg or early Fauré, they can hold their own with Saint-
Saëns and are more inventive than the *Brises d'orient* of
Félicien David. There is a quality of gentility that has lent a
certain pallor to Chaminade's charms, but both pianists here
make out a stronger case for her than most people would
imagine possible. Both are well recorded and in this respect
there is little to choose between the two. Nor is there much to
choose as far as the performances are concerned; both are
persuasive, though Parkin has a slight edge over his colleague
in terms of elegance and finesse. If you want a single-disc
collection you might choose the Chandos disc. If you seek a
complete survey, stay with Jacobs.

CHAUSSON, Ernest (1855–99)

Poème for Violin & Orchestra, Op. 25 (Original Version)
(M) *** Avie AV 2091. Graffin, RLPO, Handley – ELGAR:
Violin Concerto *******

This the first of a new series from Avie, in conjunction with
the RLPO. For this recording of the familiar *Poème*, the
French violinist Philippe Graffin and Vernon Handley have
returned to Chausson's original score, as Ysaÿe (who advised
on its composition) tinkered with the solo part afterwards.
However, for most listeners the differences are small, involving the restoration of a mere 12 bars. Graffin has an ideal
silvery tone for this work, and his performance is richly
rhapsodic, with totally idiomatic support from Handley,
whose atmospheric opening sets the scene magnetically for
his gentle entry. The recording, made in Philharmonic Hall,
Liverpool, is warmly full-bodied and very naturally balanced,
and the solo violin rides the passionate climax impressively.
The coupled Elgar concerto also goes back to the original
score.

(i; ii) *Poème for Violin & Orchestra, Op. 25;* (i) *Symphony in*
B flat, Op. 20; (iii) *Concert in D for Violin, Piano & String*
Quartet in D, Op. 21; (iv) *Piano Quartet in A, Op. 30;* (i; v)
Poème de l'amour et de la mer, Op. 19

(B) **(*) Decca (ADD/DDD) 475 6528 (2). (i) Montreal SO,
Dutoit; (ii) with Juillet; (iii) Amoyal, Rogé, Ysaÿe Qt; (iv)
Richards Piano Qt; (v) Le Roux

A useful Chausson compilation: Dutoit's version of the symphony is very well played and recorded, with elegance very
much a key feature, even if it lacks the sheer drama that the
classic Munch and Paray versions offer. The *Poème* is similarly
beautiful, if not quite reaching the intensity of the very finest
versions available. François Le Roux – usually an excellent
artist – has rather too much vibrato in his account of the
Poème de l'amour et de la mer, but it is still recommendable,
and the Decca sound brings out the sensuous beauty in
Chausson's orchestral colours.

Very enjoyable indeed (and new to CD) is the 1969 Richards version of the *Piano Quartet*: a fresh and spontaneous
performance in up-front but very warm, vintage Decca
sound. In the *Concert in D*, the natural idiomatic response of
an excellent all-French team to this high romantic work
results in a warmly spontaneous-sounding performance at
speeds rather broader than usual, made all the more involving by the full and immediate recording. Contrasts of
dynamic and texture, of light and shade, warmly and strongly
brought out, give concentration to a work which can seem
too rhapsodic. It helps too that the string quartet is given full
weight, with the Ysaÿe Quartet matching Amoyal and Rogé in
their virtuosity. This is the outstanding item on this bargain
Double.

Symphony in B flat, Op. 20
*** Universal Accord 476 8069. Liège PO, Langree –
FRANCK: *Symphony* *******

The *Symphony* of Chausson, a composer closely associated
with Franck, makes an ideal coupling for Franck's comparable work, similarly in three movements. Louis Langree draws
a persuasive, totally idiomatic performance from his finely
drilled Belgian orchestra, opting for a flowing speed in the
central slow movement, marked *Tres lent*, very slow, but never
sounding at all rushed. The clarity and immediacy of the
sound adds to the impact and, as in the Franck, Chausson's
syncopated rhythms come over most persuasively.

Piano Quartet in A, Op. 30
*** Aeon AECD 0540. Favre, Schumann Qt – FAURÉ: *Piano*
Quartet 1 *******

The first thing that strikes you on the Aeon version is the
bright, full sound of Christian Favre's piano at the start of the
Chausson, and the excellent recorded sound generally adds to
the brilliance and persuasiveness of these performances. Dating from 1896, late in Chausson's career, his *Piano Quartet* is a
fascinating work, reflecting in its hints of oriental music, both
in the rhythms and in the use of the pentatonic scale, the
impact of the celebrated Paris exhibition which influenced so
many French composers at that period. The precision of
ensemble adds greatly to the impact of the strongly rhythmic
passages, confirming the advantage of having a regular piano
quartet ensemble, rather than bringing a mixed group of
players together, however talented. What seals the quality of
the Schumann Quartet's performance is their superb reading
of the slow movement, marked *Très calme*. From the tender
and hushed opening the players build up the argument into a

towering climax, which in its passionate warmth reminds one of the climaxes in Chausson's most celebrated work, the *Poème*. Well coupled with the Fauré, this is very recommendable.

CHÁVEZ, Carlos (1899–1978)

Symphonies (i) 1; (ii) 2; (i) 4; (iii) *Baile (Symphonic Painting); The Daughter of Colchis (Symphonic Suite)*
** ASV CDCA 1058. (i) RPO; (ii) Mexico PO; (iii) Mexico State SO; Bátiz

These performances include the best known, *Sinfonia India*, which is based on true Indian melodies. It has a savage, primitive character which is very attractive.

Enrique Bátiz produces good results from his various orchestras and the sound is more than acceptable. But the older deleted Everest performances under the composer had greater character.

CHEN GANG (born 1935)

The Butterfly Lovers' Concerto
(BB) *** Naxos 8.557348. Nishizaki, New Zealand SO, Judd

The *Butterfly Lovers' Concerto* belongs to China's Communist era, when it was politically correct for a pair of composers to write music together. So in 1959 Chen Gang and his fellow student He Zhanho combined to write a violin concerto using traditional themes. The piece is based on a folk story about a pair of student comrades, one of whom is a girl dressed as a boy. They have to part, her father arranges her wedding and, too late, the hero discovers his comrade is a girl and to be married. Like a true lover he dies of unhappiness. On her wedding day the heroine insists on leaving the bridal procession to mourn at the grave. A thunderstorm breaks out, the grave opens, she leaps in, it closes again, and a rainbow appears in the sky. Two butterflies appear and fly away together, so the lovers are united for ever. It is not easy to relate the music to the narrative except for the engagingly languorous melodies, often heard on the flute as well as the violin, which frame the work and obviously relate to the lovers. There is lively dance music and passages of vigorous melodrama in the central section. But the concerto is beautifully scored, and finally the main romantic theme blossoms, first richly on the strings and then the full orchestra, to show the triumph of true love, before the delicate solo passages return on violin and flute, tenderly reflecting the sadness of the lovers' plight. Takako Nishizaki was the natural choice of soloist for this disarmingly attractive work, for she has recorded it before and became a major star in China, where over three million copies have been sold! She plays it with great tenderness and her slightly fragile (yet warm) timbre surely conjures up the prettiest pair of butterflies.

CHISHOLM, Erik (1904–65)

Scottish Airs for Children; Sonata in A ('An Riobain Dearg); Straloch Suite
** Dunelm DRD 0222. Murray McLachlan

Although this is all music with a strong Scottish flavour, and Erik Chisholm is a Scot, he chose to emigrate to Cape Town in 1946, where he became Principal of the South African College of Music. However, all the works on this CD date

from his earlier years. The *Sonata* was written in 1939 but was 'abridged' in 2004 by Murray McLachlan for the present recording. It is still pretty extended (34 minutes) and somewhat overblown, and its complexities of texture and awkward keyboard writing offer even McLachlan's skilled fingers problems of focus and clarity. Its 'piobaireachd' basis is not particularly striking and its harmonies far from adventurous. Frankly this is no masterpiece.

The *Straloch Suite* of 1933, using themes from the 'Robert Gordon of Straloch Lute Book' of 1627, is much more valuable and pianistically quite effective in preserving these folk tunes, for the original manuscript is now lost. However, by far the most important work here is the selection of 22 *Scottish Airs for Children*. Chisholm's enterprise was inspired by Bartók's *Mikrokosmos*. Bartók had visited Chisholm twice in Glasgow and apparently took bagpipe music back with him when he returned home! Chisholm's selection is taken from Patrick MacDonald's 'A Collection of Highland Vocal Airs', published in 1784, all of which are short and simply presented, and many are delightful. Murray McLachlan is obviously thoroughly at home in all this music and he is well recorded, but this is a difficult disc to recommend to the general collector rather than the specialist.

CHOPIN, Frédéric (1810–49)

Complete Chopin Editions
DG Complete Chopin Edition
(B) **(*) DG DDD/ADD 463 047-2 (17)

To commemorate the 150th anniversary of Chopin's death, DG assembled, for the first time, the complete works of Chopin – even making several new recordings to fill in the gaps. Where this edition falls down in places is in the choice of performance. There are many outstanding Chopin recordings here – notably from Argerich, Pollini and Zimerman – but there are several where DG might have made a better choice, the *Waltzes* and *Mazurkas* for example. At a bargain price and with a lavishly illustrated booklet, it is still good value and one can always supplement this set with other recordings. The merits of each volume, which are no longer available separately, are discussed below.

Volume 1: Works for piano and orchestra: *Piano Concerto* (i; ii) 1 in E min., Op. 11; 2 in F min., Op. 21; (ii; iii) *Andante spianato et Grande polonaise brillante, Op. 22;* (iv) *Grande fantasia on Polish airs, Op. 13;* (v) *Krakowiak concert rondo, Op. 14;* (iv) *Variations on 'Là ci darem la mano' from Mozart's 'Don Giovanni', Op. 2*
(M) *** DG (ADD) (IMS) 463 048-2 (2). (i) Zimerman; (ii) Concg. O, Kondrashin; (iii) LAPO, Giulini; (iv) Arrau, LPO, Inbal; (v) Askenase, Hague Residente O, Otterloo

Krystian Zimerman's Chopin concerto recordings are fresh, poetic and individual accounts, always sparkling and beautifully characterized. DG have chosen for the *E minor Concerto* to use his 'live' 1979 performance at the Concertgebouw (recorded by Hilversum Radio), rather than the studio one with Giulini, perhaps as there is a touch more spontaneity in the former. If the piano is marginally too close in both concertos, the sound is acceptable, with surprisingly little difference between the studio and concert sources. Claudio Arrau's contributions (originally Philips) are very fine too: the playing is immaculately aristocratic; but his use of rubato will not suit everyone. Askenase's *Krakowiak concert rondo* –

dating from 1959, but still sounding good – is most enjoyable, and the programme ends with a sparkling account of the *Andante spianato et Grande polonaise brillante* from Zimerman.

Volume 2: (i) *Ballades 1–4;* (ii) *Barcarolle, Op. 60; Berceuse, Op. 57; Etudes, Op. 10, 1–12; Op. 25, 1–12;* (iii) *3 Ecossaises, Op. 72/3; 3 Nouvelles études;* (i) *Fantasy in F min., Op. 49;* (iii) *Funeral March, Op. 72/2*
(M) *** DG DDD./ADD (IMS) 463 051-2 (2). (i) Zimerman; (ii) Pollini; (iii) Ugorski

Krystian Zimerman's impressive set of the *Ballades* and the *Fantasy* are touched by distinction throughout and have spontaneity as well as tremendous concentration to commend them, and the 1987 recordings are of high DG quality. Maurizio Pollini's electrifying account of the *Etudes*, from 1972, remains as satisfying as ever, with the remastering sounding fresh and full. The *Barcarolle* and *Berceuse* (1990) are hardly less impressive. This disc is completed by a series of mainly trifles, recorded in 1999 (except for the *Funeral March*, Op. 72/2) and well played by Anatol Ugorski. This is an outstanding set.

Volume 3: (i) *Mazurkas 1–49.* Mazurkas without Opus numbers: (ii) *2 Mazurkas in A min.: (ami Emile Gaillard); (notre temps); Mazurka in A flat; 2 Mazurkas in B flat; Mazurkas in C; D & G*
(M) *(*) DG (IMS) 463 054-2 (2). (i) Luisada; (ii) Zilberstein

The gifted Tunisian-born pianist Jean-Marc Luisada brings considerable elegance and finesse to the *Mazurkas* but alas, he has difficulty in finding real simplicity of expression and Chopin's line is so often the victim of wilful rubato. There are some good things during the course of this survey, but they are too few and far between to permit any but the most qualified recommendation. For the *Mazurkas* without Opus numbers, DG have made new recordings with Lilya Zilberstein which, although they are better played and have novelty value, do not compensate for the poor set of the famous ones. Good recordings, but this is the least attractive set in DG's Chopin Edition.

Volume 4: *Nocturnes 1–21*
(M) *** DG (IMS) 463 057-2 (2). Barenboim

Barenboim's playing is of considerable eloquence, the phrasing beautifully moulded, yet with undoubted spontaneous feeling. If compared with Rubinstein, these performances lack a mercurial dimension, but they have their own character, with moments of impetuosity preventing any suggestion of blandness. The 1981 recording is first class.

Volume 5: Polonaises and minor works: (i) *Andante spianato et Grande polonaise brillante, Op. 22;* (ii) *Polonaises 1–7;* (iii) *3 Polonaises, Op. 71; Polonaises (without Opus numbers): in A flat; B flat; B flat min.; G min.; G flat & G sharp min.; Album Leaf in E; 2 Bourrées; Cantabile in B flat; Fugue in A min.; Galop marquis in A flat; Largo in E flat*
(M) *** DG DDD/ADD (IMS) 463 060-2 (2). (i) Argerich; (ii) Pollini; (iii) Ugorski

Pollini offers magisterial playing, in some ways more commanding than Rubinstein (and better recorded) though not more memorable. Argerich's *Andante spianato* (1974) is everything it should be: wonderfully relaxed to start with and extrovertly sparkling in the *Grande polonaise*. Ugorski fills in

the gaps with some of Chopin's early works: interesting to hear, sometimes entertaining, but containing only glimpses of the greatness that was to emerge. Excellent value.

Volume 6: Impromptus, Preludes, Rondos and Scherzos: (i) *Impromptus 1–3; 4 (Fantaisie-impromptu);* (ii) *24 Preludes, Op. 28; Prelude in C sharp min., Op. 45; Prelude in A flat, Op. posth.;* (iii) *Rondo in C min., Op. 1; Rondo (La mazur) in F, Op. 5;* (iv) *Rondo in E flat, Op. 16;* (v) *Rondo for 2 Pianos in C, Op. posth. 73;* (vi) *4 Scherzos*
(M) **(*) DG DDD/ADD (IMS) 463 063-2 (2). (i) Bunin; (ii) Argerich; (iii) Zilberstein; (iv) Pletnev; (v) Bauer and Bung; (vi) Pollini

The *Preludes* show Martha Argerich at her finest, spontaneous and inspirational, though her moments of impetuosity may not appeal to all tastes. But her instinct is sure, with many poetic and individual touches. Stanislav Bunin follows on with the *Impromptus* and here the result is not so impressive: he is technically brilliant but can be self-aware and idiosyncratic at times. There is no want of intellectual power or command of keyboard colour in Pollini's accounts of the *Scherzi*. This is eminently magisterial playing. Zilberstein's account of two of the *Rondos* is enjoyable enough, but not as imposing as the Pletnev *Rondo in E flat* which follows, nor as beautifully recorded. This set concludes with Bauer and Bung in the *Rondo for Two Pianos*: here the recording, dating from 1958, is rather thin in sound, with noticeable tape hiss, but the performance is acceptable.

Volume 7: Piano Sonatas and Variations: (i) *Piano Sonatas 1 in C min., Op. 4;* (ii) *2 in B flat min., Op. 35; 3 in B min., Op. 58;* (iii) *Introduction & Variations on a German National Air, Op. posth.;* (iv) *Introduction & Variations on a Theme of Moore for Piano (Four Hands), Op. posth.;* (i) *Variations in A (Souvenir de Paganini);* (iii) *Variations brillantes in B flat, Op. 12;* (v) *Variation 6 from the Cycle 'Hexameron'.* Miscellaneous pieces: *Allegro de concert, Op. 46;* (vi) *Bolero, Op. 19; Tarantella, Op. 43*
(M) **(*) DG 463 066-2 (2). (i) Zilberstein; (ii) Pollini; (iii) Vásáry; (iv) Vladimir and Vovka Ashkenazy; (v) Vladimir Ashkenazy; (vi) Ugorski

This set opens with a newly recorded version of the *First Sonata*, well played by Lilya Zilberstein. Of course, having the two most famous *Sonatas* in equally famous performances following, puts it rather in the shade. Pollini's readings of the *Second* and *Third* are enormously commanding. Both works are played with great distinction, but the balance is just a shade close. The second CD is of lighter fare taken from a variety of sources: Vásáry opens with an enjoyable set of the Op. 12 *Variations*, recorded in 1965 and sounding just a little thin. The Ashkenazys are borrowed from Decca and are in excellent form. Zilberstein's and Ugorski's contributions have been newly made and are (like the sound) good without being exceptional.

Volume 8: Chamber Music and Waltzes: (i) *Cello Sonata in G min., Op. 65;* (ii) *Grand duo concertante in E for Cello & Piano;* (i) *Introduction & polonaise brillante in C for Cello & Piano, Op. 3;* (iii) *Piano Trio in G min. Op. 8;* (iv) *Waltzes 1–17;* (v) *Waltzes in E flat (Sostenuto); in A min., Op. posth*
(M) **(*) DG DDD/ADD (IMS) 463 069-2 (2). (i) Rostropovich, Argerich; (ii) Bylsma, Orkis; (iii) Beaux Arts Trio; (iv) Luisada; (v) Zilberstein

It seems a curious idea to combine the chamber music with the *Waltzes*, particularly as the recordings DG chose for the bulk of the latter are not inspired. Compared to the best available, these accounts seem pale, even though the recorded sound (1990) is good. The chamber music on the second CD is far stronger: the *Piano Trio*, an early work, is not wholly characteristic of Chopin but is certainly of interest. The Beaux Arts' performance could hardly be improved upon and the 1970 recording (originally Philips) is excellent. With such characterful artists as Rostropovich and Argerich challenging each other, a memorable account of the *Cello Sonata* is ensured. The contrasts of character between expressive cello and brilliant piano are also richly caught in the *Introduction and polonaise* and the recording is warm and vivid. In between these two works is the *Grand duo concertante*, played by Anner Bylsma and Lambert Orkis. But the performance does not have the excellence of the Rostropovich/Argerich ones which flank it, nor as flattering a recording.

Volume 9: 17 Songs, Op. posth. 74; Czary, Op. posth.; Dumka, Op. posth
(M) **(*) DG (IMS) 463 072-2. Szmytka, Martineau

The Polish soprano Elzbieta Szmytka (recorded in 1999) has the full measure of these songs and is well supported by Malcolm Martineau. If these performances don't quite come up to memories of the Söderström and Ashkenazy CD (a Decca issue that is currently withdrawn), they are well recorded and are much more than a stopgap. One is surprised how few recordings there have been of these songs, generally a neglected area of Chopin's output, for they are often surprisingly emotional; no lover of this composer or of song in general should be without them. The CD plays for under 47 minutes – Chopin disappointingly not having written enough songs to fill a CD!

Idil Biret Complete Chopin Edition

Piano Concerto 1, Op. 11; Andante spianato et Grande Polonaise brillante, Op. 22; Fantasia on Polish Airs, Op. 13
(BB) **(*) Naxos 8.550368 (with Slovak State PO, Stankovsky)

Piano Concerto 2, Op. 21; Krakowiak; Variations on Mozart's 'Là ci darem la mano'
(BB) ** Naxos 8.550369 (with Slovak State PO, Stankovsky)

Ballades 1–4; Berceuse; Cantabile; Fantaisie; Galop marquis; Largo; Marche funèbre; 3 Nouvelles études
(BB) ** Naxos 8.550508

Mazurkas, Op. posth.: in D; A flat; B flat; G; C; B flat; Rondos, Op. 1, Op. 16 & Op. 73; Rondo à la Mazurka, Op. 5; Souvenir de Paganini; Variations brillantes; (i) Variations for 4 Hands; Variations on a German Theme; Variations on Themes from 'I Puritani' of Bellini
(BB) *** Naxos 8.550367 ((i) with Martin Sauer)

Nocturnes 1–21
(BB) *** Naxos 8.550356/7 (available separately)

Polonaises 1–6; 7 (Polonaise fantaisie)
(BB) **(*) Naxos 8.550360

Polonaises 8–10, Op. 71; in G min.; B flat; A flat; G sharp min.; B flat min. (Adieu); G flat, all Op. posth.; Andante spianato et Grande Polonaise in E flat, Op. 22 (solo piano version)
(BB) **(*) Naxos 8.550361

Piano Sonatas 1, Op. 4; 2 (Funeral March); 3, Op. 58
(BB) *** Naxos 8.550363

Waltzes 1–19; Contredanse in G flat; 3 Ecossaises, Op. 72; Tarantelle, Op. 43
(BB) ** Naxos 8.550365

The Turkish pianist, Idil Biret, has all the credentials for recording Chopin. Among others, she studied with both Cortot and Wilhelm Kempff. She has a prodigious technique and the recordings we have heard so far suggest that overall her Chopin survey is an impressive achievement. Her impetuous style and chimerical handling of phrasing and rubato are immediately obvious in the *First Concerto*, and she makes a commanding entry in the *F minor Concerto*; in the *Larghetto*, too, the solo playing brings a gently improvisatory manner, and the finale really gathers pace only at the entry of the orchestra (which is recorded rather resonantly throughout). Of the other short concertante pieces, the opening of the *Andante spianato* is very delicate and there is some scintillating playing in the following *Grande Polonaise* and *Fantasia on Polish Airs* – and a touch of heaviness, too, in the former. The introductory *Largo* of the *Mozart Variations* is a bit too dreamy and diffuse but, once the famous tune arrives, the performance springs to life. Similarly, the introduction to the charming *Krakowiak Rondo* hangs fire, but again the *Rondo* sparkles, with the rhythmic rubato nicely handled, though the orchestral tuttis could ideally be firmer.

The *Ballades* bring impetuously romantic interpretations where the rubato at times seems mannered; the *Berceuse* is tender and tractable, the *Fantaisie in F minor* begins rather deliberately but opens up excitingly later; though the playing is rather Schumannesque, it is also imaginative; the three *Nouvelles études*, too, are attractively individual.

The disc called *Rondos and Variations* (8.550367) is worth anyone's money, showing Biret's technique at its most prodigious and glittering. Much of the music here is little known and none of it second rate. The *Nocturnes* are a great success in a quite different way: the rubato simple, the playing free and often thoughtful, sometimes dark in timbre, but always spontaneous. The recording is pleasingly full in timbre. The *Polonaises* demonstrate Biret's sinewy strength: the famous *A major* is a little measured but the *A flat* is fresh and exciting and the whole set commanding, while the *Polonaise fantaisie* shows imaginative preparation yet comes off spontaneously like the others. The recital ends with a fine account of the solo piano version of the *Andante spianato* (quite lovely) and *Grande Polonaise*, which is more appealing than the concertante version.

The three *Sonatas* are fitted comfortably on to one CD and, irrespective of cost, this represents one of the finest achievements in Biret's series so far. The *Waltzes* bring charismatic playing, giving opportunities for exciting bravura, but too many of these pieces are pressed on without respite. The *Ecossaises* and *Tarantelle* are also thrown off at almost breakneck speed.

Opus Chopin Edition

Piano Concerto 2 in F min., Op. 21; Fantasy on Polish Airs, Op. 13

'Chopin's Last Concert in Paris' (with music by Bellini, Donizetti, Mozart and Meyerbeer)
*** Opus 111 OP 2012. Olejniczak, Pasiechnyk, etc.

The 150th anniversary of Chopin's death brought a flurry of activity from various companies, none more original or imaginative than that of the Paris-based Opus 111 label. There are ten volumes in all (OPS 2006–15) handsomely produced and intelligently planned, two of which we list above. The first in the series, *Racines* (*Roots*) (OPS 2006), produces the traditional folk music and dances that Chopin would have heard in his youth and which played such a formative role in his musical development. Not only do we hear so much fascinating folk material – mazurkas, polkas and obereks – but we also hear instruments of the period including the suka, an eighteenth-century stringed instrument. This introduction affords a most useful insight into the world that the boy Chopin must have encountered. A second two-CD set brings 9 *Polonaises* and 23 *Mazurkas* played by Janusz Olejniczak (OPS 2007).

One of the most absorbing issues (listed above) is a reconstruction of Chopin's last concert in Paris in February 1848. Olejniczak shines in the Chopin pieces, and the Bellini, Donizetti, Meyerbeer and Mozart items are equally well served by the team that Opus 111 have assembled. Few records so successfully convey the atmosphere of this poignant occasion – and a sense of what concerts were like at that period. The remaining discs – jazz improvisations by the Andrzej Jagodzinski Trio (OPUS 2013), and 'Chopin tomorrow' (OPUS 2014) – are not mandatory purchases, though they have their rewards, as does the last CD, which presents some of the writings about Chopin by such diverse thinkers and writers as Nietzsche, Heine, Proust, Gide, Hermann Hesse and Tolstoy. An enterprising and thought-provoking set which is well worth exploring, but two of the listed discs (OPS 2008 and 2012) are outstanding.

Other Recordings

Piano Concertos 1 in E min., Op. 11; 2 in F min., Op. 21; Fantasy on Polish Airs, Op. 13; Grande Polonaise Brillante, Op. 22; Krakowiak, Op. 14; Variations on 'Là ci darem la mano', Op. 2
*** Decca 475 169-2 (2). Kun-Woo Paik, Warsaw PO, Wit

We have admired what we have heard of Kun-Woo Paik's playing either in the concert hall, in the broadcasting studio or on CD. The present set includes all of Chopin's output for piano and orchestra and does not disappoint high expectations. On the one hand this pianist has plenty of strength and character and, on the other, an abundant poetic feeling. His slow movement of the *E minor Concerto* is very broad (a minute longer than Zimerman and almost two minutes longer than Argerich) but his leisurely approach is on its own terms convincing. The comparisons that come to mind are exalted and, though one would not recommend this set in preference to Zimerman, Kun-Woo Paik's playing is touched by distinction throughout. The recording, made in the Philharmonic Hall, Warsaw, is generally admirable and the piano tone extremely clear and truthful, though there is a certain cloudiness in the bass in orchestral tuttis. Recommended.

Piano Concertos (i) 1; (ii) 2; (i) Krakowiak Rondo in F, Op. 14; Ballade 3 in A flat, Op. 47; Barcarolle, Op. 60; Berceuse, Op. 57; Impromptus 1–3 & Fantaisie-Impromptu; 4 Mazurkas, Op. 41; Nocturnes 1–20; Polonaises 1–7; Polonaise-Fantaisie; 24 Preludes, Op. 28; Scherzos 2 in B flat, Op. 31; 3 in C sharp min., Op. 31 Sonatas 2 (Funeral March) & 3; Waltzes 1–14
(B) **(*) DG stereo/mono 477 5242 (7). Askenase, with (i) Hague Residentie O, Otterloo; (ii) BPO, Lehmann (with MOZART: *Sonata 17, K.570*. LISZT: *Liebestraum 3; Valse oubliée 1*. MENDELSSOHN: *Songs without Words, Op. 19/1–2; Op. 67/4; Scherzo in E min., Op. 16/2*.

SCHUBERT: *Medley of Ländler, Waltzes & Valses sentimentales.* (arr. Askenase). SMETANA: *4 Polkas*)

Stefan Askenase was DG's key Chopin recording artist in the early days of LP, and his recording career stretched for two decades, from 1951 to 1971. Many of his finest records were made during the mono era, but the quality of DG piano recording in the 1950s was of such a high standard that all these records sound very well indeed. So, while DG have chosen here his stereo recording of the *First Piano Concerto* plus the charming *Krakowiak Rondo*, they have preferred the mono version of the *Second* because of the highly sympathetic accompaniment from the Berlin Philharmonic under Fritz Lehmann. The *Waltzes* (1951), with which this survey opens, were long regarded as a gramophone classic in their Heliodor LP format. The playing is characteristically gentle and evocative, the rubato springs naturally from the music, and the comparatively soft outline of the piano suits the music-making perfectly.

The *Second* and *Third Sonatas* (also 1951), *24 Preludes* (1953) and *Nocturnes* (1954) are also all mono recordings, although one would hardly guess it from the quality of the sound. The *Sonatas* are outstanding, showing Askenase to be a magician among Chopin pianists. With his clarity and delicacy he provides sunny, brilliant textures, and if in Chopin's largest-scale works some may find him a little lacking in weight, the sheer imagination of the playing is ample compensation. The *24 Preludes* are hardly less impressive and are played with great sympathy and insight. In the *Nocturnes* his finely graded colours and great sensitivity to dynamic are again admirably enhanced by the excellent recording.

Characteristically, there is no barn-storming in the *Polonaises* (again mono, 1951/2). As always, Askenase relies on subtlety and imagination rather than sheer volume and, being a Pole, he seems naturally to inflect the polonaise rhythms with an infectious lift. There are certainly more exciting versions of the *Polonaise-Fantaisie* than this, but all the other performances can be recommended unreservedly, and the recording withstands its age very well indeed. The *Barcarolle, Berceuse, Ballade No. 3, Scherzi, Impromptus, Op. 41,* and *Mazurkas* are among his later recordings and the stereo shows him still on top form.

Among the bonuses, the Mozart *Sonata* is memorable for its gentle simplicity of approach, and the Smetana *Polkas* are delightfully idiomatic. The Liszt, Schubert and Mendelssohn pieces come from a 1968 stereo recital. The Schubert *Ländler* and *Waltzes* are delectable; the Mendelssohn items are beautifully played too, especially the *Scherzo*, and Liszt's *Liebestraum* is given a full romantic blossoming without sentimentality. The box comes with an excellent biographical note by Jean-Charles Hoffelé.

(i) Piano Concerto 1 in E min., Op. 11: Rondo (only). Nocturne in E flat, Op. 9/2; Scherzi 1–4
*** DG **DVD** 073 4079. Yundi Li, (i) with Warsaw PO, Kord – LISZT: *Sonata* ***

Yundi Li won the Warsaw Chopin Prize in 2000 when he was only eighteen, past winners having included Pollini, Argerich and Krystian Zimerman. He was the youngest winner ever in the competition's history and the first from the People's Republic of China. In 2003 he stood in at the last minute for Mikhail Pletnev in the Philharmonie, Cologne, with the Chopin *Four Scherzi* and the Liszt *Sonata*. He repeated the programme a year later at the Festspielhaus, Baden-Baden; and this is what we are offered here, together with the finale of the Chopin *E minor Concerto*, recorded at the 2000 competition. His playing has delicacy and finesse, undoubted charm and flawless technique. He is perhaps a little headlong in the *First Scherzo*, very much in the manner of Horowitz's post-war recording, but there is a wonderful fire and freshness that carry the listener with it. So it is with the Liszt *Sonata* too. The finale of the *Concerto* makes one understand why he won first prize: it has great character and spirit, and there is poetry and at times wit. Some of the 'promotional videos' in the bonus section are embarrassingly bad (not the playing, of course) but are mercifully short. Good camera direction and excellent sound throughout. Piano fanciers should not hesitate.

Piano Concertos: (i) *1 in E min., Op. 11;* (ii) *2 in F min., Op. 21. Berceuse, Op. 57; Etudes, Op. 10/1–12; Op. 25/1–12; Impromptus 1–3; Fantaisie-Impromptu; Introduction & Variations on a German National Air, Op. posth.; Mazurkas, Op. 7/1; Op. 67/2–3; in A flat and D, Opp. posth. Polonaise in A flat, Op. 53; Sonatas 2 (Funeral March), Op. 23; 3, Op. 58*
(B) **(*) DG (ADD) 477 5510 (3). Vásáry; (i–ii) BPO; (i) Semkow; (ii) Kulka

Tamás Vásáry recorded a good deal of Chopin repertoire between 1963 and 1965 for DG, naturally following his colleague, Stefan Askenase. He is a somewhat self-effacing although always a poetic artist: in the two concertos his gentle poetry is in clear contrast with the opulent orchestral sound (especially in No. 1, where the Berlin Philharmonic recording is more resonantly expansive than in No. 2). Yet soloist and orchestra match their styles perfectly in both slow movements, which are played most beautifully, and the finales have no lack of character and sparkle. In their way these performances give considerable pleasure. So do the *Etudes*, for Vásáry's keyboard prowess is second to none, and there is both brilliance and fine taste throughout. If the *Berceuse* is just a shade deliberate and the *Impromptus* are also comparatively direct, both *Sonatas* fare admirably in Vásáry's hands. These performances are unaffected, beautifully shaped, and controlled with a masterly sense of rubato. Altogether this is highly accomplished playing, and he is accorded sound throughout that is both lifelike and natural so that one wonders why DG's reissued survey was confined to three discs and omitted the *Ballades*, *Nocturnes* and *Waltzes*.

Piano Concertos (i) *1 in E min.;* (ii) *2 in F min.*
(BB) ** HMV (ADD) 5 86719-2. Ohlsson, Polish Nat. RSO, Maksymiuk

Garrick Ohlsson's pairing of the two concertos is to be reckoned with. He is an impressive player with no lack of technical aplomb and finesse to commend him. But he is not as subtle or aristocratic as Pollini – nor, for that matter, is his conductor, who is distinctly earthbound in the tutti of the *F minor*. The recording is good, but this is not a first choice for this coupling.

Andante spianato & Grande Polonaise brillante, Op. 22; Ballades 1–4; Mazurkas, Op. 24/2; Op. 56/3; Op. 59/1–3; 3 Nouvelles Etudes; Nocturne in B, Op. 62/1; Polonaise fantaisie, Op. 61; Scherzos 1–3
(M) *** RCA 82876 72554-2 (2). Ax

Emanuel Ax is much less well-known in England than he is in the USA, where he has the highest reputatation, especially in the music of Chopin. This two-disc recital shows why. Although recorded at different times, between 1975 and 1987,

and at different venues (ranging from RCA's New York City Studio to the Henry Wood and Walthamstow Halls in the UK), the playing has the vibrant projection of a live recital, with a consistent flow of spontaneous feeling, only very occasionally affected by touches of self-consciousness. Ax's style is impulsively extrovert but with moments of affecting intimacy, as in the *Nocturne in B major* and the three *Nouvelles Etudes*, which are highlights. The *Ballades* are impetuously full of romantic flair and the *Scherzi* equally striking for their confident bravura, but there is no lack of imaginative poetic feeling, especially in the *Mazurkas*, while the closing *Polonaise-Fantaisie* is very commanding indeed. The recording is at times a little hard, but the piano is given striking presence and realism.

(i) *Andante spianato & Grande Polonaise brillante, Op. 22; Barcarolle, Op. 60; Fantaisie in F min., Op. 49; Polonaises 1–16;* (ii) *Boléro, Op. 19; 3 Ecossaises, Op. 72; Tarantelle, Op. 43; Variations brillantes on Halévy's 'Je vends des scapulaires', Op. 12*
(BB) **(*) EMI Gemini (ADD) 4 76930-2 (2). (i) Ohlsson; (ii) Ronald Smith

While still barely out of his teens Garrick Ohlsson won the 1970 Chopin Contest in Warsaw, and this début recording from 1972, a comprehensive collection of the *Polonaises*, including the juvenilia and the *Grande Polonaise brillante*, helps to explain why. The *Barcarolle* and *Fantasy in F minor* date from the following year, and are all admirably recorded at Abbey Road. Ohlsson has a weighty style and technique very much of the modern American school, but with it all he is thoughtful. When he uses a flexible beat, it is only rarely that the result sounds wilful.

Ronald Smith, who plays the rest of the programme – mostly display pieces – brilliantly, has an appropriately lighter touch.

(i) *Berceuse in D flat, Op. 57;* (ii) *Cantabile in B flat; Contredanse in G flat;* (iii) *Etudes, Op. 10/1–10; Op. 25/1–10;* (iv) *3 Nouvelles Etudes;* (v) *Impromptus 1–3; Fantaisie Impromptu, Op. 66; 19 Waltzes*
(BB) *** EMI Gemini (ADD/DDD) 3 50874-2 (2). (i) Barenboim; (ii) Barto; (iii) Gavrilov; (iv) Laval; (v) Anievas

For this anthology EMI have dipped into their archives most perceptively, and there is not an indifferent performance here. The main part of the collection is shared by Gavrilov and Augustin Anievas. Gavrilov's *Etudes* bring an exuberant virtuosity that it is impossible to resist, even if some of the tempi are breathtakingly fast, as in what Joan Chissell (in her excellent notes for the original issue) described as the 'spitfire velocity' of Op. 10/4, or the 'dancing triplets' of Op. 10/5 in G flat. Yet the sustained legato of the famous *No. 3 in E major* is lovely, and Gavrilov's poetic feeling, both here and in *No. 6 in E flat minor*, is indisputable. The impulsive bravura is often beguiling, so that one needs to take a breath on the soloist's behalf after the furious account of the *Revolutionary Study*; but this is prodigious playing, given a bold, forward, digital recording to match. For the three *Nouvelles Etudes* EMI turn to Danielle Laval, who is less extrovert than Gavrilov but not less convincing.

Anievas gives us all the *Waltzes*, including the five published posthumously. His playing is quite different from Gavrilov's and has a mellower, beautiful, analogue piano recording to match. The opening *Grande valse brillante* is a little lacking in dazzle, and Anievas is better in the reflective music than in providing glitter. Yet his technique is absolutely secure, and there is much to enjoy. He is also very successful in characterizing the three *Impromptus*, and the *Fantaisie-Impromptu* (which is used to open the second disc) certainly does not lack panache. The two miniatures, *Cantabile* and the *Contredanse in G flat*, which come at the end of the recital, are inconsequential, but Tzimon Barto brings out their guileless charm, and the second disc ends with a simple, poetic account of the lovely *Berceuse* from Daniel Barenboim, very naturally recorded.

(i) *Études, Opp. 10 & 25*; (ii) *24 Preludes, Op. 28*; (iii) *Sonata 2 in B flat min., Op. 35*
*** BBC/Opus Arte **DVD** OA 0893 D. (i) Kempf; (ii) Perl; (iii) Hewitt

These performances will be familiar to viewers of BBC Four, where they opened evening broadcasting from time to time. The *Preludes* were recorded by Alfredo Perl in Hopetoun House, Edinburgh, Kempf's *Etudes* in France at Château de Neuville, Gambais, and Angela Hewitt's Op. 35 at Wimbledon Theatre. In all three instances the performances are of quality and are free from any intrusive idiosyncrasies. Moreover, the camerawork in each location is of the old school, never fussy or wanting to draw attention to itself, but managed with discretion and taste. This DVD is very modestly priced, given the amount of music offered, and will give much pleasure.

Etudes, Op. 10/1, 2, 4–6, 12; Op. 25/5 (with transcriptions by Godowsky). Combination Godowsky transcriptions:
Op. 10/5 & Op. 25/9 combined in a G flat 'Badinage';
Op. 10/11 & Op. 15/9 combined in F; Alt-Wien
Triakontameron 11; Waltz, Op. 64/1
*** Warner 2564 62258-2. Berezovsky

It is easy to feel that Chopin's *Etudes* have enough notes, without the bravura roulades and ornamentation added by Godowsky, but he is ingenious enough to laminate more than extra decoration on the originals. Certainly, if these transcriptions are going to be recorded, Boris Berezovsky is just the man to play them; and to perform them with the added tension of live performance makes the bravura even more dazzling. In each case he presents Chopin's own piece before playing the transcription, and if in some cases – Op. 10/2, for instance – there is little advantage, in others he produces what is almost a new work, as in the two rearrangments of Op. 10/5. The transcriptions for the left hand only are certainly remarkable in the way they retain the essence of the originals, and Berezovsky places the serene Op. 10/6 at the centre of the programme. Yet even here, who would prefer the added decoration to the calmer original? The combination of Op. 10/5 and Op. 25/9 is quite witty, while the *Triakontameron* make an engaging little miniature. The closing *Minute Waltz*, is made to last 3 minutes 19 seconds by Godowsky, and it does not outstay its welcome, when Berezovsky presents it so beguilingly. Indeed, his sympathetic virtuosity is remarkable throughout, and the audience are not intrusive until at the end they rightly convey their admiration. The recording, made at Snape Maltings, is first class.

Etudes, Op. 10/6; Op. 25/3–4, 10–11; 4 Mazurkas, Op. 17;
Piano Sonata 3 in B min., Op. 58
(B) *** Virgin 4 82120-2. Andsnes

Andsnes proves as impressive an interpreter of Chopin as he is of Grieg, and here he has the advantage of state-of-the-art piano-sound. The programme here is arbitrary, but every piece is illuminatingly played.

Nocturnes, Opp. 9, 15, 27, 32, 37, 48, 55, 62 & Op. post. 72
** DG 477 4718. Pollini

Maurizio Pollini is very well recorded in the fine acoustic of the Herkulessaal, Munich, and he seems more deeply (even if less than completely) engaged in this wonderful repertoire than he was in his recent Beethoven. He is careful to eschew sentimentality – and at times sentiment itself! The pianism is often magnificent and there is much that excites admiration. All the same, he rarely touches the listener or takes us by surprise, but there are moments of tenderness.

24 Preludes, Op. 28; 25–26, Op. posth.
(M) **(*) Ph. (ADD) 475 7768. Claudio Arrau

The Arrau set, now reissued as one of Philips's Originals, is much admired, and he received a typically fine Philips recording, opulent and full-bodied, and with plenty of detail and presence; and it does justice to his subtle nuances of tone. Every prelude bears the imprint of a strong personality, to which not all listeners may respond. Yet his performances appear to spring from an inner conviction, even if the outer results will not be universally liked. Louis Lortie is a safer recommendation, the best we have had in recent years (Chandos 9597) and Ashkenazy on a Double Decca, offering also the *Scherzi* and *Waltzes*, remains a paramount interpreter of this repertoire.

RECITAL COLLECTIONS

Andante spianato et Grand polonaise brillante, Op. 22;
Ballade 1 in G min., Op. 23; Berceuse in D flat, Op. 57;
Fantasia in F min., Op. 49; Mazurkas: in D flat, Op. 30/3; in
B min., Op. 33/4; in A min., Op. 68/2; Scherzo 2 in B flat
min., Op. 31; Sonata 2 in B flat min., Op. 35; Waltzes: in A
flat, Op. 34/1; in A flat, Op. 69/1; in E flat, Op. posth.
*** Opus Arte **DVD** OA 9404D. Arturo Benedetti Michelangeli

Chopin playing of the highest artistry from Michelangeli, recorded in Milan in 1962. The visual side of the recording is in black-and-white, but his piano playing is full of colour. The clarity of articulation is phenomenal, as is the subtlety of his tone colouring. The *B flat minor Sonata* is one of the great performances on record, and the delicacy of the *Andante spianato* is pretty breathtaking. Michelangeli always insisted on a narrow range of camera angles and no facial close-ups, so that the somewhat static camera angles never intrude or disturb the extraordinary concentration he commands. Altogether outstanding performances throughout. The recorded sound is quite acceptable, if not as truthful and realistic as commercial recordings of the period.

(i) *Etudes: in G flat, Op. 10/5 & Op. 25/9;*
Fantaisie-Impromptu, Op. 66; Nocturne 10 in A flat,
Op. 32/2; Polonaise 3 in A (Military), Op. 40/1; (ii) *Préludes:*
in A & D flat, Op. 28/7 & 15; Waltzes: 1 in E flat, Op. 18; 3 in
A min., Op. 34/2; 11 in G flat, Op. 70/1; (iii) *Etude in E,*
Op. 10/3; Nocturne 2 in E flat, Op. 9/2; Polonaise 6 in A flat
(Heroic), Op. 53; Prélude in A, Op. 28/7; (iv) *Ballade 1 in G*
min., Op. 23; Etude in C min. (Revolutionary), Op. 10/12;
Waltzes: 6 in D flat (Minute); 7 in C sharp min., Op. 64/1–2
(BB) **(*) HMV (ADD/DDD) 5 86720-2. (i) Adni; (ii) Alexeev; (iii) Ogdon; (iv) Donohoe

This programme, shared by four different pianists from the EMI roster, opens with five items from Daniel Adni. He begins with an arresting account of the *Fantaisie-Impromptu*, and here, as elsewhere, his musicianship is matched by the kind of effortless technique that is essential to give Chopin's music its basic line and flow. Dimitri Alexeev then takes over, and his sensibility in this repertoire is hardly less remarkable. John Ogdon's items do not disappoint either, and the *E major Etude* is beautifully played. The recital is completed by Peter Donohoe, who is fleet-fingered and highly accomplished but more matter-of-fact, especially in the *Ballade*, which is untouched by distinction. Fine recording throughout.

CILEA, Francesco (1866–1950)

Adriana Lecouvreur (complete DVD version)
*** Opus Arte **DVD** OA LS 3011 D. Freni, Dvorský, Mingardo, Cossotto, La Scala, Milan, Ch. & O, Gavazzeni

Recorded in 1989, when Lamberto Puggelli's lavish production was new, this version of *Adriana Lecouvreur* from La Scala is far more successful than the recording of the same production made for TDK 11 years later. That is largely because the original cast is so much more assured and vocally well focused than the later replacements, and the veteran Gianandrea Gavazzeni is a masterly conductor in this music. Mirella Freni in the title-role as the great singing actress might easily have been overparted, but her projection is strong and positive, with the tenderness of her two big arias well caught. Peter Dvorský is first rate as Maurizio, strong, firm and unstrained, and Fiorenza Cossotto with her rich mezzo makes a splendid foil for Freni. Visually, with Brian Large as video director, the extravagance of the elaborate and ultra-realistic sets and costumes is wonderfully brought out.

CIMAROSA, Domenico (1749–1801)

Double Flute Concerto in G
(*) RCA 09026 63701-2. James & Jean Galway, LMP – DEVIENNE: *Flute Concertos* *

Although not momentous music, Cimarosa's concerto for a pair of flutes has undeniable charm, and its gay final *Rondo* is quite memorable. The only drawback is the composer's emphasis on florid writing, with the two solo instruments playing consistently in thirds and sixths. Here, although Galway is well up to form, the playing of his partner, Jean, while technically accomplished, is paler in timbre and personality. Even so, with good accompaniment and excellent sound this is agreeable enough.

Overtures: *La baronessa Stramba; Cleopatra; Il convito; Il credulo; Il falegname; L'impresario in angustie; L'infedelté fedele; Il matrimonia segreto; Il ritorno di Don Calendrino; Le stravaganze del conte; La vergine del sole; Voldomiro*
*(*) Marco Polo 8.225181. Esterházy Sinf., Amoretti

A disc of Cimorosa's overtures was sorely needed, but this does not fill the gap. The orchestra plays quite well for Alessandro Amoretti, and one enjoys the often witty melodic invention along the way, but it takes a Beecham or a Toscanini – with a first-class orchestra – to transform such works into something special. As it is, the collection here (which includes the first recording of the Vienna version of the *Il matrimonio segreto* overture) only intermittently displays the sparkle of Cimarosa's invention. The recording is only average, lacking

in depth and brilliance in general, with the strings in particular sounding rather thin. At Naxos price it would be more recommendable.

Il fanatico per gli antichi romani: Overture. Il matrimonio segreto: Overture; (i) *Udite, tutti udite*
(BB) **(*) Warner Apex (ADD) 2564-62418-2. Lausanne Chamber O, Jordan, (i) with Huttenlocher – DONIZETTI: *Overtures;* MERCADANTE: *Sinfonia sopra i motive dello Stabat mater di Rossini* ***

Attractive, elegant music, but the performances and recording, while good, do not quite match the sparkle of the Donizetti/Mercadante Monte Carlo recordings.

Il matrimonio segreto (opera; complete CD version)
❀ (M) *** DG 476 5303. Fischer-Dieskau, Augér, Varady, Hamari, Rinaldi, Ryland Davies, ECO, Barenboim

Restored to the catalogue as part of Universal's 'Penguin Rosette Collection', Barenboim's is a fizzing performance of Cimarosa's comic masterpiece. The setting may not have the finesse of the greatest Mozart, and in duller hands it can seem conventional – but not here, when the singing is as sparkling as the playing. The joys are similar to those of Mozart, and some of the ensembles in particular, not least the Act I finale, relate directly to *Figaro*. Fischer-Dieskau relishes the chance to characterize the old man, Geronimo, who wants to find aristocratic husbands for his two daughters, but the three principal women singers are even more compelling, with Arleen Augér and Julia Varady singing superbly. Their sisterly duets (especially the lively Act I example with its crisp triplets) are among the most captivating items in the whole work. Alberto Rinaldi as Count Robinson, secretly promised to the elder daughter, Ryland Davies as Paolino, secretly married to the younger, along with Julia Hamari as Geronimo's sister, make up an outstanding cast, and the warmly atmospheric recording has transferred vividly to CD.

CLEMENTI, Muzio (1752–1832)

(i) *Piano Concerto in C. Symphonies: in B flat & D, Op. 18; 1 in C; 2 in D; 3 (Great National) in G; 4 in D. Minuetto pastorale; Overtures in C & D*
(M) ** ASV CDDCS 322 (3). (i) Spada; Philh. O, D'Avalos

Symphonies: in B flat & D, Op. 18/1-2; 1-4. Minuetto pastorale; Overtures in C & D
(M) ** ASV CDDCS 247 (2). Philh. O, D'Avalos

Symphonies: 1 in C; 2 in D; 3 in G (Great National Symphony); 4 in D
(BB) *** Warner Apex (ADD) 2564 62762-2. Philh. O, Scimone

Clementi, publisher as well as composer, tragically failed to put most of his symphonic output into print, and it has been left to modern scholars to unearth and, in many cases, reconstruct the works which were being performed around 1800, some of them prompted by Haydn's visit to London. All four works here, made available thanks to the researches of Pietro Spada, amply explain Clementi's high reputation in his lifetime as a composer for the orchestra, not just for the piano. The most immediately striking is the *Great National Symphony*, with *God save the King* ingeniously worked into the third movement so that its presence does not emerge until near the end. Scimone's Philharmonia performances are both lively and sympathetic, the recording is excellent, and this disc is well worth its modest cost.

D'Avalos gets spirited playing from the Philharmonia, though he is not as strong on subtleties of phrasing as Scimone. The ASV performances are now available either in a three-disc set including the *Piano Concerto* (an arrangement of a piano sonata, where Piero Spada appears as the secure and accomplished soloist) or, even more economically, on a pair of CDs without the concerto. The bonus items are common to both.

Piano Sonatas: in G min ., Op. 7/3; in F min., Op. 13/6; in B flat, Op. 24/2; in F sharp min., Op. 25/5; in D, Op. 25/6
(M) **(*) Divine Art Diversions 24113. Katin

Peter Katin plays a square piano built by Clementi and Company in 1832 (the year of the composer's death) which has subsequently been restored. So the sounds he creates are as authentic as one could find. The work which comes off best in this recital is the *G minor Sonata*, Op. 7/3, with its spirited opening movement, central *Cantabile et lento* and lively finale with its gruff bass figurations, which sounds so effective on the fortepiano. So does the finale of the *D major*, Op. 25/6, very nicely articulated, and the *F minor Sonata* seems exactly suited to the instrument. Katin's approach is plainspun but sympathetic, and he is very realistically recorded.

Piano Sonatas: in F min., Op. 13/6; in F sharp min., Op. 25/5; in G min., Op. 34/2
** Häns. 98.114. Sager (piano)

Christopher Sager is less concerned than others to draw the parallel between Clementi and Beethoven. Playing with appealing gentleness, he is at his best in slow movements – the *Lento e patetico* of Op. 25/5 and the *Adagio* of the *F minor Sonata*, where he is less commanding in the *agitato* of the opening movement and the finale. The outer movements of the *G minor Sonata*, too, although presented very musically, are less than stormy. He is very well recorded, but this CD only extends to 47'40".

CLIFFE, Frederic (1857–1931)

Symphony 1 in C min., Op. 1; Cloud and Sunshine (Orchestral Picture)
✪ *** Sterling CDS 1055-2. Malmö Opera O, Fifield

Frederic Cliffe was born in Bradford in 1857 and is thus contemporary with Elgar. On the staff of the Royal College of Music, he suddenly came to the fore when his *First Symphony* was premièred in 1889, receiving enthusiastic plaudits from every quarter. The symphony is indeed an astonishing achievement for a young composer and gives absolutely no impression of inexperience. It is readily comparable in warmth and constructional skill with, for instance, the *First Symphony* of Gounod, but it has a much greater affinity with the early symphonies of Dvořák.

The stabbing opening duplet leads to a strong opening idea, and the heart-warming secondary theme is to be matched in lyrical memorability with the slow movement, which opens seductively with a cor anglais solo. Its ardent climax is to be later transformed into the powerful close of the finale. There is an engagingly pithy, syncopated Scherzo to separate the first two movements, and the finale has a Mendelssohnian sparkle and grace, producing another endearing

secondary melody, and moving through an assured contra puntal development to its expansively powerful close. The orchestration throughout is vivid, showing a natural flair especially in its richly Wagnerian scoring for the horns and brass. In short, this is a remarkably inventive and fluent work which one returns to with much pleasure.

The orchestral picture of *Cloud and Sunshine* is equally confident in its pictorial evocation, if not as memorable thematically as the symphony. Both are played with zest warmth and spontaneity by the fine Malmö orchestra, under their dedicated and understanding conductor, Christopher Fifield. In his notes he asks the obvious question why Cliffe's music has disappeared into oblivion, suggesting that (along side the rising dominance of Elgar) the all-powerful Stanford might have been jealous of Cliffe as a highly skilled potential rival. There is more of Cliffe to discover, including a *Violin Concerto*; meanwhile his *Symphony* is well worth acquiring especially in a performance and recording as red-bloodedly compulsive as this.

CLIFFORD, Hubert (1904–59)

Born in Australia, Hubert Clifford took a degree in Chemis try at Melbourne University, though he was active as a violist conductor and composer. He came to Britain in 1930 to study with Vaughan Williams and never returned home. He taught in Kent and subsequently joined the BBC, working for what is now the World Service, before becoming the BBC's Head of Light Music in the early 1950s.

String Quartet in D
(M) *** Dutton Epoch CDLX 7163. Locrian Ens. – BAINTON: *String Quartet* ***

The *String Quartet in D* comes from 1935 and was broadcast twice in the following year and again (twice) in 1946. It is a well-fashioned piece whose discourse is civilized and pleas ing, very much pre-war in feeling. There is some Gallic influence and evidence of his Irish origins, some generations back. The material does not quite sustain its length, but all the same it is well served by the Locrian Ensemble, and the Dutton recording is very truthful.

COATES, Douglas (1898–1974)

Violin Concerto in D
(M) (**) Divine Art mono 27806. Sauer, BBC N. O, Groves – MOERAN: *Violin Concerto* (***)

You won't find Douglas Coates in *Grove*, *Baker* or any other of the standard musical encyclopaedias. Coates came from Rotherham in Yorkshire and pursued a career as organist and choirmaster, alongside a working life in the Midland Bank whose choir and orchestra he also conducted. His *Violin Concerto* of 1935 is very much in the tradition of Elgar, Ireland and Finzi. Had he received encouragement and thorough schooling, he might have gained in confidence and creativity. In his fascinating notes Lewis Foreman shows how unhappy he was with this studio recording, with Charles Groves unconvinced by the piece, and the composer depressed and dispirited. Herbert Howells and Mosco Carner, writing in their confidential BBC reports, were critical of Coates's orchestral writing – and perhaps rightly so! But the idiom is very sympathetic, lyrical and warm, though the structure is very lopsided: the first movement takes over 15 minutes and he remaining two only four minutes each. Ultimately there is o sense of real mastery, or what the German call *Meister-chaft*. The music wanders and there is relatively little sense of rganic growth. However, the overall impression is congenial nd the piece is very well played by Colin Sauer. However, llowances have to be made for the recording, which derives om 78-r.p.m. acetates. Nevertheless, this is well worth hear-ng.

COATES, Eric (1886–1957)

) *By the Sleepy Lagoon;* (ii) *Calling all Workers: March;* iii) *Cinderella (Phantasy); From Meadow to Mayfair: Suite; ondon Suite; London again Suite;* (i) *The Merrymakers Overture;* (iii) *Music everywhere: March;* (iii; iv) *Saxo-Rhapsody;* (i) *The Three Bears (phantasy);* (ii) *The Three Elizabeths: Suite;* (i) *The Three Men: Man from the ea (only);* (iii) *Wood Nymphs (valsette)*

⏵ (B) *** CfP (ADD) 3 52356-2 (2). RLPO, Groves; CBSO, Kilbey; or LSO, Mackerras

t is good to welcome back this key collection of the music of ric Coates, 'the man who writes tunes', much loved by rchestral players as he also writes so gratefully for their nstruments, being an ex-orchestral player himself. On the vhole, Groves, who has the lion's share of the repertoire here, roves a persuasive advocate, although occasionally his pproach is slightly bland. Jack Brymer is the excellent soloist n the *Saxo-Rhapsody;* and the other piece with a diluted jazz lement, *Cinderella,* also goes with a swing. However, not urprisingly, the performances from Sir Charles Mackerras nd the LSO are even more lively, and there are also several eally outstanding ones from the CBSO under Reginald Kil-ey. He proves the ideal Coates conductor, with a real flair for atching the sparkle of the composer's leaping allegro figura-ions, notably in the first movement of *The Three Elizabeths,* vhere also his shaping of the central, slow movement – one f the composer's finest inspirations, dedicated to the late Queen Mother – has an affectionate grace. The marches are plendidly alive and vigorous. With good transfers this is the est Coates compilation currently available.

Calling All Workers March; Dambusters March; The Jester at he Wedding; London Suite; The Merrymakers Overture; The Elizabeths Suite. (i) *Songs: The Green hills o' Somerset; Stonecracker John*

M) ** BBC BBCM 5011-2. BBC Concert O, Boult; (i) with Wallace

An exceptionally generous collection (76 minutes) of Eric Coates favourites, including the three best-known marches: *Dambusters, Knightsbridge* and *Calling All Workers.* Most mportantly, the programme includes Coates's finest orches-ral work, *The Three Elizabeths.* The charming and little-nown ballet suite, *The Jester at the Wedding,* is played quite lelightfully and Boult sees that the marches have plenty of hythmic swing. The fine bass-baritone, Ian Wallace, is also on hand to give resonant accounts of two of Coates's most uccessful ballads. The orchestral playing is lively enough, if ot immaculate; but the recording does not flatter the violins nd suggests that there were not too many of them. Good alue, nevertheless.

The Four Centuries: Suite; The Jester at the Wedding: Ballet Suite; The Seven Dwarfs

M) **(*) ASV CDWHL 2075. East of E. O, Nabarro

Malcolm Nabarro offers a particularly delectable account of *The Jester at the Wedding Ballet Suite. The Four Centuries* is a masterly and engaging pastiche of styles from four different periods, and again it receives a performance of some subtlety, although at times one wishes for a more opulent sound from the violins, and the closing jazzy evocation of the 1930s and 1940s could be more uninhibitedly rumbustious. *The Seven Dwarfs* is an early work (1930), a ballet written for a short-lived London revue.

VOCAL MUSIC

Songs: *Always as I close my eyes; At sunset; Bird Songs at Eventide; Brown eyes I love; Dinder courtship; Doubt; Dreams of London; The Green hills o' Somerset; Homeward to you; I heard you singing; I'm lonely; I pitch my lonely caravan; Little lady of the moon; Reuben Ranzo; Song of summer; A song remembered; Stonecracker John; Through all the ages; Today is ours*

(M) *** ASV CDWHL 2081. Rayner Cook, Terroni

Eric Coates, as well as writing skilful orchestral music, also produced fine Edwardian ballads which in many instances transcended the limitations of the genre, with melodies of genuine refinement and imagination. Brian Rayner Cook, with his rich baritone beautifully controlled, is a superb advocate and makes a persuasive case for every one of the 19 songs included in this recital. His immaculate diction is infectiously demonstrated in the opening *Reuben Ranzo* (a would-be sailor/tailor), in which he breezily recalls the spir-ited projection of another famous singer of this kind of repertoire in the early days of the gramophone, Peter Daw-son. The recording is admirably clear.

COATES, Gloria (born 1938)

Symphonies (i) *1 (Music on Open Strings);* (ii) *7 (Dedicated to those who brought down the Wall in Peace;* (iii) *14 (Symphony in Microtones)*

(BB) Naxos 8.559289. (i) Siegerland O, Rotter; (ii) Bav. RSO, Henzold; (iii) Curfs, Munich CO, Poppen

It is perhaps unfortunate that this Gloria Coates listing comes near the music of Eric (no relation, of course). But she certainly is not the writer of tunes. Kyle Gann, the author of the sleeve-note of this CD, suggests (reasonably enough) that 'there is always something going on in her music. Her para-digms are few, but they are varied in ingenious ways. Coates's reliance on simple processes involving motion makes her music somehow turbulent and stable at once.'

For us, her dominating vocabulary includes weird continu-ing glissandos, upwards and downwards, which defeat the ears of someone looking for musical logic, plus the use of scordatura and divided strings, with half tuned a quarter-tone lower than the other half, and so on. In spite of the contributions of the three notable orchestras to these per-formances, we find the sounds she creates not only over-whelming but indescribable (we could add a more pejorative adjective).

To quote Gann again, 'she creates sound masses in per-petual motion that we've never heard before. It is music that in its intensity could "rive the nerves asunder". That's exactly the experience we shared, and it was not agreeable.

COLERIDGE-TAYLOR, Samuel (1875–1912)

African Dances, Op. 58; Hiawatha Sketches, Op. 16; Petite suite de concert, Op. 77; Violin Sonata, Op. 28
(M) *** Dutton Epoch CDLX 7127. Juritz, Dussek

Coleridge-Taylor's *Violin Sonata* of 1897 (premièred by Albert Sammons) has much of the easy melodic facility of the *Violin Concerto*, to come some years later, with a readily appealing central *Larghetto*. The engaging *Petite suite de concert*, familiar from its orchestral version, works just as well in this format. The *Hiawatha Sketches*, also inspired by Longfellow, pre-date the famous cantata by two years, and are pleasing light music, as are the later *African Dances*. All agreeable music, very well played by David Juritz and Michael Dussek, while the Dutton recording balance cannot be faulted.

COLES, Cecil (1888–1918)

Behind the Lines (suite): excerpts: Estaminet de Carrefour; Cortège (orch. Brabbins). Overture: The Comedy of Errors; From the Scottish Highlands (suite); Scherzo in A min.; (i) Fra Giacomo (scena for baritone and orchestra); (ii) 4 Verlaine Songs
*** Hyp. CDA 67293. BBC Scottish SO, Brabbins; with (i) Whelan; (ii) Fox

Cecil Coles, a close friend of Gustav Holst, died of wounds received on the Somme in April 1918. His career was brief but brilliant, with a period of study from 1908 on a scholarship in Stuttgart, which led to his being appointed assistant conductor at the Stuttgart Royal Opera House. As a bandmaster in the army during the war, he continued to compose, culminating in the suite *Behind the Lines*, from which the two surviving movements are included on this pioneering disc of his music. The scores were hidden away for over 80 years, until they were unearthed by his daughter, Catherine. What immediately strikes one about all the pieces is their confidence and skill, with clean-cut ideas crisply presented and beautifully orchestrated. The bustling *Comedy of Errors Overture* is typical, a piece that deserves to be in the regular repertory; and the dramatic scena, *Fra Giacomo* for baritone and orchestra to a poem by Robert Williams Buchanan, brings out the influence on Coles of Wagner, a melodramatic monologue, positive and red-blooded. The *Scherzo in A minor* is rather more adventurous stylistically, with its angular brass motif at the start, possibly a movement designed to be included in a full symphony, while the *Four Verlaine Songs*, using English translations, sound more German than French in their warmly romantic idiom. The suite *From the Scottish Highlands*, one of the earliest pieces here, dating from 1906–7, is easily lyrical, with a Scottish folk element, ending with a moving *Lament*; but it is the two movements from *Behind the Lines* that capture the imagination most. The first, *Estaminet de Carrefour*, is a jolly genre piece picturing a typical crossroads tavern, while the final *Cortège*, preserved only in short score and sensitively orchestrated by the conductor, is an elegiac piece that in this dedicated performance has a gulp-in-throat quality, bringing home more than anything the tragedy of a career cut short. Splendid performances

throughout, not least from the two singers, and warm, well-balanced recording.

COLLINS, Anthony (1893–1963)

Eire; Festival Royal Overture; The Lady with the Lamp; Louis XV Silhouettes; Symphony 1 for Strings; The Saga of Odette; Santa Cecilia; Vanity Fair; Victoria the Great
✪ (M) *** Dutton CDLX 7162. BBC Concert O, Wilson

Anthony Collins is famous mainly for his Decca LPs. He was the ideal recording conductor, as he was able to bring music vividly to life in the studio, and his Decca Sibelius cycle was a classic of the post-war LP era. This is the first CD devoted to his own highly enjoyable music. It opens with the patriotic *Festival Royal Overture* (first performed in 1956) and while it uses such obvious quotations as *God save the Queen* and the 'Big Ben' chimes, it builds its own themes into a most entertaining work. The same patriotic spirit pervades his music to the 1937 film *Victoria the Great* (Collins wrote many successful film scores and spent much of his life in Hollywood). Both the opening *Prelude* and final *Victoria Regina* have something of the spirit of Elgar and Walton in patriotic mode, with a sumptuous regal theme that is very beguiling.

Ear-tickling colours (including piquant use of the harpsichord) run through the delightful pastiche, *Louis XV Silhouettes* (1939), which culminates in the jolly *At Luciennes* portraying Madame du Barri, Louis XV's exotic mistress. The three-movement suite, *Eire*, based on Irish folk-tunes, is equally attractive, especially the toe-tapping final Reel, *Flutter's Hooley*.

The *Song of Erin*, subtitled 'Lamentation', written at the end of the Second World War, shows the composer in a more serious mood; it is a haunting and beautiful piece and deserves to be better known. *Valse Lente* is a short and nostalgic evocation, originally used in the 1950 film *Odette* and from the 1951 film *The Lady with the Lamp* the composer extracted the title theme and the music from the ball scenes to produce the *Prelude and Variations* included here.

The most recent work on the CD, *Santa Cecilia*, dates from 1959, although the composer gave no hint of its inspiration. However, Lewis Foreman, the excellent sleeve-note writer, has decided that it is a portrait of a church of the same name in Rome. In the *Symphony for Strings* (1940), Collins's penchant for pastiche is to the fore; its outer movements are witty and tuneful, and are separated by a slow movement of some charm. His most famous piece of all is the disarmingly simple *Vanity Fair*. First performed in 1952, this is the composition he most wanted to be remembered for, and indeed it is an exquisite little miniature of the sort that cheers you up every time you hear it.

John Wilson and the BBC Concert Orchestra play all his music with great affection and style, and they are well supported by Dutton's engineering team. The ✪ is for all concerned in recording this anthology, but especially for Anthony Collins, who can now be assured of being remembered for more than just *Vanity Fair*.

CONFREY, Edward (1895–1971)

African suite; Amazonia; Blue Tornado; Coaxing the Piano; Dizzy Fingers; Fourth Dimension; Jay Walk; Kitten on the

Keys; Meandering; Moods of a New Yorker (suite); Rhythm Venture; Sparkling Waters; Stumbling Paraphrase; 3 Little Oddities; Wisecracker Suite
*** Marco Polo 8.223826. Andjaparidze

Older collectors will surely remember *Kitten on the Keys* and perhaps *Dizzy Fingers* and *Coaxing the Piano* (all dazzlingly played here). Confrey established his international fame as a precocious virtuoso pianist/composer in the early 1920s. His music has a witty charm and is clearly influenced by French impressionism as well as by Gershwin and the Scott Joplin rags. The Georgian pianist Eteri Andjaparidze gives engagingly sparkling performances of the bravura pieces, including the ingenious closing *Fourth Dimension* with its amazingly virtuosic cross-hand accents, and she is equally at home in the more relaxed ragtime of *Jay Walk*, *Stumbling* and the sauntering gait of *Meandering*. But she also relishes the atmosphere and charm of the gentler pieces among the *Oddities* and the suites (two of the *Moods of a New Yorker* recall the tranquil simplicity of MacDowell's *To a wild rose*). A most entertaining collection, given excellent piano recording.

COOK, James (20th century)

We know very little about James Cook, except that he went to Oxford in 1994 to study music, and in 1998 he took a post at Eton College. He was quite prolific and has written over 100 works of various kinds, very much inspired by his religious feelings.

ORGAN MUSIC

Heaven and Hell Epitomised: 2 Sacred Lessons; Man's Fourfold State (Suite); Organ Symphony; 2 Voluntaries
*** Divine Art 25031. Hartley (organ of Manchester College Chapel)

It is always good to hear new music written for and played on an English organ, and the present repertoire was both composed for and premièred on the Manchester College Chapel instrument, a year before the composer died. As can be seen from the choral songs below, Cook's music is dominated by his powerful Christian faith, and in his organ works one might make a correlation with Messiaen, yet there is not a trace of Gallic influence in Cook's writing.

The epic programme of the *Organ Symphony*, 'an odyssey of the soul and spirit', and the *Suite, Man's Fourfold State*, are realized in the organ's rich changing colours and sonorities, rather than in virile musical arguments. Yet the underlying tension holds the listener, not least in the second movement of the symphony, which has a mesmeric forward impulse depicting 'the journey of the soul into the spiritual realm'. The following *Proem* (or preamble) is an interlude, but the finale imaginatively juxtaposes four themes representing Death, Judgement, Heaven and Hell, with Heaven winning out seraphically at the close.

The triumph of the Christian belief in heaven also dominates the other music here. The *Fourfold State of Man* is more concentrated in its invention, with the first three movements (*In Eden*, *In Nature* and *In Grace*) attractively mellow and colourful, and a triumphant mini-toccata for the celestial finale. The two *Voluntaries* bring a strong contrast, the one bold and energetic, the other dreamy and languorous; and the closing double *Epitomisation* brings a comparable dissimilarity, suggesting first the agony of the Cross (a chorale

and chaconne) and, secondly, another evocation of heaven, rocking gently and elegiacally. Myles Hartley is a very persuasive advocate on this splendid organ, and he prevents the musical flow from becoming static. He is very well recorded indeed.

VOCAL MUSIC

Choral Music: *All loves excelling; (i) Beyond the moveable heavens; Christ's blood is heaven's key. Christ's matchless love; Death is my best friend; Heavenly death; He was most lovely; If this be dying; I give to thee eternal life; In the primrose of my days; The lap of eternity; O lovely heaven; That which we call death is not death; (i) The way to heaven. When death cuts asunder; We shall meet in comfort at our journey's end*
*** Divine Art 25027. Voces Oxoniensis, Frowde; (i) with I. Evans (organ)

It is in the field of *a cappella* choral music that James Cook's musical style emerges at its most individual. Indeed it is as strikingly personal and individual as, say, the vocal writing of Britten or Tavener. All these choral songs have a pervading preoccupation with death – but not death seen as a threat, rather as a release, sometimes peaceful, often joyous, into a new life. Cook chooses texts primarily from the sixteenth and seventeenth centuries, when 'their Christian or Puritan authors may have suffered the most persecution of any minority. No wonder that the Puritans tackled the dark issues of suffering and death head-on. Their attitude to death was not to sweep it under the carpet, but to face up to it.'

Cook's music is inspired to respond to every mood, and it often moves forward in unexpected ways. *When Death cuts asunder*, for instance, is a brief canon in which the four voices enter a major third apart 'which is harmonically disorientating, an ideal way to depict the transition of the soul from the body to heaven', while *That which we call death is not death* is fugal with unpredictable progressions, yet it ends serenely.

Alternatively, his melodic lines can be simple and gently touching, as in the pair of *Lachrymae, Run sweet babe* and *If this be dying. The lap of eternity*, however (using just seven voices), has an Elysian rocking rhythm and is totally hypnotic.

He was most lovely, In the primrose of my days, and *Christ's matchless love* are described by the composer as 'hymnsongs' and, like the *Lachrymae*, share a pleasing lyrical simplicity. Only three of the songs use the organ 'to add drama and gravitas to the music'. During *In the way to heaven* and *Beyond the moveable heavens*, the organ part is orchestral, either following the voices or providing a hypnotic backdrop, with the bass pedal notes gently growling. These two are among the most memorable pieces here. But the most striking and the longest is *Christ's blood is heaven's key* (drawing on the imagery of Psalm 23's 'Valley of the Shadow of Death'), which rises to a great climax. Here Cook takes his sopranos soaring up high; elsewhere, he demands sudden upward leaps, and this presses hard on the lead singer here; otherwise the Voces Oxoniensis are on excellent form and handle the unexpected progressions confidently.

COOKE, Arnold (born 1906)

Arnold Cooke was born in Gomersal, near Leeds. He showed early musical promise and, while reading history at Cambridge, was encouraged by Professor Edward Dent to change to a music degree. In 1929 he moved on to the Berlin Hochschüle and was a pupil of Hindemith for three years. In 1933 (again through Dent's influence) he was appointed Professor of Composition at the Royal Manchester College of Music. He later moved to London and, after naval war service, in 1947 took a similar teaching post at Trinity College of Music. During the following four decades he wrote six symphonies; but after an early period of success, like many other 'traditional' composers (he was a contemporary of Rawsthorne, Benjamin Frankel and Elisabeth Lutyens) his music became unfashionable, and the last symphony was never performed.

(i) *Cello Sonata 2*; (ii) *Viola Sonata*; (iii) *Violin Sonata 2*
*** British Music Soc. BMS 432CD. Terroni, with (i) Wallfisch; (ii) Goff; (iii) Stanzelett

In the 1970s Lyrita recorded Cooke's *Third Symphony*, a well-made, enjoyable work which, like this collection of sonatas, may not break new ground but on record can provide just the sort of occasional refreshment which eludes many listeners with records of more 'advanced' music. Something of Hindemith remains in his style, most noticeably in the *Viola Sonata* of 1936/7, which is comparatively sinewy, yet has a deeply felt *Andante*, and plenty of vitality in the finale. The *Cello Sonata* was written in 1979/80 (and is due to receive its concert première by Raphael Wallfisch and Raphael Terroni on 4 November 2006, the centenary of the composer's birth). While the Hindemith influence remains, there is far more of Cooke himself here, and the first movement is positive in theme and argument. The *Lento*, improvisatory in feeling, has a touching lyricism, and the jolly, very rhythmic finale bounces along with great confidence.

But undoubtedly the most attractive of these three works is the *Violin Sonata* of 1980, which sets off with a buoyant main theme and a skipping impetus, and has a yearning melody for its *Andante*. The finale, with its cross-rhythms, also has an underlying lyrical impetus and is capped by a neatly managed fugato. All three performances are most persuasive and truthfully recorded, if lacking a little in resonant warmth.

COPLAND, Aaron (1900–90)

Billy the Kid (Ballet) *Suite & Waltz*; *Rodeo: 4 Dance Episodes & Honky Tonk Interlude*
(M) **(*) RCA SACD (ADD) 82876 67904-2. O, Gould –
GROFÉ: *Grand Canyon Suite* **(*)

Although you would never guess it from the richness of the sound of this new Living Presence SACD, Morton Gould's recordings of Copland's two cowboy ballets (in three-track stereo) date from 1957. They never made it to the British catalogue, as excellent alternative recordings by Bernstein, Ormandy and the composer himself soon became available, and this is their first appearance on CD. Gould's performances are vividly characterized and full of vitality, and the expressive music (the *Corral Nocturne* in particular) has a romantically luxuriant languor, all this emphasized by the warmly atmospheric recording. While Bernstein's versions have a more idiomatic, abrasive bite, Gould's vigour and his natural affinity (as a ballet composer himself) with Copland's rhythmic style is infectious, and he includes the *Honky Tonk* piano sequence and *Saturday Night Waltz* in *Rodeo*. The technicolor sound is gorgeous, if perhaps a shade over-resonant for music designed for the ballet pit.

Symphony 3; Music for the Theatre
(M) ** Telarc CD 80201. Atlanta SO, Levi

In brilliant Telarc sound Levi and the Atlanta Symphony Orchestra give a powerful performance of Copland's most ambitious symphony, but the weight tends to iron out imagination, making for squareness, and in thrust and urgency this cannot compare with the versions by the composer and Bernstein. The account of *Music for the Theatre* equally misses some of the jazzy vigour of Copland's inspiration.

CORELLI, Arcangelo (1653–1713)

Ciaconna, Op. 2/12; Concerto grosso, Op. 6/5; Sonate da chiesa, Op. 1/9–10; Op. 2/4; Op. 3/5; Op. 4/2; Trio Sonata, Op. 5/3
(BB) **(*) Virgin 2x1 4 82097-2 (2). L. Bar. – PURCELL: *Fantasias & In nomines* **(*)

The London Baroque collection mixes church and chamber sonatas with an impeccable feeling for the style of the period and a continuo which includes archlute and organ, appropriately. Ornamentation is judicious and intonation is secure. Though not lacking vitality, the performances here are graceful and comparatively restrained, lighter in feeling and texture than some versions, and thus providing an individual and comparatively intimate approach. The *Concerto grosso* from Op. 6 could ideally sound more robust but these performances are certainly enjoyable, and the Abbey Road recording is admirably transparent and vivid.

Concerti grossi, Op. 6/1–12
(B) ** Chan. 6663 (2). Cantilena, Shepherd

Adrian Shepherd's Cantilena are excellently recorded, but their playing is not as polished as that of Marriner and the ASMF. Their approach is genial, but slow movements are sometimes rather lazy-sounding, while the lively music lacks the pointed rhythms characteristic of the best period-instrument performances.

CORNELIUS, Peter (1824–74)

Der alte Soldat, Op. 12/1; 3 Chorgesänge, Op. 11; Die Könige, Op. 8/3; Leibe: Ein Zyklus von 3 Chorliedern, Op. 18; 3 Psalmlieder, Op. 13; So weich und warm; Requiem; Trauerchöre, Op. 9; Trost in Tränen, Op. 14; Die Vätergruft, Op. 19
*** Hyp. CDA 67206. Polyphony, Layton

Building on the German tradition of amateur choral societies, Peter Cornelius developed the genre of unaccompanied choral pieces like these, starting with the one which became by far the most famous, *Die Könige* ('The Three Kings'). Cornelius, a lifelong devotee of German verse, responded to the words with keen sensitivity, heightening the poems he set to make the genre an equivalent to Lieder, spanning a wide range of moods and atmosphere with beautifully crafted choral effects. Stephen Layton's brilliant group, Polyphony, prove ideal as interpreters, refined on detail, polished in ensemble, while giving thrust and intensity to each item. Beautifully balanced and atmospheric recording to match.

CORRETTE, Michel (1709–95)

6 Organ Concertos, Op. 26

(B) *** HM (ADD) HMA 195 5148. Saorgin (organ of L'Eglise de l'Escarène, Nice), Bar. Ens., Bezzina

These lively and amiable concertos make a very welcome return to the catalogue; they are given admirably spirited and buoyant performances, splendidly recorded using period instruments. The orchestral detail is well observed, and René Saorgin plays vividly on an attractive organ. Michel Corrette's invention has genuine spontaneity and this makes an unfailingly enjoyable collection: just play the final *Concerto in D minor* if you have any doubts.

COUPERIN, François (1668–1733)

KEYBOARD MUSIC

Harpsichord Suites, Book I: Ordre 2: Les Idées heureuses. Ordre 3: La Favorite; La Lutine; Ordre 4: Le Réveil-matin. Book II: Ordre 6: La Mézangère; Ordre 7: La Ménetou. Book III: Ordre 13: Les Lis naissans; Les Rozeaux; L'Engagement; Les Folies françoises ou Les Dominos; L'âme-en-peine; Ordre 14: Le Rossignol-en-amour; La Linote-éfarouchée; Les Fauvètes plaintives; Le Petit-rien; Ordre 15: Le Dodo, ou L'amor au Berçeau; Ordre 16: La Distraite; L'Himen-amour; Ordre 19: La Muse-Plantine

●— *** Hyp. CDA 67520. Hewitt (piano)

Angela Hewitt centres her third and last (and perhaps finest) Couperin collection on the *Treizième Ordre* of Book III, which she considers one of Couperin's finest suites. It includes *Les Folies françoises ou Les Dominos*, a miniature theme-and-variations on the famous *La Folia* bass, with each variation depicting a different character arriving at a masked ball in an invisible cloak (domino). Among the other hand-picked items are four engaging (if not scrupulously accurate) evocations of various birds and their songs from the *Quatorzième Ordre* of the same Book, and she closes with *La Ménetou* (from the *Septième Ordre*) depicting Françoise Charlotte de Ménethoud, a gifted singer, dancer and musician. Angela Hewitt comments in the excellent notes: 'The piece remains in the lower half of the keyboard giving it an extra gentleness. That is one quality that is really possible to bring out when playing Couperin on the piano.'

As before, she follows all the composer's ornamentation, and her playing is as fresh and as full of variety of colour and dynamic as ever, while the piano is very naturally recorded.

Harpsichord Suites: Prélude 3 in G; Book I: Ordre 5. Book II: Ordre 7

(M) *** DHM/BMG 82876 70000-2. Leonhardt (harpsichord)

It is good to return to distinguished performances of Couperin's keyboard music by Gustav Leonhardt on the harpsichord. There is no doubt that modern accounts on the piano have revealed new facets to this remarkable repertoire, but Leonhardt's playing has the added gravitas of a natural authority through a lifetime's experience, while the performances have no lack of life and spontaneity. He uses a 1962 copy by Martin Skowroneck of a Duelcken of 1746 which has a fine sonority in the chosen acoustic, which is not too resonant. Leonhardt's ornamentation is impeccable, his playing never rigid, yet his articulation is clean and positive. But to achieve a realistic effect it is important not to set the volume level too high. The only piece he plays in common with Angela Hewitt in her recital above is *La Ménetou*, which opens the *Septième Ordre*. A direct comparison shows their tempi to be almost identical, with the piano able to provide a rather darker atmosphere, but the harpsichord still catches the music's gentleness.

ORGAN MUSIC

Messe des Paroisses; Messe des couvents

●— (BB) *** Naxos 8.557741/42. Robin (organ of Poitiers Cathedral)

(B) *** Cal. (ADD) CAL 3907.8 (2). Isoir (organ of St Germain des Prés) (with: Jean-Henry D'ANGELBERT: Quatuor. Louis COUPERIN: Chaconne in D min.; Branle de Basque; Fantaisie; Pasacaille. Gilles JULIEN: Prélude; Cromorne en taille & Dialogue. Jehan TITELOUZE: 4 Plainsong Hymns: Ave Maris Stella; Exultet Coelum; Pange Lingua; Veni Creator)

Couperin's pair of *Organ Masses* each consist of 21 versets, which are intended to alternate with the text of the Mass, sung in plainchant. Each section is brief, and there are five versets for the *Kyrie*, nine for the *Gloria*, three for the *Sanctus* and two for the *Agnus Dei*. Only in two, for the *Offertory* and *Deo Gratias*, could the composer expand himself, and Couperin chooses to do this only in the *Offertory*. His Masses have been recorded in the past with the sung plainchant included, but the organ versets stand up well independently, and both recordings here have dispensed with the plainchant.

Of the two, the *Messe à l'usage des Paroisses* (Parishes) is the more imposing, and it especially suits the magnificent organ at Poitiers, while the *Messe à l'usage des Couvents* (Convents) is written for a more modest instrument and does not require a pedalboard with independent stops. André Isoir uses two different, completely authentic organs: at Saint Germain des Près and the J. K. Koenig instrument of SarreUnion respectively; and his recording won a Grand Prix du Disque.

The two Calliope CDs include also much other music: an attractive triptych by Gilles Julien, a brief but characterful *Quatuor* by Jean-Henry d'Angelbert, and a particularly winning suite of pieces by Louis Couperin (*Chaconne*, *Branle de Basque*, *Fantaisie* and an impressive *Pasacaille* with 39 variations) piquantly registered for the Koenig instrument. There are also four *Hymnes*, treated with variations by Jehan Titelouze, considered to be the father of French organ music. So for an overall survey of this repertoire, Isoir's set, most faithfully recorded, is an obvious primary recommendtaion. But for the general collector, Jean-Baptiste Robin's splendid performances of just the *Masses*, given magnificent, modern, digital recordings, will be an obvious choice.

Leçons de ténèbres pour le Mercredi Saint

(B) *(*) HM HMA 195113. Jacobs, Darras, Concerto Vocale, Jacobs (with PURCELL: Divine hymn; Evening hymn; CLARKE: Blest be those sweet regions **(*))

René Jacobs's singing seems emotionally overloaded and over-dramatized. Although his phrasing and intonation cannot be faulted, the result is curiously unmoving. He is joined in the Third Lesson by Vincent Darras. The other pieces on the disc are much more successful. Purcell's *Divine* and *Evening Hymns* (the latter doubtfully attributed) are sung quite eloquently, and a remarkably fine hymn from Jeremiah Clarke (of *Trumpet Voluntary* fame).

COWARD, Noël (1899–1973)

Bitter Sweet (musical play)

*** That's Entertainment CDTER 2 1160 (2). Masterson, Smith, Ashe, Maxwell, New Sadler's Wells Opera Ch. & O, Reed

The idea of writing his pastiche Viennese operetta came to Noël Coward in 1928 after hearing an orchestral selection from *Die Fledermaus* on a gramophone record. Hours later, his car parked on Wimbledon Common under the shade of a huge horse-chestnut tree, the story of its heroine, Sari Linden, was planned and some of the principal melodies began to form in Coward's sub-conscious. The score was finished a year later and the composer relates how the great hit-tune (perhaps the finest sentimental operetta melody written after Lehár's *Merry Widow Waltz*) came to him 'whole and complete', while waiting in a 22-minute traffic-jam in a London taxi.

Bitter Sweet was an enormous success in its time, but then it disappeared from the repertoire, although there have been comparatively recent revivals in Plymouth and – very appropriately – Wimbledon. The present re-creation at the New Sadler's Wells Opera, so vividly caught on this recording, could hardly be better cast. Valerie Masterson is a wholly engaging Sari and Martin Smith makes a fine partner in the delicious *Dear little café* and the famous *I'll see you again*. There are lots of fizzing ensembles, not least *Ladies of the Town* (well led by Donald Maxwell) and of course the bouncy *Ta-ra-ra-boom-de-ay*, which few realize derives from this source. But the other great number of the show – Coward at his most endearing – comes from a subsidiary character, the (appropriately named) Manon's sad little soliloquy, *If love were all*, sung with just the right blend of tenderness and philosophical resignation by Rosemary Ashe. Michael Read directs the show with fine spirit and much affection (the orchestral *Bitter Sweet Waltz* has a nice Viennese lilt) and the recording is brightly atmospheric.

(i) *Bitter Sweet* (highlights). Songs: (ii) *Dearest Love; I'll see you again; Mad dogs and Englishmen; The party's over now; The stately homes of England; Mrs Worthington; Some day; You were there*

(B) **(*) CfP (ADD) 3 35956-2. Bronhill; (i) Jason, d'Alba, Hampshire, Fyson, John McCarthy Singers, O, Johnny Douglas, or New World Show O, Alwyn; (ii) Williams, Grenfell, Lisa Gray Singers, Brian Fahey & his O

Presented in very bright and up-front 1969 sound, *Bitter Sweet* emerges vividly, and with superb diction from all concerned. June Bronhill as the Marchioness is a joy, and if Neville Jason as Carl Linden seems a little weak by comparison, there is nothing here to seriously mar one's enjoyment. Susan Hampshire's sole contribution is her little song – a peach of a number – *Bonne nuit, merci* (*Lorsque j'étais petite fille*), which is sung with delicious piquancy (seemingly recorded some years earlier). The performances have great verve as a whole, with Coward's songs sounding as wonderful as ever. The fill-ups (from 1964/5) are fascinating: while they can never compete with Coward's own unique recordings, it's great fun to hear Kenneth Williams in *Mad dogs* and *Mrs Worthington* (both very well done), June Bronhill superb in

Someday I'll find you (one of Coward's most touching numbers) and Joyce Grenfell adding her own magical twist to *The party's over*.

COWELL, Henry (1897–1965)

(i) *Symphonies: 11 (Seven Rituals of Music); 15 (Thesis);* (ii) *Hymn and Fuguing Tune 3;* (i) *Ongaku for Orchestra*

**(*) First Edition (mono/stereo) FECD 0003. Louisville O; (i) Whitney; (ii) Mester

With his use of chord clusters, and stroking and plucking the strings inside the piano, Henry Cowell was one of the pioneers of American modernism and from his earliest years was open to the influence of Asian and other musics. Like Harry Partch, he is an important figure in American music. His exploratory tastes and his appetite for the avant garde made him an ideal composer for the Louisville Orchestra's project to commission and record new repertoire. They commissioned his *Eleventh Symphony* (1954) and his *Ongaku* (1957), inspired by what Cowell calls 'the sunny splendor of Japanese music'. In its day the recording of the *Eleventh Symphony* was something of a state-of-the-art sound (when you played the mono LP, the need for stereo did not arise, so vivid and well laid out was the aural picture). Returning to this symphony after some 50 years, one realizes that, despite some striking sonic effects from bells and percussion, the invention is rather thin. The *Fifteenth Symphony* (1961) was premièred at Louisville and taken into the studio immediately afterwards. It and its companions are all likeable if insubstantial pieces. Cowell's exploratory attitude attracts one, but the music itself inspires mixed feelings. His pupil, the composer Lou Harrison, paid tribute in verse to his eclecticism and wisdom: 'he alerted ears to gamelan and/gagaku, and a thousand other joys' and also 'his advice to drink of gin in summer/and in winter to take whiskey or rum'. Sensible advice, perhaps, when playing this music!

COWEN, Frederick (1852–1935)

Symphony 3 in C min. (Scandinavian); The Butterfly's Ball; Concert Overture; Indian Rhapsody

** Marco Polo 8.220308. Slovak State PO (Košice), Leaper

The *Symphony No. 3* (1880) shows (to borrow Hanslick's judgement) 'good schooling, a lively sense of tone painting and much skill in orchestration, if not striking originality'. But what Cowen lacks in individuality he makes up for in natural musicianship and charm. His best-known work is the *Concert Overture, The Butterfly's Ball* (1901), which is scored with Mendelssohnian delicacy and skill. The *Indian Rhapsody* (1903) with its naive orientalisms carries a good deal less conviction. The performances are eminently lively. The recording is pleasingly reverberant but somewhat lacking in body.

CRAMER, John Baptist (1771–1858)

Piano Concertos 2 in D min., Op. 18; 7 in E, Op. 56; 8 in D min, Op. 70

*** Chan. 10005. Shelley, LMP

John Baptist Cramer, born in 1771 – the year after Beethoven – was brought from Mannheim to London when he was a child and became one of the influential figures in British music-making until his death, a leading virtuoso pianist as well as a composer and music-publisher. This fine disc offers superb accounts of three of his nine piano concertos, including the last two, Nos. 7 and 8. The style is like a cross between Mozart and Mendelssohn with touches of Weber, and far more than many virtuoso pianists Cramer avoids empty passagework in favour of strong arguments built on memorable ideas. Structurally, much the most striking of the three is *No. 8 in D min.*. The first movement is unceremoniously curtailed after the exposition, so that the slow movement (complete with written-out cadenza) and Spanish dance finale are made to provide the necessary resolution, helped by thematic borrowings from the first movement. Howard Shelley plays with dazzling brilliance throughout, directing the London Mozart Players from the keyboard.

CREMA, Giovanni Maria De (died c. 1550)

Con lagrime e sospiri (Philippe Verdelot); De vous servir (Claudin de Sermisy); Lasciar il velo (Jacques Arcadelt); O felici occhi mieie (Arcadelt); Pass'e mezo ala bolognesa; Ricercars quinto, sexto, decimoquarto, decimoquinto, duodecimo, tredecimo; Saltarello ditto Bel fior; Saltarello ditto El Giorgio; Saltarello ditto El Maton

(BB) *** Naxos 8.550778. Wilson (lute) – DALL'AQUILA: *Lute Pieces* ***

The pieces here are taken from a *First Lute Book*, which De Crema published in 1546. The inclusion of the dance movements alongside reflective pieces like *Con lagrime e sospiri* gives variety to an attractive programme, and the *Pass'e mezo ala bolognesa* is rather catchy. The performances are of the highest order, and Christopher Wilson is recorded most naturally. Well worth exploring, especially at such a modest cost.

CUI, César (1835–1918)

(i) *Suite concertante* (for violin & orchestra), *Op. 25. Suite miniature 1, Op. 20; Suite 3 (In modo populari), Op. 43*
**(*) Marco Polo 8.220308. (i) Nishizaki; Hong Kong PO, Schermerhorn

These pieces have a faded period charm that is very appealing (try the *Petite marche* and the equally likeable *Impromptu à la Schumann* from the *Suite miniature*) and are very well played by the Hong Kong Philharmonic. Takako Nishizaki is the expert soloist in the *Suite concertante*. An interesting issue that fills a gap in the repertoire, and very decently recorded too.

Preludes 1–25
(BB) **(*) Naxos 8.555567. Biegel

Of all the members of the 'Kutchka' or 'Mighty Handful' (Balakirev, Borodin, César Cui, Mussorgsky and Rimsky-Korsakov), Cui is by far the least well known. Born in Vilnius, the son of a French officer who had remained in Lithuania after the Napoleonic retreat, he briefly studied with Moniuszko in Warsaw before embarking on a military career (he was an authority on fortifications). His was a talent of minuscule proportions beside those of his four friends, although he was an acerbic, opinionated critic. These *Preludes* have a certain charm, though in *No. 13 in F sharp* the debt to Tchaikovsky is strong – and even stronger in its successor,

which is almost a paraphrase of the *Valse à cinq temps* of Tchaikovsky's Op. 72 set. There is also a lot of Schumann and even more Mendelssohn here. Slight and derivative though many of these pieces may be, there is still much worthwhile music among these miniatures, and Jeffrey Biegel gives decent and faithful accounts of them. The recordings come from 1992 and are perfectly acceptable, although the piano has not been perfectly conditioned.

CUVILLIER, Charles (1877–1955) & CARR, Howard (1880–1960)

The Lilac Domino (highlights)
(B) *(*) CfP (ADD) 3 35981-2. Cochrane, Young, Rita Williams Singers, O, M. Collins – KERKER: *The Belle of New York*; LEHAR: *Merry Widow* (highlights) **(*)

The Lilac Domino was first performed in 1912 in Leipzig as *Der lila Domino*; it then transferred to America in 1914 (with its English title), then to London in 1918, where numbers appended by Howard Carr added to the work's success. Five numbers of this gently pleasing music are included here, well sung and played, but with a curious recording which, although bright, places the solo voices seemingly in their own over-reverberant acoustic.

CURZON, Frederick (1899–1973)

The Boulevardier; Bravada (Paso doble); Capricante (Spanish Caprice); Cascade (Waltz); Dance of an Ostracised Imp; Galavant; In Malaga (Spanish Suite); Punchinello: Miniature Overture; Pasquinade; La Peineta; Robin Hood Suite; (i) Saltarello for Piano & Orchestra; Simonetta (Serenade)
*** Marco Polo 8.223425. (i) Cápová; Slovak RSO (Bratislava), Leaper

The best-known piece here is the *Dance of an Ostracised Imp*, a droll little scherzando. But the *Galavant* is hardly less piquant and charming, the delicious *Punchinello* sparkles with miniature vitality, and the *Simonetta* serenade is sleekly beguiling. Curzon liked to write mock Spanishry, and several pieces here have such a Mediterranean influence. Yet their slight elegance and economical scoring come from cooler climes further north. Both *In Malaga* and the jolly *Robin Hood Suite* are more frequently heard on the (military) bandstand, but their delicate central movements gain much from the more subtle orchestral scoring. The performances throughout are played with the finesse and light touch we expect from this fine Slovak series, so ably and sympathetically conducted by Adrian Leaper. The recording is admirable.

DALL'ABACO, Evaristo Felice (1675–1742)

Concerti a quattro de chiesa, Op. 2/1, 4, 5 & 7; Concerti a più instrumenti, Op. 5/3, 5 & 6; Op. 6/5 & 11
*** Teldec 3984 22166-2. Concerto Köln

Dall'Abaco's foreign travels exposed him to both French and Italian influences, and he draws on them just as it suits him. We also find him astutely keeping up with public taste and subtly modifying his style over the years. Of the four *Concerti a quattro da chiesa*, taken from his Op. 2 (1712), *No. 5 in*

G minor is a particularly fine work, worthy of Corelli. The Op. 5 set of *Concerti a più instrumenti* (*c.* 1719) brings predominantly French influences, and very appealing they are. Op. 6 (*c.* 1734) is more forward-looking, *galant* in style, with amiable allegros and nicely expressive cantabiles. All in all, this is a most stimulating collection. The Concerto Köln's virtuosity brings a sparkling response, with the group's somewhat abrasive string-timbres infectiously bending to the composer's force of personality. They are splendidly recorded. A real find.

DALL'AQUILA, Marco (*c.* 1480–1538)

Amy souffrez (Pierre Moulu); La cara cosa; Priambolo; Ricercars 15, 16, 18, 19, 22, 24, 28, 33, 70 & 101; 3 Ricercar/Fantasias; La Traditora

(BB) *** Naxos 8.550778. Wilson (lute) – CREMA: *Lute Pieces* ***

Marco dall'Aquila was a much-admired Venetian composer/lutenist in his day. These are relatively simple pieces, rhythmically active but often dolorous; *Amy souffrez* and *La cara cosa* are among the more striking, but the *Ricercars* can be haunting too. They are beautifully played by Christopher Wilson, and the recording is admirably balanced.

DAMASE, Jean-Michel (born 1928)

Quintet for Flute, Harp, Violin, Viola & Cello; Sonata for Flute & Harp; Trio for Flute, Harp & Cello; Variations 'Early Music' for Flute & Harp

*** ASV CDDCA 898. Noakes, Tingay, Friedman, Atkins, Szucs

Jean-Michel Damase was a pupil of Alfred Cortot and Henri Büsser, and his chamber music (and in particular the *Trio for Flute, Harp and Cello* and the *Quintet*) has a fluent, cool charm. It is beautifully fashioned, and those coming to it for the first time will find it very attractive, with touches of Poulenc without his harmonic subtlety. It is nicely played and very well recorded.

Piano Music: *Apparition; Introduction et Allegro; 8 Etudes; Sonate; Sonatine; Thème et Variations*

(M) *** Somm SOMMCD 034. Unwin

Damase's piano music is witty, elegant and, above all, unpredictable, with the *Apparitions* opening in a vision of delicacy and, after constantly shifting visions and textures, closing a little less enigmatically. The *Etudes* are chimerical, skipping and fluttering by turns, and with a debonair *Andantino* leading on to a glittering finale of bumble-bee bravura. The *Sonata* too, with its gruff opening toccata, moves from the bell-like sonority of the *Andante* to a turbulent finale which suddenly changes gear in midstream, to end reflectively. The *Sonatine* epitomizes the composer's finest features, neatly crafted and unostentatiously charming, especially the winningly debonair finale. The *Theme and* (fifteen) *Variations* alternate between slow and fast variants very engagingly until the penultimate good-natured *Allegro ma non troppo* returns us to a celestial restatement of the opening idea. All in all, a delectable cocktail of French pianistic *bon-bons*, played with affection and nimble dexterity by a pianist who always anticipates the surprises around the corner.

DA PONTE, Lorenzo (1749–1838)

L'ape musicale

**(*) Nuova Era 6845/6 (2). Scarabelli, Matteuzzi, Dara, Comencini, Teatro la Fenice Ch. & O, Parisi

This greatest of librettists was no composer, but he was musical enough to devise a pasticcio like *L'ape musicale* ('The Musical Bee') from the works of others, notably Rossini and Mozart. The first act – full of Rossinian passages one keeps recognizing – leads up to a complete performance of Tamino's aria, *Dies Bildnis*, sung in German at the end of the act. Similarly, Act II culminates in an adapted version of the final cabaletta from Rossini's *Cenerentola*. The sound is dry, with the voices slightly distanced. The stage and audience noises hardly detract from the fun of the performance.

DAWSON, William (1899–1990)

Negro Folk Symphony

*** Chan. 9909. Detroit SO, Järvi – ELLINGTON: *Harlem, The River; Solitude* ***

William Dawson began life the son of a poor Alabama labourer, yet he worked his way up to become Director of Music at the Tuskegee Institute. His *Negro Folk Symphony* is designed to combine European influences and Negro folk themes. All three movements are chimerical. The music is rhapsodic and has plenty of energy and ideas, but they are inclined to run away with their composer. Järvi, however, is persuasive and has the advantage of excellent orchestral playing and first-class Chandos sound.

DEBUSSY, Claude (1862–1918)

(i; ii) *Berceuse héroïque;* (ii; iii) *Danses sacrée et profane pour harpe et orchestre;* (i; iv) *Jeux;* (i; ii) *Marche écossaise;* (v) *Le Martyre de Saint-Sébastien: Fragments symphoniques;* (i; iv; vi) *Première Rapsodie pour Clarinet*

**(*) Australian Ph. Eloquence (ADD) 476 8502. (i) Concg. O; (ii) Van Beinum; (iii) Berghout, Amsterdam Chamber Mus. Soc.; (iv) Haitink; (v) LSO, Monteux; (vi) Pieterson

Monteux's classic account of music from *Le Martyre de Saint-Sébastien* offers vivid yet refined playing from the LSO in good (1962) sound. The delicacy of texture in Debussy's exquisite scoring is most perceptively balanced by Monteux and he never lets the music become static. Haitink's unsurpassed late-1970s accounts of *Jeux* and the undervalued *Première Rapsodie* are beautifully refined and atmospheric, (and very well recorded, too). Van Beinum offers distinguished performances of the *Marche écossaise* and *Berceuse héroïque* (good early stereo) as well as the *Danses sacrée et profane*, in decent enough (1952) mono (Decca) sound. An imaginative programme with equally imaginative performances.

(i) *Images;* (ii) *Jeux; Khamma;* (i) *La Mer;* (ii) *Prélude à l'après-midi d'un faune; Printemps.* (iii) *2 Arabesques;*

Children's Corner; Estampes; Images, Book 1; L'Isle joyeuse; Page d'album: Pièce pour le vêtement du blessé; La Plus que lente; Pour le piano; Préludes, Book 1
(BB) ** Virgin 562261-2 (4). (i) Rotterdam PO; (ii) Finnish RSO; Saraste; (iii) Pommier

Images; La Mer; Nocturnes: Nuages; Fêtes (only); Prélude à l'après-midi d'un faune
**(*) Australian Decca Eloquence (ADD) 476 8472. LSO, Monteux

It is good to see these excellent Monteux performances coupled together, although it was a pity that the conductor did not include *Sirènes* in his (1962, Decca) set of the *Nocturnes*. As it is, the *Nuages* drift by gently and *Fêtes* has an atmospherically luminous quality. The *Prélude à l'après-midi d'un faune* is coolly beautiful, if not the most atmospheric on disc. Monteux's *Images* is notable for its freshness and impetus. A vivid yet refined feeling for colour is found here, and the delicacy of Debussy's scoring is evocatively balanced. Very good (1963) Philips sound.

The Virgin collection is inexpensive and represents fair value. In the orchestral items, the Rotterdam acoustic brings an evocative allure to *Images*, which is played very vividly and has both sparkle and atmosphere. *La Mer* brings similar delicacy of detail and no lack of intensity at the close of the *Dialogue de vent et de la mer*. *Jeux* is not in the same league as Haitink's and, apart from a quite impressive account of *Images*, the best thing here is the *Khamma*. Altogether, these performances are eminently serviceable and certainly recommendable, even if there are better individual versions available elsewhere. The piano music offers accomplished playing from Jean-Bernard Pommier, an intelligent artist with a good feeling for Debussy and excellent technical address. He is often perceptive; but there is strong competition here and, notably in the *Préludes* (where Pommier's bold articulation brings some hardness), the good must yield to the better. The recording is basically truthful, if a little bottom-heavy at times.

Nocturnes; (i) Jeux; Prélude à l'après-midi d'un faune; Marche écossaise; (ii) La Damoiselle élue
(**) Testament mono SBT 1212. French R.O, Inghelbrecht; with (i) Chorale Marcel Briclot; (ii) Madeleine Gorge; Jacqueline Joly, and Ch.

For younger collectors, the French conductor, Désiré-Emile Inghelbrecht will hardly be a familiar name – understandably enough, as his Debussy records have not been in circulation since the 1950s. Nevertheless they have special claims on the serious collector as Inghelbrecht was closely associated with Debussy during the first decades of the century. Although the quality of the orchestral playing leaves much to be desired, there is a sense of music from another age. Among the highlights here is *Jeux*, which has a wonderful breadth and space. The singing in *La Damoiselle élue* or in *Sirènes* from the *Nocturnes* is not particularly distinguished but there is an authenticity of feeling that is rather special. Excellent transfers.

La Mer
⊕➝ (M) *** RCA (ADD) 8276 71614-2. Chicago SO, Reiner – RESPIGHI: *Fountains & Pines of Rome* ***

(M) ** Chan. 6615. Detroit SO, Järvi – MILHAUD: *Suite provençale;* RAVEL: *Boléro; La Valse* **

(**) Orfeo (ADD) C 488 981B. BPO, Mitropoulos – MENDELSSOHN: *Symphony 3;* SCHOENBERG: *Variations* (**)

(i) La Mer; (i; ii) Nocturnes; (i) Prélude à l'après-midi d'un faune; (iii) Suite bergamasque: Clair de lune (orch. Stokowski)
(BB) *** HMV 5 86722-2. (i) LSO, Previn; (ii) with Amb. S.; (iii) Phd. O, Sawallisch

Reiner's 1960 recording has all the atmosphere that makes his version of *Ibéria*, recorded at the same time (and still awaiting reissue), so unforgettable. Of course the marvellous acoustics of the Chicago Hall contribute to the appeal of this superbly played account: Reiner's record gives great pleasure: the effect is just a bit more lustrous than Karajan's remastered DG version, although the upper range is more brightly lit.

Previn's *La Mer* is not quite as fine as Karajan's, but it is a considerable achievement. His is an overtly passionate reading; his ocean is clearly in the southern hemisphere, with Debussy's orchestral colours made to sound more vividly sunlit. The playing of the LSO is extremely impressive, particularly the ardour of the strings. There is less restraint and less subtlety than with Haitink, emphasized by EMI's early (1984) digital recording, which has glittering detail and expands brilliantly at climaxes – although there is no lack of ambient atmosphere. The *Nocturnes* have even greater spontaneity. Some might feel that *Sirènes* are too voluptuous, but this matches Previn's extrovert approach. *L'après-midi d'un faune* dates from five years earlier. It is not as atmospheric as some accounts but does not lack sensuous feeling, and no version is more vividly captured by the engineers. This disc is a very real bargain in showing Previn and the LSO at the peak of their form.

Neeme Järvi's version of *La Mer* has a fair amount going for it; it has a subtle sense of flow and a good feeling for texture. There are some oddities, including a slowing down in the second part of *De l'aube à midi sur la mer* some way before the passage Satie referred to as 'the bit he liked at about quarter to eleven'. Given the sheer quantity and quality of the competition, however, this is not really a front-runner.

The Orfeo *La Mer* was recorded at the Salzburg Festival in 1960 and is a magical and atmospheric performance. Mitropoulos casts a strong spell, but the frequency range is narrow and the sound of the strings above the stave is shrill and strident.

3 Nocturnes; Pelléas et Mélisande: Concert Suite (arr. by Leinsdorf); *Prélude à l'après-mini d'un faune*
** DG 471 332-2. BPO, Abbado

In Abbado's newest collection Emmanuel Pahud is the solo flute in the *Prélude à l'après-midi d'un faune*, and the orchestral playing throughout is superb. In 1970, during his first years with Deutsche Grammophon, Abbado did a memorable and poetic account of the *Nocturnes* with the Boston Symphony, and few would fault this newcomer from Berlin. The concert suite from *Pelléas* is another matter. Beautifully played though they are, the bleeding chunks do not convince or hang together; indeed, they haemorrhage badly. So this is a rather expensive way of collecting the *Nocturnes* and the *Prélude*.

Cello Sonata in D min.
⊕➝ (M) *** Decca (ADD) 452 895-2. Rostropovich, Britten – BRITTEN: *Sonata;* SCHUMANN: *5 Stücke in Volkston* ***

*** Berlin Classics 0017832BC. Bohorquez, Groh – BRITTEN; PROKOFIEV: *Cello Sonatas* ***

This classic version of the *Cello Sonata* by Rostropovich and Britten, now restored to the catalogue in Universal's Critics' Choice series, has a clarity and point which suit the music perfectly. The recording is first class and if the couplings are suitable this holds its place as first choice.

In the Debussy *Sonata*, Bohorquez brings out the improvisational element in the writing with its sudden changes of mood, relishing the quirkiness of the pizzicato writing in the central *Serenade*, before a light and resilient account of the finale. In its scale of little more than 10 minutes overall it may seem like a miniature, but Bohorquez makes it a major statement without inflating it. This disc offers an unusual mix of works but a rewarding one.

String Quartet

** Simax PSC 1201. Vertavo Qt (with GRIEG: *String Quartet* **)

(BB) ** Warner Apex 8573 89231-2. Keller Qt – RAVEL: *Quartet* **

In neither the Debussy nor the coupled Grieg *Quartet* would the Vertavo Quartet be a first choice, although they make a logical coupling since they share the same key and the Grieg (1878) so clearly influenced the Debussy (1893). The playing is very good but nothing special.

The Keller Quartet rush and over-dramatize the first movement of the Debussy – in fact, the whole work is rather hurried along, and there is just too much paprika here to make this a three-star recommendation.

Violin Sonata

(BB) *(*) EMI Encore 5 85707-2. Zimmermann, Lonquich – JANACEK: *Violin Sonata*; RAVEL: *Violin Sonata; Sonate posthume* *(*)

Frank Peter Zimmermann projects as if he were in a large concert hall and the thoughtful intimacy of this great work eludes him. He plays with virtuosity and expressive warmth, though Alexander Lonquich is sometimes too expressively vehement. Not a realistic choice, in spite of the attractive couplings and the modest price.

PIANO MUSIC

2 Arabesques; Ballade slave; Berceuse héroïque; La Boîte à joujoux; Children's Corner; Danse (Tarantelle styrienne); Danse bohémienne; D'un cahier d'esquisses; Elégie; Epigraphs antiques; Estampes; Etudes, Books 1–2; Etude retrouvée; Hommage à Haydn; Images, Books 1–2; Images oubliées; L'Isle joyeuse; Masques; Mazurka; Morceau de concours; Nocturne; Page d'album; Le Petit Nègre; La plus que lente; Pour le piano; Préludes, Books 1–2; Suite bergamasque; Valse romantique

(BB) ** EMI 5 73813-2 (5). Ciccolini

Aldo Ciccolini's complete stereo Debussy survey is not of uniform excellence, and at times he can appear inattentive to dynamic shadings and tonal finesse, although the recording itself is a shade restricted in range. Nevertheless he brings considerable atmosphere to *Et la lune descend sur le temple qui fut* and other pieces.

2 Arabesques; Ballade slave; Berceuse héroïque; Children's corner; Danse; D'un cahier d'esquisses; Elégie; Estampes; Homage à Haydn; Images I & II; Images oubliées; L'isle joyeuse; Mazurka; Nocturne; Page d'album; Le Petit Nègre; Pièce pour piano (Morceau de concours); La plus que lente; Pour le piano; Préludes, Books I & II; Rêverie; Suite bergamasque; Valse romantique; (i) *Fantaisie for Piano & Orchestra*

**(*) Ph. 475 7301 (4). Kocsis; (i) Budapest Festival O, I. Fischer – RAVEL: *Piano Concertos* **

Zoltán Kocsis's Debussy/Ravel anthology, although superbly recorded throughout, is musically uneven. His single-disc collection (including the *Arabesques, Berceuse*, both sets of *Images*, and *L'isle joyeuse*) received a *Gramophone* Award and is still available separately (475 210-2). The *Estampes, Pour le piano* and *Suite bergamasque* all bring beautifully alert playing is which every nuance is subtly graded. Much else is of comparable distinction, especially the miniatures, and the *Fantaisie for Piano and Orchestra* is lucid and delicate and can be recommended with confidence. But the *Préludes* are much less successful. Technically, the pianism is still masterly, but too often is unexpectedly impulsive, seldom *calme*, and sometimes all but losing the feeling of impressionistic evocation.

2 Arabesques; Children's Corner; Suite bergamasque; Images Books I & II

*** HM HMC 901893. Planès

Alain Planès does not use a modern grand but rather a Blüthner of 1902 from the Giulini Collection of the Villa Medici, Briosco. (In this he follows the example of Immerseel, whose Debussy recital some years back used an Erard of much the same period.) Planès is an artist of culture and intelligence, who rarely fails to engage the listener. Although so far as the general collector is concerned, this will probably not be preferred to the excellent Debussy of Rogé, Kocsis, Thibaudet and others listed in our main volume, it should be heard by those with a specialist interest in the piano repertoire.

Berceuse héroïque; La Boîte à joujoux; Elégie; Pièce pour l'oeuvre du Vêtements du blessé. Préludes, Book II (complete)

*** BIS CD 1355. Ogawa

Her earlier Debussy recordings have left no doubt that Noriko Ogawa is a superb interpreter of this repertoire. Particularly delightful is her characterful and touching account of *La Boîte à joujoux* (comparatively rare on the piano). She also includes two wartime fragments and the *Berceuse héroïque*. The recorded sound is in the best tradition of the house, and the accompanying notes by Leif Hasselgren are first class. Strongly recommended.

Bruyères; Canope; Children's Corner; Images, Books I & II

*** Opus Arte DVD OA 0941 D. Arturo Benedetti Michelangeli (plus documentary: 'Maestro di Maestri')

This recital was filmed and recorded by RAI at Turin in 1962 and is in black-and-white. The playing is anything but. Michelangeli plays with an amazingly wide range of colour and refinement of dynamics and touch. We were not enthusiastic about the Debussy he recorded for DG later in life, but in this recital we are in a completely different world. His concentration, sense of atmosphere and pianism are at their finest. The limited camera positions he permitted make for an austere presentation, free from the restless wandering and rapid cutting so favoured nowadays, and the effect is to draw attention to the quality of Michelangeli's playing. Forget the feeble documentary of 1959 – not for the hagiography, but for the crass questions of the self-satisfied interviewer. However, it does give us a glimpse of the pianists who take part in Michelangeli's annual festival in Arrezo, including Adam Harasiewicz, who had won the Chopin Prize a few years earlier. But, as Debussy playing, Michelangeli's performances take some beating.

Children's Corner: Golliwog's Cakewalk; The little shepherd; The snow is dancing. Estampes: Pagodes. Images: Cloches à travers les feuilles; Reflets dans l'eau. Préludes: La cathédrale engloutie; La fille aux chéveux de lin; Voiles. Suite bergamasque: Clair de lune
(BB) *** HMV 5 86761-2. Ciccolini – SATIE: *Piano music* ***

Aldo Ciccolini is not the first name that comes to mind with Debussy's piano music, but he has recorded all of it quite successfully; this is a deftly chosen collection, including many 'impressionistic' favourites, in which he finds no lack of atmosphere. *La cathédrale engloutie* is particularly commanding. A good coupling for some distinguished Satie: this disc is well worth its modest cost.

Estampes; Images (1894); Images I & II
(BB) ** Warner Apex 7559 79674-2. Jacobs

Paul Jacobs has an enviable reputation, and his recordings of the *Images* and the *Estampes* have much to recommend them. They were recorded in 1978 in New York, but the sound, though generally acceptable, is a little bottom-heavy at times, unpleasingly so (try *Quelques aspects de 'Nous n'irons plus au bois'*, the third of the 1894 *Images*). It is by no means as refined sonically as, say, Zoltán Kocsis's Debussy records (Philips) or Pascal Rogé (Decca), made only a few years later.

Estampes; Images, Books I & II; Images oubliées; Masques; D'un cahier d'esquisses; L'isle joyeuse
*(*) Simax PSC 1250. Austbø

The Norwegian pianist, Håkon Austbø, based in the Netherlands since the mid-1970s, is a Debussyian *par excellence*. These are beautifully idiomatic accounts that rank along with the best, but they are badly let down by the recording, which coarsens unpleasingly at *forte* and above. Three stars for the playing, but only one for the recording.

Etudes, Books 1–2
⦿ (M) *** Ph. 475 7559. Uchida

Uchida's highly praised recording of the *Etudes*, now reissued as one of Philips's Originals, remains unsurpassed, arguably still her finest recording.

Etudes, Books 1–2; Préludes, Books 1–2
** Mer. CDE 844483–84 (2). Fou Ts'ong

Fou Ts'ong is in many ways ideally suited to this repertoire, for he has much delicacy and refinement. But the set falls short of distinction: there are some sensitive touches, offset by some curiously prosaic playing.

Préludes, Books 1–2 (complete)
*** Deux-Elles DXL 1092. Tan

Melvyn Tan recorded the Beethoven concertos and many of the sonatas on the fortepiano in the late 1980s, but he returns now to the modern grand and the recording studios with the two books of Debussy *Préludes*. The intelligence and sensitivity that made his fortepiano playing so vivid and alive are well in evidence here, and his Debussy has a refinement and imagination that will not disappoint his many admirers. We

hope to welcome further Debussy (or other repertoire) from him.

Préludes, Book 1; L'Isle joyeuse
*(*) (IMS) DG 445 187-2. Pollini

Maurizio Pollini may be Maurizio Pollini, but only 43 minutes is on the stingy side for a full-price disc. *Ce qu'a vu le vent d'ouest* sounds as if he is attacking Rachmaninov or Prokofiev. There are good things too, and the pianism and control are masterly (as in *Des pas sur la neige*), but generally speaking one remains outside Debussy's world. The recording was made in Munich's Herkulessaal and has abundant clarity and presence.

Le Martyre de Saint Sébastien; (i) 3 Ballades de François Villon
(**) Testament mono SBT 1214. Collart, Collard, Gayraud, Falcon; (i) Plantey; French R.O & Ch., Inghelbrecht

Inghelbrecht conducted the first performances of *Le Martyre de Saint Sébastien* in its concert form (André Caplet, who was responsible for putting the score into its finished shape, conducted the stage première). His performance is totally dedicated and refreshingly wanting in glamour, and such is the sense of authenticity it communicates that its want of finish seems of no account. Readers who really care about Debussy should seek this out.

OPERA

Pelléas et Mélisande (DVD versions)
(***) Warner **DVD** 504678326-2. Oelze, Croft, Tomlinson, Howell, Rigby, Arditti, Glyndebourne Ch., LPO, A. Davis (V/D: Humphrey Burton)
TDK **DVD** DVWW OPPEM. Rey, Gilfry, Volle, Kallisch, Polgár, Zurich Opera Ch. & O, Welser-Möst (Producer: Sven-Eric Bechtolf; V/D: Felix Breisach)

No challenge here to the admirable DVD of the Welsh National Opera under Boulez of the Peter Stein production (DG 073 030-9 – see our main volume), let alone to the classic CD accounts of Abbado, Baudo, Ansermet and Désormière. Those looking for the forest, the castle or the sea must look elsewhere. This production is set in a large plush *fin-de-siècle* drawing room with a glittering bejewelled floor. The production is pretty unwatchable. The singers and musicians deserve better, for Andrew Davis gets beautifully atmospheric results from his orchestra and Christine Oelze is a fine Mélisande. The three stars are for her singing and the many other musical strengths, but they are negated by the production, which is puerile and offensive.

The Zurich Opera *Pelléas* is better heard than seen. It would be an exaggeration to say that Isabel Rey is too matronly, but she is not the mysterious creature that Suzanne Danco and others created. Good though he is, Rodney Gilfry's Pelléas is no match for François Le Roux (on both Abbado's CD and Gardiner's Lyon DVD). The dark-voiced Golaud of Michael Volle is very fine. The production of Sven-Eric Bechtolf opens with Pelléas addressing a dummy seated in a rowing-boat, with the real Mélisande hovering in the background. As for the forest, needless to say there is not a tree, not even a leaf, in sight, the stage being dominated by an unsightly corrugated-iron castle. On a revolve in front of this is a lectern-shaped object, surrounded by artificial snow. All the characters are represented by dummies and are seated in wheelchairs to show the damage they have suffered from their claustrophobic environment. (What penetrating insights Sven-Eric Bechtolf offers!) Singers and musicians observe the letter and the spirit of the score: if only producers would learn to do the same for the stage directions. Recommended only to those whose tolerance can extend to these tedious conceits; others may well be less patient, given the ravishing beauty of this score and its purity of dramatic feeling. The orchestral playing is idiomatic enough, though again it rarely equals (and never surpasses) any of the rival versions listed in our main volume. One is almost tempted to say to the Glyndebourne set discussed above, 'Come back, all is forgiven!'

Pelléas et Mélisande (CD versions)

(M) (***) EMI mono 3 45770-2 [3 45782-2] (3). Joachim, Jansen, Etcheverry, Cernay, Cabanel, Leila ben Sedira, Ch. Yvonne Gouverné, Paris Conservatoire O, Désormière (with *Pelléas et Mélisande*: excerpt: *Mes longs cheveux*. Mélodies: *Ariettes oubliées 1, 3 & 5* sung by Mary Garden with composer, piano; *Ballades de François Villon 3; Chansons de Bilitis; Fêtes galantes; Le promenoir des deux amants; Proses lyriques 2* sung by Maggie Teyte with Cortot)

Roger Désormière's wartime recording (discussed in our main volume), notable for Joachim's outstanding portrayal of Mélisande, Jansen's Pelléas, and Etcheverry's unsurpassed Golaud, now arrives at mid-price as one of EMI's 'Great Recordings of the Century', including the historic recordings from Mary Garden and Dame Maggie Teyte listed above. The full documentation includes texts and translations.

DECAUX, Abel (1869–1943)

Clairs de lune
*** Hyp. CDA 67513. Hamelin – DUKAS: *Piano Sonata* ***

Abel Decaux studied the organ with Widor and Guilmant and composition with Massenet. He was organist at the Sacré-Coeur (1900–1925) and then taught the organ at the Eastman School in Rochester, New York. These four extraordinarily forward-looking and imaginative pieces are the only works of his that are known, though sketches for a fifth, *La forêt*, exist. They make a fascinating makeweight for Marc-André Hamelin's masterly account of the Dukas *Sonata*.

DE LA BARRE, Michel (c. 1675–1745)

Flute Suites 2 in C min.; 4 in G min.; 6 in C; 8 in D; Sonata 1 in B flat
**(*) ASV CDGAU 181. Hadden, Walker, Carolan, Headley, Sayce

Michel de la Barre played the transverse flute at the Court of Louis XIV with the status of *Flûte de la Chambre*. His suites are among the earliest written for the remodelled instrument, and they have a certain pale charm, balancing a pervading melancholy with brighter, more lively airs, gigues and chaconnes. The charming *Sonata* is for a pair of unaccompanied flutes, the *Suites* for solo flute with continuo, here harpsichord, viola da gamba and theorbo. These expert period-instrument performances are stylishly refined and delicate, and certainly pleasing if taken a work at a time.

DE LA RUE, Pierre (c. 1460–1518)

(i) *Missa de feria; Missa Sancta Dei gentrix;* Motet: *Pater de celis Deus;* (ii) Motets arr. for lute: *O Domine, Jesu Christe; Regina coeli; Salve Regina*
*** Hyp. CDA 67010. (i) Gothic Voices, Page; (ii) Wilson and Rumsey (lutes)

Pierre de la Rue is still an unfamiliar name, yet he was prolific. His music seems solemn, partly because he is fond of lower vocal ranges, but his ready use of intervals of the third and sixth gives it a harmonic lift and a special individuality. The *Missa de feria* is in five parts and is vocally richer than the more austerely concise *Missa Sancta Dei gentrix* in four; but they are distantly related by sharing an identical musical idea on the words '*Crucifixus*' and '*et resurrexit*'. The canonic imitation that is at the heart of Pierre's polyphony is heard even more strikingly in the superbly organized six-part motet *Pater de celis Deus*. To provide interludes, Christopher Wilson and his partner play three of his lute-duet intabulations, and their closing *Salve Regina* makes a quietly serene postlude. Christopher Page and his Gothic Voices are thoroughly immersed in this repertoire and period, and these stimulating performances could hardly be more authentic. The recording too is well up to standard.

DELDEN, Lex van (1919–88)

(i) *Concerto for Double String Orchestra, Op. 71; Piccolo Concerto, Op. 67;* (ii) *Musica sinfonica, Op. 93;* (iii) *Symphony 3 (Facets), Op. 45*
* (**) Etcetera stereo/mono KTC 1156. Concg. O; (i) Jochum; (ii) Haitink; (iii) Szell

The idiom of the Dutch composer, Lex van Delden, is predominantly tonal. The strongest of the works here are the *Third Symphony* and the brilliant *Piccolo Concerto* for twelve wind instruments, timpani, percussion and piano. Van Delden is inventive and intelligent, and these four pieces leave you wanting to hear more. The recordings, which are of varying quality, were made at various times, all in the Concertgebouw Hall and taken from various broadcast tapes, the two concertos conducted by Jochum in 1968 and 1964 respectively (the latter is mono), the *Musica sinfonica* with Haitink in 1969, and the *Third Symphony* with Szell, again mono, in 1957.

Quartet for Flute Violin, Viola & Cello, Op. 58; Sextet for Strings, Op. 97; Duo for Flute & Harp, Op. 27; Introduzione e Danza (Judith) Op. 26; Nonet for Amsterdam, Op. 101
*** MDG 603 1317-2. Viotta Ens.

The Dutch composer Lex van Delden was closely associated with the Amsterdam Concertgebouw Orchestra, whose members premièred these pieces, which range from the *Duo for Flute and Harp* of 1950, first given by Hubert Barwahser and Phia Berghout, to the *Nonet*, composed a quarter of a century later. All these pieces are expertly crafted and inventive, not dissimilar in style to Willem Pijper and, ultimately, Ravel. In the *Nonet* there are even touches of Shostakovich. A composer of culture, whose music may not plumb great depths but which has charm and offers discourse that is unfailingly civilized. The Viotta Ensemble comprises members of the Concertgebouw Orchestra, who play with all the mastery and elegance one would expect. First-rate recording.

DELIBES, Léo (1836–91)

Sylvia (ballet; complete. New choreography John Neumeier)
(**) TDK **DVD** DVWW-BLSVA. Dupont, Legris, Le Riche,
Gillet, Martinez, Nat. Op. Ballet, Paris, Connelly (Stage
Director: John Neumeier)

This is very much a 'new' version of *Sylvia*, with modern
dance choreography that Delibes would not have recognized.
The dancers perform prodigious feats of movement and
balance, most of it curiously gawky, although with moments
of surprising grace. But to our eyes it is mostly unseductive –
you can check it out by looking at the still photographs on
the outside of the box. But, curiously, in the final scene some
of the solos and the pas de deux almost become traditional!
The sparse sets by Yannis Kokkos with their Greek influence
are bleakly stylish in their way and they match the choreography, but they are totally unsuitable for Delibes's great
romantic score. The costumes, too, are little short of ridicu-
lous, with the men in Act I in bib overalls, and in the big
scene of Act II they wear suits. The only exception is Sylvia's
gorgeous deep maroon evening dress, which is very flattering.

But the biggest problem of all is following the fairly
complex plot which, as so often with classical mythology,
involves characters taking on the appearance of other characters, in this case Aminta appearing as Thyrsis. The applause at
the end showed that the audience were enraptured with this
contemporary attempt by John Neumeier (who scorns the
previous 'twee' choreography) to transform *Sylvia* into 'a
modern parable about the difficulties of loving', with the
characters 'stripped of their mythological trappings to take
on a more human, more universal dimension'. Although
admiring the extraordinary skill of the dancers and the
excellent camerawork, the only part of this production we
enjoyed was the superb performance of Delibes's score, admirably conducted by Paul Connelly, and very spectacularly
recorded.

Lakmé (complete)
(M) ** EMI 5 67742-2 [567745] (2). Mesplé, Burles, Millet,
Soyer, Paris Opéra Comique Ch. & O, Lombard

(M) (**) Decca mono 475 6793 (2). Robin, Disney, Collart,
Lemaître, Luca, Borthayre, Jansen, Perriat, Opéra Comique
O, Sébastian (with: BELLINI: Arias from: *La sonnambula*.
PROCH: *Theme & Variations, Op. 164, Deh, torna mio
bene*)

Alain Lombard's Opéra-Comique set dates from the beginning of the 1970s. Since then the *Flower Duet* has become a
top classical pop, following a British Airways TV commercial.
This is delicately sung by Mady Mesplé and Danielle Millet,
but otherwise the singing of Mesplé in the title-role is thin
and wobbly. Charles Burles sings with some charm as Gérald
and Roger Soyer offers strong support as Nilakantha. Lombard conducts with understanding, and the recording is
agreeable if rather reverberant. However, this is hardly a
suitable candidate for 'Great Recordings of the Century'!

The Sébastian performance dates from 1952 and the voices
– very much in front of the orchestra – are warmly and
vividly caught by Decca (John Culshaw was the producer).
Mado Robin's highly individual timbre is certainly affecting
and her amazing vocal agility and freak high notes are used to
predictably impressive effect in the *Bell Song*. The rest of the
cast, if not outstanding, are characterful and, with French
forces, it sounds vividly theatrical. The bonus material is well

worth having, with Robin's speciality, final high notes – and
they have to be heard to be believed – as startling as ever!

DELIUS, Frederick (1862–1934)

String Quartet; 2 Movements (1888)
** Mer. CDE 84401. Bridge Qt – GRIEG: *String Quartet* (with
GRAINGER: *Molly on the Shore*) **

Three composers linked by friendship share this Meridian
CD, which features not only Delius's *Quartet*, but two movements of a string quartet from 1888, the year in which Delius
and Grieg met in Leipzig. A few years ago Michael Schonfield,
the violist of the Bridge Quartet, discovered a manuscript of
two movements (the third and fourth) and a fragment of
another, and consequently they make their début on record
here. The musicians are totally inside the idiom and are
responsive to the ebb and flow of the musical ideas, but the
performance is a little wanting in tonal finesse and the
intonation is occasionally dry. The recording is a shade
over-reverberant.

(i) *A Mass of Life* (sung in German); (ii) *Requiem*
(M) (*(**)) Sony mono SM2K 89432 (2). Raisbeck, Sinclair,
Craig, Boyce, LPO Ch., RPO, Beecham (with introductory
talk by Beecham)

In Beecham's mono recordings the music's pantheism and
sense of ecstasy is eloquently conveyed and, whatever its odd
weakness, the performance has tremendous conviction and
authority. It brings out afresh how excellent the four soloists
are – with Bruce Boyce taking on much the biggest role – but
above all the thrust and concentration of the chorus, notably
in the opening sections of both halves, which are among the
most vigorous of all Delius's inspirations. The transfer is
generally clear and full-blooded, if with a rather glassy top-
emphasis that makes percussion sound shallow and tinny.
The first disc, offering rather short measure, includes a spoken introduction from Beecham himself, at his most endearingly pompous in trumpeting the claims of Delius as a
composer unlike any other. The booklet includes the full
German text and rather stilted English translation.

DEL TREDICI, David (born 1937)

Paul Revere's Ride
*** Telarc CD 80638. Plitmann, Clement, Polegato, Atlanta
Ch. & SO, Spano (with BERNSTEIN: *Lamentation* from
Symphony 1) – THEOFANIDIS: *The Here and Now* **(*)

David Del Tredici's dramatic – indeed thrilling – setting is
fully worthy of Longfellow's much-loved poem describing a
legendary event that took place at the very beginning of the
American War of Independence, here most vividly pictorial-
ized. Paul Revere's famous ride to warn the Massachusetts
villages of the advancing British troops is the stuff of popular
history, and this admirably crafted four-part work is all but
symphonic in form. Opening with *The Call*, a martial sum-
mons, *The Wait* is an atmospherically lyrical slow section
combined with a spooky graveyard Scherzo, while the signal
fires are lit on the Boston church towers. The frantic galloping ride itself, to Lexington and Concord, climaxes in a choral
outburst, and the three-part finale opens with a spoken
introduction, leading to a fugue pitting *Rule Britannia* against
the triumphing *Yankee Doodle* and a beautifully sustained
patriotic chorale. A valedictory epilogue reprises the poem's

opening verse. This première performance is fully worthy of Del Tredici's splendidly spontanous piece, with Hila Plitmann a most eloquent soloist, with a lovely voice, alongside a superb choral and orchestral response. It will surely be a hit wherever it is performed in the USA, and it should be included forthwith in the British *Last Night of the Proms*. The recording is spectacular, although the richly resonant chorus could be more sharply focused.

(i; ii) *Syzygy; Vintage Alice*; (ii; iii) *2 Songs on Poems of James Joyce (1958–60)*; *4 Songs on Poems by James Joyce (1959)*
*** DG 447 753-2 (2). (i) ASKO Ens., Knussen; (ii) Shelton; (iii) composer

David Del Tredici is scantily represented on disc and is probably best known for his Joyce settings and those inspired by *Alice in Wonderland*. The Schoenbergian style of the Joyce period is represented here, as is the 1972 *Vintage Alice*, drawn from the *Mad Hatter's Tea-Party*, a work of some *renommé*. It mixes the spoken text with song and musical commentary of much inventiveness and expertise, but for the present listener it has rather too high an irritation quotient. *Syzygy* is for soprano, horn and chamber orchestra and comes from 1966; it is by far the most elaborate and complex of his Joyce settings and is ingeniously crafted and expertly performed. This disc is self-recommending for, whether or not you respond to this music, it is difficult to imagine finer or more dedicated advocacy than it receives from Oliver Knussen and his artists, or better recording. The two sets of Joyce poems are accompanied by Del Tredici himself.

DETT, R. Nathaniel (1882–1943)

8 Bible Vignettes; In the Bottoms; Magnolia Suite
**(*) New World NW 367. Oldham

Robert Nathaniel Dett was the first African American to gain a Bachelor of Music degree. His writing is at times colourful and, though limited in its range of expressive devices, attractive, particularly so in the suite, *In the Bottoms*, which evokes the moods and atmosphere of life in the 'river bottoms' of the Deep South. However, this is not a disc to be taken all at once. Denver Oldham is a persuasive enough player, and he is decently recorded.

✓ DEUTSCH, Adolph (1897–1980)

Film music from: *George Washington Slept Here; High Sierra; Northern Pursuit; The Maltese Falcon; The Mask of Dimitrios*
**(*) Marco Polo 8.225169. Moscow SO, Stromberg

Adolph Deutsch's name is not as well known as that of Steiner, Korngold or Waxman, though he wrote some important scores for Warner films while he was under contract to the studio, from 1937 to 1945. (Incidentally, he later wrote the music to *Some Like it Hot*.) These scores, excellently reconstructed by John Morgan and draped in flamboyant orchestrations, are highly characteristic of Hollywood of the 1940s. Highlights include the opening flourish to *The Maltese Falcon* with its brooding *film noir* atmosphere interspersed by melodrama and highly romantic passages. *The Mask of Dimitrios* has some effective atmospheric evocation – the *Blackmail Letter* sequence, for example, where heavy brass, fluttering woodwind, and harp and celesta create plenty of dramatic

tension. *The Big Battle* from the war film *Northern Pursuit* is an exciting set-piece, a score that uses Beethoven's *Fifth Symphony* as a recurring motif, especially arresting at the end of the film. Although this music is essentially effect over substance, it is certainly presented vividly, with copious and fascinating sleeve-notes. But this is for film-music buffs rather than for the general collector.

DEVIENNE, François (1759–1803)

Flute Concertos 7 in E min.; 8 in G
*** RCA 09026 63701-2. Galway, LMP – CIMAROSA: *Double Flute Concerto* **(*)

Galway's dedication of this CD as his 'Homage à Rampal' is evidence of his regard and admiration for the great French flautist. Certainly Galway's own playing is worthy of his early mentor, celebrated with these two elegant, well-crafted works of Devienne. With performances of this calibre both concertos are worth returning to, for Galway's tone and phrasing are very persuasive. Excellent recording.

DEVREESE, Godfried (1893–1972)

(i) *Cello Concertino*; (ii) *Violin Concerto 1. Tombelène* (choreographic suite)
*** Marco Polo 8.223680. (i) Spanoghe; (ii) De Neve; Belgian R. & TV PO (Brussels), Devreese

Godfried Devreese, a Belgian composer, is imaginative as well as a gifted and colourful orchestrator, and this suite from *Tombelène* gives pleasure. His *Violin Concerto No. 1* also sounds balletic in inspiration, and if you respond to the Bloch and Delius concertos, you would find much here to engage your sympathies. The *Cello Concertino* (1930) originally appeared scored for 15 wind instruments, celesta, harp, six double-basses and variously tuned side-drums. The present version is re-scored by his son, Frédéric, for more practical forces; it, too, is imaginative without possessing a strong individual voice. Very good performances and vivid, well-detailed recording.

DIBDIN, Charles (1745–1814)

(i) *The Brickdust Man* (musical dialogue); (ii) *The Ephesian Matron* (comic serenata); (iii) *The Grenadier* (musical dialogue)
*** Hyp. CDA 66608. (i) Barclay, West; (ii) Mills, Streeton, Padmore, Knight; (iii) Bisatt, West, Mayor; Opera Restor'd, Parley of Instruments, Holman

Dibdin, best known as the composer of *Tom Bowling*, the song heard every year at the Last Night of the Proms, here provides three delightful pocket operas, two officially described as musical dialogues and *The Ephesian Matron* as a comic serenata. *The Grenadier* (dating from 1773) lasts well under a quarter of an hour, using a text that is possibly by David Garrick. The brief numbers – duets and solos – are linked by equally brief recitatives, then rounded off with a final trio. The other two pieces are just as delightful in these performances by a group that specializes in presenting just such dramatic works of this period in public. Excellent Hyperion sound.

DOCKER, Robert (1918–92)

(i) 3 *Contrasts for Oboe & Strings;* (ii) *Legend; Pastiche Variations* (both for piano and orchestra); *Air; Blue Ribbons; Fairy Dance Reel; Scènes de ballet; Scène du bal; The Spirit of Cambria; Tabarinage*
*** Marco Polo 8.223837 Dublin RTE Concert O, Knight; with (i) Presley; (ii) Davies

Robert Docker is probably best known as a composer of film music (including a contribution to *Chariots of Fire*). His *Legend*, which opens this collection, is a tuneful example of a miniature 'film-concerto'. The closing *Pastiche Variations*, opening with a horn solo, is more expansive and romantic, but witty too. Based on *Frère Jacques*, it has something in common with Dohnányi's *Nursery-Theme Variations*. William Davies proves a most persuasive soloist. In between comes an attractive lightweight suite of *Scènes de ballet*, three engaging *Contrasts for Oboe and Strings* (lovely playing from David Presley), and a series of engaging short pieces. Perhaps the best known is the catchy *Tabarinage*. The delicate *Scène du bal* is a very English waltz despite its French title. There are also some spirited folksong arrangements. *The Spirit of Cambria* (although the composer was a Londoner) was written for St David's Day in 1972 and effectively uses four different traditional Welsh melodies. All this music is played with polish and warmth by the Dublin Radio Orchestra under Barry Knight and is pleasingly recorded.

DOHNÁNYI, Ernst von (1877–1960)

(i) *Konzertstück for Cello & Orchestra, Op. 12;* (ii) *Cello Sonata in B flat min., Op. 8; Ruralia Hungarica, Op. 32d: Adagio ma non troppo*
(BB) *(*) Naxos 8.554468. Kliegel; with (i) Esterházy O, Halász; (ii) Jandó

In the *Konzertstück* Maria Kliegel proves a persuasive soloist, though the Nicolaus Esterházy Orchestra is distinctly subfusc. She is no less successful in the *Cello Sonata*, where she is well supported by the ubiquitous Jenö Jandó. The recording, particularly in the cello version of the so-called *Gypsy Andante* from the *Ruralia Hungarica*, is poor. Recommendable only for the *Cello Sonata*.

Variations on a Nursery Tune, Op. 25
** Australian Decca Eloquence 476 7671. A. Schiff, Chicago SO, Solti – LISZT: *Totentanz* **(*); LUTOSLOWSKI: *Paganini Variations* ***; RACHMANINOV: *Paganini Variations* **(*)

Solti dominates the performance of the *Nursery Tune Variations* and his vehemence in the orchestral introduction sounds as if he is trying to consign the pianist to the flames of the burning Valhalla. But this points up the contrast with the piquant piano entry and, although later Solti's lyrical climaxes have a certain pungency, there are moments of wit too, and Schiff's neat, crisp articulation makes a sparkling foil for the more aggressive orchestral response.

DONIZETTI, Gaetano (1797–1848)

Overtures: Linda di Chamounix; Maria di Rohan; Marino Faliero; Les martyres; Don Pasquale
(BB) *** Warner Apex (ADD) 2564-62418-2. Monte Carlo Op. O, Scimone – CIMAROSA: *Il fanatico per gli antichi romani; Il matrimonio segreto: Overture* **(*); MERCADANTE: *Sinfonia sopra i motive dello Stabat mater di Rossini* ***

These sprightly performances of Donizetti overtures make an attractive and entertaining collection. Both the lightness and the energy of the writing are presented with flair, with Donizetti's melodies and his rumbustious brand of drama enjoyably conveyed. The characteristic Monte Carlo acoustic adds to the theatricality of the music.

L'elisir d'amore (CD versions)
☛ (M) *** Decca 475 7514 (2). Sutherland, Pavarotti, Cossa, Malas, Amb. S., ECO, Bonynge
(M) *** Sony (ADD) S2K 96458 (2). Cotrubas, Domingo, Evans, Wixell, Watson, ROHCG Ch. & O, Pritchard
(B) *(*) Ph. Duo 475 442-2 (2). Ricciarelli, Carreras, Nucci, Trimarchi, Riagacci, Turin R. Ch. & O, Scimone

Joan Sutherland makes Adina a more substantial figure than usual, full-throatedly serious at times, at others jolly like the rumbustious Marie; in the key role of Nemorino, Luciano Pavarotti proves ideal, vividly portraying the wounded innocent. Spiro Malas is a superb Dulcamara, while Dominic Cossa is a younger-sounding Belcore, more of a genuine lover than usual. Bonynge points the skipping rhythms delectably and the recording is sparkling to match, with striking presence. Bonynge's sparkling account of *L'elisir d'amore*, with both Sutherland and Pavarotti at their best, and with Spiro Malas a superb Dulcamara, is now reissued in Decca's series of Originals, and it is offered at mid-price for the first time, with full text and translation.

Originating from a successful Covent Garden production recorded at Abbey Road, this newly remastered Sony reissue presents a strong and enjoyable performance, well sung and well characterized. Delight centres very much on the delectable Adina of Ileana Cotrubas. Quite apart from the delicacy of her singing, she presents a sparkling, flirtatious character to underline the point of the whole story. Plácido Domingo by contrast is a more conventional hero and less the world's fool than Nemorino should be. It is a large voice for the role and *Una furtiva lagrima* is not pure enough in its legato, but it is good to hear the sheer quality of Domingo's timbre as it was in 1977, and his singing is undoubtedly stylish and vigorous. Sir Geraint Evans gives a vivid characterization of Dr Dulcamara, though the microphones sometimes bring out roughness of tone. Ingvar Wixell is an upstanding Belcore; the stereo staging is effective, and the remastering has plenty of atmosphere. Alas, as with the others in this reissued Masterworks series, while the use of the original artwork from the LP sleeve is welcome, the lack of a printed libretto is not. The only way to obtain this is via a computer CD-ROM drive. Otherwise full marks.

Scimone's reissued set from the mid-1980s is disappointing. In a gentle way he is an understanding interpreter of Donizetti, but with a recording that lacks presence, the sound of the chorus and orchestra is slack next to rivals on record, and none of the soloists is on top form, with even Carreras in rougher voice than usual, trying to compensate by over-pointing. Leo Nucci as Belcore also produces less

smooth tone than usual, and Domenico Trimarchi as Dulcamara, fine *buffo* that he is, sounds too wobbly for comfort
on record. Katia Ricciarelli gives a sensitive performance,
but this is not a natural role for her and, unlike Gheorghiu,
she does not translate it to her own needs. It is the
Gheorghiu–Alagna set on Decca that remains an obvious
first choice for this opera, either on DVD (074-103-9) or CD
(455 691-2).

La Fille du régiment (CD version)
(B) * EMI 5 75260-2 (2). Anderson, Kraus, Trempont,
   T'Hézan, Garcin, Paris Op. Ch. & O, Campanella

The EMI set brings a live performance in which the applause
(as well as the stage noises) proves distractingly intrusive –
the more so when the singing is for the most part unexcep-
tional, certainly no match for the classic Decca version with
Sutherland as Marie. June Anderson is raw by comparison
and, though Alfredo Kraus cleverly husbands his voice, he is
far less convincing than Pavarotti on Decca. Nor is the
conducting as idiomatic as Bonynge's. The 1986 live recording
gives little bloom to the voices, and the CD transfer seems to
emphasize all the recording's limitations. Without doubt the
Decca Sutherland set is well worth the greater cost.

Linda di Chamonix (complete DVD version)
** TDK DVD DV-OPLDC. Gruberová, Van der Welt, Will,
   Ariostini, Kallisch, Zurich Opera Ch. & O, A. Fischer (V/D:
   A. Bernard-Leonardi)

With Edita Gruberová still in reasonably good voice in the
coloratura, undoubtedly touching in the Mad Scene
(although now no match vocally for Sutherland in her
famous early debut CD – see Vocal Recitals section, below)
this is an impressive if uneven performance, and of course
Gruberová hardly looks like a young country girl. But Deon
van der Welt looks good as Carlo and he sings ardently, and
the rest of the cast are vocally reliable, Jacob Will as the
Marquis and Cornelia Kallisch as Pieretto much more than
that. The staging with its drapes is not too distracting and the
video direction is acceptable. Best of all is the splendid
contribution of chorus and orchestra, stylishly and vividly
directed by Adam Fischer and very well recorded. A stopgap,
perhaps, but a generally enjoyable one.

Lucie de Lammermoor (complete DVD version; in French)
(*) TDK **DVD DV OPLDL. Ciofi, Alagna, Tezier, Laho,
   Cavallier, Saelens, Lyon Op. Ch. & O, Pidò (V/D: Don
   Kent)

It was bold of the Lyon Opéra to revive the French version of
Lucia di Lammermoor that Donizetti originally prepared for
Paris. The differences from the original are not great, but for
the Donizetti devotee they provide a new insight into the
working of the composer, with even some of the passage-
work in Lucia's Mad Scene modified. Patrizia Ciofi is a bright,
agile heroine who sings brilliantly, if not always with ideal
sweetness. Roberto Alagna as Edgard is outstanding and
Ludovic Tezier is impressively dark and firm as Henry, with
the rest of the cast generally reliable. The production has
traditional costumes, set against darkly sinister backgrounds,
with the Video Director tending to steal attention with his
odd camera effects. Evelino Pidò controls the ensembles well
but lets the Mad Scene drag on too slowly.

Lucia di Lammermoor: highlights
(M) ** Warner Elatus 2564 60128-2 (from complete
   recording, with Gruberová, Shicoff, Agache; cond. Bonynge)

The 72-minute Erato Elatus selection comes from a very
disappointing complete performance, with Gruberová tending to sound emotionally over the top and self-conciously so.
Shicoff is a strong but coarse Edgardo. Bonynge's alternative
Decca highlights with Sutherland and Pavarotti is far superior.

Maria Stuarda (complete CD version)
(B) ** Ph. Duo 475 224-2 (2). Baltsa, Gruberová, Vermillion,
   Araiza, Alaimo, Bav. R. Ch., Munich R.O, Patanè

Giuseppe Patanè in one of his last recordings, made in 1989,
conducts a refined account of *Maria Stuarda*, very well sung
and recorded. The manner is lighter, the speeds often faster
than in its immediate CD rival, and that makes the result less
sharply dramatic, a point reflected in the actual singing of
Gruberová and Baltsa, which, for all its beauty and fine detail,
is less intense than that of Sutherland and Tourangeau on
Decca. Whether it is Mary singing nostalgically of home in
her first cantilena, or leading the surgingly memorable Scottish prayer in Act III, or even in the confrontation between
the two queens, this account keeps a degree of restraint –
even in the thrusting insult from Mary to Elizabeth – *Vil
bastardo!* Araiza sings well enough as Leicester, but again he
gives a less rounded performance than Pavarotti with Sutherland. Not that the rivalry is exact when the Decca set uses a
slightly different text. However, Philips offer no translation
and the synopsis is not cued. The digital sound is well
balanced but there is little sense of presence.

DOPPER, Cornelis (1870–1939)

Symphony 2; Pään I in D min.; Pään II in F min. (symphonic studies)
*** Chan. 9884. Hague Residentie O, Bamert

Older readers may dimly recall an early recording of Dopper's *Ciaconna gotica*, but apart from that his music has
remained unrepresented in the catalogue. Of humble origins, Dopper rose to eminence in Dutch musical life as
Mengelberg's assistant at the Concertgebouw, where he
conducted the first Dutch performances of Debussy's *La
Mer*, Ravel's *Rapsodie espagnole* and Sibelius's *Second Symphony* as well as much else besides. During his lifetime,
Dopper's music was championed by Richard Strauss, Monteux and Mengelberg among others. He composed seven
symphonies, the *Second* dating from 1903. The writing is
cultured in the spirit of Brahms and Dvořák, although the
symphony is conservative in idiom, inclined to be diffuse
and not exhibiting strong individuality. Nor for that matter
do the two *Pääns*, composed during the First World War.
Very good performances by the fine Hague Residentie
Orchestra under Matthias Bamert. Excellent recording, too,
but this is not repertoire that we suspect will invite frequent
repetition.

Symphonies 3 (Rembrandt); 6 (Amsterdam)
*** Chan. 9923. Hague Residentie O, Bamert

We have already had a fine recording of Dopper's *Second
Symphony* from Bamert, but these are both more attractive,
and their pervading geniality is endearing. They are not really
programmatic: the title of the jolly *Third* (1905) anticipates
the third centenary of the birth of the famous Dutch painter
in 1906, which was celebrated with major compositions from
a number of Dutch composers. The work is pleasingly if
conventionally tuneful, with a strong, rhythmic Scherzo; but

the finale is perhaps the most striking movement, opening with fanfares, and with a Dvořákian lyrical flavour. The title of the *Amsterdam Symphony* relates to the finale, which celebrates a fair in Amsterdam on the queen's birthday. The Dvořákian flavour persists with the swinging secondary theme and the colourful scoring of the first movement. The contemplative Adagio makes a tranquil interlude before another bustlingly vibrant Scherzo. The engagingly jaunty finale has no lack of picaresque detail, with its popular tunes, the sounds of the bells of the tramcars, and even snatches of the national anthem. This is not great music, but it is certainly entertaining in performances as lively and well played as these. The recording is well up to the house standards, if perhaps a shade over-reverberant.

DOWLAND, John (1563–1626)

Collected Works

Volume 1: *First Booke of Songs 1597*

Volume 2: *Second Booke of Songs 1600*

Volume 3: *Third Booke of Songs 1603*

Volume 4: *A Pilgrimes Solace 1612* (beginning) *(Fourth Booke of Songs)*

Volume 5: *A Pilgrimes Solace 1612* (conclusion) *(Fourth Booke of Songs)*. Keyboard transcriptions of Dowland's music: ANON.: *Can she excuse* (2 versions); *Dowland's almayne; Frogs' galliard; Pavion solus cum sola;* BYRD: *Pavana lachrymae.* FARNABY: *Lachrimae pavan.* MORLEY: *Pavana and Galiarda.* PEERSON and BULL: *Piper's Paven and Galliard.* SCHILDT: *Paduana lachrymae.* SIEFERT: *Paduana (la mia Barbara).* WILBYE: *The Frogge* (Tilney (harpsichord))

Volume 6: *Mr Henry Noell Lamentations 1597; Lachrimae 1604*

Volume 7: Sacred songs: *An heart that's broken and contrite; I shame at mine unworthiness; Sorrow, come!.* Psalms: *All people that on earth do dwell* (2 versions); *Behold and have regard; Lord to thee I make my moan; My soul praise the Lord; Put me not to rebuke O Lord. A Prayer for the Queen's most excellent Majesty.* Instrumental music (mainly anon. arrangements): *Comagain (Comagain sweet love); Pavan lachrymae* (both arr. Van Eyck); *Earl of Essex galliard; Galliard; If my complaints; Lachrimae; Lachrimae; Lachrimae Doolande; Lady Rich galliard; Lord Willoughbie's welcome home; My Lord Chamberlaine his galliard; Pipers Pavan; Solus cum sola pavan; Sorrow stay*

Volume 8: Lute music: (i) *Almain; Almain; Can she excuse; Coranto; Dr Case's Pavan; A Dream; Fantasia; Fantasia; Lachrimae; Loth to depart; Melancholy galliard; Mr Dowland's midnight; Mrs Vaux galliard; Preludium; The Queen's galliard; Resolution; Sir John Smith, his almain;* (ii) *Aloe; Come away; Fancy (Fantasia); Galliard; John Dowland's galliard; Mr Giles Hobie's galliard; Pavan; The Earl of Essex, his galliard; The Lady Clifton's spirit (Galliard); The Most Sacred Queen Elizabeth, her galliard; What if a day.* (i) Bailes; (ii) Lindberg

Volume 9: Lute music: (i) *Complaint; A Fancy (Fantasia); The Frog galliard; Galliard on 'Walsingham'; Galliard to Lachrimae; Jig; Lachrimae; Mignarda; Semper Dowland semper dolens;* (ii) *Captain Dogorie Piper's galliard; Dowland's first galliard; Dowland's galliard; 2 Fancies (Fantasias); 2 Galliards; Go from my window; Lady*

Hunsdon's puffe; Lady Laiton's almain; Lord Willoughbie's welcome home; Mr Langton's galliard; Mrs Clifton's almain; Pavan; Piper's pavan; Sir Henry Guilforde, his almain; Tarleton's jig; Walsingham. (i) Lindberg; (ii) North

Volume 10: Lute music: (i) *Pavana Johan Douland;* (ii) *Can she excuse; Farewell Fancy; Farewell (on the 'In nomine' theme); The Frog galliard;* 2 *Galliards; The King of Denmark's galliard; Lachrimae; La mia Barbara; Lord Strang's march; Mrs Brigide Fleetwood's pavan; Mrs Nichol's almain; Mrs Norrish's delight; Mrs Vaux's jig; Mrs White's nothing; Mrs White's thing; Mrs Winter's jump; The Shoemaker's wife, a toy; Sir Henry Umpton's funeral;* (iii) *Forlorn hope fancy; Galliard; Orlando sleepeth; Robin; Solus cum sola; The Lord Viscount Lisle, his galliard.* (i) North; (ii) Rooley; (iii) Wilson

Volume 11: Lute music: *A Coy toy; Almain; Earl of Derby, his galliard; Fancy (Fantasia); Fortune my foe; Mr Knight's galliard; Sir John Langton's pavan; Sir John Souch his galliard; Tarletone's riserrectione; The Lady Rich, her galliard; The Lady Russell's pavan.* Consort music (arrangements): *Almain a 2; Can she excuse galliard; Captain Piper's pavan and galliard; Dowland's first galliard; Fortune my foe; The Frog galliard; Katherine Darcie's galliard; Lachrimae antiquae novae pavan and galliard; Lachrimae pavan; La mia Barbara pavan and galliard; Mistress Nichols alman a 2; a 5; Mr John Langton pavan and galliard; Round Battell galliard; Susanna fair; Tarleton's jigge*

Volume 12: Consort music: *Lady if you so spite me; Mistress Nichols alman; Pavan a 4; Volta a 4; Were every thought an eye. A Musicall Banquet 1610: works collected by Robert Dowland*

(B) *** O–L (ADD) 452563-2 (12). Kirkby, Simpson, York, Skinner, Hill, D. Thomas, Consort of Musicke, Rooley.

This is the full listing of the set highly praised in our main edition.

LUTE MUSIC

Complete lute works, Volume 1: *Almain, P 49; Dr Cases Pauen; A Dream (Lady Leighton's paven); A Fancy, P 5; Farewell; Frogg galliard; Galliards, P 27; P 30; P 35; P 104; Go from my windowe; The Lady Laitons Almone; Mellancoly galliard; M. Giles Hobies galliard; Mistris Whittes thinge; Mr Knights galliard; Mrs Whites nothing; Mrs Winters jumpp; My Ladie Riches galyerd; My lord Willobies wellcome home; Orlando sleepeth; Pavan P 18; Pavana (Mylius 1622); Piece without a title, P 51; What if a day*

*** HM HMU 907160. O'Dette (lute and orpharion)

Dowland wrote about 100 lute solos, using every musical form familiar at the time. Where either divisions (variations) or ornaments are obviously missing, Paul O'Dette has supplied his own – and very convincing they are. The music on this first disc is particularly rich in ideas. *Orlando sleepeth* is a hauntingly delicate miniature and it is played, like *Mrs Winters jumpp* and *Go from my window*, on the orphorion, a wire-strung instrument very like the lute but with a softer focus in sound because 'the fingers must be easily drawn over the strings, and not sharply gripped or stroken, as the lute is'. O'Dette is an acknowledged master of this repertoire: his playing, which can be robust or with the most subtle nuance, is characterized by a natural and unexaggerated expressive feeling.

Complete lute works, Volume 2: *Aloe; As I went to Walsingham; Can she excuse; Captain Candishe his galyard; Captain Digorie Piper his galliard; A coye joye; Dowlands first galliard; Dowland's galliard; Farwell (An 'In nomine'); Fantasia; Lachrimae; Mayster Pypers pavyn; Mignarda; Mounsieur's almaine; Mrs Brigide fleetwoods paven alias Solus sine sola; Mrs vauxes galliarde; Mrs vauxes gigge; My lady Hunnsdons puffe; Sir Henry Guilforde his almaine; Sir John Smith his almain; Sir John Souche his galliard; Solus cum sola; Suzanna galliard; Sweet Robyne*

*** HM HMU 907161. O'Dette (lute)

Dowland's use of other composers' music is very prevalent in Volume 2, and several of the works are not certainly his, but they are of such a quality that the attribution is just.

Complete lute works, Volume 3: *Dowlands adew for Master Oliver Cromwell; A Fancy, P 7; Forlorne hope fancye; Fortune my foe; Lord Strangs march; Mistresse Nichols almand; The most high and mightie Christianus, the fourth King of Denmark, his galliard; The most Sacred Queene Elizabeth, her galliard; Mr Dowlands midnight; Mr Langtons galliard; Mrs Cliftons allmaine; A Pavan, P 16; The Queenes galliard; The Right Honourable Ferdinando Earle of Darby, his galliard; The Right Honourable the Lady Cliftons spirit; Semper Dowland semper dolens; Sir John Langton, his pavin; Tarletones riserrectione; Tarletons Willy; Wallsingham & A galliard on Wallsingham*

*** HM HMU 907162. O'Dette

Dowland was never satisfied with his music; he was always revising and rethinking earlier works. The exotic *King of Denmark's galliard*, the opening item on Volume 3, was originally called the 'Battle galliard' because of its bugle-calls, so engagingly portrayed on the lute. *Queen Elizabeth's* not dissimilar *galliard* was originally written for someone else. Generally the third volume of this excellent series has more extrovert music, but there are still interludes of melancholy. The closing *Semper Dowland semper dolens* (extended to seven minutes) speaks for itself.

Complete lute works, Volume 4: *Almand, P 96; Awake sweet love – Galliard; Come away; Coranto, P 100; Fancy, P 6; Fantasia, P 71; Frog Galliard; Galliard, P 82; Galliard on a galliard by Daniel Bachelar; Galliard to Lachrimae; Lachrimae, P 15; The Lady Russells pavane; La mia Barbara; Loth to depart; My Lord Wilobies welcome home; Pavana; Preludium; The Right Honourable the Lord Viscount Lisle, his galliard; The Right Honourable Robert, Earl of Essex, his galliard; The shoemaker's wife - A Toy*

**(*) HM HMU 907163. O'Dette

For his fourth volume, Paul O'Dette uses two different lutes as appropriate, an 8-course and a 10-course, both after Hans Frei. For the most part this is a low-key programme, very much in the '*semper dolens*' mood. Of course there are highlights, like the famous *Fantasia, P 71*, and the mood perks up for the galliard written for the Earl of Essex, while the galliard after Daniel Bachelar is also very striking and the penultimate piece, *La mia Barbara*, is very charmingly presented. But overall this is not one of the more memorable of the O'Dette collections.

Complete lute works, Volume 5: *Almande; Captain Pipers Galliard; Doulands Rounde Battell Galyarde; Earl of Darbies Galliard; Earl of Essex Galliard; 2 Fancies; A Fantasie; Gagliarda; Galliard; Hasellwoods Galliard; A Jig; Mistris Norrishis Delight; Pavana Dowland Angli; Pavana lachrimae; Pavin; Sir Henry Umpton's Funerall; Sir Thomas Monson his Pavin and Galliard; Squires Galliard; Une jeune fillette*

*** HM HMU 907164. O'Dette

Volume 5 includes a fascinating mixture of genuine Dowland and music written by other composers very much in the Dowland manner. *Une jeune fillette* (with its extended divisions) is probably by Bachelar. The sombrely memorable *Sir Henry Umpton's Funerall* is certainly by Dowland but was originally conceived as a consort piece, as was *Hasellwood's Galliard*. Three items are probably by Dowland's son, Robert, including the rather fine *Pavin and Gaillard for Sir Thomas Monson* and the very characterful *Almande*, which appears to be derived from a piece by Robert Johnson. Dowland's own splendid closing *Fantasie* comes from a late manuscript, but in a profusely ornamented version, which suggests that it is not completely authentic. Dowland was known not to favour excessive ornamentation, which he called 'blind divisions'. Yet it makes a lively ending to a fine concert which is full of good things.

Lute Songs: *Behold a wonder here; Can she excuse; Daphne was not so chaste; Dye not before thy day; Farewell too faire; Farr from triumphing court; Fine knacks for ladies; Flow my teares; His golden locks; I saw my lady weep; It was a time; Me me and none but me; Mourne, mourne, day is with darkness; O sweet woods; Say love if ever thou didst find; Sorrow stay; Time's eldest sonne; Time stands still; When Pheobus first did Daphne love*

(*) BIS **SACD 1475. Kirkby, Rooley (lute)

If you enjoy the freshness of Emma Kirkby's singing, with its total freedom from artifice, this programme can certainly be recommended, with its naturally balanced and beautifully played accompaniments from Anthony Rooley. Songs like the opening *Can she excuse my wrongs?*, *When Phoebus first did Daphne love* and *Say love if ever thou didst find* are delightfully sung, and *I saw my lady weepe* is infinitely touching, the finest performance here. But, as with the earlier Virgin collection with Rooley, Kirkby does not find quite enough variety of expression to uncover the fullest depth of some of these songs. The recording is enhanced on surround sound SACD: if the back speakers are judiciously balanced, the sense of presence is very natural.

Can she excuse my wrongs; Come, ye heavenly states of night; Go nightly cares; In darkness let me dwell; I saw my lady weep; Me, me and none but me; Sorrow stay; Tell me, true love; Thou mighty God; Lachrimae antiquae novae; Lachrimae verae

(M) *(*) DG (ADD) 471 721-2. Von Ramm, Burgess, Rogers, Klein, Studio de Frühen Musik, Binkley

Originally issued in the mid-1960s as a solid quatercentenary tribute to Dowland, this was a curious selection to include among the first releases on DG Archiv's 'Blue' label. The anthology ranges from a pair of *Lachrimae* to a selection of the most famous lute songs. The result is a very earnest attempt to present Dowland's songs as they were meant to be sung, yet the actual quality of the solo singing leaves something to be desired. The emphasis on a flaccid, white kind of tone-production soon palls and the listener begins to long for something more lustily and ardently Elizabethan. The recording is well balanced, save for the slightly distant lute. Full texts are provided.

DRAESEKE, Felix (1835–1913)

(i) *Piano Concerto in E flat, Op. 36. Symphony 1 in G, Op. 12*
** MDG 335 0929-2. (i) Tanski; Wuppertal SO, Hanson

Felix Draeseke was best known as a critic and he is scantily represented on CD. The *First Symphony*, composed in 1873, has touches of *Lohengrin* and there are even reminders of Berlioz as well as Schumann and Brahms. The *Piano Concerto* (1885–6) is inevitably Lisztian, though much more conventional. Claudius Tanski makes out a good case for it, and the American George Hanson pilots us through these raffish backwaters with some skill. Decent sound, but not a disc that excites enthusiasm.

DUFAY, Guillaume (c. 1400–1474)

Secular Music (complete)

Volume 1: *Belle, que vous ay ie mesfait; Ce jour de l'an voudray joye mener; Entre vous, gentils amoureux; Helas, et quant vous veray?; Invidia nimica; J'ay mis mon cueur et ma pensée; Je donne a tous les amoureux; Je requier a tous amoureux; Je veuil chanter de cuer joyeux; L'alta belleza tua, virtute, valore; Ma belle dame, je vous pri; Mon chier amy, qu'aves vous empensé; Mon cuer me fait tous dis penser; Navré je sui d'un dart penetratif; Par droit je puis bien complaindre et gemir; Passato è il tempo omaj di quei pensieri; Pour ce que veoir je ne puis; Resvellies vous et faites chiere lye; Resvelons nous, resvelons, amoureux; Se madame je puis veir*

Volume 2: *Adieu ces bon vins de Lannoys; Belle plaissant et gracieuse; Belle, veullies moy retenir; Belle, vueillies vostre mercy donner; Bien veignes vous, amoureuse liesse; Bon jour, bon mois, bon an et bonne estraine; Ce moys de may soyons lies et joyeux; Dona i aredenti ray; Estrines moy, je vous estrineray; He, compaignons, resvelons nous; Helas, ma dame, par amours; J'atendray tant qu'il vous playra; J'ay grant (dolour); Je me complains piteusement; Je ne puis plus ce que y'ai peu; Je ne suy plus tel que souloye; La belle se siet au piet de la tour; La dolce uista; Ma belle dame souveraine; Portugaler; Pour l'amour de ma doulce amye (2 versions); Quel fronte signorille in paradiso; Vergene bella, che di sol vestita*

Volume 3: *Bien doy servir de volente entiere; Ce jour le doibt, aussi fait la saison; C'est bien raison de devoir essaucier; Craindre vous vueil, doulce dame de pris; Dona gentile, bella come l'oro; Donnes l'assault a la fortresse; Entre les plus plaines danoy; Hic iocundus sumit mundus; Je prens congie de vous, amours; Las, que feray? Ne que je devenray?; Mille bonjours je vous presente; Mon bien, m'amour et ma maistresse; Pouray je avoir vostre mercy?; Qu'est devenue leaulte?; Seigneur Leon, vous soyes bienvenus; Se la face ay pale*

Volume 4: *Adieu m'amour, adieu ma joye; Adieu, quitte le demeurant de ma vie; Belle, vueilles moy vangier; J'ayme bien celui qui s'en va; Je languis en piteux martire; Je n'ai doubté fors que des envieux; Juvenis qui puellam; Lamentatio sanctae matris ecclesiae constantinopolitanae; Ne je ne dors ne je ne veille; Or pleust a dieu qu'a son plaisir; Par le regart de vos beaux yeux; Puisque celle qui me tient en prison; Puisque vous estez campieur; Se la face ay pale (2*

versions); *S'il est plaisir que je vous puisse faire; Trop lonc temps ai esté en desplaisir; Va t'en, mon cuer, jour et nuitie; Vo regard et doulce maniere*

Volume 5: *De ma haulte et bonne aventure; Departes vous, male bouche et envie; Dieu gard la bone sans reprise; Du tout m'estoie abandonné; En triumphant de Cruel Dueil; Franc cuer gentil, sur toutes gracieuse; Helas mon dueil, a ce cop sui ie mort; Je ne vis onques la pareille; Je vous pri, mon tres doulx ami; Les douleurs, dont me sens tel somme; Le serviteur hault guerdonné; Malheureulx cueur, que vieulx tu faire?; Ma plus mignonne de mon cueur; Mon seul plaisir, ma doulce joye; O flos florum virginum; Resistera …; Vostre bruit et vostre grant fame*

L'Amour et La jeunesse: *Amoroso; La Danse de Cleves; Le grand desir; Salterello, estampie; Tenez ces fols en joye*

L'Arbre de Mai; *Bon jour, bon mois, Guillaume Dufay; Ce jour de l'an voudray joye mener; Parlamento, Estampe Italienne; Resvelons nous, amoureux; Vergene bella, Guillaume Dufay*

La Guerre & Le Roy: *A cheval, tout homme à cheval; Mit ganczem Willen; La Spagna (Bass danse); Vive le noble roy de France*
(B) *** O-L 452 557-2 (5). Penrose, Covey-Crump, Elwes, Elliott, Hillier, George, Medieval Ens. of L., P. and T. Davies

The above is a complete listing of the contents of a set highly praised in our main edition.

Au Soir de la Vie: *In tua memoria; Par droit he puis bien complaindre, Guillaume Dufay; Pues no mejora mi suerte; Quel fronte signorille in paradiso*
** Alpha 054. Magalhães, Ens. Allegorie

As can be seen, this collection divides into four sections, dealing with different aspects of Dufay's secular output. But in essence the programme consists of a series of mainly instrumental pieces, using conjectural collections of early instruments and percussion; every so often, an item stands out, usually a vocal number from Caroline Magalhães, whose contribution is always very attractive. The disc is handsomely produced. The documentation is excellent, but we feel this disc has a primarily exotic appeal.

Ave regina celorum; Missa Puisque je vis (attrib.)
*** Hyp. CDA 67368. Binchois Consort, Kirkman (with Loyset COMPÈRE: *Omnium bonorum plena*. ANON.: *Concede nobis domine; Salve maris stella*)

The *Missa Puisque je vis* has, for some half a century, been thought to have been written by Dufay, and recent scholarship has all but confirmed the attribution. It may well date from about the same time as the better-known *Missa Ecce ancilla domini*. It is based on a rather engaging courtly song about an unattainable lady, of which the text can be read to have a double meaning. 'Ever since I saw the gracious glance and the beauty of my lady and mistress, I am filled with joy and regain my happiness, relieved of all the ills I have suffered' could obviously refer to the Virgin Mary. It makes a useful basis for the Mass as its melody remains in the mind. It is sung here simply and beautifully by this group of eight singers. However, it does not match the richness of Dufay's *Ave regina celorum*, which was his own personal intercession with the Virgin, and he requested that it should be sung at his bedside at the moment of his death. The anonymous *Salve maris stella* is also impressive and Loyset Compère's motet, *Omnium bonorum plena*, flows agreeably, as does *Concede nobis domine*, but none of these motets, though sympathetically performed, matches the quality of the two Dufay works, authentic or not. The recording, made in All Saints, Tooting, is first class.

Missa Se la face ay pale; Hymns: In festo ominum sanctorum; In adventu Domini
(M) ** DHM/BMG 82876 69992-2. Sappl, Altmeyer, Brown, Michaelis, Rostsch, Tölz Boys' Ch., Coll. Aur., Schmidt-Gaden

This pioneering recording was made in 1964, a decade before the centenary of Dufay's death brought two further versions, both now deleted. The Collegium Aureum performance of this austere but moving work is a warmly expressive one. The soloists and chorus are excellent, but the performance is accompanied by brass instruments throughout, which is a conjectural addition and provides a continuing tutti effect. The two *Hymns* are presented more simply, and are beautifully sung. It seems likely that we shall get a more authentic version of the Mass before too long, but meanwhile this reminds us of one of Dufay's finest works, although it is a pity that the chanson on which it is based was not included.

DUKAS, Paul (1865–1935)

L'apprenti sorcier (The Sorcerer's Apprentice)
(BB) *** HMV (ADD/DDD) 5 86677-2. Oslo PO, Jansons –
BERLIOZ: *Symphonie fantastique*, etc. ***

Jansons's account of *L'apprenti sorcier* is brilliant and exciting. There is a strong sense of atmosphere and the playing of the Oslo orchestra, which is is first class in all departments, reminds us that this is now among the finest in Europe. Excellent recording, too.

(i) **L'apprenti sorcier; La Péri (with Fanfare); (ii) Polyeucte Overture; Symphony in C; (iii) Piano Sonata; La Plainte, au loin, du faune; Prélude élégiaque**
(B) *** Chan. 2 for 1 241-32 (2). (i) Ulster O; (ii) BBC PO; Y. P. Tortelier; (iii) Fingerhut

Dukas's *La Péri* was written for Diaghilev in 1912. Yan Pascal Tortelier gives a very good performance (including the introductory *Fanfare*), with plenty of atmosphere and feeling, and *L'apprenti sorcier* is equally successful. Tortelier's account of the *Symphony* is a clear primary recommendation, as is *Polyeucte*, an early piece with Wagnerian echoes. Excellent Chandos recording in all four works ensures their success.

Margaret Fingerhut's collection of the piano music is recommendable too, a distinguished survey, with the large-scale *Sonata* particularly authoritative. The Scherzo is quite dazzling, and the Lisztian finale very commanding indeed. The *Prélude élégiaque*, written in 1810 to commemorate Haydn's death, and *La Plainte, au loin, du faune* both move into the world of Debussian impressionism. Indeed, the latter piece was written a decade later as a *tombeau* for Debussy, and it even includes quotations from *L'après-midi*. They are both played very evocatively. Again very good sound.

Piano Sonata in E flat min.
*** Hyp. CDA 67513. Hamelin – DECAUX: *Clairs de lune* ***

Piano Sonata in E flat min.; La Plainte, au loin, du faune; Prélude élégiaque; Variations, Interlude and Finale on a Theme of Rameau
(BB) *(*) Naxos 8.557053. Stigliani

The Dukas *Sonata* has always hovered on the periphery of the catalogue since John Ogdon's pioneering (and long deleted) account in a five-LP HMV set called 'Pianistic Philosophies'. In our main volume we give slightly guarded recommendations to the Simax recording by the Norwegian Ketil Aspaas and the Teldec account by Dukas's pupil, Jean Hubeau. Margaret Fingerhut's fine version on Chandos is now available on a 2-for-1 Double (see above). However, with this mighty performance by Marc-André Hamelin, earlier versions are all but swept aside. Hamelin has the full measure of this extraordinary work and he is blessed with first-rate recorded sound from the Henry Wood Hall by Simon Eadon and Andrew Keener.

The French pianist Chantal Stigliani is of Venetian origin and she studied at the Paris Conservatoire and with Yvonne Lefébure. It is clear that she is an artist of quality; her finely played disc would be strongly recommended, were it not for the recording. It is made at the Atelier Philomuses, Paris, which has the acoustic of a broom cupboard. Moreover, she is closely balanced in this claustrophobic environment and the sound is horribly bass-heavy. The playing is very imaginative, but the sound really does call for much tolerance.

DUNCAN, Trevor (born 1924)

Children in the Park; Enchanted April; The Girl from Corsica; High Heels; Little Debbie; Little Suite; Meadow Mist; Maestro Variations; Sixpenny Ride; St Boniface Down; La Torrida; Twentieth-century Express; Valse mignonette; The Visionaries: Grand March; Wine Festival
*** Marco Polo 8.223517. Slovak RSO (Bratislava), Penny

Trevor Duncan is perhaps best known for the signature-tune to the TV series, 'Dr Finlay's Casebook', the *March* from the *Little Suite*, which is offered here along with the other two numbers that make up that suite. But more of his popular pieces are included: the *Twentieth-century Express*, with its spirited 'going on holiday' feel, the exotic *Girl from Corsica*, and the tunefully laid-back *Enchanted April*, which was also used in a television programme. All the music here is nostalgically tuneful, with enough invention of melody and colour to sustain interest. Andrew Penny and the Bratislavan orchestra sound as though they have played it all for years, and the recording is excellent. Full and helpful sleeve-notes complete this attractive collection of good-quality light music.

DUNSTABLE, John (d. 1453)

Very little is known about John Dunstable, the first great – indeed, very great – English composer. His musical influence was widely celebrated in his own time, and we know he lived for a period in or near St Albans, about 20 miles north of London. He appears to have spent much of his life in Europe, since the manuscripts of his music were found in a number of different places; but it was the Abbot of St Albans who wrote his epitaph.

Mass movements: Kyrie; Gloria a 4; Credo a 4 Gloria Jesus Christi Fili Dei (2 settings); Sanctus; Credo: Da gaudiorum premia; Agnus Dei; Quam pulchra es; Veni sancte spiritus; Gloria with Canon (arr. Pitts)
☛ (BB) *** Naxos 8.557341. Tonus Peregrinus, Pitts

Dunstable's music has strong individuality as well as striking richness of harmony, bringing great emotional depth. His most famous piece (and justly so) is the isorhythmic motet, *Veni sancte spiritus*, in which a comparatively enigmatic formal structure becomes totally dwarfed by the music's expressive beauty; in the way Tallis's 40-part motet, *Spem in alium*, carries the listener up, quite apart from its amazingly complex part-writing. But the Mass movements here are, if anything, more beautiful. Sample the *Gloria a 4* or the *Credo* and *Sanctus Da gaudiorum premia*, where the soprano voices soar up ravishingly to the heavens, echoing gloriously in the generous acoustic of Chancelade Abbey in the Dordogne. The eight singers of Tonus Peregrinus sing all this music with richly blended tone and deep feeling, and Antony Pitts, their director, has arranged a little encore with a performance of Dunstable's four-part *Gloria in Canon* to which he has added a two-part canon underneath, as 'in the original work there must have been some kind of harmonic support'. Altogether a superb disc, fully worthy of a great but still little-known musician from the distant past.

DUPHLY, Jacques (1715–89)

Jacques Duphly was born in Rouen, where he studied under the cathedral organist, François d'Agincourt. His talent soon became apparent, and after several other appointments he became organist at Notre-Dame-de-Ronde in his home city. But he was ambitious and in 1741 went to Paris as a harpsichordist, where his success made him give up the organ and settle in the capital city. He soon achieved an enviable reputation as teacher and composer. He published four books of *Pièces de clavecin* between 1744 and 1768, dedicated to three of his more notable patrons.

Pièces pour clavecin: *Books I–III* (complete)
⊶ *** Lyrichord LEMS 8053 (3). Paul (harpsichord)

An enterprising and important set. Duphly's music is finely wrought and enjoyably inventive, very much in the spirit of Couperin. John Paul plays it with vigour and much expressive vitality. He uses a modern Anden Houben doublekeyboard instrument, an adaptation of the often-copied Antoine Vaudry harpsichord of 1691, originally housed in the Victoria & Albert Museum. Lyrichord's producer Shawn Leopard and recording engineer Anden Houben are to be congratulated on their recording. The balance and acoustic are nigh on perfect. This is an instrument of personality, played with real understanding of its character and, indeed, the qualities of the music, and the result is most stimulating and realistic.

Pièces pour clavecin: *Allemande; La de Belombre; La du Baq; Cazamajor; Chaconne; La Forqueray; La Lanza; Médée; Menuets; La Millettina; Rondeau: Le Pothoüin; La de la Tour; La Tribolet; La de Vaucanson; La de Villeneuve*
** MDG 605 1068-2. Meyerson (harpsichord)

Mitzi Meyerson has chosen a well-contrasted and well-planned programme. In her earlier (1988) recital for ASV she used a Goble but here turns to the 1998 copy by Keith Hill of a Taskin, which she used in her recent two-CD set of Forqueray suites. Although she plays with great panache and understanding (her playing could not be more idiomatic), the balance is unpleasingly close and the aural image can only be called overbearing. One quickly tires of the sound

though Meyerson's mastery of the style is unfailingly impressive. But the Lyrichord set above is well worth having on all counts.

Pièces pour clavecin: *Chaconne; La de Drummond; La Félix; La Forqueray; Medée; Menuet; La Pothouin; La de Redemond; Rondeau; La de Vaucanson; La Victoire*
(BB) *** Warner Apex 2564 60372-2. Van Immerseel (harpsichord) – BOISMORTIER: *Pièces de clavecin* ***

Jos van Immerseel is expert in this repertoire and he is very well recorded. The *Chaconne* is very jolly in his hands and *La Victoire* is spectacular in its bravura display. An excellent introduction to rare but attractive music, if you do not want to invest in Lyrichord's complete set, for the coupled Boismortier pieces are also pleasingly presented.

DURUFLÉ, Maurice (1902–86)

Requiem, Op. 9; Messe Cum jubilo, Op. 11; 4 Motets sur les thèmes grégoriens, Op. 10; Notre père, Op. 14 (both for a cappella choir)
*** Chan. 10357. Trinity College, Cambridge, Ch., Marlow; with (i) Wilkinson; (ii) Herford; M. Williams (organ)

Requiem
*(*) DG 459 365-2. Bartoli, Terfel, Santa Cecilia Nat. Ac. Ch. & O, Chung – FAURE: *Requiem* *(*)

This Chandos CD collects together Duruflé's complete choral works, including the touching setting of *Notre Père* which the composer dedicated to his wife. The three major works are well represented on CD, but the Trinity College Choir sing very responsively, and Richard Marlow has the advantage of a very wide-ranging Chandos recording, which creates warmly atmospheric, seemingly distanced choral *pianissimos* and highly dramatic climaxes. Those who are satisfied with the organ version and who enjoy the high drama which such contrasts bring will find this very satisfying, for the soloists are excellent and Clare Wilkinson's contribution to the *Pie Jesu* is most affecting.

The characterful contributions of Cecilia Bartoli and Bryn Terfel add to the point of the newest DG coupling with Fauré. Memorably, Terfel gives the *Dies irae* section of the *Libera me* an apt violence. Sadly, the chorus is so dim and distant, with the dynamic range of the recording uncomfortably extreme, that the disc cannot be recommended.

DUŠEK, Franz Xaver (1731–99)

Sinfonias in E flat (Altner Eb3); F (Altner F4); G (Altner G2)
(BB) *(*) Naxos 8.555878. Helios 18, Oschatz

Part of Naxos's useful '18th Century Symphony' series, these three Dušek symphonies (undated) are pleasing works, with some elegant tunes and nice touches here and there, but the performances, on period instruments, are only just about serviceable, and no more than that, and the dryish sound is not particularly ingratiating.

DUSSEK, Jan Ladislav (1760–1812)

The Bohemian composer Jan Ladislav Dussek moved away from his homeland to seek his musical fortune as a celebrated virtuoso pianist, playing all over Europe (and especially as an impresario of his own concerts in London), and he met all the important musicians of his time, fom J. S. and C. P. E. Bach to Haydn, Mozart, Scarlatti and Clementi. Yet somehow his piano music remains his own.

Piano Sonatas: 18 in E flat (Grand Farewell Sonata), Op. 44; 24 in F sharp min., Op. 61; 26 in A flat (Le retour à Paris), Op. 64

*** CPO 777 020-2. Becker (piano)

The *A flat Sonata* from 1807 with its autobiographical title, which opens this triptych so agreeably, has a certain galant style to be sure, but with added depth, especially in the *Molto Adagio*, while the finale, with its hiccuping rhythm is most engaging. The *F sharp minor Sonata*, which preceded it in 1806, was an *élégie* on the death of the composer's charismatic friend, Prince Louis Ferdinand of Prussia, who had fallen in battle against Napoleon's troops. Beethoven has described him as 'not at all like a prince or king, but like a capital pianist'. There are only two movements (each just a little Beethovenian), the first combining *Lento patetico* with *Tempo agitato*, and the second moving back from a *vivace e con fuoco* to *sempre molto legato*.

The four-movement *Farewell Sonata*, Op. 44, the first of the three to be written in 1800, and the most ambitious, is again music of quality with memorable ideas throughout. Markus Becker's performances are first class in every way, and so is the truthful and present recording.

DUTILLEUX, Henri (born 1916)

Ainsi la nuit (String Quartet)

(M) *** Wigmore Hall WHLive 0003. Arditti Qt – LIGETI: *Quartet 2*; NANCARROW: *Quartet 3* ***

This is the final work in a live Wigmore Hall concert of 9 April 2005, which consisted entirely of avant-garde music, with never a tune in sight! There are seven movements in *Ainsi la nuit: Nocturne I, Miroir d'espace, Litanies I & II, Constellations, Temps suspendu* and *Nocturne II*. The composer describes them as 'a sort of nocturnal vision . . . a series of "states" with a somewhat impressionistic side to them'. But the music's essence is infinitely more fragmented than such a programme would suggest, and it is the sheer concentration of this performance that holds the music together and, on closer listening, reveals its underlying structural purpose. The audience responds enthusiastically at the close, even though the rest of the programme is equally elusive in terms of traditional music-making. The recording is very vivid and immediate.

DVOŘÁK, Antonín (1841–1904)

(i) *American Suite, Op. 98b*; (ii) *Czech Suite, Op. 39*; *Overtures:* (i) *Carnival, Op. 92*; (ii) *In Nature's realm, Op. 91*; *My Home, Op. 62*; *Otello, Op. 93*; (i) *Scherzo capriccioso, Op. 66*; *The Wood Dove* (symphonic poem), *Op. 110*

⊶ (BB) *** Virgin 2x1 3 49943-2 (2). (i) RLPO, or (ii) Czech PO; Pešek

The Czech Philharmonic always have something individual to say in Dvořák's music, and their playing here, especially in the lyrically jubilant *My Home Overture*, and the five folk-influenced pastoral movements of the *Czech Suite*, is very appealing. The other attractive feature of this two-discs-for-the-price-of-one pairing is the inclusion of all three overtures

which Dvořák wrote in 1891 and 1892 (Opp. 91, 92 and 93), contrasted musically but linked by a recurring theme.

It must be remembered that Pešek was also for a decade Musical Director of the Royal Liverpool Philharmonic Orchestra, and he left an idiomatic Czech character on their woodwind playing which one can hear in the central movements of the *American Suite*, and a certain rhythmic freshness that is very obvious in the *Carnival Overture*, with its dazzling close, and again in the sparkling *Scherzo capriccioso*, in which he observes the central repeat. Excellent recording throughout makes this a very attractive collection.

Cello Concerto in B min., Op. 104

*(*) DG 474 780-2. Maisky, BPO, Mehta – R. STRAUSS: *Don Quixote* *(*)

(M) ** Warner Elatus 0927 46727-2. Rostropovich, Boston SO, Ozawa (with TCHAIKOVSKY: *Rococo Variations*)

(M) *(*) EMI 5 67593-2 [567594]. Rostropovich, LPO, Giulini – SAINT-SAËNS: *Cello Concerto 1* **

(i) *Cello Concerto; Polonaise in A*; (ii) *Rondo in G minor*; *Silent Woods, Op. 68/5*.

(M) ** Arts 47638-2. Yang, (i) Sinfonica Helvetica; (ii) German CO; all cond. Nowak

Cello Concerto; Serenade for Wind, Op. 44

**(*) Sony 8287 682 1183. Kotova, Philh. O, Litton

Rostropovich's more recent (1987) digital Teldec version, now reissued on Elatus, is a great disappointment, and it doesn't even sound as well as the DG version, made some two decades earlier. Rostropovich is, as ever, poetic, but the flames burn much less brightly in Boston. Ozawa's accompaniment is respectful rather than stimulating his soloist to flights of inspiraton as did Karajan.

Rostropovich's 1977 version of the *Cello Concerto* (with Giulini) is his least successful on record and is a strange choice for EMI's 'Great Recordings of the Century'. He makes heavy weather of most of the concerto, and his unrelieved emotional intensity is matched by Giulini, who focuses attention on detail rather than structural cohesion. Of course there are many beauties here that compel admiration, but this does not begin to match his 1969 recording with Karajan and the Berlin Philharmonic.

'Complete Works for Cello and Orchestra' is the bold title of this disc on the Arts label, and some may query the accuracy of that, when it omits the earlier youthful *Cello Concerto*. The argument there no doubt is that Dvořák himself did not orchestrate that early concerto. In any event, the four works on the present disc make a good coupling. Wenn-Sinn Yang, of Taiwanese parentage, was born in Berne, Switzerland, and received his training in Europe, becoming principal cello of the Bavarian Radio Symphony Orchestra at the age of 24. That orchestral experience may account for the fact that there is a degree of reticence in his performances, at times amounting to a lack of bite. The conducting too of Grzegorz Nowak, with the orchestra which he himself founded, occasionally lapses into a rhythmic plod. The *Rondo in G minor* should sparkle more than it does here. That said, there is much in favour of the new issue, for Yang has an immaculate technique, with perfect intonation, and when it comes to Dvořák's warmly melodic writing, he allows himself an element of freedom that gives the performances an extra degree of persuasiveness and individuality, with fine control of tone and dynamic.

Mischa Maisky wears his heart on his sleeve (in fact nearly down to his fingertips) and lacks any kind of expressive reticence. This is an ego-centred performance that, despite good playing from the Berlin Philharmonic and an excellent DG recording, can be recommended only with caution. One critic wrote that he could not imagine returning to this very often. The present listener cannot imagine himself returning to it at all!

The Russian cellist Nina Kotova is a strong and individual soloist in this greatest of all cello concertos. The power of the performance is already established in the opening tutti in which Andrew Litton draws exceptionally passionate playing from the Philharmonia, vividly recorded. Kotova's then proves a reading of extremes, with a slowing for the great second-subject melody even bigger than usual, and with passage-work dispatched impulsively with a rapidity even greater than the movement's basic tempo would suggest. Many will find Kotova's tendency to introduce unmarked accelerandos distracting, making it something of a roller-coaster ride, but the depth of feeling and the technical control are never in doubt. The slow movement is improvisatory in its freedom, with big dynamic contrasts, and the finale is again fiery and impulsive. The *Wind Serenade* makes an unusual and attractive coupling, brisk and colourful, with the rustic element broadened out, not least in the *furiant* trio of the Minuet second movement, and with the oboe and clarinet solos of the slow movement lusciously drawn out. But first choice for the *Cello Concerto* among modern recordings remains with Rostropovich and Karajan on DG (447 413-2 – see our main volume).

(i) *Cello Concerto*; (ii) *Piano Concerto, Op. 33*

(M) (***) Sup. mono SU 3825-2. (i) Rostropovich; (ii) Maxián; Czech PO, Talich

Rostropovich has recorded the Dvořák concerto seven times in all, but he professed his 1952 collaboration with Václav Talich to be the finest – and despite the mono sound he is probably right. No one plays the concerto better than he and no one conducted Dvořák better than the great Czech conductor. František Maxián was a pupil of Vilém Kurz, whose version of the piano part he plays. Despite its age, the 1952 recording has always sounded fresh, even in its LP form, and the digital remastering enhances it further. Self-recommending.

Warner 100th Anniversary Edition: (i) *Cello Concerto*; (ii) *Piano Concerto*; (iii) *Violin Concerto*; (iv) *Romance in F min., Op. 11*; (v) *Serenade for Strings, Op. 22*; (vi) *Serenade for Wind, Op. 44*; (vii) *Slavonic Dances 1–16, Opp. 46 & 72*; (viii) *Slavonic Rhapsody 3*; (ix) *Requiem Mass*; (x) *Rusalka: 2 Arias*

(B) ** Warner 2564 61528-2 (6). (i) Rostropovich, Boston SO, Ozawa; (ii) Aimard, Concg. O, Harnoncourt; (iii) Vengerov, NYPO; (iv) Zehetmair, Philh. O, Inbal; (v) Noras, Kuopio SO, Lehtinen; (vi) St Paul CO, Wolff; (vii) COE, Harnoncourt; (viii) Czech PO, Neumann; (ix) Zylis-Gara, Toczyska, Dvorsky, Mróz, R. France Ch. & New PO, Jordan; (x) Urbanova, Prague SO, Lenárd

This is a more mixed offering than its companions: Rostropovich's account of the *Cello Concerto*, for instance, is disappointing, as is Jordan's of the *Requiem*. But the accounts of the *Piano* and *Violin Concertos* are much more recommendable and Harnoncourt's *Slavonic Dances* are very exciting.

(i) *Cello Concerto*; (ii) *Piano Trio 4 (Dumky)*

*** HMC 90 1867. Queyras; (i) Prague Philh., Bělohlávek; (ii) Faust, Melnikov

The linking of the *Cello Concerto* and the *Dumky Trio* is particularly apt when, in addition to both works dating from late in the composer's career in the 1890s, the cello plays such a salient role in the *Trio*, leading the way in each of the six movements, ahead of the violin in the slow opening sections – those which reflect the literal meaning of *Dumka*, 'lament'. The young cellist Jean-Guihen Queyras takes up that positive role with power and deep expressiveness from his very first solo, just as he does in the *Concerto*. That leads to a performance which, more than most, makes the many extreme speed changes in each of the *Dumka* movements sound totally natural and spontaneous. These may not be Czech artists, but their feeling for the idiom is unerringly magnetic. So far from the *Piano Trio* falling short in any way after the mastery of the *Concerto*, it emerges as a work of comparable stature, benefiting greatly from refined digital sound. In the *Cello Concerto* Jiří Bělohlávek and the Prague Philharmonia prove incisive and warmly sympathetic accompanists, matching the youthful urgency of Queyras's solo performance. The clarity and bite of his playing are most refreshing, with consistently clean attack and with phrasing subtly individual yet never self-conscious; as in the *Trio*, he adopts a daringly wide dynamic range.

(i) *Cello Concerto*; (ii) *Gypsy Songs, Op. 55*; (iii) *Lasst mich allein, Op. 82*

*** Sony 82876 73716-2. (i–iii) Vogler; (i) NYPO, Robertson; (iii–iv) Kirchschlager; (iv) Deutsch (with FOSTER: *Jeanie with the light brown hair; Wilt thou be gone love?*)

The title of this disc, 'The Secrets of Dvořák's *Cello Concerto*', may sound unpromisingly gimmicky, but the result is fascinating. The brilliant young German cellist Jan Vogler has collaborated with the Dvořák scholar Michael Beckerman in devising a sequence which draws attention to various aspects of Dvořák's cello masterpiece. It starts with the song, *Lasst mich allein*, from his Opus 82, which, as is clearly demonstrated, is used in the concerto at various points, culminating in the valedictory epilogue, Dvořák's expression of grief over the death of his sister. The song appears on the first track as an introduction to the concerto, beautifully sung by the mezzo-soprano Angelika Kirchschlager, with Vogler offering a cello transcription of it immediately after the main work. Two songs by Stephen Foster, the ever-popular *Jeanie with the light brown hair* with Kirchschlager and Helmut Deutsch, joined by Vogler in descant for the second, *Wilt thou be gone, love?* The seven *Gypsy Songs* from Dvořák's Opus 55, three vigorous ones sung by Kirchschlager, and four lyrical ones played in cello transcriptions by Vogler, make up the final section of the sequence, illustrating well enough the relationship of the finale of the concerto with gypsy music, something also no doubt influenced by the finale of Brahms's *Violin Concerto*. Needless to say, the ubiquitous No. 4, *Songs my Mother taught me*, is included.

Happily, the performance of the *Concerto* is a fine, dramatic one, with the conductor, David Robertson, drawing incisive playing from the New York Philharmonic. It is good to find that Vogler very much follows the pattern set by the great cellist with whom he studied, Heinrich Schiff, whose outstanding versions are even more deeply meditative than this. A fine, illuminating issue, distinctive in a now crowded field of versions of the concerto.

Piano Concerto in G min., Op. 33

** Athene CD 21. Boyle, Freiburg PO, Fritzsche – SCHOENFIELD: *Piano Concerto* **

(i) Piano Concerto in G min., Op. 33. The Golden Spinning Wheel

◑—► (M) *** (i) Aimard; Concg. O, Harnoncourt

Harnoncourt has consistently proved himself an understanding conductor of Dvořák, and here he directs an outstandingly imaginative account of the *Piano Concerto* (using the original score) in partnership with the scintillating pianism of Pierre-Laurent Aimard. There are many individual touches, including the warmly expansive opening and the delightful pointing of the secondary theme on strings and piano alike. The beginning of the *Andante*, with its romantic horn tune taken up by Aimard, then delicately on the strings, is ravishing. The *furiant* finale, marked *Allegro con fuoco*, opens and closes light-heartedly, the piano lilting delightfully. The movement is then treated very freely at the entry of the secondary theme, producing a relaxed lyrical interlude before the music again gathers sparkling momentum. *The Golden Spinning Wheel* with its opening horn fanfares, the most enticing of the composer's symphonic poems, makes an attractive coupling.

Andreas Boyle's formidable gifts and keen virtuosity are heard to good effect in Dvořák, but are perhaps not best served by the coupling. Nevertheless this is an impressive performance, but the balance places him so far forward that the Freiburg Orchestra is often masked.

Czech Suite; Polonaise in E flat; 8 Prague Waltzes
*** Sup. SU 3867-2. Prague Philh., Hrusa

This is a delightful collection of Dvořák in relaxed mood. All three works date from 1879, just when German publishers were taking note of the colourful Czech composer whose *Slavonic Dances* had been such a success. Again exploiting the Czech idiom, on the whole these are gentler, more easy-going pieces, notably the *Czech Suite*. Even the second-movement *Polka* opens very gently, with the third movement a sort of rustic Minuet, labelled *Sousedska*, and the fourth movement a lyrical *Romanza*, starting with a romantic flute solo. Only the fifth movement, a *Furiant*, relates exactly to the idiom of the *Slavonic Dances*. The *Polonaise* opens brassily, with splendid panache, introducing a strongly rhythmic piece, full of vigour. The *Eight Waltzes* then prove amazingly varied, with no sense that waltz-time is outstaying its welcome; two of them orchestrated from the piano originals by the composer, six – most imaginatively – by J. Burghauser. All the performances are excellent, with Jakub Hrusa, still in his mid-twenties, drawing colourful and alert playing from the Prague Philharmonia. First-rate sound.

The Golden Spinning Wheel; The Noonday Witch; The Water Goblin; The Wood Dove
◑—► ✿ (M) *** Teldec 2-CD 2564 60221-2 (2). Concg. O, Harnoncourt
**(*) EMI 5 58019-2 (2). BPO, Rattle
(M) (***) Sup. mono SU 3827-2. Czech PO, Talich

Harnoncourt's collection of Dvořák's four most vivid symphonic poems is one of his finest pairs of records and one of Teldec's most realistic recordings. The performances offer superlative playing from the Concertgebouw Orchestra, and Harnoncourt's direction is inspired, lyrical and dramatic by turns, ever relishing Dvořák's glowing scoring for woodwinds and, in the famous *Spinning Wheel*, the horns and, towards the close, a gloriously sonorous passage for the trombones. These are all quite long works and their colourful descriptive narrative means that they need holding firmly together. Harnoncourt does that, yet keeps the narrative flow moving along with an exciting momentum. The end of *The Water Goblin* is superbly melodramatic and *The Golden Spinning Wheel* is unsurpassed on record, even by Beecham. The recording and ambience are so believable that one feels one has the famous Dutch concert hall just beyond the speakers.

Refinement and beauty are undoubtedly the key features of Rattle's collection, with loving care given to all departments of the orchestra, and all manner of subtle detail emerges. Just occasionally his choice of tempi seems a little contrived and unspontaneous; and if the livelier sections do not quite have the idiomatic feel or characterization of classic accounts by Kubelik (DG) and Kertész (Decca), there is ample compensation in the richness of the Berlin Philharmonic playing, matched by the warm EMI sound. Rattle's way brings specially delightful results in *The Golden Spinning Wheel*, where the woodwind sparkles and the string textures glow. It is good that the rarely heard *Wood Dove* was included in this collection, as there is much beauty in this least recorded of Dvořák's tone-poems. Harnoncourt's Warner CD mirrors this programme exactly and offers performances of a more robust Czech character and spontaneous freshness (they are more vividly recorded too), but many will equally enjoy these contrasting performances for the qualities listed above.

Talich's famous mono set comes from 1950. The performances have great electricity and excitement and a uniquely idiomatic Czech feeling. The sound is fully acceptable, although the dynamic range is limited, and because Talich uses the traditional cuts in *The Golden Spinning Wheel* Supraphon have managed to fit them all on to a single disc.

Legends, Op. 59
(BB) ** Warner Apex 7559 79676-2. Rochester PO, Zinman

The Rochester performances derive from 1984 and, as far as we have been able to ascertain, have not appeared before in Britain. We are fairly close to the orchestra, and the sound needs space to expand a little more. All the same, the performances are persuasive enough, although at under 42 minutes this disc is hardly a bargain.

Slavonic Dances 1–16, Op. 46 & 72
** Sup. SU 3808-2. Czech PO, Mackerras

Slavonic Dances 1–8, Op. 46; 9–16, Op. 72
(BB) ** EMI Encore 5 86987-2. BPO, Maazel

Mackerras offers generally relaxed readings, affectionate and warm but without the brilliance and character of the finest versions available – of which there are now several, notably Harnoncourt (Teldec 8573 81032-2). The sound too lacks the sparkle this repertoire ideally needs.

Maazel's 1988 set offers fine playing, a superb body of tone from the Berlin Philharmonic and a generally sympathetic response. But the sound is slightly opaque and, although there is no lack of vigour, the overall effect tends to want that final degree of spontaneity and spirit of infectious enjoyment essential to music of the dance.

(i) Slavonic Dances 1, 3 & 8, Op. 46/1, 3 & 8; 9–10, Op. 72/1–2; (ii) Symphonic Variations, Op. 78
(M) *** Decca (ADD) 475 7730. (i) Israel PO; (ii) LSO; Kertész – SMETANA: *Bartered Bride Overture & Suite; Vltava* ***

Kertész's *Slavonic Dances* from the 1960s are here reissued for Decca's series of Originals, with the *Symphonic Variations* added for good measure. The Israel orchestra is not one of the world's finest, but here the playing is irresistible in its gaiety and vivacious colouring. The *furiants* go with the wind, but Kertész maintains the underlying lyricism of the music. The recording is marginally over-reverberant and may need a slight treble control, but it is otherwise excellent. The comparatively unfamiliar *Symphonic Variations* makes a highly desirable bonus, with playing and recording well up to the standard the LSO consistently achieved in their Dvořák series.

(i) *Symphonies 1–9; Carnival Overture;* (ii) *In Nature's Realm, Op. 91;* (i) *Scherzo capriccioso, Op. 66;* (iii) *Serenade for Strings in E, Op. 22;* (i) *Slavonic Dances 1–8, Op. 46;* (iv) *Wind Serenade in D min., Op. 44*

(B) **(*) RCA 82876 70830-2 (7). (i) Philh. O, A. Davis; (ii) SWF SO, Zinman; (iii) Munich PO, Kempe; (iv) Marlboro Festival Wind Ens., Moyse

Andrew Davis's cycle was recorded in the late 1970s and early '80s. His accounts are well played and thoughtful, with drama when required, though no individual symphony would be a top choice. The early symphonies, Nos. 1–3, are given their full weight and the playing of the Philharmonia is superb (the strings are especially enjoyable); the recording is warm, if lacking some brightness on top. In these works, where Dvořák's inspiration is not yet at its consistent best, Kertész's fresher, more earthy approach is more succesful, and in Nos. 1 and 2 he includes exposition repeats in the first movements (making them considerably longer!). Davis's opening of No. 4 gets off to a good start in its strong, direct manner, and the slow movement goes well too, but it is a pity that the recording is a bit murky; the Scherzo lacks the sheer guts of the Kertész version and, if the finale feels a bit underpowered, the sound doesn't help.

In the first properly characteristic symphony, No. 5, Davis delivers a very good, strong and honest account, without achieving the heights of the best performances available. No. 6 is also direct and strong, if not entirely idiomatic, and it is a pity that he omits the exposition repeat in the first movement. The very average recording doesn't help in No. 7, where Dvořák's dark colours are not fully brought out, and there is a feeling that, again, the symphony is a bit underpowered. In No. 8 Davis makes the most of the music's dynamic contrasts, with high drama in the climaxes of the *Adagio*, and there is certainly life in the outer movements, but it has nothing of the freshness of, for example, Kertész's Decca account, and the recording is rather thick, failing to sparkle.

In the *New World*, Davis gives a straightforward and relaxed reading, the opposite of inflated, with plenty of impulse, yet highlighting more of the folk inspiration than symphonic grandeur. The *Largo* is played with attractive simplicity; in the finale, the intensity increases and a satisfying resolution is achieved. While these performances undoubtedly offer pleasure, the generally subfusc recorded sound tends to reduce the lustre of even the best accounts here, and both the Kubelik and (especially) Kertész are more recommendable bargain sets. Of the fill-ups, the *Wind Serenade*, in up-front but dry and unsparkling sound, is somewhat charmless. Kempe's version of the *String Serenade* is fresher, and better recorded, though hardly one of the best performances the work has received on CD. *In Nature's Realm* offers more beauty of sound than spontaneous excitement. The *Slavonic Dances* are enjoyable enough, and so too are the *Scherzo capriccioso* and *Carnival Overture*, but none is especially memorable – and again the sound does not sparkle

as it might. For a complete set of the symphonies, first choice rests with Järvi's Chandos cycle (Chan. 9991), but we also have a special affection for the earlier Decca/Kertész recordings, which are available, together with the three linked overtures, *Carnival, In Nature's Realm* and *My Home*, plus the *Scherzo capriccioso*, on six bargain-price CDs (● 430 346-2).

Symphony 7 in D min., Op. 70; The Wood Dove, Op. 110
(M) **(*) Warner 3984 21278-2. Concg. O, Harnoncourt

It is easy to enjoy Harnoncourt's warmly lyrical account of the *D minor Symphony*. Like the others in his Concertgebouw series, it is a live performance, superbly played and richly recorded, the slow movement particularly affectionate, and splendidly detailed. The Scherzo lilts engagingly. But the first movement fails to develop the fullest thrust, and the finale too could use that bit more urgency, though the secondary theme flows luxuriously. The symphonic poem (see above) has that extra adrenalin flow which is less apparent in the symphony.

Symphonies 7 in D min., Op. 70; 8in G, Op. 88
●━ (M) *** EMI 86873-2. Oslo PO, Jansons
(**(*))Testament mono SBT1079. Philh. O, Kubelik

Mariss Jansons's readings of both works are outstandingly fine, with the dramatic tensions of the D minor work bitingly conveyed, yet with detail treated affectionately, and with rhythms exhilaratingly sprung. No. 8 is also given a performance of high contrasts, with the slow movement warmly expansive and the whole crowned by a winningly spontaneous-sounding account of the finale, rarely matched in exuberance. This makes a new mid-priced first choice for this coupling.

Kubelik's *D minor Symphony* first came out on HMV's mono ALP label in 1953, while its companion, also with the Philharmonia Orchestra, appeared on five plum-label 78s in 1949 and was later transferred and upgraded to the ALP label. Kubelik always brought something special to this composer, though he is very slow and deliberate in the first movement of No. 7. The authors of *The Record Guide* found it 'magnificently alive in every bar and crystal clear in the wind department'. The *G major* they found less satisfactory and thought the slow movement 'sleepy, [and] motionless'. It is a ruminative and leisurely account, with some fine playing from the Philharmonia wind and strings, though Kubelik's later versions with the Vienna Philharmonic (Decca) and the Berlin are finer. Readers interested in the Philharmonia Orchestra of this period will find many touches to reward them here. Alan Sanders's fascinating notes trace Kubelik's chequered relationship with Walter Legge, the enthusiasm of the Philharmonia, who embraced Kubelik as the finest of modern conductors after Karajan – and the subsequent cooling in their relationship.

Symphonies (i) *7;* (ii) *8; 9 (New World); Overture: Carnival; Scherzo capriccioso*
(BB) **(*) EMI Gemini (ADD) 3 50859-2 (2). (i) LPO; (ii) Philh. O; Giulini

Giulini is at his finest in both the *Seventh* and the *New World*. In the *D minor Symphony* he and the LPO players really make the music sing, and the Dvořákian sunshine keeps breaking out. The glowing (1976) recording encourages rounded textures and rounded phrases. No. 8 (like the *New World*), recorded with the Philharmonia 14 years earlier, brings a similar mellow approach, but the result is comparatively disappointing. Giulini's speeds are on the slow side, especially in the *Adagio* and rather bland *Allegretto*, while the finale opens in a somewhat subdued fashion. Frankly this does not altogether come off. The *New World* is a different matter, refreshingly direct. The remastering gives the sound plenty of warmth and projection.

Symphony 8 in G, Op. 88; The Noon Witch, Op. 108
(M) *** Warner 3984 4487-2. Concg. O, Harnoncourt

Harnoncourt's *G major* is the finest of the three Concertgebouw recordings of the late Dvořák symphonies he made between 1997 and 1999. It opens richly and expansively, yet has all the extra tension and spontaneity one expects from a live performance, and an ongoing drama, to match the underlying warmth, especially in the slow movement, which is wonderfully detailed. The Scherzo has a gracefully light touch, with the lilting tune of the Trio gently and delightfully lifted; and the finale sets off elegantly but with great brio and roistering horns at the first tutti. The reprise and coda are thrilling indeed. The orchestral playing is superb, as is the recording: rich, brilliant and ideally balanced in the glowing Concertgebouw acoustic. The tone-poem is equally fine, and this is now a top recommendation for this symphony.

Symphonies 8 in G; 9 (New World)
☛ *** Ph. **SACD** 470 617-2; 464 640-2. Budapest Festival O, I. Fischer
(M) *** Decca (ADD) 475 7517. LSO, Kertész
(BB) *** HMV 86723-2. LPO, Mackerras
(B) **(*) EMI (ADD) 4 76898-2. BPO, Karajan

Among their reissues in the Originals series, Philips and Decca vie with each other by both coupling together outstanding performances of the two favourite Dvořák symphonies. Philips have chosen a fairly recent pairing by the Budapest Festival Orchestra under Iván Fischer which combines freshness with refinement and thoughtfulness with passion, and is currently at the top of our list of recommendations, with the additional advantage of outstanding, modern, digital recording.

Decca have paired together (for the first time) Kertész's much-admired accounts of the same two symphonies with the LSO, recorded three decades earlier. Kertész's reading of the *G major Symphony* has long been famous for its freshly spontaneous excitement, with well-judged tempi throughout, and an affectionately expressive account of the slow movement. The sound-balance is forward and brightly lit, but it is notable also for the warmth of the middle and lower strings. Kertész's *New World*, too, offers one of the finest performances ever committed to disc, with a most exciting first movement (exposition repeat included, as indeed it is in Fischer's account) and a *Largo* bringing playing of hushed intensity to make one hear the music with new ears. Tempi in the last two movements are perfectly judged, and the (1967) recording quality was of Decca's finest of the period.

At bargain price Mackerras offers performances of both works which are also among the finest ever. No. 8 matches in effervescence his outstanding account of the *New World*. The colour and atmosphere of the piece are brought out vividly and with a lightness of touch that makes most rivals seem heavy-handed. In the *New World* he takes a warmly expansive view, remarkable for a hushed and intense account of the slow movement, with superb playing from the LPO, treated to a warm, atmospheric recording.

Karajan's 1979 EMI recording of the *Eighth*, although

superbly played, is disappointing. If in the much earlier Vienna performance for Decca he had moments of self-indulgence, he also projected a consistent degree of affection for the score which allows an ongoing communication with the listener. In Berlin he is straighter, and in the Trio of the Scherzo the Berlin strings achieve their portamenti with considerable subtlety. But the *Adagio*, so involving in the Vienna performance, is now curiously unaffecting, while the Scherzo's coda is rhythmically square. The *New World Symphony* (recorded two years earlier) is much more successful. A highly dramatic romantic reading, it may not have quite the polish which marked the earlier, DG version, but it is still refined and has an unselfconscious warmth. The result is more spontaneous-sounding then the *Eighth*, with the cor anglais solo of the *Largo* very fresh at a fractionally more flowing tempo. The EMI sound is warmly atmospheric but still vivid in its CD transfer.

Symphony 9 in E min. (From the New World), Op. 95
(M) *** Warner 3984 25254-2. Concg. O, Harnoncourt (with *The Water Goblin* ***)
*** Telarc CD 80616. Cincinnati SO, Paavo Järvi – MARTINU: *Symphony 2* ***
(BB) *** ASV Resonance CDRSN 3063. LPO, Bátiz (with BRAHMS: *Academic Festival Overture*; with RPO ***)

Recorded live, Harnoncourt's first movement, with its bold, clipped rhythms and a nice relaxation for the lyrical second group, generates plenty of excitement, with exposition repeat made part of the structure. The *Largo* by contrast is gentle, with the cor anglais solo very delicate, almost like an oboe, and with some superb *pianissimo* string-playing to follow. The Scherzo lilts as it should, and the finale is well thought out so that it moves forward strongly, yet it can look back to the composer's reprise of earlier themes with touching nostalgia. This CD is made the more attractive by the superbly atmospheric and magnetic account of *The Water Goblin*, one of Dvořák's most colourful symphonic poems. It is even more recommendable at mid-price.

Enrique Bátiz is a notably experienced recording conductor who has the gift of bringing virtually everything he conducts vividly alive in the recording studio. His 1989 account of the *New World Symphony* is an admirable example, a direct, enjoyably unidiosyncratic interpretation which moves forward spontaneously from the first note to the last. The LPO are kept on their toes throughout, and the slow movement has a simple, beautifully played cor anglais solo which is most affecting, while the finale brings a really thrilling finish. The Brahms *Academic Festival Overture* makes a comparably exciting coupling, and the recording throughout is first class. If you want a super-bargain *New World*, this is difficult to beat.

Having the most popular of Dvořák's symphonies in coupling with one of the most approachable of symphonies by a twentieth-century Czech composer is a neat and original idea, particularly apt when both works were written in the United States. Paavo Järvi not only reveals his own keen imagination and sharp concentration in both performances, he demonstrates consistently the excellence of the Cincinatti orchestra under his guidance: ensemble in both works is first rate, readily matching the finest rival versions, including those by Järvi's father, Neeme. The quality of the playing, warmly idiomatic both in Martinů and Dvořák, is enhanced by the refinement and clarity of the brilliant Telarc recording. With its unique coupling, this version of a much-recorded work holds a valuable place.

CHAMBER MUSIC

From the Bohemian Forest: Rondo, Op. 94; Silent Woods. Humoresque, Op. 101/7
(B) ** Cal. (ADD) CAL 3614. Navarra, Kilcher – SCHUBERT: *Arpeggione Sonata;* SCHUMANN: *Adagio & Allegro; 5 Pieces ***

These are pleasing miniatures, and of course the *Humoresque* is one of the composer's most famous tunes. But although the playing is pleasingly intimate, the recording does not give the cello a very strong profile.

Piano Quintets: in A, Opp. 5 & 81
(M) ** Ph. 475 7560-2. Richter, Borodin Qt

This was the first recording of the early *Quintet*, Op. 5, which comes from 1872. It is not fully characteristic and later Dvořák revised it, not long before composing the famous Op. 81 *Quintet*. It is good to have Sviatoslav Richter's recording back in the catalogue (as one of Philips's Originals). It was made at a public concert in Prague at the 1982 Festival. The public is eminently well behaved, but the recording does tend to give excessive prominence to the pianist, and the Borodin Quartet are not afforded the tonal opulence and bloom which they possess in reality. The performances are both good, although some may be worried by the moments of waywardnesss in the onward flow of tempi, and Op. 81 is not as fine as one might have expected. The Lindsays with Peter Frankl (coupled with Martinů's *Second Quintet* on ASV CDDCA 889) are far preferable (see our main volume) and can stand comparison with the famous early Decca account with Clifford Curzon.

Piano Trios 1 in B flat, Op. 21; 2 in G min., Op. 26; 3 in F min., Op. 65; 4 in E min. (Dumky), Op. 90
*** Simax PSC 1256 (2). Grieg Trio

The Grieg Trio is a first-rate ensemble and their accounts of the Dvořák *Trios* are lively and sympathetic, and worthy of their three-star rating. But we are very well served in this repertory and would not necessarily prefer this newcomer to the Borodins, the Beaux Arts, or the Vienna Piano Trio, all listed in our main volume. Yet no one acquiring this well-played and expertly recorded Norwegian set is likely to be disappointed.

String Quartets 10 in E flat, Op. 51; 14 in A flat, Op. 105.
** EMI 5 57013-2. Alban Berg Qt

The strengths of the Alban Berg Quartet are well known: impeccable ensemble, refined in tonal blend and superb polish. These recordings are of concert performances given in the Mozartsaal of the Vienna Konzerthaus in 1999. Surprisingly, given its provenance, the *E flat Quartet* is a little bland and uninvolved, while the great *A flat Quartet*, Op. 105, has more fire than charm. The sound is a bit close and wanting in transparency and bloom.

String Quartet 14; Terzetto in C, Op. 74
**(*) BBC Legends BBCL4180-2. Smetana Qt – JANÁČEK: *Quartet 1 (Kreutzer Sonata)* **(*)
(*) Avie AV 2092. Szymanowski Qt – BACEWICZ: *Quartet 4;* HAYDN: *Quartet *

The Smetanas are unrivalled in Czech repertoire and their account of the *A flat Quartet* was given at London's Queen Elizabeth Hall in 1975. It is as persuasive an account as any in the catalogue, and the fine BBC recording serves it well; even

if it is not as wide in range as a studio recording, the audience noise is unobtrusive. The *Terzetto* for two violins and viola is a studio recording from 1969 and makes an excellent makeweight to a rewarding and compelling recital.

The performance by the Szymanowski Quartet is excellent, sensitive and polished, with the *furiant* Scherzo full of life and the slow movement warmly played. Yet some ears may find the blend of tone these players achieve at times a little too sensuously smooth and suave, for they are very flattered by the recording.

PIANO MUSIC

Poetic Tone Pictures, Op. 85; Theme & Variations, Op. 36
(BB) **(*) Regis RRC 1171. Kvapil

Dvořák is not best known as a composer for the piano, yet his set of *Poetic Tone Pictures* has great charm. They were composed in 1889, immediately after the opera *Jacobin*, and the influences of folksong are striking. The opening *On the Road at Night* sets the scene, and these pieces have much in common with the *Lyric Pieces* of Grieg. The *Theme and Variations*, Dvořák's one major solo work, followed after the *Piano Concerto* of 1876 and is stronger and more classical in feeling. Radoslav Kvapil has the full measure of this music and plays the gentler evocations very persuasively. He is truthfully recorded, but the sound is a bit dry and *forte* passages tend to harden. Nevertheless, this disc is well worth having at its modest price. It is available either separately or within a four-CD Czech Piano Anthology, which also includes music by Janáček, Smetana and Suk (Regis 4005).

VOCAL MUSIC

4 Songs Op. 2; 3 Songs, Op. 3; 2 Songs Op. 83; 5 Biblical Songs Op. 99; 6 English Songs; 4 Gypsy Songs Op. 55; 13 Moravian Duets
*** Orfeo d'or C656 0521 (2). Bonney, Breedt, Hampson, Zeppenfeld, Rieger (with BRAHMS: *4 Serious Songs; Mainacht; Von ewige Liebe.* CADMAN: *2 Spirituals.* FARWELL: *3 Spirituals.* GRIEG: *Ein Traum.* IVES: *Songs my Mother taught me.* MAHLER: *Des Knaben Wunderhorn: Urlicht*)

Ambitiously entitled *Dvořák und seine Zeit* ('Dvořák and His Age'), this two-CD set offers over two and a half hours from a marathon Lieder recital of almost four hours, given at the Salzburg Festival in August 2004. It was the brainchild of the baritone, Thomas Hampson, who himself contributes some of the key sections in this fascinating survey of Dvořák as composer of songs, bringing out the influences both on him and from him. It was a triumph, with four well-contrasted singers making stylish contributions, the young mezzo-soprano Michelle Breedt and the bass Georg Zeppenfeld singing as sensitively as the long-established Barbara Bonney and Thomas Hampson.

The first of the four sections covers Dvořák's early work and his debt to the German Lied, with songs by Brahms and Grieg set against those of Dvořák himself. The second section deals with Dvořák's Czech inspirations, including the enchanting *Moravian Duets* for women's voices, with the selection of *Gypsy Songs* including the well-known *Songs my Mother taught me*. Ives's very different setting of the same words comes in the third section, which deals with Dvořák's American period, demonstrating the influence of spirituals and songs by MacDowell and others, and also including Dvořák's own settings of English words. As a climax, the fourth and final section introduces Dvořák's *Biblical Songs*, beautifully sung by Hampson, with Brahms's *Four Serious Songs* (Zeppenfeld singing with velvet tone) and Mahler's *Urlicht*. Wolfram Rieger at the piano battles brightly through from the beginning to the very end of the marathon. Well-balanced recording and a minimum of intrusive applause. An illuminating package. Helpfully, full texts are given, with English translations for songs with German texts, but German translations only for those with Czech texts.

Requiem, Op. 89
(BB) ** Warner Apex 0927 49922-2. Zylis-Gara, Toczyska, Dvorský, Mroz, Fr. R. Nouvel Philharmonique Ch. & O, Jordan

(i) *Requiem, Op. 89;* (ii) *6 Biblical Songs from Op. 99*
●—○ ❂ ***(M) DG 453 073-2 (2). (i) Stader, Wagner, Haefliger, Borg, Czech PO & Ch., Ančerl; (ii) Fischer-Dieskau, Demus

This superb DG set from 1959 brings an inspired performance of Dvořák's *Requiem* which here emerges with fiery intensity, helped by a recording made in an appropriately spacious acoustic that gives an illusion of an electrifying live performance, without flaw. The passionate singing of the chorus is unforgettable and the German soloists not only make fine individual contributions but blend together superbly in ensembles. DG have added Fischer-Dieskau's 1960 recordings of six excerpts from Op. 99. He is at his superb best in these lovely songs. (The numbers included are: *Rings an den Herrn; Gott, erhöre meine inniges Flahen; Gott ist mein Hirte; An den Wassern zu Babylon; Wende dich zu mir;* and *Singet ein neues Lied.*) Jörg Demus accompanies sensitively, and the recording-balance is most convincing. This superb DG set from 1959 is now reissued in Universal's 'Penguin Rosette Collection'. The performance of the *Requiem* (discussed in our main volume) is truly inspired and is well worthy of its accolade.

Jordan's 1981 Erato version on Apex is weakly characterized by comparison with its competitors, less sharply contrasted in its moods, less idiomatic. Only Zylis-Gara, more incisive than her predecessor, Pilar Lorengar on Decca, might be counted a strong plus point, although the choral singing is quite impressive and the recording is pleasingly atmospheric.

OPERA

Rusalka (sung in English) (DVD version)
*** Arthaus **DVD** 102 019. Hannan, Macann, Howard, Treleaven, Cannan, ENO Ch. & O, Elder (Stage Director: David Pountney; V/D: David Bailey)

Over the years of the so-called 'powerhouse' regime at the English National Opera, with Mark Elder as music director and David Pountney as stage director, many powerful, imaginative productions were created, of which this version of *Rusalka*, recorded here in 1986, was among the very finest. The concept was to set this fairy-tale piece in an Edwardian nursery full of toys, with the Watergnome as Rusalka's grandfather in a wheelchair, and Rusalka herself first seen on a swing with her feet bound together, very much an Alice in Wonderland figure. The Witch is a wicked aunt, dressed in sinister black as she pronounces her curses on Rusalka, as when, with Rusalka opting for human form, she snarls, 'You'll

be dumb for ever more!' On video, as in the theatre, the concept works surprisingly well, with suggestions that it is all just a dream. Motivations, characterization and story-line are, if anything, clarified, with the fantasy of the piece intensified. In the title-role Eilene Hannan sings powerfully with her clear, bright soprano, John Treleaven as the Prince sings with unstrained clarity, even if he does not cut a very romantic figure, and Rodney Macann as the Grandfather/Watergnome tends to steal the show, very characterful with his dark, incisive bass. Ann Howard is wonderfully menacing as the Aunt/Witch with her firm mezzo, while the fluttering vibrato of Phyllis Cannan as the Foreign Princess even adds to her exotic image. Unlike most of the others in Act II, who are dressed in white, she stands out in her fashionable crimson gown. The three Watersprites, Rusalka's sisters, are all wonderfully lively, and incidental characters are all very well taken. Mark Elder, an inspired conductor, draws warm, incisive playing from the orchestra, adding to the dramatic impact. A unique entertainment, well worth trying.

DYSON, George (1883–1964)

(i) *Concerto leggiero* (for piano & strings). *Concerto da camera; Concerto da chiesa* (both for string orchestra); (ii) *Violin Concerto; Children's Suite* (after Walter de la Mare)
(M) *** Chan. 10337 (2) . (i) Parkin; (ii) Mordkovich; City of L. Sinfonia, Hickox

It was an excellent idea to couple this pair of concertante discs at mid-price, the *Violin Concerto* richly inspired, the *Piano Concerto* lighter textured, the two string works in the great tradition of English string music. All are splendidly played and recorded – the two discs are discussed separately in more detail in our main volume.

EBEN, Petr (born 1929)

Job; Laudes; Hommage à Buxtehude
*** Hyp. CDA 67194. Schiager (organ of Hedvig Eleonora Kykran, Stockholm)

In his homeland this Czech composer of choral and organ music is a famous improviser/recitalist on both organ and piano. Eben is another of the East European musicians who survived Buchenwald concentration camp and emerged with his spirit unbroken. His is undoubtedly a major new voice in the field of organ music – the most exciting since Messiaen. His music is tonal but wholly original in both its complexities and mixed sonorities. Those British music-lovers who think of *Job* as synonymous only with Vaughan Williams must think again. Eben regards its theme of Job as 'the wager between Satan and God on the fate of a human being', and the eight titled movements cover what befalls Job and his personal response, ending with a set of variations on a Bohemian chorale to designate God's blessing, 'for Christ is truly the personification of the innocent sufferer to the very end'. It is an extraordinary work and sonically riveting, as indeed is the four-part *Laudes*, all based on a Gregorian melody, which reflects 'our deep ingratitude to our fellow men and to the world, and above all to its Creator'. The *Hommage à Buxtehude* alternates toccata and fugue and, although based on two quotations from that composer's music, has a quirky rhythmic individuality that would have astonished its dedicatee. This is remarkable music, superbly played and recorded. Just try the very opening of *Job* with its sombrely menacing pedal motif and you will surely want to hear the whole work (some 43 minutes long).

EBERLIN, Johann (1702–62)

Christus factus est; Cum sancto spiritu; Dextera Domini; Mass in C; Pater si non potest; Tenebrae facta sunt; Tonus octavus; Tonus secundus

*** Gaudeamus CDGAU 205. Rodolfus Ch., Allwood; Whitton (organ)

A generation younger than Bach, Johann Eberlin was the predecessor of Mozart's father, Leopold, as Kapellmeister to the Archbishop of Salzburg, so inevitably influencing the boy Mozart. Eberlin was above all a master of counterpoint, as the liturgical music here consistently demonstrates: two crisply compact settings of the Mass and three fine motets. In lively performances like these from the Rodolfus Choir, using editions prepared by the conductor, Ralph Allwood, far from sounding academic they emerge bright and refreshing, full of adventurous harmony, looking forward as well as back. The same is true of the sets of organ pieces, brief exercises in counterpoint that Bach himself would have approved. Warm, clear sound.

EINEM, Gottfried von (1918–96)

String Quartets 1, Op. 45; 3, Op. 56; 5, Op. 87
**(*) Orfeo C 098 101A. Artis Qt

String Quartets 2, Op. 51; 4, Op. 63
**(*) Orfeo C 098 201A. Artis Qt

Gottfried von Einem came into international prominence in the immediate post-war years when his opera *Dantons Tod* was mounted at the 1947 Salzburg Festival. It is a powerful work whose success put him firmly on the operatic map. In 1938, when he was twenty, he had been arrested by the Gestapo and imprisoned for some months, an experience that inspired his opera, *Der Prozess* ('The Trial'), based on Kafka and premièred in 1953. Several symphonic works were written for American orchestras, including the *Philadelphia Symphony* (1960), but he did not turn to the quartet medium until 1976 when he was in his late fifties. Four others followed, the last in 1991, some five years before his death. Michael Oliver spoke of the *First Quartet* as 'an absorbing, often beautiful and always thought-provoking work', but although there are many felicities in the others none inspires unqualified enthusiasm. They are most expertly crafted, eclectic in idiom, and products of a refined and cultured musical mind. But if the musical idiom is sympathetic and the discourse civilized, the overall impression remains less than the sum of its parts. The Artis Quartet play with total commitment and are truthfully recorded on this CD. There is little here that resonates in the memory.

EISLER, Hanns (1898–1962)

Prelude and Fugue on B-A-C-H for String Trio, Op. 46; String Quartet, Op. 75

(BB) *** CPO 999 341-2. Leipzig Qt – ADORNO: *String Quartet, etc.* ***

Hanns Eisler wrote relatively little chamber music. The *Prelude and Fugue on B-A-C-H* comes from 1934, the year after he

left Berlin for the United States, and the *String Quartet* was written four years later. Rather anonymous music, composed at the time he was renewing his faith in his teacher, Schoenberg.

'The Hollywood Songbook': Anakreontische Fragmente; An den kleinen Radioapparat; Auf der Flucht; Automne californian; 5 Elegien; Epitaph auf einen in der Flandernschlacht Gefallenen; Erinnerung an Eichendorff und Schumann; Die Flucht; Frühling; Gedenktafel für 4000 Soldaten; Die Heimkehr; Hollywood-Elégie 7; Hölderlin-Fragmente; Hotelzimmer 1942; In den Weiden; Der Kirschdieb; Die Landschaft des Exils; Die letzte Elegie; 2 Lieder nach Wofrten von Pascal; Die Maske des Bösen; Der Mensch; Nightmare; Ostersonntag; Panzerschlacht; Der Schatzgräber; Der Sohn; Speisekammer 1942; Spruch; Uber den Selbstmord; Vom Sprengen des Gartens; Winterspruch

(M) *** Decca 475 053-2. Matthias Goerne, E. Schneider

Hanns Eisler went to Los Angeles but, unlike many, reacted violently against the culture of Hollywood. So it is that the 'Hollywood Songbook', far from being a celebration, is a collection of Lieder reflecting bitterness, cynicism and disillusion. This disc offers a mixed group of 46 brief songs, mainly to words by Bertolt Brecht, which reflect both Eisler's studies with Schoenberg and a desire to communicate directly, standing very much in the central tradition of the German Lied, which Eisler felt was in direct conflict with everything that Hollywood represented. Matthias Goerne is an ideal interpreter with his incisive baritone and feeling for words, very well accompanied by Eric Schneider. The collection won the *Gramophone*'s 1999 20th-Century Vocal Award and is now welcome back to the catalogue at mid-price.

Lieder: An den kleinen Radioapparat; An den Schlaf; An die Hoffnung; An die Uberlebenden; Andenken; Auf der Flucht; Despite these miseries; Diese Stadt hat mich belehrt; Elegie (2 settings); Errinerung an Eichendorff und Schumann; Frühling; Gedenktafel für 4000 Soldaten; Hotelzimmer; In den Hügeln wird Gold gefinden; In den Weiden; In der Frühe; In der Stadt; Jeden Morgen; Die Landschaft des Exils; Die letzte Elegie; Die Maske des Bösen; Monolog des Horatio; The only thing; Die Stadt ist nach den Engeln gennant; Spruch (2 versions); Uber den Selbstmord; Uber die Dauer des Exils; Unter den grünen Pfefferbäumen; Verfehite Liebe; Zufluchtsstätte

(BB) *** Warner Apex 8573 89086-2. Fischer-Dieskau, Reimann

Eisler did more than set the words to music: he modified nearly all the texts to fit his music, and Brecht, though none too pleased, in the end accepted the alterations with good grace. With the Hölderlin settings Eisler described his versions as 'Hölderlin fragments'. But the succinct, pithy result, with most of the songs between only one and two minutes in length, increases their strength of character. Eisler's musical style is far from 'popular' but always invigorating, and it is good to have a darker-voiced Fischer-Dieskau (recorded in 1987) illuminating them with his special feeling for word-meanings, which were so important to the composer. Aribert Reimann accompanies supportively and the recording is most vivid. The translations provided refer to Brecht's original texts and do not take into account Eisler's revisions.

ELGAR, Edward (1857–1934)

Chanson de matin; Chanson de nuit; Cockaigne Overture;
Dream Children; Elegy for Strings; Enigma Variations;
Falstaff; Froissart Overture; Grania and Diarmid: Incidental
Music. In the South; Introduction and Allegro for Strings;
Pomp and Circumstance Marches 1, 3 & 4; (i) *Romance for*
Bassoon & Orchestra. Salut d'amour; Serenade for Strings;
Sospiri; Sursum corda; Symphonies 1–2; (ii) *The Music*
Makers

(BB) **(*) Warner 2564 62199-2 (5). BBC SO, A. Davis; with
(i) Sheen; (ii) Rigby, BBC Symphony Ch.

Sir Andrew Davis's Elgar survey is certainly wide-ranging,
from the earliest salon pieces to the symphonies. But by far
the most successful disc is the fourth, which includes superb
accounts of *Cockaigne*, the *Introduction and Allegro*, *Serenade*
for Strings and the *Enigma Variations*; it is available separately
on a super-bargain Apex disc (09027 41371-2). *Falstaff*, perceptively and movingly characterized and engagingly detailed,
and *Froissart* (with plenty of *nobilmente*) are also splendid,
and they have the advantage of spectacularly wide-ranging
recording. (This CD is also available separately – see below.)
But the other performances are uneven. Of the two symphonies the *First* is a broad, rather plain reading which falls short
at the very end; the *Second* is much more successful, strong
and passionate, as is *In the South*, its original coupling. *The*
Music Makers is a dedicated, refined performance with Jean
Rigby a well-focused soloist, but the rather backward balance
of the chorus prevents the performance from having the full
impact it deserves. But it comes with an imaginative collection of shorter pieces, all very attractively presented; and the
other lighter works are beautifully played and recorded, not
least the comparatively rare *Romance for Bassoon and Strings*
with Graham Sheen the excellent soloist. Throughout, the
recordings have suitable Elgarian amplitude and no lack of
range and brilliance.

Cockaigne Overture; Enigma Variations; Serenade for
Strings, Op. 20.

(M) (**) Sony mono SMK 89405 RPO, Beecham

Beecham's classic recordings of the *Cockaigne Overture*, the
Serenade for Strings and the *Enigma Variations* were made in
1954 and have been out of currency for quite some time. His
Enigma is wonderfully characterized and is among the most
thoughtful accounts in its extensive representation on disc.
Everything breathes naturally and is unerringly paced. Yet the
transfers are disappointingly poor, with a top emphasis that
makes high violins sound thin and steely. Though there has
been an attempt to make the sound more immediate than on
the original LPs, the results are generally shallow, with odd
balances, so that in the finale of *Enigma* the organ is barely
audible.

Cello Concerto in E min., Op. 85 (original version)

⊕ *** Nim. NI 5763. Wallfisch, RLPO, Dickins – BRIDGE:
Oration; HOLST: *Invocation ***

Rostropovich once said that he would never record the Elgar
Concerto again, because Jacquline du Pré in her famous
recording had 'said it all'. Yet over the years other cellists have
found fresh insights to offer in this inexhaustible work, and
Raphael Wallfisch's new recording is based on a new urtext
edition (there are, apparently, no fewer than four alternative
autograph sources for the solo part).

The edition used here is marked as carrying Elgar's final

instructions in every detail. Only a single note has had to be
corrected (and that all but inaudible), but there are many
differences in detail (dynamics, articulation, note lengths).
There is also evidence available as to the composer's wishes
concerning phrasing in the two recordings he conducted
himself with Beatrice Harrison as soloist; and in two cases
there are striking tempi changes (based on Elgar's own practice): in the *appassionato* section of the slow movement and
at the end of the main quick section of the finale. But none of
this would be effective were the soloist and conductor here
not passionately involved in the music as they feel it. After the
commanding opening flourish, Wallfisch and Dickins set off
very gently indeed, and the cello and the orchestral strings
sing their song with touching restraint. The whole movement
is infused with subtle delicacy of feeling, which carries
through to the quicksilver Scherzo, played by Wallfisch with
scurrying brilliance. Yet orchestral tutti are contrastingly
full-bodied, and the solo timbre is equally rich in the passionate interruptions and in the tenderly expressive *Adagio*. The
finale unleashes the music's energy joyously, with more brilliant solo playing; but the return to the intensity of the slow
movement has a heartfelt, elegiac feeling, before the abrupt
surge to the coda. The recording is spacious, richly realistic
and ideally balanced and, with its enterprising couplings, this
CD is very desirable indeed.

(i–ii) *Cello Concerto;* (iii) *Violin Concerto;* (ii) *Dream*
Children, Op. 43

(M) (**) Pearl mono GEM 0050. (i) Squire; (ii) Hallé O,
Harty; (iii) Sammons, New Queen's Hall O, Wood

The Pearl transfer, boomy in the bass, cannot match the Avid.
Noticeable surface hiss also exposes some 78-r.p.m. side-
joins, but with little harm done. The W. H. Squire version of
the *Cello Concerto* is far rarer, a noble reading which in the
first three movements can match almost any in its concentration, but which in the finale finds Squire's intonation less
precise in what emerges as a rougher performance. The cello
is vividly caught and, though the orchestra is relatively dim,
one quickly adjusts to the sound. The miniature, *Dream*
Children, also with Harty and the Hallé, is a charming makeweight.

Violin Concerto (original version)

*** Avie AV 2091 Graffin, RLPO, Handley – CHAUSSON:
Poème (original version) ***

It is thanks to the enterprise of the violinist Philippe Graffin
that we now also have this première recording of the Elgar
Violin Concerto in its original form. The fact that such a score
exists may surprise many (if not most) Elgarians, but it is well
known that Fritz Kreisler as the dedicatee of the concerto was
asked for his comments on the solo part at a late stage. What
Graffin has done is to consult the manuscript scores of the
work, both full score and piano score, held in the British
Library, and has compared the solo part with what was later
published by Novello, as modified by Kreisler.

It may be a disappointment to some that the differences
are very small. Maybe the most noticeable is the fact that the
double-stopped violin flourish on the final page of the finale
is less elaborate than what we know. That change, it seems, is
owed not to Kreisler but to Lady Elgar, urging such a change
on her husband, who duly responded. It was Kreisler's doing
that he cut down on the octave doubling and, far from
making the solo part technically more difficult, he generally
made the solo a little more manageable, without losing the
effects wanted. There is some evidence that Elgar himself had

eservations about some of Kreisler's suggested changes, even though he went along with them. That said, Graffin's performance with the ever-understanding backing of Vernon Handley and the Royal Liverpool Philharmonic is a most distinguished one, magically exploiting the range of *pianissimo* that the score asks for, not least in the accompanied cadenza, which is yearningly beautiful in this performance. The sound is first rate, and the disc comes with comprehensive notes, not just those of Graffin but also a reproduction of the script of a 1937 broadcast by W. H. Reed, Elgar's violinist friend, about the creation of the *Concerto*.

i) *Violin Concerto. Introduction and Allegro for Strings*
(M) *** EMI 3 45792-2 [3 45793-2]. (i) Kennedy; LPO, Handley

For many ears, Nigel Kennedy's earlier (1984) recording of the *Violin Concerto* has an even greater freshness than his later recording in Birmingham with Rattle. It is certainly commanding, and with Vernon Handley as guide it is centrally Elgarian in its warm expressiveness, but its steady pacing also brings out more than usual the clear parallels with the Beethoven and Brahms concertos. This is particularly striking in the first movement and, both here and in his urgent account of the allegros in the finale, Kennedy shows that he has learnt more than any recorded rival from the example of the concerto's first great interpreter, Albert Sammons. Yet the influence of Yehudi Menuhin is also apparent, not least in the sweetness and repose of the slow movement and in the deep meditation of the accompanied cadenza which comes as epilogue. The recording, produced by Andrew Keener, with the soloist balanced more naturally than usual, not spotlit, is outstandingly faithful and atmospheric. Interestingly (and perhaps it was Nigel Kennedy's decision), EMI have chosen this earlier recording of the *Violin Concerto* with Vernon Handley and the LPO (rather than the later version with Rattle) for their 'Great Recordings of the Century' series, coupled with Handley's passionate yet tender 1983 account of the *Introduction and Allegro*.

i) *Enigma Variations; Grania and Diarmid: Incidental Music;* (ii) *Empire March; Imperial March; Pomp and Circumstance Marches 1–5*
(BB) *** HMV (DDD/ADD) HMV 5 86725-2. (i) CBSO, Rattle; (ii) LPO, Boult

In *Enigma*, Rattle and the CBSO are both powerful and refined, overwhelming at the close, with the *Grania and Diarmid* excerpts a valuable makeweight. Boult's approach to the *Pomp and Circumstance Marches* is brisk and direct, with an almost no-nonsense manner in places. Yet the approach is naturally Elgarian, with not a hint of vulgarity, and the freshness is attractive. But it is a pity he omits the repeats in the Dvořák-like No. 2 which, with No. 5, is the highlight of the set. The *Imperial March* (1886) was an early success for the young composer, commissioned by Novello to celebrate Queen Victoria's Diamond Jubilee; the *Empire March*, written for the opening of the 1924 Wembley Exhibition, had not been recorded again since then, until Boult's present (1977) version. It is hardly a great discovery but offers a good makeweight. Warm, immediate recording, well transferred.

Enigma Variations; In the South; Introduction and Allegro for Strings
(B) **(*) CfP mono/stereo 3 52394-2. LPO, Boult

Anyone who thinks Boult could not let himself go in surging, passionate music should hear this thrilling mono version

(from 1956) of *In the South*. As sound it is pretty good too, as the recording was made in the Kingsway Hall. The stereo recording of *Enigma* (where, from the opening bars, Boult shows how naturally he can inflect and shape an Elgarian melodic line) and the athletic and thrillingly strong version of the *Introduction and Allegro* could not be more enjoyable. What a natural Elgarian Boult was! Again the sound (this time at Abbey Road) is fresh and exceptionally vivid in the string piece.

Falstaff; Froissart; (i) *Romance for Bassoon & Strings. Grania and Diarmid: Incidental Music*
⊕–• (BB) *** Warner Apex 2564 62200-2. (i) Sheen; BBC SO, A. Davis

After the superb collection comprising the *Enigma Variations* and the two key string works, this is Sir Andrew Davis's finest Elgar disc. *Falstaff* is a richly detailed, deeply affectionate performance, poignant too, and has much of the warmth of the Barbirolli version, yet it has a superbly expansive, modern, digital recording. *Froissart* too, without being pressed too hard, has a real Elgarian sweep and nobilmente. The bassoonist Graham Sheen is a most sensitive soloist in the *Romance*, and the *Grania and Diarmid* incidental music is delightfully presented, with much fine wind and string playing.

Serenade for Strings in E min., Op. 20
** Häns. 93.043. Stuttgart RSO, Norrington – HOLST: *Planets* **

Like Norrington's account of *The Planets*, with which it is coupled, his version of Elgar's *Serenade for Strings* is beautifully played and brilliantly recorded, but lacks something in expressive warmth, a little stiff rather than idiomatic.

(i) *Symphonies 1–2; Cockaigne Overture;* (ii) *Elegy, Op. 58;* (ii; iii) *Romance for Bassoon & Orchestra, Op. 62;* (iii) *Serenade for Strings, Op. 20*
(B) ** Sony (ADD) SB2K 89976 (2). (i) LPO; (ii) ECO; both cond. Barenboim; (iii) with Gatt

Symphonies 1–2; Cockaigne Overture; Sospiri
(BB) ** EMI Gemini 5 85512-2 (2). LSO, Tate

Barenboim, like Solti, studied Elgar's own recording before interpreting the *First Symphony*, and in the long first movement Barenboim overdoes the fluctuations, so losing momentum. The other three movements are beautifully performed, with the *Adagio* almost as tender as Solti's reading with the same players. The *Second Symphony* followed very much in the same path set by Barbirolli, underlining and exaggerating the contrasts of tempi, pulling the music out to the expansive limit. Yet this is still a red-blooded, passionate performance, capable of convincing for the moment at least, and the only real snag with both symphonies is that the recording is not as full and opulent or as well balanced as Elgar's orchestration really demands, and the same comment applies to *Cockaigne*. The well-played *Romance* is placed on the first disc, after the symphony and before the overture. The string pieces sound fuller and in the *Serenade* the *Larghetto* is touching. But in the *Elegy* Barenboim tends to dwell too affectionately on detail and the result is almost schmaltzy.

Jeffrey Tate conducts the LSO in expansively expressive readings of both symphonies, generally sustaining slow speeds – exceptionally slow in No. 2 – with keen concentration, but letting one or two passages sag. These are warmhearted performances nevertheless, helped by brilliant playing from the LSO and rich and full if not sharply focused recording. The *Cockaigne Overture* and brief string piece are successful too, but competition is strong and even at bargain price this coupling is hardly a first choice.

Symphony 1; Elegy; Sospiri
(BB) ** Warner Apex 0927 49021-2. BBC SO, A. Davis

With sound of demonstration quality, Andrew Davis conducts a broad, rather plain reading of the *First Symphony* which is yet highly idiomatic and is beautifully played. Sadly, the performance falls short at the very end, where the brassy coda fails to blaze as it should.

Symphony 2; In the South (Alassio)
*** Chan. **SACD** CHSA 5038. BBC Nat. O of Wales, Hickox

Hickox's version for Chandos was the first recording of an Elgar symphony in Surround Sound SACD, a very impressive pioneering effort bringing out the glory of Elgar's orchestration, not least in his writing for brass: the horns whoop magnificently, given extra separation in the opulent recording. Interpretatively, Richard Hickox with the excellent BBC National Orchestra of Wales steers a distinctive course on the key question of the tempo for the surging 12/8 rhythms of the first movement, not as alarmingly fast as Elgar himself in both his recordings but faster than those, like Vernon Handley, in the noble Boult tradition. In the slow movement, by contrast, Hickox adopts a broad tempo and sustains it well, controlling the climaxes with an idiomatic touch, graduating dynamics with the utmost care and drawing *pianissimos* of the utmost delicacy from the strings, beautifully caught in the wide-ranging recording. The transparency of sound also brings extra benefits in the Scherzo, the players unfazed by a tempo as daringly fast as Elgar's own; in the finale too, the lightness and transparency of many passages, not least the epilogue, bring out the tenderness behind this ultimately elegiac movement.

The *Overture In the South* makes a valuable supplement. The viola solo in the central Nocturne or *Canto Popolare* is beautifully done at a spacious speed, and the ripeness of the thrilling coda brings a final demonstration of this orchestra's impressive quality.

CHAMBER MUSIC

(i) Piano Quintet in A min., Op. 84. String Quartet in E min., Op. 83
(B) **(*) CfP 5 75980-2. (i) Vellinger Qt; (ii) Lane; (iii) Boyd
(M) ** Decca 473 425-2. Mistry Qt, (i) with Norris

The Vellinger Quartet is an unusually characterful group, for whom contrasts of ensemble are as important as blending. In this, their first recording, their approach to Elgar is impulsive, with allegros taken faster than in rival versions, to make the finale of the *Quintet* bold and thrusting, and the finale of the *Quartet* light and volatile. The middle movement of the *Quartet* is light and flowing too, like an interlude rather than a meditation, but the central *Adagio* of the *Quintet* is by contrast very slow and weighty, not as thoughtful as in some other versions. But what crowns the disc is the little fill-up, a ravishing performance of the magical interlude which Elgar arranged for viola and piano from the central *Nocturne* passage of his *Overture, In the South*. James Boyd, the Vellinger violist, plays with richness and firmness of tone and intonation that make one long to hear him in more solo work. However, the most recommendable couplings of the *Quintet* and *Quartet* are the exceptionally searching readings

by the Sorrel Quartet (on Chandos 9894) or the Maggir Quartet with Peter Donohoe, who offer a recommendabl budget coupling (Naxos 8.553737).

The Mistry Quartet offer enjoyable enough performance of this popular coupling, sometimes lacking in forwar impulse, but both in warm 1992 sound. However, hear alongside the reissue of the Vellinger Quartet's rival couplin on CfP, the latter is found to be consistently more imaginativ and fresher-sounding.

Violin Sonata in E min., Op. 82
(BB) **(*) ASV Resonance CD RSN 3060. McAslan, Blakely –
WALTON: *Violin Sonata* **(*)

Though Lorraine McAslan cannot match the virtuoso com mand and warmth of tone of Nigel Kennedy's Chando recording of the *Violin Sonata* (Chan. 8438), hers is an impres sive and warm-hearted version, full of natural imaginatior helped by the incisive playing of John Blakely. Good, forwar recording, which gives the violin-tone less bloom than i might. But this inexpensive disc is well worth its modest cos

Music for wind

Adagio cantabile (Mrs Winslow's Soothing Syrup); Andante con variazione (Evesham Andante); 4 Dances; Harmony Music I–IV; 5 Intermezzos; 6 Promenades
(B) *** Chan. (ADD) 241-33 (2). Athena Ens.

This is a reissue of a pair of discs which originally appeare separately at mid-price. Elgar's 'Shed Music', as he called i was written, when he was a budding young musician, fo himself and four other wind-players to perform, and here it presented very appealingly and excellently recorded.

Organ Sonata 1 in G, Op. 28; Enigma Variations (transcribed for organ by Keith John)
** Hyp. CDA 67363. John (organ of Temple Church, London)

Keith John's performance of the *Organ Sonata* is warml sympathetic, but the resonant acoustic of the Temple Chuc means that the organ itself has a comparatively diffuse pro file. Whether or not one needs an organ performance c *Enigma*, it certainly sounds spectacular here, in *Nimrod* richl sonorous, starting from a whisper and building to a hug climax, and the finale is very imposing indeed.

VOCAL MUSIC

(i; ii) Coronation Ode, Op. 44; (ii; iii; iv) The Spirit of England, Op. 80; (i) O hearken thou, Op. 64 (with (iv) Lana of Hope and Glory (arr. Elgar))
(M) **(*) EMI (ADD/DDD) 5 85148-2. (i) L. Symphony Ch.,
N. Sinfonia, Hickox; (ii) Lott; (iii) Hodgson, Morton,
Roberts, Cambridge University Musical Soc., (iv) Ch. of
King's College, Cambridge, Band of the Royal Military
School of Music, New Philh. O, Ledger – PARRY: *I Was
Glad* ***

Elgar's *Coronation Anthem Ode* is far more than a jingoisti occasional piece, though it was indeed the work which firs featured *Land of Hope and Glory*. The most tender momen of all is reserved for the first faint flickerings of that secon national anthem, introduced gently on the harp to clarine accompaniment. All told, the work contains much Elgaria treasure. Ledger is superb in capturing the swagger an panache, flouting all thoughts of potentially bad taste. Ther is excellent singing and playing, although the male soloists d ot quite match their female colleagues. The spectacular 1969) recording, made in King's College Chapel with extra rass bands, makes a splendid impact, with the resonant coustics creating a jumbo *Land of Hope and Glory* at the lose. The remastering does not seem to make the sound as deally sharp as it might be, but it remains a compulsive istening experience nevertheless. Hickox conducts a rousing igital version of *The Spirit of England*, magnificently defying he dangers of wartime bombast, with the London Symphony Chorus on radiant form. With a beautiful performance of *O earken thou*, Elgar's rousing version of the *National Anthem*, nd Parry's *I was glad*, this CD is a must for all Elgarians.

The Dream of Gerontius, Op. 38

B) (***) CfP mono 585 9042 (2). Lewis, Thomas, Cameron, Huddersfield Ch. Soc., RLPO, Sargent – WALTON: *Belshazzar's Feast*. (**)

This outstanding performance of *The Dream of Gerontius* was hosen by Alec Robertson for inclusion in *The Great Records*, nd rightly so. There is a greater spiritual perception here han in Barbirolli's stereo version, which has echoes of the opera house about it. Here, as with Boult, the closing pages of he first and second parts have a rapt intensity that is very moving, without any hint of emotional indulgence. EMI hose the excerpt of *Go Forth Upon Thy Journey* (with John Cameron in superb voice) to include in their anthology ribute to Sir Malcolm Sargent and this shows, as does the whole performance, an inspiration which this conductor only arely found in the recording studio. Richard Lewis is a fine Gerontius and his dialogues with Marjorie Thomas (in the vords of A.R. 'a Rossetti rather than a Rubens angel') have a beauty and stillness that is totally memorable. The one failure of the Sargent performance is the *Demons' Chorus*, in which he Huddersfield chorus fail to let themselves go. But every-where else the singing is magnificent, one of their finest chievements on disc, and the mono recording is generally vorthy of it.

i) *The Music Makers. Dream Children; Froissart Overture;* Bach arr. Elgar: *Fantasia and Fugue in C min.*

M) *** Hallé CD HLL 7509. Irwin, Hallé Ch. & O, Elder

The title of this disc, 'Elgar: A Self-Portrait', refers to the utobiographical element in the major work here, *The Music Makers*, but, as Michael Kennedy points out in his authorita-ive note, in many ways all of Elgar's works have an element of self-portraiture. That cantata is given a performance that bove all is refined, with the full-ranging recording bringing ut the subtlety of Elgar's orchestration. It may not be quite s warm as Boult's classic version with Janet Baker an incom-arable soloist, but the excellent Jane Irwin with her much ighter mezzo is also moving in Elder's strong and purposeful eading. The high contrasts are underlined between the eflective passages and such incisive choral outbursts as *With vonderful deathless ditties*, all sung with crisp ensemble by the Iallé Choir. Refinement also marks the performances of the ther works on the disc, and in the arrangement of Bach's reat organ *Fantasia and Fugue in C minor* Elder relishes the xotic orchestral effect to the full, helped by superb, modern, ligital sound.

EL-KHOURY, Bechara (born 1957)

i) *Piano Concerto, Op. 36. Danse des aigles, Op. 9; Image ymphonique: Les dieux de la terre.* (ii) *Méditation poétique*

(for violin & orchestra), *Op. 41*; (i) *Poèmes for piano and orchestra: 1, Op. 11; 2, Op. 22. Poème symphonique 1: Le Liban en flammes, Op. 14. Poème 2: Le regard du Christ. Requiem; Serenades for Strings 1: Feuilles d'Autumn; 2, Op. 20. Suite symphonique: La nuit et le fou, Op. 29*

(BB) *** Naxos 8.55691/2. (i) Rahman El Bacha or David Lively; (ii) Poulet; Cologne O, Dervaux

Bechara El-Khoury was born in Beirut in 1957, completed his musical training in the Paris Ecole Normale de Musique, and is now permanently resident in France, where his music has gathered a considerable reputation. He communicates readily and might be regarded as something of a crossover composer. The *Piano Concerto* is very approachable, with its varying conflicting moods well projected by the excellent soloist; it brings opportunities for virtuoso rhetoric. Both here and in the two *Poèmes* for piano and orchestra, played by a different but equally persuasive soloist, the combination of vividly coloured orchestral drama and lyricism reminds one of film music. But undoubtedly the finest concertante work here is the comparatively innocent *Méditation poétique* for violin and orchestra, which is beautifully played by Gérard Poulet. (Incidentally, these performances were recorded 'live', which accounts for a couple of slips from the horns.) The two amiable *String Serenades*, the first autumnal, the second more searching and ardent, would – like the *Méditation* – be welcome at any concert.

The companion CD of orchestral works opens with a catchy and brightly scored *Danse des aigles*, followed by the darker symphonic poem, *Les dieux de la terre*, and the suite, *La nuit et le fou*, both highly atmospheric and imaginatively scored. The other two symphonic poems, *Le Liban en flammes* (inspired by the same events as the *Requiem* below) and the shorter and much more dramatic *Regard du Christ*, are full of incident. El-Khoury's orchestral sound-world is very much his own: he uses a remarkable range of orchestral effects. Undoubtedly the finest of these orchestral works is the *Requiem* of 1980 with its subtitle ('For the Lebanese Martyrs of the War'). Opening like a traditional funeral march, it even quotes briefly the rhythm of Siegfried's funeral music and develops into an agonized lament, interrupted by warlike reminiscences; but it remains affirmative, ending with a dramatic final gesture of regret. Pierre Dervaux is a highly sympathetic exponent of this repertoire and these are all fine, dedicated performances. However, the absence of full descriptive notes in English (or French) is a drawback to this issue.

(i;ii) *Les fleuves engloutis (The engulfed rivers), Op. 64*; (i;iii) *New York, Tears and Hope, Op. 65; Sextuor (arr. for 24 violins), Op. 58.* (iv) (Piano) *Fragments oubliées, Op. 66*; (v) *Waves, Op. 60.*

(BB) *** Naxos 8.570134. (i) LSO; (ii) Harding; (iii) Brabbins; (iv) Dimitri Vassilakis; (v) Hideki Nagano

In many ways this is the finest of these three El-Khoury compilations, and in *New York, Tears and Hope* offers the first major orchestral piece concisely reflecting the human experi-ence of 9/11. Opening poignantly, it moves to a petrifying climax, and ends elegiacally, but without a trace of despair. The intensely concentrated *Sextet* (arranged for full string ensemble at the request of Shlomo Mintz) is only five min-utes in length, and might be regarded as a companion work, a wistfully dark lamentation, but suddenly quickening and moving out of the clouds. *Les fleuves englouties* is a series of impressionistic miniatures, contrasting serenity and struggle with confident life-assertion. The two closing piano pieces similarly move from reflection to responses which are more fragmented but positive. The performances are very persuasive indeed and excellently recorded.

Symphony (The Ruins of Beirut); Hill of Strangeness; Twilight Harmonies; Wine of the Clouds
(BB) **(*) Naxos 8.557043. Nat. SO of Ukraine, Sirenko

The *Symphony* was composed (in 1985) in the wake of the civil war in the Lebanon and is a powerful, tragically arresting work, laid out in four fairly traditional movements. But it is without any kind of conventional development of ideas; in essence it is a kaleidoscopic set of brief variants. Even more than the vividly scored symphony, the three shorter works rely a great deal on orchestral textures, with contrasting sonorities, dynamics, mood and colouring, all skilfully manipulated to give an illusion of forward movement (rather than development). The brass scoring is emphatic, with exuberant use of the horns. The restless symphonic meditation, *Hill of Strangeness* ('Colline de l'étrange') 'is a journey through a fog pierced by glimpses of light' and is concerned with 'solitude and the struggle of the light to come through dark clouds'. It is certainly enigmatic. *Harmonies crépusculaires* was written in memory of the conductor Pierre Dervaux and is essentially valedictory in feeling, but the finality of death is powerfully conveyed by more shattering brass interruptions, with an answering tolling bell. The dream-like *Wine of the Clouds* ('Le vin des nuages') 'is a confrontation between silence and the violence of nature', opening impressionistically and ending with a torrent of sound, including the composer's characteristic horn glissandi.

ELLINGTON, Edward Kennedy 'Duke' (1899–1974)

Harlem; The River: suite (orch. Collier); *Solitude* (trans. Morton Gould)
*** Chan. 9909. Detroit SO, Järvi – DAWSON: *Negro Folk Symphony* ***

Harlem is a wildly exuberant but essentially optimistic picture of Harlem as it used to be before the drug age. Ellington pictures a parade and a funeral, and ends with riotous exuberance. This is marvellously played by musicians who know all about the Afro-American musical tradition. The trumpets are terrific. *The River* was composed in 1970, intended as music for a ballet with choreography by Alvin Ailey, but this project proved abortive, and Ellington also saw the score as a river journey. *Solitude*, which dates from Ellington's Cotton Club days, is much more subtly scored by Morton Gould, and in its orchestral format has a haunting, almost Copland-esque flavour, although it retains Ellington's own musical fingerprints. Splendid recording.

ENESCU, Georges (1881–1955)

Violin Sonata 3 in A min., Op. 25
(BB) (***) Naxos mono 8.111127. Y. & H. Menuhin – BACH: *Unaccompnied Violin Sonata in C*; PIZZETTI: *Violin Sonata 1 in A* (***)

Yehudi Menuhin and his sister Hephzibah recorded this wonderful *Sonata* in Paris in 1936 in the presence of the composer. Their evident love for the piece shines through ('We knew it when the ink was barely dry,' Menuhin claimed, 'we almost created the work when we first learned it at the Ville d'Avrsy in 1932.') It had been premièred by the composer five years earlier, in 1927. Yehudi was 19 at the time and Hephzibah 15, and they both possess a captivating youthful ardour – and the sound is remarkably fine for the period.

Violin Sonata 3 in A min., Op. 25/1 (excerpt)
(*) EMI **DVD 4904519. Y. & H. Menuhin (bonus: MENDELSSOHN: *Variations sérieuses, Op. 54*) – BARTÓK: *Contrasts for piano, violin & cello*, etc.; FRANCK: *Violin Sonata in A*; SCHUBERT: *Piano Trio 1 in B flat* **(*)

The ORTF recording was made presumably at the Maison de la Radio in 1972 and, like the Bartók *Contrasts*, is in colour. We are given just the *Moderato malinconico*, which is a pity. On the whole the camerawork serves us well, though there is some superimposition of the two artists which may not please all tastes, and the colour is a little faded.

PIANO MUSIC

Piano Sonatas: 1 & 3, Op. 24/1 & 3; Nocturne in D flat; Pièce sur le nom de Fauré; Prelude & Fugue in C; Scherzo
*** Avie AV 2061 (2). Borac

Luiza Borac continues her traversal of Enescu's piano output with a two-CD set comprising two of his three *Piano Sonatas*, Op. 24. This repertoire is rarely (if indeed ever) encountered in the recital room or in broadcast programmes, which enhances the importance of this set. She covers the formative years in the *Prelude and Fugue* of 1903 through to the *Third Sonata* of 1934. The *First Sonata* comes from 1924 and was premièred the following year in Bucharest; it shows the influence of Debussy and Ravel, while the *Third* (written after the completion of his masterpiece, the opera *Oedipe*) will come as something of a revelation to the listener. Borac plays with total commitment and is well served by the recording, made in St Dunstan's Church, Mayfield.

ENNA, August (1859–1939)

The Little Match Girl (opera); *The Shepherdess and the Chimney-sweep* (ballet for orchestra and narrator)
** CPO 999 595-2. Bonde-Hansen, Sjöbergt, Helmuth, Danish R. Sinf., Zeilinger

The Danish composer August Enna produced a steady stream of operas and operettas throughout his career that, thanks to his melodic gift and attractive orchestration, earned him considerable success. Alas, by the end of his life his music fell out of fashion, and he died poverty-stricken and disappointed. It is good that CPO has made available these two representative works, based on Hans Andersen fairy-tales, which have never fallen completely out of the Danish repertoire. There is nothing profound here, but *The Little Match Girl* of 1897 has some charming ideas, with the influence of Wagner felt in the style though not in profundity. *The Shepherdess and the Chimney-sweep* has some engaging music, but the prominence (in volume and in quantity) of the narration will surely be too much for English-speaking listeners, although full texts and translations are offered. The performances are sympathetic, but the recording, though acceptable, lacks richness and depth.

ERSKINE, Thomas (1732–81)

Fiddler Tam: Overture in C, Op. 1/2. Overture in B flat: The Maid of the Mill; Largo; Lord Kellie's Reel; String Quartets: in C min.; in A; Trio Sonatas 5 in E; 6 in G; (i) Songs: *Death is now my only treasure; The Lover's Message*
*** Linn CKD 240. (i) Lawson; Concerto Caledonia, McGuinness

Turning his back on his aristocratic roots, Thomas Erskine, 6th Earl of Kellie, went to Mannheim to study with Johann Stamitz. Returning to Scotland, he was among the first composers in Britain to compose in the Mannheim style, even influencing J. C. Bach in London. This selection of his works gives a clear idea of the liveliness of his inspiration, starting with the exuberant *Overture in C*, in effect a symphony in three compact movements, with a central *Andantino* in C minor. One of his Mannheim characteristics is to use dramatic crescendos, not just in the overtures but in the two *Quartets*, the A major work involving a central *Adagio* in F sharp minor. The two *Trio Sonatas* are both in two movements, each ending with a Minuet. In the *Sixth* a flute takes over the violin part, as it does in the *Largo*, based on a Scottish ballad, 'The Lowlands of Holland'. Over a drone bass *Lord Kellie's Reel* typically features snapping Scottish rhythms. With Mhairi Lawson the fresh soprano in the two songs, David McGuinness draws consistently lively performances from his period players, if abrasive at times. The title, *Fiddler Tam*, was the nickname given to the Earl by his retainers. Well-balanced recording.

EYCK, Jakob van (1590–1657)

Der Fluyten Lust-hof (excerpts)
**(*) BIS CD 1375. Laurin (recorder)

According to Dan Laurin, *Der Fluyten Lust-hof* is the largest existing collection of music for a solo instrument in the world – 143 pieces in all – and a walk through the entire 'pleasure garden' would take over ten hours. In the composer's day, to carry a flute about in Holland was apparently to show that you were educated, so there was obviously a market for monodic pieces like this. They are virtually all arrangements and the opening *Engels Nachtegaeltje* ('English nightingale') was a familiar tune in the 1630s and here it is simply varied and ornamented. The variations are more elaborate for Caccini's *Amarilli mia Bella* and *Gabrielle Maditelle* (a French popular tune), where van Eyck uses a 'chain-variation' with a varied reprise. *Excusemoy* draws on John Dowland's *Can she excuse my wrongs* in a country dance version, and of course there is a *Fantasia and Echo*, a favourite device of the time. Laurin plays everything prettily enough and is at his best in *Boffons*, a catchy sword dance; but, to be honest, a series of ingenuous pieces for solo recorder, even played as well as this, rather tends to outstay its welcome.

FALLA, Manuel de (1876–1946)

Nights in the Gardens of Spain
(M) ** Warner Elatus 0927 46720-2. Argerich, O de Paris, Barenboim – ALBENIZ: *Ibéria* (suite) **

The volatile combination of the charismatic Martha Argerich and Daniel Barenboim creates a consistent electricity in the exciting Erato version, recorded at a public performance and

now reissued on Elatus. There is a degree of latitude here that would be difficult to bring off in a recording studio but, with the spur of communication from the audience, the ebb and flow of tension, with marked acceleration at climaxes, involves the listener throughout. The recording itself is somewhat restricted, but the lush orchestral textures are an admirable backcloth for Argerich's digital bravura, and much flamenco-style improvisatory feeling is engendered. The closing section provides a glowing apotheosis, almost Wagnerian in its breadth, but very telling when the whole performance has such spontaneity. However, there are reservations about the coupling.

Seite canciones populares españolas (7 **Spanish Popular Songs**)
⊕→ (BB) *** EMI Encore 5 86985-2. Monoyios, Barrueco (guitar) – GRANADOS: *12 Danzas españolas* ***

Manuel de Falla's seven *canciones populares españolas* could not be sung with greater idiomatic feeling or more charm and vivacity than they are by Ann Monoyios, and Barrueco's sparkling transcription of the piano accompaniments, superbly played, makes one feel that the guitar rather than the piano was in the composer's thoughts. A bargain reissue not to be missed.

OPERA

La vida breve (complete)
(BB) ** Naxos 8.660155 (2). Sánchez, Valls, Nafé, Echeverría, Baquerizo, Suárez, Cid, Sanz, Reyes (guitar), Prince of Asturias Foundation Ch., Asturias SO, Valdés

Having an idiomatic account of Falla's colourful opera, well cast and well recorded, makes a good bargain on the Naxos label, even if there is a serious lack of tension in much of the performance. It does not help that the story of the love between the gypsy girl Salud and Paco from a well-to-do family is too naive to be convincing. Even when Salud at the climax commits suicide in despair when Paco returns to his intended bride, neither the singer nor the orchestra sounds very involved. In the central part, Ana Maria Sánchez has a warm, well-focused voice with the right mezzo tinge, and she sings intelligently but conveys little sense of drama. As Paco, Vincente Ombuena Valls is well cast, with his pleasing, fresh tenor, while among the others Alicia Nafé is most characterful as Salud's grandmother. The two *Dances* that come as orchestral showpieces betray the relative slackness of the rest in the way they immediately raise the tension. The earlier version with Victoria de los Angeles as Salud is clearly preferable.

FANELLI, Ernest (1860–1917)

Tableaux symphoniques d'après 'Le Roman de la Momie'
**(*) Marco Polo 8.225234. Drahosova, Slovak RSO, Adriano – BOURGAULT-DUCOUDRAY: *Rhapsodie cambodgienne* **(*)

Hardly a well-known name now, but French composer Ernest Fanelli belongs to one of the great might-have-beens: if only he was born in a different time and under a different set of circumstances, he might be better known now, for he was undoubtedly a composer of some originality. It was Pierné who, in 1912, on inspecting a score submitted by Fanelli as a specimen of his musical handwriting for a job as copyist, was impressed by the music itself (Fanelli submitted his score without telling Pierné that he had written it), commenting that it 'contained all the principles and all processes of modern music used by the recognized masters of today' – remarkable, as the work was written some 29 years earlier. Through Pierné, Fanelli secured performances of some of his music, giving the composer a brief period of interest in the music world. Adriano is a strong advocate of Fanelli, and in the sleeve-notes he suggests that Fanelli invited a certain amount of jealousy from Debussy, who once walked out of a room on hearing some of Fanelli's 'advanced' harmonies; interestingly, Ravel apparently said, 'now we know where his [Debussy's] impressionism comes from'. Fanelli's life was undoubtedly difficult, and he died disillusioned and embittered. All that aside, on the strength of this disc, Adriano's championing of him is certainly worthwhile: *Le Roman de la Momie* (*Romance of the Mummy*) (1883–6) was inspired by the exotic novel of the same name by Théophile Gautier, who filled his short novel with vivid depictions of Egyptian landscapes, costumes and locations – an ideal frame for Fanelli's 'Tableaux symphoniques' (the second part of the score, *Fête dans le palais du Pharon*, is dedicated to Gautier's daughter). While it is not true to say that Fanelli has an instantly distinctive voice, his music, with the aid of a large orchestra (including a wordless soprano vocalise in Part I of *Thèbes*), enters the worlds of Rimsky-Korsakov, Ravel and Respighi, as well as encompassing whole-tone scales and polytonality. The score has plenty of atmosphere and builds up to powerful climaxes: at times the score is reminiscent of film music – an exotic/gothic production of the golden era (such as the opening of the *Fête danse le palais du Pharon*, for example) but is none the worse for that. It all makes for fascinating listening, and anyone interested in the by-ways of French music should explore this disc, especially with its rare coupling. Adriano gives an enthusiastic performance, the only reservation being that the string-tone could be sweeter, especially above the stave where they are taxed at times; the playing is not always as immaculate as it might be. The recording is well detailed and quite decent. As Adriano writes – and it must be stressed that it was he, not the writer of this note, who wrote it – 'Gautier's Mummy, in fact, returns again'!

FARNABY, Giles (1562–1640)

Giles Farnaby was born in London and began life as a joiner, but he had a cousin who played the harpsichord and who perhaps influenced the budding musician. At Oxford he gained a Bachelor of Music degree and met John Bull. In 1598 his first *Book of Madrigals* was printed and much praised, and his keyboard works were very influential and were held in great esteem, yet he retired to Lincolnshire as a teacher and church warden, and we know little else about him except what his music tells us.

Fantasias, 4/489; 5/82; 6/320; 7/333; 8/323; 9/270; 10/313; 12/343; 13/347; Canzonets: Ay me, poor heart (arr. Farnaby); *Construe my meaning; Witness, ye heavens* (both arr. Wilson); *2 Unidentified Part Songs; Variations on Loth to Depart*
(BB) *** Naxos 8. 570025. Wilson (harpsichord)

Farnaby's surviving keyboard works (53 of them) occupy one-sixth of the total content of the celebrated *Fitzwilliam Virginal Book*, compiled in the 1620s – in the company of music by Byrd, Bull, Gibbons and Tomkins. His *Fantasias*, to

quote Glen Wilson, their impressive executant here, are 'sober pieces in strict polyphony with no text and no fixed melody or *cantus firmus*', but ending with a toccata of great virtuosity. But they are by no means dull. The initially slow tempo of their presentation is explained when the extraordinary keyboard pyrotechnics begin, clusters of notes thrown off with great panache by Wilson.

The writing itself is of interest thematically (Richard Strauss used the opening theme of 4/89, and 12/343 was borrowed by Bach for the *E major Fugue* in the *Well-Tempered Klavier*) and also for its imaginative development. This is music that you have to explore, to discover Farnaby's ingenuity. The other items here are arrangements of part-songs, treated very freely, of which the most intriguing is the final song, *Loth to depart*. This CD is a most valuable addition to the catalogue, for Wilson plays on an impressive copy of a Ruckers double-keyboard harpsichord, with plenty of vitality and, at times, dazzling bravura, and he is very well recorded. But you must take care in getting the volume level right: the effect should be imposing without being overwhelming.

FARNON, Robert (born 1917)

A la claire fontaine; Colditz March; Derby Day; Gateway to the West; How Beautiful is Night; 3 Impressions for Orchestra: 2, In a Calm; 3, Manhattan Playboy. Jumping Bean; Lake in the Woods; Little Miss Molly; Melody Fair; Peanut Polka; Pictures in the Fire; Portrait of a Flirt; A Star is Born; State Occasion; Westminster Waltz
*** Marco Polo 8.223401. Slovak RSO (Bratislava), Leaper

Farnon's quirky rhythmic numbers, *Portrait of a Flirt, Peanut Polka* and *Jumping Bean*, have much in common with Leroy Anderson in their instant memorability; their counterpart is a series of gentler orchestral watercolours, usually featuring a wistful flute solo amid gentle washes of violins. *A la claire fontaine* is the most familiar. Then there is the film music, of which the *Colditz March* is rightly famous, and the very British genre pieces, written in the 1950s. All this is played by this excellent Slovak orchestra with warmth, polish and a remarkable naturalness of idiomatic feeling. The recording is splendid, vivid, with the orchestra set back convincingly in a concert-hall acoustic.

FARRANCE, Louise (1804–75)

Piano Quintets 1 in A min., Op. 30; 2 in E, Op. 31
*** ASV CDDCA 1122. London Schubert Ens.

Louise Farrance studied with Reicha, Hummel and Moscheles and became the only woman professor of the piano at the Paris Conservatoire during the nineteenth century. She composed prolifically for the piano, but her output includes three symphonies, which were given in Paris, Brussels, Geneva and Copenhagen during her lifetime, as well as a quantity of chamber music. She has fallen from view: the *Everyman Dictionary of Music* does not mention her, nor do Michael Kennedy's *Oxford Dictionary* or Alison Latham's *Oxford Companion*. All the same, there does seem to be an upsurge of interest in her on CD: two of the symphonies have been recorded, as have the *Nonet*, the *Sextet for Wind and Piano* and two of her piano trios. The *Piano Quintet in A minor* comes from 1839 and was her first chamber work of any kind, its successor following a year later. Both are scored for the same forces as the Hummel *Quintet* and the Schubert *Trout*.

Although her musical language owes much to Haydn and Hummel, there are elements of Weber, Spohr and Mendelssohn to be found, and there is considerable harmonic subtlety in her writing. Good playing from the London Schubert Ensemble and truthful recording.

FAURÉ, Gabriel (1845–1924)

Piano Quartet 1 in C min., Op. 15

*** Aeon AECD 0540. Schumann Qt – CHAUSSON: *Piano Quartet* ***

** Metronome MET CD 1048. Juno's Band – RAVEL: *Piano Trio* **

The Quatuor Schumann's precision of ensemble adds greatly to the impact of the early Fauré *Piano Quartet*, as it does with the Chausson, making an apt and attractive coupling. As in the Chausson, the most compelling playing of all comes in the Schumann Quartet's account of the *Adagio* slow movement, hushed in deep meditation, leading to an incisive account of the brilliant finale with its dashing triplet rhythms. One looks forward to more discs from this fine group.

A well-played account from the curiously named Juno's Band and decently recorded, but no match for the competition, which is abundant and of quality.

Barcarolles: 3 in G flat, Op. 42; 9 in A min., Op. 101; Impromptus: 1 in E flat, Op. 25; 2 in F min., Op. 31; 3 in A flat, Op. 34; 4 in D flat, Op. 91; 5 in F sharp min., Op. 102; Nocturne 3 in A flat, Op. 33/3; 8 Piéces brèves, Op. 84; 9 Preludes, Op. 103; Valse caprice 1 in A, Op. 30

** VAI Audio VAIA 1165. Johannesen

Grant Johannesen was one of the early champions of Fauré's piano music on LP during the 1950s. These are an admirable reminder of his artistry, though the recorded sound does not wear its years gracefully. For Johannesen's admirers rather than the music-lover starting a Fauré collection.

VOCAL MUSIC

Complete Mélodies

Vol. 1: *Accompagnement; Au bord de l'eau; Au cimetière; Barcarolle; Les berceaux; C'est la paix; Chanson du pêcheur; La fleur qui va sur l'eau; L'horizon chimérique; Les matelots; Larmes; 5 Mélodies de Venise; Mirages; Pleurs d'or; Seule!; Tarentelle*

*** Hyp. CDA 67333 Lott, J. Smith, McGreevy, Doufexis, Mark Ainsley, Maltman, Varcoe; Johnson

Vol. 2: *L'absent; Après un rêve; Automne; Chanson; Chant d'automne; Clair de lune; Dans la forêt de septembre; Dans les ruins d'une abbaye; En prière; La feé aux chansons; Il est né, le divin enfant; Le jardin clos; Lydia; Mai; Noël; Prison; Puisqu'ici-bas toute âme; Sérénade toscane; Spleen; Tristesse; Le voyageur*

*** Hyp. CDA 67334. McGreevy, J. Smith, Lott, Doufexis, Mark Ainsley, Fouchécourt, Maltman, Varcoe; Johnson

The first two volumes of Graham Johnson's Hyperion survey of the Fauré songs are quite masterly. They are shared among a distinguished team of mainly British singers. As ever in these Hyperion song surveys, the piano accompaniments are highly sensitive and imaginative in their use of keyboard

colour while, as so often, Graham Johnson provides immaculate documentation which greatly enhances the value of each volume. As usual with this company, the recording quality is very fine indeed, natural in timbre and with an excellent balance between voice and keyboard. The singing radiates a love for and dedication to these wonderful songs, and no one with an interest in Fauré (or in good singing) should miss them.

(i–iii) Requiem, Op. 48; (iv) Dolly Suite, Op. 56; (v) Pavane, Op. 50; (vi) Cantique de Jean Racine, Op. 11; (ii; vii) Messe basse

(BB) *** HMV (ADD) 5 86726-2. (i) Chilcott, Carol Case, (ii) King's College Ch., (iii) New Philh. O, Willcocks; (iv) French Nat. RO, Beecham; (v) Gareth Morris, New Philh. O, Willcocks; (vi) Winchester Cathedral Ch., Hill, with Farr (organ); (vii) with Smy, Butt (organ), cond. Ledger

Requiem (1893 version); Cantique de Jean Racine (both ed. Rutter).

⊙— *** Virgin 5 61994-2. Argenta, Keenlyside, Winchester Cathedral Ch., Bournemouth Sinf., Hill; S. Farr, organ (with Pierre VILLETTE: *O salutarus Hostia; O magnum mysterium.* Jean ROGER-DUCASSE: *Regina coeli laetare; Crux fidelis; Alma redemptoris Mater* (with Kevin Burrowes) ***)

(i–iii) Requiem, Op. 48. Mélodies: (i; iv) Aurore; Chanson d'amour; La Fée aux chansons; Notre amour; Le Secret; (ii; iv) Chanson du pêcheur; En sourdine; Fleur jetée; Nell; Poème d'un jour, Op. 21; Le Voyageur

(BB) ** RCA 82876 55303-2. (i) Bonney; (ii) Hagegård; (iii) Tanglewood Festival Ch., Boston SO, Ozawa; (iv) Warren Jones (piano)

This new Virgin recording of the Fauré *Requiem* (in the 1893 full-orchestral version) and the lovely *Cantique de Jean Racine*, with organ (both in John Rutter's editions), must now go to the top of the list of recommendations. Not only is David Hill's performance deeply felt, it is also dramatic and with a wide dynamic range, so that the opening and close are calmly atmospheric, but the climaxes are spectacular, especially the *Hosanna* at the close of *Sanctus* and the thrilling *Agnus Dei*. The singing of the Westminster trebles is Elysian, and both soloists are excellent, Nancy Argenta notably so in the *Pie Jesu*. The only slight reservation is that the articulation of the gently pointed organ accompaniment in the *Paradisum* could be clearer.

The five motets from Pierre Villette and Jean Roger-Ducasse make a perfect supplement because their musical style is similar; the climax of the *a cappella O magnum mysterium* is stirring, and the Roger-Ducasse triptych features a soaring treble soloist, here the totally secure Kenan Burrows. The recording, made in the cathedral and admirably balanced by Mike Clements, simply could not be bettered.

In their account of the *Requiem*, the King's style is very much in the English cathedral tradition. Here the solo role is taken appealingly by a boy treble, Robert Chilcott. The recording, incidentally, was made in Trinity College Chapel and is very fine and splendidly remastered. The performance is eloquent and warmly moving, although some may feel its Anglican accents unidiomatic. The *Cantique de Jean Racine* is beautifully and quite fervently sung in Winchester, with David Hill making the most of its contrasts. For the equally brief *Messe basse*, sweetly melodic, we return to King's, with the choir radiantly directed by Sir David Willcocks, and a sensitive treble soloist in Paul Smy.

The *Dolly Suite* (in Rabaud's orchestration) brings the consistently imaginative and poetic phrasing that distinguished Beecham's best performances. The delicacy of the string textures and wind playing in the *Berceuse*, *Le jardin de Dolly* and *Tendresse* is exquisite, while the closing movement, *Le pas espagnole*, has the kind of dash we associate with Beecham's Chabrier.

The final bonus is a melting version of the famous *Pavane*, with Gareth Morris playing the flute solo, given lovely, rich sound. Altogether a winning anthology.

On RCA, Ozawa uses the full score. His performance is gentle and recessive, although the performers (including the fine Boston orchestra) rise to the climaxes. The reverberation of Symphony Hall bathes the chorus in a hazy glow of resonance. However, many may like the ecceisastical, cathedral-like effect, and it ensures that the closing *In Paradisum* is tenderly ethereal. The two sensitive soloists provide the couplings, two separate groups of Fauré songs, also over-resonantly recorded (in Massachusetts and Sweden respectively) – here the piano is adversely affected. Barbara Bonney responds to Fauré's muse very pleasingly (her lively *La Fée aux chansons* and the touching *Le Secret* are highlights), Håkan Hagegård less so – his style is very forthright.

FAYRFAX, Robert (1464–1521)

Albanus Domini laudans; Ave lumen gratie; Missa Albanus; Antiphons: Eterne laudis lilium; O Maria Deo grata
*** Gaudeamus CDGAU 160. Cardinall's Musick, Carwood

The magnificent *Missa Albanus*, written for St Alban's Abbey (where Fayrfax was finally buried) is aptly coupled with two extended antiphons, just as elaborate in their polyphonic complexity. *O Maria Deo grata* is directly associated with this particular Mass, having also been written for St Alban's. *Eterne laudis lilium*, again written for St Alban's, won for Fayrfax the sum of 20 shillings from the much-loved Queen Elizabeth of York, wife of Henry VII, and is a dedicated tribute to St Elizabeth, mother of John the Baptist. Fresh and intense performances, beautifully balanced.

Antiphona Regali ex progenie; Magnificat Regali; Missa Regali ex progenie; Alas for the lak of her presens; Lauda vivi alpha et O; That was my woo
*** Gaudeamus CDGAU 185. Cardinall's Musick, Carwood

This collection is centred around the *Mass* and *Magnificat Regali ex progenie*, but opens with the extended votive antiphon, *Lauda vivi Alpha et O*. The collection also includes two rare songs, including the plangent duet, *That was my woo*. The performances are very fine and if the Mass itself is not among the composer's most ambitious works, its textures are as strongly individual as ever. Splendid recording.

Antiphon: Tecum principium (plainsong); Missa Tecum principium; Motet: Maria plena virtute; Music for recorders: Mese tenor; O lux beata trinitas; Parames tenor
*** Gaudeamus CDGAU 145. Cardinall's Musick, Carwood; Frideswide Cons.

Though the *Missa Tecum principium* is less complex than the brilliant Mass *O quam glorifica*, the argument is not just more direct but even more extended, with the four big sections lasting almost 50 minutes. The final sublime *Agnus Dei* is followed by three tiny instrumental pieces played on recorders by the Frideswide Consort. An extended votive antiphon, *Maria plena virtute*, then rounds off the disc with the most

moving music of all, a narrative on the Virgin Mary at the Cross, full of deeply personal responses to involve the modern listener immediately.

Ave Dei patris filia; Missa O quam glorifica; O quam glorifica (hymnus); Orbis factor (Kyrie). 3 secular songs: *Sumwat musyng; That was joy; To complayne me, alas*
🎧 ⊛ *** Gaudeamus CDGAU 142. Cardinall's Musick, Carwood

The Mass, *O quam glorifica*, is the most complex that Fayrfax ever wrote. The rhythmic complexities, too, sound wonderfully fresh to the modern ear, with conflicting speeds often involving bold cross-rhythms, parading the composer's closely controlled freedom, before bar-lines applied their tyranny. Above all this is music immediately to involve one in its radiant beauty. The separate antiphon or motet, *Ave Dei patris filia*, is comparably adventurous and beautiful, and is well supplemented by three secular part-songs for male voices. They even anticipate the Elizabethan madrigal, notably the third and most poignant, *To complayne me, alas*. Carwood draws inspired performances from his singers, crisp and dramatic as well as beautifully blended, and most atmospherically recorded in the Fitzalan Chapel at Arundel Castle.

FEINBERG, Samuil (1890–1962)

Piano Sonatas 1–6
*** BIS CD 1413. Samaltanos (1, 4 & 5) & Sirodeau (2, 3 & 6)

Samuil Feinberg is known as one of the greatest Soviet pianists of his day. In their anthology of the Russian Piano School issued in the mid-1990s, BMG/Melodiya included Feinberg playing his transcriptions of Bach organ pieces and some Mozart sonatas. He was a noted Bach interpreter and in his notes Christophe Sirodeau, one of the two pianists on this CD, writes that in 1958–9 Feinberg was the second pianist to record Bach's complete '48', the first being Edwin Fischer. (In fact, Rosalyn Tureck recorded a set in the early 1950s, recently reissued on DG, but let that pass.) Feinberg also championed Prokofiev, Debussy and Scriabin – his interpretation of the *Fourth Sonata* was much admired by Scriabin himself. As a composer, Feinberg wrote mainly for the piano and for the voice. During the first half of his creative life (1910–33) his output was virtuosic, rich in contrasts and (to quote Sirodeau) 'imbued with a symbolist fragility that owes something to Scriabin'. Later his style became increasingly diatonic in much the same way as had Miaskovsky and Prokofiev. Anyway, the six *Sonatas* recorded here (there are 12 in all, together with three piano concertos) come from the period 1914–23 and, with the exception of the *Third* (1916), are all in one movement and short. No. 3 takes 23 minutes but the remainder, except for No. 6, last less than ten minutes. They are all very well played and recorded.

FERRANTI, Marco Aurelio Zani de (1801–78)

Exercice, Op. 50/14; Fantaisie variée sur le romance d'Otello (Assisa a piè), Op. 7; 4 Mélodies nocturnes originales, Op. 41a/1–4; Nocturne sur la dernière pensée de Weber, Op. 40; Ronde des fées, Op. 2
*** Chan. 8512. Wynberg (guitar) – FERRER: *Collection* ***

Simon Wynberg's playing fully enters the innocently compelling sound-world of this Bolognese composer; it is wholly spontaneous and has the most subtle control of light and shade. Ferranti's invention is most appealing, and this makes ideal music for late-evening reverie; moreover the guitar is most realistically recorded.

FERRER, José (1835–1916)

Belle (Gavotte); La Danse de naïades; L'Etudiant de Salamanque (Tango); Vals
*** Chan. 8512. Wynberg (guitar) – FERRANTI: *Collection*
***

José Ferrer is a less substantial figure than Ferranti, but these four vignettes are almost as winning as that composer's music. The recording has striking realism and presence.

FERROUD, Pierre-Octave (1900–36)

Symphony in A; Sérénade; Chirurgie (opera): Suite
** Marco Polo 8.225029. Württemberg PO, Davin

This is the kind of repertoire off the beaten track that makes CD collecting these days so rewarding. Pierre-Octave Ferroud was a native of Lyons and is probably best known to collectors for the *March* he contributed to the composite ballet *L'Eventail de Jeanne* in 1927. He was a pupil of Ropartz and Florent Schmitt and a composer of sufficient merit to warrant the attention of a conductor of stature: Pierre Monteux conducted the premières of the *Symphony in A* and the one-Act comic opera *Chirurgie*, both composed in 1930. The *Sérénade* (1927) has charm and there is a hint of Roussel in the symphony. However, these performances are serviceable but no more.

FESCA, Alexander (1820–49)

Septets 1 in C min., Op. 26; 2 in D min., Op. 28
(M) *** CPO 999 617-2. Linos Ens.

Alexander Fesca's two *Septets* were written in the first half of the 1840s, each lasting around 35 minutes. While hardly profound masterpieces – though their minor key gives them a nice dash of gravitas – they are tunefully entertaining and fluent, with the composer obviously knowing how to please an audience. There are plenty of nice touches to keep the listener's ear tickled, and, as quoted in the excellent sleeve-notes (by a contemporary critic in Fesca's day), '[this music] belongs to a field of higher, nobler entertaining music'. The performances here are superb, fluent and stylish, with a recording to match. Recorded in 2001, it is now offered at mid-price.

FESCA, Friedrich Ernst (1789–1826)

Symphonies 2 in D, Op. 10; 3 in D, Op. 13; Overture: Cantemire
*** CPO 999 869-2. N. German R. Philharmonie, Beermann

Friedrich Ernst Fesca, like other composers of his generation, was overshadowed by Beethoven, and works like these disappeared from programmes after the 1840s. The two symphonies recorded here, the *Second* composed between 1809 and 1813 and the *Third* in 1816, hardly deserve to be as forgotten as they are – or, at least, were. These are very much works at the beginning of the romantic era: they are full of energy and

spirit, with the influence of Beethoven most strongly felt. With outer movements of brawling vigour and driving Scherzos contrasting with slow movements that sustain their tension – these works should be explored by anyone interested in this ever-expanding era. The *Cantemire Overture* (one of two operas he composed) makes an enjoyable bonus. The performances and recording are excellent.

FIBICH, Zdeněk (1850–1900)

Symphonies 1 in F, Op. 17; 2 in E flat, Op. 38
(BB) ** Naxos 8.553699. Razumovsky SO, Mogrelia

The Naxos issue of the first two symphonies offers fresh, clean-cut performances with transparent textures, making an attractive bargain issue, though they pale beside Järvi's Chandos performances (Chan. 9682).

Moods, Impressions & Reminiscences, Opp. 41, 44, 47 & 57; Studies of Paintings
(BB) **(*) Regis RRC 1221. Kvapil

These small vignettes are touching – they are a forerunner of Janáček's *Leaves from an overgrown path* and spring from a love affair Fibich had towards the end of his life. There are nearly 400 short, often poignant and always charming miniatures; a few are mere salon pieces (the famous *Poème* is one of them) but most are full of strong poetic feeling and beauty of melodic line. They are played with great sensitivity and subtlety by Radoslav Kvapil. The music deserves three stars, and so does the playing, which has great sensitivity and artistry. The recording is clear, but the piano-timbre is a litle hard and lacking bloom; nevertheless, the gentler pieces work their full magic and this is a worthwhile disc at its new budget price. It also comes as part of a four-disc Regis anthology of Czech piano music (RRC 4006).

FISCHER, Johann Caspar Ferdinand (c. 1670–1746)

Musical Parnassus, Volume 1: Suites 1-6 (Clio; Calliope; Melpomène; Thalia; Erato; Euterpe)
(BB) *** Naxos 8.554218. Beauséjour (harpsichord)

J. C. F. Fischer is remembered for his *Ariadne musica* (1715), a series of 20 preludes and fugues, each in a different key, thus anticipating Bach's *Wohltemperierte Klavier*. His role in music history was to fuse the style of the Lullian suite with the classical core of dance suite movements favoured by Froberger. He published his *Musicalischer Parnassus* in 1738, which comprises nine suites named after the Muses. The first six are included on this disc and are often fresh and inventive, rarely routine. The Canadian Luc Beauséjour plays them with some flair and is very vividly recorded.

FOERSTER, Josef Bohuslav (1859–1951)

After his studies at the Prague Organ School, Josef Bohuslav Foerster spent some years in Hamburg (1893–1903) and Vienna (1903–18) before returning to Prague, where he became director of the Conservatory. He received encouragement from Smetana and Tchaikovsky, and was befriended by Mahler.

Symphony 4 in C min. (Easter Eve), Op. 54; My Youth,
Op. 44; Festive Overture, Op. 70
(BB) *** Naxos 8.557776. Slovak RSO, Friedel

Foerster's *Fourth Symphony* is one of the best-kept secrets of Czech music: this is only its third recording! Kubelik recorded it in Prague in 1948 on six 78-r.p.m. discs, and Vaclav Smetáček recorded it on LP 20 years later. Composed, like its two companions on this CD, during the early part of Foerster's stay in Vienna, it shows the influence of Bruckner and Mahler. It is a long work, some 47 minutes in length, and of striking quality. Its Scherzo is worthy of Dvořák himself and is among the most captivating movements of its kind composed anywhere at this period. The opening of the work has great nobility and depth, and it leaves the listener in no doubt that this is a symphony of real substance. It is surpassed in its quality of inspiration only by Suk's *Asrael.* The *Festive Overture* of 1907 and the somewhat earlier Op. 44 symphonic poem, *My Youth*, are both first recordings and are well worth a place in the repertory. The American conductor Lance Friedel is obviously committed to this music and gets a very good response from the Slovak orchestra. Recommended with enthusiasm.

FOULDS, John (1880–1939)

April – England; (i) Dynamic Triptych (Piano Concerto),
Op. 88. Music-Pictures (Group III), Op. 33; Lament from A
Celtic Suite, Op. 29; The Song of Ram Dass
*** Warner 2564 62999-2. CBSO, Oramo; (i) with Donohoe

It is good to see the continuing interest in John Foulds, a composer who inhabits a world between Elgar's England and modern composers such as Tippett and Britten. *April – England* finds Foulds in pastoral mood, while *The Song of Ram Dass* shows something of his feeling for the East. The *Celtic Lament* was one of the few works to gain currency during his lifetime. But the most important piece here is the *Dynamic Triptych*, for piano and orchestra, deploying the composer's interest in unorthodox scales and rhythms. Donohoe's recording offers a challenge to Howard Shelley's pioneering Lyrita version and, as the latter is no longer readily available, makes a competitive alternative. The City of Birmingham Symphony Orchestra under Sakari Oramo are persuasive advocates of this highly interesting figure and in *Music-Pictures (Group III)* offer a valuable première recording. Excellent notes from Calum Macdonald and first-rate recording.

Cello Sonata
*** British Music Soc. BMS 423CD. Cole, Talbot – BOWEN;
WALKER: *Cello Sonatas* ***

Foulds wrote his *Cello Sonata* in 1905, but it was revised for publication in 1927. It is a passionately romantic work with memorable invention, notably the *dolce con semplicita* secondary theme in the first movement, and the ardent melody of the *Lento*, which is surrounded by pizzicatos. Yet structurally it is unconventional, with the closing *Molto brioso* the most original of the three movements. Rhythmically busy, it has three main themes, drawing upon an old Puritan melody which is first heard in a chordal progression on the piano. The development is succinct, and it is the coda which is the work's apotheosis, founded on a ground bass over which earlier material is reprised. Then a unison cadenza leads to a strong contrapuntal restatement of the sonata's three main

themes. The performance here could not be more expressively dedicated and, if the recording is rather over-resonant, its warmth suits the rich musical flow.

FRANCK, César (1822–90)

(i) Symphonic Variations for Piano and Orchestra; (ii)
Symphony in D minor
(*(*)) Testament mono SBT 1237. (i) Ciccolini, Paris
Conservatoire O; (ii) French Nat. R. O; Cluytens – D'INDY:
Symphonie sur un chant montagnard français (**)

Both the *Symphony* and the *Variations symphoniques* were recorded in the Théâtre des Champs-Elysées in 1953, although the former is much better balanced. Cluytens gives a dignified and finely shaped account of the piece, which is well worth hearing, even if the Orchestre National de la Radiofusion Française does not always produce a refined tone and the sound is a bit two-dimensional. The *Variations symphoniques* are well played by Aldo Ciccolini, but unfortunately the sound is dryish and the piano is too forwardly balanced to do full justice to the soloist's tone.

Symphony in D min.
*** Universal Accord 476 8069.Liège PO, Langree –
CHAUSSON: *Symphony* ***

It is apt that this excellent new version of the most important orchestral work by the greatest of Belgian composers should come from a Belgian orchestra. It is good too that the Franck *Symphony* should be coupled with another three-movement symphony by a composer closely associated with him, Chausson's Opus 20. It may come as a surprise to find on the evidence of this disc what a refined body the Liège orchestra is, and under Louis Langree the interpretation of the Franck could hardly be more idiomatic, with subtle nuances of phrasing and variations of tempo consistently reflecting the players' affection for the music. The syncopated rhythms of principal themes in both the first movement and the finale here come over with natural ease and affection, and, helped by well-balanced recording, the playing has splendid dramatic bite. Langree's tempo for the central slow movement keeps the music moving, fairly enough in reflection of the tempo marking of *Allegretto*.

Cello Sonata in A (trans. of Violin Sonata)
** DG (IMS) 471 346-2. Maisky, Argerich – CHOPIN: *Cello*
Sonata; Polonaise brillante; DEBUSSY: *Cello Sonata* **

Recorded live in Japan, this account by Maisky and Argerich of the Franck *Sonata* in its cello transcription cannot compare with the same artists' studio version made in Geneva in 1981 for EMI. Though these two highly individual artists consistently strike sparks off each other, the pulling about of phrase and tempo is so extreme it is almost grotesque, with less dedication than before. Even in the dashing Scherzo the unsteadiness of tempo is distracting, and in the finale the result is almost scrappy, even though predictably they build up to an exciting climax.

Cello Sonata in A min.; (i) Panis Angelicus; Le Sylphe
(**) Hyp. CDA 67376. Isserlis, Hough, (i) with Evans –
RACHMANINOV: *Cello Sonata, etc.* (**)

As in the great Rachmaninov *Sonata*, with which it is coupled, this Hyperion cello version of the Franck *Violin Sonata* suffers from the dimness of the recording, which seriously undermines here the expressiveness and bite of Steven Isserlis and Stephen Hough that normally mark their work. The two songs, beautifully sung by Rebecca Evans, are a small compensation.

Piano Quintet in F min.

(*(**)) Bridge mono 9185. Artur Balsam, Budapest Qt –
SCHUBERT: *Piano Quintet in A (Trout)* (**(*))

(M) ** RCA (ADD) 74321 909652. Heifetz, Baker, Primrose, Piatigorsky, Pennario – DVORAK: *Piano Quintet in A* **;
FRANCAIX: *String Trio in C* ***

Artur Balsam's artistry was never fully appreciated in England, though older readers may remember that in the late 1950s the BBC Third Programme invited him to play the six Mozart concertos of 1788 in two programmes. They left no doubt as to his mastery. As Harris Goldsmith says in his notes, 'Hearing his masterly phrasing and luminous singing tone is sufficient aural testimony to place Balsam in the highest artistic echelons.' His playing of the Franck *Quintet* has passion and eloquence but is disciplined by classical restraint. The 1953 recording, however, is very monochrome and claustrophobic and does not flatter the tone of the Budapest Quartet.

The famous Hollywood set from the 1950s is to be preferred to the rather high-powered account from Heifetz and his starry team of soloists – which is strongly projected and marvellously played, of course, but conveys little of the intimacy of chamber music. The same goes for the Dvořák coupling, but not the Françaix *Trio*, which is enchanting.

Piano Trios 2 in B flat (Trio de salon), Op. 1/2; 3 in B min., Op. 1/3; 4 in B min., Op. 2

** Chan. 9742. Bekova Sisters

These early trios come from Franck's student years and are in no way representative of his mature personality. They emanate from the world of Weber and Mendelssohn and offer little of real substance, even the fugal Op. 2, which he dedicated to Liszt. Eleonora Bekova, the pianist, proves the dominant personality in the trio and some will find her just a bit too assertive. Neither the music nor the playing is really three star but the recording is realistic in the best tradition of the house.

Violin Sonata in A min. (DVD version)

**(*) EMI DVD 4904519. Y. & H. Menuhin (bonus:
MENDELSSOHN: *Variations sérieuses, Op. 54*). – BARTÓK: *Contrasts; Violin Sonata 1: Finale*; SCHUBERT: *Piano Trio 1* **(*)

Violin Sonata in A

(M) *** DG (ADD) 477 5903. Danczowska, Zimerman – SZYMANOWSKI: *Mythes*, etc. *** ●

(BB) **(*) Naxos mono 8.110989 Y. & H. Menuhin – BEETHOVEN: *Sonata 3 in E flat*; LEKEU: *Sonata* **(*)

The Menuhins must have performed this *Sonata* many times, but they succeed in making it sound very fresh. The recording comes from the BBC studios in early 1960 and is in black-and-white. It was produced by the legendary Walter Todds, then a relative newcomer to BBC TV's music team, and the camerawork is predictably restrained and finely judged.

Kaja Danczowska's account of the Franck *Sonata* – now reissued as one of DG's Originals – is distinguishd by a natural sense of line and great sweetness of tone, and she is partnered superbly by Krystian Zimerman. Indeed, in terms of dramatic fire and strength of line, this version can hold its

own alongside the finest on record, while its Szymanowski coupling is outstanding in every way.

The Menuhins' classic pre-war account of the Franck *Sonata* deserved its high reputation, as did the early Beethoven *Sonata* with which it is coupled here. They were the first to give us the poignant Lekeu *Sonata*, and the new transfer does them all full justice.

FRASER-SIMPSON, Harold (1872–1944) & TATE, James W. (1875–1922)

The Maid of the Mountains (with James W. Tate)

** Hyp. CDA 67190. Kelly, Maltman, George, Suart, Burgess, Maxwell, Gamble, New L. Light Op. Ch. & O, Corp

The history of successful musicals is always fascinating and *The Maid of the Mountains* is no exception. Although it has a famous score accredited to Fraser-Simpson, including such a key number as the splendid 'Love Will Find a Way', when it was on its out-of-town try-out at the Prince's Theatre, Manchester, in 1916, its female lead, José Collins, decided that the score did not have enough popular hits. So her stepfather, James W. Tate, came to the rescue and wrote three of the show's most catchy numbers, 'A Paradise for Two', 'A Bachelor Gay' and the duet, 'When You're in Love'. The result was a resounding success, and the show played for 1,352 performances, its run ending only when its leading lady decided that enough was enough! It is a winningly light-hearted, cosy score and still holds up well in the amateur theatre. But it is good to have such a lively professional account as this, from principals and excellent chorus alike, conducted by Ronald Corp, with a consistently vivacious spirit and clear words. The one slight snag is that the heroine, Teresa, sung by Janis Kelly, has a rather close, soubrettish vibrato. However, Richard Suart shines in the relatively small part of Tonio, with his Gilbertian solo, 'I Understood', and the charming duet with Vittoria (Sally Burgess), 'Over Here and Over There', which also has a G&S flavour. Excellent recording and a full libretto.

The Maid of the Mountains (Musical Play): Highlights

(B) *** CfP (ADD) 3 35984-2. Kennington, Clyde/Jason, Thompson, Edwards, Mahoney, Ch. & O, Tavener – NORTON: *Chu Chin Chow* **(*)

The Maid of the Mountains was, alongside *Chu Chin Chow*, one of the two great theatrical hits during the First World War. Its gestation was typical of the musical theatre. Listening to this excellently sung collection of highlights (Gordon Clyde's *Bachelor Gay* is delightful) one can understand why *The Maid* was such a success.

FRESCOBALDI, Girolamo (1583–1643)

(i) Partita sopra passacaglia. Motets: (ii) Deus noster; (iii) O mors illa

*** Opus 111 Naïve OP 30296. (i) Fourquier; (ii) Franzetti; (iii) Van Dyck, Imboden; (ii–iii) Le Parlement de Musique, Gester (with Lelio COLISTA: *Sinfonia in D min.*) – CARISSIMI: *Sacred Oratorios* ***

This pair of beautiful motets, one solo for soprano (Elisa Franzetti) and its companion a duet for tenor (Stephan van Dyck) and bass (Stephan Imboden), plus a *Passacaglia*, played intimately on the harp by Marion Fourquier, make a splendid centrepiece in this simulated sacred concert in Rome in the middle of the seventeenth century.

FRIML, Rudolf (1879–1972)

The Firefly: excerpts

(B) ** CfP (ADD) 3 35987-2. Voss, Payne, Linden Singers, New World Show O, Braden; or Don Siegel with Ch. – ROMBERG: *Desert Song; New Moon: excerpts* **

The Firefly was premièred in New York in 1912, but it had a weak storyline so it failed to achieve much success. However, its principal hits, *Love is like a Firefly* and *Sympathy*, endured; and *Giannina mia* and especially the catchy *When a maid comes knocking on your door* are also charming in their inconsequential, period style. They are most pleasingly sung here by Stephanie Voss and Laurie Payne. Later, MGM decided to turn the show into a film, as a vehicle for Jeanette MacDonald and Alan Jones, but with a different, more exotic plot, set in Spain. To expand the film score, MGM's musical director, Herbert Stothart, transcribed a Friml piano piece into a song, for which Robert Wright and George Forrest (who later arranged Grieg's music for *The Song of Norway*) wrote the lyrics. The resulting *Donkey Serenade* became one of the most successful of all Hollywood hits. It is included here, sung by Don Siegel and chorus, but the sound is poor.

(i) *Rose Marie* (arr. Stothart; highlights); (ii) *The Vagabond King* (highlights)

(B) *(*) CfP (ADD) 3 35971-2. New World Show O, with (i) Leigh, Larner, Hughes, Cole, Croft, Fitzgibbon, Elsy, Linden Singers, cond. Douglas; (ii) Steffe, Dorow, Freda Larsen, John Larsen, Gray, Peter Knight Singers, cond. Cervenka

Somewhat over-bright and aggressive 1961 (Studio 2) sound, but the mixture of sentimental numbers and rousing choruses which make up *The Vagabond King* (1925) makes it all (lustily) enjoyable enough. The sound is slightly less wearing for *Rose Marie* (though the voices seem in a separate acoustic of their own). This was a hit in 1924, and is performed here with similar verve. This CD is mainly for aficionados of music theatre, 1920s style, who will make allowances.

FROBERGER, Johann (1616–67)

Fantasia II in E min.; Lamentation sur la mort de Ferdinand III; Suites I in A min.; XV in A min.; XX in D; III in G; X in F; XII in A min.

(M) ** DHM/BMG 82876 69999-2. Leonhardt (harpsichord)

This reissue dates back to 1962. Gustav Leonhardt is completely at home in this repertoire and his playing is authoritative and always musical. While not ideally flexible, as is an artist like Rousset (on Harmonia Mundi, HMA 1951372 – see our main volume), he is not rigid, and his relaxed performances give pleasure than their confident sense of style. He plays a copy of a 1640 Ruckers and is excellently recorded in a pleasing acoustic.

FROHLICH, Johannes (1806–60)

Symphony in E flat, Op. 33

*** Chan. 9609. Danish Nat. RSO, Hogwood – (with GADE: *Symphony 4* ***)

This delightful disc resurrects a long-buried work, which proves far more than just a curiosity. Johannes Frederik Frohlich was one of the fathers of Danish music. He wrote his *Symphony* in 1833, but it was so poorly played it sank without trace and was never given again. Yet this is a totally refreshing, beautifully written work, not unlike the symphonies of another Scandinavian, Berwald; it also owes much to Weber. The writing is inventive and full of character, and the Danish Radio Orchestra under Christopher Hogwood play it with both spirit and conviction. It is well coupled here in splendid performances with the best-known symphony by another Dane, Niels Gade, devoted follower of Mendelssohn. Good recording too, if not Chandos's very finest.

FROST, Stephen (born 1959)

(i; ii) *Bassoon Concerto;* (iii) *Oboe Concerto;* (ii; iv) *The Lesson*

**(*) Chan. 9763. (i) Birkeland; (ii) Bournemouth SO; (iii) Elmes, Ens. 2000; (iv) Bergset; cond. Harrison

The work for oboe is undoubtedly the finer of these two concertos, succinctly inventive. The *Bassoon Concerto* is perhaps somewhat over-extended when its genial opening toccata gives way to a long central soliloquy, decorated with percussion but also featuring a solo piano, which is to provide a link into the energetic finale. Both soloists are excellent players, and the performances overall are of high quality. *The Lesson* is a floating vocal melisma using the poem by W. H. Auden. The speaker is placed within the orchestra and no attempt is made to focus the words sharply (and no text is included) so one assumes they are merely a starting point for a piece that is above all evocative. Excellent recording.

FRY, William Henry (1813–64)

The Breaking Heart; Niagara Symphony; Overture to Macbeth; Santa Claus (Christmas Symphony)

(BB) **(*) Naxos 8.559057. RSNO, Rowe

William Henry Fry has a distinct place in the history of American music, for as an academic, critic and composer he was the first native-born American to write for a large symphony orchestra and also the first to write a grand opera. His music is innocently tuneful, though its roots are firmly in the European, rather than in native American soil. The longest work here is the *Santa Claus, Christmas Symphony*, written in 1853 and lasting just under 27 minutes. It is an ingenuous, episodic work, originally performed with a detailed programme of the Christmas story. The writing has a certain period charm and, if it doesn't always hold the listener's full attention, there are some attractive episodes. The finale features a sleigh-ride, followed by shimmering strings ushering in *O Come All Ye Faithful*, which is thundered out at the end.

The *Niagara Symphony* brings some quite startling passages depicting the famous Falls, with strings scurrying about in watery cascades, and with no fewer than eleven timpani to ram the effect home. This is real tempest music – and with a reflective chorale in the middle for contrast. *The Breaking Heart* is a rather sentimental 10-minute piece, which includes a lilting waltz theme, while the melodramatic *Overture to Macbeth* seems to have borrowed some of *Niagara*'s swirling strings at one point. The performances are enthusiastic, though there are signs that more rehearsal time would have been desirable. The recording is satisfactory, but this is hardly an indispensable issue.

FUCHS, Robert (1847–1927)

(i) *Piano Concerto in B flat, Op. 27. Serenade 5 in D (in Honour of Johann Strauss), Op. 53*
**(*) CPO 999 893-2. Luxembourg PO, Francis, (i) with Vorraber

The *Piano Concerto* comes from 1880, the same year as the Brahms concerto in that key. Fuchs is very heavily indebted to Brahms, and so present is this influence that it is difficult to escape. But he is a highly musicianly figure and there are some resourceful touches; but, even if the material does not sustain its 40-minutes duration, it holds the listener for much of the time by its endearing honesty. Franz Vorraber is a persuasive soloist and Alun Francis gives good support, but this is essentially of a limited and specialist interest. Good recorded sound.

Cello Sonatas 1 in D min., Op. 29; 2 in E flat min., Op. 83; Phantasiestücke, Op. 78
*** Marco Polo 8.223423. Drobinsky, Blumenthal
*** Biddulph LAW005. Green, Palmer

The *Cello Sonatas*, like the more Schumannesque *Phantasiestücke*, offer well-fashioned, cultured and civilized music (no mean virtues) which may not have a strongly original profile but are well worth investigating for all that. After long neglect these works are available in two different versions. To be frank, there is not much to choose between them; both offer very good performances; both are very well recorded and deserve their three stars, so no agonies of choice are required: you can safely invest in one or the other.

Clarinet Quintet in E flat, Op. 102
— (BB) *** Hyp. Helios CDH 55076. King, Britten Qt –
ROMBERG: *Clarinet Quintet;* STANFORD: *2 Fantasies* ***
*** Marco Polo 8.223282. Rodenhäuser, Ens. Villa Musica –
LACHNER: *Septet* ***

Fuchs completed his *Clarinet Quintet* in 1917. It has a fresh, poetic charm that is irresistible. Unlike the even more delightful Romberg *Quintet* with which it is coupled, it is without Mozartian reminiscences. It opens enticingly, and the perky scherzando second movement contrasts well with the gentle, heartfelt *Andante* and the innocent lyricism of the closing *Allegretto grazioso*, with variations. Thea King is obviously in love with the work and she plays it beautifully, receiving, warm, polished support from the Britten Quartet and first-rate recording. This disc is not to be missed.

The *Quintet* is also nicely played by the Mainz-based Ensemble Villa Musica, whose excellent clarinettist, Ulf Rodenhäuser, is worth a mention. But the Helios CD is the one to have.

String Quartets: in E, Op. 58; in A min., Op. 62
*** MDG 6031001-2. Minguet Qt

Op. 62 was composed in the late 1890s and reveals how strong Brahms's gravitational pull was on Fuchs; its Minuet bears a more than passing resemblance to Brahms's quartet in the same key, Op. 51/2. The music is fashioned expertly (although the slow movement of Op. 58 is wanting in concentration), but a distinctive voice does not emerge. Good playing and an acceptable recorded sound.

String Quartet in A min., Op. 106; in C, Op. 71
*** MDG 603 1002-2. Minguet Qt

Robert Fuchs is an interesting figure, and he numbered among his pupils composers as diverse as Wolf, Mahler and Sibelius. However, those tempted to satisfy their curiosity should know that these well-fashioned pieces are really a little too indebted to Brahms to have a strong claim on the repertoire, even in such good performances and recorded sound.

String Trio in A, Op. 94
*** MDG 634 0841-2. Belcanto Strings – REINECKE: *Trio in C min.* ***

In his day Robert Fuchs was a much admired teacher whose pupils included Franz Schmidt, Schreker and Zemlinsky! He was also a prolific composer, even if none of his works to reach the catalogues reveals evidence of a strong or original voice. Finely crafted and cultured music, very conservative for its date of composition (1910), but superbly played and recorded.

Piano Sonatas 1, Op. 19; 2, Op. 88
*** Marco Polo 8.223377. Blumenthal

The early *F minor Sonata*, Op. 19 (1877), is again heavily indebted to Brahms. All the same, it has a certain breadth and lyrical fertility that impress. The *Second Sonata*, Op. 88, is mature Fuchs. Its invention is more chromatic and there are hints of Reger and even of Debussy and Fauré. Although Fuchs may lack a strong individual voice, his musical thinking has the merit of breadth and span, and these are both rewarding works, given such masterly and persuasive advocacy as they receive at the hands of Daniel Blumenthal.

FUČIK, Julius (1872–1916)

The Bear with the Sore Head (Polka); *Donausagen Waltz; Marches: Entry of the Gladiators; Florentine; Hercegovac. Marinarella Overture; Winterstürme Waltz*
(BB) *** Warner Apex (ADD) 0927 48752-2. Czech PO, Neumann – DVORAK: *Slavonic Rhapsody 1* ***

Everyone knows Fučik's famous *Entry of the Gladiators* (here brilliantly done), but the rest of his music is now very little known. The similarly exhilarating *Florentine March* launches with a trumpet, side drum and piccolo introduction, and has a haunting central theme, before its rousing conclusion with much colourful decoration. This piece typifies the rest of the programme, which is laced with good tunes and bright orchestral colours. After studying composition with Dvořák, Fučik became Bandmaster for the Royal and Imperial Army and, while that is evident in these scores, his writing is far from being just bombastic and rhythmically square. The *Marinarella Overture*, which used to be a bandstand favourite, here features some beautifully delicate string-writing, and is one of the disc's highlights. The waltzes are very enjoyable too: there are some attractive ideas in *Donausagen*, which builds its main theme up to a fine, full-blooded, swirling climax, while *Winterstürme* has similar qualities, and is, if anything, all the more striking in its minor key. *The Bear with the Sore Head* is a comic polka with the bassoon used to amusing affect, and the concert ends with the lively *Hercegovac March*. The early 1970s sound, like the performances, is bright and brilliant.

FURTWÄNGLER, Wilhelm
(1886–1954)

Symphony 2 in E min.

(***) DG mono 457 722-2 (2). BPO, Furtwängler –
SCHUMANN: *Symphony 4.* (***) ✪

Furtwängler spoke of his *Second Symphony* as his spiritual
testament. It is Brucknerian in its dimensions and sense of
space. The first movement, lasting 24 minutes, is accommodated on the first CD, and the remaining three on the second.
Furtwängler himself thought the present studio recording,
made in the Jesus-Christus-Kirche, Berlin, in 1950 'stilted', but
it sounds amazingly clear and warm in this transfer and
readers should not be put off acquiring it. The Schumann
coupling – one of Furtwängler's very finest mono records –
makes a superb coupling.

FUX, Johann Joseph (1650–1741)

*Il Concentus musico instrumentalis, 1701: Serenada à 8 for 2
clarinos, 2 oboes, bassoon, 2 violins, viola and continuo;
Rondeau à 7 for violino piccolo, bassoon, violin, 3 violas and
continuo; Sonata à 4 for violin, cornet trombone, dulcian
and organ*

(BB) *** Warner Apex 2564 60449-2. VCM, Harnoncourt

Fux wrote a great many overtures or suites that combine the
French and Italian styles, of which the present four are lively
and quite colourful examples. They have a good deal in
common with similar works of Telemann, even if not nearly
so skilfully scored.

Harnoncourt's selection was originally issued on Telefunk-
en's Das Alte Werk series in 1970. Fux's *Serenada à 8* takes its
time – it has sixteen movements – but is amazingly inventive. It
was written for the Habsburg emperor's son in 1701 as an
outdoor entertainment. There is some highly original writing
for the high trumpets, and a most beautiful Minuet. The
Sonata is texturally even more aurally intriguing. Indeed, by
the time one has heard this CD through, one is tempted to
dismiss the common view of Fux as a dull academic. There is
nothing academic about the music, and for that matter
nothing dull about the performances. Excellent recording.

GADE, Axel (1860–1921)

Violin Concerto 2 in F, Op. 10

**(*) Danacord DACOCD 510. Astrand, Danish PO, South
Jutland, Brown (with NIELS GADE: *Capriccio; Overtures*
**(*))

Axel Gade was himself a gifted violinist who studied with
Joachim and was leader or concertmaster of the Royal Danish
Orchestra for many years. He was naturally overshadowed by
his father, but his output includes an opera, *Venetian Night*,
and a quantity of chamber music. The *Second Violin Concerto*
(1899) is expertly crafted and the solo part is very well
written. The idiom is post-romantic and the invention fluent.
It is amiable and pleasing rather than memorable or personal.
Christina Astrand plays with great conviction and is well
supported by Iona Brown and the Sønderjylland (South
Jutland) Orchestra.

GÁL, Hans (1890–1987)

PIANO MUSIC

*24 Fugues, Op. 108; 3 Sketches, Op. 7; 3 Preludes, Op. 64; 24
Preludes, Op. 83; 3 Small Pieces, Op 64; Sonata, Op. 28;
Sonatinas 1 & 2, Op. 58; Suite, Op. 24*

(M) *** Avie AV 2064 (3). McCawley

Like his slightly older contemporary, Egon Wellesz, Hans Gál
was driven from Austria to Britain by the Anschluss in 1938.
The son of a Viennese doctor, he studied the piano and
composition and (again like Wellesz) musicology with Guido
Adler. He enjoyed some considerable success with his opera,
Die heilige Ente, which was premièred by George Szell to great
acclaim. With the advent of Nazism, as a Jew he was dismissed from his position as director of the conservatoire at
Mainz and returned briefly to Vienna. Thanks to the support
of Sir Donald Tovey, he eventually settled in Edinburgh,
where he became university lecturer in music. He wrote
books on Schubert, Schumann and Brahms and Verdi and
helped to launch the Edinburgh Festival. He composed in a
wide variety of genres, and this three-CD set covers his piano
music from his earliest *Three Sketches* (1910–11) through to
the *Twenty-Four Fugues* of 1980, completed when he was
ninety. (He was active right into old age, and RL recalls
producing a perceptive talk on Schubert by him (with copious piano illustrations) when he was in his late eighties.) The
music deserves and receives dedicated advocacy from Leon
McCawley, who brings this inventive and individual body of
music to life and puts us all in his debt by so doing. The Avie
recording is lifelike and full-bodied.

GALUPPI, Baldassare (1706–85)

Piano Sonata in C

*** Opus Arte **DVD** OA 0939D. Michelangeli – BEETHOVEN:
Piano Sonatas 3 & 32; SCARLATTI: *Sonatas* ***

This slight but pleasing *bonne bouche*, played with masterly
delicacy, makes quite a contrast to the two Beethoven sonatas.

GARDINER, Henry Balfour
(1877–1950)

*Humoresque; The Joyful Homecoming; Michaelchurch; Noel;
5 Pieces; Prelude; Salamanca; Shenandoah & Other Pieces*
(suite)

*** Continuum (ADD) CCD 1049. Jacobs

Balfour Gardiner was at his finest in miniatures, and his
writing has an attractive simplicity and innocence. Most of
this music is slight, but its appeal is undeniable when it is
presented with such authority and sympathy. It is very well
recorded indeed.

GARDNER, John (born 1917)

(i) *Flute Concerto, Op. 220. Half-Holiday Overture, Op. 52;
Irish Suite, Op. 231; Prelude for Strings, Op. 148a; Sinfonia
piccola for Strings, Op. 47; Symphony 3 in E min., Op. 189*

(M) *** ASV CDWHL 2125. Royal Ballet O, Sutherland, (i)
with Stinton

John Gardner was born in Manchester. After service in the

RAF he joined the staff at St Paul's Girls' School at Hammersmith (following in famous footsteps). His *First Symphony* was premièred at the Cheltenham Festival in 1951, and the opera *The Moon and Sixpence* at Sadler's Wells in 1957.

The catchy *Half-Holiday Overture* doesn't go on a moment too long. The *Flute Concerto*, written for Jennifer Stinton in 1995, has a relaxed, conversational opening movement, followed by a poignant *Nocturne*, and the rondo finale gives the flute plenty of opportunities for sparkling virtuosity.

The *Third Symphony* suggests influences from Shostakovich, which persist in the solemn, threnodic *Adagio*. The finale restores the mood of genial humanity. The elegiac *Prelude for Strings* derives from a string quartet.

Most successful of all is the *Sinfonia piccola*. The *Andante* proves to be a searching passacaglia, always a source of stimulation in the hands of a fine composer. The finale has a touch of Britten's *Simple Symphony* about it. The *Irish Suite* genially celebrated the composer's eightieth birthday. Fine performances and an excellent recording serve to recommend this collection well, and congratulations to ASV for issuing it at mid-price.

GATES, Philip (born 1963)

Airs & Graces; Clarinet Sonata; Flute Sonata; Danzas del Sud; Mood Music; Rio Bound
(*) Priory Shellwood Productions SWCD 15. Way, Kelly, Clarke, Willox, composer

Philip Gates obviously has a special feeling for the flute and is clearly influenced by twentieth-century French writing for this instrument, including the jazzy inflexions. The engagingly cool nostalgia of the central movement of his *Sonata* has a few unpredictable interruptions from the piano, for which Gates also writes very naturally. The finale's rhythmic influences are Latin-American. The six *Airs and Graces* are lightweight vignettes, the most striking being *At Loch Leven* (with its Scottish snap in the melody) and the neatly syncopated *Rag-a-muffin*. The *Clarinet Sonata* flows amiably, with a bluesy central *Cantabile*; but it is the snappy finale that stands out. *Rio Bound* makes a good final encore. The *Mood Music* pieces for alto-saxophone are less striking. The *March Hare* gambols robustly, but *Sax-Blue* and *Soft-Shoe* are too predictable. The performances are excellent and so is the recording.

GAUARNIERI, Camargo (1907–93)

Symphonies 1; 4 (Brasília); Abertura Festiva
*** BIS CD 1290. São Paulo SO, Neschling

The Brazilian Camargo Gauarnieri was the oldest son of a poor family; his parents quickly recognized his musical gifts, moving to São Paulo so as to provide him with a good musical education. Later he was able to continue his studies both in France and in the United States. He was the most important Brazilian composer after Villa-Lobos, as well as being an influential musical educator. Young pianists have long been familiar with his *Piano Sonata*, a standby at auditions and competitions. The present disc includes the first recordings of his *First Symphony*, dedicated to Koussevitzky, and his *Fourth*, dedicated to Bernstein. Both were recorded in São Paulo by the excellent São Paulo Symphony Orchestra conducted by John Neschling. Engaging, inventive, well-wrought music, well worth investigating.

GAY, John (1685–1732)

The Beggar's Opera (arr. Pepusch and Austin)
◉━ ❂(BB) *** CfP 575 9722 (2). Morison, Cameron, Sinclair, Wallace, Brannigan, Pro Arte Ch. & O, Sargent – GERMAN: *Tom Jones* ***

The Beggar's Opera (complete; arr. Britten)
(M) *** Decca 473 088-2 (2). Murray, Langridge, Kenny, Rawnsley, Lloyd, Collins, Aldeburgh Festival Ch. & O, Bedford

The Beggar's Opera was the eighteenth-century equivalent of the modern American musical. It was first produced in 1728 and caused a sensation with audiences used to the stylized Italian opera favoured by Handel. This performance under Sargent is in every way first class, and the soloists could hardly be bettered, with Elsie Morison as Polly, John Cameron as MacHeath and Owen Brannigan a splendid Peachum. The linking dialogue is spoken by actors to make the result more dramatic, with every word crystal clear. The chorus is no less effective and the 1955 recording has a most appealing ambience. It was one of EMI's first great stereo successes and the chorus *Let us take the road* (where the singers recede into the distance) was understandably included on their Stereo Demonstration disc. It now returns to the catalogue, coupled with a delightful selection from Edward German's *Tom Jones* which is hardly less vivid.

What Britten has done is to take the simple melodies assembled by Gay and treat them to elaborate, very Brittenish accompaniments and developments that go even further in individuality than his folksong settings. It becomes very much a twentieth-century piece, starting with an overture that is pure Britten, with Gay tunes woven in. *Fill Every Glass* is then no longer a simple drinking-song but a slow contrapuntal movement, and *The Modes of the Court*, to the tune of 'Lilliburlero', becomes another elaborate mosaic. Conversely, some nostalgic arias, like *O What Pain it is to Part*, are done briskly, even abrasively.

Under Steuart Bedford this first recording is based on a staged presentation, given at The Maltings during the Aldeburgh Festival, with Declan Mulholland as an Irish beggar bluffly introducing the entertainment. Philip Langridge sings clearly and incisively as Macheath, portraying him very much as a gentleman, and Robert Lloyd is outstanding as Peachum, dark and resonant, a bluff Cockney. The team is a strong and characterful one, though neither Ann Murray as Polly Peachum nor Yvonne Kenny as Lucy Lockit is caught very sweetly. Britten's distinctive orchestration, one instrument per part, is well played by a distinguished group, including Jennifer Stinton on the flute, Nicholas Daniel on the oboe and Richard Watkins on the horn. Excellent sound, good direction of the well-edited spoken dialogue by Michael Geliot. Now offered at mid-price, it is far more than a curiosity.

GERMAN, Edward (1862–1936)

Berceuse; The Conqueror; Gipsy Suite; Henry VIII: 3 Dances. Merrie England: Suite. Nell Gwyn: Suite. Romeo and Juliet: Suite. Tom Jones: Waltz
*** Marco Polo 8.223419. Czecho-Slovak RSO (Bratislava), Leaper

Richard III Overture; The Seasons; Theme & 6 Diversions
** Marco Polo 8.223695. RTE Concert O, Penny

Symphony 2 in A min. (Norwich); Valse gracieuse; Welsh Rhapsody
*(*) Marco Polo 8.223726. Nat. SO of Ireland, Penny

Of the three Edward German CDs listed above, the first is definitely the one to go for. These suites essentially consist of a string of piquant, rustic-type dances of considerable charm. Most of the composer's most famous numbers are here: the items from *Merrie England* and *Henry VIII*, the pseudo-exotic *Gipsy Suite*, the memorable *Waltz* from *Tom Jones*, plus a few rarities. All of it is effectively presented by the ever-reliable Adrian Leaper, and his Bratislava orchestra play as though they were from the home counties. Definitely an enticing collection in Marco Polo's valuable British Light Music series, most of which shows this composer at his best.

German's 'symphonic suite', *The Seasons*, is appealingly tuneful, colourfully orchestrated and enjoyable. The darker colours in *Autumn* provide a certain gravitas, while *Winter* has plenty of scurrying strings and woodwind to paint the scene. If the *Richard III Overture* is no towering masterpiece, it is not dull either, and it has enough ideas and a certain Romantic sweep to keep it going. A robust theme in D minor on the brass opens the *Theme and Six Diversions*, and the ensuing variations are enjoyable and nicely varied. The caveat is that, although the music is well conducted and played with enthusiasm, the orchestra is a bit scrawny in the string department. Nor is the recording first class – it lacks richness and bloom. But the music's character does come through.

The *Second Symphony* was commissioned by the Norwich Festival (hence its title, 'Norwich') in 1893. It has a certain charm – the spirits of Mendelssohn and Dvořák vaguely hover around in the background – but in the last resort the writing fails to be memorable. The charming *Valse gracieuse* and the deservedly well-known *Welsh Rhapsody* show the composer on better form. The performances are committed, but the sound is only average.

Hamlet; Romeo and Juliet: Prelude. Symphony 1 in E min.; The Tempter: Overture. The Willow Song
(M) *** Dutton CDLX 7156. BBC Concert O, Wilson

This disc gets off to a splendid start with the tunefully melodramatic *Tempter Overture* of 1893, one of many successful theatre works the composer was commissioned to write. Others included here are the *Romeo and Juliet* score (1895), which also contains good ideas and atmospheric writing but, alas, is not equal to Tchaikovsky's masterpiece. *Hamlet*, based on music written for a play which never materialized, was composed in 1897. If not distinctive, this 20-minute tone-poem offers varied ideas and is suitably melodramatic, not unlike a film score. Shakespeare again provides the inspiration for *The Willow Song*, another tone-poem, composed in 1922 and based on the traditional melody, *A poor soul sat sighing* from *Othello*. It has a vaguely Elizabethan feel, often rather melancholy, but always romantic, and is a quite appealing seven minutes' listening. The *E minor Symphony* of 1890 is based on material from a student work of 1866/7. Its somewhat doom-laden introduction gives way to a brighter and busy *allegro*; the slow movement is distinctly attractive, with a powerful climax (rather Elgarian, as the sleeve-note writer observes). The *Menuetto* third movement is charming, with a slightly quirky, pastiche style, and the finale, which turns into a tarantella at one point, is infectious. None of it is great music, but it is entertaining enough, and surprisingly substantial from a composer whose reputation is in the world of light music. Performances and

recording are very good indeed and it is hoped that a second volume will follow.

Welsh Rhapsody
(BB) *** CfP (ADD) 767 7532 RSNO, Gibson – HARTY: *With the Wild Geese*; MACCUNN: *Land of Mountain and Flood*; SMYTH: *Wreckers Overture* ***

Edward German is content not to interfere with the traditional melodies he uses in his rhapsody, relying on his orchestral skill to retain the listener's interest, and in this he is very successful. The closing pages, based on *Men of Harlech*, are prepared in a Tchaikovskian manner to provide a rousing conclusion. The CD transfer is very well managed, though the ear perceives a slight limitation in the upper range.

PIANO MUSIC

Concert Study in A flat; Elegy in C min.; First Impromptu in E min.; Graceful Dance in F; Humoresque in E; Intermezzo in A min.; Mazurka in E; Melody in D flat; Melody in E flat; Polish Dance in E; Rêverie in A min.; Tarantella in A min.; Valse-caprice in A; Valse fantastique; Valsette in E min.
** Marco Polo 8.223370. Cuckston

These piano miniatures show Edward German at his best. This is unpretentious music of much charm and piquancy. The minor-key works are nostalgically disarming: sometimes quite serious, such as the seven-minute *Elegy in C*; sometimes carefree, like the *Tarantella*; but nothing outstays its welcome. Alan Cuckston's performances are good, but not outstanding, and the piano tone is a little harsh, perhaps because of the dry acoustic. Enjoyable and recommendable, nevertheless.

VOCAL MUSIC

Merrie England (complete; without dialogue)
(BB) *(**) CfP Double 575 7672 (2). McAlpine, Bronhill, Glossop, Glynne, Sinclair, Kern, Rita Williams Singers, O, Collins

Although this recording dates from 1960, it cannot compare in stereo sophistication with EMI's *Beggar's Opera* of five years earlier. All the solo voices are close-miked, usually in an unflattering way, and too often they sound edgy, while the chorus is made artificially bright; the orchestra is lively enough, but the violins are thin. However, it must be said that Michael Collins directs the proceedings in an attractively spirited fashion. Among the soloists, Howell Glynne is splendid as King Neptune, and Monica Sinclair sings with her usual richness and makes *O peaceful England* more moving than usual. Patricia Kern's mezzo is firm and forward, while William McAlpine as Sir Walter Raleigh sings with fine, ringing voice. The Rita Williams Singers are thoroughly professional even if just occasionally their style is suspect. However, another recording seems unlikely so this is acceptable, *faute de mieux*.

Tom Jones (operetta: highlights)
(BB) *** CfP 575 9722 (2). Harvey, Minty, Glover, Riley, Nigel Brooks Ch., O, Gilbert Vinter – GAY: *The Beggar's Opera*. *** ●

Listening to this sparkling selection, one's first impression is not so much that Edward German's 'Ye olde Englande' style is comparable with fake oak beams in country pubs, but how like Sullivan is the basic idiom. The opening chorus might have come straight out of *Patience*, and there are many ensembles and solos that have a distinct reminder of one or other of the Savoy operas. Of course Sullivan's mantle fell pretty easily on German's shoulders. He had in fact completed Sullivan's *Emerald Isle* in 1901, on the latter's death, and *Merrie England* and *Tom Jones* followed. The librettist here even uses one of Gilbert's rhymes '*Festina lente*' as part of a song-title. But there is music, too, that could have come only from German's own pen, the really charming *Here's a paradox for lovers* and of course the delicate *Dream O'day Jill* and the famous *Waltz Song*. They are all extremely well sung here by a solo group who, like the conductor, Gilbert Vinter, convey real enthusiasm for this tuneful score. The 1966 recording is excellent and has transferred vividly to CD. Splendidly coupled, this inexpensive set is not to be missed.

GERSHWIN, George (1898–1937)

An American in Paris; Piano Concerto in F; Rhapsody in Blue

(BB) *(*) Warner Apex 2564 60818-2. Monte Carlo PO, Foster, (i) with Tacchino

On Apex, the *Rhapsody in Blue* takes a while to warm up but turns into a reasonably enjoyable account. The *Piano Concerto*, too, is decent, but *An American in Paris* is the most enjoyable work here. However, these performances lack the zest of the best available, and the 1983 sound is not ideally atmospheric.

(i) *An American in Paris*; (i; ii) *Rhapsody in Blue*; (iii) *Porgy & Bess: Excerpts*

(BB) *** HMV (DDD/ADD) 5 86727-2. (i) Aalborg Symphony, Wayne Marshall; (ii) with Marshall (piano); (iii) White, Haymon & soloists, Glyndebourne Ch., LPO, Rattle

A superb disc, with Wayne Marshall, like Previn before him, acting as soloist and directing the orchestra with great élan. *An American in Paris* is unsurpassed – full of marvellous detail and superbly idiomatic orchestral playing, vividly projected. The great central blues tune is gorgeously yet subtly seductive. The performance of the *Rhapsody in Blue* in some ways surpasses even Bernstein's famous New York account in its audacious, glittering brilliance. Here the players of the Aalborg Symphony produce hell-for-leather pizazz in the fast brass tuttis, contrasting with the rapturously bluesy account of the big tune. With a generous selection from Rattle's complete set of *Porgy and Bess*, this is a Gershwin bargain disc not to be missed, even if duplication is involved.

(i) *Rhapsody in Blue* (orchestral version); (ii) *Rhapsody in Blue* (piano solo version); *Preludes for Piano. Songs: Do it again; I'll build a stairway to paradise; I got rhythm; Liza; The man I love; Nobody but you; Oh, lady be good; Somebody loves me; Swanee; Sweet and low down; 'Swonderful; That certain feeling; Who cares?*

(B) ** Sony (ADD) SBK 89369. (i) Entremont; Philadelphia O, Ormandy; (ii) Watts

Philippe Entremont's account of the *Rhapsody in Blue* with Ormandy is bright and attractive, marred only by the recording, which sounds over-bright and brittle in the upper register. Only the keenest Gershwin collector is likely to want the solo piano version, even though André Watts's performance is thoughtful as well as brilliant. However, the songs are ever

attractive, even without the vocals, and these assured if sometimes wilful performances have plenty of life. The recording (no dates given) is a little hard, but acceptable.

PIANO MUSIC

Piano Duet

I Got Rhythm Variations; 2nd Rhapsody; 2 Waltzes. Arrangements: *Blue Monday; Embraceable you; Our love is here to stay*

(BB) ** EMI Encore 5 74729-2. K. and M. Labéque

The Labéque sisters' usual exuberant brashness of style is matched by bright, almost metallic piano-timbre, and no one could complain of a lack of jazzy impetus – indeed the effect is often dazzling, although also a little wearing without the orchestral cushion in the two main works. The song arrangements (*Blue Monday* uses the same material that Gershwin features in *Lullaby for Strings*) have a less aggressive, more sophisticated charm that is highly communicative.

Solo Piano Music: Impromptu in 2 Keys; Jazzbo Brown Blues (from 'Porgy & Bess'); Merry Andrew; Promenade; 3 Preludes; Rialto Ripples; Three-Quarter Blues; 2 Waltzes in C. 'Gershwin Song-Book': Clap yo' hands; Do, Do, Do; Do it again; Fascinating Rhythm; I got Rhythm; I'll build a Stairway to Paradise; Liza; The Man I love; My One and Only; Nobody loves you; Oh, Lady, be good!; Somebody loves me; Strike up the Band; Swanee; Sweet and low-down; 'S Wonderful; That Certain Feeling; Who cares. Also: Bess, Oh! where's my Bess; Little Jazz Bird; Someone to watch over me

(BB) **(*) CfP (ADD) 3 52346-2 (2). Rodney Bennett (with Songs by Jerome KERN; Harold ARLEN; Richard RODGERS; Cole PORTER) – KERN: *Songs *(*)*

Richard Rodney Bennett turns a composer's ear on Gershwin's piano music, including the composer's own arrangements of his most famous songs; perhaps that is why the performances are not always fully idiomatic. Their rhythmic vigour is underpinned by considerable expressive conviction, yet the melodic exhilaration does not always come across, although there are undoubted insights. But such a comprehensive collection is welcome, especially as it is joined with a more intimate earlier collection of show tunes by other composers. The recording is very close but truthful. Unfortunately, the coupled instrumental selection of Kern songs is less succssful.

Piano Rolls

'*The Piano Rolls*' Vol. 2: FREY: *Havanola.* CONRAD/ROBINSON: *Singin' the blues.* GERSHWIN: *From now on.* AKST: *Jaz-o-mine.* SILVERS: *Just snap your fingers at care.* KERN: *Whip-poor-will.* GERSHWIN/DONALDSON: *Rialto ripples.* PINKARD: *Waitin' for me.* WENDLING/WILLS: *Buzzin' the bee.* C. SCHONBERG: *Darling.* BERLIN: *For your country and my country.* MORRIS: *Kangaroo hop.* MATTHEWS: *Pastime rag 3.* GARDNER: *Chinese blues.* SCHONBERGER: *Whispering.* GRANT: *Arrah go on I'm gonna go back to Oregon*

** None. 7559 79370-2. Gershwin

Volume 1 is included in our main volume.

As can be seen, Volume 2 includes music by others, and few of these numbers even approach the quality of Gershwin's own output. But it is all played in good, lively style, although one senses that Gershwin was doing a professional job rather than acting as an enthusiastic advocate, and some pieces come off more appealingly than others. Frankly, much of this is cocktail bar music, although Chris Schonberg's *Darling* is a rather effective exception. Again the recording cannot be faulted.

Volume 1 (1918–25): *Come to the moon; Drifting along with the tide; Fascinatin' rhythm; The half of it, Dearie, blues; Hang on to me; I'd rather Charleston; I was so young; Kicking the clouds away; Limehouse nights; The man I love; Nobody but you; Oh, lady be good; So am I; Swanee; Tee-oodle-um-bum-bo. Piano Concerto in F: slow movt. Rhapsody in Blue*

(M) **(*) ASV CDWHL 2074. Gibbons

Volume 2 (1925–30): *Clap yo' hands; Do, do, do; Embraceable you; He loves and she loves; I got rhythm (2 versions); Liza; Looking for a boy; Maybe; Meadow Serenade; My one and only; Someone to watch over me; Sweet and low-down (2 versions); 'Swonderful; Funny face; That certain feeling; When do we dance? An American in Paris (overture); Strike Up the Band (overture); Irish Waltz (Three-Quarter Blues); 3 Piano Preludes*

(M) **(*) ASV CDWHL 2077. Gibbons

Volume 3 (1931–7): *For you, for me, for evermore; Isn't it a pity; Jilted; Let's call the whole thing off; Our love is here to stay; They can't take that away from me. Cuban Overture; 2nd Rhapsody; Porgy and Bess: Suite. Good morning, Brother: excerpts. Variations on 'I got rhythm'*

(M) **(*) ASV CDWHL 2082. Gibbons

Volume 4: '*The Hollywood Years': A Damsel in Distress: I can't be bothered now; The jolly tar and the milkmaid (2 versions); Put me to the test; Stiff upper lip; A foggy day in London town; Nice work if you can get it; Things are looking up. Goldwyn Follies: I was doing all right; Love walked in. Girl Crazy: Overture. Shall We Dance: French Ballet Class; Dance of the Waves; Slap that bass; Walking the dog; I've got beginner's luck; They all laughed; They can't take that away from me; Shall we dance. The Show is on; By Strauss*

(M) **(*) ASV CDWHL 2110. Gibbons

Volumes 1–3 of Jack Gibbon's coverage of the Gershwin Piano rolls is also available in a set (ASV CDWLS 328) and is praised in our main volume.

OPERA

Porgy and Bess (opera; complete)

(M) 🔘 ⚫ *** EMI 4 76836-2 [4 76832-2] (3). White, Haymen, Blackwell, Hubbard, Baker, Clarey, Evans, Glyndebourne Ch., LPO, Rattle

On CD, Simon Rattle conducts the same cast and orchestra as in the opera house, and the EMI engineers have done wonders in establishing more clearly than ever the status of *Porgy* as grand opera. By comparison, Lorin Maazel's Decca CD version sounds a degree too literal, and John DeMain's RCA set is less subtle. More than their rivals, Rattle and the LPO capture Gershwin's rhythmic exuberance with the degree of freedom essential if jazz-based inspirations are to sound idiomatic. The chorus is the finest and most responsive of any on the three sets, and the bass line-up is the strongest. Willard White is superbly matched by the magnificent Jake of Bruce Hubbard and by the dark and resonant Crown of Gregg Baker. As Sportin' Life, Damon Evans gets nearer than any of his rivals to the original scat-song inspiration without

ever short-changing on musical values. Cynthia Haymon as Bess is movingly convincing in conveying equivocal emotions, Harolyn Blackwell as Clara relishes Rattle's slow speed for *Summertime* and Cynthia Clarey is an intense and characterful Serena. EMI's digital sound is exceptionally full and spacious. Sir Simon Rattle's superb account of Gershwin's *Porgy and Bess* now comes at mid-price as one of EMI's 'Great Recordings of the Century'.

GESUALDO, Carlo (c. 1561–1613)

The most famous aspect of the life of Don Carlo Gesualdo, Prince of Venosa, is that, having inherited the family title in 1585 and then married his cousin, Donna Maria d'Avlos, he was complicit in her murder. The marriage had proceeded normally, his young wife had borne him children, but then in 1590 she was involved in an affair with Fabrizio Carafa, Duke of Andria, and was caught *in flagranti delicto* with her lover at the court. There is no doubt that Gesualdo and his servants played their part in the brutal double murder that followed. Because of the circumstances and his exalted position, the Prince did not face legal punishment. But as a penance he built a monastery and in its chapel he was depicted as a sinner on its altarpiece. He began life again at the Court of Ferrara, a centre of art and culture, and he remarried in 1594. In 1596 Gesualdo felt able to return from Ferrara to his old home with his second wife, but not to contentment. Her depression, his remorse, and the death of their son all had their effect, and Gesualdo turned to the composition of sacred music. But the final period of his life was haunted by the past: he suffered from nightmares and delusions, and some reports suggest that before he died he turned to self-flagellation.

Madrigals, Books I–III (complete)

*** CPO 777 138-2 (2). Gesualdo Consort, Amsterdam, Van der Kamp

Madrigals, Book V (1611)

*** Glossa GCD 920935. La Venexiana

It is against the background of the peak period of his extraordinary life that Gesualdo wrote his madrigals. Their composition cannot be dated with certainty, for Books I and II had previously appeared under a pseudonym, perhaps because of the dramatic events related above. They were finally published in 1594, and the Third and Fourth Books followed in 1596. The Fifth Book arrived in 1611 but was probably written alongside the others, 15 years earlier. Obviously the 1590s were an extraordinarily creative period for Gesualdo, and the five-part madrigal settings clearly reflected the emotional turmoil of his own life. Their extraordinary unpredictability of feeling, with pain and joy side by side, was exhibited in their chromatic intensity, and the spread of dissonances, the desperation in love of many of their texts, must relate to the composer's personal experiences. We now, at last, have the beginnings of two complete collections on CD, as we assume the disc from La Venexiana is the first of a series. In each case the madrigals are sung by a beautifully blended group of five voices, with Harry van der Kamp's Amsterdam ensemble slightly more robust (and pleasingly so) in tone. Gesualdo's madrigals are essentially *a cappella* works, but in the First Book of the Amsterdam series a lute or archlute is sometimes discreetly introduced; the Second Book includes a soprano solo with harpsichord, and in the Third a harpsichord is more often featured, and a single madrigal is heard as a harpsichord solo.

The recording throughout both sets is excellent, with the acoustic very pleasing in each. Full texts and translations are included, and the documentation is first class.

GHEDINI, Giorgio Federico

(1892–1965)

Violin Concerto (Il belprato); Musica da concerto for Viola, Viola d'amore and Strings

*(*) Essay CD 1075. Tenenbaum, Pro Musica Prague, Kapp – SIBELIUS: 6 Humoresques *(*)

Giorgio Federico Ghedini belongs to the generation that came to the fore in Italy in the wake of Pizzetti and Malipiero. In the 1950s the *Concerto dell'Albatro* (1945), generally regarded as his finest work, was periodically broadcast, but he has since fallen out of the repertory. Yet he was a prolific composer: his output includes an opera on *Billy Budd* (1949), based on Melville with a libretto of Quasimodo – two years before Britten's opera of the same name. The *Concerto for Violin and Strings (Il belprato)* (1947) and the *Musica da concerto for Viola, Viola d'amore and Strings* (1953) are well worth getting to know, or would be if the performances had greater charm and were better recorded. The second movement of *Il belprato* is imaginative, even if it is reminiscent of the slow movement of the Prokofiev *G minor Violin Concerto*. Mela Tenenbaum is not particularly well served by the engineers and does not seem to possess a particularly beautiful tone; the recording is close, dry and two-dimensional. This disc is useful as a reminder that, apart from Ghedini, there is a lot of Italian repertoire waiting to be explored: Casella's *Violin Concerto*, Pizzetti's *Symphony in A* and the Petrassi *Piano Concerto*.

GIBBONS, Orlando (1583–1625)

(i) *Anthems: Almighty and everlasting God; Hosanna to the Son of David; O clap your hands together – God is gone up; O Lord increase my faith; O Lord in thy wrath rebuke me not;* (ii) *Introit: First Song of Moses; Second setting of Preces and Proper Psalm 145 for Whit Sunday.* **Second Service: Voluntary I & Te Deum; Voluntary II and Jubilate.** **Short Service: Voluntary I and Magnificat; Voluntary II and Nunc dimittis.** Verse Anthems for voices and viols: *Glorious and powerful God; See, see the word is incarnate; This is the record of John*

(M) **(*)** Decca mono/stereo 433 677-2. King's College, Cambridge, Ch., (i) with Ord; H. McLean (organ); (ii) with Jacobean Consort of Viols, Willcocks; S. Preston (organ)

Of the two groups of recordings here, the first (mono) was made under Boris Ord in 1955; the second (stereo) came three years later, directed by David Willcocks, but with Thurston Dart lending his influence and leading the consort of viols in the verse anthems (alongside Desmond Dupré). This is a most imaginative reissue for Universal to include in their 'Critics' Choice' series. The mono recordings have plenty of ambience to disguise their lack of antiphony. But generally the effect is remarkably real, although the consort of viols is not always very well balanced.

Juxtaposing the contents of two separate LPs means that there is plenty of variety, and the later, stereo collection (which comes from the old Argo catalogue) is imaginatively chosen. Gibbons is a major musical personality and it was a happy idea in each case to preface the canticles from the two Services with an organ voluntary; it was customary in the early seventeenth century to have such a voluntary before the reading of the First Lesson.

GIBBS, Cecil Armstrong (1889–1960)

Songs: *Ann's cradle song; Araby; Arrogant poppies; The Ballad of summerwater; The bells; The birch tree; By a bierside; Danger; The fields are full; Five eyes; The flooded stream; Hypochondriacus; Lullaby; In the Highlands; The mad prince; Mistletoe; Neglected moon!; Nightfall; The oxen; The rejected lover; Sailing homeward; Silver; The sleeping beauty; 4 Songs for a mad sea captain, Op. 111; The splendour falls; Summer night; Take heed, young heart; Tiger-Lily; Titania; Tom o'Bedlam; To one who passed whistling through the night; When I was one-and-twenty; The Wanderer*

*** Hyp. CDA 67337. McGreevy, Varcoe, Vignoles

Born in 1889 into the Gibbs toothpaste family, Armstrong Gibbs devoted his career above all to composing the most sensitive settings of English verse. These 36 songs offer a most attractive cross-section, including ten which set verses by his favourite poet, Walter de la Mare, a close friend whose feeling for fantasy in a child-like world was well matched by the composer. Such a lively song as *Five eyes* is nicely contrasted here with such more hauntingly poetic inspirations such as *Silver*. Otherwise Gibbs concentrated on verse by little-known poets, so that he rarely failed to heighten what might on paper seem indifferent material. Geraldine McGreevy and Stephen Varcoe are persuasive advocates (even if Varcoe has moments of roughness), with Roger Vignoles an ideal accompanist, adding to the atmosphere of each song.

GLASS, Louis (1864–1936)

Symphonies 1 in E flat, Op. 17; 5 in C, Op. 57 (Sinfonia Svastica)

** Danacord DACVO CD 544 (2). Plovdiv PO, Todorov

During the 1920s Louis Glass was acclaimed as one of the leading Scandinavian symphonists. An accomplished pianist and cellist, he appeared as a concerto soloist on both instruments, though he turned to conducting and teaching when a nervous condition in one arm forced him to give up the piano. His *First Symphony* (1894) is derivative (Schumann, Bruckner, an unusual influence for the Denmark of its day) and its thematic substance is not quite strong enough to sustain its 45 minutes. The *Fifth Symphony*, subtitled *Sinfonia svastica* alludes to the Indian wheel of life, not the later, Nazi emblem. By far the best movement is the Scherzo, where the fantasy and imaginative scoring that distinguished his masterpiece, the *Elverhøjsuite*, resurface. Neither the performance nor the recording are in the first flight and the issue is primarily of interest as a curiosity.

GLAZUNOV, Alexander (1865–1936)

Violin Concerto in A min., Op. 82

(M) *** DG 457 064-2. Shaham, Russian Nat. O, Pletnev – KABALEVSKY: *Concerto;* TCHAIKOVSKY: *Souvenir d'un lieu cher, etc.* ***

Gil Shaham gives a pretty dazzling account of the Glazunov *Concerto* with Mikhail Pletnev and the Russian National Orchestra which can well hold its own with the current opposition. It reminds us what a superb (and often touching) piece it is. The couplings are unusual, and this is an enterprising choice for Universal's 'Critics' Choice' series.

The Seasons (ballet; complete); *Scènes de ballet, Op. 52*
(M) *** Telarc CD 80347. Minnesota O, Edo de Waart

The very attractive Minnesota performances of *The Seasons* and the delightful *Scènes de ballet* make an ideal coupling, and this is doubly attractive now it has been reissued at mid-price.

Symphonies 1 in E (Slavyanskaya), Op. 5; 4, Op. 48
(BB) ** Naxos 8.553561. Moscow SO, Anissimov

In both the *First* and in the *Fourth*, Alexander Anissimov gets eminently sympathetic performances from the Moscow orchestra, though one can imagine livelier and lighter playing.

Symphony 8 in E flat; Raymonda (Ballet Suite), Op. 57a
**(*) Warner 2564 61939-2. RSNO, Serebrier

Serebrier follows up his coupling of *The Seasons* and *Fifth Symphony* by pairing the *Eighth* with an attractive selection from the *Raymonda Ballet*. The symphony comes off very well, although the Scottish performance is rather less vibrant than Polyansky's Chandos version (Chan 9961), which is coupled with an outstanding account of the *Commemorative Cantata* (for Pushkin). However, the *Raymonda Suite* shows the composer at his finest, with consistently more memorable writing than in the symphony, full of melodic charm and felicitous scoring; *Raymonda*'s *Prélude et Variation* with its harp embroidery is delightful. The orchestral playing here is most sympathetic and the sound very pleasing.

Piano Music

Piano Sonata 1 in B flat min., Op. 74; Grande valse de concert, Op. 41; 3 Miniatures, Op. 42; Petite valse, Op. 36; Suite on the name 'Sacha'; Valse de salon, Op. 43; Waltzes on the Theme 'Sabela' Op. 23
(BB) *** Hyp. Helios CDH 66833. Coombs

Easy Sonata; 3 Etudes, Op. 31; Miniature in C; 3 Morceaux, Op. 49; Nocturne, Op. 37; 2 Pieces, Op. 22; 3 Preludes-improvisations; Sonatina; Theme & Variations, Op. 72
(BB) *** Hyp. Helios CDH 55222. Coombs

Marking the start of a new Russian series, each of these two discs contains a major work, the *Piano Sonata No. 1* on the first and the *Theme and Variations*, Op. 72, on the second. For the rest, you have a dazzling series of salon and genre pieces, full of the easy charm and winning tunefulness that mark Glazunov's ballet, *The Seasons*. Stephen Coombs proves a most persuasive advocate, consistently conveying sheer joy in keyboard virtuosity to a degree rare in British pianists. Coombs plays with a natural warmth and a spontaneous feeling for line which give magic to pieces which otherwise might seem trivial. As well as the engaging *Variations*, simple in outline but elaborate and colourful in texture, the second disc offers what might be counted Glazunov's most assured piano work, the set of three *Etudes*, Op. 31. Stephen Coombs's survey of Glazunov's piano music, full of easy charm and winning tunefulness, is now appearing on the bargain Helios label. Both volumes are reviewed in our main Guide, but the second is the one to try first, as it includes the engagingly colourful *Theme and Variations*, Op. 72.

4 Preludes & Fugues, Op. 101; Prelude & Fugue in D min., Op. 62; in E min. (1926)
(BB) *** Hyp. Helios CDH 55223. Coombs

One does not think of Glazunov in terms of preludes and fugues, but these are all impressive pieces and this Helios reissue is most welcome.

GLIÈRE, Reinhold (1875–1956)

The Bronze Horseman: Suite; (i) Horn Concerto, Op. 91
** Chan. 9379. (i) Watkins; BBC PO, Downes

The Bronze Horseman is not great music – nor, for that matter, is the *Horn Concerto*. Richard Watkins is a fine soloist in the latter; Downes gets good rather than really distinguished playing from the BBC Philharmonic, though the recording is excellent.

GLINKA, Mikhail (1804–57)

PIANO MUSIC

Volume 1: Variations on an Original Theme in F; Variations on the Romance 'Benedetta sia la madre'; Variations on Two Themes from the Ballet, 'Chao-Kang'; Variations on 'The Nightingale' (by Alabyev); Variations on a Theme from 'Anna Bolena' (by Donizetti); Variations & Rondino brillante on a Theme from the Opera, 'I Capuleti e i Montecchi' (by Bellini); Variations on a Theme from 'Faniska' (by Cherubini); Variations on the Russian Folk song 'In the shallow valley'
** BIS CD 980. Ryabchikov

All these variations were written when the composer was in his twenties. Ryabchikov suggests, in his thorough and authoritative notes, that 'the music is full of tenderness and expression, elegant simplicity and nobility'. Although he plays with evident feeling, he is handicapped by a rather forward recording. When he is playing above *forte* there is a touch of glare. The recording was made in Moscow, not by the familiar BIS team, and produced by the pianist himself.

Volume 2: Andalusian Dance, Las Mollares; Bolero; Contredanse, La Couventine; Contredanse in G; Cotillon in B flat; A Farewell Waltz; French Quadrille; Galop; Grande valse in G; 6 Mazurkas; Polka; Polonaise in E; The Skylark (trans. Balakirev); Tarantella; Valse-favorite; Valse mélodique; Variations on a Theme by Mozart; Variations on the Terzetto from the Opera 'A Life for the Tsar' (trans. Alexandr Gourilyov)
** BIS CD 981. Ryabchikov

Victor Ryabchikov's second survey of Glinka's piano music includes a supplement of three alternative versions of the *Variations on a Theme by Mozart*, plus Balakirev's transcription of *The Skylark*, made a few years after Glinka's death, and the *Variations on the Terzetto from the Opera 'A Life for the Tsar'* transcribed by Alexandr Gourilyov. No masterpieces are uncovered among these salon pieces, though there are some attractive numbers such as the *Bolero* and *A Farewell Waltz*. These are the kind of dances that you might have heard at any ball in Russia, and Ryabchikov plays them in the order you might have heard them in at such a function. Three-star playing and clear, rather forward recording made in the Melodiya Studios in Moscow, but distinctly one-star music.

A Life for the Tsar (Ivan Susanin)
(BB) (***) Naxos mono 8.111078/80. Mikhailov, Spiller, Antoneva, Yelepp, Hosson, Skobtsov, Svetlanov, Bolshoi Ch. & O, Melik-Pasheyev (Acts I–IV); Nebolsin (Epilogue)

In their impressive restorations of post-war Russian opera undertaken by Ward Marston, Naxos have turned to the 1947 recording of *A Life for the Tsar (Ivan Susanin)*, conducted by the legendary Alexander Melik-Pasheyev. The bass Maxim Mikhailov was the finest Ivan Susanin of his day and he sang the role some 400 times. (Eisenstein admirers may also remember his appearance in his greatest film, *Ivan the Terrible*.) Natalia Spiller, who sings his daughter, Antonida, was one of the greatest of the Bolshoi's heroines – much admired by Stalin, she sang for him at the Kremlin. The singing is superb and it is difficult to imagine a vocally or dramatically finer cast or finer conducting. The Epilogue was recorded in 1950 and is conducted by Vasili Nebolsin. (Incidentally, the Sigismund III in this performance is sung by Fyodor Svetlanov, the father of the conductor Evgeni, who became the Bolshoi's conductor in 1962.) The third CD is completed by some isolated arias sung by Antonina Nezhdanova (1913), Chaliapin (recorded in London in 1923) and Helge Rosvænge (in Berlin, 1940). Readers who can remember what Soviet recordings sounded like in the days of 78s and LP will be amazed at the quality of this set.

GLUCK, Christoph (1714–87)

Iphigénie en Tauride (complete CD version)
(M) *(*) Sony SM2K 90463 (2). Vaness, Surian, Allen, Winbergh, La Scala, Milan, Ch. & O, Muti

Muti's set, recorded live at La Scala in 1992, is a big-scale version, a possible alternative for those who insist on modern rather than period instruments. Muti's taut direction is comparably dramatic, but with beefy orchestral sound and close-up recording it is an overweight performance that misses the essential elegance of Gluck in its lack of light and shade. Vaness's dramatic timbre is apt, but the microphone catches a flutter in the voice. Thomas Allen as Oreste is telling (as he is for Gardiner) but, thanks to the recording, his subtler shading is missing and Gösta Winbergh as Pylade sings with fine ringing tones yet lacks subtlety and variety. Moreover, the set's documentation, as in the rest of this Sony series, is hopelessly inadequate, providing neither libretto nor cued synopsis. Gardiner's set on Philips is the one to go for.

GODARD, Benjamin (1849–95)

Cello Sonata in D min., Op. 104; 2 Pieces for Cello & Piano, Op. 61
*** Hyp. CDA 66888. Lidström, Forsberg – BOELLMANN: *Cello Sonata in A min.*, etc. ***

An interesting and compellingly played disc of off-beat repertoire. Benjamin Godard was a pupil of Vieuxtemps. His *D minor Sonata* is very much in the Schumann–Brahms tradition and is beautifully crafted and powerfully shaped, as are the *Aubade and Scherzo*. Mats Lidström and Bengt Forsberg play with such passion and conviction that they almost persuade you that this piece is worthy to rank alongside the Brahms sonatas. The recording is just a trifle on the close side, but it produces eminently satisfactory results. Strongly recommended.

GOETZ, Hermann (1840–76)

Francesca da Rimini: Overture. Spring Overture, Op. 15; (i) *Nenie, Op. 10;* (i; ii) *Psalm 137, Op. 14*
(B) ** CPO 999 316-2. (i) N. German R. Ch.; (ii) Stiller; N. German R. PO, Hanover, Albert

Hermann Goetz was born in the same year as Tchaikovsky. The best piece here is *Nenie*, which has a strong sense of purpose and a genuine lyrical flow. The *Francesca da Rimini Overture* comes from an opera its composer left unfinished. The musical language is very much in the tradition of Mendelssohn and Spohr, but the invention is of some quality, even if a little bland. Good performances from all concerned and decently balanced, well-rounded sound.

GOLDBERG, Johann (1727–56)

Johann Goldberg, born in Danzig and a student in Dresden, was credited with being a pupil both of Wilhelm Friedmann and of Johann Sebastian Bach. Supposedly, at the age of 14, he was the first performer of the *Goldberg Variations* as 'house pianist' to Count Keyserlink, its commissioner. This is not very likely to be true, but it ensured that the young Goldberg, composer as well as virtuoso of the keyboard, would be remembered. He died (of consumption) when he was only 29 years old.

Harpsichord Concertos: in B flat & D min.
🎵— *** Verso VRS 2025. Ogg, Baroque O of Salamanca University

This is a fascinating disc, and one is surprised that these two enjoyable (if much too extended) concertos have not been discovered before now. Never mind, they are played here with engaging freshness by Jacques Ogg, who also directs the Orquesta Barrocca de la Universidad de Salamanca, a first-class period-instrument ensemble. The first movement of the *D minor Concerto* lasts for nearly 17 minutes! and, after the orchestral introduction, consists in the main of a fantasia for the soloist, punctuated by orchestral chords and not much else. The agreeable *Largo* is more of a dialogue and the *Allegro molto* finale is full of life, a kind of jolly shared *moto perpetuo*. Its companion work in B flat has a much shorter opening movement, with the orchestra fully integrated into the argument, and its *Largo con sordini* is gently appealing, with a bouncing finale to follow. Both performances here are so infectiously spontaneous that one cannot help responding to them, despite their longueurs. The recording is beautifully balanced, and the harpsichord itself is ideally chosen.

GOLDSCHMIDT, Berthold (1903–96)

(i) *String Quartets 2-3;* (ii) *Letzte Kapitel;* (iii) *Belsatzar*
*** Largo LC 5115. (i) Mandelring Qt; (ii) Marks; (ii; iii) Ars-Nova Ens., Berlin, Schwarz

Berthold Goldschmidt was hounded from Nazi Germany in 1935 and settled in London. This disc collects his *Letzte Kapitel* for speaker and an instrumental ensemble, very much in the style of Kurt Weill, and the *Second Quartet*, which has something of the fluency of Hindemith. It is an excellently fashioned piece with a rather powerful slow movement, an elegy subtitled *Folia*. The CD is completed by *Belsatzar*, an *a cappella* setting of Heine, and the *Third Quartet*, a remarkable achievement for an 86-year-old, the product of a cultured and thoughtful musical mind. The performances are dedicated, the recordings satisfactory.

GOLIGHTLY, David (born 1948)

Symphony 1; 3 Seascapes
*** ASC CDCS 38. Prague PO, Sutherland

It may seem extraordinary, but David Golightly's *Symphony No. 1*, written over a period of four years, was commissioned by and dedicated to Middlesbrough F. C. and its chairman, Steve Gibson. Essentially programmatic, it is effectively wrought with a first movement founded on a rhythmic ostinato (*Resoluto marcato*) 'for those who strive, knock hard on the door of fate', the Scherzo reflecting the lively optimism of visits to Wembley, the eloquent and imaginatively scored slow movement reflecting the pain of defeat in an idiom that reminded the writer a little of the spacious string-writing of Howard Hanson. The finale is a jaunty populist march, exotically scored, with the two-part structure reflecting the two halves of the game. The orchestral fanfares depict the team scoring. It is a happy, extrovert inspiration and receives a fine performance under Gavin Sutherland in Prague, and a full-blooded recording. The three *Seascapes* further demonstrate Golightly's vivid orchestral skill, using well-known folk-themes, like *Shenandoah*. The disc is available from Modrana Music Publishers Ltd, tel. 01625 875389, or Disk Imports Ltd, tel. 0161 491 6655.

Choral Music: *Frontiers (5 American Folk Songs); Rites of Passage (6 Pushkin Songs)*
*** Modrana MCD 002. St Petersburg Sogklasie Male Voice Ch., Govorov (with *14 Russian Folk Songs*)

For the recording of his choral music, the enterprising David Golightly has turned to the excellent St Petersburg Male Voice Choir, appropriately so in one sense, as his *Rites of Passage* are settings of Pushkin; oddly in another, as they are sung in an English translation by Henry Jones. Nevertheless, the six songs are magnetically presented and they sound more idiomatic with a heavy Russian accent, especially the closing *Elegy*, linking the Russian winter with life's 'final hour'. The arrangements of five American folksongs are no less beguiling, especially the lovely *Shenandoah* and the engaging *Streets of Laredo*, where the Russian singers assimilate the transatlantic style and impregnate the music with their own folksy feeling, their American English surprisingly clear. Golightly's accompaniments are full of individual touches, and Dimitri Tepliakov plays them with skilful feeling for the different colloquial rhythmic inflexions. The recording is good.

GOMBERT, Nicolas (c.1495–c.1560)

Credo; Haec dies quam fecit Dominus; Lugebat David Abalon; Meda vita in morte sumus; O beata Maria; Qui colis Ausiniam; Salve regina; Vae, vae Babylon
(BB) **(*) Hyp. Helios CDH 55247. Henry's Eight

Nicolas Gombert was born in Flanders but went to Spain to become Master of the Children of the Chapel of Emperor Charles I. Unfortunately, as a paedophile, he abused his position and was sentenced to be chained in the galleys. He was later pardoned because of the quality of his music, of which he wrote a great deal, including famous *Magnificat* settings (see our main volume) and 11 Masses. This rather bitty collection of motets and graduals does not do him full justice, though it does have some beautiful music, including the eight-part *Credo*, the *Salve regina* and the imitative five-voice *O beata Maria*. The performances by Henry's Eight are splendid and they are excellently recorded.

GÓRECKI, Henryk (born 1933)

Symphony 3 (Symphony of Sorrowful Songs), Op. 36
**(*) Naïve V 5019. Perruche, Sinfonia Varsovia, Altinoglu (with *Canticum graduum*)

(BB) **(*) Warner Apex 0927 49821-2. Woytowicz, SW SO, Baden-Baden, Bour

Górecki's *Symphony of Sorrowful Songs*, composed at Katowice in 1976 at the gates of Auschwitz, came to the wider public's attention through a television broadcast about the Holocaust which used the central movement as its background music. It has been much recorded, and these two CDs, the Naïve from 2004/5, the Apex a reissue from 1977, are the latest to come our way. Both are eloquently intense performances with fine soloists, the one French, the other Polish. Neither conductor quite gets round the problem that the arch-like opening *Lento sostenuto* is too long for its simple material, although Alain Altinoglu and the Sinfonia Varsovia at 25 minutes 39 seconds are five minutes shorter than Ernest Bour in Baden-Baden. But the solo singing in the best-known central movement is very compelling in both versions. Stefania Woytowicz has a wider, more intrusive vibrato than Ingrid Perruche and this gives a preference to the Naïve version in the closing movement. The Naïve disc also has the advantage of more modern digital recording, although its bonus of the early (1969) *Canticum graduum*, with its swathes of dissonance, was ill-chosen, as we do not feel that most admirers of the main work would wish to return to it very often. As for the *Symphony*, we continue to recommend the celebrated earlier Nonesuch version, conducted by David Zinman and crowned by the radiant singing of Dawn Upshaw (7559 79282-2). Or, if you want a bargain, Wit's Polish Naxos account, with the excellent Zofia Kilanowicz, would seem something of a best buy, for it also includes the *Three Pieces in the Olden Style*, one of the composer's most communicative and enjoyable works.

GOSSEC, François-Joseph (1734–1829)

Le triomphe de la république
*** Chan. 0727. Haller, Balducci, Sakurada, Danuser, Swiss R. Ch., Coro Calicantus, I Barochisti, Fasolis

It is sad that none of the composers who followed the great upheaval of the French Revolution came near to matching the impact of that event. Gossec here offers a delightful example of the appealing music which was being written, an opera on a patriotic theme, built on clear and direct popular tunes, often with a military flavour, with jolly choruses and rustic dances. The piece opens with an overture full of brassy fanfares and, thanks to the energy of Fasolis and his excellent team, the music over 72 minutes readily holds the attention, with excellent soloists and the Lugano Chorus of Swiss Radio a model of its kind. An attractive rarity, vividly recorded. Full text and translation included.

GOTTSCHALK, Louis (1829–69)

Louis Gottschalk was born in New Orleans of mixed German and French parentage. He studied music in Paris under Charles Hallé and then launched himself on a hugely successful career as composer/conductor/virtuoso pianist. He travelled widely (constantly moving throughout Europe and the USA), appealing to a society whose musical taste was without pretensions. As a touring star (perhaps comparable to the pop stars of today) he was to some extent an isolated figure, cut off from serious musical influences. His subservience to public taste led to a continual infusion of national and patriotic airs into his scores. The felicities of his elegant vulgarity are boundless, and his music retains a refreshing naivety to the last.

(i; ii) **Grand Tarantelle for Piano and Orchestra (arr. Hershey Kay)**; (ii) **A Night in the Tropics (Symphony 1)**; (iii; iv) **The Union: Concert Paraphrase on National Airs, for 2 pianos, Op. 48 (arr. List)**; **Music for Piano, 4 Hands: L'Etincelle; La Gallina; Jota aragonesa; Marche de Nuit; Orfa; Printemps d'amour; Radieuse; Responds-moi; Ses yeux; Souvenirs d'Andalousie; Tremolo (arr. Werner/List).**
(iii) **Solo Piano: The Banjo, Op. 15; Bamboula; La Bananier, Op. 5; Danse des nègres, Op. 2; The Dying Poet; The Last Hope, Op. 16; The Maiden's Blush; Marche des Gibaros; Ojos Criolos (Danse Cubaine); Pasquinade, Op. 59; La Savanne; Souvenir de Porto Rico; Suis Mai; Tournament Galop**
(B) *** Van. (ADD) stereo/mono ATMCD 1181 (2). (i) Nibley;
    (ii) Utah SO, Abravanel; (iii) List; (iv) Lewis/Werner

The Vanguard two-CD set includes a solo collection recorded as early as 1956; although the recording is mono, it is truthful and does not sound one-dimensional. Eugene List was just the man to choose for these solo items: he is marvellously deadpan. Whether tongue-in-cheek or not, he manages to sound stylish throughout. In the music for piano, four hands, he is joined by excellent partners; the performances have flair and scintillating upper tessitura. The opening arrangement of the Jota aragonesa heads an ear-tickling programme with a neat touch of wit in the piece called Tremolo. When the participants move to two pianos for the outrageous Union Paraphrase the effect is properly flamboyant. In the quotation from 'Hail Columbia', the second pianist enterprisingly slipped a piece of paper into the piano across the lower strings to simulate a side-drum effect with great success. The orchestral items include a so-called symphony, A Night in the Tropics, which sounds suitably atmospheric in Utah, and Rein Nibley brings plenty of bravura to the concertante Grand Tarantelle.

PIANO MUSIC

Piano music for 4 hands: (i) Le Bananier (Chanson nègre), Op. 5; La Gallina (Danse cubaine), Op. 53; Grande tarantelle, Op. 67; La jota aragonesa (Caprice espagnol), Op. 14; Marche de nuit, Op. 17; Ojos criollos (Danse cubaine – Caprice brillante), Op. 37; Orfa (Grande polka), Op. 71; Printemps d'amour (Mazurka–caprice de concert), Op. 40; Réponds-moi (Danse cubaine), Op. 50; Radieuse (Grand valse de concert), Op. 72; La Scintilla (L'Etincelle – Mazurka sentimentale), Op. 21; Ses yeux (Célèbre polka de concert), Op. 66. Solo piano music: Le Banjo; Berceuse (cradle song); The Dying Poet (meditation); Grand scherzo; The Last Hope (religious meditation); Mazurka; Le Mancenillier (West

Indian serenade); Pasquinade caprice; Scherzo romantique; Souvenirs d'Andalousie; Tournament galop; The Union: Concert Paraphrase on National Airs (The Star-Spangled Banner; Yankee Doodle; Hail Columbia)
(B) ** Nim. NI 7045/6 (2). Marks, (i) with Barrett

Much of Gottschalk's music exists in alternative two- and four-handed arrangements, and Alan Marks and Nerine Barrett make an effervescent Gottschalk partnership in the latter, playing the more dashing pieces to the manner born. The drawback is that this very personable piano duo are recorded – realistically enough – in an empty, resonant hall, and although one adjusts, the effect is not advantageous.

The solo recital is still resonant, but not exaggeratedly so, and Alan Marks plays with considerable flair: the Souvenirs d'Andalousie glitters with bravura, his felicity of touch and crisp articulation bring much sparkle to the Grand scherzo and Scherzo romantique, while he sounds like a full orchestra in the Tournament galop. Most importantly, there is not a hint of sentimentality in The Dying Poet or The Last Hope, the composer's most famous piece. For those wanting an inexpensive survey of Gottschalk, this Nimbus Double will serve well enough, but the Hyperion series is artistically and sonically preferable.

Complete solo piano music: 'An American Composer, bon Dieu!'

Volume 1: Le Bananier (Chanson nègre), Op. 5; Le Banjo; Chanson de Gitano; Columbia (Caprice américain), Op. 34; Danza, Op. 33; Le Mancenillier, Op. 11; Mazurka; Minuit à Seville, Op. 30; Romanze; Souvenir de la Havana (Grand caprice de concert), Op. 39; Souvenir de Porto Rico, marche des Gibaros, Op. 31; Les Yeux créoles (Danse cubaine), Op. 37; Union (Paraphrase de concert), Op. 48
*** Hyp. CDA 66459. Martin

Gottschalk invented the conception of the composer/recitalist in America, just as Liszt had in Europe. As a touring virtuoso he had great audience appeal, and if his music is lightweight it is well crafted and tuneful, paying homage to both Liszt and Chopin. Its exotic folk-influences are drawn colloquially and naturally from the Deep South, with syncopated rhythms the strongest feature.

Philip Martin's continuing complete survey on Hyperion is in every way distinguished. He is naturally sympathetic to the transatlantic idioms, yet he treats the music as part of the romantic mainstream, bringing out its various derivations. He plays with elegance, brilliance, style and, above all, spontaneity. He is very well recorded in an ideal acoustic. In Volume 1 he closes with the celebrated and grandiose Union (Paraphrase de concert), which Gottschalk, a dedicated abolitionist, played for President Lincoln and his First Lady in 1864.

Volume 2: Ballade; Berceuse, Op. 47; Caprice polka; Grand scherzo, Op. 57; La jota aragonesa (Caprice espagnol), Op. 14; Manchega (Etude de concert), Op. 38; Marche de nuit, Op. 17; Miserere du Trovatore (paraphrase de concert), Op. 52; Pasquinade (caprice), Op. 59; Polkas: in A flat; in B flat. La Savane (Ballade créole), Op. 3; Scherzo romantique; Souvenirs d'Andalousie (Caprice de concert), Op. 22; Souvenir de Lima (Mazurka), Op. 74; Suis-moi! (Caprice), Op. 45; Ynés
*** Hyp. CDA 66697. Martin

The Paraphrase of Verdi's Miserere all but upstages Liszt. One can imagine how the composer's contemporary audiences would have loved its melodrama, while both the *Jota aragonesa* and the similar *Souvenirs d'Andalousie* are *tours de force* of extrovert dexterity. The *Caprice polka* is polished and sparkling, while the *Souvenir de Lima* returns to an engagingly Chopinesque idiom. Again, a very good recording.

Volume 3: *Bamboula (Danse des nègres), Op. 2; La Chute des feuilles (Nocturne), Op. 42; The Dying Poet (Meditation); Hercule (Grande étude de concert); Murmures éoliens; O ma charmante, épargnes-moi (Caprice); Gottschalk's Melody; Grand fantaisie triomphale sur l'hymne national Brésilien; The Last Hope; Symphony 1 (La Nuit des tropiques)*: 1st movement: *Andante* (arr. Napoleão); *Tournament galop*
* Hyp. CDA 66915. Martin

The Dying Poet and *The Last Hope* – which the composer described, tongue in cheek, as a 'succès de larmes' (tears) – are treated with a nice discretion. *Hercule* (given a striking march theme with simple decorative variants) is built to a fine rhetorical climax, as is the slow movement of the *Symphony No. 1* (in this not entirely advantageous transcription). The closing, very orchestral *Tournament galop* is superbly thrown off. It has a Rossinian vivacity, but its roulades are very much Gottschalk's own.

Volume 4: *Apothéose (Grande marche solennelle), Op. 29; La Colombe (petite polka), Op. 49; Fantôme de bonheur (Illusions perdues), Op. 36; Forest Glade Polka (Les Follets), Op. 25; La Gitana (Caprice caractéristique), Op. 35; La Moissonneuse (Mazurka caractéristique), Op. 8; Morte!! (Lamentation), Op. 55; Ossian (2 Ballades), Op. 4/1-2; Pensée poétique; Polonia, Op. 35; Reflets du passé, Op. 28; La Scintilla (L'Etincelle: Mazurka sentimentale), Op. 20; Ricordati (Nocturne, méditation, romance), Op. 26; Le Songe d'une nuit d'été (Caprice élégant), Op. 9; Souvenir de Cuba (Mazurka), Op. 75*
* Hyp. CDA 67118. Martin

If you decide to explore this enjoyable Hyperion survey, Volume 4 is a good place to start, for much of its content is little known and every piece is enjoyable. The Lisztian *Le Songe d'une nuit d'été*, the thoughtful *Pensée poétique, La Scintilla* (with its iridescence) all have great charm. *Morte!!* brings an elegiac contrast and has a distinctly sentimental ambience. *Polonia* is a jolly peasant dance, while the *Forest Glade Polka* curiously anticipates the music of Billy Mayerl, and there is a flamboyant closing *Apothéose*, which takes a fair time to reach its zenith, but proceeds to do so with panache.

Volume 5: *Ballade 8; Bataille; La Chasse du jeune Henri; El Cocoyé; Marguerite; Orfa Polka; Polka de salon; Rayons d'azur; Réponds-moi (Dí que sí); Sospiro; Tremolo*
* Hyp. CDA 67248. Martin

Philip Martin here continues his inestimable series, playing Gottschalk with such musical feeling that he makes writing that is ingenuous and designed solely to tickle the ear sound worthy of the concert hall. Such are the opening waltzes, *Sospiro* and the very engaging *Marguerite*. The *Etude de concert* has a very striking opening theme, but its treatment is perhaps rather over-extended. The rag-like *Réponds-moi* (originally written for four hands) and *El Cocoyé*, with their Cuban rhythms, are quintessential Gottschalk, but the Chopinesque *Solitude* and the *Eighth Ballade* are both based on pleasingly serene melodies, while the ingenious *Tremolo* and the polka *Rayons d'azur*, with its leggiero repeated notes, are

both delectably virtuosic (and delightfully played here). The other polkas, notable *Orfa*, have much charm. The closing *Chasse du jeune Henri* is based on Méhul's overture to his otherwise discarded opera and soon intrigues the ear with its catchy, galloping motive. Altogether a fascinating programme, very well played and recorded.

Volume 6: *Caprice élégiaque; Le Carnaval de Venise (with Variations); Colliers d'or; Danse des sylphes; Danse ossianique; La Favorita: Grand fantaisie triomphale; Impromptu; Jeunesse; Marche funèbre; Printemps d'amour; Le Sourire d'une june fille; Vision*
* Hyp. CDA 67349. Martin

Volume 6 begins with an elaborate and scintillating treatment of the *Carnival of Venice*, followed by a droll little *Funeral March*, which Philip Martin plays charmingly. The rippling *Vision* and pretty little mazurka, *Printemps d'amour*, are more characteristic, and the *Caprice élégiaque* and *Colliers d'or (deux mazurkes)* are Chopinesque, but the very pleasing *Danse ossianique* has an even stronger flavour of that composer. The *Sylphs* dance to glittering runs in the piano's highest register, and 'The Maiden's Blush' (*Le Sourire d'une jeune fille*) was just made for Gottschalk to turn into a cute little waltz. Last comes the grandly introduced Donizetti fantasia to make a lyrically tuneful and virtuosic finale, which is presented with aplomb by Philip Martin, who continues to show such a natural flair for this writing and never makes it sound cheap.

Volume 7: *Ardennes Mazurka; Amour chevaleresque; Ballade 7; La brise; Le chant de soldat; Le cri de délivrance; Deuxième Banjo; The Dying Swan; Fairy Land; Forget me not; La Gallina; God save the Queen; Hurrah Galop; Madeleine; The Water Sprite*
* Hyp. CDA 67478. Martin

Philip Martin continues to tickle the ear in Volume 7 with the opening *Water Sprite*, and his touch is just as neat in the schottische, *Fairy Land*; then he dashes off with the *Hurrah Galop*. The Cuban dance, *La Gallina*, is catchy in the best Gottschalk manner, and Martin ensures that *The Dying Swan* is a *romance poétique* without being laden with overt sentimentality. He closes with Gottschalk's variations on 'God save the Queen' or 'My country 'tis of thee', according to your nationality. After the flamboyant introducion, the tune is repeated like a chorale, with dazzling pyrotechnics in the right hand.

Volume 8: *Chant de guerre; Chant du martyr; Dernier amour; Home, sweet home; Jérusalem; La mélancolie; Pastorella e Cavalliere; Pensive; Radieuse; Ses yeux; Variations de concert sur l'hymne portugais*
* Hyp. CDA 67536. Martin

Gottschalk loves to make the most of the piano's extreme upper register, as Philip Martin demonstrates again and again in Volume 8. *Home, sweet home*, with which he opens his programme, is played both with discretion and with some deliciously glittering bravura on top, and the delicate *Pensive Polka* is similarly seductive. Its companion, *Ses yeux*, is more rhythmically robust – in the words of the accompanying notes 'quintessential Gottschalk', and no less catchy. The large-scale piece here is the *Variations on the Portuguese National Anthem*, where the virtuosity all but needs extra fingers; but Philip Martin manages admirably with just ten. He concludes with the flamboyant operatic fantasy based on Verdi's *I Lombardi* (retitled *Jérusalem* in its 1847 revision) in which the decoration of the duo, *Une pensée amère*, is scintillating, and the paraphrase closes with the jolly *Marche des croisés*.

Piano music: Bamboula; Le Banjo; Le Bananier; Danza; Le dernier espoir: Méditation religieuse; Pasquinade; Le poète mourant: Meditation; Sixième ballade; Souvenir de Porto-Rico; Union: Paraphrase sur les airs nationaux
(BB) **(*) Warner Apex 2564 61183-2. Noël Lee

Gottschalk's light and entertaining piano music is undoubtedly distinctive, and this Warner CD is an inexpensive way to sample this composer's style. The performances are good, the sound full and vivid if just lacking a bit of atmosphere.

Bamboula; Le Banjo; Le Bananier; The Dying Poet; L'Etincelle; La Gallina; La jota aragonesa; Manchega; Pasquinade; La Savane; Souvenirs d'Andalousie; Souvenir de Porto Rico, Marche ds Gibaro; Suis-moi!; Tremolo; Tournament Galop; The Union: Paraphrase de Concert on the national airs, Star-Spangled Banner, Yankee Doodle and Hail Columbia
●━ (BB) *** Naxos 8.559145. Licad

If you want a single representative disc of Gottschalk's music, this is it. Cecile Licad is right inside this repertoire. She obviously enjoys every bar and conveys her enthusiasm to us, playing with character, polish and rhythmic gusto. *Le Banjo*, which opens the programme, has great zest, *Bamboula* (the 'Danse de nègres') thumps vigorously, and the *Tournament Galop* chases along with infectious bravura. Yet *Le Bananier* has an almost sinuous charm and *La Savane* is played with winning delicacy. Even *The Dying Poet* is made to sound delicate rather than too overtly sentimental, partly because here, as elsewhere, Licad's rubato is naturally spontaneous. The idiomatic feeling of *La jota aragonesa* and of the two *Souvenirs* is striking, for she has a real feeling for Spanish and Afro-Caribbean rhythms. The programme closes with the spectacular *Union Paraphase*, presented with genuine bravado. Very well recorded, this disc is irresistible.

GOUGH, John (1903–51)

Serenade for Small Orchestra
*** Chan. 9757. BBC PO, Handley – BAINTON: *Symphony 2 in D min.*; CLIFFORD: *Symphony* ***

John Gough worked for a time as a studio manager or balance engineer in the BBC and was later Pacific Service Music Organizer during the war years. After the war he became a features producer during the period when that BBC department was at the height of its fame. The short but charming *Serenade for Small Orchestra* reveals a genuine creative talent and was written in 1931 for Hubert Clifford's wedding. Exemplary playing and first-rate recorded sound.

GOUNOD, Charles (1818–93)

Faust: Ballet music
(B) *** Australian Decca Eloquence (ADD) 476 2724.
ROHCG O, Solti – OFFENBACH: *Gaîté Parisienne* ***;
RESPIGHI: *Rossiniana* **(*)

Solti's 1959 account of the *Faust* ballet music is undoubtedly one of the liveliest (and most vividly recorded) versions committed to disc. While Beecham *et al.* have offered more

elegance in this repertoire, no one beats Solti for sheer energy; he has a style all his own, and the final *Entrée de Phryné* almost goes off the rails with its hard-driven but exciting brilliance.

Faust (complete)
(M) **(*) Ph.475 7769 (3). Te Kanawa, Araiza, Nesterenko, Schmidt, Coburn, Bav. R. Ch. & SO, C. Davis

Sir Colin Davis, with his German orchestra and with no French singer among his principals, gives a performance which, from the very measured account of the opening onwards, relates back to the weight of Goethe as much as to French opera. As in his other recordings of French opera – notably another Goethe inspiration, Massenet's *Werther* – he removes the varnish of sentimentality. Davis's *Faust* may not always be idiomatic but, with fine singing from most of the principals, it is a refreshing version. Dame Kiri, more than you might expect, makes a light and innocent-sounding Marguerite, with the *Jewel Song* made to sparkle in youthful eagerness, leaping off from a perfect trill. Evgeni Nesterenko as Mephistopheles is a fine, saturnine tempter. Andreas Schmidt as Valentin sings cleanly and tastefully in a rather German way, while Pamela Coburn as Siebel is sweet and boyish. The big snag is the Faust of Francisco Araiza, a disappointing hero, with a voice, as recorded, gritty in tone and frequently strained. He underlines the simple melody of *Salut, demeure*, for example, far too heavily, not helped by a syrupy violin solo. The sound is first rate, with the voices cleanly focused and well balanced against the orchestra, giving a fine sense of presence, and this now returns to the catalogue at mid-price in Philips's series of Originals, with full text and translation.

GRAF, Friedrich (1727–95)

6 Flute Quartets
*** MDG 311 0520-2. Hünteler, Festetics Qt (members)

Friedrich Hartmann Graf began his musical career as a timpanist in the band of a Dutch regiment but, after being wounded in battle and taken prisoner, decided to turn to the more peaceful flute. He developed into a virtuoso, becoming a colleague of Telemann in Hamburg in 1759. In his six quartets for flute, violin, viola and cello (dating from around 1775) the flute dominates, but the ensemble is elegantly integrated. They are gently melodious and full of charm and, taken one at a time, make very pleasing listening. The performances here are beautifully turned and perfectly balanced in a warm acoustic. Undoubtedly lightweight, but beguiling.

GRAINGER, Percy (1882–1961)

PIANO MUSIC

Complete: 'Dished up for Piano', Volumes 1–5

Volume 1: Andante con moto; Bridal Lullaby; Children's March; Colonial Song; English Waltz; Handel in the Strand; Harvest Hymn; The Immovable 'Do'; In a Nutshell (Suite) (Arrival Platform Humlet; Gay But Wistful; The Gum-Suckers' March; Pastoral); In Dahomey; Mock Morris; Peace; Sailor's Song; Saxon Twi-Play; To a Nordic Princess; Walking Tune

'Volume 2: Arrangements: BACH: *Blithe Bells; Fugue in A min.* BRAHMS: *Cradle Song.* Chinese TRAD.: *Beautiful Fresh Flower.* DOWLAND: *Now, O Now, I Needs Must Part.* ELGAR: *Enigma Variations: Nimrod.* Stephen FOSTER: *Lullaby; The Rag-Time Girl.* GERSHWIN: *Love Walked In; The Man I Love.* RACHMANINOV: *Piano Concerto 2: Finale* (abridged). R. STRAUSS: *Der Rosenkavalier: Ramble on the Last Love-Duet.* TCHAIKOVSKY: *Piano Concerto 1* (opening); *Paraphrase on the Flower Waltz*

Volume 3: Folksong arrangements: *The Brisk Young Sailor; Bristol Town; Country Gardens; Died for Love; Hard-Hearted Barb'ra Helen; The Hunter in His Career; Irish Tune from County Derry; Jutish Medley; Knight and Shepherd's Daughter; Lisbon (Dublin Bay); The Merry King; Mo Ninghean Dhu; Molly on the Shore; My Robin is to the Greenwood Gone; One More Day My John* (2 versions, easy and complex); *Near Woodstock Town; The Nightingale and the Two Sisters; O Gin I Were Where Gowrie Rins; Rimmer and Goldcastle; The Rival Brothers; Scotch Strathspey; Shepherd's Hey; Spoon River; Stalt Vesselil; Sussex Mummers' Christmas Carol; The Widow's Party; Will Ye Gang to the Hielands, Lizzie Lindsay?*

Volume 4: Arrangements: ANON.: *Angelus ad Virginem.* BACH: *Toccata & Fugue in D min.* DELIUS: *Air & Dance.* FAURE: *Après un rêve; Nell.* Stephen FOSTER: *Lullaby* (Easy; Grainger). GRIEG: *Piano Concerto* (first movement). HANDEL: *Water Music: Hornpipe.* SCHUMANN: *Piano Concerto* (first movement). STANFORD: *4 Irish Dances.* GRAINGER: *At Twilight; The Bigelow March; Eastern Intermezzo; Tiger-Tiger; Klavierstücke in A min., B flat, D & E.*

Volume 5: Original works for up to six hands: BRAHMS: *Paganini Variation 12.* BYRD: *The Carman's Whistle.* (i) *Children's March;* DELIUS: *A Dance Rhapsody.* (i–ii) *English Dance.* (i) GERSHWIN: *Girl Crazy: Embraceable You.* (i–ii) *Green Bushes; Spoon River; Train Music; Up-Country Song;* (i–ii) *The Warriors* (music for an imaginary ballet); *Ye Banks and Braes o' Bonnie Doon; Zanzibar Boat-Song* (with (i) McMahon; (ii) Martin)

(B) ***Nim. NI 5767(5). Martin Jones

This is the complete listing of the Nimbus set about which we are enthusiastic in the main Guide.

GRANADOS, Enrique (1867–1916)

PIANO MUSIC

Piano Music (complete)

A la cubana; Allegro de concierto; Barcorola; Bocetos; Cantas de amor; Carezza (vals); Capricho español; Cuentos de la juventud; Danza caracteristica; 2 Danzas españolas; 12 Danzas españolas; Elisenda; Escenas poéticas I–II; Estudio; 6 Estudios espresivos en forma de piezas fáciles; 2 Gavotos; Goyescas, Books I–II; Goyescas: Intermezzo. 2 Impromptus; Libro de horas; Marche militaire; Moresque y canción arabe; Oriental, canción, variada, intermedio y final; Paisaje; Países soñados; 6 Piezas sobre cantos populares españolas; Rapsodia aragonesa; Valse de concert; Valses intimos. Reverie (Improvisation; transcribed from a Duo Art piano roll)

12 Danzas españolas (transcribed for one or two guitars by Llobet and Barrueco)

℗─ (BB) *** EMI Encore 5 86985-2. Barrueco (guitar) with Müller-Pering in Nos. 9, 13, 15–16 & 18 – FALLA: *7 canciones populares españolas* ***

These transcriptions are so skilful that one is made to feel that all this music is more naturally suited to the guitar than to the piano. Marvellous performances, most realistically recorded.

Goyescas (complete)

(BB) *(*) EMI Gemini (ADD) 4 76906-2 (2). Ciccolini – ALBÉNIZ: *Iberia* **

Aldo Ciccolini's recording of *Goyescas* is undoubtedly good value on Gemini, particularly when coupled with *Iberia*. The performances are undoubtedly idiomatic and poetic, but the recording, made in the Salle Wagram in Paris in 1966, is less than ideal, rather shallow in timbre, not showing the pianist in the best light.

GRAUPNER, Christoph (1683–1760)

Double Flute Concerto in E min., GWV.321; Overtures in E flat, GWV.429; in E, GWV.439; Sinfonias in D, GWV.538; in G, GWV.578

*** MDG 341 1121-2. Nova Stravaganza

Overture in F, GWV 451; Sinfonia in F, GWV 571; Trio in C min., GWV 203

*** MDG 341 1252-2. Nova Stravaganza, Rampe

MDG has a knack of finding these previously forgotten baroque composers. German-born Graupner was prolific, writing 113 symphonies, 50 concertos, 80 suites (overtures), operas and cantatas, as well as a vast amount of chamber music. The works recorded here are typical, showing both imagination and individuality. The three-movement *Sinfonias* demonstrate the composer's adventurous spirit, with plentiful ideas: the *Sinfonia in D* has a charming flute duet in the central movement, while the finale is both vivacious and fresh. The *G major Sinfonia* uses its two horns to good effect in the first movement, rather like a hunting concerto, contrasting with its minor-keyed central movement and the elegant, if more formal, minuet finale. Again in the *Double Flute Concerto*, while there are two quite substantial fast movements, the minor key ensures that the writing is not entirely frivolous, and the finale, with its interplay between the two soloists, is especially infectious. The *Overture/Suites* are in the late-baroque style, featuring dance movements but beginning with a more substantial introduction. They are agreeable enough, though not as striking as their companion works. Excellent performances and recording.

On Volume 2, the *F major Overture* (a première recording) is especially rich in texture, with its two chalumeaux and viola d'amore providing subtle colouring. Unusually, there is only one horn, but it is used to brilliant effect, stretching the player's virtuosity to the limit. The writing throughout this *Suite* is exceptionally inventive and colourful, but most enjoyable of all are the *C minor Trio* and the four-movement *Sinfonia in F*, which features an especially attractive slow movement (using pizzicato strings) and a jolly finale, with some engaging rustic-sounding flutes playing in thirds. Superb performances and typically well-balanced sound from MDG make these CDs an important addition to the baroque catalogue.

GRECHANINOV, Alexander
(1864–1956)

Symphonies (i) *1*; (ii) *2 in A, Op. 27 (Pastorale)*

(BB) ** Naxos 8.555410. (i) George Enescu State PO,
Edlinger; (ii) Slovak State PO (Košice), Wildner

The *First Symphony* comes from the 1890s and the *Second* from 1909, and they are typical of the post-Nationalist school. Both were recorded in the late 1980s and are well played. The Bucharest orchestra is a fine one, though the recorded sound is shallow and the acoustic resonant. The Košice orchestra is marginally better served by the acoustic though it, too, is resonant. More than serviceable performances – though, to be fair, readers are better served by the Polyansky records on Chandos.

GRIEG, Edvard (1843–1907)

Piano Concerto in A min., Op. 16

(M) *** Ph. (ADD) 478 7773. Kovacevich, BBC SO, C. Davis –
SCHUMANN: *Piano Concerto* ***

**(*) ABC Classics 476 8071. Tedeschi, Queensland O,
Bonynge – TCHAIKOVSKY: *Piano Concerto 1* **(*)

(M) ** DG (ADD) 474 838- 2. Anda, BPO, Kubelik –
BRAHMS: *Piano Concerto 2* **(*)

(B) *(*) EMI (ADD) 5 67982-2 S. Richter, Monte Carlo Op. O,
Matačić – SCHUMANN: *Piano Concerto*; *Papillons* **

*(*) Decca 467 093-2. Thibaudet, Rotterdam PO, Gergiev –
CHOPIN: *Piano Concerto 2* *(*)

(BB) * EMI Encore (ADD) 5 74567-2. Cziffra, New Philh. O,
Cziffra Jr – RACHMANINOV: *Piano Concerto 2* *

(i) *Piano Concerto. In Autumn, Op. 11; Symphony in C min.*

** BIS CD 1191. Bergen PO, Ruud, with (i) Ogawa

(i) *Piano Concerto. Lyric Suite; Peer Gynt Suites 1–2*

(M) ** Chan. 10175X. (i) Fingerhut; Ulster O, Handley

(i; ii; iii) *Piano Concerto in A min.;*(i) *Lyric Pieces: Arietta;
Elves Dance, Op. 12/1 & 4; Butterfly; To Spring;, Op. 43/1 & 6;
Notturno, Op. 54/4; Sylph, Op. 62/1; Summer Evening,
Op. 71/2;* (ii; iv) *Peer Gynt Suites 1 & 2*

(BB) **(*) Regis RRC 1218. (i) O'Hora; (ii) RPO; (iii) Judd;
(iv) Ermler

Whether in the clarity of virtuoso fingerwork or the shading of half-tone, Kovacevich is among the most illuminating of the many great pianists who have recorded the Grieg *Concerto*. He plays with bravura and refinement, the spontaneity of the music-making bringing a sparkle throughout, to balance the underlying poetry. The 1972 recording has been freshened most successfully and it returns to the catalogue, effectively remastered as one of the finest of Philips's Originals.

The Manchester pianist Ronan O'Hora, with a totally sympathetic partner in James Judd, made his recording début in 1995 with this outstanding performance of the Grieg *Concerto*. Indeed, in imagination and delicacy of feeling, combined with natural, authoritative brilliance, this perform-ance is almost unsurpassed, especially so in the melting arrival of the lovely second group in the first movement, which brings a moment of the utmost magic, matched by the gentle reverie of the *Adagio* and the tranquil, flute-led central episode in the finale. The piano is rather forwardly balanced, and some listeners may find it a little bright, but the music's gentler pages are beautifully coloured. On the original Tring CD, the programme was completed with a wholly delightful

selection of a dozen of Grieg's most cherishable *Lyric Pieces*, in which the pianist's approach is consistently disarming. However, only seven are offered in this reissue, and Regis have chosen a populist alternative of the two *Peer Gynt Suites*. Mark Ermler's accounts are well played and recorded, but they bring an element of routine to the lyrical music, and even *In the Hall of the Mountain King* fails to sound really gutsy.

Anda's 1963 account, promoted to the Originals series, is more wayward than some, but it is strong in personality and has plenty of life. Kubelik's accompaniment is also very good and, although the sound is a bit dated, it is more than acceptable.

Ogawa's performance of the *Piano Concerto* is sensitive and full of grace, and she is well supported by Ole Kristian Ruud. The solo instrument itself is beautifully recorded. *In Autumn*, too, is well played, and this new, well-shaped account of the *Symphony* from Grieg's home town is a good one, though it does not displace the finest of other versions. Overall, this full-priced CD does not seem especially competitive.

No problems with Simon Tedeschi's playing either; it brings much nuance to this often-recorded concerto. Bonynge generally favours measured tempi, but with his young soloist he revels in the intimate quality of the work, with the details emerging in a haunting, nostalgic way, the opposite of a high-powered, glossy performance. The slow movement offers a simple, straightforward approach, and the finale has a good sense of the drama within the writing, rather than merely playing it as a showpiece. This is an individual performance in good sound, but it is upstaged by Kovacevich's vintage version – to say nothing of the superb Andsnes account with Jansons, which received a ❍ in our main edition (EMI 5 57562-2).

Margaret Fingerhut has eloquently championed Bax on the Chandos label and has put us in her debt with other keyboard rarities. With the Grieg *Concerto* she enters a more competitive field and gives a thoughtful and musicianly reading that holds a fine balance between the work's virtu-osic and poetic elements. Her first-movement cadenza shows tenderness as well as brilliance, as indeed does the slow movement. Only in the finale does she fall short of distinc-tion, if we compare her, say, to Stephen Kovacevich; even so, the slow middle section has many felicitous touches and this is a far from negligible account. With its attractive couplings, this disc would seem an attractive proposition for the smaller collection, yet Vernon Handley is not at his happiest and most perceptive in the *Peer Gynt Suites*; with the *First* failing to take off and the *Second* occasionally somewhat overblown. But he gets generally sympathetic and responsive playing from the Ulster Orchestra and is very well recorded.

Richter's Monte Carlo performance is disappointingly wil-ful, with the soloist drawing out many passages self-indulgently. The recording is not very special either, and this is hardly a candidate for EMI's 'Great Recordings of the Century'.

Thibaudet's very routine performance disappoints. There are good things, notably Gergiev's contribution in the slow movement, but for the most part Thibaudet's playing is curiously monochrome and overall this never fully springs to life.

Cziffra's account of the Grieg from the early 1970s is singularly disappointing. There are moments of poetry here, but the too leisurely first movement does not hold the listener's attention and the performance overall fails to make a strong impression. The backward balance of the orchestra and the indifferent sound, shallow and thin, does not help matters. There are too many outstanding versions of this concerto to make this worth considering, even at its modest cost, especially as the coupling is hardly better.

(i) *Piano Concerto; 2 Nordic Melodies, Op. 63; Peer Gynt Suites 1 & 2*

(B) ** DG Entrée 457 5007. (i) Zilberstein; Gothenburg SO, Neeme Järvi

Lilya Zilberstein is a commanding artist with firm fingers, a good feeling for the architecture and a fine musical intelligence. In the Grieg *Concerto*, of course, flamboyance has to go hand in hand with poetic feeling, and she has that too, though not in such strong supply as Stephen Kovacevich. Zilberstein gives what one might call a good narrative performance: she holds your attention from moment to moment. Her playing could never be called routine, but her view is quite conventional, while Kovacevich brings fresh insights. Her new couplings on the Entrée label, designed to attract newcomers to Grieg, are well chosen. The *Peer Gynt Suites* are an obvious choice, but the innocent appeal of the less familiar *Nordic Melodies* is fully captured. Järvi's accounts of the *Peer Gynt* incidental music are exceptionally vivid, but one hesitates to strongly recommend a disc in which the key performance (of the *Concerto*) is not one of the finest available.

(i) *Piano Concerto in A min.;* (ii) *Peer Gynt:* extended excerpts

(BB) *** HMV (DDD/ADD) 5 86729-2. (i) Andsnes, Bergen PO, Kitayenko; (ii) Hollweg, Beecham Choral Soc., RPO, Beecham

Leif Ove Andsnes was still in his teens when he recorded the Grieg *Concerto* in the composer's home town with the Bergen Philharmonic Orchestra. Youthful virtuosi are almost two-a-penny nowadays, but Andsnes wears his brilliance lightly. There is no lack of display and bravura here, but no ostentation either. Indeed, he has great poetic feeling and delicacy of colour, and Grieg's familiar warhorse comes up with great freshness. The piano is in perfect condition (not always the case on records) and is excellently balanced in relation to the orchestra. Andsnes has since re-recorded the work, but the earlier performance is by no means put in the shade, and it comes here coupled with Beecham's vintage recording of the major items from *Peer Gynt*, which is another very special Grieg recording. (The latter is also available alternatively, coupled with other Beecham/Grieg items – EMI 5 66914-2 [5 66966-2] – see our main volume).

(i) *Piano Concerto in A min.;* (ii) *Peer Gynt* (incidental music): extended excerpts; (iii) Songs: *Haugtussa, Op. 67;* (iv) *Abschied; Das alte Lied; An Sie 1 & II; Dein Rat ist wohl gut; Des Dichters Herz; Des Dichters letztes Lied; Eingehüllt in graue Wolken; Ein Traum; Der Fichtenbaum; Gruss; Herbststimmung; Hör' ich das Liedchen klingen; Ich stand in dunkeln Träumen; Der Jäger; Jägerlied; Lauf der Welt; Mein Sinn ist wie der mächt'ge Feis; Morgenthau; Sie ist so weiss; Wo sind sie hin?; Zur Rosenzeit*

(BB) ** EMI (ADD) 5 86058-2. (i) Ogdon, New Philh. O, Berglund; (ii) Valjakka, Thaullaug, Leipzig R. Ch., Dresden State O, Blomstedt; (iii) Wennberg, Parsons; (iv) Fischer-Dieskau, Höll

John Ogdon's 1971 version of the *Piano Concerto* is not recommendable: it is indifferently played and dull, and the accompaniment is not much better. In the *Peer Gynt* music there is some splendid orchestral playing from the Dresden State Orchestra, with Joachim Ulbricht's folksy violin solos especially effective in the *Prelude.* The Leipzig chorus is spirited and vigorous, if not quite so vivid as the orchestra. The two soloists sing strongly and dramatically. The 1977 sound is good, warm and full in most respects, and this remains an enjoyable performance. In the vocal items, Siv Wennberg gives *Haugtussa* ('*The Mountain Maid*') strong characterization if not always beautiful sound: her voice has an occasional throaty quality and inclines to a slightly hard-edged timbre when pressed. The accompaniments with Parsons are beautiful. But the fascinating inclusion here is the group of songs from Dietrich Fischer-Dieskau. Recorded in 1984, the performances find his voice not at its freshest (with intrusive vibrato under pressure), but his artistry is never in question. Indeed, the simple charm found in many of these songs – such as *Der Fichtenbaum* – is touching. The freshness of Grieg's inspiration is well conveyed, helped by EMI's warm, intimate sound and excellent accompaniments by Hartmut Höll. An interesting but uneven collection, with texts available only on the EMI website.

2 Elegiac Melodies; Holberg Suite, Op. 40; 2 Lyric Pieces, Op. 68; 2 Melodies, Op. 53; 2 Nordic Melodies, Op. 63

**** BIS SACD 1491. Bergen PO, Ruud

This is simply the most beautiful record of Grieg's string music in the catalogue, and one of the most beautiful and realistic recordings of strings we have ever heard – made appropriately in the Grieg Hall in Bergen. The wonderfully vital account of the *Holberg Suite* is unsurpassed, not even by Karajan's famous account, and the gentler pieces are exquisite, especially the *Two Nordic Melodies*, which are Elysian, and the closing *At the Cradle* from the *Lyric Pieces, Op. 68.* Truly marvellous playing from the Bergen orchestra and inspired conducting from Ole Kristian Ruud, while the BIS producers, Hans Kipfer and Thore Brinkmann, and sound engineer Jens Braun deserve to share the Rosette and the fourth star unique to this volume. Try and hear the disc on SACD equipment with four speakers, and you will be amazed; but it sounds pretty marvellous through just two.

(i) *2 Elegiac Melodies, Op. 34; Holberg Suite, Op. 40;* (ii) *Lyric Pieces, Op. 54;* (i) *2 Nordic Melodies, Op. 63; Peer Gynt: The Death of Aase. Sigurd Jorsalfar, Op. 56;* (iii) *Wedding Day at Troldhaugen*

*(*) Australian Decca Eloquence (ADD) 476 8494. (i) Nat. PO, Boskovsky; (ii) LSO, Black; (iii) London Proms SO, Mackerras

Boskovsky's Grieg performances, which represents the bulk of this CD, emerge here for the first time on CD. The 1974 sound is rich and brilliant, but the performances are undistinguished, lacking the point and refinement one expects of this orchestra, formed largely for recording. Boskovsky's rhythmic flair is less apparent here than in his home repertory. Mackerras's *Wedding Day at Troldhaugen* sparkles, and in the delightful *Lyric Pieces* (in larger-than-life Phase 4 sound) Stanley Black shows a real feeling for the music's line and colour. But there are much better Grieg anthologies available than this.

In Autumn; Lyric Suite, Op. 54; Peer Gynt Suites 1 & 2. (i) *A Swan, Op. 25/2*

(*(*)) Arioso Classical mono CB 003. All Russia R. O, Golovanov, (i) with Dolidze – GLAZUNOV: *Symphonies 6–7* (*)

These familiar Grieg pieces are given with great poetic feeling and leave no doubt as to the quality of this celebrated conductor. The playing is often subtle and the phrasing quite beautiful. The 1948–9 recordings are better than many Soviet recordings of the period, but climaxes are coarse and raw. It is in any event much better than the Glazunov coupling.

CHAMBER MUSIC

Cello Sonata in A min., Op. 36; Intermezzo in A min.
(B) ** Virgin 2x1 3 49933-2 (2). Mørk, Thibaudet – BRAHMS: *Cello Sonatas 1–2*, etc.; SIBELIUS: *Malinconia*, etc. **

Truls Mørk plays the *Cello Sonata* with finesse and good poetic feeling, and he includes the rather Schumannesque *Intermezzo* that Grieg composed in 1866 for his cello-playing brother. But Jean-Yves Thibaudet, for all his flair and sensitivity, proves somewhat overbearing. The balance favours him excessively, with the result that the cello tone sounds very small.

String Quartet 1 in G min., Op. 27
** Mer. CDE 84401. Bridge Qt – DELIUS: *String Quartet* (with GRAINGER: *Molly on the Shore* **)
** DG 477 5960 Emerson Qt – NIELSEN: *At the bier of a young artist*; SIBELIUS: *Quartet (Voces intimae)* **

The Meridian issue of No. 1 celebrates the friendship between these three composers. The Bridge Quartet play with great feeling and no mean imagination, but there are better-finished and more finely tuned accounts available.

The Emersons offer little of the freshness of utterance you expect in Grieg. Nor is there much sense of repose or naturalness here. The overwhelming impression is less of the delicate colours of the Nordic landscape than the glare of Madison Avenue. It goes without saying that the playing and recording are marvellous, but these artists do not seem attuned to Grieg's sensibility. We suggest instead the Warner Apex super-bargain version by the New Helsinki Quartet, also coupled with Sibelius (0927 40601-2 – see our main volume).

PIANO MUSIC

Einar Steen-Nøkleberg Complete Naxos Series

Einar Steen-Nøkleberg has recorded every note of music Grieg composed for the piano. He has impressive musical credentials and is, among other things, the author of a book on Grieg's piano music and its interpretations. His survey displaces earlier sets in quality: he is responsive to mood and is searchingly imaginative in his approach.

Volume 1: *Funeral March in Memory of Rikard Nordraak; Humoresques, Op. 6; I love You (Jeg elsker dig), Op. 41/3; Melodies of Norway: The Sirens' Enticement. Moods (Stimmungen), Op. 73; 4 Piano Pieces, Op. 1; Sonata in E min., Op. 7.*
(BB) *** Naxos 8.550881. Steen-Nøkleberg

Volume 2: *The First Meeting, Op. 52/2; Improvisations on 2 Norwegian Folksongs, Op. 29; Melodies of Norway: Ballad to St Olaf. 25 Norwegian Folksongs & Dances, Op. 17; 19 Norwegian Folksongs, Op. 66.*
(BB) *** Naxos 8.550882. Steen-Nøkleberg

The second disc includes the remarkable *Nineteen Norwegian Folksongs*, Op. 66, which are contemporaneous with what

many would see as Grieg's masterpiece, the song-cycle *Haugtussa*, which the composer himself spoke of as full of 'hair-raising' chromatic harmonies. (One of the folksongs appears in Delius's *On Hearing the First Cuckoo in Spring*.) But the earlier set, Op. 17, written not long after the first version of the Piano Concerto, is also full of delights.

Volume 3: *4 Album Leaves, Op. 28; Ballade, Op. 24; Melodies of Norway: Iceland. Pictures from Everyday Life (Humoresques), Op. 19; Poetic Tone-pictures, Op. 3; Sigurd Jorsalfar: Prayer, Op. 56/1.*
(BB) *** Naxos 8.550883. Steen-Nøkleberg

Volume 4: *Holberg Suite, Op. 40; Melodies of Norway: I Went to Bed so Late. 6 Norwegian Mountain Melodies; Peer Gynt Suite 1: Morning. Norwegian Peasant Dances (Slåtter) Op. 72*
(BB) *** Naxos 8.550884. Steen-Nøkleberg

The third CD includes the poignant *Ballade in G min.*, Op. 24, composed by Grieg on the death of his parents. Steen-Nøkleberg is highly imaginative and, even if some may find his rubato a little extreme, the keyboard colouring is subtle and rich. He conveys a splendidly rhapsodic spontaneity and there is much feeling. This and the companion disc, with the *Seventeen Norwegian Peasant Dances (Slåtter)*, Op. 72, deserve a particularly strong recommendation. These extraordinary pieces with their quasi-Bartókian clashes are most characterful in Steen-Nøkleberg's hands.

Volume 5: *Norway's Melodies 1–63*
(BB) **(*) Naxos 8.553391. Steen-Nøkleberg

Volume 6: *Norway's Melodies 64–117*
(BB) **(*) Naxos 8.553392. Steen-Nøkleberg

Volume 7: *Norway's Melodies 118–52 (EG 108)*
(BB) **(*) Naxos 8.553393. Steen-Nøkleberg

The next three discs are devoted to *Norges Melodier* ('Norway's Melody'), an anthology Grieg made in the mid-1870s for a Danish publisher, of 'easy to play' arrangements of tunes, some of them charming, others less so. Steen-Nøkleberg plays some on the house-organ or harmonium, some on the clavichord, some on a Graf piano to match those sonorities which would have been familiar in Norwegian homes in the 1870s, and some on a Steinway.

Volume 8: *Lyric Pieces: Book I, Op. 12; Book II, Op. 38; Book III, Op. 43; Book IV, Op. 47.*
(BB) *** Naxos 8.553394. Steen-Nøkleberg

Volume 9: *Lyric Pieces: Book V, Op. 54, Book VI, Op. 57; Book VII, Op. 62*
(BB) *** Naxos 8.553395. Steen-Nøkleberg

Volume 10: *Lyric Pieces: Book VIII, Op. 65; Book IX, Op. 68; Book X, Op. 71*
(BB) *** Naxos 8.553396. Steen-Nøkleberg

Volumes 8–10 survey the delightful *Lyric Pieces*. They are admirably fresh and are presented with the utmost simplicity, yet are obviously felt. These performances come into direct competition with Daniel Adni's not quite complete but otherwise excellent set on an EMI forte double CD. Many will like to have the coverage absolutely complete, and the three Naxos discs cost about the same. The EMI piano-sound is perhaps very slightly warmer and fuller, but the Naxos recording is wholly natural and believable. Einar Steen-Nøkleberg is totally idiomatic and authoritative, and readers wanting a complete set need not hesitate.

Volume 11: *Bergliot, Op. 42; Peer Gynt Suites 1, Op. 46; 2, Op. 55; Sigurd Jorsalfar (Suite), Op. 22; (i) Olav Trygvason, Op. 50: 2 Pieces.*
(BB) *** Naxos 8.553397. Steen-Nøkleberg; (i) Norwegian State Institute of Music Chamber Ch., Schiøll

Volume 12: *Agitato, EG 106; Albumblad, EG 109; Norwegian Dances, Op. 35; (i) Peer Gynt: excerpts, Op. 23 including Dance of the Mountain King's Daughter, Op. 55/5 (Op. 23/9); 3 Piano transcriptions from Sigurd Jorsalfar. Waltz Caprices, Op. 37. arr. of HALVORSEN: Entry of the Boyards.*
(BB) *** Naxos 8.553398. Steen-Nøkleberg; (i) Norwegian State Institute of Music Chamber Ch., Schiøll

With the remaining four volumes we enter the realm of Grieg's transcriptions of his orchestral works and his juvenilia, as well as sketches for works that did not materialize. Most valuable are the *Waltz Caprices,* Op. 37, and the early *Agitato,* EG 106, and *Albumblad,* EG 109. Both these issues are recommendable but dispensable.

Volume 13: *2 Elegiac Melodies, Op. 34; 2 Melodies, Op. 53; 2 Nordic Melodies, Op. 63; Norwegian Melodies 6 & 22; 3 Piano Pieces, EG 105; 3 Piano Pieces, EG 110/112; Piano transcriptions of Songs, Op. 41*
(BB) *** Naxos 8.553399. Steen-Nøkleberg

Volume 14: *At the Halfdan Kjerulf Statue, EG 167; Canon a 4 voci for Organ, EG 179; Piano Concerto in B min. (fragments), EG 120; Larsvikspola, EG 101; Mountain Song, Norwegian Melodies 87 & 146, EG 108; 23 Small Pieces for Piano, EG 104; Piano Sonata Op. 7 (1st version: mvts 2 and 4); Piano transcriptions of Songs, Op. 52*
(BB) *** Naxos 8.553400. Steen-Nøkleberg

The last two volumes are another matter. Volume 13 brings rarities in the shape of the *Three Piano Pieces,* EG 105, and a further three, EG 110–12, all of which are otherwise available only on Love Derwinger's full-priced BIS record of the 1874 version of the *Piano Concerto.* The last volume is of particular interest in that it brings – in addition to various juvenilia – the sketches for a *Second Piano Concerto* – very Lisztian – and the first versions of the slow movement and finale of the Op. 7 *Sonata.*

Lyric Pieces, Opp. 12/1; 38/1; 43/1–2 & 6; 47/2–4; 54/1, 3–5; 57/6; 62/4 & 6; 65/5–6; 68/2–3 & 5; 71/1–4, 6–7
(BB) ** Regis RRC 1071. Austbø

Born in Norway but now based in Amsterdam, Håkon Austbø enjoyed success in Paris, where he won the Ravel Competition, and in Royan, where he won the Messiaen Competition. He is best known for his advocacy of the French master as well as Scriabin, and his command of keyboard colour and his wide dynamic range are impressive. There is no lack of tonal sophistication here, although he is rather too forwardly balanced; but, for all his unfailing accomplishment and sensitivity, he lacks the naturalness of utterance and freshness of vision that such rivals as Gilels, Andsnes and Pletnev bring to this repertoire. Theirs is the art that conceals art.

Lyric Pieces from Books III, V, VIII & IX
(BB) ** Warner Apex 2564 60070-2. Lagerspete

Johann Lagerspete opens with an over-dramatized account of Grieg's portrayal of a *Butterfly,* and elsewhere he can at times seem too forceful for these simple miniatures. However, much of his playing is very sympathetic, and he is especially

good in the pieces from Book V which are included in the orchestral *Lyric Suite.* He is very vividly recorded.

VOCAL MUSIC

Haugtussa, Op. 67; 6 Songs to Poems by A. O. Vinje, Op. 33
*(*) NMA 3. Kringelborn, Martineau

Haugtussa ('The Mountain Maid') includes the greatest of Grieg's songs and has been well served on record (Flagstad recorded it no fewer than three times). Solveig Kringelborn prefaces the cycle with *Ku-Lok* ('Cow Call') one of the five songs Grieg omitted when he finally published the set – and a very effective opening it makes to the disc. Hers is a strong musical personality, and she commands much vocal beauty, even if her expressive characterization is at times exaggerated. For example, she does not allow a song like *Blåbær-Li* ('Blueberry Slope') to speak for itself: she is too self-aware, almost arch in her approach. Throughout she gets admirable support from Malcolm Martineau. The *Twelve Settings of Aasmund Olavson Vinje,* which Grieg published as Op. 33, were composed 15 years earlier, in 1880, and are among his most poetic utterances for voice: their intensity of feeling is unmistakable. Again one is struck by the tonal beauty Kringelborn commands, but for many listeners she will seem just a bit too self-conscious, though the recording is very natural and lifelike. However, this is no match for the fine version by Anne Sofie von Otter and Bengt Forsberg on DG, which, in terms of interpretative insight and a natural unforced eloquence, remains unchallenged.

Peer Gynt (incidental music), Op. 23 (complete)
(*) BIS-SACD** 1441/2. Solberg, Kosmo, Hagegård, Vest, Bergen PO, Ruud
*(**) Aeon 3 AECD0530 (3). Dam-Jensen, Koch, Henschel, Ens. Vocal de Geneva, SRO, Tourniaire

The BIS set with Ruud and the Bergen Philharmonic, recorded live at the Bergen Festival, offers the complete incidental music, along with more spoken dialogue than has been presented on disc before. English translations of the Norwegian text are provided in the booklet, with the inflexions of spoken Norwegian clearly in tune with the cadences of the music. The production too is vividly dramatic and very well delivered. The big question mark must be how much of the dialogue one wants, for there are more tracks with dialogue than without, and many with no music at all. The characterful casting of the role of Peer Gynt himself adds to the musical strength, with Marita Solberg sweet and pure as Solveig. It is a pity that there is quite so much spoken dialogue when for most listeners the solution offered in Neeme Järvi's pioneering set with the Gothenburg Symphony Orchestra (DG 475 5433-2) will provide the ideal answer, with dialogue included only over the musical numbers.

Like the BIS set, Tourniaire's on Aeon offers not only the complete incidental music but a very full spoken text, recorded like the BIS at a staged production. One basic difference is that the dialogue comes in French with the sung numbers only in Norwegian, and with the booklet designed only for French-speakers. Happily, Aeon cleverly offers a third disc with the musical numbers shorn of any dialogue, even the dramatic shouts at the end of *In the Hall of the Mountain King.* One hopes that this will be issued separately. As Peer Gynt himself, Dietrich Henschel is outstanding, with Inge Dam-Jensen also impressive as Solveig, and the recording is full and immediate.

Arrangements

Song of Norway (Grieg, arr. WRIGHT/FORREST): **highlights**
(B) *CfP (ADD) 3 35989-2. Lawrenson, Round, Hughes, Elliot, Webb, Rita Williams Singers, O, Michael Collins – SCHUBERT: *Lilac Time* (highlights) *

Song of Norway (1944) was one of a series of musicals in the 1930s and '40s, based on the music of classical composers, arranged by Robert Wright and George Forrest. It was a big wartime hit and was even made into a film in 1970. Most collectors will find it cringingly awful, though the very brave might find this lusty 1959 set of highlights amusing in a kitsch sort of way. The damage done to Schubert (the coupling) is even worse.

GRIFFES, Charles Tomlinson
(1884–1920)

Roman Sketches: The White Peacock; Nightfall; The Fountain of the Acqua Paola; Clouds
●— *** ASV Gold GLD 4020. LSO, Pittau – KORNGOLD: *Symphonic Serenade* ***

Charles Griffes, the American impressionist composer, is most remembered for *The White Peacock*, but all four of the richly evocative miniature tone-poems here have the simmering, sensuous textures that made that piece famous, with influences from Debussy, Delius and Respighi glowingly apparent. Yet the music is still all his own, and it is very beautifully played and recorded here, with the similarly luscious Korngold *Symphonic Serenade* as an ideal coupling. Demonstration sound quality.

GRIGNY, Nicolas de (1672–1703)

5 Hymns: Veni creator; Ave maris stella; Pange lingua; Verbun supernum; A solis ortus
(B) **(*) Cal. (ADD) CAL 6912. Isoir (organ of Basilique de Saint-Maximin de Provence)

Nicolas de Grigny was born in Rheims and eventually became organist at the cathedral, which position he held until his death. His fame as a composer rests upon one book, including 49 pieces of music of which the present *Five Hymns* and the *Organ Mass* below are the most important works. The *Five Hymns* follow the style established by the so-called 'father of French organ music', Jehan Titelouz, in 1623, each based on a plainchant. This is first presented in simple harmonized form, then follows a *Fugue* using one or more motives from the chant, an independent *Duo*, and *Récit*, and a closing *Dialogue sur les Grands Jeux*. The present performances are played by André Isoir, who has already recorded Couperin's organ masses (see above) and who uses a highly suitable organ. He also includes a more elaborate hymn by Louis Marchant as it ends with a *Grand dialogue* much more spectacular than any of those by de Grigny. This is obviously a worthwhile reissue (from 1972), which is well recorded. But the documentation in English is very inadequate; one has to translate the French notes to have all the necessary information to appreciate the music.

Organ Mass
(M) *** Cal. CAL 6911. Isoir (Cliquot organ at the Cathedral of Saint-Pierre de Poitiers)

Nicolas de Grigny's Couperin-influenced *Organ Mass* was very influential in its own right. The variety of the writing is remarkable, and certainly André Isoir's performance on the Cliquot organ at Poitiers Cathedral readily demonstrates the music's imaginative range. As a double encore we are offered an *Elévation en sol* and a *Symphonie* by Nicolas LeBegue, both strong pieces. The analogue recording is of fine quality.

GROFÉ, Ferde (1892–1972)

Grand Canyon Suite
(M) **(*) RCA (ADD) 82876 67904-2. O, Gould – COPLAND: *Billy the Kid; Rodeo* **(*)

Morton Gould's account of the *Grand Canyon Suite* is as spectacular as you could want. The 1960 recording was made in RCA Victor's ballroom studio in New York's Manhattan Center, with the orchestra repositioned during the recording for maximum sonic effect. The horns, for instance, were separated and relocated round the room for the succession of horn calls which open the *Sunset movement*, and elsewhere echo-chamber effects were used, notably for the trombone duet in *On the Trail*, during which the players used megaphones. A similar treatment was given to the strings at the opening of the *Cloudburst* sequence.

GRØNDAHL, Agathe Backer
(1847–1907)

6 Etudes de concert, Op. 11; 3 Etudes, Op. 22; 3 Morceaux, Op. 15; 4 Sketches, Op. 19; Suite, Op. 20
*** BIS CD 1106. Braaten

Four years younger than Grieg, Agathe Grøndahl died only a few weeks before him. The annotator does her cause no service by placing her music on a level with Grieg and Kjerulf, for although she was much respected in her day as a concert pianist well beyond Scandinavia, her music has never escaped the shadows of Mendelssohn and Schumann. The folk-influenced Norwegian accents that inspired Nordraak, Grieg and Svendsen held little attraction for Grøndahl. Bernard Shaw hailed her as a great pianist and found some individuality in the songs but little in the piano pieces. On this disc they range from the *Concert Studies*, Op. 11, of 1881, her first published composition, through to the *Trois études*, Op. 22, of 1888; they are written capably but are wanting in originality. Geir Henning Braaten plays splendidly and is given an excellent BIS recording.

GUARNIERI, Camargo (1907–93)

Abertura Concertante; Symphonies 2 (Uirapuru); 3
*** BIS CD 1220. São Paulo City SO, Neschling

Guarnieri's vast output – albeit not as vast as that of his countryman, Villa-Lobos – is being investigated by the ever enterprising BIS label and by Marco Polo. (His parents were keen musicians who named Camargo's brothers Verdi, Rossine and Belline, though not surprisingly he dropped his own first name, 'Mozart', early in his career!) Readers who know Koechlin, with whom Guarneri studied before the war, and who play the opening of the *Third Symphony* (1952) will be reminded slightly of *La course de printemps*. Guanieri's musical language is highly colourful and appealing, the harmonies and orchestration are imaginative and hold the attention far more than does much of Villa-Lobos. The latter, incidentally, is the dedicatee of the *Second Symphony* (1945) called *Uirapuru* after an Amazonian bird which Villa Lobos celebrated with a tone-poem. Occasionally there is a reminder of Copland, who said of him, 'Guarnieri is a real composer. He has everything it takes – a personality of his own, a finished technique and a fecund imagination. His gift is more orderly than that of Villa-Lobos.' This is music of real character, and it is well played and recorded.

GUBAIDULINA, Sofia (born 1931)

In Croce for Bayan & Cello; Seven Last Words for Cello, Bayan & Strings; Silenzio for Bayan, Violin & Cello
(BB) *** Naxos 8.553557. Moser, Kliegel, Rabus, Camerata Transsylvanica, Selmeczi

In Croce is an arrangement of a work for cello and organ, composed in 1979 and arranged for bayan or push-button accordion in 1993. The *Seven Last Words*, composed in 1982 for cello, accordion and strings, is probably the best entry-point into Gubaidulina's strange world, mesmerizing for some, boring for others. Maria Kliegel is an intense and powerful cellist, and Elsbeth Moser is a dedicated player long associated with this repertoire. Good recorded sound.

GURIDI, Jesus (1886–1961)

An Adventure of Don Quixote; 10 Basque Melodies; In a Phoenician Vessel; (i) *The early cock is crowing;* (ii) *So the Boys Sing*
(BB) **(*) Naxos 8.557110. Bilbao SO, Mena, with (i) Alvarez; (ii) Bilbao Ch. Soc.

Naxos here offer a colourful and convincing survey of the unpretentious work of Jesus Guridi, a pioneer in exploiting the music of the Basque region of Spain. The *Ten Basque Melodies* of 1941 are typical in their tunefulness and bright orchestration, with vigour and haunting melancholy alternating. The fresh simplicity of the cantata, *So the Boys Sing*, with choral writing obviously designed for amateurs if not children, with popular song among the sources, is equally effective. The symphonic poem on *Don Quixote*, written in 1916, offers a nicely varied portrait of Cervantes' eccentric hero, and *In a Phoenician Vessel* of 1927 is a musical seascape inspired by the Greek myth of Telemachus, son of Odysseus. The bright soprano, Isabel Alvarez, is the soloist in the charming song, *The early cock is crowing*, like most of these pieces inspired by Basque folk music. Though the ensemble is not always ideally crisp, the performances under Juan José Mena are all warmly committed and recorded in clean if slightly distanced sound.

HAHN, Reynaldo (1875–1947)

PIANO MUSIC

L'Album d'un Voyageur: Orient. Premières Valses; Portraits de peintres, d'après les poésies de Marcel Proust; Sonatine
** ProPiano 224538. Favre-Kahn

Best known for the songs (and increasingly for his chamber music), Reynaldo Hahn composed prolifically for the piano, for which he wrote some 120 pieces, few of which have made

it to the catalogue. There is a touching quality and an innocence about many of these salon pieces composed during the period 1898–1909, and Laure Favre-Kahn conveys their grace well. She comes from Arles and studied at conservatories in Avignon and Paris. Still in her mid-twenties, she attracted attention at Carnegie Hall in 2001, and this valuable CD was the result. Unfortunately, she is balanced far too closely and recorded in a claustrophobic studio environment, and the sound is a genuine handicap. Even played at a fairly low level, it is impossible to escape the bottom-heavy sound. This is a great pity, since this charming music and sensitive pianist deserve better. There are no alternatives except in the *Sonatine* and one of the *Portraits de peintres*. Although all the pieces are slight, the engaging *Ninette* or the simple yet affecting *Berceau* from the *Premières Valses* have tremendous charm, and the haunting *Watteau* portrait from the *Portraits de peintres, d'après les poésies de Marcel Proust* (in one way not recommended since, once heard, it is difficult to get out of one's head) makes this disc well worth getting. *En caïque* from the *Album d'un voyageur* shows much inventiveness and great feeling for the atmosphere of the Bosporus and the Middle East. Recommended, with the obvious caution about the sound but with no caution about the merits of the music or its interpreter.

HALFFTER, Ernesto (1905–89)

Automne malade; Dos canciones; Rapsodia Portuguesa; Sonatina (ballet; complete)
*** ASV CDDCA 1099. Orquesta Filarmónica de Gran Canaria, Leaper

Ernesto Halffter was a pupil of Manuel de Falla. Judging from this well-played and excellently recorded issue, his music is resourceful and full of bright colours. Halffter is a good craftsman and the quality of his melodic invention is high.

Sinfonietta; (i) *Elegia;* (i; ii) *Psalms XXII & CXVI (Hymnus Laudis et gratiarum action)*
(B) *** HM HMU 987067. Tenerife SO, Pérez; with (i) Coro polifónico de la Universidad de La Laguna, Simó; (ii) Chilcott, Poell, Cabero, Carril

This recording, made in the centenary year of Ernesto Halffter's birth, celebrates a little-known but attractive composer, born in Madrid, who became a conductor in Seville. As a composer he embraced a neoclassical style, demonstrated at its most winning in the infectious and wittily scored (but by no means trivial) *Sinfonietta* (1923/5, revised 1927). It is a real find, the style all but suggesting a Spanish Ibert, though also drawing on the essence of Domenico Scarlatti's keyboard works in the *Adagio*. It is most persuasively presented here and ought to be in the repertoire. The choral *Elegia* (1966) is brief but expressively powerful, the pair of *Psalms* (1967) more concentrated still, and finely sung (though Susan Chilcott's vibrato is somewhat intrusive). Excellent recording.

HAMERIK, Asger (1843–1923)

(i) *Concert Romance for Cello and Orchestra, Op. 27. Jødisk Trilogi, Op. 19.*
**(*) Danacord DACOCD 526. (i) Steensgaard; Danish PO, South Jutland, Atzmon – EBBE HAMERIK: *Concerto molto breve, etc.* **(*)

Another issue in the 'Harmonious Families' series that the

Danish label Danacord has compiled. Asger Hamerik was a pupil of von Bülow and was befriended by Berlioz in the 1860s. He spent many years directing the Peabody Institute in Baltimore. The pieces here are new to the catalogue and are worthwhile. The performances are persuasive, and the value of the disc is enhanced by the coupling devoted to his son, Ebbe.

Symphonies 5 in G min. (Sérieuse), Op. 36; 6 in G min. (Spirituelle), Op. 38

*** dacapo 8.224161. Helsingborg SO, Dausgaard

This newcomer is every bit as fine as Johannes Goritski's CPO recording of the *Symphonie Spirituelle* (see below), and it has the benefit of a richer string sonority. The *Fifth* (1889–91), subtitled *Sérieuse*, was composed in Baltimore, as was its companion here. It is engaging, well crafted and very much in the Leipzig tradition, but it is well worth taking the trouble to know, being fresher than Gade and eminently well laid out for the orchestra. Thomas Dausgaard gets very lively performances, and there is fine recorded sound.

Symphony 6 in G min. (Symphonie spirituelle), Op. 38

(BB) *** CPO 999 516-2. German Chamber Ac., Neuss, Goritski – GADE: *Novelletter.* ***

Asger Hamerik belongs to the generation of Danish symphonists between Gade and Nielsen. His *Sixth Symphony* (*Symphonie spirituelle*) for strings comes from 1897 and is in the Gade–Schumann tradition. There is a *Seventh* and *Choral Symphony*, composed the following year, after which he gave up America and composing altogether, returning to retire in Copenhagen. No. 6 is quite an appealing work, and this is its first modern recording. First-class playing and recording.

HAMERIK, Ebbe (1898–1951)

(i) Concerto molto breve for Oboe and Orchestra; Cantus firmus V (Sinfonia breve)

**(*) Danacord DACOCD 526. (i) Frederiksen; Danish PO, South Jutland, Atzmon – ASGER HAMERIK: *Concert Romance*, etc. **(*)

In the 1950s visitors to Copenhagen would find Danish musicians speaking with some enthusiasm of Ebbe Hamerik and listening to his *Sinfonia breve*. One can see why. He had imagination and musical resource, and his almost complete disappearance from the scene is puzzling. There is a searching quality about this music and an individual voice. Well worth exploring.

HANDEL, George Frideric (1685–1759)

Concerti grossi, Op. 3/1–6

(BB) **(*) ASV (ADD) Resonance CDRSN 3065. N. Sinfonia, Malcolm

George Malcolm's performances are spirited and stylish and not lacking in polish. The 1978 recording is vivid, but the forward balance of the oboes makes them sound rather larger than life and tends to reduce the dynamic range, although the contrasts of light and shade within the strings are effective. Rhythms are sometimes jogging rather than sprightly, but this is enjoyable music-making and this inexpensive reissue is good value. Malcolm does not give us No. 4b or the revised version of No. 6, but nor do most of his competitors.

Concerti grossi, Op. 3/1–6; Concerto grosso in C (Alexander's Feast); (i) Music for the Royal Fireworks; Water Music (complete)

(BB) *(*) Virgin 2x1 5 61656-2 (2). Linde Consort; (i) with Cappella Coloniensis

These are good, quite well-characterized performances, nicely recorded, but not much more than that. This repertoire is richly covered by excellent authentic and modern-instrument versions, so we must relegate this Virgin Double – despite its bargain price – to the second division.

Concerti grossi, Op. 3/1–6; Op. 6/1–12

(M) *** Avie AV 2065 (3). Handel & Haydn Soc., Boston, Hogwood

Avie have taken over from Decca/Oiseau-Lyre Hogwood's recordings of Opp. 3 and 6, recorded in 1988 and 1991/2 respectively, and have reissued the whole series very economically on three discs. The performance of Op. 3 with his excellent Boston players has no lack of energy and life and a fairly high degree of polish. Intonation, though not always immaculate, is by no means a problem. Although the period wind instruments bring plenty of colour to Handel's scoring, the result is a little deadpan and lacking in geniality. The special interest of the reading comes with Hogwood's use of a more authentic revised score for the sixth concerto, with two new movements; the original organ concerto has been relegated to an appendix and is played as a separate encore.

Hogwood's characteristically astringent rhythmic style is then heard at its most vital in Op. 6. The playing brings bracingly brisk tempi and here there is no question of any lack of refinement, with transparency of texture rather than sonority paramount. Two harpsichords and an arch-lute are used as continuo. The playing is heard at its finest in the masterly *Fifth Concerto in D major*, with the allegros sparkling with vivacity. The sound of the solo original instruments in the lyrical writing almost suggests viols rather than violins, although the forward balance gives the concertino soloists a strikingly firm presence. Listening to this exhilarating music-making is certainly a refreshing experience, and period-instrument enthusiasts will find this set excellent value.

Concerti grossi, Op. 6/1–12

⊶ ✪ (M) *** Ph. 476 5312 (3). ASMF, I. Brown

Concerti grossi, Op. 6/1–12; Music for the Royal Fireworks; Water Music (complete)

(B) ** DG Trio 471 758-2 (3). Orpheus CO

Handel's set of *Concerti grossi*, Op. 6, is at the high-water mark of baroque orchestral music, and the return of Iona Brown's recording is most welcome, as it was one of our earlier ✪ choices. The young Iona Brown had participated in Marriner's late-1960s recording sessions. She was soloist (among others, for the solo roles were shared, Marriner himself taking part) in the *Concerto No. 10 in D minor*, and she obviously absorbed a great deal from the experience of working with Thurston Dart. Her Philips performances from the 1980s have much in common with the earlier Marriner set; tempi are sometimes uncannily alike, notably in Handel's marvellously entertaining fugues. But such similarities are deceptive, for the new readings have many new insights to offer and Brown – while always remaining entirely at the service of the composer – sets her own personality firmly on the proceedings. In the expressive music (and there are some memorable Handelian tunes here) she is freer, warmer and more spacious. Where allegros are differently paced, they are often slightly slower, yet the superbly crisp articulation and the rhythmic resilience of the playing always bring added sparkle.

On recording grounds the new set gains considerably: the sound is fuller, fresher and more transparent and the contrast between the solo group and the ripieno is even more tangible. For those wanting a modern-instrument version of these wonderfully rewarding concertos, this remains a first choice, alongside I Musici de Montréal, the aim of whose director, Yuli Turovsky, is to seek a compromise between modern and 'authentic' practice by paring down vibrato in the expressive music.

Immaculate in ensemble, with allegros crisply articulated, and offering lyrically beautiful playing from members of the concertino, the Orpheus *Concerto grosso* performances are yet disappointing. The overall impression is warm but bland. Even the best known, No. 5 in D, which Karajan did so well with larger forces, is only fitfully stimulating. The elegant finish of the playing in slow movements cannot be gainsaid, although the most famous slow movement of all, the *Larghetto e piano* in No. 12, is curiously lethargic. The recording is very truthful, even if the problem of contrast between the solo group and ripieno is not completely resolved. From DG's point of view the pairing of the reissue was obvious, and it is certainly generous. The back of the box quotes from the *Penguin Guide*'s 'rave' review of the *Fireworks* and *Water Music* (but does not quote our opinion of Opus 6!). Fortunately, the *Water* and *Fireworks* recordings are also available separately, reissued on DG's Entrée label.

Organ concertos

Organ Concertos, Op. 4/1–6; Op. 7/1–6

🔑 ✪ (BB) *** Warner Apex 2564 62760-2 (2). Koopman, Amsterdam Bar. O

Ton Koopman's paired sets of Opp. 4 and 7 now reappear on the Apex super-bargain label, complete on two CDs. They take precedence over all the competition, both as performances and as recordings. The playing has wonderful life and warmth, tempi are always aptly judged and, although original instruments are used, this is authenticity with a kindly presence, for the warm acoustic ambience of St Bartholomew's Church, Beek-Ubbergen, Holland, gives the orchestra a glowingly vivid coloration and the string timbre is particularly attractive. So is the organ itself, which is just right for the music. Koopman plays imaginatively throughout and he is obviously enjoying himslf: no single movement sounds tired and the orchestral fugues merge with genial clarity. Koopman directs the accompanying group from the keyboard, as Handel would have done, and the interplay between soloist and ripieno is a delight. The sound is first class and the balance could hardly be better.

Organ Concertos: Op. 4/1–3;* (i) *Op. 4/4;* (ii) *Op. 4/6. Op. 7/1–6

** Hyp. CDA 67291/2. Nicholson, Brandenburg Cons., Goodman; (i) with Clare College Ch., Cambridge; (ii) Kelly (harp)

Besides using Handel's own organ (still in excellent condition) in St Lawrence, Whitchurch, at Canons, near Edgware, north of London, the Nicholson–Goodman set offers a novelty in including Op. 4/4 in a 1737 version where Handel concluded the finale with an *Alleluia* chorus from *Athalia*, an eccentric idea that in the event is effective enough. Op. 4/6 i heard in the arrangement for harp, and the performanc lacks charm. In any case the performances here are at time curiously didactic. The crisp rhythms with which these work abound and that should sound amiably jaunty, are often her just that bit too rigid. Both playing and recording are other wise fresh, but the competition is fierce and this is not a firs choice.

***Music for the Royal Fireworks; Water Music* (complete)**

(BB) **(*) Naxos 8.557764. Arcadia Ens., Mallon

(BB) ** RCA 82876 55304-2. Paillard CO, Paillard

(i) *Music for the Royal Fireworks* (complete); *Water Music* (complete); (ii) *Harpsichord Suite 4: Sarabande* (arr. Hale)

(BB) *** HMV 5 86730-2. (i) LCP, Norrington; (ii) ASMF, Briger

Music for the Royal Fireworks; Water Music* (complete); (i) *Il trionfo del Tempo e del Disinganno: Sonata

(BB) ** CfP (ADD) 574 8812. Virtuosi & Wind Virtuosi of E., Davison; (i) with Kynaston (organ)

Norrington uses a full orchestra, but he highlights the brigh trumpets and braying horns to give both works a vividl open-air flavour. The dance movements have grace, but lively grace, and it is the consistent vitality which makes thes performances so stimulating. The overtures of both work bring the crispest double-dotting, while the outer movement of the *Fireworks Music* are as strong and rugged as you coul wish, without loss of polish or tuning.

What is surprising is that the EMI planners have chosen t preface Norrington's programme with an arrangement of harpsichord *Sarabande* (based on *La Folia*) in moder orchestral dress. It is attractive enough, and has been used a both a film and a TV theme, but in the present orchestratio it is far removed in style from Norrington's authenticity.

The Toronto-based period-instrument Arcadia Ensemble' performances of the three *Water Music Suites* using a rela tively small group are stylishly spick and span, alert an vivacious. The conductor, Kevin Mallon, relates in the accom panying notes how as a student he accompanied John Elic Gardiner to the Henry Watson Music Library in Mancheste to look at an eighteenth-century score of Handel's masterl work, and found that the famous *Air* in *Suite 1* was marke *Presto*. So in this music-making do not expect what he (a littl unkindly) calls the 'lugubriousness that is often heard'. Th *Fireworks Music*, appropriately, using a bigger ensemble, has proper sense of spectacle, and in the movement called *L Paix*, following that same original manuscript, he uses trans verse flutes instead of recorders. Excellent recording, but th conductor's approach with its fast speeds in the overtures an dances may not be to all tastes.

The Classics for Pleasure reissue of the complete *Wate Music* not only includes the *Fireworks Music*, but throws i for good measure the sonata that Handel wrote for hi allegorical oratorio, *Il trionfo del Tempo e del Disinganno* which is used to accompany Bellezza (who represents Beauty when she is enticed into the Palace of Pleasure. It is a engaging miniature, with an obbligato organ part, and i given a very spirited account here. Davison employs addi tional wind for his performance of the *Royal Fireworks Music* but the result rather lacks weight in the bass, although th playing is fresh and stylish and the recording crisply immedi ate. His authenticity of style is carried over into the *Wate Music*, which is well played and recorded.

Re-recording the music digitally in 1990, Paillard and hi

Chamber Orchestra fail to match the vitality and sparkle of their earlier, Erato analogue version. This is agreeable enough and is well recorded, but there is an element of routine in the playing.

CHAMBER MUSIC

Flute Sonatas: in E min., Op. 1/1; in G; in B min; in D, HWV 378; in E min., HWV 379

* MDG 311 1078-2. Hünteler, Zipperling, Lohff

The MDG CD purports to contain Handel's 'Complete Flute Sonatas' but, as can be seen above, Konrad Hünteler omits the three so-called *Halle Sonatas* and includes HWV 379 in E minor, which is not authentic: it was intended by Handel for the violin. In any case the performances on MDG, while musical enough, lack the vitality and point of those on Hyperion, and are recorded amorphously in a too resonant acoustic.

Flute Sonatas, Op. 1/1b, 2, 4, 5, 7, 9 & 11; Halle Sonatas 1–3

(M) **(*) Artemis Classics Vanguard Bach Guild (ADD) ATM CD 1494 (2). Robinson, Cooper, Eddy

These performances are stylish and pleasing, and the 1978 recording is well balanced. But the performances from Lisa Beznosiuk, Richard Tunnicliffe and Paul Nicolson on Hyperion (CDA 67278) are even finer and the recording is obviously more modern (see our main volume).

i; ii) Recorder Sonatas, Op. 1/2, 4, 7, 9 & 11; 7 in B flat; (ii) Harpsichord Suite 7 in G min.

** Guild GMCD 7301. (i) Davis; (ii) Ponsford

Alan Davis's piping recorder is robust in colour, his playing most engaging, and he does not over-ornament, so the melodic line is never fussy. He is very well accompanied by David Ponsford, who also gives a fine performance of the G minor Harpsichord Suite.

VOCAL MUSIC

Aci, Galatea e Polifemo (complete)

** Virgin 2CD 5 45557-2 (2). Piau, Mingardo, Naouri, Le Concert d'Astrée, Haïm

A delightful new version of *Aci, Galatea e Polifemo* tends to upstage the earlier, Harmonia Mundi version (HMA 901253/4). In that account Emma Kirkby as Aci sings with her usual delightful freshness, but here Sandrine Piau gives the role a stronger profile, and Sara Mingardo, a true Handelian, sings gloriously. What caps the newest version is Laurent Naouri's superbly resonant bass as the one-eyed giant, Polifemo, while Emmanuelle Haïm's direction is every bit as spirited as that of Charles Medlam, and includes an overture constructed from Handel's *Concerto grosso*, Op. 3/4. The Virgin recording is first class.

Acis and Galatea (complete)

(BB) ** Naxos 8.553188. Amps, Doveton, Davidson, Van Asch, Scholars Bar. Ens., Van Asch

On a single disc at super-bargain price, the Naxos version is well worth hearing. David van Asch, leading the Scholars Baroque Ensemble, directs a brisk and light reading with Kym Amps as Galatea, sweeter and purer than she has sometimes been on disc, and Robin Doveton a light-toned Acis, stylish if not always firm in his legato singing. The countertenor, Angus Davidson, is rather unsteady as Damon, and

though David van Asch as Polyphemus copes well with the wide range required, he is unresonant as the giant. Clear, well-balanced sound.

Alpestre monte; Mi palpita il cor; Tra le fiamme; Tu fedel? Ti costante? (Italian Cantatas)

(BB) *** Decca 476 7468. Kirkby, AAM, Hogwood

Emma Kirkby's bright, pure voice is perfectly suited to these brilliant but generally lightweight inspirations of the young Handel's Italian period. The four cantatas chosen, all for solo voice and with modest instrumental forces, are nicely contrasted, with the personality of original singer by implication identified with *Tu fedel*, a spirited sequence of mini-arias rejecting a lover. Even 'a heart full of cares' in *Mi palpita il cor* inspires Handel to a charming pastoral aria, with a delectable oboe obbligato, rather then anything more deeply expressive – and even those limited cares quickly disperse. Light-hearted and sparkling performances to match, along with superb Decca sound.

Alexander's Feast; Concerto grosso in C (Alexander's Feast)

(M) **(*) Ph. 475 7774 (2). Watkinson, Robson, Brown, Stafford, Varcoe, Monteverdi Ch., E. Bar. Sol., Gardiner

Gardiner's version of *Alexander's Feast*, recorded live at performances given at the Göttingen Festival, has now, like his set of *Solomon*, returned to the catalogue at mid-price as one of Philips's Originals. The sound is not distractingly dry, but it is still harder than usual on singers and players alike, taking away some of the bloom. What matters is the characteristic vigour and concentration of Gardiner's performance. Stephen Varcoe may lack some of the dark resonance of a traditional bass, but he projects his voice well. Nigel Robson's tenor suffers more than do the others from the dryness of the acoustic. The soprano Donna Brown sings with boyish freshness, and the alto numbers are divided very effectively between Carolyn Watkinson and the soft-grained counter-tenor Ashley Stafford. The *Concerto grosso in C* was given with the oratorio at its first performance.

(i) Coronation Anthems (complete); (ii) Dixit Dominus

(BB) ** EMI Encore (ADD) 5 85444-2. King's College, Cambridge, Ch., ECO; (i) Ledger; (ii) Zylis-Gara, J. Baker, Lane, Tear, Shirley-Quirk, Willcocks

Ledger (in 1982), using what by name are the same forces as his predecessor, Sir David Willcocks, on Decca, directs a reading that favours measured speeds, but though the choir is small the recording balance, in excellent digital sound, has the voices standing out clearly to reinforce the weight of the reading. This is a valid alternative version, for though it is perhaps not as exciting as its main competitors, it has both modern strings and admirable detail. *Dixit Dominus* was recorded a decade earlier, and this performance too is alive and spirited. But here one senses that the performers are not completely inside the work and the security that comes with complete familiarity is not always present. The intonation of the soloists is not above reproach, and the trio *Dominus a dextris* is not very comfortable, while the chorus seems not completely happy with the virtuoso running passages a little later. Willcocks might have achieved more security had he been content with a slightly slower pace. There is vigour and enthusiasm here but not always the last degree of finesse. The recording is atmospheric, and digital remastering has brought a sharper focus with hardly any loss of weight.

Coronation Anthems: Zadok the Priest; The King shall Rejoice. (i) *Israel in Egypt;* (ii) *Jephtha;* (iii) *Saul;* (iv) *Solomon* (complete)

(B) *** Ph. 475 6897 (9). Monteverdi Ch., E. Bar. Sol., Gardiner, with (i) Priday, Deam, Stafford, Collin, Kenny, Robertson, Salmon, Tindall, Tusa, Clarkson, Purves; (i; ii) Chance; (i–iii) Holton; (ii) Robson, Von Otter; (ii–iii) Dawson; (ii; iv) Varcoe; (iii) Miles, Ragin, Mark Ainsley, Mackie; (iv) Watkinson, Argenta, Hendricks, Rolfe Johnson

Any collector not already having one or more of these recordings could hardly better this bargain box. All but *Saul* (which is not available separately) are praised in our main volume; and *Saul* is hardly less recommendable, with Gardiner's performance typically vigorous. *Solomon* crowns the set and received a ✪ from us on its first issue.

(i) *Funeral Anthem for Queen Caroline: The Ways of Zion do mourn;* (ii) *Utrecht Te Deum*

(BB) ** Warner Apex (ADD/DDD) 2564 61142-2. (i) Burrowes, Brett, Hill, Varcoe, Monteverdi Ch. & O, Gardiner; (ii) Palmer, Lipovšek, Langridge, Equiluz, Moser, Naumann, Arnold Schoenberg Ch., VCM, Harnoncourt

Queen Caroline – whom Handel had known earlier as a princess in Hanover – was the most cultivated of the royal family of Hanover, and when she died in 1737 he was inspired to write a superb cantata in an Overture (Sinfonia) and eleven numbers. Gardiner directs a performance that brings out the high contrasts implicit in the music, making it energetic rather than elegiac. Excellent work from soloists, chorus and orchestra alike, all very well recorded. Handel later used the material for the first act of *Israel in Egypt*, and Erato have also coupled the piece with the complete recording of that work. However, here it is paired with the *Utrecht Te Deum*, which Handel wrote before coming to London, as a sample of his work. Harnoncourt's account offers a quite different style from Gardiner's, and in a relatively intimate acoustic he sometimes presents allegros briskly and lightly. But that is the exception; elsewhere speeds are slow and heavy, rhythms leaden, with the chorus efficient enough, but lacking the brightness and rhythmic spring that Gardiner finds in the companion work. The characterful solo singing – the murky-sounding contralto apart – makes some amends but the sound is dryish, and this cannot be counted one of Harnoncourt's more convincing ventures in the studio.

Messiah (complete DVD version)

🔑 *** Warner **DVD** 0630 17834-2. Nelson, Kirkby, Watkinson, Elliott, Thomas, Westminster Abbey Ch., AAM, Hogwood; Simon Preston (organ) (V/D: Roy Tipping)

Hogwood's DVD *Messiah* dates from 1982, the same period as his Oiseau-Lyre audio recording, and it has the appealing advantage of the warm acoustic of Wesminster Abbey. He uses a chorus of fewer than thirty, and his Academy of Ancient Music are in first-class form, with an an excellent unnamed trumpet soloist in *And the trumpet shall sound*. There is a pair of sopranos, Judith Nelson and a very young Emma Kirkby, both contributing superbly. Indeed, there is no flaw in the solo team, and David Thomas is particularly strong in the bass arias. Hogwood uses the 1754 Foundling Hospital score, and the result is an enjoyably fresh 'traditional-period' performance which is beautifully sung and a pleasure to watch, especially the choirboys, who sing with such vitality and who, one reflects, are now grown up, maybe with children of their own.

The documentation is sparse, with just 17 dividing tracks and no indication of who is singing what; but one can hear every word and the backcloth of Westminster Abbey is well used by the camera to provide a visual treat.

Messiah (complete CD versions)

(M) *** DG 477 5904 (2). Augér, Von Otter, Chance, Crook, Tomlinson, E. Concert Ch., E. Concert, Pinnock

*** DHM/BMG **SACD** Surround Sound 82876 64070-2 (2). Schäfer, Larsson, Schade, Finley, Arnold Schoenberg Ch., VCM, Harnoncourt

(M) **(*) RCA (ADD) 82876 62317-2 (2). Raskin, Kopleff, Lewis, Paul, Robert Shaw Chorale & O, Shaw

(B) ** Ph. Duo 470 044-2 (2). McNair, Von Otter, Chance, Hadley, Lloyd, ASMF Ch., ASMF, Marriner

(M) ** Westminster (ADD) 471 232-2 (3). Alarie, Merriman, Simoneau, Standen, V. Ac. Chamber Ch., V. State Op. O, Scherchen

* Teldec 9031 77615-2 (2). Gale, Lipovšek, Hollweg, Kennedy, Stockholm Chamber Ch., VCM, Harnoncourt

Trevor Pinnock presents a performance using authentically scaled forces which, without inflation, rise to grandeur and magnificence, qualities Handel himself would have relished. The fast contrapuntal choruses, such as *For unto us a Child is born*, are done lightly and resiliently in the modern manner, but there is no hint of breathlessness, and Pinnock (more than his main rivals) balances his period instruments to give a satisfying body to the sound. There is weight too in the singing of the bass soloist, John Tomlinson, firm, dark and powerful, yet marvellously agile in divisions. Arleen Augér's range of tone and dynamic is daringly wide, with radiant purity in *I know that my Redeemer liveth*. Anne Sofie von Otter sustains *He was despised* superbly with her firm, steady voice. Some alto arias are taken just as beautifully by the outstanding counter-tenor, Michael Chance. The tenor, Howard Crook, is less distinctive but still sings freshly and attractively. It is now available at mid-price on DG's Originals label.

Harnoncourt's *Messiah* is full of eccentricities, yet he is never, never dull, and his performance is endearingly enjoyable and beautifully sung, and gloriously recorded in totally believable, spectacular surround sound, with the Arnold Schoenberg Choir matching their similarly fine singing in Harnoncourt's memorable account of Haydn's *Creation*. Again, he has superb traditional soloists (no male alto) and he immediately indulges the stylish and rich-voiced tenor (Michael Schade) with a slow tempo for *Comfort ye*, so that he can offer an indulgent decorated reprise of the opening phrase. Yet *Every valley* is brisk enough, as is the jubilant *And the glory of the Lord*, and the bass (Gerald Finley) is magnificently vehement in *Thus saith the Lord*, with the contralto Anna Larsson, who takes over for *But who may abide*, equally impassioned in the 'refiner's fire'. Later, Finley is dramatically eloquent in *And the trumpet shall sound*, and the trumpet, incidentally has all the gleaming richness of a modern instrument. *And he shall purify* is again quite leisured and, more surprisingly, *For unto us a Child is born* is too slow, which one could not say about *Rejoice greatly*.

But for the most part Harnoncourt's tempi are near-traditional and the lovely duet, *He shall feed his flock*, and Larsson's *He was despised* are touching in their simplicity. The soprano Christine Schäfer is radiant throughout, and especially so in *I know that my Redeemer liveth*. Harnoncourt's accompaniments are always alive and often dramatic, as in the sharply rhythmic tenor recitative, *All that see Him, laugh Him to scorn* and the chorus *Surely He hath borne our griefs*;

yet *All we like sheep* has an engagingly light touch. *Hallelujah* brings another surprise, opening quite gently and generating a full head of steam only as it proceeds and the brass enter. It's different, but it works well, and *Worthy is the Lamb* is suitably majestic, the fugal entries all splendidly incisive, with a dramatic brass entry, and capped with a satisfying, culminating *Amen*. (It sounds overwhelming with all four speakers in action.)

Robert Shaw's *Messiah* dates from 1966, and the Webster Hall, New York City, proved an excellent venue, for this analogue recording is warmly resonant and clear in its CD transfer. It is another fairly traditional performance, using a relatively small, professionally trained chorus, and four top American soloists. We know how good Judith Raskin and Richard Lewis are from their other records, but Florence Koploff, 'a Shaw regular', is a genuine contralto with another fine voice, and the bass, Thomas Paul, is excellent too: the key solos here do not disappoint. Indeed, very little does. Shaw knew all about the move away from nineteenth-century Handelian style; his tempi have plenty of momentum and he seeks clear inner textures from his excellent choir. Altogether this is very enjoyable, and although not a first choice, will be of special interest to American listeners, for whom Shaw has been a key figure in choral performance and recording in the USA – admired by Toscanini, as well as many others.

Marriner's conception was to present *Messiah* as nearly as possible in the text followed at the first London performance of 1743. The losses are as great as the gains, but the result has unusual unity, thanks also to Marriner's direction. His tempi in the fast choruses can scarcely be counted as authentic in any way; with a small professional chorus he has gone as far as possible towards lightening them and has thus made possible speeds that almost pass belief. Although Anna Reynolds's contralto is not ideally suited to recording, this is otherwise an excellent band of soloists – and in any case Miss Reynolds sings *He was despised* on a thread of sound.

Hermann Scherchen's version is fascinatingly eccentric, notable for his erratic choice of tempi, and it is a pity that (because of a playing time of well over three hours) it comes on three mid-priced CDs, for it is a real collector's item. So we have *And the Glory of the Lord* slow and steady, while *And He shall purify* is so fast that it becomes a choral scramble, and *For unto us a Child is born* and *All we like sheep* are similarly brisk and lightly articulated, attractively so, but severely straining the resources of the Vienna Academy Choir. Scherchen has fine soloists, two of them outstanding. Beginning with a memorable *Ev'ry valley*, Léopold Simoneau's tenor contribution is very fine indeed, and throughout there is some exquisite soprano singing from Pierrette Alarie. *I Know that my Redeemer liveth* is very slow but very pure and true, and wonderfully sustained, with the orchestral accompaniment partly restricted to soloists from the first desks. *Since by man came death*, which follows, sustains the rapt atmosphere, with a spurt of energy to follow, and Richard Standen's *The trumpet shall sound* is full of robust vigour. Nan Merriman sings most sensitively too, but not all will take to her close vibrato in *He was despised*. But when Scherchen is slow he is usually very slow and, while the effect is touching in *And with His stripes we are healed*, the adagio tempo for the closing *Amen* is grotesque, providing easily the longest performance on record – taking over eight minutes to reach its marmoreal conclusion. The 1959 recording, made in the Mozartsaal of the Vienna Konzerthaus, is excellent, spacious and well transferred, giving a natural bloom to the voices, a good overall balance and a warm-textured orchestral sound.

Nikolaus Harnoncourt's Teldec version was compiled from two public concerts in Stockholm in 1982, with ill-balanced sound that puts the choir at a distance, making it sound even duller than it is. With the exception of Elizabeth Gale, the soloists are poor, and Harnoncourt's direction lacks vigour. This cannot even begin to match Scherchen's version on Westminster, let alone the top recommendations.

Messiah (sung in English): highlights
(BB) ** HMV 5 86731-2 (from complete recording, with Kirkby, Cable, Bowman, Cornwell, Thomas, Taverner Ch., & Players, Parrott)

Parrott's complete set of *Messiah* is only available coupled with *Israel in Egypt*, so a generous set of highlights (75 minutes) seems appropriate, and it features some very fine singing from the responsive Emma Kirkby, in excellent voice.

Der Messias (arr. & orch. Mozart, K.572)
☞ (M) *** Signum SIGCD 074 (2). Lott, Palmer, Langridge, Lloyd, Huddersfield Ch. Soc., RPO, Mackerras

Why did Sir Charles Mackerras choose Mozart's arrangement for a new recording of *Messiah*? Well, he hasn't told us, but he has recorded it successfully before, sung in German, for the DG Archiv label, and he is obviously happy to return to Mozart's additional orchestration (not just trombones, but flutes, clarinets, bassoons and horns, and an expanded timpani part). It certainly adds much colour to the accompaniments, and it is notable that Handel's original trumpet solo has been restored to *And the trumpet shall sound*. (Mozart only altered it to include a solo horn, an octave lower, because, by the middle of the eighteenth century, the trumpet guilds which provided the performers on high trumpets in the baroque era had all disappeared.)

Mackerras offers a more-or-less traditional approach, with a first-class team of soloists, and, like Harnoncourt, no male alto. The Huddersfield Choral Society returns to the stage, singing as richly as ever, but now more athletically and with crisper enunciation. Tempi are brisker than in Sargent's day, but not so brisk that any of the work's grandeur and nobility is lost, and there is weight without unwieldiness. Above all, Mackerras has gathered a solo team that can make the arias – taken at spacious tempi – into the radiant creations Handel envisaged. Felicity Palmer's moving *He was despised* is matched by Felicity Lott's serenely lovely *I know that my Redeemer liveth* and Philip Langridge's *Comfort ye*; while in the very first bass aria, Mackerras holds back the tempo so that Robert Lloyd's glorious runs are cleanly articulated, yet, later, *Why do the nations* rages as furiously as ever. The choruses have plenty of bite and in *Worthy is the Lamb* and the final *Amen* there is a noble majesty. The RPO accompaniments are rewarding in their own right, and altogether this is very satisfying indeed, especially when it is so splendidly recorded, with that skilful duo, Mike Hatch and Mike Clements, making the very most of the warm acoustics of London's Henry Wood Hall.

Ode for St Cecilia's Day
(BB) ** Naxos 8.554752. Mields, Wilde, Alsfelder Vokalensemble, Concerto Polacco, Helbich

Recorded in a church in Templin, Germany, the Naxos version of the *St Cecilia Ode* brings a lightweight performance, marked by some sprightly singing and playing in faster movements but with some damagingly sluggish accounts of recitative and the central soprano aria, *What passion cannot music raise*, as well as the final aria with chorus, *As from the powers*. The most celebrated movement is the aria for tenor with chorus, *The trumpet's loud clangour*, and that is admirably bright and resilient, with its 'double double double beat', with Mark Wilde the fresh, clear soloist. The bright, pure soprano is Dorothee Mields, and though the chorus is rather backwardly balanced, this adds to the liveliness of the two fast numbers to which it contributes.

Saul (complete)
**(*) HM HMC 90 1877/8. Bell, Joshua, Zazzo, Bjarnason, Ovenden, Slattery, Saks, Waddington, Berlin RIAS Chamber Ch., Concerto Köln, Jacobs

From René Jacobs a vibrant alternative performance to McCreesh's enjoyable DG set (474 510-2), well sung, especially by the chorus, and dramatically compelling. Gidon Saks' *Saul* is strongly characterized throughout, and Jeremy Ovenden is a fine Jonathan, but Laurence Zazzo's David is much less memorable than Andreas Scholl, the star of the DG set. The Harmonia Mundi version is on two discs against Paul McCreesh's three, which is a considerable price advantage, but on the whole we would prefer McCreesh, until Gardiner's Philips version is reissued.

Solomon (complete)
🠊 ❂ (M) *** Ph. 475 7561 (2). Watkinson, Argenta, Hendricks, Rolfe Johnson, Monteverdi Ch., E. Bar. Sol., Gardiner

This is among the very finest of all Handel oratorio recordings. With panache, Gardiner shows how authentic-sized forces can convey Handelian grandeur even with clean-focused textures and fast speeds. The choruses and even more magnificent double choruses stand as cornerstones of a structure which may have less of a story-line than some other Handel oratorios – the Judgement apart – but which Gardiner shows has consistent human warmth. The Act III scenes between Solomon and the Queen of Sheba are given extra warmth by having in the latter role a singer who is sensuous in tone, Barbara Hendricks. Carolyn Watkinson's pure mezzo is very apt for Solomon himself, while Nancy Argenta is clear and sweet as his Queen; but the overriding glory of the set is the radiant singing of Gardiner's Monteverdi Choir. Its clean, crisp articulation matches the brilliant playing of the English Baroque Soloists, regularly challenged by Gardiner's fast speeds, as in *The Arrival of the Queen of Sheba*; and the sound is superb, coping thrillingly with the problems of the double choruses. It is now reissued at mid-price as one of Philips's Originals, and is fully worthy of that accolade.

'Great Oratorio Duets' from Alexander Balus; Alexander's Feast; Belshazzar; Deborah; Esther; Jephtha; Joshua; Saul; Solomon; Susanna; Theodora
*** BIS SACD 1236 (Surround Sound). Sampson, Blaze, OAE, Kraemer

We usually get plenty of compilations of opera arias and duets on disc, but almost never a comparable oratorio selection. But BIS have had the inspired idea of putting together two of the finest baroque soloists of our time, and they prove a truly distinctive partnership. The voices of Robin Blaze and Carolyn Sampson were surely made for each other, and they blend quite perfectly, particularly when they trill together or answer each other in a conversational style. Sample the engaging *Where do thy ardours raise me!* from *Deborah* to hear just how effectively their voices are contrasted, while *Hail wedded love*, from *Alexander Balus*, with its dotted

rhythms, shows how charmingly they can share a dialogue. In *To thee, thou glorious sons of worth* from *Theodora* the exchanges are meltingly expressive; *Let's imitate her notes above* (from *Alexander's Feast*) brings delightful echoing of phrases; and the final item, a simple interchange between Esther and Ahasuerus, with its gentle rhythmic tread, is wonderfully poignant. Not surprisingly, Nicholas Kraemer's accompaniments are most stylish, and if you have facilities for SACD surround sound, the realism of a most vivid recording is greatly enhanced.

OPERA

Agrippina (complete DVD version)
**(*) EuroArts DVD 2054538. Daniels, Hall, Von Kannen, Kuebler, Nicolai, Hielscher, Katz, Lesbo, L. Bar. Players, Östman (Director: Michael Hampe)

Filmed at the Schwetzingen festival in 1985, the EuroArts version offers a period performance, crisply conducted by Arnold Östman, best known for his work at Drottningholm in Sweden. Michael Hampe's production involves handsome baroque sets by Mauro Pagano and traditional costumes. *Agrippina* is an opera written for Venice in 1709–10, set in the early years of Imperial Rome, with Agrippina the centre of intrigues, opposed by another great manipulator, Poppea.

Barbara Daniels is agile, bright and bright in the title-role, with Janice Hall first rate as Poppea. The snag of the performance is that two of the principal castrato roles, those of Nero and Narciso, are here taken by baritones instead of countertenors, reflecting the date of the production (before period performance was fully accepted).

Giulio Cesare in Egitto (complete DVD versions)
*** Opus Arte DVD OA 0950 D (3). Connolly, Bardon, Kirchschlager, De Niese, Dumaux, Glyndebourne Ch., OAE, Christie (Director: David McVicar; V/D: Robin Lough)
**(*) EuroArts DVD 2053599 (2). Pushee, Alexander, Gunn, Campbell, Kenny, Dalton, Bennett, Gilchrist, Australian Op. & Ballet O, Hickox (V/D: Peter Butler)
*(*) TDK DVD DVWW-OPGCES (2). Oliver, De la Merced, Podles, Beaumont, Domènech, Ch. & SO of Gran Teatre del Liceu, Hofstetter (Director: Herbert Wernicke)

Extravagantly laid out on three DVDs, the Opus Arte version is important in offering a fine period performance of this most popular of the Handel operas. William Christie conducts the Orchestra of the Age of Enlightenment and an outstanding cast in an account at once scholarly, lively and refreshing, a live recording of the 2005 production at Glyndebourne. Sarah Connolly sings superbly in the title-role, looking very boyish, opposite Danielle de Niese as Cleopatra, a soprano brighter-toned than usual for this role, a provocative figure. Patricia Bardon is an excellent Cornelia and Christophe Dumaux a characterful Tolomeo. David McVicar's production, as the publicity puts it in flattering terms, 'manages to combine serious insight with entertainment, bringing Handel's masterpiece to life in a powerful, convincing and highly intelligent way'. But, mercifully, it must be conceded that at least his production does not get in the way too much. Like most other versions, the action is updated, with the Roman army presented in the uniforms of the British army in India in the nineteenth century. Action is effectively presented against a permanent set, involving a sequence of classical arches seen in perspective.

The three DVDs offer one Act per disc, the first also including an interview with Danielle de Niese and the third a documentary called 'Entertainment is not a dirty word' by Ferenc van Damme. Apart from the excellence of much of the singing, it is the vivid and sensitive conducting of William Christie that makes this set worth investigating and leaves one feeling better than one did when the curtain went up. The performance closes in celebration, with Christie making the most of the trumpets in the final number.

Francisco Negrin's production of *Giulio Cesare* for the Sydney Opera House makes a virtue of the limited scale of the stage. With simple panels as the main background and with walls of hieroglyphics often superimposed, the setting is updated from Roman times to a kind of Ruritanian state, with colourful uniforms involving cuirasses. By contrast, the Egyptian characters, not just Cleopatra but the others too, wear timeless robes, sharply distinguishing them. With Richard Hickox conducting the orchestra in a brisk, fresh reading, taking note of many aspects of period performance, and with an excellent cast, the formula works well. The counter-tenor Graham Pushee sings powerfully in the title-role with his cleanly focused voice, offering immaculate articulation and phenomenal agility in the many formidable divisions. Opposite him is the superb Cleopatra of Yvonne Kenny, glamorous of person and voice. Happily, Hickox allows her big arias full expansiveness, bringing out their beauty. Rosemary Gunn is a fine Cornelia, statuesque in her bearing and rich of voice, with Andrew Dalton a characterful Tolomeo and the dark-toned Stephen Bennett a formidable Achilla. The Sesto of Elizabeth Campbell is bright and clear if shrill at times.

Next to the Sydney Opera House version, the production from the Liceu Theatre in Barcelona is disappointing, not so well cast and with the conductor, Michael Hofstetter, racing his soloists to have them sounding breathless. Yet the principal snag is that Herbert Wernicke, as well as directing the production, has devised a version of the score which (with no justification) introduces music from three other Handel operas, *Rinaldo*, *Orlando* and *Tolomeo*. Wernicke's own sets are handsome, but the costumes involve an updating that is less convincing than that on the rival Sydney set. The uniforms are more specifically fascist-orientated, while the Egyptian characters, including Cleopatra, have costumes similarly updated, with little hint of an Egyptian background. Flavio Oliver as Caesar and Elena de la Merced sing well enough, hampered as they are by the conductor, but the finest singing comes from Ewa Podles as Cornelia.

Radamisto (complete CD version)

*** Virgin 5 45673-2 (2). Di Donato, Ciofi, Beaumont, Labelle, Cherici, Stains, Lepore, Il Complesso Barocco, Curtis

Cast from strength, Alan Curtis's stylish reading of *Radamisto* with Il Complesso Barocco is based on a stage production at the Viterbo Festival, given in 2003. Though the acoustic is on the dry side, the richness of the central characters' voices is not compromised by a lack of bloom, with the three principal sopranos all outstanding – Joyce di Donato in the title-role powerful and agile, Patrizia Ciofi lighter and brighter and well contrasted as Polissena, and Dominique Labelle as Fraarte warm and fruity. Curtis explains his choice of the first (1720) version of the score, even though later revisions contain some magnificent extra numbers, in that the dramatic thread is tauter. Where at one point in haste Handel gave Polissena an inappropriate aria from the opera *Rodrigo*, Curtis then opts for the alternative

from the second version of the opera, *Barbaro, partiro*, effectively so.

Rinaldo (complete CD version)

(BB) **(*) Naxos 8.660165/7 (3). Barber, Whalen, Hannigan, Watson, Opera in Concert, Aradia Ens., Mallon

The Irish conductor Kevin Mallon has conducted his Toronto-based group, the Aradia Ensemble, in a number of lively performances for Naxos, and this one, the most ambitious yet, offers a totally refreshing account of *Rinaldo*, Handel's opera about the crusading knight whom the sorceress, Armida, attempts to seduce. The piece had its initial success in 1711, largely thanks to the spectacle involved, and the recording vividly simulates that, with reverberating timpani and other percussion, notably when Armida arrives in a chariot drawn by two fiery dragons. Mallon opts for the first version of the score, even though Handel later added alternative numbers. Following that decision, he has women instead of counter-tenors for the castrato roles of Rinaldo and Eustazio, giving the small castrato role of the magician, Mago, to a bass. The cast is made up of fresh, youthful-sounding singers, none of them strikingly characterful but all stylish, with clean, fresh voices and immaculate techniques. Despite the dictates of period performance Mallon takes the most famous number, the aria *Lascia ch'io pianga*, exceptionally slowly, allowing the excellent soprano Laura Whalen to ornament the reprise with great delicacy. Vivid, open sound. An excellent bargain, despite the lack of a full libretto.

Serse (complete CD version)

**(*) Virgin 5 45711-2 (3). Von Otter, Norberg-Schulz, Zazzo, Piau, Tro Santafé, Abete, Furlanetto, Les Arts Florissants, Christie

Christie and Les Arts Florissants seldom let us down, and the fact that his new recording of *Serse* is uneven is hardly his fault. Surprisingly, Anne Sofie von Otter, although she characterizes strongly in the title-role, is less sweet of tone than usual, and Elizabeth Norberg-Schulz too is not at her best as Romilda. Fortunately the counter-tenor Lawrence Zazzo is in superb voice as Arsamene, and he is much finer here than he was in *Saul* (see above); Sandrine Piau too is in excellent voice as Atalanta. Christie directs the proceedings spiritedly and you won't be disapppointed with his warmly expressive tempo for the famous *Ombra mai fù*.

Teseo (complete DVD version)

*** Arthaus DVD 100 708. Laszczkowski, Rostorf-Zamir, Riccarda Wessling, Berlin Lautten Compagney, Katschner (Director: Axel Kohler; V/D: Ute Feudel)

First given in 1713, *Teseo* was the second opera that Handel wrote for London, an adaptation of Racine's play on the confrontation of Theseus and Medea. Handel's setting crisply presents the story in a sequence of brisk arias, often with a sequence of numbers given to a particular character. In five Acts, the two protagonists do not appear until Act II, and for much of the opera Theseus hardly emerges as the central character. This Berlin production of 2004 by Axel Kohler offers a stylish reading on period instruments, with an excellent line-up of principals. As Agilea, Sharon Rostorf-Zamir with her rich mezzo establishes the quality in the first three arias, and the three counter-tenors in the cast – taking the roles of Theseus, Egeo and Arcane – are all first rate, a plus point for this version. Kohler's production involves broadly traditional costumes and the simplest of sets.

VOCAL COLLECTIONS

Operatic Duets from: *Admeto; Atalanta; Faramondo; Flavio; Muzio Scevola; Orlando; Poro, Re dell'Indie; Rinaldo; Serse; Silla; Sosarme; Teseo*
*** Virgin 5 45628-2. Ciofi, Di Donato, Il Compresso Barocco, Curtis

We have already had a stimulating and highly successful collection of duets from Handel's oratorios (see above, on BIS), and here is a comparable operatic selection, in which situations are usually more theatrical and produce dramatic or intensely expressive interchanges between the characters. So it is here, and there are plenty of novelties, not least the rewarding selection from *Poro, Re delle'Indie*, or, on a lighter note, the delightful excerpts from *Atalanta* and *Faramondo* and deeply touching ones from *Teseo and Silla*. All these duets and more are engagingly and beautifully sung by Patrizia Ciofi and Joyce Di Donato, soprano and mezzo respectively, with ornamentation nicely managed. Il Compresso Barocco, directed by Alan Curtis, provide most sensitive accompaniments, and the recording is warm and vivid.

Arias: (i) *Admeto: Cangio d'aspetto. Alexander Balus: Convey me to some peaceful shore. Ottone: La Speranzaè giunta; Vieni, o figlio. Partenope: Voglio dire. Rinaldo: Lascia ch'io pianga. Rodelinda: Dove sei. Cantata à 3: La Rodinella.* (ii) *Alcina: Pensa a chi geme. Alexander's Feast: Revenge, Timotheus cries. Ezio: Se un bell'ardier. Hercules: The God of Battle. Samson: Honour and arms. Semele: Leave me, loathsome light. Susanna: Peace crowned with roses. Theodora: Wide spread his name*
** Australian Decca Eloquence [ADD] 461 593-2. ASMF, with (i) Greevy, cond. Leppard; (ii) Robinson, cond. Ledger

This CD pairs two LPs from the mid-1960s. Bernadette Greevy's fine, rich, if sometimes unwieldy contralto voice is well caught here. She is at her best in the expansive phrases, where one is treated to a glorious stream of sound, though interpretations could be more imaginative, and it is a pity that she was reluctant to decorate the *da capo* arias. Leppard provides excellent accompaniments. Forbes Robinson had built up a formidable reputation at Covent Garden when these recordings were made, and he shows versatility in these often taxing arias. Though he fails to give them the variety one would ideally like, they are not dull, and all the items are firm favourites. This CD represents a good old-fashioned approach to Handel singing.

Arias from: *Amadigi, Ariodante, Deidamia, Giulio Cesare, Lotario, Radamisto, Rinaldo, Rodelinda, Scipione*
*** Linn CKD252. Bell, SCO, Egarr

Singing Handel has been at the centre of Emma Bell's remarkable career so far, celebrated in this superb collection of soprano arias. It covers the full span of the Italian operas that Handel wrote for London, from *Rinaldo* in 1711 to *Deidamia* 30 years later in 1741. Here is a voice of glowing quality, at once bright yet creamy in texture, weighty yet pure, which is matched by fine musical imagination and a masterly control of technique. It is a joy to hear rapid divisions sung with such perfection, with each note clearly articulated and not the least suspicion of unwanted aspirates intruding. Equally, Bell's ability in lyrical arias to float the most exposed high notes with no hint of an upward slide makes for ravishing results.

The collection begins with one of the most brilliant arias,

Destero dall empia dite from *Amadigi*, with two trumpets obbligato setting the pattern in the instrumental introduction, dazzlingly played by members of the Scottish Chamber Orchestra. Though modern instruments are used, Richard Egarr, the associate director of the Academy of Ancient Music, effectively adopts an apt degree of period style for Handel. Two of the most moving performances come in the arias from *Rodelinda*, an opera in which Bell had her first important success, and though one wishes she had included more arias from *Giulio Cesare* than Cleopatra's *Piangero*, it is good to have such adventurous rarities as *M'hai resa infelice* from Handel's very last opera, *Deidamia*, with its alternation of fast and slow. Matching Bell's impressive achievement, Linn provides beautifully balanced, cleanly focused recording.

HANSON, Howard (1896–1981)

(i; ii) *Piano Concerto, Op. 36*; (ii) *Elegy, Op. 44*; (iii) *For the First Time*; (ii) *Merry Mount: Suite; Mosaics; Symphonies 1 in E min. (Nordic), Op. 21; 2 (Romantic), Op. 30; 3*; (ii; iv) *The Lament of Beowulf; Song of Democracy* (with bonus: 'The Composer Talks')
(B) ***** Mercury (ADD) 475 6867 (4).** Composer, with (i) Mouledous; (ii) Eastman-Rochester O; (iii) Eastman Philh.; (iv) Eastman School of Music Ch.

This set features four CDs of classic Mercury recordings in benchmark performances in one box. The symphonies have a unique thrust and ardour, with the rhythm and energy of this music making a strong impression, never dull and always accessible. The *Song of Democracy* has plenty of dramatic impact and, like the symphonies, is very well recorded. The four-movement *Piano Concerto* is brilliantly played by Alfred Mouledous, especially in the *Scherzo*, marked *Allegro molto ritmico* (though they are not jazzy rhythms) and the *giocoso* finale, while the slow movement is eloquently expressive. Mercury not only pioneered many of Hanson's major works on record but also invited him to talk about his music. The three orchestral works, *For the First Time*, *Merry Mount Suite* and *Mosaics*, are ideal for the purpose and his 'guide to the instruments of the orchestra' (directly related to the scoring of *Merry Mount Suite*) is particularly instructive, the more so as microphones had been set up to project solo instruments and groupings of woodwind, brass and strings with extraordinary realism and presence.

Elsewhere, Hanson discusses orchestral colour (in relation to visual colour) and musical construction in connection with his atmospheric and vividly contrasted set of variations which he calls *Mosaics* (inspired by the mosaics in Palermo Cathedral). More controversially, he expounds on 'tone relationships' as explored in his book, *The Harmonic Materials of Modern Music*. Apparently his work method was to choose a predetermined series of notes for a given composition, rather like a tone row, but which he thinks of as circular, as it is written within the normal tonal system. This thesis is related to *For the First Time*, in essence a dozen impressionistic vignettes, evoking a day in the life of a (somewhat precocious) child. He wakes to the sound of *Bells*, watches a pair of Irish puppies at play, explores a *Deserted house*, comes across an *Eccentric clock*, meets a group of *Clowns* on their way to the circus, enjoys his mother reading to him the tale of *Kikimora*, watches a *Fireworks* spectacle, and so on; and he ends his day in the world of *Dreams*. Hanson's invention is fresh and evocative, his scoring felicitous, so all this music is made to serve a double purpose. Vivid sound from the late 1950s and 1960s in the Mercury manner.

Symphony 2 (Romantic), Op. 20; Bold Island Suite; Merry Mount Suite; Fanfare for the Signal Corps
→ *** Telarc CD 80649. Cincinnati Pops O, Kunzel

With the Delos Seattle anthologies currently unobtainable (temporarily, we hope) this must now be regarded as the key Howard Hanson CD. It is magnificently played and gloriously recorded in ideally full and spacious Telarc sound. Apart from the richly persuasive performance of the composer's most memorable symphony, so hauntingly melodic, the *Merry Mount Suite* is also played outstandingly, especially the engaging *Children's Dance* and the expansive *Love duet*. This, like the central *Summer Seascape* of the fine *Bold Island Suite* (a recording première), has the full patina of rich scoring so characteristic of this endearing composer. A splendid disc in every way.

HARBISON, John (born 1938)

(i) *Concerto for Double Brass Choir & Orchestra; (ii) The Flight into Egypt; (iii) The Natural World*
*** New World NW 80395-2. (i) LAPO, Previn; (ii) Anderson, Sylvan, Cantata Singers & Ens., Hoose; (iii) Felty, Los Angeles Philharmonic New Music Group, Harbison

These three fine works provide an illuminating survey of the recent work of one of the most communicative of American composers today. The most striking and vigorous is the concerto he wrote as resident composer for Previn and the Los Angeles Philharmonic, and for the orchestra's brass section in particular. The other two works reveal the more thoughtful Harbison, the one a collection of three songs to nature poems by Wallace Stevens, Robert Bly and James Wright. *The Flight into Egypt* is a measured and easily lyrical setting of the story of the Holy Family fleeing from King Herod. Sanford Sylvan and the choir sing the main text, with Roberta Anderson interjecting as the Angel. Excellent performances and recording.

HARRIS, Roy (1898–1979)

(i) *Violin Concerto; (ii) Kentucky Spring; Symphony 5*
(M) *(**) First Edition FECD-0005. Louisville O; with (i) Fulkerston, cond. Smith; (ii) Whitney

Only the *Third Symphony* (1938) has captured the imagination of the wider musical public – and, in a sense, rightly so. Its successors seem to be traversing much the same ground: only the *Seventh*, which Ormandy recorded in the 1950s, approaches it in eloquence. The *Fifth* of 1943, which Koussevitzky commissioned and recorded, is a good work, but the Louisville orchestral playing is not really top-drawer, as well prepared or on sufficiently good form for this reading to have an unqualified recommendation. The *Violin Concerto* (1949) is a one-movement work, lasting some 28 minutes, in which long phrases and orchestral chorales provide a bed on which 'the violin plays dance-like variations'. There are beautiful episodes but, oh dear, it seems dreadfully long and diffuse. *Kentucky Spring* (1949) is genial and full of high spirits. *Kentucky Spring* was recorded in 1960 in mono only; the *Fifth Symphony* in 1965 and the *Concerto* in 1985, both in stereo.

Symphonies 3; (i) 4 (Folk Song Symphony)
(BB) *** Naxos 8.559227. (i) Colorado Symphony Ch.; Colorado SO, Alsop

Good news. This issue heralds the appearance of a complete cycle of the 13 symphonies of Harris, which Naxos are undertaking. The *Third* gets a rousing performance, though readers who already have it should not part with the pioneering and rightly celebrated Koussevitzky set – or, for that matter, Bernstein's DG record, coupled with William Schuman's *Third*. The *Fourth, Folk Song Symphony*, offers colourful settings for chorus and orchestra of five traditional songs, with two purely instrumental numbers, livelier than the rest, as interludes. An attractive novelty, but not the equal of either of its immediate neighbours.

HARTMANN, Emil (1836–98)

(i) *Cello Concerto in D min., Op. 26. Hakon Jarl (symphonic poem); Hærmædene på Helgeland: Overture.*
**(*) Danacord DACOCD 508. (i) Dinitzen; Danish PO, South Jutland, Wallez – J.P.E. HARTMANN: *Overtures* **(*)

Emil Hartmann was naturally overshadowed in Denmark by his father, Johann Peter Emilius, who, fearing accusations of nepotism, did virtually nothing to further his son's career. He studied first with his father in Copenhagen and then in Leipzig, subsequently becoming organist at the Christianborg Slotskirke (Palace Church). He made more of a name in Germany, particularly as a conductor, where three of his seven symphonies were performed. The *Cello Concerto* is a relatively short piece, perhaps reminiscent in style of Saint-Saëns. The disc also affords an opportunity of contrasting the two composers' approach to the overture: Emil's *Overture* to Ibsen's *Hærmædene på Helgeland* is probably the most successful here.

Piano Concerto in F min., Op. 47.
*(*) Danacord DACOCD 581. Marshev, Danish PO, South Jutland, Aescbacher – WINDING: *Piano Concerto*, etc. **(*)

Emil Hartmann's *Piano Concerto*, composed in 1889, is perhaps less interesting than the *Cello Concerto* (reviewed above) and is too strongly reminiscent of Weber and Schumann to speak with a strongly individual voice. However, the Russian-born Oleg Marshev plays with such ardour and authority (and is so well supported by the Danish orchestra) that one is almost persuaded that it is better than it is. Three stars for the pianist but not for the work, which comes with a concerto by his brother-in-law, August Winding.

HARTMANN, Johann Peter Emilius (1805–1900)

4 Caprices, Op. 18/1; 6 Characteerstykker med indledende Smaavers of H. C. Andersen, Op. 50; Etudes instructives, Op. 53; Fantasiestücke, Op. 54; 2 Pièces caractéristiques, Op. 25; 6 Tonstücke in Liederform, Op. 37
**(*) dacapo 8.224162. Gade

These miniatures by Niels Gade's long-lived father-in-law are well served by Nina Gade. This is not great music, but it has a certain period charm and has not been recorded before.

Overtures: En efterårsjagt, Op. 63b; Hakon Jarl, Op. 40.
**(*) Danacord DACOCD 508. Danish PO, South Jutland,
Wallez – EMIL HARTMANN: *Cello Concerto*, etc. **(*)

Though little played nowadays, J. P. E. Hartmann composed
one fine opera, *Liden Kirsti*, and wrote excellently for the
orchestra. He became Niels Gade's father-in-law in the 1850s,
and one of his descendants, albeit remotely, was Niels Viggo
Bentzon. These two concert overtures make an admirable
introduction to his work as well as a useful foil to the *Cello
Concerto* by his son, Emil.

The Valkyrie, Op. 62
** CPO 999 620-2 (2). Frankfurt RSO, Jurowski

Written for Bournonville, Hartmann's ballet has a pretty lurid
scenario, with plenty of blood and thunder. However, *The
Valkyrie* remains curiously bland and tame, and its melodic
ideas are obstinately unmemorable. Good playing and
recording, and Bournonville fans will surely want it, but the
music itself does not represent Hartmann at his best and we
would hesitate to press its claims on non-specialists.

HARTMANN, Karl Amadeus
(1905–63)

Symphony 6; Symphony 4: Finale
(M) (***) DG mono 477 5487. RIAS SO, Berlin, Fricsay (with
BLACHER: *Variations on a Theme by Paganini, Op. 26.*
FORTNER: *Symphony: Finale*)

A welcome return to the catalogue of Ferenc Fricsay's pioneering (1955) record of Hartmann's *Sixth* and best-known
symphony – as well as his première account of Blacher's
exuberant and inventive *Paganini Variations*, which in the
1950s featured prominently in concert performances but are
now a rarity. The finales of the Hartmann *Fourth Symphony*
for strings, and Wolfgang Fortner's *Symphony*, recorded in
1949, are reminders of the explosive scene in post-war Western Germany. This is unlikely to last long in the catalogue, so
best snap it up when you can.

HARTY, Hamilton (1879–1941)

(i) *Piano Concerto. Comedy Overture; Fantasy Scenes*
(BB) *** Naxos 8.557731. Ulster O, Yuasa, (i) with Donohoe

Peter Donohoe offers a faster, fresher version of Harty's very
appealing *Piano Concerto* than the Chandos rival with Malcolm Binns, though the latter remains enjoyable in its richer
sound. Similarly, the *Comedy Overture* is much faster than on
Chandos's version, and it sparkles in its wit and easy-going
energy. The *Fantasy Scenes* is attractive, light, 'postcard' music
with a vaguely exotic feel, and prettily scored. This CD is
recommended in every way and the sound, though without
the sumptuous quality which Chandos obtained with the
same orchestra, is very good.

HASSE, Johann (1699–1783)

*Mandolin Concerto in G; Trio Sonata in G, Op. 3/4;
Harpsichord Sonata in C; (i) Cantatas: Ah, troppo è vert;
Bella, mi parto, a Dio; Se il cantor trace, oh Dio*
*** MDG 309 0944-2. (i) Wessel; Musica Alta Ripus

Johann Adolf Hasse is most celebrated for two arias from his
opera *Artaserse*, which the castrato, Farinelli, was reputed to

sing every evening for Philip V, and indeed the pair of
cantatas here, although they do not have storylines, are
imbued with a dramatic, operatic feeling. They are very
attractive indeed, *Ah troppo è vert* about the power of first
love, and the poignant *Bella, mi parto* about the sorrow of
lovers parting. The male alto, Kai Wessel, has a truly lovely
voice, and he sings them superbly, with great feeling and
expert control of vocal colour. One really feels that this is how
they might have sounded three centuries ago. In between, as
most diverting interludes, come the *Trio Sonata* for two
violins and continuo, and the similarly lightweight *Harpsichord Sonata*. But what all but steals the show is the very
engaging miniature chamber concerto for mandolin, with its
catchy finale. The recording is first class and this concert is
very diverting indeed.

HAUG, Halvor (born 1952)

(i) *Symphony 3 (The Inscrutable Life); Furuenes sang (Song
of the Pines); (ii) Silence for Strings; Insignia: Symphonic
Vision*
*** Simax PSC 1113. (i) Norrköping SO; (ii) ECO; Ruud

The Norwegian composer Halvor Haug is a composer of
substance. His sensibility is strongly Nordic and at one with
the sounds and the landscape of those latitudes. The *Third
Symphony* (1991–3) is a large-scale piece in two parts, lasting
some 36 minutes. Its subtitle incidentally alludes to the
famous *Inextinguishable* of Nielsen. This is meditative, concentrated in atmosphere and static. The ending uses a nightingale, as does Respighi in *The Pines of Rome*, but the effect
will not convince all his admirers. *Stillhet* or 'Silence' (1977) is
an evocation of tranquillity (a better translation might have
been 'stillness'); and *Song of the Pines* (1987), a threnody on
the desecration of the natural world, has real eloquence.
Insignia (1993) is a response to the other-worldly landscape of
the Lofoten islands. Ole Kristian Ruud gets good results from
the Norrköping orchestra and the sound is excellent.

HAYDN, Josef

Cello Concertos 1 in C; 2 in D, Hob VIIb/1–2
*(*) Transart TR 121. Haimovitz, O de Bretagne, Stefan
Sanderling – MOZART: *Flute Concerto 2* (arr. for cello) *(*)

The cellist Matt Haimovitz first came to prominence on disc
in recordings of Lalo and Saint-Saëns concertos for DG with
Levine and the Chicago Symphony Orchestra, and since then
has done a number of solo recordings of twentieth-century
works, also for DG. Here he gives impressive performances,
recorded live, of the two Haydn *Cello Concertos*, marred by
rhythmically stodgy playing in the slow movements and thin
orchestral sound. Set in a dry acoustic, the sound exposes
limitations in the playing of this chamber orchestra based in
Brittany, here recorded in Rheims. Though this full-price
issue cannot compare with the finest discs coupling the two
Haydn concertos, it has the unique plus-point of offering as a
bonus the first ever recording of George Szell's realization of
Mozart's *D major Flute Concerto* as a cello concerto.

(i) *Cello Concertos 1 in C; 2 in D, Hob VIIb/1–2.; (ii) Violin
Concertos in C, A & G, Hob VIIa/1, 3 & 4*
🢐➤ (BB) *** Virgin 2x1 4 82115-2 (2). (i) Mørk, Norwegian
CO, Iona Brown; (ii) Tetzlaff, N. Sinfonia, Schiff (with
MOZART: *Rondo in C, K.373* ***)

Truls Mørk gives characterful performances of both cello concertos, full of individual touches. The outer movements of the *C major* are daringly fast, though the opening movement of the *D major* brings a surprisingly relaxed approach. Both the slow movements are romantically spacious. No one could pretend that Haydn's violin concertos, early works written for Tommasini, are among his greatest music, but Christian Tetzlaff makes the most of their simple virtues. His approach is predominantly classical in feeling, though the songful slow movement of the *A major* is most engagingly phrased, and the serenade-like *Adagio* of the *C major* (the best known) is enchanting on his gentle bow. He follows with a dazzling finale. Schiff provides plenty of vitality in the accompaniments, which are crisply pointed, and appropriate bustle in the closing Rondos (that of the *A major* is one of the most impressive movements) and the recording is excellently balanced throughout.

(i) *Flute Concerto in D* (attrib., but probably by Leopold Hoffmann). *Scherzandi 1–6*
☛ (M) *** EMI 4 76863-2. (i) Pahud; Berlin Haydn Ens., Schellenberger – M. HAYDN: *Flute Concerto ***

This is an enchantingly lighthearted record, displaying the supreme musicianship of Emmanuel Pahud as one of EMI's 'Great Artists of the Century' and the Berlin Haydn Ensemble in Haydn's six *Scherzandi*, unexpected treasures, dating from Haydn's early Esterházy years.

Horn Concerto 3 in D, Hob VII/d3
(*(**)) BBC mono BBCL 4066-2. Brain, BBC Midland O, Wurmser (with instrumental recital (***)

Dennis Brain's performance brings his characteristic combination of finesse and bonhomie – but alas the BBC recording, already rough in the first movement, produces severe harmonic distortion in the *Adagio* which does not improve in the finale.

Piano Concertos: in F; in G; in D, Hob XVIII/3, 4 & 11
☛ *** HM HMC 90 1854. Staier (fortpiano), Freiburg Bar. O, Von der Golz

Piano Concertos: in F, Hob XVIII/3; in D, Hob XVIII/11
(M) ** Guild GMCD 7206. Thew, Zürich Camerata, Tschupp – KUHN: *Concierto de Tenerife ***

Andsnes has recorded these same three concertos for EMI (5 56960-2 – see our main volume) and that is a hard act to follow. However if you enjoy eighteenth-century music on a fortepiano, Staier is your man. He adds decoration and ornamentation very skilfully, especially in slow movements, and he plays his own cadenzas. So this is very much his disc. Except for one thing: the Freiburg Baroque Orchestra is the best in the authentic business, and Gottfried von der Golz's accompaniments are a joy in themselves. So this Harmonia Mundi disc has a special place in the Haydn discography and is very enjoyable indeed.

The Guild issue is a memorial to the American pianist Warren Thew, who lived in Zürich from 1956 until his untimely death in 1984. He was a composer and the author of around 200 poems in the Romansh language, which were published posthumously in 2000 to much acclaim. In the two Haydn concertos he is unfailingly musical and sensitive, though the Camerata Zürich is no match for the Norwegian Chamber Orchestra (and for Leif Ove Andsnes on EMI 5 56960-2). The recording from 1972 is acceptable and well balanced, but wanting in range and freshness.

Piano Concerto in D, Hob XVIII:11
(M) ** EMI (ADD) 5 62823-2. Michelangeli, Zurich CO, De Stoutz – MOZART: *Concertos 13 & 23.* (**)

Curiously detached playing from Michelangeli diminishes the appeal of this reissue. The great pianist adds to the range of the keyboard and thickens various chords. The piano tone could be fresher and, despite the contribution of the Zurich orchestra under Edmond de Stoutz, which is lively enough, this issue cannot be counted a great success.

Trumpet Concerto in E flat
(B) *** Ph. Eloquence 468 207-2. Hardenberger, ASMF, Marriner (with Franz Xaver RICHTER: *Trumpet Concerto*) – Michael HAYDN; HUMMEL; Leopold MOZART; Franz RICHTER: *Trumpet Concertos ***

Hardenberger's account of the Haydn *Concerto* is unsurpassed and he is equally impressive in the far lesser-known but agreeable concertos by Haydn's contemporary, Franz Xaver Richter. The other four concertos on this inexpensive Eloquence disc are also played splendidly.

24 Minuets
*** Australian Decca Eloquence (ADD) 476 7693. Philh. Hungarica, Dorati

This collection of 24 *Minuets*, amazingly varied and imaginative, was written late in Haydn's career and, though few of them have the symphonic overtones of the minuets in the late symphonies, they represent the composer at his most inspired. It is not recommended to play them all in one sitting; but this CD certainly adds point to Haydn's own definition of a good composer as 'one who can write a brand new minuet'. Dorati's classic performances are characteristically genial, and the excellent (1975) sound emerges freshly on this new CD, with plenty of weight in the orchestral sound. Well done, Australian Universal, for making them available again.

SYMPHONIES

Symphonies 1–12
(M) *(*) Chan. 6618 (3). Cantilena, Sheppard

Adrian Sheppard's set of Haydn's earliest symphonies is potentially attractive, but the playing in the first five is not well enough rehearsed, and while the named works (Nos. 6–8) have more spirit and polish, they are no match for Pinnock and Marriner. Nos. 9–11, although vigorous (except for the flaccid Minuets), still lack finesse. Pleasing sound, but although these discs do not have to compete in a crowded market even at mid-price they are too expensive to do so.

Symphony 76 in E flat
*** TDK **DVD** DV-COWAND2. NDR SO, Wand (V/D: Andreas Missler-Morell) – BRUCKNER: *Symphony 6 **(*)*

A very straight and straightforward account of this Haydn symphony both from Wand and the orchestra and from the camera team. A pleasure to watch and hear.

Symphonies 80; 83 (Hen); 84; 87–89
(BB) *** ASV Resonance CD RSB 203 (2). LMP, Glover

Jane Glover's very winning Haydn recordings with the London Mozart Players have been consistently underrated since they first appeared in the late 1980s. They are consistently strong and energetic and fully characterized. *No. 80 in*

D minor begins as though it were a throwback to the *Sturm und Drang* period, but then at the end of the exposition Haydn gives a winning smile. In No. 83 Glover neatly articulates the 'clucking' second subject which gives the symphony its nickname, and the shapely theme and variations slow movement of No. 84 is most elegantly played. Similarly, Glover finds a warm serenity for the noble slow movement of No. 88, while No. 89 ends with a dance movement which contains delectable *strascinando* (dragging) passages, neatly managed here. Throughout outer movements these modern-instrument performances are as lively as you could wish, and the recording with its warm ambience is excellent. A genuine bargain.

Symphonies 82 (The Bear); 83 (The Hen); 84; 85 (La Reine); 86; 87 (Paris)

**(*) DHM/BMG 82876 60602-2 (3). VCM, Harnoncourt
(M) ** Sony (ADD) SM2K 89566 (2). NYPO, Bernstein

Harnoncourt is nothing if not unpredictable, and this set of the Haydn *Paris Symphonies* bears this out in the most exciting fashion. First, he takes every repeat in sight (even the second parts of main movements), including of course every section of the Minuets and Trios, and even the measured introduction to *La Reine*. These performances show this always vigorous and alive conductor at his most characterful and stimulating and, above all, both dramatic and warmly expressive in Haydn's always memorable slow movements. Tempi take unexpected turns, especially in Minuets and Trios, but the individuality of this music-making and its vitality are difficult to resist. If you are attracted to the lighter, vivacious style of period-instrument Haydn playing, then you may find Harnoncourt too strong and over-emphatic, and – dare one say it? – seriously lacking in charm. In that case, Kuijken and the OAE will be a much better recommendation (Virgin 5 61659), and they cost about a third of the price of this Deutsche Harmonia Mundi set. But there is more than one way of playing Haydn, and in his own way Harnoncourt is very convincing, for there is no lack of integrity or involvement.

Bernstein offers characterful performances, full of life and zest, with great warmth and sophisticated orchestral playing. Bernstein has great dynamic nuance too, and shows much attention to detail. The main snag is the recording, which, though basically full and vivid, offers rather strident strings when under pressure, and the whole sound-picture is not as ingratiating as Dorati's Decca set. At mid-price, it is hardly a bargain, nor do Sony opt for the more convenient slim-line packaging.

Symphonies 83 (Hen); 101 (Clock): 104 (London)

(B) *(*) EMI (ADD) 4 76889-2. BPO, Karajan

Karajan's EMI Haydn symphony recordings from the 1970s do not stand up very well today. Nos. 83 and 101, recorded in St Moritz in 1971, often bring playing of characteristic finesse, as in the neatly pointed second subject of the first movement of the *Hen* and the *Andante* of the *Clock*, and the Trios of the Minuets include attractive solo contributions from the woodwind. But the resonant sound prevents the sharpness of outline from a big band that we are now used to in this repertoire. In many ways the Beethovenian account of No. 104 is the most striking, but the heaviness persists. For Karajan aficionados only.

Symphonies 92 (Oxford); 94 (Surprise). Overture La Fedelta premiata

*** MDG **SACD** Surround Sound 1325-6. Austro-Hungarian Haydn O, A. Fischer

This coupling of two of the best-known of the later nick-named symphonies is not a spin-off from this orchestra's complete set of the Haydn symphonies for Nimbus but a live recording, made in Graz in 2004. The playing is outstandingly lively and alert, bringing out the drama of both works in high dynamic contrasts. The Graz acoustic is generous rather than intimate, but textures are admirably clear. The impact of the celebrated surprise, *fortissimo* on the timpani, in the fast-flowing *Andante* of No. 94 has rarely been as great, with the vital communication of a live event vividly caught. The galloping rhythms of the overture to *La fedelta premiata* are as exhilarating as anything in the symphonies, with valveless horns braying away. As a separate showcase for the conductor and orchestra, the disc readily wins its place, vividly recorded in Hybrid Multichannel SACD.

Symphonies 93–104 (London Symphonies)

(B) *** Decca 475 551-2 (4). LPO, Solti
(B) ** Ph. Duos 468 546-2 (2) (Nos. 93–94, 97, 99, 102–103); 468 927-2 (2) (95, 96, 98, 100–101 & 104). O of 18th Century, Brüggen

A very welcome return to Solti's *London Symphonies* survey. While it might be felt that Solti's way with some of the symphonies is sometimes a bit too uptight for Haydn, others unexpectedly glow in his hands, with the coupling of Nos. 93 and 99 (recorded in 1987) proving the pick of the bunch and receiving a ❂ on their initial release. The manner in this coupling is sunny and civilized; there is no lack of brilliance – indeed, the LPO are consistently on their toes – but the music-making is infectious rather than hard-driven. The lovely slow movement of No. 93 has both delicacy and gravitas, and that of No. 99 is serenely spacious. The Minuets are shown to have quite different characters, and the finales sparkle in the happiest manner.

The earliest symphonies recorded (1981) were the *Miracle* and the *Clock* and, although brilliantly played, were rather too taut to convey all Haydn's charm. Again, in Nos. 102 and 103, recorded a year later, even though the beauty and refinement of the LPO and the fine Decca recording cannot help but give pleasure, the tensions speak of the twentieth century rather than the eighteenth, with even the lovely *Adagio* of No. 102 failing quite to relax. In the *Surprise* and *Military Symphonies* (recorded 1984), the conductor stresses the brilliance and fire of the outer movements, which are again a bit hard-driven, but there is no lack of *joie de vivre*.

The recording, hitherto excellent, approaches demonstration standard in fullness and transparency; and this is even more striking in Nos. 95 and 104. Here (in recordings made in 1986), Solti found the perfect balance between energy and repose. The pacing is admirable and the LPO playing is smiling and elegant, yet full of bubbling vitality. No. 95 has a striking sense of cohesion and purpose, and there are few finer versions of No. 104. Solti uses a full body of strings and all the resources of modern wind instruments with the greatest possible finesse, yet the spontaneity of the music-making is paramount. The final symphonies, Nos. 97 & 98, were released in 1992, and they maintained the balance between Solti's boundless energy and Haydn's warmth and humour. These symphonies, now released in a bargain box (on four instead of five CDs) make a very stimulating set.

Frans Brüggen, so successful in his early career in the world of chamber music and as a recorder player, has proved disappointing in his most recent search for authenticity on the rostrum. His approach to the last symphonies of Haydn in particular brings remarkable contradictions of style. He is not helped by the resonant acoustic, which creates weighty textures, and a focus that is not always quite clean in fortissimos. Openings and first-movement allegros are generally portentous and large scale, generating almost a Beethovenian atmosphere, and although slow movements bring the restrained 'authentic' string style, the expansive moments often seem over-inflated. Finales are usually snappily rhythmic and the orchestral playing is of high quality, with fine wind solos, but the end result fails to convince.

Symphonies 93; 96 (Miracle); 98 in B flat
●— (BB) *** EMI Encore 3 41428-2. ECO, Tate

Consistently Tate chooses speeds that allow the sparkle and wit of Haydn's writing to come out naturally, as in the first movements of Nos. 96 and 98, and the finales too. Tate's pacing brings out Haydn's humour far more than anything faster and fiercer would do, and always crisp articulation ensures that the music sounds light and springy, especially in the Minuets. Slow movements too are admirably paced and imaginative in detail, and each of these three works has a fine one, beautifully played. Warm, well-balanced sound. A most attractive triptych.

Symphonies 100 (Military); 101 (Clock)
*** BBC Legends BBCL 4176-2. LPO, Jochum – HINDEMITH: *Symphonic Metamorphoses on Themes of Weber* ***

This BBC Legends disc of Haydn (recorded in 1973) and Hindemith (recorded in 1977) neatly encapsulates the special qualities involved in Jochum's two relationships with London orchestras, the LSO and the LPO, bringing out the contrasts. These Haydn performances of the *Military* and *Clock Symphonies* were given at the Royal Festival Hall in co-ordination with a series of recording sessions that DG was holding, in which Jochum recorded all 12 of the *London Symphonies*. It is fascinating to compare the results of the studio recordings and these live versions. As one might expect, the studio recordings are a degree more polished, a fraction more precise in ensemble; yet in compensation the joy of Haydn's inspiration, above all the rhythmic lift that Jochum was able to draw from the players, is even more striking in the live accounts.

CHAMBER MUSIC

8 Notturni for the King of Naples, Hob II/25–32 (Nos. 1–6 only, Hob II/25–6; 29–32)
(M) ** CPO 999 741-2. Consortium Classicum, Klöcker

These eight divertimenti, in three or four movements (although No. 6 has only two), were commissioned by King Ferdinand IV of Naples and written for the lira organizzata or, rather, a pair of them, for the king played in duet with his friend Norbert Hadrava, an Austrian diplomat. The lira comprised a keyboard and a revolving wheel and was really a modified hurdy-gurdy. It seems a pity that someone could not have managed a reconstruction of this seemingly fascinating instrument. As rescored for wind instruments this is the nearest Haydn came to writing wind divertimenti of the calibre of those by Mozart, and although this music is slight, it has much charm, with particularly sprightly finales.

Dieter Klöcker on CPO gets round the textural problem by using a pair of chamber organs placed to the left and right of his wind and string ensemble (two violas and a double-bass), to give an antiphonal effect. The result is piquantly appealing at first, but the continuing use of the upper range of the organs loses its novelty after a time, although the music-making itself is elegant and pleasing. In any case this CPO set is incomplete.

String quartets

String Quartets 43 in D min., Op. 42; 81; 82, Op. 77/1–2; 83, Op. 103
●— ✿ *** ASV Gold GLD 4010. The Lindsays

Haydn's last three *Quartets* are exceptionally well served on CD, with outstanding versions by the Kocian Quartet (Praga PR 250157) and by the Mosaïques on period instruments (Astrée E 8800). But these 'swan song' versions by the Lindsays are outstanding in every way and, with an engaging account of Op. 42 thrown in for good measure, this is not only generous but also one of their most cherishable records. The first movement of that work (in D minor, like Haydn's very last *Quartet*) is marked *Andante ed innocentamente*, and the Lindsays catch its innocence perfectly, while the elegance of the following *Allegretto* Minuet contrasts with the tranquil, meditative *Adagio cantabile*. This is exquisitely played, followed by a finale full of imitative bustle.

But it is in the Op. 77 *Quartets* that the Lindsays' response is most fully stretched. The bouncing lift of the opening *Allegro moderato* of the G major is irresistible, and the *Adagio* has wonderful expressive delicacy and dynamic subtlety, with the buoyant Minuet producing a surge of dancing energy in the remarkable Trio, and the rustic finale brimming with imaginative contrasts. How energetically, too, do the Lindsays play the Scherzo-Minuet of the F major, following with a concentrated *sotto voce* opening for the sublime *Andante*, with the work again vivaciously rounded off by its contrapuntal finale. Only two movements of the final *Quartet* were composed by the ailing composer (who was 72), but its *Andante grazioso* has an endearingly direct communication, and the minor-key Minuet brings a certain nostalgia, sensitively caught here. Altogether this is a splendid collection that, with Opus 42 placed third in the programme, makes a very satisfying concert. The recording is very real and immediate.

String Quartets 46 in E flat; 48 in F, Op. 50/3 & 5; 76 in D min.(Fifths), Op. 76/2; 83 in B flat, Op. 103
(B) ** Cal. (ADD) CAL 6267. Suk Qt

Fine performances from the Suk Quartet, warm and polished. They have obviously lived with this music and play it with a natural impetus. The analogue recording, however, is rather recessed and though the sound is pleasing most listeners will seek better-defined detail.

String Quartet 58 in C, Op. 54/2
*** Avie AV 2092. Szymanowski Qt – BACEWICZ: *Quartet 4* ***; DVOŘÁK: *Quartet 14* **(*)

A wonderfully polished account of the *C major Quartet* from the Szymanowski Quartet; indeed, their playing in the first movement can only be described as exquisite. The *Adagio* too is gently intense, but some listeners might find here that the players' warmth of response is almost too sensuously expressive for Haydn. But they are beautifully recorded, and this is difficult to resist.

String Quartets 72–74, Op. 74/1–3

*** Sup. Praga **SACD** Surround Sound PRD/DSD 250 212. Kocian Qt

*** ASV Gold GLD 4013. The Lindsays

As usual, the Lindsays are on top form with their vital, imaginative and highly spontaneous performances, which are among the best on record, and excellently balanced.

But the Kocians are pretty marvellous too. Their blending is a joy, without any loss of individuality among the players, and they are vital too, with finales sparkling irresistibly, especially the famous *Rider* rhythm of the G major. But what caps these performances are the beautifully played slow movements, especially of Nos. 73 and 74. The F major brings a delightfully light-hearted *Andante grazioso* and the G minor a profound account of the inspired *Largo assai*, its poised gravity perfectly judged and very affecting. Moreover, the realism of the Praga recording, with the back speakers carefully balanced to add just ambient effect, is astonishingly realistic. The Kodály Quartet must not be forgotten either, long recommended by us, and their recording, too, is very naturally balanced (Naxos 8.550396).

String Quartets 75; 76 (Fifths); 77 (Emperor); 78 (Sunrise); 79; 80, Op. 76/1–6 (Erdödy Quartets)

(B) *(**) Decca 475 6213 (2). Takács Qt

No – or, at any rate – few quarrels with the playing of the Takács Quartet here; they bring vitality and polish to these wonderful *Quartets*. Alas, Nos. 75–77 were recorded in the Schubertsaal of the Vienna Konzerthaus, and the excessive reverberation – very un-Decca-like – poses problems: their dynamic range seems less wide and their colour sounds more generalized than one expects from this group: as proof, *Quartets* Nos. 78–80, recorded a year later in London in sound far more characteristically warm and vivid from Decca, does justice to the performances. The sound on CD 1 means that this set of the Op. 76 *Quartets* cannot be strongly recommended.

PIANO MUSIC

(i) Divertimento (The Master and his Pupil) for piano duet, Hob XVII/2. Arietta with 12 Variations, Hob XVII/3; Capriccio in G, Hob XVII/1; Theme & Variations in C, Hob XVII/5; 20 Variations in G, Hob XVII/2; Variations on the Austrian Anthem (after Hob XIII/77)

(BB) *** Naxos 8.553972. Jandó (piano), (i) with Kollár

A fascinatingly diverting disc in all respects. The engaging if over-long piano duet, *Il Maestro lo Scolare* (with the two-part dialogue nicely separated on a single piano in the recording) was transcribed from a baryton trio in 1766/8. It opens with an echo of Handel's *Harmonious Blacksmith* and (obviously a teacher–pupil exercise) gets progressively more difficult. The closing section is a Minuet. The *Arietta* is also based on a Minuet – from Haydn's *String Quartet No. 20, Op. 9/2*, while the *Capriccio* takes a folksong as its basis with the unlikely title of *Acht Sauschnider müssen sein* ('It takes eight to castrate a boar') and the variations on the famous *Emperor* theme are a transcription of the slow movement of the string quartet with that nickname, Op. 76/1. Jenö Jandó plays everything in his freshly direct, classical manner and he is expertly joined by Zsuzsa Kollár in the four-handed work. The recording is clear and clean.

VOCAL MUSIC

Birthday Cantatas: Destatevi o miei fidi; Qual dubbio ormai. Celebration cantata: Da qual gioia improvvisa. Symphony 12 in E flat

*** HM HMC 90 1768. Stojkovic, Sunhae Im, Ciolek, Cologne Vocal Ens., Capella Colonsiensis, Spering or Kraemer

Another Haydn CD of great interest for its novelty. Haydn was only deputy Kapellmeiser at Esterházy when he wrote the two birthday cantatas to celebrate the nameday of his princely employer – in 1763 and 1764 respectively – with the texts offering the usual unalloyed praise. *Destatevi o miei fidi* provides a demanding duet for tenor and soprano; the other birthday cantata is for soprano solo and includes a virtuoso harpsichord part; did Haydn play it himself, one wonders. The third cantata celebrates the Prince's safe return from a distant journey and even includes a welcome chorus. With good solo singing, this is enjoyable enough; and if, like the *Symphony* from the same period, it is not great music, it shows how resourceful the budding young composer was.

The Creation (Die Schöpfung; in German)

🔵 (BB) *** EMI Gemini 3 50842-2 (2). Bonney, Blochwitz, Rootering, Wiens, Bär, Stuttgart RSO & Ch., Marriner

(BB) ** Warner Apex 2564 61593-2 (2). Gruberová, Protschka, Holl, Arnold Schoenberg Ch., VSO, Harnoncourt

From Sir Neville Marriner a wholly delightful account of *The Creation*, sung in German and recorded in Stuttgart in 1989, which, curiously, we have not previously encountered. In Part I Barbara Bonney is a truly angelic Gabriel, singing radiantly and matched by a warmly lyrical tenor Uriel, Hans Peter Blochwitz, while Jan-Hendrik Rootering's resonant bass Raphael is sonorously deep in timbre. In Part III Olaf Bär and Edith Wiens are a personable Adam and Eve. Wiens is not as beaming a soprano as Bonney (whose *Auf starken Fittiche* is a highlight at the opening of Part II) but she is charming enough. The Stuttgart choral singing is first rate and, from the atmospheric introduction onwards, Marriner directs the orchestra with plenty of life and character. The recording is very good indeed, and this bargain reissue can be recommended with enthusiasm.

Harnoncourt's earlier 1986 version with the Vienna Symphony Orchestra was recorded live. It follows the first printed edition of 1800, using the same size of forces as in performances of that date, with a gentle fortepiano replacing harpsichord in recitatives. Compared with the finest versions, the ensemble is on the rough side, and the singing of the male soloists is often rough too. The tenor, Josef Protschka, shouts Uriel's first entry but settles down after that; while by far the most distinguished singing of the set comes from Edita Gruberová, dazzling and imaginative, with slightly backward balance helping to eliminate the touch of hardness that microphones often bring out in her voice. The sound otherwise is full and clear.

Masses

Masses: (i) 3 in C: Missa Cellensis (Missa Sanctae Cecilia); (ii) 10 in C (Paukenmesse): Missa in tempore belli, Hob XXII/5 & 9; (iii) 13 in B flat (Schöpfungsmesse), Hob XXII/13

(BB) ** EMI Gemini 5 86519-2 (2). (i) Speiser, Watts, Equiluz, Nimsgern, Stuttgart Hymnus-Chorknaben, Keltsch Instrumental Ens., Wilhelm; (ii) Marshall, Watkinson, Lewis, Holl; (iii) Hendricks, Murray, Blochwitz, Hölle; (ii; iii) Leipzig R. Ch., Dresden State O, Marriner

Masses:(i) 7 in B flat: Missa brevis Sancti Joannis de Deo (Little Organ Mass);(ii) 9 in B flat (Heiligmesse): Missa Sancti Bernardi von Offida;(iii) 11 in D min. (Nelson): Missa in augustiis;(ii) 12 in B flat (Theresienmesse), Hob XXII/7, 10, 11 & 12

(BB) ** EMI Gemini 5 86546-2 (2). (i) Hendricks, Murray, Blochwitz, Hölle; (ii) Vaness, Soffel, Lewis, Salomaa; (iii) Marshall, Watkinson, Lewis, Holl; Leipzig R. Ch., Dresden State O, Marriner

Marriner's project to record the late Haydn *Masses* began in the mid-1980s but was never completed; so, to fill in on these bargain Gemini reissues, EMI have added a much earlier but fully acceptable recording of the *Saint Cecilia Mass*, made in Stuttgart in 1969 and conducted by Gerhard Wilhelm. It is a straightforward and unpretentious account, well sung by both the chorus and the excellent solo team, among whom Elisabeth Speiser and Kurt Equiluz stand out.

Marriner's series, although digitally recorded, in the end fell by the wayside as the performances could not compare with the competition, notably George Guest's earlier series on Decca. In the early *Missa brevis* (the *Little Organ Mass*), the *Paukenmesse* and the later *Schöpfungsmesse*, Marriner's fast speeds defied the weight of his forces, which was increased by the bass-heavy Dresden recording. Though the Leipzig Radio Chorus was sometimes stressed, as were the soloists, these are nevertheless enjoyably vigorous readings. The *Heiligmesse* and *Theresienmesse* were recorded together, and here this highly disciplined chorus are again on top form and rise superbly to Marriner's often challengingly fast speeds. Indeed, their ensemble in slow sections is sweeter than that of the soloists or even that of the orchestra. The solo singers are close-balanced so that the vibrato of the two women is exaggerated and the full quartet makes an ill-matched ensemble. Heard like this, these voices are not well suited to Haydn and the reverberation inflates what by latter-day standards is too hefty an orchestral sound. The *Nelson Mass* brings a perfectly acceptable performance with good soloists, and the Leipzig Choir is still on excellent and vigorous form. Here the ample Dresden acoustic does not prevent internal clarity, yet overall the effect is essentially cultured and a trifle bland.

Masses 7 (Little Organ Mass); 11 (Nelson)

(BB) (*) Naxos 8.554416. Loukianetz, Sima, Azesberger, Holzer, Hungarian R. and Television Ch., Esterházy Sinf., Drahos

Welcome as it is to have a super-bargain disc of Haydn *Masses*, this Naxos issue is disappointing, lacking the bite of more expensive rivals and falling seriously short in the singing of the soprano soloist, who is hard-toned and unsteady. It is not helped by the backward placing of the chorus.

Masses 7 (Little Organ Mass); 14 (Harmoniemesse)

** Hyp. CDA 66508. Winchester Cath., Brandenburg O, Hill

The distinctive point about David Hill's Hyperion disc is the use of boys' voices in fresh, lively performances, although they do not have quite the impact of rivals like Richard Hickox in his outstanding series of all the Haydn *Masses*, despite a superb quartet of soloists. Recorded in Winchester Cathedral in 1991, the balance of the choir behind the rest, coupled with the reverberant acoustic, brings a lack of pin-point clarity in the choral sound.

Masses 9 in B flat (Missa Sancti Bernadi von Offida) (Heiligmesse); 10 in C (Missa in tempore belli) (Paukenmsse). Insanae et vanae curae

*** Ph. 470 819-2. Lunn, Mingardo, Lehtipuu, Sherratt, Monteverdi Ch., E. Bar. Sol., Gardiner

This Philips coupling follows after Gardiner's outstanding pairing of the *Nelson* and *Theresien Masses* (470 286-2 – see our main volume), similarly dramatic and incisive, and his new but equally fine team of soloists and the Monteverdi Choir are again on top form. For his bonus this time, he gives us the motet, *Insanae et vanae curae*, which originally belonged with the oratorio *Il ritorno di Tobia* and now, sung in Latin instead of German, is given a spirited, biting performance to match the two main works. The Philips recording is admirably clear and clean, bringing splendid detail.

Masses 13 in B flat: Schöpfungsmesse (Creation Mass); 14 in B flat (Harmonienmesse)

*** Ph. 470 297-2. Ziesak, Lunn, Gruffydd Jones, Fink, Spicer, Mingardo, Prégardien, Butterfield, Busher, Lehtipuu, Widmer, Sherratt, Monteverdi Ch., E. Bar. Sol., Gardiner

This was the first of Gardiner's three Philips couplings of Haydn's last six great Masses and it set the seal on the excellence of the series, with its starry group of soloists and brightly dramatic choral singing. Comparison with Hickox on Chandos shows the latter the more infectious interpreter, Gardiner the more sharply dramatic, often with faster pacing to match. Yet both are very rewarding in their own chosen ways. The recording is excellent.

Mass 14 (Harmoniemesse); Te Deum for Maria Theresia, Hob XXIIIc/2

(B) ** DHM/BMG 74321 935492. Piau, Groop, Prégardien, Van der Kamp, Namur Chamber Ch., La Petite Bande, Sigiswald Kuijken

The *Harmoniemesse* sounds pleasingly fresh in the smaller-scale chamber-styled performance from Kuijken. He has a good team of soloists and they bring out the music's devotional nature in the more intimate moments. The Namur Choir (about two dozen strong) certainly sings with conviction in both works and is given a clear projection by the recording. This is enjoyable and authentic, but less than overwhelming.

The Seasons (Die Jahreszeiten; complete; in German)

(BB) *** Naxos 8.557600/1. Rubens, Karasiak, MacLeod, Leipzig Gewandhaus Chamber Ch. & CO, Schuldt-Jensen

Naxos follow up their very successful version of *The Creation* with this equally lively account of Haydn's last oratorio. Though the performers are different, the reading has very similar qualities to that earlier one. Three fresh, young soloists are bright and cleanly focused, with well-balanced chorus and chamber orchestra, unfazed by the conductor's generally brisk speeds. The very first dramatic chord has the timbre of a period performance, but in fact the Danish conductor, Morten Schuldt-Jensen, explains in a note that he seeks with modern instruments to adopt as many traits of period performance as possible, aiming for a compromise which is near the ideal. Certainly the timbre of the horns in the final choruses of the *Autumn* section has the open ring of valveless instruments, a glorious sound; and clarity of texture is an important element all through. No text is provided, only an indication how to download it on the internet, but there is a very detailed synopsis describing each number. However, at full price our first choice remains with Jacobs with the RIAS

Chamber Choir and the marvellous Freiburg Baroque Ensemble on Harmonia Mundi (✦ HMC 801829.30).

The Seven Last Words of Our Saviour on the Cross
*** Naïve V 5045. Piau, Sandhoff, Getchell, Van der Kamp, Accentus, Akademie für alte Musik, Berlin, Equilbey

Returning from England after his second visit to London, Haydn stayed in the Bavarian city of Passau, and there he heard a performance of his own *Seven Last Words*, which he had written in orchestral form, in an arrangement by the local Kapellmeister, Joseph Friebert, for voices and orchestra. Impressed, Haydn asked for a copy of the transcription and, returning to Vienna, he set about making his own version for soloists, chorus and orchestra, adding parts for clarinets and trombones, but using Friebert's devotional texts. He also added a second instrumental *Introduzione* between the fourth and fifth 'Words', scored for wind instruments alone. Later, he asked Baron Gottfried van Swieten, director of the Imperial Library, to revise the texts for a first performance in Vienna in 1796. The result is the work on the present CD, far more eloquent and expressively powerful than the orchestral original. It is superbly sung and played here, and beautifully recorded, to make an important addition to the Haydn discography.

OPERA

L'isola disabitata (complete)
** Opus 111 OP 30319 (2). Kammerlohr, Hermann, Lee, Zinasi, Academia Montis Regalis, De Marchi

De Marchi on Opus offers a fresh, lively reading with period instruments, providing a useful alternative. As one would expect from a period performance, speeds are fast, sometimes hectic, and the strings are often edgy. With clear, young soloists, not specially characterful, it is hardly a strong recommendation.

'*Haydn & Mozart* Discoveries': Arias from: *Acide e Galatea; Il desertore; La scuola de' gelosi; La vera costanza*
(M) **(*) Decca (ADD) 475 7169. Fischer-Dieskau, V. Haydn O, Peters – MOZART: *Arias* **(*)

'Haydn and Mozart Discoveries', the disc claims – and very delightful they are too, even if Haydn gets much less attention, with comparatively lightweight and simple pieces. Fischer-Dieskau is as thoughtfully stylish as ever, though it is a pity that he did not take more advice about the inclusion of appoggiaturas. Excellent (1969) recording.

HAYDN, Michael (1737–1806)

Flute Concerto in D
🔾⇥ (M) *** EMI 4 76863-2. Pahud, Berlin Haydn Ens. – J. HAYDN: *Flute Concerto; Scherzandi* ***

Emmanuel Pahud's superbly played account of Michael Haydn's enchanting little work is now reissued to represent Pahud as one of EMI's 'Great Artists of the Century'.

Trumpet Concerto in D
(B) *** Ph. Eloquence 468 207-2. André, Munich CO, Stadlmair – Joseph HAYDN; HUMMEL; Leopold MOZART: *Trumpet Concertos* ***

Michael Haydn's concerto, a two-movement concertante section of a seven-movement *Serenade*, has incredibly high

upper tessitura, but it offers no problems for Maurice André, who plays it with aplomb.

HEBDEN, John (1712–65)

6 Concertos for Strings (ed. Wood)
**(*) Chan. 8339. Cantilena, Shepherd

These concertos are Hebden's only known works, apart from some flute sonatas. Although they are slightly uneven, at best the invention is impressive. The concertos usually feature two solo violins and are well constructed to offer plenty of contrast. The performances here are accomplished, without the last degree of polish but full of vitality.

HELY-HUTCHINSON, Victor (1901–47)

Carol Symphony
(B) ** EMI (ADD) 7 64131-2. Guildford Cathedral Ch., Pro Arte O, Rose – QUILTER: *Children's Overture;* VAUGHAN WILLIAMS: *Fantasia on Christmas Carols* **

Hely-Hutchinson's *Carol Symphony* dates from the late 1920s. His first movement could do with a little judicious pruning, the Scherzo is quite effective and in the finale he gathers all the threads together and ends with a triumphal presentation of *O come, all ye faithful*. But it is the *Andante* that remains in the memory with its deliciously imaginative gossamer texture against which the solo harp embroiders *Nowell*. The performance here is lively and sensitive if not distinctive, but the close-miked recording is curiously dry and unexpansive, bearing in mind that the 1966 venue was Guildford Cathedral.

HERBERT, Victor (1859–1924)

Auditorium Festival March; Columbus Suite; Irish Rhapsody; Natoma: excerpts
**(*) Marco Polo 8.225109. Slovak RSO (Bratislavia), Brion

The longest piece here, the *Columbus Suite*, was also the composer's last major work and was premièred in 1903. Its four movements are all descriptive and have mild moments of interest (the *Murmurs of the Sea* brings nice orchestral effects), but it's all a bit thin really. The other works are more enjoyable. The *Irish Rhapsody*, with its haunting Irish folk-tunes running throughout and alternating pastoral and vigorous episodes, is really quite fun. The selections from *Natoma* – Herbert's one foray into grand opera – sound like a mixture of Wagner and Hollywood, with a tango halfway through! Its musical inspiration, the music of Native Americans, gives it an additional dash of local colour. The *Auditorium Festival March* (1901) is an exuberant piece quoting extensively from *Auld Lang Syne*, which sounds ready made for a Hollywood film of the 1930s. Enthusiastic performances and acceptable recording.

Naughty Marietta (highlights)
(B) **(*) CfP (ADD) 3 35988-2. Voss, Egan, New World Show O, Braden – ROMBERG: *Student Prince* (highlights); O. STRAUS: *Chocolate Soldier* (highlights) **(*)

Despite a limited success at its New York opening in 1910, *Naughty Marietta* reopened in 1912 with great success, and has frequently been revived ever since. The six numbers here are all good ones. Peter Egan as Captain Dick Warrington is a bit on the weak side; but it is a lively performance in bright (1961) sound.

HÉROLD, Ferdinand (1791–1833)

La Fille mal gardée (ballet; new version adapted by Peter Hertel) (Choreography: Heinz Spoerli, after Jean Dauberval)
*** DG **DVD** 073 4158. Kozlova, Jensen, Ris, Schläpfer, Spoerli, Basle Ballet, VSO, Lanchbery (Director: José Montes-Baquer)

The ballet *La Fille mal gardée* has had a fascinatingly long and varied history, and its origins as a subject for dance panto-mime go back over two centuries. The first version was created by the French choreographer, Jean Dauberval, with the familiar plot and farmyard setting, but initially with a different title; and it was taken to London in 1791. The music included popular French folk material and operatic airs of the time. But when it reached Paris in 1828 a new score was written for it by Hérold. Much of the music was his own, but he also borrowed from Rossini and later Donizetti. In 1864 yet another new score was commissioned from Peter Ludwig Hertel, which still included a good deal of Hérold's music.

In 1960 Sir Frederick Ashton staged his now familiar version with the Royal Ballet at Covent Garden, and for this John Lanchbery newly arranged the Hérold score that we know today (both from recordings and the splendid DVD included in our main volume). But for the Spoerli Basle production, yet another score was confected by Michel Damase, based on both Hérold and Hertel; it includes some of the original French folk and 'military' music. While the story remains broadly the same, the new music allows for varied and pretty added dances with something of a pastoral French folk style, and the soldiers too make their entry. Indeed, this Spoerli version is visually most attractive, allowing the principal dancers opportunities to mime the narrative pleasingly, and it provides plenty of leeway for charming and spectacular solos and *pas de deux*. The corps de ballet have a field day. The famous drag part of the heroine's continually thwarted mother, angrier than ever, remains, as does her famous clog dance. But the part of the rich farmer's son, Alain, is expanded and he is made more appealing, an innocent rather than a simpleton. The dancing of the princi-pals is splendid throughout, the farm scene makes a convincing and beautiful backcloth, and altogether this is a most enjoyable entertainment, with quite a few differences from the Frederick Ashton version. But once again John Lanchbery conducts with flair, the orchestra plays very elegantly, and is very well recorded. With excellent video direction, this is altogether recommendable, alongside the Royal Ballet's DVD.

HERSCHEL, William (1738–1822)

Symphonies 2 in D; 8 in C min.; 12 in D; 13 in D; 14 in D; 17 in C
*** Chan. **SACD** CHSA 5005; CHAN 10048. LMP, Bamert

Sir William Herschel, the astronomer who discovered the planet Uranus, was earlier a composer, who wrote no fewer than 24 symphonies and a dozen concertos for different instru-ments, before being given an allowance by George III so that he devote himself to astronomy full time. Each of these three-movement symphonies lasts around 11 minutes, with crisp, energetic outer movements framing rather less compelling

slow movements. Born in Hanover, he served in England in the Hanover Guards and later settled in Britain, first as director of music of the Durham Militia, and it was during this period that he wrote most of these symphonies. The writing for horn in particular reflects that experience, with pairs of horns used in all but two of the works here, usually joined by pairs of wood-wind instruments in various combinations. Matthias Bamert and the London Mozart Players prove ideal advocates for music that may not be very original but that fluently exploits a winning idiom with lively writing. Full, vivid sound, and also available in compatible SACD multi-channel format.

HERZ, Henri (1803–88)

Piano concertos 3 in D min., Op. 87; 4 in E, Op. 131; 5 in F min., Op. 180
*** Hyp. CDA 63537. Shelley, Tasmanian SO

Schumann in his music-criticism loudly disparaged the music of the Paris-based Henri (born Heinrich) Herz, sug-gesting with fair justice that he was just a note-spinner. These three piano concertos, written between 1835 and 1854, rely on amiable themes, which then inspire the composer to add tinkly elaborations with little in the way of genuine develop-ment. Nevertheless, in splendid, dedicated performances from Howard Shelley with the talented Tasmanian Symphony Orchestra, they make attractive listening, as long as one does not demand too much. Vivid sound. A worthwhile addition to Hyperion's 'Romantic Piano Concerto' series.

HERZOGENBERG, Heinrich (1843–1900)

Legends, Op. 62; Piano Quartet in B flat, Op. 95; String Trio in F, Op. 27/2
(M) *** CPO 999 710-2. Frölich, Belcanto Strings

Heinrich von Herzogenberg was born in Vienna, but was descended from a French aristocratic family. A connoisseur of Baroque music, a conductor of the Leipzig Bach-Verein and then a professor of composition at the Berlin Hochschule, he figures prominently in biographies of Brahms and of Clara Schumann. His wife, Elisabet, became a close confidante of Brahms in his later years. The centenary of his death was in 2000, and the appearance of this record serves to fill in our picture of him. All three pieces are so indebted to Brahms in their musical language that they can only *just* be said to lead an independent life. They are played very well by these artists, and the recording is lifelike and well balanced.

HESS, Nigel (born 1953)

East Coast Pictures; Global Variations; Thames Journey; Scramble!; Stephenson's Rocket; (i) To the Stars!. The TV Detectives; The Winds of Power
**(*) Chan. 9764. L. Symphonic Wind O, composer; (i) with children from Daubney Middle School, Bedford

Nigel Hess has made his name primarily as a composer for television and theatre. He knows how to score, and he has a ready fund of melody. This is demonstrated in *The TV Detectives*, which brings together five rather striking TV themes, including 'Dangerfield', 'Wycliffe' and 'Hetty Wainthrop Investigates'. Of the concert music here, easily the most impressive piece is the flamboyant *To the Stars!*, which gets a real lift-off from the vocal energy of the children of Daubney Middle School. *Thames Journey* opens with trickling woodwind at its source, like Smetana's *Vltava*, and then introduces a Wiltshire folk melody on the horn as its main theme; but overall it is little more than a well-crafted potpourri, with *Greensleeves* and later *The Lass of Richmond Hill* also introduced. The three *East Coast Pictures* evoke the eastern seaboard of the USA, but are curiously without any strong American colouring. *Stephenson's Rocket* is rugged and vigorous, but not much of a train imitation. *The Winds of Power* is more evocative but rather loosely held together. *Scramble!* is more succinct and celebrates the Battle of Britain vividly enough. Indeed, all these works have plenty of vitality, even if they are not really distinctive. They are brilliantly played here under the composer, and are given excellent Chandos sound.

HILDEGARD of Bingen (1098–1179)

Chants
*** Lyrichord LEMS 8027. Gentile, Drone Ch.

The famous medieval legend of Saint Ursula, daughter of a British king, tells of a three-year pilgrimage to Rome with 11,000 other women (in fact more likely a party of 11, expanded in the storytelling), who were slaughtered on their return journey by Attila the Hun for refusing to become concubines, and were thus martyred. Hildegard's chants in this collection reflect her response to their sacrifice. Norma Gentile sings them radiantly, and they soar up over a constantly sustained drone choral pedal. Beautifully recorded, but not to be played all at once, this collection is one of the more memorable CDs of Hildegard's very remarkable and individual melismas.

Chants, Hymns and Sequences: *Ave generosa; Caritas Abundat; Columba aspexit; Et ideo; O clarissima mater; O Ecclesia; O Euchan columba; O Ierusalem, aura civitatis; O Pastor animarum; O presul vere civitatis; O virdisima virga; O virga diadema; Unde Quocumque*
*** Delos DE 3219. Theil, Montano, Eaton, Visconte, Women of the Voices of Ascension, Keene

This is a richly enjoyable compilation on all counts. Dennis Keene, the conductor, makes the point that the performances from the Voices of Ascension are 'pure, without any contemporary vocal or instrumental additions'. He has an excellent female group and his soloists sing very beautifully, bringing out the music's often richly sensuous beauty. Most of the items are sung by one or other of the soloists, the others by either a soprano or alto vocal group, producing added tonal amplitude. Many of the numbers are Marian tributes, and the most astonishing is *Ave generosa*, which portrays the Virgin as a sexual creature seducing God to be the father of her divine son: 'How he revelled in your charms! how your beauty warmed to his caresses till you gave your breast to his child.' *Ecclesia, Et ideo* and *Unde Quocumque* are all associated with the story of Saint Ursula and the martydom of the Virgin Maids. No wonder women listeners respond so readily to this rapturous music, beautifully recorded here.

'*Heavenly Revelations*': Hymns, sequences, antiphons, responds
(BB) ** Naxos 8.550998. Oxford Camerata, Summerly

The Oxford Camerata offer a simple presentation, alternating female and male voices in consecutive works. The opening female melisma, *O Euchari* ('Eucharius, you walked in the paths of happiness when you remained with the Son of God') has a striking recurring melodic line and establishes the group's unpretentious, flowing style. Then follow two eulogies to the Virgin Mary, the first a rather dark *Alleluia* from the men, followed by a soaring female tribute, *Ave generosa* ('Hail noble one, shimmering and unpolluted girl'). There is no doubt that this music suits the Oxford female voices best (the later male praise for the Trinity here lacks any sense of euphoria), and the closing accolade to the Virgin from the women certainly has a serene beauty. The conductor's restraint is palpable, there is very little feeling of ecstasy here.

Vision (The music of Hildegard; arranged and recomposed by Richard Souther)
*(**) EMI 5 55246-2. Van Evera, Sister Fritz (with chorus, instrumental contributions & synthesized rhythm)

Richard Souther's way-out recomposed versions are precociously and recklessly inauthentic, even including instrumental numbers (*The living light*, and *Only the Devil laughed* are typical titles). The sophisticated rock style amplifies the music's sensuous, hypnotic, melodic flow, adding all kinds of extra-instrumental vocal and synthesized nourishment, with echo-chamber effects plus exotic live percussion. But Souther is obviously deeply involved in this very personal enterprise, and he has the advantage of the illustrious singing of Emily Van Evera, who really understands this repertoire, having also recorded it under authentic circumstances. Her beautiful voice is close-miked, 'pop style', unabashedly flattered with an acoustic halo. The programme opens with *O virga ac diadema purpure regis*, included on the Naxos disc (8.550998 – see above), but the effect is extravagantly different. Certainly the emotional power of the music and its innate melodiousness project vividly. The CD's title number, *Vision* (*O Euchari*) (also included in Jeremy Summerly's programme on Naxos) is heard twice, ending the programme in a more elaborate, extended version. This is a disc to either wallow in or hate. Full translations are included.

HILL, Alfred (1870–1960)

Symphony 5 in A min. (The Carnival); Symphony 10 in C (Short Symphony); A rêverie; As Night Falls; Regrets; Tribute to a Musician
(BB) *** Naxos 8.223538. Queensland SO, Lehmann

The Australian composer Alfred Hill was born in Melbourne, but like most musicians of the period he studied in Leipzig. He moved to New Zealand in 1902 but returned to Australia in 1915 as a professor at the New South Wales Conservatory. His music is little known outside Australia, so this budget price disc offers an economical way of satisfying your curiosity. He is unusual in having spent various periods of his life composing exclusively in one genre – first stage works, then changing to chamber music (there are 17 string quartets) and finally turning to orchestral music. What is even more unusual is that of his 13 symphonies, 12 are orchestral versions of his string quartets. Hill was a considerable scholar who did a great deal of research into Maori and aboriginal Australian music. The writing is highly accomplished and very professional and you would be hard pressed to guess the quartet origins. The invention is fertile but not particularly memorable, and there is the occasional whiff of Delius. All the same, it is good to make the acquaintance of someone who is only a name these days, and collectors can be assured that the music is well served by both performers and engineers.

HINDEMITH, Paul (1895–1963)

(i; ii) *Piano Concerto;* (iii; iv) *Concert Music for Viola & Large Chamber Orchestra, Op. 48;* (i; ii) *Kammermusik 2, Op. 36/1*
*** First Edition (ADD) FECD 0022. Louisville O, with (i) Smith; (ii) Luvisi; (iii) Mester; (iv) Hillyer

Although the orchestral playing is not in the luxury class, it has dedication, and the repertoire is of exceptional interest. The *Piano Concerto* (1945) is never heard in the concert hall and we know of only one other recording of it. Highly imaginative and beautifully laid out, its inspiration is on a high level and textures are lucid and transparent. Lee Luvisi and the Louisville players are convincing exponents. The present issue also contains the first recording of the *Concert Music for Viola and Large Chamber Orchestra,* Op. 48, which Hindemith wrote in 1930. There are other, more recent recordings listed in our main volume, but this holds its own quite well. This valuable issue is completed by the familiar and oft-recorded *Kammermusik,* Op. 36, No. 1.

Piano Concerto
**(*) First Edition (ADD) LCD 002. Luvisi, Louisville O, Smith (with LAWHEAD: *Aleost* *(*)) – ZWILICH: *Symphony 2* **

Although the CPO recording (listed in our main volume) upstages the earlier recording by Lee Luvisi and the Louisville Orchestra, they nevertheless give a very good account of themselves and are more than adequately recorded.

Symphonic Metamorphoses on Themes of Weber
*** BBC Legends BBCL 4176-2. LSO, Jochum – HAYDN: *Symphonies 100 & 101* ***

Working with the LSO brought out quite a different aspect of Jochum's work in Britain. He was not best known for performing twentieth-century music, but here (as in Haydn) he brings out the joy of what might be regarded as Hindemith's most extrovert work. What Jochum relishes is the colour, brilliance and humour in the way Hindemith orchestrates the Weber themes, giving the music swaggering flamboyance, underlining the sharp contrasts of timbre. The LSO, then as now acknowledged as the most brilliant of the London orchestras, respond with virtuoso playing, with horn and timpani in particular having a wonderful time.

PIANO MUSIC

Berceuse; In einer Nacht, Op. 15; Kleines Klavierstück; Lied; 1922 Suite, Op. 26; Tanzstücke, Op. 19
**(*) Marco Polo 8.223335. Petermandl

Exercise in 3 Pieces, Op. 31/I; Klaviermusik, Op. 37; Series of Little Pieces, Op. 37/II; Sonata, Op. 17; 2 Little Piano Pieces
** Marco Polo 8.223336. Petermandl

Ludus Tonalis; Kleine Klaviermusik, Op. 45/4
** Marco Polo 8.223338. Petermandl

Piano Sonatas 1–3; Variations
** Marco Polo 8.223337. Petermandl

Hans Petermandl is an expert guide in this repertoire and presents it with real sympathy for, and understanding of, the idiom; his performances are very persuasive. The textures in Hindemith's piano music are often unbeautiful and less than transparent and, although neither the piano nor the acoustic of the Concert Hall of Slovak Radio is outstanding, the sound is perfectly acceptable.

HOFFMANN, E. T. A. (1776–1822)

(i) *Harp Quintet;* (ii) *Piano Trio (Grand) in E;* (iii) *6 Duettini Italiani* (for soprano, tenor and piano)
*** CPO 999 309-2. (i) Moretti, Parisii Qt; Beethoven Trio, Ravensburg; (iii) Mields, Kabow, Brunner

E. T. A. Hoffmann is indelibly linked to Offenbach's *Tales of Hoffmann,* but it is good that recordings of his music emerge from time to time. CPO have made a speciality of recording music of the early romantic era, and they always seems to come up trumps. And so they have here, in this well-produced CD, with copious and informative sleeve-notes. The *Piano Trio* of 1809 is the most meaty work here, with robust themes and dynamic contrasts; it is clear that, as on all composers of this period, Beethoven has made his influence felt here. Some will count it a weak point that it lacks a proper slow movement with an ensuing central emotional core, which we have come to expect. However, there is plenty to enjoy in the lively writing and enthusiastic playing throughout its 22 minutes. The *6 Duettini italiani,* written in 1812, with their simple and attractive vocal lines in the Italian manner, enter into the world of the fashionable drawing-room: there is lovely interplay between the tenor and soprano parts, and they are eminently entertaining: it would make a good novelty to hear in a live recital.

The *Harp Quintet* is an undemanding charmer; with its minor-key, florid writing, it is most ingratiating, with an especially attractive finale. The performances and recording are all first class.

HOFFMEISTER, Franz (1754–1812)

Clarinet Quintets: in A; B flat; D; E flat
*** CPO 999 812-2. Klöcker, Vlach Qt, Prague

Hoffmeister's *Clarinet Quintets* bubble on amiably for the duration of this 75-minute CD. There is nothing deep or profound here, but this is *galant,* light music of quality, well constructed and brimming with geniality and melodic resource. The first three *Quintets* are in three movements, each with a fairly substantial first movement, a simple *Adagio,* and fizzing finales, either allegros or Minuets. The *Adagio* of the *D major Quintet* is one of the few places where a minor key is allowed in for any length of time, and the *E flat Quintet* breaks with tradition by having five movements, but maintains the appeal of its companions. Performances are first rate, with creamy-toned Dieter Klöcker taking all the virtuosity in his stride. The recording, too, is warm and well balanced.

HOFFSTETTER, Romanus (1742–1815)

String Quartets: 1 in C; 2 E (attrib. Haydn as *Op. 3/1–2*)
(BB) *** Naxos 8.555703. Kodály Qt (with HAYDN: *Cassations, Hob II/21–22* (arr. for *String Quartet*) ***)

String Quartets 3 in G; 4 in B flat; 5 in F (Serenade); 6 in A (attrib. HAYDN, as *Op. 3/3–6*)
(BB) *** Naxos 8.555704. Kodály Qt

Romanus Hoffstetter, if it was he who composed these works, seems fated never to have his name on them, even though H. C. Robbins Landon discovered that 'Signor Hoffstetter' was inscribed on the plates from which the original parts were printed. Haydn never questioned their authenticity when Pleyel included them in the complete edition of his string quartets.

There is much to admire in these works, whoever the composer might have been. They are elegant, neatly composed works with lively outer movements, gentle, graceful slow movements and the kind of lilting, intoxicating Minuets that are an integral part of Austrian music of this period. The *C major* stands out for its resourceful opening *Fantasia con variazioni* and its charmingly wistful *Andante*. But it is the *F major* that is justly the most famous, for not only does it have the unforgettable 'Serenade' for its *Andante cantabile*, but also another *galant* lilting tune as the second subject of the opening movement, and another amiable *Scherzando* finale.

The Kodály Quartet's performances are in every way first class, treating the music with all the finesse that is its due, and winningly acknowledging its vitality and charm. The recording is most real and vivid.

HOFMANN, Leopold (1738–93)

Flute Concertos Vol. 1: in G (Badley), G2; D, D1; A, A2; D, D6
(BB) *(*) Naxos 8.554747. Seo, Nicolaus Esterházy Sinfonia, Drahos

Flute Concertos Vol. 2: in: D (Badley), D3 & D4; E min., e1; G, G3
(BB) *(*) Naxos 8.554748. Seo, Nicolaus Esterházy Sinfonia, Drahos

Hofmann's flute concertos date from the 1760s and '70s, all following the customary three-movement slow–fast–slow form. The music is as elegant and as well written as you would expect from a competent Kapellmeister and successful composer of his period (he wrote over 60 concertos). But it does not always engage the listener's attention; no great, distinctive voice emerges. As so often with works of this kind, the minor-keyed concertos are the most enjoyable. Kazunori Seo plays competently, and so, of course, does the orchestra, but a more assertive direction could be imagined – there are moments of blandness here. Decent enough sound.

Sinfonias: in B flat; in C; in D; in F; in F
(BB) **(*) Naxos 8.553866. N. CO, Ward

Leopold Hofmann was one of the earliest composers who consistently wrote four-movement symphonies with both a slow introduction and minuets. He preceded Haydn in this respect. Incidentally, for a brief period in 1791 Mozart acted as an assistant to him, doubtless in the hope of receiving preferment when Hofmann died. The five symphonies recorded here show him to be lively and fresh, though no one could pretend that his music plumbs great depths – or indeed is consistently interesting. The performances are very alert and sprightly, but the recording, though distinguished by clarity and presence, is handicapped by a rather dry acoustic.

HOL, Richard (or Rijk) (1825–1904)

Symphonies 1 in C min.; 3 in B flat, Op. 101
*(**) Chan. 9796. Hague Residentie O, Bamert

The son of an Amsterdam milkman, Richard (or Rijk) Hol was an influential figure in the second half of the nineteenth century, both as a conductor and as a teacher. He was prolific, and like Brahms he wrote four symphonies, but they are nearer to Schumann in their musical ethos, although the scoring owes more to Brahms and Mendelssohn, who provided the inspiration for the engaging Scherzo that is the highlight of the later, B flat major work. The melodic invention is somewhat conventional but is lyrical and pleasing throughout each symphony here. R. L. feels that, whatever may be said of his originality or importance, Hol was a *real* symphonist who has total command over his material and has a sense of architecture and pace. For E. G., the orchestral writing is attractive, but the musical material hardly deserves such extended treatment, with too many passages depending on empty gestures, with trite repetitions and sequences, and melodies that turn back on themselves. For I. M. this is not music he would wish to return to very often. However, we are all agreed that the performances, from a first-class orchestra who are naturally at home in the repertoire, are warmly sympathetic, and the full-bodied Chandos sound presents the composer's orchestration persuasively.

HOLBORNE, Anthony (c. 1560–1602)

Pavans, Galliards, Almains
*** HM HMX 2907238. The King's Noyse, O'Dette

In 1599 Anthony Holborne published a collection of his 'Pavans, Galliards, Almains and other Short Airs', containing 65 dances for five-part consort, which he suggested could be played on 'viols, violins, or other musical wind instruments'. Most of the pieces on this CD come from this anthology and are stylishly and warmly played by a string group, but with the occasional solo from Paul O'Dette on lute or cittern. The programme is arranged under the title 'My Self' and is subdivided into biographical sections: 'His happy youth . . . The passionate playfellow falls in love, is married and the fruit of love arrives complete with cradle and lullabie . . . He unexpectedly falls sicke, very sicke and dies . . . We follow his soul to Paradise'. But this is just a charming conceit for, although the titles of many of the pieces reflect the described events, they are not directly associated with them. Nevertheless, it makes for an attractive and varied programme, very well played and recorded.

HOLBROOKE, Joseph (1878–1958)

(i) *Piano Quartet in G min., Op. 21;* (ii) *String Sextet in D, Op. 43;* (iii) *Symphonic Quintet 1 in G min., Op. 44*
** Marco Polo 8.223736. New Haydn Qt. with (i; iii) Hegedüs; (ii) Papp, Devich

Although the music here never falls below a certain level of melodic fluency and is expertly crafted, little of it remains in the memory. The *String Sextet* makes the most immediate and positive impact but, after the CD has come to an end, one realizes why Holbrooke has not stayed the course. The fine Hungarian ensemble play these pieces with appropriate conviction and ardour. Decent recording, much better than for the orchestral disc.

HOLLOWAY, Robin (born 1943)

Second Concerto for Orchestra, Op. 40
*** NMC D015M. BBC SO, Knussen

Holloway's *Second Concerto* is a richly imaginative score and shows a sensitivity of high quality, as well as a considerable mastery of instrumental resource. The *Concerto* is a work of substance that is well worth getting to know, and it is well served by the BBC Symphony Orchestra and Oliver Knussen. The engineers produce a better sound from the Maida Vale Studios than we have heard on any other occasion.

(i) *Romanza for Violin & Small Orchestra, Op. 31;* (ii) *Sea-surface Full of Clouds, Op. 28*
*** Chan. 9228. (i) Gruenberg; (ii) Walmsley-Clark, Cable, Hill, Brett, Hickox Singers; City of L. Sinfonia, Hickox

Both works recorded here show Holloway's sensitivity to colour and marvellous feeling for the orchestra. *Sea-surface Full of Clouds* begins luminously, rather like Szymanowski, and has an at times magical atmosphere. There is an affecting and consuming melancholy about the *Romanza* for violin and orchestra. A composer of a refined intelligence and real sensibility.

HOLMÈS, Augusta (1847–1903)

Andromeda (symphonic poem); *Ireland* (symphonic poem); (i) *Ludus pro patria: Night & Love. Overture for a Comedy; Poland* (symphonic poem)
*** Marco Polo 8.223449. Rheinland-Pfalz PO, Friedmann; (i) Davin

Augusta Holmès was from an Anglo-Irish family that had settled in France. She was a person of remarkable gifts for, apart from her musical talents, she was an accomplished painter and wrote well. Although the *Overture for a Comedy* (1876) is trite, *Andromeda* is quite striking. It is by far the best piece on the disc, and the best scored, though limitations in Holmès's technique are evident. But this is music of much interest – and its composer was obviously no mean talent. She has been well served by the Rheinland-Pfalz Philharmonic under Samuel Friedmann. The recordings, too, are eminently satisfactory.

HOLST, Gustav (1874–1934)

Invocation for Cello and Orchestra, Op. 19/2
🎵 *** Nim. NI 5763. Wallfisch, RLPO, Dickins – BRIDGE: *Oration;* ELGAR: *Cello Concerto ***

Holst's *Invocation* comes from 1911 and pre-dates *The Planets.* Indeed in her book on her father, Imogen Holst spoke of it 'trying out some of the ideas for the texture of Venus'. It is a highly attractive and lyrical piece, with a big central climax, finely realized here, and a valuable addition to the catalogue. Julian Lloyd Webber recorded it for RCA some years ago, but this has long been deleted. However, the new version is in every way admirable, with some touching solo playing from Wallfisch, and it is splendidly recorded.

The Planets (suite), *Op. 32*
(BB) *** HMV (ADD) 5 86733-2. LSO & Ch., Previn –
    VAUGHAN WILLIAMS: *Serenade to Music **(*)

(B) **(*) DG Entrée 477 5010. Chicago SO & Ch., Levine –
    VAUGHAN WILLIAMS: *Greensleeves & Tallis Fantasias ***
** Häns. 93.043. Stuttgart RSO (with Ch.), Norrington –
    ELGAR: *Serenade for Strings ***

Previn's 1973 set of *Planets,* recorded in the Kingsway Hall, shows EMI's analogue engineering at its most impressive, an outstandingly attractive version, exceptionally clear and vivid, with many of Holst's subtleties of orchestral detail telling with greater point than on almost any other disc. The performance is basically traditional, yet it has an appealing freshness and is marginally more imaginative than Boult's account, with which it has much in common. Its new coupling is not particularly apt but certainly enterprising.

On DG, the sumptuous acoustics of Orchestra Hall, Chicago, make a resonantly atmospheric setting for the ferocity of the orchestral attack in Levine's exciting account of *Mars* and add bloom to the translucent purity of *Venus,* while bringing a glowing palette of colour to *Mercury,* played with graceful virtuosity and exuberance. *Jupiter,* with rollicking horns and a richly sonorous statement of the famous central melody, is also appropriately sumptuous, but the textural amplitude means that *Saturn* and *Uranus,* both weightily expansive, are less contrasted than usual. The Chicago Symphony Chorus make a bleakly atmospheric contribution to *Neptune.* An enjoyable performance then, with plenty of impact, and certainly suitable for DG's Entrée label, designed as a 'first step' into the world of classical music; but the snag is that the Vaughan Williams couplings are disappointingly unidiomatic.

Very well played and recorded, with complex textures clarified, Norrington's reading of *The Planets* is of interest as an example of a German orchestra tackling English music, but the result is literal rather than idiomatic. *Mars* is very slow and emphatic, leading to an account of *Venus* that is steady and meticulous rather than poetic. *Mercury* and *Jupiter* then sound a little cautious, with the big tune of *Jupiter* not as legato as usual, with detached phrasing. The other three movements at steady speeds are also too metrical to convey the evocative overtones that Holst requires, though the offstage chorus (unnamed) sings most beautifully in the final movement, *Neptune.*

VOCAL MUSIC

(i) *Hymns from the Rig Viga;* (ii) *6 Early Songs;* (ii; iii) *4 Songs for Voice & Violin;* (iv) *12 Humbert Wolfe settings;* (ii) *The Heart Worships; Margret's Cradle Song*
(BB) *** Naxos 8.557117. (i) Maltman; (ii) Gritton; (iii) Fuller (violin); (iv) Langridge; all with Steuart Bedford (piano)

Naxos have enterprisingly picked up a disc of rare Holst vocal repertoire, originally issued on the Collins label. Apart from the comparatively well-known, very Holstian and mystically atmospheric *Hymns from the Rig Viga,* sung sensitively (if with a slightly intrusive vibrato) by Christopher Maltman, the most striking songs are the Humbert Wolfe settings, in which Philip Langridge is in his element. But the star performer here is Susan Gritton, persuasive in the early songs but at her very finest in the *Four Songs for Voice and Violin,* set to medieval lyrics, with Louisa Fuller a responsive partner. Throughout, Steuart Bedford is thoroughly at home in the piano accompaniments, and the recording is excellent.

HOLT, Simon (born 1958)

... era madrugada ...; Shadow Realm; Sparrow Night; (i)
Canciones
*** NMC Doo8. (i) Kimm; Nash Ens., Friend

Regularly Simon Holt has found inspiration in Spanish
sources, particularly Lorca, and two of these four pieces are
fine examples – ... *era madrugada* ..., a sinister evocation of a
Lorca poem about a man found murdered in the hour just
before dawn (*madrugada*). Like the other three pieces, it was
written for the Nash Ensemble, who here under Lionel Friend
respond superbly to Holt's virtuoso demands. Fiona Kimm is
the formidable mezzo soloist in three Spanish settings, *Canciones*; but rather more approachable are the two highly
atmospheric instrumental works, *Shadow Realm* and *Sparrow
Night*, which round the disc off. These two also bring sinister
nightmare overtones. The superb recording is engineered by
Holt's fellow-composer, Colin Matthews.

HOLTEN, Bo (born 1948)

(i) *Clarinet Concerto* (1987); (ii) *Sinfonia Concertante for
Cello & Orchestra* (1985–6)
*** Chan. 9272 (i) Schou; (ii) Zeuten; Danish Nat. RSO;
cond. (i) Panula; (ii) Graf

Bo Holten's *Clarinet Concerto* is certainly appealing. The
Sinfonia Concertante comes from a broadcast of 1987 and is
long on complexity (36' 6") and short on substance, but there
are sufficient moments of poetic vision to encourage one to
return to it. It is played with great zest and conviction by
Morten Zeuten (cellist of the Kontra Quartet), and the
recording has exemplary presence and clarity.

HONEGGER, Arthur (1892–1955)

Les Aventures du Roi Pausole: Overture; Ballet. (i) *Cello
Concerto. Pastoral d'été; Pacific 231; Rugby; The Tempest:
Prélude*
(BB) (***) Dutton mono CDBP 9764. Grand SO, composer,
(i) with Marechal (with JAUBERT: *Ballade.* PIERNÉ:
Ramuntcho)

Apart from the *Cello Concerto*, which was recorded in Paris
during the war, these recordings were all made in 1930 and
have great immediacy of feeling, in particular the *Prélude* to
The Tempest, which has a frenzied intensity that is thrilling.
Maurice Marechal was the dedicatee of the concerto, composed in 1928, and he plays it committedly. After the Second
World War Honegger recorded the *Symphonie liturgique*, and
we hope that Dutton will turn their attention to that in due
course.

Cello Concerto
** MDG 0321 0215-2. Schmid, NW German PO, Roggen –
BLOCH: *Schelomo* **

Ulrich Schmid and the Nordwestdeutsche Philharmonie
under the Swiss conductor Dominique Roggen give a dedicated account of Honegger's delightful *Cello Concerto*. All the
same, at only 42 minutes' playing time, this would be distinctly uncompetitive even at bargain price, let alone premium rate.

Prélude pour Algavaine et Sélysette; (i) *Suite archaïque*
(M) **(*) First Edition mono/stereo FECD-1906. Louisville O,
Mester; (i) Robert Whitney – IBERT: *Bacchanale*, etc.

During the 1950s the Louisville Orchestra embarked on an
enlightened and ambitious scheme of commissioning and
then recording new works by contemporary composers,
including Blacher, Villa-Lobos, Henry Cowell, Hilding Rosenberg and Edmund Rubbra. The *Prélude pour Algavaine et
Sélysette* (1917) is Honegger's first orchestral piece and shows
that he is already his own man. It is highly imaginative and
exerts quite a strong spell. The *Suite archaïque* is a Louisville
commission and comes from 1951, at about the time of the
Fifth Symphony, of which there is the occasional reminder.
Rewarding pieces, and on the whole decently played: the
Prélude was recorded in 1969 (and is mono) and the *Suite* in
1961.

*Symphonies 1; 2 for Strings with Trumpet Obbligato; 3
(Symphonie liturgique); 4 (Deliciae Basiliensis); 5 (Di tre re);
Symphonic movements: 1, Pacific 231; 2, Rugby*
●─ (BB) *** Warner Apex 2564 62687-2 (2). Bav. RSO, Dutoit

Dutoit's inexpensive Apex set is an appealingly economical
way of aquiring excellent, modern, digital recordings (dating
from 1982) of the five symphonies, plus two of the *Symphonic
Movements* (recorded three years later). In Dutoit's hands the
phrasing of the Bavarian orchestra has both dignity and
eloquence. He gives thoroughly idiomatic accounts of both
the *Liturgique* and '*Di tre re*' *Symphonies*. In the *Fifth* he does
not galvanize the orchestra into playing of the same volcanic
fire and vitality that Serge Baudo secures from the Czech
Philharmonic Orchestra in the alternative Supraphon set (11
1566-2), but the Warner recording is fresher and more
detailed. Both *Pacific 231* and *Rugby* are well done; although
the latter may be found a little genteel, the playing and
recording are more than adequate compensation.

VOCAL MUSIC

Jeanne d'Arc au bûcher
** Cascavelle VEL 3024 (2). Petrovna, Lonsdale, Dominique,
Maîtrise des Haute-de-Seine, Ch. de Rouen-Haute-
Normandie, O Symphonie Français, Petitgirard

Though strong on atmosphere, Laurent Petitgirard on Cascavelle takes a rather measured approach. Although he gets
generally good results from his forces and has the benefit of
first-rate recorded sound, Ozawa is to be preferred both
artistically and as a recording. The Cascavelle set offers two
booklets, one in French, the other in German, with 36 pages
of artist and session photos but no translations into English,
Italian or Spanish. DG offered a four-language booklet as well
as an authoritative note by Harry Hallbreich. That set also
accommodates the work on one CD, while this new version
from Cascavelle runs to two. Of course, this extraordinary
piece still casts a strong spell and if you can't find the Ozawa
this is better than nothing.

HORNEMAN, Christian Frederik Emil (1840–1906)

Aladdin Overture; Ouverture héroïque: Helteliv; (i) *Gurre
(incidental music)*
*** Chan. 9373. (i) Päevatalu, Danish R. Ch.; Danish RSO,
Schønwandt

Horneman is an altogether delightful composer, and the music recorded here deserves the widest dissemination. The incidental music to Holger Drachmann's play, *Gurre*, the major work on the disc, is light-textured and full of charming, gracious invention and is beautifully scored. It is quite enchanting, particularly in such persuasive hands; and the baritone, Guido Päevatalu, sings his simple strophic songs with great character. The other two pieces, *Heltcliv* ('A Hero's Life') and the *Aladdin Overture* are the only purely orchestral works Horneman ever wrote: the *Aladdin Overture* is his first; it shows a real flair for colour. This is a most enjoyable disc, beautifully played and recorded. Strongly recommended.

HOTTETERRE, Jacques (1674–1763)

(i) *6 Trio Sonatas, Op. 3;* (ii) *Suite for 2 Treble Recorders without Continuo in D min., Op. 4*

(M) ** Teldec (ADD) 3984 26797-2. (i) Boeke, Van Hauwe, Möller, Van Asperen; (ii) Brüggen, Boeke

All the music gathered here was published in 1712. The *Trio Sonatas* are agreeable enough and are variously scored for pairs of treble recorders or voice flutes (Nos. 2 and 5), of which the latter works come off best here. Truth to tell, although the performances are authentic, complete with *notes inégales* (where the first note of two successive quavers is lengthened and the second correspondingly shortened), the sounds produced by Kees Boeke and Walter van Hauwe are somewhat pale. Their music-making is completely upstaged by the *Suite sans continuo*, where the far stronger personality of Frans Brüggen dominates the proceedings and brings this fine work vividly to life, especially its key movement, a splendid closing *Passacaille*. The recording is forward but truthful. This reissue would have been more enticing at Teldec's budget range.

HOWELLS, Herbert (1892–1983)

ORGAN MUSIC

Psalm Preludes, Sets I & II; 3 Rhapsodies, Op. 17; Rhapsody 4
B— *** Priory PRCD 480. Cleobury (organ of King's College, Cambridge)

Like so many other composer/organists before him, Herbert Howells loved to sit at the organ and improvise, but while that gives his organ music a certain freedom, it never meanders, and it is rich in colour contrasts, very like orchestral writing. That is especially so of the *Psalm Preludes*, which are rich in ideas and are powerfully communicative, each being a musical meditation on a single verse. The very *First Prelude* of Set I, based on verse 6 of Psalm 34, uses a wide range of dynamic within the arch-like structure Howells so favoured. The *Second*, however, maintains a mystically serene atmosphere throughout, but the *Third* (Psalm 23) pictures 'the valley of the shadow of death' with violent agitation and a big crescendo and, like the first, returns to calm at the close. The *Rhapsodies*, not surprisingly, are more powerfully romantic in a Lisztian way, with big, dramatic swells of tone. The *Third* was written in York during a Zeppelin raid in the First World War, and the malignant writing depicts the tumult of the experience and the composer's passionate reaction. The *Fourth* was written in 1958, some 40 years after the first three, and is actually marked *turbulento*. It opens powerfully, but

contrasting atmospheric writing follows, with a weird palette. The climax is tremendous, with thundering pedals, and as a sonic experience it is overwhelming. Stephen Cleobury's performances have great vitality and passion (and delicacy when required), and the recording is quite superb, with the gentler pages of the music beautifully clear and detailed within the King's ambience. If you enjoy the organ, this admirable CD will give much satisfaction.

VOCAL MUSIC

Anthems: *The fear of the Lord; Like as the hart;* Hymn: *All my hope on God is founded;* Sacred Part-Song; *Long, long ago; Magnificat (Gloucester Service). Requiem*
*** Coll. COLCD 118. Soloists, Cambridge Singers, Rutter; Marshall (organ) – STANFORD: *Anthems; Canticles*, etc.
***

John Rutter has had the happy idea of making up a programme from the church music of two of the finest Anglican Church composers whose careers, between them, spanned the end of the nineteenth and a good deal of the twentieth century. The programme opens with three very fine *Magnificat* settings, Howells' the most ambitious, framed by two of Stanford's, while a pair of Stanford's anthems also enclose two quite contrasted anthems of Howells: the comparatively gentle *Like as the hart*, and the more robust *The fear of the Lord*. All this music is rewarding and is capped by the lovely Howells *Requiem* for *a cappella* double choir, which above all is thoughtful and serene. Its highly unconventional layout includes Psalms 23 and 121 (*I will lift mine eyes unto the hills*), surrounded by two different settings of the *Requiem aeternam*. The work became known only in 1980, even though it was written 50 years earlier, and was probably connected with the death of the composer's son in 1935. John Rutter, too, lost a son in a car accident in Cambridge a few years ago, so it is not surprising that his performance is movingly dedicated and radiantly sung. The concert ends rousingly with a hymn, *All my hope on God is founded*. The recording is very fine.

(i) (Organ): *Master Tallis's Testament; 6 Psalm-preludes, Set 1, Op. 32/1–3; Set 2 /1–3; 3 Rhapsodies, Op. 17/1–3;* (ii) Anthems: *Behold O God our defender; Like as the hart. Collegium regale: Jubilate & Te Deum.* Motet: *Take him, earth, for cherishing. St Paul's Service: Magnificat & Nunc dimittis*
(B) ** Hyp. Dyad CDD 22038 (2). Dearnley (organ); (ii) with St Paul's Cathedral Ch., Scott

A good deal of the music here is for organ and there are only two items (about 12 minutes in all) from the *St Paul's Service*, which draws the eye as the heading on the frontispiece of this Dyad Double. Although the organ pieces provide contrast between the choral items, the *Psalm-preludes* are mostly gentle pieces, improvisatory in feeling (Op. 32/3 with its repeated bass is the most striking), and although the *Rhapsodies* are more flamboyant, their focus is not helped by the wide reverberation. The piece inspired by Tallis is the most individual, and some listeners may feel, like us, that the programme is a little overweighted with organ repertoire. Among the choral highlights are the two fine canticles associated with the *Collegium regale* and the eloquent motet, *Take him, earth*, which was dedicated to John F. Kennedy. The anthems are splendid too, and all the choral music is of high quality. The recording gives it resonance in both senses of the word, with the St Paul's acoustic well captured by the engineers.

HUBAY, Jeno (1858–1937)

Violin Concertos 1 (Concerto dramatique), Op. 21; 2, Op. 90;
Suite, Op. 5
*** Hyp. CDA 67498. Shaham, BBC Scottish SO, Brabbins

This excellent disc follows up the earlier Hyperion issue from
these same performers of Jeno Hubay's other two violin
concertos, Nos. 3 and 4 (see below). Once again the composer
demonstrates what an outstanding lyricist he was, particularly in the first of the concertos, the *Concerto dramatique*, in
which one good tune follows another, each of them a candidate for the sort of virtuoso figuration designed to show off
the brilliance of the soloist. Hubay wrote it in 1877/8 for his
former teacher, Joseph Joachim, a piece that in its lyrical
warmth has echoes of Bruch. Hubay himself was a formidable violinist who, to celebrate his fiftieth birthday in 1908,
played this concerto in a concert when his other three violin
concertos were played by his pupils, Josef Szigeti, Franz de
Vecsey, and Stefi Geyer, dedicatee of Bartók's early *First Violin
Concerto*. No. 2 dates from around 1900 and, though the first
movement is less distinguished, with a square main theme, it
too is a tuneful piece. The second movement, a charming
interlude, leads to a sparkling Hungarian dance finale.

The *Suite*, Op. 5 of 1877–8, another concertante work for
violin, starts with a gavotte, which with its hammered
double-stopping sounds more like a march. The other three
movements are freer-running in their lyricism, genre pieces,
an Idylle marked *Andantino*, an Intermezzo and a dazzling
finale, full of virtuoso writing, which opens with a brief
reminiscence of the opening movement. As in the earlier disc,
Hagai Shaham plays not just with brilliance but with great
imagination, and Martyn Brabbins and the BBC Scottish
Symphony Orchestra demonstrate what sympathetic accompanists they are. The full and vivid recording, made in Caird
Hall, Dundee, equally lives up to the high standard expected
in Hyperion's enterprising 'Romantic Concerto' series.

Violin Concertos 3; 4. Variations on a Hungarian Theme
*** Hyp. CDA 67367. Shaham, BBC Scottish SO, Brabbins

Having had outstanding success with its series of romantic
piano concertos, Hyperion here offers the third in the companion series of romantic violin concertos. Jeno Hubay represented the last of the old school of composers in Hungary,
like Liszt reflecting the gypsy tradition, before Bartók and
Kodály totally transformed ideas of Hungarian music. A
virtuoso violinist himself, he writes fluently in these two
four-movement works, like Max Bruch transforming conventional concerto form and adopting a romantic idiom not so
different from Bruch's. With compact, rhapsodic first movements (the *Introduction quasi Fantasia* of No. 3 is little more
than a brilliant clearing-of-throat), the weight of argument is
shifted to the later movements in each, notably the poignantly beautiful slow movements. The *Variations* are more
conventional but equally fun to play for a virtuoso violinist
like Hagai Shaham, based on a Hungarian theme not so
different from the Paganini theme so often used for variations.

HUME, Tobias (c. 1575–1645)

As with so many composers of Tobias Hume's era, we know
very little detail about his life. A Scot by birth, he was a
soldier/composer and must have established himself as an
officer of at least captain's rank. He served as a professional
mercenary in many European countries, but finally returned
to London, where in 1642 he petitioned parliament for support. But it seems likely that this was not forthcoming, for he
ended his life in poverty, in 1629 entering the London Charterhouse, an institution which at that time served as a refuge
for old and destitute soldiers. As a composer, he was a
champion of the viol rather than the lute, and his *Book of
Musicall Humours* for solo viola da gamba appared in 1605 (a
volume of over 100 pieces). The second volume followed in
1607, duplicating much of the music, but scored for larger
forces. Both books were designed to court favour, the first
from the Earl of Pembroke.

Musicall Humours (of Captain Hume) for Solo Bass Viol
(1605)
** AliaVox AV 9837. Savall

Musicall Humours: The First Part of Ayres (1605); *Captain
Humes Poetical Musicke, London* (1607)
(M) **(*) DHM/BMG 05472 77847-2. Figueras, Hillier,
Hespèrion XX, Savall

Captain Humes Poetical Musicke: Music for viols, lute and
voice
(BB) *** Naxos 8.55416/7 (available separately). Les Voix
Humains

Jordi Savall discovered the collection of Tobias Hume's 'Musicall Humours' in the British Library's Reading Room in 1964.
He comments: 'I began studying the *Musicall Humours (of
Captain Hume)*, each day discovering a little more about the
infinite riches of nuances and modes that the viola da gamba
was capable of creating . . . It was a musical world full of
fantasy and emotion, where the bow could be drawn across
the strings or used *col legno*, the strings sometimes plucked,
sometimes bowed, the instrument now singing, now dancing,
going from the profound melancholy to the mock martial as
in the programme pieces, with descriptive texts included.'
Savall's solo gamba collection is obviously strongly influenced by this experience. His musical response is very free
and self-absorbed: the pavans and galliards are played like
fantasias, with little rhythmic feeling of the dance. The opening 'Humorous Pavin' is not in the least humorous or light-
hearted on his bow, and the items which are the most
instantly appealing are the 'disciplined', soldierly pieces, the
lively *Souldier's Galliard* and *A Souldiers Resolution*, while
among the more expressive pieces the penultimate *Good
Againe* is quite memorable. The gamba is firmly and clearly
recorded, so admirers of this instrument may find Savall's
freely improvisatory style more appealing than we did.

For the non-specialist collector, the alternative collection
from Hespèrion XX is more recommendable. It opens attractively and robustly with a dance that really is a dance, *The
Lady of Sussex delight*, using an instrumental ensemble
including recorder, cornet, trombone, violas da gamba and
lutes, and the other instrumental items are similarly piquant.
The gamba pieces are played by a consort of several instruments, and there are two vocal numbers, *What greater griefe*
and *Fain would I change that note*, sung by the always delightfully stylish Montserrat Figueras, plus a pair of male songs,
Tobacco and *Souldiers Song*, from Paul Hillier with appropriately more robust presentation. We could wish there were
more vocal numbers, but on the whole this is a diverting
collection and is well recorded.

However, the earlier Naxos coverage, on two discs, is most
desirable of all, comprehensive and sufficiently varied in

content to show Hume as an accomplished and versatile composer. The excellently recorded Canadian Ensemble, Les Voix Humains, prove themselves persuasive advocates and this is a most welcome addition to the catalogue.

HUMMEL, Johann (1778–1837)

Piano Concerto in A; L'Enchantment d'Oberon; Rondo brilliant, 'Le Retour à Londres'; 8 Variations & Coda on 'O du lieber Augustin'
*** Chan. 10374. Shelley, LMP

Howard Shelley here adds to his formidable list of recordings of long-neglected Hummel works, three of them concertante pieces for piano, which he directs from the keyboard. By far the earliest is the *A major Piano Concerto*, written, like another unnumbered A major concerto (already recorded by Shelley) in about 1798 when the composer was still in his teens. Though the influence of Mozart is dominant, one can already detect signs that Hummel was aware of the growing influence of Beethoven. After the opening tutti, the piano instantly lightens the bold main theme with elaborate decorations typical of Hummel. It is Shelley's gift that with his phenomenal agility and clarity of articulation he can make such decorative writing a delight. Even if one were to dismiss much of this as empty note-spinning, the joyful sparkle of Shelley's playing is consistently winning. The slow movement of the concerto is a lyrical *Romanze*, again with plentiful keyboard decoration, leading to a charming Rondo finale with a lightly skipping main theme and with one more serious episode in the middle, when the key switches to the relative minor key of F sharp minor.

The other two concertante works were written much later in Hummel's career, in 1830–31, when he was planning concert tours of Britain and France. *L'Enchantment d'Oberon* (with that French word spelt incorrectly) pays an indirect tribute to Weber, who had died in London only three years before, having completed his last opera, *Oberon*, there. In structure it not only echoes Weber's one-movement *Konzertstück* of six years earlier, but in its five sections it relates to the opera, if with few direct quotations. This is unashamedly light music, designed for immediate appeal, with a march in lightly dotted rhythm leading to a storm episode, far less imaginative than Beethoven's in the *Pastoral Symphony*, but still effective.

Le Retour à Londres of 1831 was expressly designed as a tribute to the British capital on the first of his 'grand farewell tours'. A cadenza links the slow, ruminative introduction to the main body of the allegro, featuring a jaunty Rondo theme over an oompah rhythm, leading to an equally jaunty march. If anything, this is even lighter and more carefree than the *Oberon* work, and Shelley again proves an ideal soloist. As a tailpiece comes the purely orchestral set of variations and coda on the tinkling little German folksong, *O du lieber Augustin*. The tune may be unremittingly corny in its three-in-a-bar Laendler rhythms, but it is liable to stick in the mind for hours afterwards, helped by Hummel's colourful switches of instrumentation and Shelley's persuasive conducting of the London Mozart Players. First-rate recording, clear and vivid, warm and full.

Double Concerto for Piano & Violin, Op. 17; Violin Concerto
(completed by Gregory Rose)
(BB) **(*) Naxos 8.557595. Trostiansky, Osetinskaya, Russian PO, Rose

It is good to have a budget version of two of the rarer Hummel concertos, even in flawed performances. Hummel echoes Mozart's great *Sinfonia concertante* in his *Double Concerto* of 1805, a charming work with elegant interplay between the soloists, particularly in the playful Rondo finale. The great merit of this Russian performance is the piano contribution of Polina Osetinskaya, with Hummel's rippling passagework played with crystal-clear articulation. The violinist, Alexander Trostiansky, is a fluent and able artist, but sadly his tone is unpleasantly acid, a failing which also mars the *Violin Concerto*. This is a piece that the Hummel scholar, Joel Sachs, has counted 'doubtful or unverifiable', though there are plenty of characteristic touches. The rival full-price version on Chandos offers a far finer performance.

Trumpet Concerto in E flat
(B) *** Ph. Eloquence 468 207-2. Wilbraham, ASMF, Marriner – Joseph & Michael HAYDN; Leopold MOZART: *Trumpet Concertos* ***

John Wilbraham's account of the engaging Hummel *Trumpet Concerto* is among the finest ever recorded, elegant in the slow movement and with the finale sparkling irresistibly. Marriner and the ASMF, during their vintage period, accompany with comparable polish.

CHAMBER MUSIC

Cello Sonata, Op. 104
*** Hyp. CDA 67521. Barta, Milne – MOSCHELES: *Cello Sonata 2, etc.* ***

Hummel's *Cello Sonata* makes an apt coupling for the cello works of his contemporary, Moscheles. Like the Moscheles, this is a work designed for intimate music-making, opening in an easy triple-time with a movement marked *Allegro amabile* and *grazioso*. Amiable is an apt description of the piece, not just in that lyrical first movement, but in the central *Romanze*, rather like early Beethoven. Here, as in the Moscheles, there are some echoes of the music of eastern Europe in the finale, perhaps influenced by the composer's tours of Russia and Poland. Though it is a pity that Barta is not presented as a full equal to Milne (who plays brilliantly), the recording balance is largely to blame. An attractive disc nevertheless.

Piano Trios 1 in E flat, Op. 12; 3 in G, Op. 37, 4; 7 in E flat, Op. 96
*** Warner Classics 2564 62596-2. Voces Intimae Trio
Piano Trios 2 in F, Op. 22; 5 in E, Op. 83; 6
*** Warner Classics 2564 62595-2. Voces Intimae Trio

With their free flow of attractive ideas Hummel's seven *Piano Trios* are relatively well covered on disc, but this Warner Classics set from Voces Intimae breaks new ground in using period instruments. To a surprising degree there is a positive advantage in having a light and slightly twangy fortepiano in place of a modern concert grand, making for a more effective integration of the ensemble. Those who resist period performances may find that the bright tone of the violin with little vibrato is a shade aggressive, and they can turn to the MDG recordings by the Trio Parnassus (MDH 3307/8 – see our main volume). But the vigour of each performance here makes them magnetic. Consistently, the lightness of touch of this antique fortepiano allows Riccardo Cerchetti to play with phenomenal clarity of articulation, even in the fastest movements like the Presto finale of No. 1. Speeds are well chosen to allow extra lift to the rhythms with expressive pointing. So the witty finale of No. 3, in a sort of polka rhythm, is made to sound almost like an ancestor of a Gilbert and Sullivan patter song. Written over a span of about 20 years, relatively early in Hummel's career, each inhabits a similar world of chamber music designed for immediate enjoyment, with no observable stylistic deveopment. Consistently, the Voces Intimae players find an element of wit in the writing, making these into fun pieces. Significantly, not one of the seven is in a minor key. The forward recording is admirably clear and full. The two discs are available separately.

Serenades, Op. 63 & 66, Potpourri, Op. 53

*** MDG 301 1344-2. Consortium Classicum (Dieter Klocker, Helman Jung, Andreas Krecher, Sonja Prunnbauer, Thomas Duis)

This, unashamedly, is a collection of fun music, performed by the members of Consortium Classicum with the sort of exuberance that Hummel and his friends must have brought to these confections, designed for relaxed festive evenings in the Imperial Gardens in Vienna or in private houses. Though the two works for the full quintet of instruments are labelled *Grande Serenade*, all three, not just the duo for guitar and piano, are in effect pot-pourris, built on themes popular at the time. It may initially be disconcerting at the start of this disc to hear the Overture to Mozart's *La clemenza di Tito* and Tamino's Act I aria from *Zauberflöte* (which open Opus 66), as arranged by Hummel for this mixed quintet, with piano and guitar prominent. A jolly *Allegretto alla spagnola* comes next, taken from Boieldieu's *Caliph of Baghdad*, followed by a march based on a theme from Cherubini's *Les deux journées* in which the players (pianist excepted) move from one side of the stage to the other, only to return later in the piece. Rounding things off comes a jaunty contredanse-cum-waltz, evidently Hummel's own invention.

Of similar length at just under 20 minutes, the Opus 63 *Serenade* brings another jolly mix, with more quotations from *Zauberflöte* and Cherubini's *Les deux journées*, and a central set of variations on a march from *Les Abencerages*, also by Cherubini. The duo *Potpourri* for guitar and piano is less extended but just as inventive, with a darkly intense slow introduction leading to quotations from *Don Giovanni* and Spontini's *La Vestale*, rounded off brilliantly with a jolly theme from Paisiello's *Il re Teodoro in Venezia*. These evidently are the first ever recordings of light music from another age, and they can still give much pleasure in performances like these.

VOCAL MUSIC

Mass in D min., S67/W13; Salve Regina

*** Chan. 0724. Gritton, Nichols, Helen Stephen, Padmore, Varcoe, Coll. Mus. 90 Ch. & O, Hickox

Richard Hickox and Collegium Musicum 90 continue their excellent Hummel series with two more choral works far too long neglected. The *D minor Mass* of 1805 was the second of the five that Hummel wrote for Prince Esterházy in a sequence carrying on from Haydn's late masterpieces. The persistent syncopations on repeated notes at the start of the *Kyrie* directly echo Mozart's *D minor Piano Concerto*, K.466, developing from hesitancy into blazing confidence. In this and other movements Hummel seems intent on taking the

listener by surprise, with the *Credo* starting lyrically in a flowing triple time, the opposite of a positive affirmation of belief. Throughout the Mass Hummel demonstrates that he is intent on writing a thoughtful rather than a sharply dramatic setting, with the soloists generally treated as a corporate team, set against the full choir. The tenor solo for *Et incarnatus est* in the *Credo*, sung with honeyed tone by Mark Padmore, is a striking exception. The brief *Sanctus* is positive, with military overtones, and the triumphant setting of *Dona nobis pacem* ends not on a fugue such as Haydn preferred but on powerful homophonic writing. The *Salve Regina* of 1809, the year Haydn died, may have been written for a memorial event to Hummel's great predecessor, hardly elegiac in its operatic style with elaborate coloratura for the soprano soloist, here glowingly sung by Susan Gritton. Richard Hickox again proves an ideal interpreter, drawing superb playing and singing from Collegium Musicum 90.

HUMPERDINCK, Engelbert
(1854–1921)

Hänsel und Gretel (complete)

(M) *** Sony (ADD) S2K 96455 (2). Cotrubas, Von Stade, Ludwig, Nimsgern, Te Kanawa, Söderström, Cologne Op. Children's Ch., Gürzenich O, Pritchard

Beautifully cast, the Pritchard version from Sony was the first in genuine stereo (in 1978) to challenge the vintage Karajan set (now available superbly remastered by Mark Obert-Thorn on Naxos 8.110897/8). Cotrubas – sometimes a little grainy as recorded – and Von Stade both give charming characterizations, and the supporting cast is exceptionally strong, with Söderström an unexpected but refreshing and illuminating choice as the Witch. Pritchard draws idiomatic playing from the Gürzenich Orchestra, and the recording is pleasingly atmospheric. This is, however, another of those Masterwork reissues in which the libretto is only available via a CD-ROM and a personal computer.

HVOSLEF, Ketil (born 1937)

(i) *Antigone (1982);* (ii) *Violin Concerto*

*** Aurora ACD4969. (ii) Saeverud; Bergen PO; cond. (i) Eggen; (ii) Kitaienko

Ketil Hvoslef is the son of Harald Sæverud and one of the brightest and most individual figures in the Norwegian musical firmament. He has the same craggy, salty quality as his father, the same rugged independence of personality and creative resource. This CD offers *Antigone*, which comes from the early 1980s, and the *Violin Concerto*, composed almost ten years later, in which the soloist is his son, Trond.

HYDE, Miriam (born 1913)

(i) *Piano Concertos 1 in E flat min.; 2 in C sharp min.;* (ii) *Village Fair*

**(*) Australian Universal ABC Classics (ADD) 465 735-2. (i) Hyde; Australian SO, Simon; (ii) Sydney SO, Franks

Miriam Hyde is a well-respected composer and teacher in Australia, and we have here her early *Piano Concertos* written in 1932–3 and 1934–5 respectively. They are unashamedly romantic in tradition, with bold writing and rich orchestration – Brahms and Rachmaninov being obvious models. The tunes are memorable and each work has many felicities, not least in the touches of folk-like melody and colour. The finale of the *First Concerto*, with its repeated figures on the strings with the timpani, sounds rather exotic but soon becomes highly romantic, with flowing arpeggios which at times remind one of romantic film scores of the 1940s. It is all very enjoyable and the music is instantly appealing. These are excellent performances, though the 1975 recording is a little thin. With an attractive fill-up in the form of *Village Fair*, once again with folk-like themes, this is a valuable addition to the catalogue. Miriam Hyde certainly deserves wider recognition.

IBERT, Jacques (1890–1962)

Bacchanale; La Ballade de la Geôle de Reading;(i) Louisville Concerto

(M) **(*) First Edition (stereo/mono) FECD-1906. Louisville O, Mester; (i) with Whitney – HONEGGER: *Prélude pour Algavaine et Sélysette*, etc. **(*)

Ibert's reputation rests almost wholly on the *Divertissement, Flute Concerto* and *Escales*, as well of course as *Le petit âne blanc*. Robert Whitney commissioned the *Louisville Concerto* in 1953 and recorded it the following year in mono. (It was originally coupled with two other Louisville commissions, the *Eleventh Symphony* of Henry Cowell and a piece by Paul Creston.) The *Ballad of Reading Gaol* (1921) is an early work which caused quite a stir on its first appearance under the baton of Gabriel Pierné, to whom it is dedicated. It is an inventive and finely wrought score which deserves wider dissemination. The *Louisville Concerto* and the slightly later *Bacchanale* (1958) are both shorter but rumbustious and crude, even if they leave no doubt as to Ibert's skill as an orchestrator. Unusual repertoire that will appeal to those who like music well off the beaten track – where, in the case of the *Concerto*, it deserves to stay!

Bacchanale; Divertissement; Escales; Ouverture de fête; Symphonie marine

(BB) * Naxos 8.554222. LOP, Sado

Sado's *Divertissement* is without the sheer champagne fizz of Martinon's old – but exceptionally vivid – Decca recording. *Escales* also suffers from comparison with more magical accounts already available (from Munch and Paray) and, while the *Symphonie marine* is a rarity, it is musically rather thin. The *Ouverture de fête* is enjoyable enough but does rather outstay its welcome. The recording is quite good and the CD is cheap but is difficult to recommend even so.

Divertissement

(BB) **(*) Virgin 2x1 4 82103-2. City of L. Sinfonia, Hickox (with FAURÉ: *Pavane*) – BIZET: *Symphony in C*; RAVEL: *Tombeau de Couperin*; TCHAIKOVSKY: *Serenade for Strings; Souvenir de Florence* **(*)

Hickox presents the *Divertissement* with both style and gusto, and the City of London players respond with much spirit, especially in the finale, complete with police whistle. The recording is a shade over-resonant but fully acceptable when the proceedings have moments of riotous vigour. If you want the rest of the programme, this is enjoyable enough, without matching Martinon's celebrated version.

INDIA, Sigismondo d' (1582–1629)

Amico hai vinto; Diana (Questo dardo, quest'arco); Misera me (Lamento d'Olympia); Piangono al pianger mio; Sfere fermate; Torna il sereno zefiro

*** Hyp. CDA 66106. Kirkby, Rooley (chitaron) –
   MONTEVERDI: *Lamento d'Olympia*, etc. ***

Sigismondo d'India spent his childhood and was musically educated in Naples, where one of his fellow pupils was Gesualdo. He was in the vanguard of the new movement founded by Monteverdi, and his laments show him to be a considerable master of expressive resource. His setting of the *Lamento d'Olympia* makes a striking contrast to Monteverdi's and is hardly less fine. This is an affecting and beautiful piece, and so are its companions, particularly when they are sung as freshly and accompanied as sensitively as here.

Madrigals & Canzonettes: *Arditi baci miei; Cara mia cetra; Infelice Didone; Intenerite voi, lagrime mi; La mia Filli crudel; Mentre che'l cor; Mormora seco alquanto; Odi quel Rossignolo; Piange Madonna; Questa mia aurora; Scherniscimi, crudele; Sfere, fermate li giri sonori; Sù, sù prendi la cetra; Torna il sereno zfiro; Un di soletto; La Virtù; Vorrei baciarti, o Filli*

☛ *** HM HMC 901774. Kiehr, Concerto Soave, Aymes (with: Giovanni-Maria TRABACI: *Gagliarda; Partita prima sopra Ruggiero; Partita sesta Cromatica sopra Ruggiero; Seconda Stravaganza*. Ascanio MAYONE: *Toccata V per il cimbalo cromatico*)

This is a superb disc and bears out the promise of the earlier Hyperion collection, above. Sigismondo d'India's madrigals undoubtedly rank alongside those of Monteverdi, both in the quality of their melodic lines and in their expressive, chromatic richness. And there could be no more ideal performer for them than Maria Cristina Kiehr. Her vocal beauty and ravishing phrasing have long been apparent from her previous records, and the very opening canzonette here, *Cara mia cetra, andianne* ('My dear lyre, let us go'), sets the style of this superb collection; and the lute-accompanied *Un di soletto* ('One day when I was alone') is full of charm. Her vocal decoration is astonishing (sample the delightful *Vorrei baciarti, O Filli* ('I should like to kiss you, O Phyllis') or *Odi quel Rossignol* ('Do you hear the nightingale'), where her trilling would make the bird himself jealous. But she is also infinitely touching in the songs of unrequited love: *Scherniscimi, crudele!* ('Mock me, cruel one'), *Intenerite voi, lagrime mi* ('Move to pity, my tears') and the lusciously chromatic *Piange madonna* ('My lady weeps'). She closes the recital with the soaringly joyful *La Virtù*, a number to confirm D'India's mastery if one were needed. The instrumental or keyboard pieces, by contemporary composers Giovanni-Maria Trabaci and Ascanio Mayone, are used as pleasing interludes. The accompaniments, employing a small instrumental ensemble including lute, guitar, harp and organ (or one of these), are just about perfect, and the recording is first class. Full texts and translations are included. A disc to put straight away at the top of your list.

INDY, Vincent d' (1851–1931)

(i) *Fantasy on French Popular Themes* (for oboe & orchestra), *Op. 31. Saugefleurie* (Legend after a Tale by

Robert de Bonnières); *Tableaux de voyage, Op. 36;*
L'Etranger: Prelude to Act II. Fervaal: Prelude to Act I
** Marco Polo 8.223659. (i) Cousu; Württemberg PO, Nopre
or (i) Burfin

The tone-poem *Saugefleurie*, based on a tale by Robert de
Bonnières, the evocative *Tableaux de voyage* and the lovely
Prelude to Act I of *Fervaal* all offer music of quality, and
writing which also has the seeds of popularity. The *Fantaisie
sur des thèmes populaires françaises* for oboe and orchestra has
a fervent charm which is very winning. The performances of
all these pieces are variable; they fall short of distinction but
are more than routine. The recording, too, is eminently
satisfactory, and aficionados of French music need not hesitate.

*Symphonie sur un chant montagnard français (Symphonie
cévenole)*
(**) Testament mono SBT 1237. Ciccolini, Paris Conservatoire
O, Cluytens – FRANCK: *Symphonic Variations; Symphony.*
(*(*))

As with the Franck *Variations symphoniques*, d'Indy's *Symphonie sur un chant montagnard français* (sometimes known
as the *Symphonie cévenole*) was recorded in the Théâtre des
Champs-Elysées in 1953, and suffers from too forwardly
balanced a soloist and a dryish acoustic. The playing of
Aldo Ciccolini is sensitive, and André Cluytens is very
supportive.

IRELAND, John (1879–1962)

(i) *Piano Concerto in E flat.* Piano Music: (ii; iii) *April;* (iii)
*The Almond Trees; Columbine; 3 Dances; Decorations; April;
The Holy Boy; Sarnia;* (iv) *The Darkened Valley; Green
Ways; In Those Days; London Pieces; 3 Pastels; Preludes 1,
2 & 3; Sea Idyll; Summer Evening; The Towing Path*
●— (B) *** EMI (ADD/DDD) 3 52279-2 (2). (i) Horsley, RPO,
Cameron; (ii) composer (mono); (iii) Adni; (iv) Wright

John Ireland's *Piano Concerto* is unaccountably neglected in
the concert hall, for it has immediate and lasting appeal, and
it is one of the very few true masterpieces among piano
concertos by English composers. Its original interpreter was
Eileen Joyce, and her mono account remains unsurpassed.
But many listeners will prefer the later (1957) stereo recording
by Colin Horsley, with Basil Cameron, which retains the
work's original freshness and has very good sound (although
the upper violin-range has a touch of thinness). In this
performance the slow movement has a serene poise and
beauty which is ravishingly memorable. In the finale Joyce
has marginally greater dash, but Horsley still offers plenty of
sparkle, and Cameron proves a fine partner. The rest of the
programme is solo piano music, and Daniel Adni, who
provides the first group, penetrates the atmosphere of this
music to the manner born. He is characterful and accomplished and seems thoroughly inside the idiom, although,
interestingly, his performance of *April* is brisker (3′ 51″) than
the composer's own mono version (4′ 42″), which is offered
as a final encore.

Desmond Wright is not always gentle enough in his treatment of the more delicate evocations, but these too are fresh
and responsive performances which include most of the
favourite items, like *Ragamuffin* from the *London Pieces, The
Holy Boy*, hauntingly lyrical, and the third of the *Preludes.
The Darkened Valley* and *The Rowing Path* show Ireland at his

most tenderly expressive. Altogether, this includes some of
the most appealing English piano music written in the last
century, and it is very well recorded – the Adni recital is
particularly natural and truthful.

ISAAC, Heinrich (c. 1450–1517)

Missa de apostolis. Motets: *Optime pastor; Tota pulchra es;
Regina coeli laetare; Resurrexi et adhuc tecum sum; Virgo
prudentissima*
*** Gimell (ADD) CDGIM 023. Tallis Scholars, Phillips

The German contemporary of Josquin Desprez, Heinrich
Isaac has not until recently been widely appreciated. The
Mass setting is glorious, culminating in an ethereal version of
Agnus Dei, flawlessly sung by the Tallis Scholars. Among the
many striking passages is the opening of the six-part setting
of *Virgo prudentissima* for two upper voices only, with wom-
en's rather than boys' voices all the more appropriate with
such a text. Ideally balanced recording.

IVES, Charles (1874–1954)

(i; ii) *Central Park in the Dark;* (i; iii) *Symphony 2; The
Unanswered Question for Trumpet, Flute Quartet & Strings;*
(iv) *Ann Street; Chromâtomelôdtune; From the Steeples and
the Mountains; The Pond; The Rainbow; 2 Scherzi: All the
Way Around and Back; Over the Pavements. Tone Roads
1 & 3*
(M) *** Sony (ADD) SK 94731. (i) NYPO; (ii) Ozawa, Peress;
(iii) Bernstein; (iv) O, Schuller

Central Park in the Dark, as the title implies, provides a
brilliant collection of evening sounds, evocative yet bewilder-
ing. Its musical complexity ideally demands two separate
conductors and that is why Ozawa and Peress have directed
the pieces (magnetically) under Bernstein's supervision. *The
Unanswered Question* is probably the most beautiful music
Ives ever wrote, with muted strings (curiously representing
silence) set against a trumpet representing the problems of
existence. No need to worry about Ives's philosophy when the
results are so naturally moving. Bernstein's 1958 recording of
the *Second Symphony* has conviction and freshness and was
not improved upon with his later, DG remake. The sound,
too, despite the balance being too close, is excellent, full and
atmospheric, with glowing sounds from the NYPO woodwind and a satisfying depth and resonance from the strings;
the dynamics of the playing convey the fullest range of
emotion. This reading is in a class of its own. To these superb
orchestral works has been added some of Ives's music for
large chamber groups, very much in the composer's more
avant-garde, experimental style, with colour, rhythm and
dissonance all vying for attention. Not to everyone's taste, but
interesting fill-ups – brilliantly played and recorded (1969) –
to the main works on this CD. Excellent transfers.

Instrumental Pieces: *The Gong on the Hook and Ladder*
(Original version); *Hallowe'en; In Re Con Moto;* (Piano) *5
Take-offs: The Seen and Unseen? (Sweet and Tough); Rough
and Ready et al. and/or The jumping Frog; Song without
(good) Words; Scene Episode; Bad Resolutions and Good
WAN! (Jan 1, 1907). 3 Quarter-Tone Pieces;* Songs: *Aeschylus*

and Sophocles; The Housatonic at Stockbridge; On the Antipodes; The Pond; Remembrance; Soliloquy or A Study in Sevenths and Other Things; Sunrise

☺⟶ (BB) *** Naxos 8.559194. Continuum (members), Seltzer & Sachs (directors & pianists)

This fascinating collection shows Ives at his most outrageously experimental, music written in the early years of the century which upstages the work of many more recent avant-garde composers because of its originality and its abiding interest for present-day listeners.

The opening song-group, very well sung, begins lyrically with *The Housatonic at Stockbridge*, but at its climax the piano accompaniment goes wild; the following *Soliloquy* explodes similarly, and the dissonant, untamed accompaniment continues its conflict to underline *On the Antipodes*. *Sunrise* (Ives's final song) initially brings relative peace and an Elysian violin solo but still has an agitated climax. In the brief *Remembrance* (of the composer's father), the cello enters too, to create a simple eulogy in which the violin persists. In *Aeschylus and Sophocles* the wildness erupts into frenzy at the words 'Accursed be the race', but the anger subsides for the final 'Farewell', and the last word is with the cello.

The first of the instrumental pieces, *The Gong on the Hook and Ladder*, pictures the annual parade of the neighbourhood Fire Company, for the appliance was heavy and had to be held in check manually down the hill, while the violent clanging gong on the hand wheel 'must ring steady'. *Hallowe'en* is a busy, dissonant Scherzo (the strings playing in different keys), suggesting the growing flames of the bonfire, with children running round it. *In Re Con Moto et al.* brings the most ferocious dissonance of all 'to stretch ear muscles', as Ives suggested. The piano pieces, *Five Take-offs* (implying improvisatory freedom, but in fact highly organized), were published as recently as 1991, and would make a stimulating centrepiece for any modern piano recital. The untamed, feral *Jumping Frog* has an underlying boldly controlled cantus firmus. Then, astonishingly, *Song without (Good) Words* is quite beautiful – very romantic, but with wrong notes – and *Scene Episode* begins in much the same mood of emotional serenity, which is not quite sustained. *Bad Resolutions and Good WAN* opens with a hymn but once more, characteristically, the peace is boldly interrupted.

The *Three Quarter-Tone Pieces* are aurally the most fascinating of all, more remarkably so as they are very listenable. Originally written in 1924 for a double keyboard microtonal piano, they are now usually played as a simultaneous piano duo, using two pianos, tuned a microtone apart. They really do 'tweak the ear muscles', the first bell-like, the second in wild ragtime, and the third boldly fantasizing on *America 'tis of thee* or *God save the Queen* (according to your nationality). All in all, this makes a fine, characteristic anthology, splendidly realized by artists not named individually, except for the pair of director/pianists. The recording is excellent and the (essential) documentation praiseworthy, including the words of the songs.

Violin Sonatas 1–4

☺⟶ (BB) *** Naxos 8.559119. Thompson, Waters

Ives's four extraordinary *Violin Sonatas* were written between 1902 and 1906, and are quite a find. Their erratically stimulating originality is in no doubt, but they are also among his most immediately appealing works, with the usual tantalizing snatches of hymns and popular tunes to spice the melodic flow. The *First Sonata* immediately shows how well Ives can

integrate a dialogue in which violin and piano move comfortably and independently together, not always sharing the same invention. The central *Largo cantabile* is melodically nostalgic, with an idyllic violin-line and sturdier writing for the piano; the finale, a 'farmer's camp meeting', grows increasingly virtuosic but has a haunting central interlude, played quite beautifully here. The three movements of *Sonata No. 2* explain themselves: *Autumn*; *In the Barn* (where the fiddle plays for a square dance with a kaleidoscope of popular themes), while the *Revival* finale opens very gently and evocatively: its energy suddenly bursts forth and then characteristically evaporates into silence.

The *Third Sonata*, perhaps the finest of the set, has a reflective opening movement, a hymn of four verses, each with a refrain. Restless, even passionate at times, it moves forward from *Adagio* to *Andante* to *Allegretto*, and back to *Adagio*. The second movement, with its quirky syncopations, 'represents a meeting where the feet and body, as well as the voice, add to the excitement'. The extended finale, again marked *Adagio*, has a hauntingly ambiguous melodic flow and 'the tonality throughout is supposed to take care of itself'.

The last and shortest *Sonata*, subtitled *Children's Day at the Camp Meeting*, is immediately rhythmically catchy. The central *Largo* is quiet and serious, quoting the hymn, *Jesus Loves me*, with the violin ruminating in the background; and the marching finale brings one of Ives's favourite tunes, *Shall we gather at the River*, and ends in mid-phrase.

There is no doubt that the full-timbered Curt Thompson and Rodney Waters are excellent artists, and that as a duo they have completely absorbed these works into their very being. It is difficult to imagine this music being played better or more idiomatically, and the daunting bravura is readily forthcoming. The recording too is most realistic, and this is another outstanding disc in Naxos's 'American Classics' series that should be acquired forthwith.

PIANO MUSIC

(i) *Piano Sonata 2 (Concord, Mass.)*; (ii) *Three Quarter-tone Pieces*

(BB) *** Warner Apex 0927 49515-2. Lubimov; with (i) Verney, Cherrier; (ii) Aimard

Piano Sonata 2 (Concord, Mass.); *Celestial Railroad*; *Emerson Transcriptions 1*; *Varied Air & Variations*

(BB) *** Naxos 8.559127. Mayer

Ives's remarkable *Concord Sonata* was the first work he decided to publish – at his own expense, in 1920. Yet he continued working on the piece over the years in secret, increasing the dissonances, hoping 'to bring the score more up-to-date' for its second and major publication in 1947. Somehow this extraordinary work draws its tributaries from the full range of nineteenth-century music. Centring on the three 'B's, and opening with a clear allusion to Beethoven's *Fifth Symphony*, it includes references to Bach, Brahms (notably the *Second Piano Sonata*) and Chopin, to say nothing of popular influences, hymns and American folk material. As the very opening shows, it is a formidable work, yet its lyrical heart remains, in the secondary material of the first movement and in both the central movements: the hymn-like opening of the third is quite lovely, and the finale is underlyingly meditative.

After years of neglect, Ives's work is now attracting recordings from a remarkable range of pianists. But its sheer diversity brings new insights from each of them and, while Marc-André Hamelin's performance, praised in our main *Guide*, is commanding, all these new versions are highly rewarding, for the music stimulates the imagination of performers and listeners alike. So, while we have greatly enjoyed the performances by Alexei Lubimov and Pierre-Laurent Aimard (see below), both of which include Ives's brief (and optional) obbligatos for viola and flute in the first and fourth movements respectively, Steven Mayer, who omits them, is also remarkably lucid and sympathetic, and he ends the finale most movingly and memorably. As couplings he offers also the tough, though briefly soft-centred, *Varied Air and Variations* and *The Celestial Railroad*, a nightmarish, noisy train journey, a trip to a promised land which never materializes. The *Emerson Transcription* is essentially a reworking of the opening material of the *Sonata*, and of less general interest.

Lubimov on Apex offers as his bonus the remarkable *Quarter-tone Pieces*, in which he is joined by Aimard at the second piano. Whether or not they achieve identical tuning with Seltzer and Sachs on the Naxos/Continuum anthology (above), they produce a more lyrically romantic effect in the opening *Largo* and are less dauntless in the fantasia on *America/God save the King*.

(i) *Piano Sonata 2*; (ii) *Songs: Ann Street; The Cage; The Circus Band; A Farewell to Land; From The Swimmers; The Housatonic at Stockbridge; The Indians; Like a sick eagle; Memories: Very pleasant; Rather sad; 1, 2, 3; September; Serenity; Soliloquy (or A Study in 7ths and other things); Songs my mother taught me; The sound of a distant horn; The Things our Fathers Loved; Thorau*

*** Warner 2564 60297-2. Aimard, with (i) Zimmerman, Pahud; (ii) Graham

Pierre-Laurent Aimard's reading of the *Sonata* ranks with the best in all respects and it is beautifully recorded so that the work's lyrical core is fully revealed, while the brief instrumental obbligato vignettes are played by distinguished soloists. Aimard also provides outstanding accompaniments for the equally recommendable song selection. Susan Graham's voice is not quite as richly alluring as Roberta Alexander's, but her singing is truly idiomatic and has moments of real beauty; moreover, her selection is balanced to include more of the rugged numbers like the hair-raising *Soliloquy*, while she is at her best in the contrasts of *Memories, Very pleasant* and *Rather sad.*

SONGS

Ann Street; An old flame; Die Alte Mutter; At the river; At Sea; Autumn; Berceuse; The Cage; The Camp meeting; Chanson de Florian; Charlie Rutlage; The Children's Hour; The Circus Band; Down East; Dreams; Elegie; Evening; Evidence; Farewell to Land; Feldensamkeit; The Greatest Man; The Harpalus; His exaltation; The Housatonic at Stockbridge; Ich grolle nicht; Ilmenau; Immortality; Like a sick eagle; Maple leaves; Memories: Very pleasant; Rather sad. Mirage; from Night of frost in May; A Night Song; On the Counter; from Parcelsus; Qu'il m'irait bien; Remembrance; Romanzo in Central Park; Rosamunde; The see 'R'; Serenity; The Side Show; Slow March; Slugging a vampire; Songs my mother taught me; Spring Song; There's a Lane; They are there; The Things our Fathers Loved; Tom sails away; Two little flowers; Watchman; Weil'auf mir

(B) *** Etcetera 2x1 KTC 2508 (2). Alexander, Crone

With 54 out of Ives's 114 published songs included here, double the number of their previous issue, Roberta Alexander and Tan Crone seem to be making a special niche for themselves in what is rewarding repertoire. This is characterful singing from an exceptionally rich and attractive voice. As before, the overall selection is varied from lyrical and sweet, nostalgic songs (which predominate) to sharper, leaner inspirations. Roberta Alexander's manner is not always quite tough enough in those, but she is good in the folksy numbers like *The Greatest Man*, and a bravura piece like *Memories – Very pleasant* is delightfully done. Crone is the understanding accompanist, rising to the challenge of the often bravura writing. The discs come at two for the price of one, and full texts are included. Those who would prefer a shorter selection can turn to Susan Graham – see above.

JACQUET DE LA GUERRE, Elisabeth (1665–1729)

Born into a family of musicians and instrument manufacturers, Elisabeth-Claude Jacquet de la Guerre was celebrated during her lifetime as both harpsichordist and composer. She was one of four French musicians to have her keyboard works published and the only composer to secure publication in both the seventeenth and eighteenth centuries. As an instrumentalist she was a child prodigy and played for the royal family at a very early age. When the court moved to Versailles she stayed in Paris and married an organist, Marin de la Guerre. She outlived both her husband and her only son, and she continued to compose and give recitals domestically to the end of her life.

Pièces de Clavecin (1687): *Suites 1–4; Pièces de Clavecin qui peuvent se jouer sur le viollon: Suites 5–6* (1707)

(BB) *** Naxos 8.557654/5. Farr (harpsichord)

Only one copy of each of the two books of Elisabeth-Claude's *Harpsichord Suites* exists, the second of which offers the alternative possibility of being played on the solo violin. However, the writing is very keyboard-orientated. She left no ornament table, but Elizabeth Farr has researched ornamentation styles of the period, and some of the decoration is already written in. This is exceptionally attractive and spontaneous keyboard music, with each suite including the usual group of stylized dance movements, with the *Gigues* (there are two, side by side, in the *Second Suite*) very infectious, to offset the more thoughtful and expressive *Allemandes* and *Sarabandes*, while three of the suites include a *Chaconne*, and one an unusual *Toccata*. Farr's performances are full of life and character, and very stylish indeed. The recording of the harpsichord (a modern copy of a French instrument, built by Keith Hill in Michigan) is most pleasing, the sound richly resonant, bright and clear. Sample a 'gig' or two, and you will be won over. Altogether a distinguishd and rewarding set.

JADIN, Hyacinthe (1769–1800)

Piano Sonatas, Op. 4/1–3; Op. 6/3

(B) ** HM Musique d'Abord HMA 1951189. Pommier

The French composer Hyacinthe Jadin was born the year before Beethoven, and he died three years after Schubert appeared on the scene. He was thus of the in-between generation after Haydn. His Op. 4 *Sonatas* were published in 1795, and he is heard at his most classical in the artless *Andante* of the first of the set, and in the crisp Rondo finale. But the *Adagios* of both Op. 4/6 in C sharp minor and Op. 6/3 in F major are more forward-looking, and all this music is appealing, if not really distinctive. It is very well played in a crisp, direct manner by Jean-Claude Pommier, with slow movements not over-romanticized, and the Schott 1830 fortepiano obviously suits the music and is well recorded. But it would be interesting to hear the sonatas on a modern Steinway. The disc suffers from the drawback that the documentation is printed only in French and German.

JANÁČEK, Leoš (1854–1928)

Sinfonietta

(BB) ** Warner Apex 0929 48732-2. NYPO, Masur – DVORAK: *Symphony 8* *(*)

Masur's 1993 account of the *Sinfonietta*, like the Dvořák coupling, is very well played and recorded. There are some nice points of detail, and the performance has conviction. If it lacks the spark that turns a good performance into an outstanding one, it is nevertheless enjoyable. The coupling is not so recommendable.

CHAMBER MUSIC

String Quartet 1 (Kreutzer Sonata)

**(*) BBC Legends BBCL 4180-2 Smetana Qt – DVOŘÁK: *String Quartet 14*, etc. **(*)

The Smetana Quartet was recorded at London's Queen Elizabeth Hall in February 1975. The BBC recording sounds very acceptable, and the performance has a powerful involvement and intensity. We are not short of good recordings of the Janáček *Quartets*, but most are made in the studio, and the presence of an audience always draws something extra from the players.

String Quartets 1 (Kreutzer); 2 (Intimate Letters)

*** Cal. CAL 9333. Talich Qt – SCHULHOFF: *Quartet 1*

The latest coupling from the Talichs is among the very finest available. This Talich is a different ensemble from the one whose recording we list in our main volume (CAL 5699). Their leader, Jan Talich, is the son of the Talich, violist and violinist, of the previous quartet. In any event, this is big-boned and impassioned playing that carries the listener with it. The recording is a little forward, but not unacceptably so.

Violin Sonata

(BB) *(*) EMI Encore 5 85707-2. Zimmermann, Lonquich – DEBUSSY: *Violin Sonata*; RAVEL: *Violin Sonata*; *Sonata posthume* *(*)

Frank Peter Zimmermann projects this wonderful *Sonata* with conviction, though his accompanist is not exactly the last word in sensitivity. Not really recommendable, despite the attractive couplings and the modest price.

PIANO MUSIC

Along an Overgrown Path, Books I & II; In the Mists; Piano Sonata (I.X.1905); Reminiscence

(BB) *** Regis RRC 1172. Kvapil

Along an Overgrown Path: Books I & II; In the Mists; A Recollection; Piano Sonata (1.X.1905)

*(**) ECM 461 660-2. Schiff

Along an Overgrown Path: Suite 1; In the Mists; Piano Sonata (I.X.1905)

(B) *** Virgin 2x1 3 49913-2 (2). Andsnes – NIELSEN: *Chaconne*, etc. ***

Radoslav Kvapil is naturally at home in this engaging music, and he is very well recorded. So you cannot go wrong with this 1994 Regis CD (originally issued on the Unicorn label). It is also available in a first-class Regis compilation of Czech piano music, together with works by Dvořák, Smetana & Suk (RRC 4005).

Leif Ove Andsnes, too, is a first-class exponent of this repertoire and, if you are tempted by the equally fine Nielsen coupling, this can also be strongly recommended, although he offers less music.

András Schiff has great feeling for this repertoire and plays with enormous sensitivity and insight. But the recorded sound poses a real problem: there is a fair amount of reverberation, which at times smudges detail, and the instrument appears bass-heavy, ill-defined and thin on top.

OPERA

(i) *The Cunning Little Vixen* (with *Orchestral Suite*); (ii) *From the House of the Dead*; (iii) *Jenůfa*;(iv) *Káta Kabanová*; (v) *The Makropulos Affair. Sinfonietta; Taras Bulba; Zárlivost: Overture*

(B) **(*) Decca (ADD/DDD) 475 6872 (9). (i) Bratislava Children's Ch.; (i; ii) Jedlická; (ii) Zídek; (i; iii) Popp, Randová, (ii; iii) Zahradníček; (iii) Ochman; (iii; iv; v) Söderström, Dvorský; (iv) Kniplová, Krejčík, Márová; (v) Blachut; (i–v) V. State Op. Ch., VPO, Mackerras

Sir Charles Mackerras's recordings of Janáček's five key operas are one of the outstanding achivments of the Decca operatic catalogue and canot be too highly praised. In a bargain box, with three orchestral works thrown in for good measure, the attraction is obvious. However, although synopses are provided, they are not cued. These are operas where the libretti with translations are almost essential, and it is a pity that they are not made available separately – perhaps at extra cost.

Jenůfa (complete CD version)

(M) ** Sup. (ADD) SU 3869-2 (2). Beňečková, Krejčík, Kniplová, Přibyl, Pokorná, Brno Janáček Op. Ch. & O, Jílek

Handsomely repackaged, with full libretto and translation, this 1979 Supraphon set, while lacking the concentration of Mackerras's set for Decca (● 414 483-2 – see our main volume), is fresh, sharp and enjoyable. A strong cast is headed by two veteran singers, Vilém Přibyl as Laca and Nadejda Kniplová as the Kostelnička; their singing is most assured, but their voices are often raw for the gramophone. So too with most of the singers in the smaller parts, though the role of Jenůfa went to the now famous, creamy-toned Gabriela Beňečková, with no hint of a Slavonic wobble. As Steva, the tenor Vladimir Krejčík makes an excellent impression. However, the Mackerras Decca set is a far better proposition, even though it is still at full price.

(i) *Kátá Kabanová* (complete CD version); (ii) *Capriccio for Piano & 7 Instruments; Capriccio for Piano & 6 Instruments*
♦~ *** Decca (ADD) 475 7518 (2). (i) Söderström, Dvorský, Kniplová, Krejčik, Márová, V. State Op. Ch., VPO, Mackerras; (ii) Crossley, L. Sinf., Atherton

It was understandable that Decca should have chosen *Kátá Kabanová* for one of their new series of Originals, for Elisabeth Söderström dominates the opera as Káta in one of her finest and most moving recorded performances. The rest of the cast is Czech and, with Mackerras at the helm, the performance overall can hardly fail. The two concertante works, with Paul Crossley also on top form, were added for the original reissue.

JANEQUIN, Clément (c. 1485–1558)

Masses: *L'Aveuglé Dieu; La Bataille;* Motet: *Congregati Sunt*
♦~ (B) *** HM Musique d'Abord HMA 1901536. Ens. Clément Janequin, Les Sacqueboutiers de Toulouse, Visse

Of these two parody Masses – the only religious compositions by Janequin to have survived – it was *La Bataille* of 1532 (based on the catchy chanson, 'La Guerre') that helped to establish Janequin's reputation, as his lyrical yet lively setting banished any association with the original battle-song. *L'Aveuglé Dieu* dates from three decades later, and is again based on a chanson published two years earlier in 1554. Its character is graver in mood yet harmonically rich and very touching, to make a perfect foil for its companion. The performances here are admirable, *La Bataille* given instrumental support (mainly sackbutts), *L'Aveuglé Dieu* sung *a cappella*, and very beautifully, too.

JÄRNEFELT, Armas (1869–1958)

Berceuse; Korsholm; Ouverture lyrique; Praeludium; The Promised Land (Det förlovade landet): Suite; The Song of the Crimson Flower (Sången om den eldröda blomman)
** Sterling CDS-1021-2. Gävle SO, Koivula

Järnefelt is best remembered nowadays for two light classics, the *Berceuse* and *Praeludium*, which still delight music-lovers. He was one of the first Nordic composers to write for the cinema: *The Song of the Crimson Flower* dates from 1919. All this music is direct in feeling and has a touch of nobility. It is national-romantic in character, not dissimilar to, say, Sibelius's *King Christian II* music. It is appropriate that it should be played by a Swedish orchestra, as he adopted Swedish nationality in the 1920s. Hannu Koivula's conducting disappoints. There is not enough charm in these performances. Worth hearing all the same.

Songs: (i) *A Dreamer's Song to Life; A Flower is Purest when Blossoming; To the Kantele; Lullany to Breaker; The Poor One; Rock, O Cradle; Summer Shore; On Sunday; Twilight; When all the clocks have struck twelve; You;* (ii) *Dream; A Fiddling and Dancing Tune; My Hope; The Lark; Sing, sing! Soft, soft; At Sunset; Sunshine*
*** Ondine ODE 1029-2. (i) Nylund; (ii) Hynninen; Paananen

Armas Järnefelt, four years younger than his brother-in-law Sibelius, outlived him by one year. (The family enjoyed a high profile: the father was governor of Kuopio, and his sons were all gifted artistically, Eero being a fine painter and Arvid a dramatist. Their only sister, Aino, was highly cultured and a

good linguist.) Armas studied with Busoni during his Helsinki years and later with Massenet at Paris. As a conductor Järnefelt introduced the Wagner operas to Finland and in 1907 went to the Royal Opera in Stockholm, making a reputation as a fine Beethoven conductor and an authoritative Sibelius interpreter. In all there are some 60 songs of which 22 are given here. All of them are short – indeed, half are less than two minutes long, very much in the national romantic-vein idiom. Unusually for the period, half are to Finnish rather than Swedish texts. (The Järnefelts were keen advocates of the Finnish language, which during the nineteenth century enjoyed a subservient status to Swedish.) Although Järnefelt is not a great song composer, these are invariably well fashioned. Songs like *Skymning* ('Twilight'), the Fröding setting *I solnedsgången* ('At Sunset') and *Unelma* ('Dream') have a great simplicity and directness. Although Jorma Hynninen has lost the youthful timbre and bloom we remember from his records of *Kullervo* and his Kilpinen recitals, he still sings with his usual intelligence and refinement, and he still gives pleasure. Camilla Nylund is a fresh-toned and appealing interpreter, and they are well served by their accompanist and recording team.

JAUBERT, Maurice (1900–1940)

Ballade
(BB) (***) Dutton mono CDBP 9764. SO, composer – HONEGGER: *Cello Concerto*, etc. PIERNÉ: *Ramuntcho* (***)

Maurice Jaubert graduated from the Nice Conservatoire and practised law before turning to music. He is best remembered for his film music; he wrote the scores for *Un Carnet de Bal* and *La Fin du Jour* in the late 1930s. The *Ballade* was recorded in 1934. But the attraction of this issue is naturally the Honegger, for which this makes a pleasing makeweight.

JENKINS, John (1592–1678)

12 Fantasies in 6 parts; Bell Pavan in A min.; In nomines in G min. and E min., Pavan in F
*** Avie AV 2009. Phantasm

The consort of viols, Phantasm, follows up the success of its *Gramophone* award-winning disc of Gibbons's consort music (Avie 0032 – see our main volume) with this collection of consort music in six parts of John Jenkins. With their elaborate counterpoint, these pieces – all but one in the minor mode – hark back to the Golden Age of Elizabethan music, even though they probably date from the 1620s, after the great queen died, early in the long career of John Jenkins. The writing is masterly and the performances consistently sympathetic; but, with music with little variation of dynamic or texture, this is not a disc to play all the way through at one go, but to sample appreciatively. Well recorded.

JENNER, Gustave (1865–1920)

Piano Quartet in F; String Quartets 1–3; (i) *Trio for Piano, Clarinet & Horn in E flat*
*** CPO 999 699-2. Mozart Piano Qt (members); (i) with Pencz, Darbellay

We don't know much about Gustave Jenner (born in Keitum

on the Island of Sylt), though the insert notes are helpful. However, it is the music that matters, and this is another of CPO's interesting discoveries. The *Piano Quartet* begins with a lovely sweeping figure and the secondary theme is no less beguiling. The slow movement quotes Schubert's *Piano Trio in B flat* and is most attractively decorated. The lively Scherzo is then followed by a theme and variations with a diverting Hungarian sequence. The three *String Quartets* are very much in the tradition of Jenner's teacher and mentor, Brahms. They are quite spontaneous, with plenty of amiable ideas. Occasionally, too, there are darker, Hungarian colourings, notably in the *G minor Quartet*. The *Third Quartet* has a particularly attractive finale, witty and energetic and lyrically quite seductive. Though not in the league of the Brahms *Horn Trio* (Brahms apparently did not care too much for it), Jenner's differently scored work is notable for the facility and vigour of the writing, rather than any deeper qualities. But this remains an enjoyable enough collection of chamber rarities, and the performances and vivid sound make the very most of the music's felicities.

JENSEN, Ludvig Irgens (1890–1957)

Canto d'omaggio; Passacaglia; Pastorale religioso; (i) *Japanischer Frühling*
*** Simax PSC 1164. Bergen PO, Aadland, with (i) Sørensen

Ludvig Irgens Jensen belongs to the same generation of Norwegian composers as Harald Sæverud and, like Sæverud, his music is fresh, at times folk-inspired, tonal and neoclassical in feeling. The *Canto d'omaggio* (1950) is a *pièce d'occasion* but often imaginative, though there are touches of bombast. The *Passacaglia for Orchestra* (1927) is a dignified piece, which attracted the plaudits of Carl Nielsen, even if it rather outstays its welcome. The elegiac *Pastorale religioso* (1939) is an affecting piece and, like its companions, is well played here. The best thing here is the *Japanischer Frühling*, a cycle of nine songs adapted from the Japanese by Hans Begthe, whose Chinese poems Mahler had set in *Das Lied von der Erde*. Written in 1920, it is very beautiful, scored much later, in 1957, and most expertly. It has the simplicity of Mahler and Grieg, and Ragnhild Heiland Sørensen is as eloquent a soloist as Karin Langebo on an earlier LP. What we now need is Jensen's masterpiece, the unpretentious and delightful *Partita sinfonica*, which would be a popular hit if it were given the chance.

JOEL, Billy (born 1949)

Fantasies & Delusions for Solo Piano: Air (Dublinesqe); Aria (Grand Canal); Fantasy (Film Noir); Invention in C min.; Reverie (Villa d'Este); Soliloquy (On a Separation); Suite; Waltzes 1–3
*** Sony SK 85397. Joo

Billy Joel is a talented composer in the world of 'pop' music but here, in the most cultivated manner, he turns to music of a more permanent kind. His brief but memorable *Invention* certainly turns our thoughts to Bach and Scarlatti, but, although his skilful piano writing is thoroughly eclectic, Chopin is the predominating influence, especially in the *Third* of the three charming *Waltzes*, each quite different; and the *Aria* (subtitled *Grand Canal*) is like an extended nocturne. The closing, nostalgic *'Dublinesque' Air*, with its quirky mood-changes, is also most winning. Richard Joo maintains

a sense of improvisatory spontaneity throughout the recital – Joel could hardly have a more persuasive advocate – and the recording is excellent. What a pity the documentation consists only of photographs and titles.

JONES, Daniel (1912–93)

String Quartets 1–8
*** Chan. 9535 (2). Delmé Qt

The *First Quartet* is a particularly impressive work, with a certain cosmopolitanism and a distinctly French tinge to its atmosphere. But Jones is always his own man. No. 2 is exploratory and has a characteristically concentrated *Lento espressivo*. Nos. 3–5 are distinguished by seriousness of purpose and fine craftsmanship. And for the most part this is more than just expertly fashioned music: it is unflamboyant, but all three works are of substance. The last three quartets are even more succinct (each lasting about a quarter of an hour). No. 6 marked the 250th birthday of Haydn and uses two of that master's themes. Its mood is strongly focused, moving from a solemn introduction (and back again) via the Haydnesque Scherzo and a simple slow movement. No. 7 is masterly, intensely concentrated: its central movement is marked *Penseroso*. The last quartet, full of memorable ideas, was left unfinished; it was skilfully completed from the composer's sketches by Giles Easterbrook. Appropriately, it has a hauntingly elegiac close. It is played here with enormous dedication and, like No. 7, holds the listener in a powerful emotional spell. A fitting conclusion to a splendid series, given definitive readings from a quartet closely identified with the music, and first-class Chandos sound.

JONES, Sidney (1861–1946)

The Geisha (complete)
(BB) *** Helios CDH 55245. Watson, Maltman, Walker, Suart, New L. Light Op. Ch. & O, Corp

The Geisha makes a delightful, innocent romp, helped by a sparkling performance under Ronald Corp. Jones and his librettist, Owen Hall, sought to follow up the success of Gilbert and Sullivan's *Mikado*. The formula worked so well that this Japanese musical play ran for two years. Granted that Jones cannot match Sullivan in finesse or tuneful memorability, this has a striking sequence of numbers with such off-beat titles as *The amorous goldfish* and *The interfering parrot*. The choruses also work splendidly. Though Lillian Watson's bright soprano grows edgy at the top, she is charming as the heroine, Mimosa, and though Christopher Maltman's baritone grows gritty and uneven under pressure, he makes a dashing hero. Best of all is Sarah Walker, with her voice as rich and firm as ever, relishing the idiom, just as she does in cabaret songs. Richard Suart is ideal in the comic role of Wun-Hi.

JOPLIN, Scott (1868–1917)

Elite Syncopations (ballet: Rags orch. for 11-piece ensemble by Günther Schüller)
(M) **(*) CRD (ADD) CRD 3329. Gammon (piano) with members of Royal Ballet O

Kenneth Macmillan's ballet was danced to Günther Schüller's

authentic arrangements and the disc includes also three extra rags not used in the ballet. Most of the favourites are included (though not *The Entertainer*) plus some novelties, and the scoring is nicely varied, with the solo piano often left to play alone. The recording is excellent and Joplin fans will find this very enjoyable, although some might feel that the playing is *too* sophisticated.

JOSQUIN DESPREZ (died 1521)

Motets: *Ave Maria – Virgo serena; Benedicta es coelorum regina; Dominus regnavit; Inviolata, integra et casta es, Maria; Miserere mei Deus; Tu solus qui facis mirabilia*
☛ (M) *** DHM/BMG 82876 69993-2. L. Pro Cantione Antiqua, Tölz Boys' Ch., Coll. Aur., Bläserkreis für Alte Musik, Hamburg, Turner

Bruno Turner can always be relied on in repertoire from this period, and this collection of varied motets is outstanding in every way. Although the measure is comparatively short (46 minutes), the quality is very high indeed, and the choice and layout of the programme is admirable. The singing itself is superbly rich and eloquent, and there are few Josquin collections to match this one in variety. The opening *Benedicta*, which uses brass as well as voices, is quite glorious, and the *Ave Maria* also uses brass to support the choral sonority. But the unaccompanied *Tu solus qui facis mirabilia*, opening sombrely, and the glowing *Dominus regnavit* cover the widest range of mood. The setting of the penitentiary psalm, *Miserere mei Deus*, for five voices is the most ambitious motet here, 20 minutes in length, and growing out of a simple cantus firmus into a work of great beauty and power. The 1972 recording has transferred spectacularly to CD, and this disc is very recommendable indeed.

Ave Maria (for 4 voices); *Chanson: L'Homme armé; Missa l'homme armé super voces musicales; Missa l'homme armé sexti toni; Missa La sol fa re mi; Plainchant: Pange lingua; Missa pange lingua; Missa. Prater rerum serium*
(B) *** Gimell CDGIM 206 (2).Tallis Scholars, Philips

This two-for-the-price-of-one offer generously combines nearly all the contents of two outstanding Josquin CDs, including two of the most famous Mass settings of the medieval era, both based on a familar chanson, *L'homme armé*, also used by other composers. The recordings of the *Missa pange lingua* and the ingenious *Missa la sol fa re mi* are also unsurpassed and won a *Gramophone* award in 1987. The motet *Ave Maria* makes a beautiful closing item. The recordings are as outstanding as the perfectly blended flowing lines of the singing.

KABALEVSKY, Dmitri (1904–87)

Piano Concertos 1, Op. 9; 2, Op. 23
(BB) *** Naxos 8.557683. Banh, Russian PO, Yablonsky

It is good to have Kabalevsky's enjoyable *Piano Concertos* at bargain price for those who wish to explore this characterful if uneven composer. The (sub-Rachmaninov) *First Concerto* and (Prokofievian) *Second* have nice dashes of colour and melody, even if neither is a masterpiece. These performances are thoroughly committed and idiomatically Russian. Chandos is also recording the complete *Piano Concertos* with Kathryn Stott and Sinaisky, but their rather more brilliant account of the *Second* is coupled with the *Third* (CHAN

10052). The Chandos disc offers more sumptuous sound, but the Naxos coupling still has a lot going for it, including the modest price.

Violin Concerto in C, Op. 48
☛ (M) *** DG 457 064-2. Shaham, Russian Nat. O, Pletnev
  – GLAZUNOV: *Concerto*; TCHAIKOVSKY: *Souvenir d'un lieu cher*, etc. ***

Kabalevsky's *Violin Concerto* has never enjoyed the same popularity among players as either of the *Cello Concertos*. However, its effortless invention and Prokofievian charm lend it a genuine appeal. Gil Shaham's brilliant account of the piece, in partnership with Pletnev, now reissued in DG' 'Critics' Choice' series, should win it many more friends.

KAIPAINEN, Jouni (born 1956)

Trio III, Op. 29
** Simax PSC 1165. Grieg Trio – BEETHOVEN: *Piano Trio 3* etc. **

The Finnish composer Jouni Kaipainen is a contemporary of Magnus Lindberg and now in his late forties. He studied with Aulis Sallinen and Paavo Heininen at the Sibelius Academy and produced his *Trio III* (there are two others but not piano trios) in 1986–7, when he was in his early thirties. A five movement piece, some 20 minutes long, it shows evidence of a sensitive and sophisticated aural imagination, though we cannot detect an individual voice. The most compelling movement is the keenly felt central *Marcia funèbre*. But this seems a perverse coupling for Beethoven.

KAJANUS, Robert (1856–1933)

Sinfonietta in B flat, Op. 16; Finnish Rhapsody 1 in D min., Op. 5; Kullervo's Funeral March, Op. 3; (i) Aino (Symphonic Poem for male chorus and orchestra)
*** BIS CD 1223. Lahti SO, Vänskä, (i) with Helsinki University Ch.

As a conductor Kajanus was Sibelius's most fervent advocate, interpreting all his major works and directing those premières which the composer himself didn't conduct. He made the first recordings of four of the symphonies (Nos. 1, 2, 3 and 5) as well as *Pohjola's Daughter*, *Tapiola* and *Belshazzar Feast* with the LSO. It was he who founded the Helsinki Orchestra and over the years also introduced unfamiliar new music to Finnish audiences, César Franck and Ravel and, in the 1920s, Stravinsky and Hindemith. It was a performance that Kajanus gave in Berlin of his *Aino Symphony* (or, rather Symphonic Poem for male chorus and orchestra) that inspired Sibelius to compose his *Kullervo Symphony*. Before Sibelius burst on the scene with *Kullervo* and *En Saga*, Kajanus made a considerable name for himself as a composer, but his energies became increasingly consumed by conducting. His music is typical of the national romanticism of the period and, although few would make great claims for its individuality, it is always finely crafted and, in the case of the *Sinfonietta* of 1915, often arresting. Osmo Vänskä and the Lahti orchestra play it with fervour and conviction, and the BIS team serves them well.

KALLSTENIUS, Edvin (1878–1963)

Clarinet Quintet, Op. 17
*** Phono Suecia PSCD 708. Andersen, Lysell Qt –
  FERNSTROM: *Wind Quintet*; KOCH: *Piano Quintet* ***

Edvin Kallstenius was ignored in his lifetime by the record companies and his neglect by Swedish Radio was almost total. After his studies in Germany he pursued a career as a conductor, and during the 1930s he was a music librarian of Radiotjänst, as the Swedish Radio was then known. The *Clarinet Quintet* was written in 1930 and is neo-Romantic in outlook, generally Brahmsian with a touch of Reger. It is a pleasing work but does not make a really strong impression in spite of an excellent performance by Niklas Andersen and the Lysell Quartet and a first-class recording.

KÁLMÁN, Emmerich (1882–1953)

Die Csárdásfürstin (highlights)
B) *** EMI (ADD) 5 86875-2. Rothenberger, Brokmeier,
  Anheisser, Gedda, Miljakovic, Bav. State Op. Ch., Graunke
  SO, Mattes

Launching straight away into a spectacular opening number, this highly attractive operetta from 1915 is full of excellent tunes, with plenty of Hungarian spice. It is said that the hint of melancholy which runs through parts of this score was the result of the composer's grief at the death of his brother. Never mind the plot (or the lack of texts or translations here), just enjoy the tunes, some deliciously laid back, others lively; all served up, one after another, in the live (1971) performance. A bargain, even without any texts and translations. Warm yet lively sound.

Der Zigeunerprimas (complete)
** CPO 777 058-2 (2). Lienbacher, Rossmanith, Todorovich,
  Saccà, Stiefermann, Slovak R. Ch., Bav. State Op.
  Children's Ch., Munich R. O, Flor

Kálmán was appropriately described by one contemporary critic who wrote, 'He kept one foot in the Hungarian nightclub and the other in the Viennese dance hall that gave birth to the waltz'. *Der Zigeunerprimas* ('The Gypsy Princess') was his first important success (1912) when he established himself (after Lehár) as one of the most popular Austro-Hungarian composers of operetta. The composer's trademark Hungarian writing is given full rein in this operetta, a sort of Hungarian *Die Meistersinger*, of which Hungarian gypsy music is very much part of the work's essence. Kálmán supplied his operettas with attractive waltzes and other dances, but he is really seductive in such numbers as *Pali Rácz's Lied, Auf dem dolg'nem . . .* where the theme is summed over shimmering strings and a harp. There are other delightful moments too in this score, for example the woodwind and string introduction to *Aufhör'n, aufhör'n, katya láncos . . .* is deliciously piquant, as is the tune itself. None of the singers is outstanding; one or two (such as the bass) are rather wobbly, but most are acceptable. Flor conducts warmly and sympathetically, with plenty of energy in the lively numbers which, like the Act II duet, *Ich schau hin*, go with a real swing; yet he is beautifully relaxed in the lyrical central section. Similarly, the Terzett, *Und wenn mir einer tausent Franks bezahlt* (with bass drum used to telling effect), is unpretentiously enjoyable. The sound is warm and atmospheric. The main drawback is that there is no libretto,

and the track analysis is not exactly crystal clear. The notes are plentiful, but heavy-going.

KEISER, Reinhard (1674–1739)

Croesus (opera; complete)
*** HM HMC 901714/16 (3). Röschmann, Trekel, Güra,
  Häger, Berlin RIAS Chamber Ch., Akademie für Alte Musik,
  Jacobs

Reinhard Keiser, a contemporary of Bach and Handel, achieved great success early in his career as an opera-composer in Hamburg. He was acclaimed by some as the greatest opera-composer in the world, but his impresario went bankrupt, and in his absence from Hamburg his prime place was taken by the ever-inventive Telemann. In a surprisingly short time his operas were forgotten, which makes it timely that René Jacobs should demonstrate the delights of at least one Keiser opera. Written in 1710–11 at the height of his popularity, this moral tale of Croesus, King of Lydia, fabulously rich, brings the message that money does not make men happy. It was revised 20 years later, an opera in German which, adventurously for the time, leavens the sequence of short arias and recitatives with the occasional duet and ensemble.

Even though this is hardly a match for the operas which Handel was writing (in Italian) for London at the time, it is full of lively and attractive invention, with one or two more serious arias longer than the rest, and with comic servant characters to provide further contrast.

Dorothea Roschmann is superb as the heroine, Elmira, whose minor-key aria in Act I sets the pattern for her rich sequence of arias and duets. The royal characters, not just Croesus of Lydia, but Cyrus, the invading King of Persia, are well taken by the basses Roman Trekel and Johannes Manov, the latter a sinister character who is given a jolly aria towards the end of Act I. The rest make a first-rate team, with René Jacobs pacing arias and recitatives well, though it is strange that Keiser tended to end each Act in mid-air, either on recitative or with the briefest of finales. A fascinating rarity, very well recorded.

KELLY, Bryan (born 1934)

(i) *Crucifixion. Missa brevis; Magnificat from the Emanuel Evening Service; Like as the Hart; O Clap your Hands; Praise his Name in the Dance; The Lovely Lady*
*** Priory PRCD 755. (i) Manahan Thomas, Mulroy; Clare
  College, Cambridge, Ch., Brown, Reid (organ)

Bryan Kelly was born in Oxford, trained as a boy chorister at Worcester Cathedral and later studied with Gordon Jacob, Herbert Howells and Nadia Boulanger, a heady mix of influences, well absorbed. He now lives in France.

It is good to have a *Crucifixion* setting so powerful and immediate in its appeal, completely removed from the Victorian heritage of Stainer, while still featuring simple sung chorales. The work's radiantly pungent choral opening is underpinned by highly individual organ writing, which is later to demand great bravura in describing the disciples' panic. The bold contrasts between soprano and tenor soloists are a strong feature of a work which intersperses biblical texts with poems by George Herbert, the librettist, Anne Ridler and W. H. Auden's 'Shield of Achilles', and the touching solo dialogue, *A Ragged Urchin*, makes a poignant interlude after Jesus' final cry of despair to God.

Kelly's *Missa brevis* is equally compelling, with another brilliant contribution from the organ in the *Gloria in excelsis*, with the chorus later joyfully moving into waltz tempo without a suggestion of triviality. But the *Agnus Dei* ends the work in serenity. The exuberant *Magnificat* is trumped in rhythmic energy by *Praise His Name in the Dance*, and while *O Clap your Hands* is more tranquil, the use of a 5/8 time signature gives the melodic lines a subtle lift. Neither the lovely medieval carol setting, *The Lovely Lady Sat and Sang*, nor the passionate closing, *Like as the Hart*, is in the least predictable, but both show the composer at his imaginative best. The Clare College Choir have a famous association with John Rutter, and under their current conductor, Timothy Brown, they are just as naturally at home in this moving, highly communicative music, which they sing with great freshness, vigour and beauty, while the organist John Reid's contribution is in every way admirable. They are excellently recorded and those looking for choral music which tweaks the ear but which remains melodic in the best sense will find this a most rewarding collection.

KERKER, Gustave (1857–1923)

The Belle of New York (highlights)

(B) **(*) CfP (ADD) 335981-2. Thomas, Kent, Rita Williams Singers, O, Michael Collins – CUVILLIER/CARR: *The Lilac Domino* (highlights) *(*); LEHAR: *The Merry Widow* (highlights) **(*)

The Belle of New York (1897) was Gustave Kerker's one international hit, and the six numbers included here are very charming indeed. *Teach me how to kiss* has a lovely lilting melody, *La belle Parisienne* ('The American girl she walk like this') has a nice wit, and the attractive orchestrations add much to the presentation.

KERN, Jerome (1885–1945)

Songs (arr. R. R. Bennett): *All the things you are; Don't ever leave me; Go, Little Boat; I'm old-fashioned; Long ago and far away; Smoke gets in your eyes; Sure thing; Till the clouds roll by; Look for the silver lining; Up with the lark; The way you look tonight; Why do I love you; Yesterdays*

(B) *(*) CfP (ADD) 3 52346-2 (2). Tuckwell (horn), Instrumental Ens., Richardson (with Songs by Harold ARLEN; Richard RODGERS; Cole PORTER) – GERSHWIN: *Songs* **(*)

An enticing-looking collection from the great American tunesmith in the event proves most disappointing. The instrumentations chosen by Richard Rodney Bennett for Barry Tuckwell and his small accompanying group under Neil Richardson are insubstantial, and the playing itself curiously unmemorable. At best this is usable as late-evening musical wallpaper. The miscellaneous show songs played by Bennett himself are much more enjoyable – see under the Gershwin coupling

(i) *Show Boat* (highlights); (ii–v) *Music in the Air* (excerpts); (ii, v; vi) *Roberta* (excerpts)

☙–(B) *** CfP (ADD) 3 35980-2. (i) Watters, McKay, Bassey, Te Wiata, Bryan, Webb, Rita Williams Singers, O, Collins; (ii) Cole, Fitzgibbon; (iii) Grimaldi, (iv) Linden Singers; (v) New World Show O; (vi) Bronhill, Scott, O, Ornadel

Showboat opened in Manhattan in 1927 and has been going ever since. It is undoubtedly the first great musical, with its bold, even (at the time) controversial story – and, of course, its memorable score. It has been recorded several times, with various casts, as well as the famous EMI complete recording under McGlinn, given a ❂ in our main volume (7 49108-2).

These highlights from 1959 were reviewed in the first *Stereo Record Guide* in 1960. That review itself is a period piece now, with the text referring to the artists as belonging to 'the current hit parade'. There is also advice to 'sample Miss Shirley Bassey and Don McKay before purchasing the record'. Indeed, their singing style sounds more of the late 1950s than of the 1920s, but it is still very enjoyable. All the cast have music-theatre voices, and all are obviously enjoying themselves. Inia Te Wiata is outstanding in *Ol' man river*: he does not over-sentimentalize it, as many others do. Other highlights include the memorable Dora Bryan – always an entertaining actress – as Ellie, singing *Life upon the wicked stage*.

The excerpts from other two musicals are very attractive too. *Music in the Air* (1932) is a charming musical comedy with the flavour of an operetta (it was made into a film in 1934, starring Gloria Swanson). It remains one of Kern's finest lesser-known scores, with the songs worked skilfully into the plot. *I've told every little star* is one of its more famous numbers, but the four others, including *When the spring is in the air* (difficult to get out of your head) and *I'm alone*, make one long to hear the rest of the show. It is very well performed and recorded (1961).

Hardly less appealing is the music to *Roberta*, dating from 1933 (filmed in 1935 and 1952) and similarly containing some vintage hits: *Smoke gets in your eyes* and *Yesterdays* (both sung gorgeously by June Bronhill, though the latter was recorded a couple of years earlier). Again, one longs to hear more of this score. Excellent sound from 1961. This reissue is one of the great highlights in CfP's invaluable music-theatre series and should be snapped up before it disappears again.

KETÈLBEY, Albert (1875–1959)

The Adventurers: Overture. Bells across the Meadow; Caprice Pianistique; Chal Romano; The Clock and the Dresden Figures; Cockney Suite, excerpts: Bank Holiday; At the Palais de Danse. In a Monastery Garden; In the Moonlight; In a Persian Market; The Phantom Melody; Suite Romantique; Wedgwood Blue

** Marco Polo 8.223442. Slovak Philharmonic Male Ch., Slovak RSO (Bratislava), Leaper

The Marco Polo collection has the advantage of modern, digital recording and a warm concert-hall acoustic, and the effect is very flattering to *In a Monastery Garden*. Adrian Leaper's performance is romantically spacious and includes the chorus. If elsewhere his characterization is not always as apt as Lanchbery's (see below), this is still an agreeable programme. It offers several novelties and, though some of these items (for instance *The Adventurers Overture*) are not vintage Ketèlbey, there is nothing wrong with the lively Slovak account of the closing *In a Persian Market*, again featuring the chorus.

(i) *'Appy 'Ampstead*; (ii) *Bank Holiday; Bells Across the Meadows*; (i) *By the Blue Hawaiian Waters*; (ii) *The Clock and the Dresden Figures; Dance of the Merry Mascots; In a*

Chinese Temple Garden; In a Monastery Garden; (i) In the Moonlight; (ii) In the Mystic Land of Egypt; (i) A Passing Storm on a Summer Day; (ii) In a Persian Market; (i) The Phantom Melody; (ii) Sanctuary of the Heart; With Honour Crowned

(M) ** Decca mono/stereo 473 720-2. (i) New SO, Robinson; (ii) Dale, Reeves, Ambrosian Ch., L. Promenade O, Faris

The Faris recordings (originally on Philips) date from 1982 and are digital. But although they include vocal contributions, they lack the flair of the very best performances in this repertoire; occasionally the slower numbers drag a bit, although the collection is enjoyable enough. The recording is also acceptable, but lacks a bit of sparkle on top. The early Robinson performances, though mono, have more dash and brilliance in the lively numbers, as well as more atmosphere in the evocative pieces. The mono sound here is very bright, but reasonably full and warm.

'Appy 'Ampstead; Bells across the Meadows; In a Chinese Temple Garden; In a Monastery Garden; In a Persian Market; In the Mystic Land of Egypt; The Phantom Melody; Sanctuary of the Heart; Wedgwood Blue

(M) *** Decca (ADD) 444 786-2. RPO & Ch., Rogers (with Concert of Gypsy Violin Encores: Sakonov, L. Festival O. ***)

Eric Rogers and his orchestra present the more famous pieces with both warmth and a natural feeling for their flamboyant style, and the tunes throughout come tumbling out, vulgar but irresistible when played so committedly. The birds twittering in the monastery garden make perfect 'camp' but the playing is straight and committed, and the larger-than-life Phase Four recording suits the music admirably. Moreover, it was a happy idea to couple this programme with a collection of Hungarian gypsy fireworks and other favourite lollipops, played with great panache by Josef Sakonov.

Bells Across the Meadow; Chal Romano (Gypsy Lad); The Clock and the Dresden Figures; In a Chinese Temple Garden; In a Monastery Garden; In a Persian Market; In the Moonlight; In the Mystic Land of Egypt; Sanctuary of the Heart

(BB) *** CfP (ADD) 3 52399-2. Midgley, Temperley, Pearson (piano), Amb. S., Philh. O, Lanchbery (with LUIGINI: Ballet Egyptien ***)

A splendid collection in every way. John Lanchbery uses every possible resource to ensure that, when the composer demands spectacle, he gets it. In the Mystic Land of Egypt, for instance, uses soloist and chorus in canon in the principal tune (and very fetchingly too). In the Monastery Garden the distant monks are realistically distant, in Sanctuary of the Heart there is no mistaking that the heart is worn firmly on the sleeve. The orchestral playing throughout is not only polished but warm-hearted: the middle section of Bells across the Meadow, which has a delightful melodic contour, is played most tenderly and loses any hint of vulgarity. Yet when vulgarity is called for, it is not shirked – only it's a stylish kind of vulgarity! The recording is excellent, full and brilliant. Luigini's Ballet Egyptien is equally successful.

HISTORIC RECORDINGS

Aberfoyle (Waltz); Cockney Suite; Danse à la tarentelle; A Desert Romance; Fiddle Fun; Gallantry; In A Camp Of The Ancient Britons; Jungle Drums; Mind the Slide; A Musical Jigsaw; Sunset Glow; (i) With Honour Crowned; (ii) Blow, blow, thou winter wind; (iii) I call you from the shadows

(BB) (***) Naxos mono 8.110869. Various orchestras, cond. composer, except (i) Massed Bands of Aldershot & Eastern Commands, cond. Seymour; (ii) Allen; (iii) Kingston

The vibrancy of the music-making leaps out at you in these historic performances, even on the very earliest, the Danse à la tarentelle from 1909, played by the 'Empire Symphony Orchestra'. By the later 1920s, recording techniques had improved considerably so that the drums in Jungle Drums (exotic nonsense), recorded in 1929, come over reasonably well. It is very easy to respond to the rose-coloured portrayal of London in the Cockney Suite – blatant nostalgia as it is. Mind the Slide (recorded in 1916) features some wacky trombone-sliding, and plenty of whistles, too, the atmosphere of the musical hall not far away. Fiddle fun (violinist unknown, Ketèlby at the piano (1915)) is a fantasia burlesca, featuring many well-known tunes melded together in the manner of a haywire Paginini. More brilliant still is A Musical Jigsaw (1923) which comprises some 53 famous themes (cut to 44 on this recording), in what used to be known as a musical switch, here a bizarre musical jigsaw.

Norman Allen is stirring in Blow, blow, thou winter wind (recorded 1923), while Morgen Kingston in I call you from the shadows (1912) has real period atmosphere and one is reminded of Noël Coward's quip that 'there is nothing so potent as cheap music'. Many of the other numbers, such as Gallantry (1940), Sunset Glow (early 1920s) and A Desert Romance (1923), readily capture the light music style of their eras, while the Aberfoyle Waltz shows Ketèlby in Johann Strauss mode. The disc ends with the stirring With Honour Crowned (a processional march), with the massed bands of the Aldershot and Eastern Commands, conducted by Leslie Seymour – the sharp marching rhythms compensating for the rather thin, 1936 sound. Certainly recommendable, if you have a historic ear, with Naxos's transfers generally satisfactory and the sleeve-notes informative.

Canzonetta; Christmas; In Holiday Mood; Knights of the King; The Phantom Melody; Silver-Cloud; A Sunday Afternoon Rêverie; Tangled Tunes: Parts 1–4. A Vision of Fuji-San; Wildhawk; Wonga. (i; ii) In a Monastery Garden; (i) Men of England (A Short Patriotic Ode); (iii) My heart still clings to you

(BB) (***) Naxos 8.110870. O, cond. composer, with (i) Ch.; (ii) Walker; (iii) Coyle

More vintage Ketèlby, beginning with the Men of England (recorded 1929), dated patriotic music which would be very hard to bring off today; but flag waving believably here. In Holiday Mood (1938) similarly belongs to a long-gone age: the Down the Stream central section, with its gently meandering strings, is very seductive, especially when the celesta joins in at the end. Tangled Tunes (1914) – an ingenious mélange – needs some major detective work to name all the themes used. A Sunday Afternoon Rêverie is based on the musical notes DECCA 'in appreciation of the company's using Ketèlby's music on Radio Luxembourg', whom they were sponsoring. Several famous items are included here, such as The Phantom Melody (played by Jean Schwiller on the cello, recorded in 1912) and Silver-Cloud (1913), with its beating drums setting the scene for the 'Indian Maiden's Song'. Exoticism of this kind is also found in the other pseudo-oriental numbers, Wonga (1916) and Wildhawk (1913), as well as The Vision of Fuji-San, with its cymbals, gongs and harp (1933). Of the vocal items, *My heart still clings to you* (1913) suffers from poor sound, and the highlight is *In a Monastery Garden* (1927), sung by Nellie Walker, with not a dry eye in the house.

Naturally, some of the earliest recordings sound rather thin, occasionally affected by swish (such as *Tangled Tune No. 1*), but the transfers are good, with the music fighting gamely through the years.

KHACHATURIAN, Aram (1903–78)

Cello Concerto in E min.; Concerto-Rhapsody for Cello & Orchestra in D min.

(BB) **(*) Regis (ADD) RRC 1094. Tarasova, Russian SO, Dudarova

Marina Tarasova plays both works with great eloquence and expressive vehemence; she has a big tone and impeccable technique. The orchestral playing is gutsy and sturdy without, perhaps, the finesse that might have toned down some of the garishness of the orchestral colours. The recording is bright and breezy – not worth a three-star grading and nor is the orchestral contribution, though Tarasova certainly is.

Piano Concerto in D flat

⊕—➤ *** Warner 2564 63074-2. Berezovsky, Ural PO, Liss – TCHAIKOVSKY: *Piano Concerto 1* ***

(M) (**(*)) Decca mono 475 6368 (2). Lympany, LPO, Fistoulari – RACHMANINOV: *Piano Concerto 3*, etc. (**(*))

Berezovsky's is the most electrifying account of the Khachaturian *Piano Concerto* on disc, a performance that at last measures up to the famous Kapell 78-r.p.m. version. The concerto needs all the advocacy it can get, for its invention does not match that of the *Violin Concerto*. But so dazzling is Berezovsky's solo playing, and so excitingly responsive is the Ural orchestra under Liss that, while listening to this performance, one could almost think it does. For once, not only does the opening movement not sag, it moves forward irresistibly, and Berezovsky and Liss can even relax in the lyrical central section without letting the tension subside, for the orchestral playing brings out all the sinuous, Armenian colour in the scoring. The slow movement opens and closes with a creepy bass clarinet and moves towards its passionate climax with a real romantic sweep, the flexatone nicely buried in the orchestral texture so that it merely provides an added piquancy. The finale sets off thrillingly at a furious pace, and once again the performers can relax in the central cadenza-interlude before Berezovsky is dazzling us again with his digital brilliance, and the reprise of the first movement's opening theme is unashamedly raucous. Then Berezovsky, Horowitz-like, carries us impetuously through to the final bars, with the orchestra racing along beside him. One expects applause, so high is the tension. The recording is first class, too.

Moura Lympany introduced Khachaturian's *Piano Concerto* to England in 1940, and her version is certainly idiomatic. Unlike most performances, Fistoulari and Lympany never let the work sag but play it with conviction, and Fistoulari brings plenty of bite to the accompaniment. They include the flexatone in the slow movement, treating it almost like a solo instrument; no wonder the composer had second thoughts about its inclusion. But this performance is fresher than many later accounts, and Lympany's virtuosity is in no doubt.

Greeting Overture; Festive Poem; Lermontov Suite; Ode in Memory of Lenin; Russian Fantasy

** ASV CDDCA 946. Armenian PO, Tjeknavorian

Although it has plenty of characteristic Armenian colour, most of this music is routine Khachaturian, or worse: the *Festive Poem* (at nearly 20 minutes) is far too inflated for its content, and the *Ode to Lenin* is an all too typical Soviet tribute. The sub-Rimskian finale of the *Lermontov Suite* is by far the best movement. The *Russian Fantasy* uses an agreeable folk-like melody, but we hear it repeated too often before the final quickening. Good performances, but the resonant recording is acceptable rather than sparkling.

Ballet music highlights: (i) Gayaneh: Sabre Dance; (ii) Masquerade: Waltz; (i) Spartacus: Adagio of Spartacus & Phrygia

(BB) *** HMV 5 86757-2. (i) LSO, composer; (ii) Philh. O, Kurtz – BORODIN: *Polovtsian dances*; RIMSKY-KORSAKOV: *Scheherazade; Flight of the Bumble-Bee* ***

If you want recordings of Khachaturian's two most famous orchestral lollipops, plus a first-class *Scheherazade*, and Beecham's riveting choral *Polovtsian Dances* from *Prince Igor*, this super-bargain disc is not to be missed. The composer himself directs a luscious account of the famous *Spartacus Adagio* and a spectacularly vibrant *Sabre Dance*, while Kurtz contributes an appropriately stylish account of the more elegant *Waltz* from *Masquerade*. Excellent sound.

Spartacus (ballet; complete. Choreography: Yuri Grigorovich)

(***) Arthaus DVD 101 115. Mukhamedov, Verrov, Semenyaka, Belova, Bolshoi Ballet & Theatre O, Zhuraitis (V/D: Shuji Fujii)

Khachaturian's ballet *Spartacus* has had a very chequered history. The work had first been planned as early as 1940, but it was not until the composer travelled to Rome with a Soviet cultural delgation a decade later that the project was reawakened in his mind, and he decided to collaborate with Nikolai Volkov (an experienced Soviet ballet 'librettist'), and they jointly planned the scenario based on the 'proud and greatly powerful Thracian hero' who, after being sold to a gladiator school in 73 BC, led an initially successful uprising against his captors. Escaping with 70 fellow prisoners, and picking up shepherds, peasants, freed gladiators and runaway slaves on the way, he eventually created an army with which, Plutarch tells us, he defeated all nine of the legions sent by Rome to destroy him. He then planned to escape to his homeland over the Alps, but dissension among his followers thwarted this plan, and finally he was overwhelmed by a large Roman force, led by General Crassus. In the ballet scenario, Spartacus, surrounded, makes straight for Crassus himself but, missing him and deserted by his followers, he is finally killed by a large group of the centurions and raised up as a corpse on their spears.

Volkov followed this narrative to create a four-Act ballet, resourcefully adding a pair of fictitious lovers for the two main combatants, the slave girl Phrygia for Spartacus, and a self-seeking courtesan, Aegina, for Crassus. He also included a Judas-figure, Harmodius, who, having been duped by Aegina, betrays Spartacus. The historical end of the uprising was the brutal crucifixion of thousands of the rebels by the Romans along the Appian Way, and in the original synopsis that was intended as Harmodius's just punishment. However, the ballet, as the composer planned it, ended with a 'requiem' apotheosis, which portrayed Spartacus as a proletarian saviour. Khatchaturian's original score included a reference to the *Dies irae* as Spartacus died, plus a resurrection-like sunrise; and the remarkable metaphorical analogy with the Christian story was thus complete.

After four years in gestation, Khachaturian's huge score was ready in 1954. But it was never to be performed in its original form. The first choreographer, Leonid Jacobson, stripped the story to its bare essentials and, for its Leningrad première in 1956, created a stylized dance sequence of the Isadora Duncan school, with Phrygia dominating the narrative. The score was cut and amended to fit his conception of a frieze of 'pictures' that came to life as required. It did not work, and further attempts were made to use the three and a half hours of existing music for a redesigned narrative, first in Prague in 1958 and, later and more successfully, in Moscow in 1959, where the spectacle was restored and the composer was awarded a Lenin Prize. But that version also failed to sustain itself in the repertoire.

Finally, in 1968 Yuri Grigorovich started afresh. He removed the Judas character Harmodius altogether (plus a good deal of the music) and centred the narrative on the conflict between the two main characters and their lovers. The action is framed by the military scenes, with Act I opening spectacularly, Crassus and his legions filling the huge Bolshoi stage with their visceral prowess, and the choreography full of stabbing swords and goose-stepping to show they are fascists.

Alas, one wants to laugh for the wrong reasons. It is all rather crass, and one soon realizes that this is the Soviet equivalent of a second-rate Hollywood epic movie. Khachaturian's music, with its continuous sequential climaxes which almost never produce a distinctive melody, is no better than a low-grade film score, with the orchestration carrying the main interest. The dancing of the principals, however, is very impressive and their stamina extraordinary, when the choreography is so continuously athletic. Spartacus's continuous leaps are amazing, and Aegina and Phrygia's solos are as graceful as the (often curiously awkward) movements they are given to dance will allow. We get just a hint of the score's single really inspired number in Phrygia's *Monologue*, but for the ravishing full *Adagio* sequence we have to wait until Act II, and it is worth waiting for.

Act II is by far the best act, very like a major divertissement in a classical ballet, with much near-traditional choreography. The Shepherds and Slaves join Spartacus's forces, which brings some pleasing pastoral music, but the other highlight (apart for the show-stopping *Adagio*) is the memorable *Dance of the Courtesans*, where for once Grigorovich creates an inspired formal tableau to one of the composer's more simple numbers. The music of the *General Dance*, however, cannot match the famous *Sabre Dance* of *Gayaneh*, and the duel between Crassus and Spartacus is not in the same league as the duel in Prokofiev's infinitely superior *Romeo and Juliet*.

Act III is the other half of the military frame, but in the middle Grigorovich lets his hair down and Aegina has a long, slinky solo in which, after a not very erotic *Bacchanalia*, she attempts to seduce the slaves one by one, to make Crassus jealous, while they are all already busy coupling with their own women, grouped in pairs round the stage. The final battle scene has to make do with divided forces as the corps de ballet has to represent both sides (rather in the way the D'Oyly Carte chorus have to split their numbers in *The Pirates of Penzance* to represent both pirates and policemen when they have their more innocent skirmish). After the

death of Spartacus, the pyramid when he is hoisted up on the Roman swords is visually effective, but the final scene with Phrygia's despairing lament is totally let down by Khachaturian's inability to rise to the occasion with really worthy elegiac music.

The overall running time is 136 minutes, but it seems longer, for the choreography, like the music, is endlessly repetitive. But the solo dancers are magnificent and deserve their (not too obtrusive) applause, while the orchestra under Algis Zhuraitis plays this very noisy score with great feeling and passion. The camerawork is excellent, mainly close-ups, for the Bolshoi stage and proscenium are so huge that the solo dancers are dwarfed when they are shown from a distance.

VOCAL MUSIC

Ballad of the Motherland (Maybe somewhere the sky is blue); 3 Concert Arias; Ode to Joy (The Spring Sun Rises); Poem; March of Zangezur
*(*) ASV CDDCA 1087. Amirkhanian, Hatsagortsian, Vardouhi Khachaturian, Armenian PO, Tjeknavorian

Although the performances are adequate, none of this is first- or even second-class Khachaturian, although the three *Concert Arias* show a genuine operatic flair, essentially Armenian in flavour, but with a hint of Puccini too. Hasmik Hatsagortsian sings them passionately and convincingly. The *Ballad of the Motherland* was given its Russian première by six basses in unison! Here Mourad Amirkhanian sings alone, longing for his homeland. The 1936/7 *Ode to Stalin* is here revised and renamed innocuously *Poem*. It consists of a very long orchestral prelude, followed by a brief patriotic chorus with quite a good tune. The *Ode to Joy* opens with a rather engaging 16-bar *moto perpetuo* on the violins; the mezzo soloist enters with an ardent soliloquy on the joys of spring; then the chorus enters and enthusiastically takes up the melody in popular Soviet style. Texts and translations are provided only for the *Concert Arias*.

KIENZL, Wilhelm (1857–1941)

Don Quixote (opera; complete)
*** CPO 999 873-2 (3). Mohr, Wagner, Henneberg, Breedt, Hay, Berlin Radio Ch & SO, Kuhn

Wilhelm Kienzl, best known – at least in Germany – for his opera *Der Evangelimann*, followed that work up in 1897 with this ambitious opera, which is based on Cervantes' classic novel. Even in Germany it never made it into the regular opera repertory, but this fine, colourful recording demonstrates what an inspired, finely crafted piece it is, an opera that certainly deserves the occasional airing. In a warmly late romantic style, the three substantial acts, each lasting over an hour, cover a sequence of incidents in the eccentric knight's picaresque career with powerful monologues for Quixote himself. The portrait of his squire, Sancho Panza, is for a high tenor, and in some ways it echoes the portrait of David in Wagner's *Die Meistersinger*, just as there are elements in the writing for Quixote himself, notably in his final, nobly disillusioned death scene, that reflect Kienzl's admiration for Wagner's portrait of Hans Sachs. The incidental scenes involve some colourful dances and choruses, with each act well planned both overall and in detail. If none of the would-be comic sequences, with a Germanic ho-ho implied rather than achieved, emerges as genuinely funny, that in a way reflects modern responses to the original Cervantes sequences, and the final death is less rather than more moving, when Quixote no longer preserves his delusions and stoically sees his failure. The concluding scene, with Sancho reflecting on the knight's death, is then rather more moving, leading to a touching orchestral coda, as in the Strauss symphonic poem. It would be hard to imagine more convincing performances, with the principal roles very well sung, not just Thomas Mohr as a powerful, noble Quixote, but the clear-toned James Wagner as Sancho and Michelle Breedt as a fruity Mercedes. Excellent ensemble from chorus and orchestra under the incisive Gustav Kuhn and first-rate sound.

KILAR, Wajciech (born 1932)

Film scores: *The Beads of One Rosary; Bram Stoker's Dracula; Death and the Maiden; König der letzten; Pearl in the Crown*
** Marco Polo 8.225153. Cracow Phil. Ch., Polish Nat. RSO, Wit

The Polish composer Wajciech Kilar obviously knows how to handle the orchestra (he studied under Nadia Boulanger), and he wrote over 100 film scores in Poland before Coppola's *Bram Stoker's Dracula* (1992), his first American film. His 23-minute suite, complete with Gothic, doom-laden introduction, is telling enough. *The Vampire Hunters* does not lack ominously melodramatic foreboding either, and *The Party* is vaguely hypnotic with its fantasy-world celestial instrumentation. *The Storm* (with chorus) is a bit like another *Carmina Burana*, only much less memorable, while Kilar attempts to evoke a sixteenth-century atmosphere for *König der letzten* ('The King of the Last Days') (1993), about the rise and fall of John of Leyden, the false prophet, set in the short-lived New Jerusalem in Münster during 1534. Here the oppressive *Miserere* rather outstays its welcome but the melancholy *Canzona* is rather effective, and the use of a harpsichord adds a touch of piquancy. The score for *Death and the Maiden* (1994) draws on the plot's association with Schubert's famous *Quartet*. However, *Roberto's Last Chance* is reminiscent of a Nino Rota score.

None of this is anything like great music, but it is mood creation in the romantic European/Hollywood tradition. Decent performances and sound, but this issue is for film music buffs only.

KJERULF, Halfdan (1815–68)

42 Selected Norwegian Folk Tunes; 25 Selected Norwegian Folk Dances; 34 Pieces; 4 Song Transcriptions
*** Simax PSC 1228 (3). Steen-Nøkleberg

Halfdan Kjerulf was the most important Norwegian composer before Grieg, and Einar Steen-Nøkleberg, who so successfully recorded Grieg's complete piano music for Naxos, offers three CDs devoted to his keyboard output. Kjerulf's father came to Christiania (now Oslo) from Denmark in 1810 and stayed in Norway after the dissolution of the union between the two countries. Although he composed and played the piano as a boy, Halfdan Kjerulf studied law; but tuberculosis, from which he subsequently recovered, prevented him from qualifying. When he was in his early thirties he studied with Gade in Copenhagen and with E. F. Richter in Leipzig. His output is confined to piano music, songs and

music for male choir. His idiom is steeped in Mendelssohn and Schumann: the *Scherzo* (CD1, track 5) recalls the *Scenes from Childhood*, as does the *Intermezzo* (track 9). Slowly, a more distinctively Norwegian voice surfaces, and some of the dances, such as the *Springdands* (track 10), anticipate some of the keyboard devices with which we are familiar in Grieg. Steen-Nøkleberg is a highly intelligent and persuasive advocate, and the set, which has authoritative notes from Professor Nils Grinde, is beautifully recorded and elegantly presented.

4 Norwegian Folk Dances; 17 Norwegian Folk Tunes; 9 Pieces; 2 Song Transcriptions (from above)
*** Simax PSC 1225. Steen-Nøkleberg

Not everyone will want to invest in the 105 pieces in the complete works for piano by Kjerulf and will doubtless content themselves with this generous anthology of some of the most interesting. Steen-Nøkleberg shows this music in the best possible light, and although no one would claim that these miniatures have the quality or individuality of Grieg or Svendsen, they are highly rewarding and unfailingly enjoyable.

KLAMI, Uuno (1900–1961)

Kalevala Suite, Op. 23; Karelian Rhapsody, Op. 15; Sea Pictures
**(*) Chan. 9268. Iceland SO, Sakari

The *Kalevala Suite* is Klami's best-known work but, like the other two pieces on this disc, it is highly derivative. Ravel and Schmitt mingle with Falla, Sibelius and early Stravinsky; while there are some imaginative and inspired passages (such as the opening of the *Terheniemi* or *Scherzo*), there is some pretty empty stuff as well. The performances under Petri Sakari are very good indeed, and the recording has a good perspective and a wide dynamic range.

Lemminkäinen's Island Adventures; (i) Song of Lake Kuujärvi. Whirls: Suites 1 & 2
*** BIS CD 656. (i) Ruuttunen; Lahti SO, Vänskä

Klami was a master of orchestral colour. *Lemminkäinen's Island Adventures* dates from 1934 and is more Sibelian than is usual with this composer, but its musical substance does not really sustain its length. There is quite a lot of Prokofiev and Shostakovich in the ballet, *Whirls*, and in *Song of Lake Kuujärvi*, and greater depth in the orchestral song. The performances are good and Esa Ruuttunen is an excellent baritone; and the recording offers wide dynamic range and natural perspective.

Symphony 2, Op. 35; Symphonie enfantine, Op. 17
** Ondine ODE 858-2. Tampere PO, Ollila

Klami composed two symphonies, the second of which he finished at the war's end in 1945. If its tone is predominantly post-romantic in character, its musical coherence is less than impressive. It is stronger on rhetoric than on substance. The *Symphonie enfantine* is a slighter piece from the 1920s, heavily indebted to Ravel, and rather delightful. Tuomas Ollila and the Tampere Philharmonic are in good form, and the Ondine engineers produce sound of exemplary clarity and naturalness.

KLENAU, Paul von (1883–1946)

*Symphonies 1 in F min.; 5 (Triptikon); Paolo and Francesca
(symphonic fantasy)*
*** dacapo 8.224134. Odense SO, Wagner

Paul von Klenau, the son of an insurance executive, was
related on his mother's side to the composer Andreas Peter
Berggreen (1801–80). After studies in Copenhagen, he went to
Germany, where he studied with Karl Halíř (who had given
the première of Sibelius's *Violin Concerto* under Richard
Strauss) and later with the composer-conductor Max von
Schillings. He spent much of his time in Germany, travelling
widely as a conductor, returning to Denmark in 1940. In the
1920s he directed the Wiener Konzerthaus Gesellschaft, and
in Copenhagen he introduced works by Scriabin, Debussy
and Delius as well as Schoenberg, with whom he briefly
studied in the 1920s. He belonged among Alban Berg's circle
of friends.

His *First Symphony* (1908) owes something to Bruckner
and Strauss, although the orchestration is wonderfully transparent and has a Regerian delicacy. In his book, *Music in the
Third Reich*, Erik Levi describes how Klenau vigorously
responded to Nazi attacks on his opera, *Michael Kohlhaas*,
which included a tonally determined 12-note technique and
escaped serious censure. The *Fifth Symphony* of 1939 is short
and completely tonal, closer to Reger than to Schoenberg,
and is often quite beautiful, although, as with the other pieces
on this disc, the thematic material is not always memorable.
Perhaps the most imaginative work here is *Paolo and Francesca*, which is also more exploratory in idiom than the two
symphonies. The favourable impression made by these pieces
is due in no small measure to the sensitive and persuasive
direction of Jan Wagner, who conjures up fine performances
by the Odense orchestra. A most interesting issue.

KOCH, Sigurd von (1889–1919)

Piano Quintet
*** Phono Suecia PSCD 708. Negro, Lysell Qt –
FERNSTROM: *Wind Quintet.* KALLSTENIUS: *Clarinet
Quintet* ***

Little known outside Sweden, Sigurd von Koch was active as
an author and painter as well as a composer. His *Piano
Quintet* dates from 1916, and despite its length it is the least
substantial work among these rarities. Its phrase structure
tends to be square, and there is too much sequential repetition. It is played elegantly by Lucia Negro and the Lysell
Quartet but is wanting in real personality and substance.

KODÁLY, Zoltán (1882–1967)

*Dances of Galánta; Háry János Suite; Variations on a
Hungarian Folksong (The Peacock)*
(M) *** Nim. NI 7081. Hungarian State SO, A. Fischer

There are a number of highly recommended CDs of this
music in our main volume, but only the Atlanta Symphony
under Yoel Levi offer this grouping. This 1991 competitor from
Hungary has the advantage of totally idiomatic playing and a
conductor who has this repertoire in his very being. He has
already given us an integral set of the Haydn symphonies, and
these Kodály performances are no less distinguished. The
detail in *Háry János* is a delight, not least the sensitive cello

playing in the central song, while the cimbalom is perfectly
balanced. The *Galánta Dances* rise to a thrilling *vivace* close,
and the *Peacock Variations*, too, are full of colour and vitality.
An excellent collection, with demonstration sound in a
warmly resonant but unclouded acoustic.

Variations on a Hungarian Folksong (The Peacock)
(M) ** RCA (ADD) 09026 63309-2. Boston SO, Leinsdorf –
BARTOK: *Concerto for Orchestra* *(*)

Leinsdorf is more successful in this work than in the Bartók
coupling: this is a reading of genuine feeling and conviction.
Helpfully, each individual variation has been separately cued.
But it is a pity that instead of the Bartók the original coupling
of the *Háry János Suite* was not chosen. Good up-front
sound, but only a half-good disc.

KOEHNE, Graeme (born 1956)

*Elevator Music; (i) Inflight Entertainment. Powerhouse;
Unchained Melody*
(BB) *(*) Naxos 8.555847. Sydney Symphony, Yuasa, (i) with
Doherty

According to the accompanying Naxos booklet, the Australian
composer Graeme Koehne believes that 'contemporary classical music lacks the excitement and enjoyability of pop music'.
If so, why does he try and write it? While it is true that many of
the serial composers of the past 50 years – and too many
others of today – have lost the ability directly to communicate
to an audience, Koehne's easy-listening alternative is hardly
the answer. 1950s-style pop tunes, film and TV music and the
like are all fused into the suites recorded here. While the
elements are superficially attractive, the hotch-potch of ideas
makes for pretty unsatisfying listening. Real music, as Vernon
Handley likes to re-state, is primarily about structure. Koehne
makes an effort to entertain, which is something, but there is
nothing here approaching, say, a good Henry Mancini tune.
Decent sound and performances, but this shows only too
readily what happens when a composer, with the best will in
the world, dumbs down his compositions.

KOLESSA, Mykola (born 1903)

Symphony 1
** ASV CDDCA 963. Odessa PO, Earle – SKORYK:
Carpathian Concerto, etc. **

Mykola Kolessa is the grand old man of Ukrainian music.
The *First* of his two symphonies was composed in 1950 in the
immediate wake of the Zhdanov affair, when any sense of
harmonic adventure was discouraged. This piece at times
sounds like Glière or Arensky. It is expertly written and is easy
to listen to, but it could just as well have been composed in
the 1890s. Very well played and recorded. The pieces by
Kolessa's pupil, Myroslav Skoryk, are more interesting.

KOMZÁK, Karel (1850–1905)

*Edelweiss Overture; Der letzte Gruss Galopp; Louise de
Lavallière (Air). Marches: Echtes Wiener Blut; Erzherzog
Rainer; Thun-Hohenstein. Polkas: Am Gardasee; Heitere
Stunden; Volapük. Waltzes: Bad'ner Mädl'n; Maienzauber;
Neues Leben; Phantome*
**(*) Marco Polo 8.225175. Razumovsky SO, Pollack

Czech composer Karel Komzák was not only an organist for a lunatic asylum in Prague but also founded, in the same city, an orchestra in which Dvořák played the viola. He then became a highly successful bandmaster, travelling throughout Austria. He wrote around 300 works, to which this CD is an ideal introduction. It includes a nice mixture of marches, waltzes and polkas, as well as a more substantial overture. Though not quite in the Johann Strauss league, it is all tuneful music of charm, and is well played and recorded here.

KOPPEL, Herman D. (1908–98)

(i) *Piano Concerto 3, Op. 45. Prelude to a Symphony, Op. 105; Symphony 5, Op. 60*
*** dacapo 8.226027. Aalborg SO, Atzmon, (i) with Kavtaradze

We wrote with some enthusiasm of *Symphonies 1–4* in our main edition, and with even greater admiration of Koppel's *Cello Concerto*. This new disc brings the *Fifth Symphony* of 1956 and the *Third Piano Concerto* of 1948. The *Fifth* was heard at the opening of the new Tivoli Concert Hall in 1956 (the old building had been blown up by the Nazis as a reprisal for acts of the Danish resistance movement); a competition was held, which was entered by 14 composers whose names were withheld from the judges. The scores were read by three conductors (Thomas Jensen, Sixten Ehrling and Odd Grüner-Hegge) and Koppel's was their choice. It is a fine work, much of its inspiration serene, and each of its movements has the breadth and feeling of a symphony. When the 25th anniversary of the hall was celebrated in 1981, the *Fifth Symphony* was again chosen, and Koppel was commissioned to compose a short piece to open the concert. The expertly crafted five-minute *Prelude to a Symphony* was the result and it proved to be one of his last orchestral pieces. The *Third* of his four *Piano Concertos* was the most performed of his works and became the composer's calling-card (he played it extensively on tours and recorded it on LP with Vaclav Neumann and the Danish Radio Orchestra). It is fluent and inventive, and is well laid out for the instruments. Rewarding music, well played and recorded.

KOPPEL, Thomas (1944–2006)

The son of Herman Koppel, one of four children, all of them musicians, Thomas was born in a refugee camp in Sweden, and as pianist/composer/jazz musician entered the Royal Danish Academy of Music in 1962, studying piano with his father. But it soon became obvious from his early avant-garde classical compositions that he was breaking free of the traditional mould with which his family was associated, and in 1968 he and his brother Anders were at the core of a rock group called Savage Rose, whose young vocalist, Annisette, was soon to become Thomas's lifelong partner. Between 1968 and 1973 Savage Rose approached the popularity of the Beatles in Denmark, and in 1971 the Danish Royal Ballet caused a sensation by dancing naked to Koppel's ballet, *The Triumph of Death*. By 1974 Savage Rose had broken up (mainly for political reasons) and Koppel and his partner became political activists on the Left, performing in the main for disadvantaged communities. But in 1990 Koppel reactivated Savage Rose into a larger band that was once again very successful. Then Thomas and Annisette moved to Los Angeles, and he began to compose written music again, stating that 'the classical tradition serves contemporary humanity'. He died at a new home in Puerto Rico in February 2006.

(i) *Los Angeles Street Concerto* (for Sopranino Recorder, Strings & Celesta); (ii) *Moonchild's Dream* (Concerto for Recorder & Orchestra); (iii) *Nele's Dances* (for Recorder and Archlute)
*** dacapo 8.226021. Petri; (i) Kremerata Baltica; (ii) Copenhaen PO, Holten; (iii) Hannial (archlute)

The first two concertos here were written for the celebrated recorder player Michaela Petri in 1990/91, with Koppel seeking to create music 'decidedly Danish/Nordic in tone, lyrical, light and playful against a darker background'. All three works are meant to be descriptive. *Moonchild's Dream* is about a young, disadvantaged child's experience, setting innocence against darkness. *Nele's Dances*, using both sopranino and tenor recorders, portrays the picaresque lover of the legendary rogue, Till Eulenspiegel, and the composer has written poems about each of his two heroines to supplement the music. The *Los Angeles Street Concerto*, the last of the triptych to be written (in 1999), is intended to be a portrayal not of a person but of that most cosmopolitan and multicultural of American cities. The snag is that the solo recorder, engaging as it is, sounds like a solo recorder, and if it is to simulate anything at all, it is birdsong! So in listening to this undoubtedly atmospheric music, it is better to put the descriptive details to one side. Michaela Petri is a marvellous player, her virtuosity is captivating and in the closing 'Requiem' of the *Los Angeles Street Concerto*, she is very touching too.

Moonchild's Dream begins and ends boldly with percussion, but is in essence an arch-like free fantasia, dominated by a haunting, lyrical melody which we hear at the opening and which later produces dazzling virtuosity in the decorations of the third-movement Scherzo, but eventually returns to the mood of nostalgic melancholy of the opening. *Nele's Dances* brings the abrasive contrast of the strumming archlute to add spice to a series of 10 brief and often piquant variations. Each vignette illustrates a line of the linked poem, with the simple statement of the eighth movement (about the warmth of response to the birth of a child) contrasting vividly with the final 'symphony of galloping horses'. The *Los Angeles Street Concerto*, although it opens with a delicate Aria marked *Pirouette*, is much darker in mood and colour, often with complex bravura roulades. The restless third movement (of four) is marked *Inquieto – Addio fugitivo*, and the last movement brings a weird cadenza, before the final, peaceful but sudden resolution. This is remarkably individual music, superbly played, and we believe some listeners will find its easy, melodious writing and moody evocation memorable; others may find it trivial despite Petri's extraordinary virtuosity. The recording is splendidly atmospheric yet clear.

KORNGOLD, Erich (1897–1957)

Symphonic Serenade, Op. 39
●– *** ASV Gold GLD 4020. LSO, Pittau – GRIFFES: *Roman Sketches: The White Peacock* ***

Korngold's *Symphonic Serenade*, lusciously memorable, ought by now to be a repertoire work. But there is no justice in music, and dreadful stuff is regularly heard, while this small-scale masterpiece languishes unplayed in concert halls. With its sensuous, glowing textures it has much in common with its Griffes couplings, but it has great vitality too, especially in its sparkling Scherzo, while the beautiful slow movement is written in the spirit of Mahler. It is superbly played here and the recording is in the demonstration bracket.

OPERA

Die tote Stadt (complete)
** Orfeo C634 0421 (2). Kerl, Denoke, Skovhus, Denschlag, V.
State Op. Ch., VPO, Runnicles

Die tote Stadt was the surprise success of the 2004 Salzburg
Festival, and Orfeo has promptly issued the Austrian Radio
recording, made live at one of the performances. Donald
Runnicles conducts a strong and convincing reading, though
in the dry acoustic of the Kleines Festspielhaus the Vienna
Philharmonic lacks some of its bloom. Angela Denoke sings
very sweetly as Marietta, but Torsten Kerl as Paul produces a
tight tenor tone, the voice often strained and, like Bo Skovhus
as Frank, not always steady. As well as making statutory cuts –
like Segerstam on Naxos – Runnicles omits the sumptuous
prelude to Act II and substitutes a fast, brief and brilliant
prelude, presumably the composer's second thoughts. A synopsis is given, but no libretto.

KRAUS, Joseph Martin (1756–92)

*Sonatas: in E flat, VB 195; in E, VB 196; Larghetto, VB 194; 2
New Curious Minuets, VB 190; Rondo in F, VB 191; Scherzo
with Variations, VB 193; Swedish Dannce, VB 192*
**(*) BIS CD 1319. Brautigan

Though he was almost exactly contemporary with Mozart,
Joseph Martin Kraus has been left behind by musical history.
In his time he was given the sobriquet 'the Swedish Mozart';
although the little *Rondo in F* has an agreeable Mozartian
similarity, the *Sonatas*, while lively and well wrought, are
hardly worthy of such a link. But Kraus is very good at sets of
variations, and the *Andante* of the *E flat Sonata* and the
Andantino finale of the *E major* are both in this form, and
consequently are the most successful movements, while the
Scherzo with Variations is the finest of all. The two *Minuets*,
while personable, are hardly curious, and the *Larghetto* is just a
snippet to make it possible to describe this collection as the
composer's 'complete piano music'. The performances by Ronald Brautigan (who has also recorded all Mozart's solo keyboard music) are exemplary, full of life; his fortepiano, which
is attractively bright and full in timbre, is admirably recorded.

KREBS, Johann Ludwig (1713–80)

*Chorale Preludes: Ach Gott, erhör mein Seufzen; Herzlich
lieb hab ich dich, o Herr; O Ewigkeit du Donnerwort;
Fantasia à gusto italiano in F; Fugue in B flat; Preludes &
Fugues: in D; F min.; Trio in E flat; Little Prelude 3 in C*
*** MDG 331 0384-2. Krüger (Trost organ, Attenburg)

Both Naxos and Priory are currently undertaking integral
recordings of the music of Johann Krebs, favourite pupil of
Bach. But this selection is well made and played with spirit
for those wanting a single disc. The *Chorale Preludes* show
how much Krebs learned from his master, and the *Little
Prelude in C* and the miniature *Fugue in B flat*, delightfully
registered, show him at his most endearingly inventive, if
without the gravitas of Bach. Fine performances throughout
on a fascinating old organ, built by Heinrich Trost and
completed in 1739, which Bach, who was an expert in these
matters, declared was 'of good durability'. Since then it has
been much renovated and 'improved', but in 1976 it was
restored to its original form, and it sounds very well indeed.

KREISLER, Fritz (1875–1962)

*Caprice viennoise; Liebesfreud; Liebesleid; Schön Rosmarin;
Tambourin Chinoise. La gitana* (with Phd. O, O'Connell).
*Violin Concerto in C in the style of Vivaldi; Chanson Louis
XIII & Pavane; Rondino on a Theme of Beethoven. Stars in
my eyes; Marche miniature viennoise* (all with RCA Victor
SO, Voorhees). Arrangements: NEVIN: *The Rosary.*
DVOŘÁK: *Humoresque, Op. 101/7.* LEHÁR; *Frasquita:
Serenade.* FOSTER: *Old Folks at Home.* DRDLA: *Souvenir.*
BRANDL: *The Old Refrain.* HEUBERGER: *Der Opernball: Im
chambre separée.* RIMSKY-KORSAKOV: *Sadko: Chanson
hindoue.* POLDINI: *Poupée valsante.* GRAINGER: *Irish Tune
from County Derry*
(BB) (***) ASV Living Era mono AJC 8561. Kreisler, with
Lanson, Raucheisen, Rupp (or orchestras listed above)

Fritz Kreisler was not only one of the greatest (and most
popular) solo violinists of all time, but he developed a warm,
sensuous vibrato, which was to be copied by his professional
contemporaries and quite transform orchestral string-tone,
even by Casals, who adapted it to the cello. You can hear it in all
these recordings, and especially in Percy Grainger's *Irish Tune
from County Derry*. This is a particularly valuable collection in
offering the first batch of electrical recordings Kreisler made
for EMI between 1926 and 1928, all accompanied by Carl Lanson (the first nine items listed), which are not included on his
EMI mono collection (see below). The sound is dry but the
transfers are immaculate, and the violin timbre real and immediate. *The Old Refrain* and *Im chambre separée* followed in 1930,
the latter played quite magically. The other later items of great
interest are the *Violin Concerto in the Style of Vivaldi* (which it
isn't), the *Chanson Louis XIII and Pavane in the style of
Couperin, Rondino on a Theme of Beethoven*, and *Marche miniature viennoise* (all with the Victor Symphony Orchestra) and
La Gitana (with the Philadelphia Orchestra, although you'd
never guess it), all from 1945. The delightful waltz song, *Stars in
my Eyes* (which Kreisler arranged from an earlier number in his
musical play, *Apple Blossom*), appeared in the 1936 film, *The
King Steps Out* and it is played ravishingly. Excellent transfers.

*Caprice viennoise; Chanson Louis XIII & Pavane in the Style
of Couperin; La gitana; Liebesleid; Liebesfreud; Polichinelle;
La Précieuse in the Style of Couperin; Rondino on a Theme
by Beethoven; Scherzo alla Dittersdorf; Tambourin chinois;
Schön Rosmarin.* Arrangements: BACH: *Partita 3 in E, BWV
1006: Gavotte.* BRANDL: *The Old Refrain.* DVORAK:
Humoresque. FALLA: *La vida breve: Danza española.*
GLAZUNOV: *Sérénade espagnole.* HEUBERGER: *Midnight
Bells (Im chambre séparée).* POLDINI: *Poupée valsante.*
RIMSKY-KORSAKOV: *Sadko: Chanson hindoue.* SCHUBERT:
Rosamunde: Ballet Music 2. SCOTT: *Lotus Land.*
TCHAIKOVSKY: *Andante cantabile from Op. 11.* WEBER:
Violin Sonata 1 in F, Op. 10: Larghetto. TRAD.: *Londonderry
Air*
(M) (***) EMI mono 4 76840-2. Kreisler, Rupp or Rachelsein
or (in *Scherzo*) Kreisler String Qt

Impeccable and characterful performances by Fritz Kreisler of
his own lollipops, including those 'in the style of' pieces with
which – until he owned up – he fooled his audiences into
believing were actually written by the composers in question.
Most of the recordings were made with Franz Rupp in 1936 or
1938, and the transfers offer a convincingly realistic if studio-ish
balance and are of excellent technical quality; a few (the
Polichinelle, the pieces in the style of Couperin, the Schubert

Rosamunde Ballet Music, the Glazunov and Weber arrangements, *The Old Refrain* (especially) and an indulgent performance of Heuberger's *Im chambre séparée*) date from 1930, and here the piano-balance is poor, the piano badly defined. However, these were recorded before Kreisler's accident and the violin timbre is noticeably more opulent. A valuable document.

Caprice viennoise; La gitana; Liebesfreud; Liebesleid; Rondino on a Theme by Beethoven: Schön Rosmarin; Tambourin Chinoise. Arrangements: BACH: (Unaccompanied) *Violin Partita 3: Gavotte.* BRAHMS (arr. Hochstein): *Waltz in A, Op. 39/15.* CHOPIN: *Mazurka in A min., Op. 67/4.* DVOŘÁK: *Humoresque, Op. 101/7.* FALLA: *La vida breve: Spanish Dance.* MOZART: *Haffner Serenade, K.250: Rondo.* POLDINI: *Poupée valsante (Dancing Doll).* RIMSKY-KORSAKOV: *Le Coq d'or: Hymn to the Sun. Sadko: Chant Hindou.* SCOTT: *Lotus Land.* TCHAIKOVSKY: *Andante cantabile.* TRAD.: *Londonderry Air*

(BB) (***) Naxos mono 8.110992. Kreisler, Rupp

These were Kreisler's later series of recordings, made in 1936 and 1948, using EMI's No. 3 Studio at Abbey Road – all but *Caprice viennoise* and *Tambourin Chinoise*, which were made in Berlin. The recordings are technically an advance on the earlier ones listed above and are very faithful in Mark Obert-Thorn's new transfers (mostly taken from pre-war Victor 'Gold' label 78s). With excellent documentation this is thoroughly recommendable.

KREUTZER, Conradin (1780–1849)

Septet (for clarinet, horn, bassoon, violin, viola, cello & double-bass), Op. 62

*** MDG 308 0232. Charis-Ens. – WITT: *Septet* ***

A beautifully played and recorded version of Kreutzer's infectiously enjoyable *Septet*; it is full of lovely tunes and invention, all bubbling along with witty and felicitous writing for each of the seven instruments.

KROMMER, Franz (Kramář, František) (1759–1831)

Clarinet Concerto in E flat, Op. 36; (i) Double Clarinet Concertos in A flat, Opp. 35 & 91

(BB) ** Naxos 8.553178. Berkes; (i) Tsutsui; Nicolaus Esterházy Sinfonia

Both the soloists here are good players and they blend very well together; but slow movements are rather deadpan and not all the music's sense of fun comes over. Neither clarinet-tists nor orchestra are helped by the reverberant recording, which results in a forward balance for the soloists and tends to coarsen the tuttis by spreading the sound. Even so, the *Double Concerto*, Op. 91, a winner if ever there was one, is very enjoyable, with the first movement swinging along merrily and the *Polacca* finale, with its jaunty duet theme introduced against orchestral pizzicatos, equally fluent.

KUHLAU, Friedrich (1786–1832)

It has long been believed that Friedrich Kuhlau was Danish, but he was born near Hanover, moving to Denmark only when Napoleon occupied Hamburg in 1801, where Kuhlau had lived since the turn of the century. But he settled in Copenhagen, first under a pseudonym, then assuming Danish nationality in 1813. By then he had established himself as a pianist, playing both at concerts and at the Royal Court. In 1825, on a visit to Vienna, he met Beethoven and they got on well together. As a composer he was very attracted to the flute. Although not himself a professional performer on the instrument, he wrote a great deal of music for the instrument, which became highly valued. It is little known that Tchaikovsky once took part in a concert performance of Kuhlau's *Quartet for Four Flutes* in St Petersburg.

Piano Concerto in C, Op. 7

** Chan. 9699. Malling, Danish Nat. RSO, Schønwandt (with GRIEG: *Piano Concerto* *)

Kuhlau's *C major Concerto* was composed in 1810, half a century before the coupled Grieg concerto. It is pretty nondescript in character, and little of it resonates in the memory. Amalie Malling is more persuasive here than in the Grieg, of which she gives a routine account, and Michael Schønwandt gets alert and crisp playing from the Danish Radio Orchestra. Excellent sound.

Elverhøj (The Elf's Hill), Op. 100

** dacapo DCCD 8902. Gobel, Plesner, Johansen, Danish R. Ch. & SO, Frandsen

Kuhlau's incidental music to J. L. Heiberg's play *Elverhøj* is endearingly fresh. Not so the recording, however; this sounds really rather dryish, as if recorded in a fully packed concert hall. The music has great charm and the performance under John Frandsen is also very sympathetic.

CHAMBER MUSIC

Duo brillante in D, Op. 110/3; Introduction & Rondo on the Chorus 'Ah! quand il gèle', from Onslow's Opera 'Le Colporteur'; Grande Sonata concertante in A min., Op. 85

*** Globe GLO 5180. Root, Egarr (fortepiano)

Flute Sonatas in G, C & G min., Op. 83/1–3

☛ (BB) *** Naxos 8.555346. Grodd, Napoli

It seems sensible to consider these two CDs together as the music they contain was all written during the same period. The *Grand Sonata in A minor* was published in Mainz in 1827. After a leisurely opening, it has a Hummelian first movement with an engaging dotted secondary theme, followed by a bouncing Scherzo, a serene *Adagio* and a gay, chirping closing Rondo. The *Duo brillante* opens in much the same vein as the *Sonata*, and introduces an aria-like cantilena for its *Andante*, leading to another dancing Rondo finale, but with a gently lyrical secondary theme. The *Introduction and Rondo* opens dramatically and is instantly more operatic in its melodic flow. All these works are of quality but essentially lightweight. They are admirably played and recorded here. Marten Root uses a copy of an early nineteenth-century German flute, and Richard Egarr a bright-toned 1825 fortepiano.

It is when we turn to the trio of Opus 83 *Sonatas*, published in Bonn in the same year, that we discover why their composer was regarded at the time as 'the Beethoven of the flute'. The first of the set opens boldly in G major but soon moves into the minor, and its secondary theme is very striking; the slow movement then opens quite gravely, still in the minor, to introduce an *Ancien air suédois*. Again the piano writing is Beethovenian, and the following variations have real charm. The finale is Weberian in its brilliance, but it is unexpectedly interrupted by a thoughtful, nostalgic *Andante* and ends with a piano cadenza. The second of the set, in C major, has even more of a reminder of Beethoven in its dramatic, slow introduction and brings a distinctive main theme. Then follows a poetically sustained *Larghetto*, and the finale reverts to a felicitous G minor and is brilliantly decorated. The first movement of the third of the series returns to G minor. It is marked *con energia* but retains its lyrical feeling. Again the *Adagio sostenuto* has poise and no little depth, before the mood lightens for the closing *Rondo alla pollacca*.

These are three of the very finest flute sonatas of the early nineteenth century and are fully worthy of the present, highly sympathetic performances on modern instruments, which do not try to over-dramatize or trivialize the music with exaggerated bravura. The recording is excellent and this disc is another real Naxos discovery.

KUHN, Max (1896–1994)

Concierto de Tenerife for Piano & Large Orchestra
** Guild GMCD 7206. Thew, Zürich Camerata, Tschupp –
   HAYDN: *Piano Concertos* **

Max Kuhn studied with Philipp Jarnach, the Busoni pupil who completed *Doktor Faust*, and with Weingartner. He died in Ascona just a few weeks short of his 98th birthday. His *Piano Concerto* (1961–2) was composed in Santa Cruz in Tenerife – hence its title. It is a well-crafted work of modest dimensions and is pleasing, if not highly original. The opening has a touch of Reger about it, and the invention throughout shows the hand of a cultivated musician. Warren Thew is expert and sensitive, though neither the Camerata Zürich nor the recording (from 1976) are top drawer.

KUMMER, Friedrich August
(1797–1879)

Cello Duets: Op. 22/1–2; Op. 103/1 & 4; Op. 156/3: Ariosa (only); Op. 156/5
**(*) Avie AV 2060. Carri, Tomkins

Who would have thought that a collection of cello duets, not by Bach, could be so entertaining? Of course this is not a disc to be played all at one go; but, if you like the cello or – better still – a pair of them, this will give pleasure. Kummer began his career as an oboist in the Dresden Court Orchestra at the age of 15, but Weber, no less, recognized his talent and moved him over to the cello section. His *Cello Duets* are not virtuoso works but are written within the middle-to-lower range and are intended to be enjoyable to play and to listen to, and they are. Kummer's *galant* invention is attractively personable, as in the central *Andantino* of Op. 22/1, where a singing melody is supported by a pizzicato in the second part, and the scherzando finale is very jolly. The closing Rondo of Op. 22/2 is equally diverting, with the main theme heard against a galloping accompaniment. Opus 103, No. 4, opens by quoting from the finale of Beethoven's *Fifth Symphony*; the second movement is a hymn in four parts, and the finale a Spanish Bolero (but one not beyond the capabilities of a good player).

As can be seen, Kummer has no need to draw on the music of others, but the Op.156/3 *Arioso* uses an *Air* from Handel's *Water Music* and Op. 156/5 begins with variations on *See the conqu'ring hero comes* from *Judas Maccabeus* and ends by filching and elaborating another tune from the *Water Music*.

LACHNER, Franz Paul (1803–90)

Symphony 5 in C min. (Passionata), Op. 52 (Preis-Symphonie)
**(*) Marco Polo 8.223502. Slovak State PO (Košice),
   Robinson

Franz Lachner's *Fifth Symphony* is an ambitious work, lasting an hour, lyrical and well crafted. Its ideas unfold naturally and with a certain fluency; its scoring is effective and its idiom is close to the world of Schubert and Mendelssohn. It has more than mere curiosity value, and the Slovak orchestra under Paul Robinson play it with obvious enjoyment. Decent recording.

Septet in E flat
*** Marco Polo 8.223282. Ens. Villa Musica (with FUCHS:
   Clarinet Quintet ***)

Lachner's *Septet* has an easygoing charm which is quite winning. Here it is elegantly played and well recorded, as is the Fuchs coupling.

LAJTHA, László (1892–1963)

Hortobágy, Op. 21; Suite 3, Op. 56; Symphony 7, Op. 63 (Revolution Symphony)
**(*) Marco Polo 8.223667. Pécs SO, Pasquet

László Lajtha was one of the leading Hungarian composers and scholars to emerge after the generation of Bartók and Kodály. Indeed, as an exact contemporary of Honegger and Milhaud, he is separated from his compatriots by a mere decade. The *Seventh Symphony* is a well-wrought and eclectic score that is worth hearing, even if it does not possess the concentration or profile one expects of a major symphonist. The suite from *Hortobágy*, a memorable film set in the plains of Hungary, and the *Two Symphonic Portraits* are effectively scored but their material is insufficiently distinctive. Good performances and recording.

LALO, Edouard (1823–92)

Cello Concerto 1 in D min., Op. 33
(BB) ** Warner Apex (ADD) 2564 60709-2. Navarra, LOP,
   Munch – SAINT-SAENS: *Cello Concerto 1* **

André Navarra is very forwardly balanced in the Warner (originally Erato) recording but, with Munch securing some good, lively playing from his Lamoureux orchestra, it is an enjoyable, characterful account. Not a top choice, but worth considering at bargain price.

(i) Cello Concerto 1; (ii) Symphonie espagnole
(BB) ** Warner Apex (ADD) 2564 60226-2. (i) Lodéon, Philh.
   O, Dutoit; (ii) Amoyal, MonteCarlo Op. O, Paray

A musically attractive reissue is here let down by variable sound. Lodéon's performance of the *Cello Concerto* is thoroughly recommendable, with the Philharmonia under Dutoit providing excellent support. Unfortunately, the early 1980s recording was not one of Erato's best. The soloist is very forwardly balanced, and the orchestra, given a middle and bass emphasis, is muddy and opaque, although the violin timbre remains sweet. Amoyal gives an enjoyably warm and polished account of the *Symphonie espagnole*, rhythmically infectious and with many a seductive turn of phrase, but here the early 1970s recording is a little thin, and again the soloist is very forward.

(i) *Cello Concerto 1, Op. 33. Symphony in G min.; Namouna* (ballet): excerpts
*** BIS CD 1296. (i) Thedéen; Malaysian PO, Bakel

It seems remarkable that BIS needed to go to Malaysia to provide a recommendable modern recording of Lalo's *Symphony*. But Kees Bakel proves a most sensitive exponent, and he opens the work evocatively. The main allegro has plenty of impetus, and the bold chords which set off the light-hearted Scherzo are sharp and clear. After an eloquently shaped *Adagio* with fine, expressive string playing, the finale is vibrant and rhythmically not too heavy, so it does not sound Schumannesque.

Torleif Thedéen isn't a Rostropovich, but his playing is spontaneously persuasive and his wistful *espressivo* is very appealing in the secondary material of the first movement of the *Cello Concerto*. The *Intermezzo* is also touchingly responsive, after a tenderly played introduction from the Malaysian strings; and Thedéen responds to the quicksilver middle section with exquisite delicacy. His natural intensity is again telling in the ruminative opening of the finale; but then the allegro sets off with real élan, and the performance ends triumphantly.

The bonus is a suite of six movements from *Namouna*, again played with plenty of spirit and colour. But here the full and resonant orchestral sound, which has suited the other two works, is less ideal for light-textured dance music. One ideally needs a brighter, more sparkling sound, with glitter on top. Even so, this is still very enjoyable, and overall the disc is very recommendable, and especially so for the *Symphony*.

LAMBERT, Constant (1905–51)

(i; ii) *Piano Concerto* (for piano & 9 players); (iii) *The Rio Grande;* (i) *Elegiac Blues; Elegy; Old Sir Faulk* (arr. Rodney Bennett)
(B) *** EMI (ADD) 5 86595-2. (i) Bennett; (ii) E. Sinfonia (members), Dilkes; (iii) Ortiz, Temperley, L. Madrigal Singers, LSO, Previn – WALTON: *Symphony 2* ***

Originally issued on the Polydor label in 1976, Richard Rodney Bennett's solo recording of the *Piano Concerto*, with Dilkes and members of the English Sinfonia (plus the three piano pieces) has been out of the catalogue for three decades. Bennett makes the music sparkle with wit, pointing the rhythms with fractional hesitations and underlining to bring it to life. The sleight-of-hand pay-off endings to each movement are delectably done. The key item among the shorter works is the *Elegiac Blues*, which Bennett presents rather slowly and expressively; the *Elegy*, more ambitious in scale, is less sharply inspired, but *Old Sir Faulk* shines out as the finest of these three delightful genre pieces. The pairing with Previn's equally persuasive 1973 account of *The Rio Grande* could not be more apt, with its colourful and genial jazz references in a setting of Sacheverell Sitwell's exotic poem. Though Cristina Ortiz is not quite idiomatic in her playing of the central piano solo, Previn directs a strong and enjoyable performance, splendidly recorded. Lambert may not be a great composer, but this is his masterpiece.

(i) *Piano Concerto* (1924). *The Bird Actors Overture; Elegiac Blues; Prize Fight. Romeo and Juliet(ballet)*
*** Hyp. CDA 67545. (i) Plowright; E. N. Philh., Lloyd Jones

This is not the *Piano concerto with 9 players* listed above but the 1924 work, altogether more characteristically life-enhancing, which was reconstructed from the piano duet short score by Edward Shipley and Giles Easterbrook. Jonathan Plowright gave the work its first performance in 1988 and he plays it here with panache, the freshness of new discovery still permeating the music-making. All the other works are from the same period (1924/25), when Lambert's composing libido was at an early zenith. *The Bird Actors* is a mini-overture, while *Romeo and Juliet* was composed for Diaghilev. *Prize Fight* is as rumbunctious as it sounds, while the *Elegiac Blues* was a moving threnody for Lambert's favourite black singer, Florence Mills (written for piano, and not orchestrated until 1928). This is a key item in the Lambert discography, splendidly played and recorded, and highly recommended.

(i; iii) *Horoscope* (ballet suite); (iii; iv) *The Rio Grande.* Arrangements: (ii; iii) CHABRIER: *Ballabile.* LISZT: *Apparitions* (ballet): *Galop.* (iii; v) MEYERBEER: *Les Patineurs* (ballet Suite) (with (vi) WALTON: *Façade* (original version): excerpts
(BB) (***) ASV Living Era mono AJC 8558. (i) RLPO; (ii) Philh. O; (iii) cond. Lambert; (iv) Harty (piano), St Michael Singers; Hallé O; (v) Sadler's Wells O; (vi) Lambert or Dame Edith Sitwell (reciters), Ens., cond. Walton

A unique and treasurable memento of Constant Lambert as composer, conductor *and reciter* – heard alongside the equally remarkable Dame Edith Sitwell in the first recorded performance of extended excerpts from *Façade*. Every word of the daft poetry is crystal clear, and Walton himself conducts with élan, coordinating text and music with remarkable precision. That was in 1929, the same year that Lambert's masterpiece, *The Rio Grande*, was recorded with the original performers, Sir Hamilton Harty playing the solo piano part with the Hallé Orchestra, and the composer conducting. Lambert himself also conducts the sparkling account of *Horoscope*, one of I.M.'s favourite twentieth-century scores, and the jazzy syncopations are caught in both works with splendid lift and panache. Lambert's own arrangement of Meyerbeer's *Les Patineurs* follows (long a key item in the Decca ballet catalogue under Martinon), alongside Chabrier's *Ballabile*, while the *Galop* is a brief reminder of his equally colourful scoring of the Lisztian ballet, *Apparitions*, which did not work on the stage as well as it did in the orchestra. The transfers throughout are vividly clear, but with thin and scrawny violin-tone at higher dynamic levels, though the gentler music glows pleasingly. All the same, an indispensable disc for admirers of this key figure in English music-making in the first half of the twentieth century. Full texts of *The Rio Grande* and *Façade* are included. What a bargain!

LAMPE, John Frederick (1702/3–51)

(i; ii) *Pyramus and Thisbe* (A mock opera); (ii; iii) *Flute Concerto in G (The Cuckoo)*
*** Hyp. CDA 66759. (i) Padmore, Bisatt, (ii) Opera Restor'd, Holman; (iii) Brown

Pyramus and Thisbe, written in 1745, is a reworking of the entertainment given by the rude mechanicals in Shakespeare's *Midsummer Night's Dream*, with the role of the heroine, Thisbe, taken not by a man but by a soprano. The Opera Restor'd company, with Jack Edwards as stage director, here present it complete with spoken Prologue for several attendant characters. Following the overture come 16 brief numbers, with the score edited and completed by the conductor, Peter Holman. Mark Padmore is outstanding as Pyramus, with Susan Bisatt a fresh-toned Thisbe. The warm, immediate recording brings out the distinctive timbre of the period instruments, notably the braying horns. As an agreeable makeweight, the disc also offers Lampe's only surviving independent orchestral work, the *G major Flute Concerto*, with its three crisp movements lasting little more than 5 minutes.

LANE, Philip (born 1950)

3 Christmas Pictures; Cotswold Dances; Diversions on a Theme of Paganini; Divertissement for Clarinet, Harp & Strings; London Salute; A Maritime Overture; 3 Nautical Miniatures for Strings; Prestbury Park

*** Marco Polo 8.225185. Royal Ballet Sinfonia, Sutherland

Philip Lane is best known for his valuable reconstructions of film scores. His own music is tuneful and entertaining, nostalgic and very much in the British light music tradition. He offers a new slant on the Paganini theme, which has enticed so many composers before him, and the result is very enjoyable. His quietly charming set of *Cotswold Dances*, some delicately piquant writing in the *Divertissement for Clarinet, Harp and Strings*, and robust nautical writing interspersed with more melancholy sections in the *Maritime Overture*, all catch and hold the ear. The *Sleighbell Serenade*, the first of the *Three Christmas Pictures*, is his best-known work, but the central *Starlight Lullaby* is very attractive too, rather in the manner of film music. Gavin Sutherland has proved himself in this field before, and he does so again here, with the Royal Ballet Sinfonia showing an appropriately light touch. The recording and presentation are both excellent too.

LANGFORD, Gordon (born 1930)

Colour Suite: Pastorale & March; Fanfare & Ceremonial Prelude; (i) Concertino for Trumpet. Greenways; Hippodrome Waltz; 4 Movements for Strings; (ii) A Song for All Seasons (for piano & orchestra). The Spirit of London Overture; Suite of Dances 1

*** Chan. 10115. BBC Concert O, Gamba; with (i) Steele-Perkins; (ii) Stephenson

Gordon Langford had a traditional musical training at the Royal Academy, he gained orchestral experience as pianist with pier and spa orchestras, and later toured as a trombonist in the pit of an opera company. He subsequently worked for the BBC and provided orchestrations for London-produced musicals. Like Eric Coates, with whom he has much in common, Langford's orchestral scoring is winningly adroit, and the two excerpts from the *Colour Suite* show it at its most richly hued. The opening *Fanfare and Ceremonial Prelude* is contrastingly flamboyant, Elgarian/Waltonesque in derivation, with an agreeable, all-but-*nobilmente* tune in the middle.

The *Trumpet Concertino*, which Crispian Steele-Perkins plays with panache, is both cheerful and lyrical, and has an

audacious freshness. The stylish, neo-classical *Movements for Strings* are introduced by a dancing, airy-textured, opening movement, contrasting with a hauntingly delicate and agreeably atmospheric *Andante* and a pastiche Minuet. The *Song for All Seasons*, with its concertante piano (the nimble William Stephenson), has a syncopated rhythmic condiment but a lyrical core, while the *Suite of Dances* is very English, with its quaintly piping opening theme and wistful Waltz, followed by a sultry Tango and a sparkling, folksy Gigue. *Greenways* is charmingly sentimental, remembering closed railway lines, while *The Spirit of London* (very Eric Coatesian) is rumbustious and full of Cockney spirit. So too is the *Hippodrome Waltz*, composed for the BBC Concert Orchestra, which played in a north London theatre of that name, where the composer saw Christmas pantomimes as a child. All this very friendly and tuneful music is splendidly played by the BBC Concert Orchestra under Rumon Gamba and is superbly recorded. Recommended.

LANGGAARD, Rued (1893–1952)

Fra Arild (Piano Concerto)

**(*) Danacord DACOCD 535. Marshev, Danish PO, South Jutland, Aeschbacher – SIEGFRIED LANGGAARD: *Piano Concerto 1* **(*)

Rued Langgaard may well enjoy cult status at present, and at its best, such as in *The Music of the Spheres*, his music has real vision. At worst, he is a mere windbag, as in this mightily unrewarding concerto. Its genesis is somewhat complex: it draws on material by his father, Siegfried, who was working on a concerto before his death, and attempts to reproduce the feeling of the piece. Oleg Marshev despatches it with great brilliance and flair. Admirers of the composer should try it, of course, but its neglect (it has never been heard before) strikes us as unsurprising.

Symphony 1 (Klippepastoraler); Fra Dybet

*** Chan. 9249. Danish Nat. RSO & Ch., Segerstam

Rued Langgaard was a figure of undoubted but flawed talent, but as this banal, four-movement overblown sprawl slowly unwinds its 67 minutes, one realizes that the composer subjected this particular piece to no real critical scrutiny. There are some imaginative moments in the finale. *Fra Dybet* (*From the Deep*) comes from the other end of his career and was completed not long before his death: it opens rather bombastically but soon lapses into sentimentality at the entrance of the choir. Good recording.

Symphonies 4 (Løvfald: The Falling of the Leaf); 5 (Steppelands); 6 (Himmelrivende: Heaven Asunder)

*** Chan. 9064. Danish Nat. RSO, Järvi

Rued Langgaard's *Fourth Symphony*, subtitled *The Falling of the Leaf*, has retained little more than a foothold in the repertoire. The *Sixth* (*Himmelrivende*, translated as *Heaven Asunder*) is another work that hovers on the periphery of the catalogue. What is lacking in Langgaard is any real sense of organic growth and ultimately, it must be said, a distinctive and original personality. However, Neeme Järvi makes out a strong case for this music and the Danish Radio Orchestra play with conviction and sympathy. They are given excellent recorded sound.

Symphonies 4 (Løvfald); 6; (i) Sfærernas Musik
**(*) Danacord (ADD) DACOCD 340/341. (i) Guillaume,
Danish R. Ch.; Danish RSO, Frandsen

Sfærernas Musik (The Music of the Spheres), written in 1918
between the two symphonies recorded here, is an extraordinary piece of undoubted vision and originality. It has a
wild-eyed intensity and a quasi-mystical quality that is unusual in the Nordic music of its time. One has the feeling that
it could equally stop earlier or go on longer, but formal
coherence is not Langgaard's strong suit. The performances
are good and the recording eminently satisfactory without
being quite in the Chandos league.

*Symphonies 6; 7 (1926 version); (i) 8 (Minder ved
Amalienborg)*
*** dacapo 8.224180. (i) Danish Nat. R. Ch; Danish Nat.
RSO, Dausgaard

Much of the *Sixth Symphony* is ungainly and inexpert but, as
with Charles Ives and Havergal Brian, to whom he has often
been compared, there are glimpses of an original vision. It is
the most often recorded of his sixteen symphonies, though
Dausgaard holds his own with the best. The *Seventh* appears
in its 1926 version, the autograph of which Bendt Viinholt
Nielsen lists as missing in his vast, 560-page *Annotated Catalogue*! However, a score which Langgaard had printed at his
own expense has recently come to light and forms the basis of
this première recording.

The *Eighth*, which occupied him for eight years (1927–34),
honours the church at the Royal Palace at Amalienborg,
where Langgaard made his début as an organist in 1905. It
recalls Mendelssohn and Gade, and even quotes from Bruckner's *Third Symphony*. There is little in the way of real
symphonic coherence, but there is much to interest and
stimulate, alongside much that is overblown. Fine performances and recording.

*Symphonies 9 (From Queen Dagmar's City); 10 (Yon Hall of
Thunder); 11 (Ixion)*
** dacapo 8.224182. Danish Nat. RSO, Dausgaard

All three symphonies come from the war years and the Nazi
occupation of Denmark. The *Ninth (From Queen Dagmar's
City)* sounds rather Schumannesque, although there are
some queasy modulatory lurches that are vaguely Wagnerian. The Tenth, *Yon Hall of Thunder*, was inspired by the
Kullaberg peninsula in Skåne (Sweden), where Langgaard
spent many summers. Scored for a large orchestra (there is a
figure with three piccolos playing in unison and five clarinets
that is quite striking), for the most part the invention is
banal. Not as banal, however, as the *Eleventh Symphony*
(1945), subtitled *Ixion*, the figure in Greek mythology who
was fixed to an eternally rotating flaming wheel in punishment for offending the gods. Much of Langgaard's writing is
awkward and unschooled, and the waltz theme, an idea of
breathtaking mindlessness, is repeated no fewer than eleven
times in the six long minutes this 'symphony' takes. Can you
wonder that the Danish musical establishment of the day
thought him a joke? Decent performances and acceptable
recording.

Symphonies 10; 11; 12 (Helsingeborg); Sfinx (tone-poem)
** Danacord DACOCD 408. Artur Rubinstein PO, Stupel

The *Eleventh* and *Twelfth* symphonies are shorter than they
seem; in fact the *Eleventh* lasts less than six minutes but its
main theme is of awesome vapidity. The Artur Rubinstein

Philharmonic Orchestra turns in serviceable performances
and are decently enough recorded, but they do not dispel the
impression that this is music of shadows rather than substance.

*Symphonies 13 (Faithlessness); 16 (The Deluge of Sun);
Anti-Christ (opera): Prelude*
** Danacord DACOCD 410. Artur Rubinstein PO, Stupel

The *Sixteenth Symphony* opens rather like Strauss, then
comes to an abrupt stop, before launching into a short,
Schumannesque Scherzo of about one minute in the same
key, and thence into a *Dance of Chastisement*. The *Elegy*
which follows also has touches of Schumann and there is a
short and unconvincing finale. In the *Thirteenth, Undertro
(Faithlessness)*, the composer returns to material he had first
used in his *Seventh Symphony*, which he had in turn borrowed from his countryman, Axel Gade. What it lacks in
substance it makes up for in bombast. Probably the best thing
here is the *Prelude* to the opera, *Anti-Christ*, a much earlier
piece dating from the 1920s. The performances and recordings are respectable rather than distinguished.

*Humoresque (sextet for flute, oboe, cor anglais, clarinet,
bassoon and snare drum); Septet for Flute, Oboe, 2
Clarinets, 2 Horns & Bassoon; String Quartet in A flat; (i)
Lenau Moods; In Blossom Time*
*(*) dacapo 8.224139. Randers CO; (i) Simonsen

All the music on this CD belongs to Langgaard's twenties, the
same period as his *Fourth Symphony*. By far the best is the
Lenau Moods, which has poetic feeling and an appealing,
gentle melancholy. The *Quartet in A flat* sounds like pastiche
Haydn and is curiously awkward. The *Septet* is close to
Dvořák or Brahms, although not particularly expert, and the
Humoresque, with its angular wind and snare drum, was
obviously influenced by Nielsen's *Fifth Symphony*, although it
is something of a loose cannon with flashes of inspiration
side by side with bizarre and ungainly writing. Subfusc
performances except in the songs. Decent recorded sound.

VOCAL MUSIC

*Sinfonia interna: Angelus; The Dream; Sea and Sun;
Epilogue; The Star in the East, BVN 180*
**(*) dacapo 8.22413. Dahl, Hansen, Jensen, Canzone Ch.,
Aarhus SO, Rasmussen

As always with Langgaard, one senses that he is content with
the raw material of art and quite happy to pass it off as the
finished article. All the same, there are some visionary
moments in this amorphous but lush post-Wagnerian score,
and Frans Rasmussen gets very good results from his singers
and the Aarhus orchestra. Good recorded sound.

LANGGAARD, Siegfried (1852–1914)

Piano Concerto 1 in E min.
**(*) Danacord DACOCD 535. Marshev, Danish PO, South
Jutland, Aeschbacher – RUED LANGGAARD: *Fra Arild
(Piano Concerto)* **(*)

Musical dynasties, so familiar a feature of the eighteenth
century, are relatively rare in our own age but still flourished
in nineteenth-century Denmark. This is another issue in the
'Harmonious Families' series that Danacord has compiled.
Siegfried Langgaard was a pupil of Eduard Neupert, the

pianist who premièred the concertos by Grieg, Gade and Liszt, no less. His *Piano Concerto* (1885), which Bernard Stavenhagen played to Liszt when the latter's eyesight was failing, has some effective writing, but there is much over-blown, inflated Lisztian rhetoric, which Oleg Marshev des-patches with astonishing aplomb.

LANGLAIS, Jean (1907–91)

The blind Breton organist, Jean Langlais, studied at the Paris Conservatoire, first with Marcel Dupré and then with Paul Dukas. If the initial harmonic sources of his music were modal while also drawing on plainsong, he became more exploratory and adventurous during the war years and after-wards (including flirting with atonalism), and there are few, if any, twentieth-century organ composers whose palette of colour and quality of invention are more stimulating and more directly communicative.

Chant de paix; Chant héroïque; Paraphrase Grégorienne: Hymne d'Actions de grâces (Te Deum); Improvisation on Veni creator spiritus. (i) *Messe Solennelle*
⊕⟶ * Priory PRDC 597. Lee (organ); (i) with Gloucester Cathedral Ch., Briggs – VIERNE: *Messe solennelle ***

These four organ pieces sum up the style of Langlais's organ music admirably. He likes to contrast big swathes of organ sound with gentler textures – dramatically demonstrated in the *Improvisation on Veni creator spiritus* with its spectacular *fortissimos* framing the central evocation using the quiet *vox humana* stop. The *Chant héroïque* contrasts an agitated scher-zando figure with block chords on the full organ, while the *Chant de paix* brings a celestial upward movement, with a slow tread and mysterious colouring. Bold contrasts are even more striking in the *Te Deum*, with the gentle opening chords immediately interrupted by powerful *fortissimos*, and the piece is dominated by loud, gleaming fanfares.

The *Messe solennelle* is similarly dramatic, with the organ thundering out in the *Kyrie*, the choir's response ecstatic but acting as a rich emotional foil to the organ turbulence. The fugal *Gloria* is more restrained in volume, but still passionate, with a striking melodic flow, and a triumphant *Amen*. The organ is fast-moving to underpin the powerful cries of the *Sanctus*, ending with a blazing *Hosanna in excelsis*. A period of repose comes with the *Benedictus* and the opening of the *Agnus Dei*, but spectacle soon returns and, after the choral *Dona nobis pacem*, with the last word, '*pacem*', dramatically underlined, the organ concludes the work resonantly. It is remarkable that the Gloucester Cathedral organ should be so suitable for this repertoire, every bit as much as a French organ, but Mark Lee's playing is gutsy, revelling in the plan-gent registration, and the Cathedral Choir under David Briggs rises excitingly to the musical challenges. A superb disc.

5 Méditations sur l'Apocalypse; Suite Médiévale
(BB) *** Naxos 8.553190. Mathieu (Cavaillé-Coll organ at Saint-Brieuse Cathedral)

With his *Cinq Méditations* Langlais finds a partial affinity with Messiaen, although his writing is infinitely more direct and his theological conclusion, unlike Messiaen's, totally nihilistic. His inspiration to compose the *Méditations* sprang from a severe heart attack in 1973, which brought the com-poser up sharply to confront his mortality, and his reponse

was to read and re-read *The Revelation of St John the Divine* and to give expression to five of the meditations in musical terms, allotting each a title on his score. It is an extraordinary vision and one seemingly founded in despair.

Musically, the writing moves first from a mystical, fugal treatment to a minimalist evocation of eternity, using repeated notes, chords and simple ostinatos, alternating with bursts of plainsong. Then the central piece, *Visions prophé-tiques*, is a violently visceral evocation of the Apocalypse, and this is followed in turn by an intensely mystical plea for Christ's promise of salvation, the organ supplication moving up to the very top note of its range. Finally, with *The Fifth Trumpet* sounding its call, the organ pedals summon up the bottomless pit, with pungent dissonances to represent all the horrors set out in the Book of Revelations, warning mankind of the fate of those who have not accepted Christian salva-tion. The organ registrations here are extraordinarily bizarre, the picaresque grotesquerie wholly original; and it ends the work in a cruel, pessimistic nightmare. The last four chords represent sheer terror. Perhaps Langlais wrote the *Méditations* as a personal catharsis, but the result remains an extraordi-nary testament.

By its side, the *Suite Médiévale* is comparatively innocuous. It too is religious, gathering all the Gregorian themes of the Roman Catholic Mass together into a musical entity of five sections. A characteristically dramatic opening *Prélude* is followed by three meditative central movements (including a simulated *Kyrie*), luminous in colour, and ending with a powerfully confident and jubilant *Acclamations*, the very antithesis of the *Fifth Méditation*. So these two remarkable works balance each other in their opposing responses to Christian belief. Performances and recording are of the high-est quality.

(Organ) *Symphonies 1; 2 (Alla Webern); Poem of Happiness; Suite brève; Suite française: Nazard; Arabesque for flutes*
*** Nim. NI 5408. Bowyer (Carthy organ, Concert Hall, Calgary, Canada)

The *First Symphony* was composed during the dark period of the German occupation of France. Its first movement is angrily aggressive and dissonant, although its structure is comparatively traditional. The composer suggested that the second movement, *Egloque*, reflected 'consolation', yet it includes a brief scherzando section. The tension continues to haunt the arch-like, emotionally ambivalent *Choral*, but lifts in the finale, marked *Vif et joyeux*. Langlais described it as a 'celebration', obviously looking to a brighter future: the music thrillingly extrovert, brilliant in the manner of a Widor Toccata, only more astringent.

The two *Suites* were composed after the Liberation and offer a series of comfortable, engaging miniatures, delectably registered, with the four-movement *Suite brève* opening with a characteristically full-throated *Grand jeux* and closing with a jolly and very French *Dialogue sur les mixtures*. *The Poem of Happiness* (1967) is by contrast unexpectedly vigorous, scur-rying unpredictably, unfettered – exuberant rather than con-tented.

The *Second Symphony 'Alla Webern'* (1977) is a serial work with the serial theme immediately spelled out in the pedals. But (bearing in mind the sobriquet) each movement is very brief (the whole work lasts little more than five minutes). It is as if the composer was saying at the end of each miniature movement, 'enough is enough', while the listener's interest lies with the ear-tickling registration.

LA RUE, Pierre de (c. 1460–1518)

Requiem
*** ASV Gaudeamus CD GAU 352. Clerks' Group, Wickham –
BRUMEL: *Requiem* ***

Pierre de la Rue's *Requiem* is an ideal coupling for Brumel's masterpiece, for not only is it sombre, and is performed solemnly by the Clerks' Group, but it employs remarkably low ranges for the bass voices. This makes the contrasting entry of the trebles in the Gradual Psalm *Sidcut cervus* the more celestial. However, the main influences come from the *Requiem* of Ockghem (also recorded by the Clerks' Group on CDGAU 168 – see our main volume), and De la Rue's dark sonorities here are balanced by less predictable melodic writing which is both communicative and moving in its serenity. Performance and recording are outstanding, as usual from this group.

Requiem; Missa L'Homme armé
(BB) *** HM Musique d'Abord HMA 1951296. Ens. Clément Janequin, Visse

Dominique Visse's approach to the *Requiem* brings a lighter touch and considerably faster tempi throughout than the performance from the Clerks' Group. The result is still solemn but less grave, and undoubtedly freshly enjoyable. But Edward Wickham's approach is even more convincing. Similarly, the Clément Janequin Ensemble's singing of the Mass based on the chanson, *L'homme armé*, flows forward in a similar way. This is the first of two Masses De la Rue wrote using that famous chanson as his basis. The polyphony throughout is complex, but the basic theme shines through attractively, especially in the final *Agnus Deus*, where the four voices sing the same melodic line lyrically but subjecting it to different mensurations, and the result is richly mellifluous. Again, excellent recording.

LASSUS, Orlandus (1532–94)

Orlandus Lassus, born at Mons, was one of the most gifted and inspirational composers of the sixteenth century. He preceded Palestrina as maestro di capella at St John Lateran, but stayed in Rome for only a year before returning home. His first published music dates from 1555, and in 1563 he became maestro di capella at the court of Duke Albrecht in Munich, where he spent the rest of his life and career. The range of his music was extraordinarily wide, but he is best known for his Psalm and Mass settings.

Il Canzoniere di Messer Francesco Petrarca: excerpts
*** HM HMC 901828. Huelgas Ens., Van Nevel

Francesco Petrarca's fourteenth-century collection of 366 poems called *Il Canzoniere* caught the imagination of composers of the fifteenth-century Franco-Flemish school, and every one of them was set to music. The rich imagery of the poetic language, introspective and melancholy, also struck a special chord in the consciousness of Orlandus Lassus in Venice, and he set more than 60 of them. Ten of them are here. The music's richness is deeply felt in these moving performances, and the varied and refined accompaniments are part of the pleasure this collection brings: just sample the radiant opening of the lovely *Cantai, hor piango* ('I sang and now I weep') with its glowing recorders, or the similar delicacy with which the instrumental group provides the

backcloth for the closing *I'vo piangendo* ('I lament my past'). Most are in five parts, but *S'una fede amorosa* (celebrating constancy and passion in love) is in eight and is particularly rich in texture. However, a touching sadness is the pervading mood, even *Là ver l'aurora* ('Around dawn') about the coming of spring. But they are sung, played and recorded so beautifully that one's mood is elevated rather than cast down.

Lamentationes Jeremiae Prophetae (Prima Diei) (for Thursday in Holy Week). Tract: Absolve Domine. Missa pro defunctis (Requiem); Motets: In monte Oliveti; Vide homo
🟥 *** Signum SIGCD 076. Coll. Regale, Cleobury

The pairing of the *Lamentations* attributed to Jeremiah, for Maundy Thursday of 1585, with the *Missa pro defunctis* (one of three) of 1578 has been chosen by Stephen Cleobury to 'represent Lassus's treatment of death': both the sacrifice of Christ and human mortality. Of the two linked motets, the text of *In monte Oliveti* is also associated with Maundy Thursday, but the text of *Vide homo* (which closes the programme) brings a text which is the most profoundly moving of all, as Christ accuses mankind with the words, 'See, O man, what things I endure for you; To you I cry, I who am dying for you.' This beautiful setting was the composer's own swansong, for he died three weeks after he completed it, in May 1594. Performances and recording are, as to be expected with Cleobury, of the very finest quality.

Missa Bell'amfitra altera (including music by Hans Leo HASSLER & Christian ERBACH)
(BB) *** Hyp. Helios CDH 55212. Westminster Cathedral Ch., His Majesty's Sagbutts & Cornetts, O'Donnell

The Westminster Cathedral version of the glorious *Missa Bell'amfitra altera* imaginatively simulates a re-creation of how 'it might have been performed on the Feast Day of a Martyr-Bishop, around 1600', with added music by two other contemporary composers. The Mass propers are given a rich instrumental accompaniment and interspersed with organ *Toccatas* and other music, and the performance concludes with the spectacular Canzon, *La Paglia*, of Erbach and the exultant *Domine Dominus noster* of Hassler for the full ensemble. A most successful venture, on all counts.

Missa Entre vous filles; Missa Susanne un jour; Motet: Infelix ego
(BB) *** Naxos 8.550842. Oxford Camerata, Summerly

With its radiant presentation of the opening *Kyrie*, the *Missa Entre vous filles* is Lassus at his freshest and most telling, and the *Sanctus* is particularly beautiful. The *Missa Susanne un jour*, however, is more ambitious, based on what Jeremy Summerly describes as 'the most famous song of the sixteenth century – the *l'homme armé* of its day'. Moreover, as it deals with the Apocryphal Susanna who was accused of wanton behaviour by two elders after she had spurned their sexual advances, this was just the sort of parody model that had caused the Council of Trent to be upset, two decades earlier. However, it inspired Lassus to his richest polyphony, and many of his celebrants may not have been aware of the implications of the original chanson's text. The motet, *Infelix ego*, is a sombre yet very touching meditation on Psalm 51, the words of which seem appropriate under the circumstances: 'Unhappy I, of all help bereft, who, against heaven and earth have offended'. The 12 voices of the Oxford Camerata under Jeremy Summerly are beautifully blended here, and they sing with dedication and feeling throughout. Excellent recording. A bargain.

Magnificat quarti toni; Missa Surge Propera. Motets from
The *Song of Songs: Osculetur me; Quam pulchra es; Surge
propera amica mea; Tota pulchra es; Veni dilecti mi; Veni in
hortum meum; Vulnerasti cor meum*
*** ASV Gaudeamus CS GAU 310. Cardinal's Musick,
  Carwood

Andrew Carwood is very adept at arranging a programme
combining a Mass with motets, and here he has imaginatively
framed the *Missa Surge Propera* with seven motets from the
'Song of Songs', or *Canticum Canticorum*, with the eight-part
Magnificat making a rich-voiced finale. In the Mass, Lassus
uses the motet on which it is based very resourcefully and
recognizably throughout, and particularly so in the lively and
harmonious setting of the *Credo* (in triple time), musically
the climax of the work. The texts of the 'Song of Songs' revel
in the sensuous and uninhibited physical love of man for
woman, returning again and again to eulogies such as 'your
breasts are more beautiful than wine, and the fragrance of
your scent is above all perfumes'. Of course, Lassus's music is
not sensual, but he does vividly pick up the expressive feeling
of the text – just sample *Vulnerasti cor meum* ('You have
ravished my heart'). Fine singing, of course, recorded in the
warm acoustic of the Chapel at Arundel Castle. Excellent
documentation, too, and full texts and translations, especially
desirable in this instance!

7 Penitential Psalms
🅑—— (M) *** Hyp. CDD 22056 (2). Henry's Eight, Jonathan
  Brown

The *Seven Penitential Psalms* (Nos. 6, 32, 38, 51, 102, 130, 148,
150 (the last two are combined as the Laudate Psalms)) were
recited after Lauds on Fridays in Lent. Lassus's simple but
touchingly plaintive settings first appeared soon after his
appointment at the Munich court, although they were probably composed a few years earlier. Their manuscripts were
beautifully written and lavishly decorated, and they were
initially retained for the Duke's sole use. The emotional
content, while comparatively reserved, is all the more telling
for the lack of histrionics; they make perfect late-evening
listening, for there is plenty of variety in the music itself.

In praising this splendid performance from 1997 we must
quote (with a twinkle) from Denis Stevens's review in Volume
II of *The Stereo Record Guide* concerning their pioneering
stereo recording, made on the Archiv LP label at the beginning of the 1960s by the Aachen Cathedral Choir and instrumental ensemble, conducted by Rudolph Pohl. This was
described in our pages as 'a luxurious presentation which
unfortunately stepped off on the wrong foot from the word
go. Armed with vast tomes on *Aufführungspraxis* [perform-
ance practice], Deutsche Grammophon knew, as every student does, the illuminated copy of the Psalms in which Lassus
is depicted conducting his choir and chamber ensemble, and
starting from that they built an ensemble corresponding to
the one in the picture. All the authentic old instruments were
there doubling the voice parts. The only trouble is that these
are *Penitential Psalms*, written for use during Lent, and at this
time instruments were forbidden in churches throughout
Europe. The idea was that the music should sound as bare as
possible and genuinely penitential!'

Fortunately, on Hyperion Henry's Eight, directed by
Jonathan Brown, immediately set off on the right foot. They
sing unaccompanied; their ensemble, tonal blend and intonation are immaculate and the music is admirably paced;
moreover, the singing has a richness of line and tone which is

deeply felt but never overstated. The recording, made in St
Jude-on-the-Hill, Hampstead, London, is beautifully balanced and has admirable clarity within an ideal acoustic. Full
texts and translations and excellent notes accompany this
mid-priced reissue.

LECLAIR, Jean-Marie (1697–1764)
*Overture in A, Op. 3/3; Violin Sonata in E min., Op. 1/2;
Double Violin Sonata in C, Op. 6/12*
*** Astrée 8842. Kraemer, Valetti, Rare Fruit Council –
  LOCATELLI: *Sonatas* ***

Astrée have had the bright idea of combining the music of
Leclair and Locatelli on CD since, when the two virtuosi first
met and played together at Kassel for the king, the comment
was supposedly made in jest that 'this one [Leclair] plays like
an angel and that one [Locatelli] like a devil'. Hence the title
of the present disc. The *Overture* replicates in trio sonata
form the *Overture, Scylla and Glaucis*, which has a particularly fine central *Largo*. The *Double Violin Sonata* (without
continuo) brings a most winning dialogue in the second
movement, and a dancing finale; but it is the five-movement
E minor work, with its central *Sarabande*, that is most attractive of all, in these very lively and authentic performances.

Violin Sonatas, Op. 9/1, 3, 5 & 8
*** Chan. 0726. Standage, Parle (with François COUPERIN:
La Superbe ou La Forqueray. Antoine FORQUERAY PÈRE
(1672–1745): *Le Leclair*. DUPHLY: *Le Forqueray*)

This disc continues the Chandos Leclair series. We know how
attractive the Opus 9 *Sonatas* are from the coverage on
Hyperion by Convivium (CDA 67068 – see our main volume). Moreover, here Op. 9/8 ends with a splendid *Chaconne*.
No duplications are involved in investing in both discs; but in
any case we much prefer the playing of Simon Standage and
Nicholas Parle for its greater warmth. Standage's timbre is
most attractive, quite free from scratchiness. The harpsichord
pieces celebrating Leclair and his contemporaries may or may
not be an asset (the solo harpsichord does not have a very
strong presence) but can easily be programmed out if not
required.

LECUONA, Ernesto (1895–1963)
*Danzas Afro-Cubanas; Gardenia; Noche de Estrellas;
Porcelana china (Danza de muñecos); Polka de los Enanos;
(i) Rapsodia Cubana. Valses fantásticos; Vals del Nilo; Yo te
quiero siempre*
** BIS CD 794. Tirino, (i) with Polish Nat. RSO, Bartas

Ernesto Lecuona hailed from Cuba and made a career for
himself outside Latin and Central America. With the exception of the *Rapsodia Cubana*, which is conspicuously slight in
invention, this is light music in the Latin-American style but
distinguished by an inventive and resourceful use of rhythm.
Thomas Tirino's pianism is equal to its demands, although
this recording – which emanates from New York and Katowice, not BIS's usual venues – is not three-star. Nor is the
music; however, although it is all very limited, there are
rewarding moments of sophistication.

LE FLEM, Paul (1881–1984)

Symphony 4; (i) *Le Grand Jardinier de France* (film music). *7 Pièces enfantines; Pour les morts (Tryptique symphonique 1)*

** Marco Polo 8.223655. Rhenish PO, Lockhart, (i) with Nopre

Paul Le Flem is another French composer who is emerging from the shadows into which he has been so prematurely cast. The *Fourth Symphony* bears witness to an amazing creative vitality, when one thinks that its composer was just ninety years young at the time (1971–2). (As his dates will show at a glance, he lived to be 103.) The *Sept Pièces enfantines* is an orchestral transcription of a set of children's pieces for piano, and *Le Grand Jardinier de France* is a film score. Both have a certain charm and would have more, had the orchestra been allowed more rehearsal. Wind intonation is not always flawless. Le Flem is not, perhaps, a major personality, but the *Fourth Symphony* is in its way quite remarkable and, had the performance greater finesse, the disc would have rated a three-star recommendation.

LEHÁR, Franz (1870–1948)

(i) *The Count of Luxembourg:* highlights; (ii) *The Land of Smiles:* highlights; (iii) *The Merry Widow:* highlights

(B) ** CfP (ADD) 575 9962 (2). (i–iii) Bronhill; (i) Jason, Fyson, McCarthy Singers, Studio 2 Concert O; (ii) Craig, Fretwell, Grant, Sadler's Wells Op. O; (i; ii) cond. Tausky; (iii) Round, McAlpine, Lowe, Sadler's Wells Op. Ch. & O, Reid

The Sadler's Wells pioneering recording of *The Merry Widow* in English was made in 1958 after a triumphant season in the West End. It is perfectly true that this performance does not have an *echt*-Viennese flavour but, using an admirable new translation by Christopher Hassall, and with the excellent June Bronhill both stylish and charming in the lead, this can stand quite proudly alongside Stolz's Decca Viennese set with Hilde Gueden on Decca (now deleted), which was recorded at about the same time. However, although the English words (which are splendidly clear) immediately convey the point of the lighter numbers, somehow the Viennese singers can manage to convey the humour with voice inflexions alone. The Sadler's Wells cast is strongly characterized; only in Howard Glynne's Baron Zeta is there a suspicion of Gilbert and Sullivan. Thomas Round is an appropriately raffish Danilo, although it is a pity that the recording tends to accentuate the unevenness in his voice. William McAlpine as Camille de Rosillon comes over much better, and his *Red as the Rose* is exquisitely sung. The chorus is outstandingly good and these excerpts are most entertaining: the March-Septet is a riot (if a well-drilled riot), and William Reid conducts with sensitivity, obvious affection and a real feeling for the music's idiom. This is a 'Made in Britain' *Merry Widow*, but none the worse for that, and the recording is vividly atmospheric.

The Land of Smiles (again in an English version by Christopher Hassall) was recorded the following year and, if the music and performance are not quite on the level of *The Merry Widow*, there are some delightful numbers and the company sings them with an engaging freshness, if not always with the authentic Viennese ring. Here June Bronhill takes the supporting role of Mi (the heroine's sister), and though

Elizabeth Fretwell is less rich-timbred she sings sweetly enough. Charles Craig, as ever, is outstanding as Sou-Chong, with his rich, fine tenor voice sounding out gloriously in 'You are my heart's delight' (with different words) in a way that makes one forget how hackneyed it has become. The recording has a good balance between brilliance on the one hand and warmth and resonance on the other and, as with *The Merry Widow*, the CD transfer is excellent.

The Count of Luxembourg was recorded a decade later and, even though June Bronhill is most engaging as Juliette and she also sings the operatic role of Angèle Didier, this is generally less distinguished. The translation by Basil Hood and Adrian Ross, has little of Christopher Hassall's flair, and although Tausky conducts just as understandingly as he does in *The Land of Smiles*, and Neville Jason makes an engaging Count, the singing overall is less impressive than before. The recording was originally made in EMI's hi-fi-conscious Studio 2 system; although the CD transfer has managed to smooth some of the original edginess, the effect is often unflattering to the voices. Nevertheless, these excerpts offer a ~~successful reminder of a neglected score with some good~~ numbers, and altogether this inexpensive two-CD reissue makes a good sampler of a Sadler's Wells vintage period.

(i) *The Land of Smiles (Das Land des Lächelns)* (complete in German). Excerpts from: (ii) *Eva;* (iii) *Frasquita;* (iv) *Friederike;* (v) *Der Fürst der Berge;* (vi) *Giuditta;* (vii) *Das Land des Lächelns; Paganini;* (viii; ix) *Schön ist die Welt;* (viii) *Der Zarewitsch*

(BB) (***) Naxos mono 8.111016/17. (i) Schwarzkopf, Kunz, Gedda, Loose, Kraus, Philh. Ch. & O, Ackermann; (ii) Lehmann; (iii) Tauber; (iv) Aramesco; (v) Eisinger; (vi) Rosvaenge; (vii) Schwarzkopf, Glawitsch; (viii) Rethy; (ix) Wittrisch

Ackermann's mono recording of *The Land of Smiles* is available on EMI, coupled with *The Merry Widow* (see our main volume). Naxos offer it separately, together with a generous collection of Léhar arias sung by a galaxy of great operetta singers from the past. Mark Obert-Thorn's transfer is every bit as good as EMI's, but it cannot disguise the orchestral thinness in the long (too long) overture; but the voices come up well and (praise be!) the dialogue is all separately cued. Schwarzkopf not only sings delightfully in the main work but also contributes in 1939 (alongside the stirring Rupert Glawitsch) to excerpts from *Paganini* and (in 1940) *Das Land des Lächelns*, where the voice sounds young and sweet, almost soubrettish. Other highlights are provided by heady tenor contributions from Leonardo Aramesco and Marcel Wittrisch, almost trumped by Helge Rosvaenge in *Giuditta* and the delightful soprano Irene Eisinger in *Der Fürst der Berge*. But all these singers have something very special about their vocal personalities which conjures up a past era, and Ward Marston's faithful transfers show just how good were the original masters.

The Merry Widow (Die lustige Witwe): Highlights

(BB) **(*) EMI Encore (ADD) 3 41434-2. Rothenberger, Gedda, Köth, Ilsofalvy, Bav. R. Ch., Grauke SO, Mattes

When this Mattes complete set first appeared in the late 1960s it was praised by us, with the proviso that the overture was thinly recorded and that, if the spoken dialogue had been omitted, virtually all the music worth having could have been fitted on to a single disc. It is still available (EMI 5 74097-2) but the producer of this CD may have read our review, for the overture and dialogue are here cut, and the thin upper range has been smoothed. Perhaps a shade too much, as the treble is now somewhat restricted. However, although the playing time is only 45 minutes, it is an altogether delightful disc, strongly cast and vivaciously and atmospherically presented. Gedda is in excellent form (especially in the famous '*You are my heart's delight*'), and Anneliese Rothenberger sings delightfully. Her *Vilja* is a highlight and the final duet, *Lippen schweign*, is ravishing if all too short. Even if one would like a rather more sparkling treble, the ensembles come off with élan.

The Merry Widow (highlights; in English)
(B) **(*) CfP (ADD) 3 35981-2. Howard, Bronhill, Fyson, Brett, Hughes, Howlett, Fleet, John McCarthy Singers, O, Tausky – CUVILLIER/CARR: *The Lilac Domino* *(*);
KERKER: *The Belle of New York* **(*)

When the *Merry Widow* is sung in English, it tends to sound more like musical comedy than operetta, but Christopher Hassall's translation is better than most. The 1968 Studio Two sound was always a bit too bright, but the voices come over well and it is all very immediate. The singing here has a nice, light touch: June Bronhill's *Vilja* is delightful and her duet with Jeremy Brett, *Jogging in a one-horse gig*, is no less fetching. The two lovers close the operetta with equal charm in a warm and stylish account of the waltz, *Love unspoken*. It is the lyrical quality rather than any Viennese flair which makes this version a little out of the ordinary and, with rare couplings, this is one of the finest of Classic for Pleasure's operetta series. One wishes, too, that all singers today had the crisp diction found on this CD!

Arias from: *Frasquita; Friederike; Giuditta; Die lustige Witwe; Paganini; Schön ist die Welt; Der Zarewitsch.*
Overtures: *Das Land des Lächelns; Zigeunerliebe. Suite de dance*
(**(*)) CPO mono 999 781-2. Pfahl, Wittrisch, Reichssender Saarbrücken O, composer

This CD opens with a broadcast from German Radio introducing this June 1939 concert, designed to promote tuneful and edifying music to the German public girding up for war. At that time, Gustav Kneip was in charge of organizing such patriotic events, and it was he who was able to secure two of the most famous artists around to take part in the programme recorded here, preserved on shellac disc and found, quite recently, in the recording archive of the Reich Radio Society. The performances ooze period nostalgia, with Lehár extracting a large helping of sentimentality from his orchestra, as well as plenty of robust energy in the lively passages, with the idiomatic use of portamenti adding to the period flavour. Margaret Pfahl was a popular coloratura soubrette, and although she is obviously not at her best here (there is an obtrusive vocal wobble) she sings with much character. Marcel Wittrisch's contribution has a style and energy often missing in operetta recitals today, but he is capable of singing softly too – the high cadence at the end of the *Zarewitsch* is a delight, and the tenderness of the *Friederike* aria is also most affecting. With the composer directing, the Overtures are enjoyable too, especially *Zigeunerliebe* with its Hungarian flavour, and the *Suite de dance* is an unexpected bonus. The transfers seem to be very satisfactory, being warm and reasonably vivid. The wonder is these discs survived at all!

LEIGHTON, Kenneth (1929–88)

(i) *Cello Concerto;* (ii) *Symphony 3 (Laudes musicae), Op. 80*
(M) *** Chan. 10307X. (i) Wallfisch; (ii) Mackie; RSNO, Thomson

This is a straight mid-priced reissue of a disc praised in our main volume. However, many readers may prefer the alternative coupling of the fine *Cello Concerto* with the even finer concerto by Finzi, even though that is at full price (Chan. 9949).

LEMBA, Artur (1885–1960)

Symphony in C sharp min.
*** Chan. 8656. SNO, Järvi (with Concert: '*Music from Estonia*': Vol. 2 ***)

Lemba's *Symphony in C sharp minor* was the first symphony ever to be written by an Estonian. It sounds as if he studied in St Petersburg: at times one is reminded fleetingly of Glazunov, at others of Dvořák (the Scherzo) – and even of Bruckner (at the opening of the finale) and of Elgar. This is by far the most important item in an enterprising collection of Estonian music.

LEO, Leonardo (1694–1744)

Cello Concertos 1 in A; 2 in D; 3 in D min.; 4 in A; 5 in F min.; 6 (Sinfonia concertata) in C min.
*** ASV CD CDA 1169 (2). J. Knight, ECO, Gonley

The Neapolitan composer Leonardo Leo was primarily famous in the field of opera, and particularly comic opera (although he also played the organ in the Viceroy's chapel in Naples). He was celebrated for appending attractive overtures to his stage works. His six *Cello Concertos* date from 1737/8, anticipating those of C. P. E. Bach, which followed in the 1750s. They are essentially good-natured four-movement works. All the first movements are marked *Andante grazioso*, with a following scherzando (*Con bravura* or *Col spirito*) and Leo's considerable melodic gift is expressive in a reflective way, as in the engaging *Larghetto a mezza voce* of the *First*, A major *Concerto* and the charming *Amaroso* of the D minor work (No. 3). Finales are vivacious without being witty. Probably the finest of the six is not the *Sinfonia Concertata* (which is much like its companions), but *No. 2 in D major*, which, uniquely, is in five movements, with a jolly, penultimate *Fuga*. If you enjoy pre-romantic cello repertoire, these works can be cordially recommended, for Josephine Knight is a first-rate cellist; she is stylishly accompanied by Stephanie Gonley and the ECO, and the recording is most truthfully balanced. The two discs together offer 86 minutes of music, and come for the price of one.

LEONCAVALLO, Ruggiero
(1858–1919)

I Pagliacci (complete)
(BB) (***) Regis mono (ADD) RRC 1235. Callas, Di Stefano, Gobbi, Monti, Panerei, La Scala, Milan, Ch. & O, Serafin

Regis provide an excellent and inexpensive transfer of the Serafin set, where the diva is all but upstaged by Gobbi. Di Stefano too is at his finest. A bargain.

LEONIN (c. 1163–90)

Viderent omnes

⊶ (BB) *** Naxos 8.557340. Tonus Peregrinus (with
  Clausulae Motet on *Non nobis Domine*) – PEROTIN: *Beata
  viscera; Viderunt omnes ***

We are always fascinated by the richness of Leonin's two-part
organa duplum, in which the plainchant melody is slow and
the second part provides a more elaborate solo line (*organum
purum*), or with the two parts moving together sonorously in
an identical rhythm. Here, both male and female voices are
used to vary the colour, and there is nothing dull whatsoever
about the result; indeed, the bare consecutive intervals are
magnetic. The rhythm is conjectural, as there was no way of
noting it down in the twelfth century. But the presentation of
the vivid closing section here (*Factum est salutare . . . Dominus*) anticipates the motet of the future. Also included is an
earlier, simpler parallel organum, taken from the ninth-
century treatise, 'Scolica euchiriadis', setting the Psalm, *Non
nobis Domine*, which is equally magnetic, ending evocatively
with the tolling cathedral bell. The singing of Tonus Peregrinus directed by Antony Pitts is resonantly convincing, as is
the acoustic of the Abbaye de Chancelade. The superb documentation includes full texts and photographs of the original
manuscripts. Coupled with the more complex organa of
Perotin, this disc is an amazing bargain.

LESCUREL, Jehan de (early 14th century)

Ballades, Virelais & Rondeaux

(BB) *** Virgin 2x1 3 49973-2 (2). Ens. Gilles Binchois,
  Vellard – BINCHOIS: *Chansons ***

Very little indeed is known of Lescurel, except that he lived
and worked in Paris, and that he wrote poetry as well as
music. These chansons were found in the Romain de Fauvel
manuscript, dating from around 1327. All love songs, and all
monophonic (except the opening *A vous, douc debonnaire*,
which is in three parts), they are both frivolous and dolorous.
Convincingly presented here, they give us a fascinating
insight into song-writing at the beginning of the fourteenth
century, although some are presented instrumentally, like the
ballade, *Abundance de felonie*, a jolly solo for bagpipes. The
vocal items include solos with simple instrumental accompaniments (the virelai, *Dame, vo regars*, with harp) or unaccompanied ballades, but also a unison number like the spirited
Rondeau, *Bonnement m'agre*, with an accompanying tam-
bour; while the closing *Gracieuse* is a lively accompanied solo
virelai. Expert performances and recording, but this reissue is
let down by the absence of texts and translations.

LEWIS, Michael J. (born 1939)

Film scores: *Julius Caesar; The Medusa Touch; The Naked
Face; 92 in the Shade; North Sea Hijack; The Rose and the
Jackal; Sphinx; The Stick Up; Theatre of Blood; The Unseen;
Upon this Rock; The Madwoman of Chaillot; The Hound of
the Baskervilles*

*** Pen Dinas PD 951. Berlin R. SO, Los Angeles Ens.,
  composer

Welsh-born Michael J. Lewis (currently based in Los Angeles)
first came to notice with his 1969 score for *The Madwoman of
Chaillot*, the highlight of which is the romantic *Aurelia's

Theme*, though the *Palais de Chaillot*, with its battery of
percussion instruments, shows the composer's knack for
vibrant, atmospheric writing. The brooding evocation of
Dartmoor is well conveyed in *The Hound of the Baskervilles*,
while the exotically perfumed score to *Sphinx* uses authentic
Eastern instruments alongside a full modern symphony
orchestra. Lewis's ability to create an atmosphere of menace
showed his mastery in the genre of horror films. *The Unseen*,
a now largely forgotten B-movie, owes almost all its success to
the background music. The simple yet affecting *Love Theme*
and *Romance* are included here. *The Medusa Touch* gets the
full Gothic treatment, and the dramatic *Destruction of Cathedral* (London's Westminster Cathedral, no less), with its
driving rhythms and organ, is very effective. One of the most
enjoyable items, however, is the score to *Theatre of Blood*, in
which a Shakespearean actor (outrageously hammed up by
Vincent Price) wreaks revenge on all his critics by despatch-
ing them to gory deaths which correspond with the plays in
which his performances were lambasted. The mixture of
humour and horror is underlined in the score; the opening
theme begins on a single mandolin but soon expands into a
full-blooded, sweeping statement, while the fugal *Duel* (perhaps, uniquely, the only duel on film ever fought on a
trampoline) is not meant to be taken too seriously. Lewis
possesses a distinctive voice, and this CD, with excellent
performances in good sound, will be savoured by film buffs
and is worth exploring by anyone interested in film music in
general.

LIEBERMANN, Rolf (1910–99)

(i) *Concerto for Jazz Band and Orchestra. Furioso; Geigy
Festival Overture; Les Echanges;* (ii) *Medea Monolog*

(BB) *** Naxos 8.555884. Bremen PO, Neuhold; with (i) NDR
  Bigband; (ii) Tovey, Darmstadt Concerto Ch.

Rolf Liebermann had an extraordinary career, not just as a
composer – spanning the worlds of avant-garde and jazz –
but also as a radio administrator and broadcaster and for 30
years one of the leading figures in European opera as Intend-
ant, both in Hamburg and at the Paris Opera. His *Concerto*
and the *Furioso* (his best known piece) were written before
that intensive period, notably the *Concerto*, in which he
happily fused classical and jazz traditions in big, bold, energetic writing, vividly presented here. The best two movements – *Jump* and *Mamo* – are very catchy, with the NDR
Bigband on top form. The *Geigy Festival Overture*, a commission from a Basle chemical firm, to celebrate their bicentenary, was first performed in 1958. It was written for the Swiss
Tonjägerverband and recorded on tape. From this, Liebermann sketched out a score transcribed for conventional
percussion instruments.

The *Symphonie, Les Echanges*, is not to be taken too seriously either. Including local folk tunes and reflecting the
Basle tradition of a drummer marking festive occasions, this
must count as one of the very few snare-drum concertos.
(Alfons Grieder is the very occupied drummer here.) That
the composer was a pupil of Hermann Scherchen led, surprisingly, to his being accepted in the most esoteric circles of
the 1950s, then at their most rigorous, and the craftsmanship
and the vigour of his work justify that. The most ambitious
piece here, the *Medea Monolog* (some of which was used in
the composer's opera *Acquittal for Medea* in 1995), is in effect
a cantata to words by Ursula Haas and dates from after the
composer's period as an administrator, when he adopted a

powerful, less populist idiom, with the solo soprano joined by an atmospheric chorus. Excellent sound, with the conductor, Gunter Neuhold also acting as recording producer. For those who fancy the cross-over style, this CD is well worth exploring at its modest cost, and texts and translations for the *Medea Monolog* are included.

LIGETI, György (1923–2006)

String Quartet 2
(M) *** Wigmore Hall Live WHLive 003. Arditti Qt –
    DUTILLEUX: *Ainsi la nuit*; NANCARROW: *Quartet 3* ***

Ligeti's *String Quartet No. 2* opens *Allegro nervosa* with a dramatic single pizzicato pluck; then, after whistly harmonics, the figuration is spontaneously impulsive and fragmentary, but not in any way melodic. The whole of the following *Sostenuto, molto calmo* is a variation of the fabric of the first movement, and the *Presto furioso* opens with repeated pizzicatos (remembering Bartók's *First Quartet*). The composer likens this movement to the *Poème symphonique for a hundred metronomes*! Then follows a *Presto furioso, brutale, tumultuoso*, which speaks for itself. The fifth and final movement, *Allegro con delicatezza*, begins like the buzzing of flies, but then creates a remarkable atmosphere of mysticism, 'like a memory seen through mist', the composer tells us, 'the whole of the previous progress of the work is recapitulated but in a gentler form', even with wisps of what is almost, but not quite, a melodic fragment. This live Wigmore Hall performance builds up great tension so that even if you cannot follow the argument the finale is electrifying, and there is a distinct silence after the work's close, before the audience responds with applause.

LINDBERG, Magnus (born 1958)

(i) *Clarinet Concerto; Gran duo. Chorale*
*** Ondine ODE 1038-2. (i) Kriikku; Finnish RSO, Oramo

Not many composers of today can match Magnus Lindberg in the richness of the sounds he draws from the orchestra, and his *Clarinet Concerto* of 2002, inspired by the Finnish clarinettist, Kari Kriikku, is a magnificent example. The energy and thrust of the writing, as well as its richness and beauty, are what strike home from the start, fully exploited in this outstanding performance from Kriikku and the Finnish Radio Orchestra. The piece is in five linked sections, with the third and fourth much more measured than the rest. The final section, after a formidable cadenza, brings a thrilling conclusion. Like the concerto, *Gran duo* is in five linked sections, and it is a pity with both that the disc does not indicate the sections with separate tracks. *Gran duo* sets in contrast two distinct orchestral sections, a body of winds and a body of brass, the one representing the feminine side of the work (even though the sound sometimes echoes that of Stravinsky's *Wind Symphonies*) while the brass, rich and rounded, represents masculine stability. The third work, *Chorale*, much shorter, uses the chorale from Bach's cantata, *Es ist genug*, also used in the Berg *Violin Concerto*. Exceptionally vivid sound.

LINDE, Bo (1933–70)

(i) *Cello Concerto*; (ii) *Violin Concerto*
⚫ (BB) **** Naxos 8.557855. (i) Kliegel; (ii) Gomyo; Gävle SO, Sundkvist

Bo Linde is little known outside Sweden and he was only discovered there in the last couple of decades or so, but he was a composer of great talent. His native town, Gävle, has an active musical life and can boast a good concert hall and a decent orchestra. In the Sweden of the 1950s and '60s, when serial and post-serial music was all the rage, Bo Linde was left out in the cold. R.L. heard him play his *Piano Trio* in Uppsala in 1953, when he was only nineteen, a lean young man who looked a bit like Shostakovich at that age. Alas, youth is a harsh judge, and one thought it was far too heavily indebted to the Shostakovich Op. 67. It is probably far better! Linde rather disappeared from view until his *Violin Concerto* was recorded in 1972 by Karl-Ove Mannberg and the Gävle orchestra, and there was a subsequent recording in 1993 from Ulf Wallin and the Norrköping orchestra on BIS. Make no mistake this concerto, first performed in 1958, is a work of quite striking beauty and full of a gentle melancholy.

Those who respond to the Walton, Szymanowski, Britten (or the Prokofiev *D major*) concertos will feel very much at home here. Linde's craftsmanship is thoroughly assured, the invention warm and lyrical, and the writing for the orchestra highly imaginative and luminous. Its final touching coda is altogether magical. The young Tokyo-born, Canadian violinist Karen Gomyo is the elegant and expressive soloist and the orchestral playing is first class.

The somewhat later *Cello Concerto* was written for Guido Vecchi, a wonderful player and first cello of the Gothenburg orchestra, who premièred it in 1965. It is a somewhat darker but no less intense piece, with a powerful *Lento* finale. True, there is a hint of Shostakovich in the middle movement, but Linde by this stage was very much his own man. This music has real nobility and a natural eloquence, and it inspires a totally committed performance from Maria Kliegel and the orchestra, from whom Petter Sundkvist draws an excellent response. Like the *Violin Concerto*, it is beautifully laid out for the orchestra. Encountering the *Cello Concerto* was a joy – and those coming to the *Violin Concerto* for the first time are to be envied. The recording is of demonstration standard, lifelike and with a truthful perspective between soloist and orchestra. This music deserves the widest recognition and the strongest recommendation.

LISZT, Franz (1811–86)

(i–ii) *Piano Concertos 1–2; Fantasia on themes from Beethoven's 'The Ruins of Athens'; Grande fantasie symphonique on themes from Berlioz's 'Lélio'; Hungarian fantasia for Piano & Orchestra; Malédiction; Totentanz;* (i) *Ce qu'on entend sur la montagne; Die Ideale; Festklänge; 2 Episodes from Lenau's 'Faust'; Héroïde funèbre; Hamlet; Hungaria; Hunnenschlacht; Mazeppa; Mephisto Waltz 2; Orpheus; Les Préludes; Prometheus; Tasso; Von der Wiege bis zum Grabe.* (i; iii) *Dante Symphony.* (i; iv) *A Faust Symphony.* (i) *Concert Paraphrases:* SCHUBERT: *Wanderer-Fantasie.* WEBER: *Polonaise brillante*
(BB) *** EMI (ADD) 5 85573-2 (7). (i) Leipzig GO, Masur, with (ii) Béroff; (iii) Leipzig Thomaner-chor; (iv) Leipzig R. Ch. male voices

Kurt Masur's Liszt survey is perhaps his greatest recorded legacy, and it is now issued complete on seven CDs in excellent transfers – an astounding bargain. In the piano-and-orchestra works, Béroff has justly won acclaim for his superb technique and his refined poetic sense, and these recordings show him to be a Lisztian of flair. His accounts of the much-recorded concertos can hold their own with most of the competition: there is nothing routine or slapdash here, and the flair this artist shows in his Debussy and Prokofiev recordings are in ample evidence here, along with remarkable technical prowess – these are exhilarating performances and are given the extra attraction of fine orchestral playing and vivid (late 1970s) recording.

The same comments apply to the other piano concertante works: they are all superbly done, with ample brilliance, yet are musical and stylish, with a sense of fun in the virtuosic fireworks. As for the tone-poems, these 1970s performances sweep the board in almost every respect. If some of the early works suffer from formal weakness and, in some, a lack of distinctive melodic invention, Masur makes the strongest possible case for them, with works such as *Festklänge* emerging much more powerfully than usual. The well-known tone-poems – such as *Mazeppa* and *Les Préludes* – emerge very compellingly; *Hamlet* has great dramatic intensity throughout and *Die nächtliche Zug*, the first of the *Two Episodes from Lenau's 'Faust'*, strikes the listener immediately with its intense, brooding atmosphere. The performances – and, whatever one may think of it, this music – cast a strong spell and, with rare exceptions, Masur proves as persuasive an advocate as any on record. The rich sonority on the lower strings, the dark, perfectly blended woodwind tone and the fine internal balance of the Leipzig Gewandhaus Orchestra hold the listener's attention throughout – for in the weaker pieces Liszt benefits from all the help his interpreters can give him.

Only in *Orpheus* does Masur let us down: he breezes through it at record speed and misses the endearing gentleness that Beecham brought to it in the early 1960s. In the two *Symphonies*, Masur is again impressive, though even in the *Gretchen* movement of the *Faust Symphony* he moves things on, albeit not unacceptably, and there is no want of delicacy or ardour. The *Faust Symphony* can certainly hold its own, and the same may be said of the *Dante Symphony*, even though Beecham is unsurpassed in the former and Sinopoli in the latter. The recordings are well balanced and refined throughout, emerging more freshly than ever on CD. A very considerable achievement.

Piano Concertos 1–2; Concerto 3 (ed. Jay Rosenblatt);
Concerto pathétique; De profundis; Fantasia on a Theme from Beethoven's 'Ruins of Athens'; Fantasy on Hungarian Folk Tunes; Grande fantaisie symphonique on themes from Berlioz's 'Lélio'; Méditation; Polonaise brillante; Totentanz; Wandererfantaisie
(M) *** Chan. 10371X (3). Lortie, Hague Residentie O, Pehlivanian

This three-disc set gathers together at mid-price Liszt's major concertante works for piano and orchestra. Louis Lortie's accounts of the two known concertos with the Hague Residentie Orchestra under George Pehlivanian are very impressive and can hold their own with all but the very best (only the likes of Zimerman, Brendel and Richter remain unchallenged and, in No. 1, Arrau and Argerich). But these are better recorded than any of their rivals and bring poetic insights as well as virtuosity. There is less competition in the *Hungarian Fantasia* and *Totentanz*, and these Chandos versions rank with the best from the past. The so-called *Third Concerto*, first given in 1990, and the *Concerto pathétique* are reconstructions and are of interest to Lisztians rather than the wider musical public.

Liszt's transcription of Schubert's *Wanderer Fantasia* for piano and orchestra is another matter, and Lortie's performance is second to none. The transcriptions of the Weber *Polonaise brillante*, the *Fantasia on a Theme from Beethoven's 'Ruins of Athens'*, and the *Grande fantasie symphonique on Berlioz's 'Lélio'* are all equally desirable, and once again the fine playing of the Residentie Orchestra under Pehlivanian contributes to making this an exhilarating collection, with consistently excellent Chandos recording.

Piano Concertos 1–2; Hungarian Fantasia; Totentanz
(BB) ** EMI Encore (ADD) 5 74572-2. Cziffra, O de Paris, Cziffra Jr
(i) *Piano Concertos 1–2. Sonata in B min.*
(M) **(*) Sony SK 94746. Ax; (i) Philh. O, Salonen

Emanuel Ax and Esa-Pekka Salonen create a memorable partnership for a splendid modern coupling of the two Liszt *Piano Concertos*, with a spectacularly vivid recording to match performances which have all the bravura qualities one might have expected from the composer himself. Yet the lyrical interludes are played most sensitively, and in the *E flat Concerto* the slow movement is followed by a dazzling performance of the famous 'triangle' Scherzo (though the triangle is a little reticent). The more elusive *A major* work can be vulgarized, but not here. It opens atmospherically and evocatively, and the slow movement with its romantic cello solo is warmly sensitive without sentimentality. The *Allegro deciso* with its bold march rhythms then brings splendid impetus and power to the finale.

Ax's account of the *Sonata* is equally arresting, but it is a highly personal reading, impetuous and wilful. He is at its most appealing in the gently expressive *Andante sostenuto*, but his flamboyant approach is more concerned with the music's powerful romantic contrasts than in revealing Liszt's cyclic structure, with its three repeated motifs. Even so, this is a remarkable disc that cannot fail to hold the listener from the first note to the last, and the sound, though forward, is in the demonstration bracket.

These father-and-son performances on EMI Encore (Cziffra père being the pianist) emanate from the early 1970s. The playing has some flair and character, but the recording in the concertos lets the side down – the sound is opaque and shallow, with the piano inclining to brittleness. Although the *Hungarian Fantasia* and *Totentanz* have greater vividness, they are still not ideal. EMI list 12 tracks in the booklet, but in reality we have only one track per piece.

Piano Concerto 1 in E flat
(BB) **(*) Naxos 8.550292. Banowetz, Czech RSO, Bratislava, Dohnányi – CHOPIN: *Concerto 1* **(*)

A splendid, energetic account of the *First Concerto* from Joseph Banowetz, well coupled with Chopin, has the full measure of the work's flamboyance and its poetry. The wide-ranging sound is excellent, though the triangle solo in the Scherzo is only just audible.

(i) *Fantasia on Hungarian Folk Tunes. Hungarian Rhapsodies 2, 4–5; Mazeppa; Mephisto Waltz 2; Les Préludes; Tasso, lamento e trionfo*
(B) *** DG Double (ADD) (IMS) 453 130-2 (2). BPO, Karajan; (i) with Cherkassky

(i) *Fantasia on Hungarian Folk Themes; Hungarian Rhapsodies 2 in C min.; 6 (Carnival in Pest) in D. Les Préludes*

(BB) *(*) Warner Apex (ADD) 0573 89129-2. Leipzig GO, Neumann with (i) Stöckigt

Shura Cherkassky's glittering (1961) recording of the *Hungarian Fantasia* is an affectionate performance with some engaging touches from the orchestra, though the pianist is dominant and his playing is superbly assured. The rest of the programme is comparably charismatic. The cellos and basses sound marvellous in the *Fifth Rhapsody* and *Tasso*, and even the brashness of *Les Préludes* is a little tempered. *Mazeppa* is a great performance, superbly thrilling and atmospheric, with a riveting coda – worthy of a Rosette. A set showing Karajan and his Berlin orchestra at their finest.

Neumann's performances date from 1968 and are quite lively and enthusiastic, but the recording is undistinguished, lacking richness and depth.

(i–iv) *A Faust Symphony; (i; ii) Orpheus; (i; v) Les Préludes; Tasso; (i–iii; vi) Psalm XIII*

⊙→ (BB) *** EMI Gemini (ADD) 4 76927-2 (2). (i) RPO; (ii) Beecham; (iii) with Beecham Choral Soc. (iv) A. Young; (v) cond. Silvestri; (vi) W. Midgeley

Beecham's classic (1958) Kingsway recording of the *Faust Symphony*, very well transferred to CD, shows this instinctive Lisztian at his most illuminatingly persuasive. His control of speed is masterly, spacious and eloquent in the first two movements, without dragging, and with the central portrait of *Gretchen* ravishingly played. The finale is brilliant and urgent, without any hint of breathlessness. Though Barenboim's modern recording with the Berlin Philharmonic (and Domingo the soloist in the finale) must remain the primary modern choice (Warner 3984 22948-2), the sound of the Beecham CDs is unlikely to disappoint anyone wanting to enjoy a uniquely warm and understanding reading of an equivocal piece, hard to interpret. *Orpheus*, the original coupling for the two-disc LP set, is also played very beautifully, the most poetic and unaffected account yet to be committed to disc. It still sounds uncommonly fresh, and the performance is magical. The performance of *Psalm 13* is slightly less impressive. It is sung in English, with the legendary Walter Midgeley, but is drier and more monochrome.

For the additional fillers here, EMI have chosen Silvestri's highly distinguished Philharmonia accounts of *Les Préludes* and *Tasso*. *Les Préludes* is predictably fine, both dignified and exciting, but the melodramatic *Tasso* is less easy to bring off and Silvestri has its full measure and gives it great intensity. Again, the recordings from 1957/8 are amazingly full and vivid.

SYMPHONIC POEMS

Ce qu'on entend sur la montagne; Orpheus; Les Préludes; Tasso: Lamento e Trionfo (Symphonic Poems)

*** Chan. 10341. BBC PO, Noseda

In this first volume of a proposed complete coverage, Chandos's characteristically expansive sound brings a new and different dimension to Liszt's tone-poems. *Ce qu'on entend sur la montagne*, beginning with its murmuring violins, is most atmospheric, and Noseda generates plenty of inner tension in this somewhat episodic score. The huge dynamic range of the recording is very effective, with all departments of the orchestra responding to the vivid scoring with warm enthusiasm. *Tasso* brings some very beautiful playing, with

Noseda coaxing ravishing sounds in the evocative passages, but also rising to the climaxes superbly.

Les Préludes is perhaps a shade too delicate, lacking the gravitas – and, indeed, electricity – of Karajan's famous DG account, but it has an alternative subtlety of nuance to make it compelling in its own way. The richly expressive writing in *Orpheus* is much better suited to Noseda's expansive approach; one of the composer's finest tone-poems, it is full of romantic beauty, so well captured here. A promising start to the series.

Les Préludes; Tasso lamento e trionfo (symphonic poems); (i) Totantanz. Nuages gris; Unstern! (both trans. Heinz Holliger)

(BB) *(*) Arte Nova 74321 27787-2. SWR SO, Peskó with (i) Cechová

The rarities here are Heinz Hollinger's arrangement of two of Liszt's piano pieces: *Nuages gris*, with its brooding atmosphere, and *Unstern!*, with some brutal brass writing, which gives way to a quietly menacing conclusion. The well-known tone-poems suffer from inconsistent and sometimes poor orchestral playing, the brass in particular sounding insecure at times – especially in *Tasso* – and there are frequent lapses in tension. Not really recommended except to those curious about the transcriptions.

Totentanz (for piano and orchestra)

(B) (**(*)) Australian Decca Eloquence mono 476 7671. Katin, LPO, Martinon – DOHNANYI: *Variations on a Nursery Song* **(*); LUTOSLAWSKI: *Paganini Variations* ***; RACHMANINOV: *Paganini Variations* **(*)

Katin's dashing performance of the *Totentanz* with Martinon is full of demonic urgency and, despite rather thin (but not unattractive) 1954 sound, this classic account remains highly enjoyable.

PIANO MUSIC

Complete piano music (57 volumes) and supplement

Vol. 1: *Albumblatt in Waltz Form; Bagatelle Without Tonality; Caprice-valses 1 & 2; Ländler in A flat; Mephisto Waltzes 1–3; Valse impromptu; 4 Valses oubliées*
*** Hyp. CDA 66201. Howard

Vol. 2: *Ballades 1–2; Berceuse; Impromptu (Nocturne); Klavierstück in A flat; 2 Légendes; 2 Polonaises*
**(*) Hyp. CDA 66301. Howard

Vol. 3: *Fantasia & Fugue on B-A-C-H; 3 Funeral Odes: Les Morts; La notte; Le Triomphe funèbre du Tasse; Grosses Konzertsolo; Prelude on 'Weinen, Klagen, Sorgen, Sagen'; Variations on a Theme of Bach*
** Hyp. CDA 66302. Howard

Vol. 4: *Adagio in C; Etudes d'exécution transcendante; Elégie sur des motifs de Prince Louis Ferdinand de Prusse; Mariotte*
** Hyp. CDA 66357. Howard

Vol. 5: Concert paraphrases: BERLIOZ: *L'Idée fixe; Overtures: Les Francs-Juges; Le Roi Lear; Marche des pèlerins; Valse des Sylphes.* CHOPIN: *6 Chants polonais.* SAINT-SAENS: *Danse macabre*
*** Hyp. CDA 66346. Howard

Vol. 6: Concert paraphrases: AUBER: *3 Pieces on Themes from 'La Muette de Portici'.* BELLINI: *Réminiscences de*

Norma. BERLIOZ: *Benvenuto Cellini: Bénédiction et serment.* DONIZETTI: *Réminiscences de Lucia di Lammermoor; Marche funèbre et Cavatina (Lucia).* ERNST (Duke of Saxe-Coburg-Gotha): *Tony: Hunting Chorus.* GLINKA: *Ruslan and Ludmilla: Tscherkessenmarsch.* GOUNOD: *Waltz from Faust.* HANDEL: *Almira: Sarabande & Chaconne.* MEYERBEER: *Illustrations de L'Africaine.* MOZART: *Réminiscences de Don Juan.* VERDI: *Aida: Danza sacra & Duetto finale.* TCHAIKOVSKY: *Eugene Onegin: Polonaise.* WAGNER: *Tristan: Isoldes Liebestod.* WEBER: *Der Freischütz: Overture*
*** Hyp. CDA 66371/2. Howard

Vol. 7: Chorales: *Crux ave benedicta; Jesu Christe; Meine Seele; Nun danket alle Gott; Nun ruhen all Wälder; O haupt; O Lamm Gottes; O Traurigkeit; Vexilla Regis; Was Gott tut; Wer nur den Lieben; Via Crucis; Weihachtsbaum; Weihnachtslied*
** Hyp. CDA 66388. Howard

Vol. 8: *Alleluia & Ave Maria; Ave Marias 1–4; Ave Maria de Arcadelt; Ave Maris stella; Harmonies poétiques et religieuses* (complete); *Hungarian Coronation Mass; Hymnes; Hymne du Pape; In festo transfigurationis; Invocation; O Roma nobilis; Sancta Dorothea; Slavimo slavno slavenil; Stabat Mater; Urbi et orbi; Vexilla regis prodeunt; Zum Haus des Herrn*
** Hyp. CDA 66421/2. Howard

Vol. 9: *6 Consolations; 2 Elégies; Gretchen* (from *Faust Symphony*); *Sonata in B min.; Totentanz*
** Hyp. CDA 66429. Howard

Vol. 10: Concert paraphrases: BELLINI: *Hexaméron (Grand Bravura Variations* on the *March* from *'I Puritani').* BERLIOZ: *Symphonie fantastique. Un portrait en musique de la Marquise de Blocqueville*
**(*) Hyp. CDA 66433. Howard

Vol. 11: *Abschied (Russisches Volkslied); Am Grabe Richard Wagners; Carrousel de Madame P-N; Dem Andenken Petöfis; Epithalium; Klavierstück in F sharp; En Rêve; 5 Klavierstücke; Mosonyis Grabgeleit; Recueillement; Resignazione; Romance oubliée; RW (Venezia); Schlaflos! Frage und Antwort; Sospiri; Toccata; Slyepoi (Der blinde Sänger); Die Trauergondel (La Lugubre Gondola); Trauervorspiel und Trauermarsch; Trübe Wolken (Nuages gris); Ungams Gott; Ungarisches Königslied; Unstern: Sinistre; Wiegenlied (Chant de berceau)*
**(*) Hyp. CDA 66445. Howard

Vol. 12: *Années de pèlerinage, 3rd Year (Italy); 5 Hungarian Folksongs; Historical Hungarian Portraits*
** Hyp. CDA 66448. Howard

Vol. 13: Concert paraphrases: ALLEGRI/MOZART: *A la Chapelle Sistine: Miserère d'Allegri et Ave verum corpus de Mozart.* BACH: *Fantasia & Fugue in G min.; 6 Preludes & Fugues for Organ*
** Hyp. CDA 66438. Howard

Vol. 14: *Christus; Polonaises de St Stanislas; Salve Polonia; St Elizabeth*
**(*) Hyp. CDA 66466. Howard

Vol. 15: Concert paraphrases of Lieder: BEETHOVEN: *Adelaïde; An die ferne Geliebte; 6 Gellert Lieder; 6 Lieder von Goethe; An die ferne Geliebte.* DESSAUER: *3 Lieder.* FRANZ: *Er est gekommenin Sturm und Regen; 12 Lieder.*

MENDELSSOHN: *7 Lieder* including *Auf Flügeln des Gesanges.* CLARA & ROBERT SCHUMANN: 10 Lieder including *Frülingsnacht; Widmung*
**(*) Hyp. CDA 66481/2. Howard

Vol. 16: Piano transcriptions: DAVID: *Bunte Reihe* (24 character pieces for violin and piano), *Op. 30*
*** Hyp. CDA 66506. Howard

Vol. 17: Concert paraphrases: DONIZETTI: *Spirito gentil* from *'La favorita'; Marche funèbre* from *'Don Sebastien'.* GOUNOD: *Les Sabéennes (Berceuse)* from *'La Reine de Saba'.* GRETRY: *Die Rose (Romance)* from *'Zémire et Azor'.* MEYERBEER: *3 Illustrations du Prophète; Fantasia & Fugue* on *Ad nos, ad salutarem undam* on a theme from *'Le Prophète'.* MOSONYI: *Fantasy on 'Szép Ilonka'.* WAGNER: *Spinning Song & Ballade* from *'Der fliegende Hollånder'; Pilgrims' Chorus & O du, mein holder Abendstern* from *'Tannhäuser'; Valhalla* from *'The Ring'; Feierlicher Marsch zum heiligen Grail* from *'Parsifal'*
**(*) Hyp. CDA 66571/2. Howard

Vol. 18: Concert paraphrases: BEETHOVEN: *Capriccio alla turca; Fantasy* from *'Ruins of Athens'.* LASSEN: *Symphonisches Zwischenspiel zu Calderons Schauspiel über allen Zauber Liebe.* MENDELSSOHN: *Wedding March & Dance of the Elves* from *'A Midsummer Night's Dream'.* WEBER: *Einsam bin ich, nicht alleine* from *'La preciosa'.* HEBBEL: *Nibelungen*
**(*) Hyp. CDA 66575. Howard

Leslie Howard's ambitious project to record all the piano music of Liszt is now complete, and at least two of these earlier issues have already collected a Grand Prix du Disque in Budapest (Volumes 5 and 6). The performances are very capable and musicianly, and there are moments of poetic feeling, but for the most part his playing rarely touches distinction. The kind of concentration one finds in great Liszt pianists such as Arrau, Kempff and Richter (and there are many younger artists whose names also spring to mind) rarely surfaces. Howard's technical equipment is formidable, but poetic imagination and the ability to grip the listener are here less developed: his rushed account of the *Sonata* does not really stand up against the current competition. One of the most interesting issues is Volume 16, the *Bunte Reihe* of Ferdinand David (1810–70), a contemporary of Mendelssohn. These are transcriptions of music for violin and piano in which the violin seems hardly to be missed at all. Leslie Howard plays them beautifully. Certainly the coverage is remarkable and, if this playing rarely takes the breath away either by its virtuosity or its poetic insights, it is unfailingly intelligent and the recordings are first class.

Vol. 19: *Die Lorelei; 3 Liebesträume; Songs for Solo Piano, Books 1–2*
*** Hyp. CDA 66593. Howard

Vol. 20: *Album d'un voyageur: Années de pèlerinage, 1st, 2nd & 3rd Years (first versions); Chanson du Béarn; Fantaisie romantique sur deux mélodies suisses; Faribolo pastour*
*** Hyp. CDA 66601/2. Howard

Vol. 21: ROSSINI: *Soirées musicales; Grande Fantaisie on Motifs from Soirées musicales; 2nd Fantaisie on Motifs from Soirées musicales.* DONIZETTI: *Nuits d'été à Pausilippe.* MERCADANTE: *Soirées italiennes. 3 Sonetti di Petrarca* (1st version); *Venezia e Napoli* (1st set)
*** Hyp. CDA 66661/2. Howard

Vol. 22: Concert paraphrases of Beethoven symphonies: *Symphonies 1–9*
** Hyp. CDA 66671/5. Howard

Vol. 23: BERLIOZ: (i) *Harold in Italy.* LISZT: (i) *Romance oubliée.* GOUNOD: *Hymne à Sainte Cécile.* MEYERBEER: *Le Moine; Festmarsch*
**(*) Hyp. CDA 66683. Howard, (i) with Coletti

Vol. 24: Concert paraphrases: BEETHOVEN: *Septet, Op. 20.* MOZART: *Requiem Mass, K.626: Confutatis; Lacrimosa. Ave verum corpus, K.618.* VERDI: *Requiem Mass: Agnus Dei.* ROSSINI: *Cujus animam: Air du Stabat Mater; 3 Chœurs religieux: La Charité.* GOLDSCHMIDT: *7 Tödsunden: Liebesszene und Fortunas Kugel.* MENDELSSOHN: *Wasserfahrt und der Jäger Abschied.* WEBER: *Schlummerlied mit Arabesken; Leyer und Schwert-Heroïde.* HUMMEL: *Septet 1 in D min.*
** Hyp. CDA 66761/2. Howard

Vol. 25: *San Francesco: Prelude: The Canticle of the Sun; Canticle of the Sun of St Francis of Assisi. Ave maris stella; Gebet; Ich liebe dich; Il m'aimait tant; O pourquoi donc; Ora pro nobis; O sacrum convivium (2 versions); Rezignazione – Ergebung; Salve regina; Von der Wiege bis zum Grabe; Die Zelle in Nonnenwerth*
**(*) Hyp. CDA 66694. Howard

Vol. 26: *Allegro di bravura; Apparitions; Berceuse; 12 Etudes; Feuilles d'album; Galop de bal; Hungarian Recruiting Dances; Impromptu Brillant on Themes of Rossini & Spontini; Klavierstücke (aus der Bonn Beethoven-Kantatej); 2 Klavierstücke; Marche hongroise; Notturno 2; Rondo di bravura; Scherzo in G min.; Variation on a Waltz of Diabelli; Variations on a Theme of Rossini; 5 Variations on a Theme from Méhul's 'Joseph'; Waltz in A; Waltz in E flat*
**(*) Hyp. CDA 66771/2. Howard

Vol. 27: *Canzone napolitana (2 versions); La Cloche sonne; Gleanings from Woronince; God Save the Queen; Hungarian National Folk Tunes (Ungarische Nationalmelodien); Hussite Song; La Marseillaise; Rákóczi March; Szózat & Hungarian hymn; Vive Henri IV*
*** Hyp. CDA 66787. Howard

Vol. 28: *Bulow-Marsch; Heroischer Marsch im Ungarischer Geschwindmarsch; Csárdás; Csárdás macabre; Csárdás obstiné; Festmarsch zur Goethejubiläumsfeier; Festpolonaise; Festvorspiel; Galop in A min.; Grand galop chromatique; Huldigungsmarsch; Kunstierfestzug zur Schillerfeier; Marche héroïque; Mazurka brillante; Mephisto Polka; Petite valse; Rákóczy Marsch; Vorn Fels zurn Meer; La Favorite; Scherzo & March; Siegesmarsch; Ungarischer Marsch zur Krönungsfeier in Ofen-Pest; Ungarischer Stürmmarsch; Zweite Festmarsch*
**(*) Hyp. CDA 66811/2. Howard

The two Liszt *Songbooks* on Volume 19 offer 12 early Lieder in engagingly simple transcriptions. Leslie Howard plays them beautifully, as he does the three *Liebesträume*. Volume 20 centres on what Howard prefers to call *Album d'un Voyager*, the early edition of what we know as the *Années de pèlerinage*. Book I includes a flamboyant extra item, *Lyon*, inspired by a workers' uprising, and only two of the pieces in Book II, *Fleurs mélodiques des Alpes*, were retained in the final set. Apart from the *Paraphrases* in Book III, this collection also includes an unknown major improvisatory work of the same

period and inspiration, the 18-minute-long *Fantaisie romantique sur deux mélodies suisses*, with plenty of opportunities for bravura in the latter part. A fascinating collection, very well played indeed.

Volume 21 is lightweight, opening with the Rossini *Soirées musicales*, which we know from the much later Britten orchestrations, and *Soirées italiennes*, based on rather less interesting music by Mercadante. For the second disc Howard returns to the initial versions of the *Années de pèlerinage*, including the *Petrarch Sonnets* and *Venezia e Napoli*. The second CD ends with a pair of *Grand Fantasias* on themes from the *Soirées* that began the recital.

Volume 22 brings us to Liszt's paraphrases of the nine Beethoven symphonies. Leslie Howard's 'interpretations' are sound throughout; he makes more of some movements than others (the first movement of the *Eroica* could be more compelling) and the resonance of the recording is not ideal for revealing detail. The *Ninth* works impressively, if not as earth-shaking as Katsaris's version on Teldec. Overall, this is surprisingly enjoyable to listen to; without the orchestral colour, one notices the more what is happening in the internal arguments of these inexhaustible works.

Volume 23 is an effective transcription of Berlioz's *Harold in Italy* for viola and piano, and Howard takes the opportunity to include Liszt's own *Romance oubliée* for the same combination. Here Paul Coletti joins the pianist, and the performances are well played and spontaneous, if not earth-shaking. The transcriptions of the Beethoven and Hummel *Septets* in Volume 24, however, do not really work at all. This music either needs the instrumental colour or a much more witty approach (and the resonant recording is not helpful). However, there are some other paraphrases here that are much more effective, notably the excerpts from Goldschmidt's *Die sieben Todsünden* and two transcribed Mendelssohn choruses.

The *Cantico del Sol di San Francesco d'Assisi* is pleasantly based on *In dulci jubilo*. Then comes the chrysalis of the symphonic poem, *From the Cradle to the Grave*, which was greatly expanded in its orchestral form. Volume 26 is almost entirely devoted to works written when Liszt was a teenager, and the *Variations* show his mettle. Volume 27 offers patriotic songs and airs in a much more interesting and varied programme than it looks at first glance. *God Save the Queen* was written for a British tour in 1840/41 and the tune is immediately interestingly varied in the opening bars. *La Marseillaise* starts off straightforwardly and the variants come later, but the tune reasserts itself strongly. The *Ungarische Nationalmelodien* is in effect a sketch for the *Sixth Hungarian Rhapsody*. But there are plenty of enticing ideas here, notably the three-part suite, *Glanes de Woronince*, and the delightful French folksong arrangements, *Vive Henry IV* and *La Cloche sonne*. Howard is at his most imaginative. Volume 28 is essentially a collection of marches and lively extrovert pieces, but they are very well presented.

Vol. 29: *Hungarian Themes & Rhapsodies, 1–22*
** Hyp. CDA 66851/2. Howard

Here is the source material for Liszt's *Hungarian Rhapsodies* and the *Hungarian Fantasia* in earlier, more earthy form, before the dances became sophisticated concert repertoire. There is even an early version (subsequently discarded) of the *Consolation No. 3*. Of course, not all the music here is equally interesting, but Leslie Howard brings it to life fluently. His playing has convincing rubato but lacks something in flair and adrenalin.

Vol. 30: Operatic fantasies, concert paraphrases and transcriptions: DONIZETTI: *Valse de concert on 2 Motifs of Lucia di Lammermoor & Parisina.* GOUNOD: *Les Adieux (Rêverie on a Theme from 'Roméo et Juliette').* ERKEL: *Schwanengesang & March to Hunyadi László.* MEYERBEER: *Réminiscences de Robert le diable: Cavatine; Valse infernale.* MOZART: *Fantasy on Themes from 'Nozze di Figaro' & 'Don Giovanni'.* VERDI: *Ernani; Rigoletto; Il Trovatore: Miserere* (concert paraphrases); *Réminiscences de Simon Boccanegra.* WAGNER: *Lohengrin: Elsa's Bridal Procession; Wedding March; Elsa's Dream; Lohengrin's Reproof. Fantasy on Themes from 'Rienzi'.* WEBER: *Overture: Oberon*
** Hyp. CDA 66861/2. Howard

Liszt's operatic paraphrases were designed both to entertain and to remind listeners not only of the tunes that made up the best-known operas of Mozart, Verdi and Wagner but those of lesser composers too. Some of this music ideally needs a Horowitz, but for the most part Leslie Howard is up to the display and pyrotechnics which Liszt's embellishments require. However, Mozart's *Là ci darem* is heavily romanticized and the Verdi paraphrases also need more impetus. The Wagner transcriptions are more successful.

Vol. 31: 'The Schubert transcriptions' (Vol. 1): *Ave Maria; Der Gondelfahrer; Erlkönig; Märche für das Pianoforte übertragen: Trauermarsch (Grande marche funèbre); Grande marche; Grande marche caracteristique. Marche militaire* (concert paraphrase); *Mélodies hongroises; Die Rose; La Sérénade; Soirées de Vienne; 2 Transcriptions for Sophie Menter*
** Hyp. CDA 66951/3. Howard

Vol. 32: 'The Schubert transcriptions' (Vol. 2): *Die Forelle; Frühlingsglaube; Marche hongroise* (2 versions); *Meeresstille; 6 Mélodies favorites de la belle meunière; 6 Mélodies of Franz Schubert; 4 Sacred Songs; Schuberts Ungarische Melodien; Schwanengesang; 12 Songs from Winterreise; Ständchen (Leise flehen)*
** Hyp. CDA 66954/6. Howard

Vol. 33: 'The Schubert transcriptions' (Vol. 3): *Die Forelle; Die Gestirne; 2 Lieder; 12 Lieder* (2 versions); *Marche hongroise; Meerestille* (2 versions); *Müllerlieder; Die Nebensonnen; Schwanengesang; Soirées de Vienne: Valse caprice 6; 12 Songs from Winterreise*
** Hyp. CDA 66957/9. Howard

Liszt obviously admired Schubert enormously and wanted to champion him as well as play his music. The *Soirées de Vienne* really suit Howard and are played with a pleasantly Schubertian feeling and nicely judged rubato, while the *Valse caprice* is quite charming. And what of the songs? The four *Geistliche Lieder* (*Sacred Songs*) which open the collection are made to seem unremittingly sombre, and Howard has a tendency to over-characterize the darker songs elsewhere. *Die Forelle* and some of the other most famous songs are not very imaginatively done, although *Erlkönig* comes off well. But not everyone will want two complete *Schwanengesangs* without a singer. Of course, the transcriptions are free – sometimes (but not often) very free – and there is more Liszt than Schubert. Howard plays them (as Liszt surely would have done) with comparable freedom in matters of phrasing and rubato, and for the most part he is convincing, if at times his tempi seem a little too indulgent.

Vol. 34: *12 Grandes études; Morceau de salon*
*** Hyp. CDA 66973. Howard

These *Grandes études* were the pilot version of the *Etudes d'exécution transcendante* which appeared a quarter of a century later, in 1851. This (as with so much of this invaluable series) is their first recording, as the composer expressly forbade their performance. This music demands great bravura, and Leslie Howard surpasses himself in rising to the challenge with remarkable confidence. There is much to tickle the ear here, and all this music is Liszt's own and is not borrowed from others!

Vol. 35: *Arabesques* (2 mélodies russes): (ALYABIEV: *Le rossignol.* P. BULAKHOV: *Chanson bohémienne*). **Russian transcriptions:** AN AMATEUR FROM ST PETERSBURG: *Mazurka.* (Liszt's) *Prelude à la Polka de Borodin.* BORODIN: (i) *Polka.* K. BULAKHOV: *Galop russe.* CUI; DARGOMIZHSKY: *Tarentelles.* WIELHORSKY: *Autrefois.* **Hungarian transcriptions:** *Rákóczi-March.* ABRANYI: *Flower Song.* FESTETICS: *Spanish Ständchen.* SZECHENYI: *Introduction & Hungarian March.* SZABADI/MASSENET: *Revive Szegedin!.* VEGH: *Valse de concert.* ZICHY: *Valse d'Adèle*
*** Hyp. CDA 66984. Howard, (i) with Moore

Liszt was especially enthusiastic about new Russian music and, as can by seen from the piece based on the *Mazurka* of 'An Amateur from St Petersburg,' he didn't restrict his interest to famous names, although they are all here. He composed his own piano solo introduction to Borodin's engaging four-handed *Polka*, which is included here with the help of Philip Moore. Most of the Hungarian names are unfamiliar but the music itself, if slight, is often delightful. The two opening *Arabesques* are enticing; but everything tickles the ear, especially Abrányi's *Flower Song*, and no one can say that Leslie Howard does not relish its glittering colours. As usual, good recording. This is a most enjoyable collection.

Vol. 36: *Consolations 1–6; Elégie: Entwurf der Ramann; Excelsior! (Prelude to The Bells of Strasburg Cathedral); Fanfare for the Unveiling of the Carl August Memorial; Geharnischte Lieder; National Hymn (Kaiser Wilhelm!); Rosario Schlummerlied im Grabe; Die Zelle in Nonnenwerth* (2 versions); *Weimars Volkslieder 1–2*
**(*) Hyp. CDA 66995. Howard

The first version of the six *Consolations* misses out the most famous *Third in D flat* and substitutes a less memorable piece in C sharp minor, but in all other respects these earlier pieces are valid in their own right and are well worth having on disc, although the performances do tend to languish a bit. The rest of the programme consists of novelties, including cathedral bells (celebrated here by the two versions of *Die Zelle in Nonnenwerth* as well as by *Excelsior!*), all unknown, many of them occasional pieces and of no great interest except for *Rosario*, three gentle settings of *Ave Maria*, which are persuasively atmospheric.

Vol. 37: BULOW: *Tanto gentile e tanto onesta.* CONRADI: *Zigeuner-Polka.* ERNST: *Die Gräberinsel der Fürsten zu Gotha.* HERBECK: *Tanzmomente 1–8; 4* (alternative). LASSEN: *Ich weil' in teifer Einsamkeit; Löse, Himmel meine Seele* (2 versions). LESSMAN: *3 Lieder from Julius Wolff's 'Tannhäuser'.* LISZT/LOUIS FERDINAND: *Elégie sur des motifs du Prince Louis Ferdinand de Prusse*
** Hyp. CDA 67004. Howard

Johann Ritter von Herbeck was Viennese choirmaster as well as composer, and his *Tanzmomente* consists of eight dances, many of them waltzes of some charm. Liszt's transcriptions flatter them agreeably and he expands the finale considerably and to good effect. Otto Lessen was a journalist and theatre manager, and his songs also make agreeable transcriptions, as does Hans von Bülow's *Tanto gentile*. The closing *Zigeuner-Polka* of August Conradi was a pop hit in its day, and Liszt's arrangement adds a bit of spice to the melodic sequence. All this music is exceedingly rare, but its musical interest is frankly limited. The Lassen and Bülow pieces are the highlights.

Vol. 38: 'Concert études & Episodes from Lenau's Faust': Les Préludes; 3 Etudes de concert; 2 Concert Studies; 2 Episodes from Lenau's 'Faust'
*** Hyp. CDA 67015. Howard

Volume 38 is a good deal more substantial than its predecessor, starting off with the popular *Les Préludes*, which anticipates the orchestral version fairly closely, with a few minor differences near the end. The transcription is made in pianistic terms and works well. The three *Etudes de concert* continue in familiar territory, especially the third, a Lisztian romantic blossoming better known as 'Un sospiro' (which Howard presents boldly). *Waldesrauschen* and *Gnomenreigen* (beautifully done) are equally welcome, as is the opportunity of hearing the two *Faust* pieces together in their piano versions, of which the *Mephisto Waltz* is easily the more famous. A rewarding collection, very well played and recorded.

Vol. 39: Années de pèlerinage, 1st Year (Switzerland); 3 Morceaux suisses
** Hyp. CDA 67026. Howard

With Volume 39, Leslie Howard moves on to the first year of the *Années de pèlerinage*, for the most part playing the second versions. But this is music we know well in the hands of artists like Wilhelm Kempff. Howard provides thoroughly musical performances, but without finding the degree of poetry and magic that these evocative pieces deserve. The three *Morceaux suisses* come off brightly and quite spontaneously. Liszt's descriptive powers are used more literally here, with a storm graphically depicted in the second, *Un soir dans la montagne*.

Vol. 40: Ballade 2 (first version); Festmarsch zur Säkularfeier von Goethes Geburtstag; Seconde Marche hongroise; Nocturne (Impromptu); Concert paraphrases and transcriptions: Galop russe (Bulahov); Gaudeamus igitur (2 versions: Paraphrase; Humoreske); Lyubila ya (Wielhorsky); La Marche pour le Sultan Abdul Médjid-Khan (Donizetti); Seconda Mazurka di Tirindelli; Le Rossignol-Air russe (Alyabiev); Una stella amica-Valzer (Pezzini)
** Hyp. CDA 67034. Howard

This collection is described as *Pièces d'occasion*, and much of the music here is desperately trivial. Liszt's paraphrase of *Gaudeamus igitur* at nine minutes outlasts its welcome, while the second version, called *Humoreske*, is even less entertaining. Howard takes everything fairly seriously and, though his playing is secure technically, he seldom dazzles the ear, which is surely what the composer would have done.

Vol. 41: Recitations with piano: (i) *A holt költo szerelme* (The Dead Poet's Love); (ii) *Helge's Treue* (Helge's Loyalty); Lenore; Der traurige Mönch (The Sad Monk); (iii) *Slyepoi* (The Blind Man)
*(**) Hyp. CDA 67045. Howard, with (i) Eles; (ii) Kahler; (iii) Stepanov

A real curiosity, but essentially a specialist compilation. While one is willing to follow an opera libretto alongside a recording, to have to listen to a spoken poetic narrative in German, Hungarian or Russian alongside its musical illustration while following the translation is a different matter. Certainly the ballades here are not lacking in melodrama. *Lenore*, whose lover fails to come back from the wars, cries out blasphemously against God. Night falls, and she hears the sound of hooves clip-clopping: there he is on his horse to take her to the bridal bed. They travel 'a hundred miles' through the night, later followed by demons, and at the end of the journey her lover is no more than a brittle skeleton. All the lurid tales here obviously excited Liszt's imagination, and Howard rises to the occasion. But one wonders how often one would want to return to a CD of this kind.

Vol. 42: Concert paraphrases: AUBER: Tyrolean Melody from 'La Fiancée'; Tarantelle di bravura from 'Masaniello'. BELLINI: Réminiscences des Puritains; Introduction et Polonaise from 'I Puritani'; Grosse Concert-fantaisie on 'La Sonnambula'. DONIZETTI: Réminiscences de Lucrezia Borgia: Grandes fantaisies I & II. MEYERBEER: Réminiscences des Huguenots. (i) MOZART: Song of the Two Armed Men from 'Die Zauberflöte' (piano duet). RAFF: Andante finale and Marsch from 'König Alfred'. VERDI: Coro di festa e marcia funebre from 'Don Carlos'; Salve Maria de l'opéra de Jérusalem from 'I lombardi' (two versions). WAGNER: Pilgrims' Chorus from 'Tannhäuser'; Am stillen Herd - Lied from 'Die Meistersinger'
** Hyp. CDA 67101/2. Howard, (i) with Moore

Liszt's concert paraphrases need to be played with dazzling virtuosity and – above all – real charisma. Leslie Howard is reliably equal to most of their technical demands but he does not titillate the ear, and much of this music tends to lose the listener's attention. These records have been praised elsewhere, but for us they did not prove very stimulating listening. For instance, Howard takes the *Pilgrims' chorus* from *Tannhäuser* unbelievably slowly; he is at his best in the Bellini items. As a sound document to demonstrate the range of Liszt's operatic interest this is valuable, but the playing is seldom very exciting in itself.

Vol. 43: Années de pèlerinage, 1st Year, Switzerland: Au bord d'une source (with coda for Sgambati). Années de pèlerinage, 2nd Year, Italy; Supplement: Venezia e Napoli
**(*) Hyp. CDA 67107. Howard

This is one of Howard's more spontaneous recitals. *Au bord d'une source* comes off delightfully, and the brief nine-bar additional coda, which Liszt wrote for his friend, the young composer/pianist Giovanni Sgambati, makes a charming (if superfluous) postlude. Howard is also at his best in the *Venezia e Napoli Supplement*, in which the closing *Tarantella* sparkles iridescently. The earlier pieces of the Second Year come off well enough, but the *Dante Sonata* needs more grip and fire than Howard finds for it. Excellent recording.

Vol. 44: Concert paraphrases: BEETHOVEN: Symphonies 3 (Marche funèbre); 5–7 (complete) (first versions); 6 (5th

Movement) (second version); 7 (fragment); *Adelaïde* (two versions); *Fantasy* from *'Ruins of Athens'* (first version). BERLIOZ: *Marche au supplice* from *Symphonie fantastique* (second version). LISZT: *Cadenza for 1st Movement of Beethoven's Piano Concerto 3*
** Hyp. CDA 67111/3. Howard

Once again Leslie Howard seems concerned to lay the music out before us with care for every bit of detail, without seeking to create enough thrust to take the music onwards. The account of the *Fifth Symphony*, which opens the first disc, has almost no adrenalin whatsoever and proceeds onward as a very routine affair, while the *Marche funèbre* from the *Eroica* is similarly very literal in feeling. The *Pastoral Symphony* might be thought to work well with a simple, straightforward approach. But then the *Shepherd's Hymn of Thanksgiving* is presented with little warmth of feeling. The opening of the *Seventh* has a false start, for we are first given only a fragment. When Howard begins again, the *Introduction* seems to go on for a long time but the allegro has momentum, and the other movements have more life than the other symphonies. The programme ends with excerpts from Berlioz's *Symphonie fantastique*, with first the *idée fixe* languorously turned into a 'nocturne' (which does not work especially well), followed by a bold, lively *Marche au supplice* which at least ends the programme vigorously. As with the rest of this series, the recording is excellent.

Vol. 45: *Feuille morte – Elégie d'après Soriano; Grand Concert Fantasia on Spanish Themes; Rapsodie Espagnole; La romanesca* (1st and 2nd versions); *Rondeau fantastique on 'El contrabandista'*
**(*) Hyp. CDA 67145. Howard

Collecting virtually all of Liszt's Spanish-inspired solo piano music, this is one of Howard's more impressive discs. There is not quite all the necessary dash in the *Grand Concert Fantasia*, but there is some glittering fingerwork in the more familiar *Rapsodie Espagnole*. He does not find a great deal of inspiration in the alternative versions of *La romanesca*, but plays the *Feuille morte* beautifully, with just the right touch of romantic feeling. This comes as an interlude before the closing *Rondeau fantastique*, which produces arresting digital dexterity, but where one feels he could have let his hair down just a little bit more. He is excellently recorded.

Vol. 46: 'Meditations': *Responsories & antiphons*
** Hyp. CDA 67161/2. Howard

This set is in essence a series of simple chorales: settings of the matutinal plainchant responsories from the Offices for Christmas (12) and Holy Week – Maundy Thursday (22), Good Friday (19), Holy Saturday (19) – and for the Office for the Dead (24), with ('for completeness' sake') 11 alternative harmonizations. The chants are accompanied for the most part in four and occasionally three parts. Liszt's harmony is innocently simple, reflecting the Lutheran hymn tradition, without frills. Howard plays them simply too, but dedicatedly and never didactically. However, with the average timing of each item around a minute, these are not collections to listen to in bulk, for monotony inevitably sets in after just a few of these essentially ingenuous arrangements.

Vol. 47: Music intended for a first cycle of *Harmonies poétiques et religieuses* (1847): *Litanies de Marie* (1st and 2nd versions); *Miserere* (1st version); *Pater noster d'après la Psalmodie de l'Eglise* (1st version); *Hymne de l'enfant à son*

réveil (2nd version); *Prose des morts – De profundis* (2nd version); *La Lampe du temple* (1st version); *Hymne; Bénédiction* (2nd version). Earlier related pieces: *Prière d'un enfant à son réveil; Prélude* (1st version)
*** Hyp. CDA 67187. Howard

This is surely one of the most valuable of Leslie Howard's pioneering series, and all Lisztians should have it. Almost all the music recorded here is unpublished, and none of it has been previously recorded. The *Harmonies poétiques et religieuses* is one of the composer's key works and its gestation in these earlier pieces is both fascinating and musically rewarding. Howard has never played better, and his account of the remarkable *Prose de morts – De profundis* is arresting, as are both versions of *Litanies de Marie*, sombre and commanding. He shows the composer at his most flamboyantly garrulous in the *Hymne*, with its cascades of notes. But his playing in the gentler pieces is even more memorable, notably the *Hymn* and *Prière de l'enfant* and *La Lampe du temple*, while the *Bénédiction* is quite magical. Excellent recording.

Vol. 48: *Etudes d'exécution transcendante d'après Paganini* (complete); with 1 (second version); 5 (alternative); *Grandes études de Paganini* (complete); *Mazeppa* (intermediate version); *Technische Studien 62: Sprünge mit der Tremolo-Begleitung*
**(*) Hyp. CDA 67193. Howard

It would be a pity if Leslie Howard's glittering accounts of Liszt's *Grandes études de Paganini* escaped the attention of the general collector because they are 'hidden away' in this survey. He is clearly enjoying himself and his delectable digital dexterity is consistently ear-tickling, with the familiar numbers like *La campanella* sounding crisply minted. Rhythms are lifted spontaneously, even wittily, and these sparkling performances leap out of the speakers. He plays the more difficult *Etudes d'exécution transcendante d'après Paganini* with flair also, but here there are some technical smudges, although not enough to impair enjoyment; the alternative version of No. 1, incorporating a study by Schumann (Op. 10/2), is well worth having on disc. The 'intermediate' version of *Mazeppa* is structurally unconvincing yet demands enormous virtuosity; here it sounds flurried and overstressed, obviously reaching the outer limit of Leslie Howard's technique.

Vol. 49: '*Schubert & Weber Transcriptions*': SCHUBERT: *Impromptus in E flat; in G flat, D.899; Die Rose* (intermediate version); *Wanderer Fantasy in C.* WEBER: *Jubel Overture; Konzertstück; Polonaise brillante*
**(*) Hyp. CDA 67203. Howard

Liszt reorganized the pianistic layout of the Schubert *Wanderer Fantasy* with the excuse of making the score more 'pianistic'. His own version involved considerable changes in the finale, which now sounds weightily orchestral, without using an orchestra. Leslie Howard gives a commanding and convincing account. But the biggest surprise here comes in Liszt's shortened version of Schubert's famous *Impromptu in G flat*, where at the reprise of the main theme the melody is taken up an octave, with a much more elaborate accompaniment. The result is (enjoyably) highly romantic, but not at all Schubertian. Liszt's brilliant transcriptions of Weber's *Konzertstück* and *Jubel Overture* adhere fairly closely to the original texts, but demand great virtuosity. The *Polonaise brillante* (also originally for piano and orchestra) is more freely transcribed, with Weber's ideas further extended, notably in the introduction. Howard plays all this music with vigour and enthusiasm, and if at times bravura detail is lost in the pianistic stampedes, this is still impressive; the Lisztian flamboyance is well projected.

Vol. 50: 'Liszt at the opera V': Concert paraphrases: AUBER: *Souvenir de La Fiancée* (3rd version); *Tarantelle di bravura* from *'Masaniello'* (1st version). BELLINI: *Fantaisie sur des motifs favoris* from *'La sonnambula'* (2nd version). DONIZETTI: *Fantaisie sur des motifs* from *'Lucrezia Borgia'*. HALEVY: *Réminiscences de La Juive*. MEYERBEER: *Réminiscences des Huguenots* (1st version). PACINI: *Grande fantaisie sur des thèmes* from *'Niobe'*. ROSSINI: *William Tell Overture*. WAGNER: *Festspiel und Brautlied* from *'Lohengrin'; Einzug der Gäste auf der Wartburg* from *'Tannhäuser'*
(*) Hyp. CDA 67231/2. Howard

This is discussed below with Volume 54.

Vol. 51: 'Paralipomènes': *Après une lecture du Dante: Dante Sonata* (1st, 2nd and 3rd versions); *A la chapelle Sixtine – Miserere d'Allegri et Ave verum de Mozart* (1st version); *Elégie (Die Zelle in Nonnenwerth)* (1st version); *Grand solo de concert* (1st version); *Prelude & Fugue on B-A-C-H* (1st version); *Ungarische National-Melodien 1–3 & Rákóczi marsch; Romance oubliée* (draft); *Sposalizio* (1st version); *Weihnachtsbaum (Christmas Tree Suite)*
*** Hyp. CDA 67233/4. Howard

To have three different early versions of the *Dante Sonata* (altogether about an hour of music) might be thought by the average collector as being too much of a good thing, but Howard plays them all with prodigious virtuosity. This famous highlight of the second year of the *Années de pèlerinage* originally had two distinct sections, the first of which comes to a full close. It has one thematic idea which the composer later deleted. The second revised single-movement version bears the familar title, *Après une lecture du Dante – Fantasia Quasi Sonata* and this resembles the final (fourth version) fairly closely. But the third version has more additions, including a hair-raising bravura section in the final peroration, which Liszt prudently later excised. Leslie Howard plays it with thrilling abandon, and in many ways this is the most exciting of the three accounts. The first version of *Sposalizio* and the solo *Elégie*, bring calmer waters, even if the *Grand solo de concert* again shows the composer at his most rhetorically flamboyant. The second disc opens with the piano transcription of the *B-A-C-H Prelude & Fugue* for organ (technically hair-raising but less effective than the original), and includes both the ingenuous *Christmas Tree Suite*, with its series of innocent chorales, and the ear-tickling conflation of Allegri and Mozart, in which Liszt characteristically misses the simple atmospheric beauty of the originals. The Hungarian pieces make a lively and colourful interlude. A formidable achievement, splendidly recorded.

Vol. 52: *Hungarian romanzero 1–18* (complete); *2 Marches dans le genre hongrois*
** Hyp. CDA 67235. Howard

Volume 52 has greater documentary than musical interest. The *Hungarian Romances* exist only in an unpublished manuscript dating from the early 1850s, held in the Wagner Museum in Bayreuth – a volume of Hungarian dance themes arranged for piano, sometimes simply, sometimes more elaborately. They are all quite short and appear to be a kind of detailed musical notebook for future use. (Liszt had already

completed and published his set of *Hungarian Rhapsodies*.) Leslie Howard makes the most of relatively unpromising material, tickling the ear whenever he can. The two unfinished *Hungarian Marches* date from ten years earlier, and have been edited and completed by Howard himself.

Vol. 53a: Music for piano and orchestra (Vol. 1): *Piano Concerto 1; Piano Concerto in E flat, Op. posth.; Concert Paraphrase on Weber's Polonaise Brillante; Fantasy on Motifs from Beethoven's 'Ruins of Athens'; Grand solo de concert; Hexaméron; Lélio Fantasy; Malédiction (Concerto in E min. for Piano & Strings); Totentanz* (2nd version)
*** Hyp. CDA 67401/2. Howard, Budapest SO, Rickenbacher

Vol. 53b: Music for piano and orchestra (Vol. 2): *Piano Concerto 2; Concerto pathétique* (orch. Reuss); *De profundis; Hungarian Fantasia; Totentanz* (1st version). SCHUBERT, arr. LISZT: *Wanderer Fantasy*. WEBER, arr. LISZT: *Konzertstück*
*** Hyp. CDA 67403/5. Howard, Budapest SO, Rickenbacher
– MENTER: *Concerto in the Hungarian Style* ***

Crowning his monumental project to record every note of piano music that Liszt ever wrote, Leslie Howard here tackles the concertante works; not just the handful of popular pieces but no fewer than 15 works, 16 if you count the two very different versions of *Totentanz*. Each of the two volumes centres round one of the numbered concertos, and then branches out to rarities. So after a bright and sparkling account of the *First Concerto*, Volume 1 offers a sequence of eight mid-length pieces. They include not just the final version of *Totentanz*, with its grim variations on the *Dies Irae*, but *Malédiction*, a concerto for piano and strings, and the *Fantasy on Themes from Beethoven's 'Ruins of Athens'*. Rarer still, and even more interesting, are the works which Howard himself has helped to edit, usually from manuscript sources. Outstanding among these is the *Concerto in E flat*, written in the late 1830s and reconstructed only recently after much detective work by the scholar, Jay Rosenblatt, a taut sequence of five sections introduced by unaccompanied timpani. The longest work is the *Grande fantaisie symphonique on Themes from Berlioz's 'Lélio'*, which Berlioz himself conducted in 1834 with Liszt at the piano. It may be over-long for the material, but it is full of incident and, like much of this music, gives a clear idea of Liszt's style of improvisation.

Volume 2 follows up the *Second Concerto* (which Howard prefers to No. 1) with an extraordinary 36-minute piece, *De Profundis*, using a plainchant theme in a vastly expanded sonata-form. The *Concerto pathétique* is fascinating too, as not long before he died Liszt added linking passages between sections in his late, spare style. Add to that the popular *Hungarian Fantasy* and Liszt's own distinctive versions of Schubert's *Wanderer Fantasy* and Weber's *Konzertstück*. On a third bonus disc (at no extra cost) comes the oddest item of all, a colourful concert piece based on Hungarian gypsy themes by Sophie Menter, which almost certainly Liszt helped to write. Howard's dedication is clear in all his playing here, with clear, crisp articulation vividly caught in finely balanced sound.

Vol. 54: 'Liszt at the opera VI': Concert paraphrases: AUBER: *Grande fantaisie on Tyrolean melodies from 'La Fiancée'* (1st version). BELLINI: *Réminiscences des Puritains* (2nd version); *Fantaisie sur des motifs favoris* from *'La sonnambula'* (1st version). DONIZETTI: *Valse à capriccio sur deux motifs de 'Lucia et Parisina'* (1st version). GLINKA: *Marche des Tcherkesses* from *'Ruslan and Ludmilla'* (1st

version). MERCADANTE: *Réminiscences de La Scala.*
MEYERBEER: *Réminiscences des Huguenots* (2nd version).
VERDI: *Ernani: Prière paraphrase de concert.* WAGNER:
Tannhäuser Overture. WEBER: *Fantasie über Themen* from
'Der Freischütz'
*** Hyp. CDA 67406/7. Howard

Both the two-disc selections of operatic paraphrases (see
Volume 50, above) are entertaining, and in many cases they
re-serve their original purpose – to disseminate operatic
melodies to a public unlikely to hear them in the opera
house. Many of the operas here, by Auber, Donizetti, Mercadante, Halévy, Pacini and even Meyerbeer, are either forgotten or seldom performed, and Liszt's selections are often as
extended as they are elaborately set out and embroidered.
The more familiar Bellini pot-pourris are very characterful,
and Leslie Howard clearly enjoys playing them. However, he
has problems with the raging torrent of notes surrounding
the Pilgrims' chorale in the closing section of the *Tannhäuser
Overture*: surely this is only feasible in a four-handed version.
The *William Tell Overture* on the other hand is a great
success, as are the sparkling Auber *Tarantella* from *Masaniello*, and Glinka's March from *Ruslan and Ludmilla*.
Howard's vitality, commitment and strong characterization
here make up for any imprecisions in the thundering scalic
passages. This is not music to listen to all at once, but it tells
us a great deal about popular operatic taste in the mid-
nineteenth century.

Vol. 55: *Années de pèlerinage: Angelus! Prière aux anges
gardiens* (4 drafts); *Den Cypressen der Villa d'Este –
Thrénodie II; Le Lac de Wallenstadt* (early drafts). *Grand
galop chromatique; Grande fantaisie di bravura* and *Grande
fantaisie sur des thèmes de Paganini; Historische ungarische
Bildnisse; Huldigungsmarsch; Hungaria; Legend: St Francis
of Paola Walking on the Water* (simplified version); *Mélodie
polonaise; Mephisto Waltz 4; Petite valse favorite; Rákóczi
March; St Elizabeth* (excerpts); *Sunt lacrymae rerum;
Valse-impromptu; Valse mélancolique* (2 versions); *Valse
oubliée 3; Variations sur 'Le Carnaval de Venise' (Paganini)*
**(*) Hyp. CDA 67408/9/10. Howard

Leslie Howard describes the contents of this three-disc set as
'first thoughts and second drafts' and indeed there is much
here of interest which the composer discarded in later versions. And although the first draft of the *Mephisto Waltz* is
surprisingly brief, there are many delights here, especially
among the Valses, and notably among early drafts of pieces
from the *Années de pèlerinage.* Howard plays the intermediate
version of *Le Lac de Wallenstadt* beautifully, as he does the
much less familiar transcription of *The Miracle of the Roses*
from *St Elizabeth.* The *Historical Hungarian Portraits* – the
composer's last cycle of piano pieces, almost unknown in the
recital room – is remarkable for the austerity of texture and
feeling, while the rhetorical symphonic poem, *Hungaria*,
seems hopelessly inflated, for all Howard's powerful advocacy. Yet the *Huldigungsmarsch* is quite a find. The three
extended *Paganini Fantasias*, using *La campanella*, the *Carnival of Venice* or both, are rather overextended, but Howard
treats them thoughtfully and poetically rather than as vehi-
cles for mere display, and his performances have many felicities. Excellent recording, as always in this series.

Vol. 56: *'Rarities, Curiosities, Fragments'* and *23 Album
Leaves. Andante sensibilissimo; Air cosaque; Années de
pèlerinage: Canzonetta del Salvator; Il Penseroso* (1st
versions). *2 Cadenzas for Un sospiro; Concert paraphrases:*

Gaudeamus igitur (2nd version). BACH: *Fantasia & Fugue
in G min.* (1st version). CHOPIN: *Mes joies* (2nd version).
DONIZETTI: *Marche pour le Sultan Abdul Medjid-Khan.*
MEYERBEER: *Valse infernale.* NIVELLE: *La Mandragore
(ballad).* RAFF: *Waltz in D flat.* ROSSINI: *La carità; Caritas;
Harmonie on Carità La Serenata e l'orgia; Introduction &
Variations on a March from the Siege of Corinth.*
RUBINSTEIN: *Etude in D.* SCHUMANN : *Widmung* (draft).
SMETANA: *Polka.* JOHANN STRAUSS: *Waldstimmen
(Valse-caprice).* *Le Bal de Berne (Grande valse); Dante
Fragment; Dumka; En mémoire de Maximillian I (Marche
funèbre* – 1st version); *Etude in F sharp* (fragment); *
Fantasia on English Themes* (realized Howard); *Festklänge*
(1st version); *Glasgow Fragment; Korrekturblatt* (for an
earlier version of *La Lugubre Gondola); Künstlerfestzug* (1st
version); *Hungarian Rhapsodies 2, 10, 15, 16, 18* (alternative
versions); *Ländler in D; Magyar Tempo; March funèbre;
Marie-poème* (incomplete); *Mazurka in F min.* (spurious);
*Mazeppa; Mélodie in Dorian mode; Mephisto-Polka; 3rd
Mephisto Waltz* (1st draft); *Morceau in F; Operatic Aria &
Sketched Variation; Orpheus* (1879 version); *Pásztor
Lakodalmus (Mélodies hongroises); Petite Waltz* (completed
Howard); *Polnisch* (sketch); *Prometheus: Schnitterchor* (1st
version) & *Winzerchor. Rákóczi March* (1st version,
incomplete); *St Stanislaus* (fragment); *Valse in A*
*** Hyp. CDA 67414/7. Howard

For his penultimate volume (of four CDs!) Leslie Howard
clears his desk, as it were, offering all kinds of fascinating
morsels, many incomplete or early drafts, and a great many
fragmentary 'Album leaves', which the composer valued and
often dedicated to his friends. Also, more substantially, there
are six important alternative versions of six of the *Hungarian
Rhapsodies*, of which the final published works were to feature so successfully in Howard's last album, plus three complete symphonic poems prepared from manuscript sources.
Standing out among the other major pieces is the fascinating
Fantasia on English Themes (again assembled for performance by Howard himself), which combines excerpts from
Handel's *Messiah* and *Judas Maccabaeus* with Arne's *Rule
Britannia* and *God save the King.* Overall, this is perhaps a
specialist set, but there is much here to interest any admirer
of this remarkable and prolific composer. The playing consistently shows Howard at his best (especially the miniatures)
and the recording is well up to standard.

Vol. 57: *Hungarian Rhapsodies 1–19*
🕪— *** Hyp. CDA 67418/2. Howard

This splendid set represents a high artistic peak within Leslie
Howard's distinguished survey, offering as it does the final
version of material, much of which we have already heard in
Volume 29. Clearly this is music which inspires the pianist
and he plays every piece not only with great élan and virtuosity but also with an appealing sense of fantasy. His performances convey a spontaneity not always apparent in
earlier volumes, and his readings are full of imagination. The
second disc opens dramatically with a superb account of *No.
10 in E major* and Howard's rubato in *No. 12 in C sharp minor*
is most seductive. The set concludes with one of the most
impressive performances of all, *No. 19*, which is 'after the
Csárdás nobles of Abrányi'. The recording is first class. In this
repertoire György Cziffra's mono set (see below) remains
memorable for its dazzling bravura, a remarkable achievement; but Leslie Howard's technical command and control of
colour are always equal to the occasion, and in his hands

much of this writing is shown to have an unexpected depth of feeling.

Supplement

'New Discoveries': *Années de pèlerinage*: early drafts: *Aux anges gardiens; Sunt lacrymae rerum; Postludium: Nachtspiel: Sursum corda. Célèbre mélodie hongroise; From the Album of Princess Marie zu Sayn-Wittgenstein: Album-Leaf; Lilie; Hryá; Mazurek; Krakowiak. La lugubre gondola* (original Venice manuscript). *11 Zigeuner-Epos*
*** Hyp. CDA 67346 Howard

Since Leslie Howard rounded off his record-breaking Hyperion series of Liszt's complete piano music on 95 CDs in 1997, he has been searching for unconsidered trifles, newly unearthed. This supplementary disc is the result, bringing together two dozen items, many of them charming 'album-leaves', which Liszt wrote for various admirers, including the ten-year-old Princess Marie of Sayn-Wittgenstein. Such trifles, some only a few seconds long, and a series of 11 tuneful gypsy pieces reveal Liszt at his most unpretentious, fresh and direct, and so do the newly discovered early drafts of pieces, which he later elaborated, such as *La Lugubre gondola*, with strikingly bald textures. Howard is here at his warmest and most persuasive, bringing out how Liszt's genius developed.

Other recordings

(i) *Années de pèlerinage: Book 1, 1st Year: Switzerland; Book 2, 2nd Year: Italy*; (ii) *Book 3, 3rd Year: Italy*
(B) ** Ph. Duo 462 312-2 (2). (i) Brendel; (ii) Kocsis

Brendel made some of his finest conquests in the recording studio in this repertoire, and his 1959 analogue survey of the first book of the *Années de pèlerinage* was among the finest. This later, digital set of both the first and second years has many impressive moments, but also some ugly *fortissimi* that are not wholly the responsibility of the engineers. Brendel plays the *First Book* segue, without pauses, and although there is some atmospheric playing in the set, the moments of magic are relatively few. Brendel is always to be heard with respect, but this playing is out of scale and over-projected. For *Book 3*, Kocsis takes over and he gives the most compelling account of these sombre and imaginative pieces; apart from beautiful pianism, he also manages to convey their character without exaggeration. He has impeccable technical control and can convey the dark power of the music without recourse to percussive tone. He is splendidly recorded and it is a pity that Philips decided to reissue his performances in harness with those of Brendel. Readers will note that the set omits the *Book 2* supplement (*Venezia e Napoli*).

Concert Paraphrases of Schubert's Lieder: Aufenthalt; Ständchen; Das Wandern; Wohin?. Mephisto Waltz 1
** RCA 82876 58462-2. Kissin – SCHUBERT: *Piano Sonata 21*
*(*)

Kissin's pianism is second to none and serves the Liszt paraphrases effectively. At the same time, there is a certain self-consciousness and reserve. One longs for him to let rip. However, these are more satisfactory than the Schubert *B flat Sonata*, whose profundities he does not penetrate.

Hungarian Rhapsodies 1–9 (Carnaval de Pesth)
(BB) ** Naxos 8.554480. Jandó

Hungarian Rhapsodies 10–19
(BB) ** Naxos 8.554481. Jandó

This repertoire calls for great virtuosity and a musical personality of outsize stature. Jenö Jandó is not quite in that league but his performances are far from negligible. The price tag is attractive but Szidon, who is also inexpensive, rivets the attention in a way that Jandó does not (DG 453 034-2).

Piano Sonata in B min.; Concert Paraphrase on Verdi's 'Rigoletto'
*** DG **DVD** 073 4079. Yundi Li – CHOPIN: *Piano Concerto 1: Rondo*, etc. ***

Yundi Li's playing has delicacy and finesse, and a pretty flawless technique. He has an appealing personality that puts the listener very much on his side, and he gives a very fine account of the *B minor Sonata*. Nor does his version of the *Rigoletto Paraphrase* lack virtuosiy or panache. Perhaps the *Sonata* has yet to exhibit the command and personality of a great pianist, but this recital certainly indicates that his is a formidable talent with enormous potential whose future will blossom.

Piano Sonata in B min.; Fantasy & Fugue on B-A-C-H; Totentanz (arr. for piano solo by the composer)
**(*) Avie AV 2097. Groh

What makes Markus Groh's recording of the Liszt *Sonata* of extra interest is his flamboyant analysis of the work in the notes, section by section, almost page by page. The hyperbole of his language, reflecting his passionate musical response, may irritate some readers, but the appraisal of what is going on in the music is uniquely detailed. It is a great pity therefore that Avie did not offer a series of cues (to show on the display panel, without interrupting the music) for the listener to follow his comments, particularly as he numbers the principal themes on which this remarkable, cyclic work is based. As for the performance, it is arrestingly spontaneous, unashamedly romantic. Perhaps the 'exposition' carries his impulsive response to extremes, but there is no doubting the excitement of the reading, nor its poetic feeling when the *Andante sostenuto* theme is in his hands. The *Fantasia and Fugue on B-A-C-H* is equally commanding; but the highlight of the disc is his thrilling account of the *Totentanz* in the composer's own arrangement for solo piano. Groh makes it more aurally fascinating and certainly just as gripping and even more virtuosic than the concertante version. The recording, made in Germany, is excellent.

Miscellaneous recitals

Albumblatt 1 in E; Berceuse (1st & 2nd versions); Elégie sur des motifs du Prince Louis Ferdinand de Prusse; Feuilles d'album in A flat; Liebesträume 1, 2 (2nd version) & 3; Romance; Scherzo & March
(BB) ** Naxos 8.553595. Jandó

Jenö Jandó is a good pianist, but in this kind of repertoire his personality is not sufficiently compelling to put the listener under his spell. The result is more than *vin ordinaire* but less than vintage.

Années de pèlerinage: Au bord d'une source. Concert Studies 1–2: Waldesrauschen; Gnomenreigen. Concert Paraphrase: Les Patineurs (Illustration 2 from Meyerbeer's 'Le Prophète'); Etudes de Concert: La leggierezza; Un sospiro; Paganini Etudes 2 in E flat; 3 (La campanella); 5 (La Chasse). Etudes d'exécution transcendante: Feux follets
(**) Pearl mono GEM 0148. Kentner – BARTOK: *Piano Concerto 3*, etc. (*)

The Liszt performances come from 78–r.p.m. records made between 1937 and 1949 for the Columbia DX label. Louis Kentner was a Lisztian of great distinction, and these old discs testify to his finesse and sensitivity. Decent transfers, but the Bartók coupling is much less recommendable.

ORGAN MUSIC

3 Bach Bearbeitung; Prelude and Fugue on B-A-C-H; Prelude & Variations on 'Weinen, Klagen, Sorgen, Zagen'. Concert Paraphrase of Passacaglia & Fugue in C min., BWV 582
*** MDG 606 1334-2. Schönheit (Ladegast organ of Dom zu Merseburg)

Ave Maria von Arcadelt; Ave Verum of Mozart (Concert Paraphrase); Évocation à la chapelle sixtine; Fantasia & Fugue on 'Ad nos, ad salutarem undam'; Tu es Petrus (Andante maestoso out of Christus)
*** MDG 606 1352-2. Schönheit (Ladegast organ of Dom zu Merseburg)

Michael Schönheit's survey of Liszt's organ music has one great advantage in that he has the use of the magnificent organ in Merseburg Cathedral, which has a special connection with the music here. Apparently it was Liszt's pupil, Alexander Winterberger, who transcribed the piano original of the *Prelude* to 'Weinen, Klagen, Sorgen, Zagen' for organ, and he tailored it specially to the registration of the Ladegast organ; when Liszt came to write his variations, he re-used parts of his pupil's registration. Having said that, we do not find Schönheit's playing – fine as it is – as gripping as that of Andreas Rothkopf on the comparable pair of Naxos discs, praised in our main volume (8.554544 and 8.55079). The major works have fine sonority but do not generate a great deal of tension. Schönheit's account of the re-registered *Passacaglia and Fugue in C minor* begins very slowly indeed, and some of the shorter pieces, the transcription of Mozart's *Ave Verum* and the excerpt from *Cantata 38*, have a very low profile, and the *Violin and Harpsichord Sonata Adagio*, BWV 1017, although it is a straight transcription, is barely recognizable and very romantic-sounding.

VOCAL MUSIC

Lieder: *Der Alpenjäger; Anfangs wollt ist fast verzagen; Angiolin dal biodo crin; Blume und Duft; Comment, disaient-ils; Die drei Zigeuner; Du bist wie eine Blume; Der du von dem Himmel bist; Enfant, si j'étais roi; Ein Fichtenbaum steht einsam; Es muss ein Wunderbares sein; Es rauschen die Winde; Der Fischerknabe; Gastibelza; Gestoren war ich; Der Hirt; Hohe Liebe; Ich möchte hingeln; Ihr Glocken von Marling; Im Rhein, im schönen Strome; In Liebeslust; J'ai perdu ma force; Klinge leise, mein Lied; Lasst mich ruhen; Die Lorelei; Morgens steh'ich auf und frage; Oh! Quand je dors; O Lieb, so lang; Petrarch Sonnets 1–3; Schwebe, schwebe blaues Auge; S'il est un charmant gazon; Die stille Wasserose; Des Tages laute Stimmen schweigen; La Tombe et la rose; Der traurige Mönch; Uber allen Gipfeln ist Ruh; Die Vätergruft; Vergiftet sind meine Lieder; Le Vieux Vagabond; Wer nie sein Brot; Wieder möcht ich dir begegnen; Wie singt die Lerche schon*
(M) *** DG 474 891-2 (3). Fischer-Dieskau, Barenboim

This is the listing of the 43 songs enthusiastically reviewed in our main edition.

LÔBO, Alonso (c. 1555–1617)

Motets: *Ave Maria; Credo quod redemptor; Versa est in Luctum; Vivo ego, dicit Dominus*
⊕– (B) *** Gimell CDGIM 205 (2). Tallis Scholars, Philips – CARDOSO: *Requiem*; Duarte LÔBO: *Requiem*; VICTORIA *Requiem* ***

These four motets by Alonso Lôbo (not related to Duarte) include a striking setting of *Versa est in Luctum*, also set by Victoria in connection with his *Requiem*, although Lôbo's piece is not associated with a *Missa pro defunctis*. But *Credo quod redemptor* is also memorable, and so is the beautiful *Ave Maria*, which is complex in structure but sounds richly serene, with a lovely final *Amen*.

LÔBO, Duarte (c. 1565–1646)

Missa pro defunctis
(B) *** Gimell CDGIM 205 (2). Tallis Scholars, Philips – CARDOSO: *Requiem*; Alonso LÔBO: *Motets*; VICTORIA *Requiem* ***

Missa pro defunctis (Requiem); Audivi vocem de coelo
⊕– (B) *** Hyp. Helios CDH 55138 – William Byrd Ch., G. Turner – Filip de MAGALHÁES: *Missa Dilecus meus* ***

Duarte Lôbo's *Requiem* for double choir (eight voices) is an exceptionally rich and firmly harmonized work. The general effect is homophonic, but there is some simple polyphonic interplay in the *Gradual* and the *Offertory*. This is a work of dignity and deep feeling, and it is superbly sung by the William Byrd Choir, who also offer the celestial motet, *Audivi vocem de coelo*. Their coupling is music by Lôbo's Portuguese contemporary, Filip de Magalháes, which is hardly less beautiful.

Undoubtedly the Tallis Scholars are completely at home in this music, and the smaller scale of their performances brings added clarity without too much loss of atmosphere. The singing itself is radiantly pure and beautiful. If you want the Victoria *Requiem* also, this Gimell Double is the version to go for.

LOCATELLI, Pietro (1695–1764)

Concerti grossi in B flat and G min., Op. 1/3 & 12; in E flat, Op. 4/11; in F, Op. 7/4; in E flat (Il pianto d'Arianna)
(M) *** Warner Elatus 2564 60016-2. Concerto Köln

Locatelli's dramatic *E flat major Concerto grosso*, Op. 7/6 offers an instrumental paraphrase of the tragedy of Ariadne abandoned by Theseus, which inspired Monteverdi's famous *Lamento d'Arianna*. There are winds, violin recitatives, tearful laments, moments of histrionic drama and a touching *Grave* conveying the heroine's despair, before her spirited angry outburst when she calls for revenge. The six-movement work ends with an epilogue of resignation. The Cologne performance is certainly strongly characterized, but too often, both here and throughout this generous programme, the tread of the members of this celebrated group is heavy and, although the playing is polished and expert, and often very lively (especially in finales), the rhythms fail to lift off and the strong accents are abrasive. The resonant recording makes for a broad and very ample spread of sound, and slow movements are at times ungainly.

Violin Sonatas (for 1 or 2 Violins) & continuo, Op. 8/1–10

(B) *** Hyp. Dyad CDH 55226 (2). Locatelli Trio

Locatelli's Op. 8 consists of six works for solo violin, the last of which is the most impressive, its closing *Aria di minuetto* with eight variations demanding considerable bravura from the soloist. All the sonatas start with a slow, expressive introduction, with faster movements following. The remaining works are *Trio Sonatas*; with their format of (usually) four or (sometimes) five movements, they offer the composer even greater opportunities for variety and he is obviously intending to please his cultivated listeners. But the invention in the later works is deft in imaginative touches, and the contrapuntal writing is genially spirited and in that respect has no little affinity with Handel. Provided you don't respond adversely to Elizabeth Wallfisch's tendency to bulge very slightly on expressive phrasing, the performances are admirable, crisply detailed and refreshingly alive. The Hyperion recording is well up to standard, and this reissue is temptingly inexpensive.

Violin Sonata in C, Op. 8/4; Double Violin Sonata in A, Op. 8/7

*** Astrée 8842. Kraemer, Valetti, Rare Fruit Council –
LECLAIR: *Overture; Sonatas* ***

In these happily juxtaposed violin sonatas of Leclair and Locatelli it was Locatelli who was personified by a contemporary wag as 'the devil'. The story is told that he scraped his violin with such violence that the first ten rows of the audience were unable to appreciate his playing. No doubt that is a trifle exaggerated, but undoubtedly he had a lively temperament, and his music is full of imaginative and sometimes unexpected touches – like the finale of Op. 8/7, which has some witty spurts and pauses, while both the central *Adagio* and *Cantabile* demonstrate his lyrical gifts. And to show his virtuosity, the equally attractive companion work in C major has a dashing cadenza interpolated from *L'arte dell'violino* within an already sparkling allegro. Although they play with great spirit in authentic style, Pierre Valetti and Manfredo Kraemer do not scrape, and they both produce plenty of warmth in the slow movements. They are most pleasingly recorded.

LOCKE, Matthew (c. 1621–77)

Anthems: Be thou exalted Lord; How doth the city sit solitary; Lord let me know mine end; O be joyful in the Lord; all ye lands. Oxford Ode: *Descende caelo cincta sororibus.* Latin Motets: *Audi, Domine, clamantes ad te; Jesu, auctor clementie*

(B) *** Hyp. CDH 55250. New College, Oxford, Ch., Parley of Instruments, Higginbottom

We already have coverage of Matthew Locke's Consort and Theatre Music (see our main volume); now we have an excellent and inexpensive CD of his church music. Like others of his era (although he was a Catholic himself), he wrote Anglican music, including some fine anthems, as well as concerted Latin works. Apart from demands on his time at the court, he had a strong connection with Oxford and he wrote the so-called *Oxford Ode* for an academic celebration. There is plenty of variety here. *Super flumina Babylon*, a setting of Psalm 136, opens with a solemn two-movement Sinfonia. *O be joyful in the Lord* is as good-tempered as it sounds, with an attractive string accompaniment. Yet *How*

doth the city (with an almost orchestral organ accompaniment) is a melancholy setting of verses from the *Lamentations of Jeremiah. Lord let me know mine end* has a diminuendo at the close. But the collection ends on a triumphant note, with full choir and orchestra in *Be exalted Lord.* Male voices are used throughout, as women began to sing in English choirs only in the 1770s. A most worthwhile collection, well sung throughout, and recorded in a comparatively dry acoustic to match the sound the composer would have expected both in Oxford and in London.

LOEWE, Carl (1796–1869)

Ballads and Lieder: Archibald Douglas; Canzonette; Die drei Lieder; Edward; Elvershöh; Erlkönig; Freibeuter; Frühzeitiger Frühling; Der getreue Eckart; Gottes ist der Orient!; Die Gruft der Liebenden; Gutmann und Gutweib; Der heilige Franziskus; Heinrich der Vogler; Herr Oluf; Hinkende Jamben; Hochzeitlied; Ich denke dein; Im Vorübergehen; Kleiner Haushalt; Lynkeus, der Türmer, auf Fausts Sternwarte singend; Meeresleuchten; Der Mohrenfürst auf der Messe; Der Nöck; Odins Meeresritt; Prinz Eugen; Der Schatzgräber; Süsses Begräbnis; Tom der Reimer; Der Totentanz; Trommelständchen; Turmwächter Lynkeus zu den Füssen der Helena; Die Uhr; Die wandelnde Glocke; Wandrers Nachtlied; Wenn der Blüten Frühlingsregen; Der Zauberlehrling

(M) *** DG (IMS) 449 516-2 (2). Fischer-Dieskau, Demus

Like the collection of Liszt Lieder above this is one of Fischer-Dieskau's key recordings of German songs.

LOEWE, Frederick (1901–88) with
LERNER, Alan Jay (1918–86)

My Fair Lady (Musical)

(M) (***) Sony mono SMK 89997. Andrews, Harrison, Holloway, King and original cast, Ch. & O, Allers (with Post-Recording Conversations and Playback)

There are many who count *My Fair Lady* as the greatest musical of all and, with a script by George Bernard Shaw, brilliantly apt lyrics by Alan Jay Lerner, who can argue with them, for Frederick Loewe's score was no less inspired. There are sixteen numbers here, and not a dud among them, when most modern musicals manage with one or two hits, endlessly reprised.

This is not the later, stereo recording (which is far inferior) but the original mono LP, recorded in 1956 and vividly transferred to CD; moreover it includes the witty original orchestrations by Robert Russell Bennett and Phil Lang, which apparently are no longer in use today in the interests of theatrical economy and a smaller orchestra.

As the post-recording conversations reveal at the end of the disc, Julie Andrews was just 21 at the time of the recording; here she is in wonderfully fresh voice (*Show me* is dazzling); so are her colleagues. We need say no more: this is an endlessly enjoyable CD: you feel better having listened to it all the way through and glad to be alive. Why can't composers write tunes like this any more? The documentation is adequate, with a few photographs included, but this reissue was worthy of a more elaborate presentation. Snap it up before it disappears!

LOURIÉ, Arthur (1892–1966)

(i) *String Quartets 1–3 (Suite)*; (ii) *Duo for Violin & Viola*
**(*) ASV CDDCA 1020. (i) Utrecht Qt; (ii) Koskinen, Raiskin

The three quartets were composed in quick succession: the *First* is a two-movement piece lasting half an hour, whose first movement (nearly 20 minutes) is very amorphous and wanting in concentration. The *Second Quartet* (1923) is a much shorter, one-movement work with a hint of Stravinskian neo-classicism and humour. But it is the economical and well-wrought *Duo for Violin and Viola* that is most Russian. The *Third Quartet* (1924), subtitled *Suite* (its movements are called *Prélude, Choral, Hymne* and *Marche funèbre*), save for the last movement does not make as strong an impression as *A Little Chamber Music* from the same year. Nevertheless this is an interesting byway, explored with great dedication by these players.

LUDFORD, Nicholas (1485–1557)

Missa Benedicta et venerabilis; Magnificat benedicta
*** Gaudeamus CDGAU 132. Cardinall's Musick, Carwood

Ludford uses the same plainchant for both works, but the voicing has a distinct emphasis at the lower end of the range, not only adding to the weight but also bringing a certain darkness to the sonority. The performance has the same spontaneous feeling that distinguishes this magnificent series throughout, and it confirms Ludford as one of the most emotionally communicative and original musicians of his age. The plainsong Propers relate the music to the Feast of the Assumption. Excellent, full recording.

Missa Christi Virgo dilectissima; Motet: Domine Ihesu Christie
*** Gaudeamus CDGAU 133. Cardinall's Musick, Carwood

This is music of great beauty, whose expressive eloquence and floating lines quite carry the listener away. Andrew Carwood proves an excellent advocate and the sound is also spacious and well balanced.

Missa Lapidaverunt Stephanum; Ave Maria ancilla trinitatis
*** Gaudeamus CDGAU 140. Cardinall's Musick, Carwood

This Mass, celebrating St Stephen the Martyr, is thought to have been written soon after he was appointed verger and organist there in 1527. In five-part polyphony the scale is formidable, culminating in a magnificent *Agnus Dei*. The performances, fresh and stylish, are punctuated by apt plainsong.

Missa Videte miraculum; Motet: Ave cuius conceptio
*** Gaudeamus CDGAU 131. Cardinall's Musick, Carwood

The six-part *Missa Videte miraculum* brings a remarkable double treble line running together, often in thirds. Overall this work is as fine as the others in the series, and it is gloriously sung.

LUIGINI, Alexandre (1850–1906)

Ballet Egyptien, Op. 12 (suite)
(B) *** CfP (ADD) 352399-2. RPO, Fistoulari – KETELBEY: *Collection* ***

Because of its bandstand popularity, Luigini's amiable and tuneful *Ballet Egyptien* has never been taken very seriously.

However, the four-movement suite is highly engaging (both the two central sections have good tunes), especially when played as affectionately and stylishly as here under that master conductor of ballet, Anatole Fistoulari. The 195? recording has come up remarkably freshly, and this makes an excellent bonus for an outstanding Ketèlbey concert.

LULLY, Jean-Baptiste (1632–87)

Divertissements 1–3 (arr. Sempé)
(BB) ** DHM/BMG 82876 60154-2. Laurens, Capriccio Stravagante, Sempé

Skip Sempé and his chamber group have already given us a recommendable CD of the music of Buxtehude, but this collection of the music of Lully is rather disappointing. Sempé is attempting to recreate the evening concerts at the Versailles court enjoyed by the nobility, featuring a small ensemble plus a celebrated soloist. The three 'Divertissements' draw on music from several of Lully's tragédies lyriques, including *Amadis, Psyché* and *Armide*, but the authentic string-textures here are too meagre to bring out the richness of the expressive writing and, although the mezzo-soprano soloist Guillemette Laurens understands the style of the music and sings expressively, her full-bodied voice, with ample vibrato, will please some ears more than others. Overall these performances fail to seduce the ear. Texts and translations are provided.

VOCAL MUSIC

Lés Comédies Ballets: excerpts from: (i) *Les Amants magnifiques; L'Amour Médecin; Le Bourgeois Gentilhomme; George Dandin* (*Le Grand Divertissement royal de Versailles*); *Monsieur de Pourceaugnac* (*Le Divertissement de Chambourd*); *Pastoral comique; Les Plaisirs de l'ile enchantée.* (ii) *Phaëton* (tragédie en musique; complete)
☛ (BB) *** Warner Apex 2564 62184-2 (2). (i) Poulenard, Mellon, Ragon, Laplénie, Verschaeve, Delétré, Cantor; (ii) Crook, Yakar, J. Smith, Gens, Thereul, Sagittarius Vocal Ens.; Musiciens du Louvre, Minkowski

The series of comédies-ballets represented here were written between 1663 and 1670, and their tuneful and often outrageous burlesque represents an unparalleled comic partnership between composer and playwright (Molière) – French insouciance combined with witty *bucolique* music which obviously reflects the influence of Italian comic opera, yet never loses its Gallic character, especially in the charming and often beautiful pastoral airs.

The ensemble of 'Ironic salutation to Men of Medicine' (Lully despised doctors) in *L'Amour médecin* is matched by the robust male interchanges while wallowing in the hedonistic pleasures of *L'ile enchantée*, and there are similar comically boisterous ensembles in the divertissement, *George Dandin*, although they are perhaps capped by the extraordinary excerpt from *Monsieur de Pourceaugnac*, which makes fun of polygamy. The two longest selections come from *Le Bourgeois Gentilhomme*, which includes one syncopated number that anticipates *America* in Bernstein's *West Side Story*, and, finally, the masterly third *intermède* of *Les Amants magnifiques*, which combines a gentler humour with graceful lyricism. The team of soloists clearly relishes every humorous situation, and the presentation has consistent sparkle and spontaneity, while the lyrical music is most persuasively phrased by singers and orchestra alike.

Phaëton tells the famous story of the attempt of the son of Jupiter to drive across the heavens in his father's chariot. The horses bolt and Jupiter strikes him dead, to the apparent rejoicing of everyone. When Lybye can then be partnered by her beloved Epaphus, it is hardly a tragedy at all, with their love celebrated earlier in two brief but intensely beautiful duets. The cast is strong – Véronique Gens is most affecting as Lybye, with Rachael Yakar and Jennifer Smith impressive too, and Howard Crook clean-focused and stylish in the name-part. Throughout the two discs, Marc Minkowski's direction is compellingly fresh and resilient. Both recordings are co-productions between Erato and Radio France and are strikingly vivid and immediate. One laments the appalling documentation, or lack of it, but this set is not to be missed.

OPERA

Persée (complete DVD version)
*** EuroArts **DVD** 2054178. Auvity, Lenormand, Novacek, Whicher, Laquerre, Coulombe, Ainsworth, Tafelmusik Chamber Ch. & Bar. O, Niquet (V/D: Marc Stone)

Set in the historic Elgin Theatre in Toronto, Marshall Pynkoski's production for Tafelmusik under its lively music-director, Hervé Niquet, offers a staging as close as possible to the original (1682) presentation of the opera in the Palace of Versailles. Costumes are sumptuously baroque, and the sort of stage effects popular at the time, with gods coming down from the flies, add to the effectiveness. The work itself is a traditional *tragédie lyrique* in five acts, lasting just over two hours, with arioso taking the place of set numbers, punctuated in each act by dances – cue for ballet from the Atelier Company. The plot involves the linking of two classical legends, taken from Ovid's *Metamorphoses*: Perseus's slaying of Medusa, and his rescue of Andromeda, daughter of the King of Ethiopia. The title-role of Persée – who appears for the first time only in Act III – is very well taken by the high tenor, Cyril Auvity, and though the other principals are variable the piece moves swiftly. The role of Medusa is taken by a bearded baritone, Olivier Laquerre, rather roughish for this repertory, if characterful, particularly in the solo of lamentation for loss of his/her beauty.

LUMBYE, Hans Christian (1810–74)

Amelie Waltz; Britta Polka; Champagne Galop; Columbine Polka Mazurka; Concert Polka (for 2 violins and orchestra); *Copenhagen Steam Railway Galop; Dream Pictures* (fantasy); *The Lady of St Petersburg* (polka); *The Guards of Amager: Final Galop. My Salute to St Petersburg* (march); *Napoli* (ballet): *Final Galop. Polonaise with Cornet Solo; Queen Louise's Waltz; Salute to August Bournonville; St Petersburg Champagne Galop*
*** Chan. 10354X. Danish Nat. RSO, Rozhdestvensky

This Chandos reissue comes into direct competition with a similar Regis programme from the Odense Symphony Orchestra under Peter Guth (RRC 1155). Both are very entertaining and the Danish orchestra under Rozhdestvensky plays with great gusto. But in the delightful *Copenhagen Steam Railway Galop* Guth finds a period elegance which is very endearing, whereas with the Russian conductor the little train becomes more of a mainline express.

Britta Polka; Canon Galop; Cecilie Waltz; Dancing Tune from Kroll Waltz; Indian War Dance; King Christian IX

March of Honour; King George I March of Honour; Manoeuvre Galop; Memories from Vienna Waltz; Nordic Brotherhood; Pegasus Galop; Summernight at Mons Cliffe Galop; Sophie Waltz; Velocipedes Galop; Victoria Quadrille; Welcome Mazurka; Les Zouaves Galop
(BB) *** Regis RRC 1156. Odense SO, Guth

A further – essentially energetic – selection of sparkling Lumbye repertoire, splendidly played with much spirit by the excellent Odense orchestra under Guth. The *Velocipedes Galop* makes an engaging and vivacious opener, and the *Canon Galop*, which closes the concert, has properly spectacular effects, plus a final bang to make the listener jump. The *Memories from Vienna Waltz* has a particularly winning lilt, but there is nothing here that quite matches the *Copenhagen Steam Railway Galop*.

LUTOSLAWSKI, Witold (1913–94)

Paganini Variations for Piano & Orchestra
*** Australian Decca Eloquence 476 7671. Jablonski, RPO, Ashkenazy – DOHNANYI: *Variations on a Nursery Song* **(*); LISZT: *Totentanz* (**(*)); RACHMANINOV: *Paganini Variations* **(*)

The *Paganini Variations* for two pianos, one of Lutosławski's earliest works (1941), is heard here in the much later orchestral transcription, with evident pleasure and delight.

MACHAUT, Guillaume de
(c. 1300–1377)

Ballades, rondeaux, virelais: *Amours me fait desirer; Biauté qu toutes autres pere; Dame a qui; Dame, a vous sana retollir; Dame, de qui toute ma joie vent; Dame je sui cliz/Fins cuers doulz; Dame mon coeur en vous remaint; Douce dame jolie; Foy porter; Je vivroie liement; Rose, liz, printemps, verdure; Tuit mi penser;* Motet: *Inviolata genitrix/Felix virgo/Ad te suspiramus*

Ballades, motets, rondeaux & virelais: *Amours me fait desirer; Dame se vous m'estés lointeinne; De Bon Espoir – Puis que la douce rousee; De toutes flours; Douce dame jolie; Hareu! hareu! le feu; Ma fin est mon commencement; Mes esperis se combat; Phyton le mervilleus serpent; Quant j'ay l'espart; Quant je suis mis au retour; Quant Theseus – Ne quier veoir; Se ma dame m'a guerpy; Se je souspir; Trop plus est belle – Biauté paree – Je ne sui mie certeins*

Motets: *Amours/Faus samblant; Christe qui lux/Veni creator spiritus; Dame/Fins cuers doulz; Felix virgo/Inviolata genitrix; Lasse!/Se j'aime mon loyal ami; Martyrum/ Diligenter inquiramus Qui es promesse/ Ha! Fortune; Tu qui gregem/ Plange, regni respublica; Trop plus est bele/ Biaute paree de valour*

Chansons (ballades, rondeaux, viralais): *Certes mon oueil; Comment peut on; De toutes fleurs; En amer a douce vie; En vipere; De Fortune; Hel dame de valour; Je ne cuit pas; Je puis trop bien; Liement me deport; Ma fin est mon commencement; Mors sui; Se quanque amours; Tant doucement*
☛ *** Hyp. CDA 66087 Kirkby, Gothic Voices, Page

This is the full listing of titles of the CD highly praised in our main volume.

MACHY, Sieur de (died c. 1692)

Pièces de viole (1685): Suites 1–3
(M) *(*) Astrée (ADD) ES 9946. Savall

Little is known about Sieur de Machy (or Demachy) except that his published *Viol Suites* predated the first publication of the Marais suites by a year. They are the usual collection of Allemandes, Courantes, Sarabandes, Gavottes, Gigues and Minuets, but so freely improvisational is the style of Savall's performances that their rhythmic profile is often all but lost. This is simple music, and it needs a direct, clearly rhythmic approach. An interesting but essentially disappointing reissue (from the late 1970s).

MACMILLAN, James (born 1959)

The Confession of Isobel Gowdie; Symphony 3
*** Chan. 10275. BBC PO, composer

The Confession of Isobel Gowdie was the work that, at the Proms in 1990, brought James MacMillan instant success with a far wider audience than is normally attracted to new music. As the composer describes it, it is the Requiem that Isobel Gowdie, a Catholic martyr accused of witchcraft, never had. In a single 25-minute span it begins in deep meditation, then the central section, by far the longest, brings a violence reflecting the brutality with which the martyr was treated. The beauty of the final section, in which she seems to find peace, with its references to plainsong is all the more affecting here in the composer's own performance.

Symphony 3 (2002) follows a comparable pattern of slow, inexorable build-up over a massive span, this time far bigger still. The work's paradoxical subtitle, 'Silence', was inspired by the work of the Japanese author Shusaku Endo, whose novel with that title has had a profound influence on the composer. In reflection of that and the fact that the piece was commissioned by the NHK Orchestra of Japan, MacMillan introduces ideas and timbres from oriental sources. The colour of the writing and the dramatic impact of the high contrasts, which are typical of the composer, hold the massive structure together with many clear landmarks. The concentration of the playing of the BBC Philharmonic under MacMillan adds to the tautness in both works, and the performances are brilliant in every way and superbly recorded. Sadly, the different sections of each work are not marked by separate CD tracks, making it far more difficult for the listener to identify the geography of each structure, despite excellent notes by Stephen Johnson.

James MacMillan has recently won the Contemporary Music category at the Classical Brit awards for this recording of his *Symphony No. 3* ('*Silence*') and *The Confession of Isobel Gowdie.*

From Ayrshire
*** DG 476 3159 (2). Benedettti, ASMF, MacMillan –
MENDELSSOHN: *Violin Concerto;* MOZART: *Adagio & Rondo;* SCHUBERT (orch. Stephens): *Serenade* ***

The piece, written for her by her fellow Scot, James MacMillan, makes a delightful pendant to Nicola Benedetti's disc of items built round her sparkling performance of the Mendelssohn *Violin Concerto. From Ayrshire* is in two movements. The first, much the longer, is an extended cantilena with hints of Scottish folksong, prompting Benedetti to

some passionate playing, inspired by melodic lines, well geared to bringing out her special qualities. The second movement is a brisk and brilliant pay-off, relatively short, again designed to bring out magic and sparkle in the violinist's playing. Excellent sound.

Cantos Sagrados; Christus vincit; Child's Prayer; Divo Aloysio Sacrum; The Gallant Weaver; Seinte Mari mode milde; So Deep; Tremunt vidente angeli
*** Signum SIGCD 507. L. Elysian Singers, Laughton; Jackson

A fascinating pot-pourri of James MacMillan's choral music called *Santos Sagrados* ('Sacred Songs'), which ranges from Latin motets to Scottish traditional settings or arrangements, including a pair of Robert Burns songs. The two major pieces offer a striking contrast, with the title number for choir and organ (the excellent Carl Jackson) in which MacMillan brings moments of intimidating darkness to the radiantly celestial *Tremunt vidente angeli.* Fine singing throughout from the excellent Elysian Singers (appropriately named for some of these dedicated religious settings) under their persuasive conductor, Sam Laughton.

MADETOJA, Leevi (1887–1947)

Songs, Vol I: *Op. 2; Dark-hued Leaves, Op. 9/1; Serenade, Op. 16/1; Folksongs from Northern Ostrobothnia, Op. 18; Songs of Youth, Op. 20b; From Afar I Hear Them Singing, Op. 25/1–2, 4–5; I Would Build a Hut, Op. 26/3; Song at the Plough, Op. 44/1; 2 Songs, Op. 49/1–2; 2 Songs, Op. 60/2–3; Songs Op. 71/1–2; Land in Our Song; Song of the Winter Wind*
*** Ondine ODE 996-3 Suovanen, Djupsjöbacka

Songs, Vol II: *Op. 9/2–5; Op. 16/2 & 3; Op. 26/1, 2, 4 & 5; Autumn Song Cycle, Op. 68/1–6; Romance sans paroles, Op. 36; Op. 44/2–4; 2 Songs from Okon Fuoko, Op. 58; Swing Song, Op. 60/1; To an Unfaithful One*
*** Ondine ODE 995-2. Juntunen, Djupsjöbacka

These songs and their performances are discussed in full in our main *Guide.* The second volume is the more rewarding of the two discs.

MAGALHÃES, Filipe de (1571–1652)

Missa Dilecus meus; Commissa mea pavesco
⊕ (BB) *** Hyp. Helios CDH 55138 – William Byrd Ch., Gavin Turner – LÔBO: *Missa pro defunctis* ***

Filipe de Magalhães, alongside the better-known Duarte Lôbo and Cardoso, was among the names that dominated Portuguese music over the turn of the sixteenth to the seventeenth century. Most of Magalhães's surviving works are found in two books dated 1636, including the present beautiful Mass for five voices. The music flows richly but with rather more impetus than in the coupled Lôbo *Requiem,* until the simple *Benedictus* and double *Agnus Dei* which has an additional voice, with the altos divided. The following funeral motet, *Commissa mea pavesco,* is similarly serene and also richly harmonized in six parts. A splendid coupling, beautifully sung and recorded.

MAHLER, Gustav (1860–1911)

Symphonies 1–10; Das Lied von der Erde

(*) DG DVD 73 4088 (9). J. Baker, Armstrong, Ludwig, Kollo, VPO, LSO or Israel PO, Bernstein

As David Gutman points out in the perceptive essay which comes with each of these boxes of DVDs, the cycle here which Bernstein recorded for video in the early 1970s comes neatly between his early CBS cycle with the New York Philharmonic from the 1960s and the late cycle he recorded for DG with the Vienna Philharmonic in the 1980s, which is discussed further below. If the one was sharp and intense in its approach to Mahler, the later cycle represented a more reflective Bernstein. Arguably this midway view on video is the finest of the three, and certainly the addition of video to the formula adds another layer of intensity, when here is a conductor who, almost Christ-like, physically seemed to suffer as he conducted, so dedicated was he.

The four double-disc boxes contain the sequence of the symphonies, with an extra disc devoted to rehearsals with the Vienna Philharmonic in the *Fifth* and the *Ninth* and two feature films, *Four ways to say farewell*, a study of the *Ninth Symphony*, and a personal introduction to *Das Lied von der Erde*, which Bernstein regards as Mahler's greatest symphony. Those last two are wonderfully revealing of Bernstein the man, and of his intellectual brilliance, but the rehearsal sequences will be disappointing to non-German speakers, as his comments to the Vienna Philharmonic in German completely defeat the writer of subtitles, and he omits them.

Among the recordings of the symphonies, the most colourful is that of the *Resurrection Symphony* with the LSO, filmed in Ely Cathedral. Bernstein grows so involved as the choral finale reaches its conclusion that several times he makes a spectacular leap in extra emphasis, a very characteristic procedure.

Symphonies: 1 in D; (i) 2 (Resurrection).

*** Ph. **DVD** 074 3131. BPO, Haitink; (i) with McNair, Van Nes, Ernst Senff Ch. (Director: Barrie Gavin)

Symphony 3 in D min.

*** Ph. **DVD** 074 3132. Quivar, Tölz Boys' Ch., Women of Ernst-Senff Ch., BPO, Haitink (Director: Barrie Gavin)

Symphonies: (i) 4 in G. 7 in E min.

** Ph. **DVD** 074 3133. BPO, Haitink; (i) with McNair

Haitink made these, his third set of recordings of the Mahler symphonies, between 1991 and 1993, live in the Berlin Philharmonie. The Berlin Philharmonic plays superbly for him while the recording itself is very much in the demonstration bracket on CD (quite irrespective of the optional 5.1 DTS surround sound), and there is no doubt that the visual element adds enormously to their impact and communication. In the *First Symphony* Haitink builds the first-movement climax slowly, with increasing tension; and at its peak the camera focuses directly on him, and the sheer intensity of that moment is quite remarkable. There is greater gravity in his view than in earlier recordings, to bring out the full weight of this ambitious early work, and a greater freedom of expression, although Haitink was never one to wear his heart on his sleeve or even to inject charm into such a passage as the Laendler Trio of the second movement. The purity and refinement of the Berlin string-tone and the

raptness of the *pianissimo* playing is superbly caught in a recording of the widest range.

The *Resurrection Symphony* also brings one of his very finest Mahler recordings, weighty and bitingly powerful. The sound of the Berlin Philharmonic is again caught with a vividness and presence rarely matched. The equivalent CDs were studio recordings, but here all the tensions of a live performance are conveyed, leading up to a glorious apotheosis in the Judgement Day finale. The soloists are outstanding, and the chorus immaculately expands from the rapt, hushed singing of their magical first entry to incandescnt splendour.

The *Third Symphony* is no less powerful and spacious, with the Berlin Philharmonic again producing glorious sounds. Once again, the finale is a superb culmination, glowing and concentrated, and Haitink gives the work a visionary strength often lacking. The mystery of *Urlicht* is then beautifully caught by the mezzo soloist, Jard van Nes.

The key to Haitink's Mahler 4 is simplicity, and here he conducts a warm, polished reading that can hardly be faulted, except that it does not quite catch the innocent freshness lying behind all of Mahler's symphonies. The slow movement is poised and gentle, not quite as rapt as some versions but still very beautiful. The child-heaven finale, too, at a comparatively slow tempo is smoother than usual, with Sylvia McNair a light, boyish soloist.

Haitink's reading of the *Seventh* is not as evocative as others in his cycle, even the *Nachtmusiks* are less magical than they might be. The Berlin orchestra play well but there is not the conviction and concentration of the other symphonies in the cycle.

Symphonies 1 (including Blumine); 2–9 (complete); 10 (Adagio)

** Chan. 9572 (12). Copenhagen Boys' Ch., Danish Nat. Ch. & RSO, Segerstam (with Kilberg, Dolberg in 2 & 8; Gjevang in 3 & 8; Johansson in 4; Nielsen, Majken, Bonde-Hansen, Sirkiä, Hynninen, Stabell, BPO Ch. in 8)

Symphonies (i) 1 (Titan); (ii; iii; iv) 2 (Resurrection); (ii; iv; v) 3; (i; vi) 4; (i; vii) Das Knaben Wunderhorn; (viii) Lieder eines fahrenden Gesellen

(B) **(*) DG 477 5174 (6). Bernstein, with (i) Concg. O; (ii) NYPO; (iii) Hendricks; Westminster Ch.; (iv) Ludwig; (v) New York Ch. Artists, Brooklyn Boys' Ch.; (vi) Wittel, Tölz Boys' Ch.; (vii) Popp, Schmidt; (viii) Hampson, VPO

Symphonies (i) 5; 6; (ii) 7; (i; iii) Kindertotenlieder; 5 Rückert Lieder

(B) **(*) DG 477 5181 (5). Bernstein, with (i) VPO; (ii) NYPO; (iii) Hampson

Symphonies (i; ii) 8 (Symphony of 1000); (iii) 9; (i) 10; (i; iv) Das Lied von der Erde

(M) **(*) (ADD/DDD) DG 477 5187 (5). Bernstein, with (i) VPO; (ii) Price, Blegen, Schmidt, Baltsa, Riegel, Prey, Van Dam, V. State Op. Ch., V. Singverein; (iii) Concg. O; (iv) King, Fischer-Dieskau

The main advantages of the Chandos set are fine playing by a clearly committed and dedicated orchestra and superbly rich and expansive recording, notably the brass and chorus in the powerful finale of the *Resurrection Symphony*, although the vocal balance in No. 8, as so often, is less than ideal. Segerstam's is a very relaxed view of Mahler, and he takes us through the Mahlerian pastoral scenery as in an affectionate guided tour. Immediately in the *First Symphony* one notices a lack of grip in the opening evocation, and throughout the series the relaxed tempi and Segerstam's lack of firmness mean that although the playing itself is committed and always sensitive there is a loss of sustained intensity. Inner movements are often delightfully coloured, and the famous *Adagio* of the *Fifth Symphony* is warmly atmospheric but very laid back. Similarly Segerstam opens the *Fourth* in the most coaxing manner but remains very relaxed, and the explosive *fortissimo* of the slow movement could be more biting. In the great *Adagio* of the *Ninth* there is the widest range of dynamic and some beautiful *pianissimo* playing, but the final pull of tension from the conductor which makes for a compellingly great performance is missing. The layout too is less than ideal, with the first five symphonies not coming in numerical order, so initially finding one's way about the twelve CDs takes some care.

Universal has assembled Bernstein's complete DG Mahler cycle with substantial vocal couplings (including a richly enjoyable *Des Knaben Wunderhorn* and the classic (1966) Decca *Das Lied von der Erde*) in three boxes, complete with informative notes, texts and translations. In the symphonies, it is a measure of Bernstein's greatness as a Mahler interpreter that he consistently conveys in these edited live recordings a palpable and equal sense of both warmth and electricity, despite obvious shortcomings, so that they readily add up to more than the sum of their parts. The wilfulness of some of the readings, notably in Nos. 3 (the least successful of all) and 9, seems even to enrich the total experience. This is a personal statement by one great musician to another, and represents a monumental achievement.

(i) *Symphony 1 in D* (Original (1893) version with *Blumine*); (ii) *Lieder eines fahrenden Gesellen*
(M) *** RCA (ADD) 82876 76233-2. (i) Phd. O, Ormandy; (ii) Von Stade, LPO, A. Davis

The score of the early version of Mahler's *First Symphony* which contained the *Blumine* movement (which came second in the composer's original scheme) was apparently lost, then it suddenly turned up at a London auction in 1959. Ormandy's was its first recording (in 1968) and, while incorporating *Blumine* very effectively, he did not follow the original orchestration quite so completely in his recording as did Wyn Morris with the New Philharmonia Orchestra in his Pye version (long deleted). However, with Ormandy the arrival of the *Blumine* section at the close of the first movement, with its appealing trumpet melody so beautifully played, is a frisson-creating moment and, while its inclusion alters the character and scale of the work overall, any true Mahlerian should enjoy it in a performance as warm-hearted as this. Ormandy is rather relaxed at the very opening of the symphony and his tempi are very flexible elsewhere, notably in the Scherzo and finale. But the glorious playing of the Philadelphia strings is very seductive indeed, and the remastered recording has splendid richness and bloom.

The coupling (which comes from the CBS/Sony archive) is a highly enjoyable account of the *Wayfaring Lad* cycle from Frederica von Stade and Andrew Davis, recorded a decade later with a refreshing hint of youthful ardour, which contrasts with most other performances. The recording is close but has a most attractive ambience and is very well transferred.

Symphony 1 in D (Titan)
(BB) *(*) Virgin 4 82126-2. Minnesota O, Edo de Waart

Symphony 1; (i) *Lieder eines fahrenden Gesellen*
(B) **(*) DG 460 654-2. Bav. RSO, Kubelik, (i) with Fischer-Dieskau

Kubelik gives an intensely poetic reading. He is here at his finest in Mahler and though, as in later symphonies, he is sometimes tempted to choose a tempo on the fast side, the result could hardly be more glowing. The rubato in the slow funeral march is most subtly handled. In its CD reissue (originally DG) the quality is a little dry in the bass and the violins have lost some of their warmth, but there is no lack of body. In the *Lieder eines fahrenden Gesellen* the sound is fuller, with more atmospheric bloom. No one quite rivals Fischer-Dieskau in these songs, and this is a very considerable bonus. The essay is by Michael Dibdin.

Edo de Waart's performance is immaculately detailed and very well played. But Mahler's youthful inspiration is undersold and under-projected, and the work fails to spring fully to life and becomes really red-blooded only in the closing pages.

Symphonies: (i) *1 in D;* (ii) *5;* (iii) *9;* (iv; v) *Des Knaben Wunderhorn;* (iv; i) *Lieder eines fahrenden Gesellen*
(BB) ** Virgin 5 62395-2 (4). (i) RPO, Litton; (ii) Finnish RSO, Saraste; (iii) RLPO, Pešek; (iv) Murray, Allen; (v) LPO, Mackerras

The Virgin four-disc budget box is a curiously planned and uneven compilation. Vividly recorded in bright and clear rather than atmospheric sound, Andrew Litton's record of the *First Symphony* was one of the initial Virgin Classics releases in 1988. Litton's way with Mahler is fresh and generally direct, with well-chosen speeds, but the playing of the RPO strings is not always quite polished or taut enough. Pešek's *Ninth* is much more impressively played in Liverpool. The middle two movements are exceptionally light and pointed, and throughout the hushed *pianissimos* are particularly beautiful. But, compared with the very finest versions, the reading lacks a little in weight and emotional intensity. What finally lets the side down is Jukka-Pekka Saraste's *Fifth*, again well played but with tension sadly lacking throughout, so this is more like a studio play-through and without the grip of a real performance. In the *Lieder eines fahrenden Gesellen* Ann Murray's mezzo, characterful and boyish in tone, yet catches the microphone rawly at times. But she is at her best in *Des knaben Wunderhorn* (especially so in the closing *Wo die schönen Trompeten blasen*), and Thomas Allen is on fine form too, vocally and dramatically, so this to some extent compensates for the disappointing version of the *Fifth Symphony*. However, no texts and translations are included.

Symphony 2 in C min. (Resurrection)
● ❀ (M) *** EMI 3 45794-2 [3 45802-2] (2). Augér, J. Baker, CBSO Ch., CBSO, Rattle
(B) ** Sony SB2K 89784 (2). Marton, Norman, V. State Op. Konzertvereinigung, VPO, Maazel
(M) (**) Decca mono 425 970-2. Vincent, Ferrier, Amsterdam Toonkunstkoor, Concg. O, Klemperer

Sir Simon Rattle's performance, on CD an easy first choice, now re-emerges at mid-price as one of EMI's 'Great Recordings of the Century'.

With full recording, clear and atmospheric, and no lack of presence, Maazel's mid-1980s Vienna version brings impressively weighty accounts of the vocal passages in the last part of the symphony, the vision of Judgement Day. But even there Maazel's preference for a very steady pulse, varied hardly at all by rubato and tenuto, married to exceptionally slow speeds, undermines the keen intensity of the performance. Rhythmically, the first movement becomes leaden and, paradoxically with this orchestra, the Viennese element in Mahler is minimized.

Klemperer's 1951 live performance – now reissued in Universal's 'Critics' Choice' series – dates from 1951, towards the end of Kathleen Ferrier's brief career. The mono sound is limited but reasonably clear. What is disappointing is the lack of that very quality one looks for in a live performance: the drive and thrust which are often difficult to recapture in the studio. Only in the final movement, with its vision of heaven, does the magic quality at last emerge at full intensity; but, even here, the later, Philharmonia account gives a more complete idea of Klemperer's genius (EMI 5 57235-2 [5 57255-2] – see our main volume).

(i) *Symphony 3 in D min.*; (ii) *Das klagende Lied* (Published Version; complete)
(M) **(*) Ph. (ADD) 475 7564 (2). Concg. O, Haitink; with (i) Forrester, Netherlands Women's R. Ch., St Willibrord Church, Amsterdam, Boys' Ch.; (ii) Harper, Procter, Hollweg, Netherlands R. Ch.

(i) *Symphony 3. Kindertotenlieder*
(B) ** Sony SB2K 89893 (2). Baltsa, VPO, Maazel; (i) with V. Boys' Ch.; V. State Op. Ch.

In a work that can seem over-inflated, Haitink's straightforwardness as a Mahlerian makes for a deeply satisfying performance of the *Third Symphony*. Though in the first movement his rather fast speed allows for less lift in the rhythm than, say, Bernstein's, he captures to perfection the fresh, wide-eyed simplicity of the second movement and the carol-like quality of the fifth movement, *Bell Song*. Best of all is the wonderfully simple and dedicated reading of the long, concluding slow movement, which is here given an inner intensity that puts it very close to the comparable movement of Mahler's *Ninth*. Haitink's soloists are excellent, the playing of the Concertgebouw is refined and dedicated, and the 1966 recording is clean and natural. For this reissue as one of Philips's Originals, Haitink's 1972 recording of the two published sections of *Das klagende Lied* (omitting *Waldmärchen*) has been added. Here, Haitink does not quite compare in imagination or urgency with the finest versions, but the recording is virtually in the demonstration bracket and is worth considering on this basis alone.

As in his other Mahler recordings with the Vienna Philharmonic, Maazel draws beautiful, refined playing from the orchestra; however, at a time when a spacious approach to this symphony has become the norm, he outdoes others in his insistence on slow speeds until the very measured gait for the finale comes to sound self-conscious, lacking a natural forward pulse. His soloist, Agnes Baltsa, adds to the appeal of this bargain reissue by the heartfelt simplicity of her approach to the *Kindertotenlieder*, where Maazel's accompaniment is again sympathetic and warmly supportive.

Symphony 4 in G
(B) ** CfP (ADD) 574 8822. M. Price, LPO, Horenstein

Horenstein's many admirers will probably be tempted by the CfP reissue of his 1970 recording with the LPO and Margaret Price. Yet his characteristic simplicity of approach here seems too deliberate (the rhythms of the second movement, for instance, are curiously precise) and even the great slow

movement sounds didactic, though it is not without atmosphere. The solo singing in the finale is beautiful but cool, in line with the rest of the interpretation. The recording, made in Barking Town Hall (produced by John Boydon), is forwardly balanced, so the CD transfer reveals excellent detail and certainly the sound is vivid, full and rich.

(i) *Symphony 4. Symphony 5: Adagietto; (ii) Das Lied von der Erde*
(BB) ** EMI Gemini (ADD) 4 76912-2 (2). Philh. O, Kletzki; with (i) Loose; (ii) Dickie, Fischer-Dieskau (with SCHUBERT: *Rosamunde Overture, D.644; RPO*)

Despite glorious playing from the Philharmonia Orchestra, Kletzki is not entirely at home in Mahler's lovely *G major Symphony*. The first movement is made to seem episodic, nor is the tension consistently sustained in the slow movement, although the climax is impressive. In the end, the effect is unspontaneous, although the finale comes off much better, with Emmy Loose sounding delightfully innocent and girlish. The famous *Adagietto* of the *Fifth Symphony* is then presented in a warmly languorous fashion, but with great passion at the climax, helped by the richness of the recording.

Das Lied von der Erde is chiefly valuable for the singing of Fischer-Dieskau, a thoughtful and imaginative interpretation to justify this alternative use of the male voice, though Bernstein on Decca drew even more intense singing from him. Murray Dickie does not have the Heldentenor quality required, but the recording balance helps him, and Kletzki's reading with the Philharmonia at its peak has colour and imagination in plenty. The recording is resonant but well transferred, even if the focus is not as clean as in the symphony.

Symphony 5 in C sharp min. (DVD version)
*** EMI DVD 490325-2 (2). BPO, Rattle – ADÈS: *Asyla* (V/D: Bob Coles)

Rattle's fine version of Mahler's *Fifth* was recorded in November 2002 at his inaugural concert as music director of the Berlin Philharmonic. The video fully captures the atmospheric excitement of that occasion in a reading which brings out the work's lyrical qualities. It is also a version which demonstrates the joyfulness of much of the writing, notably in the finale. The DVD has a clear advantage over the CD issue in that it also contains the other work in the concert, Thomas Adès's brilliant showpiece, *Asyla*. The package also contains a second disc with an extended interview with Rattle by Nicholas Kenyon, his biographer and a former Controller of Music at the BBC.

Symphony 5 in C sharp min.
(BB) *** HMV 5 86736-2. LPO, Tennstedt
(M) ** DG Entrée 474 169-2. Chicago SO, Abbado
(B) ** Sony SBK 89289. VPO, Maazel

Tennstedt's second LPO version of the *Fifth* was recorded live at the Royal Festival Hall in 1988 at a concert which marked a happy reunion between orchestra and its music director after the conductor's long and serious illness. The emotional tension of the occasion is vividly capured. As a Mahler interpretation, it is at once more daring and more idiosyncratic than Tennstedt's earlier studio recording, but the tension is far keener. One readily accepts the expressive distortions of the moment, the little hesitations that Tennstedt introduces, when the result communicates so immediately and vividly, and the problems of recording live in this difficult acoustic have been masterfully overcome under the direction of the orchestra's managing director and former EMI recording manager, John Willan. The experience hits one at full force, whether in the exuberant, pointed account of the third-movement Scherzo, the deeply hushed, expansive one of the Adagietto, or the headlong reading of the finale which, even at thrillingly high speed, has irresistible swagger (DG 437789-2).

Abbado's readings of Mahler with the Chicago Symphony Orchestra are always refined but they are not always consistently convincing, and this 1980 version of No. 5 lacks something in spontaneity. The Adagietto, for example, is hardly slower at all than with Karajan, but the phrasing by comparison sounds self-conscious. It is a polished reading with very good recording, but Abbado's newer, Berlin version is far finer and well worth the extra cost.

Maazel draws superb playing from the VPO. His is a direct, unexaggerated approach, refreshing and clear, but, particularly in the slow movement, he misses the depth and emotional intensity that are essential elements in Mahler. A good recording, and it is inexpensive, but that's not enough in this fiercely competitive area.

(i) *Symphony 5;* (ii; iii) *Lieder eines fahrenden Gesellen;* (ii; iv) *Des Knaben Wunderhorn*

(BB) ** Virgin 2x1 5 61507-2 (2). (i) Finnish RSO, Saraste; (ii) Murray; (iii) RPO, Litton; (iv) Allen, LPO, Mackerras

Saraste and the Finnish Radio Orchestra offer a refined and well-paced reading of the *Fifth* which gives a relatively light-weight view of the symphony. Rhythms are beautifully sprung, and the *Adagietto* is the more tenderly moving for being a degree reticent and understated. The recording is refined to match, warm and naturally balanced. On the second disc Ann Murray gives a warmly responsive account of *Lieder eines fahrenden Gesellen*, and is particularly touching in the two outer songs. She is joined by Thomas Allen in *Des Knaben Wunderhorn*, directed with imagination and character by Mackerras. Two of the highlights are Allen's noble *Rheinlegendchen*, and Murray's ravishing performance of the closing song, *Wo die schönen Trompeten blasen*, here a solo rather than a duo. The recording is warmly resonant and spacious.

Symphony 6 in A min.

(B) **(*) LSO Live 0038. LSO, Jansons

(B) *(*) Telarc 3CD 80586 (3). Philh. O, Zander

(BB) ** Warner Apex 2564 62691-2. Israel PO, Mehta

Mariss Jansons, recorded live (the recording culled from a pair of performances), opens with a briskly determined first movement (with exposition repeat). He offers the *Andante* second, and counters its lyricism with a vividly pointed Scherzo and a finale full of intensity and thrust. It is certainly a spontaneous-sounding account, and the underlying feeling of some lack of depth comes partly from the vividly up-front recording balance, which does not provide the full resonant warmth one experiences in person at a Barbican concert, the acoustic of which obviously gives the LSO recording team some problems.

In such richly duplicated repertoire, Benjamin Zander's account of the *Sixth Symphony* makes few real challenges. There is an explanatory talk included – though it does not go very deep – and two alternative versions of the finale are offered, one with the three hammer-blows that Zander prefers, and the standard version with two. But the performance does not satisfy: it is limp and deficient in a sense of line. Nor

is the recording itself up to the very high standards we are used to from this source.

Mehta's account is very well played, but the briskness of the opening *Allegro energico* will not appeal to all listeners, nor will the very relaxed coda. The finale too seems over-driven. The recording is satisfactory, but this is far from a primary choice, which still rests with Karajan, with superlative playing from the Berlin Philharmonic Orchestra. Moreover, his DG 2-CD set includes Christa Ludwig's moving account of the *Kindertotenlieder* and 5 *Rückert Lieder* (DG 457 716-2).

Symphony 7 in E min.

(**) BBC mono BBCL 4034-2 (2). Hallé O & BBC N. O, Barbirolli – BRUCKNER: *Symphony 9* (**)

Sir John Barbirolli's performance received the accolade of Deryck Cooke no less, though his enthusiasm would probably not have extended to the somewhat primitive recorded quality. The playing of the combined BBC Northern and Hallé Orchestras was first class and already by this time Barbirolli was a fervent and committed Mahlerian and totally attuned to the composer's world. He is unhurried and expansive: indeed at 84 minutes, he is more leisurely than almost any other conductor, but paradoxically makes the overall performance seem more concentrated and convincing. Despite the poor sound this should be heard.

Symphony 8 (Symphony of 1000)

(M) *** Decca (ADD) 475 7521. Harper, Popp, Augér, Minton, Watts, Kollo, Shirley-Quirk, Talvela, V. Boys' Ch., V. State Op. Ch. & Singverein, Chicago SO, Solti

(**) Orfeo mono C 519 992 B. Coertse, Zadek, West, Malaniuk, Zampieri, Prey, Edelmann, Konzertvereinigung, Singverein, Wiener Sängerknaben, VPO, Mitropoulos

In interpretation, Solti's famous (1971) Mahler *Eighth* is outstanding in every way, extrovert in display but full of dark implications, and this is one of his finest Mahler records. It is reviewed in more detail in our main *Guide*, but it now comes on a single mid-priced CD as one of Decca's new series of Originals.

Dimitri Mitropoulos's acclaimed 1960 account of the *Eighth Symphony*, with a fine line-up of soloists, choirs and the Vienna Philharmonic, will doubtless be sought after by Mahlerians and Mitropoulos admirers alike. This great conductor possessed a selfless dedication to whatever work he was performing, and this certainly shines through. Artistic considerations aside, the ORF (Austrian Radio) recording lets it down. One has only to compare the sound their engineers achieved with the vivid stereo that BBC engineers produced for Horenstein in 1959 to realize how inadequate is the present engineering.

Symphony 9 in D min.

** DG (IMS) 457 581-2. Chicago SO, Boulez

Boulez's grasp of the work's architecture is impressive and he charts this territory with unfailing clarity and intelligence, without fully revealing its spiritual landscape. He seems determined to give us the facts without the slightest trace of hysteria, and his objectivity makes for a thought-provoking reading. He draws from the Chicago orchestra the most powerful playing – strong, resonant and seamless – with DG's immediate recording adding to the impact.

VOCAL MUSIC

Das klagende Lied (complete: *Part 1, Waldmärchen; Part 2,
Der Spielmann; Part 3, Hochzeitsstücke*)
(M) *(*) Warner Elatus 0927 49016-2. Urbanová, Rappé,
  Blochwitz, Hagegård, Way, Jaus, Hallé Ch. & O, Nagano

Nagano offers not just the introductory movement, *Waldmärchen*, which Mahler set aside, but the unrevised texts of
the other two movements. Snags outweigh any advantages,
and the performance cannot match its finest rivals, with
choral sound often unclear.

*Des Knaben Wunderhorn: Das irdische Leben; Wo die
schönen Trompeten blasen; Urlicht. 2 Rückert Lieder: Ich bin
der Welt abhanden gekommen; Liebst du um Schönheit*
(B) **(*) Ph. (ADD/DDD) 475 6392 (2). Norman, Gage –
  SCHUBERT: *Lieder* **(*)

Jessye Norman recorded these Mahler songs in 1971, near the
beginning of her career, but her voice was already developing
magically. There is less detail here than in more recent
performances, but the magisterial sustaining of long lines at
very measured speeds is impressive. Irwin Gage accompanies
sensitively, though he cannot efface memories of the orchestral versions. Good recording, well transferred.

Das Lied von der Erde
(M) ** Orfeo C 494 001B. Jänicke, Elsner, Stuttgart RSO,
  Fischer-Dieskau
** Sony SK 60646. Domingo, Skovhus, LAPO, Salonen

The account on Orfeo is of special interest in that Dietrich
Fischer-Dieskau conducts rather than sings. The soloists are
two German singers of the younger generation – Yvi Jänicke
and one of Fischer-Dieskau's pupils, Christian Elsner – who
are accompanied by the Stuttgart Radio Orchestra. It goes
without saying that Fischer-Dieskau knows what this music is
all about, but he is a little sluggish in *Der Einsame im Herbst*,
though not as slow as the classic Bernstein version in which
he sang. A good performance, but not the outstanding experience one might have expected. Decent sound.

  Salonen chooses speeds faster than usual, but gives a
warmly sympathetic and sensitive reading which brings out
the full emotion of the writing. There are good precedents on
record for an all-male *Das Lied*. Plácido Domingo in Heldentenor mode produces a gloriously firm and full tone, but the
subtler shadings required in Lieder-singing, even with
orchestra, rather elude him. Bo Skovhus, following Mahler's
option of using a baritone in place of the mezzo, has rarely
sounded so clear and true on disc, subtly shading his tone,
singing with perfect diction. The recording places the soloists
well forward, with the orchestra in soft focus behind so that
the violins, though refined, lack body.

MALIPIERO, Gianfrancesco
(1882–1973)

(i) *Piano Concerto 3. Fantasie di Ogni Giorno (Fantasies of
Every Day); Notturno di Canti e Balli (Nocturne of Songs
and Dances)*
(***) First Edition mono/stereo FECD 0036. Louisville O,
  Whitney, (i) with Owen

Malipiero is rarely encountered in the concert hall, though
his 11 symphonies have all been recorded by Marco Polo, and
so have his eight string quartets. André Gertler also recorded

his *Second Violin Concerto*, a beautifully relaxed and pensive
score. Music-lovers owe him a great debt, of course, for his
pioneering editions of Monteverdi. The *Fantasies* (1954) and
the *Third Piano Concerto* (1949) are both Louisville commissions and were recorded in 1954 and 1960 respectively. The
Nocturne (1957) was recorded in 1966 and is in stereo. They
are works of some quality and well worth investigating, even
if (at under fifty minutes) this is perhaps rather short measure.

MANFREDINI, Francesco (1684–1762)

Concerti grossi, Op. 3/1–12
**(*) CPO 999 638-2. Les Amis de Philippe, Rémy

This is a quite splendid set of *Concertos*, full of expressive
vitality. The most famous is No. 12, the *Christmas Concerto*,
with its *Pastorale* opening movement in Sicilian rhythm,
which here swings along rather more actively than we are
used to in modern-instrument versions. The alert, polished
playing of the period-instrument group, Les Amis de
Philippe, directed by Ludger Rémy, is very enjoyable, while
slow movements are pleasingly warm. The one snag is the
very slight edge to the violin timbre, which means that, unless
you are a very keen authenticist, the best recommendation is
the set by the Capella Istropolitana, which is outstanding in
all respects, and demonstrates how using modern instruments can be just as authentic as period manners in baroque
repertoire (❂ Naxos 8.553891 – see our main volume).

MARAIS, Marin (1656–1728)

Marin Marais was the son of a Parisian shoemaker who
became a famous viola da gamba player (perhaps the most
famous of all time) at the court of Louis XIV, and later a
celebrated composer for that instrument. He was first a
student at a church music school in Saint-Germain-
L'Auxerrois and, on leaving in 1672, became a star pupil of
Sainte-Colombe, and studied composition with Lully. Marais
played in the orchestra that performed Lully's operas, and in
1679 he was appointed Ordinaire de la Musique de la Chambre du Roy, a position he held until he died. The engaging
French film *Tous les matins du monde* brought his name
before the public, together with that of his teacher, Sainte-
Colombe, and, mainly through the influence of the gramophone, the range and quality of his music is at last being fully
appreciated.

Pièces de Viole, Book II (1701): *Suite in E min.; Book III*
(1711): *Suite in D; Book IV* (1717): *Le Labyrynth; Book V*
(1725): *Suite in D*
(B) **(*) HM Musique d'Abord HMA 1955248. Quintana,
  Costoyas, Cremonesi

These three *Suites* make a good sampler of the 41 sets of *Pièces*
for one or two violas da gamba included in Marais's five
Books. They consist of varying numbers of movements from
which the performer could make up his own selection. Apart
from the dance movements, the *D major Suite* ends with a
melancholy *Plainte* and a Chaconne; the first two movements
of the *A minor* have sobriquets (*La Soligni* and *La Facile*
respectively) which indicate something of their character.
That same suite has a striking closing *Rondeau moitié pincé et
moitié coup d'archet*, which alternates bow and pizzicato – a
real lollipop. The *E minor Suite*, in complete contrast, ends

with a dolorous *Tombeau pour Monsieur de Sainte-Columbe* (Marais's much-respected teacher). Juan Manuel Quintana's brightly focused timbre with its touches of close vibrato seems suitable for this valedictory tribute; but elsewhere we would have liked a more robust sound at times. However, he gives an impressive account of *Le Labyrinthe* (a piece discussed in more detail below), and his continuo players are well if discreetly balanced.

Pièces de Viole, Book II (1701): *Les Folies d'Espagne; Les voix humaines. Book IV* (1717): *Pièces de Caractère: Le Labyrinthe; L'Arabesque; Le Badinage; Feste Champetre; Marche Tartare; Muzette I/II; La Reveuse; La Tartarine; Le Tourbillon*
*** CPO 777 007-2. Duftschmid, Boysen, Hämmerle

Pièces de Viole, Book II (1701): *Pièces de Caractère: Chaconne en Rondeau; Cloches ou Carillon; La Polonaise; Sarabande à l'espagnole. Book III* (1711): *La Guitare; La Musette; Plainte. Book IV* (1717): *Le Bijou (Rondeau); Le Labyrinthe; Le Tourbillon. Book V* (1725): *Prélude en harpegement; Le jeu du valante; La Georgienne dite La Maupertuy; Marche Persane, dite La Savigny;* (i) *Le Tableau de l'Opération de la Taille; Tombeau pour Marais Le Cadet*
*** Glossa GCD 920404. Pandolfo, Meyerson, Boysen, with De Mulder, Fresno, Estvan; (i) Fauché

The French tradition of Lully (Marais's teacher) and, of course, Couperin was to extend suites of instrumental and keyboard pieces beyond the usual dance movements of *Sarabande, Gigue* and so on, and give them sobriquets; in the case of Marais, the names of the *Pièces de Caractère* are often programmatically significant. The two discs listed above bring a stimulating selection. The most remarkable is *Le Labyrinthe*, which is musically self-descriptive and includes seven sections: *Gayement – Gravement – Vivement – Gay – Grave – Gay*, and finally a splendid *Chaconne*. But other pieces variously simulate the deep sonority of cathedral bells (*Cloches ou Carillon*), a melancholy *Plainte* and the quaint *Musette* (hurdy-gurdy) with its underlying drone. The two sets of performances here are agreeably different. We particularly liked the sharp, pointed gamba playing of Lorenz Duftschmid, born in Linz, who negotiates the complexities of the *Labyrinthe* confidently but not over-dramatically; his *Tourbillon* is a believable whirlwind, and his account of the famous variations on *La Follia* which ends his recital is very stylish and lively, when the sound itself is so well focused.

However, the Italian, Paolo Pandolfo, is altogther more dramatically flamboyant and all but goes over the top in *La Georgienne*, ferociously picturing the cruel angst of unrequited love to the wrong woman with bold strokes of his bow, while *Le Tourbillon* almost becomes a typhoon. Yet other pieces are more restrained, the melancholy *Tombeau* for Marais himself, and *Le jeu du volant* ('Game of Shuttlecock'), which is charming. The most extraordinary piece, however, is *Le Tableau de l'Operation de la Taille* (pictured in the booklet), in which a spoken commentary in French describes the horrendous operation, without anaesthetic, for the removal of a stone from the bladder. The closing *Chaconne en Rondeau* is also given a lift here by an added percussionist. Both players have a good continuo support team; the CPO recording is crisp and clear, while Pandolfo is given a bigger, more resonant image by Glossa, who also provides especially impressive documentation.

Pièces en Trio (1692): *Suites in C; G min.; D*
(M) *** DHM/BMG 0547 77358-2. Ens. Rebel

The Italian trio sonata took hold in France in the 1690s, with Lully, the father figure, introducing the format two decades earlier. Their light, sunny atmosphere dominates throughout these three attractive *Suites*. The disc is entitled '*Fantasie champestre*', the title of the sparkling little second movement of the *D major Trio*; but the usual dance movements are present in each of them, with the *Gigues* particularly light-hearted, and the *Sarabandes* are elegant as well as expressive, without being too *Grave*. The penultimate *Passacaille* of the *G minor Suite* and closing *Chaconne* in the *C major* are just as spirited as the other movements. The performances here have just the right effervescent touch, and this is a new facet of Marais which is most rewarding and life-enhancing. Very good recording, naturally balanced in a warm acoustic.

Pièces en Trio: Sonnerie de Sainte-Geneviève du Mont de Paris (for Violin, Bass Viol & Harpsichord) (1723); *Suites: 1 in C* (for Flute, Violin, Bass Viol & Harpsichord) (1692); *Pièces de Viole, Book II* (1711): *4 in D* (for Bass Viol & Harpsichord)
(B) *** HM Musique d'Abord HMA 195414. Alice & Nikolaus Harnoncourt, Stastny, Tachezi

The *Trio Sonata* here in which the flute dominates has great charm and it includes a *Loure* and *Gavotte* as well as a *Bagatelle* among its movements which, although still dedicated to the dance, are above all delicate and elegant in feeling rather than effervescent. The *D major Viola da Gamba Suite*, played with aplomb by Nikolaus Harnoncourt (in 1973), has a dozen movements, with half of them given names, with two engaging Minuets, *La Chanterelle* and *La Trompette*, and the closing *Charivary* among them. But they are not as striking as the *Sonnerie de Sainte-Geneviève du Mont de Paris*, composed much later. This is a set of variations in the style of a chaconne, and led by a violin rather than a treble viol. It simulates church bells and also supposedly evokes city life around the church, although it is the bells which dominate. First-class performances and recording.

MARENZIO, Luca (1553–99)

Madrigals (1580): Book I: *Così moriro i fortunato amanti; Deh rinforzate il vostro pianto; Dolorosi martir, fieri tormenti; Freno Tirsi il desio; Liquide perle Amor da gl'occhi sparse; Per duo coralli ardenti; Tirsi morir volea.* Book II: *La dove sono i pargoletti Amori; E s'io mi doglio, Amor; Fuggi speme mia, fuggi; Vaghi e lieti fanciulli.* Book IV: *Caro Aminta pur vuoi; Donne il celeste lume; Nè fero sdegno mai donna mi mosse; Non puo filli più.* Book V: *Basciami mille volte; Consumando mi vo di piaggia in piaggio.* Book VI: *O verdi selv'o dolci fonti o rivi; Udite lagrimosi.* Book VII: *Cruda Amarilli; Ma grideran pur me le piagge.* Book IX: *Così nel mio parlar; Et ella ancide, e non val c'huom si chiuda.* (with PHILIPS: *Tirsi morir vola.* TERZI: *Intavolatura di liuto, libro primo: Liquide perle Amor, da gl'occhi sparse*)
*** Opus 111 OP 30245. Concerto Italiano, Alessandrini

An outstanding collection, discussed more fully in our main Guide.

MARÍN, José (1618–99)

Tonos Humanos: Caprichos de amor; Lisonjear el dolor; Mudanzas de amor
*** Alia Vox AV 9802. Figueras, Lilevand (guitar), Savall (harp), Estevan (percussion), Gonzalez-Campa (castanets)

If the biography printed in the booklet with this CD is anything to go by, José Marín, besides being a remarkable singer-composer and guitarist, was extraordinarily dynamic, high-living and totally disreputable. One could say that he took everything life had to offer. First a singer in the Spanish Royal Chapel, then a priest, he survived torture and prison more than once on charges of forgery and murder (false or not). His songs, drawing on the traditional music of his time, are exotic, passionate, richly melodious and full of the Spanish gypsy dance rhythms that were to be taken into the concert hall long after he died by composers like Falla, Albéniz and Granados.

But here the song-writing is freely spontaneous and improvisational, and Montserrat Figueras is ideally cast to sing what might be described as re-composed folk music which continually draws on the real thing. Her voice is as beautiful and naturally inflected as ever, and she has the support group listed above to give her a richly idiomatic backing. The documentation includes full texts and translations, and the warm acoustic is just right. An enterprising and beguiling issue. This is true crossover music of quality.

MARSHALL-HALL, G. W. L. (1862–1915)

Symphony in E flat; Symphony in C: Adagio
**(*) Move MD 3081. Queensland Theatre O, Bebbington

Born in London, Marshall-Hall studied under Parry and Stanford and his first song-cycle received an enthusiastic review from George Bernard Shaw. In 1892 he settled in Australia, where he became the first Professor of Music at Melbourne University. His *E flat Symphony* was premièred by Sir Henry Wood in London and by Nikisch in Berlin, before lapsing into obscurity. While highly eclectic and often Brahmsian, it still remains very much his own, and has plenty of attractively flowing ideas. The first movement surges along, the central *Largamente* is appealingly lyrical and expertly scored, and the rondo finale ends confidently. The *Adagio sostenuto* from the earlier *C minor Symphony* is gently elegiac, again attractively orchestrated. Both works are well played and quite persuasively directed by Warren Bebbington, although one feels at times that they need a stronger forward pulse. But this well-recorded CD is still enjoyable and appears on a bargain label in Australia. (Its publisher can be reached on www.move.com.au.)

MARTIN, Frank (1890–1974)

(i) *Cello Concerto; Ballade for Cello and Orchestra;* (ii) *3 Danses for Oboe, Harp & Strings. Pasacaille*
*** Etcetra KTC 1290. Netherlands R. O, Montgomery, with (i) Viersen; (ii) Swinnen, Scholten

The fine *Cello Concerto* of 1966 is a rarity. It was commissioned six years earlier by Pierre Fournier, and a recording of him playing it with Haitink and the Concertgebouw Orchestra was briefly in circulation. Quirine Viersen is a young

Dutch cellist who gives a commanding and persuasive account of this noble score and of the 1949 *Ballade*. The *Trois Danses* (1970) for oboe, harp and strings was written for Heinz and Ursula Holliger, and the two Dutch artists can hold their own alongside the Holligers' Philips recording, which in any case has been withdrawn. However, this is altogether a most desirable replacement.

PIANO MUSIC

(i) *Music for Piano Duet: Études pour 2 pianos: Ouverture et foxtrot. Pavane couleur du temps (à 4 mains); 2 pièces faciles (à 2 pianos). Piano music: Au Clair de lune. Étude rythmique; Esquisse; Guitare. Fantaisie sur des rythmes flamenco; 8 Préludes*
*** ABC Classics 476 2601 (2). Adam, (i) with Logan

Martin's music gets better and better, the more often one returns to it, and this enterprising issue brings his complete piano music, including the transcription for two pianos of the well-known *Études pour cordes* that he composed for Paul Sacher in the mid-1950s. (A fine pianist himself, he can be heard in the Westminster recording of *Le vin herbé* and accompanying Heinz Rehfuss in the *6 Jederman Monologues* as well as the *8 Préludes* written for Lipatti. They are inventive and imaginative and it is a pity that he never recovered enough to play them, any more than Segovia did the *4 pièces brèves*, by which *Guitare* is better known.) Martin was in his mid-seventies by the time he recorded the *Préludes* – a pity that he did not record them earlier, when they would have posed no technical problems. There have been other versions: Christiane Mathé (Koch Schwann CD 312212) – nothing special, very much *vin ordinaire* – and a much more distinguished account by Lucia Negro on BIS CD71. (R.L. still recalls a thrilling BBC performance given in the late 1980s by the remarkable Dutch pianist, Martijn van den Hoek which he had the privilege of producing.)

Hungarian-born but resident in Australia, Julie Adam was a pupil of Louis Kentner, Géza Anda and Paul Hamburger, and she proves a capable and convinced advocate of this music. On the second CD she is admirably partnered by Christine Logan. They sensitively convey the Ravel-like delicacy of the *Pavane couleur du temps* and the robust rhythms of the *Études*, in which they are every bit as good as the Duo Beershava (Gallo CD633). The delightful wit of *Les Grenouilles, le Rossignol et la Pluie* makes one regret that, despite his distinction as a pianist, he did not write more for the instrument. The recording, made in the Eugene Goossens Hall of the Australian Broadcasting Commission, is eminently truthful and well balanced. A rewarding issue in every respect.

VOCAL MUSIC

(i) *3 Chants de Noël; 3 Minnelieder;* (ii) *6 Monologues from 'Jederman' (Everyman);* (iii) *Poèmes de la mort*
*(*) Cantate C 58013. (i) Thomas-Martin, Kroupa; (ii) Arendts, Kroupa; (iii) Arendts, Schildt & various artists

The *Six Everyman Monologues* are among Frank Martin's finest works, and indeed among the greatest song-cycles of the twentieth century. They are heard here in their monochrome form (voice and piano) rather than in the composer's wonderful orchestration, and derive from a 1998 Sender Freies

Berlin broadcast. The performance, too, is a bit monochrome and not to be preferred to José van Dam (Virgin 5 61850-2) or David Wilson-Johnson (Chandos 9411), who are much more imaginative (alongside Fischer-Dieskau, whose DG disc is deleted). The post-war *Trois chants de Noël* for soprano, flute and piano have charm, though the *Drei Minnelieder*, written in the wake of the *Mystère de la Nativité*, have more depth. The *Poèmes de la mort* are composed for three male voices and the unusual combination of three electric guitars. The sonority is highly distinctive in Martin's hands and the songs are of both originality and quality. Decent broadcast performances but, at 48 minutes, very short measure.

(i) *In terra pax; Golgotha;* (ii) *Pilate*
*** Profil PH 04037 (3). Soloists, Bav. R. Ch., Munich R. O; (i) Viotti; (ii) Schirmer

At some time in 1944, towards the end of the Second World War, Radio Geneva approached Frank Martin with a commission for a work to be performed on the day the war ended. The result was *In terra pax*, which Ansermet conducted in 1945 and which he eventually recorded in the early 1960s with a distinguished line-up: Ursula Buckel, Martha Höngen, Ernst Haefliger, Pierre Mollet and Jakob Stämpfli. It is an eloquent and powerful work, to which the late-lamented Marcello Viotti and a fine if less well-known team of soloists bring much feeling and fine musical judgement. It shares the first CD with *Pilate*, written 20 years later and another radio commission (from the European Broadcasting Union). The last of his six oratorios, it is inventive and expressive, in every way characteristic of the master, and Ulf Schirmer's singers can hold their own against Ansermet's pioneering mono set of 1966.

However, it is *Golgotha*, occupying the remaining two CDs, which is the masterpiece here. Shortly after the war Martin saw 'The Three Crosses' at a Rembrandt Exhibition in Geneva and this triggered the composition of *Golgotha* which occupied him for some three years, 1945–8. It is of greater emotional power than *Le vin herbé* or anything else he had written before, and it can claim the distinction of being the first major Passion since Bach. Indeed, not to mince matters, it is without question one of the greatest choral works of the twentieth century! Martin was the son of a Calvinist preacher and was himself a devout Christian. Bach was a lifelong influence, and the Passions meant a great deal to him. Like them, *Golgotha* is a work of elevated feeling, and its musical language is highly personal and distinctive. For all the power of the choral writing, the orchestral textures are luminous, translucent and subtle. There is an affinity at a profound level with the Debussy of *Pelléas*, particularly in the glowing final section, *La Résurrection*. But the whole work is noble, inspired – and inspiring! These are concert performances and are excellently recorded, and they supersede earlier versions.

Le Vin herbé (oratorio)
*(**) Jecklin-Disco (ADD) JD 581/2-2. Retchitzka, Tuscher, Comte, Morath, De Montmollin, Diakoff, De Nyzankowskyi, Tappy, Jonelli, Rehfuss, Vessières, Olsen, composer, Winterthur O (members), Desarzens

On Jecklin-Disco there is some fine singing from Tuscher, Tappy and Rehfuss. The instrumental playing, though not impeccable, is dedicated (and the same must be said for the choral singing). The 1960s sound is much improved in the CD format. But this is now superseded.

MARTINŮ, Bohuslav (1890–1959)

3 Frescoes of Piero della Francesca
(**) Orfeo mono C 521 991B. VPO, Kubelik (with TCHAIKOVSKY: *Symphony 6* (**))

Martinů dedicated the *Three Frescoes of Piero della Francesca*, one of his most inspired and colourful scores, to Rafael Kubelik. This performance, recorded at the 1956 Salzburg Festival, was its première (Kubelik recorded them commercially on a mono HMV LP not long afterwards but that did not survive very long in the catalogue). His reading of the first movement is fractionally more measured than we often get nowadays and gains in its breadth. The mono sound is not bad for its period but this, of course, is a score which benefits from good modern sound. The Tchaikovsky coupling is not distinctive.

Symphony 2
*** Telarc CD 80616. Cincinnati SO, Paavo Järvi – DVOŘÁK: *Symphony 9* ***

Like Dvořák's *New World Symphony*, Martinů's *Second* was written when the composer was in the United States, making it an apt if unusual coupling for that much-recorded work. The refinement and clarity of the Telarc recording enhance an outstanding performance, with Paavo Järvi even outshining his father's excellent version of this same work, thanks to the excellence of the Cincinnati orchestra's playing. The Czech flavour in all four movements is enhanced by the genial warmth of phrasing and the rhythmic lift.

Symphony 5
** CBC Records (ADD) PSCD 2021. Toronto SO, Ančerl (with BEETHOVEN: *Symphony 6* **)

A pity that another Martinů work could not have been found for this Canadian CD, as it would make a more logical coupling than Beethoven's *Pastoral Symphony*, which is well played but in no way outstanding. Ančerl's Multisonic version of the Martinů is among the best recordings of the piece and has more breadth and sense of mystery than this Toronto account from 1971. The latter is rather fast: Ančerl takes 26 minutes 22 seconds as opposed to 30 minutes 22 seconds in 1955. There is plenty of commitment and enthusiasm from the orchestra, and the CBC sound is decent if a little top-heavy.

Symphonies 5; 6; Memorial to Lidice
(M) (***) Sup. mono SU 3694-2. Czech PO, Ančerl

These are classic accounts from the era of mono LP. The *Fifth* is the work's première recording, made in 1955, while the *Sixth*, recorded in the following year, followed close on the pioneering RCA LP made by Charles Munch and the Boston Symphony Orchestra, who commissioned it. The *Memorial to Lidice* (1943), written in the immediate wake of the Nazi atrocity (the villagers of Lidice were all massacred in response to the assassination of Heydrich), was recorded in 1957. These performances have an authenticity of feeling that still remains special, even though there are many fine new versions. The sound is better than ever.

MARTUCCI, Giuseppe (1856–1909)

(i) *Piano Concerto 1 in D min.;* (ii) *Le canzone dei ricordi*
** ASV CDDCA 690. (i) Caramiello; (ii) Yakar; Philh. O, D'Avalos

The *First Piano Concerto* (with Francesco Caramiello a capable soloist) is inevitably derivative, and it is the song-cycle that is the chief attraction here: Rachel Yakar sings beautifully and is particularly affecting in the Duparc-like *Cantavál ruscello la gaia canzone*. The recording is generally faithful.

Symphony 1 in D min., Op. 75; Notturno, Op. 70/1; Novelletta, Op. 82; Tarantella, Op. 44
** ASV CDDCA 675. Philh. O, D'Avalos

The *First Symphony* is greatly indebted to Brahms, but elsewhere there is a vein of lyricism that is more distinctive. The performances by the Philharmonia under Francesco D'Avalos are serviceable rather than distinguished, but the recording is very truthful and well balanced.

Symphony 2 in F, Op. 81; Andante in B flat, Op. 69; Colore orientale Op. 44/3
** ASV CDDCA 689. Philh. O, D'Avalos

The *Second Symphony* is a relatively late work. Though the performance falls short of distinction, it leaves the listener in no doubt as to Martucci's quality as a composer and the nobility of much of his invention. The *Colore orientale* is an arrangement of a piano work; the beautiful *Andante*, a work of depth, has a Fauréan dignity. The recording is a bit too closely balanced.

Le canzone dei ricordi; Notturno, Op. 70/1
*** Hyp. CDA 66290. Madalin, ECO, Bonavera – RESPIGHI: *Il tramonto* ***

Le canzone dei ricordi is a most beautiful song-cycle, and its gentle atmosphere and warm lyricism are most seductive. At times Carol Madalin has a rather rapid vibrato, but she sings the work most sympathetically and with great eloquence. The *Notturno* is beautifully played. Recommended with all possible enthusiasm.

MARX, Joseph (1882–1964)

Nature Trilogy: Symphonic Night Music; Idylle; Spring Music
** ASV DCA 1137. Bochum SO, Sloane

Although Marx's *Nature Trilogy* was conceived as a coherent three-movement work from the outset, no complete performance was envisaged by the composer, with each section planned and written separately. The 26-minute *Symphonic Night Music* (1922) feels rather Delian, but with no real climaxes, just drifting on and on and failing really to grip the attention. *Idylle* dates from 1925 and is loosely pastoral in character. *Spring Music* (1925) has rather more impetus and character, but there is still too little contrast, and the overall effect becomes cloying. Even so, the music is pleasing, if seemingly endless, and some might like it as agreeable late-evening backgound music. The recording and performances are satisfactory, but this is difficult to recommend without a chance to sample it first, and readers would do much better to try the disc of chamber music listed below.

Quartetto chromatico; Quartetto in modo classico; Quartetto in modo antico
*** ASV CDDCA 1073. Lyric Qt

Joseph Marx viewed serial music with disdain. Yet the influence of early Schoenberg is strong in his music, especially the luscious *Quartetto chromatico*, which opens very like *Verklärte Nacht* and sustains its chromatic sensuality almost throughout. By contrast the *Quartetto in modo antico* opens

in spring-like pastoral mood, using the Mixolydian mode for its harmonic language. The touching *Adagio* has a lovely, chorale-like theme in the Phrygian mode and, after an elegant neo-classical Minuet, the finale is light-heartedly fugal, with a song-like secondary episode. In the *Quartetto in modo classico* the sweetness of the lyricism is balanced by elegance, the Scherzo is light-hearted, the elegiac and beautiful *Adagio* is delicately refined in atmosphere. The dancing 6/8 finale introduces another fugato, but the movement closes expressively by recalling the work's opening. The performances here are persuasively committed and full of spontaneous feeling. The recording is warm, truthful and clear. Highly recommended.

MASCAGNI, Pietro (1863–1945)

L'amico Fritz (complete)
(*) Warner Fonit mono 5050466 1818-2-4 (2). Tassinari, Tagliavini, Pini, Miletti, EIAR Ch. & O, Mascagni

In November 1942, in his 79th year, Pietro Mascagni took up the baton in the Italian Radio studios, and made this recording of his second most popular opera, *L'amico Fritz*. He was following up his own recording of *Cavalleria rusticana*, made for EMI two years earlier. Interesting as it is to have the composer's own views on the work, it is very clear, here as in *Cavalleria rusticana*, that the old man was slowing down, adopting almost impossibly expansive speeds. Even the most famous number, the *Cherry Duet*, with its attractive cross-rhythms, comes to a virtual halt, and it is a measure of the artistry of Pia Tassinari as Suzel and Ferruccio Tagliavini as Fritz that they still keep the melody flowing. The recording of voices is surprisingly full and vivid, but the orchestral sound is very thin. Of historic interest only.

Le maschere (complete)
(M) * Warner Fonit 0927 43298-2 (2). Felle, Gallego, La Scola, Sabbatini, Dara, Chausson, Teatro Comunale di Bologna Ch. & O, Gelmetti

Over ten years before Strauss brought *commedia dell'arte* characters on to the operatic stage in *Ariadne auf Naxos*, Mascagni attempted a more direct approach in a full *commedia dell'arte* presentation, complete with Prologue and introduction. *Le maschere* appeared in January 1900, the same month as Puccini's *Tosca*. Such was Mascagni's fame after *Cavalleria rusticana* that no fewer than six world premières were organized on the same night in the principal Italian opera-houses. Except in Rome, where Mascagni was himself conducting to a polite reception, the performances were all fiascos, with audiences rowdily unsympathetic, even in Milan with Toscanini conducting and Caruso singing.

This live recording, made in 1988, helps to explain why. The score is skilfully written, with light textures and tripping rhythms, as one would anticipate with such a subject, but without the luscious tunes and big emotional moments that audiences had come to expect of Mascagni. One can understand audiences growing impatient, even if the total and immediate condemnation suggests some plotting.

Under Gelmetti the Bologna performance is competent enough, with a reasonable provincial cast, but what seriously minimizes enjoyment is the balance of the voices. Most of the time they are so distanced, the characters seem to be off-stage. Recommended only to Mascagni devotees.

MASSENET, Jules (1842–1912)

Cendrillon: Suite; Esclarmonde: Suite; Suite 1, Op. 13
(BB) *(*) Naxos 8.555986. Hong Kong PO, Jean

This CD, originally released in the early 1990s on full-price Marco Polo, is worthwhile for including the only recordings of the *Esclarmonde* and *Cendrillon* Suites, both attractive and colourful works in the best Massenet style. However, the performances and recording are pretty ordinary and the music fails to sparkle as it should. The *Suite No. 1* is better served on a newer Naxos recording, along with Massenet's other more famous suites for orchestra, better played and recorded (Naxos 8.553124).

Le Cid (ballet suite); *Scènes pittoresques; La Vierge: Le dernier sommeil de la vierge*
(BB) ** EMI Encore (ADD) 5 758701-2. CBSO, Frémaux –
SAINT-SAENS: *Allegro appassionato*, etc. **

Frémaux's collection was originally issued in full quadraphonic format, with Studio Two balancing, but this reissue reverts to analogue stereo, and the resonant ambience of the Great Hall of Birmingham University clouds the sound in tuttis and makes it opaque. This is a pity, for the performances, of both the ballet music and the charming *Scènes pittoresques*, are highly effective: the *Aubade* in the ballet suite is especially piquant. Frémaux also plays *The Last Sleep of the Virgin* lovingly, but the excessive resonance remains a drawback.

OPERA

Manon (complete CD version)
(BB) (**) Naxos mono 8.110003/5 (3). Sayão, Rayner, Bonelli, Metropolitan Ch. & O, Abravanel

Taken from an NBC broadcast in 1937, the other Naxos historic issue marked the début of the Brazilian, Bidú Sayão, whose light, bright soprano with a hint of rapid flutter in the tone exactly matches the role, perfectly conveying the provocative as well as the tender side of the heroine, totally at home in the French idiom. The American tenor, Sydney Rayner, makes a virile hero, using his rather baritonal voice stylishly if with occasional heaviness. Bonelli makes an excellent Lescaut too, but it is Maurice Abravanel, then in charge of the French repertory at the Met., who provides the impetus, drawing brilliant playing from the orchestra, recessed as it is behind the clearly focused voices.

Werther (complete CD version)
(M) *** Ph. 474 7567 (2). Carreras, Von Stade, Allen, Buchanan, Lloyd, Children's Ch., ROHCG O, C. Davis

Sir Colin Davis's highly recommendable set, with Frederica von Stade an enchanting Charlotte, matched by Thomas Allen as her husband, Albert, and Isobel Buchanan as her sister, Sophie, returns to the catalogue as one of Philips's series of Originals. This recording was outstanding enough to win the *Gramophone*'s Engineering Award for 1981; but in this reissue the break between the two discs remains badly placed in the middle of a key scene in Act II between Werther and Charlotte. However, a full text and translation are still provided.

MATHIAS, William (1934–92)

ORGAN MUSIC

Antiphonies, Op. 88/2; Berceuse, Op. 95/2; Chorale; Fanfare; Fantasy, Op. 78; Fenestra; Invocations, Op. 35; Jubilate, Op. 67/2; Processional; Recessional, Op. 96/4
*** Nim. NI 5367. Scott (organ of St Paul's Cathedral)

William Mathias was a most versatile musician, best known internationally, like John Rutter, for his excellent choral music (see our main volume). But, as John Scott tells us in his notes with this disc, 'He wrote gracefully and effortlessly for the (organ), and the particular ear for colour inherent in his orchestral works affords the player much opportunity for kaleidoscopic registrations, although he rarely specified anything other than the occasional timbre or manual indications in his music. These aspects he preferred to leave to the imagination of the player, in relation to the varied qualities of specific organs.'

Certainly, Scott has the full measure of the St Paul's Cathedral organ, resourcefully coping with the wide reverberation, so that his registration ensures that Mathias's bright colours and sonorities have a striking profile, while the rhythmic drive of the music comes through readily in spectacular pieces like the *Jubilate*. The *Fanfare* and the jaunty *Processional* (and its even more catchily tuneful *Recessional* counterpart) are attractive occasional pieces, and the 'trumpet' fanfares which open the *Invocations* are to lead to a complex work, offering thrilling bravura. Yet, how imaginative is the colour palette of the contrasting *Berceuse*, far more than an elegiac piece; and the *Chorale* is atmospherically introspective too, while the aurally fascinating *Fenestra* ('Window') opens in darkness but is gradually illuminated. Perhaps the most ambitious piece of all is the *Antiphonies*, which draws on two contrasting medieval themes, *L'homme armé* (a favourite basis for early Mass settings) and the plainchant, *Vexilla regis*. Altogether a thoroughly rewarding organ cornucopia: the music is never static or dull. Scott presents it all with panache and is most impressively recorded.

MAW, Nicholas (born 1935)

(i) *Dance Scenes;* (ii) *Odyssey*
(M) *** EMI 5 85145-2 (2). (i) Philh. O, Harding; (ii) CBSO, Rattle

Spanning 90 minutes, Nicholas Maw's *Odyssey* has been counted the biggest continuous orchestral piece ever written. As in Mahler, if not so readily, one comes to recognize musical landmarks in the six substantial movements. The slow movement alone lasts for over half an hour, while the allegros bring a genuine sense of speed, thrusting and energetic. It was at Rattle's insistence that this superb recording was made at live concerts. The result is astonishingly fine, with the engineers totally disguising the problems of recording in Birmingham Town Hall. For its mid-priced reissue, EMI have added his brilliantly orchestrated and virtuosic *Dance Scenes* (which at times remind one of Respighi's orchestrations), superbly played and recorded.

MAYERL, Billy (1902–59)

Billy Mayerl was a key figure in the British light music scene during a period when ragtime influences from across the Atlantic were changing the character of popular music for ever. He was an excellent pianist himself, and he gave the first public performance in England of Gershwin's *Rhapsody in Blue* at London's Queen's Hall in 1925. He established a style of writing pianistic miniatures which he called 'syncopated impressions'; they caught the public fancy and sold in their thousands, both in sheet music form and on gramophone records. If *Marigold* was the most famous, Mayerl also wrote engaging lyrical tunes like *Evening Primrose* and *Autumn Crocus*, which retain their freshness.

April's Fool; Aquarium Suite; Autumn Crocus; Bats in the Belfry; Beguine Impromptu; The Big Top (Suite); *3 Dances in Syncopation; Evening Primrose; Filigree; Four Aces; From a Spanish Lattice; From Stepping Tones (Hop-O'-My Thumb); Green Tulips; Harp of the Winds; Hollyhock; Honky-Tonk; In my Garden: Summertime; Autumntime. Insect Oddities* (Suite); *3 Japanese Pictures; Jill All Alone; The Joker; The Legend of King Arthur* (Suite); *Marigold; 3 Miniatures in Syncopation (Cobweb; Leprechaun's Leap; Muffin Man; Clockwork); Mistletoe; Nimble-Fingered Gentleman; Parade of the Sandwich-Board Men; Railroad Rhythm; Romanesque; Shallow Waters; Siberian Lament; Song of the Fir Tree; Sweet William; White Heather*

(M) *** Chan. 10324X (3). Parkin

Eric Parkin obviously enjoys this repertoire – in the notes he tells us of his delight in discovering items like the *Aquarium Suite, Harp of the Winds* and *Railroad Rhythm* as an eager schoolboy. Now, with its style fully in his being, he plays it with much sympathy and vivacious rhythmic freedom and with a ready lyrical response to the evocative tone-paintings. He is very well treated by the Chandos recording engineers, and the set is well documented.

Aquarium Suite; Autumn Crocus; Bats in the Belfry; Four Aces Suite: Ace of Clubs; Ace of Spades. 3 Dances in Syncopation, Op. 73; Green Tulips; Hollyhock; Hop-o'-my-thumb; Jill All Alone; Mistletoe; Parade of the Sandwich-board Men; Sweet William; White Heather

*** Chan. 8848. Parkin

Eric Parkin obviously enjoys this repertoire and plays the music with much sympathy and vivacious rhythmic freedom. His programme is well chosen to suit his own approach to Mayerl's repertoire, and this Chandos record is certainly very enjoyable as he is very well treated by the recording engineers.

MCDOWALL, Cecilia (born 1951)

(i; ii) *Dance the Dark Streets* (Concerto grosso for string orchestra with piano obbligato); (i; iii) *Dancing Fish* (for soprano saxophone & string orchestra); (i; iv) *Not just a Place* (for solo violin, double bass & string orchestra); (i; v) *Seraphim* (for solo trumpet, string orchestra & percussion); (vi) *The Case of the Unanswered Wire*; (vi; vii) *Dream City* (for flute, clarinet, string quartet & harp)

(M) *** Dutton CDLX 7159. (i) O Nova, Vass; with (ii) Eimer; (iii) Dickson; (iv) Ritts-Kirby, Griffiths; (v) Archibald; (vi) Tippett Qt; (vii) with K. Thomas, Scott, Willison

London-born Cecilia McDowall is another of the younger generation of musicians, who – often inspired by extramusical experiences – is highly communicative and naturally expressive. She is engagingly witty with her minimalist ostinatos, and frequently beguiles the ear with deft rhythms and colours, then readily produces an atmospheric and expressive interlude which is just as telling. Each of the individual movements within her works is titled, sometimes descriptively, at others perhaps not too seriously.

Dance the Dark Streets is a two-movement concerto grosso for strings with piano obbligato, inspired by Scottish weather, the drifting mists and gentle stillness contrasting with the wildness of the winds. *Dancing Fish* is a Russian folk fable, sung evocatively by a soprano saxophone. *Not just a Place* transports the listener to a Buenos Aires dance-hall with a complex tango in the spirit of Piazzolla. *Seraphim*, the immediately attractive trumpet concertino, has rhythmically spicy outer movements framing a hauntingly intangible centrepiece, and quotes from Handel in the finale; while *Dream City* – in four sections – for flute, clarinet, string quartet and harp, translucently draws on the paintings of Paul Klee. The lusciously ethereal third movement, *Before the snow*, is memorable in its poised, halcyon orientalism. The repetitive palpitating ostinatos of the closing work for string quartet, *The Case of the Unanswered Wire*, ingeniously draw on the Morse code sent out from a Russian ship in 1905 during the Russo-Japanese War, fading into silence as the ship is attacked and sinks into the ocean.

The resourceful solo performances here, admirably partnered by George Vass with the Orchestra Nova, are full of life and vividly project the composer's colourful detail. Not surprisingly, Mike Dutton's recordings are first class. Well worth trying if you enjoy a tangy musical vocabulary, underpinned by moments of fresh lyricism.

MCNEFF, Stephen (born 1951)

Four Tales from Beatrix Potter (adapted Adrian Mitchell): *The Tale of Jemima Puddle-Duck; The Tale of Peter Rabbit; The Tale of Samuel Whiskers;* (i) *The Tale of Squirrel Nutkin*

*** Chan. 10352. Staunton, BBC Concert O, Rundell; (i) with BBC Singers

Adrian Mitchell's adaptation of these four famous Beatrix Potter stories was originally created for the Unicorn Children's Theatre, where seven performers sang, played instruments, danced and acted throughout the narrative. Stephen McNeff's charming scores deftly follow the storylines with more than a backward glance at *Peter and the Wolf*, if without allotting each of the principal characters an individual tune and orchestral instrument. His music is winningly melodic, the orchestration is colourful and stylish. Each story is given a miniature overture, and McNeff's newly composed songs, which intersperse the narrative, are attractively sung here by the excellent narrator, Imelda Staunton, who also skilfully alters her voice to represent each of the major characters. The BBC Singers participate briefly in an atmospheric little chorus to set the scene of *The Tale of Squirrel Nutkin*, and one wonders why they were not used by the composer elsewhere. However, the orchestral contribution under Clark Rundell is beautifully played, spontaneously underpinning the whole enterprise. The Chandos recording is first class: vivid, very well balanced, with plenty of atmosphere, and every word is clear. Full texts are provided (with translations in French and German). If you are looking for an unusual gift for a young child, this could serve very well, although purists may say that the stories stand up very well on their own.

MEDTNER, Nikolai (1880–1951)

(i) *Piano Quintet in C, Op. posth.;* (ii) *Violin Sonata 2 in G, Op. 44*

** Russian Disc (ADD) RDCD 11019. Svetlanov, with (i) Borodin Qt; (ii) Labko

The *Piano Quintet*, on which Medtner laboured for so long, is played with much greater variety of tone and dynamics by Svetlanov and the Borodin Quartet than in the more recent Hyperion issue. The 1968 recording calls for tolerance, but it is worth extending for the sake of some fine music-making. Alexander Labko plays the *Second Violin Sonata* with conviction and eloquence. He is well partnered by Yevgeni Svetlanov, who proves a sensitive pianist. Unfortunately, the 1968 recording is not good, even for its age, and is wanting in frequency range.

PIANO MUSIC

Canzona matinata, Op. 39/4; Canzona serenata, Op. 38/6; Dithyrambe, Op. 10/2; Fairy Tale, Op. 20/1; Sonata elegia in D min., Op. 11/2; Sonata reminiscenza in A min., Op. 38/1; Sonata tragica in C min., Op. 39/5; Theme & Variations in C sharp min., Op. 55

** Hyp. CDA 66636. Demidenko

In the solo pieces Nikolai Demidenko sounds posturing and self-regarding. As a guide to Medtner, the less glamorous Hamish Milne (CRD) remains the truer interpreter. The quality of the Hyperion recording has also been overpraised. It is good without being distinguished and there is a lack of transparency, particularly in the middle range.

Forgotton Melodies, Cycles I & II, Opp. 38/39

(BB) ** Arte Nova 74321 93121-2. Ossipova

An inexpensive introduction to Medtner is very welcome for there is no doubting the eloquence and beauty of this music. Irina Ossipova is a respected teacher in the Moscow Conservatoire and obviously a fine player. The playing is just a little short on poetry and no one who has heard such distinguished figures as Hamelin in this repertoire will find this of comparable quality.

Forgotten Melodies, Cycles I & II Opp. 38–9; 2 Marches, Op. 8

●━ *** Hyp. CDA 67578. Hamelin

This is a reissue from Marc-André Hamelin's outstanding four-disc boxed set of Medtner's piano music which was a *Gramophone* 'Critics' Choice', and also won a Diapason d'Or. If you have not yet tried this repertoire, this is a good place to start.

Sonata-Reminiscenza in A min., Op. 38/1

**(*) RCA 82876 65390-2. Kissin – SCRIABIN: 5 *Preludes*, etc.; STRAVINSKY: 3 *Movements from Petrushka* **(*)

Kissin is a wonderful pianist, of that there is no question. However, those who recall the celebrated Gilels account of this score will find a certain self-awareness here that inhibits

him from finding the same depth. He is better in the virtuoso shallows of *Petrushka*.

MENDELSSOHN, Fanny (1805–47)

Lieder: Abenbild; Bergeslust; Bitte; Du bist die ruh; Dämmrung senkte sich von oben; Dein ist mein herz; Die ersehnte; Erwin; Ferne; Die Frühen graber; Frühling; Gondellied; Ich wandelte unter den Bäumen; Im herbste; Italien; Der Maiabend; Maienlied; Die Mainacht; Morgenständchen; Nach Süden; Nachtwanderer; Der Rosenkranz; Die Schiffended; Schwanenlied; Suleika; Traum; Vorwurf; Wanderlied; Warum sind denn Rosen so blass

*** Hyp. CDA 67110. Gritton, Asti

This is another outstanding Lieder collection for which there was not space to include titles in our main volume.

MENDELSSOHN, Felix (1809–47)

(i) *Capriccio brillante; Piano Concertos 1–2. Symphonies: 1; (ii; iii) 2 (Hymn of Praise); 3 (Scottish); 4 (Italian); 5 (Reformation); (iii: iv) A Midsummr Night's Dream: Overture & Incidental Music*

(B) (***) Warner 2564 62769-2 (5). Leipzig GO, Masur; with (i) Katsaris; (ii) Bonney, Wiens, Schreier; (iii) Leipzig R. Ch.; (iv) Wiens, Oertel, Eberle (speaker)

We discuss this box of Mendelssohn's key orchestral works (but, surprisingly, omitting the *Violin Concerto*) because the performances are of such high quality. That comment includes the complete incidental music from *A Midsummer Night's Dream*, which is very beautifully played indeed. But it is utterly perverse to offer Mendelssohn's incidental music absolutely complete, but with the original text spoken in German, at times over the music. Of course one can programme the dialogue out, but who wants to do that! Surely Warner could have afforded to re-record the text in English for the world market or, at the very least, state clearly on the box what it contained!

In the two *Piano Concertos* it is impossible not to respond to the robust vitality of Katsaris. He plays with enormous vigour in the outer movements and receives strong support from Masur. There is nothing heavy, yet the music is given more substance than usual, while the central slow movement brings a relaxed, lyrical *espressivo* which provides admirable contrast. The sheer vigour and impetus of the finale of the G minor (No. 1), with its dashing roulades from Katsaris, is exhilarating, although some may feel that all the allegros are pressed a shade too hard. The *Capriccio brillante* is done with comparable flair and the full, well-balanced recording has attractive ambience and sparkle.

Masur's mastery in Mendelssohn is due in good measure to adopting relatively fast speeds and making them sound easy and relaxed, not hurried and breathless; and in the symphonies he is faster than many of his principal rivals on disc, not just in allegros but in slower movements too. In Nos. 1 and 5 that works very well indeed, bringing an alert freshness with no hint of sentimentality, but the fast speeds in the choral *Hymn of Praise* for many be too extreme. Where Abbado on DG, no sentimentalist, takes 29 minutes over the three instrumental movements which open the work, Masur takes only 21 minutes, an astonishing difference. Nevertheless, with excellent soloists and choir freshly recorded, and with plenty of detail, this is most enjoyable.

In the *Scottish* and *Italian*, Masur observes exposition repeats in both symphonies, and his choice of speeds brings out the freshness of inspiration judiciously, avoiding any suspicion of sentimentality in slow movements, which are taken at flowing tempi. Conversely, the allegros are never hectic. The one snag is that here the reverberant Leipzig acoustic tends to obscure detail in tuttis; the Scherzo of the *Scottish*, for instance, becomes a blur, losing some of its point and charm. But the overall effect has a natural, concert-hall feel. Otherwise the sound of the orchestra has all the characteristic Leipzig bloom and beauty. Indeed, the orchestral sound is glorious and the cultured playing always a joy to listen to, while at the climax of the first movement, by bringing out the timpani strongly Masur finds a storm sequence almost to match *Fingal's Cave*.

Piano Concerto in A min; (i) Double Concerto for Violin & Piano

** Teldec 0630 13152-2. Staier, Concerto Köln; (i) with Kussmaul

As these boyhood concertos were first heard in the Sunday salons of the composer's banker father, it is logical that they should be recorded here not just on period instruments but with a small band of strings – in places one instrument per part. What is less welcome is that the strings of Concerto Köln are too acid-sounding even by period standards. By contrast, the solo violinist, Rainer Kussmaul, plays with rare freshness and purity, allowing himself just a measure of vibrato, and if Staier takes second place, that is not just a question of balance between the violin and an 1825 fortepiano, but of the young composer's piano writing, regularly built on passage-work – often in arpeggios – rather than straight melodic statements. That also applies to the piano writing in the solo concerto, and it is striking that a clear progression is revealed between 1822, the date of the solo concerto, and March 1823, when the double concerto was completed in time for his 14th birthday.

(i) Piano Concertos 1–2; Rondo capriccioso; Variations sérieuses

** Decca 468 600-2. Thibaudet; (i) Leipzig GO, Blomstedt

Jean-Yves Thibaudet's performances are well enough played, as you would expect from an artist of this calibre, and in the concertos he has admirable support from Blomstedt and the Gewandhaus Orchestra. However, there is more sparkle and sense of joy to be found in these engaging pieces than is revealed here.

Violin Concertos in D min. (for Violin & Strings); in E min., Op. 64

(BB) *(*) EMI Encore 5 74739-2. Zimmermann, Berlin RSO, Albrecht

Though it makes an apt and attractive coupling to have Mendelssohn's great *E minor Violin Concerto* coupled with his youthful essay in the genre, Zimmermann's disc has to be approached with caution. It is in the major work that he falls short. Not helped by a close balance which exaggerates the soloist's tonal idiosyncrasies, the violin sound has a distinct edge, with the melodic line often gulpingly uneven. The second subject then gives respite, but the slow movement is ungainly, and only in the finale does the playing sound happy and relaxed – though even there Zimmermann does not compare with the finest versions. Though in the youthful concerto the slow movement is delightfully persuasive, the

outer movements fail to sparkle as they should. Apart from the distractingly close balance of the soloist, the sound is full and firm.

Violin Concerto in E min., Op. 64

*** DG 476 3159. Benedetti, ASMF, MacMillan –
MACMILLAN: *From Ayrshire;* MOZART: Adagio & Rondo; SCHUBERT: (orch. Stephens) *Serenade* ***

(M) *** Telarc CD 80507. McDuffie, SCO, Swensen –
BRUCH: *Violin Concerto 1* *** ●

(M) *(*) BBC (ADD) BBCL 4050-2. Menuhin, LSO, C. Davis –
BACH: *Violin Concerto 2;* BRAHMS: *Double Concerto* *(*)

(B) *(*) CfP 574 8782. Huggett, OAE, Mackerras –
BEETHOVEN: *Violin Concerto* *(*)

Like her first, highly successful disc, this second offering from Nicola Benedetti, winner of the BBC Young Musician of the Year competition, centres round a major violin concerto. Last time it was the first Szymanowski *Concerto*, with which she had become closely associated, whereas this time she takes on an even more formidable challenge in tackling one of the central works of the repertory, the Mendelssohn *E minor*. The outer movements, taken faster than usual, have a lightness, sparkle and rhythmic resilience that are enhanced by the playing of the Academy under the composer-conductor, James MacMillan. He backs up those qualities in playing which is exceptionally transparent, bringing out the beauty and refinement of Mendelssohn's orchestration. Not that Benedetti misses the poetic qualities in her search for brilliance. For example, the key moment in the first movement where the violin has a downward sweeping arpeggio, leading to the second subject, has an ecstatic refinement and purity that makes one catch one's breath, while the central *Andante* is taken at a nicely flowing tempo, tenderly expressive and with no hint of sentimentality. The other items make up a characterful disc, not least the piece, *From Ayrshire*, specially written for Benedetti by MacMillan.

McDuffie's Mendelssohn is a performance of disarming simplicity, with natural phrasing and the most beautiful tone. This is a less passionate work than the Bruch coupling, and Swensen provides an orchestral backcloth on a comparable scale, but, as with the Bruch, the interchanges between soloist and orchestra have the natural spontaneity of live music-making, and the slow movement brings a flowing cantilena of touching beauty and raptly gentle feeling at the close, before the finale dashes off, the orchestra matching McDuffie's sparkle with comparable vivacity and colour. The Telarc recording, full textured and with a believable perspective, is well up to the high standards of the house.

In his BBC recording of the Mendelssohn *Concerto* Menuhin is on rather better form than in the Brahms coupling with Rostropovich. All the same this is not one of the most successful of the BBC 'Legends' series.

Monica Huggett's 'authentic' version is a disappointment. Without a memorably lyrical slow movement, any recording of this concerto is a non-starter.

(i) Overtures: Calm Sea and Prosperous Voyage; The Hebrides (Fingal's Cave); Ruy Blas; (ii) A Midsummer Night's Dream: Overture and Incidental Music: Scherzo; Intermezzo; Notturno; Wedding March

(BB) *(*) Naxos 8.554433. Slovak PO; (i) Bramall; (ii) Dohnányi

Leaden performances, with no magic, flair or sparkle, and with a recording to match.

(i) *Symphonies for Strings 1–12;Symphonies* (ii; iii) *1;* (ii; iv) *2 (Hymn of Praise);* (ii; v) *3 (Scottish); 4 (Italian);* (ii; vi) *5 (Reformation)*

(BB) **(*) Brilliant 99926-1/7 (7). (i) Leipzig GO, Masur; (ii) Leipzig R. O; (iii) Brüggen; (iv) with Stumphius, Kim, Bleidorn, R. PO Ch., Edo de Waart; (v) Ostman; (vi) Van Immerseel

This compilation on the super-budget label, Brilliant Classics, brings together live recordings of the mature symphonies from Dutch Radio, made in the 1990s, with a set of the youthful string symphonies, made originally for the East German record company. The radio recordings are all very lively, with such period specialists as Frans Brüggen and Arnold Ostman directing fresh and clean readings, often at brisk speeds, and Edo de Waart in the choral symphony, *Hymn of Praise*, crisp and incisive with three first-rate soloists. Though the chorus is backwardly balanced, they sing very well indeed. Kurt Masur's readings of the *String Symphonies* (which include two versions of No. 8, one just for strings, one with a fuller orchestra) cannot be bettered, and the bright, forward sound is still most acceptable.

Symphonies 1 in C min., Op. 11; 5 in D min. (Reformation)
**(*) Häns. 93 132. Stuttgart RSO, Norrington

Symphonies 3 (Scottish); 4 (Italian)
**(*) Häns. 93 133. Stuttgart RSO, Norrington

Each of these discs has a couple of speech bands after the music, in which Sir Roger Norrington gives explanations (in English) for his distinctive approach to the performances, most significantly on performance practice, not just a question of persuading the strings to play without vibrato and seeking to adopt the speeds Mendelssohn would have expected, but varying the size of the orchestra. So in No. 1 and in the slow movements of the other three symphonies Norrington uses a much-reduced ensemble, reserving for the fast movements of Nos. 3, 4 and 5 a bigger band such as Mendelssohn is known to have used for Festival performances in Leipzig. Though violin-tone is occasionally sour, the gains from his approach in clarity and textural contrast are striking. Comparing these performances of the *Scottish* and *Italian Symphonies* with those Norrington recorded in 1989 with his own period band, the London Classical Players, the gains in the *Italian* are impressive, with rhythms sprung even more infectiously, but the comparison in the *Scottish Symphony* is more problematic, with heavier rubato at broader speeds.

In the youthful No. 1, Norrington adopts a classical, even a Mozartian approach, where most modern performances more clearly reflect romantic developments. In the *Reformation*, too, Norrington's performance is less atmospheric than many modern ones, but it is as tensely dramatic as any.

(i) *Symphony 2 (Hymn of Praise); Psalm 114. A Midsummer Night's Dream: Overture*
*** EuroArts DVD 2054668. Leipzig GO, Chailly; (i) with Schwanewilms, Schnitzer, Seiffert, Leipzig Ch. (Director: Michael Beyer) (with Documentary film: *Chailly in Leipzig*; RIHM: *Verwandlung*)

The EuroArts DVD offers the same performances as on the Decca disc of the *Hymn of Praise* below, but adds the other items in the concert celebrating Riccardo Chailly's arrival in Leipzig as the new music director of the Leipzig Gewandhaus Orchestra and of the opera. The review of the CD explains why the original version of *Lobgesang* is in some ways disappointing next to Mendelssohn's own revised version. But

seeing the performance as well as hearing it in the handsome modern Gewandhaus Hall minimizes the disappointment and, though the final chorus cannot match the revision, the visible enthusiasm of the singers and of the conductor (mouthing the words) makes it much more enjoyable. The extra items are also well worth hearing, Mendelssohn's strong and forthright setting of *Psalm 114* for chorus and orchestra and the thoughtful and beautifully written orchestral work, composed expressly for this occasion by the distinguished German composer, Wolfgang Rihm. Even the sound seems better when accompanied by vision.

(i) *Symphony 2 (Hymn of Praise)* (Original Version). *Overture A Midsummer Night's Dream*
** Decca 475 4939. Schwanewilms, Schnitzer, Seiffert, Leipzig Op. Ch., Gewandhaus Ch. & O, Chailly

Recorded live in September 2005, Chailly's second version of the *Hymn of Praise* is significantly different from his first (with the LPO in 1979 for Philips). This time he performs a reconstruction of the text that was used at the very first performance of this choral symphony, in 1840. Sadly, the differences with the final, revised version normally heard are almost all to the disadvantage of the composer's first thoughts. So the soprano loses her magical response to the tenor's question, *Huter ist der Nacht bald hin?* ('Watchman, what of the night?') on the radiant phrase, *Die Nacht ist Vergangen*, ('the night is departed'), with all reference to the watchman image missing from the text. The soprano is also cheated of her contribution to the penultimate number, which here becomes a tenor solo, missing out some charming interweaving of soprano and tenor. Other smaller differences also make for disappointment for those who know the revised version, and Chailly's performance this time is less incisive than his earlier one, with Schwanewilms and Schnitzer excellent soprano soloists, but Peter Seiffert a disappointingly rough-toned tenor. The *Midsummer Night's Dream Overture* in a delightfully transparent reading makes a welcome fill-up, given in the original, 1826 version, with text virtually identical with what we know.

Symphony 3 in A min. (Scottish), Op. 56; Overture, The Hebrides
(*(*))Testament mono SBT 1377. NBC SO, Toscanini –
SCHUMANN: *Symphony 2* (**)

These 1941 studio recordings counter the myth that Toscanini was a speed merchant. Both the *Hebrides Overture* and the *Scottish Symphony* are humane and relaxed, and they are held together with all Toscanini's familiar mastery. Although the ear always accustoms itself to the sound, given a performance of great quality, it must be conceded that the recording itself is execrable and calls for great tolerance.

Symphonies 3 in A min. (Scottish); 4 (Italian)
(B) *** Virgin 2x1 3 49983-2 (2). LCP, Norrington –
SCHUMANN: *Symphonies 3 & 4* **(*)
(BB) ** EMI Encore 5 74965-2. LPO, Welser-Möst

Symphonies 3 (Scottish); 4 (Italian); Overture, Athalia
☛ (M) *** RCA 82876 76234-2. Bamberg SO, Flor

As we have said so often, Claus Peter Flor is a truly natural Mendelssohnian, and in this coupling of the two favourite symphonies he finds every bit of charm in the composer's delightful scoring, notably so in the lead-back in the first-movement exposition repeat of the *Italian*, and in the delectable Scherzo of the *Scottish*, where every detail is remarkably clear – you can even hear the horn arpeggios. He brings an easy warmth throughout, his pacing is nigh on perfect, there is sparkle and energy here, without the music ever being over-driven. Above all he understands the structure of both works and controls the inner tension of the playing marvellously. So the slow movement of the *Scottish* is richly shaped, the climax naturally placed. In the finale, the coda is beautifully prepared, then the horns sing out with great richness and dignity – not as recklessly exuberant as with Norrington, but leading firmly to the symphony's very satisfying close. The 1991/2 recordings are naturally balanced within Bamberg's Domikanerbau, glowingly resonant but with detail always fully revealed. The *Athalia Overture* makes an exciting pendant, but the symphonies are truly memorable.

When it appeared in 1990, Norrington's was the first CD to offer both the *Scottish* and *Italian Symphonies* on period instruments. As in the Schumann coupling, Norrington opts for unexaggerated speeds in the outer movements, relatively brisk ones for the middle movements. The results are similarly exhilarating, particularly the clipped and bouncy account of the first movement of the *Italian*. The *Scottish Symphony* is far lighter than usual, with no hint of excessive sweetness. The Scherzo has rarely sounded happier, and the finale closes in a fast *galop* for the 6/8 coda, with the horns whooping gloriously. Good, warm recording, only occasionally masking detail in tuttis.

Welser-Möst's are light, consciously controlled readings, very well paced, fresh and unsentimental. He brings out the finesse of the playing of the LPO, of which he had recently become music director, helped by slightly distant recording. The strings lead the ensemble in refinement, with the splendid LPO horns cutting through the texture well, though the big horn whoops in the coda of the *Scottish* are disappointingly thin and uninvolving. Elsewhere, too, Welser-Möst's concern for refinement means that in places the performances fail to lift in the way they would in a concert hall. He observes the exposition repeat in the first movement of the *Italian*, but not in the *Scottish*. Even in the bargain range this is not really competitive.

Symphonies 3 (Scottish) 4 (Italian); 5 (Reformation)
(M) **(*) DG 477 5167 (6). Israel PO, Bernstein –
  SCHUMANN: *Symphonies*, etc. **; SCHUBERT: *Symphonies 5, 8 & 9* **(*)

Bernstein's *Scottish Symphony* was recorded live in Munich in 1979; it is a loving performance, but the expansive tempi rather overload Mendelssohn's fresh inspiration with heavy expressiveness – the slow introduction and slow movement sound almost Mahlerian. The rhythmic lift in the Scherzo and finale makes some amends but, even with its good sound, this is not a performance for general recommendation. In the *Italian* and *Reformation Symphonies*, Bernstein's approach is more sparkling, never falling into the exaggerated expressiveness which in places mars the *Scottish*. As with that performance, the recordings were made at live concerts in 1978 and, though speeds are often challengingly fast, they never fail to convey the exhilaration of the occasion. In the *Reformation Symphony*, Bernstein encourages the flute to give a meditative account of the chorale, *Ein' feste Burg*, but he makes it a revelation, not a distraction. Full, close recording, not ideally clear, but atmospheric.

Symphonies 3 (Scottish); 5 (Reformation)
** Profil Median PH0 5048. Dresden State O, C. Davis

It is good to have this live recording of Sir Colin Davis conducting Mendelssohn, when this is not an area of the repertory that has figured much (if at all) in Davis's discography. His approach is warmly traditional, exploiting the resonance and natural expressiveness of this great orchestra, with slow movements rather broader than has become fashionable, if never sentimentalized. Helped by the recording, dynamic contrasts are more marked with Davis, so that the start of the allegro in the first movement of the *Scottish* sidles in with magical delicacy after the long introduction. In the delectable Scherzo, Davis's speed is challengingly fast, and the finale is thrustful and strong. The performance of the *Reformation Symphony* has similar qualities, with a hush of expectation in the slow introduction, leading up to the first *pianissimo* statement of the 'Dresden Amen' theme. Davis takes the *vivace* Scherzo relatively slowly, bringing out charm and delicacy rather than vitality. The brief slow movement is tender and refined, and Davis then rounds the *Symphony* off with tremendous swagger in the finale, which can so easily sound pompous.

Symphonies 4 (Italian); 5 (Reformation); Octet, Op. 20: Scherzo
(M) *(*) RCA (ADD) **SACD** 62876 71616-2. Boston SO, Munch

This was never one of Munch's best records. The two symphonies were recorded separately. The *Italian* (1957) is brilliant but charmless, and it misses out the all-essential first-movement exposition repeat; the *Reformation*, which is over-driven and not helped by an unrefined recording, came a year later. John Newton's SACD remastering has found more warmth on the original tape, but this is one of the few disappointing 'Living Stereo' reissues. However, these comments do not apply to the encore, a sparkling account of the Mendelssohn *Scherzo* in which the delicacy of the Boston strings is a delight. This needs adding to a different disc.

CHAMBER MUSIC

Octet in E flat, Op. 20
☙ (M) *** Wigmore Hall Live WHLive 001. Nash Ens. (with
  BEETHOVEN: *Clarinet Trio in B flat, Op. 11* ***)
(M) **(*) Decca (ADD) 475 7716. ASMF Chamber Ens. (with
  BOCCHERINI: *Cello Quintet, Op. 37/7* **(*))
(BB) ** EMI Gemini (ADD) 3 50864-2 (2). Melos Ens. of L. –
  BEETHOVEN: *Octet & Septet*; SCHUBERT: *Octet* ***

(i) Octet in E flat. String Quartet 1 in E flat, Op. 12
(BB) ** Warner Apex (ADD) 8573 89089-2. Kreuzberger Qt,
  (i) with Eder Qt – SPOHR: *Double Quartet* **

Octet in E flat, Op. 20; String Quintet 2 in B flat, Op. 87
(BB) *(*) ASV Resonance CD RSN 3066. Primavera Chamber Ens.

The Mendelssohn Octet has been chosen as the first recording for the Wigmore Hall's own mid-priced label, offering live recordings which are considered special, made at concerts there. The Nash performance is certainly that, offering the most vivid and warm-hearted playing, and all the live communication that one expects from music-making in this ideal-sized venue for chamber and instrumental music. The performance is not only spontaneous but has many imaginative insights, the most subtle interplay, and a sure control of dynamics (as the composer requested), not least in the wonderful *pianissimo* playing, and then a crescendo leading to the final section of the first movement. The *Andante* has an engagingly songful Mendelssohnian lyricism, while the delicate Scherzo truly evokes the 'swirling mists' and 'sighing breezes' that Mendelssohn pictured in his imagination. The finale has superb impetus and inner discipline, and makes a satisfyingly exuberant conclusion, even though the recording does not ideally clarify the busy contrapuntal detail. The recording's producer, Andrew Keener, obviously had balance problems. He placed his microphones fairly close, and the effect is to rob the sound of a good deal of its natural hall ambience in order to give the group a clearer projection. This is much the same effect, if on a much smaller scale, as one experiences with live LSO recordings at the Barbican.

But when one turns to the Beethoven *Clarinet Trio*, (recorded in the same hall on the same day, 19 March 2005), the change in the sound is astonishing. The natural warmth of the acoustic returns, and one immediately has an illusion of sitting in the hall, with the players out there in front, beyond the speakers. It is an Elysian performance too, with some delicious clarinet playing from Richard Hosford, and indeed from the cellist, Paul Watkins, especially in the slow movement, while the theme and variations of the finale is completely captivating.

The combined Kreuzberger and Eder Quartets give a vivacious account of the *Octet*, with the *Scherzo* the highlight, although the *Andante* is simply and affectionately played, treated like a *Song without Words*. The *First Quartet* is also brightly presented, although here the neatly pointed *Andante* loses some of its delicate fairy atmosphere. The recording, from the early 1980s, is very good, but the transfer is not entirely flattering to the upper range of the string-timbre at higher dynamic levels.

The 1966 (originally Argo) performance by the ASMF has been chosen for inclusion among Decca's Originals. The playing is fresh and buoyant, and the recording wears its years fairly lightly. It offered fine judgement in matters of clarity and sonority and the digital remastering has not lost the original ambient bloom, although the violin timbre now has noticeable thinness. The Boccherini *Cello Quintet* offered as coupling is another inspired piece: it would be worth getting to know for its own sake. Again the recording shows its age a little in the upper range, but this remains a thoroughly worthwhile reissue.

The EMI recording dates from the late 1960s, but it has a rather hard, bright edge on the leader's tone, immediately noticeable in the first movement. The stereo is remarkably clear and detailed, without loss of warmth. The first movement goes well, but the slow movement is dry until the second subject appears. The famous Scherzo, however, is played splendidly, the ensemble following Mendelssohn's instructions to the letter: *sempre pp e staccato*. The finale is bright and gains from the clear recording, but the edge on the sound remains a drawback.

With athletic opening movements, the performances by the Primavera Chamber Ensemble are efficient and well played, but they fail to charm. They are acceptably recorded.

Piano Trios 1 in D min., Op. 49; 2 in C min., Op. 66
🌐—▶ *** Hyp. CDA 67485. Florestan Trio

Dazzling playing from this ensemble puts the Florestan at the very top of the list in this repertoire. The freshness of response and the virtuosity of the pianist Susan Tomes make this pretty irresistible. Excellent recorded sound, too.

String Quartets 2; 4 in E min., Op. 44/2; 2 Pieces, Op. 81/1–2.
*(*) Chan. 8955. Sorrel Qt

The Sorrel Quartet do not produce a really beautiful sound or enough polish to be convincing candidates in these pieces. Excellent recording.

VOCAL MUSIC

Lieder: *Andres Maienlied (Hexenlied); Auf Flügeln des Gesanges; Erster Verlust; Es weiss und rät es doch keiner; Frage; Frühlingsglaube; Frühlingslied; Geständnis; Gruss; Die Liebende schreibt; Mädchens Klage; Maienlied; Minnelied; Der Mond; Nachtlied; Neue Liebe; Schilflied; Suleika (Ach, um deine feuchten Schwingen); Suleika (Wes bedeutet die Bewegung?); Sun of the Sleepless!; There be none of Beauty's Daughters; Volkslied; Das Waldschloss; Wanderlied*
(BB) *** Hyp. Helios CDH 55150. M. Price, Johnson

Lieder: *Auf Flügeln des Gesanges; Der Blumenkranz; Der Blumenstrauss; Es weiss und rät es doch Keiner; Frage; Frühlingsglaube; Herbstlied; Hexenlied; Ich hör ein Vöglein; Im Grünen; Morgengruss; Nachtlied; Neue Liebe; Reiselied; Scheidend; Die Sterne scheu'n in stiller Nacht*
🌐—▶ (B) *** EMI double forte (ADD) 5 73836-2 (2). J. Baker, Parsons – LISZT: *Lieder;* SCHUMANN: *Liederkreis, Op. 39* ***

Both these collections are not listed, but are highly recommended in our main volume.

Elijah (oratorio), Op. 70
(BB) *** EMI Gemini 3 50884-2 (2). Schmidt, Rose, Kallisch, Van der Walt, Dietzel, Düsseldorf State Musikvereins Ch., Cologne Gürzenich O, Conlon

James Conlon's *Elijah* was recorded in 1996 and, according to the booklet, first appeared in 1998. But we have not been aware of its existence until now. It comes directly into competition with the Frühbeck de Burgos New Philharmonia set, also reissued on EMI's budget Gemini label. That has rather more famous soloists, but not necesarily more successful ones, except for Dame Janet Baker, whose contribution is unique. Even so, Cornelia Kallisch's *O rest in the Lord* is beautifully sung, as is Elijah's affecting *It is enough O Lord* (the excellent Andreas Schmidt). The soprano angel, Andrea Rost, has a slightly intrusive vibrato at times, yet her *Hear ye Israel* is very impressive. Moreover, in Part II the trio, *Lift thine eyes to the mountains,* and the quartet, *O come every one that thirsteth,* are very well blended. But above all else, *Elijah* depends on the chorus and, from the opening *Help Lord!,* the choral singing in Cologne, digitally recorded and superbly present, has tremendous drama and bite. The closing choruses of both Part I (*Thanks be to God*) and Part II (*And then shall your light break break forth*) are intensely powerful. The Gürzenich Orchestra is similarly committed (and very well recorded), and throughout Conlon's vibrant direction easily matches that of Frühbeck de Burgos. So, unless the presence of Dame Janet is essential, then the newer bargain version wins on points, though first choice at premium price rests with Richard Hickox on Chandos (Chan 8774/5 – see our main volume).

(i) *Hear my Prayer. Ave Maria; Beati mortui; Die deutsche Liturgie; 100th Psalm (Jauchzet dem Herrn, alle Welt);* (i; ii)

Laudate pueri. Magnificat (My Soul doth Magnify the Lord); 3 Psalms (2, 22 & 43), Op. 78; 6 Sprüch (Maxims for the Church Year), Op. 79

✷—✷ *** Chan. 10363. Trinity College, Cambridge, Ch., Marlow; with (i) Bennett; (ii) Cheng, Wilkinson

Although *Hear my Prayer* is justly top favourite (with '*O for the wings of a dove*' sung by Rachel Bennett with glorious confidence, especially the gentle coda), there is much other truly memorable choral music here, not least the beautiful motet, *Laudate pueri*, for female choir, contrasted with a celestial trio of soloists. *Ave Maria* for eight-part choir is not in the least like the settings of Schubert or Gounod, with the opening in a lilting 6/8 rhythm, then forward to a *con moto*, with running organ accompaniment, and finally richly climaxing with the opening material.

The three sections of the *German Liturgy* for *a cappella* double choir are hardly less memorable, moving from a flowing *Kyrie*, through an expressively vigorous central section, and back to a heavenly call of *Heilig!* ('Holy'), featuring a quartet of soloists. Most ambitious of all is the *a cappella* English *Magnificat*, opening quite jauntily and, after changing mood flexibly, the penultimate section moves into a fugato, before the majestic closing *Amen*.

The present mixed Trinity College Choir was formed in 1982, following the admission of women undergraduates to the college; and what a glorious texture this creates, and how remarkably assured are the soloists from the choir. Richard Marlow, a former choirboy himself and pupil of Thurston Dart, directs this Mendelssohnian choral galaxy with sure understanding, not a hint of sentimentality and superb control. Just sample that sudden *fortissimo* at the centre of the last of the *Six Maxims* for different festivals of the Church year (*Am Charfreitage*), or the simple charm of the opening carol (*Weihnachten*), to experience the range of colour and dynamic he commands from his splendid group of singers. Needless to say, the Chandos recording is first class, and so is the documentation, with full texts and translations.

MERCADANTE, Saverio (1795–1870)

Clarinet Concertos in E flat, Op. 76; in B, Op. 101; Clarinet Concertino in C min.; (i) Concertante No. 3 (for Flute, 2 Clarinets, Horn & Orchestra) in E flat

*** Orfeo C114041A. Klöcker, Prague CO, with (i) Porgo, Schroeder

The same blend of simple yet appealing Italianate melodies we know from Mercadante's better-known *Flute Concertos* are found in his two *Clarinet Concertos*. Both offer substantial, entertaining opening movements and short yet elegant slow movements; in the finales, the Op. 76 features an infectiously enjoyable *Polacca brillante* and the Op. 101 offers an entertaining 'theme and variations' movement. The shorter *Concertinos* are hardly less attractive: the *Clarinet Concertino in C minor* offers some gentle, minor-keyed drama to its essentially sunny character, and the *Concertante No. 3*, with its various solo instruments, bubbles along in an engaging manner. The performances and recordings are excellent.

(i) Flute Concertos: in D, E & E min.; (ii) Sinfonia sopra i motive dello 'Stabat mater' di Rossini

(BB) **(*) Warner Apex (ADD) 2564 61791. (i) Rampal, ECO; (ii) Monte Carlo Op. O; all cond. Scimone

Mercadante's deliciously tuneful flute concertos, with their simple, Italianate melodies and gentle melodrama, make undemanding and enjoyable listening. The *Polacca* finales, with their catchy tunes, are especially enjoyable, and the minor-keyed concerto adds a nice touch of gravitas. The late-1970s recordings are serviceable, lacking something in depth, but perfectly acceptable. The performances are fresh and elegant, as one would expect from the aristocrat of the flute, with affectionate accompaniments. With the entertaining *Overture* (also available on another Warner collection), this bargain CD is excellent value.

Sinfonia caratteristica; Sinfonia fantastica; La danza; (i) Fantasia on 'Lucia di Lammermoor' for Cello & Orchestra; Fantasia on Themes from Rossini's Stabat Mater; Il lamento di Bardo

*(*) Fonit. 8573-81472-2 O Philharmonia Mediterranea, De Filippi

The *Sinfonia caratteristica* is delightful, very like a Rossini overture, and almost as tuneful and witty, even if Mercadante can't quite manage an authentic 'crescendo'. The episodic *Sinfonia fantastica* is less remarkable, and *Il lamento di Bardo* is melodramatic, if rather endearingly so. *La danza* is not nearly as infectious and catchy as Rossini's famous piece, and is rather like second-class ballet music; the two *Fantasias* need bolder advocacy than they receive here: the solo cello in *Lucia di Lammermoor* is wan and low-profiled. The orchestra play well enough and are pleasingly recorded, but only in the first piece does Luigi De Filippi display the kind of flair the programme needs throughout.

Sinfonia sopra i motive dello 'Stabat mater' di Rossini

(BB) *** Warner Apex (ADD) 2564 62418-2. Monte Carlo Op. O, Scimone – CIMAROSA: *Il fanatico*, etc. **(*); DONIZETTI: *Overtures* ***

An entertaining, undemanding mixture of melodrama and tunes presented with relish by Scimone. Decent sound in the characteristic Monte Carlo acoustic, more theatrical than plush.

MESSIAEN, Olivier (1908–92)

L'Ascension

* Häns. CD 93.005 (2). Baden-Baden & Freiburg SW German RSO, Cambreling – BERLIOZ: *Roméo et Juliette* *

Messiaen's four symphonic meditations make an unusual supplement for Cambreling's version of the Berlioz, but similarly bring a performance conscientious rather than convincing, lacking tension. First-rate, refined recording.

Turangalila Symphony

(M) *** RCA (ADD) 82876 59418-2. Leanne Loriod (ondes martenot), Yvonne Loriod (piano), Toronto SO, Ozawa

Ozawa's performance comes from 1967, but you would never guess that from the brilliantly atmospheric sound, which is just as vivid as some of the newer versions, such as Nagano's Erato version, and has that bit more warmth and atmosphere. Yvonne Loriod's piano is placed too forward, but her contribution is undoubtedly seminal, and the overall balance is otherwise well managed. The performance itself is brilliantly played: it has plenty of electricity, and a warm sensuality too. It was and remains one of Ozawa's best recordings and is now economically reissued on a single CD as part of RCA's 'Classic Collection'. It is also available as a part of a bargain Double

(24321 84601-2), coupled with Roussel's *Bacchus et Ariane* and *Third* and *Fourth Symphonies*.

8 Préludes pour piano; 20 Regards sur l'Enfant-Jésus
(BB) **(*) EMI Gemini (ADD) 4 76915-2 (2). Béroff

Béroff is totally at home in this repertoire and his performances are inspirational. Clean, well-focused sound – but a little wanting in richness and clarity. However, this set is very tempting at Gemini price.

MIASKOVSKY, Nikolay (1881–1950)

CHAMBER MUSIC

Cello Sonatas 1 in D, Op. 10; 2 in A min. Op. 81
** Praga PRD 250 182. Kanka, Klepáč – RACHMANINOV:
  Cello Sonata **

The *First Cello Sonata* pre-dates the First World War (though it was revised in 1931) and the *Second* comes four decades later, at the very end of Miaskovsky's career. Michal Kanka is a refined player, but the balance favours his partner, Jaromir Klepáč, far too much so that at times the cello line is swamped. Their tempo for the first movement of the *Second Sonata* is funereal: they take two minutes longer than Jamie Walton and Daniel Grimwood, and both in characterization and in expressive naturalness they are not a patch on them.

PIANO MUSIC

Piano Sonatas: 4 in C min., Op.27; 5 in B, Op. 64/1; Sonatine in E min., Op. 57
(BB) *** Regis RRC 1245. McLachlan

It is good to see that Regis are beginning to reissue (at budget price) Murray McLachlan's survey of the piano music of Miaskovsky. In a scholarly note, he also sorts out the confusion surrounding this repertoire, for some of the sonatas underwent revision at later dates and others have remained in manuscript for well over 30 years. In unravelling the numerical muddle, he tells us that No. 2 was actually the *Seventh* and that many more may come to light. If they are as interesting as the *Fourth* or the *E minor Sonatine*, so much the better. The middle movement of the latter, marked *Narrante e lugubre*, is dark and pessimistic, and quite haunting. McLachlan speaks of the 'enormous tactile pleasure' it gives to the performer, but it also grips the listener. This gifted young artist readily communicates his own enthusiasm for this music, and his playing is both authoritative and persuasive. Good recording, too.

MIELCK, Ernst (1877–99)

Symphony in F min., Op. 4; (i) Concert Piece in E min. for Piano & Orchestra, Op. 9
** Sterling CDS 1035-2. (i) Pohjola; Turku PO, Lintu

Ernst Mielck's *Symphony*, Op. 4, preceded Sibelius's *First* by two years, and its success is said to have acted as a spur to that great composer to complete his own. It is a four-movement work, some 40 minutes in length. Although it begins promisingly, neither of its main ideas can lay claim to any strong personality, though there is a genuine sense of form. Probably the best movement is the lyrical and endearing slow movement. By and large it offers promise rather than fulfilment. The Turku orchestra under Hannu Lintu plays decently. The *Concert Piece*, Op. 9, is rather dreadful, though the central *Largo* has some poetic writing. A valuable release, which will be of interest to Sibelians in deepening their historical perspective about his background, but Mielck is no Arriaga.

MILHAUD, Darius (1892–1974)

Le Bœuf sur le toit; Concertino de printemps; (i) Violin Concertos 1, Op. 93; 2, Op. 263; Op. 135
*** Orfeo C646051A. (i) Steinbacher; Munich R. O, Steinberg

The *First* and *Second Violin Concertos* were first recorded in the early days of LP by Louis Kaufman with the composer conducting; but, although André Gertler recorded the *Second*, they have been neglected since. Their return to the catalogue is to be strongly welcomed, particularly in such fluent performances by Suzanne Steinbacher and these Bavarian musicians. These are both inventive and finely wrought pieces that deserve a place in the wider concert repertoire, not just in the CD catalogue. The adorable *Concertino de printemps* and *Le Bœuf sur le toit* are splendid makeweights.

(i) Le Bœuf sur le toit (ballet), Op. 58; La Création du monde (ballet), Op. 81: Saudades do Brasil, 7–9 & 11 (only); (ii) Saudades do Brasil (complete) Op. 67
(M) *** EMI 3 45808-2 [3 45809-2]. (i) O. Nat. de France,
  Bernstein; (ii) Concert Arts O, composer

Milhaud was essentially a Mediterranean composer whose scores radiate a sunny, relaxed charm that is irresistible. The two ballet scores come from the 1920s, while the *Saudades do Brasil* come from the period when Milhaud served as Claudel's secretary in Rio de Janeiro. As one would expect, Bernstein finds this repertoire thoroughly congenial, though in *La Création du monde* the French orchestra do not respond with the verve and virtuosity that the Paris Conservatoire Orchestra gave to Prêtre in 1961 (now deleted). Nor does *Le Bœuf sur le toit* have quite the sparkle and infectious gaiety that the music ideally demands. This is not to deny that these are good performances, vividly recorded, but whether they are worthy of a place among EMI's 'Great Recordings of the Century' is another matter.

However, Milhaud's own complete recording of the carefree and catchy *Saudades do Brasil*, deriving from a 1956 Capitol LP and now appearing in stereo sounding very sprightly, rather restores the balance. The 'Concert Arts' Orchestra respond to the composer with evident delight, and they make this quite a desirable reissue.

(i) Cortège funèbre; (ii) Kentuckiana; Ouverture Méditerranéenne, Op. 330; (i) Symphony 6; (i; iii) 4 Chansons de Ronsard for Voice & Orchestra
*** First Edition stereo/mono FECD 0031. Louisville O, with
  (i) Mester; (ii) Whitney; (iii) Paula Seibel

The finest work here is the *Sixth Symphony*, composed in 1955 for Charles Munch and the Boston orchestra. Like so much of Milhaud's best music, it is sunny, lyrical and relaxed, and Jorge Mester's 1975 recording, made 11 months after the composer's death, is a beautifully natural account. It is less polished, perhaps, than the Toulouse account with Michel Plasson, coupled with No. 7 and the *Ouverture Méditerranéenne* on DG, but that is no longer readily available. Both

Kentuckiana and the *Ouverture Méditerranéenne* were commissioned by the Louisville, and both are mono recordings from the early 1950s. The *Cortège* (1939) originally formed part of a film score to 'Espoir', which portrayed a funeral procession in honour of the Republican soldiers who had destroyed the bridge at Teruel during the Spanish civil war. The *Quatre Chansons de Ronsard*, which Milhaud had presented in 1941 with Lily Pons as soloist, not long after his arrival in New York, complete this vintage portrait of an appealing and endearing composer.

(i; ii) 5 *Études for Piano & Orchestra. Op. 63;* (ii) *Sérénade, Op. 62;* (iii) *Symphony 3 (Sérénade), Op. 71;* (ii) *Suite de l'opéra, Maximilien, Op. 110b;* (iv) *Suite symphonique 2 (Protée);* (v) *Suite for Violin, Clarinet & Piano, Op. 157b;* (i) *3 Rag Caprices, Op. 78*
(M) (***) Divine Art CD 27807. (i) Badura-Skoda; (ii) VSO, Swoboda; (iii) Ens., Goehr; (iv) San Francisco SO, Monteux; (v) Parrenin, Delécluse, Haas-Hamburger

Older admirers of the composer will remember some of the 78-r.p.m. records which formed the basis of his rather slender representation in the catalogues of the 1930s. The *Sérénade*, Op. 71, with Walter Goehr conducting an eminent group of soloists including Jean Pougnet, Anthony Pini, Reginald Kell, Paul Draper and George Eskdale, was first issued in the 'Columbia History of Music' and, so far as we know, was never reissued on LP or CD. Monteux's account of *Protée* comes from his time with the San Francisco orchestra in 1945, and the Swoboda records, made in Vienna in 1950, originally appeared on Westminster and have an authentic feel to them.

Suite provençale
(M) ** Chan. 6615. Detroit SO, Järvi – DEBUSSY: *La Mer;* RAVEL: *Boléro; La Valse* **

Järvi's *Suite provençale* is very well played in Detroit and is well recorded too, but this captivating score needs greater lightness of touch if it is to charm the listener as it should. Not a first choice, and it must be conceded that neither *La Mer* nor the Ravel pieces are front-runners either, although all have their merits.

MOERAN, Ernest J. (1894–1950)

Violin Concerto
(M) (***) Divine Art mono 27806. Campoli, BBC SO, Boult – DOUGLAS COATES: *Violin Concerto* (**)

In his accompanying note, Andrew Rose makes strong claims for Alfredo Campoli's reading of the Moeran *Concerto* – and rightly so! There is an inwardness, a rhapsodic freedom and intensity about his playing which makes this a moving experience, and Sir Adrian Boult and the BBC Symphony Orchestra also play with great sensitivity. The recording comes from 1954 and calls for tolerance, but it is very acceptable, and the performance is really quite special. What a wonderful player Campoli was when he was at his best. He was never better than at this exalted level.

MOLIQUE, Bernhard (1801–69)

String Quartets, Op. 18/1–2
**(*) CPO 777 149-2. Mannheim Qt

As a teenage prodigy Bernhard Molique studied briefly under Spohr. The present works date from 1834 and, while the debt

to his mentor is obvious, there are darker undercurrents in the *Andante* of the *F major* work, which the Mannheim Quartet play most sensitively, while the main theme of the *Andante* of the *A minor* is gently disarming. These quartets also have influences from Haydn, although the Scherzo/ Minuet of Op. 18/2 has a Mendelssohnian gaiety and lightness of touch. Both are attractive and neatly constructed, and they make agreeable listening. The performances here are persuasively warm-spirited and the recording is naturally balanced. Yet a mid-price would have made this disc more recommendable still.

MONCKTON, Lionel (1861–1924)
TALBOT, Howard (1865–1928)

Lionel Monckton was born in London, the eldest son of the City's Town Clerk. Educated at Charterhouse and Oriel College, Oxford (where he helped to found the University Dramatic Society), he began a joint career of law and music criticism before, in his thirties, he established himself as a composer for the musical theatre, writing the scores for *A Country Girl* (1902) and *The Quaker Girl* (1910), before his collaboration with Howard Talbot created the outstanding score for *The Arcadians*.

Howard Talbot first studied medicine at London's King's College, before transferring to the Royal College of Music. In the 1890s he wrote several short-lived comic opera amd musical comedy scores, thus playing a distinctive role in creating a brief period of Edwardian musical comedy, quite distinct from (although influenced by) Gilbert and Sullivan, which began with Sidney Jones's *The Geisha* in 1896 and reached its zenith with *The Arcadians* in 1909, although the First World War hits of *Chu Chin Chow* (1916), written by Frederick Norton, and *The Maid of the Mountains* (another joint collaboration, between Harold Fraser-Simpson and James Tate) were still to follow.

The Arcadians: Overture (arr. Arthur Wood) & Highlights
✪ (B) *** CfP (ADD) 3 35982-2. Cynthia Glover/June Bronhill, Shirley Minty, Robert Bowman/Andy Cole, John Lawrenson/Peter Regan, Stanley Riley/Jon Pertwee, Nigel Brooks Ch., O, Gilbert Vintner or McCarthy Singers, O, Vilem Tausky (with: *Our Miss Gibbs: Moonstruck. The Quaker Girl: A Quaker girl.* Sidney JONES: *The Geisha: The Amorous Goldfish.* Paul RUBENS: *Tina: The Violin Song.* NORTON: *Chu Chin Chow: Any time's kissing-time.* MESSAGER: *Monsieur Beaucaire: Philomel* – Gwen Catley, Pro Arte O, Stanford Robinson)

Like Sullivan and, later, Ivor Novello (still underrated), Lionel Monckton was a great British tunesmith. Indeed, in *The Arcadians* the melodic flow is astonishing. Andrew Lamb (who wrote the highly informative notes for this Classics for Pleasure series) tells us that the celebrated five-minute *Overture* that is the prelude to the show was deftly put together by Arthur Wood (who also wrote an even more familiar piece, *Barwick Green*, which is BBC Radio 4's signature tune for *The Archers*). The *Arcadians Overture* is superior to all the G&S overtures, except perhaps *Iolanthe*, and immediately demonstrates the quality of Monckton's tunes, which come tumbling out, once the highlights begin.

The charming ensemble, *The Joy of Life*, is the Sullivanesque epitome of its period; then comes the prettiest tune of all, dominating the score, *The Pipes of Pan*, delightfully sung here by Cynthia Glover, complete with coloratura cadenza, followed by the warmly lyrical *To all and each*.

The problem with staging the show is that when in Act II a group of Arcadians are transported to England in a 'flying machine', we move from the Elysian Arcadia to the crass Ackwood Racecourse and meet a whole collection of unattractive, upper-class, Edwardian characters with whom it is difficult to identify. But the music is as engaging as ever, notably the catchy *Back your fancy* and the lovely *Arcady is ever young*, when the heroine, Sombra, recalls Arcadia, with a ravishing top note to finish. A trio of catchy numbers follows, the duet *Charming Weather* and, to begin Act III, *I like London, Half-past Two* and the hit of the finale, *All down Piccadilly*. But before that comes the quasi-music-hall comic song, '*I've got a motter – always merry and bright*', sung here twice, first by Stanley Riley, then, even more mournfully, by Jon Pertwee. This was Howard Talbot's novelty contribution to the score, as well as *Half-past Two* and *I like London*, showing him as a pretty good tunesmith too.

While centring on a sparkling LP of highlights conducted with élan by Gilbert Vinter, the EMI archives are also able to draw on another set of performances with June Bronhill as Sombra, plus Shirley Minty and John Lawrenson, this time conducted by Vilem Tausky. So we also get additional vivacious performances of *The Joy of Life, The Pipes of Pan, Arcady is ever young* (all with Bronhill at her freshest) as well as *My motter*. Then, as an astonishing bonus, six more songs from contemporary Edwardian musicals are included, deliciously sung by Gwen Catley. They include a pair from Monckton's other musical plays, *Our Miss Gibbs* and *The Quaker Girl*, plus *The Amorous Goldfish*, the novelty hit from *The Geisha*, Paul Rubens's *Violin Song* (both quite exquisite) and even a number from André Messager's *Monsieur Beaucaire*, in which the key female role of Lady Mary was originally sung by Maggie Teyte. But Gwen Catley is her equal.

Altogether, this is a unique cornucopia of delights. We have played it again and again, and so will you if this endearing repertoire appeals. It could not be better presented.

MONDONVILLE, Jean-Joseph Cassanéa de (1711–72)

6 Sonates en symphonies, Op. 3
𝄞— (M) *** DG 474 550-2. Les Musiciens du Louvre, Minkowski

This entirely captivating set of symphonies confirms Mondonville as a great deal more than a mere historical figure. They originated as sonatas for violin and obbligato harpsichord in 1734, but the composer later skilfully orchestrated them. Each is in three movements, with an expressively tuneful centrepiece framed by sprightly *Allegros*. Their invention is consistently fresh and they are played here with great élan and spontaneity, and they are beautifully recorded. This CD now reappears in Universal's 'Critics' Choice' series.

MONIUSZKO, Stanislaw (1819–72)

The Haunted Manor (opera; complete)
(M) *** EMI 5 57489-2 (2). Kruszewski, Hossa, Lubańska, Stachura, Nowacki, Toczyska, Polish Nat. Op. Ch. & O, Kaspszyk

Two shuddering chords at the very start reflect the title, but then the first scene sets quite a different tone of voice in a rousing military ensemble, when two brothers, Stefan and Zbigniev, on leaving their comrades, swear they will never marry, so as always to be ready to fight for their country. They find their match when they visit an old friend of their father, Miecznik, the Sword-Bearer, and meet his two daughters, Hanna and Jadwiga, each intent on finding a husband. The manner is as close to Gilbert and Sullivan as to Smetana, with a dash of Donizetti thrown in. A fortune-telling scene prompts a charming duet and ensemble for women's voices, when the sisters learn that they will marry soldiers. After that the main haunting scene anticipates the G. & S. 'Ghosts' High Noon Scene' in *Ruddigore*, with portraits coming to life. The big difference is that this is no genuine haunting but simply a ruse by Hanna and Jadwiga, themselves taking the place of the portraits. The brothers wake up to the fact that they are both in love, Stefan with Hanna, Zbigniev with Jadwiga. Though the plot rather rambles about towards the end, the dénouement is helped by the unexpected arrival of a crowd of party guests, which, however implausibly, gives Moniuszko the excuse to insert a big Mazurka number for the full ensemble, guaranteed to bring the house down.

MONTE, Philippe de (1521–1603)

The Flemish composer Philippe de Monte was much travelled, working first in Naples, then in Rome, and on to the Spanish court. After returning to Rome, in 1568 he became Kapellmeister to the Imperial Hapsburg Court in Vienna and Prague. It is remarkable that the music of such an experienced and productive composer is not better known. Seven of his Mass settings were published in Antwerp in 1597, and he wrote around 250 motets and, corresponding with Byrd in England, the two composers arranged to exchange their settings of *Super flumina Babylonis*.

Mass Si ambulavero; Motets: *Angelus Domini descendit de caelo à 6; Domine Jesus Christ à 6; Domine, quid multipicati sunt à 5; Hodie dilectissimi omnium sanctorum à 8; Miserere mei à 5; Peccavi super numerum; Spes humani generis à 6; Super flumina Babylonis à 8*
(M) *** CRD 3520. New College, Oxford, Ch., Higginbottom

In eight parts, de Monte's is a characteristically flowing setting of *Super flumina Babylonis*, richly harmonic, matching the style of the 'parody' Mass, *Si ambulavero*, in which each of the movements has a very similar and instantly recognizable opening, based on the composer's own motet of the same name. Because of this similarity, Higginbottom has chosen to intersperse the Mass movements with motets, which gives the listener more musical variety. However, separating the propers is curiously at odds with their liturgical use, where the recognizable similarity was an asset to the faithful attending the Mass.

De Monte's style is richly melismatic, yet both the lively *Spes Humani generis* and *Angelus Domini descendit di caelo* ('The Angel of the Lord came down from Heaven') bring much livelier part-writing, while the most ambitious of all is the closing *Hodie dilectissimi, omnium sanctorum* for double choir, with inceasingly complex interplay to reach a magnificent final climax.

Performances here are flowing and secure, serene rather than passionate, but with an underlying depth of feeling; and the acoustic of the Abbaye de Valloires in the Somme adds a lovely, warm resonance without impairing clarity, a credit to Mike Clements, the sound engineer responsible.

MONTEVERDI, Claudio (1567–1643)

Canzonette (1584)

(BB) *** Naxos 8.553316. Concerto delle Dame di Ferrara, Vartolo

Monteverdi's very first publication in 1582 was the *Sacrae cantiunculae tribus vocibus*, and a collection of *Madrigali spirituali* in four parts followed in 1585. The following year brought the present set of *Canzonette*, delightful works for three voices. Their title-page makes the point that Monteverdi was just 17, and they are dedicated to the composer's 'master and patron', Pietro Ambrosisi of Cremona. After a brief instrumental introduction, the opening number, *Qual si può dir*, makes a charming play on Pietro's name: 'What greater plant from Heaven can there be than sweet Ambrosia', and the music itself is fresh and engaging, as indeed are all these comparatively simple settings of poems about love (mostly unrequited) and consequent desperate longing. *La fiera vista* has another instrumental introduction, but its plangent message, 'The asp, full of death and poison, shuts its ears to the charmer's music', is not conveyed by music which is sad rather than fiercely apprehensive. But Monteverdi has a twinkle in his eye in giving *Godi pur dei bei sen* an appropriate jumping rhythm, for the poem begins: 'Delight, happy flea, in the fair bosom where you leap and ever sweetly bite.'

Other lyrics are pastoral (*Su su su che'l giorno*, about the dawn, shepherds and birdsong) and the closing *Hor care canzonette* ends the sequence, as it began, in a mood of serene happiness. This is very lightweight repertoire, to be sure, but the performances by the singers and band of Concerto delle Dame di Ferrara, directed by Sergio Vartolo, are most felicitous. A most enjoyable introduction to the early music of a composer who was later to write much greater music, but none with more charm. Excellent recording and full documentation, with texts and translations provided.

Madrigals, Book I (1587)

(BB) ** Naxos 8.555307. Delitiae Musicae, Longhini

Madrigals, Book II (1590)

(BB) ** Naxos 8.555308. Delitiae Musicae, Longhini

Madrigals, Book III (1592)

*** Glossa GCD 920910. La Venexiana, Cavina

(BB) ** Naxos 8.555309. Delitiae Musicae, Longhini

Madrigals, Book IV (1603)

(BB) ** Naxos 8.555309. Delitiae Musicae, Longhini

Madrigals, Book VI (1614)

⊕→ *** Naïve OP 30425. Concerto Italiano, Alessandrini

Madrigals, Book VII (1619)

*** Glossa GCD 920904. La Venexiana, Cavina

Apart from the distinguished earlier recordings by Anthony Rooley's Consort of Musicke (discussed in our main volume), there are now three ongoing complete cycles of the eight books of Monteverdi's madrigals, all by Italian singers, which gives them a distinct idiomatic advantage.

The performances by La Venexiana, directed by Claudio Cavina, have Italian flair and eloquence, and are strong in bringing out the rich lyricism of madrigals like *O come è gran martire* and the charming but more complex *O rossignol*. At the heart of Book III is the so-called 'nuovo stile' which anticipates operatic recitativo and aria. The two dramatically expressive highlights of the Book are *Vattene pur crudel*, the

lament of Armida, abandoned by Rinaldo, while the declamatory *Vivrò fra i mieie tormenti* (also a setting of Tasso) is the continuation of the celebrated *Combattimento di Tancredi e Clorinda*, which Monteverdi was to set in full in Book VIII. These are sung quite dramatically and with deep feeling, but their style is less histrionic than one would expect from the Concerto Italiano.

La Venexiana obviously relish the expanded 'stile concertato' of Book VII (to which, alas, we gave the wrong catalogue number in our main volume, corrected above) with its wide variety of voicing and use of an accompanying instrumental group. They also give a charming account of the final number, the pastoral dance cantata, *Tirsi and Clori*, which is delightfully sung.

However, in Book VI Rinaldo Alessandrini and the Concerto Italiano come completely into their own with their passionate account of the opening four-part scena, the famous *Lamento d'Arianna*, especially in their arrestingly plangent singing of Part 3: 'Where is the fidelity that so often you swore to me . . . Are these the crowns you place upon my brow? Are these the sceptres, these the jewels and the gold? To leave me, abandon me to be torn apart and devoured by beasts?' The second number is the equally famous *Zefiro torna*, which with its dancing rhythms provides a lighter expressive contrast, but then produces an astonishingly dissonant ending, very powerfully sung. *A Dio torna* is a superb example of the composer's concertato style, with a touching operatic dialogue between a pair of lovers at the conclusion of a passionate night together, now ready to part at daybreak, with the larger concerto group giving the central narration and an encouraging comment, before the final parting. *Batto, qui pianse Ergaste* brings even more contrasts of mood and tempo, with the heroine, Clori (represented by a pair of sopranos in duet), chasing a fleeing doe, her devoted swain following, bursting with passion; fortunately, when he catches her up, mutual love is re-kindled.

The final madrigal, *Presso un fiume tranquillo*, again combines dialogue and concertato styles. The amorous tranquillity of the loving solo exchanges between the nymph Philena and her shepherd, Eurillo, are punctuated with bolder 'choral' narration, and they have the last word, 'Let a thousand kisses heal a thousand pains.' This is an outstanding disc in every way which it will be difficult to match, let alone surpass.

The performances from Delitia Musicae, directed by Marco Longhini, are as authentic as any, with those madrigals not sung *a cappella* using a discreet *basso saguente* accompaniment, following the vocal lines. Within Book IV Longhini occasionally adds a touch of decorative improvisation, notably on cadences or long, repeated notes. The singing itself is rich-timbred, absolutely secure in intonation, perfectly blended, and distinctly sensual, sometimes making semitonal glissandi. These performances are certainly sensitive and deeply felt, but to our ears they lack the extra degree of expressive warmth offered by La Venexiana, and they are without the high drama of the Concerto Italiano. The Naxos recording is excellent, allowing for a wide dynamic range in a not too resonant acoustic, and (as always with this label) full texts and translations are included. But this series is not a strong recommendation.

Madrigals, Book VIII (Madrigali guerri ed amarosi)

*** HM HMC 90 1736/7. Kiehr, Haller, Martins, Fink, Laporte, Bowen, Ovenden, Zeffiri, Rensberg, Torres, Abete, Delaigue, Concerto Vocale, Jacobs

René Jacobs and his Concerto Vocale, with a host of outstanding singers led by Maria Cristina Kiehr, now make a major contribution in this increasingly competitive field, and they come out with flying colours. That is not to say that they surpass Alessandrini and his Italian group, but they are very impressive in their own right, even in the demanding *Lamento della Ninfa* and *Hor che'l ciel et la terra*. Jacobs and his singers are at their most dramatic in the famous opéra-ballets, *Il ballo delle ingrate* and *Il Combattimento*. But here Alessandrini and his Concerto Italiano are even finer, a clear primary choice, and their performances are available on a separate disc (Opus 111 OP 30-196). However, overall this Harmonia Mundi set is very rewarding – and, of course, it is complete as a single package, whereas Alessandrini's version is on two separate CDs (OPS 30-187 contains the remainder of the set).

Madrigals, Book 8: Opera-Ballet

(i) *Il combattimento di Tancredi e Clorinda;* (ii) *Lamento d'Arianna*
(B) ** DHM/BMG 05472 77190-2. (i) Paliatsaris, Aymonio, Malakate; (ii) Laurens; Capriccio Stravagante, Sempé (with FARINA: *Capriccio Stravagante.* Antonio il VERSO: *Lasciate mi morire.* ZANETTI: *Intrada del Marchese di Caravazzo.* Giulio MUSSI: *L'Amaltea*)

Skip Sempé's version of *Tancredi e Clorida* is both dramatic and expressive without being distinctive, and Guillemette Laurens's performance of the famous *Lamento d'Arianna* is eloquent without being memorable. For fill-ups, instrumental music by several of Monteverdi's contemporaries has been chosen, including *Capriccio Stravagante,* an eighteen-movement collection of tiny descriptive musical vignettes by Carlo Farina (1600–1640) which Sempé has chosen to provide the name of his group. The most striking movements are *Il Tremulanto, Il Gatto* (which miaows briefly) and the rather engaging *La Chitarra Spagniola,* but the other pieces are less interesting. The recording is vivid, and full texts and translations are included.

Lamento d'Olympia; Maladetto sia l'aspetto; Ohimè ch'io cado; Quel sdengosetto; Voglio di vita uscia
*** Hyp. CDA 66106. Kirkby, Rooley (chittarone) – D'INDIA: *Lamento d'Olympia,* etc. ***

A well-planned recital from Hyperion contrasts the two settings of *Lamento d'Olympia* by Monteverdi and his younger contemporary, Sigismondo d'India. The performances by Emma Kirkby, sensitively supported by Anthony Rooley, could hardly be surpassed. Her admirers can be assured that this ranks among her best records.

Church Music

Sacred Music, Vol. II: *Cantate Domino; Currite populi; Ego dormio; Exultent caeli; Laudate Dominum; Letaniae della Beata Vergine; Messa à 4 voci; O beatae viae; Venite, siccientes*
*** Hyp. **SACD** SACDA 67438 CD: CDA 67438. Sampson, Outram, Covey-Crump, Daniels, Gilchrist, Harvey, King's Consort Ch. & O, King

Sacred Music, Vol. III: *Cantate Domino; Christe, adoramus te; Confitebor tibi III alla francese; Dixit Dominus II; Ecca*

sacrum paratum; Gloria in excelsis Deo; Lauda Jerusalem; Memento Domine David; Nisi Dominus I; Salve Regina II; Sancta Maria
*** Hyp. **SACD** SACDA 67487 CD: CDA 67487. Sampson, Outram, Auchincloss, Covey-Crump, Daniels, Gilchrist, Harvey, Evans, King's Consort Ch. & O, King

Sacred Music, Vol. IV: *Adoramus te, Christe; Beatus vir II; Dixit Dominus II; Domine, ne in furore tuo; Exulta, filia Sion; Laetaus sum I; Laudate Dominum omnes gentes III; Magnificat II; Salve, o Regina, o Mater Salve Regina; Salve Regina I; Sanctorum mritis II*
*** Hyp. **SACD** SACDA 67519 CD: CDA 67519. Sampson, Outram, Osmond, Covey-Crump, Daniels, Auchincloss, Gilchrist, Harvey, Evans, King's Consort Ch. & O, King

Robert King and his King's Consort here continue their invaluable and comprehesive series of a relatively neglected part of Monteverdi's output, with masterpieces well sprinkled throughout these three volumes. Most of the works are motets, i.e. not part of the fixed church liturgy, and might be sung as interludes within a Mass or between the Psalms of a Vespers service, as with *Laetaus sum.* This is spectacularly set and, while based on a four-note ostinato, yet expands gloriously and at times reminds the listener of other, more familiar works, like the *Beatus vir* (included in Volume I) and the well-known *Gloria.* The fourth volume also includes a fascinating echo *Salve Regina,* very effectively realized here. Performances and recording throughout this fine series are of the highest quality and, as can be seen, each disc comes as an SACD with the sound further expanded.

Mass of Thanksgiving (Venice 1631)
(BB) *** Virgin 2x1 3 49993-2 (2). Taverner Consort Ch. & Players, Parrott

Following the success of his reconstruction of Handel's *Carmelite Vespers,* Andrew Parrott here presents a similar reconstruction of the *Mass of Thanksgiving* as performed in Venice on 21 November 1611. Historical records show that the Mass was then celebrated in the grandest possible way in St Mark's, in thanks to the Virgin Mary for the deliverance of the city from the plague which had raged throughout the earlier part of the year. What Parrott and his team have sought to assemble is a likely sequence of music for the liturgy, surrounding it with introits, toccatas, sonatas and recessionals, as well as linking chant. At the heart of the celebration lies Monteverdi's magnificent seven-part *Gloria* from his great collection, *Selva morale e spirituale.* The *Kyrie* sections of the *Credo* (including an amazing chromatic *Crucifixus*), the *Offertory, Sanctus, Agnus Dei* and a final *Salve regina* also come from that great collection. The only parts of the actual Mass written by another composer are the sections of the *Credo* that Monteverdi did not set. They are by Giovanni Rovetta, while other contemporaries of Monteverdi contributed the additional items, including Girolami Fantini, Giuseppe Scarani and Francesco Usper, to make a very grand whole. The recording is warmly atmospheric, with the brassy music at the opening and close approaching and receding, and with appropriate sound effects punctuating the ceremony. The performance is superb; the only reservation to make is that with only a little less linking material it would have been possible to fit the whole on to a single CD. However, this reissue is very economically priced and it is not too onerous to change from the first disc to the second after the *Et in Spiritum Sanctum.*

Vespro della Beata Vergine (Vespers)

*** Hyp. CDA 67531/2 (2). Sampson, Daniels, Gilchrist, Harvey, King's Consort and Ch., Robert King

Robert King crowns his Monteverdi series for Hyperion with an outstanding version of the *Vespers*, including not only the usual text but also the other two works that appeared in the same 1610 publication, the six-part *Magnificat* and the *Missa illo tempore*. The six-part work is less elaborate than the seven-part *Magnificat* from the *Vespers* proper, but it offers a valuable alternative. As King points out, this is a collection for choirmasters to pick and choose from in worship of the Virgin Mary, and the six-part work offers the alternative of organ accompaniment on its own, instead of orchestral accompaniment. The opening may seem disconcertingly bare, when King rejects the idea of using material from the prelude to the opera, *Orfeo*, yet the result is tautly dramatic too. The soloists make an excellent team, all singers regularly associated with King and his outstanding work, notably Carolyn Sampson and James Gilchrist. Warmly atmospheric recording, that yet allows plenty of detail to be heard.

OPERA

L'Incoronazione di Poppea (complete DVD version)

*** Warner DVD NVC Arts 0630 16914-2. Ewing, Bailey, Clarey, Duesing, Lloyd, Gale, Glyndebourne Ch., LPO, Leppard (V/D: Peter Hall & Robin Lough)

We have a very soft spot for the richly opulent Leppard version of Monteverdi's opera, at a far remove from today's scrupulously authentic versions. Here, not only are the strings gorgeous-sounding, but the castrati roles have been transposed, and the original three acts condensed into two. The cast of this faithful (1984) Glyndebourne production are watched by characters from the Prologue, Fortune, Virtue and Cupid, and, with Peter Hall directing, the drama is vividly projected (often with the camera observing the characters individually). Maria Ewing as a boldly self-confident Poppea is well matched vocally by Dennis Bailey's Nero, and Robert Lloyd is a tower of strength as Seneca. Cynthia Clarey, singing with passionate espressivo, is a sympathetic Ottavia and Dale Duesing completes a thoroughly convincing cast as Ottone. The setting is visually sumptuous, to match Leppard's luxuriant conception, and he directs the proceedings with panache. For those who don't care for authenticity in early opera, with all its visual contradictions concerning male and female personae, this well-recorded version should prove very rewarding.

Orfeo (CD versions; complete)

(M) ** Teldec (ADD) 2292 42494-2 (2). Kozma, Hansmann, Berberian, Katanosaka, Villisech, Van Egmond, Munich Capella Antiqua, VCM, Harnoncourt

(BB) ** Naxos 8.554094-2 (2). Carmignani, Pennichi, Frisani, Pantasuglia, Capella Musicale di San Petronio di Bologna, Vartolo

In Harnoncourt's version, the ritornello of the Prologue might almost be by Stravinsky, so sharply do the sounds cut. He is altogether more severe than John Eliot Gardiner. In compensation, the simple and straightforward dedication of this performance is most affecting, and the solo singing, if not generally very characterful, is clean and stylish. One exception is Cathy Berberian as the Messenger. She is strikingly successful and, though differing slightly in style from the others, she

sings as part of the team. Excellent recording. The extra clarity and sharpness of focus – even in large-scale ensembles – add to the abrasiveness from the opening *Toccata* onwards, and the 1968 recording sounds immediate and realistic.

With some first-rate solo singing and a restrained, scholarly approach, there is much to enjoy in the Naxos version. However, Sergio Vartolo's speeds are consistently slow. Alessandro Carmignani is a fine, clear Orfeo, coping splendidly with all the technical problems, and his singing in the big solos has a dedicated intensity, but at such slow speeds there is a sleepwalking quality in the results, however beautiful. More seriously, the exchanges between characters never have the dramatic intensity needed. In the instrumental numbers the strings are often uncomfortably edgy. It is as well that full text and translation are provided, when the CD tracks on the disc are radically different from those indicated in the booklet. Clear, well-balanced sound, recorded in the theatre of Puy-en-Velay in France.

Il ritorno d'Ulisse in patria (DVD versions)

**(*) Arthaus DVD 101 101. Luxon, J. Baker, Howles, Lloyd, Burrows, Popova, Caley, Glyndebourne Ch., LPO, Leppard (Director: Peter Hall; V/D: David Heather)

** Arthaus DVD 100 352. Henschel, Kasarova, Kaufmann, Bidzinsky, Scharinger, Daniluk, Scaschinger, Mayr, La Scintella O, Zurich, Harnoncourt

* Opus Arte DVD OA 0926D. Rolfe Johnson, Araya, Spence, Montague, Baroque Ens., Gen Wilson (Producer: Pierre Audi; V/D: Hans Hulscher)

Raymond Leppard's lush arrangements of Monteverdi and Cavalli operas may have fallen completely out of fashion in an age devoted to period performance but, as with *L'Incoronazione di Poppea* (above), there is a great deal to enjoy in his account, recorded in 1973, with Benjamin Luxon robust as Ulisse, still in excellent voice, and, most strikingly of all, Dame Janet Baker as the ever-patient Penelope. Hers is a deeply moving performance, masterfully acted and sung. Others making strong contribtions include Robert Lloyd as the Old Shepherd and Ian Caley as Ulisse's son, Telemaco. For Baker alone the DVD is worth hearing, and John Bury's stylized sets, with flying gods and goddesses, are a delight to the eye, backing up Peter Hall's stage direction. That said, the presentation on DVD is inadequate. There is no synopsis of a plot which involves unexpected allegorical characters; there is no indication in the list of chapters who is singing in what; and there is not even a complete cast list, except in the filmed credits at the end of the performance.

Harnoncourt's *Ritorno d'Ulisse in Patria* is in some ways just as controversial as Raymond Leppard's, with its fully scored accompaniments, including spectacular brass sonorities which hardly belong to Monteverdi's era; yet, unless you are completely attuned to authenticity, the ample scoring works well enough. The key singers give little cause for grumbles, with the baritone Ulisse, the ardent Dietrich Henschel, well matched to Vesselina Kasarova's Penelope, who is on top lyrical form. The other members of the cast, from Joseph Kaufmann's Telemaco to Paul Daniluk's characterful Neptune, are all excellent, and Harnoncourt directs the proceedings not too eccentrically, and with characteristic aplomb and energy. The sets are plain but effective enough, and the DVD direction is undistracting.

Netherlands Opera's 1998 production was conceived by Pierre Audi, using a text he himself devised. With each act starting with a prolonged silence, and musical direction that is less animated than it might be, the result hardly sustains its length, despite some excellent singing, notably from Anthony Rolfe Johnson as Ulisse and Toby Spence as Telemaco. Graziella Araya sings well as Penelope, but hers is not as moving a performance as it should be. Many of the incidental characters are taken by first-rate British singers. It does not help appreciation with such a complex and often allegorical plot that no synopsis is provided, and only a limited list of chapters and characters.

MORLEY, Thomas (1557–1602)

The First Booke of Ayres: A painted tale; Thyrsis and Milla; She straight her light greensilken coats; With my love; I saw my lady weeping; It was a lover; Who is it that this dark night?; Mistress mine; Can I forget; Love winged my hopes; What is my mistress; Come, sorrow, stay; Fair in a morn; Absence, hear thou; Will you buy a fine dog?; Sleep slumb'ring eyes

(M) ** Teldec (ADD) 3984 21334-2. Rogers, Harnoncourt, Dombois

This integral recording of Morley's *First Booke of Songs* first appeared at the beginning of the 1970s. The settings show the scope of the composer's imagination in his sensitivity to the words themselves, in the variety of style and metre, and in the diversity of manner of the accompaniments. The performances are fresh and direct and scholarly in the use of decoration.

MORRICONE, Ennio (born 1928)

Film Themes: Cinema Paradiso; Il deserto dei Tartari; Les deux Saisons de la vie; L'eredità Ferramonti; Gott mit uns; Indagine un cittadino al di sopra di ogni sospetto; Lolita; Love affair; Il Maestro e Margherita; Metti, una sera a cena; The Mission; Moss; Once upon a Time in America; Once upon a Time in the West; Per le antiche scale; Il Poteri degli angeli; Il Prato; Rampage; Romanza from Novecento; Stark System; White Dog. Piano Pieces: *4 Etudes; Rag in frantumi*

** Warner 5101 12304-2 (2). Rome Sinf. or Nat. Italian Ac. O, composer; Gilda Buttà (piano), Luca Pincini (cello), Paolo Zampini (flute); Fausto Anselmo (viola)

We were attracted to this collection because of the Academy Award-winning film, *Cinema Paradiso*, one of the finest of all Italian films, and very nostalgic for anyone who cares about the history of the cinema. It had an outstanding score by Morricone, with three memorable themes which enhanced the narrative throughout and haunted the memory afterwards. Disappointingly, the composer's brief arrangement draws on only two of them, surrounded with padding. Morricone admirers will be surprised to find that this two-disc selection does not include his most famous scores for Sergio Leone's celebrated Westerns, *For a Fistful of Dollars, The Good, the Bad and the Ugly*, and *For a Few Dollars More*. Nevertheless, he has a rare melodic gift, and the nostalgic atmosphere of his themes can be quite haunting. Unfortunately, only a few are offered here in orchestral dress, including *Deborah's Theme* from *One upon a Time in America*, and the full sweep of the strings for *Il Maestro e Margherita*. Most of the other themes are presented in simple arrangements for cello (or occasionally viola) and piano with obbligato flute, and sometimes all three instruments together. On the second of the two discs are nine more arrangements for piano alone,

plus four original avant-garde *Etudes* and a grotesque *Fragmented Rag*, which does use a film theme, appropriately taken from *Le Trio infernal*. The performances are of high quality (Gilda Buttà is a most sensitive pianist) and the recording is warm and pleasing. But this is not a disc one wants to return to very often.

MOSCHELES, Ignaz (1794–1870)

Cello Sonata 2, Op. 121; Melodic-Contrapuntal Studies, Op. 137 (after Bach's Well-Tempered Clavier 4, 8 & 9)

*** Hyp. CDA 67521. Barta, Milne – HUMMEL: *Cello Sonata* ***

Hummel and Moscheles, both keyboard virtuosos who wrote prolifically, make an apt pair of composers on this disc. Yet, where Hummel has lately been well represented on disc, Moscheles has been neglected far more, which makes this Hyperion issue especially valuable. With both, the influence is more from Mendelssohn than from Mozart. The Moscheles *Cello Sonata* of 1850–51 has one or two specific echoes of the Mendelssohn *Octet*, with a Scherzo marked *ballabile*, sparkling in the way one expects of Mendelssohn. Plainly, the younger composer as a close friend of Moscheles also influenced him in his devotion to Bach, represented here by the three *Melodic-Contrapuntal Studies*, involving easily flowing melodic writing for the cello, neatly fitted to Bach's original keyboard *Preludes*. Following tradition, Moscheles gives priority to the piano over the cello in describing the work, and this recording rather brings that out, when the balance between the instruments favours the piano, with the sensitive cellist, Jiří Barta, regularly overshadowed. What is more unexpected is that the last two movements in several ways echo Czech music, not just in the rhythms and melodic shapes of some of the themes, but in the alternation of speeds, suggesting that Moscheles was influenced by the Czech dumka.

MOSONYI, Mihály (1815–70)

(i) *Piano Concerto in E min.;* (ii) *Symphony 1 in D*

** Marco Polo 8.223539. (i) Körmendi, Slovak State Philh. O (Košice); (ii) Slovak RSO (Bratislava); Stankovsky

Despite his English origins, Mosonyi is thought of as one of the most representative nineteenth-century Hungarian composers – apart, of course, from the more obvious major figures, Liszt and Erkel. The *Symphony No. 1 in D* is an early work, composed in his late twenties and modelled on the Viennese classics in general and Beethoven in particular. The *Piano Concerto in E minor*, which comes from about the same time, shows the influence of Chopin and Weber. If, like the symphony, it is not strong on individuality, it is at least well-crafted, well-bred music and well worth an occasional airing. Klára Körmendi is the fluent soloist, and she receives decent orchestral support from Robert Stankovsky and his Slovak forces.

MOYZES, Alexander (1906–84)

Down the River Vah, Suite for Large Orchestra, Op. 26; Germer Dances, Suite for Large Orchestra, Op. 51; Pohronie Dances, Suite for Large Orchestra, Op. 43

*(*) Marco Polo 8.223278. CSR SO (Bratislava), Lenárd

This disc contains some attractive dances and colourful (not over-extended) tone-poems, which, although not great music, are yet not unappealing. Their Slavonic flavour and vivid orchestration, with considerable rhythmic interest, help to hold the listener's attention. The performances are enthusiastic, but the orchestral playing and especially the 1989 sound (which produces a scrawny effect at times) are not very inviting. At Naxos price this would be worth considering for the rare repertoire, but its full-price tag gives one pause.

Symphonies 11, Op. 79; 12, Op. 83
** Marco Polo 8.225093. Slovak RSO, Slovák

Moyzes established himself as a pioneer of Slovak national music, and both these works mix Slovakian elements into the Western Romantic tradition. Nothing is remotely atonal: it is all approachable, melodic and boldly coloured. The *Eleventh Symphony* dates from 1978 and begins ominously with repeated timpani strokes, but, from the *Allegro* onwards, the composer's penchant for lively folk material soon emerges. There is no lack of energy. The *Twelfth Symphony* was the composer's last work and follows the conventional pattern of its predecessor. The opening movement (after a slow introduction) is a kind of *moto perpetuo*, which the composer suggested represented 'contemporary living – with everyone running and hurrying, always on the move'. The central slow movement is powerfully reflective, and the finale has plenty of robust vitality. The performances are excellent, and if neither the orchestral playing nor the sound is first class, they are more than satisfactory.

MOZART, Leopold (1719–87)

Trumpet Concerto in D
(B) *** Ph. Eloquence 468 207-2. André, Rouen CO, Beaucamp – Josef & Michael HAYDN; HUMMEL: *Trumpet Concertos* ***
*** Virgin 3 32627-2. Guerrier, Ens. O de Paris, Nelson – MOZART: *Clarinet, Horn & Oboe Concertos* **(*)

Leopold Mozart's conventional but pleasing *Trumpet Concerto* is another two-movement work in which the higher solo tessitura is stratospheric and, not surprisingly, Maurice André plays it with easy confidence and style. This comes as part of a very attractive anthology which includes outstanding accounts of the masterly concertos by Hummel and Josef Haydn.

David Guerrier's performance on Virgin is also very accomplished, and is the more remarkable as on the same disc he plays Mozart's *Fourth Concerto* on the *horn* with equal confidence. He has obviously also influenced the conductor, for the bravura horn parts in the orchestral accompaniment for the Mozart work are given a bold forward balance, notably in the galumphing finale.

MOZART, Wolfgang Amadeus
(1756–91)

Adagio & Fugue in C min., K.546; 3 Divertimenti for Strings, K.136–8; Divertimenti: 10 in F; K.247; 11 in D, K.251; 15 in B flat, K.287. Serenade 13 (Eine kleine Nachtmusik), K.525
(M) ** DG (ADD) 477 5436. BPO, Karajan

Needless to say, these are beautifully played performances and, as such, prompt the liveliest admiration. At the same time, there is a predictably suave elegance that seems at times to militate against spontaneity. There is too much legato, except perhaps in *Eine kleine Nachtmusik*, on which Karajan languishes obvious warmth and affection. Cultured and

effortless readings, but the originally beautiful recordings, made betwen 1965 and 1969 and well balanced, have lost a great deal of allure in the digital transfers and even have moments of harshness, especially the three *String Divertimenti*, K.136–8, where the playing in outer movements is undoubtedly spirited.

Adagio and Fugue in C min., K.546; Violin Concerto 3 in G; Symphony 41 in C (Jupiter)
**(*) EMI 5 57418-2. Perlman, BPO

Itzhak Perlman recorded this concert live at the Berlin Philharmonie early in 2002, and the vitality of his performances, not just as violinist but as conductor too, suggests that this violin virtuoso has a second career beckoning. Recorded in up-front sound, this vividly captures the atmosphere of a great occasion, defying received taste in offering unashamedly 'big-band' performances of Mozart. Weighted with double-basses, the opening of the *Adagio and Fugue* has a magnificence worthy of Stokowski, apt enough for such a massive inspiration, and the *Jupiter Symphony*, too, is Beethovenian in scale, yet with much sparkling detail, not least from the woodwind. In the *G major Violin Concerto* Perlman is even more persuasively spontaneous, directing from the violin, than he was in his 20-year-old studio recording with a conductor. A rewarding disc then, especially for the *Adagio and Fugue*, even if some reservations are inevitable.

CONCERTOS

(i) Bassoon Concerto; (ii) Clarinet Concerto; (iii) Oboe Concerto
(BB) ** Warner Apex (ADD) 2564 60820-2. (i) Hongne, Bamberg SO, Guschlbauer; (ii) Lancelot, Paillard CO, Paillard; (iii) Pierlot, ECO, Rampal

Three highly musical performances from three different soloists, orchestras and conductors, but all with an unmistakable French accent. Jacques Lancelot's timbre is less than luscious (but he is backwardly balanced), Pierlot's playing is precise and elegant; but the most enjoyably genial soloist is Paul Hongne's woody bassoon, with some Sarastro-like low notes and touches of wit. All three accompaniments are supportive; the recordings are pleasing but not wide-ranging.

(i) Bassoon Concerto; (ii) Flute & Harp Concerto; (iii) Oboe Concerto
(M) **(*) Warner Elatus 2564 61592-2. (i) Vallon; (ii) Hazelzet, Kwast; (iii) Ponseele; Amsterdam Bar. O, Koopman

The resonant acoustic of the Elatus Amsterdam recordings suits the *Flute and Harp Concerto* best, casting a pleasingly warm atmospheric aura over the attractive partnership of William Hazelzet and Saskia Kwast, who play very beautifully. Marcel Ponseele's performance of the *Oboe Concerto* is also felicitous, but here the resonance rather clouds the focus of the accompaniment; and for similar reasons Marc Vallon's somewhat plummy but agreeably genial bassoon image is brought well forward. Koopman accompanies persuasively throughout, but this is perhaps not a first choice among such collections unless this particular group of works is wanted.

(i) Bassoon Concerto in B flat; (ii) Violin Concerto 3 in G, K.316
(M) (**(*)) Sup. mono SU 3678-2 001. (i) Bidlo; (ii) D. Oistrakh; Czech PO, Ančerl – VORISEK: *Symphony*. (**)

David Oistrakh gives a supremely poised reading of the G major Concerto, with a beautifully phrased Adagio and happy control of the changing moods of the finale. Moreover, Karel Bidlo is a most genial and stylish bassoonist with a very pleasing timbre, and he too proves an elegant Mozartian: his gently pointed tonguing in the finale is delightful. Karel Ančerl uses an orchestra of chamber size and accompanies throughout with finesse. The mono sound is resonant, the orchestral texture warm if not absolutely refined but fully acceptable when both soloists are truthfully caught.

Clarinet Concerto in A, K.622

*** Australian Decca Eloquence (ADD) 476 7404. De Peyer, LSO, Maag – WEBER: Clarinet Concerto 2 ***; SPOHR: Clarinet Concerto 1 ***

Clarinet Concerto; Overture: Die Enführung aus dem Serail

**(*) BBC (ADD) BBCM 5014-2. De Peyer, BBC SO, Sargent (with MENDELSSOHN: Midsummer Night's Dream: Nocturne & Wedding March) – SCHUBERT: Symphony 8 (Unfinished) **

Gervase de Peyer's Decca performance of the Clarinet Concerto remains among the best recorded, being both fluent and lively, with masterly phrasing in the slow movement and a vivacious finale. The superbly warm, well-balanced sound completely defies its 1959 date. An intelligent addition to the classic Weber/Spohr recordings, and well worth acquiring.

It is good, too, to hear de Peyer's 1964 performance, recorded when he was still at his peak. The first movement is highly musical but surprisingly direct, and it is in the Adagio that the magical phrasing and gentle vibrato (which influenced the style of woodwind playing in all the London orchestras) are particularly endearing, together with his gentle pianissimo reprise. The finale, too, is witty as well as vivacious, with the secondary theme delightfully pointed. Sargent accompanies supportively and provides a boisterous, big-band overture to start the proceedings, and the recording is of acceptable BBC 1960s' standard. The Mendelssohn Nocturne, surprisingly, brings a not quite secure horn solo. Perhaps Sargent had over-rehearsed it, as he was sometimes wont to do, and the principal horn became unsettled. The Wedding March, however, goes with a swing, and the Unfinished Symphony is rather successful. Good, warm, Royal Albert Hall sound.

(i) Clarinet Concerto; (ii) Horn Concerto 4, K.495; (iii) Oboe Concerto, K.271

(*) Virgin 3 32627-2. (i) P. Meyer; (ii) Guerrier; (iii) Leleux; Ens. O de Paris, Nelson – Leopold MOZART: Trumpet Concerto *

The main interest of this Virgin collection is that David Guerrier gives a very good performance of the Fourth Horn Concerto and then, at the end of the programme, picks up a trumpet and gives an equally accomplished account of the two-movement Trumpet Concerto of Leopold Mozart, with its high tessitura negotiated with equal aplomb. Paul Meyer's performance of the Clarinet Concerto is very stylish, with the reprise of the sensitive Adagio the more effective for being (as with Gervase de Peyer) played pianissimo. Here the orchestral violins sound thin in tutti, but the resulting transparency lets the vivid horn parts come through more tellingly than usual. But the most distinctive performance here is a delightfully Gallic account of the Oboe Concerto by François Leleux, the touch of plangency in his timbre adding to the piquancy, especially in the finale.

(i; ii) Clarinet Concerto in A; (iii) Flute & Harp Concerto in C; (ii) Serenade 13 (Eine kleine Nachtmusik)

(BB) **(*) HMV (ADD) 5 86737-2. (i) A. Marriner; (ii) LMP, Glover; (iii) Snowden, Thomas, LPO, Litton

Producing a beautifully even flow of warm tone, Andrew Marriner gives a distinguished reading of the Clarinet Concerto which yet lacks a feeling of spontaneity, the forward thrust, the inspiration of the moment. It would be hard to find a more beautiful timbre in the slow movement, but nevertheless the effect remains placid. The performance of the Flute and Harp Concerto is much more winning. Here the flautist Jonathan Snowden, in collaboration with Caryl Thomas on the harp, is both sparkling and sensitive, a natural soloist, regularly imaginative in his phrasing. Jane Glover's elegant and sprightly account of the Night Music, which opens the programme brightly, completes an uneven but inexpensive reissue which is certainly well recorded.

(i) Clarinet Concerto in A, K.622; (ii) Piano Concerto 27 in B flat, K.595. Symphony 25 in G min., K.183

(M) (**(*)) Dutton mono CDSJB 1026. NYPO, Barbirolli, with (i) Goodman; (ii) Casadesus

(i) Clarinet Concerto; (ii) Clarinet Quintet

(M) **(*) Ph. (ADD) 442 390-2. Brymer, (i) LSO, C. Davis; (ii) Allegri Qt

More transfers from Dutton for the Barbirolli label, rescuing valuable performances from Sir John's years with the New York Philharmonic. Both the B flat Concerto, K.595, with that great Mozartian Robert Casadesus, and the 'little' G minor Symphony, K.183, recorded on 3 November 1940, were issued commercially on 78-r.p.m. discs, but the Clarinet Concerto, with Benny Goodman as soloist, from December of that year, has not been available before. Perhaps the low rumble that affected the originals stood in the way, but all these performances are of artistic interest and, despite the 65-year-old sound, will interest Mozartians and all who care about Barbirolli's music-making in New York.

Jack Brymer's (1964) Philips account of the Clarinet Concerto has an eloquent autumnal serenity and the reading a soft lyricism that is very appealing. However, the leisurely (1970) interpretation of the Quintet is more controversial. Generally the very slow tempi throughout are well sustained, although in the finale the forward flow of the music is reduced to a near-crawl. Good transfers.

(i; iii) Flute Concerto 1 in G, K.313; Andante in C, K.315; (ii; iii) Oboe Concerto in C, K.314; (iv) Sinfonia concertante in E flat, K.297b; Serenade 10 in B flat for 13 Wind Instruments, K. 361

(BB) *** EMI Gemini 4 76918-2 (2). (i) Debost; (ii) Bourgue; (iii) O de Paris; (iv) ECO; all cond. Barenboim

Michel Debost gives a charming, sprightly account of the Flute Concerto and Maurice Bourgue is hardly less appealing in the Oboe Concerto, although the resonant sound of the string tuttis tends to spread a little too much. But the importance of this reissue lies with Mozart's less well-known Sinfonia concertante and especially the so-called 'Gran Partita'. The score of the Sinfonia concertante was lost before its first Paris performance (for which it was written) and ever since it was recovered, in the middle of the nineteenth century, doubts have been cast over its authenticity. One suspicious point is that the central slow movement fails to alter the basic tonality from E flat; whatever the source, however, there is much delightful music here and, with four fine wind soloists from the ECO and full-blooded direction by Barenboim, this is a most attractive version, particularly when it comes alongside such a splendid account of the *B flat Serenade*, which is most stylish. Here we have expertly blended wind-tone, free from the the traces of self-indulgence that occasionally mar Barenboim's music-making. Tempi are a little on the brisk side, especially in the first movement – but none the worse for that when the playing itself is so resilient and the quality of the recorded sound so well focused, with excellent body and definition.

Flute Concerto 2 in D (arr. Szell for cello)

*(*) Transart TR 121. Haimovitz, O de Bretagne, Sanderling –
HAYDN: *Cello Concertos 1–2* *(*)

The conductor George Szell had the idea that Mozart's *Oboe Concerto*, K.314, later rejigged by Mozart himself as the *D major Flute Concerto*, was originally written for cello. He transcribed the outer movements very effectively, but then found the slow movement unsuitable for cello adaptation. Instead, for a slow movement he used the *Andante in A*, K.470, for violin and orchestra, written much later, in 1785, transcribing the solo part for cello. When K.470 is a rarity, a piece thought to have been written as a substitute slow movement for a Viotti concerto, it makes an apt enough choice, even if the inconsistency of style is immediately evident. In this live recording Haimovitz gives a strong, sympathetic performance of this composite cello concerto, sadly marred by the same flaws of dry sound and insecure orchestral playing as the two Haydn concertos on the disc.

(i) Flute & Harp Concerto in C, K.299. Symphony 39 in E flat, K.543; Overture: Die Zauberflöte

** EuroArts **DVD** 2054678. (i) Gallois, Pierre; O della Svizzera Italiana, Marriner

Good performances from all concerned, though the *E flat Symphony* is not special. Recorded at the Palazzo dei Congressi, Lugano, in 2005 and broadcast on BBC4 early in 2006, one wonders whether this short concert greatly benefits from being seen as well as heard. And at 70 minutes it is rather short value, considering what DVD can now accommodate.

Horn Concertos 1–4; Concert Rondo in E flat, K.371; Fragment in E flat, K.494a; (i) Concerto 4, K.495: Rondo (transcribed Flanders & Swann): Ill Wind

(M) *** Telarc CD 80367. Ruske, SCO, Mackerras, (i) with Suart

Eric Ruske was already principal horn of the Cleveland Orchestra at the age of 20, and he gives outstandingly fresh performances of the four Mozart *Concertos*. Not only are the famous *Rondos* exceptionally buoyant and sharply rhythmic (sample the crisp little horn triplets in the finale of K.417), but first-movement allegros combine elegance with a comparatively swift pacing which is naturally Mozartian in feeling. Slow movements, too, have an equally agreeable lift, as in the *Larghetto* of K.447, while the pointed articulation in the finale is a joy. The *Concert Rondo* too has a good-humoured jubilation which is especially attractive, and the *Fragment* ends neatly in mid-air. Ruske is helped by truly vivacious accompaniments from Mackerras and the Scottish Chamber Orchestra, with crisp string articulation and equally elegant lyrical phrasing to match the solo playing, and neat touches of wit in finales. The recording is beautifully balanced, very much in the demonstration bracket. But what makes this special is the inclusion of *Ill Wind*, the famous Flanders and Swann poem, which exactly fits the *Rondo* of the *Fourth*

Concerto. Here the reciter is the celebrated Gilbertian, Richard Suart, whose vocal inflections are a joy and whose words are crystal clear (although a text is included). We feel sure that Mozart himself would have been delighted with the line 'I've lost my horn, lost my horn, found my horn . . . *gorn!*'

(i) Horn Concertos 1–4; Concert Rondo in E flat, K.371; Rondo in D, K.514; Fragments: in A flat, K.370b; in E, K.494a (all ed. Tuckwell); (i; ii) Sinfonia concertante in E flat, K.297b; (iii) Horn Quintet in E flat, K.407; (iv) Piano & Wind Quintet in E flat; K.452. Duet for 2 Horns in E flat; (v) Idomeneo: Si il padre perdei

(B) *** Decca 475 7104 (2). Tuckwell; with (i) ECO; (ii; iv) Wickens, Hill, Gatt; (iii) Gabrieli Qt; (iv) Ogdon; (v) Armstrong

Barry Tuckwell was the natural successor for the mantle of Dennis Brain, and after Dennis he was the first horn player to become a full-time professional soloist. He played a modern German wide-bore double horn, and his easy technique, smooth, warm tone and obvious musicianship command attention and give immediate pleasure.

This anthology gathers together all the major works Mozart wrote featuring the horn, even including the aria from *Idomeneo*, delightfully sung by Sheila Armstrong, in which the horn obbligato was especially provided for the celebrated principal of the Munich Orchestra, Franz Lang. The four major concertos were written for an even more famous player, Joseph Leutgeb, who moved to Vienna a few years before Mozart arrived. He had established the technique of 'stopped' notes wth the hand in the bell of the instrument, which increased the number of notes available, and this facility is apparent in the melodic lines of the concertos and the various unfinished fragments which also survive and which have been edited here for performance and recording.

Tuckwell recorded the concertos four times in all, the last for Collins (now on Regis RRC 1007), but it is the third set which is included here, in which he also directed the ECO. They were recorded, like the rest of the programme, in the Henry Wood Hall in 1983, and the playing is as fresh and spirited as ever.

He also directs the *Sinfonia concertante*, and it is an entirely beguiling performance, beautifully shaped and aptly paced, with a slow movement of radiant grace and a sparkling finale.

The same wind soloists feature in the *Piano and Wind Quintet*, which Mozart declared, when it was first performed in 1784, 'the best work I have ever composed'. The present performance is enjoyable but not distinctive. The outer movements are alert and briskly paced, but John Ogdon seems not entirely at ease in the *Larghetto*. Tuckwell also leads the *Horn Quintet* – very much like a concerto with a string quartet, instead of an orchestra. He plays with characteristic sensibility and aplomb and is at his most infectious in the finale. The contribution of the Gabrielis however is curiously severe; one would have liked the string playing to smile a bit more, but they are not helped by a grainy recording: more ambience would have helped here. In the three *Horn Duets* Tuckwell plays spiritedly against himself; with any minor reservations, this remains a thoroughly worthwhile compilation.

(i) Horn Concertos 1–4; (ii) Flute Concerto 1

(BB) **(*) HMV (ADD/DDD) 5 86738-2. (i) Tuckwell, ASMF, Marriner; (ii) Snowden, LPO, Mackerras

This is Tuckwell's second recording of the *Horn Concertos*, with pleasingly elegant accompaniments from Marriner and the ASMF. The 1972 recording sounds quite full and, though Tuckwell's later recordings were marginally finer still, these accounts are in every way enjoyable. Jonathan Snowden's persuasively fresh account of the *G major Flute Concerto* makes a fine bonus, even if here the recording (made in a church) is a shade over-reverberant.

(i) *Horn Concertos 1–4;* (ii) *Piano & Wind Quintet in E flat, K.452*

(B) (***) EMI mono 3 38603-2. Brain; (i) Philh. O, Karajan; (ii) Horsley, Brain Wind Ens. (members)

This is a bargain reissue of Dennis Brain's famous (1954) mono record of the concertos, coupled with the *Quintet*. It is also available at mid-price as one of EMI's 'Great Recordings of the Century' with fuller documentation (5 66898-2 [5569502]) and this is discussd more fully in our main volume.

Piano concertos

Piano Concertos 1–6; 8–9; 11–27; Rondo in D, K.382

(B) **(*) DG 469 510-2 (without *Rondo*) (8). Anda, Salzburg Mozarteum O

Piano Concertos 1–6; 8–9; 11–27; (i) *Double Piano Concerto, K.365;* (i; ii) *Triple Piano Concerto, K.242*

(B) ** Warner 2564 61398-2 (10). Karl Engel, Mozarteum O, Salzburg, Hager; with (i) Till Engel; (ii) Hager

Were the competition not so fierce, Anda's often very fine performances could carry a stronger recommendation. They are beautifully poised and have excellent feeling for style; some are quite memorable for their unidiosyncratic freshness. The recordings, made between 1962 and 1969, do not quite match those of Barenboim (the violin timbre is more dated) and Anda is a less individual artist, but the sound is clean and well balanced and the set gives consistent enjoyment. Where none is available by Mozart, Anda plays his own cadenzas. DG have now managed to get three concertos on each disc (with only the second split after the first movement) so the whole set comes on eight CDs, and the economy is obvious.

Karl Engel's Mozart concerto cycle with the Salzburg Mozarteum Orchestra was recorded in the mid-1970s and was rather overshadowed in the last years of LP by Murray Perahia's cycle with the ECO for CBS/Sony and by Brendel and Marriner on Philips. Not all of them were issued in Britain or America at the time, and this present compilation marks their first appearance on CD. Obviously there are many things to admire – not least the high quality of the Salzburg orchestra and the natural if reverberant sound. Karl Engel is an experienced Mozartian, but his artistry rarely touches real distinction. He is a conscientious guide rather than a pianist of great poetic insight.

Piano Concertos 5–6; 8–9; 11–27; Rondo in D, K.382

(B) **(*) Ph. 475 7306 (8). Uchida, ECO, Tate

Mitsuko Uchida's cycle, which she began in 1985, is now complete, with playing of considerable beauty and performances of the earlier concertos guaranteed never to offend and most likely to delight. (The pairing of Nos. 8 and 9, below, is a good example.) There is some lovely playing, although her cultured approach at times offers more than a hint of Dresden china. She is unfailingly elegant but a little over-civilized, consistently alive and imaginative, although at times one would welcome a greater robustness of spirit, a livelier inner current. Throughout, Jeffrey Tate draws splendid playing

from the ECO, and these artists have the benefit of exceptionally good recorded sound; although the perspective favours the piano, the timbre of the solo instrument is beautifully captured.

In the later concertos the tonal refinement and delicacy are sometimes in stronger evidence than a sense of scale. Uchida is eminently imaginative throughout the slow movement of the *C major* (No. 25, K.503). But the slow movement of No. 27, K.595, is not free from preciosity, and one has only to think of Gilels or Perahia in this work to put the undoubted tonal beauties that Uchida's playing offers into a true, Mozartian perspective. As one would expect from two artists of this calibre, there are many felicities, but individually none of the performances of the major works here would be a first choice, and No. 16 is split between two CDs after the first movement.

Piano Concertos (i) *5 in D, K.175;* (ii) *8 in C, K.246;* (iii) *17 in G, K.453;* (iv) *27 in B flat, K.595*

*** EuroArts **DVD** 2010248. (i) Frager, Swiss R. & TV O, Andreae (recorded in Teatro Bibiena, Mantua); (ii) Zacharias, Stuttgart RSO, Gelmetti (recorded at the Schwetzingen Palace); (iii) Ránki, ECO, Tate ; (iv) Aleksandar Madžar, RPO, Previn (both recorded at the Imperial Palace of Schönbrunn, Vienna) (V/D: János Darvas)

This is one of a series of DVD groups of live Mozart piano concerto recordings using different soloists, conductors, orchestras and venues, with stimulating results. The present collection happily frames early and middle-period works with the composer's very first, entirely original concerto, *No. 5 in D*, written when he was 17, and the last masterpiece, in B flat major, of the 34-year-old, composed just nine months before his death.

The partnership of Malcolm Frager and Marc Andreae seems ideal for the earliest concerto. There is the hint of a smile of pleasure on the pianist's face as he begins and Marc Andreae is similarly warm-hearted, while the playing of the Swiss orchestra is fresh, polished and vibrant, and the lively recording, brightly transferred, is just right for the music.

When we turn to the C major, the bearded conductor Gianluigi Gelmetti, has a rather imposing image, but he is a natural Mozartian and persuasively matches the warmly sensitive Stuttgart accompaniment to Christian Zacharias's comparatively intimate style, within a mellower acoustic, so suitable for the graceful *Andante* and delectable finale.

Jeffrey Tate may be seated, but he provides a strong, vivid opening ritornello for the G major work, and Desző Ránki's playing has both vitality and delicacy, especially in the exquisite *Andante*, where the fine woodwind playing of the ECO so sensitively creates the opening mood. The finale, with its winning theme and variations, has the lightest touch.

Mozart's last concerto shares the same venue but features the Royal Phiharmonic Orchestra, directed by André Previn in relaxed rather than valedictory mood. In this work, the camera often centres on the pianist, Aleksandar Madžar, who likes to keep his eyes closed; this is especially noticeable in the slow movement, which he phrases very gently, followed by orchestral playing of comparable lyrical serenity. The finale, with the tempo still not pressed too hard, makes an elegant, conclusion.

All four concertos are beautifully recorded and the camerawork varies in emphasis, but generally the shots of the orchestra, pianist and conductor are well judged. A most rewarding collection in every respect.

ano Concertos in B flat: 6, K.238; 15, K.450; 27, K.595
(*) Warner 2564 62259-2. Aimard, COE

is not often one gets three Mozart piano concertos on a
ngle disc – and all in the same key, too. They are all
gagingly spontaneous works, and the performances sunny
d cultivated to match. Darker clouds, mostly found in
595, never stay around for too long. Pierre-Laurent Aimard
rects the orchestra from the keyboard, but the only way that
ows is in the unity with the soloist; there is no scrappy
aying here. Other accounts of K.595 may find deeper under-
rrents than there are here, but this collection is very easy to
njoy.

*ano Concertos (i) 6 in B flat, K.238; (ii) 19 in F, K.459; (iii)
in D min., K.466*
** EuroArts DVD 2010238. (i) Zacharias, Stuttgart RSO,
Gelmetti (recorded at the Schwetzingen Palace); (ii) Lupu,
Deutsche Kammerphilharmonie, Zinman (recorded at the
Sophiensaal, Munich); (iii) Ivan Klánský, Virtuoso di Praga,
Jiří Bělohlávek (recorded at the Rittersaal of Palais
Waldstein) (V/D: János Darvas)

t the opening of the *B flat Concerto* the camera is at a
stance and slowly moves up to the orchestra and conductor
uring the introduction, then focuses on the pianist at his
ntry. Zacharias and Gelmetti have already given us a fine
ccount of K.246, and their performance of the compara-
vely mild K.238 is hardly less felicitous. How beautifully
elmetti introduces the theme of the *Andante un poco Adagio*
, just the right pace, and Zacharias takes it up elegantly,
llowing with a similarly leisurely finale (but with the horns
etermined to be heard with their mini-fanfares).

It is then a great pleasure to sit and identify with the
udience's welcome for Radu Lupu (whom we have enjoyed
aying so often on his Decca audio recordings) when he
mes on to the platform for his distinguished account of the
major Concerto. We see a great deal of him (and of his
ands) during the performance, and his intensity of concen-
ation is formidable. The conductor David Zinman is a
leasure to watch too, as he conjures wonderfully sensitive
aying from the Deutsche Kammerphilharmonie, strings
d woodwind alike, especially in the gracious central *Alle-
retto*. The finale then has overriding energy and purpose.
ortunately the recording in the Munich Sophiensaal is fully
orthy, very well balanced and vivid.

After this excellence, the *D minor* could well have been an
nticlimax, but Bělohlávek's intense, stormy opening sets the
cene dramatically so that Ivan Klánský's piano entry can
rovide the poetic contrast mirrored in his calm facial
xpression. The same contrast between serenity and turbu-
nce is caught in the *Romance*, and the finale then overflows
ith energy. Its engagingly sprightly secondary theme is
layed with obvious pleasure by the soloist, creating a perfect
il for the movement's darker undercurrents. Klánský plays
is own imaginative cadenzas, and altogether this is a power-
ully individual performance, again splendidly realistic as a
ecording, with the visual dimension involving the listener
iroughout: watching Klánský's face as well as his hands is a
pecial pleasure.

iano Concertos 8 in C, K.246; 9 in E flat, K.271
M) **(*) Ph. 475 777-2. Uchida, ECO, Tate

This is one of the most successful of Uchida's Mozart con-
erto couplings and, as it happens, the so-called *Jeunehomme
Concerto*, K.271, was written for a woman pianist of that

name. But these are works that suit Uchida's flowing style,
with both slow movements sensitively played and no lack of
momentum in outer movements. Some may like greater
robustness, but there is no lack of freshness or subtlety of
colour. The recording too is first class, beautifully balanced,
with a very real piano image. It is now reissued in Universal's
series of Originals.

*Piano Concertos (i) 9 in E flat (Jeunehomme), K.271; (ii) 12
in A, K.414; (iii) 26 in D (Coronation), K.537*
*** EuroArts DVD 2010218. (i) Uchida, Salzburg Mozarteum
O, Tate (recorded at the Mozarteum, Salzburg); (ii)
Ashkenazy, RPO (recorded at Hampton Court Palace,
London); (iii) Francsch, Deutsche Kammerphilharmonie,
Albrecht (V/D: János Darvas)

We already have two recordings of the *Jeunehomme Concerto*
from Uchida, on both CD and DVD, but this Salzburg
account with Jeffrey Tate is finest of all. She is at her freshest
and plays with appealing simplicity. Tate and the Salzburg
Mozarteum Orchestra are splendid partners, and Tate's shaping of the opening of the *Andantino* is memorable. The finale
has tremendous energy, with its central section neatly contrasted. Without having to worry about directing the orchestra, Uchida can concentrate on her own solo role, and here
she is a pleasure to watch.

Pianists almost always tend to look awkward conducting
from the keyboard when the camera takes a frontal view. But
Ashkenazy manages better than most in the introduction to
the *A major Concerto*, K.414, and of course the orchestra plays
very stylishly, with the full beauty of the *Andante* shared
equally by the keyboard and the orchestra. The finale is
rhythmically irresistible in its light-hearted brio, and the
recording is remarkably successful, considering the venue.

Homero Francsch is the least known of the soloists in this
series so far, but, although he is visually a little restless to
watch, he is an excellent Mozartian, and so is Gerd Albrecht,
who draws elegant and polished playing from the Deutsche
Kammerphilharmonie in the *Coronation Concerto*. The performance is beautifully proportioned, with a serene slow
movement framed by outer movements of striking vitality. In
short, this is very enjoyable in its direct, unidiosyncratic way,
and the sound is excellent.

*(i) Piano Concertos 9 (Jeunehomme), K.271; 17, K.453; 20,
K.466. Adagio & Fugue in C min., K.546*
**(*) ECM 1624/25. (i) Jarrett; Stuttgart CO, Russell Davies

Admirers of Keith Jarrett should be well satisfied with his
newest Mozartian venture, apart from the short measure. For
the *Adagio and Fugue*, well played as it is, only lasts for just
over seven minutes. Dennis Russell Davies and the excellent
Stuttgart orchestra set the scene in each of the three concertos
very impressively. Jarrett plays fluently and responsively
throughout: only in the central *Romance* of the last work does
he seem not ideally relaxed. But the *Andante* of K.453, taken
slowly and reflectively, shows him at his most thoughtful,
while the finale is delightfully light-hearted. Excellent recording, well balanced, full-bodied and clear.

Piano Concertos (i) 9, K.271; (ii) 20, K.466
(M) (**(*)) Sony mono/stereo 512863-2. Serkin; with (i)
Marlboro Festival O, Schneider; (ii) Phd. O, Ormandy

In his last years, Rudolf Serkin embarked on a Mozart concerto cycle with Abbado for DG which was remarkable for an
artist of his age. They were generally well received, but by
comparison with his earlier achievements as a Mozartian they

struck us as at times just a shade didactic, even ponderous. The *Jeunehomme Concerto*, with the Marlboro Festival Orchestra under the violinist Alexander Schneider, comes from 1956, while the *D minor* with Ormandy and the Philadelphia Orchestra was recorded in 1951, in the first years of the LP. In the 1950s Serkin's Mozart still had some of the lightness of touch and style that distinguished his pre-war collaboration with Adolf Busch. The sound is a bit opaque but there is no doubting the distinction of the music-making – not least on the part of that generally underrated maestro Ormandy.

Piano Concertos 9, K.271; 21, K.467

(B) ** CfP 575 1452. Hough, Hallé O, Thomson

On one of his early recordings (1987) Stephen Hough plays with fine freshness, point and clarity, but he tends to prettify two of Mozart's strongest concertos, minimizing their greatness. This delicate, Dresden-china treatment would have been more acceptable half a century ago, but it leaves out too much that is essential. Excellent playing and recording.

Piano Concertos 12, K.414; 14, K.449; Rondo in D, K.382

(BB) **(*) Arte Nova 74321 72117-2. Kirschnereit, Bamberg SO, Bermann

Matthias Kirschnereit's coupling is the first of a complete cycle, and he opens with an engagingly fresh account of the well-known *D major Rondo*, and follows with a warm, cultivated performance of K.414, to which Frank Bermann's elegant and supportive accompaniment makes a very considerable contribution. K.449 is characterful and enjoyable too, though it is less individual than Barenboim's version. Mozart's cadenzas are used throughout. The recording is very good and the balance realistic; but in the bargain range, Jandó's Naxos version (8.550202) includes an extra concerto (K.467) instead of the *Rondo*.

Piano Concertos 13, K.415; 20, K.466

(*) DG **DVD 073 4129. Uchida, Camerata Salzburg (Director: Horant Hohlfield) (includes Documentary featuring Uchida)

These are live performances, directed spontaneously by Uchida from the piano keyboard against the handsome backcloth of the Salzburg Mozarteum, in which the acoustic of this comparatively small hall provides excellent sound-quality and a good balance. The snag is that, while Uchida has a wonderful smile, when she begins to direct ('conduct' is hardly the word) the orchestra in the long orchestral introduction of K.415, her rather vague arm gestures are accompanied by facial grimaces which are not attractive to watch. Presumably they have the desired effect on the orchestra, who play very well indeed, although it is obvious that the musical detail and dynamics have been put in place earlier, at rehearsal. However, musically this C major performance is successful and enjoyable, if not perhaps really distinctive. The *D minor*, however, is more arresting, from the dark-hued opening onwards, and, when she is in dramatic mode, Uchida is much easier to watch during the orchestral tuttis, as she is in the solo cadenzas. The pellucid central *Romance*, simply and sensitively phrased, then brings plenty of contrast in the middle section, and the finale closes the work vigorously and spiritedly, and with a particularly attractive, artlessly managed coda. But in drama, this account does not match that of Martin Stadtfeld on CD (see below). However, the audience is very impressed, and the camera, having followed her throughout, is reluctant to leave before she has taken many bows; yet she does not respond to their enthusiasm and provide the encore they were obviously expecting.

Piano Concertos 13, K.425; 23, K.488

(M) (**) EMI mono 5 62823-2 [5 62824-2]. Michelangeli, Alessandro Scarlatti O, Caracciolo – HAYDN: *Piano Concerto 11* **

Immaculate pianism from Michelangeli, of course, but the playing in the *C major Concerto* seems a little studied, with some curious accenting. However, the simplicity of his approach in the *A major Concerto* brings its own rewards, and if the *Adagio* is a trifle cool the finale has an attractive rhythmic lift, thanks at least in part to Franco Caracciolo's contribution with the Alessandro Scarlatti Orchestra. Good, faithful, mono recording.

Piano Concertos 15 in B flat, K.450; 23 in A, K.488

(BB) **(*) Arte Nova 82876 64014-2. Kirschnereit, Bamberg SO, Bermann

The *B flat Concerto* is one of the finest performances so far in Matthias Kirschnereit's Bamberg cycle. The opening movement is attractively spirited and robust (in the latter respect different from a Uchida performance), while the central theme and variations is played with warmth and elegance and the bouncing finale is highly infectious. The first movement of the *A major*, too, is fresh and strong rather than mellow, but the lovely *Adagio*, taken very gently and slowly, makes the fullest contrast; and the finale again sparkles, with attractive woodwind detail, yet with no lack of weight. Throughout, Frank Bermann provides a vivid orchestral profile and, with a realistic balance (although the piano is quite close), this coupling is most enjoyable for its vitality.

Piano Concerto 16 in D, K.451

(M) *(*) DG 474 328-2 (2). Serkin, COE, Abbado – BEETHOVEN: *Piano Sonatas 30–32* **; BRAHMS: *Cello Sonata 1* ***

Rudolf Serkin's digital recordings of the Mozart piano concertos for DG in the 1980s showed a sad decline in his pianism. Those who are prepared to accept prosaic playing for the sake of the musical insights that do emerge will have no quarrel with this issue technically, recorded when the pianist was in his early eighties.

Piano Concertos 17 in G, K.453; 20 in D min., K.466

⊕→ *** Virgin 3 44696-2. Anderszewski, Scottish CO

This is one of the finest Mozart concerto couplings of the year. As we have seen from his other recordings, Piotr Anderszewski is an artist whose approach to music-making is fresh yet well thought out, sensitive, touched by distinction and without the slightest trace of fussiness or preciosity. There is a blend of musical imagination and pianistic finesse that makes this unfailingly illuminating. Those who have cherished Edwin Fischer and Perahia in the *G major* or Curzon and Casadesus in the *D minor* will find that this newcomer can be mentioned in their company, which is no mean compliment, although the other dramatic new version of K.466 from Martin Stadtfeld should also be considered – see below.

Piano Concertos 18, K.456; 20, K.466

(BB) **(*) Arte Nova 74321 80784-2. Kirschnereit, Bamberg SO, Bermann

The second volume in Kirschnereit's cycle, with the coupling of the *B flat* and *D minor Concertos*, once again shows him to be a Mozartian of no mean order. Well worth the cost, though not a first choice in either work.

(i; ii) *Piano Concerto 19, K.459;* **(i; ii; iii)** *Double Piano Concerto in E flat, K.365;* **(i; iv)** *Triple Piano Concerto in F, K.242*

(BB) *(*) EMI Encore (ADD) 5 854546-2. (i) Hephzibah Menuhin, (ii) Bath Festival O; (iii) Fou Ts'ong ; (iv) Yaltah & Jeremy Menuhin, LPO; all cond. Yehudi Menuhin

This family compilation from the 1960s is something of a disappointment. Hephzibah's performance of the *F major solo Concerto* is heavy-handed, her playing marred by some insensitive phrasing, and this cannot compare with other recommended versions. The *Double* and *Triple Concertos* are somewhat more successful, yet it is surprising that there is not more of a conveyed sense of enjoyment and high spirits. The playing is quite polished, but the *E flat Concerto* is careful rather than spontaneous, and K.242, not one of Mozart's best works, also lacks sparkle.

Piano Concertos 19–23

(B) **(*) Ph. Duo 468 540-2 (2). Uchida, ECO, Tate

As we have said when discussing her more complete survey, above, these are performances of grace and beauty, most naturally recorded. But on the highest level their degree of reticence – despite the superb orchestral work of the ECO under Tate – makes them at times less memorable than the very finest versions. The *F major* (No. 19) (here unfortunately divided over the two discs) is certainly very successful, with plenty of flowing lyrical momentum in outer movements, a thoughtful *Adagio* and light-hearted finale. Nos. 20 and 21, with which she began her cycle, also provides much cultivated pleasure. But her thoughtful manner is shown at its very finest in Nos. 22 *in E flat*, K.482, and its immediate successor, the beautiful *A major*, K.488. In balance, fidelity and sense of presence, few recordings can surpass these accounts, with outstanding playing from the ECO and its excellent wind soloists.

Piano Concertos 19 in F, K.459; 21 in C, K.467

(BB) **(*) Arte Nova 74321 87147-2. Kirschnereit, Bamberg SO, Bermann

Sprightly performances in Volume 3. Even in a competitive environment, Matthias Kirschnereit can hold his head high – though, given the distinction of so many rival versions, his coupling cannot be a primary recommendation. However, those who do invest in it will not be disappointed. Excellent recording, as in the earlier discs in the series.

Piano Concertos 19, K.459; 23, K.488

(*) DG **DVD 073 4097. Pollini, VPO, Boehm – BEETHOVEN: *Piano Concertos 3 & 5;* BRAHMS: *Piano Concerto 1* **(*)

Pollini's Mozart always has style and pianistic distinction, and Böhm was a wonderful Mozartian. These recordings were made at the Musikvereinssaal in April 1976 and the video direction of Hugo Käch is eminently discreet and unobtrusive, while the sound-balance by Günther Hermanns is exemplary. Together with the *Brahms B flat Concerto* they occupy the second DVD in this package, the two Beethoven concertos being accommodated on the first. It is difficult to find fault with playing of this distinction and dedication, shorn as it is of any expressive exaggeration, but it is not always possible to warm to it. There is no want of pianistic or

orchestral beauty, but there is an aloof quality to which not everyone will respond.

Piano Concerto 20 in D min., K.466

(M) (***) Westminster mono 471 214-2. Haskil, Winterthur SO, Swoboda – D. SCARLATTI: *Sonatas.* (**)

The Westminster Legacy series that DG is now issuing is not specific on this occasion in giving recording details, apart from the year. This fine 1951 performance is not to be confused with the slightly later recording Haskil made with Bernhard Paumgartner and the Wiener Symphoniker in 1954, both in mono, which was included in the Philips 'Clara Haskil Legacy'. Although the Winterthur orchestra was not the equal of the Vienna orchestra, it plays very well for Henry Swoboda, and the technical refurbishment here is really rather impressive. The sound naturally lacks the transparency of detail you find in early stereo, but it is very much more vivid than we remember.

Piano Concertos 20, K.466; 21 in C, K.467

(BB) ** EMI Encore 5 74576-2. Zacharias, Bav. RSO, Zinman

Christian Zacharias is a much-admired Mozartian in Germany. He is an artist of strong classical instinct, although less impressive in the variety and subtlety of keyboard colour he has at his command. These performances are thoroughly acceptable, but neither account challenges existing recommendations.

Piano Concertos 20, K.466; 23, K.488

**(*) Häns. CD 98.142. Moravec, ASMF, Marriner

Ivan Moravec gives fresh, thoughtful readings which never get in the way of Mozart, and Marriner and the Academy match him with playing of similar refinement. The *Romance* of the *D minor Concerto* and the *Adagio* of the *A major* are both on the slow side, sounding a little sluggish next to the outstanding performances of the same concertos with Howard Shelley as soloist-director, on Chandos. That also has a price advantage.

Piano Concertos 20, K.466; 24, K.491

⊙– *** Sony 82876 73714-2. Stadtfeld, NDR SO, Weil

(B) **(*) Virgin 4 82124-2. Pletnev, Deutsche Kammerphilharmonie

(i) *Piano Concertos 20 in D min., K.466; 24 in C min., K.491.* *Piano Sonata in C, K.545*

(BB) *** HMV (ADD) 5 86738-2. Barenboim; (i) with ECO

A superb disc. The prize-winning German pianist, Martin Stadtfeld, gives electrifying accounts of both these concertos in a true partnership with Bruno Weil and the North German Symphony Orchestra. Both concertos here have darkly dramatic openings, the *C minor* work especially so, and Weil brings out their tragic feeling with orchestral tuttis of great power and tempi which carry the music strongly forward. When Stadtfeld enters in K.491, the tension is maintained, yet the secondary theme emerges with true Mozartian lyricism. At the end of the first movement he plays a subjective and musing cadenza of his own, slowing the tempo right down, which some may feel is intrusive. But the performance has such conviction and character that it is easy to forgive this indulgence which would be fully acceptable at a concert. The *Larghetto* has an appealing simplicity, while the mood of the finale is perfectly judged.

Similarly, after the commanding first movement, the central Romance of the *D minor* is not prettified; it does not dawdle either, and the central section is boldly contrasted. Stadtfeld uses Beethoven's cadenzas in both the outer movements, which adds to the strength of the performance without imposing Beethoven's spirit on Mozart's. The recording is of the highest quality, and this is one of the most stimulating Mozart concerto couplings in the catalogue, very far removed from, say, Uchida's performances.

Barenboim's account of *No. 20 in D minor* was the first of his EMI Mozart concerto recordings with the ECO, recorded in 1967, and it remains one of his finest. The playing has all the sparkle and sensitivity one could ask for; the orchestral accompaniment too is admirably alive, and one's only serious reservation lies in the tempo he adopts in the finale. K.491 brings a more controversial performance; the very first entry of the piano shows to what a degree Barenboim wants to make it a romantic work. His conviction is unfailing, but some may find the first two movements too heavily dramatized for their taste, while the finale is compensatingly fast and hectic. The digital remastering matches the performances, with the upper range of the orchestra vividly bright, but the piano timbre remaining natural. The familiar *C major Sonata* is admirably played, the element of toughness in Barenboim's reading minimizing its 'eighteenth-century drawing-room' associations.

Pletnev and the Deutsche Kammerphilharmonie obviously established a close rapport in the 1990s when these recordings were made, and there is great personality here – whether you like everything about it or not. The opening of the *D minor Concerto* brings explosive accents in the orchestra and, in the *C minor Concerto* too, Pletnev is intensely dramatic, Beethovenian in feeling and powerful in conception: his own first-movement cadenza looks even more forward into the nineteenth century. In the *D minor* he actually uses Beethoven's cadenza, and again in the outer movements the impetus is very bold and strong, though the famous *Romanze* does not bely its title and brings contrasting delicacy. Overall there is nothing bland here: commanding playing but not to all tastes.

(i) *Piano Concerto 20 in D min., K.466. Divertimento* (for small orchestra) *1 in E flat, K.113; Symphony 41 (Jupiter)*
(*) EuroArts **DVD 2055088. (i) Vladar; C. P. E. Bach CO, Haenchen

The *Divertimento* is a comparatively large-scale performance and, though elegant, is somewhat inflated by the warm acoustic of the Berlin Konzerthaus, although it is beautifully played. The concerto and symphony have the flowing adrenalin of a live occasion; indeed, the opening movement of the concerto has all the dark atmosphere and drama you could wish for. Stefan Vladar is an excellent soloist: there is no suggestion of Dresden china in the slow movement, and the finale is vivacious. The *Jupiter Symphony*, too, is given a commanding performance, vital through and through, and with a beautifully played *Andante*. However, while the first-movement exposition repeat is observed, the repeats in the finale are not, so that, while the performance builds to an exciting climax, the full, expansive weight of the movement is unrealized.

(i) *Piano Concertos 21 in C, K.467; 23 in A, K.488. 12 Variations on 'Ah vous dirai-je maman'*
(BB) *** HMV (ADD) 5. 86740-2. Barenboim; (i) with ECO
Piano Concertos 22 in E flat, K.482; 23 in A, K.488
(BB) *** EMI Encore (ADD) 5 86982-2 [5 86983-2].
Barenboim, ECO

As can be seen here, the much-loved *A major Concerto* comes with a choice of coupling. Barenboim's performance of No. 23 is enchanting. If there are moments when his delicacy of fingerwork comes close to preciousness, it never goes over the edge. There also need be no reservations about Barenboim's account of the other top favourite concerto, K.467 (with its *Elvira Madigan* associations), which is accomplished in every way. In K.482 he is again very persuasive, if at times wilful, relishing its expansiveness with dozens of spontaneous-sounding inflexions. So choice between these two discs will depend on the coupling required. The familiar *Variations* make an added enticement on the first disc. Good remastered sound, full, firm and clear.

Piano Concertos 21 in C, K.467; 25 in C, K.503
⊕ (M) *** Ph. 476 5316. Kovacevich, LSO, C. Davis

The partnership of Kovacevich and Davis almost inevitably produces inspired music-making. Their balancing of strength and charm, drama and tenderness, makes for performances which retain their sense of spontaneity, but which plainly result from deep thought; and the weight of both these great C major works is formidably conveyed. The 1972 recording, well balanced and refined, has been newly remastered for this Universal reissue in the 'Penguin Rosette Collection'.

Piano Concertos 23, K.488; 26 (Coronation), K.537
(BB) **(*) Warner Apex 8573 89091-2. Gulda, Concg. O, Harnoncourt

Gulda discreetly participates in the orchestra ritornelli. The playing of the Concertgebouw Orchestra is careful in handling both balances and nuances, and Harnoncourt is particularly successful in his direction of the *Coronation Concerto*. Gulda gives an admirably unaffected and intelligent account of the *A major*, which is most enjoyable (as is his reading of the *Coronation*) but it does not constitute a challenge to players such as Ashkenazy, Brendel or Perahia in K.488.

Piano Concertos (i) *24, K.491;* (ii) *27, K.595*
(M) (**) Orfeo mono C 536001B. Casadesus, VPO, with (i) Mitropoulos; (ii) Schuricht

Any reminder of Casadesus's artistry is to be welcomed: his stature as a Mozartian was unquestioned, and his concerto recordings with Georg Szell were legendary in their day. The value of the present issue is somewhat diminished, however, by the inferior quality of the Austrian Radio recordings. The *C minor*, K.491, with Mitropoulos at the helm of the Vienna Philharmonic, comes from a Salzburg Festival performance in 1956 but sounds thin and shallow, almost as if it had been made on a domestic tape recorder. The *B flat*, K.595, made in 1961 with Schuricht, is better, but only marginally so. Casadesus is on characteristically good form in both works, but the disc's sonic limitations call for much tolerance.

Piano Concertos 25, K.503; 26, K.537
(**) Testament mono SBT1301. Gulda, New SO, Collins –
BEETHOVEN: (with *Piano Sonata 22* **)

When these 1955 performances first appeared on the mono Decca LXT label, there were still one or two gaps in the Mozart concerto discography, a fact which younger readers who take complete editions for granted may find it difficult to grasp. There was only one version of K.415 and none of K.451, and in these concertos only five alternative LPs. Friedrich Gulda enjoyed quite a vogue in the early 1950s, though his subsequent attention-seeking eccentricities did nothing to enhance his career. These are generally very straight performances, enlivened by moments of poetry, and Anthony Collins is admirably supportive. Few allowances need be made for the sound.

(i) *Piano Concerto 26, K.537;* (ii) *Concert Rondos for Piano and Orchestra 1 in D, K.382; 2 in A, K.386;* (i; iii) *Double Piano Concerto in E flat, K.365*

(M) (**(*)) DG mono 474 611-2. Seeman, (i) BPO; (ii) Bamberg SO; (iii) with Foldes

These mono recordings date from the early 1950s and were originally reviewed by us in the very first *Penguin Guide to Bargain Records.* About the solo concertos we said: 'An outstanding *Coronation,* with well-rounded piano tone in proportion to the work and its accompaniment.' Carl Seeman brings freshness and clarity to the finale especially and the *Concert Rondo in D major,* written to replace the rondo of an early D major concerto, is a treasure. If anything, the *A major Rondo* added here is even more elegant. Seeman's style is precise but totally Mozartian.

About the *E flat Double Concerto* (differently coupled on its original issue) we had more reservations concerning the orchestral accompaniment, but suggested that 'the pianists play it with enthusiasm and a high degree of competence'. It is perhaps a little humourless, but the finale is infectious. The recording of the pianos remains excellent; the orchestral sound is a little rougher here.

Violin concertos

Violin Concertos 1–5; Adagio in E, K.261; Rondo in C, K.373; Rondo Concertante in B flat, K.269

(B) **(*) EMI double forte 5 69355-2 (2). Zimmermann, Württemberg CO, Faerber

Violin Concertos 1–5; Adagio in E, K.261; Rondo, K.373

(B) **(*) Sony (ADD) SBK 46539/40. Zukerman, St Paul CO

Violin Concertos 1–5; Serenade in D (Haffner): Andante, Minuet & Rondo, K.250

(BB) **(*) Arte Nova 74321 72104-2 (2). Frank, Zurich Tonhalle O, Zinman

Violin Concertos 1–5; (i) *Sinfonia concertante for Violin, Viola & Orchestra, K.364*

*** DG DVD 073 4157 (2). Kremer, VPO, Harnoncourt; (i) with Kashkashian (V/D: Klaus Lindemann, Rodney Greenberg or Horant Hohfeld)

An outstanding DVD set in every respect. This is a case where watching the artists against the beautiful backcloth of Vienna's Grosser Musikvereinsaal and experiencing their direct communication adds greatly to the musical enjoyment. Gidon Kremer unites exceptionally well with the wild-eyed but visibly involved Nikolaus Harnoncourt and, with the Vienna Philharmonic playing superbly, this is exceptionally vivid music-making. The solo concertos are played simply and stylishly, but Harnoncourt's always alive and richly expressive accompaniments give the music-making the kind of lift which ensures that Kremer's playing never slips into routine.

But the highlight of the set is Mozart's masterly *Sinfonia concertante,* where Kim Kashkashian joins the partnership and adds to the intensity of feeling. She has a glorious tone and the interplay between the soloists in the slow movement is ravishing, followed by the gloriously infectious finale. She is fascinating to observe, as she watches her solo partner

closely and appears to let him lead, yet the viola response has its own individuality. The recording is splendidly balanced, the ear and eye especially taken by the contributions of the pairs of horns and oboes in the orchestra. Highly recommended.

Zukerman's set has the advantage of excellent digital recording and a good balance, the violin forward but not distractingly so. The playing of outer movements is agreeably simple and fresh, and in slow movements Zukerman's sweetness of tone will appeal to many, although his tendency to languish a little in his expressiveness, particularly in the G *major,* K.216, rather less so in the *A major,* K.219, may be counted a less attractive feature, and he is not always subtle in his expression of feeling. Nevertheless this is still enjoyably spontaneous and his admirers will certainly not be disappointed with K.219.

Frank Peter Zimmermann is also most impressive. His interpretations do not quite match those of Grumiaux (with whom, at the price, he comes into direct competition) or Perlman; but they are distinguished by fine musicianship and an effortless technical command. Zimmermann uses cadenzas by Zukerman and Oistrakh in No. 2 and Joachim in No. 4. The digital recordings have agreeable warmth and freshness and are very well balanced. Jörg Faerber is an excellent partner and gets extremely alive playing from the Württemberg orchestra. Not a first recommendation then, but certainly worth considering,

The young American violinist Pamela Frank is a strong, imaginative artist, very well matched here by the Tonhalle Orchestra under David Zinman, who shows himself just as inspired an interpreter of Mozart as he is of Beethoven. Outer movements are fresh and bright at speeds on the urgent side, while slow movements are spaciously expressive without sentimentality. As a super-bargain purchase, the two discs can be recommended, even if Frank's tone and the coloration she gives to the upper register are not ideally sweet and pure. First-rate sound. The three concertante movements from the *Haffner Serenade* provide an original and apt makeweight.

Violin Concertos 1–5; 6, K.268; 7, K.271a; in D (Adelaide; harmonized & orch. Marius Casadesus), K.Anh.294a; (i) *Concertone in C for 2 Violins, Oboe, Cello & Orchestra, K.190. Divertimento 15 in B flat, K.287; Serenade 7 in D (Haffner): 2nd–4th movements only;* (ii) *Sinfonia concertante for Violin, Viola & Orchestra in E flat, K.364*

(BB) ** EMI 5 85030-2 (5). Yehudi Menuhin, Bath Festival O, or Menuhin Festival O (K.271a & K.Anh. 294a); with (i) Lysy, Dobson, Simpson; (ii) Barshai

These recordings nearly all date from the early 1960s, although K.271a and the so-called 'Adelaide' Concerto were added a decade later, and the sound is fuller in consequence. This particular pairing is apt, for each is of doubtful origin, though both Blüme and Einstein suggest that No. 7 is largely the work of Mozart. It seems likely that he began it, lost interest in it and left it for someone else to finish off. Menuhin is just the artist to give these works persuasive performances, also inspiring his Festival Orchestra to accompany him with an infectious spring. Fascinatingly he uses cadenzas by Enescu in No. 7 and by Hindemith in the *Adelaide.* No. 6 is almost certainly the work of another composer, but if it is accepted by the listener simply as a late-eighteenth-century work of better than average quality, the music is agreeable enough, and Menuhin's affectionate warmth makes the most of it.

In the *Concertone* Mozart put his own fingerprint on the

oboe part, which, in Michael Dobson's expert hands, has nearly as much to offer the listener as the contribution from the two solo string players. The snag is that the remastering does not flatter the original recordings. Throughout the stereo has a bright sheen and the orchestral violins are made to sound thin and glassy above the stave.

For the *Divertimento* Menuhin uses a chamber orchestra rather than a chamber ensemble, yet the group is of Mozartian size and cannot be faulted in terms of style; and Menuhin makes a good job of the demanding solo fiddle section in the *Theme and Variations*. The performance is responsive and spontaneous, and the recorded sound is more agreeable than in the concertos. In the *Sinfonia concertante* again the transfer does not flatter the orchestral strings. The inclusion of only the three concertante movements (the second-movement Andante, followed by the Minuet and Trio and Rondo) from the *Haffner Serenade* makes for a curious omission, particularly as Menuhin successfully recorded the whole work, and the fifth disc, on which these excerpts appear, plays for only 57 minutes. Nevertheless, at bargain price this set might be worth considering for the three rare works of doubtful lineage. But it is a pity that the transfers were not better managed.

Violin Concertos 3 in G, K.216; 4 in D, K.218; 5 in A (Turkish), K.219
(BB) *** Virgin 4 82122-2. Tetzlaff, Deutsche Kammerphilharmonie

Christian Tetzlaff is a first-class player and a fine Mozartian. He has recorded all five concertos with great freshness, and he simultaneously directs the Deutsche Kammerphilharmonie in polished and sympathetic accompaniments. His pacing of allegros is brisk, but exhilaratingly so, and his expressive phrasing in slow movements matches the clean, positive style of his contribution to faster movements. The performances seem to get better as he works his way through the set, and this disc containing the last three works is highly recommendable, for the recording balance is excellent.

DIVERTIMENTI

Divertimenti and serenades

3 Divertimenti for Strings, K.136–8; Serenade 6 (Serenata notturna), K.239
(B) ** HM HMX 2961809. Freiburg Bar. O, Müllegans

We are great admirers of the Freiburg Baroque Orchestra (especially their DVD of the Bach *Brandenburgs*) but this beautifully packaged CD is a disappointment. In the *Serenata notturna* the timpani, played with hard sticks, dominate the music and soon become intrusive; the *Divertimenti*, although scrupulously played with undoubted finesse, are almost entirely lacking in charm, while the *Andante* which opens K.137 is over-dramatized.

Divertimento 1 in D, K.236; Serenade in D (Serenata notturna), K.239; Serenade in D (Posthorn), K.328
(BB) *** Virgin 2x1 4 82112-2 (2). Lausanne CO, Y. Menuhin
  – SCHOENBERG: *Verklaerte Nacht*; WAGNER: *Siegfried Idyll*; WOLF: *Italian Serenade* ***

An exceptionally attractive anthology of what is all essentially string music. The little *Divertimento* sparkles in Menuhin's hands and the *Serenades* are equally light-hearted and fresh, with Crispian Steele-Perkins in his element in his brief appearance in the Minuet of the *Posthorn Serenade*.

Divertimento 10 in F, K.247; Serenades 9 (Serenata notturna); 13 (Eine kleine Nachtmusik)
(BB) ** Naxos 8.557023. Swedish CO, Sundkvist

This is a curious mixture, but it is well – indeed, strongly – played by this excellent Swedish modern-instrument chamber orchestra, so that the balance with the timpani in the *Serenata notturna* is successful enough. In *Eine kleine Nachtmusik*, near the opening, a curving two-note phrase is fractionally held in a brief tenuto, and this might become irritating on repetition, but probably not; and otherwise the performances are unidiosyncratic, except that the *Adagio* of K.247 seems self-consciously slow. Good recording and enjoyably lively music-making; but there are more distinctive versions of all these pieces.

Divertimento 11 in D, K.251; A Musical Joke, K.522; Serenade 13 (Eine kleine Nachtmusik)
(M) ** Warner Elatus 2564 0123-2. VCM, Harnoncourt

Harnoncourt, it seems, cannot help parading his eccentricities, even in this music intended merely to divert. *Eine kleine Nachtmusik* is straightforward enough until the Minuet, which is taken faster than a Mozartian *Allegretto* and is then slowed down for the Trio, spoiling the intended contrast with the comparatively imperturbable finale. The *Molto allegro* which opens the *Divertimento* is taken literally – very fast and gruff – and the *Rondeau* and final *Marcia* also call for a lighter, more humorous touch. Not surprisingly, the *Musical Joke* is heavy going, that is until the horns, who bray forcefully elsewhere, play their wrong notes in the Minuet's Trio gently and reluctantly. The *Adagio*, apart from more bold accents, is comparatively elegant in its straying from the primrose path, but the closing *Presto*, although there is much deft string articulation, has a coarse vigour and a cacophanous close. For Harnoncourt aficionados only!

A Musical Joke, K.522; Notturno in D for 4 Orchestras, K.286; Serenade 9 (Serenata notturna); 13 (Eine kleine Nachtmusik)
●→ ✿ *** Alia Vox **SACD** Surround Sound AVSA 9846. Le Concert des Nations, Savall

An outstanding disc in every way, which includes (by the grace of SACD) the first really convincing recorded performance of the *Notturno for Four Orchestras*, scored for four separate groups, each consisting of first and second violins, viola and double bass, plus a pair of horns. Mozart left the first group unnamed, but called the others 'Echo Primo', 'Echo Duo' and 'Echo Trio', and the music is written so that the first orchestra announces each theme and the others repeat it in increasingly brief and shortened echoes, while it is the resonant horns that bring the remarkable atmospheric effects.

Decca made a surprisingly successful attempt to record the work with the LSO under Peter Maag in the early days of stereo, so that the left–right placing was helped out by a forward–backward placement to suggest Mozart's four groups. That is what happens if you replay the present SACD disc on ordinary stereo equipment. But with SACD surround sound, the effect is greatly enhanced and would surely have brought a twinkle of pleasure to Mozart's eye if he could have heard it.

Musically it is a very fine performance, as indeed is the *Musical Joke*, played deadpan so that the jokey dissonances are all the more arresting, and they certainly raise a smile in the closing *Presto*, when Mozart creates a hair-raising parody on the finale of his *Piano Concerto No. 19*, K.450. The performance of *Eine kleine Nachtmusik* is also refreshingly spirited and eloquent, with the use of one instrument to a part producing a pleasingly full texture; while in the equally successful *Serenata notturna* the balance with the timpani are splendidly managed, so that they outline the music without drowning it. With first-class recording and excellent documentation, this is one of the most imaginatively devised of all the new CDs to reach us during the 250th anniversary year.

Overtures: *Bastien und Bastienne; La clemenza di Tito; Così fan tutte; Don Giovanni; Die Entführung aus dem Serail; La finta giardiniera; Idomeneo; Lucio Silla; Le nozze di Figaro; Il re pastore; Der Schauspieldirektor; Die Zauberflöte*
(M) *** RCA 82876 76235-2. Dresden State O, C. Davis

A self-recommending set of Mozart overtures from Colin Davis here reappears in RCA's 'Classic Library' series at mid-price. They are thoroughly musical and have both drama and warmth, with much felicity of orchestral detail emerging from the superb Dresden orchestra throughout the programme. Davis perfectly balances the full weight of the dramatic moments with the sparkle of the lighter ones, and the dynamic contrasts are very well judged. The recording is good. If occasionally the tuttis can seem a little bass-heavy because of the resonant Dresden acoustic, this is not a serious problem, and anyone wanting a budget collection of Mozart overtures on modern instruments in digital sound cannot go far wrong here.

Serenades

Serenades 6 in D (Serenata notturna), K.239; 7 in D (Haffner), K.250
(BB) **(*) Warner Apex 2564 60712-2. Amsterdam Bar. O, Koopman

Koopman's account of the *Haffner* is bold and his accents robust, especially in Minuets; indeed, the energetic timpani are little short of explosive. But he has an excellent violin soloist in Pavlo Beznosiuk, and he ensures that the delectable *moto perpetuo* sparkles daintily. The extra transparency means that detail registers throughout. The timpani again come through strongly but cleanly in the *Serenata notturna* and they tend to dominate aurally, but the string playing remains elegantly turned.

Serenades 6 (Serenata notturna); 13 (Eine kleine Nachtmusik); Serenade for Wind 12, K.388
(M) **(*) DG (IMS) 439 524-2. Orpheus CO

The *Serenata notturna*, which can easily sound bland, has a fine sparkle here. The famous *Night Music*, however, is rather lacking in charm, with a very brisk opening movement, alert enough and very polished, but somewhat unbending. The *Wind Serenade* restores the balance of excellence, alert and sympathetic and full of character. The digital recording is first class throughout.

(i) Serenade 7 in D (Haffner); (ii) Wind Divertimento in B flat, K.186
(M) ** DG Eloquence 469 755-2. (i) Brandis, BPO, Boehm; (ii) VPO Wind Soloists

The Berlin Philharmonic plays with such polish and refinement of tone in a well-balanced (1972) recording (agreeably freshened in this remastering), with Thomas Brandis a fine soloist, that one is inclined to overlook a certain dourness on the part of Boehm. In the last analysis he is a shade wanting in sparkle and a sense of conveyed enjoyment. On the other hand, the playing of the Vienna Philharmonic Wind Ensemble is stylish, full of sparkle and wit, and the mid-1970s recording is first class.

Serenade 10 in B flat for 13 wind instruments (Gran Partita), K.361
(M) **(*) Telarc CD 80359. St Luke's O (members), Mackerras

Serenade 10 for 13 Wind Instruments, K.361; Divertimento in F, K.213
(M) **(*) Chan. 6575. SNO Wind Ens., P. Järvi

Sir Charles Mackerras has already given us fine recordings of the *Haffner* and *Posthorn Serenades* with the Prague Chamber Orchestra, and here he turns, with equal success, to an excellent group of players from Purchase, New York. They play expertly together, with good ensemble. The performance is warm and relaxed above all, with the penultimate set of variations particularly colourful and chirpy, and the closing *Rondo* (which Mozart marks *Allegro molto*) by contrast rumbustiously exhilarating. Excellent Telarc recording but, at 50 minutes 37 seconds, a coupling should surely have been added, even at mid-price.

The SNO Wind Ensemble's version under Paavo Järvi is enjoyably spontaneous-sounding, though ensemble is not quite as polished as in the finest versions. Speeds are well chosen, and the recording is warm, though the detail is sometimes masked by the lively acoustic. The little *Divertimento* makes an attractive bonus.

Serenades (i) 10 in B flat (Gran Partita); (ii) 12 in C min., K.388
(B) ** DG Eloquence (ADD) 469 763-2. (i) BPO Wind Ens., Boehm; (ii) Vienna Wind Soloists

The playing of the Berlin Philharmonic wind under Karl Boehm shows impeccable refinement, but the recording (from the early 1970s) though pleasing is not ideally detailed. The Vienna Wind are less perfectly blended; the oboe is thinner and reedier than one would like, though the clarinet is silky and rich in tone. Both these performances give pleasure, but neither is a first choice.

Serenades 10 (Gran Partita), K.361; 13 (Eine kleine Nachtmusik)
(BB) (***) Naxos mono 8.110994. VPO, Furtwängler (with GLUCK: *Overture Alceste*. BPO)

Despite its celebrity, Furtwängler's 1947 recording of the great *B flat Wind Serenade* has been reissued only once before, on LP by the short-lived Unicorn label, and its reappearance now in this excellent transfer by Ward Marston could not be more welcome. It is a performance of enormous warmth, lightness of touch and tonal richness, which we have long treasured on the five original 78s. It is a reading of depth and, although the sonorities are at times weightier than we are used to nowadays, the phrasing of the Viennese players has enormous delicacy and grace. The *Eine kleine Nachtmusik* comes from 1949 and there is a bonus in the form of the Gluck *Alceste Overture*, one of the few wartime records Furtwängler made with the Berlin Philharmonic for the Telefunken label. A must.

Sinfonias Concertantes and Epistle Sonatas

Sinfonia concertante for Violin, Viola & Orchestra, K.364
(**(*)) Testament mono SBT 1157. Brainin, Schidlof, LMP, Blech – SCHUBERT: *String Quintet in C*. (**)

The Testament version of the *Sinfonia concertante* was recorded at Abbey Road in 1953. The studio recording, cleanly transferred, focuses the soloists sharply, giving warmth and body to the tone – exceptionally rich from Peter Schidlof on the viola. If the slow movement is a degree broad and heavy with Blech, the finale is jollier, at a marginally more relaxed tempo.

(i; ii) *Sinfonia concertante for Violin, Viola & Orchestra, K.364;* (iii) *Sinfonia concertante for Oboe, Clarinet, Horn, Bassoon & Orchestra, K.297b;* (i) *Violin Concerto 5 (Turkish), K.219; Divertimento for Strings, K.136; Serenade 13 (Eine kleine Nachtmusik); Symphony 29 in A, K.201*
(BB) ** Virgin 2x1 5 62212-2. (i) Warren-Green; (ii) Chase; (iii) Hunt, Collins, Thompson, Alexander; LCO

This inexpensive reissue offers an unfortunately chosen pairing. The performances of the two *Sinfonias concertantes* are highly recommendable. In K.364 Christopher Warren-Green and Roger Chase provide a characteristically vital account of Mozart's inspired work for violin and viola: speeds for fast movements are brisk but gain in freshness when they never sound rushed. In suitable contrast the *Andante* is slow and warmly expressive, yet without a trace of sentimentality. The coupling of K.297b is even more delectable, and it would be hard to imagine a more persuasive team of wind players than those here. Gordon Hunt and Michael Collins phrase with the kind of magic one would expect from a Beecham performance, and their partners, Michael Thompson (horn) and Meyrick Alexander (bassoon), are hardly less impressive. Both performances are very satisfying, with full-timbred sound from soloists and orchestra alike.

Unfortunately, the coupled collection comprising the *Violin Concerto, Divertimento, Serenade* and the *A major Symphony* was one of Warren-Green's rare disappointing records, made during his early tenure leading the London Chamber Orchestra. The playing is as polished as ever, but tempi are so brisk that the effect is at times almost perfunctory, particularly in the *Violin Concerto*, which is undoubtedly played brilliantly. EMI should reissue the *Sinfonias concertantes* separately.

Sinfonia concertante, K.297b
*** Warner 2564 621791-2. Saleh, Azmeh, Biron, Polyak, West-Eastern Divan O, Barenboim – BEETHOVEN: *Symphony 5* ***

With the brilliantly talented young players of the West-Eastern Divan Orchestra, both Arab and Israeli, Barenboim directs an unashamedly traditional reading of Mozart's concertante masterpiece, with a relative large body of strings. In this live recording, made in the Palestinian town of Ramallah, the buoyancy of the playing is firmly established in the opening orchestral tutti, bright and brisk. The four wind soloists enhance that impression in the resilience and fine co-ordination of their interplay, led by the outstanding oboist, Mohamed Saleh. The ebb and flow of their playing in their joint cadenza bears witness not just to intensive rehearsal but to their close mutual understanding. As to the finale, it could hardly be wittier in the delicious springing of rhythm in these sparkling variations. A delectable performance. Like the orchestra's first disc, this one is backed up by a documentary on DVD, this time issued separately (see the Concerts section).

Sonatas 1–17 (Epistle Sonatas)
** MDG 605 0298. Ullman, V. Concillium Mus., Angerer

The initiator of the *Epistle Sonatas* was Archbishop Colloredo, and he similarly dispensed with them in 1783, three years after Mozart had written the present group, replacing them in the Mass with sung gradual motets.

Mozart's works are for two violins, organ and bass continuo, except for K.278 (which opens the selection here) with cello, two oboes, two trumpets and timpani added, and K.263, which retains just the trumpets and cello. The last of the series, K.329, becomes in essence a single-movement organ concerto, scored for violins, cello, two oboes, two horns, two trumpets and timpani. But the rest are written simply and scored neatly, with the organ (here, as in the Naxos alternative recording) very much in the background. They are well played and recorded.

SYMPHONIES

Symphonies 1 in E flat, K.16; in F, K.19a; 4 in D, K.19; 5 in B flat, K.22; 6 in F, K.43; 7 in D, K.45; 7a (Alte Lambacher) in G, K.45a; in B flat, K.45b; 8 in D, K.48; 9 in C, K.73; 10 in G, K.74; in F, K.75; in F, K.76; in D, K.81; 11 in D, K.84; in D, K.95; in C, K.96; in D, K.97; in C, K.102; 12 in G, K.110; 13 in F, K.112; 14 in A, K.114; in D, K.120 & K.121; 15 in G, K.124; 16 in C, K.128; 17 in G, K.129; 18 in F, K.130; 19 in E flat, K.132; 20 in D, K.133; 21 in A, K.134; in D, K.161; 22 in C, K.162; 23 in D, K.181; 24 in B flat, K.182; 25 in G min., K.183; 26 in E flat, K.184; 27 in G, K.199; 28 in C, K.200; 29 in A, K.201; 30 in D, K.202; 31 in D (Paris), K.297; 32 in G, K.318; 33 in B flat, K.319; 34 in C, K.338; 35 in D (Haffner), K.385; 36 in C (Linz), K.425; 38 in D (Prague), K.504; 39 in E flat, K.543; 40 in G min., K.550; 41 in C (Jupiter), K.551
(BB) *** EMI 5 85589-2 (11). ECO, Tate

Jeffrey Tate's survey of the Mozart symphonies is one of the finest things he has done for the gramophone. Recorded over a long period, from 1984 to 2003, his inspiration remained constant. Tate jumped in at the deep end by starting with Nos. 40 and 41, and they remain very impressive accounts. In the *Jupiter*, the apt scale of the ECO fully allows the grandeur of the work to come out: on the one hand, it has the clarity of a chamber orchestra performance, but on the other, with trumpets and drums, its weight of expression never underplays the scale of the argument, which originally prompted the unauthorized nickname. In both symphonies, exposition repeats are observed in outer movements, particularly important in the *Jupiter* finale which, with its miraculous fugal writing, bears even greater argumentative weight than the first movement, a point firmly established by Tate.

The first three CDs in the boxed set are new recordings (2003) and concentrate on his earliest symphonies, including many of the unnumbered symphonies (here given supplementary numbers, 42–52). Some of the rarer unnumbered works are adaptations of early opera overtures, and all of them are colourful pieces. These early works are full of vitality (even if the authenticity of one or two of them is doubtful). Tate finds fresh exhilaration in these scores where the young Mozart was finding his feet, exploring possibilities all the time. There is a surprising variety in Mozart's invention, often pointing to his future brilliance in the opera house. In these earlier symphonies those who like a very plain approach may find Tate's elegant pointing in the slow movements excessive, but his keen imagination on detail, as well as over a broad span, consistently conveys the electricity of a live performance. From No. 25 onwards, itself very well done, Tate's detailed articulation and fine detail are always telling. In all these works, he provides a winning combination of affectionate manners, freshness and elegance. (By the way, the alternative movements, originally included in this middle batch of symphonies, have been excised on this bargain box release.)

Both the *Linz* and the *Prague* receive strong but elegant readings, bringing out the operatic overtones in the latter, not just in the *Don Giovanni*-like progressions in the slow introduction, but also in the power of the development section and in the wonder of the chromatic progressions in the slow movement, as well as the often surprising mixture of timbres. In the *Linz*, Tate is attractively individual, putting rather more emphasis on elegance and finding tenderness in the slow movement, taken (like the Adagio of the *Prague*) at a very measured speed.

The recordings are fresh and warm throughout this stimulating and enjoyable set, which is strongly recommended, especially at super-bargain price.

Symphonies: in D, K.97; Sinfonia in D (Overture & Introduction from 'Ascanio in Alba'), K.111; 15, K.124; Sinfonia in D, K.141a: Overture 'Il sogno di Scipione', K.126 & K.161/3; 16, K.162; 25 in G min., K.183; 26, K.184; 27, K.199; in D: Overture 'La finta giardiniera', K.196; Minuet & Trio in C, K.409/383

(B) ** DHM/BMG 82876 75736-2 (2). VCM, Harnoncourt

Although in each work he temporarily relents and provides flexibly lyrical slow movements for these mostly three-part symphonies, Harnoncourt is consistently forceful and gruff in outer movements. He includes the two *Sinfonias* which are in essence Italian overtures, to make his survey all-embracing. But it is in Mozart's first out-and-out masterpiece, *No. 25 in G minor*, that he at last provides a superb performance, with the first movement electrifying with its soaring horns, a delightful *Andante*, a bold Minuet, and with the horns returning spectacularly to outline the main theme of the finale. The closing Minuet and Trio, K.409, has the same fierce vigour and delicate string and woodwind playing to provide contrast. But, overall, vitality consistently triumphs over charm here. Wide-ranging recording, resonant but clear.

Symphonies: 1; 4; K.19a; 5; 6; Alte Lambacher, K.45a; 7, K.45; in F, K.42a; in B flat, K.45b; 8; 9 (with spoken introductions in German)

(B) ** DHM/BMG 82876 58706-2 (3). VCM, Harnoncourt
(Disc 3: Letters from Leopold, Wolfgang and Nannerl Mozart, read by Nikolaus, Maximilian and Laya Harnoncourt)

In a written introduction included with this set, Harnoncourt expresses his 'flabbergasted reaction' to these works, 'written by a child aged between eight and 12'. He then goes on to give clean, relatively uneccentric performances of strong character, combining energy and attack with elegance and warmth in these remarkable early works – although, as usual, his *fortissimos* are often gruff and rhythms boldly accentuated. On the first disc he makes the most of the wind scoring in the F major, K.19a, and the delicate muted strings of the *Andante* of the so-called 'Alte Lambacher', K.45a, and the woodwind colouring of the Minuet of K.43. The orchestral playing is excellent and the presentation handsome, but the snag is that the (separately cued) spoken introductions to each of the symphonies and the fascinating excerpts from the letters which take up disc three are all in German – with no translations included!

Symphonies 7a in G, K.45a (Alte Lambacher); in G (Neue Lambacher); 12 in G, K.110; 18 in F, K.130

*** Pentatone SACD PTC 5186 112. ASMF, Marriner

Symphonies 7 in D, K.45; 8 in D, K.48; 9 in C, K.73; 19 in E flat, K.132; Andante grazioso, K.132

*** Pentatone SACD PTC 5186 138. ASMF, Marriner

Symphonies 20 in D, K.133; 45 in D, K.95; 46 in C, K.96; 47 in D, K.97; 51 in D, K.196

*** Pentatone SACD PTC 5186 113. ASMF, Marriner

Marriner and the ASMF were at the top of their form in the early 1970s when they recorded these juvenile Mozart symphonies in London (in Brent Town Hall, Wembley) as part of what was to be a complete coverage of all the Mozart symphonies for the Philips Mozart Edition (reviewed in our main volume).

The Philips recordings have long been famous for their naturalness, and now we discover that they were originally 4-channel recordings; when heard in SACD format, with the back speakers properly balanced, the spatial effect of the sound is amazing. Marriner's survey has a splendid Mozartian vitality and yet has all the grace of Karl Boehm's early DG survey of the Mozart symphonies, yet with more freedom and sparkle. The Academy play with great style, warmth and polish, and the effect with such realistic sound is splendidly alive and vivid. These delightful recordings are thus given a wholly new lease of life. It has recently been confirmed that both the *Lambach Symphonies* were written in 1766 by Mozart *père* and *fils* when the latter was ten years old. Wolfgang then wrote K.45 alone, during a trip to Vienna in 1767/8, and K.48 at the end of 1768. But as in K.132, composed in Salzburg in 1772, that Mozart's true symphonic style emerges, and included here too is its alternative slow movement, a delightful *Andante grazioso*. The symphonies on the third disc also come from the 1770s, probably written during the teenage composer's visit to Italy: distinct Italian influences can be discovered in the writing. No. 51 is identical to the *Overture La finta giardiniera*, with an added finale. It is all delightful music, and especially rewarding when played with such grace and spontaneous feeling.

Symphonies 25 in G min., K.183; 26 in E flat, K.184; 28 in C, K.200; 29 in A, K.201; 35 (Haffner) in D, K.385; 36 (Linz) in C, K.425; 38 (Prague) in D, K.504; 39 in E flat, K.543; 40 in G min., K.550; 41 (Jupiter) in C, K.551

(B) ** Teldec 5046 68288-2 (4). Concg. O, Harnoncourt

Nikolaus Harnoncourt's Mozart, for all its merits, is nothing if not wilful. He made his survey of the later Mozart symphonies between 1983 and 1988, turning from conducting an ensemble of original instruments to the glory of the Concertgebouw Orchestra and establishing his personality immediately, with strong, even gruff accents, yet at times with an approach which (notably in slow movements, with speeds rather slower than usual) is relatively romantic in its expressiveness. He consistently secures fine playing, and the Teldec engineers reward him with bright, clear, yet resonant sound. However, the results overall are of mixed appeal. No. 25 is very purposeful indeed: it opens aggressively, but the lovely slow movement lacks serenity. The unsuppressed energy in the finale brings guttural tuttis.

The opening of No. 26 is comparably pungent, tuttis emphatic and heavy, and the first movement of No. 28 is more *Molto* than *Allegro spiritoso*. Although here the gentle, muted strings in the *Andante* are beautiful, there is a feeling of restlessness too. The last two movements are crisp and fast: the finale combines lightness of articulation and great energy. No. 29 brings erratic tempi and very bold contrasts in the first movement; in the slow movement there is the most delicate string-playing, but the steady momentum reduces the feeling of repose. The performance of the *Haffner* is refreshingly direct, certainly dramatic, marked by relative unforced tempi; but charm is somewhat missing. In the *Linz* Harnoncourt observes even more repeats than are marked in the regular scores, making it a more expansive work than usual. The *Prague* is generally very successful, superbly played, and Harnoncourt is very generous with repeats (it runs for 38 minutes). Tempi are again erratic in No. 39 (the Minuet is rushed), although the first movement of this symphony is well judged; *No. 40 in G minor* has an unsettled mood overall (hardly Mozartian), with the slow movement very brisk. The *Jupiter* offers superbly disciplined playing, although the results are on the heavy side and the inclusion of all repeats gives an overall playing time of nearly 42 minutes. Nevertheless, for those wanting to try Harnoncourt's way with Mozart, this inexpensive four-CD set, which includes four of the original six CDs in the series, is fair value.

Symphonies 25 in G min., K.183; 29 in A, K.201; 35 (Haffner) in D, K.385
** Australian Decca Eloquence (ADD) 476 7401. VPO, Kertész

These are very beautifully played performances in the pre-authentic-school manner, only occasionally sounding a little heavy by today's standards. The early-1970s sound is both rich and resonant, with plushness being this CD's overall characteristic.

Symphonies (i) 26 in E flat, K.184; 32 in G, K.318; (ii) 34 in C, K.338; 36 in C (Linz), K.425; 38 in D (Prague), K.504; (i) 39 in E flat, K.543; 40 in G min., K.550; 41 in C (Jupiter), K.551; (iii) Eine kleine Nachtmusik, K.525; Serenata notturna, K.239; (ii; iv) Requiem in D min., K.626
(M) (**) DG mono/stereo 477 5296 (8). Boehm, with (i) Concg. O; (ii) VPO; (iii) BPO; (iv) V. State Op. Ch. –
R. STRAUSS: *Orchestral works*; (**(*)) WEBER: *Overtures* (**)

There are some surprises here, for those who think Boehm will be heavy by modern standards will be amazed at how sprightly the opening movement of No. 26 (the earliest symphony here) is, as is the very operatic opening of No. 32. These (Philips) recordings date from 1955 and are in acceptable sound. Nos. 34, 36 and 38 derive from two Decca LXTs from 1954; the strings here are very toppy (the *Linz* sounds more dated than the other two), but the same vitality in the playing is to be found here, with lively *Allegros*, poised *Adagios*, the Minuets slower than we are used to today but hardly weighty, and the finales always enjoyable. The later symphonies with the Concertgebouw (Philips) have more manageable string-sound, even if they still lack richness and depth. Nos. 38, 40 & 41 receive good, honest performances without being inspired. The *Serenades* (1956) have slightly better sound and are relaxed and pleasing; even though they are slower than we are used to today, one enjoys, for example, the surprising lightness of touch in the finale of K.525, while the finale of K.239 is nicely pointed.

Symphonies 29–31 (Paris); 33–34; 38 (Prague); 39
(BB) *** EMI (ADD) Gemini 3 50917-2 (2). ECO, Barenboim
Symphonies 32; 35 (Haffner); 36 (Linz); 40 in G min.; 41 (Jupiter); Divertimento 7 in D, K.205; 2 Marches in D, K.335
(BB) *** EMI (ADD) Gemini 3 50922-3 (2). ECO, Barenboim
Barenboim's recordings were made at Abbey Road over a

five-year span, between 1966 and 1971. With fine rhythmic pointing and consistently imaginative phrasing, these performances certainly still have a place in the catalogue. Nos. 29 and 34 are particularly successful, and the *Paris* (No. 31) is also given an outstanding performance, the contrasts of mood in the first movement underlined and the finale taken at a hectic tempo that would have sounded breathless with players any less brilliant than those of the ECO. The *D major Serenade* also responds well to Barenboim's affectionate treatment, while the two *Marches* are attractively jaunty and colourful.

Symphonies 29; 35 (Haffner); 38; 39; 40; 41 (Jupiter)
(M) **(*) EMI (ADD) 3 45810 2 [3 45815-2]. Philh. O or New Philh. O, Klemperer

Klemperer's monumentally characterful recordings of the key Mozart symphonies still hold their place in the catalogue and probably deserve their position among EMI's 'Great Recordings of the Century', even if there are some reservations.

Symphonies 33 in B flat, K.319; 39 in E flat, K.543; Adagio & Fugue, K.546; Serenade 13 in G (Eine kleine Nachtmusik); Divertimento for Strings in D, K.334: Adagio; Overture 'Le nozze di Figaro'
(M) (***) EMI mono 4 76876-2. VPO, Karajan

These Mozart performances were recorded immediately after the war, thanks to the flair and initiative of Walter Legge. The *B flat Symphony* (No. 33) was committed to disc in 1946 and the great *E flat* (No. 39) in 1949, and were rightly hailed in their day for their lightness of touch and perfection of style. They still sound wonderfully fresh, and the recorded sound is still impressively balanced. A very desirable reissue.

Symphonies 33 in B flat, K.319; 39 in E flat, K.543; 40 in G min., K.550
** Australian Decca Eloquence (ADD) 476 7402. VPO, Kertész

Kertész (with the help of Decca) underlines the richness of the music in his Vienna Mozart recordings, and Nos. 33 & 39, recorded in the early 1960s, lack some of the sharp contrasts we are now used to in our more 'authentic' era. However, they are still enjoyable in their well-upholstered way. No. 40 was recorded in 1973, and Kertész's generally slow tempi again underline the richness of the music, with dramatic highlighting of dynamic contrast. Not top choices in this repertoire – many will prefer performances with more character – but good to hear again.

Symphonies (i) 34; (ii) 39; 41 (Jupiter)
**(*) Testament mono/stereo SBT 1092. (i) PO, (ii) RPO, Kempe

The Testament disc of Kempe in Mozart, very well transferred, offers 1956 stereo recordings of Nos. 39 and 41 previously unissued, as well as a 1955 mono account of No. 34. Though the results initially may seem smooth and soft-grained, the conductor's warmth and understanding magnetize the ear. No. 34 has an exhilarating account of the 6/8 finale. The only reservation is over the slowness of the minuets in Nos. 39 and 41.

Symphony 35 in D (Haffner), K.385
(BB) (**(*)) Naxos mono 8.110841. NYPO & NYSO, Toscanini – HAYDN: *Symphony 101* **(*)

Toscanini conducted the amalgamated New York Philharmonic and Symphony Orchestras from 1928 to 1936 (the NBC

Symphony was created specially for him in 1937). There is a wonderful sparkle about these 1929 records which, as older collectors will recall, served as classics of the pre- and immediate post-war gramophone. In keeping with the policy of presenting all issued takes of Toscanini's New York recordings, Mark Obert-Thorn includes an alternative take of the finale. Remarkably good sound, considering their age.

Symphonies 35 (Haffner); 40 in G min.; 41 in C (Jupiter)
(B) *** DG Entrée (ADD) 477 5008. VPO, Boehm

It is always good to return to Karl Boehm's slightly mellower Mozartian world (especially after a spoonful of Harnoncourt) and here we can do so in really good sound. The performance of the *Haffner*, which first appeared in 1981, not long before Boehm's death, is distinguished by finely groomed playing from the Vienna Philharmonic. It is a comparatively athletic performance, a little lacking in charm, but still compelling; and the balance is restored in Nos. 40 and 41, dating from four years earlier. Boehm had recorded the same coupling previously with the Berlin Philharmonic; but his Vienna versions, as well as being more vividly and immediately recorded, present more alert, more spontaneous-sounding performances. He takes a relatively measured view of the outer movements of the *G minor*, but the resilience of the playing rivets the attention and avoids any sort of squareness. As a reading, No. 41 is more sharply focused, but of course there are no exposition repeats which many count desirable in Mozart's most massive symphony. The transfers are of really excellent quality, clear and clean and not dated.

Symphony 36 in C (Linz), K.425
(M) ** BBC (ADD) BBCL 4055-2. LSO, Barbirolli – R.
  STRAUSS: Ein Heldenleben **

From Barbirolli a big-band performance in the old manner – and none the worse for that! However, it must be admitted that Sir John was not in his usual robust form when this concert was recorded, and there is not much evidence of the elegance and élan which distinguished his finest work.

(i) Symphony 36 in C (Linz), K.425; March 1 in C, K.408. Overtures: (ii) La Clemenza di Tito; (iii) Così fan tutte; Idomeneo; Le Nozze di Figaro; Die Zauberflöte; (i) Serenade 13 in G (Eine kleine Nachtmusik)
** Australian Decca Eloquence (ADD) 476 7403. (i) VPO; (ii) V. State Op. O; (iii) V. Haydn O; Kertész

Kertész's VPO performances date from 1964, but they lack the character and sparkle of the best; the opening movement of the *Linz* feels a bit too slow by today's standards, but the finale is lively enough, made enjoyable by the richly vivid sound. The overtures (recorded later) are well played and recorded – if, again, they lack the character to make them truly distinctive.

Symphonies 36 (Linz); 39; Overtures: Così fan tutte; Le nozze di Figaro
** Guild GMCD 7172. Bournemouth Sinf., Frazor

These Bournemouth performances of a pair of favourite symphonies offer a model combination of warmth, elegance and finesse, though there is drama too, especially when the timpani open No. 39 so boldly. The recording is most naturally balanced. The overtures are neatly done, though they could have a shade more sparkle. But this is an enjoyable

programme, showing the conductor and orchestra as natural Mozartians.

Symphonies 38 (Prague); 39 in E flat
(M) ** Warner Elatus 0927 49828-2. Concg. O, Harnoncourt

In the *Prague*, Harnoncourt plays every possible repeat (there are over 37 minutes in this performance) and, like the *Jupiter* below, the symphony originally occupied an LP to itself. However, the Concertgebouw playing has fine spontaneity and polish that are a pleasure to listen to, and the recording is excellent. No. 39 is more uneven: the first movement is well judged, but elsewhere tempi are erratic, and the Minuet is rushed. Here the sound is resonant but very bright.

Symphonies 38 (Prague); 39; 40; 41 (Jupiter)
*** Warner 2564 63067-2 (2) + bonus sampler. COE, Harnoncourt

As a 250th anniversary gesture, Harnoncourt has re-recorded the last four symphonies of Mozart yet again, still in proper scale, but this time with the modern-instrument Chamber Orchestra of Europe, who play superbly for him. Nevertheless, Harnoncourt's period-performance influences remain, including brisk tempi, with often fierce accents, and explosive timpani with hard sticks. The performances are consistently vibrant, but with elegant playing in slow movements, the *Andante* of the *G minor* rather fast, but the *Andante cantabile* of the *Jupiter* very beautiful. The *Prague* has a feeling of bravura throughout, and No. 39 too has plenty of spirit, especially in the sparkling finale, even if Harnoncourt misses its geniality. But the first movement of the *G minor* is very successful, and the set is crowned by a thrilling account of the *Jupiter* with all repeats included (as elsewhere), to lead to a remarkably powerful final apotheosis, carrying all before it. If you enjoy Harnoncourt's sheer verve and do not react adversely to his moments of excess, this is very recommendable. There is a free bonus disc, offering samples (complete movements) from 15 of his other recordings, covering the music of eight different composers.

Symphonies 40; 41 (Jupiter)
~~*~~ *** DG 477 5798. Les Musiciens du Louvre, Minkowski
(M) *(*) Warner Elatus 0927 49622-2. Concg. O, Harnoncourt

(i) Symphonies 40–41 (Jupiter); (ii) Overtures: Così fan tutte; Le nozze di Figaro
(BB) *** HMV 5 86736-2. (i) Sinfonia Varsovia, Y. Menuhin; (ii) ASMF, Marriner

(i) Symphonies 40–41; (ii) Serenade: Eine kleine Nachtmusik
(B) **(*) DG (ADD) 439 472-2. (i) BPO; (ii) VPO; Boehm

Minkowski's coupling of the last two Mozart symphonies is truly memorable. The *G minor* opens at a brisk pace, but Minkowski's touch is warmly sympathetic. The slow movement by contrast is leisurely, but its underlying melancholy is beautifully caught, while the woodwind chirrups are delightful. The Minuet is both bold and brisk, and the more lyrical Trio brings superb horn playing. The finale makes a zestful conclusion. The *Jupiter* is equally impressive, the first movement swinging along, outlined with bold timpani strokes, the slow movement Elysian, yet flowing with dark undercurrents. Once again, the Minuet moves forward purposefully and brightly, preparing the way for the powerfully thrusting finale, again taken briskly but with plenty of weight. All repeats are taken, to build to a massive and thrilling apotheosis. In between the two symphonies comes the *Idomeneo*

Ballet Music, but treated in the spirit of a sinfonia, making an enjoyable interlude. Outstandingly vivid recording makes this a very compelling disc indeed.

Recorded in exceptionally vivid, immediate sound, Menuhin's versions of both symphonies with the Sinfonia Varsovia find a distinctive place in an overcrowded field, with playing of precision, clarity and bite, consistently refreshing, giving a feeling of live music-making. The string-tuning and refinement of expressive nuance match that of a fine string quartet, and Menuhin reveals himself again as very much a classicist, preferring speeds on the fast side, rarely indulging in romantic tricks. He is generous with repeats – observing exposition repeats in both the first movement and the finale of the *Jupiter*, for instance. With such vivid sound this stands alongside Bernstein as one of the best current recommendations for this favourite coupling, regardless of price. Not surprisingly, Marriner's accounts of the two overtures bring an appropriately light touch: the ASMF playing is characteristically spirited and stylish, with the string detail nicely clean and polished.

Harnoncourt secures fine playing from the Concertgebouw, but his *G minor Symphony* is not very successful, with a very brisk speed for the first movement and an unsettled mood overall, hardly Mozartian. The *Jupiter Symphony* originally appeared by itself on LP. All repeats are included, making a playing time of 41 minutes; but the result is on the heavy side, the style much more romantic than in this same conductor's period performances with speeds slower than usual. A stronger reading than with No. 40, but not a consistently illuminating one.

CHAMBER MUSIC

Adagio & Fugue, K.546; 3 Divertimenti, K.136–8; Serenade 13 (Eine kleine Nachtmusik); String Quartets 1–13; 14–19 (Haydn Quartets); 20 (Hoffmeister); 21–23 (Prussian 1–3). 5 4-Part Fugues from Bach's Well-Temperered Clavier, Book II, K.405
(B) **(*) DG 477 6253 (7). Hagen Qt

The survey from the Hagen Quartet finds room also for *Eine kleine Nachtmusik* and two of Mozart's arrangements, the *Adagio and Fugue* taken from his *Piano Duet*, K.426, and five *Fugues* from Book II of Bach's *Well-Tempered Clavier* (which Mozart discovered in the music library of Baron Gottfried van Swieten in 1782). The first three discs present all Mozart's music for string quartet up to the age of 17, plus the *Divertimenti*, K.136–8. In these performances the Hagens strike an excellent balance between naturalness of utterance and sophistication of tone.

When they reach the six *Haydn Quartets* (which are also available separately, see below), their ensemble playing remains impecccable, as does the level of accomplishment in terms of tonal blend and beauty of sound. But here at times they are self-conscious and overstate dynamic shading, whether marked or superimposed. Yet in No. 21 (the *First Prussian Quartet*) they are highly sensitive to dynamic markings without ever exaggerating them. Moreover, they are pensive and inward-looking (at times they seem to be viewing Mozart through Schubertian eyes) and in these last *Quartets* they can make the listener think anew about this great music. The recordings, made at various times between 1988 and 2004, are certainly exemplary, and the balance is judged expertly (as one would expect from the DG producer, Wolfgang Mitlehner).

(i) Clarinet Quartet in B flat (trans. of Violin Sonata, K.327d); (ii) Oboe Quartet in F, K.370; String Quartet 21 in D, K.575
(B) **(*) HM Classical Express HCX 3957 107. (i) Hoeprich; (ii) Schachman; Artaria Qt

The transcription of the *Violin Sonata*, K.327d, into a *Clarinet Quartet* is a surprising success, and the work sounds for all the world as if it was written for the present combination, particularly in the jocular finale. The more so as the clarinettist, Erich Hoeprich, is a most personable and musical player. Marc Schachman's creamy yet nicely pointed oboe-playing is also just right for the *Oboe Quartet*, a most spirited, expressive performance that is among the best on record. Without soloists the Artaria Quartet give an accomplished account of the *First Prussian Quartet*, enjoyable if not distinctive. But the recording is first class, and the other two works make this disc well worth investigating at bargain price

(i) Clarinet Quintet; (ii) Flute Quartet 1; (iii) Oboe Quartet
(B) **(*) EMI 5 69702-2. (i) Nicholas Carpenter; (ii) Jaime Martin; (iii) Jonathan Kelly; Brindisi Qt (members)

The three soloists introduced here in EMI's Debut series are all principals with various British orchestras. Each is a first-rate artist and all three performances are fresh and enjoyable, with the *Flute Quartet* the most successful of the three. In both the other works the slow movements, although played persuasively, are just a little plain; to make up for it, all three finales are sprightly, with that of the *Clarinet Quintet* being particularly successful. The members of the Brindisi Quartet provide admirable support, and the recording is excellent, vivid and transparent.

(i) Clarinet Quintet in A, K.581; String Quartet 19 in C (Dissonance), K.465
(*) Cal. CAL 5256. Talich Qt, (i) with Cuper

The sleevenote gets it wrong, announcing that it is the *Quintet* that comes first whereas it is in fact the '*Dissonance*' *Quartet*. Incidentally, this is not the same recording as Talich's version issued in the 1980s when Jan Kvapil was second violin. Here Vladimir Bukac replaces him, and the recording itself was made at a public performance in the Théâtre Impérial de Compiègne in 1996. The balance is very close and there is little space round the sound; nor is the tone of the leader, Petr Messiereur, exactly flattered. Similarly in the *Clarinet Quintet*, Philippe Cuper appears very much larger than life. The dry, unappealing sound rules this out of court.

(i) Clarinet Quintet. String Quartet 20 in D (Hoffmeister), K.499
(M) **(*) Whitehall Associates MQCD 600l. (i) Brymer; Medici Qt

Jack Brymer has a benign influence in a fine, mellifluous performance of the *Clarinet Quintet*. He plays the *Adagio* as a sustained half-tone and conjures from the strings comparably soft playing. The finale is delightful; there is an attractive improvisational feeling in the lyrical variation before the main theme makes its joyful return. The recording is truthful, but the close balance is more noticeable in the coupled *Hoffmeister Quartet*, which is a lively, well-integrated performance.

Divertimenti for Strings, 1–3, K.136–8. (i) Serenade 13 (Eine kleine Nachtmusik), K.525. String Quartets 1 in G, K.80; 13 in D min., K.173
* Cal. CAL 5248. Talich Qt, (i) with Dominique Serri

These performances come from 1993 and, though the actual sound is not as bad as their recording of K.465 and K.581 listed above, it is dry and unpleasing and still too forwardly balanced. No quarrels with the playing.

Divertimento 17 in D, K.334 (chamber version)

(**) Pearl mono GEM 0129. Vienna Octet (members) –
SCHUBERT: *Piano Quintet (Trout).* (**)

In the 1955 edition *The Record Guide* gave both the recordings on the Pearl disc two stars, their highest accolade. The Mozart appeared in one of Decca's earliest LP supplements at the end of 1950. The second repeat of the Trio in the Minuet is not observed and there are two cuts in the finale, one of them substantial and both unwelcome. But those who recall the Vienna Octet's broadcasts and records of this period will relish the elegance and grace of their playing. Roger Beardsley has gone to great trouble in his remastering to do justice to these performances. He claims that now for the first time they can be heard to far better effect than in the early 1950s, and those who recall hearing them will recognize a great improvement.

Flute Quartets 1 in D, K.285; 2 in G, K.285a; 3 in C, K.285b; 4 in A, K.298

(BB) ** ASV Resonance CDRSN 3064. Adeney, Melos Ens.

(i) Flute Quartets 1–4; (ii) Oboe Quartet in F, K.370

(M) **(*) DHM/BMG 05472 77846-2. (i) Hazelzet; (ii) Westermann; Les Adieux

Mozart expressed a dislike for the flute, yet these works (like the concertos, and especially the *Concerto for Flute and Harp*) have great charm, and Wilbert Hazelzet, playing a period flute, finds charm in full measure here, and an extra touch of magic in the inspired *Adagio* of the *First Quartet*. Hans Peter Westermann is equally adept in the *Oboe Quartet* and is very winning in the perky finale, but his phrasing is just a little stiff in the slow movement. Excellent recording, well balanced and with a pleasing, atmospheric warmth.

The performances by Richard Adeney, with distinguished members of the Melos Ensemble (Hugh Maguire, Cecil Aronowitz, Terence Weill) date from 1979 and were produced by John Boyden for the now long-defunct Enigma label. The balance treats the flute very much in a solo capacity and is vividly close, although the characterful playing of Adeney's colleagues is not masked. The effect is undoubtedly lively and spontaneous, but it has not the imaginative insight or persuasive charm of the best versions. However, this excellently transferred CD is in the lowest price range and represents good value.

6 Flute Sonatas, K. 10–16 (arr. from 6 Sonatas for Harpsichord, with Accompaniment for Violin or Flute by Joseph Bopp)

** Nim. NI 5754. Schmeiser, Rainer (harpsichord)

These simple works were composed by a very young Mozart and were published when he was just nine. A Swiss flautist, Joseph Bopp, published his own edition of the works in 1959, but they have been re-edited for this recording, since much of the melodic line had been adjusted by Bopp and it was thought desirable to restore Mozart's original intentions as far as possible. The *Sonatas* are each in two or three movements, with the last usually a Minuet, although the sprightly finale of K.11 has a Minuet neatly sandwiched between a pair of *Allegros*, and the last of the series is a dancing *Allegro grazioso*. At its best, the invention is surprisingly attractive,

although here the forward balance of the modern flute used by Hansgeorg Schmeiser tends at times almost to mask the lively harpsichord of Ingomar Rainer. Nevertheless, this is an attractive disc that once again makes one amazed at Wolfgang Amadeus's early melodic and harmonic facility, even if father Leopold probably helped out.

(i) Horn Quintet; (ii) Oboe Quartet in F, K.370; A Musical Joke, K.522

(BB) **(*) Naxos 8.550437. (i) Kiss; (ii) Keveházi; Kodály Qt

Highly musical if not especially individual performances of the *Horn Quintet* and *Oboe Quartet*; in the latter the oboe is balanced forwardly and seems a bit larger than life; but no matter, the recordings have a pleasingly resonant bloom. The *Musical Joke* really comes off well: the horn players have a great time with their wrong notes.

(i) Horn Quintet; (ii) Piano & Wind Quintet; (iii) String Quintets 1–3; (iv) Adagio in B flat for 2 Clarinets & 3 Basset Horns

(B) **(*) Ph. (ADD) Duo 456 055-2 (2). (i) T. Brown, ASMF Chamber Ens.; (ii) Haebler, Bamberg Wind Qt (members); (iii) Grumiaux Trio, Gérecz, Lesueur; (iv) Netherlands Wind Ens.

The *Adagio in B flat* for clarinets and basset horns is delectable in this performance. Timothy Brown is a personable soloist and the *Horn Quintet* is given a well-projected and lively account. However, in spite of Ingrid Haebler's characteristically stylish contribution to the *Piano and Wind Quintet*, the Bamberg performance does not take flight, a straightforward rather than an imaginative account. Throughout the recordings are admirably balanced and given high-quality analogue sound.

Piano Quartets 1 in G min., K.478; 2 in E flat, K.493

(BB) ** Naxos 8.554274. Menuhin Festival Piano Qt

Piano Quartets 1–2. Rondo in A min., K.411

(M) ** RCA (ADD) 09026 63075-2. Rubinstein, Guarneri Qt (members)

The Menuhin Festival Piano Quartet is an international ensemble with an excellent German pianist, Friedemann Rieger, an American violinist, Nora Chastain, the Scottish-born violist, Paul Coletti, and a French cellist, Francis Gouton. They give very spirited accounts of both quartets, observing not only the exposition but also second-time repeats in the first movements, though the brilliant pianist is a little monochrome. They are not as tonally subtle as our first recommendations, but the acoustic in which they are recorded is a bit dry and so does not flatter them.

The pity is that Rubinstein's bright and invigorating playing and indeed the string-timbre of the members of the Guarneri Quartet have been given artificial brightness and their forwardness exaggerated by the recording balance. The mercurial re-creation of two of Mozart's most delectable chamber works is here in the hands of a pianist who is nothing if not an individualist, and the liveliness of Rubinstein – even in his eighties enjoying himself with fellow-musicians – is ample reason for hearing this coupling, even if the string sound is not wholly congenial.

Piano Trios 1 in B flat, K.254; 2 in G, K.496; 3 in B flat, K.502; 4 in E, K.542; 5 in C, K.548; 6 in G, K.564

(B) **(*) EMI double forte (ADD) 5 73350-2 (2). V. Trio

(B) **(*) HM Classical Express HCX 3957033/4 or HMX 29067033/4. Mozartean Players

Claus-Christian Schuster, the pianist on the EMI Vienna set, is a stylishly elegant player. He very much dominates his colleagues, but the recording itself is smooth and natural. These performances are lightweight, but they certainly give pleasure.

Fresh, unaffected performances from the Mozartean Players, an American period-instrument group from the New York State University at Purchase. Steven Lubin leads attractively on a copy of a Viennese fortepiano of 1785, and the balance is excellent. Undoubtedly enjoyable but not especially individual. The set comes as two individual CDs or a handsomely packaged limited edition with a beautiful illustrated booklet (HMX 29067033.34).

Piano Trios 4 in E, K.542; 5 in C, K.548; 6 in G, K.564; Trio Movement in D
**(*) Signum SIGCD 081. Ambache Chamber Ens.

Diana Ambache is a most musical pianist and an affectionately stylish Mozartian. She totally dominates these performances both in temperament and in sound, for neither the violinist, Gabrielle Lester, nor (especially) the cellist, Judith Herbert, are as strong in personality or timbre. Apart from this imbalance the recording is faithful, and one cannot but respond to the spontaneity of the playing. But first choice for the *Piano Trios* rests with the budget-priced two-disc Warner Apex set by the Trio Fontenay (2564 62189-2).

Piano & Wind Quintet in E flat, K.452
(M) *(*) Telarc CD 80114. Previn, V. Wind Soloists –
BEETHOVEN: *Quintet, Op 16* *(*)

Previn leads admirably throughout this performance of one of the most engaging of Mozart's chamber works, but the wind support is robust rather than refined. The opening of the slow movement brings elegant playing from the pianist but a heavy response from his colleagues. Previn articulates the engaging main theme of the finale most attractively, and here the effect is very spirited. The resonant acoustic tends to spread the sound, but the balance is quite well managed. This CD is not strongly recommended.

String quartets

String Quartets 14–19 (Haydn Quartets)
**(*) DG 471 024-2 (3). Hagen Qt
(M) **(*) Whitehall Associates (Nos. 14 & 15: MQCD 6004; 16 & 19: MQCD 6002; 17 & 18: MQCD 6003). Medici Qt
(B) *(*) RCA (ADD) 82876 60390-2 (3). Guarneri Qt
(B) * Decca (ADD) 475 7108 (3). Esterhazy Qt

The Medici provide a polished, well-integrated set of 'Haydn' quartets, fresh and alert, if without always the touch of extra individuality that appears in their account of the *Clarinet Quintet*. The studio recordings are rather closely balanced (although they are not airless) and the leader is obviously near the microphone. These records are competitively priced and certainly give pleasure.

The Guarneri recordings prove disappointing, although they are very well transferred and the playing is highly accomplished. But this group creates much the same well-upholstered sound for Mozart as they might do for Brahms. They find little depth in slow movements, and though the textures they produce are undeniably beautiful and they are sumptuously recorded, this set gives only modified pleasure, mostly in the finales, which are consistently lively.

DG have now issued the complete survey by the Hagen Quartet of Mozart's *String Quartets* (discussed fully above)

which has many virtues, including impeccable playing and superbly natural recording. But in the *Haydn Quartets* there is at times a self-consciousness to which we do not readily respond. While in the *D minor* (No. 15) their thoughtfulness is appealing, in the *G major*, K. 387, the accents in the second movement are exaggerated. These players cannot but inspire admiration, and if at times the Hagens' sensibility is at variance with Mozart's naturalness of utterance, it is only fair to say that other respected critics have derived much pleasure from them.

The Esterhazy use period instruments and impose the restraint of no vibrato. The gain in clarity is offset by a loss of warmth and richness of feeling. This is particularly evident in slow movements. The severity of the approach is striking at first, but it soon appears inhibited and self-conscious and, though the playing itself is very accomplished indeed, it does not bring us close to Mozart, well recorded though it is.

String Quartets 14–15
(M) **(*) Telarc CD 80297. Cleveland Qt

These are engagingly warm performances by the Clevelanders, richly recorded in a warm acoustic. The playing throughout is polished, beautifully blended and affectionate, but the effect is that, at times, textures are just a trifle suave. Yet both performances are rewarding, with finales a special joy. The *Molto allegro* of K.387 brings an infectiously spirited contrapuntal interplay, with the swinging secondary theme a joy, while in K.421 the *Allegretto* siciliano finale with its variations is elegantly graceful.

String Quartets: 14 in G, K.387; 19 in C (Dissonance), K.465 (Haydn Quartets); 21 in D (Prussian I), K.575; (i) Serenade 13 (Eine kleine Nachtmusik), K.525
☇ ✿ *** EuroArts **DVD** 2054578. Gewandhaus Qt; (i) with S. Adelmann (double bass) (Director: Hans Hadulla)

Since experiencing the EuroArts DVD of the two Mozart *Piano Quartets* (DV-PQWAM – see our main volume) we have been convinced that – after opera and ballet – it was chamber music repertoire that would prove to be the most revelatory in reproduction through this visual format. And so it proves, with this treasurable set of 'Famous String Quartets' from the Leipzig Gewandhaus Quartet (who have been playing together since 1993). This comes on the same label which gave us the piano quartets and is also currently offering us a comparable series of Mozart piano concertos (see above).

The Gewandhaus Quartet is a superb group; their impeccable intonation, perfection of blending and vitality of attack remind us of the Alban Berg group at their best for, while they play with a deep seriousness of purpose, intensity of feeling is combined with spontaneity, as if they were playing to a live audience. This is helped by a beautifully balanced recording of the utmost fidelity. It is a quibble to suggest that in *fortissimos* the violins slightly outbalance the cellist, Jürnjakob Timm, for he does not make a big sound. Yet – in slow movements especially – his contribution comes through clearly and subtly, and he is obviously deeply engrossed in the music-making. The first violin, Frank-Michael Erben, is a strong leader, dominating in just the way he should, and he has an easy virtuosity at his fingertips: witness his brilliant playing in the finale of the *Dissonance Quartet*; while all the players show their paces in the fugato finale of the *G major Quartet* with its delectable swinging secondary theme. They are also in sparkling form in *Eine kleine Nachtmusik*, which is strikingly fresh; the delicacy of the *Romance* and vivacity of the finale are delightful.

The quartet is seen against the beautiful backcloth of the Barockschloss in Rammenau, Saxony, where the acoustic is not too dry and not too resonant, so that one can always hear all four players individually and watch as Mozart's inspired part-writing passes between them. But the second violin, Conrad Suske, is the player to keep one's eyes on, for his visual expressions change subtly all the time, and they tell us a great deal about the progress of the music. If one cannot get to the Wigmore Hall, this is surely the ideal way to experience Mozart's chamber music.

String Quartet 15; (i) String Quintet 5 in D, K.593
**(*) ASV CDDCA 1018. Lindsay Qt, (i) with Williams

These are perceptive, highly musical and essentially dramatic accounts, very well played. But as with the other issues in this series, accents are strong, and in the *Andante* of the *D minor Quartet*, and the *Adagio* of the *Quintet* there are dynamic surges which not all listeners will find quite comfortable. Alternative versions of the finale of the *Quintet* demonstrate how the main theme can be presented either as a descending chromatic scale or a simplified 'zigzag' rhythmic pattern. With CD cueing you can take your choice. Vividly forward sound.

String Quartets 19 in C (Dissonance), K.465; 20 in D (Hoffmeister), K.499
*** EMI 3 44455-2. Belcea Qt

After their EMI début CD, the Belcea Quartet have established themselves as one of the finest groups now before the public, and these two performances offer confirmation of their warm and penetrating response to a pair of Mozart's finest works. The playing is full of vitality, and its spontaneity is striking. The recording is faithful, although the upper range is a trifle overbright in *fortissimos*.

String Quartet 20 in D (Hoffmeister), K.499
(M) (**(*)) BBC mono BBCL 4137-2. Smetana Qt –
BEETHOVEN: *String Quartet 1* (**); SMETANA: *String Quartet 1*. (***)

The performance of the *Hoffmeister Quartet*, K.499, comes from a BBC relay from the Royal Festival Hall in June 1965. The mono sound is very good indeed, if slightly dry. The playing of the Smetanas has polish, ardour and freshness, and there is not the slightest touch of routine. Recommended.

String Quartets 20 (Hoffmeister), K.499; 22, K.589
**(*) Astrée E 8834. Mosaïques Qt

The Mosaïques' performances of the *Hoffmeister* and the second of the *Prussian* group, while as discerning and characterful as ever, are let down a little by a closer recording balance than in their previous records. All are brightly lit, but here Erich Höbarth's first violin is made fierce at climaxes, and this especially applies in the *Minuet* of the *Hoffmeister*, K.499.

String Quartets 20 (Hoffmeister); 23
**(*) Arcana A 8. Festetics Qt

These are fine, characterful performances, with splendid vigour and ensemble showing the Festetics Quartet in more relaxed form than in their coupling of K.575 and K.590. However, slow movements could still loosen up a bit more; they still sound very considered. Excellent recording.

String Quartets 21; 23 (Prussian)
**(*) Arcana A 9. Festetics Qt

The Hungarian Quatuor Festetics, who also play 'sur instruments d'époque', as the French so engagingly put it, approach Mozart with a degree of severity that not all will take to. The opening of K.575 is superbly poised, and the *Andante* is most eloquent. But never a suspicion of a smile until the arrival of the Minuet, and even this is very purposeful. Strong accents abound, and there is something a bit spare about the finale too, vital though it is. A record to be greatly admired, but not one to fall in love with.

Violin Sonatas 18 in G, K.301; 21 in G, K.304; 24 in F, K.376; 35 in A, K.526
*** DG 477 557-2. Hahn, Zhu

Elegant playing, full of sparkle and intelligence. The sound is not ideally ventilated (there is not quite enough air round the aural image) and the pianist, a vibrant player, is a bit close. But artistically this is very successful, and it would be curmudgeonly to withhold a third star.

Piano duet
Andante with 5 Variations in G, K.501; Fantasia in F min., K.608; Fugue in G min., K.401; Sonatas in B flat, K.358; in F, K.497
*** Sony 8276 782000. Tal & Groethuysen

Adagio, K.546, & Fugue, K.426 (arr. Franz Beyer); Allegro & Andante in G, K.357; (completed Julius André); Larghetto & Allegro in E flat, K.Deenst; Sonata in D (for 2 pianos), K.448; Sonata in C, K.190
*** Sony 8276 78363-2. Tal & Groethuysen

Yaara Tal and Andreas Groethuysen enjoy an enviable reputation, and it must be said that Mozart duo playing doesn't come much better than this. Apart from the vibrant intelligence and sensitivity of the playing, the sound is bright and well detailed. A model of its kind.

(i) Andante with 5 Variations, K.501; Fugue in C min., K.426; Sonatas for Piano Duet: in C, K.19d; G, K.357; B flat, K.358; D, K.381; Sonata in D for 2 Pianos, K.448; F, K.497; C, K.521 (both for piano duet)
🔗 (BB) *** Warner Apex 2564 62037-2 (2). Güher & Süher Pekinel

This excellent duo are in their element in Mozart. Their playing is full of life and spirit, yet their vigour never rides roughshod over Mozart. The *Andante* of K.381 is beautifully poised, while the *molto allegro* of its D major companion (for two pianos) is memorably bold, rhythmic and infectious. The other works are hardly less compelling and the *Andante and Variations* make an engaging counterpart. Excellent, modern, digital recording makes this a first recommendation for this repertoire. The accompanying notes tell of the historical background for these works, suggesting that it was J. C. Bach who was the 'father' of the sonata for piano duet on a single piano, and that he played the early work in C, K.19d, written about 1765, with the very young Mozart beside him.

Solo piano music
Piano Sonatas 1–18; Fantasia in C min., K.475; Adagio in B min., K.540; Eine kleine Gigue, K.574; Fantasy Fragment in D min., K.397; Klavierstücke in F, K.33b; Kleiner Trauermarsch, K.453a; Modulation Prelude in F/E min., K.6 Deest; Overture, K.399; Prelude in C, K.284a; Prelude &

Fugue in C, K.394; Rondos, K.485 & K.511; Variations, K.24; K.25; K.180; K.264; K.265; K.352; K.353; K.354; K.398; K.455; K.457; K.460; K.573; K.613

(BB) *** BIS CD 1633/36 (10). Brautigam (fortepiano)

Ronald Brautigam's set is bursting with life and intelligence. He uses a 1992 copy (made in his native Amsterdam) of a fortepiano by Anton Gabriel Walter from about 1795. It is a very good instrument and he is a very good player. Dip in anywhere in this set and you will be rewarded with playing of great imagination and sensitivity – not to mention sureness and agility of mind and fingers, and he is completely inside the Mozartian sensibility of the period. Even if you prefer Mozart's keyboard music on the piano, you should investigate this set without delay. It brings Mozart to life in a way that almost no other period-instrument predecessor has done. This series has given great pleasure, and it is beautifully recorded too. The ten discs are offered for the price of four and now come in a box with two booklets offering separate documentation for the *Sonatas* and for the *Variations* plus miscellaneous pieces.

Piano Sonatas 4 in E flat, K.282; 14 in C min., K.457; Fantasia in C min., K.457; Suite in C, K.388 with Gigue, K.574; 10 Variations in G on the Aria 'Unser dummer Pöbel meint' from Gluck's 'Die Pilgrime von Mekka'

◉─➤ (B) *** HMX 2961815. Staier (fortepiano)

There are few recitals on a fortepiano as convincing or as completely right for the music as this. We know that Andreas Staier is an outstanding artist, but on this CD he has surpassed himself. The instrument (beautifully photographed in colour in the handsome booklet which goes with this limited edition) is a copy of a fortepiano by the Viennese maker Anton Walter, very similar to an instrument he built for Mozart. It is perfect for the opening piece in the programme, a baroque-styled *Suite* that Mozart wrote in 1782 but left unfinished. Staier has completed the *Sarabande* and supplied as the missing closing movement Mozart's 'kleine Gigue', K.574, which makes a witty ending. Apart from the *Overture*, very much in the style of Handel, there is an exquisite *Allemande*, which is played here very beautifully and with every bit as much colour as could be given by a modern piano.

Staier's performance of the *E flat Sonata* is no less appealing, and the *C minor Sonata* opens and closes boldly, while its delicate *Adagio* has a captivating simplicity. The engaging *Variations* were used by Tchaikovsky in his *Mozartiana Suite* and show again the fortepiano's rich lower sonority to fine effect. But the highlight of the recital is the masterly *C minor Fantasy*, which is superbly played and leaves an unforgettable impression.

Piano Sonatas: 8 in A min., K.310; 11 in A, K.331; Fantasias: in C min., K.475; in D min., K.397

◉─➤ (M) *** DG (ADD) 477 5907. Kempff

Wilhelm Kempff's disarming simplicity of style hides great art. This is a wonderful CD, in a class of its own, and not to be missed on any account. The performance of the mature *Fantasia*, K.475, is surely one of the most beautiful pieces of piano playing on record. The 1962 recording has been admirably remastered, and this disc is most welcome back in the catalogue as one of DG's Originals.

Piano Sonatas: 10 in C, K.330; 11 in A, K.331; 12 in F, K.332; Adagio in B min., K.540; Fantasias: in C min., K.475; D min., K.385; Rondos: in D, K.485; A min., K.511; 9 Variations on a Minuet by Dupont in D, K.573

◉─➤ *** EMI 2-CD 3 36080-2 (2). Lars Vogt

In his note with this compelling recital, Lars Vogt tells us that it represents his 'personal rediscovery of Mozart's piano music, music that expresses everything of real importance that immediately touches the heart and demands of the interpreter a high degree of re-creative artistry'. Not surprisingly, this is playing of distinction, and Vogt is fortunately given an outstandingly realistic recording with a wide dynamic range.

The remarkably thoughtful and introspective *B minor Adagio* which ends the recital and the two *Fantasias* perhaps show him at his most imaginative and poetic, but the exquisite opening *Andante grazioso* of the *A major Sonata* is no less memorable, with the closing *Alla Turca Rondo* bursting in on the listener to make a thrilling, bravura finale. The two *Rondos* and the engaging *Variations* show the composer in lighter mood; but even here Vogt brings personal insights to the music, while the other two sonatas show him balancing Mozart's three-part structures with complete spontaneity and capturing every facet of the music's inner feeling.

Piano Sonata 15 in F, K.533/494

*** Calico Classics CCCR 101. Crossland – BEETHOVEN: *Sonatas 17 & 31* **(*)

Jill Crossland is a natural Mozartian and gives a delightful performance of this *F major Sonata*, compiled from a *Rondo*, K.494, and a separate *Allegro* and *Andante*, K.533, making it seem a composite whole. She is very well recorded.

VOCAL MUSIC

Concert arias: Ah, lo previdi; Nehmt meinen Dank; Ch'io mi scordi di te?; Voi avete un cor fedele, K.217. Arias from Il re pastore; Zaide

(B) *** Australian Decca Eloquence 476 7459. Kirkby, AAM, Hogwood

Recorded in 1990, this highly attractive collection of opera and concert arias is a winner. Emma Kirkby brings a lovely, intimate quality to her recordings, and her fresh, unpretentious approach is a delight. The virtuoso passages are brilliantly done (*Voi avete un cor fedele* is especially sparkling), but it is her delicate charm which makes this CD particularly memorable.

'Haydn and Mozart Discoveries': Concert Arias: *Così dunque tradisci ... Aspri rimorsi atroci, K.432; Un bacio di mano, K.541; Männer suchen stehts zu naschen; Mentre il lascio, K.513; Warnung, K.433; Ein deutsches Kriegslied, K.539: Ich möchte wohl der Kaiser sein.* Opera arias: *La finta giardiniera: Nach der welschen Art. Le nozze di Figaro: Hai già vinta la causa; Vedrò mentr'io sospiro.*

(M) **(*) Decca (ADD) 475 7169. Fischer-Dieskau, V. Haydn O, Peters - HAYDN: *Arias.* **(*)

The Mozart rarities on this disc are more numerous and more interesting than the Haydn items, and it is particularly fascinating to hear the Count's arias from *Figaro* in a version with a high vocal line which the composer arranged for performance in 1789. There is also a beautiful aria from two years earlier, *Mentre il lascio*, which reveals Mozart's inspiration at its keenest. The other items also bring their delights. Fischer-Dieskau sings most intelligently, if with some pointing of word and phrase that is not quite in character with the music.

Sacred Vocal Music

Coronation Mass: Agnus Dei. Exsultate jubilate; Regina coeli, K.107; Regina coeli, K.127; Sancta Maria, Mater Dei; Solemn Vespers: Laudate Dominum from K.321 & K.339; Sub tuum presidium
*** Hyp. CDA 67560. Sampson, King's Consort and Ch., King

Carolyn Sampson with her bright, pure soprano provides the focus of Robert King's well-compiled collection of Mozart choral works, most of them early. Sampson's singing of the showpiece, *Exsultate jubilate*, rivals Dame Kiri Te Kanawa's and Cecilia Bartoli's classic recordings in its freshness and brilliance, and her radiance in the two settings of *Laudate Dominum* is a delight too. King's Mozartian style, incisive and direct, gives vigour to even the less inspired of the early works.

Davidde penitente, K.469; Exsultate, jubilate, K.165. Così fan tutte: Temerari! . . . Come scoglio; Ei perte . . . Per pietà, ben mio; Un uomini, in soldati. Le nozze di Figaro: E Susanna non vien! . . . Dove sono; Giuse alfin il momento . . . Al desio. Don Giovanni: Batti, batti, o bel Masetto; In quali eccessi . . . Mi tradi quall'alma ingrati
(M) *** Decca 475 7526. Bartoli, V. CO, G. Fischer

'Mozart Portraits' is a truly remarkable Mozartian collection, showing that Cecilia Bartoli not only has an astonishing range – vocal and dramatic – and dazzling coloratura (as in *Exsultate, jubilate* and elsewhere), but she is also an artist who can create real operatic human characters and express their feelings vividly and touchingly. Fiordiligi's *Come scoglio* is tempestuous, her *Per pietà* ravishingly tender. For Despina the voice is much lighter (although one could have done without the 'laugh'), and her *In uomini, in soldati* charmingly displays that she has no illusions about mankind, for all her vivacious femininity; while Zerlina's *Batti, batti* is simply enchanting Mozartian lyricism. The Countess's *Dove sono* is heart-rending, but then Bartoli becomes Susanna in her supreme moments of happy expectation. The selection ends as it began, in an expression of true female ferocity from Donna Elvira, but she is still in love, and her tenderness here brings most beautiful singing on the disc. With splendid accompaniments from György Fischer and the Vienna Chamber Orchestra (the bravura horns in the *Così fan tutte* aria are really something), this excellently recorded disc returns to the catalogue as one of Decca's Originals (with full texts and translations included).

Exsultate, jubilate, K.165 (Salzburg version); Motets: Ergo interest, K.143; Regina coeli (2 settings), K.108, K.127
*** Australian Decca Eloquence 476 7460. Kirkby, Westminster Cathedral Boys' Ch., AAM Ch. & O, Hogwood

The boyish, bell-like tones of Emma Kirkby (in 1983) are perfectly suited to the most famous of Mozart's early cantatas, *Exsultate, jubilate*, culminating in a dazzling account of *Alleluia*. With accompaniment on period instruments, this is aptly coupled with far rarer but equally fascinating examples of Mozart's early genius, superbly recorded. A refreshing and enjoyable collection.

Masses 16 (Coronation); 19 (Requiem)
(BB) * Warner Apex 2564 61592-2. (i) Rodgers, Von Magnus, Protschka, Polgár, Arnold Schoenberg Ch.; (ii) Yakar, Wenkel, Equiluz, Holl, V. State Op. Ch.; VCM, Harnoncourt

In the *Coronation Mass* Harnoncourt is not entirely logical in using period instruments but women rather than boy trebles in the choir. As usual, accents are strong, dynamic contrasts are exaggerated and phrasing is somewhat eccentrically moulded, although Joan Rodgers is a fine soprano soloist, her line eloquent and without exaggerations. The recording has plenty of atmosphere but could be more clearly defined. However, in the *Requiem* there is reverberation to excess: the chorus might have been performing in a swimming bath and although the ambience lends some glamour to the solo voices – a good team – it is disconcertingly inconsistent to have an orchestra of original instruments with all its clarity set against vocal sound so vague and flabby. Not recommended.

(i) Mass 18 in C min., K.427; (ii) Vesperae de Domenica K.321 (excerpts)
(BB) ** HMV (ADD/DDD) 5 86742-2. (i) Cotrubas, Te Kanawa, Krenn, Alldis Ch., New Philh. O, Leppard; (ii) Dawson, James, Covey-Crump, Hillier, King's College Ch., Cambridge, Classical Players, Cleobury

Raymond Leppard uses the Robbins Landon Edition of the C minor Mass and a choir of comparable proportions. His manner is a degree more affectionate than some, which many will prefer, even in this comparatively dark work. The sopranos are the light-givers here, and the partnership of Ileana Cotrubas and Kiri Te Kanawa is radiantly beautiful. The best thing about the three excerpts from *Vesperae de Domenica* is Lynne Dawson's lovely account of the *Laudate Dominum*. The choral contributions tend to lack bite, not helped by a none-too-vivid balance and recording.

Mass 18 in C min., K.427; Mass 19 (Requiem), K.626
*** Ph. **DVD** 074 3121. Bonney, Von Otter, Rolfe Johnson, Miles, Monteverdi Ch., E. Bar. Sol., Gardiner (V/D: Jonathan Fulford)

What are arguably Mozart's two greatest choral masterpieces make an ideal DVD coupling in outstanding accounts by Gardiner and his team, including four star soloists. As one would expect of Gardiner, playing and singing are both brilliant and incisive, with shattering impact in the *Dies irae*, yet there is also a tenderness not always apparent in period performances. Gardiner uses the traditional completion of the Mass published in 1901 by Alois Schmitt, yet with corrections he himself has made in the *Credo*, with the string parts in the *Et incarnatus* rewritten in a truer Mozartian style. Jonathan Fulford's video direction nicely exploits the colourful qualities of the Palau de la Musica Catelana in Barcelona, where the performance was given in 1991.

Masses (i) 18 in C min. (Great); (ii) 19 (Requiem) (CD Versions)
(B) *(*) CfP 2-CD 575 7702 (2). (i) Wiens; Dale, Lloyd (i;ii) Lott; (ii) D. Jones, Lewis, White, LPO Ch. & O, Welser-Möst

Many may be attracted by this inexpensive CfP coupling, although there are no fill-ups and the playing time is ungenerous. The C minor Mass was Franz Welser-Möst's début recording in 1987, and the *Requiem* followed two years later. However, although there is some fine choral singing, especially in the *Requiem*, where Felicity Lott also shines, she is below her radiant best in the '*Great*' Mass, and here Edith

Wiens is also a disappointing first soprano. Moreover, both performances lack the extra tension that distinguishes a recorded performance from a run-through. The recording is excellent, but this is a non-starter.

Mass 19 (Requiem) in D min., K.626

(B) ** DG Entrée 474 170-2. McLaughlin, Ewing, Hadley, Hauptmann, Bav. R. Ch. & SO, Bernstein

Mass 19 in D min. (Requiem) (ed. Maunder)

(BB) ** Warner Apex (ADD) 8573 89421-2. Ameling, Scherler, Devos, Soyer, Gulbenkian Foundation, Lisbon, Ch. & O, Corboz

(i) Mass 19 (Requiem). Adagio & Fugue, K.546

(M) ** DG (ADD) 463 654-2. BPO, Karajan; (i) with Lipp, Rössl-Majdan, Dermota, Berry, V. Singverein

(i) Mass 19 in D min. (Requiem); (ii) Ave verum corpus, K.618; (iii) Exsultate jubilate, K.165

(BB) *** HMV 5 86743-2. (i) Kenny, Hodgson, Davies, Howell, L. Symphony Ch., N. Sinfonia & Ch., Hickox; (ii) V. Singverein Ch., Philh. O, Karajan; (iii) Hendricks, ASMF, Marriner

(i) Mass 19 (Requiem) in D min., K.626; (ii) Ave verum corpus, K.618; Regina coeli, K.276; Te Deum Laudamus, K.141; Venite populi, K.260

(M) **(*) RCA 82876 76236-2. (i) Blasi, Lipovšek, Heilman, Rootering, Bav. R. Ch. & SO, C. Davis; (ii) Tölz Boys' Ch., European Bar. Sol., Schmidt-Gade

At super-bargain price, Richard Hickox's excellent EMI version of the Requiem Mass on the HMV label matches almost any in the catalogue. With generally brisk speeds and light, resilient rhythms, it combines gravity with authentically clean, transparent textures in which the dark colourings of the orchestration, as with the basset horn, come out vividly. All four soloists are outstandingly fine, and the choral singing is fresh and incisive, with crisp attack. The voices, solo and choral, are placed rather backwardly; otherwise the recording is excellent, full and clean to match the performance. Of the bonuses, Karajan's account of the Ave verum corpus is suavely beautiful, and Barbara Hendricks's Exsultate jubilate is rich-timbred and fresh, though her runs are not always cleanly articulated.

Sir Colin Davis's 1991 Requiem with Bavarian forces is above all a spacious reading. But the singing of the Bavarian Chorus is eloquent and committed, and the impressive Kyrie is followed by a powerfully dramatic Dies irae and Rex tremendae. The soloists are all excellent, with each entering in turn very tellingly in the Tuba mirum, the sweet-voiced soprano Angela Maria Blasi heading a well-blended quartet both here and in the Recordare, while the chorus brings great feeling to the Lacrimosa. The tension is maintained through the Hostias and Sanctus, and the soloists are again at their best in the Benedictus. The chorus gains a lot from the acoustic of the Munich Herculessaal and the excellent support of the Bavarian Radio Orchestra, and the work moves steadily and firmly to a satisfying close, if one without the very last degree of fervour. The motets offered as a filler are also very well sung, the Te Deum illuminated by trumpets, but with the Regina coeli the finest performance of the four. After it, the lovely but gentle Ave verum corpus seems almost an anti-climax.

Bernstein, in preparation for this 1988 recording of a work he had long neglected, made a special study not only of textual problems, but also of most of the existing recordings, not least those which used period instruments. He also opted to make a recording in a church of modest size. Yet Bernstein's romantic personality engulfs such gestures towards authenticity and the result is a rich, warm-hearted reading, marked by a broad, expressive style in the slower sections. With weighty choral singing, this is a strongly characterized reading which yet hardly makes a first choice.

Karajan's earlier (1962) recording was a strange choice for reissue as one of DG's 'Originals'. There is nothing legendary here except Karajan's remarkably suave view of Mozart's valedictory work. Here detail tends to be sacrificed in favour of warmth and atmosphere. The solo quartet are wonderfully blended, a rare occurrence in this work above all, and though the chorus lacks firmness of line they are helped out by the spirited playing of the Berlin Philharmonic. However, both Karajan's later (1976) analogue and newest digital version are greatly preferable. The Adagio and Fugue offered as a make-weight, with glorious Berlin string-tone, is both refined and expansive.

Michel Corboz, an excellent choral conductor, directs a nicely scaled performance and gets some fine, and often fervent, singing from his Lisbon choir. His concern for detail is admirable. Elly Ameling is outstanding in a variable quartet of soloists, but the performance ultimately lacks the last degree of thrust, particularly in the closing Lux aeterna.

OPERA

La clemenza di Tito (complete CD versions)

*** HM HMC 901923.24 (2). Padmore, Pendatchanska, Fink, Chappuis, Freiburg Bar. O, Jacobs

*** DG 477 5792 (2). Trost, Kožená, Martinpelto, Rice, SCO, Mackerras

Two outstanding versions of this once-neglected opera seria appeared in 2006 to celebrate Mozart's 250th anniversary, providing a valuable choice. René Jacobs's version with the period instruments of the Freiburg Baroque Orchestra offers a performance of extraordinary clarity and immediacy, at once sharp in attack, yet intimate too. The fortepiano continuo illustrates that well, more elaborate than usual in recitative that can outlast its welcome (probably not by Mozart himself). Here the drama is vividly conveyed, with words crystal clear. Period performance also highlights the impact of timpani and brass, again adding to the drama, never more powerfully conveyed than here, with ensembles tautly controlled. The cast of principals is excellent, with Mark Padmore at once mellifluous and commanding as the Emperor, always imaginative and animated; and the little-known Bulgarian, Alexandrina Pendatchanska, proves an outstanding choice as Vitellia, characterful and imaginative, matched by the golden-toned Bernarda Fink as Sesto and Marie-Claude Chappuis radiant as Annio.

Sir Charles Mackerras and the Scottish Chamber Orchestra add impressively to their Mozart opera series with a warmly alert version of La clemenza di Tito that provides an ideal alternative to the Jacobs set. Modern instruments, used with concern for period-performance style, make for a weightier as well as a warmer performance, a degree more relaxed than Jacobs. Rainer Trost is an excellent, heroic Tito, even if he is not as imaginative as Mark Padmore, while the rest of the cast of principals is comparably starry, with Magdalena Kožená tough-sounding as Sesto, and Hillevi Martinpelto as Vitellia.

Così fan tutte (complete CD versions)

(B) (***) EMI mono 3 36789-2 (3). Schwarzkopf, Otto, Merriman, Simoneau, Panerai, Bruscantini, Philh. Ch. & O, Karajan

(BB) (***) Regis mono RRC 3020 (3). Schwarzkopf, Otto, Merriman, Simoneau, Panerai, Bruscantini, Philh. Ch. & O, Karajan (with Arias from: *Don Giovanni, Le Nozze di Figaro, Idomeneo, Die Zauberflöte*, sung by Schwarzkopf)

(M) *(*) Decca 473 354-2 (3). Lorengar, Berganza, Berbié, R. Davies, Krause, Bacquier, ROHCG Ch., LPO, Solti

Karajan's 1954 Kingsway Hall mono set was one of the first great LP recordings of *Così*. His cast is unsurpassed and he is personally in superb form. This outstanding performance is reissued here in EMI's Historical series, at bargain price but with a cued synopsis rather than a libretto. That is provided with the mid-priced issue in EMI's 'Great Recordings of the Century' version (5 67064-2 [567138]) – see our main volume.

The Regis super-budget transfer is also very well managed, with the recording settling down nicely after the Overture, to give plenty of bloom on the voices. It includes a cued synopsis and tends to trump the EMI sets by including seven extra arias which Schwarzkopf recorded with Pritchard in 1953, exquisitely sung, three each from *Don Giovanni* and *Le Nozze di Figaro*, including *Voi che sapete*, and one from *Idomeneo*, plus two live recordings from 1952 – *Ach, ich fühls* from *Zauberflöte* and *In quali eccessi* from *Don Giovanni* – which are all equally well transferred.

Decca have reissued Solti's earlier (1974) set in their 'Compact Opera Collection', which is attractively packaged and now includes a printed, cued synopsis plus access to the full libretto and translation via a CD-ROM. Alas, the performance does not match Solti's later (1994) version and will suit only those who want high voltage at all costs, even in this most genial of Mozartian comedies. There is little relaxation, little charm, and this underlines the shortcomings of the singing cast, notably of Pilar Lorengar, whose grainy voice is not well treated by the microphone, and who here in places conveys uncertainty. The recording is vividly atmospheric, but it is a pity that the cracking wit of Solti's Covent Garden performance of the time was not more magically captured on record. The later, Royal Festival Hall recording is the one to have.

Così fan tutte (highlights)

(M) ** Telarc CD 80399. (from complete recording, with Lott, McLaughlin, Focile, Hadley, Corbelli, Cachemaille, Edinbugh Festival Ch. & O, Mackerras)

As with the rest of this Telarc series of Mozart opera recordings, Mackerras aims to present a performance on modern instruments which echoes the practices and manner of a period performance, heightening dramatic moments, making ensembles brisk and exciting. Unfortunately the sound is too reverberant and blunts the crispness and undermines the clarity of ensembles. The cast is strong but, whether or not affected by the acoustic and recording, Mozart manners are on the rough side. A flawed set, approached best in highlights format (76 minutes in all) which are enjoyable if you can adjust to the acoustic. There is a booklet with synopsis, but it is not cued. (The complete set is available on CD 80360.)

Don Giovanni (complete DVD version)

*** Arthaus **DVD** 101 087. Luxon, Dean, Branisteani, Yakar, Gale, Goeke, Rawnsley, Thau, Glyndebourne Ch. & O, Haitink (Producer: Peter Hall; V/D: Dave Heather)

Don Giovanni (complete CD versions)

(B) (***) EMI (mono) 3 36799-2 (3). Siepi, Schwarzkopf, Berger, Grümmer, Dermota, Edelmann, Berry, Ernster, V. State Op. Ch., VPO, Furtwängler

(M) ** RCA 74321 57737-2 (3). London, Della Casa, Jurinac, Kunz, Dermota, Seefried, Berry, Weber, V. State Op. Ch. & O, Boehm

** Decca 455 500-2 (3). Terfel, Fleming, Murray, Pertusi, Lippert, Groop, Scaltriti, Luperi, L. Voices, LPO, Solti

(M) * Virgin 5 45425-2 (3). Mattei, Cachemaille, Remigio, Gens, Padmore, Larson, Fechner, Gudjon Oskarsson, Aix-en-Provence Academy Ch., Mahler CO, Harding

When in 1977 Peter Hall added *Don Giovanni* to his list of Mozart/Da Ponte productions for Glyndebourne, he took a radically different view from the ultra-realistic approach in *Figaro* and *Così*, updating the action to the Regency period and in John Bury's sets giving a picture of a dark and rainy Seville. Deliberately gloomy, it would be oppressive but for the imagination of Hall in his detailed direction, with the superb Leporello of Stafford Dean unusually positive, and the whole performance heightened by the Mozartian strength of Bernard Haitink's conducting. The weakness in the cast is the Donna Anna of Horiana Branisteani, tending to be squally in the upper register, though she gathers strength as the opera proceeds, and the big aria, *Non mi dir*, is well controlled. Benjamin Luxon as Don Giovanni was at his peak, darkly characterful and with a wide tonal range down to a seductive half-tone. Rachel Yakar, bright and fresh as Donna Elvira, and Elizabeth Gale, sweetly charming, make up the team of women principals, with Leo Goeke unstrained as Ottavio and John Rawnsley exceptionally characterful as Masetto. Camerawork on the video is imaginative too in concentrating on individual characters at key moments.

Furtwängler's 1954 performance was recorded live by Austrian Radio at the Salzburg Festival, barely three months before the conductor's death. Even though his tempi are slow, it remains a classic set and, if stage noises are a problem, voices and orchestra are vividly caught. However, the present bargain issue comes with only a cued synopsis, and many collectors will prefer the mid-priced alternative (7 63860-2) which includes a libretto – see our main volume.

The Boehm RCA version, recorded live by Austrian Radio and given in German, is a historic curiosity – a performance that in 1955 marked the reopening of the Vienna State Opera. Vocally, it is worth hearing for the contributions of the three women principals, with Lisa della Casa creamy-toned as Donna Anna, Sena Jurinac at her magical peak as Donna Elvira and Irmgard Seefried the most charming of Zerlinas. George London is a strong but sour-toned Giovanni. The others are not at their finest either, not helped by the dry acoustic and odd balances.

Recorded live at the Royal Festival Hall in London in October 1996, Solti's version is disappointing despite the promising cast-list. It lacks the keen electricity that marks his live recording of *Così fan tutte*, and not one of the singers is on top form. Even Renée Fleming's beautiful voice sounds clouded, and Ann Murray as Elvira is seriously strained. Monica Groop as Zerlina, sweet enough in her arias, is edgy elsewhere, while Roberto Scaltriti is a gritty Masetto and Michele Pertusi often rough as Leporello. Bryn Terfel, so inspired a Leporello, proves an unpersuasive lover, with the tone tending to become unfocused. Dryish sound.

Recorded live at the 1999 Aix-en-Provence Festival, Daniel

Harding's reading is an extraordinary exercise in speed. To describe it as perfunctory is to underestimate the impact of speeds that reduce the soloists to a gabble and that prompt the Mahler Chamber Orchestra to produce sounds that would seem scrawny even from an unreconstructed period band, not helped by a recording that lacks body. The cast, mainly of promising young soloists, is almost completely defeated by such wilfulness from the conductor, with even the stylish and characterful Véronique Gens sounding underpowered and uncomfortable. Only the experienced Gilles Cachemaille survives the experiment with any success, a winning and warm Leporello.

Don Giovanni (Prague & Vienna CD versions; complete)

(BB) ** Virgin 5 66267-2 (5). Schmidt, Yurisich, Dawson, Halgrimson, Argenta, Mark Ainsley, Finley, Miles, L Schütz Ch., LCP, Norrington – Die Zauberflöte. *

Norrington's version not only provides a period-instrument performance which on the orchestral side outshines earlier authentic versions (though not the newer Gardiner set) but that also ingeniously offers the alternative of hearing the original Prague score of the opera, alongside Mozart's revision for Vienna. But this is not done in the ideal way of laying out the tracks of the two versions (where they differ) side by side. Instead, the first two CDs present the opera as it would have been heard at the first performance in Prague in 1787, and the third offers the additional numbers and amendments that Mozart provided for the Vienna première the next year. So in order to switch between the two you need a pair of CD players, and many numbers are duplicated. A fascinating experiment, nevertheless, but sadly the singing cast cannot match the very finest versions. Though Lynne Dawson as Elvira, John Mark Ainsley as Don Ottavio, Gregory Yurisich as Leporello and Alastair Miles as the Commendatore all sing impressively, most of the others fall seriously short, including Andreas Schmidt as an ill-focused Don, and Amanda Halgrimson as a shrill Donna Anna. This set is now offered very inexpensively indeed (if without a libretto or cued synopsis), but it comes in harness with an unrecommendable account of Die Zauberflöte.

Don Giovanni (highlights)

(BB) **(*) EMI Encore 5 86425-2 (from complete recording, with Shimell, Ramey, Studer, VPO, Muti)

(M) ** Telarc CD 80442 (from complete set with Skovhus, Lott, Corbelli, Brewer, SCO, Mackerras)

(BB) * Warner Apex 2564 61499-2 (from complete recording, with Hampson, Gruberová, Alexander, Bonney, Blochwitz, Polgár, Scharinger, Holl, Concg. O, Harnoncourt)

Muti's Don Giovanni is on a big scale but is nevertheless refreshingly alert (using a fortepiano continuo). It is a set to sample rather than to have complete. Shimell makes a rather gruff Don, not as insinuatingly persuasive as he might be; like the others, he is not helped by the distancing of the voices. With Samuel Ramey convincingly translated here to the role of Leporello and Cheryl Studer an outstanding Donna Anna, the rest of the casting is strong and satisfying. The selection of highlights is not particularly generous but does include most of the key numbers.

Mackerras's 1995 recording of Don Giovanni is vividly dramatic and perfectly paced, with modern instruments echoing period practice. The teamwork is excellent, but individually the casting is flawed, so the performance is better approached through a highlights disc. This one is generous

enough (77 minutes), although the booklet offers only historical notes on the opera and a synopsis which is uncued. In any case Bo Skovhus as the Don may be seductive in expression but his vocal focus too often grows woolly under pressure. Felicity Lott, as recorded, is in disappointing voice as Elvira, not nearly as sweet as usual, and there is too much acid in the soprano tones of Christine Brewer as Donna Anna, though Christine Focile makes a characterful Zerlina. The sound has a pleasing ambience but does not provide much sparkle.

Harnoncourt's 1988 recording with the Concertgebouw rather fell between two stools. He persuaded the orchestra's reduced strings to play with a lighter, more detached style than usual and with little vibrato, but the heavily overreverberant recording removed any advantages. Moreover, his fast speeds tend to sound perverse rather than helpful. Thomas Hampson as Don Giovanni is predictably splendid, and the others are generally good too, but Edita Gruberová is a surprisingly squally and often raw Donna Anna. In short, this is not very tempting even in highlights format.

Die Entführung aus dem Serail (complete DVD version)

*** TDK DVD DV-OPEADS. Mei, Ciofi, Trost, Montazeri, Rydl, Markus John, Maggio Musicale Fiorentino Ch. & O, Mehta (V/D: George Blume)

One does not associate Zubin Mehta with Mozart opera, but here he is at his finest, obviously deeply involved, directing with warmth and vitality, with the orchestra on top form and providing a constantly lively backing for the singers. Eva Mei does not quite look like a Konstanze, but she sings with heartfelt passion as well as eloquence, so that the famous Martern aller Arten is a real dramatic highlight. Patrizia Ciofi is a sparkling, often fiercely vehement Blonde, and if Rainer Trost does not project as a very heroic Belmonte, he sings attractively enough. But the star of the action (as so often) is Osmin. Kurt Rydl makes the characterization deeper, more ambivalent than usual, but he sings with such brio and presence that one is capativated every time he appears. Thank goodness that, for once, the director produces no silly tricks, and the sets are visually most appealing. A real winner and most enjoyable listening and watching.

Die Entführung aus dem Serail (complete CD versions)

(M) (**) DG (IMS) mono 457 730-2 (2). Stader, Streich, Haefliger, Greindl, Vantin, Berlin RIAS Chamber Ch. & SO, Fricsay (with Exsultate, jubilate, K.165 ***)

** Telarc CD 80544 (2). Kodalli, Groves, Rancatore, Rose, Atkinson, Tobias, SCO, Mackerras

Though lacking in body, the mono sound for Fricsay's recording brings splendid detail, with voices well caught. Fricsay characteristically opts for fast, generally refreshing speeds and crisp attack, though Konstanze's great aria of lamentation, Traurigkeit, lacks tenderness. Maria Stader is appealing in that role, even though the sweet voice grows less secure on top. Haefliger as Belmonte brings weight but little lyrical beauty. Greindl is a strong but often gritty Osmin and Martin Vantin a boyish Pedrillo, while the finest singing comes from Rita Streich as Blonde. The dialogue is mainly spoken by actors. Exsultate, jubilate, with Stader, makes a welcome fill-up.

Recorded for the soundtrack of a film of Entführung, Mozart in Turkey, the Telarc version conducted by Sir Charles Mackerras offers lively conducting and a young-sounding cast. The modest string band is set in contrast against prominent percussion, with wind and brass also well to the fore. As in his other Mozart with the Scottish Chamber Orchestra, Mackerras introduces elements of period practice in light, fast allegros, fierce at times, though in slow music he allows ample relaxation. Paul Groves is a fresh, clear-toned Belmonte, not quite free enough at the very top, and Yelda Kodalli a bright, clear Konstanze, as impressive in her tender account of *Traurigkeit* as in the bravura of *Martern aller Arten*. As Blonde, Desirée Rancatore is agile too but, as recorded, there is a distracting flutter in the voice. The Osmin of Peter Rose is vocally impressive but sadly undercharacterized. There may be a point in making Osmin more serious than usual, but with the voice sounding far too young there is little or no comedy, and no feeling of anger in his rages. Lynton Atkinson makes a sparky Pedrillo, even if the voice is distractingly similar to that of Groves as Belmonte. Excellent singing from the chorus and lively playing from the orchestra. Clear recording, rather drier than some from this source. This is acceptable enough but hardly a primary recommendation.

Le nozze di Figaro (complete DVD versions)

*** NVC DVD 0630-14013-2. Finley, Hagley, Fleming, Schmidt, Rohrl, Hillhouse, Todorovitch, Tear, Adams, Glyndebourne Festival Ch., LPO, Haitink (Director: Stephen Medcalf; V/D: Derek Bailey)

**(*) TDK DVD DVWW-OPNDFF. Gallo, Gvazava, Ciofi, Surian, Comparator, Donadini, Maggio Musicale Fiorentino Ch. & O, Mehta

Though Stephen Medcalf's 1994 production of *Figaro* cannot quite match in depth of insight the classic production that Peter Hall did for Glyndebourne ten years earlier, it remains a brilliant realization, with Gerald Finley outstanding as Figaro himself, vocally strong and dramatically intense, opposite the vivacious Susanna of Alison Hagley. It was also a coup for Glyndebourne to persuade Renée Fleming to sing the role of the Countess. She had still to become an international superstar, but already hers was a moving and thoughtful characterization, beautifully sung. Other strong contributors to an excellent cast include Manfred Rohrl as Dr Bartolo and Robert Tear as an unforgettable Don Basilio. By 1994 it was fortunately no longer the Glyndebourne rule to have operas updated, and against John Gunter's toytown sets the traditional costumes work perfectly, with the action moving beautifully. The booklet provides exceptionally clear lists of chapters, set against a detailed synopsis.

Recorded at the Maggio Musicale Fiorentino in 2003, Jonathan Miller's ever-perceptive production with traditional costumes and sets has many excellent qualities, notably an outstanding Susanna in Patrizia Ciofi, bright and sparkling. Sadly, the Figaro of Giorgio Surian is on the rough side vocally, not perfectly focused, failing to bring out the full humour. Yet the young-sounding Countess of Eteri Gvazava, fresh and alert, and the strong, positive Count of Lucio Gallo make a first-rate couple. Marina Comparator is an aptly boyish Cherubino and Giovanna Donadini is outstandingly characterful as Marcellina. A pity that her aria in Act IV is omitted, as is that of Basilio. Zubin Mehta is a lively enough conductor, but the performance could be more sparkling.

Le nozze di Figaro (complete CD versions)

⊙━ *** HM HMC90 1818/20. Gens, Ciofi, Kirchschlager, McLaughlin, Keenlyside, Regazzo, Ghent Coll. Voc., Concerto Köln, Jacobs

(BB) **(*) EMI Gemini (ADD) 4 76942-2 (2). Sciutti, Jurinac, Stevens, Bruscantini, Calabrese, Cuénod, Wallace, Sinclair, Glyndebourne Ch. & Festival O, Gui

(M) ** DG 477 5614 (3). Te Kanawa, Upshaw, Furlanetto, Hampson, Von Otter, Met. Op. Ch. & O, Levine

René Jacobs conducts one of the most refreshing versions of *Figaro* to be issued in many years, with its excellent cast a worthy winner of the *Gramophone* 'Record of the Year Award' in 2004. Jacobs's approach is distinctive, not just in balancing the wind well forward of the strings, but in allowing a greater degree of freedom of tempo than is generally found in period performances. The use of fortepiano continuo, often elaborate, also adds to the individuality. It all adds up to a winning result. Véronique Gens is one of the most distinguished of Countesses, and Patrizia Ciofi is a sparkling Susanna, while Simon Keenlyside is a superb Count, well contrasted with the strongly acted Figaro of Lorenzo Regazzo. Angelika Kirchschlager sings flawlessly as Cherubino, while having Marie McLaughlin as Marcellina represents luxury casting.

Gui's effervescent 1955 Glyndebourne set was last reissued on the double forte label (see our main volume). Now it reappears on the super-budget Gemini label. It remains a classic set with a cast that has seldom been bettered, and the only regret is that there is a (very minor) cut to fit the recording on to two discs. There is no libretto, but the cued synopsis follows the narrative in detail, yet not giving the Italian titles of each item, only telling the listener what the character or characters are singing about. A pity, for this makes the set less easy to dip into.

Levine's 1990 DG recording with forces from the Met. in New York brings some outstanding individual performances – notably Anne Sofie von Otter as a delightful Cherubino – but overall it lacks the effervescence needed for this opera. Dame Kiri Te Kanawa's Countess is far better appreciated in the Decca Solti set. Dawn Upshaw is too pert a Susanna, and Ferruccio Furlanetto's resonant Figaro is not helped by the roughness of Levine's accompaniment, as in *Non più andrai*. The mid-priced reissue includes a keyed synopsis.

Le nozze di Figaro (complete; but without recitatives)

(B) (**(*)) EMI mono 3 36779-2 (2). Schwarzkopf, Seefried, Jurinac, Kunz, Majkut, London, V. State Op. Ch., VPO, Karajan

Recorded in 1950, Karajan's first recording of *Figaro*, like its mono companions *Così fan tutte* and *Don Giovanni*, offers one of the most distinguished casts ever assembled; but the absence of *secco* recitatives is most regrettable and prevents a strong recommendation, despite singing which is in every way outstanding. However, collectors might like to consider this bargain reissue, which comes on only two discs, even though it has only a cued synopsis, rather than the medium-priced set which has a full libretto and which is discussed in our main volume (5 67068-2 [567142]).

Le nozze di Figaro (highlights)

(M) **(*) Telarc CD 80449 (from complete recording, with Miles, Focile, Vaness, Corbelli, Mentzner, Murphy, R. Davies, SCO & Ch., Mackerras)

(BB) ** EMI Encore 5 74579-2 (from complete recording with Allen, Battle, M. Price, Hynninen, Murray, V. State Op. Ch., VPO, Muti)

There is much splendid singing in the Mackerras *Figaro* (discussed fully in our main volume) but at times a lack of charm. Nevertheless, this highlights disc is worth considering, even though the extensive synopsis is not cued.

Recorded in 1986, the Muti Vienna selection is disappointing for the cloudiness of the recording; and the singing, from a starry line-up of soloists, is very variable. Commanding as Thomas Allen is as Figaro, this is not a comic figure, dark rather, and less than winning. Kathleen Battle is a sparkling Susanna, but Margaret Price's Countess is not as nobly distinctive as she might be, and Ann Murray makes a somewhat edgy Cherubino. Muti's pacing is sometimes too fast to convey a feeling for the comedy. This 70-minute selection gives a good idea of the character of the set, but the sparse synopsis is barely adequate.

Die Zauberflöte (DVD versions)

⦿ *** TDK **DVD** DVWW-CLOPMF. Cotrubas, Schreier, Gruberová, Talvela, Boesch, Sieber, Hiestermann, V. State Op. Konzertvereinigung, VPO, Levine (Stage Director: Jean-Pierre Ponnelle; V/D: Brian Large)

*** Arthaus **DVD** 101 085. Lott, Goecke, Sandoz, Luxon, Thomaschke, Glyndebourne Ch., LPO, Haitink (Producer: John Cox; V/D: Dave Heather)

Jean-Pierre Ponnelle's production of *Die Zauberflöte*, with his own charming toytown sets and costumes, was the one revived more often than any other in the history of the Salzburg Festival. From the start, with James Levine at his brilliant and most perceptive as conductor, it struck an ideal between the pantomime element and the weightier implications of the Masonic background to the story. With Brian Large as video director exploiting the evocative setting in the Felsenreitschule with its series of layers of cliff recesses, it makes an ideal entertainment on film in this 1982 recording, with the possible reservation that an unusually large amount of spoken dialogue is included which, with well-chosen chapter headings, can easily be reduced on DVD.

The cast is excellent, with Peter Schreier in his prime as Tamino, Ileana Cotrubas a charming Pamina and Edita Gruberová a dazzling Queen of the Night – though the spectacle of the concentric circles of fairy-lights round her at her first appearance does not emerge on film as clearly as it should. Martti Talvela is the most resonant Sarastro, backed up by the veteran, Walter Berry, as the Speaker. Most imaginative of all is the casting of Christian Boesch as Papageno, a singing actor rather than a regular opera-singer. Few have presented the role quite so engagingly, and his duets with Pamina have a rare tenderness. The chorus and others in the cast are first rate.

What dominates John Cox's lively 1978 production of *Die Zauberflöte* for Glyndebourne are the sets and designs of David Hockney. He was following up the success of his unique designs for *The Rake's Progress*, and the vision again is striking, with stylized scenery and landscapes in false perspective, with something of a toytown atmosphere, including a delightful dragon and oriental costumes for Sarastro's followers. That puts the production firmly on the side of pantomime rather than serious drama, but the excellent casting and the powerful conducting of Bernard Haitink ensure that this is not just a trivial entertainment. Though Leo Goecke as Tamino has his roughness of voice, he sings *Dies Bildnis* beautifully, with the young Felicity Lott a charming Pamina. Benjamin Luxon is a strong and positive Papageno, with May Sandoz light, bright and agile as the Queen of the Night and Thomas Thomaschke a well-focused Sarastro, and with the young Willard White as the Speaker. A memorable version.

Die Zauberflöte (CD versions)

🅑— ⦿ **** DG 477 5789 (2). Röschmann, Miklósa, Strehl, Pape, Müller-Brachman, Kleiter, Azesberger, Georg Zeppenfeld, Arnold Schoenberg Ch., Mahler CO, Abbado

(B) (***) EMI mono 3 36769-2 (2). Seefried, Lipp, Loose, Dermota, Kunz, Weber, London, Klein, V. State Op. Ch., VPO, Karajan

(B) ** Double Decca (ADD) 448 734-2 (2). Gueden, Lipp, Simoneau, Berry, Böhme, Schoeffler, V. State Op. Ch., VPO, Boehm

As DG's wording on the box makes clear, this is Abbado's very first *Magic Flute* on record and indeed – as they claim – it is a triumphant success. Its freshness and charm, with ravishing playing from the Mahler Chamber Orchestra, reminds us of our first encounter with the celebrated Fricsay recording. But Abbado's cast is finer still, for here René Pape's magnificent Sarastro dominates the opera, just as intended. He and the superb chorus bring just the right touch of gravitas, so all the pantomime fun with Papageno and Papagena is nicely balanced. Moreover, Erika Miklósa's Queen of the Night's second aria, *Der Hölle Rache*, is quite as dazzling as Rita Streich's celebrated version, and it is slightly fuller in tone. Dorothea Röschmann and Christoph Strehl are a perfectly matched Pamina and Tamino, for both have lovely voices: Strehl is ardent, and Röschmann is infinitely touching when she mistakenly thinks Tamino is lost to her forever. The smaller parts are also without flaw. Kurt Azesberger is a splendid Monastatos, and even the Speaker, George Zeppenfeld, has a honeyed voice.

But most magical of all are the little vocal ensembles, wonderfully warm and refined, especially the numbers featuring the Three Ladies (Caroline Stein, Heidi Zehnder and Ann-Carolyn Schülter), who blend so delightfully but not suavely, and the Three Boys (from the Tölzer Knabenchor), who are just as memorable. Although the moments of drama are not lost, this is above all an affectionately relaxed performance, with Abbado continually revelling in the lyrical beauty of Mozart's wonderful score. It is, of course, a live performance, so it has the extra communicative tension that brings; but the audience are (mercifully) angelically quiet, although we are aware of their presence during the fun created by the ever-reluctant Papageno. The recording is first class and, while there is a great deal of dialogue, it can be programmed out. (In the old mono Fricsay set it was cleverly abbreviated, so DG were able to produce a famous highlights LP that contained virtually every number, sometimes very deftly truncated.)

Until now, the Vienna State Opera cast of Karajan's mono version of 1950 has not been matched on record. There is no spoken dialogue, but many may count that an advantage for repeated listening. This reissue comes with only a cued synopsis, but it is also available at medium price as another of EMI's 'Great Recordings of the Century', and as such comes with a full libretto (5 67071-2 [567165] – see our main volume).

The principal attraction of the Double Decca reissue from the earliest days of stereo, apart from its modest cost, is the conducting of Karl Boehm. That might well be counted recommendation enough, in spite of the absence of dialogue, particularly when the Tamino of Léopold Simoneau and the Papageno of Walter Berry are strongly and sensitively sung and Wilma Lipp proves an impressive Queen of the Night. But the rest of the singing is variable, with Hilde Gueden a pert, characterful Pamina, unhappy in the florid divisions, and Kurt Böhme a gritty and ungracious Sarastro. The new cued synopsis is a great improvement on the previous reissue and includes new documentation intended to offer a helpful guide for the newcomer to the opera.

Die Zauberflöte (highlights)

(M) *** Telarc CD 80345 (from complete set, with Hadley, Hendricks, Allen, Anderson, Lloyd, SCO & Ch., Mackerras)

Though the recording is rather resonant, this was the most successful of the Mackerras recordings of the four Mozart key operas for Telarc, strongly cast, and with Mackerras finding an ideal scale for the work. The 77-minute highlights disc is pretty comprehensive and the libretto has a fully cued synopsis.

Arias from: Così fan tutte; Don Giovanni; Die Entführung aus dem Serail; Idomeneo; Die Zauberflöte

(M) ** Decca Classic Recitals (ADD) 475 7168. Burrows, with LSO or LPO; Pritchard

Stuart Burrows's beautiful voice overcomes every technical problem of these demanding arias. If ultimately his recital lacks a sense of sharp characterization of the various characters, there is much to enjoy in the singing itself, and the excellent (1975, originally Oiseau-Lyre) recording and sympathetic accompaniments add to its appeal.

'Opera Festival': Arias from: Così fan tutte; Don Giovanni; Die Entführung aus dem Serail; Le Nozze di Figaro; Il re pastore; Zaide; Die Zauberflöte

** Australian Decca Eloquence (ADD) 476 7437. Popp, Fassbaender, Krenn, Krause, Jungwirth, V. Haydn O, Kertész

These are essentially concert performances, recorded in the early 1970s. There are plenty of favourite arias here and, though Kertész is not a natural Mozartian (not all his tempi are well judged), the performances are generally enjoyable. The soloists (an apparently excellent assembly) do not always sing as stylishly as they might, and there is little attempt at characterization (Fassbaender's Voi che sapete, for instance, is not very convincing) but there is a freshness to the music-making which makes it agreeable enough. Good, resonant sound from Decca.

Arias: Don Giovanni; Die Entführung aus dem Serail; Idomeneo; Le nozze di Figaro; Die Zauberflöte

(M) (***) EMI mono 4 76844-2 [4 76845-2]. Schwarzkopf (with various conductors & orchestras, including Pritchard, Krips, Braithwaite, Karajan)

This famous Schwarzkopf mono recital is reissued as one of EMI's 'Great Recordings of the Century', with two extra items added (to make 14 in all), including L'amerò sarò costante, Aminto's Act II aria from Il re pastore. This is the earliest, along with the two from Die Entführung; and one of the curiosities is a lovely account of Pamina's Ach, ich fühls, recorded in English in 1948. The majority, including those from Figaro – Susanna's and Cherubino's arias as well as the Countess's – are taken from a recital disc conducted by John Pritchard in 1953. Full translations are included.

MUDARRA, Alonso (1510–80)

Music in Tablature for Vihuela & Voice, Book 3 (1546)

(M) *** Astrée ES 9941. Figueras, Hopkinson Smith

The collection here (taken from the last of Mudarra's set of three Books) is also the third known collection of music for vihuela (following publications by Luis Milán and Luis de Nárvaez). In this repertoire Montserrat Figueras is in her element, singing these simple but beautiful melodies without artifice. She is accompanied by what many reference books have described as an obsolete instrument, the guitar's lute-like predecessor. But Hopkinson Smith plays four vihuelas (all modern reproductions) to accompany these captivating, folk-like romances and villancicos. The singing is quite lovely. A cherishable disc, beautifully recorded and with full translations included.

MUFFAT, Georg (1653–1704)

Georg Muffat was born in Megève, Savoy. As a boy he studied with Lully in Paris and he became organist at Strasbourg Cathedral, before moving on to Austria and Salzburg. From 1680 to 1682 he studied in Italy, finally returning to work in Passau. He thought of himself as a German who had mastered both the French and Italian styles of composition.

Armonico tributo (1682): Sonata V à 5; Violin Sonata

(B) *** HM Musique d'abord HMA 1951220. L. Bar., Medlam – SCHMELZER: Lament; Sonatas ***

In their somewhat melancholy atmosphere, the two works here are very like the music of Johann Schmelzer, which they follow in this excellent collection of seventeenth-century string sonatas. The Violin Sonata (the only one Muffat wrote) is cyclical, as the opening Adagio returns at the end; in between come both a fugue and a recitativo passage. The Sonata à V is in five movements, culminating in a dancing Passacaglia with 24 variations, with the theme regularly brought back. Excellent performances and recording make this a most stimulating disc.

Concerti grossi 1 in D min. (Good News); 2 in A (Watchful Heart); 3 in B (Convalescence); 4 in G min. (Sweet Sleep); 5 in D (The World); 6 in A min. (Who is This?)

(BB) ** Naxos 8.555096. Musica Aeterna Bratislava, Zajíček

Concerti grossi 7 in E (Delight of Kings); 8 in F (Noble Coronation); 9 in C min. (Sad Victory); 10 in G (Perseverance); 11 in E min. (Madness of Love); 12 in G (Propitious Constellations)

(BB) ** Naxos 8.555743. Musica Aeterna Bratislava, Zajíček

The 12 Concerti grossi of Muffat are inventive works, in which the influences of both Corelli and Lully are much in evidence. There is plenty to enjoy in these pieces, written for court entertainment, which are melodic and well contrasted, with a few unexpected quirks of harmony and rhythm adding spice. The performances are good ones, stylish and lively, with attractive embellishments, but the recording is rather strident, with the strings not very ingratiating – the effect becomes a little tiring after a while. However, this pair of CDs come at a modest price and the repertoire is certainly worth exploring. Incidentally, the intriguing titles have little to do with the actual music, but refer to the occasions of their first performances.

ORGAN MUSIC

Apparatus musico-organisticus (1690): *Toccatas 1–12; Ciacona; Passacaglia; Nova Cyclopeias Harmonica*

☞ *** Oehms **SACD** OC 604 (2). Kelemen (Freundt organ, Klosterburg Abbey, or Silberman organ, Ebersmünster)

(BB) *** Naxos 8.553917 (*Toccatas 1–8*; organ of Klosterburg Abbey); 8.553990 (*Toccatas 9–12, Ciacona, Passacaglia; Nova Cyclopeias Harmonica*; organ of Zweittl Collegiate Church). Haselböck

The *Apparatus musico-organisticus* was published in Salzburg in 1690, two years after the *Armonico tributo* mentioned above, and it was dedicated to Emperor Leopold I in Ausberg. It is a truly major collection, combining a dozen *Toccatas* of considerable variety, with three sets of variations (without pedals), for the closing *Nova Cyclopeias Harmonica* is also an air with variations.

Both sets of performances here are of high quality and both Kelemen and Haselböck have splendid organs to choose from. Joseph Kelemen alternates his two organs throughout the programme, whereas Haselböck uses the fine Klosterburg organ for the first eight *Toccatas* and the Zweittl Collegiate Church organ for the last four and the sets of variations (which call for more colour). This instrument is of special interest as it was built by Johann Egedacher, who worked in Passau, where the composer lived later in his career.

Joseph Kelemen has a great advantage over his colleague in that he is recorded in SACD, and this greatly increases both the richness and the depth of the pedals, all but shaking the floor domestically and giving one the thrilling sense of being in the church itself. However, the Naxos recordings are spectacular too, and this set is excellent value. Both recordings have good documentation.

MUNDY, William (c. 1529–c. 1591)

Vox Patris caelestis

☞ (M) *** Gimell (ADD) GIMSE 401 Tallis Scholars, Phillips – ALLEGRI: *Miserere*; PALESTRINA: *Missa Papae Marcelli* ***

Mundy's *Vox Patris caelestis* was written during the short reign of Queen Mary (1553–8). The work is structured in nine sections in groups of three, the last of each group being climactic and featuring the whole choir, with solo embroidery. Yet the music flows continuously, like a great river, and the complex vocal writing creates the most spectacular effects, with the trebles soaring up and shining out over the underlying cantilena. The Tallis Scholars give an account which balances linear clarity with considerable power. The recording is first class and the digital remastering for CD improves the focus further.

MUSSORGSKY, Modest (1839–81)

Night on the Bare Mountain; Khovanshchina: Prelude (both orch. Rimsky-Korsakov); *Pictures at an Exhibition*

(BB) **(*) EMI Gemini 3 50824-2 (2). Oslo PO, Jansons – RIMSKY-KORSAKOV: *Scheherazade; Capriccio espagnole* **(*)

The highlight of Jansons's Gemini budget reissue is the *Khovanshchina Prelude*, which is played most beautifully, yet produces a passionate climax. *Night on the Bare Mountain* is diabolically pungent; but here, as in the *Pictures*, the fiercely brilliant EMI recording with its dry bass and lack of sumptuousness brings dramatic bite and sharply etched detail, but less in the way of expansiveness.

Night on the Bare Mountain; Pictures at an Exhibition; Khovanshchina, Act IV: Entr'acte. Boris Godunov: Symphonic Synthesis (all arr. and orch. Stokowski)

❂ (BB) *** Naxos 8.557645. Bournemouth SO, Serebrier (with STOKOWSKI: *Slavic Christmas Music*; TCHAIKOVSKY: *Solitude; Humoresque ***)

This Naxos collection of Stokowski's flamboyant arrangements of Mussorgsky at budget price proves the most formidable rival for similar collections on premium-priced labels. It offers outstanding performances by the Bournemouth Symphony Orchestra, brilliantly recorded in sound if anything even more spectacular than on rival discs. Though Stokowski's arrangement of *Pictures at an Exhibition* is less refined than that of Ravel, with its weighty brass it is certainly more Russian. The most serious shortcoming is Stokowski's omission of two of the movements, *Tuileries* and *The Market Place at Limoges*, made on the grounds that they are too French. Yet Serebrier's new performance makes the result very convincing, with speeds well chosen and the brass wonderfully incisive. The atmospheric qualities of the *Boris Godunov* symphonic synthesis also come over superbly, starting with a hauntingly rarefied bassoon solo, even if the recording catches the clicking of the keys. The mystery of the chimes in the *Coronation Scene* as well as the *Death Scene* are most evocative, and in *Night on the Bare Mountain* the weight of the arrangement comes over well, and the *Khovanshchina Entr'acte*, too, has impressive weight and clarity. Among the extra items, the Tchaikovsky song, *Solitude*, explores an astonishingly wide emotional range within a tiny span, and the jolly *Humoresque* is a piano piece that Stravinsky memorably used in his ballet *The Fairy's Kiss*. The baldly effective *Slavic Christmas Music*, attributed to Stokowski himself, is based not just on a Christmas hymn but on Ippolitov-Ivanov's *In a Manger*. Altogether a treasurable collection, well worth its modest cost.

Pictures at an Exhibition (orch. Ravel)

(B) ** CfP 575 5642. LPO, Pritchard – PROKOFIEV: *Romeo and Juliet*: highlights **

A well-characterized account under Pritchard in which the personality of the orchestra comes over strongly, the players obviously enjoying themselves and their own virtuosity. The well-detailed 1970 recording, made in Barking Town Hall, makes every detail of the orchestration clear against a pleasing ambience, and the building up of *The Great Gate of Kiev* sequence provides an impressive finale.

(i) *Pictures at an Exhibition* (orch. Ravel); (ii) *Pictures at an Exhibition* (original piano version)

(M) **(*) Mercury **SACD** (ADD) 475 6620. (i) Minneapolis SO, Dorati; (ii) Janis (with CHOPIN: *Etude in F; Waltz in A min.*)

As one would expect with a 1959 Mercury recording, the sound is very upfront and vivid; the strings are practically in the room, and the brass and woodwind are clearly delineated, the percussion telling (the cymbal and bass-drum crash in *Gnomus* is spectacular). Yet, being Mercury, it is all so well balanced that it does not seem over the top and, even if the sound is a bit dry, there is plenty of warmth. Dorati's is a no-nonsense approach; it is direct and positive and makes an enjoyable recommendation, if not a top one.

Byron Janis is certainly vibrant in the original piano version of the work, with plenty of both power and subtlety. The Mercury sound is vivid, though, being so upfront, it is not always helpful to the music; *Il Vecchio Castello* is given a sympathetic reading, but the recording robs this piece of much of its haunting evocation. With Janis's crystal-clear articulation the more extrovert numbers come off well, and there is extra warmth for those with SACD systems.

(i) *Pictures at an Exhibition* (orch. Ashkenazy); (ii) *Pictures at an Exhibition* (original piano version)
(M) ** Decca 475 7717. (i) Philh. O, Ashkenazy; (ii) Ashkenazy (piano)

Ashkenazy's score cannot match Ravel's in subtlety of detail; it concentrates on broad washes of orchestral sound – helped by the richness of the Kingsway Hall acoustic – so that climaxes are massive rather than electrifying. The character of the pictures is not very individual either, although Ashkenazy undoubtedly finds plenty of Russian feeling in the music itself. The recording is opulent rather than glittering. A disappointment, even though Ashkenazy corrects a number of textual errors inherent in Ravel's version. His piano version is distinguished by poetic feeling, but lacks something of the extrovert flair with which pianists like Richter or Pletnev can make one forget all about the orchestral transcription.

Pictures at an Exhibition (original piano version)
(M) **(*) Vox (ADD) SPJ 97203. Brendel (with BALAKIREV: *Islamey*; STRAVINSKY: *3 Movements from Petrushka*)
(M) ** Sony S2K 94737 (2). Graffman – BALAKIREV: *Islamey* *(*); TCHAIKOVSKY: *Piano Concertos 1–3* **
(M) ** RCA 09026 63884-2. Evgeny Kissin (with BACH/BUSONI: *Toccata, Adagio & Fugue in C, BWV 564*; GLINKA: *The Lark* ***)
* Hyp. CDA 67018. Demidenko – PROKOFIEV: *Romeo & Juliet: 10 Pieces*, etc. **

Brendel's performance comes from the 1960s at the time when he was recording the Beethoven concertos and sonatas for Vox with such conspicuous success. It comes with a pretty electrifying *Islamey* and a hardly less exciting account of the *Three Movements from Petrushka*. The recording remains pretty shallow, but the playing is exhilarating and is a reminder of this artist at his best.

Gary Graffman takes a bold survey of Mussorgky's *Pictures* with steady tempi, except in his accelerando during the *Ballet of unhatched chickens*. In many ways it is an impressive reading, but not imaginative enough to be really individual, and the closing *Great Gate of Kiev* is rather heavy-going.

Kissin's playing is masterly but wanting in spontaneity. Every detail is carefully thought out but caution is never flung to the winds and the performance does not have the vibrant quality of a Richter or Horowitz.

No doubts about Demidenko's virtuosity and keyboard command here, or the excellence of the Hyperion sound. There are doubts, however, about many of the highly idiosyncratic touches, which are so pervasive that he attracts more attention to himself than to Mussorgsky!

Boris Godunov (arr. Rimsky-Korsakov) (complete DVD version)
*** Warner **DVD** 51011 1851-2. Nesterenko, Pyavko, Sinyavskaya, Kudryashov, Eizen, Bolshoi Theatre Ch. & O, Lazarev (Stage & Video Director: Irina Morozova)

Until the late 1960s, in the days of Christoff, the only *Boris* to be recorded (or to be seen at Covent Garden) was the edition by Rimsky-Korsakov. In recent years it has been driven from the stage in favour of Mussorgsky's original. As learned an authority as Professor Gerald Abraham was at pains to point out that the Rimsky version, recorded here, is also a masterpiece, and it is good to have it again in this 1987 staging. Nesterenko was one of the commanding exponents of the role and it is thrilling to see and hear his magisterial account. The other major roles, Vladislav Pyavko's Grigory, Tamara Sinyavskaya's Marina, Vladimir Kudryashov's Prince Shuisky and Arthur Eizen's Varlaam are pretty impressive, too. Nor are we let down by the orchestral playing under Alexander Lazarev. Of course Gergiev remains supreme, both in the DVD version of the Tarkovsky production and in the five-CD set of the 1869 and 1872 versions. However, this version of the alternative Rimsky-Korsakov score should be added to them. No booklet or notes.

Boris Godunov (arr. Rimsky-Korsakov)
(M) *** Decca 475 7718 (3). Ghiaurov, Vishnevskaya, Spiess, Maslennikov, Talvela, V. Boys' Ch., Sofia R. Ch., V. State Op. Ch., VPO, Karajan
(BB) (***) Naxos mono 8.110242. Christoff, Gedda, Zareska, Bielecki, Borg, Lebedeva, Romanova, Pasternak, Russian Ch. of Paris; French Nat. R. O, Dobrowen

With Ghiaurov in the title-role, Karajan's superbly controlled Decca version, technically outstanding, came far nearer than previous recordings to conveying the rugged greatness of Mussorgsky's masterpiece. Only the Coronation scene lacked something of the weight and momentum one ideally wants. Vishnevskaya was far less appealing than the lovely non-Slavonic Marina of Evelyn Lear on EMI, but overall this Decca set had much more to offer. This has recently been available only at bargain price, poorly documented. But this reissue, as one of Decca's Originals, comes with full text and translation. (Incidentally, the label is very appropriate in this instance for, even if the cast is flawed by Vishnevskaya's less than appealing Marina, this really was the first recording technically able to convey the rugged greatness of Mussorgsky's vision.)

It is good to welcome back the pioneering (1952) mono *Boris* in which the celebrated Christoff sang not only *Boris* himself but Varlaam and Pimen. He skilfully varies his colour in these roles, but also gives a commanding account of Boris which is a triumph in every respect, as is Dobrowen's direction – as vital and idiomatic as any version since. The youthful Nicolai Gedda is a magnificent Grigory and Eugenia Zareska is an unforgettable Marina. Kim Borg doubles as Shchelkalov and Rangoni. And there is more duplication of roles with Andrzej Bielecki as Prince Shuisky, Missail and Krushchov. The choral singing is very good and the French Radio Orchestra under Dobrowen sound as if they are all from Moscow. The set appeared briefly on EMI Références, but Mark Obert-Thorn's transfer is equally fine – if not finer.

Khovanshchina (complete CD version)
(BB) (***) Naxos 8.111124/26. Boris Freidkov, Ivan Nechayev, Mark Reizen, Vladimir Ulyanov, Sofya Preobrazhenskaya, Nina Serval, Kirov Ch. & O, Khaikin

You won't hear anything as remarkable as this *Khovanshchina* again. First of all, we have the Rimsky-Korsakov version, which has fallen completely out of favour nowadays – understandably, perhaps, given the excellence of the Shostakovich edition which all the present-day versions follow. However, Rimsky-Korsakov's scoring is absolutely wonderful and should not be allowed to pass into oblivion. Secondly, we have an incomparable cast, with Mark Reizen's Dosifey and Sofya Preobrazhenskaya as Marfa. The 1946 recording sounds surprisingly good in Ward Marston's remarkable transfer and the third CD has room for 13 songs, some from the old Mussorgsky Song Society, with Vladimir Rosing. Do not hesitate.

MUSTONEN, Olli (born 1967)

(i) *Triple Violin Concerto; Nonets 1 & 2;* (ii) *Petite Suite for Cello and Strings; Frogs dancing on water lilies*

*** Ondine ODE 9742. Tapiola Sinf., composer, with (i) P. and J. Kuusisto; (ii) Rousi

Olli Mustonen is a gifted pianist, now in his late thirties, who commands a splendid technique and considerable artistry. He also composes, and all the music here comes from 1995–2000. His *Triple Concerto for three violins and orchestra* (1998) is a neo-Baroque pastiche, and there is a strong element of pastiche in the *First Nonet*, dedicated to Steven Isserlis. Its Scherzo has a Mendelssohnian delicacy, though the repeated ostinato rhythm of the finale is too much of a not very good thing. The *Petite Suite for Cello and Strings* has a naturalness and charm that almost recall Gunnar de Frumerie's *Pastoral Suite*. Mustonen does not have a distinctive voice, but his directness and simplicity are strangely likeable. He has a natural, if at times naïve, melodic talent, and the fine musicians on this disc serve him well, as do the Ondine engineers.

NABOKOV, Nicolas (1903–78)

(i) *Ode: Méditations sur la majesté de Dieu; Union Pacific*

*** Chan. 9768. (i) Shaguch, Kisselev, Russian State Symphonic Cappella; Residentie O, The Hague, Polyansky

Nicolas Nabokov moved to Paris in 1923 where he came into contact with Prokofiev, Stravinsky and Diaghilev, and the *Ode* was one of the great successes of Diaghilev's last season. It consists of ten loosely related movements and two interludes, much in the manner of Stravinsky's *Symphony of Psalms*, and was choreographed by Massine. But in spirit it is much closer to *Les Noces*, though it does not have the inventiveness or character of Stravinsky. *Union Pacific* was commissioned for Massine and the Ballets Russes. It is on the whole attractive, diatonic music influenced by 'Les Six', Prokofiev and the spirit of the 1920s. In its use of American popular music it is reminiscent of Berners' *Triumph of Neptune*. The soloists Marina Shaguch and Alexander Kisselev are first rate, as are the Russian State Symphonic Cappella. The Hague Residentie Orchestra respond well to Polyansky's direction, and the recording is in the finest traditions of the house, with well-focused detail and totally truthful.

NANCARROW, Conlon (1912–97)

String Quartet 3

(M) *** Wigmore Hall Live WHLive 003. Arditti Qt – LIGETI: *Quartet 2;* DUTILLEUX: *Ainsi la nuit* ***

This is the formidable opening item of an extraordinary concert of avant-garde string quartets, played by the Arditti group and recorded live in April 2005. Written in 1987, after a meeting between the composer and the present players two years earlier, the *Third Quartet* has an immediately communicative opening, with a recognizable theme which is treated in strict canon, as are the themes of the two remaining movements, with the second centring on harmonics and pizzicati, while the finale includes ear-tickling glissandi. But it is essentially an angular canon fugato in which the four parts eventually end up together on the note C. As with the other works on this disc, the sheer concentration of the performance holds the listener in spite of him- or herself. A really original work, which comes off, for the sounds the quartet creates are really extraordinary. Real and vivid recording.

NAUMANN, Johann Gottlieb (1741–1801)

Aci e Galatea

*** Orfeo C222022H (2). Geller, Homrich, Häger, Libor, Bästlein, Stuttgart Chamber Ch. & Bar. O, Bernius

Naumann was one in a long line of Kapellmeisters to the Saxon court. He is represented here by his very last work, the opera he completed in the year he died. Although there is the occasional echo of Mozart, even a direct crib or two, the writing, not surprisingly, is rougher, if with some colourful orchestration on horns and even piccolo. What matters is the vigour of the piece. In telling the story of Acis and Galatea, the librettist, Giuseppe Foppa, avoids its darker side, with the predatory cyclops, Polyphemus, hardly a menace. There are even jolly numbers for a chorus of cyclopses, and Acis is brought back to life just when Galatea is contemplating suicide, bringing the necessary happy ending. The action moves swiftly, with relatively brief arias for the principals, culminating in the only long aria, when Galatea is threatening to kill herself. The music reflects little of tragedy, with a brilliant *cabaletta* fading gently into the following number, and a prompt dénouement. Neither the story nor the music needs to be taken very seriously, but in a lively performance like this under Frieder Bernius, generally well sung with Brigitte Geller and Martin Homrich excellent in the title roles, it makes a delightful entertainment. The Italian libretto comes with a German translation but only a synopsis in English.

NEBRA, Manuel Blasco de (1730–84)

Pastorellas I, VI and VII; Sonatas III; V; VI, Op. 1/1, 2 & 5

** Met. METCD 1064. Cerasi (harpsichord & fortepiano)

Born in Seville, Manuel Blasco de Nebra was seven years old when Domenico Scarlatti died, but, coming from a large musical family, he determined to carry forward the Scarlatti tradition of keyboard writing using short musical ideas which are then allowed to grow. But only 30 of the 170 keyboard works he is known to have written have survived. The *Pastorellas* are in three movements with the 'Pastorella' itself the centrepiece, followed by a Minuet. The *Sonatas* here are all two-movement works, slow and quick, and sometimes the allegros reach a virtuoso standard, as in the *Presto* of Op. 1/5, which Carole Cerasi plays brilliantly. But, alas, her rhythms are sometimes curiously jumpy, and her rubato and brief pauses in the legato lines of the *Adagios* are not always convincing. Her recordings have received considerable praise elsewhere, so if you are tempted to explore this rewarding composer, you may find her linear playing more comfortable than we do.

NEPOMUCENO, Alberto (1864–1920)

Galhofeira, Op. 13/4; Improviso, Op. 27/2; Nocturnes: 1 in C; 2 in G (for the left hand); 5 Pequenas peças (for the left hand); Nocturne, Op. 33; Sonata in F min., Op. 9; Suite antiga, Op. 11.
** Marco Polo 8.223548. Guimarães

Alberto Nepomuceno has every right to be called the father of Brazilian music. He was active as a teacher and for a time was director of the National Institute of Music in Rio de Janeiro, helping the youthful Villa-Lobos. Although he composed in most genres, little of his output has been recorded, so this disc of his piano music is welcome. Much of it is derivative – Brahmsian or Schumannesque – but it shows him to be far from negligible. Morever there is a trace of the kind of popular Brazilian music that fascinated Milhaud in his *Saudades do Brasil.* The *Cinco pequenas peças* and the *Nocturnes* of 1919 were both written for Nepomuceno's daughter, who was born without a right arm. Maria Inês Guimarães is not the most imaginative of pianists and is somewhat wanting in finesse, but those with a taste for off-beat repertoire may find this worth investigating.

NEVIN, Arthur (1871–1943)

From Edgeworth Hills
*** Altarus AIR-CD 9024. Amato – E. NEVIN: *A Day in Venice,* etc. ***

Arthur Nevin was without his older brother's melodic individuality, but he wrote spontaneously and crafted his pieces nicely. The most striking number of *From Edgeworth Hills* is the tripping *Sylphs,* very characteristic of its time, while *As the Moon Rose* has an agreeably sentimental tune, and the picaresque *Firefly* sparkles nicely here. *Toccatella* is rhythmically a bit awkward but is quite a showpiece, and Donna Amato plays it with real dash. Excellent recording.

NEVIN, Ethelbert (1862–1901)

A Day in Venice (suite), Op. 25; Etude in the Form of a Romance; Etude in the Form of a Scherzo, Op. 18/1-2; May in Tuscany (suite), Op. 21; Napoli (En passant), Op. 30/3; Mighty Lak' a Rose (after the transcription by Charles Spross); O'er Hill and Dale (suite); The Rosary (arr. Whelpley); Water Scenes, Op. 13
*** Altarus AIR-CD 9024. Amato – A. NEVIN: *From Edgeworth Hills* ***

Ethelbert Nevin was born in Edgeworth, Pennsylvania, scored his first great success when *Narcissus* became a world-wide hit, and *The Rosary* was Nevin's other success, with the sheet music selling over a million copies in the decade following its publication in 1898. Donna Amato grew up in the area where Nevin was born, and she takes care not to sentimentalize these genre pieces, which can be just a little trite but also quite engaging. *Mighty Lak' a Rose,* another favourite, retains all its charm. The recording is clear and natural in a pleasing acoustic.

NIELSEN, Carl (1865–1931)

(i) *Aladdin Suite. An Imaginary Journey to the Faeroe Islands; At the Bier of a Young Artist; Bohemian Danish Folk Tune; Helios Overture; Maskarade Overture; Pan and Syrinx; Saga-Drøm*
(M) **(*) MSR Classics MS 1150. Aarhus SO, Friedel; (i) with Jutland Op. Ch.

An attractively generous compilation of Nielsen's shorter works. The orchestral playing may not be as polished as that of the Gothenburg Symphony Orchestra in a rather similar collection (DG 447 757-2, see our main volume), but it offers 80 minutes of music, including three items not on the Gothenburg CD, *At the Bier of a Young Artist, Pan and Syrinx* (with fine contributions from the cor anglais and clarinet soloists) and the sparkling *Bohemian-Danish Folk Tune.* Although the opening *Maskarade Overture* could have had more fizz, performances are vivid and attractively atmospheric, and the *Aladdin Suite* includes a chorus who make a sudden surprise entry in *The Marketplace at Ispahan* and add to the gusto of the finale.

(i) *Commotio, Op. 48; (ii) Violin Sonata 2 in G min., Op. 35; (i) 7 Early Songs (all orch. Holten)*
*(*) Danacord DACOCD 588. (i) Hansen; (ii) Bonde-Hansen; Odense SO, Holten

These three works come from different periods of Nielsen's life. The early songs have a touching and artless simplicity that is quite special and that is lost in these orchestrations. At times *Æbleblomst* ('Appleblossom'), which has great purity and tenderness, acquires a Mahlerian lushness that changes its character. So, too, does *I Seraillets Have* ('In the Garden of the Seraglio'). Nor is the scoring always that expert: *Irmelin Rose* sounds crude. Bo Holten's orchestration of *Commotio* (1931) completely transforms its character. Instead of enhancing its majesty and splendour, it thickens Nielsen's textures; the overall effect sounds cumbersome, laboured and overblown, completely at variance with the clarity and grandeur of the original. The *G minor Violin Sonata* of 1912 is one of the composer's strangest and most haunting pieces, but its essential inwardness and feel of strangeness are lost. The character of the opening of the finale is changed beyond recognition. It all serves to show that Nielsen's thinking was keenly attuned to the medium in which it sought expression. Decent performances and recording, but not really recommendable.

Violin Concerto, Op. 33
** EMI 5 56906-2. Znaider, LPO, Foster (with BRUCH: *Violin Concerto 1 **)*

Nikolaj Znaider comes from Denmark but is of Russian parentage and made a very strong impression at the 1999 Ysaÿe Competition in Brussels, taking the first prize in a very strong field. His Nielsen concerto is very well thought out and fervent, though it lacks the total conviction and white-hot inspiration that Cho-Liang Lin and Salonen bring to it. He has very good support from Lawrence Foster and the LPO, but he is slightly self-aware and reluctant to let go. The Bruch concerto is also ardent but in the last resort not distinctive.

Symphonies: 1, Op. 7; 2 (Four Temperaments), Op. 16; 3 (Espansiva), Op. 27; 4 (Inextinguishable), Op. 29; 5, Op. 50; 6 (Sinfonia semplice)
*** Dacapo **DVD** 2.110403-05. Danish Nat. RSO, Schønwandt

These are the same performances as those discussed in our main volume, but this time with vision attached! The camera-work is tactful and restrained and it enhances our enjoyment of what are excellent performances, arguably the best since Blomstedt's San Francisco set – and perhaps even finer. The first three symphonies are accommodated on the first DVD, the remainder on the second. There is a bonus CD in the form of a film by Karl Aage Rasmussen on Nielsen's life and music called *The Light and the Darkness*, which is well worth having.

(i) *Symphonies 1 in G min., Op. 7; (ii; v) 2 (Four Temperaments), Op. 16; (iii; iv; v) 3 (Sinfonia espansiva), Op. 27; (ii; v) 4 (Inextinguishable), Op. 29; 5, Op. 50; (i) 6 (Sinfonia semplice)*
(B) ** Sony (ADD) SB3K 89974 (3). (i) Phd. O, Ormandy; (ii) NYPO; (iii) Royal Danish O; (iv) Goldbaek, Møller; (v) Bernstein

Inevitably a mixed bag, the three Sony CDs concentrate on the CBS recordings that served to blaze Nielsen's cause in the United States in the 1960s. Bernstein's account of the *Fifth Symphony* is imposing and felt; the *Espansiva* with the Royal Danish Orchestra was much admired in its day, though the main theme of the finale is laboured. Nielsen wanted it to be broad, but not that broad. The *Second* has plenty of fire, but the *Fourth Symphony* is less successful, and the recording is rather crude. Ormandy's accounts of the *First* and *Sixth* with the Philadelphia Orchestra were underrated at the time and the *Sixth* – particularly the first movement – is very impressive. This is a valuable set, historically, but now there are finer versions of all these works.

Symphonies 1 in G min., Op. 7; 2 in B min. (Four Temperaments), Op. 16
*(*) Finlandia 8573 85574-2. Finnish RSO, Saraste

There is some very good playing from the Finnish Radio Orchestra, and Saraste is generally attentive to detail and free from any kind of interpretative point-making. At the same time it makes a less strong impression than his powerful accounts of the *Fourth* and *Fifth Symphonies*. Tempi are generally well chosen (even if some may find Saraste fractionally on the fast side in the third movement of No. 1 and distinctly so in the finale of No. 2). Elsewhere, as in the finale of No. 1, he sets off at exactly the right stride. But the first movement of the *Four Temperaments* is coarse rather than choleric and its second theme wanting in nobility, as is the slow movement. The phlegmatic movement is a bit short on charm.

Symphonies: (i) 2 (Four Temperaments); (ii) 4 (Inextinguishable); Helios Overture. (iii) The Mother (Incidental Music): The Fog is Lifting
(M) *RCA (ADD) 82876 76237-2. Chicago SO, (i) Gould; (ii) Martinon; (iii) Galway, Williams

Symphonies 2 (Four Temperaments); 5
** BIS CD 1289. BBC Scottish SO, Vänskä

It is curious that BMG/RCA should have resurrected these old Chicago recordings of Nielsen symphonies which, so far as we can trace, have been out of the catalogue since we first discussed them in Volume 6 of the original *Stereo Record Guide* in the late 1960s. One does not think first of Morton

Gould as a Nielsen specialist, and surely enough his brashness of approach does little justice to the breadth and dignity of the superbly wrought *Second Symphony* with fast tempi – unacceptably fast in the second and fourth movements. More surprisingly, Martinon's performance of the *Inextinguishable* all but extinguishes it with its brutal efficiency, full of explosive brilliance, again a performance far too hard-driven to be acceptable. Of course the Chicago orchestra play efficiently enough, and the *Helios Overture*, recorded at the same time, is very well done, as of course is the miniature, *The Fog is Lifting*, from James Galway and Sioned Williams (harp), offered here as a bonus.

On the BIS CD the first movement of the *Second Symphony* needs to move a shade faster if it is to convey the choleric temperament, and the finale could also move with a brisker stride. Part of the problem with both performances is that the strings are wanting in the richness and weight that distinguish rival accounts. Decent, but not in any way outstanding, recorded sound.

(i) *Symphonies 3 (Espansiva); 4 (Inextinguishable)*
** BIS CD 1209. BBC Scottish SO, Vänskä, (i) with Komsi, Immler

Vänskä's *Espansiva* is curiously uninvolving and wanting in fire. He has not inspired his players as he did in his Sibelius cycle at Lahti. The *Fourth Symphony*, however, is another matter. This is a vital performance in every way and conveys the splendour of Nielsen's visionary score. In this the Finnish conductor gets almost everything right, though his strings could do with greater weight and body of tone. Curiously, the BIS recording, judged by the exalted standards of the house, is serviceable rather than distinguished.

CHAMBER MUSIC

String Quartets 1; 4; Little Suite for Strings (arr. Zapolski).
* Chan. 9635. Zapolski Qt
String Quartets 2 in F min., Op. 5; 3 in E flat, Op. 14
*(*) Chan. 9817. Zapolski Qt

The Zapolski Quartet is so concerned with projecting Nielsen's ideas that the music is never allowed to speak for itself. Those who know these delightful works will view both performances with some impatience, though the playing as such is accomplished and the recording more than acceptable. Just try the scherzo movement of the *E flat Quartet* and you can see for yourself. The directness of utterance of Nielsen's ideas is undermined by over-sophisticated expressive exaggeration. Perhaps the group is not quite as intrusive as it was in the *F major Quartet*, Op. 44, but it is still too studied and self-aware. Fortunately, the Oslo Quartet is available at a third of the price.

PIANO MUSIC

Chaconne; Dream of Merry Christmas; Festival Prelude; Humoresque-bagatelles, Op. 11; Piano Pieces for Young & Old, Op. 53; 3 Pieces, Op. 59; 5 Pieces, Op. 3; Luciferian Suite, Op. 45; Symphonic Suite, Op. 8; Theme & Variations, Op. 40.
(B) ** Danacord DACOCD 498/499 (2). Miller

Chaconne; Humoresque-bagatelles; Luciferian Suite; Piano Music for Young & Old, Books I–II; 5 Pieces, Op. 3; 3 Pieces, Op. 59; Symphonic Suite, Op. 8; Theme & Variations, Op. 40
*(*) da capo 8.224095/6 (2). Koppel

Chaconne; Humoresque-bagatelles, Op. 11; Luciferian Suite; 5 Pieces, Op. 3; 3 Pieces, Op. 59

(B) *** Virgin 2x1 3 49913-2 (2). Andsnes – JANACEK: *Sonata*, etc. ***

Nielsen's piano music is unmissable! The early pieces have great charm, and the later *Suite* and the *Three Pieces*, Op. 59, have great substance. Now they have found a princely interpreter in the Norwegian, Leif Ove Andsnes, who has a natural feeling for and understanding of this music. Indeed, these are performances of eloquence and nobility that are unlikely to be surpassed, while the recorded sound is vivid and lifelike.

Mina Miller is an American academic who edited the texts of the piano music for the Wilhelm Hansen Edition in 1981 and subsequently recorded them for Hyperion in 1986, of which this is a Double reissue. She really understands what this music is about but does not command the keyboard authority or range of sonority of an Andsnes.

Apart from his distinction as a composer, Herman Koppel's interpretations of Nielsen provide a link with the composer, for as a young man of 21, he played for him. He recorded the *Chaconne* and the *Theme and Variations* in 1940, and again in 1952, in the early days of LP, when he also committed the *Suite*, the *Three Piano Pieces*, Op. 59, and other important works to disc. The present set was recorded in 1982–3, when he was in his mid-seventies and beyond his prime. There is insufficient subtlety in tonal colour and dynamic shading.

NORDHEIM, Arne (born 1931)

(i) *Violin Concerto; Duplex; Partita für Paul.*
*** BIS CD 1212. (i) Herresthal; Stavanger SO, Aadland

Arne Nordheim was the pioneer of electronic music in Norway. Two of the works on this CD, the *Duplex for Violin and Viola* (1991) and the *Partita für Paul* (1985), have been recorded previously, but these new versions replace them. The Paul of the latter, incidentally, is Klee, five of whose paintings inspire these short pieces. In the last two, the player is recorded and plays, as it were, in concert with himself to quite imaginative effect. The *Duplex* is the 1999 revision of an earlier score for violin and cello. The main piece is the *Violin Concerto* of 1996, written for (and expertly played by) Peter Herresthal, who displays much virtuosity throughout. Nordheim is an eclectic with a sophisticated aural imagination and a lively musical intelligence, but the concerto itself is more arresting than satisfying: there is some beauty of incident and some striking sonorities, but the whole does not constitute the sum of the parts. Others may find more substance to this work than we do, and there is no question as to the quality of the performance or the superb recording, which can safely be recommended to Nordheim's admirers.

NØRGÅRD, Per (born 1932)

Songs: *Af Tue Bentsons viser; Året; Den jyske blaest; Det abne; Drømmesang; Du skal plante et trae; Fred; Golgatha; Landskab; Landskabsbillede; 3 Magdalene-sange; Mit lov, mit lille trae; Pa Himmelfalden; Stjernespejl; Tordenbygen; Vinternat*

(*) da capo 8.224170. Bertelsen, composer (pf)

The songs on this disc cover a period of some forty years, the three in his Op. 2, *Det åbne (The Open)*, come from the early 1950s, and the most recent, the *Three Magdalene Songs*, from

1991. The latter and the *Seven Songs*, Op. 14 (1955–7) have been recorded before, albeit very indifferently. Generally speaking, the level of inspiration is high and the music has a keen lyrical impulse and strong feeling for the poetry. As recorded here, Lars Thodberg Bertelsen's voice is wanting in bloom and richness of timbre, and he is not well served by a microphone balance that favours the piano nor by the claustrophobic studio acoustic. There are some haunting songs: *Året (The Year)* from 1976 is poignant and dignified, as is a song from the oratorio, *Golgatha (The Judgment)*, to name only two. Nørgård naturally brings authority to the proceedings, but his pianistic limitations are distinctly evident.

NØRHOLM, Ib (born 1931)

Symphonies (i) 4 (Décreation), Op. 76. 5 (The Four Elements), Op. 80.

** Kontrapunkt CD 32212. (i) Pavlovski, Dahlberg, Høyer, Nørholm, Danish Nat. R. Ch.; Danish Nat. RSO, Serov

The *Fourth Symphony (Décreation)* is highly self-conscious – the sub-title itself, *Moralities* or *There may be Many Miles to the Nearest Spider*, puts you in the picture, although there are many imaginative touches during its course. Sadly, inspiration is intermittent and the work as a whole is deficient in thematic vitality. There is a lot going on but very little actually happens. The *Fifth Symphony (The Four Elements)* is better, though again its neo-expressionism outstays its welcome. The performances under Eduard Serov are obviously committed, and in the *Fourth* the composer himself is the narrator. Decent recording.

NORMAN, Ludwig (1831–85)

Symphonies 1 in F min., Op. 22; 3 in D min., Op. 58

*(*) Sterling CDS 1038-2. Nat. SO of South Africa, Eichenholz

Ludwig Norman was an interesting figure in Swedish musical life. A champion of Berwald, whose influence can be discerned in the *First Symphony*, he was much drawn to the world of Schumann and Mendelssohn. The former remains the dominant influence not only here but elsewhere in his output. Unfortunately, the orchestral playing is wanting in finish and the strings are particularly scruffy. There is little space in which the tutti can expand and the texture lacks transparency.

NORTON, Frederic (1869–1946)

Chu Chin Chow (Musical Play): Highlights

(B) **(*) CfP 3 35984-2. Inia Te Wiata, Julie Bryan, Barbara Leigh, Marion Grimaldi, Ursula Connors, Charles Young, John Wakefield, Rita Williams Singers, O, Collins, or Linden Singers, Sinf. of L., Hollingsworth – FRASER-SIMSON & TATE: *Maid of the Mountains* ***

The two greatest theatrical hits of the First World War were *Chu Chin Chow*, which opened in London in 1916, when its companion, *The Maid of the Mountains*, was having its Manchester try-out. During the war, both were just the thing for troops returning home on leave from the trenches, and *Chu Chin Chow*, an ingenuous Arabian Nights entertainment, ran until 1921, by which time it had been performed 2,335 times.

Lancashire born, its composer, Frederic Norton, was not a romantic melodist of the calibre of Fraser-Simson, but his score contained such hits as *Any time's kissing time*, the ever-catchy *We are the Robbers of the Woods*, and the *Cobbler's Song*, here sung magificently by Inia te Wiata. This is part of an excellently cast studio recording, but the selection includes additional items from a revival production at London's Palace Theatre in 1972. Performances and recording (with just an occasional rough spot) are both excellent and this treasurable disc invites nostalgia for a long-past period in London's musical theatre, when there were still plenty of tunes around, and clever lyrics, too. Snap it up before it disappears again.

NOVÁK, Vitězslav (1870–1949)

Trio quasi una balata
*** Sup. SU 3810. Smetana Trio – SMETANA: *Piano Trio;*
SUK: *Piano Trio; Elégie ***

Novák described his *Trio quasi una balata* as a work of blackest Baudelairean pessimism, and though its themes may not be as striking as those in the other works on the disc, all but one of them darkly elegiac, it is most skilfully argued, completing an excellent programme, superbly played and very well recorded.

NYSTEDT, Knut (born 1915)

Apocalypse Joannis
**(*) Simax PSC1241 (2). Julsrud, Gilchrist, Oslo Ch. & PO, Remmereit

The Norwegian composer Knut Nystedt, now in his nineties, is best known for his choral music. He was for many years conductor of the Norsk Solistkor and as the opus number of *Apocalypse Joannis* shows (115 on the cover and 155 inside the booklet!) he is nothing if not prolific. The present work was written in response to a commission from the Oslo Philharmonic to mark his eighty-fifth birthday in 2000. It is inspired by texts from the Revelation of St John the Divine; but unlike, say, Hilding Rosenberg's *Johannes Uppenbarelse*, which is half-oratorio half-symphony, this divides into three purely orchestral movements, plus a finale for two soloists, chorus and orchestra lasting the best part of an hour (though it seems longer). For a composer in his eighties, it is undoubtedly quite an achievement. The musical language is eclectic and the writing effective and often imaginative (the third movement 'he is the Word which came forth from silence' is a case in point) and there is no doubting his skill in handling his forces. Nystedt's orchestration is masterly and resourceful, and there is a strong atmosphere at times and some arresting musical ideas. However, not all this music is touched with distinction, and to be frank the musical personality is not quite big enough to sustain a canvas of these dimensions. But we are glad to have heard the piece, and there are no quarrels with the quality of the performance or recording.

Canticles of Praise: Kristnikvede; A Song as in the Night
** Simax PSC 1190. Bergen Cathedral Ch. & O, Magnersnnes

The *Kristnikvede* or *Canticles of Praise* was commissioned in 1995 to commemorate Olav Trygvason's arrival in Norway in AD 995 and its conversion to Christianity; *A Song as in the Night* was written for a Swedish choral society in the university city of Uppsala. Nystedt's musical language is very direct in utterance, diatonic and well written. He knows exactly what voices can do. There is a faint wisp of Stravinsky and Honegger too. Worthwhile music decently performed,

though the choir is not in the first flight and neither is the orchestra. But Nystedt is a composer of substance.

OCKEGHEM, Johannes (c. 1410–97)

Missa Ecce ancilla Domini; Motet: *Intemerata Deo mater*
(M) ** DHM/BMG 82876 69991-2. L. Pro Cantione Antiqua, Coll. Aur., Turner

Ockeghem's music is comparatively austere, but its imaginative power lies beneath the surface of the music. The performances here are refined and scholarly; sometimes one feels the need for a stronger forward impulse, although the atmosphere of the music is readily communicated. Instrumental doubling is used in the Mass but not in the motet. The internal balance is not always ideal, but the 1972 recording is not too dry. Not a first choice among Ockeghem CDs, then, but a worthwhile reissue just the same.

OFFENBACH, Jacques (1819–80)

Gaîté parisienne (ballet, arr. Rosenthal; complete)
(B) *** Australian Decca Eloquence (ADD) 476 2724.
ROHCG O, Solti – GOUNOD: *Faust: ballet music ***;*
RESPIGHI: *Rossiniana **(*)*

Gaîté parisienne (ballet; complete); *Offenbachiana* (both arr. Rosenthal)
(BB) ** Naxos 8.554005. Monte Carlo PO, Rosenthal

Solti's 1959 *Gaîté parisienne* is the most brilliant version committed to disc. While some listeners may feel that the music-making is just that bit too hard-driven to be a top choice, there is no doubting the sheer virtuosity of the orchestra, and their bravura is hard to resist. Exciting music-making, and vintage Decca sound.

Naxos must have felt that it was quite a feather in their cap to get Manuel Rosenthal to record his own arrangements of these two Offenbach ballets. But alas, as he proved with his previous recording for EMI (5 85065-2), he is a less inspiring conductor than he is an arranger. He obviously chooses ballet dance tempi, and while the orchestra responds with playing of elegance and polish and the wind soloists are all very good, the absence of uninhibited zest is a great drawback, especially in the famous final *Can-can*.

Gaîté parisienne (ballet; excerpts); *Orpheus in the Underworld: Overture*
(M) ** Sony (ADD) SMK 61830. NYPO, Bernstein – BIZET: *Symphony in C *** (with SUPPE: *Beautiful Galathea: Overture ***)*

Bernstein's quite enjoyable performance of excerpts from *Gaîté parisienne* dates from 1969, and would be more recommendable if the ballet were recorded complete and the sound was less brash. The *Orpheus in the Underworld* overture comes off well, and the (1967) recording is richer here than in *Gaîté parisienne*. The Suppé Overture is superbly done.

OPERA

La Belle Hélène (complete)
(B) ** EMI (ADD) 5 74085-2 (2). Millet, Burles, Benoit, Dens, Ch. & L.O.P., Marty

Jean-Pierre Marty's 1970 recording is fair value at its bargain price, although no texts are provided. He has the advantage of

largely French cast, who generally sing their parts well
enough and with character, but Danièle Millet is not the
equal of either Norman or Lott in the other available sets (see
our main *Guide*). The recording is acceptable and would be
recommendable enough were it not for the Plasson and
Minkowski versions, which outclass it in every way and are
well worth the extra outlay.

es Contes d'Hoffmann (*The Tales of Hoffmann;* complete)
M) ** EMI 5 67979-2 [5 67983-2] (2). Gedda, D'Angelo,
  Schwarzkopf, de los Angeles, Benoit, Faure, Ghiuselev,
  London, Sénéchal, Blanc, Choeurs René Duclos, Paris
  Conservatoire O, Cluytens

everal unfortunate mistakes in casting prevent the mid-
960s EMI set from being the rare delight it should have been.
t has some fine moments, and the whole of the *Barcarolle*
cene with Schwarzkopf is memorable, but the very distinc-
ion of the cast-list makes one annoyed that the result is not
etter. Surprisingly, André Cluytens proved quite the wrong
onductor for this sparkling music, for he has little idea of
aressing the music and rarely fails to push on regardless.
Gianna d'Angelo's Olympia is pretty but shallow, George
London's Coppelius and Dr Miracle are unpleasantly gruff-
oned, and, most disappointing of all, Victoria de los Angeles
s sadly out of voice at times, with the upper register less than
 deally sweet. But with such artists, even when they are below
heir best, there are characterful moments, which take the
istener along well enough. In his ruthlessness Cluytens has a
ertain demonic energy, which has its dramatic side. The
ecording is atmospheric and has been impressively remas-
ered, but this is hardly a good choice for inclusion among
EMI's 'Great Recordings of the Century'.

es Fées du Rhin (opera; complete in German)
** Accord 472 920-2 (3). Schörg, Gubisch, Beczala, Jenis,
  Klaveness, Pepper, R. Letton Ch., Montpellier Nat. O, Layer

When, in 1863, Offenbach was commissioned to write an
opera by the director of the Hofoper in Vienna (Offenbach's
operettas were hugely popular in Vienna at that time), he
eaped at the chance, always wishing to write something more
erious than operettas. The result was *Les Fées du Rhin*, or *Die
Rheinnixen*, of which this CD set (sung in German) is its first
ecording. Into this work Offenbach poured everything that
mbodied German romanticism: from ruined castles at midnight, to soldiers, hunters, village maidens, the Rhine, of
ourse, with its water-sprites, pixies and elves, and even
psychic shock is included! Add to this elements of French and
talian grand opera, and just about everything else you can
hink of, and the result is a Weber-cum-Offenbach mélange.
f the story is a typical example of operatic hokum, one
orgives its flaws for the sake of the music, which contains
ome excellent Offenbach tunes; and if the spirit of operetta
s never too far away, there is more dramatic writing than you
night expect from this source; some of the arias and duets
re really quite impressive, and the opera includes plenty of
plendid ensembles and vibrant choruses, as well as a delight-
ul ballet and *grande valse*. The cast in this live 2002 recording
s generally very good: the heroine, Armgard, sung by Regina
Schörg, copes well with the coloratura passages: her aria in
Act I, *There, where the ancient oaks and dark pine trees grow*, is
a good example of Offenbach creating a gently eerie effect,
with wordless coloratura passages appearing throughout the
ong. Later, when she is forced to sing for the soldiers, she
delivers some even more impressive coloratura, before dropping down dead – or at least appearing to do so. The hero,

Franz, a light tenor, sung by Piotr Beczala, has an attractive
voice, coping reasonably well in the high passages and singing
with sensitivity when called for; he is well contrasted with the
baritone of Dalibor Jenis, his rival, in splendid, full-blooded
voice. Armgard's mother, Hedwig, sung by Nora Gubisch, is a
fine mezzo, and the rest of the cast is good. That the whole
thing works is a tribute to Friedemann Layer, who draws an
excellent response from his orchestra. The sound is very
good, with very little noise from the audience, and full texts
and translations are provided.

Orpheus in the Underworld (highlights in English)
** TER CDTER 1134. Kale, Watson, Angas, Squires, Bottone,
  Pope, ENO Ch. & O, Elder

After listening to Plasson's recording of *Orphée*, this version,
based on ENO's production of the mid-1980s, now seems
rather flat and dated, with Public Opinion obviously based
on the then current prime minister. Those who saw and
enjoyed the show will get more out of this than those who did
not, for while there is plenty of knock-about British humour,
little of Offenbach's French champagne comes through here.
Indeed, this kind of performance, when even Bonaventura
Bottone's hilariously camp portrait of prancing Mercury is
not nearly so much fun when simply heard, ideally needs a
DVD.

ONSLOW, Georges (1784–1853)

String Quintets in E min., Op. 19; in G min., Op. 51
*** CPO 777 187-2 Diogenes Qt, with Van Nahmer (cello)
  (with CHERUBINI: *String Quintet in E min.*)
String Quintets in B flat, Op. 33; in E min., Op. 74.
**(*) MDG 603 1233-2. Ens. Concertant Frankfurt
String Quintets in A min., Op. 34; G, Op. 35.
*** MDG 603 1253-2. Quintett Momento Musicale

Georges Onslow was one of the few French composers of his
generation who wrote a substantial amount of chamber
music, which represents his largest body of work. His quartets and quintets were published in his lifetime and reached a
wide audience in their day, although they were sometimes
criticized for a certain emotional coolness, even blandness.
The Ensemble Concertant are not quite as sweet-sounding as
the Quintett Momento Musicale and don't seem to have the
music quite under their belts as do their rivals. They still
make a good case for the Op. 33 (1827–8) and Op. 74 (1847)
Quintets, the latter being the more seductive. However, all
these works, and especially those in the hands of the Quintett
Momento Musicale, emerge as fresh, well-constructed pieces,
generally in classical tradition, not always strikingly individual but unfailingly enjoyable. The *Adagio* movements are
beautifully poised, while the lively outer movements have
plenty of life – the *Presto* of the Op. 35 is especially enjoyable
and inventive. Both CDs are beautifully recorded by MDG.

Georges Onslow's earlier *String Quintets* (using a second
cello) are written in a *galant* style, and Opus 19 has a dotted
main theme in the first movement that is very Hummelian.
The later Opus 51, after an engagingly impetuous opening,
has a galloping virtuoso Scherzo that brings a Mendelssohnian evocation, but a darkness that is also close to Berlioz. Yet
the Trio, like the slow movements in both works, is homophonic and warmly hymn-like. Cherubini's *Quintet* has a
more sensuous feel to its textures, and its sonorous *Andante*
has something of Onslow's homophonic richness, but his

Scherzo is stronger and bolder, and it is the light-hearted finale that brings a hint of Mendelssohn. The performances here are first class and, with recording that is full-bodied but clear, this is a most attractive disc.

ORFF, Carl (1895–1982)

Carmina Burana

(BB) **(*) HMV (ADD) 5 86746-2. Popp, Unger, Wolansky, Noble, Wandsworth School Boys' Ch., New Philh. Ch. & O, Frühbeck de Burgos

**(*) Telarc CD 80575. Hong, Olsen, Gwinnett, Young Singers, Atlanta Ch. & SO, Runnicles

(M) ** DG Entrée 471 739-2. Bonney, Lopardo, Michaels-Moore, Arnold Schoenberg Ch., V. Boys' Ch., VPO, Previn

Frühbeck de Burgos gives the kind of performance of *Carmina Burana* that is especially suitable for gramophone listening, scoring with his greater imagination and obvious affection for the lyrical sections of the work – and he has excellent soloists. Lucia Popp's soprano aria, *Amor volat*, is ravishing, and Gerhard Unger, the tenor, brings a Lieder-like sensitivity to his lovely singing of his very florid aria in the tavern scene. This is not to suggest that the Philharmonia account has any shortage of vitality, and the Wandsworth School Boys' Choir are not lacking either. Indeed, the gusto of the choral singing is the more remarkable when one considers the precision of both singers and orchestra alike. The brass too bring out the rhythmic pungency with splendid life and point. The slight snag lies in the recording, which has the chorus recessed in the quieter moments, and not very sharply focused in the climaxes. On earlier appearances of this 1966 recording, the digital remastering brought an unpleasant, artificial edge to the upper range. Fortunately this has now been mitigated, but the sound is still not ideal.

Any experienced CD enthusiast would guess that this Runnicles version was a Telarc recording in the very first chorus, when the spectacular bass drum thunders through the music. It is indeed a spectacular, percussion-laced recording, yet with some splendid singing from the Atlanta choristers. Runnicles's performance is imaginatively varied in mood. He uses a very wide range of dynamic, which means that the words are not always very clear in the quieter passages. Yet the gentle orchestral *Round Dance* is full of sensuality, which is taken up seductively by the female chorus, then interrupted by blazing brass fanfares, leading the way to the exuberant Tavern sequence. But it is the *Court of Love* which is at the heart of the work, and Runnicles again creates sensuously evocative textures and a languorous atmosphere, helped by the provocative solo singing of his soprano soloist, Hei-Kyung Hong. The three male soloists all characterize strongly, but none of them has a particularly beautiful voice and it is the choristers who carry the day – and they are very good indeed. The children's chorus are as eager in promiscuity as their adult counterparts and, with flashing percussion (and more hearty bass drum strokes), the final chorus brings the work to a triumphant consummation. One wishes that the *pianissimos* were sharper in focus, but otherwise this is is a most attractive version of a much-recorded work.

Previn's 1983 DG version is a disappointment and no match for the earlier, EMI analogue account. Only in the male Tavern chorus of Part I is there a reminder of the vocal swagger that makes that LSO performance so headily compulsive. Barbara Bonney, gently sensuous, is the most appealing of the three soloists, but her final submission is somewhat shrill, and th tenor sounds strained when portraying the Roasted Swan. Th Vienna Boys' Choir lack the uninhibited sexual fervour of th St Clement Dane's Grammar School youngsters, who relis every innuendo in Previn's LSO version. Both the Arnol Schoenberg Choir and the VPO make impressive contribu tions, but overall this does not have the extra spontaneity an excitement one would expect from a live performance.

OSWALD, James (1710–69)

12 Divertimentis for Guitar (1750)

*** ASV Gaudeamus CDGAU 221. Mackillop (guitar)

The Scottish musician James Oswald was born into a poor bu musical family in Crail, in eastern Fife. He made his mark fir as a fiddler and cellist and as a dancing master in Dunfermlin in 1734; then, after six years in Edinburgh, he moved London and rose to become chamber composer to George II His *Twelve Divertimentis* have a simple, ingenuous charm, th earliest with three movements, *Amoroso–Vivace–Gavotta*, the later moving on to four sections, *Affetuoso–Gavotta–Aria–Co spirito*, and introducing Minuets and the occasional *Giga*. Th is not great music, but its elegance is engaging and the tune are often quite catchy, though it is not a disc to be played all once. The guitar Ron Mackillop uses in this recording authentic, made in London in the late 1760s, and it has fou pairs of treble strings and two single bass strings, fixed with a ingenious 'watch-tuning' mechanism at one end. It certainl has a strong instrumental personality.

PAINE, John Knowles (1839–1906)

Symphony 1 in C min., Op. 23; Overture, As You Like It

*** New World NW 374-2. NYPO, Mehta

Paine's symphonies were milestones in the history of Amer can music, and it is good that at last Mehta's fine recording of both of them will allow them to be appreciated mo widely. Paine consciously inspires echoes of Beethoven, wit little feeling of dilution – though, after his dramatic C mino opening, he tends to relax into sweeter, more Mendelssoh nian manners for his second subject and the three othe movements. What is striking is the bold assurance, and th overture is also full of charming ideas. Mehta is a persuasiv advocate, helped by committed playing and full, wel balanced recording.

Symphony 2 in A, Op. 34

*** New World NW 350-2. NYPO, Mehta

Written four years after the *First Symphony*, this magnificer work is both more ambitious and more memorable than i predecessor and, far more remarkably, anticipates Mahle The idiom is notably more chromatic than that of the *Firs* and the other movements – introduced by an extended slo introduction – bring an element of fantasy, as in the frag mented rhythms and textures of the Scherzo. Mehta draws strongly committed performance from the New York Philhar monic, and the sound is first rate.

PAISIELLO, Giovanni (1740–1816)

Piano Concertos 1–8

**(*) ASV CDDCS 229 (2). Monetti, ECO, Gonley

Piano Concertos 1 in C; 5 in D; 7 in A; 8 in C
** ASV CDDCA 873. Monetti, ECO, Gonley

Piano Concertos 2 in F; 3 in A; 4 in G min.; 6 in B flat
*(*) ASV CDDCA 872. Monetti, ECO, Gonley

Mariaclara Monetti reveals herself to be an artist who can produce a silk purse out of more humble material, for her playing here is both sparkling and elegant. Paisiello obviously was primarily an opera composer, and these concertos, though not wanting grace or fluency, are often very conventional in most other respects. But with a ready facility Paisiello could certainly spin an expressive cantilena. No complaints about the recording, and on the whole the first of the two discs is the one to go for. As can be seen, the eight concertos are also available as a boxed set, though with no saving in cost.

PALESTRINA, Giovanni Pierluigi
da (1525–94)

Canticum Canticorum; 8 Madrigali spirituali (from Book I)
(BB) ** Virgin 2×1. 5 62239-2 (2). Hilliard Ens., Hillier

The 29 motets Palestrina based on the *Canticum Canticorum* (Song of Songs) include some of his most inspired writing; all are for five voices. Into these impassioned texts with their strongly erotic overtones, Palestrina poured music of great feeling, remarkable beauty and finish of workmanship. The *Song of Songs* has always been regarded as a symbolic illustration of 'the happy union of Christ and His Spouse', the spouse being the Church, more specifically the happiest part of it, namely perfect souls, every one of which is His beloved. These are beautifully shaped performances, with refined tonal blend and perfect intonation, but they are comparatively remote and ultimately rather cool in emotional temperature. Earlier recordings have, with success, adopted a more fittingly expressive and sensuous approach. The second CD includes also eight Petrarch settings from the *First Book of Madrigals*.

Canticum canticorum: Trahe me; Nigra sum, sed formosa; Surge, propera; Surge, amica mea; Quam pulchra es; Veni, dilecti mi (all a 5). Missa pro defunctis a 5 (1591, 2nd edition); Motets: Gaude Barbara a 5; Gaude gloriosa a 5; O bone Jesu a 6; Salve regina a
(M) ** Warner Elatus 0927 49619-2. Chanticleer

Chanticleer sing smoothly and beautifully (the Plainsong is especially impressive), and they are well recorded, but the performances do not produce the variety of dynamic, nor indeed the degree of expressive feeling that makes the CRD collection from New College, Oxford, so stimulating; and that comment especially applies to the *Missa pro defunctis*, which is consistently withdrawn and doleful.

MASSES

Missa Beata Mariae Virginis II; Missa Descendit angelis Domini; Jubilate Deo (for double choir); Motets: Ad te levavi oculos meos; Miserere nostri Domine; Sitivit anima mea; Super flumina Babylonis
* Paraclete Press GDCD 106. Gloria Dei Cantores, Patterson; Chant conductor: Pugsley

This fine American choir sing and blend beautifully and those looking for an essentially serene approach to these two Palestrina Masses will find much to enjoy. However, there is a distinct lack of Latin fervour, and the different sections, *Kyrie*, *Gloria* and *Credo* are sung in much the same somewhat bland style. The motets fare better, for one can sense the underlying intensity in *Super flumina Babylonis* and *Miserere nostri Domine*. The concert ends with *Jubilate Deo*, and this has more momentum, but even here the joy could be more unbuttoned. The recording is outstandingly fine.

Missa: Benedicta es (with Plainchant)
(B) *** Gimell GIMSE (DDD/AAD) 402. Tallis Scholars, Phillips (with JOSQUIN: *Motet Benedicta es*)

It would seem that this Mass was the immediate predecessor of the *Missa Papae Marcelli* and was composed while the music of *Benedictus* was still at the forefront of the composer's mind. Palestrina's *Missa Benedicta es*, coupled with the Josquin motet, *Benedicta es*, on which it is based, is here a bargain reissue to celebrate the 25th anniversary of the formation of the Tallis Scholars, with the *Missa Nasace la gioja mia* included as a special bonus. The performances are exemplary, and full documentation is included to make this a genuine bargain.

Missa Papae Marcelli
(M) *** Gimell (ADD) GIMSE 401. Tallis Scholars, Phillips – ALLEGRI: *Miserere*; MUNDY: *Vox patris caelestis* ***

The earlier Gimell alternative is an analogue recording from 1980. The performance from the Tallis Scholars has great eloquence and is now most welcome at mid-price.

PANUFNIK, Andrzej (1914–91)

(i) *Sinfonia rustica (No. 1); Sinfonia sacra (No. 3);* (ii) *Sinfonia concertante for flute, harp & strings (No. 4)*
(BB) *** EMI (ADD) 3 52289-2. (i) Monte Carlo Opéra O; (ii) Nicolet, Ellis, Menuhin Festival O; all cond. composer

The *Sinfonia rustica* was the work which first attracted attention to the Polish composer, Andrzej Panufnik, shortly after the war. It is a highly individual piece and has plenty of character, with the four movements attractively diverse, both rhythmically and in orchestral colour, though the invention is less symphonic than in the style of a sinfonietta. The *Sinfonia sacra* is based on 'the earliest known hymn in the Polish language', which in the Middle Ages was used as both a prayer and an invocation before battle. The work is in three *Visions* – the first a brass fanfare to introduce the more expressive and poignant writing which follows, while the hymn is expanded in the fourth-movement finale, which is as long as the other three movements put together, and draws on the fanfare material at its close. The *Sinfonia concertante* contrasts two movements, *Molto cantabile* and *Molto ritmico*, with the soloists well integrated to add colour and atmosphere to the texture, and it ends with a poignantly lyrical *Postscriptum*. All the performances here are directed by the composer, who also provides the notes in the accompanying booklet. The playing of the Monte Carlo orchestra is both spirited and expressive (even if the orchestra itself is not in the top flight) but the Menuhin Festival Orchestra, with its two celebrated soloists, plays with great finesse and understanding. The recording is excellent.

PARRY, Hubert (1848–1918)

(i) *Blest Pair of Sirens; I was Glad* (anthems); (ii) *Invocation to Music (An Ode in Honour of Purcell)*; (iii) *The Lotus Eaters*; (iv) *The Soul's Ransom*

🕭 (B) *** Chan. 2 for 1 241-31 (2). (i) L. Symphony Ch., LSO, Hickox; (ii) Dawson, Davies, Rayner Cook; (iii–iv) Jones; (iv) Wilson Johnson; (ii–iv) LPO Ch., LPO, Bamert

Here is an outstanding collection of some of Parry's finest choral music, with two of his most popular anthems, admirably directed by Richard Hickox, used on the second disc to frame what is perhaps his most influential and powerful vocal work, the *Invocation to Music*, a superb setting of Robert Bridges' *Ode in Honour of Purcell*. Written for the Leeds Triennial Festival in 1895 to celebrate the bicentenary of the earlier composer's death, Parry's inspiration was at its peak, and the flowing, richly melodic lyrical style was to anticipate the Elgar of the *Coronation Ode* and even *Gerontius*. The soloists here are splendid, with the passionate central soprano and tenor duet, *Love to Love calleth*, followed by the magnificent bass *Dirge*, and the very Elgarian chorus *Man, born of desire*, later to be capped by the glorious closing apotheosis, *O Queen of sinless grace*, which Bamert moves on arrestingly to its final climax.

The first disc pairs *The Lotus Eaters*, a setting for soprano, chorus and orchestra of eight stanzas from Tennyson's choric song of that name, with *The Soul's Ransom*, using a biblical text. This is subtitled *Sinfonia sacra* and forms a broadly symphonic four-movement structure with references back not only to Brahms and the nineteenth century, but to much earlier choral composers, notably Schütz. Della Jones is the characterful soloist in both works, to be joined by David Wilson Johnson in the latter piece. The singing of the London Philharmonic Chorus throughout is first class, warmly sympathetic, as is the orchestral playing, and Matthias Bamert is in his element in this repertoire, as is the Chandos recording team.

I was glad (from *Psalm 122*)

(M) **(*) EMI (ADD/DDD) 5 85148-2. Cambridge University Musical Soc., King's College, Cambridge, Ch., New Philh. O, Ledger – ELGAR: *Coronation Ode* etc. ***

This expansive version of Parry's most popular church anthem, very well recorded in 1977, makes an excellent bonus on this splendid Elgar disc.

PÄRT, Arvo (born 1935)

(i) *Cantus in Memory of Benjamin Britten; Festina lente* (for string orchestra & harp); *Summa* (for string orchestra); (ii; iii) *Fratres; Spiegel im Spiegel* (both for violin & piano); (iv; v) *The Beatitudes* (for choir & organ); (iv) *Summa* (for choir); (i; ii; v; vi) *Tabula rasa* (for 2 violins, string orchestra & prepared piano)

🕭 *** Telarc CD 80387. Manning, Springuel, Gleizes, I Fiamminghi, Werthen

Another inexpensive anthology of Pärt's music to set beside the Virgin and Classics for Pleasure collections listed in our main volume; duplicating some of the performances on those discs, it is equally recommendable.

PENDERECKI, Kryszstof (born 1933)

St Luke Passion

(BB) ** Naxos 8.557149. Klosinska, Kruszewski, Tesrowicz, Kollberger, Malanowicz, Warsaw Boys' Ch., Warsaw Philharmonic Ch., Warsaw Nat. PO, Wit

Penderecki's *St Luke Passion* is well sung here by choruses and soloists alike. But it does not wear well, its melodic invention is frankly uninspired and, although there are moments of high drama, with the crucifixion itself plangently described by the organ and brass, this is not a work one is drawn to return to very often. It is not helped by a non-English narrative with no translation provided.

PERGOLESI, Giovanni (1710–36)

(i) *Stabat mater. Salve Regina in C min.*

(BB) ** Naxos 8.557447. Waschinski; (i) Chance; Cologne CO Müller-Brühl

A disappointment. The voices of Jörg Waschinski and Michael Chance do not blend together very convincingly in the *Stabat Mater* and Waschinski's singing of the *Salve Regina* is not very attractive either.

La Morte de San Giuseppe (oratorio)

(M) * Warner Fonit 0927 43308 (2). Farruggia, Manca di Nissa, Angeles Peters, Pace, Naples Alessandro Scarlatti R. & TV O, Panni

The autograph score of Pergolesi's oratorio has only recently come to light in the New York Pierpont Library, which acquired it from a European dealer. It is a splendid work, but the present recording will not do. The singing of Maria Angeles Peters in the role of San Michelle is insecure to say the least and suffers from poor intonation. A delightful aria like *Appena spira aura soave* ('As soon as the gentle breeze blows') needs a voice like Emma Kirkby's. The contralto, Bernadette Manca di Nissa, who takes the part of Maria Santissima, is much stronger, but Patrizia Pace in the demanding coloratura role of Amor is not always accurate either, and Michele Farruggia as San Giuseppe is only adequate. Panni gets a lively and stylish response from the excellent orchestra and the digital recording is excellent, but this can only serve as a stopgap until something better comes along.

PEROTINUS, Magister (c. 1160–1225)

Beata viscera; Sederunt principes; Viderunt omnes (with Plainchant)

(BB) *** Naxos 8.557340. Tonus Peregrinus (with ANON.: *Vetus abit littera. Clausulae Motet on Dominus; Non nobis Domine*) – LEONIN: *Viderunt omnes* ***

Perotinus extended the simple polyphony of Leonin from two to three and four parts. The disc opens with a monophonic conductus, freely flowing and soaring, which reminds one of the music of Hildegard. But later in the collection we are offered *Viderunt omnes* as a four-part organum for male voices, a darkly powerful setting. Later, *Sederunt principe* brings in female voices over a drone effect; to conclude the disc, we are offered a four-part conductus for mixed voices, joyfully rhythmic in the way of a dance. The performances are first rate and the echoing acoustic is just right. If you have never heard organum with its bare intervals (octave, fourths and fifths), you will find this disc aurally fascinating.

PETTERSSON, Allan (1911–80)

Symphony 12 (Döden på torget – The Dead of the Square)
(***) CPO 777 146-2. Eric Ericson Chamber Ch., Swedish R.
   Ch. & SO, Honeck

Allan Pettersson was a prolific symphonist: he was working on his seventeenth when he died. Some of them are impressive: the *Second*, composed in the wake of his studies with Honegger and René Leibowitz in Paris, and the *Fourth* (1959) and the *Sixth* (1963–6) are dark and powerful, though wanting in concentration. It was the *Seventh* (1967) that registered with the wider musical public in Sweden, who were tiring of a diet of rebarbative post-serialism. Its Mahlerian eloquence is perhaps marred by a streak of self-pity, but it has undeniable power. But by his later symphonies Pettersson had become something of a windbag and offered little that was really new. The *Twelfth* is a choral and orchestral work, settings of Neruda, and marking contemporary developments in Allende's Chile. It caught the spirit of the armchair socialism so much in vogue in 1970s' Sweden. But, like much of Pettersson's work after the *Seventh Symphony*, it is full of rhetorical gesturing rather than real substance. Despite the high quality of the singing and the orchestral playing, we found it difficult to sit through once, let alone a second time. This work has excited much admiration from many good judges in Sweden, but we found it sadly empty.

Barfota sånger (Barefoot Songs); 6 Songs
** CPO 999499-2. Groop, Garben

These songs come from the war years when Pettersson was working as an orchestral player. The *Barefoot Songs* precede any of his seventeen symphonies and are of the utmost simplicity. They are all strophic, and few last more than a couple of minutes. They are superbly sung by Monica Groop, but not even she and her expert pianist can disguise their naïvety and in some cases emptiness. Admirers of the composer may not find their charms so eminently resistible or the melodic invention so unmemorable.

PHILLIPS, Montague (1885–1969)

*Arabesque; Moorland Idyll; The Rebel Maid: 4 Dances.
Revelry Overture; A Shakespearean Scherzo (Titania and her Elvish Court); Sinfonietta; A Surrey Suite; Symphony in C min.*
(M) *** Dutton CDLX 7140. BBC Concert O, Sutherland

Montague Phillips's name has often popped up on ASV's series of light classics recordings, and it is good that he has a disc devoted to himself. It gets off to an exhilarating start with the *Revelry Overture* of 1937, a lively six-minute piece encompassing many attractive ideas, all brightly orchestrated. The *Four Dances* from his comic-opera *The Rebel Maid* are very much in the vein of Edward German and Sullivan – and none the worse for that – with their rustic atmosphere also pervading other numbers, including the pleasing *Moorland Idyll*, which has a lilting middle section in the manner of Dvořák. The two movements which make up the *C minor Symphony* (first heard in 1912) include *A Summer Nocturne*, showing the composer in a rather deeper

emotional mood, while *A Spring Rondo* is in a more characteristic and lighter vein (the other two movements of the *Symphony* have yet to be reconstructed). The *Arabesque* of 1927 has an appealing Russian flavour, while the *Shakespearean Scherzo*, a lively and inventive mini tone-poem, is very enjoyable too. Although written during wartime Britain in 1943, the *Sinfonietta* is stiff-upper-lip heroic music rather than reflecting the horrors of war, and the slow movement is agreeably nostalgic. The Scherzo finale has a curious march motif in the middle section, which fades out on muted brass, though the work ends triumphantly. Lewis Foreman, the writer of the notes, suggests that the composer was saying in 1943, 'keep your spirits up, we've almost made it'. Excellent performances, as usual from Gavin Sutherland, well known from his ASV recordings, but here on one of Dutton's discs, superbly engineered.

Charles II Overture; Empire March; Festival Overture (In Praise of my Country); Hampton Court; In May Time; In Old Verona: a Serenade for Strings; Hillside Melody; (i) Phantasy for Violin & Orchestra, Op. 16
(M) *** Dutton CDLX 7158. BBC Concert O, Sutherland, (i) with Trusler

This second volume of Montague Phillips's orchestral music is every bit as good as the first. It starts off with the *Charles II Overture*, which is well described in Lewis Foreman's excellent sleeve-note as, 'the musical equivalent of a Gainsborough Films romanticised costume vision of seventeenth century London'. It is highly enjoyable and contains an unexpected fugue. The rest of the items sound just like their titles: the *Empire March* is suitably rousing, and both the *Festival Overture* and *Hampton Court* evoke a nostalgic and optimistic English past very strongly. *In May Time* features some especially 'rustic'-sounding music and is very prettily scored, and both the *Hillside Melody* and *In Old Verona* show the composer equally masterful in more reflective numbers. The 12-minute *Phantasy for Violin* is unpretentious and very pleasing – the main melody, played in the upper register of the violin towards the end of the work (around 8 minutes 42 seconds), is spine-tingling. All this is 'light' music of the highest order, of the sort that rarely, if ever, gets played nowadays. However, thanks to the likes of Gavin Sutherland and John Wilson on Dutton (among others), this music survives – on recordings at least – and, who knows, some of it could find its way into the odd Prom or two. Excellent performances and recording.

PIAZZOLA, Astor (1921–92)

Milonga del Angel; 3 Movimientos tanguisticos portenos; Sinfonietta; Tangazo
*** Chan. 10049. Württemberg Philharmonie Reutlingen, Castagno

Those who know Piazzola's music from popular arrangements of his tangos will be intrigued by this collection of more ambitious works, all of which demonstrate his vivid imagination in devising distinctive melody and harmonies, colourfully orchestrated. *Tangazo* is a set of strongly contrasted variations with Bartókian echoes, while the *Three Movements* are more Stravinskian in their sharpness. Written under the influence of his teacher, Ginastera, the *Sinfonietta* is one of the early works that he took to Paris, when he went to study with Nadia Boulanger. She recognized the distinctiveness of his mixture of popular dance culture and art music and encouraged him to exploit the tango, rather than reject it. *Milonga del Angel* is the only work that, in its smoochy manners, reflects Piazzola's completely popular style, seductively sensuous. The strongly committed performances are very well recorded.

PIZZETTI, Ildebrando (1880–1968)

(i) *Piano Concerto. Preludio per Fedra;* (ii) *Sinfonia del fuoco* (from the film score *Cabiria*)
** Marco Polo 8.225058. Schumann Philh. O, Caetani, with (i) Stefani; (ii) Statsenko, Städtischer Op. Ch., Chemnitz

The present issue brings the eloquent Act I *Prelude* to the opera Pizzetti composed with Gabriele d'Annunzio, plus the *Sinfonia del fuoco*, drawn from the incidental music Pizzetti wrote in 1914 for an elaborate production of *Cabiria* (again with d'Annunzio) in which silent film was used. But the most substantial work is the *Piano Concerto*, 'Song of the High Seasons', of 1930. It is a little overripe perhaps, and at times even rather like Rachmaninov. The soloist Susanna Stefani acquits herself well. The *Fedra* prelude is the finest thing here and the Robert Schumann Philharmonie of Chemnitz give decent, serviceable performances. However, at less than 50 minutes' playing time this CD is over-priced.

PLEYEL, Ignaz (1757–1831)

String Quartets, Op. 2/1–3
(BB) *** Naxos 8.557496. Enso Qt

String Quartets, Op. 2/4–6
(BB) *** Naxos 8.557497. Enso Qt

When in 1784 Mozart came across the newly published set of six quartets, Opus 2, by Ignaz Pleyel, he commended them to his father, saying how well written they were and how agreeable to listen to. He noted the influence of Pleyel's teacher, Haydn, the dedicatee of the six; but, as these brilliant and understanding performances by the Enso Quartet demonstrate, there is much more to them than echoes of Haydn. They are full of good ideas, expressed robustly (with octave doubling used most effectively), yet with refinement. The bluff finale of No. 2 suggests some influence from folk music, but each movement is in its way bold and inventive, and Pleyel's structures are often quite original. All the quartets save No. 4 come in three movements, with No. 3 reversing the usual layout of fast-slow-fast, starting with an *Adagio* in G minor, leading to a central *Allegro*, much the most substantial movement, and ending with a charming *Grazioso* movement. The American Enso Quartet make use of the Artaria Editions of these fine works, prepared by the scholar, Dianne James, which with any luck will help to bring them back into the repertory. Clear, well-balanced sound.

PONCE, Manuel (1882–1948)

Concierto del sur
*** Warner 2564 60296-2. Isbin, NYPO, Serebrier –
RODRIGO: *Concierto de Aranjuez;* VILLA-LOBOS: *Guitar Concerto ***

As Sharon Isbin suggests in her notes to this CD, Ponce has 'a magical gift of lyricism, counterpoint and colour', and this is a delightful, lightweight concerto, scored with a delicate palette and engaging transparency. Throughout, the guitar, in free fantasia, embroiders the glowing orchestral texture. The themes are gentle but soon insinuate themselves into the listener's consciousness, while Isbin's subtle guitar frescos and roulades captivate the ear. She plays marvellously and is accompanied by Serebrier with great skill. He is always there with the composer's charming orchestral comments but never for a moment submerges the guitar, which is also a tribute to the finely balanced recording.

PÓRARINSSON, Leifur (1934–c. 1994)

A Dream of the House; In Cyprus; Rent; Spring in my Heart;
(i) *Angelus Domini; Styr: Notturno Capriccioso*
** Smekkleysta SMK 27. Reykjavík CO; (i) Gunnarsdóttir

Born in 1934, Leifur Pórarinsson studied in Vienna in the mid-1950s with Hanns Jelinek, a pupil of Alban Berg, and then with Wallingford Riegger and Gunther Schuller in the United States. He subsequently lived for some years in Denmark and, in the early 1990s, in Nicosia. In his work there are traces of Bartók, Stravinsky and Schoenberg, and his adherence to serial technique remained strong until the very end. He died in the mid-1990s, though the notes do not give the exact date. This CD collects six pieces for various chamber combinations; they are eclectic in spirit and idiom, and show a keen aural imagination and an awareness of sonority. (*Rent* is so called because it was a commission from the Örebro Orchestra, which paid his rent for a month!) Among the strongest pieces here is *Angelus Domini*, a setting of Laxness's translation of a medieval Latin poem published in his novel, *The Great Weaver of Kashmir*. All six pieces are resourceful and well crafted, though it is possible to imagine more polished performances. Accomplished and often arresting music, then, albeit one in which it is difficult to discern a strongly distinctive voice.

PORPORA, Nicola (1686–1768)

Sinfonia a tre 5 in E min.; 6 in B. (i) *Lamentazione il del Mercoledi; Salve Regina in F*
(M) **(*) Somm SOMMCD 232. (i) Andalò; Cappella Teatina

Nicola Porpora was born in Naples, the son of a bookseller and something of an infant prodigy, beginning musical training at the age of ten. As well as being a choirmaster, he was to become one of the most celebrated singing teachers of his time. This enterprising Somm collection confirms his considerable talents as a composer. The four-movement *Sinfonie* for three instruments were published in London in 1736. Their style is halfway between church and chamber sonata, and each is inventively fresh and has a vocal-styled expressive *Affettuoso* movement. They are splendidly played here by this excellent period-instrument group (using archlute or baroque guitar continuo). The *Salve Regina* and Porpora's setting of the second *Lamentation* for the Wednesday in Holy Week are also deeply expressive, and genuinely touching as sung by the counter-tenor, Michele Andalò. He phrases most musically, but there has to be a reservation here, for not all may take to his individual vocal timbre, especially in conjunction with his fairly close vibrato. The recording throughout is truthful and well balanced, and texts and translations are included.

POULENC, Francis (1899–1963)

ORCHESTRAL MUSIC

Aubade; Piano Concerto; (i) Double Piano Concerto in D min.

⊕— (BB) *** Warner Apex 2564 62552-2. Duchable, Rotterdam PO, Conlon; (i) with Collard

This Apex CD is one of the most attractive of all the issues in this enterprising series. The *Aubade* is an exhilarating work of great charm; the *Piano Concerto* evokes the faded charms of Paris in the 1930s. The performance of these two solo works by François-René Duchable and the Rotterdam orchestra have a certain panache and flair that are most winning. Perhaps in these works Duchable is a shade too prominent, but not sufficiently so to disturb a strong recommendation, for the sound is otherwise full and pleasing. The *Double Concerto* too captures all the wit and charm of the Poulenc score, and the 'mock Mozart' slow movement is particularly elegant.

Concerto in G min. for Organ, Strings & Timpani

** René Gailly CD 87 162. Michiels, Brugense Coll., Peire – FAURE: *Requiem.* **

(BB) Warner Apex 8573 89244-2. Alain, O. Nat. de l'ORTF, Martinon – SAINT-SAENS: *Symphony 3, etc.* (***)

Ignace Michiels is an excellent soloist for the Brugense performance, and the orchestra has plenty of fire. However, it is obvious that there are few players, and there is a want of body and weight. Not a first choice, although the Fauré is not unappealing.

Marie-Claire Alain's performance of the *Organ Concerto* is exhilarating and can be compared with the best. Unfortunately, the CD transfer has brightened the original analogue sound unmercifully and the organ is made to sound very ugly indeed – harsh and brash, indeed virtually unlistenable. The Saint-Saëns couplings, while more acceptable, are still disagreeably over-bright. But it is disgraceful that Warner Classics should not have sampled and remastered the Poulenc!

'Francis Poulenc and Friends': (i) Double Piano Concerto in D min.; (ii) Concerto in G min., for organ, timpani & strings; (iii) Dialogues des Carmélites; La voix humaine; Les Mamelles de Tirésias; La Courte Paille; (iv) Flute Sonata; (v) Pastourelle; Toccata; (vi) 3 Mouvements perpétuelles; (vii) Banalités; Chansons villageoises; Chansons gaillardes; (viii) Sarabande

*** EMI **DVD** DVB 3102009. Composer, with (i) Février, O Nat. de l'ORTF, Prêtre; (ii) Grunewald, PO de l'ORTF, Prêtre; (iii) Duval; (iv) Rampal, Veyron-Lacroix; (v) Tacchino; (vi) Février; (vii) Bacquier, Février; (viii) Gendron, Ivadli

An indispensable item for admirers of this inspiriting and life-loving composer. Much of this DVD derives from a concert in the Salle Gaveau to mark Poulenc's sixtieth birthday, where he is seen in conversation with Bernard Gavoty. (He is as entertaining a speaker as he is witty a composer.) The two concertos come from 1962 and 1968 respectively, the former at about the time when these artists recorded it commercially. Poulenc's score is both witty and at times profound, though he is by no means as elegant or polished at the keyboard as, say, Britten or for that matter his partner here, Jacques Février. It is good to see and hear the delightful Denise Duval, who sings with great artistry; small wonder that Poulenc adored her so much. The picture quality is variable but acceptable and, though the camerawork in the first movement of the *D minor Concerto* is a bit fussy, it is otherwise exemplary both in the other movements and elsewhere in this compilation.

CHAMBER MUSIC

(i; ii) Cello Sonata; Chanson Galliarde 8: Sérénade (arr. Gendron); Song Transcriptions: C; C'est ainsi que tu es (arr. York); Suite française (arr. composer); (ii; iii) Sonata for 2 Pianos

*(*) ASV Gold GLD 4014. (i) Wallfisch; (ii) J. York; F. York

Raphael Wallfisch's account of the *Cello Sonata* (from 2000) is here recoupled with more music arranged for cello and piano. Although the composer himself transcribed the *Suite française*, it sounds more piquant and witty in his scoring for wind, and the songs too are more effective vocally. Wallfisch plays sympathetically and turns in a good performance of the *Cello Sonata*, but next to Fournier's EMI version (available only in a boxed set) the ASV version sounds more efficient than inspired. Perhaps the effect is exacerbated by the recording, which tends to iron out the dynamic range. The lively account of the *Two-piano Sonata* is also let down by the sound, which is too resonant and without enough point.

CHORAL MUSIC

Ave verum corpus; Exultate Deo; Figure humaine; 4 petites prières de Saint François d'Assise; Un soir de neige; 4 Motets pour le temps de Noël; Salve Regina; 7 Chansons

** ASV CDDCA 1067. Joyful Company of Singers, Broadbent

Poulenc's choral music is very well represented on disc. This newcomer from the Joyful Company of Singers and Peter Broadbent is not without merit but, in terms of ensemble, chording and tonal blend it does not outclass other recordings.

Chanson à boire; 7 Chansons; Chansons françaises; Figure humaine; Petite voix; Un soir de neige

(BB) ** Hyp. Helios CDH 55179. New L. Chamber Ch., Wood

A collection devoted entirely to Poulenc's *a cappella* secular vocal music is welcome, especially one as well sung and recorded as this, and with full translations provided. The snag is the Anglican style of the French pronunciation. This is fully acceptable in the delightful *Chansons*, some of which sound very like carols, but less convincing elsewhere – and particularly so in Poulenc's 1943 wartime setting of the Paul Éluard poems, *Figure humaine*. This was Poulenc's own musical 'résistance', and he proudly displayed a copy of his work in his window as the liberating Allied troops marched through Paris. James Wood and his singers convincingly convey the darkness of the penultimate section, *La menace sous le ciel*, but in the finale, with its calls for Liberté: '*J'écris ton nom*' they are unable to project a full-throated French fervour.

PROCTOR-GREGG, Humphrey
(1895–1980)

(i) *Clarinet Sonata;* (ii) *Horn Sonata in A;* (iii) *Violin Sonata 3 in F. 4 Westmorland Sketches for Piano (23–26)*
(M) *** Dutton CDLX 7165. Buckle, with (i) Cox; (ii) Ashworth; (iii) Howarth

When I.M. was a student at the Royal Manchester College of Music in the late 1950s and early 1960s (before it was amalgamated into the Royal Northern School of Music) Humphrey Proctor-Gregg was the College Bursar and Chief Administrator, his role as a fine composer unsuspected by most of us. Born in the delightful Lakeland town of Kirkby Lonsdale, he had enjoyed a very considerable career in the field of opera, a friend and colleague of Beecham.

This admirable collection shows the range and sheer quality of his compositions over six decades, from the charming pastoral piano sketches of the First World War years, evoking the colourings of the Lake District, to the all-but-heroic *Horn Sonata,* dedicated in 1980 to Robert Ashworth, who plays it eloquently here with a very full broad tone.

The clarinet seems to bring out the best in most composers, and so it is with Proctor-Gregg's *Sonata* (1943), immediately appealing with its yearning *lusingando* melodic style. But all this music is rewardingly melodic, deftly structured and never predictable, not least the *Violin Sonata* (written for Thomas Matthews, who gave the first performance of Britten's *Violin Concerto*). Linked throughout by a descending arpeggio, it is again fluently enticing from the very opening bars; it has a memorable slow movement and a soaring finale, the whole work essentially English in feeling. The performances here are surely definitive, played with great warmth and spontaneity, and the beautifully balanced Dutton recordings are in the demonstration bracket. A disc not to be missed if you love English composers like Butterworth, Moeran and Ireland.

PROKOFIEV, Serge (1891–1953)

Warner Prokofiev Edition:
(B) ** Warner (ADD/DDD) 0927 49147-2 (24)

Vol. I: *Symphonies: 1–7* (complete, including both 1930 & 1947 versions of 4)
(M) * Warner 0947 49634-2 (4). O Nat. de France, Rostropovich

Although Rostropovich's authority in this repertoire is beyond doubt, he makes heavy weather of most of the symphonies. There is a tendency to linger and labour, even in the *Classical Symphony,* and although the 1930 version of the *Fourth Symphony* is much tauter than the 1947 revision, taut is not the word that springs to mind when listening to this great musician's reading. It is painfully slow, and even though he adopts much the same tempi as his rivals on record he somehow sounds slower thanks to his heavyweight accentuation. Of course, there are good things here (the first movement of the *Sixth,* perhaps), but the expressive vehemence of the *Fourth* and *Seventh Symphonies* is very hard to take. Neeme Järvi's Chandos cycle remains a much better bet, as did Rozhdestvensky's now deleted analogue set from the early 1970s.

Vol. II: Concertos: (i) *Piano Concertos 1–5; Violin Concertos* (ii–iv) *1, Op. 19;* (v) *2, Op. 63;* (iii; iv; vi) *Symphony-Concerto for Cello and Orchestra, Op. 125*
(M) ** Warner 0927 49635-2 (4). (i) Krainev, Frankfurt RSO, Kitaenko; (ii) Vengerov; (iii) Rostropovich; (iv) LSO; (v) Repin, Hallé O, Nagano; (vi) Ozawa

Vladimir Krainev is a Neuhaus pupil, and there is some virtuoso pianism and much excitement in his accounts of the piano concertos. The *First* and *Fifth* are very impressive, though the *Third* is rather less subtle. Generally speaking, there is sensitive and well-prepared orchestral support from the Frankfurt orchestra under Dmitri Kitaenko and very acceptable sound. Maxim Vengerov's record of the *First Violin Concerto* with Rostropovich conducting was much admired by us on its original release, although it is less poetic (but more dazzling) than some rivals. Vadim Repin's account of the *Second* with Nagano and the Hallé Orchestra is also magnificent, though full justice is not done by the engineers to his sweetness of tone. In the *Sinfonia concertante,* which Prokofiev fashioned from his *Cello Concerto* after hearing Rostropovich play it, the great cellist is hardly less stunning than he was in his pioneering set in the West with Sir Malcolm Sargent. Ozawa shows much sensitivity to dynamic nuance, and the recorded sound is distinguished by a truthful perspective and transparency of texture. However, this is now available in an even more electrifying account on DVD. Rostropovich apart, none of these recordings would necessarily be a first choice when, in the piano concertos, the likes of Ashkenazy, Béroff and Toradze are available, and, in the violin concertos, Sitkovetsky, Kyung-Wha Chung and Cho-Liang Lin.

Vol. III: Stage Works & Film Scores: (i) *Cinderella* (excerpts); (ii) *Lieutenant Kijé: Suite, Op. 60;* (iii) *The Love for Three Oranges: Suite, Op. 33b;* (iv) *Peter and the Wolf, Op. 67* (in English, German, French and Spanish); (iii) *The Prodigal Son: Suite, Op. 64b;* (v) *Romeo and Juliet: Suites, Op. 64;* (vi) *The Steel Step: Suite, Op. 41b.* (vii) *Alexander Nevsky, Op. 78*
(M) ** Warner (ADD/DDD) 0927 49636-2 (6). (i) Strasbourg PO, Lombard; (ii) LPO, Tennstedt; (iii) Monte-Carlo PO, Foster; (iv) Lyon Op. O, Nagano (Narrators English: Patrick Stewart. German: Marius Müller-Westernhagen. French: Jacques Martin. Spanish: Miguel Bose); (v) OSR, Jordan; (vi) Philh. O, Markevich; (vii) Watkinson, Latvija Ch., Leipzig GO, Masur

None of these performances is top drawer. In *Romeo and Juliet* the Suisse Romande is alert enough and their rhythms are well defined, but there are occasional lapses of intonation and the clarinets do not exactly produce a beautiful sound. Masur's *Alexander Nevsky* and the *Scythian Suite* were recorded in Leipzig in 1991 and are both ultimately a little too civilized and wanting in the atmosphere that such rivals as Gergiev, Abbado and Järvi can muster. The *Prodigal Son,* on which the *Fourth Symphony* draws, and the *Three Oranges Suite* come from an Erato issue of the early 1980s and are both well enough played and recorded. Markevich's *Le Pas d'acier* (called here *The Steel Step*) with the Philharmonia comes from 1954 (previously available on EMI's Rouge et Noir series, though its provenance is not acknowledged) and has much to recommend it. *Peter and the Wolf* is included with the narration spoken in English, French, Spanish and German. The documentation is good, though the provenance and dates of the recordings are not given.

Vol. IV: Instrumental & Chamber Music: (i) *Overture on Hebrew Themes, Op. 34b.* (ii) *Cello Sonata in C, Op. 119;* (iii) *Flute Sonata in D, Op. 94;* (iv) *Overture on Hebrew Themes, Op. 34* (chamber version); *Quintet in G min., Op. 39;* (v; vi) *Sonata for Two Violins, Op. 6;* (v; vii) *Violin Sonatas 1–2; 5 Melodies for Violin & Piano;* (viii) *Tales of the Old Grandmother for Violin and Piano* (trans. Milstein). *Piano Sonatas* (ix) *2, Op. 14;* (x) *7, Op. 83;* (xi) *8, Op. 84.* (xii) *Music for Children;* (xiii) *10 Pieces for Piano, Op. 12: Prelude.* (xi) *Romeo and Juliet: Suite for Piano, Op. 75; Toccata for Piano*

(M) *** Warner (ADD/DDD) 0927 49637-2 (5). (i) Monte-Carlo PO, Foster; (ii) Noras, Heinonen; (iii) Rampal, Veyron-Lacroix; (iv) Berlin Soloists; (v) Repin; (vi) Barachovsky; (vii) Berezovsky; (viii) Milstein, Pludermacher; (ix) Devoyon; (x) Sultanov; (xi) de Groote; (xii) Sebok; (xiii) Katsaris

This is one of the best volumes in this edition. It brings us Vadim Repin and Boris Berezovsky in the two violin sonatas and the *Cinq mélodies*, one of the very finest modern versions of these magnificent works and almost alone worth the price of the set. The Finnish cellist Arto Noras gives an eloquent account of the late *Cello Sonata,* and there is the welcome *Quintet, Op. 39,* for oboe, clarinet, violin, viola and double bass, which Prokofiev wrote in Paris in 1924 as a ballet for the Romanov company, inspired by circus life and entitled *The Trapeze.* A good choice, particularly in such a fine performance as this by the Berlin Soloists. (It originally appeared coupled with the Hindemith *Octet,* which may have inhibited its wider dissemination.) The *Overture on Hebrew Themes for Piano, String Quartet and Clarinet* was composed in Chicago in 1919 for a group of Jewish students Prokofiev had known during his years at the St Petersburg Conservatoire, and whom he had met in New York (and the version for small orchestra that he made in 1934 is also included here). The Berlin Soloists play marvellously and are beautifully recorded. Of the piano sonatas, the *Eighth* is represented in the late Steven de Groote's 1979 performance, which, like the *Romeo and Juliet* transcription, is vital, expertly characterized and thoroughly compelling. So, too, is Pascal Devoyon's *Second.* The notes throughout are very good, though once again the documentation does not give the dates and provenance of the performances.

Vol: V: *War and Peace, Op. 91* (complete opera)

👂 (M) *** Warner 0927 49638-2 (4). Vishnevskaya, Miller, Ochman, Gedda, Ghiuselev, Ciesinski, Paunova, Toczyska, R. France Ch., O Nat. de France, Rostropovich

Rostropovich tells us that during his last illness Prokofiev begged him to make *War and Peace* better known. It had a chequered history during the Soviet era, but Rostropovich, who conducted it at the Bolshoi in 1970, does the composer outstanding service in this fine Paris account from 1988. The recording is very good indeed, and the set will be treasured for the Natasha of Vishnevskaya (who also sang the role in the pioneering but cut 1962 Melodiya set), the magisterial Kutuzov of Nicolai Ghiuselev, Wieslaw Ochman's Pierre and so much else besides. The choral singing and orchestral playing are very impressive indeed. For those who are attached to the Philips set with the Kirov Opera under Gergiev, the Rostropovich still has special claims, particularly now that it is competitively priced.

Bonus CD with complete edition only: Piano Rolls recordings made by the composer: PROKOFIEV: *The Love*

for Three Oranges: March & Intermezzo; 10 Pieces for Piano, Op. 12: March; Tales of Old Grandmother; Toccata.* RACHMANINOV: *Prelude in G min., Op. 23/5.* SCRIABIN: *Prelude, Op. 45/3.* MUSSORGSKY: *Pictures at an Exhibition: Ballet of the Unhatched Chicks & Promenade.* PROKOFIEV/RIMSKY-KORSAKOV: *Fantasia* (improvisation). Prokofiev singing: *Ivan the Terrible: Song of Praise* & *Canon Founders*

(***) Warner mono (ADD) 0927 49819-2. composer

Those buying the complete edition – and it has the advantage of a highly competitive price-tag, good presentation and, with the exception of the symphonies, serviceable performances at worst and some outstanding ones at best – have an additional bonus in the form of some archival material. Listening to the sonatas and concertos, it becomes obvious that Prokofiev must have been an impressive pianist, as those who have the Dutton or Pearl transfers of the *Third Concerto* with Piero Coppola and the LSO (recorded in 1933) will already know. These afford an additional glimpse of his pianism and greatly enhance the value of this set.

Other Recordings

(i) *Autumnal, Op. 8; Dreams, Op. 6; Cello Concertino in G min., Op. 132;* (ii; iii) *Piano Concertos 1–5;* (iii; iv) *Violin Concertos 1 in D, Op. 19; 2 in G min., Op. 63;* (i) *The Prodigal Son, Op. 46; 2 Pushkin Waltzes, Op. 120;* (i; v) *Sinfonia concertante in E min. Op. 125;* (i) *Symphonies 1–7; Waltzes, Suite, Op 110; The Year 1941, Op. 90;* (iii) *Sonata for Solo Violin, Op. 115*

(BB) ** Naxos White Box 8.509001 (9). (i) Nat. O of the Ukraine, Kuchar; (ii) Paik; (iii) Polish Nat. R.O, Wit; (iv) Papavrami; (v) Rudin

On the face of it a bargain, even if few of these performances would be a first choice. The symphonies do not compete with many of their CD rivals: the *Classical Symphony* is very heavy-handed and the quality of the playing is not particularly distinguished in the remainder. There are some deeply felt things in the *Sixth,* whose tempi are eminently well judged, but the horns call for some tolerance. Kuchar gives us the post-war version of the *Fourth Symphony* but he also includes *The Prodigal Son,* from which the original Op. 47 drew so heavily. The *Piano Concertos* are much more successful. Kun Woo Paik is an impressive and commanding soloist who is thoroughly inside the idiom. His virtuosity is imposing and he enjoys excellent support from the Polish National Radio Orchestra under Antoni Wit. In the *Violin Concertos* Tedi Papavrami proves a formidable soloist. Brought up in Albania, he became a pupil of Pierre Amoyal and an admired competition winner; he has real temperament and lyrical feeling. With Alexander Rudin we return to the Ukraine orchestra, who are not the most subtle of accompanists, but the Russian cellist is a powerful player, and, although this is not a flawless reading, he brings conviction and feeling to the score. A serviceable box and a useful introduction to this fascinating repertoire.

Cinderella (ballet; complete), Op. 87

** CPO 999610-2 (2). Cologne WDR SO, Jurowski

Michail Jurowski's recording of *Cinderella* is in no sense the equal of his account of *The Tale of the Stone Flower* with the Hanover Radio Philharmonic Orchestra, which was distinguished by refined orchestral playing and a pleasingly natural sound. It is soon evident that the characterization and the quality of the orchestral playing do not begin to approach either Pletnev or Previn. This is a studio performance with no sense of the footlights or atmosphere. Good though the Cologne orchestra is, the LSO outclass it in every way, as do the Cleveland Orchestra for Ashkenazy. Moreover, these competitors offer more music.

(i) Concertino in G min. for Cello & Orchestra, Op. 132 (completed and orch. Kabalevsky & Rostropovich); Sinfonia concertante in E min. for Cello & Orchestra, Op. 125; (ii) Cello Sonata in C, Op. 119

(M) (**) Revelation mono RV10102. Rostropovich, (i) USSR SO, Rozhdestvensky; (ii) Richter

Rostropovich's performances of this coupling were made at public concerts in 1964 and 1960 respectively (the performance is a composite one). Some allowance must be made for the sound here and in the 1951 recording of the Cello Sonata, once briefly available on the Monitor label, but what a performance!

Piano Concerto 1 in D flat; Suggestion diabolique, Op. 4/4

(BB) *** EMI Encore 5 86881-2. Gavrilov, LSO, Rattle – BALAKIREV: Islamey; TCHAIKOVSKY: Piano Concerto 1 etc. ***

A dazzling account of the First Concerto from Andrei Gavrilov. This version is second to none for virtuosity and sensitivity. Apart from its brilliance, it scores on other fronts too. Simon Rattle provides excellent orchestral support and the EMI engineers offer the most vivid recording, while the Suggestion diabolique makes a hardly less brilliant encore after the concerto.

Piano Concerto 3 in C, Op. 26 (DVD version)

(***) EMI mono **DVD** DVB 3 101989. Janis, O. Nat. de l'ORTF, Paray (with bonus: BRAHMS: Piano Sonata 2 in F sharp min., Op. 2; Hungarian Dances 4 & 5 – Julius Katchen) – RACHMANINOV: Rhapsody on a Theme by Paganini (***)

Byron Janis was recorded by French Radio in 1963 in a black-and-white film, and the mono sound ought to be better than this. But if the violins sound thin and pinched, the piano tone is acceptable and, not surprisingly, Janis's virtuosity is dazzling. He is fascinating to watch, while the concerto's full lyricism is caught in the orchestra, thanks to Paray: it just gets dehydrated by the inadequate microphones. The Brahms works are played commandingly by Katchen, and here the 1968 sound is much better.

Piano Concerto 3 in C, Op. 26

(M) **(*) RCA **SACD** (ADD) 82876 67894-2. Van Cliburn, Chicago SO, Hendl – RACHMANINOV: Piano Concerto 3 **(*)

The Third Concerto had its first performance with the Chicago Symphony Orchestra (the composer as soloist) in December 1921 and it was appropriate that the first stereo recording should have been made there four decades later, in 1960. Van Cliburn plays the work, not only with astonishing digital brilliance but also with much sympathetic warmth. With a forward balance for the piano, the bold projection of both orchestra and soloist is undoubtedly telling, and especially so in the sharply characterized slow movement. But then the new compatible SACD transfer brings out the background Chicago ambience and the result is more flattering, less brittle than the original LP, even if the piano timbre is less than ideally sonorous.

Piano Concerto 5 in G, Op. 55

(BB) *(*) EMI Gemini (ADD) 3 50849-2. S. Richter, O de Paris, Maazel – BARTÓK: Piano Concerto 2 *(*); TCHAIKOVSKY: Piano Concertos 1–3 **

Richter is his own keenest rival in this 1970 performance of the last of the Prokofiev concertos. His much earlier version for DG with Rowicki (449 744-2) was presented in sharper focus – not just a question of recording acoustic – and the newer account is not its match. The EMI recording balance favours the soloist.

(i) Violin Concerto 1. Symphony 1 (Classical); Visions fugitives (orch. Barshai)

* Chan. 9615. (i) Grubert; Moscow CO, Orbelian

All these pieces date from 1917 but, the Classical Symphony apart, they receive pretty lacklustre performances. Ilya Grubert undergoes too close a scrutiny from the recording engineers, and in the Visions fugitives their American conductor sets somewhat slow tempi. Subfusc recording.

Violin Concertos 1, Op. 19; 2, Op. 63

(M) *** Decca (ADD) 476 7226. Chung, LSO, Previn – STRAVINSKY: Concerto ***

Kyung Wha Chung's performances emphasize the lyrical quality of these concertos with playing that is both warm and strong, tender and full of fantasy. Previn's accompaniments are deeply understanding, while the Decca sound has lost only a little of its fullness in the digital remastering, and the soloist is now made very present. The Stravinsky coupling is equally stimulating. This is now reissued in Universal's 'Critics' Choice' series.

Violin Concerto 2 in G min., Op. 63

(B) ** Ph. 2-CD 475 7547 (2). Mullova, LAPO, Salonen – BARTOK: Violin Concerto 2 **; SHOSTAKOVICH: Violin Concerto 1 *(*); STRAVINSKY: Violin Concerto ***

Mullova's reading is pretty dazzling. She is very well balanced and is given altogether first-class sound and predictably idiomatic support from Salonen. However, as an overall package this set is difficult to recommend.

Ivan the Terrible (Complete ballet, arr. Tchulaki)

** Arthaus **DVD** 101 107. Bolshoi Ballet & Theatre O, Zhuraitis (V/D: Motoko Sakaguchi)

The composer Mikhail Tchulaki was asked by the Bolshoi company to adapt the film score that Prokofiev wrote for the Eisenstein film, Ivan the Terrible, into a two-act ballet. Cunningly, he used not only 377 fragments from the original score, but also various extracts from other works of Prokofiev, including Symphony No. 3 and the Alexander Nevsky Cantata. In the lavish Bolshoi production it works well, with spectacular dancing, atmospheric sets and costumes, a welcome addition to the list of the composer's ballets, well conducted here by Algis Zhuraitis.

Peter and the Wolf, Op. 67

(B) Virgin 5 61782-2. Henry, RLPO, Pešek – BRITTEN: Young Person's Guide **(*); SAINT-SAENS: Carnival of the Animals (chamber version) ***

Lenny Henry's colloquial narration is enthusiastic, clear and communicative. Children will certainly respond to his individual 'voices' for the characters in the tale and also his additional vocalized effects. But the record's appeal is reduced to virtually nil by the extraordinarily inept new instrumental characterization for each of the characters in the tale. The piece was specifically designed by Prokofiev to introduce young listeners to the orchestral palette, and the dumbing-down here robs his score of its primary purpose, plus almost all its elegance and wit. Peter stays with the strings; but, instead of a flute, the bird is portrayed by a Chinese 'mouth organ', the duck is a squealing Catalan 'tiple'. Even more unfortunately, the wolf is represented by three very bland accordions; and, worst of all, the engagingly feline clarinet with which Prokofiev identified the cat is changed to an oboe d'amore in order to produce a semblance of a 'miaow'.

Romeo and Juliet, Op. 64: (ballet; highlights)
(BB) *** HMV (ADD) 5 86750-2. LSO, Previn

(B) ** CfP 575 5642. LPO, Pritchard – MUSSORGSKY: *Pictures at an Exhibition* **

This selection from Previn's complete 1973 recording was originally entitled 'Scenes and Dances' and was chosen fairly arbitrarily. But this inexpensive reissue has been expanded to 75 minutes and follows through the action of all three Acts; besides giving a birds-eye picture of the complete work, it shows marvellously the diversity of Prokofiev's inspiration.

Pritchard's selection is not always predictable in its content, but it follows the narrative until the fight between Tybalt and Mercutio, then moves straight to the *Death of Juliet*. He is rhythmically positive, yet most effective in the gentler lyrical music, as is shown by his sensitive rubato in the atmospheric introduction, and his picture of *Juliet as a Young Girl*, delicately evoked. The LPO play with colour and commitment, although the passion of the lovers has been depicted with even greater intensity in other selections. The 1975 recording, made in Barking Town Hall, is certainly vivid.

Romeo and Juliet (ballet): *Suites 1–3: excerpts*
(B) *** DG Entrée 477 5011. Concg. O, Myung-Whun Chung

Romeo and Juliet (ballet; excerpts including *Suites 1–3*)
** DG 453 439-2. BPO, Abbado

Romeo and Juliet (ballet): *Suites 1 & 2, Op. 64*
(BB) ** EMI Encore CDE5 75226-2. Oslo PO, Jansons

We wrongly listed the contents of Chung's admirable disc in our main *Guide*, for it includes excerpts from all three suites from the ballet, 63 minutes of music. Myung-Whun Chung draws playing of great atmosphere, virtuosity and dramatic fire from the Royal Concertgebouw Orchestra, and DG provide a recording of great range and presence, comparable with the best now available. At its new price, the disc is a genuine bargain and is especially suitable for the Entrée label, aimed at collectors finding their way into this repertoire.

Abbado's selection from *Romeo* has some exemplary playing from the Berlin Philharmonic, and the DG engineers offer us very well-balanced recorded sound. This 70-minute anthology is assembled from the three published concert suites, as well as the ballet itself. Everything is well shaped and finely characterized, but Chung's Concertgebouw selection has greater atmosphere and dramatic flair.

Jansons secures playing of alert sensibility, discipline and refinement from the Oslo Philharmonic and has the advantage of a naturally balanced and vividly present recording, but the performance as a whole is wanting in a sense of the theatre.

Sinfonia concertante for Cello & Orchestra in E min., Op. 125
*** Avie AV 2090. Harrell, RLPO, Schwarz –
  SHOSTAKOVICH: *Cello Concerto 2* ***

Lynn Harrell recorded the *Sinfonia concertante* with the RPO under Ashkenazy for Decca some years ago, but here he is captured live with the excellent Liverpool orchestra under Gerard Schwarz to hardly less impressive effect. The performance has great ardour and intelligence and those who do not possess the earlier account should invest in this, not only for its artistic quality but for the valuable coupling which Harrell has not given us before.

SYMPHONIES

Symphonies 1, Op. 25 (Classical); 2, Op. 40; 3, Op. 44; 4, Opp. 47 & Op. 112(rev. 1947); 5, Op. 100; 6, Op. 111; 7, Op. 131
*** Ph. 475 7655. LSO, Gergiev
*** Chan. 8931/4. RSNO, Järvi

Symphonies 1–7; Lieutenant Kijé: Suite
(B) * DG 463 761-2 (4). BPO, Ozawa

Gergiev's Prokofiev cycle took place at the Barbican Hall, London, between 1 and 8 May 2005 to much (and deserved) acclaim and to packed houses – hence a certain dryness in the acoustic caused by the fairly close microphones. The performances were in every way admirable and the sound offered here is very much as one remembers it in the hall itself, full of presence and with very well-detailed textures, with astringent upper strings and rich, full-bodied wind and brass. Fine though Neeme Järvi's set with the Royal Scottish National Orchestra is (see our main edition), this newcomer must now take pride of place as a first recommendation.

Ozawa's BPO set of Prokofiev symphonies is a non-starter. The performances are well played, but are very routine: without looking at the documentation, it would be hard to recognize this celebrated orchestra, which here produces a general-purpose sonority which Karajan would never have countenanced in his day. *Lieutenant Kijé* is sadly lacking in sparkle.

Symphonies: 1 (Classical); 5. Lieutenant Kijé (Suite)
(M) ** RCA 82876 62319-2. St Petersburg PO, Temirkanov

The St Petersburg Philharmonic, as we must now learn to call the great (formerly Leningrad) ensemble, is still a magnificent orchestra, even if it does not produce quite the same special sound one recalls from the days of Mravinsky. Nevertheless they play the *Classical Symphony* with élan and good humour. Temirkanov does not hurry the first movement and the *pianissimo* string entry in the *Larghetto* is exquisite. He is a touch laboured at the opening of the Scherzo, but the finale sparkles vivaciously. However, in the *Fifth Symphony* pleasure is somewhat diminished by one or two mannerisms which Temirkanov indulges in. At the very opening theme matters almost come to a stop as early as bar 7, and in the Trio section of the Scherzo each four-bar phrase is broken by a disruptive little pause which inhibits the flow of the line. Needless to say, there are many good things here, but this performance as a whole offers no serious challenge to existing recommendations. *Lieutenant Kijé*, however, is a different matter, very well played and with the recording in the demonstration bracket (bass-drum fanciers will be especially impressed), and with the nostalgic closing section wonderfully atmospheric.

Symphonies (i) *1 (Classical)*; (ii) *5. Lieutenant Kijé, Op. 60*; (iii) *Romeo and Juliet* (excerpts). (iv) *Alexander Nevsky, Op. 78*
(B) ** RCA mono/stereo 74321 88684-2 (2). (i) Boston SO, Koussevitzky; (ii) St Petersburg PO, Temirkanov; (iii) NBC SO, Stokowski. (iv) Elias, Chicago SO & Ch., Reiner

A mixed bag. Koussevitzky's 1947 *Classical Symphony* is sparkling, although the mono sound is limited, and Stokowski's *Romeo and Juliet* with NBC forces (from 1954) is highly charged. Termikanov is better in the *Lieutenant Kijé Suite*, which is well characterized, than in the *Fifth Symphony*, which is mannered and pulled around. Reiner's 1959 *Alexander Nevsky* is one of the very finest versions of the cantata, but this is also available separately, differently coupled. As with the rest of this two-CD RCA series, the documentation and presentation leave much to be desired.

Symphonies 3 in C min., Op. 44; 4 in C, Op. 112 (revised 1947 version)
(M) * Warner Elatus 2564 60020-2. O. Nat. de France, Rostropovich

These Elatus recordings derive from Rostropovich's complete cycle, in which he offered both the original 1930 version of the *Fourth Symphony* and also the longer, revised 1947 score; it is the latter that is included here. The playing of the Orchestre National is first class, and the recording has impressive body and good range, but Rostropovich is terribly heavy-handed. The *Andante* of the *Third Symphony* comes off well enough, but the finale is very emphatic. One longs for a lighter touch, both here and in No. 4, in which tempi are again all on the slow side.

Symphony 5; Romeo and Juliet: excerpts
** Teldec 4509 96301-2. NYPO, Masur

In Kurt Masur's live account, the playing is eminently cultured, and the performance would be enjoyable in the concert hall were it not for the abrupt hiatus at the *l'istesso tempo* section of the Scherzo which will rule it out of court for many collectors. The recording is very full-bodied and well detailed. The six movements from *Romeo and Juliet* are studio recordings and, paradoxically enough, sound more spontaneous.

Symphonies 6; 7 in C sharp min., Op. 131
(M) * Warner Elatus 0927 49826-2. Fr. Nat. O, Rostropovich

These performances formed part of the Warner Prokofiev Centenary set (see above). Rostropovich makes heavy weather of both masterpieces, and even at mid-price they are not really recommendable.

CHAMBER MUSIC

Cello Sonata in C, Op. 119
*** Berlin Classics 0017832BC. Bohorquez, Groh – BRITTEN; DEBUSSY: *Cello Sonatas* ***

Under the title 'Modern Milestones' Claudio Bohorquez, with a fine fellow artist at the piano, brings together three twentieth-century cello sonatas that work well as a nicely contrasted programme on disc. Of Peruvian and Uruguayan parentage, Bohorquez was born and raised in Germany, and is currently based in Berlin. The Prokofiev owes much to the help and inspiration of the then young Mstislav Rostropovich, and though this late work, written at a time when the composer's health was failing him, has its gritty moments,

Bohorquez brings out the power of the first movement, measured until the final *animato* section. His account of the central *Moderato* movement is built on high contrasts between the wit of the opening and the lyricism of the later passages, while power again dominates in his weighty reading of the strongly rhythmic Allegro finale.

PIANO MUSIC

10 Pieces from Romeo and Juliet, Op. 75; Toccata in D min., Op. 11
** Hyp. CDA 67018. Demidenko – MUSSORGSKY: *Pictures* *

No doubts about Demidenko's virtuosity and keyboard command, particularly in the *Toccata*, or the excellence of the Hyperion sound. His playing in the *Romeo and Juliet* often delights, but there are exasperating mannerisms that attract attention to the pianist rather than to Prokofiev.

Piano Sonata 7 in B flat, Op. 83
(BB) *(*) Warner Apex 0927 40830-2. Sultanov – RACHMANINOV: *Piano Sonata 2*; SCRIABIN: *Piano Sonata 5* *(*)

A strongly muscular and powerful account of the *Seventh Sonata* comes from Alexei Sultanov, although it is too crude and aggressive to disturb allegiance to such recommendations as Argerich, Pollini and Pletnev.

Piano Sonatas 7–9
*** ASV CDDCA 755. Lill

This disc, coupling the last three *Sonatas*, offers exceptionally good value, and the excellent ASV recording was made in Henry Wood Hall. All three performances are of high quality, and John Lill is never less than a thoughtful and intelligent guide in this repertoire.

OPERA

The Love for three Oranges (CD version in English)
*** Chan. 10347 (2). Humble, MacMaster, Tahu Rhodes, Arthur, Whitehouse, Op. Australia Ch., Australian Op. & Ballet O, Hickox

There have been recordings of Prokofiev's wryly humorous opera in the original Russian and in French, the language in which it was first performed; but with such a lively and complex piece there is every advantage in having it in English, particularly when the deft translation by Tom Stoppard is used. Recorded live, the humour comes over naturally, helped by the crispness of ensemble, even in the most complex passages. This company is built on its fine ensemble work, and Richard Hickox proves the liveliest interpreter, securing excellent playing from the orchestra, brilliantly recorded, with crisp and incisive singing from the chorus. The singing of the principals is consistently strong and positive, even if the voices are not specially distinctive, with Teddy Tahu Rhodes as Leandro, William Ferguson as Truffaldino, John MacMaster as the Prince, and Elizabeth Whitehouse as Fata Morgana all first rate. Above all, with a recording like this in the vernacular and based on stage performances (here recorded in concert), the humour of the piece comes over as the composer clearly intended. The set also scores over its rivals in the full, atmospheric, well-focused sound.

PUCCINI, Giacomo (1858–1924)

Capriccio sinfonico; Crisantemi; Minuets 1–5; Preludio sinfonico; Edgar: Preludes, Acts I & III. Manon Lescaut: Intermezzo, Act III. Le Villi: Prelude. La Tregenda (Act II)
(M) *** Decca 475 7722. Berlin RSO, Chailly

In a highly attractive collection of Puccinian juvenilia and rarities, Chailly draws opulent and atmospheric playing from the Berlin Radio Symphony Orchestra, helped by outstandingly rich and full recording. The *Capriccio sinfonico* brings the first characteristically Puccinian idea in what later became the opening Bohemian motif of *La Bohème*. There are other identifiable fingerprints here, even if the big melodies suggest Mascagni rather than full-blown Puccini. *Crisantemi* (with the original string quartet version expanded for full string orchestra) provided material for *Manon Lescaut*, as did the three little *Minuets*, pastiche eighteenth-century music.

OPERA

La Bohème (complete DVD version)
*** Arthaus **DVD** 100 054. Barker, Hobson, Douglas, Roger and David Lemke, Rowley, Ewer, Australian Op. Ch. & O, J. Smith (V/D: Geoffrey Nottage)

An up-to-date, with-it *La Bohème* DVD from Australia, with mixed modern sets and a young cast, makes a good deal of Puccini's opera in contemporary terms, though this is not for traditionalists. David Hobson's Rodolfo and Cheryl Barker's Mimì are well cast: they fit togther and they can sing, although they are not what Puccini had in mind. Christine Douglas and Roger Lemke are down-to-earth visions of Musetta and Marcello. Julian Smith conducts with conviction and the production works well, but it is more like a musical than an opera.

La Bohème (complete CD versions)
(M) **(*) RCA (ADD) 82876 70784-2 (2). Caballé, Domingo, Milnes, Raimondi, Alldis Ch., Wandsworth School Boys' Ch., LPO, Solti

(M) ** RCA (ADD) 09026 63179-2 (2). Moffo, Tucker, Costa, Merrill, Tozzi, Rome Op. Ch. & O, Leinsdorf

(BB) (**) Naxos mono 8 110072/3. Albanese, Gigli, Poli, Menotti, La Scala Milan Ch. & O, Berrettoni

(M) (**) Nim. mono NI 7862/3. Albanese, Gigli, Poli, Menotti, Baracchi, Baronti, La Scala, Milan, Ch. & O, Berrettoni

(M) DG (ADD) 477 5618 (2). Scotto, Poggi, Meneguzzer, Gobbi, Modesti, Maggio Musicale Fiorentino Ch. & O, Votto

(BB) EMI 4 76921-2 (2). Dessi, Sabbatini, Scarabelli, Gavanelli, Antoniozzi, Colombara, Piccolo Coro dell'Antoniano, Bologna Teatro Comunale Ch. & O, Gelmetti

Solti's 1974 set is not a top choice, but is worth considering for the glorious singing of Montserrat Caballé as Mimì. Domingo is unfortunately not at his most inspired, but the recording is both vivid and atmospheric (see our main volume).

On the Leinsdorf set Anna Moffo is an affecting Mimì, Mary Costa a characterful Musetta, while Merrill and Tozzi provide strong support. Tucker gives a positive characterization as Rodolfo, though he has lachrymose moments. Sadly, Leinsdorf's rigid direction, with speed fluctuations observed by instruction and never with natural expression, sets the singers against a deadpan, unsparkling accompaniment. Dated recording, impressively remastered.

Gigli was always at his most winning in the role of Rodolfo in *La Bohème*, and here opposite Licia Albanese he is the central focus of a warmly enjoyable version, recorded in 1938 at La Scala. Gigli indulges at times in his cooing manner, but it is a powerful as well as a charming assumption, with humour well caught. In the next decade Albanese was Toscanini's choice for Mimì, and she went on singing the role at the Met. in New York until the mid-1960s, a role she made her own. The others are reliable if not comparably characterful, with Umberto Berrettoni as conductor. First-rate Naxos transfers from 78s and a bonus of ten extra arias from Albanese.

The Nimbus transfer process works well here too, with plenty of body in the sound, without too much masking of reverberation, and with a bloom on the voices. The glory of the set is Gigli's Rodolfo, with a chuckle in the voice bringing out the fun, and he uses his pouting manner charmingly, with the occasional sob adding to the charm. He adds little touches, as when he murmurs '*Prego*' when ushering Mimì out, before she discovers she has lost her key. He dwarfs the others, with even Albanese a little shrill as Mimì.

We wonder why DG decided to reissue their Florence recording of *La Bohème*, and we only list it in case any collector might be tempted by the cast. Scotto's voice is not caught at all well, and Gobbi is less than a success as Marcello. As for Poggi, he makes the most frightful noises! Do we really want to hear a Bohemian snarling? No stars.

Similarly the Gelmetti EMI set, recorded live in Bologna in 1990, has little going for it. When Giuseppe Sabbatini sings above a cooing *mezzo voce* his tenor becomes strangulated, while Daniela Dessi makes a colourless Mimì, fluttery and effortful. Gelmetti's conducting brings rough-and-ready ensemble in the larking of the Bohemians, with the score alternately overdriven and languorously soupy. Add to that a vinegary Musetta and a Marcello who blurts like a foghorn and one wonders how this set ever came to receive its original premium-priced issue. The only possible excuse is that the revised Ricordi score was used here for the first time on record, and now the set comes in EMI's lowest price bracket. The voices are balanced behind the orchestra, which may be just as well when the singing is so indifferent. Again no stars.

La Bohème (highlights)
(M) (**) EMI mono 5 66670-2 (from complete recording with Callas, di Stefano; cond. Votto)
(BB) ** EMI Encore (ADD) 5 74985-2. Scotto, Kraus, Milnes, Neblett, Plishka, Manuguerra, Amb. Op. Ch., Trinity Boys' Ch., Nat. PO, Levine

The set of excerpts from the Callas recording is little more than a sampler. Although it includes the Love duet from Act I, and the closing scene, the overall playing time is only 54 minutes. There is a cued synopsis.

With Levine's 1979 complete set currently unavailable, collectors might consider this highlights disc, even though the singing is flawed. Alfredo Kraus's relatively light tenor is no longer as sweet as it was and Scotto is not flatteringly recorded here. Milnes makes a powerful Marcello and Neblett a strong Musetta, but Levine could be more persuasive in the big melodies.

La fanciulla del West (The Girl of the Golden West; CD versions)

☞ (M) *** DG (ADD) 474 840-2 (2). Neblett, Domingo, Milnes, Howell, ROHCG Ch. & O, Mehta

(M) (*(*)) Warner Fonit mono 8573 87488-2 (2). Gavazzi, Campagnano, Savarese, Caselli, RAI Ch. & O of Milan, Basile

On DG, Mehta's manner – as he makes clear at the very start – is on the brisk side, even refusing to let the first great melody, the nostalgic *Che faranno i viecchi*, linger into sentimentality. Sherrill Milnes as Jack Rance makes that villain into far more than a small-town Scarpia, giving nobility and understanding to the Act I arioso. Domingo, as in the theatre, sings heroically, disappointing only in his reluctance to produce soft tone in the great aria, *Ch'ella mi creda*. The rest of the team is excellent, not least Gwynne Howell as the minstrel who sings *Che faranno i viecchi miei*; but the crowning glory of a masterly set is the singing of Carol Neblett as the Girl of the Golden West herself, gloriously rich and true, with formidable attack on the exposed high notes. Full, atmospheric recording to match, essential in an opera that is full of evocative offstage effects. With its new 'Originals' transfer and at a new mid-price, with texts and translations included, this set deserves upgrading to a full three stars.

Recorded in 1950 for Cetra in collaboration with Italian Radio, this Warner Fonit set was the first ever commercial recording of *La fanciulla del West*, an opera for long unfairly ignored outside Italy. It yields to later versions both in recorded sound – limited mono with clear voices but dim orchestra – and in the casting, which features a team of singers from a generation that built up opera in Italy after the war without making an impact outside. All the principals have powerful voices but, as recorded, their singing is fluttery, maybe in part a question of recording balance. What makes the performance convincing nonetheless is the conducting of Arturo Basile, totally idiomatic, pressing home the great lyrical and dramatic moments with a conviction born of familiarity. An Italian libretto is provided, but no translation. A historic document rather than a serious contender.

Gianni Schicchi (CD version)

(M) ** Orfeo (ADD) C546 001B. Fischer-Dieskau, Schary, Mödl, Ahnsjö, Thaw, Fahberg, Auer, Engen, Grumbach, Wewezow, Bav. State Ch. & O, Sawallisch

Gianni Schicchi recorded live in German makes little sense outside Germany, but this is well worth hearing for the powerful contribution of Dietrich Fischer-Dieskau in the title-role. He takes a freer view than you would expect of so meticulous a musician, resorting to parlando at times, but in that he is responding to the joy of the piece as a member of a strong team. The trouble is that Gunther Rennert's lively production involves stage noises – often sounding louder than the music. The balance of voices is very variable, too, with the orchestra set behind. One result of the dryness and Sawallisch's incisive conducting is that the dissonant modernity of Puccini's writing in places is brought out the more. Fischer-Dieskau is well supported by a delightful pair of young lovers. As Lauretta, Elke Schary is fresh and girlish, ending her celebrated aria (in German *O du, mein lieber Vater*) with a tender diminuendo. As Rinuccio, the Swedish tenor Claes-Haakan Ahnsjö sings with a bright, clear tone. Among the others one cherishes most of all the characterful contribution of Martha Mödl, then over sixty, as a formidable Zita.

Madama Butterfly (CD versions)

(BB) (***) Regis mono RRC 2070 (2). De los Angeles, Di Stefano, Gobbi, Canali, Rome Op. Ch. & O, Gavazzeni

(M) (*) Warner Fonit mono 0927 43551-2 (2). Petrella, Tagliavini, Taddei, Cetra Ch., RAI SO of Turin, Questa

Victoria de los Angeles' first recording of *Madama Butterfly*, a role which for a decade or more she made her own, was done in mono in 1954. On Testament (SBT 2168) in the days of LP, it was first reissued at full price on a pair of EMI CDs, and now reappears on the super-budget Regis label, faithfully transferred. The performance has many advantages over the later, stereo version. De los Angeles' tone is even more beautiful, Di Stefano is a more ardent Pinkerton, and Tito Gobbi, unexpectedly cast as a rugged Sharpless, uses that small role to point some of the set's most memorable moments, notably the Act I toasting duet with Pinkerton and the Act II confrontation with Butterfly. The mono transfer is kind to the voices, which are given a full presence, and if the orchestra sounds a bit dry it still makes a vivid backcloth. There is a cued synopsis and good documentation.

Recorded in 1954, the old Cetra set of *Butterfly*, now reissued on Warner Fonit, brings perfunctory conducting from Angelo Questa and a flawed cast. Ferruccio Tagliavini as Pinkerton sets out loud and hectoring in the opening scene, only to be transformed by the sight of Butterfly, becoming from then on seductively honey-toned. Giuseppe Taddei is an impressive Sharpless, while Clara Petrella is an idiomatic if hardly distinctive Butterfly. Not a viable set with its limited, mono sound, with voices balanced so close that even Goro sounds loud.

Madama Butterfly: highlights

(BB) **(*) HMV (ADD) 5 86751-2 (from complete recording, with Scotto, Bergonzi, Di Stasio, Panerai, Rome Opera Ch. & O, Barbirolli)

It is a pity that the selection from the Barbirolli set is disappointingly short (54 minutes) and does not include any of the music before Butterfly's entrance (outstandingly done); but each item here demonstrates the glories, vocal and orchestral, of the performance, which has a dedication and intensity comparatively rare in opera recordings made in Italy. Those who have invested in another complete version, will find this a satisfying and inexpensive supplement. Barbirolli joins in the enjoyment with great groans of pleasure in places. Excellent analogue recording (from 1966).

Manon Lescaut (complete CD version)

(BB) (***) Naxos mono 8.111030/1 (2). Albanese, Bjoerling, Merrill, Calabrese, Rome Op. Ch. & O, Perlea (with Arias from BOITO: *Mefistofele*. CATALANI: *La Wally*. CHARPENTIER: *Louise*. CILEA: *Adriana Lecouvreur*. VILLA-LOBOS: *Bachianas Brasileiras 5*)

With Bjoerling as des Grieux giving one of his very finest performances on disc and with Robert Merrill in glorious voice as Lescaut, the Romanian conductor Jonel Perlea conducts one of the most passionate performances of this opera ever recorded. Timing is masterly, and, though Licia Albanese no longer sounded girlish in 1954, she has the deepest understanding of the role of Manon. The transfer is bright and clear, with an edge that can readily be tamed. This was one of the very first complete operas recorded by RCA in Italy, and the thrust and enthusiasm of the whole company reflect that. As a bonus comes a valuable collection of Albanese's solo recordings, including most of the arias for which she was especially famous. Also the celebrated *Aria* from Villa-Lobos's *Bachianas brasileiras No. 5* with Leopold Stokowski conducting.

Tosca (complete CD versions)

(M) *** Decca 475 7522 (2). L. Price, di Stefano, Taddei, V. State Op. Ch., VPO, Karajan

(M) *** RCA 82876 70783-2 (2). L. Price, Domingo, Milnes, Plishka, Alldis Ch., Wandsworth Schol Boys' Ch., New Philh. O, Mehta

(BB) (**) Naxos mono 8.110256–57 (2). Callas, Di Stefano, Gobbi, Calabrese, Mercuriali, La Scala, Milan, Ch. & O, De Sabata

(M) (**) Warner Fonit mono 8573 87479-2 (2). Frazzoni, Tagliavini, Guelfi, RAI Ch. & O of Turin, Basile

* Decca 473 710-2 (2). Cedolins, Bocelli, Guelfi, Coro Polofonico, Maggio Musicale Fiorentino Ch. & O, Mehta

Karajan's 1962 Vienna *Tosca* (discussd in our main volume) is now reissued as one of Decca's Originals, so it still includes a full libretto and translation. It remains one of the finest versions, with Leontyne Price at the peak of her form and di Stefano singing most sensitively. But Karajan deserves equal credit with the principal singers, and the sound is first class.

Leontyne Price made her second complete recording of *Tosca* (for RCA) ten years after the first under Karajan, and the interpretation remained remarkably consistent, a shade tougher in the chest register – the great entry in Act III a magnificent moment – and a little more clipped of phrase. That last modification may reflect the relative manners of the two conductors – Karajan more individual in his refined expansiveness, Mehta more thrustful. On balance, taking Price alone, the preference is for the earlier set, but Mehta's version also boasts a fine cast, with the team of Domingo and Milnes at its most impressive. The recording, too, is admirable, even if it yields to the Decca in atmosphere and richness.

Though the historic mono recording from Warner Fonit is uncompetitive in a crowded field, it is worth hearing for the mellifluous Cavaradossi of Ferruccio Tagliavini, at his peak in 1956 when the recording was made. Also for the stentorian Scarpia of Gian Giacomo Guelfi, dark and powerful rather than convincingly villainous. It was recorded for Cetra by Italian Radio, which accounts for the absence of stereo in a 1956 recording, but the voices are well caught. The Tosca of Gigliola Frazzoni is totally idiomatic but not very distinctive.

Though it is understandable that the companies should want to exploit the popular appeal of Andrea Bocelli, with his sweet, smooth tenor timbre, the Decca set of *Tosca* is misguided. The recording balance favours the voices to an absurd degree, with the orchestra – so necessary in Puccini for evoking atmosphere – consigned to the half-distance, adding to the limpness of Mehta's direction, with tensions low. Worse still, Bocelli is coarse and loud throughout – allowing a moment or two of cooing half-tone in *E lucevan le stelle* – with phrasing square and unimaginative. As Tosca Fiorenza Cedolins is more imaginative, but the voice is edgy and unsteady under pressure, and although Carlo Guelfi makes a clear-toned, virile Scarpia, he does not sound very sinister. The recording dampens down even the confrontation of Scarpia and Tosca in Act II. For unquestioning devotees of Bocelli only.

Tosca: highlights

(BB) ** EMI Encore 5 87009-2 (from complete recording, with Scotto, Domingo, Bruson; cond. Levine)

(M) ** EMI (ADD) 5 66666-2 (from complete recording with Callas, Bergonzi, Gobbi, Paris Op. Ch., Paris Conservatoire O, Prêtre)

Scotto, in generally good voice, makes a highly convincing Tosca, and Domingo is among the very finest Cavaradossis of our time. Bruson is a powerful if rather young-sounding Scarpia, and Levine's direction is suitably red-blooded. With 65 minutes offered and a simple cued synopsis, this is certainly good value, and the digital recording provides excellent presence for the singers.

Even to Callas admirers her stereo remake of *Tosca* must be a disappointment when it fails so obviously to match the dramatic tension of the first version under de Sabata. This is another sampler-length selection with only 56 minutes of music.

Il Trittico: (i) Il Tabarro; (ii) Suor Angelica; (iii) Gianni Schicchi (complete DVD version)

*** Warner **DVD** 5050467 0943-2. (i) Cappuccilli, Sass, Martinucci, Bertocchi, Bramante, Jankovic; (ii) Plowright, Vejzovic, Allegri, Verri, Santelli, Spezia, d'Amico; (iii) Pons, Gasdia, Marusin, Jankovik, Poggi; La Scala, Milan, Ch. & O, Gavazzeni (V/D: Brian Large)

We need an *Il Trittico* on DVD, and if this La Scala production brings a fairly traditional approach to a stage production (*Il Tabarro* is realistic but over the top) it will do very well, as the casting does not disappoint either. Piero Cappuccilli as the bargemaster is well supported by the believably hard-voiced Sylvia Sass as Giorgetta, and the melodrama is brought off effectively. In the title-role of *Suor Angelica*, Rosalind Plowright is at her finest, both vocally and in commanding our sympathy; Dunja Vejzovic's Princess is not as intimidating as she should be, but she sings well enough. The set for *Gianni Schicchi* is unrealistically spacious but Cecilia Gasdia is a rich-voiced Lauretta and, at the centre of the story, Juan Pons is a firm and believable Schicchi, although the staging of his final solo as a devil from hell is totally misguided in just the way that producers refuse to let well alone. But the veteran Gianandrea Gavazzeni conducts throughout with vitality and warmth, and altogether this has much to offer.

Turandot (complete DVD version)

*(*) TDK **DVD** DV-OPTURSF. Schnaut, Gallardo-Domâs, Botha, Ombuena, Davislim, Boaz, Tear, Burchuladze, V. State Op. Ch. & O, Gergiev (V/D: Brian Large)

David Pountney's lavish production of *Turandot* was staged for the 2002 Salzburg Festival, creating a ruthless visual background of death and torture for the opera. As usual with way-out modern productions, not all of it can be taken seriously, and it has nothing to do with Puccini's vision. The cast is equally flawed, with Gabriele Schnaut's Turandot neither convincing (she is simply not glamorous enough) nor comfortably sung and, although Johan Botha is a much more pleasing Calaf, he has very little charisma. The smaller supporting roles are well cast, but the star of the show is Cristina Gallardo-Domâs's Liù. Gergiev conducts confidently and with passion, including Berio's not very satisfactory completion. Brian Large, as usual, gets the video angles right, but this is not really recommendable.

Turandot (complete CD versions)

*(*) RCA 74321 60617-2 (2). Casolla, Larin, Frittoli, Maggio Musicale Fiorentino Ch. & O, Mehta

(M) *(*) Sony (ADD) SM2K 90444 (2). Marton, Carreras, Ricciarelli, Kerns, V. State Op. Ch. & O, Maazel

(BB) * Naxos 8.660089/90 (2). Casolla, Bartolini, Deguci, Bilbao Choral Society, Malaga PO, Rahbari

The RCA recording offers a strong performance under Zubin Mehta in beefy, if at times abrasive, sound, with ample space round the voices. The casting of the principals is seriously flawed. Sergei Larin sings with fine dramatic thrust, though his voice grows strained towards the end. Giovanna Casola has a big voice with a pronounced flutter, so that the tone grows sour, and at the top pitching becomes vague under stress, so that In questa reggia ends with a squeal. Barbara Frittoli is even less well cast as Liù, with her heavy vibrato and reluctance to sing softly.

Turandot brings the warmest and most sensuous performance in Maazel's Sony Puccini series, thanks in good measure to its being a live recording, made in September 1983 at the Vienna State Opera House. Applause and stage noises are often distracting, and the clarity of CD tends to make one notice them even more. Recording balances are often odd, with Carreras – in fine voice – suffering in both directions, sometimes disconcertingly distant, at others far too close. Katia Ricciarelli's Liù is predictably heavyweight, though the beat in her voice is only rarely apparent. The strengths and shortcomings of Eva Marton as the icy princess emerge at the very start of In questa reggia. The big, dramatic voice is well controlled, but there is too little variation of tone, dynamic or expression; she rarely shades her voice down. In the closing act, during the Alfano completion, Marton's confidence and command grow impressively, with her heroic tone even more thrilling. But the presentation of this reissue prevents any kind of general recommendation. Not only are there no dividing bands within the acts, but no libretto is provided either, nor any kind of cued synopsis, and only a single paragraph to summarize the plot!

The central problem of the Naxos set under Alexander Rahbari lies with the casting of Giovanna Casolla in the title role. She is the same dramatic soprano as appeared as the Icy Princess in the 1998 RCA set of this opera, recorded live in Beijing with Zubin Mehta as conductor. Sadly, since then, the marked judder that Casolla kept more or less under control in 1998 has developed alarmingly, and the very opening of Turandot's big opening aria, In questa reggia, starts with such squally singing, loud, gusty and uneven, that it is unlikely to give pleasure to anyone. It is true that when she is singing softly the production is far firmer, but power is what one needs in this role, and Casolla's squally singing is not helped by the close balance of voices. The singing of Lando Bartolini as Calaf is seriously flawed, too, when he belts everything out with unremitting coarseness, often sliding up to notes. The Japanese soprano Masako Deguci is far finer as Liù, for hers is a sweet, pure, well-controlled voice, even if she could be more characterful. Though the baritone taking the role of Ping is gritty and ill-focused, there is little to complain of among the others, with Pang and Pong typical comprimario tenors. The opening scene is impressive too for the singing of the Bilbao Choral Society, so important when at that point the chorus is protagonist, responding well to the vigorous conducting of Alexander Rahbari, who tends to favour speeds on the brisk side. When Naxos also offers the historic first recording of 1938, there is much to be said for remaining faithful to that earlier set, which not only brings far better singing, but on the two discs offers as a substantial bonus a fascinating collection of early recordings from the opera (8.110193/4).

Arias from: Gianni Schicchi; Madama Butterfly; Manon Lescaut; Suor Angelica; Turandot

(M) *** Decca Classic Recitals (ADD) 475 7167. Weathers, V. Op. O, Quadri – VERDI: Arias **(*)

This 1966 recital does not appear to have seen the light of day for some years, and its reissue is very welcome. Felicia Weathers had a beautiful voice, not always totally under control in this 1966 recording, but – and most importantly – she is commanding enough to make one sit up at these well-known arias. No singer can sing each of these roles equally well, but Weathers made an impressive showing. The Decca sound is very good indeed, and Quadri is a sympathetic accompanist.

PURCELL, Henry (1659–95)

Fantasias 1–3 in 3 Parts; 4–12 in 4 Parts; in 5 Parts in F 'upon one note'; in 6 Parts in G min. (In nomine); in 7 Parts in G min. (In nomine)

(BB) **(*) Virgin 2x1 4 82097-2 (2). L. Bar. – CORELLI: Ciaconna etc. **(*)

The Purcell Fantasias are among the most searching and profound works in all music and the London Baroque do them fair justice. They are a very accomplished group and their intonation and blend are impeccable. The resonance of the recording, made in London's Temple Church in 1983, may trouble some collectors, but we did not find the halo round the aural image unpleasing. At the same time, it is possible to feel that in music so highly charged with feeling and so richly imbued with melancholy, the constraints exercised by these artists result in playing that at times is close to understatement.

(i) 12 Fantasias in 3 Parts; Fantasia on One Note; In Nomines in 6 Parts & 7 Parts; (ii) Abdelazar: Overture & Suite. The Gordian Knott Untied: Overture and Suite. The Married Beau: Overture and Suite. Music's Handmaid: Lessons 1–12. The Virtuous Wife: Overture and Suite. (iii) Harpsichord Suite 6 in D

(M) ** Van. Artemis (ADD) ATMCD 1522 (2). (i) VCM, Harnoncourt; (ii) Hartford CO, Fritz Mahler; (iii) Malcolm (harpsichord)

A fascinating collection – much fine music offered with different degrees of authenticity. Harnoncourt's Fantasias come from the earlier years of the Vienna Concentus Musicus (1965). The string playing is without vibrato but warm and mellow. The theatre music is played very pleasingly by a modern chamber orchestra, with no attempt at period-instrument manners. The great joy is the Harpsichord Suite from George Malcolm, which is irresistible. Good recording, but the list of works is reproduced from the original LP sleeve and the type is minuscule.

VOCAL MUSIC

Odes for the Birthday of Queen Mary (1692 & 1694); Music for the Funeral of Queen Mary (1695); Funeral Anthem; Funeral Sentences; Praise the Lord, O Jerusalem

(*) * EMI 3 444138. Soloists, King's College, Cambridge, Ch., AAM, Cleobury

Purcell composed some of his very finest vocal works for these royal celebrations, and the joyful Odes, Come ye sons of Art and Love's Goddess sure, are among them. By contrast, the Funeral Music is infinitely touching in a quite different way.

The performances here are authentic, superbly sung and played, full of life, and very well recorded. A disc to treasure.

Odes for Queen Mary's Birthday: Come Ye Sons of Art; Love's Goddess Sure was Blind; Now Does the Glorious Day Appear
(B) ** Virgin 5 61844-2. Gooding, Bowman, Robson, Crook, Wilson-Johnson, George, OAE Ch. & O, Leonhardt

A happy triptych on Virgin, but Leonhardt's personality is firmly stamped on all three works here. The orchestral texture has the less than fully nourished sound of period stringed instruments, and Leonhardt's jogging rhythm at the opening of *Now Does the Glorious Day Appear* seems a little too circumspect for that joyful ode. Indeed, his sobriety tends to override the music's character. He has a splendid chorus and superb soloists, and they are in excellent voice. James Bowman stands out, as does Julia Gooding (most winning, both in *Love's Goddess Sure* and in her lovely duet with the oboe, *Bid the Virtues*, in *Come Ye Sons of Art*). But Leonhardt's restraint prevents Purcell's inspired settings from taking the fullest flight.

STAGE WORKS AND THEATRE MUSIC

Dido and Aeneas (complete)
(B) **(*) HM HMX 2991683. Dawson, Joshua, Finley, Bickley, Clare College Chapel Ch., OAE, Jacobs

(BB) ** Warner Apex 8573 89242-2. Troyanos, Stilwell, Johnson, Ch. & CO, Leppard

René Jacobs directs a characterful and dramatic reading of *Dido and Aeneas*, with Lynne Dawson a pure and refined heroine leading an excellent cast. Speeds tend to be extreme in both directions, with Dido's *Lament* and final chorus very slow indeed, with some heavy underlining. Happily Dawson sustains her line very well in the *Lament*, deeply affecting in her noble dedication. What is more controversial is Jacobs's tendency in choruses not just to underline individual notes – as in the final chorus – but to pull the tempo around outrageously, particularly in the Witches' choruses. So both *Harm's Our Delight* and *Destruction's Our Delight* start very slowly indeed, and then have sudden bursts at high speed, with phrasing pulled around too. Many will accept such quirks as part of a characterful experience, particularly when the Sorceress (Susan Bickley) and the two counter-tenors who take the roles of the first two witches (Dominique Visse and Stephen Wallace) are hilariously characterful in a way that Purcell would certainly have relished. Rosemary Joshua as Belinda, golden in tone, and Gerald Finley as a virile Aeneas are also ideally cast. Well-balanced recording, if with a reverberation that gives some of the choruses a religious flavour. This CD is now reissued inexpensively and comes handsomely packaged with a Harmonia Mundi catalogue.

On Apex Leppard directs a consistently well-sprung and well-played performance, as one would expect, but the overall impression is disappointing, largely because the climax of the opera fails to rise in intensity as it should. Tatiana Troyanos, stylish elsewhere, misses the tragic depth of the great lament of Dido, and without that focus the impact of the rest falls away. However, it is interesting to have a baritone (Richard Stilwell), instead of a tenor, singing the *Sailor's song*. The recording is excellent.

QUANTZ, Joseph Joachim (1697-1773)

Flute Concertos: in C; in D (For Potsdam); G; G min.
*** RCA RD 60247. Galway, Württemberg CO, Heilbron, Faerber

Quantz was a skilled musician and all four concertos here are pleasing, while their slow movements show a genuine flair for melody. Quantz also wrote well-organized allegros, and the opening *Allegro assai* of the *G major* shows him at his most vigorous, even if perhaps the *Potsdam Concerto* is overall the best of the four works here. The thoroughly musical James Galway is most winning in the lyrical cantilenas, and the Württemberg group accompany with polish and much vitality. Excellent sound.

Flute Sonatas (for transverse flute & continuo) *in C, D, G min., QV 1:9, 42, 116 & 128;* (i) *Trio Sonatas in D & E flat, QV 2:15 & 17*
(BB) ** Naxos 8.555064. Oleskiewicz; Vial, Schulenberg; (i) with Beaudin

As can be heard at the opening of the *D major Sonata*, Mary Oleskiewicz's baroque flute is rather pale and watery, and although these performances are well played, they are lacking in real personality and will appeal mostly to those wedded to period instruments. Apart from odd individual movements, such as the Minuet that closes the *G minor* work, Quantz's invention fails to be memorable.

QUILTER, Roger (1877–1953)

A Children's Overture
(B) ** EMI (ADD) CDM7 64131-2. Light Music Society O, Dunn (with TOMLINSON: *Suite of English Folk Dances*) – HELY-HUTCHINSON: *Carol Symphony;* VAUGHAN WILLIAMS: *Fantasia on Christmas Carols* **

The neglect of this charming overture, skilfully constructed from familiar nursery rhymes, is inexplicable. Sir Vivian Dunn gives a good if not remarkable performance and the recording too is pleasing rather than outstanding. But the music itself is a delight. Ernest Tomlinson's suite of six folk-tunes, simply presented and tastefully scored, makes an attractive bonus. Again the sound is acceptable but could be richer.

(i) *A Children's Overture;* (ii) *3 English Dances; Where the Rainbow Ends* (Suite). (iii) *The Fuchsia Tree; Now sleeps the crimson petal; Weep you no more.* (iv) *Come away, death;* (v) *7 Elizabethan Lyrics;* (vi; vii) *Go, lovely rose. It was a lover and his lass* (two versions, with viii; ix & x); (viii; ix) *Love's Philosophy;* (xi) *Non nobis, Domine;* (iv) *Now sleeps the crimson petal;* (vi; ix) *O mistress mine*
(B) *** EMI (ADD/DDD) 5 85149-2. (i) Light Music Soc. O, Dunn; (ii) N. Sinfonia, Hickox; (iii) Hough; (iv) Bostridge, Drake; (v) Allen, Parsons; (vi) Harvey; (vii) Byfield; (viii) Baker; (ix) Moore; (x) Lott, Murray, Johnson; (xi) Finchley and Barnet & District Choral Societies, Central Band of the RAF, Wing. Cdr J. L. Wallace

Beginning with Quilter's masterly *A Children's Overture*, in Sir Vivian Dunn's bright performance from 1969, this delightful anthology is a worthy tribute to this master of short and unpretentious composition. Richard Hickox's digital accounts of the three *English Dances* and *Where the Rainbow Ends* are charmingly done, unashamedly simulating all the rustic qualities of 'old England'. There are some real gems in the vocal items: Janet Baker bringing characteristic richness to *Love's Philosophy* and *It was a lover and his lass*, which is also heard in a quite different version for duet with Felicity Lott and Ann Murray which is utterly delightful. Baritone Trevor Harvey certainly invests passion in *O mistress mine*, but he sings *Go, lovely rose* with more tenderness. In Ian Bostridge's two numbers, the sheer beauty of his tenor makes one readily forgive any reservations of over-interpretation, and what lovely songs they are, too! With three very attractive piano pieces, sensitively played by Stephen Hough, and a rousing performance of *Non nobis, Domine*, this CD is thoroughly recommended. The sound-quality throughout is excellent, only the Frederick Harvey items, dating from the mid-1960s, sounding a bit dated.

RABAUD, Henri (1873–1949)

Divertissement sur des chansons russes, Op. 2; Eglogue, Op. 7; Mârouf, savetier du Caire: Dances; Symphonic Poem after Lenau's Faust (Procession nocturne), Op. 6; Suites anglaises 2–3

** Marco Polo 8.223503. Rheinland-Pfalz PO, Segerstam

The *Eglogue* was Rabaud's first orchestral piece and derives its inspiration from the first *Eclogue* of Virgil. The dances from *Mârouf, savetier du Caire* have an appropriately oriental flavour since the opera itself is based on an episode from the *Arabian Nights*. The *Procession nocturne* is a tone-poem based on the same Lenau poem which inspired Liszt's *Nächtlige Zug* and is the most atmospheric of the pieces on this disc. The *Suites anglaises* are arrangements of Byrd, Farnaby and other Elizabethan composers that Rabaud made for a 1917 production of *The Merchant of Venice*. Like Roger-Ducasse, Rabaud's music is not strongly personal, but it is distinctly Gallic and well worth investigating. Segerstam and his orchestra show a real sympathy with this turn-of-the-century French repertoire, and they are decently recorded too.

RACHMANINOV, Sergei (1873–1943)

Piano Concertos: (i; ii) 1 in F sharp min., Op. 1; (i; iii) 2 in C min., Op. 18 (2 versions); (i; ii) 3 in D min., Op. 30; 4 in G min., Op. 40; (i; iii) Rhapsody on a Theme of Paganini, Op. 43; (iv) Isle of the Dead, Op. 29; Symphony 3 in A min., Op. 44. Vocalise, Op. 34/14; (v) Piano (4 Hands) Polka Italienne; (Solo Piano) Barcarolle, Op. 10/2; Daisies (song transcription); Etudes-tableaux, Op. 33/2 & 7; Op. 39/6; Humoresque, Op. 10/3; Lilacs (song transcription; 2 versions); Mélodie, Op. 3/3; Moment musical, Op. 16/2; Oriental Sketch; Polichinelle, Op. 3/4; Polka de V. R. (3 versions); Preludes: in C sharp min., Op. 3/2 (3 versions); in G min.; in G flat, Op. 23/5 & 10; in E, G, F min., F, G sharp, Op. 32/3, 5–7, 12; Serenade, Op. 3/5 (2 versions).

Other Performances: (vi) BEETHOVEN: *Violin Sonata 8, Op. 30/3.* SCHUBERT: *Violin Sonata in A, D.574.* GRIEG: *Violin Sonata, Op. 45.* BACH: *Partita 4, BWV 828: Sarabande.* BEETHOVEN: *32 Variations in C min.* BORODIN: *Scherzo in A flat.* CHOPIN: *Ballade 3; Mazurkas, Op. 63/3; Op. 68/2; Nocturnes, Op. 9/2; Op. 15/2; Scherzo 3; Sonata 2 (Funeral March); Waltzes, Op. 18; Op. 34/3; Op. 42; Op. 64/1 (2 versions); Op. 64/2; Op. 64/3 (2 versions); Op. 60/2; Op. 70/1; in E min., Op. posth.; Ballade 3.* DAQUIN: *Le coucou.* DEBUSSY: *Children's Corner: Dr Gradus ad*

Parnassam; Golliwog's Cakewalk. DOHNÁNYI: *Etude, Op. 28/6.* GLUCK: *Orfeo ed Euridice: Mélodie.* GRIEG: *Lyric Pieces: Waltz; Elfin Dance.* HANDEL: *Suite 5: Air & Variations (Harmonious Blacksmith).* HENSELT: *Etude (Si oiseau étais), Op. 2/6.* LISZT: *Concert Paraphrases: Chopin: Polish Songs (Return home; The maiden's wish); Schubert: Das Wandern; Serenade; Concert Study: Gnomenreigen; Hungarian Rhapsody 3.* MENDELSSOHN: *Song without Words: Spinning Song, Op. 67 (2 versions); Etudes, 104b/2–3.* MOSZKOWSKI: *Etude (La jongleuse), Op. 52/4.* MOZART: *Sonata in A, K.331: Theme and Variations; Rondo alla Turca.* PADEREWSKI: *Minuet, Op. 14/1.* SAINT-SAËNS: *Le Cygne (arr. Siloti).* D. SCARLATTI: *Pastorale (arr. Tausig).* SCRIABIN: *Prelude, Op. 11/8.* SCHUBERT: *Impromptu in A flat, Op. 90/4.* SCHUMANN: *Carnaval, Op. 9; Der Kontrabandiste (arr. Tausig).* Johann STRAUSS Jr: *One Lives but Once (arr. Tausig).* TCHAIKOVSKY: *Humoresque, Op. 10/2; The Seasons: November: Troika (2 versions); Waltz, Op. 40/8. Piano Transcriptions:* BACH (Violin) *Partita 3, BWV 1003: Preludio; Gavotte & Gigue.* BEETHOVEN: *Ruins of Athens: Turkish March.* BIZET: *L'Arlésienne: Minuet.* KREISLER: *Liebesfreud (3 versions).* MENDELSSOHN: *A Midsummer Night's Dream: Scherzo.* MUSSORGSKY: *Gopak.* RIMSKY-KORSAKOV: *Flight of the Bumble bee.* SCHUBERT: *Wohin?* TCHAIKOVSKY: *Lullaby, Op. 16/1.* (viii) TRAD.: *Powder and Paint*

⚫ (B) (★★★) RCA mono 82876 67892-2 (10). Composer; (i) with Phd. O; (ii) Ormandy; (iii) Stokowski; (iv) cond. composer; with (v) Natalie Rachmaninov; (vi) Kreisler; (vii) Nadejda Plevotskaya

This reissued RCA collection originally appeared for the 50th anniversary of the composer's death, and it encompasses all the recordings Rachmaninov made from 1919, the time his arrived in America, until 1942, the year before his death. These include all four of his *Piano Concertos* (No. 3 irritatingly cut) as well as the *Paganini Rhapsody*, the *Third Symphony* and the tone-poem, *The Isle of the Dead* (also with cuts). The recordings were of high quality, the piano tone is firm and the orchestral sound full, if acoustically dry. You will not be disappointed with Stokowski's Philadelphia strings in the famous 18th variation of the *Rhapsody*. The *Symphony* too, unsurpassed as a performance, sounds splendid, the Philadelphia strings again covering themselves with glory.

When one turns to the solo performances, the acoustic recordings made between 1920 and 1925 are on balance the most cherishable of all, with the sound again astonishingly full and the readings sparkling and vivid. That is true even of the 1924 recording of the *Piano Concerto No. 2*, here for the very first time issued complete. As in the classic electrical recording of five years later, he is partnered by Stokowski and the Philadelphia Orchestra, but the earlier one had a more volatile quality, with the fingerwork remarkably clear.

Interpreting Chopin, Rachmaninov was also at his freshest and most imaginative in the early recordings, yet many of the items here bear witness to the claim often made that he was the greatest Golden Age pianist of all. The delicacy of his playing in Daquin's little piece, *Le coucou*, shows how he was able to scale down his block-busting virtuosity, and though in Beethoven's *32 Variations in C minor* he omitted half a dozen variations so as to fit the piece on two 78 sides, it is full of flair.

There is magic too in the collaboration with Fritz Kreisler, not just in Beethoven, but also in the Grieg and Schubert *Sonatas*, and in the private recordings, when he accompanies a gypsy singer in a traditional Russian song or plays a piano duet, the *Polka Italienne*, with his wife Natalie. Transfers are commendably clean and truthful, and the ten discs come in a box with good documentation.

Piano Concertos (i) 1 in F sharp min.; (ii) 2 in C min.; (iii) 3 in D min.; (i) 4 in G min.; (ii) Rhapsody on a Theme of Paganini, Op. 43

(BB) *** EMI Gemini (ADD) 4 76948-2 (2). Anievas, New Philh. O, Frühbeck de Burgos, Atzmon, or Ceccato

(B) **(*) Chan. 2 for 1 241-30. Shelley, RSNO, Thomson

Piano Concertos 1–4; Rhapsody on a Theme of Paganini; (i) Vocalise (trans. Kocsis)

(M) ** Ph. 468 921-2 (2). Kocsis, San Francisco SO, De Waart

Anievas cannot match Ashkenazy or Rudy as a searching or individual interpreter of Rachmaninov (see our main volume), but his youthful freshness makes all these performances highly enjoyable. He plays the *Third Concerto* uncut and the EMI recording is bright, full and vivid. Excellent value at Gemini price.

Howard Shelley's performances are sumptuously recorded (in Caird Hall, Dundee) with rich strings, powerfully resonant brass and a bold, truthful piano image projected out in front. There is some lovely playing from the orchestra and the performances do not lack adrenalin, although their ebb and flow of tension is not consistent, and at times the music-making almost tends to run away with itself. Undoubtedly the finales have great dash and much charisma from Shelley, but Bryden Thomson seems less assured in the idiom. Just after the opening of the *Rhapsody* he produces a curious echo effect (in which his soloist joins) but the *Eighteenth Variation* could have more fervour, as could the climax of the finale of the *Second Concerto*. The *Fourth Concerto* has some spectacular moments but lacks a really firm profile. Even so, there is much to enjoy here, and Shelley's contribution is always distinguished.

Zoltán Kocsis has fleet fingers and dashes through the first two concertos with remarkable panache and striking brilliance. But in No. 2 he gives the listener too little time to savour incidental beauties or surrender to the melancholy of the slow movements. He is just a little too carried away with his own virtuosity, and, although this is thrilling enough, it is not the whole story. Similarly, he rushes through the first movement of No. 3, opting for the shorter cadenza in the first movement, which he plays with electrifying brilliance. The *Fourth Concerto* is a good deal less rushed, though it is full of excitement and virtuosity when required, which is perhaps even more suited to the *Paganini Rhapsody*. But there are moments in both concertos when one feels Kocsis should rein in his fiery high sprits. The Philips recording places him rather far forward, but there is no lack of orchestral detail and there is plenty of range. However, first choice rests with Ashkenazy (Decca 444 839-2).

Piano Concerto 2 in C min., Op. 18

(BB) ** Warner Apex 0927 40835-2. Sultanov, LSO, Shostakovich – TCHAIKOVSKY: *Piano Concerto 1* **

(BB) ** EMI Encore 5 85705-2. Weissenberg, BPO, Karajan – TCHAIKOVSKY: *Piano Concerto 1* *(*)

(BB) * EMI Encore (ADD) 5 74567-2. Cziffra, New Philh. O, Cziffra Jr – GRIEG: *Piano Concerto* *

(BB) * Virgin 4 82128-2. Pommier, Hallé O, Foster – TCHAIKOVSKY: *Piano Concerto 1* *

Sultanov's recording was made in the immediate aftermath of his success at the eighth Van Cliburn Competition. There is plenty of exuberance and brilliance and an impressive range of tonal colour. Whatever reservations one may have, this is an eminently serviceable account, even if this would hardly be a first choice. The balance places the soloist too far forward, and the recording does not do justice to the LSO strings, which sound lustreless.

The Weissenberg–Karajan partnership dates from 1972. The performance rises splendidly to the climaxes, notably in the first movement and finale, but elsewhere tension is less consistently sustained. Weissenberg's thoughtful manner often seems too deliberate, although the slow movement produces some hushed playing which has undoubted magnetism. Taken as a whole, even though the recording is vivid, this is not entirely satisfying, and the new Tchaikovsky coupling provided for this reissue is even less so.

Though not entirely lacking poetic feeling, Cziffra's early 1970s account brings a general lack of passion and brilliance (mainly the fault of the conductor), though the finale does catch fire in the right places. The sound is below 1970s standards, with the orchestra sounding scrawny at times. Not recommended, even at budget price, with so much white-hot competition.

Neither soloist Jean-Bernard Pommier nor conductor is at their best in this Virgin coupling of two famous concertante warhorses, and there is nothing to detain the collector here.

Piano Concertos (i) 2; (ii) 3

(B) ** DG Entrée (ADD) 474 171-2. Vásáry, LSO, Ahronovich
** BIS CD 900. Ogawa, Malmö SO, Arwel Hughes

Tamás Vásáry and the impetuous Yuri Ahronovich are not dull but one does not feel they form an entirely convincing partnership. The *Second Concerto* is effective enough, with a fine climax in the first movement. But after that the tension is allowed to drop, and the languorous *Adagio* does not distil the degree of poetry that makes the Ashkenazy–Previn performance so beautiful. The recording is bold and colourful. Vásáry uses the longer version of the first movement cadenza in the *Third Concerto*. The slow movement is indulgent and lacks momentum. Vásáry's playing itself is clear and often gentle in style, but the conductor's extremes of tempi are inappropriate here.

Norika Ogawa is a cultured and musical artist but she does not have quite the tempestuous, barnstorming brilliance that any pianist aspiring to the *Third Piano Concerto* must command if he or she is to convince. She gives us the bigger cadenza, which seems to have replaced the more exhilarating one that Rachmaninov and Horowitz recorded. This is all rather low-voltage, though the Malmö orchestra under Owain Arwel Hughes are very supportive and the BIS recording is first class.

Piano Concertos 2 in C min.; 4 in G min., Op. 40

(M) **(*) Decca 475 7550. Ashkenazy, Concg. O, Haitink

Now reissued as one of Decca's Originals, this account of the *Second Concerto* cannot match the poetic reading Ashkenazy recorded earlier with Previn. Here the opening theme is a touch more ponderous, and elsewhere too the yearning passion of the work is rather muted, even in the lovely reprise of the main theme in the slow movement. Fortunately, Ashkenazy gives a superb account of the *Fourth Concerto*, strong and dramatic and warmly passionate, with Haitink and the Concertgebouw establishing the work as more positively characterful than is often appreciated. Splendid Deccca sound, with the Concertgebouw acoustics making a warmly resonant framework.

(i) *Piano Concerto 2;* (ii) *Rhapsody on a Theme of Paganini*
(BB) ** EMI Encore 5 86993-2. Gavrilov, Phd. O, Muti
(B) ** CfP 585 6232. Fowke, RPO, Temirkanov

Gavrilov's playing here is distinguished by flamboyant virtuosity and a self-regarding brilliance that are not wholly pleasing. In both performances there is finely shaped and responsive orchestral support, but neither in the concerto nor in the *Rhapsody* does the pianist bring the aristocratic distinction of naturalness of utterance that he commanded in his earlier recordings.

Philip Fowke gives tasteful, well-mannered performances, ultimately lacking the bravura needed in both these display works, although the recording is excellent.

Piano Concerto 3 in D min., Op. 30
☉⟶ (M) *** EMI (ADD) 3 45819-2 [3 45820-2] . Gilels, Paris Conservatoire O, Cluytens – SAINT-SAËNS: *Piano Concerto 2;* SHOSTAKOVICH: *Preludes & Fugues* ***
(M) **(*) RCA **SACD** (ADD) 82876 67894-2. Van Cliburn, Chicago SO, Hendl – PROKOFIEV: *Piano Concerto 3* **(*)
(BB) (***) Naxos mono 8.110787. Horowitz, RCA Victor SO, Reiner – BEETHOVEN: *Piano Concerto 5* (***)

(i) *Piano Concerto 3 in D min., Op. 30. 24 Preludes*
(M) (***) Decca mono 475 6368 (2). Lympany, (i) with New SO of London, Collins – KHACHATURIAN: *Piano Concerto* (**(*))

Gilels's 1955 performance of the *Third Concerto* (miraculously recorded in very satisfactory stereo) can readily be placed alongside Horowitz. As Bryce Morrison comments in the note with this reissue as one of EMI's 'Great Recordings of the Century': 'not even Rachmaninov played the concerto with such sovereign ease'. Like Horowitz, Gilels plays the simpler first cadenza, yet he still dazzles the ear with his virtuosity, as he does in the thrilling finale, where the climax (with Cluytens moved to an unexpected degree of passion) is overwhelmingly intense. Yet this performance is not just about passion or bravura, but about the glowing feeling of Russian nostalgia with which the whole concerto is imbued. Truly a great performance, and a very acceptable and certainly vivid transfer to CD.

In this remarkable 1958 live Carnegie Hall recording, which is new to CD, Van Cliburn fulfilled absolutely the promise of his earlier RCA record of the Tchaikovsky *First Concerto*. This remains one of the very finest accounts of the *D minor Concerto* on record, and it has much in common with Horowitz's classic 1941 mono version with Reiner. There is the same balance between delicate lyricism and power, and the slow movement is ravishingly played. Van Cliburn's exciting bravura in the outer movements has to be heard to be believed, not in any freakish sense, but because of the pleasure given by his complete technical and musical mastery. The dainty scherzando section is captivating and the final peroration has never sounded more exciting in its growth and full flowering at the climax. Alas, the recording leaves much to be desired. The balance is dry and close and the piano *fortissimos* unflattering, for the engineers make little use of the background ambience of the hall. Nevertheless, this is a performance for all time and, with its distinguished Prokofiev coupling, is true treasure trove.

On Naxos comes the second account Horowitz made of the *D minor Concerto* and, like its coupling, it remains one of the classics of the gramophone. Horowitz was unrivalled in this

concerto and it is good to have the first cadenza which Rachmaninov recorded rather than the second, a barn-storming volley of octaves that Ashkenazy first recorded in the 1960s and which unfortunately seems to have become standard ever since. It is among the most classical of readings and Reiner is a totally like-minded partner. Good new transfers.

The combination of Moura Lympany and Anthony Collins in Rachmaninov's *Third Piano Concerto* produces a strikingly passionate and very sympathetic performance indeed. The soloist's delicate opening contrasts with the splendid way she controls the climax of the first movement, and she makes the closing pages meaningful. Collins begins the slow movement with a singular depth of feeling, and the exultant finale is superb, with the final climax tremendously exciting. The string-sound is a bit over-bright and strident (it always was) but the overall sound is generally full and good for its period (1952). In the *Preludes*, Lympany reveals the latent beauty found in these works in a series of highly musical performances, without resorting to vulgar or showy playing for cheap effect. The 1951 sound is more than acceptable. Bryce Morrison in his sympathetic sleeve-notes sums it up in the final paragraph: 'Moura Lympany's Rachmaninov is both a classic and romantic experience. Like Lipatti, Solomon and Clara Haskil before, she is one of those artists who, in Charles Rosen's words, "invites admiration by appearing to do nothing while achieving everything".'

The Isle of the Dead, Op. 29; Symphonic Dances, Op. 45
(M) **(*) LPO 1004. LPO, Jurowski

As the Principal Guest Conductor of the LPO, the dynamic young Vladimir Jurowski on the orchestra's own label conducts high-powered readings of these two Rachmaninov works. The dramatic tension in the *Symphonic Dances* leads up to a thrilling close, and though the hushed sequence of *The Isle of the Dead* does not bring an equivalent rush of adrenalin, the mystery of this piece inspired by Böcklin's great painting (reproduced in the booklet) is perfectly caught. These are fine performances, marked by clean textures, which gain in tension from being recorded live.

***Rhapsody on a Theme of Paganini* (DVD version)**
(***) EMI mono **DVD** DVB 3 101989. Janis, O Philharmonique de l'ORTF, Froment – PROKOFIEV: *Piano Concerto 3* (***)

When one turns to Byron Janis, we hear and see (in black and white) playing of an entirely different order, and not just virtuosity either (although there is plenty of that). But Janis and Froment between them reveal much detail that often passes by unnoticed, and they do not fall short in the passionate 18th variation either. The snag is that the string-tone is thin and meagre: it is curious to watch a large orchestra produce tone which is entirely lacking in voluptuousness. But the recording of the piano is fully acceptable.

***Rhapsody on a Theme of Paganini* (CD versions)**
(*) Australian Decca Eloquence mono/stereo 476 7671. Jablonski, RPO, Ashkenazy – DOHNÁNYI: *Variations on a Nursery Song;* LISZT: *Totentanz* ((*)); LUTOSLOWSKI: *Paganini Variations* ***
(M) ** Telarc CD 80193. Gutiérrez, Baltimore SO, Zinman – TCHAIKOVSKY: *Piano Concerto 1* **

Jablonski's is a thoroughly recommendable version of the *Rhapsody* with Ashkenazy and the RPO. There is sparkle and virtuosity, if not the high-voltage lyricism of the very best versions available. But there is an enjoyably varied collection of works on this CD.

Horatio Gutiérrez's fingerwork in the *Rhapsody* and his virtuosity are both impressive. But the best is the enemy of the good, and there are more imaginative and poetic accounts to be had. The Baltimore orchestra give him firm support under David Zinman; but neither here nor in the Tchaikovsky coupling could one point to qualities which would warrant a three-star rating.

SYMPHONIES

Symphony 1 in D min., Op. 13; Caprice bohémien, Op. 12
(BB) ** Naxos 8.550806. Nat. SO of Ireland, Anissimov

Taken on its own merits, the budget account from Alexander Anissimov and the National Symphony Orchestra of Ireland is more than adequate and can be recommended. The recording is very good.

Symphony 2 in E min., Op. 27
(BB) * Naxos 8.554230. Nat. SO of Ireland, Anissimov
Symphony 2; (i) 3 Russian Songs, Op. 41.
*(*) Chan. 9665. Russian State SO, Polyansky; (i) with Russian State Symphonic Capella

Valéry Polyansky's account is far from negligible, but it is equally far from distinguished. The most attractive feature of the disc is the Op. 41 set of *Three Russian Songs*, a glorious triptych, full of character, which are given decent, full-blooded performances.

Though the Naxos version is well played and recorded, the conductor, Alexander Anissimov, tends to make heavy weather of the outer movements, with boldly underlined rubato in the big melodies and with a final climax in the fourth movement which fails to lift as it should. Even in the super-bargain category there are preferable, more idiomatic versions, including the earlier Naxos issue with Gunzenhauser, which also boasts *The Rock* as a coupling.

(i) Symphony 3; The Rock, Op. 7; (ii) The Isle of the Dead; (iii) Preludes, Opp. 23 & 32; Op. 3/2
(B) ** RCA (ADD) 74321 88679-2 (2). (i) Stockholm PO, Berglund; (ii) Chicago SO, Reiner; (iii) Weissenberg
Symphony 3; Symphonic Dances
(M) **(*) Telarc CD 80331. Baltimore SO, Zinman

David Zinman has already given us a fine account of the *Second Symphony*. His reading of the *Third* is similar, warmly relaxed, with glorious string playing from the Baltimore orchestra and the most affectionate detail throughout. Climaxes are dramatic, helped by the superb demonstration-quality recording from Telarc, and the finale makes a real apotheosis, as long as you are not looking for the highest degree of tension and drama. The *Symphonic Dances* are also very attractively done, full of colour, with the closing number especially benefiting from the splendidly vivid sound.

The best thing by far on the RCA disc is Reiner's classic account of *The Isle of the Dead*. Only Rachmaninov himself and Koussevitzky surpassed this marvellously controlled and beautifully recorded 1957 account. Why RCA have chosen to bury it with Berglund's earthbound 1988 version of the *Third Symphony* when they have the composer's own in their archives is puzzling. The Stockholm Philharmonic is a fine orchestra but does not play with any great enthusiasm for Berglund and does not command the Rachmaninov sonority

or idiom. Alexis Weissenberg's *Preludes* are much better but would not necessarily be a first choice.

CHAMBER MUSIC

Cello Sonata in G min., Op. 19
** Praga PRD 250 182. Kaňka, Klepáč – MIASKOVSKY: *Cello Sonatas 1 & 2* **
Cello Sonata in G min.; Oriental Dance, Op. 2/2; Prelude, Op. 2/1
(**) Hyp. CDA 67376. Isserlis, Hough – FRANCK: *Cello Sonata, etc.* (**)

On the face of it, the Praga disc offers an attractive coupling, but the *G minor Sonata* suffers, as do the two Miaskovsky works, from an ill-balanced recording. Michal Kaňka is a refined player but there is not enough projection or eloquence here to balance Jaromír Klepáč's pianism.

On Hyperion, in the Rachmaninov as in the cello version of the Franck, the expressiveness and subtlety of Steven Isserlis and Stephen Hough is seriously – unexpectedly with such a duo – undermined by the dim recording, making the music seem small-scale and lacking in bite.

PIANO MUSIC

Piano duet

Suites 1–2, Opp. 5 & 17; Symphonic Dances Op. 45
(B) ** Warner 0927 49611-2. Argerich, Rabinovitch

Very good recorded sound in this Warner coupling, which conveys the full range of touch and colour and has just the right amount of atmosphere. In the *First Suite* Argerich and Rabinovitch strive a bit too hard for effect and don't get far under the surface. The *Second Suite* and the *Symphonic Dances* are less self-conscious, but readers who want this repertoire are really far better off musically with the Ashkenazy and Previn set on Decca (444 845 2).

Solo piano music

(i) 24 Preludes; (ii) Suite 2 for 2 pianos, Op. 17
(BB) **(*) Warner Apex 2564 62036-2. (i) Lympany; (ii) Katia & Marielle Labèque

Moura Lympany's 1993 Warner Erato recording of Rachmaninov *Preludes* repeated an early success. While the pieces that need bravura seem to offer her no problems, she is at her best in the lyrical pieces, which truly blossom in her hands, and the famous *G minor* and *A flat major* from Op. 23 are memorable. The whole series moves forward spontaneously and, with full, vivid piano recording, this makes a good budget set, with the Labèques' account of the two-piano *Suite* an acceptable bonus.

Piano Sonata 2, Op. 36
(BB) ** Warner Apex 0927 40830-2. Sultanov – PROKOFIEV: *Piano Sonata 7; SCRIABIN: Piano Sonata 5* *(*)
Piano Sonata 2 in B flat min., Op. 36 (original version); Etudes-tableaux, Op. 33/1, 39/4; 7 Morceaux de fantaisie, Op. 3/3 & 5; Preludes, Op. 23/1 & 7; 32/2, 6, 9 & 10
(M) *** Ph. 475 7779. Zoltán Kocsis

Now reissued as one of Philips's Originals, this is one of the finest of all Rachmaninov recital discs. Be it in the smaller, reflective pieces or in the bigger-boned *B flat minor Sonata*,

Zoltán Kocsis's piano speaks with totally idiomatic accents, effortless virtuosity and a keen poetic feeling. This is a most distinguished offering and it is once more recommended with enthusiasm. Excellent recording.

Even at its modest price, Alexei Sultanov's Apex CD is of questionable value. There is no want of virtuosity, but it is of the designed-to-dazzle variety. Sultanov gives a pretty aggressive account of the *Sonata*, very brightly lit and fiery. Some readers may respond more warmly to his showmanship than others, but he is essentially brilliant but brash and no challenge to the top recommendations.

VOCAL MUSIC

(i) *The Bells, Op. 35; The Rock, Op. 7*
(BB) ** Naxos 8.550805. Nat. SO of Ireland, Anissimov; (i) with Field, Choupenitch, Meinikov, RTE Philharmonic Ch.

A far from negligible account of *The Bells* from this Russo-Irish partnership on Naxos, and *The Rock* is well played too.

Mass in B flat (arr. Vale); Ave Maria; 2 Benediction Hymns (O Salutaris; Tantum ergo); Evening Canticles on B flat; Hymn of the Cherubim (arr. Arnold)
**(*) Priory PRCD 860 All Saints, Margaret Street, Ch., Brough – VALE: *Requiem Mass in D flat* **(*)

In October 1924 Rachmaninov, on tour in Britain, went to the church of All Saints, Margaret Street, in central London, to hear what was described as his *Mass in B flat*. What the Director of Music, Dr Walter Vale, had done was to take five of the movements from Rachmaninov's great 18-movement *Liturgy of St John Chrysostom* and fit to them the words of the Mass in the translation prescribed by Cranmer in the Church of England Prayerbook – *Gloria, Credo, Sanctus/Benedictus* and *Agnus Dei*, leaving the opening *Kyrie* in Greek. Much more recently, Vale's successor, Eric Arnold, has followed up that example by similarly adapting Rachmaninov choral pieces by fitting English words to them, using not only other movements from the *Liturgy* but also from the *Vespers* (or All-Night Vigil) with which in 1915 Rachmaninov followed up the *Liturgy* of 1910. So in this collection, the Evening Canticles – *Magnificat* and *Nunc dimittis* – as well as the *Ave Maria* were taken from the Vespers. The result, as atmospherically recorded by Priory, is most impressive, with fine, incisive choral singing from the small mixed choir of professional singers. It is true that the hypnotic quality of the original sequences of the *Liturgy* and *Vespers*, each roughly an hour long, is diluted in these much shorter works. It is also true that, despite the efforts of the basses, required to plumb subterranean depths, the sound is very English, with the tenor, Julian Smith, and the soprano, Amy Moore, impressive soloists in the beautiful setting of the *Nunc dimittis*.

As a half-hour supplement, the disc also includes the *Requiem Mass* setting in D flat by Walter Vale, written even before he had adapted Rachmaninov.

RAFF, Joachim (1822–82)

Symphony 1 in D (An das Vaterland), Op. 96
(BB) ** Naxos 8.555411. Rhenish PO, Friedman

Symphony 2 in C, Op. 140; Overtures: Macbeth; Romeo and Juliet
(BB) ** Naxos 8.555491. Slovak State PO (Košice), Schneider

Symphonies 3 in F (Im Walde), Op. 153; 10 in F min. (Zur Herbstzeit), Op. 213
(BB) ** Naxos 8.555 491. Slovak State PO (Košice), Schneider

Symphonies 3; 4 in G min., Op. 167
(BB) ** Hyp. Helios CDH 55017. Milton Keynes City O, Davan Wetton

Symphonies 4; 11 in A min. (Winter), Op. 214
*(*) Marco Polo 8.223529. Slovak State PO (Košice), Schneider

Symphony 5 in E (Lenore), Op. 177; Overture, Ein feste Burg ist unser Gott, Op. 127
*(*) Marco Polo 8.223455. Slovak State PO (Košice), Schneider

Raff enjoyed enormous standing during his lifetime, though nowadays he is best remembered for a handful of salon pieces. However, he composed no fewer than eleven symphonies between 1864 and 1882, some of which have excited extravagant praise. Yet generally speaking, Raff's music is pretty bland, if far from unambitious. His *First Symphony (An das Vaterland)* takes itself very seriously and its 70-minute duration invites longueurs. However, now it has been reissued at Naxos price admirers of this uneven composer might feel it is worth trying. It is well enough played and recorded.

Although the *Symphony No. 2 in C* – also well played and recorded – has a certain charm, it is predominantly Mendelssohnian and, while outwardly attractive, it remains pretty insubstantial.

The *Third (Im Walde)* and *Tenth Symphonies* are also now available on Naxos and might be a good starting point for collectors wishing to explore this repertoire.

Of the eleven symphonies it is the *Fifth (Lenore)* which has captured the imagination of many. No doubt this may be accounted for by the somewhat macabre programme that inspired its finale. Although the symphony itself is more inspired than some of its companions (it has a particularly eloquent slow movement), it does need rather better advocacy than it receives from the Slovak Philharmonic under Urs Schneider. The Overture, *Ein feste Burg ist unser Gott*, is hardly sufficient to tip the scales in its favour.

The *Eleventh Symphony in A minor* was left incomplete on Raff's death in 1882 and is not otherwise available; the *Fourth* of 1871, available on the Hyperion version under Hilary Davan Wetton, is insufficiently persuasive. This music has moments of charm but is essentially second-rate and must have the most expert advocacy and opulent recorded sound if it is to be persuasive; neither of these two versions is really first class. One needs a Beecham to work his magic on these scores. In these performances they are merely amiable but insignificant.

RAMEAU, Jean Philippe (1683–1764)

Les Indes galantes: Suites for Orchestra
(M) **(*) Ph. 475 7780. O of 18th Century, Brüggen

Brüggen's account of the *Prologue* and four suites from *Les Indes galantes* is alive and responsive. But the measure is short, only 44 minutes, and Philips should have found a coupling for this reissue. Readers would do far better to invest in the DVD of the complete opéra-ballet from Les Arts Florissants under William Christie (Opus Arte OA 0923D – see our main volume).

KEYBOARD MUSIC

Pièces de clavecin: Suite in E min.; Nouvelles Suites de Pièces de clavecin (1738): Suite in A min.; La Poule; L'Enharmonique; L'Egyptienne

●━ *** Avie AV 2056. Trevor Pinnock (harpsichord)

Pinnock has already recorded three discs of Rameau's harpsichord suites for CRD. But this generous (80-minute) collection is played on a particularly attractive, authentic, two-manual instrument, built in Paris in 1764 and modified by Taskin 20 years later. Pinnock opens with a dazzling bravura piece called *Les Cyclopes* which gives the disc its title, but he follows immediately with the plaintive *L'entretien des Muses*. In the *A minor Suite*, *Les trois Mains* is particularly engaging, as is the *Fanfarinette* (using a mute stop) while *Le Rappel des Oiseaux*, *Musette en Rondeau*, *Tambourin* and *La Villageoise* (from the *E minor Suite*) are all attractively picturesque. The recital closes with the famous clucking *La Poule* and the hardly less characterful *L'Enharmonique* and *L'Egyptienne*, all from the *Nouvelles Pièces*. Altogether a most refreshing collection, and the recording gives the harpsichord splendid presence. But don't have the volume level too high.

Pièces de clavecin (1706): Excerpts: Prélude; Allemande; Sarabandes I & II; Gavotte; (1724): Suite in E. Suite in D: Excerpts. Nouvelles Suites (1728): Suite in A

** Ondine ODE 1067-2. Barto (piano)

It is almost a truism to say that Rameau sounds utterly different on the piano, but in Tzimon Barto's hands the difference is more striking than with Angela Hewitt playing Bach or Couperin. This recital is called 'A Basket of Wild Strawberries', but they are undoubtedly supplied with a little sweetening. Barto dallies self-consciously over the opening *Prélude* from Book I and the *Sarabandes* and *Gavotte* are played very freely. Yet *Le Rappel des Oiseaux* is most engagingly imitative, and *Tambourin* and *La Villageoise* are very delicately coloured. But *Les Soupirs* from the *D major Suite* is surely too expressively slow and, while *La joyeuse* is refreshingly like a peal of bells, after a while one finds that Barto's playing is too idiosyncratic to be idiomatically satisfying.

RAMIREZ, Ariel (born 1921)

Missa Criolla; Navidad Nuestra

(BB) *** Naxos 8.557542. Rheams, Melendez, Sacin, Talamante, Washington Choral Arts Soc. Chamber Ch. & Ens., Holt (with Father Guido HAAZEN: *Missa Luba*)

We are often asked about finding a good recording of the *Missa Criolla*, and understandably so, for it is spontaneously tuneful. A folk Mass, written by Ariel Ramirez in 1964, it draws on Argentinian folk tunes and idioms, but in most respects is wholly original. The opening *Kyrie* and closing *Agnus Dei* are lyrical and reflective, the central *Gloria*, *Credo* and *Sanctus* are dynamic and full of dancing rhythms. The Mass is written for tenor celebrant, chorus, percussion, Andean instruments, including a notched flute or *quena*, a *charango* (small guitar), double bass and percussion, with a pair of tom-toms in the *Credo*. The closing section brings a haunting, reflective passage for *quena* and *charango*.

This is genuine crossover music of real quality, but it is obviously difficult to perform live, as it needs a group of specialist performers who are immersed in the idiom, which is exactly what we have here, and the Washington Choristers are for the most part beyond praise.

The *Navidad Nuestra* ('Our Nativity') is a Creole tableau in six episodes (with a Spanish text by Félix Luna), telling the Christian Nativity story from the annunciation to the birth of Jesus, the venue relocated to northern Argentina, and ending with the family's flight. Ramirez again bases his music on dances and songs from the Argentinian folk tradition, this time even more unashamedly popular: the second part of the work, *La Peregrinación* ('The Pilgrimage'), has become famous on the hit parade.

The music of the *Missa Luba* comes from the Belgian Congo, and was arranged by a missionary, Father Guido Haazen, from the improvisations of the local singers and musicians, so the accompaniment consists entirely of local percussion sounds which create the rhythmic framework for the popular melodies. The performance here is entirely choral and has a haunting, lyrical core. With such excellent, idiomatic performances and good documentation, this is a disc to recommend unreservedly if you enjoy exotic, folk-derived music.

RANGSTRÖM, Ture (1884–1947)

Symphonies 3; (i) 4 in E flat (Invocation)

(BB) ** CPO 999 369-2. (i) Fahlsjö; Norrköping SO, Jurowski

The *Third Symphony* (1929) takes one of Rangström's songs, *Bön till natten* ('Prayer to the night') as its starting point, but the result is terribly inflated. The *Fourth Symphony* (1933–6) is best described as a suite for orchestra and organ. Its invention is very uneven, though there is a charming Intermezzo, which forms the central movement. Good performances and recordings, but neither work is remotely convincing symphonically.

RAUTAVAARA, Einojuhani (born 1928)

Adagio Celeste (for string orchestra); Book of Visions; Symphony 1

*** Ondine **SACD** ODE 1064-5. Belgian Nat. O, Franck

We have already had the first three symphonies from Ondine, well played by the Leipzig Radio Symphony Orchestra under Max Pommer. But this looks like the first of a new series, recorded in spacious four-channel SACD, which admirably suits Rautavaara's rich orchestral textures, and immediately so in the sumptuously powerful string cantilena which opens the *First Symphony*, written in two movements in 1955, but with a third added in 2003. Rautavaara acknowledged his debt to Shostakovich in this work, partly because of its string writing, but also because of the 'grotesque and ironic' Scherzo which closes the work.

The *Adagio Celeste* then follows. Inspired by a poem by Lassi Nummi which begins, 'Then, that night, when you want to love me in the deep of night, wake me,' it makes an ecstatic interlude between the *Symphony* and the imaginatively scored four chapters of the *Book of Visions*, each telling a *Tale*: darkly of *Night*, feverishly of *Fire*, warmly and sensuously of *Love*, and dramatic and apprehensive in *Fate*. The performances throughout are superbly played by this fine orchestra and, whether using two or four speakers, the sound is richly opulent, and in the demonstration bracket for its superb recording of the strings.

RAVEL, Maurice (1875–1937)

Boléro; La Valse

(M) ** Chan. 6615. Detroit SO, Järvi – DEBUSSY: *La Mer;*
MILHAUD: *Suite provençale* **

Järvi's *La Valse* opens atmospherically but is fairly brisk and
not without its moments of exaggeration – indeed, affectation unusual in this conductor. There is no lack of tension,
either here or in *Boléro*, although this is not a first choice for
either piece. Very natural recorded sound.

Piano Concerto in G; Piano Concerto in D for the Left Hand

(M) ** Ph. 475 7301 (4). Kocsis, Budapest Festival O, I.
Fischer – DEBUSSY: *Fantaisie for Piano and Orchestra &*
Solo Piano Music **(*)

Zoltán Kocsis offers some superb pianism in his accounts of
the two concertos; although the orchestral response is spirited, he is, surprisingly, not always responsive to the wide
range of colour and dynamic in both scores, and the
glorious slow movement of the *G major Concerto* is curiously wanting in that dreamy, sensuous quality which
Zimerman (DG 449 213-2) or Argerich (DG 447 438-2) bring
to it.

Daphnis et Chloé (complete); *Ma Mère l'Oye: suite*

(*(*)) Testament mono SBT 1264 O. French Nat. RO,
Inghelbrecht

Daphnis et Chloé (complete); *Pavane pour une infante*
défunte; Rapsodie espagnole

🔹━ (M) *** Decca 475 7525. LSO, Monteux

Monteux conducted the first performance of *Daphnis et*
Chloé in 1912 and it is a matter for gratitude that his poetic
and subtly shaded reading should have been recorded in such
astonishingly realistic sound which hardly sounds dated even
now. It was made in the Kingsway Hall in 1959, with John
Culshaw the producer. The performance was one of the finest
things Monteux did for the gramophone, and the sensuous
and atmospheric orchestral and choral sheen Decca provided
is fully worthy of such distinguished music-making. The
Pavane and *Rapsodie espagnole* came two years later, in 1961,
with Erik Smith in charge. The LSO again play superbly for
Monteux and he achieves a balance and a contrast between a
mood of quiet introspection for the opening of the *Rapsodie*
and a vivid, flashing brilliance for the *Féria*. The *Pavane* is
wonderfully poised, and is played most beautifully. An ideal
choice for Decca's Originals label.

Inghelbrecht's complete *Daphnis* was recorded in 1953, not
long after Ansermet's pioneering LP and a year or so before
Münch's famous Boston Symphony disc. It does not with-
stand comparison with them either in terms of conception or
execution. The playing of the French Radio Orchestra is at
times scruffy, and there is none of the distinctive authority
that can be discerned in other records by this (rightly)
admired conductor. The Testament transfer does its best for a
recording that fell far below those the French engineers gave
André Cluytens. Most, if not all, of Testament's reissues from
this period in the French catalogue are self-recommending
but this is an exception.

Ma Mère l'Oye: Suite; La Valse

** Chan. 9799. Danish Nat. RSO, Termirkanov –
TCHAIKOVSKY: *The Nutcracker* ** (with GADE: *Tango:*
Jalousie)

It is difficult to know quite for whom this Chandos recording
is designed. Recordings of the *Ma Mère l'Oye* suite and *La*
Valse are hardly in short supply and most collectors will want
a more logical coupling than bits of Act II of *Nutcracker*.
Including the Gade item was a curious idea. No complaints
about the sound.

Le tombeau de Couperin

(BB) **(*) Virgin 2x1 4 82103-2. City of L. Sinfonia, Hickox
(with FAURÉ: *Pavane*) – BIZET: *Symphony in C;* IBERT:
Divertissement; TCHAIKOVSKY: *Serenade for Strings;*
Souvenir de Florence **(*)

There is much elegant playing here from the City of London
Sinfonia, especially from the woodwind, and this is perhaps
the most successful overall performance on this bargain
double, alongside the delicate Fauré *Pavane*. It you want all
the music, this reissue is certainly value for money.

CHAMBER MUSIC

Piano Trio in A min.

** Metronome MET CD 1048. Juno's Band – FAURE: *Piano*
Quartet 1 **

A good account from Juno's Band on Metronome, though
without being in any way distinguished, and decently
recorded. But there is nothing special here.

String Quartet in F

(BB) ** Warner Apex 8573 89231-2. Keller Qt – DEBUSSY:
Quartet **

The Keller Quartet are tauter and more dramatic than some
of their rivals but, for all its merits, their performance does
not match those rivals in terms of subtlety and tonal finesse.

Violin Sonata (1897); *Violin Sonata in G*

(BB) *(*) EMI Encore 85708-2. Zimmermann, Lonquich –
DEBUSSY, JANACEK: *Violin Sonatas* *(*)

Frank Peter Zimmermann plays with virtuosity and warmth,
though Alexander Lonquich is not the most sensitive of
partners. Readers who recall Augustin Dumay and Jean-
Philippe Collard on this label will wonder why EMI's choice
fell on these recordings.

PIANO MUSIC

A la manière de Borodine; A la manière de Chabrier;
Menuet sur le nom d'Haydn; Pavane pour une infante
défunte; Prélude, Postlude; Sonatine; Le Tombeau de
Couperin; Valses nobles et sentimentales

(*) Channel CCS 17598. Lazic

Now in his mid-twenties, Dejan Lazic is a formidable artist.
Born in Zagreb, he divided his talents between the piano and
the clarinet, and by the time he was thirteen he had already
made a record with the Solisti di Zagreb coupling the Mozart
E flat Concerto, K.449, with the *Clarinet Concerto*. He also
composes and wrote a work for Rostropovich's seventieth
birthday celebrations. However, this Ravel recital is unrecommendable. He pulls everything, even the *Sonatine*, completely
out of shape. Nothing is left to speak for itself and the *Valses*
nobles et sentimentales are treated in the same wilful fashion,
one phrase is lingered over and the next gabbled. The recording is satisfactory. For a fine coverage of the piano music we
suggest Angela Hewitt (Hyperion CDA 67341/2).

Shéhérazade (song-cycle)

➤— ✪ (M) *** Decca 475 7712. Crespin, SRO, Ansermet (with Recital of French Songs ***) – BERLIOZ: *Nuits d'été* ***

Crespin is right inside these songs and Ravel's magically sensuous music emerges with striking spontaneity. She is superbly supported by Ansermet who, aided by the Decca engineers, weaves a fine tonal web round the voice. Her style has distinct echoes of the opera house; but the richness of the singer's tone does not detract from the delicate languor of *The Enchanted Flute*, in which the slave-girl listens to the distant sound of her lover's flute playing while her master sleeps. The new transfer of the 1963 recording adds to the allure of the remarkably rich and translucent Decca sound. The remastered reissue is now elevated to 'Originals' status and includes full documentation.

READE, Paul (20th century)

Hobson's Choice (ballet; complete; orchestrated by Lawrence Ashmore; devised and choreographed by David Bintley from the play by Harold Brighouse) (Director: Tom Gutteridge)

✪ **** Arthaus **DVD** 100 442. Karen Donovan, Michael O'Hare, Desmond Kelly, Sandra Madgwick, Chenca Williams, Joseph Cipolla, Stephen Wicks; Birmingham Royal Ballet O, Wordsworth

David Bintley's ballet *Hobson's Choice* was created in 1989 for Sadler's Wells Royal Ballet in London, and it quickly became a box-office hit. However, it was first (at the turn of the century) a famous Lancashire play, then a book, and finally a film; and Bintley has obviously drawn on all three for his scenario for a story which popularized an old phrase in the English language.

The setting in Salford, Lancashire, is very truthful and the narrative is followed in faithful detail. It was a brilliant idea to have a central scene in the park, where in the late 1800s the whole town would have walked on a fine Sunday afternoon, with the bandstand and Salvation Army band bringing an opportunity for a particularly attractive divertissement.

The scene where Hobson senior gets very drunk casts a backward look at the David Lean movie and recalls Charles Laughton. But here Desmond Kelly is his match, a splendidly pompous old soak. The simple but engaging Willie Mossop, the hero of the piece (with Michael O'Hare perfectly cast), at first innocent and 'gormless', is transformed into a man by the superbly characterized Maggie, Karen Donovan. Perhaps she is not plain enough for a true Maggie, but one can readily believe that Willie can fall under her authoritative but charming spell. Maggie's two sisters and their swains are all four fine actors and dancers, and at the key moments, when Hobson has to make his choices, are both dramatically and humorously convincing.

The dancing itself is a delight, the choreography, like Paul Reade's brilliant and tuneful score, endlessly witty and inventive. Willie's engaging Dance with the Shoes at the end of Act I evokes Chaplin, and the solo Clog Dance which follows is a bravura highlight; and there is an ensemble clog encore in the park in Act II.

The authenticity of the period and of Lancashire middle-class culture is confirmed at the family high tea after the impecunious Maggie and Willie have taken their wedding vows with simple nods. They enjoy bread-and-butter, cake and tea, and the wedding toast is made with raised teacups, followed by a song round the upright piano (which no middle-class home would be without).

With splendid sets and fine continuity, this is a wonderfully warm and repeatable entertainment, and the music, full of melody and attractive orchestral effects and cleverly drawing on popular folk themes, is a pleasure in itself, for the composer's ideas never flag. Surely Harold Brighouse would have been delighted with it.

REBEL, Jean-Féry (1661–1747)

Les Caractères de la danse; Les Elémens; Le Tombeau de M. Lully

*** Erato 2292 45974-2. Musiciens du Louvre, Minkowski

The eloquent trio sonata, *Le Tombeau de M. Lully* was written on the death of the great French composer whose pupil Rebel had become as a boy of eight and *Les Elémens* is one of the most original works of the period. With its representation of chaos in which all the notes of the harmonic scale are heard simultaneously, it is certainly quite astonishing in effect. The performance and recording are of the highest quality.

REED, W. H. (1875–1942)

Andante con moto; Andante tranquillo; 2 Chinese Impressions; Fantaisie brillante; The Gentle Dove (Welsh Folksong); Lento and Prelude; Luddi Dance; On Waterford Quay (An Irish Impression); Punjabi Song; Reverie; Rhapsody for Viola and Piano; Rhapsody in E min. for Violin and Piano; Spanish Dance (Fragment); Toccata

(M) *** Dutton CDLX 7135. Gibbs, Mei-Loc Wu

This Dutton compilation is illustrated with an engaging picture of W. H. Reed and Elgar, two English gentlemen complete with walking sticks, standing on the bank of the River Severn. Reed was a great friend of Elgar as well as being his musical colleague and adviser, and he assisted Elgar with violin figuration for the latter's *Concerto* and chamber music. He was well equipped to do so as leader of the London Symphony Orchestra from 1912 to 1935, as a Professor of the Violin at the Royal College of Music, and as a composer of unadventurous, but very well-written music of his own, in which the violin (or viola) took the leading role. Many of these pieces are romantic vignettes, which have something in common with Kreisler's miniatures, if without being quite so sharply memorable. But they include a pair of more ambitious *Rhapsodies* and a lighthearted, dancing *Andante tranquillo*, all of which display an easy-going fluency and genuine musical craftsmanship. The more extended *Fantaisie brillante*, with its agreeable central *Andante* and virtuoso *moto perpetuo* finale, was dedicated to Reed's teacher, Emile Sauret.

The advocacy here of the sweet-toned Robert Gibbs, partnered by Mary Mei-Loc Wu (who is much more than an accompanist), is very persuasive throughout this programme, and they play the longer works with conviction and style. But the genre pieces are also often appealing and are thrown off with aplomb. The *Toccata* has a cascading, Elgarian felicity, the *Chinese Impressions* are quaint without being trivial, while the *Punjabi Song* is quite memorable in its simplicity, and the *Luddi Dance* is certainly catchy. Excellent recording too, natural and very well balanced.

REICH, Steve (born 1936)

Different Trains; Duet; Triple Quartet

*** Signum SIGCD 004. Smith Qt; composer

The music of Steve Reich is wholly original and exists in an unpredictable sound-world of its own, with repetitions and constant ostinatos a basic feature – indeed, part of the very fabric of the music. You will find it either fascinatingly hypnotic, or inexplicable, or boring. But it is highly imaginative.

Different Trains is in three sections, evoking (but not describing) three different railway networks and their sounds – *America before the war*, *Europe during the war*, and *After the war*. The train rhythms and siren sounds are created by a string quartet, over which are superimposed speaking voices constantly repeating phrases.

Duet and the three-movement *Triple Quartet* use quartet sonorities alone, but they expand the sounds available by using pre-recorded tapes so that three and sometimes four groups can be heard playing together. The haunting central movement of the *Triple Quartet* is lyrical, even elegiac; the outer movements are abrasive and incisive. The effect in these performances is both spontaneous and original.

Drumming

*** Cantaloupe CA 21026. So Percussion

This version of *Drumming* by So Percussion (with Rebecca Armstrong and Jay Clayton, vocals and whistling, and Eric Lesser, piccolo) lasts 73 minutes and is certainly hypnotic, but we would not like to say that it is more or less effective than the performance under the composer (on DG 474 323-2) listed in our main volume.

Variations for Wind, Strings & Keyboards

(M) *** Ph. 475 7551. San Francisco SO, Edo de Waart –
ADAMS: *Shaker Loops* ***

The *Variations*, written for the San Francisco orchestra in 1980, marked a new departure in Reich's writing, using a large orchestra instead of a small chamber scale. The repetitions and ostinatos which gradually get out of phase (like *Drumming*) are used most skilfully to produce a kind of hypnotic poetry, soothing rather than compelling.

REICHA, Antonín (1770–1836)

Requiem

(M) *** Sup. SU 3859-2. Hrubá-Freiberger, Barová, Doležal, Vele, Prague Philharmonic Ch., Dvořák CO, Mátl

Antonín Reicha is best known for his instrumental and chamber music, so the comparatively recent discovery of this substantial and ambitious *Requiem* (written when the composer was living in Vienna) was a surprise. It is above all a choral work, with the soloists often acting together as a contrasting mini-chorus, as in the *Liber scriptus* and the *Recordare*. There are moments of incisive drama in the *Dies irae*, *Rex tremendae* and the swift-moving *Lacrimosa*, while the *Tuba mirum* is introduced boldly by the brass, bringing the first of the vocal solos. The *Benedictus* is led by the soprano soloist, but the beautiful *Agnus Dei* again brings back the vocal group. The closing *Lux aeterna* caps the work richly and contrapuntally with an extended fugue, with everyone singing their hearts out. Though not an out-and-out masterpiece, the work is well worth hearing in a performance as dedicated and vital as this, and the recording is full and clear.

RESPIGHI, Ottorino (1879–1936)

The Fountains of Rome; The Pines of Rome

☞ (M) *** RCA **SACD** (ADD) 82876 71614-2. Chicago SO, Reiner – DEBUSSY: *La Mer* ***

Reiner's classic recording has now been given RCA's SACD facelift and sounds more vividly brilliant than ever. It is presumably still to remain available, alternatively coupled with Mussorgsky's *Pictures at an Exhibition* (0926 61401-2 – see our main volume), but Reiner's account of *La Mer* on the present disc is also pretty riveting.

Rossiniana (arr. Respighi)

(*) Australian Decca Eloquence (ADD) 476 2724. SRO, Ansermet – OFFENBACH: *Gaîté parisienne*; GOUNOD: *Faust: ballet music* *

It is perhaps curious that this work is usually catalogued under Respighi, whereas *La boutique fantasque*, which Respighi also based on Rossini's music, is more often found under Rossini. *Rossiniana* is not as inspired as that score but there is still much to enjoy. Ansermet's performances are the very opposite of the Solti items on this CD, and it is the delicate colour and balance of these scores (rather than immaculate orchestral playing) that Ansermet fans will most admire. The final *Tarantella* is especially enjoyable here. Vintage Decca sound.

REYNOLDS, Alfred (1884–1969)

Alice Through the Looking Glass: Suite. The Duenna: Suite of Five Dances. Festival March; Marriage à la mode: Suite. Overture for a Comedy; 3 Pieces for Theatre; The Sirens of Southend; The Swiss Family Robinson: Swiss Lullaby and Ballet. The Taming of the Shrew: Overture. 1066 and All That: Suite (inc. Ballet of the Roses). The Toy Cart: Suite

**(*) Marco Polo 8.225184. Royal Ballet Sinf., Sutherland

Born in Liverpool, the son of waxwork museum proprietors, Alfred Reynolds studied music in Liverpool, Heidelberg, and then for six years in Berlin under the guidance of Humperdinck. His name is largely associated with the stage, with much of the music here written as incidental music for plays. It is all spontaneously tuneful in the best British light music tradition, occasionally more substantial, but never attempting profundity. The more substantial overtures are highly enjoyable: the *Overture for a Comedy* has some diverting episodes and, like the rest of the programme, makes one nostalgic for the past. *Alice Through the Looking Glass* features some nice, piquant numbers (especially the *Jabberwocky* and *March of the Drums*), and Reynolds's interest in eighteenth-century music is felt sporadically throughout the programme, including the *Entr'acte* from *The Critic* (*Three Pieces for Theatre*), a charming minuet with a gentle hint of pomposity. The excerpts from his most famous work, *1066 and All That*, are highly enjoyable, as is the splendidly rousing *Festival March*. Dance rhythms make up a fair proportion of the content – a lively tarantella here, a nostalgic waltz there, plus a rustic jig and a Spanish fandango. Gavin Sutherland is as reliable as ever in securing the right style from his orchestra, though occasionally the sound isn't as sweet as it might be. Lovers of light music should consider this CD, as Alfred Reynolds deserves to be remembered.

REZNIČEK, Emil von (1860–1945)

Raskolnikov (Phantasy Overture); (i) Schlemihl (A Symphonic Life Story)

*** CPO 999 795-2. WDR SO, Cologne, Jurowski, (i) with Yamamasu

It is good to have more music from the composer of the brilliant *Donna Diana Overture*, and it is immediately striking to hear the Richard Strauss parallels (a composer who often entrusted performances of his tone-poems to Reznicek) in *Schlemihl, A Symphonic Life Story*, first performed in 1912. It is loosely autobiographical, and the sleeve-note writer at one point suggests it might be entitled 'Not a Hero's Life'. The events of this 45-minute work (which contains plenty of hints of Mahler, Wagner and Shostakovich, too, along with Strauss) are written out in exhaustive detail, down to the last minute, and are included in the extensive booklet. It makes for very enjoyable listening, especially Reznicek's gift for bright orchestrations; with seemingly every conceivable emotion and orchestral gesture contriving to make an appearance, there is no lack of variety. This committed performance makes a fair case for this work, though Nobuaki Yamamasu is a little unsteady in his short solo. The 22-minute *Raskolnikov Overture* (1932) is, once again, very much in the vein of Richard Strauss (if without the genius), and has some fine passages in it, but in its meandering way it does not always sustain interest. However, it is interesting to hear, especially in this excellent performance. Good recording.

Symphonies 2 (Ironic); 5 (Dance Symphony)

** CPO 777 056-2. Berne SO, Bermann

Reznicek originally described the *Second Symphony* as a sinfonietta, and it does have something of the lively mood of the famous *Donna Diana Overture*. The *Fifth Symphony* is a quartet of dance movements (*Polonaise, Czárdás, Laendler* and *Tarantella*). So this whole CD ought to be a bundle of fun, and it is not; the invention is not up to it. One cannot say that Frank Bermann and the Berne orchestra lack vigour, but maybe their touch is not light enough, and that is the more ironic in the *Second Symphony* which, one feels, ought to be thoroughly entertaining.

RIMSKY-KORSAKOV, Nikolay (1844–1908)

Capriccio espagnol; May Night Overture; Russian Easter Festival Overture; Sadko, Op. 5

(BB) *(*) ASV Resonance CD RSN 3044. Mexico City PO, Bátiz

This is a useful budget collection but, although Bátiz's performances have plenty of spirit, in the mid-1980s when these recordings were made the Mexico City Philharmonic Orchestra could not produce a rich enough body of string timbre to do justice to the *Capriccio*, though the horns are good and there is a fine trombone solo in the *Russian Easter Festival Overture*. *Sadko* comes off best, with Bátiz obviously in sympathy with its atmosphere. The digital recording is brilliant, but artificially balanced, with sometimes fierce brass, and the *Festival Overture* is dominated by the percussion.

Christmas Eve: Suite; Le Coq d'Or: Suite; Legend of the Invisible City of Kitezh: Suite; May Night: Overture; Mlada:
Suite; The Snow Maiden: Suite; The Tale of Tsar Saltan: 3
Musical Pictures; The Flight of the Bumblebee

(M) *** Chan. 10369X (2). SNO, Järvi

Originally on three full-priced discs, this selection is now offered on a pair of mid-priced CDs, a remarkable saving. Neeme Järvi draws the most seductive response from the SNO; he continually creates orchestral textures which are diaphanously sinuous. Yet the moments when the brass blazes or the horns ring out sumptuously are caught just as strikingly, and the listener is assured that here is music which survives repetition very well.

Christmas Eve: Suite; Le Coq d'or: Suite; The Tale of Tsar
Saltan: Suite; Flight of the Bumble-Bee

*** ASV CDDCA 772. Armenian PO, Tjeknavorian

Tjeknavorian and his fine Armenian orchestra are completely at home in Rimsky's sinuous orientalism, with its glittering, iridescent wind-colouring. The racy vigour and sparkle of the playing brings a jet-setting bumble-bee and the carolling horns and bold brass add to the vividness. The Tchaikovskian *Polonaise* music from *Christmas Eve* exudes similar sparkling vitality within a glowing palette. In short this is one of the most desirable and generous Rimsky-Korsakov collections in the current catalogue, and only a degree of thinness in the violin timbre above the stave prevents the use of the adjective, sumptuous. In all other respects this is in the demonstration bracket.

Christmas Eve: Suite; Overture on Russian Themes, Op. 28;
Pan Voyevoda: Suite; The Snow Maiden: Suite; The Tsar's
Bride: Overture

🅑→ *** BIS CD 1577. Malaysian PO, Bakels

A superb collection, even more seductive than Järvi's compilation, above, and including several novelties. The Malaysian Philharmonic Orchestra under its excellent conductor, Kees Bakels, is comparable with the finest European orchestras, and they play this exotic Russian music with great finesse, warmth and sparkle. *The Tsar's Bride Overture* ought to be better known; it is most vividly scored and has a gorgeous secondary theme on the strings, while the *Pan Voyevoda Suite* is very rare and yet also includes some of Rimsky's most colourful ideas. It opens mysteriously and evocatively and, after the deliciously scored *Krakowiak*, dancing like the breeze, there is a truly lovely *Nocturne* (subtitled *Clair de lune*) which deserves to be a familiar lollipop, as do the closing *Mazurka* and *Polonaise*.

The more familar *Christmas Eve Suite* (a favourite of Ansermet's) opens with a glowing horn solo, and the three central dances of the stars and comets are played with much delicacy, while the following *Polonaise* has splendid rhythmic lift. The *Overture on Russian Themes* is also most imaginatively presented, opening atmospherically, while the closing *maestoso* has great flair. Here and in *The Snow Maiden Suite* Rimsky's orchestral palette glitters and glows iridescently, the *Dance of the Birds* is delightful, and the famous closing *Dance of the Clowns* has real rhythmic panache. The BIS recording is very much in the demonstration bracket.

Fairy Tale (Skazka), Op. 29; Fantasia on Serbian Themes,
Op. 6; Legend of the Invisible City of Kitezh (symphonic
suite); The Maid of Pskov (Ivan the Terrible): Suite

(BB) ** Naxos 8.553513. Moscow SO, Golovchin

This is a very attractive compilation containing some of Rimsky's lesser-known music, often languorous in feeling and displaying a characteristically glowing orchestral palette. The Moscow Symphony Orchestra are obviously at home in this repertoire and they play it very beguilingly (apart from occasional rasping trombones), and the recording is warmly atmospheric. But the effect is very relaxed and in music which is atmospherically sustained one needs more internal tension. The narrative of *Skazka*, too, lacks a positive momentum. Even so, this is still desirable and worth its modest price.

Scheherazade (ballet; complete; with choreography by Michael Fokine and costumes and sets adapted from the original Ballets Russes production by Anatoly and Anna Nezhny)

❀ *** Decca DVD 079 322-9. Ilze Liepa, Andris Liepa, Victor Yeremenko, Bolshoi State Academic Theatre O, Chistiakov (Director: Andris Liepa) – STRAVINSKY: *Petrushka; The Firebird* ***

This indispensable DVD offers re-creations of three key Diaghilev productions from the peak era of the Ballets Russes, with choreography, décor and costumes as near as possible to the original staging. In its day *Scheherazade* (with the heroine renamed Zabeida) was something of a *coup de théâtre*, because its climax was a bacchanalian orgy, with Zabeida and her Golden Slave lover caught *in flagrante delicto* by the sudden return of her master, Sultan Shakhriar, from a supposed hunting expedition. At the beginning of the ballet, after reluctantly leaving the seductive Zabeida's caresses, the Sultan greets Shah Zeman, who warns his friend that his favourite slave is unfaithful. They depart, and the pompous Chief Eunuch provides an entertainment, which brings a colourful divertissement. But the harem slaves have other ideas; they bribe him with jewels to unlock the door and let in their lovers, and Zabeida is reunited with her Golden Slave.

All this happens to edited sections of the first movement of Rimsky's suite. Then the slow movement is played in its entirety for the vividly sensuous *pas de deux* of Zabeida and her lover, which becomes increasingly erotic. With the opening of the finale the whole company has joined them, and the dancing becomes riotously orgiastic. Zabeida and her lover become more and more abandoned, but at the climax, just as they are discovered, the Russian cameraman takes care not to show a close-up, so the intended consummation remains unexplicit. But the Sultan and his friend have no doubt as to what is going on, and with their armed entourage they promptly slaughter all the slaves, though it is Shah Zeman who cuts down Zabeida's lover. Zabeida pleads for her own life very enticingly, and Shakhriar relents, until his friend reminds him of his honour. But before he can take any further action, Zabeida steals his knife and stabs herself to death. He is left devastated as Rimsky's closing bars act as a threnody rather than the peaceful, much happier ending the composer intended. But what makes this melodramatic ballet so enjoyable is the luxurious décor and costumes, and the excitement and overt eroticism of the dancing itself. Moreover, the principals are believably, ethnically real in a way that a European ballet company would find difficult to cast. The Bolshoi State Academic Theatre Orchestra plays voluptuously and excitingly throughout under Andrey Chistiakov and the recording is vividly wide-ranging and full-blooded, if not entirely refined. Moreover, this DVD also includes *The Firebird* and *Petrushka*.

Scheherazade (symphonic suite), *Op. 35*

(M) *** Ph. 475 7570. Concg. O, Kondrashin (with BORODIN: *Symphony 2* *(*))

(i) *Scheherazade;* (ii) *Capriccio espagnol, Op. 34*.

(BB) **(*) EMI Gemini 3 50824-2 (2). Oslo PO, Jansons – MUSSORGSKY: *Night on the Bare Mountain*, etc. **(*)

Scheherazade; Russian Easter Festival Overture
** Telarc CD 80568. Atlanta SO, Spano

(i) *Scheherazade, Op. 35;* (ii) *Tsar Saltan: Flight of the Bumble-Bee*

(BB) *** HMV 5 86757-2. (i) LPO, Yuasa; (ii) ASMF, Marriner – BORODIN: *Polovtsian dances;* KHACHATURIAN: *Ballet music* ***

Takuo Yuasa's *Scheherazade* is a recommendable version in every way, a romantically compulsive account very responsively played by the LPO. There is a freshness and absence of routine in the music-making, and the sinuously supple contribution of the orchestral leader Stephen Bryant in the role of the heroine is believably placed in the orchestral texture. Yuasa's reading is more spacious and less urgent than Mackerras's – another top recommendation – but his evocation of the sea in the first movement is very compelling, and the central movements are full of colour and warmth, with a burst of passion to climax the idyllic rapture of the slow movement. The finale brings grippingly animated orchestral viruosity and a powerful climax, with the tam-tam flashing out at the moment of the shipwreck. The poetic close has a lustrous rapture, even if it is not as enchanting as on the Mackerras disc. Marriner's *Bumble-Bee* then whizzes past dazzlingly, yet is evoked with a delicacy suggestive of Mendelssohn. At super-bargain price, coupled with Beecham's thrilling *Polovtsian Dances* and three Khachaturian lollipops, this is very recommendable indeed, although Reiner's RCA Chicago version makes an even finer mid-priced recommendation (SACD 82876 66377-2).

Kondrashin's 1980 *Scheherazade* has stood the test of time and, with Hermann Krebbers' exquisitely seductive portrayal of its heroine, and with superb recording, in many respects it remains unsurpassed. Unfortunately, for this reissue among their Originals, Philips have chosen an unrecommendable coupling with Borodin's *Second Symphony*.

Jansons gives us a very well-played and warmly characterized account with much to recommend it. What distinguishes it from other versions is the way he points rhythms in all four movements – lilting, bouncy and affectionate – before bringing a satisfying resolution at the great climax, towards the end of the finale. The *Capriccio espagnol* brings a similar combination of warmth and exuberance.

Robert Spano in his first recording as music director draws clean, polished playing from the Atlanta orchestra, which yet lacks the forward thrust and improvisatory freedom needed in the episodic structure of *Scheherazade*. The violin soloist, Cecylia Arzewski, similarly plays with precision but too stiffly. The *Russian Easter Festival Overture*, too, brings a note of caution. The Telarc recording is unobtrusively brilliant, with brass very well caught.

Symphonies: 1, Op. 1; 3, Op. 32; Fantasia on Serbian Themes
*** BIS CD 1477. Malaysian PO, Bakels

This is the third of a trio of issues from BIS, collecting the principal orchestral works of Rimsky-Korsakov. It may still seem surprising that Kuala Lumpur, for all its oil riches, should spawn an orchestra of unmistakable international quality like the Malaysian Philharmonic. Founded as recently as 1998, it was built up by the music director, Kees Bakels, drawing on 105 players from many different countries. Here, in the two less well-known symphonies of Rimsky-Korsakov

(*Antar* was earlier coupled with *Scheherazade*), Bakels offers performances of admirable point and refinement, particularly in the strings, with the slow movement of No. 3, for example, tender in its delicate phrasing, and with the 5/4 rhythms of the Scherzo delectably pointed.

The *Fantasia on Serbian Themes* makes an attractive supplement. Starting with a warm horn solo, it leads up to an *Allegro* which inspires Bakels to a sparkling performance, again with textures light and clear. Like the *First Symphony*, it is an early work, directly prompted by Rimsky's mentor, Balakirev. Clear, well-balanced recording, with air round the sound.

OPERA

Mlada (complete DVD version)

*** Teldec **DVD** 4509-92052-3. Nina Ananiashvili (dancer), Oleg Kulko, Maria Gavrilova, Gleb Nikolsky. Galina Borisova, Mikhail Maslov, Lyudmila Nam, Olga Velichko, Vladimir Kudriashov, Bolshoi Ballet, Bolshoi Ch. & O, Lazarev (Stage/Video Director: Boris Pokrovsky)

Mlada is a curious hybrid, half choral ballet and half opera with dancing. The score is full of colour, and so is this Bolshoi production, expertly directed by Boris Pokrovsky. It is best known to most music lovers for the *Procession of the Nobles*. The scoring is lavish even by Rimsky's own standards: the wind, brass and percussion are all expanded, and there are three harps and an organ. On stage there is a stage band in Act III which includes two pan-pipes (ancient Slavonic instruments) and eight lyres. The plot is flimsy, but it was the elaborate scoring which held up the production. Composed in 1890, it was not produced at the Maryinsky until 1892. One of the singers was Fyodor Stravinsky, father of the composer, who was obviously inspired by one of the episodes in Act III which immediately brings to mind *Katschei's Dance* from *The Firebird*. A wonderful performance from Nina Ananiashvili, dancing the role of Princess Mlada, and impressive singing from the imposing cast. A highly enjoyable rarity which we can strongly recommend.

RODGERS, Richard (1902–79)

Ballet Scores: *Ghost Town; On Your Toes: La Princesse Zenobia; Slaughter on Tenth Avenue*
*** TER CDTER 1114. O, Mauceri

Richard Rodgers often wrote quite extensive ballets for his Broadway output, the best known being *Slaughter on Tenth Avenue*, first heard in the 1936 musical *On Your Toes*, which also presented *La Princess Zenobia* for the first time. However, *Ghost Town*, an American folk ballet about the Gold Rush, was commissioned by the Ballet Russe de Monte Carlo in 1939 and produced at the Metropolitan Opera that year. All three ballets have their fair share of good tunes – *Slaughter on Tenth Avenue*, easily the best of them, has three superb melodies (among Rodgers's finest) – and there is no doubting that the colourful orchestrations of Hans Spialek go a large way towards making these scores as sparkling as they are. The performances under John Mauceri are first rate, as is the vivid and bright recording, which admirably catches the Hollywoodesque orchestrations. The fine orchestra is presumably a pick-up ensemble as, curiously, it is not credited with a name.

Carousel (film musical)

*** EMI (ADD) 5 27352-2. Film soundtrack recording with MacRae, Jones, Mitchell, Ruick, Turner, Rounseville, Christie, 20th Century Fox Ch. & O, Newman

The King and I (film musical)

*** EMI (ADD) 5 27351-2. Film soundtrack recording with Nixon/Kerr, Brynner, Gordon/Moreno, Saunders, Fuentes/Rivas, 20th Century Fox Ch. & O, Newman

Oklahoma! (film musical)

*** EMI (ADD) 5 27350-2. Film soundtrack recording with MacRae, Jones, Greenwood, Grahame, Nelson, Steiger, 20th Century Fox Ch. & O, Newman

In these days when so many twentieth-century composers of so-called 'serious' music and opera seem unwilling, or unable, to write hummable melodies, it seems worth while to celebrate again the achievement of three great Rodgers and Hammerstein musicals of the 1940s and early 1950s. The sheer tunefulness of the music is of the kind which, once lodged in the memory, is impossible to erase. And Richard Rodgers had the good fortune to collaborate with a librettist who showed not only a natural feeling for a melodic line, but also an inspired ear for the vernacular. The Rodgers and Hammerstein love songs communicate directly and universally, while in the case of 'I can't say no' and 'With me it's all or nothin'' (from *Oklahoma!*) there is an attractive colloquial realism. When Carrie Pipperidge (Barbara Ruick) in *Carousel* sings her charming song about her beloved fisherman, Mr Snow, she tells us engagingly 'my heart's in my nose', while 'June is bustin' out all over' conveys the burgeoning fecundity of spring with an elemental exuberance seldom matched elsewhere.

In *The King and I* author and composer were faced with a seemingly unromantic widow-heroine, who had become an impecunious schoolteacher. Yet in 'Hello young lovers' (with its graceful shifts between duple and waltz time) they triumphed over the problem with one of their loveliest songs, as Anna remembers and communicates her past happiness with her husband, Tom. Later, the underlying tension between Anna and the King underpins the apparently lighthearted number, 'Shall we dance'.

In short, these are masterly scores, with masterly lyrics and, as the recent outstanding National Theatre revival of *Oklahoma!* demonstrated, this is a work of classic stature, with much greater depth of characterization than had been hitherto realized.

We discussed the original Capitol soundtrack LPs of these three spectacular wide-screen movies in the very first volume of our hardback *Stereo Record Guide* (1960), where our response was mixed. In spite of often surprisingly good stereo effects, the sound was often coarse, and unnecessary musical cuts were made. The new digital transfers show how extraordinarily rich and vivid was the quality of the original film tracks, and what gorgeous sounds were made by the superb 20th Century Fox studio orchestra under Alfred Newman. The chorus is pretty good too.

The dubbing of Deborah Kerr's songs in *The King and I* by the sweet-voiced Marni Nixon, and Tuptim's 'We kiss in the shadow' by the sultry Leonora Gordon (originally undisclosed) is now part of the current documentation, although Rita Moreno herself narrates the highly dramatic ballet sequence, *The Small House of Uncle Tom*. In *Carousel* and *Oklahoma!* Gordon MacRae and Shirley Jones make a delightfully fresh-voiced pair of lovers, and the smaller parts are all full of character.

Much that was previously omitted has now been restored, including items which did not appear in the final edited films. This means that there is a good deal of repetition and reprises. Never mind, these three discs are very enjoyable, and you may even find yourself humming along. The documentation is excellent, so a final word from Oscar Hammerstein about the gestation of the famous *Carousel Waltz* seems appropriate: 'I'd become weary – and am still weary – of the sound that comes out of an orchestral pit during the "Overture". All you can hear is the brass, because you never have a sufficient number of strings; and the audience must make a concerted effort to pick up any melody that is not blasted. I wanted to avoid this. I wanted people to start paying attention to what came out of the pit with the very first sound they heard.' He succeeded.

'*Rodgers & Hammerstein Songs*' from: *Allegro; Carousel; The King and I; Me and Juliet; Oklahoma!; The Sound of Music; South Pacific; State Fair*
*** DG 449 163-2. Terfel, Opera North Ch., E. N. Philh., Daniel

Bryn Terfel masterfully embraces the Broadway idiom, projecting his magnetic personality in the widest range of songs, using a remarkable range of tone, from a whispered head voice (as he does magically at the end of 'Some enchanted evening') to a tough, almost gravelly *fortissimo* at climaxes, from the biting toughness of 'Nothing like a dame' or Billy Bigelow's big soliloquy in *Carousel* (using a very convincing American accent) to the warmth of 'If I loved you' and 'You'll never walk alone' (with chorus). Specially welcome are the rarities, including one number from *Me and Juliet* and four from the stylized and underprized *Allegro*, including the powerfully emotional 'Come home'. With excellent sound and fine playing from Opera North forces under Paul Daniel, this is a wide-ranging survey. It deserves the widest circulation.

RODRIGO, Joaquín (1901–99)

Naxos Complete Rodrigo Edition

Complete Orchestral Works, Vol. 1: *Soleriana* (ballet, arr. from Soler's keyboard music); 5 *Piezas infantiles; Zarabanda lejana y Vallancico*
(BB) **(*) Naxos 8.555844. Asturias SO, Valdés

Rodrigo's delightfully imagined eighteenth-century picture of Spain is the essence of *Soleriana*, which is based on the keyboard works of Antonio Soler and consists of eight dances, lasting some 40 minutes in all. The *Pastoral* has a lovely melancholy beauty, though most of the movements are relatively lively and portray a picturesque, rococo image of the local scene in music, which displays both charm and piquancy. The *Zarabanda lejana* ('Distant Sarabande') is a haunting work, its two movements displaying some lovely string-writing, and the highly engaging *Cinco piezas infantiles* are characteristically brightly coloured. The performances are good; the massed strings sound a bit thin above the stave, but the overall sound-picture is very acceptable.

Complete Orchestral Works, Vol. 2: (i) *Concierto Andaluz for 4 Guitars and Orchestra*; (ii) *Concierto de Aranjuez; Fantasía para un gentilhombre*
(BB) **(*) Naxos 8.555841. Asturias SO, Valdés, with (i) EntreQuatre Guitar Qt; (ii) Gallén

The popular *Concierto de Aranjuez* and *Fantasía para un gentilhombre* are given very decent performances, but they lack the last ounce of polish and, in terms of recording and performance, cannot match the very best versions, such as Bonell–Dutoit on Decca. The *Concierto Andaluz*, with its *Tempo di boléro* opening movement and use of Andalusian folk tunes, makes an enjoyable companion-piece.

Complete Orchestral Works, Vol. 3: (i) *Concerto in modo galante* (for cello & orchestra); *Concierto como un divertimento* (for cello & orchestra); (ii) *Concierto de estío* (for violin & orchestra); *Cançoneta* (for violin & string orchestra)
(BB) *** Naxos 8.555840. Castile and León SO, Darman, with (i) Polo; (ii) Ovrutsky

Volume 3 plunges into rarer Rodrigo: in the jolly *Concerto in modo galante*, written in 1949 for cellist Cassadó, Rodrigo's easy-going manner has an eighteenth-century Spanish spirit. The *Concierto como un divertimento*, written in 1981, is another agreeable cello concerto, peppered with all sorts of Spanishry and brightly orchestrated; the slow movement features the cello playing against flute, clarinet and celesta, creating a very pleasing effect. Rodrigo looked to Vivaldi (in structural form, at least) in his *Concierto de estío* for violin and orchestra: the two lively outer movements are separated by an especially attractive central Siciliana *adagio*. The *Cançoneta for Violin and String Orchestra* is short and pleasurable.

Complete Orchestral Works, Vol. 4: (i) *Concierto para piano y orquesta* (rev. Achúcarro). *Homenaje a la tempranica; Juglares; Música para un jardín; Preludio para un poema a la Alhambra*
(BB) **(*) Naxos 8.557101. Castile and León SO, Darman, (i) with Ferrandiz

Starting dramatically, the *Concierto para piano y orquesta* soon enters familiar Rodrigo territory, with some attractive episodes, but not really having enough inspired music to sustain its 30 minutes. The *Música para un jardín*, written in 1935, depicts the growth of a garden throughout the year. It's a slight work, with one or two nice touches, but hardly another *Nights in the Gardens of Spain*. More successful and more deeply reminiscent of Falla is the *Preludio para un poema a la Alhambra*, a mini tone-poem: 'At twilight, the guitar sighs, and beyond, almost within the Alhambra, rings out the rhythms which drive the dance.' It was first performed in 1930. Similarly, the *Homenaje a la tempranica* and *Juglares* find the composer at his best in short, undemanding movements. Lively performances and good sound.

Complete Orchestral Works, Vol. 5: *Concierto Madrigal; Concierto para una fiesta*
(BB) **(*) Naxos 8.555842. Gallén, Clerch, Asturias SO, Valdés

The *Concierto Madrigal*, a suite of movements with the common link of the Renaissance madrigal *O felici ocche*, is one of the composer's finest compositions, with a real piquancy. It has been recorded several times of course, and this performance is a good, warmly relaxed one, though other versions, such as the Yepes on DG, are livelier, with more character and flair. The *Concierto para una fiesta* has a slow movement not unlike that of the *Concierto de Aranjuez*, if not so inspired. The outer movements are predictably tuneful and undemanding. The orchestral playing and the recordings are both up to standard.

Complete Orchestral Works Vol. 6: *A la busca del más allá; Dos danzas españolas; Palillos y panderetas; Per la flor del lliri blau; Tres viejos aires de danza*

(BB) ** Naxos 555962. Castile and León SO, Darman

Plenty of light, undemanding Spanishry here, not all of it showing the composer at his best, some of the movements here being a bit noisy and empty (the opening of *Palillos y panderetas*, for example), and showing melodic weakness. The pair of *Spanish Dances* are pleasing enough, and so too are the three *Traditional Dance Airs* (*Tres viejos aires de danza*). For the Flower of the Blue Lily (*Per la flor lliri blau*) is a colourful tone-poem dating from 1936 and is admirably inventive. *A la busca del más allá* ('In Search of What Lies Beyond') was written in 1976 in response to a commission from the Houston Symphony Orchestra, and dedicated to NASA. It is undoubtedly one of the composer's most modern-sounding works, with the orchestra's fullest resources used to good effect, though there is no great substance in the work. The performances are enthusiastic, but the violin sound is somewhat under-nourished when exposed, with signs of under-rehearsal in a few sloppy entries. Otherwise, good sound.

Complete Orchestral Works, Vol. 7: *Cántico de San Francisco de Asis; Himnos de los neófitos de Qumrán; Música para un códice salmantino; Retable de Navidad*

(BB) ** Naxos 8.557223. Lojendio, Prieto, Marchante, Allende, Rubiera, Comunidad Ch. & O, Encinar.

Volume Seven concentrates on Rodrigo's works for chorus and orchestra. *Retablo de Navidad* (*Christmas Carols and Songs*) (1952) are really simple folksongs dressed up in orchestral colours, but with more restraint than one expects from this composer. *Himnos de los neófitos de Qumrán* (*Hymns of the Neophytes of Qumran*), for three sopranos, male chorus and chamber orchestra, using texts from the Dead Sea scrolls, was written in 1975. Here the composer reduces the orchestral forces to a minimum, and it is hard to guess that this was written by Rodrigo – it has a far more eerie sound-world than usual. A more familiar style returns for *Música para un códice salmantino*, a commission from Salamanca University in 1953, though its 11 minutes (for bass soloists and mixed chorus) are not especially gripping, and the chorus is not especially refined. The *Cántico de San Francisco de Asis* ('Canticle of St Francis of Assisi') was written in 1982 to mark the 800th anniversary of the birth of the saint. As ever with this composer, it has some good episodes, though it only just holds the listener's interest through its (almost) 19 minutes. Again the recording is good but, like the orchestral playing, not exceptional, and the chorus is a bit approximate at times. Texts and translations are helpfully included.

Complete Orchestral Works, Vol. 8: (i) *Concierto pastoral* (for flute & orchestra); *Fantasía para un gentilhombre* (arr. Galway for flute & orchestra). *Dos miniaturas andaluzas; Adagio para instrumentos de viento*

(BB) ** Naxos 8.557801. Asturias SO, Valdés, (i) with G'froerer

Top-notch light music in the form of Rodrigo's *Fantasía para un gentilhombre*, but here presented in Sir James Galway's arrangement for flute and orchestra. It is an enjoyable performance, even if it doesn't quite gel in the way the best performances do: occasionally the soloist's playing seems a bit too literal, not helped by the closely

miked flute, robbing the music of some of its dynamic range. The *Concierto pastoral* is another of the composer's best works, undemanding but inventive, and the *Dos miniaturas andaluzas* make an attractive five-minute bonus. The *Adagio para instrumentos de viento* ('Adagio for Wind Instruments') features unexpectedly loud and lively music for an adagio!

Other recordings

Concierto de Aranjuez (for guitar & orchestra)
🎵 *** Warner 2564 60296-2. Isbin, NYPO, Serebrier – PONCE: *Concierto del sur;* VILLA-LOBOS: *Guitar Concerto* ***

(i) *Concierto de Aranjuez;* (ii) *Fantasia para un gentilhombre*
(BB) *** HMV 5 86758-2. Angel Romero, LSO, Previn – ALBÉNIZ: *Suite española 1,* etc. ***

(i) *Concierto de Aranjuez; Fantasia para un gentilhombre. En los trigales; Pastoral; Sonata a la española*
(BB) ** EMI Encore 5 86989-2. Bitetti; (i) Philh. O, Ros-Marbá

Sharon Isbin is an ideal exponent of this concerto. Winner of the Queen Sofia competition in Madrid, she also enjoyed a twenty-year friendship with Rodrigo and his wife during the last period of the composer's life. A quite exceptional guitarist, she has the gift of creating a musing, improvisatory feeling which is seemingly totally spontaneous and is heard at its most magical in the famous slow movement. In a chamber-styled performance Serebrier accompanies with comparable delicacy, ensuring that the orchestral detail is vividly realized, but always in scale with the soloist. Yet the climax is full of yearning passion. The recording is outstanding and perfectly balanced.

The Romero/Previn recording of the *Concierto* is undoubtedly very successful and can be recommended to those who like a recording which favours atmosphere and warmth over crystal clarity. Angel Romero does not emerge as such a strong personality as, say, Julian Bream or John Williams, but the skill and sensibility of his playing are in no doubt, and Previn is obviously so delighted with the orchestral scores that he communicates his enthusiam with loving care for detail. Thus although the guitar is slightly larger than life in relation to the orchestra, Previn is still able to bring out the engaging woodwind chatter in the outer movements of the *Concierto*. The famous slow movement is very beautifully played indeed: the opening is especially memorable. The approach to the *Fantasia* is vividly direct, missing some of the Spanish graciousness, but its infectious quality is more than enough compensation. The encores by Albéniz and others are superbly played too (mostly by Julian Byzantine).

Ernesto Bitetti is a lively exponent of the *Concierto*, and the *Fantasia* is especially successful, with Ros-Marbá and the Philharmonia Orchestra providing a brilliantly coloured orchestral backing, full of bracing rhythmic vitality. The solo items, too, are very well played; indeed, the *Sonata a la española*, which ends the programme, is dedicated to Bitetti. He gives a rather introspective performance of it, but the music responds to his thoughtfulness. While not being a top choice, this well-recorded collection is good value.

ROGER-DUCASSE, Jean-Jules
(1873–1954)

Au jardin de Marguérite: Interlude; Epithalame; Prélude d'un ballet; Suite française
*** Marco Polo 8.223641. Rheinland-Pfalz Philh. O, Segerstam

Le Joli jeu de furet: Scherzo; Marche française; Nocturne de printemps; Orphée: 3 Fragments symphoniques; Petite suite
*** Marco Polo 8.223501. Rheinland-Pfalz Philh. O, Segerstam

The music of Roger-Ducasse has both elegance and atmosphere. The *Nocturne de printemps* and the fragmentary but imaginative *Prélude d'un ballet* show a post-impressionist, Debussy-like figure with a refined feeling for the orchestra; elsewhere, in *Orphée* for example, the influence of d'Indy can be discerned. There are touches of Ravel and in the *Epithalame* something of the high spirits of Les Six. Segerstam has a good feeling for this repertoire and gets atmospheric and sensitive performances from his Baden-Baden forces and good, serviceable recordings from the Marco Polo and radio engineers.

ROMBERG, Sigmund (1887–1951)

(i) *The Desert Song*: highlights; (ii) *The New Moon*: highlights
(B) *** CfP (ADD) 3 35987-2. (i) Hockridge, Bronhill, Julie Dawn, Bruce Forsyth, Leonard Weir; (ii) Andy Cole, Elizabeth Larner; Rita Williams Singers, O, Collins –
FRIML: *The Firefly*: excerpts **

Of all the American musical plays pre-dating the musical's golden era, *The Desert Song* (1927) was the longest-lasting (alongside *The Student Prince*). John Hanson was able to go on touring with it after virtually all its predecessors had been relegated to theatrical history. It has a splendid score, teeming with memorable tunes, the *Riff Song* balanced by the *French Military Marching Song*, the delightful romantic numbers, *Romance, I want a kiss* and, of course, the *Desert Song* itself, the unforgettable *Blue Heaven*. Then there are the usual novelty numbers, '*It*' (quite sexy for its time), and *One good boy gone wrong* (both marvellously put over here by Bruce Forsyth) and, of course, the pseudo-Oriental songs, reflecting a popular and misguided vision of *Eastern and Western Love*.

But, as Peter Gammond has written elsewhere, a musical play depends above all on a good book if it is to enjoy lasting success, and Oscar Hammerstein II had a hand in this one. Its story, with its Robin Hood hero, the 'Red Shadow', who sympathizes with and leads the anti-French Arab guerrillas but is himself a Frenchman in disguise, worked well in the late 1920s. The idea of being carried off by an Arab sheikh was a Rudolph Valentino-inspired female fantasy, and was now given a happy ending, as he turns out to be a completely eligible husband at the end of the story.

The present selection of highlights, recorded in the late 1950s, is quite admirably sung. It was produced by EMI's pop music department, hence the schmaltzy orchestra and close microphones, which are not flattering to June Bronhill's pretty voice. But she is a charming Margot, and Edmund Hockridge is a suitably ardent 'Red Shadow', alias Pierre Birabeau.

Oscar Hammerstein also collaborated in writing *The New Moon*, which had to be withdrawn at first, for Romberg to add more hits. The result was another group of memorable numbers like *One Kiss, Wanting You, Lover come back to me* and, of course, *Softly as in a morning sunrise*, all delightfully sung here by Elizabeth Larner and Andy Cole. The chorus contributes with sparkle and gusto in both shows, and Michael Collins directs the proceedings with much spirit. Both *The Desert Song* and *The New Moon* were twice made into films, which confirmed the durability of their scores, and this excellent disc, vividly recorded, readily demonstrates just how good the tunes are.

The Student Prince (musical play/operetta; complete)
*** TER CDTER 1172 (2). Bailey, Hill-Smith, Montague, Rendall, Ambrosian Ch., Philh. O, Edwards

The Student Prince (orchestrated by Emil Gerstenberger) is Romberg's most famous score and was first performed in New York in 1924. The story of a young prince who falls in love with a barmaid but is forced to give her up for the sake of duty gives it a bittersweet quality, while Romberg's music all but redeems its sentimentality. The melodic invention is very strong indeed, with colourful orchestrations adding to the impact, and this (1990) recording presents the music complete for the first time on CD. John Owen Edwards directs an enthusiastic yet polished performance, and with a fair sprinkling of star performers, notably Marilyn Hill-Smith as the heroine Kathy – completely at home in this repertoire – and David Rendall as her lover, the result is most enjoyable. There are excellent contributions, too, from Norman Bailey and Diana Montague, and the heady if somewhat dated atmosphere of the operetta-musical play style of the 1920s is vividly conveyed.

The Student Prince (highlights)
(B) **(*) CfP (ADD) 335988-2. Wakefield, Grimaldi, McCue, Keyte, Brooks, Linden Singers, Sinfonia of L., Hollingsworth
– HERBERT: *Naughty Marietta*; O. STRAUS: *The Chocolate Soldier* **(*)

The Student Prince fared well for many years, thanks to the Mario Lanza film, and also to the 1968 revival with added songs. It is old-fashioned music theatre, but the mixture of lively numbers, such as the drinking songs, and a string of romantic hits – all with memorable tunes – such as *Golden Days, Just we two, Thoughts will come to me* and *Deep in my heart*, has ensured that the work has not completely faded. This selection of the hits, recorded with a good theatrical cast (not all first-rate singers, but more than adequate), was recorded in 1960. Like many of these Studio Two recordings in the CfP re-releases, it is in rather too bright, but theatrical sound.

ROPARTZ, Joseph Guy (1864–1955)

From 1905 Ropartz headed the conservatoire of Nancy and then Strasbourg. On retirement he returned to his Breton roots. He was at one time loosely paired with his immediate contemporary, Albéric Magnard, just as Debussy was with Ravel.

(i) *Rhapsody for cello & orchestra. Œdipe à Colone* (incidental music); *Pêcheurs d'Islande*
*** Timpani TC 1095. (i) Demarquette; O de Bretagne, Karabits

The discovery here is the *Rhapsody for Cello and Orchestra*, written in 1928, whose pensive style and restrained eloquence are quite haunting. Henri Demarquette is a highly sympathetic and musical soloist. The early *Pêcheurs d'Islande*, composed in 1891, shows him still under the influence of Franck and his circle, and the modal touches to be found here and in the incidental music to *Œdipe à Colone* bear occasional reminders of d'Indy. This music is cultured and finely wrought and, though the Breton orchestra is not the Orchestre de Paris, they give dedicated performances of all three pieces.

Symphonies 1 (Sur un choral breton); 4
*** Timpani 1C 1093. Nancy SO, Lang-Lessing

Ropartz was a dedicated pupil of Franck, and everything about the *First Symphony* (based on a Breton chorale) directly reflects his mentor's *D minor Symphony*. The measured introduction, the obvious chromaticism, the first movement's half-familiar secondary theme, and its sequential development are all directly absorbed from that obvious source. The five-part central slow-movement-and-Scherzo combined again discloses its sources, and so does the finale, although here the Breton folk-element brings a light-hearted character, further away from the organ loft, which is the composer's own contribution. But the grandiloquent reprise of the hymn-like Breton chorale at the close is again very Franckian.

Perhaps even more surprisingly, the similarly cyclic *Fourth Symphony*, composed in 1910, retains the Franckian undercurrents. Ropartz even uses the cor anglais for the central movement's doleful cantilena (again interspered with two more lively *Allegretto* sections). The symphony then has a more vigorous finale, yet ends gently. But despite these Franckian fingerprints (indeed, perhaps because of them), both works are enjoyable and they are certainly well structured; any Franck admirer will enjoy spotting their source material. Sebastian Lang-Lessing and his excellent Nancy orchestra respond to the ebb and flow of this music spontaneously, generating plenty of adrenalin too, and they are very well recorded.

ROREM, Ned (born 1923)

(i) *Flute Concerto;* (ii) *Violin Concerto. Pilgrims*
(BB) *** Naxos 8.559278. (i) Khaner; (ii) Quint; RLPO, Serebrier

Ned Rorem is already a celebrated composer of the newer generation in America; he writes tonally and without the need to shock his listeners into submission. On this well-planned Naxos disc we are transported into his refined, often elegiac sound-world by the opening *Pilgrims* for string orchestra, which evokes a quiet feeling of 'remembrance'.

Each of the two concertos is programmatic, the work for flute offering a series of vignettes with often virtuosic embroidery. It is superbly played by Jeffrey Khaner. The arresting opening drum-command introduces the haunting five-note motif on which the six movements all draw. So the work is almost a set of variations, ending with a catchy *False Waltz* and on to the refined mood of the closing *Résumé and Prayer*. The result is highly imaginative and full of variety, if perhaps a little over-extended.

The *Violin Concerto* opens dramatically and ardently and is a true interplay between soloist and accompaniment, its second movement an unlikely *Toccata-Chaconne* built over a jagged timpani rhythm. But the heart of the work is lyrically heart-warming in its gentle beauty, first a simple *Romance*

without Words, followed by the serene *Midnight*, 'a microsonic variation'. Then comes the witty, carolling *Toccata-Rondo* ('a waltz in 4/4'); and the closing ecstatic *Dawn* recalls the opening and then the *Romance*, and ends idyllically. Philippe Quint is a deeply responsive soloist, playing with silvery timbre: the composer could not have asked for better, and throughout Serebrier directs the accompanying RLPO most sympathetically. First-class recording. A disc well worth exploring.

Songs: *Alleluia; Clouds; Do I love you more than a day?; Early in the morning; Little elegy; Far far away; Ferry me across the water; For Poulenc; For Susan; I am rose; I will always love you; I strolled across an open field; A journey; Jeannie with the light brown hair; Look down fair moon; The Lordly Hudson; Love; Now sleeps the crimson petal; Ode; O do not love too long; O you, whom I often and silently come; Orchids; Santa Fé, Op. 101/Nos. 2, 4, 8 & 12; The serpent; The tulip tree; Sometimes with one I love; Stopping by woods on a snowy evening; To a young girl; That shadow, my likeness*
*** Erato 8573 80222-2. Graham, Martineau

Ned Rorem spent many of his formative years in Paris during the 1950s, when he came to know Poulenc and Auric, but he never lost the American flavour that makes his style so distinctive. This recital, encompassing settings of English, American and French verse, gives a good idea of his melodic resource and feeling for words. His songs, such as the *Santa Fé* series and the setting of Tennyson's *Now sleeps the crimson petal*, bear witness to a rich imagination and a marvellous feel for both the voice and the piano. Susan Graham does them all proud, and Malcolm Martineau gives impeccable support.

ROSENBERG, Hilding (1892–1985)

PIANO MUSIC

Improvisationer; Plastiska Scener; Små föredragsstudier; Sonatas 1 & 3
** Daphne 1001. Widlund

Sonatas 2 & 4; Sonatina; Suite; Tema con variazioni
** Daphne 1003. Widlund

The musical quality of Rosenberg's piano music is variable: the cosmopolitan influences are obvious and Rosenberg is at his best in the smaller-scale miniatures such as the *Små föredragsstudier* ('Small Performing Studies'). He obviously knew his Ravel and Honegger, and in the *Largamente* from the *Plastiska Scener* there are hints of Schoenberg. The *Third Sonata* in particular is arid and its companions are not uniformly rewarding. But the smaller pieces are well worth having and, like the sonatas, are new to the catalogue. Mats Widlund is a dedicated advocate and the recordings are very natural.

Christmas Oratorio: Den heliga natten (The Holy Night)
** Marco Polo 8.225123. Inglebäck, Anna & Anders Larsson, Elby, Amadel Chamber Ch., Swedish Chamber O, Sundkvist
− LARSSON: *Förklädd Gud (God in Disguise), Op. 24* **

Rosenberg's *Christmas Oratorio* was composed in 1938, the year before the *Third Symphony*, and was recorded both in the days of 78s and again by Eric Ericsson and Swedish Radio forces in the 1960s. Like Lars-Erik Larsson's *Förklädd Gud*, it is a setting of poems by Hjalmar Gullberg, who enjoyed much standing in the 1930s and 1940s. At one time it was a regular fixture in the Swedish Radio Christmas schedules but has fallen out of favour in recent years.

Understandably perhaps, since it is not one of Rosenberg's strongest or most inventive pieces, and in many of its sections his muse seems to be on auto-pilot. There are, of course, good things (*Herod's Song* is one) and Petter Sundkvist gets good results from his chorus and orchestra. Not essential listening and by no stretch of the imagination as rewarding as the *Third Symphony* listed in our main volume.

ROSETTI, Antonio (c. 1750–92)

Flute Concertos in C, RWV C16; F, RWV C21; G, RWV C22; G, RWV C25

*** Orfeo C095 031A. Meier, Prague CO

Charming, unpretentious music of the sort we expect from this composer: full of tunes and elegance, offset with gentle drama. These flute concertos, each lasting 18 or 19 minutes, with lively outer movements flanked with slow movements of pastoral charm, receive their première recording here. The performances (on modern instruments) are as unselfconscious as the music itself, and give unfailing pleasure.

ROSLAVETS, Nikolai (1881–1944)

Cello Sonatas 1 & 2; Dance of the White Girls; Meditation; 5 Preludes for Piano

*** Chan. 9881. Ivashkin, Lazareva

Roslavets was one of the leading avant-garde figures in the 1920s Soviet Union and the first to experiment with atonality. He soon fell foul of official orthodoxy, and, while his work was known in specialist quarters, he never gained wide recognition in either the Soviet Union or the West. In fact he is known for his reputation rather than the music itself.

The *Dance of the White Girls* is an early piece with a strong whiff of impressionism, while the two one-movement *Cello Sonatas* and the *Meditation* come from the early 1920s. Alexander Ivashkin speaks of the *Second* as a mixture of late Scriabin and early Messiaen, and the *Five Preludes for Piano* are certainly indebted to Scriabin's Op. 74. Both the cellist and pianist make out a strong case for this music, and they are well served by the recording.

Piano Trios 2–4

** Teldec 8573 82017-2. Fontenay Trio

The Fontenay give a strong account of the three *Trios* but, interesting though this music is, it conveys little real feeling of mastery.

ROSSETER, Philip (1567–1623)

Lute Pieces: Almayne; Fantasia; Galliard; 3rd Galliard for the Countess of Sussex; Pavin; Pavin by Rossesters; Prelude. Lute Songs: And would you see my Mistress' face; If she forsake me; Kind in unkindness; No grave for woe; Reprove not love; Shall I come if I swim?; Sweet come again; Though far from joy; What heart's content; What then is love but mourning?; When Laura smiles; Whether men do laugh or weep

**(*) Avie AV 2074. Gilchrist, Wadsworth (lute)

James Gilchrist has just the right warm vocal timbre for these songs and he sings them eloquently, and Matthew Wadsworth plays the lute pieces as interludes. They are beautifully recorded and the opening *Sweet come again* is quite lovely. But this is a collection to dip into rather than to play all at once, for Rosseter's songs (and, to a lesser extent, his instrumental writing) bring a pervading melancholy, so that one is very glad to welcome lively numbers like *When Laura smiles* or *If she forsakes me*.

ROSSINI, Gioachino (1792–1868)

String Sonatas 1–5 (arr. for wind quartet by Berr)

(BB) ** Naxos 8.554098. Michael Thompson Wind Qt

The considerable charm of Rossini's delightful early *String Sonatas* is the more remarkable when one realizes that they are the work of a 12-year-old: their invention is consistently on the highest level and their bubbling humour is infectious. This wind arrangement adds another dimension to these works and is highly enjoyable, with the quartet of soloists (horn, flute, clarinet and flute) providing felicitous interplay and it shows considerable resource of colour with only four instruments. The performances here are spontaneous, stylish and lively, with plenty of sparkle. Alas, the very forward recording is set in a too dry and unatmospheric acoustic, and the effect is rather unyielding after a while, with a lack of bloom and an inadequate ambience.

CHORAL MUSIC

Messa di gloria

(M) *** Ph. 475 7781. Jo, Murray, Giménez, Araiza, Ramey, Ch. & ASMF, Marriner

This is a surprisingly neglected work, considering its excellence. There have been only two recordings of it, both from Philips, the first directed by Herbert Handt, who was responsible for rescuing it from oblivion, and this 1992 Marriner version, which now returns to the catalogue as one of Philips's Originals. Rossini's *Messa di gloria* is in nine movements, offering appropriately ambitious but never heavy settings of the *Kyrie*, deeply expressive, and a jauntily operatic *Gloria*, products of Rossini's first full maturity at a time (1820) when he was otherwise totally occupied with writing operas. There are links between the tenor duet which starts the *Christe* (beautifully sung by Giménez and Araiza) and Mathilde's aria in *William Tell*, but the delight is that so much unknown Rossini contains so much new to charm us, including the beautiful *Gratias*, with its obbligato cor anglais. Marriner's account replaces Handt's version, good though that was, for he has a starry team of soloists, Sumi Jo notably fresh-voiced and Giménez equally memorable. The St Martin's Chorus predictably matches the ASMF in excellence rising exultantly to the closing contrapuntal *Cum sancto spirito*, which incidentally may not have been wholly Rossini's work. First class recording.

Overtures: Il barbiere di Siviglia; La cambiale di matrimonio; L'inganno felice; L'Italiana in Algeri; La scala di seta; Il Signor Bruschino; Tancredi; Il Turco in Italia

❂ (M) *** DG 416 5317. Orpheus CO

Overtures (as above); (i) *Introduction, Theme & Variations for Clarinet & Orchestra in E flat*
→ (B) *** DG Entrée 477 5012. Orpheus CO; (i) with Neidich

The Orpheus Chamber Orchestra displays astonishing unanimity of style and ensemble in this splendid collection of Rossini overtures, played without a conductor. Not only is the crispness of string phrasing a joy, but the many stylish wind solos have an attractive degree of freedom, and one never senses any rigidity in allegros, which are always joyfully sprung. *La scala di seta* is an especial delight, and the opening string cantilena of *Il Barbiere* is agreeably gracious. These are performances that in their refinement and apt chamber style give increasing pleasure with familiarity. The DG recording is marvellously real, with the perspective perfectly judged. However, extraordinarily, the Orpheus collection of Rossini overtures is also reissued on a bargain Entrée CD, including also Charles Neidich's lively account of the *Introduction, Theme and Variations* for clarinet and orchestra, which must be the best buy.

Overtures: (i) *Il barbiere di Siviglia; La gazza ladra*; (ii) *L'Italiana in Algeri; La scala di seta*; (i) *Semiramide; Il Signor Bruschino; Tancredi; Il viaggio a Reims*
(M) (***) DG mono 477 5908. Fricsay, with (i) RIAS SO, Berlin; (ii) BPO – BIZET: *Carmen: Suite* (**(*)

Taut, dramatic performances from Fricsay in generally full and vivid 1950s mono sound; only in the earliest performances does the quality feel noticeably dated. In *Semiramide* here is electrifying excitement from the word go, but adrenalin runs freely throughout these performances. There is elegance, too, and nicely pointed strings: the jaunty tune in *Il viaggio a Reims* (deliciously done), the main allegro subject in *La gazza ladra*, and the delightful *Il Signor Bruschino* are just three examples. The woodwind sparkles with wit, and altogether this CD is a must for all Fricsay admirers.

OPERA

Il barbiere di Siviglia (complete CD versions)
(B) *(*) DG (ADD) 477 5634. Gianna d'Angelo, Capecchi, Monti, Cava, Taddei, Bav. R. Ch. & O, Bartoletti
(BB) * EMI (ADD) 585523-2 (2). Sills, Gedda, Milnes, Capecchi, Raimondi, Barbieri, John Aldis Ch., LSO, Levine

Bartoletti's DG reissue is not a serious contender. Gianna d'Angelo is a sweet enough Rosina, but not especially individual. Capecchi gives an over-respectable portrait of the barber himself, sometimes a little like a pompous politician. The recording favours the voices unduly.

Levine conducts vigorously in his EMI version, but the singing of neither Beverly Sills nor Nicolai Gedda can be recommended with any enthusiasm, the one unpleasant in tone, for all its brilliance, the other seriously strained – a reminder, no more, of what Gedda's voice once was. Sherrill Milnes makes a strong, forthright Figaro, in every way the centre of attention here, and Ruggero Raimondi is a sonorous Basilio. Even though it is now offered at bargain price, in good mid-1970s sound, this set can hardly be recommended with such strong competition around. A synopsis is included. But the Decca set with Bartoli is the one to go for (425 520-2).

La Cenerentola (complete CD version)
(M) *(*) Sony (ADD) SM2K 90419 (2). Valentini Terrani, Araiza, Trimarchi, Dara, Ravaglia, West German R. Ch., Capella Coloniensis, Ferro

On Sony, Gabriele Ferro, one of the ablest of Rossini scholars, who earlier recorded *L'Italiana in Algeri* impressively, conducts an easy-going, but at times pedestrian account of *La Cenerentola*, well played and well sung, but lacking some of the fizz essential in Rossini. Even the heroine's final brilliant aria hangs fire, and that despite warm, positive singing from Lucia Valentini Terrani, whose stylish contribution is spoilt only by a high quota of intrusive aitches. The rest of the cast is strong and, apart from the backward placing of the orchestra, the digital transfer is full and realistic. However, as in the other operas in this series of Sony reissues, the documentation is unacceptably sparse, with neither libretto nor cued synopsis, and once again the Bartoli Decca set is the one to have (436 902-2).

La donna del lago (complete DVD version)
(*) Opus Arte **DVD OA LS 3009 J. Anderson, Blake, Merritt, La Scala Ch. & O, Muti (Director: Werner Herzog; V/D: Ilio Catani)

It was on the initiative of Riccardo Muti as music director that La Scala, Milan, extended its range of Rossini productions to the relatively rare *La donna del lago*, an opera first heard in 1819, based on *The Lady of the Lake* by Sir Walter Scott. With lavish sets by Maurizio Balo, evocative and realistic, it establishes the period atmosphere well; but it is Muti's evident enthusiasm for the piece in his taut and exciting conducting that above all brings out the drama of conflict in sixteenth-century Scotland, with the melancholy Elena, the heroine, caught between rival forces. June Anderson in that role sings very reliably, but it is hardly a characterful performance, and it is left to the two principal tenors, both with an impressive upper rage so necessary in Rossini, to make the most striking vocal contributions, Rockwell Blake as Giacomo V (James V) of Scotland and Chris Merritt as Rodrigo di Dhu. Though Merritt has the weightier voice, he produces astounding top notes out of the blue, while Blake with sweeter tone is amazingly agile, relishing the most taxing divisions. The others make a strong, consistent team. A complete libretto is provided and a good synopsis of the plot, but no information on the opera's history.

Ermione (complete DVD version)
*** Warner **DVD** 0630 1012-2. Antonacci, Montague, Ford, Lopez-Janez, Austin Kelly, Howell, Glyndebourne Ch., LPO, A. Davis (Director: Graham Vick; V/D: Humphrey Burton)

Recorded live in the new Glyndebourne Opera House in 1995, the Warner DVD offers a Rossini rarity in a striking production by Graham Vick. It updates the action – in a plot based on Racine's tragedy, *Andromaque* – to the early twentieth century, with colourful military uniforms to the fore. Fascinatingly, the set represents sections of an eighteenth-century theatre with its galleries and boxes, a device that works flexibly enough. As usual in an *opera seria* of Rossini, the mixture of jolly music may seem incongruous, bringing unexpected lurches of mood, but it is always lively and it offers the three principal tenors some spectacular vocal challenges. Bruce Ford as Oreste sings powerfully, producing penetrating top notes out of the blue, while Jorge Lopez-Janez as Pyrrhus sings more gently and with a sweeter tone, also coping well with the high tessitura. Oddly, this adaptation of *Andromaque* slants the story away from her – superbly played here by Diana Montague – towards Ermione, whose Act II aria provides an emotional high point in the piece. Excellent contributions too from the third tenor, Paul Austin Kelly, as Pilade and from Gwynne Howell as Phoenix. Andrew Davis, Glyndebourne music director at the time, draws fresh, incisive performances from chorus and orchestra. As so often with Warner DVDs, there is no booklet, only a synopsis and a list of chapters – a pity when such a rarity really requires some background information.

Guglielmo Tell (complete CD version in Italian)
(M) *** Decca (ADD) 475 7723 (3). Pavarotti, Freni, Milnes, Ghiaurov, Amb. Op. Ch., Nat. PO, Chailly

This now arrives at last at mid-price as one of Decca's Originals, with Milnes a heroic Tell, and, although Pavarotti has his moments of coarseness, he sings the role of Arnoldo glowingly. Mirella Freni as the heroine, Matilde, provides strength as well as sweetness, and Chailly controls this massive opera purposefully, with the many ensembles particularly impressive, especially when the Decca analogue recording is so fine.

Il Turco in Italia (complete CD version)
(BB) (**) Naxos 8.660183/4 (2). De Carolis, Papatanasiu, Pinti, Gagliardo, Moretti, Chieti Teatro Marrucino Ch. & O, Conti

It is good to have a lively account of *Il Turco in Italia*, one of the rarer Rossini comic operas, on Naxos's super-budget label. The Italian theatre where the performance was recorded has a relatively dry acoustic, which is no help to the voices, but the results are clean-cut and fresh, with a fortepiano imaginatively providing the recitative. The singing is very acceptable if hardly distinguished, with Myrto Papatanasiu as the heroine, Fiorilla, bright-toned and reasonably agile, and the tenor Amedeo Moretti as Narciso, clean-cut, though the voice is hardly beautiful, with elaborate vocal divisions treated heavily. The vocal ensemble of the company is first rate, which ensures that overall the result is readily enjoyable. There is no libretto, but one can get a text via the internet, and the description of plot for each track is very helpful in telling a story with many oddities.

Il viaggio a Reims (complete DVD version)
** TDK **DVD** DV OPVAR (2). Merced, Rasmussen, Cantarero, Bayo, Bros, Tarver, Orfila, Ulivieri, Dara, Gran Theatre Del Liceu Ch. & SO, Lopez Cobos (V/D: Toni Bargalló; Director: Sergi Belbel)

It was only in 1984 at the Pesaro Festival that *Il viaggio a Reims* was given its first modern revival, a piece originally written as a one-off celebration for the coronation of Charles X, drawing on a whole team of star singers. Since then it has been revived a number of times, not always with stars but sometimes (as here) with a good team of repertory singers. Under Jesus Lopez Cobos's crisp direction it still works well, though as always the most striking numbers are those that Rossini re-used in 1828 for his French comic opera, *Le Comte Ory*, often with different voices involved and to different effect.

In Sergi Belbel's production, with stylized but lavish sets, the scene, updated to the Edwardian period, is not in a hotel but in a spa sanatorium, with a swimming pool prominent at the back. The simple idea of a group of travellers waiting to be taken to Rheims for the coronation remains, with one would-be traveller after another doing his or her party piece, and with a whole range of nationalities involved. In this performance there are few outstanding singers, though all give good, characterful performances, with Kenneth Tarver and the Russian Conte di Libenskof standing out. Unnecessarily this allegedly one-act piece spreads to two discs, with the first half ending – as in *Comte Ory* – with one of the most sparkling ensembles that even Rossini ever wrote.

COLLECTIONS

'Bi-centennial Gala, Avery Fisher Hall, 1992': Overture: La gazza ladra; (i) La donna del lago: Mura felici; (ii) Stabat Mater: Inflammatus (iii) La Cenerentola: Nacqui all'affano. Zelmira: (iv) Terra amica; (ii; v) Perché mi guardi e piangi; (i; vi) Bianca e Falliero: Cielo, il mio labbro ispiri; (vi) Guillaume Tell: Asile héréditaire; (vii) Il barbiere di Siviglia: Largo al factotum; (v) Petite messe solennelle: Agnus Dei; (iv) L'Italiana in Algeri: Pappatachi! che mai sento; (viii) Le siège de Corinthe: La gloire et la fortune; (i–vii) Il viaggio a Reims: A tal colpo inaspettato
(M) **(*) Virgin 3 49953-2 (2). (i) M. Horne; (ii) Voigt; (iii) Von Stade; (iv) Blake; (v) Kuhlmann; (vi) Merritt; (vii) Hampson, Ramey; NY Concert Chorale, O of St Lukes, Norrington

Operatic galas can often be a mixed bag, but not this one with virtually every number a winner, and plenty of novelties too. Norrington gets the proceedings off to a lively start with the *Overture, La gazza ladra*, and he keeps the pot boiling admirably throughout, with excellent support from the New York chorus and orchestra. Marilyn Horne is immediately arresting, showing her range, with dramatic and vocal skills undiminished. Of course Thomas Hampson brings the house down with his *Largo al factotum* sung hair-raisingly fast, and Frederica von Stade's *Cenerentola* showpiece is predictably seductive. But the dramatic surprise of the first half of the concert is Deborah Voigt's thrilling *Inflammatus*, while in complete contrast, Kathleen Kuhlmann is very touching in the *Agnus Dei* from the *Petite Messe solennelle*. Later, she joins with Deborah Voigt in a moving excerpt from *Zelmira*. After Samuel Ramey has done his bit, the programme ends spectacularly with the great ensemble from *Il viaggio a Reims*. A splendid entertainment – but, alas, neither texts and translations nor any kind of synopses are provided, only a list of titles and singers.

ROUSSEL, Albert (1869–1937)

Aeneas; Bacchus et Ariane, Op. 43: Suites 1 & 2
● (M) *** Erato (ADD) 2564 60576-2. ORTF Nat. O, Martinon

Erato have at long last released Martinon's classic 1969 version of *Bacchus et Ariane* (1930) on CD. It's a thrilling performance, and comparing it to Dutoit's version on the same label, one finds the latter sounding tame by comparison. Martinon's energy and drive do not smudge the Roussel dense orchestration, and there is both inner life and outer drive here, and the quiet passages are held with both tension and atmosphere. Splendid remastered sound, too, much better than it ever was on LP. The coupling of *Aeneas* – a much rarer work – is ideal: composed after *Bacchus* and based on a libretto by the Belgian poet Joseph Weterings, depicting the destiny of the founder of Rome, the work is equally compelling and undeniably powerful. It is full of Roussel's characteristic rich textures and orchestrations, with the chorus playing an important role. There is no lack of vigorous imagination, both rhythmically and harmonically, during its 40 minutes, ending with a triumphant hymn 'to his glory and the glory of Rome'. The only reservation is that *Aeneas* has only one cue. Along with the companion disc and Munch's accounts of the *Third* and *Fourth Symphonies*, also on Erato, this is a must for anyone interested in this composer.

Symphony 2 in B flat, Op. 23; Bacchus et Ariane: Suites 1 & 2, Op. 43
*** Ondine ODE1065-2. O de Paris, Eschenbach

Roussel's *Second Symphony* has been recorded most notably by Jean Martinon on Erato (see below). That remains perhaps its most distinguished and idiomatic performance, and the sound remains very good for its period. Christoph Eschenbach's new record with the Orchestre de Paris, the first we have had for some two decades, is a welcome addition to the Roussel discography and, in addition to the symphony, also brings well-prepared and vital accounts of the *Bacchus et Ariane* ballet. Not only does Eschenbach show obvious sympathy with this repertoire, but he gets absolutely first-class recorded sound, too. The *Second Symphony* is a powerful score and we must hope that this recording will make many new friends for it.

Symphony 2 in B flat, Op. 23; Le festin de l'araignée, Op. 17
(M) *** Erato (ADD) 2564 60577-2. ORTF Nat. O, Martinon

Martinon fully captures the brooding atmosphere of the slow sections of Roussel's *Second Symphony*, and from the opening bars the listener's attention is caught. This is one of the finest accounts available, with the richness of the score fully realized and an inner vitality ensuring total conviction. The lighter score to the magical *Le festin de l'araignée* provides the perfect contrast, and it receives a similarly superb performance, with all the subtleties and nuances vividly caught. The remastered sound is very good for its date (1969), and this CD should be snapped up quickly by fans of Roussel: these Martinon performances never seem to remain in the catalogue for long.

RUBBRA, Edmund (1901–86)

(i) *Violin Concerto, Op. 103; Improvisation for Violin & Orchestra, Op. 89. Improvisations on virginal pieces by Giles Farnaby, Op. 50*
(BB) *** Naxos 8.557591. (i) Osostowicz; Ulster O, Yuasa

Rubbra is largely identified in the popular mind with the symphony and with choral music – and rightly so. By their side the concertos take a back seat in his output, and his three essays in this genre are rarities in the concert hall. Although it was with a concerted work, the *Sinfonia concertante for Piano and Orchestra*, that he first came to prominence in the 1930s, all his concertos come from the 1950s, the *Violin Concerto* coming from the end of the decade, 1959. The *Improvisation for Violin and Orchestra* (1956), commissioned by the Louisville Orchestra and subsequently recorded by them with their leader, Sidney Harth, as soloist, no doubt stimulated his interest in the idea of a full-blown concerto. Malcolm Macdonald reminds us that much of the invention derives from a fantasia he had sketched out 20 years earlier. It is difficult to understand its neglect. It unfolds with a seeming inevitability and naturalness and, above all, an eloquence which speaks directly to the listener.

This is its first recording since the Louisville account (issued in Britain on RCA GL 25096) and Krysia Osostowicz

and the Ulster Orchestra really get to its heart. Her noble account of the *Violin Concerto* is hardly less persuasive. The piece may not have the dramatic contrasts of Bartók, Walton or Prokofiev, nor their vocabulary of dissonance. Indeed, one is reminded of a remark of Egon Wellesz: 'novelties in harmonic writing are the most dangerous things because they fade so soon, [while] part-writing is something that remains'. And the satisfaction this concerto gives resides primarily in the subtlety with which its lines evolve and grow. There have been two earlier accounts, by Carl Pini and Melbourne forces under David Measham (Unicorn-Kanchana DKPCD 9056) and by Tasmin Little with the RPO under Vernon Handley (Conifer CDCF 225). Osostowicz is more than their equal, and she engages with the score at the deepest level. Some music lovers are worried by Rubbra's opaque orchestral textures, but in Takuo Yuasa's hands they are sensitively laid out and the reading finely paced. The *Farnaby Improvisations*, at one time a regular feature of BBC programmes, has never sounded better. As always with Rubbra, there is little surface glamour but great musical substance. A self-recommending issue.

RUBINSTEIN, Anton (1829–94)

Piano Concertos 1 in E, Op. 25; 2 in F, Op. 35
** Marco Polo 8.223456. Banowetz, Czech State PO, A. Walter

Piano Concertos 3 in G, Op. 45; 4 in D min., Op. 70
** Marco Polo 8.223382. Banowetz, Slovak State PO (Košice), Stankovsky

Piano Concerto 5 in E flat, Op. 94; Caprice russe, Op. 102
**(*) Marco Polo 8.223489. Banowetz, Slovak RSO (Bratislava), Stankovsky

Rubinstein was the first composer of concertos in Russia and was enormously prolific. His *First Piano Concerto in E major*, dating from 1850, is greatly indebted to Mendelssohn though it is more prolix. The *Third Piano Concerto in G* (1853–4) is more concentrated, and there is a recording of the *Fourth in D minor* (1864) by his pupil, Josef Hofmann; no later pianist has equalled that. By the mid-1860s Rubinstein's perspective had broadened (rather than deepened), and the *Fifth Piano Concerto in E flat* (1874) is an ambitious piece, longer than the *Emperor* and almost as long as the Brahms *D minor*. No doubt its prodigious technical demands have stood in the way of its wider dissemination. It has all the fluent lyricism one expects of Rubinstein, though most of its ideas, attractive enough in themselves, overstay their welcome.

Joseph Banowetz has now recorded all the concertos for Marco Polo and, although the orchestral support and the recording do not rise much above routine, there is nothing ordinary about Banowetz's pianism. The *Fifth*, at least, is worth investigating (for the *Fourth*, one should turn to Cherkassky). The *Caprice russe* was written four years after the concerto, but the fires were obviously blazing less fiercely. All the same, this is an issue of some interest, and the solo playing has conviction.

Symphony 1, Op. 40; Ivan the Terrible, Op. 79.
(BB) *(*) Naxos 8.555476. Slovak State PO (Košice), Stankovsky

Naxos are presumably going to reissue on their bargain label all six of the Rubinstein symphonies previously available at full price on Marco Polo (They were originally discussed in our 1996 edition.) The *First* – a young man's work – comes from 1850 and is coupled with the tone-poem *Ivan the Terrible* of 1869, which draws its inspiration from the same source as did Rimsky-Korsakov's opera of the same name (also known as *The Maid of Pskov*). Tchaikovsky, incidentally, made the piano score of it. Rubinstein's language is completely and utterly rooted in Mendelssohn, and David Brown's verdict on the *Second Symphony (Ocean)* as 'watery and Mendelssohnian' applies equally here. Music of lesser stature calls for interpreters of quality and flair if it is to have the slightest chance of success, and neither of these performances is much more than routine. However, given the modest outlay involved, readers may be inclined to give these pieces a try.

Symphony 3 in A, Op. 56; Eroica Fantasia, Op. 110.

(BB) * Naxos 8.555590. Slovak RSO, Stankovsky

The *Third Symphony* is not endowed with ideas of interest or even with personality, and although it is not entirely without merit it is mostly predictable stuff. The playing by the Bratislava Radio Orchestra is fairly routine and Robert Stankovsky brings few insights to the score. The *Eroica Fantasia*, as its high opus number suggests, is a later and, if anything, less inspired work.

Symphony 4 in D min. (Dramatic), Op. 95

(BB) * Naxos 8.555979. Slovak PO, Stankovsky

The Rubinstein symphonies are perhaps more enticing on a budget label. The *Fourth*, the *Dramatic* of 1874, runs to some 65 minutes and is not a strong work. Its thematic substance is pretty thin and, despite its epic proportions, there is little sense of sweep or consistency of inspiration. The performance is acceptable but no more, as is the recording.

Piano Sonatas 1 in E min., Op. 12; 2 in C min., Op. 20; 3 in F, Op. 41; 4 in A min., Op. 100

(B) *** Hyp. Dyad CCD 22007 (2). Howard

Leslie Howard proves highly persuasive in all four works. The 1981 recordings sound excellent, and this set is more enticing as a Dyad, with two discs offered for the price of one. Returning to these works, one is surprised to find how enjoyable the music is, with some good lyrical ideas, phrased romantically, to balance the arrestingly flamboyant rhetoric which Leslie Howard obviously relishes.

RUTTER, John (born 1945)

Gloria; Magnificat; Psalm 150

☞ *** EMI 5 57952-2. Treble soloists from the Choirs of King's College & Gonville and Caius College, Cambridge, CBSO, composer; T. Winpenny or A. Grote (organ)

John Rutter's choral music is the most widely performed of any contemporary English composer, not only in England and the Commonwealth, but in North America too; listening to the *Gloria*, one can understand why. With its Waltonesque opening and thrilling use of the brass, it communicates immediately and directly; the central section is touchingly elegiac, and the closing *Amens* are exultant. It makes you feel good. It was commissioned by Mel Olson for his choir in the American Mid-West; Mr Olson gave clear directions to the composer: 'Something short, sharp and festive, with a familiar text; and say whatever you have to say up front.' It was originally written with an accompaniment for brass ensemble (a practical solution to ensure easy performance) but it

sounds wonderful in the present full-orchestral version with the King's choristers responding jubilantly and sensitively.

In the *Magnificat* setting, Rutter characteristically uses a recognizable four-note motif to fit the word itself, and the lovely second movement, *Of a Rose, a lovely rose*, is memorable enough to be extracted for separate performance. Some might feel that, for a *Magnificat*, the setting is a little soft-centred, as both the *Misericordia* and the *Esurientes* are gently lyrical, each featuring a diminutive solo treble, but the closing *Gloria Patri* is triumphant.

The closing *Psalm 150*, where the words actually invite an instrumental response, brings sounding brass, organ, full choir and percussion, and again it is spectacular, with the *Laudate Dominum* giving contrast by using a distanced group of singers. But the closing *Alleluia . . . Amen* is Rutter at his most extravagantly exuberant. The performances here are quite splendid in every respect, with the King's acoustic adding a glowing aura to the music-making.

(i–iv; vii) Mass of the Children; (ii; v) Shadows (Song-cycle with Guitar); (iii; v; vi) Wedding Canticle

(BB) **(*) Naxos 8.557922. (i) Gruffydd-Jones; (ii) Huw Williams; (iii) Clare College, Cambridge, Ch.; (iv) Farnham Youth Ch., Clare Chamber Ens.; (v) French (guitar); (vi) Pailthorpe (flute); (vii) McVinnie (organ), T. Brown

John Rutter tells us that he wrote the *Mass of the Children* to join together children's and adults' voices, remembering his own boyhood experience, singing in the choir for the Decca recording of Britten's *War Requiem*: 'I wanted to write a work that would bring them [adults and children] together in a more joyful context than a requiem.' His opening *Kyrie* is full of good spirits, but it is in the bouncing *Gloria* that his younger participants will surely revel most, as they do here. The *Sanctus* and *Benedictus* bring a gentler mood, created by intertwining flute and oboe; but the *Agnus Dei* is darker in mood, to be resolved in the lyrical finale (*Dona nobis pacem*). The brief *Wedding Canticle* is written serenely for mixed choir, flute and guitar, and is directly and beautifully presented here as a closing bonus.

But it did not seem an ideal choice to include on this CD Rutter's song-cycle, *Shadows*, which apparently attempts to re-create the tradition of the melancholy lute songs of the Elizabethan era. They are sung simply and often mournfully by Jeremy Huw Williams, accompanied most delicately by Stewart French on the guitar. But it is the lively songs, like *Gather ye rosebuds* and *In a goodly night*, which come off best.

COLLECTION

'The Gift of Music': Sacred: *All things bright and beautiful; Be Thou my vision; A Clare Benediction; For the beauty of the earth; Hymn to the Creator of Light; Look at the world; The Lord bless you and keep you; Lord, make me an instrument of Thy Peace; Magnificat; Of a Rose, a lovely Rose. Requiem: Pie Jesu; Sanctus.* arr. Rutter: Spiritual: (i) *Deep River.* Shaker Song: *Lord of the Dance.* TRAD.: *Gaelic Blessing.* Secular: (ii) *The Gift of Music; Mary's Lullaby.* Arrangements: *Golden slumbers; I know where I'm going; The keel row; O waly waly; Sans Day Carol; Willow Song*

☞ (M) *** Universal 476 3068. Cambridge Singers, City of L. Sinfonia (or BBC Concert O), composer; (ii) with Melanie Marshall

Universal have had the bright idea of asking Rutter to choose an anthology of some of the many original compositions and arrangements which he has recorded on his own Collegium label with the excellent Clare College Choir. The result is a generous, 78-minute cornucopia of musical delights, opening with a happy *Look at the world* and going on immediately to *Of a rose, a lovely rose*, which is the second movement of his *Magnificat*, and the characteristic flowing melody of *For the beauty of the earth*, liltingly decorated with Rutter's familiar flute cascades. But then comes the masterly *Hymn to the Creator of Light*, with its thrilling dissonances, which out-Taveners Tavener.

There are some attractive arrangements included, too, from the Shaker song, *The Lord of the Dance*, to a group of English folksongs, including *O waly waly* (very different from Britten's setting), *The keel row* and the haunting *I know where I'm going*. Finally there are two of Rutter's delectable carols (his speciality): the traditional Cornish *Sans Day* (with more decorative flutes) and Rutter's own enchantingly simple *Mary's Lullaby*. Superb singing and first-class recording.

SABATA, Victor de (1892–1967)

Gethsemani; Juventus; La notte di Plàton
*** Hyp. CDA 67209. LPO, Ceccato

Most conductors from Furtwängler to Pletnev compose, though few reach the record catalogues. As you might expect, Victor de Sabata shows himself a master of the orchestra and these scores have the opulence and extravagance of Respighi and Strauss. The three pieces recorded here comprise the bulk of his orchestral output. *Juventus* (1919) was championed by Toscanini and its two companions are also virtuoso orchestral showpieces. *La notte di Plàton* (1923) is an evocation of Plato's last feast and its opening portrayal of night is highly imaginative. So is *Gethsemani* (1925), which makes some use of Gregorian melody. The LPO under Aldo Ceccato respond well to these scores, as will those who take the trouble to investigate this impressively recorded disc.

SÆVERUD, Harald (1897–1992)

Symphonies: 2, Op. 4 (1934 version); 4, Op. 11; Cinquante variazioni piccole, Op. 8; (i) Romanza for violin & orchestra, Op. 23a. Sumarnat-Båtsong (Barcarola d'una notte d'estate), Op. 14/6
**(*) BIS CD 1262. (i) Buvaarp; Stavanger SO, Ruud

In terms of sheer personality Harald Sæverud is a figure unique in Norway: his dry, laconic wit and rugged features and the strong sense of the Norwegian character and landscape mark him out from most of his contemporaries. BIS continue their survey of Sæverud's output with the *Second* and *Fourth Symphonies* and three other pieces. His *First Symphony* had begun life as a student work but he returned to it after studies in Berlin, where it was first performed in 1921. Its success prompted him to return to the genre immediately and write the *Second*, but he overhauled the score in 1934 and it is in this form that it is given here. Like so much of his later music, it speaks with completely personal accents even if it does not match the later pieces in concentration. The *Fourth* from 1937 is in one movement and is full of atmosphere and a sense of mystery. There is at times something of the feeling of strangeness that distinguishes *Fartein Valen*, as if one is exploring the landscape of a different planet. It is highly imaginative, though the journey is a little discursive and the invention is by no means even in quality;

but overall it casts a strong spell. This music has lots of character and a dogged individuality, that will appeal to admirers of Robert Simpson. The wartime *Sumarnat-Båtsong* is also a haunting piece which inhabits a special bucolic sound-world that is quite unlike anyone else's. Although the sad, gentle world of *Fartein Valen* is highly distinctive, there is no more original Norwegian composer than Sæverud, whose craggy independence of outlook makes him so attractive.

The BIS sound offers no lack of detail, though the acoustic of the Stavanger Hall is a bit dry. The performances are dedicated and totally inside the idiom, but it must be conceded that they want the last ounce of polish and the strings could do with greater opulence and bloom. But don't be deterred from investigating this music. It is both rewarding and strange, intriguing and imaginative.

SAINT-SAËNS, Camille (1835–1921)

(i) Allegro appassionato (for cello and orchestra), Op. 43; (ii) Caprice in D for violin and orchestra (arr. Ysaÿe); (i) Carnival of the animals: Le cygne. (ii) Le Déluge: Prélude, Op. 45; (iii) Wedding-cake (Caprice-valse) for piano and orchestra, Op. 76
(BB) ** EMI Encore (ADD) 5 75871-2. (i) Paul Tortelier; (ii) Yan Pascal Tortelier; (iii) De la Pau; CBSO, Frémaux – MASSENET: *Scènes pittoresques; Le Cid*, etc. **

Paul Tortelier fails to make much of the busy but uninspired *Allegro appassionato* but is more persuasive in the famous portrayal of *Le cygne*, which has a harp accompaniment. Yan Pascal Tortelier plays with charm in the *Caprice* and catches the salon element in the music without vulgarizing it. He also plays with pleasing simplicity in the *Prélude* to the oratorio, *Le Déluge*, which has a concertante part for solo violin. The *Wedding-Cake Caprice* is also nicely done, even though Maria de la Pau does not reveal a strong musical personality. However, the drawback to this collection, as with the Massenet couplings, is the very resonant sound, which is far from ideal for this music.

(i) Cello Concertos 1; 2; (ii) Cello Sonata 1; Le Cygne
*** Quartz QTZ 3029. Walton, with (i) Philh. O, Briger; (ii) Grimwood

Shrewdly, the talented young British cellist, Jamie Walton, offers a coupling of Saint-Saëns cello works that is near ideal, vying with the outstanding series of Saint-Saëns cello pieces from Steven Isserlis on RCA (82876 65845-2 – see our main volume), both of the *Cello Concertos* and the first of the *Cello Sonatas*, with the most popular of all Saint-Saëns's works, *Le Cygne*, for bonus. It says much for Walton that in every way his readings stand the closest comparison with those of Isserlis, both in expressive imagination and in virtuosity. Helped by rather fuller recording, the Walton performances are even a shade warmer than those of Isserlis, notably in slow movements, and though the cello is balanced well forward the playing of the Philharmonia under Alex Briger has an impact to enhance Walton's playing, as at the sharply rhythmic opening of the *Concerto 2*. That work may not have the attractions of the more popular No. 1, largely because the thematic material is not so memorable, but it remains a powerful piece. The disc also reminds us of the comparable power of the *First Cello Sonata* from the striking, vigorous opening onwards, in every way a work of comparable stature. Daniel Grimwood proves an excellent partner for Walton.

Cello Concerto 1 in A min., Op. 33

(M) ** EMI 5 67593-2 [567594]. Rostropovich, LPO, Giulini – DVORAK: *Cello Concerto* *(*)

(BB) ** Warner Apex (ADD) 2564 60709-2. Navarra, LOP, Munch – LALO: *Cello Concerto* **

(i) *Cello Concerto 1; Suite, Op. 16;* (ii) *Allegro appassionato, Op. 43; Carnival of the Animals: The Swan's Romance 1 in F; Cello Sonata 1*

** DG (IMS) 457 599-2. Maisky, (i) Orpheus CO; (ii) Hovora

Rostropovich's 1977 recording serves as a pairing for the Dvořák concerto and is more successful than its coupling, though not as successful as his earlier version (currently withdrawn). There is less rhetorical intensity here than in the Dvořák, and the performance is warmly and atmospherically recorded, with an impresssive CD transfer.

Mischa Maisky plays with great virtuosity and brings splendid vitality as well as brilliance to the quicker movements of the *A minor concerto*. But for all his virtuosity and beauty of tone, expressive exaggeration is not alien to his nature and he is prone to emote heavily at the slightest pretext. Of course he makes a glorious sound, and the Orpheus Chamber Orchestra play with splendid attack. One longs for the finesse and understatement of a Fournier.

As in the Lalo coupling, Navarra is too forwardly balanced, sometimes masking the orchestral detail, which is a pity as the playing of the Lamoureux Orchestra is lively and characterful. However, at bargain price, this CD is worth considering as the overall effect is enjoyable.

Piano Concerto 2 in G min., Op. 22

☞ (M) *** EMI (ADD) 3 45819-2 [3 45820-2]. Gilels, Paris Conservatoire O, Cluytens – RACHMANINOV: *Piano Concerto 3*; SHOSTAKOVICH: *Preludes & Fugues* ***

(M) ** Chan. 6621 (2). Margalit, LSO, Thompson (with MENDELSSOHN: *Capriccio brillant* **) – BRAHMS: *Concerto 1*; SCHUMANN: *Concerto* **

With Gilels, Saint-Saëns's most popular piano concerto becomes a bigger, more commanding work than usual. The opening movement is remarkably serious, with genuine depth of feeling to balance the sparkling Scherzo and even more dazzling finale. Cluytens is a splendid partner, investing the orchestral accompaniment with both gravitas and bravura as needed, and the 1954 recording sounds remarkably good in this new transfer. This account is utterly different from Rubinstein's, yet many will find it even more rewarding. A truly 'Great Recording of the Century'.

Israela Margalit's version of the concerto has no want of abandon, but it lacks the aristocratic distinction that Rubinstein brings to it. The recording is resonant, but the piano is rather forward in the aural picture. The two-CD format does not enhance the attractions of this reissue.

(i) *Violin Concerto 3; Havanaise, Op. 83; Introduction & Rondo capriccioso, Op. 28;* (ii) *Le Déluge: Prelude*

(BB) ** EMI 585699-2. Dumay, Monte Carlo PO; with (i) Yazaki; (ii) Rosenthal (with FAURE: *Berceuse*; LALO: *Symphonie espagnole: Intermezzo* **)

The characteristic Monte Carlo acoustic isn't always ideal, and on EMI the soloist is placed a bit too far forward. But these straightforward, idiomatic accounts of works for violin and orchestra (recorded in 1983) with admirable pacing and plenty of life are all enjoyable, even if some other versions of this much-recorded repertoire offer even greater polish. The three short items conducted by Rosenthal don't have quite the same level of tension as the rest of the programme, but it is good that the comparatively rare *Prelude* to *Le Déluge*, with its violin obbligato, is included.

Javotte (ballet; complete); *Parysatis* (ballet; introduction & 3 scenes)

** Marco Polo 8.223612. Queensland O, Mogrelia

It is a pity that Saint-Saëns didn't write more ballet music outside his operas – his natural gift for melody and colour suits the medium perfectly. *Javotte* (1896) seems to be his only full-length ballet and one can find out very little about its history – nothing is mentioned in the booklet, although a detailed synopsis is provided. The rustic story, in the manner of *La Fille mal gardée*, provides plenty of opportunity for Saint-Saëns to prove that at the end of his career he had lost none of his ability to write witty and tuneful music, all of it charmingly orchestrated. Curiously, the composer regarded this work as 'the *post scriptum* to my musical career', though in the event it proved nothing like it. The eight-minute *Parysatis* suite, incidental music for the play first performed in 1902, shows the composer in exotic mode, reflecting both the romantic nature both of the story and of the country, Egypt, where the music was mainly written (during 1901). Excellent performances, though the recording is pretty average: the strings lack glow, with Saint-Saëns's colours slightly muted by the sound in general.

Symphony 3 in C min., Op. 78

(M) *** Decca 475 7728. (i) Hurford, Montreal SO, Dutoit (with POULENC: *Organ Concerto* ***)

(*) Testament mono SBT 1240. Roget, Paris Conservatoire O, Cluytens – FAURE: *Requiem* (*)

Dutoit brings to the symphony his usual gifts of freshness and a natural sympathy for Saint-Saëns's attractive score. There is a ready spontaneity here. The recording is very bright, with luminous strings given a thrilling brilliance above the stave, perhaps a shade too much at times, but there is a balancing weight, and the reading effectively combines lyricism with passion. In the finale Hurford's entry in the famous chorale melody is more pointed, less massive than usual, although Dutoit generates a genial feeling of gusto to compensate. With its wide range and bright lighting, this is a performance to leave one tingling after Dutoit's final burst of adrenalin. The Poulenc *Organ Concerto*, now offered as coupling for the Originals reissue, also sounds very convincing in Peter Hurford's hands, but independently would not be a first choice.

André Cluytens recorded Saint-Saëns's *Third Symphony* at the Salle de la Mutualité in 1955 – and, of course, in mono. Cluytens gives a generally well-paced and finely conceived account of it, although the playing of the Paris Conservatoire Orchestra falls short of distinction.

Piano Trios 1 in F, Op. 18; 2 in E min., Op. 92

☞ *** Hyp. CDA 67538. Florestan Trio

These are such captivating performances that they must take preference even over those listed in our main volume. They radiate a vital intelligence that shows both scores to best effect. All three players are superb, and Susan Tomes's pianism is particularly rewarding and virtuosic. The Hyperion recording serves them excellently.

ORGAN MUSIC

Bénédiction nuptial, Op. 9; Cyprès et Lauriers, Op. 156;
Élévation, ou Communion, Op. 13; Fantaisies 1–3; 7
Improvisations; Marche religieuse, Op. 107; Offertoire in E;
O salutaris hostia; 9 Pièces for Organ or Harmonium;
Prédication aux oiseaux; Préludes in C, C min. & F; 6
Préludes & Fugues, Opp. 99 & 109; 3 Rhapsodies (on Breton
folksongs), Op. 7; Thème, Variations et Choral de Dies irae
(BB) *** Arte Nova 74321 35088-2 (4). Bleichen (organ of
Church of St Johann, Schaffhausen)

We already have an outstanding SACD of some of Saint-
Saëns's organ music on Capriccio, but if you want everything
he wrote, then this Arte Nova set will do nicely. Stefan
Bleichen has a fine organ at his disposal and he plays this
music, all of it attractive and much admired in its day, very
persuasively. The *Preludes and Fugues* are very diverse, and
the *Theme, Variations and Choral on the Dies irae*, which the
composer never finished, is worthy of Liszt; and it is Liszt's
music which inspired the *Prédication aux oiseaux de St
François d'Assise*. Fine recording, but not as spectacular as the
Capriccio disc (SACD 71 046).

SAINTE-COLOMBE (died c. 1700)

*Concerts for 2 Bass Violas da gamba: III (Le Tendre); VIII
(La Conférence); XLII (Dalain); LI (La Rougeville); LXVII
(Le Figure)*
**(*) Naïve Astrée ES 9933. Savall, W. Kuijken

*Concerts: Excerpts: Le Changé; La Conférence (complete);
Les Couplets; Le Varié; La Raporté; Le Retrouvé: Gigue
caprice. Les Majestueux; La Précipité; Tombeau: Les Regrets;
Le Varié*
**(*) DHM/BMG 05472 77373-2. Perl, Duftschmidt, Santana,
Lawrence-King

The notes with the Astrée CD describe Saint-Colombe's
music as 'strange, somehow distant and aloof, grave and
erudite, impossible to relate either to a particular school or a
specific type of composition'. It is certainly austere and
uncompromising, but if you want to hear it without frills
then the combination of Jordi Savall and Wieland Kuijken is
as authentic and responsive as you will get, and they are
recorded vividly.
But this is not music which is easy to come to terms with,
so Hille Perl and Lorenz Duftschmidt, also excellent gamba
players, have added a continuo to some of the pieces, often
writing the necessary bass lines. Certainly this is easier listening; but both collections need perseverance for the music to
communicate, unless you are a viola da gamba addict.

SALIERI, Antonio (1750–1825)

*Overtures: L'Angiolina, ossia Il matrimonio per sussurro;
Armida; Axur, re d'Ormus; Cesare in Farmacusa (Tempesta
di mare); Les Danaïdes; Don Chisciotte alle nozze di
Gamace; Eraclito e Democrito; La grotta di Trofonio; Il
moro; Il ricco d'un giorno; La secchia rapita; Il talismano*
(**) Marco Polo 8.223381. Czech-Slovak RSO (Bratislava),
Dittrich

In his day Salieri was a highly successful opera composer in
both Vienna and Paris, and this collection of overtures covers
his output from the one-act opera-ballet *Don Chisciotte* of

1770 to *L'Angiolina, ossia Il matrimonio per sussurro* of 1800, of
which a complete recording exists. The overtures are often
dramatic, *Armida* and *Les Danaïdes* especially so, while *La
grotta di Trofonio* begins by depicting the magician's cave
where the two male heroes are put under a spell to interchange
their characters, much to the annoyance of their prospective
brides. *Cesare in Farmacusa* is entirely taken up by the standard opening storm sequence. Elsewhere there is plenty of
bustle and vigour, and some agreeable lyrical ideas, but also
much that is conventional. The performances are lively and
well played but not distinctive, and the recording is more than
acceptable. But this cannot match the Chandos collection and
would have been more attractive as a budget Naxos issue.

SAMMARTINI, Giuseppe
(c. 1693–1750)

Concerti grossi 6 & 8; (i) Recorder Concerto in F
(B) *** HM Musique d'Abord HMA 1951245. (i) Steinmann;
Ens. 415, Banchini – Giovanni SAMMARTINI: *Sinfonias*
***

Giuseppe Sammartini was celebrated in his time as an oboist
and so, not surprisingly, his little *Recorder Concerto* with its
Siciliano centrepiece has much charm. His loyalty to the
Corelli-styled concerto grosso was encouraged by his moving
to London, where he became a chamber musician to the
Prince of Wales, and the manuscripts of these two attractively
inventive examples (both of which have Handelian style
fugues, and end with *galant* Minuets) were found in the
British Library in London. Performances here could hardly be
bettered and, with the programme laid out to intersperse
works by each composer in turn, this is a most rewarding disc.

SAMMARTINI, Giovanni Battista
(1700–1775)

Sinfonias in D & G; String Quintet 3 in G
(B) *** HM Musique d'Abord HMA 1951245. Ens. 415,
Banchini – Giuseppe SAMMARTINI: *Concertos* ***

A most attractive and well-planned disc to introduce the
listener virtually simultaneously to the music of the two
brothers Sammartini, born in Milan scarcely five years apart,
whose musical output and style went in different directions.
Giovanni Battista was essentially a composer of string sinfonias – 67 of them exist. Here are two, both unambitious but
spontaneously full of life, the *D major* in the usual three-
movement Italian style, the *G major* with an added Minuet
(though not perhaps part of the composer's original score).
The *String Quintet* is (obviously) a more mature piece and
has much greater depth. In fact, it is altogether finer music,
Excellent performances and recording.

SARMANTO, Heikki (born 1939)

*'Meet the Composer': (i; ii) Kalevala Fantasy: Return to Life;
(iii) Max and the Enchantress; Sea of Balloons; (iv; v; ii)
Suomi (A Symphonic Jazz Poem for Orchestra); (iii; vi) The
Traveller: Northern Atmosphere. (Instrumental): (iv; vii)
Distant Dreams: Tender Wind. Pan Fantasy: The Awakening;*

In the Night. (Vocal) (viii) *Carrousel;* (ix) *Light of Love;* (x)
New England Images; (xi; iii) *New Hope Jazz Mass: Have
Mercy on Us.* (x) *Northern Pictures*

(B) ** Finlandia 0630 19809-2 (2). (i) UMO Jazz O; (ii) dir.
composer; (iii) Heikki Sarmanto Ens.; (iv) with Aaltonen;
(v) with O; (vi) with Pantir, Rainey; (vii) composer
(keyboards); (viii) Merrill, Tapiola Sinf., Zito; (ix) Parks,
McKelton, Opera Ebony, Haatanen; (ix; x) Sarmanto Jazz
Ens.; (x) Finnish Chamber Ch., Eric-Olof Söderström; (xi)
Hapuoja, Gregg Smith Vocal Qt, Long Island Symphonic
Choral Assoc., Smith

Heikki Sarmanto firmly 'eludes all attempts at categorization,'
writes Antti Suvanto in his notes for this set. Sarmanto was a
theory pupil of Joonas Kokkonen, and he went on to further
studies in the United States. The main influence on the music
that represents him here is Duke Ellington, though few of the
pieces here rival his model. He is accomplished and inventive,
though the choral pieces really do strike us as having more
facility than taste. There is some good playing from the
various artists involved, and Sarmanto is obviously a skilled
as well as a prolific musician. On the whole, however, his
music strikes us as deeply unappealing.

SATIE, Erik (1866–1925)

Erik Satie was born of a Scottish mother and a French father
who was himself a composer of musical inconsequentia. He
later set up a sheet-music emporium with his second wife,
another composer of salon music, and it was she who
ensured that her stepson entered the Paris Conservatoire,
where his teachers formed a very low opinion of his musical
dedication! But the young musician was soon composing
light music in his own right, the first really individual piece of
which was the *Valse ballet* of 1885. His unconventional style
and the bizarre titling of his works did not endear him to his
potential public, and as a result it was well into the twentieth
century before his special, quirky style began to be celebrated
and his music published. Meanwhile he made a living as a
cabaret pianist. It was the *First Gymnopédie* that (understandably) established his reputation as a composer and in 1896 it
was orchestrated, together with No. 3, by Debussy. It slowly
became obvious that, underneath the surface whimsy, in
much of his writing there was a subtle richness of poetic
melancholy that is altogether unique. But he remained
throughout his life a true eccentric. When he died (of alcohol
poisoning) his cellar revealed remnants of his numerous
collections of trivia, among them many of the hundred
umbrellas he owned (he was obsessed with rain), over 80
handkerchiefs, and a dozen, identical, grey suits.

Gymnopédies 1 & 3 (orch. Debussy); *Relâche* (Ballet);
Parade (Ballet); *Gnossienne 3* (orch. Poulenc); *La belle
excentrique;* 5 Grimaces pour le songe d'une nuit d'été* (orch.
Milhaud)

(BB) **(*) EMI Encore 3 41444-2. Toulouse Capitole O,
Plasson

Plasson gets sensitive and lively performances from the Toulouse orchestra, though in *Parade* they do not have quite the
same circus spirit and abandon as did the LSO for Dorati in
the 1960s. However, few collectors will quarrel with these
performances at this modest cost, and the music has much
gamin-like charm. Moreover, this is better than many recent
recordings from the Salle-aux-Grains in Toulouse; detail is
more transparent and the textures somewhat better observed.

PIANO MUSIC

*Avant-dernières pensées; Chapitres tournés en tous sens;
Gnossiennes 1–5; 5 Grimaces; 3 Gymnopédies; Je te veux
(Valse); Nocturnes 1, 3 & 5; Passacaglia; Pièces froides (Airs à
faire fuir 1–3); Le piège de Méduse; Ragtime Parade; Rêverie
du pauvre; Sonatine Bureaucratique; Sports et
divertissements; Valse-ballet*

(BB) *** Regis (ADD) RRC 1327 McCabe

This attractive and generous (77 minutes) anthology draws
on a pair of Saga records which have been much praised by us
over the years. John McCabe has the full measure of Satie's
understated melancholy and lyrical nostalgia, and he also has
insights of his own to offer. His style might be described as
gently cool: the three *Gymnopédies*, for instance, are played a
little slower than usual, and the *Gnossiennes* are very delicately evoked. His programme ranges from the simple,
almost Chopinesque *Valse-ballet*, Satie's first published piano
piece, to the three *Nocturnes* of 1919–20, which are exquisitely
played. The hauntingly simple valse, *Je te veux*, the quietly
nostalgic elegy of the *Rêveries du pauvre*, and the two sets of
miniatures, *Le Piège de Méduse* and *Avant-dernières pensées*,
are particularly memorable here, while the *Cinq Grimaces*
end the recital with robust geniality. The *Ragtime Parade* is a
transcription from his ballet *Parade*, in which his collabora-
tors were none other than Diaghilev, Massine and Picasso,
but its style is not unlike Gottschalk. The intelligent planning
of this recital and the penetrating response of the pianism
place this inexpensive CD among the most desirable Satie
collections, and the recording, though not vividly present like
the HMV Queffélec disc below, is natural and intimate,
within a highly appropriate ambience.

(i) *Chapitres tournés en tous sens; Croquis et agaceries d'un
gros bonhomme en bois; Le fils des étoiles (Act II Prélude);
Gnossiennes 2 & 4; 3 Gymnopédies; Heures séculaires et
instantanées; Nocturnes 2 & 4; Nouvelles pièces froides; Piège
de Méduse; Passacaille; Sonata bureaucratique;* (ii) *Embryons
desséchés; Fantaisie et divertissements 11, 13 & 15–21;
Gnossiennes 1 & 3; Je te veux; Le Piccadilly (La
Transatlantique); Valse-ballet*

(B) ** CfP (ADD/DDD) 575 147-2. (i) Lawson; (ii) Brownridge

This Classics for Pleasure CD draws on two LPs, Peter Lawson's from 1979 (all of it included) and around half of Angela
Brownridge's compilation from 1985 (digital). Lawson's
recital opens with the famous *Gymnopédies*, played coolly but
not ineffectively. The highlight is a perceptive and articulate
characterization of *Le piège de Médusa* – seven epigrammatic
morceaux de concert. Elsewhere his account is quietly tasteful,
and though he catches something of Satie's gentle and wayward poetry, he is less successful in revealing the underlying
sense of fantasy. Angela Brownridge's playing is bright and
stylish, sensitively reflecting the sharply changing moods and
lacking only the last touch of poetry.

*Descriptions automatiques; Embryons desséchés;
Gnossiennes; 3 Gymnopédies*

(BB) *** HMV 5 86761-2. Queffélec – DEBUSSY: *Piano music*
***

Anne Queffélec is exceptionally well served by the engineers,
who produce as good a piano-sound as almost any to have
appeared on CD: it is firm, fresh and clean, with a splendid
tonal bloom. Their dedication is not misplaced, for her
playing has great tonal subtlety and character. Nor does she

possess less charm than Pascal Rogé. The famous *Gymnopédies* and *Gnossiennes* are predictably seductive, but the three *Embryons desséchés* are also very compelling, particularly the centrepiece, *d'Edriophthalma*. About them Satie wrote, 'This work is absolutely incomprehensible, even to me. Of singular profundity, it never ceases to astonish me. I wrote it despite myself, driven by fate.'

Embryons desséchés; 6 Gnossiennes; 3 Gymnopédies; Je te veux; Nocturne 4; Le Piccadilly; 4 Préludes flasques; Prélude et tapisserie; Sonatine bureaucratique; Vieux sequins et vieilles cuirasses
(M) *** Decca 475 7527. Rogé

Pascal Rogé gave Satie his compact disc debut with this fine recital which is splendidly caught by the microphones. So this is a perfect candidate for Decca's series of Originals. Rogé has a real feeling for this repertoire and he conveys its bittersweet quality and its grave melancholy as well as he does its lighter qualities. He produces, as usual, consistent beauty of tone, and this is well projected by the recording. The disc appears at medium price for the first time.

SCARLATTI, Alessandro (1660–1725)

Missa ad Usum Cappellae Pontificiae. Motets: *Ad te Domine levavi; Domine vivifica me; Exaltabo te Domine quoniam; Exultate Deo adjutori; Intloige clamorem meum; Salvum fac populum tuum*
(BB) ** Warner Apex (ADD) 2564 60522-2. Ens. Vocal de Lausanne, Corboz

An acceptable rather than an outstanding collection, rare though it is. All the works here are *a cappella* and for four voices. The Mass is comparatively austere, but the motet settings are varied and attractive. However, while the choral intonation is true, the style of the singing with its noticeable vibrato seems out of character, in the Mass especially.

Stabat Mater
** ATMA ACD2 2237. Kirkby, Taylor; (ii) Colpron; Theatre of Early Music

Emma Kirkby does not often disappoint, and her fresh voice blends well with the alto of Daniel Taylor. But their performance of the *Stabat Mater* fails to move the listener as it should. The *Flute Concerto* (played on the recorder) offered as a meagre coupling is pleasing enough, and is most notable for its *Veloce* central movement, which takes just 12 seconds!

SCARLATTI, Domenico (1685–1757)

Keyboard Sonatas, Kk.10, 46, 54, 69–70, 105, 119, 126, 201, 203, 212, 261, 444, 447, 525, 537
(BB) ** Naxos 8. 555047. Jandó (piano)

Jenö Jandó's Scarlatti style is brisk, crisp and clean. His articulation at times offers remarkable bravura (witness Kk.10 in D minor or Kk.212 in A major). The E minor Kk.203 and G major Kk.105 are certainly characterful, while the C minor Kk.126 has an appropriate pensive quality. Yet other performers find more diversity of colour and delicacy of feeling in this music. He is very well recorded.

Keyboard Sonatas, Kk. 11, 27, 159 & 322
*** Opus Arte DVD OA 0939D. Michelangeli – BEETHOVEN: *Piano Sonatas 3 & 32*; GALUPPI: *Sonata* ***

Recorded at a recital in Turin in 1962, these are a model of delicacy and refinement. Michelangeli always played Scarlatti with a special distinction that only Horowitz and Pletnev have matched in recent times. Very good sound.

Keyboard Sonatas, Kk.69, 108, 126, 202, 206, 278, 384, 402–403, 406, 434, 450, 518–19
** MDG 340 1162-2. Zacharias (piano)

Christian Zacharias plays Scarlatti with expressive elegance, but he uses rather a lot of pedal and the rich sonority he provides often makes the music sound out of period, indeed at times more like Mozart.

Keyboard Sonatas, Kk.115–16, 144, 175, 402–3, 449–50, 474–5, 513, 516–17, 544–5
(M) **(*) Decca 475 7729. Schiff (piano)

Exquisite and sensitive playing, full of colour and delicacy. As always, András Schiff is highly responsive to the mood and character of each piece. At times one wonders whether he is not a little too refined: in some pieces, one would have welcomed more abandon and fire. However, for the most part this is a delightful recital, and the Decca recording is exemplary in its truthfulness. This now returns to the catalogue at mid-price as one of Decca's Originals.

Salve Regina
*** Analekta FL 2 3171. Lemieux, Tafelmusik, Lamon (with AVISON: *Concerto grosso after Scarlatti 7*) – VIVALDI: *Stabat Mater, etc.* ***

Domenico Scarlatti's beautiful setting of the *Salve Regina* is gloriously sung here and is paired with an equally fine performance of Vivaldi's *Stabat Mater*, plus some attractive Vivaldi string concertos to make up a balanced concert. The performances by Tafelmusik are second to none, and the inclusion of one of Avison's concertos transcribed from Scarlatti sonatas seems rather appropriate.

SCHILLINGS, Max von (1868–1933)

(i) *Violin Concerto, Op. 23. King Oedipus* (tone-poem), *Op. 11; Moloch: Harvest Festival Scene*
*** Marco Polo 8.223324. (i) Rozsa; Czecho-Slovak RSO (Košice), Walter

Max von Schillings' *Violin Concerto* is a beautifully crafted and highly accomplished score in the post-Romantic style. Although it reveals no strong individuality, it has a certain rhetorical command and lyrical warmth to commend it, and its masterly handling of the orchestra will make a strong appeal to those with a taste for turn-of-the-century music. The eloquent soloist plays marvellously and inspires the Košice Orchestra under Alfred Walter to great heights. Neither the excerpt from the opera *Moloch* (1906) nor the *Symphonic Prologue to the Oedipus Tyrannus of Sophocles* (1900) makes anywhere near as strong an impression. The Marco Polo recording is very well detailed and has plenty of warmth and presence.

SCHMELZER, Johann (c. 1620–80)

Lament on the Death of Ferdinand III (a tre); Sonata a tre (Lamentation); Sonata (Lanterly a tre) Sonata IX
(B) *** HM Musique d'Abord HMA 1951220, L. Bar., Medlam – MUFFAT: *Sonatas* ***

Johann Schmelzer, whom we know best for his ballet and sacred music, turns out to be also an adept composer of chamber music, often of a touchingly melancholy disposition. The two *Laments*, one written for the king, one as part of a *Sonata a tre* (actually in four parts) are both in the form of a funeral oration, and both have a descriptive passage (named in the Royal elegy as *Die Todtenglockh* – 'Death Bells'). The *Sonata for three violins* is a most attractive work, a genuine trio of equals in four elegant movements. The *'Lanterly' Sonata* features florid variations on an engaging folksong, and all the works have passages of real bravura to alternate with the fine, expressive writing. The performances and recording are first class (no scratchiness) and this collection is unexpectedly enjoyable.

SCHMIDT, Franz (1874–1939)

(i) *Quintet in B flat for Clarinet, Piano & Strings;* (ii) *3 Fantasy Pieces on Hungarian National Melodies.* (Piano) *Romance in A; Toccata in D min.*
** Marco Polo 8.223415. Ruso, with (i) Janoska, Török, Lakatos; (i; ii) Slávik

The *Quintet*, like so much of Schmidt's music with piano, was composed with the left-handed pianist Paul Wittgenstein (brother of the philosopher) in mind. The piano part was subsequently rearranged for two hands by Friedrich Wührer. Its character is predominantly elegiac; it was composed after the death of Schmidt's daughter and can best be described as having something of the autumnal feeling of late Brahms, the subtlety of Reger and the dignity and nobility of Elgar or Suk. The players sound pretty tentative at the very start but soon settle down, though their tempo could with advantage have been slower. All the same it is a thoroughly sympathetic, recommendable account. The *Drei Phantasiestücke* and the two piano pieces, the *Romance* and the *D minor Toccata*, are earlier and less interesting, though they are well enough played.

SCHMITT, Florent (1870–1958)

La tragédie de Salomé (ballet): Suite. (i) *Psalm 47, Op. 38*
(BB) *** Warner Apex 2564 62764-2. (i) Sweet, Fr. R. Ch.; Gill, Fr. R. Philh. O, Janowski

Perhaps Schmitt's best-known work is his colourful and atmospheric ballet, *La tragédie de Salomé,* composed in 1907, two years after Strauss's opera on the same theme. Martinon recorded it in 1973, and more recently Davin and the Rheinland-Pfalz Philharmonic Orchestra have recorded the complete score (on Marco Polo 8223448 – see our main volume). The score, like Dukas's *La Péri*, is full of Art Nouveau exoticism and heady atmosphere. Schmitt's setting of *Psalm 47* dates from his last year as a Prix de Rome scholar at the Villa Medici, and is a stirring and imposing piece which contrasts two aspects of the great books of exaltation and jubilation: the tenderness and voluptuousness of the *Song of Songs*. Good performances from the Orchestre Philharmonique de Radio France under Marek Janowski which are eminently recommendable at Apex price – save for Sharon Sweet's wide and ugly vibrato.

SCHOENBERG, Arnold (1874–1951)

5 Orchestral Pieces
*** Ideale-Audience **DVD** 3. Netherlands R. PO, Gielen –
    STRAVINSKY: *'The Final Chorale'* – a documentary about the *Symphony of Wind Instruments* ***

This is a most illuminating feature by Frank Scheffer that follows the genesis and musical development of the *Five Orchestral Pieces* of Schoenberg. Michael Gielen rehearses and performs this revolutionary piece, and there are contributions from Carl Schorske and Charles Rosen, as well as some archival footage. There is nothing dumbed-down here: it is real Third Programme stuff, and it pays the viewer the compliment of assuming he or she is reasonably knowledgeable. A fascinating study (available from www.ideale-audience.dot.com.) that will deepen your understanding of this strange and disturbing music.

(i) *Suite in G for String Orchestra;* (ii) *String Quartet 2, Op. 10;* (iii) *6 A cappella Mixed Choruses*
(BB) *** Naxos 8.557521. (i) Twentieth Century Classics Ens.; (ii) Fred Sherry Qt, with Welch-Babbage; (iii) Simon Joly Singers; Craft

Schoenberg famously said that there is plenty of music still to be written in C major, and here in his six *A cappella Choruses* he deliberately relaxes in setting sixteenth-century German folksongs, harmonizing them in his own distinctive way. Three were written in 1948, not long before he died, following up the three he had composed 20 years earlier, all superbly sung here by the Simon Joly Singers. The *String Quartet No. 2* is distinctive in having a vocal part in the last two of the four movements, with Jennifer Welch-Babbage ideally cast, her fresh, clear soprano as precise as any instrument. The texts of the poems by Stefan George are provided, as are the words for the six *A cappella Choruses*. The *Suite in G* of 1934, less demanding, makes an apt coupling. The vocal pieces were recorded in London, the instrumental in New York, both in superb sound.

Verklaerte Nacht
(BB) *** Virgin 2x1 4 82112-2 (2). Sinfonia Varsovia, Y. Menuhin – MOZART: *Divertimento 1*, etc.; WAGNER: *Siegfried Idyll*; WOLF: *Italian Serenade* ***

In a passionately volatile performance, Menuhin encompasses the changing moods of Schoenberg's masterpiece with wonderful spontaneity and ardour. The fourth section, *Sehr breit und langsam*, is particularly eloquent, but the closing *Sehr ruhig* is also deeply felt, with superbly responsive playing from members of the Sinfonia Varsovia, and the work closes in a mood of gently sensuous nostalgia. Textures are rich yet they never clot, a tribute to the unnamed Virgin balance engineer.

VOCAL MUSIC

Erwartung
*** Decca 417 348-2 (2). Waechter, Silja, Laubenthal, Jahn, Malta, Sramek, VPO, Dohnányi – BERG: *Wozzeck* ***

Schoenberg's searingly intense monodrama makes an apt coupling for Dohnányi's excellent version of Berg's *Wozzeck*; it has now been reissued in Universal's 'Critics' Choice' series. As in the Berg, Silja is at her most passionately committed, and the digital sound is exceptionally vivid.

(i) *Erwartung, Op. 17;* (ii) Cabaret Songs: *Arie aus dem Spiegel von Arkadien; Einfältiges Lied; Galathea; Der genügsame Liebhaber; Gigerlette; Jeden das Seine; Mahnung; Nachtwandler* (with trumpet, piccolo & snare drum)

(B) *** Ph. 475 6395. Norman, with (i) Met. Op. O, Levine; (ii) Levine (piano) – STRAVINSKY: *Oedipus Rex* **

The monodrama, *Erwartung* ('Expectation') may not be among the most appealing of Schoenberg's formidable oeuvre, but Jessye Norman and James Levine present it on this 1993 Philips CD recording in a way which could win it new friends. She herself has said that *Erwartung* is 'technically the most difficult thing [she] has ever sung', but that, having learned it, she found it 'immensely singable'. That clearly accounts for the warmth, intensity, range of expression and sheer beauty that she and Levine bring to this score. Levine draws ravishing sounds from the Metropolitan Opera Orchestra; Norman's singing, beautiful and totally secure over the widest range of expression and dynamic, is also a revelation. The impact of *Erwartung* is heightened by the total contrast of the *Cabaret Songs*. Accompanied by Levine on the piano – a sparkily individual partner – Norman sings all eight of the *Cabaret Songs* that Schoenberg wrote when he was in Berlin. In these witty, pointed, tuneful numbers, Schoenberg was letting his hair down in a way that must be surprising to his detractors. These are art songs that yet completely belong to the half-world of cabaret, and Norman projects her personality as masterfully as a latter-day Marlene Dietrich. Texts and translations are included.

(i) *Erwartung;* (ii) *Pierrot lunaire, Op. 21*

(M) ** Warner Elatus 0927 49017-2. (i) Castellani, Lucchesini, members of Dresden State O; (ii) Marc; Dresden State O, Sinopoli

Sinopoli, a sympathetically persuasive interpreter of Schoenberg who brings out any underlying romanticism, offers an apt coupling not otherwise available – but the results are flawed. The live recording of *Erwartung* has Alessandra Marc as a warm-toned soloist with a rich chest register, who sings well, but conveys little of the horror behind this monodrama. Luisa Castellani in *Pierrot lunaire* is intimately confidential in her sing-speech recitations, but too often is masked by the instruments, which are balanced too far forward.

Gurrelieder

(M) *** Ph. 475 7782 (2). McCracken, Norman, Troyanos, Tanglewood Festival Ch., Boston SO, Ozawa

Ozawa's gloriously opulent live performance of *Gurrelieder*, with a ravishing contribution from Jessye Norman, which won the *Gramophone* Choral Award in 1979, now returns to the catalogue as one of Philips's Originals, with text and translation included.

SCHOENFIELD, Paul (born 1947)

Piano Concerto (Four Parables)

** Athene CD 21. Boyde, Dresden SO, Nott – DVORAK: *Piano Concerto* **

The American composer Paul Schoenfield is now in his fifties and has made few inroads into the concert hall outside the USA. This CD is of the 1998 European première of his *Piano Concerto (Four Parables)*, which draws on a variety of styles – popular music, vernacular and folk traditions and 'the normal historical traditions of cultivated music often treated

with sly twists'. It has some degree of flair, but from the multiplicity of styles no distinctive personality emerges. Very brilliant playing from the talented Andreas Boyde but this is not music which arouses enthusiasm.

SCHREKER, Franz (1878–1934)

Die Gezeichneten (opera): complete

(M) *(*) Orfeo C584 0222. Adam, Martin, Becht, Riegel, Meven, Moser, ORF & Arnold Schoenberg Ch., V. RSO, Albrecht

Schreker's sumptuously scored *Die Gezeichneten* ('The Branded' or 'The Marked One') is a blend of post-Straussian luxuriance and exoticism, with more than a dash of Puccini, Korngold, Scriabin and Szymanowski. Its colours and textures intoxicated its first audiences in 1918 and they still sound pretty dazzling. The Orfeo set is an Austrian Radio relay from the 1984 Salzburg Festival. Its strong points are the Alviano of Kenneth Riegel and the Duke Adorno of Theo Adam, and Gerd Albrecht paces the work expertly and obtains sensitive orchestral playing. The recording is natural, with good perspective and a decent balance. But there are serious drawbacks. First, it is cut: Lothar Zagrosek's deleted Decca set ran to 170 minutes – almost half an hour longer. Secondly, the sound does not match the Decca in terms of detail, transparency and definition. Thirdly, it offers inferior documentation, giving only the German libretto and a cursory English summary; the Decca gave copious notes, and the libretto appeared in four languages.

SCHUBERT, Franz (1797–1828)

(i) *Concerto Movement for Violin and Orchestra in D, D.345;* (i;ii) *5 German Dances; 5 Minuets, D.89;* (i) *Polonaise for Violin and Orchestra in B flat; Rondo for Violin and String Orchestra, D.438;* (iii) *Octet in F, D.803;* (iv) *Violin Sonatinas 1–3, D.384/5 & D.408;* (v) *Violin Sonata in A, D.574;* (iv) *Der Erlkönig* (trans. Ernst); (v) *Fantasia in C, D.934; Rondo in B min., D.895;* (iv) *Valse-Caprice 6* (trans. Liszt); *Variations for Violin and Piano on 'Trockne Blumen'*

(M) ** DG 469 837-2 (4). Kremer, with (i) COE; (ii) Gabrielle & Richard Lester, Poppen; (iii) Keulen, Zimmerman, Geringas, Posch, Brunner, Vlatkovic, Thunemann; (iv) Maisenberg; (v) Afanassiev

This four-CD set collects performances recorded by Gidon Kremer and various other musicians of distinction between 1987 and 1993. Schubert's music here has a complete naturalness of expression, free of either artifice or artificiality. The excellence of these performances is not in question, but there are too many touches of over-sophistication which seem out of place in Schubert's world. Many music-lovers find Kremer a shade self-regarding; others may be bowled over by the sheer quality of sound he produces. The *Octet* sounds a bit too 'all-star' and, while enjoyable, does not convey the sense of effortless geniality that lies at its heart. Of course, there is much fine musicianship and playing of strong personality to be found here, but the interpretative care lavished on the *Sonata* (or *Sonatinas*) tends to overlay the naturalness and innocence of Schubert's inspiration.

Symphonies 1–6; 8 (Unfinished); 9 (Great); 2 Overtures in the Italian Style

(B) **(*) Warner 2564 62323-2 (4). Concg. O, Harnoncourt

Harnoncourt takes a relatively severe view and, significantly, he is at his finest in the darkness of the *Tragic Symphony*. There is little of Schubertian charm here, with his eccentrically slow tempo for the finale of No. 6 in its lumbering gait missing the pure sunlight of the piece which Beecham displayed so well (EMI 5 66984-2, coupled with Nos. 3 and 5). Harnoncourt's preference for short phrasing also tends to make slow movements less songful, though equally it adds to the bite and intensity of other movements, notably Scherzos with their sharp cross-rhythms. However, there is a lighter touch in the *Italian Overtures* and even moments of charm, with the introductions (especially the quote from *Rosamunde*) affectionately done. Though the reverberance of the Amsterdam Concertgebouw obscures detail in tuttis, as well as reinforcing the weight of sound, the recording is warm and otherwise helpful. Harnoncourt, like Abbado, has used specially prepared texts, but they avoid the radical changes that spice the Abbado set (DG 423 651-2).

Symphonies 1; 8 (Unfinished)
(BB) ** EMI Encore 5 87005-2. VPO, Muti

Muti's robust approach is not endearingly Schubertian, even though he has the Vienna Philharmonic at his disposal. With playing relatively routine, despite the conductor's natural electricity and his preference for urgent speeds, there is nothing here to set the blood tingling or charm the ear.

Symphonies 5; 8 (Unfinished); 9 in C (Great)
(M) **(*) DG 477 5167 (6). Concg. O, Bernstein –
MENDELSSOHN: *Symphonies 3–5* **(*); SCHUMANN: *Symphonies*, etc. **

Though in Nos. 5 & 8 there is some inconsistency between Bernstein's brisk and fresh treatment of fast movements and his spacious, moulded style in the two slow movements, these are distinguished performances, beautifully played and recorded, conveying well the tension of live music-making. Apart from the woodwind, which is a little distant, the sound is good. In the *Great C major*, Bernstein's speeds are on the fast side, and it is typical of the superb playing which he draws from the Concertgebouw that the *sempre piano* of the recapitulation has exceptional delicacy. The slow movement is fast and cleanly articulated, the Scherzo is tough rather than charming, and the finale brings exceptionally crisp articulation of triplets. Exposition repeats are omitted in the outer movements, as well as the second repeat in the Scherzo. Full, warm recordings from 1987.

Symphony 8 in B min. (Unfinished), D.759
(M) ** DG (IMS) (ADD) 463 609-2 (2). Chicago SO, Giulini –
MAHLER: *Symphony 9* **
** BBC (ADD) BBCM 5014-2. BBC SO, Sargent (with
MENDELSSOHN: *Midsummer Night's Dream: Nocturne &
Wedding March*) – MOZART: *Clarinet Concerto*, etc. **(*)

There are some very good things in Giulini's deeply felt 1978 reading of the *Unfinished*, with much carefully considered detail. But the Mahler coupling is not a prime recommendation.

Sargent's *Unfinished* is a direct, flowing account, not lacking in drama, with some notably sensitive playing from the BBC Orchestra woodwind in the second movement. Acceptable BBC sound; but the main interest of this record is Gervase de Peyer's fine account of Mozart's *Clarinet Concerto*.

Symphonies 8 (Unfinished); 9 in C (Great)
(M) ** Sony (ADD) SMK 61842. NYPO, Bernstein

Bernstein gives a dramatic account of the *Unfinished*, with a great surge of energy in the first-movement development. Yet there is lyrical warmth too and at times a sense of mystery. The playing of the NYPO is first class and the recording from 1963 is acceptable. The account of the *C major Symphony* is less consistent. There is plenty of vitality, but it lacks the unforced spontaneity which can make this symphony so exhilarating. The finale charges along like a runaway express train, exciting and brilliant, yes, but a bit charmless too.

Symphony 9 in C (Great), D.944
*** EMI 3 39382-2. BPO, Rattle
(M) ** Sup. (ADD) SU 3468-2 011. Czech PO, Konwitschny

When Sir Simon Rattle over the years has regularly conducted orchestras of period instruments, it may come as a surprise that with his own Berlin Philharmonic he takes a relatively free and romantic view of this massive symphony, perhaps reflecting in part the fact that this is a live recording. Not only are his speed on the broad side, he allows marked rallentandos at the ends of sections. His moulding of phrases too seems to reflect the older traditions of this great orchestra rather than those of his predecessor as music director, Herbert von Karajan, who in his 1978 recording for EMI is altogether more severe. One key passage in the symphony comes in the middle of the slow movement where, on repeated phrases in crescendo, Schubert builds up the movement's biggest climax, resolved after a sudden pause on an affectionate cello melody: here Rattle lingers lovingly. What emerges from this relatively relaxed approach is an extra sense of joy in Schubert's inspiration, with rhythms lifted infectiously. Not that the playing lacks bite or precision, far from it, with many counter-motifs brought out that are too often hidden by the main melodies. The recording also has an admirably wide range, down to magical *pianissimos* from the strings.

Konwitschny's *Ninth* dates from 1962. It is a straightforward, simple and warmly relaxed reading, Viennese in feeling. In that, it has a good deal in common with Krips's early Decca version with the VPO, although without the level of concentration that makes that performance so totally compelling; Konwitschny is more easy-going. The first movement's development has a pleasing jaunty progress and the return to the opening theme is deftly managed. The *Andante* is beautifully played (the principal oboe's contribution a highlight). Only the Scherzo, with all repeats included, brings a nagging suggestion of 'heavenly length', and the finale, although not pressed hard, makes an agreeable conclusion. The analogue recording is warm and naturally balanced.

CHAMBER MUSIC

Arpeggione sonata, D.821 (arr. for cello)
(B) **(*) Cal. (ADD) CAL 3614. Navarra, D'Arco – DVOŘÁK: *Humoresque*, etc.; SCHUMANN: *Adagio & Allegro*, etc. **(*)

A warm-hearted, rather old-fashioned performance from Navarra, rather discreetly accompanied by Annie d'Arco. The cello itself is richly caught, the piano truthful but a little backward.

Octet in F, D.803
🎵 *** Onyx ONYX4006. Mullova, Moraguès, Postinghel, Cori, Chamorro, Krüger, M. Fischer-Dieskau, Stall

*** ASV Gold GLD 4005. Nash Ens.

*** Cal. CAL 9314. Octuor de France

(BB) *** EMI Gemini (ADD) 3 50864-2 (2). Melos Ens. of L.
 – BEETHOVEN: *Octet*, etc.; MENDELSSOHN: *Octet* **

This newest version of the *Octet* from Onyx is not only the best since the celebrated 1957 Vienna Octet version on Decca, it actually surpasses it. These artists find a greater depth than their predecessors in a work that we all think we know well. There is not only grace, pathos and tenderness here, but also a thoughtful attention to details of phrasing and internal balance. Tempi are generally on the slow side, but the listener's attention is compelled throughout. Musically, a most satisfying and revealing account – and a moving one too. Very fine recording.

But no single version has a monopoly on interpretation of any work, and the other two new versions are also very fine. The Nash players have insights of their own to offer, with many subtle touches of light and shade, especially in the first movement, which is tauter than usual, but still eminently Schubertian. The performance as a whole is beautifully played and truthfully balanced as a recording.

The French performance is appealing in a different way, warmly relaxed and easier-going than the Nash, but certainly not lacking concentration. Their star player is the luscious toned, seductive clarinettist, Jean-Louis Sajot, who time and again provides a magical solo. But this performance is very enjoyable overall, and is certainly well recorded in a very pleasing acoustic.

Another very fine account comes from the Melos group. Although made in the late 1960s, this is still one of the best versions available, and is especially welcome at budget price. The playing is fresh and spontaneous, yet polished, with excellent ensemble. The recording is splendidly detailed and truthful. It is a pity that the couplings are not caught as sweetly by the engineers.

(i) *Piano Quintet in A (Trout), D.667. Quartettsatz in C min., D.703* (DVD Version)

*** Testament **DVD** SBDVD1001 (i) Clifford Curzon;
 Amadeus Qt – BRITTEN: *String Quartet 2* ***

The performance tele-recorded in Aldeburgh was part of a week-long celebration of Schubert and Britten staged in September 1977. It was recorded by a team that included John Culshaw, previously of Decca but by then Head of Music at BBC Television. It is superbly and simply directed, with totally unobtrusive camerawork and expertly balanced sound, with the legendary Jimmy Burnett in charge. Curzon is wonderfully natural yet patrician in the *Trout Quintet* and the playing throughout gives unalloyed pleasure.

Piano Quintet in A (Trout), D.667 (CD Versions)

(M) **(*) Ph. (ADD) 475 7574. Brendel, Cleveland Qt

(**) Pearl mono GEM 0129. Panhofer, Vienna Octet
 (members) – MOZART: *Divertimento 17* (**)

(M) (**(*)) Bridge mono 9185 Balsam, Budapest Qt, Julius
 Levine – FRANCK: *Piano Quintet in F min.* (**(*))

The Brendel/Cleveland performance, from the late 1970s, may lack something in traditional Viennese charm, but it has a compensating vigour and impetus, and the work's many changes of mood are encompassed with finesse and subtlety. This is now reissued (yet again) in Philips's series of Originals and the recording is well balanced and truthful. But it would have benefited from a coupling, and it can no longer be considered a top choice.

The Record Guide gave the early Decca mono recording on the Pearl disc two stars – in those days the Guide listed only two versions! The *Trout* was reissued on Decca's Ace of Clubs economy label in the early 1960s, by which time Curzon's set with the same artists had supplanted it. Curzon brings greater subtlety and tonal refinement to the piano part, though Panhofer has undeniable sparkle and style. The original sounded wiry and unpleasing (particularly in its ACL format), but Roger Beardsley has gone to great trouble to find a stylus that would do justice to these performances. The sound is far richer and better defined. An affecting reminder of performance style fifty years back and well worth hearing fifty years on!

Artur Balsam's artistry was never fully appreciated in England, though older readers may remember that in the late 1950s the BBC Third Programme invited him to play the six Mozart concertos of 1788 in two programmes; they left no doubt as to his mastery. As Harris Goldsmith says in his notes, 'hearing his masterly phrasing and luminous singing tone is sufficient aural testimony to place Balsam in the highest artistic echelons'. His playing of the Franck *Quintet* has passion and eloquence but is disciplined by classical restraint. However, the 1956 recording calls for some tolerance.

(i) *Piano Quintet in A (Trout). String Quartets 13 in A min., D.804; 14 (Death and the Maiden); 15 in G, D.887;* (ii) *String Quintet in C, D.956*

(M) ** EMI (ADD) 5 66144-2 (4). Alban Berg Qt, with (i)
 Leonskaja, Hörtnagel; (ii) Schiff

The Alban Berg *Trout* (in which the quartet are joined by Elisabeth Leonskaja and Georg Hörtnagel) brings keen disappointment. Despite the excellence of the recording and some incidental beauties, it remains a curiously uninvolving performance with routine gestures. The *A minor Quartet*, however, is beautifully managed, though the slow movement is very fast indeed. The exposition repeat is omitted in the first movement of *Death and the Maiden*, but otherwise this, too, is a very impressive performance. The playing is breathtaking in terms of tonal blend, ensemble and intonation throughout both these works; if one is not always totally involved, there is much to relish and admire. In the *G major* the Alban Berg players are most dramatic. They are strikingly well recorded, and beautifully balanced; but the sense of over-projection somehow disturbs the innocence of some passages. In the great *C major Quintet*, where they are joined by Heinrich Schiff, they produce a timbre which is richly burnished and full-bodied. Once more there is no first-movement exposition repeat, but theirs is still a most satisfying account, strongly projected throughout. The recording is admirable, but as a collection this is a mixed success.

Piano Trios 1–2; Notturno, D.897; Sonata (Trio Movement) in B flat, D.28

🠔 *** MDG 342 1166-2 (*Trio 1*); 342 1167-2 (*Trio 2; Notturno; Sonata*). V. Piano Trio

(M) *** Ph. 475 7571 (2). Beaux Arts Trio

The new set of the *Piano Trios* from the Vienna Piano Trio on MDG is outstanding in every way. Their playing is wonderfully fresh and spring-like, and the contribution of the pianist, Stefan Mendl, is ear-catchingly crisp (sample the opening of the *Andante* or the brilliant finale of the *E flat Trio*). The cellist Matthias Gredler is warmly sensitive, and the violinist Wolfgang Redik soon asserts his authority at climaxes. This is true chamber music-making by a beautifully matched team, dramatic and expressive by turns, with remarkable ongoing spontaneity, yet full of incidental subtleties. The recording is in the demonstration class, perfectly balanced. The two CDs are available separately; the first includes the alternative version of the finale, which Schubert composed first, as an appendix.

The much-praised Beaux Arts performances are an obvious choice for Philips's Originals label. The performances combine impeccable ensemble with simple dedication. However, on their last appearance on a Philips Duo there was a bonus of the two much rarer *String Trios*, D.471 and D.581, beautifully played by the Grumiaux Trio, so readers may feel that they are being short-changed by the current reissue, which offers no extras and is at mid-price.

Piano Trio 1 in B flat
(*) EMI **DVD 4904519. Y. & H. Menuhin, Gendron –
  BARTÓK: *Contrasts*, etc.; ENESCU: *Sonata 3*; FRANCK:
  Violin Sonata in A (***)

Recorded in rather grainy black-and-white at the Bath Festival in 1964, this is still a rewarding account, thanks to the rapport between the players. It serves as a reminder not only of the two Menuhins but of the wonderful artistry of Maurice Gendron. For all the frailty of the sound, this is a thoroughly enjoyable experience.

Piano Trio 2 ; Notturno, D.897
*(*) ECM 453 300-2. Schneeberger, Demenga, Dähler

The fine players on ECM do not help themselves by choosing an all too leisurely tempo in the first movement. They are just a shade ponderous and heavy-handed at times in both pieces, though the actual quality of the recorded sound is more than serviceable.

String quartets
String Quartets 10, D.87; 14 (Death and the Maiden)
** BIS CD 1201. Yggdrasil Qt

The fine Swedish quartet on BIS bring elegance and straightforwardness to these two quartets, but their emotional reticence and want of the depth that *Death and the Maiden* calls for counters the directness of their playing. They are well enough recorded but this is not really very recommendable.

String Quartet 14 in D min. (Death and the Maiden)
*** EMI **DVD** 0946 3 38446 9 2. Alban Berg Qt (with
  documentary by Bruno Monsaigeon)

A very well-thought-out reading of *Death and the Maiden* by the Alban Berg Quartet, recorded in 1995 in the Mozartsaal, Vienna, and played with their usual mastery. Bruno Monsaigeon's documentary is very largely a masterclass by the members of the quartet with the Artemis Quartet. The celebrated Lied on which the slow movement is based is sung by Julia Varady, with her husband, Dietrich Fischer-Dieskau, as pianist.

String Quartet 15, D.887 (arr. Kissine)
**(*) ECM 476 1939. Kremerata Baltica, Kremer

Unlike most orchestral transcriptions of string quartets, this one involves a constant interchange, bar by bar, between the full string ensemble of 25 players and a string quartet, with Kremer joined by the leaders of the relevant sections. The solo quartet is not set in contrast with the main body of strings so much as forming a part of it. The contrast of timbre between solo and tutti passages is further reduced by the warmly reverberant recording, which gives substantial weight to the quartet, to match that of the full ensemble. With a full string orchestra reinforcing the heavier passages the power of this masterpiece is formidably presented, most strikingly in the first movement, for Kremer inspires a deeply felt and expressive performance. Yet, next to the finest performances of the original quartet, the result tends to sound fussy. Despite those reservations, it is an alternative well worth hearing, recorded in full, warm sound.

String Quintet in C, D.956 (DVD version)
*** Testament **DVD** SBDVD1002. Amadeus Qt, Pleeth –
  BRITTEN: *String Quartet 3* ***

Many listeners find Norbert Brainin's sound a little over-sweet, but this performance is in many respects superior to the earlier commercial versions (and certainly to the DG set), the whole concert is rewarding to listen to and follow or screen. It comes with an authoritative version of Benjamin Britten's *Third Quartet*, composed for the Amadeus Quartet in the last months of his life. As with its companion, the camerawork is unobtrusive and never attracts attention to itself.

(i) String Quintet in C, D.956. String Quartet 12 (Quartettsatz)
(M) *RCA (ADD) 82876 6310-2. Guarneri Qt, (i) with Leonard
  Rose

This recording dates from 1970, and in its new digital transfer the sound is immediately aggressive and overbright. Not recommended for such an Elysian work as the Schubert *Quintet*.

PIANO MUSIC

Piano duet
Music for piano, four hands: *Allegro in A min., D.947; Fantasy in F min., D.940; Marche caractéristique 1 in C, D.968b; Marche militaire 1 in D, D.733; Sonata in C (Grand Duo), D.812*
*** RCA 82876 69283-2 (2). Kissin, Levine

This set provides a record of the recital that Evgeny Kissin and James Levine gave in Carnegie Hall on 1 May 2005. Their programme draws on Schubert's work for piano, four hands, or, in the case of the *Grand Duo*, two keyboards. For the sake of both comfort and sonority, they use two pianos throughout. All this music comes from the late 1820s and it is difficult to find fault with this distinguished partnership, in terms of either spontaneity or sensitivity.

Solo piano music
Fantasia in C (Wanderer), D.760 (DVD version)
*** EMI **DVD** (ADD) 4 901229. Katchen – BEETHOVEN:
  Piano Sonata 29 ***

Like his celebrated recording of the Ravel *Left-hand Concerto*, this was made in the shadows of the illness that claimed Katchen some months later. It is a poignant and impressive reading, and its appearance here is a cause for celebration for all his admirers.

Fantasia in C (Wanderer), D.760 (CD version)
(M) (**) BBC mono BBCL 4126-2. Richter (with CHOPIN:
  Etude in F sharp min., Op. 10/4) – BEETHOVEN: *Piano
  Sonatas 9–10*; SCHUMANN: *Abegg Variations*, etc. **

The *Wanderer Fantasy* was one of the first works that Richter took into his repertoire while he was still studying with Neuhaus and this BBC recording, as one might expect, is a performance of stature. Richter himself said that it was only in later life that he succeeded in playing it with the freedom it needs. Such are its almost orchestral demands that Schubert himself broke down when he came to the concluding fugue. Richter recorded it commercially in 1963; but the present magisterial account has the compelling quality of a live concert occasion. Very acceptable sound, although the EMI studio recording is finer still.

Fantasia in C (Wanderer Fantasy), D.760; Piano Sonata 19 in G, D.894

(BB) *(*) Warner Apex 0927 40831-2. Leonskaja

Even at budget price Elisabeth Leonskaja's account of the *Wanderer Fantasy* and the *G major Sonata*, D.894, would not be a strong recommendation. There is something four-square about her playing, and she does not fully convey the vulnerability and tenderness of Schubert's art. The Warner recording is a bit hard, which does not help.

Impromptus 1–4, D. 899; 5–8, D.935

*** Sony SK 94732. Perahia (with LISZT: *Concert paraphrases of Schubert Lieder: Auf dem Wasser zu singen; Erlkönig; Ständchen – Leise flehen meine Lieder ***)

(BB) ** EMI (ADD) Encore 5 75883-2. Ciccolini

Perahia's account of the *Impromptus* is very special indeed. Directness of utterance and purity of spirit are of the essence here, with articulation of sparkling clarity. The CBS recording is very good and truthful in timbre. Perahia's set of *Impromptus* remains at the top of the recommended list (see our main volume) and now has three Liszt/Schubert song transcriptions as a tempting bonus, played equally perceptively.

Aldo Ciccolini was not always lucky in his recorded sound, which often gave his piano tone a rather hard, brittle quality. This 1972 release has only a touch of this, but the piano is too forwardly balanced. The performances are unsentimental and direct, but much less memorable than classic accounts by Arrau, Perahia and Kempff.

4 Impromptus 1–4, D.899; 5–8, D.935; Moments musicaux, D.780; Piano Sonatas 13 in A, D.664; 21 in B flat, D.960

🔷 (M) *** DG (ADD) 459 412-2 (2). Kempff

Kempff always had something special to say in Schubert. The *Impromptus* are beautifully done, especially the D.899 set, and in his hands the *Moments musicaux* range so much further than one expects. Kempff characteristically gives intimate performances. His allegros are never very fast and the results sing in the most relaxed way. The *B flat Sonata* is the highlight of the collection, and it is a tribute to Kempff's artistry that, with the most relaxed tempi, he conveys such consistent, compulsive intensity. Hearing the opening, one might feel that it is going to be a lightweight account, but in fact the long-breathed expansiveness is hypnotic so that, as in the *Great C major Symphony*, one is bound by the spell of the heavenly length. Rightly, Kempff repeats the first-movement exposition with the important nine bars of lead-back, and though the overall manner is less obviously dramatic than is common, the range of tone colour is magical, with sharp terracing of dynamics to plot the geography of each movement. Though very much a personal utterance, this interpretation is no less great for that. It belongs to a tradition of

pianism that has almost disappeared, and we must be eternally grateful that its expression has been so glowingly captured on this reissue.

Piano sonatas

Piano Sonatas 1 in E, D.157; 5 in A flat D.557; 13 in A, D.664; 14 in E min., D.784; 16 in A min., D.845; 18 in G, D.894; 19 in C min., D.958; 20 in A, D.959; 21 in B flat, D.960; Moments musicaux, D.780; 2 Scherzos, D.593

(B) *** Decca (ADD/DDD) 475 7074 (4). Lupu

Radu Lupu obviously intended to record a complete cycle but it was never completed; the recordings arrived individually between 1971 and 1994. He was a true Schubertian, sensitive and poetic throughout, and this box is cherishable. He strikes the perfect balance between Schubert's classicism and the spontaneity of his musical thought, and at the same time he leaves one with the impression that the achievement is perfectly effortless, with an inner repose and depth of feeling that remain memorable long after the performances have ended. This especially applies to the *C minor*, D.958, which has a simple eloquence that is most moving as indeed has the late *A major* work, D.959. The peak of the survey was perhaps reached with the original coupling of Nos. 16 and 18 to which we gave a 🔷 on its initial issue. Lupu brings both tenderness and classical disciplines to bear on the structure of the *A minor Sonata* of 1825, while the *Fantasy Sonata in G major* has a compulsion which reveals the artist at full stretch, a superb reading, relatively straight in its approach but full of glowing perception on points of detail; moreover, he observes the exposition repeat in the first movement. The last to be recorded, in December 1991, was the great final *B flat Sonata*; one of the most searching of available recordings, it again finds this masterly pianist at his most eloquent and thoughtful. But the earlier works are very appealing too: in the little three-movement *A flat Sonata*, D.557, the *Andante* unfolds with pleasing delicacy and the finale combines gentleness with strength. The *Moments musicaux* are very fine indeed and the two *Scherzi* are hardly less successful, the first particularly light and airy. The recordings are generally of Decca's finest, with timbre of warm colour yet with a striking sense of presence overall.

Piano Sonatas 7 in E, D.568; 16 in A min., D.845

(BB) *(*) Naxos 8.553099. Jandó

These are decent performances from Jenö Jandó but ultimately plain and unmemorable. Not a patch on Schiff, Kempff or Lupu.

Piano Sonatas 13 in A, D.664; 17 in D, D.850

** HM HMC 901713. Planès

The French pianist Alain Planès is currently embarked on a project to record all the Schubert sonatas. A sensitive and perceptive artist, he proves an authoritative guide and holds the right balance between beauty of detail and the overall architecture. The sunny *A major Sonata* comes from 1819, the same year as the *Trout* quintet, and the *D major* of 1825 paves the way for the big late sonatas. Planès is handicapped by his recording acoustic, so that the piano seems dry and brittle. However, it is worth making allowances for there are real musical rewards here. Planès is a Schubertian of real quality, and his interpretations are far more satisfying than some of his more celebrated rivals.

Piano Sonatas 13 in A, D.664; 20 in A, D.959

(BB) ** Warner Apex 0927 40832-2. Leonskaja

The two *A major Sonatas* coupled here find Elisabeth Leonskaja much more attuned to the Schubertian sensibility, though in neither would her performances be a first choice. Were this on the shelf alongside the likes of Lupu, Brendel or Kempff, it would be to them rather than to Leonskaja that you would turn.

Piano Sonata 21 in B flat, D.960; Impromptus 1–4, D.935
(M) ** Warner Elatus 0927 49838-2. Barenboim

Barenboim's are live performances at the Vienna Musikverein in 1992, marking the fortieth anniversary of the pianist's debut there and his own fiftieth birthday. There is some point-making in the sublime *B flat Sonata* (the C sharp minor theme which opens the slow movement would be more effective if given without expressive underlining). Of course there are perceptive and insightful touches, but on the whole this does not do full justice to this exalted Schubertian, nor really does the recording quality. The *Impromptus* fare better and have a welcome spontaneity.

Complete Waltzes: 36 Dances (Erste Walzer), D.365; Scherzos, D.593; 12 Valses nobles, D.969; 34 Valses sentimentales, D.779; 2 Waltzes, D.980; 12 Waltzes, D.145; 12 (Graz) Waltzes, D.924; 20 Waltzes (Letzte Walzer); Waltzes with Trios in E flat, D.146; F, D.146
(BB) *** EMI Gemini (ADD) 350894-2 (2). Bordoni

A first look at this two-disc Gemini set brings an astonished double-take, for it contains no fewer than 132 waltzes (or pieces in waltz format). How could such a collection hold the interest? But it does – partly because Schubert was a master of the form (very popular in his day), and partly because Paolo Bordoni is such a sympathetic exponent, and he is very well recorded. Of course we are not suggesting they should all be played at once but in groups. That is what Schubert planned; if you heed our advice, you will find that they follow each other very pleasingly – then suddenly there is a Schubertian jewel.

If for instance one begins with the second disc (which is a good place to start) and the *12 Waltzes*, D.145, published in 1823, you will suddenly encounter the lilting *No. 5 in G*, which Bordoni plays most expressively, while *No. 7 in E flat* sounds almost like Chopin. Yet *No. 10* is more like a folk Laendler, and the miscellaneous group which follows includes the delightful and familiar *C Sharp major Waltz*, D.139.

The Deutsch catalogue numbers appear to be no positive guide to when the waltzes were written. Schubert's first attempts at the genre are the *36 Waltzes*, D.365, composed between 1818 and 1821, and the *36 Valses sentimentales* date from 1823. As can be seen from the listing, Schubert much preferred the shorter, independent waltz form rather than the waltz with trio which had evolved from the minuet. So, by composing in groups, Schubert prepared the way for the Viennese waltzes of the Strauss family, for each of those is a string of short waltzes, with perhaps one recurring to create a unified structure. But Schubert's waltzes are special in their own way, and this remarkable anthology provides an opportunity to explore them at leisure.

VOCAL MUSIC

DG Fischer-Dieskau Schubert Lieder Edition with Gerald Moore

Song-cycles: *Die schöne Müllerin; Winterreise; Schwanengesang* (complete) & *405 key Lieder*
(B) *** DG 477 5765 (21). Fischer-Dieskau, Moore

Fischer-Dieskau's monumental survey of all the Schubert songs suitable for a man's voice (some of the longer ones excepted) was made over a relatively brief span, with the last 300 songs concentrated in a period of only two months in 1969; yet there is not a hint of routine. No fewer than 405 songs are included here, plus the three song-cycles, which were also new recordings, made in 1971/2. If anything, these performances – notably that of the darkest and greatest of the cycles, *Winterreise* – are even more searching than before, with Moore matching the concentration of the singer in some of the most remarkable playing that even he has put on record. As in the miscellaneous songs (which we do not have space to list), Fischer-Dieskau is in wonderfully fresh voice, and the transfers to CD have been managed very naturally. The documentation includes full texts and translations and an essay by André Tubeuf. The one serious omission is an alphabetical list of titles. This makes it unnecessarily hard to find a particular song – much the most likely way of using so compendious a collection.

The Graham Johnson Schubert Lieder Edition
(B) **** Hyp. CDS 44201/40 (40). 60 soloists, including Ian Bostridge singing *Die schöne Müllerin* and Matthias Goerne singing *Winterreise*

Hyperion's complete coverage of Schubert's Lieder is a monumental achievement. The individual discs are still all available separately (see below) but now come in a box presented in chronological order of composition. Three bonus CDs now complete the survey by adding 81 further songs by Schubert's friends and contemporaries. There is a handsome book, including complete texts and translations which is also available separately (BKS 44201/40).

When it comes to background information, Graham Johnson's Schubert Lieder Edition for Hyperion using some of the greatest singers of the day – is unmatchable. With each disc devoted to a group of songs on a particular theme, Johnson provides notes that add enormously to the enjoyment, heightening the experience of hearing even the most familiar songs.

Lieder Vol. 1: Der Alpenjäger; Amalia; An den Frühling; An den Mond; Erster Verlust; Die Ewartung; Der Fischer; Der Flüchtling; Das Geheimnis; Der Jüngling am Bache; Lied; Meeres Stille; Nähe des Geliebten; Der Pilgrim; Schäfers Klagelied; Sehnsucht; Thekla; Wanderers Nachtlied; Wonne der Wehmut
♦── *** Hyp. CDJ 33001. Baker, Johnson

Hyperion's complete Schubert song edition was masterminded by the accompanist, Graham Johnson, and this first volume sets the pattern of mixing well-known songs with rarities. Dame Janet's whole collection is devoted to Schiller and Goethe settings, above all those he wrote in 1815, an exceptionally rich year for the 18-year-old; one marvels that, after writing his dedicated, concentrated setting of *Wanderers Nachtlied*, he could on that same day in July write two other equally memorable songs, *Der Fischer* and *Erster Verlust* (*First loss*). Dame Janet is in glorious voice, her golden tone ravishing in a song such as *An den Mond* and her hushed tone caressing the ear in *Meeres Stille* and *Wanderers Nachtlied*. Presented like this, the project becomes a voyage of discovery.

Lieder Vol. 2: Am Bach im Frühling; Am Flusse; Auf der Donau; Fahrt zum Hades; Fischerlied (two settings); Fischerweise; Der Schiffer; Selige Welt; Der Strom; Der Taucher; Widerschein; Wie Ulfru fischt
*** Hyp. CDJ 33002. Varcoe, Johnson

Graham Johnson with the baritone, Stephen Varcoe, devises a delightful collection of men's songs, culminating in the rousing strophic song, *Der Schiffer*, one of the most catchily memorable that Schubert ever wrote, here exhilaratingly done. Otherwise the moods of water and wave, sea and river, are richly exploited. The last 28 minutes of the collection are devoted to the extended narrative, *Der Taucher* (*The Diver*), setting a long poem of Schiller which is based on an early version of the Beowulf saga. Varcoe and Johnson completely explode the long-accepted idea that this is overextended and cumbersome, giving it a thrilling dramatic intensity.

Lieder Vol. 3: *Abschied; An die Freunde; Augenlied; Iphigenia; Der Jüngling und der Tod; Lieb Minna; Liedesend; Nacht und Träume; Namenstagslied; Pax vobiscum; Rückweg; Trost im Liede; Viola; Der Zwerg*
*** Hyp. CDJ 33003. Murray, Johnson

This is one of Ann Murray's finest records, with the intimate beauty of the voice consistently well caught and with none of the stress that the microphone exaggerates on record. Like the songs that Johnson chose for Ann Murray's husband, Philip Langridge, these too represent Schubert in his circle of friends, with their poems his inspiration, including a long flower ballad, *Viola*, by his close friend, Franz von Schober, which Murray and Johnson sustain beautifully.

Lieder Vol. 4: *Alte Liebe rostet nie; Am See; Am Strome; An Herrn Josef von Spaun (Epistel); Auf der Riesenkoppe; Das war ich; Das gestörte Glück; Liebeslauschen; Liebesrausch; Liebeständelei; Der Liedler; Nachtstück; Sängers Morgenlied* (2 versions)*; Sehnsucht der Liebe*
*** Hyp. CDJ 33004. Langridge, Johnson

Philip Langridge brings a collection to illustrate Schubert's setting of words by poets in his immediate circle, ending with *Epistel*, a tongue-in-cheek parody song addressed to a friend who had left Vienna to become a tax collector, extravagantly lamenting his absence. It is Johnson's presentation of such rarities that makes the series such a delight. Langridge has rarely sounded so fresh and sparkling on record.

Lieder Vol. 5: *Die Allmacht; An die Natur; Die Erde; Erinnerung; Ferne von der grossen Stadt; Ganymed; Klage der Ceres; Das Lied im Grünen; Morgenlied; Die Mutter Erde; Die Sternenwelten; Täglich zu singen; Dem Unendlichen; Wehmut*
*** Hyp. CDJ 33005. Connell, Johnson

Thanks in part to Johnson's choice of songs and to his sensitive support at the piano, Connell has rarely sounded so sweet and composed on record, yet with plenty of temperament. The collection centres round a theme – this time, Schubert and the countryside, suggested by the most popular song of the group, *Das Lied im Grünen*. As ever, the joy of the record is enhanced by Johnson's brilliant, illuminating notes.

Lieder Vol. 6: *Abendlied für die Entfernte; Abends unter der Linde* (two versions)*; Abendstern; Alinde; An die Laute; Des Fischers Liebesglück; Jagdlied; Der Knabe in der Wiege (Wiegenlied); Lass Wolken an Hügeln ruh'n; Die Nacht; Die Sterne; Der Vater mit dem Kind; Vor meiner Wiege; Wilkommen und Abschied; Zur guten Nacht*
*** Hyp. CDJ 33006. Rolfe Johnson, Johnson (with chorus)

The title of Anthony Rolfe Johnson's contribution is 'Schubert and the Nocturne'. Two items include a small male chorus, a group of individually named singers. *Jagdlied* is

entirely choral, and the final *Zur guten Nacht*, a late song of 1827, has the 'Spokesman' answered by the chorus, ending on a gentle *Gute Nacht*. Rolfe Johnson's voice has never sounded more beautiful on record, and the partnership of singer and accompanist makes light even of a long strophic song (using the same music for each verse) like *Des Fischers Liebesglück*, beautiful and intense.

Lieder Vol. 7: *An die Nachtigall; An den Frühling; An den Mond; Idens Nachtgesang; Idens Schwanenlied; Der Jüngling am Bache; Kennst du das Land?; Liane; Die Liebe; Luisens Antwort; Des Mädchens Klage; Meeres Stille; Mein Gruss an den Mai; Minona oder die Kunde der Dogge; Naturgenuss; Das Rosenband; Das Sehnen; Sehnsucht* (2 versions)*; Die Spinnerin; Die Sterbende; Stimme der Liebe; Von Ida; Wer kauft Liebesgötter?*
🎵 *** Hyp. CDJ 33007. Ameling, Johnson

An extraordinarily rewarding sequence of 24 songs, all written in the composer's *annus mirabilis*, 1815. With Ameling both charming and intense, Johnson's robust defence in his ever-illuminating notes of the first and longest of the songs, *Minona*, is amply confirmed, a richly varied ballad. Here too is a preliminary setting of *Meeres Stille*, less well-known than the regular version, written a day later, but just as clearly a masterpiece, sung by Ameling in a lovely intimate half-tone at a sustained pianissimo. It is fascinating too to compare the two contrasted settings of Mignon's song *Sehnsucht*, the first of five he ultimately attempted.

Lieder Vol. 8: *Abendlied der Fürstin; An Chloen; An den Mond; An den Mond in einer Herbstnacht; Berthas Lied in der Nacht; Erlkönig; Die frühen Gräber; Hochzeitslied; In der Mitternacht; Die Mondnacht; Die Nonne; Die Perle; Romanze; Die Sommernacht; Ständchen; Stimme der Liebe; Trauer der Liebe; Wiegenlied*
*** Hyp. CDJ 33008. Walker, Johnson

For Sarah Walker, with her perfectly controlled mezzo at its most sensuous, the theme of the disc, 'Schubert and the Nocturne', leads from the first, lesser-known version of the Goethe poem, *An den Mond*, to two of the best-loved of all Schubert's songs, the delectable *Wiegenlied* ('Cradle-song'), and the great drama of *Erlkönig*, normally sung by a man, but here at least as vividly characterized by a woman's voice.

Lieder Vol. 9: *Blanka; 4 Canzonen, D.688; Daphne am Bach; Delphine; Didone abbandonata; Gott! höre meine Stimme; Der gute Hirt; Hin und wieder Fliegen Pfeile;* (i) *Der Hirt auf dem Felsen. Ich schleiche bang und still (Romanze). Lambertine; Liebe Schwärmt auf allen Wegen; Lilla an die Morgenröte; Misero pargoletto; La pastorella al prato; Der Sänger am Felsen; Thekla; Der Vollmond strahlt (Romanze)*
🎵 *** Hyp. CDJ 33009. Augér, Johnson; (i) with King

'Schubert and the Theatre' is the theme of Arleen Augér's contribution, leading up to the glories of his very last song, the headily beautiful *Shepherd on the rock*, with its clarinet obbligato. The *Romanze, Ich schleiche bang* – adapted from an opera aria – also has a clarinet obbligato. Notable too are the lightweight Italian songs that the young Schubert wrote for his master, Salieri, and a lovely setting, *Der gute Hirt* ('The good shepherd'), in which the religious subject prompts a melody which anticipates the great staircase theme in Strauss's *Arabella*.

Lieder Vol. 10: *Adelwold und Emma; Am Flusse; An die Apfelbäume, wo ich Julien erblickte; An die Geliebte; An*

Mignon; Auf den Tod einer Nachtigall; Auf einen Kirchhof; Harfenspieler I; Labetrank der Liebe; Die Laube; Der Liebende; Der Sänger; Seufzer; Der Traum; Vergebliche Liebe; Der Weiberfreund
*** Hyp. CDJ 33010. Hill, Johnson

Graham Johnson here correlates the year 1815 with what has been documented of Schubert's life over those twelve months, which is remarkably little. So the songs here form a kind of diary. The big item, overtopping everything else, is the astonishing 38-stanza narrative song, *Adelwold and Emma*, with Hill ranging wide in his expression. It is almost half an hour long, from the bold march-like opening to the final happy resolution.

Lieder Vol. 11: An den Tod; Auf dem Wasser zu singen; Auflösung; Aus 'Heliopolis' I & II; Dithyrambe; Elysium; Der Geistertanz; Der König in Thule; Lied des Orpheus; Nachtstück; Schwanengesang; Seligkeit; So lasst mich scheinen; Der Tod und das Mädchen; Verklärung; Vollendung; Das Zügenglöcklein
*** Hyp. CDJ 33011. Fassbaender, Johnson

Starting with a chilling account of *Death and the Maiden*, the theme of Brigitte Fassbaender's disc is 'Death and the Composer'. Fassbaender's ability precisely to control her vibrato brings baleful tone-colours, made the more ominous by the rather reverberant, almost churchy, acoustic. So in *Auf dem Wasser zu singen* the lightly fanciful rippling-water motif presents the soul gliding gently 'like a boat' up to heaven, and the selection ends astonishingly with what generally seems one of the lightest of Schubert songs, *Seligkeit*. This, as Johnson suggests, returns the listener from heaven back to earth. In this, as elsewhere, Fassbaender sings with thrilling intensity, with Johnson's accompaniment comparably inspired.

Lieder, Vol. 12: Adelaide; An Elise; An Laura, als sie Klopstocks Auferstehungslied sang; Andenken; Auf den Sieg der Deutschen; Ballade; Die Betende; Don Gayseros I, II, III; Der Geistertanz; Lied an der Ferne; Lied der Liebe; Nachtgesang; Die Schatten; Sehnsucht; Trost; Trost in Tränem; Der Vatermörder
** Hyp. CDJ 33012. Thompson, Johnson

Adrian Thompson's disc brings the only disappointment in Graham Johnson's outstanding Schubert series. As recorded, the voice sounds gritty and unsteady, with the tone growing tight and ugly under pressure, yet this collection of early songs, all teenage inspirations, still illuminates the genius of Schubert at this earliest period of his career.

Lieder, Vol. 13: (i) Eine altschottische Ballade. Ellens Gesang I, II & III (Ave Maria); Gesang der Norna; Gretchen am Spinnrade; Gretchens Bitte; Lied der Anna Lyle; Die Männer sind méchant; Marie; Das Marienbild; (i) Normans Gesang; Szene aus Faust. Shilrik und Vinvela; Die Unterscheidung
*** Hyp. CDJ 33013. McLaughlin, Johnson; (i) with Hampson

The theme for Marie McLaughlin's contribution to the Hyperion Schubert edition is broadly a survey of Schubert's inner conflicts and contradictions. The Goethe settings are crowned by one of the most celebrated of all Schubert songs, *Gretchen am Spinnrade*. McLaughlin gives a fresh and girlish portrait, tenderly pathetic rather than tragic. Fascinatingly the selection also includes *Gretchens Bitte*, an extended song that Schubert left unfinished and for which Benjamin Britten in 1943 provided a completion of the final stanzas. The translations of Scottish ballads cover a wide range. *Eine*

altschottische Ballade is one of the three dramatic items involving the baritone, Thomas Hampson, which also include a sinister dialogue for Gretchen and an evil spirit, *Szene aus Faust*. McLaughlin's voice comes over sweetly, with brightness and much charm.

Lieder, Vol. 14: Amphiaraos; An die Leier; (i) Antigone und Oedip. Der entsühnte Orest; Freiwilliges Versinken; Die Götter Griechenlands; Gruppe aus dem Tartarus; Fragment aus dem Aeschylus; (i) Hektors Abschied. Hippolits Lied; Lied eines Schiffers an die Dioskuren; Memnon; Orest auf Tauris; Philoktet; Uraniens Flucht; Der Zürnenden Diana
*** Hyp. CDJ 33014. Hampson, Johnson; (i) with McLaughlin

Thomas Hampson's theme here is 'Schubert and the Classics', mainly Ancient Greece. Matching the hushed intensity of the opening song, *Die Götter Griechenlands*, singer and accompanist give a rapt performance, and Hampson's ecstatically sweet tone, with flawless legato, contrasts with the darkly dramatic timbre – satisfyingly firm and steady – that he finds for later songs and dialogues, including the finale *Hektors Abschied*. In that dialogue Marie McLaughlin sings the part of Andromache to Hampson's Hector.

Lieder, Vol. 15: Am Fenster; An die Sonne; An die untergehende Sonne; Der blinde Knabe; Gondelfahrer; Im Freien; Ins stille Land; Die junge Nonne; Klage an den Mond; Kolmas Klage; Die Mainacht; Der Mondabend; Der Morgenkuss; Sehnsucht; Der Unglückliche; Der Wanderer an den Mond; Der Winterabend
⊶ ✿ *** Hyp. CDJ 33015. M. Price, Johnson

In the fifteenth disc of his Hyperion series, Graham Johnson, accompanying Dame Margaret Price in songs on the theme of 'Night', achieves a new peak. One winning rarity is *Klage an den Mond* ('Lament to the Moon'), gloriously fresh and lyrical. Price and Johnson find here a distinctive magic so that its simple melody rings through the memory for hours. The other Holty setting on Margaret Price's disc is of *Die Mainacht*, much better known in Brahms's raptly beautiful setting. The young Schubert simply lets his lyricism flower as no one else could. Johnson and Dame Margaret match that with folk-like freshness, concealing art. In the best-known song, *Der Wanderer an den Mond*, Price is light and crisp, but she finds extra mystery in the moonlight scene of *Am Fenster*, poignantly reflecting the lover's sadness.

Lieder, Vol. 16: An die Freude; An Emma; Die Bürgschaft; Die Entzückung an Laura I & II; Das Geheimnis; Der Jüngling am Bache; Laura am Clavier; Leichenfantasie; Das Mädchen aus der Fremde; Die vier Weltalter; Sehnsucht; Der Pilgrim
*** Hyp. CDJ 33016. Allen, Johnson

Following the pattern of Graham Johnson's unique Schubert series, Thomas Allen in Schiller settings is challenged to some of his most sensitive singing, using the widest tonal range. They include two extended narrative songs that are a revelation, one of them, *Leichenfantasie* ('Funereal fantasy'), written when Schubert was only fourteen. As before, Johnson's notes and commentaries greatly heighten one's understanding both of particular songs and of Schubert generally.

Lieder, Vol. 17: Am Grabe Anselmos; An den Mond; An die Nachtigall; An mein Klavier; Aus 'Diego Manazares' (Ilmerine); Die Einsiedelei; Frühlingslied; Geheimnis; Der Herbstabend; Herbstlied; Die Herbstnacht; Klage; Klage um

Ali Bey; Lebenslied; Leiden der Trennung; Lied; Lied in der Absehenheit; Litanei; Lodas Gespenst; Lorma; Minnelied; Pflicht und Liebe; Phidile; Winterlied
*** Hyp. CDJ 33017. Popp, Johnson

It was fitting that one of the last recordings which Lucia Popp made, only months before her tragic death in the autumn of 1993, was her contribution to Graham Johnson's Schubert series. These songs, written in 1816 and almost all of them little known, inspire all her characteristic sweetness and charm. They include an extended narrative song to a text from Ossian, *Lodas gespent*, which, like others resurrected by the indefatigable Johnson, defies the idea that long equals boring. She also relishes two of Schubert's rare comic songs, pointing them deliciously. As ever, Johnson's notes are a model of fascinating scholarship.

Lieder, Vol. 18: *Abendlied; An den Schlaf; An die Erntfernte; An die Harmonie; An mein Herz; Auf den Tod einer Nachtigall; Auf der Bruck; 'Die Blume und der Quell'; Blumenlied; Drang in die Ferne; Erntelied; Das Finden; Das Heimweh (2 versions); Im Frühling; Im Jänner 1817 (Tiefes Lied); Im Walde; Lebensmut; Der Liebliche Stern; Die Nacht; Uber Wildemann; Um Mitternacht*
*** Hyp. CDJ 33018. Schreier, Johnson

This eighteenth disc in Graham Johnson's masterly series represents the halfway point, with Peter Schreier providing a keenly illuminating supplement to his prize-winning recordings with András Schiff of the great Schubert song-cycles for Decca. The challenge is just as great here, when this particular group centres on strophic songs. The first nine songs are all early ones, dating from 1816, leading to just one extended non-strophic song, *Das Heimweh*, D.851, of 1825. Its weight and complexity come over the more powerfully after such a preparation. Johnson then delivers a master-stroke by devising for Schreier what amounts to a new Schubert song-cycle, presenting in sequence ten settings of poems from the *Poetisches Tagebuch* ('Poetic Diary'), by the obsessive, unstable poet, Ernst Schulze, all written in 1825 and 1826. Quoting the first song, Johnson calls the cycle *Auf den wilden Wegen* ('On the wild paths'), with the sequence following the poet's madly fanciful love-affair with a beloved who, in real life, rejected him as a mere stranger. Schreier and Johnson in their imaginative treatment present clear parallels with *Winterreise*, offering one momentary haven of happiness, instantly shattered. That comes in the best-known song, *Im Frühling*, among the most haunting that even Schubert ever wrote. Johnson's comprehensive notes, as in previous discs of the series, intensify enjoyment enormously.

Lieder, Vol. 19: *Abendlied; Am See; Auf dem See; Auf dem Wasser zu singen; Beim Winde; Der Blumen Schmerz; Die Blumensprache; Gott im Frühling; Im Haine; Der liebliche Stern; Nach einem Gewitter; Nachtviolen; Die Rose; Die Sterne; Suleika I & II; Die Sternennächte; Vergissmeinicht*
*** Hyp. CDJ 33019. Lott, Johnson

Graham Johnson's theme for Felicity Lott's disc is 'Schubert and Flowers', prompting a sequence of charming, ever-lyrical songs, mostly neglected but including such a favourite as *Nachtviolen* (raptly sung) and – less predictably – *Auf dem Wasser zu singen*, all enchantingly done. Lott's soprano is not caught quite at its purest, but the charm and tender imagination of the singer consistently match the inspired accompaniments. In his detailed notes Johnson manages to include a

'Schubertian florilegium', listing several hundred of the songs inspired by particular flowers.

Lieder, Vol. 20: *'Schubertiad' (1815)* Songs and part-songs: *Abendständchen (An Lina); Alles um Liebe; Als ich sie errötten sah; Begräbnislied; Bergknappenlied; Der erste Liebe; Die Frölichkeit; Geist der Liebe; Grablied; Heidenröslein; Hoffnung; Huldigung; Klage um Ali Bey; Liebesrausch; Die Macht der Liebe; Das Mädchen von Inistore; Der Morgenstern; Nachtgesang; Ossians Lied nach dem Falle Nathos; Osterlied; Punschlied (Im Norden su singen); Schwertlied; Schwanengesang; Die Tauschung; Tischerlied; Totenkranz für ein Kind; Trinklied (2 versions); Trinklied vor der Schlacht; Wiegenlied; Winterlied; Der Zufriedene*
*** Hyp. CDJ 33020. Rozario, Mark Ainsley, Bostridge, George, Johnson; L. Schubert Ch., Layton

The twentieth volume of the Hyperion Schubert series brings a different kind of recital disc, with a range of singers performing no fewer than 32 brief songs and ensemble numbers, all written in 1815. Johnson conceives that this might well have been the sort of Schubertiad to take place towards the end of that year and, aptly for the opening and closing numbers, chooses drinking songs. In between, the vigorous and jolly songs are effectively contrasted with a few darker ones, such as a burial song. The team of singers has the flair one expects of Johnson as founder of the Songmakers' Almanac, with the young tenor, Ian Bostridge, appearing in one of his first recordings.

Lieder, Vol. 21: *Songs from 1817–18: Die abgeblühte Linde; Abschied von einem Freunde; An die Musik; An eine Quelle; Erlafsee; Blondel zu Marien; Blumenbrief; Evangelium Johannes; Der Flug der Zeit; Die Forelle; Grablied für die Mutter; Häßflings Liebeswerbung; Impromptu; Die Liebe; Liebhaber in allen Gestalten; Lied eines Kind; Das Lied vom Reifen; Lob der Tränen; Der Schäfer und der Reiter; Schlaflied; Schweizerlied; Sehnsucht; Trost; Vom Mitleiden Mariä*
*** Hyp. CDJ 33021. Mathis, Johnson

Instead of adopting a particular theme for this sequence, sung with characteristic sweetness by the Swiss soprano, Edith Mathis, Graham Johnson has devised a delectable group of 24 songs written in 1817–18, including a high proportion of charmers. Two of them are among the best known of all Schubert's songs, *Die Forelle* ('The trout') and *An die Musik*, here sung with disarming freshness and given extra point through Johnson's inspired playing. The songs in swinging compound or triple time are particularly delightful, as are the often elaborately decorative accompaniments, which Johnson points with winning delicacy.

Lieder, Vol. 22: *'Schubertiad II': Der Abend; Das Abendroth; An die Sonne; An Rosa I & II; An Sie; Das Bild; Cora an die Sonne; Cronnan; Die drei Sänger; Die Erscheinung; Furcht der Geliebten; Gebet wahrend der Schlacht; Genugsamkeit; Das Grab; Hermann und Thusnelda; Das Leben ist ein Traum; Lob des Tokayers; Lorma; Das Mädchen aus der Fremde; Morgenlied; Punschlied; Scholie; Selma und Selmar; Die Sterne; Trinklied; Vaterlandslied*
*** Hyp. CDJ 33022. Anderson, Wyn-Rogers, MacDougall, Keenlyside; Johnson

The year 1815 was an *annus mirabilis* for Schubert, and Graham Johnson here, from the wealth of songs written in those twelve months, devises a sequence such as the composer might have performed with friends in an intimate Schubertiad. So the solo items are punctuated by three male-voice quartets and one trio for female voices in which the main soloists, listed above, are joined by four other distinguished singers: Patricia Rozario, Catherine Denley, John Mark Ainsley and Michael George. Though most of the 28 items are brief, they include one more-extended song, *Die drei Sänger* ('The three minstrels'), in which Schubert adventurously illustrates the narrative in an almost operatic way. The final page is missing from the manuscript, which is here sensitively completed by Reinhard von Hoorickx.

Lieder, Vol. 23: Songs from 1816: *Abendlied; Abschied von der Harfe; Am ersten Maimorgen; An Chloen; Bei dem Grabe meines Vater; Edone; Der Entfernten; Freude der Kinderjahre; Die frühe Liebe; Geist der Liebe; Gesänger des Harfners aus 'Wilhelm Meister' (Wer sich der Einsamkeit ergibt; Wer nie sein Brot mit Tränen ass; An die Türen will ich schleichen); Das Grab; Der Hirt; Julius an Theone; Der Jüngling an der Quelle; Klage; Die Knabenzeit; Der Leidende* (2 versions); *Die Liebesgötter; Mailied; Pflügerlied; Romanze; Skolie; Stimme der Liebe; Der Tod Oscars; Zufriedenheit*

⊶ *** Hyp. CDJ 33023. Prégardien, Johnson

The German lyric tenor, Christoph Prégardien, uses his lovely voice with its honeyed tone-colours through a wide expressive range in a very varied selection of songs from 1816. It is his artistry as well as Johnson's that makes the opening item so riveting, a long narrative song to words by Ossian in translation, which Prégardien's feeling for word-meaning helps to bring to life. That is followed by a brief chorus, *Der Grab*, sung by the London Schubert Chorale, which Johnson intends as a comment on that narrative. The poet is Johann von Salis-Seewis, who is also represented by four solo songs, including the ravishing *Der Jungling an der Quelle*, one of the most haunting that Schubert ever composed. In that year Schubert was expanding the range of poets he chose to set, including Johann Mayrhofer for the first time, here represented by the little-known *Der Hirt* ('The shepherd'). The selection of 19 items is rumbustiously rounded off by a drinking-song, *Skolie*.

Lieder, Vol. 24: *Goethe Schubertiad: An Mignon; An Schwager Kronos; Bundeslied; Erlkönig; Ganymed; Geistes-Gruss; Gesang der Geister über den Wassern* (2 versions); *Der Goldschmiedsgesell; Der Gott und die Bajadere; Hoffnung; Jägers Abendlied* (2 versions); *Mahomets Gesang; Mignon (So lasst mich scheinen); Rastlose Liebe; Der Rattenfänger; Schäfers Klagelied; Der Schatzgräber; Sehnsucht* (2 versions); *Sehnsucht (Nur wer die Sehnsucht kennt); Tischlied; Wer nie sein Brot mit Tränen ass*

*** Hyp. CDJ 33024. Schäfer, Mark Ainsley, Keenlyside, George, L. Schubert Ch., Layton; Johnson

This collection, drawn from Schubert's many settings of Goethe, aims to celebrate the important role the poet's works played in the composer's life. Graham Johnson in his notes makes high claims: 'It was the collaboration between Schubert and Goethe which allowed song with piano to become an enduring and valid means of musical expression on a large emotional scale.' Sadly, Goethe himself was indifferent to the inspired efforts of this then-obscure composer, but it did not affect the intensity of Schubert's response to the words. This selection, like that of Volume 28, devoted to Schiller, is related

to the life of the poet and includes many fascinating items, not least those in which Schubert set a text more than once. There are half a dozen of them here, including two quite different settings of *The Song of the Spirits over the Waters*, each completed by other hands. The second, for male chorus, is particularly powerful. Also fascinating is the version of *Erlkönig* here, with three singers taking part, characterizing the different voices in the story, a practice which Schubert himself sanctioned. (This is also included in Volume 2 of EMI's historical Lieder collection, with Georges Thill leading a performance in French.) All the singers here are ideally responsive, with Michael George reining in a voice weightier than the rest.

Lieder, Vol. 25: (i) *Die schöne Müllerin* (song-cycle); **(ii) with additional poems by Wilhelm Müller**

⊶ ✿ *** Hyp. CDJ 33025 (i) Bostridge, Johnson; (ii) read by Fischer-Dieskau

For this first of the big song-cycles in his comprehensive Schubert edition for Hyperion, Graham Johnson could not have chosen his singer more shrewdly. It is a delight to have in Ian Bostridge a tenor who not only produces youthfully golden tone for this young man's sequence but who also gives an eagerly detailed account of the 20 songs, mesmeric at the close, to match even the finest rivals. With the help of Johnson's keenly imaginative accompaniment, Bostridge's gift for changing face and conveying mood makes the story-telling exceptionally fresh and vivid. The bonus is also to have Dietrich Fischer-Dieskau (now retired from singing) reciting the Müller poems which Schubert failed to set. Johnson is at his most inspired too in his detailed notes, which will be a revelation even to experienced Schubertians.

Lieder, Vol. 26: 'An 1826 Schubertiad': *2 Scenes from Lacrimas* (Schauspiel); **4 Mignon Lieder of Wilhelm Meister. Lieder:** *Abschied von der Erde; An Sylvia; Das Echo; Der Einsame; Grab und Mond; Mondenschein; Nachthelle; Des Sängers Habe; Ständchen; Totengräberweise; Trinklied; Der Wanderer an den Mond; Widerspruch; Wiegenlied*

*** Hyp. CDJ 33026. Schäfer, Mark Ainsley, Jackson. L. Schubert Ch., Layton; Johnson

Starting with *Der Einsame*, sung by Richard Jackson, one of the most haunting of Schubert songs, here is a Schubertiad that brings its measure of darkness, relying entirely on Lieder which Schubert wrote in 1825 and 1826. By then he was writing fewer songs than before, but was hitting the mark every time. It ends in sombre tones with *Abschied von der Erde* ('Farewell to the Earth'), not a song at all but a melodrama for reciter and piano, which Richard Jackson narrates as effectively as one could imagine. Christine Schäfer and Richard Jackson between them perform most of the programme, with John Mark Ainsley contributing just one or two, including *To Sylvia*. That is one of the three Shakespeare settings which come as a lightweight interlude. Schäfer's contributions shine the most brightly, not least the hypnotic *Wiegenlied*, to words by Seidl. Graham Johnson's notes include a survey of Schubert's career in 1825–6, a list of the songs written then, and his brilliant analysis of each item.

Lieder, Vol. 27: *Abendröte cycle of Friedrich von Schlegel* (complete). **Other settings of Friedrich von Schlegel:** *Blanka; Fülle der Liebe; Im Walde; Der Schiffer.* **Settings of August von Schlegel:** *Lebensmelodien; Lob der Tränen; Sonnets I–III; Sprache der Liebe; Wiedersehn*

*** Hyp. CDJ 33027. Görne, Schäfer, Johnson

When the young German baritone, Matthias Görne, made his début at Wigmore Hall, deputizing on a gala occasion, it was instantly obvious that here was a major new Lieder singer. He makes an inspired choice for this fine disc in Graham Johnson's collected edition of the Schubert songs, firmly established as one of the most important recording projects of the nineties. With a masterly feeling for words and vocal line Görne brings out the full charm of these settings of poems by the von Schlegel brothers, Friedrich as well as August, the translator of Shakespeare. The seven songs to words by August are rounded off with three settings of his translations of Petrarch sonnets, while Johnson, prompted by circumstantial evidence, has ingeniously assembled a cycle of 11 Friedrich von Schlegel settings, Abendröte ('Sunset'), with Christine Schäfer as soloist in three of them, though not in the best-known of them, Die Vogel ('The Bird'), a favourite with both Elisabeth Schumann and Elisabeth Schwarzkopf. Görne and Johnson regularly demonstrate what masterpieces even some of the least known and briefest songs are. Johnson's notes are, as ever, a model, explaining why belated publication of particular songs has unfairly brought about neglect.

Lieder Vol. 28: 'Schubertiad' (1822): Am Flusse; An die Entfernte; Du liebst mich nicht; Frülingsgesang; Geheimes; Geist der Liebe; Ihr Grab; Im Gegenwärtigen Vergangenes; Johanna Sebus; Die Liebe hat gelogen; Mahomets Gesang; Mignon (Heiss mich nicht reden); Der Musensohn; Die Nachtigall; Schatzgräbers Begehr; Sei mir gegrüsst!; Selige Welt; Des Tages Weihe; Todesmusik; Versunken; Der Wachtelschlag; Willkommen und Abschied

*** Hyp. CDJ 33028. Schäfer, Mark Ainsley, Koningsberger, Ch., Johnson

Described as an 1822 Schubertiad, this volume offers an attractively varied collection of items, not just songs from the principal tenor and baritone, both sensitive singers, but concerted numbers, ending with a solemn quartet, a miniature cantata, Des Tages Weihe. Settings of Goethe predominate, with Christine Schäfer a very welcome contributor in the first version of Der Musensohn, made to sparkle in a higher key than usual. The sound between items is not always consistent, when the chorus is set in a more reverberant acoustic.

Lieder Vol. 29: Abendbilder; Blondel zu Marien; Einsamkeit (cantata); Frühlingsglaube; Himmelsfunken; Hoffnung; Hymne I–IV; Im Walde (Waldesnacht); Der Jüngling auf dem Hügel; Die Liebende schreibt; Morgenlied; Nachthymne; Trost

*** Hyp. CDJ 33029. Lipovšek, Berg, Johnson

Though Marjana Lipovšek with her warm, velvety mezzo, is the central soloist in this collection of songs from 1819 and 1820, the young Canadian baritone, Nathan Berg, takes on the biggest challenge here. That is the cantata, Einsamkeit, in twelve sections, setting words by Mayrhofer, with whom Schubert at that time shared a small room. The beauty and range of tone, with flawless legato, make one want to hear more of Berg, but Lipovšek's contribution is equally persuasive in a wide range of songs including five settings of metaphysical poems by Novalis, distinctive in Schubert's oeuvre. Like his playing, Johnson's sleeve notes are revelatory, both on the music and Schubert's life and character.

Lieder, Vol. 30: Winterreise (song cycle), D.911

○— *** Hyp. CDJ 33030. Görne, Johnson

For this greatest of song-cycles Graham Johnson has boldly turned not to a staid, long-experienced artist but to Matthias Görne, the young baritone who is rapidly proving himself the most exciting and inspired Lieder-singer since Dietrich Fischer-Dieskau. Görne movingly brings out the point that this is the tragedy of a young lover, not an old one. He sings not just with velvety beauty of tone in every register but with a rapt dedication that forces you to rethink each poem in the cycle, ending with a chill that is all-involving. At every point Graham Johnson heightens the experience with his subtly pointed playing. His commentary in a massive booklet not only illuminates the musical inspiration, but invaluably puts the work in its historical context, showing how profoundly Schubert's reordering of the songs, different from that of the poet, Müller, heightens their tragic impact.

Lieder, Vol. 31: Die Allmacht (2nd version for chorus); Die gestirne; Hagars Klage; Himmelsfunken; Im Abendrot; Das Mädchens Klage (1st version); Mirjams Siegergesang; Psalms 13; 23 (both trans. Mendelssohn); Psalm 92 (unacc. in Hebrew); Dem Unendlichen

*** Hyp. CDJ 33031. Brewer, Holst Singers, Layton; Johnson

In Graham Johnson's superb series covering all of Schubert's songs, this disc devoted to sacred songs is quite distinct from previous issues, offering not only those for solo voice, but some with chorus too. With the sensitive and powerful American soprano, Christine Brewer, as the central soloist, joined by the Holst singers and other soloists in the concerted numbers, this provides a fascinating survey of Schubert's equivocal approach to religious inspiration, too individual to follow Catholic dogma precisely. Schubert may not have been devout, but the plight of Hagar and Ishmael in the desert, as told in Genesis, led him as a mere 14-year-old to write an extended 16-minute sequence. It is good to have this big religious narrative piece – Hagars Klage and Mirjams Siegesgesang, a cantata on the Exodus story of Miriam, from the last year of his life – so strongly and persuasively performed, defying length. There is also some electrifying chorus work from the Holst Singers in the Psalm settings. The first two come in translations by Moses Mendelssohn, grandfather of the composer, while Schubert set the third in the original Hebrew, responding sensitively to a commission from a Jewish friend. The solo songs, often simple and hymn-like, are also beautifully sung by the rich-toned mezzo, Christine Brewer. As ever in this series, Johnson's brilliant notes are an inspiration.

Lieder, Vol. 32: 'An 1816 Schubertiad': An die Sonne; Beitrag zur Fünfzigjährigen Jubelfeier des Herrn von Salieri: Der Entfernten; Entzückung; Der Geistertanz; Gott der Weltschöpfer; Gott im Ungewitter; Grablied auf einen Soldaten; Das grosse Halleluja; Licht und Liebe; Des Mädchens Klage; Naturgenuss; Ritter Toggenburg; Schlachtgesang; Vedi quanto adoro (Dido Abbandonata); Die verfehlte Stunde; Der Wanderer; Das war ich; Zufriedenheit; Zum Punsche

*** Hyp. CDJ 33032. Dawson, Schäfer, Murray, Ainsley, Norman, Prégardien, Schade, Spence, Maltman, Varcoe, L. Schubert Ch. & Soloists, Layton; Johnson

With the exception of Der Wanderer, few items in this '1816 Schubertiad' are well known yet it makes for fascinating listening, with Graham Johnson's illuminating notes providing an ideal commentary. Solitary but substantial contributions from such artists as Christine Schäfer and Christoph Prégardien come as bonuses from earlier sessions in the series, and the collaborations of various artists on ensemble pieces bring just the right atmosphere for a Schubertiad. A trivial but charming sequence of four items was written in celebration of the 50th anniversary of the arrival in Vienna of Schubert's evidently much-loved teacher, Salieri. The brief, trivial canon, *Unser aller Grosspapa* is a special delight. Full, warm sound.

Lieder, Vol. 33: (i) *Lebenstraum (Gesang in C min.); Lebenstraum; Pensa, che questo istante; Totengräberlied;* (ii) *Entra l'uomo allor che nasce (Aria di Abramo); L'incanto degli occhi; Misero pargoletto; O combats, o désordre extrême!; Ombre amene, amiche piante (La serenata); Quelle' innocente figlio (Aria dell' Angelo); Rien de la nature; Son fra l'onde;* (iii) *Klaglied;* (iv) *Entra l'uomo allor che nasce (Aria di Abramo); Erinnerungen; Geisternähe;* (v) *Serbate o dei custodi;* (vi) *Die Befreier Europas in Paris;* (vii) *Der abend;* (viii) *Ammenlied; Die Nacht;* (ix) *Dithyrambe; Trinklied; Viel tausend Sterne prangen*

*** Hyp. CDJ 33033. McLaughlin, Murray, Wyn-Rogers, Langridge, Norman, Thompson, Koningsberger, Varcoe and soloists, L. Schubert Ch., Layton; Johnson

Entitled 'The Young Schubert', this volume brings together a mixed bag of songs from the years of the composer's boyhood, 1810–14, which for various reasons have not been included in previous volumes. Thanks to Graham Johnson and his powers of coordination, the result is intensely compelling; it even offers what, through scholarly detective work, is now thought to be the very first Schubert song: probably written before 1810, an extended piece of 394 bars, previously described simply as 'Gesang in C minor', when the words were unknown. Now, as *Lebenstraum* ('Life's dream'), it has been persuasively fitted with words from a poem by Gabriele von Baumberg, which Schubert also used in another song on the disc. It is fascinating too to find the boy Schubert doing arrangements of arias by Gluck, and no fewer than ten of these early songs set Italian words. Standing out among the original songs is the tenderly beautiful *Klaglied* lament of 1812, magically sung by Marie McLaughlin. Though the recordings were made from a whole sequence of sessions between 1990 and 1999, Johnson and his chosen singers offer performances of consistent excellence, very well recorded.

Lieder, Vol. 34: (i) *Abend;* (ii) *Das Abendrot;* (iii) *Der Alpenjäger;* (iv) *Atys;* (v) *Kantate zum Geburtstag des Sängers Michael Vogl;* (vi) *Das Dörfchen;* (vii) *Die Einsiedelei;* (viii) *Frohsinn;* (ix) *Die gefangenen Sänger;* (x) *Die Gesellkeit (Lebenslust);* (xi) *Das Grab;* (xii) *Grenzen der Menschheit; Der Kampf;* (xiii) *Das Mädchen;* (vi) *La pastorella al prato;* (xiv) *Prometheus;* (xv) *Sing-Ubungen;* (xvi) *Uber allen Zauber Liebe;* (iii) *Wandrers Nachtlied II*

*** Hyp. CDJ 33034. Anderson, Dawson, Rozario, Lipovšek, Hill, Langridge, Norman, Schade, Finley, Görne, Hampson, Keenlyside, Loges, Maltman, Davies (with Denley, Mark Ainsley, Bostridge, MacDougall, George); Johnson; L. Schubert Ch., Layton

It is one of the great merits of Graham Johnson's inspired method of presenting the collected Schubert songs that he gives such a clear perspective on Schubert's career over each year of his short working life. This thirty-fourth volume brings together the songs that Schubert wrote between 1817 and 1821 not previously included in the edition. As Johnson explains, the years 1815 and 1816 were the most productive for songs, leading to the present years when other commitments left him with fewer opportunities for songwriting. The nineteen items here, presented in chronological order, offer a wide range of pieces, including several vocal quartets, one of them

the delectable *Die Geselligkeit* ('Zest for Life'), and a ten-minute cantata written for the birthday of his singer-friend and advocate, Michael Vogl. Other jewels include some fine Goethe settings, notably the dramatic *Prometheus*, and the second version of the *Wandrers Nachtlied*, a miniature of just a few bars that delves astonishingly deep. Consistently fine performances from sessions recorded between 1991 and 1999.

Lieder, Vol. 35: (1822–25): *Bootgesang; Coronach; Dass sie hier gewesen!; Du bist die Ruh; Gebet (Du Urquell aller güte); Gondelfahrer; Gott in der Natur; Greisengesang; Lachen und Weinen; Lied des gefangenen Jägers; Lied eines Kriegers; Pilgerweise; Schwestergruss; Der Sieg; Der Tanz; Totengräbers Heimwehe; Die Wallfahrt; Der zürnende Barde*

*** Hyp. CDJ 33035. Dawson, McGreevy, Langridge, Hampson, Konigsberger, Maltman; Johnson

Rounding off his magnificent project of recording all Schubert's songs, Graham Johnson gathers together what might have seemed loose ends, concentrating on songs from the years of the composer's late twenties. It was a period which, as Johnson explains in his ever-informative notes, brought more extreme highs and lows in the composer's life than ever before.

Central to the scheme are the five settings of poems by Rückert, four of them masterpieces including two of the best-known songs here, the playful *Lachen und weinen*, lightly touched by Geraldine McGreevy, and the glorious *Du bist die Ruh*, with Lynne Dawson rapt and dedicated in its soaring vocal line.

Also from the Rückert group are the tenor song, *Dass sie hier gewesen*, winningly sung by Philip Langridge, and a fine sixteen-bar fragment only recently discovered. Another song to note is *Totengräbers Heimwehe*, a baritone song which in its marching tread seems to anticipate *Winterreise*, powerfully sung by Christopher Maltman, if with gritty tone on sustained notes.

Rarities that prove a revelation include the poised *Schwestergruss* (McGreevy again), with four fine ensemble pieces framing the collection, starting with *Gott in der Natur*, written at the time of the *Unfinished Symphony*, and ending with the exuberant quartet, *Der Tanz* ('The Dance'). Recordings from different periods are all beautifully balanced.

Lieder, Vol. 36: *'Am 1827 Schubertiad': Cantata zur Feier der Genesung der Irene Kiesewetter; Fröhliches Scheiden; Frühlingslied; Heimliches Lieben; Der Hochzeitsbraten; Il mondo di prender moglie; Il traditor deluso; L'incanto degli occhi; Jägers Liebeslied; Der Kreuzzug; Romanze des Richard Löwenherz; Schiffers Scheidelied; Sie in jedem Liede; Die Sterne; Das Wallensteiner Lanznecht beim Trunk; Das Weinen; Wolke und Quelle*

*** Hyp. CDJ 33036. Banse, Schade, Finley, Dawson; Johnson; Holst Singers, Layton; Asti

This penultimate volume brings together miscellaneous songs from the year preceding the composer's death, ending with one of his very rare pieces, an extended comic dialogue for three singers, *Der Hochzeitsbraten* ('The Wedding Roast'), designed to raise a laugh. That is just the sort of item which might have rounded off a Schubertiad in that year, leading to a final brief chorus from the Holst Singers, misleadingly entitled *Cantata*.

The major vocal contribution here comes from the baritone, Gerald Finley, in magnificent voice, clear, firm and dark. As well as the comic trio, he sings eight of the songs, three of them settings of Italian, sounding very Schubertian rather than Italianate. Juliane Banse, with her light, bright soprano, sings five songs and Michael Schade just two. Though none of them is well known, Johnson and his colleagues make them magnetic, also thanks to his detailed, revelatory notes. Excellent sound.

Lieder, Vol. 37: 'The final year': Schwanengesang, Parts I & II. (i) *Auf der Strom. Bei dir allein!; Herbst; Irdisches Glück; Lebensmut*

🎵— *** Hyp. CDJ 33037. Mark Ainsley, Rolfe Johnson, Schade; (i) with Pyatt

Graham Johnson here rounds off his comprehensive Schubert Edition with a magnificent final offering. Whether in scholarship or breadth of musical imagination no single recording project can quite match it, covering every one of the many hundreds of songs. Not only does it include the last song-cycle, *Schwanengesang*, presented by Johnson with new insight, but a carefully chosen group of other songs from 1828, the year Schubert died. Poignantly after the darkness of the final songs of *Schwanengesang* – with *Der Döppelganger* stark and bare as though in anticipation of death – comes the last song that Schubert ever composed, *Die Taubenpost* ('Pigeon post'), seemingly trivial. Here finally happy lyricism blossoms gloriously over an exhilarating accompaniment, representing the clip-clopping of a horse.

As in the previous 36 volumes Johnson's notes (112 pages) are both searching and original, exploiting with daunting scholarship themes which bring the composer vividly to life. So the extended first song on the disc, *Auf dem Strom* ('On the river'), with opulent horn obbligato from David Pyatt, was written for a memorial concert exactly a year after Beethoven died, with Schubert both paying a heartfelt tribute to that master and laying claim to be his successor. Johnson then explores the way that many of these songs echo the theme of Beethoven's late song-cycle, *An die ferne Geliebte* ('To the distant beloved'), ever more intensely pursuing an aching realization that true love is all too seldom encountered this side of the grave.

It was shrewd to choose three fine Lieder-tenors as the soloists here. So after Michael Schade's refreshing and thoughtful singing of the introductory songs Johnson divides the *Schwanengesang* cycle between the two other tenors, for once using Schubert's original keys – John Mark Ainsley, ardent in the seven Rellstab settings (the hackneyed *Serenade* sounding totally new at a broad tempo), and Anthony Rolfe Johnson, weightier and darker-toned in the six Heine settings. All three singers – who together give a joint performance of the bizarre *Glaube, Hoffnung und Liebe* ('Faith, Hope and Love') – excel themselves in bringing out word-meaning and in tonal shading, while Johnson in his accompaniments consistently revels in Schubert's joyfully original piano writing. Few series of recordings so richly repay detailed study, and no disc from it more than this culminating issue.

Hyperion Schubert Edition sampler. Lieder: (i) *Die Allmacht;* (ii) *Alinde;* (iii) *Als ich sie erröten sah;* (iv) *Am Bach im Frühling;* (v) *Am See;* (vi) *Am Strome;* (vii) *An den Frühling;* (viii) *An die Sonne;* (ix) *An Emma;* (x) *An Silvia;* (xi) *Auflösung;* (xii) *Blondel zu Marien;* (xiii) *Erlkönig;* (xiv) *Jüngling an der Quelle;* (xv) *Der liebliche Stern;* (xvi) *Lied, D.284;* (xvii) *Lied eines Schiffers an die Dioskuren;* (xviii)

Lob der Tränen; (iii) *Mein;* (xix) *Romanze;* (xx) *Rückweg;* (xxi) *Sehnsucht;* (xxii) *Seufzer;* (xiii) *Ständchen;* (xxiii) *Tost im Tränen;* (xxiv) *Unterscheidung*

(BB) *** Hyp. HYP 200. (i) Connell; (ii) Rolfe Johnson; (iii) Bostridge; (iv) Varcoe; (v) Lott; (vi) Langridge; (vii) Ameling; (viii) Price; (ix) Allen; (x) Mark Ainsley; (xi) Fassbaender; (xii) Mathis; (xiii) Walker; (xiv) Prégardien; (xv) Schreier; (xvi) Baker; (xvii) Hampson; (xviii) Görne; (xix) Augér, King; (xx) Murray; (xxi) Schäfer; (xxii) Hill; (xxiii) Thompson; (xxiv) McLaughlin; all with Johnson

This is a delightful sampler, featuring the widest range of the fine Lieder singers whom Graham Johnson has assembled for his magnificent project, which is covered in depth in our main *Guide*. Dame Janet Baker, Dame Margaret Price and Dame Felicity Lott are on the list, with Peter Schreier, Christoph Prégardien, Brigitte Fassbaender, Elly Ameling and the late Arleen Augér among the distinguished singers from outside Britain. Inspired newcomers include Christine Schäfer, Matthias Görne and, in some ways most striking of all, Ian Bostridge, who contributes three songs. Sarah Walker has the longest item, a serenade, *Ständchen*, quite different from the famous one, with male chorus as backing. What – understandably – are missing are the texts and detailed notes which Johnson provides for the individual discs, but the booklet includes full details of each of the first 27 discs.

Miscellaneous vocal recitals

Lieder: *Abschied; Abenstern; Der Alpenjäger; Antigone und Oedip; Atys; Auf der Donau; Auflösung; Der entsühne Orest; Der Fahrt zum Hades; Fragment aus dem Aeschylus; Freiwillges Versinken; Gondelfahrer; Lied eines Schiffers an die Dioskuren; Memnon; Nach einen Gewitter; Nachtstück; Nachtviolen; Philoktet; Der Schiffer; Der Sieg; Die Sternennächte; Wie Ulfru fischt; Der zürnendeden Diana*

**(*) Teldec 8573 85556-2. Prégardien, Staier (fortepiano)

Christoph Prégardien opts for accompaniment by a fortepiano rather than a modern grand, presenting the songs on a scale such as the composer might have expected. This collection to lyrics by Mayrhofer finds him and his accompanist, Andreas Staier, unfailingly responsive to the words, even if the singer too often attacks notes from below, with intonation questionable at times. Moreover, the sound of a fortepiano is an acquired taste in such repertory.

Die Allmacht; An die Natur; Auf dem See; Auflösung; Ellens Gesänge; Erlkönig; Ganymed; Gretchen am Spinnrade; Der Musensohn; Rastlose Liebe; Schwestergruss; Suleika I; Der Tod und das Mädchen; Der Zwerg

(B) **(*) Ph. (ADD/DDD) 475 6392 (2). Norman, with Moll or Gage – MAHLER: *Lieder* **(*)

The bulk of the Schubert items date from a 1985 recital with Moll (a fine, sympathetic accompanist) and it was noted in the original review that, with so magnificently large a voice, Jessye Norman manages to scale it down for the widest range of tone and expression in this beautifully chosen selection of Schubert songs. The characterization of the four contrasting voices in *Erlkönig* is powerfully effective, and the reticence which once marked Norman in Lieder has completely disappeared. The poignancy of *Gretchen am Spinnrade* is exquisitely touched in, building to a powerful climax; throughout, the breath control is a thing of wonder, not least in her surpassing account of *Ganymed*. The five songs with Irwin Gage, dating from 1971, are all sensitively done, but with less detail than she would have later provided (as the later recordings show) but they are very well worth hearing. Good sound in both vintages, though the piano is fuller in the later recording.

(i) *Am grabe Anselmos; An die Musik; An die Nachtigall; An Sylvia; Auf dem See; Auf dem Wasser zu singen; Dass sie hier gewesen; Die Forelle; Die junge Nonne; Du bist die Ruh'; Ganymed; Geheimes; Gretchen am Spinnrade; Heidenröslein; Lachen und Weinen; Der Musensohn; Rastlose Liebe; Sei mir gegrüsset; Seligkeit; Ständchen; Suleika I & II; Wiegenlied.* (ii) *Winterreise* (song-cycle), *D.911*

(BB) **(*) Virgin 2x1 5 61457-2 (2). (i) Augér, Orkis (fortepiano); (ii) Allen, Vignoles (piano)

This Virgin Double joins up Arleen Augér's collection of favourite Lieder with Thomas Allen's *Winterreise*, dating from 1991 and 1994 respectively. The distinctive point about Arleen Augér's collection of Schubert songs – which includes a high proportion of favourites – is that the accompaniment is played by Lambert Orkis on a fortepiano. Though Augér's voice is caught most beautifully, with the tone consistently sweet and pure, the scale of the accompaniment intensifies a lightweight feeling, with beauty of tone given higher priority than word-meaning.

On the second disc Thomas Allen, understandingly supported by Roger Vignoles, tackles this Everest of the Lieder repertory with a beauty of tone and line that sets his reading apart. Allen's concentration on purely musical qualities, far from watering down word-meaning, is used to intensify the tragic emotions of the wandering lover. Allen uses a wider dynamic range than most of his direct rivals, shading the voice down to a half-tone for intimate revelations, then expanding dramatically, using the art of the opera-singer. In the two final songs, *Die Nebensonnen* and *Der Leiermann*, he is very restrained, keeping them hushed instead of underlining expressiveness. The poignancy of Schubert's inspiration is allowed to speak for itself. The one serious reservation here is the lack of translations.

Vocal Quartets

Vocal Quartets: *An Die Sonne; Gebet; Geist der Liebe; Gott der Weltschöpfer; Hymn an den Undenlichen; Die Nacht; Die Nachtigall; Psalm XXIII; Schicksalslenker; Widerspruch*

*(*) Ara. Z 6689. NY Vocal Arts Ens., Beegle (cond. & piano) (with Brecher & Cudlip)

A collection like this needs very fine vocal blending, and this is forthcoming (more or less) in the simpler lyrical settings like *Gebet* ('Prayer'), *Geist der Liebe* and the *Psalm* or the more lively *Widerspruch*, which is sung with fervour. But elsewhere individual voices extrude, notably that of the lead soprano, who has a noticeable vibrato, while the male soloist in *Schicksalslenker* is not distinctive. The singers certainly convey their joy in the closing *Gott der Weltschöpfer* but overall, although quite enjoyable, this is not a collection to recommend with real enthusiasm, especially as the playing time is only 47 minutes.

Song-cycles

Die schöne Mullerin (complete DVD version)

*** TDK **DVD** DV-CODSM. Fischer-Dieskau, Schiff (V/D: Fritz Jurmann)

Dietrich Fischer-Dieskau was filmed by Austrian Radio singing *Die schöne Mullerin* in 1991. He was 66, yet the voice is still in remarkable shape, and he compensates for any lack of bloom by dramatizing the cycle with facial expression and body language. With a superb partnership established with András Schiff, the performance has great concentration and spontaneity, leading invitably on to the closing three songs, which are most movingly sung. As a bonus there is a short portrait of the singer, filmed at the 1985 Schubertiade, in which we learn a great deal about him and his approach to interpretation.

Die schöne Müllerin (song-cycle), *D.795* (see also above, under Graham Johnson Schubert Lieder Edition, Vol. 25)

** Decca 470 025-2. Görne, Schneider

Die schöne Müllerin (complete); *Die Forelle; Frühlingsglaube; Heidenröslein*

(M) ** DG 447 452-2. Wunderlich, Geisen

Fritz Wunderlich had one of the most heavily beautiful voices among German tenors and that alone makes his record cherishable. But when he recorded the cycle (and the three favourite songs are also included here), he had still to develop as a Lieder singer, and for so subtle a cycle the performance lacks detail. He was not helped either by a rather unimaginative accompanist, and the recording is unflattering to the piano.

The German baritone, Matthias Görne, as one of the most searching of our younger Lieder-singers, follows up his masterly reading of *Winterreise* for Graham Johnson's Schubert Edition on Hyperion with this recorded account of Schubert's other great song-cycle, *Die schöne Müllerin*. Surprisingly, when this is manifestly less demanding than the later, darker cycle, his reading, always beautiful and finely detailed, lacks the same concentration, self-indulgently at the end getting slower and slower.

Schwanengesang, D.957. Lieder: (i) *Auf dem Strom. Herbst; Lebensmut*

(BB) ** Naxos 8.554663. Volle, Eisenlohr; (i) with Scott

In Naxos's enterprising Schubert Lieder Edition, Michael Volle adds three settings of poems by Ludwig Rellstab to the seven which come in the late collection of songs, *Schwanengesang*. It is an imaginative bonus, when they include the extended song with horn obbligato, *Auf dem Strom* ('On the River'). Volle is as yet a rather cautious Lieder singer, not always avoiding the squareness that can overtake strophic songs, and he seems unable to convey a smile in his voice, with the tone growing plaintive at the top. Yet with his clear diction, this is still a disc worth hearing and, as in the rest of the series, full words and translations are provided.

Winterreise (song-cycle), D.911

** EMI CDC5 56445-2. Hampson, Sawallisch

(BB) ** Naxos 8.554471. Trekel, Eisenlohr

(BB) *(*) ASV Resonance CDRSN 3053. Tear, Ledger

Though Hampson produces a stream of distinctively velvety tone, his account of this challenging song-cycle is too easy and undetailed, even bland, with Wolfgang Sawallisch uncharacteristically square and unimaginative in his playing. The experience is observed in detachment, where above all it should be involving.

Roman Trekel's baritone is more remarkable for sensitive inflection than for beauty, and though the tone grows fluttery under pressure of emotion, as in the last two songs of this supreme song cycle, the concentration and intelligence of the performance are considerable compensation. This may not rival the finest available versions of this challenging work, but it is good to hear a German singer towards the beginning of his career giving a young man's view. Ulrich Eisenlohr, one of the two pianists who have masterminded the Naxos series, does not always help with accompaniments that are too square at times. Full texts and translation as in the rest of the series.

The 1982 performance from Robert Tear and Philip Ledger is disappointing from two artists who might have been expected to follow in the inspired tradition of Pears and Britten. It is partly the dryness and lack of bloom in the recording – with the piano sounding like a cottage upright recorded too close – that underlines a degree of squareness in the slower songs. The vigorous songs go much better, but persuasiveness is undermined.

Arrangements

Lilac Time (arr. Clutsam): Highlights

* (B) CFP (ADD) 3 35989-2. Bronhill, Grimaldi, Osborne, Round, Kent, Rita Williams Singers, Michael Collins & His O – GRIEG: *Song of Norway* *

Lilac Time (*Blossom Time* in the USA) was a musical based on an idealized biography dating from 1916, also released as a lavish film version as a vehicle for Tauber in 1936. Adaptations of classical composers' music rarely (if ever) work, and G. H. Clutsam's arrangements, curiously enough, failed to improve on Schubert's invention! This dated piece of nostalgia, although it is pseudo-biographical, has very little to do with Schubert's art; but in these brightly performed highlights (recorded in 1959) it might raise a smile or two, especially at the tasteless lyrics. June Bronhill, as always, is a delight. (The film, with the exception of its star, is hilariously dreadful.) A piece of trivia: the lead in the 1922 London version of *Lilac Time* was the wife of the composer Montague Phillips (who wrote some delightful light music, so do look under his entry); her name was Clara Butterworth and she died in 1997 (outliving all her family) at the age of 109!

SCHULHOFF, Erwin (1894–1942)

String Quartet 1

*** Cal. CAL 9333. Talich Qt – JANÁČEK: *Quartets 1 & 2* ***

Erwin Schulhoff was a prolific composer, eclectic in outlook and very typical of the 1920s. After his studies at the Prague Conservatoire, he served in the First World War and was scarred for life by it. Before the war he had studied briefly with Reger and Debussy, and he was later much influenced by Mahler and early Schoenberg, 'Les Six', jazz, Bartók and Stravinsky. As a communist and a Jew, he was vulnerable after the Nazi occupation, and when he tried to flee to the Soviet Union in 1941 he was arrested. He was among the many who were murdered in a concentration camp in Wulzburg, Bavaria. The vehement and Bartókian *First Quartet* has been frequently recorded in recent years (by the Kocian and Petersen Quartets) but the Talich do it with authority and passion. An interesting makeweight to the Janáček *Quartets*.

SCHUMAN, William (1910–92)

Symphonies 4 & 9 (*Le Fosse Ardeatine*)

(BB) *** Naxos 8.559254. Seattle SO, Schwarz

Symphonies 7 & 10 (*The American Muse*)

(BB) *** Naxos 8.559255. Seattle SO, Schwarz

These two issues are part of a projected cycle of the complete Schuman symphonies. The *Third* and *Sixth* are two of the greatest American symphonies, and their appearance is impatiently awaited. In the meantime, Gerard Schwarz and the Seattle orchestra give finely prepared and totally committed accounts of the present four. After the success of the wartime symphonies, Schuman became President of the Juilliard School of Music in 1945, and by the time he had completed the *Eighth* in 1962 he was President of the new Lincoln Center. He is said to have composed early in the morning and then turned to musical education and administration for the rest of the day. The *Fourth Symphony* followed its famous predecessor within a few months, and its première was conducted by Koussevitzky. It was recorded by the Louisville Orchestra in 1990 on the Albany label, but this newcomer easily supersedes it. The *Ninth* was written in 1967, when Schuman had visited Rome and seen the memorial *Le Fosse Ardeatine* that commemorates a random massacre by Nazi forces. It is a dark and powerful score. The *Seventh* (1960) marks Schuman's return to the symphony after a gap of 11 years, while the *Tenth* was commissioned for the bicentennial celebrations of 1975. No one investigating these works will be disappointed.

String Quartet 3

*** Testament 1374. Juilliard Qt – BERG: *Lyric Suite*; CARTER: *Quartet 2* ***

It was William Schuman who, when he became President of the Juilliard School, made plans for a resident quartet, and he who hailed their debut concert: 'I'll never forget it if I live to be a thousand, it was greater than anything I'd ever dreamed of.' They recorded Schuman's own *Quartet* (1940) in 1958 and play it with consistent fervour and the deep understanding that they show in the companion works. The *Third* is a powerful and strongly original piece which alone is worth the price of this record.

SCHUMANN, Clara (1819–96)

3 Romances, Op. 22

*** Avie AV 2075. Khaner, Abramovic – BRAHMS: *Clarinet Sonatas 1–2*; Robert SCHUMANN: *Romances* ***

Though Clara Schumann's charming *Romances* were originally written for violin, they make an apt and attractive fill-up to the flute transcriptions of the other works on the disc, rarities that deserve to be heard more often, here most sensitively performed.

SCHUMANN, Robert (1810–56)

(i) *Cello Concerto*; (ii) *Piano Concerto; Introduction & Allegro appassionato, Op. 92*

(BB) ** EMI (ADD) 5 74755-2. (i) Du Pré, New Philh. O, Barenboim; (ii) Barenboim, LPO, Fischer-Dieskau

The most attractive performance here is Jacqueline du Pré's 1968 recording of the *Cello Concerto*. Her spontaneous style is strikingly suited to this most recalcitrant of concertos and the slow movement is particularly beautiful. She is ably assisted by Daniel Barenboim and the only snag is the rather faded orchestral sound, unflattered by the present transfer, though the cello timbre is realistically focused.

The coupling was recorded in the mid-1970s; the sound is somewhat firmer and the balance lets the piano dominate but, with the LPO below its best under Fischer-Dieskau (a good but not outstanding conductor), this is probably just as well. Barenboim is brisk and not particularly poetic, and these performances lack what he usually achieves on record: a sense of spontaneity, a simulation of live performance.

(i) *Cello Concerto;* (ii) *Piano Concerto. Symphonies 1–4*
(M) ** DG 477 5167 (6). VPO, Bernstein; with (i) Maisky; (ii) Frantz – MENDELSSOHN: *Symphonies 3–5;* SCHUBERT: *Symphonies 5, 8 & 9* **(*)

These recordings were made at live concerts in the mid-1980s and there is no doubting the extra voltage that provided. It is a pity, however, that Bernstein, who displays a natural response to Schumann, imposes personal idiosyncrasies on the performances less convincingly than Karajan or Furtwängler, with tempos not always perfectly controlled. The opening of the *Spring Symphony* is pushed hard, while the outer movements of the *Fourth* are not allowed to move forward at a steady pulse. There is always much to admire, of course, and the slow movements have striking warmth, even if, for example, the opening *Romance* in No. 4 sounds a little self-conscious. The *Rhenish* is full of nobility, even if there is a tendency towards exaggeration.

The *Piano Concerto* is a little wanting in spontaneity and does not have the delicacy of feeling or subtlety of nuance that the best versions possess. In the *Cello Concerto*, both artists have moments of self-indulgence and, like the *Second Symphony*, with which it was originally coupled, there is a feeling that the music is rarely allowed to speak for itself.

Piano Concerto in A min., Op. 54
(M) *** Ph. (ADD) 478 7773. Kovacevich, BBC SO, C. Davis – GRIEG: *Concerto* ***
(M) ** DG (IMS) 471 353-2. Pollini, BPO, Abbado – BRAHMS: *Piano Concerto 1* **
((M) ** Chan. 6621 (2). Margalit, LSO, Thompson (with MENDELSSOHN: *Capriccio brillant* **) – BRAHMS: *Concerto 1;* SAINT-SAENS: *Concerto 2* **
(i) *Piano Concerto in A min. Papillons, Op. 2*
(M) ** EMI (ADD) 5 67982-2. S. Richter, Monte Carlo Op. O, Matačić – GRIEG: *Piano Concerto* *(*)

Kovacevich and Davis give an interpretation fresh and poetic which is still unsurpassed and is now reissued as one of Philips's Originals.

Pollini's account of the *Concerto* is not without tenderness and poetry, but he is at times rather businesslike and wanting in freshness. He is handicapped by rather unventilated recording and an inconsistent balance. The Schumann coupling is every way successful: the *Symphonic Studies* has a symphonic gravitas and concentration; it also has the benefit of excellent recorded quality. The Brahms alternative coupling is less recommendable.

Richter's Monte Carlo reading of the Schumann, like that of the Grieg coupling, is extraordinarily wayward. Though with this composer he can hardly help bringing occasional illumination, this remains on the whole a disappointing version and is hardly well chosen for inclusion among EMI's 'Great Recordings of the Century'. *Papillons*, a live recording made in Florence in 1962, is in quite a different class, chimerical and wholly spontaneous, even if the piano recording is somewhat hard.

Israela Margalit brings no lack of warmth or poetic feeling to the concerto, but she is somewhat idiosyncratic. The central A flat section of the first movement is very measured and she is not averse to point-making by means of rubati. The recording is resonant, with the piano well forward. This offers no serious challenge to the front-runners in the catalogue (Andsnes and Kovacevich), and the two-disc format is uneconomical.

Introduction & Allegro appassionato in G, Op. 92
(BB) *(*) Naxos 8.554089. Biret, Polish Nat. RSO, Wit – BRAHMS: *Piano Concerto 2* **

As with the companion work below, Biret's playing is romantically full-blooded, and she receives warm support from Wit and the Polish orchestra. However, a tighter overall grip would have made the performance even more effective. No complaints about the recording, which is resonantly full and well balanced.

Introduction & Concert-allegro, Op. 134
(BB) ** Naxos 8.554088. Biret, Polish Nat. RSO, Wit – BRAHMS: *Piano Concerto 1* *(*)

Idil Biret plays with no mean virtuosity and brilliance, and this performance is more successful than its coupling. The recording is spacious.

SYMPHONIES

Symphonies 1; 4 (original, 1841 version)
(BB) ** Warner Apex 0927 49585-2. LPO, Masur
Symphonies 2; 3 (Rhenish)
(BB) ** Warner Apex 0927 49814-2. LPO, Masur
Symphonies 1–4; Scherzo in G min. (ed. Draheim)
**(*) Classico CLASS CD 431/2. Czech Chamber PO, Bostock

On Apex is a reissue of Masur's complete set of the early 1990s. The recording is full-blooded and the performances are sound but not distinctive. Slow movements lack something in romantic expansiveness, and the second movement of the *Rhenish* is comparatively brusque. The main interest of the first disc is that Masur offers the 1841 version of the *Fourth Symphony*, which was admired by Brahms; the differences are most marked in the finale. This set cannot compete with Zinman on Arte Nova (8287657743-2).

It is fascinating to hear the versions of the symphonies that Douglas Bostock has recorded for Classico with the Czech Chamber Philharmonic Orchestra using a very modest band of strings recorded in a modestly sized hall. It is he too who orchestrated the extra item, the *Scherzo in G minor*. It makes an attractive miniature. In the regular symphonies the interpretative approach is consistently plain, almost metrical at times, with melodies less affectionately phrased than they might be. These are not in any way chilly readings, and they will appeal to anyone who wants a lighter approach to these works.

Symphony 2 in C
(**) Testament SBT 1377. NBC SO, Toscanini – MENDELSSOHN: *Symphony 3; Hebrides Overture* (**)

This 1941 studio recording, together with the Mendelssohn couplings, counters the myth that Toscanini was a speed merchant. The *Second Symphony* is humane and is held together with all Toscanini's familiar mastery. Given a performance of great quality, the ear tends to accustom itself to poor recorded sound; but here the recording itself really is quite awful and calls for great tolerance.

Symphonies 3 in E flat (Rhenish); 4 in D min., Op. 120
(BB) **(*) Virgin 2x1 3 49983-2 (2). LCP, Norrington –
MENDELSSOHN: *Symphonies 3; 4* ***

With Schumann's orchestration usually accused of being too thick, there is much to be said for period performances like this. Norrington not only clarifies textures, with natural horns in particular standing out dramatically, but, at unexaggerated speeds for the outer movements – even a little too slow for the first movement of No. 3 – the results are often almost Mendelssohnian, to make a clear link with the coupling. Middle movements in both symphonies are unusually brisk, turning slow movements into lyrical interludes. Warm, atmospheric recording.

CHAMBER MUSIC

Adagio and Allegro, Op. 70; 5 Pieces in Popular Style
(B) **(*) Cal. (ADD) CAL 3614. Navarra, Annie d'Arco –
DVOŘÁK: *Humoresque*, etc.; SCHUBERT: *Arpeggione
Sonata* **(*)

Navarra plays the *Adagio* very romantically and then finds ready bravura for the *Allegro*. But it is the five miniatures in which he is most eloquent, playing them very appealingly.

Fantasiestücke, Op. 73; (i) Märchenerzählungen (Fairy Tale), Op. 132 (for clarinet & piano)
(B) ** CfP (ADD) 5 87023-2. De Peyer, Crowson; (i) with
Aronowitz – BRAHMS: *Clarinet Sonatas 1–2* ***

The *Fantasy Pieces* begin well in strong, romantic vein, but the *Fairy Tales* are not very magical and, for all Gervase de Peyer's persuasive advocacy, the music here is not very memorable. Excellent recording.

5 Stücke in Volkston (5 Pieces for cello & piano)
(M) *** Decca (ADD) 452 895-2. Rostropovich, Britten –
BRITTEN: *Cello Sonata*; DEBUSSY: *Sonata* ***

Though simpler than either the Britten or Debussy sonatas with which it is coupled, this is just as elusive a work. Rostropovich and Britten show that the simplicity is not as square and solid as might at first seem and that, in the hands of masters, these *Five Pieces in Folk Style* have a rare charm, particularly the last with its irregular rhythm. The excellent recording justifies the reissue.

(i) Piano Quintet in E flat, Op. 44. String Quartets 1–3, Op. 41/1–3
(BB) **(*) EMI Gemini 3 50819-2 (2). (i) Zacharias; Cherubini
Qt

The account of the *Piano Quintet* is first class in every way, with Christian Zacharias dominating and taking the string players with him. It has splendid vigour and spirit, with the *In modo d'una Marcia* very characterfully done. The recording is excellent. The three *String Quartets* were recorded in a different venue, and both performances and sound are slightly drier. Without Zacharias, the Cherubini Quartet seem slightly more inhibited, less spontaneous, though they still play very well indeed.

3 Romances Op. 95
*** Avie AV 2075. Khaner, Abramovic – BRAHMS: *Clarinet
Sonatas 1–2*; Clara SCHUMANN: *3 Romances* ***

When Schumann gave the option of playing these pieces on violin or clarinet in place of the oboe, which he originally had

in mind, there is a strong case for welcoming Jeffrey Khaner's arrangements for flute, ideal fill-ups for his transcriptions of the two Brahms *Clarinet Sonatas*, the main works on the disc. As in the other items, Khaner's performances could not be more sensitive.

PIANO MUSIC

Abegg Variations, Op. 1; Faschingsschwank aus Wien, Op. 26
(M) (**) BBC mono BBCL 4126-2. Sviatoslav Richter (with
CHOPIN: *Etude in F sharp min., Op. 10/4*) – BEETHOVEN:
Piano Sonatas 9–10; SCHUBERT: *Wanderer Fantasy* (**)

It was with an LP of Schumann's *Waldszenen* and some of the *Fantasiestücke* on DG that Richter first made his entry into the catalogues. His affinity with the composer is soon communicated, though the bronchial audience is tiresome. As always with this great artist, his readings are the product of much thought and the mono sound is perfectly acceptable.

Arabeske, Op. 18; Bunte Blätter; Etudes symphoniques, Op. 13 (1832 & 1852 versions, with 1873 appendix); Fantasie in C, Op. 17
*** DG 474 817-2. Pletnev

Mikhail Pletnev has a uniquely distinctive keyboard sonority and his pianistic prowess is almost unrivalled. He gave three of the *Bunte Blätter* and the *C major Fantasy* at the Barbican Centre in London, early in 2003, which viewers of BBC Four will have seen. Wonderful though his pianism is, it must be conceded that the *C major Fantasy* has some disruptive, agogic touches which impair its natural flow. Even so, Pletnev has remarkable powers of artistic persuasion, and his Schumann has a compelling quality that mostly silences some of the doubts listeners might initially feel. This finely recorded issue should be heard by all Schumanniacs, for although Perahia remains a first choice Pletnev always has interesting thoughts, whatever the repertoire he chooses.

Carnaval, Op. 9; Fantasiestücke, Op. 12; Papillons, Op. 2
(M) ** Somm SOMMCD 024. Lazaridis

George-Emmanuel Lazaridis was perhaps unwise to choose this very demanding Schumann programme for his début CD. The moments of gentle poetry show that he has a feeling for the composer, even if his tempi and phrasing are somewhat indulgent, especially in *Papillons*. But for the most part his impulsive tendency to press ahead, seeking to convey a spontaneous forward impulse, serves Schumann less well. Even in *Carnaval*, the most successful performance here, one sometimes feels the piano hammers being applied too percussively, although the playing has plenty of spirit. Fine recording, its brightness partly accounted for by Lazaridis's bold articulation.

Impromptus on a Theme of Clara Wieck, Op. 5; Variations on a Theme of Beethoven; Variations on an Original Theme (Geistervariationen); Variations on a Theme of Schubert
** Athene ATHCD 23. Boyde – BRAHMS: *Variations on a
Theme of Schumann* **

An intelligently planned recital, which brings repertoire little-known even to those who know their Schumann. The ten *Impromptus on a Theme of Clara Wieck* of 1833 are well represented in the catalogue but the remainder are relatively neglected. The Beethoven variations of 1830 are based on the slow movement of the *Seventh Symphony*. The *Geistervariationen* was Schumann's very last work. Andreas Boyde has reconstructed the *Variations on a Theme of Schubert*, which Schumann began in 1829 and to which he returned five years later. Accomplished but not highly sensitive playing, though this impression may in part be due to the close and two-dimensional recording.

VOCAL MUSIC

Frauenliebe und Leben, Op. 42
*⊶ ☉ (BB) ***** Regis (ADD) RRC 1225. J. Baker, Isepp – Vocal Recital, including Brahms & Schubert Songs* ***

Dame Janet's famous early (1966) Saga recording of Schumann's great song-cycle at last re-emerges on another budget label, Regis, carefully remastered and sounding remarkably real and vivid. As we said in our original review, her range of expression runs the whole gamut, from a joyful golden tone-colour in the exhilaration of *Ich kann's nicht fassen*, through an ecstatic half-tone in *Süsser Freund* (the fulfilment of the line '*Du geliebter Mann*' wonderfully conveyed), to the dead, vibrato-less agony at the bereavement in the final song. A performance that should be in every collection.

Frauenliebe und Leben, Op. 42; Liederkreis, Op. 39
(B) ***** Ph. ADD 475 6374 (2). Norman, Gage – BRAHMS: *Lieder* **(*)

The richness and power of Jessye Norman's voice are well caught in this 1975 recital, but in *Frauenliebe* she is not quite at her happiest or most spontaneous. It has its quota of mawkish words, and Norman does not seem naturally to identify. Richer in poetry, the Eichendorff *Liederkreis* is more sympathetic to her; but other versions are even more sensitive. Accompaniments and recordings are most refined.

(i; ii) Mass, Op. 147; (ii–vi) Requiem für Mignon; (ii; iv–viii) Requiem, Op. 148; (ii; v; vii; x; xi) Der Rose Pilgerfahrt
(BB) ******* EMI Gemini 3 50900-2 (2). (i) Shirai, Seiffert, Rootering, BPO, Sawallisch; (ii) Ch. of the State Musikvereins, Düsseldorf; (iii) Lindner, Andonian, Georg, Welchhold; (iv) Fischer-Dieskau; (v) Düsseldorf SO; (vi) Klee; (vii) Donath; (viii) Soffel; (vix) Gedda; (x) Lövaas, Hamari, Altmeyer, Pola; (xi) De Burgos

Sawallisch's dedicated performance of Schumann's long-neglected and under-prized setting of the Mass was recorded live in Düsseldorf in September 1987. Schumann himself only heard the *Kyrie* and *Gloria* of this late work of 1853; but some of his finest flights of invention – not at all the tailing-off which has been ascribed to him in the period leading up to his mental illness – come in the *Sanctus* and *Agnus Dei*. Of the soloists, only the soprano has much to sing (the delectable Mitsuko Shirai, sensuously beautiful in the *Offertorium* solo) and the weight of the work rests on the chorus, a fine body here, warmly rather than clinically recorded.

Like Mozart, Schumann was unable to shake off the conviction that the *Requiem* was for himself. The opening *Requiem aeternam* is affecting and dignified, and the final *Benedictus* has a haunting eloquence. Bernhard Klee extracts a very sympathetic response from his distinguished team of soloists and the fine Düsseldorf chorus and orchestra. They also give an attentive and committed account of the 1849 *Requiem for Mignon*, and the attractive cantata, *Der Rose Pilgerfahrt*, is equally successful. The EMI recording is natural and well balanced.

Das Paradies und die Peri, Op. 50
(BB) ****** Arte Nova 74321 87817-2 (2). Kernes, Wollitz, Paulsen, Dewald, Fernández, Schulte, Cechova, Zabala, Europa ChorAkademie, Pforzheim Wind Ens., SW German CO, Daus

Recorded live at performances in Wiesbaden and Bremen, Joshard Daus's version of Schumann's secular oratorio offers a serviceable version at super-budget price, generally well recorded and with Simone Kernes sweet-toned as the Peri, only occasionally overstressed. As a more traditional, heavier-handed reading than Gardiner's on DG Archiv, it cannot match that full-price version. It comes with the German text but no translation.

SCHÜTZ, Heinrich (1585–1672)

Der Schwanengesang (reconstructed Wolfram Steude)
(BB) ***(*)** Virgin 2x1 4 82100-2 (2). Hannover Boys' Ch., Hilliard Ens., L. Bar., Hillier – BACH: *Motets* ***

Schütz's *opus ultimum* is a setting of Psalm 119 (The longest psalm in the psalter), which he divides into 11 sections. He finishes off this 13-part motet cycle with the final setting of Psalm 100, which he had originally composed in 1662, and the *Deutsches Magnificat*. Wolfram Steude's note recounts the history of the work, parts of which disappeared after Schütz's death; and his reconstruction of two of the vocal parts is obviously a labour of love. The performance is a completely dedicated one, with excellent singing from all concerned and good instrumental playing, and the conductor, Heinz Hennig, secures warm and responsive singing from the Hannover Knabenchor. The acoustic is spacious and warm and the recording balance well focused. The sound is firm, clear, and spacious.

SCOTT, Cyril (1879–1970)

(i) Piano Concerto 1; 'Early One Morning' for Piano & Orchestra. Symphony 4
*** Chan. 10376. BBC PO, Brabbins, (i) with Shelley

Scott's *First Piano Concerto* was premièred by Beecham in 1915, when the composer, who took the solo role, was at the height of his early fame. It is not a work offering a traditional dialogue between piano and orchestra, for the pianist hardly pauses to take a breath, nor is it clearly structured (apart from the separation into movements), the music changing from mood to mood; yet there is a chromatic lusciousness about the texture that is appealing, especially in the slow movement. The *Fourth Symphony* is similarly exotic, flowing forward with a tidal surge and a chromatic impressionistic atmosphere to make up for the structural ambiguity. The central movements form a distinct kernel, with a sensuous *Molto tranquillo* contrasting with an uninhibited Scherzo with its main theme in 15/8, and the finale ends ecstatically. After all this fluidity, the concertante *Variations on 'Early One Morning'* are joyfully explicit, though still never predictable. Excellent performances throughout, with Shelley obviously completely at home in the concertante works, which he plays with great flair.

SCRIABIN, Alexander (1872–1915)

(i) *Piano Concerto in F sharp min., Op. 20; Le Poème de l'extase, Op. 54;* (i; ii) *Prometheus*
** DG (IMS) 459 647-2. (i) Ugorski; (ii) Chicago Symphony Ch.; Chicago SO, Boulez

Boulez's second recording of *Le Poème de l'extase* is short on ecstasy and not too strong on poetry either; ultimately it is analytical and detached. Boulez does restrain Anatole Ugorski's propensity to pull things out of shape, and both the *Piano Concerto* and *Prometheus* receive straightforward and at times elegant performances with excellent recorded sound. All the same, this is not a first choice for any of these pieces.

Symphony 3 (Le Divin Poème); Le Poème de l'extase
(M) ** Warner Elatus 2564 60812-2. O de Paris, Barenboim

Barenboim's performances were recorded live at the Salle Pleyel, Paris, in 1986 and 1987. The *Symphony* sprawls in his hands and is far from a first choice, although the Orchestre de Paris plays with evident relish. The *Poème de l'extase* is much more successful, a ripely atmospheric reading emphasizing the composer's debt to Wagner, and to *Tristan* in particular. The orchestra produces warm, well-integrated textures, and that is stressed by the mellow, slightly recessed quality of the recording.

Symphony 3 (Le Divin Poème); Le Poème de l'extase (arr. Konyus for piano, 4 hands)
(BB) ** Naxos 8.555327. Prunyi, Falvai

In the early years of the twentieth century piano reductions were the only way for most music lovers to get to know the repertoire. Nowadays such arrangements of complex orchestral scores seem much less useful. As transcriptions go this is expert enough, and the playing and recording are fully acceptable, but it is far more sensible to get a coupling of the real thing!

PIANO MUSIC

5 Preludes, Op. 15; Sonata 3, Op. 23
*** RCA 82876 65390-2. Evgeny Kissin – MEDTNER: *Sonata-Reminiscenza* **(*); STRAVINSKY: *Movements from 'Petrushka'* ***

Kissin is a wonderful pianist who is in his element in Scriabin. He is attuned to the pianistic flair and keen narcissism of the composer and surmounts the formidable difficulties of the big-boned *Third Sonata* with great aplomb.

Piano Sonata 5 in F sharp, Op. 53
(BB) *(*) Warner Apex 0927 40830-2. Sultanov – PROKOFIEV: *Piano Sonata 7*; RACHMANINOV: *Piano Sonata 2* *(*)

Alexei Sultanov has great brilliance and a formidable technical address, which is heard to considerable effect here. But the concentration is largely on virtuosity, dazzle and gloss.

Piano Sonata 9 (Black Mass)
*RCA 82876 64561-2. Luisada – CHOPIN: *Sonata 3*; LISZT: *Sonata* *
  Jean-Marc Luisada's account of the *Ninth Sonata* is curiously unidiomatic and wanting in both keyboard authority and artistic conviction.

SEIBER, Mátyás (1905–60)

String Quartet 3 (Quartetto lirico)
(M) (***) EMI mono/stereo 5 85150-2. (i) Amadeus Qt – TIPPETT: *String Quartet 2*, etc. (***)

Hungarian composer Mátyás Seiber's *Third String Quartet* was completed in 1951 and dedicated to the Amadeus Quartet, who recorded this performance in 1954. It employs serial technique, with plenty of *glissandi* and *sul ponticello* and, if this style will not be to all tastes, the music obviously comes from intense emotion, although it is the Tippett *Second String Quartet* on this CD which more readily communicates. This performance is a very good one indeed, and one enjoys the often very beautiful sounds for their own sake. The recording is astonishingly rich and full, with virtually no background noise at all.

SESSIONS, Roger (1896–1985)

String Quartet 1 in E min.; String Quintet; Canons to the memory of Stravinsky for String Quartet; 6 Pieces for Cello
(BB) *** Naxos 8.559261. The Group for Contemporary Music

Sessions was an uncompromising figure who composed absolute music and eschewed any obvious American influences. He was an influential teacher, whose pupils included Milton Babbitt. Thanks to the gramophone, he is best known here for his *Second Symphony* and his ballet, *The Black Maskers*, an early work reflecting the influence of Bloch, with whom he studied, and Prokofiev. The *E minor String Quartet* of 1936 (not 1938 as stated on the sleeve – it was first performed in 1937) belongs to his neo-classical period. The form of the first movement is modelled on the corresponding movement of Beethoven's *A minor Quartet*, Op. 132. So, too, is that of the *String Quintet* of 1958 which derives from the Schoenberg of the *Third* and *Fourth Quartets*. The solo cello *Pieces* are from 1966, and the *Canons* for Stravinsky come from the year of his death. The Group for Contemporary Music is a New York ensemble, and a very expert one. The recording dates from 1993 and first appeared on the Koch label.

SHOSTAKOVICH, Dmitri (1906–75)

(i; ii) *Alone: Suite, Op 26;* (i; iii) *The Bolt: Suite, Op. 27a* (1934 version); (iv) *The Bolt: Suite, Op. 27a* (1931 version); (v) *Chamber Symphony (String Qt 4), Op. 83a; Chamber Symphony (String Quartet 8), Op. 110a;* (vi) *Cello Concertos 1–2. Piano Concertos* (i; ii; vii) *1 in C min. for Trumpet & Strings.* (viii; ix) *2 in F, Op. 102. Violin Concertos* (x) *1 in E min., Op. 99;* (xi) *2 in C sharp min., Op. 129;* (i; ii) *The Counterplan: Suite;* (viii) *Festive Overture, Op. 96. 5 Fragments, Op. 42. Funeral and Triumphal Prelude;* (i; iii) *The Gadfly (excerps);* (iv) *The Golden Age: Suite, Op. 22;* (i; ii) *The Great Citizen: Funeral March;* (iv) *Hamlet: Suite, Op. 32a;* (i; ii) *Hamlet (excerpts), Op. 116; Jazz Suites 1 & 2;* (i; iii) *Moscow-Cheryomushki: Suite, Op. 105;* (viii) *October, Op. 131;* (ii; xii) *Overture on Russian and Kirghiz Folk Themes, Op. 115;* (i; ii) *Pirogov: Scherzo & Finale. Sofia Perovskaya: Waltz;* (v) *Symphony for Strings, Op. 118a; Symphony for Strings and Woodwinds, Op. 73a;* (i; ii) *Tahiti Trot (Tea for Two); The Tale of the Silly Little Mouse* (arr. Cornall), *Op. 56;* (xiii) *The Execution of Stepan Razin;* (viii; xiv) *The Song of the Forests*
(B) Decca 475 7431 (9). (i) Chailly; (ii) Concg. O; (iii) Philh. O; (iv) Gothenberg SO, Järvi; (v) COE, Barshai; (vi) Schiff,

Bav. RSO, Maxim Shostakovich; (vii) Brautigam, Masseurs; (viii) RPO, Ashkenazy; (ix) Ortiz; (x) Mullova, RPO, Previn; (xi) Kremer, Boston SO, Ozawa; (xii) Haitink; (xiii) Vogel, Leipzig Ch. & RSO, Kegel; (xiv) Kotliarov, Storojev, New London Children's Ch., Brighton Festival Ch.

This feast of Shostakovich includes Chailly's three famous CDs of ballet and film suites and the supremely delightful *Jazz Suites* – some of the most appealing music Shostakovich ever wrote. All sorts of intriguing repertoire is here, and Shostakovich's ready fund of melody and his exotic orchestral palette, spiced with touches of wit, make for a kaleidoscope of memorable vignettes. The delightful opening *Presto* in the music from *The Counterplan* leads to a wistful romantic concertante violin episode, not unlike the more famous *Romance* from *The Gadfly*, which is also included (in its original orchestration). *The Tale of the Silly Little Mouse* (an animated cartoon) is full of delicate charm, and the engaging *Valse* from *Pirogov* is rather more robust. *Hamlet* (there are two versions of the music here) brings music of more pungency and dramatic power, while the composer's instantaneous and irresistible arrangement of Youmans's 'Tea for Two', the *Tahiti Trot*, almost upstages everything.

One of the most substantial film scores, *Alone*, brings a wide range of picaresque and touching evocations, describing a barrel organ, schoolchildren and a tempest, and ending with an eerie calm after the storm. Other highlights include the opening number from *Moscow-Cheryomushki*, which has great energy and élan, and the luscious violins in the *Tango* from *The Bolt* are a joy. In fact, the full body of tone from the Philadelphia Orchestra in melancholy response to *The Slap in the Face* (*The Gadfly*) and the soft-voiced cellos and violas in *Gemma's Room* recall Stokowski. Chailly plays this repertoire superbly and receives magnificent orchestral playing from both the Concertgebouw and Philadelphia orchestras, with Decca sound to match.

In the concertos, the *Cello Concertos* with Schiff are superbly recorded and the *First* can hold its own with the finest. The *Second* is a haunting piece, essentially lyrical; it is gently discursive, sadly whimsical at times, and tinged with smiling melancholy that hides deeper troubles. The recording (Philips) is enormously impressive. There's a perfectly enjoyable account of the *Piano and Trumpet Concerto* from Brautigam and his excellent trumpet partner, Peter Masseurs, vividly accompanied by Chailly, but this in the last resort is not the most memorable account the work has received.

The *Second Piano Concerto* with Ortiz is very successful: she gives a sparkling account of the jaunty first movement and brings out the fun and wit in the finale with fluent, finely pointed playing. The *First Violin Concerto* is disappointing: Viktoria Mullova does not penetrate far below the surface in the poignant opening *Nocturne* and, although it is all very expert, the performance is ultimately routine and wanting in atmosphere. Gidon Kremer's DG account of the *Second Violin Concerto* is played with his customary aplomb, but the recording is not really in the demonstration bracket.

The *Chamber symphony* is an arrangement for full strings of the *Eighth Quartet* and the *Symphony for Strings* is a similar transcription of the *Tenth*. Both were made by Rudolf Barshai, and he directs them with the authority of the composer and bears his imprimatur. These are strong performances and are excellently recorded (DG). With two substantial choral rarities – Ashkenazy's *The Song of the Forests* (a freshly tuneful and enjoyable work that would have pleased the Soviet authorities) and Kegel's dramatic 1972 recording of the red-blooded *The Execution of Stepan Razin* –

this bargain set is well worth considering. Only the *First Concerto* disappoints here, a small complaint among these riches. Texts and translations included.

(i) *Chamber Symphonies: in D, Op. 83a; in C min., Op. 110a* (arr. of *String Quartets 4 & 8*); *Symphonies: for Strings & Woodwind, Op. 73a; for Strings, Op.118a* (arr. of *String Quartets 3 & 8*) (all orch. Barshai).(ii) *Symphony 15 in A, Op. 141bis* (arr. for violin, cello, piano, celesta & percussion by Viktor Derevianko)

(M) *** DG 2-CD 477 544. (i) COE, Barshai; (ii) Kremerata (with SCHNITTKE: *Prelude in memory of Shostakovich*)

This DG Double usefully gathers together Rudolf Barshai's distinguished arrangements for orchestra of four of Shostakovich's string quartets. He sustained a long friendship with the composer, and he directs these performances with the latter's authority and imprimatur. The players of the Chamber Orchestra of Europe excel themselves in the tonal beauty, refinement and responsiveness of their playing, here recorded in the smaller Philharmonie in Berlin. But inevitably, with the fuller string sound (although it is not lush), some of the darkness of the music disappears: notably the chill of much of the writing in No. 8, inspired by memories of the war and the bombing of Dresden. In compensation, the added weight of sound gives greater impact to such movements as the *Allegro molto* of Op. 110a. These are strong performances of real eloquence and power, very well recorded, and can be confidently recommended to those who prefer the brooding transcriptions to the inward-looking originals.

Viktor Derevianko's remarkably successful transcription of the *15th Symphony* for a chamber quintet (essentially a piano trio plus percussion) makes a surprise bonus, bringing out the quirkiness of the pair of *Allegrettos* (movements 1 and 3), yet by no means missing the expressive depth of the *Adagio/ Largo* and questioning ambivalence of the finale. The sound is again first class.

Alfred Schnittke's *Prelude* (for two violins, with Gidon Kremer playing with his own pre-recorded tape, as the composer directed) makes a strikingly stark *In memoriam*, being placed between Op. 73a and the *Symphony*.

Cello Concertos 1; 2 in G, Op. 126

(M) *** Ph. 475 7575. Schiff, Bav. RSO, Maxim Shostakovich

Heinrich Schiff was the first cellist to couple these two concertos, which certainly makes him a perfect choice for Philips's Originals collection. The *Second Concerto* is the more elusive of the two. A haunting piece, essentially lyrical, it is gently discursive, sadly whimsical at times and tinged with a smiling melancholy that hides deeper troubles. Schiff has its full measure, as indeed he has of the more direct *First Concerto*, and this has long been a favourite coupling of ours. The recording is enormously impressive.

Cello Concerto 1 in E flat, Op. 107; (i) Cello Sonata in D min., Op. 40

*** EMI 332 4222. Han-Na Chang, LSO, Pappano; (i) with Pappano (piano)

A highly impressive account of the *First Concerto* from Han-Na Chang, which can hold its own in the most exalted company. The same can be said of the *Sonata*, in which Pappano abandons the baton for the keyboard. He is a very fine pianist and gives Han-Na Chang excellent support.

Cello Concerto 2, Op. 126

*** Avie AV 2090. Harrell, RLPO, Schwarz – PROKOFIEV: *Sinfonia concertante* ***

(i) *Cello Concerto 2; Symphony 12 (The Year 1917), Op. 112*

** Chan. 9585. (i) Helmerson; Russian State SO, Polyansky

Avie offer a strong coupling and a welcome addition to the catalogue. Although Lynn Harrell recorded the *First Concerto* for Decca with the Concertgebouw Orchestra and Bernard Haitink, he has not committed the *Second* to disc before. Here he is captured live in performances from May 2005, and he gives (as one would expect) a masterly account of this elusive score and one which has all the electricity of live music-making. And what good results Gerard Schwarz gets from the Liverpool orchestra. Very acceptable recording quality.

This fine Swedish cellist on Chandos plays with eloquence and authority in the *Second Cello Concerto* but the orchestral response is a little disappointing. Moreover, the *Twelfth Symphony* calls for the advocacy of an outsize personality if it is to make a really positive impression.

Violin Concerto 1 in A min., Op. 99

** EMI 3 46053-2. Chang, BPO, Rattle – PROKOFIEV: *Violin Concerto 1* **(*)

(B) *(*) Ph. 2-CD 475 7547 (2). Mullova, RPO, Previn – BARTÓK: *Violin Concerto 2* **; PROKOFIEV: *Violin Concerto 2*; STRAVINSKY: *Violin Concerto* ***

Although Sarah Chang and Simon Rattle have a good rapport in the *First Violin Concerto*, the rather forward balance of the soloist is a bit troubling. There is some coarseness of tone as a result and, although there is considerable finesse from the orchestra, Chang is a little too closely observed for real comfort and her vibrato is at times a little excessive.

Viktoria Mullova does not penetrate far below the surface in the poignant opening *Nocturne* of the concerto. It is all very expert, but ultimately the performance is routine and wanting in atmosphere.

Violin Concertos 1; 2 in C sharp min., Op. 129

⊶ *** Warner 2564 62546-2 Hope, BBC SO, M. Shostakovich

Daniel Hope is a brilliant and thoughtful soloist in both the familiar *First Concerto* and its underrated successor. Maxim Shostakovich gets good results from the BBC Symphony Orchestra, and the recording team offer excellent and natural sound. This is as good as any rival coupling on the market.

Symphonies

Symphonies 1–2; (i) 3.4–13 (Babi Yar); (i; ii) 14; (iii) 15

⊶ (B) *** Cap. **SACD** 71029 (12). (i) Prague Ph. Ch; (iii) Shaguch; (ii; iii) Kotchinian; Gürzenich O, Cologne, Kitajenko

Here is a competitively priced survey of the Shostakovich canon from Dmitri Kitajenko and the Cologne Gürzenich Orchestra. Kitajenko won the Karajan Competition in 1969 but has not, as far as we know, recorded any Shostakovich commercially before. His orchestra, the Gürzenich Orchestra, takes its name from the historic ballroom in the centre of Cologne where concerts have been held since 1857. It has witnessed the first performances of such famous works as the Brahms *Double Concerto*, Strauss's *Till Eulenspiegel* and *Don Quixote* and Mahler's *Fifth Symphony*; and the orchestra's conductors have included Abendroth, Fritz Steinbach, Günter Wand and, in the last decade or so, James Conlon. Nos. 1, 4, 7,

8, 11 and 15 were recorded at live concerts at the Cologne Philharmonic in 2003–4 and the remaining nine at the Stolberger Straße Studios. Kitajenko has the measure not only of the tauter works such as Nos. 1 and 9, but also of the epic canvases of Nos. 8 and 11. His *Tenth* has the tragic power and concentration that this great symphony calls for. Memories of Mitropoulos or Mravinsky are not eclipsed, and the latter's electrifying *Eighth*, recorded when the Leningrad orchestra came to Britain in 1959 (BBC Legends 4002-2), still remains in a class of its own. Many great performances still have special claims: Stokowski and Reiner in No. 6, Kondrashin in No. 4 and Ormandy in Nos. 1 and 13; but readers needing a complete survey, recorded in magnificent and finely detailed sound, with performances that rarely fall short of distinction, can invest in this set with confidence.

Symphonies 1, Op. 10; 9 in E flat, Op. 70

(M) ** EMI 557855-2. Munich PO, Celibidache (with BARBER: *Adagio for Strings* *)

Celibidache made an early recording of No. 9 with the Berlin Philharmonic which enjoyed a short life on three plum-label 78-r.p.m. discs. This 1990 performance is by no means as 'idiosyncratic' (shorthand for 'pulled about') as some of his readings, but he cannot let the finale alone. The *First Symphony* is well played and, for the most part, well characterized, though there is inevitably some expressive exaggeration. These Munich recordings are not ideally balanced and are a little bottom-heavy, with prominent percussion.

Symphonies 2, Op. 14 (To October); 12 in D min., Op. 112 (The Year 1917)

*** EMI 3 55994-2. Bav. RSO, Jansons

By general consent the *Twelfth* is the emptiest and weakest of the Shostakovich symphonies, yet in the hands of a Mravinsky it can exert a strange and compelling fascination. Mariss Jansons and the wonderful, rich-toned Bayerisches Rundfunk Orchestra do their very best for the piece and for the *Second*, also inspired by the October revolution. The latter never really lives up to the promise of its opening, but there is no question that Jansons secures first-class performances of both and that the recording quality does full justice to the Munich players.

'The War Symphonies': Documentary on Symphonies 4–9 by Larry Weinstein. (Prod.: Niv Fichman)

*** Ph. **DVD** 074 3117. Kirov O or Rotterdam PO, Gergiev

Don't be put off by the tabloid-like title 'Shostakovich against Stalin', for there is nothing glib or crude about this remarkable and searching documentary. Anyone who cares about the Shostakovich symphonies should lose no time in getting this DVD. It includes contributions from Shostakovich's circle of family, including his daughter Galina, friends and colleagues. They and the widow of the composer Shebalin all bear witness to what life was like during the terrible Stalinist years. The programme has a unique authority – as one would expect, given the participation of Gergiev, whose brainchild it was, and the collaboration of Elizabeth Wilson, daughter of a former British Ambassador to Moscow and author of an excellent biography of the composer. There is even an appearance by Khrennikov, who launched the attack on 'formalism' during the 1948 Congress of Soviet Composers presided over by Zhdanov. There is a great deal of rare archive material.

(i) *Symphony 5 in D min., Op. 47*; (ii) *Chamber Symphony in C min.* (arr. of *String Quartet 8*)

(M) *** Sony SK 94733. (i) NYPO, Bernstein; (ii) MITD SO, Barshai

(i) *Symphony 5*; (ii) *Hamlet* (film incidental music), *Suite, Op. 116*

☛ (M) *** RCA (ADD/DDD) 82876 55493-2. (i) LSO, Previn; (ii) Belgian RSO, Serebrier

Previn's RCA version, dating from early in his recording career (1965), remains among the top of the list for this much-recorded symphony, sounding excellent in this new transfer. This is one of the most concentrated and intense readings ever, superbly played by the LSO at their peak. In the third movement, Previn sustains a slower speed than anyone else, making it deeply meditative in its dark intensity, while the build-up in the central development section brings playing of white heat. The bite and urgency of the second and fourth movements are also irresistible. Only in the hint of tape-hiss and a slight lack of opulence in the violins does the sound fall short of the finest modern recordings, but it is more immediate than most. The coupling is appropriate. *Hamlet* obviously generated powerful resonances in Shostakovich's psyche and he produced vivid incidental music: the opening Ball scene is highly reminiscent of *Romeo and Juliet*. The playing of the Belgian Radio Orchestra under Serebrier is eminently serviceable without being really distinguished but, with an atmospheric recording, this 28-minute suite makes a considerable bonus.

Recorded in Tokyo in 1979 when Bernstein and the New York Philharmonic were on tour there, the Sony version is rich and weighty, partly because of the interpretation, but also because of the digital sound, which is particularly rich in the bass. Unashamedly, Bernstein treats the work as a romantic symphony. The very opening makes a strong impact and then, exceptionally, in the cool and beautiful second-subject melody Bernstein takes a slightly detached view, though as soon as that same melody comes up for development after the exposition the result is altogether more warmly expressive. Yet the movement's central climax, with its emphasis on the deep brass, injects a powerful element of menace, and the coda communicates a strongly Russian melancholy, which is perhaps why the composer admired Bernstein above other American interpreters of his music. The *Allegretto* becomes a burlesque, but here its Mahlerian roots are strongly conveyed. The slow movement is raptly beautiful (marvellously sustained *pianissimo* playing from the New York strings) and the finale is brilliant and extrovert, with the first part dazzlingly fast and the conclusion one of unalloyed triumph, even if its very vehemence suggests a hollow victory. The performance of the *Chamber Symphony* under Barshai is no less intense and deeply expressive in its essential melancholy, but more austere in texture and refined in feeling. It is superbly played and recorded.

Symphony 7 in C (Leningrad), Op. 60
(BB) *(*) Warner Apex 0927 41409-2. Nat. SO (of Washington), Rostropovich

Rostropovich's account is eminently well prepared and springs from undoubted feeling, but he is often a bit heavy-handed, rarely letting the music speak for itself, and the overall effect is studied. The engineers provide him with a recording of impressive dynamic range. However there is a literal feeling here – all i's are dotted and t's crossed.

Symphony 8 in C min., Op. 65
(M) * RCA 82876 76238-2. (i) St Louis SO, Slatkin; (ii) St Petersburg PO, Temirkanov

Slatkin gives a very disappointing account of the *Eighth*, a reading which lacks the necessary weight and intensity – fatal in the long first movement – even though he draws refined playing from the Saint Louis orchestra. The recording too could be richer.

Symphony 9 in E flat, Op. 70
*** Arthaus DVD 100 302. Bav. RSO, Solti (V/D: Klaus Lindemann) – TCHAIKOVSKY: *Symphony 6* **(*)

Solti's performance of the *Ninth Symphony* (filmed in 1990) is admirable. He catches its wit and humour readily (one responds to the occasional half-smile on his face) and, with his economical, purposive gestures, he is a pleasure to watch. The Bavarian Radio Orchestra play marvellously and obviously are enjoying themselves too, appreciating the yearning lyricism of the second movement as well as the humour. The camera observes everything without moving about excessively.

Symphony 10 in E min., Op. 93
☛ (M) *** DG 477 5909. BPO, Karajan
(BB) ** EMI Encore 5 86871-2. Philh. O, Rattle – BRITTEN: *Sinfonia da Requiem* ***

Already in his 1967 recording Karajan had shown that he had the measure of this symphony; this newer version is, if anything, even finer. In the first movement he distils an atmosphere as concentrated as before, bleak and unremitting, while in the *Allegro* the Berlin Philharmonic leave no doubts as to their peerless virtuosity. Everything is marvellously shaped and proportioned, and the early (1981) digital sound is made firmer by this 'original-image' bit re-processing. Now (at last) it is reissued at mid-price as one of DG's 'Originals'. The performance is peerless, and this remains an obvious primary recommendation.

Rattle's Philharmonia version is curiously wayward in the two big slow movements, first and third in the scheme. In the first, Rattle is unexpectedly slow, and the tension slips too readily. So too in the third movement. The Scherzo and energetic finale are much more successful. The recording does not help, with strings sounding thin and lacking body.

Symphony 11 (The Year 1905), Op. 103
(M) ** Warner Elatus 2564 60443-2. Nat. SO of Washington, Rostropovich

There is atmosphere in Rostropovich's account with the Washington orchestra but, as can easily happen in this score, the listener can soon wool-gather if the conductor does not have tremendous grip. The out-of-tune timpani have been commented on elsewhere, but for many this will not be as disturbing as the lack of narrative drive. No challenge here to the finest versions.

Symphony 15; (i) *Cello Concerto 1*
*(*) Chan. 9550. (i) Helmerson; Russian State SO, Polyansky

Valery Polyansky and the Russian State Symphony give a straightforward but ultimately rather undistinguished account of the *Fifteenth Symphony*. The slow movement in particular is lacking in atmosphere. In the *First Cello Concerto*, the distinguished Swedish soloist plays well, but ensemble is not impeccable.

CHAMBER MUSIC

(i; ii) *Cello Sonata in D min., Op. 40;* (i; iii) *Piano Quintet in G min., Op. 57;* (i; iv) *Piano Trio 2 in E min., Op. 67;* (iii) *2 Pieces for String Quartet.* Piano music: (i) *Aphorisms, Op. 13; 3 Fantastic Dances, Op. 5; Lyric Waltz; Nocturne; Polka; 5 Preludes;* (v) *24 Preludes, Op. 34;* (i) *24 Preludes & Fugues, Op. 87; Piano Sonatas* (vi) *1;* (i) *2; Short Piece & Spanish Dance*

(B) Decca 475 7425 (5). (i) Ashkenazy; (ii) Harrell; (iii) Fitzwilliam Qt; (iv) Beaux Arts Trio; (v) Mustonen; (vi) Zilberstein

There is little to cavil at in Ashkenazy's Shostakovich: in the *Preludes and Fugues* his playing is very fine indeed, as is the excellent sound. If Ashkenazy does not find as much in this music as the best recorded accounts (such as Tatiana Nikoayeva's RCA/Melodiya's version), his version is still very recommendable. Likewise, in the shorter piano pieces, Ashkenazy is always a trusted guide in this repertoire, and if the *Second Sonata* does not surpass Gilels's classic account, it is still excellent by any standards. The *First Piano Sonata* is a radical piece with something of the manic, possessed quality of Scriabin and the harmonic adventurousness of Berg. Lilya Zilberstein rises triumphantly to its formidable demands, and she makes a strong case for it; she is recorded with striking immediacy and impact by (originally) DG.

Olli Mustonen's version of the Op. 34 *Preludes* is extremely good, both artistically and technically. The *Cello Sonata* with Ashkenazy and Lynn Harrell is convincingly done; though they slow down rather a lot for the second group of the first movement, their brisk tempi and freedom from affectation are refreshing. The *Piano Quintet* with the Fitzwilliam Quartet could hardly be faulted, and the *Two Pieces* for string quartet (one based on Katerina's aria at the end of *Lady Macbeth of Mtsensk*, the other the *Polka* from *The Age of Gold*) are superb. The Beaux Arts Trio give a pure and intense reading of the *Piano Trio*, in which all the technical difficulties are overcome. The *Scherzo* is rarely played as fast as it is here – and certainly not with such meticulous ensemble – and the 1974 Philips recording is very good indeed. An excellent bargain collection.

String Quartets 1–15
(B) *** Fuga Libera FUG512. Danel Qt

String Quartets 1–15;(i) *Piano Quintet, Op. 57; Piano Trio 2, Op. 67*
(B) **(*) Hyp. CDS 44091/6. St Petersburg Qt; (i) with Igor Uryash

The Danel Quartet is based in Brussels and, after winning first prize at the International Shostakovich Competition in 1993, they have gone on to study with the Beethoven and Borodin Quartets. Their survey, recorded by Bayerisches Rundfunk over the period 2001–5 is of the highest quality, thoughtful and inward. There are a number of fine complete cycles now before the public, but this must be preferred to many (if not most) of them. Of course, the Borodins have special claims, but the Danel offer searching, private musings, humane and fully attuned to this composer's sensibility. They are worlds removed from the brilliant, 'public' statements of the Emersons, wonderfully efficient though they are; these are far more natural in feeling. The recordings too are very good, though in some instances there is

not quite enough air round the sound. But this is a distinguished cycle, offered with exemplary presentation and at budget price. Strongly recommended.

The St Petersburg Quartet's performances display appropriate intensity and enthusiasm, even if *piano* and *pianissimo* markings are sometimes a little exaggerated. Some of the tempi are less than ideal and sometimes the playing can be a little bit rough. They are not free from expressive exaggeration and the leader's rapid vibrato will not give universal pleasure. That sounds damning, but these are Russian players: they perform with impressive virtuosity, and they understand what this music is all about; and that applies to the *Piano Quintet* and *Piano Trio* also.

Violin Sonata; Jazz Suite 1
*** BIS CD 1592. Glutzman, Yoffe – AUERBACH: *Lonely Suite; Violin Sonata 2* ***

Vadim Glutzman and Angela Yoffe, who make a splendid team, have a sure grip on the Shostakovitch *Violin Sonata*, notably so in the passacaglia-styled opening movement, where Yoffe makes the twelve-tone motif immediately lyrically communicative, rather than a stark, serial row. The central *Allegretto* erupts powerfully, and the variation finale, with its bizarre pizzicato theme arriving after another bold introduction, is most satisfyingly linked cyclically to the opening movement. The *Jazz Suite* works very well in Glutzman's excellent transcription and it is played with charm, humour, and obvious relish. The recording is alive and present, and the coupling (by another Russian composer) is as intriguing as it is stimulating.

PIANO MUSIC

24 Preludes; Piano Sonata 2, Op. 61
** Cyprès CYP 2622. Schmidt

Johan Schmidt is a young Belgian pianist with good fingers and clean articulation. He is fluent and intelligent but is let down by the synthetic-sounding recording, which is very two-dimensional. The piano is too close and the acoustic dry.

Preludes & Fugues, Op. 87/5 & 24
(M) *** EMI (ADD) 3 45819-2 [3 45820-2]. Gilels – RACHMANINOV: *Piano Concerto 3*; SAINT-SAËNS: *Piano Concerto 2* ***

These two *Preludes and Fugues* make a fine contrasting encore for Gilels's Rachmaninov and Saint-Saëns concertos; the second, the last of the 24, brings a tremendous crescendo and is very commanding indeed. Good recording too.

24 Preludes & Fugues, Op. 87: excerpts
** Ondine ODE 1033-2 (2). Mustonen (piano) – BACH: *Well-Tempered Clavier, Book 1: excerpts* **

Olli Mustonen intersperses the Shostakovich *Preludes and Fugues* with those of Bach. His playing is impressive, yet we find the result curiously unsatisfying, in that he seems very concerned with personal point-making rather than letting the music speak for itself.

24 Preludes & Fugues, Op. 87, 2–4, 8–10, 14–16, 20–22
*(*) RCA 74321 61446-2 (2). Mustonen (with BACH: *Preludes & Fugues* *(*))

Olli Mustonen has again chosen here a dozen of the Shostakovich Op. 87 set of *Preludes and Fugues* and juxtaposes them with half of *Book I* of the Bach *Well-Tempered Clavier*. The eccentricities – exaggerated staccatos picked from the keyboard – and his narcissistic attention-seeking detract from the half of Shostakovich he does give us.

VOCAL MUSIC

The Execution of Stepan Razin, Op. 119; October: Five fragments
(BB) *** Naxos 8.557812. Charles Robert Austin, Seattle Ch. & SO, Schwarz

The Execution of Stepan Razin is a setting of Yevtushenko and comes two years after the *Thirteenth Symphony*. It does not have the concentration or emotional intensity of the symphony, but it is well worth hearing. Kondrashin's pioneering recording of 1969 is no longer in circulation; until it returns, this well-played and expertly recorded version will serve well, particularly at its modest price.

Songs: (i) *2 Fables of Krylov; From Jewish Folk Poetry, Op. 79a; 6 Poèmes d'Alexandre Blok, Op. 127; 6 Poems of Marina Tsvetayeva, Op. 143; 3 Romances on Poems by Pushkin, Op. 46; 6 Romances, Op. 62/140; 6 Romances on Texts by Japanese Poets, Op. 21; Suite of Verses of Michelangelo Buonarroti, Op. 145a; 4 Verses of Captain Lebyadkin;* (ii) *Lady Macbeth of Mtsensk District* (complete opera)
(B) Decca 475 7441 (5). (i) Leiferkus, Orgonasova, Levinsky, Zaremba, Fischer-Dieskau, Söderström, Shirley-Quirk, with Ashkenazy (piano) or Gothenburg SO, Järvi; (ii) Ewing, Haugland, Langridge, Larin, Ciesinski, Zednik, Bastille Op. Ch. & O, Chung

An outstanding compilation of Shostakovich's songs, as well as Myung-Whun Chung's superb version of *Lady Macbeth of Mtsensk*. Shostakovich's songs brim with character and nuance: the first two CDs are with Neeme Järvi and the Gothenburg orchestra, and the accompaniments are of as much interest and importance as the vocal lines themselves. Järvi coaxes playing which is both atmospheric and sensitive and this is very much one of the main joys of these recordings. The soloists are characterful and distinguished, and all Shostakovich fans will gain much from listening to this repertoire, much of which is comparatively little known. There is the full range of Shostakovichian expression found here, from the spikily acerbic to the hauntingly moving; nothing here is dull, and there are surprises everywhere. Ashkenazy provides excellent accompaniments for both the Fischer-Dieskau and John Shirley-Quirk items on the third CD and, like the performances, the sound is very vivid (especially so in the 1977 Shirley-Quirk items). The Söderström recordings, with violin, cello and piano, are quite superb, with haunting, spine-tingling atmosphere in the quiet numbers and plenty of drama in the lively ones.

Myung-Whun Chung's performance of *Lady Macbeth of Mtsensk* is very successful too and the most moving account on disc. Maria Ewing gives a vulnerable portrayal of her character in this 1992 (originally) DG recording – unlike Vishnevskaya's aggressive, fire-eating portrayal in the classic EMI/Rostropovich account – with moods and responses subtly varied. As a heroine, she is insinuatingly seductive and by the last Act one comes to pity her much more than Vishnevskaya; with a younger voice too, the heroine's feminine charms are more vividly conveyed in singing that is far more sensuous, with the beauty of tone and hushed *pianissimos* most tenderly affecting. The vocal challenges stretch the voice

to the very limit and beyond, but that itself adds to the vulnerability. Sergei Larin as Katerina's labourer-lover equally gains over the EMI rival, Nicolai Gedda, by sounding more aptly youthful, with his tenor sounding both firm and clear yet Slavic-sounding. His touch is lighter than Gedda's, with a nice hint of irony. Aage Haugland is magnificent as Boris, Katerina's father-in-law, and Philip Langridge sings sensitively as her husband, Zinovi, while Kurt Moll as the Old Convict provides emotional focus in his important solo at the start of the last Act. The recording is atmospheric. An excellent contrasting performance to Rostropovich's more overtly dramatic version. Texts and translations are provided in this handsome, bargain set.

SIBELIUS, Jean (1865–1957)

Andante festivo (for strings & timpani); *The Bard;* (i) *Violin Concerto, Op. 47. En Saga* (revised 1902); (ii) *Karelia Suite* (includes *Ballade*). *Kuolema: Valse triste; The Oceanides; Pohjola's Daughter; Porilaisen Marssi* (arr. Sibelius); *Tapiola; The Wood Nymph*
(M) *** BIS CD 1557/8. Lahti SO, Vänskä; with (i) Kavakos; (ii) Laukka

This is the third collection of Sibelius's shorter orchestral works from Osmo Vänskä, plus of course the mature *Violin Concerto* of 1905, which he and Kavakos have already recorded successfully, coupled to the earlier, 1903/4 version. Some of the other works here are also duplicated on the earlier discs, including *En Saga, The Oceanides, Pohjola's Daughter, Tapiola,* and *The Wood Nymph. The March of the Pori Regiment* is orchestrated from a traditional melody used by the Finnish armed forces for their parades. *Karelia* comes with a sung version of the *Ballade* by Raimo Laukka. While not all these performances are first choices (notably *The Oceanides*), Vänskä and his fine orchestra are thoroughly at home in this repertoire, and the recording is first class. If you want this particular group of works, this set is excellent value.

(i) *The Bard;* (ii) *Violin Concerto, Op. 47;* (i) *En Saga; Kuolema: Valse triste; The Oceanides; Pohjola's Daughter; Tapiola; Symphony 2 in D, Op. 43*
(B) ** RCA 74321 88685-2 (2). (i) Finnish RSO, Saraste; (ii) Kremer, LSO, Rozhdestvensky

The orchestral pieces and the symphony under Saraste are on the whole better than serviceable, though less than distinguished, except in the case of *The Oceanides* and *The Bard,* which are very fine indeed. Kremer's account of the *Violin Concerto* with Rozhdestvensky and the LSO is slick and self-regarding. Very good sound throughout, though poor documentation.

Violin Concerto in D min., Op. 47
(M) *** Decca 475 7734. Chung, LSO, Previn –
TCHAIKOVSKY: *Violin Concerto* ***
(M) (***) EMI mono 4 76830-2 [4 76831-2]. Neveu, Philh. O, Susskind – BRAHMS: *Violin Concerto* (***)
(B) *(*) RCA (ADD) 82876 59419-2. Perlman, Boston SO, Leinsdorf – TCHAIKOVSKY: *Violin Concerto* *(*)

Kyung Wha Chung's feeling for the Sibelius *Concerto* is second to none, and Previn's accompanying cannot be praised too highly: it is poetic when required, restrained and full of controlled vitality and well-defined detail. The Kingsway Hall recording is superbly balanced, and this altogether most beautiful account is fully worthy of reissue as one of Decca's Originals.

Ginette Neveu's celebrated performance – her first concerto recording, from 1945 – is magnetic from the opening phrase onwards. It now finds a place among EMI's 'Great Recordings of the Century' in this perfectly acceptable transfer.

Perlman's performance on RCA is a good one, but this reading has neither the character nor the personality of his later, EMI version. The over-bright sound and the close balance of the soloist don't help matters either.

Six Humoresques, Opp. 87 & 89

*(*) Essay CD 1075. Tenenbaum, Pro Musica Prague, Kapp – GHEDINI: Violin Concerto, etc. *(*)

Sibelius was toying with the idea of a second violin concerto in 1915, and it is not too fanciful to imagine that some of its ideas could have found their way into the two sets of Humoresques. They are rarely heard in the concert hall, thanks partly to their dimensions and the technical demands they make. Mela Tenenbaum is no match for the likes of Dong-Suk Kang (BIS CD 472), Aaron Rosand or Accardo (now deleted). She inserts all sorts of little expressive hesitations and does not produce a particularly beautiful sound, though to be fair the close balance and unglamorous studio acoustic do not help her. The liner notes are uninformed on matters Sibelian and are marred by factual errors. Nor are they well written: we learn at one point that Sibelius at the time of the Humoresques 'found himself prematurely obsolesced'!

SYMPHONIES

Symphonies 1–7
*** DG SACD/CD (compatible) 477 5688. Gothenburg SO, Neeme Järvi
*(*) Finlandia 3984-23389-2 (4). COE, Berglund

Symphonies 1–4
(BB) *** EMI Gemini 4 76963-2 (2). Helsinki PO, Berglund

Symphonies 5–7; Finlandia; The Oceanides; Tapiola
(BB) *** EMI Gemini 4 76951-2 (2). Helsinki PO, Berglund

Symphonies 1–7; Karelia Overture, Pohjola's Daughter, Nightride and Sunrise, Pelléas et Mélisande: excerpts
(BB) (***) Beulah mono 14PD 8 (4). LSO, Collins

Gothenburg has a strong Sibelius tradition. During his time as its Chief Conductor, Stenhammar brought Sibelius to the 'Goteborg Symfoniker', both during the 1914–18 war and in the 1920s when he conducted the Sixth Symphony. It is now two decades since Neeme Järvi recorded his Sibelius cycle with them. The new Nos. 1 and 2 were recorded at concerts in 2001–2 and the remainder later under studio conditions. There is no want of intensity in any of them. Järvi's 1983 version of the Second was distinguished by a very brisk first movement (almost as fast as the famous old Kajanus set, though Sibelius himself is said to have taken it even faster in a 1916 performance). Järvi is much more measured, and the same goes for most of these performances, in particular the Seventh Symphony. Järvi conveys its sense of awe and of vision, and he shows his usual feeling for the Sibelian sound-world; however, we feel that it could do with a little more forward movement.

The Sixth is both thoughtful and powerful, dark in feeling – albeit less subtle in colouring and atmosphere than Karajan or Colin Davis. What strikes one about this partnership is the blend of freshness and enthusiasm, as well as a complete lack

of self-regard. These readings are straight and natural without a trace of ego. (Only in the Scherzo of the Fourth are there some moments of expressive or agogic exaggeration, though the performance as a whole is very powerful in conception and has a marvellous slow movement.)

These artists have an additional advantage, of course, in the wonderful acoustic of the Gothenburg Concert Hall, which presents orchestral detail with great vividness and presence and which the new recording (made in the 1980s by the Lennart Dehn–Michael Bergek team) brings into one's room with great realism. Surround sound enhances its impact. Järvi is a dedicated guide in the Sibelian terrain and his is a rewarding, satisfying cycle. Let us hope DG will encourage him to revisit some of the Tubin symphonies, given this magnificent sound. It is a useful complement to the splendid RCA box, which collects not only the seven symphonies, Tapiola and Kullervo but also all the tone-poems and orchestral pieces, that Sir Colin Davis recorded with the LSO in the 1990s and which remains a first recommendation (82876 55706-2).

Berglund's Helsinki cycle, recorded in 1986/7, now comes on a pair of EMI super-bargain doubles. His are rugged, sober but powerful readings which maintain a high standard of performance and recording. The tone-poems are also very tellingly played and highly atmospheric. These performances are all fully discussed in our main volume and this set is now very competitively priced, although the Colin Davis cycle with the Boston Symphony on a pair of Philips Duos, which includes Accardo's estimable account of the Violin Concerto (446 157-2 and 446 160-2), is worth its extra cost.

Anthony Collins (1893–1963) is remembered these days almost solely for these Decca recordings. His was the first integral set of the symphonies to appear in this country, though Sixten Ehrling and the Stockholm Radio Orchestra preceded them on Metronome in Scandinavia (and on the Mercury label in the USA). Collins has an instinctive feeling for pace, with the sole exception of the second movement of the Third Symphony, which is far too fast. In terms of sheer electricity, his 1952 account of the First Symphony remains pretty well unsurpassed, even by the likes of Karajan, Sir Colin Davis or Bernstein. It is taut and concentrated, yet full of feeling and wonderfully paced. Forty years on, in a dissertation for Indiana University, Guy Thomas could call it 'the most consistently successful series ever recorded', though present-day collectors will rightly prefer Sir Colin Davis's cycle with the LSO on RCA, which also includes masterly accounts of Kullervo, En Saga, the Lemminkäinen Legends, Tapiola and other works (RCA 82876 54034-2).

Collins's accounts of Nightride and Sunrise and Pohjola's Daughter are hardly less impressive: the former can hold its own alongside the Jochum and Davis versions. Collins was in some ways the ideal recording conductor, for he could combine an unerring sense of style with a natural gift for spontaneity. It is good to see these authoritative accounts returning to circulation at bargain price, for they have a prized and special place in the Sibelius discography and still sound remarkably vivid.

Berglund's COE survey is available not only as a complete set but also broken down into separate formats. Nos. 1–3 are offered together on two discs: 3984-23388-2; Nos. 4 and 6 on 0630 14951-2; and Nos. 5 and 7 on 0630 17278-2. They are the product of an enthusiastic collaboration with the Chamber Orchestra of Europe. Berglund knows this music as intimately as anyone alive. He offers the scores plain and unadorned. There are good things, namely a sober and vigorous *Third* and a finely paced and sensitively moulded *Sixth*, as well as one or two ugly details, such as the ungainly stress he gives to the rhetorical string passage in the first movement of the *Second* (1 minute 35 seconds, five bars before letter B).

One has to decide whether these performances, good though they are, convey enough new insights to justify displacing his earlier cycles with the Bournemouth and Helsinki orchestras. Those earlier sets, though they have solid merits, fall short of the ideal in terms of poetic imagination, but the same goes for this new set. In some ways Berglund's very first, 1969 recording of the *Fourth Symphony*, issued in 1973, remains the freshest and most keenly felt of his Sibelius recordings!

Symphonies 1; 7; Karelia Overture
* Ondine ODE 1007-2. Helsinki PO, Segerstam

Leif Segerstam's Sibelius cycle with the Danish National Radio Symphony Orchestra on Chandos was made in the early 1990s. The present issue is a little less self-conscious than that earlier set, but not enough to make the new performances a serious contender. In the second theme of the finale of the *First Symphony*, Segerstam emotes heavily, and the closing paragraphs are pulled around and horribly bombastic. The *Seventh* is more successful than in the earlier set: the opening has an impressive breadth and grandeur, though some ideas are slightly cosseted and pulled out of shape. But by the side of the finest versions this is all too self-aware and crude. Decent playing and recording.

Symphony 2 in D, Op. 43
(M) *** Royal Concg. O RCO 05005. Concg. O, Jansons
*** Profil Median PHo 5049. (i) Selbig; Dresden State O, C. Davis

Symphony 2 in D, Op. 43; En Saga, Op. 9
(BB) *** EMI Encore 3 41441-2. BPO; Karajan

(i) Symphony 2; (ii) Karelia Suite; (i) Legend: The Swan of Tuonela
(BB) **(*) Regis RRC 1220. (i) LSO; (ii) RPO, Mackerras

Mariss Jansons recorded the *Second* with the Oslo Philharmonic in 1992, and this new account is broadly consistent with its predecessor (the middle movements differ in timing by only one second) but there is the same passion and commitment, with an additional gravitas and depth. There is not a strong Sibelius tradition in Amsterdam, though Eduard van Beinum recorded *En Saga* and *Tapiola* for Decca in the early 1950s and George Szell recorded the *Second Symphony* with them in the 1960s. Jansons's approach to the opening is not dissimilar to Karajan's, that is to say, fairly broad and relaxed. Kajanus's première recording of 1930 was altogether brisker and more urgent and, according to Erik Furuhjelm, when Sibelius himself conducted in 1916 it was even faster and had tremendous dynamic thrust.

Be that as it may, Jansons is a totally committed and authoritative Sibelian and throughout the performance he holds the listener totally in his grip. It is a joy to hear this wonderful orchestra in all its tonal opulence and splendour. Collectors are spoilt for choice in this repertoire: Karajan and Sir Colin Davis (LSO) among newer versions, Beecham, Barbirolli (RPO) and Stokowski among earlier ones. However, Jansons's reading is splendidly fresh and at times makes you feel that you are listening to this familiar music for the first time. At its modest price, a fraction of the cost of a concert ticket, this disc, one of the first on the Concertgebouw's own label, is well worth adding to your collection, even if rival versions offer couplings.

Karajan's 1980 digital version of the *Second Symphony* with the Berlin Philharmonic is more spacious than his earlier reading with the Philharmonia. Tempi in all four movements are fractionally broader; nevertheless, the first movement is still a genuine *Allegretto* – much faster than with Maazel or Ashkenazy, among others – basically in the brisker tradition of Kajanus, whose pioneering 1930 records were probably closer to Sibelius's intentions than most. Throughout all four movements there is a splendour and nobility here – and some glorious sounds from the Berlin strings and brass. The oboe theme in the trio section of the Scherzo is most expressively moulded, and the finale is slower and grander than most of its rivals. This is a performance of stature, and is well recorded, too. In *En Saga* Karajan is a brisk story-teller, more concerned with narrative than with atmosphere at the beginning, but the *lento assai* section and the coda are quite magical. The EMI recording has plenty of body and presence. A remarkable bargain.

Taken from German radio broadcasts, these live Dresden recordings give a vivid idea of the impact Sir Colin Davis had on the venerable Staatskapelle Dresden. It is fascinating to register the way that the ripe Dresden sound modifies his interpretation, faster, smoother, warmer than with the LSO in his RCA recording. In its extra clarity and directness the LSO version is more authentically Sibelian, but it is good to have such a warmly persuasive and dramatic reading as this, with the players giving heartfelt commitment to repertory not likely to be very familiar to them. *En Saga* in this version is less magically transparent, less mysterious than with the LSO, but it is still a powerfully convincing performance, while the elusive tone-poem, *Luonnotar*, benefits greatly from the girlish freshness of the soprano, Ute Selbig, in the haunting vocal solo, though, sadly, the booklet gives neither text nor translation.

Sir Charles Mackerras gives an eminently well-judged account of the *Second Symphony*. The tempo of the first movement is apt, a real *Allegretto*, fast but without going to extremes. There is no lack of tenderness and he shapes phrases with sensitivity. The *Swan of Tuonela* too has no lack of atmosphere. The 1988 recording (originally from the Pickwick label) was made in the EMI Abbey Road studio and is bright and clean. The lively RPO account of *Karelia* was made five years later.

Symphonies 2; 5 in E flat, Op. 82
(BB) * Warner Apex 8573 88434-2. Finnish RSO, Saraste

Saraste's performances are well played and acceptably recorded, but considering these were concert performances there is a remarkable absence of real grip and forward thrust here.

Symphonies 4 in A min., Op. 63; 6 in D min., Op. 104
(***) Somm-Beecham mono 16. (i) BBC SO; (ii) RPO; Beecham

R.L. remembers hearing the Beecham broadcast of the *Fourth Symphony* on 4 October 1951; it seemed very different from his pre-war records with the LPO with which R.L. had grown up. That has a cool, austere chamber-music feeling, while the studio performance had a more full-bodied sound and an altogether greater intensity. Sir Adrian Boult had not long retired from the BBC Symphony, to be succeeded by Sir Malcolm Sargent, and this comes from the brief period that

Sir Thomas spent as guest conductor in the early autumn of 1951. He brought some adventurous programme planning, including some Vincent d'Indy, then as now a rarity. It is obvious that the orchestra welcomed the transformation in sonority that Beecham's presence achieved. The performances are immaculately prepared and, as in the case with the *Second Symphony* three years later, the orchestra play as if their very lives depend on it.

Beecham's commercial recording of the *Sixth* was said to be the composer's favourite (a fact which Eva Paloheimo, Sibelius's eldest daughter, confirmed to R.L. in the early 1960s). This present version has all the vision and authority that his commercial discs had, and the sound (apart from a problem with the level at the very outset) is eminently acceptable. The closing section of the finale has great feeling and poignancy. The recording is transferred from acetates and shows some signs of wear, particularly in the *Fourth Symphony*. However, it is good to have these performances, whatever their sonic limitations.

CHAMBER MUSIC

Malinconia, Op. 20; 2 Pieces, Op. 77; 4 Pieces, Op. 78 (for cello and piano)

(B) ** Virgin 2 CD. 3 49933-2 (2). Mørk, Thibaudet –
  BRAHMS: *Cello Sonatas 1–2; 7 Lieder* (arr. Mørk); GRIEG:
  Cello Sonata; Intermezzo **

Like Grieg, Sibelius also had a cello-playing brother, which is probably why the Opp. 77 and 78 pieces for violin and piano are marked as playable by the cello. *Malinconia* was written for the cellist and conductor Georg Schnéevoigt and his wife Sigrid, and is emphatically not top-drawer Sibelius. Truls Mørk and Jean-Yves Thibaudet play these pieces well enough, but the balance is unsatisfactory and favours the pianist excessively, with the result that Mørk's tone sounds very small.

String Quartet in D min. (Voces intimae), Op. 56

** DG 477 5960. Emerson Qt – NIELSEN: *At the bier of a young artist*; GRIEG: *Quartet* **

No one can deny the sheer mastery of the Emersons as a well-nigh perfect ensemble. But they do not seem really inside the *Voces intimae Quartet*. There is little of the fragrance and delicacy of colouring of the Sibelian landscape and more of the glare of strip-lighting and high-rise towers.

Music for violin and piano: (i) Sonatina in E, Op. 80; (ii) Berceuse, Op. 79/6; Danse caractéristique, Op. 116/1 & 2. 4 Pieces, Op. 78; 4 Pieces, Op. 81; 4 Pieces, Op. 115; Scène de danse

** Finlandia 4509 95853-2. (i) Arai, Tateno; (ii) Yaron, Sharon

Sibelius was of course an accomplished violinist in his youth and never lost his feeling for the instrument. Most of the violin pieces, with the exception of Opp. 115 and 116, come from the war years, when Sibelius was cut off from the great European orchestras and from his livelihood, namely his royalties from Breitkopf in Leipzig. He wrote a large number of instrumental pieces to generate the income his isolation cost him. In the first decade of the century Breitkopf also published arrangements of some of his smaller orchestral scores (the *Elégie* from *King Christian II* was made by the conductor, Georg Schnéevoigt). Although many of these pieces are slight, they are (for the most part) of quality and are presented as such.

PIANO MUSIC

10 Bagatelles, Op. 34; 10 Pieces, Op. 58; 13 Pieces, Op. 76; 2 Rondinos, Op. 68; March of the Finnish Jaeger Battalion, Op. 91a

*(*) Ondine ODE 1014-2. Mustonen

Olli Mustonen is an individual player: he makes the most of tonal and colouristic refinements and is often imaginative in matters of characterization. But his staccato articulation is exaggerated and self-aware and, the longer one listens, the more self-regarding his playing seems, and the greater the strain on one's tolerance. The sleeve prints the pianist's name in larger type than the composer's, and the booklet and presentation give us four pictures of Mustonen against one of Sibelius! He is very well recorded, but any of his rivals are to be preferred.

VOCAL MUSIC

Finlandia (version for orchestra and mixed chorus); Homeland (Oma maa), Op. 92; Impromptu, Op. 19; (i) Snöfrid, Op. 29; Song to the Earth (Maan virsi), Op. 95; Song to Lemminkäinen, Op. 31; Väinö's Song, Op. 110

** Ondine ODE 754-2. (i) Rautelin (reciter); Finnish Nat. Op.
  Ch. & O, Klas

While most of Sibelius's songs are to Swedish texts, the choral music is predominantly Finnish. *Oma maa* ('Homeland') is a dignified and euphonious work and includes a magical evocation of the wintry nights with aurora borealis and the white nights of midsummer. *Väinö's Song* is an appealing piece which bears an opus number between those for *The Tempest* and *Tapiola* – though it is not really fit to keep them company. The performances and the recording are decent rather than distinguished.

Kullervo Symphony, Op. 7

☛ (B) *** LSO Live 0574. Groop, Mattei, L. Symphony Ch.,
  LSO, C. Davis

It is puzzling that Sibelius should have entertained such strong doubts about *Kullervo* as to discourage all performances during his lifetime. Fortunately, he never got round to destroying it, as he did the *Eighth Symphony*, but was forced to sell the manuscript in the early 1920s. Sir Colin Davis did a very fine set in 1992 with the LSO; this new disc, recorded at the Barbican Hall in autumn 2005, is every bit as magisterial. Sir Colin's first movement is spacious – certainly broader than the 1958 performance by Sibelius's son-in-law, Jussi Jalas, which brought this piece alive again after its long slumber. There is the same epic sweep and iron control, and the passion which was so impressive in the earlier version. What a remarkable and imaginative movement it is, too. The slow movement, *Kullervo's Youth*, is powerfully characterized, as indeed is the central *Kullervo and his Sister* movement. The general flow and dramatic thrust of this remarkable scena, Sibelius's first setting of the *Kalevala*, the repository of Finnish mythology, is wonderfully conveyed. Sir Colin is a Sibelian of commanding stature, and the LSO and London Symphony Chorus give of their finest. Both soloists have recorded *Kullervo* before: Monica Groop with Saraste (Finlandia) and Peter Mattei with Paavo Järvi (Virgin), both in the mid-1990s, and they are in fine voice here. Good recording, though the acoustic is just a little dry, thanks to the full house. This is arguably the finest *Kullervo* now before the public and is a first recommendation.

SILLÉN, Josef Otto af (1859–1951)

(i) *Violin Concerto in E min.; Symphony 3 in E min.*
** Sterling CDS 1044-2 (i) Bergqvist; Gävle SO, Nilson

Josef Otto af Sillén is a very minor figure and is not listed in *Grove* or *Bakers*, nor even in *Sohlman*, the Swedish equivalent. As a young man he pursued a military career and then turned to insurance, while at the same time being active in the Philharmonic Society: he was briefly in charge of the Stockholm Opera and held a court appointment as a royal chamberlain. He composed for much of his life, though performances were not always under his own name as he felt his aristocratic name might work to his disadvantage. His *Violin Concerto* probably dates from the early 1920s, and he wrote the *Third Symphony* in his late seventies (it was premièred in 1937). A musician of culture rather than originality, he conveys little feeling of real mastery. The *Violin Concerto*, dedicated to his daughter, Greta af Sillén Roos, an Auer pupil who, alas, never played it, opens like Bruch, and in the symphony there is a lot of Tchaikovsky: the Scherzo is Mendelssohnian, albeit somewhat heavy-handed. There are moments here and there which are rather endearing. Christian Bergqvist is the persuasive soloist in the concerto and the performance and recording are perfectly acceptable. Of interest for its curiosity value.

SILVESTROV, Valentin (born 1937)

Metamusik (Symphony for Piano & Orchestra); Postludium
*** ECM 472 081-2. Lubimov, V. RSO, R. Davies

Silvestrov has been hailed in extravagant terms as one of the legends of the former Soviet avant garde: David Fanning called his *Fifth Symphony* one of 'the best-kept secrets of the ex-Soviet symphonic repertoire', and nominated it as 'the finest symphony composed in the former Soviet Union since the death of Shostakovich'. The notes speak of the relationship between the two pieces as that of a sketch and its execution. The earlier *Postludium* for piano and orchestra, now almost 20 years old, is the terser; the *Metamusik* of 1992 lasts nearly 50 minutes! It casts a strong spell and the heady atmosphere is tremendously powerful; one's thoughts turn to late Scriabin or the most hothouse Szymanowski, though they sound positively austere by comparison! Whether or not you respond to Silvestrov, there is no doubting the qualities of imagination and the richness of invention that his music possesses. The scoring, particularly in the bass end of the spectrum, is wonderfully rich and the heavy, dark and oppressive textures are at times almost suffocating. The post-Scriabinesque moments are offset by the occasional dream-like (some might say sickly) hints of Mahlerian warmth. This is strong stuff, an undeniably powerful vision to which listeners will react strongly. As with any composer of vision, Silvestrov creates a world that is distinctively his own, though not everyone will want to enter it and some ears may have difficulty sitting this music out! Expert and authoritative playing, and superb recorded sound.

SIMPSON, Robert (1921–97)

String Quartets 1–3
(**) Pearl mono GEM 0023. Element Qt

These are off-air recordings from the composer's own collection of the première broadcast performances in the Third Programme in the 1950s. They have a certain gutsy quality, a total and impassioned commitment that more than compensates for the odd rough edges.

SJÖGREN, Emil (1853–1915)

Violin Sonatas 1, Op. 19; 2 in E min., Op. 24; 2 Lyric Pieces; Poème, Op. 40
*** BIS CD 995. Enoksson, Stott

Emil Sjögren belongs to the generation of Swedish composers before Stenhammar, though he is not in the same league and his attainments are more modest. He never tried his hand at orchestral music or opera, though he wrote some fine songs. The two *Violin Sonatas* come from the 1880s and are finely crafted, and the *Second Sonata* is generally thought of as his masterpiece. It is certainly the work of a cultured and inventive composer with strong classical instincts and is served excellently by Per Enoksson and Kathryn Stott. The recording is in the best traditions of the house.

SKORYK, Myroslav (born 1938)

Carpathian Concerto; Hutsul Triptych
** ASV CDDCA 963. Odessa PO, Earle – KOLESSA: *Symphony 1* **

Myroslav Skoryk teaches composition at Lvov and has a considerable output to his credit, including two piano concertos, two violin concertos and a good deal of music for the theatre. The *Hutsul Triptych* (1965) derives from a score Skoryk composed for the film, *Shadows of Forgotten Ancestors*, by Sergei Paradzhanov. It is colourful, often atmospheric and inventive, not unlike some Shchedrin. The *Carpathian Concerto* (1972) is an expertly scored orchestral piece with strong folkloric accents – and some cheap orientalism. Not a good piece nor strongly individual, but the centrepiece of the *Hutsul Triptych* is worth hearing.

SLAVICKY, Klement (1910–99)

Moravian Dance Fantasies; Rhapsodic Variations
(M) (***) Sup. mono SU 3688-2. Czech PO, Ančerl – NOVÁK: *In the Tatras* (***)

Klement Slavicky was Moravian (his father had been a pupil of Janáček) and served until 1951 on the staff of the Czechoslovak Radio, ending up as its head of music. The *Moravian Dance Fantasies* come from 1951 and its companion here from 1953. Ančerl conducted the première the following year. They are both folkloric in feeling and are scored with great expertise and a feeling for colour. Well worth seeking out.

SMETANA, Bedřich (1824–84)

Má Vlast (complete)
(B) *** LSO Live SACD LSO 0516. LSO, C. Davis

Sir Colin Davis has long been noted as an interpreter of Czech music, particularly that of Dvořák, but this is his first recording of Smetana's great cycle of six programme works, completed at the very end of the composer's tragic life. Recorded live at the Barbican in May 2005, the disc offers a warm, incisive reading which brings out the drama as well as the poetry behind each portrait of Smetana's homeland, clearly integrating the final two symphonic poems, *Tábor* and *Blaník*, noisier than the rest and written rather as an afterthought. It is true that the limited Barbican acoustic does not make for the very finest sound, yet it is well detailed, and there are advantages of having a slightly more distanced sound in places, as in the evocative central section of *Vltava*, when the shimmering repeated figure on woodwind, representing the play of nymphs in the river, is given more mystery. The clinching point in favour of the new disc, as with all the LSO Live issues, is the very reasonable price, making it in every way a first-rate bargain.

Má Vlast: Vltava. The Bartered Bride: Overture; Polka; Furiant
(M) *** Decca (ADD) 475 7730. (i) Israel PO; (ii) LSO; Kertész – DVOŘÁK: *Slavonic Dances; Symphonic Variations* ***

With Kertész, these pieces are exceptionally vivid. The separate entries in the *Overture* are beautifully positioned by the stereo, and the ambience makes the background rustle of all the strings weaving away at their fugato theme sound quite captivating. *Vltava*, too, is very brilliant, with fast tempi, yet not losing its picturesque qualities. The 1960s recording is perhaps somewhat over-bright and over-reverberant, but it glows in Decca's best analogue fashion.

CHAMBER MUSIC

Piano Trio in G min., Op. 15
*** Sup. SU 3810. Smetana Trio – NOVAK: *Trio quasi una balata*; SUK: *Elegie; Piano Trio* ***

(BB) ** Warner Apex 0927 40822-2. Trio Fontenay – CHOPIN: *Piano Trio* **

(i) *Piano Trio in G min., Op. 15*; (ii) *Fantasy on a Bohemian Song; From my Homeland*
(M) ** Sup. (ADD) SU 3449-2 131. (i) Klánsky; (i; ii) Pavlík, Jerie

Written as an elegy after the death of the composer's four-year-old daughter, Smetana's *Piano Trio* is a darkly reflective work, despite the lack of a slow movement. It ends with an urgent Rondo finale which seems to reflect the composer's anger over his loss. Like the other works on this fine disc, it is given a strongly characterized, idiomatic and finely polished reading by the eponymous Smetana Trio, a re-formed group whose cellist, Jan Paleníček, is the son of Josef Paleníček, pianist in the original Smetana Trio, founded in the 1930s.

The Trio Fontenay take a comparatively extrovert view and, while it is good to hear it played as if they believe every note, they tend rather to dramatize its emotions too much and do not allow the work's dignified, elegiac quality to speak as naturally as it might. Good recording.

Idiomatic performances on Supraphon of the *G minor Piano Trio* and of the *Fantasy on a Bohemian Song* and *From my Homeland*, both for violin and piano. Decent recording, too, but at only 47 minutes' playing time, it is hardly good value, even at mid-price.

PIANO MUSIC

Czech Dances I & II; 8 Bagatelles and Impromptus
(BB) *** Regis RRC 1223. Kvapil

Radoslav Kvapil is entirely inside this music, even if his account of the *F major Polka* from the first book of *Czech Dances* does not eclipse memories of Firkušný's celebrated mono LP account, which had great exuberance and dash! All the same, Kvapil is a highly sensitive exponent of this repertoire. The recording is good, too. The disc also comes as part of a four-disc survey of Czech piano music (Regis RRC 4006).

OPERA

The Bartered Bride: highlights (in Czech)
(M) ** Sup. SU 3708-2 (from recording, with Beňačková, Dvorský; cond. Košler)

A well-made if not strikingly generous set of highlights from Košler's sparkling complete set. But the documentation includes only a list of excerpts unrelated to any synopsis, and there is no translation.

The Bartered Bride (complete in English)
🔢 (M) *** Chan. 3128 (2). Gritton, Clarke, Robinson, Rose, Davies, Montague, Moses, Bonner, Leggate, Hesketh-Harvey, ROHCG Ch., Philh. O, Mackerras

This outstanding new version of Smetana's *The Bartered Bride* comes in a crisp new English translation, very clear and lively, by Kit Hesketh-Harvey, half of the popular cabaret duo, 'Kit and the Widow'. What makes this translated version so successful is not just the brilliant conducting of Sir Charles Mackerras and the scintillating playing of the Philharmonia Orchestra, with an exceptionally strong team of soloists working well together, but also the extra impact of the comedy made by a performance in the vernacular. The echoes of G & S, with double-rhymes given a jolly, Gilbertian ring, distracting in many operas, for once seem entirely appropriate, adding to the joy of the piece. That is all the more evident when Kecal, the marriage-broker, has so many patter numbers in which Peter Rose is wonderfully agile, characterfully establishing himself as the key figure in the story. Even the chorus has rapid tongue-twisters to cope with, crisply performed by the Covent Garden Chorus. The impact of the performance is instantly established in Mackerras's sparkling performance of the overture, taken at headlong speed. Susan Gritton is a radiant heroine, producing golden tone and rising superbly to the challenge of the poignant numbers when it seems that Jeník has betrayed her, moments also intensified in translation, with the twists and turns of the plot so well clarified. Paul Charles Clarke as Jeník is less successful when his tenor grows uneven under pressure, though his characterization is first rate. The two other tenor roles are both superbly taken by Timothy Robinson as the stuttering simpleton, Vašek, and Robin Leggate as the Ringmaster in Act III. Robinson not only sings immaculately but characterizes brilliantly, a comic figure who brings out an element of pathos. Strong casting too for Mařenka's parents, Neal Davies as Krušina and Yvonne Howard as Ludmila, clearly establishing their contrasted responses to the proposed marriage of Marenka and Vašek. Vašek's parents, Toby Micha and Hata, have far less to do, but there too the set has splendid casting in Geoffrey Moses and Diana Montague. This is among the finest of all issues in Sir Peter Moores' 'Opera in English' series.

The Bartered Bride: (i) Overture and (ii) highlights (sung in English)
(B) ** CfP (ADD) 585 010-2. (i) Pro Arte O, Mackerras; (ii) Robson, Drake, June, Stannard, Miller, Holmes, Sadler's Wells Op. Ch. & O, Lockhart

Sparked off by Mackerras's brilliantly zestful (earlier) recording of the *Overture*, this is another of the jolly Sadler's Wells productions from the early 1960s. The tone is set by the superb chorus work at the opening, and the rest follows infectiously. The soloists are not individually very striking, but Ava June is a fresh, if lightweight Mařenka and Kevin Miller an appealing Vašek. John Holmes makes a lively and resonant Marriage Broker, without effacing memories of Owen Brannigan, who used to steal the show with *Just a moment if you please*. But the singers work well as a team, as is shown by the Act III Sextet, *Think it over*, and the opera itself gains from this concentration. The jollity is inescapable when the orchestra plays the dance music with such spirit, and the recording is well up to the high standard of the series. The only drawback is that the result, while very enjoyable, doesn't sound very Czech!

The Bartered Bride (sung in German)
(M) (**) Somm Beecham (mono) 14-2. Konetzni, Tauber, Jarred, Tessmer, Ch., LPO, Beecham

Here is the first of three performances of Smetana's masterpiece that Beecham conducted at Covent Garden in his last pre-war opera season. It was recorded on 1 May 1939, only a few weeks after the Nazi annexation of Czechoslovakia, but such were the problems of assembling a cast at short notice (the Nazis had forbidden the Prague Opera from travelling) that they had to settle, ironically enough, on giving it in German. However, Beecham managed to assemble a pretty stellar line-up, including the glorious Hilda Konetzni, Richard Tauber, Mary Jarred and Marko Rothmüller. As the notes explain, Sir Thomas had all too little time for rehearsal and there is less of the sparkle and finesse we associate with him. But there is an exhilarating sense of occasion, plenty of spirit and, despite the many intrusive sonic imperfections, the glories of the singing comes across. Singers of this period possessed the most extraordinary diction and presence, and what vocal distinction there is! The sound quality calls for a tolerance that is well worth extending.

SMITH, Alice Mary (1839–84)

Symphonies in A min.; C min.; (i) *Andante for Clarinet & Orchestra*
*** Chan. 10283. LMP, Shelley, (i) with Malsbury

Alice Mary Smith was the first British woman to have composed a symphony and had it performed, and it seems ironic that her surname was a different spelling of the name of the woman composer who was really to make it, towards the end of the nineteenth century. Alice studied privately at the Royal Academy of Music, and her *Symphony in C minor*, written at the age of 24, was premièred at a London Musical Society in November 1863, and received a good press. And what a fine work it is, attractively tuneful throughout and with a fine grasp of orchestration and form. It has a particularly delightful second-movement *Allegretto amorevole*, with a folksy principal melody of real memorability. The Scherzo opens

with rollicking horns, and even the Victorian *maestoso* finale lightens up after a bit.

The *A minor Symphony* is immediately Mendelssohnian in its richly lyrical forward impetus, and the romantic *Andante* opens with the horns and then offers a flowing cantilena. The third movement is a little like a Laendler; the finale is boisterous and confident. There are a lot of symphonies which are heard occasionally and yet which are not as enjoyable as Smith's pair.

Her *Andante for Clarinet and Orchestra*, delicately scored and persuasively played here by Angela Malsbury, again demonstrates Smith's easy melodic gifts, very songlike and pleasing. Howard Shelley and the London Mozart Players are admirable advocates throughout, and this CD is most enjoyable.

SOLER, Antonio (1729–83)

Harpsichord Sonatas 1; 15; 18–19; 43; 54; 85; 90–91; 101; 110
(BB) ** Naxos 8.553462. Rowland (harpsichord)

Harpsichord Sonatas 16–17; 35; 42; 46; 52; 83; 87; 92; 106; 116
(BB) ** Naxos 8.553463. Rowland (harpsichord)

Harpsichord Sonatas 28–29; 32–34; 50; 55; 57; 69; 93; 117
(BB) ** Naxos 8.553464. Rowland (harpsichord)

A new series of the Soler keyboard sonatas from Naxos is played with sensibility and often real panache by Gilbert Rowland on a modern copy of a French two-manual harpsichord. The snag is that while he is truthfully and not too forwardly recorded, the acoustic of Epsom College Concert Hall (Surrey) is over-resonant and spreads the sound somewhat uncomfortably in the fast bravura passages. In the more reflective minor-key works (*17 in D minor* and *52 in E minor*, for instance) there are no grumbles, and often the brilliance of the playing (as in the romping *No. 43 in G*, the sparkling *No. 69 in F* and *No. 106 in E minor*, with its crisp articulation) projects through the resonance. The discs have really excellent documentation, describing each individual work in detail.

Keyboard Sonatas: 18 in C min.; 19 in C min.; 41 in E flat; 72 in F min.; 78 in F sharp min.; 84 in D; 85 in F sharp min.; 86 in D; 87 in G min.; 88 in D flat; 90 in F sharp; Fandango
(B) *** Virgin 5 62199-2. Cole (harpsichord or fortepiano)

Maggie Cole plays a dozen Soler pieces, eleven *Sonatas* and the celebrated *Fandango*, half of them on harpsichord and the remainder on the fortepiano; she gives altogether dashing performances on both. The fortepiano is a Derek Adlam copy of a Viennese instrument of the 1790s by Anton Walther and the harpsichord is a Goble. Good pieces to sample are *No. 87 in G minor* (track 5) and, on the harpsichord, *No. 86 in D major* (track 9) or the *Fandango* itself. The playing is all very exhilarating and inspiriting. Played at a normal level setting, both instruments sound a bit thunderous but, played at a lower level, the results are very satisfactory.

SOUSA, John Philip (1854–1932)

The Bride Elect (including ballet: *People Who Live in Glass Houses*); *El Capitan; Our Flirtations*
**(*) Marco Polo 8.223872. Razumovsky SO, Brion

John Philip Sousa's Band was the first great commercial success of American popular music. Sousa became its primary focus in the last decade of the nineteenth century. He toured the American continent every year, and took his Band across the Atlantic on four European tours in the first five years of the new century. His quick marches and two-steps (danced as well as marched to) had a unique transatlantic rhythmic vitality. One tends to forget that Sousa wrote things other than marches, and here we have some music from his operettas. Though successful in their day, like so many other stage works of their kind they did not have the staying power of Gilbert and Sullivan, but the dances and incidental music from them remain fresh. *The Bride Elect* was written in 1897, but Sousa's ballet *People Who Live in Glass Houses* was used in the 1923 revival and is included here. It seems like a ballet for alcoholics, with its dances entitled *The Champagnes, The Rhine Wines, The Whiskies* ('*Scotch, Irish, Bourbon and Rye!*'), and is highly entertaining. The waltzes and marches from *El Capitan* and *Our Flirtations* are enjoyable too, and display imaginative touches of orchestration. Keith Brion, musicologist, Pops Director of the Harrisburg Symphony, also leads his own touring Sousa band, so it is not surprising that he is thoroughly at home in this repertoire. Under his direction the Razumovsky orchestra plays this music brightly and idiomatically, and the recording is good.

Caprice: The Coquette; Circus Galop; The Gliding Girl (tango); *The Irish Dragoon: Myrrha Gavotte; On Wings of Lightning; Peaches and Cream* (foxtrot); *Presidential Polonaise; 3 Quotations; Sandalphon Waltzes; Silver Spray Schottische.* Marches: *Belle of Chicago; Fairest of the Fair; Federal; Gladiator; Hail to the Spirit of Liberty; Venus*
**(*) Marco Polo 8.223874. Razumovsky SO, Brion

The present Sousa survey provides a fair degree of variety by including an attractive *Gliding Girl* tango, a flimsy *Caprice* and a disarming *Gavotte*, plus a slightly grander *Presidential Polonaise*, as well as the usual marches and waltzes at which Sousa excelled. As usual on this label, helpful notes are included, and this CD should not disappoint those drawn to this repertoire.

Colonial Dames Waltz; Humoresque on Gershwin's *Swanee; Looking Upwards* (suite). Marches: *Daughters of Texas; Foshay Tower; Hail to the Spirit of Liberty; Hands across the Sea; Imperial Edward; Invincible Eagle; Kansas Wildcats; Manhattan Beach; Power and Glory*
(BB) *** Naxos 8.559058. Royal Artillery Band, Brion

Naxos provide here a superb new collection of Sousa's wind band music, presented with tremendous vigour and panache by the Royal Artillery Band, directed by Keith Brion, who knows just how to play this repertoire. The old favourites – as well as some of the rarer items – come up as fresh as paint. The recording is very good – perhaps a little lacking in opulence, but vivid enough.

Dwellers of the Western World (suite); *Humoresque* on Gershwin's *Swanee; Humoresque* on Kern's *Look for the Silver Lining; The Irish Dragoon: Overture; Rêverie: Nymphalin; Semper fidelis; Songs from Grace and Songs for Glory.* Marches: *Bullets and Bayonets; The Daughters of Texas; Jack Tar; Invincible Eagle; Power and Glory; Stars and Stripes Forever*
** Marco Polo 8.223873. Slovak RSO (Bratislava), Brion

Opening with the bright and breezy *Irish Dragoon Overture*, the ensuing programme is laced with bracing marches, but balanced out with more reflective music, such as the *Rêverie*, and fantasias on famous popular songs, plus arrangements of

popular religious themes. The three movements of *The Dwellers of the Western World* are entitled *Red Man, White Man* and *Black Man*. This is agreeable enough with its dashes of folksy colour, though much of the writing is less than first rate. Keith Brion persuades his Slovak orchestra to play it all convincingly enough, while the famous *Stars and Stripes Forever* generates plenty of gusto. The sound is fully acceptable, but lacks ultimate range and richness. The documentation is good.

MARCHES

The Complete 116 Known Published Marches
ⓞ– *** Walking Frog Records (ADD) WFR 300 (5). Detroit Concert Band, Smith (available from PO Box 680, Oskaloosa, Iowa 52577, USA www.walkingfrog.com)

We are greatly indebted to an American reader who not only pointed out the omission of this key set of recordings from our survey, but subsequently arranged for Walking Frog Records (wonderful name) to send us the CDs for review. Their excellence is almost beyond compare. The Detroit Band is a superb ensemble in all departments, and Leonard B. Smith (distinguished cornet soloist and ex-member of the Goldman Band and later the US Navy Band) proves to be an outstandingly persuasive exponent of Sousa marches. In his hands they swing along without any feeling of being pressed too hard; indeed, their gait and their sheer bonhomie bring an instant smile of pleasure. The playing is not only crisp and polished, but it has a consistent zest and spontaneity.

The recordings too are consistently demonstration-worthy. We were not surprised to discover that they have analogue masters. They were made between 1973 and 1979 in the main auditorium of the Masonic Temple in Detroit, Michigan, using a classic stereo microphone coverage without gimmicks, and the recording team was led by none other than Jack Renner (of Telarc); his colleagues were Robert Woods and James Schulkey. Tony Schmitt's digital remastering for CD calls for equal praise: nothing has been lost. The percussion (wonderful snare drums) and the full, clear bass line are equally real. As the documentation truly claims: the sound you hear is what the listener would hear having 'the best seat in the house'.

We have not space to list the entire contents, but each of these five CDs is led by one of the most famous marches: Volume 1, *The Thunderer*; Volume 2, *El Capitan*; Volume 3, *The Washington Post*; Volume 4, *Hands across the Sea*; while Volume 5 offers a double whammy, opening with a riveting *Semper fidelis*, with a splendidly built climax, and ending with the greatest march of all, *The Stars and Stripes Forever*. This is music-making that cannot but help but cheer you up.

The Complete Commercial Recordings of 60 Marches by the Sousa Band (1897–1930)
(**(*)) Crystal CD 461-3 (3). Introductory speech by Sousa. Sousa Band, Sousa; Pryor; Higgins; Rodgers; Shillkret; Bourdon; Herbert L. Clarke; Edwin G. Clarke; Pasternack

Sousa himself briefly introduces this anthology, in a recording taken from a 1929 NBC broadcast celebrating his seventy-fifth birthday, and he follows, of course, by conducting *The Stars and Stripes Forever*. These recordings, made over a period of 33 years, are an integral part of the history of the gramophone, for before the coming of the electric process a woodwind and brass concert band was the only instrumental ensemble which could be captured with a reasonable degree of realism by the acoustic recording process.

If the recordings deriving from early 7-inch Berliner discs are often of very poor quality, with more background noise than music, a cheerful 1899 record of *The Mikado March* (well laced with Sullivan tunes), conducted by Arthur Pryor, is an honourable exception, and Sousa's own later RCA recordings are often of surprising fidelity. In his historical note, Keith Brion reminds us that the musicians used for these RCA Camden sessions included many members of the Philadelphia Orchestra, plus a smattering of Sousa Band players who lived in the Philadelphia area.

Arthur Pryor usually got good results, too, although not all the playing here is immaculate. The ensemble slips badly at the opening of *Jack Tar*, yet the performance is redeemed by the middle section, which briefly quotes the *Sailor's Hornpipe* and has almost hi-fi percussion effects. However, the recordings Sousa himself made in 1917–18 bring some particularly crisp ensemble and tempi that, in *Sabre and Spurs* and *Solid Men to the Front*, for instance, are surprisingly relaxed.

Joseph Pasternack, who conducted the band in the 1920s, also did not press forward as forcefully as some modern American performances do, but followed Sousa's style, with a swinging pace that would have been ideal for marching. Rosario Bourdon, who followed in the late 1920s (and had the benefit of fuller, though not necessarily clearer electric recording), added a little more pressure, and Arthur Pryor, who has the last word here with a 1926 Camden recording of *The Stars and Stripes*, certainly doesn't look back: the piccolo solo is a joy. Excellent documentation, with photographs

Marches: *The Ancient and Honorable Artillery Company; The Black Horse Troop; Bullets and Bayonets; The Gallant Seventh; Golden Jubilee; The Glory of the Yankee Navy; The Gridiron Club; High School Cadets; The Invincible Eagle; The Kansas Wildcats; The Liberty Bell; Manhattan Beach; The National Game; New Mexico; Nobles of the Mystic Shrine; Our Flirtation; The Piccadore; The Pride of the Wolverines; Riders for the Flag; The Rifle Regiment; Sabre and Spurs; Sesqui-centennial Exposition; Solid Men to the Front; Sound off*

➛– *** Mercury (ADD) **SACD** 475 6182. Eastman Wind Ens., Fennell

Fennell's collection of 24 Sousa marches derives from vintage Mercury recordings of the early 1960s. The performances have characteristic American pep and natural exuberance; the zestfulness of the playing carries the day. One of the more striking items is *The Ancient and Honorable Artillery Company*, which incorporates *Auld lang syne* as its middle section. Reissued as an SACD, it sounds even better than in its former incarnation on CD.

Marches: *The Beau Ideal; The Belle of Chicago; The Black Horse Troop; The Charlatan; The Crusader; Daughters of Texas; The Diplomat; El Capitan; The Fairest of the Fair; Le Flor de Sevilla; From Maine to Oregon; The Gallant Seventh; The Gladiator; The Glory of the Yankee Navy; Golden Jubilee; The Gridiron Club; Hail to the Spirit of Liberty; Hands Across the Sea; The High School Cadets; The Invincible Eagle; Jack Tar; Kansas Wildcats; King Cotton; The Lambs; The Legionnaires; The Liberty Bell; Manhattan Beach; Marquette University; The National Game; New York Hippodrome; The Northern Pines; Nobles of the Mystic Shrine; On the Campus; Powhatan's Daughter; The Pride of*

the Wolverines; *The Rifle Regiment; The Royal Welch Fusiliers; Semper fidelis; Solid Men to the Front; Sound Off; The Stars and Stripes Forever; The Thunderer; The Washington Post*

➛– (BB) *** EMI Gemini 5 85535-2 (2). Band of HM Royal Marines, Lt-Col. Hoskins

Originally issued on three CDs, these are the most convincing performances of Sousa marches yet to appear from a British Band. Lt-Col. Hoskins liltingly catches their breezy exuberance and his pacing is consistently well judged. While many of the favourites are included, there is plenty of unfamiliar material here too; while the music-making still retains the sense that the performances emanate from this side of the Atlantic, the Royal Marines Band plays with style as well as enthusiasm. The digital recording is very much in the demonstration class. EMI have a long history of recording military bands and know how to balance them properly; the result is stirringly realistic, with cymbal transients telling and the side-drum snares crisp without exaggeration. Excellent value.

SPERGER, Johannes (1750–1812)

Symphonies in B flat; C; F

(BB) ** Naxos 8. 554764. Musica Aeterna Bratislava, Zajíček

Johannes Sperger was a famous double-bass player in his day and, apart from appearing as a soloist, found his main livelihood playing in various court orchestras, including that of the Cardinal Primate of Hungary. His symphonies are stylized works in three movements, the centrepiece in one instance here being a simple *Andante*; in each of the other two it is a *Minuet* and *Trio*. The most striking movement is the first of the *F major*, relatively (only relatively) strong and turbulent. But these are in essence undemanding works, well crafted, but with nothing very individual to say, and they never reveal that their composer was a virtuoso of the double-bass. They are very well played by this excellent period-instrument chamber orchestra, and the recording cannot be faulted. But, alas, Johannes Sperger deserves his obscurity.

SPOHR, Ludwig (1784–1859)

Clarinet Concerto 1 in C min., Op. 26

*** Australian Decca Eloquence (ADD) 476 7404. De Peyer, LSO, C. Davis – MOZART: *Clarinet Concerto in A;* WEBER: *Clarinet Concerto 2* ***

Gervase de Peyer's (1961) Spohr and Weber coupling now has classic status: the warmly intimate and exceptionally vivid sound adds much to one's pleasure (even the strident tuttis give it a not unattractive 'edge') and, of course, the music is highly appealing. The main theme of the first movement, besides being the kind that stays in the memory, is perfectly conceived for the instrument, and the *Adagio* is charming, too. The finale is a captivating rondo: it chuckles away in sparkling fashion, then surprises the listener by ending gently. Superb support from Colin Davis and the LSO.

String Quartets 32 in C, Op. 141; 34 in E flat, Op. 152

**(*) Marco Polo 8.225307. Moscow Philharmonic Concertino Qt

In continuing their string quartet cycle, Marco Polo appear to have left Budapest in favour of Moscow, not entirely to advantage. These are enjoyable performances, with the *Larghetto* and Scherzo of No. 32 standing out, alongside the perky Minuet of No. 34. But there is a touch of astringency on the leader's tone that is pretty certainly due to the microphones; the recording balance otherwise is good.

String Quintets 3 in B min., Op. 69; 4 in A min., Op. 91

(BB) *** Naxos 8.555966. Augmented New Haydn Qt

This coupling was previously available on Marco Polo and as such was reviewed in our main *Guide* with the performances wrongly attributed to the Augmented Danubius Quartet. These two minor-key works have much of the wistful mood for which the composer is noted, especially the *Adagio* of the B *minor*, which is rather memorable, while there is also a rocking barcarolle finale. The quality of Spohr's invention is well maintained throughout, and they are warmly played and pleasingly recorded, to be very enticing at their new Naxos price.

String Quintet 7 in G min., Op. 144; Potpourri (for solo violin & string quartet), Op. 22; Sextet in C, Op. 140

(BB) *** Naxos 8.555968. Augmented New Haydn Qt

Like the CD above, this disc was first issued on the Marco Polo label, when it was praised in our main volume. The three works are admirably contrasted, the *Quintet* uncertain in mood, often permeated with a feeling of unease, and the *Sextet* much sunnier, while the *Potpourri* combines a Russian folk tune with Mozart's *Là ci darem la mano* to form a showoff piece, suitable as an encore. Very good performances and first rate recording.

STANFORD, Charles (1852–1924)

(i) *Piano Quintet in D min.; (ii) String Quintet 1*

*** Hyp. CDA 65505. Vanbrugh Qt, with (i) Lane; (ii) Knox

The *Piano Quintet* comes from 1886, when Stanford was 33, and is an ambitious and powerfully argued score, beautifully laid out for the medium. Although Brahms and Schumann are always in the background, the musical ideas are strong and sweep the listener along with a sense of purpose. Although Stanford's music may not possess the strong individuality of Fauré or any comparable contemporary, it is powerful music and its neglect unaccountable. The *First String Quintet* (1903), with second viola, is hardly less persuasive. The ideas are keenly lyrical and their quality distinguished, and the overall flow of the music is extraordinarily natural. Excellent music that will delight and give pleasure; and both the performances and recording, produced by Andrew Keener, are of real excellence. Not to be missed.

Anthems: I heard a voice from heaven; O for a closer walk. *Canticles: Magnificat in G; Magnificat & Nunc Dimittis in B flat; Te Deum in C; When Mary thro' the garden went*

*** Coll. COLCD 118. Cambridge Singers, Rutter; Wayne Marshall (organ) – HOWELLS: *Church music* ***

Stanford's *Magnificat in G* opens this disc seductively, with an Elysian soprano solo from Caroline Ashton and some delightful organ colouring, while the B flat setting is full-throated, with a more restrained *Nunc Dimittis* following. The two Anthems are both simple, *O for a closer walk* reflective, while *I heard a voice from heaven* brings another lovely soprano solo from Karen Kerslake, with the choir entering elegiacally. *When Mary thro' the garden went* is a part-song with something of the memorability of Stanford's famous *Blue Bird*. But the *Te Deum* moves forward swiftly

and is exultant without being too overwhelming. All this music is effectively interspersed with contributions from Herbert Howells to make a contrasted and thoroughly satisfying programme. If you need a single disc to cover both these fine composers, this splendidly sung and recorded collection is very recommendable.

The Revenge: A Ballad of the Fleet, Op. 24; Songs of the Fleet, Op. 117; Songs of the Sea, Op. 91

✪ **** Chan. **SACD** CHSA 5043. Finley, Welsh Nat. Ch. & BBC SO of Wales, Hickox

It is surprising that this is the first new recording of Stanford's glorious *Songs of the Sea* and *Songs of the Fleet* since Benjamin Luxon's 1982 EMI account. These inspired works are immediately memorable, with *The Old Superb* and *Drake's Drum* being real hits. There is much here that is genuinely touching, such as *Homeward Bound* from the *Songs of the Sea*; the more moody and brooding items from *The Songs of the Fleet* offer contrast to the extrovert numbers, but throughout, Stanford's briny inspiration always comes up as fresh as the sea air.

This new recording is valuable for including the première recording of *The Revenge: A Ballad of the Fleet*. It is hard to understand why this work is unknown – maybe, since all three works would have been too long for one LP, it missed its chance of being revived earlier. *The Revenge* tells the story of Richard Grenville's heroic 1591 battle against the Spanish fleet, and it was a huge success at its 1886 première. It is just as entertaining as the more famous works on this CD, and hopefully this recording may spark off the odd live performance. Gerald Finley's golden tone is superb and he rises to both the heroic and tender passages with total conviction. With equal dedication from the chorus – not to mention the orchestra, which offers both enthusiasm and sensitivity – this CD is an outstanding success. The Chandos recording is warm and detailed, offering plenty of spine-tingling atmosphere, which is even more impressive when played through an SACD system. This new version is a clear winner for this repertoire and another triumph for Richard Hickox.

STEFFANI, Agostini (1654–1728)

Stabat Mater

(B) *** DHM/BMG 82876 60149-2. Alamanjo, Van der Sluis, Elwes, Padmore, Van der Kamp, Netherlands Bach Festival Ch. & O, Leonhardt – BIBER: *Requiem à 15 in A* ***

Agostino Steffani was diplomat and priest as well as a composer, but his music has a strongly individual character. His serene, melancholy *Stabat Mater* has moving and expressive content and much imaginative word-setting, while the *Cujus animam* and *Pro peccatis* are glorious in their expressively rich harmonies. The solo writing is imaginative and the layering of parts in the closing *Quando corpus*, which gathers pace as it proceeds, is very telling. The performance could hardly be bettered, with soloists and chorus equally dedicated. First-rate recording.

STEINBERG, Maximilian (1883–1946)

Symphony 1 in D, Op. 3; Prélude symphonique, Op. 7; Fantaisie dramatique, Op. 9

*** DG 457 607-2. Gothenburg SO, Järvi

The *First Symphony* (1905–6) is very much influenced by Glazunov and is in no way inferior: indeed, Steinberg's scoring is more transparent and less congested. The melodic invention is perhaps less distinguished but, without making excessive claims, the music is well worth reviving. The *Fantaisie dramatique* (1910) is inspired by Ibsen's *Brand* and like its companions on this enterprising disc bears witness to Steinberg's continuing debt to his mentors and his feeling for the orchestra is little short of remarkable. Neeme Järvi proves an invigorating and refreshing guide in these genial and sympathetic pieces, and the fine Gothenburg orchestra respond to his enthusiasm. The recording is absolutely state-of-the-art, beautifully defined and present, yet transparent in detail.

STENHAMMAR, Wilhelm (1871–1927)

CHAMBER MUSIC

(i) *Allegro brillante in E flat; Allegro ma non tanto;* (ii; iii) *Violin Sonata in A min., Op. 19;* (iii) *Piano Sonata in A flat, Op. 12*
** BIS CD 764. (i) Tale Qt (members); (ii) Olsson; (iii) Negro

All this music comes from the 1890s, before Stenhammar's personality was fully formed. The *A flat Sonata*, written in the same year (1895) as the better-known and somewhat Brahmsian *Three Fantasies*, Op. 11, though derivative has some pleasing invention and a good feeling for form. Lucia Negro plays it with great authority and sensitivity. The *Violin Sonata* comes from 1899 and was written for Stenhammar's chamber-music partner, the composer Tor Aulin. The *Allegro ma non tanto* is the first movement of a projected piano trio (1895); and little is known about the even earlier *Allegro brillante* fragment. The pianist, who is unfailingly responsive, rather swamps her partners here and in the *Violin Sonata*, thanks to a less than satisfactory balance.

STEVENS, Bernard (1916–83)

(i) *Cello Concerto; Symphony of Liberation*
*** Mer. (ADD) CDE 84124. (i) Baillie; BBC PO, Downes

Bernard Stevens came to wider notice at the end of the war when his *Symphony of Liberation* won a *Daily Express* competition. What a fine work it proves to be, though the somewhat later *Cello Concerto* is even stronger. Dedicated performances from Alexander Baillie and the BBC Philharmonic. Good recording.

(i) *Violin Concerto; Symphony 2*
*** Mer. (ADD) CDE 84174. (i) Kovacic; BBC PO, Downes

The *Violin Concerto* is a good piece and well worth investigating. Stevens is a composer of real substance, and the *Second Symphony* (1964) is impressive in its sustained power and resource. Ernst Kovacic is persuasive in the *Concerto*, and Downes and the BBC Philharmonic play well. Good (but not spectacular) recording.

STOCKHAUSEN, Karlheinz (born 1928)

(i) *Mikrophonie 1; Mikrophonie 2;* (ii) *Klavierstücke 1–11*
(M) *** Sony (ADD) S2K 53346 (2). (i) Members of W. German R. Ch. & Studio Ch. for New Music, Cologne, Kontarsky, Alings, Fritsch, Bojé, cond. Schernus; supervised by composer; (ii) Kontarsky (piano)

This reissue combines two important Stockhausen recordings from the mid-1960s. *Mikrophonie 1* is electronic music proper; *Mikrophonie 2* attempts a synthesis of electronic music and choral sounds, and it is the vocal work that is the more immediately intriguing. It may be in dispute just how valid performances like these are when the composer's score allows many variables, but at least it is the composer himself who is supervising the production. Outstanding recording-quality for its time – as, of course, it should be with so many musician-engineers around in the Cologne studios.

The *Klavierstücke* provide a stimulating coupling. Aloys Kontarsky plays these eleven pieces – arguably the purest expression yet of Stockhausen's musical imagination – with a dedication that can readily convince even the unconverted listener. Seven of the pieces are very brief epigrammatic utterances, each sharply defined. The sixth and tenth pieces (the latter placed separately on the second disc) are more extended, each taking over 20 minutes. The effect at the beginning of the ninth piece provides a clear indication of Stockhausen's aural imagination. The pianist repeats the same, not very interesting discord no fewer than 228 times, and one might dismiss that as merely pointless. What emerges from sympathetic listening is that the repetitions go nagging on so that the sound of the discord seems to vary, like a visual image shimmering in heat-haze. The other pieces, too, bring similar extensions of musical experience, and all this music is certainly communicative. Excellent if forward recording and extensive back-up notes. A good set on which to sharpen avant-garde teeth.

Stimmung (1968)
*** Hyp. CDA 66115. Singcircle, Rose

Gregory Rose with his talented vocal group directs an intensely beautiful account of Stockhausen's 70-minute minimalist meditation on six notes. Though the unsympathetic listener might still find the result boring, this explains admirably how Stockhausen's musical personality can hypnotize, with his variety of effect and response, even with the simplest of formulae. Excellent recording.

STOJOWSKI, Zygmunt (1870–1946)

Piano Concertos 1 in F sharp min., Op. 3; 2 in A flat (Prelude, Scherzo & Variations), Op. 32
*** Hyp. CDA 67276. Plowright, BBC Scottish SO, Brabbins

The Polish-born pianist and composer, Zygmunt Stojowski, emigrated to the United States in 1905 where, despite early success, he found his unashamedly romantic style irrevocably overtaken and submerged. Even in Poland he is almost entirely forgotten, but this charming disc of his first two piano concertos demonstrates that such easily fluent, lyrical music has much to offer even today. It is true that none of his thematic material can quite match that of a contemporary like Rachmaninov, whose late-romantic style is similar, but the tunes are there and in brilliant performances like those given by Jonathan Plowright, with warmly committed accompaniment from the BBC Scottish orchestra, both works are well worth hearing.

The structure of the *First Concerto*, written in 1890, is relatively conventional with a delightful central Andante in which the cello and cor anglais are given solo roles alongside the piano, and a '*Dance of Death*' finale. The *Second Concerto*, dating from between 1909 and 1910, is unconventional in its structure – a Prologue, Scherzo and Variations in which the model of Liszt is more striking than in No. 1. The most memorable section is the *Presto Scherzo*, with echoes of Litolff and Saint-Saëns in its galloping rhythms, but until the substantial closing section the final set of variations is rather too full of stopping and starting. Nevertheless this is most enjoyable. Warm, well-balanced recording.

STRAUS, Oscar (1870–1954)

Marches: *Einzugs; Bulgaren; Die Schlossparade. Menuett à la cour.* Polka: *G'stellte Mäd'ln. Rund um die Liebe* (Overture); Waltzes: (i) *L'Amour m'emporte. Alt-Wiener Reigen; Eine Ballnacht; Der Reigen; Didi;* (i) *Komm, komm, Held meiner Träume; Tragante; Valse lente; Walzerträume*

*** Marco Polo 8.223596. (i) Kincses; Budapest Strauss SO, Walter

Although Oscar Straus is no relation to the famous Strauss family, his style of writing echoed theirs, also absorbing influences from Lehár. His great hit was the operetta, *A Waltz Dream* (1907), which had a first run in Vienna of 500 performances. His *Walzerträume* is deftly based on the main theme from the operetta, and the *Einzugs-Marsch* comes from the same source. But he could also manage a neat polka and score it very prettily, as is instanced by *G'stellte Mäd'ln*, while the *Alt-Wiener Reigen Waltz* is also full of charm and is played here very seductively. *Komm, komm, Held meiner Träume* is, of course, the famous 'Come, Come, my Hero', which comes from a parody operetta based on George Bernard Shaw's *Arms and the Man*. In 1908 it was a flop in Vienna, under its title *Der tapfere Soldat* ('The Brave Soldier') but was a resounding success in England and the USA later, when its title was changed to *The Chocolate Soldier* and its hit song took the world by storm. It is nicely sung here in soubrette style by Veronika Kincses.

After the Second World War, Straus wrote an engaging hit, sung first by Danielle Darrieux in a 1952 French film, *Madame de ...*, and here by Kincses, and he capped his movie career with a Parisian-style waltz, *Der Reigen*, for the famous Max Ophüls film, *La Ronde*, the song eventually becoming better-known than the movie. The programme opens with a pot-pourri overture irresistibly full of sumptuous and lighthearted melody. It is infectiously played here, like the rest of the programme, by the first-class Budapest Strauss Symphony Orchestra, conducted with affection and great élan by Alfred Walter – easily the best CD he has made so far. The recording, too, is gorgeously sumptuous, and this is a marvellous disc to cheer you up on a dull day. Highly recommended.

***The Chocolate Soldier* (highlights)**

(B) **(*) CfP (ADD) 335988-2. Voss, Payne, Stevens, Elsy, Linden Singers, New World Show O, Braden – HERBERT: *Naughty Marietta* **(*); ROMBERG: *The Student Prince* (highlights) **(*)

The Chocolate Soldier, based on a George Bernard Shaw play, was a satirical look at war and its consequences. It was first performed in Vienna in 1908 and was revived many times and turned into a film in 1947. It contained several popular numbers, five of which, including the most famous, *My Hero*, are included here. *Ti-ra-la-la* (*Three women sighing alone one night*) is rather fetching in its sentimental way, as is the catchy title-number, *The Chocolate Soldier*. The collection ends with the lively *Forgive, forgive, forgive!*, sung by the Barbarians, which turns into a gently lilting waltz. A good music-theatre cast and lively performances and 1962 sound.

STRAUSS Family, The

Strauss, Johann Sr: The Complete Edition

Volume 1: *Alte und neue Tempête* (includes: *Altdeutscher Postertanz; Altvatr Galoppade; Altvater Marsch; Sauvage).* Galops: *Alpenkönig, Op. 7/1–2; Champagner; Schauer; Seufzer; Stelldichein.* Waltzes: *Döblinger Réunion; Gesellschafts; Kettenbrücke; Täuberin; Wiener-Carneval; Wiener Launen*

*** Marco Polo 8.225213. Camerata Cassovia, Pollack

Marco Polo's all-embracing survey of the music of the Strauss family now turns to the least-known repertoire of all, that written by Johann Senior, beginning in the third decade of the nineteenth century. Until the arrival of Johann the Elder, Viennese dance music had been in the hands of Joseph Lanner, and Johann began his career as a viola player in Lanner's small café orchestra. But he was already composing and arranging, and although his *Täuberin-Walzer* of 1826, published as his Op. 1, was not his very first waltz, no earlier examples have survived and it is now regarded as his first major composition. It has distinct charm but is of modest scale, and with the solo violin introducing the main theme a Ländler flavour remains, as it does in the *Döblinger Réunion-Walzer*, written for Lanner's ensemble that same year, and very simply scored for flute, two clarinets, two horns, trumpet and strings.

But in 1827 Strauss struck out on his own and gave his first concert with his own orchestra at the Zu den zwei Tauben (Two Doves tavern). No doubt *Täuberin* was included in that programme. The agreeable *Vienna-Carnival Waltz* appeared the following year and was intended as a tribute to Weber, who had just died. It quotes from an aria from *Oberon*, but its style remains predictable.

The *Alpine Galop* (which appears here in two versions, differently scored, brought about by a change of the composer's publisher) spiritedly connects a series of motives from Wenzel Müller's incidental music for a play of the time, but the *Champagne Galop* of 1828 has rather more individuality and its principal motif was quoted by the composer again in his later waltz of the same name.

But it is with the *Kettenbrüke Waltz* that Strauss (then still only 24) gives us his first really striking string of tunes to establish a format which was to be the pattern for the finest Viennese works in this form. Similarly, the *Seufzer-Galoppe*, sparkles with personality, and appropriately it originally included a vocal 'sigh' in which the breathless dancers were invited to join. Its scoring, although still modest in scope, is certainly vivid, and the *Stelldichein-Galoppe* with its bouncing horn theme is also charmingly infectious. Perhaps most fascinating of all is Strauss's 1827 pot-pourri of old and new dances, individually primitive but agreeably diverse and including the *Old German Pillow Dance*, a round dance for courting couples, which Tchaikovsky included in the Act I party scene of his *Nutcracker Ballet*.

Christian Pollack is a master of this repertoire and his Camerata Cassovia gives a perfect simulation of the small Viennese ensembles of the period. They play with a polished, infectious stylishness that gives much pleasure, and they are well recorded in a pleasing acoustic.

Volume 2: Galops: *Carolinen; Chineser; Erinnerungs; Gesellschafts; Kettenbrücke.* Ländler: *Die so sehr beliebten Erinnerung.* Waltzes: *À la Paganini; Die beliebten*

Trompetenwalzer; Champagne; Fort nacheinander! Krapfen-Waldel; Lieferung der Kettenbrücke Lust-Lager
*** Marco Polo 8.225252. Camerata Cassovia, Pollack

Volume 2 remains mainly in the more intimate world of Viennese Schrammeln music, scored for modest resources, which spawned the early Strauss output. Paganini caused a sensation when he visited Vienna in March 1828, so Strauss's *Paganini* selection begins with *La Campanella* (which was the talk of the city) but after that is a rather routine affair. The highlights are the relatively familiar *Chinese Galop* with its piquant piccolo and the lesser-known *Carolinen* and *Kettenbrücke Galops*, which both have infectious galloping rhythms. *Erinnerungs* is bouncy too. The *Die so sehr beliebten Erinnerung* Ländler, charmingly scored, shows that Johann Senior was still happiest in this earlier triple-time format. The 'Popular Trumpet Waltz' is enterprising only for the signal calls from its named brass soloist, but *Fort nacheinander* ('Off after One Another!'), as the title suggests, is the most varied and inventive waltz here. Fine performances from Pollack and his chamber group.

Volume 3: *Contredanses par Jean Strauss. Galops: Einzugs; Hirten; Sperl; Ungarische Galoppe oder Frischka Nos.1–3; Wettrennen; Wilhelm Tell. Waltzes: Es ist nur ein Wien! Frohsinn im Gebirge; Hietzinger-Reunion (or Weissgärber-Kirchweih-Tänz) Josephstädler; Es ist nur ein Wein!; Dies Verfassers beste Laune*
*** Marco Polo 8.225253. Slovak Sinf., Zilina, Märzendorfer

By 1829 Strauss's scoring was growing more ambitious, and the lively 'There is Only One Vienna! Waltz' is given its winning character from its chirpy scoring for a pair of clarinets and a flute (besides two horns and a trumpet), while the delectable *Hirten-Galoppe* expands the orchestral complement to flute, oboe, bassoon, two clarinets, two horns (used simply and effectively) plus a pair of trumpets; and the *Races Galop* uses the brass wittily. The *Hietzinger-Reunion-Walzer* returns to a simple, Ländler style, but retains the fuller scoring. The *William-Tell Galoppe* is an unashamed crib, but skilfully put together; while the three *Hungarian Dances* draw on the same material used by Brahms. The finest of the waltzes here is appropriately 'The Composer's Best Fancy', but this collection is most notable for its galops, in particular the irresistible *Sperl*, which is delightfully scored and draws on a familiar Rossini motif to spirited effect. The *Contredanses for Jean Strauss* is a quadrille, drawing on lively French melodies but retaining much of the Viennese Schrammeln style, even when the music is fully scored. Excellent performances throughout, even if the playing is spirited rather than very polished.

Volume 4: *Cotillons on Motives from Bellini's opera, 'La Straniera'; Schwarz'sche Ball-Tänz in Saul zum Sperl (Cotillons based on Motives from Auber's 'La Muette de Portici'). Galops: Galop 1 & 2 from Auber's 'La Muette de Portici'; Fortuna; Venetianer. Polkas: Charmant; Launen. March: Wiener Bürger-Marsch 1: Original Parademarsch. Waltzes: Bajaderen; Heiter auch in ernster Zelt; Hof-Ball-Tänzer; Das Leben ein Tanz oder Der Tanz ein Leben!; Vive la Danse!*
*** Marco Polo 8.224254. Slovak Sinf., Zilina, Märzendorfer

The cotillons from Auber's *La Muette de Portici* open zestfully with the jolly tune, famous from the Overture, better known as *Masaniello*. You can't go wrong with Auber, and this is most enjoyable, as are the pair of galops using material fom

the same opera. The carefree *Bajaderen-Walze*, equally agreeable, draws on Auber's *Le Dieu et la Bayadère*. The *Charmant Polka* really is charming, and this extends to the lighthearted waltz, *Viva la Danse!* The follow-up was 'Cheerful too, at a serious time', badly needed in Vienna, as in 1830 the Danube flooded its banks and in 1831 the city was suffering a cholera epidemic. *Das Leben ein Tanz* thus opens mournfully on the brass to signify Strauss's acknowledgement of the disaster, but the waltz itself is lighthearted. The cheerful *Parade March* of 1832 must also have been much appreciated. We move on to 1834 for the delicately effervescent *Venetian Galope* which completes a particularly generous programme.

Vol. 5: *Contratänze; Contredanses; Der Raub der Sabinerinnen, Charakteristisches Tongemälde; Tivoli Frudenfest-Tänze. Galopps: Bayaderen; Der Fest der Handwerker; Montecchi; Zampa. Waltzes: Benefice; Gute Meinung für die Tanzlust; Souvenir de Baden (Helenen-Walzer); Tivoli Rutsch; Wiener-Damen*
** Marco Polo 8.225281. Slovak Sinfonietta Zilina, Pollack

The problem for the compilers of this series is that Johann Senior was quite happy to turn out strings of potboiler waltz themes, for his patrons always wanted something new, and although they must be agreeable to dance to they are not memorable. The performances here, especially those conducted by Christian Pollack, are most sympathetic and the recording is excellent; but you cannot make much of a really routine genre piece.

Volume 5 does not contain any really outstanding pieces, although the opening *Contredanses* draw engagingly on Rossini. All three waltzes are simple and simply structured, the scoring of *Gute Meinung* quaint, and the *Souvenir de Baden* bringing chattering woodwind. The surprise is the virtually non-danceable tone-poem, *The Abduction of the Sabine Women*, which was a hit in its day. This consists of a march, a galopp and a six-section waltz, followed by an extended coda suggesting reconciliation, a remarkable epilogue for abuse.

Vol. 6: *Fra Diavolo-Cotillons. Galopp: Reise. Marches: Wiener Bürgermarsch 2. Polkas: in Es; Jäger. Quadrille nach Motiven aus der Oper 'Anna Bolena'. Waltzes: Alexandra; Carnevals; Mein schönster Tag in Baden; Die vier Temperamente*
** Marco Polo 8.225282. Slovak Sinf. Zilina, Pollack

Volume 6 gets off to a good start with the *Fra-Diavolo Cotillons* – Strauss was at his best when purloining other composers' tunes, and there is some nice scoring in both the *Zampa Waltz* and the *Quadrille*, which uses themes from Donizetti. The other *Waltzes* are agreeable enough (*Mein schönster Tag* has a catchy main theme), and the *Jäger Polka* and *Reise-Galopp* are both quite lively and inventive.

Vol. 7: *Mittel gegen den Schlaf. Galopps: Boulogner; Cachucha; Der Carneval in Paris; Jugendfeuer. Original-Parade-Marsch. Waltzes: Emlék Pestre; Erinnerungen an Berlin; Gabrielen; Iris; Pfennig*
**(*) Marco Polo 8.225283. Slovak Sinf. Zilina, Märzendorfer

Volume 7 is one of the most striking collections, with the *Cachucha Galopp* really sparkling, as is the *Parade March*; and all the waltzes have their share of charm, especially *Erinnerungen an Berlin* and *Iris*.

Vol. 8: *Cotillons nach beliebten Motiven aus der Oper 'Der Zweykiampf'; Militär Quadrille; Robert-Tänze. Galopps:*

Ballnacht; Versailler; Gitana. Polkas: *Maruanka; Paris*. Waltzes: *Elisabethen; Der Frohsinn, mein Ziel; Rosa; Tausendsapperment*
**(*) Marco Polo 8.225284. Slovak Sinf. Zilina, Pollack

Volume 8 is another better-than-average collection, opening with the charming *Tausendsapperment Waltz*, followed by the *Ballnacht-Galopp* with carolling horns. The *Paris Polka* too is one of Strauss's best and the *Cotillons* from a now unknown opera show it had some good tunes. The programme ends with the attractive *Versailler-Galopp*, the *Rosa Waltz* and the relatively well-known *Gitana-Galopp*.

Johann Strauss Jr: The Complete Edition

Vol. 1: Mazurka: *Veilchen, Mazur nach russischen motiven.* Polkas: *Fledermaus; Herzenslust; Zehner.* Quadrilles: *Debut; Nocturne.* Waltzes: *Bei uns z'Haus; Freuet euch des Lebens; Gunstwerber; Klangfiguren; Maskenzug française; Phönix-Schwingen*
**(*) Marco Polo 8.223201. A. Walter

Vol. 2: *Kaiser Franz Josef 1, Rettungs-Jubel-Marsch.* Polkas: *Czechen; Neue Pizzicato; Satanella; Tik-Tak.* Polka-Mazurka: *Fantasieblümchen.* Quadrilles: *Cytheren; Indra.* Waltzes: *Die jungen Wiener; Solonsprüche; Vermälungs-Toaste; Wo die Zitronen blüh'n*
** Marco Polo 8.223202. A. Walter

Vol. 3: Polkas: *Aesculap; Amazonen; Freuden-Gruss; Jux; Vergnügungszug.* Quadrilles: *Dämonen; Satanella.* Waltzes: *Berglieder; Liebslieder; Lind-Gesänge; Die Osterreicher; Wiener Punsch-Lieder*
**(*) Marco Polo 8.223203. A. Walter

Vol. 4: Polkas: *Bürger-Ball; Hopser; Im Krapfenwald'l (polka française); Knall-Kügerin; Veilchen.* Marches: *Austria; Verbrüderungs.* Quadrille: *Motor.* Waltzes: *Dividenden; O schöner Mai!; Serail-Tänze*
**(*) Marco Polo 8.223204. Edlinger

Vol. 5: *Russischer Marsch Fantasie.* Polkas: *Eilsen (polka française); Heiligenstadt Rendezvous; Hesperus; Musen; Pariser.* Quadrille: *Sur des airs français.* Waltzes: *Italienischer; Kennst du mich?; Nachtfalter; Wiener Chronik*
*** Marco Polo 8.223205. O. Dohnányi

Vol. 6: *Caroussel Marsch.* Polkas: *Bluette (polka française); Camelien; Warschauer.* Quadrilles: *Nach Themen französischer Romanzen; Nordstern.* Waltzes: *Concurrenzen; Kuss; Myrthen-Kränze; Wellen und Wogen*
** Marco Polo 8.223206. O. Dohnányi

Vol. 7: *Deutscher Krieger-Marsch; Kron-Marsch.* Polkas: *Bacchus; Furioso; Neuhauser.* Polka-Mazurka: *Kriegers Liebchen.* Quadrille: *Odeon.* Waltzes: *Ballg'schichten; Colonnen; Nordseebilder; Schnee-Glöckchen; Zeitgeister*
**(*) Marco Polo 8.223207. Polish State PO, O. Dohnányi

Vol. 8: *Banditen-Galopp; Erzherzog Wilhelm Genesungs-Marsch.* Polkas: *Leichtes Blut; Wiedersehen; Pepita.* Quadrilles: *Nach Motiven aus Verdi's 'Un ballo in maschera'; Saison.* Waltzes: *Cagliostro; Carnevals-Botschafter; Lagunen; Die Sanguiniker; Schallwellen*
**(*) Marco Polo 8.223208. Polish State PO, O. Dohnányi

This extraordinary Marco Polo enterprise – to record the entire output of the Strauss family – began in 1988. All these volumes centre on the music of Johann Junior. Johann and his orchestra were constantly on the move and, wherever they

travelled to play, he was expected to come up with some new pieces. While obvious 'hits' and favourites stayed in the repertoire, often the novelties were treated as ephemeral and in many instances only the short piano-score has survived. It was necessary – for the purpose of the recording – to hire professional arrangers to make suitable orchestrations; from these, new orchestral parts could be copied. Such is the perversity of human experience that quite regularly the original orchestral parts would suddenly appear for some of the pieces – after the recording had been made! It is therefore planned to have an appendix and to re-record those items later, from the autographs. So far the recordings have been made in Eastern Europe. Apart from cutting the costs, the Slovak Bohemian tradition provides a relaxed ambience, highly suitable for this repertoire. Much of the music is here being put on disc for the first time, and indeed the excellent back-up documentation tells us that three items on the first CD were part of the young Johann's first concert programme: the *Gunstwerber* ('Wooer of Favour') *Waltz, Herzenslust* ('Heart's Desire') polka and, even more appropriately, the *Debut-Quadrille,* so that makes Volume 1 of the series something of a collectors' item, while Volume 3 also seems to have above-average interest in the selection of its programme.

Evaluation of these recordings has not been easy. The first three CDs were made by the Slovak State Philharmonic under Alfred Walter. The mood is amiable and the playing quite polished. With the arrival of Richard Edlinger and Oliver Dohnányi on the scene, the tension seems to increase, and there is much to relish. Of this second batch we would pick out Volumes 5, 7 and 8, all representing the nice touch of Oliver Dohnányi, with Volume 5 perhaps a primary choice, although there are many good things included in Volume 8.

Vol. 9: *Habsburg Hoch! Marsch; Indigo-Marsch.* Polkas: *Albion; Anen; Lucifer.* Polka-Mazurka: *Nachtveilchen.* Quadrille: *Festival Quadrille nach englischen Motiven.* Waltzes: *Carnevalsbilder; Gedanken auf den Alpen; Kaiser*
** Marco Polo 8.223209. Polish State PO, Wildner

Vol. 10: *Pesther csárdas.* Polkas: *Bauern; Blumenfest; Diabolin; Juriston Ball.* Quadrille: *Nach beliebten Motiven.* Waltzes: *Feuilleton; Morgenblätter; Myrthenblüthen; Panacea-Klänge*
** Marco Polo 8.223210. Polish State PO (Katowice), Wildner

Vol. 11: *Revolutions-Marsch.* Polkas: *Frisch heran!; Haute-volée; Hermann; Patrioten.* Polka-Mazurka: *Waldine.* Quadrilles: *Die Afrikanerin; Handels-élite.* Waltzes: *Aus den Bergen; Donauweibchen; Glossen; Klänge aus der Walachei*
**(*) Marco Polo 8.223211. A. Walter

Vol. 12: *Krönungs-Marsch.* Polkas: *Auora; Ella; Harmonie; Neues Leben (polka française); Souvenir; Stürmisch in Lieb' und Tanz.* Quadrille: *Fest.* Waltzes: *Aus den Bergen; Donauweibchen; Glossen; Klänge aus der Walachei*
**(*) Marco Polo 8.223212. A. Walter

Vol. 13: *Egyptischer Marsch; Patrioten-Marsch.* Polkas: *Demolirer; Fidelen; Nur fort!; Tanzi-bäri; was sich liebt, neckt sich (polka française).* Quadrilles: *Nach Motiven aus der Oper 'Die Belagerung von Rochelle'; Neue Melodien.* Waltzes: *Sirenen; Thermen; Die Zillerthaler*
**(*) Marco Polo 8.223213. A. Walter

Vol. 14: *Romance 1 for Cello & Orchestra.* Polkas: *Champagne; Geisselhiebe; Kinderspiele (polka française); Vöslauer.* Quadrilles: *Bal champêtre; St Petersburg*

(*Quadrille nach russischen Motiven*). Waltzes: *Du und du; Ernte-tänze; Frohsinns-spenden; Grillenbanner; Phänomene*
**(*) Marco Polo 8.223214. A. Walter

Vol. 15: *Jubelfest-Marsch.* Polkas: *Bijoux; Scherz.*
Polka-Mazurkas: *Lob der Frauen; La Viennoise.* Quadrilles: *Alexander; Bijouterie.* Waltzes: *Die Jovialen; Kaiser-Jubiläum; Libellen; Wahlstimmen*
** Marco Polo 8.223215. CSR SO (Bratislava), Wildner

Vol. 16: *Fürst Bariatinsky-Marsch.* Polkas: *Brautschau* (on themes from *Zigeunerbaron*); *Eljen a Magyar!; Ligourianer Seufzer; Schnellpost; Studenten. La Berceuse Quadrille; Zigeuner-Quadrille* (on themes from Balfe's '*Bohemian Girl*'). Waltzes: *Bürgerweisen; Freuden-Salven; Motoren; Sangerfährten*
**(*) Marco Polo 8.223216. A. Walter

With Volume 9, we move to Poland and a new name, Johannes Wildner. He has his moments, but his approach seems fairly conventional. He does not make a great deal of the famous *Emperor Waltz*, which closes Volume 9, although he does better with *Gedanken auf den Alpen*, another unknown but charming waltz. Alfred Walter – who began it all – then returns for Volumes 11–14. Of this batch, Volume 11 might be singled out, opening with the jolly *Hermann-Polka*, while the *Klänge aus der Walachei, Aus den Bergen* ('From the Mountains') and *Donauweibchen* ('Nymph of the Danube') are three more winning waltzes; but the standard seems pretty reliable here, and these are all enjoyable discs. Volume 16 has another attractive batch of waltzes, at least two winning polkas and a quadrille vivaciously drawing on Balfe's *Bohemian Girl.* It also includes the extraordinary *Ligourian Seufzer-Polka,* in which the orchestra vocally mocks the Ligourians, a despised Jesuitical order led by Alfonso Maria di Ligouri. Another good disc.

Vol. 17: *Kaiser Franz Joseph-Marsch.* Polkas: *Armen-Ball; 'S gibt nur a Kaiserstadt! 'S gibt nur a Wien; Violetta (polka française);* Quadrille: *Melodien.* Waltzes: *Adelen; Bürgersinn; Freiheits-Lieder; Windsor-Klänge*
*** Marco Polo 8.223217. CSR SO (Bratislava), Eschwé

Vol. 18: *Alliance-Marsche; Studenten-Marsch.* Polkas: *Edtweder-oder!; Invitation à la polka mazur; Leopoldstädter; Stadt und Land; Cagliostro-Quadrille.* Waltzes: *Grössfürstin Alexandra; Lava-Ströme; Patronessen; Die Pulizisten; Rathausball-Tänz*
**(*) Marco Polo 8.223218. A. Walter

Vol. 19: *Hoch Osterreich! Marsch.* Polkas: *Burschenwanderung (polka française), Electro-magnetische; Episode (polka française).* Quadrilles: *Le Premier Jour de bonheur; Opéra de Auber; Seladon.* Waltzes: *Dorfgeschichten (im Ländlerstil); Novellen; Rosen aus dem Süden; Seid umschlungen, Millionen; Studentenlust*
**(*) Marco Polo 8.223219. A. Walter

Vol. 20: *Dinorah-Quadrille nach Motiven der Oper, 'Die Wallfahrt' nach Meyerbeer. Kaiser-Jäger-Marsch. Slovianka-Quadrille, nach russischen Melodien.* Polkas: *Auf zum Tanze; Herzel.* Polka-Mazurkas: *Ein Herz, ein Sinn; Fata Morgana.* Waltzes: *Aurora-Ball-Tänze; Erhöhte Schwärmereien* (concert waltz)
** Marco Polo 8.223220. A. Walter

Vol. 21: *Ottinger Reiter-Marsch.* Polkas: *Figaro (polka française); Patronessen (polka française); Sans-souci.*

Polka-Mazurka: *Tändelei.* Quadrilles: *Orpheus; Rotunde.* Waltzes: *Cylcoiden; G'schichten aus dem Wienerwald; Johannis-Käferin*
** Marco Polo 8.223221. Wildner

Vol. 22: *Klipp-Klapp Galopp. Persischer Marsch.* Polkas: *L'Inconnue (polka française); Nachtigall.* Polka-Mazurka: *Aus der Heimat.* Quadrilles: *Carnevals-Spektakel; Der lustige Krieg.* Waltzes: *Controversen; Immer heiterer (im Ländlerstil); Maxing-tänze; Ninetta*
** Marco Polo 8.223222. Wildner

Vol. 23: *Deutschmeister-Jubiläumsmarsch.* Polkas: *Maria Taglioni; Die Pariserin (polka française); Rasch in der Tat!* Polka-Mazurka: *Glücklich ist, wer vergisst.* Quadrilles: *Le Beau Monde; Indigo.* Waltzes: *Gross-Wien; Rhadamantus-Klänge; Telegramme; Vibrationen; Wien, mein Sinn!*
** Marco Polo 8.223223. Wildner

Vol. 24: *Gavotte der Königin. Viribus unitis, Marsch.* Polkas: *Demi-fortune (polka française); Heski-Holki; Rokonhangok (Sympathieklänge); So ängstlich sind wir nicht!* Polka-Mazurka: *Licht und Schatten.* Quadrille: *Streina-Terrassen.* Waltzes: *Idyllen; Jux-Brüder; Lockvögel; Sinnen und Minnen*
** Marco Polo 8.223224. A. Walter

Volume 17 introduces another new name, Alfred Eschwé. It is a particularly good collection, one of the highlights of the set, and is beautifully played. Volume 18 brings back Alfred Walter and another very good mix of waltzes and polkas. Johannes Wildner then directs Volumes 21–23, and it must be said that the middle volume shows him in better light than the other two, and with a well-chosen programme.

Vol. 25: *Grossfürsten Marsch.* Polkas: *Bonbon (polka française); Explosions; Lustger Rath (polka française); Mutig voran!.* Polka-Mazurka: *Le Papillon.* Quadrilles: *Künstler; Promenade.* Waltzes: *Frauen-Käferin; Krönungslieder; Spiralen; Ins Zentrum!*
** Marco Polo 8.223225. Wildner

Vol. 26: *Es war so wunderschön Marsch.* Polkas: *Elektrophor; L'Enfantillage (polka française); Gut bürgerlich (polka française); Louischen (polka française); Pásmán.* Quadrilles: *Industrie; Sofien.* Waltzes: *Juristenball-Tänze; Künstlerleben; Pasman; Sinngedichte*
*** Marco Polo 8.223226. Austrian RSO, Vienna, Guth

Vol. 27: *Spanischer Marsch.* Polkas: *Drollerie; Durch's Telephon; Express; Gruss an Wien (polka française).* Polka-Mazurka: *Annina.* Quadrilles: *Künstler; Sans-souci.* Waltzes: *Aeolstöne; Souvenir de Nizza; Wein, Weib und Gesang; Frühlingsstimmen*
❀ *** Marco Polo 8.223227. Austrian RSO, Vienna, Guth

Vol. 28: *Freiwillige vor! Marsch (1887). Frisch in's Feld! Marsch.* Polkas: *Unter Donner und Blitz; Pappacoda (polka française).* Polka-Mazurkas: *Concordia; Spleen.* Quadrille: *Tête-à-tête.* Waltzes: *Einheitsklänge; Illustrationen; Lebenswecker; Telegraphische Depeschen*
** Marco Polo 8.223228. Wildner

Vol. 29: *Brünner-Nationalgarde-Marsch. Der lustig Krieg, Marsch.* Polkas: *Die Bajadere; Hellenen; Secunden (polka française).* Polka-Mazurka: *Une bagatelle.* Quadrille: *Waldmeister.* Waltzes: *Deutsche; Orakel-Sprüche; Schatz; Tausend und eine Nacht; Volkssänger*
** Marco Polo 8.223229. A. Walter

Vol. 30: *Fest-Marsch. Perpetuum mobile.* Polkas: *Alexandrinen; Kammerball; Kriegsabenteuer; Par force!* Quadrille: *Attaque.* Waltzes: *Erinnerung an Covent Garden; Kluh Gretelein; Luisen-Sympathie-Klänge; Paroxysmen; Reiseabenteuer*
** Marco Polo 8.223230. A. Walter

Vol. 31: *Napoleon-Marsch.* Polkas: *Husaren; Taubenpost (polka française); Vom Donaustrande.* Polka-Mazurka: *Nord und Süd.* Quadrilles: *Bonvivant; Nocturne.* Waltzes: *Gambrinus-Tänze; Die ersten Curen; Hochzeitsreigen; Die Unzertrennlichen; Wiener Bonbons*
** Marco Polo 8.223231. A. Walter

Vol. 32: *Wiener Jubel-Gruss-Marsch.* Polkas: *Auf der Jagd; Olge; Tritsch-Tratsch.* Polka-Mazurka: *An der Wolga.* Quadrilles: *Methusalem; Hofball.* Waltzes: *Fantasiebilder; Ich bin dir gut!; Promotionen. Wiener Blut*
** Marco Polo 8.223232. Wildner

Volume 26 brings another fresh name, Peter Guth, and fresh is the right word to describe this attractive programme. From the bright-eyed opening, *Elektrophor Polka schnell*, this is winningly vivacious music-making, and the waltz that follows, *Sinngedichte*, makes one realize that there is something special about Viennese string-playing, for this is the orchestra of Austrian Radio. Volume 27 features the same orchestra and conductor and opens with the delectable *Künstler-Quadrille*. After the aptly named *Drollerie* polka comes the *Aeolstöne* waltz with its portentous introduction, and the waltz itself is heart-warming. The *Souvenir de Nizza* waltz is hardly less beguiling; and *Wine, Women and Song* and, to end the disc, *Frühlingsstimmen* – two top favourites – simply could not be better played. These two Peter Guth CDs are the finest of the series so far, and we award a token Rosette to the second of the two, although it could equally apply to its companion. After those two marvellous collections it is an anticlimax to return to the following volumes. There is much interesting music here, but the performances often have an element of routine.

Vol. 33: *Saschen-Kürassier-Marsch.* Polkas: *Etwas kleines (polka française); Freikugeln.* Polka-Mazurka: *Champêtre.* Quadrilles: *Bouquet; Opern-Maskenball.* Waltzes: *Abschieds-Rufe; Sträusschen; An der schönen blauen Donau; Trau, schau, wem!*
** Marco Polo 8.223233. Wildner

Vol. 34: (i) *Dolci pianti* (Romance for Cello & Orchestra). *Im russischen Dorfe, Fantasie* (orch. Max Schönherr). *Russischer Marsch. Slaven-potpourri.* Polkas: *La Favorite (polka française); Niko.* Polka-Mazurka: *Der Kobold.* Quadrille: *Nikolai.* Waltzes: *Abschied von St Petersburg; Fünf Paragraphen*
** Marco Polo 8.223234. Dittrich

Vol. 35: *Zivio! Marsch.* Polkas: *Jäger (polka française); Im Sturmschritt! Die Zeitlose (polka française).* Polka-Mazurka: *Die Wahrsagerin.* Quadrilles: *Der Blitz; Der Liebesbrunnen.* Waltzes: *Accelerationen; Architecten-Ball-Tänze; Heut' ist heut' Königslieder*
** Marco Polo 8.223235. Wildner

Vol. 36: *Matador-Marsch.* Polkas: *Bitte schön! (polka française); Diplomaten; Kreuzfidel (polka française); Process.* Polka-Mazurka: *Der Klügere gibt nach.* Quadrilles: *Elfen;*

Fledermaus. Waltzes: *D'Woaldbuama (im Ländlerstil)* (orch. Ludwig Babinski); *Extravaganten; Mephistos Höllenrufe; Neu-Wien*
** Marco Polo 8.223236. A. Walter

Among the following batch, the CD that stands out features another new name, Michael Dittrich. Working with the Slovak Radio Symphony Orchestra, he produces a splendid collection to make up Volume 34. The flexible handling of the *Slav Pot-pourri* shows his persuasive sympathy for Strauss, while the *Fünf Paragraphen* waltz has an equally delectable lilt. There is great charm in the elegant *La Favorite* polka and the *Abschied von St Petersburg* waltz has a nicely beguiling opening theme.

Vol. 37: *Triumph-Marsch* (orch. Fischer). Polkas: *Das Comitat geht in die Höh!; Sonnenblume; Tanz mit dem Besenstiel!* (all arr. Pollack); (i) *Romance 2 in G min.* for *Cello & Orchestra, Op. 35* (arr. Schönherr). Quadrilles: *Die Königin von Leon* (arr. Pollack); *Spitzentuch. Neue Steierische Tänze* (orch. Pollack); *Traumbild II.* Waltzes: *Jugend-Träume* (orch. Pollack); *Schwungräder*
*** Marco Polo 8.223237. Pollack; (i) with Jauslin

Volume 37 is among the most interesting and worthwhile issues so far. It includes the waltz with which the nineteen-year-old Johann Junior created his first sensation at Zum Sperlbauer in Vienna. He had taken over the orchestra's direction in February 1845, and during a summer's night festival in August of that same year *Jugend-Träume* was introduced. It received five encores! The waltz is entirely characteristic, opening with a lilting theme on the strings and moving from one idea to another with the easy facility that distinguishes his more famous waltzes. Christian Pollack is a Strauss scholar, and in almost every case here he has worked from piano scores or incomplete scoring. Particularly delectable is the set of *New Styrian Dances*, seductively written in the Ländler style of Lanner's *Steyrische Tänze*. Here an almost complete piano version was available, while the orchestral parts end with the third dance; Pollack has therefore scored the fourth dance (very convincingly) in the style of the other three. While the *Romance for Cello and Orchestra* is agreeably slight, the other striking novelty here is *Traumbild II*, a late domestic work in two sections, the first of which is a gentle and charming 'dream-picture' of Strauss's wife, Adèle; the second shows the other side of her nature – more volatile and capricious. Both are in waltz time. Christian Pollack is not just a scholar but an excellent performing musician, and the playing here is polished, relaxed and spontaneous in an agreeably authentic way.

Vol. 38: *Wiener Garnison-Marsch* (orch. Babinski); *Ninetta-Galopp.* Polkas: *Damenspende; Lagerlust; Maskenzug* (2nd version); *Nimm sie hinn!; Zehner* (2nd version). Quadrilles: *Eine Nacht in Venedig; Serben* (orch. Babinski). Waltzes: *An der Elbe; Faschings-Lieder* (orch. Kulling); *Leitartikel*
**(*) Marco Polo 8.223238. A. Walter

An der Elbe is a real find among the waltzes, a charming melodic sequence with a striking introduction. But the *Ninetta-Galopp* with its perky main theme and swirling woodwind answer has the potential to become a Strauss lollipop, while the more sedate *Maskenzug-polka française* closes the programme engagingly. This is one of Alfred Walter's better programmes, nicely played and well recorded.

Vol. 39: *Ninetta-Marsch.* Polkas: *I Tipferl; Sylphen; Unparteiische Kritiken.* Quadrilles: *Jabuka; Slaven-Ball* (both orch. Pollack). Quodlibet: *Klänge aus der Raimundzeit.* Waltzes: *Abschied; Irenen* (orch. Babinski); *Hell und voll*

**(*) Marco Polo 8.223239. Pollack

The two most interesting items here both date from Johann's last years, the *Abschied* ('Farewell') *Waltz* and the *Klänge aus der Raimundzeit* (1898), an affectionate pot-pourri, including tunes by Johann Senior and Lanner. Johann originally called this good-humoured quodlibet *Reminiscenz. Aus der guter alten Zeit* ('from the good old days'). The score of the waltz is written in the composer's own handwriting; his widow, Adèle, offered it to be performed posthumously in 1900. The *I Tipferl-polka française* is based on a popular comic song from Strauss's *Prinz Methusalem*, and the couplet: 'The man forgot – the little dot, the dot up on the i!' is wittily pointed in the music. Christian Pollack directs excellent performances of all the music here which, although of varying quality, is never dull.

Vol. 40: *Hochzeits-Praeludium.* Polkas: *Herzenskönigin; Liebe und Ehe; Wildfeuer.* Quadrilles: *Ninetta; Wilhelminen* (orch. Babinski). Waltzes: *Heimats-Kinder* (orch. Babinski); *The Herald* (orch. Schönherr); *Irrlichter; Jubilee* (orch. Cohen)

*(*) Marco Polo 8.223240. Slovak RSO (Bratislava), Bauer-Theussl

Vol. 41: March: *Wo uns're Fahne weht.* Polkas: *Newa; Shawl.* Quadrilles: *Martha; Vivat!.* Waltzes: *Burschen-Lieder; Gedankenflug; Lagunen. Traumbild* (symphonic poem). *Aschenbrödel (Cinderella): Prelude to Act III*

** Marco Polo 8.223241. Slovak RSO (Bratislava), Dittrich

Vol. 42: *Hommage au public russe.* March: *Piccolo.* Polkas: *An der Moldau; Auroraball; Grüss aus Osterreich; Sängerlust; Soldatespiel.* Waltzes: *Gartenlaube; Hirtenspiele; Sentenzen*

**(*) Marco Polo 8.223242. Slovak RSO (Bratislava), Pollack

For Volumes 40 to 42 Christian Pollack returns, but we also meet a new conductor, Franz Bauer-Theussl. As it turns out, the music-making in Volume 40 under Bauer-Theussl immediately proves heavy-handed in the opening waltz, and the feeling throughout is that he is conducting for the commercial ballroom rather than the concert hall. As Pollack demonstrates in Volume 42, much more can be made of relatively strict tempo versions than Bauer-Theussl does with the *Irrlichter* and *Herald* Waltzes. The *Jubilee Waltz* was written for the Strausses' American visit in 1872, when in Boston he conducted its première, played by a 'Grand Orchestra' of 809 players, including 200 first violins! With this kind of spectacle it is not surprising that he chose to end a not particularly memorable piece by including a few bars of the American national anthem in the coda.

Without being exactly a live wire, Michael Dittrich makes a good deal more of Volume 41. He is able to relax and at the same time coax the orchestra into phrasing with less of a feeling of routine, as in the *Shawl-Polka*, which lilts rather nicely, and the comparatively sprightly *Vivat!* Dittrich fails to make a great deal of the one relatively well-known waltz here, *Lagunen*, but he manages the *Aschenbrödel Prelude* colourfully and does very well indeed by the *Traumbild I* ('Dream Picture No. 1'), a warmly relaxed and lyrical evocation, quite beautifully scored. It was written towards the end of the composer's life, for his own pleasure.

But when we come to Volume 42, so striking is the added vivacity that it is difficult to believe that this is the same orchestra playing. The opening *Piccolo-Marsch* and the *Auroraball polka française* are rhythmically light-hearted, as are all the other polkas in the programme, and if the *Hirtenspiele* (or 'Pastoral play') *Waltz* is not a masterpiece, it is still freshly enjoyable in Pollack's hands, despite the demands of a ballroom tempo. The *Gartenlaube-Walzer* is a real find; it has a charming introduction with a neat little flute solo, then the opening tune, lightly scored, is very engaging indeed. It is a great pity that Marco Polo did not hire the services of Christian Pollack much earlier in the series. Even the recording sounds better focused here.

Vol. 43: *An dem Tanzboden* (arr. Pollack); *Reitermarsch.* Polkas: *Herrjemineh; Postillon d'amour; Die Tauben von San Marco.* Quadrilles: *Simplicius; Des Teufels Antheil* (arr. Pollack). Waltzes: *Trifolien; Walzer-Bouquet 1; Wilde Rosen* (arr. Babinski & Kulling)

**(*) Marco Polo 8.223243. Pollack

Vol. 44: Polkas: *Auf freiem Fusse; Nur nicht mucken* (arr. Peak); *Von der Börse.* Quadrilles: *Hinter den Coulissen; Monstre* (with J. STRAUSS SR). *Maskenfest; Schützen* (with J. and E. STRAUSS). Waltzes: *Altdeutscher* (arr. Pollack); *Aschenbrödel (Cinderella); Strauss' Autograph Waltzes* (arr. Cohen)

**(*) Marco Polo 8.223288. Pollack

Vol. 45: Ballet music from *Der Carneval in Rom* (arr. Schönherr); *Ritter Pásmán. Fest-Marsch. Pásmán-Quadrille* (arr. Pollack); *Potpourri-Quadrille; Zigeunerbaron-Quadrille.* Waltzes: *Eva; Ischler*

**(*) Marco Polo 8.223245. A. Walter

With Christian Pollack directing with his usual light touch, Volume 43 is one of the best of the more recent Marco Polo issues, even if the *Walzer-Bouquet* is less winningly tuneful than its title suggests. *Wilde Rosen* is rather better, though not really memorable like *An dem Tanzboden* ('On the Dance Floor'), which was inspired by a painting. It is a real lollipop with a charming introduction (with clarinet solo) and matching postlude. The main waltz-tune is captivating and Pollack plays it exquisitely. Strauss originally intended to feature a zither in his scoring, but later indicated a pair of flutes instead, which sound delightful here. This is a prime candidate for a New Year concert. The polkas and *Simply Delicious Quadrille* are amiably diverting too, but the *Trifolien Waltz*, though lively enough, is a run-of-the-mill piece.

Volume 44 includes the brief (three-minute) but pleasant *Altdeutscher Waltz*, arranged by the conductor, and the relatively familiar *Aschenbrödel*, which is attractive but not one of Strauss's vintage waltzes. As usual with Pollack, the various quadrilles and polkas are agreeably relaxed but never dull, and the recording is up to standard.

Alfred Walter returns to conduct Volume 45, and he is at his finest in the lively and tuneful waltz that is the central movement of the *Ritter Pásmán Ballet.* The other ballet music, from *Der Carneval in Rom*, is scored by Schönherr – and very vividly too. The *Eva Waltz* is brief but delightfully graceful; *Ischler*, however, is more conventional. The quadrilles are nicely managed and the sound is very good.

Vol. 46: March: *Vaterländischer.* Polkas: *Pawlowsk; Pizzicato* (with Josef); *Probirmamsell.* Quadrilles: *Marien; Annika.*

Romance: *Sehnsucht*. Waltzes: *Cagliostro; Engagement;
Greeting to America*. (i) Gradual: *Tu qui regis totum orbem*.
SCHUMANN (arr. J. Strauss): *Widmung*
*** Marco Polo 8.223246. Slovak RSO (Bratislava), Dittrich;
(i) with Slovak Philh. Ch. (members)

Michael Dittrich is on top form in Volume 46 of this
ongoing series, opening vivaciously with a musical switch in
march form, beginning with the *Radetzky* 'fanfare' and proceeding to quote intriguing snippets from all kinds of
sources, including the Austrian national anthem. The *Greeting to America Waltz* has a very appropriate and recognizable
introduction and is as attractive as the delightfully scored
Engagement Waltz, also written for America. The *Marien-
Quadrille* is another charmer, and we learn from the excellent notes that the famous *Pizzicato Polka*, a joint effort
between Johann and Josef, was composed in Pavlovsk on a
Russian tour in 1869. The transcription of Schumann's love
song, *Widmung*, was made by Johann in 1862 as a tribute to
his new bride, Jetty, who was a singer, but the *Romance
(Sehnsucht)* was written as a more robust cornet solo. The
Gradual, *Tu qui regis totum orbem* ('Thou who rulest the
whole world'), is a surprise inclusion from the eighteen-
year-old composer – an offertory sung in conjunction with
the performance of a Mass by his teacher, Professor Dresch-
ler – and very pleasing it is. The concert ends with one of the
deservedly better-known waltzes, taken from the operetta
Cagliostro in Wien and played in an elegantly vivacious but
nicely flexible style, like the rest of this very appealing
programme, one of the very best of the Marco Polo series.
The recording is excellent.

**Vol. 47: Ballet music from *Die Fledermaus*; from *Indigo und
die vierzig Räuber* (arr. Schönherr). *Eine Nacht in Venedig:
Processional March*. GOUNOD (arr. J. Strauss): *Faust
(Romance)*. *Quadrille on themes from 'Faust'*. Marches:
*Kaiser Alexander Huldinungs; Kaiser Frans Joseph
Jubiläums; Der Zigeunerbaron*. Waltzes: *Coliseum Waltzes;
Farewell to America; Sounds from Boston***
*** Marco Polo 8.223247. Bratislava City Ch., Slovak RSO,
Wildner

This is another very attractive compilation with many beguiling novelties. After the brief but lively march from *Der
Zigeunerbaron* comes *Farewell to America*, an agreeable pastiche waltz, which waits until its coda to quote *The Star-
spangled Banner*. The following *Faust Romance* is a robust
flugelhorn solo, based on an aria which was later to disappear
from Gounod's revision of his score. The lively *Quadrille*,
however, includes many favourite tunes from the opera and
climaxes genially with the *Soldiers' Chorus*. Strauss's own
ballet-music, written to be played during Orlofsky's supper
party in *Die Fledermaus*, is today almost always replaced by
something briefer. It includes a number of short national
dances (not forgetting a *Schottische*) and the *Bohemian Dance*
is in the form of a choral polka, actually sung here ('Mari-
anka, come here and dance with me'), while the Hungarian
finale reprises the music from Rosalinde's *Csárdás*. On the
other hand, Schönherr's audaciously scored (some might say
over-scored) 11-minute *mélange* of tunes from *Indigo and the
Forty Thieves* is at times more like Offenbach than Strauss: it
coalesces the good tunes and presents them in a glittering
kaleidoscope of orchestral colour. The engaging *Coliseum
Waltzes* that follow uncannily anticipate the *Blue Danube*,
complete with an opening horn theme. *Sounds from Boston*,
written for the composer's Boston visit in 1872, is another

pastiche waltz of considerable charm, resulting as much from
its delicacy of scoring as from its ready melodic flow: the
orchestra parts were discovered, hidden away in the music
library of the Boston Conservatory. The ideas come from
earlier waltzes and almost none of them are familiar. All this
music is liltingly and sparklingly presented by the Slovak
Radio Orchestra, and no one could accuse the conductor,
Johannes Wildner, of dullness.

**Vol. 48: Complete Overtures, Vol. 1: *Concert Overture:
Opéra comique* (arr. Pollack). *Intermezzo* from '*Tausend
und eine Nacht*'. Overtures: *Blindekuh; Cagliostro in Wien;
Der Carneval in Rom; Die Fledermaus; Indigo und die
vierzig Räuber. Prince Methusalem; Das Spitzentuch der
Königen***
**(*) Marco Polo 8.223249. A. Walter

Collections of operetta overtures are almost always entertainingly tuneful, and this one is no exception. It begins with a
curiosity that may or may not be authentic, an *Overture
comique* written by the young Johann Jr for large harmonium
(a kind of orchestrion) and piano, and afterwards arranged
by the Strauss scholar, Fritz Lange, for violin and piano. None
of the ideas it contains can be traced to the composer's
notebooks, but the piece is attractive and is well put together
in the form of a concert overture. It is heard here in a new
arrangement (following the Lange manuscript) by Christian
Pollack. *Indigo und die vierzig Räuber* ('Indigo and the Forty
Thieves') is also interesting in that Strauss omits the waltz
rhythm altogether, which makes its lightly rhythmic progress
seem rather Offenbachian. The *Intermezzo* from *Thousand
and One Nights* is a just favourite, although Walter's languorous performance could use a little more lift, and *Die Fledermaus* is a fairly routine performance. However, Walter
conducts the other overtures very agreeably and makes the
most of their pretty scoring. The waltzes are always coaxed
nicely, particularly that in *Cagliostro in Wien*, and the playing
has charm; yet one feels that some of the livelier ideas might
have been given a bit more zip.

**Vol. 49: Complete Overtures, Vol. 2: *Aschenbrödel
(Cinderella)*: *Quadrille*. Overtures: *Die Göttin der Vernunft
(The Goddess of Reason); Der lustige Krieg. Jabuka: Prelude
to Act III. Eine Nacht in Venedig: Overture* and *Prelude to
Act III*. Overtures: *Simplicius; Waldmeister; Der
Zigeunerbaron***
**(*) Marco Polo 8.223275. A. Walter

Alfred Walter's second collection of overtures has distinctly
more sparkle than the first. He is always good with waltzes
and there are quite a few here, if only in snippet form. The
pair included in *A Night in Venice* are presented with appealing delicacy, while *The Goddess of Reason* brings a waltzing
violin solo complete with cadenza and, at the close, another
waltz which swings splendidly. *Zigeunerbaron* is the best-
known piece here, and it is laid out elegantly and is beautifully played. But Walter is inclined to dally by the wayside: in
the theatre a performance like this would not hold the
attention of the audience. *Simplicius* is much more lively,
with a march near the beginning, and *Waldmeister* has real
verve, with the horns skipping along nicely towards the end.
What one rediscovers on listening through this pair of discs is
not only the fecundity of Johann's invention and the charm
of his orchestration, but also the felicitous way he turns a
pot-pourri into a naturally spontaneous sequence of ideas.
The recording throughout both collections is first class, spacious and with a ballroom warmth.

Vol. 50: (i) *Am Donaustrand;* (i) *Erste Liebe (Romanze);* *Erster Gedanke;* (i) *Ein gstanzi von Tanzl; Die Fledermaus; Csárdás. Frisch gewagt* (Galop); *Da nicken die Giebel* (Polka-Mazurka); *Die Göttin der Vernunft* (Quadrille); (i) *Dolci pianti.* Waltzes: (i) *Frühlingsstimmen;* (i) *King Gretelein; Nachgelassener; Odeon-Waltz;* (i) *Wo die Citronen blüh'n;* (i) *Wenn du ein herzig Liebchen hast*
*** Marco Polo 8.223276. (i) Hill Smith; Slovak RSO (Bratislava), Pollack

Marilyn Hill Smith was on hand for this collection, so one wonders why the opening *Csárdás* from *Die Fledermaus* is the orchestral version (arranged by Hans Swarowsky); but the excellent Christian Pollack makes a good case for it, his ebb and flow of mood and tempo very engaging. Hill Smith sings a number of items, and her light soubrette is just right for this repertoire. She presents *Wo die Citronen blüh'n* with much vivacity and is hardly less sparkling in the famous *Voices of Spring.* Moreover she offers as a charming vignette *Dolci pianti* (a song that Strauss composed for his singer-wife, Jetty) for which she has also provided the accompanying translation. The rest of the programme is agreeable, but there are no lost masterpieces here. Pollack makes the most of the waltzes and is especially characterful in the polka-mazurka, *Da nicken die Giebel,* which sounds a bit like a slow waltz with extra accents. Again, first-rate recording.

Vol. 51: *Auf der Alm* (Idyll); *Fürstin Ninetta* (Entr'acte). Galop: *Liebesbotschaft.* (i) Choral polka: *Champêtre (Wo klingen die Lieder).* Polka-Mazurka: *Promenade-Abenteuer.* (ii) *Romance 2 for Cello & Orchestra.* Choral waltz: (i) *An der schönen, blauen Donau.* Waltzes: *Centennial; Enchantment; Engagement; Farewell to America; Manhattan; Tauben.* Songs: (iii) *Bauersleut' im Künstlerhaus; D'Hauptsach* (both arr. Rott)
✹ *** Marco Polo 8.223279. Slovak RSO (Bratislava), Cohen; with (i) Slovak Philharmonic Ch.; (ii) Tvrdik; (iii) Eröd

It is rather appropriate that Volume 51 should be special, and so it is. It opens with the enchanting choral *Polka mazurka champêtre,* introduced by the horns and gloriously sung by a male chorus with a nicely managed diminuendo at the coda. And it ends with Strauss's masterpiece, the *Blue Danube,* also for male-voice choir and sung with an infectious lilt, to leave the listener in high spirits. All the other half-dozen waltzes here are virtually unknown, and every one is delightful. The opening strain of *Manhattan* is ear-catching and Cohen later (rarely in this series) indulges himself in some affectionate rubato, which is most seductive. The *Centennial* and the (well-named) *Enchantment Waltzes* are again most affectionately presented, and their beguiling introductions are in each case followed by a string of good tunes. The *Engagement Waltz* opens more grandly, but then the atmosphere lightens, and there is plenty of sparkle. *Farewell to America* (a pot-pourri) brings the American national anthem delicately and nostalgically into the coda. The *Romance No. 2 for Cello and Orchestra,* tastefully played by Ivan Tvrdik, is surprisingly dolorous at its opening, then produces a romantic flowering, before ending nostalgically. The *Liebesbotschaft Galop* then arrives to cheer us all up, and it is followed by yet another unknown waltz, *Tauben,* in which Cohen coaxes the opening quite ravishingly. Of the two brief baritone solos, the second, *D'Hauptsach,* has a most pleasing melody. No other record in the series so far offers such a fine package of unexpected delights or more hidden treasure, and there could be no better advocate than the present conductor, Jerome Cohen.

He has the advantage of spacious, naturally balanced recording. A Rosette then for the sheer enterprise of the first half-century of this series and also for the special excellence of this collection with its discovery of six remarkably fine waltzes.

Pot-pourris, Vol. 1: *Cagliostro in Wien; Indigo und die vierzig Räuber; Der lustige Krieg; Eine Nacht in Venedig; Prinz Methusalem; Das Spitzentuch der Königin*
*(*) Marco Polo 8.225074. Pollack

Pot-pourris, Vol. 2: *Fürstin Ninetta; Die Göttin der Vernunft; Jabuka (Das Apfelfest); Ritter Pásmán; Simplicius*
*(*) Marco Polo 8.225075. Pollack

Even today, selections from musical shows are the mainstay of the bandstand, and so it was in the days of the Strauss family. However, although they include a fair smattering of good tunes, some of the pot-pourris here outlast their welcome (*Indigo und die vierzig Räuber* runs for over 18 minutes) and the scoring of the vocal numbers is seldom very imaginative. Curiously, even Christian Pollack, usually an inspired Straussian, is below his best form, and he fails to make a case for them. In the end this becomes nothing more than wallpaper music. So this pair of discs, although well enough played, is of documentary interest only.

STRAUSS, Johann Sr (1804–49),

STRAUSS, Johann Jr (1825–99),

STRAUSS, Josef (1827–70),

STRAUSS, Eduard (1835–1916)

2006 New Year's Concert': *Auf's Korn!; Künstler Quadrille.* Galopps: *Banditen; Liebesbotschaft.* Marches: *Spanischer; Der Zigeunerbaron.* Polkas: *Diplomaten; Eljen a Magyar!; Furioso; Im Krapfenwald'l; Lob der Frauen; Neue Pizzicato.* Waltzes: *An der schönen, blauen Donau; Du und Du; Frühlingsstimmen; Künsterleben; Lagunen.* STRAUSS, EDUARD: Polka: *Telephon.* STRAUSS, JOHANN SR: March: *Radetzky.* STRAUSS, JOSEF: Polkas: *Eingesendet; Ohne Sorgen!* (with MOZART: *Le nozze di Figaro* Overtures. LANNER: Waltz: *Die Mozartisten*)
(M) *** DG 477 5566 (2). VPO, Jansons

After New Year's Concerts conducted by Harnoncourt and Muti, Jansons is altogether mellower. Not, of course, with the lively Marches (*Auf's Korn* and *Zigeunerbaron*) and fast Polkas (*Ohne Sorgen!* with its vocal interjections, which swings along). But in the Waltzes, Jansons has a lilting, coaxing style and *Du und Du, Voices of Spring, Lagunen* and, of course, the *Blue Danube* are very seductively phrased by the Viennese strings. One of the more appealing novelties is Lanner's *Die Mozartisten,* a pot-pourri with some very familiar operatic melodies. Altogether a very enjoyable and relaxing programme, spread over two discs (for the price of one) but not one that makes you sit up, except in response to beautiful orchestral playing.

(i) *Le Beau Danube* (ballet suite, arr. Désormière); (ii) *Graduation Ball* (ballet, arr. Dorati)
*** Australian Decca Eloquence (ADD) 476 7522. (i) Nat. PO, Bonynge; (ii) VPO, Dorati

t is a pity that this kind of repertoire has fallen out of favour these days as it really is sparklingly entertaining from beginning to end. Antal Dorati described his arrangement of generally lesser-known Strauss pieces as 'a youthful prank' or 'escapade', and his musical direction follows this mood. It is immensely spirited and exhilarating and, while Boskovsky's earlier Decca version offered more charm, there is no doubting the vibrancy of the music-making. The flamboyant solo dances come off vividly, and zestful exuberance is the keynote of this 1976 recording – with sound to match. Equally brilliant is Richard Bonynge's 1974 version of *Le Beau Danube* where, once again, Strauss is raided to produce another delightful confection. It is all tunefully bright and vivacious, and the finale, aided by the exceptionally vivid sound, builds up to a frenzy of excitement. A sensible coupling from Australian Decca which puts Dorati's *Graduation Ball* on CD for the first time.

The Strauss family in London': J. STRAUSS SR: *Almack's Quadrille; March of the Royal Horse Guards* (orch. Georgiadis); *Huldigung der Königen Victoria Grossbritannien* (waltz). Polkas: *Alice; Exeter-Polka; Fredrika.* EDUARD STRAUSS: *Greeting Waltz, on English Airs; Old England for Ever* (polka, orch. Georgiadis). J. STRAUSS II: *Erinnerung an Covent-Garden* (waltz); *Potpourri-Quadrille* (orch. Peak). J. STRAUSS III: *Krönungs-Walzer*

(M) *** Chan. (ADD) 7128. LSO, Georgiadis

A waltz which starts with *Rule, Britannia* and ends with *God save the Queen* may seem unlikely, but that's exactly how *Huldigung der Königen Victoria Grossbritannien* goes. The music here is the result of visits made to England by the Strausses, the first one instigated by one of their greatest admirers: Queen Victoria. Like Jack Rothstein's companion set, this disc is full of delightful surprises and, with idiomatic playing from the LSO, fine Chandos sound, and excellent sleeve-notes by Peter Kemp, it is surely an essential purchase for all Straussians. The most striking novelty is the inclusion of a waltz by the now virtually forgotten Johann Strauss III.

Galops: *Banditen; Cachucha.* Marches: *Egyptyscher; Kaiser Franz Josef.* Polkas: *Annen; Auf der Jagd; Eljen a Magyar; Fata Morgana; Furioso; Tritsch-Tratsch.* Quadrille nach *Motiven der Operette 'Der lustige Krieh'.* Waltzes: *An der schönen blauen Donau; Morgenblatter; Rosen aus dem Süden; 1001 Nacht; Wiener Blut; Wiener Bonbons.* JOSEF STRAUSS: Polkas: *Farewell; Die Libelle; Moulinet; Ohne Sorgen.* Waltzes: *Aquarellen; Perlen der Liebe.* EDUARD STRAUSS: March: *Weyprecht-Payer.* Polka: *Saat und Ernte.* Waltzes: *Leuchkäferin; Schleier un Krone*

(B) ** Chan. 6687 (2). Johann Strauss O, Rothstein

This generous two-disc compilation is assembled from recordings made between 1981 and 1992. It includes a number of attractive novelties, among them rare items from Josef and Eduard, although Josef's *Perlen der Liebe* is a shade disappointing. Otherwise there is no lack of spontaneity here: the polkas are infectious and cheerful, there is no lack of lilt in the waltzes, and the bright digital sound has plenty of bloom. However, good though Rothstein is, he does not equal John Georgiadis among other British conductors in this repertoire.

Banditen-Galopp; Quadrille nach Motiven der Operette. Marches: *Egyptischer; Kaiser Franz Josef.* Polkas: *Annen-Polka; Auf der Jagd; Eljen a Magyar; Fata Morgana; Furioso-Polka quasi Galopp; Tritsch-Tratsch; Unter Donner*

und Blitz. Waltzes: *An der schönen, blauen Donau; Morgenblatter; Rosen aus dem Süden; Tausend and eine Nacht; Wiener Blut; Wiener Bonbons.* EDUARD STRAUSS: *Weyprecht-Payer* (march); *Saat und Ernte* (polka). Waltzes: *Leuchtkäferlin; Schleir und Krone.* JOSEF STRAUSS: Polkas: *Die Libelle; Farewell!; Moulinet; Ohne Sorgen.* Waltzes: *Aquarellen; Perlen der Liebe.* J. STRAUSS SR: *Cachucha-Galopp*

(M) **(*) Chan. (ADD) 7129 (2). Strauss O, Rothstein

These are relaxed, enjoyable performances, which are hard to fault. If they lack the Viennese distinction of Boskovsky or the individuality of Karajan, the varied programme, with plenty of novelties, makes up for it. There are several agreeable surprise items in this two-CD set, and the sound is very good.

(i) *Egyptischer Marsch.* Overtures: *Die Fledermaus; Der Zigeunerbaron.* Polkas: *Kreuzfidel; Leichtes Blut;* (ii) *Lob der Frauen;* (i) *Pizzicato* (with Josef); (ii) *Die Tauben von San Marco; Tritsch-Tratsch;* (i) *Unter Donner und Blitz;* Waltzes: *An der schönen blauen Donau; Geschichten aus dem Weiner Wald; Wiener Bon Bons*

(BB) **(*) Warner Apex 0927 49981-2. (i) Concg. or (ii) BPO; Harnoncourt

Until he had such a great success with the 2003 New Year Concert, Nikolaus Harnoncourt was not the first conductor to spring to mind in connection with a Strauss concert, but he shows here in the pair of Overtures (*Die Fledermaus* particularly volatile and diverting) that he has the full measure of the vivacity and character of the idiom, and he secures very polished and responsive playing from both the Concertgebouw and Berlin Philharmonic Orchestras, with plenty of attack when needed. Elsewhere his care for detail sometimes seems to concentrate on the trees at the expense of the wood. The *Egyptian March* (complete with chorus) could have more verve, and the waltzes too are more easily flexible in other hands. A highlight is the very gentle *Pizzicato Polka*, but the other three polkas played by the Berlin Philharmonic, which have been added on for this reissue, are also among the most successful items.

Polka: *Unter Donner und Blitz.* Waltzes: *An der schönen, blauen Donau; Kaiser; Morgenblätter; Rosen aus dem Süden; Treasure; Wiener blut.* Josef STRAUSS: *Dorfschwalben aus Osterreich*

(M) *** RCA SACD 82876 671615-2. Chicago SO, Reiner (with WEBER: *Invitation to the Dance.* Richard STRAUSS: *Der Rosenkavalier: Waltzes*)

Reiner's collection was recorded in 1957 and 1960, but the new SACD transfer restores the voluptuousness to the sound. Although the *Thunder and Lightning Polka* has an unforgettable explosive exuberance, these performances are memorable for their Viennese lilt, especially the *Emperor Waltz* and Josef's *Village Swallows.* Reiner is especially persuasive in the introductory interchanges of Weber's *Invitation to the Waltz*, while the *Der Rosenkavalier* Waltz sequence brings a passionate surge of adrenalin.

OPERA AND OPERETTA

Die Fledermaus (complete)

(M) (**) RCA mono 74321 61949-2. Gueden, Streich, Waechter, Zampieri, Berry, Stolze, Kunz, Klein, Ott, Meinrad, V. State Op. Ch. & O, Karajan

(M) *(*) DG (ADD) 457 765-2 (2). Varady, Popp, Prey, Kollo, Weikl, Rebroff, Kusche, Bav. State Op. Ch. & O, C. Kleiber

Recorded live by Austrian Radio at the Vienna State Opera on New Year's Eve, 1960, the RCA set gives a vivid picture of the event, warts and all. For the non-German speaker, the acres of dialogue will be a serious deterrent, notably in Act III with only 15 minutes of music out of 40. This is still a cherishable issue for capturing the atmosphere and special flavour of a great Viennese occasion. Hilde Gueden is the complete charmer (as on her early Decca set, a very Viennese heroine), with Walter Berry as Falke, Giuseppe Zampieri as Alfred and Peter Klein as Dr Blind, also relishing the comedy all the more. The party junketings in Act II include not just Erich Kunz singing the *Fiakerlied* by Gustav Pick, but a special guest, Giuseppe di Stefano, singing *O sole mio* and Lehár's *Dein ist mein ganzes Herz* (Italy's tribute to Vienna prompting wild cheering). Also a ten-minute ballet, *Schottisch, Russisch, Hungarisch und Polka*.

The glory of the Kleiber set is the singing of the two principal women – Julia Varady and Lucia Popp, magnificently characterful and stylish as mistress and servant – but much of the set is controversial, to say the least. Carlos Kleiber is certainly exciting at times and rejects many older conventions in performing style, which some will find refreshing, but he is not at all easy-going. Other conductors allow the music's intrinsic charm to bubble to the surface like champagne; with Kleiber, one feels the charm, if one can call it that, being rammed down one's throat. But that is nothing compared to the falsetto of Ivan Rebroff, which has to be heard to be believed – it sounds grotesque and is likely to put most listeners off this recording. Full texts and translations are included.

(i) *Die Fledermaus*: highlights; (ii) *The Gypsy Baron*: highlights (both sung in English) (iii) *Tritsch-Tratsch Polka*
(B) ** CfP (ADD) 585 0022. (i) Elliott, Studholme, Heddle Nash, Young, Pollak; (ii) Bronhill, Howard, Douglas, Eddy; (i;ii) Sadler's Wells Ch. & O; (iii) Studio 2 SO; Tausky

While Christopher Hassall's English version of *Die Fledermaus* is effective enough and Geoffrey Dunn's translation of *The Gypsy Baron* is neat and witty, these two selections of Sadler's Wells productions from 1959 and 1965 do not enjoy the same success as the Offenbach operettas praised above. While the Company showed in the theatre that it is second to none in capturing Viennese gaiety, and the chorus in particular has an incisiveness which will disappoint no one, it must be admitted that the soloists, while always reliable, are not particularly memorable in their singing. In *Die Fledermaus* Marion Studholme, for example, as Adele sings with great flexibility, but there is a 'tweety' quality to her voice as caught by the microphones which prevents the final degree of enjoyment. Anna Pollak as Orlofsky sounds too old-womanly by far, and her attempts at vocal acting seem over-mannered and only add to the womanliness. In the *Gypsy Baron*, June Bronhill sings appealingly, but she is no match for the adorable Saffi of Elisabeth Schwarzkopf. Vilem Tausky conducts throughout with spirit, and the singing cast is never less than good, but one had better put memories of refined Viennese performances to the back of one's mind. No complaints about the recordings, which have transferred vividly to CD.

STRAUSS, Richard (1864–1949)

An Alpine Symphony, Op. 64
☛ (BB) *** Naxos 8.557811. Weimar Staatskapelle, Wit
**(*) EMI 3 34569-2. Gustav Mahler Jugendorchester, Welser-Möst

Wit's highly imaginative performance, with the remarkably fine Weimar orchestra, is in the class of Kempe, having something in common with the analogue performances of Strauss by the Dresden Staatskapelle, both in the radiance of the orchestral sounds and the warm acoustic of the Weimarhalle (not unlike the Dresden Lukaskirche). Wit's tempi, too, are often unhurried; his overall performance takes 54 minutes against Welser-Möst's 46, but it gives the Weimar experience an extra spaciousness, and the panoramic sweep of the strings is rapturously beautiful in the opening *Night* and *Sunrise* sequences. Yet the forward flow is not consistently measured. It is during the moments of scenic splendour that Wit, always flexible, pulls back gently to evoke the sensuous beauty of what his orchestra is describing: the *Entry into the Forest*, the pause on the *Alpine pasture* and, most of all, the thrilling radiance *On the summit*. The storm on the way down is thunderingly real, and in the moments before it breaks Wit creates a subtle feeling of apprehension; then, as the descent nears safety, the orchestra mirrors a glorious sunset and evokes a sense of thankfulness for past excitement, and an elegiac contemplation of the natural wonders experienced. In that '*Ausklang*' the organ steals in gently and magically, and night falls in peace and tranquillity. Throughout, the Naxos recording is wonderfully vivid and spectacular, and the disc is a well-documented one, too.

Franz Welser-Möst is also a fine Straussian, here readily catching the music's romantically sensuous surge, creating tension and excitement. After the sonorous brass at the opening, he builds a superbly graduated climax, and the music flows forward, the impetus quickening as the ascent begins. Every detail of the score is heard in perspective, and the string playing of the Gustav Mahler Jugendorchester is richly exciting. The Epilogue is very serene, the orchestra gentle. With recording which is very spectacular indeed, this is very recommendable, except for the playing time: 46 minutes is short measure for a premium-priced CD.

(i) *An Alpine Symphony*; (ii) *Also sprach Zarathustra*; (i) *Death and Transfiguration; Don Juan; Ein Heldenleben; Till Eulenspiegel; Tod und Verklärung*; (iii) *4 Last Songs* (with bonus CD: 'A Life Retold')
(M) (**(*)) DG mono/stereo 477 5296 (8). Boehm, with (i) Dresden Staatskapelle; (ii) BPO; (iii) Della Casa, VPO – MOZART: *Symphonies*; WEBER: *Overtures* (**)

Boehm was an excellent Straussian and there is very little to complain about the performances here, and much to praise. *Don Juan* receives a fresh and lively account which grips from beginning to end, despite the limited mono (1957) sound. Similarly, *Death and Transfiguration* has high tension from the outset and, despite what sounds like a little tape flutter, one's attention is caught, and there is a certain nobility here, yet plenty of drama in the climaxes. The sound is more of a problem in the *Alpine Symphony*, a work that depends a great deal on its panoply of orchestral sound to make its full effect; while it is marvellously played and dramatically sculptured, the recording, though clear, lacks the necessary opulence. Boehm's extremely lively portrait of *Till* comes off well, but he recorded it again in stereo (the later BPO characterization has more of the peasant about him, less of the irrepressible rogue). *Ein Heldenleben* is very good indeed, though it is not as fine as the classic Reiner and Krauss accounts from the same period. Lisa Della Casa sings beautifully in the *Four Last Songs* and (unlike so many singers today) there is no distracting vibrato – very refreshing. This derives from a 1953 Decca LP and is very well worth having, with Boehm's warmly sympathetic support another plus factor. *Also sprach Zarathustra* is in early and good stereo: it is a distinguished account, passionate and finely structured. As a bonus, a CD of Boehm narrates 'A life retold'; an outline of it in English is included in the booklet. This set is not perhaps for the general collector, but more for those especially interested in Boehm's unique way with Strauss's music, despite the sometimes limited sound-quality.

An Alpine Symphony; Death and Transfiguration; Don Juan; Ein Heldenleben

(M) ** Chan. 10199 X (2). RSNO, Järvi

Neeme Järvi's version of the *Alpine Symphony* is roundly enjoyable, ripely recorded in a helpfully reverberant acoustic; his approach is warm and genial, if without the electricity of the finest performances. *Ein Heldenleben* is strongly characterized, warmly sympathetic, with the RSNO giving a powerful thrust throughout, lacking only the last degree of refinement in tone and ensemble. There are few complaints to be made about *Don Juan*, even if, again, it is not quite in the league of the very best versions available. *Death and Transfiguration* comes off very well, with the RSNO standing up remarkably well by comparison with its Dresden and Berlin rivals – one of Järvi's best Strauss performances.

An Alpine Symphony; (i) Oboe Concerto; (ii) Duet Concertino for Clarinet, Bassoon & Strings. Symphonia Domestica, Op. 53

(M) **(*) Avie AV 2071 (2). RLPO, Schwarz; with (i) Small; (ii) Stewart, Pendlebury

Gerard Schwarz's performances are attractively idiomatic. Indeed, the *Symphonia Domestica* has been as convincingly presented on record only by Karajan. With Schwarz, the richly exprssive *Adagio* is affectionately serene, then bursting into passion as the romantic tryst between husband and wife ('*scène d'amour*', Strauss called it) becomes sexually charged. As for the *Alpine Symphony*, it is impressively detailed (though the distant horns in the forest don't come off as atmospherically here as in Wit's version), but while Schwarz celebrates the vision of the summit, he holds back the real spectacle for the horrendous storm on the descent.

Jonathan Small is a stylishly expressive soloist in the *Oboe Concerto*, and Malcolm Stewart and Alan Pendlebury find plenty of charm in the *Duet Concertino*. But there is a snag to this otherwise recommendable issue: the recording lacks the sumptuousness of orchestral texture that the two major works demand, and the violins in their upper range sound rather thin. One needs more ambient warmth, less clarity in this repertoire.

An Alpine Symphony; Die Frau ohne Schatten: Symphonic Fantasy

(M) *(*) Warner Elatus 0927 49837-2. Chicago SO, Barenboim

By the side of the finest recordings of the *Alpine Symphony* by Karajan, Kempe and others, Barenboim and his Chicago forces have little new to report. Indeed, he does not even get the kind of high orchestral voltage or sense of atmosphere which he can often be counted on to command. By the side of Karajan his grip is loose and in comparison with Kempe there is little of *echt*-Straussian atmosphere. Not even the inducement of a bonus in the orchestral fantasy on themes from *Die Frau ohne Schatten* enhances this disc's claims for a high star rating among the best.

An Alpine Symphony; Der Rosenkavalier: Suite

** DG 469 519-2. VPO, Thielemann

Thielemann's are live recordings made in the Grosser Saal of the Musikverein in October 2000, offering brilliant VPO playing, and these performances certainly do not lack tension. However, in the *Alpine Symphony* the conductor's scrupulous concern for pictorial detail means that we receive a series of vividly colourful pictures of each segment of the ascent and descent, rather than an overall impression of a continuing journey, although the closing nocturnal sequence is movingly gentle. The digital recording is very spectacular, immensely so in the *Thunderstorm* sequence, but the ear senses the presence of the close microphones, so a natural concert-hall effect is less readily conveyed. The *Rosenkavalier Suite* is again superbly played, but its sensory romantic atmosphere, and the perception of a lilting masquerade, eludes Thielemann. Moreover, the vivid recording lacks the necessary lusciousness of string texture.

Also sprach Zarathustra; (i) Don Quixote. Macbeth; Sinfonia domestica; Till Eulenspiegel

(M) ** Chan. 10206 X (2). RSNO, Järvi, (i) with Wallfisch

Neemi Järvi's well-regarded Strauss recordings, dating from the 1980s, are now being released at mid-price in slim-line packaging. Although this is a step in the right direction, they are competing with Karajan and Reiner – as well as Kempe's magnificent Dresden survey – and are therefore not the value they might once have been. *Also sprach Zarathustra* is one of the least successful performances in his Strauss survey for Chandos. The reverberant acoustic (characteristic of Caird Hall in Dundee) here muddies the sound without giving it compensating richness. *Till* is much better, however, and Järvi brings out the work's joy admirably. The *Symfonia domestica* is a good-natured and strongly characterized account, gutsy and committed to remove any coy self-consciousness from this extraordinarily inflated but delightful musical portrait of Strauss's family life. *Macbeth*, not one of Strauss's masterpieces, gets as good a performance here as you're likely to get.

Le Bourgeois gentilhomme: incidental music; (i) Ein Heldenleben

*** EMI 3 39339-2. BPO, Rattle; (i) with Braunstein

It says much for Sir Simon Rattle's achievement in Berlin that the result in this live recording offers the keenest rivalry for the recordings of his great predecessor, Herbert von Karajan, for whom *Ein Heldenleben* was a favourite work. The heroic opening section already establishes the extra warmth and expressive flexibility of Rattle's approach and, typically, he treats the violinist, Guy Braunstein, as a genuine concerto soloist, encouraging him to play with the sort of expressive freedom one expects in a concerto. What remains constant is the opulence of the Berlin Philharmonic sound, the more glorious in modern digital recording, covering a formidable dynamic range, bringing out the subtlety of Rattle's control and the refinement of the orchestra's playing. *Le Bourgeois gentilhomme* is a generous coupling, bringing the overall timing of the disc to an exceptional 82 minutes. The engineers, though working in the Philharmonie as in *Heldenleben*, have rightly balanced the microphones to give a much more intimate result with this chamber ensemble in a performance that delightfully captures the light-heartedness of this music.

(i) *Horn Concerto 1. Death and Transfiguration; Don Juan*
(BB) **(*) ASV Resonance CDSN 3061. (i) Lloyd; Philh. O,
Kashif

Frank Lloyd's is the finest account of the *First Horn Concerto*
on record since Dennis Brain's famous version: full of style
and verve, with a stirringly bold central section in the
Andante and a bravura coda from the soloist in the sparkling
rondo finale. Tolga Kashif provides matching accompaniments, and the Philharmonia Orchestra is on top form in
these thrillingly direct accounts of the pair of symphonic
poems, which, if not subtle, are not lacking in atmosphere
either. The 1990 recording is a bit fierce in climaxes and one
could do with more opulence from the violins, but this is still
a bargain.

*Don Juan; Metamorphosen; Der Rosenkavalier: Waltzes; Till
Eulenspiegel*
(M) *** EMI 3 45826-2 [3 45827-2]. Dresden State O, Kempe

These performances are drawn from a whole series of recordings of Strauss's orchestral music which Kempe made in the
mid-1970s, glowingly recorded in the Dresden Lukaskirche.
The Dresden Staatskapelle produces marvellously luxuriant
tone, especially from the strings in *Metamorphosen*, a great
performance. Kempe's *Till* and *Don Juan* are also magnificent
and his control of rubato in the *Rosenkavalier Waltzes* is
wholly idiomatic. A worthy reissue for EMI's 'Great Recordings of the Century'.

Don Quixote, Op. 35
*(*) DG 474 780-2. Maisky, B PO, Mehta – DVOŘÁK: *Cello
Concerto* *(*)

Don Quixote is so richly eloquent a score that its narrative
needs no expressive adornment. As in the Dvořák *Concerto*,
Mischa Maisky is all too prone to wear his heart on his sleeve
and he emotes all too readily. When there are so many
marvellous versions around there is no reason for this to
detain readers, good though the Berlin orchestra's playing
and the DG recording are.

Ein Heldenleben, Op. 40
(M) ** BBC (ADD) BBCL 4055-2. LSO, Barbirolli – MOZART:
Symphony 36 (Linz) **

This BBC recording from 1969 documents one of Sir John's
last concert appearances. Made in the Royal Festival Hall, it
shows considerable vitality and zest, although it is far from
being an ideal testimony to his art and career. The sound is
very good and not greatly inferior to that in the studio
recording.

Till Eulenspiegel (Rehearsal)
*(*) Arthaus **DVD** 100 286 Israel PO, Mehta (rehearsal only)

Here is Zubin Mehta rehearsing (but not performing)
Strauss's *Till* with the Israel Philharmonic who have –
incredibly – not played it since the war for political reasons.
Strauss's political record during the war is well documented
(see Michael Kennedy's masterly biography – OUP, 1999)
when the composer had to protect his Jewish daughter-in-
law and his two half-Jewish grandsons. But so often judge-
ments rest on prejudice rather than knowledge and reason as
Barenboim discovered when he tried to conduct the *Prelude
to Tristan* in Israel. Mehta takes the players through this
wonderful score which is (naturally enough) unfamiliar to
them as orchestral musicians, and virtually teaches them.
Mehta has both tact and charm, and gets a good response

even when the players show boredom (the clarinet impatiently watches the time). Generally speaking Mehta tells you
nothing you don't already know and the 55 minutes of
rehearsal does not lead to a performance. Were we observing
a great orchestra unfamiliar with this classic, going through
their paces in a complete performance it would be another
matter, but as it is there seems little point in this exercise.
The camera work is perfectly well managed as indeed is the
sound.

VOCAL MUSIC

(i) *4 Last Songs; Cäcilie; Morgen; Meinem Kinde; Ruhe,
meine Seele!; Wiegenlied; Zueignung.* (ii) *Ach Lieb, ich muss
nun scheiden; Allerseelen; Befreit; Du meines Herzens
Krönelein; Einerlei; Heimliche Aufforderung; Ich trage meine
Minne; Kling!; Lob des Leidens; Malven; Mit deinen blauen
Augen; Die Nacht; Schlechtes Wetter; Seitdem dein Aug';
Ständchen; Stiller Gang; Traum durch die Dämmerung; Wie
beide wollen springen; Wir sollten wir geheim sie halten; Die
Zeitlose*
✪ (B) *** Ph. 475 6377 (2). Norman, with (i) Leipzig GO,
Masur; (ii) Parsons

Two classic recordings here from the 1980s. Strauss's publisher Ernest Roth says in the score of the *Four Last Songs* that
this was a farewell to 'serene confidence', which is exactly the
mood Jessye Norman conveys. The power of her singing
reminds one of the first ever interpreter, Kirsten Flagstad
(with Furtwängler and the Philharmonia at the Royal Albert
Hall in May 1950). The start of the second stanza of the third
song, *Beim Schlafengehen*, brings one of the most thrilling
vocal crescendos on record, expanding from a half-tone to a
glorious, rich and rounded *forte*. In concern for word detail
Norman is outshone by Schwarzkopf (unique in conveying
the poignancy of old age), but in the *Four Last Songs* and in
the orchestral songs the stylistic as well as the vocal command
is irresistible, with *Cäcilie* given operatic strength. The radiance of the recording (1982) matches the interpretations. In
the 1985 recital with Geoffrey Parsons, Norman brings heartfelt, deeply committed performances, at times larger than life,
which satisfyingly exploit the unique glory of her voice. Quite
apart from such deservedly popular songs as *Heimliche Aufforderung*, it is good to have such a rarity as Strauss's very last
song, *Malven*, which with Norman is utterly compelling.
Some of the songs bring extreme speeds in both directions,
with expression underlined in the slow songs, but *Ständchen*
is given exhilarating virtuoso treatment at high speed. The
magnetism of the singer generally silences any reservations,
and Geoffrey Parsons is the most understanding of accompanists, brilliant too. Excellent recording, and this bargain
two-CD set is one of the must-haves in Philips's 'Jessye
Norman' collection.

Songs: *Ach, was Kummer, Qual und Schmerzen; Allerseelen;
Blauer Sommer; Cäcilie; Des Dichters Abendgang; Einerlei;
Ich wollt ein Sträusslein binden; Leises Lied; 3 Lieder Der
Ophelia, Op. 67; Meinem Kinde; Morgen!; Muttertändelei;
Die Nacht; Das Rosenband; Ruhe, meine Seele!; Schlechtes
Wetter; Ständchen; Der Stern; Die Verschwiegenen;
Waldseligkeit; Wiegenlied; Winterweihe; Die Zeitlose;
Zueignung*
** ASV CD DDCA 1155. Lott, Johnson

A disc of Strauss songs sung by Dame Felicity Lott accompanied by Graham Johnson is self-recommending, and there is

much to enjoy on this issue, recorded in 2002. Lott's insights and those of her accompanist are consistently revealing, not least in the three Ophelia songs, which come at the climactic point of the recital, just before the final item, *Morgen*. She and Johnson bring out the other-worldly quality which Strauss evokes in these offbeat evocations of Ophelia's madness. The snag is that the odd recording quality is not kind to the singer's voice, betraying the fact that her characteristic creamy sound-quality is not as pure as it once was, with vibrato often intrusive. More seriously, the odd recording-balance is flattering neither to the singer nor to the pianist, with a slight distancing in an odd acoustic that makes one want to clear away a gauze.

OPERA

Arabella (complete DVD version)

(M) ** DG **DVD** (ADD) 477 5625 (2). Della Casa, Rothenberger, Fischer-Dieskau, Malaniuk, Paskuda, Bav. State Op. Ch. & O, Keilberth

Keilberth's set was taken from a live performance celebrating the 1963 opening of the Munich Opera House, and inevitably there are the usual noises and distractions that tend to disfigure theatre performances. The sound is no better and probably not as convincing as the earlier Decca set, made in 1957, and the conducting of Keilberth is considerably less crisp than Solti's. Moreover, Lisa Della Casa had in the meantime lost a great deal of the bloom from her voice. Fischer-Dieskau, however, gives a masterly account of the part of Mandryka, far fuller, more mature and beautiful than George London's on Decca. There are a number of minor cuts and the Munich version is used, telescoping Acts II and III together in a way approved by the composer.

Arabella (complete CD version)

(M) *** Decca 475 7731 (2) Della Casa, Gueden, London, VPO, Solti

On the Decca CD set Della Casa soars above the stave with the creamiest, most beautiful sounds and constantly charms one with her swiftly alternating moods of seriousness and gaiety. Perhaps Solti does not linger as he might over the waltz rhythms, and it may be Solti too who prevents Edelmann from making his first scene with Mandryka as genuinely humorous as it can be. Edelmann otherwise is superb, as fine a Count as he was an Ochs in the Karajan *Rosenkavalier*. Gueden, too, is ideally cast as Zdenka and, if anything, in Act I manages to steal our sympathies from Arabella, as a good Zdenka can. George London is on the ungainly side, but then Mandryka is a boorish fellow anyway. Dermota is a fine Matteo, and Mimi Coertse makes as much sense as anyone could of the ridiculously difficult part of Fiakermilli, the female yodeller. The sound is brilliant. It has now been impressively remastered onto two discs with the break coming just before Milli begins her yodelling song. Solti's *Arabella* now returns to the catalogue, offered at mid-price for the first time (with full libretto) as one of Decca's Originals.

Daphne (complete; CD version)

*** Decca 475 6926 (2). Fleming, Botha, Schade, Youn, Larsson, WDR Ch. & O, Cologne, Bychkov

The freshest of Strauss's later operas with its pastoral overtones, *Daphne* really requires a girlish-sounding soprano in the title-role, and Renée Fleming might in principle seem too mature-sounding a singer. In fact, she copes beautifully with the high tessitura of the role, and she produces her clearest, brightest tone, making this a very enjoyable version of an opera which exploits her acting powers. The casting in this co-production with West German Radio may not rival that of Haitink's Munich set for EMI with Lucia Popp as Daphne and a starry line-up of supporting characters, but that is currently not available and in this Decca set, with bright, cleanly focused sound backing Bychkov's urgent and sensuous reading, the result is very convincing. Johan Botha as Apollo sings with a rather pinched sound, but the notes come over cleanly and powerfully enough, and he is well contrasted with the mellifluous tenor of Michael Schade as Leukippos, and the mezzo, Anna Larsson, brings out rich tones in the role of Gaea.

(i) Elektra: Soliloquy; Recognition scene; Finale. Salome: Dance of the seven veils; Finale

(M) *** RCA **SACD** (ADD) 82876 67900-2. Borkh, Chicago SO, Reiner; with (i) Schoeffler, Yeend, Chicago Lyric Theatre Ch.

With Borkh singing superbly in the title-role alongside Paul Schoeffler and Francis Yeend, this is a real collector's piece. Reiner provides a superbly telling accompaniment; the performances of the Recognition scene and final duet are as ripely passionate as Beecham's old 78-r.p.m. excerpts and outstrip the complete versions. The orchestral sound is thrillingly rich, the brass superbly expansive (those with SACD equipment will hear even greater ambient effect). Reiner's full-blooded account of *Salome's Dance* is very exciting too, and Borkh is comparably memorable in the final scene. No Straussian should miss this disc.

Der Rosenkavalier (complete CD versions)

(M) ** DG (ADD) 463 668-2 (3). Schech, Seefried, Streich, Böhme, Fischer-Dieskau, Unger, Wagner, Dresden State Op. Ch., Saxon State O, Dresden, Boehm

(M) *(*) Decca 473 361-2 (3). Lear, Von Stade, Welting, Bastin, Hammond Stroud, Netherlands Opera Ch., Rotterdam PO, de Waart

There is much that is very good indeed about the Boehm Dresden performance. Yet here is undoubtedly a set that elusively fails to add up to the sum of its parts. It is partly Boehm's inability to generate the sort of power and emotional tension that are so overwhelming in the Karajan–Schwarzkopf set on EMI. More importantly, the Feldmarschallin of Marianne Schech is decidedly below the level set by Seefried as Octavian and Streich as Sophie. Schech just does not have the strength of personality that is needed if the opera's dramatic point is to strike home. We cannot feel the full depth of emotion involved in her great renunciation from the performance here.

The glory of the 1976 set conducted by Edo de Waart is the singing of Frederica von Stade as Octavian, a fresh, youthful performance full of imagination. Next to her the others are generally pleasing but hardly a match for their finest rivals, though it is good to have a characterful vignette from Derek Hammond Stroud as Faninal. Evelyn Lear, hardly dominant as the Marschallin, produces her creamiest tone for most of the time but falls seriously short in the great Trio of Act III. Jules Bastin gives a virile performance as Baron Ochs, but the serious blot is Sophie Welting, shallow of tone and technically flawed. The Rotterdam Philharmonic plays well for its then principal conductor, but the warm recording is not as detailed as it might be. The compact Decca package comes at mid-price, but there is no printed libretto, only an access to libretto and translation via computer.

Salome (complete DVD version)

*** Warner NVC Arts **DVD** 9031 73827-2. Malfitano, Estes, Rysanek, Hiestermann, Deutsche Op. Ch. and O, Sinopoli (Director: Petr Weigl; V/D: Brian Large)

Recorded in 1990 at the Deutsche Opera in Berlin, the Warner DVD offers a powerful and warmly expressive performance under Giuseppe Sinopoli, the counterpart of his outstanding CD recording. Catherine Malfitano is an abrasive Salome, confident from the start, knowing exactly what she wants, and not at all girlish as she snarls out her demands or curiously asks the age of the prophet imprisoned in the cistern below. Simon Estes in his prime is a powerful Jokanaan, noble and handsome as he stands tall. Horst Hiestermann characterizes well as Herod and sings accurately, even if his voice is never beautiful, while Leonie Rysanek – earlier a great Salome – here gives a classic performance as Herodias, searingly compelling in her imperious way. The others make a first-rate team, well directed against the stylized white sets like great blocks of concrete. Malfitano is seductive in the *Dance of the Seven Veils*, and grows obsessively lascivious when fondling the head of the Baptist, repulsively so.

Salome (complete CD version)

(M) *** Decca 475 7528 (2). Nilsson, Hoffman, Stolze, Waechter, VPO, Solti

Birgit Nilsson is splendid throughout; she is hard-edged as usual but, on that account, more convincingly wicked: the determination and depravity are latent in the girl's character from the start. Of this score Solti is a master. He has rarely sounded so abandoned in a recorded performance. Waechter makes a clear, young-sounding Jokanaan. Gerhardt Stolze portrays the unbalance of Herod with frightening conviction, and Grace Hoffman does all she can in the comparatively ungrateful part of Herodias. The vivid CD projection makes the final scene, where Salome kisses the head of John the Baptist in delighted horror (*I have kissed thy mouth, Jokanaan!*), all the more spine-tingling, with a close-up effect of the voice whispering almost in one's ear. Like *Arabella*, above, Solti's classic set of *Salome*, reissued as one of Decca's Originals, now appears for the first time at mid-price (with full documentation).

Salome: Dance of the Seven Veils; Closing Scene. Lieder: Cäcile; Ich liebe dich; Morgen; Wiegenlied; Zueignung

(M) **(*) DG (ADD) 477 5910. Caballé, O Nat. de France, Bernstein (with BOITO: *Mefistofele: Prologue.* Ghiaurov, V. State Op. Ch., VPO)

One of Caballé's earliest and most refreshingly imaginative opera sets was *Salome* with Leinsdorf conducting. This version of the final scene, recorded over a decade later with a very different conductor, has much of the same imagination, the sweet, innocent girl still observable next to the bloodthirsty fiend. The rest of the programme is less recommendable, partly because Caballé underlines the expressiveness of works that remain Lieder even with the orchestral accompaniment. Bernstein, too, directs an overweighted account of the *Dance of the Seven Veils*. For the reissue as one of DG's Originals, the *Prologue* to Boito's *Mefistofele* has been added. Both Ghiaurov and the VPO with chorus are in excellent form, and the cataclysmic effects at the opening are well brought off.

STRAVINSKY, Igor (1882–1971)

Apollo (ballet; complete); (i) *Capriccio for Piano and Orchestra. Le Chant du rossignol; Circus Polka;* (ii) *Concerto for Piano & Wind;* (iii) *Violin Concerto. Petrushka* (complete; original (1911) ballet); *Symphony in E flat, Op. 1; Symphony in C; Symphony in Three Movements;* (iv) *Symphony of Psalms;* (iv; v) *Oedipus Rex*

(B) ** Chan. 6654 (5). SRO, Järvi, with (i) Tozer: (ii) Berman; (iii) Mordkovitch; (iv) Chamber Ch., Lausanne Pro Art Ch., Société Ch. de Brassus; (v) Schnaut, Svensson, Amoretti, Grundheber, Kannen, Rosen, Plat

Neeme Järvi offers typically red-blooded readings in his five-disc collection of symphonies, concertos and ballets, plus *Oedipus Rex*. His performances do not always have the refinement and sharpness of focus that one ideally wants, but the thrust of the music comes over convincingly, even if some of the slow movements – as in the *Symphony in Three Movements* – grow curiously stodgy rhythmically at relatively slow speeds. However, the *Violin Concerto* is beautifully played by the warm-toned Lydia Mordkovitch, with the romantic expressiveness of the two central *Arias* an apt counterpart to the vigour and panache of the outer movements. The string playing in *Apollo* has plenty of warmth, and Järvi's vivid *Petrushka* is particularly winning. Using the 1911 score, he finds an attractive sparkle at the opening and in the *Shrovetide Fair*, with the *Russian Dance* given a superb bounce. Some of the subtlety of Stravinsky's scoring in the central tableaux may be missing, but such characterful playing is most attractive, both here and in the *Circus Polka* on the same disc. Generally speaking the symphonies and concertos are all very successful in their outer movements and disappointing in their slow ones, and both Geoffrey Tozer and Boris Berman are convincingly muscular soloists in the two concertante works with piano. The performance of the youthful *Symphony, Op. 1,* is particularly convincing in its warmth and thrust. *Oedipus Rex*, with a good narrator in Jean Piat, receives the same sort of full-blooded approach, but the cast is uneven, with Gabriele Schnaut wobbly and shrill as Jocasta and with *pianissimos* sadly lacking, partly a question of recording balance. The sound throughout the five discs is generally warm and full, although the resonance means that inner detail often lacks sharpness of focus, and in the *Symphony of Psalms* the chorus is rather backwardly balanced. The texts for the vocal items are not included, but these CDs remain individually available at mid-price (including texts, where applicable).

(i) *Apollo; Dumbarton Oaks Concerto; Concerto in D;* (ii) *Le Chant du rossignol; Symphony in C; Symphony in Three Movements*

(BB) *(*) Virgin 5 62022-2 (2). Saraste, with (i) Scottish CO; (ii) Finnish RSO

There is nothing really wrong with the Scottish performances but, on the other hand, there is nothing especially brilliant about them either. The Scottish Chamber Orchestra offer some impressive and sometimes beautiful playing in *Apollo*, but in some of the slow sections of the score the tension is not well maintained. The neo-classical *Concertos* are quite lively, but their effect is dampened down by the rather over-reverberant acoustic. *Le Chant du rossignol*, which opens the Finnish CD, is played with considerable finesse, but here the sound is undistinguished, with a limited dynamic range, the bright orchestral colours blunted by the flat, under-recorded sound. The two *Symphonies* suffer much the same fate.

Le Baiser de la fée (divertimento)
*** Pentatone **SACD** PTC 5186 061. Russian Nat. O, Jurowski
 – TCHAIKOVSKY: *Suite 3* ***

The young Russian, Vladimir Jurowski, currently the Glyndebourne Music Director, offers performances of both works that are as near ideal as one can imagine, electric in tension to give the illusion of live music-making. The Stravinsky *Divertimento*, its four movements taken from the ballet, *Le Baiser de la fée*, may make an unexpected coupling for the Tchaikovsky, but it is an apt and illuminating one. Jurowski steers a nice course between bringing out the romantic warmth of the Tchaikovsky sources from which Stravinsky took his material (songs and piano pieces) and the neo-classical element in his style of the 1920s. So the chugging rhythms on horns in the most memorable section of the second movement convey jollity in their springing step, while the pointing of contrasts in the final *Pas de deux*, the longest of the four movements, brings yearning warmth in the big lyrical moments and wit in the faster sections. Exceptionally vivid sound, recorded by Pentatone's Dutch engineers in Moscow.

(i) *Ebony Concerto; L'Histoire du soldat* (ballet suite); *Octet for Wind; Symphonies of Wind Instruments;* (ii) *Piano Rag-Music;* (ii; iii) *Ragtime for 11 Instruments*
(M) ** Sup. SU 3168-2 911. (i) Prague Chamber Harmony, Pešek; (ii) Novotný, (iii) Zlatnikova

These Prague performances from the 1960s are no match for the finest versions in their characterization and finesse or the quality of the recorded sound. However, given the moderate price-tag, they remain very serviceable.

Violin Concerto in D
(M) *** Decca (ADD) 476 7226-2. Chung, LSO, Previn –
 PROKOFIEV: *Violin Concertos 1–2* ***
(B) *** Ph. 2-CD 475 7547 (2). Mullova, LAPO, Salonen –
 BARTOK: *Violin Concerto 2* **; PROKOFIEV: *Violin Concerto 2;* SHOSTAKOVICH: *Violin Concerto 1* *(*)

Kyung-Wha Chung is at her most incisive in the spicily swaggering outer movements which, with Previn's help, are presented here in all their distinctiveness, tough and witty at the same time. In the two movements labelled *Aria*, Chung brings fantasy as well as lyricism, conveying an inner, brooding quality. This pairing with Prokofiev is now reissued in Universal's 'Critics' Choice' series – and worthily so.

The Stravinsky *Concerto* also suits Viktoria Mullova and her brilliant partners in Los Angeles rather well, and this version can certainly be recommended if you want all four of these works. The Philips recording is first rate in every respect. But this is a very uneven collection.

The Firebird; Petrushka (complete ballets; with choreography by Michel Fokine and costumes and sets adapted from the original Ballets Russes production by Anatoly and Anna Nezhny)
⬤ *** Decca **DVD** 079 322-9. Nina Ananiashvili, Andris Liepa, Ekatrina Liepa, Victor Yeremenko, Tatiana Beltskaya, Gediminas Taranda, Sergey Petukhov, Vitaly Breusno, Bolshoi State Academic Theatre O, Andrey Chistiakov (Director: Andris Liepa) – RIMSKY-KORSAKOV: *Scheherazade* ***

Both the authentic Bolshoi productions of *The Firebird* and *Petrushka* are very spectacular indeed, as are the costumes

and sets. *The Firebird* is in reality a folk tale about the power of love and the triumph of good over evil, with a glittering fairy figure in the Firebird and a demonic villain in Katshchei. The presentation is vividly and colourfully handled, and Nina Ananiashvili is a truly sparkling Firebird, dancing very gracefully. The handsome Prince Ivan, Andris Liepa (who later transforms himself into the puppet, Petrushka), has little to do but be resourceful and court his beautiful Princess who, like her royal companions, is held captive by a spell; and it is they who do most of the dancing, with the golden apples from a truly fairyland tree and to the prettier parts of Stravinsky's delightful score. The entry of Katshchei (Sergey Petukhov) is truly demonic: the grotesque make-up and bizarre costumes create a gothically evil atmosphere, and he is a wonderfully malignant ogre. When the Prince finds the huge golden egg that contains Katshchei's soul and smashes it, all the stone images around become human again and can be the guests at Ivan's wedding to the most radiant tune of all.

In *Petrushka* the opening Shrovetide Fair scene fills the huge Bolshoi stage with a myriad different characters and vividly colourful events, all happening simultaneously; but at the centre is the Magician/Showman's stage, from which Petrushka, the Moor and the Ballerina emerge to dance into the audience. The drama of Petrushka's unrequited love for the Ballerina, who prefers the Moor, begins almost immediately and reaches its peak in Petrushka's cell. This is the one miscalculation of the production, for the cell scene is not nearly claustrophobic enough. However, Andris Liepa is a very touching Petrushka, and his murder (and the puppet substitution) is effectively managed, while the final ghost appearance is splendidly dramatic. Both ballets are entertaining to watch, but one continually reflects that Stravinsky's music is far, far greater and more imaginative than the choreography.

(i) *The Firebird* (Original, 1910 version); (ii) *The Rite of Spring;* (i) *Symphonies of Wind Instruments;* (ii; iii) *Perséphone* (complete)
(B) *** Virgin 2x1 4 82106-2 (2). (i) LSO; (ii) LPO; Nagano; (iii) with Anne Fournet (narrator), Rolfe Johnson, LPO Ch. & Tiffin School Boys' Ch.

Kent Nagano's vividly detailed LSO recording of the original *Firebird* score is highly praised in our main volume as a top recommendation, with its apt coupling of the original (1920) score of the *Symphonies of Wind Instruments,* divertingly cool, with sonorities and textures keenly balanced. Nagano's reading of *The Rite of Spring* has similar qualities. If it is less weightily barbaric than many, the springing of rhythm and the clarity and refinement of instrumental textures make it very compelling, with only the final *Danse sacrale* lacking something in dramatic bite.

The only rival for Nagano's *Perséphone* – with its spoken narration described by the librettist, André Gide, as 'a melodrama in three scenes' – is the composer's own version, and the contrasts are extreme. Where Stravinsky himself – at speeds consistently more measured than Nagano's – takes a rugged, square-cut view, Nagano, much lighter as well as more fleet, makes the work a far more atmospheric evocation of spring. The playing and singing are consistently more refined, and the modern digital recording gives a warm bloom, while the sung French sounds far more idiomatic for everyone. The narration of Anne Fournet brings out all the beauty of Gide's words, with Anthony Rolfe Johnson free-toned in the taxing tenor solos. All in all, a highly recommendable Virgin double.

(i) *The Firebird* (suite; 1919 score). (ii) *The Rite of Spring;*
** Delos DE 3278. Oregon SO, DePreist

The Oregon Symphony under James DePreist give a sumptuously romantic account of the *Firebird Suite*, helped by the warm acoustics of the Baumann Auditorium, at the George Fox University in Newberg. But although the mystic atmosphere of the lyrical pages of *The Rite of Spring* is hauntingly conveyed, the score's inherent violence and sacrificial brutality are under-emphasized, and there is a lack of pungent rhythmic bite.

Petrushka (1911 score; complete)
(M) (*) Westminster mono 471 245-2. RPO, Scherchen –
HONEGGER: *Chant de joie,* etc. (*(*))

With a sprinkling of Scherchen eccentricities to remind one who is at the helm, it is hard to recommend his otherwise rather flaccid 1954 account to the general collector with so many excellent and less idiosyncratic performances available.

Petrushka (ballet; complete 1947 version); *The Rite of Spring; Circus Polka*
** Australian Decca Eloquence (ADD) 460 509-2. LAPO, Mehta

(i) *Petrushka* (1947 score); (ii) *The Rite of Spring; Fireworks, Op. 4*
(M) ** RCA (ADD) 09026 63311-2. (i) Boston SO; (ii) Chicago SO, Ozawa

Mehta's Los Angeles *Rite of Spring*, despite extreme tempi, some very fast, others slow, is an interesting and individual reading, very well recorded. *Petrushka* is played superbly, but lacks the character of the finest versions. What makes it compelling, in its way, is the astonishingly brilliant recording, which startlingly brings the Los Angeles orchestra into your sitting room. The *Circus Polka* makes a sparkling bonus, but this CD is primarily recommendable to audiophiles.

Recorded in 1968 and 1969 respectively, Ozawa's accounts of *Petrushka* and *The Rite of Spring* are unequal in appeal. *Petrushka* is a lightweight interpretation in the best sense, with Ozawa's feeling for the balletic quality of the music coming over, sometimes at the expense of dramatic emphasis. However, he is at times too dainty, and the underlying tension suggesting the strong feelings of the puppet characters is not always apparent. There are certainly more earthy accounts of *The Rite of Spring* available, even if the Chicago acoustic adds to the weight of the performance. Curiously, the early *Fireworks,* which one would have thought suited Ozawa's talents best of all, sounds rather aggressive.

'*The Final Chorale*' – a documentary about the *Symphony of Wind Instruments*
*** Ideale-Audience **DVD** 3. Netherlands Wind Ens., de Leeuw – SCHOENBERG: *5 Orchestral Pieces* ***

This is a most illuminating feature (available from www.ideale-audience.dot.com.) that follows the musical development of the *Symphonies of Wind Instruments,* composed in 1920 in memory of Debussy, and explores what makes them so profoundly original. The exposition by Frank Scheffer has clarity and insight, and there is some archival material and a highly interesting interview with

Robert Craft. Splendid playing, as one might expect, from the Netherlands Wind Ensemble under Reinbert de Leeuw.

PIANO MUSIC

Solo piano music

3 Movements from Petrushka
*** RCA 82876 65390-2. Evgeny Kissin – MEDTNER: *Sonata-Reminiscenza* **(*); SCRIABIN: *5 Preludes; Sonata 3* ***

Kissin is a wonderful pianist – of that there is no question. However, those who recall the celebrated Gilels recording of *Petrushka* may find some touches here just a shade self-regarding. Even so, this is pretty memorable.

3 Movements from Petrushka; Piano Rag Music; Serenade in A; Sonata; Tango
(BB) ** Warner Apex (ADD) 0927 40911-2. Ranki – BARTOK: *Out of Doors, Sz 81; Suite, Op. 14* **

This Apex reissue comprises all Stravinsky's solo music except the early *Sonata* and the Op. 7 *Studies*. Ranki recorded this recital in 1979 in a rather dry studio that may not be wholly inappropriate to Stravinsky's music. (The composer's own pioneering record of his *Capriccio* was even drier than this.) However, it does Ranki less than full justice and prevents his normally wide dynamic range making its full effect. The CD transfer increases the sense of presence and makes one even more aware of the acoustic. The playing is excellent, but the recording is a serious handicap.

VOCAL MUSIC

(i) *Cantata on Old English Texts. Mass;* (ii) *Les Noces*
☛ *** HM HMC 801913. Sampson, Parry & soloists, RIAS Kammerchor, MusikFabrik, Reuss
(M) * Sup. SU 3692-2. (i) Robotham, English; (ii) Czech Vocal Soloists & 4 Pianists; Prague Philharmonic Ch., Czech PO, Ančerl

Here are three little-known but inspired works by Stravinsky that few people know at all, and they have long been waiting for recorded performances of this calibre. Stravinsky, an ardent believer and a member of the Russian Orthodox Church, wrote the *Mass* for himself and for liturgical rather than concert use. It has an archaic feeling, but it is gloriously lyrical and inspired, the plangent harmonies giving it dramatic bite, especially in the thrilling *Sanctus,* while the *Agnus Dei* is raptly beautiful in the same way that the 'Alleluias' at the end of the *Symphony of Psalms* are so memorable.

The *Cantata,* too, opens unforgettably and is lyrically inspired throughout, using four verses from *A Lyke-Wake Dirge,* interspersed with polyphonic *Ricercari* allotted to solo voices and accompanied by celestial flutes, oboe, cor anglais and cello.

Stravinsky's own recording of *Les Noces* is notably ruthless, but the work simulates a folk wedding, and its special feature is exuberant rhythmic joy, which is just what this new Harmonia Mundi performance so exhilaratingly captures. The rhythms are remorseless, spell-binding, only pausing for the Blessing, the Lament of the two mothers, and the bride's mother's poignant moment, letting her daughter go.

Then, of course, there is that haunting tolling bell at the end, which somehow confirms that the ritual is archaic but eternal. The performance here is directed with superb exuberance by Daniel Reuss; when listening to it, you'll also discover where Orff's *Carmina Burana* came from. The *Cantata* and *Mass* are equally beautifully sung, with the glorious Carolyn Sampson standing out among the excellent soloists. The recording is in the demonstration class. This triptych again confirms Stravinsky as one of the greatest and most original composers of the whole of the twentieth century.

This is not one of Karel Ančerl's more memorable records. In *Les Noces* the resonant recording lacks crispness and (apart from the supreme wobble of the soprano, Libuse Domaninská) his account is noticeably lacking in the rhythmic bite so necessary if these Orff-like ostinatos are to be effective. The performance of the *Cantata* is red-blooded enough, but here the degree of deliberate expressiveness detracts markedly from the impact of the music. Barbara Robotham and Gerald English are perhaps an exception in that their expressiveness goes with crisp enunciation of these bizarre stylized settings of medieval English. But again the accompaniment lacks bite, and the *Mass* with its expressive coverage of the Latin liturgy loses its point with soggy choral tone and poor rhythm such as that provided by the Prague Philharmonic Chorus.

OPERA

Oedipus Rex

(B) ** Ph. 475 6395. Norman, Schreier, Terfel, Peeters, Swensen, Saito Kinen O, Ozawa – SCHOENBERG: *Cabaret Songs; Erwartung* ***

Where the prize-winning stage production of *Oedipus Rex* from Japan has Philip Langridge in the title-role, the CD offers a similar cast, with Peter Schreier as Oedipus. Ozawa's conducting is just as warmly dramatic and powerful, and Jessye Norman's Jocasta has a commanding intensity never surpassed, with a relatively short role assuming key importance. Yet Schreier sounds too old and strained to be convincing, robbing the rest of the impact it should have. Only in his final hushed *Lux facta est* does Schreier convey full intensity, but that is hardly enough. However, the coupling on this bargain CD is superb.

Stravinsky Edition, Vol. 9: *The Rake's Progress* (complete)

*** Warner DVD 3984 22352-2. Fedderly, Hendricks, Hagegård, Asawa, Swedish R. Ch. & O, Salonen (V/D: Inger Aby)

The Warner DVD version offers not a regular staging but a filmed version, made in Sweden with a strong trio of principals. The tenor Greg Fedderly makes a handsome Tom, with a clean, well-focused voice, opposite the provocative soprano, Barbara Hendricks, not quite the innocent maiden of an ideal casting, but vocally strong. Hakan Hagegård on his home territory is a formidable Nick Shadow, smooth and sinister. Exceptionally, the bearded lady, Baba the Turk, is played by a man, Brian Asawa, certainly characterful. The sound is bright and forward to reinforce the incisiveness of Esa-Pekka Salonen's conducting. Documentation is poor, with only a synopsis and a brief list of chapters.

Le Rossignol (complete)

**(*) Virgin Classics DVD 5 44242. Dessay, Simcic, McLaughlin, Urmana, Grivnov, Scjagidulli, Naouri, Mikhailov, O & Ch. de l'Opéra de Paris, Conlon (a film by Christian Chaudet)

This is very much a film – and not a filmed performance of the opera. Christian Chaudet is inventive – perhaps too inventive, as he draws attention away from the music and towards the visual presentation. Natalie Dessay makes a splendid nightingale, and the remainder of the cast is very good, too. James Conlon gets a sensitive response from the fine Orchestre de l'Opéra de Paris. It can certainly be enjoyed without the distraction of vision, but we can imagine others preferring the wonderful post-war account by Janine Micheau, conducted by André Cluytens and available on Testament, which still sounds marvellous. Not even Stravinsky's own recording surpasses it.

SUK, Josef (1874–1935)

Piano Trio; Elegie

*** Sup. SU 3810. Smetana Trio – NOVAK: *Trio quasi una balata;* SMETANA: *Piano Trio* ***

Unlike the other items on this disc, which are darkly elegiac, Suk's *Piano Trio* is a miniature work, its three movements lasting less than a quarter of an hour. Originally written when the composer was only 15, it was twice revised, the second time under the tutelage of Dvořák; it stands as a delightful piece, full of light and shade, built on clear, memorable themes, with a wonderfully compact, sonata-form finale. Following that, the *Elegie* is a far deeper composition, opening with a violin melody which inspires Jana Novakova to playing of an other-worldly delicacy, rapt (like so much of the playing here), building into a passionate central climax.

About Mother, Op. 28; Piano Pieces, Op. 7; Spring, Op. 22a; Summer Impressions, Op. 27b

(BB) *** Regis RRC 1174. Kvapil

A most attractive anthology, beautifully played and well recorded. The disc also comes with three others, devoted to Czech piano music, including music by Dvořák, Smetana and Janáček (Regis RRC 4005).

SULLIVAN, Arthur (1842–1900)

(i) *Henry VIII* (incidental music): *March; Graceful Dance. Overtures:* (ii) *Di ballo;* (i) *Macbeth; Marmion.* (iii) *Pineapple Poll suite* (arr. Mackerras; for band: Duthoit); (i) *Victoria and Merrie England suite 1.* (iv) *The Lost Chord;* (v) *My dearest heart;* (vi) *Onward Christian Soldiers* (arr. Rogers)

(M) ** Decca (ADD) 468 810-2. (i) RPO, Nash; (ii) Philh. O, Mackerras; (iii) Eastman Wind Ens., Fennell; (iv) Burrows, Ambrosian Singers, Morris; (v) Palmer, Constable; (vi) Rogers Ch. & O, Rogers

The highlight here is Mackerras's account of the delightful *Overture di ballo*, showing more delicacy of approach than usual, though certainly not lacking sparkle. The *Macbeth Overture* is dramatic and brightly coloured, but not inspired, worthier of another Savoy opera rather than Shakespeare. *Marmion* too is not really distinctive. The two excerpts from *Henry VIII* are agreeable enough and the selection from

Victoria and Merry England also includes some pleasing ideas, but with only eleven minutes of music included collectors would do far better to investigate the complete ballet on Marco Polo. The selection from *Pineapple Poll*, however, makes an engaging novelty as it is heard in a military band arrangement and is superbly played by an American ensemble of the highest calibre directed with élan by Frederick Fennell. Of the vocal items Felicity Palmer sings the ballad *My dearest heart* with an appropriate degree of sentimentality, *The Lost Chord* is presented in an elaborate arrangement with luscious chorus, and *Onward Christian Soldiers* as a patrol. The sound throughout is variable, always good but only outstanding in *Di ballo* and the Mercury recording of *Pineapple Poll*.

(i) *The Merchant of Venice (Masquerade); Henry VIII* (incidental music): suite. *Overture: The Sapphire Necklace; Overture in C (In Memoriam)*
** Marco Polo 8.223461. RTE Concert O, Dublin, Penny; (i) with Lawler

Here is a comparatively extended suite from *Merchant of Venice* which includes a solo tenor *Barcarolle* with a strong flavour of *The Gondoliers*. There are plenty of good ideas here, and nice orchestral touches, and a grand G&S-style finale to round things off spiritedly. The *Henry VIII* incidental music opens with regal trumpet fanfares and the scoring is well laced with brass (which made it popular on the bandstand) but it is also notable for a pleasing tenor contribution, *King Henry's song* (well sung here by Emmanuel Lawler). The *Sapphire Necklace overture* is a re-arrangement of the military band score. The piece is well constructed and has a rumbustious ending, but it would have been more effective had it been shorter. Andrew Penny secures lively, well-played performances throughout; but in the last resort this is a disc for curious Sullivan fans rather than for the general collector.

Symphony in E (Irish); Imperial March; Overture in C (In Memoriam); Victoria and Merrie England Suite
* CPO 999 171-2. BBC Concert O, Arwel Hughes

On CPO the first movement of the *Irish Symphony* obstinately refuses to take off and, as Owain Arwel Hughes observes the exposition repeat, its 16 minutes' length seems like a lifetime. The other movements are rather more successful, but in almost every way this performance is inferior to the new Chandos version. The other items here pass muster, with the ballet suite easily the most enjoyable item, especially the finale, *May Day Festivities*, which might well have been an undiscovered interlude from *The Yeomen of the Guard*.

SZYMANOWSKI, Karol (1882–1937)

Mythes, Op. 30; Nocturne & Tarantella, Op. 38
❂ (M) *** DG (ADD) 477 5903. Danczowska, Zimmerman –
FRANCK: *Violin Sonata in A* ***

Kaja Danczowska brings vision and poetry to the ecstatic, soaring lines of the opening movement of *Mythes*, and there is a sense of rapture throughout that is totally persuasive. This is now understandably included in Universal's 'Penguin Rosette Collection'.

TAILLEFERRE, Germaine
(1892–1983)

(i; iv) *Chansons populaires françaises*; (ii) *Forlane*; (iii) *Galliarde*; (iv) *Images*; (v) *Sonata for Harp*; (vi) *String Quartet*; (vii) *2 Valses*
**(*) Helicon HE 1008. (i) Maginnis, (ii) Miller, Herrmann; (iii) Baccaro, McGuishin; (iv) Ens., Paiement; (v) Cass; (vi) Porter Qt; (vii) Herrmann, McGuishin

Germaine Tailleferre was born in the same year as Milhaud and Honegger, but outlived them both; indeed, she lived into her nineties and died in the same year as Georges Auric, the last remaining member of *Les Six*. Her music is slight but well wrought and civilized. The *Sonata for Harp* of 1957 is cool and elegant. The *String Quartet* was written 40 years earlier, when Satie proclaimed her his 'daughter in music' having heard *Jeux de plein air*. It is rather charming. Overall this is smiling music, but of no great substance. The performances are dedicated and well performed, and the recording is serviceable, though nowhere near the demonstration bracket.

TALBOT, Howard *See* Lionel MONCKTON.

TANEYEV, Sergei (1856–1915)

Symphonies (i) *2 in B flat* (ed. Blok); (ii) *4*
** Russian Disc (ADD) RD CD11008. (i) USSR R. & TV Grand SO, Fedoseyev; (ii) Novosibirsk PO, Katz

In the *Fourth Symphony* Arnold Katz and the Novosibirsk orchestra give a spirited, characterful reading, which can hold its own against Järvi's excellent account. The recording is very good, though not quite in the three-star bracket. This version of the *Second Symphony in B flat* seems to be identical with Fedoseyev's 1969 LP; climaxes are a bit raw and raucous. The performance itself is satisfactory, and there is at present no alternative.

Piano Quintet, Op. 10; Piano Trio. Op.22
*** DG 477 5419. Pletnev, Repin, Gringolts, Imai, Harrell

We have had performances of these two impressive works separately but not together. So the present DG disc (82 minutes) rather upstages the opposition. The *Piano Quintet* is a particularly strong and enjoyable work. Pletnev and his colleagues make it sound like a true masterpiece, and they are nearly as convincing in the *Trio*. Excellent recording, too.

TANSMAN, Alexandre (1897–1986)

Symphonies 4–5; (i) *6*
*** Chan. CHSA 5041. Melbourne SO, (i) & Ch.; Caetani

The Polish-born Alexandre Tansman spent the greater part of his life in Paris – apart from the war years, the period of the *Fifth Symphony* (1942) and the *Sixth* (1944), which he spent in the United States. During these years he also wrote a biography of Stravinsky for which he was briefly better known than as a composer. But he was a composer of real quality with a sophisticated aural imagination. Works like *Le Serment* ('The Solemn Oath'), an opera for radio composed for the French Radio, and *Isaiah* show a certain indebtedness to Szymanowski, particularly in their heady orchestral textures, but they still leave no doubt that he is very much his own man. The

Fourth Symphony (1936–9) has a Gallic finesse, not surprisingly, given that he spent so much of his life in France. Eminently acceptable and committed playing by the Melbourne orchestra under Oleg Caetani, and good Chandos recording.

Symphony 5 in D min.; 4 Movements for Orchestra; Stèle in memoriam d'Igor Stravinsky
**(*) Marco Polo 8.223379. Slovak PO (Košice), Minsky

Alexandre Tansman was a prolific composer. His craftsmanship is fastidious and his command of the orchestra impressive. His music is highly atmospheric, with shimmering textures enhanced by celesta, piano and vibraphones and sensitively spaced pianissimo string chords, plus poignant wind writing. The *Quatre mouvements pour orchestre* is impressive and resourceful. The *Fifth Symphony*, which dates from his Hollywood years, is less successful. The ideas are pleasing without being as memorable or as individual as the two companion works. The performances are very serviceable and the recordings decent.

TARP, Svend Eric (born 1908)

(i) *Piano Concerto in C, Op. 39;* (ii) *Symphony 7 in C min., Op. 81;* (iii) *The Battle of Jericho, Op. 51;* (iv) *Te Deum, Op. 33*
**(*) da capo DCCD 9005. Danish Nat. RSO, with (i) Per Solo; (i; iii) Schønwandt; (ii) Schmidt; (iv) Danish Nat. R. Ch., Nelson

The only familiar work here is the neo-classical, Françaix-like *Piano Concerto*, a light, attractive piece. There is a distinctively Danish feel to the *Te Deum*, though the piece is eclectic and owes a lot to Stravinsky and may even at times remind English listeners of Walton. The *Seventh Symphony* is neo-classical in feeling, very intelligent music, and only occasionally bombastic. The performances, which come from 1986–90, are enthusiastic and committed, and the recordings are serviceable without being top-drawer.

TAVENER, John (born 1944)

Lament for Jerusalem
(BB) *** Naxos 8.557826. Gryffydd Jones, Crawford, Ch. & O of L., Summerly

Written in 2002 and lasting almost an hour, *Lament for Jerusalem* is one of the most tautly conceived of Tavener's essays in spiritual minimalism. It consists of seven cycles, each beginning with a quotation from Psalm 137, 'By the Waters of Babylon', and each following a similar layout, with an instrumental texture, solos for counter-tenor and soprano, and a final choral lament. What is specially impressive is the juxtaposition of vocal forces of varying sizes, with Summerly drawing incandescent singing from his choir of just over 30 singers, sounding far bigger than that thanks to the warmly atmospheric recording, made in the church of All Hallows, Gospel Oak. Equally, the cycles expand as the work progresses, making it more than just a repetitive litany. Outstanding solo singing too from Angharad Gryffydd Jones and Peter Crawford.

TCHAIKOVSKY, Peter (1840–93)

Andante cantabile; Nocturne, Opus 19/4; 10 Romances (arr. Stetsuk); *Variations on a Rococo Theme*
** Warner 1564 62061-2. Kniasev, Moscow CO, Orbellian

Alexander Kniasev is a prize-winning young Russian cellist with an opulent tone. He demonstrates here what a fullblooded romantic he is in performances of all these Tchaikovsky works, marked by a free, almost improvisatory, expressive style, a preference for a generous vibrato and generally broad speeds. The *Nocturne* is taken from his Op. 19 piano pieces, while the *Andante cantabile* is the ever-popular slow movement from the *First String Quartet*. The performance of the *Rococo Variations* tends to be rather heavy-handed, though always compelling. The so-called *Romances* are arrangements for cello and orchestra by Evgeni Stetsuk of ten songs, including many favourites. A pity that some of the orchestrations of the original piano parts tend to be fussy. The Moscow Chamber Orchestra under Constantine Orbellian offers sympathetic support, well recorded, if from a rather backward position. The recording, favouring the soloist, does bring out the exceptionally wide dynamic range that Kniasev employs, regularly resulting in magical echo effects.

Capriccio italien; (i) *1812. Festival Coronation March; Marche slave; Eugene Onegin: Polonaise; Waltz. Mazeppa: Cossack Dance*
(*) Telarc **Audio DVD DSD DVDA 70541; CD 80541. Cincinnati Pops O, Kunzel; (i) with Kiev Symphony Ch., Cincinnati Children's Ch., Cannon & Cleveland carillon

The Telarc CD is aimed straight at audiophiles and is additionally available in surround sound (Discrete Multichannel Surround). But the snag is that the real cannon, spectacularly reproduced, the carillon and choruses singing the folktunes in *1812* very freshly cannot turn a good performance into a thrilling one, and here the adrenalin does not run as free as it should. *Marche slave*, however, is much more successful. The other works, too, are very well played, but there are more sparkling versions available elsewhere, and though the recording is sumptuous, the frequent presence of the bass drum thundering away eventually becomes too much of a good thing. We found ourselves unable to reproduce the DVD Audio version on a British DVD player.

(i) *Concert Fantasy in G, Op. 56;* (ii) *Symphony 4, Op. 36*
(BB) *(*) Warner Apex 0927 49545-2. (i) Leonskaja, NYPO; (ii) Leipzig GO; Masur

The arresting fate motive that opens Tchaikovsky's *Fourth Symphony* fails to make the dramatic impact it should in Masur's Leipzig recording, and the performance as a whole fails to catch fire as it continues. The recording is somewhat muted too, and there are plenty of more recommendable versions available. The *Concert Fantasy* is much more successful as a performance, with more animated and lively orchestral playing from the New York orchestra and an enthusiastic response from the soloist. The recording has more brilliance too. This is worthy of a recoupling.

Piano Concertos: (i) *1;* (ii) *2* (with abridged Siloti version of *Adagio*); *3*
(BB) ** EMI Gemini (ADD) 3 50849-2 (2). Gilels, O de Paris, Maazel – BARTÓK: *Piano Concerto 2;* PROKOFIEV: *Piano Concerto 5* *(*)

(M) ** Sony S2K 94737 (2). Graffman; (i) Cleveland O, Szell;
(ii) Phd. O, Ormandy – BALAKIREV: *Islamey* *(*);
MUSSORGSKY: *Pictures at an Exhibition* **

Gilels's 1972 set of the three Tchaikovsky *Piano Concertos* with
Maazel is not as attractive as it looks because, alas, it includes
the Siloti version of No. 2. The performances are distinguished and undoubtedly have freshness. No. 3 in particular
has a poetic quality which is highly rewarding, despite some
lack of robustness. The account of No. 1, however, is lightweight. It has a very fast opening, exhilarating in its way, but
Tchaikovsky's famous introductory melody needs a broader
treatment. The balance places the piano well forward, and the
orchestral recording, though good, is not as refined and
lustrous as it might be.

Graffman's set of the three Tchaikovsky concertos is disappointing, not least because of indifferent sound. His partnership with Szell in the *First Concerto* produces a performance
in which the electricity crackles, with the spirit of Horowitz
and Toscanini evoked in the finale. One senses Szell's personality strongly throughout, alongside that of his soloist. The
impact is undeniable, producing a combination of power and
breadth in the first movement, with lyrical contrast not
forgotten, and an engaging delicacy for the outer sections of
the *Andantino*. The snag is the recorded sound, full-bodied
certainly, but unrefined, closely balanced, with an edge on
top. Surprisingly, the partnership with Ormandy works much
less well in the other two concertos, Graffman used Tchaikovsky's original score for the outer movements of the *Second
Concerto*, but he reverts to Siloti's abridged version of the
Andante. Perhaps this was a sensible decision, for the orchestral cello and violin soloists find little charm in the passages
that remain. The outer movements are played strongly but
aggressively and there is no sense of geniality in the finale,
belying the amiable picture of Ormandy included in the
booklet. The *Third Concerto* fares no better, and the recording
is excessively resonant, with clattery piano-timbre and poor
orchestral definition.

Piano Concerto 1 in B flat min., Op. 23; (ii) 2 in G, Op. 44 (arr. Siloti)

(M) (**) DG (IMS) mono 457 751-2. Cherkassky, BPO; (i)
Ludwig; (ii) Kraus

Cherkassky's were famous performances in their day. Some
might find the opening of the *First Concerto* too slow and
massive, but the performance soon settles down to offer
plenty of thrills and, in the second subject (and later in the
slow movement), sensitive playing from all concerned. There
is also the kind of spontaneity one enjoys at a live performance. The DG sound is clear and well balanced, with excellent
piano image. The upper strings, however, are less smooth
than usual.

The *Second Concerto* was recorded before conductors had
discovered that the first movement is split in common time,
and meant to be taken at two-beats-in-a-bar. Richard Kraus
plods along emphatically using four, and Tchaikovsky's opening is immediately bogged down. Cherkassky's playing is
superb throughout, but he uses the truncated Siloti edition.
Some will feel that his flair and poetry more than compensate
– but not the present writer. This recording comes in excellent mono sound.

Piano Concerto 1 in B flat min., Op. 23

**(*) Warner 2564 63074-2. Berezovsky, Ural PO, Liss –
KHACHATURIAN: *Piano Concerto* ***

**(*) ABC Classics 476 8071. Tedeschi, Queensland O,
Bonynge – GRIEG: *Piano Concerto 1* **(*)

(M) ** Telarc CD 80193. Gutiérrez, Baltimore SO, Zinman –
RACHMANINOV: *Rhapsody on a Theme of Paganini* **

(BB) ** Warner Apex 0927 40835-2. Sultanov, LSO,
Shostakovich – RACHMANINOV: *Piano Concerto 2* **

(BB) *(*) EMI Encore 5 85704-2. Weissenberg, O de Paris,
Karajan – RACHMANINOV: *Piano Concerto 2* **

(BB) * Virgin 4 82128-2. Pommier, Hallé O, Foster –
RACHMANINOV: *Piano Concerto 2* *

Berezovsky's new recording of the *B flat minor Concerto*
should have been a world-beater. It is the very opposite of
routine and is full of imaginative touches, seeking, rather like
Ashkenazy's Decca version, to move away from a barnstorming approach and bring out the concerto's lyrical core.
The opening is properly flamboyant and the *Allegro con
spirito* sets off with fine impetus. But when the second-
subject group arrives, both pianist and conductor combine to
produce the utmost delicacy. The recording has a very wide
dynamic range, and the result is that their joint image recedes
and all but loses its tangibility. However, as the movement
progresses, the performance gathers impetus and power, and
the cadenza is most poetically done. The pizzicato opening of
the slow movement brings another *pianissimo* from the
orchestra which is only just audible; but the movement
brings more refined delicacy from Berezovsky and a dazzling
scherzando centrepiece. The finale then sets off in sparkling
fashion, and Liss gives the secondary lyrical tune a lighter
dancing rhythmic profile than usual. This remains at the
climactic reprise, giving the end of the work an added freshness, without losing the pianistic bravura. In spite of the
idiosyncrasies, this remains a real three-star performance,
well worth hearing, while the coupled Khachaturian *Concerto*
is amazingly transformed by this new approach, sounding
quite different from any previous account, yet still producing
an exciting, very Russian brilliance.

Perhaps it is Bonynge's experience as a ballet conductor –
without any sense that this warhorse is being played as a
showpiece – that gives this Queensland version a distinctive,
ultra-romantic feel. Simon Tedeschi seemingly has no problems negotiating the work's virtuosic passages, but it is his
poetic qualities which are especially enjoyable. The recording
is basically good, but the strings could have done with a bit
more 'oomph' from the engineers, especially at the opening.

Horace Gutiérrez has a dazzling technique and there is no
questioning his effortless virtuosity. At the same time, there is
a certain lack of freshness and spontaneity, and the razzle-
dazzle brilliance of the pianist and the routine responses of
the conductor do not make for a front recommendation. The
sound is excellent, but the performance is far from earth-
shaking.

There is some fiery playing from Alexei Sultanov, which
testifies to a considerable technique; but compare his handling of the *prestissimo* episode in the slow movement with
someone like Argerich and he emerges as rather coarse-
grained, and the second group of the finale is crudely handled. However, there is much more that excites admiration,
and it is only the indifferent accompanying and the less than
ideal recording balance that inhibit a strong recommendation, even at bargain price.

The Weissenberg Karajan account dates from 1970. The
opening is very slack and while the languorous approach to
the allegro finds the poetic element of the secondary material, the main climax of the first movement lacks impetus

and thrust. The *Andante cantabile* too is similarly lacking in magnetism, and even at budget price this coupling with Rachmaninov provides no real competition. Indeed alongside Horowitz the Weissenberg Tchaikovsky performance sounds positively anaemic.

Jean-Bernard Pommier plays this famous showpiece confidently but has no individual insights to offer, and the orchestral support is not memorable either. There are much more rewarding accounts of both these works in the catalogue.

(i) *Piano Concerto 1*; (ii) *Violin Concerto in D, Op. 35*
(BB) ** EMI Encore (ADD) 7243 574591 2 9. (i) Cziffra, Philh. O, Vandernoot; (ii) Kogan, Paris Conservatoire O, Silvestri

In the famous Tchaikovsky warhorse, Cziffra displays a prodigious technique, but during the first movement he and Vandernoot seem not wholly to agree on the amount of forward thrust the music needs and, despite the use of Kingsway Hall, the strings tend to shrillness. Kogan's performance of the *Violin Concerto* is a different matter. Enjoyment and spontaneity are written in every bar of his interpretation. His account of the finale is especially infectious, with a lilt to the rhythm to really make it a Russian dance. In the first two movements, where he and Silvestri are more concerned with the architecture, he is steadier, but the build-up of tension when the main theme is developed is most exciting through his very refusal to slacken the basic speed. His tone is gloriously rich, and only occasionally does he mar a phrase with a soupy swerve. He rarely achieves a true *pianissimo*, but that may be the fault of the early stereo recording, which is very good, fuller and warmer than many Paris issues of this period.

Piano Concerto 1 in B flat min.; Theme and Variations, Op. 19/6
(BB) *** EMI Encore 5 86881-2. Gavrilov – BALAKIREV: *Islamey*; PROKOVIEV: *Piano Concerto 1*, etc. ***

Gavrilov is stunning in the finale of the concerto; however, the final statement of the big tune is broadened very positively so that one is not entirely convinced. Similarly in the first movement, contrasts of dynamic and tempo are extreme, amd the element of self-consciouness is apparent. The *Andante* is full of tenderness and the *prestissimo* middle section goes like quicksilver, displaying the vein of spontaneous imagination that we recognize in Gavrilov's other records. The recording is full and sumptuous. In the *Variations, Op. 19*, Tchaikovsky's invention has great felicity. Gavrilov's playing is stylishly sympathetic here, and the Balakirev and Prokofiev couplings are dazzling.

Violin Concerto in D, Op. 35
(M) *** Decca 475 7734. Chung, LSO, Previn – SIBELIUS: *Violin Concerto* ***
(M) *** DG (ADD) 477 5914. Milstein, VPO, Abbado (with 'Encores' (with Georges Pludermacher, piano): GEMINIANI: *Sonata in A*. SCHUBERT: *Rondo brilliant in B min*. MILSTEIN: *Paganiniana*. LISZT: *Consolation 3 in D flat*. STRAVINSKY: *Chanson russe*. KODALY: *Il pleut dans la ville*. MUSSORGSKY: *Hopak*)
(B) *(*) RCA (ADD) 82876 59419-2. Perlman, Boston SO, Leinsdorf – SIBELIUS: *Violin Concerto* *(*)

Violin Concerto; Meditation; Swan Lake, Op. 20: Danse russe
*** Sony SH 94829. Bell, BPO, Tilson Thomas

Kyung Wha Chung's earlier recording of the *Violin Concerto* with Previn conducting now returns to the catalogue as one of Decca's Originals; it has remained one of the strongest recommendations for a much-recorded work ever since it was made, right at the beginning of her career. Although she recorded it later with Dutoit, anyone should be well satisfied with Chung's 1970 version with its Sibelius coupling. With Previn a most sympathetic and responsive accompanist, this has warmth, spontaneity and discipline, every detail is beautifully shaped and turned without a trace of sentimentality. The recording is well balanced and detail is clean.

Recorded in the Berlin Philharmonie in January 2005, Joshua Bell's new version is freer, more volatile and even more affectionate than his studio account of 1988 for Decca, yet he never indulges in excessive mannerism. Though speeds this time tend to be a degree faster than before, it is typical that in the cadenza of the first movement Bell this time takes over 30 seconds longer than before, confident in sustaining pauses of far greater length, giving an impression of improvisation more clearly than before, persuasive as his youthful performance was. In the central *Canzonetta* Bell is this time even more tender and more individual in his phrasing, despite a more closely balanced sound, and, as before, he achieves a genuine *pianissimo* without using a mute. In the finale he opens up the brief traditional cuts that he allowed in his 1988 performance, an obvious advantage, and he adopts a marginally faster speed with more exciting results, particularly at the end, where the Berlin audience understandably responds with great enthusiasm. The coupling this time is not generous but is still valuable, particularly when the *Meditation* – the first of the three pieces labelled *Souvenirs d'un lieu cher* – was originally designed as the slow movement for the *Concerto*.

Milstein's 1972 recording of the *Violin Concerto* still remains among the top versions available. He plays beautifully, Abbado secures playing of genuine sensitivity and scale from the VPO, and the recording is first class. A 1984 collection of encores makes an unusual and attractive coupling, with plenty of contrasting and thoroughly entertaining pieces: the Liszt is very effective when played so seductively and, if the Geminiani is not successful stylistically, Milstein comes into his own in his own arrangement of Paganini's most famous *Caprice* and the vivacious *Hopak* of Mussorgsky. Excellent 1975 sound.

Perlman provides a good performance with Leinsdorf but, in a field as competitive as this, his RCA version cannot figure high in the lists of recommendations. As in the Sibelius coupling, his later, EMI recording is far preferable.

Fatum (Symphonic Poem). Dances and Overtures from Operas: Cherevichki ('The Slippers'): Cossack Dance; Russian Dance. The Enchantress: Introduction; Dance of the Histrions. The Maid of Orleans: Entr'acte between Acts I & II; Dance of the Bohemians; Dance of the Polichinelles and Histrions. Mazeppa: Gopak. The Oprichnik: Dances, Act IV; The Queen of Spades: Overture. The Voyevoda: Overture
(BB) *** Naxos 8.554845. Ukraine Nat. SO, Kuchar

A fascinating disc containing much unknown Tchaikovsky, opening with the histrionic *Overture* to *The Queen of Spades*, followed by the even more melodramatic early symphonic poem, *Fatum*, of 1868, which Tchaikovsky later destroyed and which was reassembled only after his death. What redeems both works is the undeniably Tchaikovskian lyrical inspiration, and the characteristic scoring. The same comments might apply to the *Voyevoda Overture*, written in the same year as *Fatum* and belonging to the one opera the composer destroyed. The other operas had greater or lesser success. *The Maid of Orleans* has now been recorded, and we know it contains some fine music. The excerpts here are attractive, as is the *Cossack Dance* from *Cherevichki* which, like the similar dance from *Mazeppa*, is the one familiar item. Performances are first class, full of Russian vitality, and the recording most vivid. An unmissable bargain for keen Tchaikovskians.

Francesca da Rimini

(M) ** Virgin 5 61837-2. Houston SO, Eschenbach –
DVORAK: *Symphony 9 (From the New World)* **

Francesca da Rimini; Romeo and Juliet (fantasy overture)

(M) ** BBC (ADD) BBCB 8012-2. ECO, Britten – FALLA: *El amor brujo* **(*)

Eschenbach's performance of *Francesca da Rimini* has similar qualities to those in the Dvořák symphony with which it is coupled. With clean textures and ensemble, with rhythms crisply resilient and with the brass section gloriously ripe, it is a refreshing performance, which yet lacks Tchaikovskian passion. It makes a generous and unusual fill-up for the *New World Symphony*.

Britten's love of the music of Tchaikovsky may seem strange when he was so vitriolic about other high romantics like Puccini. He conducted these live performances at the Aldeburgh Festival – *Romeo* in 1968 and *Francesca* in 1971. Although the lack of weight in the ECO strings (not helped by recording balances) and the overall lack of brilliance tells against these pieces being as dramatic as they might be, the warmth of feeling in spontaneous expressiveness is never in doubt. But this is for Britten's admirers rather than Tchaikovskians.

Manfred Symphony, Op. 58

(M) **(*) LPO 0009. LPO, Jurowski

(*(*)) Testament mono SBT 1129. Fr. Nat. R. O, Silvestri (with LISZT: *Tasso* ***)

(M) * Warner Elatus 0927 46751-2. Leipzig GO, Masur

With a work as episodic as the *Manfred Symphony*, particularly in the long first movement, there is much to be said for a live recording, with dramatic tension more readily sustained. Vladimir Jurowski, the LPO's brilliant young music director, directs a powerful performance which presses the music hard, rather too much so in the second-movement Scherzo. At Jurowski's hectic speed it loses some of its sparkle, and the ensemble is not as crisp as in the finest studio recordings, like those of Jansons (Chandos 8535) and Pletnev (DG 439 891-2). The live recording offers ample compensation, with the engineers securing well-balanced sound, recorded in the Royal Festival Hall.

In the earlier *Manfred Symphony* he recorded with the Orchestre National de France, Silvestri tarted up Tchaikovsky's orchestration, but it is not that so much as the moments of sour intonation and agogic distortion that diminish the appeal of his recording. The Bournemouth broadcast is to be preferred (see our main *Guide*), but the Testament does have the benefit of a first-class fill-up in Liszt's *Tasso*.

Masur's 1991 account of the *Manfred Symphony* is a pretty dreary affair, with very ordinary sound. The performance at last gets going in the finale, but there are just too many outstanding accounts available to make this one recommendable, even at bargain price.

(i) The Nutcracker, Op. 71; (ii) The Sleeping Beauty, Op. 66; (iii) Swan Lake, Op. 20 (complete ballets)

(B) ** RCA 82876 55707-2 (6). St Louis SO, Slatkin

Slatkin recorded the three great Tchaikovsky ballets over seven years, from the middle and late 1980s to the early 1990s, with uneven success. In *The Nutcracker* his brightly paced reading keeps the action moving in Act I, and the orchestral playing has plenty of character throughout. Other versions have more charm but are not more vivid. The lively St Louis recording, though spacious, is a little lacking in sumptuousness and richness of woodwind colour, but here Slatkin's vitality is a plus point.

The same briskness of approach works less well in *Swan Lake*; these are far from ballet tempi, and the relative thinness of the RCA sound, with dry violin timbre, is unalluring, increasing the feeling of unyielding forward motion.

Sleeping Beauty, the last to be recorded, in 1990–91, offers superior sound-quality, fuller than the earlier *Nutcracker*, with the hall ambience well conveyed. Here the vitality is less pressured, while there is plenty of drama and colour, and the Act III *Divertissement* brings both sparkle and grace. But the sound lacks that degree of glowing warmth and expansiveness in the bass that one would expect from, say, a Decca recording. Previn or Bonynge prove more satisfying guides in this repertoire.

The Nutcracker, Op. 71 (ballet; complete)

*** Ph. **DVD** 070 173-2 (Choreography by Petipa, adapted Vasily Vainonen). Larissa Lezhnina, Victor Baranov, Piotr Russanov, Kirov Ballet at Mariinsky Theatre, St Petersburg, Kirov O, Victor Fedotov (Director: Oleg Vinogradov)

The Kirov *Nutcracker* is a delight, following the story simply, with wonderful sets and superb dancing. We see the guests for the party arriving through the snow (a huge number of them, but then it's a big stage) and meet Drosselmeyer (the excellent Piotr Russanov) at the very beginning, while the Mice make their appearance earlier than usual and frighten Clara (Masha in the Russian production) before the very well-staged battle.

The production is traditional and no attempt is made to explain the background to the story, as in Peter Wright's Royal Ballet production. But that is unimportant when the dancing is of the highest quality, both from the principals and from the corps de ballet. The *Waltz of the Snowflakes* is a highlight, and the Russians know how to produce plenty of snow. In the final divertissement the costumes are unadventurous, but the Mirlitons, Chinese Dancers and the Sugar Plum Fairy are enchanting; and the grand *Pas de deux* is really spectacular. The orchestra plays marvellously and the recording is first class. Altogether a wonderful entertainment.

(i) The Nutcracker (complete), Op. 71; (ii) Serenade in C for Strings, Op. 48

(M) *** Mercury **SACD** (ADD) 475 6623 (2). (i) LSO; (ii) Philharmonia Hungarica; Dorati

Dorati's classic version of the *Nutcracker* remains among the most lively and characterful on disc, with both warmth and bloom balancing the vivid Mercury sound. The main set-pieces, such as the *Journey through the Pine Forest*, expand magnificently, while the choral delicacy of the *Waltz of the Snowflakes* is full of charm. The Act II characteristic dances have much colour and vitality. This new CD release offers even greater ambience for those with an SACD set-up, but it is impressive on any equipment. The *Serenade for Strings* is less compelling (the Mercury sound is not so flattering here) but this is just a bonus for the main work of this release.

The Nutcracker: Extended Suite

(B) ** Sony (ADD) 517482-2. Phd. O, Ormandy –
RIMSKY-KORSAKOV: *Christmas Eve; Mlada:* excerpts **

Although Ormandy's 1963 recording is described as the *Suite*, it obviously derives from a more complete version, as there are additional items and the Sugar Plum Fairy is given her extended exit music as in the ballet, rather than the coda which Tchaikovsky provided for the concert suite. The Philadelphia Orchestra know just how to play this music and the music-making has suitable moments of delicacy (as in the *Ouverture miniature*) as well as plenty of flair. In the *Waltz of the Flowers* Ormandy blots his copybook by taking the soaring violin tune an octave up on its second appearance and in the reprise. Here the Philadelphia strings create such a brilliant effect that one can almost forgive the excess, were it not that, although the recording is warmly atmospheric, the violins are glassy in their upper register. The four Rimsky bonuses are all brilliantly played.

Serenade for Strings; Souvenir de Florence. Op. 70

(BB) **(*) Virgin 2x1 4 82103-2. City of L. Sinfonia, Hickox (with FAURÉ: *Pavane*) – BIZET: *Symphony in C;* IBERT: *Divertissement;* RAVEL: *Tombeau de Couperin* **(*)

Serenade for Strings; Suite 4 in G (Mozartiana), Op. 61; (i) Nocturne in C sharp min., Op. 19/4 (arr. for cello and orchestra); (ii) Legend: Christ in his Garden

(M) ** BBC stereo/mono BBCB 8002-2. ECO, Britten; with (i) Rostropovich; (ii) Pears

The coupling of the *Serenade* and the hardly less delectable *Souvenir de Florence* is surprisingly rare. Hickox's well-played performances are both vivacious and nicely detailed, with Tchaikovsky's contrasts of mood in the *Souvenir* well observed. The recording is full and resonant, with the upper range perhaps lacking the last touch of refinement. But overall this is a worthwhile bargain package.

Britten's relaxed accounts of the *Serenade* and *Suite* are warmly persuasive but not distinctive. The solo contributions from Rostropovich and Pears add to the character of the programme, but there are more memorable recordings available of both the major works.

The Sleeping Beauty, Op. 66 (ballet; complete)

❀ *** Arthaus **DVD** 101 113 (Choreography: Marius Petipa; staged Yuri Grigorovich). Nina Semizorova, Aleksei Fadeyechev, Nina Speranskaya, Yuri Vetrov, Maria Bilova, Bolshoi Ballet & Theatre O, Aleksander Kopilov (V/D: Shuji Fujii)
*** DG 457 634-2 (2). Russian Nat. O, Pletnev

Of the three great Tchaikovsky ballets, *The Nutcracker* has the most delightful and engaging music, and the most magical scenario, while *Swan Lake* is the most powerfully dramatic and the most symphonic in structure. But in the view of the composer's biographer, David Brown (with whom we agree), the greatest score of all is the *Sleeping Beauty*, if only for its sheer fecundity – well over two hours of continuous melodic inspiration – and incredibly imaginative scoring. Tchaikovsky, too, thought it was among his best works. 'The subject is so poetic and so well suited to music,' he wrote, and he was very disappointed when, at its first performance, it received a

lukewarm reception. But, of course, it has survived, although even today one of the problems of production is that Petipa's highly demanding choreography needs not just two or four but a whole group of leading dancers, with both Princess Aurora and the Lilac Fairy major female roles.

The story, histrionic as it is, occupies very little of the scenario – one of the weaknesses of the original 'libretto'. All three Acts have divertissements, and both the outer Acts include variations for the key fairy attendants and solos for the Lilac Fairy. But in the extended third Act not only are there characteristic dances by Little Red Riding Hood and the Wolf, and by Puss-in-Boots and the White Cat (exquisitely danced here), but a big, demanding number for the Blue Bird, while the Prince and Princess (separately, and together) have a whole series of bravura dances, all to marvellous music.

The 1989 Bolshoi production offered here is as lavish as one could wish, and historically traditional in the sense that Yuri Grigorovich has rescued a very high proportion of Petipa's original choreography and scenario so that, as nearly as possible, we are seeing what Tchaikovsky envisaged, produced with a large cast in terms of the huge stage of the Bolshoi Theatre.

One of the most magical scenes is when the Lilac Fairy takes the Prince in her boat to meet his sleeping princess, while the orchestra plays one of the most beautiful of all Tchaikovsky's melodies, the *Panorama*, with its rocking bass. The size of the stage means that a huge revolve can give the impression of the boat slowly floating to its destination. As for the dancing, not surprisingly it is quite fabulous, with the key characters matched in their virtuosity by the many ensemble dances for the corps de ballet, but with Nina Semizorova outstanding in the role of Princess Aurora, matched by the incredibly virile (and good-looking) Prince, Aleksei Fadeyechev. Nina Speranskaya is a delectably graceful Lilac Fairy, given another of Tchaikovsky's most memorable tunes whenever she appears. Even so, Yuri Vetrov as the grotesquely malignant Carabosse nearly steals the show in his two main appearances.

The orchestra shows great stamina and plays with vigour, passion and much charm throughout, although one has the feeling that the performance takes a little while to warm up – which it certainly does at the first great *Adagio*, the fifth number of Act I. With traditional sets, one cannot think that we will see Tchaikovsky's and Petipa's masterpiece more effectively staged or better danced, and the cameras follow the dancers in close-up or long shot very perceptively. The lavish period costumes are based on the illustrations which accompanied the original story, reflecting the court of the Sun King, where Charles Perrault's fairytale was first heard and where, in the book, his original heroine, on being awakened by the Prince's kiss, said precociously 'Is it you, dear Prince? You have been long in coming!' (Only 100 years!)

One last piece of advice. The action is continuous for 145 minutes, so have a glass of wine ready for the interval between each of the three Acts, and especially before the longest, Act III, and you will enjoy the final divertissement as much as the live audience (who have obviously also used the intervals to advantage).

Pletnev's is a performance of individuality and high quality. It is a strongly narrative and dramatic account that has tenderness and much the same virtuosity that Pletnev exhibits at the keyboard. It is now offered at mid-price for the first time.

Souvenir d'un lieu cher, Op. 42; Valse scherzo in C, Op. 34 (orch. Glazunov)

(M) *** DG 457 064-2. Shaham, Russian Nat. O, Pletnev – GLAZUNOV; KABALEVSKY: *Concertos.* ***

Eloquent and dazzling playing of these two Tchaikovsky pieces by Gil Shaham are an additional inducement to get this fine coupling of the Glazunov and Kabalevsky *Concertos.*

Suite 3 in G, Op. 55

☛ *** Pentatone **SACD** PTC 5186 061. Russian Nat. O, Jurowski – STRAVINSKY: *Le Baiser de la fée (divertimento)* ***

The young Russian, Vladimir Jurowski, offers a brilliant performance, electric in tension, to give the illusion of live music-making. The *Third Suite* with its extended set of variations for finale can seem rather square under some conductors, but Jurowski, maybe influenced by his conducting of opera and ballet, brings out the surging lyricism of all four movements. So the opening *Elégie* is warmly moulded without ever sounding fussy, with phrasing that seems totally idiomatic. The rhythmic lightness of the second-movement *Waltz* leads to a dazzling account of the third-movement Scherzo, taken at a genuine Presto, yet with no feeling of breathlessness, while the *Variations* have rarely seemed so attractive in their breadth of ideas, leading to a thrilling build-up and conclusion. Exceptionally vivid sound, recorded by Pentatone's Dutch engineers in Moscow.

Swan Lake, Op. 20 (ballet; complete)

(B) ** Sony SB2K 89735 (2). LSO, Tilson Thomas

Unlike his splendid version of the *Nutcracker*, there is a slight wanting of character in Tilson Thomas's Sony recording, and the performance does not feel especially theatrical in impact. The opening lacks the atmosphere that implies a great romantic drama to follow and the music is not sustained at the highest level of tension. There is little to complain of in terms of the orchestral playing and recorded sound, but the end result is disappointing.

Swan Lake (highlights)

(M) (**(*)) Cala mono CACD0543. NBC SO, Stokowski (with STRAUSS: Waltzes: *An der schönen blauen Donau; Geschichten aus den Wiener Wald.* BEETHOVEN: *Ruins of Athens: Turkish March.* MOZART: *Turkish March (arr. Stokowski from Piano Sonata 11: Alla Turca))*

Stokowski's 1954/5 set of highlights from *Swan Lake* (more than an hour of music) was a recording première; hitherto only the suite had been readily available (although some extended excerpts of little-known passages from the score had been issued on four Columbia 78s in the 1940s). Most of the music here comes from Acts II and III, but the sequence is Stokowski's own, and includes one of the composer's piano pieces from Op. 72, orchestrated by Drigo and used in performances at that time.

The response of the NBC Orchestra has both panache and excitement, with fine woodwind playing. A reduced string section was used at the time for economic reasons, but the hall resonance pretty well disguises that; indeed, at times one might almost think that the vivid sound was stereo. (There was a stereo tape master but it was apparently lost.) An enjoyable selection, then, and not at all predictable. The Johann Strauss *Waltzes* are well played but less individual (except for the contrived effect at the beginning of *Tales from*

the Vienna Woods). The two marches sparkle, especially the ebullient Mozart *Alla Turca*, which Stokowski transcribed himself. The transfer to CD is remarkably good and this is well worth having, if not one of the maestro's very finest records from this era.

SYMPHONIES

Symphonies 1–6; Capriccio italien; Fatum; Francesca da Rimini; Marche slave; Romeo and Juliet (Fantasy Overture); Swan Lake (ballet suite)

(B) ** RCA 82876 55781-2 (6). RPO, Temirkanov

Temirkanov is a wilful Tchaikovskian. In concert his free approach on questions of tempo, with exaggerated speed-changes, can result in exciting performances. In the studio it is harder to get the necessary adrenalin working, and, even with the RPO in first-rate form, the wilfulness quickly comes to sound mannered or contrived, not spontaneous. These discs are inexpensive but can be recommended only to devotees of the conductor.

Symphony 1; Francesca da Rimini

(BB) * Warner Apex 2564 61141-2. Leipzig O, Masur

Though there is something to be said for bringing out the symphonic weight of Tchaikovsky's writing, Masur and his superb Leipzig orchestra with their smooth manner and rhythmically four-square approach go too far in removing all hints of Slavonic temperament. Even in this first and lightest of the Tchaikovsky cycle, the result is heavy, and *Francesca da Rimini* also lacks excitement.

Symphonies 4–6 (Pathétique)

☛ (B) *** Ph. 475 6315 (3). VPO, Gergiev

If you want a box offering the three last symphonies of Tchaikovsky, Gergiev's VPO set is now an indisputable first choice. The recordings are all in the front rank, and Gergiev's accounts of Nos. 4 and 5 are very highly praised by us in our main *Guide*, with the *Fifth* given a ✿. The VPO *Pathétique* is very fine too, and the orchestra is obviously highly involved throughout. But Gergiev's reading has one or two moments of self-consciousness in the opening movement; and, overall, the performance is without that degree of riveting thrust and passion found in his account with his own Kirov orchestra. In Vienna, the fast, lilting tempo for the 5/4 movement does not make the same contrast with the Scherzo/March as it does in the Russian account, where the adrenalin flow at the end of the third movement is almost overwhelming. However, those readers for whom the Kirov performance feels too hard-driven will surely find that this Vienna performance makes a very satisfying alternative, for its depth of feeling in the finale is in no doubt.

(i) Symphony 4; (ii) Francesca da Rimini

*** EMI **DVD** DVB 5 996899. (i) Leningrad PO, Rozhdestvensky (colour); (ii) Leningrad PO, Mravinsky (black and white) – see under Documentaries: 'Yevgeny Mravinsky – Soviet Conductor, Russian Aristocrat'. A documentary by Dennis Marks

These memorable performances are a bonus for a documentary about Mravinsky – see DOCUMENTARIES below.

Symphony 4; Capriccio italien

*** HM HMU 90 7393 RPO, Gatti

Symphony 4; Romeo and Juliet (fantasy overture)
(M) ** Warner Elatus 2564 60027-2. Chicago SO, Barenboim
(BB) * Naxos 8555714. Colorado SO, Alsop

Gatti's interpretation, as in his memorable version of the *Fifth Symphony*, often favours tempi which press the music on more swiftly than usual. In the opening movement, after the introductory Fate theme, he immediately takes the music forward, underlining its agitation. But this means that there is less contrast than usual when the balletic secondary theme arrives, trickling on the woodwind. Yet Gatti's momentum is compulsive and he finds his contrast in the rocking string melody, played so beautifully by the RPO strings. The nostalgic second movement is also beautifully played, yet the melancholy oboe melody is again taken a little faster than usual. But here the vigorous middle section makes a spontaneous contrast, and the decorated reprise shows the RPO woodwind at their most sensitive. After the balalaika pizzicato Scherzo, the finale bursts in on the listener and, with the dramatic re-entry of the fatal fanfare, Gatti carries forward to a spectacular coda. His performance of the *Capriccio italien* is vigorously enjoyable, if not as distinctive as the symphony. The Walthamstow recording is full-blooded and realistic, but could perhaps be more expansive.

From Barenboim on Elatus come good, well-prepared and spirited accounts of both the *Fourth Symphony* and *Romeo and Juliet*. At the same time this does not challenge – let alone displace – primary recommendations. These are not the kind of performances that invite frequent re-hearing, though neither the performances nor the recording could be called second rate.

After her excitingly committed recordings of Samuel Barber's music and her fine Brahms *First Symphony* for Naxos, Marin Alsop's first Tchaikovsky CD is a great disappointment. Although the Colorado orchestra plays very well indeed and is meticulously rehearsed, the performance of the *Fourth Symphony* is passionless and entirely without flair. The opening of *Romeo and Juliet*, too, is totally unatmospheric and lacking tension and the appearance of the great love theme is entirely without magic.

Symphony 5 in E min., Op. 64
*** Warner **DVD** + CD 2564 62190-5. West-Eastern Divan
Orchestra, Barenboim (with SIBELIUS: *Valse triste*. VERDI:
La Forza del destino Overture ***)

The West-Eastern Divan Orchestra – the name taken from Goethe – was the amazing inspiration of Daniel Barenboim and his Palestinian philosopher-friend, the late Edward Said. The idea was to bring together in direct collaboration young Arab musicians and young Israelis, for them to make music together, sharing at every level, so that each would more readily come to understand the other. As Said says in a long conversation with Barenboim, contained on the DVD (which comes as a supplement to the CD), 'Their lives have been changed.'

The result, inspired above all by Barenboim's dynamic leadership, has been an unqualified success musically. Their performance of the Tchaikovsky, recorded live in Geneva in 2004, is electrifying from beginning to end, remarkable not just for the weight of the string-tone but for its refinement in *pianissimos*; also for the subtlety and warmth of the wind solos and the biting attack of the brass. The finale is thrilling, and though on the CD applause has been eliminated, the DVD version brings out on video what an ecstatic reception the Geneva audience gave, ending with a prolonged standing ovation after the encore, Verdi's *Forza del destino Overture*, dazzlingly done. The DVD omits the other encore, Sibelius's *Valse triste*, but includes the symphony and overture complete, as well as the 75-minute conversation between Barenboim and Said, recorded in Weimar in 1999, and a documentary, 'Lessons in Harmony', vividly illustrating the orchestra's preparations in sessions in Seville and the way the young musicians work together. An inspiring issue.

(i) *Symphony 5;* (ii) *The Seasons, Op. 37b/1–6*
** Ondine 1076-5. (i) Phd. O, Eschenbach; (ii) Eschenbach
(piano)

(i) *Symphony 5;* (ii) *Variations on a Rococo Theme for Cello*
& *Orchestra*
(B) **(*) CfP 586 1682. LPO; (i) Edwards; (ii) Del Mar

The still much-underrated Sian Edwards is a natural Tchaikovskian, and on CfP she conducts an electrifying and warm-hearted reading of Tchaikovsky's *Fifth*. With refined playing from the LPO and brilliant recording, it matches any version in the catalogue. Her control of rubato is exceptionally persuasive, notably so in moulding the different sections of the first movement, while the great horn solo of the slow movement is played with exquisite delicacy by Richard Bissell. The Waltz third movement is tenderly done, as though for a ballet, while the finale brings a very fast and exciting allegro, challenging the orchestra to brilliant, incisive playing. By the side of Edwards's natural vitality, Norman Del Mar's warmly agreeable account of the *String Serenade* seems just a little bland, although it is well played and the 1978 recording is warm and pleasing. But the original coupling of *Tatiana's Letter Scene* was far more stimulating.

The interpretation of Christoph Eschenbach, the Philadelphia Orchestra's latest music director, could hardly provide a stronger contrast with those of his great predecessors, Stokowski and Ormandy. This is a live recording, yet until the finale, when the performance really takes off in a thrilling account, the result is curiously muted. Speeds are consistently slow, so that at over 51 minutes it is one of the slowest ever; too often the conductor seems to be spelling things out in heavy detail, steady and plain. What makes the reading of the symphony the more puzzling is the playing of Eschenbach as pianist in the charming account he gives of the first six movements of Tchaikovsky's piano suite, *The Seasons*, celebrating the months January to June. His touch is magical, with rippling passagework that tickles the ear, and a natural feel for the flexible phrasing that the music calls out for. These are performances that characterize each movement brilliantly, full of fantasy and charm, with contrasts strongly established. What a pity that Eschenbach evidently finds it hard to persuade orchestral players to follow similar patterns of interpretation.

Symphony 6 in B min. (Pathétique), Op. 74
(*) Arthaus **DVD 100 302. Bav. RSO, Solti (V/D: Klaus
Lindemann) – SHOSTAKOVICH: *Symphony 9* ***
(**) Ondine ODE 1002-2. Swedish RSO, Franck –
RAUTAVAARA: *Apotheosis* **
(BB) * Warner Apex (ADD) 0927 49604-2. NW German Phil.
O, Lindenberg

(i) *Symphony 6 (Pathétique);* (ii) *Romeo and Juliet (Fantasy Overture)*
(M) ** RCA 82876 62320-2. (i) St Petersburg PO; (ii) RPO;
Temirkanov

Symphony No.6, 'Pathétique'. Serenade for Strings
*** HM HMU90 7394. RPO, Gatti

Symphony 6 (Pathétique); The Storm: Overture
(BB) *** Regis RRC 1214. LSO, Rozhdestvensky

Solti's *Pathétique*, even with the extra involvement of visual communication, is not the overwhelming experience one might have expected. We watch him shape the opening movement and the arrival of the great second subject, which is played with real tenderness; and again we watch as he directs the Scherzo/March crisply and builds the big climax at the end, which is inevitably exciting but not overwhelming. Then the finale, although it is played very beautifully, is curiously low-key, and we are left without the lift that comes with a powerful communication of Tchaikovsky's deeply felt but resigned despair. The recording is excellent, and so is the camerawork. But there are many CD performances that are more moving than this.

Following up their recordings of Tchaikovsky's *Fourth* and *Fifth Symphonies* for Harmonia Mundi, this completes the RPO's trio of lively versions under their music director, Daniele Gatti. If the opening *Adagio* of the *Pathétique* seems rather staid, slow and very steady, and the flexible rubato of the great second-subject melody itself sounds rather studied at a slow tempo, a total transformation comes with the shattering *fortissimo* that opens the development section. From then on, through all four movements the performance is magnetic, with Gatti consistently conveying the white heat of Tchaikovsky's inspiration. In retrospect one can readily justify the relative reticence of the opening as a desire not to give too much too soon in this deeply emotional work. The Harmonia Mundi recording, made at the Colosseum, Watford, offers the widest dynamic range and brings out the clarity of texture and of articulation that Gatti draws from his players. Gatti and the RPO also hold a trump card in their exceptionally generous coupling, a warmly persuasive reading of the *Serenade for Strings* which builds on the ripe resonance of the RPO string section, again with clear textures and articulation and a wide dynamic range. Altogether an excellent recommendation.

Rozhdestvensky's 1987 performance with the LSO, originally on Pickwick, now perceptively reissued by Regis, is generously coupled with a fine version of the comparatively little-known symphonic poem, *The Storm*. His passionate reading of the symphony fails to match the finest in precision of ensemble – the slow finale is warm rather than tense or tragic – but the sense of spontaneity is most compelling, and the digital recording is impressive still.

Temirkanov is a sympathetic Tchaikovskian in his Slavic volatility, but his self-conscious phrasing brings a degree of wilfulness. This is a pity, for there is plenty of excitement here, both in *Romeo and Juliet* and in the *Symphony*, with both the St Petersburg and RPO strings making a passionate response in both works, and the brass (and timpani) impressive in the third movement of the symphony. The finale, too, is moving in a genuinely Russian way, even though Temirkanov's rubato is very free.

In his introductory note Mikko Franck tells us that Tchaikovsky's *Pathétique* has had great personal significance for him since he was a child and so one would expect a distinctive performance. Alas, it is individual in a highly self-indulgent way. The first movement is dangerously slow as it opens, and after the climax the very measured trombones are emphatically heavy. The theme of Scherzo/March is introduced in sprightly fashion, but the movement fails to reach a

compulsive climax, and in the finale, at the introduction of the descending scalic theme, Franck slows the music nearly to a halt. Although very well played and recorded, this interpretation is a non-starter.

Lindenberg's 1970 account of the *Pathétique* is well played and has reasonable sound; however, it lacks the dramatic thrust and depth of emotion that the best performances of this work convey.

CHAMBER MUSIC

String Quartets 1 in D, Op. 11; 2 in F, Op. 22; 3 in E flat min., Op. 30; Adagio molto for String Quartet & Harp; 5 Early Pieces for String Quartet; Souvenir de Florence: Adagio cantabile e con moto
(BB) **(*) Regis (ADD) RRC 2071 (2). Shostakovich Qt

These performances by the Shostakovich Quartet, which derive from Moscow Radio broadcasts in the 1970s, are masterly and, if not in the league of the Borodin or Brodsky Quartets, this set is value for money. The recordings sound a shade strident at the upper end of the spectrum, though this is easily tamed. Indeed, in the *Third Quartet* this is barely noticeable; the sound has warmth and presence. The *Adagio for String Quartet and Harp* is one of the few Tchaikovsky rarities that is not of real interest; but the early pieces, dating from the composer's student years at the St Petersburg Conservatory, are – though they are not masterpieces.

String Quartets 1 in D; 3 in E flat min.
** Cedille CDR 90000056. Vermeer Qt

Recorded in 1999–2000 at the WFMT radio studios in forwardly balanced sound, this Vermeer coupling of Tchaikovsky's *First* and *Third Quartets* offers strong, positive performances, fresh and totally unsentimental, with emotions held in check. That the recording balance tends to preclude full pianissimo reinforces that impression, though the subtlety and refinement of the Vermeer's control of dynamic compensates for that. Although they miss some of the lighter qualities that others find in these two fine works – both from Tchaikovsky's early, exuberant creative period – the combination of power and polish is consistently impressive.

OPERA

Eugene Onegin (complete DVD version)
*** Warner DVD 0630-14014-2. Prokina, Drabowicz, Thompson, Winter, Minton, Filatova, Olsen, LPO, A. Davis (Stage Director: Graham Vick; V/D: Humphrey Burton)

Eugene Onegin (complete CD version)
(M) ** Ph. 475 7017 (2). Hvorostovsky, Focile, Shicoff, Borodina, Anisimov, St Petersburg Chamber Ch., O de Paris, Bychkov

We are well served on both DVD and CD in this opera, but this recording of Graham Vick's acclaimed Glyndebourne production from 1994 is a welcome addition. Not only is the production convincing but the cast is, too. But it is Elena Prokina's magnificent portrayal of Tatiana that makes this so desirable. The video direction is admirably discreet, with no intrusive camerawork and with the eye being directed where one feels it ought to be. Among the Onegins now before the public, this ranks high.

Dmitri Hvorostovsky makes a strong, heroic Onegin in the Philips set, though Bychkov's conducting does not always encourage him to be as animated as one wants, and the voice at times comes near to straining. Nuccia Focile also emerges at her most convincing only in the final scene of confrontation with Onegin. Earlier her voice is too fluttery to convey the full pathos of the young Tatiana in the *Letter Scene*, edgy at the top. Neil Shicoff as Lensky also suffers, though he sings with passionate commitment, conveying the neurotic element in the poet's character. As Gremin, Alexander Anisimov also has a grainy voice. Olga Borodina sings impressively as Olga, but on balance the other characters are much better cast in the DG and Decca sets. However, this mid-priced reissue comes with libretto and translation.

The Maid of Orleans (complete DVD version)

(*) Warner **DVD** 4509-94191-2. Rautio, Kulko, Gavrilova, Krutikov, Redkin, Nikolsky, Bolshoi Theatre Ch. & O., Lazarev (Director: Boris Pokrovsky; V/D: Brian Large)

Tchaikovsky embarked on his own adaptation of Zhukovsky's translation of Schiller's *Jungfrau von Orleans* immediately after *Eugene Onegin*, with the intention of composing a score that would succeed on the Paris stage. Hence the crowd effects, coronation scene, and so on. Not only Meyerbeer but Gounod, whose scores he had been studying, were his models. In his *Master Musicians* study, Edward Garden calls the result 'colourless, with an almost total lack of that subjectivity which was vitally necessary if he was to compose convincing music'. The exception is Joan herself, where Tchaikovsky carried over identification with his heroine from *Onegin*. It is her music, and that of her beloved but ill-fated Lionel, that gives us the best music. And it is these roles that are the most memorable in this Bolshoi performance, recorded in 1993 without an audience present. Gerald Abraham once spoke of the rest of the cast as merely characters in fancy dress. This set is worth having for the sake of Nina Rautio's superb Joan – beautifully rounded in tone and finely shaped phrasing, and with excellent acting. The staging is somewhat stiff and traditional, and the orchestral response decent rather than distinguished. All the same, although this is not top-drawer Tchaikovsky it is well worth seeing, and there is after all Joan's narrative in Act II and other set pieces that are worthy of the master.

Mazeppa (complete DVD version)

*** Ph. **DVD** 074 1949. Putilin, Loskutova, Alexashkin, Dyadkova, Lutsiuk, Kirov Op. Ch. & O., Gergiev

This performance was recorded live from performances at the Maryinsky Theatre, St Petersburg, during May 1996 – like the Philips three-CD set which we reviewed some years ago. In both this set and the DG rival from Gothenburg with Sergei Leiferkus in the title-role, the erudite essay by Richard Taruskin was included, but in the present DVD and the DG reissue (see below) it is not included. Nikolai Putilin's Mazeppa is weightier than his DG counterpart, Leiferkus, though not perhaps as subtle. However, as there is no video of the DG set, the comparison is irrelevant. The production is in the best spirit of the Maryinsky, sumptuous to look at and full of period atmosphere. No dustbins in the Gorbals, no t-shirts or pairs of holed jeans in sight but a faithful attempt to match what the composer might have expected to see on stage. Putilin scores over Leiferkus in terms of range and is the more credible tyrant. Irina Loskutova's Maria does not obliterate memories of Gorchakova in terms of tonal lustre or beauty of line, but she is more dramatically convincing. No complaints about the remainder of the cast and the wonderful, full-throated singing of the chorus and the magnificence of the Kirov orchestra under Gergiev. This is a very distinguished production and a hugely enjoyable evening.

Mazeppa (complete CD version)

(M) ******* DG 477 5637 (2). Leiferkus, Gorchakova, Larin, Kotscherga, Dyadkova, Stockholm Royal Op. Ch., Gothenburg SO, Järvi

Here Sergei Leiferkus sings the role of Mazeppa superbly, with his very Russian-sounding tone a little grainy and tight in the throat, entirely apt for the character. There is no flaw either among the other principals. Sergei Larin, in what might seem the token part of Andrey, sings with such rich, heroic tone and keen intensity that the character springs to life. Equally, the magnificent, firm-toned bass, Anatoly Kotscherga, as the father of the heroine, Maria, confirms the high impressions he created in his *Boris* recording with Abbado. As Maria, Galina Gorchakova also emerges as one of the latter-day stars among Russian singers, with her rich mezzo gloriously caught, even if the final lullaby for her dead lover, Andrey, could be more poignant. Järvi draws electric playing from the Gothenburg orchestra, not least in the fierce battle music which opens Act III. The only disappointment is that the opportunity was not taken of also recording the conventional finale to the opera which Tchaikovsky originally wrote. There is no libretto, only a simple cued synopsis.

TCHEREPNIN, Alexander (1899–1977)

Piano Concertos 2, Op. 26; 4 (Fantaisie), Op. 78; 6, Op. 99

(BB) ******* Regis RRC 9110. McLachlan, Chetham's SO, Clayton

A most attractive disc, with brilliant playing from Murray McLachlan in all three works, while the young orchestra is highly responsive – just sample the cello solo which opens the central section of the lively one-movement *Second Concerto*, directly popular in its appeal. The *Fourth Concerto* is exotically programmatic (a bit like a Chinese opera) with the three movements subtitled *Eastern Chamber Dream, Yan Kuei Fei's Love Sacrifice* (a set of variations), and *Road to Yunnan*. In McLachlan's hands the piano writing glitters and the Eastern influence is in no doubt, while the orchestral woodwind playing ensures that the finale is charmingly pentatonic. The *Sixth Concerto* was written many years later, in 1965, and is more Prokofievian, with the opening movement bringing a long, unstoppable toccata before the lyrical material enters. The *Andantino* is simpler but still exotic, and soon leads to more brilliant playing from the soloist; while the finale, opening with the bass drum, brings greater weight, with a curious main theme, and later powerfully quoting the Russian folk-song, *Do not flood, my quiet Don*. None of this is great music, but all three concertos are entertaining when presented with such panache, for the Chetham's Orchestra plays throughout with remarkably spontaneous brilliance, the players obviously enjoying themselves. Excellent recording, too.

TELEMANN, Georg Philipp
(1681–1767)

Concertos and Overtures: (i) 5 Concertos for 2 Flutes, with Lute, Bassoon & Strings (10 284); (ii) Chamber Concerto for Alto Recorder in G min., TWV 43:G3; (iii) Double Concerto in E min. for Recorder & Flute; (iv) Concerto for 3 Trumpets & 2 Oboes in D; (ii) Sonata in A for Recorder, 2 Scordato

Violins & Continuo, TWV 43:A7; (v) Tafelmusik II: Trio in E min. for Recorder, Oboe & Continuo (49 431); (vi) *2 Overtures (Suites): in C, TWV 55:C3 (Hamburg Ebb and Flow) & C6; Overture in E min.,TWV 55:C5* (10 625); *Overtures: in D* (connected with a *Tragicomical Suite); in F (Alster Echo), TVW 55:F11; in D, TWV 55:D15* (49 428); (vii) *3 Overtures (Suites) in D, TWV D18; TWV 55:D6 & D7; in F* (49 429)

(B) *** Cap. 49 426 (5). (i) Dresden Bar. Soloists, Haupt; (ii) Huntgeburth, Berlin Bar. Company; (iii) Höller, Hünteler, Capella Colonsiensis, G. Fischer; (iv) Friedrich & soloists, Budapest Strings; (v) Passin, Gütz, Leipzig Bach Coll.; (vi) Capella Colonsiensis, Linde; (vii) Deutsch Bach Soloists, Winschermann

If you want a representative collection of Telemann at his best, this Capriccio box (with the five CDs in a slip case) is hard to better. The *Concertos* for a pair of flutes are continually inventive and the two compilations of miscellaneous concertos and chamber music offer plenty of variety, not only in the music but also the performances, although all are authentic in the best possible way. The *Suites* (Overtures) are all among the composer's best, including the two most famous, both pictorial or programmatic, the *Alster Echo* and the *Hamburg Water Music*. The performances and recordings are excellent, as is the documentation. As far as we know, the discs are not currently available separately.

Flute Concerto in B min.; Double Concertos: in A min. for 2 Recorders; in E min. for Recorder & Flute; in C min., for Violin & Oboe; in D for 2 Oboes d'amore; Chamber Concerto in B flat for Oboe, Violin, 2 Flutes, 2 Violins & Continuo

(M) *** DHM/BMG 05472 77367-2. Camerata Köln

A very winning collection of mostly *Double Concertos*, of which the *E minor Concerto for Recorder and Flute* is perhaps the most winning as it has a *Largo* slow movement which recalls Handel's *Where'er you walk* and a bustling finale using a drone bass. The closing *Chamber Concerto* for six soloists is also very diverting, but the whole programme offers playing and recording of high quality. However, the documentation is inadequate, with no TWV identification.

Oboe Concertos: in C min., D min., E min., F min.

(BB) *** EMI Gemini (ADD) 3 50905-2 (2). De Vries (baroque oboe), Amsterdam Alma Musica, Van Dael – BACH; VIVALDI: *Oboe Concertos* ***

These four *Oboe Concertos* of Telemann are beautifully played by Han de Vries on a piquant baroque oboe; if their sprightly invention does not quite match that of Bach, the *C minor Concerto* is a piece of more than usual depth of imagination, and the wistful central *Largo* of the *E minor* work is quite memorable. Excellent recording, but with the oboe dominating the sound-picture. Altogether this is an excellent and inexpensive anthology for those who love the oboe, for the coupled concertos are played stylishly on a modern instrument.

Oboe Concerto in D min., TWV 51:d2; Violin Concerto in E, TWV51:E3; Double Violin Concerto in A, TWV 52:A2; Overture in C, TWV 55:c4; Sinfonia melodica for 2 Oboes & Strings; Sonata (Concerto ripieno) for Strings, TW 43:Es1

◑─⟶ *** DG 477 5923. Berlin Barock Soloists, Kussmaul

Here is splendid example of a well-planned Telemann programme, played by a modern-instrument ensemble, with all the added warmth of tone that implies, yet whose conductor,

Rainer Kussmaul, understands and accepts period-instrument style. The brief *Overture* here is a reconstruction and sets the concert off to a lively start, and all the concertos are attractive in their various ways. The most interesting work is the *Sinfonia melodica*, which turns out to be a French Suite with a brilliant *Vivace* in place of the usual Overture, followed by a plaintive *Sarabande* and other dances, including a *Chaconnette*, and ending with a delightful, bouncing *Gigue en Canarie*. With a pair of oboes used concertante style, this is similar to the better-known *Suite in A minor for Recorder* (or *Flute) and Strings*, only that does have an Overture. A most enjoyable disc, very well recorded.

Recorder Concerto in C, TWV 51:C1; Suite for Recorder in A min., TWV 55:a2; C (Hamburger Ebb und Flut), TWV 55:C3

◑─⟶ *** HM HMC 901917. Maurice Steger, Akademie für Alte Musik, Berlin

This recording offers a triptych of three of Telemann's finest works, the well-known *Suite for Recorder and Strings in A minor*, played with virtuosity and élan by Maurice Steger (sample the *Réjouissance* for an astonishing example of his bravura) plus the *Concerto in C*, which has a similarly dazzling finale, and the celebrated *Hamburg Water Music*, in which all the movements are associated with mythology, except for the finale, which is a *Jolly Sailors' Dance*. A first-class collection, splendidly recorded.

Don Quixote (Suite burlesque) in G; Overture in D min; Suite in E flat (La Lyra)

(BB) ** Naxos 8.554019. NCO, Ward

The performances on Naxos by the Northern Chamber Orchestra are warm and polished, and pleasingly recorded. But in the *Don Quixote Suite*, there is little sense of witty burlesque: the musical characterization is not as strong as in the competing period-instrument versions, and in the *Lyra Suite* the hurdy-gurdy simulation is rather bland.

Die Kleine Kammermusic, Orchestral Suites 1–6

*** CPO 999 994-2. La Stagione, Frankfurt, Schneider

Telemann had great success with the *6 Partitas* which made up the second part of his *Kleine Kammermusik* which he published in 1716. So he decided to compose an orchestral version of the whole series, scored for two oboes, strings and continuo, although he omitted the woodwind in Nos. 2 and 3 of the set. During the reworking he left the upper part and bass line unchanged but rewrote the middle parts, and in each work he added a newly composed French overture, lasting about six minutes, which altered the scale of the *Suites* altogether. They are most agreeable and entertaining works and, as played here by the excellent period-instrument Frankfurt chamber orchestra, make enjoyably elegant listening. Some listeners may find them a little bland alongside the original *Partitas* (available from the Camerata Köln on CPO 999 497-2 – see our main volume). Even so, the present disc will give much pleasure, for it is beautifully recorded.

CHAMBER MUSIC

Flute Quartets: Concert 3 in A (1734); Nouveaux Paris Flute Quartets 1 & 2 (1738); Tafelmusik: Quartet in E min.

(BB) ** Warner Apex 2564 60636-2. Punder, with Hortus Musicus, Mustonen

As can be seen, these simply scored works are hand-picked from three different sources, so anyone wanting a sampler of

Telemann's *Flute Quartets* will find this inexpensive collection neatly played and well recorded. The excerpt from the *Tafelmusik* stands out, but the opening movement of the Second *Nouveau Quartet*, marked *Allégrement*, is inviting too, and this is also one of the composer's most engaging works in this form. The agreeable *Concert* which closes the programme derives from the *Six Concerts and Suites* published in 1734.

Quadros (Flute or Recorder Quartets) *in B flat, for 2 Violins, Viola & Continuo, G 43:B2; in A min. for Recorder, Oboe, Violin & Continuo, TWV 43:a3; in D min. for Flute, Violin, Cello & Continuo, TWV 43:d3; in G min., for Recorder, Violin, Viola & Continuo, TWV 43:g4; in G, for Recorder, Oboe, Violin & Continuo, TWV 43:G6; in G, for Flute, 2 Violins & Continuo, TWV 43:G10; for Flute, Violin, Cello & Continuo, TWV 43:G11; for Flute, 2 Violins & Continuo, TWV 43:G12*

⊕→ *** DG 477 5379. Mus. Ant. Köln, Goebel

These *Quadros* are among Telemann's very finest chamber music and, offered in a group like this, the changing instrumentation brings plenty of variety. Although the flute or recorder tends to dominate, these are not concertante works, as Telemann writes parts of equal interest for each of the grouped instruments. The playing here is expert and full of life, and the balance and recording are very realistic, so this is a very recommendable disc.

Sonatas Corellisante 1–6; Canonic Duos 1–4

** Chan. 0549. Standage, Comberti, Coe, Parle, Coll. Mus. 90

The six (Trio) *Sonatas Corellisante* of 1735 are not transcriptions, as might at first be expected, but original works 'in the Italian style', although it is essentially an overlay rather than intrinsic to Telemann's invention. Frankly, this is too often routine and fails either to sparkle or to have the sunshine sonority of the real thing. Perhaps it might sound better on the fuller sound of modern instruments. These performances are alert but hardly beguiling, and the simpler *Canonic Duos*, which are played with sprightly vivacity, completely upstage them.

Sonata Metodiche 1–6 (1728); 7–12 (1732)

** MDG 311 1110-2 (2). Hünteler, Zipperling, Lohff

We are inclined to prefer the Kuijkens' performances to the new set from Konrad Hünteler. He plays well enough but his early flute seems to offer performance problems, for there are just occasionally moments when the intonation is slightly insecure.

COLLECTIONS

Chamber Concertos, Overtures & Sonatas, Vol. 1: Concertos: for Recorder in C, TWV51:C1; for Viola in G, TWV51:G9; Overture in F sharp min., TWC55:bis; Quadro in G min., TWV 43:g4; Sonata in F, TWV 43:F1.

** MDG 309 1189-2. Musica Alta Ripa

Chamber Concertos, Overtures & Sonatas, Vol. 2: Concertos: for Recorder Bassoon in F, TWV 52:F1; for Strings in D min., TWV43:d2; Overture in B min., TWV55:h4; Sonatas: in D, TWV 41:D6; in F min., TWV44:f32.

** MDG 309 1250-2. Musica Alta Ripa

In theory, Musica Alta Ripa offer an ideal way to present collections of Telemann works – in the form of a concert with

mixed genres. But one needs an ongoing feeling of spontaneity as on a live occasion, and here the warm and relaxed style of the music-making at times seems too easy-going. The playing itself is of high quality, as is the recording, but on the first disc the opening of the familiar *Viola Concerto*, for instance, is comparatively lethargic. On the second, where there is a lot of music for strings alone, one welcomes the work for recorder and bassoon for its geniality; elsewhere one would have liked more extrovert vitality.

Music for Oboe, Recorder & continuo: Darmstadt *Concerto in A min., for Treble Recorder, Oboe & Violin.* Darmstadt *Quartets in F for Treble Recorder, Oboe & Violin; in G min. for Violin, Oboe & Viola da gamba.* Darmstadt *Trio Sonata in G min. for Oboe & Violin. Esercizi Musicale: Trio Sonata in F for Treble Recorder, Viola da gamba.* Brussels *Trio Sonata in D min. for Treble Recorder & Violin*

(BB) ** Hyp. Helios CDH 55108. Chandos Baroque Players

Almost all the chamber works here were found in a manuscript in the Hessian State Library at Darmstadt, although the *G minor Trio Sonata* was also discovered in another copy at Dresden and the *D minor* was found in Brussels. All are typically inventive works, if none is especially distinctive. The performances, too, are musical enough and pleasing but somewhat lacking in personality.

Music for Oboe & Continuo: (i) *'Dresden' Sonata for Oboe & Bassoon, TWV 41:g10. Esercizi musici: Sonatas in B flat, TWV 41:B6; E min., TWV 41:e6. Trio Sonata in E flat. Der getrue Musikmeister: Sonata in A min., TWV 41:a3. Tafelmusik: Sonata in G min. for Oboe & Bassoon, TWV 41:g6*

⊕→ (BB) *** Regis RRC 1240. Francis, Dodd, Powell, Jordan; (i) with Beach

Originally issued by Somm, this admirable collection in which Sarah Francis is the star performer draws on both the *Esercizi musici* and *Der getreue Musikmeister*, and includes an extra sonata, found in a Dresden manuscript. The performances are first class in every way and the recording is very well balanced (see our main volume) and this is even more recommendable on the Regis budget label.

VOCAL MUSIC

Das befreit Israel (oratorio; complete); Der May (Eine musicalische Idylle). Overture in F min. for 2 Recorders, 2 Oboes, Bassoon & Strings, TWV 55:f1

⊕→ *** CPO 999 673-2. Schmithüsen, Schubert, Crook, Mertens, Abele, Rheinisch Kantorei, Kleine Konzert, Max

Handel's *Israel in Egypt* was possibly the source of inspiration for Telemann's much briefer (27 minutes) and less complex, but cheerfully melodic and appealing oratorio, which was premièred in 1759. It is very well sung here and makes a fine contrast with the pastoral idyll *Der May*, in which the scoring for flutes, horns and bassoons is used very effectively to colour the text. It forms a charming series of arias and duets gently extolling the joys of spring. Phillis (the soprano, Ingrid Schmithüsen) and Daphnis (the bass, Klaus Mertens), who has already made a strong impression in the oratorio, both sing very pleasingly. In between the vocal works comes a fine performance of one of Telemann's most inventive Suites (Overtures). A most engaging disc, very well recorded.

THEOFANDIS, Christopher
(born 1967)

The Here and Now
(*) Telarc CD 80638. Plitmann, Clement, Polegato, Atlanta Ch. & SO, Spano (with BERNSTEIN: *Lamentation (from Symphony 1)*) – DEL TRIDICI: *Paul Revere's Ride* *

Christopher Theofandis has been composer-in-residence with the California and Pittsburgh Symphony Orchestras, and he was commissioned to compose *The Here and Now* by Roberto Spano for the Atlanta Symphony. The work, which has something in common with Orff's *Carmina Burana*, is based on twelfth-century love poems by Jelaluddin Rumi, who lived on the Anatolian peninsula (now Turkey). But Rumi's poems are not about the hedonistic joys of the tavern and sexual gratification but about love in its deepest sense as a transcendent mutual human experience. The poetic imagery is sensitively transcribed in Cleman Bark's translation and the sensuousness, urgency and possessive passion are powerfully captured in *The one who pours is wilder than we*; yet there us much wisdom in *Hear blessings dropping their blossoms around you* and 'the touch of the spirit on the body'. In the powerful *Drumsound rises* and *The urgency of love* (a soprano/tenor duet with chorus) there is a distinct affinity with Orff's cantata, but it is the luminescence of *Spreading radiance* for overlapping female voices which is the kernel of the work: 'The stars come up spinning every night, bewildered in love ... Everything has to do with love, and not loving.' One's only real criticism is that the spirited ostinatos of the closing section, *The music of our final meeting*, do not match what has gone before in intensity. This is not the fault of the excellent Atlanta performance, so stirringly sung and played under Robert Spano. Moreover, as it happens, the touching performance of Bernstein's *Lamentation* from his *First Symphony* acts as a telling Epilogue, even though soloist Nancy Maultsby's vibrato is rather fluttery. The Telarc recording is full and vivid, but the resonance tends to blunt the bite of the orchestral sound.

THUILLE, Ludwig (1861–1907)
(i) *Piano Concerto in D. Symphony in F*
** CPO 777 008-2. (i) Triendl; Haydn O of Bolzano & Trento, Francis

Ludwig Thuille, pupil of Rheinberger and friend of the young Richard Strauss, was an accomplished if hardly forward-looking composer. His is an agreeable concerto (remarkably mature for a student diploma work), in style an amalgam of Chopin and Mendelssohn. It has amiable themes in the first movement and its flowing passages are here fully alive in the hands of Olivier Triendl. The *Andante*, although nearer Mendelssohn in melodic facility, brings a recognizably Chopinesque touch, and the flowing finale (with plenty of glittering bravura scales) completes a work that was described by the composer's biographer as 'serene and untroubled'. The *Symphony* is similarly fluent and elegant, but with a rather overextended first movement. The *Largo* alternates charm (with neat writing for the oboe) with a bolder, march-like theme, with brassy interludes. But the charm returns fully in the Minuet with its lighter, Mendelssohnian touch. The finale then picks up the stronger material of the slow movement to make a more extrovert finale. Not a masterpiece, then, but quite winningly orchestrated. Both works are played with warmth and spirit. Alun Francis conveys his affection for the music, and the

Haydn Orchestra plays impressively throughout; the pianist is confident and makes the most of his lyrical and bravura opportunities. Good, well-balanced recording. But the music's conventionality prevents a strong recommendation.

TIPPETT, Michael (1905–98)
Concerto for Double String Orchestra
(B) *** CfP 5 75978-2. LPO, Pritchard – BRITTEN: *Violin Concerto; Serenade* ***

This Classics for Pleasure reissue is a first-rate bargain, well recorded, and coupling one of the warmest and most memorable string works of the twentieth century with two key works of Britten. In Handley's fine performance no one could miss the passion behind the sharp, rhythmic inspirations of the outer movement and the glorious lyricism of the central slow movement.

Concerto for Double String Orchestra; Little Music for Strings
(BB) *** ASV Resonance CD RSN 3057. E. Sinfonia, Farrer – VAUGHAN WILLIAMS: *Dives & Lazarus; Partita* ***

John Farrer conducts strong, athletic performances, very well played and recorded, with slow movements touching but not over-ripe. If you want the fine Vaughan Williams coupling, this is excellent value.

(i) *String Quartet 2 in F sharp*; (ii; iii) *Boyhood's End; The Heart's Assurance*; (ii; iv) *Songs for Ariel*
(M) (***) EMI mono/stereo 5 85150-2. (i) Amadeus Qt; (ii) Pears; (iii) Wood; (iv) Britten – SEIBER: *String Quartet No.3* (***)

A fascinating disc in which some historic Decca recordings (the vocal items) seem to have escaped on to EMI. *Boyhood's End* is a setting of a passage from W. H. Hudson's autobiography, *Far Away and Long Ago*. Its evocation of Hudson's boyhood past – seen from the perspective of him as an old man – in which he recalls his fear of losing his close contact with nature is subtly done, with the vocal line in very expressive arioso style, with much florid decoration. There is great atmosphere, too, with Pears making the very most of all the nuances. *The Heart's Assurance* occupies very much the same world, though with even more brilliant and difficult accompaniments, and the tragic spirit of the poems is beautifully caught. These historic recordings (Pears premièred both these works) dating from 1953 suffer from a little distortion, but are perfectly acceptable. The three short *Songs for Ariel*, written for a 1962 production of *The Tempest*, are short but effective, and are recorded here in stereo. Tippett's *Second String Quartet*, with its opening movement rich in polyphony, a very haunting fugal second movement, a bracing Scherzo and the emotional fervour of the finale, has much to recommend it. This very eloquent performance, in amazingly good (1954) sound, makes a welcome return to the catalogue. An important historical disc, with an unusual coupling.

TOCH, Ernst (1887–1964)
Symphonies 1, Op. 72; 2, Op. 73; 3, Op. 75; 4, Op. 80; 5, Op. 89 (Jephtha); 6, Op. 93; 7, Op. 95
*** CPO 777 191-2 (3). Berlin RSO, Francis

Like his contemporary, Egon Wellesz, Toch came late to the symphony. He enjoyed some success in 1920s' Germany, and the *Geographical Fugue* (1930) gained much admiration. As a teacher he attracted some distinguished pupils, including Vagn Holmboe. He escaped just before Hitler came to power, but it took a long time before he could establish himself in the United States, where he settled in 1940. His *First Symphony* was written at the age of 61 in 1948, not long after he had suffered a heart attack. The *Third Symphony* won a Pulitzer Prize and was recorded in the mid-1950s by William Steinberg and the Pittsburgh orchestra on Capitol. His later music was relatively ignored, though the ever-enterprising Louisville Orchestra recorded the *Fifth*. Toch certainly made up for his neglect of the symphony (a genre which came so naturally to him), for the last three were written in under a year and a half, shortly before his death from cancer in October 1964. The *First* and *Fourth* share the first disc and the *Second* and *Third* the second, while the presentation offers the notes accompanying the individual releases (Nos. 1 and 4 are discussed in our main volume). It is amazing how, when we think there are no composers of the twentieth century left to rediscover, an unfamiliar – and major – figure surfaces. Those investing in this set will be well rewarded.

Tanz-Suite, Op. 30.
** Edition Abseits EDA013-2. Kammersymphonie Berlin,
  Bruns – SCHREKER: *Der Geburtstag der Infantin* **

Ernst Toch's *Dance Suite* comes from 1923. It is an expertly crafted piece, inventive and resourceful. The playing of the Kammersymphonie Berlin under Jürgen Bruns is first rate, and the recording is eminently serviceable.

TOMKINS, Thomas (1572–1656)

ANTHEMS AND MOTETS

Above the Stars; Almighty God, the fountain of all wisdom; Behold, the hour cometh; Glory be to God on high; My Shepherd is the living Lord; O God the proud are risen against me; O sing unto the Lord a new song; Sing unto God; Then David mourned; My beloved spake; When David heard; Third Service: Magnificat and Nunc dimittis
(BB) ** Hyp. Helios CDH 55066. St George's Chapel,
  Windsor, Ch., Robinson, R. Judd (organ)

A varied programme here of anthems, canticles and collects, well sung with good soloists. But the choir is backwardly balanced in a very resonant acoustic, which means that words are not very clear and the singers not well projected. However, the beauty of the music still comes across.

TOMLINSON, Ernest (born 1924)

Aladdin: 3 Dances (Birdcage Dance; Cushion Dance; Belly Dance); Comedy Overture; Cumberland Square; English Folk-Dance Suite 1; Light Music Suite; Passepied; (i) Rhapsody & Rondo for Horn & Orchestra. Brigadoon; Shenandoah (arrangement)
*** Marco Polo 8.223513. (i) Watkins; Slovak RSO
  (Bratislava), composer

The opening *Comedy Overture* is racily vivacious, and there are many charming vignettes here, delectably tuneful and neatly scored, and the pastiche dance movements are nicely elegant. The *Pizzicato humoresque* (from the *Light Music*

Suite) is every bit as winning as other, more famous pizzicato movements, and in the *Rhapsody and Rondo* for horn Tomlinson quotes wittily from both Mozart and Britten. The composer finally lets his hair down in the rather vulgar *Belly Dance*, but the concert ends well with the charming *Georgian Miniature*. The playing is elegant and polished, its scale perfectly judged, and the recording is first class.

An English Overture; 3 Gaelic Sketches: Gaelic Lullaby. Kielder Water; Little Serenade; Lyrical Suite: Nocturne. Nautical Interlude; 3 Pastoral Dances: Hornpipe. Silverthorne Suite; 2nd Suite of English Folk Dances; Sweet and Dainty; arr. of Coates: The Fairy Coach; Cinderella Waltz
*** Marco Polo 8.223413. Slovak RSO (Bratislava), composer

Ernest Tomlinson's orchestral pieces charm by the frothy lightness of the scoring. The winningly delicate *Little Serenade*, which opens the disc, is the most famous, but the gentle, evocative *Kielder Water*, the captivating *Canzonet* from the *Silverthorne Suite* and the *Nocturne* are hardly less appealing. *Love-in-a-mist* is as intangible as it sounds, with the most fragile of oboe solos, and it is not surprising that *Sweet and Dainty* has been used for a TV commercial. There is robust writing, too, in the *Folk Dance Suite* – but not too robust, although the jolly *English Overture* begins with *Here's a Health unto His Majesty* and certainly does not lack vitality. The music is played with much grace and the lightest possible touch by the remarkably versatile Slovak Radio Orchestra under the composer, and the vivid recording has delightfully transparent textures, so vital in this repertoire.

TORCH, Sidney (1908–90)

All Strings and Fancy Free; Barbecue; Bicycle Belles; Comic Cuts; Concerto Incognito; Cresta Run; Duel for Drummers; Going for a Ride; London Transport Suite; Mexican Fiesta; On a Spring Note; Petite Valse; Samba Sud; Shooting Star; Shortcake Walk; Slavonic Rhapsody; Trapeze Waltz
*** Marco Polo 8.223443. BBC Concert O, Wordsworth

Sidney Torch worked frequently with the BBC Concert Orchestra (the orchestra on this CD), and for many he is remembered for his weekly broadcasts 'Friday Night is Music Night'. The *London Transport Suite* was commissioned by the BBC for their Light Music festival of 1957 and was inspired by the withdrawal of the 'Brighton Belle' on the London-to-Brighton railway service. Each of its three movements represents a mode of transport: *The Hansom Cab, Rosie, the Red Omnibus* and *The 5:52 from Waterloo*. All the music here is tuneful, at times wistful and nostalgic, at others bright and breezy – *All Strings and Fancy Free* is both. *Barbecue* sounds like a Scottish snap, while the *Trapeze Waltz* is reminiscent of the circus music of Satie. The *Concerto Incognito* is very much in the *Warsaw Concerto* mould, and the *Petite Valse* (also with piano) is more robust than its title suggests. The *Mexican Fiesta* and *Samba Sud* produce some fine local colour and are very jolly, while the *Slavonic Rhapsody* (with two pianos) is a fun work, drawing on the music of Rimsky-Korsakov, Tchaikovsky, Knipper, Borodin and Khachaturian, to form an entertaining if outrageous pastiche. The longest work is the *Duel for Drummers*, which, as its title suggests, is a *tour de force* for the percussion department; it has some ideas which are reminiscent of Eric Coates and a few surprises, including a cockerel crowing, and a desert-island storm in the central movement. It ends with a lively *galop*. Barry Wordsworth conducts with flair, and the recording is excellent.

TOVEY, Donald (1875–1940)

Symphony in D, Op. 32; The Bride of Dionysis: Prelude
** Toccata TOCC 0033. Malmö Op. O, Vass

It is enterprising of the Toccata company to offer the first modern recording of Tovey's *Symphony*, a massive work lasting nearly an hour. When Tovey wrote so perceptively about other composers' music, including that of contemporaries of his like Sibelius, it is disappointing to find that he seems to have learned little from his many searching analyses. The musical material is deeply unmemorable and the treatment heavy-handed and generally four-square, while the work is not helped by a performance that sounds as though the players are simply sight-reading. The *Prelude* to the opera, *The Bride of Dionysus*, is more overtly Wagnerian in its style, but hardly more memorable. Yet it is fascinating to have an insight into the work of one of the great figures in British music-making from the first half of the twentieth century.

TRIMBLE, Joan (born 1915)

(i) *Phantasy Trio*; (ii; iii) *Music for 2 pianos: The Baird of Lisgoole; Buttermilk Reel; The Green Bough; The Humours of Carrick (Hop-jig); Pastorale: Homage à Poulenc; Puck Fair; Sonatina. 3 Traditional songs: The cows are a-milking; Gartan Mother's lullaby; The heather glen*; (iv; iii) *County Mayo Song Cycle: The County Mayo; Peggy Mitchell; Inis Fail; In the poppy field*; (v; iii) *3 Songs: Girl's song; Green rain; My grief on the sea*
**(*) Marco Polo 8.225059. (i) Dublin Piano Trio; (ii) Hunt; (iii) Holmes; (iv) Corbett; (v) Bardon

In the 1930s, at the suggestion of Arthur Benjamin, Joan and Valerie Trimble established a celebrated piano duo, and in turn he wrote for them the *Jamaican Rumba*, which they made world famous. But Joan proved a talented composer in her own right, drawing on the rich vein of Irish folksong and composing her own pieces in a similar style. Their simplicity and freshness of inspiration give much pleasure, as does the deft keyboard writing. There are other influences too, from the French school in the *Sonatina* and the *Pastorale* and from Vaughan Williams, who suggested the composition of the passionate, yearning *Piano Trio* (*Phantasy*), which is very English in feeling. But it is for the winning Irish keyboard duo pieces that Joan Trimble will be remembered, and they are played here with just the right lightness of touch. The songs are certainly worth preserving on disc, although their performances are less so. Joe Corbett is a sympathetic 'Irish' interpreter of the *County Mayo Cycle*, but his presentation is really distinctive only in the lively final song, *In the poppy field*, with the *Buttermilk Reel* piano duo making a sparkling postlude. The soprano songs, although eloquently sung, are let down by Patricia Bardon's intrusively wide vibrato.

TUBIN, Eduard (1905–82)

Symphonies 1 in C min.; 8
** Alba ABCD 163. Estonian Nat. SO, Volner

The *Eighth* is the darkest and most powerful of Tubin's symphonies, and in it he perhaps permits himself a strain of

bitterness at the shameful neglect he suffered in his adopted Sweden. The *First* is an astonishingly assured work for a young man still in his twenties. Welcome though this coupling is, neither the performance nor the recording is in any way a match for Neeme Järvi's records with the Swedish Radio Symphony Orchestra on BIS.

TURINA, Joaquin (1882–1949)

Danzas fantásticas, Op. 22; La Procesión del Rocio, Op. 9; Ritmos (Fantasia correográfica); Sinfonia sevillana, Op. 17
(BB) ** Naxos 8.555955. Castile & León SO, Bragado-Darman

The Castile & Léon Symphony Orchestra play with relish and enthusiasm for Max Bragado-Derman, and this makes a good and inexpensive entry point for someone investigating Spanish music of the first half of the twentieth century. It is very well recorded, but the Telarc collection is well worth the extra cost.

VALE, Walter (1875–1939)

Requiem Mass in D flat; Hosanna filio David
**(*) Priory PRCD 860 All Saints', Margaret Street, Ch., Brough – RACHMANINOV: *Mass in B flat; Evening Canticles*, etc. **(*)

In 1907, even before Walter Vale as Director of Music at All Saints', Margaret Street, in central London, adapted Rachmaninov's choral pieces for use in the Anglican liturgy, he wrote this *Requiem Mass* in the warm key of D flat. It is a skilful blend of Anglican chant, plainsong and motets in an early twentieth-century style. At the end comes an exuberant setting by Vale of a brief motet, designed for use on Palm Sunday, *Hosanna filio David*, 'Hosanna to the Son of David', making a triumphant conclusion.

VAUGHAN WILLIAMS, Ralph (1872–1958)

Fantasia on Greensleeves; Fantasia on a Theme of Thomas Tallis
(B) * DG Entrée 477 5010. Chicago SO & Ch., Levine – HOLST: *The Planets* **(*)

Alas, the Orpheus performance of the *Tallis Fantasia* suggests a lack of the kind of familiarity and innate understanding of the music which comes with frequent performance. Though there are moments of passion, they are short-lived, and the overall pacing is unconvincing. The bright, vividly clear recording confirms the need for a greater weight and body of tone to help the work expand emotionally.

Fantasia on a Theme of Tallis
◉─▶ ◉(B) (***) EMI mono 4 76880-2. Philh. O, Karajan (with HANDEL (arr. Harty): *Water Music Suite*) – BRITTEN: *Variations on a Theme of Frank Bridge* *** ◉

Karajan's version of the *Tallis Fantasia*, coupled with Britten's *Variations on a Theme of Frank Bridge*, is one of his greatest records, sounding as fresh and sonorous today as it did in the 1950s, when it first appeared. Sonically it is little short of amazing, and artistically it is no less impressive. The playing of the Philharmonia strings for Karajan is altogether superlative, and the *Tallis Fantasia* sounds both idiomatic and vivid, rather like a newly cleaned painting. Recordings of this work are legion, and stereo undoubtedly brings an added dimension, but this mono version ranks among the best. The *Water Music* is an unexpected but welcome bonus, also superbly played.

Fantasia on a Theme by Thomas Tallis; In the Fen Country;
(i) *The Lark Ascending. Norfolk Rhapsody 1;* (ii) *On Wenlock Edge*
(M) **(*) EMI 5 85151-2. LPO, Haitink; with (i) Chang; (ii) Bostridge

These orchestral works were originally fill-ups to Haitink's symphony-cycle, and it was a good idea to reissue them on a single CD. Haitink's way with Vaughan Williams may not always be the most perfectly idiomatic, but his ear for colour and texture is always telling. A good example would be in the *Tallis Fantasia*, where the straight rhythmic manners do sound somewhat unidiomatic; but it is certainly powerful in its monumental directness, especially with the wide-ranging recording. In the *Norfolk Rhapsody* there is also a direct quality which is certainly appealing, especially with the beautiful playing of the LPO; the same comments apply to *In the Fen Country*, even if it doesn't have quite the spontaneous, surging qualities in the climaxes which mark the very best accounts. Sarah Chang proves an intensely poetic soloist in *The Lark Ascending*, volatile at the start in the bird-like fluttering motif and magnetically concentrated throughout. Ian Bostridge is the sensitive, honey-toned soloist in the Housman song-cycle, *On Wenlock Edge*, which ends this disc.

Five Variants on Dives and Lazarus; Partita for Double String Orchestra
(BB) *** ASV Resonance CD RSN 3057. E. Sinfonia, Farrer – TIPPETT: *Concerto for Double String Orchestra,* etc. ***

John Farrer conducts a particularly fine account of *Dives and Lazarus,* opening delicately and finding plenty of contrast between the five variants, leading to a richly eloquent conclusion. The underrated *Partita* too is very persuasively played, again opening seductively, providing a brilliant *Scherzo ostinato* and finale, athletic yet full of lyrical fervour.

5 Variants of Dives and Lazarus; (i) *The Sons of Light; Toward the Unknown Region; The Voice out of the Whirlwind;* (ii) *Willow-Wood*
(BB) *** Naxos 8.557798. (i) RLPO Ch.; RLPO, Lloyd-Jones; (ii) with Williams

Toward the Unknown Region, like the glorious *Dives and Lazarus,* is comparatively well known, but *The Sons of Light* less so. It is a setting of three poems about the creation by Vaughan Williams's wife, Ursula. *The Voice out of the whirlwind* draws on the magical *Galliard for the Songs of the Morning* from *Job.* But the real novelty here is *Willow-Wood,* which lasts about a quarter of an hour and is a setting of Rossetti for baritone, optional female chorus and orchestra; and it is really rather beautiful. Altogether an unexpectedly attractive disc, very well sung and played and recorded.

Symphonies 1–9; Fantasia on Greensleeves; Fantasia on a Theme by Thomas Tallis; Job; (i) *The Lark Ascending; The Wasps: Overture*
(B) ** Warner 2564 51730-2 (6). Soloists, including (i) Tasmin Little; BBC SO, A. Davis

Helped by clear, finely focused sound, Andrew Davis's account of the *Sea Symphony* is a performance that can hardly be faulted on any detail whatsoever but which fails quite to add up to the sum of its parts: it is a degree too literal. So while in Amanda Roocroft and Thomas Hampson you have two of the finest international soloists available, yet they convey too little of the mystery behind these settings of Walt Whitman, and even with bright, clean choral sound one is less involved than with the finest of rival versions. In Nos. 4 and 5 Davis draws beautiful, refined playing from the BBC orchestra, yet again there is a lack of dramatic tension, which – particularly in the violent No. 4 – prevents the performance from catching fire. One can pick out many passages which, with the help of superb recorded sound, are as beautiful as any ever recorded, but the parts do not add up to a satisfying whole.

By contrast, the reading of the *Sixth* is taut and urgent, yet still with emotions kept under firm control. But here Warner's wide-ranging sound, setting the orchestra at a slight distance, blunts the impact in the first three movements somewhat, but then works beautifully in the chill of the hushed *pianissimo* meditation of the finale. No. 9 is attractively coupled with Vaughan Williams's early ballet score, *Job* (intended for Diaghilev but rejected as being 'too English'). The BBC Symphony Orchestra play both scores splendidly and the recording is spacious. However, the orchestra is again set back and some of the impact is lost, especially in the nightmarish Scherzo: the performance too, though finely shaped, again lacks the ultimate degree of concentration. *Job* is very successful and no one could say that the spectacular organ entry (recorded earlier by Andrew Davis in King's College Chapel and effectively dubbed in) does not make a huge impact, while Job's comforters are strongly characterized and the serene closing music, including the lovely *Pavane of the Sons of the Morning,* is radiantly presented. The shorter works are all successful, with Tasmin Little an immaculate soloist in *The Lark Ascending,* playing very beautifully indeed.

Symphonies 2 (London); 6 in E min.; (i) *Prelude & Fugue in C min.*
(B) *** EMI (ADD) 5 86592-2 (2). LPO, Handley; (i) with Bell

These recordings of Vaughan Williams's *Second* and *Sixth,* reissued in a two-disc package in EMI's 'British Composers' series, were made by Vernon Handley and the London Philharmonic in the late 1970s, not long before digital recording took over from analogue. When Handley went on to record a complete cycle of the nine Vaughan Williams symphonies for CfP in digital sound, these earlier versions were put to one side and largely forgotten. Yet this compilation, with excellent transfers, demonstrates that they stand up extraordinarily well, and in some ways are even preferable to the rightly praised CfP versions. That is especially so of the wonderfully rich and evocative *London Symphony,* which benefits from the fuller-bodied, analogue recording, here transferred more immediately and at a higher level. Though the interpretation is very little different, there is more mystery and hushed intensity in this earlier account. The advantages of late analogue sound over early digital are not so great in the *Sixth Symphony.* Again, the differences in interpretation are minimal, though the LPO performance is more polished, if less elemental. As fill-up, the rare *Prelude and Fugue in C minor,* originally written for organ in 1921 and orchestrated a decade later, makes a relatively brief but worthwhile supplement, pointing forward to the later symphonies.

VOCAL MUSIC

(i) *Fantasia on Christmas Carols*. Arr. of carols: *And all in the morning; Wassail Song* (also includes: TRAD., arr. Warlock: *Adam lay y-bounden; Bethlehem down*)
(B) ** EMI (ADD) 7 64131-2. Guildford Cathedral Ch., Pro Arte O, Rose; (i) with Barrow – HELY-HUTCHINSON: *Carol Symphony;* QUILTER: *Children's Overture* **

Vaughan Williams's joyful *Fantasia on Christmas Carols* is comparatively short. It was written for performance in 1912 in Hereford Cathedral, so the acoustic at Guildford Cathedral is apt. The performance here is suitably exuberant, and John Barrow is a good soloist, but not everyone will respond to his timbre and style, and the King's performance with Hervey Alan (currently unavailable) is marginally preferable. But the Christmas carol arrangements are delightful, beautifully sung and recorded. Valuable couplings too.

Serenade to Music
(BB) **(*) HMV (ADD) 5 86733-2. 16 vocal soloists, LPO, Boult – HOLST: *The Planets* ***

The *Serenade to Music*, written in honour of Sir Henry Wood, makes a curious coupling for *The Planets*, but it is good to have a performance which, following the original idea, uses 16 solo singers, though these cannot (except in one or two instances) match the quality of the originals whose initials were placed on the score. The violin soloist disappointingly uses too sweet a style in his important part in the introduction. The recording, however, has fine, atmospheric warmth and the performance overall is beautiful.

The Wasps (complete recording of Aristophanes' play with Overture and incidental music; English translation by David Pountney)
(M) *** Hallé HLD 7510. Henry Goodman (nar.), Hallé Ch. & O, Elder

Vaughan Williams composed his score for Aristophanes' satirical comedy *The Wasps* for a production of the play in Greek at Cambridge University in 1909. Since then the justly famous *Overture* and a 1912 suite (admittedly containing almost all the best music) is all that has been heard of the score, which for the most part is folksy and light-hearted and includes witty quotations from other composers' works. But the choral writing itself is splendid, and the most ambitious part of the score is the *Parabasis* (a diatribe on human behaviour, drawing a parallel with the conduct of wasps, sung directly by the chorus to the audience). In effect this is an ambitious choral scena, which almost immediately quotes from Debussy's *L'après-midi*, and draws from the composer some of his most atmospheric and forward-looking music.

The original play had three characters, but David Pountney's translation reduces the text to a narration from just one, Procleon, a 'curmudgeonly old codger, an old soldier, and a bigot', a part which Henry Goodman takes with relish. A full text is included, but if you do not want to repeat the dialogue it is cued separately; you can programme your player accordingly and just enjoy the superb singing and playing of the Hallé Chorus and Orchestra, vividly directed by Mark Elder, and excellently recorded. A major scoop for the Orchestra's own record label.

OPERA

The Poisoned Kiss (complete)
*** Chan. **SACD** 5020 (2); CD 10120 (2). Jo Watson, Gilchrist, Helen Stephen, Williams, N. Davies, Collins, Adrian Partington Singers, BBC Nat. O of Wales, Hickox

This recording helps towards rehabilitating the opera by eliminating virtually all the spoken dialogue, including it is merely in the libretto, printed in shaded sections. Prefacing the libretto comes a very helpful detailed synopsis, describing each of the 39 numbers and the story in between. One trouble is that neither Vaughan Williams nor Sharp could quite work out the right balance between comedy and the central romance, the love between Tormentilla, brought up on poison by her magician father, Dipsacus, and Prince Amaryllus, son of the Empress Persicaria. Despite the irritations of the libretto, repeated hearings bring out how rich this score is in vintage Vaughan Williams inspiration, with mere doggerel prompting one delectable musical idea after another, and with each number beautifully tailored, never outstaying its welcome. Plainly, Vaughan Williams took the story of forbidden love much more seriously than he perhaps realized even himself. The inspiration never flags, charm predominating, with tenderly beautiful melodies like that in the Act I duet of Amaryllus and Tormentilla, *Blue Larkspur in a Garden*, and a surgingly emotional climax in the ensemble which crowns Act II, when their love leads passionately to the poisoned kiss and the threat of death to Amaryllus.

VELASQUEZ, Glauco (1884–1914)

Album-leaves 1–2; Brutto Sogno; Canzone Strana; Danse de silphes; Devaneio; Divertimento 2; Impromptu; Melancolia; Minuetto e Gavotte Moderni; Petite Suite; Prelúdios 1–2; Prelúdio e Scherzo; Rêverie; Valsa lenta; Valsa romântica
*** Marco Polo 8.223556. Sverner

Glauco Velasquez was an illegitimate child, born in Naples to a Brazilian mother and fathered by a Portuguese singer. When their relationship collapsed, his mother took the boy to Brazil, where he was brought up in ignorance of his father's identity. He soon showed musical aptitude, and by his mid-twenties he had attracted some attention in musical circles with his piano miniatures, recorded here. Their heady melancholy, often in Scriabinesque chromatic writing, is most beguiling. Clara Sverner brings out the personality and charm, and they are very well recorded.

VERACINI, Francesco Maria (1690–1768)

Violin Concertos: a cinque in A & D; a otto stromenti in D. Aria schiavona in B flat for Orchestra (attrib.); *Overture 5 in B flat*
(BB) *** Naxos 8.553413. Accademia I Filarmonici (Verona), Martini

Veracini's *Violin Concerto a otto stromenti* is endearingly ambitious in its scoring, and the brilliant opening, with its two trumpets and oboes, must have made quite an impression when it was first heard in Venice in 1712 at a concert to celebrate the visit of the ambassador of the new Holy Roman Emperor.

Tartini's influence is apparent. The decorative figurations in the outer movements rise and fall in scalic sequence. Some solo passages are left to the soloist to fill in and the unusual minor-key slow movement is very improvisatory in feeling.

The two earlier *Concerti a cinque* are more modest, closer to Vivaldi, although Veracini's own presence is very apparent at times and especially in the finale of the A major work. The *Overture in B flat* is one of the finest of the complete set discussed below, and the *Aria schiavona* is an engaging minuet lollipop, very *galant* in feeling and almost certainly not by Veracini at all. First-class performances throughout with fine solo contributions, presumably from Alberto Martini, the leader of the Accademia I Filarmonici, which claims to have no conductor. The recording is excellent.

Overtures (Suites) 1–6

(BB) *** Naxos 8.553412. Accademia I Filarmonici (Verona), Martini

These overtures were composed for the Dresden court orchestra, probably around 1716. Their character brings a curious amalgam of Italian volatility and German weight, and they have something in common with the orchestral suites of Telemann. Yet Telemann loved instrumental light and shade, whereas Veracini favoured tutti scoring. The music is strong in personality and there is no shortage of ideas, but energy is more important than expressive lyricism, with usually a single brief sarabande to provide contrast as the centrepiece of up to half-a-dozen dance movements.

The Accademia I Filarmonici claim to use the original manuscripts, but they play on modern instruments, and their bright, gleaming sound is full of Italian sunshine. The performances are Italianate and they play the *Sarabandes* of Nos. 1 and 2 with an attractive air of relaxed graciousness, while the sparkling opening movement of No. 6 is made to seem almost a tarantella. So at Naxos price this could well be a first choice.

12 Sonate accademiche, Op. 2

*** Hyp. CDA 66871/3 (3). Locatelli Trio

Alongside his fame as a composer, Veracini was renowned as a master of the violin: he boasted that there 'was but one God and one Veracini', so that even Tartini was intimidated by his prowess. The twelve *Sonate accademiche* date from 1744. They are much more Italianate than the overtures, though German influence remains strong. The writing has a rhapsodic exuberance and drive, and, as with the overtures, dance movements predominate. But there are touching lyrical interludes and some lovely slow movements. The last *Sonata* is masterly, opening with a descending minor scalic theme, which is first used for a *Passacaglia*, then for a *Capriccio cromatico*, and finally provides the basis for an ambitious closing *Ciaccona*. The Locatelli Trio, led by Elizabeth Wallfisch, are a first-class group, and their authentic style, strongly etched, is full of joy in the music's vitality, while the composer's lyrical side is most persuasively revealed. Paul Nicholson's continuo is very much a part of the picture, especially in the works using an organ, which is very pleasingly balanced. The recording is vivid and immediate.

VERDI, Giuseppe (1813–1901)

Requiem Mass

(BB) *** HMV (ADD) 5 86780 (2). Scotto, Baltsa, Luchetti, Nesterenko, Amb. Ch., Philh. O, Muti

(i) *Requiem Mass*; (ii) *4 Sacred Pieces*

(M) *** Decca (ADD) 475 7735 (2). (i) Sutherland, Norman, Pavarotti, Talvela; VPO, Solti

(M) *(*) Warner Elatus 2564 60119-2 (2). Marc, Meier, Domingo, Furlanetto, Chicago Ch. & SO, Barenboim

With spectacular sound – not always perfectly balanced but vividly wide in its tonal spectrum – Muti's 1979 Kingsway Hall recording has tremendous impact. Characteristically, he prefers fast speeds, and in the *Dies irae* he rushes the singers dangerously, making the music breathless in its excitement rather than grandly dramatic in its portrayal of the Day of Wrath. It is not surprising that Muti opted for a professional choir rather than the Philharmonia Chorus, and the engineers are able to give it fine impact. Unashamedly, this is an operatic performance from first to last, with a passionately committed quartet of soloists, underpinned by Nesterenko in glorious voice, giving priestly authority to the *Confutatis*. Scotto is not always sweet at the top, but Baltsa is superb, and Luchetti sings freshly. Generally this Muti recording must be counted first choice among bargain versions – excellent value.

Solti's Decca performance, now reissued as one of Universal's series of Originals, is not really a rival to any other. He plays up the dramatic side of the work at the expense of the spiritual, his conception very operatic. The team of soloists is strong, so if you want an extrovert performance with spectacular recording, you could hardly do better.

Daniel Barenboim conducts a warm, powerful performance, which is not helped by a lack of weight in the recording, made in Orchestra Hall, Chicago. With the chorus less well focused than it should be, the glory of the set lies in the solo singing from an exceptionally starry quartet, all individually characterful, yet well matched as a team. Ensemble is often less crisp than one would expect from this source, so this version must be relegated to the also-rans.

4 Sacred Pieces (Quattro pezzi sacri)

(M) ** Sony SMK 89619. Sweet, Ernest Senff Ch., BPO, Giulini – VIVALDI: *Credo, RV 591* (revised Malipiero) *(*)

Giulini's Berlin account of the *Quattro pezzi sacri*, mystical and serene, is beautiful in its way. Tempi are leisurely, and the distanced chorus in a warm acoustic provides the widest dynamic contrast at the opening of the *Te Deum*, moving from *pianopianissimo* to a *fortefortissimo* at the *Sanctus*. Yet the performance overall sadly lacks vitality and does not compare in intensity with his earlier EMI recording.

OPERA

Aida (complete; CD version)

(M) (**) EMI mono 5 56316-2 (3). Callas, Tucker, Barbieri, Gobbi, La Scala, Milan, Ch. & O, Serafin

The Nile Scene has never been performed more powerfully and characterfully on record than in this vintage La Scala set. Though Callas is not a sweet-toned Aida, her detailed imagination is irresistible, and she is matched by Tito Gobbi at the very height of his powers. Tucker gives one of his very finest performances on record, and Barbieri is a commanding Amneris. The mono sound is greatly improved in the latest transfer.

Attila (complete DVD version)

*** Opus Arte DVD 09478 03010. Ramey, Zancanaro, Studer, Kaludov, Gavazzi, Luperi, La Scala, Milan, Ch. and O, Muti

The 1991 production of *Attila* from La Scala with Riccardo Muti taut and incisive in this strong, compact piece is outstandingly dramatic. It helps that the chorus takes a vital part, rather as it does in the even earlier *Nabucco*. There are also anticipations of later Verdi operas like *Rigoletto*, notably in the storm scene. The relative brevity of the piece, with one key number following promptly on another, makes a strong impact on DVD, in a production with traditional costumes and using minimal but atmospheric sets. Samuel Ramey in the title-role and Giorgio Zancanaro as the Roman general, Ezio, both at their peak, in their nicely contrasted ways firm and dark, are ideally cast, with Cheryl Studer also outstanding as Odabella.

Un ballo in maschera (complete CD version)
(M) *** DG 477 5641 (2). Domingo, Barstow, Nucci, Quivar, Jo, V. State Op. Konzertvereinigung, VPO, Karajan

Recorded in Vienna early in 1989, *Un ballo in maschera* was Karajan's last opera recording. It was done in conjunction with the new production at that year's Salzburg Festival, which Karajan was scheduled to conduct. He died only days before the first night, while the production was already in rehearsal. The recording makes a fitting memorial, characteristically rich and spacious with a cast – if not ideal – which still makes a fine team, responding to the conductor's single-minded vision. Karajan's understanding of dynamic contrasts in the final assassination scene, for example, is thrilling, demonstrating his undiminished sense of drama. Standing out vocally is the Gustave of Plácido Domingo, strong and imaginative, dominating the whole cast. He may not have the sparkle of Pavarotti in this role, but the singing is richer, more refined and more thoughtful. Karajan's unexpected and controversial choice of Josephine Barstow as Amelia certainly makes for a striking and characterful performance, even if it is flawed vocally, with the tone growing raw under pressure. Nevertheless, this is Barstow's finest achievement on record, and she is most compelling dramatically. Leo Nucci, though not as rough in tone as in some of his other recordings, is over-emphatic, with poor legato in his great solo, *Eri tu*. Sumi Jo, a Karajan discovery, gives a delicious performance as Oscar, the page, coping splendidly with Karajan's slow speed for her Act I solo. Florence Quivar produces satisfyingly rich tone as Ulrica. Though the sound is not as cleanly focused as in the Decca recording for Solti, it is warm and full.

Un ballo in maschera: highlights
(BB) * Warner Apex 2564 61504-2 (from complete recording, with Leech, Chernov, Crider, Zaremba, Bayo, Welsh Nat. Ch. & O, Rizzi).

Carlo Rizzi draws crisp, amiably relaxed performances from his Welsh National Opera forces, yet the result is disappointing. Too many of the cast have voices which do not take easily to recording, with wobbles and vibrato exaggerated by the microphones. That is especially true of the soprano, Michele Crider, who sings Amelia – although neither the Russian baritone (Vladimir Chernov) as Renato nor the Russian mezzo (Elena Zaremba) as Ulrica are ideally steady. Most successful among the soloists is the bright, clear Spanish coloratura, Maria Bayo, as Oscar. The ensembles come over well, thanks largely to the conductor, but this is not really a satisfying selection.

Ernani (complete DVD version)
*** Warner DVD 4509 99213-2. Domingo, Freni, Bruson, Ghiaurov, La Scala, Milan, Ch. & O, Muti

Although the cast is starry, it is Muti who ensures that this live La Scala, Milan, production of *Ernani* is so gripping, as we know from the CD set (EMI 7 47083-2 – see our main volume). Even if Mirella Freni at the opening sounds strained, it is still a powerful, rich-voiced performance, and Bruson is here on better form than on the CD set and he makes a superb contribution as Don Carlo, while Ghiaurov, as on CD, is a characterful Silva. But it is Domingo's set and he sings magnificently, while the staging is traditional, thank goodness, though not unimaginative. Good camera angles, too.

Ernani (complete CD version)
🔊 (M) *** Decca 475 7008 (2). Pavarotti, Sutherland, Nucci, Burchuladze, Welsh Nat. Op. Ch. & O, Bonynge

Bonynge's celebrated Decca (late 1990s) recording now returns to the catalogue at mid-price (with libretto included). Sutherland gives a commanding account of the role of Elvira, and though the beat in her voice betrays her age, the challenging aria, *Ernani involami*, brings not just power but all the old flexibility. Helped by the sympathetic conducting of her husband, Richard Bonynge, she endearingly throws caution to the winds. Pavarotti too, balanced rather close, gives a vividly characterful portrait of Ernani himself, always ready to shade down his tone, characteristically bringing out the word-meaning. Leo Nucci as Don Carlo, the King, his rival in love, is also firmer and more characterful than others on disc, and Paata Burchuladze as the vengeful de Silva was caught here at the brief peak of his career, his dark, sinister bass well controlled. On sound terms, this reissue easily outshines its CD rivals.

Falstaff (complete DVD versions)
*** TDK DVD DV-OPFAL. Maestri, Frontali, Frittoli, Mula, Flórez, Di Nissa, Antonacci, Gavazzi, Barbacini, Roni, La Scala, Milan, Ch. & O, Muti (V/D: Pierre Cavasillas)
**(*) BBC Opus Arte DVD OA 0812D. Terfel, Frittoli, Rancatore, Manca di Nissa, Montague, Frontali, Tarver, Leggate, Howell, ROHCG Ch. & O, Haitink
(**(*)) Arthaus DVD mono 101 083. Gramm, Luxon, Griffel, Gale, Cosotti, Condo, Fryatt, Dickerson, Trama, Glyndebourne Ch., Philh. O, Pritchard (V/D: Dave Heather)

Muti's *Falstaff* was recorded at the Teatro Verdi, Busseto, in 2001 to celebrate the centenary of the composer's death, acted out against copies of the same sets usd by Toscanini in 1913. With Muti on his best form, the performance is warmly and sparklingly worthy of the occasion, with a Falstaff who looks the part, and has the size of voice and personality to carry this lovable Shakespearean character naturally without any hamming or exaggeration. The lively ladies of the cast are equally personable: Barbara Frittoli's resourceful Alice is matched by Roberto Frontali's very believable Ford, while Juan Diego Flórez (Fenton) and Inva Mula (Nannetta) are a charming pair of lovers who sing as attractively as they look. With excellent sound and fine video direction, this *Falstaff* goes to the top of the DVD list and it will be hard to beat.

Graham Vick's provocative DVD production with crudely-coloured toy-town sets by Paul Brown was the opening attraction in the newly refurbished Covent Garden opera-house. It is powerfully conducted by Bernard Haitink as Music Director who, in a brief interview, rightly suggests that this is a score with not a superfluous note. The production's principal asset is the strong, characterful Falstaff of Bryn Terfel, musically and dramatically most satisfying despite his grotesquely exaggerated costume and pot-belly. In the tradition of the finest Falstaffs, he is at once comic and dignified and ultimately moving, while the voice is in splendid form. Barbara Frittoli also makes an excellent Alice, and the rest of the cast is consistently fine. The problem lies in the sets with their aggressive primary colours and simplistic lines, though the false perspectives have a vaguely medieval look.

The costumes, although equally garish, are in Elizabethan style, and Vick allows Falstaff to be tipped into the Thames in a genuine laundry basket, but he removes all magic from the final Windsor Forest scene, with a tower of bodies (intrepid members of the chorus) taking the place of Herne's Oak. In an interview (one of the extra features) Vick explains that he wanted to bring out the physicality of the piece, emphasizing that this is an Italian opera, not a Shakespeare play. The interview with Terfel is not helped by the questioner who is rather too pleased with himself, but the singer's warm personality overrides that drawback. There is also a 10-minute tour backstage of the newly-refurbished opera-house, and an illustrated synopsis of the opera. Unlike many operas on DVD this one has ample index points, with 31 chapters or tracks.

Donald Gramm's *Falstaff* is well (if not memorably) sung and elegantly characterized and with a proper touch of dignity; and he gets excellent support from a fine cast, notably from Benjamin Luxon as Ford and Kay Griffel's bright-eyed portrayal of Alice. Elizabeth Gale's fresh Nannetta and Max-René Cosotti's very eligible Fenton make a delightful pair of lovers, silhouetted behind sheets in Act I, an example of Jean-Pierre Ponnelle's engaging production, typical of Glyndebourne at its finest in 1976. The lesser characters, John Fryatt's Dr Caius, Bernard Dickerson's Bardolph and Ugo Trama's Pistol, are all well observed, and there are nice touches of humour. Pritchard keeps the action sparkling and the cameras seem always to be in the right place. The sound is mono, but very acceptable.

La forza del destino (1862 version; complete CD version)
(M) ***** DG 477 5621 (3). Plowright, Carreras, Bruson, Burchuladze, Baltsa, Amb. Op. Ch., Philh. O, Sinopoli

Sinopoli's *Gramophone* award-winning set is here reissued at mid-price (with a keyed synopsis instead of a libretto). Sinopoli's performance is notable for the creamy soprano of Rosalind Plowright, Agnes Baltsa's splendidly assured Preziosilla and Paata Burchuladze's resonant portrayal of the Padre Guardiano. Although this recording won the *Gramophone* Opera Reward in 1987, it is not now a first choice. Sinopoli draws out phrases lovingly, sustaining pauses to the limit, putting extra strain on the singers. Happily, the whole cast thrives on the challenge, and the spaciousness of the recording acoustic not only makes the dramatic interchanges the more realistic, it brings out the bloom on all the voices. Though José Carreras is sometimes too conventionally histrionic, even strained, it is a strong, involved performance. Renato Bruson is a thoughtful Carlo, while some of the finest singing of all comes from Agnes Baltsa as Preziosilla.

Macbeth (complete DVD version)
* Opus Arte **DVD** OA 0922 D (2). Alvarez, Guleghina, Scandiuzzi, Berti, Liceu Ch. and O, Campanella (Director: Phyllida Lloyd; V/D: Toni Bargallo)

Extravagantly spread over two DVDs, the production from the Liceu in Barcelona offers a striking version, set on a bare stage with stylized geometric squares taking the place of scenery. It works surprisingly well, with the opening chorus of witches – a large contingent – singing powerfully, dressed

in black with vermilion turbans. Otherwise costumes are relatively conventional. The drama of the piece is intensified by the sharp attack and crisp ensemble secured by the conductor, Bruno Campanella, though the dryness of the Liceu acoustic is no help for the atmospheric moments. Even more than Carlos Alvarez as a fine Macbeth, Maria Guleghina dominates the performance as Lady Macbeth, singing with a generous vibrato, well controlled, and staring hypnotically with wide, madly obsessed eyes. She rises well to the challenge of her sleepwalking scene, even if her final top note develops into a scream. Roberto Scandiuzzi is first rate as Banquo, but Marco Berti makes a coarse if confident Macduff.

Nabucco (complete DVD version)
* TDK **DVD** DVWW OPNAB. Nucci, Dvorský, Prestia, Guleghina, Domashenko, V. Op. Ch. & O, Luisi (Director: Gunter Kraker; V/D: Anton Reitzenstein)

Recorded at the Vienna State Opera in 2001, the TDK disc offers a spectacular production, which makes full use of the very large stage. At the opening, the enormous chorus instantly establishes the dominance of choral music in this work, not just the ever-popular *Chorus of Hebrew Slaves* but in key numbers throughout the piece. This biblical story is updated to the 1940s, bringing out the parallels with the plight of the Jewish people in Europe at that time. The costumes are drab and dark, with the men in trilbies or bowler hats, with Abigaille providing a contrast in her elaborate costumes, reflecting her association with Nabucco and the Babylonian court. Maria Guleghina sings compellingly; but it is the two bass roles that provide the key to any performance and, though Giacomo Prestia is not always ideally steady, his is a powerful performance, a good match for the strong Nabucco of Leo Nucci. Marina Domashenko as Fenena and Miroslav Dvorský as Ismaele are well cast, too; but it is the chorus that dominates, with Fabio Luisi securing splendid ensemble. Sadly, there is no synopsis of the plot, but instead a good essay about the background to this first of Verdi's big successes.

Otello (complete DVD version)
* TDK **DVD** DV-OPOTEL. Domingo, Frittoli, Nucci, Catani, Ceron, La Scala, Milan, Children's Ch., Ch. & O, Muti (V/D: Carlo Battistoni)

Imaginatively overseen by Graham Vick, who never seems to let his personal conception override Verdi's intentions, and with an imaginative set and traditional costumes, this *Otello* is very recommendable, with Domingo and Frittoli always singing and acting movingly, to create a real-life situation of passion and tenderness ruined by unthinking jealousy. By their side, Leo Nucci's Iago is disappointingly low-key, and Cesare Catani's Cassio is not memorable either. But Muti directs with his usual brio and the video presentation is admirable. Even with the disappointing Iago, this still projects Verdi's great opera very powerfully, for the sound is first class.

Rigoletto (complete CD version)
(M) ***(**)** RCA (ADD) 82876 70785-2 (2). Merrill, Moffo, Kraus, Flagello, Elias, RCA Italiana Op. Ch. & O, Solti

Robert Merrill sang Rigoletto in a very early RCA LP version of the opera but, if anything, this reissued set from 1963 is even more impressive, with its rich flow of tone and clean-styled musical strength. The Gilda of Anna Moffo is enchanting and, aided by the rest of the production, gives a firm interpretation. Admittedly she is not always helped by Solti's conducting, for he seems determined to rush everyone on, and his beat is often too stiff for middle-period Verdi. But that is a comparatively small drawback, for the briskness brings a consistent intensity to the interpretation, and there are only the barest 'statutory' cuts. The recording too, like the rest of this series, is very good for its period. The snag is that while the reissue reproduces the original LP artwork, a libretto with translation is accessible (using the second disc) only via a CD-ROM drive which 'may not work on all computers'.

(i) *Rigoletto*: highlights; (ii) *La Traviata*: highlights; (iii) *Il Trovatore*: highlights (all sung in English)

(B) *(*) CfP 2-CD 585 0052 (2). (i) Harwood, Smith; (i; iii) Glossop; (ii) June, Wakefield, Easton; (iii) Fretwell, Craig, Johnson; Sadler's Wells Op. Ch. & O, (i) Lockhart; (ii) Matheson; (iii) Moores

Early Verdi is very difficult to bring off in English, and none of these excerpts can be counted a complete success, even though the Sadler's Wells teamwork is excellent as ever. In *Rigoletto* James Lockhart tends to race things through in what sounds like an intended imitation of Toscanini-methods. It can come off in the theatre, but here the effect is rather too hard for comfort. Elizabeth Harwood's Gilda is disappointing, and Peter Glossop is not at his best either. Only Donald Smith as the Duke acquits himself really well, and even he is adversely affected by the absurdities of the translation.

The collection of *La Traviata* highlights only serves to emphasize the stiffness that sometimes seemed to afflict Sadler's Wells singers in the early 1960s, and although it is good to have reminders of John Wakefield as Alfredo Germont and Ava June as Violetta, it would be idle to pretend that her performance matches today's international standards.

With *Il Trovatore* the best items are the ensembles, the *Miserere* and the finale to the Convent Scene, which have splendid attack. The solo singing stands up less well. Elizabeth Fretwell is rather shaky in *Tacea la notte*, and it is left to Charles Craig to stand out as Manrico – as ringing and well-controlled a tenor as any of his generation. Neither Patricia Johnson as Azucena nor Peter Glossop as the Count is up to their stage form. All in all, this reissue is a disappointment.

Simon Boccanegra (complete CD version)

(M) ** Decca 475 7011 (2). Nucci, Te Kanawa, Burchuladze, Aragall, Coni, La Scala, Milan, Ch. & O, Solti

The glory of Solti's reissued set from the late 1980s is the singing of Kiri Te Kanawa as Amelia, a beautiful, touching performance. The freedom and absence of strain in the voice go with an almost Straussian quality in her characterization, with the widest dynamic and expressive range. Giacomo Aragall makes a strong, unforced Gabriele, but the others are less distinguished. As a cast, this line-up hardly matches that of Abbado on the rival DG set (449 752-2). Leo Nucci is most disappointing, the voice showing signs of wear, not nearly steady enough. He sings powerfully, but Boccanegra's solo in the great Council Chamber scene finds the voice spreading. Burchuladze also is surprisingly less steady than usual, and Paolo Coni as Paolo is capable but undistinguished. What also makes this a less compelling reading compared with the DG is Solti's obsession with observing the metronome markings in the score very precisely – laudable in theory, but often questionable in practice; so the great recognition scene between Boccanegra and his daughter is powerfully dramatic at a speed faster than usual, but it lacks tenderness and fails to

convey the joy of recognition which Abbado finds so movingly. The sound of the DG analogue version is also preferable, less wide-ranging, but with the voices more realistically focused.

La traviata (complete CD versions)

(M) ** RCA (ADD) 82876 70778-2 (2). Caballé, Bergonzi, Milnes, RCA Italiana Op. Ch. & O, Prêtre

(M) *(*) Sony SM2K 90457 (2). Fabbricini, Alagna, Coni, La Scala, Milan, Ch. & O, Muti

Caballé, in her 1967 RCA recording, gives a wonderfully poised and pure account of Violetta's music, but this was one of her earlier complete-opera sets, and she still had to learn how to project depth of emotion. Vocally, with such fine technicians as Bergonzi and Milnes as her colleagues, this set is satisfying but does not add up as a dramatic experience. One is rarely moved, and that is also partly the fault of the conductor, Georges Prêtre, a degree too detached for Verdi. Good recording for its period, and an absolutely complete text. The reissue reproduces the original LP cover picture; but, alas, a libretto with translation is accessible (using the second disc) only via a CD-ROM drive, which 'may not work on all computers'.

Response to Muti's Sony version will depend greatly on the ear's response to the voice of Tiziana Fabbricini as Violetta. Its Callas-like tang goes with many of the same vocal flaws which afflicted that supreme diva, but Fabbricini has nothing like the same musical imagination or charisma. The effort is hardly worth it for, although she produces one or two impressive top notes in *Sempre libera* at the end of Act I, the edge on the voice is genuinely unattractive. Muti, always a taut Verdian, does not pace the opera any more sympathetically here than in his earlier, EMI set, and in a live performance the flaws of ensemble are distracting, with the dry La Scala acoustic generally unhelpful, despite clever balancing by the Sony engineers. Paolo Coni is a strong, smooth-toned Germont but not very imaginative, and the main enjoyment in the set comes from the fresh, virile singing of the tenor Roberto Alagna as Alfredo. However, this is another of those Sony reissues with neither a libretto nor a cued synopsis.

La traviata (highlights)

(BB) ** EMI Encore (ADD) 5 74760-2 (from complete recording, with Sills, Gedda, Panerai, John Alldis Ch., RPO, Ceccato)

Beverly Sills makes an affecting Violetta, producing much lovely singing, although when she is pressed her voice grows shrill and unfocused. The character of an older woman knowing what suffering is to come remains firm, however, and with a fine Alfredo in Gedda this is a very acceptable set of highlights, when Panerai is a strong-voiced, if not subtle Germont and Aldo Ceccato proves an alert and colourful conductor. The RPO play well for him, and the closely miked recording is almost too vivid in its CD transfer. It is a pity that the selection (only 59 minutes) is not more generous, and the synopsis is sparsely inadequate.

Il trovatore (complete DVD version)

*** TDK **DVD** DV-CLOPIT. Kabaivanska, Domingo, Cappuccilli, Cossotto, Van Dam, V. State Op. Ch. & O, Karajan (V/D: Günther Schneider-Siemssen)

Domingo joined the production only at the last moment and so ensured that this 1978 *Il Trovatore* was all but ideally cast and with Karajan returning to the Vienna State Opera to rect an undoubtedly great performance. How lucky we are that the cameras were there and that the staging was traditional, with no silly quirks, indeed nothing to mar an evening of glorious singing, with Cappuccilli in first-class voice as Count de Luna matching his famous troubadour adversary. As for Fiorenza Cossotto's Azucena, it is surely unsurpassable in our own time. And José van Dam is there too, to sing one of Verdi's finest arias at the opening of the opera. Perhaps Raina Kabaivanska does not quite match the others in sheer beauty of voice, but dramatically she is a very convincing Leonora indeed, so one can see why Manrico and the Count are willing to fight to the death to win her. It is a live performance, so understandably the audience applause interrupts at times, but their presence adds to the adrenalin flow. Fortunately, Günther Schneider-Siemssen's video direction is very well managed, and the sound is first class.

Il trovatore (complete CD versions)

M) *** DG 477 5915 (2). Plowright, Domingo, Fassbaender, Zancanaro, Nesterenko, Ch. & O of St Cecilia Ac., Rome, Giulini

3B) ** Arte Nova (ADD) 74321 72110-2 (2). Bogza, Svetanov, Alperyn, Morosow, Bratislava Nat. Op. Ch., Bratislava Slovak RSO, Anguelov

3) *(*) Double Decca 460 735-2 (2). Sutherland, Pavarotti, Wixell, Horne, Ghiaurov, L. Op. Ch., Nat. PO, Bonynge

*) Sony S2K 89533 (2). Frittoli, Licitra, Urmana, Nucci, La Scala Ch. & O, Muti

As it so happens, DG have also re-released, as one of their Originals, Domingo's later (1984) portrayal of Manrico on CD, perhaps even more heroic and only very occasionally showing signs of vocal strain. Giorgio Zancanaro matches him with a firmly resonant Count, but the special joy of this set is Rosalind Plowright's Leonora, the singing not just having sweetness and purity (one can imagine her ending up in a convent) but with spirited and brilliantly flexible coloratura. Giulini's tempi are measured, but the intensity of concentration is in no doubt, and the recording is both naturally balanced and vivid.

The Arte Nova version, an enjoyable super-bargain issue, stems from a live concert performance, well recorded, with a good team of young soloists and fresh, vigorous playing and singing from the Bratislava choir and orchestra under the conductor Ivan Anguelov. This may not be a subtle performance, but the dramatic bite of a live occasion, well rehearsed, comes over very well. Anda-Louise Bogza makes a strong, vehement Leonora with plenty of temperament, and Boiko Svetanov as Manrico sings with clean, firm tone, if explosively from time to time. Shining out even from the others is Graciela Alperyn as Azucena, with a firm, strong mezzo and splendid chest register, well controlled, attacking notes fearlessly. As the Conte di Luna, Igor Morosow is strong and clear except under strain on top. A full libretto in Italian is provided, but no translation.

Bonynge in most of his opera sets has been unfailingly urgent and rhythmic, but his account of *Il trovatore* is at an altogether lower level of intensity. Nor does the role of Leonora prove very apt for Sutherland late in her career; the coloratura passages are splendid, but a hint of unsteadiness is present in too much of the rest. Pavarotti for the most part sings superbly, but he falls short in, for example, the semiquaver groups of *Di quella pira* and, like Sutherland, Marilyn Horne as Azucena does not produce a consistently firm tone. Wixell as the Count sings intelligently, but a richer tone is needed. The CD transfer cannot be faulted.

When there are many fine versions of this opera, it seems a waste to have a live recording from Muti and La Scala forces which might just pass muster in a radio broadcast, but which is far too flawed for repeated listening. Even Barbara Frittoli is well below form as Leonora, not as steady as usual, and though Salvatore Licitra as Manrico has a ringing tenor, he uses it with little subtlety, while Leo Nucci is a mere shadow of his former self, singing coarsely throughout, too often failing to pitch notes at all, resorting to a sort of sing-speech. By far the best soloist is Violeta Urmana as Azucena, even if she sounds too young for the role. Muti is at his least sympathetic, forcing the pace so as to make the music sound breathless and brutal, and though five performances were edited together for the recording, the musical imprecisions and stage noises counterbalance any of the advantages of a live event. The sound too has little bloom on it.

I vespri siciliani (complete DVD version)

*** Opus Arte **DVD** OALS 3008D. Studer, Zancanaro, Merritt, Furlanetto, La Scala, Milan, Ch. & O, Muti (V/D: Preben Montell)

As with *Ernani*, we have had this production already on CD (EMI 7 54043-2 – see our main volume) and again it is Muti who, conducting tautly, ensures that this live performance carries high drama, with the orchestra too playing splendidly. Cheryl Studer sings gloriously as Elena and Chris Merritt (as Arrigo) is in even better form here than on the CD set. They get excellent support from Giorgio Zancanaro as Montfort, the Governor of Sicily who also turns out to be Arrigo's father – while Ferruccio Furlanetto, who is vocally less strong than his colleagues, still cuts a convincing figure as Procida. As with *Ernani*, the production is straightforward, with no crazy impositions from a self-conscious stage director. The ballet is included, but it is presented effectively and danced well, and the music is tuneful enough. Excellent sound, too.

'Verdi Heroines': Arias from: *Aida; Un ballo in maschera; Ernani; La forza del destino; Macbeth (Sleepwalking scene); Otello; La Traviata; Il trovatore*

(M) *** RCA (ADD) 82876 7629-2. Leontyne Price (with various orchestras and conductors)

A famous collection from the 1960s, issued without additions. However, Leontyne Price, peerless in her generation, is here at her finest in virtually all these arias, recorded between 1959 and 1967, at the peak of her career, with the glorious voice well caught in the transfers. Full texts and translations included.

Arias from: *Don Carlo; Otello*

(M) **(*) Decca Classic Recitals (ADD) 475 7167. Weathers, V. Op. O, Quadri – PUCCINI: Arias ***

Felicia Weathers had a glorious tone-quality, which comes over well in this 1966 recital, and her Verdi singing is most beautiful. Next to the Puccini items, the Verdi is not quite so polished: the *Willow Song* and *Ave Maria* are not quite as poised as they might be, and *Tu che la vanità* clearly taxes her to the limit; but none of these points seriously distract from one's pleasure. With the excellent Puccini items, very good sound and conducting, this is a very worthy addition to Decca's Classic Recitals series.

'Nilsson Sings Verdi'. Arias from: *Don Carlo; La forza del destino; Macbeth; Nabucco*

(M) **(*) Decca Classic Recitals (ADD) 475 6413. Nilsson, ROHCG Ch. & O, Quadri

This Verdi recital dates from 1962 and opens with Nilsson's impressive Lady Macbeth arias, in which her sharp-toned voice is most impressive. She is less successful in the *La forza del destino* arias, and *Pace Pace* is too hard to make it truly convincing. If Nilsson fails to make the mezzo aria from *Don Carlo* an attractive vehicle for a soprano (largely because her chest register is so un-Italian), there is no doubting her distinctive character and personality (not to mention a huge voice), and Nilsson fans will especially enjoy this recital – if only we had singers of such commanding power today! Vivid recording and conducting.

Arias from: *Macbeth; Nabucco; Simon Boccanegra; I vespri siciliani*

(M) *** Decca Classic Recitals (ADD) 475 6280. Ghiaurov, Amb. S., LSO, Abbado

By any standards, this is an impressive recital – though, when released in 1970, obvious comparisons were made with the great singers of the 78-r.p.m. period, whose memory is still very much with us. But make no mistake, Ghiaurov was a wonderful bass who produced a marvellous tone, and he sings beautifully and stylishly throughout this recording: we would be lucky to hear a singer of this distinction in any opera house today. This highly enjoyable (if short) CD is well worth buying, especially as the recording and conducting are equally fine.

Choruses from: *Aida; La battaglia di Legnano; Don Carlos; I Lombardi; Macbeth; Nabucco; Otello; Il trovatore*

(BB) ** Warner Apex 0927 40836-2. St Cecilia Ch. & O, Rizzi

These are certainly very well-sung accounts of Verdi's most popular choruses, but Rizzi concentrates on refinement rather than on drama. The result lacks the raw energy that can make these warhorses so exciting. Compared with Decca's rival (1960s) recording with the same orchestra under Franci (now on Opera Gala 458 237-2), these digital performances feel a little anaemic. Side by side, the ubiquitous *Anvil Chorus* and *Grand March* from *Aida* sound tame compared to the Decca set, which has more character and excitement. Even if there is some tape hiss, the Decca sound is palpably more vivid and theatrical too, and if it costs a little more, there are almost 15 minutes' extra music, and full texts and translations are provided.

VICTORIA, Tomás Luis de
(c. 1548–1611)

Officium defunctorum (Requiem, 1605); Motet: Versa est in luctum

☛ (B) *** Gimell CDGIM 205 (2). Tallis Scholars, Philips – CARDOSO: *Requiem*; Duarte LOBO: *Requiem*; Alonso LOBO: *Motets* ***

The Tallis Scholars achieve great clarity of texture in this masterly work; they are 12 in number and, as a result, the polyphony is clearer and so are the words. They embrace also the motet, *Versa est in luctum*, which Victoria included as an appendix to his score. This outstanding performance of the *Requiem* is also available on a single disc with Alonso Lôbo's setting of the same motet text (see our main volume), but the

present two-CD set includes Duarte Lôbo's *Requiem* as we as more motets by Alonso.

VIERNE, Louis (1870–1937)

Messe solennelle

*** Priory PRDC 597. Mark Lee (organ); (i) with Gloucester Cathedral Ch., David Briggs – LANGLAIS: *Organ Pieces* & *Messe solennelle* ***

Vierne's setting of the *Messe solennelle* is less dependent o dramatically turbulent organ contrasts with the choir tha the coupled work of Langlais, with the organ's role he more fully integrated. But it is still a Mass setting which both thrilling and full of cantabile melody, and the *Sanct* builds richly and climactically to the closing *Hosanna*. T Benedictus is full of gentle radiance, while the *Agnus D* brings a moving tranquillity, the *Donna nobis pacem* qui magical. The performance here could not be more symp thetic and is not in the least Anglican-sounding. It remarkable that an English cathedral choir and organ should be able to capture the music's essence so moving Congratulations to all concerned, including the recordir producer, Caroline Paschalides.

VILLA-LOBOS, Heitor (1887–1959)

Bachianas brasileiras (i) *1;2;* (ii) *3–4;* (iii) *5;* (iv) *6–9*

*** Naxos 8.557460 (3). (ii) Feghali, (iii) Lamosa, (iv) Gratton; Nashville SO, (i) Mogrelia, (ii–iv) Schermerhorn

Villa-Lobos is enjoying some considerable exposure on C these days. Both the symphonies and the string quartets ar rewarding: none of the 17 quartets finds him repeating him self in any way. The present issue makes an excellent intro duction to the composer, and its three CDs assemble the nir *Bachianas brasileiras* he composed between 1930 and 194 They were conceived as homage to Bach and range fro instrumental and chamber pieces (like the *First* for an orches tra of cellos, the *Fifth* for voice and eight cellos, and the *Six* for flute and bassoon) to larger orchestral forces (the *Nin* for strings and the *Third* for piano and orchestra and Nos. and 8 for orchestra). They are all highly original and most colourful, and they are very well played. José Feghali is a excellent soloist in the *Third*, as is Rosana Lamosa in th well-known *Fifth*. The Nashville orchestra respond wit enthusiasm to Kenneth Schermerhorn who, alas, died befor he could complete all nine pieces, and the *First*, which ha been left to last, was conducted by Andrew Mogrelia.

Bachianas brasileiras: (i) *1* (for 8 cellos); *2 (Little Train of the Caipira);* (ii; iii; iv) *5 (Aria & Dança);* (iv; v) *Forest of the Amazon*

(BB) **(*) HMV (stereo/mono) 5 86718-2. (i) RPO, Bátiz; (ii) De los Angeles; (iii) French Nat. R. O; (iv) composer; (v) Bidú Sayäo, Symphony of the Air – CANTELOUBE: *Chants d'Auvergne* ***

Bátiz gives characterful performances of No. 1 (with its eigh cellos) and No. 2 with its famous portrayal of a train, and h has the advantage of modern, digital recording. But it is fo Victoria de los Angeles's contribution to No. 5 that this disc most notable, together with the composer's vivid portrait o the Amazon Forest, complete with forest fire, and bringin another, somewhat wilder, vocal contribution from Bid yäo. Both are directed by the composer himself. The sound good but variable (No. 5 is mono).

uitar Concerto

* *** Warner 2564 60296-2. Isbin, NYPO, Serebrier –
PONCE: *Concierto del sur;* RODRIGO: *Concierto de Aranjuez* ***

illa-Lobos's *Concerto* has been recorded often, but never ith such a magical effect as here. From the very opening, rebrier spins a web of vividly colourful sounds from the chestra, which Sharon Isbin gently dominates. The lyrical condary theme floats enticingly by, but the effect in the ening movment is of a free fantasia in which guitar and chestra find true serendipity. The *Andantino* is charmingly mantic, the finale with its playful touches from the bassoon zestful but rhythmically graceful. The recording is first class d beautifully balanced.

ISÉE, Robert de (1650?–1732)

uites de dances (for theorbo): *in A min.; B min.; C min.; D in.*

B) *** Virgin 2x1 4 82094-2 (2). Monteilhet – BACH: *Cello Suites* (trans. for theorbo) *1–3* ***

he theorbo could be supplemented by a set of very low-unding strings which added support to the harmony with eir rich tone and added resonance, as Pascal Monteilhet ows here in these remarkably evocative performances, armly recorded, which transport the listener back to a fferent age. Here they are coupled with Pascal Monteilhet's anscriptions of three of Bach's *Suites for Unaccompanied ello,* and very successfully too. The result is attractively timate and most beguiling.

IVALDI, Antonio (1678–1741)

he Trial between Harmony and Invention (12 Concertos), p. 8

) ** Chan. 6697 (2). Thomas, Digney, Bournemouth Sinf.

he Bournemouth Sinfonietta set on Chandos is beautifully corded and has much in its favour. The use of modern struments does not preclude a keen sense of style. Allegros e alert without being rigid and the balance is convincing, ith the continuo coming through not too insistently. The ter concertos are particularly successful: Nos. 5 (*La tempesta mare*) and 6 (*Il piacere*) are excellent, and there is some electable oboe playing from John Digney in the final group. he drawback for most listeners will be the account of *The our Seasons,* which is seen as part of the whole cycle rather an as individually dramatic. Ronald Thomas's approach mphasizes the music's breadth and lyricism rather than its lourful pictorialism, so that the shepherd's dog barks gently nd the winds blow amiably, certainly never reaching gale rce. In its way this is pleasing, but there remains an element f disappointment in the under-characterization.

he Four Seasons, Op. 8/1–4 ((i) DVD and (ii) CD cordings)

M) * DVD ; *** CD Ph. 475 6940. (i) Agostini; (ii) Carmirelli; I Musici

(i) *The Four Seasons, Op. 8/1–4;* (ii) *Bassoon Concerto in A min., RV 498;* (iii) *Double Concerto for 2 Oboes in D min., RV 535;* (iv) *Piccolo Concerto in C, RV 443*

●— (M) *** 475 7531. ASMF, Marriner; with (i) Loveday; (ii) Gatt; (iii) Black, Nicklin; (iv) Bennett

(i) *The Four Seasons, Op. 8/1–4.* (ii) *Violin Concertos: in E flat (La tempesta di mare); in B flat (La Caccia), Op. 8/5 & 10;* (iii) *Mandolin Concerto in C, RV 425; Double Trumpet Concerto in C, RV 537*

(BB) *** HMV (DDD/ADD) 5 86783-2. (i) Warren-Green, LCO; (ii) Menuhin, Polish CO, Maksymiuk; (iii) Soloists, Toulouse CO, Auriacombe

The DVD performance of *The Four Seasons* is accompanied by the camera's tour of Venetian scenes, after I Musici have begun their performance in the open air by the side of the lagoon. As the recorded sound has the warm resonance of a hall, it must be presumed that they are miming to a pre-recording, and very accurately, too; but we see so little of them, it is difficult to be exactly sure. The performance itself is a routine one, with nothing new or imaginative to offer, and one would not want to return to it. Moreover, the Venetian scenes have no connection with the seasons, except for the brief appearance of masked and costumed visitors to the winter carnival.

Pina Carmirelli's CD account is a different matter. The third out of four made in stereo by I Musici, it is undoubtedly much, much finer than the DVD account. Musical values are paramount; this time, however, there is more vitality and the programmatic implications are more strikingly realized. Yet Carmirelli's playing maintains the lyrical feeling and beauty of tone for which I Musici performances are remembered, and combines it with attractively alert and nimble bravura in the allegros. The gentle breezes are caught as effectively as the summer storms, and the slow movement of *Autumn* (helped by especially atmospheric recording) makes an elegiac contrast. The opening of *Winter* is certainly chilly. The recording is outstandingly natural.

Marriner's 1969 recording of *The Four Seasons* with Alan Loveday has been our top recommendation for nearly four decades and is still unsurpassed. Its stylish success on modern instruments makes one wonder what all the fuss about period performance is all about. It now comes back into the catalogue with three bonus concertos which are hardly less enjoyable.

Christopher Warren-Green makes a brilliantly charismatic soloist with the London Chamber Orchestra (which he also directs), providing delectably pointed bird-imitations in *Spring* and *Summer.* Tempi of allegros are very brisk, and the effect is tinglingly exhilarating when the soloist's bravura is so readily matched by the accompanying ensemble. Certainly this account of Vivaldi's *Four Seasons* is memorable, and its sheer brio is impossible to resist. Slow movements offer the widest contrast, with delicate textures and subtle use of the continuo, as in *Winter,* where Leslie Pearson makes a delightful surprise contribution to the finale, having already embroidered in the opening allegro and prevented it from being too chilly. Needless to say, the storms approach gale force, while the peasants are hardly less rumbustious, enjoying their autumn hunting and bacchanal. The recording, made in All Saints' Church, Wallingford, has plenty of ambient fullness, but remains bright and fresh.

Four extra concertos have been added for this reissue. Menuhin's contribution of a pair of violin concertos, both with nicknames, dates from 1983 and brings some of the freshest and most intense playing from his later years. Particularly in slow movements, he again shows his unique insight in shaping a phrase. Fresh and alert accompaniments, and full digital recording. The piquant *Mandolin* and more robust *Double Trumpet Concerto* are analogue, and come from Toulouse (in 1968). They are vividly played and excellently recorded.

The Four Seasons, Op. 8/1–4; Concerto alla rustica in G, RV 151; Quadruple Violin Concerto in B flat, RV 553; Sinfonia in G, RV 146 Disc 2: Flute Concerto in G (La notte), RV 439; Concerto per l'Orchestra de Dresden in G, RV 577; Concerto per la Solennità di S. Lorenzo, RV 556; Chamber Concerto in D (La pastorella), RV 95; Concerto for Strings (Sinfonia) in C, RV 114; Quadruple Concerto in G, for 2 Violins, 2 Cellos, RV 575
(BB) *** Virgin 2x1 4 82088-2 (2). Soloists, Taverner Players, Parrott

The Taverner Players offer an authentic version which stimulates the ear without acerbity. They are not the first group to use a different soloist for each of Vivaldi's *Four Seasons*, and this works well, with plenty of tingling vitality overall and a good deal of imaginative freedom from each player in turn, with Chiara Banchieri setting the style in her duets with the leader in her volatile account of *Spring*. In the Adagio of *Summer*, Alison Bury's timbre is pure with a minimum of vibrato, yet the playing is appealingly expressive. There is no lack of sensuous lustre in the hazy evocation of the slow movement of *Autumn* (the brooding harpsichord continuo particularly effective) and Elizabeth Wallfisch's contribution to the outer movements gleams with bravura. John Holloway's upper tessitura is suitably mercurial. To complete the first disc, the four players join together to provide much virtuosity for the *Quadruple Violin Concerto in B flat*, while the *Sinfonia* and *Concerto alla rustica* bring much energy and tonal bite from the orchestral strings.

The second disc, recorded four years earlier, is a particularly winning collection. *La Notte* is (by common consent) among Vivaldi's most imaginative works for flute: its descriptive evocations are atmospherically caught by the Taverner Players, notably 'Ghosts' and 'Sleep', which is so reminiscent of the *Four Seasons*. The *Dresden Concerto*, with its interplay between wind groups, but including also violin obbligati, is particularly original. The grand opening of the *Concerto per la Solennità di S. Lorenzo* is Handelian, but Vivaldi's own personality asserts itself firmly in the following allegro. The work is richly scored and, apart from the main protagonists – a pair of solo violins – features recorders, oboes and (a great novelty at the time) clarinets, with ear-catching results. The delightfully pastoral *Chamber Concerto*, with its rustic woodwind charm, has a particularly engaging siciliano for the solo recorder as its central *Largo*, so nicely played (and decorated) here by Marion Verbruggen, while the imitative finale is hardly less endearing. The two-movement *Sinfonia*, RV 114, is also notable for its inventive finale – in the form of a ciaconna, while the concerto for the pair each of violins and echoing cellos at times sounds more like a concerto grosso. Altogether an outstanding hour-long concert, very well laid out, beautifully and authentically played and excellently recorded.

(i) *Flute Concertos, Op. 10/1–6;* (ii) *L'estro armonico: Triple Violin Concerto in D min., RV 565; Quadruple Violin Concerto in B min., RV 58, Op. 3/10–11*
(BB) **(*) Regis RRC 1243. (i) Hall, Divertimenti of L., Barritt; (ii) Laredo & soloists, SCO

Judith Hall's set of the Op. 10 *Flute Concertos* is fresh an[d] brightly recorded. She plays with considerable virtuosity an[d] a great deal of taste. The Divertimento of London i[s a] modern-instrument group and the players are both sensitiv[e] and alert, and this is most enjoyable on all counts.

The two accompanying *Violin Concertos* from *L'estr[o] armonico*, for three and four violins respectively (althoug[h] this is not made clear on the disc's packaging), are amon[g] Vivaldi's finest; they receive vigorous, spontaneous perform[-] ances from the Scottish Chamber Orchestra, led from th[e] bow by Jaime Laredo. While the solo playing occasionall[y] lacks the last touch of polish, there is excellent team spir[it] here and the phrasing has light and shade. However, th[e] recording of the solo violins is a shade overbright and thin[ly] focused and, although there is a firm supporting bass line, th[e] upper range is less attractive than on the flute concertos. A[t] Regis price, a fair bargain.

Flute Concertos, Op. 10/1–6; Flute Concertos in D, RV 429; A[ ] min., RV 440
*** EMI 3 4212-2. Pahud, Australian CO, Tognetti

Needless to say, the virtuosity of Emmanuel Pahud is dazzlin[g] in the first concerto of Opus 10, *La tempesta di mare*, whil[e] the two *Largo* movements of *La notte* show his legato tone a[t] its most beguiling. The Australian Chamber Orchestra accom[-] pany spiritedly, and they come into their own in the bustle [of] the finale, and Pahud chirrups with the best in the finale of [*Il] gardellino*, after a delicious *Siciliano Cantabile* central move[-] ment. The *Largo e cantabile* of Op. 10/5, too, is quite haunting[,] while the theme and variations finale of the last concerto i[n] the set brings more charming birdsong. The other two con[-] certos here are well up to Vivaldian form, with the perk[y] finale of RV 429 particularly diverting. Strangely, the sleeve[-] note mentions another track, a slow movement from RV 226[,] which does not appear to be on the disc at all. Truthfu[l] recording.

Oboe Concertos: in C, RV 178 & RV 450; in D, RV 453; in D min., RV 454; in F, RV 456; in A min., RV 461; in B flat, RV 465
(BB) **(*) EMI Gemini (ADD) 3 50905-2 (2). De Vries, I Solisti di Zagreb – BACH & TELEMANN: *Oboe Concertos* ***

Han de Vries, playing a modern instrument, here offers n[o] fewer than seven of Vivaldi's *Oboe Concertos*, and thei[r] variety of invention completely contradicts Stravinsky'[s] famous remark that Vivaldi 'wrote the same concerto si[x] hundred times'. The central group here are particularl[y] varied, even though many of the slow movements ar[e] played with a delicate organ continuo. The outer move[-] ments of the C major Concerto, RV 450, are strikingl[y] prolix, demanding (and here receiving) considerable virtu[-] osity from the soloist; the *D major* and *D minor* works ar[e] more robust, but with pensive central *Largos*. The *F majo[r]* opens gravely, with a beautiful solo cantilena following[;] then comes a sparkling bravura *Allegro*, which suddenl[y] changes in mid-movement to a gentle but brief *Adagio* t[o] provide contrast, before the roulades of the spirited closin[g] movement. All the performances are first class, spirited an[d] expressive by turns, freshly accompanied by the Zagre[b] players, and the recording is excellent, with the soloi[st] dominating the sound-picture.

Concertos for Strings: in C, RV 115; in C min., RV 120; in D, RV 121 & 123; in D min., RV 129; in F, RV 141; in F min., RV 143; in G min., RV 153, 154 & 156; in A, RV 158 & 159

*** Opus 111 OP 30377. Concerto Italiano, Alessandrini

Until now, these attractive and lively string concertos have been the province of Simon Standage and Collegium Musicum 90 on Chandos (see our main volume). But now Rinaldo Alessandrini and his Concerto Italiano have come to give them a run for their money, offering 12 concertos played with great brio and expressive sensibility. They content themselves with strings alone, and you have only to sample the first or the last of the concertos here, RV 159 and RV 123 respectively, to hear how deeply expressive are the brief slow movements, and how infections are the *Allegros*. First-class recording ensures that this new series gets the strongest recommendation.

'Violin Concertos for the Emperor': 2 in C, RV 189; 3 in C min., RV 202; 4 in F, RV 286; 7 in C, RV 183; 10 (L'amoroso) in E, RV 271; 11 (Il favorito) in E min., RV 277

⊕ *** HM HMU 907332. Manze, E. Concert

This CD brings together (in some cases reconstructed from the original manuscript) six of the violin concertos which Vivaldi presented to the Holy Roman Emperor, Charles VI, in 1728. One assumes they were among the composer's most valued works (because he was hoping for a position at court) and several are otherwise well known, especially *L'amoroso* with its celestially gentle opening movement and touching *Cantabile* and diaphanous finale, all exquisitely played. *Il Favorito* also has a memorable central *Andante*, but the other works are generally more robust, though their central movements are played with comparable sensitivity. In the *Largo* of the *F major*, RV 286 (also known as the *Concerto per la solennità di San Lorenzo*), and in the finale of the opening *C major* work, RV 189, Andrew Manze improvises his own cadenzas. His playing throughout is of the very highest quality, with memorably characterful accompaniments from the English Concert, of which Manze is now musical director. The recording is very truthful, and this is a very distinguished CD indeed.

Violin Concertos: in C, RV 190; in D, RV 217; in G, RV 303; in G min., RV 325 & RV 331

**(*) DG 477 6005 Carmignola, Venice Bar. O, Marcon

These are all characteristic Vivaldi concertos of quality, with the *Largo* movements of the *D minor* and *C major* (with its gentle plucked accompaniment) particularly memorable. Giuliano Carmignola plays them beautifully, with a superb sense of style, and he is given equally distinguished accompaniments and excellent recording. But this premium-priced CD is short measure, with only five concertos included.

Violin Concertos (for Anna Maria): in D, RV 229; in D min., RV 248; in A, RV 343 & RV 349; in B flat, RV 366 & RV 387

*** CPO 777 078-2. Guglielmo, L'Arte dell'Arco

Anna Maria was the most brilliant of all Vivaldi's pupils, and he was so impressed with her talent that he purchased a personal violin for her. She was to become one of the most celebrated of female violinists in Italy, and Vivaldi wrote a great deal of music especially for her to play. A volume still exists with her name on it, listing some of these works, but including only the violin solo parts. However, research has provided the orchestral accompaniments, which were found in libraries either in Turin or Dresden. They are all bravura

works, attesting to her virtuosity, but expressive too, and they are played most impressively here. They make a surprisingly impressive group, full of unpredictable features, and the present performances do them full justice.

(i) Violin Concertos: in D, RV 230; in A min., RV 356; (i; ii) Double Concerto for Oboe & Violin in B flat, RV 548; (i; iii) Double Violin Concertos: in A, RV 519; C, RV 507; (i; iii; iv) Triple Concerto for 2 Violins & Cello in G min., RV 578; (iv; v) Violin Sonata 2 in D min., RV 12

*** EMI 5 57859-2. Kennedy, (i) BPO (members); (ii) Mayer; (iii) Stabrawa; (iv) Maninger; (v) Mayerson,Takeuchi

Nigel Kennedy is back in the studio to play Vivaldi – and with the Berlin Philharmonic, no less, which he apparently directs from the bow. As one immediately discovers from the opening *Double Violin Concerto in A major*, performances are rhythmically sharp-edged and full of zest, yet lyrically free, and his partnership with his colleague on the violin, Daniel Stabrawa, is beautifully matched, whereas the oboist, Albrecht Mayer, is more delicately balanced. There is a particularly lovely oboe solo in the central *Largo* of RV 548, which Kennedy decorates ethereally. When the cellist, Olaf Maninger, joins them in the *Triple Concerto*, which opens with commanding spiccato chords, they play most subtly as a group, and the dynamic contrast inherent in the playing is most sensitive throughout. Altogether a most stimulating collection.

Violin Concerto in D (per Pisendel), RV 242

(M) *** EuroArts Invitation DVD 2050746. Onofri, Il Giardino Armonica, Antonini (V/D: Karina Fibich) – C. P. E. BACH: Sinfonia in G ***; J. S. BACH: Double Clavier Concerto 2; Triple Clavier Concerto ** (*)

This *Violin Concerto* is a most agreeable work, if not one of Vivaldi's finest, and it is very well played by Enrico Onofri, being placed after the C. P. E. Bach *Sinfonia* and before the closing Bach *Triple Keyboard Concerto*, the highlight of this well-planned concert.

Bassoon Concerto in B flat, RV 502; Cello Concerto in C min., RV 501; Oboe Concerto in C, RV 447; Double Trumpet Concerto in C, RV 537. L'estro armonico: Double Violin Concerto in A min., RV 522; Quadruple Violin Concerto in B min., RV 580. Triple Violin Concerto in F, RV 551

(BB) *** Virgin 4 82136-2. Soloists, LCO, Warren-Green

Christopher Warren-Green and his LCO have already given us a splendid account of the *Four Seasons*, and this generous (75-minute) collection is another fine example of their vividly spontaneous music-making. The opening *Double Trumpet Concerto* is brightly arresting, and in the works for oboe and bassoon both soloists (Gordon Hunt and Merrick Alexander, respectively) play with much character and elegance and, in the latter, also a touch of humour. The lovely slow movement of the *C minor Cello Concerto* is warmly sympathetic on André Schulman's bow. For some reason, a continuo is used only in the two woodwind concertos. The harpsichord swirls are rather effective in the first movement of the *Oboe Concerto*, and in the *Largo* of the *Bassoon Concerto* a chamber organ piquantly introduces the solo entry. The excerpts from *L'estro armonico* are gleamingly strong and expressive, and one senses an added energy, possibly deriving from the musicians standing while they play. Excellent recording, made in All Saints', Petersham, yet with the resonance never becoming oppressive.

CHAMBER MUSIC

Cello Sonatas: in E flat, RV 39; in E min., RV 40; in F, RV 41; in G min., RV 42; in A min., RV 43 & 44

(M) *** DHM/BMG 74321 93561-2. Bylsma, Suzuki, Ogg

Cello Sonatas: in E flat, RV 39; in E min., RV 40; in F, RV 41; in G min., RV 42; in A min., RV 43 & 44; in B flat, RV 45, 46 & 47

**(*) TDK TDK-AD 012 (2). Suzuki, Zipperling, Palviainen

Vivaldi was addicted to instruments playing in the middle and lower register and, as we already know, he wrote more concertos for the bassoon and cello than for any other instrument except the violin. He wrote ten *Sonatas for Cello and continuo*, of which one is lost. Hidemi Suzuki offers them all, but spread over two discs. Anner Bylsma and his companions content themselves with six of the best, and there is no question that the Deutsche Harmonia Mundi performances are preferable. Bylsma's tone is firm and full, with eloquent phrasing, and the continuo group is well balanced; although Suzuki plays very musically, his performances have a less strong profile and are rather less spontaneously enjoyable.

Chamber Concertos for Recorder: in C, with Oboe, 2 Violins & Cello, with Harpsichord Continuo, RV 87; in D, with Violin & Cello Continuo, RV 92; in D, with Oboe, Violin & Bassoon, RV 94; in G, with Oboe, Violin & Bassoon, with Cello & Harpsichord Continuo, RV 101; in G min., with Oboe, Bassoon & Harpsichord, RV 103; in G, with Oboe, Violin & Bassoon, with Cello Continuo, RV 105; in A min., with 2 Violins, with Cello & Harpsichord Continuo, RV 108

(BB) *** Naxos 8.557215. Kecskeméti, Hadady, Falvay, Párkányi, Olajos, Kertész, Doboszy

For the latest issue in the ongoing Naxos cycle of Vivaldi concertos, these excellent Hungarian soloists offer a group of chamber works for various instruments, all dominated by the recorder, here László Kecskeméti, a brilliant player, matched by an impressive number of his colleagues. They play with great freshness and rhythmic zest, with the *Largo* central movements pleasingly expressive. It is the range of contrasting woodwind colour that makes these works so ear-tickling, especially those featuring the bassoon. Excellently balanced recording.

Complete Sacred Music

Volumes 1–10

(BB) *** Hyp. CDS 44171/81 (11). Soloists, King's Consort, King

Sacred music, Vol. 8: *Cur sagittas, cur tela, RV 637; Laudate pueri, RV 600; Salve Regina, RV 616; Sanctorum meritis, RV 620; Sum in medio tempestatum, RV 632*

*** Hyp. CDA 66829. Gritton, Semmingsen, Stutzmann, Ch. & King's Consort, King

Sacred music, Vol. 9: *Ascende laeta, RV 635; Gaude mater Ecclesia, RV 613; Gloria Patri, RV 602a; Salve Regina, RV 618; Vos aurae per montes, RV 634*

*** Hyp. CDA 66839. Sampson, Gritton, Lunn, DiDonato, Stutzmann, Ch. & King's Consort, King

Sacred music, Vol. 10: *Gloria, RV 589; Nisi Dominus, RV 803; Ostro picta, RV 642*

*** Hyp. CDA 66849. Ch. & King's Consort, King (with RUGGIERI: *Gloria*)

With the last three volumes appearing in a group, Robert King's coverage of Vivaldi's key sacred choral works is now the most complete survey in the catalogue, and this admirable set now appears in a box (with a booklet including full texts and translations), at what appears to be budget price, and as such receives the strongest recommendation, for the quality of Vivaldi's sacred music is amazingly high and the performances and recordings are equally consistent, with superb solo contributions from all concerned and especially Carolyn Sampson.

Volumes 1–7 are discussed in detail in our main volume. Volume 8 opens with a thrilling virtuoso performance from the agile, light-voiced mezzo, Tuva Semmingsen, of *Sum in medio tempestum* ('I am·in the midst of stormy weather'), bringing tender melancholy to '*Semper maesta*', and sparkling in the closing '*Alleluia*'. Susan Gritton responds to the greater expressive range of *Laudate pueri*, while the darker-voiced Nathalie Stutzmann finds plenty of venomous character in *Cur saggitas, cur tela* ('Why oh terrible hobgoblins') and is very touching in the closing section, *In te, beate Pater*, and again in the following *Salve Regina*, with a delicate flute obbligato from Christine Garratt in *Ad te suspiramus*.

Carolyn Sampson frames the programme of Volume 9, a particularly rich collection. She opens with a gloriously sung *Laudate pueri*, in which she is joined in duet in several movements by the well-matched soprano voice of Joanne Lunn, with the chorus adding weight at the opening and close. A very nimble oboe obbligato from Alexandra Bellamy adds much to the interest of the *Gloria Patri*. She then ends the programme with an expressive *Vox aurae per montes* ('You breezes through the mountains') with its lively final *Alleluia* and as a postlude a more gentle alternative setting of *Gloria Patri* (RV 602a) with an engaging flute obbligato. As a centrepiece, Stutzmann's darker contralto is heard at her most eloquent in the Salve *Regina*, RV 618, and especially in the mournful closing *O clemens, o pia*; and then Joyce DiDonato (mezzo) brings bright contrast with her bravura in another venture into the mountains, *Ascende laeta montes et colles*.

Volume 10 rounds off Robert King's magnificent survey by opening very appropriately with Vivaldi's most famous choral work, the *Gloria*, RV 589. It is a splendid performance on every count, with soloists, chorus and orchestra all shining. Then the following *Nisi Dominus* proves an ideal showcase for many of the soloists, all on top form, and often with accompanying instrumental obbligato, including *Cum dederit* (chalumeau), *Sicut sagittae* (violin 'in tromba marina'), *Beatus vir* (cello), and *Gloria Patri* (a delicately played chamber organ). The range of vocal and instrumental colour shows Vivaldi at his most imaginatively inspired. After Carolyn Sampson has made her distinguished final solo contribution in the touching *Ostro picta* we are offered a *Gloria* setting by Giovanni Ruggieri (1690–1720), about whom the accompanying notes are unhelpful. This is not as original as Vivaldi's settings and it offers a stylistic mixture, but it is still a fine work and is splendidly sung here.

Philips Vivaldi Edition: Sacred music: *Beatus vir* (2), RV 597 & 598; *Canta in prato, RV 623; Confitebor tibi, RV 596; Crediti propter quod, RV 605; Credo* (2), RV 591 & 592; *Deus tuorum militum, RV 612; Dixit Dominus* (2), RV 594 & 595; *Domine ad adiuvandum me, RV 593; Gaude Mater ecclesia, RV 613; Gloria in D* (2) RV 588 & 589; *In exitu Israel, RV 604; In furore, RV 626; Introduzione al Dixit* (2), RV 635 & 636; *Introduzione al Gloria* (2), RV 639 & 642; *Juditha triumphans* (Oratorio), RV 644; *Kyrie, RV 587; Laetatus*

um, RV 607; Lauda Jerusalem, RV 209; Laudate Dominum,
RV 606; Laudate pueri Dominum (3), RV 600, 601 & 602;
Magnificat (2), RV 611 & 610/11; Nella in mundo pax, RV
630; Nisi Dominus, RV 608; O qui coeli, RV 631; Regina coeli,
RV 615; Sacrum, RV 586; Salve Regina (3), RV 616, 617 & 618;
Sanctorum meritis, RV 620; Stabat Mater, RV 621

B) **(*) Ph. (ADD) 462 234-2 (10). Marshall, Lott, Finnie,
Murray, Finnilä, Collins, Burgess, Ameling, Springer,
Hamari, Burmeister, Kowalski, Van de Meel, Rolfe Johnson,
Holl, Thomaschke, Scharinger, Alldis Ch., Berlin R.
Soloists' Ens., ECO, Concg. CO, Berlin CO, Negri

Mostly recorded between 1974 and 1979, but concluded in
1990, this Philips box gathers together Vittorio Negri's
recordings of Vivaldi's sacred music. He does not make use
of period instruments, but he penetrates as deeply into the
spirit of this music as many who do, and the CD transfers
are of high quality. Any lover of Vivaldi is likely to be
astonished that not only the well-known works but the
rarities show him writing with the keenest originality and
intensity. There is nothing routine about any of this music,
nor are any of the performances either. However, Robert
King's more modern Hyperion set is even finer, it costs
about the same, and it includes one or two recent discoveries
that are missing here. Michael Talbot writes excellent notes
for both sets, and full texts and translations are also
included.

An excellent Philips Duo listed in our main volume (462
170-2) offers a fine selection from Negri's survey. It includes
the two Glorias, the double-choir version of the Magnificat,
and a fine account by Jochen Kowalski of the Stabat Mater.

Credo, RV 591 (revised Malipiero)

(M) *(*) Sony SMK 89619. Ernest Senff Ch., BPO, Giulini –
VERDI: 4 Sacred Pieces **

Giulini presents Vivaldi's four-section Credo in a late
nineteenth-century arrangement by Malipiero. It is lovely
music richly sung, and beautifully recorded but as with the
Verdi coupling the performance lacks vitality, notably so in
the closing Et resurrexit.

Gloria in D, RV 589

*** Telarc SACD 60651. Tamara Matthews, Deanne
Meek, Mary Phillips, Boston Bar., Pearlman – BACH:
Magnificat ***

(BB) *** HMV (DDD/ADD) 5 86784-2. Hendricks, Murray,
Rigby, Heilman, Hynninen, ASMF Ch., ASMF, Marriner –
BACH: Magnificat; Cantata Chorales, etc. ***

Pearlman sets off energetically into the famous opening of
Vivaldi's Gloria, and concludes the work equally spiritedly.
But then in the Et in terra pax, the chorus sings with appealingly relaxed, expressive warmth; and the jaunty tempo for
the engaging soprano duet, Laudamus te, again contrasts
most tellingly with the opening of the Gratias agimus. The
Domine Deus, with its sensitive oboe obbligato, is beautifully
sung by Tamara Matthews; and the later sequence, by the fine
alto, Mary Phillips, shared with the chorus (Domine Deus,
Agnus Dei – Qui tollis peccata mundi – Qui sedes) is equally
moving. In short, this performance is splendidly sung and
sensitively paced, and the surround sound recording is in
every way first class.

Marriner, too, very successfully couples Vivaldi's Gloria
with Bach's Magnificat. With fine soloists and an excellent
choral response this can be recommended on all counts, and
the Bach chorales added as a bonus increase the appeal of this
inexpensive disc.

(i) Stabat Mater in F min., RV 621. Concerto for Strings in A
min., RV 158; Sinfonia for Strings in G, RV 149

*** Analekta FL 2 3171. (i) Lemieux; Tafelmusik, Jeanne
Lamon (with AVISON: Concerto grosso after Scarlatti 7) –
Domenico SCARLATTI: Salve Regina ***

Marie-Nicole Lemieux's performance of the Stabat Mater is
very moving, her rich contralto voice just right for this
intensely expressive setting. Tafelmusik provide an imaginative accompaniment, and also lively performances of a Concerto and Sinfonia for strings which are most stimulating. The
Andante of the Sinfonia is particularly diverting, its sharp
principal rhythmic figure deliciously pointed.

VOLANS, Kevin (born 1949)

String Quartets 1 (White Man Sleeps); 2
(Hunting-Gathering); & 6

*** Black Box BBM 1069. Duke Quartet

Born in South Africa, Kevin Volans in his First Quartet (White
Man Sleeps), dating from 1982, ingeniously uses fragments of
African music, translating it with its different scales into Western terms in a sequence of five dance-movements. In his Second
Quartet (Hunting-Gathering), dating from 1987, the debt to
African music is much more incidental, yet the use of the
medium is just as striking and original, a collage of contrasted
ideas over two extended movements and a brief third movement of summary. The Sixth Quartet of 2000 is much tougher
and more severe, using no African material at all, and points
forward to further developments in his highly original use of a
traditional genre. The Duke Quartet, very well recorded, give
totally committed performances which bring out the underlying emotional intensity behind Volans' inspiration.

WAGNER, Richard (1813–83)

American Centennial March (Grosser Festmarsch);
Kaisermarsch; Overtures: Polonia; Rule Britannia

(BB) ** Naxos 8.555386. Hong Kong PO, Kojian

The Polonia Overture (1836) is the best piece here. Although
its basic style is Weberian, there is a hint of the Wagner of
Rienzi in the slow introduction. The Grosser Festmarsch
(American Centennial March) was commissioned from Philadelphia, and for this inflated piece Wagner received a cool few
thousand dollars! The Rule Britannia Overture is even more
overblown, and the famous tune, much repeated, outstays its
welcome. The Kaisermarsch is also empty and loud. The
Hong Kong orchestra play all this with great enthusiasm, if
without much finesse. The recording is vividly bright, but on
CD it is not a priority item, even for the most dedicated
Wagnerian. However, at the Naxos price it is more enticing
for the curious collector than the original issue was on Marco
Polo.

(i) Die Feen: Overture. Grosser Festmarsch (American
Centennial March); Huldigungsmarsch; Kaisermarsch; Das
Liebesverbot: Overture. (ii) Lohengrin: Preludes to Acts I &
III. Die Meistersinger: Preludes to Acts I & III; Dance of the
Apprentices; Finale. Tannhäuser: Overture. Tristan und
Isolde: Prelude

(BB) ** Virgin (ADD/DDD) 5 62034-2 (2). (i) R. France PO;
(ii) LSO; Janowski

This two-CD compilation combines two unequal Wagner
collections. One CD contains a not terribly distinguished

group of operatic preludes and orchestral excerpts, but they generate no real excitement or tension, and the digital recording is disappointing. But the paired CD, recorded by EMI in 1972, makes this collection worth considering. It consists of early, rarely heard works and occasional pieces, none of them great music, but all of them at the very least interesting. Indeed, it is quite a surprise to hear Wagner's music sounding not too different from Offenbach, as in the racy *galop* – complete with glittering castanets – which opens the Overture *Das Liebesverbot* (a failed Wagner operetta, dating from 1836). Elsewhere, the marches such as the *Huldigungsmarsch (Homage March)* and the *Grand Festival March* (written to celebrate the centenary of American independence in 1876) have a pomp more associated with Meyerbeer, while *Die Feen* resides in the world of Weber. It is all eminently enjoyable and enthusiastically played by the LSO, with the analogue recording much more vivid than its digital companion.

Symphony in C

(BB) ** Warner Apex 2564 60619-2. Norwegian R.O, Rasilainen – WEBER: *Symphonies 1 & 2* **

A useful and inexpensive way to explore Wagner's early *Symphony*, composed at the age of nineteen, and very much indebted to Beethoven and even Mendelssohn. It's no masterpiece, of course, but fascinating to hear and reasonably rewarding. The performance and recording are good, but not outstanding.

Siegfried Idyll

(B) *** Virgin 2x1 4 82112-2 (2). Sinfonia Varsovia, Y. Menuhin – MOZART: *Divertimento 1*, etc.; SCHOENBERG: *Verklaerte Nacht;* WOLF: *Italian Serenade* ***

The members of the Sinfonia Varsovia play beautifully. Menuhin opens in a warmly relaxed manner but the performance gathers impetus and is most sensitively shaped. Fine recording, too.

Siegfried idyll; Preludes: Die Meistersinger, Act I; Parsifal, Act I; Lohengrin, Act III; Rienzi Overture; Tristan und Isolde: Prelude & (i) Liebestod

(BB) **(*) Virgin 2x1 4 82091-2 (2). LCP, Norrington; (i) with Eaglen – BRUCKNER: *Symphony 3* **

By traditional standards of Wagnerian interpretation, Norrington's tempi here are eccentric, but the *Meistersinger Prelude*, swinging off joyfully, two-in-a-bar, has the imprimatur of the composer's own treatise, 'On Conducting'. Wagner tells us that his own tempo for this piece was 'a few seconds over eight minutes'. Norrington's timing is 8 minutes 28 seconds. On the other hand, the performance here of the *Rienzi Overture* is, above all else, grandly spacious, and this certainly brings more gravitas, with the bandstand flavour all but banished. Anyone used to Bruno Walter's gentle treatment of the *Siegfried Idyll* will surely be disconcerted by the way Norrington presses forward, beautifully though it is played; and in the *Parsifal Prelude* he is very different from Jochum. Certainly the ardent thrust works well in *Tristan*, and Jane Eaglen rises to the occasion in the *Liebestod*. So these performances are all refreshingly different; the orchestral response is impressive, committed and spontaneous, while detail is sophisticated. The Abbey Road recording is superb, and it is a pity that this reissue is linked to a much less convincing Bruckner performance.

(i) *Der fliegende Höllander: Overture.* (ii) *Götterdämmerung: Dawn; Siegfried's Rhine Journey & Funeral March.* (i) *Lohengrin: Prelude to Act III. Die Meistersinger: Preludes to Acts I & III. Tannhäuser: Overture and Venusberg Music. Die Walküre: Ride of the Valkyries*

(B) ** CfP (DDD/ADD) 575 5682. LPO, (i) Elder; (ii) Rickenbacher

Most of the excerpts here are conducted by Mark Elder, who provides well-played but unmemorable performances, brightly but not particularly richly recorded. The *Ride of the Valkyries* comes off best, but it seems a curious plan to include the *Venusberg Music* from *Tannhäuser* without the chorus. The *Götterdämmerung* excerpts conducted by Karl Anton Rickenbacher, added as a makeweight, are altogether superior, and it was a pity that EMI did not choose to reissue the complete collection from which they derive, instead of the Elder disc.

OPERA

Overture, Der fliegende Holländer. Lohengrin: Preludes to Acts I & III. Die Meistersinger: Overture; (i) *Tannhäuser: Overture and Venusberg Music. Tristan und Isolde: Prelude & Liebestod*

B—** (M) *** EMI (ADD) 4 76896-2. BPO, Karajan; (i) with Deutsche Oper Ch.

All in all, Karajan's 1974 collection is perhaps the finest single disc of miscellaneous Wagnerian overtures and preludes in the catalogue, recommendable alongside Szell's Cleveland collection of orchestral music from the *Ring*. Karajan's CD is fully worthy of inclusion as one of EMI's 'Great Recordings of the Century' and this CD reissue in EMI's Karajan Collection is equally recommendable. The body of tone produced by the Berlin Philharmonic gives a breathtaking amplitude at climaxes and the electricity the conductor generates throughout the programme is unforgettable. As with the other EMI Audio DVDs the recording was originally made in quadrophony, and there is a choice between multi-channel surround sound or high-resolution stereo. The results are spectacular with greater depth, a wider dynamic range and a remarkable sense of the ambience of the Berlin Philharmonie. But this much less expensive CD can be recommended with equal enthusiasm.

(i) *Götterdämmerung: Siegfried's Rhine Journey & Funeral March;* (ii) *Die Meistersinger: Prelude to Act III; Procession of the Meistersingers;* (iii) *Das Rheingold: Entrance of the Gods into Valhalla;* (ii) *Rienzi: Overture. Tristan und Isolde: Prelude and Liebestod. Die Walküre:* (ii) *Magic Fire Music;* (iii; iv) *Ride of the Valkyries*

(M) *(**) RCA (ADD) 82876 55306-2. Stokowski, with (i) LSO; (ii) RPO; (iii) Symphony of the Air; (iv) Arroyo; Ordassy; Parker

Three orchestras, unified by Stokowski's brand of magic crackling throughout this programme. At a flick of the wrist, Stokowski creates electricity, the large dynamic contrasts and climaxes made all the more effective, heard alongside the richly luscious playing in the slow numbers, adopting tempos which might seem indulgent in less gifted hands. The opening of the *Die Meistersinger Prelude* is beautifully done, with a glowing atmosphere in the high strings, while the *Tristan* items are saturated with Stokowskian/Wagnerian atmosphere. The *Entry of the Gods into Valhalla* and the *Ride of the Valkyries* are predictably exciting, as is the *Rienzi Overture*, which builds up to a fine passion. The two *Götterdämmerung* items with the LSO bring excellent moments of frisson in the climaxes, while *Siegfried's Funeral March* is suitably sombre, with the dramatic interjections from the orchestra effectively timed. The sound is surprisingly uniform throughout the programme (dating from 1961–74), generally full and certainly vivid, but not always refined, especially with the brass under pressure, though Stokowski's string sound comes over well. A must for all Stokowski fans.

Der fliegende Holländer (complete CD version)

(M) *** Decca 436 418-2 (2). Hale, Behrens, Rydl, Protschka, Vermillion, Heilman, V. State Op. Konzertvereinigung, VPO, Dohnányi

Curiously, Decca have reissued the Dohnányi set in their 'Critics' Choice' series. Despite the promising cast, it is disappointing. The sound is rich and full, if not completely clear on detail, but Dohnányi's relatively sluggish speeds go with rhythms too often square and unsprung. In all, he takes ten minutes longer than Nelsson in his Bayreuth set on Philips – on balance, still the finest mid-price version. Nor does his cast fulfil expectations. Robert Hale is a powerful, intense Dutchman but, as recorded, the voice is ill-focused, lacking necessary firmness. Hildegard Behrens too has trouble with vibrato, which is intrusive except when her voice opens out richly at the top, and she offers a far less satisfying performance than those she gives as Brünnhilde in the Levine *Ring* cycle. The others are more satisfying, though in various degrees they also have voice-production problems, even Kurt Rydl, whose ripely characterful Daland is not as steady as it might be.

Die Meistersinger von Nürnberg (complete DVD versions)

*** DG DVD 0730949-2 (2). Morris, Heppner, Mattila, Pape, Allen, Polenzani, Met. Op. Ch. & O, Levine (V/D: Brian Large)

*** EMI DVD 599736-9 (2). Van Dam, Salminen, Volle, Seiffert, Strehl, Schnitzer, Pinter, Zürich Op. Ch. & O, Welser-Möst (V/D: Andy Sommer)

James Levine has already given us an outstanding traditional *Ring* cycle, and here he matches it with an expansive and warm-hearted *Meistersinger*. The production is again traditional, which is what his New York audience wants. Thank goodness for no quirky ideas. The singers are all outstanding, led by James Morris's warmly genial Sachs, matched vocally by René Pape's Pogner, and by Ben Heppner, who is an equally convincing Walther. Karita Mattila not only looks gorgeous but sings ravishingly as Eva, while Sir Thomas Allen's characterization of Beckmesser is all his own. Matthew Polenzani's David too is quite agreeable, but not charismatic. Levine's conducting holds the performance together richly, and the chorus is superb, vividly recorded (like the orchestra); and Brian Large comes up trumps with the video direction. Choice between this DG set and the fine EMI version below will not be easy to determine.

Though the performance lacks a little in weight, Franz Welser-Möst conducts a fresh and incisive reading, with another excellent cast. José van Dam gives a noble account of the role of Hans Sachs, his voice firm and unstrained as it always has been. Beardless, he cuts a less elderly figure than usual, but that goes with the freshness of the voice. The other masters are first rate too, with Matti Salminen a superb Pogner and Michael Volle a Beckmesser who with his firm, resonant voice refuses to guy the role, making the character more convincing than if he emerges as simply a comic figure. Petra-Maria Schnitzer sings with golden tones as Eva, and

Peter Seiffert makes a lusty Walther, more mellifluous than most Heldentenors, while Christoph Strehl is clear and youthful as David. Nikolaus Lehnhoff's production for the Zurich Opera opens with an ultra-realistic court-room set, and goes on to an impressionistic, shadowy set for Act II, with barely any stage furniture, while the first scene of Act III is similarly economical, with a pile of books representing Sachs's dwelling. That leads on to a direct setting for the second scene of Act III, with the chorus in rows as if in choir stalls. Inconsistently, they wear modern dress, while the main characters have Victorian costumes, with the Masters emerging in black robes and tall, stove-pipe hats. The impression of space is created by an atmospheric backcloth. Though one can criticize detail and inconsistencies, the production works well.

Die Meistersinger von Nürnberg (complete CD versions)

(BB) (***) Naxos 8.111128/31 (4). Schoeffler, Edelmann, Treptow, Dermota, Gueden, Donch, V. State Op. Ch., VPO, Knappertsbusch

** Teldec 3984 29333-2 (4). Holl, Seiffert, Magee, Schmidt, Wottrich, Bayreuth Festival Ch. & O, Barenboim

When in February 1951 Decca issued Act II of *Die Meistersinger* in this recording, it was a breakthrough not just for that company but for the development of opera recording on LP. Decca went on to an elaborate programme of recording opera, not least Wagner, and the success of this first sample led to the other two Acts being recorded almost immediately. The result stands the test of time extremely well, when the cast from the Vienna State Opera is so strong. It centres round the noble Hans Sachs of Paul Schoeffler in one of his very finest recordings, opposite the totally enchanting Eva of Hilde Gueden, with her golden tone. Otto Edelmann (already the Hans Sachs in the Bayreuth *Meistersinger* being recorded live in 1951 for EMI with Karajan) is a superb Pogner, and Karl Donch as Beckmesser has the right, mean-sounding voice, which he uses intelligently without guying the role. Gunther Treptow, with his clean-cut, baritonal Heldentenor, is a fine, unstrained Walther and Anton Dermota a glowing David, with Else Schurhoff a strong but mature-sounding Magdalene. Knappertsbusch's direction is spacious and intense, and the transfer of the original mono recording is first rate, with ample body.

Recorded live at the 1999 Bayreuth Festival, Barenboim's version starts well with a thrustful account of the Overture, helped by full, immediate sound, but problems develop rapidly from then on, with the orchestra close but the voices set in a far more spacious acoustic, with the chorus distant and ill-defined. Too often over the great span of the three acts, Barenboim's direction grows uncharacteristically stodgy and square, with jog-trot rhythms evenly stressed. Vocally the great glory of the set is the singing of Peter Seiffert as Walther, amply heroic in scale but clear-toned and never strained. His feeling for words is always illuminating, and his performance is crowned by a superb account of the Prize Song in Act III. Emily Magee is an impressive Eva too, the voice warm, the manner fresh and girlish. Both of them are sharply contrasted with the pedestrian Hans Sachs of Robert Holl, lacking weight, with the voice no longer cleanly focused and with little feeling for the character. This is a dull dog of a Sachs with little or no sense of humour. Andreas Schmidt sings well as Beckmesser in a clean-cut, unexaggerated reading, but that minimizes the sparkle of the inspiration.

Parsifal (complete CD versions)

✓ ⊕━ ✱ *** DG 477 6006 (4). Domingo, Struckmann, Meier, Selig, Bankl, Anger, V. State Op. Ch. & O, Thielemann

(M) (***) Ph. mono 475 7785 (4). Thomas, Dalis, Hotter, London, Neidlinger, Talvela, Bayreuth Festival Ch. & O, Knappertsbusch

Christian Thielemann conducts an incandescent account of *Parsifal*, recorded live at a sequence of performances at the Vienna State Opera in June 2005. The performance is crowned by the magnificent singing and acting of Plácido Domingo in the title-role. It is astonishing that in his sixties he can produce such glorious, cleanly focused tone, powerful and even youthful-sounding, in keeping with the character of the young hero. Even in a live account, his voice remains fresh to the end of this long opera. Comparably fine is the Kundry of Waltraud Meier, in glorious voice, attacking even the most exposed top notes with freshness, clarity and precision. Though the others are rather less impressive, they all sing well, with Franz-Josef Selig darkly powerful, if occasionally unsteady, as Gurnemanz, and Falk Struckmann as Amfortas initially gritty-toned, later focusing more cleanly in Act III. Wolfgang Bankl is an excellent Klingsor, attacking the role incisively, while Ain Anger as Titurel completes a well-balanced team. Thielemann remains the hero alongside Domingo, bringing dedication to this quasi-religious score, combined with passion and dramatic bite. He keeps speeds flowing well, while letting the music breathe spaciously, with the choral singing magnificent throughout, and with the recording – made in collaboration with Austrian Radio – vividly atmospheric. This now takes pride of place for this opera, even ahead of Karajan's deeply spiritual and equally dedicated account.

Knappertsbusch's expansive and dedicated 1962 reading is caught superbly in this reissued set as one of Philips's Originals. It is arguably the finest live recording ever made in the Festspielhaus at Bayreuth, with outstanding singing from Jess Thomas as Parsifal and Hans Hotter as Gurnemanz. Though Knappertsbusch chooses consistently slow tempi there is no sense of excessive squareness or length, so intense is the concentration of the performance, its spiritual quality; and the sound has undoubtedly been further enhanced in the new remastering for this reissue. The snag is that stage noises and coughs are also emphasized, with the bronchial afflictions particularly disturbing in the *Prelude*.

The Ring (Das Rheingold; Die Walküre; Siegfried; Götterdämmerung): Highlights

(BB) *** HMV 5 86786-2. Marton, Jerusalem, Morris, Studer, Goldberg, Lipovšek, Bav. RSO, Haitink

Haitink's *Ring* cycle (from 1989/1992) has no lack of tension and power, but it is unevenly cast. However, the disappointing Brünnhilde (Eva Marton) does not appear in these highlights until *Götterdämmerung*, and before that James Morris as Wotan is very impressive in the *Fire Music* scene. Of course this can be little more than a sampler, but it includes key items like the *Entry of the Gods into Valhalla*, the *Ride of the Valkyries*, *Siegfried's Rhine Journey*, and the closing scene of *Götterdämmerung*, which all show Haitink's superb pacing and control; and there is a cued synopsis which places the various excerpts in context.

Siegfried (complete CD version)

✱ **** Testament (ADD) SBT4 1392 (4). Windgassen, Kuen, Hotter, Varnay, Neidlinger, Bayreuth Festival O, Keilberth

Fine as the recording of the 1955 *Walküre* is in the Testament processing, the *Siegfried* of that year is even more impressive, with even greater weight in the orchestral sound, with the brass and timpani astonishingly vivid. In this section of the *Ring* cycle, that is particularly important, when Wagner relies more than ever on darkened orchestration. The voices are vividly caught too, with a wonderful sense of presence, and Wolfgang Windgassen as Siegfried (also the Siegfried of the Solti cycle) is in gloriously fresh voice, superbly contrasted with the mean-sounding but comparably well-focused tenor of Paul Kuen as Mime. Gustav Neidlinger too is clear and incisive as Alberich, with Josef Greindl darkly majestic as Fafner. The duetting of Varnay and Windgassen as Siegfried and Brünnhilde then makes a thrillingly passionate conclusion in Keilberth's thrustful reading.

Tristan und Isolde (complete CD versions)

⊕━ *** EMI 3 52423-2 (3). Stemme, Domingo, Fujimora, Pape, Bär, ROHCG Ch. & O, Pappano

(M) **(*) Ph. 475 7020 (4). Hofmann, Behrens, Minton, Weikl, Sotin, Bav. R. Ch. & SO, Bernstein

The Pappano *Tristan und Isolde*, with Domingo magnificent in the title-role is praised at length in our main edition. It came at a special price, complete with an Audio DVD of the complete performance in Surround Sound, with an on-screen libretto. The present listing is of just the normal three-CD set of the opera, which is recommendable in its own right. However, while the sparse documentation contains just a list of scenes, if you want text and translation you need to go to www.emiclassics.com.

Bernstein's early 1980s set, originally on five CDs, is now reissued on four medium-priced discs with libretto included. The fine quality of the recording is all the more appealing in the new transfer, a tribute to the Bavarian engineers working in the Herkulessaal in Munich. The surprise is that Bernstein, over-emotional in some music, here exercises restraint to produce one of the most spacious readings ever put on disc, more expansive even than Furtwängler's. His rhythmic sharpness goes with warmly expressive but unexaggerated phrasing, to give unflagging concentration and deep commitment. The Love duet has rarely if ever sounded so sensuous, with supremely powerful climaxes. Nor in the *Liebestod* is there any question of Bernstein rushing ahead, for the culmination comes naturally and fully at a taxingly slow speed. Behrens makes a fine Isolde, less purely beautiful than her finest rivals, but with reserves of power giving dramatic bite. The contrast of tone with Yvonne Minton's Brangäne (good, except for flatness in the warning solo) is not as great as usual, and there is likeness too between Peter Hofmann's Tristan, often baritonal, and Bernd Weikl's Kurwenal, lighter than usual. The King Mark of Hans Sotin is superb. A reissue well worth exploring.

Die Walküre (complete DVD version)

(*) Warner **DVD 2564 6319-2. Emeling, Secunde, Evans, Tomlinson, Finnie, Hölle, Bayreuth Festival O, Barenboim

(V/D: Horant Hohlfeld)

John Tomlinson's Wotan, singing magnificently, dominates Barenboim's *Die Walküre* against a stage as bare as Bayreuth has ever seen. However, colour is provided by the Wälsungs, who are all red-headed, while for contrast Brünnhilde (Ann Evans), also on fine vocal form, and Fricka (Linda Finnie) are in black. Vocally and musically this is strong, but, although the cameras are usually in the right place, visually we shall stick to Levine (or Boulez).

Die Walküre (complete CD version)

*** Testament SBT4 1391 (4). Varnay, Hotter, Brouwenstijn, Vinay, Greindl, Bayreuth Festival O, Keilberth

This pioneering recording, taken live from the 1955 *Ring* cycle at Bayreuth, was the very first to be done in stereo, several years ahead of the great Solti cycle for Decca, which was recorded in the studio. This one has been languishing in the archives, and it was thanks to the enterprise of Stewart Brown of Testament that finally, after much negotiation, the cycle has begun to appear. When Wieland Wagner invited Joseph Keilberth to conduct *The Ring* at Bayreuth, he was consciously aiming to present a reading manifestly contrasted with that of Hans Knappertsbusch, spacious and contemplative. Keilberth, by contrast, is urgent and passionate, and the thrust of the performance makes the result intensely exciting, inspiring the great Wagnerian singers in the cast to give of their finest. Hans Hotter's interpretation of the role of Wotan is well known from a number of versions; but here he not only sings with urgency, his voice is in wonderfully fresh condition, perfectly focused. *Wotan's Farewell* has never been more powerfully presented, with his agony over having to punish his favourite daughter conveyed most movingly. Astrid Varnay as Brünnhilde is similarly moving, and so are Gre Brouwenstijn as Sieglinde and the darkly baritonal Ramon Vinay, Toscanini's choice as Otello, singing Siegmund, with Josef Greindl massive of voice as Hunding. The end of Act I, when the twins fall into each other's arms, brings another great orgasmic moment; the recording, originally made by Decca and now beautifully reprocessed, far outshines in quality the radio recordings of Bayreuth that have appeared on various labels.

Die Walküre: Act I (complete); Act II, Scenes 3 & 5

(M) (***) EMI mono 3 45832-2 [3 458352]. Lehmann, Melchior, List, VPO, Walter

Bruno Walter's 1935 recording of Act I and scenes from Act II of *Die Walküre* has been transferred to CD with astonishing vividness in this reissue for EMI's 'Great Recordings of the Century'. Though in the days of 78s the music had to be recorded in short takes of under five minutes, one is consistently gripped by the continuity and sustained lines of Walter's reading, and by the intensity and beauty of the playing of the Vienna Philharmonic. Lotte Lehmann's portrait of Sieglinde, arguably her finest role, has a depth and beauty never surpassed since, and Lauritz Melchior's heroic Siegmund brings singing of a scale and variety – not to mention beauty – that no Heldentenor today begins to match. Emanuel List as Hunding is satisfactory enough, but his achievement at least has been surpassed.

WALDTEUFEL, Emile (1837–1915)

Polkas: *Les Bohémiens; Retour des champs; Tout ou rien.* Waltzes: *Ange d'amour; Dans les nuages; España; Fontaine lumineuse; Je t'aime; Tout-Paris*

** Marco Polo 8.223438. Slovak State PO (Košice), Walter

Polkas: *Camarade; Dans les bois; Jeu d'esprit.* Waltzes: *Bien aimés; Chantilly; Dans tes yeux; Estudiantina; Hommage aux dames; Les Patineurs*

** Marco Polo 8.223433. Slovak State PO (Košice), Walter

Polkas: *L'Esprit français; Par-ci, par-là; Zig-zag.* Waltzes: *Hébé; Les Fleurs; Fleurs et baisers; Solitude; Toujours ou jamais; Toujours fidèle*

**(*) Marco Polo 8.223450. Slovak State PO (Košice), Walter

Invitation à la gavotte; Polkas: *Joyeux Paris; Ma Voisine.* Waltzes: *Pluie de diamants; Les Sirènes; Les Sourires; Soirée d'été; Très jolie; Tout en rose*

** Marco Polo 8.223441. Slovak State PO (Košice), Walter

Béobile pizzicato. Polka-Mazurka: *Bella.* Polka: *Château en Espagne.* Waltzes: *Acclamations; La Barcarolle; Brune ou blonde; Flots de joie; Gaîté; Tout à vous*

**(*) Marco Polo 8.223684. Slovak State PO (Košice), Walter

Grand vitesse galop. Mazurka: *Souveraine.* Polka: *Les Folies.* Waltzes: *Amour et printemps; Dolorès; Mello; Mon rêve; Pomone; Sous la voûte étoilée*

** Marco Polo 8.223451. Slovak State PO (Košice), Walter

Galop: *Prestissimo.* Polkas: *Bella bocca; Nuée d'oiseaux.* Waltzes: *Au revoir; Coquetterie; Jeunesse dorée; Un Premier Bouquet; Rêverie; Trésor d'amour*

** Marco Polo 8.223685. Slovak State PO (Košice), Walter

Grand galop du chemin de fer. Polkas: *Désirée; Jou-jou* (all arr. Pollack). Waltzes: *La Berceuse: Entre nous; Illusion; Joie envolée; Mariana; Sur le plage*

** Marco Polo 8.223686. Slovak State PO (Košice), Walter

Waldteufel's music, if not matching that of the Strauss family in range and expressive depth, has grace and charm and is prettily scored in the way of French ballet music. Moreover, its lilt is undeniably infectious. The most famous waltz, *Les Patineurs*, is mirrored in style here by many of the others (*Dans les nuages*, for instance), and there are plenty of good tunes. *Pluie de diamants*, with lots of vitality, is among the more familiar items, as is the sparkling *Très jolie*, but many of the unknown pieces are equally engaging. Like Strauss, Waldteufel usually introduces his waltzes with a section not in waltz-time, and he is ever resourceful in his ideas and in his orchestration. The polkas are robust, but the scoring has plenty of character. The performances here are fully acceptable.

March: *Kamiesch* (arr. Pollack). Polkas: *Bagatelle; En garde!; Trictrac.* Waltzes: *Etincelles; Idyll; Naples; Nid d'amour; Roses de Noël; La Source*

**(*) Marco Polo 8.223688. Slovak State PO (Košice), Walter

For this latest in the ongoing Marco Polo series, Christian Pollack made the arrangement of the opening *Kamiesch March* and one could wish he had also conducted the disc, for Alfred Walter is often rather metrical. Yet he opens the charming *Bagatelle* and *Trictrac* Polkas flexibly enough and the closing polka militaire, *En garde!*, suits him admirably. But the main attraction here is the inclusion of half a dozen waltzes, most of them unknown. Walter opens each affectionately enough (none actually begins in waltz tempo), is distinctly beguiling in both *Nid d'amour* and *Roses de Noël* and phrases the horn solo at the beginning of *Naples* very pleasingly. When each gets under way he is spirited; but a little more subtlety, a little less gusto, would have been welcome. Nevertheless the Slovak playing is full of spirit and the recording excellent.

Waltzes: *Acclamations; España; Estudiantina; Les Patineurs*

(BB) ** EMI Encore (ADD) 5 85065-2. Monte Carlo PO, Boskovsky – OFFENBACH *Gaîté Parisienne* (ballet) **

It is good to have this inexpensive reissue of Boskovsky's performances, well recorded in 1976. *Les Patineurs* is the composer's finest waltz, and it is the highlight here, given a splendidly affectionate and sparkling account. *Estudiantina* is similarly vivacious, and *Acclamations* opens very invitingly too; in *España* one feels that Boskovsky could have alluded more subtly to Chabrier's original.

WALKER, Ernest (1870–1949)

Cello Sonata

*** British Music Soc. BMS 423CD. Cole, Talbot – BOWEN; FOULDS: *Cello Sonatas* ***

Ernest Walker was to centre his whole life and career on Oxford's Balliol College, which he entered at the age of 17 and where he eventually became a 'musical don'. He organized chamber music concerts at the college and in 1907 wrote a *History of Music in England*. His compositions were small-scale and his *Cello Sonata* dates from 1914. It is a profoundly lyrical work, the first movement passionate, followed by a deeply felt but calmer *Adagio*, marked *serioso*. The mood lightens in the finale – but not entirely, for it is marked *con fuco*. It is a personal work and a match for its companions on this disc by Bowen and Foulds, even if the composer's voice is less individual than theirs. It is very well played here by Jo Cole and John Talbot, as if they believe in every note, as well they might.

WALLACE, William Vincent (1812–65)

Celtic Fantasies: Annie Laurie; Auld Lang Syne and The Highland Laddie; The Bard's Legacy; Charlie is my Darling and The Campbells are Coming; Coolun, Gary Owen and St Patrick's Day; Homage to Burns: Impromptu on Somebody and O for Ane and Twenty Tam; Kate Kearney and Tow, row, row; The Keel Row; The Last Rose of Summer; The Meeting of the Walters and Eveleen's Bower; Melodie Irlandaise; The Minstrel Boy and Rory O'More; My Love is like a Red Red Rose and Come o'er the Stream Charlie; Comin' through the Rye; Robin Adair; Roslin Castle and A Highland Lad my Love was Born; Ye Banks and Braes

(M) ** Cala CACD 88042. Tuck

William Wallace was born in Waterford, Ireland, and began his career as a bandmaster, later concentrating on the violin, leading the Adelphi Theatre Orchestra in Dublin. In 1829 he heard Paganini and was so mesmerized that he 'stayed up all night' practising that composer's more dashing pieces. When he went to Tasmania (for his health) in 1836, his virtuosity caused a sensation, and moving on to Sydney, he was dubbed the 'Australian Paganini'. He subsequently travelled the world; in New Orleans he met and befriended Gottschalk, and in the early 1840s his playing was to be acclaimed in New York, Boston and Philadelphia. But when he returned to London in 1845 he made his name not with his fiddling, but with his first opera, *Maritana*, the work by which he is now chiefly remembered, although his ballads and songs also became very popular. His *Celtic Fantasias* for piano, based on traditional melodies, are little more than elaborate arrangements, with bravura embellishments which add little except surface gloss. Rosemary Tuck plays them with accomplished sympathy, but cannot make them more than showpieces: the tunes are far more indelible than Wallace's embellishments. She is well recorded.

WALTON, William (1902–83)

Cello Concerto

** Orfeo C621 061A. Müller-Schott, Oslo PO, Previn – ELGAR: *Cello Concerto*

Daniel Müller-Schott gives a passionate performance of the Walton *Cello Concerto*, matching his equally compelling account of the Elgar in this ideal coupling. Significantly, Müller-Schott writes his own liner-notes, clearly demonstrating his warm affection and understanding of both works. His passionate response comes across in every movement of both works, fast as well as slow, making this a formidable rival to Yo-Yo Ma's similar coupling, with Previn also conducting. Sadly, the recording balance is seriously at fault, with the cello balanced so close that one hears the orchestra through a haze, obscuring the subtlety of Walton's orchestration. Even so, this is well worth investigating for the quality of the performances.

Viola Concerto

*** ASV CD DCA 1181. Callus, New Zealand SO, Taddei (with YORK BOWEN: *Viola Concerto;* HOWELLS: *Elegy;* VAUGHAN WILLIAMS: *Suite for Viola* ***)

Helen Callus, British-born but nowadays based in America, gives the most beautiful account of the Walton *Viola Concerto* on disc. With sumptuous viola tone and flawless intonation, not only does she bring out the warmth of Walton's lyricism, with one memorable theme after another, she discovers a hushed beauty in those passages which find mystery in half-tones, as in the link leading to the reprise in the first movement and, above all, in the haunting epilogue, which she takes expansively, with the music fading to nothingness. Add to that the incisiveness of her playing – and that of the orchestra in excellent form – in Walton's characteristically syncopated writing, helped by a recording which allows the fullest dynamic range to be appreciated, with the soloist very well balanced, not too close. The result is an account to match and outshine any that have appeared in many years. The coupling is generous, with the York Bowen *Concerto* strong and lyrical, the Vaughan Williams and Howells valuable rarities as makeweights, making this an outstanding recommendation.

Violin Concerto

☛ (M) *** Decca 475 7710 – Bell, Baltimore SO, Zinman – BLOCH: *Baal Shem;* BARBER: *Violin Concerto* ***

From an American perspective, Walton's *Violin Concerto* can well be seen as a British counterpart of the Barber, similarly romantic, written at exactly the same period. This prize-winning Decca disc has Bell giving a commanding account of the solo part of Walton's *Concerto*, even matching Heifetz himself in the ease of his virtuosity, and playing with rapt intensity. Rich and brilliant sound. The disc won a *Gramophone* Concerto award and is now placed among Decca's Originals.

Sonata for Strings

*** Channel Classics CCSSA 23005. Amsterdam Sinf. – BEETHOVEN: *String Quartet 16* ***

The Walton *Sonata for Strings*, an arrangement of his *A minor String Quartet* of 1945–7, has become a favourite work with this superb Dutch ensemble and was an automatic choice for a recording by them. It was felt appropriate to couple it with another arrangement of a string quartet, Opus 135, the last that Beethoven wrote. This is an ensemble that aims to conceive the orchestra in terms of a string quintet, remaining small in size 'for the exact purpose of preserving the intimate character of works such as these'. So the reading is more intimate than most, sharp and incisive in the fast movements, but warmly lyrical too, with the heart of the performance coming in the lovely slow movement, which here matches the *Lento* slow movement of the Beethoven in its dedication, with one yearning melody after another.

Symphony 1
(M) ***** LSO Live **SACD** LSO 0576. LSO, C. Davis

Symphony 1; Variations on a theme by Hindemith
(B) ***(*)** EMI 5 86596-2. Bournemouth SO, Handley

When towards the end of 2005 Colin Davis conducted this performance of Walton's *First Symphony* at the Barbican, it was greeted with ecstatic notices in the press, and rightly so. It was as though the critics involved had suddenly rediscovered this iconic work, reflecting the mood of uncertainty and tension of the 1930s. The very opening enters in such hushed tones, it is almost as though the music has only just come into human hearing. That atmosphere of mystery quickly evaporates, as the nagging syncopations of the repeated ostinato figure become ever more insistent, quickly developing into a powerful climax. The clarity of the textures and the sharpness of the attack add to the impact, with Colin Davis plainly at ease with the jazz element, finding more light and shade than is common in this bitingly intense movement. The Scherzo with its equally insistent syncopations brings big contrasts too, with textures again clarified, and the slow movement hauntingly once more plays on the feeling of music just coming into human hearing, this time in warmly lyrical ideas. The finale, altogether more extrovert, again brings clarity in the contrapuntal writing of successive fugatos, leading to a ripe conclusion. This first SACD version finds a welcome place, even though the 40-year-old benchmark performance from the same orchestra under the youthful André Previn has a sharpness and bite marginally even greater.

With a more sumptuous sound than in many versions, Handley's reading is above all red-bloodedly romantic, with Walton's melodies given their full expressive warmth. Equally, the jazzy spring that Handley gives to the rhythms, with their jaggedly misplaced accents, conveys a consistent buoyancy; nerves jangle less than usual, and the *Presto con malizia* of the Scherzo has a *Till*-like sense of fun about it. The lovely flute melody of the slow movement is not as cool as it usually is, leading on warmly to a climax that is weighty rather than bitingly tragic. It is a very valid view, beautifully achieved by Handley and the Bournemouth orchestra. Before the symphony, Handley presents what in 1989 was the first CD version of Walton's *Hindemith Variations*, one of the most satisfying of his later orchestral works, full of strong invention and finely wrought.

Symphony 2
(M) ***** EMI (ADD) 5 86595-2. LSO, Previn – LAMBERT: *Piano Concerto*, etc. *****

If Walton's *Second Symphony* prompted George Szell to direct the Cleveland Orchestra in one of its most spectacular performances on record (now deleted), André Previn and the LSO give another brilliant performance which in some ways gets closer to the heart of the music with its overtones of the composer's romantic opera, *Troilus and Cressida*. Previn is less literal than Szell, more sparkling in the outer movements,

more warmly romantic in the central slow movement. The 1973 Abbey Road recording is outstandingly fine and the coupling with Lambert could not be more imaginative.

Violin Sonata
(BB) ***(*)** ASV Resonance CD RSN 3060. McAslan, Blakely – ELGAR: *Violin Sonata* ***(*)**

Lorraine McAslan gives a warmly committed performance of Walton's often wayward sonata. The romantic melancholy of the piece suits her well and, though the recording does not make her tone as rounded as it should be, she produces some exquisite *pianissimo* playing. John Blakely is a most sympathetic partner, particularly impressive in crisply articulated passages. A disc that is worth its modest cost.

WARLAND, Bill (born 1921)

Amaro dolce; Bossa romantica; Brighton Belle; Dreaming Spires; Happy Hacienda; In the Shadows of Vesuvius; It's Spring Again; Latin Lover; Leeds Castle; Millennium: A Celebration March; Pepita; Rhapsodie Tristesse; Scottish Power; Shopping Spree; 3 Señoritas (suite); *Sombrero; To Eleanor*
* Marco Polo 8.225161. Dublin RTE Concert O, Sutherland

An excellent addition to Marco Polo's 'British Light Music' series. The composer himself wrote the sleeve notes – making some interesting comments on 'the death of light music in popular culture'. Still, it thrives on CD, for which Marco Polo, ASV and others have done splendid work. If none of the music here is momentous, it is thoroughly enjoyable and tuneful. There are nice splashes of local colour here and there (the rumbustious *Latin Lover* is especially enjoyable) and sentiment as well as humour are represented, and it's good to see that Bill Warland is still composing; his *Millennium March* was written for the January celebrations. In case you are thinking the Gaelic flavoured *Scottish Power* has something to do with the electricity supply, it was actually written, the composer tells us, 'as a dedication to a Scots lassie I know so well, with whom there was a magnetic attraction, and whose maiden name was Power'. Excellent performances and recording.

WAXMAN, Franz (1906–67)

Film Suites: (i) *The Bride of Frankenstein;* (ii) *The Invisible Ray; Prince Valiant; Rebecca; Suspicion; Taras Bulba*
* Silva Screen FILMCD 726. Westminster PO, Alwyn; (ii) City of Prague PO, Bateman

With a flamboyant introduction that sweeps you into 1930s Hollywood, *The Bride of Frankenstein*, still regarded as one of the finest horror films ever made, brings one of Waxman's most enjoyable scores. There is plenty of exciting, dramatic music here, very colourfully orchestrated, including the use of whole-tone scales and an ondes martenot (a synthesizer is used here to create supernatural effects). It's not all horror hokum music though, there's wit and parody too (Gounod's *Faust* crops up), and one especially enjoys the *Minuet*, most charmingly orchestrated by Clifford Vaughan, himself an organist, an instrument used effectively in this score, as in the delightfully quirky *Dance Macabre* – a number that should have a lease of life on its own. This well-arranged suite marks this score's début on CD, with Kenneth Alwyn and his orchestra fully at home in Waxman's musical world. The more famous suites of *Prince Valiant, Taras Bulba* and *Suspicion* are included, as well as *Rebecca* (his finest score), and the less well-known *The Invisible Ray*, another enjoyable horror score, dating from 1936, with the suite assembled by the composer's son, John Waxman, and with Stephen Bernstein having to orchestrate it completely by ear as none of the original survives. Very good recordings and performances, too – a must for film-music buffs.

Rebecca (complete film score)
(BB) *** Naxos 8.557549. Slovak RSO, Adriano

Rebecca (1940) is regarded as Waxman's finest score, and it is easy to see why: as soon as the splendid Selznick International trademark theme is played (composed by Newman), Waxman sweeps you into the world of Daphne du Maurier's bestseller *Rebecca*. The score is an integral part of Hitchcock's film, with the Rebecca theme used to portray the ghostly presence of Max De Winter's dead first wife (Rebecca) and, throughout, the music brilliantly portrays the often haunting and creepy atmosphere of this gothic fantasy. It is not all gloomy though, with numbers such as the *Lobby Waltz* providing a gorgeous, haunting piece of nostalgia. Adriano (and others) has made a splendid job of assembling this score, some of which had to be reconstructed from the soundtrack while other music, not used in the final film, is restored here. Both the performance and recording are very good and, at bargain price, this is essential for all film music fans.

WEBER, Carl Maria von (1786–1826)

Clarinet Concerto 2 in E flat, Op. 74
*** Australian Decca Eloquence (ADD) 476 7404. De Peyer, LSO, C. Davis – MOZART: *Clarinet Concerto in A;* SPOHR: *Clarinet Concerto 1* ***

De Peyer is fully up to the bravura in Weber's splendidly tuneful *Second Clarinet Concerto*, especially in the infectious finale, packed with fireworks. The exceptionally warm, vivid Decca recording adds to the vibrant quality of the music-making and, with buoyant support from Colin Davis and the LSO, this CD makes a very welcome return to the catalogue.

Overtures: Euryanthe; Oberon; Peter Schmoll und seine Nachbarn; Preciosa
(M) (**) DG mono/stereo 477 5296 (8). VPO, Boehm – MOZART: *Symphonies* (**); R. STRAUSS: *Tone-poems* (**(*))

These Weber overtures date from a 1951 Decca LP (last seen on ACL 28) and, as often with Decca's recordings of that period, the treble is bit toppy, though there is some compensation in the depth of the overall sound-picture. The performances are robustly enjoyable, with Boehm taking care in the Spanish rhythms of *Preciosa*, and one enjoys his considered – though not too considered – approach. It is, as always, hard not to listen to the delightful bassoon tune in *Peter Schmoll* without smiling!

Symphonies 1 in C; 2 in C, J.50/51
(BB) ** Warner Apex 2564 60619-2. Norwegian RO, Rasilainen – WAGNER: *Symphony in C* **

On Apex, an inexpensive way of acquiring Weber's two very attractive *Symphonies*, with a Wagner curiosity. The performances are lively and committed, but the recording is not much above average.

OPERA

Euryanthe (complete DVD version)
* Dynamic **DVD** DV 33408. Prohinka, Fogašová, Yikun Chung, Cernoch, Scheibner, Salsi, Savoia, Cagliari Teatro Lirico Ch. & O, Korsten

Weber's libretto for *Euryanthe* is pretty feeble to say the least, and so the fine music goes unperformed. The story, with an unlikely ghost haunting the hero and heroine, needs someone to try and do a rewrite. Meanwhile, Gérard Korsten and his Cagliari company take the work at face value and he keeps the music spiritedly alive. There are no outstanding singers or actors here, but the company does its best and the production is traditional and natural. Of mainly novelty value.

Oberon (complete CD recording)
(M) *** DG 477 5644 (2). Grob, Nilsson, Domingo, Prey, Hamari, Schiml, Bav. R. Ch. & SO, Kubelik

We owe it to Covent Garden's strange ideas in the mid-1820s as to what 'English opera' should be, that Weber's delicately conceived score is a sequence of illogical arias, scenas and ensembles, strung togther by an absurd pantomime plot, nearly as bad as the one for *Euryanthe*, but not quite! Though even on record the result is slacker because of the loose construction, one can appreciate, in a performance as stylish and refined as this, the contribution of Weber. The original issue included dialogue and a narrative spoken by one of Oberon's fairy characters. In the LP reissue this was cut, but the dialogue has now been restored (although it is separately cued, so it can be programmed out). With Birgit Nilsson commanding in *Ocean thou mighty monster* and excellent singing from the other principals, helped by Kubelik's ethereally light handling of the orchestra, the set can be recommended without reservation, for the 1970 recording, made in the Munich Herculessaal, is of excellent quality. The reissue comes with a cued synopsis of the story.

WEILL, Kurt (1900–50)

(i; ii) *Die sieben Todsünden (The Seven Deadly Sins);* (i) Songs: *Berlin im Licht; Complainte de la Seine; Es regnet; Youkali; Nannas Lied; Wie lange noch?*
(B) **(*) HM Musique d'Abord HMA 1951420. (i) Fassbaender; (ii) Brandt, Sojer, Komatsu, Urbas, Hanover R. PO, Garben

This Harmonia Mundi set stars Brigitte Fassbaender, who, using the original pitch, brings a Lieder-singer's feeling for word detail and a comparable sense of style. Her account is obviously less street-wise than Lemper's, but there is a plangent feeling that is highly appropriate. The songs are equally impressive, mainly connected in one way or another with the main piece. The vocal quartet makes an idiomatic team, but the conductor Cord Garben at times seems on the leisurely side in his choice of tempi. Excellent, vivid recording.

WEISS, Silvius (1686–1750)

Lute Sonatas: 2 in D; 27 in C min.; 35 in D min.
(BB) *** Naxos 8.554350. Barto (Baroque lute)

Lute Sonatas: 5 in G; 25 in G min.; 50 in B flat
(BB) *** Naxos 8.553988. Barto (Baroque lute)

Lute Sonatas: 7 in C min.; 23 in B flat; 45 in A
(BB) *** Naxos 8.555772. Barto (Baroque lute)

Lute Sonatas: 21 in F min.; 37 in C; 46 in A
(BB) *** Naxos 8.554557. Barto (Baroque lute)

Lute Sonatas: 36 in D min.; 42 in A min.; 49 in B flat
(BB) *** Naxos 8.553773. Barto (Baroque lute)

Lute Sonatas: 38 in C; 43 in A min.; Tombeau sur la mort de M. Cajeran Baron d'Hartig
(BB) *** Naxos 8.554833. Barto (Baroque lute)

Lute Sonatas 15 in B flat; 48 in F sharp min.
(BB) *** Naxos 8.557806. Barto (Baroque lute)

On Naxos, Robert Barto, playing a baroque lute, shows us the breadth of Weiss's achievement and how naturally the music suits the lute, rather than the guitar. On almost all the discs offered so far he combines one early, one mid-period and one late sonata. He begins Volume I (8.553773) with the *D minor Sonata* from the 1720s (No. 36), opening with a short *Fantasia* which immediately invites an improvisatory freedom leading us naturally into the *Allemande*. Like the expansive *Sarabande*, this demonstrates the composer's celebrated Italianate cantabile style. Yet the *Bourrée* and, especially, the lively closing *Gigue* bring plenty of bubbly virtuosity. Both Sonatas 42 (probably a later work from the 1730s) and 49 open with pensive *Allemandes*, but there is plenty of variety later, and No. 42 has two consecutive fast movements (including a vigorous *Bourrée* marked 'Posato'), the essence of which reappears in the *moto perpetuo* finale.

The manuscript of the *Sonata in G major* (No. 5), which opens the second disc, was found in London. It is a most winning work, spontaneously integrating its basic musical material throughout, with the central *Courante* and *Bourrée* particularly infectious, and a jaunty finale. The opening *Prelude* of *No. 25 in G minor* is no more than a very brief introduction to the *Allemande* and, after the lively *Passepied* and *Bourrée*, its *Sarabande* is nobly serene. However, No. 50 is a late work, and it has an extended *Introduzzione* which acts as Prelude and *Allemande* combined. After the light-hearted central movements, the *Sarabande* is thoughtful and searching, one of the composer's finest; the work ends with a brilliant finale which in its harmonic progressions is compellingly unpredictable.

No. 2, which begins Volume 3 (8.554350), is another early work, found in the London manuscript. It too is all of a piece, so that the continued use of the basic musical idea found in the Prelude follows through the remaining six movements very neatly. No. 27 must have been written on a rainy day. Weiss omits the Prelude and it is the *Allemande* which sets the doleful character of this C minor work; neither the following *Gavotte*, written in the lower register, nor the Rondeau lifts the mood, and while the *Sarabande* moves into the relative major key, the closing movements maintain the sonata's curiously melancholy atmosphere. No. 35, written in D minor (the natural key of the baroque lute), is one of the composer's last and most ambitious works, probably dating from the 1740s. The measured *Allemande* is harmonically exploratory, and even the finale, by use of the instrument's lower tessitura, provides virtuosity without loss of gravitas.

No. 46 in A major, which opens Volume 4, is another late work; it begins unusually, with a French Overture (though without the usual reprise of the opening section). This is another of Weiss's most inspired and varied sonatas, very outgoing, with a lively *Bourrée*, followed by a halcyon *Sarabande*, a pair of Minuets (in A minor and A major) effectively contrasted in mood, and one of the composer's bravura moto perpetuo finales. By contrast *No. 21 in F minor* (written in 1719) is one of the composer's more melancholy sonatas, but the bright sound of the instrument's upper register prevents the music from becoming mournful. A pleasing balance is struck by ending the disc with the *C major Sonata* (No. 37) from the same period, which is altogether more cheerful throughout.

No. 43, in Volume 5 (8.554833), is one of the composer's last works – and one of his finest. On the disc it follows immediately after the solemn *Tombeau for Count Jan Anton Losy* (a celebrated Bohemian nobleman and lutenist), and the sonata's dignified opening *Allemande* might almost be a funeral march for the lamented Count. The sixth disc spans the whole range of Weiss's career, with the early *C minor Sonata* (No. 7) actually dated 1706 by the young composer in pencil on the manuscript. The writing has a youthful preciosity, and the grave opening *Allemande* leads into an easy-going *Courante* and a charming *Gavotte*. *Sonata 23 in B flat* probably dates from around 1720, and is unusual in having a pair each of *Bourrées*, *Gavottes* and *Menuets*, of which the second in each case is rather more demanding of the player than the first. The solemn single *Sarabande* counters the graceful levity of the movements which surround it, but the sonata ends with a delightful *Saltarella*. The *A major Sonata* (No. 45) is one of Weiss's most mature works, coming from the 1740s. Like No. 50, it has an *Introduzzione*, but this time in the form of a French Ouverture which introduces a theme a little like Handel's *Harmonious Blacksmith*. The following *Courante* is remarkably extended, and the *Bourrée* and *Sarabande* are similarly spacious, to be followed by a memorable *Sarabande* and a finale of comparable scope and interest.

But the quality of Weiss's invention seems inexhaustible throughout all these works, and he has a worthy exponent in Robert Barto, a virtuoso lutenist of a high order and a fine musician. He understands this repertory perfectly, never seeking to impose his personality over that of the composer, and the first-class Naxos recording gives him a natural presence.

The two large-scale *Sonatas*, Nos. 15 and 48 in Volume 7, come from the middle and late periods of Weiss's output. Both have solemn opening *Allemandes*, while the *Sarabande* in the B flat Sonata is described as a *Plainte*. This is the more serious and reflective of the two works, *No. 48 in B flat* brings a greater variety of feeling, notably in the *Courante*, while the *Sarabande* has a resigned melancholy. Then the mood of the music lightens attractively for the closing *Minuet* and *Presto* (no longer a gigue). Robert Barto's performances meet every challenge with confidence and sensitivity.

WEISSENBERG, Alexis (born 1929)

(i) *4 Improvisations on Songs from La Fugue. Le Regret; Sonata en état de jazz*
*(**) Nim. NI 5688. Mulligan; (i) with Walden

As with other composer-pianists who have a wide repertoire, Weissenberg's own music does not project a strong individuality. *La Fugue* was a musical comedy for which he wrote the score in Paris in the 1960s. It was revived as a 'surrealistic musical' in Darmstadt in 1992, with the new name *Nostalgia*. The first of the *Four Improvisations* is a jazzy, jittery tarantella, brilliantly played here; the other three bear out the title admirably, with Frank Walden on saxophone joining the pianist to create the smoky, late-evening atmosphere in the second piece, *Mon destin*. *Le Regret* is also written in a gentle, improvisatory style, which seems to be the composer's forte, for it is the third movement of the *Jazz Sonata*, the rather haunting *Reflets d'un blues*, which is the most beguiling. The other three, which in turn supposedly embody the spirit of the tango, charleston and samba, are somewhat intractable, and not very successful in their evocation, although the final *Provocation de samba* is the most rhythmically inventive. Weissenberg could not have a more committed advocate than Simon Mulligan, who plays with great flair and conviction, and is very well recorded. But this is not a disc for the general collector.

WELLESZ, Egon (1885–1974)

Symphonies 1, Op. 62; 8, Op. 110; Symphonic Epilogue, Op. 108
*** CPO 999 998-2. V. RSO, Rabl

During the war years Wellesz wrote very little, but towards the end of the war and with the prospect of an allied victory his muse was reawakened with his setting of Gerard Manley Hopkins's 'The Leaden Echo and the Golden Echo'. Wellesz was in awe of the symphonic form and his *First Symphony* (1945–6) was written relatively late in life, when he was 60, and was premièred by Celibidache and the Berlin Philharmonic in 1948; a recording of their performance was broadcast in the Third Programme later that year. The first movement is in strict sonata form and there is an inventive and animated Scherzo. The finale, also in sonata form, owes much to Mahler, then slowly surfacing in England. After completing his one-movement *Symphonic Epilogue* Wellesz changed his mind and wanted to preface it with two other movements and call it the *Symphony No. 8*. His publisher, who had already prepared the Epilogue for the press, persuaded him to write a new finale for the two movements, and this became the *Eighth*. Both works were composed in 1969 when he was 84, two years before he was incapacitated by a stroke.

Symphonies 3; 5
*** CPO 999 999-2. V. RSO, Rabl

The *Third Symphony* was composed in Oxford between 1949 and 1951, and the *Fifth*, which comes in 1955–6, returns to the dodecaphony of Schoenberg, which had occupied Wellesz before the war. The *Third* was not premièred until 2000; but while he was a student, R.L. was privileged to hear the composer playing it for him on the piano with the sustaining pedal held down pretty well throughout, plus vocalizations added when necessary! Recollections of the occasion were dashed upon hearing this performance – which shows just how unreliable memory can be. But one thing stands: the sheer sense of sweep, the real stamp of the symphonist, and the quality of the ideas and their development. As this series has developed, it has shown Wellesz to be a powerful symphonic thinker. The *Fifth* is a tougher nut, but one well worth cracking. The Vienna Radio Symphony Orchestra plays well for Gottfried Rabl and the ORF engineers get well-balanced sound.

WHITLOCK, Percy (1903–46)

Ballet of the Wood Creatures; Balloon Ballet; Come Along, Marnie; Dignity and Impudence March. The Feast of St

Benedict: Concert Overture. Holiday Suite; Music for Orchestra: Suite. Susan, Doggie and Me; Wessex Suite
**(*) Marco Polo 8.225162. Dublin RTE Concert O, Sutherland

Percy Whitlock's style is attractive and easy-going, with quite imaginative orchestration and nice touches everywhere. The marches are jolly and the waltzes nostalgic – *The Ballet of the Wood Creatures* is especially charming. Gavin Sutherland directs the RTE Orchestra with his usual understanding. The sound is good, but occasionally the strings sound a little scrawny (the opening of *Waltz* in the *Holiday Suite*, for example).

WIDOR, Charles-Marie (1844–1937)

Piano Quintet in D min., Op. 7; Piano Trio in B flat, Op. 19
(BB) *** Naxos 8.555416. Prunyi, New Budapest Qt

This is quite a find. Widor as a composer of chamber music comes from an altogether different musical species than the writer of spectacular organ symphonies. The *Piano Trio* is early. Composed in 1875, it is a charming, lightweight work, with a romantic first movement with a pleasingly elegant secondary theme. There is a debt to Mendelssohn in the *Andante*, which is like a song without words. The Scherzo and rondo finale have attractive ideas too, besides freshness and vitality.

The *Piano Quintet*, although shorter in length, is a bigger work, more concentrated in conception and style, with the piano dominating the bold opening movement. Once more the *Andante* brings elegance, but it is the *Molto vivace* Scherzo that looks back to Mendelssohn. The polyphonic development in the finale then brings added gravitas. Both works are played here with fluent spontaneity and plenty of spirit, and the recording is excellent. This is not great music, but admirers of Widor's organ music may find it a refreshing change.

Organ Symphonies: 1 in C min.: Méditation (only). 2 in D; 3 in E min.: Prélude, Adagio & Final. 4 in F min., Op. 13/1–4; 5 in F min.; 6 in G min., Op. 42/1–2; 9 in C min. (Gothique), Op. 70
(BB) *** Warner Apex 2564 62297-2 (2). Marie-Claire Alain (Cavaillé-Coll organs, St-Etienne de Caen & Eglise de St-Germain-en-Laye)

Fot this Apex reissue Warner have combined two sets of recordings, from 1970 and 1977, which jointly offer an impressive overall coverage of this repertoire. Marie-Claire Alain contents herself with playing just the *Méditation* from the uneven *First Symphony*, and only three movements from the *Third*. Here the St Germain organ sounds very orchestral and the colouring of the gentle *Adagio* (a perpetual canon) is very effective. If its spectacular Wagnerian finale, with cascading sextuplets, is not musically as well focused as the more famous *Toccata* from No. 5, it sounds very exciting here. As it ends gently, the opening movement of No. 4 makes a bold contrast, while the *Andante cantabile* is quite haunting. The later symphonies are more impressive works than the earlier group of Op. 13. No. 5 is justly the most famous, but the *Gothic Symphony* has a specially fine third movement in which a Christmas chant (*Puer natus est nobis*) is embroidered fugally. The final section is a set of variations, and the Gregorian chant is reintroduced in the pedals. These are classic, authoritative performances, given spacious analogue sound with just a touch of harshness to add a little edge in *fortissimos*. Excellent value.

(i) *Symphonies 9 in C min. (Gothique), Op. 70; (ii) 10 in D (Romane), Op. 73*
*** ASV CDDCA 1172. Fisell (organs of (i) St George's Chapel, Windsor; (ii) Liverpool Metropolitan Cathedral)

An outstanding and apt coupling (for both works are based on Gregorian chant), one of the best in the ASV series. Perhaps surprisingly, the St George's Chapel organ at Windsor suits the *Gothique Symphony* admirably. The warm acoustic and clarity of detail mean that the plainchant, *Puer natus et nobis*, which dominates the third and fourth movements (with the finale a quasi-passacaglia) always emerges from the texture, while the pedals in the closing toccata are as thunderous as the composer could possibly want.

The *Symphonie Romane* is based on a single Easter gradual, *Haec dies*, and it is subject to both a series of variations and what the organist in the notes suggests is 'a Lisztian/ Franckian thematic metamorphosis'. It needs just the wide range of colour, atmosphere and reedy bite that the Liverpool organ can provide, and the cathedral resonance adds spectacle to the thrilling cascades of the finale, with its long, sustained closing chord. Jeremy Fisell gives outstanding performances of both works, splendidly recorded; for once, one does not long for a Cavaillé-Coll; these two English organs suit the music admirably.

WILLIAMS, Charles (1893–1978)

The Bells of St Clements; Blue Devils; Cross Country; Cutty Sark; Destruction by Fire; Devil's Galop; (i) The Dream of Olwen. The Girls in Grey; High Adventure (Friday Night is Music Night); The Humming Top; Jealous Lover; Little Tyrolean; London Fair; Model Railway; (i) The Music Lesson. The Night Has Eyes; Nursery Clock; The Old Clockmaker; Rhythm on Rails; Sally Tries the Ballet; Starlings; Throughout the Years; The Voice of London; Young Ballerina (The Potter's Wheel)
(M) *** ASV WHL 2151. BBC Concert O, Wordsworth, (i) with Elms

Rather like Henry Mancini and his *Pink Panther* theme, if Charles Williams had written only *Devil's Galop* (aka the *Dick Barton* theme), he would certainly be remembered, and it is brilliantly done here. Older listeners will surely recognize *Girls in Grey* and *The Potter's Wheel* from early 1950s television, and also *High Adventure* (used for *Friday Night Is Music Night* on Radio 2). Film buffs will know the themes from *The Apartment* and the pseudo-romantic piano concerto *The Dream of Olwen* – not in the league of the *Warsaw Concerto* but curiously haunting nevertheless, and certainly more durable than the film for which it was written (*While I Live*). Williams wrote a great deal of attractive, unpretentious music, much of it included on this generously filled CD. There are plenty of 'character' numbers, such as *The Music Lesson*, with metronome and scales interspersed with a most attractive theme, and *The Nursery Clock*, a perky little vignette, just on the right side of twee. *The Little Tyrolean* gently evokes the world of the Strauss family, while *The Humming Top* is reminiscent of Bizet's *Jeux d'enfants*. England of the 1950s is evoked in *Cross Country* (1954) and *London Fair* (1955), while railway travel of the period is recalled in *Model Railway* (1951) and the even better remembered *Rhythm on the Rails* (1950). *The Bells of St Clements* is a charming fantasy based on the popular nursery rhyme, while the composer is in more dramatic mode for *Destruction by*

Fire, depicting the wartime Blitz. In the 1960s, Oxford University invited Williams to receive an honorary doctorate. He declined, considering himself unworthy. It's hard to imagine too many composers of popular music doing that today! Recording and performances are both excellent.

WILLIAMSON, Malcolm (1931–2003)

Concerto grosso; Our Man in Havana: Suite; Santiago de Espada Overture; Sinfonietta
*** Chan. 10359. Iceland SO, Gamba

Our Man in Havana, based on Graham Greene's novel, is among the most colourful of post-war British operas, with its catchy Cuban rhythms and its tunes first-cousin to those in Broadway musicals. Until this excellent disc, the first of a projected Williamson series, not a note of it had been recorded, and this suite of four substantial movements makes one long for a full-scale stage revival. The *Concerto grosso* and *Sinfonietta* are both exercises in Williamson's attractive brand of neo-classicism, and the *Overture, Santiago de Espada*, written in 1956, well before the rest, is even more approachable, one of Williamson's first essays in tonality after his early experiments with serialism. Rumon Gamba conducts fresh, crisp performances with the Iceland Symphony Orchestra, very well recorded.

WINDING, August (1835–99)

Piano Concerto in A min., Op. 19; Concert Allegro in C min., Op. 29
**(*) Danacord DACOCD 581. Marshev, Danish PO, South Jutland, Aeschbacher – E. HARTMANN: *Piano Concerto* *(*)

August Winding belonged to Grieg's circle of Copenhagen friends (Grieg introduced his *Overture to a Norwegian Tragedy* to Christiania, as Oslo was then known). He studied with Gade, Reinecke and Dreyschock and had a flourishing but short career as a virtuoso pianist before a nervous complaint in his arm forced him to give up concert work. His *Piano Concerto* shares the same key but not the same opus number as the Grieg. The concerto is small talk, very derivative and much indebted to Gade and Mendelssohn. It has a certain charm, even if the ideas are pretty unmemorable. The *Concert Allegro* is eminently Schumannesque, but is so brilliantly played by the Russian virtuoso Oleg Marshev and the Danish orchestra that one is almost tempted to believe that it is better than it is. Winding shares the disc with his brother-in-law, Emil Hartmann.

WITT, Friedrich (1770–1836)

Septet (for Clarinet, Horn, Bassoon, 2 Violins, Viola, Cello & Double bass)
*** MDG 308 0232. Charis-Ens. – KREUTZER: *Septet* ***

There is much attractive interplay between the instruments in Witt's pleasing *Septet* and, if it isn't quite as inspired as the sparkling Kreutzer work, it is still enjoyable, with its attractive melodies, a nicely varied *Adagio* and an easy-going manner – the finale especially so. It receives a first-class performance and recording.

WOLF, Hugo (1860–1903)

Italian Serenade in G

(BB) *** Virgin 2x1 4 82112-2 (2). Sinfonia Varsovia, Y.
Menuhin – MOZART: *Divertimento 1*, etc.; SCHOENBERG:
Verklaerte Nacht; WAGNER: *Siegfried Idyll* ***

Seldom heard in the concert hall (it is too short to fit in
today's sparse two- and three-work programmes), Wolf's
Italian Serenade used to be more familiar as it fitted neatly on
two 78 r.p.m. sides. Menuhin's vivacious performance of the
chamber orchestral version is full of charm and vivacity, and
is vividly recorded.

YSAŸE, Eugène (1858–1931)

Violin Sonata 1 in G min.

*** Sony SK 92938. Skride – BACH: *Partita 2;* BARTÓK: *Solo
Violin Sonata* ***

Baiba Skride is a Latvian violinist, now in her mid-twenties,
who won the *Prix Concours* at the Queen Elisabeth Competition in Brussels in 2001 when she was 19. She has a flawless
technique and makes a wonderful sound, and it is evident
from all these pieces that she is a musician first and a virtuoso
second: in short, an artist first and foremost. In the Ysaÿe *G
minor Sonata* she is highly persuasive.

ZEMLINSKY, Alexander von
(1871–1942)

Alexander Zemlinsky, although influential in his lifetime as
an apostle of Mahler and teacher of Webern, Korngold and
Schoenberg – who greatly admired his music – spent his
career mainly as an opera conductor. He emigrated to
America in 1938, where he only survived four more years,
virtually forgotten as a composer. But in recent years his star
has risen, mainly through the influence of recordings.

Symphonies (i) 1 in D min.; (ii) 2 in B flat

(BB) **(*) EMI Encore 3 41446-2. Cologne Gürzenich O,
Conlon

The early symphonies are comparatively conventional works
and give little idea of the originality and luxuriant textures of
Zemlinsky's later works. The *D minor Symphony* was the
confident work of a 20-year-old student; the *B flat Symphony*
is rather more exploratory, with a striking Scherzo and a
strongly lyrical slow movement leading to a passacaglia finale
which brings a flavour of Brahms, a wayward middle section
where the tension drops, but it ends boldly and vigorously.
Both works are scored in a post-Brahmsian way. Conlon is a
highly sympathetic advocate and makes a good case for the
Second Symphony, especially the quite memorable slow
movement, which the Cologne orchestra play ardently and
sympathetically, with a very touching closing section. The
recording is full-bodied and quite well detailed. But neither
of these works is destined to enter the concert repertory.

ZIEHRER, Carl Michael (1843–1922)

Auersperg-Marsch; Landstreicher-Quadrille. Polkas:
Burgerlich und romantisch; Pfiffig; Die Tänzerin; Loslassen!

Waltzes: *Clubgeister; Diesen Kuss der ganzen Welt;
Libesrezepte; Osterreich in Tönen; Wiener Bürger*
**(*) Marco Polo 8.223814. Razumovsky Sinfonia, Walter

Fächer-polonaise; Mein Feld ist die Welt-Marsch. Polkas:
*Endlich allein! Im Fluge; Lieber Bismarck, schaukle nicht;
Matrosen.* Waltzes: *Heimatsgefühle; Herreinspaziert!; Sei
brav; In der Sommerfrische; Tolles Mädel*
**(*) Marco Polo 8.223815. Razumovsky Sinfonia, Dittrich

Ziehrer's style is very much in the Johann Strauss tradition
but, unlike many of Strauss's rivals, Ziehrer's music has a
distinctive, robust quality, probably attributable to his career
as a military band leader for many years. His music overflows
with tunes, is thoroughly entertaining, and will disappoint no
one who responds to the Viennese tradition.

Volume 1 opens with his most famous piece, *Wiener
Bürger*, a delightful waltz that rivals the best of Strauss. The
Die Tänzerin polka uses as its basis themes from the opera of
the same name – to invigorating effect; the *Landstreicher-
Quadrille* is composed in the same way, and contains some
particularly jaunty numbers. Not surprisingly, Ziehrer was
adept at writing marches, and the *Auersperg-Marsch* is one of
his best – it had to be repeated several times at its première.
The almost forgotten *Osterreich in Tönen Waltz (Melodies of
Austria)* is another highlight: all its melodies are in fact
original, but it has an agreeably localized ethnic flavour.

Volume 2 offers more of the same: it begins with the fine
Herreinspaziert Waltz, which soon lunges into a richly contoured theme to rival *Wiener Bürger*. The *Fächer* ('Fan')
polonaise is memorable, and is still used to introduce the
prestigious annual Philharmonic Ball in Vienna. The polkas
are wittily crafted, and none of the waltzes here is without at
least one memorable theme. The *Tolles Mädel* ('Crazy Girl')
waltz even begins to look forward to the American musical
and is a winner in every way, as is the *Sei brav* ('Be Good')
waltz – a lively confection of music from Ziehrer's operetta
Fesche Geister ('Lively Spirits').

The performances from both conductors are lively and
sympathetic, the recordings bright and vivid (the second disc
a little less so), and the sleeve-notes helpful and informative.

Marches: *Auf! in's XX; Freiherr von Schönfeld; Wen mann
Geld hat, ist man fein!* Polkas: *Ballfieber; Ein Blich nach
Ihr!; Cavallerie; Wurf-Bouquet.* Styrien Tänze: *D'Kermad'ln;*
Waltzes: *Auf hoher See!; Gebirgskinder; Ich lach'!; O, dies
Husaren!; Zichrereien*

☞ *** Marco Polo 8.225172. Razumovsky Sinfonia, Pollack

Volume 3 is easily the finest Ziehrer collection so far, and one
laments again that Christian Pollack, who is a master of
Viennese rhythmic inflexion, did not direct the other two
(and indeed all the Strauss family collections). The three
marches have a light-hearted zest (*Wenn man Geld hat* almost
sounds like Lehár). *Auf hoher See* opens with a trumpet/
cornet solo, and not surprisingly the brass take the lead in the
Cavallerie Polka, while the *Ballfieber* polka français is also
most beguiling, and Pollack's bold accents in *Wurf-Bouquet*
add lift rather than heaviness. The charming waltzes bounce
along engagingly. *O, dies Husaren!* has been rescued from its
surviving piano score and orchestrated jointly by Martin Uhl
and Pollack with idiomatic skill; and how beautifully Pollack
opens the *Gebirgskinder*, with a zither solo reminiscent of
Johann's *Tales from the Vienna Woods*. Indeed this is another
of Ziehrer's waltzes with a string of melodies all but worthy
of that master. The orchestra responds with lilt and sparkle
throughout, and the recording cannot be faulted.

CONCERTS OF ORCHESTRAL AND CONCERTANTE MUSIC

Art of conducting

The Art of Conducting: Vol. 1: 'Great Conductors of the Past' (Barbirolli, Beecham, Bernstein, Busch, Furtwängler, Karajan, Klemperer, Koussevitzky, Nikisch, Reiner, Stokowski, Richard Strauss, Szell, Toscanini, Walter, Weingartner): BRUCKNER: *Symphony 7* (rehearsal) (Hallé O, Barbirolli). GOUNOD: *Faust: ballet music* (with rehearsal) (RPO, Beecham). Silent film (BPO, Nikisch). RICHARD STRAUSS: *Till Eulenspiegel* (VPO, Richard Strauss). WEBER: *Der Freischütz: Overture* (Paris SO, Felix Weingartner). WAGNER: *Tannhäuser: Overture* (Dresden State O, Fritz Busch). MOZART: *Symphony 40* (BPO, Bruno Walter). BRAHMS: *Symphony 2* (rehearsal) (Vancouver Festival O, Bruno Walter). BEETHOVEN: *Egmont: Overture; Symphony 5* (Philh. O, Klemperer). WAGNER: *Die Meistersinger: Overture.* SCHUBERT: *Symphony 8* (*Unfinished*). BRAHMS: *Symphony 4* (both rehearsals) (BPO, Furtwängler). VERDI: *La forza del destino: Overture; La Traviata: Coro di zingarelle*. RESPIGHI: *The Pines of Rome* (NBC SO, Toscanini). PURCELL (arr. Stokowski): *Dido and Aeneas: Dido's lament*. RESPIGHI: *The Pines of Rome* (BBC SO). CHAIKOVSKY: *Symphony 5* (NYPO) (all cond. Stokowski). BEETHOVEN: *Egmont overture* (Boston SO, Koussevitzky). CHAIKOVSKY: *Violin Concerto* (Heifetz, NYPO, Reiner). BEETHOVEN: *Symphony 7* (Chicago SO, Reiner). BRAHMS: *Academic Festival Overture*. BEETHOVEN: *Symphony 5* (Cleveland O, Szell). BEETHOVEN: *Symphony 5*. DEBUSSY: *La Mer* (BPO, Karajan). SHOSTAKOVICH: *Symphony 5* (rehearsal and performance) (LSO). MAHLER: *Symphony 4* (VPO) (both cond. Bernstein). BEETHOVEN: *Symphony 9* (Philh. O, Klemperer). (Commentary by John Eliot Gardiner, Isaac Stern, Jack Brymer, Beecham, Menuhin,

Oliver Knussen, Suvi Raj Grubb, Szell, Walter, Klemperer, Hugh Bean, Werner Thärichen, Richard Mohr, Stokowski, Julius Baker, Karajan)
✪ *** Teldec **DVD** 0927 42667-2

This extraordinary DVD offers a series of electrifying performances by the great conductors of our century, all seen and heard at their very finest. Enormous care has been taken over the sound, even in the earliest recordings, for it is remarkably full-bodied and believable. But most of all it is to watch conductors weaving their magic spell over the orchestra which is so fascinating. And sometimes they do it imperceptibly, like Richard Strauss conducting *Till Eulenspiegel* with apparent nonchalance, yet making music with the utmost aural vividness; Fritz Busch creating great tension in Wagner; Bruno Walter wonderfully mellow in Brahms; Klemperer in Beethoven hardly moving his baton and yet completely in control; Furtwängler rehearsing the finale of Brahms's *Fourth Symphony* with a tremendous flow of adrenalin; Toscanini the martinet in Verdi; Stokowski moulding gloriously beautiful sound with flowing movements of his hands and arms; and, most riveting of all, Bernstein creating enormous passion with the LSO in Shostakovich's *Fifth Symphony*.

Of the many commentaries from other artists and various musicians, the experience of Werner Thärichen stands out. He was participating in a Berlin performance when he suddenly realized that the sound around him had changed: it had become uncannily more beautiful. Not understanding why, he looked to the back of the hall . . . and saw that Furtwängler had just walked in. The great Nikisch is seen conducting (on silent film) but not heard – and no one knows what the music was!

The collection opens fascinatingly with Toscanini (1952), Karajan (1957), Klemperer and Szell (1961) heard consecutively conducting an excerpt from Beethoven's *Fifth Symphony*.

Ančerl, Karel

SHOSTAKOVICH: *Festive Overture.* NOVAK: *In the Tatra Mountains.* KREJCI: *Serenade.* JANACEK: *Taras Bulba.* MACHA: *Variations on a Theme by and on the Death of Jan Rychlík* (all with Czech PO). SMETANA: *Má Vlast: Vltava.* DVORAK: *Slavonic Dance 8, Op. 46/8* (with VSO). *Symphony 8 in G.* (with Concg. O). MARTINU: *Symphony 5* (with Toronto SO)

(B) (***) EMI mono/stereo 5 75091-2 (2)

The earliest recording in this Ančerl anthology is the Novák, made in 1950 and familiar to LP collectors from the old mono Supraphon catalogue. It sounds very good here, though naturally it is lacking the transparency of a more modern recording. The *Serenade for Orchestra* of Iša Krejčí is extrovert and diatonic; the composer was a school friend of Ančerl and, subsequently, a colleague in pre-war Prague Radio. Recorded in 1957, it is unremittingly cheerful but completely unmemorable. The transfer of Ančerl's classic (1959) account of *Taras Bulba* is excellent and the *Variations on a Theme by and on the Death of Jan Rychlík* by Otmar Mácha – whose representation in the catalogue is slender – is rather haunting. The 1958 *Vltava*, recorded in Vienna, is first rate both as performance and as sound. The Dvořák *Eighth Symphony* is relatively late, coming from a 1970 guest appearance with the Concertgebouw, and there is a bright and vital account of the Martinů *Fifth Symphony* from a 1971 Toronto concert. Even if the quality of the Canadian strings is not as fine-grained or as well blended as the Czech Philharmonic in the earlier commercial records, this is still well worth having. The presentation is exemplary, with authoritative notes from Patrick Lambert. Incidentally there is a misprint on the back of the disc, which gives Ančerl's date of death as 1967.

Argenta, Ataúlfo

LISZT: *A Faust Symphony.* RAVEL: *Alborada del gracioso.* FALLA: *El amor brujo* (with Ana Maria Iriate; all with Paris Conservatoire O). SCHUBERT: *Symphony 9 in C (Great)* (with O des Cento Soli)

(B) (**(*)) EMI mono/stereo 5 75097-2 (2)

Whether or not this set does full justice to Ataúlfo Argenta is a moot point. His mono account of the *Faust Symphony* was made in 1955 without the choral ending Liszt added later. It was soon superseded by the Beecham, which was in stereo and which had Liszt's choral afterthoughts. This is a performance of some merit but it does not have the imaginative flair and dramatic fire of Argenta's *Symphonie fantastique*, which soon acquired cult status after its appearance in 1958. (It may even reissued in an LP custom pressing a few years ago.) His Schubert *Great C major* with the Orchestre des Cento Soli, made for the Club Français du Disque and available in England only from one of the then emerging LP clubs, was also stereo. It is a spirited account though not perhaps with the natural flair he brought to early twentieth-century music, as evinced in the 1951 *El amor brujo* (mono) and the Ravel. Sadly, his early death at only forty-four brought to an end a career of already some fulfilment but even more exceptional promise.

Barbirolli, Sir John (cello and conducting various orchestras)

(See also under HALLÉ ORCHESTRA)

'*Glorious John*': Barbirolli centenary collection (1911–69): Disc 1: (1911–47): VAN BIENE: *The Broken Melody* (Barbirolli, cello). MOZART: *String Quartet in E flat, K.428: Minuet* (with Kutcher Qt). MASCAGNI: *Cavalleria rusticana: Santuzza's aria* (with Lilian Stiles-Allen). VERDI: *Otello: Niun me tema* (with Renato Zanelli). PUCCINI: *Tosca: Tre sbirri, una carozza* (with Giovanni Inghilleri). JOHANN STRAUSS JR: *Die Fledermaus: Brother dear and sister dear.* SAINT-SAENS: *Valse-caprice, Op. 76* (with Yvonne Arnaud, piano). BALFE: *The Bohemian Girl: Overture* (with SO). COLLINS: *Overture.* WEINBERGER: *Christmas* (with NYPO). WEBER: *Euryanthe: Overture.* DELIUS: *Walk to the Paradise Garden* (with VPO)

Disc 2: (1948–64) (all with Hallé O): STRAVINSKY: *Concerto in D.* MOZART: *Cassation in G, K.63: Andante; Divertimento No. 11 in D, K.251: Minuet.* GRIEG, arr. Barbirolli: *Secret.* VILLA-LOBOS: *Bachianas brasileiras 4.* FALLA: *Seguidilla murciana* (with Marina de Gabarain). LEHAR: *Gold and Silver Waltz.* BACH, arr. Barbirolli: *Sheep may Safely Graze.* BERLIOZ: *Damnation of Faust: rehearsal sequence.* Interview: Barbirolli and R. Kinloch Anderson

(B) (***) Dutton mono/stereo CDSJB 1999 (2)

It was Vaughan Williams who referred to Barbirolli as 'Glorious John', hence the title of this budget-priced compilation to celebrate the great conductor's centenary: twenty historic items, five of them previously unpublished, plus a rehearsal sequence and an interview full of reminiscences. From 1911 you have the eleven-year-old Giovanni Barbirolli playing the cello, swoopy but perfect in intonation.

As a budding conductor he accompanies star soloists, including Yvonne Arnaud in Saint-Saëns's charming *Valse-caprice*, while items from his underprized New York period include a delightful Weinberger piece, otherwise unavailable, *Christmas*. Also unexpected is Barbirolli's pioneering account with the Hallé of Stravinsky's *Concerto in D*, recorded in 1948, two years after the work first appeared. And how revealing to have the Vienna Philharmonic heartfelt in Delius's *Walk to the Paradise Garden*!

The rehearsal of the *Dance of the Sylphs* dates from 1957, and in many ways most endearing of all is the 1964 conversation between the gravel-voiced Barbirolli and his recording producer Roland Kinloch Anderson, covering such subjects as Mahler, the Berlin Philharmonic and Elgar – a splendid portrait.

ELGAR: *Enigma Variations.* RAVEL: *Ma Mère l'Oye* (suite) (both with Hallé O). WAGNER: *Die Meistersinger: Prelude* (with LSO). MAHLER: *Symphony 2 (Resurrection)* (with Donath, Finnilä, Stuttgart R. Ch. & SO). PUCCINI: *Madama Butterfly: Love Duet* (with Scotto, Bergonzi, Rome Op. O)

(B) (***) EMI mono/stereo 5 75100-2 (2)

This valuable set brings out of limbo Barbirolli's 1956 Pye version of Elgar's *Enigma Variations* – his first in stereo but largely forgotten thanks to the excellence of his EMI recording of six years later – and offers for the first time a radio recording from Stuttgart of a Mahler symphony Barbirolli never otherwise put on commercial disc, No. 2. This radio recording of the Mahler dates from April 1970, the year Barbirolli died, and although dynamic contrasts tend to be ironed out a little, the warmth and concentration of Barbirolli in Mahler come over from first to last, leading up to a thrilling account of the choral finale, with the re-creation of Judgement Day thrillingly caught. The acoustic seems to open up the moment the voices enter, with the excellent soloists, Helen Donath and Birgit Finnilä, and the massed chorus all sounding full and vivid. The *Meistersinger Prelude*, recorded by EMI the previous year with the LSO, brings a weighty reading at broad speeds. After that the Pye recordings both of *Enigma* and of the Ravel *Mother Goose Suite* are more limited in different ways. The Ravel brings up-front sound with good, bright reproduction of percussion. In the Elgar the playing may not be as refined as in the much-loved EMI stereo version with the Philharmonia of 1962, but the Hallé with Barbirolli somehow convey an extra emotional tug, whether in *Nimrod* or the passionate climax of the finale. As a welcome supplement comes the heart-warming extract from Barbirolli's Rome recording for EMI of Puccini's *Madama Butterfly* with Renata Scotto and Carlo Bergonzi, as loving an account of the Act I duet as you will ever hear.

Beecham, Sir Thomas

ROSSINI: *Overture: William Tell.* DVORAK: *Legend in G, Op. 59/2.* WEBER: *Der Freischütz: Overture.* DELIUS: *Appalachia* (with Cuthbert Matthews and Royal Op. Ch.) (all with LPO). WAGNER: *Das Rheingold: Entry of the Gods into Valhalla* (with Walter Widdop, Theo Hermann & soloists). MOZART: *Divertimento 15 in B flat, K.287: Theme and Variations; Minuet* (only). RIMSKY-KORSAKOV: *Symphony 2 (Antar), Op. 9.* MENDELSSOHN: *Songs Without Words 44 & 45, Op. 102/3* (orch. Del Mar). TCHAIKOVSKY: *Symphony 4 in F min., Op. 36.* HANDEL: *Amaryllis (Suite, arr. Beecham): Sarabande* (all with RPO)
(B) (***) EMI mono/stereo 5 75938-2 (2)

An impressive selection of recordings made in 1934/5 with the LPO and between 1947 and 1957 with the RPO. There were 17 78-r.p.m. side takes for the opening *William Tell Overture* and the earliest three have been chosen here for their extra spontaneity, yet the string playing in the very spirited galop is flawless. The ensemble in the Dvořák *Legend* is not quite so fine (it was never issued) and the horns are not immaculate in *Der Freischütz*. But this is a live performance, recorded in the Queens Hall in 1935 alongside *Appalachia*, which displays all the Beecham Delian magic in the atmospheric horn solos at the very opening, and later in some fine *pianissimo* choral singing. An exciting finale triumphs over the two-dimensional sound, with shrill violins. It is good to have the Wagner excerpt (with text and translation included), notable mainly for Walter Widdop's memorable contribution as Loge, and the two movements from the Mozart *Divertimento* are engagingly urbane.

Beecham's warmly sensuous, richly coloured, yet highly animated 1951 performance of *Antar* is unsurpassed and, together with his thrilling reading of Tchaikovsky's *Fourth Symphony*, provides the highlight of the set. Fortunately both recordings offer glowing sound, with alluring strings and rich colouring given to the RPO woodwind. Curiously, only the

first movement of the Tchaikovsky *Fourth* was recorded in stereo, in the Kingsway Hall in 1958. It sounds marvellous. But the other three movements do not disappoint, recorded a year earlier in Paris in the resonant Salle Wagram. Beecham's reading is full of individual touches (with some lovely gentle woodwind and string playing in the first movement's second subject), but they never hold back the music's spontaneous onward flow. The close of the *Andantino* is particularly beautiful, and after the vibrant pizzicato the finale generates plenty of excitement.

Two of Mendelssohn's *Songs Without Words*, charmingly scored by Norman Del Mar, make an elegant interlude between the two symphonies, and Sir Thomas's own arrangement of the lovely *Sarabande* from Handel's *Amaryllis Suite* makes a fitting final encore.

Beinum, Eduard van

THOMAS: *Mignon: Overture.* SCHUBERT: *Symphony 6 in C.* BRAHMS: *Symphony 2 in D.* NICOLAI: *The Merry Wives of Windsor Overture.* R. STRAUSS: *Don Juan.* RIMSKY-KORSAKOV: *Scheherazade* (all with Concg. O). ELGAR: *Cockaigne Overture* (with LPO)
(B) (**(*)) EMI mono 5 75941-2 (2)

Eduard van Beinum inherited the Concertgebouw Orchestra from Mengelberg immediately after the war, and he also became a regular visitor to London, becoming conductor of the LPO for a time (1950–53). He made numerous commercial records in Amsterdam, including some memorable Bruckner with Decca and then with Philips. Like Sir Adrian Boult, he was dedicated to the letter and the spirit of the score; expressive self-indulgence and interpretative flamboyance were foreign to his muse. As this compilation shows, he never fell below a high standard and (despite assertions to the contrary) was rarely dull. He recorded the Brahms *First* no fewer than three times, but the Brahms *Second* and *Don Juan* are live performances, made when the Concertgebouw Orchestra was visiting Stuttgart (he never recorded any Strauss commercially).

Bonynge, Richard

(See also under NEW PHILHARMONIA ORCHESTRA and BALLET MUSIC)

MASSENET: *Cigale* (ballet, with Nat. PO); *Fantasy for Cello and Orchestra* (with Silberman, SRO). Songs: *Les amoureuses sont des folles; Ce que disent les cloches; Elle s'en est allée; L'éventail; Je t'aime; L'âme des fleurs; La mélodie des baisers; Nuit d'Espagne; On dit! Passionnément; Pensée d'automne; Le petit Jésus; Pitchounette; Printemps dernier; Rose d'Octobre; Le sais-tu?; Sérénade d'automne; Souhait; Souvenance; Les yeux clos* (with Huguette Tourangeau, Bonynge, piano). AUBER: *Cello Concerto 1* (arr. Gamley). POPPER: *Cello Concerto in E min., Op. 24* (with Silberman, SRO). J. C. BACH: *Sinfonia concertante in C* (for flute, oboe, violin, cello & orchestra); *Symphony in E flat, Op. 9/2.* SALIERI: *Double Concerto in C* (for flute & oboe); *Sinfonia in D (Veneziana)* (with ECO). 'Arias from Forgotten Operas': Arias from: BALFE: *Ildegonda nel Carcere.* BIZET: *Djamileh.* DONIZETTI: *L'assedio di Calais.* AUBER: *Le Cheval de bronze.* MASSENET: *Hérodiade.* VERDI: *Oberto.* VACCAI: *Giulietta de Villars.* MAILLART: *Les Dragons de*

Villars (with Huguette Tourangeau, SRO). '*Arie Antiche*': MARTINI: *Piacer d'amor*. SARTI: *Lungi dal caro bene*. BONONCINI: *Deh più a me non v'ascondete*. HANDEL: *Verdi prati, selve amene*. A. SCARLATTI: *Le violette*. GLUCK: *Divinités du Styx; Frondi tenere Ombra mai fù; O del mio dolce ardor*. PAISIELLO: *Chi vuol la zingarella; Nel cor più non mi sento*. PERGOLESI: *Stizzoso, mio Stizzoso*. CIAMPI: *Tre giorni son che Nina*. VIVALDI: *O del mio dolce ardour* (with Renata Tebaldi, New Philh. O)

✪ *** Universal Classics Australian Heritage (ADD) ABC 475 070-2 (4)

A diverse collection, to say the least, with the attraction that much of it has never been released on CD before. One of the most striking LPs to be transferred is Huguette Tourangeau's vividly recorded 1970 recital disc, '*Arias from forgotten operas*'. Hers was a controversial voice in some ways, but a distinctive and characterful one: rare qualities these days. The vivid colour photograph on the original LP sleeve (reproduced in the booklet) certainly suggests an artistic personality of character, and the recital does not disappoint. The dark, lower register of the voice, with its ability to bring a sudden change of character to the melodic line, coupled to the crisp, accurate coloratura of the upper register, is especially effective in the Donizetti excerpt (which has a swinging *cabaletta*), while the dramatic bite and secure technical control make the very most of the opening Balfe aria, which is of unexpectedly high quality. Bizet's lyrical scene is beautifully sung, and the excerpt from Vaccai's *Giulietta e Romeo* is very attractive too.

One of the highlights here is a vivacious aria by Maillart, which has a finale worthy of Offenbach, and another is the little-known but sparkling aria from Auber's *Le Cheval de bronze*. Enjoyable as is the excerpt from Verdi's *Oberto*, not even the exciting *stretta* in the orchestra near the end of the aria prepares one for Tourangeau's unexpected and thrilling final D – electrifying in its impact.

If her style is unashamedly histrionic for the bold romantic arias, she is wonderfully intimate in Massenet's charming songs. Here, in this 1975 recital disc, she knows just how to inflect her voice in the right way to bring out the full range of colour in these varied mélodies, from the playful *Pitchounette* to the long sweeping phrases in such songs as *Sérénade d'automne*. Three are heightened by cello obbligati, which brings an added frisson, especially effective in the impassioned *Je t'aime!* Other highlights include *Ce que disent les cloches*, with its haunting, bell-like accompaniment (superbly done by Bonynge throughout), and Massenet's *Nuit d'Espagne*, which uses the delightful *Air de ballet* from his *Scènes pittoresques*, with a suitably Spanish accompaniment, to great effect.

The third vocal LP included here was Renata Tebaldi's final recording, *Arie Antiche*, recorded in 1973. It was a clever programme in choosing songs which did not tax a great voice that was no longer in its prime. However, Tebaldi's artistry – and her (and Bonynge's) love for the music – is never in doubt, and Douglas Gamley's ear-tickling (if not exactly authentic) orchestrations are a delight. Throughout the programme, Tebaldi maintains a beautiful legato line in both the dramatic and pastoral items, and in Vivaldi's melancholy *Piango, gemo, sospiro*, she draws the voice into the deep, chest mezzo to great effect. Two favourites are included: the well-known *Plaisir d'amour* and the delightful Paisiello song, *Nel cor più non mi sento*, with flutes adding rustic piquancy, as they do in the Bononcini aria.

In the orchestral items, the highlight is undoubtedly Massenet's ballet *Cigale* (1978), full of memorable tunes, colourfully orchestrated and brilliantly played and recorded. Of the three *Cello Concertos*, Auber's is a pleasing work of which the jolly finale is the most enjoyable movement; the Popper is nicely lyrical too and, once again, the rustic-sounding finale is the best. But the finest of the trio is Massenet's: its richly lyrical nature, very rhapsodic in feeling, is obviously by the composer of *Manon*. There are many delights along the way, not least the gypsy-flavoured passage in the central movement, a jaunty gavotte, its quirky harmonies adding to the memorability of the piece.

The baroque and classical items are all extremely well played and recorded. They are fresh and enjoyable, and Salieri's *Double Concerto* is a real charmer of a work. The vigorous writing of J. C. Bach can't fail to give pleasure, even if these works are not in the authentic style of today (they were recorded in the late 1960s). Our ✪ is given to this set for two reasons: as an overall accolade to Richard Bonynge, who has been indefatigable over the past 40 years in bringing out so many enterprising recordings, orchestral and operatic, and for Huguette Tourangeau's brilliant recital. The sleeve-notes are lavish, although no texts are provided. Although this is an Australian issue it seems to be readily available in the UK.

Boult, Sir Adrian

BERLIOZ: *Rob Roy Overture*. TCHAIKOVSKY: *Suite 3 in G: Theme and Variations*. WALTON: *Portsmouth Point: Overture*. SCHUMANN: *Symphony 4 in D min*. SCHUBERT: *Symphony 4 in C min*. SIBELIUS: *The Tempest, Prelude* (all with LPO). FRANCK: *Symphony in D min*. (with L. Orchestral Soc.). BEETHOVEN: *Coriolan Overture* (with New PO). WOLF: *Italian Serenade* (with PO)

(B) *** EMI 5 75459-2 (2)

This EMI series usually mixes live or studio performances that are not otherwise available with commercial recordings; but the set devoted to Sir Adrian Boult does not include any of his concerts with the BBC Symphony Orchestra which ought to survive in the BBC's Archives. Instead it concentrates on the commercial LPs he made for Pye or Nixa, which he made in his sixties with the LPO. The Franck is given an unsentimental and well-held-together reading and the players were drawn from various London orchestras, including the Philharmonia. He recorded *Portsmouth Point* on a 10-inch HMV record before the war and remade it with the LPO for Decca, but this 1967 account comes from a series of recordings made for the World Record Club, as do the Franck and Schubert symphonies. The Schumann symphony is no less finely shaped and sounds very good indeed – and in every way an improvement over the original LPs. Sir Adrian was much underrated in both Berlioz and Sibelius. He never recorded the symphonies commercially but made a fine set of the tone-poems in 1956, also including this powerfully atmospheric *Tempest Prelude*, which did not last very long in the catalogue. A useful set that pays tribute to a master conductor whose interpretative range went much further than Elgar and Vaughan Williams. Very good transfers by Paul Baily.

Busch, Fritz

BEETHOVEN: *Leonora Overture 2*. BRAHMS: *Tragic Overture; Symphony 2*. HAYDN: *Sinfonia concertante in B lat.* MENDELSSOHN: *Symphony 4 in A (Italian).* MOZART: *Symphony 36 in C (Linz).* WEBER: *Overture, Der Freischütz* (all with Danish State RSO). R. STRAUSS: *Don Juan* (with LPO)

B) (***) EMI mono 5 75103-2 (2)

It is a revelation that Fritz Busch, the musical founder of Glyndebourne and normally regarded as just a Mozartian, conveys such authority in this wide range of works. They are superbly played, consistently reflecting the joy that the players had in renewing their relationship with a conductor who, from 1933, when he was sacked by the Nazis from his post in Dresden, was their great orchestral trainer in the classical and romantic repertory.

With the exception of the Strauss *Don Juan*, which was made in 1936 with the LPO, all these performances come from 1947–51, the heyday of the Danish State Radio Symphony Orchestra, which Busch brought to a level unrivalled in the other Scandinavian countries. They had greater personality as well as greater virtuosity and finesse than the Stockholm and Oslo orchestras of the day, as witness the 1949 *Linz Symphony* (the 78s were treasurable and still are) and the superb Brahms *Second Symphony*, which is also available on the Dutton anthology issued to mark the orchestra's 75th anniversary; the Dutton transfer is in every way superior. This is also valuable for the first reissue of the Haydn *Sinfonia concertante in B flat*, which features their celebrated oboist, Waldemar Wolsing, and three other first-desk players. The *Leonora 2 Overture* and the *Italian Symphony* are new to the catalogue and come from a 1950 concert in Copenhagen.

Cluytens, André

BIZET: *Symphony in C.* BERLIOZ: *Symphonie fantastique* (with French RO). DEBUSSY: *Images* (with Paris Conservatoire O). MUSSORGSKY: *Boris Godunov: Coronation Scene* (with Christoff, Sofia Opera Ch.) RAVEL: *La Valse* (with Philh. O). SCHUMANN: *Manfred Overture.* WAGNER: *Lohengrin, Act III: Prelude* (with BPO)

B) *** EMI (ADD) 5 75106-2 (2)

As far as British and American audiences are concerned, André Cluytens (pronounced Klwee-tunss) came to prominence only in the early 1950s: he accompanied Solomon in the *Second* and *Fourth* Beethoven *Concertos* in 1952, but he made few appearances in England, although he was the first Belgian conductor to appear at Bayreuth (in 1955). Bizet was one of the first composers he recorded, and his 1953 account of the *Symphony in C* with the Orchestre National de la Radiodiffusion Française was highly thought of in its time – and rightly so. There is a straightforward quality about it, totally unconcerned with effect. It is also available in Testament's Bizet anthology. Also included here is the Coronation Scene from Mussorgsky's *Boris Godunov* with Boris Christoff in the title-role – naturally in Rimsky-Korsakov's opulent scoring – and a relatively little-known account of *La Valse* with the Philharmonia Orchestra from 1958, which is more polished than his later recording, although the warmer acoustic of the Salle Pleyel shows the Parisians to better advantage.

The highlights of the set are the atmospheric accounts of the Debussy *Images*, quite unjustly overshadowed at the time by the Monteux (though that was admittedly better played) and the *Symphonie fantastique*, a different account from that issued on Testament. This was recorded at a 1964 concert in Tokyo while the Conservatoire Orchestra was on tour, and is new to the catalogue. A strongly narrative performance, it grips and holds the listener, not so much through its virtuosity as through its sense of forward movement and line. Cluytens knew what this music was all about, and though it lacks the polish of the very finest versions, there is a splendid sense of involvement. A most valuable issue, which gives a good picture of a much underrated maestro.

Coates, Albert

WEBER: *Oberon Overture.* LISZT: *Mephisto Waltz 1.* BORODIN: *Symphony 2 in B min.* RIMSKY-KORSAKOV: *Mláda: Procession of the Nobles.* MUSSORGSKY: *Sorochinsky Fair: Gopak.* TCHAIKOVSKY: *Francesca da Rimini.* RAVEL: *La Valse.* WAGNER: *Tannhäuser Overture; Das Rheinhold: Entry of the Gods into Valhalla; Die Walküre: Magic Fire Music; Götterdämmerung: Siegfried's Rhine Journey* (all with LSO). HUMPERDINCK: *Hänsel und Gretel: Overture.* R. STRAUSS: *Death and Transfiguration.* WAGNER: *Tristan und Isolde: Love Duet* (with Frida Leider, Lauritz Melchior, Berlin State Op. O)

B) (***) EMI mono 5 75486-2 (2)

Albert Coates was old enough to have met Tchaikovsky when he was a small boy and to have studied composition with Rimsky-Korsakov. He began his career on the podium in Elberfeld, Mannheim and Dresden, before conducting *Siegfried* in St Petersburg, where he was immediately engaged by the Imperial Opera House. After the First World War he began his long association with the London Symphony Orchestra, which he had first conducted in 1910. After 1926, pretty well all his HMV records were made with them, though he was in demand as a guest conductor on the continent, in America and the Soviet Union. All these performances come from 1926–32 and display much of the zest and fire for which he was celebrated. The Borodin *Second Symphony* was for long the classic of its day, and as he championed so much Russian music and made a first recording of Tchaikovsky's *Polish Symphony*, it is a pity that his pioneering (1932) set of Prokofiev's *Le Pas d'acier*, which sounds quite astonishing for its day, was not included. This is a valuable reminder of a conductor of stature whose work spanned the first decades of the century. Good transfers and excellent notes by Alan Sanders.

Dorati, Antal

Mercury Recordings: STRAVINSKY: *4 Etudes for Orchestra* (with LSO); *Petrushka; Le Sacre du printemps* (with Minneapolis SO). PROKOFIEV: *The Love for Three Oranges: Suite; Scythian Suite* (with LSO); *Symphony 5, Op. 100.* GERSHWIN: *An American in Paris.* COPLAND: *Rodeo: 4 Dance Episodes.* SCHULLER: *7 Studies on Themes of Paul Klee.* BLOCH: *Sinfonia Breve.* R. STRAUSS: *Don Juan; Till Eulenspiegel; Tod und Verklärung.* ALBENIZ: *Iberia: Suite.* FALLA: *La vida breve: Interlude & Dance.* MUSSORGSKY: *Khovanshchina: Prelude & Dance of the Persian Slaves.* SMETANA: *The Bartered Bride: Overture; Polka; Furiant; Dance of the Comedians* (with Minneapolis SO)

B) **(*) Mercury (ADD) 475 6856 (5)

An inexpensive way to sample Dorati's Mercury legacy in bold and colourful music to suit Mercury's bold recording style. Highlights include the exciting Prokofiev suites (the opening of the *Scythian Suite* is almost maniacal!) and *Fifth*

Symphony, a vivid *Petrushka* and violent *Rite of Spring*; the bright and breezy Gershwin items go very well and there are no complaints about the lively Copland items; Dorati and Mercury enjoy bringing out all the colours in Albéniz's *Iberia Suite*. If the Strauss tone poems lack the depth and richness, as interpretations and recordings, of the great performances, there is something fresh and enjoyable in Dorati's no-nonsense approach. With the interesting Schuller and Bloch items, this set is recommendable.

'A Celebration': COPLAND: *Appalachian Spring* (1945 ballet suite); *El salón México; Dance Symphony; Fanfare for the Common Man; Rodeo: 4 Dance Episodes.* STRAVINSKY: *Apollon musagète* (ballet: 1947 version); *Scherzo fantasque, Op. 3; The Rite of Spring.* DVOŘÁK: *Slavonic Rhapsody in A flat min., Op. 45/3.* TCHAIKOVSKY: *Capriccio italien.* RICHARD STRAUSS: *Don Juan* (with Detroit SO). BARTÓK: *Concerto for Orchestra; Portraits* (with Concertgebouw O); *Dance Suite.* WEINER: *Hungarian Folk Dances, Op. 18.* KODÁLY: *Háry János Suite* (with Philh. Hungarica). DORATI: *Trittico* (for oboe d'amor, oboe, cor anglais & strings; with Heinz Holliger, oboe, and Basle SO). BIZET: *Carmen: Suites 1 & 2* (with Lamoureux O of Paris). DEBUSSY: *Nocturnes; Ibéria.* WAGNER: *Die Walküre: Wotan's Farewell and Magic Fire Music* (with National SO of Washington, DC). JOHANN STRAUSS JR; Waltzes: *An der schönen blauen Donau; Wein, Weib und Gesang* (with LPO)
(B) *** Decca (ADD/DDD) 475 7615 (6)

The Hungarian musician, Antal Dorati (1906–88), was perhaps not one of the very greatest conductors of the twentieth century. But – as R.L. puts it in the notes accompanying this box – 'in his catholicity of tastes and dedication to musical truth, as he saw it, he was second to none'. Moreover, he was one of the key figures in establishing the claims of twentieth-century orchestral repertoire, both in the concert hall and, more importantly, on the gramophone. He made more than 600 recordings.

As a student in the Franz Liszt Academy in Budapest his professors included Bartók, Kodály and Leó Weiner, all of whose causes he later championed, and each of whom is represented in this anthology. He first recorded the *Concerto for Orchestra*, thrillingly, for Mercury, but his later Concertgebouw recording is a more lyrical account, bringing out the folk-dance character in the score. On the other hand, his *Háry János Suite*, although folksy, has plenty of bite and sparkle.

He later conducted for the Ballet Russe de Monte Carlo and the American Ballet Theatre, so it is not surprising that, when contracting to record with Mercury in the late 1950s, he pioneered some of the first complete major recordings of ballet music, from Tchaikovsky to Stravinsky and Copland. There is a bright, extrovert brilliance about his recordings of Copland's 'cowboy' ballets, bringing out their cheerful, wide-open-space qualities, but not emphasizing their jazzy syncopations. Yet in the masterly *Appalachian Spring*, while not missing its touches of rhythmic wit, his performance is wonderfully evocative of the Appalachian backcloth at the opening and it brings a feeling of serene acceptance at the close.

Stravinsky, too, was to remain important in his schedules. He recorded the *Rite of Spring* very successfully three times, and the present, exuberant (1981) Detroit version was awarded a Grand Prix du Disque, while his vivid account of *Apollon Musagète* is just as notable for its sheer vitality. But he was nothing if not versatile, and the fifth disc here shows him donning his best Gallic style, both in the sparkle of

Bizet's *Carmen Suites* (with the appropriately chosen Lamoureux Orchestre of Paris) and finding plenty of atmosphere and glitter in Debussian impressionism. Here, as throughout, he was helped by the vividly atmopheric sound the Decca engineers always gave him.

Like many conductors, Dorati considered himself a composer first and a conductor second, and his concertante *Trittico* (with the three movements featuring solo oboe d'amore, oboe and cor anglais in turn, all beautifully played by Heinz Holliger) shows his feeling for orchestral colour and rhythm, if less in the way of a melodic flair.

Many would regard his complete Decca recording of the Haydn *Symphonies*, made between 1971 and 1974, to be his finest achievement on disc, and it is astonishing that not one is included here. But maybe Decca are planning a second box to demonstrate further his remarakable versatility.

Fricsay, Ferenc

'A Life in Music' (with BPO, or Berlin RIAS SO):
BEETHOVEN: *Symphony 1 in C.* MENDELSSOHN: *Midsummer Night's Dream: Overture and Incidental Music* (with Streich, Eustrati, Berlin RIAS Ch.; all with BPO). PROKOFIEV: *Symphony 1 in D (Classical).* MAHLER: *Rückert Lieder* (with Forrester). TCHAIKOVSKY: *Symphony 6 in B min. (Pathétique).* ROSSINI–RESPIGHI: *La Boutique fantasque.* RIMSKY-KORSAKOV: *Scheherazade.* Concertante works: FALLA: *Nights in the Gardens of Spain.* FRANÇAIX: *Concertino for Piano and Orchestra.* HONEGGER: *Concertino for Piano and Orchestra.* FRANCK: *Symphonic Variations.* RACHMANINOV: *Rhapsody on a Theme of Paganini* (all five with M. Weber). VON EINEM: *Dantons Tod: Interlude.* HINDEMITH: *Symphonic Dances.* HARTMANN: *Symphony 6.* MARTIN: *Petite symphonie concertante* (with Herzog, Kind, Helmis). HAYDN: *The Seasons (Die Jahreszeiten)* (with Stader, Haefliger, Greindl & St Hedwig's Cathedral Ch.). JOHANN SR & JR AND JOSEF STRAUSS: *Waltzes and Overtures* (all above with Berlin RIAS SO)
(B) (***) DG mono/stereo 474 383-2 (9)

Some years ago Deutsche Grammophon issued a ten-CD box devoted to Ferenc Fricsay – plus a bonus rehearsal disc of Smetana's *Vltava*. Readers who have it may easily be tempted to brush the present nine-CD set aside, fearing that it would entail inevitable duplication. But DG have kept faith with collectors by ensuring that there is none. Even Gottfried von Einem, represented in the larger box by his *Piano Concerto* and *Ballade for Orchestra*, is appropriately (since he conducted the opera's première) served by the inclusion of the *Interlude* from *Dantons Tod*. Many performances that have been out of circulation for many years, like the Frank Martin *Petite symphonie concertante* or the *Sixth Symphony* of Karl Amadeus Hartmann, make a long overdue and welcome comeback. Honegger's delightful and unjustly neglected *Concertino for Piano and Orchestra* and Jean Françaix's captivating essay in that form are expertly handled. The earliest performances here (the Martin and *Midsummer Night's Dream* music with the Berlin Philharmonic) are from 1950; the noble account of Haydn's *Die Jahreszeiten* with a particularly distinguished line-up of soloists was made in 1961, only 14 months before his death. And of course his Tchaikovsky *Pathétique* should not be forgotten; but this is not the 1953 recording with which he created such a sensation when Deutsche Grammophon began issuing mono LPs in the UK, but a superb stereo version, full of volatile intensity, made in 1959 and never approved for issue by Fricsay himself.

Golovanov, Nikolai

GLAZUNOV: *Symphony 6.* LISZT: *Symphonic Poems: Festklänge; Héroïde funèbre; Mazeppa; Orpheus; Prometheus.* MENDELSSOHN: *A Midsummer Night's Dream: Overture; Scherzo.* TCHAIKOVSKY: *1812 Overture* (all with Moscow RSO)

(B) (*) EMI mono 5 75112-2 (2)

Nikolai Golovanov, an exact contemporary of Prokofiev, brought the Moscow Radio Orchestra to a high pitch in the difficult post-war years. He gets playing of much sensitivity and vitality from the strings in Glazunov's endearing *Sixth Symphony* – a very spirited account. In the Liszt tone poems the playing is handicapped by ill-tuned, raw wind tone and blowsy horns. He sets a very fast tempo for the Mendelssohn *Scherzo*, and the results sound scrambled. The recording quality ranges from the just acceptable to the rough.

Jensen, Thomas

'*Scandanavian Classics*' (with (i) Copenhagen PO, (ii) Royal Danish O; (iii) Tivoli Concert Hall O; (iv) Eskdale; (v) Danish State R. O; (vi) Andersen): (i) GADE: *Echoes of Ossian Overture, Op. 1.* J. P. E. HARTMANN: *Triumphal March of the Nordic Gods.* HENRIQUES: *Voelund the Smith: Prelude.* HOFFDING: *Det er ganske vist (Once Upon a Time).* LANGE-MULLER: *Prelude to Renaissance.* NIELSEN: (ii) *Little Suite for Strings, Op. 1; Helios Overture, Op. 17;* (iii) *Saul & David, Act II Prelude.* RIISAGER: *Little Overture for Strings;* (iv; v) *Concertino for Trumpet and Strings;* (ii) *Slaraffenland (Fools' Paradise).* (iii) SIBELIUS: *Finlandia, Op. 26; Valse triste, Op. 44/1; Valse lyrique, Op. 96a.* (v; vi) SVENDSEN: *Romance for Violin & Orchestra, Op. 26.* TARP: *Mosaik Suite*

(***) Danacord mono DACOCD 523/524 (2)

Thomas Jensen's post-war Nielsen LPs are well represented on CD. This generously filled two-CD set collects some of his pre-vinyl records from the late 1930s and 1940s, including Nielsen's *Little Suite for Strings,* Op. 1, eloquently played by the Royal Danish Orchestra, and the *Helios Overture.* Jensen himself played under Nielsen and also heard Sibelius conduct *Finlandia* and *Valse triste* when he visited Copenhagen in 1925 to give the first Danish performance of the *Seventh Symphony.* His pioneering (1939) account of Svendsen's *Romance* with Carlo Andersen, leader of the Royal Orchestra, as soloist – recorded, incidentally, the day before the German invasion of Poland – is refreshingly free from cloying sentiment. It is a measure of the popularity of Riisager's *Slaraffenland (Fools' Paradise)* in the 1940s that there were two versions of it on 78s. *Slaraffenland* inhabits the vaudeville world of Satie or *Les Six* and was perhaps an echo of the days Riisager spent in Paris in the 1920s. (Jensen's 1937 recording omits three movements.) George Eskdale, whose Haydn concerto was one of the mainstays of the shellac catalogue, recorded Riisager's *Concertino for Trumpet and Strings* in 1949, and it was not seriously challenged until Håkan Hardenberger came along. Finn Høffding, whose pupils, incidentally, included Vagn Holmboe, lived to be 98 and is best known by his short

tone-poem, *Det er ganske vist,* a brilliant orchestral show-piece, which, in a just world, would be a well-known repertory piece. Not everything here is of interest: the *Prelude* to *Vølund Smed* by Fini Henriques is pretty thin stuff, and the same goes for the Lange-Müller and J. P. E. Hartmann pieces. A very welcome issue all the same, with admirably straightforward, no-nonsense transfers.

Karajan, Herbert Von

(See also under BERLIN PHILHARMONIC and PHILHARMONIA ORCHESTRAS)

J. STRAUSS: *Tritsch-Tratsch Polka* (with VPO). WALTON: *Symphony 1* (with Rome R. O). MUSSORGSKY: *Pictures at an Exhibition* (orch. Ravel). WALDTEUFEL: *Les Patineurs Waltz.* SIBELIUS: *Symphony 4.* LISZT: *Hungarian Rhapsody 2.* WEINBERGER: *Schwanda the Bagpiper: Polka.* OFFENBACH: *Contes d'Hoffmann: Barcarolle.* CHABRIER: *España; Joyeuse Marche* (with Philh. O). WAGNER: *Tristan und Isolde: Liebestod* (with BPO)

(B) (***) EMI stereo/mono (ADD) 5 62869-2 (2)

The main point of interest here is the Walton *Symphony,* which is new to the catalogue. Walton often asked Karajan to record the work but, for a variety of reasons, it never worked out. The 1953 account by the Rome Orchestra of the Italian Radio is pretty electrifying and makes one regret that Walter Legge did not schedule the symphony with the Philharmonia. Transferred from acetates, it still sounds very impressive. It alone is worth the price of the set. Sibelius spoke of the 1953 *Fourth Symphony* with the Philharmonia as the best he had ever heard, and although it has been available in other couplings (and in some territories still is) it is a classic of the gramophone. The whole compilation is well worth having, and the Walton *Symphony* makes it a must.

Kleiber, Erich

'*Decca Recordings, 1949–1955*': BEETHOVEN: *Symphonies 3 in E flat (Eroica), Op. 55;* (2 versions, with Concg. O and VPO); *5 in C min., Op. 67; 6 in F (Pastoral), Op. 68* (both with LPO); *7 in A, Op. 92* (with Concg. O); *9 in D min. (Choral), Op. 125* (with Gueden, Wagner, Dermota, Wever, Singverein der Gesellschaft der Musikfreunde, VPO). WEBER: *Symphony 1 in C, Op. 19.* MOZART: *Symphonies Nos. 39 in E flat, K.543; 4 German Dances* (with Cologne RSO); *40 in D min., K.550* (with LPO). SCHUBERT: *Symphony 9 in C (Great), D.944*

(M) (**(*)) Decca mono 475 6080 (6)

Kleiber's series of legendary Beethoven recordings was one of the highlights of the early LP era: indeed, the 1953 performance of the *Fifth Symphony* was virtually top choice until his son Carlos made his famous stereo version for DG, recording some 20 years later. Erich Kleiber's vision of Beethoven is profoundly classical, taut but never hard-driven, and he always leaves the listener feeling that his is the only possible way of playing these masterpieces. If many European orchestras in the immediate post-war period and up to the mid-1950s were not at their peak, any blemishes are swept away by the power of the music-making. Two versions of the *Eroica* are included here; the Vienna account dates from 1955 but was not issued until 1959 because the woodwind balance was imperfect and the horns were also backward. That said, no

418 GREAT CONDUCTORS OF THE TWENTIETH CENTURY

other apologies need be made, and the spacious acoustics of the Musikvereinsaal spread the sound and help cushion the rather thin violins above the stave. The performance is in every way outstanding – even more intense and dramatic than his earlier, Concertgebouw version (good though it is to have and to compare) – and it includes the repeat of the exposition in the first movement, making the whole structure more powerfully monumental. The electricity of the performance is maintained throughout, with the *Funeral March* deeply felt, the mood lightened in the Scherzo, and the finale making an apotheosis.

Decca released Erich Kleiber's 1953 accounts of the *Fifth* and *Sixth Symphonies* on CD in 1987, but this new transfer is much better, with greater warmth and richness. The *Seventh* was recorded in 1950 and is a little thin in sound, with the string-tone a shade astringent, as many recordings of this period were, but not too bad. In the slow movement Kleiber uses a controversial pizzicato ending, a curious effect (also adopted by his son); the Scherzo has an exhilarating bounce, and throughout this symphony the right sort of tension is maintained.

The *Choral Symphony* dates from 1952 and, with an excellent team of soloists, has the same clear-eyed conception as the rest of the symphonies.

Mozart's *Symphony 40* dates from 1949, and here the string-sound is both richer and warmer than in the Beethoven – no doubt largely thanks to the (much missed) Kingsway Hall acoustics. The performance is spontaneous and has the humanity and life for which Kleiber was famous. The orchestral playing is not immaculate: the horns in the third movement and the discipline in the finale can be faulted, but the music-making, as always here, is so alive and sympathetic to make one forgive all.

Symphony 39 and the *Four German Dances*, along with the charming Weber *Symphony*, derive from a recorded live broadcast dating from 1956, and although the sound-quality (and sometimes the playing) is not of the best, the music-making is alive, even though the *Four German Dances* are taken a bit too fast: the famous sleigh ride is positively reckless!

The sound, too, in Schubert's *Great C major Symphony*, also taken from a live broadcast in 1953, is not ingratiating (nor is one of the horn notes in the terrifyingly exposed introduction, which goes a little sharp near the end – we are so used to it being heard in perfect studio conditions), but it is good to have Kleiber's impressive conception all the same; unlike many conductors who vary the tempi of this work throughout, especially those who are romantically inclined, Kleiber manages to vary the tension without any slowing down or speeding up and he achieves the same result with no violation of the score whatsoever. The strength of Kleiber's interpretation comes over again and again with a multitude of interpretative problems solved as it they didn't exist. If only he had recorded the work a few years later in stereo with the VPO, it would surely be a legendary account, never out of the catalogue. An important historical set.

BEETHOVEN: *Symphony 6 (Pastoral), Op. 68* (with Czech PO). DVORAK: *Carnaval Overture.* MOZART: *Symphony 40 in G min., K. 550.* JOSEF STRAUSS: *Waltz: Spharenklänge.* JOHANN STRAUSS JR: *Der Zigeunerbaron Overture* (all with LPO); *Du und Du Waltz* (with VPO). SCHUBERT: *Symphony 5 in B flat.* R. STRAUSS: *Till Eulenspiegel* (with N. German R. O)

(B) (***) EMI mono 5 75115-2 (2)

Often the most valuable items on the two-disc sets so far issued in this EMI 'Great Conductors' series are radio recordings never previously published. In the superb set representing the work of Erich Kleiber (father of the elusive Carlos Kleiber, and, many would say, even greater), the most exciting performances are indeed those on radio recordings. The recording he made with the Czech Philharmonic in Prague in 1955 (less than a year before his death) of Beethoven's *Pastoral Symphony* is at once glowingly incandescent and refined, with radiant string tone and rollicking Czech wind and horn playing in the Scherzo. Kleiber's readings for North German Radio of Schubert's *Fifth Symphony* and Strauss's *Till Eulenspiegel* are also outstanding, the Schubert sunny and full of character, the Strauss racily exciting. Though the transfer engineers have not tamed the fierce string sound of the Decca recordings included here, it is good to have from that source Kleiber's powerful, dramatic reading of Mozart's *G minor Symphony*, No. 40, and engaging trifles by the other Strausses, presented with warmth and a degree of indulgence.

Koussevitzky, Serge (double-bass and conductor)

(See also under BOSTON SYMPHONY ORCHESTRA)

'Collection' (with (i) Pierre Luboshutz; (ii) Boston SO; (iii) Bernard Zighera, Pierre Luboshutz): BEETHOVEN: (i) *Minuet in G* (arr. Koussevitzky) (ii) *Symphony 6 in F (Pastoral).* (iii) ECCLES: *Largo.* (i) LASKA: *Wiegenlied.* (ii) KOUSSEVITZKY: *Concerto, Op. 3: Andante; Valse miniature.* JOHANN STRAUSS JR: *Wiener Blut; Frühlingsstimmen* (M) (***) Biddulph mono WHL 019

In his youth and before he was established as a conductor of international celebrity, Koussevitzky was regarded as the greatest double-bass virtuoso of the age. In 1928–9, in his mid-fifties, he was enticed into the New York studios to record the above with the pianist Bernard Zighera, but he then re-recorded everything with Pierre Luboshutz the following year. These performances confirm that he brought to the double-bass the same lyrical intensity and feeling for line and sonority that distinguished his conducting.

Judging from the two concerto movements included here, he was no great composer, but the 1928 recording of the *Pastoral Symphony* with the Boston Symphony Orchestra is little short of a revelation. As an interpretation it feels just right; generally speaking, it is brisk but totally unhurried, each phrase wonderfully shaped. Given the fact that he never lingers, the paradox is that this performance seems strangely spacious. One young and knowledgeable collector to whom we played this thought it quite simply 'among the best *Pastorals* ever'; moreover the recorded sound is remarkable for its age and comes up very freshly. This disc, though comparatively expensive, is worth it.

BEETHOVEN: *Symphony 5 in C min.* (with LPO). SIBELIUS: *Symphony 7* (with BBC SO). HARRIS: *Symphony 3.* TCHAIKOVSKY: *Symphony 5 in E min.* RACHMANINOV: *The Isle of the Dead* (all with Boston SO)

(B) (**(*)) EMI mono 5 75118-2 (2)

The two discs devoted to Serge Koussevitzky are variable in content, but among the treasures is the revelatory first recording, made live with the BBC Symphony in 1933, of Sibelius's *Seventh Symphony*. By comparison his 1934 studio recording of Beethoven's *Fifth* with the LPO is disappointingly heavy, while all the rest, recorded later with his own Boston Symphony Orchestra, bring superb playing, not least in Roy Harris's powerful, single-movement *Third Symphony*. This account of Rachmaninov's *Isle of the Dead*, never issued in Europe in the 78 era, even rivals the composer's classic account.

Krips, Josef

MOZART: *Symphonies Nos. 31 in D (Paris), K.297; 39 in E flat, K.543; 40 in G min., K.550* (with LSO); *41 in C (Jupiter)* (with Israel PO). BRAHMS: *Symphony 4 in E min., Op. 98.* SCHUBERT: *Symphony 8 (Unfinished).* SCHUMANN: *Symphony 4 in D min., Op. 120.* MENDELSSOHN: *Symphony 4 (Italian).* DVORAK: *Cello Concerto in B min., Op. 104* (with Nelsova; all with LSO). BEETHOVEN: *Ah! Perfido!.* R. STRAUSS: *Salome: Closing Scene* (both with Borkh). TCHAIKOVSKY: *Symphony 5 in E min., Op. 64.* HAYDN: *Symphonies Nos. 94 in G (Surprise); 99 in E flat*

(B) (**) Decca mono/stereo 473 121-2 (5)

This is a disappointing set which does not do Krips full justice. It is not the fault of the (mostly mono) Decca recordings, which are of quality and have been well transferred. But in the 1950s Krips seemed to be able to create spontaneous vitality in his studio recordings only sporadically. Of the Mozart *Symphonies*, the *Paris* is the most lively; but No. 39 is routine. The *Fortieth in G minor* is just about adequate, but the tension in the *Jupiter*, recorded in Israel, is again held very slackly. The slow movement refuses to blossom, while the finale lacks grip. The Brahms *Fourth Symphony* is more successful. It is a straightforward, no-nonsense reading, and the first two movements are very satisfying, with Krips showing that the emotion of the slow movement can speak for itself. But the Scherzo is too straitlaced and the passacaglia finale hardly has the strength that the greatest conductors have brought to it.

The *Unfinished* is one of the highlights of the collection, finely played and full of drama and atmosphere, to anticipate Krips's later, outstanding, stereo version. He also offers a colourful and lively account of Mendelssohn's *Italian Symphony*, making the most of the flowing, sunlit phrases. The LSO plays the tarantella finale with great gusto and crisp staccato – a performance that is as alive to colour as it is to rhythm. The Schumann *Fourth* is also animated, if lightweight.

Zara Nelsova is the passionate soloist in the Dvořák *Cello Concerto*, producing a gloriously radiant sound at any speed, and at any part of the compass. But Krips's accompaniment is far behind her in quality – though, fortunately, not as regards ensemble. So with the soloist carrying the day, this is still very enjoyable. The vocal items with Inge Borkh depend on how you take to this very individual voice, but when we move on to the Vienna Philharmonic's Tchaikovsky *Fifth* – superbly recorded – the symphony refuses to hang together properly under Krips's baton, and the result is frankly dull.

Fortunately, the paired Haydn *Symphonies*, the *Surprise* and No. 99, show Krips back on top form. They are played in the very finest Viennese manner. Krips extracts the very best from his players, and his performances are matched by excellent, early stereo recording, and an ideal balance between wind and strings. Perhaps the performances reach their peak in the beautiful slow movement of the *E flat Symphony* (No.

99), which is especially rich in melodic ideas and in depth of musical thought, but the *Surprise*, too, is highly infectious, and the bright, vivid sound presents both works in their best light.

Kubelik, Rafael

'*Rare Recordings, 1963–1974*': MOZART: *Serenade 7 in D (Haffner), K.250* (with Bav. RSO). DVORAK: *Serenade for Strings in E, Op. 22* (with ECO). BEETHOVEN: *Symphonies 1 in C, Op. 21* (with LSO); *2 in D, Op. 36* (with Concg. O); *3 in E flat (Eroica), Op. 55* (with BPO); *7 in A, Op. 92* (with Bav. RSO). TCHEREPNIN: *Piano Concertos 2, Op. 26; 5, Op. 96* (with composer (piano), Bav. RSO). MARTINON: *Violin Concerto 2, Op. 51* (with Henryk Szeryng, Bav. RSO). HARTMANN: *Symphonies 4 & 8 for String Orchestra* (with Bav. RSO). STRAVINSKY: *Circus Polka; Scherzo à la russe* (with BPO). WEBER: *Overtures: Abu Hassan; Jubel; Preciosa* (with Bav. RSO). KUBELIK: *Quattro forme per archi* (with ECO). MENDELSSOHN: *A Midsummer Night's Dream* (+ rehearsal) (with Edith Mathis, Ursula Boese, Bav. R. Ch. & SO). SCHOENBERG: *Gurrelieder* (with Herbert Schachtschneider, Inge Borkh, Hertha Töpper, Kieth Engen, Lorenz Fehenberger, Hans Fiedler, Bav. R. Ch. & SO)

(M) *** DG (ADD) 477 5838 (8)

Rafael Kubelik rarely went awry in the recording studio: his performances were imbued with warmth and sensitivity, never becoming mannered or eccentric. This DG Originals set (graced with understanding biographical sleeve-notes by Patrick Lambert) includes many of his lesser-known recordings, highlighting the breadth of his repertoire, especially in relation to twentieth-century music (including one of his own works) and his special relationship with the Bavarian Radio Symphony Orchestra.

Many recordings make a welcome return to circulation here: Jean Martinon's *Second Violin Concerto* is an attractive work from the early 1960s; it is beautifully scored, full of interesting detail, and is very well recorded and played. Alexander Tcherepnin's style is cosmopolitan but eclectic. His piano concertos are undoubtedly entertaining: the *Second* is colourful and direct, the *Fifth* more angular (but enjoyable with it) and these performances with the composer as soloist have integrity. The 1968 recording is up-front and vivid. Kubelik was a strong advocate of the music of Karl Amadeus Hartmann and premièred his *Eighth Symphony*, recorded here. This is a complex, challenging score but, like the Bartókian *Fourth Symphony* (for strings) on this disc, it receives an intense reading, and the 1967 recording is full and warm.

Kubelik's 1964 *Gurrelieder* won golden opinions (and rightly so) for the eloquence of the performance and the excellence of the recording. The balance is musically done and Kubelik's approach shows sympathy and insight, while his team of artists work well together. In the last analysis, Kubelik's coolness of manner misses some of the music's red-blooded, dramatic qualities, but this performance will best suit those for whom refinement is more important than dynamism.

Kubelik had an original idea to record each of Beethoven's symphonies with different orchestras, the first three of which are included here. Kubelik was a lyrical Beethovenian, and Richard Osborne's original *Gramophone* review well sums up this project: 'a valuable undertaking – sanely, humanely, at times gloriously realised. In an often troubled and divided world, its message, quite literally, crosses frontiers.' The 1970 Bavarian performance of the *Seventh Symphony* was not part of (but was eclipsed by) that cycle: it is a sparkling yet relaxed account, even warmer than the later, VPO version and very much worth hearing.

The *Haffner Serenade* is robust and lively in the fast movements, warmly romantic in the slow ones and, if the *Menuettos* are not at the expected tempos of today, they work well with Kubelik's approach. The Dvořák *Serenade* is very lovingly done, almost gentle, and though the *Scherzo* and *Finale* are full are life, there is nothing showy or high-powered about the playing here, just sincere warmth. The Weber overtures receive splendidly consistent performances, and the sparkle of the colourful *Abu Hassan* is especially enjoyable. Mendelssohn's *Midsummer Night's Dream* shows the Bavarian orchestra on top form (only the *Nocturne* disappoints a little) with the *Overture* straightforward but fresh (a rehearsal sequence of this is also included). There is much magical playing throughout and vocal and choral sections go splendidly.

Kubelik's own composition, *Quattro forme per archi*, was premièred by the ECO in 1968 and recorded by the same players a year later. It is a personal, thoughtful work, quite knotty but with a compensating warmth and liveliness of ideas. The recordings throughout this set are consistently warm and vivid, and it is thoroughly recommendable.

DVOŘÁK: *Slavonic Rhapsody in A flat, Op. 45/3* (with RPO). MARTINŮ: *Symphony 4* (with Czech PO). BERLIOZ: *Damnation de Faust: Ballet des sylphes.* HINDEMITH: *Symphonic Metamorphosis on themes by Carl Maria von Weber* (with Chicago SO). JANÁČEK: *Sinfonietta.* SCHUBERT: *Symphony 3 in D* (with VPO); MAHLER: *Symphony 10: Adagio* (with Bav. R. O.). MENDELSSOHN: *Midsummer Night's Dream Overture* (with Philh. O). SCHUMANN: *Genoveva Overture* (with BPO)

(BB) (***) EMI stereo/mono (ADD) 5 62863-2 (2)

Of the great conductors included in this series, Rafael Kubelik enjoyed less renown among the wider musical public than his peers. Perhaps something of the misfortune he suffered in Chicago in the early 1950s rubbed off. Yet his musicianly accounts of the Dvořák symphonies and his performance of *Les Troyens* at Covent Garden linger in the memories of all who heard them. The present set makes a fitting tribute, bringing as it does one of his finest Chicago performances, the Hindemith *Symphonic metamorphosis on themes by Carl Maria von Weber*, together with an eminently persuasive Martinů *Fourth Symphony*. This he recorded in 1948, way back in the days of 78s, and it shows his natural feeling for his great countryman, as does the Janáček *Sinfonietta*. We are offered here the second of his three recordings, this time with the Vienna Philharmonic, just before Decca had installed stereo equipment in the Musikverein. Very informative notes by Patrick Lambert.

Mackerras, Sir Charles

'A Knight at the Ballet': SULLIVAN/MACKERRAS: *Pineapple Poll.* DELIBES: *La Source.* COPLAND: *El salon México.* REZNICEK: *Donna Diana Overture.* BERLIOZ: *The Damnation of Faust: Ballet des sylphes; Marche hongroise; Menuet des follets.* MEYERBEER/LAMBERT: *Les Patineurs.* ROSSINI: *William Tell: Ballet Music.* STRAUSS/DORATI:

Graduation Ball. MUSSORGSKY: *Gopak.* GLIERE: *Russian Sailor's Dance.* BURKHARD: *The Hunting Parson Overture*
✹ (B) *** CfP mono/stereo 344123-23 (2)

This is the best CD set released to coincide with Sir Charles Mackerras's 80th birthday celebrations from any record company. (CfP even made each CD last 80 minutes – one minute for each of the conductor's years!) It includes Mackerras's first version of *Pineapple Poll* and, although he recorded it in stereo for both EMI and Decca, neither quite captures the exhilarating freshness of this 1951 version. The stereo items (which form the bulk of the programme) are astonishingly warm and vivid for their date: *La Source* has great charm and piquancy, with stylish pointing (especially from the strings) throughout. The marvellous *Donna Diana Overture* is both fluffy and furious; but all the show-pieces, such as the *Russian Sailor's Dance, Gopak* and the Berlioz items come off splendidly. In *Les Patineurs*, Mackerras plays with a delightful, unforced charm, and this relaxed yet lively manner makes for very good results in the sparkling confection which makes up the *Graduation Ball.* The very rare overture, *The Hunting Parson*, is very welcome indeed, with all its hunting horns and galloping themes; once again, the 1954 recording is unbelievably good. To make this bargain set even more attractive, the Classics for Pleasure team have included some attractive photos of Mackerras, along with colour pictures of the beautiful original LP covers.

VORISEK: *Symphony in D, Op. 24.* DVORAK: *Czech Suite, Op. 39* (with ECO). *Romance in F min. for Violin & Orchestra, Op. 11.* SUK: *Fantastic Scherzo, Op. 25; Fantasy for Violin & Orchestra, Op. 24; Summer Tale* (with Pamela Frank (violin), Czech PO). JANACEK: *Zarlivost: Overture* (with VPO). DELIUS: *A Song of the Hills; Brigg Fair – An English Rhapsody; On Hearing the First Cuckoo in Spring* (with Welsh Nat. Op. Ch. & O). ELGAR: *Enigma Variations* (with RPO)

(M) **(*) Decca (ADD/DDD) 475 7061 (3)

A good compilation from Decca again celebrating Mackerras's 80th birthday. New to CD is the attractive Vorisek *Symphony in D* (described as the nearest the Czechs came to producing a Beethoven), though this performance, elegant and enjoyable though it is, has not the drive of the old Supraphon recording with the Prague Chamber Orchestra. The *Czech Suite* (Dvořák) with which it was originally coupled is very good, and the 1969 sound is excellent. The rest of this collection is generally first class: the Suk items – all of them very attractive pieces – go especially well, with plenty of bite and dynamic expression in repertoire for which Sir Charles is famous. The Delius items receive warmly sympathetic performances, even if the Branwyn Hall acoustics are not always ideal for the Delian sound-world, lacking some of the atmosphere which is part of the composer's mystery. There is much to enjoy in the *Enigma Variations* after the rather sluggish start (*Nimrod* is a bit slow, too) but it erupts in a superb, impulsive finale, bold and brassy. Apart from the reservation about the Delius sound, the rest is of first-class Decca/Argo quality.

Malko, Nicolai

BORODIN: *Symphony 2.* DVORAK: *Symphony 9 (New World).* GLINKA: *Ruslan and Ludmilla – Overture.* PROKOFIEV: *Symphony No 7.* RIMSKY-KORSAKOV: *Tsar Sultan: Dance of the Tumblers.* SUPPE: *Poet and Peasant: Overture.* TCHAIKOVSKY: *Nutcracker: excerpts.* (all with

Philh. O). HAYDN: *Symphony 92* (with Royal Danish O).
NIELSEN: *Maskarade: Overture* (with Danish State R. O)
(B) (***) EMI mono/stereo 5 75121-2 (2)

Nicolai Malko conducted the première of Shostakovich's *First Symphony* in 1926 and was an eminent teacher, numbering Evgeni Mravinsky among his pupils. But when Soviet policy towards the Arts became less liberal, he decided to emigrate and take his chance as a freelance conductor. His recording career began in the days of shellac, and the present compilation ranges from Nielsen's *Maskarade Overture* (1947), thoroughly idiomatic and vital, through to Prokofiev's *Seventh Symphony* (1955) and Glinka's *Ruslan Overture* (1956), a spirited account but not breathless and headlong. He is at his best in Borodin's *Second Symphony* (the second of his two recordings) and the Prokofiev *Seventh Symphony*, whose first British performance he gave. Both have great clarity of texture and momentum, and in charm and finesse the *Seventh* has rarely been equalled. His Haydn with the Royal Danish Orchestra ('Det Kongelige') has great lightness of touch and, in the finale, wit. There is not the slightest trace of affectation, and the same goes for the *New World Symphony*, which is not a great performance, perhaps, but is lively and enjoyable. Malko was not a charismatic conductor, but he was always at the service of the composer and not his own ego. The sound is consistently good for its period.

Markevitch, Igor

(See also under PHILHARMONIA ORCHESTRA)

BEETHOVEN: *Symphony 3 in E flat (Eroica), Op. 55* (with Symphony of the Air); *Symphony 6 in F (Pastoral), Op. 68; Overtures: Coriolan; Leonore 3; Fidelio; Zur Namensfeier, Op. 115; Consecration of the House.* BIZET: *Suite: Jeux d'enfants.* BRAHMS: *Symphonies 1 in C min., Op. 68; 4 in E min., Op. 90; Tragic Overture.* DEBUSSY: *La Mer.* GOUNOD: *Symphony 2 in E flat.* GLUCK: *Sinfonia in G.* HAYDN: *Sinfonia concertante in B flat, Hob. I:105.* MOZART: *Symphony 38 (Prague).* SCHUBERT: *Symphony 3 in D, D.200.* TCHAIKOVSKY: *Francesca da Rimini Op. 32.*
WAGNER: *Preludes: Lohengrin: Acts I & III; Tannhäuser: Overture and Bacchanale* (all with LOP). BRAHMS: *Alto Rhapsody, Op. 53* (with Arkhipova). KODÁLY: *Psalmus Hungaricus, Op. 13* (with Ilosfalvy; both with Russian State Ac. Ch., USSR State SO). CIMAROSA: *Double Concerto for 2 Flutes in G* (with Nicolet, Demmler). MOZART: *Symphonies 34; 35 (Haffner).* TCHAIKOVSKY: *Symphony 6 in B min. (Pathétique).* WAGNER: *Siegfried Idyll* (all with BPO)
(B) *** DG 474 400-2 (9)

Markevitch's eminence as a conductor was a post-war phenomenon. Before the war he was known primarily as a composer and composer–conductor, making his début as a teenager with his *Piano Concerto* during Diaghilev's last London season. During the war he took part in the Italian resistance, but after the early 1940s his creative fires had burned out. It was Nadia Boulanger who encouraged him to take up conducting, and this occupied him until deafness struck him in the last years of his life. He conducted in Berlin, Paris, Moscow, London and Stockholm; and his repertoire was exploratory, ranging from Berwald to Roussel. This set includes almost all the Berlin Philharmonic recordings that have not been available from other sources. The notes speak of his translucent and intense dramatic style and his generally unsentimental approach. At times this led some listeners to

find him 'cool' in some of the cycle of Tchaikovsky symphonies he recorded with the LSO for Philips – but this stricture certainly does not apply to his 1953 *Pathétique* included here. His Brahms *Alto Rhapsody* with Irina Arkhipova at her prime is very powerful, as is his very dark *Tragic Overture*. His Gounod *E flat Symphony* has charm, a quality which we don't normally associate with him; and the clarity of his mind is evident in the Debussy he also recorded with the Orchestre Lamoureux de Paris. There are some memorable things here, and this impeccably produced set provides a valuable opportunity to rediscover a many-faceted and highly individual artist.

CHABRIER: *España* (with Spanish R. & TV SO). DEBUSSY: *La Mer.* GLINKA: *A Life for the Tsar: Overture and 3 Dances* (with LOP). RAVEL: *Daphnis et Chloë: Suite 2* (with Hamburg NDR O). R. STRAUSS: *Till Eulenspiegel* (with French Nat. R. O). TCHAIKOVSKY: *Manfred Symphony* (with LSO). VERDI: *La forza del destino: Overture* (with New Philh. O)
(B) ** EMI (ADD) 5 75124-2 (2)

An enormously gifted man and a composer of substance, Igor Markevitch gave us relatively few great recordings. His first *Rite of Spring* was certainly one, and his Berwald symphonies with the Berlin Philharmonic were very fine, too. None of the performances here falls below a certain standard, but nearly all have been surpassed elsewhere: his somewhat cool *Manfred Symphony* is not a patch on the electrifying Toscanini, Jansons or Pletnev accounts, and his *Daphnis* is no match for the likes of Ormandy or Karajan. As is the case with other issues in this series, the performances derive not only from commercial recordings but from broadcasts. Trouble has been taken over the transfers, so Markevitch's admirers need not hesitate on that score.

Martinon, Jean

'Complete Decca Recordings' (with Paris Conservatoire O): ADAM: *Giselle.* PROKOFIEV: *Russian Overture, Op. 72; Symphonies 5 in B flat, Op. 100; 7 in C sharp min., Op. 131.* BIZET: *Jeux d'enfants, Op. 22.* BERLIOZ: *Béatrice et Bénédict; Benvenuto Cellini; Le Carnival Romain; Le Corsaire; Hungarian March.* IBERT: *Divertissement.* SAINT-SAËNS: *Dance macabre; Rouet d'Omphale* (with LPO, Lympany). *Piano Concerto 2 in G min., Op. 22* (with LPO, Long). FAURÉ: *Ballade for Piano & Orchestra, Op. 19.* FRANCAIX: *Concertino for Piano & Orchestra* (with LPO, Katin). MENDELSSOHN: *Capriccio Brillant.* LISZT: *Totentanz* (with LPO). STRAUSS: *Le beau Danube* (arr. Désormière). WEINBERGER: *Schwanda The Bagpiper: Polka & Fugue.* ROSSINI: *Guillaume Tell: ballet music.* LALO: *Namouna: Ballet Suites 1 & 2.* OFFENBACH: *Overtures: La belle Hélène; Barbe-Bleu; La Grande Duchesse de Gérolstein; Le Mariage aux lanterns.* HEROLD: *Overture: Zampa.* BOIELDIEU: *Overtures: Le Calife de Bagdad; La Dame Blanche* (with LSO). DVOŘÁK: *Slavonic Dances 1–8, Op. 46.* RIMSKY-KORSAKOV: *Capriccio espagnol, Op. 34.* SHOSTAKOVICH: *The Age of Gold: Suite, Op. 22; Symphony 1 in F min., Op. 10.* BORODIN: *Symphony 2 in B min.* RIMSKY-KORSAKOV: *The Tale of Tsar Saltan: March* (with LPO). MEYERBEER: *Les Patineurs: ballet music* (arr. C. Lambert; with Israel PO). MASSENET: *Le Cid: ballet music.* TCHAIKOVSKY: *Symphony 6 in B min., Op. 74* (with VPO)
☻(B) *** Decca mono/stereo 475 7209 (9)

Jean Martinon was one of the last proponents of the great French tradition – a tradition wherein rhythmic point, clarity of texture and lightness of touch are the most obvious hallmarks. This can be especially revealing in non-French repertoire: in Tchaikovsky's *Pathétique Symphony*, the famous Scherzo makes its impact by rhythmic point rather than frenetic playing, and the impassioned Vienna Philharmonic Orchestra, in both texture and rhythmic pulse, give a fresh tint to this much-recorded work.

Martinon's famous (1959) LSO account of Borodin's *Second Symphony*, with its arresting (almost startling) opening theme and the Scherzo's dazzling orchestration, is as electrifying as ever: it knocks spots off most other recordings, both as a performance and in recorded sound. Similarly, one basks in the vibrant colours brought out in *Capriccio espagnol* and the piquant *Tsar Saltan March*. Brahms's *Hungarian Dances*, imbued with Gallic wit, go like the wind, and the 1958 recording sounds only slightly dated.

If bright colours and vivid sound are paramount, try Martinon's famous coupling of the *Les Patineurs* and *Le Cid* ballet music; the rhythmic vitality and the Decca sound grab you immediately (though in a charming, French way, of course) and the Israel Philharmonic play as if they had lived in the Champs-Elysées all their lives. No less vivacious playing – and brimming with French *esprit* – are the (originally) two mono LPs of French overtures – the first is the finest of all collections of Offenbach overtures – exploding like a bottle of ice-cold champagne – while the second LP, containing the once-popular war horses *Zampa*, *Si J'étais Roi*, *Le Calife de Bagdad* and *La Dame Blanche*, comes up as fresh as paint. The latter was aptly described in the *Guide*'s original review as 'four French soufflés, served up by a conductor who obviously relishes every moment and the orchestra giving of their very best'.

If these LPO mono recordings lack the depth Decca achieved in very quickly in stereo, they are more than acceptable (if a bit thin on top). The Fauré *Ballade* and Françaix *Concertino* (both with Kathleen Long) are beautifully done, the former quite haunting and the latter deliciously fragile, both full of atmosphere. The dashing Mendelssohn items are well known, though the 1954 sound lacks the sparkle of the playing. The earlier (1951) recording of Saint-Saëns's *Second Concerto* (which 'begins like Bach, ends like Offenbach') is fuller, and the performance (with Moura Lympany) is as brilliant as can be. In Désormière's Strauss confection, *Le beau Danube*, there is a wonderful sense of enjoyment; the playing in this elegantly light-hearted repertoire is always sophisticated, and the close of the works is as exhilarating as a *can-can* can ever be!

In the recordings with the Paris Conservatoire Orchestra we hear the distinctive sound of a true French orchestra (now all but lost), most notably in the woodwind and brass, with the vibrato deemed unacceptable to modern tastes. Dancers may not wish to tackle Martinon's *Giselle* – at his fast tempi, they'd soon be in casualty – but what a superb concert performance it is, exciting from beginning to end, with Martinon's striking rhythmic point all but turning it into an orchestral showpiece. Just sample *La chasse*, where the vibrancy of the music is very theatrical, while the 1959 (stereo) Decca recording is warm and vivid throughout. Martinon chose the Büsser edition, which includes much of the best music (and which conveniently fitted on to a single LP). The individual sections are also helpfully and properly cued.

In that same year, another famous early stereo recording was made, now providing the most exhilarating performance of Ibert's *Divertissement* on CD. No other version can match the fizzing high spirits found here (just play the finale). It was coupled with stylish accounts of *Danse macabre*, *Le Rouet d'Omphale* and Bizet's *Jeux d'enfants*. The delicacy of the playing is worthy of Beecham, though the CD transfer has lost a little in amplitude, compared with the LP. In the collection of Berlioz overtures the adrenalin does not flow as grippingly as in the rest of the items, but the performances have a genuine French accent and are most memorable for their orchestral colour. We are indebted to Decca's Raymond McGill for compiling this boxed set. Martinon's Decca legacy is of the best vintage in the house. His Gallic style of conducting has largely vanished, as has the sound of the Paris Conservatoire Orchestra, and the recording world is the poorer for it.

Mitropoulos, Dimitri

MAHLER: *Symphony 6* (with West German RSO, Cologne). BERLIOZ: *Roméo et Juliette: excerpts*. DEBUSSY: *La Mer*. R. STRAUSS: *Salome: Dance of the Seven Veils* (with NYPO) (B) (**(*)) EMI mono 575471-2 (2)

The Mahler symphony comes from a 1959 concert in the WestDeutscher Rundfunk studio in Cologne, a year before the conductor's death. This was a period when the Mahler symphonies were rarities and the LP catalogue listed only one commercial recording of the *Sixth* (by the Rotterdam Philharmonic Orchestra under Eduard Flipse on Philips). As one might expect, Mitropoulos brings great intensity and tremendous grip to this mighty score. The New York recordings were made when he was conductor-in-chief of the Philharmonic: the Debussy in 1950, the Berlioz in 1952 and the Strauss four years later. All were issued in the USA and the Berlioz appeared on a 10-inch Philips LP in Britain. Both that and the Debussy were still to be found in specialist outlets in Britain in the 1970s. The recorded sound is very much of its day but the performances are pretty electrifying.

Mravinsky, Yevgeny

(see also under LENINGRAD PHILHARMONIC ORCHESTRA)

'*Yevgeny Mravinsky – Soviet Conductor, Russian Aristocrat*' (documentary by Dennis Marks). Includes WEBER: *Oberon: Overture*. TCHAIKOVSKY: *Francesca da Rimini* (Leningrad PO)
*** EMI **DVD** DVB 5 996899 (black-and-white) (with bonus: TCHAIKOVSKY: *Symphony 4*. Leningrad PO, Rozhdestvensky)

Yevgeni Mravinsky made few recordings, and he worked with the same orchestra and in the same acoustic for the best part of half a century. His talent was recognized in the 1930s and, after his appointment to the Leningrad Philharmonic, the Soviet regime gave him carte blanche to build up the orchestra into one of the finest in the world. At first his aristocratic background told against him and he was rejected by the Leningrad Conservatoire. His early career was with the ballet as a rehearsal pianist and then conductor, and we even catch a glimpse of him as a dancer. He enjoyed a privileged position in terms of preparation and rehearsal time and had a freedom and power unheard of elsewhere. Dennis Marks's remarkable portrait of the great Russian conductor reveals much about his relationship with the Soviet authorities and his profoundly religious nature. His performances were dedicated to the deity and not to the public. Indeed, when he once programmed Bruckner's *Seventh Symphony*, having lavished enormous time and preparation on it, the final run-through was such an inspired and intense performance that he cancelled the concert itself, feeling he could never match it! We see him meticulously rehearsing the Schubert *Unfinished* and Shostakovich's *Eighth*, and we hear from the members of his orchestra. There are recordings of the *Oberon Overture* and *Francesca da Rimini* and, as a bonus, an outstanding film of a Prom appearance the orchestra made in 1971 with Rozhdestvensky conducting Tchaikovsky's *Fourth Symphony*. An exceptional and inspiring document.

Münch, Charles

SAINT-SAËNS: *La Princesse jaune, Overture.*
MENDELSSOHN: *Octet: Scherzo* (◉). MARTINU: *Symphony 6 (Fantaisies symphoniques).* PROKOFIEV: *Romeo and Juliet:* excerpts. BEETHOVEN: *Symphony 9 in D min. (Choral)* (with L. Price, Forrester, Poleri, Tozzi, New England Conservatoire Ch.; all with Boston SO). BERLIOZ: *Le Corsaire Overture* (with Paris Conservatoire O). BIZET: *Symphony in C* (with Fr. Nat. R. O)
(B) (***) EMI mono/stereo 5 75477-2 (2)

This is of exceptional interest in that it restores to circulation the Martinů *Sixth Symphony (Fantaisies symphoniques)*, written for Münch, which has never been available in Britain on CD. (Indeed, we are not sure that it was ever available in stereo.) The 1956 recording which was rather hard in its mono LP form has splendid tonal refinement and openness. It is superbly balanced and has good detail and a wonderful sense of space. It is the definitive performance and recording, if there could ever be such a thing. The collection ranges from a 1948 *Corsaire* with the Orchestre de la Société des Concerts du Conservatoire to the 1966 Bizet *Symphony*. (It would have been good if his fine *Queen Mab Scherzo* from the same period could have been included, or his glorious Mendelssohn *Reformation Symphony*, but perhaps next time ...).

Ormandy, Eugene (conductor and violinist)

(See also under PHILADELPHIA ORCHESTRA)

'The Art of Eugene Ormandy': Ormandy as violinist: RIMSKY-KORSAKOV: *Le Coq d'Or: Hymn to the Sun. Sadko: Song of India.* VICTOR HERBERT: *Mlle. Modiste: Kiss Me Again.* DRDLA: *Souvenir.* DVORAK: *Humoresque.* Ormandy and his Salon O: BRAHMS: *Hungarian Dance 2 in D min..* HOSMER: *Southern Rhapsody.* With Dorsey Brothers' Concert O: COSLOW-SPIER-BRITT: *Was it a Dream?.* With Minneapolis SO: ZEMACHSON: *Chorale and Fugue in D min., Op. 4.* ZADOR: *Hungarian Dance.* GRIFFES: *The Pleasure Dome of Kubla Khan, Op. 8.* HARRIS: *When Johnny Comes Marching Home.* With Phd. O: BARBER: *Essay 1, Op. 12.* MENOTTI: *Amelia Goes to the Ball: Overture.* MIASKOVSKY: *Symphony 21 in F sharp min., Op. 51.* R. STRAUSS: *Symphonia domestica, Op. 53.* With Yeend, Beech, Coray, Kullman, Harrell, London, Los Angeles Ch., Hollywood Bowl SO: MAHLER: *Symphony 8: 1st movt only*
(***) Biddulph mono WHL 064/5

This two-disc set gives a fascinating profile of Ormandy's early career. He arrived in America seeking a career as a

violinist and in the first five tracks we hear him as a good deal more than capable in that role. These recordings, dating from the 1920s, have a warm nostalgic glow and the sound is generally good.

His next progression was conducting light classical and salon music for radio, of which there are three examples from the late 1920s, including a characteristic 1920s account (with vocals) of *Was it a Dream?*

Ormandy's great turning point came when he stood in for Toscanini, who sudddenly pulled out of a Philadelphia Orchestral engagement and Ormandy took over. His concerts were a triumph and, thanks to a talent scout, resulted in a series of recordings with the Minneapolis Symphony Orchestra, of which four (from the mid-1930s) are included here. The repertoire is comparatively rare today, which makes their inclusion valuable, especially as they are so enjoyable.

But it is the Philadelphia recordings which are the glories of this set: Barber's *Essay 1* has rarely been equalled in performance, while the Menotti overture is brilliant as it could be. The Miaskovsky is magnetic in concentration and atmosphere, and one just has to hear the sumptuous string-tone to appreciate why the Philadelphia sound is legendary. The *Symphonia domestica* is also perceptively characterized and, again, there is something quite magnetic about the performance.

The first movement of Mahler's *Eighth Symphony* is an interesting reminder of Ormandy's pioneering importance in this repertoire, but the recorded sound, from a live broadcast in 1948, leaves something to be desired. A fascinating collection just the same, with helpful sleeve-notes and convenient slim-line packaging.

BRAHMS: *Symphony 4.* RACHMANINOV: *Symphony 2.* SIBELIUS: *Legend: Lemminkäinen's Homeward Journey, Op. 22/4.* WEBERN: *Im Sommerwind* (all with Phd. O). KABALEVSKY: *Colas Breugnon: Overture.* R. STRAUSS: *Don Juan* (both with Bav. RSO)
(B) *** EMI (ADD) 5 75127-2 (2)

All these recordings, except for the brilliantly played Kabalevsky *Colas Breugnon Overture* and Strauss's *Don Juan*, are with the Philadelphia Orchestra, over whose fortunes Ormandy presided for the best part of half a century. Since theirs was one of the most prolific recording partnerships, selection must have presented a problem, although it is natural that Rachmaninov, with whom Ormandy was so closely associated, should feature. He recorded that composer's *Second Symphony* four times, and it is the fourth version, in which he opened out all the old traditional cuts, that is offered here. The 1973 performance sails forth with consistent ardour, but for all the splendour of the rich, massed Philadelphia strings, the continuous intense expressiveness, with relatively little light and shade, almost overwhelms the listener. What a pity the 1956 CBS version was not chosen, cuts and all, for that is much fresher and more spontaneous sounding.

The performance of Brahms's *Fourth Symphony*, another work that Ormandy recorded more than once, brings a similar problem. The performance has great forward thrust, and the passionate progress of the music certainly holds the listener, but at the end one is left emotionally spent, craving more subtle detail and greater dynamic contrast.

Ormandy's recordings of Shostakovich's *First* or *Fifteenth*, both peerless, his wonderful Prokofiev *Fifth* or either of his magical accounts of the *Daphnis et Chloé Suite 2* would have done his art greater justice.

Undoubtedly the highlight of the first disc is Webern's rarely heard early work, *Im Sommerwind*, an evocation of a summer day spent in the countryside. Its vivid impressionism obviously fired Ormandy, and he conducted its première in 1962. The recording followed a year later, and like most first recordings the performance has constant freshness and is most stimulating and enjoyable. Fortunately, the second disc closes with an excerpt from the *Lemminkäinen Legends* of Sibelius, one of Ormandy's finest late recordings for EMI, dating from 1978. Throughout these Philadelphia sessions the sheer orchestral opulence and dazzling virtuosity of the players and the control exercised by this great conductor (whose powers were so often taken for granted in his lifetime) still put one under his spell, and the sound is certainly full blooded.

For the brashly exciting Kabalevsky overture and Strauss's *Don Juan* Ormandy turned to the Bavarian Radio Symphony Orchestra, and in an exciting live recording of Strauss's tone-poem they provide a balance between passion and strong characterization.

Rosbaud, Hans

BEETHOVEN: *Piano Concerto 5 (Emperor), Op. 73* (with Casadesus, Concg. O). BLACHER: *Concertante Musik, Op. 10* (with BPO); *Piano Concerto 2* (with Herzog, BPO). HAYDN: *Symphonies 92 in G (Oxford); 104 in D (London)* (with BPO). MOZART: *Violin Concerto 4 in D, K.218* (with Schneiderhan (violin), BPO). RACHMANINOV: *Piano Concerto 2* (with Karolyi (piano), Munich PO). SIBELIUS: *Festivo; Finlandia; Karelia Suite; Tapiola; Valse triste* (with BPO). STRAVINSKY: *Petrushka* (with Concg. O); *Agon.* BERG: *3 Pieces, Op. 6.* WEBERN: *6 Pieces, Op. 6* (with SWF SO, Baden-Baden)

(M) *(**) DG mono/stereo 477 0892 (5)

Hans Rosbaud (1895–1962) was one of the most respected conductors of his day, but he was rarely invited into the recording studio. As a champion of modern music in general and of Schoenberg in particular, he lavished generous rehearsal time on his chosen repertoire during his days with the Frankfurt and Baden-Baden orchestras. All the performances recorded here are meticulously prepared and given masterly and insightful interpretations. In commenting on his fine Haydn no less a scholar than H. C. Robbins Landon wrote, 'During the next few years another dozen accounts of the "Oxford" and no doubt two dozen of the "London" will appear but this DG issue will go down in gramophone history as *the* perfect Haydn interpretation.' Fifty years on, this still holds good. His Berg is superlative and so, too, is the Blacher. When invited to conduct the BBC Symphony Orchestra in 1961, he insisted on programming Sibelius's *Fourth Symphony* despite pressure from William Glock, the BBC's Controller of Music, to drop it in favour of other repertory. Such was his dedication to the Sibelius cause – and his quality as a Sibelius interpreter can be heard in his 1957 *Tapiola*, one of the most terrifying and intense accounts ever committed to disc. Indeed, everything in this five-CD set is pretty special and we cannot recommend it too strongly. On the sticker on the front of the box, the once-dignified Deutsche Grammophon company has descended to Anglo-American standards of advertising vulgarity: 'hear how a master-conductor delivers the goods!' However, nothing else in the presentation of these performances, long absent from the catalogue (with the exception of the Sibelius), is out of key or lets Rosbaud down.

Schuricht, Carl

BEETHOVEN: *Symphony 1 in C* (with Paris Conservatoire O). BRUCKNER: *Symphony 8 in C min.* MENDELSSOHN: *Overture: The Hebrides.* MOZART: *Symphony 35 in D (Haffner).* SCHUBERT: *Symphony 8 (Unfinished)* (all with VPO)

(B) *** EMI (ADD) 5 75130-2 (2)

Carl Schuricht was a conductor of the old school, a wholly dedicated and thoughtful musician, unconcerned with image or publicity. Although Testament reissued his glorious Bruckner *Ninth* with the Vienna Philharmonic some years back (in a special vinyl pressing), his *Eighth* (in the Haas Edition) with the same orchestra has not been available since the 1960s. It never received its proper due at the time, but it is every bit as glorious a performance, finely proportioned and noble, and sounds pretty sumptuous in this splendidly restored 1963 recording. It can challenge many of its more celebrated rivals. Yet, starting with an account of Mendelssohn's *Hebrides Overture* that is thrusting and not at all atmospheric, there is a penny-plain element in Schuricht's approach to these masterpieces that makes one hanker after more idiosyncratic touches. In Schubert's *Unfinished Symphony*, recorded for Decca in 1956, there is none of the magic one finds, for example, in the earlier Decca mono version from Josef Krips and the Vienna Philharmonic. As in the Mendelssohn, Schuricht is strong and rugged with no attempt at charm, and it is much the same in both Mozart's *Haffner Symphony* and Beethoven's *First*; there is no lingering by the wayside. That comes closer to latterday taste than the more romantically expressive manner often favoured at the time, with the slow movement of the Beethoven crisp and clean with relatively little moulding. When Schuricht varies tempo, it tends to be towards an accelerando rather than an easing up, with the fundamental impression being one of ruggedness, with textures clarified. Except for the Beethoven, all these performances are with the Vienna Philharmonic.

Stokowski, Leopold (with various orchestras)

(See also under HILVERSUM RADIO PO, NEW YORK PHILHARMONIC ORCHESTRA, PHILADELPHIA ORCHESTRA and STOKOWSKI SYMPHONY ORCHESTRA)

'*Decca Recordings 1965–1972*': Orchestral transcriptions: BACH: *Toccata and Fugue in D min., BWV 565; Well-Tempered Clavier: Prelude in E flat min., BWV 853.* Chorales: *Mein Jesu was für Selenweh, BWV 487; Wir glauben all'einen Gott, BWV 680. Easter Cantata: Chorale: Jesus Christus, Gottes Sohn, BWV 4. Passacaglia and Fugue in C min., BWV 582.* RACHMANINOV: *Prelude in C sharp min.* (all with Czech PO). BYRD: *Earl of Salisbury Pavan; Galliard (after Tregian).* CLARKE: *Trumpet Voluntary* (with Snell, trumpet). SCHUBERT: *Moment musical in F min., D.780/3.* CHOPIN: *Mazurka in A min., Op. 17/4.* TCHAIKOVSKY: *Chant sans paroles, Op. 40/6.* DUPARC: *Extase* (with LSO). DEBUSSY: *La Cathédrale engloutie* (with New Philh. O). TCHAIKOVSKY: *Symphony 5, Op. 64.* BERLIOZ: *Symphonie fantastique* (with New Philh. O) *Damnation de Faust: Ballet des Sylphes.* SCRIABIN: *Poème de l'extase.* ELGAR: *Enigma Variations* (with Czech PO). FRANCK: *Symphony in D min.* RAVEL: *L'Éventail de Jeanne*

with Hilversum R. PO). *Daphnis et Chloé: Suite 2.* (with
LSO Ch.). STRAVINSKY: *Firebird Suite* (1919 version).
DEBUSSY: *La Mer; Prélude à l'après midi d'un faune.*
MESSIAEN: *L'Ascension: 4 Méditations symphoniques* (all
with LSO)
(B) **(*) Decca (ADD/DDD) 475 145-2 (5)

The five Stokowski CDs included here were all made in
Decca's hi-fi-conscious Phase 4 system which, by close microphoning and the use of a 20-channel mixer, created exceptionally vivid projection and detail. None was more
spectacular than the 1968 Kingsway Hall *Symphonie fantasique*, with the New Philharmonia Orchestra, in which the
brass have satanic impact in the *Marche au Supplice* and
finale. The performance is as idiosyncratic as it is charismatic
and is thrilling in every way. Stokowski's warmth of phrasing
is aptly romantic, but generally the most surprising feature is
his meticulous concern for the composer's markings. The
Danse des Sylphes makes a ravishing encore.

Elgar's *Enigma Variations* also shows Stokowski at his most
persuasive, richly phrased by the Czech players and completely spontaneous-sounding. Equally, the Czech account of
Scriabin's *Poème de l'extase* (edited from more than one
performance) has all the passionate commitment of the live
concert hall, with the ebb and flow of tension and the
flexibility of the phrasing again captured compellingly.

Among the LSO recordings, *La Mer* has surprisingly slow
basic tempi, but the effect is breathtaking in its vividness and
impact, and the *Prélude à l'après-midi d'un faune* is richly
languorous, yet has a wonderful intensity. The account of the
second *Daphnis et Chloé Suite* is comparably glowing, with
sumptuous playing, and the multi-channel technique is used
here to produce exactly the right disembodied, ethereal effect
for the offstage chorus. Stokowski takes the choral parts from
the complete ballet and adds a *fortissimo* chord at the very
end; but after such involving music-making few will
begrudge him that.

The *Firebird Suite* is similarly sumptuous, and the gentler
music shows the wonderful luminosity Stokowski could
command from a first-class orchestra. Rich-textured violins
dominate the beginning of the final climax. Messiaen's
L'Ascension is tonally hardly less opulent, yet Stokowski is
characteristically persuasive in developing the smooth flow
of the music. Though some may feel that the final sweet
meditation for strings alone, *Prayer of Christ ascending to
the Father*, lacks true spirituality, it is played very beautifully.

The most controversial performance here is of Tchaikovsky's *Fifth Symphony*. Although there is no doubting the
electricity of the music-making, Stokowski tends to languish
rather than press forward. Yet he also creates some thrilling
climaxes and certainly holds the listener throughout. However, he makes a number of small cuts in the outer movements, and dispenses with the pause before the finale. In the
César Franck *Symphony* the Hilversum orchestra plays with
tremendous energy and warmth. The problem is that
Stokowski's reading, though moulded with conviction,
underlines vulgarities in the score that most conductors try
to minimize.

The transcriptions, without which no Stokowski anthology
would be complete, range from thrilling technicolor Bach to
the extraordinarily imaginative arrangement of Debussy's *La
Cathédrale engloutie*, which has a wholly different sound-
world from the original piano version. The sheer force of

Stokowski's orchestral personality makes all this music very
much his own.

Szell, George

AUBER: *Fra Diavolo: Overture.* DVORAK: *Symphony 8 in G.*
DELIUS: *Irmelin: Prelude.* ROSSINI: *L'Italiana in Algeri:
Overture* (all with Cleveland O). DEBUSSY: *La Mer.*
TCHAIKOVSKY: *Symphony 5* (with West German RSO,
Cologne). WAGNER: *Die Meistersinger: Prelude.* JOSEF
STRAUSS: *Delirien Waltz* (with NYPO)
(B) *** EMI 5 75962-2 (2)

The Dvořák symphony is the version EMI recorded three
months before Szell's death in 1970. The sound is more
spacious and natural than the quality which the CBS engineers used to give him in Cleveland. This is one of Szell's
finest performances, he gives the phrases time to breathe, the
slow movement is relaxed and has charm (not a quality one
normally associates with him), and he never rushes the
music, either in the Scherzo or in the finale. In short, a lovely
performance and arguably the best thing in the set. The two
live studio performances come from Cologne: the Tchaikovsky *Symphony* was recorded in 1966 and *La Mer* four years
earlier. They bear all the hallmarks of the conductor: finely
balanced textures, clarity, excellence of execution and a complete absence of interpretative idiosyncrasy. We don't associate Szell with Delius, but the inclusion of his 1956 account of
the *Prelude to Irmelin*, played with a fine sense of atmosphere,
serves as a reminder that he spent 1937–9 in Glasgow as
conductor of the BBC Scottish Orchestra. A valuable set.

Walter, Bruno

BEETHOVEN: *Symphony 6 in F (Pastoral).* MAHLER:
*Symphony 5: Adagietto; Kindertotenlieder: Nun will die
Sonn' so hell aufgeh'n* (with Ferrier) (all with VPO).
BRAHMS: *Symphony 2 in D* (with NYPO). HAYDN:
Symphony 92 in G (Oxford). JOHANN STRAUSS JR: *Die
Fledermaus: Overture* (both with Paris Conservatoire O).
MOZART: *Le nozze di Figaro: Overture.* WAGNER: *Die
Meistersinger: Overture; Die Walküre: Act II, Scene 5* (with
Lehmann, Melchior & soloists) (both with British SO)
(B) (***) EMI mono 5 75133-2 (2)

The value of this Bruno Walter set lies in its pre-war rarities: his
1936 account of the Beethoven *Pastoral*, which has great freshness and warmth, and one of the Haydn symphonies he
recorded in 1938 during his days with the Paris Conservatoire, a
performance of great elegance, treasured by all who have them
in their shellac form. The radiance of the *Adagietto* from
Mahler's *Fifth Symphony* is richly caught in a reading that is by
no means slow – it had to fit on two 78-r.p.m. sides! – yet
because of the expansive phrasing, it still sounds relaxed, and
the recording is remarkably warm and spacious.

Walter's partnership with Kathleen Ferrier was certainly
worth remembering, and she is in superb voice in this finely
transferred excerpt from the *Kindertotenlieder*. Walter also
championed Wagner on his regular London visits, and his
Meistersinger overture, where the sound is less flattering, comes
from 1930, as does the *Figaro* overture, brilliantly done by the
British Symphony Orchestra. The excerpt from *Die Walküre*
with Lotte Lehmann and Lauritz Melchior among others is
almost worth the price of the whole disc. The only post-war
recording is a fine New York Brahms *Second* from 1946 – once

again given a first-class transfer. Definitely worth having, not least for the sake of the *Pastoral*, which he never surpassed.

Weingartner, Felix

BEETHOVEN: *The Creatures of Prometheus Overture, Op. 63* (with VPO). *Symphony 2 in D* (with LSO). BERLIOZ: *Marche troyenne.* WAGNER: *Rienzi Overture* (with Paris Conservatoire O). WEBER/BERLIOZ: *Invitation to the Dance.* BRAHMS: *Symphony 3 in F, Op. 90.* MOZART: *Symphony 39 in E flat, K.543.* WAGNER: *Siegfried Idyll.* LISZT: *Les Préludes; Mephisto Waltz* (all with LPO)

(B) (***) EMI mono 5 75965-2 (2)

Weingartner is thought of as the supreme classicist, the conductor who served (in Peter Stadlen's memorable phrase) 'lean-beef' Beethoven in Vienna's Sunday morning concerts. His Beethoven, now restored on the Naxos Historical label, is pretty well unsurpassed, and the LSO records of the *Second Symphony* are included here, 'a paradigm of Weingartner's greatness', as the notes put it. The Brahms *Third Symphony*, recorded with the LPO in 1938, is wonderfully sinewy but at the same time warm, and the remaining performances have the ring of truth. Here is a conductor who is totally dedicated and self-effacing. Though he was not identified with Berlioz, his *Marche troyenne* serves as an admirable reminder of his credentials in this repertoire: he made an impressive recording of the *Symphonie fantastique* with the LSO in the late 1920s, though the sound was distinctly frail. No quarrels with any of the sound here — quite the reverse. *Les Préludes* and the *Mephisto Waltz* were recorded with the LSO during the war (Weingartner was based in Basle during his last decades). His Liszt carries special authority as he was close to the composer during 1883–6. As Christopher Dyment's authoritative notes remind us, Weingartner was known as the 'prince of guest conductors', for he appeared with most major European orchestras after his long tenure of the Vienna Philharmonica, and this set offers examples of his work in London and Paris as well as Vienna. Very successful transfers.

Academy of Ancient Music, Pavlo Beznosiuk

Live Wigmore Concert, 24 January 2005 (with Rachel Podger, violin, Frank de Bruine, oboe): HANDEL: *Concerti grossi, Op. 6/1 & 10.* VIVALDI: *Double Violin Concerto in B flat, RV 524; Double Concerto for Oboe & Violin in B flat, RV 548.* BACH: *Double Violin Concerto in D min., BWV 1043*
(M) **(*) Wigmore Hall Live WHLive 005

John Gilhooly, the Director of the Wigmore Hall Trust, has decided to follow the example of the managements of the LPO and LSO, who have now established their own independent CD labels and are recording some of their most important concerts live. But, as John Newton, the distinguished sound engineer who records all the concerts in Boston's Symphony Hall, has told us, this offers great problems for the unwary. To capture the hall acoustics at a live performance requires much aural skill and technical experience, and frankly the present example is not a great success. The Wigmore Hall is famous for its perfect resonance for chamber and instrumental music, and solo performances. But on this CD one is only aware of its effect during the audience applause! The microphones are too close to the players. Not close enough to prevent an accurate portrayal of the ensemble, nor to spoil the internal balance, (although the dynamic range is reduced), but too close to capture also the small decay', which is what gives a live recording an added dimension. The performances are all stylish and pleasing, but the overall effect is bland.

Academy of Ancient Music, Christopher Hogwood

PACHELBEL: *Canon & Gigue.* HANDEL: *Water Music: Air; Berenice: Overture; Minuet; Gigue.* VIVALDI: *Flute Concerto in G min. (La notte), Op. 10/2.* BACH: *Christmas Oratorio, BWV 248: Sinfonia; Quadruple Harpsichord Concerto in A min., BWV 1065.* CORELLI: *Concerto grosso (Christmas Concerto), Op. 6/8.* A. MARCELLO: *Oboe Concerto in D min.*
(M) **(*) O-L ADD/DDD 443 201-2

It seems a curious idea to play popular baroque repertoire in a severe manner; Pachelbel's *Canon* here sounds rather abrasive and lacking in charm. But those who combine a taste for these pieces with a desire for authenticity should be satisfied. The selection for this reissue has been expanded and altered. Handel's *Queen of Sheba* no longer arrives – and she is not missed (for she was much more seductive in Beecham's hands) – and the highlight of the original, full-priced compilation (a pair of Gluck dances) is no longer present! Instead, we get several new items taken from another Academy of Ancient Music compilation of baroque music associated with Christmas, notably Corelli's splendid Op. 6/8, in which the playing has a suitably light touch, and Vivaldi's engaging *La notte Flute Concerto*, while Bach's *Quadruple Harpsichord Concerto* substitutes for the famous Vivaldi work for four violins (Op. 3/10). On the whole an enjoyable mix. The new playing time is 67 minutes.

Academy of St Martin-in-the-Fields, Sir Neville Marriner

'The Best of the Academy': SUPPE: *Overture: Light Cavalry.* GRIEG: *2 Elegiac Melodies, Op. 34; Holberg Suite, Op. 40: Prelude.* TCHAIKOVSKY: *Andante cantabile (from String Quartet 1).* DVORAK: *Nocturne in B, Op. 40.* PONCHIELLI: *La Gioconda: Dance of the Hours.* NICOLAI: *The Merry Wives of Windsor: Overture.* FAURE: *Pavane, Op. 50.* BOCCHERINI: *String Quintet in E, Op. 13/5: Minuet.* WAGNER: *Siegfried Idyll.* HANDEL: *Solomon: Arrival of the Queen of Sheba.* J. S. BACH: *Cantata 208: Sheep may safely graze; Cantata 147: Jesu, joy of man's desiring; Christmas Oratorio: Pastoral Symphony.* HANDEL: *Berenice: Minuet; Messiah: Pastoral Symphony.* SCHUBERT: *Rosamunde: Entr'acte 3 in B flat.* GLUCK: *Orfeo ed Euridice: Dance of the Blessed Spirits.* BORODIN: *String Quartet 2 in D: Nocturne.* SHOSTAKOVICH: *The Gadfly: Romance.* MUSSORGSKY/RIMSKY-KORSAKOV: *Khovanshchina: Dance of the Persian Slaves.* RIMSKY-KORSAKOV: *Tsar Saltan: The Flight of the Bumble-bee; The Snow Maiden: Dance of the Tumblers*
(B) *** CfP 585 6242 (2)

This reissued CfP bargain double draws on the contents of three different (HMV) digital collections, recorded between 1980 and 1987. The first included the *Siegfried Idyll*, in which Marriner uses solo strings for the gentler passages, a fuller ensemble for the climaxes, here passionately convincing. Delicately introduced by the harp and the gentle striking of the morning hour, the account of the *Dance of the Hours* has characteristic finesse and colour, while there is comparably gracious phrasing in *The Merry Wives of Windsor Overture*. The other, mainly gentle, pieces by Tchaikovsky, Fauré, Boccherini and Grieg are given radiant performances. To open the second disc, Handel's *Queen of Sheba* trots in very briskly and here the noble contour of Handel's famous *Berenice* melody is the first thing to strike the ear; but it is the Schubert *Entr'acte* from *Rosamunde* and the passionately expressive Borodin *Nocturne* that resonate in the memory. With the Shostakovich *Barrel Organ Waltz* providing a touch of piquancy and Mussorgsky's *Persian Slaves* suitably sinuous and sentient, this makes a most agreeable entertainment, ending with gusto with Rimsky's *Tumblers*. The digital sound is excellent throughout.

'Fantasia on Greensleeves': VAUGHAN WILLIAMS: *Fantasia on Greensleeves; The Lark Ascending* (with Iona Brown); *English Folksongs Suite.* WARLOCK: *Serenade; Capriol Suite.* GEORGE BUTTERWORTH: *A Shropshire Lad; Two English Idylls; The Banks of Green Willow.* DELIUS: *A Village Romeo and Juliet: The Walk to the Paradise Garden; Hassan: Intermezzo and Serenade; A Song before Sunrise; On Hearing the First Cuckoo in Spring; Summer Night on the River; La Calinda.* ELGAR: *Serenade for Strings, Op. 20; Sospiri for Strings, Harp & Organ; Elegy for Strings, Op. 58; The Spanish Lady (suite); Introduction and Allegro, Op. 47*
(B) *** Double Decca (ADD) 452 707-2 (2)

This exceptionally generous programme, mainly of English pastoral evocations but including Iona Brown's Elysian account of *The Lark Ascending* and Elgar's two string master-pieces in not wholly idiomatic but very characterful perform-ances, is self-recommending, for the Academy are thoroughly at home here and play with consistent warmth and finesse, while the vintage Decca sound never disappoints. Marvellous value for money.

'A Celebration': VIVALDI: *The Four Seasons: Spring.* HANDEL: *Water Music: Suite 2 in D.* BACH: *Brandenburg Concerto 4 in G.* AVISON: *Concerto grosso 7 in G min.* BOYCE: *Symphony 5 in D.* MOZART: *Eine kleine Nachtmusik.* BIZET: *Symphony in C.* WAGNER: *Siegfried Idyll.* BRAHMS: *Hungarian Dance 5.* ROSSINI: *Overture: William Tell.* BEETHOVEN: *Wellington's Victory.* BARBER: *Adagio for Strings.* FALLA: *Ritual Fire Dance.* DELIUS: *The Walk to the Paradise Garden.* VAUGHAN WILLIAMS: *Fantasia on a Theme by Thomas Tallis.* WALTON: *Sonata for Strings.* TIPPETT: *Fantasia Concertante on the Theme of Corelli* (includes a bonus DVD with: TCHAIKOVSKY: *Serenade for Strings in C, Op. 48.* GRIEG: *At the Cradle, Op. 68/5; Holberg Suite, Op. 40)*

(M) **(*) Ph. (ADD/DDD) 475 6117 (4)

So vast and ubiquitous is Sir Neville Marriner's output, it is only too easy to take for granted what he has contributed to the recorded repertoire. Yet this three-CD set offers plenty of evidence as to why he has been such a successful recording artist: the classic account of the Bizet *Symphony* remains one of the best ever recorded – it has all the polish and elegance characteristic of vintage ASMF records of the early 1970s: the slow movement has a delectable oboe solo and the finale is irrepressibly high-spirited. Walton expanded his *Sonata for Strings* at the suggestion of Marriner in 1947, and for the bigger ensemble Walton tautened the argument, while expanding the richness of texture, frequently relating the full band to the sound of four solo instruments. Though some-thing of the acerbity of the original is lost, the result was another in the sequence of great British string works, warmly romantic in lyricism in the first and third movements, spikily brilliant in the Scherzo and finale. The performance here is superb, as is the 1973 recording, and it makes its CD debut. From the same Argo era there are vintage performances of Delius's *A Walk to the Paradise Garden* and Tippett's *Corelli Variations*, as well as a compilation disc devoted mainly to some of his classic Argo baroque recordings (Vivaldi, Bach, Avison, Boyce and Handel) which remain as fresh-sounding as ever.

Understandably, Universal wanted to include some of his later, digital accounts on Philips and, while these are very good by any standards, they don't quite capture the magic of the earlier ones: the *Tallis Fantasia*, for example, is beautiful but lacks the last degree of emotional intensity. Similarly too, while the original Argo recording of Barber's *Adagio* received a ✪ in our main volume; the later, digital version featured here does not have the gripping intensity of that classic account. The same comments also apply to the *Siegfried Idyll*, which is again very beautiful but does not create the emo-tional pull of the very best accounts. Unexpectedly included is Beethoven's *Wellington's Victory* (recorded 1990) with a battery of sound effects. That goes well, as does a warm and vividly recorded *Eine kleine Nachtmusik*, dating from 1984, and the *William Tell Overture* also finds the conductor on top form, with the finale going like the devil. The bonus DVD, '*From Penshurst Place, 1989*', offers attractive music-making from Marriner and the ASMF, but also lots of pretty film of the countryside. It is a bit twee, really, and when the orchestra

plays outside, after the Tchaikovsky, with the sound dubbe on afterwards, the effect is not quite so convincing. Still, as free bonus DVD it's acceptable, and it does include, of course some gorgeous music. A good, enjoyable collection, if no quite full to the brim with the very best that Marriner ha given us.

'*Academy in Concert*': MOZART: *Serenade 13 in G (Eine kleine Nachtmusik), K.525; German Dance: Sleigh Ride, K.605/3.* ALBINONI: *Adagio in G min.* (arr. Giazotto). MENDELSSOHN: *Octet, Op. 20: Scherzo.* PACHELBEL: *Canon in D.* BACH: *Orchestral Suite 3, BWV 1068: Air.* FAURÉ: *Pavane, Op. 50.* BOCCHERINI: *String Quintet, Op. 13/5: Minuet.* TCHAIKOVSKY: *Andante cantabile, Op. 11.* GRIEG: *Elegiac Melodies*

(BB) *** EMI Encore (ADD/DDD) 5 86998-2 [5 86999-2]

The Academy are for the most part on top form here. The most famous of Mozart's serenades is graciously played, i with a hint of blandness, while the account of the Albinoni Giazotto *Adagio* (with Iona Brown the violin soloist) must be the most refined in the catalogue, as is the Pachelbel *Canon* Excellent analogue sound. The other, mainly gentle, pieces by Fauré, Boccherini, Tchaikovsky and Grieg enjoy radiant per-formances and are given excellent digital sound.

Adni, Daniel (piano), Bournemouth Symphony Orchestra, Kenneth Alwyn

Film Concertos: ADDINSELL (arr. DOUGLAS): *Warsaw Concerto* (from 'Dangerous Moonlight'). CHARLES WILLIAMS: *Dream of Olwen* (from 'While I Live'). ROZSA: *Spellbound Concerto* (from 'Spellbound'). HUBERT BATH: *Cornish Rhapsody* (from 'Love Story'). GERSHWIN: *Rhapsody in Blue.* (with RICHARD RODNEY BENNETT: *Murder on the Orient Express* (Overture & excerpts; composer (piano), ROHCG Orchestra, Marcus Dods)

(B) *** CfP (ADD) 3 52392-2

By far the finest of these early film concertos is the *Warsaw Concerto*, for which Addinsell provided the melodic line (the main theme totally memorable) and Roy Douglas put together the succinctly structured concert piece in the style of Rachmaninov (who had refused the original commission). There is no better performance on record. The following pieces are less distinctive but, at this distance, are endearing. The performance of *Rhapsody in Blue* (also used in the Gershwin biopic of the same title) is not special, but what makes the disc irresistible is Richard Rodney Bennett's deli-cious pastiche score for *Murder on the Orient Express*, full of melody, with the composer at the piano in the catchy waltz in the concertante section and with Marcus Dods and the Covent Garden Orchestra in their element throughout. Superb sound too.

Algarve Orchestra, Alvaro Cassuto

ARRIAGA: *Overture: Los esclavos felices; Symphony in D.* SEIXAS: *Sinfonia in B flat.* CARVALHO: *Overture: L'amore industrioso.* MOREIRA: *Sinfonia.* PORTUGAL: *Overture: Il Duca di Foix*

(BB) **(*) Naxos 8.557207

An attractive collection of Spanish and Portuguese music from the eighteenth century, the most famous work being

Arriaga's splendid *D major Symphony*, along with his delightfully bubbly *Los esclavos felices Overture*. The *Sinfonia* of Moreira is another highlight, with its sunny Italian disposition, qualities also found in Portugal's *Il Duca di Foix Overture*. The rest of the programme is similarly pleasing and undemanding. The performances are lively, and if sometimes (such as in the *Los esclavos Overture*) the strings are not quite able to take the fast tempi in their stride, it is a minor point compared to the overall vitality and enjoyment of the music-making. Good sound.

American Horn Quartet

Concertos for Four Horns (with Sinfonia Varsovia, Dariusz Wišniewski): SCHUMANN: *Konzertstück for 4 Horns.* HANDEL: *Concerto in F.* TELEMANN: *Overture (Suite) in F (Alster).* HAYDN: *Symphony 31 in D (Horn Signal)*
(BB) *** Naxos 8.557747

Schumann's Quadruple *Horn Concerto*, written in 1849 for the newly developed valve horn, is all but impossible to sustain at a live performance, although we have recently heard it played very successfully in both London and France. The problem lies not just in the extreme bravura writing, especially for the first horn, but that the writing continually reaches up to the instrument's stratospheric register, and in the original version (recorded here) includes several high concert 'A's (a major third above the normal register of the instrument). This is very tiring on the lips for a virtuoso work that lasts 17 minutes. However, at a recording, it is possible to rest between movements and this is obviously one reason why the present performance, featuring the superb American Horn Quartet, which has all the ebullience one could wish for, is so securely successful.

The Handel *Concerto*, dating from around 1746 and contemporary with the *Royal Fireworks Music*, is of uncertain provenance and may be an arrangement. It is pleasing enough, but not nearly so stimulating as the more familiar Telemann descriptive *Alster Suite* with its bold *Prelude* and bizarre characterization. After the *Echo* movement, the portraits include a *Concert of Wailing Frogs and Crows*, *Dorfmusik* ('shepherds' music, complete with drone) and a more delicate portrayal of Pan.

The equally celebrated *Horn Signal Symphony* was especially written by Haydn in 1765 for the virtuoso horn section of the orchestra at that time, soon after his appointment as Vice-Kapellmeister at Esterházy. There is plenty for them to do, not least in the Minuet and finale, while in the opening movement the principal horn continually soars up with an octave leap.

Throughout the concert, the splendid solo playing is well supported by the stylish contribution of the excellent Sinfonia Varsovia, directed by Dariusz Wišniewski.

American masterpieces

'*American Masterpieces*' (with (i) Cleveland O, Louis Lane; (ii) Phd. O, Eugene Ormandy; (iii) NYPO, André Kostelanetz): (i) BERNSTEIN: *Candide: Overture.* (ii) IVES: *Variations on 'America'.* (iii) WILLIAM SCHUMAN: *New England Triptych.* (ii) BARBER: *Adagio for Strings.* GOULD: *American Salute.* (iii) GRIFFES: *The Pleasure Dome of Kubla Khan.* (ii) MACDOWELL: *Woodland Sketches: To a Wild Rose.* (iii) GERSHWIN: *Promenade.* (ii) GOTTSCHALK:

Cakewalk: Grand Walkaround (arr. Hershy Kay). (i) BENJAMIN: *Jamaican Rumba.* RODGERS: *On Your Toes: Slaughter on 10th Avenue.* VIRGIL THOMSON: *Louisiana Story* (film score): *Arcadian Songs and Dances*
(B) **(*) Sony (ADD) SBK 63034

Not everything here is a masterpiece, and Arthur Benjamin, who makes the wittiest contribution, was an Australian! But there are some obvious favourites included and one or two novelties, among them the attractively folksy *Arcadian Songs and Dances* of Virgil Thomson, affectionately directed in Cleveland by Louis Lane. He is well recorded, and so, on the whole, is Ormandy, who presents the Ives *Variations* with charm as well as panache, while the Philadelphia strings are powerfully eloquent in Barber's *Adagio* and warmly persuasive in MacDowell's engaging *To a Wild Rose*. Kostelanetz conducts with plenty of personality and zest and is at his best in the Gershwin *Promenade* and the touching central movement of Schuman's *New England Triptych*. But here the up-front recording of the NYPO is overlit and the climaxes of the otherwise atmospheric *Kubla Khan* sound aggressive. A stimulating programme, just the same.

André, Maurice (trumpet)

Trumpet Concertos (with BPO, Karajan): HUMMEL: *Concerto in E flat.* LEOPOLD MOZART: *Concerto in D.* TELEMANN: *Concerto in D.* VIVALDI: *Concerto in A flat* (ed. Thilde)
(M) **(*) EMI (ADD) 5 66909-2 [5 66961]

A key collection of trumpet concertos, brilliantly played by André. His security in the upper register in the work by Leopold Mozart and the fine Telemann concerto is impressive, with Karajan and the BPO wonderfully serene and gracious in the opening *Adagio* and the *Grave* slow movement of the latter. The jaunty quality of the Hummel is not missed, and the finale of this work, taken at breakneck pace, is certainly exhilarating, while the cantilena of the *Andante* is nobly contoured.

The Vivaldi work is arranged from the *Sonata in F major for Violin and Continuo*, RV 20, and makes a very effective display piece. The 1974 recording has generally been well transferred to CD. Although the trumpet timbre is very bright and the violins are not absolutely clean in focus, there is plenty of ambience. However, this reissue has a playing time of only 47 minutes and hardly seems an apt choice for EMI's 'Great Recordings of the Century' series.

'*Trumpet Concertos*' (with ASMF, Marriner): STOLZEL: *Concerto in D.* TELEMANN: *Concerto in D.* VIVALDI: *Double Trumpet Concerto in C, RV 537* (with Soustrot); *Double Concerto in B flat for Trumpet and Violin, RV 548* (with I. Brown). TORELLI: *Concerto in D*
(B) *** EMI Encore 5 86645-2 [5 86646-2]

Maurice André is peerless in this kind of repertoire and the accompaniments under Marriner are attractively alert and stylish. The Academy provides expert soloists to match André on the concertante works by Telemann (in D) and Vivaldi (RV 548) which offer much the most interesting invention. The concerto by Stölzel is conventional, but has a fine slow movement. Throughout, André's smooth, rich timbre and highly musical phrasing give pleasure. The recording is first class, with the CD transfer adding extra definition and presence.

Music for Trumpet and Organ (with Jane Parker-Smith or Alfred Mitterhofer): CHARPENTIER: *Te Deum: Fanfare.* ALBINONI: *Adagio* (arr. Giazotto). BACH: *Violin Partita in E: Gavotte & Rondeau; Orchestral Suite 3: Air; Cello Suite 4: Bourrée; Cantata 147: Chorale: Jesu, joy of man's desiring.* CLARKE: *Trumpet Voluntary.* SENAILLÉ: *Allegro spiritoso.* STANLEY: *Trumpet tune.* BACH/GOUNOD: *Ave Maria.* MOZART: *Exsultate jubilate: Alleluja.* PURCELL: *The Queen's dolour* (aria). Music for trumpet and orchestra: HANDEL: *Concerto in D min.* (arr. Thilde from *Flute Sonata in B min.*). ALBINONI: *Concertos: in B flat and D, Op. 7/3 & 6* (arr. of *Oboe Concertos*). TELEMANN: *Concerto in D for Trumpet & Oboe* (all with ECO, Mackerras). HERTEL: *Concerto in E flat.* HAYDN: *Concerto in E flat.* TELEMANN: *Concerto in F min.* (arr. of *Oboe Concerto*). ALBINONI: *Concerto in D min.* (arr. of *Chamber Sonata for Violin & Continuo, Op. 6/4*). ALESSANDRO MARCELLO: *Concerto in C* (originally for oboe) (all with LPO, Jesús López-Cobos)
(B) *** EMI Double fforte (ADD) 5 73374-2 (2)

Both these discs open with a series of famous tunes arranged for trumpet and organ, which for baroque repertoire works well enough. Played with rich tone, cultured phrasing, and, when needed, dazzling bravura, they are sumptuously presented, if you don't mind an excess of resonance. The programme begins with a larger-than-life account of the famous Charpentier *Te Deum*, and includes Clarke's famous *Voluntary* and the comparable trumpet piece by Stanley.

But otherwise the repertoire ranges wide, encompassing music originally written for other, very different instruments. These include pieces by Bach for solo violin and cello, by Albinoni and others for oboe, a famous bassoon encore by Senaillé and even (in the case of Mozart) a display-piece for the soprano voice. But André's presentation is so assured that one could be forgiven at times for thinking that they were actually conceived for the trumpet. Indeed the Bach *Gavotte* and *Rondeau* are most attractive on the trumpet.

Much the same applies to the concertos. The first group, vivaciously conducted by Mackerras, includes an ingenious Handel concoction, which even brings a brief reminder of the *Water Music*, and the Telemann multiple concerto is also very diverting. Then André negotiates the Hertel concerto, with its high tessitura, with breathtaking ease.

The second group, also given lively accompaniments, by the LPO under López-Cobos, are particularly successful, with the famous Haydn concerto most elegantly played, and in the transcriptions of works by Albinoni and Marcello slow movements are warmly phrased and André's stylishness and easy execution ensure the listener's enjoyment. Throughout, the analogue recording from the mid- to late 1970s is of high quality and very well transferred to CD. It is a pity that room was not found for the Hummel concerto, but this is undoubtedly excellent value.

Music for Trumpet and Organ (from above two-disc set with Jane Parker-Smith or Alfred Mitterhofer). Music (as listed) by CHARPENTIER; ALBINONI; BACH; CLARKE; SENAILLÉ; STANLEY; BACH/GOUNOD; PURCELL; also HANDEL: *Serse: Largo; Gloria in excelsis Deo.* MOZART: *Exsultate jubilate; Alleluia.* KREBS: *Chorales: In allen meinen Taten; Jesu meine Freude.* ALBINONI: *Violin Sonata in A: Adagio.* BACH: *Chorales: Mein gläubiges Herz, from BWV 68; Wachet auf, BWV 645*
(BB) *** EMI Encore 5 86882-2 [5 86883-2]

Those seeking just the arrangements for trumpet and organ should be well satisfied with this single-CD selection, which duplicates much of the repertoire above, but adds some extra items, notably *Chorales* by Bach and Krebs and a brilliant transcription of Mozart's *Exsultate jubilate.*

Music for Trumpet and Organ, and Concertos (from above one- or two-disc set, with Jane Parker-Smith or Alfred Mitterhofer). Music (as listed) by CHARPENTIER; ALBINONI; BACH; CLARKE; SENAILLÉ; STANLEY; BACH/GOUNOD; PURCELL; HANDEL; MOZART. *Trumpet Concertos* (with ECO, Mackerras; or LPO, López-Coboz) by HANDEL: *in D min.* ALBINONI: *in B flat & D, Op. 7/3 & 6; in D min.* TELEMANN: *in D & F min.* HERTEL: *in E flat.* HAYDN: *in E flat.* MARCELLO: *in C min.*
(BB) ***EMI Gemini 4 76954-2 (2)

Similarly, those wanting the fuller collection would do best with this inexpensive Gemini Double, which includes three more concertos than the Double fforte set.

'The Trumpet Shall Sound' (a 70th birthday tribute): TELEMANN: *Concertos: in E min., TWV51:e1; in G, TWV Anh.51:G1; in C min., TWV51:c1.* HANDEL: *Concertos 1 in B flat, HWV 301; 2 in B flat, HWV 302a; 3 in G min., HWV 287; Messiah: The Trumpet Shall Sound* (with Franz Crass, bass) (all with Munich Bach O, Karl Richter). JOSEPH HAYDN: *Concerto in E flat.* MICHAEL HAYDN: *Concerto in D.* Franz Xaver RICHTER: *Concerto in D* (all with Munich CO, Hans Stadlmair). ALESSANDRO SCARLATTI: *Sinfonia Concertata con ripieni 2 in D for Flute, Trumpet & Strings* (with Hans-Martin Linde, flute, & Zurich Coll. Mus.). VIVALDI: *Double Trumpet Concerto in C, RV 537.* VIVIANI: *Sonata 1 in C for Trumpet & Organ* (with Hedwig Bilgram, organ). TORELLI: *Concerto in D.* STOLZEL: *Concerto in D.* TELEMANN: *Concerto Sonata in D, TWV44:1* (all with ECO, Mackerras)
(B) **(*) DG Double (ADD) 474 331-2 (2)

DG have gathered together on this Double all Maurice André's recordings made for that label between 1965 and 1977, with splendidly sustained solo playing throughout. It includes, of course, the greatest trumpet concerto of all, by Haydn, and here André takes the *Andante* in a rather leisurely fashion; but he is gracious and serene, and most listeners will respond to his elegance. Michael Haydn's concerto, a two-movement concertante section of a seven-movement *Serenade*, has incredibly high tessitura but, characteristically, André reaches up for it with consummate ease. Most of the Baroque concertos (notably those by Telemann and Handel) were originally written for oboe, tempering virtuosity in outer movements with very agreeable central *Andantes*, but André makes them sound custom-made for the trumpet. The Torelli (with its fine slow movement) is an exception. In the Vivaldi *Double Concerto* André plays both solo parts (by electronic means). The *Sonata* by Giovanni Buonaventura Viviani (1638–c. 1692) is a very attractive piece, comprising five brief but striking miniatures, each only a minute or so in length. Alessandro Scarlatti's engaging *Sinfonia* is also in five movements and incorporates a solo flute; the latter is all but drowned out in the *Spiritoso* first movement but takes the solo role in the two brief *Adagios* (the second quite touching); the trumpet returns to echo the flute in the central *Allegro*, and they share the *Presto* finale. The recording usually catches the solo trumpet faithfully throughout, but the earlier, Munich recordings show their age in the string-tone and occasionally a certain lack of refinement, though those conducted by Stadlmair are smoother. The later recordings with Mackerras and the ECO are obviously more modern.

Andsnes, Leif Ove (piano & conductor) with the Norwegian Chamber Orchestra

'Andsnes Plays Bach and Mozart'. Excerpts from: BACH: *Keyboard Concerto 5 in F min., BWV 1056.* MOZART: *Piano Concertos 9 (Jeunehomme) in E flat, K.271; 18 in B flat, K.456; 20 in D min., K.466*

(*) EMI **DVD** 310436 9 (V/D: Espen Dyring Skau)

A promotional DVD which gives us some 48 minutes of music (but no complete works), impeccably played by these wonderful artists, plus shortish interviews with Andsnes himself in English and Norwegian. As one might expect, the music-making is touched by distinction and keen intelligence throughout. However, the visual side is unworthy of it, full of all sorts of tricks and silliness, superimpositions and the like. The incessantly restless and intrusive camerawork never ceases to draw attention to itself. Its director, Espen Dyring Skau, has previously been exclusively involved with pop – and it shows! He should return to that world with the most urgent expedition, for this narcissistic video production is unwatchable. For the musical side: three stars; for the video: absolute zero. This kind of attempt to appeal to a wider audience rarely succeeds, for it betrays a lack of respect for the viewer. Andsnes admirers should buy his CDs and give this a wide berth.

Argerich, Martha (piano), with other artists

Martha Argerich Collection
(M) **(*) DG ADD/DDD 453 566-2 (11)

Volume I: Concertos: BEETHOVEN: *Piano Concertos 1 in C, Op. 15; 2 in B flat, Op. 19* (with Philh. O, Sinopoli). CHOPIN: *Piano Concertos 1 in E min., Op. 11* (with LSO, Abbado); *2 in F min., Op. 21.* SCHUMANN: *Piano Concerto in A min., Op. 54* (both with Nat. SO, Rostropovich). TCHAIKOVSKY: *Piano Concerto 1 in B flat min., Op. 23* (with RPO, Dutoit). LISZT: *Piano Concerto 1 in E flat* (with LSO). PROKOFIEV: *Piano Concerto 3 in C, Op. 26.* RAVEL: *Piano Concerto in G* (with BPO) (both cond. Abbado)
(M) **(*) DG ADD/DDD 453 567-2 (4)

The chimerical volatility of Martha Argerich's musical personality comes out again and again in this impressive survey of her recorded repertory. Her ability in concertos to strike sparks in a musical partnership with the right conductor (Giuseppe Sinopoli in Beethoven and Abbado in Chopin's *First Concerto*) brings characteristically spontaneous music-making, bursting with inner life.

If Chopin's *F minor Concerto*, recorded ten years later in 1978, is rather less successful, she is back on form again in Tchaikovsky (with Dutoit), to produce a performance which has a genuine sense of scale and which balances poetry with excitement. Her temperament takes less readily to the Schumann *Concerto* (here with Rostropovich), a performance which has dynamism, vigour and colour, and delicacy in the slow movement, but which does not quite capture the work's more refined romantic feeling in the outer movements.

Yet her Liszt *E flat Concerto* is surprisingly restrained, gripping without any barnstorming. She is perhaps at her very finest in Prokofiev's *Third Concerto* and hardly less impressive in the Ravel *G major*, a performance full of subtlety, but vigorous and outgoing too. Abbado was again her partner in the three last-mentioned works and together they found a rare musical symbiosis. DG have generally given Argerich's concertos excellent recording, and there is nothing here which will not provide stimulating repeated listening. All these performances (except the Chopin *Second Concerto*) are discussed in greater depth under their composer entries in our main volume.

Volume II: Chopin and Bach: CHOPIN: *Piano Sonatas 2 in B flat min., Op. 35; 3 in B min., Op. 58; Barcarolle in F sharp, Op. 60; Scherzos 2 in B flat min., Op. 31; 3 in C sharp min., Op. 39; 24 Preludes, Op. 28; Preludes in C sharp min., Op. 45; in A flat, Op. posth.; Andante spianato & Grande polonaise brillante, Op. 22; Polonaise 6 in A flat, Op. 53; Polonaise-Fantaisie in A flat, Op. 61; 3 Mazurkas, Op. 59.* BACH: *Toccata in C min., BWV 911; Partita 2 in C min., BWV 826; English Suite 2 in A min., BWV 807*
(M) **(*) DG (ADD) 453 572-2 (3)

Argerich's accounts of the two Chopin *Sonatas* are fiery, impetuous and brilliant, with no want of poetic vision to discommend them. Both, however, have a highly strung quality that will not be to all tastes. The *Preludes* show Argerich at her finest, full of individual insights. The *Scherzo No. 3* and *Barcarolle* are taken from her remarkable début LP recital of 1961 and are very impetuous indeed, and are also less easy to live with. She seems not to want to provide a firm musical control, but is carried away on a breath of wind. Many of the other pieces are played splendidly, with the *Scherzo No. 2* impressively demonstrating her technical command. Her Bach, too, is lively but well conceived. The digital remastering gives the piano-image striking presence, and the recording is resonant and full in timbre, although at *fortissimo* levels the timbre becomes hard.

Volume III: Music for piano solo and duo: SCHUMANN: *Kinderszenen, Op. 15; Kreisleriana, Op. 16; Piano Sonata 2 in G min., Op. 22.* LISZT: *Piano Sonata in B min.; Hungarian Rhapsody 6.* BRAHMS: *Rhapsodies, Op. 79/1–2.* PROKOFIEV: *Toccata, Op. 11.* RAVEL: *Gaspard de la nuit; Jeux d'eau; Sonatine; Valses nobles et sentimentales; Ma Mère l'Oye; Rapsodie espagnole* (arr. 2 pianos & percussion). BARTOK: *Sonata for 2 Pianos & Percussion* (with Freire, Sadlo, Guggeis). TCHAIKOVSKY: *Nutcracker Suite, Op. 71a* (arr. 2 pianos). RACHMANINOV: *Symphonic Dances for 2 Pianos, Op. 45* (with Economou)
(M) **(*) DG ADD/DDD 453 576-2 (4)

The third box contains much of interest. There is no doubting the instinctive flair or her intuitive feeling for Schumann. However, she is let down by an unpleasingly close recording of *Kinderszenen* and *Kreisleriana*. Her Ravel again shows her playing at its most subtle and perceptive, yet with a vivid palette, even if at times a little more poise would be welcome. Taken from her début recital of 1961, the Brahms *First Rhapsody* is explosively fast; then suddenly she puts the brakes on and provides most poetic playing in the central section. Such a barnstorming approach is more readily at home in the Prokofiev *Toccata*, and she goes over the top in the Liszt *Hungarian rhapsody* with a certain panache.

In the Liszt *Sonata*, although the playing demonstrates an impressively responsive temperament, the work's lyrical feeling is all but submerged by the brilliantly impulsive virtuosity. The Ravel arrangements (with percussion!) are done with eminently good taste, restraint and musical imagination but, all the same, is there a need for them at all? They are more interesting to hear once or twice than to repeat.

The Bartók, though, has tremendous fire and intensity. The aural image is very good and discreetly balanced. The Tchaikovsky *Nutcracker* arrangement of Nicolas Economou works well. The playing is of a very high order. The Rachmaninov *Dances* are played with great temperament, and everything is marvellously alive and well thought out. There is much sensitivity and a lively sense of enjoyment in evidence, as well as great virtuosity. The recording is good.

Ashton, Graham (trumpet)

CD 1 (with Irish Chamber Orchestra): PURCELL: *Trumpet Sonata in D.* CORELLI: *Trumpet Sonata in D.* VIVALDI: *Double Trumpet Concerto* (with Ruddock). TELEMANN: *Trumpet Concerto in D.* ALBINONI: *Trumpet Sonatas 1 in C; 2 in D.* STRADELLA: *Sinfonia 'Il Barcheggio' in D.* TORELLI: *Sonata 5 for Trumpet and Strings in D.* HANDEL: *Suite for Trumpet and Strings in D*

CD 2 (with John Lenehan (piano)): MAXWELL DAVIES: *Trumpet Sonata.* JOLIVET: *Heptade for Piano & Percussion* (with Gregory Knowles, percussion). NYMAN: *Flugal Horn & Piano Sonata.* HENZE: *Sonatina for Solo Trumpet.* BERIO: *Sequenza X for Solo Trumpet.* FENTON: *Five Parts of the Dance*

(BB) ** Virgin 2x1 5 62031-2 (2)

This inexpensive set combines two recital CDs, one devoted to baroque trumpet repertoire, the other to more contemporary works. The baroque items are well enough played by the soloist, but his orchestral support is indifferent, and the reverberant recording is poorly detailed. The avant-garde works on the second CD are altogether more sharply performed and are given better sound. Maxwell Davies's *Trumpet Sonata* echoes the layout of the baroque concertos, though the harmonic language is of an entirely different world. Jolivet's *Heptade* has a battery of percussion instruments to support the myriad effects the soloist achieves on his instrument, and after this generally spiky work, Michael Nyman's lyrical writing is welcome. The longest piece here is Berio's *Sequenza*. It is everything one expects of this composer, and if there is no melody to speak of, the effects are aurally fascinating, even if some may feel that twenty minutes of them is too much of a good thing. Fenton's *Five Parts of the Dance* begins rather hauntingly, with the trumpet placed in the distance, and the ensuing movements with piano and percussion are quite imaginative. This set will be of greatest appeal to those interested in the contemporary items (which would be better off on a separate issue and with more helpful documentation).

Australian Chamber Orchestra, Richard Tognetti

HAAS: *String Quartet 2 (From the Monkey Mountains, Op. 7).* JANACEK: *String Quartet 1 (Kreutzer Sonata).* SZYMANOWSKI: *String Quartet 2, Op. 56* (all. arr. Tognetti) *** Chan. 10016

The fashion for arranging string quartets for full orchestral strings seems to have caught on, even if much of the music's intimacy is lost. The Australian performance of Janáček's *First Quartet* does not lose out in passionate feeling, positive or negative, but the sudden contrasts of mood are less easily conveyed by a bigger, less intimate string group. However, the sensuous Szymanowski string-writing suits a fuller, richer texture and the music's unsettled mood, its bittersweet nostalgia and hints of desolation, are not negated. This is a powerful performance which is very convincing. So also is the Haas pictorial *Second Quartet* with the opening *Landscape* evocation followed by a boisterous *Driver and Horse* sequence (created with pulsing glissandi) contrasting with a 'cool play of moonbeams' and a 'Wild Night' finale, vividly rhythmic. The performances of all three works are appropriately volatile and spontaneous-sounding, and the Chandos recording first rate.

Ballet Music

'Fête du Ballet' (played by the ECO, LSO, New Philh. O, ROHCG O, Bonynge): ROSSINI: *Matinées musicales; Soirées musicales; William Tell: Ballet Music.* CHOPIN: *Les Sylphides.* STRAUSS (arr. Desormière): *Le Beau Danube.* SAINT-SAENS: *The Swan.* TCHAIKOVSKY: *Pas de deux from The Black Swan, Sleeping Beauty and Swan Lake; Melody; December.* RUBINSTEIN: *Danses des fiancées de Cachemir.* CZIBULKA: *Love's Dream after the Ball.* KREISLER: *The Dragonfly.* ASAFYEV: *Papillons.* LINCKE: *Gavotte Pavlova.* DELIBES: *Naïla: Intermezzo.* CATALANI: *Loreley: Danza delle Ondine.* KUPRINSKI: *Polish Wedding.* TRAD.: *Bolero, 1830; Mazurka.* DRIGO: *Le Flûte magique: Pas de trois; Le Réveil de Flore; Pas de deux from Le Corsaire, Diane et Actéon and La Esmeralda.* MINKUS: *Pas de deux from La Bayadère, Paquita (including Grand pas) and Don Quixote.* ADAM: *Giselle* (excerpts). LOVENSKJOLD: *La Sylphide: Pas de deux.* PUGNI: *Pas de quatre.* HELSTED: *Flower Festival at Genzano: Pas de deux.* MASSENET: *Le Cid: Ballet Music; La Cigale: Valse très lente; Le Roi de Lahore: Entr'acte (Act V) and Waltz (Act III); Méditation de Thaïs; Cendrillon; Scènes alsaciennes; Scènes dramatiques.* MEYERBEER: *Les Patineurs.* LUIGINI: *Ballet égyptien.* AUBER: *Pas classique; Marco Spada; Les Rendez-vous.* THOMAS: *Françoise de Rimini.* SCARLATTI: *The Good-humoured Ladies.* DONIZETTI: *La Favorite: Ballet Music.* BERLIOZ: *Les Troyens: Ballet Music.* LECOCQ (arr. Jacob): *Mam'zelle Angot.* OFFENBACH: *La Papillon: Suite.* BURGMÜLLER: *La Péri.*

❂ (BB) *** Decca (ADD/DDD) 468 578-2 (10)

This set is a perfect and well-conceived tribute to Richard Bonynge's indefatigable quest to resurrect forgotten treasures: it's a feast of some of the most delightful and piquant ballet music of the (mainly) nineteenth century. It includes two major ballets not released on CD before: Auber's *Marco Spada*, which is full of the catchy tunes we know from his overtures, and Burgmüller's *La Péri*, a work steeped in the romantic ballet tradition. Other highlights include Lecocq's deliciously witty *Mam'zelle Angot*; the rarely heard and effervescent *Le Beau Danube*; Luigini's *Ballet égyptien* (still the only recording of the complete work and originally part of a two-LP set, 'Homage to Pavlova', of which all the charming vignettes are included here); the only recordings of Auber's *Pas classique* and *Les Rendez-vous*; plus a string of vivacious and colourful *pas de deux*. Other unexpected delights are the perky *Bolero, 1830*; the once-popular coupling of *Le Cid* and *Les Patineurs* ballet music (here in exceptionally vivid sound); the luscious

Waltz from Massenet's *Le Roi de Lahore;* the same composer's *Scènes dramatiques* (first time on CD) and *Scènes alsaciennes,* along with the sparkling *March of the Princes* from *Cendrillon.* Bonynge's supremacy in this repertoire is obvious: through his well-sprung rhythms and elegant pointing of the melodic line, the music glows. With excellent sleeve notes and vintage Decca sound, this set is highly recommended.

'*Bonynge Ballet Festival*' (played by LSO or Nat PO):

Volume 1: WEBER (orch. Berlioz): *Invitation to the Dance.* CHOPIN (arr. Douglas): *Les Sylphides.* J. STRAUSS JR (arr. Gamley): *Bal de Vienne.* LUIGINI: *Ballet égyptien*

Volume 2: TRAD. (arr. O'Turner): *Bolero 1830.* PUGNI: *Pas de quatre.* MINKUS: *La Bayadère* (excerpts). DRIGO: *Pas de trois.* ADAM: *Giselle* (excerpts). LOVENSKJOLD: *La Sylphide* (excerpts)

Volume 3: '*Homage to Pavlova*': SAINT-SAENS: *The Swan.* TCHAIKOVSKY: *Melody; Noël.* RUBINSTEIN: *Danses des fiancées de Cachemir.* CZIBULKA: *Love's dream after the ball.* KREISLER: *The Dragonfly (Schön Rosmarin).* ASSAFYEV: *Papillons.* LINCKE: *Gavotte Pavlova (Glowworm idyll).* DELIBES: *Naïla: Intermezzo.* CATALANI: *Danza delle Ondine.* KRUPINSKI: *Mazurka (Polish Wedding)*

Volume 4: '*Pas de deux*': AUBER: *Pas classique.* MINKUS: *Don Quixote: Pas de deux; Paquita: Pas de deux.* TCHAIKOVSKY: *The Nutcracker: Pas de deux. Sleeping Beauty: Pas de deux.* DRIGO: *Le Corsaire: Pas de deux; La Esmeralda; Pas de deux.* HELSTED: *Flower Festival at Genzano*

Volume 5: '*Ballet Music from Opera*': ROSSINI: *William Tell.* DONIZETTI: *La Favorita.* GOUNOD: *Faust; La Reine de Saba (waltz).* MASSENET: *Ariane; Le Roi de Lahore.* BERLIOZ: *Les Troyens.* SAINT-SAENS: *Henry VIII*
*** Australian Decca (ADD/DDD) 452 767-2 (5)

This less comprehensive set of Richard Bonynge's ballet recordings also includes much music not otherwise available. Volume 1 has two rarities: *Bal de Vienne* – a particularly felicitous arrangement of Johann Strauss's lesser-known works, with an exhilarating finale, and (surprisingly) the only complete recordings of Luigini's delightful *Ballet égyptien* (Fistoulari only recorded the four-movement suite).

Volume 2 draws from Bonynge's '*The Art of the Prima Ballerina*' set: each of the rarities by Minkus, Drigo and Pugni has at least one striking melody, and all are vivacious and colourfully orchestrated; the *Bolero 1830* is short but piquant.

Volume 3, '*Homage to Pavlova*', is more reflectively nostalgic and has delightful rarities: many are just salon pieces but show their worth when played so beautifully on a full orchestra.

Volume 4's collection of *Pas de deux* is both elegantly and robustly enjoyable, with the Auber, Minkus and Drigo numbers especially lively and memorable.

Volume 5 comprises generally better-known ballet music from operas. It includes the lovely Massenet ballet music from *Le Roi de Lahore,* which starts off ominously in a minor key, before a theme, magically introduced on the saxophone, builds up into a magnificent full orchestral waltz swirling around the whole orchestra. *The Dance of the Gypsy* from Saint-Saëns's *Henry VIII* is another gem: it begins sinuously, but ends in a jolly *valse macabre.*

This is music in which Bonynge excels: he has exactly the right feel for it and produces an infectious lift throughout. The recordings are in Decca's best analogue tradition – vivid, warm and full (though a few are from equally fine digital

sources), and all sound pristinely fresh in these transfers. With full sleeve-notes included, this is a splendid bargain collection of highly entertaining music well worth seeking out.

Baltimore Symphony Orchestra, David Zinman

'*Russian Sketches*': GLINKA: *Overture: Ruslan and Ludmilla.* IPPOLITOV-IVANOV: *Caucasian Sketches.* RIMSKY-KORSAKOV: *Russian Easter Festival Overture.* TCHAIKOVSKY: *Francesca da Rimini, Op. 32. Eugene Onegin: Polonaise*
**(*) Telarc CD 80378

Opening with a fizzingly zestful performance of Glinka's *Ruslan and Ludmilla Overture,* with impressively clean articulation from the violins, this remarkably well-recorded concert of Russian music readily demonstrates the excellence of the Baltimore Symphony in every department.

The *Caucasian Sketches* are a disappointment, but only because Zinman's conception of the evocative first three movements (*In the Mountain Pass, In the Village* and *In the Mosque*) is too refined, not Russian enough in feeling; but the famous *Procession of the Sardar* has plenty of piquant colour and impetus. *Francesca da Rimini* brings the most brilliant playing and the middle section, with its rich, Tchaikovskian woodwind palette, is glowingly beautiful. However, the impact of the closing pages here depends more on the spectacular Telarc engineering than on the conductor, who does not generate the necessary degree of passionate despair in the work's great climax. Rimsky-Korsakov's *Russian Easter Festival Overture* is a different matter, generating considerable excitement. It is superbly done, with lustrous colours from every section of the orchestra and a memorable solo contribution from the trombones (who are also very impressive in *Francesca*). The recording here is very much in the demonstration bracket and shows Telarc engineering at its most realistic, thrilling in its breadth and body of orchestral tone, with excellent detail and a convincing presence in a natural concert-hall acoustic.

Baroque Favourites

(with Academy of St Martin-in-the-Fields, Sir Neville Marriner or Sir Philip Ledger; LCO, Christopher Warren-Green; Bath Festival O, Lord Yehudi Menuhin; Toulouse CO, Louis Auricombe; ECO, Raymond Leppard)

'*Baroque Favourites*': HANDEL: *Solomon: Arrival of the Queen of Sheba. Berenice: Minuet; Serse: Largo.* BACH: *Cantata 147: Jesu, joy of man's desiring; Cantata 203: Sheep may safely graze; Christmas Oratorio: Pastoral Symphony; Orchestral Suite 3, BWV 1068: Air.* GLUCK: *Orpheus and Eurydice: Dance of the Blessed Spirits.* CHARPENTIER: *Te Deum: Prelude.* ALBINONI/GIAZOTTO: *Adagio in G min.* PURCELL: *King Arthur: Trumpet Tune; Air; Sinfonia; Passacaglia; Abdelazar: Rondo.* CORELLI: *Concerto grosso, Op. 6/8: Allegro.* RAMEAU: *Les fêtes d'Hébé: Musette et tambourin en roundeau.* PACHELBEL: *Canon.* Bonuses: BACH: *Flute Sonata 3, BWV 1031: Siciliano* (Michel Debost,

Lionel Rogg). CLARKE: *Trumpet Voluntary (Prince of Denmark's March)* (Ole Edvard Antonsen & Wayne Marshall)

☞ (BB) *** HMV (ADD) 5 86747-2

A splendid, imaginatively chosen anthology that surely cannot be bettered in its field, specially as it is so inexpensive. Marriner and his Academy have the lion's share of the performances – and very good they are, too – though Ledger directs the engaging Rameau rondeau and also the Charpentier *Prelude* (better known as the European Anthem) to provide an up-beat ending for the programme.

The Pachelbel *Canon* and the famous Albinoni *Adagio* are allotted to Christopher Warren-Green and his excellent London Chamber Orchestra, who present them stylishly and without romantic excess, while it is Menuhin and the Bath Festival Orchestra who give us the Purcell items (including the *Abdelazar* Rondo on which Britten based his *Young Person's Guide to the Orchesra*) plus one of the most tasteful and memorable performances in the catalogue of the Bach *Air* from the *D major Orchestral Suite*.

The two bonuses are a superb account of the *Trumpet Voluntary* by the excellent Ole Antonsen with Wayne Marshall (organ) and the delightful Bach *Siciliana* for flute (Michel Debost) and harpsichord (Lionel Rogg). The recording and CD transfers are excellent throughout; only the Menuhin/Purcell suite from the 1960s sounds a little dated. This would make an ideal present for a friend who 'doesn't like classical music'.

BBC Philharmonic Orchestra, Matthias Bamert

'*Stokowski Encores*': HANDEL: *Overture in D min.* GABRIELI: *Sonata piano e forte.* CLARKE: *Trumpet Prelude.* MATTHESON: *Air.* MOZART: *Rondo alla turca.* BEETHOVEN: *Adagio from Moonlight Sonata.* SCHUBERT: *Serenade.* FRANCK: *Panis Angelicus.* CHOPIN: *Funeral March.* DEBUSSY: *The Girl with the flaxen hair.* IPPOLITOV-IVANOV: *In the manger.* SHOSTAKOVICH: *United Nations March.* TCHAIKOVSKY: *Andante cantabile.* ALBENIZ: *Festival in Seville.* SOUSA: *The Stars and Stripes forever.* (all arr. Leopold Stokowski)

*** Chan. 9349

However outrageous it may seem to take a tiny harpsichord piece by a contemporary of Bach and Handel, Johann Mattheson, and inflate it on full strings, the result caresses the ear, and the Chandos engineers come up with recording to match. Amazingly, Mozart's *Rondo alla turca* becomes a sparkling moto perpetuo, Paganini-like, with Stokowski following Mozart himself in using 'Turkish' percussion, *Entführung*-style.

The opening *Adagio* of Beethoven's *Moonlight Sonata* with lush orchestration then echoes Rachmaninov's *Isle of the Dead*, with menace in the music. Stokowski's arrangement of the Handel *Overture in D minor* (taken from the *Chandos Anthem 2*) is quite different from Elgar's transcription of the same piece, opulent in a different way, with timbres antiphonally contrasted.

If Bamert cannot match the panache of Stokowski in the final Sousa march, *The Stars and Stripes forever*, that is in part due to the recording balance, which fails to bring out the percussion, including xylophone. The least attractive item is Schubert's *Serenade*, given full Hollywood treatment not just

with soupy strings but with quadruple woodwind trilling above. Hollywood treatment of a different kind comes in the *United Nations March* of Shostakovich, in 1942 used as the victory finale of an MGM wartime musical, *Thousands Cheer.* Stokowski promptly cashed in with his own, non-vocal arrangement. A disc for anyone who likes to wallow in opulent sound.

BBC Philharmonic Orchestra, Yan Pascal Tortelier

'*French Bonbons*': Overtures: ADAM: *Si j'étais roi.* AUBER: *Le Cheval de bronze (The Bronze Horse).* HEROLD: *Zampa.* MAILLART: *Les Dragons de Villars.* THOMAS: *Mignon: Gavotte.* OFFENBACH: *La Belle Hélène* (arr. Haensch); *Contes d'Hoffmann: Entr'acte & Barcarolle.* CHABRIER: *Habanera; Joyeuse marche.* GOUNOD: *Marche funèbre d'une marionette.* MASSENET: *Thaïs: Méditation* (with Yuri Torchinsky, violin; both with Royal Liverpool PO Ch.); *Mélodie: Elégie* (with Peter Dixon, cello); *Les erinnes: Tristesse du soir; La Vierge: Le Dernier sommeil de la Vierge*

☞ *** Chan. 9765

As Sir Thomas Beecham well knew, there is something special about French orchestral lollipops and this is a superb collection, beautifully played and given demonstration-standard recording – just sample the brass evocation of Maillart's Dragoons, and in *La Belle Hélène*, which is played with much warmth and style. Gounod's whimsical *Funeral March of a Marionette*, which Hitchcock has made famous, is delightfully done, and the other bandstand overtures have plenty of sparkle and zest, yet are not driven too hard – the galop which climaxes *The Bronze Horse* is exhilaratingly jaunty. Highly recommended.

BBC Symphony Orchestra, Sir Adrian Boult

'*Boult's BBC Years*': BEETHOVEN: *Symphony 8 in F, Op. 93.* HUMPERDINCK: *Overture: Hansel and Gretel.* TCHAIKOVSKY: *Capriccio italien, Op. 45; Serenade for Strings, Op. 48*

(***) Beulah mono 1PD12

These recordings return to the catalogue for the first time since the days of shellac and will almost certainly be new to the majority of younger collectors. The Beethoven is a strong, sturdy performance which gives a good idea of the excellence of the BBC Symphony Orchestra in the early days of its existence. It comes from 1932 and the strings produce an opulent, weighty sound without having the opaque quality they developed in the post-war years. The recording is not at all bad for the period, and the transfer does it justice. The Tchaikovsky *Serenade* was recorded five years later in the same Abbey Road studio but with the acoustic sounding much drier. A patrician account with no nonsense about it that may since have been surpassed by many other great partnerships but which will give pleasure to those old enough to remember Sir Adrian's pre-war and wartime broadcasts. The Colston Hall, Bristol, in which the orchestra recorded the *Capriccio italien* in 1940, has the richer acoustic, and the performance combines dignity and freshness.

'*Boult Conducts the BBC Symphony Orchestra*': AUBER: *Overture: Masaniello.* BERLIOZ: *Overtures: King Lear; Les*

francs juges. BORODIN: *Prince Igor: Polovtsian March.*
HOLST: *Scherzo* (from an unfinished symphony).
MENDELSSOHN: *Overtures: The Hebrides; Ruy Blas.*
MOZART: *Overture: Così fan tutte; Symphony 32 in G, K.318.*
TCHAIKOVSKY: *Eugene Onegin: Polonaise*
⏺ (B) (***) Dutton mono CDBP 9763

All these recordings (with the exception of the Mozart symphony and the Holst) were made in the 1930s, when the orchestra was in its infancy. Only collectors now in their seventies will be likely to have the originals, so these superb transfers will be new to most readers. Only the Berlioz *Les francs juges* has been reissued since the 1940s, in an LP anthology commemorating the BBC Symphony Orchestra's fiftieth anniversary in 1980. These records show the quality of the orchestra with which Toscanini, Bruno Walter and Fritz Busch were pleased to appear, and act as a reminder of the excellence of Sir Adrian as a selfless interpreter. We don't associate him with Berlioz, but he had a great feeling for him, and we recall a superb BBC studio account of *Harold in Italy* from the late 1950s–early '60s. We treasured (and R.L. still possesses) his *Hebrides Overture* on DB2100, and its understated yet strong poetic feeling still impresses. This alone is worth a ⏺. The Dutton transfers are extremely faithful and vivid.

BBC Symphony Orchestra & Chorus, Sir Andrew Davis

'*Last Night of the Proms 2000*': BACH: *Fantasia and Fugue in C min., BWV 537.* MOZART: *Violin Concerto 4 in D, K.218* (with Hahn, violin). R STRAUSS: *Salome: Dance of the Seven Veils: Final Scene* (with Eaglen, soprano). SHOSTAKOVICH: (orch. McBurney) *Jazz Suite 2.* GRAINGER: *Tribute to Foster* (with Watson, Murray, Spence, Tear, Davies). DELIUS: *A Village Romeo and Juliet: Walk to the Paradise Garden.* ELGAR: *Pomp & Circumstance March 1.* WOOD: *Fantasia on British Sea Songs.* ARNE: *Rule Britannia!* (with Eaglen). PARRY (orch. Elgar): *Jerusalem. National Anthem* (with introductions, interviews with soloists, laying of the wreath; speech by Sir Andrew Davis and presentation by Nicholas Kenyon. Producer: Peter Maniura)
*** BBC **DVD** WMDVD 8001-9

Watching an old Last Night of the Proms programme on DVD might seem like eating half-warmed-up soup, but the year 2000 had some special claims – not just marking the Millennium but also in celebrating Sir Andrew Davis. He said goodbye after eleven consecutive Last Nights, as well as giving his final concert as Chief Conductor of the BBC Symphony Orchestra. The programme itself reflects Davis's own preferences, when, as he explains in an interview, three of his favourite composers are represented: Elgar, with his sumptuous arrangement of Bach organ music, the *Fantasia and Fugue in C minor*; Mozart, with the *Violin Concerto 4 in D* featuring the brilliant young American, Hilary Hahn, as soloist; and Richard Strauss, with the *Dance of the Seven Veils* and the final scene from *Salome*, in which Jane Eaglen is the soprano, producing the most opulent tone, a commanding figure in every way.

Special facilities on the DVD consist of options on subtitles and an ability to limit the playing to music only, without introductions. What is infuriating and pure sloppiness over the transfer, however, is that tracking is so limited, so that the

Mozart *Violin Concerto*, 25 minutes long, is on a single track, with no separation of movements.

BBC Symphony Orchestra & Chorus, Sir Andrew Davis (with other artists)

'*Prom at the Palace*' (The Queen's Golden Jubilee concert): WALTON: *Anniversary Fanfare.* HANDEL: *Music for the Royal Fireworks:* excerpts (both with Band of Royal Marines, Col. Richard Waterer); *Coronation Anthem: Zadok the Priest.* BIZET: *Carmen: Micaëla's Aria.* GERSHWIN: *Porgy and Bess: Summertime* (Dame Kiri Te Kanawa). TRAD., arr. BURTON: 2 *Spirituals* (London Advent Chorale, Ken Burton). MESSAGER: *Solo de Concours for Clarinet & Piano* (Julian Bliss, Ashley Wass). HOLST: *The Planets: Jupiter.* TCHAIKOVSKY: *Swan Lake; Black Swan pas de deux* (danced by Roberto Bolle & Zenaida Yanowsky). ROSSINI: *Il barbiere di Siviglia: Largo al factotum.* GERMAN: *Merrie England: The Yeomen of England* (Sir Thomas Allen). ARNOLD: *Irish Dance; 2 Scottish Dances; Welsh Dance.* VILLA-LOBOS: *Bachianas Brasileiras 1* (Rostropovich & Cellos of LSO). PUCCINI: *Tosca: Vissi d'arte; 'E lucevan le stelle.* VERDI: *La Traviata: Brindisi* (Angela Gheorghiu & Roberto Alagna). ELGAR: *Pomp and Circumstance March 1.* ARNE: *God Save the Queen* (DVD introduced by Michael Parkinson. TV Producer: Ben Weston; Director: Bob Coles; DVD Producer: James Whitbourn)
*** BBC Opus Arte **DVD** OA 0844 D. CD: VTCDX 42

The DVD offers a straight repeat of the BBC's television relay of the concert in the grounds of Buckingham Palace, celebrating the Queen's Golden Jubilee in June 2002. Introduced by Michael Parkinson, it offers a sequence of short items, not all of them predictable, performed by an excellent choice of artists, with none of the media-boosted, middle-of-the-road performers who in too many so-called classical events represent a degrading of standards. Gheorghiu and Alagna may have been glamorized, but in musical terms they are outstanding, and here offer arias from Puccini's *Tosca* and the *Brindisi* duet from Verdi's *La Traviata.* Sir Thomas Allen, as well as singing Figaro's aria from Rossini's *Barbiere*, gives the *Yeomen of England* from Edward German's *Merrie England*, nowadays a rarity, and as an encore to Micaëla's aria from Bizet's *Carmen* Dame Kiri Te Kanawa sings *Summertime* from Gershwin's *Porgy and Bess.* A charming interlude has the 13-year-old clarinettist Julian Bliss performing a *Solo de Concours* by Messager (an item that specially delighted the Queen) and Rostropovich with the cellos of the LSO plays the *Prelude* from Villa-Lobos's *Bachianas Brasileiras 1*, not on the outdoor stage but more intimately in the Music Room of Buckingham Palace. In the Ballroom of the Palace, the dancers Roberto Bolle and Zenaida Yanowsky perform the *Black Swan pas de deux* from Tchaikovsky's *Swan Lake*, and Sir Andrew Davis and the BBC Symphony Orchestra crown their many contributions with Handel's *Fireworks Music*, joined by the Royal Marines Band and prompting a cracking firework display in *La Réjouissance* just as dusk gives way to night. The concert ends in true Proms-style with *Land of Hope and Glory* and the *National Anthem.* Though the amplified sound is aggressive at times, the wonder is that it comes over so well.

The CD version simply includes most of the musical items with the Parkinson introductions omitted as well as the *Fireworks Music.*

BBC Symphony Orchestra, Jac van Steen

'British Film Scores': BRITTEN: Love from a Stranger. GERHARD: This Sporting Life. LUTYENS: The Skull. R. R. BENNETT: The Return of the Soldier
*** NMC D 073

Benjamin Britten's scores for pre-war GPO documentary films have long been recognized – notably the two with words by Auden, Night Mail and Coal Face – but his one score for a feature film, the thriller Love from a Stranger, has been buried for almost 70 years. The six fragments on this fascinating disc show that, even working at high speed, he wrote music consistently striking and inventive. Temperamental, he swore afterwards he would never again have anything to do with the film world (nor did he), when in addition to cuts being made, some of his music was ditched. The other three composers are all serialists, with the exiled Catalan, Roberto Gerhard, a strange choice for David Storey's This Sporting Life, with its background of mining and rugby league football. The result is fluent if unrelievedly dark. Elisabeth Lutyens, equally uncompromising in her idiom, is much more attuned to the needs of the medium in the horror film, The Skull, at once vigorous and sinister. Richard Rodney Bennett, far more adaptable, remains one of our most successful film composers, here splendidly represented by his evocative music for Alan Bridge's neglected film, The Return of the Soldier, an adaptation of a novel by Rebecca West. Excellent performances throughout, well recorded.

Beckett, Edward (flute), London Festival Orchestra, Ross Pople

'Fantaisie (Romantic French Flute Music)': HUE: Gigue; Nocturne. VILLETTE: Complainte. SAINT-SAENS: Romance, Op. 37; Odelette, Op. 162. RAVEL: Pièce en forme de habanera (orch. Hoérée). GODARD: Suite, Op. 116. BUSSER: Andalucia, Op. 86. FAURE: Fantaisie, Op. 111. PERILHOU: Ballade. WIDOR: Suite for Flute & Piano, Op. 34: Scherzo; Romance (orch. Beckett & Widor)
*** Black Box BBM 1049

French composers instinctively write flute music to tickle the ear, with Gallic elegance in the way of the Gigue and Nocturne of Georges Huë. His sprightly Gigue blithely erupts with triple-tongued bravura, while the Nocturne, a languorous barcarolle, is hardly less enticing.

The most subtle music here is by Fauré and Ravel, but Pierre Villette's Complainte has a Ravelian atmosphere and a gentle melancholy. The two morceaux by Saint-Saëns are characteristically charming, with Odelette bringing a brief central burst of virtuoso roulades. On the other hand, Benjamin Godard's Suite is very operatic: one could imagine the pirouetting opening Allegretto and the chirruping Waltz being used as a duet with a coloratura soprano; in between comes the ingenuous Idylle to remind us that Godard was the composer of the Berceuse de Jocelyn.

Büsser's Andalucia has Mediterranean charm and a whiff of voluptuousness, though it remains more French than Spanish, and Widor's Scherzo and Romance display a thistledown lightness, unexpected from an organ composer. Edward Beckett, Irish born, yet a pupil of Rampal, has a lovely tone and phrases with style. He is persuasively accompanied by Pople, but the orchestra has comparatively little to

contribute, except support. The sound is warmly atmospheric, the flute not too forward. Altogether a most enticing lightweight collection.

Bergen Philharmonic Orchestra, Dimitri Kitaienko

'French & Russian Orchestral Favourites': DUKAS: The Sorcerer's Apprentice. RAVEL: Ma Mère l'Oye Suite; Boléro. DEBUSSY: Prélude à l'après-midi d'un faune. MUSSORGSKY: Night on the Bare Mountain (original version). LIADOV: The Enchanted Lake; 8 Russian Folk Songs; Kikimora; A Musical Snuffbox; Baba-Yaga. STRAVINSKY: The Firebird (suite, 1919); 4 Norwegian Moods
(BB) ** Virgin 2×1 5 61901-2 (2)

This is an attractive programme, but the two CDs were recorded five years apart, in 1991 and 1996 respectively, and are uneven in appeal. The inclusion of the original score of Mussorgsky's Night on a Bare Mountain is particularly welcome. It is much cruder, more rambling than Rimsky's later revision, but it sounds strikingly primitive and bizarrely individual. The opening Dukas showpiece is glowingly animated, and the works by Debussy and Ravel also come off well. The approach is direct and atmospheric, while Boléro moves forward to produce a strong climax. On the second disc, however, while Kitaienko's Liadov performances are not without atmosphere, they lack sparkle. Stravinsky's Norwegian Moods bring a pleasingly folksy evocation, but the Firebird Suite, though similarly colourful, seriously lacks a vibrant dramatic profile. The recording is pleasingly lively and evocative, but this is not distinctive music-making.

Berlin Philharmonic Orchestra, Claudio Abbado

'New Year's Gala 1997': BIZET: Carmen: excerpts (with Von Otter, Alagna, Terfel). BRAHMS: Hungarian Dance 5 in G min.. FALLA: El amor brujo; Ritual Fire Dance. RACHMANINOV: Rhapsody on a Theme of Paganini (with Pletnev). RAVEL: Rapsodie espagnole. SARASATE: Carmen Fantasy, Op. 25 (with Shaham)
*** Arthaus DVD 100 026

A concert that takes Bizet's Carmen as a theme, or point of departure. The sound is very good indeed and naturally balanced, and the camerawork discreet and unobtrusive. The excerpts from the opera come off very well, but easily the best thing on the disc is the Paganini Rhapsody, played effortlessly by Mikhail Pletnev. Rachmaninov playing does not come better than this. It is every bit as strongly characterized and brilliant in execution as his CD recording and must be numbered among the very finest on disc. The individual variations do not have access points. Gil Shaham's performance of the Sarasate Fantasy is also played with virtuosity and panache. A rather strangely designed programme, but well worth having, purely for the sake of Pletnev's dazzling Rachmaninov.

'New Year's Gala Concert' (with Swedish R. Ch.): BRAHMS: Hungarian Dances 1, 5, 7, 10, 17, 21; Gypsy Songs, Op. 103; Liebesliederwalzer 1, 2, 4, 5, 6, 8, 9, 11; Es tont ein voller, Op. 17. BERLIOZ: Hungarian March. RAVEL: Tzigane (with Maxim Vengerov); La Valse
*** Arthaus DVD 100 042

The Berlin Philharmonic in this 'New Year's Gala' puts up a direct challenge to Vienna, using Brahms pieces very much as the Vienna Philharmonic uses Johann Strauss, concentrating on the *Hungarian Dances* and the *Liebesliederwalzer*. As in Vienna it makes for a fun occasion, with Abbado at his most relaxed, smiling as he conducts. The theme of dances and gypsy tunes then extends to Ravel in two major items, *Tzigane* and *La Valse*, while Berlioz is finally brought in with the *Hungarian March* from the *Damnation of Faust* as an obvious equivalent of Vienna's *Radetsky March*, though happily no one in the Berlin audience dares to clap to it.

One great bonus of this programme is the inclusion of Maxim Vengerov as a masterly soloist in the *Tzigane*, as well as in Brahms's *Hungarian Dance 7*, which comes as his encore. Just as striking is the contribution of the Swedish Radio Chorus, not just visually with the ladies sporting velvet stoles over their black dresses in brightly contrasted primary colours, but in their obvious affection for Brahms. The *Liebeslieder Waltzes* are charmingly done, as is the lovely song for women's chorus with horn and harp accompaniment, *Es tont ein voller*, though one is sorry not to have the other three songs in that Opus 17 group. The only extra item is a brief tourist sequence on Berlin and its attractions, *Kunst und Genuss* ('Arts and Delights').

DEBUSSY: *Nocturnes.* VERDI: *4 Sacred Pieces* (both with Swedish R. Ch.); TCHAIKOVSKY: *The Tempest, Op. 18.*
WAGNER: *Overture: The Flying Dutchman*
*** TDK **DVD** DV-STOCK (Director: Bob Coles)

Abbado's records of the Debussy *Nocturnes* have always been among the very finest in the catalogue, and this DVD (made in 1998) is no exception. *Nuages* is particularly evocative and the playing of the flautist, Emanuel Pahud, particularly expressive. There is a highly poetic account of *Sirènes* too, with the female voices of the Swedish Radio Choir sounding agreeably seductive. The concert is given in the concert hall built at the Vasa museum, which houses the battleship of that name that sank on her maiden voyage in 1628 and was lovingly restored in the 1960s. In the past, the Swedish Radio Choir and Eric Ericsson's Choir have collaborated in Berlin with the Philharmonic Orchestra; now the roles are reversed, with the orchestra making the journey to Stockholm. The Verdi comes off splendidly, and the attractiveness of the concert is enhanced by an informative feature on Stockholm which is sumptuously visually and offers a glimpse of the treasures of the Royal Palace.

Berlin Philharmonic Orchestra, Daniel Barenboim

'Invitation to the Dance' (New Year's Eve concert in the Philharmonie): BACH: *Orchestral Suite 3: Gavotte.* MOZART: *Divertimento 17 in D, K.334: Menuetto; Rondo for Piano & Orchestra, K.382* (with Barenboim, piano). VERDI: *Aida: Dance of the Moorish Slaves.* TCHAIKOVSKY: *The Nutcracker: Waltz of the Flowers.* SIBELIUS: *Kuolema: Valse triste.* JOHANN STRAUSS, JR: *Kaiser (Emperor) Waltz; Unter Donner und Blitz (Thunder and Lightning) Polka.* ❂ KODÁLY: *Dances from Galánta.* BRAHMS: *Hungarian Dance 1.* SALGÁN: *A fuego lento (Tango).* DE ABREU & OLIVEIRA: *Tico Tico.* CARLI: *El firulete*
*** TDK **DVD** DV-SG 2001;105184-9. (Director: Hans Hulscher)

This is the Berlin Philharmonic's equivalent of the Vienna New Year Concert, and very enjoyable it is. The music is all strikingly well played, and in the Mozart *Rondo*, with its neat interchanges between piano and orchestra of a simple but most engaging theme, Barenboim directs from the piano. Tchaikovsky's *Waltz of the Flowers* is lush but a trifle cosy, but it sparks up nicely for the coda, and the following *Valse triste* is played very beautifully indeed. Then suddenly, and electrifyingly, the music-making is transformed with a superb, wonderfully spontaneous performance of Kodaly's *Dances from Galánta*. The musicians play with enormous intensity, the lyrical solos richly glowing, with even a brief flash of irony at one point. Barenboim's up-and-down conducting style is transformed with kinetic energy, and one can feel his powerful communicative force. The tension builds up and the end is riveting, and superbly timed. The audience reaction is tumultuous, as well it might be. This is a wonderful example of the way a DVD can be far more exciting than a CD. You sit in your chair and the full force of the inspirational playing jumps out and engulfs you thrillingly. Whew!

After that, the popular encores seem a little cheap, until the electricty sparks again in the *Thunder and Lightning Polka*, and the concert ends with Brahms, played with great warmth. Fortunately, the recording is in the demonstration bracket, and the camera is almost always in the right place. A very entertaining DVD, both to enjoy and to demonstrate to your friends.

'1997 *European Concert at the Opéra Royal de Château de Versailles':* RAVEL: *Le tombeau de Couperin.* ❂ MOZART: *Piano Concerto 13 in C, K.415* (with Barenboim, piano). BEETHOVEN: *Symphony 3 in E flat (Eroica)*
*** TDK **DVD** DV-VERSA

Another oustanding example of the way DVD video can enhance one's enjoyment of a live concert. All the performances here are of the highest calibre, and although the cameras are at times restless, and the back-of-the-hall perspective is too distant, the close-ups of the conductor and players communicate the music visually as well as aurally, with members of the orchestra projecting as individual personalities. Ravel's *Le tombeau* is played with engaging freshness and luminous beauty, and one identifies especially here with the principal oboe.

One turns the disc over for Barenboim's *Eroica*, which is very strong indeed, the climaxes gripping, the Funeral March powerfully moving. In the Scherzo the horns dominate visually, as they should, and the finale, with its visually fascinating variations and fugue, ends the work with an explosion of joy.

But the highlight of the concert is the captivating account of the early Mozart *Concerto*, when Barenboim, like the composer before him, directs from the keyboard. Here the empathy between soloist and players is magical and this communicates to the viewer, raptly so in the concentration of the lovely slow movement and the light-hearted finale, with its intriguing changes of tempo and mood. The recording throughout is first class, very naturally balanced with a dramatic but not exaggerated dynamic range, and a full, clean bass response. The piano too is naturally focused. This is a DVD to return to, and it is enhanced by the glorious visual backcloth of the Opéra Royal de Château de Versailles.

'1998 *Concert at the Berlin State Opera, Unter den Linden':*
BEETHOVEN: *Symphony 8 in F.* SCHUMANN: *Konzertstück in F for 4 Horns & Orchestra, Op. 86* (with Dale Clevenger,

Stefan Dohr, Ignacio Garcia, George Schreckenberger, horns). LISZT: *Les Préludes.* WAGNER: *Die Walküre: Ride of the Valkyries*
*(*) TDK **DVD** DV-LINDE

After Barenboim's 1997 Berlin Philharmonic concert at the Opéra Royal de Château de Versailles this is a great let-down. It opens with a comparatively routine account of Beethoven's *Eighth Symphony*, while Liszt's *Les Préludes* is lacking in flamboyance and adrenalin, though in both the Berlin Philharmonic playing cannot be faulted for poor tone or ensemble. The great highlight of the concert is the superb performance of the Schumann *Konzertstück for Four Horns.* This work is not only technically very demanding, but lies very high in the horn register, with continually repeated passages where the soloists are taken up into the the stratosphere, which is very tiring on the horn-player's lip muscles, something Schumann did not seem to understand. With fine players a studio recording is feasible as the work can be recorded in sections. But this is a live performance by a superb quartet, led by Dale Clevenger, one of America's most distinguished orchestral principals, and the spirited bravura of all four players (to say nothing of their stamina) throughout the work's 21 minutes is as exhilarating as it is astonishing, while Barenboim accompanies zestfully. The horn quartet returns for the final item in the programme and lines up behind the orchestra as the extras in Wagner's *Ride of the Valkyries.* But that performance, well played as it is, only serves to emphasize the other drawback to the audio recording throughout this DVD – its very limited dynamic range. This has a damping-down effect in both the Beethoven and Liszt, and when the extra brass is visibly seen to enter in Wagner's famous galloping show piece and the music fails to increase in volume, the effect is bizarre.

Berlin Philharmonic Orchestra, Plácido Domingo

'Spanish Night': CHABRIER: *España.* LINCKE: *Berliner Luft.* LUNA: *Cancion Espanola.* SERRANO: *Romanza.* TORROBA: *La Petenara* (all with Ana Maria Martinez). MASSENET: *Thaïs: Méditation.* SARASATE: *Carmen Fantasy; Zigeunerweisen* (all with Sarah Chang). MONCAYO: *Huapango.* RIMSKY-KORSAKOV: *Capriccio espagnol.* J. STRAUSS JR: *Spanish March.* VIVES: *Fandango*
*** TDK Euro Arts **DVD** 10 5123 9

The Waldbühne (Woodland Stage) in Berlin where the open-air concert on this DVD took place in July 2001 is like a cross between the concert venue at Kenwood in north London and the Hollywood Bowl. With an audience of 22,000 this performance rounded off the orchestra's season and, following tradition, ended with Lincke's rousing Prussian song, *Berliner Luft*, with Domingo finally persuaded to sing as well as conduct, and with the audience flashing lights and waving sparklers. The focus of the whole event this time was Spanish, with Plácido Domingo as conductor putting together a delightful sequence of Spanish-inspired pieces, including three songs from his favourite genre of the distinctive Spanish form of operetta, the zarzuela, in which Martinez's warm, throaty soprano is ideal.

Sarah Chang makes just as glamorous a figure, playing with masterly point in the two Sarasate works, *Zigeunerweisen* and the *Carmen Fantasy*, as well as sweetly and tenderly in the *Méditation* from Massenet's *Thaïs*. Besides the purely Spanish items, such orchestral show pieces as Chabrier's *España* and Rimsky-Korsakov's *Capriccio espagnol* are self-recommending, and loyally Domingo includes a colourful piece, *Huapango*, by the Mexican composer Moncayo, well worth hearing. Of particular interest is the rarity by Johann Strauss, the *Spanish March*, with its sharply varied sections. One of the 'Special Features' of the disc is an interview session with both Chang and Domingo. Considering how dry the sound can be in the open air, the quality here is first rate, no doubt helped by the canopy over the orchestra resembling an extended crusaders' tent.

Berlin Philharmonic Orchestra, Wilhelm Furtwängler

Wartime Concerts, 1942–4

Vol. 1: BEETHOVEN: *Coriolan Overture, Op. 62; Symphonies 4, 5 & 7; Violin Concerto* (with Röhn). HANDEL: *Concerto grosso in D min., Op. 6/10.* MOZART: *Symphony 39 in E flat, K.543.* SCHUBERT: *Symphony 9 in C (Great).* WEBER: *Der Freischütz: Overture*
(B) (***) DG mono 471 289-2 (4)

Vol. 2: BRAHMS: *Piano Concerto 2 in B flat, Op. 83* (with Fischer). BRUCKNER: *Symphony 5 in B flat.* RAVEL: *Daphnis et Chloé: Suite 2.* SCHUMANN: *Cello Concerto in A min., Op. 129* (with de Machula); *Piano Concerto in A min., Op. 56* (with Gieseking). SIBELIUS: *En saga.* R. STRAUSS: *Don Juan, Op. 20; Till Eulenspiegel, Op. 28; Symphonia Domestica, Op. 53*
(B) (***) DG mono 471 294-2 (5)

Hans Werner Henze once recalled how during the war he came to associate music-making with danger, having played chamber music with some Jewish friends who were in continual fear of discovery and arrest. And there is certainly a heightened intensity and an urgent, emotional charge about performances given in wartime conditions, as we can hear in the astonishing recordings Furtwängler made with the Berlin Philharmonic in 1942–4, which DG have just repackaged. British Intelligence was puzzled by the sheer quality of wartime German broadcast concerts, which were technically far ahead of their time, thanks to the excellence of the recordings, which were made on 14-inch reels of iron-oxide tape running at 30 inches per second. There are performances of great stature in these inexpensive boxes, including a Brahms *Second Piano Concerto* with Edwin Fischer, and an imposing Mozart *Symphony 39 in E flat*, as well as repertoire that one does not associate with Furtwängler: Sibelius's *En saga*, full of atmosphere and mystery, and a magical account of the Second Suite from Ravel's *Daphnis et Chloé*. Strauss's *Symphonia Domestica*, Furtwängler's only recording of a longer Strauss tone-poem, is superbly shaped and vividly characterized: it comes from the last concert before the Philharmonie was destroyed by Allied bombs. The other work in the same 1944 concert was the Beethoven *Violin Concerto*, seraphically played by the Berlin Philharmonic's leader, Erich Röhn – a very special performance indeed. Not everything is inspired (Gieseking's Schumann *Concerto* is curiously prosaic by his standards), but there is much that is, including an incandescent and noble Bruckner *Fifth Symphony*, and some powerful Beethoven.

Berlin Philharmonic Orchestra, Mariss Jansons

'A Night of Encores: Summer Concert at the Berlin Waldbühne'* (with Vadim Repin, violin): MONIUSZKO: *Halka: Mazurka.* WIENIAWSKI: *Polonaise, Op. 4.* TCHAIKOVSKY: *Souvenir d'un lieu cher: Mélodie. Valse-Scherzo, Op. 34. The Nutcracker: Pas de deux.* CHAPI Y LORENTE: *Overture: Le revoltosa.* LYAN JOON KIM: *Elegy.* LUMBYE: *Champagne Galop.* TOYAMA: *Dance of the Celestials.* SIBELIUS: *Kuolema; Valse triste.* ELGAR: *Wand of Youth; Wild Bears.* WAGNER: *Lohengrin: Prelude to Act III.* KREISLER: *Tambourin Chinois.* GARDEL: *Por una cabezza.* PAGANINI: *The Carnival of Venice* (with encore). ZIEHRER: *Wiener Burger.* MASCAGNI: *Cavalleria Rusticana: Intermezzo.* DVORAK: *Slavonic Dance 15 in C, Op. 72/7.* BIZET: *L'Arlésienne: Farandole.* MASSENET: *Le Cid: Aragonaise; Navarraise.* LINCKE: *Frau Luna: Berliner Luft

(*) TDK **DVD 10513-9; DV-WBONE (Producer: Dorothy Dickmann; Director: Bob Coles)

The Berlin Walbühne is a huge open space, able to take a very large audience indeed, with the orchestra accommodated in a shell. As some of the distant shots demonstrate, if you are at the back, the orchestra is very far away indeed. Presumably there is amplification for the audience: what we hear is not an open-air sound; instead, there is an agreeable ambience. The programme offers a nice mixture of favourites and novelties. The *Overture Le revoltosa* has attractive writing for the woodwind and bouncy dance rhythms, Lyan Joon Kim's *Elegy* has a rich melody introduced on the cor anglais and taken up warmly by the strings. Toyama's *Celestials* dance nostalgically and gracefully on the flute, and Lumbye's *Champagne Galop* is complete with a 'popping cork'. The standard items in the programme are very well played indeed, with Elgar's *Wild Bears* a rumbustious novelty. The soloist Vadim Repin has plenty of chances to show his virtuosity and his warm, lyrical playing in the two Tchaikovsky miniatures. *The Carnival of Venice* is treated as a fun piece but, as the camera is not in right place, the DVD viewer misses the joke. Otherwise the camera angles are well managed, and this is undoubtedly a very enjoyable concert of its kind.

Berlin Philharmonic Orchestra, Herbert von Karajan

'New Year's Eve Concert, 1985'*: LEONCAVALLO: *I Pagliacci: Intermezzo.* LISZT: *Hungarian Rhapsody 5 in E min.* PUCCINI: *Manon Lescaut: Intermezzo.* RAVEL: *Boléro.* WEBER: *Overture: Der Freischütz

*** Sony **DVD** SVD 46402

The passion behind Karajan's conducting in this celebratory concert comes over very clearly on DVD, as though he realizes that this may be the last time he ever conducts these favourite works. That gives an emotional tug to such a piece as the *Interlude* from Puccini's *Manon Lescaut,* where his facial expression, generally grim and mask-like, clearly indicates the depth of his feelings, always a great interpreter of this composer. Unlike the New Year's Day concerts in Vienna, the New Year's Eve events in Berlin span the widest range of repertory. This time he starts with the Weber overture, not just refined and beautifully shaded but with high dramatic contrasts. The two Italian opera interludes follow, with Karajan quickly silencing threatening applause between them, leading to an affectionately lyrical reading of the least Hungarian and least dramatic of Liszt's *Hungarian Rhapsodies.* The final item, which inevitably brings the house down, is Ravel's *Boléro,* offering a superb demonstration not just of the virtuosity of individual players and of the different sections in this great orchestra but also of the deftness of the television directors, picking out the relevant players in close-up. If Karajan's reading of this obsessively repetitive piece is far less boring than it can be, the explanation lies not just in the technical brilliance of the players but in the subtlety of the conductor's pointing of rhythm, lifting music that can so easily become merely metrical. Significantly, for this piece Karajan abandons his baton, merely giving restrained indications with gesturing hands.

'Overtures and Intermezzi'*: JOHANN STRAUSS JR: *Overture: Zigeunerbaron.* MASSENET: *Thaïs: Méditation* (with Anne-Sophie Mutter, violin). CHERUBINI: *Overture: Anacréon.* WEBER: *Overture: Der Freischütz.* SCHMIDT: *Notre Dame: Intermezzo.* PUCCINI: *Suor Angelica: Intermezzo; Manon Lescaut: Intermezzo.* MASCAGNI: *L'amico Fritz: Intermezzo.* HUMPERDINCK: *Overture: Hänsel und Gretel.* MENDELSSOHN: *Overture: The Hebrides (Fingal's Cave)

(BB) ** EMI Encore (ADD/DDD) 5 74598-2

A curiously planned programme. It opens with a brilliantly played and indulgently seductive account of the *Gypsy Baron Overture*; then comes the *Méditation* from *Thaïs* (a young Anne-Sophie Mutter the gentle soloist) played very romantically, immediately followed by Cherubini's *Anacréon Overture.* The performances of the Weber and Humperdinck overtures are disappointing, the first lacking electricity, the second charm. Best are the intermezzi, played with the utmost passion. The digital recording here is very brightly lit and there is a fierce sheen on the strings, but the closing *Fingal's Cave Overture* is played most beautifully, generating plenty of excitement, its effect enhanced by the resonantly spacious acoustic.

CHOPIN: *Les Sylphides* (orch. Roy Douglas). DELIBES: *Coppélia: Ballet Suite.* GOUNOD: *Faust: Ballet Music and Waltz.* OFFENBACH: *Gaîté parisienne* (ballet, arr. ROSENTHAL): extended excerpts. TCHAIKOVSKY: *Sleeping Beauty: Suite.* PONCHIELLI: *La Gioconda: Dance of the Hours*

🔑 ✿ *** DG (ADD) 459 445-2 (2)

This scintillating collection of ballet music is superbly played, and every item shows Karajan and his great orchestra at their finest. The very beautiful performance of Roy Douglas's exquisite arrangement of *Les Sylphides* – with its ravishing string playing and glowingly delicate woodwind solos – has never been matched on record. It is also available on a single bargain disc together with the exhilaratingly racy *Gaîté parisienne* selection (which includes most of the ballet) and the *Coppélia Suite*; but the latter is cut. The missing movements are restored here and sound marvellous, as does the vivacious *Faust Ballet Music* and *Waltz,* the latter played with irresistible panache. Another riveting moment comes in the thrilling crescendo at the climax of the *Introduction* to the *Sleeping Beauty Ballet Suite,* yet there is much elegance and delicacy of colour to follow. The closing *Dance of the Hours* – so affectionately phrased – also sparkles as do few other recorded performances, and throughout, these excellent CD transfers demonstrate DG's finest analogue quality from the 1960s and 1970s.

WEBER: *Invitation to the Dance.* BERLIOZ: *Damnation de Faust: Ballet des Sylphes; Menuet des feux follets.* LISZT: *Mephisto Waltz.* SMETANA: *The Bartered Bride: Furiant, Polka & Dance of the Comedians.* BORODIN: *Prince Igor: Polovtsian Dances.* VERDI: *Otello: ballet music.* PONCHIELLI: *La Gioconda: Dance of the Hours*
(M) *** DG (ADD) 474 617-2

With panther-like smoothness, Karajan and his Berlin orchestra purr their way through these popular orchestral pieces. Not that in their smoothness they lack vitality: the lively numbers are superbly done too (the Liszt is wonderfully romantic in style); indeed, these are vintage performances in every respect, with every item given the full Karajan treatment – even the hardly subtle Verdi ballet music is given greater dignity than usual, and the result is highly enjoyable. The delicacy of the strings in the *Invitation to the Dance* and the *Ballet des Sylphes* is spine-tingling, while *The Dance of the Hours* have never passed the time more magically. Well-remastered sound from 1971. This CD is worth anyone's money.

Berlin Philharmonic Orchestra and (i) Wind Ensemble, Herbert von Karajan

'Christmas Concert': CORELLI: *Concerto grosso in G min. (Christmas), Op. 6/8.* MANFREDINI: *Concerto grosso in C (Christmas), Op. 3/12.* LOCATELLI: *Concerto grosso in F min., Op. 1/8.* TORELLI: *Concerto a 4 (Pastorale), Op. 8/6.* (i) GIOVANNI GABRIELI: *Canzona a 8.* SCHEIDT: *In dulci jubilo.* ECCARD: *Chorales: Vom Himmel hoch, da komm ich her; Es is ein Ros entsprungen.* GRUBER: *Stille Nacht*
(M) ** DG 474 556-2

Karajan's '*Christmas Concert*' combines a collection of Christmas concertos, played exquisitely (especially the *Pastorales*) in the conductor's perfumed baroque style, interspersed with more robust items from the Berlin Philharmonic Wind Ensemble. However, the lack of bite in the faster movements of the string works, partly brought about about by the balmy resonance of the 1970s analogue recording, damps down the music's vitality. Karajan is pictured looking grey and old in a series of family snapshots with his wife.

Berlin Philharmonic Orchestra, Georges Prêtre

'Concert at the Waldbühne': BERLIOZ: *Overture: Le Carnaval romain.* BIZET: *Carmen Suite; L'Arlésienne: Farandole.* DEBUSSY: *Prélude à l'après-midi d'un faune.* RAVEL: *Concerto for Piano Left Hand* (with Leon Fleischer); *Boléro.* JOHANN STRAUSS SR: *Radetzky March.* (Director & Video Director: Hans-Peter Birke-Malzer.)
*** TDK **DVD** DV-WBFRN.

This is a 1992 outdoor concert recorded at the Waldbühne in Berlin with the Berlin Philharmonic in splendid form under the vivacious Georges Prêtre. The Berlioz *Carnaval romain* is wonderfully spirited and there seems to be an excellent rapport between the Berliners and their French guest. The DVD is worth acquiring for the rare opportunity of seeing and hearing Leon Fleisher play the Ravel *Left Hand Concerto* with impressive authority. The camera-work is unobtrusive and expert.

Berlin Philharmonic and Israel Philharmonic Orchestras; Zubin Mehta

'Joint Concert, Tel Aviv (1990)': BEN-HAIM: *Symphony 1, 2nd Mov.: Psalm;* SAINT-SAENS: *Introduction & Rondo capriccio, Op. 28* (with Hagner, violin). WEBER: *Clarinet Concertino in E flat, Op. 67* (with Kam, clarinet). RAVEL: *La Valse.* BEETHOVEN: *Symphony 5*
*(*) Arthaus **DVD** 100 068

The visit of the Berlin Philharmonic had been keenly awaited in Tel Aviv, and this joint concert in the Mann Auditorium should have been an electrifying occasion. The two soloists are very good, and there is some excellent orchestral playing, with the two orchestras combined in the *Psalm* and the Beethoven and sounding pretty splendid in the Ravel, in spite of the less than ideal acoustics. However, the account of Beethoven's *Fifth* simply fails to spark into life until the finale, and even then it is hardly earth-shaking. Certainly the DVD gives one a sense of being there, but the concert remains a disappointment.

Berlin State Opera Orchestra, Daniel Barenboim

'Berliner Luft' (Gala concert from the State Opera, Unter den Linden): NICOLAI: *Overture: The Merry Wives of Windsor.* MOZART: *Don Giovanni: Là ci darem la mano* (with Pape, Röschmann). SAINT-SAENS: *Introduction & Rondo capriccioso, Op. 28* (with Christ, violin). TCHAIKOVSKY: *Swan Lake: Dance of the Little Swans* (with ballet); *Waltz.* SHOSTAKOVICH: *Tahiti Trot.* WEILL: *Berlin im Licht* (Gruber, Barenboim, piano). KOLLO: *Untern Linden* (Vocal Ens.). LINCKE: *Glow-Worm Idyll* (Nold); *Berliner Luft.* J. STRAUSS JR: *Unter Donner und Blitz.*
*** Arthaus **DVD** 100 094

This is obviously the Berliners' equivalent of the Last Night of the Proms and the well-dressed audience clearly have a wonderful evening. The DVD has tremendous spirit and atmosphere, Barenboim and the orchestra are obviously enjoying themselves and there are even magicians doing party tricks to add to the revels. Everyone joins in the closing popular numbers, and although it is not as uninhibited as at the Proms (the audience is much older for one thing), it is still very infectious and enjoyable. The recording obviously came from a broadcast, for it is compressed here and there, but it does not affect the sense of spectacle. One could criticize the cameras for being too volatile in moving around the orchestra, but it suits the occasion, especially in the delightful account of Shostakovich's *Tahiti Trot* (based on Vincent Youmans's *Tea for Two*).

Bezaly, Sharon (flute), Tapiola Sinfonietta, Jean-Jacques Kantorow

GOUNOD: *Concerto for Flute & Small Orchestra.* DEVIENNE: *Flute Concerto 7 in E min.* SAINT-SAENS: *Airs de ballet d'Ascanio: Adagio & Variation; Odelette; Romance; Tarentelle* (for flute, clarinet and orchestra). FAURE: *Fantaisie*
*** BIS CD 1359

A delightful disc this, with Sharon Bezaly on sparkling form. The longest work here is Devienne's *Flute Concerto*, most appealing in its minor-keyed *galant*-style writing – elegant melody interspersed with not-too-serious drama, and a lilting finale. Fauré's *Fantaisie* is as beautiful as ever, and one doesn't resent Yoav Talmi giving it – with the aid of added final chords – a more emphatic ending than Fauré wrote. Both the Gounod *Concertino* and the Saint-Saëns *Romance* are slight, but utterly charming – and the same goes for the latter's *Odelette*, written just a year before the composer's death. However, the six-minute *Tarentelle* is perhaps the gem of these rarer works, with flute and clarinet skipping along together over the tarantella rhythm with infectious insouciance. Although Bezaly is quite closely recorded, the sound is full and rich, as well as cleanly focused. Jean-Jacques Kantorow conducts with both enthusiasm and sensitivity throughout, adding much to the success of this disc.

Bolister, Ruth (oboe), Elgar Chamber Orchestra, Stephen Bell

'*English Oboe Concertos*': JACOB: *Oboe Concerto 1*. ELGAR: *Soliloquy* (orch. Jacob). HOLST: *A Fugal Concerto for Flute & Oboe* (with Kate Hill, flute). GOOSSENS: *Concerto in One Movement*. VAUGHAN WILLIAMS: *Concerto in A min.*
✪ *** ASV CDDCA 1173

This is just about the most desirable collection of English oboe concertos in the catalogue. Ruth Bolister's delicate timbre and refined phrasing are captivating throughout, and especially so in the delicate Elgar *Soliloquy* (a fragment of an *Oboe Suite*, scored by Gordon Jacob). His own *First Concerto* is the most substantial work in the programme, and is given its première here. It was written for Evelyn Rothwell, and in Bolister's hands the neo-classical first movement is most diverting and the yearning *Andante* quite lovely. In the Holst *Fugal Concerto*, Kate Hill's contribution is equally felicitous; the opening *Moderato* brings a perky interplay and the *Adagio*, with its flowing line reminding one of Bach, has surely never been played more beautifully on record, capped by the witty, folksy finale. The Goossens *Concerto*, succinctly structured, is yet a kaleidoscope of diverse invention, its spicy and unpredictable moments of astringency aurally stimulating and making a foil for the other music here; the piece has a sombre lyrical core, yet it ends genially. The closing work by Vaughan Williams then makes a delightful finale, its pastoral feeling perfectly caught. Throughout Stephen Bell's accompaniments with the excellent Elgar Chamber Orchestra could not be more stylish or polished, with the string playing especially fine; the lustrous recording, warm, natural and transparent, is very much in the demonstration bracket. Very highly recommended.

Boston Pops Orchestra, Arthur Fiedler

'*Pops Caviar*': BORODIN: *In the Steppes of Central Asia*. RIMSKY-KORSAKOV: *Russian Easter Festival Overture; Tsar Saltan: Flight of the Bumblebee*. BORODIN: *Prince Igor: Overture and Polovtsian Dances*. KHACHATURIAN: *Gayaneh: Suite; Masquerade; Galop*. TCHAIKOVSKY: *Eugene Onegin: Polonaise; Sleeping Beauty Waltz*
(M) *** RCA **SACD** (ADD) 82876 71618-2

A superb disc, as much a tribute to the excellent acoustics of Boston's Symphony Hall and the skill of the original recording team as to the performers, with the balance absolutely natural. Yet Fiedler and his excellent Boston players are right on the ball throughout this highly entertaining concert. The translucence of the woodwind colouring helps to bring magic to the Borodin (including a fine horn solo in the Overture) and the Rimsky-Korsakov works, but the sparkling Tchaikovsky *Polonaise* and *Waltz* and Khachaturian's *Gayaneh* (Fiedler at his most ebullient) are as vibrant as anyone could wish. The new SACD transfers from the original three-tracks by John Newton of Soundmirror are masterly.

Boston Symphony Orchestra, Serge Koussevitzky

COPLAND: *El salón México*. FOOTE: *Suite in E min., Op. 63*. HARRIS: *Symphony (1933); Symphony 3*. MCDONALD: *San Juan Capistrano – Two Evening Pictures*
(M) (***) Pearl mono GEMMCD 9492

Koussevitzky's performance of the Roy Harris *Third Symphony* has never been equalled in intensity and fire – even by Toscanini or Bernstein – and Copland himself never produced as exhilarating an *El salón México*. The Arthur Foote *Suite* is unpretentious and has great charm. Sonic limitations are soon forgotten, for these performances have exceptional power and should not be missed.

PROKOFIEV: *Symphony 1 in D (Classical), Op. 25; Chout, Op. 21 bis: Danse finale*. SHOSTAKOVICH: *Symphony 9 in E flat, Op. 70*. TCHAIKOVSKY: *Francesca da Rimini, Op. 32*
(***) Biddulph mono WHL 058

Koussevitzky is in a class of his own. His premier recordings have great freshness and authority. His Shostakovich *Ninth Symphony*, recorded in 1946–7, was a rarity and never appeared in Britain in the days of shellac. The pre-war set of the Prokofiev *Classical Symphony* has even greater sparkle than the 1947 version included here, but this will do very nicely too! An electrifying *Francesca da Rimini*. Very good notes by David Gutman and decent transfers by Mark Obert-Thorn.

Boston Symphony Orchestra, Charles Munch

SAINT-SAËNS: *Symphony 3*. IBERT: *Escales*. D'INDY: *Symphonie sur un chant montagnard (Symphonie cévénole)* (with Nicole Henriot-Schweitzer). FRANCK: *Symphony in D min.* ROUSSEL: *Bacchus et Ariane: Suite 2*. HONEGGER: *Symphony 5 (Di Tre Re)*
(BB) (***) RCA mono/stereo 74321 98715-2

This is one of the 50-odd two-CD Artistes-Repertoires series that RCA France are marketing, and it collects well-known recordings from Munch's Boston years including a brilliant (1952) mono record of Honegger's *Fifth Symphony* which still remains unsurpassed, an exhilarating *Suite* from *Bacchus et Ariane* (with which it was originally coupled), as well as other classic French scores including an atmospheric and seductive *Escales*. The set is decently transferred and well worth acquiring if you haven't already got these recordings, though the presentation is printed in minuscule type. The notes are in French only, but that should not deter the serious collector.

Bournemouth Sinfonietta, Richard Studt

'*English String Music*': BRITTEN: *Variations on a Theme of Frank Bridge, Op. 10.* HOLST: *St Paul's Suite, Op. 29/1.* DELIUS: *2 Aquarelles.* VAUGHAN WILLIAMS: *5 Variants of Dives and Lazarus.* WARLOCK: *Capriol Suite*
(BB) *** Naxos 8.550823

This is the finest of the concerts of string music recorded for Naxos by Richard Studt and the excellent Bournemouth Sinfonietta. The Britten *Frank Bridge Variations* is particularly memorable, showing easy virtuosity yet often achieving the lightest touch, so that the Vienna waltz movement sparkles in its delicacy. The *Funeral March* may not be so desperately intense as Karajan's famous mono version with the Philharmonia, but it is still very touching; and the following *Chant* is ethereal in its bleakly refined atmosphere.

The sprightly Holst *St Paul's Suite* and Warlock's *Capriol*, agreeably robust, could hardly be better played, while Vaughan Williams's *Dives and Lazarus* is especially fresh and conveys the famous biblical story of the rich man and the beggar most evocatively, especially in the very beautiful closing section, when Lazarus finds himself in heaven. The recording, made in St Peter's Church, Parkstone, is full-bodied, immediate and real – very much in the demonstration bracket.

'*20th-century String Music*': BARTOK: *Divertimento.* BRITTEN: *Simple Symphony, Op. 4.* WALTON: *2 Pieces from Henry V: Death of Falstaff (Passacaglia); Touch her Soft Lips and Part.* STRAVINSKY: *Concerto in D*
(BB) ** Naxos 8.550979

This is the least successful of the three concerts of string music recorded by Naxos in Bournemouth. The Sinfonietta players do not sound completely at ease in the shifting moods of the Bartók *Divertimento* and their ensemble could be crisper in the Stravinsky *Concerto*. The *Simple Symphony* comes off brightly, with a gently nostalgic *Sentimental Sarabande* and a brisk, alert finale, but the *Playful Pizzicato* could be more exuberant, especially in its famous trio which the composer wrote so joyously. The two Walton pieces are warmly atmospheric, and there are no complaints about the sound.

'*Scandinavian String Music*': GRIEG: *Holberg Suite.* DAG WIREN: *Serenade, Op. 11.* SVENDSEN: *2 Icelandic Melodies; Norwegian Folksong; 2 Swedish Folksongs, Op. 27.* NIELSEN: *Little Suite in A min., Op. 1*
(BB) *** Naxos 8.553106

The liltingly spontaneous account of the Dag Wirén *Serenade* ensures a welcome for this enjoyable collection of Scandinavian music. The performance of Grieg's perennially fresh *Holberg Suite* is hardly less successful in its combination of energy and polish, folksy charm and touching serenity in the famous *Air*. Nielsen's *Little Suite* also has plenty of style and impetus, the changing moods of the finale neatly encompassed. The Svendsen folksong arrangements belong to the 1870s. The two *Icelandic Melodies* are melodically robust but the *Norwegian Folksong* is gentler and quite lovely. Yet it is the second of the two *Swedish Folksongs* that most reminds the listener of Grieg. All are played with a natural expressive feeling, and the recording, made in the Winter Gardens, Bournemouth, has a fine, full sonority to balance its natural brilliance.

Brain, Dennis (horn)

BEETHOVEN: *Horn Sonata in F, Op. 17* (with Denis Matthews). MOZART: *Horn Concertos Nos. 2 in E flat, K.417* (with Philh. O, Susskind); *4 in E flat, K.495* (with Hallé O); *Horn Quintet in E flat, K.407* (with Griller Qt). RICHARD STRAUSS: *Horn Concerto 1 in E flat, Op. 11* (with Philh. O, Galliera)
(M) (**(*)) Pearl mono GEM 0026

Dennis Brain recorded the Beethoven *Sonata* with Denis Matthews in February 1944 on a simple, valved Boosey and Hawkes French horn (which legend has it cost £12). Because of its valve system, this was a more flexible instrument than the Viennese hand-horns used in Mozart's own time, but also a more imperfect one, with a few insecure upper harmonics Brain's timbre is unique, his articulation is endearingly musical, his technique phenomenal but never showy; even so, there is the occasional slightly insecure note. Yet the passage-work in both Beethoven and Mozart is full of imaginative touches In the Beethoven *Sonata* Denis Matthews provides an elegant Mozartian-styled partnership, his lightness of touch balancing nicely with Brain's elegance. How beautifully they exchange the question and answer of the briefly melancholy *Andante* and then launch into the robust finale so spiritedly!

The programme opens with the lovely Mozart *Quintet* (recorded eight months later). The Grillers play very sweetly and adroitly for the dominating horn, and the finale sparkles but remains elegant. The two Mozart concertos followed. K.495 came first in 1943 (with the Hallé Orchestra – the strings in rather indifferent form, conducted by their leader, Laurence Turner), K.417 (with the Philharmonia under Susskind) in 1946. In both, Brain's phrasing of the lovely slow-movement melodies is Elysian and the jaunty finale of K.417 remains unforgettable. When he came to re-record the Mozart *Horn Concertos* with Karajan in 1953 (reissued in EMI's 'Great Recordings of the Century' series – 5 66898-2) he had adopted the wide-bore German double horn, which has a fatter, more spreading sound, not a timbre Mozart would have recognized. So there is a case for preferring Brain's earlier performances because Mozart simply sounds better on the narrower-bore instrument, and that is not to disparage the marvellous playing on the Karajan disc.

It is not certain which instrument Brain used for the present 1947 recording of the Richard Strauss, but the playing is wonderfully ebullient and crisply articulated, all difficulties swept aside: it sounds like a French rather than a German horn. The effect is to echo the work's Mozartian inspiration, and in the great soaring romantic theme at the centre of the slow movement – here, unfortunately affected by intrusive, uneven, scratchy surface noise – the lyrical surge is thrilling but not inflated, and this is one of his very finest solo performances on record. The Pearl transfers are faithful and agreeable (there is no edginess on the strings). But it surely ought to have been possible to diminish the background surface noise.

Brass Partout

'*Playgrounds for Angels*': GRIEG: *Sorgemarsj over Rikard Nordraak.* NYSTEDT: *Pia Memoria.* RAUTAVAARA: *A Requiem in our Time; Playgrounds for Angels.* SIBELIUS: *Overture in F min.; Allegro; Andantino and Menuett; Förspel (Preludium); Tiera*
*** BIS CD 1054

rass Partout (or rather brass partout, all fashionably lower
ase), is a virtuoso group of brass and percussion players,
rawn from the Berlin Philharmonic and other major
erman orchestras. The disc takes its title from the ingenious
iece the Finnish composer Einojuhani Rautavaara com-
osed for the Philip Jones Brass Ensemble. The *Requiem in
ur Time* put Rautavaara on the map in 1953 and is only
vailable in one other version.

All the Sibelius rarities are from 1889, before *Kullervo*,
xcept only *Tiera* (1899).They fill in our picture of his growth
uring those formative years, though none is a masterpiece.
he splendid *Pia Memoria*, a requiem for nine brass instru-
nents by the Norwegian, Knut Nystedt, has nobility and
ignity. So, too, does Grieg's *Sorgemarsj over Rikard Nordraak*
> whose strains the composer himself was buried. The
laying is pretty stunning and so, too, is the superb BIS
ecording.

British Light Music

British Light Music' (with (i) Light Music Society O, Sir
ivian Dunn; (ii) Pro Arte O, George Weldon; (iii) Studio
wo Concert O, Reginald Kilbey; (iv) Eric Coates and his
)): (i) DUNCAN: *Little Suite: March.* CURZON: *The
oulevardier.* BINGE: *The Watermill.* DOCKER: *Tabarinage.*
OPE: *The Ring of Kerry Suite: The Jaunting Car.* (ii)
OATES: *Springtime Suite: Dance in the Twilight.* COLLINS:
anity Fair. CURZON: *Punchinello: Miniature Overture.*
OMLINSON: *Little Serenade.* BINGE: *Miss Melanie.* Alan
ANGFORD: *Waltz.* BAYCO: *Elizabethan Masque.* DEXTER:
iciliano. HAYDN WOOD: *Moods Suite: Joyousness.* (iii) *Paris
uite: Montmartre.* BINGE: *Elizabethan Serenade.* VINTER:
ortuguese Party. OSBORNE: *Lullaby for Penelope.* FARNON:
ortrait of a Flirt. HARTLEY: *Rouge et noir.* (iv) COATES:
mpression of a Princess; Wood Nymphs; The Dam Busters
March

M) *** EMI stereo/mono 5 66537-2

)bviously inspired by the great success of the programmes of
ritish light music recorded (at premium price) by Ronald
orp for Hyperion, EMI have delved into their archives and
rought out this equally attractive selection, drawing on four
ifferent sources, all of the highest quality. Moreover this
MI CD is offered at mid-price and includes 76 minutes of
ar-catching melody. The obvious favourites are here, from
onald Binge's famous *Elizabethan Serenade* to his delectable
ignette evoking *The Watermill*, Anthony Collins's *Vanity Fair*
he popularity of which he valued above his fame as a
onductor) and Robert Farnon's witty *Portrait of a Flirt*.

But also included are many more novelties of equal charm:
ayco's winning pastiche, *Elizabethan Masque*, Binge's wistful
ortrait of *Miss Melanie*, Alan Langford's pastel-shaded
Waltz, Harry Dexter's lilting *Siciliano*, Leslie Osborne's gently
ouching *Lullaby for Penelope*, and the delicious Irish whimsy
f Peter Hope's *Jaunting Car*. To bring lively contrast come
obert Docker's roisterous *Tabarinage* and Gilbert Vinter's
qually vivacious *Portuguese Party*. The stereo recordings,
nade at Abbey Road between 1963 and 1970, are excellent and
ery pleasingly transferred. Appropriately, the programme
pens and closes with the music of Eric Coates, and the last
hree items are conducted by the composer, ending with a
igorous account of *The Dam Busters March*. These are mono
ecordings, but of high quality.

'*British Light Music'* (played by the Slovak or
Czecho-Slovak RSO, Andrew Penny, Adrian Leaper (with
male chorus), Ludovit Raijter or Ernest Tomlinson; BBC
Concert O, Kenneth Alwyn; Dublin RTE Concert O, Ernest
Tomlinson or Proinnsias O Duinn):

Volume 1: COATES: *By the Sleepy Lagoon.* QUILTER:
Children's Overture. ADDINSELL: Film music: *Tom Brown's
Schooldays.* CURZON: *Robin Hood Suite.* HAYDN WOOD:
Sketch of a Dandy. DUNCAN: *Little Suite.* COLLINS: *Vanity
Fair.* KETELBEY: *Suite romantique.* (8.554709)

Volume 2: KETELBEY: *In a Monastery Garden.* FARNON:
Colditz March. GERMAN: *Gypsy Suite.* HAYDN WOOD: *Roses
of Picardy; Serenade to Youth.* DUNCAN: *Enchanted April.*
CURZON: *La Pienneta.* QUILTER: *Rosmé Waltz.* ELLIS:
Coronation Scot. (8.554710)

Volume 3: ADDINSELL: Film music: *Goodbye Mr Chips.*
GERMAN: *Romeo and Juliet* (incidental music):
DUNCAN: *20th-century Express.* HAYDN WOOD: *The Sea-
farer.* FARNON: *Pictures in the Fire.* COATES: *The Selfish
Giant.* QUILTER: *As You Like It: Suite.* BENJAMIN: *Jamaican Rumba.* KETELBEY: *Bells across the Meadow.*
(8.554711)

Volume 4: ADDINSELL (arr. Roy Douglas): *Warsaw
Concerto.* BATH: *Cornish Rhapsody.* RICHARD RODNEY
BENNETT: *Murder on the Orient Express: Theme and Waltz.*
CHARLES WILLIAMS: *Dream of Olwen* (with Philip Fowke).
FARNON: *Lake in the Woods; Westminster Waltz.* DUNCAN:
Girl from Corsica; Visionaries' Grand March. CURZON:
Bravada: Paso doble. HAYDN WOOD: *Evening Song.*
TOMLINSON: *Little Serenade.* (8.554712)

Volume 5: COATES: *Dam Busters March.* ADDINSELL: Film
music: *Fire over England.* GERMAN: *Nell Gwynn: 3 Dances;
Tom Jones: Waltz.* KETELBEY: *In the Moonlight.* BINGE:
Elizabethan Serenade. FARNON: *Peanut Polka.* QUILTER: *3
English Dances.* HAYDN WOOD: *May-Day Overture.*
MAYERL: *Marigold.* KETELBEY: *In a Persian Market.*
(8.554713)

(BB) *** Naxos 8.505147 (5)

Unlike the Naxos set of '*British Orchestral Masterpieces'*
(listed in our previous edition of the *Yearbook*), in which
five existing CDs are offered in a slipcase, '*The Best of British
Light Music'* has been specially compiled, with items selected
from a number of Naxos CDs. It offers a wide selection, well
over five hours of music, so is less selective than the
full-priced Hyperion CDs of the New London Orchestra
under Ronald Corp. The NLO are also rather more characterful and even better recorded (see below) but the Naxos
set remains excellent value. Although Kenneth Alwyn directs
most of the film music, much of the rest is played, surprisingly idiomatically, by the Slovak Radio Symphony Orchestra, usually conducted by Adrian Leaper, although Ernest
Tomlinson directs his own music (including his delicate
lollipop, *Little Serenade*). The highlights include Roger Quilter's lovely *Children's Overture*, Anthony Collins's *Vanity Fair*
(which he greatly prized), Binge's *Elizabethan Serenade* and
Sailing By, Benjamin's *Jamaican Rumba* and mostly familiar
items by Eric Coates. Robert Farnon is well represented by
Colditz, his charming *Westminster Waltz* and the catchy
Peanut Polka, as well as two rather effective tone-pictures,
Lake in the Woods and *Pictures in the Fire*, and there are
other obvious hits like Vivian Ellis's *Coronation Scot* and of
course the '*film concertos'*. Not everything else is quite so

memorable, but Edward German, Haydn Wood and Ketèl-bey are all well represented and everything is brightly played and well recorded. The five records come for the price of four, and all are quite well documented.

'British Light Music Festival' (played by various orchestras & conductors): FANSHAWE: *Fanfare To Planet Earth; Millennium March.* LANGFORD: *Petite Promenade.* HOPE: *Irish Legend; Petit Point; Playful Scherzo; Ring of Kerry.* TOMLINSON: *Cantilena.* ABBOTT: *London Fragments.* TURNER: *Countrywise; Passepied des enfants.* KELLY: *Dance Suite; Comedy Film.* LYON: *Dance Prelude; Divertimento.* VINTER: *April Shower; March Winds; Mayflowers; Song – Dance Suite; Tenderfoot.* JOSEPHS: *Aeolian Dance; Ecossaise; March Glorious.* ARNOLD: *Sarabande.* DYER: *Marche Vive.* PERRY: *Lonely Journey.* DRING: *Danza Gaya.* SAUNDERS: *Badinage; Kanikani.* DOCKER: *Commemoration March*
(M) **(*) ASV (ADD) CDWLS 250 (2)

An excellent anthology of performances drawn from various sources, mainly from the 1960s, though David Fanshawe's were recorded as recently as 2000. All of the music is in the best British light-music tradition, which flourished especially well in the 1950s and 1960s. If it is not all first rate, it is often nostalgically enjoyable just the same. Helpful sleeve-notes, as usual from this source.

'Halcyon Days: A Treasury of British Light Music': PHILIPS: *Hampton Court Overture.* DELIUS: *2 Aquarelles.* TOMLINSON: *Cantilena.* RUTTER: *Vivace.* BRIDGE: *Miss Melanie.* DAVIES: *RAF March Past.* WARLOCK: *4 Folksong Preludes.* J. GARDINER: *Half Holiday.* VAUGHAN WILLIAMS: *Fantasia on Greensleeves.* ELGAR: *The Spanish Lady (Suite), Op. 90.* FIELD: *Rondo.* HOROVITZ: *Sinfonietta.* ARNOLD: *The Padstow Lifeboat.* ANSELL: *Plymouth Hoe.* HAYDN WOOD: *London Landmarks.* MORLEY: *Rotton Row.* COATES: *By the Sleepy Lagoon; The Dam Busters March; Halcyon Days; London Suite.* LANE: *3 Spanish Dances; Suite of Cotswold Folk Dances (excerpts).* GLYN: *Anglesey Seascapes (excerpts).* CURZON: *March of the Bowmen.* GOODWIN: *City of Lincoln March.* MACCUNN: *Land of the Mountain and Flood Overture.* HARTY: *Londonderry Air.* CHARLES WILLIAMS: *The Devil's Galop; Girls in Grey; High Adventure.* BINGE: *Sailing By; The Watermill.* MATHIESON: *Loch Laggan.* GOODALL: *Ecce Homo; Psalm 23.* ADDINSELL: *Southern Rhapsody.* JOSEPHS: *March Glorious.* LEWIS: *An English Overture.* WALTON: *Spitfire Prelude and Fugue.* MONTGOMERY: *Carry On Suite.* ERIC ROGERS: *Carry On Up the Khyber* (arr. Sutherland). BLAKE: *Andante Expressivo.* FANSHAWE: *Tarka the Otter.* GRAY: *The African Queen.* BLEZARD: *Caramba.* SMYTH: *2 Interlinked French Melodies.* SAUNDERS: *Kanikani.* KELLY: *Divertissement.* R. R. BENNET: *Suite Française.* SUMSION: *A Mountain Tune.* HOPE: *4 French Dances.* LANGFORD: *Petite Promenade.* MACDONALD: *Cuban Rondo.* VINTER: *Song – Dance Suite.* ADDINSELL: *Greengage Summer (excerpts).* TCHAIKOVSKY (arr. Wilkinson): *Beatlecracker Suite.* ARNOLD: *Sarabande.* GORDON: *2 Dances.* DRING: *Danza Gaya.* TOYE: *The Haunted Ballroom.* READE: *2 Dances.* LYON: *3 Dances.* STANFORD: *Celestial Fire (excerpts).* JOSEPHS: *Aeolian Dances*
(B) *** ASV (ADD/DDD) WLS 501 (5)

A positive cornucopia of British light music, taken from the myriad of CDs in the ASV White Line catalogue, mostly conducted by Gavin Sutherland, along with Barry Words-worth, Kenneth Alwyn, *et al.*, and a sprinkling of vintage

performances from the 1960s. With compositions ranging from Elgar and Dame Ethel Smyth, right up to the *Carry On* films, there is no lack of variety here, with pretty much all the famous numbers – *The Devil's Galop, Sailing By*, the *Dam Busters March*, etc., included. The pleasure of this set lies in rediscovering so much long-forgotten, undemanding and tuneful music which has slipped from the repertoire over the years but has been rescued, on recordings at least, for the twenty-first century. The five CDs are very well planned, mixing the more substantial compositions of MacCunn and Walton and the like with the various suites, overtures, dances and novelty numbers, with the sound consistently fine. This feast of light music is a great way to acquire a lot of good tunes in one go!

Camden, Anthony (oboe)

'Italian Oboe Concertos' (with City of London Sinfonia, Nicolas Ward): CIMAROSA, arr. Arthur BENJAMIN: *Concerto in C.* BELLINI: *Concerto in E flat.* RIGHINI: *Concerto in C.* FIORILLO: *Sinfonia concertante in F* (with Julia Girdwood). CORELLI, arr. BARBIROLLI: *Concerto in A.* PERGOLESI/BARBIROLLI: *Concerto in C min.*
(BB) **(*) Naxos 8.553433

This collection recalls the series of outstanding recordings made by Evelyn Rothwell for Pye/PRT with her husband, Sir John Barbirolli, conducting. He specially arranged the highly engaging pastiche works of Corelli and Pergolesi for her to play and put his signature firmly on the *Sarabanda* of the Corelli *Concerto*, which he scored as a duet for oboe and cello, his own instrument. Lady Barbirolli's recordings have just been restored to the catalogue, but at full price.

Meanwhile these sympathetic and stylishly played performances from Anthony Camden will suffice admirably, particularly at Naxos price. He has a most attractive timbre, and Nicholas Ward's accompaniments are impeccable. There are two very small reservations. The Fiorillo *Sinfonia concertante*, which features a pair of oboes (the second part is neatly managed by Julia Girdwood), although nicely written for the two soloists, is very conventional in its material and the first movement is a shade too long. The other point concerns the delightful five-note opening phrase of Arthur Benjamin's delicious Cimarosa confection, which Camden plays curiously lethargically, echoed by Ward. It is a small point, but Lady Barbirolli's account still lingers in the memory. The Naxos recording is excellently balanced and truthful.

'The Art of the Oboe' (with (i) London Virtuosi, John Georgiadis; (ii) City of L. Sinfonia, Nicholas Ward): (i) ALBINONI: *Oboe Concertos: in C, Op. 7/12; in D min., Op. 9/2; in C, Op. 9/5.* (ii) HANDEL: *Concerto 3 in G min.; Rondo in G; Rigaudon.* RIGHINI: *Idomeneus Concerto.* CORELLI: *Concerto.* CIMAROSA: *Concerto in C min.* BELLINI: *Concerto in E flat*
(BB) *** Naxos 8.553991

This collection again has something in common with Evelyn Rothwell, Lady Barbirolli's collection of oboe concertos with her husband directing, but has the advantage of modern digital sound of high quality. Anthony Camden is a first-class soloist and these are vividly played performances, stylishly accompanied by both groups. Camden's tempi are not always quite so apt as his predecessor but slow movements are always sensitive and finales sparkle. Most enjoyable.

Capella Istropolitana, Adrian Leaper

'English String Festival': DOWLAND: *Galliard a 5*. ELGAR: *Elegy, Op. 58; Introduction and Allegro, Op. 47; Serenade, Op. 20*. BRIDGE: *Lament*. PARRY: *An English Suite; Lady Radnor's Suite*

(BB) **(*) Naxos 8.550331

It is fascinating and rewarding to hear these excellent Slovak players turn their attention to essentially English repertoire, and with a considerable degree of success. The brief Dowland *Galliard* makes a strong introduction, and the attractive pair of neo-Baroque Parry suites of dance movements, played with warmth, finesse and spirit, are given bright and lively sound. In the Elgar *Introduction and Allegro* the violins above the stave have their upper partials over-brilliantly lit by the digital recording, the focus not quite sharp; but otherwise the sound is full, with plenty of resonant ambience. The playing is strongly felt, but the fugue is a bit too measured, and the great striding theme, played in unison on the G string, could also do with more pace, especially when it returns. Otherwise this is persuasive, and the *Serenade* is presented simply, combining warmth and finish. At super-bargain price, this is worth exploring.

Capuçon, Renaud (violin)

'Le Boeuf sur le toit' (with Bremen Deutsche Kammerphilharmonie, Harding): BERLIOZ: *Rêverie et caprice*. MASSENET: *Thaïs: Méditation*. MILHAUD: *Le Boeuf sur le toit, Op.58*. RAVEL: *Tzigane*. SAINT-SAENS: *Danse macabre; Havanaise; Introduction and Rondo capriccioso; Etudes, Op. 52* (arr. YSAYE): *En forme de valse*

*** Virgin 5 45482-2

This is a violin-and-orchestra recital with an attractive theme that fills a neat gap. Featuring the brilliant young French virtuoso, Renaud Capuçon, masterly throughout, this collection of short concertante pieces by French composers offers such predictable items as the Massenet *Méditation*, the Ravel *Tzigane* and the Saint-Saëns *Havanaise* and *Introduction and Rondo capriccioso*, but also includes the less well-known Berlioz piece and other related items. *Danse macabre* makes an obvious extra, although it features the solo violin more as an orchestral leader than as a main soloist, while the fourth Saint-Saëns item, described as *Valse-caprice* on the disc, is an arrangement made by Ysaÿe of the most popular of Saint-Saëns's piano études.

Most intriguing is the longest item, which provides the title for the whole disc, *Le Boeuf sur le toit*. This is one of two current versions of the arrangement which Milhaud himself made for the violinist, René Benedetti, of his Brazilian-inspired 'cinema-fantasy'. He characteristically takes the opportunity to emphasize the bizarre character of this suite of jazzy dances with its rondo theme inspired by Charlie Chaplin, making the solo violin the prime mover in bringing out the comic 'wrong-note' writing and clashing polytonality. Capuçon and Harding together make a strong case for this alternative version, relishing to the full the wit of the piece.

Carmignola, Giuliano (violin), Venice Baroque Orchestra, Andrea Marcon

'Concerto veneziana': VIVALDI: *Violin Concertos: in B flat (in due cori), RV 583; in E min., RV 278*. LOCATELLI: *Violin Concerto in G, Op. 3/9*. TARTINI: *Violin Concerto in D, D.96*
✿ *** DG **SACD** Surround Sound (compatible) 474 8952

An outstanding disc in every way. This may be an arbitrary collection, but each work represents the composer at his finest and most resourceful. Vivaldi's emotionally charged *Concerto a due cori* (with its special tuning for the solo violin) and Locatelli's *G major* work appear to be contemporaneous, and there is much affinity between the styles of the latter composer and Tartini. The performances are superb. Giuliano Carmignola is a wonderful soloist, finding the music's drama and expressive eloquence in equal measure. He ends the concert with the alternative slow movement of the Tartini concerto, a ravishing bonus. The Venice Baroque Orchestra must be placed alongside the Freiburg group as one of the finest period-instrument groups now before the public, and the recording is very real indeed. It is admirable on CD, but if you have SACD facilities the subtle addition of the sound from the rear speakers provides a real sense of 'being there'.

Casals, Pablo (conductor & cello)

SCHUBERT (with Prades Festival O): *Symphony 5 in B flat; String Quintet in C, Op. 163, D.956* (with Stern, Schneider, Katims, Tortelier)
(M) (***) Sony mono SMK 58992 [id.]

The Schubert *Fifth Symphony*, recorded in 1953, omits the first-movement exposition repeat but, as with everything this great musician does, is full of musical interest. It has not been issued in the UK before, eclipsed by the later (and perhaps even finer) performance by the 1970 Marlboro Orchestra in stereo. However, this earlier account boasts a particularly eloquent reading of the slow movement. The Casals account of the sublime Schubert *C major String Quintet* has rarely been absent from the catalogue: it first appeared on Philips and then CBS, and is too familiar to require detailed comment. Recorded in 1952, it sounds as marvellous as ever. This coupling is surely a must for all Casals admirers.

Chang, Han-Na (cello), Philharmonia Orchestra, Leonard Slatkin

'The Swan: Classic Works for Cello & Orchestra':
SAINT-SAENS; *Le Cygne*. BRUCH: *Ave Maria, Op. 61*. DVOŘÁK: *Silent Woods*. FAURÉ: *Sicilienne, Op. 78; Après un rêve, Op. 7/1*. GLAZUNOV: *Chant du Ménestrale, Op. 71*. KIM: *Korean Elegy*. RACHMANINOV: *Vocalise, Op. 14/14*. RESPIGHI: *Adagio con variazioni*. TCHAIKOVSKY: *Nocturne, Op. 11*
*** EMI 5 57052-2

Han-Na Chang, protégé of Rostropovich, is a naturally gifted artist with a lovely tone, and she plays with a simple eloquence that suits all these small-scale concertante works perfectly. The delicacy of Fauré, especially the delightful *Sicilienne*, is matched by the Russian nostalgia of Tchaikovsky. She is at her most passionate in the Bruch (with which the concert ends), but it is in the Rachmaninov *Vocalise* that her gentler approach is even more poignant. Slatkin accompanies her most sympathetically, and the mellow recording is just right for the repertoire. A disc that will give much pleasure.

Chang, Sarah (violin), Berlin Philharmonic Orchestra, Plácido Domingo

'*Fire and Ice*': BACH: *Orchestral Suite 3 in D, BWV 1068: Air.* BEETHOVEN: *Romance 2 in F, Op. 50.* DVORAK: *Romance in F min., Op. 11.* MASSENET: *Thaïs: Méditation.* RAVEL: *Tzigane.* SARASATE: *Concert Fantasy on Carmen, Op. 25; Zigeunerweisen, Op. 20*
*** EMI 5 57220-2

Don't be put off by the silly title of the disc – '*Fire and Ice*'! We have here a collection of rightly popular violin virtuoso pieces played with terrific panache and splendid style by this still young player. It is only ten years since Chang's last record of the Sarasate, although it was made some years earlier (when she was nine) and played on a smaller-sized instrument. Since then she has gone on to record concertos by Paganini, Tchaikovsky, Sibelius and Vieuxtemps, all of which have been acclaimed. In the early 1990s Miss Chang was hailed by Menuhin as 'the most ideal violinist I have ever heard', and now, ten years later, her prowess and virtuosity are never in doubt here. Those attracted to this repertoire can be assured that the playing from all concerned is pretty dazzling, and there are no reservations about the quality of the recording, made in the Philharmonie, Berlin. The balance is very acceptable and places the soloist firmly in the spotlight without in any way allowing her to mask the orchestral detail.

Chicago Symphony Orchestra

'*Historic Telecasts*', Volume 1 (1954): **Fritz Reiner**
BEETHOVEN: *Symphony 7 in A, Op. 92; Egmont Overture, Op. 84.* HANDEL: *Solomon: Arrival of the Queen of Sheba*
(***) VAI Video VAI 69601
'*Historic Telecasts*', Volume 2 (1961): **Georg Szell**
MUSSORGSKY: *Prelude to Khovanshchina.* BEETHOVEN: *Symphony 5 in C min., Op. 67.* BERLIOZ: *Le Carnaval romain Overture, Op. 9*
(***) VAI Video VAI 69602
'*Historic Telecasts*', Volume 3 (1962): **Leopold Stokowski**
BACH, arr. Stokowski: *Toccata and Fugue in D min.* BRAHMS: *Variations on a Theme of Haydn (St Anthony chorale).* RIMSKY-KORSAKOV: *Capriccio espagnol, Op. 34*
(***) VAI Video VAI 69603
'*Historic Telecasts*', Volume 4 (1961): **Pierre Monteux**
BEETHOVEN: *Symphony 8 in F, Op. 93.* WAGNER: *Die Meistersinger: Prelude to Act III.* BERLIOZ: *Le Carnaval romain Overture, Op. 9*
(***) VAI Video VAI 69604

The above four videos are even more valuable than the wider but more piecemeal coverage of the '*Art of Conducting*', above. They offer us four great conductors at the height of their powers directing a great orchestra, and every performance is memorable. We even have a chance to compare Szell's and Monteux's interpretations of Berlioz's supreme orchestral masterpiece, *Le Carnaval romain*, Szell the more electrifying, Monteux the more colourful.

These telecasts are part of a series inaugurated in Chicago in 1951 (under Kubelik). But when Reiner took over the orchestra in 1953 the programmes were extended to 45 minutes, broadcast first on Sunday afternoons, and subsequently (in 1959) at 8 p.m. on Sunday evenings, with Deems Taylor as initial host. The list of guest conductors who joined the series is wide-reaching, including Barbirolli, Beecham, Copland, Hindemith, Martinon, Munch and Previn. Announcements and commentaries are omitted from the published videos and the music is presented without introductions.

It was right that Reiner should carry on the series, at a live concert in Symphony Hall in 1954. With the bold swathe of his strong, clear up-and-down beat, a serious mien, and frowning gaze, he establishes total control of the orchestra. Although the early recording quality brings the usual soundtrack discoloration of woodwind upper partials, with moments of distortion in the wide amplitude of string sound, the warmth of the playing projects readily, as does its spontaneous feeling (after the single hour-long run-through rehearsal, which was standard for the series).

It is a pity that no Richard Strauss was included, but the Beethoven performances generate enormous electricity. The camera-work is fairly primitive, and it is interesting that the producer misses the dominating role of the horns in the thrilling furioso close of the outer movements of the *Seventh Symphony* and focuses instead on the woodwind, whereas in *Egmont* the horn section is portrayed at the key moments. Reiner, stiff and unrelenting in manner throughout, permits himself a half smile to acknowledge the applause, and even gives the oboes a bow – after the Queen of Sheba has arrived and departed rather fiercely.

Szell's clear beat is hardly less concentrated, achieving extraordinary precision and powerful clipped rhythms in Beethoven's *Fifth*; but he uses his left hand much more subtly than Reiner. It is a great performance, creating and gathering intensity in a formidable progress to its gripping finale. The first-movement repeat is observed (as it is later by Monteux in the *Eighth*) and the strings flowingly decorate the main theme of the slow movement with appealing warmth. Before that comes the evocatively detailed Mussorgsky *Khovanshchina Prelude*, with the delectable Rimsky-Korsakov orchestration glowing in the coda, and the following Berlioz overture is quite riveting in its orchestral bravura, almost upstaging the symphony in sheer adrenalin.

Reiner, Monteux and Szell conduct from memory, but Stokowski uses scores throughout, even in his famous Bach arrangement. Here the remarkably imaginative orchestration is made to seem the more vivid by camera close-ups, which even feature the glockenspiel and show the great horn entry at the climax of the fugue, before the thrilling upward rushes of strings. Where his colleagues favour batons, Stokowski uses his ever-supple hands to shape the music. This means slightly less precision of ensemble in the Bach (where he is concerned with the range of sonority and colour) but not in the Brahms, a richly idiomatic account, in no way idiosyncratic, although the lyrical warmth of the string writing is brought out in the closing variations. Rimsky's *Capriccio* is then played with enormous virtuosity (especially at the close) and the camera relishes the opportunity to portray each of the orchestral soloists in turn. As with the Szell concert, this is a studio recording, with a much drier acoustic, but the middle strings still glow as Stokowski coaxes their phrasing affectionately.

For the Monteux concert we return to Symphony Hall, with an audience, and this tape offers the best sound of the four – warm and well-detailed. Monteux's dapper, genial manner is deceptive, yet it brings the most relaxed atmosphere of all and at one endearing moment the camera catches one of the violin players on the back desks turning to his companion and smiling. The performance of Beethoven's *Eighth* is superb, polished, wonderfully detailed, and with a perfectly judged forward flow. When Monteux wants to be forceful he clenches his left fist, and the result catches the music's full intensity without fierceness. The glorious horn playing (on which the camera dwells indulgently) gives great warmth and nobility to the following Wagner *Prelude*, and the Berlioz overture ends the programme with a fizzing burst of energy at its very close.

Historic Telecasts', Volume 5 (1963): **Charles Munch**
RAMEAU/D'INDY: *Dardanus Suite.* BERLIOZ: *Les Troyens: Royal Hunt and Storm.* RAVEL: *Valses nobles et sentimentales; La Valse*
***) VAI Video VAI 69605

Historic Telecasts', Volume 6 (1963): **Paul Hindemith**
HINDEMITH: *Concert Music for Strings and Brass.*
BRUCKNER: *Symphony 7: first movement* (only). BRAHMS: *Academic Festival Overture*
⊕ (***) VAI Video VAI 69606

Historic Telecasts', Volume 7 (1961): **George Szell**
MOZART: *Overture: Le nozze di Figaro; Violin Concerto 5 in A (Turkish), K.219* (with Erica Morini). BEETHOVEN: *Overture: Leonora 3*
***) VAI Video VAI 69607

This second batch of videos includes the most valuable of all, a video of Paul Hindemith conducting 'live' in Chicago's Orchestra Hall, where understandably the privileged audience give him a hero's welcome. With his lips pursed seriously throughout, and using a clear, purposeful stick technique, he directs an electrifying account of his own *Concert Music for Strings and Brass*, with the Chicago strings and brass responding with the most glorious sounds. One might even use the adjective voluptuous in relation to the strings, except that, rich though the textures are, Hindemith's lyricism remains sinewy – for that is its strength. The fugato (nicely observed by the camera) also has splendid bite. He also conducts a superbly paced account of the first movement of Bruckner's *Seventh*, full of humanity. This follows a brief filmed interview when he is suitably articulate on the music's universality to a not very imaginative TV interviewer. The closing overture, spacious and exciting, is richly Brahmsian. The sound really is remarkably good.

By the side of this, Munch's concert is just a shade disappointing. The Rameau/D'Indy suite is elegant enough, but, lacking the incandescence of a Beecham touch, sounds anachronistic, and the *Royal Hunt and Storm*, beautifully played as it is, takes a little while to warm up. However, the climax when it comes does not disappoint (with the camerawork among the brass adding a great deal to the visual effect), and the closing horn solo is poetically atmospheric. The Ravel performances are warmly idiomatic, but here the sound lacks enough transparency to bring out the lustrous detail.

Szell, after a brilliant, if ungenial *Nozze di Figaro Overture*, has the advantage of a very stylish soloist, Erica Morini, in Mozart's most popular violin concerto. She plays with beautiful tone, splendid assurance and a disarming simplicity of line, and only the three cadenzas (rather too much of a good

thing) give any cause for criticism. *Leonora 3* makes a meticulously detailed but exciting finale. Good sound, with the solo violin well caught, although balanced very forwardly.

Chicago Symphony Orchestra, Daniel Barenboim or Pierre Boulez

'Musik Triennale Cologne 2000'

DVD 1 (cond. Pierre Boulez): BERG: *Lulu Suite.* DEBUSSY: *Le jeu d'eau; 3 Ballades de François Villon* (with Christine Schäfer). STRAVINSKY: *The Firebird* (ballet; complete)
*** TDK **DVD** DV-MTKBO

DVD 2 (cond. Daniel Barenboim). BOULEZ: *Notations I–IV.* CARLI: *El firulete.* DEBUSSY: *La Mer.* FALLA: *El sombrero de tres picos (The Three-cornered Hat)* (ballet; complete; with Elisabete Matos)
*** TDK **DVD** DV-MTKBA

In April 2000 the Chicago Symphony Orchestra visited the Cologne Triennial Music Festival of 20th-century Music, with these two concerts conducted respectively by Pierre Boulez and Daniel Barenboim. On each DVD comes a ten-minute excerpt, one following from the other, of a conversation between the two conductors, both of them worthwhile supplements. The music-making in both concerts is persuasive, brilliant and warm, the more compelling when seen as well as heard.

It is Barenboim who conducts the Boulez work, the one example of music from after the Second World War. Not that these four *Notations* are typical of Boulez when they are basically orchestrations, made in maturity with revisions and development, of early piano pieces he wrote as a student of René Leibowitz. The first, with its evocative orchestral writing, here sumptuously performed, has one thinking of Debussy, while the energetic fourth piece brings echoes of *The Rite of Spring*, with Barenboim momentarily echoing Boulez's crisp 'tic-tac' style of conducting. The Barenboim programme then goes on to a sensuous account of Debussy's *La Mer* and a vigorously dramatic one of the complete Falla ballet, with the Chicago players warmly idiomatic in the Spanish dance-rhythms. Elisabete Matos is the fine mezzo soloist in the vocal introduction, with the members of the orchestra enthusiastically clapping and shouting '*Ole!*' They equally let their hair down when, at the end of the concert, Barenboim concedes an encore, a jolly dance by José Carli, *El firulete*, a frill or bit of nonsense.

The Boulez offering is even more striking, when Christine Schäfer is such an inspired soloist both in Berg's *Lulu Suite* and in the Debussy songs with orchestral accompaniment. Schäfer not only sings Lulu's Song in the second movement but the lament of Countess Geschwitz after Lulu's murder in the final movement, though she does not attempt a scream at the moment prescribed. When heard live, Schäfer's voice may seem relatively small, but as balanced here it is full, firm and sensous, ideal both for Berg in such a warm performance and for Debussy in the subtleties of the *Villon* songs with their echoes of early music. A pity though that the camera often takes you so close to her you practically see down to her tonsils. The orchestral sound is full-bodied on both discs, with solo instruments brought forward in reflection of the camera-work. An auspicious introduction to twentieth-century music on DVD.

Chicago Symphony Orchestra, Sir Thomas Beecham

HAYDN: *Symphony 102 in B flat.* MOZART: *Symphony 38 in D (Prague), K.504*
** NCV Arts Video 8573 84095-3

DELIUS: *Florida Suite: By the River.* HANDEL, arr.
BEECHAM: *Love in Bath* (Suite). MENDELSSOHN: *Hebrides Overture.* SAINT-SAENS: *Le Rouet d'Omphale*
** NCV Arts Video 8573 84096-3

Beecham is not generously represented on film, and these performances given in Chicago in March 1960 are the only colour images to survive. The colour is admittedly not very good; nor, for that matter, is the sound. Moreover, the dynamic range is not as wide as we are accustomed to in Beecham's commercial recordings, so the rapt magical *pianissimo* tone is less in evidence. Of course, there are moments when the Beecham magic works, but they surface only intermittently. The camera-work is rather stiff and wooden, with none of the flexibility you would expect from a BBC telecast of the period. We often focus on lines of string players, and Beecham himself gets far less attention from the camera than one might expect. Recommended, then, but with only modified rapture.

Chicago Symphony Orchestra, Carlo Giulini

'The Chicago Recordings': MAHLER: *Symphony 1 in D.*
BERLIOZ: *Roméo et Juliette, Op. 17:* orchestral music.
BEETHOVEN: *Symphony 7 in A, Op. 92.* BRUCKNER:
Symphony 9 in D min. BRAHMS: *Symphony 4 in E min., Op. 98.* STRAVINSKY: *Firebird Suite* (1919); *Petrushka Suite* (1947)
(M) *** EMI 5 85974-2 (4)

To mark the great Italian conductor's ninetieth birthday EMI have collected the recordings he made with the Chicago Symphony Orchestra in 1969–71 (save for the Bruckner *Symphony*, which comes from 1976). They have been out of circulation since the days of LP, apart from the Beethoven and Bruckner symphonies, which have briefly appeared on CD. They are all performances of some stature, in particular the collection of orchestral excerpts from *Romeo and Juliet*, which alone is worth the price of the set. This is playing of rapt poetic feeling and intensity, which shows the Chicago orchestra at its very finest. The Bruckner *Ninth*, too, is very fine and arguably more spontaneous than the later, DG account with the Vienna Philharmonic, though the orchestral playing was particularly sumptuous. The sound in most of these recordings is very vivid and truthfully balanced, though we regret that EMI have split the Berlioz over two discs, though that matters less perhaps than putting the first movement of the Brahms on disc 3 and the rest on disc 4. Never mind, these are very impressive performances and it is good to have them all back.

Chicago Symphony Orchestra, Rafael Kubelík

MOZART: *Symphony 38 (Prague) in D, K.504.* DVORAK:
Symphony 9 in E min. (From the New World), Op. 95.
SMETANA: *Ma Vlast.* MUSSORGSKY: *Pictures at an*

Exhibition. BARTOK: *The Miraculous Mandarin: Suite; Music for Strings, Percussion & Celesta.* HINDEMITH:
Symphonic Metamorphosis on Themes by Carl Maria von Webber. SCHOENBERG: *5 Pieces for Orchestra, Op. 16.*
KODALY: *Peacock Variations*
(M) (**) Mercury stereo/mono 475 6862 (4)

Kubelik's 1951 mono version of Ravel's masterly scoring of Mussorgsky's *Pictures at an Exhibition* was the Mercury recording which coined the term 'Living Presence'. The realism of the recording (in spite of some thinness in the top range of the strings) still has the power to astonish; it conveys much of the splendid acoustic of Chicago's Symphony Hall. The performance has great freshness, with not a hint of any routine anywhere; there are many subtleties, particularly as one picture or promenade is dovetailed into the next. The *New World Symphony*, also from 1951, was almost as celebrated as the *Pictures.* The Chicago orchestra are kept constantly on their toes. There is no first-movement exposition repeat, but the *Largo* is played most beautifully, with the one proviso that the cor anglais soloist is not ripe-toned and comes across as a rather nervous vibrato. The sparkling Scherzo, crisply rhythmic and full of idiomatic character, then leads to a thrilling finale, where the tension is held at the highest level until the very last bar. Here the sound, hitherto remarkably good for its age, tends to become a bit shrill. The 1953 account of the *Prague Symphony* is splendid: the outer movements are alert and sparkling, and the *Andante* is ideally paced, gracefully and beautifully placed. The effect is undoubtedly refreshing; the ambience of Chicago's Symphony Hall adds warmth, and the only snag is the consistent edge imparted by the single Telefunken microphone to the violin timbre. This poses a far more serious problem in the Bartók items, and the *Miraculous Mandarin* really does require a degree of tolerance, being very strident and lacking body in its CD incarnation – a pity, as the performance is superbly exciting. Famous too in its day was the LP of Hindemith, Schoenberg and Kodály, and while the performances remain compelling, the fiercely bright mono sound does take some getting used to.

Chicago Symphony Orchestra, Frederick Stock

WAGNER: *Die Meistersinger Overture.* BRAHMS: *Hungarian Dances 17-21.* GOLDMARK: *In the Springtime Overture.* SUK:
Fairy-Tales: Folkdance (polka). GLAZUNOV: *Les Ruses d'amour: Introduction and Waltz.* TCHAIKOVSKY:
Symphony 5 in E min. PAGANINI: *Moto perpetuo, Op. 11* (orch. Stock). WALTON: *Scapino: Comedy Overture.*
DOHNANYI: *Suite for Orchestra, Op. 19.* R. STRAUSS: *Also sprach Zarathustra.* STOCK: *Symphonic Waltz. Op. 8*
⚫ (M) (***) Biddulph mono WHL 021/22

Frederick Stock, born in Germany in 1872, studied composition and violin at the Cologne Conservatoire; among his teachers was Humperdinck, and Mengelberg was a fellow student. He began his career as an orchestral violinist, and in 1895 he emigrated to America to join the ranks of the Chicago Symphony as a viola player. The orchestra was then four years old. In 1905 he was hired on a temporary basis as its musical director; but he stayed on for nearly forty years until he died in October 1942.

He built the orchestra into the splendid ensemble which Fritz Reiner was eventually to inherit and established its world reputation, especially for its brass playing, although (on the evidence of these recordings) the strings were equally impressive. Like Reiner, he had the advantage of the marvellous acoustics of Chicago's Symphony Hall in which to make his records, which, alongside Stokowski's Philadelphia recordings, are technically among the finest to come out of America in the late 1920s.

Indeed, the sound in Tchaikovsky's *Fifth* (1927) is so warm and full-bodied that in no time at all one forgets one is listening to an old recording and simply revels in the rich string patina and fine woodwind colours (heard at their best in the elegantly played waltz movement). The brass come fully into their own in the finale. Stock's interpretation is endearingly wilful, very like Mengelberg's more famous reading, which was made only six months later. Stock pulls back at the entry of the secondary group in the first movement. The effect is emphasized because of a side change but is consistent in the recapitulation. The slow movement is very much *con alcuna licenza* (Tchaikovsky's marking) and the horn soloist must have needed immense nerve to sustain his great solo at the chosen spacious tempo. But Stock has that supreme gift of being able to create the feeling of a live performance while making a recording, and this *Fifth*, for all its eccentricities, is very enjoyable. The finale has the traditional cut which was so often observed at that time, but the effect is seamless and the final brass peroration has only ever been topped by Stokowski's 78-r.p.m. Philadelphia set.

The programme opens with a thrillingly sonorous account of *Die Meistersinger Overture* (1926), with the tension held right to the end, in spite of the big rallentando at the majestic reprise of the introductory 'fanfare'. The Brahms dances, played with virtuosity and considerable panache, were recorded in 1925 but never issued, and both the Suk *Polka* (1926) and the charming Glazunov *Waltz* (1929) show the colourful palette of Stock's Chicago woodwind section, while Goldmark's *In the Springtime Overture* sounds uncommonly fresh in this early (1925) performance. The Dohnányi suite too (1928) is stylishly and pleasingly done, with nice touches of wit and plenty of lilt in the waltz featured in the closing movement, where Stock handles the tempo changes with affectionate sophistication. But here for some reason the recording is very closely miked and dry; was it actually recorded in Symphony Hall, one wonders, for there is little ambient effect?

Stock's most famous record is of Walton's *Scapino Overture*, which he commissioned for the orchestra's fiftieth-anniversary celebrations. It is played here with fizzing virtuosity and much élan and is particularly valuable in being the only existing recording of Walton's original score before the composer made his revisions. This and an equally brilliant account of Paganini's *Moto perpetuo*, deftly played in unison by the orchestral violins, were recorded in 1941, the sound brightly lit (the violins are closely miked in the Paganini) but retaining underlying warmth.

The set ends appropriately with a work indelibly associated with Chicago because of Reiner's superb, later, stereo version: Strauss's *Also sprach Zarathustra*. But Stock's account certainly does not come under its shadow. The spectacular opening is remarkably well caught and the passion of the violins is thrilling. This was made in 1940, and here the Columbia engineers made a compromise between brilliance and richness of timbre, with the hall ambience adding a natural breadth. The range of dynamic is striking, and Stock's reading must be placed among the finest, for it is seemingly completely spontaneous, yet splendidly controlled and shaped. The orchestral concentration is held at the highest level throughout, and particularly so during the darkly dormant section of the score on the lower strings associated with '*Science*' and the later passage on the high violins; Stock then follows with an exciting accelerando to reach the spectacular climax in '*The Convalescent*'. He maintains this thrust through to the closing pages, with the tolling bell coming through plangently, and the coda very touching. Then for an encore the conductor provides a charmingly tuneful *Symphonic Waltz* of his own composition, endearingly inflated but not boring when presented with such zest, and sumptuously recorded in 1930. Yet there is nothing 'historic' about live music-making of this calibre, and this fascinating set is very highly recommended. It certainly does Stock's reputation full justice.

(i) Chicago Symphony Orchestra, Frederick Stock; (ii) Cincinnati SO, Eugene Goossens

'*English Music*': (i) BENJAMIN: *Overture to an Italian Comedy*. ELGAR: *Pomp and Circumstance March 1*. (ii) VAUGHAN WILLIAMS: *A London Symphony* (No. 2; original version); WALTON: *Violin Concerto* (with Jascha Heifetz (violin))

(***) Biddulph mono WHL 016

This superbly transferred Biddulph issue celebrates the fact that some of the very finest recordings of British music have come from America. Heifetz's historic first recording of the Walton *Violin Concerto* is imaginatively coupled with the pioneering recording (also by Goossens and the Cincinnati orchestra, immediately following the Walton sessions in 1941) of the 1920 version of Vaughan Williams's *London Symphony*. As welcome fill-ups come Elgar's *Pomp and Circumstance 1* and Arthur Benjamin's *Overture to an Italian Comedy*, brilliantly played by the Chicago orchestra under Frederick Stock.

Chung, Kyung Wha (violin)

'*The Great Violin Concertos*': MENDELSSOHN: *Concerto in E min., Op. 64* (with Montreal SO, Dutoit). BEETHOVEN: *Concerto in D, Op. 61* (with VPO, Kondrashin). TCHAIKOVSKY: *Concerto in D, Op. 35*. SIBELIUS: *Concerto in D min., Op. 47* (both with LSO, Previn)

(B) **(*) Double Decca ADD/DDD 452 325-2 (2)

This Double Decca begs comparison with Grumiaux's Philips Duo, called, more sensibly, '*Favourite Violin Concertos*' (see below). Grumiaux offers Brahms instead of Sibelius and concentrates on repertoire in which his refined, poetic style produces satisfying results in all four works. Chung only scores three out of four. Her collection is let down by the 1979 account of the Beethoven which, measured and thoughtful, lacks the compulsion one would have predicted, due largely to the often prosaic conducting of Kondrashin. There is poetry in individual movements – the minor-key episode of the finale, for example, which alone justifies the unusually slow tempo – but, with too little of the soloist's natural electricity conveyed and none of her volatile imagination, it must be counted a disappointment, despite the first-class digital sound.

The Mendelssohn, made two years later, could not be more different. Chung favours speeds faster than usual in all three movements and the result is sparkling and happy, with the lovely slow movement fresh and songful, not at all sentimental. With warmly sympathetic accompaniment from Dutoit and the Montreal orchestra, amply recorded, the result was one of her happiest recordings.

The Sibelius/Tchaikovsky pairing (from 1970) is highly praised in our main volume. She brings an equally sympathetic and idiomatic response to both concertos, and Previn's accompaniments are of the highest order. The latter is a much better investment than the latest format, unless the Mendelssohn is essential.

Cincinnati Pops Orchestra, Erich Kunzel

'Favourite Overtures': SUPPE: Light Cavalry; Poet and Peasant. AUBER: Fra Diavolo. HEROLD: Zampa. REZNICEK: Donna Diana. OFFENBACH: Orpheus in the Underworld. ROSSINI: William Tell

*** Telarc CD 80116

In this spectacularly recorded (1985) collection of favourite bandstand overtures the playing has fine exuberance and gusto (only the galop from William Tell could perhaps have had greater impetus) and the resonant ambience of Cincinnati's Music Hall lends itself to Telarc's wide-ranging engineering, with the bass drum nicely caught. Perhaps the opening of Fra Diavolo would have benefited from a more transparent sound, but for the most part the opulence suits the vigorous style of the music-making, with Zampa and the Suppé overtures particularly successful.

'Pomp and Pizazz': J. WILLIAMS: Olympic Fanfare. SUK: Towards a New Life. ELGAR: Pomp and Circumstance March 1. IRELAND: Epic March. TCHAIKOVSKY: Coronation March. BERLIOZ: Damnation de Faust: Hungarian March. J. F. WAGNER: Under the Double Eagle. FUCIK: Entry of the Gladiators. SOUSA: The Stars and Stripes Forever. HAYMAN: March Medley

*** Telarc CD 80122

As enjoyable a march collection as any available, with characteristically spectacular and naturally balanced Telarc recording, with its crisp transients and wide amplitude. The performances have comparable flair and sparkle. The inclusion of John Ireland's comparatively restrained Epic March and the Tchaikovsky Coronation March, with its piquant trio and characteristic references to the Tsarist national anthem, makes for attractive contrast, while the Hayman medley (including Strike up the Band, 76 Trombones, South Rampart Street Parade and When the Saints go Marching in) makes an exuberant, peppy closing section. By comparison the Berlioz Rákóczy March is quite dignified. The sound is in the demonstration class. Most entertaining.

'Symphonic Spectacular': SHOSTAKOVICH: Festival Overture, Op. 96. WAGNER: Die Walküre: Ride of the Valkyries. FALLA: El amor brujo: Ritual Fire Dance. BIZET: L'Arlésienne: Farandole. JARNEFELT: Praeludium. CHABRIER: España. TCHAIKOVSKY: Marche slave, Op. 31. HALVORSEN: Entry of the Boyars. ENESCU: Romanian Rhapsody 1, Op. 11. KHACHATURIAN: Gayaneh: Sabre Dance (M) *** Telarc CD 80170

With spectacular recording, well up to Telarc's best standards, this is a highly attractive collection of orchestral lollipops.

Everything is played with the special flair which this orchestra and conductor have made their own in this kind of repertoire. Most entertaining, and technically of demonstration standard.

'The Fantastic Leopold Stokowski' (transcriptions for orchestra): BACH: Toccata & Fugue in D min., BWV 565; Little Fugue in G min., BWV 578. BOCCHERINI: Quintet in E flat: Minuet. BEETHOVEN: Moonlight Sonata: adagio sostenuto. BRAHMS: Hungarian Dance 6. DEBUSSY: Suite bergamasque: Clair de lune; Prélude: La Cathédrale engloutie. ALBENIZ: Fête-Dieu à Seville. RACHMANINOV: Prelude in C sharp min., Op. 3/2. MUSSORGSKY: Night on the Bare Mountain; Pictures at an Exhibition: The Great Gate of Kiev

✹ (M) *** Telarc CD-80338

Stokowski began his conducting career in Cincinnati in 1909, moving on to Philadelphia three years later; so a collection of his orchestral transcriptions from his first orchestra is appropriate, particularly when the playing is so committed and polished and the recording so sumptuous. Indeed, none of Stokowski's own recordings can match this Telarc disc in sheer glamour of sound. The arrangement of La Cathédrale engloutie is very free and melodramatically telling. Most interesting is Night on the Bare Mountain, which has a grandiloquent brass chorale added as a coda. Any admirer of Stokowski should regard this superbly engineered CD as an essential purchase. It is now reissued with two extra items added, the Brahms Hungarian Dance No. 6 and Stokowski's extraordinary transcription of The Great Gate of Kiev from Mussorgsky's Pictures at an Exhibition. Kunzel has the advantage of Telarc's bass-drum recording, and at the very close there is a highly imaginative added touch as the old magician introduces an evocation of Moscow cathedral bells.

City of Prague Philharmonic Orchestra, Gavin Sutherland

'Carry On Album: Music from the Films': Carry on Camping; Carry on Suite (music from Carry on Sergeant, Teacher and Nurse); Carry on Cabby; Carry on Cleo; Carry on Jack; Carry on Behind; Raising the Wind; Carry on at Your Convenience; Carry on Up the Khyber; Carry on Doctor Again

(M) *** ASV CDWHL 2119

Some readers may raise a quizzical eyebrow at the inclusion of this collection, for the famous 'Carry On' series of films is the epitome of British vulgarity. Yet their incidental music shows the British light-music tradition at its best. The early scores were written by Bruce Montgomery (Carry on Teacher, Nurse, Cabby, etc.) where a flavour of the late 1950s is evoked: the main 'Carry On' theme is unashamedly jazzy, yet has a central counter-theme which is delightfully nostalgic and totally British. For the later films, Eric Rogers took over – he peppered the films with quotes from famous classical pieces, whilst his own melodies are distinctly appealing, reflecting the 'swinging sixties'. The Carry on Camping and Carry on Doctor suites are perhaps the best, not just for their vivaciousness, but also for the remarkably piquant and deft orchestration throughout. Carry on at Your Convenience evokes the production line of a toilet-bowl factory, and the Prague orchestra respond with enthusiasm (the timpani are especially impressive); then there is an unexpectedly charming romantic passage which is quite touching, before the riotous ending. The imperial opening music of *Carry on Up the Khyber* (perhaps the wittiest of the series) is strongly characterized, and the *Carry on Cleo* suite, with a Hollywood-style opening march à la Rozsa, is also effective. Altogether the invention is surprisingly varied. The orchestra perform as though they have played it all their lives, no doubt a tribute to the conductor, Gavin Sutherland, and the producer, Philip Lane. The recording is also superb. Thoroughly recommended for those on the 'Carry On' wavelength, and for other lovers of this musical genre who are simply curious.

'British by Arrangement': TCHAIKOVSKY: *Beatlecracker Suite* (arr. Wilkinson). BORODIN: *Nocturne* (arr. Sargent). GRAY: *The African Queen: Suite* (arr. Lane). LANE: *Mendelssohniana.* PRAETORIUS: *Dances from Terpsichore* (arr. Lane). DONIZETTI: *Donizetti Variations* (arr. Irving)
(M) ** ASV WHL 2142

The Beatlecracker Suite is an ingenious – if curious – working of Beatles' themes in the style of Tchaikovsky. It was written at the suggestion of the ballet star, Doreen Wells, for her personal use and is recorded here in its expanded eight-movement form. Whatever one thinks of the result, it is cleverly done, a homage to both Tchaikovsky and the Beatles. Philip Lane's *Mendelssohniana* for strings (based on his *Children's Pieces*) is distinctly attractive, as is his colourful arrangement of Praetorius's *Dances from Terpsichore*, which is audaciously un-period in style. Allan Gray's amalgam of romantic themes from the film *The African Queen* makes another unexpected item, though here the high strings sound pinched and under-nourished at times; and a similar problem affects the lovely Borodin *Nocturne*. Donizetti wrote much jolly and vivacious ballet music, and this suite, the *Donizetti Variations*, as arranged by Robert Irving, is certainly enjoyable, even if the performance lacks the brilliance of Antonio de Almeida's Philips recording with the Philharmonia Orchestra (now on a bargain Duo release). Good performances and recording, as one expects from this source, but the exposed strings do sound uncomfortable from time to time.

'British Light Music Discoveries', Vol. 5: HOPE: *Kaleidoscope.* FOX: *A Pastoral Reflection.* LEWIS: *Inauguration.* LYON: *Adagio Serioso; Rondoletta.* DOUGLAS: *Music for Strings.* G. SUTHERLAND: *Capriol Overture.* HANDEL (arr. BARBIROLLI): *Clarinet Concerto.* TOYE: *The Haunted Ballroom: Waltz.* PITFIELD: *Overture on North-Country Tunes*
(M) **(*) ASV WHL 2144

Peter Hope's colourful *Kaleidoscope* is aptly described by Philip Lane, the disc's producer, as 'a mini-concerto for orchestra', and this disc offers a varied programme of mainly rare items. It is good that we can hear something of Gavin Sutherland's own compositions, with his tunefully attractive *Capriol Overture* of 2001. John Fox's *Pastoral Reflection* and David Lyon's *Adagio Serioso* offer a quiet nostalgia, though the latter's *Rondoletta* is a contrasting bright and perky number. Entertaining, too, is Barbirolli's arrangement of Handel to form this clarinet concerto, originally written for oboe. Of the other works, Thomas Pitfield's *Overture on North-Country Tunes* offers some familiar, attractively scored folk tunes; Paul Lewis's *Inauguration* is suitably festive, but with more reflective interludes; while Brian Douglas's *Music for Strings* is more unusual in drawing its influences from Elizabethan church music. Geoffrey Toye's lovely *Haunted*

Ballroom Waltz is hardly a rarity, but its inclusion here is a highlight. Excellent performances and recording, but with the violins sounding a bit taxed in the upper registers under pressure.

City of Prague Philharmonic Orchestra, with (i) Gavin Sutherland or (ii) Christopher Phelps

'Entente Cordiale': (i) WARLOCK: *Capriol Suite* (orchestral version). SMYTH: *Two Interlinked French Melodies.* HOPE: *4 French Dances.* JONGEN: *2 Pieces, Op. 53a.* LECOCQ: *The Lady and the Maid: Overture.* LEWIS: *A Paris.* GABRIEL-MARIE: *Mireio (Suite Provençale).* (ii) FRANCK: *Choral 2 in B min.* (orch. Phelps)
(M) *** ASV CD WHL 2147

A typically felicitous programme from ASV, opening with a robust performance of Warlock's splendid *Capriol Suite*, in full orchestral dress. Peter Hope's *Four French Dances* similarly employ ancient dance-metres, dressed up in modern orchestrations. Jean Gabriel-Marie's *Mireio*, incidental music written in 1930 for an adaptation of a poem by Paul Giran (which also was the basis of Gounod's *Mireille*), is all prettily rustic-sounding, slight but undeniably charming. The *Lady and the Maid Overture* is not quite authentic Lecocq: it was put together by Havelock Nelson, using various scores found in Cramer's *Opéra-Comique Cabinet*, mainly using a work by Lecocq called *My New Maid*. It makes an enjoyable three minutes and sounds like a number left over from *La Fille de Madame Angot*. Dame Ethel Smyth's *Two Interlinked Melodies* feature genuine folk melodies: the first 'Melody' is a Burgundian vintage song, the second is Breton in origin, and they make for pleasing listening. Joseph Jongen's *Two Pieces* were originally organ works, somewhat impressionistic in style, and this is also true in their orchestral guise: the first, *Chant de mai*, is essentially a solo line with accompaniment, and has an appealingly quirky nature which is nicely contrasted with the more robust *Menuet-Scherzo*. By far the longest track on this disc (and rather more serious than the rest of the programme) is an arrangement of César Franck's organ *Choral 2 in B minor* for full orchestra. It is an excellent arrangement, with Christopher Phelps capturing the sound-world of Franck admirably, and is most enjoyable, especially for those who enjoy Stokowski-like transcriptions. The performances and recordings, while they do not have the last word in refinement, are still very good.

Cleveland Symphonic Winds, Fennell

'Stars and Stripes': ARNAUD: *3 Fanfares.* BARBER: *Commando March.* LEEMANS: *Belgian Paratroopers.* FUCIK: *Florentine March, Op. 214.* KING: *Barnum and Bailey's Favourite.* ZIMMERMAN: *Anchors aweigh.* J. STRAUSS SR: *Radetzky March.* VAUGHAN WILLIAMS: *Sea Songs; Folksongs Suite.* SOUSA: *The Stars and Stripes Forever.* GRAINGER: *Lincolnshire Posy*
*** Telarc CD 80099

This vintage collection from Frederick Fennell and his superb Cleveland wind and brass group is one of the finest of its kind ever made. Severance Ethel Hall, Cleveland, has ideal acoustics for this programme and the playing has wonderful virtuosity and panache. Add to all this digital engineering of Telarc's highest calibre, and you have a very special issue.

worth investigating and with an admirably annotated 150-page booklet in five languages.

(Royal) Concertgebouw Orchestra, Eduard van Beinum

'The Radio Recordings': ANDRIESSEN: Miroir de Peine (with Kolassi); Symphony 4. BACH: Cantata 56 (with Harrell); Clavier Concerto in D min., BWV 1052 (with Lipatti); Double Concerto in C min., BWV 1060 (with van Beinum, den Hertog). BADINGS: Cello Concerto 2 (with Leeuwen Boomkamp). BARTOK: Concerto for Orchestra. BEETHOVEN: Egmont Overture, Op. 84; Piano Concerto 3 in C min., Op. 37 (with Solomon); Violin Concerto in D, Op. 61 (with Francescatti). BRAHMS: Symphony 1 in C min., Op. 67. DEBUSSY: La Mer; Images pour orchestre; Printemps. DIEPENBROCK: Te Deum (with Spoorenberg, Merriman, Haefliger, Bogtman; Toonkunstkoor Amsterdam). ESCHER: Musique pour l'esprit en deuil. FRANCK: Psyché (excerpts); Symphonic Variations (with Hengeveld). HENKEMANS: Viola Concerto (with Boon). LISZT: Piano Concerto 2 in A (with Pembauer). RUDOLF MENGELBERG: Salve Regina (with van der Sluys). MOZART: Violin Concerto 4 in D, K.218 (with Menuhin). PIJPER: Symphony 3. RAVEL: Daphnis et Chloé: Suite 2; Piano Concerto in G (with de Groot). REGER: Eine Ballet Suite, Op. 130. RESPIGHI: Fountains of Rome. SCHOENBERG: 5 Orchestral Pieces, Op. 16. SCHUBERT: Der Hirt auf dem Felsen (with Vincent). STEPHAN: Musik für Geige und Orchester (with Kulenkampff). STRAVINSKY: Firebird Suite. TCHAIKOVSKY: Romeo and Juliet (Fantasy Overture); Symphony 4 in F min. VERDI: Don Carlos: Dormirò sol nel manto mio regal (with Christoff)

DVD: BEETHOVEN: Symphony 3 in E flat (Eroica).
(**(*)) One for You Q-Disc (mono) 97015 (11 CDs + 1 **DVD**)

Eduard van Beinum presided over the Concertgebouw Orchestra in the post-war years when Willem Mengelberg was in disgrace because of his collaboration with the Nazis. Van Beinum was a most civilized and selfless artist, who never enjoyed the renown of some of his contemporaries but who, like Sir Adrian Boult in England, put the cause of the composer above all else. Although the Dutton label has brought us transfers of the Symphonie fantastique, the Brahms First Symphony and his amazing Bartók Concerto for Orchestra, this 11-CD set enables a generation for whom he is only a name to assess the quality of his contribution to Dutch musical life. Enterprising collectors will welcome the opportunity of having such rarities as Willem Pijper's Third Symphony, the Fourth of Hendrik Andriessen and the Viola Concerto of Hans Henkemans, all of which are rewarding scores (neither the Pijper nor the Henkemans is otherwise available). Van Beinum was a conductor of classical instinct, whose performances are perfectly straight yet infused with poetic feeling. Of particular interest are the concerto appearances of Solomon and Dinu Lipatti and, in the Bach C minor Concerto for two pianos, van Beinum himself. What a fine Debussy conductor he was too. This valuable set also comes with a black-and-white DVD of the Eroica Symphony, gripping and exhilarating, recorded from a TV broadcast in May 1957, which gives a rare glimpse of his technique and mastery. Naturally, the quality of these radio recordings, which come from the late 1940s and early 1950s, is variable, although generally much better than you might reasonably expect. Well

(Royal) Concertgebouw Orchestra, Bruno Walter

MAHLER: Symphony 4 in G (with Schwarzkopf). BRAHMS: Symphony 4 in E min., Op. 98. MOZART: Symphony 40 in G min., K.550. R. STRAUSS: Don Juan
(**) Music & Arts mono CD 1090

Music & Arts offers the whole of a 1952 Bruno Walter/Concertgebouw concert with Elisabeth Schwarzkopf. Egon Wellesz, who often heard Mahler conducting in the first decade of the last century, spoke of the composer as having 'the fire and electricity of Toscanini and the warmth of Bruno Walter', and it was Walter he thought of as being, as it were, the keeper of the seal. Even now, when there is a superabundance of CDs of the Fourth Symphony, Walter's Mahler is still something special and carries an authenticity of feeling that comes across half a century. The sound is not up to the standard of commercial recordings of the 1950s but is perfectly adequate.

Concerto Copenhagen, Andrew Manze

'Swedish Rococo Concertos' (with soloists): AGRELL: Flute Concerto in B minor (with Bania); Oboe Concerto in B flat (with Henriksson). HEINRICH PHILIP JOHNSEN: Double Bassoon Concerto in F (with Klingfors & Beuse). FERDINAND ZELLBELL: Bassoon Concerto in A minor: Allegro (with Klingfors). Cello Concerto in D (with Åkerberg)
*** Musica Sveciae Dig. MSCD 411

These composers inhabit the outer fringes of the catalogue. None is represented by more than one work. Heinrich Philip Johnsen (1717–79) was born in northern Germany and came to Stockholm with his princely employer, Adolf Frederik of Holstein-Gottorp, who was elected to the Swedish throne. Johan Agrell (1701–65) was born in Sweden but spent the bulk of his life in Germany, and of the three only Ferdinand Zellbell (1719–80) was born, bred and died in Sweden.

With the exception of the Handelian Oboe Concerto of Agrell, all these pieces are in manuscript. The F major Concerto for Two Bassoons by Heinrich Philip Johnsen is rather delightful. It is fresh and entertaining, and played with polish and elegance. (Johnsen enjoys the distinction of having written an opera, The Bartered Bride.)

Zellbell was a pupil of Roman and went to Hamburg, where he studied with Telemann, and to Hanover, where in 1741 he composed this cello concerto. He spent the bulk of his life in Stockholm, where he succeeded to his father's position as organist of the Storkyrkan (cathedral) but he was unpaid for many years and died heavily in debt. The movement from his A minor Concerto is a witty piece, and the Cello Concerto is inventive and at times touching. Andrew Manze and the Concerto Copenhagen give first-class support to the talented soloists and the aural perspective is eminently truthful. Impeccable scholarly notes by Martin Tegén.

Crowther, Jill (oboe), English Northern Philharmonia, Alan Cuckson

'English Oboe Concertos': HURD: *Concerto da camera.* LEIGHTON: *Concerto, Op. 23.* BLEZARD: *2 Celtic Pieces.* GARDNER: *Concerto, Op. 193.* LANE: *3 Spanish Dances*
(M) *** ASV CDWHL 2130

A highly delectable collection of oboe concertos by 20th-century English composers, immediately inviting, full of melody, and diverse enough to make a stimulating concert. Jill Crowther, principal of the Royal Ballet Orchestra and subsequently of the RPO, is a highly sensitive artist with an agreeably succulent tone which she can fine down with the utmost delicacy, as in the solo filigree of the opening movement of the very striking Gardner *Concerto*, heard against a backcloth of dancing violins. Michael Hurd's *Concerto da camera* is romantically rich-textured, but its English pastoralism soon peeps through, and the syncopated finale is infectiously winning. Kenneth Leighton's work is altogether more searching (and affecting), with an unusual degree of angst for an oboe concerto. The elegiac slow movement has a bleak flavour of Shostakovich; however, the clouds lift for the finale. The two *Celtic Pieces* of William Blezard are hauntingly folksy, and Philip Lane's *Spanish Dances* close the concert in holiday mood by taking the listener into a diverting Mediterranean atmosphere. Excellent, spacious recording well balanced, although the high violins are not always in perfect focus.

Curzon, Clifford (piano)

Decca recordings, Volume 1: 1949–1964: BEETHOVEN: *Piano Concerto 5 (Emperor) in E flat, Op. 73* (with LPO, Szell). TCHAIKOVSKY: *Piano Concerto 1 in B flat min., Op. 23* (with New SO, Szell). SCHUBERT: *4 Impromptus, D.935; Piano Sonata 17 in D, D.850.* FRANCK: *Symphonic Variations.* LITOLFF: *Concerto Symphonique: Scherzo* (with LPO, Boult). FALLA: *Nights in the Gardens of Spain* (with New SO, Jorda). RAWSTHORNE: *Piano Concerto 2* (with LSO, Sargent). MOZART: *Piano Concertos 23 in A, K.488; 27 in B flat, K.595* (with VPO, Szell)
⊛ (B) *(**) Decca mono/stereo 473 116-2 (4)

The two volumes dedicated to Clifford Curzon in Decca's 'Original Masters' series are very special indeed. One must acknowledge Raymond McGill who, as Product Manager for the series, has ensured that all these boxes skilfully chosen repertoire to show Curzon at his most characteristic, including some rare performances. In this case, we have two magnificent Mozart *Piano Concertos*, K.488 and K.595, which have never been released before. Curzon was notoriously fussy – even neurotic – about what was released on LP, and if he felt they were not good enough, they could not be issued, however unreasonable their rejection seemed to be. But it really is hard to know why he withheld these two recordings. His playing is as stylish as ever, aristocratic and elegant, framed by Szell's alert and sympathetic accompaniments, more relaxed than one might expect from this conductor. The opening allegros are perfectly proportioned, full of little felicities which delight the ear, though never fussy in detail; the finale of K.595 has a wonderfully lilting quality, and the playing throughout sparkles.

It is as rare as it is rewarding to hear Curzon in twentieth-century repertoire, and the inclusion of Rawsthorne's vigorously inventive *Second Piano Concerto* is especially welcome. It was written for the Festival of Britain and recorded in 1951, and it is given a highly persuasive performance, with Curzon bringing out all the colour and vitality of the writing. The sound is vivid for its period, too. Other classic mono recordings include the 1949 *Emperor Concerto* where, bar the odd bit of distortion, the sound is good, with the performance more fiery under Szell than in Curzon's later, stereo account with the magisterial Knappertsbusch. The Tchaikovsky concerto with Szell is also arguably more successful than the later, stereo version with Solti – fine though that is – in as much as soloist and conductor are seemingly more in tune with one other here, and the sound is again excellent for its vintage (1950). In the *Nights in the Gardens of Spain*, Curzon excels with his ability to change in a flash from the flamboyant to the introspective. This dates from a year later and, with bright mono sound – full of colour and atmosphere – it makes a welcome return to the catalogue, as do the poised, masterly accounts of the Schubert *Impromptus* (1952), recorded in a studio-ish acoustic but with reasonably full sound. Back in stereo, we have a glittering account of the Litolff *Scherzo*, Franck's *Symphonic Variations* – still among the best versions available – and a spontaneously relaxed account of Schubert's *D major Sonata*, D.850 – all classics of the gramophone.

Decca recordings, Volume 2: 1941–1972: SCHUBERT: *4 Impromptus, D.899; Piano Sonata 21 in B flat, D.960.* MOZART: *Piano Concertos 23 in A, K.488; 24 in C min., K.491* (with LSO, Josef Krips). BRAHMS: *Piano Concerto 1 in D min., Op. 15* (with Concg. O, Eduard van Beinum). *Piano Sonata 3 in F min., Op. 5; Intermezzi: in E flat, Op. 117/1; in C, Op. 119/3.* GRIEG: *Piano Concerto in A min., Op. 16* (with LSO, Anatole Fistoulari). DVORAK: *Piano Quintet in A, Op. 8.* FRANCK: *Piano Quintet in F min.* (with V. Philharmonic Qt)
⊖ ⊛ (M) *** Decca mono/stereo (ADD) 475 084-2 (4)

This treasurable second anthology, which won the *Gramophone* 'Historical Instrumental Award' in 2003, surveys some of the very finest of Clifford Curzon's recordings for Decca made over three decades, including the early Schubert *Impromptus* (1941) and the remarkably beautiful performances of the two Mozart *Piano Concertos* (1953) with Josef Krips. Curzon was to record them again later in stereo, but the *C minor* (No. 24) in particular, with its exquisite *Larghetto*, remains very special. It appears here in its first international CD release.

Curzon was also to record the Brahms and Grieg *Concertos* again in stereo, the Brahms famously with Szell in 1962. But the earlier account with Van Beinum is no less fine, if different in character, less pungently arresting, more warmly relaxed, the music's nobility brought out, especially in the slow movement. With the Grieg, Fistoulari proved a volatile partner, and again the slow movement is memorable, although in this instance the later, stereo version with Fjelstad brought a specially idiomatic character to the orchestral playing. Both these earlier performances (from 1951) are also appearing on CD for the first time.

In chamber music Curzon's playing was no less magnetic, and the stereo coupling of the utterly seductive Dvořák and Franck *Piano Quintets* was another landmark; the stereo recordings, made in the Sofiensaal (in the early 1960s), still sound very impressive.

But it is the Brahms and Schubert *Sonatas* that sum up

perfectly all that is uniquely cherishable in Curzon's art. The playing has great humanity and freshness. Both interpretations are wonderfully sensitive and totally spontaneous-sounding; yet in the Brahms, despite the underlying intensity, nothing is overstated, and in the Schubert, (as with the *Impromptus*) detail is finely drawn but never emphasized at the expense of the architecture as a whole. The stereo recording too is first class and balanced most naturally. A set (described as a Limited Edition) which is not to be missed.

Czech Philharmonic Orchestra, Gerd Albrecht

HAAS: *Studies for String Orchestra*. SCHULHOF: *Symphony 2*. ULLMANN: *Symphony 2*. KLEIN: *Partita for Strings*
*** Orfeo C 337941 A

Like the issues in Decca's *Entartete Musik* series, this Orfeo disc features music dismissed by the Nazis as decadent, all here by Jewish composers from Czechoslovakia slaughtered in the Holocaust. Pavel Haas, often counted as Janáček's most important pupil, wrote his *Studies* in Theresienstadt, the prison camp where the Nazis assembled Jewish intellectuals, later to be killed in death camps. Tautly argued in four sections lasting eight minutes, it was given its first performance in the camp under one of the then inmates who happily managed to survive, Karel Ančerl, later the conductor of the Czech Philharmonic. Albrecht and today's Czech Philharmonic bring out the vitality of the writing, with no hint in it of self-indulgence or self-pity. This is a composer writing in sight of death simply because he has to, relishing a last opportunity.

The *Symphony No. 2* of Erwin Schulhof was written in 1932, long before the Germans invaded Czechoslovakia, a work very much of its period with a charming *Scherzo alla Jazz* influenced by Stravinsky's *Soldier's Tale*. The *Symphony 2* of Viktor Ullmann, also in four crisp movements, was one of no fewer than twenty-five works that he wrote in Theresienstadt, including the opera *The Emperor of Atlantis*, also on disc. Though he was a pupil of Schoenberg, he here returned to tonality, communicating directly.

The youngest of the four, Gideon Klein from Moravia, more specifically drew inspiration from folk roots, very much in the way that Bartók did in Hungary. His *Partita for Strings*, like the Pavel Haas *Studies*, has darkness in it, notably in the central variation movement, but here too the piece culminates in a mood of energetic optimism, a heart-warming expression of defiance. Very well played and recorded, the four works are the more moving for giving only momentary hints of what the composers were going through. First-rate sound.

Czech Philharmonic Orchestra, Karel Ančerl

'*Celebrated Overtures*': SHOSTAKOVICH: *Festive Overture, Op. 96*. MOZART: *Die Zauberflöte*. BEETHOVEN: *Leonora 3*. WAGNER: *Lohengrin: Prelude to Act I*. SMETANA: *The Bartered Bride*. GLINKA: *Ruslan and Ludmilla*. BERLIOZ: *Le Carnaval romain*. ROSSINI: *William Tell*. WEBER/BERLIOZ: *Invitation to the Dance*
(M) *** Sup. (ADD) SU 3689-2

Karel Ančerl and the Czech Philharmonic Orchestra have never sounded better on record than in this thrilling collection of overtures. Admirably played and recorded in the Prague Rudolfinum Dvořák Hall, in the early to mid-1960s, the recording is now so expertly transferred (by Stanislav Sýcora) to CD that the sound at times reaches demonstration quality. The excessive resonance that had previously dogged Supraphon recordings is now controlled, yet the hall ambience remains. The witty Shostakovich *Festive Overture* sparkles irresistibly, followed by a crisply stylish *Zauberflöte* and a compulsive *Leonora 3*, where the allegro skips along unstoppably to reach a powerful climax at the coda. Not surprisingly, *The Bartered Bride* has a real Slavonic fizz: those stabbing string entries are superbly clear, and *Ruslan and Ludmilla* demonstrates similar virtuosic élan, yet with the lyricism nicely balanced. For some reason, one has to turn up the volume slightly for the virtuosic *Le Carnaval romain*, and then down a little for the superb *William Tell*, elegant at the opening, chirping merrily in the pastoral scene, and with barnstorming trombones at the close. Only the *Lohengrin Prelude* is a fraction below par, yet it is still well played and has a fine climax. The elegant Weber/Berlioz piece acts as a successful opening *Invitation* to the programme.

Daniel, Nicholas (oboe), Peterborough String Orchestra

'*Italian Oboe Concertos*': VIVALDI: *Concerto in C, RV 44*. ALBINONI: *Concerto in D min., Op. 9/2*. BELLINI: *Concertino in E flat*. MARCELLO: *Concerto in D min*. CIMAROSA: *Concerto in C* (arr. Arthur Benjamin)
(BB) **(*) Hyp. Helios CDH 55034

All the music here is tunefully undemanding, with the minor-key concertos adding a touch of expressive gravitas. Arthur Benjamin's arrangement of the charming Cimarosa concerto is always a delight, and the lovely Bellini *Concertino* sounds like one of his operatic arias arranged for oboe – complete with cabaletta finale. Nicholas Daniel is closely miked, but is a stylish performer and draws lively support from the Peterborough orchestra. The disc plays for just under 55 minutes, but is offered at budget price.

Danish State Radio Symphony Orchestra

'*75th Anniversary Concert*': BRAHMS: *Symphony 2* (cond. Busch). HAYDN: *Symphony 91 in E flat; 12 German Dances* (cond. Wöldike). BEETHOVEN: *Funeral March*. NIELSEN: *Overture Maskarade*. DEBUSSY: *Prélude à l'après-midi d'un faune*. SÆVERUD: *Galdreslåtten*. STRAVINSKY: *Suite 2* (cond. Malko). GLINKA: *Ruslan and Ludmilla: Overture* (cond. Dobrowen). LUMBYE: *Dream Pictures*. NIELSEN: *At the Bier of a Young Artist* (cond. Grøndahl). RIISAGER: *Trumpet Concertino* (with Eskdale; cond. Jensen). NIELSEN: *Little Suite for Strings* (cond. Tuxen). MOZART: *Divertimento 12 in E flat, K.252* (orchestral wind soloists)
● (B) (***) Dutton mono 2CDEA 5027 (2)

Issued to celebrate the splendid Danish orchestra's 75th anniversary, these excellent recordings, mainly from the late 1940s, demonstrate what a superb band had developed in Copenhagen during and just after the Second World War. The late 1940s and early 1950s were the heyday of the orchestra, and the acoustic of the Concert Hall of the Radio House was, before its later refurbishment, altogether superb, bright yet warm and full bodied.

Nikolai Malko's account of the Stravinsky *Suite 2* and Sæverud's *Galdreslåtten* were demonstration 78-r.p.m. discs in their day, and this early 1950s account of Brahms's *Second Symphony*, urgent and direct under Fritz Busch's direction, was a revelation (particularly its thrilling finale), at a time when choice was limited to Beecham, Weingartner or Stokowski. In his admirable note Lyndon Jenkins calls it 'civilized, exhilarating, yet full of humanity'. The sound, as transferred by Dutton, is still vivid, as it is in all these varied items.

Mogens Wöldike's wonderfully sprightly and stylish recording of Haydn's *Symphony 91 in E flat* is its first and arguably best recording, not even forgetting Jochum's glorious version with the Bavarian Radio Orchestra from 1958, while the little Riisager *Trumpet Concertino* is a delight, as is Nielsen's vigorous *Overture to Maskarade*. The *Deutsche Tänze* are absolutely captivating.

The *Funeral March* is, incidentally, a transcription and transposition Beethoven made of the first movement of the *Sonata in A flat*, Op. 26, for the play, *Leonora Prohaska*. As far as we know, neither the Haydn nor the Brahms symphonies was ever transferred to LP and make their first appearance since the 1950s. The same goes for most of the other material.

The original sound is so good that collectors will be amazed at its quality and presence. The transfers are really excellent with no trace of surface noise, although with a fractional loss of the body compared with the originals, which were probably bottom-heavy. A very special set, which for those who do not know these performances will bring unexpected musical rewards and which deserves the widest currency.

Davies, Philippa (flute), Thelma Owen (harp)

'The Romance of the Flute and Harp': HASSELMAN: *La Source, Op. 44; Feuilles d'automne.* GODARD: *Suite, Op. 16: Allegretto.* GODEFROID: *Etude de concert.* FAURE: *Berceuse, Op. 16; Impromptu, Op. 86.* DOPPLER: *Mazurka.* MENDELSSOHN: *Spring Song, Op. 62/3.* THOMAS: *Watching the Wheat.* SAINT-SAENS: *Carnival of the Animals: The Swan.* BIZET: *Fair Maid of Perth: Intermezzo.* PARISH-ALVARS: *Serenade.* DEBUSSY: *Syrinx; Suite bergamasque: Clair de lune*

(BB) *** Regis RRC 1085

An unexpectedly successful collection which effectively intersperses harp solos with music in which the flute takes the leading role. The playing is most sensitive and the recording is very realistic indeed. The programme, too, is well chosen and attractively laid out and is fairly generous in playing time (59 minutes). Highly recommended for a pleasant summer evening.

Detroit Symphony Orchestra, Neeme Järvi

'Favourite Encores': CHABRIER: *Fête polonaise.* GLINKA: *Kamarinskaya; Valse fantaisie.* SIBELIUS: *Andante festivo for Strings.* BOLZONI: *Minuet.* DVORAK: *Humoresque.* DARZINS: *Valse mélancolique.* ELLINGTON: *Solitude* (trans.

for strings). SHOSTAKOVICH: *The Gadfly: Romance.* MUSSORGSKY: *Gopak.* DEBUSSY: *Suite bergamasque: Clair de lune.* SCHUMANN: *Abendlied, Op. 107/6.* MEDINS: *Aria.* GERSHWIN: *Promenade: Walking the Dog.* SOUSA: *The Stars and Stripes Forever*

(M) **(*) Chan. 6648

The acoustics of Detroit's Orchestra Hall, made famous by the Mercury engineers at the end of the 1950s, remain impressive and the Detroit orchestra is flattered here by opulently glowing sound, which especially suits the Glinka pieces and the lovely Sibelius *Andante festivo*. The rest of the programme is rather slight, consisting entirely of lollipops, some well known, plus a few engaging novelties. All are presented with Järvi's customary flair and are very well played. If you enjoy this kind of concert, there is no need to hesitate, for the programme is generous at 73 minutes.

Detroit Symphony Orchestra, Paul Paray

'French Orchestral Music': SAINT-SAENS: *Symphony 3 in C min. (Organ); Samson and Delilah: Bacchanale.* PARAY: *Mass for the 500th Anniversary of the Death of Joan of Arc.* LALO: *Namouna: Suite 1; Le Roi d'Ys: Overture.* BARRAUD: *Offrande à une ombre.* CHAUSSON: *Symphony in B flat, Op. 20.* IBERT: *Escales.* RAVEL: *Alborada del gracioso; Pavane pour une Infante défunte; Rapsodie espagnole; Le Tombeau de Couperin; La Valse.* BIZET: *Carmen: Suite; L'Arlésienne: Suites 1 & 2.* THOMAS: *Mignon: Overture & Gavotte; Raymond: Overture.* HEROLD: *Zampa: Overture.* AUBER: *The Crown Diamonds: Overture.* GOUNOD: *Faust: ballet music.* BERLIOZ: *Royal Hunt and Storm.* MASSENET: *Phèdre: Overture*

✪ (B) *** Mercury (ADD) 475 6268 (5)

Paul Paray's style of conducting has virtually vanished today: it represents what is often referred to as the 'French style of conducting': clear, elegant, superbly balanced and – what will instantly strike listeners – often very fast. This repertoire shows the conductor at his best and includes many of his most famous recordings: the Chausson *Symphony* is thrilling in its drive, as is the *Organ Symphony* of Saint-Saëns, where the Mercury sound still amazes. The rhythmic point of the playing is a source of delight: try the strings after the opening of the *Raymond Overture* or in the *Mignon Minuet*; the playing throughout is consistently stylish and, in music such as the *Namouna Suite*, Paray brings out all colour and wit with delicious piquancy. The once-popular warhorses of *Zampa* and the *Crown Dimonds* (not to mention Lalo's striking *Le Roi d'Ys Overture*) make one lament their disappearance in concert halls, while Massenet's melodramatic overture, *Phèdre*, makes a welcome rarity. Rare, too, is Paray's enjoyable *Mass* and Barraud's effective *Offrande à une ombre*. The Ravel items represent some of the most exciting of his recordings on disc: the *Alborada* glitters and the *Pavane* is glowingly elegiac; *Le Tombeau de Couperin* has great refinement and elegance: the solo oboist plays beautifully. Paray's *Rapsodie espagnole* can be spoken of in the same breath as the Reiner/RCA and Karajan/EMI versions, with its languorous, shimmering textures and sparkling *Féria*. Hardly less impressive is Berlioz's *Royal Hunt and Storm* music, almost (though not quite) rivalling Munch's incandescent version. The recordings are brilliant in the Mercury manner (only in the Bizet items do they sound a little thick in texture) and their famous vividness remains striking. More than the sound, though, it is the exhilarating and unique performances which make this set valuable – and make so many performances of today seem dull.

Du Pré, Jacqueline (cello)

'The Art of Jacqueline du Pré' (with (i) LSO, Sir John Barbirolli; (ii) RPO, Sir Malcolm Sargent; (iii) New Philh. O; (iv) Chicago SO; (v) ECO; (vi) Daniel Barenboim; (vii) Valda Aveling; (viii) Gerald Moore; (ix) Ernest Lush; (x) Steven Bishop): (i) ELGAR: Cello Concerto in E min., Op. 85. (ii) DELIUS: Cello Concerto. (iii; vi) SAINT-SAENS: Cello Concerto 1 in A min., Op. 33. (iv; vi) DVORAK: Cello Concerto in B min., Op. 104; Waldesruhe, Op. 68. (iii; vi) SCHUMANN: Cello Concerto in A min., Op. 129. (i; vii) MONN: Cello Concerto in G min. HAYDN: Cello Concertos: in (i) C and (v; vi) D, Hob VIIb/1-2. (vi) CHOPIN: Cello Sonata in G min., Op. 65. (vi) FRANCK: Cello Sonata in A. (viii) FAURE: Elégie in C min., Op. 24. (viii) BRUCH: Kol Nidrei, Op. 47. BACH: (Unaccompanied) Cello Suites 1-2, BWV 1007/8. (ix) HANDEL: Cello Sonata in G min. BEETHOVEN: (vi) Variations in G min. on Judas Maccabaeus: See the conqu'ring hero comes, WoO 45; (x) Cello Sonatas 3, in A, Op. 69; 5 in D, Op. 102/2. (vi) Variations on Themes from 'The Magic Flute': 7 Variations in D, WoO 46 (Bei Männern, welche Liebe fühlen); 12 Variations in F, 66 (Ein Mädchen oder Weibchen)
(B) *** EMI (ADD) 5 68132-2 (8)

Admirers of this remarkably gifted artist, whose career ended so tragically, will welcome this survey of her major recordings, made over the incredibly brief period of a single decade. Her first recordings (1961) have a BBC source and her last (the Chopin and Franck Sonatas) were made at Abbey Road in 1971. But of course she made her real breakthrough in 1965 with the justly famous Kingsway Hall recording of the Elgar Concerto with Barbirolli. Some items included here are not otherwise currently available and, with excellent transfers, this set is an admirable and economical way of exploring her art. There are good, if brief, notes and some heart-rending photographs showing this young prodigy playing with characteristic concentration and joyously in conversation with her equally young husband, Daniel Barenboim.

'Cello Concertos': BOCCHERINI: Concerto in B flat (arr. GRUTZMACHER). HAYDN: Concertos in C & D, Hob VIIb/1-2 (with ECO, Barenboim or LSO, Barbirolli). SCHUMANN: Concerto in A min., Op. 129. SAINT-SAENS: Concerto 1 in A min., Op. 33 (with New Philh. O, Barenboim). DVORAK: Concerto in B min., Op. 104; Silent Woods, Op. 68/5 (with Chicago SO, Barenboim). DELIUS: Concerto (with RPO, Sargent). MONN: Concerto in G min. ELGAR: Cello Concerto in E min., Op. 85 (both with LSO, Barbirolli). R. STRAUSS: Don Quixote, Op. 35 (with New Philh. O, Boult)
(B) *** EMI (ADD) 5 67341-2 (6)

Those not wanting the chamber music on the above eight-disc coverage of the 'Art of Jacqueline du Pré', will find that this six-disc set is no less desirable, adding as it does the Boccherini/Grützmacher Concerto, most endearingly played, plus the recently remastered 1968 Don Quixote (with Boult), which is particularly fine. Good transfers and excellent value.

'A Lasting Inspiration' (with Daniel Barenboim, cond. or piano): BOCCHERINI: Cello Concerto in B flat (arr. GRUTZMACHER). DVORAK: Cello Concerto (Adagio); Silent woods, Op. 68/5. HAYDN: Cello Concerto in C. BEETHOVEN: Piano Trio 5 in D (Ghost), Op. 70/1; 7 Variations on 'Bei Männern' (both with Pinchas Zukerman). BRAHMS: Cello Sonata 1 in E min., Op. 38. FRANCK: Sonata in A (arr. DELSART) (Allegro ben moderato)
(M) **(*) EMI (ADD) 5 66350-2 (2)

A medium-priced anthology that is self-recommending if the more comprehensive programme is of appeal. The chamber-music performances have the same qualities of spontaneity and inspiration that have made du Pré's account with Barbirolli of Elgar's Cello Concerto come to be treasured above all others. Any tendency to self-indulgence, plus a certain leaning towards romantic expressiveness, is counterbalanced by the urgency and intensity of the playing. In the Brahms Sonata it is hard to accept the blatant change of tempo between first and second subjects, but here too there is warmth and flair. If some find du Pré's approach to Haydn too romantic, it is nevertheless difficult to resist in its ready warmth. The Beethoven Ghost Trio is comparably individual and inspirational. The sound-quality is fairly consistent, for all the remastered transfers are successful.

Ehnes, James (violin), Orchestre Symphonique de Québec, Yoav Talmi

'French Showpieces: Concert Français': SAINT-SAENS: Introduction and Rondo capriccioso. BERLIOZ: Le Corsaire: Overture; Rêverie et Caprice. CHAUSSON: Poème. DEBUSSY: Tarantelle Styrienne. MILHAUD: Le Boeuf sur le toit (cinéma fantasie). MASSENET: Thaïs: Méditation
*** Analekta Fleur de Lys FL 2 3151

By a remarkable coincidence James Ehnes and the Quebec Symphony Orchestra under Yoav Talmi have recorded a very similar programme to the young French virtuoso, Renaud Capuçon with the Bremen Chamber Philharmonique (see above) featuring Le Boeuf sur le toit in the weird but ear-tweaking jazzy arrangement of this Brazilian-inspired 'cinema-fantasy' which Milhaud himself made for the violinist, René Benedetti. James Ehnes plays the solo part with much dash and relish and the Quebec orchestra obviously enjoy its more outlandish elements and witty polytonal acerbity.

Ehnes is also a memorable soloist in the two Saint-Saëns showpieces, with dazzlingly brilliant articulation of the pyrotechnics and a seductive response to the lyrical melodies, a response which he also extends to an all but voluptuous account of Chausson's Poème. For all his extrovert bravura he is above all a very stylish player, which shows in the Berlioz and Massenet pieces. His timbre is not as expansive as some, but perfectly formed and nicely coloured, with a wide range of dynamic: his intonation is impeccable, his playing involved and involving, the result is very appealing indeed. The orchestra also show their paces not only in the lively accompaniments but in a wildly uninhibited account of Berlioz's Le Corsaire Overture and are no less exhilarating in the Debussy Danse.

Elizabethan Serenade

'Elizabethan Serenade' (played by (i) Slovak RSO, Penny; (ii) Czecho-Slovak RSO, Leaper; (iii) RTE Concert O or zecho-Slovak or Slovak RSO, Tomlinson; (iv) Slovak RSO, arpenter): (i) COATES: *By the Sleepy Lagoon;* (ii) *London uite: Knightsbridge March; Dam Busters March.* CURZON: *obin Hood Suite: March of the Bowmen.* KETELBEY: *Bells cross the Meadows; In a Monastery Garden; In a Persian Market* (both with chorus). (iii) ELLIS: *Coronation Scot.* (ii) AYDN WOOD: *Sketch of a Dandy;* (iii) *Roses of Picardy.* (ii) ARNON: *Westminster Waltz.* (i) DUNCAN: *Little Suite: March.* (iii) BINGE: *Sailing By; Elizabethan Serenade.* BENJAMIN: *Jamaican Rumba.* TOMLINSON: *Little Serenade.* WHITE: *Puffin' Billy.* (ii) GERMAN: *Tom Jones: Waltz.* (iii) OLLINS: *Vanity Fair.* (iv) MAYERL: *Marigold*

BB) *** Naxos 8.553515

his Naxos collection is in effect a super-bargain sampler for a worthwhile (full-priced) Marco Polo Light Music composer eries, and it inexpensively duplicates a great deal of the reper- oire included on other, similar programmes by various rchestras (see above and below). Our allegiance to their excellence remains, but the strong appeal of the present collec- ion is obvious. The performances are a little more variable but re always very good, and those conducted by Ernest Tomlin- on, who includes his own delightful *Little Serenade*, are excel- ent, notably Edward White's *Puffin' Billy*, Arthur Benjamin's amaican Rumba and the morceau by Anthony Collins. There re no complaints about the recording either. Excellent value.

English Chamber Orchestra, Daniel Barenboim

'*English Music*' (with (i) Black; (ii) Zukerman): DELIUS: *On Hearing the First Cuckoo in Spring; Summer Night on the River; 2 Aquarelles; Fennimore and Gerda: Intermezzo.* VAUGHAN WILLIAMS: *Fantasia on Greensleeves;* (i) *Oboe Concerto;* (ii) *The Lark Ascending.* WALTON: *Henry V* (film incidental music): *Passacaglia; The Death of Falstaff; Touch her Soft Lips and Part*

M) *** DG (ADD) 439 529-2

We have always had a soft spot for Barenboim's warmly evocative ECO collection of atmospheric English music. Even if the effect is not always totally idiomatic, the recordings have a warmth and allure that are wholly seductive.

English Chamber Orchestra, Richard Bonynge

Handel Overtures and Overtures of the 18th century': HANDEL (ed. Bonynge): *Solomon: Overture and Arrival of he Queen of Sheba. Overtures: Berenice; Teseo; Ariodante; Jephtha (Sinfonia); Esther; Rinaldo* (with *March and Battle*)*; Sosarme; Faramondo; Judas Maccabaeus; Radamisto; Arminio; Deidamia; Scipio; Belshazzar (Sinfonia); Julius Caesar* (with Act I *Minuet*)*; Semele: Sinfonia* (Act II). 18th-century overtures: J. M. KRAUS: *Olympia.* FLORIAN GASSMANN: *L'amore artigiano.* BOIELDIEU: *Zoraime et Zulnar.* FERDINANDO PAER: *Sargino.* GRETRY: *Le Magnifique.* SACCHINI: *La Contadina in Corte (Sinfonia).* HAYDN: *Orlando Paladino.* SALIERI: *La fiera di Venezie*

*** Double Decca (ADD) 466 434-2 (2)

This remarkably generous Double (150 minutes) covers the contents of three LPs from 1968–71. The Handel collection

may include the *Arrival of the Queen of Sheba,* but much of the rest has been left unheard, and all credit to Bonynge for resurrecting it with such vigour. Handel's cosmopolitan qualities give such music the benefit of all the traditions of the time – French finesse, Italian elaboration, English plain- spokenness. Bonynge uses his scholarship to produce results that are the very opposite of the dry-as-dust approach which can affect hard-line authenticists.

He may use double-dotting, *notes inégales* and added *appoggiaturas* beyond what other scholars would allow, but the baroque elaboration is justified in the exuberance of the end result. The rarities included here are all delightful and if the English Chamber Orchestra fields a larger body of strings than we expect today, the playing is splendidly alert, and the recording is exceptionally vivid.

The overtures by lesser names are much less inspired, but they undoubtedly have an aural fascination. *Olympia* is like Gluck without the inspiration, and *L'amore artigiano* is con- ventional, if with an attractive middle section. *Zoraime et Zulnar,* an early work of Boieldieu, shows something of the wit and melodic flair of the better-known overtures. But *Sargino* is altogether more striking, offering more in the way of memorable tunes, and a distinct flavour of Rossini.

Grétry's *Le Magnifique,* if somewhat optimistically titled, is also quite memorable. Unexpectedly opening with a side- drum like Auber's *Fra Diavolo,* it gradually builds up to its middle section, a hauntingly serene and rather beautiful minor-keyed passage, before concluding as it began in mili- tary style. The Salieri piece, too, is pleasingly fresh, helped like the rest by first-class advocacy from conductor, orchestra and recording engineers alike. The CD transfers are excellent.

English Chamber Orchestra, Sir Benjamin Britten

'*English Music for Strings*': PURCELL (ed. Britten): *Chacony in G min.* ELGAR: *Introduction & Allegro, Op. 47.* BRITTEN: *Prelude & Fugue for Strings, Op. 47; Simple Symphony, Op. 4.* DELIUS: *2 Aquarelles.* BRIDGE: *Sir Roger de Coverley for String Orchestra*

B— ✪ (M) *** Decca (ADD) 476 1641

This rich-toned recording, still sounding extraordinarily real and vivid, was surely a prime candidate for reissue in Univer- sal Classics' mid-priced 'Penguin ✪' Collection. It was one of the first made at The Maltings, Snape, in 1968 (although the *Prelude and Fugue,* which has been added to fill out the CD, dates from three years later). The warm acoustic gives the strings of the English Chamber Orchestra far greater weight than you would expect from their numbers. Britten drew comparably red-blooded playing from his band, whether in his own *Simple Symphony* (a performance unsurpassed on disc), the engaging Bridge dance or the magnificent Purcell *Chacony,* which has never sounded more imposing. It is good to find him treating his own music so expressively. In the Delius, the delicacy of evocation is delightful, while the Elgar is in some ways the most interesting performance of all, moving in its ardour yet with the structure of the piece brought out far more clearly than is common. An indispen- sable reissue to set alongside Barbirolli's coupling of the string music of Elgar and Vaughan Williams.

'*Britten at the Aldeburgh Festival*': BEETHOVEN: *Coriolan Overture.* DEBUSSY: *Prélude à l'après-midi d'un faune.*

HAYDN: *Symphony 95 in C min.* MENDELSSOHN: *Overture: Fingal's Cave.* MOZART: *Symphony 35 in D (Haffner)*
(M) **(*) BBC Music (ADD) BBCB 8008-2

Though this is a strange mixture, Britten as conductor brings to each item a striking freshness, giving a vivid idea of the electricity he conveyed in his performances at the Aldeburgh Festival. Mendelssohn's *Hebrides Overture* – the item which opens the sequence – is urgent and vigorous, giving a storm-tossed view of the Hebrides, while bringing out the strength of the musical structure. That and the Beethoven overture, given a similarly alert and dramatic reading in a 1966 performance at Blythburgh church, are especially valuable, as Britten otherwise made no commercial recordings of either composer's music.

The Debussy too is wonderfully fresh, with Richard Adeney's mistily cool flute solo at the start, presenting the whole score with a rare transparency, leading to a passionate climax. The recording, also made at Blythburgh, is a degree more immediate, less atmospheric than those from the Maltings, but the extra impact is an advantage – as it is in Britten's account of the Haydn symphony, which in its C minor angularity at the start has the biting toughness of *Sturm und Drang*. Mozart's *Haffner Symphony*, recorded in the Maltings in 1972, brings sound rather less focused than on the rest of the disc, but it is an amiable performance, energetic in the outer movements, warmly affectionate in the slow movement.

English Northern Philharmonia, David Lloyd-Jones

'*Victorian Concert Overtures*': MACFARREN: *Chevy Chase.* PIERSON: *Romeo and Juliet, Op. 86.* SULLIVAN: *Macbeth.* CORDER: *Prospero.* ELGAR: *Froissart, Op. 19.* PARRY: *Overture to an Unwritten Tragedy.* MACKENZIE: *Britannia, a Nautical Overture, Op. 52*
(BB) *** Hyp. Helios CDH 55088

Sir George (Alexander) Macfarren (1813–87) was an English composer of Scottish descent who taught at and eventually became Principal of the Royal Academy of Music. His music was very successful in its day; he was a distinguished early editor of Purcell's *Dido and Aeneas* and of major stage works of Handel. Many of his own operas were produced in London, including one based on the story of Robin Hood.

A CD showing us a wider range of his music is overdue; meanwhile he makes a strong contribution to this collection of Victorian concert overtures with *Chevy Chase*, a spirited, tuneful piece that was admired by Mendelssohn. Pierson's *Romeo and Juliet* hardly explores its theme with any substance but Frederick Corder's *Prospero* has a certain flamboyant gravitas. Mackenzie's *Britannia* is a pot-boiler featuring a borrowed tune now famous at the Proms. Against all this and more, Elgar's *Froissart* stands out as the early masterpiece it was. The whole concert is persuasively performed by the excellent Northern Philharmonia under the versatile David Lloyd-Jones, and this reissue is even more tempting at budget price.

'*English String Miniatures*', Volume 2: BRIDGE: *Sally in our Alley; Cherry Ripe; Sir Roger de Coverley.* ELGAR: *Sospiri.* HAYDN WOOD: *Fantasy Concerto.* IRELAND: *The Holy Boy.* VAUGHAN WILLIAMS: *Charterhouse Suite.* DELIUS: *Air and Dance.* WARLOCK: *Serenade for the 60th Birthday of Delius.* BUSH: *Consort Music*
(BB) *** Naxos 8.555068

A wholly delightful record, even more winning than th highly recommendable Volume 1 from the same source, which Lloyd-Jones conducted the Royal Ballet Orchest (Naxos 8.554186 – see below). Opening with Frank Bridge exquisitely tender arrangement of *Sally in our Alley*, fo lowed by the charmingly witty *Cherry Ripe*, Lloyd-Jon moves on to give a very touching performance of Elga lovely *Sospiri*, then brings a comparable delicacy of feelin to John Ireland's *Holy Boy*. The Haydn Wood *Fantas Concerto* is in the best tradition of lyrical English strir music and has a splendidly pulsing finale, with a memor ble secondary tune. The title of Vaughan Williams's *Cha terhouse Suite* reflects the composer's schooldays. It w originally written for piano, and has been effectively orche trated by James Brown. It is unassertive, the pastoral *Slo Air* engagingly English, with a lively closing *Pezzo ostinat* Warlock's *Serenade* and Delius's *Air and Dance* are so alik in harmonic character that they might well have bee written by the same composer. Geoffrey Bush's *Conso Music* is not remotely Elizabethan, but it is very entertai ing, especially the quirky *Caprice* and the lusciously expa sive *Cradle Song*. The spiritedly robust finale is high! contagious. Then Bridge's *Sir Roger de Coverley* ends th programme with sparkling virtuosity, with *Auld Lang Syr* making a surprise appearance at the close. Altogether marvellous concert, given first-class recording – a splendi bargain by any standards.

European Community Chamber Orchestra, Eivind Aadland

'*Concertos for the Kingdom of the Two Sicilies*':
A. SCARLATTI: *Concerto 6 in E (for strings). Sinfonia di concerto grosso 12 in C min.* PERGOLESI: *Flute Concerto in G (both with Giulio Viscardi).* PORPORA: *Cello Concerto in G (with Giovanni Sollima).* DURANTE: *Concerto per quartetto 1 in F min.*
(BB) *** Hyp. Helios CDH 55005

This most engaging and beautifully recorded collection i centred on Naples, the musical focus of the so-called 'Tw Sicilies', which once embraced southern Italy. The pro gramme is lightweight but played – on modern instruments with an airy lightness. Whereas Scarlatti's E major work is concerto grosso, the *Sinfonia di concerto* features a solo flu and matches the concerto attributed to Pergolesi in charn when the flute playing is so nimble. In Porpora's *Cello Co certo* (again with an impressive soloist) exuberantly vivaciou *Allegros* frame an eloquent central *Largo*. Durante's splendi little concerto grosso has a sombre introduction and is com paratively serious in mood; even the *Amoroso* third move ment, using the solo quartet, is touching rather tha romantic, but the tension lifts in the gay, rhythmicall pointed finale. Excellent value.

European Union Chamber Orchestra, Dmitri Demetriades

'*The Concerto in Europe*': PAISIELLO: *Harp Concerto in D.* GRETRY: *Flute Concerto in C.* GARTH: *Cello Concerto 2 in E flat.* STAMITZ: *Viola Concerto in D, Op. 1*
(BB) **(*) Hyp. Helios CDH 55035

A collection of quietly attractive and tuneful, rarely heard

ncertos. The Paisiello *Harp Concerto*, originally a keyboard
ork, is graceful and elegant, with a touching central move-
ent and a jolly, if brief, finale. Grétry's operatic leaning is
t at the opening of his *Flute Concerto*, and at intervals
roughout; the central movement flirts with minor keys, but
is generally a sunny work. The English are represented by a
llo concerto by John Garth: it is an interesting piece with
me robust cello writing, stylistically a bit earlier than the
her concertos (more baroque in flavour) but no less enjoy-
le for that. Stamitz's *Viola Concerto* is the most substantial
ork, with some nice ideas, especially in the slow movement,
d has secured a place in the viola concerto repertoire. The
rformances and recordings are good, though at times a
nt of blandness creeps in. The CD, which plays for just
der an hour, is worth considering if the programme
peals.

oundation Philharmonic Orchestra, avid Snell

ILLIAMS: *Tuba Concerto* (with Easler). TAILLEFERRE:
arp Concerto* (with Dall'olio). TOMASI: *Saxophone
ncerto* (with Ashby). MAYUZUMI: *Xylophone Concertino
ith May)

(*) ASV CDDCA 1126

n enterprising, if uneven, disc of twentieth-century concer-
s. There cannot be too many xylophone concertos; that by
e Japanese composer Toshirô Mayuzumi dates from 1965,
d although no masterpiece, it has its entertaining
oments, if inevitably it sounds a bit 'Tom and Jerryish' at
nes. John Williams wrote his *Tuba Concerto* in 1985. His
tractive film-music style provides a backcloth for his unu-
al soloist, though the piece is musically pretty thin, espe-
ally the slow middle section, which goes on for too long.
enri Tomasi's *Saxophone Concerto* of 1949 is more substan-
al; its full, colourful orchestration has atmosphere and
agination, suggesting at times a score for a *film noir* of the
40s. But perhaps the best concerto here is Germaine Taille-
rre's unpretentious work for harp of 1928, a piece that mixes
pressionistic and classical influences with much charm.
e performances cannot be faulted, the recording is good,
d if the strings occasionally sound a little undernourished,
e actual balance is well judged.

ournier, Pierre (cello)

ristocrat of the Cello': VIVALDI: *Cello Concerto in E
in.* COUPERIN: *Pièces en Concert for Cello & Strings.* C.
E. BACH: *Cello Concerto in A.* BOCCHERINI: *Cello Con-
rto in B flat.* HAYDN: *Cellos Concertos 1 in C; 2 in D
ith Lucerne Festival Strings, Baumgartner).* DVORAK:
ello Concerto in B min., Op. 104 (with BPO, Szell).*
LGAR: *Cello Concerto in E min., Op. 85 (with BPO, Wal-
nstein).* STRAVINSKY: *Suite Italienne from 'Pulcinella';
hanson russe from 'Mavra' (with Lush (piano)).*
RAHMS: *Cello Sonatas 1 in E min., Op. 38; 2 in F, Op. 99
ith Firkušný (piano)).* FRANCK: *Violin Sonata in A
rans. for cello).* SCHUBERT: *Arpeggione Sonata in A
in., D.821a.* MENDELSSOHN: *Variations concertantes,
p. 17.* SCHUMANN: *Adagio & Allegro, Op. 70; Fantasie-
ücke, Op. 73; 5 Stück im Volkston, Op. 102.* CHOPIN:
ello Sonata in G min., Op. 65; Nocturne in E flat,
p. 9/2 (with Fonda (piano)).* FRANCOEUR: *Cello Sonata

in E. HAYDN: *Cello Sonata in C: Minuetto.* WEBER: *Violin
Sonata, Op. 10/3.* RIMSKY-KORSAKOV: *Flight of the Bum-
ble Bee; Hymne au soleil from 'Le Coq d'or'.* BACH: *Ave
Maria.* TCHAIKOVSKY: *Pezzo capriccioso, Op. 62; Valse
sentimentale.* BRAHMS: *Feldeinsamkeit, Op. 86/2.* POPPER:
Elfentanz. DVORAK: *Rondo.* SAINT-SAËNS: *The Swan.*
PAGANINI: *Variations on a Theme from Rossini's 'Moses'
(with Crowson (piano))

(M) **(*) DG (ADD) 477 5939 (6)

It was not for nothing that Fournier was called 'The
Aristocrat of the Cello', and this six-CD set makes a superb
collection of his art. Many of Fournier's famous recordings
are included here, such as the superb Dvořák *Cello Concerto*,
with its ravishing phrasing in the slow movement and an
ideal balance between nobility and tension in the outer
ones. The Elgar is played with passion and conviction,
though here his close balance is not ideal, with the orchestra lacking weight. The beauty of tone and phrasing is very
telling in the great nineteenth-century chamber repertoire
of Brahms, Schumann and Chopin, with the personality of
the performer emerging but never overpowering the music.
If the Franck doesn't always have the total conviction of the
other repertoire, there is no doubting the quality of the
playing. The baroque and classical items are richly attractive
and, if they are obviously not in the authentic style of
today, they are lively and enjoyable nevertheless. The final
CD is a collection of short, varied pieces for cello and piano
and it makes a good collection, especially with the unexpected items. Generally excellent recordings and transfers
throughout.

French Orchestral Favourites

'*French Orchestral Favourites*': CHABRIER: *España; Joyeuse
marche* (Hallé O, James Loughran). RAVEL: *Rapsodie
espagnole* (LPO, Sir John Pritchard). BERLIOZ: *Overture: Le
Carnaval romain.* SAINT-SAËNS: *Symphony 3 (Organ),
Op. 78* (RLPO, Andrew Litton)

(BB) **(*) CfP (ADD/DDD) 5 87025-2

A surprisingly impressive collection, well worth its modest
cost. Loughran's Chabrier has plenty of life and sparkle, and
Pritchard's *Rapsodie espagnole* is a good one, poised and
with a sense of atmosphere, and very well played. Again the
1970s recording sparkles, the castenets coming over exotically. Litton then keeps the Royal Liverpool Philharmonic
Orchestra on their toes in a brilliant and exciting account of
Le Carnaval romain. The resonant acoustics of Liverpool
Cathedral, in which both this and the symphony were
recorded (much later, in 1986), suit Berlioz, bringing a
resplendent sonority to the brass and making the thrilling
final chord a moment to relish, as the reverberation ebbs
away naturally. However, the generous cathedral ambience
offers problems that are not entirely solved in the *Organ
Symphony*. Litton cleverly times the music to take the
acoustic into effect, with relatively steady tempi throughout,
and his lyrical feel for the work is attractive. The detail
registers amazingly well, but the finale – after the hugely
spectacular opening – becomes a swimming bath of sound,
especially in the closing bars, where the echoing resonance
undoubtedly brings a physical frisson which is undoubtedly
exhilarating, despite the problems.

(i) French Radio Orchestra,
(ii) Philharmonia Orchestra,
Igor Markevitch

PROKOFIEV: (i) *Love for 3 Oranges (suite), Op. 33;* (ii) *Le Pas d'acier (suite), Op. 41;* (i) *Scythian Suite, Op. 20.*
STRAVINSKY: (i) *Le Baiser de la fée (Divertimento);* (ii) *Petrushka: Suite;* (i) *Pulcinella (suite);* (ii) *The Rite of Spring* (B) (**(*)) EMI mono/stereo 5 69674-2 (2)

Igor Markevitch was the last and most unusual of Diaghilev's protégés and married the daughter of his first, Nijinsky. Markevitch's career initally took off as a composer and pianist. However, after the end of the Second World War, during which he served in the Italian resistance, he gave up composition to concentrate on conducting full time. He was an excellent ballet conductor whose cool elegance can be readily observed in these recordings. His mono (1952) account of *Le Sacre* with the Philharmonia Orchestra caused quite a stir in its day, but this 1959 stereo re-make, undertaken at very short notice when Klemperer was taken ill, has much to recommend it, even if the former has perhaps the greater atmosphere.

Markevitch gets good results from the Philharmonia Orchestra throughout and a very professional response from the French Radio Orchestra, which was in better shape than the Conservatoire Orchestra at this period. *Le Pas d'acier* is a rarity these days and is hardly ever encountered in the concert hall; it sounds to excellent effect here. The Paris recordings come from 1954–5 and the Philharmonia *Petrushka* and *Pas d'acier* from 1954. Only the 1959 *Le Sacre* is in stereo.

French Radio Philharmonic Orchestra, Paavo Järvi

'*Ballets Russes*': TCHAIKOVSKY: *Eugene Onegin: Polonaise & Waltz; The Nutcracker: Waltz of the Flowers.* GLINKA: *Valse-fantasia.* GLAZUNOV: *Raymonda: Entr'acte.* LIADOV: *Dance of the Amazon, Op. 65.* KHACHATURIAN: *Gayaneh: Sabre Dance; Masquerade: Waltz.* PROKOFIEV: *Love for 3 Oranges: March; Romeo and Juliet; Dance of the Knights.* SHOSTAKOVICH: *Jazz Suite 2: Waltz 2; Tahiti Trot, Op. 16; Golden Age, Op. 22: Polka.* BORODIN: *Prince Igor: Polovtsian Dances* (with Mariinsky Choir)
*** Virgin 5 45609-2

Collections of orchestral dance movements like this do not always work as a satisfying listening experience; but this one does, not only because the orchestral characterzation is vivid and alive, but also because the programme surveys both the history of Russian ballet (even beyond the coverage of Diaghilev's Ballets Russes, which also gives the collection its title) and nineteenth- and twentieth-century Russian orchestral writing which, as Tchaikovsky himself acknowledged with fervour, began with Glinka. The only obvious (and surprising) omission is Stravinsky. But it remains a very attractive anthology, with the wit of Shostakovich and Prokofiev nicely balanced by romantic lyricism, so one can enjoy this disc as an ongoing concert or simply select favourite items, like the pair of Tchaikovsky dances from *Eugene Onegin,* the *Polonaise* opening the programme with a fine rhythmic lift, and the *Waltz* later on inviting an elegant response from the violins.

The central sequence, with the erupting Khachaturian

Sabre Dance followed by the warmly lyrical Glazunov *Raymonda Entracte* and then the exotically colourful and rare Liadov *Dance of the Amazon,* works particularly well, while the delectable Shostakovich arrangement of *Tea for two* is most delightfully played. The concert ends with a zestful account of Borodin's *Polovtsian Dances,* thrilling in its final build-up of excitement, with plenty of idiomatic fervour from the Russian choir. Excellent recording throughout.

Fröst, Martin (clarinet), Malmö Symphony Orchestra, Lan Shui

'*Clarinet Concertos*': ARNOLD: *Concerto 2, Op. 112.* COPLAND: *Concerto for Clarinet & String Orchestra, with Harp & Piano.* HINDEMITH: *Concerto*
*** BIS CD 893

Three first-class performances of three outstanding twentieth-century concertos, all originally written for Benny Goodman. Fröst is an eloquently spontaneous soloist, stealing in gently against a magical orchestral *pianopianissimo* at the opening of the Copland; and he is equally at home in Hindemith's more sinewy lyricism. Both he and the persuasive conductor, Lan Shui, obviously relish the verve and energy of the Malcolm Arnold *Concerto* and they play the slow movement very seductively, before romping away into the rooty-tooty finale, with its audacious orchestral whoops, the kind of music to bring the house down at a Promenade concert. The recording is splendid in every way and this can receive the strongest recommendation.

Galway, James (flute)

'*Pachelbel's Canon and other Baroque Favourites*' (with various orchestras & conductors): VIVALDI: *Concerto in D (Il Gardellino), Op. 10/3:* 1st & 2nd movts; *Four Seasons: Spring* (arr. GALWAY). TELEMANN: *Suite for Strings in A min.: Réjouissance; Polonaise.* PACHELBEL: *Canon.* HANDEL: *Sonatas in A min., Op. 1/4:* 4th movt; *in F, Op. 1/11: Siciliana; Allegro* (both with Cunningham, Moll). *Solomon: Arrival of the Queen of Sheba* (arr. GERHARDT). *Messiah: Pifa (Pastoral Symphony); Xerxes: Largo.* BACH: *Suites 2 in B min., BWV 1067: Minuet & Badinerie; 3 in D, BWV 1068: Air; Trio Sonata 2 in G, BWV 1039:* 4th movt (with Kyung Wha Chung, Moll, Welsh); *Flute Sonatas 2 in E flat, BWV 1031: Siciliano* (with Maria Graf, harp); *4 in C, BWV 1033:* 2nd movt (arr. GERHARDT for flute & O); *Concerto in E min., BWV 1059/35* (ed. Radeke): 3rd movt. ALBINONI: *Adagio.* QUANTZ: *Concerto in C: Finale.* MARAIS: *Le Basque* (arr. GALWAY/GERHARDT)
*** BMG/RCA DDD/ADD 09026 61928-2

If the famous Bach *Air* from BWV 1068 is spun out somewhat romantically and the *Siciliano* from BWV 1031 (with harp accompaniment) is too solemn, Handel's famous *Largo* is gloriously managed, completely vocal in feeling. Galway certainly dominates Pachelbel's *Canon* in a way not intended by the composer, but his elegant line and simple divisions on the lovely theme are very agreeable.

Any of the composers included here would surely have been amazed at the beauty of his tone and the amazing technical facility, always turned to musical effect. He is a wonderful goldfinch in Vivaldi's Op. 10/3, while Gerhardt's arrangement of Handel's *Arrival of the Queen of Sheba,* which exchanges oboes for flutes, is ear-tickling. The engaging Quantz concerto movement is as sprightly in the strings (of the Württemberg Chamber Orchestra) as it is in the feliciously decorated solo part. The Bach and Handel sonata excerpts are refreshing and the (Handel) Siciliana from Op. 1/11 is matched in pastoral charm by the beautiful account of the *Pifa* from *Messiah*, but is not more engaging than the lollipop of the whole concert: the delicious *Le Basque* of Marais, one of Galway's most endearing arrangements. The recording naturally balances the soloist forward, but the sound is first class throughout. This is a full-price record but it includes 68 minutes of entertainment, perfect for a fine summer evening.

Galway, James (flute), Berlin Philharmonic Orchestra, Herbert von Karajan or Karl Boehm

'I was a Berliner'. Excerpts from: GRIEG: *Peer Gynt.* BIZET: *L'Arlésienne.* BACH: *Mass in B min.: Domine Deus* (with Gundula Janowitz & Peter Scheier). VERDI: *Aida: Dance of the Princesses; Dance of the Young Maidens.* R. STRAUSS: *Salome: Dance of the Seven Veils* (all with Karajan). MOZART: *Posthorn Serenade: Concertante & Rondeau* (with Boehm). DANZI: *Wind Quintets* (excerpts): *in B flat, Op. 56/1: Allegretto & Allegro; in C, Op. 91/1: Menuet & Rondo Finale* (with Lothar Koch, Karl Leister, Günther Piesk, Gerd Seifert)

(M) **(*) DG (ADD) 477 6077

It was not generally realized at the time that, during the early 1970s, before he became a famous international soloist, James Galway was principal flute in Karajan's Berlin Philharmonic, although Galway once related in a broadcast interview that at the audition for the post (in front of the whole orchestra) he was expected to play *all* the most famous orchestral solos (including Ravel's *Daphnis and Chloé*) on the spot, from memory.

DG have now had the bright idea of making an anthology of some of the recordings in which he played. However, in Grieg's *Morning* from *Peer Gynt* the oboe is just as important as the flute, and in many of the other items the flute is prominent only briefly. But it is the *Menuet* from Bizet's *L'Arlésienne* and the seductive *Aida* dance music that certainly show his individuality, and many other examples are enjoyable for their own sake, especially the beautifully played excerpts from the Danzi and Reicha *Wind Quintets*. Moreover, the new transfers show all the recordings in the best possible light. But the choice of *Salome's Dance* to end the programme, luscious as it is, was a curious one.

Il Giardino Armonico, Giovanni Antonini

'The Italian Bach in Vienna': J. S. BACH: *Double Clavier Concerto in C, BWV 1061; Triple Clavier Concerto in D min., BWV 1061* (both with Katia and Marielle Labèque (fortepianos); BWV 1061 also with Danone (harpsichord)). C. P. E. BACH: *Sinfonia in G, Wq.182/1.* VIVALDI: *Il cimento dell'armonia e dell'inventione: Violin Concerto in D min., Op. 8/7, RV 242* (with Onofri (violin))

**(*) TDK DVD DV-BACON

The Musikverein provides an attractive backcloth and an appealing ambience for this programme which centres on the music of Bach and Vivaldi. The novelty here is the performance of Bach's *Triple Keyboard Concerto* on a pair of fortepianos plus a harpsichord, which works surprisingly well. With a microphone given to each soloist, the engineers are able to achieve a satisfactory balance, but the snag in the *Double Concerto*, with such a close balance and the two keyboards side by side, is that the movement of Bach's solo line from one fortepiano to another is achieved electronically, and the effect is curiously unnatural. Moreover the close balance reveals an obbligato vocalise from one of the soloists, very audible in the Adagio of BWV 1061. The performances are certainly brilliant, with both finales very lively indeed. Enrico Onofri (the orchestra's leader) also plays with much bravura in the Vivaldi *Concerto*, especially in his first-movement cadenza, but his performance is without charm.

Il Giardino Armonico and its young and dynamic conductor, Giovanni Antonini, have made their name by a bravura period-instrument style, and that is very much to the fore in the *G major Sinfonia* of C. P. E. Bach, visually overflowing with energy, with sharply articulated, very brisk outer movements and staccato articulation in the *Poco Adagio*. But their ensemble cannot be faulted and no one could suggest their music-making was lacking in spirit.

CASTELLO: *Sonata concertante, Op. 2/4 & 10.* MARINI: *Sonata, 'Sopra la Monica'.* MERULA: *Ciaconna.* SPADI: *Dominuziono;* SOPRA: *Anchor che co'l partire.* VIVALDI: *Lute Concertos in D, RV 93; in D (Il gardellino), Op. 10/3. Recorder Concerto in G min. (La notte), RV 104*
* Arthaus **DVD** 100 010

Il Giardino Armonico is a brilliant group which performs this repertoire with stunning virtuosity and imagination. Musically, there are no quarrels here except, perhaps, for the over-bright sound. Moreover, the DVD facilities offer the scores, though when they are superimposed the visual image is masked – indeed, it virtually disappears. The text in the Vivaldi is, of course, the Ricordi short score. Although the performances are expert enough, though very brightly recorded, the visual direction is irritatingly hyperactive. The musicians are superimposed on all sorts of Sicilian backdrops but never for more than a few seconds at a time. The empty 'cleverness' of the director, who cannot leave anything to speak for itself, is very tiresome to start with and insufferable after a few minutes. Two stars for the brilliant if exhibitionist music-making, but none for the distracting visual antics.

Gould, Glenn (piano)

Glenn Gould Edition

BACH: *Harpsichord Concertos 1–5; 7, BWV 1052–6 & BWV 1058* (with Columbia SO, Bernstein (No. 1) or Golschmann)
(M) (**) Sony mono (No. 1)/stereo SMK 87760/61 (2)

BACH: *Well-tempered Clavier, Book I, Preludes and Fugues 1–24, BWV 846–69*
(M) (**) Sony (ADD) SM2K 52600 (2)

BACH: *Well-tempered Clavier, Book II, Preludes and Fugues 25–48, BWV 870–93*
(M) (**) Sony (ADD) SM2K 52603 (2)

BEETHOVEN: *7 Bagatelles, Op. 33; 6 Bagatelles, Op. 126; 6 Variations in F, Op. 34; 15 Variations with Fugue in E flat (Eroica), Op. 35; 32 Variations on an Original Theme in C min., WoO 80*

(M) (**) Sony (ADD) SM2K 52646 (2)

BRAHMS: *4 Ballades, Op. 10; Intermezzi, Op. 76/6–7; Op. 116/4; Op. 117/1–3; Op. 118/1, 2 & 6; Op. 119/1; 2 Rhapsodies, Op. 79*

(M) (**) Sony ADD/DDD SM2K 52651 (2)

Glenn Gould is an artist who excites such strong passions that guidance is almost superfluous. For his host of admirers these discs are self-recommending; those who do not respond to his pianism will not be greatly interested in this edition. For long he enjoyed cult status, enhanced rather than diminished by his absence from the concert hall. There is too much that is wilful and eccentric in these performances for any of them to rank as a sole first recommendation. Yet if for his devotees virtually all his recordings are indispensable, for the unconverted a judicious approach is called for. There is no questioning Gould's keyboard wizardry or his miraculous control of part-writing in Bach, for which he had much intuitive feeling. The majority of his Bach discs evidence strong personality and commitment throughout, even though the tiresome vocalise (which became an increasing source of frustration, particularly later in his recording career) is a strain. However, the sound generally has insufficient freshness and bloom, and the eccentricity (some might say egocentricity) of some of Gould's readings and the accompanying vocalise are often quite insupportable.

Graffin, Philippe (violin), Ulster Orchestra, Thierry Fischer

'Rare French Works for Violin and Orchestra': FAURE: *Violin Concerto in D min., Op. 14.* SAINT-SAENS: *Morceau de concert, Op. 62.* LALO: *Fantasie norvégienne.* GUIRAUD: *Caprice.* LALO: *Guitarre, Op. 28.* CANTELOUBE: *Poème*

*** Hyp. CDA 67294

This attractive compilation is worth having for the Fauré *Concerto* alone, which the composer never completed. The existing two movements are full of delightful ideas and Philippe Graffin is a most sympathetic exponent. The Saint-Saëns *Morceau* is a working of the *Caprice brillant* for violin and piano and shows all the composer's tuneful facility and flair. Lalo's *Fantasie norvégienne* uses what he thought was a folksong, but was in fact a melody of Grieg's – and a very delightful one too. *Guitarre* is essentially an instrumental piece, engaging enough, and orchestrated by Pierné for his own use as an encore. It recalls the *Symphonie espagnole*, but is altogether slighter. The surprise here is the two-movement *Caprice* of Ernest Guiraud, who we remember as the composer of recitatives for Bizet's *Carmen*. The gently seductive *Andante* is followed by a sparkling *Allegro appassionato*, after the fashion of the Saint-Saëns *Introduction and Rondo capriccioso*. The Canteloube *Poème* is passionately languorous, richly orchestrated: its composer was afraid his scoring was too opulent and would drown its soloist, but that is not a problem here and one revels in its sumptuousness and orchestral colour. Altogether a most worthwhile collection, very well played and recorded.

Grumiaux, Arthur (violin)

'Favourite Violin Concertos' (with (i) Concg. O; (ii) New Philh. O; (iii) Sir Colin Davis; (iv) Bernard Haitink; (v) Jan Krenz): BEETHOVEN: (i; iii) *Concerto in D*; (i; iv) *Romance 2 in F.* (ii; iii) BRAHMS: *Concerto in D.* (ii; v) MENDELSSOHN: *Concerto in E min.* TCHAIKOVSKY: *Concerto in D*

⊖ ❋ (B) *** Ph. Duo (ADD) 442 287-2 (2)

Another extraordinary Duo bargain set from Philips, containing some of the great Belgian violinist's very finest performances. He recorded the Beethoven twice for Philips, and this is the later account from the mid-1970s with Sir Colin Davis. Grumiaux imbues this glorious concerto with a spirit of classical serenity and receives outstanding support from Davis. If we remember correctly, the earlier account with Galliera had slightly more of a sense of repose and spontaneous magic in the slow movement, but the balance of advantage between the two versions is very difficult to resolve, and the Concertgebouw recording is fuller and richer and (even if there is not absolute orchestral clarity) there is less background noise.

The performance of the Brahms, it goes without saying, is full of insight and lyrical eloquence, and again Sir Colin Davis lends his soloist the most sympathetic support. The (1973) account of the Mendelssohn is characteristically polished and refined, and Grumiaux, even if he does not wear his heart on his sleeve, plays very beautifully throughout: the pure poetry of the playing not only lights up the *Andante* but is heard at its most magical in the key moment of the downward arpeggio which introduces the second subject of the first movement.

Similarly in the Tchaikovsky his playing – if less overtly emotional than some – has the usual aristocratic refinement and purity of tone to recommend it. His reading is beautifully paced and has a particularly fine slow movement; both here and in the brilliant finale he shows superb aplomb and taste. With excellent accompaniments in both works from Krenz this adds to the attractions of the set, for the 1970s recording has a wide range and is firmly focused in its CD format.

Concert (with LOP, Rosenthal): LALO: *Symphonie espagnole, Op. 21.* SAINT-SAENS: *Introduction and Rondo capriccioso, Op. 28; Havanaise, Op. 83.* CHAUSSON: *Poème, Op. 25.* RAVEL: *Tzigane*

**(*) Australian Ph. Eloquence (ADD) 462 579-2

A worthwhile collection of French music. Grumiaux's playing is always individual, not showy or extrovert, but with plenty of colour and relaxed bravura. The orchestral support is lively and sympathetic, and lets the soloist dominate in the right way. The Lamoureux Orchestra is not the most refined of instruments but is reasonably stylish, with a French timbre which is nice to hear in these conformist times. The recording is a little thin-sounding (it dates from the mid-1960s), but is acceptable and well balanced.

Hallé Orchestra, Sir John Barbirolli

BAX: *Oboe Quintet* (arr. Barbirolli; with Evelyn Rothwell). VAUGHAN WILLIAMS: *Symphony 8 in D min.* DELIUS: *On Hearing the First Cuckoo in Spring.* RAWSTHORNE: *Street Corner Overture.* WALTON: *Coronation March: Crown Imperial.* ELGAR: *Land of Hope and Glory* (with Kathleen

Ferrier & Hallé Ch.). *National Anthem* (with Trumpeters & Band of Royal Military School of Music, Kneller Hall)

(M) (***) BBC mono/stereo BBCL 4100-2

On the BBC Legends label these radio recordings of British music, all but one from the late 1960s, offer a delightful selection of Barbirolli favourites, including his own arrangement of Bax's *Oboe Quintet* for oboe and strings, with his wife Evelyn Rothwell as the expressive soloist. Written for Rothwell's teacher, Leon Goossens, it originally involved writing for the string quartet that Barbirolli found awkward with its double-stopping, something that his arrangement clarifies. Vaughan Williams's *Eighth Symphony*, dedicated to him as 'Glorious John', was always a work he specially enjoyed, and this live performance from a 1967 Prom is both broader and warmer than his studio recording, if not quite so clean of texture. That and Rawsthorne's rumbustious *Overture, Street Corner*, are the only stereo recordings here. Walton's *Crown Imperial* is also given with plenty of panache, and Delius's *First Cuckoo* could not be more warmly done. The National Anthem, recorded at the same Royal Albert Hall concert, is an oddity, with voices inaudible, and *Land of Hope and Glory*, also taken very slowly, is a much older recording, taken from a severely damaged shellac disc, with Kathleen Ferrier the radiant soloist. This was recorded at the opening of the rebuilt Free Trade Hall in Manchester in 1951.

BEETHOVEN: *Symphony 7 in A, Op. 92*. MOZART: *Symphony 35 in D (Haffner)*; WAGNER: *Siegfried Idyll*

(M) (**(*)) BBC Legends stereo/mono BBCL 4076-2

Barbirolli never made a commercial recording of Beethoven's *Seventh Symphony* (in fact he recorded only Nos. 1, 3, 5 and 8), so this Festival Hall account is more than welcome. One senses straight away that there is a strong personality in command, and one that is wholly dedicated to Beethoven. In this mighty work Sir John is totally straightforward and unfussy, yet attentive to every detail of phrasing, and there is a fine sense of momentum. The only slight reservation lies in the finale, which is not quite headlong enough. But this is a performance of stature, and the sound is remarkably good for its period and venue: the balance is excellently judged, with every detail coming across, even if tuttis sound a bit fierce. The Mozart symphony has plenty of spirit and warmth; tempi are brisk but the phrasing is always alive. The Albert Hall sound, though not as finely detailed or as present as in the Beethoven, is more than acceptable. Sir John also never recorded the *Haffner Symphony* for his record companies, nor did he commit the *Siegfried Idyll* to disc. As you would expect, he shapes it beautifully, though the playing is generally less polished than in either of the symphonies. The strings sound vinegary at times, although their quality and timbre were not flattered by the acoustic of the BBC Manchester Studios. The mono recording is less rich and detail less transparent. All the same, this set is a valuable addition to the Barbirolli discography.

'Barbirolli at the Opera': RICHARD STRAUSS: *Die Liebe der Danae* (symphonic fragments; arr. Krauss); *Der Rosenkavalier: Suite*. WEBER: *Der Freischütz; Euryanthe: Overtures*. VERDI: *La traviata: Preludes to Acts I & III*. MOZART: *Le nozze di Figaro: Overture*. WAGNER: *Lohengrin: Preludes to Acts I & III*

(M) (***) Dutton Lab. mono CDSJB 1004

Hearing these glowing performances, full of Barbirollian expressiveness and panache, brings home how sad it is that he recorded so few complete operas in the studio. It is tantalizing to realize what a great interpreter of *Rosenkavalier* he would have been, when his account of the much-maligned suite is so warm and persuasive, a première recording of 1946. Every item demonstrates the quality of the Hallé as trained by Barbirolli in the immediate post-war period, notably the strings. The Dutton transfers are first rate, though the original recordings used here were obviously more limited than those on some earlier Barbirolli Society issues, and this collection is too highly priced.

'Hallé Favourites – 2': SUPPE: *Overture: The Beautiful Galatea*. TURINA: *Danzas fantásticas*. CHABRIER: *España*. LEHAR: *Gold and Silver Waltz*. SIBELIUS: *Valse triste*. WALDTEUFEL: *The Skaters' Waltz*. GRIEG: *Two Elegiac Melodies; Peer Gynt Suite 1*

(M) (***) Dutton Lab. mono/stereo CDSJB 1013

Some of the recordings here have an EMI mono source from the 1950s; the rest, including the Sibelius and Grieg items (which are particularly warmly played), were early stereo with a Pye source. All the transfers are up to Dutton's standard and Chabrier's *España* and the two waltzes have plenty of lilt and sparkle. It is a pity that – as it is sponsored by the Barbirolli Society – this disc is comparatively expensive.

'Barbirolli's English Music Album': BARBIROLLI: *An Elizabethan Suite*. BAX: *The Garden of Fand*. BUTTERWORTH: *A Shropshire Lad*. ELGAR: *Three Bavarian Dances: Lullaby; Enigma Variations*. IRELAND: *The Forgotten Rite; Mai-Dun; These Things Shall Be* (with Parry Jones, tenor, Hallé Ch.). PURCELL (arr. Barbirolli): *Suite for Strings*. VAUGHAN WILLIAMS: *Fantasia on Greensleeves; Fantasia on a Theme by Thomas Tallis*

(M) (***) Dutton mono CDSJB 1022 (2)

The long-buried treasure here is Barbirolli's very first recording of Elgar's *Enigma Variations*, never previously issued. As Michael Kennedy's authoritative note explains, it was recorded in Manchester in May 1947, only months before he went on to make his first published recording in October of that year, an inexplicable duplication when if anything this earliest version is even finer than the published one, certainly more spontaneously expressive at key points such as *Nimrod* and the finale variation, while the opening statement of the theme is more flowing and less emphatic.

There is much else to cherish on the two discs for any devotee of English music, let alone Barbirolli enthusiasts. The two Vaughan Williams items, the *Tallis Fantasia* dating from 1946 and *Greensleeves* from 1948, both recorded in Houldsworth Hall, Manchester, have never previously appeared on CD, and both are very welcome. In mono sound they may be less rich-textured than Barbirolli's stereo remakes, but the *Tallis Fantasia*, featuring a vintage quartet of Hallé principals, separates the quartet more clearly from the main body than the version with the Sinfonia of London, and again is more warmly expressive. The extra lightness of *Greensleeves* too sounds more easily spontaneous.

Those performances are contained on the second of the two discs, with the shorter works of Bax, Butterworth and Ireland on the first. The exotic orchestration of Bax's *The Garden of Fand* is well detailed, as are the evocative textures of the Butterworth orchestral rhapsody, recorded for Pye like Barbirolli's own *Elizabethan Suite*, all of them stereo recordings. The EMI mono recordings of the two Ireland orchestral pieces, dating from earlier, have comparable weight. In the

Ireland choral work, *These Things Shall Be*, the dynamic range is again wider than one expects in mono recordings of this vintage. The performances all have a passionate thrust typical of Barbirolli, with the tenor, Parry Jones, and the Hallé Chorus matching the orchestra in their commitment. The two suites devised by Barbirolli himself emerge as curiosities in an age devoted to period practice. It is striking that Purcell survives the romanticizing involved rather better than Byrd, Farnaby and Bull.

Hälsingborg Symphony Orchestra, Okko Kamu

'*Swedish Orchestral Favourites*': SODERMAN: *Swedish Festival Music.* STENHAMMAR: *The Song (cantata): Interlude.* LARSSON: *Pastoral Suite; A Winter's Tale: Epilogue.* PETERSON-BERGER: *Frösöblomster: 4 Pieces.* ALFVEN: *Roslagspolka; Midsummer Vigil; Gustavus Adolphus II suite.* WIREN: *Serenade for Strings: Marcia*
(BB) *** Naxos 8.553115

A useful anthology of popular favourites from the Swedish repertory, nicely played by the Hälsingborg orchestra and Okko Kamu, which should have wide appeal, not only in but outside Sweden. The playing is lively, the performances of the Alfvén and Lars-Erik Larsson pieces are as good as any in the catalogue, the recording is excellent and the price is right.

Hanover Band, Graham Lea-Cox

'*18th-Century British Symphonies*': ABEL: *Symphony in E, Op. 10/1.* ARNE: *Symphony 4 in C min.* COLLETT: *Symphony in E flat, Op 2/5.* ERSKINE: *Periodical Overture 17 in E flat.* MARSH: *A Conversation Symphony in E flat.* SMETHERGELL: *Symphony in B flat, Op. 5/2*
⚙ *** ASV CDGAU 218

This collection of six British symphonies dating from the late eighteenth century could not be more refreshing, brilliantly played and recorded. Hardly anything is known of John Collett, not even his dates, but his four-movement *Symphony in E flat*, Op. 2/5, published in 1767, is a delight, its eager energy echoing the new Mannheim school, with brazen horn writing. His patron, Thomas Erskine, the Earl of Kelly, studied for years in Mannheim, but his *Periodical Overture 17*, briefer and bluffer, is less striking. It is in three movements only, as are all the rest, including John Marsh's elegant *Conversation Sinfonie* for two orchestras from 1778, which was influenced by J. C. Bach. With such bright, carefree inspiration running through all these works, the old idea that Handel stifled British composers needs revising.

Hanslip, Chloé (violin)

'*Chloé*' (with LSO, Mann): PAGANINI (arr. KREISLER): *La Campanella.* BLOCH: *Nigun.* GADE: *Capriccio.* J. WILLIAMS: *Theme from 'Schindler's List.* MUSSORGSKY (arr. Rachmaninov & Ingman): *Gopak;* BRUCH: *Adagio appassionato.* GLAZUNOV: *Meditation.* TCHAIKOVSKY: *Valse-scherzo.* SHOSTAKOVICH: *The Gadfly: Romance.* SARASATE: *Romanza andaluza.* WAXMAN: *Carmen Fantasy*
*** Warner 8573 88655-2

Chloé Hanslip was 13 years old when she recorded this impressive recital disc. Although there is only limited evidence of distinctive artistry, it makes a formidable display, very well recorded. Hanslip, born and brought up in Surrey, gives formidably mature performances of all 11 pieces here, marked by dazzling virtuosity, flawless intonation, phenomenal attack in virtuoso showpieces like the Sarasate, and, above all, a genuine depth of expression that is sensitively matched to the style of each piece. So in Bloch's *Nigun*, with its subtitle of improvisation, she is uninhibitedly free in her warm phrasing, freer than in the Shostakovich, where the haunting melody is played with tender restraint. What are especially welcome are the rarities. Bruch's *Adagio appassionato*, written in 1891, the same year as the *Third Violin Concerto*, is a violin equivalent of *Kol Nidrei*. Niels Gade's *Capriccio*, too, which was written in his sixties and has rarely appeared on disc, is here played with all the sparkle that is slightly lacking from the brilliant but literal account of the opening item, Kreisler's arrangement of the Paganini *Campanella* study, which is a little too metrical. By contrast, Tchaikovsky's *Valse-scherzo*, another rarity, sounds a little unsteady, with tenutos not quite spontaneous sounding.

Hardenberger, Håkan (trumpet)

'*Famous Classical Trumpet Concertos*': HUMMEL: *Concerto in E.* HERTEL: *Concerto 1 in E flat.* STAMITZ: *Concerto in D.* HAYDN: *Concerto in E flat* (all with ASMF, Marriner). RICHTER: *Concerto in D.* LEOPOLD MOZART: *Concerto in D.* MOLTER: *Concerto 1 in D.* MICHAEL HAYDN: *Concerto 2 in C* (all with LPO, Howarth). CORELLI: *Sonata for Trumpet, 2 Violins & Continuo.* ALBINONI: *Concerto in B flat, Op. 7/3* (with I Musici). ALBINONI/GIAZOTTO: *Adagio in G min.* CLARKE: *Trumpet Tune* (attr. PURCELL). BACH: *3 Chorale preludes.* BACH/GOUNOD: *Ave Maria* (all with Simon Preston, organ)
θ⟶ ⚙ (B) *** Ph. Duo 464 028-2 (2)

This is simply the finest collection of concertante music for trumpet in the catalogue. Hardenberger's playing in the famous Haydn concerto, with his noble line in the *Andante* no less telling than his sparkling bravura in the finale, is matched by his account of the Hummel which he plays in E, rather than the expected key of E flat, which makes it sound brighter than usual. Neither he nor Marriner misses the galant lilt inherent in the dotted rhythm of the first movement, while the slow-movement cantilena soars beautifully over its jogging pizzicato accompaniment, and the finale captivates the ear with its high spirits and easy virtuosity. The Stamitz concerto is a comparatively recent discovery. The writing lies consistently up in the instrument's stratosphere and includes some awkward leaps. It is inventive, however, notably in the exhilarating finale. There is no lack of panache here or in the lesser concerto by Hertel, and throughout Marriner's accompaniments are consistently elegant and polished. Apart from these obvious highlights there is much to enjoy in the lesser works too. The wealth of melody is apparent, and if not all the music here is in the masterpiece league, it is played as if it were. Hardenberger is as brilliant in the fast movements as he is sensitive in the slow ones, and his phrasing and tone are superb in both. In the two attractive baroque concertos by Albinoni and Marcello he plays with similar flair and gleaming tone, and he is a dab hand at embellishment, without overdoing things. The recordings nd accompaniments are comparably fine, and it is difficult o imagine a better programme of this kind at any price.

Harle, John (saxophone), Academy of St Martin-in-the-Fields, Sir Neville Marriner

DEBUSSY: *Rapsodie for Alto Saxophone and Orchestra.* BERT: *Concertino da camera.* GLAZUNOV: *Concerto.* R. R. BENNETT: *Concerto.* HEATH: *Out of the Cool.* VILLA-LOBOS: *Fantasia*
(B) *** EMI Red Line 5 72109

A first-class disc in every way. These are all attractive and well written for their instrument, and John Harle is its master. The Debussy, Ibert and Glazunov are all works well worth getting to know. The recording is excellent.

Harp Concertos

'Harp Concertos' (played by: (i) Robles; (ii) ASMF, Brown; (iii) Ellis, LSO, Bonynge; (iv) Tripp, Jellinek, VPO, Münchinger; (v) Philh. O, Dutoit): (i; ii) BOIELDIEU: *Harp Concerto in C.* DITTERSDORF: *Harp Concerto in A* (arr. PILLEY). (iii) GLIERE: *Harp Concerto, Op. 74.* (i; ii) HANDEL: *Harp Concerto, Op. 4/6.* (iv) MOZART: *Flute & Harp Concerto in C, K.299.* (i; v) RODRIGO: *Concierto de Aranjuez*
(B) *** Double Decca (ADD) 452 585-2 (2)

Boieldieu's *Harp Concerto* has been recorded elsewhere but never more attractively. The (originally Argo) recording is still in the demonstration class and very sweet on the ear. Dittersdorf's *Harp Concerto* is a transcription of an unfinished keyboard concerto with additional wind parts. It is an elegant piece, thematically not quite as memorable as Boieldieu's, but captivating when played with such style. Glière's is an unpretentious and tuneful work, with Osian Ellis performing brilliantly. Excellent (1968) Kingsway Hall recording.

Handel's Op. 4/6 is well known in both organ and harp versions. Marisa Robles and Iona Brown make an unforgettable case for the latter by creating the most delightful textures while never letting the work sound insubstantial. The ASMF accompaniment, so stylish and beautifully balanced, is a treat in itself, and the recording is well-nigh perfect. The much earlier, Vienna recording of Mozart's *Flute & Harp Concerto* is played stylishly and has stood the test of time, the recording smooth, full, nicely reverberant and with good detail. Refinement and beauty of tone and phrase are a hallmark throughout, and Münchinger provides most sensitive accompaniments.

The glowing acoustic of St Barnabas's Church, London, creates an attractively romantic aura for Marisa Robles's magnetic and highly atmospheric account of the composer's own arrangement for harp of his *Concierto de Aranjuez*. Robles is so convincing an advocate that for the moment the guitar original is all but forgotten, particularly when, with inspirational freedom, she makes the beautiful slow movement sound like a rhapsodic improvisation. It is a haunting performance, and the digital sound is first rate. Altogether an excellent anthology; however, the Boieldieu, Dittersdorf and Handel concertos on the first disc are also available separately

at mid-price, and we gave a Rosette to this disc in our main volume (Decca 425 723-2).

Hauk, Franz (organ), Ingolstadt Philharmonic, Alfredo Ibarra

Music for Organ and Orchestra (Klais Organ in Liebfrauenmünster Ingolstadt): WIDOR: *Symphony 3 for Organ and Grand Orchestra, Op. 42.* JONGEN: *Alleluja, Op. 112; Hymne, Op. 78* (both for organ and orchestra). HORATIO PARKER: *Organ Concerto in E flat, Op. 55*
**(*) Guild GMCD 7182

In terms of sheer hyperbole Widor does this better than almost anyone. His *G minor concertante Symphony* is made up from two solo organ symphonies: the spectacular outer movements, including the brilliant closing *Toccata*, well laced with brass, are drawn from the *Sixth*, Op. 42/2, and the central *Andante* from the *Second*, Op. 13/2, composed ten years earlier.

The Jongen works are both lyrically colourful. The nobilmente *Alleluja* was composed to inaugurate a new organ in the concert hall of Belgian Radio in 1940, and with its closing fanfares sounds rather like wartime film music. The *Hymne* (for organ and strings) is a threnody of some character, well sustained and making a welcome contrast with the surrounding flamboyance.

The American Horatio Parker earned the contempt of his pupil Charles Ives for 'imposing second-hand German romanticism on the patriots of New England'. But his readily tuneful if at times overblown edifice is endearing for its somewhat sentimental romantic feeling, symbolized by the violin and horn solos in the *Andante*. The work was modelled on a concerto of Rheinberger, and its third-movement *Allegretto* is also lightly scored and has charm. The finale includes a fugato, a vigorous pedal cadenza, a bit like a recitative, and a resounding close to bring the house down. Here the final cadence echoes away in the long reverberation period of the Liebfrauenmünster. The organ itself is a magnificent beast and is played with great bravura and expressive flair by Franz Hauk; the orchestra accompany with spirit and enthusiasm, even if at times they are all but drowned in the resonant wash of sound. The recording copes remarkably well, although it is hardly refined.

'Triumphal Music for Organ and Orchestra': GOUNOD: *Fantaisie on the Russian National Hymne; Suite concertante.* DUBOIS: *Fantaisie triomphale.* GUILMANT: *Adoration.* GIGOUT: *Grand choeur dialogue*
*** Guild GMCD 7185

Gounod's *Fantaisie* on the Tsarist anthem is imposing enough, if a bit repetitive. The Dubois *Fantaisie* is suitably grand and pontifical, to be followed by Guilmant's very romantic *Adoration*, a rather beautiful soliloquy for organ and strings. After more pomp from Gigout, we return to Gounod, and an amiably attractive four-movement suite, with hunting horns setting off the jolly Scherzo, followed by a songful *Andante* (nicely registered here). But, not surprisingly, it is the catchy vivace finale that steals the show: a bouncy tune that could become a hit if it got more exposure. It is most winningly played and completes an attractive concertante programme that does not rely on decibels for its main appeal. The performances are excellent and here the very reverberant acoustic seems for the most part under control.

Heifetz, Jascha (violin)

'*Centenary Memorial Edition*' (*1901–2001*): BEETHOVEN: *Concerto* (with NBC SO, Toscanini). BRAHMS: *Concerto*. PROKOFIEV: *Concerto 2, Op. 63* (both with Boston SO, Koussevitzky). SIBELIUS: *Concerto* (with LPO, Beecham). GLAZUNOV: *Concerto*. TCHAIKOVSKY: *Concerto*. WIENIAWSKI: *Concerto 2*. VIEUXTEMPS: *Concertos 4, Op. 31; Op. 37*. ELGAR: *Concerto* (both with LSO, Sargent). SAINT-SAENS: *Introduction & Rondo capriccioso* (all with LPO, Barbirolli); *Havanaise*. SARASATE: *Zigeunerweisen* (both with LSO, Barbirolli). WALTON: *Concerto* (original version; with Cincinnati SO, Goossens). BRAHMS: *Double Concerto for Violin & Cello* (with Feuermann, O, Ormandy). BRUCH: *Scottish Fantasia* (with RCA Victor SO, Steinberg). MENDELSSOHN: *Concerto, Op. 64*. MOZART: *Concertos 4, K.218* (with RPO, Beecham); *5 (Turkish), K.219* (with LPO, Barbirolli). GRUENBERG: *Concerto, Op. 47* (with San Francisco SO, Monteux). WAXMAN: *Carmen Fantasy* (with RCA Victor O, Voorhees)

(BB) (***) Naxos mono 8.107001 (7)

The seven Naxos discs of Heifetz's mono recordings of concertos are available in a boxed set as above, as well as separately. The transfers are of a good standard, mellower than the RCA originals, although the EMI alternative remastering is rather more sophisticated, and the EMI separate discs have less background hiss. They are also far more expensive. This Naxos box is certainly highly recommendable in its own right.

'*Heifetz the Supreme*': BACH: (Unaccompanied) *Violin Partita 2, BWV 1004: Chaconne*. BRAHMS: *Violin Concerto in D, Op. 77*. TCHAIKOVSKY: *Violin Concerto in D, Op. 35* (with Chicago SO, Fritz Reiner). BRUCH: *Scottish Fantasy, Op. 46* (with New SO of London, Sargent). SIBELIUS: *Violin Concerto, Op. 47* (with Chicago SO, Hendl). GLAZUNOV: *Violin Concerto, Op. 82* (with RCA Victor SO, Hendl). GERSHWIN (trans. Heifetz): *3 Preludes* (with Brooks Smith, piano)

(M) *** RCA (ADD) 74321 63470-2 (2)

For once the hyperbole of a record company's title is not exaggerated: truly Heifetz is the supreme virtuoso among violinists, and this generously compiled two-disc set shows him at his very finest. The performance of the great Bach *Chaconne* is not only technically phenomenal, it has an extraordinary range of feeling and dynamic, while Heifetz exerts a compelling grip over the structure. The performances of the five concertante works (discussed more fully in our main volume) are not only inspired and full of insights, they show how well Heifetz chose his accompanists, notably Fritz Reiner in Brahms and Tchaikovsky. Sargent too gives most sensitive support in the Bruch *Scottish Fantasy* – the atmospheric opening is most evocative. Finally come the dazzling and touching Gershwin showpieces, showing that quicksilver bow arm at its most chimerical, even if here the recording is much too closely observed.

'*The Unpublished Recordings*': BEETHOVEN: *Romances 1 and 2*. LALO: *Symphonie espagnole* (both with Philh. O, Susskind). CHAUSSON: *Poème* (with San Francisco SO, Monteux)

(***) Testament mono SBT 1216

It seems astonishing that any recordings by Heifetz, let alone performances as fine as these, should have slipped through the net and never been issued. The Lalo and Beethoven were recorded at EMI's Abbey Road studios in June 1950, just at the time when the long-time alliance between EMI in Britain and RCA Victor in America was slackening. Heifetz went on to record both the *Romances* and the Lalo again for RCA in America the following year, but the EMI sound is warmer and more helpful to the violin. In both (with the central *Intermezzo* of the Lalo omitted, as was then the custom) Heifetz also sounds more flexibly spontaneous. The Chausson, with Monteux and the San Francisco orchestra, was recorded by RCA five years earlier, in 1945, with limited sound and a dry, unhelpful acoustic, making even Heifetz's violin-tone sound rather fizzy at the start, and with the orchestra backwardly placed. The performance itself is magnificent, warmly expressive, with the structure tautly held together.

(i) Hilversum Radio PO or (ii) London Symphony Orchestra, Leopold Stokowski

(i) FRANCK: *Symphony in D min.* RAVEL: *L'éventail de Jeanne.* (ii) CHOPIN: *Mazurka in A min., Op. 17/4* (orch. Stokowski). MESSIAEN: *L'Ascension.* DUPARC: *Extase* (orch. Stokowski)

(M) ** Cala CACD 0526

These recordings were made in the early 1970s in Decca's hi-fi-conscious Phase Four system, and the exaggerated sound goes with the flamboyance of Stokowski's interpretations. The Franck *Symphony* is the most controversial reading on this disc. The conviction with which Stokowski moulds a romantic symphony like this is always striking. But here, by underlining the vulgarities in this score which most conductors seek to conceal, the overall balance of the work is disturbed, and the reading is less than satisfying. Of course it has its moments, but Stokowski too often ventures perilously close to the cliff edge. The Hilversum orchestra does not have the virtuosity of the LSO in the companion pieces, but plays with energy as well as warmth. The rest of the programme is much more successful. After the Ravel *Fanfare* which is startling in its vividness, the following Chopin and Duparc pieces are richly atmospheric and show Stokowski at his most magical. Messiaen's *L'Ascension* is an early work, written first for organ, but then orchestrated in 1935 with a different third movement. Stokowski is characteristically persuasive in developing the smooth flow of the music, though some will object to the opulence of the sound he (and the engineers) favour in the sweet meditation for strings alone, *Prayer of Christ ascending to the Father*.

Hofmann, Josef (piano)

'*The Complete Josef Hofmann*', Vol. 2 (with Curtis Institute Student O, cond. Reiner or Hilsberg): BRAHMS: *Academic Festival Overture*. RUBINSTEIN: *Piano Concerto 4 in D min*. CHOPIN: *Ballade 1 in G min., Op. 23; Nocturne in E flat, Op. 9/2; Waltz in A flat, Op. 42; Andante spianato et Grande polonaise brillante in E flat, Op. 22* (2 versions); *Nocturne in F sharp, Op. 15/2; Waltz in D flat, Op. 64/1; Etude in G flat, Op. 25/9; Berceuse in B flat, Op. 57; Nocturne in C min.,*

Op. 48/1; Mazurka in C, Op. 33/3; Waltz in A flat, Op. 34/1.
HOFMANN: *Chromaticon for Piano & Orchestra* (2 versions). MENDELSSOHN: *Spinning Song in C, Op. 67/4.* RACHMANINOV: *Prelude in G min., Op. 23/5.* BEETHOVEN–RUBINSTEIN: *Turkish March.* MOSZKOWSKI: *Caprice espagnole, Op. 37*
⊕ (***) VAI Audio mono VAIA/IPA 1020 (2)

Josef Hofmann's amazing 1937 performance of Rubinstein's *Fourth Piano Concerto* has long been a much-sought-after item in its LP format, and those who possess it have treasured it. The performance was attended by practically every pianist around, including Rachmaninov and Godowsky. (It was the latter who once said to a youngster who had mentioned a fingerslip in one of Hofmann's recitals, 'Why look for the spots on the sun!') In no other pianist's hands has this music made such sense: Hofmann plays his master's best-known concerto with a delicacy and poetic imagination that are altogether peerless.

Olin Downes spoke of his 'power and delicacy, lightning virtuosity and the capacity to make the keyboard sing, the richness of tone colouring and incorruptible taste'. The 1937 concert included the Brahms overture, a speech by Walter Damrosch, the incomparable performance of the Rubinstein concerto and, after the interval, a Chopin group. One is tempted to say that the *G minor Ballade* has never been surpassed. The second CD includes four later items, recorded in 1945. Once again – and it can't be said too often – the Rubinstein is phenomenal.

Horowitz, Vladimir (piano)

'*The First Recordings*': CHOPIN: *Etude in F, Op. 10/8; Mazurka 21 in C sharp min., Op. 30/4.* DEBUSSY: *Children's Corner: Serenade for the Doll.* SCARLATTI: *Capriccio in E, L. 375.* BIZET/HOROWITZ: *Variations on Themes from 'Carmen'.* DOHNANYI: *Capriccio (Concert Etude in F min., Op. 28/6).* LISZT: *Concert Paraphrase of Schubert's Liebesbotschaft; Paganini Etude 5 in E (La chasse); Valse oubliée 1 in E flat (Octave).* RACHMANINOV: *Piano Concerto 3 in D min., Op. 30* (with LSO, Coates)
(BB) (***) Naxos mono 8.110696

Horowitz's pioneering 1930 account of the Rachmaninov *Third Concerto* with Albert Coates conducting the LSO last appeared on the Biddulph label (coupled with Rachmaninov's own version of the *Second* with Stokowski). An earlier transfer on EMI Références came in a three-CD set with all his recordings from 1930–51. This Naxos transfer comes with the early records Horowitz made for Victor between 1928–30, when he would have been twenty-five to twenty-seven. When in 1928 he first ran through the concerto, with Rachmaninov at the second piano, the composer famously told friends that 'Horowitz pounced with the voraciousness of a tiger: he swallowed it whole'. One can hear this in the Coates partnership – and even more, perhaps, in the electrifying 1941 account with Barbirolli on APR. The Coates version (with its memory lapse in the finale to testify that Horowitz was after all human) is so well known as to need no further comment, except to say that Coates is a marvellously supportive accompanist and that the Obert-Thorn transfer is very successful. It is good to have the cadenza Rachmaninov himself played, too, rather than the

combative (and ugly) one now generally favoured by pianists. Three of the other pieces here have never been released before: two of them, *Liebesbotschaft* and the 1838 version of *La chasse*, Horowitz dropped from his repertoire after 1930. Obert-Thorn uses vinyl pressings for the unpublished takes and has taken great trouble over the transfer. A feast of superb playing from a unique pianist and an invaluable supplement to the Horowitz discography.

'*Legendary RCA Recordings*': RACHMANINOV: *Piano Concerto 3* (with RCA SO, Reiner); TCHAIKOVSKY: *Piano Concerto 1* (with NBC SO, Toscanini): Recital: CHOPIN: *Polonaise-Fantaisie; Mazurka in C sharp min., Op. 30/4. Nocturne in E flat, Op. 9/2.* SCHUMANN: *Kinderscenen: Träumerei. Sonata 3 in F min., Op. 14: Wieck Variations.* SCRIABIN: *Preludes: in D flat, Op. 48/3; in G flat, Op. 11/13; in F sharp min., Op. 15/2; Etude in D sharp min., Op. 18/12.* MOSZKOWSKI: *Etincelles.* BIZET: *Variations on a Theme from 'Carmen'.* PROKOFIEV: *Toccata.* CLEMENTI: *Sonata, Op. 47/2: Rondo.* POULENC: *Presto.* RACHMANINOV: *Prelude in G, Op. 32/5.* DOMENICO SCARLATTI: *Sonatas, L. 189 & L. 494.* LISZT: *Mephisto Waltz*
⊕→ (B) (***) RCA mono 82876 56052-2 (2)

The two famous concerto performances are discussed under their respective composer entries. The solo recital is of hand-picked items spanning Horowitz's RCA recording career after the early years. Most were recorded between 1947 and 1957, although the beautifully played Rachmaninov *Prelude*, Schumann's *Wieck Variations* and the dazzling Liszt *Mephisto Waltz* come from the late 1970s, and the Scarlatti *Sonatas* and Scriabin *D sharp minor Etude* from the early 1980s. There is some prodigious virtuosity here, notably in the Bizet, Clementi and Poulenc encores, but some lovely lyrical playing too, in Schumann and Rachmaninov, and delectable delicacy of articulation in Scarlatti. The sound for the most part is very acceptable.

Hungarian State Orchestra, Mátyás Antal

'*Hungarian Festival*': KODALY: *Háry János: Suite.* LISZT: *Hungarian Rhapsodies for Orchestra 1, 2 & 6* (arr. DOEPPLER). HUBAY: *Hejre Kati* (with Ferenc Balogh). BERLIOZ: *Damnation de Faust: Rákóczy march*
(BB) *** Naxos 8.550142

The Hungarian State Orchestra are in their element in this programme of colourful music for which they have a natural affinity. There are few more characterful versions of the *Háry János Suite* and Hubay's concertante violin piece, with its gypsy flair, is similarly successful, even if the violin soloist is not a particularly strong personality. The special interest of the Liszt *Hungarian Rhapsodies* lies in the use of the Doeppler orchestrations, which are comparatively earthy, with greater use of brass solos than the more sophisticated scoring most often used in the West. The performances are suitably robust and certainly have plenty of charisma. The brilliant digital recording is strong on primary colours but has atmosphere too, and produces plenty of spectacle in the Berlioz *Rákóczy march*.

Jansen, Janine (violin), Royal Philharmonic Orchestra, Barry Wordsworth

KHACHATURIAN: *Masquerade: Nocturne.* RAVEL: *Tzigane.* SAINT-SAENS: *Havanaise; Introduction and Rondo capriccioso.* SHOSTAKOVICH: *The Gadfly: Romance.* TCHAIKOVSKY: *Swan Lake: Danse russe.* VAUGHAN WILLIAMS: *The Lark Ascending.* JOHN WILLIAMS: *Schindler's List: Theme*
**(*) Decca 475 011-2

This brilliant young Dutch violinist made an impressive British début, playing *The Lark Ascending* at the second Prom of 2003. She is an artist of exceptional magnetism, as this mixed bag of a recital demonstrates in every item, from her flamboyant account of the *Danse russe* from *Swan Lake* onwards. With close recording balance for both orchestra and soloist, these are larger-than-life performances, with the two Saint-Saëns showpieces, *Havanaise* as well as the *Introduction and Rondo capriccioso*, prompting the widest expressive and dynamic range. Vaughan Williams's *Lark Ascending* is fresh and open rather than meditative, while Ravel's *Tzigane* in its concentration has the feeling of an improvisation. It will be good to hear Jansen in more substantial works.

Johnson, Emma (clarinet)

Disc 1: *Concertos* (with ECO): MOZART: *Concerto in A, K.488* (cond. Leppard). CRUSELL: *Concerto 2 in F min., Op. 5.* BAERMANN (attrib. WAGNER): *Adagio in D* (both cond. Groves). ARNOLD: *Concerto 2, Op. 115* (cond. Bolton)

Disc 2: *Recital*: READE: *The Victorian Kitchen Garden (suite)* (with Kanga, harp). RIMSKY-KORSAKOV: *Flight of the Bumblebee.* RACHMANINOV: *Vocalise, Op. 34/12.* MILHAUD: *Scaramouche.* SATIE: *Gymnopédie 1.* GERSHWIN (arr. Cohn): *3 Preludes.* MACDOWELL (arr. Isaac): *To a Wild Rose.* BLAKE: *The Snowman: Walking in the Air.* BENJAMIN: *Jamaican Rumba* (all with Drake, piano). SCHUMANN: *Fantasiestücke, Op. 73.* DEBUSSY: *La fille aux cheveux de lin.* RAVEL: *Pavane pour une infante défunte* (with Black, piano). FINZI: *5 Bagatelles, Op. 23* (with Martineau, piano)
(M) *** ASV CDDCS 238 (2)

Emma Johnson's recording of Bernhard Crusell's *Second Concerto* made her a star and earned a Rosette for the original disc (ASV CDDCA 559), coupled with Baermann's rather beautiful *Adagio* (once attributed to Wagner) and music of Rossini and Weber. In return she put Crusell's engagingly lightweight piece firmly on the map, and later went on to record its two companion works (ASV CDDCA 784 – see our main volume). Here it comes coupled with Malcolm Arnold and her magnetic performance of the greatest clarinet concerto of all, by Mozart.

The solo pieces on the second CD derive from several compilations recorded over the last decade, two of which are listed below under Instrumental Recitals. But many will find the present collection works well as an ongoing recital, as it covers such a wide range. Highlights include her heartfelt account of the Schumann *Fantasy Pieces*, and the 5 *Bagatelles* of Gerald Finzi. The charming – almost Ravelian – douceur of Paul Reade's *Victorian Kitchen Garden Suite* is matched by the simplicity of MacDowell's *To a Wild Rose*; and the famous *Snowman* theme is hauntingly presented. There is plenty of virtuosity too – *Scaramouche* is uninhibitedly scatty – the

rhythmic sparkle here and in the *Jamaica Rumba* is delightful, and Rimsky's *Bumblebee* is almost jet-propelled. The various pianists all accompany helpfully and the recording is excellent.

Katchen, Julius (piano)

'Decca Recordings, 1949–1968': RAVEL: *Piano Concerto for the Left Hand; Piano Concerto in G.* GERSHWIN: *Rhapsody in Blue.* PROKOFIEV: *Piano Concerto 3 in C, Op. 26* (with LSO, Kertész); *Piano Concerto 2 in C min., Op. 18* (with New SO, Fistoulari); *Rhapsody on a Theme of Paganini.* DOHNANYI: *Variations on a Nursery Tune, Op. 25* (with LPO, Boult). BARTOK: *Piano Concerto 3* (with SRO, Ansermet); *Mikrokosmos* (excerpts). BRITTEN: *Diversions for Piano & Orchestra, Op. 21* (with LSO, Britten). BEETHOVEN: *Diabelli Variations, Op. 120; Piano Sonata 32 in C min., Op. 111; Polonaise in C, Op. 89.* SCHUBERT: *Fantaisie in C (Wanderer), D.760.* SCHUMANN: *Carnival, Op. 9; Etudes Symphonique; Toccata in C, Op. 7.* CHOPIN: *Piano Sonatas 2 in B flat min., Op. 35; 3 in B min., Op. 58; Ballade 3 in A flat, Op. 47; Fantaisie in F min., Op. 49; Fantaisie-Impromptu in C sharp min., Op. 66; Polonaise in A flat, Op. 53.* MENDELSSOHN: *Auf flügeln des Gesanges* (arr. Liszt); *Prelude & Fugue in E min., Op. 35/1; Rondo capriccioso in E, Op. 14; Scherzo in E min., Op. 16/2.* FRANCK: *Prélude, Choral et Fugue.* BRAHMS: *Piano Sonata 3 in F min., Op. 5; Variations & Fugue on a Theme by Handel, Op. 24; Variations on a Theme by Paganini, Op. 35; Violin Sonatas 2 in A, Op. 100; 3 in D min., Op. 108.* ROREM: *Piano Sonata 2*
(M) *(**) Decca mono/stereo 475 7221 (8)

Jeremy Hayes, in his perceptive sleeve-notes, describes Katchen as a 'natural extrovert and born communicator' and, unlike many artists, these qualities were as apparent in the recording studio as in live concerts. Katchen's fame rests mainly on his stereo recordings made during the late 1950s and '60s, notable for their brilliance both as performances and as recordings. In the items conducted by Kertész, the Grieg, Prokofiev, Gershwin and, especially, the Ravel *Concertos* remain fresh and exciting, with Decca's sound still impressing. What will be of special interest to piano devotees are the mono solo recordings, most of which haven't been available for many years. The Rachmaninov *Concerto 2* (the work's first LP recording) still impresses with its fire and romantic ardour, and the famous coupling of the *Rhapsody on a Theme of Paganini* and *Variations on a Nursery Tune* remains one of classic accounts of all time. With Ansermet, interesting detail is brought out in the Bartók *No. 3*, while Britten's masterly conducting in the *Diversions* makes for compelling listening. Included is Katchen's first LP for Decca, the 1949 account of Brahms's *Piano Sonata 3*, in which, as Hayes writes, 'a young man playing another young man's music'. Brahms was a Katchen speciality in the stereo years, and those recordings have tended to eclipse the mono accounts: the mono *Violin Sonatas* with Ricci have all the brilliance of his more famous stereo versions with Suk, and they are very enjoyable indeed. Katchen's vitality, as well as his imagination, shines in Schumann's *Carnival*, where the contrasts of each number are sharply brought out. The pianist's virtuosity is stupendous in the *Paganini Variations* and there is always a sense of live music-making in these performances, unfailingly exciting in effect: the bravura in Schumann's *Toccata* is electrifying – but never at the expense of musical beauty (one critic wrote, 'Anyone could be forgiven for assuming that he had four hands'). In the same way, although the *Diabelli Variations* are fast by any standard, the style and elegance squash any feeling of 'fast for fast's sake'. As Jeremy Hayes notes, the account of Beethoven's *C minor Sonata*, Op. 111, may not offer the most profound slow movement on disc, but the first movement offers a 'fiery impulse' which is far preferable to many more mundane accounts that have been committed to disc. Katchen's spontaneous passion makes both the Schumann and Chopin items sound as fresh and exciting as newly minted works, and throughout these recordings there is a sense of enjoyably urgent music-making. A must for piano buffs and, with rarer items such as the Ned Rorem *Piano Sonata 2*, as well as some impressive Bartók solo piano music, you can't accuse Decca of lacking imagination.

King, Thea (clarinet)

'*The Clarinet in Concert*': BRUCH: *Double Concerto in E min. for Clarinet, Viola and Orchestra, Op. 88* (with Imai). MENDELSSOHN: *2 Concert Pieces for Clarinet and Basset Horn in F min., Op. 113; in D min., Op. 114* (with Dobrée). CRUSELL: *Introduction and Variations on a Swedish Air, Op. 12* (all 4 works with LSO, Francis). SPOHR: *Variations in B flat for Clarinet and Orchestra on a Theme from Alruna*. RIETZ: *Clarinet Concerto in G min., Op. 29*. SOLERE: *Sinfonie Concertante in F for 2 Clarinets* (with Dobrée). HEINZE: *Konzertstück in F* (all with ECO, Judd or Litton)
(B) *** Hyp. Dyad CDD 22017 (2)

A thoroughly engaging programme of little-known music (the Bruch is not even listed in the *New Grove*), all played with skill and real charm, and excellently recorded. The Bruch *Double Concerto* is particularly individual, but the two attractive Mendelssohn concert pieces (each in three brief movements) and the quixotic Crusell *Variations* are by no means insubstantial. They are discussed more fully under their composer entries in our main volume. The novelties on the second disc are slighter but no less entertaining: the jaunty Spohr *Variations* followed by the galant concerto by Julius Rietz (1812–77) with its engaging lyrical flow. In Etienne Solère's *Sinfonie concertante*, one cannot help but smile at the garrulous chatter between the two solo instruments, which evokes the clinking of teacups, while Gustav Heinze's warmly tuneful *Konzertstück* has a jocular, Hummelian finale to match the bouncing closing Rondeau of the Solère. The playing brings many chortling roulades and a seductive timbre from the ever-stylish Thea King, and Georgina Dobrée is a nimble partner in the *Sinfonie concertante*. The accompaniments are excellent too, while the recording has fine range and presence.

Kraggerud, Henning (violin), Razumovsky Symphony Orchestra, Bjarte Engeset

'*Norwegian Violin Favourites*': BULL: *The Herd-girl's Sunday; La Mélancholie* (arr. Kraggerud); *Concerto in E min.: Adagio*. SINDING: *Suite im alten Stil, Op. 10*. SVENSEN: *Romance in G, Op. 26*. HALVORSEN: *Norwegian Dances 1-2; Maiden's Song; The Old Fisherman's Song; Wedding March; Andante religioso*. GRIEG: *I Love Thee* (arr. Kraggerud); *Elegiac Melody: The Last Spring*
(BB) *** Naxos 8.554497

Ole Bull, born in Bergen in 1810, was a virtuoso of the traditional Norwegian 'Hardanger' fiddle, which he took to Europe, where he achieved a considerable success in Paris. He was one of the first gatherers of Norwegian folk tunes, which he used in his own music. The opening piece here, *The Herd-girl's Sunday*, with its charming melancholy, is characteristic, but the touching *Adagio* from his *Violin Concerto* shows that he also used his folk material more ambitiously and his influence remained. The best-known piece here, Svensen's disarmingly memorable *Romance*, although more sophisticated in construction, is in a similar melodic vein. Johan Halvorsen continued this tradition and his miniatures are equally attractive, as is the Sinding *Suite*. Henning Kraggerud plays a modern violin, and invests all these pieces with a simplicity of style and a beauty of tone that gives great pleasure, ending with two Grieg favourites, including a transcription of his most famous song. With excellent accompaniments and a most natural sound-balance this collection gives much pleasure.

Larrocha, Alicia de (piano)

'*The Art of Alicia de Larrocha*' (with various orchestras and conductors):

Disc 1: BACH: *Italian Concerto in F, BWV 971; French Suite No. 6 in E, BWV 817; Chorales: Beloved Jesus, We Are Here; Sanctify Us with thy Goodness* (both arr. Cohen); *Chaconne in D min. from BWV 1004* (arr. Busoni). *Concerto 5 in F min., BWV 1056*. HAYDN: *Concerto in D, Hob XVIII/2* (both with London Sinf., David Zinman)

Disc 2: HAYDN: *Andante with Variations in F min., Hob XVII/6*. MOZART: *Sonatas: in A, K.331; in D, K.576*. BEETHOVEN: *7 Bagatelles, Op. 33*. MENDELSSOHN: *Variations sérieuses, Op. 54*

Disc 3: CHOPIN: *24 Preludes, Op. 28; Berceuse, Op. 57; Piano Concerto 2 in F min., Op. 21* (with SRO, Comissiona)

Disc 4: LISZT: *Sonata in B min.* SCHUBERT: *Sonata 21 in B flat, D.960; Impromptu in A flat, D.899/4*

Disc 5: SCHUMANN: *Fantaisie in C min., Op. 17; Allegro, Op. 8; Romance, Op. 28/2; Concerto in A min.* (with RPO, Dutoit)

Disc 6: SOLER: *Sonatas: in G min., SR 42; in D min., SR 15; in F, SR 89*. TURINA: *Zapateado, Op. 8/3*. GRANADOS: *Danzas españolas, Book 2; El pelele*. MONTSALVATGE: *Sonatina para Yvette*. MOMPOU: *Prélude 7 (for Alicia de Larrocha)*. ALBENIZ: *Tango, Op. 165/2; Iberia, Book 1*. FALLA: *Fantasia béatica*

Disc 7: FALLA; *Nights in the Gardens of Spain* (with SRO, Comissiona). KHACHATURIAN: *Concerto* (with LPO, Frühbeck de Burgos). RAVEL: *Piano Concerto for the Left Hand* (with LPO, Foster)
(B) **(*) Decca (ADD/DDD) 473 813-2 (7)

The 2002/3 concert season marked Alicia de Larrocha's eightieth birthday and also her farewell to the concert hall, so Decca's anthology covering her peak years from 1970 onwards is opportune. She usually combined the gift of spontaneity in the studio with excellent support from the Decca engineers. However, at times she could be idiosyncratic, and not all the recordings chosen here show her at her very best.

The programme opens well with her solo Bach recital, for the most part recorded in Decca's West Hampstead studio in 1970. The sound is clear and clean, reflecting her simple style and her desire to present Bach effectively in pianistic terms.

The great *Chaconne*, however, recorded two years later in Kingsway Hall, is expansive and romantically very free, reflecting her response to the transformation of Busoni's flamboyant transcription. Then in the Haydn *Concerto*, which completes the first disc, her crisp, clean articulation obviously seeks to evoke the fortepiano, and the sharp rhythmic snap of the 'gypsy' finale is a joy, when David Zinman's accompaniment is excellent and the scale of the recording is so well judged.

She was a natural classicist and Haydn's *Andante and Variations* are thoughtfully played, while in the Mozart *Sonatas* her balance between warmth and poise shows a ready sensibility; phrasing is always intelligently pointed and there is an admirable sense of flow. She is equally accomplished in the Mendelssohn *Variations sérieuses*, but here some of her rubati are a shade unconvincing, and this comment could also be applied to her set of Chopin *Préludes*. Yet there is some poetic and imaginative playing too, and the *F minor Concerto* is also attractive and poetic; throughout, the analogue recording is first class.

The Liszt *Sonata* brings some formidable playing, yet, for all the many perceptive touches, she is a little too idiosyncratic for her reading to be included among the finest available versions. However, her performance of the great *B flat major Sonata* of Schubert shows her at her finest. The heart of her reading lies in the slow movement, played introspectively with great poetic feeling. Her poise and crisp articulation in the final two movements also give much pleasure, and if she is rather less successful than, say, Curzon or Kempff in finding the spiritual serenity of the large span of the first movement, hers is still a memorable account, beautifully recorded.

The Schumann *Fantasia in C minor* again brings a very personal reading, perhaps too personal, yet there are many good things in its favour. She is very relaxed indeed in the *A Minor Concerto*, and there are more touches of wilfulness, as in the ritenuto before the recapitulation of the first movement. Poetry is certainly not absent: the interchanges between piano and clarinet are beautifully done, but the lack of overall vitality becomes enervating in the finale, where the basic tempo is too lazy to be convincing.

The encores on the sixth disc are entirely delightful; the *Sonatas* of Soler and the works of Turina, Granados, Albéniz and Falla are her home territory, and Mompou's *Seventh Prelude* was written for her. The final disc brings a distinguished account of Ravel's *Left-Hand Concerto* and an unsurpassed reading of Falla's *Nights in the Gardens of Spain*, and she then makes the slow movement of the Khachaturian *Concerto* sound evocatively like Falla. The finale too is infectiously jaunty. Not so the first movement, however, which is disappointingly slack in rhythm at a dangerously slow tempo.

The seven records in their cardboard sleeves each carry a different photograph of the pianist, taken over the years during which the recordings were made, which will make this set doubly attractive for her admirers.

Lawson, Colin (clarinet or basset horn), Parley of Instruments, Peter Holman

'*English Classical Clarinet Concertos*': JOHN MAHON: *Concerto 2 in F; Duets 1 & 4 in B flat for 2 Basset Horns* (with Harris). J. C. BACH: *Concerted Symphony in E flat.* JAMES HOOK: *Concerto in E flat*
** Hyp. CDA 66869

The clarinet (invented around 1700) did not achieve a strong solo profile until well into the eighteenth century, and even then it was not favoured by amateurs. Mozart remains the only composer of that period to have written really great music for it. Thus, even more than in his companion disc of violin concertos (listed under Wallfisch), Peter Holman has had to scrape the barrel a bit and even include a *Concerted Symphony* by J. C. Bach, which in the event is the most enterprising work here but which features (besides a pair of clarinets) two oboes, a bassoon and two horns. It has a very striking first movement and a touching *Larghetto*, which opens with a bassoon solo; the flute then takes over, and the clarinets enter much later. The most unusual scoring is in the closing Minuet, where in the Trio the woodwind take over entirely.

John Mahon's *Duos* for basset horns are agreeable but sub-Mozart. His *Concerto*, however, goes even further than the contemporary violin concertos (see below), by using a complete Scottish folksong for his ingenious *Andante* and another popular tune (*The wanton God*) for the Rondo finale. James Hook's *Concerto* has little that is individual to say in its conventional and rather long opening movement, yet it includes the prettiest roulades for the clarinet soloist. However, the composer reserves the real fireworks for the final Rondo, especially in the spectacular closing episode, introduced by the horns, where the clarinet ripples hectically up and down its register in a quite abandoned manner. Colin Lawson is fully equal to such bravura and he plays with fine style throughout. Holman provides excellent accompaniments, but it is a pity that the music itself is so uneven.

Lefèvre, Alain (piano), Quebec Symphony Orchestra, Yoav Talmi

20th-Century Piano Concertos: MATHIEU: *Concerto de Québec.* ADDINSELL: *Warsaw Concerto.* GERSHWIN: *Concerto in F*
** Analekta AN 29814

André Mathieu's *Concerto de Québec*, written in 1943, in time for the composer's fourteenth birthday, exists in six different scores(!), out of which Alain Lefèvre has fashioned this performing version. It is prodominently romantic, with the undoubtedly memorable slow movement sounding very like film music, yet somehow curiously distinctive in its melodic lyricism. The finale has a perkily rhythmic main theme, and again brings a memorable secondary idea with a distinctly Rachmaninovian flavour, and its passionate climax on the strings is truly in the Rachmaninov/Tchaikovsky concerto tradition. This is not great music, but it is very persuasively played here: Lefèvre is obviously committed to the music and Talmi provides excellent support.

The *Warsaw Concerto* is given an expansive, at times very languorous performance, again very well played, and certainly producing a luscious climax. But some may want more ongoing thrust in the performance overall. Similarly the first movement of the Gershwin is very relaxed, not without its nice touches of rhythmic pointing, but minus the exhilaration one expects from North American performances. This means that the evocative slow movement, warmly played though it is, does not bring the proper degree of contrast, and it is in the zestful finale that Gershwin's witty crossover rhythms come fully into their own. The recording is very good without being in the demonstration bracket.

Leningrad Philharmonic Orchestra, Evgeni Mravinsky

'*Mravinsky in Prague*': BARTOK: *Music for Strings, Percussion and Celesta.* SHOSTAKOVICH: *Symphonies 5 in D min., Op. 47; 6 in B min., Op. 54; 11 in G min. (The Year 1905), Op. 103; 12 (The Year 1917), Op. 112; Violin Concerto 1 in A min., Op. 77* (with Czech PO & D. Oistrakh). PROKOFIEV: *Symphony 6 in E flat min., Op. 111*

(M) (***) HM/Praga mono/stereo PR 256016/19 (4)

The performances in this set have been issued previously in various combinations and formats. The first disc couples the Bartók and the Shostakovich *Fifth* in 1967 performances recorded at the Prague Spring Festival. The *Music for Strings, Percussion and Celesta* has suitable intensity, although not as much as that in the Shostakovich *Eleventh Symphony*, recorded in the same year, which occupies the third CD. This is one of the finest performances Mravinsky gave on disc, and it is played flat out with such electricity that criticism is silenced. The second CD brings a 1955 performance of the *Sixth Symphony*, a work he did with extraordinary concentration. It is not the equal of his Melodiya version from the 1960s and, quite apart from the limited mono sound, suffers from intrusive audience noise. The *Twelfth Symphony* comes from 1962, the same year as his Melodiya recording, and gives it with 500 per cent conviction and frenetic but wonderfully controlled energy. The Shostakovich *First Violin Concerto* with David Oistrakh comes fresh from the press as it were, in 1957, when the piece was being introduced to the world, and, like its pioneering accounts under Mitropoulos and Mravinsky himself, is in mono. His first mono version of the Prokofiev *Sixth* was a classic of the LP catalogue, and this 1967 version, though not perhaps as intense, is still one of the most impressive on CD. The sound is of variable quality throughout, but the playing is mostly in a class of its own.

Lindberg, Christian (trombone)

'*American Trombone Concertos*' (with BBC Nat. O of Wales, Llewellyn): CHAVEZ: *Concerto.* ROUSE: *Concerto in Memory of Leonard Bernstein.* AUGUSTA READ THOMAS: *Meditation*

(***) BIS CD 788

By the time he started writing his *Concerto*, Chavez was already in the terminal stages of cancer and his wife had just died. The work opens with an extended morose soliloquy in which the orchestra provides dissonantly pungent support; at times the pacing quickens, but the disconsolate atmosphere remains and, though some percussive intrusions towards the end provide more lively contrast, this music undoubtedly brings longueurs and is essentially depressing.

The *Meditation* by Augusta Read Thomas opens much more positively, with the soloist proceeding over a series of lively orchestral interjections. Bell effects (echoed by the strings) and a percussive spicing add variety, and there is a final eruption of energy. But the meagre musical invention is unenticing.

Easily the finest work here is the concerto by Rouse, which, though darkly atmospheric, readily holds the listener most compellingly. The music climbs up from the lower depths (the opening evocation rather like that at the beginning of the Ravel *Left-hand Piano Concerto*). After an exciting climax the soloist has a ruminative cadenza, before dashing off in a dazzling Scherzo (superb bravura from Lindberg), with the

orchestra just about managing to keep up, yet doing so with some panache. There is a series of hair-raising orchestral explosions, followed by a mêlée of urgently volatile brass figurations, which then die away slowly, leading to the touching finale, marked *Elegiaco, lugubre.*

This is designated by Rouse as a memorial to Leonard Bernstein and quotes what is described as the 'Credo' theme from Bernstein's *Third (Kaddish) Symphony*. The movement has an unrelenting thrust and the central orchestral declamation of grief makes a powerful statement, before the soloist steals in with his own gentle and moving valedictory lament. Then, Orpheus-like, he returns into the depths. Superb solo playing throughout this disc, and very fine recording. But the Rouse is the only piece here of real memorability, and it badly needs new couplings.

'*Classical Trombone Concertos*' (with Australian CO, Richard Tognetti): MICHAEL HAYDN: *Concerto in D.* LEOPOLD MOZART: *Concerto in D.* WAGENSEIL: *Concerto in E flat.* ALBRECHTSBERGER: *Concerto in B flat.* LINDBERG: *Dreams of Arcadia* (for flute and orchestra) (Bezaly, Swedish CO, Lindberg). GOTHE: *Prelude and Dance* (Swedish Wind Ensemble, Lindberg)

*** BIS CD 1248

These concertos by Michael Haydn and Leopold Mozart are *not* transcriptions of horn concertos, they are genuine classical trombone concertos, almost certainly written for a celebrated Austrian trombone virtuoso, Thomas Gschladt, who was a contemporary and friend of horn player Joseph Leutgeb, for whom Mozart wrote his four horn concertos. The presence of lip trills in the solo parts fooled scholars, as they were not thought possible on a trombone. But subsequently it became clear that such trills were indeed part of the eighteenth-century trombonist's expertise and, as Christian Lindberg demonstrates here with flair, he positively relishes them.

Michael Haydn's *Concerto* dates from 1764 and was almost certainly written for Gschladt. It consists of three movements of a ten-movement work which included a solo trombone in three of them, and was later published as a *Divertimento in D*. The brilliant opening *Allegro spiritoso* is very spirited, the thoughtful central *Andantino* (with plenty of trills) was admired by Mozart, and it is followed by a sprightly closing *Presto*, where the orchestra's principal horn (probably Leutgeb at the first performance) joins the trombone in amiable duetting.

Leopold Mozart's three concertante movements are also part of a larger work, a *Serenade* which already (in 1755) had two movements for trumpet, to which (on hearing Gschladt play) Leopold added three more especially for this astonishing early virtuoso. He included a spectacular cadenza in the first movement and an all but Romantic central *Andante*, which Lindberg plays very beautifully. The closing *Presto* skips along winningly and the clipped solo articulation here is most diverting.

Wagenseil's *Two Movements for Trombone* are of more doubtful origin (although Gschladt may have been associated with their provenance). They are agreeable enough, the first a modest march, the second more animated and demanding. But neither this nor the three-movement *Concerto* by Johann Albrechtsberger rises much above a routine level, except for the brief, jolly finale of the latter, which would make a good encore.

Christian Lindberg's performances of all four works are outstanding. He shows total mastery of his instrument and his virtuosity is audacious, while his elegant phrasing and stylish use of dynamic contrast conquers the more conventional writing. The accompaniments from Richard Tognetti and his Australian Chamber Orchestra are admirable, and the recording is most convincingly balanced. The two bonus items are samplers of two other CD collections, where Christian Lindberg takes over the conductor's podium. The excerpt from his own concertante work for flute (sensitively played by Sharon Bezaly) introduces some seductive bird-sounds; the *Prelude and Dance* by Mats Larsson Gothe is altogether less genial, rhythmically persistent but with a wide range of sonority and colour. It is presented with great conviction, and both are very well recorded.

'Trombone Concertos' (with São Paolo SO, John Neschling): SHILKRET: *Trombone Concerto.* HÖGBERG: *Concerto 1 ('The Return of Kit Bones').* LINDBERG: *Helikon Wasp*
(*) BIS compatible Surround **SACD BIS-SACD 1448

Nathaniel Shilkret (1889–1992) was a distinguished crossover musician during the great days of Hollywood: directing, composing and conducting music for over 600 films and being associated with artists as diverse as Glenn Miller, Benny Goodman and Fred Astaire and Ginger Rogers, and even working in the world of opera. In 1927 he also conducted the famous Paul Whiteman record of *Rhapsody in Blue* (though, at the time, the credit on the disc was given to Whiteman, for commercial reasons). Shilkret wrote his *Trombone Concerto* for Tommy Dorsey, who first performed it in New York with Stokowski (who greatly admired it) in 1945. The score has been retrieved from the composer's estate and restored by Brian Free – and it is well worth restoring: a true crossover work, exuberantly jazzy in the outer movements, with a remarkable cadenza and a richly enjoyable *Andante* that is pure Gershwin pastiche – almost, but not quite, a crib. At 23 minutes it could do with a little judicious pruning, but the performance here is superb, with the jazzy 'big band' orchestration obviously relished by John Neschling and his excellent São Paolo Orchestra. Needless to say, Christian Lindberg's solo playing is superlative, as it is in the other two works.

Especially is it so in the extreme bravura of his own concerto, *Helikan Wasp*, which follows after Fredrik Högberg's work in being associated with a poem about 'a funny, funny little creature who can sing and play' and who is ready to sting those who 'hide behind intellectual mannerism'. Högberg's *Concerto* is inseparable from his epic poem, 'The Return of Kit Bone', who 'ruled the West with a slide trombone' and who, in the course of an ingenuous narrative, first 'shoots' the orchestra's first trumpet, then is himself 'shot' and wounded by the principal trombone, before the conductor succumbs in the final 'gunfight' and Kit himself directs the work's conclusion. It is difficult to take the piece seriously, but it is certainly depicted vividly in SACD surround sound, and Lindberg's contribution is peerless.

Lipatti, Dinu (piano)

'The Legacy of Dinu Lipatti' (with Boulanger; Philh. O, Zürich Tonhalle O, Lucerne Festival O; Galliera, Ackermann, Karajan): BACH: *Chorale: Jesu, Joy of Man's Desiring* (arr. Hess, from BWV 147); *Chorale Preludes, BWV 599 & 639* (both arr. Busoni); *Partita 1, BWV 825; Siciliana* (arr. Kempff, from BWV 1031). D. SCARLATTI: *Sonatas, Kk. 9 & 380.* MOZART: *Piano Concerto 21 in C, K.467; Piano*

Sonata 8 in A min., K.310. SCHUBERT: *Impromptus 2–3, D.899/2 & 3.* SCHUMANN: *Piano Concerto in A min., Op. 54.* GRIEG: *Piano Concerto in A min., Op. 16.* CHOPIN: *Piano Concerto 1 in E min., Op. 11; Barcarolle, Op. 60; Etudes, Op. 10/5 & 25/5; Mazurka 32, Op. 50/3; Nocturne 8, Op. 27/2; Piano Sonata 3 in B min., Op. 58; Waltzes 1–4.* LISZT: *Années de pèlerinage, 2nd Year: Sonetto 104 del Petrarca.* RAVEL: *Alborada del gracioso.* BRAHMS: *Waltzes (4 hands), Op. 39/1–2, 5–6, 10, 14–15.* ENESCU: *Piano Sonata 3 in D, Op. 25*
✹ (M) (***) EMI mono 7 67163-2 (5)

This set represents Lipatti's major recording achievements. Whether in Bach (*Jesu, joy of man's desiring* is unforgettable) or Chopin – his *Waltzes* seem to have grown in wisdom and subtlety over the years – Scarlatti or Mozart, these performances are very special indeed. The remastering is done well, and this is a must for anyone with an interest in the piano.

Lloyd Webber, Julian (cello)

'Favourite Cello Concertos': DVORAK: *Concerto in B min., Op. 104* (with Czech PO, Neumann). TCHAIKOVSKY: *Variations on a Rococo Theme* (original version), *Op. 33* (with RPO, Cleobury). FAURE: *Elégie, Op. 24.* SAINT-SAENS: *Concerto 1 in A min., Op. 33; Allegro appassionato, Op. 43* (with ECO, Yan Pascal Tortelier); *Carnaval des animaux: Le cygne* (with ECO, Cleobury). ELGAR: *Concerto in E min., Op. 68* (with RPO, Menuhin); *Romance in D min., Op. 62* (with ASMF, Marriner); *Idylle, Op. 4/1* (arr. for cello and organ). ALBINONI: *Adagio* (arr. GIAZOTTO). SCHUMANN: *Kinderszenen: Träumerei* (arr. PARKER). BACH: *Cantata 147: Jesu, Joy of Man's Desiring.* RIMSKY-KORSAKOV: *Flight of the Bumblebee.* BACH/GOUNOD: *Ave Maria* (all with ECO or RPO, Cleobury). J. LLOYD WEBBER: *Jackie's Song.*
(M) *** Ph. (ADD) 462 115-2 (2)

Lloyd Webber is at his finest in the Elgar *Concerto.* Nor is there any lack of intensity in the Dvořák, a strong and warmly sympathetic reading. He has the advantage of Menuhin to direct the RPO most idiomatically in the former, and the Dvořák specialist, Neumann, with the Czech Philharmonic to accompany him in the latter. The Czech orchestral attack has fine bite and the clipped style of articulation brings out the folk element. The horn soloist plays the great second-subject melody with a degree of vibrato but he is a fine artist, and Lloyd Webber's playing is marked by a ripe, rich tone. Intonation is excellent, but the soloist's occasional easing of tempi may not appeal to some listeners.

Both Saint-Saëns works are played with considerable virtuosity, and again there is the advantage of a first-class accompaniment, from Yan Pascal Tortelier and the ECO. Tchaikovsky's original score is used for the *Rococo Variations,* which is presented affectionately and elegantly. All in all, if the various encores also appeal, this is an attractive enough package, very well recorded in Philips's most natural manner. *Jackie's song,* Lloyd Webber's catchy little tribute to Jacqueline du Pré, is added as an ardent postscript.

'Cello Moods' (with RPO, James Judd): FRANCK: *Panis angelicus.* ELGAR: *Chanson de matin; Salut d'amour.* J. LLOYD WEBBER: *Jackie's song.* DEBUSSY: *Rêverie.* BACH: *Suite 3: Air.* MASSENET: *Thaïs: Méditation.* CACCINI: *Ave Maria.* BORODIN: *Nocturne.* GLAZUNOV: *Mélodie,*

Op. 20/1. CHOPIN: *Nocturne, Op. 9/2.* BOCCHERINI: *Cello Concerto: Adagio.* RHEINBERGER: *Cantilena.* BRUCH: *Kol Nidrei*
*** Ph. 462 588-2

Decorated with extraordinary artwork by Jane Powell which shows an unclothed cellist covered only with shadowy music staves (the cello hiding any suggestion of immodesty), this collection of lollipops is obviously aimed at the crossover market. The playing is of high quality, with none of these famous tunes sentimentalized. Franck's *Panis angelicus* and Massenet's *Méditation* here sound almost noble on the cello. The other highlights are the charming Glazunov *Mélodie*, the Rheinberger *Cantilena*, and the very eloquent Max Bruch *Kol Nidrei*. If you enjoy this kind of programme it couldn't be better played or recorded.

London Gabrieli Brass Ensemble, Christopher Larkin

Original 19th-century Music for Brass: BEETHOVEN: *3 Equales for 4 Trombones.* CHERUBINI: *Trois pas redoublés et la première marche; Trois pas redoublés et la seconde marche.* DAVID: *Nonetto in C min.* DVORAK: *Fanfare.* LACHNER: *Nonet in F.* RIMSKY-KORSAKOV: *Notturno for 4 Horns.* SIBELIUS: *Overture in F min.: Allegro; Andantino; Menuetto; Praeludium*
*** Hyp. CDA 66470

'From the Steeples and the Mountains': IVES: *From the Steeples and the Mountains; Let there be Light.* BARBER: *Mutations from Bach.* HARRIS: *Chorale for Organ and Brass.* VIRGIL THOMSON: *Family Portrait.* COWELL: *Grinnell Fanfare; Tall Tale; Hymn and Fuguing Tune 12; Rondo.* GLASS: *Brass Sextet.* RUGGLES: *Angels.* CARTER: *A Fantasy upon Purcell's Fantasia about One Note*
(BB) *** Hyp. Helios CDH 55018

It is difficult to decide which of these two programmes is the more enterprising and the more rewarding. If you are responsive to brass sonorities and you acquire one of them, you will surely want its companion. Beethoven's *Equales* were used at the composer's funeral. They are brief, but noble and dignified. The Sibelius suite is folksy, uncharacteristic writing, but has genuine charm.

The second concert opens and closes with the always stimulating music of Charles Ives. *From the Steeples and the Mountains* is scored for four sets of bells, trumpet and trombones, and its effect is clangorously wild! Elliott Carter's Purcell arrangement also has tolling bells, and is quite haunting. Of the other pieces the most striking is the Barber *Mutations*, which draws on the chorale *Christe du Lamm Gottes* to highly individual effect. Most passionate of all is Ruggles's pungently compressed, muted brass *Angels*, yet the piece is marked 'Serene'! The brass playing throughout the two discs is as communicative as it is expert and the recording is splendidly realistic and present.

London Baroque, Terence Charlston
(harpsichord/chamber organ)

'The Trio Sonata in 17th-Century England': GIBBONS: *3 Fantasias a 3.* COPRARIO: *Fantasia Suite.* LAWES: *Sett 1.*

JENKINS: *Fancy & Ayre; Fantasia a 3.* LOCKE: *Suite in D min.* SIMPSON: *(Suite) in D.* BLOW: *Ground in G min.; Sonata in A.* PURCELL: *Sonata XX in D*
**(*) BIS CD 1455

A well-played and -recorded collection of trio sonatas from the seventeenth century. It is all gently pleasing but, with a preponderance of generally quite slow music, not desperately exciting. The chamber organ contributions in some of the items make for a nice tonal contrast, and overall this makes for ideal 'relaxing' listening, perhaps best not played all in one go.

London Philharmonic Orchestra, Sir Thomas Beecham

'The Founding Years': CHABRIER: *España.* SIBELIUS: *The Tempest (Incidental Music): Suite.* MOZART: *Symphony 35 (Haffner); Mass in C min. (Great), K.427: Kyrie; Qui tollis.* HANDEL: *Israel in Egypt: But as for his people; The Lord is a Man* (with Dora Labette (soprano), Leeds Festival Ch.))
Ⓜ (M) (***) LPO (mono) LPO 0006

The highlight of this disc, and a quite indispensable one, is Beecham's fizzing (1939) recording of Chabrier's *España*, which has never been surpassed for sheer *joie de vivre*. Who would guess that the first side of this famous 78-r.p.m. performance was recorded in one day, and the second three weeks later? Dutton joins them up perfectly and his superb transfer restores all the warmth and bloom of the Kingsway Hall recording with its lustre and glittering castanets. The rest of the concert is hardly less enticing, especially the pioneering recording of a suite from Sibelius's incidental music for *The Tempest*, then virtually new music. Beecham works his magic on *The Oak Tree*, the lovely and delicate *Berceuse* and especially the dramatic closing *Storm* with its anticipation of *Tapiola*. This comes from the Leeds Festival in 1934, when Beecham also made a recording of Borodin's *Polovtsian Dances* from *Prince Igor*, which became famous. But the Sibelius was never released, even though it had the composer's imprimatur.

Further recordings from that occasion, released here for the first time, include excerpts from the Mozart *C minor Mass* (with Dora Labette the soloist) and, more importantly, splendid excerpts from *Israel in Egpt*, especially the thrilling chorus, *'The Lord is a Man of War'* which has a characteristic Beecham swagger, with the Leeds Town Hall acoustic giving the full-toned Festival Chorus a rich, ambient setting.

The Mozart *Haffner Symphony* is another delight, especially the 'pomposo' Minuet with its very winning Trio, and for the way Beecham points that bouncy Mozartian tune in the *Andante*. There is a slight edge on the violins here, but otherwise the sound is again full and pleasing. Altogether an unmissable CD, and the Dutton transfers offering an amazing degree of realism.

HANDEL, arr. Beecham: *The Great Elopement* (ballet).
HAYDN: *Symphony 97 in C.* MOZART: *Serenade (Eine kleine Nachtmusik); La clemenza di Tito: Overture*
(**) Biddulph mono WHL 041

BEETHOVEN: *Symphony 4 in B flat, Op. 60.* MOZART: *Die Entführung aus dem Serail: Overture.* SCHUBERT: *Symphony 6 in C, D.589*
(**) Biddulph mono WHL 042

BERLIOZ: *Les Troyens: Royal Hunt and Storm; Trojan March.* BORODIN: *Prince Igor: Overture.* MENDELSSOHN: *Symphony 5 in D min. (Reformation), Op. 107.*
RIMSKY-KORSAKOV: *May Night: Overture.* TCHAIKOVSKY: *Eugene Onegin: Waltz; Polonaise*
(**) Biddulph mono WHL 043

These three discs are most welcome for filling in the least-known period of Beecham's recording activities, towards the end of the Second World War, working with the newly self-governing LPO, before he founded the RPO. These recordings had a sadly brief period in the catalogue and, unlike Beecham's pre-war recordings, have remained in limbo ever since.

The second of the three discs, coupling Mozart, Beethoven and Schubert, is the most substantial. Beecham's account of Beethoven's *Fourth Symphony* – a work he never returned to on record – has great flair and vitality, with fierceness set alongside elegance. The *Entführung Overture* here is very similar to the one in his classic recording of the complete opera, but with a concert ending.

This 1944 version of Schubert's *Sixth* was a first recording, differing from his RPO remake in that the outer movements are faster, and the middle two broader, notably the *Andante*. On the first disc, the finale of *Eine kleine Nachtmusik* in this 1945 version is more an *Allegretto* than an *Allegro*, idiosyncratically slow but deliciously sprung. In the *Clemenza overture*, originally issued by Victor, not HMV, Beecham takes a lightweight view, as though this is early Mozart, but the Haydn *97th Symphony* comes in a typically alert reading, with fierceness and elegance set in contrast, rather as in the Beethoven. The Biddulph transfers here lack sufficient body to sustain the top emphasis. That is very evident when one compares this transfer of the Handel–Beecham *Great Elopement* recording with the Dutton version.

On the third disc the sound for the Beecham lollipops – delectably done – is still thin, but the 1945 version of Mendelssohn's *Reformation Symphony* is generally better, with brass full, bright and well separated, and with gentle string *pianissimos* (as in the '*Dresden Amen*') beautifully caught. A valuable trio of discs which should be considered by Beecham devotees despite the reservations over the transfers and the fact that they are not inexpensive.

(i) London Philharmonic Orchestra or (ii) BBC Symphony Orchestra, Sir Thomas Beecham

(i) RIMSKY-KORSAKOV: *May Night Overture.* BERLIOZ: *The Trojans: Royal Hunt and Storm; Trojan March.*
MENDELSSOHN: *Symphony 5 in D min. (Reformation), Op. 107.* BORODIN: *Prince Igor: Overture.* (ii) SIBELIUS: *Karelia Suite, Op. 11.* REZNICEK: *Donna Diana: Overture*
(B) (***) Dutton Lab mono CDEA 5508

All these excellent transfers come from 1945, before Beecham had formed the RPO. The *Royal Hunt and Storm* from the *The Trojans* and Rimsky-Korsakov's *May Night Overture* are characteristic of Beecham, and his guest appearances with the BBC Symphony Orchestra produced excellent accounts of the *Intermezzo* and *Alla marcia* from the *Karelia Suite* and the delightful *Donna Diana Overture* of Rezniček, which has not appeared before. Was its release delayed because, a year or so

later, Karajan recorded it with the Vienna Philharmonic for Columbia? Sir Thomas's account of the *Reformation Symphony* does not, however, show him at his very best (the *Allegro vivace* movement is just a bit too fast). Excellent transfers.

London Philharmonic Orchestra, Sir Adrian Boult

'*The Boult Historic Collection*'

GEORGE BUTTERWORTH: *A Shropshire Lad* (rhapsody); *The Banks of Green Willow* (idyll). BAX: *Tintagel* (tone-poem). HOLST: *The Perfect Fool* (ballet suite). VAUGHAN WILLIAMS: *Old King Cole* (ballet). ELGAR: *Chanson de nuit; Chanson de matin, Op. 15/1–2*
(BB) (***) Belart mono 461 354-2

Butterworth's two beautiful evocations of the English countryside have wonderful delicacy of texture and feeling, while Bax's *Tintagel* is both evocative and passionately full-blooded at its climax. Holst's *Perfect Fool* ballet suite sounds remarkably fresh and vivid, and Vaughan Williams's *Old King Cole* (taken from another ballet, of 1923) is both jolly and boisterous, as befits the image of that famous nursery-rhyme monarch. Elgar's paired miniatures of morning and night have characteristically affectionate warmth, and here the full ambience of the recording might almost be mistaken for stereo.

London Symphony Orchestra, Karl Boehm

'*In Salzburg 1973/7*': BEETHOVEN: *Symphony 7 in A.*
BRAHMS: *Symphony 2.* MOZART: *Symphonies 28 in C, K.328; 38 in D (Prague); Violin Concerto 7 in D, K.271* (with Szeryng, violin); SCHUMANN: *Symphony 4; Piano Concerto in A min.* (with Gilels, piano); R. STRAUSS: *Death and Transfiguration*
(M) **(*) Andante RE-A-4030 (4)

It was the most unexpected of musical love-affairs – between Karl Boehm, fierce upholder of the German-Austrian tradition, and the London Symphony Orchestra, in 1973 riding high to the point of arrogance. The rehearsal of the very first item, Brahms's *Second Symphony*, set the pattern, and after the concert, which also included Mozart's *Haffner Symphony* and the doubtfully authentic *Violin Concerto 7*, with Henryk Szeryng as soloist, the message came back from Boehm that he had rarely known an orchestra so warmly responsive. He conducted the LSO again on their next Salzburg visit in 1975, and a third time in 1977, by which time the love affair had so developed that the players voted to have the old man as their honorary president.

Those seminal occasions are now preserved on these four discs in excellent transfers of Austrian Radio recordings. Consistently there is an extra warmth and a degree more flexibility in the performances compared with those that Boehm made in the studio, usually with the Berlin Philharmonic or the Vienna Philharmonic. In the Brahms (which Boehm never recorded in the studio) the recording reveals a crescendo of tension, while Boehm's Mozart with the LSO is lighter and more elegant than in his studio recordings, and in Beethoven's *Seventh Symphony* the Salzburg performance is markedly more joyful in the fast movements and less square in the *Allegretto* slow movement. In Schumann's *Fourth Symphony* Boehm's measured speeds are controlled so subtly that again squareness is avoided, while Emil Gilels gives a warmly magisterial account of the *A minor Piano Concerto*, crisply lightened in the central intermezzo. Strauss's *Death and Transfiguration*, in the 1977 concert, has an irresistible glow. What consistently emerges throughout is not just the brilliance of the LSO woodwind and brass but the refinement and the resonance of the strings.

London Symphony Orchestra, Skitch Henderson

'*Children's Classics*' PROKOFIEV: *Peter and the Wolf, Op. 67* (narrative revised). SAINT-SAENS: *Carnival of the Animals* (with verses by Nash, and animals from the London Zoo; both with Lillie). TRAD. (arr. Sharples): '*Uncle Ken's Nursery Rhymes*' (with McKellar, and orchestral accompaniment directed by Sharples)

**(*) Australian Decca Eloquence (ADD) 466 673-2

This collection includes a fascinating early LP version of *Peter and the Wolf* involving a 'cabaret act' by Beatrice Lillie to words by 'Bidrum Vabish' (a pseudonym for John Culshaw), full of asides and additions like 'The cat climbed up the tree before you could say Prokofiev'. The original LP was most notable for the correspondence it provoked (after the record's review in *The Gramophone*) between Mr Culshaw Vabish and Vetrov Hayver (Guess who!). Curious older readers are referred to the issues of November and December 1960.

The orchestral part of the performance is rather less than distinguished, but the conductor adopts a determined and unflagging pace, and after all it is Miss Lillie's record, and its enjoyment depends on whether or not you take to her rather arch contribution and the new text which she undoubtedly points up in lively fashion, as she does with the words (by Ogden Nash) which are a superfluous addition to Saint-Saëns's witty menagerie.

The grafted-on animal noises which set the scene for the *Carnival* were recorded at London Zoo: the lion's roar at the beginning is startling to say the least! What also makes this disc of interest is that Julius Katchen and Gary Graffman, no less, are the pianists, and the Decca sound from the early 1960s, which is remarkably vivid. The fill-up is a charming medley of the A–Z of nursery rhymes, inimitably sung by Kenneth McKellar, with nicely detailed orchestral accompaniments by Robert Sharples – it will appeal to children of all ages. A collectors' item.

London Symphony Orchestra, Sir Georg Solti

'*Romantic Russia*': GLINKA: *Ruslan and Ludmilla Overture.* MUSSORGSKY: *Khovanshchina: Prelude; Night on the Bare Mountain* (arr. RIMSKY-KORSAKOV). BORODIN: *Prince Igor: Overture and Polovtsian Dances* (with LSO Ch.). TCHAIKOVSKY: *Symphony 2 (Little Russian), Op. 17* (with Paris Conservatoire O)

❂ (M) *** Decca Penguin Rosette Collection (ADD) 476 5310

This was a demonstration record in its day and the analogue recording remains of Decca's vintage quality, with marvellous detail and a warm ambience. The account of the *Ruslan and Ludmilla Overture* is justly famous for its sheer brio, and Solti's

Polovtsian Dances are as exciting as any in the catalogue with a splendid contribution from the LSO Chorus. The *Prince Igor Overture* is warmly romantic, yet has plenty of fire and spontaneity, and a lovely horn solo. *Night on the Bare Mountain* makes a forceful impact, but brings a tender closing section.

Solti also recorded the evocative *Khovanshchina Prelude* with the Berlin Philharmonic Orchestra around the same time, and that had marginally more lustre, but the LSO create plenty of atmospheric tension. The performance of Tchaikovsky's *Little Russian Symphony* has been added for this reissue. It dates from the late 1950s and the recording is noticeably less opulent. After a commanding opening, there is no lack of vitality, and the delightful slow movement is affectionately shaped. The Scherzo lacks something in elegance and charm (partly the fault of the French orchestral playing) but the finale certainly does not lack adrenalin. Overall this is surprisingly memorable and makes a splendid addition to Decca's 'Penguin Rosette Collection'.

(i) London Symphony Orchestra; (ii) Royal Philharmonic Orchestra, (iii) Anatole Fistoulari; (iv) Gaston Poulet

'*French Favourites*': (i; iii) POULENC: *Les Biches (ballet suite).* (ii-iii) *Aubade (choreographic concerto for piano and 18 instruments).* DEBUSSY: *Fantaisie for Piano and Orchestra* (both with Jacquinot, piano). (i; iv) RAVEL: *Alborada del gracioso; Une barque sur l'océan*

(B) (***) Dutton Lab. mono CDEA 5501

Here are some splendidly fresh performances from the early-1950s Parlophone label. Expert and attractive accounts of *Alborada del gracioso* and *Une barque sur l'océan* from the LSO under Gaston Poulet are coupled with two Poulenc works: a sparkling and vivacious *Les Biches* from Fistoulari and the same orchestra, and a captivating *Aubade* with Fabienne Jacquinot. She is hardly less persuasive in Debussy's neglected *Fantaisie*, both with the RPO (billed on the LP at the time, as older collectors will remember, as the Westminster Symphony Orchestra for contractual reasons). In any event, these are thoroughly delightful performances and few allowances need be made, for the recorded sound is little short of amazing.

Long Beach Symphony Orchestra, JoAnn Falletta

'*Impressions of the Sea*': MENDELSSOHN: *The Hebrides Overture (Fingal's Cave).* DEBUSSY: *La Mer.* LIADOV: *The Enchanted Lake.* BRIDGE: *The Sea (suite).* DEBUSSY: *Prélude: La Cathédrale engloutie* (arr. BUSSER)

*** LBSO 6698-1

It is good to find an orchestra of this calibre, under the excellent JoAnn Falletta, producing playing of such high quality, especially in an often thrilling and certainly evocative account of *La Mer* where the body of orchestral tone is most impressive. Liadov's *Enchanted Lake* is also atmospherically evoked, but best of all is Frank Bridge's *Suite* with the opening *Seascape* and penultimate *Moonlight* scenes pictured with memorable vividness of colour. Finally comes Henri Büsser's orchestration of Debussy's *La Cathédrale engloutie*, not as outrageously original as the celebrated Stokowski version, but still imaginative, and richly sonorous in its scoring. The recording is excellent, spacious and well detailed. The CD is available from the orchestra direct, whose website is www.lbso.org

Los Angeles Philharmonic Orchestra or Chamber Orchestra, Zubin Mehta

'Concertos in Contrast' (with soloists): HAYDN: Trumpet Concerto in E flat. VIVALDI: Piccolo Concerto in A min., P.83. WEBER: Concertino for Clarinet and Orchestra, Op. 26. WIENIAWSKI: Polonaise de concert, Op. 4; Scherzo-Tarantelle, Op. 16. BLOCH: Schelomo (with Janos Starker (cello), Israel PO)

**(*) Australian Decca Eloquence (ADD) 466 683-2

Contrasting concertos indeed – but the programme works. All are played with polish and sparkle, with the soloists (except in Schelomo) principals of the Los Angeles orchestra. The Wieniawski showpieces are brilliant rarities, and the delightful Weber piece has all the melodic freshness of his better-known concertos. The famous Haydn and Vivaldi concertos receive beefy performances, but not at all heavy, and it is a pleasure to hear them in such a rich sound. The recordings throughout are particularly full, though the Israeli strings in Schelomo cannot quite match those of the American orchestra. But the performance with Starker is very fine indeed.

Ma, Yo-Yo (cello)

'The Essential Yo-Yo Ma' (with various accompanists): Disc 1: BACH: (Unaccompanied) Cello Suite 1 in G, BWV 1007: Prelude; Chorale: Jesu, joy of man's desiring; Sheep may safely graze; Sleepers awake. VIVALDI: Four Seasons: Winter: Largo (with Amsterdam Baroque Orchestra, Koopman). SAINT-SAËNS: Carnival of the Animals: The Swan (with Philippe Entremont & Gaby Casadesus, piano duo); Havanaise, Op. 83. MASSENET: Thaïs: Méditation (both with Kathryn Stott). KREISLER: Liebesfreud (with Patricia Zander). GERSHWIN: Prelude 1 (with Jeffrey Kahane). RACHMANINOV: Vocalise (with Bobby McFerrin). SHOSTAKOVICH: Cello Sonata, Op. 69: 4th movt (with Emanuel Ax). TCHAIKOVSKY; Andante cantabile (with Pittsburgh SO, Maazel). BRAHMS: Piano Quartet 1, Op. 25: Rondo alla Zingarese (with Stern, Laredo, Ax). DVOŘÁK: Cello Concerto, Op. 104: Finale (with NYPO, Masur)

Disc 2: MARIANO: Cristal (with composer, piano). VILLA-LOBOS: A lenda do cabocio (with Assad Guitar Duo). JOBIM: Chega de saudade (with Ross Passos). D'RIVERA: Wapango (both with Kathryn Stott & percussion). PIAZZOLLA; Libertango (with Ensemble). O'CONNOR: Appalachia Waltz; Butterfly's Day Out (with composer, mandolin). MEYER: 18 (with Mark O'Connor, violin & bass). JOHN WILLIAMS: Pickin' (for solo cello). TRAD.: Simple Gifts (with Alison Krauss). MORRICONE: Film music: The Mission (excerpts) (Rome Sinfonietta, composer). TAN DUN: Film music: Crouching Tiger, Hidden Dragon: The Eternal Vow (Shanghai SO, composer). WILDE: The Cellist of Sarajevo: A Lament in Rondo (for solo cello). AZZAIOLO: Chi passa per'sta strada. TRAD. (Chinese): Mido Mountain. SANDEEP DAZ & INDRAJIT DREY: Mohini (Enchantment) (all with Silk Road Ensemble). BOLLING: Suite for Cello & Jazz Piano Trio: Baroque in Rhythm (with

composer & Rhythm). PORTER: Anything Goes (with Stefane Grapelli Ens.). LOEWE: My Fair Lady: I could have danced all night (with Steven Prutsman, piano)

(M) *(**) Sony S2K 63927 (2)

While Yo-Yo Ma is one of the world's outstanding cellists, for us this collection is very far from 'essential'. The key classical works included are represented only by single-movement excerpts, and while Ma plays transcriptions (like the Saint-Saëns Havanaise, Massenet's Méditation and Kreisler's Liebesfreud) gorgeously, they all sound more effective on the violin. Rachmaninov's Vocalise is taken literally and presented with a curious wordless contribution from Bobby McFerrin. The second disc is given over to crossover and world music, which is not our province. But this second collection acts well as a sampler for the various CDs from which the excerpts are taken.

Marches

'40 Famous Marches' (played by various ensembles, including the Philip Jones Brass, VPO, Boskovsky and Knappertsbusch, Curley, organ): ALFORD: Colonel Bogey. C. P. E. BACH: March. BEETHOVEN: Turkish March. BERLIOZ: Damnation de Faust: Hungarian March. BIZET: Carmen: Marche des contrebandiers. BLISS: Things to Come: March. CHABRIER: March joyeuse. CLARKE: Trumpet Voluntary. COATES: The Dambusters March. ELGAR: Pomp and Circumstance Marches 1 and 4 in D. FUCIK: Entry of the Gladiators. GOUNOD: Funeral March of a Marionette. HANDEL: Occasional Oratorio: March; Rinaldo: March; Saul: Dead March. KARG-ELERT: March triomphale. MENDELSSOHN: Athalie: War March of the Priests; Midsummer Night's Dream: Wedding March. MEYERBEER: Coronation March. NIELSEN: Oriental Festive March. PROKOFIEV: The Love for 3 Oranges: March. PURCELL: Funeral March. RIMSKY-KORSAKOV: The Procession of the Nobles; The Tale of Tsar Saltan: March. SCHUBERT: March militaire. SIBELIUS: Karelia Suite: All marcia. SOUSA: Stars and Stripes Forever; Washington Post. J. STRAUSS JR: Egyptian March; Jubel March; Napoleon March; Persian March; Russian March; Spanish March. J. STRAUSS SR: Radetzky March. TCHAIKOVSKY: The Nutcracker: March Miniature. VERDI: Aida: Grand March. WAGNER: Tannhäuser: Grand March. WALTON: Crown Imperial (Coronation march)

⊕↝ (B) *** Double Decca (ADD) 466 241-2 (2)

Most of the obvious marches are here, but this splendid collection is made all the more interesting by a shrewd choice of imaginative repertoire and performance, often in unexpected arrangements – the Philip Jones Brass Ensemble in the Aida and Tannhäuser marches (played with considerable brilliance), Carlo Curley's organ arrangement of Beethoven's Turkish March, and so on. Highlights include a string of J. Strauss's most exotic marches (Egyptian, Persian, Russian and Spanish) under Boskovsky, a crisply executed example from The Tale of Tsar Saltan by Martinon, Ansermet's hi-fi demonstration version of Chabrier's Marche joyeuse, a simple but striking march by C. P. E. Bach, arranged by the late Philip Jones, and many others. The Nielsen march is another unexpected choice, and no Decca collection of marches would be complete without Knappertsbusch's noble account of the March militaire. This is one of the best collections of its kind, and with recordings ranging from good to spectacular it will not fail to lift the spirits.

Marsalis, Wynton (trumpet)

Trumpet Concertos (with ECO or Nat. PO, Raymond Leppard): PURCELL: *The Indian Queen: Trumpet Overture.* HAYDN: *Concerto in E flat.* HUMMEL: *Concerto in E.* FASCH: *Concerto in D for Trumpet and 2 Oboes.* MOLTER: *Concerto 2 in D.* TORELLI: *2 Sonatas à 5 for Trumpet and Strings in D, t.v. 3 & 7*

🎵➡ ⦿ (M) *** Sony SMK 89611

The brilliant American trumpeter, Wynton Marsalis, recorded the Haydn, Fasch and Hummel concertos with the ECO over a period of a week in 1993 at St Giles Church, Cripplegate, in London. The playing is as expert and stylish as we have come to expect from this remarkable player. His approach is just a little cool, but none the worse for that, for there is also admirable poise, and in the finale of the Hummel he lets himself go with the most infectious bravura. Incidentally, there is no improvising in cadenzas: 'I don't feel comfortable enough to improvise in music of this period', Marsalis told us in the notes with the original full-priced issue.

The other recordings date from a year later, with the Purcell *Trumpet Overture* from *The Indian Queen* used to open the programme arrestingly. So often in a trumpet anthology the ear wearies of the timbre, but never here. Marsalis scales down his tone superbly to match the oboes in the delightful Fasch *Concerto* (especially as they are backwardly balanced) and he plays the *Sonatas* of Torelli with winning finesse. The recording gives him a striking (but not too exaggerated) presence in relation to the orchestra, making the trumpet very tangible, especially in the upper tessitura of the Molter *Concerto*, where the solo playing makes the hairs at the nape of one's neck tingle.

Mewton-Wood, Noel (piano)

BEETHOVEN: *Piano Concerto 4 in G, Op. 58* (with Utrecht SO, Goehr); *Violin Sonata 8 in G, Op. 30/3.* ALBENIZ (arr. Kreisler): *Malagueña* (both with Haendel). CHOPIN: *Tarantelle in A flat, Op. 43.* WEBER: *Piano Sonata 1 in C, Op. 24.* LISZT: *Années de pèlerinage: Petrarch Sonnets 44 & 104.* TCHAIKOVSKY: *Piano Concerto 2 in G, Op. 44* (with Winterthur SO, Goehr). SHOSTAKOVICH: *Concerto 1 for Piano, Trumpet & Strings, Op. 35* (with Sevenstern, Concert Hall SO, Goehr). SCHUMANN: *Kinderszenen, Op. 15.* BUSONI: *Violin Sonata 2 in E min., Op. 36a* (with Rostal). TIPPETT: Songs: *Boyhood's End; The Heart's Assurance* (with Pears)

⦿ (***) Australian Universal Heritage ABC Classic mono 461 900-2 (3)

An invaluable reissue, impressively produced and presented, this three-CD set comprises one of three in the launch of the Australian Heritage Series. No effort has been spared in presentation, and the set pays tribute to an almost forgotten but outstanding artist, Noel Mewton-Wood. Born in Melbourne, Australia, he had a highly successful career in England, favoured by, among others, Beecham, Sargent, Henry Wood and Britten. His recordings have long been sought after by collectors, and this anthology presents him in solo and concertante repertoire. Several performances are especially worth pointing out: his sleight of hand in one of the silveriest performances of the Beethoven *G major Violin Sonata* on record, with a 13-year old Ida Haendel; a magnificent

Beethoven *Fourth Concerto*; a corruscating Shostakovich *Concerto* (the finale is electrifying); two searing Liszt *Petrarch Sonnets*; and a memorable recording of *Kinderszenen* (though with some surface noise) never before issued. The two Tippett song-cycles were the first recordings of any of the composer's vocal works (originally issued on Argo) with Peter Pears sounding admirably fresh and Mewton-Wood's accompaniments full of insight. His playing is consistently suffused with vitality and warmth, ranging from the imperceptibly delicate to the overwhelmingly powerful. Tchaikovsky's *Second Concerto*, brought off with enormous aplomb, is highly charged emotionally and remains among the finest versions available. The sound ranges from acceptable to good, but this set is indispensable and well worth seeking out.

Minimalism

'The World of Minimalism': GLASS: *'Heroes' Symphony: V2 Schneider* (with American Composers O, Davies). REICH: *Drumming:* excerpts (with Steve Reich and Musicians). MORAN: *Points of Departure* (with Baltimore SO, Zinman). FITKIN: *Frame* (Fitkin and Sutherland). ADAMS: *Shaker Loops: Shaking and Trembling* (with San Francisco SO, de Waart). NYMAN: *The Cook, the Thief, his Wife and her Lover: Memorial* (Michael Nyman Band). RILEY: *In C* (with Davidson-Kelly, Harris, Heath, Richter, Strawson, Wood)

(M) **(*) Decca (ADD/DDD) 470 125-2

Minimalist music has a small yet sturdy following, but some of the music here will test all but its most devoted advocates. The excerpts from Steve Reich's *Drumming* is hypnotic to some but is undoubtedly monotonous to others. Fitkin's *Frame*, played on two keyboards, merely grates from the first note. Repetition is taken to extreme in Riley's infamous *In C* – a 20-minute composition, based on the repeated playing of the octave C, for concert grand and upright piano, Rhodes piano, two harpsichords and vibraphone. Moran's mythical ballet *Points of Departure* offers far more attractive and colourful symphonic scoring and, like Glass's *V2 Schneider*, sounds not unlike many contemporary American film-scores. Nyman's *Memorial* is perhaps the most approachable work here, with an easy listening quality that has made his film music so successful. However, it is John Adams who shines as the strongest and most original composer in this collection. Superb recordings and, as far as one can tell, performances.

Minnesota Orchestra, Eije Oue

'Orchestral Fireworks': KABALEVSKY: *Overture Colas Breugnon.* DEEMS TAYLOR: *Through the Looking Glass: Looking Glass Insects.* RIMSKY-KORSAKOV: *Tsar Sultan: Flight of the Bumblebee.* LISZT: *Les Préludes.* BRAHMS: *Hungarian Dance 3 in F.* DINICU: *Hora staccato.* DVORAK: *Slavonic Dance, Op. 71/2.* JARNEFELT: *Praeludium.* BERLIOZ: *Damnation de Faust: Danse des sylphes.* KLEMPERER: *Merry Waltz.* CHABRIER: *Habanera.* RAVEL: *Boléro*

*** Reference Dig. RR-92 CD

From the evidence of this enjoyable concert the Minneapolis Orchestra is in excellent shape under its new conductor, Eije Oue, and they play with refinement as well as virtuosity. *Les Préludes*, for instance, is a particularly impressive performance, entirely without vulgarity, with a dignified opening, yet the closing pages generate much excitement and the final peroration is really powerful. The slightly bass-heavy recording adds to the weight of the piece. And how warmly and elegantly does the orchestra play the Brahms and Dvořák dances, while the slinky Chabrier *Habanera* is very seductive. An attractive novelty here is the Deems Taylor *Scherzo*, reminiscent of early Stravinsky, but very colourful in its own right.

Hora staccato and Rimsky's *Bumblebee* are both played with the lightest touch, the orchestral virtuosity sparkling throughout, while it is good to welcome the charming Jarnefelt *Praeludium*. But the surprise is the Klemperer *Waltz*, turned into a real lollipop, and more persuasive here than the conductor/composer's own version. *Boléro* is very well played indeed (the opening woodwind solos especially so), but it is also very relaxed until a sudden burst of adrenalin at the close. The recording is spacious and full, with warm, pleasing string-quality, but the bass is at times a trifle boomy.

Molnar, Jozsef (alphorn)

Alphorn Concertos (with Capella Istropolitana or Slovak PO, Urs Schneider): LEOPOLD MOZART: *Sinfonia pastorella.* JEAN DAETWYLER: *Dialogue avec la nature; Concerto.* FERENC FARKAS: *Concertino rustico*
(BB) *** Naxos 8. 555978

The Alphorn (pictured on the front of the CD) has a fine fat timbre, but its natural harmonics produce a basic range of only five notes. Leopold Mozart uses them robustly in various permutations and most successfully in his ingenuously jolly rondo finale. But a good deal of the melodic action goes on in the orchestra, and the *Andante* omits the soloist altogether. For all its naivety the result is rather endearing.

The *Concerto rustico* of Ferenc Farkas is much more ingenious in using and extending the instrument's range. The slow movement, *Rubato, a piacere,* is surprisingly successful in its doleful *espressivo,* unashamedly featuring the instrument's out-of-tune harmonics, and in the finale the alphorn almost manages a tune rather like a garbled version of '*Poor Jennie is A-weeping*'.

The Swiss composer, Jean Daetwyler, gets round the minimalistic problem even more enterprisingly by adding in a piccolo to portray the birds in his *Dialogue avec la nature,* while his orchestral scoring is rich in atmosphere and colour. The alphorn and piccolo duet together piquantly in the charming rondo finale, which is not too extended.

Daetwyler's four-movement *Concerto* is much more ambitious, opening with a soliloquy taking his soloist up to his highest harmonics, and, like Farkas, not shunning those notes that are inherently out of tune. Again the tangy orchestral colouring makes a rich backcloth for the soloist, especially in the razzle-dazzle *Scherzo* and the *Misterioso pastorale.* The *Furioso* finale makes even more virtuoso demands, which Jozsef Molnar clearly relishes. Indeed his playing throughout is astonishingly secure and full of character. The accompaniments are supportive and the recording excellent. This is a collection which would have been a doubtful recommendation at its original Marco Polo premium price, but on Naxos it is well worth trying – although not all at once!

Musica da Camera, Robert King

Baroque Chamber Works: BACH: *Cantata 42: Sinfonia.* CORELLI: *Concerto grosso in G min. (Christmas), Op. 6/8.*
PACHELBEL: *Canon and Gigue.* HANDEL: *Concerto grosso in B flat, Op. 3/2.* VIVALDI: *L'Estro armonico: Concerto in D min., Op. 3/11.* ALBINONI (arr. GIAZOTTO): *Adagio for Organ and Strings*
*** Linn CKD 012

An exceptionally successful concert of baroque music, with a very well-chosen programme, presented on an authentic scale, with what appears to be one instrument to a part. Phrasing is thoroughly musical and the intimacy and transparency of sound are achieved without loss of sonority or disagreeable squeezing of phrases. The familiar *Largo* of the Corelli *Christmas Concerto* is particularly fresh, and the opening of the famous Pachelbel *Canon* on a sombre solo bass-line is very telling. The colour of the lively Bach and Handel works (using wind as well as strings) is attractively realized. Excellent, realistic recording.

I Musici

ALBINONI: *Adagio in G min.* (arr. GIAZOTTO). BEETHOVEN: *Minuet in G, WoO 10/2.* BOCCHERINI: *Quintet in E, Op. 11/5: Minuet.* HAYDN (attrib.): *Quartet, Op. 3/5; Serenade.* MOZART: *Serenade 13 in G (Eine kleine Nachtmusik), K.525.* PACHELBEL: *Canon*
*** Ph. (IMS) 410 606-2

A very enjoyable concert, recorded with remarkable naturalness and realism. The effect is very believable indeed. The playing combines warmth and freshness, and the oft-played Mozart *Night Music* has no suggestion whatsoever of routine: it combines elegance, warmth and sparkle. The Boccherini *Minuet* and (especially) the Hoffstetter (attrib. Haydn) *Serenade* have an engaging lightness of touch.

Mutter, Anne-Sophie (violin)

MOZART: *Violin Concertos 2 in D, K.211; 4 in D, K.218* (with Philh. O, Muti). BACH: *Concertos 1 in A min., BWV 1041; 2 in E, BWV 1042; Double Violin Concerto in D min., BWV 1043* (with ECO, Accardo). LALO: *Symphonie espagnole, Op. 21.* SARASATE: *Zigeunerweisen, Op. 20* (with O Nat. de France, Ozawa)
(M) *** EMI 5 65538-2 (3)

Anne-Sophie Mutter followed up her celebrated early coupling of Mozart's *G major, K.216,* and *A major, K.219, Violin Concertos* (now reissued as a DG Original – see under the Composer entry in our main volume) with the two *D major Concertos* on HMV, and a different orchestra and conductor. The results are hardly less successful. Her variety of timbre as well as the imagination of her playing is extremely compelling, and while the degree of romantic warmth she adopts in her Bach playing is at odds with today's 'authentic school', her performance of the slow movement of the *E major Concerto* is finer than almost any other version except Grumiaux's, with marvellous shading within a range of hushed tone.

Accardo's accompaniment here (as throughout the collection) is splendidly stylish and alert. In principle the slow movement of the *Double Concerto* – where Accardo takes up his bow to become a solo partner, scaling down his timbre – is too slow, but the result could hardly be more beautiful, helped by EMI recording which gives body to the small ECO string band. The account of Lalo's Spanish showpiece makes an excellent foil, with its dazzling display of bravura offset by Mutter's delicacy of phrasing, although there is no lack of passionate eloquence in the central movements. Here the balance is a shade too forward, and the digital recording brings a touch of digital edge to the sound. The Sarasate offers more violinistic fireworks, but some may find Mutter's playing of the famous principal lyrical melody a little chaste. Overall, however, this makes a fine showcase for a splendid artist.

'Carmen-fantasie' (with VPO, James Levine): SARASATE: *Zigeunerweisen; Carmen Fantasy.* WIENIAWSKI: *Légende.* TARTINI: *Sonata in G min. (Devil's Trill).* RAVEL: *Tzigane.* MASSENET: *Thaïs: Méditation.* FAURE: *Berceuse*
*** DG 437 544-2

This is an unashamedly fun record, with Mutter playing with freedom and warmth and obviously enjoying herself. Comparing the *Carmen Fantasy* of Sarasate with Perlman shows Mutter as equally sharp in characterization, yet in the end Perlman's easy style is the more beguiling. But Mutter's Ravel *Tzigane* is made stunningly Hungarian in its fiery accelerando at the end, while Tartini's famous *Devil's Trill Sonata* is played as a virtuoso piece, rather than placed back in the eighteenth century – no harm in that in the present context. The recording is vividly close.

Nakariakov, Sergei (trumpet)

Concertos (with Lausanne CO, López-Cobos): JOLIVET: *Concertino for Trumpet, Piano & Strings* (with Markovich, piano). HUMMEL: *Concerto in E flat.* HAYDN: *Concerto in E flat.* TOMASI: *Concerto in D*
(M) *** Warner Elatus 0927 49831-2

The very gifted young Russian trumpeter makes a brilliant contribution to the Jolivet *Double Concerto.* His partner, the pianist Alexander Markovich, plays very well too, but the balance is less than ideal. Yet, at under ten minutes, the work does not outstay its welcome and it has a catchy, angular main theme. The Tomasi solo concerto is more kaleidoscopic, with lyrical and rhythmic elements alternating and a whiff of jazz in the melodic style.

In the Haydn and Hummel *Concertos* Nakariakov does not quite match the famous Hardenberger performances, and the orchestral playing in Lausanne is serviceable rather than outstanding. Nakariakov plays the Hummel in the key of E flat, rather than the brighter E major favoured by Hardenberger, but both this and the Haydn bring a superb solo contribution from the young Russian virtuoso, and the lovely *Andante* of the latter work is memorably warm and graceful, before a sparkling finale which matches that of the Hummel in high spirits.

'No Limit' (playing trumpet and flugel horn, with Philh. O, Ashkenazy; arrangements by Nakariakov & Dokshitser): Trumpet: SAINT-SAENS: *Introduction and Rondo capriccio.* GERSHWIN: *Rhapsody in Blue.* Flugel horn: TCHAIKOVSKY: *Andante cantabile; Variations on a Rococo Theme.* BRUCH: *Canzone.* MASSENET: *Thaïs: Méditation*
(***) Teldec 8573 80651-2

Sergei Nakariakov's tone is so beautiful, his phrasing so naturally musical, his virtuosity so effortless and dazzling, that he almost reconciles one to these arrangements. Certainly the Saint-Saëns display-piece is presented with great flair – and Nakariakov's breathtakingly fast tonguing at the close is extraordinary.

But Tchaikovsky's *Andante cantabile*, on the flugel horn instead of the cello, just will not do. For all the warmth of line and tasteful vibrato, the atmosphere of the bandstand remains. The *Rococo Variations* works rather better, played very stylishly, with the melodic line here often lying higher up. But again it sounds far better on a cello.

Max Bruch's *Canzone* and Massenet's *'Méditation'* are effective enough, and undoubtedly Nakariakov is a natural in Gershwin, where he returns to the trumpet. It is a brilliant performance, with a strong jazzy inflection. The instrument's middle and lower range is used to good effect, and there is a touch of humour when the bassoon makes a solo entry. The big tune is introduced delicately and played with a cup mute; but in the following string climax the saxes fail to come through (if they are there). Throughout Ashkenazy provides good support, although the balance makes his contribution no more than an accompaniment. But that Gershwin opening should have been left to the clarinet.

NBC Symphony Orchestra, Guido Cantelli

'The NBC Broadcasts 1951': BARTOK: *Concerto for Orchestra.* BRAHMS: *Tragic Overture.* DEBUSSY: *Le Martyre de Saint-Sébastien: Symphonic Fragments.* GHEDINI: *Concerto dell'Albatro* (with Mischakov, Miller, Balsam, Grauer). GILLIS: *Prairie Sunset.* MENDELSSOHN: *Symphony 4 (Italian).* MOZART: *Le nozze di Figaro: Overture. Symphony 29 in A, K.291.* RAVEL: *La Valse; Pavane pour une infante défunte.* ROSSINI: *Overture: The Siege of Corinth.* SCHUBERT: *Symphony 2 in B flat, D.125.* STRAVINSKY: *Fireworks.* VIVALDI: *Concerto grosso in A min., Op. 8/3* (with Mischakov, Hollander)
(M) (***) Testament mono SBT4 1336 (4)

On these four discs we have broadcasts from five concerts Cantelli conducted in New York with the NBC Symphony Orchestra, four in January 1951 and one in the December of that year. None are from the notoriously dry Studio 8-H; the January concerts are from the Manhattan Center and the December one from Carnegie Hall. Although the set includes pieces that he recorded commercially, such as the *Italian Symphony* and the *Symphonic Fragments* from *Le Martyre de Saint-Sébastien* (which incidentally was broadcast by the BBC Third Programme as a tribute during the evening after his death was announced), he never recorded the Bartók *Concerto for Orchestra* or the *Concerto dell'Albatro* by his compatriot and teacher, Giorgio Federico Ghedini. The Bartók is atmospheric and sensual. Ghedini's almost forgotten score used to be broadcast quite frequently in the 1950s; with its austere neoclassicism and eloquence (the idiom is indebted to Bartók, Hindemith and Frank Martin) it is very well served by the orchestra and its fine soloists. The quotations from Melville featured in the finale are spoken in the civilized American English which was in wide currency in the 1950s. The Schubert *Second Symphony* is absolutely exhilarating and wonderfully light and vibrant. Cantelli's NBC producer was Don Gillis (of *Symphony No. 5-and-a-half* fame) whose short *Prairie Sunset* makes a welcome appearance. Leaving aside the quality of the playing, the mono recordings are a very pleasant surprise and have been expertly remastered by Paul Baily.

Neveu, Ginette (violin)

Concert: BRAHMS: *Violin Concerto* (with Philh. O, Dobrowen). **CHOPIN:** *Nocturne 12 in C sharp min.* **FALLA:** *Danse espagnole.* **RAVEL:** *Tzigane.* **SUK:** *4 Pieces.* **DINICU:** *Hora staccato* (with Jean Neveu, piano)

(BB) (***) Dutton mono CDEP 9710

No sooner had Ginette Neveu established her claims as a great artist, mainly in her recordings in the immediate post-war period, than she was taken from us, together with her brother, Jean, in a tragic air accident. It makes these fine recordings the more precious, and they have been superbly transferred by Dutton, with the Brahms *Violin Concerto* sounding a degree more refined than in the earlier, EMI transfer. Some of Neveu's recordings of the other items are new to CD, as for example the imaginative *Four Pieces* of Suk, with Neveu displaying her virtuoso flair in such showpieces as Dinicu's *Hora staccato*.

New London Orchestra, Ronald Corp

'British Light Music Classics': Vol. 1: **COATES:** *Calling All Workers.* **TOYE:** *The Haunted Ballroom.* **COLLINS:** *Vanity Fair.* **FARNON:** *Jumping Bean.* **BAYNES:** *Destiny.* **CURZON:** *The Boulevardier.* **LUTZ:** *Pas de quatre.* **BINGE:** *The Watermill; Elizabethan Serenade.* **WILLIAMS:** *The Devil's Galop.* **GIBBS:** *Dusk.* **WHITE:** *Puffin' Billy.* **KETELBEY:** *Bells across the Meadows.* **CHARLES WILLIAMS:** *The Old Clockmaker.* **JOYCE:** *Dreaming.* **ELLIS:** *Coronation Scot.* **ANCLIFFE:** *Nights of Gladness*

*** Hyp. CDA 66868

Almost as soon as it was issued, Ronald Corp's stylish and beautifully played collection of inconsequential but engaging English miniatures rose up and held its place in the bestseller lists. This was the kind of music that used to be heard on seaside piers and which was played by spa orchestras in the years between the two World Wars – orchestras that have long since disappeared.

The robust *Nights of Gladness* (1912) was composed by Charles Ancliffe on return from service as a bandmaster in India, while Sydney Baynes's *Destiny Waltz*, from the same year, has a cello solo which, years later, was played by Sir John Barbirolli at Hallé balls; Archibald Joyce's *Dreaming* dates from the previous year, while two other hauntingly atmospheric pieces, *Dusk* by Armstrong Gibbs and Geoffrey Toye's *Haunted Ballroom*, were both written in 1935. Vivian Ellis's *Coronation Scot*, a catchy sound-picture of a steam locomotive, dates from 1939 and became famous when it was used as the signature tune for BBC radio's 'Paul Temple' detective series. More recently, Ronald Binge has added his engaging *Elizabethan Serenade* (1951) and a delicate portrait of *The Watermill* (1958). It was the famous Sibelius conductor, Anthony Collins, who wrote the delectable morsel, *Vanity Fair*, and he once said in a radio interview that he valued its composition above all his other achievements 'because it will keep my name alive long after my records have been forgotten'. The affectionate, polished performances here will certainly help to do that: they give much pleasure, and Tony Faulkner's recording balance is beautifully judged.

'British Light Music Classics', Vol. 2: **COATES:** *London Suite: Knightsbridge.* **FLETCHER:** *Bal masqué.* **BUCALOSSI:** *Grasshopper's Dance.* **ARTHUR WOOD:** *The Archers Theme: Barwick Green.* **HARTLEY:** *Rouge et Noir.* **FARNON:** *Peanut Polka; Westminster Waltz.* **FRANKEL:** *Carriage and Pair.* **HAYDN WOOD:** *The Horse Guards, Whitehall (Down Your Way Theme).* **DUNCAN:** *Little Suite: March (Dr Finlay's Casebook Theme).* **BINGE:** *Sailing By.* **VINTER:** *Portuguese Party.* **RICHARDSON:** *Beachcomber.* **FINCK:** *In the Shadows.* **DOCKER:** *Tabarinage.* **KETELBEY:** *Sanctuary of the Heart.* **ELGAR:** *Carissima.* **CHARLES WILLIAMS:** *Girls in Grey.* **WHITE:** *The Runaway Rocking Horse.* **CURZON:** *Robin Hood Suite: March of the Bowmen*

*** Hyp. CDA 66968

Ronald Corp's second collection of popular evergreens is just as delightful as the first, for the supply of catchy and popular numbers shows no sign of drying up. Radio and television signature-tunes provide the cornerstones, with *Barwick Green* (*The Archers*) by Arthur Wood pointing the way, a piece inspired not by the West Country or the fictional world of Ambridge, but by a village near Leeds. From Eric Coates's *Knightsbridge March* onwards, chosen in the early 1930s to introduce the pioneering radio magazine programme *In Town Tonight*, here is a rich source of nostalgia, including Haydn Wood's *Horse Guards March (Down Your Way)*, Ronald Binge's *Sailing By* (Radio 4 signing off) and Trevor Duncan's catchy *March (Dr Finlay's Casebook)*, which reminds one a little of the *Marcia* of Dag Wirén and is here played most delicately.

What comes out from every one of these 20 pieces is not just their catchy memorability and tunefulness, but the brilliance and subtlety of the instrumentations. They are full of the sort of effects that only a really practical musician, close to players, could think up; and they are here made the more enjoyable by the warmth and clarity of the sound. It is welcome that Elgar is this time included with one of his lesser-known pieces, *Carissima*, not to mention Ben Frankel with the jaunty *Carriage and Pair*, with its clip-clopping rhythm vividly evoking the period Parisian atmosphere of the film *So Long at the Fair*. A must for anyone at all given to nostalgia.

'British Light Music Classics', Vol. 3: **HAYDN WOOD:** *Montmartre.* **CLIVE RICHARDSON:** *Melody on the Move.* **TREVOR DUNCAN:** *The Girl from Corsica.* **LIONEL MONCKTON:** *Soldiers in the Park.* **FELIX GODIN:** *Valse septembre.* **BINGE:** *Miss Melanie.* **IVAN CARYLL:** *Pink Lady Waltz.* **FARNON:** *Portrait of a Flirt.* **DEXTER:** *Siciliano.* **KETELBEY:** *In a Persian Market* (with chorus). **JACK STRACHEY:** *Theatreland.* **ARCHIBALD JOYCE:** *Songe d'automne.* **VIVIAN ELLIS:** *Alpine Pastures.* **TOMLINSON:** *Little Serenade.* **MELACHRINO:** *Woodland Revel.* **TOLCHARD EVANS:** *Lady of Spain.* **ANCLIFFE:** *Smiles, then Kisses.* **TORCH:** *On a Spring Note.* **COATES:** *Rediffusion March: Music Everywhere*

*** Hyp. CDA 67148

Volume 3 is well up to the standard of its attractive predecessors, warmly and sparklingly played, with the orchestra clearly enjoying the melodic profusion. Haydn Wood's opening *Montmartre* would cheer anyone up, and the following *Melody on the Move* and *In the party mood* maintain the spirited forward momentum. Many of the later items are justly famous. No collection of British light music would be complete without Ketèlbey, and the New London Light Opera Chorus makes a lusty contribution in the *Persian Market*.

Farnon's *Portrait of a Flirt*, Harry Dexter's delectably fragile *Siciliano* and Tomlinson's equally charming *Little Serenade* are all winningly personable, while Melachrino's *Woodland Revel* begins wittily with a simple interplay on a melodic fragment, which then flowers romantically, generating a rumbustious climax. The Ancliffe waltz is delightfully English in rhythmic inflection, and after Sidney Torch's catchy reminder of spring, Eric Coates provides a rousing conclusion. The recording is crisp and clear within a pleasingly warm ambience. Most refreshing.

'European Light Music Classics': JESSEL: *Parade of the Tin Soldiers.* LEHAR: *Gold and Silver* (waltz). PIERNE: *Album pour mes petits amis: Marche des petits soldats de plomb.* JOHANN STRAUSS JR: *Tritsch-Tratsch Polka.* LINCKE: *Glow Worm Idyll.* ALFVEN: *Swedish Polka.* GOUNOD: *Funeral March of a Marionette.* WALDTEUFEL: *The Skaters Waltz.* HEYKENS: *Serenade.* PADILLA: *El relicaro.* BECUCCI: *Tesoro mio!* HELLMESBERGER: *Ball Scene.* WEINBERGER: *Schwanda the Bagpiper: Polka.* FETRAS: *Moonlight on the Alster.* HALVORSEN: *Entry of the Boyars*
**(*) Hyp. CDA 66998

Although there is much to enjoy here, this is a less enterprising collection than usual in this series. The highlights are what one might call the Palm Court trifles, the two evocations of miniature soldiers (Pierné's unmistakably French), Lincke's exquisite *Glow Worm Idyll*, the Heykens *Serenade* and the *Entry of the Boyars*, which is most winningly played. *Moonlight on the Alster*, too, is a famous waltz by an unfamous composer and Waldteufel's *Skaters* are always welcome. But why choose the *Tritsch-Tratsch Polka* and *Gold and Silver*, which are readily available elsewhere; the latter is one of Barbirolli's specials? Performances and recordings are pretty well up to standard.

'American Light Music Classics'; SOUSA: *Washington Post.* KERRY MILLS: *Whistling Rufus.* GOULD: *American Symphonette 3: Pavane.* FELIX ARNDT: *Nola (A Silhouette).* PRYOR: *The Whistler and his Dog.* LEROY ANDERSON: *Belle of the Ball; Plink, plank, plunk.* TRAD.: *The Arkansas Traveller (The Old Fiddler's Breakdown).* BRATTON: *Teddy Bears' Picnic.* MACDOWELL: *Woodland Sketches: To a Wild Rose.* HOLZMANN: *Blaze Away!* FRIML: *In Love (Chanson).* RAYMOND SCOTT: *The Toy Trumpet.* GERSHWIN: *Promenade.* HERBERT: *Babes in Toyland: March of the Toys.* ROSE: *Holiday for Strings.* NEVIN: *Water Scenes: Narcissus.* DON GILLIS: *Symphony 5½ (A Symphony for Fun).* RODGERS: *Carousel Waltz*
*** Hyp. CDA 67067

The surprise here is instantly to recognize so many catchy tunes, and then find they come from the other side of the Atlantic. After the familiar Sousa march (played with spirit and a touch of panache, rather than Yankee pizazz), Kerry Mills's *Whistling Rufus*, with its cakewalk rhythm, is unmistakably American. Abe Holzmann's *Blaze Away!*, complete with piccolo solo, is equally identifiable. So is the engaging Gould *Pavane* and the two witty Leroy Anderson encore pieces, while the New Yorker Edward MacDowell's tender little portrait of a wild rose, delightfully played here, remains his most famous piece. But *Nola*, *The Whistler and his Dog* (complete with 'barking' coda), *Narcissus* and David Rose's winning pizzicato *Holiday for Strings* all seem so familiar that they feel more like local items.

The *Teddy Bear's Picnic*, was an American instrumental piece but became a British song, and a huge hit in England. Rudolf Friml's *Chanson (In Love)* also became famous when words were added to it – for its appearance in the Hollywood film *The Firefly*, and it was renamed the *Donkey Serenade*.

I.M. has a treasured childhood memory of seeing another 1930s film, *Babes in Toyland*, in which Laurel and Hardy helped to defeat the evil Bogeymen to the strains of Victor Herbert's famous *March*. In that instance the toy soldiers were six feet tall, as Stanley, who had ordered them for Father Christmas, unfortunately got the measurements wrong! The music sounds as piquant as ever. Don Gillis's *Symphony for Fun* doesn't seem as audacious as it once did, but it still enjoyably bears out its descriptive title. As in the rest of this splendid Hyperion series, performances are as polished as they are spontaneous, and the recording is first class.

(i) New Philharmonia Orchestra, (ii) London Symphony Orchestra, Richard Bonynge

'Overtures and Ballet Music of the Nineteenth Century':
Disc 1: (i) Overtures: AUBER: *Marco Spada; Lestocq.* ADAM: *Giralda; La Poupée de Nuremburg.* LECOCQ: *La Fille de Madame Angot.* THOMAS: *Mignon.* PLANQUETTE: *Les Cloches de Corneville.* BOIELDIEU: *Le Calife de Bagdad; La Dame blanche.* (ii) Ballet Music: MEYERBEER: *Le Prophète: Coronation March.* MASSENET: *La Navarraise: Nocturne.* GOUNOD: *La Reine de Saba, Act II: Waltz.* BIZET: *Don Procopio, Act II: Entr'acte*

Disc 2: (ii) Overtures: DONIZETTI: *Roberto Devereux.* ROSSINI: *Torvaldo e Dorliska.* MAILLART: *Les Dragons de Villars.* OFFENBACH: *La Fille du tambour-major.* VERDI: *Giovanna d'Arco.* HEROLD: *Zampa.* WALLACE: *Maritana.* AUBER: *La Neige.* MASSENET: *Cherubin, Act III: Entr'acte. Don César de Bazan: Entr'acte Sevillana; Les Erinnyes: Invocation.* GOUNOD: *Le Tribut de Zamora, Act III: Danse grecque.* SAINT-SAENS: *Henry VIII, Act II: Danse de la gypsy.* DELIBES: *Le Roi l'a dit, Act II: Entr'acte*
⊖– ✪ *** Double Decca (ADD) 466 431-2 (2)

By delving further into the back catalogue, Decca have come up with an even more delectable collection of overtures and orchestral sweetmeats than in the companion ECO eighteenth-century compilation, above. The programme is again based on three Bonynge LPs, two from the LSO and one from the New Philharmonia Orchestra, again from the late 1960s and early 1970s. The format of the nineteenth-century overture is a pretty standard one, usually a potpourri, but sometimes more sophisticated in layout, as with Thomas's *Mignon* and, to a lesser extent, Hérold's *Zampa*. But it is the tunes that count.

Of the three Auber overtures *Marco Spada* has a wonderfully evocative opening, suggesting a sunrise, before bursting champagne-like into one of his typical galloping allegros; *Lestocq* contains a memorably wistful tune for the oboe, while *La Neige*, more subtle than usual, shows the composer's gift for writing catchy tunes quite early in his career. Adam's *Giralda* and *La Poupée de Nuremburg* display all the delicacy and skill we know from his ballet scores; the former features glittering castanets, the latter an unexpected passage for string quartet. Boieldieu's charming *La Dame blanche* is as light as thistledown and *The Caliph of Bagdad* has never sounded more resplendent. Lecocq's *La Fille de Madame Angot* is quite delicious.

Among the LSO performances, *Maritana* stands out. Bonynge does this gorgeously, the melodramatic opening arresting, and the shaping of the hit tune 'Scenes that are

Brightest' lusciously presented. Rossini's *Torvaldo e Dorliska* is interesting in including the second subject of the *Cenerentola Overture*, while Donizetti's *Roberto Devereux* flagrantly draws on '*God Save the King*'. Offenbach's winning *La Fille du tambour-major*, piquantly scored, ends with an exuberant can-can played with superb gusto.

We also turn to the LSO for the ballet music. Besides a brilliant account of Meyerbeer's *Coronation March*, there is a series of delightful *bon bouches* including a famous Massenet cello solo (the *Invocation* from *Les Erinnyes*) and the *Nocturne* from *La Navarraise*. Gounod's *Grande valse* from *La Reine de Saba* sounds as though it has been left over from the *Faust* ballet music, while Saint-Saëns's *Gypsy Dance* from *Henry VIII*, with its ominous timpani strokes, turns into a tuneful valse-macabre. The programme ends with a charming pastiche *Minuet* from Delibes's *Le Roi l'a dit*. Bonynge is a complete master of this repertoire, which he clearly loves, and all this music is so chic and poised in his hands and so brilliantly played and recorded, that enjoyment is assured.

New World Symphony, Michael Tilson Thomas

CHAVEZ: *Symphony 2 (Sinfonia india)*. COPLAND: *Danzón cubano*. ROLDAN: *Suite de 'La rebambaramba'*. REVUELTAS: *Sensemayá*. CATURLA: *Tres danzas cubanas*. ROLDAN: *Ritmica V*. PIAZZOLLA: *Tangazo*. GINASTERA. *Estancia, Op. 8a: 4 Dances*
*** Australian Decca Eloquence (ADD) 467 603-2

This disc seems to have had a short life in its full-price incarnation, but returns in Australian Decca's Eloquence series. It demonstrates a titillating mixture of South American influences, from the unashamedly jazzy *Danzón cubano* of Copland to more substantial works, such as Chávez's *Second Symphony*. Its exotic rarities include Revueltas's *Sensemayá*. This has a delightfully quirky opening with the bass drum, gong and bassoon; then an ever-increasing collection of instruments create an impressive cumulative effect. The longest work here is *Tangazo*, first heard in 1988. A celebration of the famous South American dance, it begins slowly and broodingly, but gradually becomes more vigorous and sensual. All the music here is colourful and vivid, and the performances and recordings are excellent.

New York Philharmonic Orchestra, Leopold Stokowski

'The Classic 1947–49 Columbia Recordings and Live Broadcasts'

Volume 1: GRIFFES: *The White Peacock*. IPPOLITOV-IVANOV: *Caucasian Sketches, Op. 10: In a Village*. MESSIAEN: *L'Ascension*. TCHAIKOVSKY: *Francesca da Rimini, Op. 32*. VAUGHAN WILLIAMS: *Fantasia on Greensleeves*. WAGNER: *Der fliegende Höllander: Overture*. *Die Walküre: Wotan's Farewell and Magic Fire Music* (arr. Stokowski)
(***) Cala mono CACD 0533

Volume 2: COPLAND: *Billy the Kid: Prairie Night; Celebration*. KHACHATURIAN: *Masquerade: Suite*. SCHOENBERG: *Gurrelieder: Song of the Wood-Dove* (arr. Stein). SIBELIUS: *Swanwhite, Op. 54: The Maiden with the Roses*. TCHAIKOVSKY: *String Serenade, Op. 48: Waltz*. WAGNER; *Götterdämmerung: Siegfried's Rhine Journey; Siegfried's Funeral March. Rienzi Overture*
(***) Cala mono CACD 0534

When Stokowski made the first of these recordings with the New York Philharmonic, it was with an orchestra whose playing and image had been greatly improved after a three-year period with Artur Rodzinski as Musical Director. The latter resigned unexpectedly around the time of Stokowski's first concert as guest conductor over the Christmas/New Year period of 1946/7. The recordings followed; the more expansive 1947 recordings were made in Carnegie Hall, while the 1949 sessions were studio-bound; each disc offers a combination of both.

Stokowski premièred Griffes's intoxicating, impressionistic *White Peacock* in 1919, and here he creates a wonderfully sensuous sheen of sound, with lovely wind solos. He seduces the ear too in the brief Sibelius and Copland miniatures, while the sinuous *In the Village* from the *Caucasian Sketches*, with a beautifully played cor anglais solo from Michel Nazzi, is made just as memorable. Not unexpectedly, the vivid recording of Messiaen's *L'Ascension* concentrates on the orchestral colour, yet (surprisingly) the *Waltz* from the Tchaikovsky *String Serenade* has less charm than one would expect.

But it is the Wagner repertoire, with splendid wind and brass playing, that is finest of all. The Shawe-Taylor *Record Guide* reckoned the rumbustious *Overture Rienzi* as 'most exciting and well contrived' and Stokowski's flair is again shown in the equally brilliant *Der fliegende Höllander*. The characteristically opulent *Wotan's Farewell and Magic Fire Music* was recorded in Carnegie Hall, where the intensity and following tenderness of the string playing are matched by excellent sound. Hardly less memorable are the two (studio) *Götterdämmerung* excerpts, truncated by Stokowski from the complete score: the *Funeral Music* bursts in at the actual stabbing of Siegfried, and again brings radiant strings as well as sonorous brass.

But the only real disappointment here is the admittedly spectacular but overdriven account of Tchaikovsky's *Francesca da Rimini*, where the tempi and pulse throughout are less convincing than in Stokowski's classic later account on Everest (currently withdrawn), in which, incidentally, he also reinstated the brief cuts made in this comparatively unsatisfactory first recording. Even so, this pair of discs is well worth exploring.

Volume 3: VAUGHAN WILLIAMS: *Symphony 6*. TCHAIKOVSKY: *Romeo and Juliet*. MOZART: *Symphony 35 (Haffner)*. SCOTT: *From the Sacred Harp*. WEINBERGER: *Schwanda the Bagpiper: Polka and Fugue*
(***) Cala mono CACD 0537

The main item here is the electrifying account of Vaughan Williams's *Sixth Symphony*, which Stokowski recorded in New York in February 1949, only nine months after the first performance – a première recording made ahead even of EMI's first version with Sir Adrian Boult. Stokowski's speeds are consistently on the fast side, but that brings a thrilling intensity, magnetic from first to last. This has appeared on CD from Sony, but the Cala version, with digital mastering by Paschal Byrne and Craig Thompson, brings sound more vivid and more open. This version of the Tchaikovsky overture, recorded in New York in November 1949, is similarly high-powered, marked by Stokowski's preference for a *pianissimo* ending, avoiding the *fortissimo* chords added by the composer. The *Haffner Symphony*, brisk and alert in the outer movements, is, amazingly, the only commercial issue of Stokowski conducting a Mozart symphony, taken from a broadcast in November 1949 with obviously rougher sound than in the Columbia studio recordings. The swaggering account of the Weinberger showpiece is also taken from a broadcast, while the piece by Thomas Jefferson Scott is based on two Southern American hymns which the composer found in a collection called *The Sacred Harp* and which Stokowski encouraged him to write. A recording of the broadcast was put on a wartime V-disc, distributed for entertaining members of the American forces, few of which have survived.

Northern Ballet Theatre Orchestra, John Pryce-Jones

'Twentieth-century English Ballets': FEENEY: *Cinderella.* MULDOWNEY: *The Brontës.* CARL DAVIS: *A Christmas Carol*

(BB) *** Naxos 8.553495

This enterprising disc is of music taken from full-length ballet scores commissioned by the Northern Ballet Theatre. The most instantly appealing work is Carl Davis's *A Christmas Carol*, delightfully nostalgic with its mixture of sentimental and vigorous numbers – these include a lively, rustic-sounding dance as some poor Londoners try to keep themselves warm. It is an appealing score, with much piquant orchestration and a neat use of the harpsichord. Davis introduces well-known Christmas carols to present the story of Scrooge in a fresh way.

Philip Feeney's *Cinderella* is more severe, reflecting the story as told by the Brothers Grimm, rather than the more romanticized version by Perrault. Feeney uses a battery of percussion instruments to tell the tale, and the result lacks really memorable tunes. But it is not at all dull and has plenty of rhythm and colour. The *Courtly Dances* begin with an array of bells, percussion instruments and a gong, then the composer switches to the harpsichord halfway through to striking effect. *The Red Ball*, where the prince introduces himself, is quirky in a haunting way, and the finale brings an up-beat conclusion.

The Brontës, with music by Dominic Muldowney, is a series of vignettes portraying the Brontë family, as seen through the eyes of the father, Revd. Patrick Brontë, who outlived all his six children. The opening *Toy Soldiers' Fantasy* is charming, with its trumpet fanfares set against a robust marching tune; *The Moors* and *Wuthering Heights* numbers are appropriately broody, while *Charlotte in Brussels* is a jaunty little waltz with witty writing throughout the orchestra. It is thoroughly entertaining. The performances and recording are outstanding.

Northern Philharmonia Orchestra of England, Leeds Festival Chorus, Paul Daniel

'Rule, Britannia – The Last Night of the Proms': WALTON: *Coronation Marches: Crown Imperial; Orb and Sceptre.* PARRY: *Jerusalem.* ELGAR: *Enigma Variations: Nimrod;*

Pomp and Circumstance March 1. WOOD: *Fantasia on British Sea Songs* (including *Rule, Britannia*). ARNOLD: *Overture Tam O'Shanter.* PARRY: *I was Glad*

(BB) **(*) Naxos 8.553981

If it seems a little perverse to record such a programme without the contribution of the Prommers and the heady last-night atmosphere, it has to be said that this is a very good concert in its own right, and the Leeds Chorus makes an impressive contribution in *Rule, Britannia* and especially in the reprise of the great *Pomp and Circumstance* melody (which is the more effective at Paul Daniel's spacious tempo). The two Walton marches have panache and Arnold's *Tam O'Shanter* is splendidly done. Here the recording is of spectacular demonstration quality. Excellent value.

Northern Sinfonia, David Lloyd-Jones

'English String Miniatures': HOPE: *Momentum Suite.* BRIDGE: *2 Pieces* (arr. Hindmarsh). CARSE: *2 Sketches.* TOMLINSON: *Graceful Dance.* HOLST: *A Moorside Suite.* DELIUS: *2 Aquarelles.* LEWIS: *English Suite*

(BB) *** Naxos 8.555070

Another enterprising programme of light but never trivial English music, all with a distinct pastoral feel. In Philip Hope's *Momentum Suite* the first movement, *Dance*, a lively rustic-sounding piece, has an especially attractive middle section, while the last movement, which gets faster and faster, gives the work its title. Paul Lewis's *English Suite* balances its lively *March, Jig* and *Jaunt* movements with a reflective *Meditation*. The two Frank Bridge *Pieces* are highly contrasted. The humour of the *Scherzo Phantastick* comes over well in Paul Hindmarsh's arrangement, including the 'sneeze' at the end of the mock *Trio* section; the *Valse-intermezzo* is delightful, too. *A Northern Dance* from Adam Carse's *Two Sketches* has a quite haunting melancholy feel (with a tune rather similar to 'Danny Boy'). Tomlinson's *Graceful Dance* is slight, but pleasing. The better-known Holst and Delius works are beautifully played, with the *Nocturne* from Holst's *A Moorside Suite* especially atmospheric. The recording is resonant but well detailed, and the performances are first class, as one might expect from Lloyd-Jones and his excellent northern players. Strongly recommended at super-bargain price.

Oistrakh, David (violin)

'The Originals' (with (i) VSO; (ii) Igor Oistrakh; (iii) RPO, Goossens; (iv) Dresden State O, Konwitschny): BACH: (i) *Violin Concertos 1 in E; 2 in A min;* (ii-iii) *Double Violin Concerto in D min., BWV 1041-3.* (iii) BEETHOVEN: *Romances 1 in G, 2 in F, Opp. 40 & 50.* (iv) BRAHMS: *Violin Concerto, Op. 77.* TCHAIKOVSKY: *Violin Concerto, Op. 35*

(M) (***) DG stereo/mono 447 427-2 (2)

In 'The Originals' series at mid-price, DG here offers reissues of classic Oistrakh recordings, unavailable for years in any format. Rarest are the 1954 mono recordings of the Brahms and Tchaikovsky *Concertos*, more relaxed, more volatile readings than those Oistrakh recorded later in stereo. Oistrakh moves effortlessly from dashing bravura to the sweetest lyricism, the complete master.

The Bach and Beethoven offerings are hardly less welcome. Allowing for the practice of the time, these Bach performances are all strong and resilient, consistently bringing out the sweetness and purity of Oistrakh's playing, not least in the rapt accounts of the slow movements. Directing the Vienna Symphoniker from the violin, Oistrakh may make the tuttis in the two Bach solo concertos rather heavy, but he then transforms everything the moment he starts playing. The Bach *Double Concerto* with Oistrakh father and son, accompanied by Goossens and the RPO, is more magnetic still, and they accompany him no less sympathetically in the warm, poised readings of the two Beethoven *Romances*.

Orchestre National de France, Charles Munch

'*Hommage à Charles Munch*'

BEETHOVEN: *Symphonies 4 in B flat; 7 in A; Overture: Consecration of the House* (*(*) V 4825)

BERLIOZ: *Symphonie fantastique, Op. 14; Overtures: Le Corsaire, Op. 21; Benvenuto Cellini, Op. 23* (* V 4826)

BRAHMS: *Symphony 2 in D, Op. 73.* SCHUMANN: *Symphony 4 in D min., Op. 120* (** V 4827)

DEBUSSY: *Images: Iberia; La Mer; Fantaisie for Piano & Orchestra* (with Nicole Henriot) (** V 4828)

FRANCK: *Symphony in D min.* FAURE: *Pelléas et Mélisande: suite* (** V 4829)

HONEGGER: *Symphony 1.* DUTILLEUX: *Symphony 2* (**(*) V 4830)

HONEGGER: *Symphonies 2 (for strings & trumpet obbligato); 5 (Di tre re); Le chant de Nigamon; Pastorale d'été* (** V 4831)

ROUSSEL: *Symphonies 3 in G min., Op. 42; 4 in A, Op. 53; Bacchus et Ariane: Suite 2* (** V 4832)

'*Hommage à Charles Munch*' (complete)

(BB) ** Auvidis Valois (ADD) V 4822 (8) (with the complete set: SIBELIUS: *Legends: The Swan of Tuonela; Lemminkäinen's Return*)

An eight-CD set called *Hommage à Charles Munch* commemorates his work with the Orchestre National after his return from Boston. If you buy the whole set – and it is very inexpensive – you get a 1964 recording of two of the *Four Legends*, made while the orchestra was on tour in Finland. The discs are available separately and bring some outstanding performances, albeit in variable sound.

The Beethoven *Fourth* (V 4825) was recorded in Stockholm on the same Scandinavian tour; and the *Seventh* and, appropriately enough, *The Consecration of the House* come from the inaugural concert in the *Maison de la Radio* in Paris in 1963. Not first-class but acceptable sound, as is the Berlioz (V 4826). The *Symphonie fantastique*, recorded in a rather dry acoustic in Lisbon in 1963, is a bit hard-driven, as was his Boston account. *Un bal* is horribly rushed.

Good though his Franck, Brahms and Schumann may be, it was for his Honegger and Roussel that Munch is best remembered. Always a champion of good contemporary music, he conducted the Honegger and Dutilleux (V 4830) in 1962. Both works are closely associated with Boston. Koussevitzky commissioned the Honegger *First Symphony* (along with the Roussel *Third*) for the 50th anniversary of the founding of the Boston Symphony and Munch conducted the première of the Dutilleux *Symphony* during his Boston years. The Honegger recording is not absolutely first class – a bit strident and narrower in frequency range than some of its

companions – but the Dutilleux is very good, and what a performance!

Two other Honegger symphonies, Nos. 2 and 5 (V 4831), come from performances taken from the orchestra's 1964 European tour, the *Symphony for Strings* in San Sebastián in Spain and the *Fifth* from Helsinki. The early *Le chant de Nigamon*, an amazingly original piece, was recorded at the Théâtre des Champs-Elysées two years earlier and, though not first-class sound, is perfectly acceptable (it briefly captures the conductor's vocalise!). Neither of the symphonies is superior to his Boston performances from the 1950s and the rather shrill-sounding *Symphony for Strings* is nowhere near as impressive as his 1969 EMI recording with the Orchestre de Paris. The Helsinki recording of the *Fifth* sounds better.

The Roussel *Third* (V 4832) has plenty of drive, too, but the recording balance is poor. It comes from the 1964 Edinburgh Festival and the string melody at the opening has to struggle to make itself heard against the percussive accompaniment. The *Fourth Symphony*, recorded two years later at the Théâtre des Champs-Elysées, is better, though the *Bacchus et Ariane* suite, whose provenance is not given, is more transparent and present than either. Munch was closely identified with Roussel all his life and, though this disc is better than nothing, if you can get hold of his commercial recording of the symphonies on Erato they are better served in terms of sound. All the same, despite its sonic limitations this is a set to have. Munch was a conductor of stature and his work with the Orchestre National is well worth commemorating.

Paris Conservatoire Orchestra, Albert Wolff

MASSENET: *Scènes alsaciennes; Scènes pittoresques.* Overtures: ADAM: *Si j'étais roi.* AUBER: *Le domino noir.* HEROLD: *Zampa.* REZNICEK: *Donna Diana.* SUPPE: *Pique Dame*

**(*) Testament (ADD) SBT 1308

Never mind the bracket round the third star – that merely acknowledges the odd orchestral blemish – for this disc offers full three-star enjoyment. These recordings from the 1950s simply ooze with a Gallic style of orchestral playing which has now all but disappeared, with performances of much character and personality. Just listen to the delicious way Wolff points the strings in *Si j'étais roi*, and the genial vitality which pervades the music-making throughout – a long way from the bland brilliance of many of today's performances. The Massenet *Suites* could hardly sound more picturesque – why are these charming works so rarely heard nowadays? – and the sound of the French orchestra, especially the brass, makes one regret the more or less uniform quality of international orchestras today. Even the obvious fluff in the brass in *Zampa* [3'25"] seems to add to the charm of this disc. The overtures, originally released in 1958 under the title 'Overtures in Hi-Fi', have never sounded better, full and vivid, with only a certain tubbiness betraying their age. The Massenet items were recorded in 1955 and the excellent sound-quality, though a bit thin by modern standards, is even more remarkable. Well done to Testament for restoring these recordings to us, and hopefully more will follow.

Pekinel, Güher and Süher (piano duo)

'*French Music for Piano Duo*': SAINT-SAËNS: *Carnival of the Animals*. POULENC: *Double Piano Concerto in D min.* (both with Fr. R. Philh. O, Marek Janowski). MANUEL INFANTE: *Danses Andalouses*. RAVEL: *Rapsodie espagnole; La Valse*

℗→ ❂ (BB) *** Warner Apex 2564 62125-2

The piano duo, Güher and Süher Pekinel – of mixed Turkish/Spanish parentage – have already given us an outstanding set of Mozart's music for piano duo. Here they make a sparkling contribution to Saint-Saëns's zoological fantasy, readily dominating the performance with their scintillating pianism. Saint-Saëns's portrait gallery comes vividly and wittily to life, and the gentle dignity of Eric Levionnais's *Le Cygne* makes a touching highlight, leading on to an exhilarating finale. They play with comparable dash and sparkle in Poulenc's *Double Concerto*, relishing the Mozartian pastiche of the *Larghetto* and the sensuous Ravelian/Satiesque nostalgia of the other lyrical ideas. In both works Janowski contributes a lively and thoroughly supportive backcloth, and the recording balance is excellent.

Manuel Infante (1883–1958) provides a perfect encore with his glittering *Danses Andalouses* (written in 1971), and this superb concert is rounded off with unsurpassed accounts of Ravel's *Rapsodie espagnole*, luminous, glittering, and subtle, and a dazzling *La Valse* with a thrilling climax, both works every bit as enticing as the orchestral versions. A bargain of bargains.

Perkins, Laurence (bassoon)

'*Bassoon Concertos*' (with Manchester Camerata, Douglas Boyd): M. HAYDN: *Concertino in B flat*. MOZART: *Concerto*. STAMITZ: *Concerto*. WEBER: *Concerto; Andante and Rondo ungarese*

*** Hyp. CDA 72688

If the bassoon has often been cast as the clown of the orchestra, the five concertante works on this disc demonstrate how much wider its role is, with Laurence Perkins as soloist bringing out the tender beauty of the muted slow movement of the Mozart *Bassoon Concerto*, an early work too often dismissed, but full of charm. The Stamitz *Concerto*, elegant in the slow movement, vigorous in the outer movements, is equally attractive, and the two Weber concertante works show him in relaxed mood, with the *Hungarian Rondo* and the finale of the *Concerto* winningly rumbustious. The *Concertino* by Michael Haydn is the slow movement of one of his orchestral *Serenades*. Perkins, with his crisp articulation, brings out the fun in much of the inspiration as well as the lyrical beauty, warmly accompanied by the Manchester Camerata (of which he is principal bassoon) under another leading wind-player, the oboist, Douglas Boyd.

Perlman, Itzhak (violin)

'*The Perlman Edition*':

BEETHOVEN: *Piano Trios 5 (Ghost); 7 (Archduke); in E flat (from Septet), Op. 38* (with Ashkenazy & Harrell) (5 62588-2)

BRUCH: *Concerto 2; Scottish Fantasy, Op. 46* (with New Philh. O, Lopez-Cobos) (5 62589-2)

KORNGOLD: *Concerto in D, Op. 35*. SIBELIUS: *Concerto in D min., Op. 47*. SINDING: *Suite in A min., Op. 10* (with Pittsburgh O, Previn) (5 62590-2)

MENDELSSOHN: *Concerto in E min., Op. 64* (with LSO, Previn). TCHAIKOVSKY: *Concerto in D, Op. 35* (with Phd. O, Ormandy) (5 62591-2)

PROKOFIEV: *Concertos 1–2* (with BBC SO, Rozhdestvensky); *Sonata for 2 Violins* (with Zukerman) (5 62592-2)

GLAZUNOV: *Concerto in A min., Op. 82*. SHOSTAKOVICH: *Concerto 1 in A min., Op. 99* (with Israel PO, Mehta); *3 Violin Duets* (with Zukerman) (5 62593-2)

PAGANINI: *Concerto 1 in D, Op. 6*. SARASATE: *Carmen Fantasy, Op. 25; Introduction et Tarantelle, Op. 43; Zigeunerweisen* (with RPO or Abbey Road Ens., Foster) (5 62594-2)

DVORAK: *Concerto in A min., Op. 53; Romance in F min., Op. 11* (with LPO, Barenboim); *Sonatina in G, Op. 100; 4 Romantic Pieces, Op. 75* (with Sanders, piano) (5 62595-2)

'*Encores*' (with Sanders, piano) (5 62596-2)

'*Tradition*': Familiar Jewish Melodies (with Zohar, clarinet, and Israel PO, Seltzer) (5 62597-2)

BRAHMS: *Concerto in D, Op. 77* (with BPO, Barenboim). *Sonatensatz in C min. (Scherzo); Hungarian Dances 1, 2, 7 & 9* (with Ashkenazy, piano) (5 62598-2)

CHAUSSON: *Poème*. RAVEL: *Tzigane*. SAINT-SAENS: *Introduction & Rondo capriccioso, Op. 28; Havanaise, Op. 83* (with O de Paris, Martinon). MASSENET: *Thaïs: Méditation* (with Abbey Road Ens., Foster) (5 62599-2)

BARBER: *Concerto, Op. 14*. BERNSTEIN: *Serenade after Plato's Symposium*. FOSS: *3 American Pieces* (all with Boston SO, Ozawa) (5 62600-2)

KREISLER: *Encores: Andantino in the Style of Martini; Caprice Viennoise; Liebeslied; Recitative & Scherzo capriccioso, Op. 6; Schön Rosmarin; Siciliano & Rigaudon in the Style of Francoeur; Tempo di minuetto in the Style of Pugnani; Syncopation; Toy Soldiers' March; Tambourin chinoise*. Arrangements: ALBENIZ: *Tango*. CHAMINADE: *Sérénade espagnole*. DVORAK: *Slavonic Dances 2 in E min.; 3 in G; Songs My Mother Taught Me*. GLUCK: *Mélodie*. GRAINGER: *Molly on the Shore*. GRANADOS: *Spanish Dance 5*. CHOPIN: *Mazurka 45 in A min., Op. 67/4*. LEHAR: *Frasquita: Serenade*. SCHUMANN: *Romance in A, Op. 94/2* (with Sanders, piano) (5 62601-2)

BACH: *Concertos 1 in A min., BWV 1041; 2 in E, BWV 1042; Double Concerto in D min., BWV 1043* (with Zukerman, ECO, Barenboim); *Concerto for Violin & Oboe in C min., BWV 1060* (with Black (oboe), Israel PO) (5 62602-2)

(B) *** EMI (ADD/DDD) 5 85083-2 (15)

Itzhak Perlman was born in Tel Aviv in 1945; he taught himself to play the violin and, despite being stricken by polio (and thus obliged always to play sitting down), he began his concert career at the age of ten. Undoubtedly the supreme master of his instrument in our time, he has seemed a natural successor to Heifetz, and has recorded virtually all the key concertos for his instrument with consistent success. If his technique is dazzling, it is always put at the service of the composer, and his extraordinary sophistication of bow technique and rich yet often subtle control of colour and dynamic often add a new dimension to music which we know well. He chose always to make his recordings in a microphone spotlight, which detracts to some extent from the orchestral balance; but in the end the listener is disarmed by the glorious sounds he conjures from his 1714 Stradivarius violin.

He worked with many different conductors on record, but undoubtedly his most successful concerto records were made mainly with André Previn, while he has a similarly close relationship with Pinchas Zukerman in instrumental music. The somewhat self-effacing Samuel Sanders was his chosen accompanist in solo repertoire, and they achieved a genuine duo in music in which the piano played an equal role with the violin. Each of these CDs is available separately at mid-price and (apart from the two recital collections) each is reviewed separately under its various conposer entries. All in all, this slip-case compilation – the CDs are in separate jewel-cases – is a fabulous achievement; the current transfers, even if at times the analogue recordings have lost just a little of their atmospheric allure, are generally excellent.

'A la carte' (with Abbey Road Ens., Foster): MASSENET: *Thaïs: Méditation.* GLAZUNOV: *Mazurka-Obéreque; Méditation, Op. 32.* RACHMANINOV: *Vocalise, Op. 34/14.* SARASATE: *Zigeunerweisen, Op. 20; Introduction and Tarantelle, Op. 43.* RIMSKY-KORSAKOV: *Russian Fantasy* (arr. KREISLER). TCHAIKOVSKY: *Scherzo, Op. 42/2* (orch. Glazunov). WIENIAWSKI: *Légende, Op. 17.* KREISLER: *The Old Refrain; Schön Rosmarin*
**(*) EMI 5 55475-2

Perlman is in his element in this luscious concert of mostly Russian lollipops – although, as it happens, the most delectable playing of all comes in the Sarasate *Zigeunerweisen.* But the pieces by Glazunov, Tchaikovsky's sparkling *Scherzo* and the Rimsky-Korsakov *Fantasy* also show the extraordinary range of colour and sheer charisma of this fiddling. Alas, as always, the violin is too closely balanced, and this is most disadvantageous in the Wieniawski *Légende,* which loses much of its romantic atmosphere. Perlman's closing solo encore, Kreisler's *Schön Rosmarin,* ends the programme with extraordinary panache. Otherwise Lawrence Foster accompanies discreetly.

'Concertos from my Childhood' (with Juilliard O, Foster): RIEDING: *Violin Concerto in B min., Op. 25.* SEITZ: *Schuler-Konzert 2, Op. 13* (orch. ADOLPHE). ACCOLAY: *Violin Concerto 1 in A min.* BERIOT: *Scenes de ballet, Op. 100.* VIOTTI: *Violin Concerto 22 in A min.*
*** EMI 5 56750-2

Itzhak Perlman here returns in nostalgia to the concertos which, from the age of six onwards, helped to shape his phenomenal technique. None of this is great music, not even the longest and best-known piece, the Viotti *Violin Concerto 22.* But playing with obvious love, Perlman brings out freshness and sparkle in each of them. He turns even passing banalities into moments of joy. Oscar Rieding and Friedrich Seitz are so obscure that even their dates seem to be unknown, yet their miniature concertos here are totally charming, with Perlman springing rhythms infectiously. The student orchestra plays brilliantly too.

'Encores' (with Sanders, piano): NOVACEK: *Perpetuum mobile.* BEN-HEIM: *Berceuse sfaradite.* DEBUSSY: *La Fille aux cheveux de lin.* SARASATE: *Zapateado.* PONCE: *Estrellita.* MOSZKOWSKI: *Guitarre, Op. 45/2.* CHOPIN: *Nocturne in E flat, Op. 55/2.* POULENC: *Presto.* SAINT-SAENS: *Le Cygne.* PARADIES: *Toccata.* ELGAR: *La Capricieuse.* FOSTER: *Old Folks at Home.* VIEUXTEMPS: *Souvenir d'Amérique.* PARADIES: *Sicilienne.* RAFF:

Cavatina, Op. 85/3. SARASATE: *Malagueña, Op. 21/1; Caprice basque, Op. 24; Romanza andaluza, Op. 22/1.*
(M) *** EMI 5 62596-2

Perlman's supreme mastery of the violin has never been demonstrated more endearingly than in this collection of encores, recorded over two decades between 1972 and 1989. Brilliant showpieces vie with gentler inspirations which touch the heart by their refined delicacy, like the performance of Ben-Heim's dainty *Berceuse* and Debussy's delicate evocation of *La Fille aux cheveux de lin* with their veiled tonal beauty – framed as they are by Nováček's dazzling *Perpetuum mobile* and Sarasate's coruscating *Zapateado.* The wistful sentimentality of Ponce's *Estrellita* (which actually derives from a forgotten violin concerto) is perfectly caught, while Poulenc's spiccato *Presto* and the Paradies *Toccata* similarly offer contrast to a charmingly fragile portrayal of *Le Cygne.*

Tully Potter in the notes tells us that Elgar's *La Capricieuse* 'demands a good up-bow staccato': it is managed here with aplomb, while the Paradies *Sicilenne* and the more luscious Raff *Cavatina* make a charming foil for the witty Vieuxtemps *Souvenir d'Amérique,* which must surely raise a smile of recognition. The recital ends with Spanishry: three pieces by Sarasate, with whom Perlman has already shown a great affinity in his recordings of the concertante *Carmen Fantasy* and *Zigeunerwiesen.* Samuel Sanders accompanies with discretion but is a true partner where necessary. For the most part he is backwardly balanced, but he makes his initial entry strongly, before Perlman, in the opening *Perpetuum mobile.* The recording is very truthful and immediate.

'Tradition': Familiar Jewish Melodies (with Israel Zohar, clarinet, and Israel PO, Seltzer): *A Yiddishe Mamme; As der Rebbe Elimelech is gevoyrn asoi freylach; Reyzele; Oif'n Pripetchik brennt a feier; Doyna; Rozhinkes mit Mandelen; Oif'n Weyg steyt a Boim; A Dudele; Viahin soll ich geyn?*
(M) *** EMI 5 62597-2

Perlman spent his childhood years in Israel, and this affectionately played programme reflects his familiarity with traditional Jewish melodies, always warmly seductive in melodic outline and 'poised', as Tully Potter comments in the notes, 'between joy and sadness, sentiment and sentimentality'. There are also the occasional accelerando features that we recognize from the Brahms *Hungarian Dances.* Dov Seltzer has scored these pieces concertante fashion, but leaving plenty of opportunities for Perlman to carry the luscious melodies, gently and tastefully (as in *Oif'n Weyg steyt a Boim*). The principal clarinettist of the Israel Philharmonic also makes a modest solo contribution to three numbers. However, despite the conductor's surname, his chosen programme concentrates on slow, languorous melodies, rather than adding an element of sparkle. The recording is richly textured, with Perlman flatteringly profiled.

'The Art of Itzhak Perlman' (with Israel PO, Mehta; Pittsburgh SO, Previn; LPO, Ozawa; RPO, Foster; also Ashkenazy, Canino, Sanders, Previn (piano) and other artists): BACH: *Concerto, BWV 1056; Partita 3, BWV 1006.* VIVALDI: *Concerto, RV 199.* MOZART: *Oboe Quartet, K.370.* BRAHMS: *Sonata 3; Hungarian Dances 1–2, 7 & 9.* SINDING: *Suite, Op. 10.* WIENIAWSKI: *Concerto 1.* SIBELIUS: *Concerto.* KHACHATURIAN: *Concerto.* KORNGOLD: *Concerto.* STRAVINSKY: *Suite italienne.* ANON.: *Doyna.* YELLEN/POLLACK: *My Yiddishe Momma.* FOSTER (arr. HEIFETZ): *The Old Folks at Home.* PONCE (arr. HEIFETZ): *Estrellita.* JOPLIN: *The Rag-time Dance; Pineapple Rag.*

SMETANA: *Z domoviny.* KREISLER: *Liebesfreud; Liebesleid.* RACHMANINOV (arr. PRESS/GINGOLD): *Vocalise.* GRAINGER: *Molly on the Shore.* PREVIN: *Look at him; Bowing and Scraping.* TRAD. (arr. KREISLER): *Londonderry Air.* SARASATE: *Carmen Fantasy*

(M) *** EMI ADD/DDD 7 64617-2 (4)

This box contains a feast of this great violinist's recordings. He made the choice himself and, while the concertos, particularly the Wieniawski, Sibelius, Khachaturian and Korngold (and not forgetting the dazzling concertante *Carmen Fantasy* of Sarasate or the *Suite* of Sinding), are all indispensable, the shorter pieces on the last disc just as readily display the Perlman magic. They include the delectable jazz collaboration with Previn, the beautifully played Kreisler encores, and many popular items which are readily turned into lollipops. The stylish account of the Stravinsky *Suite italienne* which ends disc three is also one of the highlights of the set. For the most part the recordings have the violin very forwardly balanced, but that was Perlman's own choice; the sound is otherwise generally excellent. The discs are also currently available separately at mid-price.

'*Great Romantic Violin Concertos*' (with (i) Chicago SO or (ii) Philh. O, Giulini; (iii) Concg. O, Haitink; (iv) RPO, Foster; (v) Phd. O, Ormandy): (i) BRAHMS: *Concerto in D, Op. 77.* (iii) BRUCH: *Concerto 1 in G min., Op. 26.* (ii) BEETHOVEN: *Concerto in D, Op. 61.* (iv) PAGANINI: *Concerto 1 in D, Op. 6.* (iii) MENDELSSOHN: *Concerto in E min., Op. 64.* (v) TCHAIKOVSKY: *Concerto in D, Op. 35*

(M) **(*) EMI ADD/DDD 7 64922-2 (3)

These major Perlman recordings include his earlier (1980) studio recording of the Beethoven *Concerto*; it is among the most commanding of his readings and the element of slight understatement, the refusal to adopt too romantically expressive a style, makes for a compelling strength, perfectly matched by Giulini's thoughtful, direct accompaniment. The (1976) Brahms is also a distinguished performance, again finely supported by Giulini, this time with the Chicago orchestra, a reading of darker hue than is customary, with a thoughtful and searching slow movement rather than the autumnal rhapsody which it so often becomes. The (1983) Bruch *G minor Concerto* must be counted a disappointment, however, not helped by the harsh, early digital recording which gives an edge to the solo timbre. The performance is heavily expressive and, like the Mendelssohn (recorded at the same time), is not nearly as spontaneous as Perlman's earlier, analogue recording with Previn. The Paganini (1971) is one of Perlman's very finest records and, although the traditional cuts are observed, the performance has irresistible panache and has been transferred to CD very well. In the Tchaikovsky (1978) the soloist is placed less aggressively forward than is usual. Perlman's expressive warmth goes with a very bold orchestral texture from Ormandy and the Philadelphia Orchestra. However, admirers of these artists are unlikely to be disappointed.

Petri, Michaela (recorder)

'*The Ultimate Recorder Collection*': VIVALDI: *The Four Seasons: Spring* (with Guildhall String Ens., Malcolm). *Concerto in D (Il gardellino), Op. 10/3: Finale; Concerto in G min. (La Notte), Op. 10/2, RV 439.* SAMMARTINI: *Recorder Concerto in F* (all with Moscow Virtuosi, Spivakov). SATIE: *Gymnopédie 1.* GLUCK: *Orfeo: Melody & Dance of the*

Blessed Spirits. BACH: *Suite in D, BWV 1067: Air.* SCHEINDIENST: *Variations.* TARTINI: *Sonata in G min. (Devil's Trill).* KOPPEL: *Nele's dances 15–18.* JACOB: *An Encore for Michaela* (all with Hannibal, arr. for recorder and guitar). GRIEG: *Peer Gynt: Solveig's Song; Anitra's Dance.* Lyric pieces: *Butterfly; Little Bird, Op. 43/1 & 4; March of the Trolls, Op. 54/3; Once Upon a Time, Op. 71/1; 2 Norwegian Dances, Op. 35/1-2* (all arr. Langford). KOPPEL: *Moonchild's Dream: Conclusion.* ARNOLD: *Recorder Concerto, Op. 133: Lento.* CHRISTIANSEN: *Dance suite, Op. 29: Molto vivace* (all with ECO, Okko Kamu). HANDEL: *Sonata in G min., Op. 1/2.* BACH: *Sonata in E flat (transposed G), BWV 1031* (with Jarrett, harpsichord). TELEMANN: *Trio sonata 3 in F min.* (with Hanne Petri, harpsichord, David Petri, cello); *Sonata 5 in D min. for 2 recorders* (with Selin). CORELLI: *Concerto grosso, Op. 6/8 (Christmas): Finale including Pastorale* (with Nat. PO, Neary). BACH: *Cantata 140: Chorale: Wachet auf* (with Westminster Abbey Ch., Ross, organ; cond. Neary)

(B) ** RCA Twofer 74321 59112-2 (2)

This is a collection that will best appeal to amateur recorder players, and might make a good birthday present for a young beginner, who will surely be impressed by Michaela Petri's easy virtuosity and will respond to a string of such famous melodies. Not all of them transcribe too well, and many are far more effective on the instruments for which they were written. Vivaldi's *Spring* from *The Four Seasons* is indestructible, but Bach's famous *Air* sounds puny, while Grieg's *Second Norwegian Dance* is much better suited to the oboe. However, there is quite a lot of genuine recorder repertoire here, stylishly presented, which hopefully should tempt any budding young soloist to explore further. The recording balance is generally well managed and the effect is truthful and not overblown.

Philadelphia Orchestra, Leopold Stokowski

(see also under STOKOWSKI SYMPHONY ORCHESTRA below)

'*Fantasia*': BACH, orch. Stokowski: *Toccata and Fugue in D min.* DUKAS: *L'Apprenti sorcier.* MUSSORGSKY, arr. Stokowski: *Night on the Bare Mountain.* STRAVINSKY: *The Rite of Spring.* TCHAIKOVSKY: *Nutcracker Suite*

(M) (***) Pearl mono GEMMCD 4988

A self-recommending disc. *The Rite of Spring* comes from 1929–30 and the *Nutcracker* from as early as 1926, though one would never believe it. Everything Stokowski did at this period was full of character, and the engineers obviously performed miracles. The latest recording is Stokowski's amazing arrangement of *Night on the Bare Mountain*, which dates from 1940. Such is the colour and richness of sonority Stokowski evokes from the fabulous Philadelphians that surface noise and other limitations are completely forgotten. The transfers are very good.

'*Philadelphia Rarities*' (1928–1937): arr. Stokowski: *2 Ancient Liturgical Melodies: Veni, Creator Spiritus; Veni, Emmanuel.* FALLA: *La vida breve: Spanish Dance.* TURINA: *Gypsy Dance, Op. 55/5.* DUBENSKY: *Edgar Allan Poe's 'The Raven'* (narr. de Loache). arr. Konoye: *Etenraku: Ceremonial Japanese Prelude.* MCDONALD: *The Legend of the Arkansas Traveller; The Festival of the Workers (suite): Dance of the*

Workers; Double Piano Concerto (with Behrend & Kelberine). EICHHEIM: *Oriental Impressions: Japanese Nocturne; Symphonic Variations: Bali.* SOUSA: *Manhattan Beach; El Capitan*

(M) (***) Cala mono CACD 0501

All these recordings show what splendid recorded sound Stokowski was achieving in Philadelphia as early as 1929. The opening Stokowski liturgical arrangements show how that master of orchestral sonority could make liturgical chants his very own, with a discreet tolling bell to indicate their source. Falla's *Spanish Dance* shows him at his most sparklingly chimerical. Dubensky's music does not add a great deal to Edgar Allan Poe, but the narrator, Benjamin de Loache, certainly does, presenting the narrative with the essentially genial, melodramatic lubricity of Vincent Price.

Hidemaro Konoye and Stokowski and his players conspire between them to provide an extraordinarily authentic Japanese sound in *Etenraku*, and then in *The Legend of the Arkansas Traveller* we have a complete change of local colour for Alexander Hilsberg's folksy, sub-Country-and-Western violin solo. Henry Eichheim's Japanese and Balinese impressions are suitably exotic, but not music one would wish to return to. As for Harl McDonald's *Double Piano Concerto*, the piano writing is splashy and the finale is spectacularly based on the *Juarezca*, a jazzy Mexican dance. The two soloists provide convincing, extrovert dash, and Stokowski obviously revels in what Noël Coward might have described as 'potent cheap music' if with nothing like the melodic appeal of Coward's own work. The two Sousa marches have both poise and élan, but here the sound is barely adequate – not the fault of the CD transfer. The programme lasts for 78 minutes and Stokowksi aficionados need not hesitate.

Philadelphia Orchestra, or (i) Minneapolis Orchestra, Eugene Ormandy

BEETHOVEN: *Piano Concertos 3 in C min., Op. 37* (with Arrau); *4 in G, Op. 58* (with Casadesus). BARBER: *Essay 1 for Orchestra, Op. 12.* BRAHMS: *Double Concerto in A min., Op. 102* (with Heifetz & Feuermann). BRUCKNER: *Symphony 7 in E.* DVORAK: *Cello Concerto in B min., Op. 104* (with Piatigorsky). (i) GRIEG: *Piano Concerto in A min., Op. 16* (with Rubinstein). GRIFFES: *The Pleasure Dome of Kubla Khan, Op. 8.* (i) MAHLER: *Symphony 2 in C min. (Resurrection)* (with Frank, O'Malley Gallogly; Twin City Symphony Ch.). MIASKOVSKY: *Symphony 21 in F sharp min. in One Movement, Op 51.* MUSSORGSKY: *Pictures at an Exhibition* (orch. Caillet). RACHMANINOV: *Piano Concertos 1 in F sharp min., Op. 1; 3 in D min., Op. 30* (with composer). RAVEL: *Piano Concerto for the Left Hand* (with Casadesus). (i) SCHOENBERG: *Verklaerte Nacht, Op. 4.* SIBELIUS: *Symphony 1 in E min., Op. 39; Legend: Lemminkäinen's Homeward Journey, Op. 22/4.* R. STRAUSS: *Don Quixote, Op. 35* (with Feuermann); *Symphonia domestica, Op. 53.* TCHAIKOVSKY: *Piano Concerto 1 in B flat min., Op. 23* (with Levant); *Symphony 6 in B min. (Pathéthique)*

(BB) (***) Brillante Maestro (mono) 205236/240-303 (10)

This is an amazing cornucopia of classic performances given by the Philadelphia Orchestra, presided over by Eugene Ormandy. The Minneapolis Orchestra is represented by the electrifying 1935 Mahler *Second Symphony* and the 1934 Schoenberg *Verklaerte Nacht*, its première recording in the version for full strings. The earliest of the Philadelphia performances are *The Pleasure Dome of Kubla Khan* (1934) and the Bruckner *Seventh Symphony* (1935), the last being the Tchaikovsky *B flat minor Concerto* with Oscar Levant. Speaking of which, what a line-up of soloists is on offer: Jascha Heifetz and Emanuel Feuermann in the Brahms, and the legendary 1940 *Don Quixote* also with Feuermann. Those who remember the Mahler will know how dramatic and intense was this performance. It is particularly good to have Robert Casadesus in Beethoven's *G major Concerto* and Louis Caillet's scoring of *Pictures at an Exhibition* recorded in 1937. Some of these performances (the Barber *Essay for Orchestra* and the Miaskovsky *Symphony*) are already available in alternative transfers, but many are not. As far as we know, the *Verklaerte Nacht* makes its first appearance since the 1930s. It was a much-sought-after import after the war and commanded what was then an astronomic price: £1 a disc! The whole treasure-house of ten CDs is marketed at under £20 (£2 a disc, each of which would encompass eight or nine 78s). Generally speaking the transfers are serviceable rather than distinguished: the Schoenberg does not noticeably improve on the original shellac discs, and the Rachmaninov concertos are not better than either the RCA or Naxos transfers. No matter; this is an incredible bargain, and some of the performances are alone worth the price of the whole box. Ormandy was taken for granted in the 1950s and 1960s, but he got a wonderful sound from his Philadelphia Orchestra; none of these performances falls below distinction.

Philharmonia Orchestra, Herbert von Karajan

'*Philharmonia Promenade Concert*': WALDTEUFEL; *Les Patineurs (Skaters' Waltz)*. JOHANN STRAUSS JR: *Tritsch-Tratsch; Unter Donner und Blitz Polkas.* JOHANN STRAUSS SR: *Radetzky March.* CHABRIER: *España; Joyeuse Marche.* SUPPÉ: *Overture: Light Cavalry.* WEINBERGER: *Schwanda the Bagpiper: Polka.* OFFENBACH: *Orpheus in the Underworld.* BERLIOZ: *Le carnaval romain: Overture.* LEONVACALLO: *Pagliacci: Intermezzo.* BORODIN: *Prince Igor: Polovtsian Dances*

⊝— (M) *** EMI (ADD) 4 76900-2

A superb reissue from the late 1950s, splendidly recorded in the Kingsway Hall when the Philharmonia players were at their peak, and the whole collection has the proper infectious 'fun' quality. Perhaps the Chabrier items don't quite have the swagger of Beecham, but the concert certainly does not lack élan, and overall this is an exhilarating experience, with the elegant Waldteufel *Waltz*, the grand Suppé *Overture* and the lively *Schwanda Polka* standing out. The last three items have been added for the reissue and the *Polovtsian Dances* make for a sumptuous and exciting finale.

Philharmonia Orchestra, Constant Lambert

'*The Last Recordings*': CHABRIER (orch. Lambert): *Ballabile.* SUPPÉ: *Overtures: Morning, Noon and Night in*

Vienna; Pique dame. WALDTEUFEL: Waltzes: *Estudiantina, Les Patineurs, Pomone, Sur la plage.* WALTON: *Façade Suites 1 and 2*

(M) (***) Somm Celeste mono SOMMCD 023

This charming disc offers a generous collection, very well transferred, of the recordings Constant Lambert made just before his death. Lambert's flair as a ballet conductor is reflected in all the items here. Whether in Waldteufel waltzes, Suppé overtures or the orchestral *Façade* pieces (source of the highly successful ballet) Lambert is masterly at giving a spring to the dance-rhythms, while never indulging excessively in rubato. Lambert rivals even the composer himself in bringing out the fun of *Façade*. He was, after all, almost the work's surrogate creator – the friend of Walton who, alongside him, discovered the joys of jazz and syncopated rhythms in the early 1920s. It is remarkable too that even with the limitations of mono recording of 1950 Lambert keeps textures ideally clear and transparent, helped by the refined playing of the Philharmonia Orchestra, adding to the freshness of all these performances. As part of the documentation, Alan Sanders provides a most illuminating essay on Lambert's life and recording career.

Philharmonia Orchestra, Nicolai Malko

BORODIN: *Prince Igor: Overture; Polovtsian Dances; Polovtsian March. Symphony 2 in A min.*
RIMSKY-KORSAKOV: *Maid of Pskov (Ivan the Terrible): Overture.* LIADOV: *8 Russian Folksongs.* GLAZUNOV (with Sokolov and Liadov): *Les vendredis: Polka*

(**) Testament mono/stereo SBT 1062

Nicolai Malko, from 1926 the chief conductor of the Leningrad Philharmonic and the first interpreter of Shostakovich's *First Symphony*, made all too few recordings; though some of these with the Philharmonia lack tautness, his feeling for the Slavonic idiom is unerring. This reading of the *Prince Igor Overture* is light and transparent (in newly unearthed stereo) but lacks dramatic bite, and so do the *Polovtsian Dances*, polished but not involving. The *Polovtsian March* is quite different: a tense, swaggering performance which reveals the true Malko. Then after an amiable, low-key account of the first movement of the Borodin *Symphony*, the Scherzo second movement brings a virtuoso performance. Best of all is the Rimsky-Korsakov overture, in full-bodied stereo. After a relaxed, colourful account of the Liadov *Folksongs*, the corporately written *Polka* makes a charming encore, an Elgar-like salon piece.

Philharmonia Orchestra, Igor Markevitch

'*Orchestral Portrait*': BARTOK: *Dance Suite.* RAVEL: *La Valse.* SATIE: *Parade.* BUSONI: *Tänzwalzer.* LIADOV: *Kikimora.* CHABRIER: *Le Roi malgré lui: Fête polonaise.* LISZT: *Mephisto Waltz*

(***) Testament (mono) SBT 1060

The seven varied items here make an illuminating portrait of a conductor who at the time seemed destined to be more central in the world of recording than he became. With immaculate transfers, the 1950s mono recordings have astonishing vividness and presence. In the effervescent account of Satie's *Parade* (sadly cut in the last movement) the brass and

percussion (including the celebrated typewriter) have wonderful bite, and so have the joyful brass fanfares at the start of the Chabrier *Polonaise*, done in Viennese style. Perhaps most vivid of all is the virtuoso performance of the *Mephisto Waltz*.

Pollini, Maurizio (piano)

'*The Pollini Edition*':

BARTOK: *Piano Concertos 1–2* (with Chicago SO, Claudio Abbado). STRAVINSKY: *3 Movements from Petrushka* (471 360-2)

BEETHOVEN: *Piano Concertos 3–4* (with BPO, Abbado) (471 352-2)

BEETHOVEN: *Piano Concerto 5 (Emperor).* MOZART: *Piano Concerto 23 in A, K.488* (with VPO, Karl Boehm) (471 351-2)

BEETHOVEN: *Piano Sonatas 13 in E flat; 14 (Moonlight), Op. 27/1–2; 17 in D min. (Tempest), Op. 31/2; 21 in C (Waldstein), Op. 53* (471 354-2)

BEETHOVEN: *Piano Sonatas 29 (Hammerklavier); 32 in C min., Op. 111* (471 355-2)

BOULEZ: *Sonata 2.* DEBUSSY: *12 Etudes* (471 359-2)

BRAHMS: *Piano Concerto 1 in D min., Op. 15.* SCHUMANN: *Piano Concerto in A min., Op. 54* (with BPO, Abbado) (471 353-2)

CHOPIN: *Berceuse; 12 Etudes, Op. 25; Piano Sonata 2, Op. 35* (471 357-2)

LISZT: *Sonata in B min.; La Lugubre gondola.* SCHUMANN: *Fantasy in C, Op. 17; Arabesque, Op. 18* (471 358-2)

MANZONI: *Masse: Omaggio a Edgard Varèse* (with BPO, Giuseppe Sinopoli). NONO: *Como una ola de fuerza y luz* (with Taskova, Bav. RSO, Abbado); . . . *soffrte onde serene* (471 362-2)

SCHOENBERG: *The Works for Solo Piano; Piano Concerto* (with BPO, Abbado). WEBERN: *Variations for Piano, Op. 27* (471 361-2)

SCHUBERT: *Piano Sonata 20 in A, D.959; Allegretto in C min., D.915; 3 Klavierstücke, D.946* (471 356-2)

Bonus CD: CHOPIN: *Piano Concerto 1 in E min., Op. 11* (with Warsaw PO, Katlewicz). SCHUMANN: *Piano Concerto in A min., Op. 54* (with VPO, von Karajan)

(B) **(*) DG (ADD/DDD) 471 350-2 (12 + bonus CD)

Pollini's impeccable keyboard mastery dominates this collection. His Beethoven recordings have been highly praised, yet they have had variable success on records. Here DG have chosen the later (1992) recordings of Beethoven's *Third* and *Fourth Piano Concertos*, recorded live. But the balance of advantage does not always favour these later versions, and wisely Pollini's earlier, analogue recording of the *Emperor* with Boehm has been preferred, for although it is a studio recording it is seemingly more spontaneously expressive.

When they were first issued in 1977, Joan Chissell spoke of the 'noble purity' of Pollini's performances of the late Beethoven *Sonatas*, and that telling phrase aptly sums them up, if also hinting perhaps at a missing dimension of deep feeling which the CD transfer seems to emphasize. Yet Pollini's performances are undoubtedly eloquent and have great authority and power. His Chopin playing is cool and elegant, his Schubert strong and commanding. Both have superb precision, but his technical mastery is even more impressive in the music of Liszt. With any minor reservations noted, taken overall this collection is very impressive, with his records of twentieth-century repertoire outstanding in every way. Yet in some ways the bonus CD is finest of all, combining a spendid account of Chopin's *E minor Concerto* with a superb performance of the Schumann *Piano Concerto* in which his partnership with Karajan produces results that are dazzling, touchingly poetic and, above all, freshly spontaneous.

Radio Television Eireann Concert Orchestra, Dublin, Ernest Tomlinson

'*British Light Music - Miniatures*': COLLINS: *Vanity Fair.* LUBBOCK: *Polka Dots.* GIBBS: *Dusk.* FRANKEL: *Carriage and Pair.* ELLIS: *Coronation Scot.* BENJAMIN: *Jamaican Song; Jamaican Rumba.* DOCKER: *Tabarinage.* ELGAR: *Beau Brummel.* DEXTER: *Siciliano.* WARNER: *Scrub, Brothers Scrub!* JACOB: *Cradle Song.* ARNE, arr. TOMLINSON: *Georgian Suite: Gavotte.* VINTER: *Portuguese Party.* TOYE: *The Haunted Ballroom* (concert waltz). WHITE: *Puffin' Billy.* MELACHRINO: *Starlight Roof Waltz.* RICHARDSON: *Beachcomber*

**(*) Marco Polo 8.223522

Anthony Collins was right to be proud of his delightful vignette, 'Vanity Fair', for its theme is indelible, and it comes up very freshly here in a programme of unassuming orchestral lollipops, including many items with almost equally catchy musical ideas, even a *Gavotte* by Thomas Arne, arranged by the conductor to sound just a little like a caricature. The tunes are usually pithy and short, like Harry Dexter's daintily wispy *Siciliano*, but sometimes the writing is gently evocative, like the two romantic waltzes, *Dusk* by Armstrong Gibbs, and Geoffrey Toye's *Haunted Ballroom*, and Gordon Jacob's delicate *Cradle Song*.

Novelties like Benjamin Frankel's clip-clopping *Carriage and Pair*, Edward White's *Puffin' Billy*, and Ken Warner's moto perpetuo, *Scrub, Brothers Scrub!* readily evoke the world of Leroy Anderson, while Clive Richardson's quirky *Beachcomber* makes one want to smile. The conductor, Ernest Tomlinson, understands that their very slightness is part of the charm of nearly all these pieces, and he presents them with a simplicity that is wholly endearing. The only relative disappointment is Vivian Ellis's wittily evoked *Coronation Scot*, which needs much more verve than it receives here. Good playing and good recording, although the acoustic effect becomes noticeably more brash for the second item, Mark Lubbock's breezy *Polka Dots.*

Rahbari, Sohre (saxophone), Belgian Radio and TV Orchestra, Brussels, Alexander Rahbari

'*Music for Saxophone and Orchestra*': MILHAUD: *Scaramouche (suite).* GLAZUNOV: *Concerto in E flat, Op. 109.* DEBUSSY: *Rapsodie.* IBERT: *Concertino da camera.* MUSSORGSKY: *Pictures at an Exhibition: The Old Castle.* SOHRE RAHBARI: *Japanese Improvisation for Solo Saxophones*

(BB) ** Naxos 8.554784

The Ibert is the most successful piece here, and the concertante version of *Scaramouche* works well too, with its lively quotation of 'Ten green bottles', but the Glazunov rather outstays its welcome. Sohre Rahbari is a fine player and responds to Debussy's exoticism with an attractive freedom of line. Alexander Rahbari is at his best and the Belgian orchestra gives quite persuasive support, although their playing could be more refined. The recording is good, but rather resonant. Value for money, but not distinctive.

Rampal, Jean-Pierre (flute)

'*20th-century Flute Masterpieces*' (with (i) LOP, Froment; (ii) O de l'ORTF, Martinon; (iii) LOP, Jolivet; (iv) Robert Veyron-Lacroix): (i) IBERT: *Concerto.* (ii) KHACHATURIAN: *Concerto* (arr. from *Violin Concerto*). (iii) JOLIVET: *Concerto.* (iv) MARTINU: *Sonata.* HINDEMITH: *Sonata.* PROKOFIEV: *Sonata in D.* POULENC: *Sonata*

(M) **(*) Erato (ADD) 2292 45839-2 (2)

The concertos on the first CD have less than perfectly focused orchestral strings, and the Khachaturian arrangement is dispensable. But the Ibert *Concerto* is winning and the more plangent Jolivet not inconsiderable. The highlights of the collection are all on the second disc, three out of the four of them inspired works, delightfully written for the instrument and marvellously played. Only the first movement of the Hindemith is a bit below par in its utilitarian austerity; the cool slow movement and more vigorous finale have something approaching charm. The Prokofiev *Sonata* (also heard in a version for violin – but the flute is the original) is a masterpiece, and Rampal makes the very most of it. Then comes the delightful Poulenc piece with its disarmingly easy-flowing opening, delicious central cantilena and scintillating finale with hints of *Les Biches*. The recording of the sonatas, made in 1978, is vividly firm and realistic. If this set is reissued later on a Bonsai Duo, it will be well worth seeking out.

Reilly, Tommy (harmonica)

'*Harmonica Concertos*' (with (i) Munich RSO, Gerhardt; (ii) Basel RSO, Dumont; (iii) SW German R. O, Smola; (iv) Munich RSO, Farnon; (v) Farnon O, Farnon): (i) SPIVAKOVSKY: *Harmonica Concerto.* (ii) ARNOLD: *Harmonica Concerto, Op. 46.* (iii) VILLA-LOBOS: *Harmonica Concerto.* (iv) MOODY: *Toledo (Spanish Fantasy).* (v) FARNON: *Prelude and Dance*

*** Chan. 9248

This most attractive. The Spivakovsky is a particularly winning piece, with a catchy tune in the first movement, rather like a Leroy Anderson encore, a popular, romantic central interlude, marked *Dolce*, and a delicious moto perpetuo finale. Not surprisingly, the Malcolm Arnold is very appealing too, one of this composer's best miniature concertos, written in 1954 for the BBC Proms. The Villa-Lobos, written in 1955, should be much better known. Scored for a small orchestra of strings, single wind, harp, celesta and percussion, it has a neoclassical character. It produces a quite lovely melody for the *Andante*; only the finale, which moves along at a genial pace, has piquant hints of the composer's usual Brazilian preoccupation. James Moody's *Spanish Fantasy* might be described as good cheap music, and it offers the soloist a glittering chance to demonstrate his bravura with

...fectious panache. Farnon's hauntingly nostalgic *Prelude ...nd Dance* (a charmingly inconsequential little waltz) brings ...felicitous interleaving of both themes. The recording bal-...nce is surely as near perfect as one could wish.

...icci, Ruggiero (violin)

...ecca Recordings, 1950–59': PAGANINI: *Violin Concertos ...los. 1 in D, Op. 6; 2 (Campanella) in B min., Op. 7* (with ...SO, Collins); *24 Caprices for Solo Violin, Op. 1*. RAVEL: *...zigane* (with SRO, Ansermet). R. STRAUSS: *Violin Sonata ...1 E flat, Op. 18*. WEBER: *6 Sonatas Progressives, J99–104 ...with Bussotti)*. SARASATE: *Fantasia on Bizet's 'Carmen', ...p. 25; Zigeunerweisen, Op. 20*. SAINT-SAENS: *Havanaise, ...p. 83; Introduction & Rondo capriccioso, Op. 28* (with LSO, ...amba). LALO: *Symphonie espagnole, Op. 21* (with SRO, ...nsermet). HINDEMITH: *Solo Violin Sonatas, Op. 31/1 & 2*. ...ROKOFIEV: *Solo Violin Sonata, Op. 115*. KHACHATURIAN: *...iolin Concerto* (with LPO, Fistoulari)

...) *(**) Decca mono/stereo 475 105-2 (5)

...: is good that Ruggiero Ricci has been included in the ...Original Masters' series. He was an important recording ...rtist in the early years of the Decca company, and this set, ...ompiled by Raymond McGill, contains a wide range of ...oth expected and unexpected items. The Paganini *Caprices ...re the mono accounts dating from 1950, rather than Ricci's ...ater stereo version (already released). It is fascinating to ...ompare the two versions, some numbers faster in one, ...lower in the other, though the later accounts shave off ...round 4 minutes from the overall time. However, this ...nono set – in vividly bright, if rather dry sound – emerges ...s the fresher of the two, and it is now available on CD for ...he first time. The Paganini *Concertos* are brilliantly done, ...ull of life, with Ricci making the most of Paganini's *bel ...anto*-like melodies, as well as the dazzling virtuosity of the ...ravura writing. Anthony Collins's lively and stylish accom-...animents are of enormous help. The mono sound (1955) is ...trikingly full and vivid, but of course the soloist is very ...losely miked.

...The pianist Carlo Bussotti is the accompanist for the ...nexpected repertoire on the third disc, with the Strauss *...iolin Sonata* a good if not totally convincing account, and ...he rare Weber *Sonatas Progressives* one of this set's high-...ghts: charming, unpretentious works, with delightful ...nelodic invention. The sound for this disc is a little two-...imensional, but more than acceptable. Ricci's 1960 (stereo) ...ecital of twentieth-century solo violin works stands up very ...vell: the Prokofiev *Sonata* is the most approachable by reason ...f its neo-baroque spirit and easy contours; and if the Hin-...lemith *Sonatas*, as always, show the workings of a vigorous ...nd inventive mind, the music does not readily hold the ...ttention throughout.

...Ricci's classic (1956) account of the Khachaturian *Concerto ...s still one of the best-sounding and most exciting versions ...oday, with Fistoulari's lively and incisive support. Ricci again ...rovides plenty of colour and sparkle in Lalo's *Symphony ...spagnole* and Ravel's *Tzigane*, even if the ensemble of Anser-...net's Suisse Romande Orchestra at that time was hardly the ...ast word in refinement. Ricci's classic accounts of the Saras-...te and Saint-Saëns showpieces with the LSO and Gamba are ...haracteristically brilliant, sounding as fresh and exciting as ...ver: in terms of bravura these 1959 versions remain in the ...irst division.

Roscoe, Martin (piano), Guildhall Strings, Robert Salter

'Peacock Pie': JACOB: *Concertino*. ARMSTRONG GIBBS: *Concertino; Peacock Pie (suite)*. ROOTHAM: *Miniature Suite*. MILFORD: *Concertino in E*. DRING: *Festival Scherzo*
*** Hyp. CDA 67316

A wholly delectable disc of piano concertinos with string orchestra, very English in character. The opening work by Gordon Jacob, characteristically well crafted, sets the scene with its spirited neoclassical outer movements, and a delicate morsel of a central *Andante*. Armstrong Gibbs opens and closes his *Concertino* (written at Windermere, in the Lake District, in 1942) jauntily and is more romantic in the *Andante*, which yet has an English pastoral flavour. *Peacock Pie* is no less infectious, taking its title and inspiration from Walter de la Mare's book of rhymes; again the lyrical style is folksy, but the central picture of a *Sunken Garden* is mysteri-ously evocative and the *Ride-by-Nights* finale gallops along with witches in tow, although there is nothing spooky in the music. Cyril Rootham's *Miniature Suite* is again very English in atmosphere, with a dainty opening *Allegretto*, a tripping third movement in a neatly contrived 5/4 rhythm and a distinct folksong idiom coming to the fore in the finale. Robin Milford's *Concertino* has a pleasing insouciance and a charming siciliano as its central *Poco adagio*, which is recalled in the last movement. Madeleine Dring's *Festival Scherzo* makes a sparkling, debonair encore. Performances are light-hearted and polished, and beautifully recorded.

Rostropovich, Mstislav (cello and conductor)

'The Russian Years' (1950–1974): SHOSTAKOVICH: *Cello Concertos 1 in E flat, Op. 107* (with Moscow PO, Rozhdestvensky); *2 in G, Op. 126* (with USSR State SO, Svetlanov); *Cello Sonata in D min., Op. 40* (with composer, piano). KABALEVSKY: *Cello Sonata in B flat, Op. 71* (with composer, piano). KAREN KHACHATURIAN: *Cello Sonata* (with composer, piano)
(M) (**(*)) EMI mono 5 72295-2 (2)

In 1997 EMI marked the 70th birthday of Mstislav Rostropo-vich with an ambitious, celebratory survey called 'The Rus-sian Recordings – 1950–74', which consisted of 13 discs (EMI CZS5 72016-2, now withdrawn) from which the present two-CD set is drawn. Rostropovich chose them himself from archival recordings in Russia. All the performances are three star, but the sound does not always do justice to his glorious tone.

EMI 5 72295-2 concentrates on Shostakovich and includes a 1961 concert performance of the *First Cello Concerto* and the very first performance of the *Second*, in 1966, given under Svetlanov and in the presence of the composer, who was celebrating his 61st birthday. The accompanying sonatas were all recorded with their respective composers, though no date is given for the Shostakovich. Rostropovich recalls that some tempi are on the brisk side: 'it was a beautiful day and Shostakovich was anxious to visit friends in the country'. The performance sounds identical to the one issued in the USA in 1958 on the Monitor label (MC 2021), though the sound has been rebalanced.

'Slava 75' (75th Birthday Edition): Cello: BACH: *Suite 3 in C BWV 1003*. HAYDN: *Concertos 1–2* (with ASMF). DVORAK:

Concerto (with LPO, Giulini). BEETHOVEN: *Triple Concerto, Op. 56* (with Oistrakh, Richter, BPO, Karajan). Conducting: DVORAK: *Symphony 9 (New World)* (LPO). GLINKA: *Overture: Ruslan and Ludmilla; Valse-fantaisie.* BORODIN: *In the Steppes of Central Asia* (O de Paris).
SHOSTAKOVICH: *Symphony 8* (Nat. SO of Washington)
(M) **(*) EMI (ADD/DDD) 5 67807-2 (4)

This is a more ambitious coverage than that offered by DG below and, while its range is wider, not everything shows the great Russian musician at his finest and most illuminating. He is at his most brilliant and responsive in Bach's *Third Cello Suite*, and the recording is vividly present. The pair of Haydn concertos bring comparable virtuosity and, even if his style is rather romantic, it is only too easy to be seduced by such genial and commanding music-making. The Beethoven *Triple Concerto* is a classic account which remains unsurpassed, and the 1969 recording, made in the Berlin Jesus-Christus-Kirche, is generous in resonance and yet remains clear. It is rightly one of EMI's 'Great Recordings of the Century'. The Dvořák *Concerto* is another matter. Although it is beautifully recorded, it is much too indulgently idiosyncratic to be really satisfying for repeated listening.

Turning now to Rostropovich as conductor, we find his interpretations consistently more wilful than his solo playing. He directs the weightiest reading possible of the *New World Symphony*. The very opening chords of the slow introduction suggest an epic view, and from then on, with generally expansive tempi, the performance presents this as a genuine 'Ninth', a culmination to the cycle. In the first movement the exposition repeat brings a slight modification of treatment the second time round, and some will resist such inconsistencies as this. The conscious weight of even the *Largo* is controversial too, though in all four movements Rostropovich contrasts the big tuttis – almost Straussian at times – with light pointing in woodwind solos. The recording is richly ample to match, and certainly this account is an engulfing experience.

Of the Russian items, the most attractive is the Glinka *Valse-fantaisie*, which is both elegant and lilting; the *Ruslan Overture* is very well played too but lacks the kind of zest which makes it unforgettable. *In the Steppes of Central Asia* is poetically shaped, but here the kind of heaviness experienced in the *New World Symphony* returns in the brass, the phrasing becomes too broad and the music's onward flow loses its simple forward impetus.

Fortunately the Shostakovich *Eighth* is in every way a success. This is a Teldec recording, licensed to EMI for the occasion, and here Rostropovich's intensity and that of his American players does not spill over into excess. This is a gripping account that can rank alongside the best performances one has heard on or off record – Mravinsky, Rozhdestvensky, Kondrashin and the excellent Haitink – and it is very well recorded too.

'*Rostropovich Mastercellist (Legendary Recordings 1956–1978)*': DVORAK: *Concerto.* TCHAIKOVSKY: *Andante cantabile for Cello & String Orchestra* (with BPO, Karajan). SCHUMANN: *Concerto* (with Leningrad PO, Rozhdestvensky). GLAZUNOV: *Chant du ménéstral* (with Boston SO, Ozawa). RACHMANINOV: *Cello Sonata, Op. 19; Vocalise, Op. 34/14.* CHOPIN: *Introduction & Polonaise brillante, Op. 3.* SCHUBERT: *Impromptu in D flat, D. 899/3.* SCHUMANN: *Kinderszenen: Träumerei* (all with Alexander Dedyukhin, piano).
☞ (M) *** DG stereo/mono DG 471 620-2 (2)

Of the two celebratory compilations issued to celebrate Rostropovich's 75th birthday, the DG two-disc package is undoubtedly the one to go for, unless you already have his incomparable 1969 recording of the Dvořák *Concerto* with Karajan or indeed the hardly less memorable account of the Schumann, imaginative and ever-communicative. The slighter, nostalgic Glazunov piece is also disarmingly attractive, and the great cellist can be readily forgiven for indulging himself a little in two of Tchaikovsky's loveliest lyrical melodies which together form the *Andante cantabile*. But what makes this programme even more enticing and valuable is the inclusion of the works with piano.

Recorded in Warsaw in 1956, with Alexander Dedyukhin, who was Rostropovich's regular partner in recitals over many years, these pieces have not been published in the UK before. They include a truly outstanding account of Rachmaninov's *Cello Sonata*, a romatically vibrant work in which a stream of irrepressible lyrical melodies constantly rise to the surface and blossom. Rostropovich plays with a rapt delicacy of feeling, his timbre in the upper range quite lovely, his phrasing at times slightly more restrained than in later years, echoed by the ever-poetic Dedyukhin.

However, there is plenty of flair and gusto in the Chopin *Introduction and Polonaise brillante*, and here the pianist lets himself go brilliantly in the more extrovert bravura. The encores are played affectionately, with the Schubert *Impromptu* (transcribed first by Heifetz and then arranged by Rostropovich) quite unlike the piano original. The recordings are mono and truthful, closely but faithfully balanced.

Rotterdam Philharmonic Orchestra, Valéry Gergiev

STRAVINSKY: *Fireworks; Piano Concerto* (with Toradze). PROKOFIEV: *Scythian Suite, Op. 20* (with rehearsal feature). DEBUSSY: *Le Martyre de Saint-Sébastien: Symphonic Fragments.* (Director: Rob van der Berg. Video Director: Peter Rump)
☻ *** Arthaus DVD 100 314

The concert itself is just under an hour but the DVD also includes a rehearsal feature in which Gergiev discusses Prokofiev and the *Scythian Suite*. What a relief to find a conductor championing this score with such eloquence! For too long it has been compared unfavourably with *The Rite of Spring* by English and American critics when no such comparison is called for. There are few pieces in twentieth-century music that are as imaginative as its third movement, *Night*, or as inventive as the first, *The Adoration of Vélès and Ala*, with its extraordinarily lush contrasting group (fig. 8 onwards). There have been some fine CD versions, by Markevitch and Abbado, albeit none with the fervour of Koussevitzky and Désiré Defauw in the late 1940s. Gergiev comes nearest to them in his fervour and conviction, and it is good to hear him speak of the music with such warmth in the accompanying hour-long documentary. This includes some valuable archive material of Prokofiev himself and a contribution from his second son, the painter Oleg. (The programme was recorded in 1997, some time before Oleg's death.) The concert itself is imaginatively planned and Alexander Toradze is as impressive an exponent of the Stravinsky *Concerto* as he was of the Prokofiev concertos he recorded with Gergiev and the Kirov Orchestra for Philips. The camera-work is unobtrusive and intelligent, though one could do without some of the aerial shots of the orchestra. The *Scythian Suite* is difficult to balance, and some of the detail emerges in greater prominence than the main lines, but for the most part the sound-balance is vivid and very present. This is an outstanding and valuable issue that is hugely enjoyable.

Rousseau, Eugene (saxophone), Paul Kuentz Chamber Orchestra, Kuentz

Saxophone Concertos: IBERT: *Concertino da camera for Alto Saxophone and 11 Instruments.* GLAZUNOV: *Alto Saxophone Concerto in E, Op. 109.* VILLA-LOBOS: *Fantasia for Soprano Saxophone, 3 Horns and String Orchestra.* DUBOIS: *Concerto for Alto Saxophone and String Orchestra*
(M) *** DG (ADD) 453 991-2

An enterprising anthology. The Glazunov is a late work and the best known and most often recorded of the pieces here. However, both the Villa-Lobos *Fantasia* and the Ibert *Concertino da camera* are as appealing and exotic, and there is much to give pleasure. The longest work is the *Concerto for Alto Sax* by Max-Pierre Dubois, a pupil of Milhaud: fluent, well crafted and civilized. Eugene Rousseau is an expert and persuasive soloist and the recording, which dates from the early 1970s, is first class.

Royal Academy of Music Brass Soloists, John Wallace or James Watson

'World Tour': ARNOLD: *Flourish for a 21st Birthday, Op. 44.* DUKAS: *La Péri: Fanfare.* ELGAR: *Severn Suite, Op. 87.* GLAZUNOV: *In modo religioso, Op. 38.* SCHULLER: *Symphony for Brass, Op. 16.* SIBELIUS: *Petite Suite.* R. STRAUSS: *Festmusik der Stadt Wien*
*** Cantoris CRDC 6064

An imaginative collection, worthy of its opening fanfares. The key work for most collectors will be the Elgar *Severn Suite*, which is played splendidly, with the reprise of the swinging main theme at the end brought off most tellingly. But the surprising highlight is the attractive Sibelius *Suite* for brass septet, written at the end of the 1880s, with few Sibelian fingerprints, but full of attractive ideas. The opening *Prelude*, with its staccato triplets and responding lower sonorities, shows the composer's natural feeling for the brass medium, and the richer texture of the central *Andantino* is also most agreeable.

Glazunov's *In modo religioso*, led by the expressive solo trumpet of Adam Wright, shows the composer's mellow, romantic, melodic facility, so that the fierce opening discords of the Schuller *Symphony*, which follows, make an effective contrast. But this is an ingeniously inventive work, especially in the technically demanding *Scherzo*, and the evocative *Lento desolato*.

The Strauss *Festmusik* is brilliantly played and detailed, but this is not the composer at his best, a little underwhelming, until the flamboyant closing climax. Throughout, the excellent playing and ensemble of this student group is fully professional, and the recording combines sonority with brilliance.

Royal Academy of Music Symphonic Winds, Keith Bragg

'Sounding Out': MOZART: *Serenade 10 in B flat (Gran Partita), K.161.* R. STRAUSS: *Sonatina 2 in E flat for Wind (The Happy Workshop).* BEETHOVEN: *Symphony 7* (arr. for wind ensemble)
** Royal Academy of Music RAM 020 (2)

It seems strange that the Royal Academy of Music Symphonic Winds chose to record a programme that would not fit on a single CD. But as it happens, by far the most impressive performance here is of the genial Richard Strauss *Sonatina* (more a wind symphony – 35 minutes long) which is alone on the second disc (presumably with the two CDs offered for the cost of one). This is in every way a 'happy workshop'. The opening movement has great vigour and spirit, yet every detail of its complex scoring comes through, every sonority is beautifully judged. The *Andantino* has genuine charm (an unexpected dimension with Richard Strauss) and the Minuet has just the right touch of robust humour. The dazzling yet essentially lyrical finale brings some aurally captivating woodwind textures. An appealing lyrical feeling predominates, even when considerable virtuosity is demanded and provided. There is some particularly fine playing from the clarinets and much nimble bravura from the horns, the solo flute and oboe. The climax is joyously resounding, to cap a superb account overall.

Alas, the rest of the programme is less appealing. Clearly Keith Bragg (the Academy's Professor of the Piccolo) has trained his players to a very high standard of excellence, but in Mozart he favours a very brisk, direct performance style that fails to to capture the convivial spirit of the great *B flat major Serenade*, and in the finale his tempo is simply too fast to find the music's wit. The *Allegretto* of the Beethoven symphony is pressed on somewhat unrelentingly and, while the Scherzo is infectious, the finale, although undoubtedly physically exciting, is *vivace* rather than *con brio*. Throughout, the Royal Academy of Music Symphonic Winds is a very impressive ensemble indeed, both in matching of timbres and in solo individuality, but in the Mozart *Serenade* they do not seem to be encouraged to play with a great deal of personal flexibility. The recording is excellent.

Royal Ballet Orchestra, David Lloyd-Jones

'English String Miniatures', Volume 1: RUTTER: *Suite.* ORR: *Cotswold Hill Tune.* MELACHRINO: *Les Jeux.* DODD: *Irish Idyll.* ARMSTRONG GIBBS: *Miniature Dance Suite.* CORDELL: *King Charles's Galliard.* LYON: *Short suite.* DOUGLAS: *Cantilena.* LANE: *Pantomime*
(BB) *** Naxos 8.554186

A delightful collection. John Rutter shows how artfully he can write for strings, using traditional tunes: the invigorating *A-Roving*, the gentle *I Have a Bonnet Trimmed with Blue*, the touchingly simple *O, Waly, Waly* and the fizzing energy of *Dashing Away with the Smoothing Iron*. Much of the other music is permeated with influences from British folksong. Orr's *Cotswold Hill Tune* and Charles Peter Dodd's flimsy *Irish Idyll* have much in common melodically, while George Melachrino's *Les Jeux* makes an engaging contrast, a gossamer dance tapestry, alternating with a semi-luscious lyrical tune. Frank Cordell's melancholy *Galliard*, of noble contour, and the *Miniature Dance Suite* of Armstrong Gibbs both have a hint of the pastiche flavour of Warlock's *Capriol Suite*. The serene *Aria*, the penultimate movement of the equally attractive *Short Suite* of David Lyon, shares an evocative link with the longer, gentle *Cantilena* of Roy Douglas. Philip Lane's *Pantomime* is another three-movement miniature suite of dainty charm and energy: its bouncing closing *Vivace* ends the concert winningly. Performances are persuasively polished and vivacious, and the Naxos recording is excellent: this disc is rewarding value for money.

'*English String Miniatures*', Vol. 3: BLEZARD: *Duetto*. FINZI: *Prelude, Op. 25; Romance, Op. 11*. HOLST: *Brook Green Suite*. MARTELLI: *Persiflage*. MONTGOMERY: *Concertino*. HURD: *Sinfonia concertante* (both with Robert Gibbs). HAYDN WOOD: *An Eighteenth-Century Scherzo*
(BB) *** Naxos 8.555069

Volume 3 is well up to the standard of its predecessors. There are some unfamilar names here, but Carlo Martelli's *Persiflage* and Haydn Wood's *Dancing Scherzo* (a period piece in name only) are equally felicitous. Finzi's nostalgic *Prelude* makes a neat contrast, as does his nostagic, yearning *Romance*. Holst's more familiar *Brook Green Suite* is newly minted and fresh, while William Blezard's *Duetto* is an easygoing canon, opening pizzicato. But the highlights are the concertante works with violin by Michael Hurd and Bruce Montgomery, both with memorably expressive slow movements, which are played most sympathetically by the soloist, Robert Gibbs. With David Lloyd-Jones in charge, the performances are predictably polished and alive, and the Naxos recording is excellent.

Royal Ballet Orchestra, Andrew Penny

'*Welsh Classical Favourites*': WILLIAMS: *Fantasia on Welsh Nursery Rhymes*. WALFORD DAVIES: *Solemn Melody*. WALTERS: *Overture Primavera; A Gwent Suite*. ROBERTS: *Pastorale*. HODDINOTT: *Folksong Suite*. BURTCH: *Aladdin: Overture*. MATHIAS: *Serenade*. PARROTT: *Fanfare Overture (for a Somerset Festival)*
(BB) *** Naxos 8.225048

The Welsh have a long and enduring vocal and choral heritage. But only in the twentieth century has there been an orchestral tradition, and so Welsh folk melodies had not received the concert-hall exposure of comparable English tunes. Then, in 1940, Grace Williams completed her *Fantasia*, using eight very attractive ideas, arranging them into a kind of pot-pourri, winningly scored. Walford Davies had preceded her in the 1930s, and he left us the famous hymn-like *Solemn Melody*. Trevor Roberts's delicate *Pastorale* readily evokes the Pembrokeshire countryside, with a lovely oboe solo and an expressive string climax, somewhat in the manner of George Butterworth. Alun Hoddinott's *Folksong Suite* is similarly felicitously scored. Mervyn Burtch's *Aladdin* concert overture has a syncopated main theme of considerable character, and Gareth Walters's vigorous spring-inspired overture is hardly less spontaneously inventive. The colourful orchestration of the latter's set of dances is matched in the extrovert finale of Mathias's *Serenade*, where the main theme is presented in constantly changing colours, and in the exuberant opening and closing movements of the Walters *Gwent Suite*. All this music is vividly played by Penny and his Royal

Ballet Orchestra and given excellent recording, with a flattering ambience. The disc is generously full and good value. Worth exploring.

Royal Ballet Sinfonia, Gavin Sutherland

'*Brian Kay's British Light Music Discoveries*': ARNOLD: *The Roots of Heaven Overture*. ALWYN: *Suite of Scottish Dances*. SARGENT: *An Impression on a Windy Day*. PARKER: *Overture: The Glass Slipper*. LANGLEY: *The Coloured Counties*. JACOB: *Overture: The Barber of Seville Goes to Town*. JOHNSTONE: *Tarn Hows (Cumbrian Rhapsody)*. LANGFORD: *Two Worlds (Overture)*. R. R. BENNETT: *Little Suite*. DYON: *Joie de vivre*
(M) *** ASV CDWHL 2113

Brian Kay (of BBC Radio 3) has certainly made some felicitous discoveries here: this is a most entertaining programme, summed up perfectly by Ernest Tomlinson's quoted definition of light music as 'where the melody matters more than what you do to it'. There are plenty of melodies here, and the opening rumbustious Malcolm Arnold *Overture* (a concert work based on film music) has a characteristic share. William Alwyn's *Scottish Dances* are charmingly scored, with *Colonel Thornton's* elegant *Strathspey* a highlight. Sir Malcolm Sargent's breezy *Scherzo An Impression on a Windy Day* follows, and after the frothy *Glass Slipper Overture*, James Langley's *Coloured Counties* (which describes the spectacular English view from Bredon Hill) brings an engaging oboe solo. Gordon Jacob's pastiche is agreeable enough and the whimsy of Langford's *Two Worlds Overture* leads neatly into Sir Richard Rodney Bennett's *Little Suite* with its charming bird-imagery and delicate *Ladybird Waltz*. The only disappointment is Maurice Johnstone's *Tarn Hows*, a pleasantly evocative pastoral idyll, but unworthy of that man-made gem, up in the hills above Hawkshead, perhaps the most beautiful tarn in the whole English Lake District.

'*British Light Music Discoveries*', Vol. 2: ARNOLD: *Little Suite 4, Op. 80a* (orch. Lane). BLEZARD: *The River*. CRUFT: *Hornpipe Suite*. FENBY: *Overture: Rossini on Ilkla Moor*. WARREN: *Wexford Bells - Suite on Old Irish Tunes*. ARTHUR BUTTERWORTH: *The Path across the Moors*. HEDGES: *An Ayrshire Serenade, Op. 42*. LEWIS: *An English Overture*. LANE: *Suite of Cotswold Folkdances*
(M) *** ASV CDWHL 2126

An excellent collection of British light music, all imbued with a strong rustic flavour, and valuable for rarities. Adrian Cruft's *Hornpipe Suite* is nautically enjoyable, with each dance nicely contrasted; Raymond Warren's *Wexford Bells Suite* draws on traditional melodies, yet with modest orchestral forces, each movement nicely atmospheric.

Arthur Butterworth's *The Path across the Moors* is highly enjoyable – its title perfectly describing its content – and Fenby's witty *Rossini on Ilkla Moor* gives us an idea of what Rossini might have sounded like had he been a Yorkshireman! Robustly enjoyable is *An English Overture* by Paul Lewis, written in 1971 for the opening of Westward TV in the west of England; it uses folksongs from that area.

William Blezard's *The River* is a beautiful, haunting, slightly melancholy piece, while Anthony Hedges's three-movement *Ayrshire Serenade*, with its breezy outer movements and nostalgic centrepiece, is a good find. Philip Lane's superb arrangements and reconstructions of film music are greatly valued, and it is good to hear some of his own music:

his suite of *Cotswold Folkdances* is piquantly orchestrated, as is his arrangement of Arnold's *Little Suite*. Gavin Sutherland understands exactly how this music should go, and the recording is excellent.

'British Light Music Discoveries', Vol. 4: RUTTER: *Partita.* R. R. BENNETT: *Suite française.* ARNOLD: *The Padstow Lifeboat: March.* FANSHAWE: *Fantasy on Dover Castle.* BLEZARD: *Battersea Park Suite.* HURD: *Dance Diversions.* LEWIS: *Miniature Symphony*
(M) *** ASV CDWHL 2131

John Rutter's opening *Partita* is comparatively ambitious, with a gently elegiac *Aria* framed by a brightly syncopated *Vivace* – perhaps a shade overlong – and a finale which unashamedly borrows the celebratory regal manners and characteristic harmonic progressions of Walton's *Crown Imperial*. Less imposing but no less appealing is Richard Rodney Bennett's charming *Suite française*, which uses traditional French melodies made distinctive by refined, often Ravelian scoring.

Arnold's exuberant *Padstow* march brings an almost bizarre domination from the local foghorn, while David Fanshawe's historical evocation of *Dover Castle*, although impressively scored, is not underpinned by really memorable musical material. That could not be said of William Blezard's *Battersea Park*, which vividly evokes the Festival of Britain funfair of the early 1950s, which he enjoyed with his children. *On the Lake* and *Child asleep* make charming nostalgic interludes.

Charming ideas are certainly not lacking in Michael Hurd's set of five *Dance Diversions*, often pastel-coloured and reminding one a little of the Malcolm Arnold *English Dances*. Each of the four movements of Paul Lewis's *Miniature Symphony* lasts barely over a minute, and this piece is most memorable for its finale – a galumphing horn tune. Excellent performances and first-rate recording, but overall this programme seems a little lacking in more robust items.

'British Light Overtures': BLEZARD: *Caramba.* BLACK: *Overture to a Costume Comedy.* LANGLEY: *Overture and Beginners.* DUNHILL: *Tantivy Towers.* CHAPPELL: *Boy Wizard.* CARROLL: *Festival Overture.* HURD: *Overture to an Unwritten Comedy.* MONCKTON: *The Arcadians* (arr. Wood). LANE: *A Spa Overture.* PITFIELD: *Concert Overture.* LEWIS: *Sussex Symphony Overture*
(M) *** ASV CD WHL 2133

A very promising start to an ASV series of British light overtures and including a modern recording of Stanley Black's delightful *Overture to a Costume Comedy*, a work of considerable charm, deftly scored. But there are many such delights in this programme: Michael Hurd's *Overture to an Unwritten Comedy* was written in 1970, yet sounds as though it could slot into an Ealing comedy of the 1950s. Lionel Monckton's *The Arcadians* is particularly tuneful and lively, while William Blezard's *Caramba*, which opens the programme, has a distinct Latin-American flavour, and is well laced with rumba rhythms. Thomas Pitfield's *Concert Overture*, the longest work here, makes charming use of French folk tunes (real or not) and is prettily orchestrated. Paul Lewis describes his *Sussex Symphony Overture* as 'seven minutes of joyful noise with a quiet bit in the middle'. This refers to some lovely nostalgic episodes, very imaginatively orchestrated, and proves that there are still composers who can write tunes (it was composed in 2000). Even more recent is Herbert Chappell's *Boy Wizard* overture from 2001, which is

great fun. Philip Lane's *A Spa Overture* dates from 1982 and was written for the Cheltenham Ladies' College. It creates a romantic picture of that town, with a middle section evoking the spirit of Edward Wilson, Cheltenham's Antarctic explorer, whose statue looks down on the main Promenade. James Langley's *Overture and Beginners* has a theatrical atmosphere and a galumphing main theme. Thomas Dunhill's *Tantivy Towers* (reconstructed by Philip Lane from the piano score, plus a tape of a BBC broadcast from the 1970s) well captures the spirit of the early 1930s, when it was written. Gavin Sutherland secures an excellent response from the orchestra, and the sound is just right for the music: bright, not too reverberant, warm, with plenty of detail emerging. Most entertaining!

'British Light Overtures, Vol. 2': ANSELL: *Plymouth Hoe (A Nautical Overture).* GOW: *Overture One-Two-Five.* R. R. BENNETT: *Farnham Festival Overture.* ALWYN: *The Moor of Venice.* JOHN GARDINER: *A Scots Overture.* GRYSPEERDT: *The Lamprey.* HOPE: *Scaramouche.* HEDGES: *A Cleveland Overture.* GLYN: *A Snowdon Overture*
(M) *** ASV WHL 2137

The second volume of British overtures kicks off with John Ansell's briny *Plymouth Hoe Overture*, full of traditional sea-songs and ending with Arne's *Rule Britannia*. From the sea we move to the land-locked railway with David Gow's *One-Two-Five Overture*, written in 1976 to celebrate the launch of British Rail's 125 train. But there have been more memorable musical evocations of the railways from other composers. Richard Rodney Bennett's unpretentious *Farnham Festival Overture* is not unrelated to his film music, and none the worse for that: the main theme is particularly winning. Gareth Glyn's *A Snowdon Overture* is the longest and most recent work here (2001), pleasingly episodic, with an evocatively nostalgic middle section. Anthony Hedges' *Cleveland Overture* was written 'to provide a showpiece for the enthusiasm, exuberance and artistry of the Cleveland Youth Orchestra players', and here its five minutes' playing time tests the resources of the Royal Ballet Sinfonia. They come through with flying colours, as they do in the spirited *Scaramouche Overture* of Peter Hope and John Gardiner's equally lively *Scots Overture*, featuring bagpipe tunes, brightly orchestrated.

William Alwyn's *The Moor of Venice* – a character study of Othello, and more of a mini tone-poem – was originally a piece for brass band, but it is here heard in Philip Lane's excellent orchestral arrangement, moving from the stormy music which heralds Othello himself to the melancholy of Desdemona's haunting 'Willow Song'. Not a masterpiece, perhaps, but, like the rest of this composer's music, very well crafted. Sympathetic performances throughout and bright recording.

'British Light Overtures, Vol. 3': CURTIS: *Open Road.* BLYTON: *The Hobbit.* PHILLIPS: *Hampton Court.* FOX: *Summer Overture.* MONTGOMERY: *Overture to a Fairy Tale.* SAUNDERS: *Comedy Overture.* QUILTER: *A Children's Overture.* LANE: *Celebration Overture.* LANGLEY: *The Ballyraggers.* TAYLOR: *The Needles*
(M) **(*) ASV WHL 2140

The obvious highlight of the third volume in ASV's enterprising 'British Light Overtures' series is Roger Quilter's enchanting *Children's Overture*, a brilliant weaving together of the finest nursery rhyme tunes you can think of, superbly orchestrated and wonderfully crafted, not for a second outstaying its 11-minute duration. None of the rest of the music here is of this inspirational quality, although Matthew Curtis's breezy *Open Road*, as its title suggests, effectively evokes a feeling of driving away from it all – even if its sense of freedom gives the impression of driving in the 1950s rather than in 2004!

Bruce Montgomery (who wrote the music to the early *Carry On* films) is represented by his *Overture to a Fairy Tale*, a substantial work, completed in 1946, in which the spirit of Elgar is pleasingly evoked. Carey Blyton (nephew of the children's author, Enid Blyton) has chosen *The Hobbit* for his miniature, whizzing through the characters of the J. R. R. Tolkein classic in four and a half minutes – quite different in character from the recent block-buster films! Montague Phillips's *Hampton Court Overture* is light-heartedly regal in spirit, while John Fox's *Summer Overture* has an especially attractive middle section, flanked by lively but less distinctive outer sections. Philip Lane's *Celebration Overture* lives up to its name in style, if perhaps not entirely in content, and Adam Saunders' *Comedy Overture* would not sound out of place as background to a 1950s Ealing comedy. Nor, for that matter, would James Langley's *The Ballyraggers*. (A Ballyragger is a person who indulges in violent language, practical jokes and horseplay.) But this scallywag music is no match for Malcolm Arnold's *Beckus the Dandipratt*. The most recent work here is Matthew Taylor's *The Needles* (2001), which is a pretty empty, orchestral showpiece. Indeed, quite a lot of the music on this disc has an element of routine, despite the usual sympathetic advocacy and bright recording (with the upper strings sounding a little under-nourished at times).

'**British String Miniatures, Vol. 1**': WALTERS: *Divertimento*. ELGAR: *Elegy*. ROBERTS: *Suite*. DELIUS: *2 Aquarelles* (arr. Fenby). HEDGES: *Fiddler's Green*. WALTON: *Henry V: The Death of Falstaff; Touch Her Soft Lips and Part*. ADDISON: *Partita*
(M) **(*) ASV WHL 2134

ASV's prodigious White Line series has now tapped into the rich vein of British string music and has come up with three programmes which attractively mix the familiar with the unfamiliar, often exploring byways of this repertoire with entertaining results. Apart from the well-known Elgar, Delius and Walton items here (all receiving sensitive performances), the majority of the items in Volume 1 are rarities. Gareth Walters' *Divertimento* is an inventive five-movement suite, lively and expressive by turns. Michael Roberts's *Suite* draws on music written for TV in the 1960s and 1970s, all tuneful and easy-going. John Addison's *Partita*, by contrast, is much grittier, but appealing in its amalgam of Englishness with a touch of acerbity. Anthony Hedges' *Fiddler's Green* was written as recently as 2001, but it slots in well to the light music world of the 1950s. Splendid performances and recordings, the strings only slightly taxed in high-lying fast passages.

'**British String Miniatures, Vol. 2**': PURCELL: *Set of Act Tunes and Dances* (arr. Bliss). WARLOCK: *Serenade for the Birthday of Frederick Delius*. GLYN: *Anglesey Sketches*. DELIUS: *Air and Dances*. CURTIS: *Serenade*. ELGAR: *The Spanish Lady (Suite), Op. 69*. LANE: *Serenata concertante*
(M) *** ASV WHL 2136

Volume 2 carries forward the repertoire combination of Volume 1, with Bliss's slight but charming arrangements of Purcell's *Act Tunes and Dances* and better-known items such as Elgar's engaging music for *The Spanish Lady*, and the very

welcome Delius and Warlock miniatures – all lovingly played here. Matthew Curtis's *Serenade* is a further fine example of English string writing, as are the *Anglesey Sketches* of Gareth Glyn. Philip Lane's *Serenata concertante* was originally a brass band piece, but it is doubly effective in this string arrangement, written in the manner of an eighteenth-century *concerto grosso*, with a string quartet concertino contrasting with the ripieno of the main body of strings. Its slow central movement is especially haunting and, with fine playing and recording, this is one of the most rewarding of Gavin Sutherland's exploratory compilations.

'**British String Miniatures, Vol. 3**': VINTER: *Entertainments*. ELGAR: *Sospiri*. WARLOCK: *4 Folksong Preludes*. FOX: *Countryside Suite*. MARSHALL: *Elegy*. CYRIL SCOTT: *First Suite for Strings*. WALTERS: *Sinfonia breve*
(M) *** ASV WHL 2139

With only Elgar's *Sospiri* really well known, this is perhaps the most enterprising of Gavin Sutherland's collections of English string music. The programme gets off to a bright and breezy start with Gilbert Vinter's *Entertainments*, originally a brass band work, but sounding very much at home here. It includes an amusing *Taproom Ballad*, with a solo viola portraying a somewhat inebriated singer. Philip Lane's transcription from piano to strings of Peter Warlock's haunting *Folksong Preludes* is just as telling in its new format, while John Fox's *Countryside Suite* is very much music of the open air – a pastoral suite, dating from 1975. A valedictory mood comes with Haigh Marshall's deeply felt *Elegy*, dedicated to the memory of Sir John Barbirolli, but contrast is again provided by Cyril Scott's folksy *First Suite for Strings*, written in the composer's highly chromatic style and wittily including 'Oh, dear, what can the matter be' in the finale. Gareth Walters' *Sinfonia breve* is the longest and most recent work (1998) in the programme, the 'breve' acknowledging that it has only three movements instead of the usual four of the classical symphony. The writing is more abrasive than the rest of the programme, not so obviously tuneful, but making an agreeably astringent diversion and a satisfying end-piece. Throughout the programme there is some especially delightful string-playing from the Royal Ballet Sinfonia, and this disc is well worth seeking out.

'**British Clarinet Concertos**' (with Scott, clarinet): PAUL: *Clarinet Concerto*. HOROVITZ: *Concertante for Clarinet & Strings*. WOOLFENDEN: *Clarinet Concerto*. G. BUSH: *Rhapsody for Clarinet & Strings*. MACDONALD: *Cuban Rondo*. CRUFT: *Concertino for Clarinet & Strings*. RIDOUT: *Concertino for Clarinet & Strings*
(M) **(*) ASV WHL 2141

All the works here are rarities and are presented on CD for the first time. Scottish composer Alan Paul's *Concerto* (1958) is dedicated to Jack Brymer. It begins with a tuneful opening movement, followed by a richly romantic central *Adagio* and a jolly finale, with some pleasing touches of baroque pastiche, as well as a lilting waltz. But its overall profile is not very individual. Geoffrey Bush's nostalgically dreamy *Rhapsody* (1940), however, is one of the disc's highlights. It has a haunting atmosphere, which is not matched in Joseph Horovitz's similarly paced *Concertante for Clarinet and Strings* of 1948. By the side of this, Adrian Cruft's reflective (1955) *Concertino* is quite compelling, well constructed and with plenty of imaginative touches. It is a more interesting work than Guy Woolfenden's *Concerto* (1985) which, though amiable enough, is not really memorable. Alan Ridout's *Concertino* (1978) is short and pleasing, and Malcolm MacDonald's *Cuban Rondo* (1960) makes an enjoyable lollipop, with an appropriate Cuban percussion backing. Excellent performances from soloist and orchestra alike, and very good recording; but most of this music is pleasing without being really distinctive.

'British Film Composers in Concert': PARKER: 2 *Choreographic Studies; Thieves' Carnival.* LUCAS: *Ballet de la reine.* COLLINS: *Eire Suite.* MONTGOMERY: *Scottish Aubade; Scottish Lullaby.* ERIC ROGERS: *Palladium Symphony*
(M) *** ASV WHL 2145

It is almost always rewarding to hear film-music composers' concert music. Both Bruce Montgomery and Eric Rogers are famous for their background music for the *Carry On* films, but here their style is more reflective than expected. Montgomery's Scottish works are actually derived from his film-scores and are vignettes, giving a popular romantic evocation of picturesque Caledonia, well leavened with attractive folk themes in nicely clothed orchestrations. Rogers' *Palladium Symphony*, on the other hand, was inspired by his experiences as an orchestral pit player, but the feeling throughout its four movements is one of nostalgia for a past era, rather than a gaudy musical representation of the musical hall. Clifton Parker's *Thieves' Carnival Overture* is light-heartedly swashbuckling, while his two very pleasing *Choreographic Studies – Alla spagnola* and *Alla cubana* – create local colour without recourse to a battery of percussion instruments. Leighton Lucas's unrealized ballet on the subject of Queen Mary, *Ballet de la reine*, appealingly infuses sixteenth-century styles with modern, piquant orchestrations. Last and not least is Anthony Collins' *Eire Suite*, full of Irish whimsy, and especially infectious in the *Fluter's Hooley* (Reel). Excellent recording to match the highly persuasive performances.

Royal Ballet Sinfonia, John Wilson

'Scottish Light Music': DAVIE: *Royal Mile.* DODS: *Highland Fancy.* HAMILTON: *Scottish Dances.* MACCUNN: *The Land of the Mountain and Flood (overture); Highland Memories.* MATHIESON: *From the Grampians (suite).* ORR: *Fanfare and Processional; Celtic Suite.* ROBERTON: *All in the April Evening*
(M) *** ASV CDWHL 2123

What a good idea to assemble a disc of comparatively rare light Scottish music, which with its characteristic folksy influences proves most entertaining. The most famous piece here, MacCunn's *The Land of the Mountain and Flood Overture*, begins the programme robustly, while the same composer's *Highland Memories* (1897) for strings offers contrast: two rather nostalgic movements followed by a more lively *Harvest Dance* (which is curiously reminiscent of the second movement of Schubert's *Ninth Symphony*). Muir Mathieson is widely known for his work in countless films and the opening of the *Grampians Suite* (1961) could well begin some Scottish swashbuckler; the rest of the *Suite* is thoroughly diverting too.

Buxton Orr's *Fanfare and Processional* (1968) is more angular than its companion pieces, while in his *Celtic Suite* (1968), a four-movement work using dance rhythms as a basis, he

pays tribute to his Celtic origins (the last movement, *Port-a-Beul*, means 'mouth music'). Cedric Thorpe Davie's robustly enjoyable *Royal Mile* (recorded complete for the first time) is subtitled 'a coronation march' and was written in 1952 for one of a series of concerts leading up to that celebrated event. Iain Hamilton's *Scottish Dances* were, like Sir Malcolm Arnold's, composed for the BBC Light Music Festival and premièred on St Andrew's Day, 1956. They are comparably enjoyable. Marcus Dods' amusing *Highland Fancy* and Sir Hugh Roberton's touching *All in the April Evening* complete the programme. Full marks for an original collection, committed performances, a vibrant recording – and all at mid-price.

Royal Ballet Sinfonia, Barry Wordsworth

'Tribute to Madame': Ballet Music: BLISS: *Checkmate.* BOYCE-LAMBERT: *The Prospect Before us.* GORDON: *The Rake's Progress.* TOYE: *The Haunted Ballroom*
(M) *** ASV CDWHLS 255

'Madame' was of course Dame Ninette de Valois, the 'mother' of British ballet, and she is rightly celebrated with these fine scores by Bliss and Gavin Gordon and Constant Lambert's elegant pastiche drawing on the music of Boyce. The surprise is Toye's *Haunted Ballroom*, much more than just a (very memorable) waltz. First-class performances and fresh, bright recording.

'Tribute to Sir Fred': MESSAGER: *Les Deux pigeons* (arr. Lanchbery). LISZT: *Dante Sonata* (arr. Lambert). RAWSTHORNE: *Madame Chrysanthème* (ballet). COUPERIN: *Harlequin in the Street* (arr. Jacob)
(M) **(*) ASV CDWLS 273 (2)

These four contrasting ballets are gathered together here as a tribute to choreographer, Sir Frederick Ashton. *Les Deux pigeons* is a charming score, and it is brightly played in a slightly truncated version by John Lanchbery (the complete original version is offered by Bonynge on Decca). Liszt's *Dante Sonata* is very telling in Lambert's orchestration, sounding very gothic in its high-flown romanticism. *Madame Chrysanthème* is presented here complete, rather than the suite we know from the old EMI recording conducted by the composer. Rawsthorne's vividly energetic score was first performed in 1955. It is colourfully orchestrated, featuring a large percussion section, including piano, and beginning unusually and hauntingly with a wordless mezzo-soprano voice. The music is full of imaginative touches, with subtle devices used to evoke the oriental flavour of the story. Much lighter in tone is *Harlequin in the Street*, with Couperin's short pieces strung together in Gordon Jacob's colourful and witty orchestrations. The performances throughout are lively and sympathetic, bar the odd slip in the orchestra, and the recorded sound is vivid, though the strings lack richness in the upper register – the violins sound a little pinched at times.

(i) Royal Ballet Sinfonia or (ii) BBC Concert Orchestra, Barry Wordsworth

'British Light Music, Volume 3': (i) ARNOLD: *HRH The Duke of Cambridge March, Op. 60a.* KELLY: *Divertissement.* LAMBERT: *Elegiac Blues.* LYON: *3 Dances.* RAWSTHORNE:

Overture for Farnham. (ii) LAMBERT: *Romeo and Juliet:*
Second Tableau. MARTELLI: *Promenade.* STANDFORD:
Celestial Fire
(M) *** ASV CD WHL 2128

This concert gets off to a rousing start with a swaggering
march by Sir Malcolm Arnold, complete with a stirring central
theme. Much of this music comprises short dance movements
and, as such, makes attractive, undemanding listening. Constant Lambert's *Romeo and Juliet* is a shade more serious to
balance the programme; it has a particularly haunting *Adagietto*, and elsewhere Lambert shows much imagination as well
as wit. Martelli's cheeky *Promenade* almost sounds as though
it has come out of a *Carry On* film, while the old dance forms
parodied by David Lyon, Bryan Kelly and Patric Standford all
have piquant charm. There is enough quirky writing, wit and
humour to hold the listener's attention, and this disc of
rarities is certainly recommendable.

Royal Liverpool Philharmonic Orchestra, Sir Charles Groves

'Rule Britannia': ELGAR: *Pomp and Circumstance Marches
1 & 4; Imperial March; Empire March.* HOLST: *Song without
Words 2: Marching Song.* TRAD.: *The British Grenadiers*
(arr. Stanford Robinson); *Hornpipe* (arr. Wood). VAUGHAN
WILLIAMS: *Coastal Command: Dawn Patrol* (film score).
WALFORD DAVIES: *Royal Air Force March Past.* WALTON:
Henry V (film music): *Touch her Soft Lips; Agincourt Song.*
COATES: *Dam Busters March.* BLISS: *Processional.* ALFORD:
On the Quarter Deck. ARNE: *Rule Britannia* (arr. Sargent)
(B) **(*) CfP (ADD) 3 52407-2

A genial collection of traditional favourites. Groves's way with
the music is affectionately relaxed but agreeably fresh. The most
memorable items are the *Dam Busters March* (full of patriotic
life) and the breezy Walford Davies *Royal Air Force March Past*
with its winningly lyrical central section (added by a later RAF
Director of Music). The Elgar marches have a spacious nobility
(the lesser-known *Imperial March* is especially attractive) and
Anne Collins is an ideal soloist for the closing *Rule Britannia*,
taken by Sargent very grandly; but with this, like the famous
Hornpipe, one misses the ambience of the Proms. Very good
analogue sound throughout, well transferred.

Royal Northern College of Music Wind Orchestra, Timothy Reynish

'French Wind Band Classics': SCHMITT: *Dionysaques,
Op. 62.* SAINT-SAËNS: *Orient et Occident, Op. 25.* BOZZA:
Children's Overture. MILHAUD: *Suite française, Op. 248.*
BERLIOZ: *Grande symphonie funèbre et triomphale, Op. 15*
(with Joseph Alessi, trombone)
**(*) Chan. 9897

A well-planned and very well-played anthology, full of character, but let down somewhat by the performance of the
Berlioz *Grande symphonie funèbre*, which is certainly grand
and nobly dignified, with an eloquent if not very French
trombone solo; but it is rather slow and lacking in Gallic
gusto, and it has no closing chorus like the highly idiomatic
version by the Musiques des Gardiens de la Paix and the
Chorale Populaire de Paris, directed by Désiré Dondeyne

(Warner Apex 2564 6183-2). However, the rest of the pro-
ramme is very successful, notably the ebullient Bozza *Children's Overture*, which opens like Respighi and then wittily
incorporates a clutch of French nursery rhymes and folk
tunes. It is a little bit like the *English Overture* by Roger
Quilter, only more boisterous. Milhaud's *Suite française* is
equally entertaining, with its five colourfully scored movements named after French provinces, and again using folk
material. The second movement, *Bretagne*, with its horn
chorale, is particularly engaging, and the faster numbers
representing the Ile de France and Provence are vivaciously
folksy. The Saint-Saëns *Grande marche* is agreeable, if not as
spectacular as it sounds, but Schmitt's tone-poem *Diony-
siaques*, written for the Garde Républicain, brooding and
intense in its sonorities, is very telling, if not melodic. Excellent, top-quality Chandos sound.

Royal Philharmonic Orchestra, Clio Gould

'English String Classics', Volume 2: DELIUS: *2 Aquarelles.*
ELGAR: *Introduction & Allegro for Strings; Sospiri.* HOLST:
Brook Green Suite. TIPPETT: *Little Music for Strings.*
VAUGHAN WILLIAMS: *5 Variants of Dives and Lazarus.*
WARLOCK: *Capriol Suite*
⊕→ (BB) **(*) Warner Apex 2564 62114-2

Clio Gould, violinist-turned-conductor, directs a most enjoyable disc of favourite string works, recorded in full, well-
balanced sound, and here issued at budget price on Warner
Apex, a label normally associated with reissues. When all but
one of the performances are excellent, with crisp ensemble
and well-sprung rhythms, it is sad that the exception, a
plodding account of the Vaughan Williams *Variants on Dives
and Lazarus*, should come first on the disc. With its slower
than usual speeds and sluggish rhythms it is totally different
from the rest, as one promptly appreciates in the second item,
a light and crisp account of the *Capriol Suite*, with a hint of
period style in the *Pavane*. The Delius *Aquarelles* are then
warmly idiomatic, with rubato finely controlled; the Tippett
is positive and incisive, and the Holst *Brook Green Suite* is
fresh and refined. Both the Elgar pieces are again warmly
idiomatic in their control of rubato. *Sospiri* is taken at a
flowing speed, with the tender poignancy of the piece building in tragic intensity, a work far bigger than its scale in
minutes. The *Introduction and Allegro*, the final item, makes a
superb climax when textures are so clean, with the separation
of the solo strings beautifully caught in the recording. In spite
of the disappointnment of the Vaughan Williams piece. the
disc is still worth having.

Royal Philharmonic Orchestra, Sir Charles Groves

'English String Masterpieces': ELGAR: *Serenade for Strings,
Op. 20.* BRITTEN: *Variations on a Theme by Frank Bridge,
Op. 10.* VAUGHAN WILLIAMS: *Fantasia on a Theme by
Thomas Tallis.* TIPPETT: *Fantasia Concertante on a Theme
of Corelli*
✪ (BB) *** Regis RRC 1138

With gloriously full and real recording, providing the most
beautiful string-textures, this is one of Sir Charles Groves's
very finest records, and it makes a worthy memorial to the

achievement of the closing decade of his long career. The RPO players give deeply felt, vibrant accounts of four great masterpieces of English string music.

Royal Philharmonic Orchestra, Adrian Leaper

'*Orchestral Spectacular*': CHABRIER: *España.*
RIMSKY-KORSAKOV: *Capriccio espagnol.* MUSSORGSKY: *Night on the Bare Mountain* (arr. Rimsky-Korsakov).
BORODIN: *Prince Igor: Polovtsian Dances.* RAVEL: *Boléro*
(BB) *** Naxos 8.550501

Recorded in Watford Town Hall by Brian Culverhouse, this concert would be highly recommendable even if it cost far more. All these performances spring to life, and the brilliant, full-bodied sound certainly earns the record its title. The brass in the Mussorgsky/Rimsky-Korsakov *Night on the Bare Mountain* has splendid sonority and bite, and in the *Polovtsian Dances* the orchestra 'sings' the lyrical melodies with such warmth of colour that the chorus is hardly missed. Leaper allows the *Capriccio espagnol* to relax in the colourful central variations, but the performance gathers pace towards the close. Chabrier's *España* has an attractive rhythmic lilt, and in Ravel's ubiquitous *Boléro* there is a strong impetus towards the climax, with much impressive playing on the way (the trombone solo, with a French-style vibrato, is particularly strong).

Royal Philharmonic Orchestra, Barry Wordsworth

'*British Light Classics*': ARNOLD: *English Dance, Set 2, Op. 33/1.* COATES: *Calling All Workers; The Dam Busters March; The Sleepy Lagoon.* A. WOOD: *Barwick Green.* ELLIS: *Coronation Scot.* HAYDN WOOD: *The Bandstand, Hyde Park.* BATH: *Cornish Rhapsody.* FARNON: *Portrait of a Flirt; Westminster Waltz.* DUNCAN: *Little Suite: March.*
C. WILLIAMS: *Devil's Galop; Heart O' London; Rhythm on Rails.* BENJAMIN: *Jamaican Rumba.* WHITE: *Puffin' Billy.*
COLLINS: *Vanity Fair.* ELGAR: *Chanson de nuit*
**(*) Warner 2564 61438-2

A very well-played collection of British light classics in warm and detailed sound: the percussion is clear and sharp, and the strings and brass are warm and vivid. These are essentially genial performances, and if other versions have offered more sheer excitement one finds oneself readily responding to the warmth of the music-making. Almost everything here is well known, from Arthur Wood's *Barwick Green* (*The Archers* theme), to Anthony Collins's delicious *Vanity Fair*. There is a lovely swagger in *The Bandstand* of Haydn Wood and no lack of drive in Charles Williams's inspired *Devil's Galop*, which ends the CD. If the programme appeals, don't hesitate.

Rubinstein, Artur (piano)

'*Piano Concertos*' (with LSO, Previn): GRIEG: *Concerto in A min., Op. 16.* CHOPIN: *Concerto 2 in F min., Op. 21.*
SAINT-SAËNS: *Concerto 2 in G min., Op. 22*
(*) DG **DVD 073 4195 (includes conversation with Robert MacNeil) (V/D: Hugo Käch)

When Rubinstein made these recordings he was 89 and possessed only peripheral vision. Because of this, he seems

relatively impassive and only occasionally glances at conductor and orchestra. But his prodigious technique seems unimpaired, and the glittering brilliance of his right hand, which is fascinating to watch in close-up, is undiminished. Fortunately the camera dwells mostly on his hands, which will make this DVD indispensable for his admirers, even though the continually changing orchestral close-ups, with constant shifts, fades and dissolves, become less appealing to watch.

The three concertos were recorded in the Fairfield Hall, Croydon, in April 1975 without an audience. This was a pity, because, almost certainly, had they been caught 'live' on the wing, the performances would undoubtedly have been even more rewarding. Audience communication (as Rubinstein tells us himself) was a key to his interpretative projection. What comes over at first is Rubinstein the patrician. Certainly, the opening of the Grieg is a little cool and circumspect, and although the moments of poetry are well observed throughout, and the finale has plenty of dash, there is not the degree of spontaneous, surging espressivo that this great pianist usually created in the recording studio.

This is perhaps the more surprising as Rubinstein makes the point in his post-concert talk with Robert MacNeil that he discovered Grieg's *Concerto* comparatively late in his career, but then embraced it with much affection and admiration. The Chopin performance brings much exquisite lyrical embroidery, but again not that last touch of expected spontaneous magic. One wonders if Previn was partly responsible, for his direction never seems to rise to an inspirational level. That is, until the final work on the programme, the Saint-Saëns *Second Concerto*, which Rubinstein says he found technically 'difficult', but mastered it early in his career, and with which he had great and continuing success.

He called it his 'warhorse', and plays it with great brilliance and panache, grabbing the viewer/listener from the commanding opening and, with Previn a passionate partner, holding the tension at the highest level throughout all four movements. Like Gilels, he reveals it as a work of considerable depth and emotional power, with the quicksilver brilliance of the famous Scherzo a corruscating and genial interlude between the impressive outer movements. Later he relates to Robert MacNeil that Ravel, who also greatly admired the work, told him that he himself learned how to orchestrate from studying this concerto. It certainly sounds superb here.

The interview which follows is treasurable too, revealing the great pianist to be not only a connoisseur of all the arts, but a thinking, feeling human being, completely free from artifice, with a remarkable, life-assertive philosophy to underpin his musical genius, which humbly acknowledges the greatness of the music he is privileged to play.

Salvage, Graham (bassoon)

'*English Bassoon Concertos*' (with Royal Ballet Sinfonia, cond. (i) Sutherland (ii) Butterworth): (i) FOGG: *Concerto in D.* ADDISON: *Concertino.* HOPE: *Concertino.* (ii)
A. BUTTERWORTH: *Summer Music, Op. 77*
(M) *** ASV CD WHL 2132

The three concerto/concertinos by John Addison, Eric Fogg and Peter Hope are all most enjoyable and are played with elegance, warmth and style by Graham Salvage, an outstandingly sensitive soloist, with lively and sympathic accompaniments from Gavin Sutherland and the Royal Ballet Sinfonia.

The Addison *Concertino* opens in a mood of gentle melancholy, soon wittily dispelled but returning later, and is quietly enjoyable. It is notable for the droll waltz that forms the second movement and the humorously quirky finale. Fogg's *Concerto* (1931) is essentially light-hearted and rhythmically sparkling, although there is a balancing dolour and solemnity in the central movement. The first-movement cadenza is too long, but the rest of the movement, like the finale, is certainly entertaining. Peter Hope's *Concertino*, written as recently as 2000, opens in a mood of romantic reverie. It is rather like a period-film score (the composer worked with John Williams and James Horner), with gentle string ostinatos creating a haunting evocation, contrasted with a more lively middle section. But it has a blues centrepiece, replete with a 'walking bass' and vibraphone, while the finale delectably evokes a Latin-American fiesta.

But these very personable works are completely upstaged by Arthur Butterworth's masterly *Summer Music*, written in 1985, which is discussed under its separate composer entry. This work alone is well worth the cost of this disc. You will surely be drawn back to it, as we were. The other very entertaining pieces make an attractive programme overall. The performances and recordings are excellent, and this is a valuable addition to the catalogue.

Sargent, Sir Malcolm

'*Sir Malcolm Sargent Conducts British music*' (with (i) LPO; (ii) LSO; (iii) Mary Lewis, Tudor Davies & O; (iv) Royal Choral Soc.; (v) New SO): (i) HOLST: *Perfect Fool: Suite.* (ii) BRITTEN: *Young Person's Guide to the Orchestra.* (iii) VAUGHAN WILLIAMS: *Hugh the Drover: Love Duet.* ELGAR: (iv) *I Sing the Birth*; (ii) *Pomp & Circumstance Marches 1 & 4.* (v) COLERIDGE-TAYLOR: *Othello: Suite.* (ii) BAX: *Coronation March*
(***) Beulah mono 1PD13

Sargent was at his finest in this repertory, and it is very welcome to have his personal electricity so vividly conveyed throughout the disc, and most of all in the recording, taken from the sound-track of the original COI film, of Britten's *Young Person's Guide.* The optical transfer by Martin Sawyer produces far more vivid and satisfyingly weighty results than one would ever expect. The *Love duet* from *Hugh the Drover* was recorded in 1924 in limited pre-electric sound, but the Elgar part-song, recorded live at the Royal Albert Hall in 1928, also soon after the first performance, is vividly atmospheric. The *Othello Suite* of Coleridge-Taylor, another première recording, is a sequence of brief genre pieces, with recording more than lively and colourful enough to make one forget the high surface-hiss. The three marches at the end were recorded for the Queen's coronation in 1953, with Sargent taking an uninhibitedly broad view of the great tunes in both the Elgar favourites, and with Bax doing a fair imitation of Walton.

Schuricht, Carl (conductor)

'*The Decca Recordings, 1949–1956*': BEETHOVEN: *Symphonies 1 in C, Op. 21; 2 in D, Op. 36* (with VPO); *5 in C min., Op. 67* (with Paris Conservatoire O). MENDELSSOHN: *Overtures: The Hebrides (Fingal's Cave); Calm Sea and Prosperous Voyage; The Fair Melusine; Ruy Blas* (with VPO). BRAHMS: *Piano Concerto 2 in B flat, Op. 83* (with

Backhaus, VPO); *Violin Concerto in D, Op. 77* (with Ferras, VPO); *Symphony 2 in D, Op. 73.* SCHUMANN: *Overture, Scherzo and Finale, Op. 52; Symphonies 2 in C, Op. 61; 3 (Rhenish) in E flat, Op. 97* (with Paris Conservatoire O). SCHUBERT: *Symphony 8 in B min. (Unfinished)* (with VPO). TCHAIKOVSKY: *Capriccio italien; Suite 3 in G: Theme and Variations* (with Paris Conservatoire O)
(M) (**) Decca mono 475 6074 (5)

It is good that Decca have devoted one of their 'Original Masters' boxes to Carl Schuricht, for many of these recordings haven't been in circulation since their last resurrection on Ace of Clubs LPs, of which they formed a large part. Straight away one notices the sharp difference in the sound of the orchestras between those recordings made in Vienna and those in Paris, with the latter's distinctive reedy oboes and the brass with pronounced vibrato, characteristics all now gone. Character these French performances may have, but not orchestral brilliance: the Schumann symphonies are given straightforward accounts, but the playing lacks polish throughout. The *Rhenish*, curiously, isn't as well recorded as the *Second*, though it dates from a year later (1953); in the finale of the *Rhenish*, Schuricht does not adopt the usual rallentando at the end of the final movement with the glorious brass chords, but he cranks up the tempo at the end, which is unexpected but quite exciting. In Brahms's *Second Symphony*, Schuricht's sense of rhythm is more erratic than usual; nor is the *Violin Concerto* the most exciting or imaginative version from this period, and the 1954 sound is also below Decca's best. All are back on form for the 1952 account of the *Second Piano Concerto*, always a work which Backhaus did well (he later made an even finer account in stereo with Boehm), even if the strings sound a bit papery. 'Good but not outstanding performances' was how the 1966 *Penguin Guide* described the Mendelssohn overtures when they lived on ACL 33, and that assessment holds, pleasant though it is to hear them again (*Ruy Blas* and *Calm Sea* come off best). Beethoven's *First Symphony* is unfussy and direct, but the 1952 recording is not terribly comfortable, the strings rather too bright and acidic. The *Fifth*, recorded in 1949, is better recorded, sounding good for its age, and the performance is direct and honest – if again not the last word in precision of ensemble and intonation. As for the Tchaikovsky items (in quite vivid (1952) sound), *Capriccio italien* is quite exciting (and what vibrato on the opening brass fanfare!), but in the *Theme and Variations* the playing of the woodwind lets things down too much for comfort, though the performance itself goes quite well. The *Unfinished Symphony*, recorded in 1957, is excellent and was much admired in its day; it is an affectionate reading, warmly played (the best playing and recording in this set) with a good forward impulse. In short, recommendable to admirers of Schuricht interested in his historical performances, rather than to the general collector, and certainly not a choice for those who insist on flawless orchestral refinement!

Scottish Chamber Orchestra, Jaime Laredo

'*String Masterpieces*': ALBINONI: *Adagio* (arr. Giazotto). HANDEL: *Berenice: Overture; Solomon: Arrival of the Queen of Sheba.* BACH: *Suite 3, BWV 1068: Air; Violin Concerto 1 in*

A min., BWV 1041: Finale (with Laredo, violin).
PACHELBEL: *Canon in D.* PURCELL: *Chacony; Abdelazar: Rondeau*
(BB) *** Regis RRC 1160 (with VIVALDI: *The Four Seasons* *** – see above)

An excellent popular collection, the more attractive for being at budget price and coupled with a first-rate performance of Vivaldi's *Four Seasons*. The playing of the Scottish Chamber Orchestra is alive, alert, stylish and committed, without being overly expressive; yet the famous Bach *Air* has warmth and Pachelbel's *Canon* is fresh and unconventional in approach. The sound is first class, spacious and well detailed but without any clinical feeling. The Purcell *Rondeau* is the tune made familiar by Britten's *Orchestral Guide*; the superb *Chaconne* is presented with telling simplicity.

Scottish National Orchestra, Neeme Järvi

'*Music from Estonia*': RUDOLF TOBIAS: *Julius Caesar.*
ARTUR LEMBA: *Symphony in C sharp min.* HEINO ELLER: *Twilight; Dawn; Elegia for Harp & Strings; 5 Pieces for Strings.* RAID: *Symphony 1.* VELJO TORMIS: *Overture 2.*
ARVO PÄRT: *Cantus in memoriam Benjamin Britten*
(B) *** Chan. 2 for 1 241-26 (2)

A most enterprising and rewarding reissue of a pair of discs from the late 1980s. Arvo Pärt's *Cantus in memoriam Benjamin Britten*, an effective and haunting little work, is the only piece to have become comparatively well known since then, but there is much else of interest here. Heino Eller was an Estonian composer and teacher whose pupils included Pärt, Tubin and Raid. *Dawn*, a tone-poem written at the end of the First World War, is frankly romantic – with touches of Grieg and early Sibelius as well as the Russian nationalists. The *Five Pieces for Strings* are transcriptions of earlier piano miniatures and have a wistful, Grieg-like charm. *Twilight* (another tone-poem) is rather less impressive, but the *Elegy for Harp and Strings* of 1931 strikes a deeper vein of feeling and casts a strong spell. It has nobility and eloquence, tempered by quiet restraint; there is a beautiful dialogue involving solo viola and harp which is gently memorable.

The *Julius Caesar Overture* by Rudolf Tobias (1873–1918) – the very first Estonian orchestral piece – is of less interest, as is the repetitive Tormis work (inspired by the opening of Tubin's *Fifth Symphony*). But these works are all short, and the two symphonies by Artur Lemba (1885–1963) and Kaijo Raid (1922–2005) are much more substantial. Raid fled to Sweden in 1944 but soon afterwards emigrated to the United States, where he studied with Milhaud and Ibert. He has written in all manner of styles and is highly prolific. His *First Symphony* of 1944 was written when he had just pased 21 and was still studying with Eller; it shows a genuine feeling for form and a fine sense of proportion, even though the muiscal personality is not fully formed. Well worth hearing.

Lemba's work, the first symphony ever written by an Estonian, is however astonishingly accomplished for a 23-year-old; the invention is fresh and memorable. It sounds as if he studied in St Petersburg: at times one is fleetingly reminded of Glazunov, at others of Dvořák (the Scherzo) – and even of Bruckner (at the opening of the finale) and of Elgar. This is by far the most important item in this enterprising collection and it is played here with evident enthusiasm. Indeed, Neeme Järvi gets very committed playing from the Scottish National Orchestra throughout and the recording is warm and well detailed.

Scottish National Orchestra, Sir Alexander Gibson

ETHEL SMYTH: *The Wreckers: Overture.* HARTY: *With the Wild Geese.* MACCUNN: *The Land of the Mountain and Flood.* GERMAN: *Welsh Rhapsody*
⊕– (B) *** CfP (ADD) 3 52405-2

Recorded in the Usher Hall in Edinburgh in April 1968, and almost never out of the catalogue since, this enterprising collection of British tone-pictures remains one of Sir Alexander Gibson's finest records. Dame Ethel Smyth's opera, *The Wreckers*, was first performed in England in 1909. The story concerns the wrecking of ships by false signal lights on the Cornish coast. Its *Overture* is a strong, meaty piece which shows the calibre of this remarkable woman's personality – the first emancipated English feminist. While the material itself is not memorable, it is put together most compellingly and orchestrated with real flair.

With the Wild Geese was written a year later for the Cardiff Festival. It is another melodramatic piece, this time about soldiers fighting on the French side in the Battle of Fontenoy. The ingredients – a gay Irish theme and a call to arms among them – are effectively deployed and, though the music does not reveal a strong individuality in Harty as a composer, it is carried along by a romantic sweep which is well exploited here.

Edward German's *Welsh Rhapsody* was also written for the Cardiff Festival (in 1904) and makes a colourful and exciting finale for this well-chosen programme. German is content not to interfere with the traditional melodies he uses, relying on his orchestral skills to retain the listener's interest, in which he is very successful. The closing pages, based on *Men of Harlech*, are prepared in a Tchaikovskian manner to build to a rousing conclusion.

But undoubtedly Hamish MacCunn's descriptive Scottish overture is the highlight of the disc, and it has become better known by its use on TV. It is well crafted, has a memorable tune and is attractively atmospheric. Gibson's performances are outstanding throughout in their combination of warmth, colour, drama and atmosphere, and the recording still sounds very well indeed.

Serenades for Strings

Israel PO: DVORAK: *Serenade in E, Op. 22* (cond. Kubelik). TCHAIKOVSKY: *Serenade in C, Op. 48* (cond. Solti). ASMF, Marriner: ELGAR: *Serenade in E min., Op. 20.* WARLOCK: *Serenade*
*(*) Australian Decca Eloquence (ADD) 466 665-2

Decca's early recordings in Israel were not of their finest vintage, suffering from the difficult hall acoustics, and this 1958 pairing of the Dvořák and Tchaikovsky *Serenades* with the Israeli orchestra sounds a bit aggressive and bright in the upper registers, and rather tubby in the bass. Kubelik is sensitive and musical in the Dvořák, and the performance emerges fresher than we had remembered. Solti's hurricane-like Tchaikovsky has to be heard to be believed – the finale almost flies off with the gale. However, Marriner's trusty accounts of the Elgar and Warlock are always a joy to hear, and here the recorded sound is beautiful.

Slovak Philharmonic Orchestra

'*Russian Fireworks*' (cond. (i) Hayman; (ii) Jean; (iii) Gunzenhauser; (iv) Halász): (i) IPPOLITOV-IVANOV: *Caucasian Sketches: Procession of the Sardar.* (ii) LIADOV: *8 Russian folksongs.* KABALEVSKY: *Comedians' Galop.* MUSSORGSKY: *Sorochintsy Fair: Gopak; Khovanshchina: Dance of the Persian Slaves.* (iii) LIADOV: *Baba Yaga; The Enchanted Lake; Kikimora.* (iv) RUBINSTEIN: *Feramor: Dance of the Bayaderes; Bridal Procession; The Demon: Lesginka.* (ii) HALVORSEN: *Entry of the Boyars*

(BB) *** Naxos 8.550328

A vividly sparkling concert with spectacular digital sound, more than making up in vigour and spontaneity for any lack of finesse. The Liadov tone-poems are especially attractive and, besides the very familiar pieces by Ippolitov-Ivanov, Halvorsen and Mussorgsky, it is good to have the Rubinstein items, especially the *Lesginka*, which has a rather attractive tune.

Slovak State Philharmonic Orchestra (Košice), Mika Eichenholz

'*Locomotive Music (A Musical Train Ride), Vol. 1*': LANNER: *Ankunfts Waltz.* JOHANN STRAUSS SR: *Reise Galop; Souvenir de Carneval 1847 (quadrille); Eisenbahn-Lust (waltz).* HOYER: *Jernban Galop.* JOHANN STRAUSS JR: *Reiseabenteuer Waltz.* MEYER: *Jernvägs-Galop.* EDUARD STRAUSS: *Glockensignale Waltz; Mit Dampf Polka; Lustfahrten Waltz; Tour und Retour Polka.* JOSEF STRAUSS: *Gruss an München Polka.* GRAHL: *Sveas helsning till Nore Waltz.* LUMBYE: *Copenhagen Steam Railway Galop*

** Marco Polo 8.223470

'*Locomotive Music, Vol. 2*': LANNER: *Dampf Waltz.* FAHRBACH: *Locomotiv-Galop.* JOHANN STRAUSS JR: *Wilde Rosen Waltz; Vergnügungszug Polka; Spiralen Waltz; Accelerationen Waltz.* GUNGL: *Eisenbahn-Dampf Galop.* EDUARD STRAUSS: *Polkas: Reiselust; Ohne Aufenthalt; Treuliebchen; Ohne Bremse; Von Land zu Land; Bahn frei; Feuerfunken Waltz.* ZIEHRER: *Nachtschwalbe Polka*

** Marco Polo 8.223471

This seems a happy idea on which to base a two-CD collection of Viennese-style dance music, but in the event the only piece which celebrates the effect of a train journey really successfully is the *Copenhagen Steam Railway Galop.* The Slovak performance has rather a good whistle but seems more concerned with rhythm than with charm and cannot compare with the account included in the splendid Unicorn collection of Lumbye's dance music, so beautifully played by the Odense Symphony Orchestra under Peter Guth (DKPCD 9089 – see our main volume). The first Marco Polo disc opens with Lanner's *Ankunfts* ('Arrival') *Waltz*, which ironically dates from before the railway had even arrived in Vienna. It is enjoyable for itself; the other highlights are more descriptive. Frans Hoyer's *Jernban Galop* makes a fair shot of a train starting up and has a rather engaging main theme, while Jean Meyer's *Jernvägs-Galop* follows Lumbye's pattern of an elegant opening and a whistle start, with the side-drum snares giving a modest railway simulation. This too is attractive melodically, but the coda is too abrupt. Eduard Strauss's *Mit Dampf Polka* has a rather half-hearted whistle but plenty of energy, and his *Lustfahrten Waltz* is lyrically appealing. The second disc opens with Lanner again, but the *Dampf*

refers to the steam of a coffee house! It is followed by Fahrbach's jolly *Locomotiv-Galop*, where the effects are minimal and primitive. However, Joseph Gungl does better, with an opening whistle which returns on a regular basis against supporting bass-drum beats. Johann Strauss's *Vergnügungszug Polka* concentrates on the exhilaration of a day out on an excursion train, but Eduard Strauss's *Bahn frei*, comparably zestful, manages a cleverly brief introductory train imitation, and *Ohne Aufenthalt* has a gentle bell to set off. If most of this repertoire is unadventurous in terms of evocation, it is all tuneful and brightly presented; the playing is not without finesse and has plenty of zest, and the orchestra is very well recorded – and not in a train shed either. But these are full-priced CDs and plainly one is not travelling in a first-class carriage with the VPO.

Steele-Perkins, Crispian (trumpet)

'*Six Trumpet Concertos*' (with ECO, Anthony Halstead): J. HAYDN: *Concerto in E flat.* TORELLI: *Concerto in D.* M. HAYDN: *Concerto 2 in C.* TELEMANN: *Concerto for Trumpet, 2 Oboes & Strings.* NERUDA: *Concerto in E flat.* HUMPHRIES: *Concerto in D, Op. 10/12*

(BB) *** Regis (ADD) RRC 1053

Collectors who have relished Håkan Hardenberger's famous collection of trumpet concertos might well go on to this equally admirable concert, which duplicates only the Joseph Haydn – and that in a performance hardly less distinguished. Crispian Steele-Perkins has a bright, gleaming, beautifully focused timbre and crisp articulation, with easy command of the high tessitura of the Michael Haydn work and all the bravura necessary for the sprightly finales of all these concertos. His phrasing in the slow movement of Joseph Haydn's shapely *Andante* is matched by his playing of the *Largo* of the Neruda and the *Adagio-Presto-Adagio* of the Torelli, another fine work. Anthony Halstead with the ECO gives him warmly sympathetic support. The recording balance gives the soloist plenty of presence, but the orchestra is recorded rather reverberantly, an effect similar to that on the Hardenberger record.

Stinton, Jennifer (flute)

20th Century Flute Concertos (with SCO, Bedford): NIELSEN: *Flute Concerto.* HONEGGER: *Concerto da camera for Flute, Cor Anglais & Strings* (with Brown, cor anglais). IBERT: *Flute Concerto.* POULENC: *Flute Sonata* (orch. Berkeley)

(BB) *** Regis RRC 1126

Honegger's *Concerto da camera* comes from the same period as the *Fourth Symphony*, and the slow movement is strikingly reminiscent of it. It is an enticing work and very nicely played (with a most sensitive cor anglais contribution from Geoffrey Brown), as is the Poulenc, an effective transcription by Lennox Berkeley of the *Sonata for Flute and Piano*. The Nielsen, too, is a fine performance, although its contrasts could be more strongly made. Ibert's charming and effervescent piece comes off even better, though the orchestral playing is not particularly subtle. The whole concert is beautifully recorded, and this remains a very enjoyable concert, well worth exploring at budget price.

Stockholm Sinfonietta, Esa-Pekka Salonen

'*A Swedish Serenade*': WIRÉN: *Serenade for Strings, Op. 11.*
LARSSON: *Little Serenade for Strings, Op. 12.* SÖDERLUNDH: *Oboe Concertino* (with A. Nilsson). LIDHOLM: *Music for Strings*
**(*) BIS CD 285

The most familiar piece here is the Dag Wirén *Serenade for Strings*. Söderlundh's *Concertino for Oboe and Orchestra* has a lovely *Andante* whose melancholy is winning and with a distinctly Gallic feel to it. It is certainly played with splendid artistry by Alf Nilsson and the Stockholm Sinfonietta. The Lidholm *Music for Strings* is somewhat grey and anonymous, though it is expertly wrought. Esa-Pekka Salonen gets good results from this ensemble and the recording lives up to the high standards of the BIS label. It is forwardly balanced but has splendid body and realism.

Stockholm Sinfonietta, Jan-Olav Wedin

'*Swedish Pastorale*': ALFVÉN: *The Mountain King, Op. 37: Dance of the Cow-girl.* ATTERBERG: *Suite 3 for Violin, Viola & String Orchestra.* BLOMDAHL: *Theatre Music: Adagio.* LARSSON: *Pastoral Suite, Op. 19; The Winter's Tale: 4 Vignettes.* ROMAN: *Concerto in D for Oboe d'amore, String Orchestra & Harpsichord, BeRI 53.* ROSENBERG: *Small Piece for Cello & String Orchestra*
*** BIS CD 165

In addition to affectionate accounts of the *Pastoral Suite* and the charming vignettes for *The Winter's Tale*, the Stockholm Sinfonietta include Atterberg's *Suite 3*, which has something of the modal dignity of the Vaughan Williams *Tallis Fantasia*. It has real eloquence and an attractive melancholy, to which the two soloists, Nils-Erik Sparf and Jouko Mansnerus, do ample justice. The Blomdahl and Roman works are also given alert and sensitive performances; they make one realize how charming they are. Hilding Rosenberg's piece is very short but is rather beautiful. A delightful anthology and excellent (if a trifle closely balanced) recording. Confidently recommended.

Stokowski Symphony Orchestra, Leopold Stokowski

HAYDN: *Symphony 53 in D (Imperial).* HUMPERDINCK: *Hänsel und Gretel: Prelude.* MOZART: *German dance (Sleigh Ride), K.605/3.* SCHUMANN: *Symphony 2 in C, Op. 61.* JOHANN STRAUSS JR: *An der schönen blauen Donau; G'schichten aus dem Wienerwald*
(M) (***) Cala mono CACD 0532.

All these recordings date from 1949, except the Schumann, which followed a year later. They were made at the RCA studios with 'his Symphony Orchestra' which, to save money, used a much smaller string section than the Philadelphia Orchestra. He hand-picked the very finest players; but in Humperdinck and Haydn the violins, even though they obviously play beautifully, at times sound thin in their upper register. Nevertheless, because the underlying sound is basically full-bodied, with a weighty bass, the Humperdinck *Prelude* is vigorously enjoyable, with the brass and percussion well caught.

The Haydn is the only recording Stokowski made of any of this composer's symphonies. The first movement races along with gusto, but Stokowski really comes into his own in the theme and variations of the *Andante*, elegantly and charismatically full of instrumental charm. The Minuet is strongly rhythmic, but the urbane, flute-led Trio is reminiscent of Beecham. Stokowski used a 1939 edition of the score, using one of four available finales, which it is now thought may be spurious. But it has a dancing main theme and there is plenty of spirited dynamic contrast and a Haydnesque flavour. Mozart's *Sleigh Ride* is again strongly rhythmic, but the Trio has a lilting charm, especially the reprise, with its closing diminuendo.

But the highlight of the disc is the Schumann *Symphony*, the first movement bold and purposeful, with affectionate warmth for the lyrical material, and the tempo accelerating naturally to a thrilling close. The brilliant playing in the Scherzo shows the excellence of the string group, and there are touches of nicely judged rubato for the woodwind in the Trio. Stokowski is at his very finest in the string cantilena of the glorious *Adagio*. His magnetism and intensity are fully at Schumann's service – the result, with such responsive playing, is enormously passionate and involving. Fortunately the recording of the strings here has much more body and the warm acoustic is quite flattering. The finale then rounds the symphony off with robust vigour, but again with affectionate flexibility for the lyrical sections of the score, and the final quickening sounds completely spontaneous.

The two Strauss *Waltzes* act as a pair of encores. They were truncated (each tailored to fit a 78-r.p.m. side) and have characteristic luscious strings, but their panache carries the day. The resonant recording here is not always ideally focused, especially in the *Vienna Woods*. An indispensable disc, nevertheless, for all Stokowski aficionados.

Stuttgart Radio Symphony Orchestra, Sir Georg Solti

'*Solti in Rehearsal*': BERLIOZ: *Damnation of Faust: Hungarian March.* WAGNER: *Overture: Tannhäuser*
*(**) Arthaus **DVD** 101068

These rehearsal sequences, recorded in black and white in 1966 (Wagner) and 1968 (Berlioz) give an illuminating idea of Sir Georg Solti's approach at that period when, in his mid-fifties, he was emerging as one of the world's leading conductors. Though his reputation at that time – at least with British orchestral players – was one of impatience and even irascibility, the opposite is the case here. The vast majority of his instructions involve subtle gradations, a dominant concern not with the brilliant or extrovert qualities one might have expected, but with the shading of *pianissimos* and the moulding of legato phrases.

So in the *Tannhäuser Overture* he spends almost all of the 45 minutes of the first rehearsal sequence getting the slow introduction as he wants it, notably the hushed opening on the horns, then letting the players off the rein with a cry of release when the great trombone theme enters. He also makes a point of quoting, when the relevant theme arrives, the words of Tannhäuser himself in the opera, that the burden of his sins is weighing him down. The fast sections he tends to leave alone in his instructions, relying on fierce information from his baton.

The Berlioz similarly finds Solti concentrating on refined points, and charmingly he goes into some detail about how Berlioz was given the theme by Liszt and was instantly magnetized. It is, Solti explains, an old Hungarian song of liberation, a joyful march associated with Rákóczy as a freedom fighter. That leader failed – but then, 'Hungarians always fail', says Solti with a grin.

The big limitation, needless to say, is that the rehearsal sequences are conducted in German. Though, as always with DVDs, one has the option of having subtitles in English, the translation involved inevitably dilutes the experience. The performances themselves are as polished and refined as the rehearsals promise. The only surprise is that at the end of each performance the applause is so feeble.

Swedish Chamber Orchestra, Petter Sundkvist

'*Swedish Orchestral Favourites, Vol. 2*': LARSSON: *Lyric Fantasy, Op. 54; Little Serenade, Op.12; Adagio for String Orchestra, Op. 48.* FRUMERIE: *Pastoral Suite, Op. 13b* (with Lindloff). BLOMDAHL: *The Wakeful Night: Adagio.* ATTERBERG: *Suite 3 for Violin, Viola & Orchestra, Op. 19/1* (with Tröback & Persson). RANGSTROM: *Divertimento elegiaco for Strings*
(BB) *** Naxos 8.553715

All the music on this inexpensive issue exerts a strong appeal. It is worth the modest outlay for just Atterberg's poignant *Suite 3 for Violin, Viola and Orchestra*, Op. 19, which is one of his most poignant utterances, and for Gunnar de Frumerie's perennially fresh *Pastoral Suite* for flute and strings. Having been resistant over the years to Rangström's overblown symphonies but captivated by his songs, it is also a pleasure to welcome a new account of the *Divertimento elegiaco*, whose eloquence is well conveyed in this fine performance. Indeed, throughout this disc the Swedish Chamber Orchestra under Petter Sundkvist are first class.

Symphonies: 'Great Symphonies'

BEETHOVEN: *Symphony 5 in C min., Op. 67* (Philh. O, Ashkenazy). BRAHMS: *Symphony 3 in F, Op. 90.* DVORAK: *Symphony 9 in E min. (From the New World), Op. 95.* (VPO, Kertész). HAYDN: *Symphony 94 in G (Surprise)* (Philh. Hungarica, Dorati). MENDELSSOHN: *Symphony 3 in A min. (Scottish), Op. 56* (LSO, Abbado). MOZART: *Symphony 40 in G min., K.550* (VPO, Karajan). SAINT-SAENS: *Symphony 3 in C min. (Organ), Op. 78* (LAPO, Mehta). SCHUBERT: *Symphony 9 in C (Great), D.944* (Israel PO, Mehta). SIBELIUS: *Symphony 7 in C, Op. 105* (VPO, Maazel). TCHAIKOVSKY: *Symphony 4 in F min., Op. 36* (LSO, Szell).
**(*) Australian Decca ADD/DDD 466 444-2 (5)

This set contains two really outstanding recordings: Szell's Tchaikovsky *Fourth* and Maazel's Sibelius *Seventh*, with the Kertész *New World* not far behind. There is nothing substandard about anything else in this set either – most of the performances are well worth hearing, not least Ashkenazy's superbly recorded Beethoven *Fifth*, Dorati's Haydn *Surprise* and Mehta's vintage Decca version of the Saint-Saëns *Organ Symphony*. He is less successful in Schubert's *Ninth*. The set includes excellent sleeve-notes.

Tancibudek, Jiri (oboe)

HAYDN: *Oboe Concerto in C, Hob. VIIg/C1* (with Adelaide CO, Duvall). MARTINU: *Oboe Concerto for Small Orchestra* (with Adeleide SO, Shapirra). BRITTEN: *6 Metamophoses after Ovid.* FELD: *Sonata for Oboe & Piano* (with Blumenthal). SUTHERLAND: *Sonatina for Oboe & Piano* (with Stokes)
**(*) Australian Universal Heritage ABC Classics (ADD) 461 703 2

Part of the brief of the Australian Heritage series is to include recordings by important Australian residents even if they were not Australian born. One such is oboist Jiri Tancibudek, who was principal oboist for the Czech Opera and then the Czech Philharmonic under Kubelik. The Second World War caused him and his family to flee in a desperate night-time trek across the mountains, and they finally settled in Australia. This anthology is valuable for his agile playing of the Martinů *Oboe Concerto*, a work dedicated to him, as well as the Bartók-influenced *Sonatine* for oboe and piano by the Australian composer Margaret Sutherland, although the Haydn *Concerto* and the Britten pieces also receive fine performances. The 1970s sound is good, but not outstanding.

Thames Chamber Orchestra, Michael Dobson

'*The Baroque Concerto in England*' (with Black, Bennett): ANON. (probably HANDEL): *Concerto grosso in F.* BOYCE: *Concerti grossi in E min. for Strings; in B min. for 2 Solo Violins, Cello & Strings.* WOODCOCK: *Oboe Concerto in E flat; Flute Concerto in D*
(M) *** CRD (ADD) CRD 3331

A wholly desirable collection, beautifully played and recorded. Indeed, the recording has splendid life and presence and often offers demonstration quality – try the opening of the Woodcock *Flute Concerto*, for instance. The music is all highly rewarding. The opening concerto was included in Walsh's first edition of Handel's Op. 3 (as No. 4) but was subsequently replaced by another work. Whether or not it is by Handel, it is an uncommonly good piece, and it is given a superbly alert and sympathetic performance here. Neil Black and William Bennett are soloists of the highest calibre, and it is sufficient to say that they are on top form throughout this most enjoyable concert.

Tokyo Metropolitan Orchestra, Ryusuke Numajiri

'*Japanese Orchestral Favourites*': TOYAMA: *Rhapsody for Orchestra.* KONOYE: *Etenraku.* IFUKUBE: *Japanese Rhapsody.* AKUTAGAWA: *Music for Symphony Orchestra.* KOYAMA: *Kobiki-Uta for Orchestra.* YOSHIMATSU: *Threnody to Toki for String Orchestra & Piano, Op. 12*
(BB) *** Naxos 8.555071

There are now plenty of CDs devoted to British light classics, but this one of Japanese favourites is the first of its kind. It is everything one imagines Japanese light orchestral music to be: full of glittering percussion instruments, folk melodies and dance rhythms interspersed with more exotic elements. All these composers are professionals, writing for a modern symphony orchestra, so the music is well constructed and readily accessible. It is all entertainingly colourful, and well worth Naxos price for anyone wanting something fresh and off the beaten track. The performances and recordings are first class.

Toulouse Capitole Orchestra, Michel Plasson

French Symphonic Poems: DUKAS: *L'Apprenti sorcier.* DUPARC: *Lénore; Aux étoiles.* FRANCK: *Le Chasseur maudit.* LAZZARI: *Effet de nuit.* SAINT-SAENS: *Danse macabre*
(*) EMI 5 55385-2

An interesting and (on the whole) successful programme, let down by the brilliant but unbeguiling account of *The Sorcerer's Apprentice*. There is more fun in this piece than Plasson finds. Similarly, the humour of *Danse macabre* is not within Plasson's perceptions, although he gives an excitingly dramatic account of the piece and there is a seductive violin solo from Malcolm Stewart. There is plenty of gusto in *Le Chasseur maudit*, where the opening horn-call is arresting, the chase is properly demonic and the malignant middle section masterful, when Christian stalwarts are sinisterly warned of the Satanic welcome waiting for those choosing the hunt rather than the church for their Sunday morning occupation.

Hardly less telling is Duparc's *Lénore*, an equally melodramatic scenario (also espoused by Liszt, with narrative included). This concerns a ghoulish midnight embrace with a skeleton after the eager heroine has been carried off on horseback by her dead lover. But the two most memorable pieces here are the radiantly serene *Aux étoiles* ('The astral light of dawn'), also by Duparc, and – most haunting of all – Sylvio Lazzari's impressionistic *Effet de nuit*, with its bleakly sinuous evocation on the bass clarinet of the scaffold silhouetted in the rain against the darkening evening sky. Its climax depicts 'three ghastly prisoners marching dejectedly' in the pitiless downpour, urged on by 225 halberdiers. The recording is excellent: spacious, yet vivid; it is a shame about *L'Apprenti sorcier*.

Trudel, Alain (trombone), Northern Sinfonia

Trombone Concertos by ALBRECHTSBERGER: *in B flat;* WAGENSEILL: *in E flat;* LEOPOLD MOZART: *in G;* MICHAEL HAYDN: *in D*
(BB) *** Naxos 8.553831

This must be a unique recording début, for Alan Trudel not only takes the solo trombone part here, he also directs the polished orchestral accompaniments. He is a very stylish player with a cleanly focused timbre and warm legato. Indeed, these performances are very enjoyable, and the recording balance is excellent. As we have stated above when discussing Christian Lindberg's CD, which includes the same four works, these are all genuine trombone concertos, not transcriptions, and Alain Trudel plays them just as appealingly as his more famous competitor. The BIS CD contains some bonus items (but not for trombone), so if you want just these four works, the Naxos disc has a clear price advantage, and musically the performances are a match for those of Lindberg.

Trumpet: 'The Sound of the Trumpet'

'The Sound of the Trumpet': CLARKE: *Trumpet Voluntary.* M.-A. CHARPENTIER: *Te Deum: Prelude* (arr. Hazel). PURCELL: *Trumpet Tune and Air* (arr. Hurford) (all with Hurford, organ, Michael Laird Brass Ens.). HAYDN: *Trumpet Concerto in E flat* (Stringer, trumpet, ASMF, Marriner). BACH: *Christmas Oratorio: Nun seid ihr wohl gerochen* (arr. Reeve). SCHEIDT: *Galliard battaglia.* HANDEL: *Occasional Oratorio: March* (arr. Hazel); *Royal Fireworks Music: Overture* (arr. & cond. Howarth) (all with Philip Jones Brass Ens.); *Messiah: The Trumpet Shall Sound* (with Howell, bass). VIVALDI: *Double Trumpet Concerto in C, RV 537* (with Wilbraham, Jones, trumpets). HUMMEL: *Trumpet Concerto in E* (with Wilbraham, trumpet) (all three with ASMF, Marriner). STANLEY: *Trumpet Tune in D* (arr. Pearson; with Pearson, organ). ARBAN: *Carnival of Venice* (arr. & cond. Camarata; L. Festival O) (both with Wilbraham, trumpet)
☞ ✹ (M) *** Decca (ADD/DDD) 476 1644

The Decca production team are particularly adept at compiling an anthology like this, and there is simply no better single-disc recommendation for those who enjoy the sound of trumpets – regal and exciting – on the lips of true virtuosi. Such indeed are John Wilbraham and the individual players of the Michael Laird and Philip Jones Ensembles (especially in Elgar Howarth's highly effective brass arrangement of the *Overture* from Handel's *Royal Fireworks Music*). The popular favourites by Jeremiah Clarke, once attributed to Purcell, and Purcell's own *Trumpet Tune and Air* are equally appealing. Wilbraham's account of the Hummel *Concerto* is among the finest ever recorded, elegant in the slow movement and with the finale sparkling irresistibly. Marriner and the ASMF, during their vintage period, accompany with comparable polish, as they do Alan Stringer, who plays the Haydn *Concerto* excellently, with a bolder and more forthright open timbre which is undoubtedly authentic. Peter Hurford, when he participates, is similarly stylish. Almost every item here is a winner, and the stereo interplay in Scheidt's *Galliard battaglia* is indicative of the demonstration standard of many of the recordings included. The programme ends with a dazzling display from John Wilbraham in Camarata's lollipop arrangement of the most famous of all cornet solos, Arban's variations on the *Carnival of Venice*. It is an excellent and unexpected addition to Universal's 'Penguin Rosette' Collection and, especially at mid-price, fully deserves its accolade.

Tuckwell, Barry (horn)

(with Academy of St Martin-in-the-Fields, Iona Brown or Sir Neville Marriner; London Symphony Orchestra, Peter Maag or István Kertész; Royal Philharmonic Orchestra, Andrew Davis or Vladimir Ashkenazy)

'The Art of Barry Tuckwell' (75th Birthday Tribute): JOHANN KNECKTL: *Concerto in D.* CHERUBINI: *Sonata (Etude) 2.* MICHAEL HAYDN: *Concertino in D.* MOZART: *Concerto 4 in E flat, K.495.* FRANZ STRAUSS: *Concerto in C min., Op. 8.* R. STRAUSS: *Concertos 1 in E flat, Op. 11; 2 in E flat.* HODDINOTT: *Concerto, Op. 6; Sonata for Horn & Piano.* BEETHOVEN: *Sonata in F, Op. 17.* DANZI: *Sonata in E flat, Op. 28.* SAINT-SAËNS: *Romance, Op. 67.* R. STRAUSS: *Andante, Op. posth.*
(B) *** Decca (ADD/DDD) 475 7463 (2)

Barry Tuckwell readily inherited Dennis Brain's mantle and held his place as Britain's pre-eminent solo horn player, before finally retiring in 1997, after being the first musician to earn a full-time living as an international soloist on this instrument. His first series of recordings was with Decca, beginning with the four Mozart concertos, with Peter Maag and the LSO, in 1961. About this début we commented: 'His easy technique, smooth warm tone and obvious musicianship command attention and give immediate pleasure.' He was to record them again later but it is good to have the favourite *Fourth Concerto* in this anthology.

Two of the other pieces here, the virtuoso Cherubini *Etude* and Michael Haydn's *Concertino* (which opens with a slow movement), are also available in the HMV compilation below. But he recorded the other key works for Decca, notably the two Richard Strauss *Concertos*, where he is especially successful in the brilliant finale of the *Second* but does not quite match Dennis Brain in the Mozartian *First*.

The collection opens with an attractive eighteenth-century work by Johann Knechtl, in which the high tessitura is negotiated with aplomb. The other novelty, by Franz Strauss (1822–1905), Richard's father, has some bright ideas but has a rather distressing tendency to fall into the style of a cornet air with variations. Nevertheless, Tuckwell makes the most of it. The *Concerto* by Alun Hoddinott is one of the few really memorable twentieth-century works for the instrument, not obviously melodic, but inventive, atmospheric and dramatic, with a powerful cadenza in the finale.

The unsurpassed account of the Beethoven *Sonata* stands out among the repertoire for horn and piano, but the Danzi *Sonata*, too, is a first-class little piece, and the Saint-Saëns *Romance* is most engaging, ending on a high *pianissimo*, beautifully sustained. Altogether a rewarding collection to celebrate the 75th birthday of a remarkable British musician, backed up by a historical note by our own I.M. – an ex-horn player himself.

Tuckwell, Barry (horn),

(with Academy of St Martin-in-the-Fields, Sir Neville Marriner or (i) English Chamber Orchestra)

'Horn Concertos': TELEMANN: *Concerto in D.* CHERUBINI: *Sonata 2 in F for Horn & Strings.* CHRISTOPH FORSTER: *Concerto in E flat.* WEBER: *Concertino in E min., Op. 45.* LEOPOLD MOZART: *Concerto in D.* GIOVANNI PUNTO: *Concertos 5 in F; 6 in E flat; 10 in F; 11 in E.* (i) MICHAEL HAYDN: *Concertino in D* (arr. SHERMAN). (i) JOSEPH HAYDN: *Concerto 1 in D*

☞ (BB) *** EMI Gemini (ADD) 5 86558-2 (2)

Barry Tuckwell here celebrates his supreme achievement in nearly a dozen of the finest concertos for his instrument; the Tuckwell recordings of the key works by Wolfgang Amadeus and Richard Strauss are of course available on Decca. His mastery and ease of execution, his natural musicality and warm lyricism of line – to say nothing of his consistent beauty of tone – make every performance here memorable, and he has the advantage of polished, graceful accompaniments from the ASMF under Marriner, except in the works by Michael and Joseph Haydn, in which he directs the ECO himself with comparable elegance.

The *Concerto* of Telemann opens with a catchy moto perpetuo, despatched with aplomb; then comes a fine *Adagio* which often moves to the very top of the horn's upper range,

before the tension is released in the buoyant finale. The Cherubini *Sonata* opens with a melancholy *Largo*, then erupts into joyous high spirits, while the racing opening arpeggios of the *Concerto* by Leopold Mozart and the tight trills in the finale (with harpsichord echoes) are managed with comparable exuberance. The Weber is an attractively diverse and extensive (17 minutes) set of variations and includes a good example of horn 'chords', where the soloist plays one note and hums another; it also has an exceptionally joyful finale.

One of the novelties is a delightful concerto by the virtually unknown Christoph Forster (1693–1745) with its amiably jogging first movement marked *Con discrezione* and its brief, disconsolate *Adagio* followed by a closing Rondo in which, though the clouds clear away, the lyrical feeling remains. In some ways, most striking of all is the collection of four concertos by the Bohemian virtuoso Giovanni Punto, a successful and highly cultivated composer whose music is enjoyably distinctive, a mixture of Mozartian influences and Hummelian *galanterie*. The individual CD of these four works was issued to celebrate Barry Tuckwell's fiftieth birthday, and the performances show him at his finest. The recording throughout is of EMI's finest analogue quality, and the remastering retains the warmth and beauty of the originals.

Turner, John (recorder)

'British Recorder Concertos' (with Camerata Ens., Philip McKenzie, Eira Lynn Jones (harp), Richard Howarth (violin), Janet Fulton (percussion)): PETER HOPE: *Birthday Concerto for Recorder, Strings, Harp & Percussion.* DAVID BECK: *Flûte-à-Beck (Concerto for Recorder, Strings & Harp).* HANS GAL: *Concertino for Recorder & Strings.* DAVID ELLIS: *Divertimento elegiaco (in Memoriam Ida Carroll)* (for recorder, strings, harp & marimba). IAN PARROTT: *Sinfonia Concertante for Recorder, Solo Violin, Strings & Percussion.* DAVID DUBARRY: *Mrs Harris in Paris* (for recorder & strings)

☞ (M) *** Dutton CDLX 7154

This is John Turner's third concertante recorder collection. His first, on Olympia OCD 657 (containing works by Malcolm Arnold, Philip Lane, Thomas Pitfield, Edward Gregson David Lyon and others) is withdrawn, awaiting reissue. But the present Dutton compilation is very enticing in its own right, for the solo playing is wonderfully assured, and the Camerata Ensemble provide warmly polished accompaniments. Remarkably, the concert introduces five new composer names to this specialist repertoire, for it seems English musicians are especially drawn to this endearing and surprisingly versatile group of solo instruments. Morover, all six works here are distinctive.

The first two make a neatly contrasted pair. Peter Hope's *Concerto* (written to celebrate the soloist's 60th birthday) is instantly appealing. It has perkily vivacious outer movements, the first showcasing both the treble and descant recorders, while the catchily syncopated bravura finale features the sopranino instrument. Hope is a genuine tunesmith and the lyrical material is as appealing as the virtuoso roulades, not least the sultry central *Intermezzo* given to the bass recorder, with a contrasting middle section inviting florid bird calls from the sopranino. The work is wittily scored, using tuned percussion instruments to add to the piquancy of colour. Most diverting.

David Beck's *Concerto* is essentially evocative and atmos-pheric, the first movement using haunting string chords to contrast with the 'anxious' tenor recorder, which soliloquizes against a gentle harp accompaiment. The effect is enigmatic, and the misty central movement continues to sustain the restrained pastoral mood, but now in its turn introduces both the descant and sopranino recorders. The finale, for treble recorder, is more lively, but the music's evocation is not entirely disturbed.

Hans Gal's inventive four-movement *Concertino* opens with a theme of simple charm. It is engagingly lyrical, and deftly structured, with a delectable, lightweight Scherzo, fol-lowed by a nocturnal serenade and ending with a sprightly closing *Rondo capriccioso*.

David Ellis's *Divertimento elegiaco* is a musical portrait of a dear friend, kaleidoscopic in style and mood, ending with an impressive *Chaconne* as a closing epitaph to a lady, obviously of substance.

Ian Parrott's *Sinfonia concertante* then opens with a touch-ing, rocking theme, a *Reverie*, but one not lacking passion. The flowing, energetic *Ritornello* follows, with the solo recorder and violin alone in duet, leading to a a surprise virtuoso cadenza for the xylophone. The intensity grows in the third movement *Rhapsody*, but 'thunder and lightning' from the percussion introduce the gay, march-like finale, which reprises earlier material before its lively conclusion.

David Dubarry then closes the programme with his por-trait of *Mrs Harris* (from Paul Gallico's novel), choosing a temptingly elegant new gown in the House of Dior in Paris to a gracefully debonair *valse français*, so urbanely phrased by the soloist, to make a perfect tail-piece for a collection which is marvellously played and beautifully recorded. Strongly recommended.

English Recorder Concertos' (with Royal Ballet Sinfonia, Gavin Sutherland): GARDINER: *Petite Suite, Op. 245.* McCABE: *Domestic Life.* LAWSON: *Song of the Lesser Twayblade.* LEIGHTON: *Concerto, Op. 88.* LANE: *Suite champêtre.* MELLERS: *Aubade.* MILFORD: *2 Pipe Tunes* (arr. Lane). KAY: *Mr Pitfield's Pavane.* DODGSON: *Concerto Chacony*

(M) *** ASV WHL 2143

Opening with John Gardiner s delightful *Petite Suite,* this disc of English recorder concertos also proves diverting. There are plenty of similarly attractive concertante pieces here: Philip Lane's *Suite champêtre,* Wilfrid Mellers' colourfully scored *Aubade* (which has some lovely sonorities, especially in the *Cantilena*), and Robin Milford's *Two Pipe Tunes,* simple but effective as heard in Philip Lane's arrangement.

There is nothing like a chaconne for bringing out the best in a composer, and Stephen Dodgson's *Concerto Chacony,* with its baroque overtones, is an intriguing score, as is Kenneth Leighton's *Concerto,* one of the finest works included. It is especially notable for its vivid harpsichord writing, neatly played by Keith Elcombe. Indeed, at times it seems almost like a harpsichord concerto!

John McCabe aptly describes his *Domestic Life* as 'a very light *pièce d'occasion*', while *The Song of the Lesser Twayblade* of Peter Lawson was written in 2000 as part of a series of musical portraits dedicated to the 48 wild orchids of Britain. It is easy-going and agreeably evocative, rather in the manner of film music. Norman Kay's *Mr Pitfield's Pavane* also has its moments. Excellent performances from John Turner, backed up by the ever-reliable Gavin Sutherland, and very good

sound too, with a convincing balance; plus useful and copi-ous notes by the brilliant soloist.

Turovsky, Yuli (cello), I Musici di Montreal

'*Violonchelo Espagñol*': ALBENIZ: *Malagueña.* BORODIN: *Serenata all spañola.* CASSADO: *Requiebros; Sonata nelo stile antico spagnolo.* FALLA: *7 Cançiones populares espanoles; El amor brujo: Ritual Fire Dance.* GLAZUNOV: *Chant du Ménestral; Sérénade espagnole.* GRANADOS: *Goyescas: Intermezzo.* SHCHEDRIN: *A la Albéniz*
*** Analekta AN 29897

The alternative Spanish spelling of 'violonchelo' in the title signals an attractive sequence of musical lollipops with a strong Spanish flavour. This is plainly favourite repertory with Yuli Turovsky, founder-conductor of I Musici di Mon-treal, who here resumes his original role of virtuoso cellist, playing *con amore* throughout. Russian-born, he divides his collection between pieces written by Spanish composers and those written by Russians in reflection of Spanish music. The sequence opens with a jolly and brilliant piece by the Spanish cellist-composer Gaspar Cassado, *Requiebros,* and it is Cas-sado who provides the only multi-movement item, 'Sonata in the Old Spanish Style', baroque pastiche. The best-known items are those by Manuel de Falla, the *Ritual Fire Dance* from *El amor brujo* and the *Seven Spanish Popular Songs,* ably arranged, like most of the other items, by Madeleine Messier. The cello similarly takes on a quasi-vocal role in Albéniz's *Malagueña* and the Granados *Intermezzo,* yearningly atmos-pheric in imitating the voice, while the two Glazunov pieces are nicely contrasted. As a tail-piece Turovsky offers a work written in imitation of Albéniz by Rodion Shchedrin, colour-ful but with too many stops and starts for it to sound like the genuine article. Warm, full sound and strongly committed playing.

'Twilight Memories'

'*Twilight Memories*': WILLIAMSON: *Curtain Up.* WILLIAMS: *They Ride by Night; The Young Ballerina.* YORKE: *Fireflies.* ELLIS: *Muse in Mayfair.* TORCH: *Fandango; Wagon Lit* (with Queen's Hall Light O, Sydney Torch). VAUGHAN WILLIAMS: *Sea Songs: Quick March* (with New Concert O). FLETCHER: *Fiddle Dance; Folk Tune* (with Jay Wilbur O). COATES: *The 3 Bears: Waltz* (with Queen's Hall Light O, composer). STRACHEY: *Ascot Parade.* BRIDGEWATER: *Prunella.* WHITE: *Caprice for Strings.* W. COLLINS: *Cumberland Green.* BANTOCK: *Twilight Memories* (L. Promenade O, W. Collins). RICHARDSON: *Shadow Waltz.* CAMPBELL: *Cloudland.* MORLEY: *Mock Turtles.* SIDAY: *Petticoat Lane.* MACKINTOSH: *Strings on Wings* (with Queen's Hall Light O, King). CURZON: *Dance of an Ostracised Imp* (New Concert O, Wilbur). MILNER: *Downland* (with L'Orchestra de Concert, O'Henry). FARNON: *Goodwood Galop.* THOMAS: *Looking Around* (with Queen's Hall Light O, Farnon)
(M) (***) ASV mono CDAJA 5419

Another collection of vintage nostalgia, dating from the late 1940s. The programme opens appropriately with Lambert Williamson's *Curtain Up,* a charming example of period writing, and a lively account of the *Quick March* from

Vaughan Williams's *Sea Songs* follows. Percy Fletcher's *Folk Tune*, a piece of much charm, and Sidney Torch's catchy percussion rhythms in the jazzy *Fandango* are offset by Richardson's dainty *Caprice for Strings*. Farnon's *Goodwood Galop* races along without a care in the world, and Angela Morley shows her gift for orchestral colour in the amusing *Mock Turtles*. Peter Yorke's *Fireflies* with its scurrying woodwind writing brings slinky strings into the middle section. Walter Collins's *Cumberland Green* is another joyful piece of tuneful writing, while Bantock's *Twilight Memories*, which gives this collection its title, is a rather haunting waltz. The recordings vary in quality, though none is below a decent standard for the period, and this disc is certainly recommended to those collectors with a nostalgic affection for the British light music tradition.

Vengerov, Maxim (violin)

'Vengerov and Virtuosi' (with Papian, piano, or Virtuosi):
BAZZINI: *Le Ronde des lutins, Op. 25*. BRAHMS: *Hungarian Dances 1, 5 & 7*. DVORAK: *Humoresque 7 in G flat*.
KHACHATURIAN: *Gayaneh: Sabre Dance*. MASSENET:
Thaïs: Méditation. MONTI: *Csárdás*. NOVACEK: *Perpetuum mobile*. PONCE: *Estrellita*. RACHMANINOV: *Vocalise, Op. 34/14*. TCHAIKOVSKY: *Souvenir d'un lieu cher, Op. 42*.
SCHUBERT (arr. Wilhelmi): *Ave Maria*
*** EMI 5 57164-2

With its odd accompaniment from Vengerov's chosen band of 11 Russian solo violins and piano, recorded live in the Musikvereinsaal in Vienna in April 2001, Vengerov's recital of violin lollipops is very much a fun record for those with a sweet tooth. The opening item, Rachmaninov's *Vocalise*, heavily inflected, leads to an account of Ponce's *Estrellita* that echoes Palm Court in its sweetness. Vengerov, full of spontaneous flair and encouraged by a live audience, allows himself extreme rhythmic freedom. Cheering greets the last item, Monti's famous *Csárdás*, with a big laugh from the audience as Vengerov plays around with bird imitations, but otherwise there is little evidence of the audience's presence. Tempo changes in almost every bar witness a young violinist at the peak of his form, enjoying himself from first to last in music that is undemanding on the ear if not on the technique, and outrageously showing off in a way that for many will be very endearing. Not that the playing is extrovert all the time. Vengerov's account of the *Méditation* from Massenet's *Thaïs* conveys a rare depth of feeling, making it more than just a lyrical interlude. Curiously, the coagulation of 11 solo violins often sounds rather like an accordion.

Vienna Philharmonic Orchestra, Valéry Gergiev

'Salzburg Festival Concert': PROKOFIEV: *Symphony 1 in D (Classical) Op. 25*. SCHNITTKE: *Viola Concerto* (with Yuri Bashmet). STRAVINSKY: *The Firebird* (complete ballet). plus feature: Stravinsky and Prokofiev (interview with Gergiev) and Schnittke (interview with Bashmet).
(Director/Video Director: Brian Large)
*** TDK DVD DV-VPOVG

Gergiev and the Vienna Philharmonic are recorded at the Salzburg Festival in 2000 in an all-Russian programme. The excellence of the performances is enhanced by the visual

direction, which, as so often with Brian Large, directs th listener's eyes where his ears want them to be. Gergiev has a excellent rapport with his Viennese players, and *The Firebir* for which most collectors will want this concert, is impressiv both musically and, thanks to an excellent balance, aurall There are times when one feels he could give his players just little more time (the *Dance of the Princesses*) and conversel the first movement of the Prokofiev feels a little staid. However, for the most part these are very fine readings, wit superb playing from the Viennese.

Schnittke's *Viola Concerto*, completed not long before hi stroke, is generally thought to be among his most powerfu compositions. Yuri Bashmet, who is the dedicatee, ha recorded the concerto twice before, with Rozhdestvensky anc Rostropovich. It is made up of two *Largos* surrounding a fas central movement, the mood swinging between a pensiv brooding and a kind of frenetic activity. Whether one warm: to Schnittke or not, it is a powerfully communicative per formance. The TDK notes, incidentally, tell us that the *'Fire bird Suite* exists in three versions ... the second, *to be heard i the present recording* contains only seven numbers of the original 19 in the two-act (sic!) ballet version'. Not so, fortunately! The title-page lists the 19 numbers of the full versior and it is the complete score that is recorded here. TDK mus look to their presentation.

Vienna Philharmonic Orchestra, Nikolaus Harnoncourt

'Vienna New Year's Concert 2001': J. STRAUSS SR: *Radetzky March* (original and revised versions). J. STRAUSS JR:
Overture: Eine Nacht in Wien (Berlin version). Polkas:
Electrofor; Electro-magnetic; Vergnügungzug (Excursion Train); Der Kobold; Luzifer. Waltzes: *Morgenblätter; Seid umschlungen Millionen; An der schönen Blauen Donau (Blue Danube)*. JOSEF STRAUSS: Polkas: *Harlekin; Ohne Sorgen*. Waltz: *Dorfschwalben aus Osterreich (Village Swallows)*. LANNER: *Jägers Lust (galop); Die Schonbrunner Waltz; Steyrische Tanze*
*** Teldec 8573 83563-2

Harnoncourt may still be best known as a pioneer of period performance, but he is also dedicatedly Viennese, someone who as a young cellist once played in the orchestra. True to character, he introduces a fair sprinkling of novelties, starting with the original version of what by tradition has become the concert's final encore, the *Radetzky March*. Far more plainly orchestrated, it offers little rivalry for the established version. Other items new to the concerts include the *Electro-magnetic Polka* and *Electrofor Polka*, nicely contrasted, and the Polka-mazurka, *Der Kobold* ('The Goblin'), with charming pizzicato effects and a *pianissimo* coda. The three items by Joseph Lanner, stylistically well differentiated, celebrate that composer's bicentenary and include a jolly rarity, *Jägers Lust* ('Huntsman's Delight'), with hunting horns prominent and a shot simulated by the timpani. In a fascinating note on the history of the concerts the orchestra's chairman, Dr Clemens Hellberg, makes an illuminating comment on Harnoncourt from the players' point of view: that they were delighted to 're-examine the Philharmonic's Strauss tradition through the eyes of this analytical yet so impulsive conductor'. A vintage year, presented in sparklingly clear sound.

Vienna Philharmonic Orchestra, Rudolf Kempe

'The Vienna Philharmonic on Holiday': MASCAGNI: Cavalleria rusticana: Intermezzo. PONCHIELLI: La Gioconda: Dance of the Hours. SCHMIDT: Notre Dame: Intermezzo. GOUNOD: Faust: Waltz. BAYER: Die Puppenfee: Suite. OFFENBACH: Orpheus in the Underworld: Overture. GOTOVAC: Ero the Joker (dance). SCHUBERT: Rosamunde: Overture (Die Zauberharfe); Entr'acte in B flat; Ballet in G. GLUCK: Orfeo et Euridice: Dance of the Blessed Spirits

*** Testament (ADD) SBT 1127

It is good to be reminded so vividly of an aspect of Rudolf Kempe's mastery too easily forgotten – his Beechamesque charm in light music. Waltz rhythms are given a delicious lilt, not just in Viennese items like the delightful Josef Bayer suite, Die Puppenfee, but in Gounod too, with Kempe bringing out the delicacy as well as the vigour. Kempe's use of rubato is often extreme – arguably too much so in the Schubert Rosamunde music – but it never fails to be winning in a very Viennese way, as in the rare Franz Schmidt Intermezzo. The Ponchielli, once so popular, now neglected, sparkles with uninhibited joy, as does the Offenbach, and it is good to have such a rarity as the Kolo by the Zagreb conductor and composer Jakob Gotovac, rhythmic and colourful. The recordings were all made in the Musikvereinsaal in Vienna in December 1961, with the glowing EMI recording well caught in Testament transfers which bring out both warmth and depth of focus.

Vienna Philharmonic Orchestra, Riccardo Muti

'New Year's Concert, 2004': JOHANN STRAUSS JR: Waltzes: Accelerationen; An der schönen, blauen Donau. Champagne Polka; Die Fledermaus: Csádás. Es war so wunderschön March; Im Sturmschritt Polka; Satanella Polka; Das Sitzentuch der Königin Overture; Zigeunerola Quadrille. JOHANN STRAUSS SR: Beliebte-Sperl Polka; Cachucha-Galopp; Frederika Polka; Indianer Galopp; Philomelen Waltz; Radetzky March. LANNER: Hofball-Tänze Waltz; Tarantel Galopp. JOSEF STRAUSS: Eislauf Polka; Sphären-Klänge Waltz; Stiefmütterchen Polka. EDUARD STRAUSS: Mit Vergnügen Polka

*** DG DVD 073 097-9 (V/D: Brian Large); CD 474 900-2 (2)

It is fascinating how the New Year's Day concert in Vienna seems to mellow even the severest disciplinarians among conductors. Lorin Maazel has never been so warm as when conducting this annual event; and here Riccardo Muti once again presents his programme with an authentic Viennese glow. The concert in 2004 was designed to celebrate the bicentenary of Johann Strauss I, father of the waltz-king we most revere. Normally the final encore, the Radetzky March, is his most notable contribution, but on the first of these two discs we have four rare pieces by him, including the delectable Philomela Waltz, leading to two seductive items by his contemporary, Joseph Lanner, presented with an endearing' gentle touch of Viennese schmalz in the more modest Schrammeln style that we remember from the early recordings of the Boskovsky Ensemble.

Johann Strauss II and his siblings, Josef and Eduard, take over again in the second half, with more rarities and an ecstatic account of the Sphärenklänge Waltz, to match an equally ravishing account of the Accelerationen Waltz in the first half, where the increase of tempo at the opening is managed most engagingly.

While the Champagne Polka fizzes appropriately, it cannot be said that visually the 2004 concert is as electrifying as Harnoncourt's 2003 proceedings (see our main volume, p. 1264). Muti's visual image is dapper; curiously, his bespectacled countenance reminds one a little of Glenn Miller, although there is nothing jazzy about his affectionately cultivated conducting style. With Brian Large in command, the camera angles are almost always impeccable and only very occasionally do we leave the auditorium. With DVD one feels part of the proceedings, and the sound is excellent. There are optional filmed sequences of the Vienna State Opera Ballet for Accelerations and the Champagne Polka; and for Josef Strauss's Eislauf Polka, we are offered a choice of figure-skating impressions. But it is much more rewarding to watch and be caught up in the music-making itself.

Vienna Philharmonic Orchestra, Seiji Ozawa

'New Year Concert 2002': JOHANN STRAUSS SR: Beliebte Annen Polka, Radetzky March. JOHANN STRAUSS JR: Carnevalbotschafter Waltz; Zivio! March; Kunstlerleben Waltz; Die Fledermaus Overture; Perpetuum mobile; Elisen-Polka; Waltz: Wiener Blut; Tik-tak Polka; Waltz: An die schönen Blauen Donau. JOSEF STRAUSS: Die Schwatzerin, Vorwarts!, Arm in Arm, Aquarellen Waltz, Die Libelle, Plappermaulchen, Im Pfluge. HELLMESBERGER: Danse diabolique

*** TDK DVD Mediactive DV-WPNK02 (V/D: Brian Large)

With a large Euro sign in flowers on the organ pipes behind the orchestra in the Vienna Musikvereinsaal, this was a special New Year's concert, signalling the arrival that day of the new currency. One of the extra items in the 'Special Features' section of the disc is an alternative version of Johann Strauss's Perpetuum mobile, showing what is described as the 'Dance of the Machines' with illustrations of Euro notes being printed and Euro coins being minted and stamped. Other additional items include alternative accounts of the Blue Danube, with the ballet company of the Vienna State Opera, and of two polkas, Beliebte Annen by Johann Strauss Senior and the Elisen Polka by Junior, with the Spanish Riding School performing wonders of equitation, a delightful extra.

Those extra items allow the main concert to be presented with no visual distraction from shots of the players, conductor, hall and audience, with almost every advantage for the DVD over the equivalent CD. Quite apart from the bonus of visual presentation the DVD offers five numbers omitted from the CD – two pieces by Josef Strauss, celebrating his 175th anniversary, the polkas Arm in Arm and Im Pfluge, and three Johann Jr numbers, the Carnevalbotschafter Waltz, the Beliebte Annen Polka and Perpetuum mobile.

Ozawa at his most relaxed is naturally idiomatic in his pauses and warm rubato, helped by not using a baton, relying on the innate expressiveness of the Viennese players to mould in perfect time. More than anyone since Karajan in his single New Year concert, Ozawa controls the clapping of the audience, limiting it to the proper passages in the final Radetzky March. The international credentials of the orchestra are demonstrated in the multilingual new year greetings from a dozen and more players, just before the traditional *Blue Danube*.

Vienna Philharmonic Orchestra, Christian Thielemann

German Overtures: MARSCHNER: *Hans Heiling*.
MENDELSSOHN: *The Hebrides (Fingal's Cave); A Midsummer Night's Dream*. NICOLAI: *The Merry Wives of Windsor (Die lustigen Weiber von Windsor)*. WAGNER: *Rienzi*. WEBER: *Euryanthe; Oberon*
** DG 474 5022

There is much to admire in this collection of German overtures from Christian Thielemann, not least the refinement of the Vienna Philharmonic's playing. These are performances of extremes, not only in the range of dynamic – arguably too much for comfortable home listening – but also in contrasts of tempo, both fast and slow. That works very well in the opening item, Mendelssohn's *Midsummer Night's Dream*, where the lightness of the fairy music is a delight, though the humour of the piece is missing. Similarly, at the end of the well-paced account of the *Hebrides Overture*, the final string pizzicatos are so literally in tempo that there is no sense of a pay-off. The amiability of the other works too is reduced by a heavy-handed treatment, though in Wagner's *Rienzi* Thielemann's approach brings out the links with later Wagner. Next to the rest, the Marschner piece falls rather short, interesting though it is as a rarity. The playing of the Vienna Philharmonic, recorded in the Musikverein in Vienna, is a delight to the ear, even if inner clarity is limited in some of the heavier tuttis.

(i) Vienna Philharmonic Orchestra, or (ii) Berlin Philharmonic Orchestra, Bruno Walter

(i) MAHLER: *Symphony 4 in G* (with Seefried). (ii) R. STRAUSS: *Don Juan*
(**) Urania mono URN 22156

One of the glories of the post-war catalogue was Mahler's *Fourth Symphony* with Bruno Walter and the New York Philharmonic. Although the *Second* and *Ninth Symphonies* had been available, the latter, together with a Vienna *Das Lied von der Erde*, was a Society issue, available only by subscription. The appearance of the *Fourth* enthused music-lovers, but Walter's singer was Desi Halbein, whose colouring and timbre were somewhat uninviting. The Urania set comes from 1950 and has a rich-toned Irmgard Seefried and the Vienna Philharmonic. There is another Walter recording with her in New York in 1953, while Music & Arts (see above) offers a 1952 live Concertgebouw recording with Elisabeth Schwarzkopf.

Wallfisch, Elizabeth (violin), Parley of Instruments, Peter Holman

'English Classical Violin Concertos': JAMES BROOKS: *Concerto 1 in D*. THOMAS LINLEY JR: *Concerto in F*. THOMAS SHAW: *Concerto in G*. SAMUEL WESLEY: *Concerto 2 in D*
**(*) Hyp. CDA 66865

Peter Holman and his Parley of Instruments expend much energy and Elizabeth Wallfisch considerable musical sensibility to bring these concertos from the late eighteenth century fully to life. They succeed admirably in that, working hard over music which is usually felicitous and always well crafted but too often predictable. In first movements one keeps getting the impression of second-rate Haydn. However, the opening movement of the James Brooks *Concerto* is amiably pleasing in its melodic contours and offers the soloist plenty of lively bravura. Its brief *Largo affettuoso* is agreeable too, and the dancing finale sparkles on the Wallfisch bow, and she produces a neat cadenza.

Thomas Linley offers a *galant* Moderato first movement, another all-too-brief but graceful slow movement with a nice rhythmic snap; the finale is a charming gavotte. But Thomas Shaw goes one better in his *Adagio*, creating the best tune on the disc, for his slow movement, again with a Scottish snap, is most winning, very like a folksong. The finale bounces and the horns hunt boisterously. Wesley's first movement is vigorous and assured, if too long; and in the slow movement a pair of the orchestral violins join the soloist in a trio. The finale is very jolly and buoyant. The recording is excellent and, dipped into, this collection will give pleasure, providing you do not expect too much.

'Wedding Classics'

'Wedding Classics': Prelude: BACH: *Orchestral Suite 3: Air* (Noel Rawsthorne, organ). HANDEL: *Water Music: Air* (Prague CO, Sir Charles Mackerras). ALBINONI/GIAZOTTO: *Adagio* (Maurice André (trumpet), Jane Parker-Smith (organ)). PACHELBEL: *Canon* (ASMF, Sir Neville Marriner)

Processional: WAGNER: *Lohengrin: Bridal Chorus* (Fredric Bayco (organ)). CLARKE: *Trumpet Voluntary*. STANLEY: *Trumpet Tune in D* (André, Parker-Smith). CHARPENTIER: *Te Deum: Prelude* (ASMF, Sir Philip Ledger)

Ceremony and Signing of the Register: BACH/GOUNOD: *Ave Maria* (Dame Janet Baker). BACH: *Chorale: Jesu, joy of man's desiring* (Temple Church Ch., George Thalban-Ball). VAUGHAN WILLIAMS: *The Call* (John Shirley-Quirk). VIVALDI: *Four Seasons: Spring* (Krzysztof Jakowicz, Polish CO, Jerzy Maksymiuk). SCHUBERT: *Ave Maria* (Anneliese Rothenberger). HANDEL: *Serse: Largo* (André, Parker-Smith). FRANCK: *Panis angelicus* (Hallé Ch. & O, Maurice Handford)

Recessional: MENDELSSOHN: *Midsummer Night's Dream: Wedding March* (Rawsthorne). HANDEL: *Arrival of the Queen of Sheba* (ASMF, Marriner). KARG-ELERT: *Now that we all our God* (Ledger, organ). HANDEL: *Royal Fireworks Music: Réjouissance* (Bamberg SO, Rudolf Kempe). WIDOR: *Organ Symphony 5: Toccata* (Parker-Smith)
(B) ** CfP (ADD/DDD) 5 86659-2

Classics for Pleasure has sensibly divided the chosen music into four sections, covering each part of the wedding service, but, curiously, the *Arrival of the Queen of Sheba* is placed among the recessional items! And who would want the ubiquitous *Spring* from Vivaldi's *Four Seasons* at their wedding, or choose *The Call* from Vaughan Williams's five *Mystical Songs*, even though it is impressively sung by John Shirley-Quirk? The collection has obviously also been planned either as a guide to pre-wedding choice of music, or for use on the day at a venue where no organ or organist could be present; hence the prevalence of performances on the solo organ, or

1 duet with a trumpet. However, the disc does include the lorious Mendelssohn *Wedding March*, Wagner's (now nfashionable) *Bridal March* from *Lohengrin*, a gorgeous horal performance of Franck's *Panis angelicus*, and the bra-ura Widor *Toccata*, which not all local organists may be able o play comfortably.

Wedding Classics': MENDELSSOHN: *Midsummer Night's Dream: Wedding March* (OAE, Mackerras). ALBINONI: *Adagio* (L. CO, Warren-Green). FAURE: *Pavane* (City of L. inf., Hickox). MARCELLO: *Oboe Concerto: Adagio* (Ray till, L. Academy, Stamp). MOZART: *Ave verum Corpus* with Schütz Ch.). PURCELL: *The Fairy Queen, Part II: Overture* (both with LCP, Norrington); *The Indian Queen: Trumpet Overture*. PACHELBEL: *Canon*. HANDEL: *Messiah: Hallelujah Chorus; Dixit Dominus: excerpt*. BACH: *Jesu, joy of man's desiring* (all by Taverner Players & Ch., Parrott). uite 3: *Overture; Air; Gavottes I & II* (ECO, Ledger); *Wedding Cantata (No. 202): Gavotte* (Nancy Argenta, Ens. onnerie, Huggett). BARBER: *Agnus Dei* (arr. of *Adagio for Strings*) (Winchester Cathedral Ch., Hill). MOZART: *Alleluia* (Monika Frimmer); *Serenata notturna: Minuet* (Lausanne CO, Y. Menuhin). BACH/GOUNOD: *Ave Maria* (Sister Marie Keyrouz, Auvergne CO, Van Beck). ROSSINI: *Petite Messe olennelle: Prelude religioso* (Wayne Marshall, organ). RACHMANINOV: *Gloria in excelsis* (Swedish R. Ch., Kaljuste). FRANCK: *Cantabile for organ* (Nicholas Danby). HAYDN: *The Seasons: excerpt* (La Petite Bande, Kuijken). ALLA: *Three-Cornered Hat (ballet): Miller's Dance* Aquarius, Cleobury). HOLST: *The Planets; Venus* (RLPO, Mackerras). GRIEG: *Olav Trygvason: excerpts* (Trondheim Ch. & SO, Ruud). BORODIN: *Prince Igor: Polovtsian Dance* RLPO Ch. & O, Mackerras). POULENC: *Organ Concerto: xcerpts* (Weir; cond. Hickox). ORFF: *Carmina Burana: O Fortuna* (Bournemouth Ch. & SO, Hill)

B) ** Virgin 2x1 5 61890-2 (2)

This curious Virgin collection of wedding music ('spiritual, contemplative or festive') was originally compiled in 1989, which perhaps accounts for the omission of the Widor *Organ Toccata*. But one wonders where music from Falla's *Three-Cornered Hat* ballet or Grieg's *Olav Trygvason* will fit into an English wedding celebration? However there are quite a number of more suitable items, and the performances and recordings are of a high standard. No doubt the inclusion of Orff's *O Fortuna* as the final item is intended to celebrate the luck' of the bride, and she will be glad to know that Holst's *Venus* represents 'the bringer of peace' rather than extra-marital temptation.

West-Eastern Divan Orchestra, Daniel Barenboim

The Ramallah Concert: Knowledge is the Beginning' (a film by Paul Smaczny): includes: BEETHOVEN: *Symphony 5*. MOZART: *Sinfonia concertante, K.297b* (with Mohamed Saleh (oboe), Kinan Azmeh (clarinet), Mor Biron (bassoon), Sharon Polyak (horn)). ELGAR: *Enigma Variations: Nimrod* (only)

*** Warner Music Vision DVD/CD 2564 62792-2 (2)

The Palestinian town of Ramallah on the West Bank of the Jordan was the venue where Barenboim's reconciliation through music, overcoming towering logistic difficulties, achieved this concert in August 2005. Not only was the hall packed to the doors, with hundreds sitting in the aisles, the performances on this live recording bear powerful witness to the deep emotional qualities inspired by Barenboim with his young players. One might have expected nineteenth-century romantic works like Tchaikovsky's *Fifth Symphony* to draw out powerful emotions, but here in Mozart and Beethoven the emotion is just as intense, not in any way through inappropriately romantic interpretations, but in thrust, energy and drive. So, in the thrilling account of the finale of Beethoven's *Fifth*, which crowns the concert, few will fail to register the gulp-in-throat quality that plainly came over not just the players but the audience too, vividly conveyed in warm, full and immediate recording. So, too, in the moving account of Elgar's *Nimrod*, given as an encore.

The first of the two discs offers a 90-minute film about the orchestra, including many interviews with the players, as well as with Barenboim and co-founder Edward Said. A visit to the Buchenwald Concentration Camp is also shown. The second disc offers a video of the whole concert, prefaced by a 17-minute Prologue, in which the formidable logistic prob-lems of getting the players to Ramallah are explored: the Israelis went by way of Tel Aviv, while the Arabs and others arrived via Amman in Jordan. They hated being separated and were visibly relieved to be reunited. For security reasons the Israeli players had to depart in a long convoy to Jerusalem within minutes of the end of the concert. During the fare-wells one player says, 'How hard it is not to cry.' The DVD also includes half a dozen speeches, most of them in English, and that is perhaps excessive. It is good to have the concert on DVD as well as CD.

Williams, John (guitar)

'The Seville Concert' ((i) with Orquesta Sinfónica de Sevilla, José Buenagu): ALBENIZ: *Suite españolas: Sevilla; Asturias; Torre Bermeja; Granada; Cadiz; Cordoba*. BACH: *Lute Suite 4, BWV 1006a: Prelude*. D. SCARLATTI: *Keyboard Sonata in D min., Kk. 13* (arr. WILLIAMS). (i) VIVALDI: *Concerto in D, RV 93*. YOCUH: *Sakura Variations*. KOSHKIN: *Usher Waltz, Op. 29*. BARRIOS: *Sueño en la Floresta*. (i) RODRIGO: *Concierto de Aranjuez: Adagio*
*** Sony SK 517488-2

It is good to have a first-rate, modern (1992) recital from the estimable John Williams. It was recorded in Spain (in the Royal Alcázar Palace) as part of a TV programme, which accounts for its hour-long duration and the inclusion of the ubiquitous Rodrigo *Adagio* as the closing item. The recording is very realistic and present, yet the balance is natural and the effect not jumbo-sized. John Williams's intellectual concen-tration is as formidable as his extraordinary technique. This playing comes as much from the head as from the heart. He is first rate in the Bach and brings a sense of keyboard articula-tion to the engaging *D minor Sonata* of Scarlatti (who was Bach's almost exact contemporary). His strength is felt in the flamenco accents of Albéniz's *Asturias*; a sense of the darkly dramatic is powerfully conveyed in Koshkin's *Usher Waltz* (after Edgar Allan Poe). Yet his playing can be charmingly poetic, as in the delicate account of the *Largo* of the Vivaldi concerto; touchingly gentle, as in Yocuh's charming penta-tonic evocation of cherry blossoms; or thoughtfully improvi-sational, as in the Barrios *Sueño en la Floresta*. The reissue is especially welcome in including four more evocations of Spanish cities by Albéniz not included on the original disc.

World Orchestra for Peace, Sir Georg Solti or Valery Gergiev

'The First Ten Years 1995–2005': CD: DEBUSSY: *La Mer.* MENDELSSOHN: *A Midsummer Night's Dream: Scherzo.* STRAVINSKY: *Petrushka* (ballet; 1911 version)

DVD: BARTÓK: *Concerto for Orchestra.* BEETHOVEN: *Fidelio*: Act II, finale (with Evelyn Herlitzius, Stig Andersen, Andreas Kohn, London Voices). ROSSINI: *William Tell: Overture*

*** Ph. CD + **DVD** 475 6937 (2)

The World Orchestra for Peace was founded in 1995 by Sir Georg Solti, who was inspired by the idea of bringing together leading musicians from great orchestras all over the world. Charles Kaye, Solti's assistant and later director of the World Orchestra, brought together an ensemble of players drawn from 13 of the orchestras, world wide, with which Solti had a special relationship. The concert here on the supplementary DVD, recorded in Victoria Hall, Geneva, in 1995 celebrated the 50th anniversary of the United Nations Organization. Preceded by clips from the rehearsals and comments from Solti himself on the role of music in the search for peace, the concert is electrifying from beginning to end. It opens with a heart-warming cello solo at the start of the *William Tell Overture.* The thrilling conclusion of the piece, sharply detailed, then defies its hackneyed reputation, leading to a dazzling, intense account of Bartók's *Concerto for Orchestra*, a work perfectly designed to bring out the combination of brilliance and refinement which marks the playing of this orchestra of stars. The finale from Beethoven's *Fidelio* makes the most satisfying conclusion, with a thrilling orchestral crescendo leading into the first choral section, very well sung by London Voices. The fine team of soloists is led by the cleanly focused bass, Andreas Kohn, as Don Fernando, Evelyn Herlitzius as Leonore and Stig Andersen as Florestan.

Sadly, Solti died just before a planned concert for the year 2000 in Baden-Baden, but Valery Gergiev was able to step in, conducting a phenomenal account of the *Midsummer Night's Dream Scherzo*, with astonishingly agile playing from the first flute. There follows a strong, darkly atmospheric account of Debussy's *La Mer*, recorded in 2000 at the BBC Proms in London, with Gergiev electrically intense. Stravinsky's *Petrushka*, in the original (1911) scoring, was recorded in Moscow in 2003, wonderfully idiomatic and persuasive as a performance, but with sound that could be more sharply defined internally. It adds to the impression of liveness in all these performances that applause is included at the end of each.

Zabaleta, Nicanor (harp)

'Harp Concertos': (i) BOIELDIEU: *Harp Concerto in 3 tempi in C* (with Berlin RSO, Märzendorfer). SAINT-SAENS: *Morceau de concert in G, Op. 154.* TAILLEFERRE: *Concertino for Harp & Orchestra* (with ORTF, Martinon). RAVEL: *Introduction & Allegro for Harp, Flute, Clarinet & String Quartet* (with members of the Kuentz CO)

(M) **(*) DG (IMS) (ADD) 463 084-2

Two rarities – the Tailleferre and Saint-Saëns – make this collection interesting. Germaine Tailleferre's *Concertino* dates from 1927 and contains influences of Ravel, Poulenc and even Stravinsky peeping over the composer's shoulder. It is elegantly written and not without its own degree of urbanity, even if the lyrical element is comparatively diffuse. The three movements have an attractive impetus, with the jolly finale developing real exuberance. Saint-Saëns's *Morceau de concert* was written when he was 83 years old. Its four miniature movements – the dainty Scherzo only runs for 1'54" – have a structure which has much in common with that of the *Second Piano Concerto.* But the work's charm rests on its delicacy of texture and the skill with which the accompaniment is tailored, so that it supports but never overwhelms the soloist. Yet the invention has characteristic facility. Both performances are superb, with Martinon providing stylish accompaniments in good (1969) DG sound. The Ravel and Boieldieu performances are both stylish, but neither is quite the finest available, and the sound is not ideally full either. A pity that the Ginastera *Concerto*, originally on the Martinon disc, was dropped, for this disc plays for under 65 minutes.

INSTRUMENTAL RECITALS

The Art of the Piano

'*The Art of the Piano*': *Great Pianists of the 20th Century*: (Paderewski; Hofmann; Rachmaninov; Moiseiwitsch; Horowitz; Cziffra; Myra Hess; Rubinstein; Planté; Cortot; Backhaus; Edwin Fischer; Gilels; Richter; Michelangeli; Gould; Arrau)
(*) Warner/NVC Arts **DVD 3984 29199-2; Video 3984 29199-3

This fascinating DVD and video is in the line of '*The Art of Conducting*'. Unfortunately it is musically flawed because so many of the most interesting visual images are taken from old films and cinema sound-tracks which, with their inherent unsteadiness and fluctuations of timbre and pitch, have in the past been notoriously unkind to the piano. Most of the examples here offer marbled tone and harmonic distortion to varying degrees. However, the video's introduction still brings a spectacular display of technical wizardry. We see and hear a kaleidoscope of stormy performances of Beethoven's *Appassionata Sonata* edited together in a rapid ongoing sequence, with Solomon first (in 1956), swiftly followed by Arrau (1983), then Dame Myra Hess (1945), Sviatoslav Richter (1992) and finally the aristocratic Artur Rubinstein (1975). Even with such short snippets, the different pianistic personalities of the five players emerge vividly.

We next focus on Paderewski, Prime Minister as well as a somewhat eccentric musician, but an artist whose personal magnetism projected strongly. Like Liszt, whose music he plays, he was irresistible to women; hence his success in a 1936 Hollywood movie, *Moonlight Serenade*. Josef Hofmann, a legend among fellow pianists, is much more patrician: his approach to the ubiquitous Rachmaninov *C sharp minor Prelude* has no nonsense about it. Rachmaninov follows on, playing his own music with natural authority, and then we meet one of his greatest contemporary interpreters, Moiseiwitsch. A pity there is not more of the *Second Piano Concerto* (conducted by Constant Lambert) as the plum-label HMV records of this work were considered by some collectors even finer than the composer's own set with Stokowski.

The extraordinary dash of Horowitz (filmed in the Carnegie Hall in 1968) is seen in Scriabin and Bizet, his hands (to quote Támás Vásáry) 'like race horses!' virtually matched by those of the underrated Cziffra in Liszt.

Dame Myra Hess always felt intimidated by the recording studio, but here her performance of the first movement of Beethoven's *Appassionata Sonata* (of which we have previously heard a brief excerpt) demonstrates the full power and concentration of her live performances. Rubinstein follows magisterially with Chopin's *A flat Polonaise* (in 1953), then creates magic in the closing pages of the first movement of Beethoven's *Fourth Concerto*, with Antal Dorati 15 years later; and here the recording is faithful enough to make a real highlight.

But perhaps it is Cortot who provides the most intriguing cameo in the first part of the video. We see and hear him playing *The poet speaks* from *Kinderszenen* to a 1953 masterclass, commenting throughout Schumann's intimate reverie,

and suggesting that the performer's aim should be 'to dream the piece rather than play it'.

Backhaus (filmed during his Decca recording sessions) now plays the slow movement of his favourite concerto, Beethoven's *Fourth*. He quotes Hans Richter who called it the 'Greek' concerto. In this central movement, Backhaus tells us, 'Orpheus pleads to set Eurydice free; he meets with fierce resistance before his entreaties are answered'.

We move on to Edwin Fischer's pioneering Bach with its 'luminous' sound-quality and intellectual spontaneity and then meet a very young Gilels in a Soviet wartime propaganda film playing Rachmaninov to a carefully staged group of Russian service personnel. Cut to his electrifying and extraordinarily imaginative 1959 performance of the cadenza from the first movement of Tchaikovsky's *B flat minor Piano Concerto* (conducted by André Cluytens). This is followed immediately by Sviatoslav Richter, with his 'overwhelming presence' and extraordinary visceral bravura in the finale of the same work, and a comparable 'transcendental virtuosity' in a performance of Chopin's *Revolutionary* study.

After that, Michelangeli's narcissistically self-aware keyboard personality makes a strange contrast, but his immaculate performance of a Scarlatti sonata is blurred by poor sound. Glenn Gould makes his entry playing Bach eccentrically, with intrusive vocalise, but is then heard at his most magnetically inspirational in partnership with Bernstein in the closing part of the first movement of the *D minor Clavier Concerto*, where he is totally absorbed in creating an extraordinary diminuendo. But it is Claudio Arrau who has the last word, and he is just as articulate talking about music-making as he is at the keyboard, where his closing excerpt from Beethoven's last, *C minor*, *Piano Sonata* is played with a beauty and concentration to transcend the recorded sound.

The Golden Age of the Piano

'*The Golden Age of the Piano*' (Documentary written and narrated by David Duval) including excerpts from performances by **Claudio Aurau** (LISZT; MENDELSSOHN); **Rudolf Serkin** (BEETHOVEN; SCHUBERT); **Vladimir Horowitz** (SCRIABIN); **Glenn Gould** (BACH); **Wanda Landowska** (Folk Dance); **Dame Myra Hess** (BEETHOVEN); **Artur Rubinstein** (MENDELSSOHN); **Alexander Brailowsky** (CHOPIN); **Ignacy Paderewski** (PADEREWSKI; CHOPIN); **Josef Hofmann** (RACHMANINOV); **Percy Grainger** (GRAINGER); **Alfred Cortot** (DEBUSSY); **Van Cliburn** (TCHAIKOVSKY; SCHUMANN). **Bonus:** BEETHOVEN: *Piano Concerto 4 in G, Op. 58* (Arrau, Phd. O, Riccardo Muti)
*(*) Ph. **DVD** 075 092-9 (Director: Clark Santee; Producer: Peter Rosen)

A great disappointment. Although David Duval's narrated history of the piano is sound enough and is quite well illustrated with vintage film, the illustrating musical excepts are tantalizing snippets, usually with voiceover, and often the sound-quality is poor, while the picture-quality is variable. Few would want to watch this through more than once.

The Art of the Violin

'The Art of the Violin' (Written and directed by Bruno Monsaingeon). With Elman, Enescu, Ferras, Francescatti, Goldstein, Grumiaux, Heifetz, Kogan, Kreisler, Menuhin, Milstein, Neveu, Oistrakh, Rabin, Stern, Szeryng, Szigeti, Thibaud, Ysaÿe; and with commentaries by Perlman, Gitlis, Haendel, Hahn, Rostropovich and Menuhin
*** Warner/NVC Arts **DVD** 5 8573-85801-2

Bruno Monsaingeon made a strong impression with his revealing studies of Sviatoslav Richter and David Oistrakh. As a glance at the list of artists here shows, he offers a glimpse of some of the great violinists of the last century and includes archival footage that will not only be new to many but, since some has only just come to light, new to all.

Virtuosity is common to all and transcendental in many, but it is the originality of their sound-world that is at the centre of Monsaingeon's opening argument, which explores the expressive individuality and sonority of great violinists.

No one listening to Szigeti or Kreisler, Oistrakh or Elman – and above all Heifetz – is ever in the slightest doubt as to who was playing. There are excellent commentaries by Itzhak Perlman, Ida Haendel and the splendid Ivry Gitlis; only Hilary Hahn is completely out of her depth in their company.

There is rare footage of Thibaud and Ginette Neveu playing the closing bars of the Chausson *Poème* in Prague and an interesting montage of part of the Mendelssohn *Concerto* in which the soloists (Oistrakh, Stern, Christian Ferras, Milstein, Menuhin, Grumiaux, Heifetz and Elman) change, thus bringing home their differences in tonal production and their rich diversity of approach.

Other rarities include a glimpse of Ysaÿe from 1912, looking like an emperor! This thoughtful and intelligent production can be warmly recommended. Incidentally, on the credits nearly every European TV station is listed as supporting this venture, but neither the BBC nor Channel 4 is among them – further evidence, perhaps, of the declining cultural ambition of British television in the last decade.

Other Instrumental Recitals

Amadeus Quartet

Westminster, DG and EMI Recordings (1951–7): HAYDN: *The Seven Last Words of our Saviour on the Cross; String Quartets 57 in G; 58 in C, Op. 54/1–2; 67 in B flat, Op. 64/3; 72 in C; 74 in G min. (Rider), Op 74/1 & 3; 81 in G, Op. 77/1; 83 in B flat, Op. 103.* HOFFSTETTER: *String Quartet in F (Serenade)* (attrib. HAYDN, *Op. 3/5*). SCHUBERT: *String Quartets 10 in E flat, D.87; 8 in B flat, D.112; 13 in A min., D.804; 14 in D min. (Death and the Maiden); 15 in G, D.887; Quartettsatz, D.703.* MENDELSSOHN: *Capriccio in E min., Op. 81.* BRAHMS: *String Quartets 1 in C min.; 2 in A min., Op. 51/1–2; 3 in B flat, Op. 67*

☛ ✿ (B) (***) DG mono/stereo 474 730-2 (7)

These superb performances were originally issued on either the Westminster or DG labels, and were recorded at Conway Hall, in Hanover's Beethovensaal, or by an EMI recording team at Abbey Road. The performances are of consistently superb quality (*The Seven Last Words* of Haydn is particularly fine), immaculate in ensemble and with a freshness, intensity and spontaneity which the Amadeus players did not always maintain in their later, stereo recordings for DG. Their Haydn *Quartets* are wonderfully refreshing, their Schubert appealingly combines drama with humanity, and their Brahms has the lyric feeling and warmth that make this composer special. The recordings, partly mono, partly stereo, have only the slightest hint of thinness on top, and plenty of body, and the acoustic has a pleasing spaciousness. A superb set in every way.

Anda, Géza (piano)

Edinburgh Festival Recital, 23 August 1955: BEETHOVEN: *Piano Sonata 7 in D, Op. 10/3.* SCHUMANN: *Etudes symphoniques, Op. 13.* BARTOK: *Suite, Op. 14.* BRAHMS: *Variations on a Theme by Paganini, Op. 35*

(M) (***) BBC mono BBCL 4135-2

Géza Anda made a number of records on the blue Columbia label during the 1950s, including a memorable 'Bartók For Children', before migrating to Deutsche Grammophon in the 1960s. (His Bartók and Schumann have reappeared in excellent transfers on the Testament label.) This BBC recording was made when he was at the height of his powers and brings an account of the *Etudes symphoniques* that does him – and Schumann – proud, and the Bartók *Suite* is hardly less fine. The recording shows its age a little, but the recital offers playing of such pianistic finesse and poetic feeling that few will be troubled by sonic shortcomings.

Anderson, John (oboe), Gordon Back (piano)

'*Capriccio*': PONCHIELLI: *Capriccio.* HUE: *Petite pièce.* PALADILHE: *Solo.* KALLIWODA: *Morceau de salon, Op. 228.* PASCULLI: *Concerto sopra motivi dell'opera 'La Favorita' di Donizetti.* FAURE: *Pièce.* DONIZETTI: *Solo.* SCHUMANN: *3 Romances, Op. 94.* FRANCK: *Pièce 5.* SINIGAGLIA: *Variations on a Theme of Schubert, Op. 19*

(M) **(*) ASV CDWHL 2100

The three *Romances* by Schumann are the highlight of the programme: they have more substance than the rest and are beautifully played, while Sinigaglia's ingenious variations on one of Schubert's most charming melodies make for an engaging finale. The decoratively florid *Capriccio* of Ponchielli which opens the recital receives the most stylish bravura from the soloist; but it is completely inconsequential. The *Petite pièce* of Georges Hüe is more distinctive and Paladilhe's *Solo* (in fact a duo with piano) is amiable too, as is the Kalliwoda *Morceau*, although it is rather longer than a morceau.

When we come to Pasculli's cleverly contrived fantasia on Donizetti's *La Favorita*, the tunes are more indelible, and the resulting virtuosity is impressive. Donizetti's own *Solo* is another attractive miniature, as is the lilting Franck *Pièce*. John Anderson is a first-rate oboist and he is persuasively supported throughout by Gordon Back. The recording is very real and immediate. But this lightweight 75-minute concert needs to be dipped into rather than taken all at once.

Andreasen, Henri Wenzel (flute), Anna Oland (piano)

'*Flute Music of the Danish Golden Age*': HARTMANN: *Sonata in B flat, Op. 1; Prelude in G min.* FROLICH: *Sonata in A min.* WEYSE: *Rondeau in D min.* KUHLAU: *Duo brillant, Op. 110/1*

(BB) *** Naxos 8.553333

The Danish Golden Age is, roughly speaking, the period of the artists C. W. Eckersberg and Christen Købke (the first half of the nineteenth century) and it was then that the present repertoire was composed. It is best summarized as slight but pleasing music, and the performances are alert and fresh with good, bright – but not overbright – sound.

Andsnes, Leif Ove (piano)

'*The Long, Long Winter Night*': GRIEG: *Norwegian Folksongs, Op. 66; Peasant Dances, Op. 72.* TVEITT: *Fifty Folktunes from Hardanger, Op. 150.* JOHANSEN: *Pictures from Nordland: Suite 1, Op. 5.* VALEN: *Variations for Piano, Op. 23.* SÆVERUD: *Tunes and Dances from Siljustøl, Opp. 22, 24, 25; Peer Gynt: Hymn against the Boyg, Op. 28*

✿ *** EMI 5 56541-2

A recital of unusual excellence and distinction from Leif Ove Andsnes, devoted to his fellow countrymen. The disc takes its title, 'The Long, Long Winter Night', from one of the *Hardanger Folktunes* by Geirr Tveitt. His programme ranges widely from some of the late and extraordinarily characterful *Slåtter* or *Peasant Dances* of Grieg to the *Variations* by Fartein Valen, the pre-war Norwegian apostle of dodecaphony. Grieg's biographer David Monrad Johansen (best known perhaps for his tone-poem, *Pan*) is represented by two early piano pieces that are of more than passing interest. He also includes seven of the Op. 150 set of *Hardanger Folktunes*, which could be as popular here as they are in Norway if they were given the chance.

Although his symphonies are now gaining ground on CD, Harald Sæverud was arguably at his best as a miniaturist, and Andsnes gives us a handful of his distinctive, original *Slåtter og stev fra Siljustøl*, which have such winning titles as 'The cotton grass plays on a moonbeam fiddle' (variously translated as 'The windflowers twiddle the moonbeam fiddle'). He also includes *Kjæmpeviseslåtten* ('The Ballad of Revolt') that came to symbolize Norwegian resistance to the Nazis during the occupation. A well-planned and imaginative recital, and an exhibition of masterly pianism. Very good recording indeed.

Anraku, Mariko (harp)

'*Music for Harp*': FAURÉ: *Impromptu, Op. 86; Après un rêve.* SAINT-SAËNS: *Le Cygne.* HANDEL: *Prelude & Toccata in C min.* SALZEDO: *Variations on a theme in Ancient Style.* ROTA: *Saraband & Toccata* (the above five items with William De Rosa (cello)). SATIE: *Gymnopédie 1.* HINDEMITH: *Sonata.* DOMENICO SCARLATTI: *Sonatas in C min. & G.* (unidentified). DEBUSSY: *La fille aux cheveaux de lin*
(BB) *(*) EMI Encore 5 85710-2 [5 85711]

There have been few solo harp CDs over the years, so this one is welcome, despite its limitations, the main problem being that the recording is so resonant that sharpness of articulation is blunted, which adversely affects the classical pieces by Scarlatti and Handel. The music which is most effective is atmospheric: Satie, Debussy, Fauré and (more surprisingly) the finale of the Hindemith *Sonata*, which is magical. The Salzedo and Rota works are also enjoyable. However, it was a curious idea to include five items which require a cello to play the melodic line. The documentation, too, is poor.

Antonelli, Claudia (harp)

Music for Harp and Violin: CLEMENTI: *Andante and Variations.* VIOTTI: *Harp Sonata.* POLLINI: *Capriccio and Aria with Variations; Theme and Variations.* ROSSINI: *Allegretto; Harp Sonata; Violin and Harp Sonata.* DONIZETTI: *Violin and Harp Sonata* (both with Alberto Ambrosini, violin). BOCHSA: *Fantasia on Bellini's 'I Capuleti e Montecchi'.* ROCCHIS: *Fantasia on Bellini's 'Casta Diva'*
(BB) * Naxos 8.554252

For the most part this is prettily attractive music, the most substantial work being the 16-minute Viotti *Sonata*, which gives the programme a bit of weight. Claudia Antonelli plays well enough, though from time to time a hint of blandness creeps in, and, although the two short sonatas with violin add tonal variety, Alberto Ambrosini's timbre is hardly beautiful, with unstable intonation, and one or two really disagreeable passages. The harp is recorded adequately, but with the higher registers leaning towards harshness.

Argerich, Martha (piano)

CHOPIN: *Scherzo 3 in C sharp min., Op. 39; Barcarolle in F sharp min., Op. 60.* BRAHMS: *2 Rhapsodies, Op. 79.* PROKOFIEV: *Toccata, Op. 11.* RAVEL: *Jeux d'eau.* LISZT: *Hungarian Rhapsody 6; Piano Sonata in B min.*
(M) (**) DG 447 430-2

This particular 'Legendary Recording' in DG's series of 'Originals' presents Argerich's remarkable début LP recital, recorded for DG in 1961. The phenomenal technique (she was twenty-one at the time) is as astonishing as the performances are musically exasperating. This artist's charismatic impulsiveness is well known, but in presenting Chopin and Brahms she is too impetuous by half, although *Jeux d'eau* brings a certain Ravelian magic. The Liszt *Sonata* has been added on; it dates from a decade later and yet again, although the bravura is breathtaking and there is no lack of spontaneity, the work's architecture and indeed its breadth are to some extent sacrificed to the insistent forward impulse of the playing. Good but not exceptional recording, a bit hard in the Liszt, though that may well reflect faithfully the percussive attack of Argerich's powerful hands.

'*Live from the Concertgebouw 1978 & 1979*'
Disc 1: BACH: *Partita 2 in C min., BWV 826; English Suite 2 in A min., BWV 807.* CHOPIN: *Nocturne 13 in C min., Op. 48/1; Scherzo 3 in C sharp min., Op. 39.* BARTOK: *Sonata.* GINASTERA: *Danzas argentinas, Op. 2.* PROKOFIEV: *Sonata No. 7, in B flat, Op. 83.* D. SCARLATTI: *Sonata in D min., Kk.141*
*** EMI 5 56975-2

Disc 2: RAVEL: *Sonatine; Gaspard de la Nuit.* SCHUMANN: *Fantaisiestücke, Op. 12*
*** EMI 5 57101-2

Electrifying playing, even by Argerich's own standards. The Prokofiev *Seventh Sonata* is given with demonic abandon, and the commanding performances by Horowitz, Pollini and Pletnev seem almost measured by comparison. The Bartók is hardly less astonishing, and the same must be said of Ginastera's *Danzas argentinas.* The Scarlatti is wonderfully elegant, and the Bach and Chopin are gripping. Fine though her studio recordings are, these have an inflammable quality that is special. The recordings are a bit forward, but with playing like this, who cares!

Art of Brass, Copenhagen

'*From the Merry Life of a Spy*' (Music for Brass Quintet): HOLMBOE: *Quintets 1, Op. 79; 2, Op. 136.* NORHOLM: *From the Merry Life of a Spy. Op. 156.* NORDENTOFT: *3 Studies.* JORGENSEN: *Quintet.* ANDRESEN: *3 Norwegian Dances*
*** dacapo 8.226001

The Art of Brass, Copenhagen, was formed in 1996 and won first prize in the Eighth International Brass Quintet Competition in Narbonne four years later. Small wonder, for they are technically immaculate and their virtuosity is lightly worn in this record of Danish music for brass. By far the most substantial pieces here are the two *Brass Quintets* by Vagn Holmboe, the *First* commissioned in 1960 by the New York Wind Quintet and the *Second* written in 1979 for the tenth anniversary of the Copenhagen Brass Quintet. The writing is masterly and always both individual and vital. The disc takes its title, '*From the Merry Life of a Spy*', from Ib Nørholm's short piece whose inspiration derives, the composer tells us, from the many different muting possibilities of the ensemble, which prompted him to try and write a spy story on the John Le Carré model 'with a hush-hush conspiracy in the first movement and a shoot-out in the last'. The *Three Norwegian Dances* of 1990 by Mogens Andresen are inventive and entertaining (the composer, born in 1945, is himself a trombonist) and the companion pieces, the amiable wartime *Quintet* by Axel Jørgensen and the far less amiable *Studies* by Anders Nordentoft, complete a stimulating and brilliantly played disc.

Barere, Simon (piano)

'The Complete HMV Recordings, 1934–6': LISZT: Etude de concert (La leggierezza), G.144/2. Années de pèlerinage, 2nd Year (Italy): Sonetto 104 del Petrarca, G.161/5. Gnomenreigen, G.145/2; Réminiscences de Don Juan, G.418 (2 versions); Rapsodie espagnole, G.254; Valse oubliée 1, G.215. CHOPIN: Scherzo 3 in C sharp min., Op. 39; Mazurka 38 in F sharp min., Op. 59/3; Waltz 5 in A flat, Op. 42. BALAKIREV: Islamey (2 versions). BLUMENFELD: Etude for the Left Hand. GLAZUNOV: Etude in C, Op. 31/1. SCRIABIN: Etudes: in C sharp min., Op. 2/1; in D sharp min., Op. 8/12 (2 versions). LULLY/GODOWSKI: Gigue in E. RAMEAU/GODOWSKI: Tambourin in E min. SCHUMANN: Toccata in C, Op. 7 (2 versions)
⊙ (***) Appian mono CDAPR 7001 (2)

This two-CD set offers all of Barere's HMV recordings, made in the mid-1930s, including the alternative takes he made in the studio. What can one say of his playing without exhausting one's stock of superlatives? His fingerwork is quite astonishing and his virtuosity almost in a class of its own. The set contains an absolutely stunning account of the Réminiscences de Don Juan, and his Islamey knocks spots off any successor's in sheer virtuosity and excitement; it is altogether breathtaking, and much the same might be said of his Rapsodie espagnole. Nor is there any want of poetry – witness the delicacy of the Scriabin C sharp minor Etude or Liszt's La leggierezza. Readers wanting to investigate this legendary artist should start here. One of the most important functions of the gramophone is to chart performance traditions that would otherwise disappear from view, and this set is one to celebrate.

Barrueco, Manuel (guitar)

VILLA-LOBOS: Preludes 1–5; Chôros 1 in E min. BROUWER: Danza caracteristica; Canticum; Canción de cuna (Berceuse); Elogio de la danza; Ojos brujos; Guajira criolla; Julián orbon: Preludio y danza
(M) *** EMI 5 66576-2

The Cuban guitarist Manuel Barrueco is the latest star in the line of great guitarists which began with Segovia and includes, of course, both John Williams and Julian Bream. His breadth of repertoire is remarkable and his playing is often electrifying, yet showing the most subtly imaginative touches in the control of rhythm, colour and dynamics. Barrueco is naturally at home in the music of his compatriots Leo Brouwer and the young Julián Orbon. The latter was a pupil of Aaron Copland, but his Preludio y danza comes nearer to the world of Villa-Lobos, with which Barrueco also has a ready affinity.

The Brouwer pieces, including the Canticum (dazzlingly vibrant and evocative by turns), the deliciously seductive Canción de cuna, the haunting Elogio de la danza and the Guajira criolla with its enticing opening pizzicatos (violin style), are all marvellously done. Barrueco is perhaps not quite as winningly flexible as Bream in the famous Third Prelude of Villa-Lobos, but he makes No. 4 totally his own with a magical vibrato on the repeated tenutos. The Chôros is played with engaging intimacy, and the recording cannot be faulted.

'Cantos y danzas' (with (i) Barbara Hendricks (soprano), (ii) Emmanuel Pahud, flute): TRAD.: Danza del altipiano. BARRIOS: Cueca danza chilena; Danza para guaya; Una Limosa por el amor de Dios; La Catedral (Preludio; Andante religioso; Allegro solemne). PONCE: Estrellita; Scherzino mexicano. (i) VILLA-LOBOS: Bachianas brasileiras 5: Aria. GNATTALI: Dansa brasileira. GRENET: Drume negrita. LAURO: Vals criollo (Natalia).(ii) PIAZOLLA: La Muerte del angel; Histoire du tango
(M) *** EMI 5 56578-2

Manuel Barrueco is a master guitarist if ever there was one. His superb technique is matched by the most subtle inflexions of rubato and light and shade. The present disc is his finest so far. He opens with the traditional Peruvian Dance of the High Plain, which has total spontaneity of feeling, and he continues with music of Augustin Barrios Mangoré, to which he is naturally attuned. The fluttering tremolo of Una Limosa is particularly dazzling, but the three pieces which evoke the Cathedral in Montevideo are even more compelling. Ponce's seductive Estrellita and delicious Scherzino mexicano bring a light-hearted interlude, before he is joined by Barbara Hendricks for a sensuously passionate account of the famous Aria in Villa-Lobos's Fifth Bachiasas brasileiras.

But in many ways the highlight of the programme lies with the music of Piazzolla. In the four contrasted movements of the Histoire du tango their Argentinian composer attempts to enhance that dance form for concert music in the way that Chopin re-created the Polish mazurka. Here Emmanuel Pahud's radiant flute joins him in the evocations of Argentinian night life, to colourful and sparkling effect.

'Cuba!': LECUONA: La Comparsa; Dana Lecami; A la Antiga. BROUWER: Preludio; Rito de los Orisbas. FARINAS: Cancón triste; Preludio. UBIETA: New York Rush (Theme from El Super). ANGULO: Cantos Yoraba de Cuba. ARDEVOL: Sonata
(M) **(*) EMI 5 56757-2

Manuel Barrueco, Cuban by birth, is clearly at home in this late-evening programme of mostly gentle music. The three opening Lecuona pieces are totally seductive, as is Brouwer's lovely Preludio and the haunting Theme from El Super, which is built on a rhythmic bass ostinato of Caribbean extraction. Even the series of nine brief vignettes which make up Angulo's Cantos Yoraba, and which are based directly on folk melodies, are primarily evocative (No. 4, Borotití, is like a berceuse). And it is only in Ardévol's Sonata with its central variations and vibrant closing Danza that the music becomes really animated.

This is maintained in the closing group of five Dances and Evocacións from Brouwer's Rito de los Orisbas, which bring plenty of chances for rhythmic bravura. (They should have been individually cued, however.) Barrueco plays with a spontaneous, ruminative style, and he is most naturally recorded (at Abbey Road).

Bate, Jennifer (organ)

'From Stanley to Wesley' (Eighteenth-century organ music on period instruments from Adlington Hall, the Dolmetsch Collection, St Michael's Mount, Kenwood House, Killerton House, Everingham Chapel)
(BB) **(*) Regis RRC 5002 (5)

Volume 1: READING: Airs for French Horns & Flutes. STANLEY: Voluntaries, Op. 5/7 & 10; Op. 6/5 & 8; Op. 7/3. HANDEL: Fugues in G min.; in B flat. ROSEINGRAVE:

Voluntary in G min. TRAVERS: *Voluntary in D min. & major.* WALOND: *Voluntary in A min.* RUSSELL: *Voluntary in E min.* S. WESLEY: *Short Pieces 7 & 12; Voluntary, Op. 6/1*

(BB) *** Regis RRC 1113

Volume 2: GREENE: *Voluntary in C min.* STANLEY: *Voluntaries, Op. 5/6 & 9; Op. 6/7 & 9; Op. 7/2.* HANDEL: *Voluntary in C; Fugue in A min.* LONG: *Voluntary in D min.* WALOND: *Voluntary in B min.* NARES: *Introduction & Fugue in F.* RUSSELL: *Voluntary in A min.* S. WESLEY: *Short Piece 9 in F; Voluntaries, Op. 6/3 & 9*

Volume 3: GREENE: *Voluntary in B min.* STANLEY: *Voluntaries, Op. 6/1, 6 & 10; Op. 7/1 & 6.* WALOND: *Voluntary in G.* HANDEL: *Fugue in B min.; Voluntary in C.* BURNEY: *Voluntary 1: Cornet Piece in C.* RUSSELL: *Voluntary in A.* DUPUIS: *Voluntary in B flat.* S. WESLEY: *Short Pieces 6 & 8; Voluntary, Op. 6/6*

(BB) **(*) Regis RRC 2058 (2)

Volume 4: CROFT: *Voluntary in D.* GREENE: *Voluntary in E flat.* STANLEY: *Voluntaries, Op. 5/1 & 8; Op. 6/4; Op. 7/8.* WALOND: *Voluntary in G.* HANDEL: *Fugue in C min.; Voluntary in G min.* BURNEY: *Fugue in F min.* KEEBLE: *Select Piece 1 in C.* S. WESLEY: *Voluntary, Op. 6/10*

Volume 5: BOYCE: *Voluntary in D.* STANLEY: *Voluntaries, Op. 6/2; Op. 7/4, 7 & 9.* STUBLEY: *Voluntary in C.* HANDEL: *Fugue in G; Voluntary in C.* ROSEINGRAVE: *Fugue 8 in E min.* HERON: *Voluntary in G.* RUSSELL: *Voluntary in F.* HOOK: *Voluntary in C min.* S. WESLEY: *Voluntaries in B flat; in E flat, Op. 6/7*

(BB) **(*) Regis RRC 2059 (2)

Jennifer Bate's survey of eighteenth-century English organ music uses six different organs from stately homes to secure maximum variety of presentation. But these instruments are without pedals, and each produces a sonority that is relatively light-textured, bright and sweet. The five programmes are each made up in the same way, usually opening with a voluntary by Maurice Greene (or alternatively Croft or Boyce), then offering a clutch of voluntaries by John Stanley, followed in most cases by music by Walond and Handel, among others, and usually ending with pieces by Samuel Wesley.

None of these are great composers, save Handel of course, and his chosen examples are extremely minor works. Jennifer Bate did much initial research into available instruments before undertaking the original project for Unicorn, and she plays all this music in impeccable style and is beautifully recorded. So the particular attractions of each volume depend on the items included. Easily the most engaging are the works which use cornet or trumpet stops, which are colourful and jolly, while the *Vox humana* stop, as in the finale of Stanley's Op. 6/5 of the first disc, is also ear-tickling.

Indeed the first volume is a good place to start, with Op. 5/7 by the same composer also proves quite engaging. The voluntaries are usually in two sections, but William Russell's E minor piece is in three, with an imposing opening, and the fugue used as a centre-piece. Samuel Wesley's *Short Piece 12* is a contrapuntal moto perpetuo.

The second volume offers more examples of Stanley's ready facility, notably Op. 7/2 and Op. 5/6, but on the whole this is a less interesting programme than the third, which again shows Stanley at his more inventive in Op. 7/1, while Op. 6/1 begins with a pleasing *Siciliano*, and the trumpet

theme of Op. 6/6 might have been written by Purcell. Handel's *Voluntary in C* brings an attractive interplay of parts in its second movement, while Burney's *Cornet Piece* has a whiff of the *Hallelujah Chorus*.

In Volume 4 Jennifer Bate registers Stanley's Op. 5/8 with piquant skill (this is a three-part work), and Volume 5 brings new composer names, adding music of Heron, Hook and Stubley, although the idiom remains much the same. Volume 1, however, is the CD to try first, and if you enjoy this go on to the two-CD set including Volumes 3 and 4. But only the dedicated enthusiast attracted by the sounds of early English organs will want the complete set, for much of the music here is conventional.

Beaux Arts Trio

'*1967–74 Recordings*': MENDELSSOHN: *Piano Trios 1 in D min., Op. 49; 2 in C min., Op. 66.* SCHUMANN: *Piano Trios 1 in D min., Op. 63; 2 in F, Op. 80; 3 in G min., Op. 110.* CLARA SCHUMANN: *Piano Trio in G min., Op. 17.* CHOPIN: *Piano Trio in G min., Op. 8.* TCHAIKOVSKY: *Piano Trio in A min., Op. 50.* SMETANA: *Piano Trio in G min., Op. 15.* IVES: *Piano Trio.* SHOSTAKOVICH: *Piano Trio 2, Op. 67*

⊶ (B) *** Ph. (ADD) 475 171-2 (4)

It is right that the achievement of the Beaux Arts Trio in the late 1960s and early 1970s should be celebrated. The Schumann *Piano Trios*, for instance, were recorded in 1971, and still remain the safest recommendation in this repertoire, sounding good over 30 years later. Following on in the same year, Clara Schumann's attractive *G minor Piano Trio*, though not in the same league as her husband's, is still very welcome. If in the past we have favoured the EMI Chung/Tortelier/Previn version of the Mendelssohn *D minor Trio* – one of his most richly inspired chamber works – the Beaux Arts are hardly far behind, with playing that is always splendidly alive and musical. Chopin's *Piano Trio* is an early work and not wholly characteristic, but it would be hard to imagine a more persuasive performance. The original coupling of the Smetana *Piano Trio* is included and is given powerful advocacy here; the 1970 sound remains fresh and vivid. It is good, too, to hear the Beaux Arts Trio in some twentieth-century repertoire, and the 1974 pairing of Ives and Shostakovich was an apt choice. Written between 1904 and 1911, Ives's *Piano Trio* is a powerful and memorable work, ending with a strikingly beautiful *Moderato* movement. There is a fascinating contradiction between the superb polish of the Beaux Arts ensemble and the characteristic oddity of Ives's inspiration, with its separation of individual parts. But the result here is splendidly convincing, with the toughness of the first movement and the exuberance of the central Scherzo (a typical collage of popular tunes) presented at full intensity. The Beaux Arts also give a pure and intense reading of the Shostakovich *Piano Trio 2*, in which all the technical difficulties are overcome. The Scherzo has rarely if ever been played so fast as here, and certainly not with the same meticulous ensemble – a tribute to the players' collective virtuosity, developed over many years of corporate performance. The Tchaikovsky *Trio* is as polished and eloquent as one would expect, though some collectors may prefer a bolder approach. On the whole an impressive achievement, with the excellent recordings impressively transferred throughout.

Bergen Wind Quintet

BARBER: *Summer Music, Op. 31.* SÆVERUD: *Tunes and Dances from Siljustøl, Op. 21a.* JOLIVET: *Serenade for Wind Quintet with Principal Oboe.* HINDEMITH: *Kleine Kammermusik, Op. 24/2*

*** BIS CD 291

Barber's *Summer Music* is a glorious piece dating from the mid-1950s; it is in a single movement. Sæverud's *Tunes and Dances from Siljustøl* derive from piano pieces of great charm and sound refreshing in their transcribed format. Jolivet's *Serenade* is hardly less engaging, while Hindemith's *Kleine Kammermusik*, when played with such character and finesse, is no less welcome. Throughout, the fine blend and vivacious ensemble give consistent pleasure.

Bloch, Thomas (ondes martenot)

'*Thomas Bloch Performs*' (with (i) Bernard Wisson, piano): (i) MESSIAEN: *Feuillet inédit 4.* BLOCH: *Formule; Lude 9.6* (with Thomas Bloch Waves O); *Sweet Suite* (both for 9 ondes martenot). WISSON: (i) *Kyriades* (with Paderewski Philh. O, Quattrochi). REDOLFI: *Mare Teno* (with composer, electroacoustic & voice of Susan Belling). LINDSAY COOPER/ABDULLAH SIDRAN: *Nightmare* (with voices & percussion). MARTINŮ: (i) *Fantaisie* (with Marek Swatowaki (oboe), Pomeranian Qt). OLIVIER TOUCHARD: *Euplotes* (with composer, electroacoustic). ROLIN: *Space Forest Bound* (with composer (alto flute or soprano saxophone)): *Heterodyne; Jungle Jingle; Creature Beat*

(BB) (**) Naxos 8.555779

We are familiar with the weird sound of the ondes martenot – one of the oldest of all electronic instruments (invented in 1919) – from the music of Messiaen, and indeed it is he who provides here in the *Feuillet inédit 4* one of the two pieces on this disc which are of real memorability. The other is the Martinů *Fantasie*, an inspired and evocatively imaginative piece which shows the instrument's full potent.

For the rest, Thomas Bloch has resourcefully gathered round him a group of excellent musicians to explore the efforts of contemporary composers to provide musical back-cloths which further exploit his instrument. Bernard Wisson's *Kyriades*, a double concerto for ondes martenot, piano and percussion, sets off with side drum and a rhythmic figure obviously drawn from Stravinsky's *Rite of Spring*, but then the rhythm frees up and becomes more jazzy, tuned percussion join in, and the music becomes first lyrical in a crossover way and then exotic in the ostinatos and glissandi of the finale, ending with a return to the jagged Stravinskian manner of the opening.

Michel Redolfi electronically provides atmospheric textures, but no musical argument, and in the joint piece by Lindsay Cooper and Abdullah Sidran the ondes martenot presides over a mêlée of sounds and voices speaking in English against a backing with a vaguely Eastern ambience. It is all a bit like Steve Reich. In Olivier Touchard's *Euplots*, the most memorable sound is of waves breaking on the seashore, and Etienne Rolin's *Space Forest Bound* apparently simulates a series of animal noises and bird calls from the jungle.

Bloch himself provides several works, including the bravura minimalist throbbing *Formule*, and the two pieces using no fewer than nine ondes martenot, of which the three-movement *Sweet Suite*, which ends the programme, is aurally the most appealing. But it is very difficult to take most of this avant-garde electronics music seriously, and I.M. is reminded of a very quotable American phrase used in one of his favourite movies: 'You can't kid a kidder'. Thomas Bloch tries hard. But he would have done better to have found more Messiaen, and perhaps included some arrangements of real music to demonstrate the potentiality of his instrument, which he plays marvellously and which is very well recorded throughout.

Bok, Henri (bass clarinet), Rainer Klaas (piano)

20th-century Music for Bass Clarinet and Piano: HINDEMITH: *Sonata.* SCHOECK: *Sonata, Op. 41.* SLUKA: *Sonata.* REHAK: *Sonnet III.* HEUCKE: *Sonata, Op. 23.* SOLL: *Lumen*

*** Clarinet Classics CC 026

A remarkably stimulating collection with a group of four diverse sonatas which between them explore every lyrical and virtuosic possibility of the bass clarinet's colour spectrum and virtuosic range. From Hindemith comes an unexpectedly enticing mixture of wit and wan pastoralism, while Rehak's *Sonnet III* is a darkly atmospheric interlude before the most ambitious piece here, by Stefan Heucke. It is in three sections, a *Ballade*, an extraordinary set of central *Variations*, full of original and unexpected rhythms and sounds, followed by a plangent closing *Elegie*. Soll's *Lumen* then acts as a lighter, entertaining encore. The performances throughout are in every way superb and the recording excellent.

Bowyer, Kevin (organ)

'*A Feast of Organ Exuberance*' (Blackburn Cathedral organ): LEIDEL: *Toccata Delectatione, Op. 5/35.* SWAYNE: *Riff-Raff.* BERVEILLER: *Suite; Cadence*

(M) *** Priory Dig. 001

The spectacular sound made by the magnificent 1969 Walker organ in Blackburn Cathedral is well demonstrated by this first-rate recital. Leidel is from the former East Germany, and his acknowledged influences from Messiaen and Scriabin are well absorbed into his own style. The *Toccata for Pleasure* is titillating in its colouring and certainly exuberant in its extravagant treatment of its basic idea, which goes far beyond the minimalism achieved by many of his contemporaries. Giles Swayne is Liverpool-born and his quirky *Riff-Raff*, in the words of the performer, suggests 'isolated flashes of light of varying intensity'. Berveiller comes from the traditional French school of Dupré. His *Suite* is eminently approachable music, with a whimsical second-movement *Intermezzo* to remain in the memory, and a smoothly rich *Adagio*, before the Widorian finale. His *Cadence* provides a lightweight but by no means trivial encore. What one remembers most of all from this concert is the magnificent sonority of the organ, beautifully captured within its natural ambience, and that in itself shows how well composers and performer have combined their talents.

Brain, Dennis (horn)

Chamber Music: BEETHOVEN: *Piano and Wind Quintet in E flat, Op. 16* (with Dennis Brain Wind Ensemble). BRAHMS: *Horn Trio in E flat, Op. 40* (with Salpeter & Preedy).

DUKAS: *Villanelle.* MARAIS: *Le Basque* (both with Parry). MOZART: *Horn Quintet in E flat, K.407* (with English String Qt)

⊶ ✺ (***) BBC mono BBCL ADD 4048-2

This is an indispensable record which does full justice to the art of Dennis Brain in the key classical chamber works featuring the horn. The undoubted highlight of the programme is the Beethoven *Piano and Wind Quintet* in which Dennis shows himself to be the perfect chamber-music partner who yet cannot help drawing the ear at every entry.

This recording (like the Dukas and Marais) was made in the Ulster Hall at the 1957 Edinburgh Festival, in front of a live audience. But they are mercifully unintrusive, and the balance is quite perfect. The recording too is astonishingly real and immediate. It might even be stereo: one can visualize the five players sitting just behind one's speakers: Leonard Brain (oboe), Steven Waters (clarinet), Cecil James (who is recognizably playing a French bassoon), Wilfrid Parry (piano) and, of course, Dennis. The blending is nigh perfect, and Parry's pianism is not only the bedrock of the performance, but the playing itself is very elegant and communicative, particularly the way in which the players echo one another in the development section of the first movement – and how splendidly they play the coda (with a superb flourish of triplets from the horn).

The Mozart *Horn Quintet* is hardly less felicitous. Brain has warm support from the English String Quartet, notably in the lovely slow movement, but here his playing consistently dominates the ensemble, particularly in the joyful closing Rondo. Needless to say, the performance of the Brahms *Horn Trio* is very fine indeed. The withdrawn atmosphere of the slow movement created by the horn's gentle soliloquy is unforgettable; and again the infectious hunting-horn whooping of the finale carries all before it. The recording is distanced in a resonant acoustic and is not ideally clear, but one soon forgets this. Brain's ardour all but convinces us that the Dukas *Villanelle* is first-rate music, and he uses Marais's sprightly *Le Basque* as a witty encore, his articulation dazzling in its easy poise.

BEETHOVEN: *Sextet in E flat for String Quartet & 2 Horns, Op. 81b* (with Civil & English String Qt). SCHUBERT: *Auf dem Strom* (with Pears, Mewton-Wood). HAYDN: *Horn Concerto 1* (with BBC Midland O, Wurmser). MOZART: *Wind Divertimento (Sextet) 14 in B flat, K.270.* IBERT: *3 Pièces brèves.* MILHAUD: *La Cheminée du roi René* (with Brain Wind Quintet). ARNOLD COOKE: *Arioso and Scherzo* (with Carter String Trio). Illustrated talk: Dennis Brain demonstrates the sounds of different horns

(M) (**(*)) BBC mono BBCL 4066-2

It is the three recordings by the Dennis Brain Wind Quintet (Brain himself, Gareth Morris, Leonard Brain, Stephen Waters and Cecil James) which make this collection indispensable. The delectable Mozart *B flat Divertimento* could not sound fresher, and the geniality of Ibert's witty *Trois Pièces brèves* and Milhaud's *Cheminée du roi René*, with its piquant Provençal colouring, is sheer delight. In the Beethoven *Sextet* Dennis chooses to play the second horn part, giving Alan Civil the upper line: the result is a felicitously characterful bravura interplay, well supported by the English String Quartet. Unfortunately the recording of the Haydn *Concerto*, which Dennis plays with characteristic finesse and spirit, produces severe harmonic distortion which gets worse as the

work proceeds. However, in the attractive occasional piece by Arnold Cooke the sound is excellent.

In Schubert's *Auf der Strom*, Brain and Pears offer a memorable partnership, but here the voice is rather too closely miked, and Noel Mewton-Wood's piano contribution is relegated to the background, although artistically he remains very much in the picture. As a bonus Dennis gives an engagingly laid-back demonstration of the different timbres of an 1812 French hand-horn, a modern Alexander wide-bore double horn, and – on his lips – an amazingly effective 'garden' hose-pipe. He ends with the *Prologue* from Britten's *Serenade*, played on the hand-horn, which demonstrates – as the composer intended – the horn's not-quite in-tune upper harmonics.

More Chamber Music: BEETHOVEN: *Piano & Wind Quintet in E flat, Op. 16* (with Benjamin Britten (piano), Leonard Brain (oboe), Stephen Waters (clarinet), Cecil James (bassoon)). HINDEMITH: *Horn Sonata* (with Noel Mewton-Wood (piano)). JACOB: *Piano & Wind Sextet* (with George Malcolm (piano), Dennis Brain Wind Quintet). VINTER: *Hunter's Moon* (with BBC Concert Orchestra, Vilem Tausky)

(**) BBC mono BBCL 4164-2

This recording of the Beethoven *Piano and Wind Quintet* was made during the Aldeburgh Festival in 1955 and, although Britten leads throughout at the keyboard very engagingly, and especially so in the slow movement, the subfusc, poorly balanced BBC mono recording means that the later (1957) performance (see above) is in every way preferable. The Gordon Jacob *Piano and Wind Sextet* fares much better technically, although here the balance is rather too immediate, especially in the Scherzo. The performance is still enjoyable for the gentle melancholy of its slow movment, a charming Minuet and the spirited, syncopated finale. The highlight of the disc, however, is the Hindemith *Horn Sonata* which Dennis plays superbly, with Noel Mewton-Wood an ideal partner. Here the recording is well balanced, as it is in Gilbert Vinter's *Hunter's Moon*, one of Dennis's favourite showpieces, which is presented with characteristoc panache.

Bream, Julian (guitar or lute)

✺ 'The Julian Bream Edition' (BMG/RCA)

The Julian Bream Edition once ran to some 30 CDs, representing three decades of a remarkably distinguished recording career on RCA. Nearly all of these were withdrawn when Bream later moved over to EMI. However, as we go to press, RCA have re-released five of his key discs of Spanish music in a budget box. On the first of these Bream plays the lute. Three of the discs are available separately.

'The Music of Spain'

*** RCA 82876 67889-2 (6)

Disc 1: Lute Music: LUIS DE MILÁN: *El Maestro: Fantasias 8, 9, 12 & 16; Pavanas 1, 4, 5 & 6; Tento 1.* LUYS DE NARVÁEZ: *El Delphin de Musica,* Book 1: *Fantasia 5;* Book 2: *Fantasias 5 & 6;* Book 3: *La canción del Emperador;* Book 4: *O Glorisa Domina (seys differencias);* Book 5: *Arde coraçón arde; Ya se asiente el Ray Ramiro;* Book 6: *Conde claros; Guárdame las vacas; Tres differencias por otra parte; Baxa de contrapunto.* MUDARRA: *Fantasia*

This music was originally written for the vihuela, a hybrid instrument popular in sixteenth-century Spain which looked ke a guitar but tuned like a lute. It was Milán who produced the first published book of vihuela music in 1535, calling it *El Maestro*, and including also instruction. Julian Bream seeks and achieves nobility of feeling in this repertoire and often chooses slow, dignified tempi.

Luys de Narváez followed Milán's first book of music for the vihuela with his *Los seys libros del Delphin de Musica* of 538, which included songs as well as instrumental pieces. The collection Bream plays here is more diverse than the Milán items and he includes some arrangements of the popular songs of the time and some of the earliest know *differencias* (variations). Bream is undoubtedly in his element in this repertoire and each piece is eloquently felt and strongly characterized and, as with Milán, the music's nobility is readily conveyed. It all sounds splendid here on a proper lute, specially when so beautifully recorded.

Disc 2: SOR: *Fantaisies, Op. 7 & Op. 30; Variations on a Theme by Mozart, Op. 9.* AGUADO: *Pieces: Adagio, Op. 2/1; Polonaise, Op. 2/2; Introduction & Rondo, Op. 2/3*

Both Sor *Fantaisies* are ambitious, and each has a central set of variations. Bream's approach is spacious, and his deliberation – for all the variety and skill of the colouring – means that the listener is conscious of the music's length, although it is all agreeable enough. The more concise *Mozart Variations* remain Sor's most famous piece, and the variety and flair of the playing demonstrate why.

Aguado was a contemporary of Sor; the two composers played duets together in Paris. The *Adagio* is the most striking piece, serene and introspective; it might have been even more effective had Bream been slightly less deliberate and reflective and had chosen to move the music on a little more. However, the other pieces have plenty of life, and all are played with Bream's characteristic feeling for colour. The New York recording is truthful and realistic.

Disc 3: GRANADOS: *Cuentos para la juventud: Dedicatoria; La Maja de Goya (Tonadilla); Danzas españolas: Villanesca; Andaluza, Op. 37/4 & 5; Valses poéticos.* ALBÉNIZ: *Mallorca, Op. 202; Suite española, Op. 47: Cataluña; Granada; Sevilla; Cádiz; Cantos de España: Cordoba, Op. 232/4*

This is easily the finest of the five solo recitals here, showing Bream at his most inspirational, and the recording too is particularly realistic. Fotunately it is also available separately on a budget RCA disc (74321 68016-2) with some extra pieces added.

Disc 4: TÁRREGA: *Mazurka in G; Etude in A; Marieta; Capricho árabe; Prelude in A min.; Recuerdos de la Alhambra.* MALATS: *Serenata.* PUJOL: *Tango español; Guajira.* LLOBET: *Canciones populares catalanas: La nit de Nadal; Lo rossinyol; El mestre; La filadora; El testament d'Amelia; Canço del lladre; Plany; El Noi de la Mare; L'heuru Riera.* TURINA: *Fandanguillo, Op. 36; Sevillana, Op. 29; Homanaje a Tárrega, Op. 69*

Disc 5: MUDARRA: *Fantasias 10 & 14.* MILÁN: *Fantasia 22.* NARVAÉZ: *La canción del Emperador; Conde claros.* DE MURCIA: *Prelude & Allegro.* BOCCHERINI: *Guitar Quintet, G.448: Fandango (arr. Bream, for 2 Guitars).* SOR: *Grand Solo, Op. 14.* AGUADO: *Rondo in A min., Op. 2/3.* SOR: *Variations on a Theme by Mozart, Op. 9; Fantasie, Op. 7: Sonata, Op. 25: Minuet*

Discs 4 and 5 were originally Volumes 26 ('*La guitarra romantica*') and 27 ('*Guitarra*') of the Bream Edition. The latter disc

is still available separately and is discussed below. Volume 4 is a mainly digital recital which opens with an attractive light-weight Tárrega group, including the *Capricho árabe* and his most famous evocation, the tremolo study, *Recuerdos de la Alhambra*, which in Bream's hands is curiously muted and withdrawn.

Then, after works by Malats and Pujol (his *Guajira* has some fine special effects), there follows a delightful Llobet suite of nine varied *Canciones populares catalanas*. The programme ends with vibrant, flamenco-inspired music of Turina, including the composer's last (two-part) guitar work, the *Homenaje a Tárrega*. Bream's dynamism in these performances makes one almost believe he was Spanish-born. The final work (consisting of a *Garrotin* and *Soleares*) was recorded at Kenwood House in 1962 and is exceptional in that here the resonance inflates the guitar image; for the rest of the recital the recording is ideal in all respects.

Disc 6: RODRIGO: *Concierto de Aranjuez* (with COE, John Eliot Gardiner); *Fantasia para un gentilhombre* (with RCA Victor CO, Leo Brouwer). *3 Piezas españolas; Invocation and Dance (Hommage à Manuel de Falla)*

This concertante disc is also available separately at mid-price (82876 60870-2) and is discussed in our main volume. With Gardiner in charge of the Chamber Orchestra of Europe, the *Concierto de Aranjuez* has plenty of dash, with the *Adagio* played in a very free, improvisatory way. The *Fantasia para un gentilhombre* is conducted by Leo Brouwer, himself both a composer and a guitarist, and it also has plenty of colour and vitality. Bream is on top form throughout, and the solo bonus pieces again show him at him at his most spontaneous.

Bream, Julian (lute)

Volume 1. '*The Golden Age of English Lute Music*': ROBERT JOHNSON: *2 Almaines; Carman's Whistle.* JOHN JOHNSON: *Fantasia.* CUTTING: *Walsingham; Almaine; Greensleeves.* DOWLAND: *Mignarda; Galliard upon a Galliard of Daniel Bachelar; Batell Galliard; Captain Piper's Galliard; Queen Elizabeth's Galliard; Sir John Langton's Pavan; Tarleton's Resurrection; Lady Clifton's Spirit.* ROSSETER: *Galliard.* MORLEY: *Pavan.* BULMAN: *Pavan.* BACHELAR: *Monsieur's Almaine.* HOLBORNE: *Pavan; Galliard.* BYRD: *Pavana Bray; Galliard; Pavan; My Lord Willoughby's Welcome Home*
(M) *** BMG/RCA (ADD) 09026 61584-2

Bream is a natural lutenist and a marvellously sensitive artist in this repertoire, and here he conjures up a wide range of colour, matched by expressive feeling. Here Dowland is shown in more extrovert mood than in many of his lute songs, and overall the programme has plenty of variety. The CD combines two recitals, the first 15 items recorded by Decca in London in September 1963, and the rest of the programme in New York City two years later. The recording is exemplary and hiss is minimal.

Bream, Julian (guitar)

'*Guitarra*' (Music of Spain): MUDARRA: *Fantasias X & XIV.* LUIS DE MILAN: *Fantasia XXII.* LUIS DE NARVAEZ: *La canción del Emperador; Conde claros; Santiago de murcia: Prelude & Allegro.* BOCCHERINI: *Guitar Quintet in D, G.448 (arr. for 2 guitars): Fandango.* SOR: *Gran solo, Op. 14; Variations on a Theme of Mozart, Op. 9; Fantasie, Op. 7;*

Sonata, Op. 25: Minuet. AGUADO: *Rondo in A min., Op. 2/3.*
TARREGA: *Study in A; Prelude in A min.; Recuerdos de la
Alhambra*

(M) *** BMG/RCA (DDD/ADD) 09026 61610-2

An admirable survey covering 400 years and featuring several
different instruments, all especially built by José Ramanillos
and including a Renaissance guitar and a modern classical
guitar. Bream's natural dexterity is matched by a remarkable
control of colour and unerring sense of style. Many of the
earlier pieces are quite simple but have considerable magnetism. The basic recital was recorded digitally in 1983 at Bream's
favourite venue, Wardour Chapel, Windsor, and is laid out
chronologically. Two additional Sor items, the *Fantasie*, Op. 7,
and the *Minuet* from Op. 25, were made 18 years earlier in
New York and, as they are analogue, have sensibly been added
at the end.

'*Popular Classics for Spanish Guitar*': VILLA-LOBOS: *Chôros
1; Etude in E min.* TORROBA: *Madroños.* TURINA: *Homenaje
a Tárrega, Op. 69: Garrotín; Solearas; Fandanguillo.*
ALBENIZ: *Suite española, Op. 47: Granada; Leyenda
(Asturias).* FALLA: *Homenaje pour le tombeau de Debussy.*
TRAD., arr. LLOBET: *Canciones populares catalanas: El
testament d'Amelia*

(M) **(*) RCA (ADD) 09026 68814-2

This outstanding early recital, recorded at Kenwood House in
1962, was one of Bream's very finest LP collections. The
electricity of the music-making is consistently communicated, and all Bream's resources of colour and technical
bravura are brought into play. The Villa-Lobos pieces are
particularly fine, as is the Turina *Fandanguillo* (which comes
at the end), and the Albéniz *Leyenda* is a *tour de force* and
makes an almost orchestral effect. The recording (originally
produced by James Burnett, with Bob Auger the engineer)
has been splendidly remastered for RCA's 'Living Stereo'
series (the equivalent of Decca's 'Classic Sound') and Bream
is given a remarkable presence, with the analogue background noise all but vanquished. However, the playing time is
only 42 minutes, while that earlier reissue included most of
the present items, plus a great deal more music.

'*Baroque Guitar*': SANZ: *Pavanos; Canarios.* J. S. BACH:
*Prelude in D min., BWV 999; Fugue in A min., BWV 1000;
Lute Suite in E min., BWV 996.* SOR: *Fantasy and Minuet.*
WEISS: *Passacaille; Fantaisie; Tombeau sur la mort de M.
Comte de Logy.* VISEE: *Suite in D min.*

(BB) *** RCA Navigator (ADD) 74321 24195-2

This is a shorter version of the baroque recital which formed
Volume 9 of the 'Julian Bream Edition'. It still includes well
over an hour of music as Bream's superb account of Bach's E
minor *Lute Suite* has been added. The recording is very
natural, and this makes a fine recital in its own right, realistically recorded. A very real bargain in RCA's bargain-basement
Navigator series.

Bream, Julian (guitar and lute)

'*The Ultimate Guitar Collection*' ((i) with Monteverdi O,
Gardiner): (i) VIVALDI: *Lute Concerto in D, RV 93* (ed.
Bream). Lute Pieces: CUTTING: *Packington's Round;
Greensleeves.* DOWLAND: *A Fancy (Fantasia).* Guitar Pieces:
SANZ: *Canarios.* M. ALBENIZ: *Sonata in D* (arr. PUJOL). I.
ALBENIZ: *Suite española, Op. 47: Cataluña; Granada;
Sevilla; Cádiz; Leyenda (Asturias); Mallorca, Op. 202;*

Cantos de España: Córdoba, Op. 232/4. FALLA:
Three-cornered Hat: Miller's Dance. TARREGA: *Recuerdos d*
la Alhambra. VILLA-LOBOS: *Chôros 1; Preludes 1 in E min.;*
in D. RODRIGO: *En los trigales;* (i) *Concierto de Aranjuez; 3*
Piezas españolas. GRANADOS: *Cuentos para la juventud:*
Dedicatoria. Tonadilla: La Maja de Goya; Danzas españolas
4 (Villanesca); 5 (Valses poéticos)

●─→ ❂ (B) *** RCA (DDD/ADD) 74321 33705-2 (2)

The extraordinary achievement of RCA's 'Julian Bream Ed
tion' is admirably summed up by this inexpensive pair
CDs which include two and a half hours of the most popul
repertoire for guitar, plus a small group of lute pieces f
good measure. There is not a single item here that is n
strong in musical personality, and every performance spring
vividly and spontaneously to life. John Eliot Gardiner pr
vides highly distinguished accompaniments for the two just
famous concertos by Vivaldi (for lute) and Rodrigo (f
guitar).

The first of the two CDs provides a well-planned historic
survey, opening with Elizabethan lute music and progressi
through to include three magnetic pieces by Villa-Lobo
Highlights include an electrifying performance of Fall
Miller's Dance from *The Three-cornered Hat* and, of cours
the most famous guitar piece of all, the *Recuerdos de*
Alhambra of Tárrega.

The second collection, which is entirely digital (from 198
3), concentrates mainly on Isaac Albéniz and Granados (n
forgetting the superb accounts of the *Córdoba* by the forme
and the *Danza española 5* by the latter, which are high
praised in our Composer section). It ends appropriately wi
Rodrigo's *Tres Piezas españolas*, with its remarkable centr
Passacaglia. The recordings are of the highest quality and a
excellently transferred to CD.

Bream, Julian and John Williams
(guitar duo)

'*Together*': Disc 1: CARULLI: *Serenade in A, Op. 96.*
GRANADOS: *Danzas españolas: Rodella aragonesa; Zambra,*
Op. 37/6 & 11. ALBENIZ: *Cantos de España: Bajo la palmera*
Op. 232/3; Ibéria: Evocación. GIULIANI: *Variazioni*
concertanti, Op. 130. JOHNSON: *Pavan & Galliard* (arr.
BREAM). TELEMANN: *Partie polonaise.* DEBUSSY: *Rêverie;*
Children's Corner: Golliwog's Cakewalk. Suite bergamasque
Clair de lune

Disc 2: LAWES: *Suite for 2 Guitars* (arr. BREAM). CARULLI:
Duo in G, Op. 34. SOR: *L'encouragement, Op. 34.* ALBENIZ:
Cantos de España: Córdoba, Op. 232/4. Suite española:
Castilla (Seguidillas). GRANADOS: *Goyescas: Intermezzo*
(arr. PUJOL). *Danzas españolas: Oriental, Op. 37/2.* FALLA:
La vida breve: Spanish Dance 1. RAVEL: *Pavane pour une*
infante défunte. FAURE: *Dolly (suite), Op. 56* (both arr.
BREAM)

(B) *** RCA (ADD) 74321 84589-2 (2)

The rare combination of Julian Bream and John William
was achieved by RCA in the studio on two separate occa
sions, in 1971 and 1973, providing the basic contents of thes
two recitals. Further recordings were made live in Bosto
and New York in 1978, during a North American concer
tour.

Curiously, it is the studio programmes which seem th
more spontaneous, and Fauré's *Dolly Suite*, which sounds
little cosy, is the only disappointment (it also brings som

dience noises). Highlights are the music of Albéniz and ...anados (notably the former's haunting *Evocación* from ...ria, and *Córdoba*, which Bream also included on a very ...ccessful solo recital). The transcription of the *Goyescas* ...termezzo is also very successful, as is Debussy's *Golliwog's* ...kewalk, in a quite different way. Giuliani's *Variazioni concer-* ...nti, actually written for guitar duo, brings some intimately ...ntle playing, as does the Theme and variations which forms ...e second movement of Sor's *L'encouragement*, while the ...ntabile which begins this triptych is delightful in its simple ...icism.

The Carulli *Serenade* opens the first recital very strikingly, ...ile on the second disc the performance of Ravel's *Pavane*, ...ry slow and stately, is memorable. The Elizabethan lute ...usic by Johnson and Lawes and the Telemann *Partie polo-* ...ise (written for a pair of lutes) bring a refreshing change of ...yle in what is predominantly a programme of Spanish ...usic. The concert ends with Albéniz's *Seguidillas*, and an ...propriately enthusiatic response from the audience. With ...e overall timing at a very generous 149 minutes, the pair of ...scs comes for the cost of a single premium-priced CD and ...n be recommended very strongly indeed. This is music-...aking of the very highest order, and the CD transfers bring ...e presence and a natural balance.

rodsky Quartet

Music from Vienna, Volume I': SCHOENBERG: *String* ...uartet in D. WEBERN: *Langsamer Satz (Slow Movement)*. ...MLINSKY: *String Quartet 1 in A*
...) *** Van. 99208

...the first of two discs titled 'Music from Vienna', the ...odsky Quartet have devised a fascinating grouping of early ...orks by musical pioneers which give little idea of radical ...velopments to come. The Schoenberg offers a surprising ...nge of Dvořákian echoes from the opening onwards, and ...vořák is one of the influences too in the early Zemlinsky ...uartet, again with Brahms part of the mixture. The Webern ...ated 1905, the same year as his earliest atonal works) is ...en more ripely romantic, with echoes of Schoenberg's ...rklärte Nacht and little astringency. The Brodsky Quartet ...ve flawless performances, at once stirring and subtle, with ...perbly polished ensemble in deeply expressive music. For ...olume 2, see our main volume under composers Korngold ...d Kreisler.

rowns, The Five (five pianos)

...ebut Recital: RIMSKY-KORSAKOV: *Tsar Saltan: Flight of* ...e Bumblebee. BERNSTEIN: *West Side Story: Scenes*. ...UKAS: *The Sorcerer's Apprentice*. GRIEG: *Peer Gynt: In the* ...all of the Mountain King. Desirae & Deondra Brown: ...AVEL: *La Valse*. Melody Brown: FRIEDMAN: *Musical Box*, ...p. 33/3. DEBUSSY: *L'isle joyeuse*. Ryan Brown: ...ACHMANINOV: *Moment musicaux, Op. 16/4*. PROKOFIEV: ...onata 3 in A min, Op. 28: excerpt. Gregory Brown: ...Morceaux de concert, Op. 3: Elégie. BOWEN: *Toccata, Op. 133* ...*(*) Sony CADV 66007-2

...he Five Browns are a very talented family group (brothers ...d sisters) – all Juilliard trained – from Utah, who play five ...einway pianos together, in duet or singly. We heard them ...ve, at their London début in the Steinway Hall, playing in ...e round, and were very impressed. When they work

together, they share the music, passing phrases from one to another, as well as playing in tutti, and the result is visually, as well as musically, engaging. It is perhaps surprising that Sony have not issued this début recital in surround sound SACD or video DVD; but perhaps that is to follow.

In ordinary stereo, with close microphoning, the result, although truthful, is at times a little overwhelming. But the composite performances are spontaneous and exciting, especially *In the Hall of the Mountain King*. Among the solo performances, Gregory Brown's account of the Rachmaninov *Elégie* and the dazzling York Bowen *Toccata* stand out, but Melody provides an engaging *Musical Box* simulation and proves up to the virtuosity of Debussy's *L'isle joyeuse*. The duo account of Ravel's *La Valse* is stimulating, but here the textures are not always ideally balanced; and why did Ryan Brown choose only an excerpt from the Prokofiev *A minor Sonata*, which does not stand up very well on its own? But this CD entered the crossover arena in America and, when it appeared, went straight into the charts, for it clearly has popular appeal on all counts.

Bylsma, Anner (cello)

'*The Violoncello in the 17th Century*' (with Lidewy Scheifes (cello), Bob van Asperen (organ & harpsichord)): FRESCOBALDI: *Canzoni VIII, XV & XVI*. DOMENICO GABRIELI: *Canzon for 2 Cellos in D. Ricercari I–VII for Solo Cello; Sonata in A.* JACCHINI: *Cello Sonatas in A min. & B flat, Op. 1/7–8; in G, Op. 3/9; in C, Op. 3/10*. ANTONII: *Ricercar III in F; X in G min.*
☛— (M) *** DHM/BMG 82876 60160-2

The cello was a new instrument in the seventeenth century, gradually replacing the viola da gamba in favour. The earliest cellos were comparatively large (and were used to play the bass parts in Lully's orchestra in France). By the second half of the century, the instrument had become considerably smaller and more portable, and the strings were tuned C-G-D-G, as favoured by Bach and as used in the present recordings. The music written for this instrument is direct and appealing, the *Ricercari* usually brief and improvisatory in style, sometimes virtuosic, as in the *Third F major* example of Giovani Antonii, but also expressive, as in the *D minor* work of Domenico Gabrieli. The *Canzoni* of Frescobaldi, for one or two celli and continuo, are simple and melodic, with varying tempi. But easily the most attractive music here is the series of *Sonatas* by Giuseppe Jacchini, through composed, using the same melodic material and usually including a brief, fast, virtuosic movement (*Prestissimo* or *Spiritoso*) plus an *Aria* and a finale (in Op. 3/9 a Minuet). Anner Bylsma ('the Rostropovich of the baroque cello') is the superbly eloquent soloist here, given excellent support by her colleagues, notably Bob van Asperen, whose organ continuo richly fills out the harmony. These artists are beautifully recorded, and this is a very attractive disc indeed, backed by the soloist's informative notes

Byzantine, Julian (guitar)

ALBENIZ: *Rumores de la Caleta; Suite española 1; Torre bermeja*. TORROBA: *Madroños*. TARREGA: *La Alborada; Capricho árabe*. LAURO: *Vals venezolano 3*. VILLA-LOBOS: *Chôros 1 in G; 5 Preludes; Study 1 in E min*. RODRIGO: *En los*

trigales. BORGES: *Vals venezolano.* GRANADOS: *Adaluza.*
MALATS: *Serenata española.* FALLA: *The Three-cornered
Hat: Corregidor's Dance; Miller's Dance*
(B) **(*) CfP (ADD/DDD) 575 140-2

Julian Byzantine is a thoroughly musical player; his rubato
and control of light and shade are always convincing. The
playing may lack the last degree of individuality and electricity, and sometimes the listener may feel that the flow is too
controlled, not absolutely spontaneous, but this remains an
impressive recital, generous and varied in content and well
recorded.

Campoli, Alfredo (violin)

'*Homage to Kreisler*' (with Gritton or Wada, piano):
KREISLER: *Praeludium and Allegro; Liebesleid; Liebesfreud;
Polichinelle-serenade; Schön Rosmarin; Caprice viennois;
Tamborin chinois; Rondo on a Theme by Beethoven; La
Chasse; La Gitana.* Arrangements: PADEREWSKI: *Minuet in
G.* WIENIAWSKI: *Caprices: in E flat; A min.* GRANADOS:
Dance espagnole. TARTINI: *Variations on a Theme of
Corelli.* ALBENIZ: *Tango.* BRAHMS: *Waltz in A flat.*
YAMADA: *Akatonbo; Jogashima no ame.* BACH: *Arioso.*
SCHUBERT: *Ave Maria.* MOZART: *Divertimento 17: Rondo*
(***) Australian Decca Eloquence mono/stereo 466 666-2

This disc not only pays 'Homage to Kreisler', but also to
Alfredo Campoli. None of the music here is deeply profound,
but it is all very entertaining – whether it be breathtakingly
showy or charmingly sentimental. Many of Kreisler's encore
hits are included and Campoli's performances are full of flair,
while the Decca recordings, both mono and stereo, are all
characteristically vivid, though the stereo brings greater
depth and richness.

Cann, Claire and Antoinette (piano duo)

'*Romantic Favourites on 2 Pianos*': SAINT-SAENS: *Danse
macabre.* DEBUSSY: *Petite suite.* TCHAIKOVSKY (arr.
CANN): *Nutcracker Suite: excerpts.* BRAHMS: *Variations on a
Theme of Haydn (St Anthony Chorale), Op. 56b; Waltzes,
Op. 39/1–2, 5–6, 9–11 & 15.* MACDOWELL (arr. NIEMANN):
Hexentanz. LISZT (arr. BRENDEL): *Hungarian Rhapsody 2*
✿ (M) *** Apollo Recordings ARCD 961

We are glad to welcome the début recital of the Cann duo
back to the catalogue. With the demise of the Pianissimo
label it was unavailable for some time but it now returns on
the Apollo label, distributed in the UK by Canterbury Classics. It is difficult to imagine a more scintillating piano duet
record than this. Saint-Saëns's skeletons – summoned by an
evocative midnight bell – dance as vigorously as do MacDowell's witches in the brilliant *Hexentanz*, while Debussy's
delightful *Petite suite* – played here very effectively on two
pianos, rather than with four hands on one – is full of charm.
The Cann sisters then produce a rich-textured fullness of
tone for the Brahms *Haydn Variations*, which are every bit as
enjoyable here as in their orchestral dress. Most remarkable
of all are the excerpts from the *Nutcracker Suite*, conceived
entirely pianistically and glittering with colour. Indeed, the
Sugar Plum Fairy has a much stronger profile than usual and
the *Chinese Dance* an irresistible oriental glitter. The *Hungarian Dances* bring beguiling variety of mood and texture and
display an easy bravura, ending with a lovely performance of
the famous *Cradle Song (No. 15 in A flat)*, while the dazzling

Liszt *Hungarian Rhapsody* ends the recital with great exube
ance and much digital panache. The recording, made i
Rosslyn Hill Chapel, is exceptionally real and vivid, and
ideally balanced.

'*Fantasy – Classics on 2 Pianos*': RIMSKY-KORSAKOV (arr.
RACHMANINOV): *Flight of the Bumblebee.* RACHMANINOV
Rhapsody on a Theme of Paganini: Variation 18.
TCHAIKOVSKY (arr. RACHMANINOV): *Sleeping Beauty:
Suite.* ELLIOT: *Berceuse pour deux.* RAVEL: *Ma Mère l'oye*
(excerpts). BORODIN (arr. CANN): *Polovtsian Dances.*
OWENS: *Pianophoria 3.* GERSHWIN (arr. GRAINGER):
Fantasy on 'Porgy and Bess'
*** Apollo ARCD 011

A delightful and generous follow-up recital. There is plenty
virtuosity and, as usual with this very musical duo, they a
especially enjoyable when playing transcriptions; both th
Sleeping Beauty Suite and the *Polovtsian Dances* are sparklin
examples. Elliot's *Berceuse* is quite memorable, but Owen
Pianophoria seems to meander. However, Grainger's Gersh
win *Fantasy* ends the programme with much flair. Excellen
recording.

Capuçon, Renaud and Gautier (violin and cello)

'*Face à Face*' (Duos for Violin and Cello): HALVORSEN:
Passacaille after Handel (Suite 7 in G min.). KODALY: *Duo,
Op. 7.* TANGUY: *Sonata for Violin & Cello.* SCHULHOFF:
Duo. GHYS/SERVAIS: *Variations brillantes sur 'God Save th
King', Op. 38*
*** Virgin 5 45576-2

A showcase for the Capuçon brothers, who hail from Cham
béry and who have won various prestigious awards an
competitions. Renaud studied with Stern, Shlomo Mintz an
Dumay, while the cellist Gautier won the André Navarra priz
in Toulouse. It is not perhaps ideal as a calling-card, as
would have been if it had been able to include the Rav
Sonata, which they recorded on an earlier Virgin antholog
They are impressive artists and their programme is reward
ing, particularly the Kodály *Duo* and Halvorsen's engagin
Variations.

Casals, Pablo (cello)

'*Song of the Birds*': TRAD.: *Song of the Birds; Sant Mari del
Canigo* (with Prades Festival O). FALLA: *Nana* (with
Eugene Istomin, piano). BEETHOVEN: *7 Variations on
Mozart's 'Bei Männern'; 12 Variations on Mozart's 'Ein
Mädchen'* (both from *Die Zauberflöte*; with Rudolph
Serkin, piano); *Minuet in G* (with Otto Schulhoff, piano);
Piano Trio in B (Archduke): Scherzo & Trio. HAYDN: *Piano
Trio in G: Rondo all'Ongarese* (with Alfred Cortot &
Jacques Thibaud). BACH: (Unaccompanied) *Cello Suites: 1
in G: Prelude; 3 in C: Prelude; 6 in D: Gigue.* SAINT-SAËNS:
Le Cygne (with Nicolai Mednikov, piano). BRUCH: *Kol
Nidrei* (with LSO, Sir Landon Ronald)
(BB) (**) Regis mono RRC 1193

It is good to have a sound-portrait of the 'pre-war' Casal
from a time when he was one of the most popular an
celebrated of all international musicians. He had a great h
with the public with his arrangement of an old Catala
Christmas tune, the *Song of the Birds*, and one can hear hir

emoting as he plays it. But his two greatest recording achievements were the pioneering set of the Bach *Cello Suites* in the mid-1930s and his accounts of the Haydn and Schubert and Beethoven *Piano Trios* with Cortot and Thibaud; they have stood the test of time and still sound surprisingly well. The transfers here are clean and serviceable, if the effect is sometimes dated. But this is a good, inexpensive memento.

Cherkassky, Shura (piano)

'*80th Birthday Recital from Carnegie Hall*': BACH (arr. BUSONI): *Chaconne*. SCHUMANN: *Symphonic Etudes, Op. 13*. CHOPIN: *Nocturne in F min., Op. 55/1; Tarantelle, Op. 43*. IVES: *3-Page Sonata*. HOFMANN: *Kaleidoscope, Op. 40/4*. PABST: *Paraphrase on Tchaikovsky's 'Eugene Onegin'*. GOULD: *Boogie Woogie Etude*
(M) *** Decca 475 040-2

It is rare for a miscellaneous piano recital, even a live one, to win a *Gramophone* award, but Cherkassky did so in 1993 with his 80th-birthday programme at Carnegie Hall. The content has a wide range, including several novelties, and the Bach/Busoni *Chaconne* and Schumann *Symphonic Studies* show him at his most commanding. There are few examples of a live recital captured more succssfully on disc than this, and the Decca recording is most real and vivid.

Clarion Ensemble

'*Trumpet Collection*': FANTINI: *Sonata; Brando; Balletteo; Corrente*. MONTEVERDI: *Et e pur dunque vero*. FRESCOBALDI: *Canzona a canto solo*. PURCELL: *To Arms, Heroic Prince*. A. SCARLATTI: *Si suoni la tromba*. BISHOP: *Arietta and Waltz; Thine Forever*. DONIZETTI: *Lo L'udia*. KOENIG: *Posthorn Galop*. ARBAN: *Fantasia on Verdi's 'Rigoletto'*. CLARKE: *Cousins*. ENESCU: *Legende*
✪ *** Amon Ra (ADD) CD-SAR 30

The simple title 'Trumpet Collection' covers a fascinating recital of music for trumpet written over three centuries and played with great skill and musicianship by Jonathan Impett, using a variety of original instruments, from a keyed bugle and clapper shake-key cornopean to an English slide trumpet and a posthorn. Impett is a complete master of all these instruments, never producing a throttled tone; indeed, in the Purcell and Scarlatti arias he matches the soaring soprano line of Deborah Roberts with uncanny mirror-image precision. Accompaniments are provided by other members of the Clarion Ensemble. The Frescobaldi *Canzona* brings a duet for trumpet and trombone, with a background harpsichord filigree, which is most effective. With demonstration-worthy recording, this is as enjoyable as it is interesting, with the *Posthorn Galop* and Arban's *Rigoletto Variations* producing exhilarating bravura.

Cleobury, Stephen (organ of King's College, Cambridge)

'*Organ Favourites*': VIERNE: *Carillon, Op. 31/21*. BACH: *Toccata and Fugue in D min., BWV 565; Chorale Preludes: Herzlich tut mich verlangen, BWV 727; In dulci jubilo, BWV 808*. MESSIAEN: *L'Ascension: Transports de joie*. PRIZEMAN: *Toccata*. KARG-ELERT: *Nun danket alle Gott, Op. 65/69*. MENDELSSOHN: *Sonata in D min., Op. 65/6: Finale; Prelude and Fugue in C min., Op. 37/1*. LISZT: *Prelude and Fugue on Bach*. PACHELBEL: *Ciacona in F min*. JONGEN: *Chant de mai, Op. 53/1*. WIDOR: *Symphony 5: Toccata*
(B) **(*) CfP 585 6172

A well-balanced and generous recital. Perhaps the opening Vierne *Carillon* does not suit the King's College organ as well as it would a Cavaillé-Coll instrument, but the Messiaen *Transports de joie* certainly does, and so does the engaging *Chant de mai* of the Belgian composer, Joseph Jongen. Cleobury is flamboyant enough in Liszt, using the widest dynamic range, but the most famous Bach *D minor Toccata and Fugue* (which the accompanying notes suggest may not be by Bach at all!) is a rather laid-back performance which some listeners might find a bit tame. The *Chorale Preludes*, however, are beautifully played and Cleobury makes Robert Prizeman's *Toccata* (familiar as the signature-tune for the BBC's '*Songs of Praise*') into a catchy neo-lollipop. His closing Widor *Toccata* is magnificent in every way. The recording cannot be faulted and this is excellent value.

Cohler, Jonathan (clarinet)

'*Cohler on Clarinet*' (with Gordon, piano): BRAHMS: *Sonata 1 in F min., Op. 120/1*. WEBER: *Grand duo concertante, Op. 48*. BAERMANN: *Quintet 3, Op. 23: Adagio* (arr. for clarinet & piano). SARGON: *Deep Ellum Nights* (3 Sketches)
*** Ongaku 024-101

This fine collection marks the recording début of an outstanding, Boston-born, American clarinettist. He has a splendid technique and a lovely tone, and he is already master of an extraordinarily wide range of repertoire. The opening Brahms *F minor Sonata* is a supreme test, and he passes with distinction. The Weber *Grand duo concertante* is suitably good-natured, with a songful central cantilena and plenty of wit in the finale.

The Baermann *Adagio* shows how ravishingly Cohler can shape a melting legato line with a breath-catching *pianissimo* at its peak. He then throws his hat in the air in the three exuberant *Sketches* of Simon Sargon, where sultry melodic lines are interrupted by all kinds of jazzy glissandos and uninhibited syncopations, notably an explosive burst of energy intruding into the *Quiet and easy* central section. The finale is like a flashy cakewalk. The recording is truthful, but the piano is placed behind in a too resonant acoustic (the empty Paine Concert Hall at Harvard University), which is a tiresome misjudgement. Even so, Judith Gordon provides sympathetic support, and the playing more than compensates.

'*More Cohler on Clarinet*' (with Hodgkinson, piano): BRAHMS: *Sonata 2 in E flat, Op. 120/2*. POULENC: *Sonata*. SCHUMANN: *Fantasiestücke, Op. 73*. MILHAUD: *Sonatina, Op. 100*. STRAVINSKY: *3 Pieces* (for solo clarinet)
*** Ongaku 024-102

Cohler's second disc is much more satisfactorily balanced. His excellent partner, Randall Hodgkinson, is fully in the picture. The opening of the Brahms *E flat Sonata* is agreeably warm and relaxed, and the Theme and variations finale brings a pleasing interplay between the two artists. Poulenc's *Sonata* is beautifully done, the lovely *Romanza (Très calme)* is cool in the way only a player who knows about jazz can manage, while the fizzing finale also brings a hint of rapture in its contrasting lyrical theme. The warmth of the Schumann pieces, for which Cohler imaginatively modifies his timbre, contrasts with the outrageous Milhaud *Sonatina*, with both outer movements marked *Très rude* but the *Lent* centrepiece quite magical. The three dry Stravinsky fragments make a perfect close to a disc which is outstanding in every way.

Coletti, Paul (viola), Leslie Howard (piano)

'*English Music for Viola*': BRITTEN: *Elegy for Solo Viola*. VAUGHAN WILLIAMS: *Romance*. CLARKE: *Lullaby 1; Morpheus; Sonata*. GRAINGER: *Sussex Mummers' Carol; Arrival Platform Humlet for Solo Viola*. BAX: *Legend*. BRIDGE: *Pensiero; Allegro appassionato*
(BB) *** Hyp. Helios CDH 55085

This attractive and important collection went unnoticed on its first issue and we are happy now to give it the strongest recommendation as an unmissable bargain. Paul Coletti is a first-rate violist and a fine artist, and he opens with an intensely compelling account of the *Elegy* which Britten wrote when he was only sixteen, but which was only recently discovered and premièred at the Aldeburgh Festival in 1984 by Nobuko Imai. The moving Vaughan Williams *Romance* was another posthumous discovery, found among the composer's effects after his death.

Like Vaughan Williams, Bax had a special feeling for the viola and his elegiac *Legend* is imbued with a mysterious Celtic atmosphere. The two folk inspirations of Grainger certainly suit the viola's rich cantilena, and Frank Bridge's *Pensiero* and *Allegro appassionato* make a perfect foil for each other. But the major work here and the most ambitious (21 minutes long) is Rebecca Clarke's three-movement *Sonata*. Not for nothing is the first movement marked *Impetuoso*, and this mood interrupts and engulfs the lyrical *Adagio* finale. Here (as elsewhere), Leslie Howard proves his mettle. Clarke's two shorter pieces, the lovely *First Lullaby* and the similarly reflective *Morpheus*, are, like the *Sonata*, underpinned with English pastoral feeling. All in all a most stimulating and rewarding programme, played with great commitment by both artists, and vividly recorded.

Cortot, Alfred (piano), Jacques Thibaud (violin), Pablo Casals (cello)

BEETHOVEN: *Variations on 'Ich bin der Schneider Kakadu'*. HAYDN: *Piano Trio 39 in G (Gypsy)*. SCHUBERT: *Piano Trio 1 in B flat*
(BB) (***) Naxos mono 8110188

Although the piano trio Alfred Cortot formed with Pablo Casals and Jacques Thibaud was perhaps the most famous pre-war trio, it was extraordinarily short lived – in fact it lasted barely a decade, unlike the Beaux Arts, which cover the best part of half a century, and (again unlike them) had a small repertoire and made few records. The claims of their solo careers meant that they had virtually stopped playing together by the mid-1930s. They are technically immaculate, supremely lyrical and with a spontaneity of feeling underpinned by firm yet flexible rhythm. Ward Marston's transfers give these exalted performances a new lease of life.

Cortot, Alfred (piano)

'*The Master Classes*': BACH: *Partita 1, BWV 825*. MOZART: *Fantasy in C min., K.475; Sonatas: 8, K.310; 11, K.331*. BEETHOVEN: *Sonatas 26 (Les Adieux), Op. 81a; 27, Op. 90; 28, Op. 101; 30, Op. 109; 31, Op. 110*. SCHUMANN: *Sonata 2, Op. 22 (2nd movt); Fantasy in C, Op. 17 (1st movt)*. CHOPIN: *Sonatas 2, Op. 35; 3, Op. 58; Ballades 1–4; Scherzo 3, Op. 39. Mazurkas, Op. 24/1, 2 & 4; Op. 30/1–2; Préludes, Op. 28/2, 4, 5, 8, 17 & 20; Nocturne in F min., Op. 55/1; Waltz 1 (Grande valse brillante) Op. 18*
(M) (***) Sony mono S3K 89698 (3)

This remarkable set offers recordings made during Alfred Cortot's Master Classes at the École Normale de Musique in Paris between 1954 and 1960. Murray Perahia, who produced the CD issue, comments: 'This documents one of the great musicians of the twentieth century playing in an intimate, relaxed setting – not so much "teaching" in the conventional sense of the word, but rather sharing his thoughts about the music he plays. These recordings are rare, not only for the light they shine on his musical thoughts, but also because they are the only recordings of Cortot playing solo music of Bach, Mozart and Beethoven ever to have been released.'

Although the Bach is remarkable in its special individuality, it is the Chopin repertoire on the third disc that is most illuminating of all. Of course there is a great deal of voiceover in French (with translations provided). And there are clumsy moments and scrambled notes. But that does not seem to matter. Even when Cortot in playing a short section of a piece as he works his way through it with comments (as in the *Ballades*), the music springs spontaneously to life, for his playing is totally unselfconscious. The recording is basically good, although there are moments of distortion; but this remains a totally fascinating experience, and pianists will surely consider the set 'a must'.

Crabb, James and Geir Draugsvoll (accordions)

Début Recital: STRAVINSKY: *Petrushka* (ballet; complete). MUSSORGSKY: *Pictures at an Exhibition* (both arr. CRABB/DRAUGSVOLL)
(B) **(*) EMI Début 5 69705-2

It seems impossible to believe that Stravinsky's brilliantly scored ballet, played on a pair of piano accordions, could sound remarkably like the orchestral version; but this phenomenal transcription brings all the colours of the Stravinskian palette vividly before the listener. Only the bold sound of unison horns and the bite of massed strings eludes these virtuosi, and they bring the ballet's drama and pathos fully to life. This is an extraordinary listening experience. Mussorgsky's *Pictures at an Exhibition* is equally ingenious but is far less consistently effective, for one's ear is used to bold brass sonorities and spectacle. *Catacombs* and the big finale do not really come off, although the grotesque *Baba-Yaga* certainly does, played with proper rhythmic venom; otherwise the most effective pictures are those in which we normally expect woodwind chattering: *Tuileries, Limoges* and the cheeping chicks. Nevertheless it's a good try, and the playing itself has astonishing bravura. Well worth sampling on EMI's bargain Début label. The recording cannot be faulted.

Curzon, Clifford (piano)

'Edinburgh Festival Recital': HAYDN: Andante and Variations in F min. LISZT: Années de pèlerinage: Sonetto del Petrarca 104; Berceuse (2nd version); Valse oubliée 1; Piano Sonata in B min.; SCHUBERT: Impromptus, D.899/2, 3 & 4.

(M) (***) BBC Legends mono BBCL 4078-2

When Clifford Curzon was always so reluctant to work in the recording studio, such a collection as this of live performances is most treasurable, despite any flaws. Curzon's account of the Liszt Sonata, given at the 1961 Edinburgh Festival, has obvious slips of finger but is even more persuasively spontaneous than the Decca studio version of only a couple of years later. The impulsive energy lets us appreciate a side of Curzon's genius rarely revealed in his official recordings, the daring of the virtuoso. As for the other Liszt items, they reveal Curzon's magic at its most intense, so that in the Petrarch Sonnet his velvet legato has one imagining a voice singing the words. In the Haydn Variations, a piece that can seem too formal and painstaking, Curzon similarly finds sparkle and fantasy, and the Schubert Impromptus – for him core repertory – show him at his happiest, though his breathtakingly fast tempo for No. 2 with its rippling scales in triplets may initially seem disconcerting. The singing legato of No. 3 is then all the more soothing, and the textural contrasts of No. 4 the more dramatic. The mono sound may be limited but is very acceptable. An excellent note by Jonathan Dobson movingly quotes a remark made by Curzon in 1981 that in his boyhood playing the piano became 'a lonely child's retreat from a happy family'. That sense of wonder was a quality he kept throughout his life.

Daniel, Nicholas (oboe), Julius Drake (piano)

(See below under SNOWDEN, Jonathan (flute))

Danish National Symphony Orchestra Wind Quintet

'French Music for Wind Quintet': POULENC: Sextet for Piano & Wind Quintet (with Ralf Gothóni (piano)). IBERT: Trois Pièces brèves. MILHAUD: La Cheminée du roi René. FRANÇAIX: Wind Quintet 1

(BB) **(*) Naxos 8.557356

The playing of the celebrated Danish Quintet is of superlative quality, remarkably vivid and polished. They catch the gentle melancholy of the central Andantino of the Poulenc Sextet and the quirky virtuoso wit of the outer movements, where the pianist, Ralf Gothoni, is very much part of the ensemble. The music of Milhaud's Cheminée du roi René is not quite at this level but is still full of pleasing and attractive ideas, and the air of easy-going pleasure is well caught here. The Françaix is delightful, but perhaps a shade over-projected. The recording is outstandingly clear and immediate – perhaps a little too immediate, for the Copenhagen recording studio is just a little dry. But this remains a first-class collection, if somewhat overbright.

Danish Radio Wind Quintet

NIELSEN: Wind Quintet, Op. 43. MORTENSEN: Wind Quintet. JERSILD: Serenade for Wind Quintet. WELLEJUS: Wind Quintet

*** dacapo 8.224151

Recordings of the Nielsen Quintet, all variously coupled, are relatively plentiful. The fine wind players of the Danish Radio Orchestra give an expertly shaped and well-characterized account of the piece. In the finale the clarinet variation was not more vividly portrayed even by Aage Oxenvad himself, whose character it was supposed to enshrine. The expressive emphasis a few bars into the first movement and some rather too affectionate phrasing in the Trio of the minuet must be mentioned, but one cannot imagine them causing serious concern. The Nielsen can be recommended alongside the Oslo Quintet on Naxos. Jørgen Jersild was born in 1913 and spent some years in France, studying briefly with Roussel. The Serenade (1947) confirms the positive impression so much of his music makes; it is impeccably crafted, intelligent and of some wit. The Quintet of 1944 by Otto Mortensen (1907–86) is pleasing, not wildly original perhaps, but civilized. The same goes for Henning Wellejus's slight and short Quintet from the mid-1960s. The performances are carefully prepared and strongly profiled, and the disc is worth having for the Nielsen and the Jersild. Good recording.

Claude Debussy Wind Quintet

'The New Interpreters': LIGETI: 6 Bagatelles; 10 Pieces. JANACEK: Mládí; Concertino (with Cassard, piano, Martinez & members of Parish Qt)

(B) *** HM HMN 911624

Anyone who thinks of Ligeti as a 'difficult' composer should sample this infectious performance of the Six Bagatelles, especially the riotous élan of the opening Allegro con spirito and the more wry wit of the finale. There is unexpected melodic charm too in the Allegro grazioso (No. 3), and the sombre tribute to Bartók is darkly memorable. The Ten Pieces are thornier, but still stimulating. The penultimate number is marked Sostenuto stridente and the finale Presto bizzare, but the music remains ear-catching. The two better-known Janáček works are also played with keen rhythmic feeling and, although this is in essence a sampler, it makes a highly enjoyable concert; the recording gives these excellent players a very tangible presence within a nicely judged acoustic.

Demidenko, Nikolai (piano)

'Live at Wigmore Hall': VORISEK: Fantasia in C, Op. 12. HAYDN: Variations in F min., Hob XVII/6. D. SCARLATTI: Sonatas, Kk. 11, 377. SCHUMANN: Variations on a Theme of Clara Wieck. MENDELSSOHN: Fantasy in F sharp min., Op. 28. KALKBRENNER: Nocturne in A flat, Op. 129. LISZT: Concert Paraphrase of Beethoven's 'An die ferne Geliebte'. BERG: Sonata in B min., Op. 1. BUXTEHUDE/PROKOFIEV: Prelude & Fugue in D min., BuxWV 140. GUBAIDULINA: Ciacona. LISZT: Funérailles. SCHUBERT: Impromptu, D.899/4

(B) **(*) Hyp. Dyad CDD 22024 (2)

With the advantage of the superb Wigmore Hall acoustics, Nikolai Demidenko, recorded live at a series of concerts between January and June 1993, comes over charismatically, and the programme is certainly diverse. Mendelssohn's *Fantasy* could hardly be played more brilliantly and this set, which has received an enthusiastic press, is a must for the pianist's admirers, even if perhaps the general collector would not be drawn to hearing some of this music very often. The Liszt/Beethoven song-cycle transcription, for instance, has not very much to offer compared with a vocal version. The Gubaidulina *Ciacona* is a stunning, indeed overwhelming, example of extrovert bravura and (like the spectacular Liszt *Funérailles*) receives a deserved ovation. But it leaves the listener somewhat battered! One welcomes the simpler appeal of the Schubert *Impromptu* with which the recital closes.

Drake, Susan (harp)

'*Echoes of a Waterfall*': HASSELMANS: *La Source, Op. 44; Prelude, Op. 52; Chanson de mai, Op. 40*. ALVARS: *Divertissement, Op. 36*. GODEFROID: *Bois solitaire; Etude de Concert in E flat min., Op. 193*. GLINKA: *Variations on a Theme of Mozart*. THOMAS: *Echoes of a Waterfall; Watching the Wheat; Megan's Daughter*. SPOHR: *Variations on 'Je suis encore', Op. 36*
(BB) *** Hyp. Helios CDH 55128

The music here is lightweight but full of charm. Susan Drake is a beguiling exponent and her technique is as impressive as her feeling for atmosphere. Those intrigued by the title of the collection will not be disappointed by the sound here (the recording is excellent) which balances evocation with a suitable degree of flamboyance when the music calls for it. The evocation of watery effects is certainly picturesque in the Hasselmans *La Source* and Thomas's *Echoes of a Waterfall* (which is exquisitely played), while the Spohr and (especially) the Glinka *Variations* have considerable musical appeal. So have the arrangements of Welsh folk tunes. The definition is very good, while the acoustic remains warmly resonant. A most enjoyable disc.

'*Arabesque*': (*Romantic Harp Music of the 19th Century*): DEBUSSY: *Arabesque 1; La Fille aux cheveux de lin*. HASSELMANS: *Feux follets (Will-o'-the-Wisp)*. TRAD.: *All Through the Night* (arr. Drake). PARISH-ALVARS: *Romance in G flat, Op. 48/3; La Mandoline, Op. 84*. SCHUBERT: *Ave Maria*. ZABEL: *Am Springbrunnen, Op. 23; Marguerite douloureuse au rouet, Op. 26*. POSSE: *Variations on The Carnival of Venice*. ANON.: *Romance (Jeux interdits)*. DIZI: *Etude 21*. SAINT-SAENS: *Le Cygne* (arr. Hasselmans)
(BB) **(*) Hyp. Helios CDH 55129

Susan Drake's second recital, although attractive, is not quite as successful as her first, and the recording, though still warmly atmospheric, has a mistier focus. Having said this, many of the items are very attractive, not least her free approach to Debussy's *Arabesque*, with its element of fantasy, and her exquisite portrayal of *The Girl with the Flaxen Hair*. The Parish-Alvars miniatures, and the delightful Hasselmans *Feux follets* are also very pleasing, and if the anonymous *Romance* is more familiar as a guitar solo, it is equally effective on the harp, as is, more surprisingly, her arrangement of Saint-Saëns's gliding *Swan*.

Duo Mandala (Alison Stephens (mandolin), Lauren Scott (harpsichord))

'*Tapestry*': CONNOR: *Krug*. DAWES: *3 Pieces for Mandolin & Harp*. MITCHELL-DAVIDSON: *Tapestry*. SUTTON-ANDERSON: *Mandalas*
*** Black Box BBM 1088

All the works here have been written especially for this remarkable duo – the gentler harp contrasting and blending with the more tangy mandolin – an ear-tickling texture, with surprising potential for variety. Bill Connor's minimalist *Krug* is dominated by a single rhythmic idea, in circular momentum. The *Three Pieces* of Julian Dawes bring first a mellow *Waltz*, drawing for its mood on Satie's most famous *Gymnopédie*, and the rhapsodic *Phantasy* which follows is ingeniously based on a pair of decorated arpeggio chords; the third piece is a dazzling carillon.

David Sutton-Anderson's aurally intriguing set of eight *Mandalas* is the centrepiece of the programme. Each is brief and concentrated, and together they display a magically glowing range of textures and colours with an exotic flavour of orientalism. A 'Mandala' is a Buddhist symbol of both a deity and the universe itself. It is essentially contemplative, and this mood is immediately created by the work's mysterious opening, with its suggestion of water droplets. The second piece is lively and explorative; the third, featuring the solo mandolin, is improvisational. The delectable No. 4 is like an angelic music-box, while No. 5 contrasts resonant harp chords with glittering mandolin figurations. No. 6 is more meditative, but using a wide variety of textures; No. 7 darts about iridescently, and at the close the work returns to its opening idea, culminating in a mood of gentle serenity.

Paul Mitchell-Davidson's colourful four-movement suite, *Tapestry*, is more richly romantic, especially in the opening *Dance of Limewood*, *Smile of Ash*, and the moments of 'polytonal dissonance' in the jumpy second movement tickle the ear rather than bringing discomfort, even in the atonal obbligato for the central processional Chopinesque chorale. The closing *Full Moon Rising Red* is the most virtuosic and complex, demanding great bravura from the players to sustain its kaleidoscopic mood-changes. But they do so with panache. The whole programme is brilliantly played, providing a continuing sense of spontaneity, and given a recording that is extremely real and present. A most stimulating CD!

Du Pré, Jacqueline (cello)

BACH: *Cello Suites 1 in G; 2 in D min., BWV 1007–8*. BRITTEN: *Cello Sonata in C, Op. 65 (Scherzo and Marcia)* (with Kovacevich). FALLA: *Suite populaire espagnole*. BRAHMS: *Cello Sonata 2 in F, Op. 99*. HANDEL: *Sonata in G min.* (all with Lush). F. COUPERIN: *Treizième concert (Les goûts-réunis)* (with Pleeth)
(B) (***) EMI Double fforte mono 5 73377-2 (2)

Here are some of the radio performances which Jacqueline du Pré gave in her inspired teens. Her 1962 recordings of the first two Bach *Cello Suites* may not be immaculate, but her impulsive vitality makes phrase after phrase at once totally individual and seemingly inevitable. In two movements from Britten's *Cello Sonata in C*, with Stephen Kovacevich as her partner, the sheer wit is deliciously infectious, fruit of youthful exuberance in both players. The first of the two discs is completed by Falla's *Suite populaire espagnole*, with the cello matching any singer in expressive range and rhythmic flair. The second has fascinating Couperin duets played with her teacher, William Pleeth; the Handel *Sonata* is equally warm and giving. Best of all is the Brahms *Cello Sonata No. 2*, recorded at the 1962 Edinburgh Festival.

Fanning, Diana (piano)

'*Musical Treasures*': JANACEK: *On an Overgrown Path* (1911). DEBUSSY: *L'isle joyeuse*. CHOPIN: *Piano Sonata 3 in B min., Op. 58* ***

The American pianist Diana Fanning is a member of the music faculty at Middlebury College in Vermont and also a well-known soloist and chamber-music performer in her native state. She has that special gift of being able to bring music spontaneously to life in the recording studio. The highlight of this recital is a splendidly alive and romantically compelling account of the Chopin *B minor Sonata*, which exerts more magnetism than many accounts by more famous artists. Her account of *L'isle joyeuse* is compellingly exciting too, and yet *On an overgrown path* has a pleasingly poetic intimacy. The recording is real and vivid, the ambience attractive, although a shade over-resonant for the fullest detail to emerge in the Debussy piece. The CD appears to have no catalogue number, but is available direct from Franck Publications, PO Box 96, Middlebury, Vermont 05753, USA.

Fergus-Thompson, Gordon (piano)

'*Reverie*': DEBUSSY: *Rêverie; Arabesque 1; Suite bergamasque: Clair de lune*. SCRIABIN: *Etude, Op. 42/4*. BACH: *Chorales: Wachet auf* (trans. Busoni); *Jesu, joy of man's desiring* (trans. Hess). GLINKA: *The Lark* (trans. Balakirev). GODOWSKY: *Alt Wien*. SAINT-SAENS: *The Swan* (arr. GODOWSKY). SCHUMANN: *Arabeske in C, Op. 18; Kinderszenen: Träumerei*. BRAHMS: *Intermezzo in A, Op. 118*. GRIEG: *Lyric Pieces: Butterfly, Op. 43/1; Nocturne, Op. 54/4*. RAVEL: *Le tombeau de Couperin: Forlane; Pavane pour une infante défunte*
(M) *** ASV CDWHL 2066

This 76-minute recital fills a real need for a high-quality recital of piano music for the late evening, where the mood of reverie is sustained without blandness. Gordon Fergus-Thompson's performances are of high sensibility throughout, from the atmospheric opening Debussy items to the closing Ravel *Pavane*. Perhaps his Bach is a little studied but the rest is admirably paced, and the two favourite Grieg *Lyric Pieces* are particularly fresh. Excellent recording.

Fernández, Eduardo (guitar)

'*The World of the Spanish Guitar*': ALBENIZ: *Sevilla; Tango; Asturias*. LLOBET: *6 Catalan Folksongs*. GRANADOS: *Andaluza; Danza triste*. TARREGA: *Estudio brillante; 5 Preludes; Minuetto; 3 Mazurkas; Recuerdos de la Alhambra*. SEGOVIA: *Estudio sin luz; Neblina; Estudio*. TURINA: *Fandanguillo; Ráfaga*
(M) *** Decca 433 820-2

Fernández is most naturally recorded in the Henry Wood Hall. His programme is essentially an intimate one and centres on the highly rewarding music of Tárrega, although opening colourfully with items from Albéniz's *Suite española*.

The Llobet group of *Folksongs*, and Segovia's hauntingly atmospheric *Neblina* ('Mist'), make further highlights. Later there is bravura from Turina, notably the spectacular *Ráfaga* ('Gust of wind') but even here, though the playing is vibrant, there is no flashiness. With an hour of music and digital sound, this well-chosen programme is excellent value.

Finch, Catrin (harp)

'*Live*': BACH: *Toccata and Fugue in D min.* (arr. Erdelli & Finch); GLINKA: *The Lark*. LISZT: *Le Rossignol* (arr. Renié). WILLIAM MATHIAS: *Improvisations for Harp (Movements I–III)*. PATTERSON: *Bugs! (Mosquito Massacre)*. ALBÉNIZ: *Cantos de España: Asturias*. SALZEDO: *Fantasy on 'Granada'*. PARISH-ALVARS: *Grand Study in Imitation of the Mandoline*. David HELLIWELL: *Kentucky Fried Chicken Rag* (arr. Finch)
*** Kissm KISSANCD 007

Bach's *D minor Toccata and Fugue* introduces this programme rather seductively, an unexpected but surprisingly successful piece on the harp which gives it an altogether more delicate image than a keyboard instrument. Catrin Finch studied at the Royal Academy, she has won several awards and aims to make the harp more familiar as a solo instrument. Her début programme is imaginatively planned and, by being a live recital, has an appealing spontaneity, for the audience response is palpable. Her technique is unostentatiously dazzling. Salzedo's rhapsodic *Fantasy* is entertaining enough, and Glinka's portrait of *The Lark* and Liszt's of *Le Rossignol* are pleasingly evocative, while the Parish-Alvars *Study* is an impressive showpiece. But the highlights are William Mathias's *Improvisations*, slightly ingenuous music but brought colourfully to life, while the climax of the recital is the Albéniz *Asturias*, which is magnetically compelling, with something of the bolder profile of the guitar. Paul Patterson's *Bugs! Mosquito Massacre* and David Helliwell's *Kentucky Fried Chicken Rag*, which is the final encore, are fun pieces, and the audience obviously enjoys the joke. The recording is excellent: the ambience is just right, with an excellent focus.

Firkušný, Rudolf (piano)

BRAHMS: *4 Piano Pieces, Op. 119*. HAYDN: *Piano Sonatas 33 in C min., Hob.XVI:20; 59 in E flat, Hob.XVI:49*. SCHUBERT: *Piano Sonata 21 in B flat, D960*
*** BBC (ADD) BBCL 4173-2

Some memorable playing from the great Czech pianist, Rudolf Firkušný, captured at a recital in the Queen Elizabeth Hall, London, on 4 January 1968. Like Gilels or Solomon, Firkušný was an aristocrat of pianists who eschewed display and ostentation: every note is invested with its proper meaning and beauty of tone. He had a devoted following but never enjoyed the wider popularity of a Rubinstein or Ashkenazy. His selflessness, dedication and artistry shine through every phrase. An altogether outstanding recital.

Fischer, Annie (piano)

BRAHMS: *Piano Sonata 3 in F min., Op. 5*. BARTOK: *15 Hungarian Peasant Songs*. LISZT: *3 Etudes de concert*. DOHNANYI: *Rhapsody in C, Op. 11/3*
(M) (***) BBC mono BBCL 4054-2

Annie Fischer is captured here in an Usher Hall recital at the 1961 Edinburgh Festival, albeit in mono sound. She was an artist of great musical insight who steeped herself in each composer's sound-world. Probably the best thing is the Bartók, which has never been played with greater imagination or sympathy (except, perhaps, by Kocsis). The Dohnányi encore is a delight. Such is the quality of Fischer's playing that the odd smudge or finger-slip to which she was prone in the concert hall do not disturb more than marginally.

Fox, Virgil (organ of Riverside Church, New York City)

'Encores': BACH: *Fugue in G min., BWV 578; Chorales: Jesu, joy of man's desiring; Now thank we all our God; Trio Sonata 6 in G, BWV 530; Suite 3 in D, BWV 1068: Air.* HANDEL: *Organ Concerto in F: 1st Movt. Concerto grosso: Aria.* BOYCE: *Ye Sweet Retreat (arr. Bauer).* MULET: *Thou Art the Rock.* CLARKE: *Trumpet Voluntary.* SCHUMANN: *Canon in B min.* WIDOR: *Symphony 5: Toccata.* ELGAR: *Pomp and Circumstance March 1*
(M) **(*) RCA 82876 71626-2

A fascinating disc in every way – in effect a resurrection of brilliant playing from the past (late 1950s) by a true virtuoso, Virgil Fox, born in 1912, who in his day was the most celebrated organist in America, playing to over six million people. His career at the Riverside Church lasted for 19 years and he made many records; most of his LPs were on the Capitol label and were reviewed by us in the early volumes of the *Stereo Record Guide*. Surprisingly, none appear to have been reissued, but this restored Living Presence RCA disc will do well enough to demonstrate Fox's remarkable virtuosity and the brilliantly clear sound of the Aeolian-Skinner double organ at the Riverside Church (complete with echo-effects). The church ceiling was also treated at the time of the installation of the organ in order to minimize the original absorbent qualities of the surfaces and convert them into sound reflectors, while the recording itself appears to add a degree of harshness in *fortissimos* and to emphasize the dry clarity of the pedals.

Virgil Fox undoubtedly has a fabulous technique and, although the programme itself is not outstandingly interesting, his bravura in Mulet's chorale variations on *Thou Art the Rock* is remarkable enough; yet it is surpassed by the Widor *Toccata*, surely the fastest on record. The tempo of the Bach 'Little' *Fugue* is nicely judged, and the excerpt from the Handel *Organ Concerto* uses the organ's colourful stereoscopic interplay to light-hearted effect. Otherwise the music is given the full sentimental treatment, with slow tempi predominant, even in the very grand *Trumpet Voluntary*, while both the Handel and Bach *Airs* are lush and phlegmatic. Elgar's *Pomp and Circumstance* omits the allegro opening and begins with the *Land of Hope and Glory* tune, which is given a grandiloqent reprise.

Fretwork

'In nomine': 16th-century English Music for Viols: TALLIS: *In nomine a 4, 1 & 2; Solfaing song a 5; Fantasia a 5; Libera nos, salva nos a 5.* TYE: *In nomine a 5 (Crye); In nomine a 5 (Trust).* CORNYSH: *Fa la sol a 3.* BALDWIN: *In nomine a 4.* BULL: *In nomine a 5.* BYRD: *In nomine a 4, 2. Fantasia a 3, 3.* TAVERNER: *In nomine; In nomine a 4.* PRESTON: *O lux beata Trinitas a 3.* JOHNSON: *In nomine a*

4. PARSONS: *In nomine a 5; Ut re mi fa sol la a 4.* FERRABOSCO: *In nomine a 5; Lute fantasia 5; Fantasia a 4*
*** Amon Ra (ADD) CD-SAR 29

This was Fretwork's début CD. The collection is not so obviously of strong popular appeal as the later collections for Virgin but is nevertheless very rewarding and distinguished, and it includes the complete consort music of Thomas Tallis. The sound is naturally pleasing in a fairly rich acoustic and readers can be assured that there is no vinegar in the string-timbre here; indeed, the sound itself is quite lovely in its gentle, austere atmosphere.

'Heart's Ease': HOLBORNE: *The Honiesuckle; Countess of Pembroke's Paradise; The Fairie Round.* BYRD: *Fantasia a 5 (Two in One); Fancy in C.* DOWLAND: *Mr Bucton, his Galliard; Captaine Digorie Piper, his Galliard; Ye sacred muses.* FERRABOSCO: *In nomine a 5.* GIBBONS: *In nomine a 5; Fantasia a 4 for the Great Dooble Base.* LAWES: *Airs for 2 division viols in C: Pavan of Alfonso; Almain of Alfonso. Consort Sett a 5 in C: Fantasia; Pavan; Almain*
*** Virgin 7 59667-2

An outstanding collection of viol consort music from the late Tudor and early Stuart periods; the playing is both stylish and vivacious, with a fine sense of the most suitable tempo for each piece. The more lyrical music is equally sensitive. This is a tuneful entertainment, not just for the specialist collector, and Fretwork convey their pleasure in all this music. The William Byrd *Fancy* (from *My Ladye Nevells Booke*) is played exuberantly on the organ by Paul Nicholson, to bring some contrast before the closing Lawes *Consort sett*. The recording is agreeably warm, yet transparent too.

'Portrait: Music for Viols' ((i) with Chance (counter-tenor), Wilson (lute), Nicholson (organ)): BYRD: *Pavan a 6; Galliard a 6; (i) Come to me, grief for ever; Ye sacred muses.* BEVIN: *Browning a 3.* GIBBONS: *Go from My Window a 6; Fantasy a 6; In nomine a 5.* DOWLAND: *Lachrimae Antiquae; Lachrimae Coacte; Mr John Langtons Pavan; The Earl of Essex Galliard; Mr Henry Noell his Galliard. (i) Lasso vita mia.* LAWES: *Pavan a 5 in C min.; Fantasy a 6 in F; Aire a 6 in F min.* HOLBORNE: *The Honiesuckle; The Fairie Round*
(M) *** Virgin 5 61402-2

A quite outstanding concert, with the consort music nicely leavened by three vocal solos. Much of the atmosphere is melancholic, but with the arrival of the two dances by Holborne the mood (and timbre) changes completely, while the following Dowland *Galliards*, if less upbeat, bring yet another change of character. The two vocal highlights are by Byrd, *Come to me, grief for ever*, in which he outflanks Dowland in dolour, and the beautiful *Ye sacred muses*, both sung ravishingly by Michael Chance. Lawes's *Pavan a 5 in C minor* which follows embroiders a particularly memorable theme and features the use of the chamber organ subtly to fill out the sonority, as it does the touching Gibbons *In nomine a 5*, while in the Lawes *Fantasy a 6* the organ has a delicate contrapuntal role. Excellent – if close – recording.

Friedman, Ignaz (piano)

Vol. 1: LISZT: *Concert Paraphrase of Schubert's 'Hark Hark, the Lark'.* CHOPIN: *Ballade in A flat, Op. 47/3; Etudes, Op. 10/7 & 12 (Revolutionary); Op. 25/6; Mazurka in D; Mazurka in B min.; Mazurkas in D, Op. 33/2; C sharp,*

Op. 63/3; Minute Waltz; Preludes in D flat, Op. 25/15 (Raindrop); E flat, Op. 28/19; Waltz in A min., Op. 34/2. GAERTNER-FRIEDMAN: *Viennese Dance 1.* HUMMEL: *Rondo in E flat.* MOZART: *Rondo alla Turca.* SCARLATTI: *Pastorale.* MOSZKOWSKI: *Serenata, Op. 15/1.* MENDELSSOHN: *Scherzo in E min., Op. 16/2.* BEETHOVEN: *Sonata 14 in C sharp min. (Moonlight), Op. 27/2.* LISZT/BUSONI: *La Campanella.* FRIEDMAN: *Elle danse, Op. 10*

(BB) (***) Naxos mono 8.110684

Vol. 2: MENDELSSOHN: *Scherzo in E min., Op. 16/2.* FRIEDMAN: *Elle danse, Op. 10; Marquis et Marquise; Tabatière à musique.* BEETHOVEN: *Piano Sonata 14 in C sharp min. (Moonlight), Op. 27/2.* CHOPIN: *Berceuse, Op. 57; Etudes: in G flat, Op. 10/5 & Op. 25/9; Mazurka in B flat, Op. 7/1; Polonaise in A flat, Op. 53; Sonata 2 in B flat min., Op. 35: Funeral March and Finale.* GRIEG: *Piano Concerto in A min.* (with O, Gaubert). RUBINSTEIN: *Romance in E flat, Op. 44/1.* SUK: *Suite, Op. 21: Minuet.* MITTLER: *Music Box for the Little Nana, Op. 2/2*

(BB) (***) Naxos mono 8.110686

Vol. 3: CHOPIN: *Mazurkas: in B flat, Op. 7/1; in A min., Op. 7/2; in F min., Op. 7/3; in B flat, Op. 24/4; in D, Op. 33/2; in B min., Op. 33/4; in C sharp min., Op. 41/1 (twice); in A flat, Op. 50/2; in C sharp, Op. 63/3; in C, Op. 67/3; in A min., Op. 67/4; in A min., Op. 68/2; Polonaise in B flat, Op. 71/2.* GLUCK/BRAHMS: *Gavotte.* GLUCK/FRIEDMAN: *Menuet (Judgement of Paris).* LISZT: *Concert Paraphrase of Schubert's 'Hark Hark, the Lark'.* SCHUBERT/FRIEDMAN: *Alt Wien* (plus Friedman talking about Chopin (from New Zealand Radio, 1940))

(BB) (***) Naxos mono 8.110690

When Ignaz Friedman first approached Leschetizky in 1901, the great pianist, then a seventy-year-old, advised him to give up any thought of being a pianist. Naturally he was fired to pursue his goal and perfect his technique, and he was eventually acknowledged as being among Leschetizky's greatest pupils. There is the very occasional reminder that articulation is less than perfect but, the odd inaccuracy apart, this is fabulous playing. The rich and subtle range of sonority he could produce from the instrument is splendidly conveyed in Ward Marston's superb transfers. In terms of virtuosity, Friedman was one of the old school and he did not hide just how masterly was his technique. Listen to his extraordinary brilliance and, above all, delicacy in Liszt's *La Campanella.* Delicacy and imagination are there in abundance, and the three discs offer a treasure house of great playing. Friedman recorded only one concerto, the Grieg, which is let down by poor piano sound and less than distinguished orchestral support from an unnamed ensemble under Philippe Gaubert. But these are records that no piano buff will want to pass over.

Fromentin, Lawrence and Domenique Plancade (piano duo)

Début: 'French Piano Duets': POULENC: *Sonata.* DEBUSSY: *Petite suite.* RAVEL: *Ma Mère l'Oye suite.* FAURE: *Dolly (suite), Op. 56.* BIZET: *Jeux d'enfants (complete)*

(B) *** EMI Début 5 72526-2

Lawrence Fromentin and Domenique Plancade, both Gold Medal winners at the Paris Conservatoire and pupils of Pascal Devoyon, decided to join together as a duo in 1992, and this is their recording début. The results are very impressive indeed. They encompass the wide stylistic contrasts of their programme with sympathy and panache, from the brittle wit of Poulenc and its underlying innocence, to the exquisitely delicate Ravelian atmosphere of *Ma Mère l'Oye* and the gentle charm of Fauré's *Dolly.* Debussy's *Petite suite* is winningly spontaneous, while the perceptively characterized *Jeux d'enfants* of Bizet is the more valuable for being complete, including all 12 movements, not just those familiar in the orchestral suite. The recording is excellent. A genuine bargain in every sense.

Galimir Quartet

BERG: *Lyric Suite.* MILHAUD: *String Quartet 7 in B flat.* RAVEL: *String Quartet in F*

(**) Rockport RR 5007

Like the Hagens, the Galimir was a family *Quartet*, founded in 1929 by Felix Galimir with his three sisters. They recorded the Milhaud and Ravel quartets in 1934 in the presence of their respective composers, and the *Lyric Suite* in 1935 just before Berg's death. Felix Galimir emigrated to the United States just before the outbreak of the Second World War and taught at the Juilliard School until his death. The performances naturally carry authority, though the somewhat dry acoustic of the Berg calls for tolerance. The present transfer of the latter is much better than the Continuum version coupled with Louis Krasne's broadcast of the *Violin Concerto,* with Webern conducting.

Gallois, Patrick (flute), Lydia Wong (piano)

'French Flute Music': POULENC: *Sonata.* MESSIAEN: *Le Merle noir.* SANCAN: *Sonatine.* JOLIVET: *Chant de Linos.* DUTILLEUX: *Sonatine.* BOULEZ: *Sonatine*

(BB) *** Naxos 8.557328

French composers have shown a particular affinity for the flute throughout the twentieth century. The note on the back of this Naxos compilation suggests that one of the reasons for this has been the availability of a group of highly gifted flautists, associated in one way or another with the Paris Conservatoire. They include the soloist on this recording, Patrick Gallois (a pupil of Jean-Pierre Rampal), whose delicacy of execution is the epitome of the insouciant Gallic style, whether in melancholy cantabile or rapid figuration. This is immediately apparent in the masterly Poulenc *Sonata* and comparable *Sonatine* of Pierre Sancan. These are also included on another outstanding collection of French repertoire by the American Flautist, Jeffrey Khaner, whose tempi are very little different and whose phrasing is certainly no less sensitive, but whose timbre is fractionally richer in texture. Patrick Gallois's sound is more silvery, and rapid passages have an attractive, will-o'-the-wisp fragility. He has Lydia Wong as a fine (and by no means always reticent) partner, and passionate too, as in Jolivet's *Chant de Linos* (a touching, very French threnody, interrupted by wild cries). The Dutilleux *Sonatine* also requires great virtuosity in its outer movements, but its central *Andante* is poignantly Ravelian, before the mood lightens for the jauntily capricious finale.

Messiaen's *Le Merle noir* (taken from the *Catalogue d'oiseaux*) creates a poetic affinity with the call of the blackbird. Boulez studied under Messiaen and his *Sonatine* also opens with a simulation of birdsong, before its progress becomes more intractible. It is meticulously performed, to match its intellectual structure, but is not a piece distinguished by melodic lines of the kind found in the other works here. But overall this is as authentic a French collection as you will find anywhere, and even if it is not perhaps as diverting throughout as its Avie competitor, it is most realistically recorded.

(i) Goldstone, Anthony & (ii) Caroline Clemmow (piano duo)

'Explorations': (i; ii) LEIGHTON: Prelude, Hymn & Toccata, Op. 96. HOLST: Japanese Suite, Op. 33 (for 2 pianos). STEVENSON: 2 Chinese Folk-Songs (for piano duet). Solo piano music: HEDGES: (i) Sonata, Op. 53; (ii) 3 Explorations, Op. 45; 5 Aphorisms
*** Divine Art 25024

The key work here is Kenneth Leighton's Prelude, Hymn and Toccata, an immensely impressive and commanding antiphonal work for two pianos. The Hymn, on which Leighton provides a kind of fantasia, is 'Abide with me', but it is so heavily disguised that one has to listen out for it as it enters. After its serene close comes the Toccata, erupting into a characteristically powerful and abandoned Presto precipitoso climax, and ending with surprising abruptness. The works by Anthony Hedges are also exploratory and stimulating, the Explorations based on a single concentrated motif, the Aphorisms producing a fine Lento slow movement, and the Sonata (also with a memorable Adagio) concentrated in structure, with the brilliant Rondo finale nostalgically recalling material from the first two movements, before the animated closing section. Lighter, exotic contrast is provided by the enticing oriental pastiches of Holst and Stevenson, with the latter's Song of the Crab Fisher something of a lollipop. Altogether a stimulating collection, played with commitment and understanding by these two fine artists, and very well recorded.

Goossens, Leon (oboe)

'The Goossens Family' (with Lloyd, piano, Marie & Sidonie Goossens, harps, Fitzwilliam Qt): BACH: Easter Oratorio: Sinfonia. SOMER-COCKS: Three Sketches: 1. STANTON: Chanson pastorale. RICHARDSON: Scherzino. HENSCHEL: Shepherd's Lament. PITFIELD: Rondo Lirico. HUGHES: Bard of Armagh. DUNHILL: Romance. BOYCE: Matelotte. FINZI: Interlude. KREIN: Serenade for Oboe & 2 Harps. NICHOLAS: Melody. SAUNDERS: A Cotswold Pastoral. ELGAR (arr. Jacob): Soliloquy (with Bournemouth Sinf., Del Mar)
(M) *** Chan. (ADD) 7132

This touching tribute to Leon Goossens, a superstar among oboists long before that term was invented, is the more welcome when he made relatively few recordings over his long career. The harpists, Marie and Sidonie Goossens, accompany their brother in two of the most charming items, the Krein Serenade and Morgan Nicholas's Melody, but the rest of the programme is devoted to Leon. These are mainly recordings (first issued on RCA in the late 1970s) which Goossens made after his amazing rehabilitation following a serious car accident. Although the technical facility may not be quite the same as earlier, the warmth of tone and the ability to charm are undiminished. That he was in his late seventies at the time only adds to the marvel. The two most extended items are the Soliloquy which Elgar wrote for Goossens right at the end of his life, and the Finzi Interlude,

superbly played by the Fitzwilliam Quartet, with contrasted sections covering a wide emotional range. Specially welcome is the carefree little Rondo by Thomas Pitfield with its witty pay-off.

Gourlay, James (tuba), Royal Ballet Sinfonia, Gavin Sutherland

'British Tuba Concertos' by EDWARD GREGSON; ROGER STEPTOE; VAUGHAN WILLIAMS: in F min.; and JOHN GOLLAND : Op. 46
⊕→ (BB) *** Naxos 8.55754

A superb – indeed, unmissable – disc. In spite of the moments of bluff good humour in the Vaughan Williams concerto, who would have thought that four such works in a row could be so consistently entertaining? The most ambitious and probably the finest is the Gregson, for it has a real romantic sweep, with a nod to its Vaughan Williams predecessor. The striking, contrasted themes of the first movement are linked, both together and with the finale, which gives the soloist plenty of opportunities for thrilling virtuosity, yet the slow movement, with its string chorale, is contrastingly evocative. The resouceful and inventive Steptoe work is also highly effective, if it is most memorable for its molto calmo finale. The Vaughan Williams we know well and it is characteristically pastoral in its melodic flow, especially in the central Romanza, beautifully played here. The Golland Concerto has a boldly rhythmic opening movement and a catchy, bravura 7/8 finale to contrast with the lovely central Adagio, which pits the soloist against a vibraphone. Yet there is a fine lyrical theme to match that light-hearted virtuosity at the close. The performances are superb. James Gourlay plays with incredible nimbleness and the fullest expressive feeling, and, not surprisingly, Gavin Sutherland and the Royal Ballet Sinfonia give him rumbustious support. The recording is spectacular, to match the size of the soloist's instrumental personality.

Green, Gareth (organ)

'English Organ Music' (organ of Chesterfield Parish Church): LANG: Tuba Tune, Op. 15. HOWELLS: 3 Psalm Preludes, Op. 32. ELGAR: Sonata 1, Op. 28. VAUGHAN WILLIAMS: Rhosymedre (Hymn Prelude). WHITLOCK: Hymn Preludes: on Darwell's 148th; on Song 13. COCKER: Tuba Tune
(BB) *(*) Naxos 8.550582

The organ as recorded here has no clarity of profile, and even the two characterful Tuba Tunes fail to make their full effect. The sound in the Hymn and Psalm Preludes is washy and indistinct. Gareth Green plays the early Elgar Sonata very well but it makes an impact only in its more powerful moments, and it is difficult to find a volume level which reveals the unfocused, quieter detail while not having the climaxes too loud.

Grumiaux, Arthur (violin), István Hajdu (piano)

'Favourite Violin Encores': PARADIS: Sicilienne. MOZART: Rondo, K.250; Divertimento in D, K.334: Minuet. GLUCK: Mélodie. GRANADOS: Danza española 5. KREISLER: Schön

Rosmarin; Liebesleid; Liebesfreud; Rondino on a Theme of Beethoven; Andantino in the Style of Padre Martini. VERACINI: *Allegro; Largo* (arr. CORTI). VIVALDI: *Siciliano* (arr. from Op. 3/11). LECLAIR: *Tambourin.* BEETHOVEN: *Minuet in G.* SCHUBERT: *Ave Maria; Ständchen.* DVORAK: *Humoresque in G flat, Op. 101/7; Songs My Mother Taught Me, Op. 55/4; Sonatine in G, Op. 100: Larghetto.* MASSENET: *Thaïs: Méditation.* TCHAIKOVSKY: *Valse sentimentale, Op. 51/6.* ELGAR: *La Capricieuse.* FAURE: *Après un rêve, Op. 7/1; Les berceaux, Op. 23/1.* ALBENIZ: *Tango, Op. 165/2.* PONCE: *Estrellita.* SIBELIUS: *Nocturne, Op. 51/3.* PERGOLESI: *Andantino.* SCHUMANN: *Kinderszenen: Träumerei.* BACH/GOUNOD: *Ave Maria.* PAGANINI: *Sonata 12 in E min., Op. 3/6.* WIENIAWSKI: *Souvenir de Moscou, Op. 6.* RAVEL: *Pièce en forme de habanera; Tzigane.* SARASATE: *Zigeunerweisen, Op. 20/1.* FIOCCO: *Allegro.* BLOCH: *Baal Shem: Nigun.* KODALY: *Adagio*
(B) *** Ph. (IMS) Duo (ADD) 446 560-2 (2)

Marvellous fiddler as he is, Grumiaux is not an extrovert in the manner of a Perlman who likes to dazzle and be right on top of the microphones; instead, these are essentially intimate performances. Yet when fire is needed it is certainly forthcoming, as in the superb account of Ravel's *Tzigane.* But Grumiaux is completely at home in what are mostly elegant *morceaux de concert,* and especially the Kreisler encores. He brings a particularly nice touch of rubato to *Schön Rosmarin* and produces a ravishingly stylish *Liebesleid,* while the *Andantino in the Style of Martini* is engagingly ingenuous. Schumann's *Träumerei* is made to sound as if originally conceived as a violin solo. The *Méditation* from *Thaïs* is delectably romantic without being oversweet, and the following *Valse sentimentale* of Tchaikovsky has just the right degree of restraint.

But Grumiaux's simplicity of style is heard at its most appealing in Wieniawski's *Souvenir de Moscou,* with its warm melody elegantly decorated and then let loose in a burst of Paganinian fireworks. István Hajdu accompanies with comparable taste, notably in Bach's unwitting contribution to Gounod's *Ave Maria,* while his simple introduction to Elgar's *La Capricieuse* is a model of how to set the scene for a salon piece of this kind. He is equally helpful in echoing Grumiaux in Schubert's lovely *Serenade* and in his discreet backing for Ponce's gently voluptuous *Estrellita.* The recording is most natural, without any edginess on the violin-tone, and the piano is pleasingly balanced within a warm acoustic.

Hamelin, Marc-André (piano)

'Live at Wigmore Hall': BEETHOVEN (arr. ALKAN): *Piano Concerto 3:* first movt. CHOPIN (arr. BALAKIREV): *Piano Concerto 1: Romanza.* ALKAN: *3 Grandes études.* BUSONI: *Sonatina 6 (Chamber Fantasy on 'Carmen').* MEDTNER: *Danza festiva, Op. 38/3*
🔊 ⭕ *** Hyp. CDA 66765

This is among the most spectacular piano issues of the last decade. It captures live one of the programmes given in June 1994 at Wigmore Hall by the French-Canadian pianist Marc-André Hamelin, in a series called 'Virtuoso Romantics'. Bizarre as the mixture is, it works magnificently, thanks not only to Hamelin's breathtaking virtuosity, finger perfect, but to his magnetism. As well as the *Trois Grandes études* of Alkan, he plays Alkan's arrangement of the first movement of

Beethoven's *Third Piano Concerto.* Thanks to his sharp clarity, one marvels afresh at the purposefulness of the writing, and he revels in Alkan's manic six-minute cadenza, which in dotty inspiration even quotes the finale of Beethoven's *Fifth Symphony.* Balakirev's arrangement of the Romanza from Chopin's *First Piano Concerto* then offers yearning poetry, with two flamboyant display-pieces as encores: Busoni's *Carmen Fantasy* and Medtner's *Danza festiva.*

'Kaleidoscope': WOODS: *Valse phantastique.* BEHR (trans. RACHMANINOV): *Polka de W.R.* HOFMANN: *Kaleidoskop; Nocturne.* HAMELIN: *Etudes 3 (d'après Paganini-Liszt) & 6 (Essercizio per pianoforte).* BLUMENFELD: *Etude pour la main gauche seule.* OFFENBACH: *Concert Paraphrase of 'The Song of the Soldiers of the Sea'.* MASSENET: *Valse folie.* MOSZKOWSKI: *Etude in A flat min, Op. 72/13.* POULENC: *Intermezzo in A flat.* GODOWSKY: *Alt Wien.* MICHALOWSKI: *Etude d'après l'Impromptu en la bémol majeur de Fr. Chopin.* LOURIE: *Gigue.* BLANCHET: *Au jardin du vieux sérail, Op. 18/3.* CASELLA: *2 Contrastes.* VALLIER: *Toccatina.* GLAZUNOV (trans. HAMELIN): *Petit adagio.* KAPUSTIN: *Toccatina*
*** Hyp. CDA 67275

This collection of encores, most of them rarities, is a box of delights, with Marc-André Hamelin bringing out the fun as well as the brilliance. Consistently, one marvels that ten fingers can possibly play the notes involved, when the virtuosity demanded is almost beyond belief. Yet Hamelin is masterly at bringing out the wit of each piece, as in the opening item by a virtually unknown composer, Edna Bentz Woods, with waltz rhythms naughtily pointed. Hamelin's own tribute to Scarlatti in his *Etude 6* is in fact an amusing parody, very much tongue-in-cheek, and it is pure fun to have the American Marines' Hymn (drawn from Offenbach) elaborated as a virtuoso keyboard study. Hamelin also brings out the keyboard magic of such a piece as Blanchet's evocation of the garden of the seraglio or the transcription from Glazunov's ballet, *The Seasons,* with beauty as well as brilliance part of his message. Vivid recorded sound.

Hardenberger, Håkan (trumpet)

'The Virtuoso Trumpet' (with Pöntinen): ARBAN: *Variations on Themes from Bellini's 'Norma'.* FRANCAIX: *Sonatine.* TISNE: *Héraldiques.* HONEGGER: *Intrada.* MAXWELL DAVIES: *Sonata.* RABE: *Shazam!.* HARTMANN: *Fantasia brillante on the Air 'Rule, Britannia'*
*** BIS CID 287

This collection includes much rare and adventurous repertoire, not otherwise available and very unlikely to offer frequent access in live performance. Moreover, Hardenberger plays with electrifying bravura in the Maxwell Davies *Sonata* and the virtuoso miniatures. Antoine Tisné's five *Héraldiques* are eclectic but highly effective on the lips of such an assured player; *Scandé* and the following *Elégiaque* are notably characterful. But easily the most memorable item is the Françaix *Sonatine* (originally for violin and piano) in which two delicious brief outer movements frame a pleasing central *Sarabande.* Honegger's improvisatory *Intrada* is an effective encore piece. The recording is eminently realistic, with the CD giving superb presence.

Harle, John (saxophone), John Lenehan (piano)

Sonatas: R. R. BENNETT: *Soprano Saxophone Concerto.* MICHAEL BERKELEY: *Keening.* DENISOV: *Alto Saxophone Sonata.* HEATH: *Romania.* WOODS: *Alto Saxophone Sonata*
(*) Clarinet Classics CC 0048

It is primarily French composers who have adopted the timbre of the saxophone as an additional orchestral colour, not forgetting its jazz associations but incorporating it into the wider orchestral field. British composers have been slower to integrate it into mainline repertoire, but Richard Rodney Bennett's *Sonata* for soprano saxophone shows it can be done, a convincing piece of genuine concert music. The first movement is plaintively nostalgic, if not without its light-hearted moments, and it has a touching close. The second is a brightly rhythmic Scherzo, yet with a whiff of lyrical melancholy peeping out from behind the lively syncopations. The *Andante* is based upon the Harold Arlen song, *Once I had a sweetheart*, but Bennett refines the melody without losing its romantic kernel. The bravura finale is a rondo, drawing on previous ideas for its episodes.

Michael Berkeley's *Keening*, for the throatier, vocally poignant alto sax, draws its title from its Irish usage of the word: wailing bitterly for the dead (in this instance the dedicatee, the oboist Janet Craxton). Its grief is deeply expressed, its style virtuosic, yet leading to an increasingly poignant lament which moves into painful upward glissando cries in the desperate melancholy of its closing section.

The opening mood of the Denisov *Sonata* is dry and jocular, and even the *Lento* (though expressively dark in colour) with its sudden sforzandos becomes ambivalent in mood. The bravura finale then moves over directly to the world of jazz and the brilliance of bebop. An entertainingly contradictory piece, mavellously brought off here.

Dave Heath's *Romania* and the Phil Woods *Sonata* are even more obviously crossover works. Heath uses the 'chords and rhythms of modern Jazz, in particular Miles Davis and McCoy Tyner'; in the exotic lyrical writing John Harle at times creates an instrumental colour rather like a cor anglais. Phil Woods's less individual *Sonata* opens simply and reflectively, and the allegro unfolds effortlessly into a free (if not especially original) jazz style, which then permeates the two contrasted central movements, with the finale uninhibited. John Harle obviously relishes the bravura and the lyrical flavour of all these pieces, and John Lenehan is an impresssive partner: both play brilliantly. They are truthfully recorded, but this is a disc for saxophone admirers: there is no real masterpiece here.

Headington, Christopher (piano)

British Piano Music of the 20th Century. BRITTEN: *Holiday Diary.* DELIUS: *3 Preludes.* ELGAR: *Adieu; In Smyrna; Serenade.* HEADINGTON: *Ballade-image; Cinquanta.* IRELAND: *The Island Spell.* MOERAN: *Summer Valley.* PATTERSON: *A Tunnel of Time, Op. 66*
*** Kingdom KCLD 2017

The novelties here are fascinating. The Delius *Preludes* (1923) have much of the luminous atmosphere of the orchestral music, while Britten's *Holiday Diary* (what a happy idea for a suite!), written when he was just twenty, is most winning. The Elgar pieces are well worth having, and Headington again reveals himself as an appealing composer. Both his pieces were written for fiftieth-birthday celebrations and the *Ballade-image* expressly seeks to conjure up an atmosphere combining the influences of Chopin and Debussy. It is most engaging. John Ireland's *Island Spell* is beautifully played. A 69-minute recital which is skilfully planned to be listened to in sequence. Good, if not outstanding, recording.

Heifetz, Jascha (violin)

'*Hora Staccato and Other Favourites*' (with Emmanuel Bay or Arpad Sandor (piano)): MOSZKOWSKI: *Guitarre.* FALLA: *Spanish Dance 1; Jota.* BAZZINI: *La Ronde des lutins.* WIENIAWSKI: *Polonaise brillante 1 in D, Op. 4.* KORNGOLD: *Much Ado About Nothing:* excerpts. ACHRON: *Hebrew Melody.* PROKOFIEV: *Gavotta, Op. 32/3; March in F min., Op. 12/1.* RACHMANINOV: *Daisies; Oriental Sketch in B flat.* KROLL: *Banjo and Fiddle.* BIZET/WAXMAN: *Carmen Fantasia* (with RCA Victor SO, Donald Voorhees). SAINT-SAËNS: *Introduction & Rondo capriccioso; Havanaise* (with LPO, Barbirolli)
(B) **(**(*))** ASV mono AJC 8553

Many of Heifetz's most celebrated miniatures from the 78-r.p.m. era offered in this collection come from the 1930s and 1940s. The mono recordings are studio-bound, but those made in London in the 1930s, the first nine items (including the Saint-Saëns *Introduction and Rondo capriccioso* and *Havanaise* showpieces in partnership with a warmly responsive Barbirolli), are well balanced. The later recordings, made in Hollywood, are more variable but still capture Heifetz's uniquely seductive timbre, especially the Achron *Hebrew Melody* and the Rachmaninov song transcription, *Daisies*, while Kroll's sparkling *Banjo and Fiddle* is a demonstration track. The transfers are not flattering but they are rather better than the earlier, EMI transfers below.

'*The Legendary Heifetz*' (with Bay or Sandor, piano): BAZZINI: *La Ronde des lutins, Op. 25.* WIENIAWSKI: *Scherzo-tarantelle in G min., Op. 16.* DEBUSSY: *L'enfant prodigue; Prélude.* ALBENIZ: *Suite española: Sevillañas.* ELGAR: *La Capricieuse, Op. 17.* MOSZKOWSKI: *Guitarre, Op. 45/2.* FALLA: *Danza española 1.* CYRIL SCOTT: *Tallahassee Suite: Bygone Memories.* DOHNANYI: *Ruralia hungarica, Op. 32a: Gypsy Andante.* CASTELNUOVO-TEDESCO: *Valse.* POULENC: *Mouvements perpétuelles 1.* VIVALDI: *Sonata in A, Op. 2/2.* PAGANINI: *Caprice, Op. 1/13.* BACH: *English Suite 3 in G min., BWV 808: Gavottes 1 & 2 (Musette).* FRANCK: *Sonata in A: First Movement Mosso* (with Rubinstein)
(M) **(**)** EMI mono 5 67005-2

Although the playing here offers the sophistication of bow-arm technique, and fabulous assurance for which Heifetz is famous, the recorded sound detracts very considerably from the listener's pleasure. All these recordings were made at Abbey Road (for the most part in 1934, and a few in 1937) but they are a credit neither to the original EMI engineers nor to the current EMI remastering process. The acoustic is dry, the violin uncomfortably close to the microphone, minimizing the breadth of tone, making it sound top-heavy and peaky. It is surely possible to do better than this! As it is, the extraordinary virtuosity of *La Ronde des lutins*, Wieniawski's *Scherzo-tarantelle* and famous *Hora staccato*, the veiled beauty of tone in the Debussy *Prélude* to *L'enfant prodigue* and the evocation of Cyril Scott are all but lost. The Vivaldi *Sonata*, superbly stylish, and the excerpt from the Franck *Sonata* (with Rubinstein) seem almost to triumph over the sound, but, even so, one needs to replay this disc with the aural equivalent of top-quality dark glasses to enjoy the music-making.

'*Heifetz Rediscovered*' (with (i) Emanuel Bay; (ii) Isidor Achron; (iii) Samuel Chotzinoff, (piano)): (i) Violin Sonatas: GRIEG: *Sonata 3 in C min., Op. 45.* BRAHMS: *Sonata 1 in G, Op. 78.* (ii) WIENIAWSKI: *Etude alla saltarella in E flat, Op. 10/5.* RAMEAU: *Tambourin* (arr. Achron, from *Pièces de clavecin*). BACH: *Sicilienne in C* (arr. Auer from *Flute Sonata in E flat, BWV 1041*). SARASATE: *Zapateado, Op. 23/2.* (iii) TCHAIKOVSKY: *Lenski's Aria* (from *Eugene Onegin*). Bonus: PADILLA: *Valencia* (Heifetz & Isidor Achron, (piano, 4 hands))
(M) (**(*)) RCA mono 0906 63097-2

Although the most recent recordings here are 60 years old, and the other items date from between 1922 and 1928, this is still worth having. The debonair young Heifetz (confidently pictured in the booklet) already demonstrates the superlative technique that caused Kreisler to comment in despair, 'We might as well break our fiddles over our knees.' The balance is close (piano as well as violin) and the studio-sound dry, but both *Sonatas* are unique treasure trove, particularly the slow movment of the Grieg. Of the shorter encore pieces, Heifetz plays the Bach *Sicilienne* exquisitely and the recording producer reckons that among his three recordings of *Zapateado* this is most notable, 'for its devilish abandon'. The unexpected bonus of *Valencia* (piano, four hands) in which Heifetz is joined at the keyboard by his accompanist also has plenty of gusto.

Hilton, Janet (clarinet), Keith Swallow (piano)

'*Rhapsodie*': POULENC: *Clarinet Sonata.* RAVEL: *Pièce en forme d'habanera.* DEBUSSY: *Première rhapsodie.* SAINT-SAENS: *Clarinet Sonata, Op. 167.* ROUSSEL: *Aria.* MILHAUD: *Duet concertante, Op. 351*
(M) ** Chan. 6589

There are some highly beguiling sounds here, and the languorous style adopted throughout is emphasized by the reverberant acoustic which is less than ideal, creating the feeling of an empty hall. The Ravel and Debussy are given an evocative sentience and the Poulenc comes off very well too; overall, however, there is a feeling that a little more vitality and a more sharply focused sound-picture would have been advantageous.

Horowitz, Vladimir (piano)

'*Horowitz in Moscow*' (1986): D. SCARLATTI: *Sonatas, Kk.87, 380 & 135.* MOZART: *Piano Sonata 10 in C, K.330.* RACHMANINOV: *Preludes: in G and G sharp, Op. 32/5 & 12.* SCRIABIN: *Etudes in C sharp min.,Op. 2/1 & D sharp min., Op. 8/12.* SCHUBERT: *Impromptu in B flat, D.395/3.* LISZT: *Concert Paraphrase of Schubert's Valse Caprice 6 from* '*Soirées de Vienna'; Années de pèlerinage,* 2nd Year: *Sonetto 104 del Petrarcha.* CHOPIN: *Mazurkas: in C sharp min.,Op. 30/4; in F min., Op. 7/13; Polonaise in A flat, Op. 53.* SCHUMANN: *Kinderszenen: Träumerei.* MOSZKOWSKI: *Morceaux caractéristiques: Etincelles, Op. 36/6.* RACHMANINOV: *Polka de W.R.*
*** Sony **DVD** SVD 64545

This DVD celebrates Horowitz's return to Moscow in 1986 after a sixty-year absence. We first meet him at home, reading a letter from his family who are looking forward to the reunion, then his arrival in Moscow and walking the streets, and finally quite casually on to the stage. The programme he has chosen is core repertoire which we know well from his CDs, and which he plays magnificently. His audience is obviously as much moved by the occasion as by his music-making, so this is a truly memorable recital, quite well recorded and sensitively photographed, showing the audience response as well as well-judged shots of the pianist himself. At the close of the recital, he takes the applause with characterstic modesty, informally waving to individuals all over the hall. In the interval we hear him reminisce about his early life, including his meeting, when a young boy, with Scriabin, who was to become his mentor briefly during the year before the composer died.

Complete DG Recordings: BACH/BUSONI: *Chorale Prelude, Nun komm, der Heiden Heiland.* MOZART: *Piano Sonatas: in B flat, K.281; in C, K.330; in B flat, K.333. Adagio in B min., K.540; Rondo in D, K.485; Piano Concerto 23 in A. K.488* (with La Scala, Milan, O, Giulini). CHOPIN: *Mazurkas: in A min., Op. 17/4; in C sharp min., Op. 30/4; in F min., Op. 7/3. Scherzo 1 in B min., Op. 20; Polonaise 6 in A flat, Op. 53.* SCHUBERT: *Impromptus: in A flat, D.899/4; in B flat, D. 935/3. Marche militaire in D flat, D.733/1; Moment musical in F min., D.780/3; Piano Sonata 21 in B flat, D.960.* LISZT: *Consolation 3 in D flat; Impromptu (Nocturne) in F sharp; Valse oubliée 1; Soirées de Vienne: Valses-Caprices 6, 7 & 8; Années de pèlerinage: Sonetto 101 del Petrarca; Concert Paraphrase of Schubert's 'Ständchen'.* SCHUMANN: *Novelette in F, Op. 21/1; Kreisleriana, Op. 16; Kinderszenen, Op. 15* (complete) & excerpt: *Träumerei.* RACHMANINOV: *Preludes: in G sharp min., Op. 32/12; in G, Op. 32/5; Polka de W. R.* SCRIABIN: *Etude in C sharp min., Op. 2/1; in D sharp min., Op. 8/12.* MOSZKOWSKI: *Etude in F, Op. 72/6; Etincelles, Morceau caractéristique, Op. 36/6.* D. SCARLATTI: *Sonatas: in B min., Kk. 87; in E, Kk. 135; in E, Kk. 380*
(B) *** DG 474 370-2 (6)

This set of six CDs collects all the recordings Horowitz made for Deutsche Grammophon between 1985 and 1989, when he was in his early eighties. The first was made in his Manhattan home and is taken from the soundtrack of the video, 'Vladimir Horowitz – The Last Romantic'. Other recordings come from Moscow, Vienna and Milan. Although, judged by the standards of the youthful Horowitz, there is less of the demonic virtuoso, there is still plenty of brilliance, combined with introspective sensitivity. We have lavished plaudits on each of these recordings in their first incarnations. There is much vintage Horowitz: the Bach/Busoni arrangement, which he had not committed to disc since his 1947 RCA recording, has a seamless legato that is almost in a class of its own. Some of the stormier passages in *Kreisleriana* are not as effortless as they would have been in his youth, but it is still an astonishing achievement. Some have complained that, in his desire to shed new light, there are touches that are a little forced. Yet he evokes a Schumann who sounds wholly possessed. And as Joan Chissell so aptly put it, his Scriabin *Etude in D sharp minor* 'shows how he can still kindle glowing embers into scorching flame'. The Scarlatti and Mozart are marked by exquisite delicacy, and his feeling for sonority and his magisterial authority leave a profound impression. And it is good to hear the great pianist in truthful recorded sound. This is a set to cherish – and in its new edition a bargain as well.

Recital: BACH/BUSONI: *Chorale Prelude: Nun komm, der Heiden Heiland.* MOZART: *Piano Sonata 10 in C, K.330.* CHOPIN: *Mazurka in A min., Op. 17/4; Scherzo 1 in B min., Op. 20; Polonaise 6 in A flat, Op. 53.* LISZT: *Consolation 3 in D flat.* SCHUBERT: *Impromptu in A flat, D.899/4.* SCHUMANN: *Novellette in F, Op. 21/1.* RACHMANINOV: *Prelude in G sharp min., Op. 32/12.* SCRIABIN: *Etude in C sharp min., Op. 2/1.* MOSZKOWSKI: *Etude in F, Op. 72/6* (recording of performances featured in the film *Vladimir Horowitz – The Last Romantic*)
*** DG (IMS) 419 045-2

Recorded when he was over eighty, this playing betrays remarkably little sign of frailty. The Mozart is beautifully elegant and the Chopin *A minor Mazurka*, Op. 17, No. 4, could hardly be more delicate. The only sign of age comes in the *B minor Scherzo*, which does not have the leonine fire and tremendous body of his famous 1950 recording. However, it is pretty astonishing for all that.

'The Studio Recordings': SCHUMANN: *Kreisleriana, Op. 16.* D. SCARLATTI: *Sonatas in B min., Kk. 87; in E, Kk. 135.* LISZT: *Impromptu (Nocturne) in F sharp; Valse oubliée 1.* SCRIABIN: *Etude in D sharp min., Op. 8/12.* SCHUBERT: *Impromptu in B flat, D.935/3.* SCHUBERT/TAUSIG: *Marche militaire, D.733/1*
*** DG (IMS) 419 217-2

The subtle range of colour and articulation in the Schumann is matched in his Schubert *Impromptu*, and the Liszt *Valse oubliée* offers the most delicious, twinkling rubato. Hearing Scarlatti's *E major Sonata* played with such crispness, delicacy and grace must surely convert even the most dedicated authenticist to the view that this repertoire can be totally valid in terms of the modern instrument. The Schubert–Tausig *Marche militaire* makes a superb encore, played with the kind of panache that would be remarkable in a pianist half Horowitz's age. With the passionate Scriabin *Etude* as the central romantic pivot, this recital is uncommonly well balanced to show Horowitz's special range of sympathies.

'The Indispensable Horowitz': CHOPIN: *Polonaise-fantaisie in A flat, Op. 61; Scherzi 1 in B min., Op. 20; 2 in B flat, Op. 31; Etudes in C sharp min., Op. 10/4; in C sharp min., Op. 25/7; Nocturnes in B, Op. 9/3; in C sharp min., Op. 27/1; in E min., Op. 72/1; Barcarolle, Op. 60; Polonaise in A flat, Op. 53; Ballade 1 in G min., Op. 23.* D. SCARLATTI: *Keyboard Sonatas, Kk. 87, 127, & 135.* RACHMANINOV: *Humoresque, Op. 10/5; Preludes in G min., Op. 23/5; in G, Op. 32/5; Barcarolle, Op. 10/3.* MOSZKOWSKI: *Etincelle, Op. 36/6; Etude in F, Op. 72/6.* LISZT: *Hungarian Rhapsodies 2 & 15 (Rákóczy March)* (both arr. HOROWITZ); *Mephisto Waltz 1.* BIZET/HOROWITZ: *Variations on a Theme from 'Carmen'.* SCRIABIN: *Etudes: in C sharp min., Op. 2/1; in B flat min., Op. 8/7; in D sharp min., Op. 8/12; in C sharp min., Op. 42/5.* SOUSA/HOROWITZ: *The Stars and Stripes Forever*
✆ ✿ (B) *** RCA stereo/mono, 74321 63471-2 (2)

The notes with this remarkably generous collection include a quote from Neville Cardus, who once described Horowitz as 'the greatest pianist alive or dead'. Later he added that this comment 'perhaps was not positive enough about pianists still unborn'. His eulogy still holds true at the time of writing, and the programme here demonstrates why. If you look for astonishing, barnstorming virtuosity you will find it in Horowitz's own *Carmen Variations*, the Liszt *Hungarian Rhapsody* 'arrangements' or the closing *Stars and Stripes*; but if you seek bravura delicacy, the Moszkowski *F major Etude* is a supreme example, while his Scarlatti is unforgettable. Romantic poetry constantly illuminates his Chopin (the *Barcarolle* and *G minor Ballade* are especially memorable) and his Rachmaninov (the *G major Prelude* is exquisite), while throughout this is playing of unique distinction which offers infinite rewards.

Scriabin, another of Horowitz's special composers, is generously represented, not only by Horowitz's favourite, *D sharp minor Etude* (taken from a 1982 live recital) but also by the more prolix *C sharp minor*, recorded three decades earlier. What is surprising is the fairly consistent quality of the sound: one of the earliest mono recordings (from 1950), of Scriabin's Op. 2/1, is remarkably warmly coloured. Of course, the later, stereo recordings are ever finer, as the commanding opening *Polonaise-fantaisie* of Chopin (1982) readily shows. But on sonic grounds there is little to criticize; artistically this pair of discs are in a class of their own.

'Favourite Encores': SCHUMANN: *Toccata in C, Op. 7; Arabeske in C, Op. 18; Kinderszenen, Op. 5: Träumerei.* CHOPIN: *Etudes: in E; G flat (Black Key); C min. (Revolutionary); Op. 10/3, 5 & 12; in A flat & E min., Op. 25/1 & 5; Polonaise in A flat (Heroic), Op. 53.* SCRIABIN: *Etudes: in C sharp min., Op. 2/1; in D sharp min., Op. 8/12.* MOSZKOWSKI: *Etude in A flat, Op. 72/11.* SCHUBERT: *Impromptu in G flat, D.899/3.* DOMENICO SCARLATTI: *Sonatas in E, K.531; in A, K.322.* MOZART: *Sonata 11 in A, K.331: Rondo alla Turca.* RACHMANINOV: *Prelude in G sharp min., Op. 32/12; Etude-Tableau in C, Op. 33/2.* DEBUSSY: *L'isle joyeuse; Children's Corner: Serenade for the Doll.* HOROWITZ: *Variations on a theme from Bizet's 'Carmen'* (abridged)
(M) *** Sony 516232

These are all items with which Horowitz chose to end his recitals. Many are recorded live, but only one or two include applause. It was perhaps a mistake to open the programme with the Schumann *Toccata*, well played though it is, but the following Chopin *E major Etude* then instantly melts the ear, followed by Horowitz'a favourite Scriabin *Etude* (in D sharp minor) and a scintillating acount of Moszkowski's *A flat major Study*. Schumann is heard to more persuasive effect in the lovely flowing *Arabeske* and, late in the recital, *Träumerei*, another of the pianist's favourites. The two Scarlatti *Sonatas* are presented with predictable finesse, with the famous *Alla Turca Rondo* of Mozart following effectively; but the highlight of the collection is a magical account of Schubert's glorious *G flat major Impromptu*, with the two Rachmaninov pieces and the dazzling Debussy *L'isle joyeuse* hardly less memorable. The recordings, nearly all from the 1960s and 1970 and made in a variety of venues, are always good, sometimes a little dry and close, but never unacceptably so. The final pair of Chopin Etudes (Op. 25/1 and 5) (1989) are digital and end the programme in satisfying realism.

Horszowski, Mieczyslaw (piano)

J.S. BACH: *French Suite 6 in E, BWV 817.* BEETHOVEN: *Piano Sonata 6 in F, Op. 10/2.* SCHUMANN: *Papillons, Op. 2; Kinderszenen: Träumerei.* CHOPIN: *Etude in F min., Op. 25/2; Impromptu in F sharp, Op. 36; Nocturne in E flat, Op. 9/2; Scherzo 1 in B min., Op. 20; Waltz in C sharp min., Op. 64/2*

⊕ (M) *** BBC BBCL (ADD) 4122-2

Extraordinary playing. This is a recording of a recital given in London's Wigmore Hall on 21 June 1990, when Horszowski was two days short of his 98th birthday. The playing is radiant and the quality of sound he produces has an almost disembodied, luminous quality that was so special. Older collectors will remember the famous Vox LPs he made of the *Hammerklavier Sonata* and the *Diabelli Variations*, and they will find that he was still active and better than ever, forty years later. As those who heard his wonderful Szymanowski *Mazurkas* at Aldeburgh seven years earlier will remember, there is not the slightest trace of age in his playing. Magical playing that is to be treasured.

Hough, Stephen (piano)

'*Piano Album*':

Disc 1: MACDOWELL: *Hexentanz, Op. 12.* CHOPIN: *Chant polonaise 1.* QUILTER: *The Crimson Petal; The Fuchsia Tree.* DOHNANYI: *Capriccio in F min., Op. 28/8.* PADEREWSKI: *Minuet in G, Op. 14/1; Nocturne in B flat, Op. 16/4.* SCHLOZER: *Etude in A flat, Op. 1/2.* GABRILOVICH: *Mélodie in E; Caprice-burlesque.* RODGERS: *My Favourite Things.* WOODFORDE-FINDEN: *Kashmiri Song.* FRIEDMAN: *Music Box.* SAINT-SAENS: *Carnival of the Animals: The Swan* (arr. GODOWSKY). ROSENTHAL: *Papillons.* GODOWSKY: *The Gardens of Buitenzorg.* LEVITZKI: *Waltz in A, Op. 2.* PALMGREN: *En route, Op. 9.* MOSZKOWSKI: *Siciliano, Op. 42/2; Caprice espagnol, Op. 37*

Disc 2: CZERNY: *Variations brillantes, Op. 14.* LEVITZKI: *The Enchanted Nymph.* SCHUMANN: *Der Kontrebandiste.* RUBINSTEIN: *Melody in F.* LIEBERMANN: *Gargoyles, Op. 29.* REBIKOV: *The Musical Snuffbox.* RAVINA: *Etude de style (Agilité), Op. 40/1.* WOODFORDE-FINDEN: *Till I Wake.* QUILTER: *Weep You No More.* RODGERS: *March of the Siamese Children.* MOSZKOWSKI: *Valse mignonne; Serenata, Op. 15/1.* BACH: *Violin Sonata 2: Bourrée.* GODOWSKY: *Erinnerungen.* BIZET: *L'Arlésienne: Adagietto.* TAUSIG: *Ungarische Zigeunerweisen*

(BB) *** Virgin 5 61498-2 (2)

There are few young pianists who can match Stephen Hough in communicating on record with the immediacy and vividness of live performance; this dazzling two-disc recital of frothy showpieces presents the perfect illustration. Indeed, this Virgin Classics bargain Double captures more nearly than almost any other record – even those of Horowitz – the charm, sparkle and flair of legendary piano virtuosos from the golden age of Rosenthal, Godowsky and Lhévinne.

So many of the items are frivolous that it may be surprising that any serious pianist can stomach them; yet on the first disc the very opening item, MacDowell's *Hexentanz* ('Witches' dance'), launches the listener into pure pianistic magic, and the second, with Czerny's fizzing *Variations brillantes*, similarly offers totally uninhibited playing, with articulation and timing that are the musical equivalent of being tickled up and down the spine.

One would hardly expect Hough's own arrangements of sentimental little songs by Roger Quilter or Amy Woodforde-Finden to be memorable – yet, in their tender expressiveness, they are most affecting. In the grand tradition, Hough does a Valse-caprice arrangement he himself has made of *My Favourite Things* from *The Sound of Music*, as well as an equally attractive but simpler arrangement of Rodgers's *March of the Siamese Children*. Firework pieces by Rosenthal and Moszkowski, among others, go along with old-fashioned favourites like Paderewski's *Minuet in G*, Rubinstein's *Melody in F* (here sounding fresh and unfaded) and Godowsky's arrangement of the Saint-Saëns *Swan*.

Not all of Lowell Liebermann's *Gargoyles* are menacing (there is a charming *Adagio semplice*) but the *Feroce* marking for the closing number is pungently realized. Then follow two different miniature portrayals of a *Musical Snuffbox*, the first, by Vladimir Rebikov, not a whit less delightful than the more famous version by Liadov. The programme ends with an arresting account of Tausig's *Ungarische Zigeunerweisen*. Altogether it is a feast for piano lovers, very well recorded: the first disc in 1986 (in London and New York), the second in 1991 using the BBC's Manchester studio.

'*New Piano Album*': LISZT: *Concert Paraphrase of Schubert: Soirées de Vienne.* SCHUBERT (arr. GODOWSKY): *Moment Musical in D min., D.780/3; Die schöne Müllerin: Morgengrüss.* GODOWSKI: *Alt Wien.* MOSZKOWSKI: *Etincelle, Op. 36/6.* PADEREWSKI: *Mélodie in G flat, Op. 16/2.* CHAMINADE: *Pierrette (Air de ballet), Op. 41; Autrefois, Op. 87/4.* KALMAN (arr. HOUGH): *Hello Young Lovers; Carousel Waltz.* TRAD. (arr. HOUGH): *Londonderry Air.* RACHMANINOV: *Humoresque, Op. 10/5; Mélodie, Op. 3/3* (revised, 1940 version). TCHAIKOVSKY: *Humoresque, Op. 10/2.* TCHAIKOVSKY, (arr. WILD): *Swan Lake: Pas de quatre.* TCHAIKOVSKY/PABST (arr. HOUGH): *Sleeping Beauty Paraphrase*

*** Hyp. CDA 67043

In his latest collection, Stephen Hough demonstrates yet again the flair with which he tackles trivial party pieces like the 20 varied items here. Such encore material has in his hands a sparkle and point that magick the ear, whether in the virtuoso display of pieces by Godowsky, Moszkowski and Rachmaninov or in the loving lyricism of pieces by Chaminade, Kalman and Rodgers. As well as offering two witty showpieces of his own, Hough also plays his arrangements of two Richard Rodgers numbers and the *Londonderry Air*. Among the four Tchaikovsky items, it is good to have the haunting little *Humoresque*, best known through Stravinsky's ballet, *The Fairy's Kiss*. Vivid sound.

'*English Piano Album*': RAWSTHORNE: *Bagatelles.* REYNOLDS: *2 Poems in Homage to Delius; 2 Poems in Homage to Fauré.* HOUGH: *Valses enigmatiques 1–2.* ELGAR: *In Smyrna.* BANTOCK: *Song to the Seals.* BOWEN: *Reverie d'amour, Op. 20/2; Serious Dance, Op. 51/2; The Way to Polden, Op. 76.* BRIDGE: *The Dew Fairy; Heart's Ease.* LEIGHTON: *6 Studies (Study-Variations), Op. 56.*

*** Hyp. CDA 67267

This recital disc from Stephen Hough has a different aim from his previous collections of charmers, starting with four gritty and tough miniatures of Rawsthorne, thoughtful and intense, balanced at the end by Kenneth Leighton's *Study Variations*. Those do not make for easy listening either, inspiring Hough to superb pianism over six sharply characterized pieces, at times echoing Bartók in their angry energy, at others full of fantasy, with the second a slow and concentrated piece full of harmonic clusters, and with the final *Study* a breathtaking virtuoso exercise. What all these very varied items demonstrate is Hough's profound love of keyboard sound and textures, and his rare gift of bringing out the full beauty of that sound. His own pieces, the two *Valses enigmatiques*, each based on his own initials linked to those of friends, both bear that out, the one with light textures, the other with Debussian parallel chords. He also offers a warmly sympathetic arrangement of a song he recorded earlier with the tenor, Robert White, on a Hyperion disc of ballads, Bantock's *Song to the Seals*.

It is evidence too of Hough's wizardry that he makes the Elgar piece, *In Smyrna*, sound so bewitching, with echoes of the lovely solo viola serenade in the overture, *In the South*, written some two years before in 1903 and also with a Mediterranean inspiration. The four pieces by Stephen Reynolds, two with echoes of Delius, two of Fauré, are consciously relaxed exercises outside the composer's more astringent idiom. The two pieces by Frank Bridge bring out his love of delicate keyboard textures, while the three York Bowen pieces are simple and song-like, using an almost cabaret-style of piano writing. In all this music Hough's magic is presented in full, clear Hyperion sound.

Howard, Leslie (piano)

'*Rare Piano Encores*': ROSSINI: *Petite caprice.*
MOZART/BUSONI: *Serenade: Deh vieni alla finestra* from '*Don Giovanni*'. GERSHWIN: *Promenade.* REGER: *Maria Wiegenlied, Op. 76/52.* GRAINGER (after Bach): *Blithe Bells.* WAGNER: *Albumblatt.* FRIEDMAN: *Viennese Dance 2.* RACHMANINOV: *Romance in E flat, Op. 8/2.* MOSZKOWSKI: *Concert paraphrase of Chanson bohème from Bizet's 'Carmen'.* LISZT: *Valse oubliée 4; Soirées de Vienne 6 (Valse-caprices, after Schubert); Concert Paraphrase (Valse de concert) on motifs from Donizetti's 'Lucia and Parisina'.* RUBINSTEIN: *Valse-caprice.* GRIEG: *Ich liebe dich.* BRUCKNER: *Erinnerung.* HOWARD: *Yuletide Pastorale, Op. 33a; Concert Paraphrase: Reminiscences on the opera 'La Wally' of Catalani*
(BB) *** Hyp. Helios CDH 55109

A most winning collection. Leslie Howard is on top form, not just in Liszt (for which he is justly famous) but in the gentle pieces by Reger, Wagner and Bruckner, although Grieg's *Ich liebe dich* is given the full romantic treatment. Elsewhere there is plenty of charm and sparkle too. The opening Rossini *Caprice* is instantly familiar from Respighi's transcription in *La boutique fantasque*, and Busoni's delicately pointed treatment of the famous *Don Giovanni Serenade* is matched by Grainger's bell-like arrangement of equally familiar Bach. Perhaps it was a mistake for Howard to end with his own concert paraphrase of Catalani's *La Wally*, which is melodically less strong than the rest; but overall this is most entertaining, crisply and elegantly played and very well recorded.

Hurford, Peter (organ)

'*Great Romantic Organ Works*' (played on organs at Ratzeburg Cathedral, the Royal Festival Hall, in the Basilica of Saint-Sermin, Toulouse): WIDOR: *Symphony 5: Toccata; Symphony 6, Op. 42: Allegro.* FRANCK: *Chorals 1–3; Pièce héroïque.* MENDELSSOHN: *Preludes and Fugues: in C min., Op. 37/1; D min., Op. 37/3; Sonata in A, Op. 65/3.* GIGOUT: 10 *Pièces: Scherzo.* KARG-ELERT: *March triomphale: on 'Nun danket alle Gott'.* VIERNE: *24 Pièces en style libre: Berceuse; Symphony 1, Op. 14: Final.* BRAHMS: *Choral Preludes: Es ist ein Ros entsprungen; Herzlich tut mich verlangen; Schmücke dich.* LISZT: *Prelude and Fugue on B-A-C-H.* SCHUMANN: *4 Sketches, Op. 58/4: Allegretto.* REGER: *Introduction and Passacaglia in D min.* BOELLMAN: *Suite gothique, Op. 25*
(B) *** Double Decca 466 742-2 (2)

A self-recommending set of organ favourites at bargain price in splendid digital sound, for the most part played on the magnificent organ at Ratzeburg Cathedral. Not many collections of Romantic organ music match this in colour, breadth of repertoire and brilliance of performance. Hurford's playing defies all considerations of Victorian heaviness, and the programme includes many key repertoire works. You cannot go wrong here.

'*Organ Favourites*': Sydney Opera House organ: BACH: *Toccata and Fugue in D min., BWV 565; Jesu, joy of man's desiring.* ALBINONI: *Adagio* (arr. GIAZOTTO). PURCELL: *Trumpet Tune in D.* MENDELSSOHN: *A Midsummer Night's Dream: Wedding March.* FRANCK: *Chorale 2 in B min.* MURRILL: *Carillon.* WALFORD DAVIES: *Solemn Melody.* WIDOR: *Organ Symphony 5: Toccata.* Royal Festival Hall organ: FRANCK: *Pièce héroïque.* Ratzeburg Cathedral organ: BOELLMANN: *Suite gothique*
(B) **(*) Decca 452 166-2

Superb sound here, wonderfully free and never oppressive, even in the most spectacular moments. The Widor is spiritedly genial when played within the somewhat mellower registration of the magnificent Sydney instrument (as contrasted with the Ratzeburg Cathedral organ), and the pedals have great sonority and power. The Murrill *Carillon* is equally engaging alongside the Purcell *Trumpet Tune*, while Mendelssohn's wedding music has never sounded more resplendent. The Bach is less memorable, and the Albinoni *Adagio*, without the strings, is not an asset to the collection either. The *Pièce héroïque* and the *Suite gothique* have been added for the Eclipse reissue.

Isbin, Sharon (guitar)

'*Latin Romances*': DE LA MAZA: *Zapateado.* RODRIGO: *Invocación y Danza.* BARRIOS: *La Catedral.* ABREU: *Quejas (Lament).* JOBIM: *Estrada do Sol.* TARREGA: *Capricho árabe.* BROUWER: *El Decameron negro.* VILLA-LOBOS: *Sentimental Melody; Etude 8.* ALBENIZ: *Mallorca; Asturias*
(BB) *** Virgin 2x1 5 61627-2 (2) (with RODRIGO: *Concierto de Aranjuez; Fantasia para un gentilhombre ***. SCHWANTNER: From afar . . . (fantasy) ***)

Sharon Isbin is a masterly guitarist and has inherited Segovia's gift of achieving natural spontaneity in the recording studio, so that this solo recital is consistently fresh and communicative, the playing brilliant and evocative by turns. Rodrigo's *Invocación y Danza* and Tárrega's *Capricho árabe*

re only two of the familiar pieces which project magneti-
ally, as does the Albéniz *Asturias*, which ends the recital so
ibrantly. The novelty is *The Black Decameron* of Leo Brou-
ver, a programmatic triptych which is sharply characterized
nd atmospherically realized. Isbin is given great presence by
he recording, and he plays the key Rodrigo concertante
vorks with no less distinction. The Schwantner piece is less
ecommendable, but this two-disc set remains a bargain.

Isoir, André (organ)

French Renaissance Organ Music (Koenig organ at Bon
Pasteur, Angers): Bransles, Galliards and other dances by
GERVAIS; FRANCISQUE; ATTAIGNANT. JANEQUIN: *Allez
my fault.* SANDRIN: *Quand ien congneu.* Eustache du
CAURROY: *Fantaisie sur une jeune fillette.* ATTAIGNANT: *3
Versets du Te Deum; Prélude aux treize motets; Kyrie
cunctipotens.* Fantaisies by GUILLET; LE JEUNE; RACQUET.
RICHARD: *Prélude in D min.* THOMELIN: *Duo.* LA BARRE:
Sarabande. Henri du MONT: *Prélude 10 in D min.; Pavane
in D min.* ANON.: *Fantaisie; Ave Maris Stella.* ROBERDAY:
*Fugue et caprice 3 in C; Fugues 10 in G min.; 12 in D
B)* ******* Cal. CAL 6901

The Angers organ has a spicy régale stop which is used
ellingly in several of the dance movements included in the
programme, notably Gervaise's *Bransle de Bourgogne* and a
Basse danse, Bransle and *Gaillarde* of Attaignant and also in
Sandrin's *Quand ien congneu.* A warmer palette is found for
Eustache du Caurroy's agreeable *Fantaisie sur une jeune
fillette.* This is a French equivalent to the divisions found in
Elizabethan music, whereas the piquant *Fantaisie sur orgue
ou espinette* of Guillaume Costeley is very succinct.
Attaignant's *Kyrie cunctipotens* and the *Third Fantaisie* of
Charles Guillet are essentially chorale preludes, as is the
more elaborate *Fantaisie* of Charles Racquet, but the *Second
Fantaisie* of Claude Le Jeune, a remarkable piece, anticipates
the chorale variations of Bach, but using two different fugal
subjects. Joseph Thomelin's (two-part) *Duo* is a winning
miniature and Joseph de la Barre's *Sarabande* also has a
gentle charm, while the three *Fugues* of François Roberday
show impressive craftsmanship. No. 12, which ends the
recital resplendently, is a good example of Isoir's imaginative
registrations, which find ear-tickling contrasts between the
plangent and mellow timbres that this organ offers, while the
music is kept very much alive. A generous (76 minutes) and
stimulating recital, although not to be played all at one
sitting.

(i) Jackson, Francis (organ of York Minster), (ii) Michael Austin (organ of Birmingham Town Hall)

Pipes of Splendour': (i) COCKER: *Tuba Tune.* PURCELL:
Trumpet Tune and Almand. JACKSON: *Division on 'Nun
Danket'.* LEIGHTON: *Paean.* DUBOIS: *Toccata in G.*
GUILMANT: *Allegretto in B min., Op. 19.* GIGOUT: *Scherzo in
E.* MULET: *Carillon-Sortie.* (ii) REGER: *Toccata and Fugue in
D min./major, Op. 59/5–6.* DUPRE: *Prelude and Fugue in B,
Op. 7.* FRANCK: *Final in B flat
(M)* ******* Chan. (ADD) 6602

It was Francis Jackson who made Cocker's *Tuba Tune* (with
its boisterous, brassy principal theme) justly famous, and it
makes a splendid opener. But the entire programme shows

that it is possible to play and record an English organ without
the result sounding flabby. The *Toccata* of Dubois is very
winning and, in its quieter central section, the detail is
beautifully clear, as it is in the charming Guilmant *Allegretto*
and the lightly articulated Gigout *Scherzo.* Mulet's *Carillon-
Sortie* rings out gloriously and Leighton's *Paean* brings a blaze
of tone. The items played in Birmingham by Michael Austin
are no less stimulating, especially the two French pieces,
which have a fine piquant bite, while the Reger isn't in the
least dull. Superb transfers of demonstration-standard analogue recording from the early 1970s.

Jacoby, Ingrid (piano)

MUSSORGSKY: *Pictures at an Exhibition.* PROKOFIEV: *Piano
Sonata 7.* TCHAIKOVSKY: *The Seasons:* excerpts
*** Dutton CDSA 6802

There are few keyboard warhorses to compare with Mussorgsky's *Pictures at an Exhibition.* Quite apart from the virtuoso
demands of piano writing with its chunky chords that rarely
fit under the fingers, there is always the colourful rivalry of the
ever-popular orchestral arrangement by Ravel. It says much
not just for the brilliant technique but also the artistry of the
American pianist, Ingrid Jacoby, that she so clarifies textures,
with pedal lightly used, making the writing seem far more
pianistic than usual, yet retaining the vivid pictorial detail and
the tension and excitement of the final sequence leading to the
culminating evocation of *The Great Gate at Kiev.* The
Prokofiev *Sonata,* another warhorse, arguably his most striking piano work, demands great virtuosity, yet brings similar
clarity and incisiveness, with four of the most memorable
movements from Tchaikovsky's suite, *The Seasons,* as an
agreeable interlude. Exceptionally vivid piano-sound.

John, Keith (organ)

'Great European Organs 10': Tonhalle, Zurich:
MUSSORGSKY (trans. John): *Pictures at an Exhibition.*
ALAIN: *3 Danses (Joies; Deuils; Luttes)*
*** Priory PRCD 262

Keith John has made his own transcription of Mussorgsky's
Pictures – and pretty remarkable it sounds. Only the pieces
like *Tuileries* that require pointed articulation come off less
well than on orchestra or piano, but *Gnomus* and *Bydlo*
and, especially, the picture of the two Polish Jews are all
remarkably powerful, while the closing sequence of *Catacombs, The Hut on fowl's legs* and *The Great Gate of Kiev* are
superb. The three Alain pieces make a substantial encore.
This is as much a demonstration CD as an orchestral
version of the Mussorgsky.

'Great European Organs 26': Gloucester Cathedral:
STANFORD: *Fantasia and Toccata in D min., Op. 57.* REGER:
Prelude and Fugue in E, Op. 56/1. SHOSTAKOVICH: *Lady
Macbeth of Mtsensk: Passacaglia.* SCHMIDT: *Chaconne in C
min.* RAVANELLO: *Theme and Variations in B min.*
*** Priory PRCD 370

Keith John, having shown what he can do with Mussorgsky,
turns his attention here to little-known nineteenth- and
twentieth-century organ pieces. The programme is imaginatively chosen and splendidly played – indeed, the bravura is
often thrilling – and most realistically recorded on the superb
Gloucester organ. Both the Schmidt *Chaconne* and Ravanello

Theme and Variations are fine works, and the Shostakovich *Passacaglia*, an opera entr'acte, was originally conceived as a work for organ.

'*Toccata!*' (organ of St Mary's, Woodford): BACH/BUSONI: *Partita 2 in D min., BWV 1004: Chaconne* (trans. K. John). BACH/RACHMANINOV: *Partita 3 in E, BWV 1006: suite* (trans. K. John). GUILLOU: *Sinfonietta.* HEILLER: *Tanz-Toccata*
(M) *** Priory PRCD 002

It was a most imaginative idea to use Busoni's arrangement of Bach's famous *D minor Partita for Unaccompanied Violin* as a basis for an organ transcription, and the result is like nothing you have ever heard before – especially when Keith John gets cracking on the pedals. The three excerpts from the *E major Partita* (as originally transcribed by Rachmaninov) are hardly less successful: how well the opening *Prelude* sounds on the organ, and one can forgive Keith John's affectionately mannered touch on the famous *Gavotte*. We then have a dramatic, almost bizarre change of mood and colour with Jean Guillou's 'neoclassical' (more 'neo' than 'classical') *Sinfonietta*. Even though it opens with a Bachian flourish, its colouring and atmosphere are highly exotic, the austere central *Allegretto* leading to a somewhat jazzy but naggingly insistent, partly contrapuntal and plangent *Gigue*. Heiller's *Tanz-Toccata*, with its complex rhythms and chimerical changes of time-signature, finally brings a positive link with Stravinsky's *Rite of Spring* during the insistent motoric final pages. After his remarkable Bach performances, Keith John's kaleidoscopic registration here shows how adaptable and versatile is the modern (1972) organ at St Mary's, Woodford.

Johnson, Emma (clarinet)

'*A Clarinet Celebration*' (with Back, piano): WEBER: *Grand duo concertante; Variations concertantes.* BURGMULLER: *Duo.* GIAMPIERI: *Carnival of Venice.* SCHUMANN: *Fantasy pieces, Op. 73.* LOVREGLIO: *Fantasia de concerto, La Traviata*
*** ASV CDDCA 732

ASV have reissued and repackaged Emma Johnson's outstanding 72-minute collection, dating from 1990. It is still at full price but is worth it. These are party pieces rather than encores, all of them drawing electric sparks of inspiration from this winning young soloist. Even in such virtuoso nonsense as the Giampieri *Carnival of Venice* and the Lovreglio *Fantasia* Johnson draws out musical magic, while the expressiveness of Weber and Schumann brings heartfelt playing, with phrasing creatively individual. Gordon Back accompanies brilliantly, and the sound is first rate.

'*British Clarinet Music*' (with Martineau (piano); (i) Howard (soprano)): IRELAND: *Fantasy Sonata in E flat.* VAUGHAN WILLIAMS: *6 Studies in English Folksong;* (i) *3 Vocalises for Soprano Voice & Clarinet.* BAX: *Clarinet Sonata.* BLISS: *Pastoral;* (i) *2 Nursery Rhymes.* STANFORD: *Clarinet Sonata*
*** ASV CDDCA 891

Stanford's *Sonata* has the usual Brahmsian flavour but uses an Irish lament for the expressive central *Adagio*; then the finale has the best of both worlds by combining both influences. Vaughan Williams's *Six Studies in English Folksong* (1927) are beguilingly evocative, while the *Vocalises* for soprano voice and clarinet are brief but rather touching; they

were written in the last year of the composer's life. Both the Bax two-movement *Sonata* and the Ireland *Fantasy Sonata* are fine works, and Bliss's *Pastoral* is wartime nostalgia written while the composer was in France during the First World War. Needless to say, Emma Johnson plays everything with her usual spontaneity and musicianship, and she has a fine partner in Malcolm Martineau, while Judith Howard's contribution is pleasingly melismatic. Excellent, atmospheric recording, made in the London Henry Wood Hall.

Kang, Dong-Suk (violin), Pascal Devoyon (piano)

'*French Violin Sonatas*': DEBUSSY: *Sonata in G min.* RAVEL: *Sonata in G.* POULENC: *Violin Sonata.* SAINT-SAENS: *Sonata 1 in D min.*
☛ (BB) *** Naxos 8.550276

One of the jewels of the Naxos catalogue, this collection of four of the finest violin sonatas in the French repertoire is self-recommending. The stylistic range of this partnership is evident throughout: they seem equally attuned to all four composers. This is warm, freshly spontaneous playing, given vivid and realistic digital recording in a spacious acoustic. A very real bargain.

Katchen, Julius (piano)

The Art of Julius Katchen

Volume 1: BEETHOVEN: *Piano Concertos 1–3; 5 (Emperor), Rondo in B flat for Piano & Orchestra* (with LSO, Piero Gamba)
(B) *** Double Decca 460 822-2 (2)

Volume 2: BEETHOVEN: *Piano Concerto 4, Op. 58* (with LSO, Gamba); *Choral Fantasia, Op. 80* (also with LSO Ch.). MOZART: *Piano Concertos 13 in C, K.415* (with New SO of London, Maag); *20 in D min., K.466; 25 in C, K.503* (with Stuttgart CO, Karl Münchinger)
(B) *** Double Decca 460 825-2 (2)

Volume 3: BRAHMS: *Piano Concertos 1* (with LSO, Monteux); *2* (with LSO, Ferencsik). SCHUMANN: *Piano Concerto in A min.* (with Israel PO, Kertész); *Fantasia in C, Op. 17.*
(B) *** Double Decca 460 828-2 (2)

Volume 4: LISZT: *Piano Concertos Nos. 1-2* (with LPO, Argenta); *Mephisto Waltz 1; Harmonies poétiques et religieuses; Funérailles; Hungarian Rhapsody 12.* GRIEG: *Piano Concerto in A min., Op. 16* (with Israel PO, Kertész). BALAKIREV: *Islamey.* MUSSORGSKY: *Pictures at an Exhibition.*
(B) *** Double Decca stereo/mono 460 831-2 (2)

Volume 5: TCHAIKOVSKY: *Piano Concerto 1 in B flat min., Op. 23.* LISZT: *Hungarian Fantasia* (both with LSO, Gamba). PROKOFIEV: *Piano Concerto 3 in C, Op. 26* (with LSO, Kertéz). RACHMANINOV: *Piano Concerto 2 in C min., Op. 18* (with LSO, Solti). *Rhapsody on a Theme of Paganini, Op 43.* DOHNANYI: *Variations on a Nursery Theme* (both with LPO, Boult)
(B) *** Australian Double Decca mono/stereo 460 834-2 (2)

Volume 6: GERSHWIN: *Piano Concerto in F* (with Mantovani and his Orchestra). BARTOK: *Piano Concerto 3.*

RAVEL: *Piano Concerto in G; Piano Concerto for the Left Hand* (all with LSO, Kertész). BRITTEN: *Diversions for Piano (left hand) & Orchestra, Op. 21* (with SO, composer)
(B) *** Australian Double Decca 460 837-2 (2)

Katchen's very distinguished 15-year recording career spanned the end of the mono LP era and the first decade of stereo. He was for most of that time Decca's star pianist, and these six Double Deccas are part of a complete survey of his Decca recordings on a series of well-filled Doubles with the brightly lit transfers adding to the vividness, and the piano timbre of consistent high quality. However, as yet, the last two volumes are only available in their original Australian issues. Katchen's range of repertoire was as wide as his technique was brilliant, and he never delivered an unstimulating or unspontaneous performance. For his concerto recordings Decca provided him with a fine roster of conductors. The unexpected choice of Mantovani for the early LP of Gershwin's *Concerto in F* worked quite well, for he had fine soloists in his orchestra, and many will relish the compilations offered here on Volumes 5 and 6, particularly as the wonderfully imaginative performance of Britten's *Diversions* (with the composer conducting) is an indispensable highlight.

In the Beethoven concertos Katchen's partnership with Gamba worked particularly well, and the performances are fresh and commanding. Tempi are often on the fast side, but Katchen keeps a classical firmness and provides the necessary contrast in relaxed, poetic accounts of slow movements and sparkling readings of finales. In No. 1 he uses the longest and most impressive of Beethoven's own cadenzas for the first movement. The opening atmosphere of No. 4 is beautifully caught, while the *Emperor* is characteristically full of animal energy. The first and last movements are taken at a spanking pace, but not so that Katchen sounds at all rushed. Plainly he enjoyed himself all through, and in the very relaxed slow movement he seems to be coaxing the orchestra into matching his own delicacy, with the tension admirably sustained. The *Rondo* and the *Choral Fantasia*, too, are both very successful.

In the Brahms *First Concerto* the solo playing is superb, especially in the first movement, and Katchen is well partnered by Monteux (with the LSO), as he is by Ferencsik in No. 2, where he again gives an impassioned and exciting account of the solo piano part, here combining tremendous drive with the kind of ruminating delicacy Brahms so often calls for. These recordings are less successfully balanced than the Beethoven. However, in the Grieg and Schumann *Concertos* the sound is clear and brilliant, with both performances strong, any wilfulness tempered by a natural flexibility and the feeling for the music's poetry. Kertész provides plenty of life in the accompaniments. In Schumann, Katchen's virtuosity does not eschew romantic charm, the first movement more rhapsodical than usual, and throughout there is a pervading freshness. The Mozart performances, with Münchinger not always an ideally resilient conductor, yet have character (as does the solo sonata), and in the *D minor* there is strength as well as plenty of life and spirit.

In Liszt, Katchen is in his element. He is superb in the *E flat Concerto* and by any standards these are commanding performances. The Bartók, Prokofiev and Ravel *Concertos* are among his finest records, with Kertész especially compelling in his native Hungarian music, the playing combining intensity with brilliance and sparkle, and the Rachmaninov and Dohnányi performances are hardly less celebrated. The Tchaikovsky *Piano Concerto* offers equally prodigious

pianism, but is alas mono, and although the recording is basically rich and full, and the piano timbre is real and well balanced, the high violin timbre is thin and glassy, though not disastrously so, except perhaps at the very opening. Some might feel that in the finale Gamba broadens the reprise of the grand tune rather more than necessary. An exciting account just the same. Of the other solo performances Katchen's almost unbelievable technique is well demonstrated in Balakirev's *Islamey*. Even in an age of technicians few pianists could play the piece like this. The *Mephisto Waltz* and Mussorgsky *Pictures* are also pretty remarkable, but in the latter the rather dry mono sound does not help Katchen to colour the music as he might. *Goldenberg and Schmuyle* and the *Chicks* are highlights, but the finale could ideally be more expansive.

Volume 7: BEETHOVEN: *Piano Sonatas 23 in F min. (Appassionata), Op. 57; 32 in C min., Op. 111. 33 Variations on a Waltz by Diabelli, Op. 129; 6 Bagatelles, Op. 126; Polonaise in C, Op. 89* MOZART: *Piano Sonatas 13 in B flat, K.388; 16 in C, K.545.*
*** Australian Decca Double mono/stereo 466 714-2 (2)

Katchen recorded his impressive (mono) *Appassionata* in 1956 and his sparkling account of the *Diabelli Variations* (a work that proved ideal for his pianistic talents) in 1961, but Opus 111 dates from the year before his death. Already the cancer which would kill him was taking its toll, for the playing, although still prodigious, is no longer immaculate. But the performance has great power, total spontaneity and a profound searching inner quality in the *Adagio*. The Mozart sonatas, also from 1956 and mono, are sheer delight, wonderfully crisp and stylish, yet with just the right degree of underlying expressive feeling. All the recordings have come up well and Katchen is given a very real presence.

Volume 8: SCHUBERT: *Fantasy in C (Wanderer), D.760.* SCHUMANN: *Carnaval, Op. 9; Toccata in C, Op. 7; Arabeske in C, Op. 18.* DEBUSSY: *Suite bergamasque: Clair de lune.* FALLA: *El amor brujo: Ritual Fire Dance.* CHOPIN: *Piano Sonatas 2 in B flat min. (Funeral March), Op. 36; 3 in B min., Op. 58; Fantaisie-impromptu, Op. 66; Polonaise 6 in A flat (Heroic), Op. 53.* MENDELSSOHN: *Rondo capriccioso, Op. 14.* LISZT: *Concert Paraphrase of Mendelssohn's On Wings of Song.* BACH, arr. HESS: *Jesu, joy of man's desiring*
*** Australian Decca Double mono/stereo 466 717-2 (2)

Volume 8 is another Double showing the remarkable range of a great pianist who died sadly young at the age of 42. The performance of *Carnaval* is striking for its skittishness as well as its infinite variety of mood and colour, while the *Arabeske* has a delightful sense of fantasy. The *Wanderer Fantasia* also shows both Katchen's imaginative range and his feeling for Schubert. But what stands out here is the Chopin, powerful yet with a natural lyrical feeling. His virtuosity comes into play too in the dazzling account of the *Fantaisie-impromptu*, while the finale of the *B flat minor Sonata* is quite breathtaking in its evenness and clarity, and the *Scherzo* of the *B minor* is just as remarkable in its clean articulation. Yet both slow movements are deeply felt. The famous *A flat Polonaise* is arresting and the two Mendelssohn pieces which follow show in turns sparkling dexterity and an unsentimental bold romantic impulse, while Debussy's *Clair de lune* has an exquisite simplicity. The sound throughout is excellent.

Kayath, Marcelo (guitar)

'Spanish Guitar Music': TARREGA: *Prelude in A min.; Capricho arabe; Recuerdos de la Alhambra.* GRANADOS: *La Maja de Goya.* ALBENIZ: *Granada; Zambra; Granadina; Sevilla; Mallorca.* TORROBA: *Prelude in E; Sonatina; Nocturno.* RODRIGO: *Zapateado.* TRAD.: *El Noy de la mare*
(BB) *** Regis RRC 1122

Following the success of his first Latin-American recital (see below), Marcelo Kayath gives us an equally enjoyable and spontaneous Spanish collection, full of colour. By grouping music by several major composers, he provides a revealing mix. The three fine Tárrega pieces include the famous *Recuerdos*, played strongly; then come five of Granados's most evocative and tuneful geographical evocations, while the Tórroba group includes the attractive three-movement *Sonatina*. After the vibrant Rodrigo miniature, he closes with the hauntingly memorable *El Noy de la mare*. The recording affords him a realistic presence in a pleasing acoustic.

'South American Guitar Classics': PONCE: *Valse; Preámbulo e allegro; Gavotte.* PIAZZOLA: *La muerte del angel.* BARRIOS: *Mazurka appassionata; Danza Paraguaya; Tremolo, Una limosna por el amor de Dios; Tango 2; Study in A (Las abejas); Vals, Op. 8/3; Choror de Saudade; Julia Florida.* LAURO: *Vals Venezolanus 2; El negrito; El marabino.* REIS: *Si eia preguntar.* VILLA-LOBOS: *5 Preludes*
(BB) *** Regis RRC 1149

Marcelo Kayath's inspirational accounts of the Villa-Lobos *Preludes* can stand comparison with the finest performances on record, and he is equally at home in the extended programme of the distinctive music of Barrios, playing with the lightest touch and a nice feeling for rubato, notably so in the *Vals*. He is a fine advocate too of the engaging Lauro pieces. Indeed, he plays everything here with consummate technical ease and the most appealing spontaneity. The recording, made in a warm but not too resonant acoustic, is first class.

Kempff, Wilhelm (piano)

'Classic Archive': Recitals at the Paris ORTF, and Besançon: SCHUMANN: *Arabeske in C, Op. 18; Papillons, Op. 2; Davidsbündlertänze, Op. 6.* BEETHOVEN: *Piano Sonatas 14 in C sharp min. (Moonlight), Op. 27/2; 17 in D min. (Tempest), Op. 31/2; 27 in E min., Op. 90*
⊕ *** EMI DVD DVB 490447-9. (Directors: Gérard Herzog, Denise Billon, Claude Ventura & Yvonne Courson). Bonus: SCHUMANN: *Novelleten, Op. 21/1.* BARTOK: *Out of Doors, Nos. 4 & 5* (Dino Ciani)

This DVD is pure gold. Even though the Schumann items (from 1961 and 1963) and the Beethoven *Tempest Sonata* (1969) are in black and white, the latter has a brief voice-over as Kempff begins to play, and by some oversight the recording misses out most of the exposition of the first movement. Yet the visual images are very remarkable; and when we see the *Moonlight Sonata* and the *E minor, Op. 90*, in colour, the effect is totally compelling. As we guessed from his records, Kempff's concentration is visionary: he is utterly held inside the music; there is absolutely no attempt to play to the audience. He plays for the composer, his *pianissimos* raptly gentle, his *fortissimos* unexpectedly strong. His affinity with both Schumann and Beethoven is legendary, and now we can

enjoy the unassertive genius of his art and watch his curiously stubby fingers coaxing magical sounds from the keyboard. His face is often almost expressionless, yet with just occasionally a hint of a smile of pleasure at a special turn of phrase or modulation. The recording is generally very good, catching a full range of dynamic, and the camera angles are simple, with the changes of perspective sensibly managed. There is a curious black-and-white bonus of Dino Ciani playing (and playing very well) Schumann and Bartók, but neither the photography or the sound is distinguished.

Recital in Queen Elizabeth Hall, London, 5 June 1969: BACH: *Chromatic Fantasia and Fugue, BWV 903.* BEETHOVEN: *Sonata 22 in F, Op. 54.* SCHUBERT *Sonata 11 in F min., D.625; 3 Klavierstücke, D.946; Impromptus 3 & 4, D.899/3–4*
(M) *** BBC (ADD) BBCL 4045

This recital was one of the finest examples of Kempff's inspired pianism that London ever heard. He was still at the height of his powers, and inspiration did not desert him on this occasion. Brendel spoke of his *cantabile* with reverence as being the essence of his art, which made him such a great Schubert interpreter and makes his *Klavierstücke* so special. (Oddly enough, the cover does not refer to the *F minor Sonata*.) But the Bach and Beethoven are hardly less magnificent, and they enhance the value of this invaluable BBC archive series. This playing really is the stuff of legends.

Broadcast Recital, 7 October 1967: MOZART: *Sonata 12 in F, K.332.* SCHUBERT: *Sonata 21 in B flat, D.960.* BEETHOVEN: *Sonata 12 in A, Op. 101.* BRAHMS: *Intermezzi, Op. 119/1–2*
(***) BBC mono BBCL 4169

What can one say about a recital as unforgettably fine as this? Kempff's Beethoven is very special: unforced, lyrical. Sample the opening of Op. 101 or the lovely *Adagio* of Mozart's K.332 for perfect simplicty. We already know his Schubert *B flat Sonata* from his studio recording. This is just as haunting but interpretatively not identical; and the Brahms *Intermezzi* make an ideal epilogue. Very good mono sound. Not to be missed.

Piano Transcriptions (arr. Kempff): BACH: *Chorale Preludes: Es ist gewisslich an der Zeit, BWV 307 & 734; Nun komm der Heiden Heiland, BWV 659; Befehl du deine Wege, BWV 727; In dulci jubilo, BWV 751; Wachet auf, BWV 140; Ich ruf' zu dir, BWV 639; Jesus bleibet meine Freude, BWV 147/6; Cantatas 29: Sinfonia, BWV 147: Herz und Mund und Tat und Leben: Jesu, joy of man's desiring; Flute Sonata in E flat, BWV 1031: Siciliano. Harpsichord Concerto 5 in F min., BWV 1056: Largo.* HANDEL: *Minuet in G min.* GLUCK: *Orfeo ed Euridice: ballet music.* J. S. BACH: *English Suite 3 in G min.; French Suite 5 in G, BWV 816*
**(*) Australian DG Eloquence (ADD) 457 624-2

The Kempff magic is never entirely absent from any of this pianist's recordings, but some may feel that it makes its presence felt rather unevenly in this recital. Several of the *Chorale Preludes* are played in a rather studied way. The presentation of *Wachet auf* is very firm and clear, the background embroidery precisely articulated, and *Jesu, joy of man's desiring* has more extrovert projection than usual. The *Siciliano* from BWV 1031, however, is given an appealing lyrical flow, and the *Orfeo* excerpts are very beautiful. For this bargain release, the *English Suite 3* and the *French Suite 5* have been added, and they are first class in every way.

Kennedy, Nigel (violin), Lynn Harrell (cello)

'Duos for Violin and Cello': RAVEL: *Sonata.* HANDEL:
Harpsichord Suite 7 in G min.: Passacaglia (arr.
HALVORSEN/PRESS). KODALY: *Duo.* BACH: *2-Part
Invention 6 in E*
→ ❀ *** EMI 5 56963-2

An extraordinarily successful collaboration between the
extrovert Kennedy and the more reticent Harrell, in which
the listener has the constant impression of inspirational live
intercommunication, and no suggestion whatsoever of the
recording studio. The Ravel *Sonata* opens with disarming
simplicity and immediately takes off, producing an enormous
intensity of feeling – whether in the sheer gutsy energy and
fireworks of the *Très vif Scherzo*, or the veiled delicacy of the
slow movement, begun very gently by Harrell.

The playing in the first movement of the masterly Kodály
Duo is so closely and powerfully intertwined, so completely
integrated in its ebb and flow of phrasing, dynamic and
tension, that it is as if violin and cello were the flip sides of
the same coin. The superb Handel *Passacaglia* is played with
confident and captivating bravura and the programme ends
coolly and satisfyingly with simple Bach polyphony, the
interchange quite perfectly balanced. The recording is forward and gives the illusion of an extremely vivid presence,
within an open acoustic.

Khaner, Jeffrey (flute) Sung, Hugh (piano)

'American Flute Music': ELDIN BURTON: *Sonatina.*
COPLAND: *Duo.* PISTON: *Sonata.* BERYL RUBINSTEIN:
Sonata. LIEBERMANN: *Sonata.* JENNIFER HIGDON:
Autumn Reflection
(M) *** Avie 0004

A most attractive anthology (with only two really well-known
names included) to suggest that twentieth-century American
composers understand the flute just as well as the French (see
below). The *Sonatina* of Georgia-born Eldin Burton is immediately lyrically diverting, the *grazioso* first movement leading
to a dreamy *Andante* (with cascading flute runs at its reprise)
and a lilting *Fandango* for Finale.

Beryl Rubinstein was also born in Georgia, and her 1941
Sonata is just as immediately attractive as that of her fellow
Georgian. The titles of the three eminently tuneful movements are self-explanatory: *Cheerful and with motion* (one
might add 'jaunty'), *Lyrical* (one might add 'songful, and a
touch modal'), *but not dragging*; and *Spirited and very rhythmic* (but with a tinge of lyricism too).

Copland's splendid *Duo* (1971) ought to be a repertoire
work. The first movement has a flowing, gentle progress,
happily remembering familar ideas from his early ballet
scores; the second movement is even more wistful and the
finale, *Lively, with bounce*, may be rhythmically jagged but it
has a splendidly confident dénouement. Piston's *Sonata* is
simultaneously modern and neoclassical, introspective and
sombre in the *Adagio*, then with a sparkling change of heart
in the bubbly finale.

Lowell Liebermann is another considerable American figure, whose music has not so far exported readily. Yet here he
writes engagingly, breaking the mould by constructing a
two-movement *Sonata* (1988) in which the thoughtful first
movement jogs along amiably but memorably (*Lento con
rubato*), until interrupted by a brief *fortissimo* outburst, after
which the pensive mood returns. By contrast, the virtuoso

finale goes even faster than the wind, and is full of passionate
feeling.

After that, Jennifer Higdon's *Autumn Reflection* (1994),
inspired by the Appalachian fall colours, is a free soliloquy,
rather angular in outline but deeply felt, ending in nostalgia.
All these works are superbly played by Jeffrey Khaner who,
American by birth and training, knows just what they are
about. His accompanist is first rate too, and the recording is
excellent.

'French Flute Music': DUBOIS: *Sonata.* GAUBERT: *Sonata 1
in A.* FAURÉ: *Fantasie.* TANSMAN: *Sonatine.* POULENC:
Sonata. SANCAN: *Sonatine.* DEBUSSY: *Syrinx*
(M) *** Avie 0027

A wholly delightful record in every respect. Every one of the
seven works here demonstrates the special fascination of the
modern flute for French composers, who found a way to cool
its intrinsic sensuality when required and refine its agility, yet
always seduce the listener's ear. If the key work here is
Poulenc's masterpiece, with its immediately engaging *Allegro
melancolico* and chirpy *Presto giocoso* framing an exquisite
central *Cantilena*, the opening *Sonata* of Pierre-Max Dubois
is also full of sparkle and wit, with a comparable balancing
Andante nostalgico.

Phillipe Gaubert's piece is more restrained, taking the stage
with a gentle *Modéré*, followed by a hauntingly delicate *Lent*,
modal in harmonic inflexion, while its finale, for all its
romantic flair, retains its moderation without losing its magnetism.

Fauré's *Fantasie* has much in common with Debussy's
subtly understated, unaccompanied *Syrinx*, imbued with
comparably delicate lyrical feeling. Alexandre Tansman, on
the other hand, was Polish born but moved to Paris. His style
is correspondingly eclectic, with a foxtrot Scherzo at the
centre of his five-movement *Sonatine*, framed by a wistful
Intermezzo and a melancholy *Notturno.*

Pierre Sancan, a gifted pianist and teacher at the Conservatoire, wrote his *Sonatine* in a three-movements-in-one formation, its central section full of nostalgia, while in the finale
the flute seems to be happily chasing its tail.

All these works are superbly played by Jeffrey Khaner who,
though American by birth and training, is totally at one with
the French sensibility. His technique is dazzling and his
timbre glows luminously, while his partner, Hugh Sung,
matches his every turn of phrase very musically indeed. The
recording is very real and beautifully balanced.

King, Thea (clarinet), Clifford Benson (piano)

English Clarinet Music: STANFORD: *Sonata, Op. 29.*
FERGUSON: *4 Short Pieces, Op. 6.* FINZI: *5 Bagatelles, Op. 23.*
HURLSTONE: *4 Characteristic Pieces.* HOWELLS: *Sonata.*
BLISS: *Pastoral.* REIZENSTEIN: *Arabesques.* COOKE: *Sonata
in B flat*
(B) *** Hyp. Dyad CDD 22027 (2)

This Hyperion Dyad aptly combines two separate recitals,
now offered for the price of one. They were recorded at the
beginning of the 1980s and are in many ways complementary.
Stanford's *Clarinet Sonata* is clearly influenced by Brahms but
has plenty of character of its own. The other works on the
first disc are all appealingly communicative, lighter in texture
and content, but well crafted.

The second CD opens with the Howells *Sonata*, among the

finest written since Brahms, a warmly lyrical piece in two extended movements that bring out the instrument's varied colourings. Bliss's early *Pastoral* follows, thoughtful and unassuming, improvisatory in feeling. Reizenstein's short piece then acts as an interlude before the Cooke *Sonata*, strong but undemanding, with a darkly nostalgic *Adagio* and a chirpy finale. Thea King's warm, naturally expressive playing makes her an ideal advocate, not only for the music, but for her instrument; and her partner, Clifford Benson, is no less eloquent. Smooth, natural, analogue recording.

Kipnis, Igor (harpsichord)

'*First Solo Recordings (1962)*': BACH: *French Suite 6 in E, BWV 817; Fantasia in G min., BWV 917; Prelude, Fugue and Allegro in E flat, BWV 998. Toccata in E min., BWV 914.* HANDEL: *Suite 5 in E (HWV 430).* SOLER (attrib.): *Fandango in D min.* DUSSEK: *The Sufferings of the Queen of France*
*** VAI Audio VAIA 1185

With a photo of the young Kipnis as the frontispiece, this superb recital demonstrates a prodigious keyboard talent, and playing that is thoughtful, scholarly yet alive. His Bach is of a high calibre, and equally impressive is the Handel suite (which includes a breathtaking account of the *Harmonious blacksmith*). Soler's extended *Fandango* is equally brilliant and diverting, and he ends with his own edition of Dussek's vividly pictorial programmatic fantasia, describing the suffering, imprisonment and execution of Marie Antoinette – played with great imaginative flair, and bravura. The harpsichord is not named, but it is a most attractive instrument, with a wide range of colour, and is most naturally recorded.

Kissin, Evgeni (piano)

'*Carnegie Hall Début*' (30 September 1990), *Highlights*: LISZT: *Etude d'exécution transcendante 10; Liebestraum 3; Rhapsodie espagnole.* SCHUMANN: *Abegg Variations, Op. 1; Etudes symphoniques, Op. 13; Widmung* (arr. LISZT)
*** BMG/RCA 09026 61202-2

Evgeni Kissin has phenomenal pianistic powers; this is a *tour de force* not only in terms of technical prowess but also in sheer artistry. Both sets of Schumann *Variations* are remarkable. The Liszt *Rhapsodie espagnole* is played with superb bravura. Kissin's range of colour and keyboard command throughout are dazzling. The Carnegie Hall was packed and the recording balance, while a bit close, is perfectly acceptable. The excitement of the occasion is conveyed vividly.

BEETHOVEN: *Piano Sonata 14 in C sharp min. (Moonlight), Op. 27/2.* BRAHMS: *Variations on a Theme of Paganini, Op. 35.* FRANCK: *Prélude, choral et fugue*
*** RCA 09026 68910-2

Strongly projected playing from this outstanding (and still young) artist. There is impressive concentration in the Beethoven, an effortless virtuosity in the Brahms, and great poetic feeling in the Franck. Everything here bears witness to a powerful musical mind allied to consummate pianistic mastery. Excellent recorded sound.

Kocsis, Zoltán (piano)

BEETHOVEN: *Sonata 27 in E min., Op. 90.* SCHUBERT: *Sonata 7 in E min., D.566.* BARTOK: *Sonata, Sz80; For Children: excerpts.* KURTAG: *Games: excerpts.* LISZT: *Hungarian Rhapsody 5 in E min.; Années de pèlerinage: Les Jeux d'eau à la Villa d'Este; Sunt lacrymae rerum; Czárdás macabre*
*** Naïve DVD DR 2100 AV103 (Recorded live at La Roque d'Anthéron, France, 29 July 2002; V/D: János Darvas)

Kocsis may have lost his youthful appearance but certainly none of his ability to mesmerize an audience. At 90 minutes this recital is more generous in length than Lugansky's but no less rewarding musically. Recorded at La Roque d'Anthéron in the heart of Provence when Kocsis had just turned fifty, his Bartók has tremendous fire and virtuosity, while the Beethoven and Schubert exhibit a satisfying blend of classicism and sensitivity. The Liszt, too, has effortless technique and naturalness of utterance to commend it. As with the other recitals we have heard in this series, the sound has superb clarity and definition, and the camerawork is altogether exemplary. A most worthwhile issue that can be recommended to all admirers of this artist and to all lovers of the piano.

Kogan, Leonid (violin)

'*Classic Archive*': BACH: *Violin Partita in D min., BWV 1004: Sarabande.* HANDEL: *Violin Sonata in E, HWV 373.* DEBUSSY: *Beau soir.* SHOSTAKOVICH: *Preludes, Op. 24/10, 15, 16 & 24* (with Andrei Mytnik). BRAHMS: *Hungarian Dance 17.* PAGANINI: *Cantabile.* FALLA: *Suite populaire espagnole* (with Naum Walter, piano). LECLAIR: *Sonata for 2 Violins in C, Op. 3/3* (with Elizaveta Gilels-Kogan)
(***) EMI DVD 492834-9 – BEETHOVEN: *Violin Concerto* (**(*))

This is even more rewarding than the Beethoven *Concerto*, because the BBC recordings from 1962 do full justice to the great tonal refinement Kogan commanded. They were produced by Walter Todds, whose direction of the cameras is a model of unobtrusiveness and discretion. The Handel has seamless phrasing and a musicality that is a joy in itself, and *Beau Soir* and the four Shostakovich *Preludes* in Dmitri Tziganov's transcriptions are no less beguiling. Andrei Mytnik is a splendid partner, and the overall sound is hardly less refined in the 1968 Paris recordings (Brahms, Falla and Paganini). Kogan's stage presence may lack charm but he saves that quality for his music-making. There is a bonus in the form of a 1963 recording of a Leclair *Sonata for Two Violins* which he recorded with his wife (the sister of Emil Gilels). There is a good accompanying essay from Tully Potter.

Koh, Jennifer (violin), Reiko Uchida (piano)

'*Violin Fantasies*': ORNETTE COLEMAN: *Trinity.* SCHOENBERG: *Phantasy, Op. 47.* SCHUBERT: *Fantasy in C, D.934.* SCHUMANN: *Fantasie in C, Op. 131*
*** Cedille CDR 90000 073

Jennifer Koh, winner of the 1994 Tchaikovsky Competition, offers an unusual and attractive grouping of works, based on the idea of a Fantasy, the most flexible of forms. The warmth and imagination of her playing consistently illuminate pieces that by the very freedom of their structure need a positive hand to hold them together. This she does admirably, with the help of an ideally matched partner in he pianist, Reiko Uchida, wonderfully crisp and agile in piano writing that is not always grateful for the player. The Schubert, with its central set of variations on the song, 'Sei mir gegrüsst', fares least well, partly because of the ungainly piano part; but that leads to magnetic, often passionate accounts of the other three pieces. The Schumann *Fantasie in C* was one of his last works, written for the young Joachim, and here played in the composer's own piano transcription of the orchestral part, while Schoenberg's *Phantasy* was the last of his instrumental works, for which the piano part was added almost as an afterthought. *Trinity*, for unaccompanied violin, has the jazz musician Ornette Coleman forsaking his usual idiom in a lyrical meditation with folk-like overtones. Excellent recording.

Kremer, Gidon (violin)

Violin Sonatas: BEETHOVEN: *Sonatas 1–10* (complete).
SCHUMANN: *Sonatas 1–2.* BARTOK: *Sonata for Violin & Piano 1.* JANACEK: *Sonata.* MESSIAEN: *Theme and Variations for Violin & Piano.* PROKOFIEV: *Sonatas 1–2; 5 Mélodies, Op. 35 bis* (all with Argerich). BRAHMS: *Sonatas 1–3.* BUSONI: *Sonata 2 in E min., Op. 36a* (both with Afanassiev). R. STRAUSS: *Sonata in E flat, Op. 18* (with Maisenberg)
(B) ** DG 474 648-2 (8)

Kremer's partnership with Martha Argerich proved to be very propitious in Beethoven and Schumann, and their volatile Beethoven cycle is highly praised in our main volume, notably for its freshness and spontaneity, as are the Schumann *Sonatas*, which are reflective and mercurial by turns.

The triptych of Bartók, Janáček and Messiaen is also very successful, the Bartók played with great expressive intensity, enormous range of colour and effortless virtuosity, while the Janáček again displays great imaginative intensity and power. The Messiaen *Variations*, an early work, is rarer, and here the music's fervour is well captured.

However, these artists are less successful in Prokofiev, where subtle differences of dynamics or characterization do not detain them more than cursorily and Prokofiev's lyricism takes second place to considerations of virtuosic display. The recordings, however, are excellent.

For the Brahms and Busoni *Sonatas* Kremer formed a partnership with Valery Afanassiev which proved much less fortunate. Not that there is any doubt as to their artistry and accomplishment, but their approach is so studied as to be self-conscious; in the opening of the *A major Sonata*, for example, the playing has enormous tonal refinement, but the expressive hesitations in the lead into the second subject group are surely excessive. The first three minutes of the *G major* are beautifully played, it is true, but the way in which these artists hold back just before the end of the exposition through to the return of the G major theme is unacceptably wilful. There is little difference between the *Allegro* and the ensuing *Adagio* of the *G minor*, so disruptive are the rubati and so slow the tempi that the music is robbed of any sense of forward movement.

These artists then follow on with another indulgent performance – of Busoni's *Second Sonata*, which is a one-movement piece, dating from 1898, with a *Langsam* opening (though not as langsam as it is in their hands), a *Presto*, and a most beautiful *Andante* section leading to a set of variations, where they are heard at their best.

Fortunately, Kremer's partnership with Oleg Maisenberg in the Richard Strauss *Sonata* is more successful. If these artists fail to find the fullest romantic intensity which distinguishes both the Repin/Berezovsky and Kyung Wha Chung versions, their performance is still enjoyable – and especially so in the brilliant finale. As throughout, the recording is excellent, but this compilation is difficult to recommend as a whole, except to Kremer's admirers.

Kvapil, Radoslav (piano)

'*Czech Piano Anthology*': The Music of Dvořák, Janáček, Smetana, Suk
(BB) *** Regis RRC 4005 (4)

The separate CDs in this outstanding anthology are all reviewed individually under their composer entries, but this makes a most attractive package.

Landowska, Wanda (harpsichord)

'*Portrait*': F. COUPERIN: *La favorite; Les moissonneurs; Les Langueurs-Tendres; Le Gazouillement; La Commère; Le Moucheron; Les Bergeries; Les Tambourins; Les Fastes de la grande ménestrandise; Le Dodo, ou l'amour au berceau; Musette de Taverny; Les Folies françaises ou les Dominos; Les Calotins et les calotines; Les Vergers fleuris; Soeur Monique.* RAMEAU: *Suite in G min.* BACH: *Goldberg Variations, BWV 988.* HANDEL: *Suites 2 in F, HWV 427; 5 in E, HWV 430; 7 in G min., HWV 432*
(M) (***) Grammofono 2000 mono AB 78715/6

It is good to have a representative collection of the art of Wanda Landowska, who put the harpsichord back on the musical map in the twentieth century. She was not the first to try to do so; Violet Gordon Woodhouse actually made earlier acoustic recordings of some distinction, but it was Landowska's larger-than-life personality that soon made her a star. She gave her first performances on this instrument in 1903, and she toured Europe over the next two decades, visiting the United States from 1923 onwards. She persuaded Falla and Poulenc to write concertos (in 1926 and 1927 respectively) and had Pleyel build a large, modern instrument especially for her concerts.

Yet, as is readily apparent here, in the music of Couperin and Rameau she could articulate with the greatest delicacy (*La Poule* is delightful), and she kept her big guns in reserve for appropriate moments. Her *Goldberg Variations* was rightly celebrated, the playing robust when required but suitably restrained at other times. Her overall timing is surprisingly close to Leonhardt's but her approach, without any loss of seriousness of purpose, is freer and more imaginative, and her reprise of the *Aria* reminds one of Rosalyn Tureck in its delicacy of feeling.

The recordings of French music were made in 1934, the *Goldberg* in 1933, and the quality is excellent, although in the French *pièces de clavecin* there are pitch differences between some items. The Handel *Suites* are a little more variable in sound, but still impressive, and in No. 5 *The Harmonious Blacksmith* (1935) strikes his anvil at first robustly but later with varying degrees of delicacy: there is no more spontaneous account in the catalogue. In the *Overture* which opens Handel's *Seventh Suite*, Landowska flamboyantly sounds like a full orchestra, and she plays the closing *Passacaglia* with similar satisfying weight, but in between there is a wider range of dynamic. Above all, this great artist communicated her joy in everything she played, and these excellent transfers ensure that we fully share it.

LaSalle Quartet

Chamber Music of the Second Viennese School: BERG: *Lyric Suite; String Quartet, Op. 3.* SCHOENBERG: *String Quartets: in D; 1 in D min., Op. 7; 2 in F sharp min., Op. 10/3* (with Price); *No. 3, Op. 30; 4, Op. 37.* WEBERN: *5 Movements, Op. 5; String Quartet* (1905); *6 Bagatelles, Op. 9; String Quartet, Op. 28*

(M) *** DG (IMS) 419 994-2 (4)

DG have compressed their 1971 five-LP set on to four CDs, offering them at a reduced and competitive price. They have also retained the invaluable and excellent documentary study edited by Ursula Rauchhaupt – which runs to 340 pages! It is almost worth having this set for the documentation alone. The LaSalle Quartet give splendidly expert performances, even if at times their playing seems a little cool; and they are very well recorded. An invaluable issue for all who care about twentieth-century music.

Lawson, Peter, and Alan MacLean

(piano duet)

English Music for Piano Duet: BERNERS: *Valses bourgeoises; Fantasie espagnole; 3 Morceaux.* LAMBERT: *Overture* (ed. Lane); *3 Pièces nègres pour les touches blanches.* RAWSTHORNE: *The Creel.* WALTON: *Duets for Children.* LANE: *Badinages*

*** Troy TROY 142

This collection centres on Lord Berners, who had a recurring twinkle in the eye and loved to parody; moreover his inspiration regularly casts a glance in the direction of Satie and Poulenc, as the *Trois Morceaux* readily demonstrate. Both Walton and Constant Lambert were his friends, admired his individuality and came under his influence. Lambert's *Trois Pièces nègres* have a Satiesque title, yet they are all the composer's own work: the *Siesta* is quite haunting and the catchy *Nocturne* brings sparkling Latin-American rhythmic connotations, far removed from Chopin.

The four engaging Rawsthorne miniatures, inspired by Izaak Walton's *Compleat Angler*, fit equally well into the programme. The Walton *Duets for Children* have a disarming simplicity and often a nursery rhyme bounce: *Hop Scotch* is particularly delightful, and vignettes like *The Silent Lake* and *Ghosts* will surely communicate very directly to young performers. Walton's final *Galop* was arranged by Philip Lane, who also provides four of his own pieces to close the concert with a strongly Gallic atmosphere. The performances by Peter Lawson and Alan MacLean are strong on style yet also convey affection. Excellent recording in a nicely resonant but not muddy acoustic.

Leach, Joanna (piano)

'Four Square': SOLER: *Sonata 90 in F sharp.* HAYDN: *Sonata in C, Hob XVI/1.* J.S. BACH: *Partita 1 in B flat: Prelude; Minuets I & II; Gigue.* MOZART: *Fantasia in D min., K.397; Sonata 11 in A, K.331.* SCHUBERT: *Impromptu in A flat, D.899/4.* MENDELSSOHN: *Songs Without Words, Op. 19/1*

*** Athene CD 3

There is no more convincing fortepiano recital than this. Joanna Leach uses an 1823 Stodart with its effectively dark lower register for the Soler *Sonata*, then plays the same instrument later to show its attractive upper range in an almost romantic performance of Mozart's *Fantasia in D minor*, she ends the recital with the *A major Sonata*, K.331, with the introductory variations particularly inviting. For the Haydn, she chooses a 1789 Broadwood, a more brittle sound, and for the Bach a very effective 1787 instrument made by Longman & Broderip. In the Schubert and Mendelssohn pieces an 1835 D'Almaine brings us that bit nearer a modern piano. Fine performances throughout, and excellent recording. A fascinating way of discovering what the modern piano's ancestors could best do.

Léner Quartet

HAYDN: *String Quartets: 76 in D min., Op. 76/2: Andante; 77 in C (Emperor), Op. 76/3; 79 in D, Op. 76/5* (2 versions)
(**) Rockport mono RR 5004

HAYDN: *String Quartets 17 in F, Op. 3/5* (2 versions); *67 in D (Lark), Op. 64/5: Minuet.* MOZART: *Divertimento 17 in D, K.334* (with Aubrey & Dennis Brain)
(**) Rockport mono RR 5006

SCHUBERT: *Octet in F, D.803* (with Draper, Aubrey Brain, Hinchcliff, Hobday). SCHUMANN: *String Quartet 3 in A, Op. 41/3*
(**) Rockport mono RR 5008

MOZART: *Oboe Quartet in F, K.370* (with Goossens); *String Quartet 17 in B flat (Hunt), K.458; String Quintet 3 in G min., K.516* (with d'Oliviera)
(**) Rockport mono RR 5010

These are the first four CDs in what is to be a complete reissue of all the Léner Quartet recordings on CD. The scale of the enterprise is daunting, as the Léners recorded no fewer than 210 shellac discs. The planners of the series estimate that the final set will run to 30 CDs. Only a few of their recordings are currently available: the Brahms *Quartets*, the Mozart and Brahms *Clarinet Quintets* and the Mozart *Oboe Quartet* with Leon Goossens (also included here). The Léners began recording in 1924 and were the first to record a complete Beethoven cycle. One unusual feature of this venture is to juxtapose their acoustic recordings with later, electrical versions on the same CD. The first disc brings Haydn's *Emperor Quartet*, Op. 76, No. 3, made in 1935, and contrasts their 1924 and 1928 versions of the *D major Quartet*, Op. 76, No. 5. Similarly, the third disc brings two versions of the Op. 3, No. 5 (now attributed to Roman Hoffstetter).

Those who think of the Léner as oversweet in tone with too much vibrato and cloying portamento should hear the *Hunt Quartet*, recorded in 1924. The sound is frail and wanting in body, but the quartet's purity of style is quite striking. Later on, in the 1930s, Jenö Léner developed a much wider vibrato, witness the *D major Divertimento*, K.334, from 1939 (with Aubrey and Dennis Brain) and again in the *G minor Quintet*, K.516, of 1930, with Louis d'Oliviera as second viola. Contrasts between their approach in the same works are often quite marked. In the first movement of Op. 3, No. 5 they are faster in their 1924 acoustic recording, although the famous *Serenade* movement is slower in 1928 and much pulled around. The Schumann Quartet in A, Op. 41, No. 3, is wonderfully rhapsodic in feeling, with little sense of the bar-line. Indeed, this is the sort of approach that seems totally idiomatic. Léner shows great imagination and poetic feeling in the *Adagio*, and there is an aristocratic poise that distinguishes his playing throughout. His style is very personal, whether or not you like it, and, on its own terms, is completely natural in approach, with, above all, no playing to the gallery. The Schubert *Octet*, with such distinguished figures as Charles Draper and Aubrey Brain, has some lovely playing, though the sound is pretty frail. Allowances have to be made for the actual quality, but then that is the case throughout the set. Robert Philip in his *Grove* article rightly speaks of the 'unusually homogeneous blend' of the Léners and the 'extraordinary smoothness and finish of their performances'. What is equally striking are their matchless sense of legato, a sophisticated lyricism (some might say over-sophisticated) and a generally unhurried and civilized approach. An important project.

Lidström, Mats (cello), Bengt Forsberg (piano)

'*Smörgåsbord*': KORNGOLD: *Mummenschant; Romance Impromptu in E flat.* GRAINGER: *Sussex Mummers' Christmas Carol.* SIBELIUS: *Rondino; Berceuse.* GODOWSKY: *Larghetto lamentoso.* JONGEN: *Valse; Habanera.* MONTSALVATGE: *Canto negro.* HALFFTER: *Habanera.* MOERAN: *Prelude.* KREISLER: *Liebesleid.* SCRIABIN: *Poème in F sharp, Op. 32/1; Romance in A min.* MARTINU: *Arabesque 1.* TORTELIER: *Pishnetto.* HAGG: *Andante; Albumblatt.* LENNOX BERKELEY: *Andantino, Op. 21/2a.* LIDSTRÖM: *The Sea of Flowers is Rising Higher (Elegy).* RAMEAU: *Air vif; 'Torture d'Alphise'.* TILLE: *Courante.* OFFENBACH: *Souvenir du val, Op. 29/1.* FAURE: *Pièce (Papillon), Op. 77.* STENHAMMAR: *Adagio*
*** Hyp. CDA 67184

This fine Swedish partnership has given us some enterprising issues, ranging from Saint-Saëns to Boëllmann and Benjamin Godard, but on this disc they assemble some 25 *bonnes bouches* lasting in all not much longer than an hour. They call it '*Smörgåsbord*' (the table of Scandinavian hors d'oeuvres that used to precede but sometimes also comprises the main course) although many of the pieces here, such as Ernesto Halffter's *Habanera* and Kreisler's *Liebesleid* could just as well be petits fours. In any event, whether they be sweet or savoury, they are all delicious as served here. As a glance at the listing above shows, their choice of repertoire is highly enterprising and ingenious. The thought of hearing so many miniatures puts one in mind of Bernard Shaw's celebrated remark about Grieg: 'His sweet but very cosmopolitan modulations, and his inability to get beyond a very pretty snatch of melody do not go very far with me – give me a good, solid, long-winded classical lump of composition with time to go to sleep and wake up two or three times in each movement.' Well, there is no time to doze off here, and no inducement to do so either. Everything is compellingly and exquisitely played, and beautifully recorded too. Almost all these pieces are worthwhile, though one is not altogether sure about Lidström's own work, written soon after the death of Diana, Princess of Wales. But that is the single exception and this is a highly enjoyable issue.

Lim, Dong-Hyek (piano)

CHOPIN: *Ballade 1 in G min., Op. 23; Etude in C, Op. 10./1; Scherzo 2 in B flat min., Op. 31.* RAVEL: *La Valse* (trans. composer); SCHUBERT: *Four Impromptus, D.899/1–4*
● (M) *** EMI 5 67933-2

Magnificent! This recital by the South Korean pianist Dong-Hyek Lim is as virtuosic as were some of his footballing countrymen at the World Cup. He was seventeen last year when this recital was recorded, and is presently studying in Moscow with Lev Naumov. From the very first bar to the last, he has the listener in his grip, such is the strength of his musical personality. A real artist and not just a brilliant pianist, he brings a commanding narrative power to this repertoire. The Chopin is electrifying, sensitive, poetic and has an authority that is unexpected in one so young, and the Schubert has depth and poignancy. He is one of the artists who appear under Martha Argerich's banner and has the same youthful flair she had at the beginning of her career as well as ardour, effortless technique and sensitivity.

Lindsay Quartet

'*The Art of the Lindsays*': String Quartets: MOZART: *19 in C (Dissonance), K.465.* SCHUBERT: *13 in A min., D.804.* RAVEL: *in F.* HAYDN: *68 in E flat, Op. 64/6.* MENDELSSOHN: *6 in F min., Op. 80.* DVOŘÁK: *12 in F (American), Op. 96.* BEETHOVEN: *11 in F min., Op. 95.* BORODIN: *2 in D.* JANÁČEK: *1 (Kreutzer Sonata).* TIPPETT: *5.* BARTOK: *6 in D.* SCHUBERT: *Piano Quintet in A (Trout)* (with Kathryn Stott (piano), Leon Bosch (double bass)). BRAHMS: *Clarinet Quintet in B min.* (with Janet Hilton (clarinet))
(B) *** ASV CDRSB 404 (5)

This five-CD bargain box admirably surveys the achievement of the Lindsays over the widest range of repertoire, and they are never found wanting. All these recordings have been reviewed by us over the years with enthusiasm; and where this box does not cause too much duplication it can receive the strongest recommendation.

Lipatti, Dinu (piano)

Besançon Festival Recital (1950): BACH: *Partita 1 in B flat, BWV 525.* MOZART: *Piano Sonata 8 in A min., K.310.* SCHUBERT: *Impromptus, D. 899/2 & 3.* CHOPIN: *Waltzes 1; 3–14*
(M) (***) EMI mono 5 62819-2 [5 82820-2]

Like Lipatti's representation in EMI's 'Great Recordings of the Century' (see below) these recordings derive from the pianist's Besançon Festival recital, and the incomplete set of the Chopin *Waltzes* has been added from the same source, the recording different from the complete set, recorded by Walter Legge in a Geneva studio.

Recital: BACH: *Partita 1 in B flat, BWV 825. Chorale Preludes: Nun komm, der Heiden Heiland; Ich ruf zu dir, Herr Jesu Christ; Jesu, joy of man's desiring; Flute Sonata 2 in E flat, BWV 1031: Siciliana* (arr. KEMPFF). D. SCARLATTI: *Sonatas, Kk. 9 & 380.* MOZART: *Sonata 8 in A min., K.310.* SCHUBERT: *Impromptus, in E flat; G flat, D.899/2–3*
(M) (***) EMI mono 5 66988-2 [5 67003-2]

No collector should overlook this Lipatti CD. Most of the performances derive from the pianist's last recital in Besançon and have scarcely been out of circulation since their first appearance in the 1950s: the haunting account of the Mozart *A minor Sonata* and the Bach *B flat Partita* have both had more than one incarnation on LP and CD. The

Schubert *Impromptus* are equally treasurable, and the Scarlatti *Sonatas* have been added for the present reissue in EMI's 'Great Recordings of the Century' series. The remastering is well done; and one notices that, among his other subtleties, Lipatti creates a different timbre for the music of each composer.

Recital: CHOPIN: *Sonata 3 in B min., Op. 58.* LISZT: *Années de pèlerinage; Sonetto del Petrarca 104.* RAVEL: *Miroirs: Alborada del gracioso.* BRAHMS: *Waltzes, Op. 39/1, 2, 5, 6, 10, 14 & 15* (with Boulanger). ENESCU: *Sonata 3 in D, Op. 25*
(M) (***) EMI mono 5 67566-2 [567567-2]

The Chopin *Sonata*, the Liszt and the Ravel were recorded in 1947–8, the Brahms *Waltzes*, with Nadia Boulanger, as long ago as 1937; while the Enescu *Sonata* comes from a 1943 wartime broadcast from Swiss Radio. The Chopin is one of the classics of the gramophone and it is good to have it again on CD. The Brahms *Waltzes* are played deliciously, with tremendous sparkle and tenderness; they sound every bit as realistic as the post-war records. The Enescu *Sonata* is an accessible piece with an exuberant first movement, a rather atmospheric *Andantino* and a sparkling finale, and that too sounds fresher in this latest transfer, though not as impressive as the Brahms. A must for all those with an interest in the piano and an obvious 'Great Recording of the Century'.

Little, Tasmin (violin), Piers Lane (piano)

'*Virtuoso Violin*': KREISLER: *Prelude and Allegro in the style of Pugnani; Caprice viennois.* BRAHMS: *Hungarian Dances 1 & 5.* SHOSTAKOVICH: *The Gadfly: Romance.* DRIGO: *Valse bluette.* FIBICH: *Poème.* FALLA: *La vida breve: Spanish Dance.* WIENIAWSKI: *Légende, Op. 17.* SARASATE: *Introduction and Tarantelle, Op. 43.* BLOCH: *Baal Shem: Nigun.* DEBUSSY: *Beau soir.* RIMSKY-KORSAKOV: *Flight of the Bumblebee* (both arr. HEIFETZ). DELIUS: *Hassan: Serenade* (arr. TERTIS). KROLL: *Banjo and Fiddle.* RAVEL: *Tzigane*
(B) *** CfP 574 9492

A pretty dazzling display of violin fireworks from a brilliant young fiddler who conveys her delight in her own easy virtuosity. The opening Kreisler pastiche, *Prelude and Allegro*, is presented with real style, and later the *Caprice viennois* has comparable panache and relaxed charm. The schmaltzy daintiness of Drigo's *Valse bluette* is followed by an unexaggerated but full-timbred warmth in Fibich's *Poème*. The gypsy temperament of the Falla and the ready sparkle of Sarasate's *Tarantelle* and Kroll's *Banjo and Fiddle* are offset by the lyrical appeal of the more atmospheric pieces. The violin is very present – perhaps the microphones are a fraction too close, but the balance with the piano is satisfactory and there is not an exaggerated spotlight here.

Lloyd Webber, Julian (cello)

'*British Cello Music*' ((i) with McCabe, piano): (i) RAWSTHORNE: *Sonata for Cello & Piano.* ARNOLD: *Fantasy for Cello.* (i) IRELAND: *The Holy Boy.* WALTON: *Passacaglia.* BRITTEN: *Tema (Sacher); Cello Suite 3*
*** ASV CDDCA 592

A splendid recital and a most valuable one. Julian Lloyd Webber has championed such rarities as the Bridge *Oration* at a time when it was unrecorded and now devotes this present issue to British music that needs strong advocacy there is no alternative version of the Rawsthorne *Sonata*, in which he is most ably partnered by John McCabe. He gives this piece – and, for that matter, the remainder of the programme – with full-blooded commitment. Good recording.

'*British Cello Music*', Vol. 2 (with McCabe, piano): STANFORD: *Sonata 2, Op. 39.* BRIDGE: *Elegy; Scherzetto.* IRELAND: *Sonata in G min.*
✪ *** ASV CDDCA 807

The Stanford *Second Cello Sonata* (1893 – written between the *Fourth* and *Fifth Symphonies*) is revealed here as an inspired work whose opening theme flowers into great lyrical warmth on Lloyd Webber's ardent bow. The focus of the recording is a little diffuse, but that serves to add to the atmosphere. Ireland's *Sonata*, too, is among his most richly inspired works, a broad-spanning piece in which ambitious, darkly intense outer movements frame a most beautiful *Poco largamente*. Again Lloyd Webber, who has long been a passionate advocate of the work, conveys its full expressive power. The Bridge *Elegy* (written as early as 1911) is another darkly poignant evocation, which points forward to the sparer, more austere style of the later Bridge, and the *Scherzetto* (even earlier, 1902) makes a winning encore: it should ideally have been placed at the end of the recital. John McCabe is a sympathetic partner – in spite of the balance – but this collection offers what are among Lloyd Webber's finest performances on disc.

London Wind Trio

'*20th-century Miniatures*': IBERT: *5 Pièces en trio.* MILHAUD: *Pastorale; Suite d'après Corrette, Op. 161b.* TOMASI: *Concert champêtre.* POULENC: *Sonata for Clarinet & Bassoon.* VILLA-LOBOS: *Trio*
(M) *** Somm SOMMCD 013

The personnel of the London Wind Trio consists of Neil Black, Keith Puddy and Roger Birnstingl, who are as adroit individually as they are perfectly matched as a team. They give attractively deft and fresh performances of these finely crafted French works, conveying their enjoyment of the music's melodic felicity. The wit, charm and nostalgia of Ibert's *Cinq Pièces* contrast with Milhaud's *Pastorale*, which is more brazenly prolix, yet his *Suite d'après Corrette* has an ingenuous simplicity, while offering a neat condiment of dissonance in its Menuet, before the chirping of 'Le coucou'.

No less diverting is the cheeky Poulenc duo *Sonata* with its rueful central 'Nocturne' (*très doux*). Tomasi's rustic *Concert champêtre* is hardly less engaging, with its droll *Nocturne* temporarily interrupting the good humour before the folksy closing 'Vif'. The Villa-Lobos *Trio* is the most ambitious piece, fascinatingly intricate in its rhythmic and harmonic texture, evoking the exotic, vividly colourful sounds of the Brazilian jungle, with the central *Languissamente* a darker, but still restless, tropical nocturnal. It is played with great character and unforced virtuosity. The well-balanced, natural recording gives these artists a fine presence, and altogether this is a most diverting and rewarding recital.

Lugansky, Nikolai (piano)

BRAHMS: *6 Pieces, Op. 118.* WAGNER: *Götterdämmerung Paraphrase* (arr. Lugansky). RACHMANINOV: *Moment Musical in E min., Op. 16/4; Preludes, Op. 23/5 & 7*
*** Naïve **DVD** DR 2105 AV103 (Recorded live at La Roque d'Anthéron, France, 6 August 2002. V/D: Pernoo)

Very impressive playing by this masterly Russian pianist. His Brahms is thoughtful and full of musical insight, while the highly successful Wagner transcription (which includes *Siegfried's Journey down the Rhine*, the *Funeral March* and the closing *Immolation*) is imaginative and compelling. The three Rachmaninov pieces serve as a reminder that among pianists of his generation Lugansky is second to none. This recital was captured live at the piano festival at La Roque d'Anthéron, near Aix-en-Provence; the camera-work is unobtrusive and the sound excellent.

Marleyn, Paul (cello), John Lenehan (piano)

From Jewish Life': BERNSTEIN: *Mass: Meditations 1 & 2.* BLOCH: *Baal Shem: Nigun; Méditation hébraïque; From Jewish Life: Prayer; Supplication; Jewish Song. Cello Sonata.* BRUCH: *Kol Nidrei, Op. 47.* SHCHEDRIN: *Cardil.* STUTSCHEWSKY: *Kinah.* TRAD.: *Avremi, the pickpocket; Chanukah Oy Chanukah; Dona, Dona*
*** Signum Two SIGCD 505

While this collection centres on the more familiar music of Ernest Bloch, the programme opens with Max Bruch's even better-known *Kol Nidrei*, which the pianist John Lenehan introduces sensitively, before Paul Marleyn takes up Bruch's passionate soliloquy with its memorably warm *Adagio* main theme. Bloch's contribution includes a fine early (1897) *Cello Sonata*, a cyclic work in which the principal ideas only slightly anticipate his mature Hebrew melodic style. But it is freshly enjoyable here, given such ardent advocacy, and this is also extended to the *Méditation hébraïque*; and if the three pieces *From Jewish Life* (*Prayer, Supplication*, and *Jewish Song*) are more restrained, they are not less deeply felt.

The pair of Bernstein *Meditations* are used as interludes in his *Mass*, and they act similarly here. With the cello part originally written for Rostropovich, and improvisational in feeling, Bernstein poignantly explores the instrument's fullest range, while the piano role is by no means just an accompaniment.

Stutschewsky's heartfelt lament, *Kinah*, has much in common with the characteristic traditional numbers, as has Rodion Shchedrin's *Cardil*, all of which which alternate Hebrew irony and nostalgia with sudden accelerandos into cheerful dance music.

The penultimate popular song, *Chanukah Oy Chanukah*, celebrates a family festival of candles, presents and goodwill, and gathers momentum infectiously. Here John Lenehan provides his own spontaneous version of the piano part. The closing Bloch *Nigun*, taken from *Baal Shem*, then makes a touchingly sombre coda. It was written for violin and piano, but Paul Marleyn's cello sings the fervent melodic line with deeply lyrical feeling to make the transcription just as convincing. The playing of both artists throughout is naturally idiomatic, and the recording too is very vivid and present within an attractive acoustic. A most rewarding concert if you enjoy the special melodic tang of Hebrew music.

Mayer, Albrecht (oboe), Markus Becker (piano)

COSSART: *Liebesgedicht, Op. 23/4.* DAELLI: *Fantasy on Themes from Verdi's 'Rigoletto'.* KOECHLIN: *Le Repos de tityre – Monodie, Op. 216/10.* NIELSEN: *2 Fantasy Pieces, Op. 2.* SCHUMANN: *Abendlied, Op. 107/6; Ihre Stimme, Op. 96/3; Romanzen, Op. 94; Stille tränen, Op. 35/10.* YVON: *Sonata in F*
✪ (B) *** EMI Début 5 73167-2

Albrecht Mayer is an artist of exceptional quality and his partnership with Markus Becker the meeting of true minds. Their playing on this EMI Début recital gives enormous pleasure for its subtlety, refinement and musicianship. Their choice of repertoire is unfailingly enterprising and the Schumann and Nielsen are played as well as we have ever heard. Mayer is principal oboe of the Berlin Philharmonic and will obviously be one of the great players of the next decade or so. Excellent recording.

Melos Ensemble

18th- and 19th-century Chamber Music: MOZART: *Piano & Wind Quintet in E flat, K.452.* BEETHOVEN: *Piano & Wind Quintet in E flat, Op. 16; Sextet in E flat for 2 Horns, 2 Violins, Viola & Cello, Op. 81b; March for Wind Sextet in B flat, WoO 29; Rondino in E flat, WoO 25; Duo 1 for Clarinet & Bassoon, WoO 27.* SCHUMANN: *Fantasiestücke for Clarinet & Piano, Op. 73. Märchenerzählungen, Op. 132.* BRAHMS: *Clarinet Quintet in B min., Op. 115.* REGER: *Clarinet Quintet in A: 2nd Movt: Vivace*
(B) *** EMI Double fforte (ADD) 5 72643-2 (2)

This collection, like its companion below, dates from the late 1960s when the Melos Ensemble gathered together some of London's finest orchestral musicians to make a series of recordings for EMI. There is plenty of individual personality in the music-making here, but how beautifully these fine musicians blend together as a group! The polished elegance and charm of their playing cannot be heard to better effect than in the Mozart *Piano and Wind Quintet*, dominated by the splendid musicianship of the pianist, Lamar Crowson, and with some particularly felicitous oboe playing from Peter Graeme. Its Beethoven successor follows on naturally, played with a lighter touch than usual to emphasize the Mozartian influences.

The *Sextet* brings some splendid bravura from the two horn players, Neil Sanders and James Buck, while the *March* (for wind alone) is very jolly. The *Duo* for clarinet and bassoon is now thought not to be by Beethoven but is very agreeable nevertheless. Schumann's rarely heard *Märchenerzählungen* ('Fairy-tales') is late (1853) and is almost unique in being scored for the same combination as Mozart's *Trio* for clarinet, viola (here Gervase de Peyer and Cecil Aronowitz) and piano. The *Fantasiestücke*, for clarinet and piano, was written four years earlier. Both performances are persuasively warm and mellow, although Lamar Crowson again achieves a strong backing profile. For all their lyricism, these artists don't miss Schumann's marking, '*mit Feuer*', in the finale of Op. 73, and the second movement of Op. 132 is strongly accented to make a bold contrast with the flowingly romantic third, before the similarly bold finale. Gervase de Peyer then relaxes completely to present an essentially lyrical view of the Brahms *Clarinet Quintet*. It is a lovely performance, achieving a wistful nostalgia in the slow movement, but it is perhaps in the rippling execution of the arpeggios of the finale that his playing is particularly individual. The Reger lollipop *Scherzo*, which acts as an encore, may be as light as thistledown, but its central *Trio* has a beguiling richness of style in the post-Brahms tradition. All the recordings were made at Abbey Road, and the sound is excellent throughout; only in the Beethoven *Sextet* is there a hint of thinness in the violins. Overall this will give much refreshment and pleasure.

Menuhin, Yehudi and Stéphane Grappelli (violins)

'*Menuhin and Grappelli play*' (with rhythm group; Alan Clare Trio; Orchestral Ens.; cond. Nelson Riddle and Max Harris): GERSHWIN: *Fascinatin' rhythm; Soon; Summertime; Nice work if you can get it; Embraceable you; Liza; A foggy day; 'S wonderful; The man I love; I got rhythm; He loves and she loves; They can't take that away from me; They all laughed; Funny face; Our love is here to stay; Lady be good.* STRACHEY: *These foolish things.* RASKIN: *Laura.* HARBURG & DUKE: *April in Paris.* KOSMA, PREVERT & MERCER: *Autumn leaves.* DUKE: *Autumn in New York.* BERLIN: *Cheek to cheek; Isn't this a lovely day; Change partners; Top hat, white tie and tails; I've got my love to keep me warm; Heat wave.* KERN: *The way you look tonight; Pick yourself up; A fine romance; All the things you are; Why do I love you?* PORTER: *I get a kick out of you; Night and day; Looking at you; Just one of those things.* RODGERS & HART: *My funny Valentine; Thou swell; The lady is a tramp; Blue room.* GADE: *Jealousy.* CARMICHAEL: *Skylark*

(B) *** EMI Double fforte (ADD/DDD) 5 73380-2 (2)

The partnership of Menuhin and Grappelli started in the television studio, many years before Menuhin was ennobled. Their brief duets (tagged on to interviews) were so successful that the idea developed of recording a whole recital (and then several), with each maestro striking sparks off the other in style, but matching the other remarkably closely in matters of tone and balance. One of the secrets of success of this partnership lies in the choice of material. All these items started as first-rate songs, with striking melodies which live in whatever guise, and here with ingenious arrangements (mostly made by Max Harris, but some by Nelson Riddle) which spark off the individual genius of each violinist, acting as a challenge, and inviting the players' obvious enjoyment. The result is delightful, particularly in numbers such as *Pick yourself up*, where the arrangement directly tips a wink towards Bachian figuration. The CD transfers are immaculate and the high spirits of the collaboration are caught beautifully.

Michelangeli, Arturo Benedetti (piano)

Recital in the RTSI Auditorium, Lugano, Switzerland on 7 April 1981: BEETHOVEN: *Piano Sonatas 11 in B flat, Op. 22; 12 in A flat, Op. 26.* SCHUBERT: *Piano Sonata 4 in A min., D.537.* BRAHMS: *4 Ballades, Op. 10*

*** Euro Arts TDK **DVD** 10 5231 9 DV MPSR (TV Director: János Darvas)

It is really something to come almost face to face with this legendary pianist and to realize that the sense of aloofness that his recordings often engender is indeed part of his personality. As for instance here, when he takes his bow impassively at the end of the recital. The programme too demonstrates his apparent degree of involvement, less so in Beethoven's Op. 26, which offers beautiful, refined pianism but in which the *March funèbre* seems almost stoic, although the Scherzo is lively enough. The more extrovert account of the *B flat Sonata*, Op. 22, communicates more directly: here the *Adagio* has feeling as well as refinement, and he almost gets carried away in the closing Rondo.

But when he begins the early Schubert *A major Sonata*, one is immediately conscious of being in the presence of a great artist, not least in the beautifully articulated *Allegretto* which is utterly enchanting. The Brahms *Ballades*, too, from the very opening of the *First in D minor*, command the attention and hold the listener raptly in their spell.

The colour photography is excellent and the camera angles well judged, not intrusive, with the changes of shot always achieved at appropriate moments in the music. The close-ups subtly reveal the pianist's degree of involvement in his facial gestures, which communicate to us, even though he is always totally absorbed in the music. The piano sound lacks a little in range, but is real – full in sonority and timbre. Altogether a success: Michelangeli admirers need not hesitate.

BEETHOVEN: *Piano Sonatas 4 in E flat, Op. 7; 12 in A flat, Op. 26.* DEBUSSY: *Hommage à Rameau.* RAVEL: *Gaspard de la nuit*

(M) *** BBC Legends (ADD) BBCL 4064-2

The Ravel *Gaspard de la nuit* has been in circulation on various labels, most recently in the Philips 'Great Pianists of the Twentieth Century' series. Recorded in the Concert Hall of Broadcasting House in 1959, it was a legendary account of *Gaspard* which left all who heard it spellbound. But, of course, there have been many *Gaspard*s: the balance renders Michelangeli's enormous dynamic range less wide than usual (the opening of *Ondine* is not as *pianissimo* as one remembers it being in the Concert Hall). Those who recall Michelangeli's marmoreal account of the *E flat Sonata*, Op. 7, which bestrode two sides of a DG LP way back in the early 1970s, will find the 1982 Festival account more involving – but then, it had to be! Generally speaking, Michelangeli is commanding in both *Sonatas* and produces some lovely sounds in the Debussy *Hommage à Rameau*. Admirers of the great pianist will want this, and the sound is very acceptable indeed.

BACH/BUSONI: *Chaconne* from *Violin Partita 2 in D min., BWV 1004.* BRAHMS: *Variations on a Theme by Paganini, Op. 35.* SCHUMANN: *Carnaval, Op. 9. Album für die Jugend, Op. 68,* excerpts: *Winterzeit I & II; Matrosenlied*

(M) ** EMI mono/stereo 5 62740-2 [5 62757-2]

'Few pianists have provoked greater awe and controversy than Michaelangeli,' writes Bryce Morrison in his note for this reissue among EMI's 'Great Recordings of the Century', 'through his crystalline perfection, controversy through interpretations that ranged from the chilly to the sublime.' One could add to this, interpretative linear eccentricity, which rears its head here both in Schumann and the otherwise very impressive Brahms *Variations*. The *Chaconne* is certainly a remarkable display of freely romantic Bach and some prodigious pianism, even if the recording is only fair. But the Schumann performances are strangely idiosyncratic. Beautiful pianism, of course (and good recording), but far from self-effacing. The opening of *Carnaval* is portentous and there is far too little spontaneity. Of all the recordings of this work by major arists this is the least consistent, and the excerpts from the *Album für die Jugend* could ideally sound more light-hearted.

SCARLATTI: *Keyboard Sonatas: in D min., Kk. 11; B flat, Kk. 172, B flat; Kk. 332.* BEETHOVEN: *Piano Sonata 32 in C min., Op. 111.* CLEMENTI: *Piano Sonata in B flat, Op. 12/1.* CHOPIN: *Piano Sonata in B flat min., Op. 35*

(M) (**(*)) BBC mono BBCL 4128-2

Michelangeli recorded Op. 111 for Decca in the early 1960s, but this studio recording was made in 1961 at the BBC's Maida Vale studios some few years later. Magisterial pianism, but we somehow remain outside Beethoven's world (as we did in the commercial recording). All the same, the piano sound is remarkably good for its age. The Scarlatti, Clementi and Chopin are another matter, and no admirer of great piano playing should miss them.

Miolin, Anders (ten-stringed guitar)

'The Lion and the Lute': WALTON: *5 Bagatelles.* RAWSTHORNE: *Elegy.* LENNOX BERKELEY: *Sonatina, Op. 51; Theme and variations, Op. 77.* TIPPETT: *The Blue guitar.* BRITTEN: *Nocturnal, Op. 70*

*** BIS Dig. CD 926

Anders Miolin, born in Stockholm, designs his own guitars, allowing a greater compass and creating a richer palette. That is well borne out here by this unsurpassed collection of British twentieth-century guitar music; indeed, the colour inherent in the five Walton *Bagatelles* has never glowed so brightly, and this comment might also be applied to the whole programme, so attractively recorded in an open acoustic. The Rawsthorne *Elegy* is darkly expressive and both the Tippett and Britten works are highly charged and atmospheric. The Tippett was inspired indirectly by a Picasso painting, which stimulated Wallace Stevens to write a poem called 'The man with the blue guitar'. The Britten night music is a set of seven variations and a passacaglia on Dowland's song *Come heavy sleep*. Both make considerable imaginative as well as technical demands on the player, and they could hardly be more persuasively presented or recorded. If you enjoy guitar music, this is not to be missed.

Mitchell, Madeleine (violin), Andrew Bell (piano)

English Violin Sonatas: GOOSSENS: *Sonata 1 in E min., Op. 21.* HURLSTONE: *Sonata in D min.* TURNBULL: *Sonata in E min.*

(M) *** Somm SOMMCD 031

Of these three fine *Violin Sonatas* (all new to CD) that by Eugene Goossens (1918) is the most commanding. The style is thoroughly romantic, but Goossens also draws eclectically on the musical background of the period. Yet the music's underlying lyrical feeling predominates, and there is fine craftsmanship too, as in the beautifully managed close of the first movement. The *Adagio* features an appealing folk theme, and the sparkling *Con brio* finale centres on a lolloping principal rhythmic figure, also with a folksy flavour. There is also a passionate secondary melody to again bring contrast. The piano writing throughout the work is just as demanding as the violin contribution, and both these artists enter fully into the music's spirit, as they do in the other two works included here.

Hardly less appealing is the Hurlstone *D minor Sonata* of

1897, comparably lyrical and inventive and bringing another sprightly scherzando finale (which again produces a memorable second subject). Percy Turnbull's *E minor Sonata* of 1925 also has a friendly opening movement: its *Andante* is thoughtful, and the lively finale is imbued with a Ravelian purity of feeling in the piano writing, with the violin soaring freely above in richly lyrical response. In short these works make a most attractive triptych, and the recording is excellent, naturally balanced and clear within a warm acoustic.

Moiseiwitsch, Benno (piano)

1938–1950 Recordings: MUSSORGSKY: *Pictures at an Exhibition.* BEETHOVEN: *Andanti favori, WoO 57; Rondo in C, Op. 51/1.* WEBER: *Sonata 1: Presto; Invitation to the Dance* (arr. TAUSIG). MENDELSSOHN: *Scherzo in E min., Op. 16.* SCHUMANN: *Romanzen: 2, Op. 28/2.* CHOPIN: *Nocturne in E flat, Op. 9/2; Polonaise in B flat, Op. 71/2; Barcarolle, Op. 60.* LISZT: *Liebestraum 3; Etude de concert: La leggierezza. Hungarian Rhapsody 2 in C sharp min. Concert Paraphrase of Wagner's 'Tannhäuser' Overture.* DEBUSSY: *Pour le piano: Toccata. Suite bergamasque: Clair de lune. Estampes: Jardins sous la pluie.* RAVEL: *Le tombeau de Couperin: Toccata*

(**(*)) APR mono CDAPR 7005 (2)

Moiseiwitsch never enjoyed quite the exposure on records to which his gifts entitled him, though in the earlier part of his career he made a great many. Later, in the electrical era, he was a 'plum-label' artist and was not issued on the more prestigious and expensive 'red label'. In this he was in pretty good company, for Solomon and Myra Hess were similarly relegated. This anthology gives a good picture of the great pianist in a wide variety of repertory: his *Pictures at an Exhibition*, made in 1945, was for some time the only piano version; and those who identify him solely with the Russians will find his Chopin *Barcarolle* and Debussy *Jardins sous la pluie* totally idiomatic. The transfers are variable – all are made from commercial copies, some in better condition than others.

Mordkovitch, Lydia (violin), Gerhard Oppitz (piano)

BRAHMS: *Violin Sonatas Nos. 1–3.* PROKOFIEV: *Violin Sonatas 1–2.* SCHUBERT: *Fantasie in C, Op. post. 159 D.934; Violin Sonata in A, Op. post. 162 D.574.* R. STRAUSS: *Violin Sonata in E, Op. 18.* SCHUMANN: *Violin Sonatas 1–2.* FAURÉ: *Violin Sonata in A, Op. 13*

(M) ** Chan. 6659 (4)

Chandos has collected Lydia Mordkovitch's sonata recordings made with Gerhard Oppitz in the 1980s into this one bargain box. It is an inexpensive way of acquiring this artist's often exciting violin playing, very Russian, full of temperament, and never dull. The Brahms *Sonatas* are without question among the finest performances of this repertoire, with Mordkovitch's imaginative and subtle phrasing a constant source of pleasure. Both she and Oppitz give authoritative and perceptive accounts of all three *Sonatas*, which could almost be a top choice, were it not for the over-reverberant sound. If her accounts of the Prokofiev *Sonatas* do not displace versions by Oistrakh and Perlman, they can be placed alongside them. These are thoughtful readings with vital contributions from both partners. They have the measure of the darker, more searching side of the *F minor*, and are hardly less excellent in the companion work. The recording is excellent and the insights both artists bring to this music make these performances well worth exploring. The popular Fauré *Sonata* is given a sensitive account by Mordkovitch, but her other-worldly, disembodied *pianissimo* tone does not always draw comparable playing from the pianist, though the acoustic may have posed problems. All the same, the performance gives pleasure. The Strauss *Sonata* is certainly compelling, though here too the recording, which tends to make the piano a little overpowering, is not ideal. The Schubert pieces receive lovely performances, though yet again the over-reverberant recording, which draws attention to the fact that it was recorded in an empty church, does not help – for this is above all intimate music, and the sound – which even blurs details in places – precludes that. The quality for the Schumann is much better, and one enjoys the rich colours Mordkovitch finds in these richly rewarding *Sonatas*.

Murray, Michael (organ of the Cathedral of St John the Divine, New York City)

'*The Great Organ*': DUNSTABLE: *Agincourt Hymn.* SOLER: *The Emperor's Fanfare.* MARCELLO: *Psalm 19.* PURCELL: *Trumpet Tune.* WIDOR: *Symphony 6: Finale.* BACH: *Prelude and Fugue in E min., BWV 533.* VIERNE: *Meditation; Prelude.* FRANCK: *Chorale 2 in B min.* DUPRÉ: *Cortege and Litany, Op. 19/2; 7 Pieces, Op. 27: Final*
(M) **(*) Telarc CD 80169

The cathedral organ in New York City is a magnificent instrument and Michael Murray is undoubtedly its master. He conjures up an attractively tangy registration for the *Agincourt Hymn* and *Emperor's Fanfare*, then in the two lyrical Vierne pieces and the Franck *Chorale* there is some delightful 'woodwind' colouring. If the Marcello and especially the Purcell item seem a little too grandly solid, the registration is again pungent. But Murray seems especially at home in the French repertoire, and the Dupré *Final* could hardly be more spectacularly arresting. Not surprisingly, the Telarc recording is first class, never for a moment lacking sharpness of focus despite the obvious resonance.

Mutter, Anne-Sophie (violin)

'*Tango, Song and Dance*' (with André Previn or Lambert Orkis, piano): PREVIN: *Sonata drammatica; Tango, Song & Dance.* FAURE: *Violin Sonata 1.* Music by: BRAHMS; GERSHWIN; KREISLER
**(*) DG 471 500-2

Celebrating the marriage of Anne-Sophie Mutter and André Previn, this collection of songs and dances, for which Previn's *Tango, Song and Dance* provides the title, is as near as anything to a direct expression of love. Mutter is inspired to play with uninhibited freedom, both with her new husband (in Heifetz's Gershwin arrangements as well as his own piece) and with Lambert Orkis, her accompanist in the other pieces. The Fauré *Violin Sonata 1* is the most substantial work, like the rest at once songful and dance-like, and Previn's three-movement *Sonata drammatica*, written for Mutter in 1996, starts like Piazzola observed through a distorting lens, before developing into a haunting song and a final jazz-based dance, 'like Boogie on speed' as Mutter says. Three of Brahms's *Hungarian Dances* are so uninhibitedly free that rhythms are undermined, but the three Kreisler pieces are magnetic.

Nakariakov, Sergei (trumpet), Alexander Markovich (piano)

ARBAN: *Variations on a Theme from Bellini's 'Norma'; Variations on a Tyrolean song.* BIZET, arr. WAXMAN: *Carmen Fantasy.* BRANDT: *Concert Piece 2.* FALLA: *Spanish Dance.* FAURE: *Le réveil.* PAGANINI: *Caprice, Op. 1/17; Moto perpetuo, Op. 11.* SARASATE: *Zigeunerweisen, Op. 20/1.* SAINT-SAENS: *Le Cygne*
**(*) Teldec 4509 94554-2

Sergei Nakariakov exhibits some stunning technique in this Teldec recital, coupling various trifles, including Franz Waxman's *Carmen Fantasy* and Paganini's *Moto perpetuo*, as well as the remainder of his programme. He was only seventeen when this recording was made and, although not many will want to hear more than a few of these pieces at a time, there is much to enjoy. He is a veritable Russian Håkan Hardenberger, save for the fact that, on the evidence of this disc, he does not always command the latter's extraordinary variety of tonal colour or his impeccable taste.

Nash Ensemble

Live Wigmore Hall Concert, 8 October 2005: SCHUMANN: *Märchenerzählungen (Fairy Tales) for Clarinet, Viola & Piano.* MOSCHELES: *Fantasy, Variations & Finale for Clarinet, Violin, Cello & Piano, Op. 46.* BRAHMS: *Clarinet Quintet in B min., Op. 115*
(M) *** Wigmore Hall Live WHLive 0007

With Andrew Keener producing, it is not surprising that this concert is a great success, admirably capturing the so friendly Wigmore Hall acoustic and the natural clarity of detail heard within its ambience. Moreover, the Nash Ensemble are on excellent form and play with great spontaneity throughout. It cannot be said that Schumann's *Märchenerzählungen* is one of his finest works, and it probably stays in the repertoire only because of its unusual instrumentation. Indeed, it can easily be boring, but here the performance makes the very most of it, particularly the third-movement *Ruhiges Tempo, mit zarten Ausdruck*.

The amiable Moscheles *Fantasy* immediately makes amends, with its *galant* charm, sustained enteraininly throughout. The composer teases the listener with a long preamble before the *Theme* arrives. But when it does, it is a very engaging one, as are the resourceful six variations and finale which follow. It is played with great freshness. The Nash players are obviously enjoying themselves and this is readily communicated to us.

But the highlight of the concert is still to come, a superb account of the Brahms *Clarinet Quintet*, with the clarinettist Richard Hosford in inspired form, with his rich, limpid tone and beautiful legato phrasing. The very opening is magical, and there is some exquisite *pianissimo* string playing in the *Adagio*, the clarinet line wonderfully fluid; and the final variations are winning in their warm lyricism. Altogether a memorable occasion, so truthfully caught on the wing by the excellent recording team.

Navarra, André (cello), Erika Kilcher (piano)

recital: Sonatas by: LOCATELLI; VALENTINI; BOCCHERINI: *1 A & G.* GRANADOS: *Goyescas: Intermezzo.* FALLA: *Suite populaire espagnole* (arr. Maurice MARECHAL). NIN: *Chants d'Espagne: Saeta; Andalousie*

M) *** Cal. (ADD) CAL 6673

Navarra's recital dates from 1981 and shows this fine cellist in top form. He is splendidly partnered by Erika Kilcher, who, though she is backwardly balanced in relation to the up-front cello (recorded somewhat dryly), makes a highly artistic contribution with her sympathetic accompaniments. This is immediately noticeable in the splendid opening Sonata of Locatelli. But it is the four-movement work by Giuseppe Valentini which is the highlight of the Italian repertoire, a most engaging piece with an elegant *Gavotte* and an aria-like *Largo*, framed by two energetic outer movements in which Navarra's spiccato-like articulation of moto perpetuo allegros is most infectious. He is equally at home in the Spanish half of the programme, and Kilcher joins him in providing colourful characterization of the five miniatures which make up the Falla suite. In the second of the two Nin pieces, *Andalousie*, Navarra's cello sounds like a larger-than-life Spanish guitar. However, it is a pity that the documentation does not identify the Italian sonatas more positively.

New Century Saxophone Quartet

'Main Street USA': GOULD: *Pavane; Main Street Waltz; Main Street March.* GERSHWIN: *Promenade; Three Quartet Blues; Merry Andrew; Porgy and Bess: Clara, Clara; Oh, I got plenty o' nuttin'; Bess, you is my woman now; Oh, I can't sit down; It ain't necessarily so; Summertime; There's a boat dat's leavin' for New York; Oh Lawd, I'm on my way.* BERNSTEIN: *West Side Story: I feel pretty; Balcony scene; Tonight; Cha-cha/Meeting scene; Jump; One hand, one heart; Gee, officer Krupke; Scherzo; Somewhere*

*** Channel Classics CCS 9896

Uncommonly fine playing, with superbly blended timbres and a subtly appealing melodic lead from Michael Stephenson on the soprano saxophone, means that this collection of famous show melodies is very appealing. Gould's delightful *Pavane* is presented with a neat degree of whimsy and the three Gershwin instrumental numbers have a pleasing sophistication. Stephenson's line in the songs is quite remarkably vocal in feeling. 'It ain't necessarily so' recalls Fats Waller, and the Balcony scene from *West Side Story* is really touching. Steven Kirkman gives admirably restrained support on percussion, when needed, and the balance and recording could hardly be bettered.

Nishizaki, Takako (violin)

Romantic Violin Favourites': trans. Kreisler (with Harden, piano): SCHUBERT: *Rosamunde: Ballet Music.* BIZET: *L'Arlésienne: Adagietto.* RIMSKY-KORSAKOV: *Le coq d'or: Hymn to the Sun; Sadko: Hindu Song; Scheherazade: Oriental Dance.* DVORAK: *Songs my Mother Taught Me.* GLUCK: *Orfeo ed Eurydice: Dance of the Blessed Spirits.* HAYDN: *Piano trio in G: Hungarian Rondo; Austrian Imperial Hymn.* MOZART: *Haffner Serenade: Rondo.* SCHUMANN: *Romance, Op. 94.* GRIEG: *Lyric Piece: To the*

Spring. RAMEAU: *Tambourin.* GRAINGER: *Molly on the Shore.* TRAD.: *Song of the Volga Boatmen; Londonderry Air*

(BB) **(*) Naxos Dig. 8.550125

'Violin Miniatures' (with Jandó, piano): KREISLER: *Schön Rosmarin; Rondino; Liebesleid; Liebesfreud; Caprice viennois.* RACHMANINOV: *Rhapsody on a Theme by Paganini: Variation 18.* FIBICH: *Poème.* ELGAR: *Salut d'amour.* GRANADOS: *Spanish Dance: Andaluza, Op. 37/5.* BRAHMS: *Hungarian Dance 1.* SCHUBERT: *Moment musical in F min.* DVORAK: *Humoresque, Op. 101/7; Slavonic dance 1 in G min.* (all trans. Kreisler). BOCCHERINI: *Minuet.* DEBUSSY: *Clair de lune.* MASSENET: *Thaïs: Méditation.* TCHAIKOVSKY: *Chant sans paroles, Op. 2/3; Chanson triste, Op. 40/2*

(BB) **(*) Naxos 8.550306

Takako Nishizaki is a highly accomplished player who has recorded prolifically on the Marco Polo and Naxos labels. She has recorded Mozart sonatas with Jenö Jandó and a host of rare works, from Respighi's *Concerto gregoriano* to César Cui's *Suite concertante.* She delivers these miniatures with considerable charm and aplomb. Good recording – no one investing in these CDs is likely to be disappointed and, were there not even more virtuosic and authoritative versions in the catalogue, they would warrant an unqualified three stars.

O'Dette, Paul (lute, archlute, baroque guitar)

'Ancient Airs and Dances' (with (i) Rogers Covey-Crump; (ii) Christel Thielmann): Suite 1: MOLINARO: *Ballo dello il Conte Orlando; Saltarello del predetto ballo.* GALILEI: *Polymnia.* ANON.: *Italiana; Villanella 'Orlando fa'che ti raccordi'; Italiana; Passo mezzo bonissimo; Mascherada*

Suite 2: CAROSO: (i; ii) *Laura soave.* BESARD: *Bransles de village.* ANON.: *Campanae Parisiensis.* BOËSSET: *Divine Amaryllis.* GIANONCELLI: *Tasteggiata; Bergamasca*

Suite 3: ANON.: *Italiana.* DA PARMA: *Le Cesarina.* BESARD: (i) *Airs de cour: C'est malheur; Adieu, bergère; Beaux yeux; La voila la nacelle d'amour; Quelle divinité; Si c'est pour mon pucellage.* ANON.: *Spagnoletta.* RONCALLI: *Passacaglia*

⊖— (B) *** Hyp. Helios CDH 55146

Lutenists don't come any finer than Paul O'Dette, and in this delightful collection he proves that his resourcefulness is the equal of his remarkable musical and instrumental skills. What he has done is to research the original manuscripts of the three suites of *Ancient Airs and Dances* which Respighi drew upon and scored for his *Suites.* These, in turn, drew upon transcriptions made by the Italian musician, Oscar Chilesotti. The detective work was a considerable challenge, as Respighi did not name his sources, with the anonymous pieces coming from a sixteenth-century manuscript, held in a private library. All this music had to be carefully edited and the many errors excised. The resulting three suites follow Respighi's layout, with some items played in fuller versions than in the orchestral score. *Laura soave,* in the *Second Suite* (originally a *ballo*), is more appropriately transcribed more fully for violin, lute and viola da gamba.

Respighi's borrowing also drew on vocal *Airs de cour* attributed to Jean-Baptiste Besard, and here Rogers Covey-Crump sings six of them most stylishly. (Full texts and translations are provided.) The overall result, expertly presented and beautifully recorded, is entertaining in a delightfully spontaneous way, and collectors who already have the

Respighi suites will surely be fascinated to match their movements to the originals.

'Alla Venetiana': DALZA: Pavana alla veneziana; Saltarello; Piva I; Piva II; Piva III; Ricercar; Calata ala spagnola ditto terzetti; Tastar de corde – Recercar dietro; Pavana alla ferrarese; Saltarello. ANON., arr. DALZA: Laudate Dio. CAPIROLA: Recercar primo; Recercar secondo; Recercar quinto; Non ti spiaqua l'ascoltar; La vilanela; Padoana belissima; Spagna seconda; Tientalora (Balletto da ballare). VAN GHIZEGHEM: De tous bien playne; De tous bien playne nel ton del primo recercar. CARA: O mia ciecha, e dura sorte. PESENTI: Che farala. SPINACINO: Recercare I; Recercare II. MARTINI: Malor me bat. JOSQUIN DESPREZ: Adieu mes amours; Qui tolis pechata mondi
⊶ *** HM HMU 907215

The expert lutenist Paul O'Dette seldom disappoints. He draws here mainly on the very first Venetian books of solo lute music to be published, by Francesco Spinacino (1507) and Joan (Zuan) Ambrosio Dalza (1508). Lively dance pieces by the latter, who has a comparatively strong musical personality, are used to frame this varied 73-minute programme. The early repertory comes in three main categories, the improvisatory ricercare, and arrangements of vocal music and dances. O'Dette shows himself a master of the ruminative improvisatory style, but adding some splendid bravura flourishes, as in the first of Spinacino's Recercare, and his virtuosity is just as striking in the Spagna seconda of Capirola and Dalza's sparkling Calata ala spagnola (which must have been a hit in its day).

One of the most touching pieces is Martini's melancholy Malor me bat, which is followed by a most extrovert Piva by Dalza, and the darker mood then returns with the reflective anonymous Laudate Dio. Capirola's haunting La vilanela is matched by the two reflective vocal transcriptions from Josquin Desprez.

This discerningly selected recital is beautifully played and recorded, and admirably documented. A sample page (in colour) from Capirola's richly illuminated Lute Book is upstaged by the frontispiece (taken from a miniature by Philippe de Mazerolles) elegantly picturing a Venetian brothel. A colourfully garbed lutenist is accompanying the less venial pleasures: the naked men are clearly enjoying themselves, the young ladies are hardly more modest in their apparel, but look more circumspect.

Ogden, Craig (guitar), Alison Stephens (mandolin)

'Music from the Novels of Louis de Bernières': VIVALDI: Concerto in C, RV 425 (arr. BEHREND). HUMMEL: Mandolin Concerto in G: Andante with Variations. GIULIANI: Grand duo concertante. PERSICHINI: Polcha variata. CALACE: Amor si culla, Op. 133. PALUMBO: Petite bolero. SAGRERAS: El Colibri (The Humming Bird). LAURO: 4 Venezuelan Waltzes. BARRIOS: Choro de Saudade; Las Abejas. LLOBET: El noi de la mare; El testament d'Amelia; El mestre. ANON.: Mis dolencias. Celedonio ROMERO: Suite andaluza: Soleares. TURINA: Homenaje a Tárrega: Soleares
*** Chan. 9780

Not many gimmicky discs work as well as this. It makes a delightful mixture having the metallic 'plink plonk' of the mandolin set against the rich twanging of the guitar. The author of Captain Corelli's Mandolin has helped the two talented young performers here, Craig Ogden and Alison Stephens, in making a wide selection of music from Vivaldi to Villa-Lobos, mainly of works specifically mentioned in de Bernières' novels – not just Captain Corelli's Mandolin but also the Latin trilogy – as well as of related pieces. Starting with Vivaldi's Mandolin Concerto with the string accompaniment arranged for solo guitar, each of the 23 items is a charmer, not least those from unknown composers like Persichini, Calace and Sagreras.

Ogdon, John and Brenda Lucas (pianos)

RACHMANINOV: Suites for 2 Pianos 1 (Fantasy), Op. 5; 2 in C, Op. 17; Six Pieces for Piano Duet, Op. 11; Polka italienne. ARENSKY: Suite for 2 Pianos, Op. 15. KHACHATURIAN: Sabre Dance. SHOSTAKOVICH: Concertino, Op. 94. DEBUSSY: Petite Suite; Fêtes. BIZET: Jeux d'enfants
(B) **(*) EMI (ADD) Double fforte 5 69386-2 (2)

John Ogdon and Brenda Lucas's readings of the two Rachmaninov Suites, not ideally imaginative but enjoyable nevertheless, are aptly coupled with other duet recordings made by them, including the delightful Arensky Suite which includes the famous waltz. It is good too to have the long-neglected Concertino of Shostakovich and the anything-but-neglected Sabre Dance, which is rather heavy-going here. However, the Debussy Petite suite is very engaging, and most valuable of all is the complete recording of Bizet's Jeux d'enfants – all twelve movements. Only the five included by the composer in his orchestral suite are at all well known, and many of the others are equally charming, not least the opening Rêver (L'Escarpolette), the Scherzo (Les chevaux de bois) and the Nocturne (Colin-Mainard – 'Blind man's buff'). Fine ensemble and sparkling fingerwork, but just occasionally a touch of rhythmic inflexibility. Good, mid-1970s recording.

Oslo Wind Ensemble

Scandinavian Wind Quintets: FERNSTROM: Wind Quintet, Op. 59. KVANDAL: Wind Quintet, Op. 34; 3 Sacred Folktunes. NIELSEN: Wind Quintet, Op. 43
(BB) ** Naxos 8.553050

A super-bargain account of the Nielsen Quintet, more relaxed in its tempi and measured in approach than the account by the Scandinavian Quintet on Marco Polo. Very decently recorded, too. The Swedish musician John Fernström was a prolific composer whose output runs to 12 symphonies and much else besides. He was for years solely represented in the catalogue by a Concertino for Flute, Women's Choir and Small Orchestra. This Wind Quintet is not quite so charming, but is well worth hearing – as, for that matter, is the Wind Quintet by the Norwegian Johan Kvandal, a thoughtful figure who is a composer of imagination and substance.

Oxalys (group)

'Voyage au pays du tendre et de l'effroi': DEBUSSY: Sonata for Flute, Viola & Harp. MARTIN: Pavane couleur du temps (for string quintet). CAPLET: Conte fantastique d'après E. A. Poe (for harp & string quartet). PIERNÉ: Variations libres et Finale, Op. 51; Voyage au pays du tendre (for flute, string trio & harp)
*** Fuga Libra FUG 511

special, unique and intangibly sensuous atmosphere distin-
uishes French chamber music composed in the half-century
urrounding the year 1900. It is here evoked magically and
mmediately by the haunting *Pastorale* which opens the
ebussy Sonata, and which helped to encapsulate the idiom
1915.

At times in these six varied pieces, often impressionistically
nked by flute or harp, one might mistake the sound-world
f one composer for another. The title of the collection is
rawn from Pierné's *Voyage au pays du tendre* (1935) in which
combination of flute, harp and string trio takes the listener
eguilingly on the river of 'Inclination', passing by various
llages, including 'Protective Care', 'Tenderness', 'Submission'
nd 'Pretty Couplets', across the 'Sea of Eternity' to the
estination, the 'City of Tender-on-Inclination'.

The following Pierné *Variations* are more lively, less volup-
uous, even playful, but a more sinister mood haunts Caplet's
Conte fantastique. This explains the additional *l'effroi* of the
isc's title, suggesting dismay or terror, but its underlying
mbience is still sensuous, for it is a melodramatic yet imagi-
ative setting of Poe's *Mask of the Red Death*, complete with
he striking of the midnight hour as the disguised spectre
ppears.

Of the two Jongen pieces the first has a diaphanous aura,
ut the second is an exotic dance, and the influence of Ravel
nd Debussy is strong in both. But perhaps the surprise here
s the lovely, restrained *Pavane couleur du temps* of Frank
Martin.

The Oxalys group play all this music with deep under-
tanding. Their blending and ensemble are as perfect as their
ontrol of nuance and colour, yet the effect is always warmly
pontaneous. Altogether this is a captivating disc, beautifully
ecorded in an atmospheric acoustic which is ideal.

Pahud, Emmanuel (flute)

French Connection' (with Paul Meyer, Francis Meyer, Eric
e Sage): EMMANUEL: *Sonata Trio 1.* JOLIVET: *Sonatine.*
CHMITT: *Sonatine en trio, Op. 85.* SHOSTAKOVICH: *The
Return of Maxim, Op. 45: Valse 3; The Gadfly, Op. 97a:
Waltz.* VILLA-LOBOS: *Choros 2*
** EMI 5 57948-2

he flautist Emmanuel Pahud has here devised a delightful
isc exploiting the distinctive combination of flute and clari-
et, something evidently fascinating to French composers in
articular. The sequence of compact multi-movement works
y Florent Schmitt, Darius Milhaud, André Jolivet and Mau-
ice Emmanuel is framed by waltzes by Shostakovich, both of
hem deliciously lilting, and a chattering and quirky duo by
Villa-Lobos, his *Choros 2*. It is a fun disc that plainly gave joy
o the performers, as it will to listeners. That these are friends
f Pahud helps to bring the sort of give-and-take between the
erformers that results in musical magic.

The Schmitt *Trio* for flute, clarinet and piano (or harpsi-
hord) is a charmingly neoclassical piece in four very com-
act movements, leading to the most substantial piece on the
isc, the Milhaud *Sonata*, which adds an oboe to the basic
rio of instruments. This is a piece dating from 1918 when he
was attached to the French legation in Rio and, like other
works of the period, picks up echoes of Brazilian folk music
n melody and rhythm, while also paying the occasional
ribute to the Stravinsky of *Petrushka* and the *Rite of Spring* in
olytonal writing.

Paik, Kun Woo (piano)

Recital: LISZT: *Années de pèlerinage: Au bord d'une source;
Au lac de Wallenstadt; Les jeux d'eau à la Villa d'Este.
Harmonies poétiques et religieuses: Bénédiction de Dieu
dans la solitude. Liebestraum 3; Mephisto Waltz 1;
Hungarian Rhapsody 12; Variations on B-A-C-H.* French
music: POULENC: *Nocturnes 1, 5 & 6; Presto; Improvisations
10, 12 & 15; Intermezzo 2; Mouvements perpétuels 1–3.*
DEBUSSY: *Pour le piano; Suite bergamasque: Clair de lune.*
SATIE: *Gnossiennes 4 & 5; Ogives 1–2; Descriptions
automatique: Sur un vaisseau; Sur un casque. Chapitre
tourné en tous sens: Celui qui parle trop; Croquis et
agaceries d'un gros bonhomme en bois: España; Embryons
desséchés: D'Edriophtalma; De Podophtalma; Gymnopédies
1–3*
(BB) *** Virgin Classics 2×1 5 61757-2 (2)

This Virgin 2×1 reissue pairs two outstanding individual
recitals, a distinguished Liszt collection already discussed
under the composer, and the present grouping of French
repertoire, which is slightly more idiosyncratic, even including individual movements from suites of miniatures meant to
be played as a group. However, the mixture works well when
the playing is consistently magnetic. There is much to relish,
notably Poulenc's *Mouvements perpétuels* and indeed other
pieces by this composer. Kun Woo Paik's withdrawn performance of *Clair de lune* is a little indulgent and the *Gnossiennes*
also find him a shade mannered, while the *Gymnopédies* are
very languorous. But the outer movements of Debussy's *Pour
le piano* bring some electrifying bravura and his imagination
is given full rein in the quirkier Satie miniatures. There are
154 minutes of music here and, even if the back-up documentation is fairly sparse, the value is obvious, for the recording is
excellent.

Parker-Smith, Jane (organ)

'Popular French Romantics' (organ of Coventry Cathedral):
WIDOR: *Symphony 1: Marche pontificale; Symphony 9
(Gothique), Op. 70: Andante sostenuto.* GUILMANT: *Sonata
5 in C min., Op. 80: Scherzo.* GIGOUT: *Toccata in B min.*
BONNET: *Elfes, Op. 7.* LEFEBURE-WELY: *Sortie in B flat.*
VIERNE: *Pièces de fantaisie: Clair de lune, Op. 53/5; Carillon
de Westminster, Op. 54/6*
*** ASV CDDCA 539

The modern organ in Coventry Cathedral adds a nice bite
to Jane Parker-Smith's very pontifical performance of the
opening Widor *March* and creates a blaze of splendour at
the close of the famous Vierne *Carillon de Westminster*, the
finest performance on record. The detail of the fast, nimble
articulation in the engagingly Mendelssohnian *Elfes* of
Joseph Bonnet is not clouded; yet here, as in the splendid
Guilmant *Scherzo* with its wider dynamic range, there is also
a nice atmospheric effect. Overall, a most entertaining
recital.

'Popular French Romantics', Vol. 2 (organ of Beauvais
Cathedral): FRANCK: *Prélude, fugue et variation, Op. 18.*
GUILMANT: *Grand choeur in D (after Handel).* MULET:
Carillon-Sortie. RENAUD: *Toccata in D min.* SAINT-SAENS:
Prelude and Fugue. VIERNE: *Symphony 1: Finale. Stèle pour
un enfant défunt.* WIDOR: *Symphony 4: Andante and
Scherzo*
*** ASV CDDCA 610

With his *Prelude and Fugue*, Saint-Saëns is in more serious mood than usual but showing characteristic facility in fugal construction; Widor is first mellow and then quixotic – his *Scherzo* demands the lightest articulation and receives it. High drama and great bravura are provided by the Vierne *Finale* and later by Albert Renaud's *Toccata* and Henri Mulet's *Carillon-Sortie*, while Franck's *Prélude, fugue et variation* and the poignant Vierne *Stèle pour un enfant défunt* bring attractive lyrical contrast: here Jane Parker-Smith's registration shows particular subtlety. The organ is splendidly recorded.

'Romantic and Virtuosos Works', Vol. 1 (Goll organ of St Martin Memmingen): MARCEL LANQUETUIT: *Toccata*. JOSEPH BOULNOIS: *Choral in F sharp min*. MULET: *Esquisses Byzantines: Rosace*. JONGEN: *Sonata Eroica, Op. 94*. WHITLOCK: *Fantasie choral 1*. DEMESSIEUX: *Répons pour le Temps de Pâques*. YORK BOWEN: *Melody in G min*. MIDDELSCHULTE: *Passacaglia in D min*.

*** Avie AV 0034

The new organ at St Martin's Memmigen was built by the Lucerne firm of Goll and inaugurated in 1998. This is an organ in the 'French symphonic style', drawing its weight and projection from the reeds and not the mixtures, while the church acoustic provides a magnificent sonority for the pedals, without overall clouding. Jane Parker-Smith has chosen a rewarding programme to demonstrate the organ's very wide range of dynamic and rich palette of colour, alternating feisty bravura pieces with gentle, touching interludes, with the flutes often creating a delightful radiance. It is difficult to believe that Lanquetuit's opening *Toccata in D* is not by Widor, so strong is the latter's influence, with a brilliant semi-quaver figure underpinned by the pedals and overlaid with a lyrical theme. It certainly makes an arresting opening. The flowing Boulnois *Choral* also has a dynamic climax before its closing *Tranquillo* prepares us for the gentle Mulet *Rosace* ('Rose Window').

Jongen's single-movement *Eroica Sonata*, with a bravura introduction (including a fanfare), is in linked sections with a set of variations, concluding with a spectacular fugato. Then Percy Whitlock's pastoral *Fantasie Choral* brings a peaceful interlude before we are carried off on Jeanne Demessieux's galloping *Répons pour le Temps de Pâques* with its rhythmic, tangy chorale, drawn from the principal theme, and then gently subdued at the coda.

York Bowen's engagingly ingenuous *Melody in G minor* then lets us relax before Wilhelm Middleschulte's arresing four-bar introduction announces the familiar B-A-C-H motif and leads into his ambitious *Passacaglia*. It has 62 variants, of which No. 42 introduces *Ein' feste Burg*, and a paean of virtuoso energy follows, before a chordal B-A-C-H thunders out three times to make a grandiloquent close. We know from her past records what an exciting organist Jane Parker-Smith is, and the spectacular recording is worthy of the performances. But you need good speakers for this and indulgent neighbours.

Perlman, Itzhak (violin)

Encores (with Samuel Sanders (piano)):

Disc 1: ELGAR: *Salut d'amour, Op. 12*. SUK: *Un poco triste, Op. 17/2; Burleska*. DE TAYE: *Humoresque*. RACHMANINOV: *Prelude, Op. 23/5; It's peaceful here; Melody, Op. 21/7 & 9*. MENDELSSOHN *Song without Words, Op. 19/1: Sweet Remembrance*. FIOCCO: *Allegro*. DEBUSSY: *La plus que lente*

(Valse); Petite suite: Minuet. Children's Corner: Golliwog's Cakewalk. SARASATE: *Jota Navarra, Op. 22/2*. FAURÉ: *Berceuse, Op. 16*. GERSHWIN: *Porgy & Bess: It ain't necessarily so; Preludes 1–3*. ARENSKY: *Serenade in G, Op. 30/2*. RIMSKY-KORSAKOV: *Tsar Saltan: Flight of the Bumblebee*. DRIGO: *Valse bluette*. RAVEL: *Valses nobles et sentimentales 6 & 7*. ALBÉNIZ: *Sevilla*. SCHUMANN: *Prophe Bird, Op. 82/7*. RAMEAU: *Rigaudon*. ACHRON: *Hebrew Melody*

Disc 2: BAZZINI: *La ronde des lutins*. WIENIAWSKI: *Polonaise brillante 2 in A, Op. 21; Obertass-Mazurka, Op. 19 Polonaise de concert, Op. 4; Scherzo-tarantelle, Op. 16*. STRAVINSKY: *Chanson russe*. FOSTER; *Jeannie with the light brown hair*. TRAD.: *Deep River*. TCHAIKOVSKY: *Mélodie*. GODOWSKY: *Alt-Wien*. CASTELNUOVO-TEDESCO: *Tango*. DEBUSSY: *Petite suite: En bateau*. EDGAR DANIEL DEL VALLE: *Ao pé da fogueira (Prelude XV)*. RACHMANINOV: *Vocalise, Op. 34/14*. PAGANINI: *Sonata 12, Op. 3/6*. GRASE: *Wellenspiel*. HALFFTER: *Danza de la gitana* SARASATE: *Habanera, Op. 21/2; Playera, Op. 23; Spanish Dance, Op. 26/8*

🎵 (BB) *** EMI Gemini (DDD/ADD) 4 76957-2 (2)

Perlman is a violinist who even on record demonstrates hi delight in virtuosity in every phrase he plays, and there are plenty of examples in this pair of recitals, notably on the firs in the jet-propelled bumblebee and, more strikingly in the second, with the dazzling account of *La ronde des lutins*, and the Wieniawski and Sarasate dance-movements. But as the gentle opening *Salut d'amour* on disc one shows, there is plenty to charm and seduce the ear by the sheer style of the playing and the subtlety of bowing, notably in the often exquisite Rachmaninov miniatures (mostly transcribed by Heifetz himself), the two engaging transcriptions from Debussy's *Petite suite*, and the seductive Achron *Hebrew Melody*, while the trifle by Drigo and the little moto perpetuo *Allegro* by Fiocco are captivating. If you enjoy violin encores, they don't come any better than this. Samuel Sanders accompanies judiciously, somewhat backwardly balanced, less so in the Kingsway Hall recordings and (especially) the Abbey Road sessions, which come on the second disc and are analogue. But throughout, the EMI engineers give Perlman the kind of vivid presence he always seeks on record.

'Violin Sonatas Rediscovered' (with David Garvey, piano): PAGANINI: *Caprices, Op. 1/1, 16 & 24*. BEN-HAIM: *Berceuse Sfaradite*. SARASATE: *Navarra, Op. 33*. HANDEL *Sonata 15 in E, Op. 1/15*. HINDEMITH: *Sonata 1 in E flat, Op. 11*. LECLAIR: *Sonata in D, Op. 9/3*. BLOCH: *Nigun (Baal Shem 2)*. FALLA: *Spanish Dance 1*. BAZZINI: *La Ronde des lutins, Op. 25*

(M) *(**) RCA 82876 6517-2

As the notes on the cover tell us, this is a 'dazzlingly delayed' RCA recording début, from 1965. Perlman (pictured youthfully on the front) was 20, and he could already throw off brilliant showpieces with easy aplomb. The disc is framed with three of Paganini's solo *Caprices* (including the most famous) and a sparkling account of the Heifetz favourite encore, *La Ronde des lutins*. In these items he is balanced far too close, but when the piano enters for the luscious accounts of Ben-Haim's *Berceuse* and Sarasate's seductive *Navarra*, while the violin is still on top of the listener, the piano is still in the picture. The two Baroque sonatas are played with genuine style, but the surprise is the Hindemith, where the second, slow movement is magically nostalgic, not a description one often applies to this composer's music. The passionate highlight of the recital is Bloch's *Nigun*, a superb account.

Peyer, Gervase de (clarinet), Gwenneth Pryor (piano)

French Music for Clarinet and Piano: SAINT-SAENS: *Sonata, Op. 167.* DEBUSSY: *Première rhapsodie; Arabesque 2; Prélude: La Fille aux cheveux de lin.* POULENC: *Sonata.* SCHMIDT: *Andantino, Op. 30/1.* RAVEL: *Pièce en forme de habanera.* PIERNE: *Canzonetta, Op. 19*

⏻ ⊙ *** Chan. 8526

A gorgeous record. The Saint-Saëns *Sonata* is an attractively crafted piece, full of engaging invention. Poulenc's *Sonata* is characteristically witty, with contrast in its lovely central *Romanza* (*très calme*); and the other short pieces wind down the closing mood of the recital, with de Peyer's luscious timbre drawing a charming portrait of *The Girl with the Flaxen Hair* before the nimbly tripping closing encore of Pierné. This is a quite perfect record of its kind, the programme like that of a live recital and played with comparable spontaneity. The recording is absolutely realistic; the balance could hardly be improved on.

'Piano Favourites' (Various artists)

'Piano Favourites', played by: (i) Dame Moura Lympany; (ii) Kun Woo Paik; (iii) Leif Ove Andsnes; (iv) Joshua Rifkin; (v) Daniel Adni & Bournemouth SO, Kenneth Alwyn; (vi) John Ogdon, CBSO, Louis Frémaux

(i) BEETHOVEN: *Für Elise.* CHOPIN: *Fantasie-impromptu, Op. 66.* BRAHMS: *Waltz in A flat.* SCHUMANN: *Kinderszenen: Träumerei.* RUBINSTEIN: *Melody in F.* DVOŘÁK: *Humoresque.* MACDOWELL: *To a Wild Rose.* DEBUSSY: *Suite bergamasque: Clair de lune.* RACHMANINOV: *Prelude in C sharp min.* GRANADOS: *Goyescas: The Maiden and the Nightingale.* (ii) LISZT: *Liebesträume 3.* (iii) GRIEG: *Weddding Day at Troldhaugen.* (iv) JOPLIN: *Maple Leaf Rag; The Entertainer.* (v) ADDINSELL, arr. Roy Douglas: *Warsaw Concerto.* WILLIAMS: *Dream of Olwen.* (vi) LITOLFF: *Concerto Symphonique 4: Scherzo*

(BB) *** HMV (ADD/DDD) 5 86799-2

It would be difficult to imagine a more comprehensive collection of favourite piano items than this, and EMI have a strong roster of pianists to draw upon. The 78-minute collection centres on a particularly successful recital, recorded by Dame Moura Lympany at Abbey Road in 1988. She had lost none of the flair and technical skill which earned her her reputation: all the pieces have the spontaneity of a live recital. *Träumerei* and *Clair de lune* emerge the more freshly through a total absence of sentimentality, and the boldly romantic account of Granados's *Maiden and the Nightingale* is particularly fine. The other contributions are skilfully chosen to show their exponents at their most perceptive, Leif Andsnes in Grieg, Joshua Rifkin perfectly at home in Scott Joplin. The two 'film concertos' come off well, though the *Warsaw Concerto*, crafted by Roy Douglas out of Addinsell's music, is much more distinctive. John Ogdon's closing account of the vivacious Litolff *Scherzo* is rather too determinedly brilliant: a lighter and more graceful approach would have been more

exhilarating. But overall this is a most successful and enjoyable programme, well recorded.

Pine, Rachel Barton (violin), Scottish Chamber Orchestra, Alexander Platt

'Scottish Fantasies': BRUCH: *Scottish Fantasy.* MACKENZIE: *Pibroch.* MCEWEN: *Scottish Rhapsody (Prince Charlie).* SARASATE: *Airs écossais.* TRAD.: *Medley of Scottish Tunes* (arr. Pine/Fraser)

*** Cedille CDR 90000 083

Rachel Barton Pine had the idea of assembling this colourful collection of works on a Scottish theme after being asked to do a recital entitled 'Scotland'. She points out that even the best-known work on the disc, Bruch's *Scottish Fantasy*, now a regular repertory piece, was seriously neglected until after the Second World War, when it was impressively taken up both in concert and on disc by Jascha Heifetz. With her flawless intonation, crisp rhythmic attack and gift of drawing out the full tenderness of the many lyrical passages, it is a warm and moving performance, as are the performances of the other works on this disc, with the fun of the Sarasate medley brilliantly caught. Alexander Platt draws persuasively alert playing from the Scottish Chamber Orchestra, with clear, well-balanced recording.

The McEwen *Rhapsody, Prince Charlie,* written in 1915 for violin and piano, was orchestrated and drastically revised by the composer in 1941, but was not performed until this present recording. The final item is a medley devised by the violinist in collaboration with the Scottish fiddle-player, Alasdair Fraser, who joins her on his traditional instrument in similarly clean attack and with no folk-like rasping.

Pinnock, Trevor (harpsichord or virginals)

'At the Victoria and Albert Museum': ANON.: *My Lady Wynkfylds Rownde.* BYRD: *The Queens Alman; The Bells.* HANDEL: *Harpsichord Suite 5 in E.* CROFT: *Suite 3 in C min.* ARNE: *Sonata 3 in G.* J. C. BACH: *Sonata in C min., Op. 5/6*

(M) *** CRD (ADD) CRD 3307

Trevor Pinnock recorded for CRD before he moved over to the DG Archiv label and this was his first solo recital, made at the Victoria and Albert Museum using virginals and other period harpsichords. He opens with three very colourful pieces played on an instrument originally belonging to Queen Elizabeth I, who was an accomplished virginals player. It is in splendid condition and has a most attractive sound. Pinnock plays it with enthusiasm and his performance of Byrd's extraordinarily descriptive *The Bells* is a *tour de force.* For the rest of the recital he uses two different harpsichords. His style in the works of Handel, Croft, Arne and J. C. Bach is less flamboyant, more circumspect, but the music is strongly characterized and boldly recorded. The Handel suite is the one which has the *Harmonious blacksmith* as its finale, which is played with considerable flair.

16th-Century Harpsichord and Virginals Music:
Harpsichord: BYRD: *Walkin's Ale; La Volta; Lord Willoughby's Welcome Home; The Carman's Whistle.* Virginals: *My Lady Carey's Dompe.* TALLIS: *O ye Tender Babes.* Harpsichord: GIBBONS: *The Woods so Wild; The Fairest Nymph; The Lord of Salisbury his Pavin and Galliard.* BULL: *The King's Hunt; My Grief; My Self.*

Virginals: DOWLAND: *Lachrimae and Galliard: Can she excuse.* **Harpsichord:** FARNABY: *Muscadin or Kempe's Morris; Loath to depart.* TOMKINS: *Barafostus' Dream*
🎵▬ (M) *** CRD 3350

This programme is cleverly arranged into two groups of pieces so that in each a central section for virginals is framed by major items on the harpsichord. In the first group the two virginals pieces nearly steal the show, for the engaging *My Lady Carey's Dompe* is beautifully set off by Tallis's *O ye Tender Babes.* There is some superb bravura from Pinnock in the harpsichord music. John Bull's *The King's Hunt* is splendidly vigorous and *Lord Salisbury's Pavin and Galliard* (Gibbons) bring comparable poise and elegance. Everything springs vividly to life and Pinnock's decoration is always well judged, adding piquancy and zest to the fast pieces. The recording (produced by Simon Lawman and balanced by Bob Auger) is outstandingly real in a perfectly chosen acoustic. Early keyboard records don't come any better than this, and one can imagine the illusion of Queen Elizabeth (a celebrated performer on the virginals) herself sitting at the keyboard enjoying this attractive programme.

Pletnev, Mikhail (piano)

'*Hommage à Rachmaninov*': RACHMANINOV: *Variations on a Theme of Corelli, Op. 42; 4 Etudes-tableaux, Op. 39/5; Opp. 44/6, 8–9.* BEETHOVEN: *Piano Sonata 26 (Les Adieux), Op. 81a.* MENDELSSOHN: *Andante cantabile & Presto agitato; Andante & Rondo capriccioso, Op. 14.* CHOPIN: *Andante spianato et Grande polonaise brillant, Op. 22*
🌑 *** DG 459 634-2

Way back in 1982, when Pletnev was in his early twenties, Dr Mark Zilberquist (in *Russia's Great Modern Pianists*) noted the young pianist's affinities with his aristocratic and patrician compatriot, Rachmaninov: 'discreet, reserved, outwardly restrained in showing emotion'. Pletnev certainly has something of the same commanding keyboard authority, the extraordinary range of colour and clarity of articulation of Rachmaninov. This recital is recorded at Rachmaninov's own summer home, the Villa Senar on the Vierwaldstätter See, near Lake Lucerne, using the composer's newly restored American Steinway. The playing is breathtaking, worthy of the composer at his best, and dazzling but never ostentatious. The delicacy of the Mendelssohn and the introductory *Andante cantabile* to the Chopin is magical. A quite exceptional recital even by the standards of this exceptional pianist.

'*Carnegie Hall Recital*' (1 November 2000): BACH/BUSONI: *Chaconne in D min., BWV 1004.* BEETHOVEN: *Sonata 32 in C min., Op. 111.* CHOPIN: *4 Scherzi: Op. 20; Op. 31; Op. 39; Op. 54.* Plus encores: BALAKIREV: *Islamey.* MOSZKOWSKI: *Etude de virtuosité, Op. 72/6.* RACHMANINOV: *Etude-tableau, Op. 39/5.* SCARLATTI: *Sonata in D min., Kk 9.* SCRIABIN: *Poème, Op. 32/1*
🌑 *** DG 471 157-2 (with encores bonus CD)

Mikhail Pletnev made his Carnegie Hall début when he was in his early forties, relatively late in his career, but the wait should not have disappointed his many American admirers. 'He links arms with such stalwarts of the Russian school as Horowitz, Richter and Gilels,' wrote the *New York Times*, and his programme has all the dazzling command and authority, not to mention virtuosity, we would expect. The Beethoven Op. 111 *Sonata* has tremendous power and concentration and

comes up sounding altogether fresh, while the four Chopin *Scherzi*, which comprised the second half, are quite thrilling and brought the house down. The five encores that followed come on an extra CD, and the *Islamey* belongs among the great performances of this work. Some recital this, and very decently recorded too!

Pollini, Maurizio (piano)

STRAVINSKY: *3 Movements from 'Petrushka'.* PROKOFIEV: *Piano Sonata 7 in B flat, Op. 83.* WEBERN: *Variations for Piano, Op. 27.* BOULEZ: *Piano Sonata 2*
(M) *** DG 447 431-2

The Prokofiev is a great performance, one of the finest ever committed to disc; and the Stravinsky *Petrushka* is electrifying. Not all those responding to this music will do so quite so readily to the Boulez, fine though the playing is; but the Webern also makes a very strong impression. This is the equivalent of two LPs and is outstanding value. It is a natural candidate for reissue in DG's set of 'Originals' of legendary performances.

Preston, Simon (organ)

'*The World of the Organ*' (organ of Westminster Abbey): WIDOR: *Symphony 5: Toccata.* BACH: *Chorale Prelude, Wachet auf, BWV 645.* MOZART: *Fantasia in F min., K.608.* WALTON: *Crown Imperial* (arr. MURRILL). CLARKE: *Prince of Denmark's March* (arr. PRESTON). HANDEL: *Saul: Dead March.* PURCELL: *Trumpet Tune* (arr. TREVOR). ELGAR: *Imperial March* (arr. MARTIN). VIERNE: *Symphony 1: Finale.* WAGNER: *Tannhäuser: Pilgrims' Chorus.* GUILMANT: *March on a Theme of Handel.* SCHUMANN: *Study 5* (arr. WEST). KARG-ELERT: *Marche triomphale (Now Thank We All Our God)*
(M) *** Decca (ADD) 430 091-2

A splendid compilation from the Argo catalogue of the early to mid-1960s, spectacularly recorded, which offers 69 minutes of music and is in every sense a resounding success. Simon Preston's account of the Widor *Toccata* is second to none, and both the Vierne *Finale* and the Karg-Elert *Marche triomphale* lend themselves admirably to Preston's unashamed flamboyance and the tonal splendour afforded by the Westminster acoustics. Walton's *Crown Imperial*, too, brings a panoply of sound which compares very favourably with an orchestral recording. The organ has a splendid trumpet stop which makes both the Purcell piece and Clarke's *Prince of Denmark's March*, better known as the 'Trumpet Voluntary', sound crisply regal.

Prometheus Ensemble

'*French Impressions*': RAVEL: *Introduction & Allegro for Harp, Flute, Clarinet & String Quartet.* DEBUSSY: *Danses sacrée et profane; Sonata for Flute, Viola & Harp.* ROUSSEL: *Serenade*
*** ASV CDDCA 664

This young group gives eminently well-prepared and thoughtful accounts of all these pieces. The *Danse sacrée* and *Danse profane* sound particularly atmospheric and the Debussy *Sonata* is played with great feeling and sounds appropriately ethereal. The Roussel, too, is done with great style and, even if the *Introduction and Allegro* does not supersede the celebrated Melos account, the Prometheus do it well.

Purcell Quartet, Purcell Band, with Robert Woolley (harpsichord)

'*La Folia (Variations on a Theme)*': CORELLI: *Violin Sonata in D min., Op. 5/12.* MARAIS: *Les folies d'Espagne.* VIVALDI: *Trio Sonata in D min. (Variations on 'La Folia'), Op. 1/12 (RV 63)* (Purcell Quartet). GEMINIANI: *Concerto grosso (La Folia)* (after Corelli) (Purcell Quartet & Purcell Band). ALESSANDRO SCARLATTI: *Toccata 7 (Primo tono): Folia.* C. P. E. BACH: *12 Variations on Folies d'Espagne, Wq.118/9 (H.263)* (Wooley)

🎵 *** Hyp. CDA 67035

Just as the chanson *L'homme armé* was popular among composers as a basis for Mass settings in the fifteenth and early sixteenth centuries, so at the very end of the seventeenth and throughout the eighteenth, *La Folia* was in constant use for instrumental variations. The word '*folia*' is Portuguese in origin and means 'empty-headed', but also refers to a dance in triple time, which originated around the same time as that famous chanson. It changed its rhythmic accents over the years, and the special character of the format we now recognize seems to have first come into use by Lully for an oboe tune around 1672.

Corelli probably appropriated it from Lully in 1700, resourcefully turning the piece into a chaconne, but Marais probably beat him to it: even though his *Folies d'Espagne* was not published until 1701, it was probably written some years earlier. Thereafter composers seemed to almost fall over each other to put it to good use in their instrumental music. The above six listings are excellent examples, among which Vivaldi's highly entertaining *Trio Sonata* stands out alongside Carl Philipp Emanuel Bach's superb set of variations for the keyboard, which ought to be much better known. But all the versions here are stimulating, and played with fine, expressive vitality. The recording too is excellent. This is not a recital to play continuously, but, dipped into a version at a time, it will give much pleasure.

Ragossnig, Konrad (Renaissance lute)

'*Renaissance Lute Music*': Disc 1: England: DOWLAND: *King of Denmark's Galliard; Lachrimae antiquae pavan; Fantasia; My Lady Hunsdon's Puffe; Melancholy Galliard; Mrs Winter's Jump; Semper Dowland, semper dolens; Earl of Essex his Galliard; Forlorne Hope Fancy.* BATCHELAR: *Mounsiers almaine.* BULMAN: *Pavan.* CUTTING: *Almain; Greensleeves; Walsingham; The Squirrel's Toy.* ANON.: *Sir John Smith his Almain.* MORLEY: *Pavan.* JOHNSON: *Alman.* HOLBORNE: *Galliard.* Italy: CAPIROLA: *Ricercars 1, 2, 10 & 13.* SPINACINO: *Ricercar.* FRANCESCO DA MILANO: *Fantasia*

Disc 2: Italy (continued): MOLINARO: *Fantasias 1, 9 & 10. Saltarello – Ballo detto Il Conte Orlando – Saltarello.* BARBETTA: *Moresca detta le Canarie.* TERZI: *Ballo tedesco e francese – Tre parti di gagliarde.* NEGRI: *La spagnoletto – Il bianco fiore.* SANTINO GARSI DE PALMA: *Aria del Gran Duca – La Cesarina – La Mutia – La ne mente per la gola – Gagliarda Manfredina – Ballo del Serenissimo Duca di*

Parma – Corenta. Spain: MILAN: *Pavanas 1–6; Fantasias 10–12 & 16.* MUDARRA: *Pavana de Alexandre; Gallarda; Romanesca: O guárdame las vacas; Diferencias sobre Conde claros; Fantasia que contrahaze la harpa en la manera de Luduvico.* LUIS DE NARVAEZ: *Diferencias sobre Guádame las vacas; Milles regres. La canción des Emperador del quarto tono de Jusquin; Fantasia; Baxa de contrapunto*

Disc 3: Poland & Hungary: CEDA: *Praeludium; Galliarda 1 & 2; Favorito.* ANON.: *Balletto Polacho.* POLAK: *Praeludium.* DLUGORAJ: *Chorea polonica.* BAKFARK: *Fantasia; Finale; Villanella; Finale; Kowaly; Finale; 4 Fantasies.* Germany: JUDENKUNIG: *Hoff dantz.* NEWSIDLER: *Ellend bringt peyn; Der Juden Tantz; Preambel; Welscher tantz Wascha mesa.* LANDGRAF MORITZ VON HESSEN: *Pavane.* ANON.: *Der gestraifft Danntz – Der Gassenhauer darauff.* WAISSEL: *Fantasia; Deutscher Tantz.* OCHSENKHUN: *Innsbruck, ich muss dich lassen*

Disc 4: Netherlands: ADRIAENSSEN: *Fantasia; Courante; Branle simple de Poictou.* HOWET: *Fantasie.* SWEELINCK: *Psalms 5 & 23.* Joachim van den HOVE: *Galliarde.* VALLET: *Prelude; Galliarde; Slaep, soete, slaep.* France: ATTAIGNANT: *Chansons: Tant que vivray; Destre amoureux. Basse dances: Sansserre; La Magdelena; Branle gay: C'est mon amy; Haulberroys.* ADRIEN LE ROY: *Passemeze.* BALLARD: *Entrée de luth; Corante; Branle de village.* BESARD: *Branle; Gagliarda; Branle gay; Gagliarda vulgo dolorata; Allemande; Air de cour: J'ai trouvé sur l'herbe assise; Volte; Branle – Branle gay; Guillemette; Ballet; Pass' e mezo; Chorea rustica*

⊙ (M) *** DG (ADD) 476 1840 (4)

This admirable four-disc Archiv set gives us a comprehensive survey of the development of lute music throughout Europe in the fifteenth, sixteenth and the first half of the seventeenth century. English lute music came to its peak at the end of the Elizabethan and beginning of the Jacobean eras and is well represented by that master of melancholy, John Dowland – although he could also be spirited, witness *My Lady Hunsdon's Puffe*. But the oldest-known (written-down) lute music came from Italy, and the remarkably flexible *Ricercars* of Vincenzo Capirola (born in 1474) make an ideal example of music which is essentially improvisatory in feeling yet settling down into formal shape. The equivalent of the lute in Spain was the vihuela de mano (an ancestor of the guitar), and it was in Spain that the variation form was born, using the term 'diferencias'. Here, besides the solemn music and dances, we have fine examples of *Diferencias* by Mudarra and Narvaéz.

Polish and Hungarian lute music is comparatively little known, but, as the four late-sixteenth-century pieces by Diomedes Cato demonstrate, its manner closely reflects the Renaissance style in the rest of Europe. The Hungarian, Valentin Bakfark, however, is revealed as a composer of considerable individuality and his two *Villanellas* are particularly haunting. The German repertoire, too, is particularly strong in character and it brings some novelties, like Newsidler's extraordinarily exotic *Juden Tanz*. In the Netherlands programme, Sweelinck's music (two beautiful Psalm evocations) catches the ear, while the *Galliarde* and the touching *Slaepe, sote slaep* draw the listener's attention to his little-known contemporary, Nicolas Vallet.

The programme of French music which concludes the survey is hardly less rich in fine invention, and this is obviously because Pierre Attaignant and Robert Ballard were publishers first and foremost, and they both clearly had an ear for a hit number. Thus all the anonymous pieces listed under their names are full of character: sample the *Branle gay: C'est mon amy*, the charming *La Magdalena* or the rustic *Branles de village* with its drone imitation suggesting a hurdy-gurdy. Jean-Baptiste Besard, however, was an outstanding French lutenist (also a doctor of law and a physician) and his music is of the highest quality: the *Gagliarda vulgo dolorata*, *Air de cour*, *J'ai trouvé sur l'herbe assise*, *Branle gay* and sad little *Guillemette* can be spoken of in the same breath as the best Dowland pieces. Throughout his long programme, recorded between 1973 and 1975, Konrad Ragossnig plays with impeccable style. His spontaneous feeling brings all this music vividly to life and his variety of timbre and subtle use of echo dynamics always intrigue the ear. The recording is very fine indeed, giving his period lute a natural presence and very slightly more body than RCA provide for Julian Bream, who nevertheless can continue to be recommended alongside the present set: he is especially at home in the English repertoire. Ragossnig's set is now available in Universal's 'Penguin Rosette' Collection and is especially welcome at mid-price, with full documentation.

Rév, Lívia (piano)

'*For Children*': BACH: *Preludes in E, BWV 939; in G min., BWV 930*. DAQUIN: *Le Coucou*. MOZART: *Variations on 'Ah vous dirai-je maman', K.265*. BEETHOVEN: *Für Elise*. SCHUMANN: *Album for the Young, Op. 63: excerpts*. CHOPIN: *Nocturne in C min., Op. posth*. LISZT: *Etudes, G. 136/1 & 2*. BIZET: *Jeux d'enfants: La Toupie*. FAURE: *Dolly: Berceuse*. TCHAIKOVSKY: *Album for the Young, Op. 39: Maman; Waltz*. VILLA-LOBOS: *Prole do bebê: excerpts*. JOLIVET: *Chansons naïve 1 & 2*. PROKOFIEV: *Waltz, Op. 65*. BARTOK: *Evening in the Country; For Children: excerpts*. DEBUSSY: *Children's Corner: excerpts*. MAGIN: *3 Pieces*. MATACIC: *Miniature Variations*
*** Hyp. CDA 66185

A wholly delectable recital, and not just for children either. The whole is more than the sum of its many parts, and the layout provides excellent variety, with the programme stimulating in mixing familiar with unfamiliar. The recording is first class. Highly recommended for late-evening listening.

Reykjavik Wind Quintet

JEAN-MICHEL DAMASE: *17 Variations*. DEBUSSY (arr. BOZZA): *Le Petit nègre*. FAURE (arr. WILLIAMS): *Dolly Suite: Berceuse, Op. 56/1*. FRANCAIX: *Quintet 1*. IBERT: *3 Pièces brèves*. MILHAUD: *La Cheminée du Roi René, Op. 205*. PIERNE: *Pastorale, Op. 14/1*. POULENC (arr. EMERSON): *Novelette 1*
*** Chan. 9362

Another delightful recital for late-night listening. Elegant, crisp playing from this accomplished Icelandic ensemble. The Damase *Variations* are delightful, as indeed are the Françaix and Milhaud pieces, and the Chandos recording is in the best traditions of the house.

'*Nordic Music for Wind Quintet*': RASMUSSEN: *Quintet in F*. LARSSON: *Quattro tempi (Divertimento), Op. 55*. NIELSEN: *Quintet, Op. 43*. HALLGRIMSSON: *Intarsia*
*** Chan. 9849

The *Quintets* by Peter Rasmussen and Haflidi Hallgrímsson are new to CD. Rasmussen comes between Gade and Nielsen,

though if you heard this music without knowing what it was, you could be forgiven for thinking it was by Reicha and Danzi or one of their contemporaries. It is well written for the instruments but pleasingly inconsequential. Haflidi Hallgrímsson, who was born in 1941, is Icelandic. His *Intarsia* is a witty and inventive score, expertly laid out for wind. Its title derives from knitting, and the ideas bubble away in a diverting and inventive way. Well worth trying out. Lars-Erik Larsson's evocation of the four seasons, *Quattro tempi*, is an imaginative and individual score. This version more than holds its own against the earlier (1983) version by the Stockholm Wind Quintet (Caprice). With the Nielsen *Quintet*, competition is very stiff, and though the Reykjavik players do it well, the Oslo Quintet (Naxos) and the Wind Quintet of the Danish Radio Orchestra (dacapo – see above) have the greater personality and finesse. Enjoyable and recommendable, though the sound is a bit upfront.

Ricci, Ruggiero (violin), Louis Persinger or Ernest Lush (piano)

PAGANINI: *Witches Dance, Op. 8; Fantasia on the G string after Rossini's 'Mosè in Egitto'; Moto perpetuo in C; Variations on 'Nel cor più mi sento' from Paisiello's 'La Molinara'; Variations on 'God Save the Queen'; La Campanella (from Violin Concerto 2); Sonata 12 in E min, Op. 3/6; I Palpiti: Variations after Rossini's 'Tancredi'* (arr. KREISLER). WIENIAWSKI: *Scherzo-Tarantelle in G min*. ELGAR: *La Capricieuse*. VECSEY: *Caprice 1 (Le vent)*. KROLL: *Banjo and Fiddle*. CHOPIN: *Nocturne 20 in C sharp min.* (arr. MILSTEIN). SMETANA: *Má Vlast: Andantino*. SARASATE: *8 Spanish Dances; Caprice basque; Introduction et Tarantelle; Zigeunerweisen; Jóta Aragonesa*. SUK: *Burleska*. ACHRON: *Hebrew Melody*. HUBAY: *The Zephyr*. MOSZKOWSKI: *Guitarre*. BAZZINI: *La Ronde des lutins: scherzo fantastique*
(B) *** Double Decca (IMS) mono/stereo 458 191-2 (2)

Ricci gives us a dazzling display of violin pyrotechnics in all these pieces which are much prized by violinists from Heifetz downwards – music to show off the virtuoso possibilities (and improbabilities) of the instrument, and this they surely do. Ricci uses every trick in the book to make one gasp at the sheer technical brilliance – try the final Bazzini number first, and then the music of Sarasate, in which he was a specialist. The mono sound is naturally a little thin, but has transferred very well to CD, and half the programme is in excellent stereo. As much of this repertoire is rare in the concert hall these days, this collection is especially valuable, and this is now available as a Double Decca, thanks to Australian Decca (who compiled the original issue). Thoroughly recommended.

Richter, Sviatoslav (piano)

Recital: BACH: *Well-tempered Klavier: Preludes and Fugues 1–6, BWV 846–53*. HAYDN: *Piano Sonata in G min*. SCHUBERT: *Allegretto in C min., D.915; Ländler in A, D.366*. CHOPIN: *Polonaise-fantaisie, Op. 61; Etudes: in C; in C min. (Revolutionary), Op. 10/7 & 12*. SCHUMANN: *Abegg Variations, Op. 1*. DEBUSSY: *Estampes; Préludes: Voiles; Le Vent dans la plaine; Les Collines d'Anacapri*. SCRIABIN:

Sonata 5 in F sharp min., Op. 53. RACHMANINOV: *Prelude in G sharp min., Op. 32/12*. PROKOFIEV: *Visions fugitives, Op. 22/3, 6 & 9; Sonata 8 in B flat, Op. 84*

➝ ✹ (M) *** DG (ADD) 476 2203 (2)

This remarkable Richter treasury collects many of the stereo recordings he made for DG (or which were licensed to DG) between 1962 and 1965. They are all of good quality and often the sound is excellent, if a little dry. The recordings, taken from live recitals during his Italian tour, bring a cough or two. The opening Bach *Preludes and Fugues* immediately bring rapt concentration. The Chopin selection opens with a wonderfully poetic account of the *Polonaise-fantaisie*, and the *Revolutionary Study* is almost overwhelming in its excitement. The audience noises may be found intrusive both here and in the superb Debussy performances, yet *Jardins sous la pluie* is quite magical, as is the gentle exoticism of *Pagodes* (both from *Estampes*). Richter's Schumann is no less special, and in the delicious account of the Schubert *Ländler* one can sense the smile in his eyes. Both in the Scriabin and Prokofiev *Sonatas* it is the powerful dynamism of Richter's technique that projects the music so vividly, but of course there is much poetic feeling too. An inexpensive cross-section of his art, this could hardly be bettered. A splendid addition to Universal's Penguin Rosette' Collection, at mid-price.

Sviatoslav Richter in the 1950s, Volume 1: PROKOFIEV: *Cinderella: 5 Pieces; Visions fugitives, Op. 22: excerpts; Piano Sonata 7 in B flat, Op. 83*. SCHUMANN: *Toccata in C, Op. 7*. DEBUSSY: *Images, Book II: Cloches à travers les feuilles* (2 performances). CHOPIN: *Etudes in C & E* (2 performances), *Op. 10/1 & 3*. RACHMANINOV: *Preludes: in F sharp min., Op. 23/1; in B flat, Op. 23/2; in D, Op. 23/4; in G min., Op. 23/5; in C min., Op. 23/7; in A flat, Op. 23/8; in A, Op. 31/9; in C, Op. 32/1; in B flat min., Op. 32/2; in F, Op. 32/7; in B min., Op 32/10; in G sharp min., Op. 32/12; in G sharp min., Op. 32/15*. TCHAIKOVSKY: *Piano Sonata in G, Op. 37*. LISZT: *Valse oubliée 1*

(M) (***) Parnassus mono PACD 96-001/2 (2)

We owe this double-pack of Richter to the dedication of some enthusiasts who have tracked down a considerable number of live performances from the 1950s, before his star had risen in the West, recordings which have never been issued before. The unsigned liner-note claims that Richter was at this time 'perhaps even more of a virtuoso than the more mature artist' and that 'he was more willing to dazzle audiences with his facility'. Another claim the producer makes, and one that must be upheld, is that 'the recorded sound while not the ultimate in fidelity is superior to what we might have expected from early Russian tapes'.

The first CD brings some dazzling Prokofiev, recorded in Moscow in April 1958. The transcriptions from *Cinderella*, the excerpts from *Visions fugitives* and the *Seventh Sonata* are little short of amazing. (The sonata was recorded two months before the BMG/Melodiya version made at a recital in the Great Hall of the Moscow Conservatoire, and is every bit as electrifying, though the BMG is better recorded.) The producer's claim that Richter took more risks in this concert performance of the Schumann *Toccata* than in the safer but still stunning DG studio recording later the same year is also on target.

The Tchaikovsky *G major Sonata*, Op. 37, comes from another Moscow recital, in December 1954, two years before the BMG account, as do two other pieces also played at that later recital, the *Cloches à travers les feuilles* and the Chopin E

major *Study*, Op. 10, No. 3. Richter also recorded the Tchaikovsky *Sonata* in the studio in the mid-1950s (it was issued in the UK on Parlophone). We would not wish to choose between the two presently before the public; what is undeniable is that both are pretty sensational. (There are some barely discernible bumps in the slow movement but the transfers are otherwise excellent.) So, for that matter, are the 13 Rachmaninov *Preludes* in this recital. What pianism!

Sviatoslav Richter in the 1950s, Volume 2: MUSSORGSKY: *Pictures at an Exhibition*. SCHUMANN: *Abegg Variations, Op. 1; 3 Fantasiestücke, Op. 12; Humoreske in B flat, Op. 20*. SCRIABIN: *12 Preludes, Op. 11; Sonatas 2 in G sharp min., Op. 19; 6, Op. 62*. TCHAIKOVSKY: *Piano Concerto 1 in B flat min., Op. 23* (with USSR State SO, Rachlin)

(M) (**(*)) Parnassus mono PACD 96-003/4 (2)

The earliest performances here are the Mussorgsky *Pictures* and the Scriabin *Sixth Sonata*, which come from a 1952 Moscow recital. The BMG/Melodiya account comes from 1958, the same year as the famous Sofia recital, while their recording of the Scriabin comes from three years later, in 1955. The other Scriabin repertoire, along with the Schumann pieces, come from June 1955 and the Tchaikovsky concerto with Nathan Rachlin from 1957. Though the playing is again dazzling, the orchestral recording is coarse and climaxes discolour, and in the climaxes the engineers can be heard reducing the level to avoid overloading. Apart from this, Richter is in a class of his own, and *aficionados* will surely want this.

'In Memoriam - Legendary Recordings (1959–1962)': BACH: *Well-tempered Clavier, Book I: Preludes and Fugues 1, 4–6 & 8, BWV 846, 849–51 & 853*. HAYDN: *Sonata in G min., Hob XVI/44*. CHOPIN: *Ballades 3 in A flat, Op. 47; 4 in F min., Op. 52; Polonaise-fantaisie in A flat, Op. 61; Etudes in C; C min. (Revolutionary), Op. 10/1 & 12*. SCHUBERT: *Allegretto in C min., D.915. Ländler, D.366/1, 3 & 4–5*. SCHUMANN: *Abegg Variations, Op. 1*. DEBUSSY: *Estampes; Préludes; Voiles; Le Vent dans la plaine; Les Collines d'Anacapri*. RACHMANINOV: *Preludes 3 in B flat; 5 in D; 6 in G min.; 8 in C min., Op. 23/2, 4–5 & 7; 12 in C; 13 in B flat; 23 in G sharp min., Op. 32/1–2 & 12*. PROKOFIEV: *Visions Fugitives, Op. 22/3, 6 & 9*

(B) *** DG Double 457 667-2 (2)

Over the years DG have made a number of different collections from the recordings Richter made at live recitals while on tour in Europe between 1959 and 1962. The present programme extends the Chopin coverage to include two *Ballades*, volatile, highly individual performances; the number of Rachmaninov *Preludes* is also increased to cover virtually all the favourites. The remastered recordings – the quality varies somewhat between items – are for the most part very good, though audience noises inevitably intrude at times.

The compelling accounts of the Scriabin and Prokofiev *Sonatas* previously included have been omitted. Each disc is generously full and the set is highly recommendable. The discography details are as follows: Rachmaninov *Preludes* (except Op. 32/12): Warsaw, 1959; Haydn *Sonata*, Chopin Op. 47, Debussy *Préludes*: Wembley Town Hall, 1961; Bach, Prokofiev, Chopin (except Op. 47), Debussy *Estampes*, Rachmaninov Op. 32/12, Schubert, Schumann: Italian tour, 1962.

CHOPIN: *Ballade 3 in A flat, Op. 47; Barcarolle in F sharp, Op. 60; Etudes, Op. 10/12 (2 versions) 1; 4; 6; & 10; Mazurkas, Op. 24/1–4; Scherzo 4 in E min., Op. 54*.

DEBUSSY: *Images, Book II: Cloches à travers les feuilles. L'Isle joyeuse; Préludes, Book I: I Danseuses de Delphes; II Voiles; III Le Vent dans la plaine; IV Les Sons et les parfums tournent dans l'air du soir; VI Des pas sur la neige; IX La Sérénade interrompue* (2 versions); *V Les Collines d'Anacapri; XI La Danse de Puck; VII Ce qu'a vu le vent d'ouest; X La Cathédrale engloutie. Préludes, Book II: I Brouillards; II Feuilles mortes; III La Puerta del Vino; IV Les Fées sont d'exquises danseuses; Bruyèrea; VI General Lavine – eccentric; VII La Terrasse des audiences du clair de lune; VIII Ondine; IX Hommage à Pickwick Esq. P.P.M.P.C.; X Canope; XI Les tierces alternées; XII Feux d'artifice.* PROKOFIEV: *Dance, Op. 32/1*

(M) (✱✱✱) BBC mono BBCL 4021-2 (2)

These archive recordings offer a unique glimpse of Richter's art in the early 1960s. The Chopin and the ten *Préludes* from Book I plus *L'Isle joyeuse* and *Cloches à travers les feuilles* come from a 1961 relay of his Festival Hall recital, while Book II is from a 1967 recital at The Maltings, Snape. He was very much at his peak at this time, and no Richter admirer or lover of the piano will want to be without this invaluable memento. As a Debussy interpreter, Richter gave a powerfully concentrated distillation that brought the atmosphere of these miniature tone-poems before our eyes with greater refinement of colour and touch than almost all his colleagues. Sonic limitations are surprisingly few and matter little, given the distinction and stature of this playing.

BEETHOVEN: *Piano Sonata 11 in B flat, Op. 22; Eroica Variations, Op. 35.* CHOPIN: *Nocturnes, Op. 15/1; Op. 72/2.* HAYDN: *Piano Sonata 37 in E, Hob.XVI/22.* RACHMANINOV: *12 Preludes, Op. 23/1, 2, 4, 5 & 8; Op. 32/1, 2, 6, 7, 9, 10 & 12.* SCHUMANN: *Etudes Symphoniques*

(M) ✱✱✱ BBC (ADD) BBCL 4090-2

These performances are assembled from various broadcasts: the Rachmaninov from the Free Trade Hall, Manchester, in 1969; the Beethoven and Schumann from a Festival Hall recital in the previous year, and the Haydn *Sonata* and one of the Chopin *Nocturnes* from the Snape Maltings in 1967. This was a period when Richter was at the height of his powers: the Rachmaninov *Preludes* particularly draw from him playing of exceptional eloquence and concentration. However, the Beethoven and Schumann are hardly less impressive, and the Haydn *E major Sonata* (No. 37 in E, Hob.XVI/22) has tremendous character too. The recordings are excellent for their period and enhance the attractions of a most distinguished compilation.

Robles, Marisa (harp)

'*The World of the Harp*': FALLA: *Three-cornered Hat: Danza del corregidor.* ALBENIZ: *Rumores de la Caleta; Torre Bermeja.* BIDAOLA: *Viejo zortzico.* EBERL (attrib. Mozart): *Theme, Variations and Rondo pastorale.* BEETHOVEN: *Variations on a Swiss Song.* BRITTEN: *Ceremony of Carols: Interlude.* FAURE: *Impromptu, Op. 86.* PIERNE: *Impromptu-caprice, Op. 9.* SALZEDO: *Chanson de la nuit.* BRAHMS: *Lullaby.* BACH: *Well-tempered Clavier: Prelude 1.* CHOPIN: *Mazurka, Op. 7/1; Prelude, Op. 28/15 (Raindrop).* HASSELMANS: *La Source*

⊶ (M) ✱✱✱ Decca (ADD) 433 869-2

The artistry of Marisa Robles ensures that this is a highly attractive anthology and the programme is as well chosen as it is beautifully played. As ex-Professor of the harp at the Madrid Conservatory, Robles has a natural affinity for the Spanish music that opens her programme, and other highlights include a magnetic account of the Britten *Interlude* and the Salzedo *Chanson de la nuit* with its bell-like evocations. The Eberl *Variations* are highly engaging. The excellent recordings derive from the Argo catalogue of the 1960s and '70s, except for the Chopin, Brahms, Bach and Hasselmans pieces, which have been added to fill out the present reissue (75 minutes). The delicious Hasselmans roulades are the epitome of nineteenth-century harp writing. The CD has a most realistic presence.

Los Romeros

'*Spanish Guitar Favourites*' (with Pepe Romero, Celín Romero, Celedonio Romero, Celino Romero): GIMENEZ: *La boda de Luis Alonso: Malagueña – Zapateado; El baile de Luis Alonso: Intermedio.* BOCCHERINI: *Guitar Quintet 4 in D, G.448: Grave – Fandango.* CELEDONIO ROMERO: *Fantasia Cubana; Malagueñas.* FALLA: *El amor brujo: Ritual Fire Dance.* SOR: *L'encouragement, Op. 34.* PRAETORIUS: *Bransle de la torche; Ballet; Volta.* TARREGA: *Capricho árabe.* TURINA: *La oración del torero.* TORROBA: *Estampas*

✪ ✱✱✱ Ph. 476 2265

The famous Los Romeros guitar quartet (father Celedonio and three sons, led by Pepe) have never sounded quite like this before on record. The playing throughout is both vibrant and seemingly totally spontaneous, although the group were in fact recorded under studio conditions in the San Luis Rey Mission in California. Opening with a compelling *Malagueña – Zapateado* of Jerónimo Giménez and closing with an engaging and lighter *Intermedio* encore by the same composer, both from zarzuelas, this 74-minute collection of mainly Spanish music grips and entertains the listener as at a live concert. Celedonio contributes two pieces of his own, a charming solo lightweight *Fantasía Cubana*, and the others join him for his glittering flamenco *Malagueñas*, which has an improvisatory central section before the dashing coda with castanets. Among the more famous pieces arranged for the four players are the very effective Falla *Ritual Fire Dance* and Turina's *La oración del torero* (full of evocation), while Sor's *L'encouragement*, with its ingenuous lilting *Cantabile*, a simple but artful *Theme and variations* and elegant closing *Valse*, is played as a duet by Pepe and Celino. Tárrega's haunting *Capricho árabe* is exquisitely phrased by Celino. The arrangement of the three Praetorius dances, with an added condiment of percussion, is colourfully in period. The title of Torroba's collection of *Estampas* recalls the little Japanese prints which also inspired Debussy, and these eight sharply etched vignettes bring a highly imaginative response from the group, making this a highlight of the concert. The recording gives the guitars splendid presence against the attractively warm ambience, which in no way blurs the sharpness or focus of the players' attack. It is most welcome at mid-price in Universal's 'Penguin Rosette' Collection.

Rosenthal, Moritz (piano)

CHOPIN: *Piano Concerto 1 in E min., Op. 11* (with Berlin State Opera O, Weissmann); *Romanze only* (with NBC SO, Black). *Berceuse, Op. 57; Chants polonais* (arr. LISZT);

Etudes, Op. 10/1; 10/5 (twice); *Mazurkas, Opp. 63/3* (three versions); *67/1; Waltz in C sharp min., E min. Op. posth.*
(***) Biddulph mono LHW 040

Rosenthal was a pupil of Karl Mikuli, who was himself a Chopin pupil, and his Chopin is quite out of the ordinary. The *E minor Concerto* was made in 1930 and the ritornello is cut, but what pianism! (The alternative slow movement was recorded in New York on Rosenthal's 75th birthday.) Rosenthal's effortless virtuosity, lightness of touch, legatissimo and tonal subtlety are altogether remarkable. Playing of great culture from a distant age and beautifully transferred by Ward Marston.

Rossetti-Bonell, Dario (guitar)

'Début': BARRIOS: *2 Valses, Op. 8/3–4; Mazurka appassionata; Aconquija.* VIVALDI: *Mandolin Concerto in C, RV 425* (trans. for solo guitar by Rossetti-Bonell). VILLA-LOBOS: *Preludes 1–5.* GRANADOS: *Valses poéticos*
(B) **(*) EMI 5 73499-2

Dario, son of Carlos Bonell, proves to be a masterly guitarist, and by no means in the shadow of his father. His technique is consummate and he knows just how to seduce the ear with subtle rubato, as in the Barrios *Mazurka appassionata*, or with a magnetically gentle melodic ebb and flow, as in the *A minor* or *E major* Villa-Lobos *Preludes*, and how to hold the listener with dramatic use of light and shade as in *No. 4 in E minor.* The engaging closing Granados *Valses poéticos* are presented with charm and much expertise in the matter of colour. However, the inclusion of the Vivaldi *Mandolin Concerto*, arranged for guitar without orchestra, was a curious indulgence. It is very well played, of course, but fails to make a case for a guitar taking over the orchestral as well as solo mandolin roles. The recording, made in Forde Abbey, Somerset, is wholly natural with a most pleasing acoustic.

Rothwell, Evelyn (oboe)

Recital: C. P. E. BACH: *Sonata in G min.* TELEMANN: *Sonata in E flat.* M. HEAD: *Siciliana* (all with Aveling, harpsichord, Nesbitt, viola da gamba). LOEILLET: *Sonata in C* (arr. ROTHWELL). HANDEL: *Air & Rondo* (arr. & ed. ROTHWELL). MORGAN: *Melody* (all with Parry, piano)
(M) ** Dutton Lab./Barbirolli Soc. (ADD) CDSJB 1016 (with CORELLI; HAYDN; MARCELLO: *Oboe concertos ***)

Evelyn Rothwell, as always, plays expressively with charm and poise. But the recording of Valda Aveling's harpsichord seems unnecessarily recessed and insubstantial. Even so the Telemann *Sonata* is enjoyable enough, and the Michael Head *Siciliana* brings a more positive effect. The items accompanied on the piano by Wilfrid Parry are more successful. He is still rather backwardly placed but emerges with a stronger personality, and the delightful Handel titbits and the Nicholas Morgan *Melody* are the highlights of the recital.

Russell, David (guitar)

'Spanish Legends': REGINO SAINTZ DE LA MAZA: *Zapateado; Rondeña.* LLOBET: *10 Canciones populares Catalanas.* SEGOVIA: *Estudio Sin Luz; Anécdotas 2 & 5; Remembranza (Estudio II).* PUJOL: *Seguidilla; Impromptu; Triquilandia (Jugando al Escondite); El Abejorro; Canción*

Amatoria; Festvola (Danza Catalina de Espiritu popular); Tango; Tonadilla (Manola de Lavapiés); Guajira
*** Telarc CD 80633

David Russell studied at the Royal Academy of Music and, having twice won the Julian Bream Guitar Prize, seems fitted to take on that great guitarist's mantle. Like Bream, he seems to have a natural feeling for the special idiom of Spanish repertoire, and the sheer, joyous verve of the opening *Zapateado* here is matched by his brilliant performances of the two closing Pujol pieces, the catchy *Tonadilla* and *Guajira*. In between comes a programme of diverse miniatures, played with much individuality and character and, to quote an accolade from elsewhere, he coaxes a magnificent range of colours from his instrument. He is very vividly, if perhaps a little too forwardly recorded, which gives him great presence but robs him of the widest range of dynamic, which certainly exists in his playing. But the vitality of his music-making is matched by fine musicianship and a concern for detail, so this recital can be highly recommended.

Salomon Quartet

'The String Quartet in 18th-century England': ABEL: *Quartet in A, Op. 8/5.* SHIELD: *Quartet in C min., Op. 3/6.* MARSH: *Quartet in B flat.* WEBBE: *Variations in A on 'Adeste fidelis'.* S. WESLEY: *Quartet in E flat*
** Hyp. CDA 66780

A good idea, let down by the indifferent invention of much of the music itself. The amateur, John Marsh, stands up very well alongside his professional companions, and his five-movement *Quartet in B flat* (modelled on Haydn's Op. 1/1 and almost as pleasing) is the first piece to catch the listener's attention, for Abel is a very dull dog indeed. Samuel Webbe's *Variations on 'O come all ye faithful'* does little but repeat the melody with decorations. Samuel Wesley begins conventionally and agreeably, then produces a real lollipop as the Trio of the Minuet and a similarly winning finale. No complaints about the performances: the Salomon Quartet play everything freshly and with total commitment, using original instruments stylishly and in the sweetest possible manner. They are very realistically recorded, too. Three stars for the performers but not for the programme.

Satoh, Toyohiko (lute)

'Gaultier and the French Lute School': E. GAULTIER: *Tombeau de Mezangeau; Courante; Carillon; Rossignol; Testament de Mezangeau; Canarie.* D. GAULTIER: *Tombeau de Mademoiselle Gaultier; Cleopâtre amante (Double).* J. GALLOT: *Prélude; Le Bout de l'an de M. Gaultier; Courante la cigogne; Sarabande la pièce de huit heures; Volte la Brugeoise.* DUFAUT: *Prélude; Tombeau de M. Blanrocher; Dourante; Sarabande (Double); Gigue.* MOUTON: *Prélude. Tombeau de Gogo (Allemande); La Belle homicide/Courante de M. Gaultier (Double de la belle homicide); Gavotte; La Princesse sarabande; Canarie.* DE VISEE: *Tombeau de M. Mouton (Allemande)*
*** Channel Classics Dig. CCS 8795

Toyohiko Satoh has already given us a collection of the music of Robert de Visée (CCS 7795), whose *Tombeau de M. Mouton* provides one of the most affecting pieces here, to close a recital which is in essence a survey of French lute music of the seventeenth century.

Satoh is clearly an expert in this field, and he plays an original lute made by Laurentius Grieff of Ingolstadt in 1613, which was modified into an eleven-course French baroque instrument around 1670. It took four years for the Dutch lute-maker Van der Waals to restore it to playing condition, and its gut strings create a pleasingly warm sonority.

Satoh's playing is robust yet thoughtful and it has an improvisatory freedom which extends even to the dance movements. (Dufaut's *Gigue*, for instance, is jolly enough but would be difficult to dance to.) This is apparently possible because, around 1630, a new French tuning was developed within the lute school centring round Gaultier le Vieux (Ennemond Gaultier of Lyon, 1575–1651). This allowed more freedom for the fingers of the left hand, enabling lutenists to write their music in a *style brisé* (broken style), which was later to spread across Europe.

Gaultier and his cousin Denis (Gaultier le Jeune) were important innovators in their time and they also introduced the idea of the dignified 'tombeau' mementos, as well as vignettes with sobriquets like *Le Rossignol* and *Carillon*, yet which are in no way imitative. The two versions of the *Canarie* (by Ennemond Gaultier and Mouton respectively) are based on the same melody and dance form, with a dotted rhythm, and both are among the more striking items here, alongside the expressive *Sarabande* of Dufaut and Mouton's *La Princesse*, which features the famous *La Folia*. Rather unexpectedly, the same composer's *La Belle homicide* is a cheerful piece.

Scandinavian Wind Quintet

Danish Concert: NIELSEN: *Wind Quintet, Op. 43.*
HOLMBOE: *Notturno, Op. 19.* NORGARD: *Whirl's World.*
ABRAHAMSEN: *Walden*
*** dacapo 8.224001

The Scandinavian Wind Quintet give an eminently acceptable account of the Nielsen which can stand up to most of the competition. The Holmboe *Notturno* is a beautiful piece from 1940 whose language blends the freshness of Nielsen with the neoclassicism of Hindemith yet remains totally distinctive. The Nørgård is less substantial but is not otherwise available; Hans Abrahamsen's *Walden* is thin but atmospheric. Very present and lifelike recording.

Schiff, András and Peter Serkin (piano duo)

Music for 2 Pianos: MOZART: *Fugue in C min., K. 426; Sonata in D, K.448.* REGER: *Variations and Fugue on a Theme of Beethoven, Op. 86.* BUSONI: *Fantasia contrappuntistica*
*** ECM 465 062-2 (2)

András Schiff and Peter Serkin join here in a symbiotic partnership to give a quite superb and certainly gripping account of Busoni's formidable *Fantasia contrappuntistica* in which they find as wide a range of mood and colour as in Max Reger's *Variations* (on a Beethoven *Bagatelle* from Op. 119). The theme is presented with a disarming simplicity, but Reger soon introduces characteristically florid textures, yet returning to simplicity in the *Andante* and *Sostenuto* variations. These alternate with *Agitato* and *Vivace* sections, leading to the spirited closing *Fugue*. The pair of early twentieth-century works are framed by two-piano music of Mozart. Here the opening *Fugue in C minor* is strong and positive, and the first movement of the D major Sonata, too,

is taken very seriously, not emphasizing what Alfred Einstein called its 'gallant character' until the arrival of the second subject, and then only momentarily. However, the mood lightens in the central *Andante*, in which the two players exchange phrases very beguilingly, and the finale is rhythmically most winning. Excellent, well-focused and not too resonant recording.

Segovia, Andrés (guitar)

American Decca Recordings (1952–1969) (previously released by MCA): RODRIGO: *Fantasia para un gentilhombre.* PONCE: *Concierto del Sur.* BOCCHERINI: *Cello Concerto 6 in D* (arr. Cassadó in E for guitar) (with Symphony of the Air, Enrique Jorda). Solo music: TORROBA: *Castillos de España.* MOMPOU: *Suite Compostelana.* CASTELNUOVO-TEDESCO: *Sonata Omaggio a Boccherini, Op. 77.* PONCE: *Allego in A.* ESPLA: *Impresiones musicales 5: Estampa* (arr. for guitar). RODRIGO: *3 Piezas españolas: 1: Fandango.* DE MERCIA: *Praeludium & Allegro.* RONCALLI: *Passacaglia; Capricci armonici: Suite in G: Gigue; Suite in E min.: Gavotte.* MILAN: *6 Pavanes.* SANZ: *Suite española: Galliarda y Villano; Españoletas.* AGUADO: *8 Lessons.* SOR: *Minuets in C and C min. Etudes, Op. 6/1, 3 & 17; Op. 29/19–20; Op. 31/9 & 10; Op. 35/6 & 15.* ALBENIZ: *Suite española, Op. 47: Granada; Danza española, Op. 37: Andaluza; Danza triste. Tonadilla 1: La Maja de Goya.* BACH: *Lute Suite in E min., BWV 996: Allemande; Bourrée. Partita for Lute in C min., BWV 997* (both transposed to A min.); *Sarabande; Gigue; Prelude for Lute in C min., BWV 999* (trans. D min.); *Fugue for Lute in G min., BWV 1000* (trans. A min.); *Cello Suite 3 in C, BWV 1009* (trans. A); *Cello Suite 1 in G, BWV 1007* (trans. D): *Prelude; Cello Suite 6 in D, BWV 1012* (trans. E): *Gavottes I & II; Violin Partita 1 in B min., BWV 1002: Sarabande; Bourrée; Double. Violin Partita 2 in C min., BWV 1004: Chaconne; Violin Partita 3 in E, BWV 1006: Gavotte and Rondo; Violin Sonata 1 in G min.* (trans. to F sharp min.): *Siciliano*
(M) *** DG stereo/mono 471 430-2 (4)

A set which has taken us by surprise. Although reissued by Deutsche Grammophon, and remastered at the Emil Berliner Studios, the recordings derive from American Decca and are of extraordinarily high quality. Segovia's guitar is beautifully caught, and in the solo music one might often feel that he is sitting out there behind the speakers. The concerto recordings are also first class and, with Enrique Jorda directing the accompanying Symphony of the Air, the results are very appealing indeed. Rodrigo's *Fantasia para un gentilhombre* is most characterfully done, and if the Ponce *Concierto del Sur* is a bit long-winded, it is in persuasive hands. The slow movement of Cassadó's transcription of Boccherini's *Concerto* is particularly warm-hearted. As for the rest of the repertory, it is predictably wide-ranging and includes complete sets of the pieces by the most familiar composers, but plenty of novelties too. The last of the four discs is devoted to Bach and is particularly treasurable, including as it does a complete recording of the transcribed *Third Suite for Unaccompanied Cello*, and Segovia's most familiar encore, the *Gavotte and Rondeau* from the *E major Violin Partita*. Segovia's playing is incomparable. Highly recommended.

'*Dedication*': More American Decca/MCA recordings (1954–1959): PONCE: *Sonata romántica (Homage to Schubert); Sonata clásica (Homage to Sor); Sonata 1*

(Mexicana); Sonata 3; Mazurka; Canción 3. VILLA-LOBOS: *Prelude 1 in E min.* TANSMAN: *Cavatina* (Suite). CASTELNUOVO-TEDESCO: *5 Pieces from 'Platero and I'.* MANÉN: *Fantasia (Sonata).* HARRIS: *Variations & Fugue on a Theme of Handel.* JOHN DUARTE: *English Suite, Op. 31*

(M) **(*) DG stereo/mono 477 6050 (2)

These were all pieces specially written for Segovia, the *English Suite* by John Duarte dedicated to the guitarist and his wife 'on the occasion of his marriage', and a very pleasing little triptych is is. Otherwise it is the Castelnuovo-Tedesco and (especially) Tansman *Suites* that stand out for musical interest. Joan Manén's *Fantasia* is anonymous sounding and lacking in melodic interest, and Albert Harris's *Variations* are inventive only in a conventional way. The first disc is given over to the music of Ponce, whose *Sonatas* are relatively simplistic and do not seek to simulate the composing style of their dedicatees. But Segovia, who plays everything with the 'dedication' of the disc's title, makes the central *Canción* of the *Third Suite* sound quite magical. The recording, as before, is most realistic.

'*The Legendary Segovia*': BACH: *Cello Suite in G, BWV 1007: Prelude* (arr. PONCE); (Unaccompanied) *Violin Partita 3 in E, BWV 1006: Gavotte & Rondo; Prelude in C min. for Lute, BWV 999* (both arr. SEGOVIA). SOR: *Thème varié, Op. 9.* ROBERT DE VISEE: *Minuet.* FROBERGER: *Gigue.* CASTELNUOVO-TEDESCO: *Hommage à Boccherini: Vivo e energico.* MENDELSSOHN: *String Quartet 1 in E flat, Op. 12: Canzonetta* (arr. SEGOVIA). MALATS: *Serenata.* ALBENIZ: *Suite española: Granada; Sevilla.* GRANADOS: *Danza española 10 in G, Op. 37.* TURINA: *Fandanguillo.* TORROBA: *Suite castellana: Fandanguillo; Sonatina in A: Allegretto. Preludio; Notturno.* PONCE: *Petite valse; Suite in A.* TARREGA: *Recuerdos de la Alhambra*

(M) (***) EMI mono 5 67009-2

It was Segovia's pioneering recitals in the 1930s that re-established the guitar in the public mind as a serious solo instrument. This collection consists of his early recordings, made over a span of 12 years from 1927 to 1939 either at Abbey Road or the Small Queen's Hall in London. There are quite a few transcriptions, including several Bach items, where the style of the playing is romantic (though never showing lapses of taste). However, the second part of the programme includes a high proportion of Spanish repertoire either written for or naturally suited to the guitar. What is so striking throughout this collection is the way all the music, slight or serious, springs vividly to life. Segovia had the gift of natural spontaneity in all he played, and he was in his prime at this period, so that technically this is wonderfully assured. His performance of Tárrega's famous *Recuerdos* is quite individual, with the underlying melodic line shaped like a song, rather than treated seamlessly. Guitar fans will find this generous 74-minute recital an essential purchase; others will be surprised to discover that no apologies need be made for the sound, which is natural in timbre and gives the instrument a ready projection.

Shaham, Gil (violin), Jonathan Feldman (piano)

'*Devil's Dance*': BAZZINI: *Ronde des lutins.* BOLCOM: *Graceful Ghost.* BRAHMS: *Walpurgisnacht, Op. 75/4.* GRIEG: *Puck, Op. 71/3* (arr. Achron). KORNGOLD: *Caprice fantastique* (arr. Révay). MENDELSSOHN: *Hexenlied,*

Op. 8/8. MORRIS: *Young Frankenstein (Transylvanian Lullaby).* PAGANINI (arr. Schumann): *Caprice 13 in B flat.* SAINT-SAËNS: *Danse macabre, Op. 40.* SARASATE: *Concert Fantasy on Gounod's 'Faust'.* TARTINI (arr. Kreisler): *Violin Sonata in G min. (Devil's Trill).* WILLIAMS: *The Witches of Eastwick: Devil's Dance.* YSAŸE: (Solo) *Violin Sonata in A min., Op. 27: 1st movt.*

*** DG 463 483-2

The whimsical red caution notice provided on this disc suggests that the listener approach the opening track on this CD at his or her peril. But John Williams's title-piece is much less demonic than the closing excerpt from Ysaÿe's *Solo Violin Sonata 2*, which has the *Dies irae* as a source for Gil Shaham's dazzlingly fiendish decorations. Tartini's *Devil's Trill Sonata*, heard in Kreisler's arrangement, opens with a disarming graciousness: the devil's voice here being entirely seductive. Shaham makes light of the once much-feared trills; so if you need to be petrified by this piece, you have to turn to Andrew Manze's record. But overall this is a most engaging collection, ingeniously devised, played with panache and given demonstration sound-quality. There are quite a few novelties too, including Grieg's delectably sparkling *Puck* and Korngold's impish *Wichtenmänchenn*, with its unexpected coda, while Mendelssohn's *Hexenlied* has a sprightly charm. Bazzini's *Ronde des lutins* remains one of the most hair-raising of all violinistic showpieces and here it is dazzling, while William Bolcom's *Graceful Ghost* brings a wraith-like interlude. Saint-Saëns's *Danse macabre* works well enough as a violin solo, and Feldman provides a colourful backcloth, using the composer's own piano transcription. It was an excellent idea to include in the documentation the whole Cazalis poem which inspired this piece; but David Lawrence's somewhat high-flown essay, which replaces individual notes on each piece in the documentation, is less appealing. However, this is presumably intended as a crossover record, and it is a very good one. Paganini (who takes a back seat in the programme, with only one of his *Caprices* included) would surely have approved of the stylish presentation by Gil Shahan, who is a devilishly fine fiddler and is well partnered, too, by Jonathan Feldman.

Shifrin, David (clarinet), Lincoln Center Chamber Music Society

Five American Clarinet Quintets: CORIGLIANO: *Soliloquy for Clarinet & String Quartet.* ZWILICH: *Clarinet Quintet.* TOWER: *Turning Points.* SHENG: *Concertino for Clarinet & String Quartet.* ADOLPHE: *At the Still Point there the Dance Is*

*** Delos DE 3183 (2)

A remarkable group of five surprisingly lyrical works, often searching and all readily approachable. John Corigliano's *Soliloquy*, adapted from the second movement of his *Concerto*, is essentially a haunting interplay between solo clarinet and violin. It was written in memory of his father, who was concertmaster of the New York Philharmonic, and is passionately elegiac. While sustaining its mood of desolation throughout, it leaves the listener uplifted rather than depressed.

Ellen Zwilich's *Quintet* opens with stabbing aggression from the strings and a continuing restlessness from the soloist, with moments of wildness carried through into the pungent second movement. Finally, a degree of calm is reached in the third, but its language becomes increasingly plangent, until relative serenity returns towards the close. The brief Scherzo is ironically jocular, followed by an atmospheric epilogue.

Joan Tower's *Turning Points* immediately features the device of a long slow crescendo for the soloist: its style is at first rhapsodic, with a central cadenza-like virtuoso display for the soloist and increasing agitation towards the end. The remaining two works are primarily atmospheric. Bright Sheng's attractively lyrical *Concertino* brings an exotic influence from Chinese folk music. It opens and closes reflectively, but its serenity does not run an even course, with energetic bursts from the clarinet. The Chinese influence is most strongly felt in the repeated scherzando ostinatos of the second movement.

Bruce Adolphe's *At the Still Point* is also ruminative, the first two movements, *Aria* and *Meditation*, move hauntingly towards the 'still point', though not without interruption, and then are released into the dance, which swirls, but in a relatively gentle, minimalist manner. It is a work of immediate appeal. David Shifrin's performances are masterly and the recording is excellent. A most stimulating collection.

(i) Snowden, Jonathan (flute), Andrew Litton (piano), (ii) Nicholas Daniel (oboe), Julius Drake (piano)

'*French Music for Flute and Oboe*': (i) WIDOR: *Suite for Flute and Piano, Op. 34.* FAURE: *Fantaisie, Op. 79; Morceau de concours.* DEBUSSY: *Syrinx.* HONEGGER: *Danse de la chèvre.* ROUSSEL: *Jouers de flûte, Op. 27.* MESSIAEN: *Le Merle noir.* POULENC: *Flute Sonata.* (ii) SAINT-SAENS: *Oboe Sonata.* DUTILLEUX: *Oboe Sonata.* KOECHLIN: *Oboe Sonata, Op. 28.* POULENC: *Oboe Sonata*
(BB) *** Virgin 2x1 5 61495-2 (2)

This Virgin Double aptly and inexpensively pairs two outstanding recitals of French instrumental music, originally issued separately, but which in this format complement each other admirably. Jonathan Snowden, deftly accompanied by Andrew Litton, a formidable pianist, first gathers a vintage collection of French works for flute. The Poulenc *Sonata* is dazzlingly done, and so are the other virtuoso pieces, all strongly characterized. The surprise is the opening item, by Widor, delicate and pointed, charmingly lyrical, a suite by a composer now remembered for his heavyweight organ works.

On the second disc Nicholas Daniel and Julius Drake concentrate equally persuasively on four major French oboe sonatas. Once again the Poulenc proves highly diverting, its outer movements, *Elégie paisiblement* and *Déploration: très calme*, proving as unpredictable as ever. The opening piece, by Saint-Saëns, is captivating but by no means trivial, with its central *Allegretto* framed by two sections giving the soloist a great deal of freedom. Dutilleux's *Sonata* typically combines subtlety of colour and expressive depth with ingenuity. However, the most ambitious work is by Koechlin, its four movements running for 28 minutes. It opens in pastoral evocation, but afterwards the writing often becomes very prolix, the range of mood remarkably wide. The Daniel/Drake duo play it expertly and sympathetically, but they do not entirely erase one's suspicion that it would have been a stronger piece if more concise. Yet overall these paired recitals, well balanced and truthfully recorded, give much pleasure.

Söllscher, Göran (guitar)

'*Entrée*': ALBÉNIZ: *Granada.* BROUWER: *Berceuse.* BARRIOS: *Vals, Op. 8/3; La Catedral.* TORROBA: *Toriija.* SOR: *Sonata in C, Op. 15b.* VILLA-LOBOS: *Preludes 1–5.* RODRIGO: *Concierto de aranjuez* (with Orpheus CO)
(B) ** DG Entrée 474 74-2

Göran Söllscher, DG's star guitarist, has been too long absent from the catalogue until relatively recently, when this collection brought about his bargain re-Entrée. The shorter pieces are beautifully played; but, before choosing the Rodrigo *Concierto* for inclusion, DG should have read its review in the June 1990 issue of *The Gramophone*. We agree with John Duarte's assessement there, that the performance has 'something of Scandinavian cool' and that 'seekers after Spanish fire will not find it here, and may too be impatient with some easygoing tempos'. We found the playing of the Orpheus Chamber Orchestra excellent and unusually well detailed here. But this is a performance in which the head controls the heart, and for us that is not enough.

'*Eleven String Baroque*': WEISS: *Passacaille in D; Tombeau sur la mort de Me Compte de Logy.* PACHELBEL: *Lute Suite in F sharp min.* KELLNER: *Fantasia in F.* BACH: *Orchestral Suite 3, BWV 1068: Air;* (Unaccompanied) *Violin Sonata 1, BWV 1001; Menuets in G & G min.* (from Anna Magdalena Notebook) *BWV Anh., 114/115.* ROMAN: *Assagio 1: Andante; Assagio 2: Bourrée.* BARON: *Lute Sonata in B flat: Aria.* COUPERIN: *Pièces de clavecin: Les barricades mistérieuses.* LOGY: *Suite in G*
**(*) DG 474 815-2

As we have discovered above, Göran Söllscher is a very fine player, but he can sometimes be a little positive, and not relaxed enough to charm, and so it is in the opening Weiss *Passacaille* here and in Pachelbel's *Lute Suite*. But he brings an improvisatory feeling to David Kellner's *Fantasia*, and he is at his finest in Bach. How simply he plays the celebrated *Air*, and the pair of *Menuets* from Anna Maddelena's Notebook are most engaging. After the transcribed unaccompanied *Violin Sonata* which is perhaps just a fraction didactic, he is again pleasingly spontaneous in the two Roman miniatures, although the Couperin keyboard piece is not very effective on the guitar. But Weiss's valedictory lute piece certainly is, and it makes an affecting close. The resonant 11-stringed instrument (modelled after a lute) sounds wonderfully rich-timbred, and is most naturally recorded, in an ideal acoustic.

'*The Renaissance Album*': MUDARRA: *Fantasia which imitates the harp in the manner of Ludovico; Pavana de Alexandre; Gallarda.* PHILIPS: *Chromatic Pavan (Pavan Dolorosa); The Galliard to the Chromatic Pavan.* FRANCESCO DI MILANO: *Fantasias: in C; C min.; in F 1 & 2; Ricercare in G min.* DOWLAND: *My Lady Hunsdon's Allmande; A Piece without Title; The Shoemaker's Wife (A Toy); He who spoils Grace by Gossip; Mr Dowland's Midnight; Sir John Smith, his Allman; Semper Dowland, Semper Dolens; Forlorn Hope Fancy.* NEUSIDLER: *The Queen's Dance (Italian Dance); Ach Eiselein; In Love's Ardour; An Italian Dance with After-Dance.* MOLINARO: *Ballo detto 'Il Conte Orlando': Saltarello del predetto ballo.* MILÁN: *Fantasia of Chords and Scale Passages; Pavana V & VI.* NARVÁEZ: *The Song of the Emperor; 4 Variations on 'Guádame las vacas'.* HOLBORNE: *Hartes ease; The Fairy Round.* BALLARD: *Branles de village*
☛ *** DG 477 5726

This is a superb disc in every way and one of the finest collections of its kind in the catalogue. Söllscher again uses his specially built 11-string guitar (the six highest strings tuned like a Renaissance lute) to admirable effect. The added sonority adds much to the music, and it certainly suits the opening Mudarra *Fantasia in imitation of a harp*, written, of course, for the vihuela. Narváez's *Song of the Emperor* is also a highlight of the programme, alongside Molinaro's catchy *Ballo* and Milán's *Fantasia of chords and scales* (much more interesting than the title suggests), and the dances by Hans Neusidler are equally rewarding and full of life and character.

But while the Spanish, Italian and German repertoire is splendidly played, it seems to be the music from the 'golden age' of English lute music (at the turn of the sixteenth into the seventeenth century) that has obviously caught Söllscher's imagination, and he is often inspired in his playing of the music of Dowland, who gets the lion's share of the programme (*Semper Dowland, Semper Dolens* is wonderfully touching), Peter Philips and Holborne. But there is not a single performance here that is not highly spontaneous, and this compilation is truly treasurable. The recording is in the demonstration bracket.

Staier, Andreas (harpsichord)

'*Variaciones del fandango español*': SOLER: *Fandango.*
ALBERO: *Recercata, fuga y sonata in G; Recercata, fuga y sonata in D.* GALLES: *Sonatas 9 in C min.; 16 in F min.; 17 in C min.* LOPEZ: *Variaciones del fandango español.* FERRER: *Adagio in G min.; Sonata, Andantino in G min.*
BOCCHERINI: *Fandango, Grave assai* (with Schornheim (harpsichord) & Gonzáles Cámpa (castanets))
*** Teldec 3984 21468-2

Framed by two great *Fandangos* by Soler and Boccherini, and with a sparkling further set of *Fandango Variations* by Félix López as centrepiece, this is a fascinatingly conceived recital, superbly played on an ideal harpsichord – a modern French copy of an early eighteenth-century German instrument (associated with Silbermann). The rest of the programme includes a pair of inventive triptychs by Sebastián de Albero (1722–56) – 'polyphony used in a very Mediterranean way' (to quote Staier) – and three delightful miniature sonatas by Joseph Gallés: *No. 16 in F minor* (a single movement) is particularly winning, as are the two short pieces by José Ferrer.

Staier plays with fine sensibility and great virtuosity, always retaining the listener's interest. For the spectacular finale (which he has freely arranged from the finale of Boccherini's *D major Guitar Quintet*, G.448) Staier is joined by an excellent second player, with a third artist to decorate the thrilling climax with castanets. The result is a semi-improvisational *tour de force*. The only small snag is that the recording is somewhat over-resonant – thus setting a modest volume level is important, though not, of course, in the *Fandangos*.

Steele-Perkins, Crispian (trumpet), Stephen Cleobury (organ)

'*The King's Trumpeter*': MATHIAS: *Processional.* L. MOZART: *Concerto in E flat.* BOYCE: *Voluntaries in D.* ANON.: *3 16th-century Dances.* TELEMANN: *Concerto da caccia in D.* GOUNOD: *Méditation: Ave Maria.* STEELE: *6 Pieces, Op. 33*
**(*) Priory PRCD 189

Crispian Steele-Perkins is here given a chance to show his paces on a modern trumpet. The programme opens with Mathias's distinctly catchy *Processional* and covers a fairly wide range of repertoire, ending with the six characterful pieces by Christopher Steele. The disc is relatively short measure (53 minutes), but the playing is first class and the balance most convincing.

Stringer, Alan (trumpet), Noel Rawsthorne (organ)

'*Trumpet and Organ*' (organ of Liverpool Cathedral): M.-A. CHARPENTIER: *Te Deum: Prelude.* STANLEY: *Voluntary 5 in D.* PURCELL: *Sonata in C; 2 Trumpet Tunes and Air.* BOYCE: *Voluntary in D.* CLARKE: *Trumpet Voluntary.* BALDASSARE: *Sonata 1 in F.* ROMAN: *Keyboard Suite in D: Non troppo allegro; Presto (Gigue).* FIOCCO: *Harpsichord Suite 1: Andante.* BACH: *Cantata 147: Jesu, joy of man's desiring.* attrib. GREENE: *Introduction and Trumpet Tune.* VIVIANI: *Sonata 1 in C*
(M) **(*) CRD 3308

This collection is extremely well recorded. The reverberation of Liverpool Cathedral is under full control and both trumpet and organ are cleanly focused, while the trumpet has natural timbre and bloom. Alan Stringer is at his best in the classical pieces, the *Voluntary* of Boyce, the *Trumpet Tunes* and *Sonata* of Purcell and the stylishly played *Sonata* of Viviani, a most attractive little work. He also gives a suitably robust performance of the famous *Trumpet Voluntary*. Elsewhere he is sometimes a little square: the Bach chorale is rather too stiff and direct. But admirers of this repertoire will find much to enjoy, and the *Andante* of Fiocco has something in common with the more famous *Adagio* attributed to Albinoni in Giazotto's famous arrangement.

Tetzlaff, Christian (violin), Lars Anders Tomter (viola), Leif Ove Andsnes (piano)

JANACEK: *Violin Sonata.* DEBUSSY: *Violin Sonata.* RAVEL: *Violin Sonata.* NIELSEN: *Violin Sonata 2, Op. 38.* BRAHMS: *Viola Sonatas 1 & 2.* SCHUMANN: *Märchenbilder*
(BB) *** Virgin 5 62016-2 (2)

Virgin has here brought together two outstanding recital discs from the 1990s, of which the Brahms and Schumann coupling originally received a Rosette. There is no need to modify that judgement, and in view of the overall excellence of this combined release, it is extended to this double-CD as a whole. In the Janáček *Sonata*, Christian Tetzlaff and Leif Ove Andsnes show a complete understanding of the score. They play with commitment and dedication, while there are no more imaginative accounts of either the Debussy or Ravel couplings.

Nielsen's *G minor Sonata* is a transitional work in which the composer emerges from the geniality of the *Sinfonia espansiva* into the darker, more anguished world of the *Fourth Symphony*. It has much of the questing character of the latter and much of its muscularity, and Tetzlaff and Andsnes give a very distinguished – at times inspired – performance. They also provide one of the best accounts in the catalogue of the Brahms *Sonatas* in their viola form. Theirs is playing of great sensitivity and imagination. These Norwegian artists bring a wide range of colour to this music and they phrase with an unforced naturalness that is very persuasive, and their fresh account of the Schumann gives much pleasure too. The sound is natural and well balanced throughout this programme (in the Brahms and Schumann, there is a slight bias towards the piano), and this is altogether a rather special CD Double and remarkably inexpensive.

Thurston Clarinet Quartet

'*Clarinet Masquerade*': FARKAS: *Ancient Hungarian Dances from the 17th Century.* MOZART (arr. WHEWELL): *Divertimento 2.* TOMASI: *3 Divertissements.* GARNER (arr. BLAND): *Misty.* JOBIM (arr. BLAND): *The Girl from Ipanema.* DESPORTES: *French Suite.* ALBINONI (arr. THILDE): *Sonata in G min.* STARK: *Serenade.* GERSHWIN (arr. BLAND): *Rhapsody: Summertime.* PHILLIPS (arr. HARVEY): *Cadenza*; (arr. FERNANDEZ): *Muskrat Sousa*
(M) *** ASV CDWHL 2076

A light-hearted concert, but an entertaining one which will especially appeal to those who like the clarinet's sonority, reedier than the flute's and with more character. The opening suite of *Hungarian Dances* (with the chirps and cheeps in the finale very engaging) leads on to a Mozart *Divertimento* for basset horns. The other pieces, the insouciant Tomasi and the Desportes *Suite* (full of Ravelian elegance) are all amiable, and the arrangement of Gershwin's *Summertime* has the famous opening swerve of *Rhapsody in Blue* as its introduction. Finally there is the exuberant *Muskrat Sousa* which features a combination of *12th Street Rag* and *South Rampart Street Parade*. The recording is immaculately vivid.

Tracey, Ian (organ of Liverpool Cathdral)

'*Bombarde!*': GIGOUT: *Grand choeur dialogué.* BOËLLMANN: *Suite Gothique, Op. 25.* PIERNÉ: *3 Pièces.* BONNET: *Variations de concert, Op. 1.* DUBOIS: *In paradisum.* WIDOR: *Symphony 6 in G, Op. 42/2*
*** Chan. 9716

Readers unfamiliar with the meaning of the organ term used for the title of this collection will probably have guessed (correctly) that it is an organ builder's *pièce de résistance*, designed to hit the listener in the solar plexus. In Liverpool it is a recently added division of 61 pipes, arrayed 175 feet above the floor and played from the keyboard's top manual (of five). It features a Trompete Militaire stop, operated by its own separate blower motor, and it includes a Tuba Magna, a subdivision of smaller Tubas, and a Grand Choir. This is its first appearance on record, and its magnificence of amplitude is well demonstrated in the opening *Grand choeur dialogué* of Eugène Gigout, which Ian Tracey plays with great aplomb.

Of course, this programme is nearly all repertoire for which the French Cavaillé-Coll organs are intended, with their bright, sharply focused reeds. The panoply of the Liverpool organ sound is far from sharp in focus, so that Tracey's dazzling bravura in scalic passages (as in the closing *Toccata* of the Boëllmann *Suite gothique*), inevitably become blurred. But the organ's range of colour in the gentler items – the central *Cantilène* of the *Three Pièces* of Pierné and the engagingly delicate Dubois *In paradisum* – is very seductive. The dynamic range here is also remarkable: the massive opening of the Bonnet *Variations* gives way immediately to the gentle

first variation, and this contrast is also very effective in the five-movement Widor *Sixth Symphony*, which ends with characteristic rumbustious hyperbole.

Troussov, Kirill (violin), Alexandra Troussova (piano)

BEETHOVEN: *Violin Sonata 5 in C min., Op. 30/2.* BRAHMS: *Violin Sonata 3 in D min., Op. 108.* WIENIAWSKI: *Fantaisie brillante on Themes from Gounod's 'Faust'.* ZIMBALIST: *Fantasy on Rimsky-Korsakov's 'The Golden Cockerel'*
(B) *** EMI Début 5 73212-2

One of the best of the valuable EMI Début series. Kirill Troussov and Alexandra Troussova are a brother-and-sister team of remarkable skill. They are Russian and were both in their teens when this outstanding recital was recorded. Vibrant and committed playing from both artists and excellent recordings.

Trpčeski, Simon (piano)

PROKOFIEV: *Piano Sonata 6 in A.* SCRIABIN: *Piano Sonata 5.* STRAVINSKY: *3 Movements from 'Petrushka'.* TCHAIKOVSKY (trans. PLETNEV): *Nutcracker Concert Suite*
(B) *** EMI Début 5 75202-2

Simon Trpčeski is Macedonian-born and in his early twenties, making his record début in virtuoso Russian repertoire. He is obviously a pianist of awesome technical prowess, and it is a tribute to his pianism and artistry that only the most exalted comparisons come to mind. The Scriabin *Sonata 5* is very impressive indeed, it sounds freshly experienced and has great inner vitality. The Prokofiev *Sixth* does not have quite the abandon of Kissin's Tokyo version (at least in the finale) but is among the very finest all the same. Trpčeski plays the Stravinsky with great abandon and does very well in Mikhail Pletnev's arrangement of movements from the *Nutcracker*, though without perhaps having quite the range of colour and dynamics that the latter demands.

Tureck, Rosalyn (piano)

'*Live at the Teatro Colón*': BACH: *Adagio in G, BWV 968; Chromatic Fantasia and Fugue, BWV 903; Partita 1, BWV 825: Gigue; Goldberg Variation 29, BWV 988; Klavierbüchlein for Anna Magdalena Bach: Musette in D.* MENDELSSOHN: *Songs Without Words, Op. 19/1.* SCHUBERT: *Moments musicaux 2 in A flat; 3 in F min.* BACH/BUSONI: *Chaconne (from BWV 1004).* BRAHMS: *Variations and Fugue on a Theme by Handel, Op. 24*
**(*) VAI Audio VIAI 1024-2 (2)

Rosalyn Tureck has lost none of her magic, as this Buenos Aires (1992) live recital demonstrates, and it is good to find her so sympathetic in Schubert and Mendelssohn, as well as in Bach. Her articulation in the Brahms *Handel Variations* suggests she is thinking as much of Handel as of Brahms, but that is a comment, not a criticism. The Bach/Busoni *Chaconne* is splendid. Excellent recording, but there are two snags: the almost hysterical applause which bursts in as soon as a piece has ended and the fact that this recital would almost have fitted on one CD. These two play for just 83 minutes 31 seconds.

Uchida, Mitsuko (piano)

'*Perspectives*': MOZART: *Piano Sonata 8 in A min., K.310;
Piano Concerto 20 in D min., K.466* (with ECO, Tate).
DEBUSSY: *Etudes 1, 3, 6, 11 & 12.* SCHUMANN: *Carnaval,
Op. 9.* BEETHOVEN: *32 Variations on an Original Theme,
WoO 80.* SCHUBERT: *Moment musical 3 in F min., D. 780;
Impromptus D.899/1, 3 & 4.* SCHOENBERG: *6 Little Pieces,
Op. 19*
(M) **(*) Ph. 473 686-2 (2)

This admirably recorded two-disc set certainly offers a well-
judged perspective on Mitsuko Uchida's impressive but somewhat inconsistent achievement in the recording studio. She
established her reputation in the mid-1980s with a stylish and
sensitive set of the complete Mozart *Piano Sonatas*, but when
she came to tackle the concertos her success was uneven. The
D minor work was the first of the series, a beautiful performance, guaranteed never to offend and, like much of her playing, most likely to delight; but on the highest level her
characteristic degree of reticence – despite the superb orchestral contribution of the ECO under Tate – makes the reading
less memorable than the very finest versions.

In 1989 she had another great success with the Debussy
Etudes, undoubtedly her finest recording to date, and there
are five well-chosen examples here. But Schumann's piano
music is not repertoire with which we have normally associated her, and the impulsive performance of *Carnaval* explains
why. She seems too anxious to make points and is unwilling
to allow the invention to flow naturally.

The Beethoven *Variations*, however, are a distinct success
and have something of the simplicity of her Mozart sonata
performances, while the Schoenberg *Pieces* are also very
impressive in their directness. Her Schubert is again highly
individual, undoubtedly poetic and always distinctive. But
there is a degree of delicacy and charm about the *G flat
Impromptu* which perhaps underestimates its profundity. Yet
throughout this programme her gift for creating spontaneity
in the recording studio is apparent, and she always enjoyed a
first-class sound-balance from the Philips engineers, so this
survey has much to offer her admirers.

Vieaux, Jason (guitar)

Recital: MERLIN: *Suite del recuerdo.* PUJOL: *Preludios 2, 3 ,
& 5.* ORBON (de SOTO): *Preludio y Danza.* KROUSE:
Variations on a Moldavian hora. BARRIOS: *Valses,
Op. 8/3 & 4; Julia Florida; Barcarola.* MOREL: *Chôro; Danza
Brasileira; Danza in E min.* BUSTAMENTE: *Misionera*
⌾ (BB) *** Naxos 8.553449

Jason Vieaux is a young American musician, already a prizewinner – and no wonder. This Latin-American repertoire is
unfailingly diverting in his hands: there are no familiar names
here except that of Barrios, yet almost every item is either
memorably evocative or it makes the pulse quicken. Vieaux's
completely natural rubato at the opening *Evocación* of José
Luis Merlin's *Suite del recuerdo* is quite masterly and the slow
crescendos in the final *Carnavalito* are thrilling; there then is
a complete change of mood and the *Evocación* makes a
haunting return before the final *Joropo.* The *Preludios* of Pujol
are quite magical; Vieaux then lets his hair down for the
Candombe. The two *Valses* of Barrios are deliciously fragile,
with the central *Barcarola* hardly less subtle, while the more
robust Brazilian dances of Jorge Morel have real panache. The

Naxos recording has good ambience and is present yet not
too closely balanced. Unforgettable.

Wagler, Dietrich (organ)

'*Great European Organs 24*': Freiberg Dom, Silbermann
organ: SCHEIDT: *Magnificat Noni toni.* CLERAMBAULT:
Suite de premier ton. BUXTEHUDE: *Prelude and Fugue in D
min.* KREBS: *Choral Preludes: Mein Gott, das Herze bring
ich dir; Herr Jesus Christ, dich zu uns wend; Herzlich tut
mich verlangen; O Ewigkeit, du Donnerwort.* J. S. BACH:
Fantaisie in G; Prelude and Fugue in C
**(*) Priory PRCD 332

The organ, rather than the player, is the star of this record;
the latter's performances are sound but very much in the
traditional German style. But he knows his instrument and
the opening *Magnificat Noni toni* of Scheidt sounds resplendent, with the following Clérambault *Suite* also very effectively
registered. A well-balanced programme, lacking only the last
degree of flair in presentation.

Watson, James (trumpet), Simon Wright (piano)

'*Trumpet Masterpieces*': ENESCU: *Legend.* HANSEN: *Sonata,
Op. 18.* HINDEMITH: *Sonata.* MARTINŮ: *Sonatina.* PILSS:
Sonata. RAVEL: *Mélodies hébraïque: Kaddisch*
**(*) Deux-Elles DXL 1109

The Hindemith *Sonata* is a splendid work, opening with a
robust, stalking trumpet tune, and with a central movement
that is a shade offbeat, but which affords some demanding
writing for the piano, playing in direct dialogue with the
brass instrument. The *Trauermusik* which ends the work,
with its little fanfare figure and solemn processional, is puis-
sant indeed. Martinů's *Sonatina* is another fine work, declamatory and energetic, but lyrical too, with both virtuoso
writing and a chorale, its ending triumphant. The two
melodic miniatures by Ravel and Enescu make a C minor
partnership. Then come a pair of traditional works, the
Hansen easy-going with strong ideas, the Pilss more romantic, less distinctive in its melodic flow but enjoyably fluent.
The performances throughout are excellent and, especially in
the piano parts of the Hindemith and Martinů works, Simon
Wright makes a major contribution. Truthful recording, well
balanced in a suitable acoustic.

Weir, Gillian (organ)

'*King of Instruments: The Art of Dame Gillian Weir (A feast
of Organ Music from the 16th to 20th Centuries)*'

Volume I: BACH: *Toccata, Adagio and Fugue in C, BWB 564;
Fantasia in G, BWV 572; Trio Sonata 1 in E flat, BWV 525;
Passacaglia in C min., BWV 582* (Organ of St Lawrence,
Rotterdam). MARCHAND: *Pièces d'Orgue, Premier Livre:
Dialogue sur les grands jeux; Récit de tierce en taille; Basse
et dessus de trompette et de cornet; Récit de voix humaine;
Cinquième Livre: Bass de coumorne ou de trompette; Duo;
Récit; Plein-jeu; Fugue; Basse de trompette ou de cromorne;
Récit de tierce en taille* (Organ of St Maximin, Thionville,
France). BULL: *Dr Bull's my selfe; Dr Bull's jewell* (Organ of
Hexham Abbey)

Volume II: CLERAMBAULT: *Suite de premier ton; Suite de deuxième ton* (Organ of St Leonard Kirche, Basel, Switzerland). BRUHNS: *Praeludium 1–3; Chorale: Nun komm, der Heiden Heiland* (Organ of Clare College, Cambridge)

Volume III: ROBERDAY: *Fuges et caprices pour orgue 1–12* (Organ of St Leonhardkirche, Basel, Switzerland). LANGLAIS: *Dialogue sur les mixtures* (Organ of Hexham Abbey). SCHEIDT: *Passamezzo* (Variations 1–12) (Organ of Clare College, Cambridge)

Volume IV: DANDRIEU: *Premier Livre de Pièces d'Orgue: Pièces en A, Mi, La; Magnificat* (Organ of St Leonard, Basel, Switzerland); *Pièces en G, Ré, Sol minuer; Magnificat II.* MARCHAND: *Pièces d'Orgue, Troisième Livre: Dialogue sur les grands jeux; Quatrième Livre: Duo; Fugue; Trio; Récit; Duo; Basse et trompette; Récit de tierce en taille* (Organ of St Maximin, Thionville, France). DE GRIGNY: *Tierce en taille.* MULET: *Toccata Tu es Petrus* (Organ of Hexham Abbey)

Volume V: CAMILLERI: *Missa Mundi* (Organ of Royal Festival Hall). WIDOR: *Symphony 6: Allegro.* VIERNE: *Impromptu.* DAQUIN: *Noël suisse.* DUPRE: *La Fileuse.* TOMKINS: *Worcester braules.* SWEELINCK: *Chorale: Mein junges Leben hat ein End.* DUBOIS: *Toccata* (Organ of Hexham Abbey)

*** Australian Argo/Decca (ADD) 460 185-2 (5)

Gillian Weir made her début at the 1965 season of Proms, and soon established a formidable reputation over the widest range of organ repertoire, but especially in music of the French school. Over a period of five years in the latter half of the 1970s, she made a series of major recordings for Decca's Argo label and it is good that this logo has been retained for the present superbly remastered five-disc survey.

Her Bach, recorded on an ideal Dutch organ in Rotterdam, is cool and poised. The bravura in the deliciously registered *Fantasia in G* cannot escape the listener, yet there is no sense of the virtuosity being flaunted. The *Trio Sonata* is equally colourful, but the remorseless tread of the *Passacaglia in C minor*, taken very steadily, is undoubtedly compelling, and the *Toccata, Adagio and Fugue* is hardly less telling in its sense of controlled power.

Louis Marchand (1669–1732) was Bach's French contemporary: his suites are not learned but meant to divert, which they certainly do here and especially the delectably registered *Basse et dessus de trompette et de cornet* from the first book and the comparable pieces in the second, again played on a highly suitable organ in France. The brief encores by John Bull are equally tangy and spirited.

Clérambault's *Livre d'orgue* dates from 1710 and follows the same layout as those of Marchand: the music has slightly more formality, yet the influences of French dance music remain, and once again Weir's sparkling registration tickles the ear. The Swiss organ also features an authentic 'tremblant fort' stop, used in the piece called *Flûtes*, with a suprisingly modern effect, followed by the charming dialogue of the *Récit de Nazard* and a powerful closing *Caprice*.

Nikolaus Bruhns (1665–97) died young and left only five organ works, of which four are recorded here. His individuality is striking, and so is the quirky originality of his musical style, which freely interchanges fugal passages and sections of the most florid bravura. The *First Praeludium in G major* has

the kind of immediate appeal which could make it famous if regularly heard; its memorable fugal subject is even more jaunty than Bach's *Fugue à la gigue*. Gillian Weir has the full measure of this music, finding a perfect balance between the fantasy and the structural needs of each piece. She dazzles the ear not only with her vigour and virtuosity but also with some quite scrumptious registration on an organ at Clare College, Cambridge, that seems exactly right for the music. The recording is marvellous, a demonstration of clarity and sonority admirably combined.

François Roberday (1624–80) will be little more than a name – if that – to most readers. He is a *petite maître* who occasionally figures in recitals, but has until now not made a very striking presence in the CD catalogue. This recording of his 12 *Fugues et caprices* (over an hour of music) is made on a modern instrument in Basel which produces very authentic-sounding timbres. As usual Gillian Weir plays with enormous style and aplomb, but it would be idle to maintain that this is music of more than passing interest, except to the specialist collector. Once again the Argo recording has splendid range and presence.

On the other hand, Samuel Scheidt's *Passamezzo Variations*, taken from the first Volume of his *Tablatura nova* has a more general appeal, readily demonstrating the composer's mastery of variation technique, with imaginative invention throughout. Gillian Weir helps a great deal, not only by playing the music splendidly but by again choosing registrations with great flair and a marvellous sense of colour. The piquancy of several of her combinations is unforgettably apt and she is superbly recorded. This music was originally coupled with the Bruhns *Preludes* above, but now it is joined with Roberday, with Langlais's rhythmically quirky *Dialogue for the mixtures* used as a colourful intermezzo.

Dandrieu was a younger contemporary of Couperin le Grand and, like him, came from a musical family. He spent most of his life as organist at Saint-Barthélemy in Paris and at the Royal Chapel. The First Book of organ pieces, published in 1739 a year after his death, contains a number of suites; two are recorded here, consisting of an offertory, several other short movements, and a series of couplets which comprise the organ's contribution to a pair of settings of the *Magnificat*. The music is more than just historically interesting; the invention is full of individual character and resource. Weir plays each *Suite* and *Magnificat* on a different instrument, both of them recorded in a lively acoustic, and her interpretations are marked by a vivid palette, authority and taste. There follows a further selection of *Pièces* by Louis Marchand and a move forward in time for Nicolas de Grigny's serene *Tierce en taille* (effectively decorated). The programme of this most stimulating disc ends with a famously brilliant twentieth-century Toccata, *Tu es Petrus*, by Henri Mulet.

The composer who dominates the final disc, Charles Camilleri, is Maltese, but his background influence comes as much from the East as the West. The (45-minute) *Missa Mundi* is a highly mystical work, inspired by a meditative prose-poem by Teilhard de Chardin, *La Messe sur le Monde*, written in the middle of the Ordos Desert area of China in 1923. The music follows the five sections of the meditation: *The offering; Fire over earth; Fire in the earth; Communion; Prayer.* The poem introduces an astonishing range of organ technique and sonority from the frenzied *Fire in the earth* to the simplistic closing *Prayer*. Weir gives a thrillingly dedicated performance which immediately grabs the listener. Certainly this playing offers both a personal identification with the music and great bravura in equal measure; at times it is as overwhelming as the composer envisaged, at others its simple statements show an eloquence that is notable for its gentleness. The recording is superb. It is as clear and clean as a whistle, immensely wide in dynamic range, and there is not a ripple of distortion of any kind.

The rest of the programme is made up of a skilfully chosen selection of genre pieces, among which Vierne's rippling *Impromptu*, Daquin's charming fanfare-like *Noël suisse* and Dupré's delicate evocation of *La Fileuse* stand out. The jolly closing *Toccata* of Theodor Dubois (which has a whiff of Widor) makes an exhilarating finale.

Almost all this repertoire is most rewarding and can be cordially recommended even to those who normally fight shy of early organ composers. It could hardly be played more masterfully and the engineers provide first-class sound throughout. Readers interested in this repertory (and even those who are not) should investigate this thoroughly satisfying survey.

'*The Grand Organ of the Royal Albert Hall*': LISZT: *Fantasia and Fugue on 'Ad nos salutarem undam'; Legend: St Francis of Paola walking on the waves* (arr. Lionel Rogg). HOWELLS: *Rhapsody 3 in C sharp min.* PARRY: *Toccata & Fugue (The Wanderer).* COOKE: *Fanfare.* ELGAR: *Enigma Variations: Nimrod; Pomp and Circumstance March 1.* LANQUETUIT: *Toccata in D*
*** Priory PRCD 859

One can imagine the diminutive Gillian Weir sitting at the massive console of the Royal Albert Hall. But there is nothing diminutive about the sounds she conjures from this huge instrument. Indeed, the climax of Liszt's *Fantasia and Fugue, Ad nos salutarem undam*, is overwhelming and this is surely the finest and most thrilling performance of this flamboyant work on reord. Lionel Rogg's arrangement of the *Legend* about St Francis on the waves is rather less successful as a transcription but, even though it suits the piano better, it is still very impressive here. The organ has the widest possible range of dynamic and this is consistently demonstrated throughout the programme. Elgar's *Nimrod* is appropriately noble and dignified, but the great tune of *Pomp and Circumstance* is given an arresting and quite overpowering projection. The final item, Lanquetuit's *Toccata*, which is a direct crib from the famous piece by Widor, steals the show as the final spectacular climax. Throughout, Weir is on her finest form, and the recording has extraordinary range and power.

'*On Stage at The Royal Festival Hall*': IVES: *Variations on 'America'.* DANDRIEU: *3 Noëls.* BACH: *Prelude & Fugue in C, BWV 547.* GRISON: *Toccata.* REGER: *Fantasia & Fugue in D min., Op. 135b.* DUPRÉ: *Variations sur un Noël.* GUY BOVET: *3 Préludes Hambourgeois*
*** Priory PRCD 866

For her programe on the Royal Festival Hall organ, which has fine sonority but a much crisper projection than the instrument in the Royal Albert Hall, Gillian Weir has chosen a consistently rewarding programme, opening with Ives's characteristically imaginative variations on *America*, immediately followed by the three Dandrieu *Noëls*, which have piquant charm. Bach's *C major Prelude and Fugue* makes a lively baroque centrepiece, but John Grison's bouncing *Toccata* is no less exhilarating, and Max Reger's extended *Fantasia and Fugue* is the epitome of sonority, weight, spectacle and dynamic contrast. Guy Bovet's three *Preludes*, which use the

organ's registration to produce an orchestral range of colours, are all but matched by Dupré's extended *Variations on a Noël*. In short, there are few organ recitals which offer more variety of texture than this, and there is plenty of high-quality melodic invention here too. The playing is superbly assured and the recording in the demonstration bracket. If you want a single organ disc for your collection, this would be ideal: it will surely tempt you to explore further. Very highly recommended.

Whiteley, John Scott (organ)

'*Great Romantic Organ Music*' (organ of York Minster): TOURNEMIRE: *Improvisation on the Te Deum.* JONGEN: *Minuet-Scherzo, Op. 53.* MULET: *Tu es Petrus.* DUPRÉ: *Prelude and Fugue in G min., Op. 3/7.* R. STRAUSS: *Wedding Prelude.* KARG-ELERT: *Pastel in B, Op. 92/1.* BRAHMS: *Chorale Prelude: O Gott, du frommer Gott, Op. 122/7.* LISZT: *Prelude and Fugue on B-A-C-H, G.260*
*** York CD 101

A superb organ recital, with the huge dynamic range of the York Minster organ spectacularly captured on CD and *pianissimo* detail registering naturally. John Scott Whiteley's playing is full of flair: the attractively complex and sparklingly florid *Prelude and Fugue* of Marcel Dupré is exhilarating and reaches a high climax, while the grand Liszt piece is hardly less overwhelming. The opening Tournemire *Improvisation* is very arresting indeed, while Jongen's *Minuet-Scherzo* displays Whiteley's splendidly clear articulation.

Williams, John (guitar)

'*Spanish Guitar Music*': I. ALBENIZ: *Asturias; Tango; Córdoba; Sevilla.* SANZ: *Canarios.* TORROBA: *Nocturno; Madroños.* SAGRERAS: *El Colibri.* M. ALBENIZ: *Sonata in D.* FALLA: *Homenaje; Three-cornered Hat: Corregidor's Dance; Miller's Dance. El amor brujo: Fisherman's Song.* CATALAN FOLKSONGS: *La Nit de Nadal; El noy de la mare; El testamen de Amelia.* GRANADOS: *La Maja de Goya: Spanish Dance 5.* TARREGA: *Recuerdos de la Alhambra.* VILLA-LOBOS: *Prelude 4 in E min.* MUDARRA: *Fantasia.* TURINA: *Fandanguillo, Op. 36*
☐— (B) *** Sony (ADD) SBK 46347

John Williams can show strong Latin feeling, as in the vibrant *Farruca* of the *Miller's Dance* from Falla's *Three-cornered Hat*, or create a magically atmospheric mood, as in the hauntingly registered transcription of the *Fisherman's Song* from *El amor brujo*. He can play with thoughtful improvisatory freedom, as in the Villa-Lobos *Prelude*, with its *pianissimo* evocation, or be dramatically spontaneous, as in the memorable performance of Turina's *Fandanguillo*, which ends the recital magnetically. The instinctive control of atmosphere and dynamic is constantly rewarding throughout a varied programme, and the technique is phenomenal yet never flashy, always at the service of the music. The remastering brings a clean and truthful, if very immediate, image. Background is minimal and never intrusive.

Winters, Ross (recorder), Andrew Ball (piano)

English Recorder Music: JACOB: *Variations.* SCOTT: *Aubade.* RUBBRA: *Sonatina, Op. 128; Passacaglia sopra*

'Plusieurs regrets', Op. 113; Meditation sopra 'Coers désolés', Op. 67. ANTONY HOPKINS: *Suite.* JOHN GARDNER: *Little Suite in C, Op. 60.* COLIN HAND: *Sonata breve.*
REIZENSTEIN: *Partita*
**(*) British Music Soc. BMS 425CD

This collection has been recorded by the British Music Society specifically to explore contemporary repertoire associated with the pioneering recorder virtuoso, Carl Dolmetsch, for whom all these works were written. What seems perverse however is that many of these pieces (notably those by Gordon Jacob, Rubbra and John Gardner) were intended to be partnered by a harpsichord and, while they are highly effective heard with piano, a special enterprise like this deserves total authenticity. Nevertheless, Ross Winters and Andrew Ball create a symbiotic partnership.

The ten Jacob *Variations* on a delicately pastoral melody are most engaging, including both a siciliana and a tarantella, but in the languorous piece by Cyril Scott it is the lusciousness of the piano harmonies that catch the ear.

Undoubtedly the three works by Rubbra are the highlight of the recital, the *Passacaglia* and the resonantly noble *Meditazioni* both drawing on themes by Josquin. The *Sonatina* with its long, winding central melody, followed by variations on a jolly Spanish dance, *En la fuente del rosel*, clearly has the harpsichord in mind.

The witty *Sonatina* of Antony Hopkins and the piquant *Sonata breve* of Colin Hand are succinct and diverting, but the wayward harmonic progressions of Reizenstein's *Partita* work better in the dance movements than in the rather wan lyricism. Excellent recording and a very good balance.

Yates, Sophie (virginals)

English Virginals Music: BYRD: *Praeludium – Fantasia; The Barley Breake; The Tennthe Pavan (Sir William Petre); Galliard to the Tennthe Pavan; The Woods so Wild; Hugh Aston's Ground; The Bells.* DOWLAND: *Lachrymae Pavan* (arr. BYRD). HARDING: *Galliard* (arr. BYRD). GIBBONS: *Fantasia.* ANON.: *My Lady Careys Dompe.* TOMKINS: *Barafostus's Dreame.* ASTON: *Hornepype.* BULL: *In nomine*
** Chan. 0574

Sophie Yates is a thoughtful and accomplished player and she uses a modern copy by Peter Bavington of an Italian instrument made at the very beginning of the seventeenth century. Her programme is well thought out and, even though it is dominated by the music of Byrd, it is musically well balanced. The snag is the resonant recording, which gives a larger-than-life impression of the instrument which even the lowering of the volume control does not entirely diminish.

Yepes, Narciso (guitar)

'Guitarra española': RODRIGO: *Fantasia para un gentilhombre.* BACARISSE: *Concertino for Guitar and Orchestra, Op. 72* (both with Spanish R. and TV SO, Odón Alonso). RODRIGO: *Concierto madrigal* (with Godelieve Monden, Philh. O, García Navarro); *Concierto de Aranjuez.* RUIZ-PIPÓ: *Tablas for Guitar and Orchestra.* OHANA: *Concierto: Tres gráficos for Guitar and Orchestra* (with LSO, Rafael Frühbeck de Burgos). Solo music: ALBÉNIZ: *Suite españolas: Asturias. Legenda; Recuerdos de viaje: Rumores de la caleta; Malagueña; Piezas caracteristicas: Torre bermeja;*
Serenata; Malahueña, Op. 164/3. GRANADOS: *Danza española 4 (Villanesca).* TÁRREGA: *Alborada; Capriccio; Danza mora; Sueno; Recuerdos de la Alhambra; Marieta (Mazurka); Capricho árabe (Serenata); Tango.* FALLA: *El amor brujo: El círculo mágico; Canción del fuego fatuo. El sombrero de tres picos; Danza del molinero (Farruca). Homenaje: Le tombeau de Claude Debussy.* TURINA: *Sonata, Op. 61; Fandanguillo, Op. 36. Garrotin y soleares; Ráfaga.* BACARISSE: *Passpie.* YEPES: *Catarina d'Alió.* ANON.: *Jeux interdits: Romance.* SANZ: *Suite española.* MUDARRA: *Fantasia que contrahaze la harpa en la manera de Ludvico.* NARVÁEZ: *Diferencias sobre 'Guádame las vacas'.* SOLER: *Sonata in E.* SOR: *10 Etudes; Theme and Variations, Op. 9.* RODRIGO: *En los trigales.* ANON., arr. LLOBET: *4 Canciones populares catalanas.* PUJOL: *El abejorro.* TORROBA: *Madroños.* MONTSALVATGE: *Habanera.* O'HANA: *Tientos.* RUIZ-PIPÓ: *Canción y danza 1*
(B) *** DG (ADD/DDD) 474 666-2 (5)

This collection admirably celebrates Narciso Yepes's long-lived and distinguished recording achievement in music from his own country. He had a prodigious technique, but it was in harness to a fine intellect plus an instinctive feeling for the colourful emotions and Spanish dance-rhythms expressed in this repertoire. It was inevitable that the three most famous concertante works of Rodrigo should be included, plus other similar works of varying attractiveness. But the solo repertoire is all marvellously played, for Yepes had no difficulty in creating electricity in the recording studio, and many of these performances – with their vivid palette and high level of concentration – constantly remind us of Beethoven's assertion that a guitar is an orchestra all by itself.

'Malagueña' (Spanish Guitar Music): ALBENIZ: *Malagueña, Op. 165/3; Suite española: Asturias (Leyenda).* TÁRREGA: *Recuerdos de la Alhambra; Marieta (Mazurka); Capricho árabe.* RODRIGO: *En los trigales.* RUIZ-PIPO: *Cancion y danza 1.* SOR: *Introduction & Variations on a Theme of Mozart, Op. 9.* SANZ: *Suite española: Españoletas; Gallarda y villano; Danza y villano; Danza de las hachas; Rujero y paradetas; Zarabanda al ayre español; Passacalle; Folias; La miñona de Cataluña; Canarios.* MUDARRA: *Fantasia que contrahaza la harpa en la manera de Ludovico.* SOLER: *Sonata in E.* GRANADOS: *Danza española 4 (Villanesca).* FALLA: *El sombrero de tres picos: Danza del mólinero (Farruca).* ANON.: *Romance* (from the film: *Forbidden Games*)
◷ ✹ (BB) *** DG Eloquence (ADD) 469 649-2

With repertoire recorded between 1968 and 1977, this Eloquence reissue is based on a long-standing DG recital showing this great Spanish guitarist at his very peak, which now has been expanded to a playing time of 76 minutes. Yepes was not only an outstanding exponent of this repertoire but also had that rare gift of constantly creating electricity in the recording studio, no more thrillingly than in Falla's *Miller's Dance* from the *Three-cornered Hat*, in which he creates an orchestral range of colour. But all this music springs vividly to life and popular favourites like Tárrega's *Recuerdos de la Alhambra* (presented with unostentatious bravura) and the engagingly ingenuous *Mozart Variations* of Sor are wonderfully fresh. The earlier music is also very appealing, the Sanz *Suite* – ten through-composed miniatures of which *Canarios* is probably the best known – is delightful. The final item, an anonymous *Romance* used in the film, *Forbidden Games*, makes a real lollipop encore. Throughout, Yepes's assured, vibrant and always stylish advocacy brings consistent pleasure and stimulation: there are few solo guitar records to match this, particularly as the Eloquence transfers are so present and realistic and the cost so reasonable.

Zabaleta, Nicanor (harp)

'Arpa española': ALBENIZ: Malagueña, Op. 165/3; Suite española: Granada (Serenata); Zaragoza (Capricho); Asturias (Leyenda). Mallorca, Op. 202; Tango español. FALLA: Serenata andaluza. TURINA: Ciclo pianistico 1: Tocata y fuga. GOMBAU: Apunte bético. GRANADOS: Danza española 5. HALFFTER: Sonatina (ballet): Danza de la pastora. LOPEZ-CHAVARRI: El viejo castillo moro
⬤ (M) *** DG (IMS) (ADD) 435 847-2

A good deal of the music here belongs to the guitar (or piano) rather than the harp, but Nicanor Zabaleta, with his superb artistry and sense of atmosphere, makes it all his own. Throughout this delightful programme, Zabaleta gives each piece strong individuality of character. In the Granados Spanish Dance 5 he matches the magnetism of Julian Bream's famous recording, and Manuel de Falla's Serenata andaluza is hardly less captivating. DG's sound-balance is near perfection, as is the choice of acoustic, and the magic distilled by Zabaleta's concentration, often at the gentlest levels of dynamic, is unforgettable.

VOCAL RECITALS AND CHORAL COLLECTIONS

The 'Art of Singing'

Video: 'Golden Voices of the Century' (Björling, Callas, Caruso, Chaliapin, Christoff, Corelli, De los Angeles, De Luca, Di Stefano, Flagstad, Gigli, Martinelli, Melchior, Olivero, Pinza, Ponselle, L. Price, Schipa, Stevens, Supervia, Sutherland, Tauber, Tebaldi, Tetrazzini, Tibbett, Vickers, Wunderlich): Excerpts: PUCCINI: *La Bohème.* SAINT-SAENS: *Samson et Dalila.* VERDI: *Rigoletto.* LEONCAVALLO: *Pagliacci* (all silent film excerpts with Caruso). DONIZETTI: *Lucia di Lammermoor:* sextet with Caruso, mimed. DE CURTIS: *Torna a Surriento* (song) (Giovanni Martinelli). HANDEL: *Xerxes: Ombra mai fù* (Beniamino Gigli). FLOTOW: *Martha: M'appari* (Tito Schipa). ROSSINI: *Il barbiere di Siviglia: Largo al factotum* (Giuseppe de Luca). FLOTOW: *Martha: M'appari* (Luisa Tetrazzini). PUCCINI: *La Bohème: Quando me'n vo* (Conchita Supervia). BIZET: *Carmen: Chanson Bohème; Habanera* (Rosa Ponselle). SCHUBERT: *Ständchen* (Richard Tauber). RIMSKY-KORSAKOV: *The Maid of Pskov.* IBERT: *Chanson du duc* (both with Fyodor Chaliapin). WAGNER: *Die Walküre: Hojotoho!* (Kirsten Flagstad). BIZET: *Carmen: Chanson du toréador* (Lawrence Tibbett). SAINT-SAENS: *Samson et Dalila: Mon coeur s'ouvre* (Risë Stevens). WAGNER: *Die Walküre: Winterstürme* (Lauritz Melchior). MUSSORGSKY: *Boris Godunov: Coronation scene* (Ezio Pinza). PUCCINI: *La Bohème: Che gelida manina; Mi chiamano Mimì; O soave fanciulla* (Jussi Björling, Renata Tebaldi). FALLA: *La vida breve: Vivan los que rien* (Victoria de los Angeles). MEYERBEER: *Les Huguenots: O beau pays* (Joan Sutherland). VERDI: *Aida: O patria mia* (Leontyne Price). MUSSORGSKY: *Boris Godunov: Death scene* (Boris Christoff). PUCCINI: *Tosca: Vissi d'arte;* (i) *Act III duet* (Magda Olivero, (i) with Alvinio Misciano). MOZART: *Die Zauberflöte: Dies Bildnis ist bezaubernd schön* (Fritz Wunderlich). BEETHOVEN: *Fidelio: In des Lebens* (Jon Vickers). PUCCINI: *Turandot: Non piangere, liù* (Franco Corelli). LEONCAVALLO: *I Pagliacci: Vesti la giubba* (Giuseppe di Stefano). (i) VERDI: *La traviata: Parigi, o cara.* (ii) PUCCINI: *Tosca: Duet and Vissi d'arte* (both Maria Callas, with (i) Alfredo Kraus, (ii) Tito Gobbi). (Commentary by Magda Olivero, Thomas Hampson, Schuyler Chapin, Kirk Browning, Nicola Rescigno)
*** Teldec **DVD** 0630 15896-2

This is Teldec's vocal equivalent of 'The Art of Conducting'. While almost all the film excerpts included here are fascinating, this comparable vocal survey proves less uniformly compulsive than its orchestral equivalent. Moreover, while almost all the comments on the earlier video concerning the conductors themselves and their various idiosyncrasies proved very perceptive, the commentaries here, especially the contributions by the singers themselves, seem much less illuminating. Thomas Hampson's definition of the meaning of *legato*, a term which almost explains itself, is perversely over-complicated. But now to the singing.

Two performances stand out above the rest in magnetism. A live telecast, with good sound, from the Met. in 1956 brought Renata Tebaldi and Jussi Björling together in virtually the whole of the great Act I love scene in *La Bohème*, from *Che gelida manina* to their final exit, with their glorious voices ending the act from offstage. They are dressed in a curiously formal way – one might even say overdressed – and Tebaldi is not shown to be the greatest actress in the world, but their voices match superbly. The other scene is even more electrifying – a live telecast made in December of the same year for which obviously no expense was spared, and the set and production were fully worthy. Boris Christoff's Death scene from *Boris Godunov* is deeply moving; Nicola Moscona is a hardly less resonant Pimen, and an unnamed boy is very touching as Boris's young son. Hardly less impressive is the great Kirsten Flagstad (at her vocal peak), introduced by Bob Hope, who manages to keep a straight face, in a Paramount movie, *The Big Broadcast of 1938*. She sings *Hojotoho!* thrillingly from *Die Walküre*, waving her spear with remarkable conviction.

Risë Stevens, Lauritz Melchior, Victoria de los Angeles in Falla and Joan Sutherland in Meyerbeer coloratura add to the vocal pleasures, and Leontyne Price's gloriously full-voiced *O patria mia* from *Aida* is engulfing. What a stage presence she has! Another highlight is Magda Olivero's charismatically seductive *Vissi d'arte* from *Tosca*. The great Callas ends the programme by singing the same aria (in 1964) but, although her presence is commanding, the actual singing, with its wobbling vibrato, is no match for Olivero.

The early recordings are interesting, but the sound is such that they are usually less than overwhelming vocally, with Gigli and Tito Schipa possible exceptions. A hilarious interlude is provided by a 1908 silent film with professional actors hopelessly overacting and miming the words of the Sextet (*Chi mi frena*) from *Lucia di Lammermoor*, designed to accompany the famous 1911 RCA recording by Caruso, Daddi, Journet, Scotti, Sembrich and Severina. Another smile comes when Rosa Ponselle is shown singing *Carmen* for an MGM screen test in 1936 and her fan gets in the way of the camera! All in all, this is a considerable entertainment, but one hoped, unrealistically perhaps, for more items like *Boris* and *Bohème*.

Historical Vocal Recitals

'The EMI Record of Singing'

Volume 3 (1926–39): Part 1: The German school: Arias and excerpts from WAGNER: *Tannhäuser* (Lauritz Melchior; Göta Ljungberg with Walter Widdop); *Die Walküre* (Max Lorenz; Kirsten Flagstad); *Lohengrin* (Franz Völker); *Die Meistersinger* (Rudolf Bockelmann; Delia Reinhardt); *Das Rheingold* (Hans Hermann Nissen); *Der fliegende Holländer* (Elizabeth Ohms); *Siegfried* (Nanny Larsen-Todsen). WILLIE: *Königsballade* (Helge Rosvaenge). D'ALBERT: *Tiefland* (Torsten Ralf). JOHANN STRAUSS JR: *Die Fledermaus* (Richard Tauber with Vera Schwarz). KIENZL: *Der Evangeligmann* (Marcel Wittrisch with Children's chorus). RICHARD STRAUSS: *Der Rosenkavalier* (Herbert Ernst Groh; Lotte Lehmann); *Arabella* (Alfred Jerger with Viorica Ursuleac; Tiana Lemnitz); *Daphne* (Margarete Teschemacher); *Die ägyptische Helena* (Rose Pauly). KORNGOLD: *Die tote Stadt* (Joseph Schmidt; Karl Hammes). MOZART: *Die Entführung aus dem Serail* (Julius Patzak). HUMPERDINCK: *Hänsel und Gretel* (Gerard Hüsch). KREUTZER: *Das Nachtlager in Granada* (Willi Domgraf-Fassbaender). MENDELSSOHN: *Elijah* (Friedrich Schorr); *Saint Paul* (Jo Vincent). LORTZING: *Zar und Zimmermann* (Heinrich Schlusnus; Leo Schützendorf); *Der Wildschütz* (Alexander Kipnis). NICOLAI: *Die lustigen Weiber von Windsor* (Wilhelm Strienz). VERDI: *Macbeth* (Ivar Andresen); *Un ballo in maschera* (Adele Kern). MEYERBEER: *Le Prophète* (Sigrid Onegin); *L'Africaine* (Elisabeth Rethberg). PONCHIELLI: *La Gioconda* (Karin Branzell). SAINT-SAENS: *Samson et Dalila* (Kerstin Thorborg). MOZART: *La clemenza di Tito* (Rosette Anday). FLOTOW: *Alesandro Stradella* (Fritz Jold). RIMSKY-KORSAKOV: *The Tsar's Bride* (Miliza Korjus; Meta Seinemeyer). ADAM: *Le Postillon de Longumeau* (Felicie Hüni Mihacsek). PUCCINI: *Turandot* (Luise Helletsgruber); *La Bohème* (Maria Cebotari). GOLDMARK: *Die Königen von Saba* (Maria Nemeth). Lieder: BEETHOVEN: *Der Wachtelschlag* (Karl Erb). SCHUMANN: *Liederkreis: Mondnacht* (Leo Slezak); *Die Lotusblume* (Ursula van Diemen). WOLF: *Vers hwiegene Liebe* (Heinrich Schlusnus). SCHUBERT: *Die Stadt* (Herbert Jannsen); *Aufenthal* (Maria Olczewska); *Die Allnacht* (Marta Fuchs). BRAHMS: *Nicht mehr zu dir zu gehen* (Margarete Klose); *Feldeinsamkeit* (Elena Gerhardt); *Volkslieder: Schwesterlein* (Lulu Mysz-Gmeiner). SCHOECK: *Mit einem gemalten Bande* (Ria Ginster); *Nachtlied* (Margherita Perras). MARX: *Marienlied* (Elisabeth Schumann). ROSSINI: *Soirrées musicales; L'invito.* (Lotte Schöne). OBOUSSIER: *Weine du nicht* (Erna Berger). LISZT: *Es muss ein Wunderbares sein* (Emmy Bettendorf). REGER: *Waldeinsamkeit; Zum Schlafen* (Maria Müller). WAGNER: *Wesendonck Lieder: Schmerzen* (Frida Leider)

Part 2: The Italian school: Arias and excerpts from: PAISIELLO: *I zingari infiera* (Conchita Supervia). BIZET: *Carmen* (Giannina Pederzini). VERDI: *Requiem* (Irene Minghini-Catteneo; Ezio Pinza); *I Lombardi* (Giannina Aranji-Lombardi); *La forza del destino* (Dusolina Giannini); *Ernani* (Iva Pacetti). *Otello* (Hina Spani; Renato Zanelli); *Rigoletto* (Lina Pagliughi); *Falstaff* (Mariano Stabile).

SAINT-SAENS: *Samson et Dalila* (Ebe Stignani). DONIZETTI: *La Favorita* (Florica Cristoforeanu); *Don Pasquale* (Afro Poli with Ernesto Badini). BOITO: *Mefistofele* (Pia Tassinari; Nazzareno de Angelis). CATALANI: *Loreley* (Bianca Scacciati). GIORDANO: *Siberia* (Maria Caniglia); *Andrea Chénier* (Lina Bruna Rasa; Cesare Formichi; Benvenuto Franci; Antonio Cortis); *Il Re* (Mercedes Capsir). PUCCINI: *La fanciulla del West* (Gina Cigna); *Madama Butterfly* (Margaret Sheridan); *Turandot* (Maria Zamboni; Magda Oliviero; Alessandro Ziliani); *Manon Lescaut* (Licia Albanese; Francesco Merli; Giacomo Lauri-Volpi); *La Bohème* (Tancredi Pasero); *Tosca* (Giovanni Inghilleri). PIETRI: *Maristella* (Rosetta Pampanini). MASCAGNI: *Iris* (Maria Farneti); *Lodeletta* (Malfada Favero; Galliano Masini); *Guglielmo Ratcliffe* (Carlo Galeffi). GOMES: *Il Guarany* (Bidù Sayão). CILEA: *Adriana Lecouvreur* (Adelaide Saraceni; Aurelio Pertile). RICCI: *Crispino e la comare* (Salvatore Baccaloni). PONCHIELLI: *Il figliuol prodigo* (Mario Basiola). LEONCAVALLO: *Zazà* (Apollo Granforte). BELLINI: *La sonnnambula* (Dino Borgioli with Maria Gentile, Ida Mannarini, Gina Pedroni; also Enzo de Muro Lomanto). MASSENET: *Werther* (Tito Schipa). GUERRERO: *Los Gavilanes* (Tino Folgar). VITTADINI: *Anima allegra* (Luigi Fort). OFFENBACH: *La Belle Hélène* (Jussi Bjoerling). Songs: TRAD.: *Have you seen but a whyte lilie grow?* (Conchita Supervia); BUZZI-PECCIA: *Colombetta* (Claudia Muzio). GRANADOS: *Tonadillas: El majo discreto; El majo timido* (Conchita Badia). JAMES: *Maori lullaby* (Toti da Monte). TIRINDELLI: *Mistica* (Carlo Tagliabue). TOSTI: *Ideale* (Riccardo Stracciari); *Aprile* (Beniamino Gigli); *Do not Go, my Love* (Dino Borgioli). HAGEMAN LONGAS: *En effeuillant la marguerite* (Tito Schipa)

Part 3: The French school: Arias from: RAMEAU: *Hippolyte et Aricie* (Leila Ben Sedira). OFFENBACH: *Les Brigands* (Emma Luart); *Contes d'Hoffmann* (André Pernet); *La Grande Duchesse de Gérolstein* (Yvonne Printemps); *Le Boulangère a des écus* (Reynaldo Hahn). DELIBES: *Lakmé* (Germaine Feraldy). ROSSINI: *Guillaume Tell* (Eidé Norena). MASSENET: *Marie-Magdeleine* (Germaine Martinelli); *Hérodiade* (René Maison). GOUNOD: *Sapho* (Suzanne Cesbron-Viseur; Germain Cernay); *Polyucte* (José Luccioni); *Mireille* (Gaston Micheletti). DUKAS: *Ariane et Barbe-Bleu* (Suzanne Balguerie). WAGNER: *Lohengrin* (Germaine Lubin). GLUCK: *Orphée* (Alice Raveau). REYER: *Sigurd* (Georges Thill; César Vezzani). HALEVY: *La Juive* (René Verdière). LAPARRA: *L'Illustre Fregona* (Miguel Villabella). BAZIN: *Maître Pathelin* (André d'Arkor). VERDI: *Luisa Miller* (Giusppe Lugo). LALO: *Le Roi d'Ys* (Joseph Rogatchewsky). LEROUX: *L'Ombre* (Lucien Fugère). BERLIOZ: *L'Enfance du Christ* (Jean Planel); *La Damnation de Faust* (Charles Panzéra). MAGNARD: *Guercoeur* (Arthur Endrèze). PALADILHE: *Patrie!* (Robert Couzinou). BERTHOMIEU: *Robert Macaire* (André Balbon). Songs: SAINT-SAENS: *Le Rossignol et la rose* (Lily Pons). FAURE: *Les berceux* (Ninon Vallin); *Aurore* (Pierre Bernac); *Lydia* (Roger Bourdin). TORELLI: *Tu lo sai* (Povla Frijsh). DEBUSSY: *Chansons de Bilitis: Le Chevelure* (Jane Bathori). RAVEL: *Chants hébraïques: Kaddisch* (Madeleine Grey);

Don Quichotte à Dulcinée: Chanson épique (Martial Singher). DE BREVILLE: *Une jeune fille parle* (Claire Croiza). HAHN: *D'un prison* (Charles Panzéra). MARTINI: *Plaisir d'amore* (Jean-Emil Vanni-Marcoux).

Part 4: The Anglo-American school: Arias and excerpts from: VERDI: *Falstaff* (Lawrence Tibett). THOMAS: *Hamlet* (John Charles Thomas; John Brownlee). ROSSINI: *Il barbiere di Siviglia* (Dennis Noble); *Stabat Mater* (Florence Austral). Songs: COWAN: *Onaway, awake, beloved* (Harold Williams). HANDEL: *Messiah* (Peter Dawson). OFFENBACH: *Contes d'Hoffmann* (Charles Kullman). BIZET: *La Jolie fille de Perth* (Heddle Nash); *Carmen* (Marguerite D'Alvarez). Goring THOMAS: *Esmeralda* (Thomas Burke). PUCCINI: *Tosca* (Richard Crooks); *La Bohème* (Grace Moore; Ina Souez); *Madama Butterfly* (Joan Cross); *Turandot* (Eva Turner). HANDEL: *Acis and Galatea* (Walter Widdop). PURCELL: *The Tempest* (Norman Allin). MENDELSSOHN: *St Paul* (Muriel Brunskill). HANDEL: *Theodora* (Isobel Baillie). DELIUS: *Irmelin* (Dora Labbette). SPONTINI: *La Vestale* (Rosa Ponselle). REYER: *Sigurd* (Marjorie Lawrence). Songs: DUNN: *The Bitterness of Love* (John McCormack). MONTEVERDI: *Maladetto sia l'aspetto* (Roland Hayes). MARTINI: *Minuet* (Mme Charles Cahier). SULLIVAN: *The Lost Chord* (Dame Clara Butt). SCHUBERT: *Der Tod und das Mädchen* (Marian Anderson). FAURE: *Le Secret* (Susan Metcalfe-Casals). CANTELOUBE: *Baïlero* (Gladys Swarthout). PALADILHE: *Psyché* (Maggie Teyte). HAYDN: *My Mother Bids me Bind My Hair* (Florence Easton).

Part 5: The East European/Slavic school: Arias and excerpts from: DVORAK: *Rusalka* (Jarmila Novotná; Ada Nordenova). RIMSKY-KORSAKOV: *The Tsar's Bride* (Nathalie Vechor). GOMES: *Salvator Rosa* (Mark Reisen). KODALY: *Háry János* (Imry Palló). Songs: GRETCHANINOV: *The Wounded Birch; Snowflakes* (Maria Kurenko with Composer, piano); *Lullaby* (Oda Slobodskaya). RIMSKY-KORSAKOV: *The Rose and the Nightingale* (Xenia

Belmas). KARLOWICZ: *I Remember Golden Days* (Ada Sari). DVORAK: *Leave me Alone* (Maria Krasová). arr. BARTOK: 2 *Hungarian Folksongs* (Maria Basildes). DARGOMIJSKY: *Bolero* (Feodor Chaliapin). CUI: *Hunger* (Vladimir Rosing). KASHEVAROV: *Tranquility* (Sergei Lemeshev).

☉ (M) (***) Testament mono SBT 0132 (10)

The importance of EMI's monumental series 'The Record of Singing' cannot be exaggerated, and it is sad that although the fourth volume was issued on CD, covering the period from the start of electrical recording up to the end of the 78rpm era, the others have been allowed to languish. That fact makes it all the more creditable that Stewart Brown of Testament has boldly issued this beautifully produced CD reissue of the third volume, the work of Keith Hardwick, both in the selection of items, often unexpected but always keenly perceptive, and in the actual transfers, which set standards in clarity and accuracy too rarely matched by others. Inevitably in a very compact format, the background material is not quite so lavish as in the original LP issue, with separate booklets included covering details of recording and biographies of the 200 or so singers covered. Even so, essential details are all here, and the methodical covering of so many singers from so many different schools, divided mainly by nationality, could not be more illuminating. In a note written especially for this CD reissue Hardwick confesses that though initially he had misgivings over following up the earlier two volumes of golden age material with recordings from a period generally regarded as one of decline, he has more and more come to revise that opinion. Certainly, thanks to his brilliant choice of items, one has much to admire in every school represented, with reservations not so much over quality of singing as of performance style, where inevitably modern taste differs greatly, notably on such composers as Mozart. A magnificent achievement. One hopes that Testament may have the courage to bring out CD versions of the first two volumes of this indispensable series.

Nimbus Prima Voce Series

Introduction

The Nimbus company have taken a radical view of transferring historic 78rpm vocal recordings to CD. The best possible copies of shellac originals have been played on an acoustic machine with an enormous horn, one of the hand-made Rolls-Royces among non-electric gramophones of the 1930s, with Thorn needles reducing still further the need to filter the sound.

'The Golden Age of Singing' (50 Years of Great Voices on Record)

Volume I (1900–10): TCHAIKOVSKY: *Queen of Spades: Forgive Me, Heavenly Being* (Nicolay Figner). FLOTOW: *Marta: Chi mi dirà* (Edouard de Reszke). BELLINI: *La sonnambula: Vi ravviso, o luoghio ameni* (Pol Plançon); *Ah, non credea mirarti* (Adelina Patti). VERDI: *Otello: Niun mi tema* (Francesco Tamagno); *Era la notte* (Victor Maurel); *Credo in un Dio crudel* (Eugenio Giraldoni). *Aida: Fuggiam gli ardori inospiti* (Celestina Boninsegna). *Ernani: O sommo Carlo* (Mattia Battistini). *Luisa Miller: Quando le sere al placido* (Alessandro Bonci). *Rigoletto: Caro nome* (Nellie Melba). *Simon Boccanegra: Il lecerato spirito* (Francesco Navarrini). *Falstaff: Quand' ero paggio* (Antonio Scotti). DONIZETTI: *L'elisir d'amore: Una furtiva lagrima* (Enrico Caruso). *Chiedi all'aura lusinghiera* (Maria Galvany; Aristodemo Giorgini). *Don Pasquale: So anch'io la virtu magica* (Rosina Storchio); *Sogno soave e casto* (Giuseppe Anselmi). *La favorita: A tanto amor* (Mario Ancona). *Lucrezia Borgia: Di pescatore ignobil* (Francesco Marconi); *Il segreto per esser felice* (Clara Butt). WAGNER: *Lohengrin: Elsa's Dream* (Félia Litvinne). *Rienzi: Gerechter Gott!* (Ernestine Schumann-Heink). *Götterdämmerung: Fliegt heim ihr Raben*; GOUNOD: *Roméo et Juliette: Je veux vivre dans ce rêve* (Emma Eames). MOZART: *Die Zauberflöte: O Isis und Osiris* (Wilhelm Hesch). *Le nozze di Figaro: Heil'ge Quelle* (Lilli Lehmann). GLINKA: *A Life for the Tsar: They guess the truth* (Vladimir Kastorsky). MASSENET: *Le Roi de Lahore: Promesse de mon avenir* (Maurice Renaud). *Manon: Il sogno (en fermant les yeux)* (Fernando de Lucia). *Le Cid: O souverain! ô juge! o père!* (Vilhelm Herold). MEYERBEER: *Le prophète: Sopra Berta l'amor mio* (Francesco Vignas). *Les Huguenots: A ce mot* (Olimpia Boronat); *O beau pays de la Touraine* (Antonina Nezhdanova). PONCHIELLI: *La Gioconda: Ebbrezza! Delirio!* (Eugenia Burzio and Giuseppe de Luca). BIZET: *Carmen: Habanera* (Emma Calvé). ERKEL: *Hunyadi László: Ah rebéges* (Lillian Nordica). THOMAS: *Hamlet: O vin, discaccia la tristezza* (Titta Ruffo). PUCCINI: *Madama Butterfly: Con onor muore* (Emmy Destinn). ROSSINI: *Il barbiere di Siviglia: La calunnia è un venticello* (Adamo Didur). *Semiramide: Bel raggio Lusinghier* (Marcella Sembrich). GOLDMARK: *Die Königin von Saba: Magische Töne* (Leo Slezak). BOITO: *Mefistofele: Giunto sul passo estremo* (Dmitri Smirnov). RIMSKY-KORSAKOV: *May Night: Sleep, My Beauty* (Leonid Sobinov). HATTON: *Simon the Cellarer*, (Sir Charles Santley)
(B) (***) Nimbus Double mono NI 7050/1 (2)

For the ordinary collector without a specialist interest in historical vocal repertoire this bargain Double should prove an ideal way of making an initial exploration. There are some 44 widely varied items sung by as many outstanding singers. Some of the names will be unfamiliar – it is not always the most famous that make the greatest initial impression, although Tamagno's *Otello* aria (from 1902) is immediately commanding, Caruso is very winning in Donizetti, Battistini is joined by other singers and the La Scala Chorus in a splendid 1906 scene from Verdi's *Ernani*. But it is the second disc that is particularly well planned, with a whole stream of superb performances that project vividly, from Melba's *Caro nome* and Tito Ruffo's *Hamlet*, to Emmy Destinn's thrilling acount of Butterfly's final aria. Amor Didur's solemn *La culunnia* and Vilhelm Herold in *Massenet* are both memorable, and with Gadski in *Götterdämmerung*, the orchestra may sound puny, but not the glorious flow of vocal tone. One of the surprises is the lightly pointed coloratura of Clara Butt in Donizetti, the big voice fined down, yet the lower register still ringing out. Scotti's Falstaff, Leo Slezak in *Die Königen von Saba* are both highlights, and the programme ends in light-hearted vein with Sir Charles Santley's clear yet resonant 'Simon the Cellarer'. The transfers almost all show the Nimbus process at its best; only occasionally is the surface noise slightly intrusive.

Battistini, Mattia (baritone)

Arias from: TCHAIKOVSKY: *Eugene Onegin.* VERDI: *Un ballo in maschera; Ernani; La traviata; Macbeth; Don Carlos.* FLOTOW: *Marta.* DONIZETTI: *La favorita; Don Sebastiano; Linda di Chamounix.* HEROLD: *Zampa.* BERLIOZ: *La Damnation de Faust.* MASSENET: *Werther.* THOMAS: *Hamlet.* NOUGUES: *Quo Vadis?*
(M) (***) Nimbus mono NI 7831

As with other Nimbus issues, the transfers are remarkably kind to the voice and are probably nearer to how Battistini sounded 'live'. It is a remarkable voice, with a fine, clear upper range. The programme is well chosen and the recordings date from between 1902 and 1922. While obviously the Verdi excerpts are essential to show the calibre of any baritone, it is good to have the rare *Pourquoi tremblez-vous?* from Zampa.

Björling, Jussi (tenor)

'*The First Ten Years*': Arias from: VERDI: *Il trovatore; Rigoletto; Aida; Requiem.* PUCCINI: *Tosca; La fanciulla del West; La Bohème.* BORODIN: *Prince Igor.* LEONCAVALLO: *Pagliacci.* MASCAGNI: *Cavalleria rusticana.* RIMSKY-KORSAKOV: *Sadko.* MEYERBEER: *L'Africana.* PONCHIELLI: *La Gioconda.* MASSENET: *Manon.* ROSSINI: *Stabat Mater.* Song: FANAL: *I maünner oüver lag och raütt*
(M) (***) Nimbus mono NI 7835

Volume 2, 1911–1960: Arias from: PUCCINI: *Tosca; La Fanciulla del West; La Bohème.* VERDI: *Rigoletto.* FLOTOW: *Martha.* GOUNOD: *Faust.* BIZET: *Carmen.* OFFENBACH: *La Belle Hélène.* J. STRAUSS JR: *Der Zigeunerbaron.* MILLOCKER: *Der Bettelstudent.* Songs: BEETHOVEN:

Adelaide. SCHUBERT: *Ave Maria; Ständchen; An die Leier.*
R. STRAUSS: *Cäcile.* SIBELIUS: *Svarta rosor; Säv, säv, susa.*
ALFVEN: *Skogen sover.* EKLOF: *Morgon.* SJOBERG: *Tornerna.*
TOSTI: *Ideale*
(M) (***) Nimbus mono NI 7842

'Bjoerling in song': LEONCAVALLO: *Mattinata.* TOSELLI:
Serenata. DI CAPUA: *O sole mio.* Songs by: ENDERS;
CHRISTGAU; PETERSON-BERGER; ARTHUR; ELGAR; DE
CURTIS; BALL; RAY; DAHL; SCHRADER; PEREZ-FREIRE;
STENHAMMAR; ALTHEN; CARUSO; WIDESTEDT. TRAD.:
Tantis serenade. Arias from LEHAR: *Das Land des Lächelns.*
KALMAN: *Das Veilchen von Montmartre*
(M) (***) Nimbus mono NI 7879

'Jussi Bjoerling in Opera and Song'
(M) (***) Nimbus NI 1776 (3) (NI 7835; 7842 & 7879)

The three Bjoerling discs above are brought together in a
box, giving a comprehensive view of his early years, when
from the age of nineteen (in 1930) he recorded regularly for
the Swedish branch of HMV. That means that most of the
items, including the early recordings of opera and all the
operetta, are done in Swedish. Not that lovers of vocal art
will worry overmuch, when even in 1930 the headily golden
voice is both distinctive and rich, fully developed even then.
Volume 2 covers recordings that Bjoerling made between
1936 and 1940, not just in Sweden but in 1939–40 in New
York, when Victor recorded him in Lieder, not just Schubert, Strauss and Beethoven but Swedish song, in which he
sounds even more at home. All but one of the items in the
song disc are Swedish domestic recordings, but they lead in
1937 to his first red-label recording of song, sung in Italian,
di Capura's *O sole mio.* The Nimbus process gives a vivid
idea of the voice with ample bloom on it, but the surfaces
are marked by a very noticeable but even swish, rather than
a hiss.

Bjoerling, Jussi, Enrico Caruso, Beniamino Gigli (tenors)

'Three Legendary Tenors in Opera and Song'

Caruso: Arias from: BIZET: *Carmen.* MASSENET: *Manon.*
VERDI: *Otello; La forza del destino; Aida.* GIORDANO:
Andrea Chénier. PUCCINI: *Tosca*

Gigli: Arias from: LEONCAVALLO: *I Pagliacci* (also song:
Mattinata). BIZET: *Les Pêcheurs de perles* (also duet: *Del
tempo al limitar,* with Giuseppe de Luca). VERDI: *La
Traviata.* PUCCINI: *Tosca.* Song: DI CAPUA: *O sole mio*

Bjoerling: Arias from VERDI: *Rigoletto.* PUCCINI: *La
Bohème; Turandot.* RIMSKY-KORSAKOV: *Sadko.*
MEYERBEER: *L'Africana.* MASSENET: *Manon.* Song: TOSTI:
Ideale
(M) (***) Nimbus mono NI 1434

Nimbus caught on to the idea of promoting a selection from
three legendary tenors from their archives and they decided
that a single disc (75 minutes) would be the best proposition.
Their system of playing-back 78rpm originals through a big
fibre horn and re-recording them works very well here with
the three voices naturally caught, but the orchestral backing is
more variable. The documentation is poor and no recording
dates are given, but the excerpts are obviously hand-picked
and recorded over a fairly wide time-span. Items which

obviously stand out are Caruso's *Un dì, all'azzurro spazio*
from *Andrea Chénier* and of course *Celeste Aida* (with a
remarkably believable brass fanfare); Gigli's honeyed *E
lucevan le stelle* from *Tosca* and his thrilling *O sole mio*; and
Bjoerling's *Che gelida manina* from *Bohème,* the seductive
Sadko 'Song of India' and his glorious *Nessun dorma.* The
collection ends splendidly with Caruso and De Luca matching their voices sensationally in the frisson-creating *Pearl
Fishers* duet.

Caruso, Enrico (tenor)

'Caruso in Opera', Volume I: Arias from: DONIZETTI:
L'Elisir d'amore; Don Sebastiano; Il duca d'Alba.
GOLDMARK: *La regina di Saba.* GOMEZ: *Lo schiavo.*
HALEVY: *La Juive.* LEONCAVALLO: *Pagliacci.* MASSENET:
Manon. MEYERBEER: *L'Africana.* PUCCINI: *Tosca; Manon
Lescaut.* VERDI: *Aida; Un ballo in maschera; La forza del
destino; Rigoletto; Il trovatore*
(M) (***) Nimbus mono NI 7803

The Nimbus method of transfer to CD, reproducing ancient
78s on a big acoustic horn gramophone of the 1930s, tends to
work best with acoustic recordings, when the accompaniments then emerge as more consistent with the voice. There
is an inevitable loss of part of the recording range at both
ends of the spectrum, but the ear can often be convinced.
This Caruso collection, very well-chosen to show the development of his voice, ranges from early (1904) recordings of
Massenet, Puccini and Donizetti with piano accompaniment
to the recording that the great tenor made in 1920, not long
before he died, of his very last role, as Eleazar in Halévy's *La
Juive,* wonderfully characterized.

Chaliapin, Feodor (bass)

Excerpts from: MUSSORGSKY: *Boris Godunov.* RUBINSTEIN:
The Demon. VERDI: *Don Carlos.* RIMSKY-KORSAKOV:
Sadko. BORODIN: *Prince Igor.* GOUNOD: *Faust.* MOZART:
Don Giovanni. GLINKA: *A Life for the Tsar; Ruslan and
Ludmilla.* PUCCINI: *La Bohème.* BOITO: *Mefistofele.*
MASSENET: *Don Quichotte.* RACHMANINOV: *Aleko.*
DARGOMYZHSKY: *Rusalka*
(M) (**(*)) Nimbus mono NI 7823/4 (2)

As recorded by the Nimbus process Chaliapin's unique bass
sounds sepulchral – partly due, no doubt, to the resonating
effect of the horn gramophone on which the 78s are played.
The EMI issues of many of the same items as here on his disc
of Russian arias (now deleted), including his recordings of
Boris, are much fuller and more immediate (as transferred by
Keith Hardwick). However, this two-disc collection includes
valuable items outside the Russian repertory, including Leporello's catalogue aria from *Don Giovanni* (taken very fast,
with detail only sketched though very characterful) and
Beethoven's song, *In questa tomba,* not helped by a heavy
surface-noise, but bringing a thrilling expansion. In every
item, one is aware that this is not just one of the great voices
of the twentieth century but also one of the most characterful
singers; compassing not just the darkness and tragedy of
Boris, but the sparkle and humour of such an item as Farlaf's
Rondo from Glinka's *Ruslan and Ludmilla* with its dauntingly
rapid patter.

Divas

'*Divas*', Volume 1: 1906–35: (Tetrazzini; Melba; Patti; Hempel; Galli-Curci; Ponselle; Lehmann; Turner; Koshetz; Norena; Nemeth; Muzio): Arias from: VERDI: *Un ballo in maschera; Rigoletto; Aida; Il trovatore.* THOMAS: *Mignon.* MOZART: *Die Zauberflöte.* ROSSINI: *Il barbiere di Siviglia.* MASSENET: *Manon.* PUCCINI: *Madama Butterfly.* BEETHOVEN: *Fidelio.* RIMSKY-KORSAKOV: *Sadko.* BORODIN: *Prince Igor.* GOUNOD: *Roméo et Juliette.* BOITO: *Mefistofele.* Songs: YRADIER: *La Calesera.* DENAUDY: *O del mio amato ben*
(M) (***) Nimbus mono NI 7802

The six supreme prima donnas on this compilation are all very well represented. The soprano voice benefits more than most from the Nimbus process, so that with extra bloom Tetrazzini's vocal 'gear-change' down to the chest register is no longer obtrusive. She is represented by three recordings of 1911, including Gilda's *Caro nome* from *Rigoletto*; and Galli-Curci has three items too, including Rosina's *Una voce poco fa* from *Il barbiere di Siviglia*. The tragically short-lived Claudia Muzio and the Russian Nina Koshetz have two each, while the others are each represented by a single, well-chosen item. They include Melba in *Mimi's farewell*, the 60-year-old Patti irresistibly vivacious in a Spanish folksong, *La calesera*, and Frida Hempel in what is probably the most dazzling of all recordings of the Queen of the Night's second aria from *Zauberflöte*.

'*Divas*' Volume 2, 1909–40: (Hempel, Galli-Curci, Farrar, Kurz, Garrison, Gluck, Ivogün, Onegin, Schoene, Norena, Ponselle, Leider, Vallin, Teyte, Koshetz, Flagstad, Favero): Arias from: BELLINI: *I Puritani.* MOZART: *Le nozze di Figaro; Die Entführung aus dem Serail.* PUCCINI: *Tosca.* VERDI: *Rigoletto; La forza del destino.* OFFENBACH: *Les contes d'Hoffmann; La Périchole.* GODARD: *Jocelyn.* BIZET: *Carmen.* JOHANN STRAUSS JR: *Die Fledermaus.* THOMAS: *Hamlet.* WAGNER: *Tristan und Isolde; Die Walküre.* MASSENET: *Werther.* PONCE: *Estrellita.* MASCAGNI: *Lodoletta*
(M) (***) Nimbus mono NI 7818

As in the first *Divas* volume, the choice of items will delight any lover of fine singing, a most discriminating choice. Maria Ivogün, the teacher of Schwarzkopf, contributes a wonderfully pure and incisive *Martern aller Arten* (*Entführung*) dating from 1923, and Lotte Schoene is unusually and characterfully represented by Adele's *Mein Herr Marquis* from *Fledermaus*. Frida Leider's *Liebestod* is nobly sung but is surprisingly fast by latterday standards. Maggie Teyte sings delectably in an aria from *La Périchole*; and though some of the pre-electric items in Nimbus's resonant transfers suggest an echo chamber, the voices are warm and full.

Farrar, Geraldine

Arias from: MOZART: *Le nozze di Figaro; Don Giovanni.* WOLF-FERRARI: *Le donne curiose; Il segreto di Susanna.* PUCCINI: *La Bohème* (with Caruso, Scotti and Viafora); *Tosca; Madama Butterfly* (with Josephine Jacoby, Caruso and Scotti)
(M) (***) Nimbus mono NI 7857

Geraldine Farrar, born in 1882, was in almost every way an ideal recording soprano. Though she retired from the stage

before the arrival of electrical recording, these acoustic recordings give a wonderful idea of the glorious voice. Almost three-dimensional in the way they convey the warmth and firmness combined with power, it is a delight to register the clarity of attack on even the most exposed notes. The Mozart and Wolf-Ferrari items provide a charming introduction to the range of Puccini recordings here, recorded between 1908 and 1912 when she was at the peak of her powers. Most valuable of all are the items from *Madama Butterfly*, with two duets for Caruso and Scotti interspersed with those of Farrar, making it clear why this was one of her two most celebrated roles, at once tenderly expressive, yet powerfully dramatic.

French opera: Arias from: MASSENET: *Manon; Thaïs.* THOMAS: *Mignon.* GOUNOD: *Roméo et Juliette* (with Clément). OFFENBACH: *Contes d'Hoffmann* (with Scotto). BIZET: *Carmen* (extended excerpts with Martinelli, Amato)
(M) (***) Nimbus mono NI 7872

This fine selection of Farrar's recordings of French opera concentrates on her most celebrated role as Carmen. Though nowadays it is almost always sung by a mezzo, Farrar demonstrates, by the dramatic intensity of her singing, with fine detail and flawless control, what benefits there are from having a full soprano in the role. The fourteen items from that opera include not only Carmen's principal solos and ensembles but Micaela's aria, and – setting the rest in context – the Toreador's song, José's 'Flower Song' and the 'Prelude to Act IV', in a rare acoustic recording conducted by Toscanini. The voice, bright, sweet and full, comes over vividly in these Nimbus transfers.

Flagstad, Kirsten (soprano)

Arias from: WAGNER: *Die Walküre; Tannhäuser; Lohengrin; Tristan und Isolde; Götterdämmerung.* WEBER: *Oberon.* BEETHOVEN: *Fidelio.* Concert aria: BEETHOVEN: *Ah! perfido!*
(M) (***) Nimbus mono NI 7847

The eleven items here are drawn from the recordings that Flagstad made between 1935 and 1939. Five of them, dating from 1937, are with Eugene Ormandy and the Philadelphia orchestra, including commanding accounts of the 'Abscheulicher' from Beethoven's *Fidelio* and his concert aria, *Ah! perfido!*. Four more items, including Isolde's *Liebestod* were recorded in 1935 with Hans Lange conducting, but the most substantial item is the fine, clean-cut account of Brünnhilde's Immolation scene from Wagner's *Götterdämmerung* with Edwin McArthur (her regular piano accompanist) and the San Francisco Orchestra. The Nimbus transfers superbly convey the bloom and heroic power of the unique voice in its prime, full and even throughout its range, but the orchestral accompaniments are unpleasantly thin.

Galli-Curci, Amelita

Arias from: AUBER: *Manon Lescaut.* BELLINI: *I puritani; La sonnambula.* DONIZETTI: *Don Pasquale; Linda di Chamounix; Lucia di Lammermoor.* GOUNOD: *Roméo et Juliette.* MEYERBEER: *Dinorah.* ROSSINI: *Il barbiere di Siviglia.* THOMAS: *Mignon.* VERDI: *Rigoletto; La traviata*
(M) (***) Nimbus mono NI 7806

'Like a nightingale half-asleep,' said Philip Hope-Wallace in a memorable description of Galli-Curci's voice, but this vivid

Nimbus transfer makes it much more like a nightingale very wide-awake. More than in most of these transfers made via an acoustic horn gramophone, the resonance of the horn itself can be detected, and the results are full and forward. Galli-Curci's perfection in these pre-electric recordings, made between 1917 and 1924, is a thing of wonder, almost too accurate for comfort; but tenderness is there too, as in the Act II duet from *La traviata* (with Giuseppe de Luca) and the *Addio del passato*, complete with introductory recitative, but with only a single stanza. Yet brilliant coloratura is what lies at the root of Galli-Curci's magic, and that comes in abundance.

Volume 2: Arias from: DELIBES: *Lakmé.* DONIZETTI: *Lucia di Lammermoor.* VERDI: *Rigoletto; Il trovatore; La traviata.* DAVID: *La Perle du Brésil.* BIZET: *Les Pêcheurs de perles.* RIMSKY-KORSAKOV: *Le Coq d'or; Sadko.* GOUNOD: *Philémon et Baucis.* THOMAS: *Hamlet.* PROCH: *Air & Variations*
(M) (✶✶✶) Nimbus mono NI 7852

This second Galli-Curci selection from Nimbus offers recordings from the pre-electric era between 1917 and 1924, as well as six electrical recordings from 1925–30, four of them in ensembles, the celebrated ones of the Lucia Sextet and Rigoletto quartet with Gigli, as well as the magical *Traviata* duets with Tito Schipa. The reproduction of the voice in both pre-electric and electric recordings is astonishingly vivid. The Nimbus 'Prima Voce' transfers give the voice more bloom, recorded from 78rpm discs in a helpful acoustic, but the surface-hiss has a swishy quality, easily forgotten, which not everyone will like.

Gigli, Beniamino (tenor)

Volume 1, 1918–24: Arias from: BOITO: *Mefistofele.* CATALANI: *Loreley.* DONIZETTI: *La favorita.* FLOTOW: *Martha.* GIORDANO: *Andrea Chénier.* GOUNOD: *Faust.* LALO: *Le Roi d'Ys.* LEONCAVALLO: *Pagliacci.* MASCAGNI: *Iris.* MEYERBEER: *L'Africana.* PONCHIELLI: *La Gioconda.* PUCCINI: *Tosca.* Songs
(M) (✶✶✶) Nimbus mono NI 7807

Gigli's career went on so long, right through the electrical 78rpm era, that his pre-electric recordings have tended to get forgotten. This collection of twenty-two items recorded between 1918 and 1924 shows the voice at its most honeyed, even lighter and more lyrical than it became later, with the singer indulging in fewer of the mannerisms that came to decorate his ever-mellifluous singing. In aria after aria he spins a flawless legato line. Few tenor voices have ever matched Gigli's in its rounded, golden beauty, and the Nimbus transfers capture its bloom in a way that makes one forget pre-electric limitations. In the one item sung in French, by Lalo, he sounds less at home, a little too heavy; but the ease of manner in even the most taxing arias elsewhere is remarkable, and such a number as the *Serenade* from Mascagni's *Iris* is irresistible in its sparkle, as are the Neapolitan songs, notably the galloping *Povero Pulcinella* by Buzzi-Peccia. One oddity is a tenor arrangement of Saint-Saëns's *The Swan*.

Volume 2, 1925–40: Arias from: DONIZETTI: *L'elisir d'amore; Lucia di Lammermoor.* PUCCINI: *Manon Lescaut; La Bohème; Tosca.* VERDI: *La forza del destino; La traviata; Rigoletto.* THOMAS: *Mignon.* BIZET: *I pescatori di perle.*

PONCHIELLI: *La Gioconda.* MASSENET: *Manon.* GOUNOD: *Faust.* RIMSKY-KORSAKOV: *Sadko.* GLUCK: *Paride ed Elena.* CILEA: *L'Arlesiana.* Song: CACCINI: *Amarilli*
(M) (✶✶✶) Nimbus mono NI 7817

Issued to celebrate the Gigli centenary in 1990, the Nimbus selection concentrates on recordings he made in the very early years of electrical recording up to 1931, when his voice was at its very peak, the most golden instrument, ideally suited to recording. The items are very well chosen and are by no means the obvious choices, though it is good to have such favourites as the *Pearl Fishers* duet with de Luca and the 1931 version of Rodolfo's *Che gelida manina.* The Nimbus transfers are at their best, with relatively little reverberation.

Great Singers

'*Great Singers*', 1909–38: (Tetrazzini; Caruso; Schumann-Heink; McCormack; Galli-Curci; Stracciari; Ponselle; Lauri-Volpi; Turner; Tibbett; Supervia; Gigli; Anderson; Schipa; Muzio; Tauber): Arias from: BELLINI: *La sonnambula; I Puritani; Norma.* LEONCAVALLO: *Pagliacci.* DONIZETTI: *Lucrezia Borgia.* MOZART: *Don Giovanni; Die Zauberflöte.* ROSSINI: *Il barbiere di Siviglia.* PUCCINI: *Turandot.* VERDI: *Un ballo in maschera.* BIZET: *Carmen.* PUCCINI: *La Bohème.* SAINT-SAENS: *Samson et Dalila.* MASCAGNI: *L'amico Fritz.* Song: REFICE: *Ombra di Nube*
(M) (✶✶✶) Nimbus mono NI 7801

The Tetrazzini item with which the selection opens – *Ah non giunge* from Bellini's *La Sonnambula* – is one of the supreme demonstrations of coloratura on record; the programme goes on to a magnificent Caruso of 1910 and an unforgettable performance of the coloratura drinking-song from Donizetti's *Lucrezia Borgia* by the most formidable of contraltos, Ernestine Schumann-Heink. Then follows John McCormack's famous account of *Il mio tesoro* from Mozart's *Don Giovanni*, with the central passage-work amazingly done in a single breath. Other vintage items include Galli-Curci's dazzling account of *Son vergin vezzosa* from Bellini's *I Puritani*, Eva Turner in her incomparable 1928 account of Turandot's aria, Gigli amiably golden-toned in *Che gelida manina* from *La Bohème*, and a delectable performance of the Cherry duet from Mascagni's *L'amico Fritz* by Tito Schipa and Mafalda Favero – riches indeed!

'*Great Singers*' Vol. 2, 1903–39: (Tamagno; Clavé; Plançon; Farrar; Ruffo; Gluck; De Luca; Garden; Martinelli; Onegin; Pinza; Ivogu'n; Chaliapine; Rethberg; Melchior; Flagstad; Bjoerling; Favero): Arias from: VERDI: *Otello; Ernani.* FLOTOW: *Marta.* PUCCINI: *Madama Butterfly; Manon Lescaut.* MEYERBEER: *L'Africana; Les Huguenots.* HANDEL: *Atalanta.* BELLINI: *I Puritani.* ALFANO: *Resurrection.* R. STRAUSS: *Ariadne aux Naxos.* JOHANN STRAUSS JR: *Die Fledermaus.* WAGNER: *Rienzi; Lohengrin.* Songs by: MARIO; MASSENET; BEETHOVEN; TRAD.
(M) (✶✶✶) Nimbus mono NI 7812

This was the first of Nimbus's series of archive recordings, taking a radical new view of the problem of transferring ancient 78rpm vocal recordings to CD. The best possible copies of shellac originals have been played on an acoustic machine with an enormous horn, one of the hand-made Rolls-Royces among non-electric gramophones of the 1930s, with thorn needles reducing still further the need to filter the sound electronically. The results have been recorded in a small hall, and the sound reproduced removes any feeling of boxy closeness. Those who have resisted the bottled or tinny sound of many historic recordings will find the Nimbus transfers more friendly and sympathetic, even if technically there is an inevitable loss of recorded information at both ends of the spectrum because of the absolute limitations of the possible frequency range on this kind of reproducer.

Whether in Donizetti or Meyerbeer or, indeed, in the Strauss waltzes (*Frühlingsstimmen, G'schichten aus dem Wiener Wald* and the *Blue Danube*), this is singing to give great refreshment. The recordings were for the most part made between 1917 and 1925, and these respond especially well to the Nimbus transferring system, but the folksongs were electrical, and were her very last records, made in 1932.

Hempel, Frieda (soprano)

Arias from: VERDI: *Rigoletto; La traviata; Ernani; Un ballo in maschera.* DONIZETTI: *Lucia di Lammermoor.* ROSSINI: *Il barbiere di Siviglia.* MOZART: *Le nozze di Figaro; Die Zauberflöte.* MEYERBEER: *Les Huguenots; Robert le Diable.* GOUNOD: *Mireille.* OFFENBACH: *Les Contes d'Hoffmann.* LORTZING: *Der Wildschütz.* Song: MANGOLD: *Zweigesang.* JOHANN STRAUSS JR: *Waltz: Wein, Weib und Gesang*
● (M) (***) Nimbus mono NI 7849

This is one of the very finest of all the Nimbus 'Prima Voce' series. The 78rpm sources are immaculate, background noise is steady and no problem. The recordings are nearly all early, mostly made between 1910 and 1913, the rest in the following four years, except for the final song which was much later (1935). It is an extraordinary voice, with an almost unbelievably free upper tessitura. The divisions in the Adam *Variations* (on 'Twinkle, Twinkle Little Star') make you want to laugh, they are so outrageous, taking off into the vocal stratosphere like a series of shooting stars. *Caro nome*, too, which opens the programme arrestingly, is wonderfully free and open, and the final cadence is taken up. Even more than the Lucia Mad scene, Rossini's *Una voce poco fa*, with its added decorations, shows how a soprano voice can sparkle when the intonation is spot-on. Both are sung in German.

Frieda Hempel's Mozart is less stylish; the famous *Der Hölle Rache* almost runs away before the end. But the ravishing vocal line in *Ah fors' è lui*, with a deliberate tenuto on the cadence, is followed by a wonderfully frivolous cabaletta. The recording quality is astonishingly consistent and the vocal richness comes across with uncanny realism, while the decorations in Strauss's *Wine, Women and Song* make one's hair stand on end. Not to be missed!

Ivogün, Maria (soprano)

Arias from: HANDEL: *L'allegro, il penseroso ed il moderato.* DONIZETTI: *Don Pasquale; Lucia di Lammermoor.* ROSSINI: *Il barbiere di Siviglia.* VERDI: *La traviata.* MEYERBEER: *Les Huguenots.* NICOLAI: *Die lustigen Weiber von Windsor.* JOHANN STRAUSS JR: *Die Fledermaus;* also Waltzes: *An der schönen blauen Donau, Geschichten aus dem Wienerwald* and *Frühlingsstimmen.* Songs: SCHUBERT: *Horch, horch, die Lerche; Winterreise: Die Post;* KREISLER: *Liebesfreud;* CHOPIN: *Nocturne in E flat, Op. 9/2.* 2 Folksongs, arr. GUND: *O du liabs ängeli; Z'Lauterbach hab' i'mein Strumpf velor'n*
(M) (***) Nimbus mono NI 7832

Maria Ivogün is a less familiar name today than in the 1920s when she took Covent Garden by storm. Hers was a small voice but enchantingly focused; in that, she has much in common with a more familiar recent name, Rita Streich. Ivogün sang with both charm and sparkle, and the present Nimbus transfers show just what a delightful artist she was.

Luca, Giuseppe de (baritone)

Arias from: VERDI: *Don Carlos, Ernani, Il trovatore, La traviata, Rigoletto.* ROSSINI: *Il barbiere di Siviglia.* DONIZETTI: *L'elisir d'amore.* BELLINI: *I Puritani.* DIAZ: *Benvenuto Cellini.* PUCCINI: *La Bohème.* PONCHIELLI: *La Gioconda.* WOLF-FERRARI: *I gioielli della madonna.* Songs: DE LEVA: *Pastorale.* ROMILLI: *Marietta*
(M) (***) Nimbus mono NI 7815

There has never been a more involving account on record of the Act IV Marcello–Rodolfo duet than the one here with de Luca and Gigli, a model of characterization and vocal art. The baritone's mastery emerges vividly in item after item, whether in the power and wit of his pre-electric version of *Largo al factotum* (1917) or the five superb items (including the *Bohème* duet and the *Rigoletto* numbers, flawlessly controlled), which were recorded in the vintage year of 1927. Warm Nimbus transfers.

Martinelli, Giovanni (tenor)

Volume 1, Arias from: GIORDANO: *Andrea Chénier; Fedora.* LEONCAVALLO: *Pagliacci.* MASCAGNI: *Cavalleria Rusticana; Iris.* TCHAIKOVSKY: *Eugene Onegin.* VERDI: *Aida; Ernani; La forza del destino; La traviata*
(M) (***) Nimbus mono NI 7804

This collection of seventeen fine examples of Martinelli's very distinctive and characterful singing covers his vintage period from 1915 to 1928, with one 1927 recording from Verdi's *La forza del destino* so clear that you can hear a dog barking outside the studio. The other two items from *Forza* are just as memorable, with Martinelli joined by Giuseppe de Luca in the Act IV duet, and by Rosa Ponselle and the bass, Ezio Pinza, for the final duet, with the voices astonishingly vivid and immediate.

Volume 2, Arias from: PUCCINI: *La Bohème; Tosca; Madama Butterfly* (with Frances Alda). PONCHIELLI: *La Gioconda.* VERDI: *Aida; Un ballo in maschera; Rigoletto; Don Carlos; Il trovatore.* LEONCAVALLO: *Pagliacci.* MEYERBEER: *L'Africana.* BIZET: *Carmen.* ROSSINI: *Guillaume Tell.* MASSENET: *Werther*
(M) (***) Nimbus mono NI 7826

Martinelli's second collection is hardly less distinctive than the first, and admirers of this great tenor should not be disappointed with the transfers, which are well up to the convincingly natural standard now being achieved by the Nimbus process.

McCormack, John (tenor)

Arias and excerpts from: DONIZETTI: *Lucia di Lammermoor; L'elisir d'amore; La figlia del reggimento.* VERDI: *La traviata; Rigoletto.* PUCCINI: *La Bohème.* BIZET:

Carmen; I pescatore di perle. DELIBES: *Lakmé.* GOUNOD: *Faust.* PONCHIELLI: *La Gioconda.* BOITO: *Mefistofele.* MASSENET: *Manon.* MOZART: *Don Giovanni.* WAGNER: *Die Meistersinger.* HERBERT: *Natomah.* HANDEL: *Semele; Atalanta*

(M) (***) Nimbus mono NI 7820

With the operas represented ranging from Handel's *Atalanta* and *Semele* to *Natomah*, by Victor Herbert, the heady beauty of McCormack's voice, his ease of production and perfect control are amply illustrated in these twenty-one items. His now legendary 1916 account of *Il mio tesoro* from *Don Giovanni*, with its astonishing breath control, is an essential item; but there are many others less celebrated, which help to explain his special niche, even in a generation that included Caruso and Schipa. Characteristic Nimbus transfers.

McCormack, John and Fritz Kreisler

(violin)

'*McCormack and Kreisler in Recital*': Arias from: GODARD: *Jocelyn.* BENEDICT: *Lily of Killarney.* Songs: RACHMANINOV: *O, Cease thy Singing, Maiden Fair; When Night Descends.* R. STRAUSS: *Morgen.* TOSTI: *Goodbye.* KREISLER: *Liebesfreud; Caprice viennoise* and *Cradle Song* arr. from *Caprice viennoise.* SCHUBERT: *Rosamunde: Ballet music 2.* BRAHMS: *Hungarian Dance 5.* BRAGA: *Angel's serenade.* Songs by: COTTENET; PARKYNS; LEROUX; BALOGH; MOSZKOWSKI; LARCHET; TRAD.

(M) (***) Nimbus mono NI 7868

This is a delightful disc of two great artists enjoying themselves in undemanding repertory. On one occasion, when McCormack and Kreisler were both recording in the Victor studios in Camden, New Jersey, the tenor asked the violinist's advice on the tempo for a Rachmaninov song. Whereupon Kreisler provided an impromptu obbligato which McCormack sang. Happily the engineer had switched on his machine, and this recording is included here. Roughly half the items are of McCormack and Kreisler together. Others include McCormack's solo recordings of Kreisler pieces, including a cradle song arranged from *Caprice viennois*. There are also solo recordings of Kreisler playing favourite pieces of his, including arrangements. Recordings, all acoustic, date from between 1914 and 1924 when both artists were at their peak.

Melba, Nellie (soprano)

Arias from: MOZART: *Le nozze di Figaro.* HANDEL: *L'allegro, il pensero ed il moderato.* CHARPENTIER: *Louise.* MASSENET: *Don César de Bazan.* GOUNOD: *Faust.* THOMAS: *Hamlet.* LOTTI: *Armino.* VERDI: *Otello.* PUCCINI: *La Bohème; Tosca.* Songs: BISHOP: *Lo, Here the Gentle Lark.* BEMBERG: *Sur le lac.* DEBUSSY: *Romance; Mandoline.* CHAUSSON: *Poème de l'amour et de la mer: Le Temps des Lilas.* HAHN: *D'une prison.* TRAD.: *Swing Low, Sweet Chariot*

(M) (***) Nimbus mono NI 7890

Though Melba among golden age sopranos is the one who even today is most regularly bracketed with Caruso as a legendary singer, her discs can seem disappointing, with a hardness regularly developing in the bright, clear voice. It says much for the Nimbus transfer process that this varied selection of songs as well as arias conveys a fullness, even a

sweetness, alongside consistent purity and precision, with the voice less edgy than in most transfers. It is thrilling to hear her riding easily over the voices of McCormack and Sammarco in the final trio from Faust, and in some ways most revealing of all is a brief collection of distance tests, recorded in 1910, with Melba repeating a couple of phrases from Ophelia's aria in Thomas's *Hamlet* at different distances. As John Steane's illuminating note points out, one can then appreciate the star-like splendour of the voice. It is also good to have Melba's very last recording, made in 1928 at the age of 65, of the spiritual *Swing Low, Sweet Chariot*, with amazingly full tone.

Melchior, Lauritz (tenor)

Arias from: WAGNER: *Siegfried; Tannhäuser; Tristan und Isolde; Die Walküre; Die Meistersinger; Götterdämmerung.* LEONCAVALLO: *Pagliacci.* MEYERBEER: *L'Africana.* VERDI: *Otello*

(M) (***) Nimbus mono NI 7816

The Nimbus disc of Melchior, issued to celebrate his centenary in 1990, demonstrates above all the total consistency of the voice between the pre-electric recordings of *Siegfried* and *Tannhäuser*, made for Polydor in 1924, and the *Meistersinger* and *Götterdämmerung* extracts, recorded in 1939. Of those, the Siegfried–Brünnhilde duet from the *Prologue* of *Götterdämmerung* is particularly valuable. It is fascinating too to hear the four recordings that Melchior made with Barbirolli and the LSO in 1930–31: arias by Verdi, Leoncavallo and Meyerbeer translated into German. As a character, Otello is made to sound far more prickly. Characteristic Nimbus transfers.

Muzio, Claudia (soprano)

Arias from: MASCAGNI: *Cavalleria rusticana.* VERDI: *La forza del destino; Otello; Il trovatore; La traviata.* PUCCINI: *Tosca; La Bohème.* GIORDANO: *Andrea Chénier.* BOITO: *Mefistofele.* CILEA: *Adriana Lecouvreur; L'Arlesiana.* BELLINI: *La sonnambula.* Songs by BUZZI-PECCIA; PERGOLESI; REGER; DELIBES; REFICE

(M) (***) Nimbus mono NI 7814

This Nimbus collection of recordings by the sadly short-lived Claudia Muzio duplicates much that is contained on the deleted EMI Références CD of her. The main addition here is the Act III duet from *Otello* with Francesco Merli, but some cherishable items are omitted. The Nimbus acoustic transfer process sets the voice more distantly as well as more reverberantly than the EMI, with its distinctive tang less-sharply conveyed.

Patti, Adelina (soprano), and other singers

'*The Era of Adelina Patti*' ((i) Adelina Patti; (ii) Victor Maurel; (iii) Pol Plançon; (iv) Mattia Battistini; (v) Mario Ancona; (vi) Lucien Fugère; (vii) Francisco Vignas; (viii) Emma Calvé; (ix) Maurice Renaud; (x) Fernando de Lucia; (xi) Francesco Tamagno; (xii) Nellie Melba; (xiii) Félia Litvinne; (xiv) Wilhelm Hesch; (xv) Lillian Nordica; (xvi) Mario Ancona; (xvii) Edouard de Reszke; (xviii) Marcella Sembrich; (xix) Francesco Marconi; (xx) Mattia Battistini; (xxi) Lilli Lehmann; (xxii) Sir Charles Santley): Arias from:

VERDI: (ii) *Falstaff;* (i, iii) *Don Carlos;* (iv, xx) *Ernani;* (v, xiv) *Otello.* ADAM: (iii) *Le Chalet.* GLUCK: (vi) *Les Pèlerins de la Mecque.* MOZART: (i, ii, xx) *Don Giovanni;* (i, vii, xxi) *Le nozze di Figaro.* MEYERBEER: (vii) *Le Prophète.* BIZET: (viii) *Carmen.* MASSENET: (ix, xi) *Hérodiade;* (x) *Manon.* THOMAS: (xii) *Hamlet.* WAGNER: (xiii) *Lohengrin;* (xiv) *Die Meistersinger von Nürnberg.* ERKEL: (xv) *Hunyadi László.* DONIZETTI: (xvi) *La favorita;* (xix) *Lucrezia Borgia;* (xii) *Lucia.* BELLINI: (i) *La sonnambula;* (xviii) *I Puritani.* FLOTOW: (xvii) *Martha.* ROSSINI: (x) *Il barbiere di Siviglia.* GOMES: (xx) *Il Guarany.* Songs by TOSTI; (vi) RAMEAU: (i, vi) YRADIER; (i) HOOK; (i) BISHOP; (ix) GOUNOD; (xv) R. STRAUSS; (xxii) HATTON
(M) (***) Nimbus mono NI 7840/41 (2)

The very first item on this wide-ranging collection of historic recordings has one sitting up at once. The voice ringing out from the loudspeakers prompts cheering from the singer's little audience. The clear-toned baritone is singing *Quand'ero paggio* from Verdi's *Falstaff* and, encouraged, he repeats it. Then, more cheering and a third performance, this time in French, to cap the occasion. The singer is Victor Maurel, the baritone whom Verdi chose as his first Falstaff in 1893 and, before that, his first Iago in *Otello.* The recording dates from 1907, and many lovers of historic vocal issues will remember it well. Yet hearing it on the Nimbus transfer to CD brings a sense of presence as never before.

That company's controversial technique of playing an ancient 78rpm disc with a thorn needle on the best possible acoustic horn gramophone is at its most effective here, with exceptionally vivid results on these acoustic recordings. They not only convey astonishing presence but also a sense of how beautiful the voices were, getting behind the tinny and squawky sounds often heard on old 78s. This is an ideal set for anyone not already committed to historic vocals who simply wants to investigate how great singing could be ninety years ago, providing such an unexpected mix of well-known items and rarities, to delight specialists and newcomers alike.

The first of the two discs offers recordings that Nimbus regards as technically the finest of their day, including Patti in 1906, not just singing but shouting enthusiastically in a Spanish folksong, *La Calesera*, 'Vivan los españoles!' Recorded much later in 1928 comes the French baritone, Lucien Fugère, eighty at the time but singing with a firm focus that you might not find today in a baritone in his twenties.

The second of the two discs has just as fascinating a mixture, but the recordings 'have not survived the decades so well'. Even so, it is thrilling to hear Sir Charles Santley, born in 1834, the year after Brahms, singing 'Simon the Cellarer' with tremendous flair at the age of seventy-nine, and the coloratura Marcella Sembrich sounding even sweeter in Bellini than on previous transfers.

Pinza, Ezio (bass)

Arias duets and scenes from: VERDI: *Il trovatore; I vespri siciliani; Don Carlos; Aida* (with Grace Anthony and Giovanni Martinelli); *Attila.* DONIZETTI: *Lucia di Lammermoor.* HALEVY: *La Juive.* BELLINI: *I Puritani; Norma.* GOUNOD: *Faust* (with Aristodemo Giorgini). PUCCINI: *La Bohème.* MOZART: *Die Zauberflöte; Don Giovanni.* MEYERBEER: *Robert le Diable.* THOMAS: *Mignon; Le Caïc*
(M) (***) Nimbus mono NI 7875

This very well-chosen selection of Pinza recordings concentrates on those he made early in his career, starting in 1933 when, at the age of 31, he demonstrates the already extraordinary richness and clarity of focus which made him pre-eminent among operatic basses of the inter-war period. Fine as his later recordings are, notably those with Toscanini, or even his characteristic contribution to the musical *South Pacific*, these early discs have an extra freshness. The subtlety with which Pinza shades his phrases using rich, firm tone and flawless legato is a constant delight. Philip II's aria from Verdi's *Don Carlos* has rarely been so nobly sung as here, and it is a mark of Pinza's sense of style that he is comparably commanding in the Mozart, Bellini and Donizetti arias. As well as the six acoustically recorded items, you have fourteen electrical recordings made between 1927 and 1930, all presenting the voice vividly in warm Nimbus transfers.

Ponselle, Rosa (soprano)

Arias from: BELLINI: *Norma.* PONCHIELLI: *La Gioconda.* SPONTINI: *La vestale.* VERDI: *Aida; Ernani; La forza del destino; Otello.* Songs by: ARENSKY; RIMSKY-KORSAKOV; DE CURTIS; DI CAPUA, JACOBS-BOND
(M) (***) Nimbus mono NI 7805

One of the most exciting American sopranos ever, Rosa Ponselle tantalizingly cut short her career when she was still at her peak. Only the Arensky and Rimsky songs represent her after her official retirement, and the rest make a superb collection, including her classic accounts of *Casta diva* from Bellini's *Norma* and the duet, *Mira o Norma*, with Marion Telva. The six Verdi items include her earlier version of *Ernani involami*, not quite so commanding as her classic 1928 recording, but fascinating for its rarity. Equally cherishable is her duet from *La forza del destino* with Ezio Pinza.

Volume 2: Arias from: PUCCINI: *Madama Butterfly; Tosca; Manon Lescaut.* VERDI: *Il trovatore; Aida.* MASCAGNI: *Cavalleria rusticana.* HERBERT: *Mademoiselle Modiste.* RIMSKY-KORSAKOV: *Sadko.* HALEVY: *La Juive.* Songs by: TOSTI; MASSENET; BACH/GOUNOD; CHARLES
(M) (***) Nimbus mono NI 7846

This second volume of Nimbus's Ponselle collection is mainly devoted to her early acoustic recordings, made for Columbia between 1918 and 1924 when she was still in her early twenties. Hers is a flawless voice, which takes very well to the Nimbus process, when just as in her later electrical recordings the pure creamy quality comes over vividly with ample bloom, set in a lively acoustic. With not a hint of strain she subtly shades her tone in such an aria as Tosca's *Vissi d'arte*, underlining the emotion. The poise and flawless legato of Leonora's *La vergine degli angeli* from *Forza del destino*, the earliest recording here, explains why from the start this taxing role was one for which she was specially renowned; at the other extreme she gives a sparkling account of the Victor Herbert number 'Kiss me Again'. The electrical recordings then include her early recordings of Aida, notably the whole of the death scene with Martinelli, a classic recording. The discs ends with a touchingly apt song, recorded in 1939 after her retirement at the age of forty, 'When I have sung my songs to you, I'll sing no more'.

Volume 3: Arias from: VERDI: *Aida; Ernani; Il trovatore; La forza del destino.* ROSSINI: *William Tell.* MEYERBEER: *L'Africana.* PUCCINI: *La Bohème.* LEONCAVALLO: *Pagliacci.* Songs: DI CAPUA: *Maria, Mari!.* TOSTI: *Serenade; 'A Vucchella; Luna d'estate; Si tu le voulais;* and by: BLAND; FOSTER
(M) (***) Nimbus mono NI 7878

In this third Ponselle volume from Nimbus, the only electrical recordings are of ballads by Tosti, Stephen Foster and James Bland, which Ponselle magically transforms, giving distinction to trivial material. The acoustic recordings of arias include Aida's *Ritorna vincitor*, sung even more commandingly in 1923 than in her electrical recording of 1928 in Volume 2. The poise and flawless control in each are as remarkable as in the two earlier discs, and the nine operatic items plus two ballads include four recorded for Victor in 1923–5 but never released.

Rethberg, Elisabeth (soprano)

Arias from: VERDI: *Aida; Otello; Un ballo in maschera.* GIORDANO: *Andrea Chénier.* PUCCINI: *La Bohème; Madama Butterfly.* WAGNER: *Tannhäuser; Lohengrin.* MOZART: *Le nozze di Figaro; Die Zauberflöte.* JOHANN STRAUSS JR: *Der Zigeunerbaron.* BIZET: *Carmen*
(M) (***) Nimbus mono 7903

Elisabeth Rethberg, counted by Toscanini as his favourite soprano, was once voted 'the most perfect singer in the world'. This excellent selection of her recordings, drawn from the years 1924–30, helps to explain why. Consistently she was flawless in controlling her full, firm, finely projected voice both in phrase and dynamic over the widest expressive range. No recording of Aida's *O patria mia* can quite match the subtlety of this pre-electric version, recorded for Brunswick in 1924 – one of the few where the culminating top C is sung *dolce*, as marked. Her characterizations of each role may not be the most individual, but few singers have matched her in these arias, whether in Verdi, Puccini, Mozart or the Wagner of *Tannhäuser* and *Lohengrin*. The Nimbus transfers give a vivid idea of the voice, if not of the instrumental accompaniment, with six pre-electric items, twelve electrically recorded.

Royal Opera House, Covent Garden

Royal Opera House Covent Garden: (An Early History on Record)'. Singers included are: Melba, Caruso, Tetrazzini, McCormack, Destin, Gadski, Schorr, Turner, Zanelli, Lehmann, Schumann, Olczewska, Chaliapin, Gigli, Supervia, Tibbett, Tauber, Flagstad, Melchior. Arias from: GOUNOD: *Faust.* VERDI: *Rigoletto; Otello.* DONIZETTI: *Lucia di Lammermoor.* VERDI: *La traviata.* PUCCINI: *Madama Butterfly; Tosca.* WAGNER: *Götterdämmerung; Die Meistersinger; Tristan und Isolde.* R. STRAUSS: *Der Rosenkavalier.* MUSSORGSKY: *Boris Godunov.* GIORDANO: *Andrea Chénier.* BIZET: *Carmen.* MOZART: *Don Giovanni*
(M) (***) Nimbus mono NI 7819

Nimbus's survey of great singers at Covent Garden ranges from Caruso's 1904 recording of *Questa o quella* from *Rigoletto* to the recording of the second half of the *Tristan* love duet, which Kirsten Flagstad and Lauritz Melchior made in San Francisco in November 1939, a magnificent recording, never issued in Britain and little known, which repeated the partnership initiated during the 1937 Coronation season at Covent Garden. The Vienna recording of the *Rosenkavalier* Trio with Lehmann, Schumann and Olczewska similarly reproduces a classic partnership at Covent Garden, while Chaliapin's 1928 recording of the *Prayer* and *Death of Boris* was actually recorded live at Covent Garden, with the transfer giving an amazingly vivid sense of presence. Those who like Nimbus's acoustic method of transfer will enjoy the whole disc, though the reverberation round some of the early offerings – like the very first, Melba's Jewel Song from *Faust* – is cavernous. Particularly interesting is the 1909 recording of part of Brünnhilde's Immolation scene, with Johanna Gadski commandingly strong.

Schipa, Tito (tenor)

Arias from: MASCAGNI: *Cavalleria rusticana; L'amico Fritz.* VERDI: *Rigoletto; Luisa Miller.* DONIZETTI: *Lucia di Lammermoor; Don Pasquale; L'elisir d'amore.* LEONCAVALLO: *Pagliacci.* MASSENET: *Manon; Werther.* ROSSINI: *Il barbiere di Siviglia.* THOMAS: *Mignon.* FLOTOW: *Martha.* CILEA: *L'Arlesiana.*
(M) (***) Nimbus mono NI 7813

The first nine items on this well-chosen selection of Schipa's recordings date from the pre-electric era. The voice is totally consistent, heady and light and perfectly controlled, between the *Siciliana* from Mascagni's *Cavalleria*, recorded with piano in 1913, to the incomparable account of more Mascagni, the Cherry Duet from *L'amico Fritz*, made with Mafalda Favero in 1937. It says much for his art that Schipa's career continued at full strength for decades after that. The Nimbus transfers put the voice at a slight distance, with the electrical recordings made to sound the more natural.

Schumann-Heink, Ernestine (contralto)

Arias from: DONIZETTI: *Lucrezia Borgia.* MEYERBEER: *Le Prophète.* WAGNER: *Das Rheingold; Rienzi; Götterdämmerung.* HANDEL: *Rinaldo.* Songs by: ARDITTI; BECKER; SCHUBERT; WAGNER; REIMANN; MOLLOY; BRAHMS; BOEHM; TRAD.
(M) (***) Nimbus mono NI 7811

Ernestine Schumann-Heink was a formidable personality in the musical life of her time, notably in New York, as well as a great singer. 'I am looking for my successor,' she is reported as saying well-before she retired, adding, 'She must be the contralto.' Schumann-Heink combines to an astonishing degree a full contralto weight and richness with the most delicate flexibility, as in the *Brindisi* from Donizetti's *Lucrezia Borgia*. This wide-ranging collection, resonantly transferred by the Nimbus acoustic method, presents a vivid portrait of a very great singer.

Sembrich, Marcella (soprano)

Arias from: DONIZETTI: *Don Pasquale; Lucia di Lammermoor.* MUNIUSZKO: *Halka.* ROSSINI: *Semiramide; Il barbiere di Siviglia.* VERDI: *La traviata; Ernani; Rigoletto.* BELLINI: *Norma.* THOMAS: *Hamlet.* VERDI: *I vespri siciliani.* FLOTOW: *Martha.* BELLINI: *La sonnambula.* Songs: JOHANN STRAUSS JR; ARNE; ARDITI; BISHOP; HAHN; SCHUBERT; CHOPIN; TRAD.
(M) (***) Nimbus mono NI 7901

Now that the four discs of the complete Romophone edition of Sembrich are deleted, this Nimbus issue is very welcome. Her reputation as the supreme coloratura of her day may be undermined, but the choice of twenty-one items is first-rate, with only three recordings from before 1907. The Nimbus transfer method, with 78rpm discs played in front of a modern stereo recording machine, presents the voice in a flattering three-dimensional setting, but with focus less sharp than on Romophone.

Supervia, Conchita (mezzo-soprano)

'In Opera and Song': BIZET: Carmen: excerpts (with Micheletti, Vavon, Bernadet). Arias from: ROSSINI: L'Italiana in Algeri; Il barbiere di Siviglia; La Cenerentola. GOUNOD: Faust. THOMAS: Mignon. SAINT-SAENS: Samson et Dalila. SERRANO: La Alegría del Batallón; El mal de amores. Songs: FALLA: 7 Canciones populares españolas. BALDOMIR: Meus amores. YRADIER: La paloma. VALVERDE: Clavelitos
(M) (***) Nimbus mono NI 7836/7 (2)

Readers who remember the 78s of Conchita Supervia, especially in Rossini – and in particular her dark, brittle mezzo with its wide vibrato ('like the rattle of shaken dice', as one critic described it) sparkling in the divisions of Una voce poco fa – may be astonished to discover the degree of vocal charm in other roles. Her reputation for dazzling the ear in Rossini was surely deserved (and she helped to restore La Cenerentola and L'Italiana in Algeri to the repertoire). Her Carmen, too, is unforgettable, as is her Delilah – but, more unexpectedly, her Mignon is also a highlight here, as is the brief Delibes item. As usual, the Nimbus transfers are kind to the voice (there is no suggestion of the 'death rattle' of one unkind description) and almost certainly more truthful than the edgier, brighter quality we have had from some other sources. The recordings date from between 1927 and 1935.

Tauber, Richard (tenor)

Arias from: R. STRAUSS: Der Rosenkavalier. WAGNER: Die Walküre; Die Meistersinger. KIENZL: Der Evangelimann. PUCCINI: Tosca; La Bohème; Madama Butterfly; Turandot. VERDI: Il trovatore. MOZART: Don Giovanni; Die Zauberflöte. TCHAIKOVSKY: Eugene Onegin. BIZET: Carmen. KORNGOLD: Die tote Stadt. LORTZING: Undine. OFFENBACH: Les Contes d'Hoffmann
(M) (***) Nimbus mono NI 7830

The Nimbus transfers for both this and the operetta excerpts (see below) come from between 1919 and 1929, and, although there is some duplication of repertoire, Tauber admirers will probably want both CDs. The effect of Nimbus transfers is always most impressive in the pre-electric recordings, which predominate here, but the voice is always naturally focused, even in the 1929 excerpt from Offenbach's Tales of Hoffmann. The effect is mellower, more rounded than in the EMI transfers.

Tauber, Richard (tenor), and Lotte Schöne (soprano)

Operetta arias from LEHAR: Paganini; Zigeunerliebe; Der Land des Lächelns; Die lustige Witwe. SUPPE: Die schöne Galatea. SCHUBERT/BERTE: Das Dreimäderlhaus (Lilac Time). JOHANN STRAUSS JR: Die Fledermaus; Der lustige Krieg; Indigo und die vierzig Räuber; Cagliosto in Wien. KALMAN: Gräfin Mariza; Die Zirkusprinzessin. MILLOCKER: Der arme Jonathan. ZELLER: Der Vogelhändler; Der Obersteiger. NESSLER: Der Trompeter von Säckingen
(M) (***) Nimbus mono NI 7833

These imaginatively chosen operetta excerpts, recorded over the same period (1919–29) as the operatic collections above, explain Tauber's phenomenal popularity over so many years. The collection is the more tempting for its inclusion of the contributions of Lotte Schöne, a delightful artist. Moreover, there is much here that is very rare, and it is a pity that no duets were available – these are all solo items. The transfers are most successful.

Tetrazzini, Luisa (soprano)

Arias from: BELLINI: La sonnambula. DONIZETTI: Lucia di Lammermoor. ROSSINI: Il barbiere di Siviglia. THOMAS: Mignon. VERACINI: Rosalinda. VERDI: Un ballo in maschera; Rigoletto; La traviata; Il trovatore; I vespri siciliani
(M) (***) Nimbus mono NI 7808

Tetrazzini was astonishing among coloratura sopranos not just for her phenomenal agility but for the golden warmth that went with tonal purity. The Nimbus transfers add bloom to the sound, with the singer slightly distanced. Though some EMI transfers make her voice more vivid and immediate, one quickly adjusts. Such display arias as Ah non giunge from La sonnambula or the Bolero from I vespri siciliani are incomparably dazzling, but it is worth noting too what tenderness is conveyed through Tetrazzini's simple phrasing and pure tone in such a tragic aria as Violetta's Addio del passato, with both verses included. Lieder devotees may gasp in horror, but one of the delightful oddities here is Tetrazzini's bright-eyed performance, with ragged orchestral accompaniment, of what is described as La serenata inutile by Brahms – in fact Vergebliches Ständchen, sung with a triumphant if highly inauthentic top A at the end, implying no closure of the lady's window!

Volume 2: Arias from: BELLINI: I Puritani; La sonnambula. DAVID: Le Perle du Brésil. DONIZETTI: Linda di Chamounix. ROSSINI: Semiramide; Il barbiere di Siviglia. GOUNOD: Roméo et Juliette. BIZET: Carmen. MEYERBEER: Dinorah; Les Huguenots. VERDI: Il trovatore; La traviata. Songs: TOSTI: Aprile. GRIEG: Peer Gynt: Solveig's song. BRAGA: La Serenata. BENEDICT: Carnevale di Venezia
(M) (***) Nimbus mono NI 7891

Tetrazzini's bright clear soprano with its characteristic touch of gold is ideally suited to the Nimbus process, and with ample bloom on the sound these early acoustic recordings made between 1910 and 1914, give one a vivid idea not only of the beauty and brilliance but of the scale of the voice. Nor that they disguise the technical shortcomings, such as her tendency to attack the exposed start of florid runs fearlessly with a little squawk, endearing as it may be, or the way that some of the coloratura here is on the sketchy side, as in the Queen's aria from Meyerbeer's Les Huguenots. The disc ends with three Zonophone recordings made in 1904 with piano accompaniment, including an early version of her party piece, Ah non giunge, from Sonnambula and the first half only of Rosina's Una voce poco fa from Il barbiere di Siviglia.

Tibbett, Lawrence (baritone)

'Tibbett in Opera': excerpts from: LEONCAVALLO: *Pagliacci.*
BIZET: *Carmen.* PUCCINI: *Tosca.* VERDI: *Un ballo in
maschera; Simon Boccanegra; Rigoletto; Otello.* ROSSINI: *Il
Barbiere di Siviglia.* GOUNOD: *Faust.* WAGNER: *Tannhäuser;
Die Walküre*

M) (***) Nimbus mono NI 7825

The scale and resonance of Lawrence Tibbett's voice come
over vividly in this fine selection of his recordings made
between 1926 and 1939. The Nimbus process allows the rapid
vibrato in his voice to emerge naturally, giving the sound a
thrilling richness in all these varied items. Particularly interesting is the longest, the whole of Wotan's Farewell, with
Stokowski conducting the Philadelphia Orchestra in 1934. It is
an over-the-top performance that carries total conviction,
even if the sheer volume produces some clangorous resonances in the Nimbus transfer. Also memorable is the celebrated *Boccanegra* council chamber sequence, recorded in
1939 with Martinelli and Rose Bampton in the ensemble.

Other Historical Reissues

Caruso, Enrico (tenor)

The Naxos Complete Recordings Edition

The Complete Recordings of Enrico Caruso, Vol. 1 (1902–3 recordings): Arias from: FRANCHETTI: *Germania*. VERDI: *Aida; Rigoletto*. MASSENET: *Manon*. DONIZETTI: *L'elisir d'amore*. BOITO: *Mefistofele*. PUCCINI: *Tosca*. MASCAGNI: *Cavalleria Rusticana; Iris*. GIORDANO: *Fedora*. PONCHIELLI: *La Gioconda*. LEONCAVALLO: *Pagliacci*. CILEA: *Adriana Lecouvreur*. Songs: DENZA: *Non t'amo più*. TOSTI: *La mia canzone*. ZARDO: *Luna fedel* (2 versions). TRIMARCHI: *Un bacio ancora*

(BB) (***) Naxos mono 8.110703

The Complete Recordings of Enrico Caruso, Vol. 2 (1903–6 recordings): Arias from: PUCCINI: *La Bohème; Tosca*. MEYERBEER: *Les Huguenots*. VERDI: *Aida; Rigoletto; Il trovatore*. DONIZETTI: *Don Pasquale; L'elisir d'amore: La favorita*. MASCAGNI: *Cavalleria rusticana*. LEONCAVALLO: *Pagliacci*. MASSENET: *Manon*. BIZET: *Carmen; Les pêcheurs de perles*. PONCHIELLI: *La Gioconda*. FLOTOW: *Martha*. GOUNOD: *Faust*. Songs: PINI-CORSI: *Tu non mi vuoi più bene*. LEONCAVALLO: *Mattinata*

(BB) (***) Naxos mono 8.100704

The Complete Recordings of Enrico Caruso, Vol. 3 (1906–7 recordings): Arias from: VERDI: *Aida; La forza del destino; Rigoletto*. GIORDANO: *Andrea Chénier*. LEONCAVALLO: *Pagliacci*. PUCCINI: *La Bohème; Madama Butterfly*. BIZET: *Les Pêcheurs de perles*. MEYERBEER: *L'Africana*. DONIZETTI: *Don Sébastien; Lucia di Lammermoor*. Songs: BARTHELEMY: *Adorables tourments; Triste ritorno*. TOSTI: *Ideale*

(BB) (***) Naxos mono 8.110708

The Complete Recordings of Enrico Caruso, Vol. 4 (1908–10 recordings): Arias from: VERDI: *Aida; La forza del destino; Rigoletto; Il trovatore*. PUCCINI: *Tosca*. GOLDMARK: *Regina di Saba*. BIZET: *Carmen*. MEYERBEER: *Les Huguenots*. FLOTOW: *Martha*. Songs: BUZZI-PECCIA: *Lolita*. DONCIEUX-TOSTI: *Pour un baiser*. RUSSO-NUTILE: *Mamma mia, che vo' sapè*

(BB) (***) Naxos mono 8.110719

The Complete Recordings of Enrico Caruso, Vol. 5 (1908–10 recordings): Arias from GOUNOD: *Faust*. FRANCHETTI: *Germania*. PUCCINI: *Madama Butterfly*. PONCHIELLI: *La Gioconda*. LEONCAVALLO: *Pagliacci*. VERDI: *Otello*

(BB) (***) Naxos mono 8.110720

The Complete Recordings of Enrico Caruso, Vol. 6. (1911–12 recordings): Arias from: VERDI: *Aida; Un ballo in maschera; La forza del destino*. DONIZETTI: *L'elisir d'amore*. LEONCAVALLO: *La Bohème*. GOMES: *Lo Schiavo*. MASSENET: *Manon*. FLOTOW: *Martha*. Songs: MASSONI-MASCHERON: *Eternamente*. CORDIFERRO-CARDILLO: *Core 'ngrato*. BOVIO DE CURTIS: *Canta pe'me*. TESCHEMACHER-GARTNER: *Love is Mine*

(BB) (***) Naxos mono 8.110721

The Complete Recordings of Enrico Caruso, Vol. 7 (1912–13 recordings). Arias from: VERDI: *Don Carlos; I Lombardi;*

Rigoletto; Il trovatore. DONIZETTI: *Lucia di Lammermoor*. MASSENET: *Manon*. PUCCINI: *La Bohème; Manon Lescaut*. Songs: J.-B. FAURE: *Crucifix*. DE CRESCENZO: *Tarantella sincera*. ROSSINI: *La danza*. CARUSO: *Dreams of Long Ago*. SULLIVAN: *The Lost Chord*. D'HARDELOT: *Because*. GRAINGER: *Hosanna*. TCHAIKOVSKY: *Pimpimella*. BIZET: *Agnus Dei*. KAHN: *Ave Maria*. MASSENET: *Elegy*

(BB) (***) Naxos mono 8.110724

The Complete Recordings of Enrico Caruso, Vol. 8 (1913–14 recordings). ROSSINI: *Stabat Mater*. Arias from: MASCAGNI: *Cavalleria rusticana*. VERDI: *Un ballo in maschera; Otello*. Songs: LEONCAVALLO: *Lasciati amar*. DE CRESCENZO: *Guardann 'a luna*. O'HARA: *Your Eyes have Told me What I Did Not Know*. COTTRAU: *Fenesta che lucive*. FAURE: *Les Rameaux* (2 versions). TCHAIKOVSKY: *Sérénade de Don Juan*. RICCIARDI: *Amor mio*. VALENTE: *Manella mia*. GARTNER: *Trusting Eyes*. RONALD: *Sérénade espagnole*. TOSTI: *Parted*. ALVAREZ: *La partida*. CHAPI: *El milagro de la Virgen purisima*

(BB) (***) Naxos mono 8.110726

The Complete Recordings of Enrico Caruso, Vol. 9 (1914–16 recordings): Arias from: VERDI: *Requiem; La traviata; Macbeth*. GOMES: *Il Guarany*. BIZET: *Carmen*. DONIZETTI: *Il Duca d'Alba*. MASSENET: *Le Cid*. GOUNOD: *La reine de Saba*. PUCCINI: *La Bohème*. Songs: SZULC: *Hantise d'amour*. TOSTI: *La mia canzone; Luna d'estate*. PENNINO: *Pecchè?* CIOCIANO: *Cielo turchino*. DENZA: *Si vois l'aviez compris*. LEONCAVALLO: *Les Deux Sérénades*. FRANCK: *La Procession*. DI CAPUA: *O sole mio*. ROTOLI: *Mia sposa sarà la mia bandiera*. ADAM: *Cantique de Noël*

(BB) (***) Naxos mono 8.110750

The Complete Recordings of Enrico Caruso, Vol. 10 (1916–17 recordings): Arias from: TCHAIKOVSKY: *Eugene Onegin*. GIORDANO: *Andrea Chénier*. SAINT-SAENS: *Samson et Dalila*. BIZET: *Les Pêcheurs de perles*. VERDI: *Rigoletto*. DONIZETTI: *Lucia di Lammermoor*. FLOTOW: *Martha*. RUBINSTEIN: *Nero*. Songs: FAURE: *Sancta Maria*. CARUSO: *Tiempo antico*. FOLK SONG (arr. COTTRAU): *Santa Lucia*. TCHAIKOVSKY: *Porquoi?* GODARD: *Chanson de juin*. TOSTI: *L'alba separa dalla luce l'ombra* (2 versions)

(BB) (***) Naxos mono 8.110751

The Complete Recordings of Enrico Caruso, Vol. 11 (1918–19 recordings): Arias from: VERDI: *La forza del destino*. SAINT-SAENS: *Samson et Dalila*. DONIZETTI: *L'elisir d'amore*. Songs: MICHELENA: *A la luz de la luna*. COSTA: *Sei morta ne la vita mia*. ALVAREZ: *La partida*. COHAN: *Over There*. NIEDERMEYER: *Pietà, Signore*. ALVAREZ: *A Granada*. BILLI (arr. MALFETTI): *Campane a sera 'Ave Maria'*. OLIVIERI: *Inno di Garibaldi*. ARONA: *La Campana di San Giusto*. PLANQUETTE: *Le Régiment de Sambre et Meuse*. TOSTI: *'A Vucchella*. TRAD.: *Vieni sul mar*. DE CURTIS: *Tu, ca nun chiagne*. COTTRAU: *Addio a Napoli*

(BB) (***) Naxos mono 8.110752

The Complete Recordings of Enrico Caruso, Vol. 12 (1902–20 recordings): Arias from: GOMES: *Salvador Rosa*. HANDEL: *Serse*. HALEVY: *La Juive*. MEYERBEER: *L'Africana*. LULLY: *Amadis de Gaule*. ROSSINI: *Petite Messe Solennelle*. FRANCHETTI: *Germania*. Songs: CIAMPI: *Nina*. DE

CRESCENZO: *Première caresse.* DE CURTIS: *Senza nisciuno.*
BRACCO: *Serenata.* FUCITO: *Scordame.* SECCHI: *Love Me or Not.* PASADAS: *Noche feliz.* GIOE: *I' m'arricordo 'e Napule.*
DONAUDY: *Vaghissima sembianza.* BARTLETT: *A Dream.*
CARUSO: *Liberty Forever.* EDWARDS: *My Cousin Caruso*
(BB) (***) Naxos mono 8.110753

The role of the great tenor Enrico Caruso is unique in the history of recorded music. The recordings he made in the early years of the twentieth century more than anything transformed what was regarded as a toy into an important and popular branch of the media. In the age of CD that role has been recognized in repeated attempts to renovate those recordings, starting with those made by Thomas G. Stockham and his Soundstream organization for RCA, successor of the Victor Company, which made most of the original recordings. Indeed, it was specifically to improve the sound of pre-electric Caruso recordings that Stockham devised the first commercial digital recordings, scarcely realizing that digital techniques would quickly take over recording generally. Sixteen of these digitally enhanced recordings with modern orchestral accompaniments rather incongruously laminated on are now available on RCA (82876 64165-2) at mid-price.

Masterminded by Ward Marston, artist as well as technician, who supervised these 12 discs, the Naxos series offers CD transfers that achieve new degrees of fidelity. With meticulous care Marston has used mint copies of the 78rpm originals, reduced the surface hiss, clarified the voice and taken great care to restore the original pitch – not easy when recording speeds were variable in the early years of the century. The discs can all be warmly recommended, particularly when each comes with a comment by Marston himself, as well as a note by Hugh Griffith, which not only comments on the specific recordings but gives an illuminating account of developments in the singer's life, as well as the background in the opera world, not least at the Metropolitan Opera in New York. In direct comparison with the RCA transfers, the voice is less forward but clearer, with less distortion, and with lighter surface noise behind.

In Volume 1 the Griffith note is especially illuminating, when it highlights the flaws and mistakes in the first batch of Caruso recordings, made by the HMV recording manager, Fred Gaisberg, in a hotel room in Milan on 11 April 1902. He notes that Caruso funks the final top note of *Celeste Aida*, using a falsetto instead, condemning the practice even though the falsetto is extremely beautiful. Gaisberg's bosses in London objected to his paying the singer £100 for the first ten recordings, but they quickly realized how profitable the results were going to be.

It was not until the second series, in November 1902, that Caruso made his first recording of *Vesti la giubba* from *Pagliacci*, with its laughter at the beginning and sob at the end, an aria that became the singer's calling-card. He also re-recorded *Celeste Aida*; but, to avoid the final top note, cut the aria short, omitting the coda. All these early recordings have piano accompaniment, with Giordano taking over as accompanist from the staff pianist for *Amor ti vieta* from his opera, *Fedora*, and Cilea taking over for an aria from his *Adriana Lecouvreur*. A series of seven recordings was also made for the Zonophone Company, and Volume 2 starts with three recordings, also made in Milan, originally for issue on cylinders and later issued on disc by the Pathé Company, inevitably less clear than the HMV recordings.

It was when (in February 1904) Caruso started making recordings for the Victor Company in New York (associated company of British HMV) that the American engineers wanted to improve on the standards of recording. It shows the astronomic rise in Caruso's popularity that in his first contract with Victor he was guaranteed at least $2,000 a year, very different from the contested £100 of two years earlier. The first batch of American recordings concentrated on repertory Caruso had already recorded in Milan, generally with improved results not just in sound quality but also in artistic assurance. In April 1904 he made two more recordings in Milan, one of them with Leoncavallo accompanying him splashily in his song, *Mattinata*; but from then on, Caruso made all his recordings in the United States, for he was spending six months of each year in New York, singing at the Met.

It was in February 1906 that Victor made the first Caruso recordings with orchestra, a strange band based on wind and brass, and technical improvements meant that arias of over four minutes could be recorded complete, one of the first being Rodolfo's *Che gelida manina* from Puccini's *La Bohème*, beautifully shaped. The singer's artistic development can also be measured, as Griffith points out, by the differences between his 1906 recording of *Cielo e mar* from Ponchielli's *La Gioconda* and the far less imaginative one made in Milan in 1902. He also made his first recording in French, Faust's *Salut demeure*.

Volume 3 brings Caruso's earliest recordings, also from 1906, with other singers, first his fellow Neapolitan, the baritone Antonio Scotti. Then, in February 1907, came the first of his four recordings of the *Quartet* from *Rigoletto*, again with Scotti, as well as Bessie Abbott and Louise Homer. Ward Marston deduces from the sound-quality and technical details that, unlike his later versions, this one was recorded a semitone down; and it is a measure of Marston's thoroughness that he appends at the end of the volume a transfer at the score-pitch, which, as he says, makes the opening solo sound not quite true to Caruso. Volume 3 also brings Caruso's first account of *Vesti la giubba* with orchestra, the one which became a runaway bestseller and has remained so ever since.

Volume 4 brings more Neapolitan songs and two versions of Don José's Flower Song from *Carmen*, one in French, one in Italian; while Volume 5 marks another departure, with no fewer than nine items from Gounod's *Faust* recorded in 1910, with Caruso joined by Geraldine Farrar as Marguerite, Gabrielle Gilibert, Scotti again and Marcel Journet as Mephistopheles. For this series Ward Marston has not kept strictly to chronological order of recording but has arranged them in musical sequence, a sensible course. At this period there was no question of recording complete operas with star singers like Caruso, but Victor devised this sequence as a compromise, the choice of opera reflecting the reputation of the Met. at the time as being the 'Faustspielhaus'.

Where in 1907 Caruso dominated the Met.'s season, the arrival of Toscanini as conductor, with a broadening of the repertory, meant that the tenor was not so dominant. By this time, the changes of colouring in Caruso's voice are more marked, when it was growing weightier and more baritonal, as in the March 1910 version of *Cielo e mar*. Volume 6 brings a recording of Riccardo's Act I aria with chorus from *Ballo in maschera*, and when Caruso was spending so much of the year in New York it was relatively easy to get singers at the Met., soloists as well as chorus, to record either in New York or in the Victor studios in Camden, New Jersey. Volume 6 also contains a sequence of items from Flotow's *Martha* with Frances Alda, Josephine Jacoby and Marcel Journet.

Volume 7 brings Caruso's 1912 version of the *Rigoletto*

Quartet, this time with Tetrazzini (who at the time even threatened to rival Caruso as the Met.'s top vocal attraction), Jacoby and Pasquale Amato. Songs were playing an increasing role in the singer's recording programme, including at this period Sullivan's 'The Lost Chord', the ballad 'Because' by Guy d'Hardelot, sung in French as *Parceque*, and a ballad by Caruso himself, 'Dreams of Long Ago'. There is also a memorable account of *O soave fanciulla* from Act I of *La Bohème* with Geraldine Farrar who, unlike some other prima donnas, notably Nellie Melba, became a great friend.

Volume 8 not only brings more songs like *Les Rameaux* by Jean-Baptiste Faure (not to be confused with Gabriel Fauré), Massenet's *Elégie*, with Mischa Elman playing the violin solo, *Cuius animam* from Rossini's *Stabat Mater*, and *Don Juan's Serenade* by Tchaikovsky. Most memorable of all is the Oath Duet from Act II of Verdi's *Otello*, with Caruso at his most heroic matched against the magnificent Titta Ruffo as Iago, who sadly made too few recordings with Caruso when his American visits were based on Chicago, not New York. Volume 8 also contains ensembles from *Ballo in maschera* with the soprano Frieda Hempel, among the other singers.

Volume 9 brings the *Brindisi* from *La Traviata* with Alma Gluck as Violetta, and two versions, both unpublished at the time, of the Don José–Micaela duet from *Carmen* with Frances Alda. The curiosity in this volume is Caruso's recording of Colline's Coat Song from Act IV of *La Bohème*, with Caruso singing like a *basso cantante*, having in 1913 stepped in impromptu at a live performance when his colleague, Andres de Segurola, lost his voice. Volume 10 finds the voice even darker and richer, and the 1917 account of the Quartet from *Rigoletto* was made this time with the young diva of the moment, Amelita Galli-Curci. Interestingly, there is an unpublished alternative take of the opening tenor solo.

Volume 11 brings a sequence of patriotic songs, recorded in 1918 to help the war effort, not only the celebrated account of George M. Cohan's 'Over There', but Garibaldi's *Hymn* and the jaunty *La campana di San Giusto* to encourage his fellow Italians and Planquette's marching song, *Le régiment de Sambre et Meuse*, for the French. Increasingly over the years, it had become difficult to find new repertory for the great tenor, and the final volume brings such unexpected repertory as Handel's *Ombra mai fú*, complete with recitative, weightily done in the manner of the time. The two operatic items are an aria from Meyerbeer's *L'Africana* sung in Italian and the big aria from the last opera Caruso added to his repertory, *La Juive* by Halévy, the voice still heroic and full. That was among the recordings he made in September 1920 at his last session, and within a year he was dead.

That penultimate volume ends with a fascinating appendix, a march, *Liberty Forever*, by Caruso himself, played by the Victor Military Band, and a music-hall number, 'My Cousin Caruso', from 1909, sung by Billy Murray. Finally there is yet another example of Ward Marston's thoroughness – an improved transfer of Caruso's very first recording, the aria, *Studente, udite*, from *Germania* by Franchetti. This is a model series, and the only disadvantage of having these Naxos discs separately is that one lacks a composite index, making it harder to find particular items.

Other Caruso CDs

'*The Legendary Caruso*': Opera arias and songs: Arias from: MASCAGNI: *Cavalleria rusticana; Iris.* PONCHIELLI: *La Gioconda.* LEONCAVALLO: *Pagliacci*; and song: *Mattinata.* BOITO: *Mefistofele.* PUCCINI: *Tosca.* GIORDANO: *Fedora.*

CILEA: *Adriana Lecouvreur.* VERDI: *Rigoletto; Aida.* BIZET: *Les Pêcheurs de perles.* MASSENET: *Manon.* DONIZETTI: *L'elisir d'amore.* MEYERBEER: *Les Huguenots.* Songs: TOSTI: *La mia canzone.* DENZA: *Non t'amo più*; and by ZARDO; TRIMARCHI

(M) (***) EMI mono 5 67006-2

The EMI collection was originally on the Références label and has now been again remastered. It brings together Caruso's earliest recordings, made in 1902, 1903 and 1904 in Milan with at times misty piano accompaniment. The very first pieces were done impromptu in Caruso's hotel, and the roughness of presentation reflects that; but the voice is glorious in its youth, amazingly well caught for that period and now remarkably fresh and free from horn resonances, even if the background noise, not always regular, is still obvious.

Christoff, Boris (bass)

'*The Early Recordings (1949–52)*': excerpts from: MUSSORGSKY: *Boris Godunov; Khovanshchina.* BORODIN: *Prince Igor.* RIMSKY-KORSAKOV: *Sadko; The Legend of the Invisible City of Kitezh.* TCHAIKOVSKY: *Eugene Onegin.* MUSSORGSKY: *Songs; Russian folksongs*

(M) (***) EMI mono CDH7 64252-2

The magnetic quality of Christoff's singing is never in doubt here, and the compulsion of the singer's artistry as well as the vivid individuality of his bass timbres make this a real portrait, not just a collection of items. These were his first recordings of the *Boris Godunov* excerpts (in which he assumes three different characters), and in musical terms probably never surpassed them. But his characterization here is just as impressive as the singing itself, full of variety. The EMI transfers are bold and brightly focused, with the most vivid projection.

Gigli, Beniamino (tenor)

The Gigli Edition, Volume 1: BOITO: *Mefistofele.* PUCCINI: *La Bohème; Tosca.* DONIZETTI: *La favorita.* PONCHIELLI: *La Gioconda.* MASCAGNI: *Cavalleria rusticana; Iris; Lodoletta.* GOUNOD: *Faust.* Arias: CANNIO: *O surdato 'nnamurato*

(BB) (***) Naxos mono 8.110262

Beniamino Gigli, the uniquely honeyed-toned tenor, made his first recordings for HMV in Milan in the autumn of 1918. These excellent transfers have been master-minded by Mark Obert-Thorn and were originally issued on the Romophone label, but this time they have been upgraded. The surface noise remains high on the earliest items – *Dai campi, dai prati* from *Mefistofele* and Cavaradossi's two arias from *Tosca*. Even so, the distinctive timbre, which gave Gigli the title of Caruso's successor, is already clear, and in these earliest recordings, made when the singer was 28, the mannerisms which tended to mar his later work – aspirated lines and cooing tone – are largely absent. Already he revealed a musical imagination greater than that of most Italian tenors, and the head-tone he uses in *Apri la finestra* from Mascagni's *Iris* has rarely been matched by any rival. The poise and purity of his singing also comes out in his account of *Spirto gentil* from Donizetti's *La favorita*, and the clarity of his diction is exemplary, as in his performance of Faust's aria, in Italian translation, *Salve dimora.* *Cielo e mar* from Ponchielli's *La Gioconda* then reveals his open, heroic tone, all well caught on these pre-electrics, even if the orchestral accompaniment conducted by Carlo Sabajno is necessarily thin.

The Gigli Edition, Volume 2: BIZET: *Les Pêcheurs de perles.* GIORDANO: *Andrea Chénier; Fedora.* BOITO: *Mefistofele.* PUCCINI: *Tosca.* DONIZETTI: *La favorita.* PONCHIELLI: *La Gioconda.* MASCAGNI: *L'amico Fritz; Iris.* DRIGO: *I milioni d'Arlecchino.* LALO: *Le roi d'Ys.* GOUNOD: *Faust.* PUCCINI: *La Bohème.* Arias: CURTIS: *Tu sola.* MARIO: *Santa Lucia luntana.* TOSELLI: *Serenata*
(BB) (***) Naxos mono 8.110263

This second volume of Naxos's 'Gigli Edition', like the first, was originally issued on Romophone, but with Mark Obert-Thorn again upgrading his original transfers. It opens with five items from his Milan sessions in 1919 not included in Volume 1, starting with the delectable Cherry Duet from Mascagni's *L'amico Fritz*, with Nerina Baldisseri as Gigli's partner. Then in January 1921 he made his first recordings for Victor in the United States, then the associate company of HMV in Europe. As Obert-Thorne suggests, the quality of recordings made in Camden, New Jersey and New York was higher than those made in Milan, so that many of the earliest recordings made there were remakes of what he had already done. Not that the differences are all that great in these transfers, except that surface noise is generally less obtrusive, notably in the Mefistofele aria, with the voice clearer. Faust's aria – in Italian *Salve dimora* – is here more robust and less delicate than it was in the Milan version of two years earlier, but the absence of strain in everything Gigli sings is a delight. Interestingly, he did not make his first recording of *Vesti la giubba* from *Pagliacci* – the aria than more than any of his recordings made Caruso a superstar – until March 1922, six months after his great predecessor had died, presumably not wanting to make his challenge while Caruso was still alive.

Volumes 3 (Naxos 8.110264) and 4 (8.110265) covering the Camden and New York recordings of 1923–5 and 1926–7 respectively and there are approximately a dozen volumes in all, which we hope to discuss in our next volume.

Opera arias from: GOUNOD: *Faust.* BIZET: *Carmen; Les Pêcheurs de perles.* MASSENET: *Manon.* HANDEL: *Serse.* DONIZETTI: *Lucia di Lammermoor; L'elisir d'amore.* VERDI: *Rigoletto; Aida.* LEONCAVALLO: *Pagliacci.* MASCAGNI: *Cavalleria rusticana.* PUCCINI: *La Bohème; Tosca.* GIORDANO: *Andrea Chénier.* PIETRI: *Maristella*
(M) (***) EMI mono CDH7 61051-2

Beniamino Gigli's status in the inter-war period as a singing superstar at a time when the media were less keenly organized is vividly reflected in this Références collection of eighteen items, the cream of his recordings made between 1927 and 1937. It is especially welcome to have two historic ensemble recordings, made in New York in 1927 and originally coupled on a short-playing 78rpm disc – the Quartet from *Rigoletto* and the Sextet from *Lucia di Lammermoor.* In an astonishing line-up Gigli is joined by Galli-Curci, Pinza, De Luca and Louise Homer. Excellent transfers.

Melba, Nellie (soprano)

Arias from: VERDI: *Rigoletto; La traviata.* DONIZETTI: *Lucia di Lammermoor.* HANDEL: *Il penseroso.* THOMAS: *Hamlet.* MOZART: *Le nozze di Figaro.* PUCCINI: *La Bohème.* Songs: TOSTI: *Goodbye; Mattinata.* BEMBERG: *Les Anges pleurent; Chant vénitien; Nymphes et sylvains.* TRAD.: *Comin' thro' the Rye.* ARDITI: *Se saran rose.* D'HARDELOT: *Three Green Bonnets.* HAHN: *Si mes vers avaient des ailes.* BACH/GOUNOD: *Ave Maria*
(BB) (***) Naxos mono 8.110737

From the moment she made her debut in Brussels as Gilda in *Rigoletto* in 1887 Helen Porter Mitchell, better known as Nellie Melba, became an operatic star of stars, particularly at Covent Garden, but also at the Met. and in Europe. She retired in 1926. Her first records, of which nineteen items are included here, were made privately at her home in 1904, when she was forty-three. They were not originally intended for public release, but later she approved fourteen for publication, though in the case of the Act I *La traviata* aria she only permitted the release of *Ah! fors è lui* (simply and beautifully sung) and not the cabaletta, though both are included here. Another fascinating item from those first sessions is Handel's 'Sweet Bird' from *Il penseroso*, where during the first take the flautist played incorrectly, causing Melba to stop and say 'Now we'll have to do it over again'. Fortunately the second take is flawless, for she was good at trilling with a flute, as is shown in the brief excerpt from Donizetti's Mad scene (*Lucia de Lammermoor*). Although the voice is obviously showing signs of wear, the agility is unimpaired, as the arias from Thomas's *Hamlet* demonstrate. *Et maintenant, écoutez ma chanson!* is a real bravura example. Some of the items suffer from distortion or excess, uneven surface noise, but not this, and *Caro nome* (with more background and some slight distortion) is also pretty impressive. Mozart's *Porgi amor* is not really stylish by today's standards but shows Melba's quality of tone and line. Ward Marston's fine transfers certainly bring this legendary figure fully to life, and the Naxos documentation is well up to standard for this enterprising series.

Opera Arias and Excerpts from: DONIZETTI: *Lucia di Lammermoor.* VERDI: *Rigoletto; La traviata* (with Brownlee)*; Otello.* GOUNOD: *Roméo et Juliette; Faust.* PUCCINI: *La Bohème* (excerpts: with Caruso & others). Songs: TOSTI: *La serenata.* BEMBERG: *Chant hindou.* BISHOP: *Lo, Here the Gentle Lark; Home, Sweet Home.* BACH/GOUNOD: *Ave Maria* (with W. H. Squire, cello). CHAUSSON: *Le Temps de lilas.* SZULC: *Claire de lune*
(M) (***) EMI mono 5 85826-2

Puccini disparagingly called Melba 'the Centenarian'. That was long before she retired in 1926 at the age of sixty-five, and, as the excerpts here from her Covent Garden Farewell demonstrate, the voice remained astonishingly bright, firm and true. Yet equally it shows very clearly how little emotion she seems to have felt – or at least was able to convey. There is that same limitation throughout these twenty items (including the two done with piano accompaniment after her retirement). But the security of her technique and the clarity and precision of her voice are amazing in one dazzling performance after another. Excellent transfers.

Piccaver, Alfred (tenor)

'The Son of Vienna' Arias and Duets from: VERDI: *Rigoletto; Il trovatore; Un ballo in maschera; Aida.* MEYERBEER: *L'Africaine.* MASCAGNI: *Cavalleria rusticana.* LEONCAVALLO: *Pagliacci.* WAGNER: *Die Meistersinger; Lohengrin.* GOUNOD: *Faust.* PONCHIELLI: *La Gioconda.* PUCCINI: *Tosca; Turandot.* Song: GEEHL: *For You Alone*
(BB) (***) Dutton mono CDPB 9725

Though born in England, Alfred Piccaver was brought up in the United States, and then in his mid-twenties settled permanently in Vienna, where he was a stalwart of the Vienna State Opera for almost thirty years. This disc of his relatively rare recordings in every item explains his success. His was a ringingly clear tenor, with no hint of strain even in the high registers. His style was Germanic, at times suggesting similarities with his Viennese contemporary, Richard Tauber, yet Piccaver's repertory was far wider, extending to most of the principal lyrico-dramatic tenor parts, as the items here suggest. The recordings are divided sharply into two sections, the first eight numbers recorded in 1923 by the acoustic process – with the voice yet ringingly clear – and eight recorded electrically in 1928. The Dutton transfers are excellent, though it is a pity that background details of each recording are very limited.

Schmidt, Joseph (tenor)

Complete EMI Recordings: Arias (sung in German) from: MEYERBEER: *L'Africaine.* FLOTOW: *Martha; Alessandro Stradella.* KIENZL: *Der Evangelimann.* KORNGOLD: *Die tote Stadt.* ADAM: *Der Postillon von Longjumeau.* MASSENET: *Manon; Der Cid.* TCHAIKOVSKY: *Eugene Onegin.* MORY: *La Vallière.* GOTZE: *Der Page des Königs.* JOHANN STRAUSS JR: *1001 Nacht; Der Zigeunerbaron; Simplicus.* LEHAR: *Zigeunerliebe.* TAUBER: *Der Singende Traume.* DONIZETTI: *Der Liebestrank (L'elisir d'amore).* VERDI: *Rigoletto; Der Troubadour (Il trovatore).* LEONCAVALLO: *Der Bajazzo (Pagliacci).* PUCCINI: *La Bohème; Tosca; Das Mädchen aus dem Goldenen Westen (La fanciulla del West); Turandot.* SERRANO: *El Trust de Los Tenorios.* SPOLIANSKY: *Das Lied einer Nacht* (film). Lieder & Songs: SCHUBERT: *Ständchen; Ungeduld.* BENATZKY: *Wenn du treulos bist.* NIEDERBERGER: *Buona notte, schöne Signorina.* LEONCAVALLO: *Morgenständchen.* LABRIOLA: *Serenata.* BISCARDI: *L'ariatella.* DENZA: *Funiculi, funicula.* BUZZI-PECCIA: *Lolita.* DI CAPUA: *O sole mio*
(M) (***) EMI mono 7 64676-2 (2)

Joseph Schmidt, born in 1904 in what is now Romania, studied in Berlin, and developed what by any standards is one of the most beautiful German tenor voices ever recorded, less distinctive than that of Richard Tauber, but even more consistently honeyed and velvety in the upper registers, exceptionally free on top, so that the stratospheric top notes in *Le Postillon de Longjumeau* have never sounded so beautiful and unstrained. This is the ideal lyric tenor voice, not just for the German repertory, including operetta, but for the Italian; it was tragic that, standing less than five feet high, he was precluded from having an operatic career. Nevertheless, he was most successful in his concert work as well as in his recording career, as this glowing collection demonstrates. He even had a brilliantly successful American tour in 1937; but sadly, as a Jew, he got caught up in Europe during the Second World War and died from a chest complaint in a Swiss refugee camp in 1942. The records – with informative notes – make a superb memorial, here at last given full prominence in excellent transfers.

Tauber, Richard (tenor)

Arias from: AUBER: *Fra Diavolo.* FLOTOW: *Martha.* KORNGOLD: *Die tote Stadt.* KIENZL: *Der Evangelimann.*

PUCCINI: *La Bohème; Tosca.* ROSSINI: *Il barbiere di Siviglia.* SMETANA: *The Bartered Bride.* RICHARD STRAUSS: *Der Rosenkavalier.* TCHAIKOVSKY: *Eugene Onegin.* THOMAS: *Mignon.* VERDI: *La forza del destino; La traviata; Il trovatore.* WOLF-FERRARI: *Jewels of the Madonna*
(B) (***) Naxos mono 8.110729

These acoustic recordings, made between 1919 and 1926, offer a totally different view of Richard Tauber and his art from the usual one, revealing the range of his sympathies in the world of opera. A complete musician, an excellent pianist and conductor as well as singer, he here tackles a formidable list of arias, including even Siegmund's *Wintersturme* solo from Wagner's *Die Walküre*, not a role he ever sang on stage. While in the 1920s he was establishing his unique reputation in operetta, he was also much admired for his performances in opera, a career that had begun in 1913, first in Chemnitz with *Zauberflöte* and then on contract in Dresden with Thomas's *Mignon*. The distinctive warmth of Tauber's tenor was ideally suited to recording, and though these acoustic examples do not generally capture the timbre we associate with his singing of Lehár, the sweetness is beautifully caught in Ward Marston's fine transfers. It is good too to be without the kind of distortion characteristic of some of his later electric recordings. The disc comes with a highly informative note by Peter Dempsey.

'**The Legendary Richard Tauber**': MOZART: *Don Giovanni: Il mio tesoro; Die Zauberflöte: Dies Bildnis.* Arias from: PUCCINI: *La Bohème; Madama Butterfly; Tosca; Turandot.* LEONCAVALLO: *Pagliacci.* VERDI: *Il trovatore.* MEHUL: *Joseph in Aegypten.* OFFENBACH: *Les Contes d'Hoffmann.* THOMAS: *Mignon.* TCHAIKOVSKY: *Eugene Onegin.* SMETANA: *Bartered Bride* (all sung in German). WEBER: *Der Freischütz.* LORTZING: *Undine.* KIENZL: *Der Evangelimann.* WAGNER: *Die Meistersinger.* RICHARD STRAUSS: *Der Rosenkavalier.* KORNGOLD: *Die tote Stadt.* LEHAR: *Die lustige Witwe (Lippen schweigen; Vilja-Lied); Paganini; Friederike (O Mädchen, mein Mädchen); Das Land des Lächelns (4 excerpts, including Dein ist mein ganzes Herz); Giuditta; Die Zarewitsch.* KALMAN: *Die Zirkusprinzessin; Gräfin Mariza.* HEUBERGER: *Der Opernball (Im chambre séparée).* STOLZ: *Adieu, mein kleiner Gardeoffizier; Im Prater blühn wieder die Bäume.* SIECZYNSKY: *Wien, du Stadt meiner Träume.* JOHANN STRAUSS JR: *Geschichten aus dem Wienerwald; Rosen aus dem Süden.* ZELLER: *Der Vogelhändler.* DOELLE: *Wenn der weisse Flieder wider blüht.* ERWIN: *Ich küsse Ihre Hand, Madame.* Lieder: SCHUBERT: *Ständchen; Der Lindenbaum*
(M) (*(**)) EMI mono 5 66692-2 (2)

If one begins with the second of these two CDs, it becomes immediately obvious why Tauber established his reputation with the wider public largely in the field of operetta. The uniquely honeyed voice makes simple melodies like *Lippen schweigen* from *The Merry Widow*, with its magical final cadence, or the *Vilja-Lied* utterly seductive, and that despite often inadequate transfers, with thin, whistly orchestral sound and plenty of distortion, even on the voice itself. One wonders why Tauber, more than most singers of his generation, so regularly suffers from this problem. It isn't that the basic recordings are bad, except for the thin orchestra (though there are frequent moments of blasting); usually the magic and power of the voice are well conveyed; yet the original sources too often seem prone to distortion. The first disc concentrates on opera and opens with a glowingly lyrical 1939 *Il mio tesoro*, but again there is distortion. *Dies Bildnis* (from *Die Zauberflöte*) is acoustic (1922) and rather better, and Tauber then makes 'Your Tiny Hand is Frozen' sound beguiling even in German! – the chosen language for most of his records. There are many remarkable performances here, from the lilting *Legend of Kleinsach* (1928) to a stirring *Di quella pira* (1926) with a comic wind band accompaniment; there are also equally moving versions of Lenski's aria from *Eugene Onegin* (1923), when the band is less clumsy, and the ardent 'On with the Motley' (recorded in London in 1936 and sung in English). It is a pity the recordings are technically so inadequate, but the voice still enthrals the listener.

Teyte, Maggie (soprano)

'The Pocket Prima Donna' (with various accompanists): RAVEL: *Shéhérazade*. BERLIOZ: *Nuites d'été: Le Spectre de la rose; Absence*. DUPARC: *L'Invitation au voyage; Phidylé*. DEBUSSY: *Proses lyriques*. Arias from: PERGOLESI: *La serva padrona* (in French); MONSIGNY: *Rose et Colas; Le Déserteur*; GRETRY: *Zémire et Azore; Le tableau parlant*; DOURLEN: *Les Oies de Frère Philippe*. OFFENBACH: *La Périchole*

(BB) (***) Dutton mono CDBP 9724

Maggie Teyte, born in Wolverhampton, made a speciality of the French repertory. In 1908 at the age of twenty she sang Mélisande in Debussy's opera with great success, the second singer after Mary Garden to tackle the role. Though there was a gap in her career after she got married, she returned, and made most of her recordings – including the majority of those here – in the 1940s. Hers is an exceptionally sweet soprano, ideally suited to the microphone in its purity, while her sense of style is unerring, whether in the songs of Ravel, Berlioz and Debussy or the lighter operatic and operetta repertory represented here, always sung with character and vivacity. The Dutton transfers are first-rate.

Other Vocal and Choral Recitals

Alagna, Roberto (tenor)

'French Opera Arias' (with ROHCG O, de Billy) from:
BAZIN: *Maître Pathelin.* BERLIOZ: *La Damnation de Faust.*
BIZET: *The Pearl Fishers.* BRUNEAU: *L'Attaque du Moulin.*
CHERUBINI: *Les Abencerrages.* GLUCK: *Iphigenie en
Tauride.* GOUNOD: *Mireille.* GRETRY: *L'Amant jaloux.*
HALEVY: *La Juive.* LALO: *Le Roi d'Ys.* MASSENET: *Le Cid.*
MEHUL: *Joseph.* MEYERBEER: *L'Africaine.* SAINT-SAENS:
Samson et Dalila (with London Voices). THOMAS: *Mignon*
*** EMI 5 57012-2

It was a bold venture for such a leading tenor as Roberto
Alagna to present such a formidable collection of fifteen
arias, many of which are rarities. From the start his forte has
been the French repertory, and here he displays his versatility
in operatic excerpts that cover the widest range of styles and
periods. They also make dauntingly contrasted demands on
any single tenor, from the lyric purity of Bizet's *Pearl Fishers*
aria to the heroic scale of Samson's aria in the Saint-Saëns
opera, the longest item here, with Alagna's singing not just
powerful but finely shaded. The title role in an earlier
biblical opera, Méhul's *Joseph*, also demands a heroic style,
yet Alagna, a devoted admirer of the legendary French tenor
Georges Thill, copes superbly both stylistically and vocally.
The high tessitura of some of these arias, demanding in
quite a different way, has Alagna producing beautiful head-
tones when required. It is especially good to hear the work of
such little-known composers as François Bazin (1816–78) and
Massenet's pupil, Alfred Bruneau (1857–1934), while other
charming rarities include the Lalo aria and Grétry's
Sérénade, with its accompanying mandolin. The warmly
understanding accompaniment is from the Covent Garden
Orchestra under the brilliant young French conductor, Bertrand de Billy.

Allen, Sir Thomas (baritone)

'Songs My Father Taught Me' (with Martineau, piano):
PURCELL: *Passing By.* TATE: *The Lark in the Clear Clean
Air.* SULLIVAN: *The Lost Chord; My Dearest Heart.*
SANDERSON: *Until.* HAYDN WOOD: *Bird of Love Divine; A
Brown Bird Singing; It is Only a Tiny Garden; Love's Garden
of Roses.* QUILTER: *Drink to Me Only.* CAPEL: *Love, Could I
Only Tell Thee.* TRAVERS: *A Mood.* PENN: *Smilin' Through.*
S. ADAMS: *The Holy City.* ROBSON: *The Cheviot Hills.*
DRESSER: *On the Banks of the Wabash, Far Away.*
LAMBERT: *God's Garden; She is Far from the Land.* PEEL: *In
Summertime on Bredon.* DIX: *The Trumpeter.* NOVELLO:
Till the Boys Come Home. RASBACH: *Trees.* O'CONNER: *The
Old House.* COATES: *Bird Songs at Eventide.* MURRAY: *I'll
Walk Beside You*
*** Hyp. CDA 67290

Sir Thomas Allen explains that in this collection of drawing-
room ballads he has tried to 'recapture memories of amateur
singers coming to our house in Seaham Harbour', when his
father would supervise at the piano. The disc, he says, marks

something of a watershed for him, with 'nostalgia and sentiment almost entirely responsible'. Thanks to the singer's
mastery and his winningly intimate, intense manner, speaking from the heart, there is not a suspicion of sentimentality
even in such numbers as 'Love's Garden of Roses', 'Smilin'
Through' or 'The Lost Chord', which could so easily have
seemed mawkish. Instead through his magnetism, as Allen
intends, one wonders at the simple beauty of the melodies in
these once-popular songs. Malcolm Martineau is the most
understanding accompanist, equally sensitive in taking a
fresh, unexaggerated approach.

'More Songs My Father Taught Me' (with Martineau,
piano): TRAD.: *She Moved thro' the Fair* (unaccompanied);
The Star of County Down (arr. Hughes); *Water o'Tyne.*
COATES: *The Green Hills o'Somerset; I Heard you Singing;
Star of God.* MURRAY: *Will you Go with Me?.* SHELDON: *A
Cradle Song.* SOMERSET: *Echo; A Song of Sleep.* SQUIRE:
Mountain Lovers. CLAY: *I'll Sing thee Songs of Araby.* BALL:
Mother Machree. WOOD: *Roses of Picardy.* ELLIOT: *There's a
Long Long Trail a-Winding.* BARRI: *The Old Brigade.*
WALLACE: *Yes! Let me Like a Soldier Fall.* D'HARDELOT:
Because. MOLLOY: *Love's Old Sweet Song.* SANDERSON:
Friend o'Mine. HATTON: *Simon the Cellarer; Time to Go.* S.
BENNETT: *The Songs of Today.* JACOBS-BOND: *Just
a-Wearyin' for You; Perfect Day.* HUGHES: *Down by the
Sally Gardens.* SULLIVAN: *Orpheus with his Lute.*
WOODFORDE-FINDEN: *Kashmiri Song.* F. HARRISON: *In the
Gloaming*
*** Hyp. CDA 67374

Sir Thomas Allen's first collection of drawing-room ballads
for Hyperion had immediate success. In this second instal-
ment, Allen's artistry once again transforms music, popular
long ago, that latterly has come to be dismissed as cheap and
sentimental. The melodies of such songs as 'Roses of Picardy',
'Love's Old Sweet Song' and 'Because', not to mention dozens
of less well-known items, have a winning ease and freshness
when sung with such warmth and fervour, with Malcolm
Martineau the ever-sensitive accompanist. Many of the songs
this time are Irish, reminding one of the vital role played by
the great tenor John McCormack in popularizing such ballads, while the inclusion of Sullivan's Shakespeare setting,
'Orpheus with his Lute', gives a reminder that the unquenchable melodic world of Gilbert and Sullivan is very close.

Allen, Sir Thomas (baritone), Malcolm Martineau (piano)

'Wigmore Hall Recital, 29 March 2005': BEETHOVEN:
*Maigesang; Adelaide; Marmotte; L'amante impatiente; Der
Kuss.* WOLF: *Harfnerspieler I–III; Anakreons Grab; Wie viele
Zeit verlor ich; Schon streckt ich aus; Ein Ständchen Euch zu
bringen kam.* Readings from A. E. Housman.
BUTTERWORTH: *A Shropshire Lad* (cycle). VAUGHAN
WILLIAMS: *Let beauty awake; The roadside fire; The infinite
shining heavens; Silent Noon.* BRIDGE: *So perverse;
Adoration; The Devon Maid*
(M) *** Wigmore Hall WHLive 002

This is easily the most successful of the three live vocal recitals issued so far on the Wigmore Hall's own label. Sir Thomas Allen not only sings beautifully but his warm baritone is naturally, often ravishingly, caught by the recording. Moreover, he has planned his programme admirably so that it can be listened to in entirety with continuing pleasure. He opens in romantic mood with Beethoven, and the last two songs of the group, *L'amante impaziente* and *Der Kuss*, are charmingly light-hearted. By contrast, the Wolf items are more serious, with the three *Harfnerspieler* particularly moving.

You may not always want the A. E. Housman poems with which he introduces each number of the lovely *Shropshire Lad* cycle – the epitome of English song-writing – but they can be programmed out, and the following Vaughan Williams and Frank Bridge songs follow in much the same style. His closing encore is *Silent Noon*, and very touching it is. Full texts (and, where necessary, translations) are included.

Alva, Luigi (tenor)

'*Spanish & Latin American Songs*' (arr. Pattacini) (with the New SO of L, Iller Pattacini): *Granada; Sevilla; Toledo; Valencia; Ay-Ay-Ay; Princesita; Estrellita; Sin tu amor; Te quiero, dijiste; La partida; Amapola; El trust de los tenorios*
(M) *** Decca Classic Recitals (ADD) 475 6410

These popular and gorgeously tuneful songs are presented with colourful orchestrations, stylish singing and idiomatic flair. The 1964 sound is exceptionally warm and vivid, bringing out all the bright colours and vivid orchestrations (the opening snare drum in *Granada* is arresting) and this collection is highly desirable in every way.

Ameling, Elly (soprano)

'*The Artistry of Elly Ameling*': BACH: Excerpts from: *St Matthew Passion; St John Passion; Christmas Oratorio.* HAYDN: *Die Schöpfung* (with Stuttgart CO, Münchinger). *Orlando Paladino* (with Lausanne CO, Dorati). HANDEL: *Messiah* (with Reynolds, ASMF, Marriner). Cantatas: *Crudel tiranno amor* (with ECO, Leppard). VIVALDI: *Juditha triumphans, RV 644* (with Berlin CO, Negri). Songs: HAYDN: *Das strickende Mädchen; Der erste Küss; An Iris; Liebeslied; Geistliches Lied; Das Leben ist ein Traume Abscheidslied* (with Demus). MOZART: Arias from: *Le nozze di Figaro. Misera! Dove son! Exsultate, jubilate, K.165* (with ECO, Leppard). *Ch'io mi scordi, K.505.* SCHUBERT: *Der Musensohn; Die Forelle; Aus dem Wässer zu singen* (with Jansen); *Die Sterne; Der Einsamel; An Sylvia; Minnelied; An die Laute; Seligkeit; Das Lied im Grünen; Im Freien; Kennst du das Land; Heidenröslein; Die junge Nonne; Gretchen am Spinnrade; Ave Maria; An die Musik; Der Knabe.* SCHUMANN: *Frauenliebe und Leben, Op. 42.* BRAHMS: *Heimweh; Der Jäger; Agnes; In den Beeren; Der Frühling; Die Trauernde; Vergebliches Ständchen; Spanische Lied; Von waldbekränzter Höhe; Wiegenlied; Immer Leiser wird mein Schlummer.* WOLF: *20 Mörike Lieder* (all with Baldwin). FAURE: *Après un rêve.* DEBUSSY: *Beau soir; Mandoline.* HAHN: *L'Amité; La Vie est belle.* SATIE: *La Diva de 'L'Empire'* (with Jansen). GERSHWIN: *Embraceable You; The Man I Love; I've Got a Crush on You; But not for Me.* GOEMANS: *Aan de Amsterdamse grachten.* PORTER: *I Get a Kick out of You; What is This Thing Called Love?; You do*

Something to Me; Begin the Beguine; Night and Day. KERN: *All the Things You Are.* SONDHEIM: *Can that Boy Foxtrot!.* GIMBEL: *Garota de Ipanema.* DRÉJAC: *Sous le ciel de Paris.* ELLINGTON: *Caravan; Sophisticated Lady; Solitude; It don't Mean a Thing; In a Sentimental Mood* (all with Van Dijk)
(BB) **(*) Ph. (ADD/DDD) 473 451-2 (5)

The Dutch soprano Elly Ameling was launched on her career in 1956 when she so impressed the judges at an international competition that they created a special new award for her: 'First Prize with Distinction'. Her recording career with Philips spanned the next two decades and covered a remarkably wide musical range. The beauty of her voice is never in doubt, and the first CD here concentrates on her eighteenth-century repertoire, drawing on her complete sets, with several items recorded in the 1960s when her voice was at its brightest and her technique ideally fluent. However, Vivaldi's *Juditha triumphans* dates from the mid-1970s and shows her in maturity. Here she takes only a servant's role, though that is one which demands more brilliant technique than any.

Many of the Haydn songs so charmingly sung on disc 2 have clear anticipations of nineteenth-century Lieder, and Ameling, with her simple style, projects them to perfection, with Joerg Demus a brightly sympathetic accompanist. There are also Mozart performances of a very high order, and in *Exsultate, jubilate* the bravura is marvellously secure technically, while the singing itself has a simple radiance.

The Schubert Lieder on disc 3 make a delightful recital in themselves, with Ameling at her freshest and Dalton Baldwin accompanying with unfailing sensitivity. In the strophic songs she is a persuasive interpreter, gently pointing each verse. The early setting of Mignon's *Kennst du das Land* is charmingly simple, in contrast to the great Wolf setting. The performance of *Frauenliebe und Leben* has freshness and girlishness on its side, but this is a cycle which demands deeper tones in the later songs, so, while this is attractive, it is only a partial view.

The Brahms songs are sung with spirit and feeling, and the readings are unfailingly musical. *Die Trauernde* is very touching. However, in Wolf's *Mörike Lieder*, while the diction is clean and her interpretations intelligent, there is a certain uniformity of colour and mood that makes listening to the whole collection less satisfying than picking out individual songs. Needless to say, there is much to enjoy and, while Baldwin is a bit prosaic at times, against this must be balanced some highly musical and carefully thought-out details.

The popular collection on disc 5 is particularly treasurable. One expects the French mélodies to be a success, though the nice hint of irony in Satie's *La Diva de 'L'Empire'* is a neat touch. But anyone who thinks of Elly Ameling as a rather demure singer will be surprised at the magnetism with which she can bring out the beauty of melodies by Gershwin or Cole Porter. The introduction to 'Night and Day' is particularly seductive, and she is especially good in one of the most memorable of Gershin's songs, 'The Man I Love'; and she is very stylish in the Ellington numbers. Loius van Dijk's pointed accompaniments often have a flavour of Debussy or Ravel. Throughout all five discs the recording is most natural and beautifully balanced. However, there are no texts and translations, and the notes are sparse and mainly biographical.

Renaissance Christmas Music and Motets (with Bernard Michaelis (alto), Tölz Boys' Ch., Instrumental Ens.,

Gerhard Schmidt-Gaden): Music by PRAETORIUS, ECCARD, SCHEIDT and others. *Alpine Christmas Carols.*
(B) ** BMG/DHM 82876 69996-2 (2)

This set combines two quite separate discs, recorded in 1961 and 1965 respectively. The first includes quite a few familiar pieces by Praetorius, and the performances, led by Elly Ameling, are warmly refined. The second collection, from the Tölz Boys' Choir, is livelier, bringing more Christmas motets and some charming Alpine Christmas folk carols. The period instrumental ensemble provides good support and the recording is warmly atmospheric. The overall effect is pleasing, but not really distinctive.

American Boychoir, Atlantic Brass Quintet, James Litton

'*Trumpets Sound, Voices Ring: A Joyous Christmas*': arr. WILLCOCKS: *O Come All Ye Faithful; Once in Royal David's City.* RUTTER: *Angel Tidings; Star Carol; The Lord Bless You and Keep You.* BRAHMS: *Regina coeli.* ELGAR: *The Snow.* GAWTHROP: *Mary Speaks.* MENDELSSOHN, arr. WILLCOCKS: *Hark! the Herald Angels Sing.* VAUGHAN WILLIAMS: *Hodie; Lullaby.* FRASER: *This Christmastide (Jessye's Carol).* CORELLI: *Concerto grosso in G min. (Christmas), Op. 6/8.* MANZ: *E'en so, Lord Jesus, Quickly Come.* TELEMANN: *Lobet den Herrn, alle Heiden; Meine Seele, erhebt den Herrn.* CASALS: *Nigra sum.* Spiritual: *Go Tell it on the Mountain*
*** MusicMasters 01612 67076-2

Gleaming brass fanfares introduce this lively and attractively diverse American collection featuring a gleaming treble line against full brass sonorities. The Americans follow the English King's College tradition at the opening of 'Once in Royal David's City' but cap its climax resplendently. The three Rutter carols are ideal for boy trebles and the infectious *Star Carol* brings an engagingly light rhythmic touch. Elgar's much less well-known portrayal of 'The Snow' is very touching, while 'Jessye's Carol' has one of those gentle but haunting melodies that persist in the memory: its descant is particularly apt, and it builds to an expansive climax. Both 'Mary Speaks' and Paul Manz's 'E'en so, Lord Jesus' are modern carols with an appealing simplicity, matched by Pablo Casals's better-known *Nigra sum.* The two Telemann items featuring famous chorales are both floridly testing of the boys' resources, and here the faster passages are not always completely secure. But they provide a nice baroque contrast, and it was a happy idea to include a brass transcription of Corelli's famous *Christmas Concerto grosso,* which, if sounding comparatively robust, is still highly effective when played so well. The choral singing is generally of a high calibre and the recording has a natural, warm ambience and is admirably clear.

Ampleforth Schola Cantorum, Ian Little

'*Carols from Ampleforth*': arr. WILLCOCKS: *O Come All Ye Faithful; Once in Royal David's City; Unto us a Son is Born; Sussex Carol; God Rest you Merry, Gentlemen.* arr. HOLST: *Personent Hodie.* arr. JACQUES: *Good King Wenceslas.* arr. STAINER/WILLCOCKS: *The First Nowell.* PRAETORIUS: *A Great and Mighty Wonder.* arr. RUTTER: *Angel Tidings.*

STEWART: *On this Day Earth shall Ring.* WARLOCK: *Adam Lay Ybounden.* MATHIAS: *Sir Christèmas.* arr. WOOD: *Past Three o'Clock; Ding, Dong! Merrily on High.* arr. SULLIVAN: *It Came upon the Midnight Clear.* arr. LEDGER: *Still, Still, Still.* arr. LITTLE: *Come with Torches.* arr. PETTMAN: *The Infant King.* GRUBER, arr. LITTLE: *Silent Night.* MENDELSSOHN, arr. WILLCOCKS: *Hark! the Herald Angels Sing*
*** Ampleforth Abbey Records Dig. AARCD 1

A splendidly robust selection of favourites, with the expansive abbey acoustic and the superb organ adding much to the listener's pleasure. The sound itself is often thrilling with men and boys both singing ardently; there are a few minor blemishes of ensemble, but nothing to worry about when the projection is so vigorously communicative. Perhaps the rhythm of Mathias's 'Sir Christémas' is a bit heavy, but 'On this Day Earth shall Ring' makes a magnificent effect, with the organ adding a final blaze of sound at the close. There are gentler carols too, of course, though not all will like Ian Little's added harmonies at the end of 'Silent Night'.

Angeles, Victoria de los (soprano)

French Songs: (with Paris Conservatoire O, Georges Prêtre, or Gonzalo Soriano (piano)): RAVEL: *Shéhérazade; 5 Mélodies populairs grecques; 2 Mélodies hébraïques; Chants populaires.* DEBUSSY: *3 Chansons de Bilitis; Fêtes galants; Noël des enfants qui n'ont plus de maisons; L'enfant prodigue: Récit et Air de Lia.* DUPARC: *L'invitation au voyage; Phidyle*
☞ (M) *** EMI (ADD) 3 45821-2 [3 45822-2]

This treasurable collection last appeared in a four-disc compilation rghtly called '*The Fabulous Victoria de los Angeles*' and has not been available separately for many years. The recordings were made in the 1960s, when the voice was at its freshest, and these French classics give special delight. They are well worthy of a place among EMI's 'Great Recordings of the Century'.

'*Songs of Spain*': Disc 1: *Traditional songs* (arr. Graciano Tarragó; with Renata Tarragó & Graciano Tarragó, guitars); *Medieval songs* (early 14th century); *Renaissance and Baroque songs* (15th–18th centuries; with Ens., José María Lamaña)

Disc 2: *Medieval and Renaissance songs of Andalusia; Renaissance songs* (with Ars Musicae de Barcelona, Enrique Gisbert & José María Lamaña)

Disc 3: *19th- and 20th-century arrangements and art songs: Canciones Sefardies* (arr. Valls; with Gérard, flute, & Ghighia, guitar); *Canciones populares españoles* (arr. Lorca; with Miguel Zanetti, piano). Songs by MOMPOU; TOLDRA; MONTSALVATGE; RODRIGO (all with Soriano, piano); GRANADOS; GURIDU; HALFFTER; TURINA; NIN; VALVERDE (all with Gerald Moore, piano); BARRERA & CALLEJA (arr. Los Angeles, guitar); MONTSALVATGE: *Madrigal* (with Barcelona City Orchestra, Navarro)

Disc 4: *Songs and opera arias:* GRANADOS: *Colección de tonadillas; 3 majas dolorosa* (with Gonzalo Soriano, piano); *Goyescas: La Maja y el ruiseñor.* FALLA: *La vida breve:* excerpts (with New Philh. O or Paris Conservatoire O, Rafael Frühbeck de Burgos). 1971 New York Recital (with

De Larrocha, piano): Songs by LITERES; DE LASERNA; GIMENEZ. GRANADOS: *Canciones amatorias.* FALLA: *7 Canciones populares españolas*

(M) *** EMI mono/stereo 5 66937-2 (4)

Issued to celebrate the singer's seventy-fifth birthday in November 1998, this four-disc compilation of Los Angeles in her native Spanish repertory is a delight. Two of the four discs are devoted to traditional, medieval and renaissance songs, accompanied by the guitarist Renata Tarragó, as well as by her mentor in early music, José María Lamaña, with his own Ars Musicae of Barcelona and a British group. Recorded over two decades between 1950 and 1971, the set also includes de los Angeles's contribution to the closing ceremony of the 1992 Barcelona Olympic Games (the folk/madrigal *El cant dels ocells* of Montsalvatge), the voice carefully husbanded but still golden.

Overall, this lavish survey represents a cross-section of the varied types of art song which were current in the rich period of Spanish music between the thirteenth and sixteenth centuries, and then moves on to include key nineteenth- and twentieth-century repertoire. Earliest are monodic cantigas associated with the Virgin Mary, but most of the rest are secular, including a group of songs of the Sephardic Jewish tradition, also romances and villancicos (brief ballads), songs with vihuela accompaniments and madrigals – one might quibble about their presentation by a solo voice – of a later period. The first disc opens with eighteen traditional songs arranged by Graciano Tarragó, with guitar accompaniments, and the result has a captivating simplicity; moreover the mono recordings (from 1950–52) give a most natural presence for the voice.

Since the early days of her career, Los Angeles has been associated with the Ars Musicae ensemble of Barcelona. They play here on authentic instruments – fidulas, recorders, lute, vihuela de mano, viols and lira da braccio – and if the more complex later songs from the Courts of Charles V and Philip II hardly match the finest of our own Elizabethan songs, they are exquisitely done by Los Angeles and her friends. The Spanish folksongs arranged by the poet Lorca are mainly dance-songs, while the main Sephardic collection, arranged by Valls, gives an admirable sample of the music which was developing among Spanish Jews in the late Middle Ages, exotic and individual. The later Granados and Falla items are better known and no less winning.

Los Angeles made her recording début with the two Falla arias years ago; these later versions come from 1962. The collection ends with her live New York recital of 1971, where she forms a symbiotic partnership with her Catalan contemporary, Alicia de Larrocha, as accompanist, including the best loved of her encore numbers, Valverde's *Clavelitos* and *Adios Granada*, and ending with a riotous *Zapateado*. The voice is as fresh as ever. What matters most is that this is all music which inspires the singer to her fullest, most captivating artistry. The documentation could be more extensive, but full texts and translations are included.

Anonymous Four

'*The Lily and the Lamb*' (chant and polyphony from medieval England): *Conducti, Hymns, Motets, Sequences; Antiphon: Ave regina coelorum*

*** HM HMU 907125

The Anonymous Four (Ruth Cunningham, Marsha Genensky, Susan Hellauer and Johanna Rose) are an American vocal quartet whose voices merge into a particularly pleasing blend. They came together in 1986, bringing with them a variety of musical skills, including instrumental proficiency and a musicological background. The group focuses on medieval music, mainly sacred, spanning 500 years, from the eleventh to the fourteenth century. It is perhaps appropriate that this first collection should be devoted to hymns, sequences and motets dedicated to the Virgin Mary.

Women in medieval times identified with Mary and in particular her suffering as she saw her son dying on the cross. The second item in this programme, a monodic hymn, begins with the words 'The gentle lamb spread on the cross, hung all bathed with blood'. For women of those times, death was an everyday event, especially since only a small proportion of their many children survived into adulthood and they saw their young loved ones succumb to disease and other causes. The singers here blend their voices into one, whether singing monody or in simple polyphony, as in the sequence *Stillat in stelam radium*, or the beautiful motet *Veni mater gracie*. The voices are heard floating in an ecclesiastic acoustic and the effect is mesmeric.

'*An English Ladymass*' (13th- and 14th-century chant and polyphony in honour of the Virgin Mary): *Alleluias, Gradual, Hymn, Introit, Kyrie, Motets, Offertory, Rondellus, Sequences, Songs*

**(*) HM HMU 907080

In medieval times most large churches and cathedrals had a lady chapel, where a Ladymass could be sung regularly to the Virgin Mary. And these still exist today in larger Catholic cathedrals, like Chartres in France. They usually have an extraordinary atmosphere and one watches with respect as young mothers not only attend alone but also bring their children to present to the statue of the Virgin. Here the Anonymous Four have arranged their own Mass sequence with the Propers interspersed with appropriate motets, hymns, a Gradual and Alleluia, finally concluding with the hymn *Ave Maris stella*. In doing so they make their own homage to the Virgin Mother which is well planned. The music is beautifully sung, although this is perhaps not one of their most potent collections.

'*Miracles of Sant'Iago*' (medieval chant and polyphony for St James from the Codex Calixtinus): *Agnus dei trope, Benedicamus tropes, Kyrie trope, Antiphon, Conducti, Hymns, Invitatory, Offertory, Prosae, Responsories*

*** HM HMU 907156

The Cathedral of Santiago in Compostela is the home of a manuscript of five books called collectively *Jacobus*, and its music was designed to be sung by groups of young French boy-trebles. It proves ideal material for the Anonymous Four and its musical interest is immediately demonstrated by the brilliantly decorated Benedicamus trope *Vox nostra resonet*. Much of the music is plainchant, but the early examples of two-part polyphony are very striking. Again the singing here is magnetic and the warm resonance of the recording very flattering.

'*Love's Illusion*' (French motets on courtly love texts from the 13th-century Montpellier Codex): *Plus bele que flor / Quant revient / L'autrier joer; Puisque bele dame m'eime; Amours mi font souffrir / En mai; Ne sai, que je die; Si je chante / Bien doi amer; Or ne sai je que devenir / puisque d'amer; Hé Dieus, de si haut si bas / Maubatus; Celui en qui / La bele estoile / La bele, en qui; Qui d'amours se plaint;*

Amours, dont je sui / L'autrier, au douz mois / Chose Tassin; Au cuer ai un mal / Ja ne m'en repentirai / Jolietement; Quant voi la fleur; Quant se depart / Onques ne sai amer; Joliement / Quant voi la florete / Je sui joliete; Amor potest conqueri / Adamorem sequitur; Ce que je tieng / Certes mout / Bone compaignie; J'ai si bien mon cuer assiz / Aucun m'ont; Ne m'oubliez mie; J'ai mis toute ma pensee / Je n'en puis; Blanchete / Quant je pens; Dame, que je n'os noumer / Amis donc est / Lonc tans a; Li savours de mon desir / Li grant desir / Non veul mari; Entre Copin / Je me cuidoie / Bele Ysabelos; S'on me regarde / Prennés i garde / Hé, mi enfant; Quant yver la bise ameine; Ne m'a pas oublié; On doit fin[e] Amor / La biauté; Ja n'amerai autre que cele; Quant je parti de m'amie
*** HM HMU 907109

For this programme the Anonymous Four have moved away from liturgical music and chosen twenty-nine thirteenth-century motets from the Montpellier Codex, setting courtly love texts with simple and affecting polyphony. It is remarkable how the atmosphere of this music brings a more secular, plaintive quality. The means are the same but the expressive result is different, for the words are about the joys and regrets and the feelings of love. Many of these songs are dolorous but *Ne sai, que je die* (about pride, hypocrisy and avarice) and *Qui l'amours se plaint* are both dance songs. This is one of the most attractive of this fine group's collections. They are obviously moved, as women, by the words they sing, and they find remarkable variety of expressive feeling here. Occasionally a drone is added under the melodic line to telling effect, and one never misses an instrumental backing. The recording is well up to standard. A splendid disc.

'*On Yoolis night*' (medieval carols and motets): *Antiphons, Carols, Hymns, Motets, Responsory, Rondella, Songs*
*** HM HMU 907099

This is a delightful collection. The carol *Alleluia, A New Work* and the anonymous setting of *Ave Maria* are both enchanting discoveries, and many of these items have that curious, Christmassy colouring. The dance song *Gabriel from Heaven-king* and the lovely *Lullay: I Saw a Sweet Seemly Sight* are matched by *As I Lay on Yoolis Night*, while the closing *Nowel* is wonderfully joyful. The simple medieval implied harmonies in no way inhibit the character but increase the special colour of these carols, which are sung tenderly or with great spirit by this excellent group. Here is a record to lay in store for next Christmas, but to play at other times too.

'*A Star in the East*' (medieval Hungarian Christmas music): *Alleluias, Antiphons, Communion, Evangelium, Gradual, Hymns, Introit, Lectio, Motet, Offertory, Sanctus, Songs, Te Deum*
*** HM HMU 907139

The repertoire here is comparatively unsophisticated but full of charm, and the singing has the right kind of innocence. The programme came about by accident. While one of the group was researching the music of Hildegard of Bingen at Columbia University Library, a book of Hungarian Christmas music fell off the shelf at the researcher's feet, inviting its performance. There is not a great deal of polyphony here, but that is not a feature of many of our own favourite Christmas carols either. There is no lack of melody. Excellent recording and splendid documentation.

'*Wolcum Yule*' (Celtic and British Songs and Carols): TRAD. English: *Awake and Join the Cheerful Choir; The Holly and the Ivy; I Saw Three Ships; Cherry Tree Carol.* TRAD. Irish: *Good People All; The Seven Rejoices of Mary; Air: On a Cold Winter's Day; Flight into Egypt.* TRAD. Scottish: *Balulalo; The Reel of Tullochgorum.* TRAD. Welsh: *Behold Here is the Morning.* TRAD. Cornish: *Wassail Song.* R. R. BENNETT: *Balulalow.* MAXWELL DAVIES: *Calendar of Kings.* BURGON: *A God, and yet a Man.* HENRY VIII (attrib.): *Grene Growith the holy.* BRITTEN: *A New Year Carol*
*** HM HMU 907325

Anonymous Four have come up trumps again with their latest Christmas collection. Johanna Maria Rose has researched her repertoire with characteristic skill, drawing on early folk collections by Scotsman Alan Ramsay, Northern Irishman Edward Bunting, and the pair of Cornishmen, Davies Gilbert and William Sandys. The resulting programme is delightfully fresh and varied, with the folk items interwoven with more modern carols, notably the highly individual *Calendar of Kings* by Peter Maxwell Davies, newly commissioned for this antholgy. As usual the layout is as impeccably planned as it is diverse, and the *a cappella* singing and playing as polished as it is consistently engaging (with Andrew-Lawrence King using – variously – Irish harp, baroque harp, and psaltery). The recording is first class, as is the documentation, with full texts ornamented by soft-grained woodcuts. A Christmas concert that can be listened to as a whole entity or dipped into at pleasure, and also making a perfect Christmas gift.

'*A Portrait*': excerpts from '*Miracles of Sant'Iago*'; '*The Lily and the Lamb*';'*A Star in the East*'; '*Love's illusion*'; '*An English Ladymass*';'*On Yoolis Night*'
(B) *** HM HMX 2907210

Here is a carefully chosen selection of highlights from the six CDs listed above. It's well worth sampling to find out whether the pure yet richly expressive vocal style of this remarkable female group will tempt you to explore further in one direction or another.

Ars Nova, Bo Holten

'*Portuguese Polyphony*': CARDOSO: *Lamentatio; Magnificat secundi toni.* LOBO: *Audivi vocem de caelo; Pater peccavi.* MAGALHAES: *Vidi aquam; Missa O Soberana luz; Commissa mea pavesco.* MANUEL DA FONSECA: *Beata viscera.* BARTOLOMEO TROSYLHO: *Circumdederunt.* PEDRO DE ESCOBAR: *Clamabat autem mulier*
(BB) *** Naxos Dig. 8.553310

In every respect this is an outstanding anthology. Apart from the major items from the Portuguese 'famous three' contemporaries, Cardoso, Lôbo and (the least-known) Filippe de Magalhães, which are discussed above under their respective composer entries in our main volume, the motets by the earlier figures, Pedro de Escobar (c. 1465–1535), Bartolomeo Trosylho (c. 1500–c. 1567) and Manuel da Fonseca (*maestre da capela* at Braga Cathedral in the mid-sixteenth century), are all touchingly, serenely beautiful, if perhaps less individual. The singing of this Danish Choir is superb and so is the Naxos recording. Texts and translations are provided, although for some reason they are printed separately. A unique bargain of the highest quality.

Atlanta Symphony Orchestra Chamber Chorus, Norman Mackenzie

20th Century Choral Music: MESSIAEN: *O sacrum convivium.* TAVENER: *Song for Athene.* VAUGHAN WILLIAMS: *Mass in G min.* DURUFLÉ; *4 Motets on Gregorian Theme, Op. 10.* COPLAND: *4 Motets, Op. 20.* TALLIS: *O sacrum convivium*

⊕ *** Telarc CD 80654

Formed by Robert Shaw to replace his own Chorale, the Atlanta Symphony Orchestra Chamber Chorus is among the finest semi-professional vocal groups in the world. It numbers from 40 to 60 voices, depending on the repertoire to be performed, and has been under the direction of the present conductor, Norman Mackenzie, since Shaw's death in 1999. This is the chorus's first *a cappella* compilation – and very fine it is. The blending of voices is matched by the most subtle control of dynamic and colour, well shown by the two contrasting settings of *O sacrum convivium* by Messiaen and Tallis which frame the programme so richly and expressively. The climax of Tavener's *Song for Athene* is quite remarkably intense, and the account of the Vaughan Williams *Mass* could not be more sensitive or richly appealing; the *Sanctus* is wonderfully radiant. The third of the Duruflé *Motets, Tu es Petrus,* also has an exhilarating climax, and the *Four* (early) Copland *Motets,* if not typical of the composer, are most lively and stimulating. A splendid disc in every way, given sound-quality of demonstration calibre in its naturalness and ambient warmth.

Augér, Arleen (soprano)

'Love songs' (with Baldwin, piano): COPLAND: *Pastorale; Heart, we will Forget Him.* OBRADORS: *Del Cabello más sutil.* OVALLE: *Azulao.* R STRAUSS: *Ständchen; Das Rosenband.* MARX: *Selige Nacht.* POULENC: *Fleurs.* CIMARA: *Stornello.* QUILTER: *Music, when Soft Voices Die; Love's Philosophy.* O. STRAUS: *Je t'aime.* SCHUMANN: *Widmung; Du bist wie eine Blume.* MAHLER: *Liebst du um Schönheit.* TURINA: *Cantares.* LIPPE: *How do I Love Thee?* COWARD: *Conversation Piece: I'll Follow my Secret Heart.* GOUNOD: *Serenade.* SCHUBERT: *Liebe schwärmt auf allen Wegen.* BRIDGE: *Love Went a-Riding.* FOSTER: *Why, No One to Love.* DONAUDY: *O del mio amato ben.* BRITTEN (arr.): *The Salley Gardens.* LOEWE: *Camelot: Before I Gaze at you Again*

✿ *** Delos D/CD 3029

This extraordinarily wide-ranging recital is a delight from the first song to the last. Arleen Augér opens with Copland and closes with *Camelot,* and she is equally at home in the music by Roger Quilter (*Love's Philosophy* is superbly done), Noël Coward and the *Rückert* song of Mahler. Britten's arrangement of *The Salley Gardens,* ravishingly slow, is another highlight. The layout of the recital could hardly have been managed better: each song creates its new atmosphere readily, but seems to be enhanced by coming after the previous choice. Dalton Baldwin's accompaniments are very much a partnership with the singing, while the playing itself is spontaneously perceptive throughout. With a good balance and a very realistic recording, this projects vividly like a live recital.

Baker, Dame Janet (mezzo-soprano)

'Philips and Decca Recordings, 1961–79': CD 1: *'Aria amorose'* (arr. Preston) (with ASMF, Marriner): GIORDANI: *Caro mio ben.* CACCINI: *Amarilli mia bella.* STRADELLA: *Region sempre addita.* SARRI: *Sen corre l'agnelletta.* CESTI: *Intorno all'idol mio.* LOTTI: *Pur dicesti, o bocca bella.* A. SCARLATTI: *Già il sole Gange; Selve amiche; Sento nel core; Spesso vibra per suo gioco.* CALDARA: *Come raggio di sol; Sebben, crudele, mi fai languir.* BONONCINI: *Deh più a me non v'ascondete.* DURANTE: *Danza fanciulla gentile.* PERGOLESI: *Ogni pena più spietata.* MARTINI: *Plaisir d'amour.* PICCINNI: *O notte, o dea del mistero.* PAISIELLO: *Nel cor più non mi sento.* Arias from: CAVALLI: *La Calisto* (with James Bowman, LPO, Raymond Leppard)

CD 2: HANDEL: *Lucrezia* (cantata). Arias from: *Ariodante; Atalanta; Hercules; Joshua; Rodelinda; Serse* (with ECO, Leppard). Arias from: BACH: *Cantata 170* (with ASMF, Marriner). PURCELL: *Dido and Aeneas* (with St Anthony Singers, ECO, Lewis)

CD 3: HAYDN: *Arianna a Naxos* (cantata); *Berenice, che fai?* (*Scena di Berenice*) (with ECO, Leppard). MOZART: Arias from: *La Clemenza di Tito; Così fan tutte* (with ROHCG O, C. Davis). SCHUBERT: *Ständchen; Lazarus: So schlummert auf Rosen.* BEETHOVEN: *Ah Perfido!* (with ECO, Leppard)

CD 4: Arias from: RAMEAU: *Hippolyte et Aricie* (with St Anthony Singers, ECO, Lewis). GLUCK: *Alceste; Orfeo ed Euridice* (with ECO, Leppard). BERLIOZ: *Cléopâtre; Herminie.* Excerpts from: *Béatrice et Bénédict* (with LSO, C. Davis)

CD 5: RAVEL: *Chansons Madécasses; 3 Poèmes de Stéphane Mallarmé.* CHAUSSON: *Chanson perpétuelle.* DELAGE: *4 Poèmes Hindous* (with Melos Ens.). BRITTEN: Arias from: *The Rape of Lucretia* (with Shirley-Quirk, ECO, Britten); *Owen Wingrave* (with Luxon, Douglas, ECO, Britten); *Phaedra* (with ECO, Steuart Bedford)

(B) *** Ph. (ADD) 475 161-2 (5)

A self-recommending treasure trove. The contents of Dame Janet Baker's rare 1978 LP *Arie amorose* is included complete, a delightful anthology, with the programme cleverly arranged to contrast expressive with sprightly music, and the wide range of tonal gradation and beautiful phrasing matched by an artless lightness of touch. The accompaniments are intimate and tasteful: there is no more engaging example than Pergolesi's *Ogni pena più spietata,* with its deft bassoon obbligato, or the short closing song with harpsichord, Paisiello's *Nel cor più non mi sento.* Warm, well-focused sound, too.

Disc 2 (1972) includes Dame Janet's Handel recital – with the cantata *Lucrezia* and various arias, ranging from the pure gravity of *Ombra mai fù* to the passionate commitment and supreme coloratura virtuosity in *Dopo notte* from *Ariodante.* Leppard gives sparkling support, and the sound emerges freshly on CD.

On the third CD, recorded in 1973 with the same conductor, the two Haydn cantatas (*Arianna a Naxos* and *Scena di Berenice*) communicate the same warm intensity, transcending the formality of the genre, making them miniature operas in all but name. Also included are Mozart arias and key recordings of music by Schubert and Beethoven.

The fourth CD ventures into French opera and also includes Berlioz's two dramatic scenas, *Cléopâtre* and *Herminie,* which were both written as entries for the *Prix de Rome;* both give many hints of the mature Berlioz, even presenting specific foretastes of material later used in the *Symphonie fantastique* (the *idée fixe*), and the *Roman Carnival Overture* (the melody of the introduction). Dame Janet sings with passionate intensity, while Sir Colin Davis draws committed playing from the LSO, all in fine (1979) sound.

Disc five brings Baker's classic (1966) Oiseau-Lyre recital of French mélodies, with superb playing from the Melos group. Chausson's cycle of a deserted lover has a direct communication, which Baker contrasts with the subtler beauties of the Ravel songs. She shows great depth of feeling for the poetry here, and an equally evocative sensitivity to the songs about India written by Ravel's pupil, Maurice Delage, in 1912. Filling up this disc are powerful reminders of Baker's association with Benjamin Britten, and the selection includes her 1977 recording of *Phaedra*, written for her at the very end of the composer's life. Setting words from Robert Lowell's fine translation of Racine's play, the composer encapsulated the character of the tragic heroine and provided vocal writing which brings out every glorious facet of her voice. The use of the harpsichord in the recitative linking the sections of this scena is no mere neo-classical device, but a sharply dramatic and atmospheric stroke. Altogether this is a feast of great performances offered for little money, and the only quibble is the lack of texts. The sound is excellent throughout.

Lieder (with Martin Isepp (piano)): SCHUMANN: *Frauenliebe und Leben (Song Cycle), Op. 42.* BRAHMS: *Die Mainacht; Das Mädchen spricht; Nachtigall; Von ewiger Liebe.* SCHUBERT: *Heimliches Lieben; Minnelied; Die Abgeblühte Linde; Die Musensohn*
♦—• (BB) *** Regis RRC 1225

Janet Baker's famous (1966) – originally Saga – Lieder recital has been out of the catalogue for far too long. Her elysian, intensely poignant account of Schumann's *Frauenliebe und Leben* is discussed under its composer entry. The Brahms songs are also beyond praise. The Schubert songs are not quite on this level (*Der Musensohn* is a little jerky) but this is singing of a quality that you find only once or twice in a generation. The recording is not perfect: the balance favours the piano and the loud passages strain the resources of the engineers. But Baker's artistry quickly distracts attention from any such minor techincal defects.

Radio Recordings (with various accompanists): HAYDN: *Arianna a Naxos (cantata).* SCHUMANN: *Frauenliebe und Leben, Op. 42.* SCHUBERT: *Der blinde Knabe; Totengräber-Weise.* WOLF: *Die ihr schwebet; Geh', Geliebter, geh'jetzt!* SCHUMANN: *Meine Rose; Der Page.* R. STRAUSS: *Befreit; Heimliche Aufforderung; Morgen!*
(M) *** BBC (ADD) BBCL 4049-2

These vintage radio recordings from 1968–70 find Dame Janet Baker in glorious voice. Both the Haydn scena and Schumann song-cycle were recorded live at Snape Maltings, while the mixed Lieder recital was done in the studio, with all three conveying the urgency and spontaneity of live performance. Compared with Dame Janet's other studio recordings of this same repertory they bring out even more strikingly the vehement intensity of her singing as well as its heart-stopping beauty and glorious contrasts of tone-colour. Never have the changing emotions of *Frauenliebe und Leben* been so vividly conveyed on disc, from ecstasy to exhilaration to agony. It is a pity no texts are given.

HAYDN: *19 Scottish Folksongs* (with Menuhin & Malcolm, harpsichord). BEETHOVEN: *5 Scottish Folksongs* (with Ross Pople). CAMPIAN: *Never Love Unless you Can; Oft have I Sighed; If Thou Longest so Much to Learn; Fain Would I Wed;* DOWLAND: *Come Again* (with Spencer, lute). ARNE: *Where the Bee Sucks* (with Spencer & Whittaker, flute). BOYCE: *Tell me Lovely Shepherd.* MONRO: *My Lovely Celia.* PURCELL: *Sleep, Adam, Sleep, Lord, What is Man?* (with Isepp & Gauntlett)
*** Testament SBT 1241

This Testament issue, superbly transferred, generously brings together two of Dame Janet Baker's most charming discs, long neglected. The Haydn and Beethoven folksong settings accompanied by Yehudi Menuhin and George Malcolm (on the harpsichord in Haydn, on the piano in Beethoven) stem from a project at the Windsor Festival in the 1970s, when Menuhin was music director. These studio recordings reflect the joy of discovery and corporate music-making on the highest level. The English songs come from a recording which Dame Janet made earlier in 1967 with the Elizabethan songs by Dowland and Campian accompanied on the lute by Robert Spencer and with the flautist, Douglas Whittaker joining the team in the popular Arne setting of *Where the Bee Sucks.* Dame Janet is in glorious voice, with well-balanced EMI sound still very vivid.

RAVEL: *Shéhérazade* (with New Philh. O, Barbirolli). CHAUSSON: *Poème de l'amour et de la mer.* DUPARC: *Phidylé; La Vie antérieure; Le Manoir de Rosamonde; Au pays où se fait la guerre; L'Invitation au voyage* (all with LSO, Previn). SCHUMANN: *Frauenliebe und Leben* (with Barenboim). BRAHMS: *Vier ernste Gesänge, Op. 121* (with Previn); *2 Lieder, with Viola, Op. 91* (with Aronowitz, Previn); *4 Duets, Op. 28* (with Fischer-Dieskau, Barenboim)
♦—• (B) *** EMI Double fforte (ADD) 5 68667-2 (2)

Dame Janet Baker was always at her finest in French music, and with her 1967 performance of *Shéhérazade* she inspired Barbirolli to one of his most glowing performances in this atmospherically scored music; her range of tone and her natural sympathy for the French language make for heart-warming singing which has a natural intensity. The account of Chausson's *Poème de l'amour et de la mer* is comparably glorious and heartfelt, both radiant and searching, so that this picture of love in two aspects, first emergent, then past, has a sharpness of focus often denied it; in this she is superbly supported by Previn and the LSO. Their partnership is hardly less persuasive in the five Duparc *mélodies,* which the composer orchestrated himself – each a jewelled miniature of breathtaking beauty, with the extra richness and colour of the orchestral accompaniment adding to the depth and intensity of the exceptionally sensitive word-settings, especially in the greatest of them all, *Phidylé.*

It was Schumann's *Frauenliebe und Leben* that helped to establish Dame Janet's early reputation, and she returned to this favourite cycle in early maturity with renewed freshness in the light of deeper experience. Where on her Saga record (now on Regis) she transposed most of the earlier songs down a full tone, the later version keeps them in the original keys. Then by contrast it is the later songs which she transposes, reserving her warmer tones for those expressions of motherhood. The wonder, the inwardness, are even more intense, while the final song in some ways brings the most remarkable performance of all ('Now you Have Hurt me'), not at all a conventional expression of mourning. With Barenboim an endlessly imaginative – if sometimes reticent – accompanist, this is another classic example of her art.

The Brahms Lieder were the last to be recorded, in 1977, and the gravity and nobility of her singing in the *Four Serious Songs* underline the weight of the biblical words while presenting them with a far wider and more beautiful range of tone-colour than is common. André Previn's piano is placed rather backwardly, but his rhythmic control provides fine support, and in the two viola songs, which are ravishingly sung and played, these artists are partnered by Cecil Aronowitz, making his last appearance on record.

To cap the recital come the four varied duets of Op. 28, in which Baker is joined by Dietrich Fischer-Dieskau, recorded at a live recital at London's Queen Elizabeth Hall in 1969. The vivacious closing *Der Jäger und sein Liebchen* makes a spiritedly vivacious coda to a collection which could hardly be bettered. Even if the presentation here omits texts and translations, this set still makes an amazing bargain.

'*The Very Best of Janet Baker*': BACH: *Christmas Oratorio: Bereite dich, Zion* (with ASMF, Marriner). HANDEL: *Messiah: He Was Despised* (with ECO, Mackerras). MENDELSSOHN: *Elijah: O Rest in the Lord* (with New Philh. O, Burgos). *On Wings of Song* (with Parsons, piano). BRAHMS: *Alto Rhapsody* (with John Aldis Ch., LPO, Boult); *Geistliches Wiegenlied* (with Previn, piano & Aronowitz, viola). MAHLER: *Rückert Lieder: Ich bim der Welt abhanden gekommen* (with Hallé O, Barbirolli). DUPARC: *L'Invitation au voyage* (with LSO, Previn). DURUFLÉ: *Requiem: Pie Jesu* (with Butt, organ, cond. Ledger). ELGAR: *The Dream of Gerontius: Angel's Farewell* (with Ambrosian Singers, Sheffield Philh. Ch., Hallé O, Barbirolli); *Sea Pictures* (with LSO, Barbirolli). VAUGHAN WILLIAMS: *Linden Lea.* BRITTEN: *A Boy was Born: Corpus Christi Carol.* WARLOCK: *Pretty Ring Time.* FAURE: *Clair de lune; Prison; Soir.* SCHUBERT: *Ave Maria; Gretchen am Spinnrade; Wiegenlied* (with Moore, piano); *An die Musik; An Sylvia; Auf dem Wasser zu singen; Du bist die Ruh'; Die Forelle; Heidenröslein; Nacht und Träume* (with Parsons, piano). SCHUMANN: *Du Ring an meinem Finger; Mondnacht* (with Barenboim, piano). R. STRAUSS: *Befreit; Morgen* (with Moore, piano)

☛ (B) *** EMI (ADD) 5 75069-2 (2)

A self-recommending recital, imaginatively chosen and well assembled, logically progressing from Bach and Handel, to her incomparable accounts of Elgar's *Sea Pictures* and the *Angel's Farewell* from *Gerontius* – both offering the finest accounts yet committed to disc – as well as some of her finest Lieder performances. Her extraordinary ability to communicate is apparent throughout this programme and as gives the music a fresh perspective; her strongly characterized reading of *Die Forelle* makes it much more of a fun song than usual, and similarly Geoffrey Parsons's naughty springing of the accompaniment of *An Sylvia* (echoed by the singer) gives a twinkle to a song that can easily be treated too seriously. Her heartfelt expressiveness in such numbers as *Gretchen am Spinnrade* and her equal mastery of the French repertoire complete the picture. There are no texts or translations, but a well-written biography relevant to the music is included, and the CD is inexpensive and the transfers are excellent.

Bartoli, Cecilia (mezzo-soprano)

Italian songs (with Schiff): BEETHOVEN: *Ecco quel fiero istante!; Che fa il mio bene?* (2 versions); *T'intendo, si, mio cor; Dimmi, ben mio; In questa tomba oscura.* MOZART: *Ridente la calma.* HAYDN: *Arianna a Naxos.* SCHUBERT: *Vedi quanto adoro ancora ingrato!; Io vuo'cantar di Cadmo; La pastorella; Non t'accostar all'urna; Guarda, che bianca luna; Se dall'Etra; Da quel sembiante appresi; Mio ben ricordati; Pensa, che questo istante; Mi batte'l cor!*

*** Decca 440 297-2

Bartoli and András Schiff make a magical partnership, each challenging the other in imagination. These seventeen Italian songs and one cantata by the great Viennese masters make a fascinating collection, not just Haydn and Mozart but Beethoven and Schubert as well. Beethoven's darkly intense *In questa tomba oscura* is well enough known but, as sung by Bartoli, with Schiff adding sparkle, the lighter songs are just as magnetic, with Beethoven showing his versatility in two astonishingly contrasted settings of the same love-poem.

'*A Portrait*': Arias from: MOZART: *La clemenza di Tito; Così fan tutte; Le nozze di Figaro; Don Giovanni. Concert aria: Ch'io mi scordi di te?* ROSSINI: *Semiramide; Maometto II; La Cenerentola.* Songs: ROSSINI: *Bella crudèle.* PARISOTTI: *Se tu m'ami.* GIORDANI: *Caro mio ben.* CACCINI: *Amarilli.* SCHUBERT: *La pastorella;* Metastasio: *Vedi quanto adoro ancora ingrato!*

☛ *** Decca 448 300-2

Cecilia Bartoli's portrait, covering a recording period from 1991 to 1995, could hardly be more enticing. Every lyrical aria displays her truly lovely voice with astonishing consistency. The very opening *Parto, parto, ma tu ben mio* from *La clemenza di Tito* could hardly be more inviting, with its engaging basset clarinet obbligato from Lesley Schatzberger, and *Come scoglio* shows her dramatic and vocal range to powerful and moving effect.

There is a delicious combination of charm and sparkle in Despina's *In uomini, in soldate* (wonderfully crisp trills echoing the orchestral violins), while Cherubino's *Voi che sapete* brings delightful innocence, and Susanna's *Deh vieni* the sunny joy of loving anticipation, which ravishes the ear, especially at the leisurely close. The simpler classical songs bring contrast, with the silken line of *Caro mio ben* followed by the very touching and gloriously sung *Amarilli* of Caccini.

Finally Rossini, where Bartoli is unsurpassed among the present generation of mezzos (and measures up impressively to famous names from the past). After the beautifully spun line of the aria from *Maometto II* (with choral support) she captivates with a fizzing, crisply articulated and joyfully humorous *Non più mesta*. Top-class Decca recording throughout ensures the listener's pleasure and this hugely enjoyable collection would have earned a Rosette but for the totally inadequate documentation, with no translations – unacceptable in a premium-priced record.

'*Chant d'amour*' (with Myung-Whan Chung, piano): BIZET: *Mélodies: Adieux de l'hôtesse arabe; Chant d'amour; La Coccinelle; Ouvre ton coeur; Tarantelle.* BERLIOZ: *La Mort d'Ophélie; Zaïde.* DELIBES: *Les Filles de Cadix.* VIARDOT: *Les Filles de Cadiz; Hai luli!; Havanaise.* RAVEL: *4 Chansons populaires; 2 Mélodies Hébraïques; Tripatos; Vocalise-etude en forme de Habanera*

*** Decca 452 667-2

This is a delectable disc, a winning collection of French songs, many of them unexpected, which inspire Bartoli to the most seductive singing. One would have predicted that Delibes's sparkling setting of Musset's poem *Les Filles de Cadix* would draw out Carmen-like fire from her, but here that charming song is set alongside the setting of the same poem made by the great prima donna Pauline Viardot, giving a refreshingly different view. The other Viardot items too come as a delightful surprise, as do the Bizet songs, including *La Coccinelle*, ('The Ladybird'), a sparkling waltz, superbly characterized here. The better-known Berlioz and Ravel songs are beautifully done too, with Myung-Whun Chung revealing himself just as inspired in the role of pianist as of conductor. Excellent sound.

'Live from Italy' (with Thibaudet (piano), Sonatori de la gioiosa marca): BELLINI: *Malinconia ninfa gentile; Ma rendi pur contento.* BERLIOZ: *Zaïde.* BIZET: *Carmen: Près des ramparts de Séville.* CACCINI: *Al fonte al prato; Tu ch'hai le penne; Amarilli mia bella.* DONIZETTI: *La conocchia; Me voglio fa'na casa.* GIORDANI: *Caro mio ben.* HANDEL: *Il trionfo del tempo e del disinganno: Lascia la spina.* MONTSALVATGE: *Canto negro.* MOZART: *Le nozze di Figaro: Voi che sapete. Concert aria: Oiseaux, si tous les ans.* ROSSINI: *Mi Lagnerò tacendo, Book I/2, 3 & 4; L'Orpheline du Tyrol; Zelmira: Riedi al soglio; Canzonetta spagnuola.* SCHUBERT: *La pastorella al Prato.* VIARDOT: *Havanaise; Hai luli!* VIVALDI: *Griselda: Agitata da due venti*
*** Decca 455 981-2

Recorded live at the Teatro Olimpico in Vicenza, this recital vividly conveys the high-powered magnetism of Cecilia Bartoli. Encouraged by the rapturous audience, Bartoli may in some items go over the top in her individual characterization, but magic is there from first to last. The opening group of baroque items comes with string accompaniment, but then Jean-Yves Thibaudet at the piano takes over as the most sympathetic partner, whether in the characterful little Schubert song, *La pastorella*, the tango-like *Havanaise* of Pauline Viardot or Berlioz's *Zaïde*, with Bartoli herself playing castanets. It is fascinating to have three widely contrasted settings by Rossini of the same Metastasio text, and crowning the whole recital – before a sparkling sequence of encores – is the longest item, a spectacular aria from Rossini's *Zelmira* with a breathtaking display of coloratura at the end. A fun disc, atmospherically recorded.

'The Art of Cecilia Bartoli': Arias from: HANDEL: *Rinaldo* (with AAM, Hogwood). VIVALDI: *Bajazet; Dorilla in Tempe; Farnace* (with Arnold Schoenberg Ch., Il Giardino Armonico, Antonini). GLUCK: *La clemenza di Tito; Il Parnaso confuso* (with Akademie für Alte Musik, Berlin, Forck). MOZART: *Don Giovanni; Le nozze di Figaro; Die Zauberflöte* (with Santa Cecilia Academy O, Chung or VPO, Abbado); ROSSINI: *La Cenerentola* (with Teatro Comunale de Bologna O, Chailly); *Il barbiere di Siviglia* (with Santa Cecilia Academy O, Chung); *Il Turco in Italia* (with La Scala, Milan, O, Chailly). DONIZETTI: *L'elisir d'amore.* VERDI: *La traviata* (with Giuseppe Verdi Ch. & O, Chailly)
**(*) Decca 473 380-2

This is in many way an excellent disc, in repertoire for which Cecilia Bartoli has become famous. There is much beautiful singing here, such is in the lovely aria, *Di Questa centra in seno* (Gluck), and the famous *Lascia ch'io pianga* (Handel), as well, of course, as brilliant coloratura passages of Rossini. Occasionally, however, her coloratura is marred by a machine-gun-type quality, such as in the aria, *Anch'il mar per che sommerga* (Vivaldi), though it is undoubtedly exciting. Hers is a small voice, though on a recording that is no problem, of course. However, with brilliant Decca sound,

excellent orchestral support, and a varied programme, Bartoli admirers need not hesitate. Full texts and translations and deluxe packaging complete the picture.

Bartoli, Cecilia (mezzo-soprano), Bryn Terfel (baritone)

'Cecilia and Bryn': Duets (with Santa Cecilia National Academy O, Chung) from: MOZART: *Le nozze di Figaro; Così fan tutte; Don Giovanni; Die Zauberflöte.* ROSSINI: *Il barbiere di Siviglia; L'Italiana in Algeri.* DONIZETTI: *L'elisir d'amore*
*** Decca 458 928-2

The friendly title, *Cecilia and Bryn*, though suggesting a crossover disc, is well justified when in each of these operatic duets these two charismatic singers are so characterful in their performances, both musically and dramatically. At times they come near to overacting but, with brilliant support from Myung-Whun Chung and the orchestra, that goes with the virtuoso flair. Warm, full sound, though Bartoli is made to sound breathy.

BBC Singers, Stephen Cleobury

'Illuminare: Carols for a New Millennium' (with Quinney, organ): HOLTEN: *Nowell Sing we Now.* MARTLAND: *From Lands that See the Sun Arise; Make we Joy; There is no Rose of such Virtue.* RUTTI: *I Wonder as I Wander.* WEIR: *Illuminare.* BINGHAM: *The Shepherd's Gift.* GRIER: *Corpus Christi Carol.* ADES: *Fayrfax Carol.* SUSA: *Shepherds Sing.* BELMONT: *Nativitas.* MACMILLAN: *Seinte Mari Moder Milde.* TAVENER: *Today the Virgin.* KORNOWICZ: *Waiting.* R. R. BENNETT: *Carol.* MAXWELL DAVIES: *One Star, at Last.* HARBISON: *O Magnum Mysterium.* PANUFNIK: *Sleep, Little Jesus, Sleep.* GOODALL: *Romance of the Angels.* HARLE: *Mrs Beeton's Christmas Plum Pudding*
*** BBC WMEF 0063-2

This immensely varied collection includes eight brand-new carols, from British, European and North American composers, six of them commissioned by the BBC. Many are unaccompanied but some use the organ very effectively. The penultimate 'Romance of the Angels' is the obvious 'hit' of the programme, an ebullient melody carried by a vigorous organ toccata, but Bo Holten's lovely opening echoing 'Nowell Sing we Now' creates the right atmosphere, and Steve Martland's triptych frames a vigorous scherzando, 'Make we Joy', with two more gentle settings.

Carol Rütti's 'I Wonder as I Wander' swings along with the organ, while Judith Weir's title-piece brings celestial trebles and intriguing dissonance, and this mood continues in Francis Grier's 'Corpus Christi', with more floating soloists, and also in the very striking Adès setting. Jean Belmont's 'Nativitas' rocks ethereally, but not all will take to the moments of sharp dissonance in James MacMillan's 'Seinte Mari Moder Milde', which opens so passionately.

We come back to earth with John Tavener's strophic dance, 'Today the Virgin', with its catchy medieval rhythm over a drone bass. The most extended carol is from Jerzy Kornowicz; 'Waiting', with a rocking motion and curiously intrusive solo voices, is strangely hypnotic. Richard Rodney Bennett's simple melisma is more appealing than Peter Maxwell Davies's equally lyrical but sombre 'One Star, at Last'; but Panufnik's

'Sleep, Little Jesus, Sleep' brings gentle balm. John Harle's catchy 'Christmas Pudding', with slick rhythm and barber-shop harmonies, is a closing fun item, not meant to be taken seriously at all. Performances throughout are first class, as is the recording.

Berganza, Teresa (mezzo-soprano)

'A Portrait': Arias from: ROSSINI: Il barbiere di Siviglia; La Cenerentola; L'Italiana in Algeri (with LSO, Gibson). MOZART: Così fan tutte; Le nozze di Figaro (with LSO, Pritchard). GLUCK: Alceste. CHERUBINI: Medea (with ROHCG O, Gibson). HANDEL: Alcina (with LSO, Bonynge). BIZET: Carmen (with LSO, Abbado). Songs/Arias: MOZART: Ch'io mi scordi di te? ... Non temer, amato bene (with LSO, Pritchard). CHERUBINI: Ahi! Che forse ai miei di. CESTI: Intorno all'idol mio. PERGOLESI (attr.): Confusa, smarrita. SCARLATTI: Chi vuol innamorarsi; Elitropio d'amor; Qual mia colpa, o sventura ... Se delitto è l'adorarvi; La Rosaura. LAVILLA: 4 Canciones vascas. TURINA: Farruca. Saeta en forma de Salve a la Vergen de la Esperanza. GRANADOS: La maja dolorosa; El majo timido; El tra-la-la y el punteado (with Lavilla, piano). FALLA: 7 Canciones populares españolas. GUERRERO: Sagrario's Romanza. MARQUES: Margarita's Romanza (with O, cond. Lauret). ARAMBARRI: Canciones vascas (O, cond. Gombau)

— (B) *** Decca (ADD) 475 518-2 (2)

A truly recommendable Teresa Berganza compilation. Natu-rally, there is a sprinkling of her classic early operatic record-ings of Rossini and Mozart, which sparkle as brightly as ever and have rarely been out of the catalogue. But all the other items on this disc, from the Gluck and Handel to the Bizet, also show her on top form, a real star mezzo of character and style. The second CD is full of her native Spanish repertoire, most of which has not been widely available on CD before, some being transferred for the first time. Her recordings with Felix Lavilla, made at the beginning of the 1960s, are highly enjoyable, and on their original release it was to Victoria de los Angeles that she was compared. Perhaps the arias by Cherubini and Scar-latti, and others, would have gained from more than piano accompaniment, but the classical quality of the singing is most beautiful, and the sound has transferred well to CD. The Ocho canciones vascas ('Eight Basque Songs') and Sagrario's Romanza and Margarita's Romanza, derive from two EPs from the late 1950s, and these simple, naïve songs are sung to perfection. The group of Basque songs is especially captivat-ing: they were arranged in their present form by Jesús Arám-bareri in 1931, and the discreet and delicate orchestral accompaniment he has provided subtly underlines the mood of each item. The sound is a little dated, with the odd bit of distortion, but they are warm and highly atmospheric. At bargain price, this is one of the best in Decca's 'Portrait' series.

'Brava Berganza – a Birthday Tribute': FALLA: The Three-Cornered Hat: excerpts (with Boston SO, Ozawa); El amor brujo: excerpts (with LSO, Garcia Navarro); 7 Popular Songs (with Narciso Yepes (guitar)); La Vida breve (with Alicia Nafé, Paloma Perez Iñigo, José Carreras, Yepes, Ambrosian Op. Ch., LSO, Navarro). Arias from: PENELLA: El gatomontés (with Veronica Villarroel, Plácido Domingo, Mabel Perelstein, Carlos Alvarez, Coto Titular del Teatro Lírico Nacional La Zarzuela, Madrid SO, Miguel Roa). BIZET: Carmen (with Domingo, Ileana Cotrubas, Nafé, Yvonne Kenny, Ambrosian Singers, LSO, Claudio Abbado).

ROSSINI: Il barbiere di Siviglia (with Hermann Prey, Luigi Alva, LSO, Abbado); La Cenerentola (with Margherita Guglielmi, Laura Zannini, Renato Capecchi, LSO, Abbado). MOZART: La clemenza di Tito (with Rufus Müller, Dresden Staatskapelle, Karl Boehm). PUCCINI: Madama Butterfly (with Mirella Freni, Juan Pons, Carreras, Philh. O, Giuseppe Sinopoli). STRAVINSKY: Pulcinella (with Ryland Davies, John Shirley-Quirk, LSO, Abbado). CAVALLI: Lamento di Cassandra; Son ancor pargoletta. CARISSIMI: No, non si speri; Vittoria, mio cuore. ALESSANDRO SCARLATTI: Canzonetta – Chi vuole innamorasi; Se delitto è l'adorati ... Qual mia colpa, o sventura; Se Florindo è Fedele; Le violette – Rugiadose, odorose violette graziose. CALDARA: Come raggio di sol; Selve amiche. VIVALDI: Piango, gemo; Un certo non so che. PERGOLESI: Aria di Martia – Confusa, smarrita; Se tu m'ami (with Ricardo Requejo (piano)). SABIO: Rosa das rosas. FUENLLANA: Pérdida de Antequera. ANON.: Dindirindin. TORRE: Dime, triste corazón. VALDERRABANO: De dónde venís, amore?. MILÁN: Toda vida os amé. DE TRIANA: Dinos, madrew del donsel. MUDDARA: Claros y frescos ríos; Si me llaman del donsel; Triste estaua el rey David; Ysabel, perdiste la tu faxa. ENCINA: Romerico. VAZQUEZ: En la fuente del rosel; Vos me matastes. NAVAREZ: Con qué la laveré?. SABIO: Santa Maria. LORCA: 13 Old Spanish Songs (with Yepes (guitar)). GRANADOS: La maja dolorosa. TURINA: Cantares; El Fantasma; Saeta en forma de Salve a la Virgen de la Esperanza. GURIDI: 6 Castilian Songs (excerpts). MONTSALVATGE: Canciones negras (with Félix Lavilla (piano))

(B) DG *** (ADD/DDD) 477 5489 (4)

DG have ungallantly put a sticker on the front of this CD revealing Teresa Berganza's age but, apart from that, they have served her well in this birthday tribute. Excerpts from her famous DG complete opera recordings – Carmen, Il barbiere de Siviglia, La Cenerentola, La Clemenza, etc. – are all included and it is a tribute to this artist that they remain top or near-top choices in these popular operas. There may be the odd quibble here and there (the Carmen is a bit straight-laced) but in that work, as in her Rossini characterizations, the agility and reliability of the singing give much pleasure. Much of this set is devoted to music of her native Spain; included is a complete recording of Falla's La Vida breve, a sort of Spanish Cavalleria Rusticana, though less melodra-matic and lumbered with a weak plot. The story of the heroine who dies of a broken heart when her lover deserts her for another is hardly compelling dramatically, but Berganza's strong, earthy performance helps to compensate for Falla's dramatic weakness, even though memories of her compa-triot, Victoria de les Angeles, in this role are not eclipsed. The rest of the cast is good, though the recording is not always ideal, or consistent; but it is well conducted and has a certain atmosphere, vital in this work. In the same composer's Seven Popular Songs, Berganza provides the right balance between sophistication and an earthy, folk music style, helped by the superb guitar accompaniment of Narciso Yepes. Yepes is also the vibrant guitar accompanist to the 'Spanish Songs from the Middle Ages and Renaissance' from 1974 – a delectable recital in every way; Berganza is on top form and sings with disarm-ing eloquence in repertoire which she obviously loves. The two artists are naturally balanced and the music communi-cates in a direct way – this is not just repertoire for the specialist. The Thirteen Old Spanish Songs, recorded two years later, are equally delightful in their easy-going freshness and seductive melody. The Spanish songs with the pianist Félix Lavilla (1975) inhabit the same world, and again we find the singer throughout performing with great spirit and with an ideal collaborator in her pianist. The first of Granados's *Tonadillas*, *La maja dolorosa*, is particularly moving in its range of expressiveness, but there are many pleasant surprises throughout; although Berganza may not always match Victorias de los Angeles in this repertoire, few CDs of Spanish songs are more attractive than this. With a modern piano, the Italian Baroque arias (with Ricardo Requejo) may not be the last word in authenticity, but with very attractive accompaniments (most arranged by more recent hands such as Leppard, Dallapiccola and the pianist on this CD) it works well with Berganza's concept: there is much beautiful singing here and the music-making is warmly expressive and well recorded (in 1978). Quite a contrast is the lively *El gato montés* ('The Wildcat'); with its captivating tunes and bold – if obvious – colours it makes one want to hear more of her recordings of zarzuela. Alas, no texts, but an excellent interview with Berganza as well as a short biography are included.

Berger, Erna (soprano), Sebastian Peschko (piano)

Arias from: PERGOLESI: *Il Flaminio*. VERACINI: *Rosalinda*. HANDEL: *Semele*. GLUCK: *Die Pilger von Mekka*. Arias: CACCINI: *Amarilli mia bella*. A. SCARLATTI: *La Violetta*. TELEMANN: *Trauer-Music eines kunstverfahrenen Canarienvogels*. J. C. BACH: *Midst Silent Shades*. MOZART: *Abendempfindung; Oiseaux, si tous les ans; Ridente la calma; Der Zauberer*. SCHUBERT: *Im Abendrot; An die untergehende Sonne; Am Grabe; Schäfers Klagelied; Suleika I & II*

(M) (**) Orfeo mono C 556021B

This recital was recorded in Hanover in 1962. Erna Berger too, was 62, and while the voice still sounds remarkably fresh, a close vibrato is used to maintain the tonal bloom. There is more than a hint of strain in Johann Christian Bach's 'Midst Silent Shades'. However, she is at her charming best in the Italian arias (especially the Veracini and Scarlatti) and still impresses in Mozart and Schubert. But the highlight is the winning Telemann cantata about the canary's funeral. It is a great pity that no texts and translations are provided, either here or elsewhere, and the notes are entirely biographical. Handel's famous aria from *Semele* is engagingly listed (although not sung) as 'Wher'are you Walking'. However, this is a recital for Berger admirers, rather than the general collector.

Bergonzi, Carlo (tenor)

'The Sublime Voice of Carlo Bergonzi' (with various orchestras and conductors): Arias from: PUCCINI: *La Bohème; Madama Butterfly; Manon Lescaut; Tosca*. MASCAGNI: *Cavallieria rusticana*. LEONCAVALLO: *Pagliacci*. VERDI: *Aida; Un ballo in maschera; Don Carlo; Otello; Rigoletto; La traviata; Il trovatore*. PONCHIELLI: *La Gioconda*. CILEA: *Adriana Lecouvreur*

⊕→ (B) *** Decca (ADD) 476 1858 (2)

Carlo Bergonzi won the *Gramophone* Magazine's Lifetime Achievement Award in 2000 and on that occasion appeared at the Festival Hall and sang two numbers (conducted by Pappano), including the Brindisi from *La traviata* with Angela

Gheorghiu. It was undoubtedly the highlight of that occasion, Bergonzi's star quality shining through and himself sounding in remarkably fine voice. This collection is a splendid representation of his career, as well as good tenor collection in its own right. The arias are mainly from Decca's vintage recordings of the 1960s and, as one would expect, offer first-class sound. This excellent anthology appears in the *Gramophone* Awards Collection; (texts and translations are not included, however).

Arias (with Santa Cecilia Ac. O, Gavazzeni) from: VERDI: *Aida; Un ballo in maschera; La forza del destino; Luisa Miller; Il trovatore*. MEYERBEER: *L'africana*. GIORDANO: *Andrea Chénier*. CILEA: *Adriana Lecouvreur*. PUCCINI: *Manon Lescaut; Tosca*

(M) **(*) Decca Classic Recitals (ADD) 475 392-2

Decca's 'Classic Recitals' use the original artwork – both the front and back of the LPs, quite attractively reproduced, but in a flimsy cardboard case. Only the LP's original contents are included, making the timing rather shorter than we are used to today, and the reproduction of the LP's notes is in a disgracefully reduced typeface, not always clear. However, many collectors will be glad to have the repertoire available again.

This recital of Bergonzi's early stereo recordings shows him on peak form. Although he does not attempt the rare *pianissimo* at the end of *Celeste Aida*, all the Verdi items in this 1957 recording show the true heroic quality of his voice, a voice still baritonal enough (he started his career as a baritone) to sound completely happy in the wide range demanded of Manrico in *Il trovatore*. Bergonzi's is a remarkable voice and this is a consistently enjoyable recital, especially as the sound is exceptionally vivid and Gianandrea Gavazzeni's conducting is incisive and dramatic.

Bernac, Pierre (baritone)

'The Essential Pierre Bernac' (with Poulenc, Moore, Johnson, piano): GOUNOD: *Sérénade; Ce que je suis sans toi; Au rossignol; 6 Mélodies (cycle)*. DUPARC: *Soupir; L'Invitation au voyage*. CHABRIER: *L'Ile heureuse*. CHAUSSON: *Le Colibri*. ROUSSEL: *Le Jardin mouillé; Coeur en péril*. SCHUMANN: *Dein Angesicht; Dichterliebe (cycle), Op. 48*. LISZT: *Freudvoll und Leidvoll; Es muss ein Wunderbares; Nimm einen Strahl der Sonne*. MILHAUD: *La Tourterelle*. VELLONES: *A mon fils*. BEYDTS: *La Lyre et les amours (cycle)*. FAURE: *Après un rêve; Le Secret; Aurore; Prison; Soir; Jardin nocturne*. DEBUSSY: *3 Chansons de France; Fêtes galantes: Colloque sentimental; 3 Ballades de François Villon*. SATIE: *Mélodies Nos. 1 & 3*. RAVEL: *Don Quichotte à Dulcinée (cycle)*. POULENC: *2 Chansons gailliards; Métamorphoses; Le Bestiaire (cycles); 2 Mélodies de Guillaume Apollinaire: Montparnasse; 2 Poèmes de Guillaume Apollinaire: Dans le jardin d'Anna; 2 Poèmes de Louis Aragon (with O, Beydts); Telle jour telle nuit (cycle); Le Travail du peintre (cycle); L'Histoire de Babar, le petite éléphant*

(***) Testament mono SBT 3161 (3)

When the duo of Pierre Bernac and Francis Poulenc provided a French equivalent of Pears and Britten, it is especially valuable to have this distinctive and often magical collection of recordings, made between 1936 and 1958. Most were recorded for EMI, notably those made in London just after the end of the Second World War. But the core of the collection, the late recordings made in 1957–8, come from BBC sources, recorded from broadcast concerts.

The distinctive voice, with its flicker of vibrato, was not quite so evenly produced as earlier, but the artistry remains magical. As a supplement comes a broadcast interview, with Bernac questioned by Graham Johnson, and finally comes a performance of Poulenc's *Babar the Elephant* with Johnson at the piano and Bernac a magnetic narrator. On the first disc as a sample of Bernac's Lieder-singing comes an EMI recording with Gerald Moore of Schumann's *Dichterliebe*, while as the perfect introduction there is Bernac's uniquely charming account with Poulenc of Gounod's *Sérénade*. Most moving of all are their readings of such deeper Poulenc songs as the first of the two *Poèmes de Louis Aragon*, 'C', inspired by the Nazi occupation of France.

Björling, Jussi (tenor)

Bjoerling Edition: (Studio recordings 1930–59; with O, Grevillius): Disc 1 (1936–41): Arias from VERDI: *Aida; Rigoletto; Requiem; La traviata; Il trovatore*. PUCCINI: *La Bohème; Tosca; La fanciulla del West*. PONCHIELLI: *La Gioconda*. MEYERBEER: *L'Africaine*. MASSENET: *Manon*. BIZET: *Carmen*. GOUNOD: *Faust*. FLOTOW: *Martha*. ROSSINI: *Stabat Mater*. FRIML: *The Vagabond King*. Songs by TOSTI; DI CAPUA; GEEHL. Disc 2 (1941–50): Arias from: PUCCINI: *La Bohème; Turandot; Manon Lescaut; Tosca*. VERDI: *Rigoletto; Un ballo in maschera*. GIORDANO: *Andrea Chénier; Fedora*. MASCAGNI: *Cavalleria rusticana*. LEONCAVALLO: *Pagliacci* (also song: *Mattinata*). DONIZETTI: *L'elisir d'amore*. BIZET: *Les Pêcheurs de perles*. GOUNOD: *Roméo et Juliette*. MASSENET: *Manon*. CILEA: *L'Arlesiana*. GODARD: *Jocelyn (Berceuse)*. Song: TOSTI: *L'alba separa*. Disc 3: Arias (sung in Swedish) from: GOUNOD: *Roméo et Juliette*. VERDI: *Rigoletto; Il trovatore*. LAPARRA: *L'illustre Fregona*. BORODIN: *Prince Igor*. PUCCINI: *Tosca; La fanciulla del West*. LEONCAVALLO: *Pagliacci*. MASCAGNI: *Cavalleria rusticana*. ATTERBERG: *Fanal*. RIMSKY-KORSAKOV: *Sadko*. OFFENBACH: *La Belle Hélène*. JOHANN STRAUSS JR: *Der Zigeunerbaron*. MILLOCKER: *Der Bettelstudent*. Trad. songs (in Swedish) and by PETERSON-BERGER; SJOBERG; SCHRADER; STENHAMMAR; ALTHEN; WIDE. Disc 4: Lieder and songs (1939–59): BEETHOVEN: *Adelaide*. R. STRAUSS: *Morgen; Cäcile*. RACHMANINOV: *In the Silence of the Night; Lilacs*. FOSTER: *Jeannie with the Light Brown Hair*. D'HARDELOT: *Because*. SPEAKS: *Sylvia*. CAMPBELL-TIPTON: *A Spirit Flower*. BEACH: *Ah, Love but a Day*. SJOBERG: *I Bless Ev'ry Hour*. SIBELIUS: *The Diamond in the March Snow*. ADAM: *O Holy Night*. Songs by NORDQVIST; SALEN; PETERSON-BERGER; SODERMAN; ALFVEN

(M) (***) EMI mono/stereo 5 66306-2 (4)

All admirers of the great Swedish tenor should consider this comprehensive compilation, eighty-nine items chosen by Harald Henrysson from EMI's Swedish archives and admirably remastered at Abbey Road. The voice is caught freshly and truthfully. Björling's wife, Anna-Lisa, also participates in duets from *La Bohème* and *Roméo et Juliette*, towards the end of the second disc. The selection of arias is almost entirely predictable (and none the worse for that); a number of the key items are offered twice, and sometimes again in Swedish (where they sound surprisingly effective, even an excerpt from Offenbach's *La Belle Hélène*). All the songs have a direct popular appeal. Björling opens Disc 4 with a winning account

of Beethoven's *Adelaide*, and many will welcome the lighter songs, and particularly the English ballads. However, the closing group of eight Scandinavian songs is memorable: romantic and dramatic by turns, and closing with a bold final contrast, 'The Diamond in the March Snow' of Sibelius, which is capped by Björling's ardent version of Adam's *Cantique de Noël* in Swedish. Excellent documentation, with photographs and full translations.

Opera arias from: DONIZETTI: *L'elisir d'amore*. VERDI: *Il trovatore; Un ballo in maschera; Aida*. LEONCAVALLO: *Pagliacci*. PUCCINI: *La Bohème; Tosca; La fanciulla del West; Turandot*. GIORDANO: *Fedora*. CILEA: *L'arlesiana*. MEYERBEER: *L'Africana*. GOUNOD: *Faust*. MASSENET: *Manon*. FLOTOW: *Martha*. ROSSINI: *Stabat Mater*

(M) (***) EMI mono CDH7 61053-2

The EMI collection on the Références label brings excellent transfers of material recorded between 1936 and 1947 on the tenor's home-ground in Stockholm. The voice was then at its very peak, well caught in those final years of 78rpm discs, with artistry totally assured over this wide range of repertory.

'Great Opera Arias' (with RCA Victor O, Robert Shaw Chorale, Cellini or Rome Op. O, Perlea or Leinsdorf or (i) Schauwecker (piano)): MEYERBEER: *L'Africana: O paradiso*. VERDI: *Aida*: excerpts. *Il trovatore*: excerpts (with Milanov, Barbieri, Warren). *Rigoletto*: excerpts (with Peters, Merrill, Rota). PUCCINI: *La Bohème: Che gelida manina*. *Tosca: E lucevan le stelle; Amaro sol per te* (with Milanov). *Manon Lescaut: Ah! Manon mi tradisce* (with Albanese); *No! no! pazzo son!* (with Campo). MASCAGNI: *Cavalleria rusticana*: excerpts (with Milanov). (i) BIZET: *Carmen: Flower Song*. (i) MOZART: *Don Giovanni: Il mio tesoro*. (i) MASSENET: *Manon: Instant charmant; En fermant les yeux*. (i) GIORDANO: *Fedora: Amor ti vieta*. (i) PUCCINI: *Turandot: Nessun dorma*

🎧 (M) *** RCA mono/stereo 09026 68429-2

If you want a single disc to represent Jussi Björling, this is the one to have. The recordings date from between 1951 and 1959, the last decade of his life, when the voice was still astonishingly fresh. Most of the excerpts come from distinguished complete recordings, when the great tenor was partnered by artists of the calibre of Zinka Milanov and Licia Albanese (the duets from *Tosca* and *Manon Lescaut* are electrifying and the excerpts from *Aida, Il trovatore* and *Cavalleria rusticana* are hardly less thrilling). The recordings, splendidly transferred, are all of high quality and show the great tenor in the very best light: even the 1958 live recital, with just a piano accompaniment, is treasurable for its famous arias from *Carmen* and *Manon*, and the closing, passionate *Nessun dorma*.

Opera arias (HMV recordings 1936–45, with SO or RPO, Grevillius): Arias from: DONIZETTI: *L'elisir d'amore*. VERDI: *Rigoletto; Il trovatore; Aida*. PONCHIELLI: *La Gioconda*. MEYERBEER: *L'Africana*. FLOTOW: *Martha*. GOUNOD: *Faust; Roméo et Juliette*. BIZET: *Carmen*. MASSENET: *Manon*. MASCAGNI: *Cavalleria rusticana*. LEONCAVALLO: *Pagliacci*. PUCCINI: *Manon Lescaut; La Bohème; Tosca; Turandot*

(BB) (**(*)) Naxos mono 8.110701

This Naxos programme is generous (78 minutes) and is certainly value for money. The transfers are made by Mark Obert-Thorn from clean shellac originals, and the voice is faithfully caught: some of the transfers are smoother than others. The orchestral sound can be a bit thin, irrespective of the recording date (the 1944 *Amor ti vieta* from *Fedora*, for instance), whereas the splendid *O Lola* aria from *Cav.* is much warmer because of the resonance. The Flower Song from *Carmen*, the aria from *Romeo and Juliet* and the closing *Nessun dorma* are examples where there seems to be extra bloom. Background noise is not entirely vanquished but is not a problem. However, the mid-priced RCA collection, including recordings from the last decade of the tenor's life and which includes many of the items above, sung just as passionately and offering much better sound, is well worth its extra cost (RCA 09026 68249-2 – see above).

Bocelli, Andrea (tenor)

Operatic arias (with Maggio Musicale Fiorentino O, Noseda): PUCCINI: *La Bohème, Tosca, Madama Butterfly.* LEONCAVALLO: *La Bohème.* CILEA: *Adriana Lecouvreur.* BELLINI: *I Puritani.* R. STRAUSS: *Der Rosenkavalier.* DONIZETTI: *La Fille du régiment.* BIZET: *Carmen.* .MASSENET: *Werther*
**(*) Ph. 462 033-2

Andrea Bocelli here shows his paces in a formidable collection of arias, including the tenor's aria from *Der Rosenkavalier*. Bocelli's great natural gift is a tenor of very distinctive timbre, not conventionally rounded in a Pavarotti-like way but above all virile with a baritonal tinge, used over a wide tonal range with not a suspicion of strain. He soars readily to a top C or even a C sharp, as in *A te o cara* from Bellini's *I Puritani*.

There is fair evidence too of lessons well learnt. Werther's *Pourquoi me reveiller* – among the most testing of French arias – inspires Bocelli to produce very refined mezza voce, beautifully sustained, and the Flower Song from *Carmen* too is subtler than most. Yet there is a sequence of Puccini arias – the two from *Tosca*, one from *Butterfly* – which are disappointingly slow and heavy, though *Che gelida manina* is nicely detailed. And though in the nine top Cs of Tonio's *Pour ton âme* from *La Fille du régiment* – the final rip-roaring item here – he cannot quite match the flamboyance of Pavarotti, there are all too few recording tenors who could do it so confidently, or even at all.

Bolshoi Opera

'*Russian Opera at the Bolshoi – The Vintage Years*': Arkhipova, Bolshakov, Guesuelnikova, Kozlovsky, Krivchenia, Lemeshev, Lisitzian, Maslennikova, Mikhailov, Nortzov, Obrastsova, Ognivtsev, Petrov, Petrova, Piavko, Pirogov, Preobrazhenskaya, Reizen, Shalyapin, Sololov, Vishnevskaya
*** Warner DVD 5050467 4772-2-3

Here is a cornucopia of riches from the Bolshoi archives which will be self-recommending to all interested in Russian opera. The great basses tend to dominate and astonish, from Chaliapin (or Shalyapin, which is the currently favoured transliteration) to Ivan Petrov and Mark Reizen; but such legendary tenors as Ivan Kozlovsky and Sergei Lemeshev are strongly featured. Had it not been for the repressive regime they would surely have been commanding figures on the international stage, but they were not allowed to travel. The

excerpts range from Pavel Lisitzian in Tchaikovsky's *Mazeppa*, both Kozlovsky and Lemeshev in *Onegin* and Vishnevskaya in *Queen of Spades*. Also film of Alexander Melik-Pashayev in the same opera, unforgettable for those who were privileged to see his Covent Garden appearances. There is so much outstanding singing that superlatives soon run out.

Bonney, Barbara (soprano)

'*Diamonds in the Snow*' (with Pappano, piano): GRIEG: *Spring; I Love You; With a Water-lily; The Princess; A Swan; From Monte Pincio; 6 Lieder, Op. 48; Peer Gynt: Solveig's Song.* SIBELIUS: *The Diamond in the Snow; Lost in the Forest; Sigh, Rushes, sigh; Was it a Dream?; The Girl Came Home from Meeting her Lover.* STENHAMMAR: *The Girl Came Home from Meeting her Lover; Adagio; Sweden; Guiding Spirit; In the Forest.* ALFVEN: *Take my Heart; The Forest Sleeps.* SJOBERG: *Music*
🔊 *** Decca 466 762-2

Barbara Bonney, with her warm understanding of Scandinavia and its music, offers the most seductive choice of songs in this inspired collection. The Grieg group includes most of the well-known favourites, but with Antonio Pappano proving just as understanding a piano accompanist as he is a conductor, they all emerge fresh and new, animated and strongly characterized. There is a sensuousness and passion behind the love songs in particular, with free rubato sounding spontaneous, never studied. The Sibelius set brings ravishing tonal contrasts too, and it is fascinating to hear the settings of the same Swedish poem, first by Sibelius, then more simply but with warm feeling by Stenhammar. More than anything the disc disproves the idea of coldness in the Nordic make-up. Warm, full sound with Bonney's lovely voice glowingly caught.

Bostridge, Ian (tenor), Julius Drake (piano)

'*The English Songbook*': STANFORD: *La Belle Dame sans merci.* GURNEY: *Sleep; I will Go with my Father a-Ploughing.* DUNHILL: *The Cloths of Heaven.* WILLIAM DENIS BROWN: *To Gratiana Dancing and Singing.* SOMERVELL: *To Lucasta, on Going to the Wars.* DELIUS: *Twilight Fancies.* GERMAN: *Orpheus with his Lute.* WARLOCK: *Jillian of Berry; Cradle Song.* FINZI: *The Dance Continued (Regret not me); Since we Loved.* VAUGHAN WILLIAMS: *Linden Lea; Silent noon.* Irish air, arr. STANFORD: *My love's an Arbutus.* Irish tune, arr. BRITTEN: *The Salley Gardens.* TRAD./ANON.: *The Death of Queen Jane; The Little Turtle Dove.* PARRY: *No Longer Mourne for Me.* WARLOCK: *Rest, Sweet Nymphs.* QUILTER: *Come Away Death; Now Sleeps the Crimson Petal.* GRAINGER: *Bold William Taylor; Brigg Fair*
🔊 *** EMI 5 56830-2

Ian Bostridge with his clear, honeyed tone is in his element in this collection of twenty-four English songs, almost all of them neglected. He and his keenly responsive accompanist, Julius Drake, have made an imaginative, far from predictable choice of items, with only the two Vaughan Williams songs, 'Linden Lea' and 'Silent Noon', qualifying as popular favourites. It is good to find the collection delving as far back as Parry and Stanford (the first and most ambitious of the songs, memorably setting Keats's 'La Belle Dame sans merci'), and including composers like Edward German, generally celebrated for his light music. It is a reflection on the singer's personality too that there is a high proportion of thoughtful, introspective songs, most sensitively matched by Drake in his accompaniments. One hopes that EMI's inclusion of French and German translations alongside the English texts will encourage new discovery outside Britain of a genre seriously underappreciated, one which directly reflects the magic of English lyric poetry.

Bott, Catherine (soprano)

'Mad Songs' (with New London Consort, Pickett): PURCELL: *From Silent Shades; From Rosy Bow'rs; Not All my Torments can your Pity Move; Don Quixote: Let the Dreadful Engines; A Fool's Preferment: I'll Sail upon the Dog Star.* ECCLES: *The Mad Lover: Must then a Faithful Lover Go?; Let's all be Gay; Cease of Cupid to Complain; She ventures and He Wins: Restless in Thought; Don Quixote: I Burn, my Brain Consumes to Ashes; Cyrus the Great: Oh! Take him Gently from the Pile. The Way of the World: Love's but the Frailty of the Mind.* WELDON: *Reason, What art Thou?; While I with Wounding Grief.* D. PURCELL: *Achilles: Morpheus, thou Gentle God.* BLOW: *Lysander I Pursue in Vain.* ANON.: *Mad Maudlin; Tom of Bedlam*
(M) *** Decca 476 2099

Purcell and his contemporaries, including his brother Daniel, John Eccles, John Blow and others, in such mad-songs as these, devised a whole baroque genre. The best-known song here is Purcell's 'I'll Sail upon the Dog Star', but mostly these are miniature cantatas in contrasted sections of recitative and aria, displaying a refreshingly unclassical wildness, often set against pathos. They make a marvellous vehicle for the soprano Catherine Bott, who in this and other discs emerges as an outstanding star among early-music performers, with voice fresh, lively and sensuously beautiful.

'London Pride – A Celebration of London in Song' (with Owen Norris, piano): MONCKTON: *Chalk Farm to Camberwell Green.* DRING: *Business Girls.* WILSON: *A Room in Bloomsbury.* GERSHWIN: *A Foggy Day in London Town.* WALTON: *Rhyme.* DAVID OWEN NORRIS: *Big Ben Blues.* MACCOLL: *Sweet Thames, Run Softly.* BOYCE (arr. Franklin): *The Pleasures of Spring Gardens.* DOVE: *Five Am'rous Sighs.* HESKETH-HARVEY/SISSON: *Wimbledon Idyll.* FRASER-SIMPSON: *They're Changing Guard at Buckingham Palace.* KENNEDY/CARR/MAYERL: *Mayfair Merry-go-round.* DASCRE: *While London's Fast Asleep.* R. R. BENNETT: *Let's Go and Live in the Country.* SHERWIN: *A Nightingale Sang in Berkeley Square.* SCOTT: *Take me in a Taxi, Joe.* SWANN: *Joyful Noise.* COWARD: *London Pride*
*** Hyp. CDA 67457

This is a fun disc, with Catherine Bott – best known as a baroque and early music specialist – demonstrating her mastery in a programme of cabaret numbers recorded live before an audience. With the help of her accompanist, David Owen Norris, she has devised a formidably wide-ranging programme in celebration of London in song. She starts in the world of the musical with Lionel Monckton and Sandy Wilson ('A Room in Bloomsbury' from *The Boy Friend*) and leads via a number from Walton's *Song for the Lord Mayor's Table* to 'A Nightingale Sang in Berkeley Square' and Noel

Coward's 'London Pride'. On the way there is an eighteenth-century interlude with a Boyce song celebrating Vauxhall Gardens and a sequence by Jonathan Dove setting poems evoking eighteenth-century town life. Bott brilliantly adapts her vocal technique to each, with precise control of vibrato, timbre and phrasing. Best of all is Joyce Grenfell's 'Joyful Noise', in which a lady chorister celebrates the Royal Albert Hall. Bott puts her own delicious slant on a number that one would have thought nobody but Grenfell could ever bring off.

Bott, Catherine (soprano), The Parley of Instruments, Peter Holman

'Music for Shakespeare from Purcell to Arne': WELDON: *Dry Those Eyes which are O'erflowing; Take, O Take those Lips Away.* ECCLES: *Can Life be a Blessing?.* CHILCOT: *Hark, Hark, the Lark; Orpheus and his Lute; Pardon, Goddess of the Night.* GREENE: *Orpheus and his Lute.* ARNE: *Honour, Riches, Marriage-blessing; To Fair Fidele's Grassy Tomb; When Daisies Pied and Violets Blue; When Icicles Hang on the Wall; Where the Bee Sucks, There Lurk I.* LEVERIDGE: *When Daisies Pied and Violets Blue.* SMITH: *Full Fathom Five; You Spotted Snakes.* DE FESCH: *All Fancy Sick.* PURCELL: *Dear Pretty Youth.* Orchestral: CLARKE: *Titus Andronicus: Overture and Minuet.* WOODCOCK: *Concerto 9 in E min. for Flute & Strings* (with Brown)
*** Hyp. CDA 67450

In the late seventeenth through into the eighteenth century, when Shakespeare's plays were regularly presented in 'improved' versions, often radically different from the original, the revised texts gave plenty of scope for musical items. This attractive collection, characterfully sung by Catherine Bott, includes varied settings of such favourite Shakespeare songs as 'Orpheus with his Lute' and 'When Daisies Pied'. So Maurice Greene's setting of the *Orpheus* song is tricked out with delicate trills and, even more memorably, Thomas Chilcot's extended setting has a haunting flute (beautifully played by Rachel Brown) over a trotting accompaniment. The collection is introduced by Jeremiah Clarke's two-movement overture to *Titus Andronicus*, with a string concerto by Robert Woodcock punctuating the song-sequence, which culminates in two fine songs by Thomas Arne, 'Honour, Riches, Marriage-blessing' and 'Where the Bee Sucks'.

Bott, Catherine (soprano), New London Consort, Philip Pickett

'Music from the Time of Columbus': VERARDI: *Viva El Gran Re Don Fernando.* ANON.: *A los Maytines era; Propinan de Melyor; Como no le andare yo; Nina y viña; Calabaza, no sé, buen amor; Perdí la mi rueca; Al alva venid buen amigo; Dale si la das.* URREDA: *Muy triste.* J. PONCE: *Como esta sola mi vida.* ANCHIETA: *Con amores mi madre.* ENCINA: *Triste españa; Mortal tristura; Mas vale trocar; Ay triste que vengo; Quedate carillo.* MEDINA: *No ay plazer en esta vida.* DE LA TORRE: *Danza alta.* DE MONDEJAR: *Un sola fin des mis males*
*** Linn CKD 007

The songs offered here are broadly divided into two groups, the romantic ballads, usually of a melancholy disposition (the word 'triste' occurs frequently), and the usually jollier *villan-cico* form, which brings a repeated refrain. Catherine Bott is the most delightful soloist, singing freshly and simply, often with a ravishing tone, and there is much to give pleasure. In the anonymous songs it is fascinating to discover just how international medieval folk music was, for more than once the listener is reminded of the Auvergne songs collected later in France by Canteloube. The two most delightful items are saved until the end, first a truly beautiful love song, *Al alva venid buen amigo* ('Come at Dawn my Friend'), in which a young woman reflects on her lover's visits, and then lets her thoughts change to consider the birth from the Virgin Mary of 'him who made the world'. In complete contrast is the robust and charmingly naughty villancio, *Dale si das* ('Come on, Wench of Carasa'). The recording is first class, naturally balanced in a pleasing acoustic, and full documentation is provided.

Bowman, James (counter-tenor)

'*The James Bowman Collection*' (with the King's Consort, Robert King): BACH: *Erbarme dich; Stirb in mir.* HANDEL: *Almighty Power; Crueltà nè lontananza; Impious Mortal; Tune your Harps; Welcome as the Dawn of Day; Thou shalt Bring them in; Or la tromba; Eternal Source of Light.* PURCELL: *Britain, Thou Now art Great; O Solitude; By Beauteous Softness Mixed; An Evening Hymn; On the Brow of Richmond Hill; Vouchsafe, O Lord.* ANON.: *Come Tread the Paths.* GABRIELI: *O magnum mysterium.* FORD: *Since I Saw your Face.* F. COUPERIN: *Jerusalem, convertere*
(BB) *** Hyp. KING 3

Apart from the opening Bach item, which has not previously been published and which is not entirely flattering, this admirable 78-minute sampler will delight fans of James Bowman as it shows his art and fine vocal control over a wide range of repertoire at which he excelled. Robert King and his Consort provide admirable support.

Callas, Maria (soprano)

'*La Divina I*': Arias from: PUCCINI: *Madama Butterfly; La Bohème; Gianni Schicchi; Turandot; Tosca.* BIZET: *Carmen.* CATALANI: *La Wally.* ROSSINI: *Il barbiere di Siviglia.* BELLINI: *Norma.* SAINT-SAENS: *Samson et Dalila.* VERDI: *Rigoletto; La traviata.* GOUNOD: *Roméo et Juliette.* MOZART: *Don Giovanni.* MASCAGNI: *Cavalleria rusticana.* PONCHIELLI: *La Gioconda*
**(*) EMI stereo/mono 7 54702-2

'*La Divina II*': Arias from: GLUCK: *Alceste; Orphée et Eurydice.* BIZET: *Carmen.* VERDI: *Ernani; Aida; I vespri siciliani; La traviata; Don Carlos.* PUCCINI: *Manon Lescaut; La Bohème.* CHARPENTIER: *Louise.* THOMAS: *Mignon.* SAINT-SAENS: *Samson et Dalila.* BELLINI: *La sonnambula.* CILEA: *Adriana Lecouvreur.* DONIZETTI: *Lucia di Lammermoor*
*(*) EMI stereo/mono 5 55016-2

'*La Divina III*': Arias and duets from: GIORDANO: *Andrea Chénier.* SPONTINI: *La Vestale.* MASSENET: *Manon.* PUCCINI: *Manon Lescaut; La Bohème* (with di Stefano); *Madama Butterfly* (with Gedda); *Turandot.* BIZET: *Carmen*

(with Gedda). ROSSINI: *Il barbiere di Siviglia* (with Gobbi). DELIBES: *Lakmé.* VERDI: *Aida; Il trovatore.* LEONCAVALLO: *Pagliacci.* MEYERBEER: *Dinorah*
*** EMI stereo/mono 5 55216-2

These three recital discs (with nearly four hours of music) cover Callas's recording career pretty thoroughly, although the first two are inadequately documented, giving only the date each recording was published. *La Divina III*, however, provides both the actual dates and venues of the recordings and details of the other artists involved. Throughout the three programmes, results are inevitably uneven, and if at times the rawness of exposed top-notes mars the lyrical beauty of her singing, equally often her dramatic magnetism is such that many phrases stay indelibly in the memory.

Each disc has its share of highlights, with the earlier recordings usually the more memorable. What is perhaps surprising are the omissions: nothing, for instance, from the collection of 'mad scenes' she recorded with Rescigno. However, many of the choices are apt. *La Divina I*, for instance, includes her sharply characterful, early 1954 recording of *Una voce poco fa* from Rossini's *Barbiere*, and *La Divina III* draws on the later, complete set for the duet *Dunque io son*, with Tito Gobbi. *La Divina II* consistently shows her at her finest or near it. The recordings cover a decade from 1954 to 1964 and include much that is arrestingly dramatic (Gluck and Verdi) and ravishing (Puccini and Cilea), while everything shows that special degree of imagination which Callas brought to almost everything she did. The *Mignon* Polonaise is not ideally elegant but it has a distinctive character and charm, and it is almost irrelevant to criticize Callas on detail when her sense of presence is so powerful. The excerpt from *La traviata* was recorded live in Lisbon in 1958 and even the audience noises cannot detract from its magnetism. All three recital discs are available separately at full price, with the third certainly the place to start, as it centres on early recordings, including the excerpt from *La Vestale*, and opens with the movingly intense *La mamma morta* from *Andrea Chénier*. However, it is astonishing that, having provided so much information about the singer, EMI chose not to include any translations, resting content with a brief synopsis of each aria.

Callas Edition

'*Callas at La Scala*' (with La Scala, Milan O, Serafin): CHERUBINI: *Medea: Dei tuoi figli.* SPONTINI: *La Vestale: Tu che invoco; O nume tutelar; Caro oggetto.* BELLINI: *La sonnambula: Compagne, teneri amici ... Come per me sereno; Oh! se una volta solo ... Ah! non credea mirati*
(M) (***) EMI mono 5 66457-2

These recordings were made at La Scala in June 1955 and feature extracts from three operas which at the time Callas had made all her own. However, for some unexplained reason, the diva refused to sanction publication of the *Sonnambula* items, so the original LP was released in 1958 with substituted performances, taken from her complete set, made the previous year. Yet, with Callas in her prime, if anything more relaxed than in those later versions, the remarkable quality is the total consistency: most details are identical in both performances. *Aficionados* will surely be delighted that the original performances have been restored alongside the Cherubini and Spontini arias. Throughout, Callas is heard at her most magnetic. As usual in this series, the CD transfers are very impressive.

'*Lyric and Coloratura Arias*' (with Philh. O, Serafin): CILEA: *Adriana Lecouvreur: Ecco, respiro appena ... Io son l'umile; Poveri fiori.* GIORDANO: *Andrea Chénier: La mamma morta.* CATALANI: *La Wally: Ebben? Ne andrò lontana.* BOITO: *Mefistofele: L'altra notte.* ROSSINI: *Il barbiere di Siviglia: Una voce poco fa.* MEYERBEER: *Dinorah: Shadow Song.* DELIBES: *Lakmé: Bell Song.* VERDI: *I vespri siciliani: Bolero: Mercè, dilette amiche.* CHERUBINI: *Medea: Dei tuoi figli la madre.* SPONTINI: *La vestale: Tu che invoco con orrore; O Nume, tutelar; Caro ogetto*

(M) (***) EMI mono 4 76842-2 [4 76843-2]

Recorded at the same group of sessions in September 1954 as her very first (Puccini) recital for EMI, this is another of the classic early Callas records, ranging extraordinarily widely in its repertory and revealing in every item the uniquely intense musical imagination that set musicians of every kind listening and learning. Coloratura flexibility here goes with dramatic weight. Not all the items are equally successful: the Shadow Song from *Dinorah*, for example, reveals some strain and lacks charm, but these are all unforgettable performances. Callas's portrait of Rosina in *Una voce poco fa* was never more viperish than here, and she never surpassed the heartfelt intensity of such numbers as *La mamma morta* and *Poveri fiori*. This mono reissue is well balanced and cleanly transferred with the voice vividly projected against a convincing orchestral backdrop. It now reappears as one of EMI's Great Recordings of the Century with bonus arias from Cherubini's *Medea* and Spontini's *La Vestale*.

'*Lyric and Coloratura Arias*' from: CILEA: *Adriana Lecouvreur.* CATALANI: *La Wally.* BOITO: *Mefistofele.* ROSSINI: *Il Barbiere di Siviglia; Il Turco in Italia; Armida.* MEYERBEER: *Dinorah.* DELIBES: *Lakmé.* VERDI: *I vespri siciliani.* MOZART: *Die Entführung.* CHARPENTIER: *Louise*

(BB) (**) Regis mono RRC 1233

This is much the same collection as the EMI disc above, again with extra items added, notably *Depuis le jour* from *Louise*. However, surprisingly for this label, although the voice is often beautifully caught, the transfers are not always well managed, with occasional insecurity in the sound, and some uncomfortable moments of blasting on *fortissimos*.

'*Mad Scenes*' (with Philh. Ch. & O, Rescigno): DONIZETTI: *Anna Bolena: Piangete voi? ... Al dolce guidami castel natio.* THOMAS: *Hamlet: A vos jeux ... Partagez-vous mes fleurs ... Et maintenant écoutez ma chanson.* BELLINI: *Il pirata: Oh! s'io potessi ... Cor sorriso d'innocenza*

⚬━ (M) *** EMI (ADD) 5 66459-2

Recorded in the Kingsway Hall in September 1958, this is the record which, Desmond Shawe-Taylor suggested, more than any other summed up the essence of Callas's genius. If the rawness of exposed top notes mars the sheer beauty of the singing, few recital records ever made can match – let alone outshine – this collection of 'mad scenes' in vocal and dramatic imagination.

'*Callas à Paris*', Volume I (with Fr. Nat. R. O, Prêtre): GLUCK: *Orphée et Euridice: J'ai perdu mon Euridice.* *Alceste: Divinités du Styx.* BIZET: *Carmen: Habanera; Seguidilla.* SAINT-SAENS: *Samson et Dalila: Printemps qui commence; Amour! viens aider ma faiblesse! Mon coeur s'ouvre à ta voix.* GOUNOD: *Roméo et Juliette: Ah! je veux vivre dans ce rêve.* THOMAS: *Mignon: Ah, pour ce soir ... Je*

suis Titania. MASSENET: *Le Cid: De cet affreux combat ... pleurez.* CHARPENTIER: *Louise: Depuis le jour*

(M) *** EMI (ADD) 5 66466-2

'*Callas à Paris*', Volume II (with Paris Conservatoire O, Prêtre): GLUCK: *Iphigénie en Tauride: O malheureuse Iphigénie.* BERLIOZ: *La Damnation de Faust: D'amour l'ardente flamme.* BIZET: *Les Pêcheurs de perles: Me voilà seule ... Comme autrefois.* MASSENET: *Manon: Je ne suis que faiblesse ... Adieu notre petite table. Suis-je gentille ainsi? ... Je marche sur tous les chemins.* WERTHER: *Werther! Qui m'aurait dit ... Des cris joyeuse (Air des lettres).* GOUNOD: *Faust: Il était un Roi de Thulé ... O Dieu! que de bijoux ... Ah! je ris*

(M) ** EMI (ADD) 5 66467-2

The first LP collection, *Callas à Paris*, dating from 1961, has the singer at her most commanding and characterful. The sequel disc was recorded two years later when the voice was in decline. The vocal contrast is clear enough, and the need at the time to patch and re-patch the takes in the later sessions makes the results sound less spontaneous and natural. But the earlier portraits of Carmen, Alceste, Dalila and Juliette find Callas still supreme, and her mastery of the French repertoire provides a fascinating slant on her artistry.

'*Romantic Callas*': Arias from: PUCCINI: *La Bohème; Madama Butterfly; Manon Lescaut; Tosca.* BELLINI: *La sonnambula.* VERDI: *Aida; Un ballo in maschera; La traviata; Il trovatore.* LEONCAVALLO: *Pagliacci.* DONIZETTI: *Lucia di Lammermoor.* SAINT-SAENS: *Samson et Dalila.* BIZET: *Carmen; Les Pêcheurs de perles.* BERLIOZ: *La Damnation de Faust.* MASSENET: *Werther.* MOZART: *Don Giovanni.* SPONTINI: *La Vestale.* MASCAGNI: *Cavalleria rusticana.* CILEA: *Adriana Lecouvreur*

(M) *(**) EMI mono/stereo 5 57205-2 (2)

There have probably been more Maria Callas compilations than of any other female opera singer, and in the two-CD set listed above, there is nothing that has not been compiled several times before. However, never have they been presented more extravagantly. This release features a lavish booklet in hardback containing over 45 high-quality photographs (in black and white and colour), biographical information, full texts and translations, a discography and something of the opera's plots, which places each aria in context. There are plenty of examples of Callas at her commanding best. The majority of items are from her classic complete opera recordings and recital discs from the 1950s. The transfers are excellent.

'*Live in Hamburg 1959*' (with N. German RSO, Rescigno): Arias from: SPONTINI: *La Vestale.* VERDI: *Don Carlo; Macbeth.* ROSSINI: *Il barbiere di Siviglia.* BELLINI: *Il pirata*

(M) (***) EMI mono 5 62681-2

This is the most consistent of the live recordings of Callas recitals latterly issued by EMI. The programme is identical with that on the Stuttgart disc, recorded four days later in May 1959. Not only is the Hamburg recording fuller and firmer, the orchestral playing is a degree more polished. There is little to choose between Callas's performances in each. This is a programme which allows her to display her fire-eating qualities to the full as she portrays a sequence of formidable heroines, with the voice still at its peak, commanding in every way. Curiously, in Lady Macbeth's Letter aria her reading of the letter finds her speaking voice far less menacing than her magnetic singing. Only the slightest flicker on culminating top notes forecasts the flaw that would seriously develop over the following years. This is Callas at her finest, making this a valuable addition to her discography.

'*Live in Paris 1963 & 1976*' (with O Nat. de l'RTF, Prêtre): Arias from: ROSSINI: *La Cenerentola; Semiramide.* MASSENET: *Manon; Werther.* VERDI: *Nabucco.* PUCCINI: *La Bohème; Gianni Schicchi; Madama Butterfly* (with Tate, piano). BEETHOVEN: *Ah! perfido!*
(M) (**(**)) EMI mono 5 62685-2

By the time Callas gave this Paris recital in 1963 the unsteadiness in her voice had developed to the point of being obtrusive. There is still much to enjoy here, and not just for Callas devotees, for the programme ranges wide, from the brilliant Rossini arias from *Cenerentola* and *Semiramide* to Massenet, poignantly done, Verdi (the Act II aria from *Nabucco*) and Puccini. The fire-eating Callas here portrays two of the composer's tender 'little women', Lauretta pleading with her father in *Gianni Schicchi* and *Butterfly* in her suicide aria, formidably intense. Also – unexpectedly – Musetta in her waltz song from *Bohème* and not Mimì. The oddity is the seriously flawed private recording of Beethoven's concert aria, *Ah! perfido!*, here cut off before the end, with Jeffrey Tate's piano accompaniment fuzzy and close and Callas's voice ill-focused behind. By 1976 Callas's career was almost over but, whatever the vocal flaws, the power of her personality still shines through in repertory she did not otherwise record.

'*Live in Amsterdam 1959*' (with Concg. O, Rescigno): Arias from: SPONTINI: *La Vestale.* VERDI: *Don Carlo; Ernani.* BELLINI: *Il pirata*
(M) (**) EMI mono 5 62683-2

Recorded two months after the Hamburg and Stuttgart recitals in this same series of Callas singing live, this programme overlaps with those, but with one important exception. Here, instead of Lady Macbeth's Act I aria, she sings the big aria from Verdi's *Ernani*, again in a fire-eating performance. Neither the sound nor the playing quite matches that on the Hamburg disc.

'*Live in London 1961 & 1962*' (with Philh. O, Prêtre): Arias from: WEBER: *Oberon.* MASSENET: *Le Cid.* ROSSINI: *La Cenerentola.* DONIZETTI: *Anna Bolena.* VERDI: *Macbeth.* (with ROHCG O, Prêtre): BIZET: *Carmen.* VERDI: *Don Carlo.* (with Sargent, piano): MASSENET: *Le Cid.* BOITO: *Mefistofele*
(M) (*(*)) EMI mono 5 62684-2

The items with Georges Prêtre and the Philharmonia recorded live at the Royal Festival Hall bring unsteady, crumbly sound with the voice 'off-mike', set at a distance. Aficionados will readily listen through the limitations to hear bold, thrusting performances, with Callas in formidable voice, even if the definition of coloratura is inevitably restricted by the sound. The items recorded at Covent Garden come in far better sound, even if it seems a waste to have orchestral items punctuating Carmen's *Habanera* and *Seguidilla*, both wonderfully characterized. Best of all is Leonora's aria from *Don Carlo*, even if there is some unsteadiness at the top of the ever-distinctive Callas voice. A truncated version of Leonora's aria also comes in the curious items recorded live at St James's Palace in 1961, along with another version of the Massenet aria and Margarita's aria from Boito's *Mefistofele*. The piano accompaniment by Sir Malcolm Sargent is so poorly recorded it sounds like a harp.

'*Live in Stuttgart 1959*' (with South German RSO, Rescigno): Arias from: SPONTINI: *La Vestale.* VERDI: *Don Carlo; Macbeth.* ROSSINI: *Il barbiere di Siviglia.* BELLINI: *Il pirata*
(M) (**) EMI mono 5 62682-2

Recorded four days after the Hamburg recital in this same series (see above) and offering an identical programme, the results are similarly electrifying, though recorded in thinner sound, with the orchestra less polished. The Hamburg disc has every advantage.

Calleja, Joseph (tenor)

Tenor Arias (with Milan SO, Chailly) from: CILEA: *L'Arlesiana; Adriana Lecouvreur.* DONIZETTI: *L'elisir d'amore; Lucia di Lammermoor.* PUCCINI: *Madama Butterfly.* VERDI: *Macbeth; Rigoletto; La traviata*
*** Decca 475 250-2

Among the latest contenders in the top tenor stakes Joseph Calleja from Malta stands out for relating more closely than usual to examples set by tenors from the early years of recording. His very distinctive timbre, with a rapidly flickering vibrato, brings a reminder of such a 'golden age' singer as Alessandro Bonci. Calleja's technique, with fine control down to the most delicate half-tones, finds him just as happy in the bel canto of Donizetti as in the warm verismo phrases of Cilea and Puccini. The choice of items is imaginative too, helped by the purposeful conducting of Riccardo Chailly. So Alfredo's aria, *De' miei bollenti spiriti*, in Act II of Verdi's *La traviata* is set in context, and though the Duke's *Questa o quella* and *La donna è mobile* from *Rigoletto* come as brief separate items, his *Parmi veder* is presented as part of a complete scene, as is Arturo's big aria in Donizetti's *Lucia di Lammermoor*.

Cambridge Singers, John Rutter

'*Flora Gave me Fairest Flowers*' (English madrigals): MORLEY: *My Bonny Lass she Smileth; Fyer, Fyer!; Now is the Month of Maying.* EAST: *Quick, Quick, Away Dispatch!* GIBBONS: *Dainty Fine bird; Silver Swan.* BYRD: *Though Amaryllis Dance in Green; This Sweet and Merry Month of May; Lullaby.* WEELKES: *Hark, All ye Lovely Saints.* WILBYE: *Weep, Weep, Mine Eyes; Flora Gave me; Draw on Sweet Night; Adieu Sweet Amaryllis.* TOMKINS: *Too Much I Once Lamented; Adieu ye City-prisoning Towers.* FARMER: *Little Pretty Bonny Lass.* BENNETT: *Round About.* WEELKES: *Ha ha! This World doth Pass; Death hath Deprived me.* RAMSEY: *Sleep, Fleshly Birth*
*** Coll. COLCD 105

John Rutter's Cambridge Singers bring consistent unanimity of ensemble and a natural expressive feeling to this very attractive programme of madrigals. Perhaps the first group, devoted to love and marriage, may be thought rather too consistently mellifluous; but the second, 'Madrigals of Times and Season', is nicely contrasted, with the clean articulation of Morley's 'Now is the Month of Maying' made the more telling by the lightness of the vocal production. John Wilbye's lovely 'Draw on Sweet Night', which follows, makes a perfect contrast. After two items about 'Fairies, Spirits and Conceits', the concert closes in a mood of moving Elizabethan melancholy with a group devoted to mourning and farewell. Superb recording in a most flattering acoustic makes this collection the more enjoyable, though one to be dipped into rather than heard all at once.

'Faire is the Heaven' (music of the English Church): PARSONS: *Ave Maria.* TALLIS: *Loquebantur variis linguis; If ye Love me.* BYRD: *Misere mei; Haec dies; Ave verum corpus; Bow Thine Ear.* FARRANT: *Hide not Thou Thy Face; Lord for thy Tender Mercy's Sake.* GIBBONS: *O Clap your Hands; Hosanna to the Son of David.* PURCELL: *Lord, How Long wilt Thou be Angry; Thou Knowest, Lord; Hear my Prayer, O Lord.* STANFORD: *Beati quorum via.* arr. WOOD: *This Joyful Eastertide.* HOWELLS: *Sing Lullaby; A Spotless Rose.* WALTON: *What Cheer?* VAUGHAN WILLIAMS: *O Taste and See.* BRITTEN: *Hymn to the Virgin.* POSTON: *Jesus Christ the Apple Tree.* HARRIS: *Faire is the Heaven*
*** Coll. COLCD 107

These recordings were made in the Lady Chapel of Ely Cathedral, and the ambience adds beauty to the sound without in any way impairing clarity of focus. The music ranges from examples of the Roman Catholic Rite as set by Tallis, Byrd and Robert Parsons (with a touch of almost Latin eloquence in the presentation), through widely varied Reformation music, to the Restoration, represented by three Purcell anthems, and on to the Anglican revival and the twentieth century. The Reformation group is particularly successful, with the opening Tallis and closing Gibbons works rich in polyphony and Byrd's 'Bow Thine Ear' wonderfully serene. Of the modern items, the Howells pieces are quite lovely and Walton's 'What Cheer?', with its engaging imitation, is attractively genial. The Britten and Poston items, both well known, are hardly less engaging; and the concert ends with the ambitious title-number, William Harris's 'Faire is the Heaven', sung with great feeling and considerable power. There is no more successful survey of English church music in the current catalogue and certainly not one presented with more conviction.

'Hail Queen of Heaven' (Music in Honour of the Virgin Mary): Plainchant: *Alma Redemptoris Mater.* GUERRERO: *Ave Virgo sanctissima.* TRAD.: *There is no rose of such virtue.* VICTORIA: *Ave Maria (for 4 voices).* Plainchant: *Ave Regina caelorum.* PALESTRINA: *Stabat Mater.* BRUCKNER: *Ave Maria.* VERDI: *Laudi alla Vergine Maria.* STRAVINSKY: *Ave Maria.* TCHAIKOVSKY: *Dostoino Yest.* Plainchant: *Regina caeli laetarre.* HOWELLS: *Regina caeli.* ANON.: *Hail Blessed Virgin Mary.* VILLETTE: *Hymn à la Vierge.* SWAYNE: *Magnificat.* Plainchant: *Salve Regina.* BYRD: *Alleluia, Ave Maria.* VICTORIA: *Vidi speciosam; Ave Maria (for double choir).* HOLST: *Ave Maria*
(M) *** Coll. CSCD 508

'Hail, Queen of Heaven' was also recorded very appropriately in the glowingly resonant acoustics of the Lady Chapel in Ely Cathedral. It might be thought that with 23 works, all inspired by the Virgin Mary, there would be a lack of variety, but that is not so. The programme is divided into four groups, each one centring on a different period of the church year (Advent to Candlemas; Candlemas to Holy Week; Easter to the Sunday after Pentecost; and Trinity to Advent), and each section is introduced by an appropriate Gregorian Chant.

All this music is beautiful and rewarding, and the order of presentation brings continuing contrast. But certain works stand out, not least the lovely fifteenth-century English carol, *There is no rose of such virtue,* sung with wonderful purity,

and featuring two fine soloists, Caroline Ashton, soprano, and Andrew Gant, tenor. Victoria's *Ave Maria* also stands out in the first section, as does Palestrina's infinitely touching *Stabat Mater* in the second. But Verdi's richly operatic *Laudi* and Stravinsky's passionately brief *Ave Maria* are equally memorable in a different way.

The third group brings Herbert Howells' unforgettably exuberant *Regina caeli* with its radiant 'Alleluias', and it closes with Giles Swayne's bouncing *Magnificat*, while the fourth juxtaposes two *Ave Marias*, a simple setting by Holst, and another, much more complex, by Victoria for double choir, which ends the programme superbly, when singing and recording are of the very highest standard.

'A cappella': BRITTEN: *Hymn to St Cecilia.* BRAHMS: *4 Lieder aus dem Jungbrunnen.* SCHUMANN: *4 Songs for Double Choir, Op. 141.* PEARSALL: *Lay a Garland.* DELIUS: *The Splendour falls on Castle Walls.* RAVEL: *3 Chansons.* DEBUSSY: *3 Chansons de Charles d'Orléans.* POULENC: *8 Chansons françaises*
(M) *** Coll. CSCD 909

A cappella (unaccompanied) choral singing came into its own in the nineteenth and twentieth centuries, with composers often creating antiphonal effects to add interest to the internal part-writing, when there was to be no accompanying instrumental group. Britten planned his two early choral masterpieces, the *Ceremony of Carols* (which uses a harp backing) and the *Hymn to St Cecilia*, with their lyricist, W. H. Auden, when they were together in the United States in 1940. They were completed during the voyage home in 1942.

The *St Cecilia Hymn* is in three sections, using three different poems, and the format is like a miniature choral sinfonietta (*Tranquillo*; scherzando and a closing *Andante*). The result, with its complex interweaving of parts, is a glorious tribute to the patron saint of music and it opens this prgramme arrestingly. The works that follow, from the rich sonorities of Brahms and Schumann (the music both serene and vigorous), the very English and very touching valedictory *Lay a Garland* of Pearsall, and Delius's delightful chromatic evocation, where the voices simulate the 'blowing bugle, echoes dying' are hardly less memorable.

The French group have their own special individuality by looking backwards in time for their inspiration. Ravel's *Chansons* (using his own texts), and Debussy's too, re-create an earlier Renaissance tradition, none more so than Debussy's drummer playing in *Quant j'ai ouy le tabourin*. Ravel's *Trois beaux oiseaux du Paradis* is quite ravishing, and the following *Ronde* is wonderfully exuberant.

Poulenc (who had had the traumatic experience of living in occupied France during the Second World War) asserted his national identity by setting traditional folk-rhymes to his own melodies – of simple beauty (*La belle se sied au pied de la tour* and *Ah! mon beau laboureau*) or with infectious folksy exuberance, as in the sparkling simulation of dancing clogs (*Clic clac*) and the closing *Les tisserands* (Weavers 'who are worse than bishops – every Monday they celebrate'). Performances, as usual from Rutter, are superb, and the recording equally so.

'The Lark in the Clear Air' (trad. songs; with members of the London Sinfonia): *I Know Where I'm Going; She Moved through the Fair; The Lark in the Clear Air; Down by the Salley Gardens; Dashing Away with the Smoothing Iron; The Sprig of Thyme; The Bold Grenadier; The British Grenadiers; The Keel Row; The Girl I Left behind me; The Cuckoo; O*

Waly Waly; Willow Song; The Willow Tree; The Miller of Dee; O Can ye Sew Cushions; Afton Water. arr. VAUGHAN WILLIAMS: *The Spring Time of the Year; The Dark-eyed Sailor; Just as the Tide was Flowing; The Lover's Ghost; Wassail Song*
**(*) Coll. COLCD 120

Most of these songs are arranged by Rutter himself, often with simple and characteristic instrumental backings – the opening 'I Know Where I'm Going' has an oboe introduction, 'Down by the Salley Gardens' a clarinet, and 'The Miller of Dee' a genial bassoon. 'The Cuckoo' brings a harp, and in 'The Keel Row' the woodwind interjections are delightful, while the evocative introduction to *Afton Water* is particularly beautiful. Even so, several more memorable items, 'O Waly Waly' for instance, are unaccompanied. The five arrangements by Vaughan Williams bring welcome contrast. The choir sings beautifully, but most of the programme is flowing and mellifluous and one would have welcomed more robust items like 'Dashing Away with the Smoothing Iron' and 'The British Grenadiers'. The recording is richly atmospheric.

'*Christmas Day in the Morning*' (with City of London Sinfonia; (i) Varcoe): TRAD., arr. RUTTER: *I Saw Three Ships; Sans Day Carol; Un flambeau, Jeannette, Isabelle; Wexford Carol; Quittes pasteurs; Go Tell it on the Mountain; Deck the Hall; We Wish you a Merry Christmas; (i) Riu, riu, chiu.* RUTTER: *Mary's Lullaby; Star Carol; Jesus Child; Donkey Carol; Wild Wood Carol; The Very Best Time of Year; Shepherd's Pipe Carol; Christmas Lullaby.* WILLAN: *What is this Lovely Fragrance?* WARLOCK: *Balulalow; I Saw a Fair Maiden.* TAVENER: *The Lamb.* VAUGHAN WILLIAMS: (i) *Fantasia on Christmas Carols.* TRAD., arr. WILLCOCKS: *Blessed be that Maid Mary*
**(*) Coll. COLCD 121

Admirers of Rutter's own carols will certainly be drawn to his latest Christmas collection, for alongside the favourites there are several new ventures in his inimitably lively rhythmic style. The 'Donkey Carol', too, becomes more passionate than in previous accounts. But in general, although the whole programme is enjoyable, beautifully sung and smoothly recorded, the feeling of spontaneous freshness, so enticing on his earliest Decca collection (currently withdrawn), made with the choir from Clare College, is less apparent here, and at times there is a hint of blandness (noticeable with the ritardando at the close of Tavener's 'The Lamb'). 'Go Tell it on the Mountain' does not sound entirely idiomatic, and while 'We Wish you a Merry Christmas' ends the concert spiritedly, the Vaughan Williams *Fantasia*, even though it has a fine climax, does not quite match the King's College version (see below) in robust, earthy vigour.

'*A Banquet of Voices*' (music for multiple choirs): GUERRERO: *Duo seraphim.* ALLEGRI: *Miserere.* CALDARA: *Crucifixus.* SCHEIDT: *Surrexit pastor bonus.* TALLIS: *Spem in alium* (40-part motet). PHILIPS: *Ave Regina caelorum.* BRAHMS: *3 Fest- und Gedenksprüche.* MENDELSSOHN: *Mitten wir im Leben sind; Heilig.* BACH: *Motet: Singet dem Herrn, BWV 225*
** Coll. COLCD 123

The resonant acoustic of the Great Hall of University College, London, does not really suit the complex early polyphonic music here, often clouding the detail of writing for double or triple choir and producing a poorly focused climax in the spectacular Tallis *Spem in alium*. The singing too could be more robust in the Scheidt motet. The choir seem much more at home in Brahms and Mendelssohn, and the closing section of the Bach motet *Singet dem Herrn* is vigorously joyful.

'*Portrait*': BYRD: *Sing Joyfully; Non vos relinquam.* FAURE: *Cantique de Jean Racine; Requiem: Sanctus.* RUTTER: *O be Joyful in the Lord; All Things Bright and Beautiful; Shepherd's Pipe Carol; Open Thou Mine Eyes; Requiem: Out of the Deep.* PURCELL: *Hear my prayer, O Lord.* STANFORD: *Beati quorum via; The Blue Bird.* TRAD.: *This Joyful Eastertide; In dulci jubilo.* HANDEL: *Messiah: For unto us a Child is Born.* FARMER: *A Pretty Bonny Lass.* MORLEY: *Now is the Month of Maying.* DELIUS: *To be Sung of a Summer Night on the Water I & II.* VICTORIA: *O magnum mysterium.* TERRY: *Myn Lyking*
(M) *** Coll. DDD/ADD CSCD 500

John Rutter has arranged the items here with great skill so that serene music always makes a contrast with the many exuberant expressions of joy, his own engaging hymn-settings among them. Thus the bright-eyed hey-nonny songs of John Farmer and Thomas Morley are aptly followed by the lovely wordless 'To be Sung of a Summer Night on the Water' of Delius, and Stanford's beautiful evocation of 'The Blue Bird' (one of Rutter's own special favourites). The sound, vivid and atmospheric, suits the colour and mood of the music quite admirably. Not to be missed!

'*The Cambridge Singers Collection*' (with Marshall, City of L. Sinf.): DEBUSSY: *3 Chansons d'Orléans.* Folksongs (arr. RUTTER): *The Keel Row; The Willow Tree.* Gregorian chant: *Regina caeli laetare.* BRUCKNER: *Ave Maria.* VERDI: *Laudi alla Vergine Maria.* STANFORD: *Magnificat in D; Te Deum in C.* PURCELL: *Remember not, Lord, our Offences.* TAVERNER: *Christe Jesu, pastor bone.* PHILIPS: *O Beatum et sacrosanctum diem.* PEARSALL: *Lay a Garland.* RUTTER: *Riddle Song; Waltz; Magnificat* (1st movement); *The Wind in the Willows* (excerpt, with The King's Singers, Baker, Hickox). TRAD. (arr. RUTTER): *Sing a Song of Sixpence*
(M) Coll. CSCD 501

Here is an attractively chosen, 64-minute sampler, including a wide range of tempting repertoire from arrangements of folksongs to Stanford and Verdi. The Taverner and Philips items are particularly welcome. Rutter includes a fair proportion of his own music, but the opening (only) from his setting of *The Wind in the Willows* will not be something one would want to return to very often.

'*There is Sweet Music*' (English choral songs): STANFORD: *The Blue Bird.* DELIUS: *To be Sung of a Summer Night on the Water I & II.* ELGAR: *There is Sweet Music; My Love Dwelt in a Northern Land.* VAUGHAN WILLIAMS: *3 Shakespearean Songs: Full Fathom Five; The Cloud-capp'd Towers; Over Hill, over Dale.* BRITTEN: *5 Flower Songs, Op. 47.* Folksongs: arr. MOERAN: *The Sailor and Young Nancy.* arr. GRAINGER: *Brigg Fair; Londonderry Air.* arr. CHAPMAN: *Three Ravens.* arr. HOLST: *My Sweetheart's Like Venus.* arr. BAIRSTOW: *The Oak and the Ash.* arr. STANFORD: *Quick! We Have but a Second*
☞ ✸ (M) *** Coll. COLCD 505

Opening with an enchanting performance of Stanford's 'The Blue Bird' followed by equally expressive accounts of Delius's two wordless summer evocations, this most attractive recital ranges from Elgar and Vaughan Williams, both offering

plendid performances, to various arrangements of folk-
ongs, less fashionable today than they once were, but giving
much pleasure here. The recording, made in the Great Hall of
University College, London, has an almost ideal ambience:
words are clear, yet the vocal timbre is full and natural. A
highly recommendable anthology.

Carewe, Mary (soprano)

'Tell me the Truth about Love' (with Blue Noise, Mayers,
piano): GERSHWIN: Blah, Blah, Blah; Embraceable You;
They All Laughed; Summertime; Love is Here to Stay; By
Strauss. WAXMAN: Alone in a Big City. HOLLAENDER:
Chuck out the Men. SPOLIANSKY: The Smart Set. WEILL:
Speak Low; The Saga of Jenny; It Never was You.
MULDOWNEY: In Paris with You. BRITTEN: Tell me the
Truth about Love; Funeral Blues; Johnny; Calypso; When
You're Feeling like Expressing your Affection

(M) *** ASV CDWHL 2124

In her brilliantly chosen collection of cabaret songs, Mary
Carewe hits an ideal balance between cabaret style – with a
touch of the old-fashioned 'belter' – and art-song style – with
clean, firm vocal attack. Too often, Britten's five settings of
Auden poems emerge as too refined. Carewe's full-blooded
approach brings them to life in a new way, not just as
anaemic pastiche. The first and longest of them is what gives
the collection its title, but the six Gershwin numbers which
frame the programme at beginning and end are just as
stylish, though Philip Mayers' sophisticatedly smoochy
arrangement of 'Summertime' from Porgy and Bess makes it
almost unrecognizable. In some ways the most moving item
is one of the three Kurt Weill songs, 'It Never was You', and it
is good to have Dominic Muldowney represented in nicely
turned pastiche, the more impressive when set against numbers by such exiles in Hollywood as Waxman, Hollaender and
Spoliansky. The only snag is the overblown recording, which
emphasizes the pop style in aggressive closeness for voice and
instruments.

Cathedral Choirs of Winchester, St Paul's and Christ Church, Oxford

English Cathedral Music. PURCELL: Rejoice in the Lord
Always (with Brandenburg Consort). SCHUBERT: German
Mass: Sanctus. LOTTI: Crucifixus. ALLEGRI: Miserere mei.
HAYDN: Missa Rorate coeli desuper: Kyrie; Gloria; Credo
(with Academy of Ancient Music, Preston). BYRD: Bow
thine Ear, O Lord; Turn Our Captivity, O Lord. WEELKES:
Alleluia, I Heard a Voice; Lord Arise into Thy Resting-Place
(with London Cornet & Sackbut Ens.). VAUGHAN
WILLIAMS: O Clap Your Hands. SAINT-SAENS: Messe à
quatre voix, Op. 4: Sanctus; Benedictus; O salutaris.
WALTON: Coronation Te Deum (with Bournemouth SO,
Hill)

(B) **(*) Decca (ADD/DDD) 470 124-2

This collection, though diverse, works well as a 70-minute
anthology of choral favourites, plus a few less familiar pieces.
Mixing organ-accompanied items with the full orchestral
numbers, as well as others with baroque orchestral accompaniments, means that the results are well contrasted. The
performances range from good to outstanding, and the
recordings are all excellent. At bargain price this is attractive
enough.

Chadwell, Tracy (soprano), Pamela Lidiard (piano), John Turner (recorders)

'Songbook': MACONCHY: Sun, Moon and Stars; Three Songs.
LEFANU: I am Bread; A Penny for a Song. WHITEHEAD:
Awa Herea. CRESSWELL: Words for Music. LUMSDAINE:
Norfolk Songbook (with Turner, recorders). LILBURN: 3
Songs. FARQUHAR: 6 Songs of Women. JOUBERT: The
Turning Wheel. BENNETT: A Garland for Marjory Fleming

*** British Music Society BMS 420/1 (2)

Tracey Chadwell, whose career was tragically cut short by
leukaemia when she was still in her mid-thirties, was an
exceptional singer, as this generous two-disc collection of
songs makes plain. Hers was a light, bright soprano of
extraordinary flexibility and sweetness. She might have
become an operatic coloratura, but her special love was for
new music. She had an extraordinary gift for making the
most impossibly craggy vocal lines sound grateful and
expressive, as she does in many of the challengingly difficult
songs here. Three of the song-cycles in the collection, by
Elizabeth Maconchy, David Lumsdaine and the new Zealand
composer, Gillian Whitehead, were specially written for her,
as well as one of the separate songs, and one can understand
the enthusiasm of composers to write for a singer so responsive. Not only did she sing with keen musical imagination,
she projected her sparkling personality with a zest that
matched the sparkle in her voice.

The recordings, drawn from BBC sources, are all first-rate,
with Pamela Lidiard as her understanding piano accompanist, and with the recorder-player, John Turner, as her partner
in the Lumsdaine cycle. The collection comes to a charming
conclusion with Richard Rodney Bennett's settings of poems
by an early-nineteenth-century child-poet, A Garland for
Marjory Fleming. An illuminating collection of modern songs
as well as a fitting memorial.

Chanticleer

'Sing we Christmas': M. PRAETORIUS: Es ist ein Ros'
entsprungen. VICTORIA: O magnum mysterium. TRAD.: In
dulci jubilo (with verse 2 arr. M. PRAETORIUS; verse 3 arr.
H. PRAETORIUS; verse 4 arr. BACH). O Jesulein süss, O
Jeuslein mild (verse 1 arr. SCHEIDT; verse 2 arr. BACH).
JOSQUIN DES PRES: O virgo virginum. HANDL: Hodie
Christus natus est; Mirabile mysterium. ANON.: Verbo caro
factum est; Y la Virgen le dezia. GUERRERO: A un niño
llorando. HOWELLS: Here is the Little Door. SAMETZ: Noel
Canon. arr. WILLCOCKS: Quelle est cette odeur agréable. arr.
RIBO: El noi de la mare. IVES: A Christmas Carol.
BILLINGS: A Virgin Unspotted. HOLST: In the Bleak
Midwinter. arr. JENNINGS: Glory to the Newborn King
(fantasia on four spirituals). GRUBER: Stille Nacht

**(*) Teldec 4509 94563-2

The rich sonority of the very familiar opening Praetorius
carol immediately demonstrates the body and homogeneity
of the singing of this fine choral group of a dozen perfectly
matched male voices; but while the choir's dynamic contrasts are not in question, the close balance prevents an
absolute pianissimo, and the resonance brings a degree of
clouding when lines interweave swiftly, as in Jacob Händl's
Hodie Christus natus est. The lush blend of the slowly
flowing Mirabile mysterium, with its haunting momentary
stabs of dissonance, shows the choir at its finest, as does

Victoria's contemplatively gentle setting (*O magnum myste-rium*) and the rapt, interweaving polyphony of Josquin's *O virgo virginum*, where the depth of sonority is extraordinary.

If Herbert Howells's 'Here is the Little Door' and Holst's 'In the Bleak Midwinter' are made to seem too static, the Ives 'Christmas Carol' suits the sustained style, while Sametz's ingenious 'Noel Canon' is admirably vigorous, as is William Billings's 'A Virgin Unspotted'. The extended sequence of four traditional gospel songs, arranged by Joseph Jennings, is perhaps the highlight of the concert, sung colloquially with some fine solo contributions, especially from the bass; and the closing *Stille Nacht* brings an unforgettably expansive resonance, with the voices blending like a brass chorale.

'Christmas' (also with Upshaw, soprano): Arr. VAUGHAN WILLIAMS: *This the Truth Sent from Above.* TAVENER: *A Christmas Round; Today the Virgin.* DISTLER: *Es ist ein Ros entsprungen (Fantasy).* Arr. HUMPHRIES: *Noël nouvelet.* BOLD/KIRKPATRICK: *Lullaby/Away in a Manger.* Arr. WILLCOCKS: *The First Nowell.* WILLAN: *Three Kings.* MANTYJARVI: *Die Stimme des Kindes.* TRAD. Welsh: *Sio Gân.* GRUBER: *Silent Night.* TRAD.: *Mary and the Baby Medley*
*** Teldec 8573 85555-2

An essentially intimate collection, beautifully sung and recorded. But the mixture, with its fair sprinkling of favourites, does not always gell readily. John Tavener, as always, manages stimulatingly to look backwards in time, with his bare medieval harmonies; but some of the other modern settings are quite luscious, notably Hugo Distler's vocal divisions on *Es ist ein Ros entsprungen* and Jaakko Mäntyjärvi's *Die Stimme des Kindes.* Healy Willan's 'The Three Kings' is refreshingly original, and Dawn Upshaw contributes serenely to Vaughan Williams's lovely arrangement of 'This is the Truth Sent from Above' and vivaciously to the Spanish carol. However not all will want the elaborate treatment of Grüber's 'Silent Night', and the American gospel sequence, *Mary and the Baby Medley*, spirited as it is, does not fit readily into the programme's overall mood.

Chiara, Maria (soprano)

'The Decca Recitals': Arias from: DONIZETTI: *Anna Bolena.* BELLINI: *I puritani.* VERDI: *Aida; I masnadieri; I vespri siciliani; Otello* (with Rosanne Creffield, mezzo, John Alldis Ch.); *Giovanna d'Arco; Simon Boccanegra; La forza del destino.* BOITO: *Mefistofele.* PUCCINI: *La Bohème; Suor Angelica; Manon Lescaut; Turandot.* MASCAGNI: *Lodoletta* (all with Vienna Volksopernorchester or ROHCG, Nello Santi). CILEA: *Adriana Lecouvreur.* GIORDANO: *Andrea Chénier.* MASCAGNI: *L'amico Fritz; Iris.* LEONCAVALLO: *Pagliacci.* CATALANI: *La Wally; Loreley* (with Nat. Philh. O, Kurt Adler)
✪ (BB) *** Decca (ADD) 475 6250 (2)

Few if any début recitals of lyric soprano operatic arias can match the first of these two discs, which originally appeared in 1972 but, incredibly, had a very limited catalogue life. Such was the rich sweetness of Maria's Chiara's voice, the feeling of youthful freshness, the sense of line and control of phrase, that one immediately hailed this young Italian soprano as a successor to Tebaldi. John Steane thought well enough of the original disc to add a complimentary footnote to his book on *The Grand Tradition.*

Surprisingly, apart from the second group of *verismo* arias on the second disc, made in 1977, which were slightly – but only slightly – less suited to her voice, Decca did not take an option to feature her in major recordings. After she had appeared as a much praised Liù at Covent Garden in 1973 she seemed to disappear from the recording scene altogether. Yet she had already made her stage début in Venice as Desdemona in *Otello* in 1965 and this is well reflected by her ravishingly lovely account here of the *Willow Song* and *Ave Maria*, heartrendingly poignant, and touchingly accompanied by Nello Santi. She went on to make a distinguished stage career, taking most of the leading roles in the major operatic centres of Europe and especially Verona, where a recently issued DVD (Warner 0630 18389-2) shows her in 1981 in her most celebrated role as Aida, her vocal powers undiminished.

But there is something very special indeed about this first recital, gloriously recorded in the Sofiensaal by Gordon Parry and Kenneth Wilkinson. She is the Mimì of one's dreams, her Liù is exquisite, pure and effortless, and *O patri mia* from *Aida* is, not suprisingly, quite glorious, as is the excerpt from *Mefistofele,* while the relatively unfamiliar aria from Mascagni's *Lodoletta* brings a frisson of pleasure for its sheer style. Many collectors who knew the original SXL LP will have been impatient for its reissue after three decades in the vaults. It is for I.M. the most beautiful single disc of lyrical soprano arias in the catalogue.

Christchurch Cathedral Choir, Oxford, Francis Grier

'Carols from Christchurch' (with Bicket, organ): GARDNER: *Tomorrow shall be My Dancing Day.* TRAD.: *O Thou Man; In dulci jubilo.* HADLEY: *I Sing of a Maiden.* HOWELLS: *Sing Lullaby; Here is the Little Door; A Spotless Rose.* WARLOCK: *Bethlehem Down.* MATHIAS: *Sir Christèmas.* arr. BACH: *O Little One Sweet.* TCHAIKOVSKY: *The Crown of Roses.* WISHART: *Alleluya, a New Work is Come on Hand.* BRITTEN: *A Ceremony of Carols* (with Kelly, harp); *Shepherd's Carol; A Boy was Born: Jesu, as Thou art our Saviour*
(M) *** ASV (ADD) CDWHL 2097

This is among the most attractive of mid-priced reissues of carol collections, the more particularly as it includes not only a first-class account of Britten's *Ceremony of Carols*, plus 'Jesu, as Thou art our Saviour', with its piercing momentary dissonances, but also the dialogue 'Shepherd's Carol', so effectively featuring four soloists. The dozen other carols also bring some radiantly expressive singing, particularly in the three inspired Howells works; the Hadley carol, too, is delightful. They are framed by the admirably lively items by Gardner and Wishart, with Mathias's buoyant Sir Christémas as a centrepiece. Generally good, analogue sound from the early 1980s.

'Christmas from a Golden Age' (various artists)

'Christmas from a Golden Age' (original recordings from 1925–50): HANDEL: *Messiah: Comfort ye ... Ev'ry valley* (Schiøtz); *He shall Feed his Flock* (Matzenauer). ANON.: *Adeste Fidelis* (with chorus). EASTHOPE MARTIN: *The Holy*

Child. Arr. BURLEIGH: *Little Child of Mary* (all McCormack). BACH/GOUNOD: *Ave Maria* (Ponselle). LUCE: *O salutaris* (Journet). REGER: *The Virgin's Lullaby* (Muzio). YON: *Gesù bambino* (Martinelli with chorus). TRAD.: *Der Tannenbaum* (Lashanska and Reimers). HUMPERDINCK: *Weinachten.* GRUBER: *Stille Nacht* (both Schumann-Heink). ADAMS: *The Star of Bethlehem.* REDNER: *O Little Town of Bethlehem* (both Crooks). TRAD.: *Coventry Carol* (Schumann); *Go Tell it to the Mountain* (Maynor with chorus). Catalonian Carol: *El Cant de Ocells* (de los Angeles). Arr. NILES: *I Wonder as I Wander* (Swarthout). WARREN: *Christmas Candle* (Thomas). DEL RIEGO: *A Star was his Candle* (Tibbett). ADAM: *Cantique de Noël* (Thill with chorus). BERLIN: *White Christmas* (Tauber with chorus)

(BB) (***) Naxos mono 8.110296

A fascinating collection of voices from Christmas past, which emerge here with startling individuality in these excellent transfers. Highlights include Aksel Schiøtz's *Messiah* excerpts, Rosa Ponselle's *Ave Maria*, and Marcel Journet's very characterful *O salutaris*, with a quaint violin and harmonium accompaniment. Finest of all are Claudia Muzio's lovely Reger 'Lullaby', Martinelli's stirring *Gesù Bambino* and, predictably, Elisabeth Schumann's ravishing 'Coventry Carol' and Victoria de los Angeles's delightful contribution from Catalonia, 'The Song of the Birds'. Ernestine Schumann-Heink's *Stille Nacht* is indulgently drawn out, but Dorothy Maynor's 'Go Tell it to the Mountain', with an excellent male choir, is memorable, as is John McCormack's 'Little Child of Mary' while Gladys Swarthout's Appalachian folksong is very touching. There are strong contributions too from Richard Crooks, Lawrence Tibbett and Georges Thill, who delivers a commanding account of Adam's *Cantique de Noël*. The selection ends, unexpectedly, with Richard Tauber's stylishly elegant 'White Christmas'. Well worth having.

City Waites, The

(or The Musicians of Grope Lane)

'*Bawdy Ballads of Old England*': *The Beehive; Blue Petticoats or Green Garters; Diddle Diddle or the Kind Country Lovers; The Disappointment; A Ditty Delightful of Mother Watkin's Ale; The Fair Maid of Islington; The Frolic; The Gelding of the Devil; Greensleeves and Yellow Lace; Green Stockings; The Husband who met his Match; The Jolly Brown Turd; The Jovial Broom Man; The Jovial Lass or Dol and Roger; Lady Lie Near Me; Lady of Pleasure; The Lusty Young Smith; The Maid's complaint for Want of a Dil Doul; Miss Nelly; Mundanga Was; Oh how you protest; The Old Wife; Oyster Nan; 2 Rounds (Tom Making a Manteau; When Celia was Learning)*

(B) *** Regis RRC 1175

There really was a Grope Lane, which meant exactly what it says. In this collection, it is the words rather than the music which count, for it is no good having lewd words that one cannot hear, even if they are all included in the booklet. And ballads like *The jovial lass* and *The Lusty young smith* are unequivocally lewd; others use metaphor more tastefully and also have a touch of wit, like the 'Ditty delightful', in which the young maid tells her lover, 'I am afraid to die a maid'. He promises to give her Watson's ale and when, after her first draught, she innocently asks for a second, she is disconcerted when she has to wait a little. 'Let us talk a while,' he suggests.

So full marks to the City Waites for their diction and also for their swinging dialect style with ballads that usually fall far short of being art songs. The items here are sometimes accompanied, sometimes not, but they are made into a lively entertainment by being interwoven with instrumental pieces from Playford's *Dancing Master*. Now issued at bargain price with full texts, this is a must for all lovers of naughtyness in ye olde style!

Clare College, Cambridge, Choir and Orchestra, John Rutter

'*Christmas from Clare*': TRAD.: *King Jesus hath a garden; Up! Good Christian folk, and listen; Gabriel's Message; Wexford Carol; Ding! dong! merrily on high; Quelle est cette odeur agréable; I saw a maiden; In dulci jubilo; I saw three ships; The Holly and the Ivy.* RUTTER: *Donkey Carol; Mary's Lullaby; Cradle Song; Child in a Manger.* DARKE: *In the bleak mid-winter.* TCHAIKOVSKY: *The Crown of Roses.* POSTON: *Jesus Christ the Apple Tree.* PRAETORIUS: *The noble stem of Jesse; Omnis mundus jocundetur.* arr. VAUGHAN WILLIAMS: *Wassail Song*

⟿ ✹ (B) *** Decca (ADD) 425 500-2

When asked recently why he liked to write carols, John Rutter replied, 'Because for a carol it is still permissible to write a tune.' Melody is his very special gift as a composer, in an age when there are too few real tunes about; there is no better example than his gently syncopated *Donkey Carol*, full of charm and a sense of Christmas celebration. *Mary's Lullaby* is quite lovely too, but Rutter's joyful spirit permeates this whole collection for he has made many of the arrangements himself. They present a more colourful and romantic image than usual, with orchestrations often in keeping with the Christmas tree lights. He loves the sound of cascading flutes, and the opening arrangement of *King Jesus hath a garden* sets the mood with pretty flute decorations. The programme is not especially ecclesiastical in character; he has chosen carols primarily for their melodic character – some of the finest are here – but he has not forgotten the 'bleak midwinter' scene at Bethlehem.

The singing and playing are full of feeling, both exuberant and deeply expressive, and the (originally Argo) recording is first class, warm and clear, with a most attractive ambience. There are few issues that will give more pleasure than this in the late evening over the Christmas period. I.M. has been playing this LP, cassette or CD over the years (every year) with the greatest pleasure.

'Coloratura Spectacular'

'*Coloratura Spectacular*' (with (i) Sutherland; (ii) Jo (sopranos); (iii) Horne (mezzo)): (i) OFFENBACH: *Les Contes d'Hoffmann: Doll Song.* (ii) *Un Mari à la porte: Valse tyrolienne.* (iii) PERGOLESI/LAMPUGNANI: *Meraspe o l'Olimpiade: Superbo di me stesso.* (i) VERDI: *Attila: Santo di patria ... Allor che i forti corrono.* (ii) AUBER: *Le Domino noir: La Belle Inès fait florès; Flamme vengeresse.* (i; iii) ROSSINI: *Semiramide: Serbami ognor si fido il cor.* (ii) MASSE: *La Reine Topaze: Ninette est jeune et belle.* (iii) ARDITI: *Bolero: Leggero, invisibile qual aura sui fiori.* (i)

GLIERE: *Concerto for Coloratura Soprano, Op. 82; (iii)*
DONIZETTI: *Lucrezia Borgia: Il segreto per esse felici.* (ii)
MOZART: *Die Zauberflöte: Der Hölle Rache*
🎵— (M) *** Decca ADD/DDD 476 7231

'Coloratura Spectacular' is a dazzling display of vocal *feux d'artifice* from Decca's three top female vocal virtuosi, opening appropriately with Sutherland's sparklingly precise 'Doll Song', followed by Sumi Jo's glittering and no less charming displays in Offenbach and Auber, plus an amazing *Carnaval de Venise*, where the flexibility of her upper tessitura has to be heard to be believed. Vibrant drama comes from Sutherland in Verdi's *Attila*, and Marilyn Horne shows her vocal range and fire-eating strength in a thrilling pastiche Pergolesi aria, Arditi's *Bolero* and *Il segreto per esse felici* from Donizetti's *Lucrezia Borgia*. The two divas then join together for a famous duet from Rossini's *Semiramide*, while Glière's two-movement *Concerto for Coloratura Soprano* again shows Sutherland at her most nimble and personable. Overall this is a remarkable demonstration to confirm that the present-day coloraturas can hold their own with the best from the so-called Golden Age. Full translations are included. This has been reissued in Universal's 'Critics' Choice' series.

Columbus Consort

'Christmas in Early America' (18th-century carols and anthems): BELCHER: *How Beauteous are Their Feet.* HOLYOKE: *How Beauteous are Their Feet; Th'Almighty Spake and Gabriel Sped; Comfort ye My People.* CARR: *Anthem for Christmas.* STEPHENSON: *If Angels Sung a Saviour's Birth.* HUSBAND: *Hark! The Glad Sound.* HEIGHINGTON: *While Shepherds Watched their Flocks by Night.* FRENCH: *While Shepherds Watched their Flocks by Night.* BILLINGS: *While Shepherds Watched their Flocks by Night.* PETER: *Unto us a Child is Born.* ANTES: *Prince of Peace, Immanuel.* MICHAEL: *Hail Infant Newborn.* HERBST: *To us a Child is Born.* SCHULZ: *Thou Child Divine.* DENCKE: *Meine Seele erhebet den Herrn.* GREGOR: *Hosanna! Blessed he that Comes in the Name of the Lord.* Charles PACHELBEL: *Magnificat anima mea Dominum*
*** Channel Classics Dig. CC 5693

A fascinating look back at the celebration of Christmas in the New World in the late eighteenth century, both by the British colonial settlers in New England and by their Moravian counterparts in Pennsylvania and North Carolina, where the inheritance was essentially in the European tradition. The English style is usually fairly simple and hymn-like, but with overlapping part-writing and occasional solo dialogues (as in the rhythmically interesting 'Th'Almighty spake').

Samuel Holyoke shows himself to be a strikingly fresh melodist; while, of the three settings of 'While Shepherds Watched' to different tunes, William Billings's emerges as the most striking and imaginative. Benjamin Carr's *Anthem for Christmas* is a musical pastiche (indeed, a kind of 'musical switch' with brief quotations from Corelli's *Christmas Concerto* and Handel's *Messiah* among other works). The Moravian/German music is usually more elaborate. Johann Peter's delightful motet-like carol, 'Unto us a Child is Born', has characteristically resourceful accompanying string-writing and those who follow him – David Moritz Michael, Johannes Herbst, J. A. P. Schulz and Jeremiah Dencke – all write in a tradition descended from the great German composers, capped by Charles Pachelbel (son of the Johann Pachelbel of

Canon fame). He played the organ in Boston, New York and Charleston in the 1730s and 1740s, and his *Magnificat* for double chorus celebrates a much more florid style, utterly different from the music which opens this programme.

The surprise is that this concert is performed not by American singers but by a Dutch group of expert vocal soloists, with a choral and string ensemble who sing and play with convincing authenticity and an agreeably stylish spontaneity. The recording is realistic and clear and made within a perfectly judged acoustic.

Corena, Fernando (bass)

Arias from: ROSSINI: *La Cenerentola; L'italiana in Algeri.* MASSENET: *Grisélidis* (with Maggio Musicale Fiorentino O, Gavazzeni). THOMAS: *Le Caïd.* OFFENBACH: *La Grande Duchesse de Gérolstein.* SAINT-SAËNS: *Les pas d'armes du roi Jean.* GOUNOD: *Philémon et Baucis* (with Suisse Romande O, Walker)
(M) (***) Decca Classic Recital mono 475 7170

Fernando Corena was an unfailingly impressive bass whose appearance in recordings was always something to look forward to. He was especially outstanding in the *buffo* repertoire, where he raised a smile by stylish pointing of the voice, rather than resorting to crude slapstick (he is also the superb Leporello in Decca's classic (1956) stereo *Don Giovanni*). There are some fine examples of his *buffo* bravura here in the Rossini items and the Cimarosa excerpt, as well as the delightfully blustering Général Boum aria from Offenbach's *La Grande Duchesse de Gérolstein*. It is good to hear him in more French repertoire as well, where he sings with style and character, nicely pointing the words in the *Grisélidis* aria and in the exotic-sounding Gounod rarity. The mono sound is superb in the Italian numbers, both warm and full (and very well conducted by Gavazzeni); although the Swiss items with Walker are vivid (Corena's voice is very well captured), the orchestra is not so refined nor as well recorded. Well worth acquiring.

Crespin, Régine (mezzo-soprano)

'French Songs': BERLIOZ: *Les Nuits d'été.* RAVEL: *Shéhérazade* (with Suisse Romande Orchestra, Ansermet). DEBUSSY: *3 Chansons de Bilitis.* POULENC: *Banalités: Chanson d'Orkenise; Hôtel; La Courte Paille; Le Carafon; La Reine de coeur. Chansons villageoises: Les Gars qui vont à la fête; 2 Poèmes de Louis Aragon: C; Fêtes galantes* (with Wustman, piano)
🎵— ❀ (M) *** Decca (ADD) 475 7712

Régine Crespin's recordings with Ansermet of the Berlioz and (especially) Ravel song-cycles are classics of the gramophone and sound marvellous in these new Decca transfers. The other songs were originally part of a 1967 song-cycle recorded in the Kingsway Hall with John Wustman. Crespin cleverly chose repertoire to suit her voice and all come over vividly, particularly the Debussy *Chansons de Bilitis* and the charming Poulenc song about *Le Carafon* ('The Little Water Jug') who wants (like the giraffe at the zoo) to have a baby water jug and, with the magical assistance of Merlin, succeeds, much to the astonishment of the lady of the house.

Italian Operatic Arias' (with ROHCG O, Downes): Arias from: VERDI: *Un ballo in maschera; Otello; Il trovatore.* PONCHIELLI: *La Gioconda.* MASCAGNI: *Cavalleria rusticana.* PUCCINI: *Madama Butterfly.* BOITO: Mefistofele
(M) **(*) Decca Classic Recitals (ADD) 475 393-2

The richness of Crespin's voice is well caught in this 1963 recital, with a fine, steady *Suicidio* and an affecting account of the heroine's prison aria in Boito's *Mefistofele*. More controversial are the Verdi items: the lack of a trill in the cabaletta to the *Trovatore* aria, the occasional sliding into the notes in the *Ballo* aria, and too many intrusive aitches. But Crespin devotees will not mind any of this, and one forgives much because of her sheer personality; she is that now rare thing: a distinctive and easily recognizable voice. Good, rich sound for this recent Classic Recital release.

Cura, José (tenor)

Anhelo': Argentinian songs (with Bitetti, guitar; Delgado, piano; and orchestra)
*(*) Erato/Warner 3984-23138-2

In his disc of Argentinian songs José Cura not only sings but directs the performances – seven of them involving a small orchestra – and arranges some of the pieces, two of them his own compositions. It makes a crossover disc that is not just 'middle-of-the-road' but 'easy listening', evidently designed to provide a sweet and unobtrusive background. The bright little Ginastera song is one of the few which, with its tango rhythm, has a Hispanic flavour. Most of the rest are yearningly melancholy, with *La campanilla*, the fifth of eight songs by Carlos Guastavino, a charming exception. In face of the general mood, the title, *Anhelo* ('Vehement Desire'), taken from the last of the Guastavino songs, seems hardly appropriate. Though the recording acoustic and close balance do not allow the full bloom of Cura's fine tenor to come out, these are warmly expressive performances, not just from him but from his associates too.

Daniels, David (counter-tenor),
Orchestra of the Age of Enlightenment,
Harry Bicket

Sento amor': Operatic arias from: MOZART: *Mitridate; Ascanio in Alba* (also concert aria: *Ombra felice ... Io ti lascio,* K.255). GLUCK: *Telemaco; Orfeo ed Euridice.* HANDEL: *Tolomeo; Partenope*
*** Virgin 5 45365-2

There are few discs of counter-tenor arias to match this. The American David Daniels uses his exceptionally beautiful and even voice with flawless artistry and imagination, whether in Handel, Gluck or Mozart. Even such a well-known aria as *Che faro* from Gluck's *Orfeo* emerges with fresh individuality, and the coloratura is breathtaking in its precision and fluency throughout, not just a brilliant technical exercise but a musical delight. One can imagine singing like this from castratos of the time delighting eighteenth-century audiences. Even those who usually resist the falsetto voice will find Daniels on this disc an exception in his naturalness and freshness. Excellent sound.

Danish National Radio Choir, Stefan Parkman

'Scandinavian Contemporary a cappella': TORMIS: *Raua needmine.* NORGARD: *And Time shall be no More.* RAUTAVAARA: *Suite de Lorca,* Op. 72. SANDSTROM: *A Cradle Song.* JERSILD: *3 Romantike korsange*
*** Chan 9264

Tormis is an honorary Scandinavian: he hails from Estonia. Jørgen Jersild and Per Nørgård are both Danish, Sven-David Sandström is Swedish (and mightily overrated in his homeland), and Einojuhani Rautavaara comes from Finland. Stefan Parkman has brought the Danish National Radio Choir to considerable heights and now it almost (but not quite) rivals the Swedish Radio Choir in its heyday under Eric Ericsson. None of the music is quite good enough to enter the permanent repertory in the way that the sublime motets of Holmboe's *Liber canticorum* should and doubtless will. By their side, this is all pretty small beer, but the Jersild and Rautavaara are worth investigating.

Dawson, Lynne (soprano), Malcolm Martineau (piano)

'On this Island': BRITTEN: *On this Island.* WARLOCK: *Lilligay My Own Country; The Night.* QUILTER: *Fair House of Joy; My Life's Delight.* PARRY: *Armida's Garden; My Heart is like a Singing Bird.* STANFORD: *La Belle Dame sans merci; 3 Edward Lear Limericks; Limmerich ohne Worte* (piano solo). GURNEY: *Sleep.* HOWELLS: *King David.* VAUGHAN WILLIAMS: *Silent Noon; The Lark in the Clear Air; Through Bushes and Through Briars.* FINZI: *Oh Fair to See; Since we Loved; As I Lay in the Early Sun*
*** Hyp. CDA 67227

Lynne Dawson, singing with golden tone and sparklingly clear diction offers one of the most delectable recitals of English song. In addition to well-known favourites like Vaughan Williams's 'Silent Noon' and Howells's 'King David', Dawson and Martineau include a whole sequence of brief, intensely tuneful songs that are totally charming and deserve to be far better known, from Parry's 'Armida's Garden' to Gurney's rapt setting of John Fletcher's, 'Sleep'. Stanford is represented not only by the substantial 'La Belle Dame sans merci', but by three witty settings of Edward Lear limericks, which he used as comic party-pieces, full of parodies, together with a brief piano solo designed as an accompaniment to any other limerick required. The recital ends with the Britten cycle of Auden settings that gives the disc its title; this is tougher, more incisive music than most of the rest. Dawson and Martineau are inspired throughout and beautifully recorded.

Robert DeCormier Singers and Ensemble, Robert DeCormier

'Children Go Where I Send Thee' (*A Christmas Celebration around the World*) (with soloists from the choir): Traditional songs and carols from: Sweden (arr. DECORMIER): *Ritsch, ratsch, filibon.* Italy: *Dormi, dormi, O bel bambin.* Austria: *Da Droben vom Berge.* Nigeria:

Betelehemu. Spain: *A la nanita, nanita;* (Catalonia): *El noi de la mare*. USA: *Children go where I send thee; Poor little Jesus;* (Appalachian): *In the valley*. Puerto Rico: *La Trulla*. Germany: *Es ist ein' Ros' entsprungen*. France: *Ecoutons donc les aubades*. India: *Lína avatárá*. Canada: *Huron Carol*. Syria: *Miladuka*. Argentina: *La peregrinacion*. West Indies: *The Virgin Mary had a Baby Boy*
*** Arabesque Z 6684

The excellent Robert DeCormier Singers have already recorded a number of fine collections, including a John Dowland anthology ('Awake Sweet Love': Z 6622) and two previous Christmas collections ('A Victorian Christmas': Z 6525 and 'The First Nowell': Z 6526), but none has been more attractive than this geographically wide-ranging programme of Christmas songs with children in mind. The arrangements are simple, for every number has great character and needs no embellishment.

The programme opens enticingly with a tick-tock (*Ritsch, ratsch*) Swedish carol, which is immediately captivating; it is followed with an exquisite Italian lullaby. The oldest item is a Syrian Christmas hymn, *Miladuka* ('The Nativity'), which, based on plainchant, is thought to be more than 1,000 years old. It is presented here in harmonized form and is quite haunting, as is the example from northern India, *Lína avatárá* ('He Chose to be Among Us'), which is introduced softly on flute and chiming percussion. When the voices enter, the harmonies are bare, whereas the Nigerian song about Bethlehem has rich upper intervals above the sonorous repeated bass and soon becomes exultant. The Argentinian carol, 'The Pilgrimage', is lusciously Latin, while the Spanish examples are simpler but lilting. The only really familiar carol is from Germany and it is beautifully and serenely presented. The concert ends swingingly with the more familiar West Indian 'The Virgin Mary had a Baby Boy', which is given the lightest, most infectious rhythmic touch. Altogether this splendidly recorded anthology, with its nicely judged instrumental accompaniments, will give great pleasure – to grown-ups as well as to children.

Deller, Alfred (counter-tenor)

'Portrait of a Legend' (with various artists, including Dupré, lute): PURCELL: Excerpts from *The Fairy Queen; King Arthur; The Indian Queen; Olinda; The Old Bachelor; Dioclesian.* Sacred music: Gregorian Chant: *Ténèbres: Dernière Leçon du Samedi Saint.* TALLIS: *Te lucis ante terminum.* COUPERIN: *Deuxième Leçon de Ténèbres pour le Mercredy.* BUXTEHUDE: *Cantate Domino.* PURCELL: *In Guilty Night.* GIBBONS: *Great King of Gods.* PALESTRINA: *Ave verum.* GRANDI: *Cantabo Domine.* Songs: ANON.: *The Wind and the Rain. Othello: Willow Song. Calleno Custure Me.* *Misere my Maker.* MORLEY: *It was a Lover and his Lass.* CAMPION: *I Care not for These Ladies.* BARTLET: *Of All the Birds.* ROSSETER: *What then is Love?* BLOW: *The Self-banished.* CLARKE: *The Glory of the Arcadian Groves.* DOWLAND: *Fine Knacks for Ladies; Flow my Tears.* PURCELL: *If Music be the Food of Love; From Rosy Bow'rs. O Solitude.* CACCINI: *Pien d'amoroso affretto; Amarilli, mia bella.* SARACINI: *Pallideto quai viola.* A. SCARLATTI: *Infirmata vulnerata.* Folksongs: *The Three Ravens; Black is the Colour of my True Love's Hair; The Oak and the Ash; Barbara Allen; Lord Rendall; The Water is Wide; The Tailor and the Mouse; Down by the Salley Gardens; I will Give my Love an Apple; Bushers and Briars; The Foggy, Foggy Dew;*

She Moved through the Fair; Evening Prayer. MORLEY: *Swee[t] Nymph, Come to thy Lover; I Go before My Darling; Miraculous Love's Wounding.* R. JONES: *Sweet Kate*
(BB) **(*) HM (ADD) HMC 290261.4 (4)

This a valuable survey of the latter part of Deller's caree[r] from 1967 to 1979. He was joined by many other artists o[f] distinction, including Desmond Dupré, David Munrow, Wil[-] liam Christie and his own Consort. As can be seen above, th[e] range of his recordings was wide, and he contributed som[e] important Purcell repertoire to the French Harmonia Mund[i] catalogue. But the collection of this composer's musi[c] although vivid, is piecemeal, and Deller is heard at his ver[y] best in the solo songs and folksongs, where his turn of phras[e] can often be quite ravishing. He sings some of the latter i[n] duet with his son, Mark Deller. It is a pity that these wel[l] recorded discs are not available separately. Texts are include[d] and this anthology is still very recommendable, although th[e] earlier, Vanguard series needs to be reissued in a new, accessi[-] ble format.

'O Ravishing Delight' (with Munrow, Lee, Dupré, Elliott): ANON.: *Miserere my Maker.* DOWLAND: *Shall I Sue?; Come Heavy Sleep; I Saw my Lady Weep; Wilt thou Unkind; Fine Knacks for Ladies; Flow My Tears.* CAMPION: *I Care not for These Ladies; The Cypress Curtain.* BARTLET: *Of All the Birds.* ROSSETER: *What then is Love; What then is Love but Mourning.* FRANCIS PILKINGTON: *Rest, Sweet Nymphs.* BLOW: *The Fair Lover and his Black Mistress; The Self-banished.* CLARKE: *The Glory of the Arcadian Groves; In her Brave Offspring.* ECCLES: *Oh! the Mighty Pow'r of Love.* CROFT: *My Time, O ye Muses.* DANIEL PURCELL: *O Ravishing Delight.* HUMFREY: *A Hymne to God the Father*
(B) **(*) HM Musique d'abord (ADD) HMA 190215

Deller's recording contract with Vanguard lasted from 1954 t[o] 1965 and he made more than sixty LPs for this label, whic[h] are no longer available. Then he had a second, shorter record[-] ing period with Harmonia Mundi. The present collectio[n] dates from 1969 and one can hear him husbanding his voic[e] using it lightly where possible.

Many of the songs here are available in earlier perform[-] ances, but they still sound pleasingly fresh, and as can b[e] heard in the very lovely opening 'Miserere my Maker', he ha[s] not lost his magic touch. Dowland's 'Come Heavy Sleep' an[d] 'I Saw My Lady Weep' and Campion's 'Cypress Curtain of th[e] Night' certainly bring the 'ravishing delight' of the title. It i[s] good to have also a pair of songs from Jeremiah Clarke (o[f] *Trumpet Voluntary* fame), and 'The Glory of the Arcadia[n] Groves' features a charming recorder obbligato. The pro[-] gramme closes with a beautifully refined performance o[f] Dowland's famous 'Flow My Tears'. Throughout, the accom[-] paniments are of the highest quality, as is the recording, an[d] as texts are included, this makes a fine bargain sampler o[f] Deller's later achievement.

Folksongs (with Mark Deller, counter-tenor, Dupré, lute): *The Three Ravens; Black is the Colour of My True Love's Hair; The Oak and the Ash; Barbara Allen; Lord Rendall; The Water is Wide; The Tailor and the Mouse; Down by the Salley Gardens; I will Give My Love an Apple; Bushes and Briars; The Foggy Foggy Dew; She Moved Through the Fair; Evening Prayer.* MORLEY: *Sweet Nymph, Come to thy Lover; I go before My Darling; Miraculous Love's Woundings.* JONES: *Sweet Kate*
(B) ** HM (ADD) HMA 195226

riginally published by RCA, this 1972 collection shows eller in peak vocal form, but not all will respond to his very ee, art-song style in this repertoire. This is shown in the very pening number, 'The Three Ravens', where very free rubato nd self-conscious control of the dynamic become exaggerized into excess refinement, and the earthiness which is a asic element of folk music is all but submerged. Of course eller's singing is often beautiful, the phrasing of 'Down by ne Salley Gardens' is lovely; but many will feel that when he joined in duet by Mark Deller (their voices match admiraly) this is too much of a good thing. The recording is good, Deller *aficionados* need not hesitate, although the disc is ort measure.

)iDonato, Joyce (mezzo soprano), Julius)rake (piano)

Journey through Venice' (Wigmore Hall Recital, 16 nuary 2006): ROSSINI: *La regata veneziana; La enerentola: Non più mesta*. HEAD: *3 Songs of Venice*. AURÉ: *5 Mélodies de Venise*. HAHN: *Venezia*. HANDEL: *iulio Cesare: Care speme*

M) **(*) Wigmore Hall WHLive 009

his is certainly a happily planned recital, centring on Venice, ut it is curiously disappointing. The recording appears to apture Joyce Di Donato's often lovely voice faithfully, yet her ersonality does not always emerge fully in the first part of ne recital. The Michael Head triptych is undoubtedly beauful, as is the Fauré group, but there is also a certain blandess. This lifts entirely in the engaging Hahn cycle *L'avertimento* is delightful and the closing *La primavera* parkles). The two encores show her at her very best, the Iandel *Cara speme* ravishing, and the coloratura in Rossini's *Jon più mesta* combines bravura with a nicely infectious buch, which Julius Drake obviously appreciates. He accomanies supportively throughout, and full texts and translaons are included.

)omingo, Plácido (tenor)

Domingo Sings Caruso' (with various orchestras and onductors): arias from: LEONCAVALLO: *La Bohème; 'agliacci*. DONIZETTI: *L'elisir d'amore*. MASSENET: *Le Cid; Janon*. CILEA: *L'Arlesiana*. FLOTOW: *Martha*. PUCCINI: *La anciulla del West; La Bohème*. VERDI: *Aida; Rigoletto*. IEYERBEER: *L'Africana*. GOUNOD: *Faust*. HALEVY: *La uive*. MASCAGNI: *Cavalleria rusticana*

M) *** RCA (ADD) 82876 59407-2

)omingo's heroic stage presence comes over well in this Caruso' anthology, the ringing tone able to impress in a yrical phrase, even though more fining down of the tone and willingness to sing really softly more often would enhance he listener's pleasure. But in the theatre this is obviously a oice to thrill, and the engineers have captured it directly and ealistically, from the sobbing verismo of *Pagliacci* to the crisp ristocracy in *Rigoletto*. The selection is an interesting one, pening with an aria from Leoncavallo's *Bohème* that suggests hat this opera is worth reviving (it has since been recorded). he bulk of this recording derived from a 1972 LP with the ame name as this release (with the LSO, conducted by Santi), vhich was expanded from various other recordings in RCA's CD catalogue. Texts and translations are now included in its

latest mid-price release for RCA's 'Classic Collection'.

'Vienna, City of My Dreams' (with Ambrosian Singers, ECO, Rudel): arias from: LEHAR: *Das Land des Lächelns; Die lustige Witwe; Paganini*. ZELLER: *Der Vogelhändler*. KALMAN: *Gräfin Mariza*. FALL: *Der fidele Bauer; Die Rose von Stambul*. SIECZYNSKI: *Wien, du Stadt meiner Träume*. O. STRAUS: *Ein Walzerstaum*. JOHANN STRAUSS JR: *Eine Nacht in Venedig*

(BB) *** EMI Encore 5 75241-2 [5 75242-2]

Having such a golden tenor sound in Viennese operetta makes a winning combination, and Domingo, always the stylist, rebuts the idea that only a German tenor can be really idiomatic. A delightful selection, including one or two rarities, which is very well recorded and now offered at budget price.

'Domingo Favourites' (with various orchestras and conductors): arias from: DONIZETTI: *L'elisir d'amore*. VERDI: *Ernani; Il trovatore; Aida; Nabucco; Don Carlos*. HALEVY: *La Juive*. MEYERBEER: *L'Africaine*. BIZET: *Les Pêcheurs de perles; Carmen*. PUCCINI: *Tosca; Manon Lescaut*

(M) *** DG 445 525-2

The greater part of this collection is taken from a 1980 digital recital, recorded in connection with yet another gala in San Francisco. The result is as noble and resplendent a tenor recital as you will find. Domingo improves in detail even on the fine versions of some of these arias he had recorded earlier, and the finesse of the whole gains greatly from the sensitive direction of Giulini. Though the orchestra is a little backward, the honeyed beauty of the voice is given the greatest immediacy. The other items are taken from Domingo's complete sets of *Don Carlos* (with Abbado), *Nabucco, Manon Lescaut* and *Tosca* (with Sinopoli), and are well up to the high standards this great tenor consistently sets for himself.

Early Music Consort of London, David Munrow

'Music of the Gothic Era'; LEONIN: *Viderunt omnes; Alleluya Pascha nostrum; Gaude Maria Virgo; Locus iste*. PEROTIN: *Viderunt omnes; Sederunt principes*. ANON.: *Alle, psallite cum luya; Amor potest; S'on me regarde; In mari miserie; On parole de batre; En mai, quant rosier sont flouri; Dominator Domine; El mois de mai; O mitissima; Hoquentus I–VII; La Mesnie fauveline; Quant je le voi; Zelus familie; Quasi non ministerium; Clap, clap, par un matin; Lés l'ormel a la turelle; O Philippe, Franci qui generis; Febus mundo oriens; Degentis vita; Inter densas deserti meditans*. PETRI DE CRUCE: *Aucun ont trouvé*. ADAM DE LA HALLE: *De ma dame vient; J'os bien a m'amie parler*. PHILIPPE DE VITRY: *Impudenter circumivi; Cum statua*. BERNARD DE CLUNY: *Pantheon abluitur*. HENRI GILLES DE PUSIEUX: *Rachel plorat filios*. MACHAUT: *Lasse! comment oublieray; Qui es promesses; Hoquetus David; Christe, qui lux es*. ROYLLART: *Rex Karole, Johannis genite*

(M) *** DG Blue (ADD) 471 731-2 (2)

In the 1970s David Munrow was pioneering repertoire by composers who are now much more readily accessible. But Munrow's gift of bringing early music consistently to life for the non-specialist listener and finding ear-catching ways to present the instrumental pieces is as valid today as it was then. 'Music of the Gothic Era' is particularly valuable in providing a remarkably lively survey of medieval music during the two centuries when it was developing at a comparatively swfit rate from early organa to the thirteenth-century motet, 'from the monumental to the miniature', as David Munrow says in his notes. So the choice of music moves from Léonin's organum to the *Rex Karole* of Philippe Royllart, dating from the second half of the fourteenth century. The set was originally on three LPs (now reduced to a pair of CDs), so the music comes in three groupings – I, Notre Dame period, II, Ars Antiqua Motetti and III, Ars Nova Motetti – although there are instrumental items included among the vocal works. Munrow projects this music with characteristically buoyant rhythms and expressive liveliness. Its presentation is essentially conjectural, but to bring the music back to life is the most important thing, and Munrow certainly does that, and most entertainingly too. The recording is excellent.

'*The Art of the Netherlands*': secular songs (vocal and instrumental versions): JOSQUIN DESPREZ: *Scaramella va alla guerra; Allegez moy, doulce plaisant brunette; El grillo è buon cantore; Adieu mes amours.* ISAAC: *Donna di dentro della tua casa.* VAN GHIZEGHEM: *De tous biens plaine.* BRUMEL: *Du tout plongiet – Fors seulement l'attente.* OCKEGHEM: *Prenez sur moi vostre exemple amoureux; Ma bouche rit.* BUSNOIS: *Fortuna desperata* (with others by GHISELIN; ANON.). Sacred music: TINCTORIS: *Missa sine nomine: Kyrie.* BRUMEL: *Missa et ecce terrae motus: Gloria.* JOSQUIN desprez: *Credo super De tous biens; De profundis; Benedicta es caelorum regina.* DE LA RUE: *Missa Ave sanctissima Maria: Sanctus.* ISAAC: *Missa la bassadanza: Agnus Dei.* OBRECHT: *Haec Deum caeli; Laudemus nunc Dominum.* MOUTON: *Nesciens mater virgo virum.* OCKEGHEM: *Intemerata Dei mater* (with anon.)
(M) *** Virgin (ADD) 5 61334-2 (2)

The coverage here concentrates on the latter half of the fifteenth century, and the first disc is devoted to secular songs and instrumental arrangements. Josquin immediately makes his presence felt with an ear-catching opening item, 'Scaramella is off to War', for vocal quartet with recorders, bass viol, guitar, harp and tambourine, and later he is to return with the unaccompanied *El grillo*, where the vocal interchanges are equally lively. As most of these vocal numbers are short, what follows is a kaleidoscope of concerted and solo items, alongside instrumental arrangements (for lute duet, recorder consort, broken consorts or keyboard), providing plenty of contrast. Heinrich Isaac's jubilant quodlibet feaures nine singers, while Hayne van Ghizeghem's touching chanson, *De tous biens plaine*, is first sung as an accompanied counter-tenor solo, and then heard in three different instrumental arrangements. Many of the songs are richly expressive, Ockeghem's canon *Prenez sur moi vostre exemple amoureux* and Brumel's *Du tout plongiet* are memorably poignant examples. Busnois's *Fortuna desperata* is first presented in a three-part vocal presentation, then in six parts (three singers with a trio of viols), and finally on a combination of tenor dulcian, recorder, rebec and two lutes.

The second section, a group of Mass movements, immediately brings a greater degree of gravitas with Johannes Tinctoris's *Kyrie*, solemnly presented by four low male voices, yet Brumel's robust *Gloria* is memorably gutsy. Pacing never drags; indeed, Isaac's six-part *Agnus Dei* flows

forward strongly. The motets in the third section, many o them Marian, are more consistently expressively solemn, bu all are strikingly beautiful, with Josquin's *De profundis*, with its firm bass line, particularly eloquent. Full texts an translations are included and this seems an excellent way t explore this repertoire as a prelude to acquiring CDs con centrating on a single composer. The standard of singing and playing is high, and the recording is as vivid as yo could wish.

'*The Art of Courtly Love*' (with Bowman, Brett, Hill, Shaw): I: '*Guillaume de Machaut and his Age*': JEHAN DE LESCUREL: *A vous douce debonaire* (chanson). MACHAUT: *Amours me fait desirer; Dame se vous m'estés lointeinne; De Bon Espoir – Puis que la douce rousee; De toutes flours; Douce dame jolie; Hareu! hareu! le feu; Ma fin est mon commencement; Mes esperis se combat; Phyton le mervilleus serpent; Quant j'ay l'espart; Quant je suis mis au retour; Quant Theseus – Ne quier veoir; Se ma dame m'a guerpy; Se je souspir; Trop plus est belle – Biauté paree – Je ne sui mie certeins.* P. DES MOLINS: *Amis tout dous vis.* ANON.: *La Septime estampie real.* F. ANDRIEU: *Armes amours – O flour des flours.* II: '*Late fourteenth-century Avant-garde*': GRIMACE: *A l'arme a l'arme.* FRANCISCUS: *Phiton Phiton.* BORLET: 2 *Variants on the tenor 'Roussignoulet du bois'; Ma tedol rosignol.* SOLAGE: *Fumeux fume; Helas! je voy mon cuer.* JOHANNES DE MERUCO: *De home vray.* ANON.: *Istampitta Tre fontane; Tribum quem; Contre le temps; Restoés restoés.* HASPROIS: *Ma douce amour.* VAILLANT: *Trés doulz amis – Ma dame – Cent mille fois.* PYKINI: *Plasanche or tost.* ANTHONELLO DE CASERTA: *Amour m'a le cuer mis.* MATTEO DA PERUGIA: *Andray soulet; Le greygnour bien.* III: '*The Court of Burgundy*': DU FAY: *Ce moys de may; La Belle se siet; Navré ju sui d'un dart penetratif; Lamention Sanctae Matris Ecclesiae Constantinopolitaine (O tres piteulx – Omnes amici); Par droit je puis bien complaindre; Donnés l'assault; Helas mon dueil; Vergine bella.* BINCHOIS: *Je ne fai tousjours que penser; Files a marier; Amoreux suy et me vient toute joye; Je loe Amours et ma dame mercye; Vostre trés doulx regart; Bien puist.* ANON.: *La Spagna* (basse danse) *Variants I & II*
(M) *** Virgin (ADD) 5 61284-2 (2)

David Munrow's two-disc set 'The Art of Courtly Love' span the period 1300–1475 in some depth. The survey is divided into three sections: 'Guillaume de Machaut and his Age', 'Late fourteenth-century Avant-garde' and 'The Court of Burgundy'. The first section is introduced arrestingly by two cornetts and an alto shawm, who accompany a striking chanson of Jehan de Lescurel (died 1304), which must have had 'hit' status in its time (*A vous douce debonaire*). The bare harmonies give a real tang to the tune. Then comes the first o many numbers by the justly famous Guillaume de Machaut Hareu! hareu! le feu ... le feu d'ardant desir, which one hardly needs to translate, and it is certainly ardent!

But it is the expressive romantic chansons of Machaut that make one appreciate how readily the composer came to dominate the combination of lyric poetry and music in fourteenth-century France and to epitomize the title, 'The Art of Courtly Love'. The virelais *Se ma dame m'a guerpy* ('If My Lady has Left Me') and *Quant je suis mis au retour*, for solo tenor and chorus, with its sad introductory bass rebec solo, surely anticipate the melancholy eloquence of Dowland, while Machaut could also be attractively lighthearted as in *Se je souspir* ('If I Sigh'), or robustly jolly and spiritedly extrovert (*Douce dame jolie*).

The second CD opens with a particularly lovely vocal trio by Jehan Vaillant (?1360–90), which anticipates 'The First Nowell' in its vocal line, and a following ballade, *Amour m'a la cuer mis*, by Anthonello de Caserta (whose career spanned the turn of the century) demonstrates how forward-looking were other composers of 'the late fourteenth-century avant-garde', while Solage (flourished 1370–90) is no less enterprising in providing lugubrious humour with his baritone solo *Fumeux fume* ('He who fumes and lets off steam provokes hot air') with its unlikely melodic line. (Not surprisingly, Munrow gives this rondeau an appropriately bizarre instrumental backing.) 'A Man's True Worth' (*De home vray*), a ballade by the late-fourteenth-century Johannes de Meruco, also brings lively melodic twists and turns.

Gilles Binchois (*c.* 1400–60) was another leading figure of the time, well represented here, and, like Machaut, he had a wide range. But it is the lovely rondeau duet *Amoreux suy et me vient toute joye* ('Filled with love, I am overjoyed, hoping that your kindness might bring sweet comfort') that one especially remembers. With its expressive pleading so direct in its appeal, it is one of the set's highlights and is ravishingly sung here. With the music from 'The Court of Burgundy' we also meet the remarkable Guillaume Du Fay, with his exhilarating rondeau *Ce moys de may*, so different in mood from his Masses, followed by an engagingly melancholy echoing duet for two counter-tenors, *La Belle se siet au piet de la tour* ('The maiden sits ... weeping, sighing and venting her grief'), while the virelai *Helas mon dueil*, a rejected lover's lament, is infinitely touching.

However, the collection ends in lively fashion with the anonymous basse danse *La Spagna*, and here (as in the other instrumental items) Munrow's choice of colour brings an extra dimension to what is basically a very simple dance. All the soloists are distinguished and at their finest. Incidentally, although the translations are not affected, the documentation for this set has the list of titles for the second disc mixed up, starting with bands 12–15, then following with 1–11, but they are all there.

Elysian Singers, Sam Laughton

'*Peacocks and Pirahnas*': MUSGRAVE: *On the Underground*. HINDEMITH: *La Biche; Un Cygne*. ARCADELT: *Il bianco e dolce cigno*. GIBBONS: *The Silver Swan*. DAVIES: *O magnum mysterium*. BULLARD: *Choristers of Flight*. VAUTOR: *Sweet Suffolk Owl*. STANFORD: *The Blue Bird*. TAVENER: *The Lamb*. FINZI: *Nightingales*. RAVEL: *3 Chansons*
*(*) Elysian ES 1202

This is an attractive, imaginative collection of *a cappella* songs devoted to birds and beasts. The Elysian Singers of London are well known for their splendid concerts, as well as making some good recordings, notably a disc of Delius's partsongs for Somm. There is some interesting repertoire here, with some good, modern, choral writing, such as Thea Musgrave's 'On the Underground', as well as the more familiar territory of Finzi and Stanford. The short Renaissance items, such as Arcadelt's *Il bianco e dolce cigno* and Gibbons's 'The Silver Swan', are enjoyable, as is the brief but catchy 'Sweet Suffolk Owl'. The later works of Ravel and Hindemith are well done too, and this would make a pleasant 45-minute concert. The snag is the unflattering recording, which places the choir backwardly and, with the relatively dry-sounding acoustic, the result lacks warmth and intimacy and fails to show the choir at their best.

Emmanuel College, Cambridge, Chapel Choir, Timothy Prosser

'*Carols from Cambridge*': TRAD.: *Veni, veni Emmanuel; The Angel Gabriel; In dulci jubilo*. RUTTER: *What Sweeter Music*. GAUNTLETT: *Once in Royal David's City*. arr. WILLCOCKS: *Ding Dong! Merrily on High; O Come All Ye Faithful*. BRITTEN: *A Hymn to the Virgin; Friday Afternoons, Op. 7: New Year Carol*. arr. JACKSON: *Noël Nouvelet*. arr. VAUGHAN WILLIAMS: *This is the Truth Sent from Above; Wither's Rocking Hymn*. MATHIAS: *Sir Christèmas*. WARLOCK: *Bethlehem Down; Benedicamus Domino*. arr. HAMMOND: *Swete was the Song the Virgin Soong*. GARDNER: *Tomorrow shall be my Dancing Day*. BERLIOZ: *L'Enfance du Christ: Shepherds' Farewell*. LEIGHTON: *Lully, Lulla, Thou Tiny Child*. RAVENSCROFT: *Remember, O Thou Man*. HOPKINS: *We Three Kings*. ORD: *Adam Lay y-Bounden*. GRUBER: *Stille Nacht*. arr. RUTTER: *Wexford Carol*
(M) *** ASV CDWHL 2104

Opening with the famous melodic chant *Veni, veni Emmanuel*, which turns out to be medieval in origin and not a Victorian hymn, this is a particularly appealing mid-priced collection, beautifully recorded. Although it includes (as the third item) 'Once in Royal David's City, sung in crescendo in the Willcocks arrangement, a strongly expressed 'O Come All Ye Faithful', and Mathias's jovial 'Sir Christèmas', as outgoing and vigorous as one could wish, the style of performance, as befits a smaller chapel choir, is for the most part a pleasingly intimate one.

Unlike King's College, Emmanuel uses women's voices, but they are as sweet and pure as any boy trebles', the overall blending and ensemble are nigh perfect and the effect is disarmingly simple, notably so in the lovely *Shepherds' Farewell* from Berlioz's *L'Enfance du Christ*. Anna Dennis is a pleasingly fragile soloist in Vaughan Williams's setting of Wither's 'Rocking Hymn'; Rutter's 'What Sweeter Music' and Warlock's 'Bethlehem Down' are especially lovely.

Enterprisingly, the famous *Stille Nacht* is presented in its charming original version for two solo voices (Julia Caddick and Sarah Fisher) and guitar. Grüber hastily scored it in this fashion when the organ broke down just before its first performance on Christmas Eve 1818 – in the appropriately named Church of St Nicholas (Oberndorf, Austria). Not all the choices are obvious, and Britten's 'New Year Carol', taken from *Friday Afternoons*, is an engaging novelty. Prosser and his splendid singers are equally impressive in the livelier carols: the rhythmic syncopations of Gardner's 'Tomorrow shall be My Dancing Day' are as sparkling as the bounce of 'We Three Kings', and the choir's lightness of touch is equally appealing in Warlock's *Benedicamus Domino*, which ends the concert joyfully.

English Song

'*The Very Best of English Song*' (Various Artists):

Disc 1: VAUGHAN WILLIAMS: *Linden Lea*. IRELAND: *The Salley Gardens*. PARRY: *O Mistress Mine*. QUILTER: *Love's Philosophy* (Baker, Moore); *Now Sleeps the Crimson Petal*. PEEL: *Bredon Hill* (Allen, Parsons). BUTTERWORTH: *A Shropshire Lad: Loveliest of Trees*. GURNEY: *Down by the Salley Gardens; Black Stichel*. WARLOCK: *My Own Country; Passing by; Pretty Ring Time* (Rolfe Johnson, Willison).

VAUGHAN WILLIAMS: *The Lamb; The Shepherd* (Partridge, Craxton, oboe); *Silent Noon.* QUILTER: *Come Away, Death.* FINZI: *Since we Loved* (Bostridge, Drake). FINZI: *Rollicum-rorum.* IRELAND: *Sea Fever.* KEEL: *Trade Winds* (Lemalu, Vignoles). STANFORD: *Sea Songs: Drake's Drum; The Old Superb* (Lloyd, Walker). WOODFORDE-FINDEN: *Indian Love-Lyrics: Kashmiri Song* (Harvey, Byfield). BRAHE: *Bless this House.* WARLOCK: *Balulalow* (Baker, Ledger, organ). DIBDIN: *Tom Bowling.* BISHOP: *Home! Sweet Home!* BALFE: *Come into the Garden, Maude* (Tear, Previn). BRITTEN: *The Foggy, Foggy Dew; The Plough Boy* (Tear, Ledger). WALTON: *Façade: Popular Song* (Flanders, ASMF, Marriner)

Disc 2: TRAD.: *Greensleeves.* MORLEY: *It was a Lover and his Lass; O Mistress Mine.* ANON.: *The Willow Song.* JOHNSON: *Where the Bee Sucks; Full Fathoms Five* (Deller, Dupré, lute). BYRD: *Lullaby, My Sweet Little Baby; Elegy on the Death of Thomas Tallis; Ye Sacred Muses* (Chance, Fretwork). DOWLAND: *Sorrow Stay!; Can she Excuse My Wrongs; Awake Sweet Love; Woeful Heart* (Kirkby, Rooley, lute and orpharion); *Shall I Sue; Me, and None but Me; Flow My Tears* (Daniels, Miller, lute). PURCELL: *Fairest Isle; Music for a While; I Attempt from Love's Sickness; If Music be the Food of Love; An Evening Hymn* (Argenta & various accompanists). WARLOCK: *Yarmouth Fair.* MORTIMER: *Smuggler's Song.* CARTER: *Down Below* (Brannigan, Lush or Moore). SWANN: *A Transport of Delight; The Wart Hog* (Wallace, Swann); *The Hippopotamus Song* (Flanders and Swann)

☞ ✹ (B) *** EMI (ADD/DDD) 5 75926-2 (2)

This must easily be judged the finest and most comprehensive recital of English songs ever put on record – 57 in total – offering just about as much music as can be placed on a pair of CDs; each plays for just under eighty minutes. But not only is the quality remarkable, so too is the consistent quality. The concept was apparently Ray Hammond's, but the compilation was made and assembled by Richard Abram with unerring skill. Every item is a gem, every performance masterly, and the aligning of artist to repertoire is equally prescient.

There are of course two separate recitals here: the first offers a broad swathe of many of the greatest nineteenth- and twentieth-century English songs, the second looks back to the era of Elizabathan lute songs, juxtaposing the art of two celebrated counter-tenors (opening with Alfred Deller's lovely, artless account of 'Greensleeves') one tenor, Charles Daniels, and two sopranos, with Emma Kirkby nearly stealing the show with her infinitely touching account of Dowland's 'Woeful Heart', just as Dame Janet Baker does on the first disc with her lovely performance of Warlock's 'Balulalow'.

But, apart from Dame Janet (who opens the first collection enticingly), here it is the men who make their special mark – Sir Thomas Allen glowing-voiced in Quilter's 'Now Sleep the Crimson Petal', Anthony Rolfe Johnson memorable in Warlock, Ian Bostridge ravishing in Vaughan Williams's 'Silent Noon', and Jonathan Lemalu's rich-toned 'Rollicum-rorum' of Finzi and Ireland's 'Sea Fever'. Robert Lloyd's pair of *Sea Songs* of Stanford could perhaps have been even more boisterous in the way John Shirley-Quirk presented them, but they are still irresistibly vigorous.

There are some inspired individual selections too: Frederick Harvey's 'Kashmiri Song', Robert Tear's Victorian ballads and his ravishingly sung 'Tom Bowling', while the two Britten folksong arrangements, the seductive 'Foggy, Foggy Dew' and

infectiously spirited 'Plough Boy' are sheer joy. It is good that Geordie Owen Brannigan was not forgotten, a larger-than-life vocal personality with a richly resonant voice who often sang with a twinkle in his eye: he is heard at his finest here.

The inestimable Flanders and Swann are used to provide witty end-pieces for each disc: the 'Popular Song' from Walton's *Façade* for the first, and 'The Hippopotamus Song' as the grand finale, with an appropriately enthusiastic audience response. The remastering by John Hadden is first class and there is an excellent note by John Steane; this is a set which should be in every collection, however large or small.

'The Very Best of English Song with Orchestra' (Various Artists): Disc 1: ELGAR: *Sea Pictures* (J. Baker, LSO, Barbirolli); *2 Songs: The Torch; The River, Op. 60.* BUTTERWORTH: *Love Blows as the Wind Blows* (Tear, CBSO, Handley). VAUGHAN WILLIAMS: *Songs of Travel* (Allen, CBSO, Rattle); *5 Mystical Songs* (Shirley-Quirk, King's College, Cambridge, Ch., ECO, Willcocks); *On Wenlock Edge* (Bostridge, LPO, Haitink). BRITTEN: *Serenade for Tenor, Horn & Strings* (Tear, Civil, N. Sinfonia, Marriner); *Les Illuminations* (Mark Ainsley, Britten Sinfonia, Cleobury); arr. of Folksongs: *The Bonnie Earl o'Moray; Oliver Cromwell* (Mackie, Scottish CO, Bedford). FINZI: *Dies natalis* (W. Brown, ECO, Finzi). STANFORD: *Songs of the Sea* (Luxon, Bournemouth Ch. & SO, Del Mar). DELIUS: *Sea Drift* (Noble, RLPO Ch. & O, Groves). PEEL: *In Summertime on Bredon.* SANDERSON: *Devonshire Cream and Cider* (Harvey, PO, Weldon)

☞ (B) *** EMI (ADD/DDD) 5 85896-2 (3)

Richard Abram's excellent compilation of English orchestral songs is complementary to his inspired selection of songs with piano. The programme is framed by two of the most beautiful English cycles on record. Dame Janet Baker's *Sea Pictures* with Barbirolli comes up as richly and memorably as ever, and Ian Bostridge's magically atmospheric performance of Vaughan Wlliams's *On Wenlock Edge* is ravishingly delicate in colour and accompanied with matching sensitivity by Bernard Haitink. John Shirley-Quirk, too, is at his finest in the Vaughan Williams *Mystical Songs*, and if in the *Songs of Travel* Sir Thomas Allen's voice is not as warmly flattered as with his recordings in the companion set with piano, his singing is both understanding and characterful.

In the two Britten cycles, *Les Illuminations* finds John Mark Ainsley echoing the example of Peter Pears, and in the *Serenade* Robert Tear is also very much in the Aldeburgh tradition while bringing a new and positive slant to each of the songs, with the Jonson 'Hymn to Diana' given extra jollity, thanks partly to the brilliant galumphing of Alan Civil on the horn. Neil Mackie then sings Britten's arrangement of 'The Bonny Earl o'Moray' with real passion, then throws off 'Oliver Cromwell' with lighthearted zest. Wilfred Brown richly captures the meditative mood of Finzi's *Dies natalis*, and if alongside this Sir Charles Groves's Liverpool account of Delius's *Sea Drift*, with John Noble as soloist, lacks something in evocation, Benjamin Luxon is in his element in all five of Stanford's *Songs of the Sea.* 'The Old Superb' is wonderfully boisterous, gaining much from the richly resonant contribution of the Bournemouth Chorus. Frederick Harvey provides the postlude with a characterful account of Graham Peel's setting of Housman's 'Summertime on Bredon', leading to a final vigorous lollipop, infectiously giving praise in a colloquial West Country accent to 'Devonshire Cream and Cider'.

Estampie, John Bryan

'*Under the Greenwood Tree*' (with Catterall, Derrick): WALTHER VON VOGELWEIDE: *Palästinalied.* RICHARD COEUR DE LION: *Ja nuis homs pris.* BLONDEL DE NESLE: *A l'entrant d'este.* DE VAQUERIAS: *Kalenda Maya.* CORNYSHE: *Ah! Robin.* STONINGES: *Browning my Dear* (on the theme *The Leaves be Green*). GERVAISE: *4th Livre de Danceries: La Venissienne; 6th Livre de Danceries: Gailliarde.* PLAYFORD: *The Dancing Master: Greenwood; Nottingham Castle; Green Goose Fair; The Green Man.* SIMPSON: *Ricercar on Bonny Sweet Robin.* WEELKES: *When Kempe did Dance Alone, or Robin Hood, Maid Marian and Little John are Gone.* ANON.: *Novus miles sequitur; Estampie; Clap, clap un matin s'en aloit Robin; The Wedding of Robin Hood; Under the Greenwood Tree; Sellenger's Round; Greensleeves* (lute and vocal versions); *Robin Hood and the Curtal Friar; Robin Hood and the Tanner; Robin Hood and Maid Marian; Sweet Angel of England* (to the tune *Bonny Sweet Robin*); *O Lusty May*
(BB) ** Naxos 8.553442

With John Bryan as music director and Graham Derrick as arranger and main performer, the early-music group Estampie here offer a well-devised group of dances and instrumental pieces, interspersed with songs, broadly inspired by the legend of Robin Hood and the ballad 'Robin is to the Greenwood Gone' in its various forms. That in turn leads to celebrations in song and dance of Maytime and the annual revival of the Green Man. Items range from a song attributed to King Richard the Lionheart in the twelfth century to four items drawn (in arrangements by Graham Derrick) from John Playford's collection *The Dancing Master*, in the seventeenth.

The sequence is most illuminating, but the performances, always tasteful, rather lack the bite and earthiness which can make medieval music so invigorating. The final item, a Scottish song, 'O Lusty May', is anything but that, though there and in the other songs the mezzo, Deborah Catterall, sings with a fresh, clear tone. Aptly intimate recorded sound.

Evans, Sir Geraint (baritone)

'*Arias and Sacred Songs*' (with (i) SRO, Balkwill; (ii) Shelley Singers, Lyrian Singers, Glendower Singers, BBC Welsh SO, Mansel Thomas). (i) HANDEL: *Berenice: Si trai ceppi. Semele: Leave me Radiant Light.* MOZART: *Le nozze di Figaro: Non più andrai. Don Giovanni: Madamina, il catalogo. L'oca del Cairo: Ogni momento. Die Zauberflöte: Der Vogelfänger.* BEETHOVEN: *Fidelio: Ha! welch'ein Augenblick!* LEONCAVALLO: *Pagliacci: Prologue.* DONIZETTI: *Don Pasquale: Un fuoco insolito.* VERDI: *Otello: Credo. Falstaff: Ehi! Paggio ... l'onore! Ladri.* BRITTEN: *A Midsummer Night's Dream: Bottom's Dream.* MUSSORGSKY: *Boris Godunov: Tchelkalov's Aria.* (ii) MENDELSSOHN: *Elijah: Lord God of Abraham; Is not His Word like a Fire?* HANDEL: *Judas Maccabaeus: Arm, Arm ye Brave. Messiah: The Trumpet shall Sound.* ROSSINI: *Requiem: Pro peccatis*
(BB) *** Belart (ADD) 461 492-2

This is a marvellous display of wide-ranging virtuosity, of artistic bravura such as we know from almost any performance that this ebullient and lovable singer gave. Part of Evans's mastery lay in the way he could convey the purest

comedy, even drawing laughs without ever endangering the musical line through excessive buffoonery. His Mozart characters are almost unmatchable – Figaro, Leporello, Papageno – while it is good to be reminded that here is a singer who could be a formidable Iago as well as the most complete Falstaff of his day. Good accompaniment and recording, with a richly atmospheric orchestral backing, of one of Britain's greatest singers at the peak of his form.

Evans, Nancy (mezzo-soprano)

'*The Comely Mezzo*' (with various accompanists including Newton, Moore, Foss, piano): A. BEECHAM: *Outward Bound; Otello: Willow Song; O Mistress Mine.* DELIUS: *Indian Love Song; Irmelin Rose.* PARRY: *Armida's Garden.* BURY: *There is a Lady.* VAUGHAN WILLIAMS: *The Water Mill; How Can the Tree but Wither?* WARLOCK: *Rest, Sweet Nymphs; St Anthony of Padua.* HAGEMAN: *Do not Go my Love.* GURNEY: *The Scribe; Nine of the Clock O; All Night Under the Moon; Blaweary; You are my Sky; Latmian Shepherd.* FALLA: *7 Spanish Popular Songs.* BLISS: *Pastoral: Pigeon Song.* D'HARDELOT: *Wait.* FISHER: *An Old Violin.* ELGAR: *Land of Hope and Glory* (with Noble & chorus)
(BB) (**(*)) Dutton mono CDBP 9723

As Alan Blyth's note rightly says, Nancy Evans was for sixty years 'one of the best-loved personalities on the British musical scene', one who followed up her singing career with untiring work as a teacher, administrator and adjudicator, helping generations of young singers. She was married in turn to the recording producer Walter Legge and to Eric Crozier, collaborator with Britten on such operas as *Albert Herring* and *Billy Budd*. It was for Nancy Evans that Britten wrote the role of Nancy in *Albert Herring*, and in his preceding chamber opera, *The Rape of Lucretia*, Evans alternated with Kathleen Ferrier in the title role. When far too few of her recordings have appeared on CD, it is good to welcome this collection of rarities, even though the close balance of most of the pre-war recordings takes the bloom from the voice, giving it a raw quality in places and undermining the beauty. Nonetheless, the artistry and technical security come out from first to last, whether in the songs by Adrian Beecham (with the composer's father, Sir Thomas, at the piano), a sequence of songs by Ivor Gurney or the well-known Falla songs, which she delivers with Spanish fire. Most beautiful is 'The Pigeon Song' from Bliss's *Pastoral*, with accompaniment for flute and strings, set in a more open acoustic, and the programme ends with two ballads and a stirring account of Elgar's *Land of Hope and Glory* with chorus and military band accompaniment.

I Fagiolini, Robert Hollingsworth with David Miller (lute)

'*The Triumphs of Oriana*' (compiled by Thomas Morley): WILBYE: *The Lady Oriana.* NICHOLSON: *Sing, Shepherds All.* MUNDY: *Lightly she Whipped o'er the Dales.* CARLTON: *Calm was the Air and Clear the Sky.* HOLBORNE: *Lute Fantasias Nos. 2 & 3; Galliard 8 (Clark's Galliard).* EAST: *Hence Stars too Dim of Light.* CAVENDISH: *Come, Gentle Swains and Shepherds' Dainty Daughters.* KIRBYE: *With Angel's Face and Brightness.* MARSON: *The Nymphs and Shepherds Danced.* HOLBORNE: *Galliard.* BENNET: *All Creatures Now are Merry Minded.* FARMER: *Fair Nymphs, I*

Heard Calling. R. JONES: *Fair Oriana, Seeming to Wink at Folly.* TOMKINS: *The Fauns and Satyrs Tripping.* E. GIBBONS: *Round About her Cherret; Long Live Fair Oriana.* COBBOLD: *With Wreaths of Rose and Laurel.* HOLMES: *Thus Bonny-boots the Birthday Celebrated.* MORLEY: *Arise, Awake, Awake; Hard by a Crystal Fountain.* HUNT: *Hark! Did ye Ever Hear so Sweet a Singing?* MILTON: *Fair Oriana in the Morn.* NORCOME: *With Angel's Face and Brightness.* JOHNSON: *Come Blessed Bud.* BYRD: *Galliard.* HILTON: *Fair Oriana, Beauty's Queen.* LISLEY: *Fair Cytherea Presents her Doves.* WEELKES: *As Vesta was from Latmos Hill Descending* *** Chan. 0682

This outstanding collection of madrigals in praise of Oriana (a poetic image for Queen Elizabeth I), compiled by Thomas Morley in 1601, has been seriously neglected on disc for many years, making this fine new version from I Fagiolini very welcome. Drawing on the talents of a wide range of his friends and contemporaries, including Wilbye, Tomkins and Weelkes, as well as his own work, Morley presents a superb overview of the art of the Elizabethan madrigal at its peak. Though the talented singers of I Fagiolini have a tendency to squeeze notes in pursuit of authenticity, this is refined singing, polished and expressive. The sequence of twenty-five madrigals is nicely punctuated by lute solos played by David Miller, four by Holborne, one by Byrd. The recording is both warm and immediate in an intimate acoustic.

Ferrier, Kathleen (contralto)

Kathleen Ferrier Collection (complete on 10 CDs)

Volume 1: GLUCK: *Orfeo ed Euridice* (abridged) (with soloists, Glyndebourne Festival Ch., Southern PO, Stiedry)

Volume 2: BACH: *St Matthew Passion:* Arias & choruses (with soloists, Bach Ch., Jacques O, Jacques)

Volume 3: PERGOLESI: *Stabat Mater* (orch. Scott) (with Taylor, Nottingham Oriana Ch., Boyd Neel String O, Henderson). Arias: GLUCK: *Orpheus and Euridice: What is Life?* HANDEL: *Rodelinda: Art thou Troubled? Serse: Ombra mai fu.* BACH: *St Matthew Passion: Have Mercy, Lord, on me* (all with LSO or Nat. SO, Sargent). *Cantata 11: Ah, Tarry Yet, my Dearest Saviour.* MENDELSSOHN: *Elijah: O Woe unto Them; O Rest in the Lord*

Volume 4: Lieder: SCHUMANN: *Frauenliebe und Leben* (song-cycle); *Volksliedchen; Widmung* (with Newmark, piano). BRAHMS: *Sapphische Ode; Botschaft.* SCHUBERT: *Gretchen am Spinnrade; Die junge Nonne; An die Musik; Der Musensohn* (with Spurr, piano); *Ganymed; Du liebst mich nicht; Lachen und Weinen* (with Britten, piano). GRUBER: *Silent Night.* TRAD.: *O Come All Ye Faithful* (with Boyd Neel String O, Neel)

Volume 5: BBC Broadcasts (1949–53): BRAHMS: *4 Serious Songs, Op. 121* (with BBC SO, Sargent). CHAUSSON: *Poème de l'amour et de la mer, Op. 19* (with Hallé O, Barbirolli). Recital (with Lush, piano): FERGUSON: *Discovery* (song-cycle). WORDSWORTH: *Red Skies; The Wind; Clouds.* RUBBRA: *3 Psalms: 6, O Lord rebuke me not; 23, The Lord is my shepherd; 150, Praise ye the Lord*

Volume 6: Broadcast recitals: English and German songs: STANFORD: *The Fairy Lough; A Soft Day.* PARRY: *Love is a Bable.* VAUGHAN WILLIAMS: *Silent Noon.* BRIDGE: *Go not, Happy Day.* WARLOCK: *Sleep; Pretty Ring-time.* Folksongs, arr. BRITTEN: *O, Waly, Waly; Come you not from Newcastle?*

arr. HUGHES: *Kitty, my Love* (with Stone, piano). PURCELL: *From Silent Shades: Mad Bess of Bedlam. The Fairy Queen: Hark! the Echoing Air.* HANDEL: *Atalanta: Like as the Love-lorn Turtle. Admeto: How Changed the Vision.* Lieder: WOLF: *Verborgenheit; Der Gärtner; Auf ein altes Bild; Auf einer Wanderung.* JENSEN: *Altar* (with Spurr, piano). BACH: *Vergiss mein nicht; Ach dass nicht die letzte Stunde* (with Silver, harpsichord). *Bist du bei mir* (with Newmark, piano)

Volume 7: Bach and Handel arias (with LPO, Boult): Arias from BACH: *Mass in B min.; St Matthew Passion; St John Passion.* HANDEL: *Samson; Messiah; Judas Maccabaeus*

Volume 8: *'Blow the Wind Southerly'* British songs & folksongs (with Spurr or (i) Newmark, piano): TRAD., arr. WHITTAKER: *Ma Bonny Lad; The Keel Row; Blow the Wind Southerly.* arr. HUGHES: *I have a Bonnet Trimmed with Blue; I Know Where I'm Going; I will Walk with my Love; The Stuttering Lovers; Down by the Salley Gardens; The Lover's Curse.* arr. SHARP: *My Boy Willie.* arr. ROBERTON: (i) *The Fidgety Bairn.* arr. JACOBSON: (i) *Ca' the Yowes.* arr. BRITTEN: *O Waly, Waly.* arr. WARLOCK: *Willow, Willow.* arr. GREW: *Have you Seen but a Whyte Lillie Grow?.* arr. QUILTER: *Ye Banks and Braes; Drink to me Only; Now Sleeps the Crimson Petal; The Fair House of Joy; To Daisies; Over the Mountains*

Volume 9: Broadcast Edinburgh Festival recital, 1949: Lieder (with Walter, piano): SCHUBERT: *Die junge Nonne. Rosamunde: Romance. Du bist mich nicht; Der Tod und das Mädchen; Suleika; Du bist die Ruh'.* BRAHMS: *Immer leiser wird mein Schlummer; Der Tod das ist die kuhle Nacht; Botschaft; Von ewiger Liebe.* SCHUMANN: *Frauenliebe und Leben* (song-cycle), *Op. 42*

Volume 10: MAHLER: *3 Rückert Lieder* (with VPO, Walter). BRAHMS: *Alto Rhapsody, Op. 53* (with LPO Ch., LPO, Kraus); *2 Songs with Viola, Op. 91* (with Spurr, piano, Gilbert, viola). *Vier ernste Gesänge, Op. 121* (with Newmark, piano)

(B) (**(*)) Decca mono 475 6060 (10)

Decca's first Ferrier anthology was on seven LPs, and later a shorter survey appeared on four cassettes. The CD coverage, which first appeared in the early 1990s at mid-price, is on ten CDs, which now come in a Collector's Edition at bargain price, although now the discs are no longer available separately. Curiously, Mahler's *Das Lied von der Erde* is not included, but that is available separately in an improved transfer, and the disc includes the three *Rückert Lieder* (466 576-2).

Unfortunately Decca seemed not always to be able to preserve their 78rpm masters without deterioration, which the CD transfers can sometimes emphasize. Even so, there is much treasure here, and these records readily demonstrate not only Ferrier's star quality and amazing range but also the consistency with which the radiant vocal quality lit up almost everything she recorded.

The single-disc selections from Bach's *St Matthew Passion* and Gluck's *Orfeo ed Euridice* (recorded in 1947–8) are a mixed blessing – of interest only for her personal contribution, and it might have been better to extract the individual arias, which are sung in English with radiant vocal freshness. The Bach items include 'Master and my Lord ... Grief for Sin', 'Have Mercy, Lord on Me' and 'O Gracious God ... If my Tears be Unavailing'. They show that from the start there was a projection of forceful personality and a natural musicianship that was uniquely powerful. The soprano/alto duet with Elsie

Suddaby ('Behold my Saviour now is Taken') is interrupted by a mushy chorus, and the arias, 'Ah! now my Saviour is Gone ... Have Mercy, Lord on Me', 'Ah Golgotha! ... See Ye!' and 'Sweet the Saviour's Outstretched Hands' again bring the ill-focused choral sound, although here Ferrier's contribution rides over everything. Whatever the recording flaws, the singer's commanding presence lights up the performances, and it is fascinating to play these excerpts alongside the inspired performances recorded only five years later with Boult in order to see the development.

Similarly, the much-abridged version of Gluck's opera, recorded soon after the Glyndebourne performances of 1947, is valuable only for Ferrier's magnificent contribution, even if it is obvious that this was only a first attempt by a great artist to scale a formidable part. At that time she was not entirely at ease singing in Italian, and when Fritz Stiedry chose an absurdly fast tempo for the big aria, *Che farò*, she was less impressive – in spite of the vocal freshness – than in the later version with Sargent, which is included in Volume 3.

The 1946 Pergolesi *Stabat Mater* comes off remarkably well, mainly because of Roy Henderson's excellence as a choral trainer, and the recording was good for its period and still sounds lively. This is included on Volume 3, with more Ferrier favourites, reasonably well transferred, including Gluck's 'What is Life?' (*Che farò*), Handel's 'Art thou Troubled?' and Mendelssohn's 'O Rest in the Lord' (from *Elijah*), all showing the glorious voice at its most nobly resonant.

As Volume 4 demonstrates, Ferrier was a deeply impressive Lieder singer. Had she lived, her art would undoubtedly have deepened considerably beyond what is displayed here. There are more tender, more loving emotions in Schumann's *Frauenliebe und Leben* than Ferrier was able to convey in 1950, and she is not helped by the limited accompaniment of John Newmark. Yet she is never less than compelling, and her Schubert and Wolf bring a natural warmth and dedication and a lightness of touch that are disarming; any shortcomings are here outweighed by the beauty of the voice. She identifies readily with *Die junge Nonne* and there is a special glow for *An die Musik*, while the Brahms songs are beautifully sung. Generally the sound here is very good and background noises are not too distracting. The three items accompanied by Benjamin Britten come from a BBC broadcast of 1952: the sound here is more opaque, and in *Du liebst mich nicht* the recording fades out before the end. Kathleen Ferrier had a marvellously robust Lancashire sense of fun and she would surely have found a natural riposte to suit such a minor calamity. The recital ends with two very touching carols, recorded with Boyd Neel for the Christmas market in 1948.

Volume 5 is very much a curate's egg. The performance of the *Four Serious Songs* in English with Sargent comes from a BBC broadcast of 1949, while the Barbirolli/Hallé performance of Chausson has a similar 1951 source. The quality is poor, the surfaces are noisy; indeed, the general effect in the Chausson is little short of execrable. But the rest of the CD offers a broadcast recital of 12 January 1952 with results that are more than acceptable. The rare Howard Ferguson cycle, the even rarer Wordsworth songs, of which 'Clouds' is totally memorable, and the very characteristic Rubbra Psalm settings show the singer at her most searching and imaginative, and they are well accompanied by Ernest Lush. Here the voice has excellent presence, and there are only occasional clicks from the acetate original.

Volume 6 is also strongly recommendable. Again one discovers that the magic of Ferrier's voice was never so potent as when she was singing English songs, and the opening group, with the highly sympathetic Frederick Stone – taken from a broadcast recital given just over a year before the singer's untimely death – brings a natural spontaneity and projection of warm feeling that are irresistible, especially when the transfers are generally of such vivid immediacy. The second recital on this disc derives from a Norwegian broadcast, made three years earlier, with a rather noisier background, but this group is famous for Jensen's *Altar*, which Ferrier introduces herself with apologetic charm. The bonuses include private recordings of two rare Bach items with harpsichord, where the surface noise is very distracting, and then the programme end with a glorious *Bist du bei mir*, where the background miraculously abates. (This comes, remarkably, from a 1950 Voice of America recording held in the Library of Congress.)

Ferrier's superb (1952) recording swansong, combining Bach and Handel arias (in Volume 7), was lovingly accompanied by Boult and the LPO. John Culshaw produced this disc and ensured that at least one Decca CD was technically fully worthy of Kathleen's art. This disc and Volume 8 were each given a ❂ when they were available separately.

The other collection which is unmissable (and which is generally well engineered) is her recital of British songs and folksongs. It is given the title of the unaccompanied lyric by which she is most fondly remembered by the greater musical public, 'Blow the Wind Southerly'. Even that transfer is not completely free from distortion, but the sense of the singer's presence is unforgettable. That recital contains much that is utterly magical – Ferrier's way with folksongs brought a simple innocence that few other singers have approached – but it is a very special, wonderfully tender performance of 'I will Walk with my Love', in which the gloriously gently vocal halo she places gently round the climactic word, 'boy', is achingly beautiful.

The 1949 Edinburgh Festival recital is technically less than perfect but still makes enjoyable listening. The piano sound may be a bit hazy, but this historic occasion gives a wonderful idea of the intensity of a live Ferrier recital. Her account here of *Frauenliebe und Leben* is freer and even more compelling than the performance she recorded earlier. Walter's accompaniments may not be flawless, but they are comparably inspirational. The recital is introduced by a brief talk on Walter and the Edinburgh Festival given by Ferrier, so welcome when the *Altar* introduction is so brief. The CD transfer does not seek to 'enhance' the sound, but most of the background has been cleaned up; there are moments when the vocal focus slips, but the ear readily adjusts.

The vintage Brahms/Mahler coupling on Volume 10 brings together Ferrier's 1948 recording of the *Alto Rhapsody*, a glowing performance which culminates in a heart-warming final section. The *Four Serious Songs*, issued three years later, are even more intense, with the voice more suited to these dark, weighty songs than to most Lieder; and this comment applies also to the three *Rückert Lieder*, heartfelt and monumental, exploratory in the world of Mahler. Here the voice emerges realistically, but the CD transfer is less kind to the orchestral strings. Throughout the series back-up documentation is adequate rather than generous, but the set remains a splendid tribute to one of the greatest English singers whose career was tragically cut off by cancer when she was at the height of her powers.

'*The World of Kathleen Ferrier*', Volume 1: TRAD.: *Blow the Wind Southerly; The Keel Row; Ma Bonny Lad; Kitty my love.* arr. BRITTEN: *Come you not from Newcastle.* HANDEL: *Rodelinda: Art thou troubled? Serse: Ombra mai fù.* GLUCK: *Orfeo ed Euridice: What is life?* MENDELSSOHN: *Elijah: Woe unto them; O rest in the Lord.* BACH: *St Matthew Passion: Have mercy, Lord, on me.* SCHUBERT: *An die Musik; Gretchen am Spinnrade; Die junge Nonne; Der Musensohn.* BRAHMS: *Sapphische Ode; Botschaft.* MAHLER: *Rückert Lieder: Um Mitternacht*

⊶ ❂ (M) (***) Decca mono 430 096-2

This selection, revised and expanded from the original LP issue, admirably displays Kathleen Ferrier's range, from the delightfully fresh folksongs to Mahler's *Um Mitternacht* in her celebrated recording with Bruno Walter and the VPO. The noble account of 'O Rest in the Lord' is one of the essential items now added, together with an expansion of the Schubert items (*Die junge Nonne* and *An die Musik* are especially moving). The CD transfers are remarkably trouble-free and the opening unaccompanied 'Blow the Wind Southerly' has uncanny presence. The recital plays for 65 minutes and fortunately there are few if any technical reservations to be made here about the sound quality.

'*The World of Kathleen Ferrier*' , Volume 2: TRAD.: *Ye Banks and Braes; Drink to me Only* (both arr. QUILTER); *I have a Bonnet Trimmed with Blue; Down by the Salley Gardens; The Stuttering Lovers* (all arr. HUGHES). PURCELL: *The Fairy Queen: Hark! the Echoing Air.* HANDEL: *Atalanta: Like the Love-lorn Turtle.* GLUCK: *Orfeo ed Euridice: Che puro ciel.* MAHLER: *Rückert Lieder: Ich bin der Welt abhanden gekommen.* SCHUMANN: *Frauenliebe und Leben: Er, der Herrlichste von allen.* BRAHMS: *Geistliches Wiegenlied; Von ewiger Liebe.* SCHUBERT: *Du bist die Ruh'; Rosamunde: Romance.* BACH: *Mass in B min.: Agnus Dei.* HANDEL: *Messiah: He was Despised*

(M) (***) Decca mono 448 055-2

Volume 2 offers a comparable mixture, opening with more delightful folksongs, notably the charming 'Stuttering Lovers', although it is 'Ye Banks and Braes' and 'Drink to me Only' that show the full richness of this glorious voice. *Che puro ciel* stands out among the opera arias for its simple eloquence, and the Brahms *Geistliches Wiegenlied*, with its somewhat wan viola obbligato, is gently ravishing. The passionate *Du bist die Ruh'*, the *Rosamunde Romance* and *Von ewiger Liebe* come from a BBC acetate disc of her 1949 Edinburgh Festival recital with Bruno Walter at the piano, and here there is some uneven background noise and the quality deteriorates in the Brahms song. But the CD closes with one of her very last recordings, her unforgettably poignant 'He was Despised', with those words given an uncanny presence.

'*A Tribute*': Arias from: BACH: *St Matthew Passion* (with National Symphony Orchestra, Sir Malcolm Sargent); *Mass in B min.; St John Passion; Judas Maccabaeus; Messiah* (with LPO, Sir Adrian Boult). HANDEL: *Rodelinda; Serse.* GLUCK: *Orfeo ed Euridice* (two excerpts, with LSO, Sargent & Southern PO, Fritz Stiedry). MENDELSSOHN: *Elijah* (with Boyd Neel O, Boyd Neel). MAHLER: *3 Rückert-Lieder* (with VPO, Bruno Walter). Songs & Lieder: TRAD.: *Down by the Salley Gardens; Drink to Me Only; Hark! The Echoing Air; I Have a Bonnet Trimmed with Blue; The Keel Row; Ma Bonny Lad; The Stuttering lovers; Ye Banks and Braes.* BRAHMS: *Botschaft; Geistliches Wiegenlied; Sapphische Ode.* HANDEL: *Atalanta.* SCHUBERT: *An die Musik; Gretchen am*

Spinnrade; Die junge Nonne; Der Musensohn (with Phyllis Spurr, piano). *Du bist die Ruh; Romance* (from *Rosamunde*) (with Walter, piano). SCHUMANN: *Er, der Herrlichste von allen* (with John Newmark, piano). STANFORD: *A Soft Day.* BRIDGE: *Go not Happy Day.* TRAD.: *Come you not from Newcastle; Kitty my Love* (with Frederick Stone, piano). *Blow the Wind Southerly*

❂ (B) (***) Decca mono 475 078-2 (2)

This is now the best Kathleen Ferrier collection available and includes many of her famous recordings, from the delightfully fresh folksongs (the haunting, unaccompanied version of *Blow the wind southerly* has uncanny presence) to her celebrated recordings of Bach and Mahler. The noble account of *O rest in the Lord* is another highlight, along with the Schubert lieder (*Die junge Nonne* and *An die Musik* are especially moving). Even better, Decca have remastered and improved the sound for this bargain two-CD set, and the booklet includes many fascinating pictures of the great contralto.

Bach and Handel Arias (with the LPO, Adrian Boult) from: BACH: *Mass in B min.; St John Passion; St Matthew Passion.* HANDEL: *Judas Maccabaeus; Messiah; Samson.*

(M) *** Decca Classic Sound (ADD) 475 6411

This is something of a sonic wonder: Kathleen Ferrier recorded these arias in 1952 (sadly, her last recordings) and it became one of her most famous recital discs. However, in 1960, under the supervision of the legendary John Culshaw for Decca, the same orchestra and conductor re-recorded the accompaniments, synchronizing and then superimposing them over the original recording, so that we now have the orchestra in (very good) stereo. It works remarkably well, and there is little discrepancy in sound, from the point of view of recorded dates, between the orchestra and soloist. The performances are among the best Ferrier committed to disc, and this is its first international release on CD.

'*What is Life?*' (with Spurr or Newmark, piano; Jacques O, Jacques; Nat. SO or LSO, Sargent; Boyd Neel O, Neel or Henderson): TRAD.: *Blow the Wind Southerly; The Keel Row; Down by the Salley Gardens; Ma Bonny Lad; Ca' the Yowes.* SCHUBERT: *Die junge Nonne; Gretchen am Spinnrade.* SCHUMANN: *Volksliedchen; Widmung.* BACH: *St Matthew Passion; Grief for Sin; Have Mercy Lord; Cantata 11: Ah, Tarry Yet, my Dearest Saviour.* GLUCK: *Orfeo: What is Life?* HANDEL: *Xerxes: Ombra mai fu; Rodalinda: Art thou Troubled?* PERGOLESI: *Stabat Mater; Fac et portem.* MENDELSSOHN: *Elijah: Woe unto Them; O Rest in the Lord.* GRUBER: *Silent Night*

(BB) (***) Regis mono RRC 1057

This disc does not replace the two Decca Volumes of *The World of Kathleen Ferrier*, where the recordings have been transferred with greater range and, as in the first item, a remarkable presence. But for the Regis anthology, offering many of the same recordings, Tony Watts has taken great care to smooth out the sound from the original masters: it is always warm and pleasing, the vocal quality rich, and the extraneous noises have been virtually eliminated. So if you want an inexpensive single disc assembling some of the very finest records made by this great artist, comfortably presented (and in some items, *Ombra mai fu* for instance, the quality is particularly warm and beautiful), this disc can be cordially recommended. And it is good to have Ferrier's lovely performance of the most magical carol of all, Grüber's 'Silent Night'.

Fischer-Dieskau, Dietrich (baritone)

'Early Recordings': J. S. BACH: Cantatas 56; 82 (with Karl Ristenpart CO, Ristenpart); Christ lag in Todesbanden, BWV 4 (with Bach Festival O, Fritz Lehmann). HANDEL: Giulio Cesare (excerpts) (with Berlin RSO, Karl Boehm). HENZE: 5 Neapolitan Songs (with BPO, Richard Kraus). FORTNER: The Creation (with North German R. O, Hans Schmidt-Isserstedt). MARTIN: 6 Monologues from 'Jedermann'; Der Sturm (3 excerpts) (with BPO, composer). GLUCK: Orpheus und Eurydice (with Maria Stader, Rita Streich, RIAS Chamber Ch., Berlin RSO, Ferenč Fricsay). Arias from: VERDI: Falstaff; La forza del destino; La traviata. ORFF: Carmina burana. GIORDANO: Andrea Chénier. LEONCAVALLO: Pagliacci (all with Berlin RSO, Fricsay). Lieder: WOLF: The Italian Songbook (excerpts). BRAHMS: 4 Serious Songs, Op. 121 (with Hertha Klust (piano)); Die schöne Magelone; Es liebt sich so lieblich im Lenze; Es schauen die Blumen; Meerfahrt; Mondenschein; Sommerabend; Der Tod, das ist die kühle Nacht. REICHARDT: An Lotte; Canzon, s'al dolce loco la donna nostra; Di tempo in tempo mi si fa mem dura; Einschränkung; Erano I capei d'oro; Eunziger Augenblick; Aus Euphrosyne; Feiger Gedanken; Gott; Mut; O poggi, o valli, o fiume, o selve, o campi; Or ch 'l ciel e la terra, e 'l vento tace; Più volte già dal bel sembiante umano; Die schöne Nacht. ZELTER: Gleich und gleich; Rastlose Liebe; Um Mitternacht; Wo geht's Liebchen. PREISSEN: Auf dem Lande in der Stadt. SECKENDORFF: Romanze. NEEFE: Serenade. BEETHOVEN: Mit Mädeln sich vertragen. KREUTZER: Ein Bettler vor dem Tor. HUMMEL: Zur Logenfeider. ARNIM: Aus 'Faust'. WAGNER: Branders Lied; Lied des Mephistopheles. SCHUMANN: Dichterliebe (with Jörg Demus (piano)); 12 Gedichte, Op. 35 (Kerner-Lieder); Freisinn; Schneeglöckchen; Des Sennen Abschield I; Ständchen; Talismane; Venezianisches Lied I & II (with Günther Weissenborn (piano)). MEYERBEER: Cantique du Trappiste; Le Chant du dimanche; Der Garten des Herzens; Hör ich das Liedchen klingen; Komm; Menschenfeindlich; Mina; Le Poète mourant; Die Rose, die Lillie, die Taube; Der Rosenblätter; Scirocco; Sicilienne; Sie und ich; Ständchen (with Karl Engel (piano))

(M) *(**) DG mono/stereo 477 5279 (9)

A self-recommending set and a must for Fischer-Dieskau fans, especially for including so many unexpected and rare items – and, remarkably, no Schubert! Fischer-Dieskau was at his freshest in the 1950s and '60s, as can be instantly heard in his youthful account of Brahms's Die schöne Magelone (1957), where the excitement of the music-making vividly brings the music to life. It is fascinating to have his first DG recording, which was Brahms's Four Serious Songs (O Tod, woe bitter bist du is gorgeously done) in astonishingly vivid (if a little dry) sound for its date (1949). Both this and his next DG recording, 16 songs from Wolf's Italienisches Liederbuch, make their début on CD; all are most impressive and set the high standard which was to follow. Schumann's Dichterliebe (1957) is similarly fresh, with the voice beautifully captured in excellent mono sound (he sounds as if in the room at times) and the intimate quality of the songs themselves is conveyed touchingly.

Indeed, it is the spontaneous quality of the singing, with few if any distracting mannerisms, which is one of this set's most appealing characteristics. Fischer-Dieskau's repertoire was enormous, not only in the expected eighteenth- and

nineteenth-century repertoire (with many appealing, tuneful items here by Hummel, Kreutzer, Preussen, Zelter, Reichardt and the like), but also in those from the twentieth century: he sings the somewhat austere Frank Martin items with a superb sense of character (in good, 1963 stereo), while the Henze Neapolitan Lieder (mono, 1956) have great atmosphere. Taken from a live concert in 1957, Fortner's The Creation is a real rarity and if it is hardly as tuneful as Haydn's work of the same name it is worth a hearing and makes its first appearance on CD (in decent sound, too).

Another unexpected item is the collection of Meyerbeer songs (from 1974), and if that composer's operas are notable for their sheer massiveness his songs are fresh and direct, with the simplest possible accompaniment. Occasionally Fischer-Dieskau may be a bit heavyweight for this unassuming music, but such point and charm as they contain is beautifully brought out. The Bach cantatas are hardly in the style of today's modern performances, but Fischer-Dieskau fans are not likely to worry too much about this. The early 1950s mono sound is full but suffers from a touch of distortion under pressure. The 1960 Giulio Cesare excerpts offer plenty of red-blooded singing, with Boehm providing more lively support than might be expected in the fast items (which also come off best), but the stereo sound here also suffers from moments of distortion.

In the complete Orfeo ed Euridice with Fricsay, (recorded in 1956) the fact that a baritone is featured in the main role, singing a part written for alto (or for tenor in the Paris version), means that Fischer-Dieskau's recording is always ruled out of court in 'Building a Library'-type surveys. However, his ready expressiveness and his response to word meanings bring sure rewards, and those not wedded to historical performance will enjoy this (now very inauthentic) version, with its excellent cast. Unfortunately, the sound is not of DG's best: the orchestra sounds muddy and the overall effect is lustreless, though the voices are reasonably clear. However, all goes very well in the group of opera arias conducted by Fricsay, who is on much firmer ground stylistically and conducts with style and energy, and the 1961 stereo is good (if not outstanding).

To top off this collection, an interview with the soloist is included and, although in German (or course), there is also a summary of the interview in English. There are no texts but there are some interesting photographs, and each CD's sleeve reproduces the original covers – and how appealing they are too!

'Fischer-Dieskau Lieder Edition'

SCHUBERT: Lieder, Volume 1 (1811–17): Ein Leichenfantasie; Der Vatermörder (1811); Der Jüngling am Bache (1812); Totengräberlied; Die Schatten; Sehnsucht; Verklärung; Pensa, che questo istante (1813); Der Taucher (1813–15); Andenken; Geisternähe; Erinnerung; Trost, An Elisa; Die Betende; Lied aus der Ferne; Der Abend; Lied der Liebe; Erinnerungen; Adelaide; An Emma; Romanze: Ein Fräulein klagt' im finstern Turm; An Laura, als sie Klopstocks Auferstehungslied sang; Der Geistertanz; Das Mädchen aus der Fremde; Nachtgesang; Trost in Tränen; Schäfers Klagelied; Sehnsucht; Am See (1814); Auf einen Kirchhof; Als ich sie erröten sah; Das Bild; Der Mondabend (1815); Lodas Gespenst (1816); Der Sänger (1815); Die Erwartung (1816); Am Flusse; An Mignon; Nähe des Geliebten; Sängers Morgenlied; Amphiaraos; Das war ich; Die Sterne; Vergebliche Liebe; Liebesrausch; Sehnsucht der Liebe; Die erste Liebe; Trinklied; Stimme der Liebe; Naturgenuss; An die

Freude; Der Jüngling am Bache; An den Mond; Die
Mainacht; An die Nachtigall; An die Apfelbäume; Seufzer;
Liebeständelei; Der Liebende; Der Traum; Die Laube; Meeres
Stille; Grablied; Das Finden; Wanderers Nachtlied; Der
Fischer; Erster Verlust; Die Erscheinung; Die Täuschung; Der
Abend; Geist der Liebe; Tischlied; Der Liedler; Ballade;
Abends unter der Linde; Die Mondnacht; Huldigung; Alles
um Liebe; Das Geheimnis; An den Frühling; Die Bürgschaft;
Der Rattenfänger; Der Schatzgräber; Heidenröslein;
Bundeslied; An den Mond; Wonne der Wehmut; Wer kauft
Liebesgötter? (1815); Der Goldschmiedsgesell (1817); Der
Morgenkuss; Abendständchen: An Lina; Morgenlied:
Willkommen, rotes Morgenlicht; Der Weiberfreund; An die
Sonne; Tischlerlied; Totenkranz für ein Kind; Abendlied; Die
Fröhlichkeit; Lob des Tokayers; Furcht der Geliebten; Das
Rosenband; An Sie; Die Sommernacht; Die frühen Gräber;
Dem Unendlichen; Ossians Lied nach dem Falle Nathos; Das
Mädchen von Inistore; Labetrank der Liebe; An die Geliebte;
Mein Gruss an den Mai; Skolie – Lasst im Morgenstrahl des
Mai'n; Die Sternenwelten; Die Macht der Liebe; Das gestörte
Glück; Die Sterne; Nachtgesang; An Rosa I: Warum bist du
nicht hier?; An Rosa II: Rosa, denkst du an mich?;
Schwanengesang; Der Zufriedene; Liane; Augenlied;
Geistes-Gruss; Hoffnung; An den Mond; Rastlose Liebe;
Erlkönig (1815); Der Schmetterling; Die Berge (1819);
Genügsamkeit; An die Natur (1815); Klage; Morgenlied;
Abendlied; Der Flüchtling; Laura am Klavier; Entzückung an
Laura; Die vier Weltalter; Pflügerlied; Die Einsiedelei; An die
Harmonie; Die Herbstnacht; Lied: Ins stille Land; Der
Herbstabend; Der Entfernten; Fischerlied; Sprache der Liebe;
Abschied von der Harfe; Stimme der Liebe; Entzückung;
Geist der Liebe; Klage: Der Sonne steigt; Julius an Theone;
Klage: Dein Silber schien durch Eichengrün; Frühlingslied;
Auf den Tod einer Nachtigall; Die Knabenzeit; Winterlied;
Minnelied; Die frühe Liebe; Blumenlied; Der Leidende;
Seligkeit; Erntelied; Das grosse Halleluja; Die Gestirne; Die
Liebesgötter; An den Schlaf; Gott im Frühling; Der gute Hirt;
Die Nacht; Fragment aus dem Aeschylus (1816); An die
untergehende Sonne (1816–17); An mein Klavier; Freude der
Kinderjahre; Das Heimweh; An den Mond; An Chloen;
Hochzeitlied; In der Mitternacht; Trauer der Liebe; Die Perle;
Liedesend; Orpheus; Abschied; Rückweg; Alte Liebe rostet
nie; Gesänge des Harfners aus Goethes Wilhelm Meister:
Harfenspieler I: Wer sich der Einsamkeit ergibt;
Harfenspieler II: An die Türen will ich schleichen;
Harfenspieler III: Wer nie sein Brot mit Tränen. Der König
in Thule; Jägers Abendlied; An Schwager Kronos; Der Sänger
am Felsen; Lied: Ferne von der grossen Stadt; Der Wanderer;
Der Hirt; Lied eines Schiffers an die Dioskuren; Geheimnis;
Zum Punsche; Am Bach im Frühling (1816); An eine Quelle
(1817); Bei dem Grabe, meines Vaters; Am Grabe Anselmos;
Abendlied; Zufriedenheit; Herbstlied; Skolie: Mädchen
entsiegelten; Lebenslied; Lieden der Trennung (1816); Alinde;
An die Laute (1827); Frohsinn; Die Liebe; Trost; Der Schäfer
und der Reiter (1817); Lob der Tränen (1821); Der Alpenjäger;
Wie Ulfru fischt; Fahrt zum Hades; Schlaflied; Die
Blumensprache; Die abgeblühte Linde; Der Flug der Zeit;
Der Tod und das Mädchen; Das Lied vom Reifen; Täglich zu
singen; Am Strome; Philoktet; Memnon; Auf dem See;
Ganymed; Der Jüngling und der Tod; Trost im Liede (1817)
(B) *** DG (ADD) 437 215-2 (9) (with Gerald Moore, piano)

SCHUBERT: Lieder, Volume 2 (1817–28): An die Musik; Pax
vobiscum; Hänflings Liebeswerbung; Auf der Donau; Der
Schiffer; Nach einem Gewitter; Fischerlied; Das Grab; Der

Strom; An den Tod; Abschied; Die Forelle; Gruppe aus dem
Tartarus; Elysium; Atys; Erlafsee; Der Alpenjäger; Der
Kampf; Der Knabe in der Wiege (1817); Auf der Riesenkoppe;
An den Mond in einer Herbstnacht; Grablied für die Mutter;
Einsamkeit; Der Blumenbrief; Das Marienbild (1818);
Litanei auf das Fest Allerseelen (1816); Blondel zu Marien;
Das Abendrot; Sonett I: Apollo, lebet noch dein Hold
verlangen; Sonett II: Allein, nachdenken wie gelähmt vom
Krampfe; Sonett III: Nunmehr, da Himmel, Erde schweigt;
Vom Mitleiden Mariä (1818); Die Gebüsche; Der Wanderer;
Abendbilder; Himmelsfunken; An die Freunde; Sehnsucht;
Hoffnung; Der Jüngling am Bache; Hymne I: Wenige wissen
das Geheimnis der Liebe; Hymne II: Wenn ich ihn nur hab;
Hymne III: Wenn alle untreu werden; Hymne IV: Ich sag es
jedem; Marie; Beim Winde; Die Sternennächte; Trost;
Nachtstück; Prometheus; Strophe aus Die Götter
Griechenlands (1819); Nachthymne; Die Vögel; Der Knabe;
Der Fluss; Abendröte; Der Schiffer; Die Sterne; Morgenlied
(1820); Frühlingsglaube (1822); Des Fräuleins Liebeslauschen
(1820); Orest auf Tauris (1817); Der entsühnte Orest;
Freiwilliges Versinken; Der Jüngling auf dem Hügel (1820);
Sehnsucht (1817); Der zürnenden Diana; Im Walde (1820);
Die gefangenen Sänger; Der Unglückliche; Versunken;
Geheimes; Grenzen der Menschheit (1821); Der Jüngling an
der Quelle (1815); Der Blumen Schmerz (1821); Sei mir
gegrüsst; Herr Josef Spaun, Assessor in Linz; Der
Wachtelschlag Ihr Grab; Nachtviolen; Heliopolis I: Im kalten,
rauhen Norden; Heliopolis II: Fels auf Felsen hingewälzet;
Selige Welt; Schwanengesang: Wie klage'ich's aus; Du liebst
mich nicht; Die Liebe hat gelogen; Todesmusik;
Schatzgräbers Begehr; An die Leier; Im Haine; Der
Musensohn; An die Entfernte; Am Flusse; Willkommen und
Abschied (1822); Wandrers Nachtlied: Ein Gleiches; Der
zürnende Barde (1823); Am See (1822/3); Viola; Drang in die
Ferne; Der Zwerg; Wehmut; Lied: Die Mutter Erde; Auf dem
Wasser zu singen; Pilgerweise; Das Geheimnis; Der Pilgrim;
Dass sie hier gewesen; Du bist die Ruh'; Lachen und Weinen;
Greisengesang (1823); Dithyrambe; Der Sieg; Abendstern;
Auflösung; Gondelfahrer (1824); Glaube, Hoffnung und Liebe
(1828); Im Abendrot; Der Einsame (1824); Des Sängers Habe;
Totengräbers Heimwehe; Der blinde Knabe; Nacht und
Träume; Normans Gesang; Lied des gefangenen Jägers; Im
Walde; Auf der Bruck; Das Heimweh; Die Allmacht; Fülle
der Liebe; Wiedersehn; Abendlied für die Entfernte; Szene I
aus dem Schauspiel Lacrimas; Am mein Herz; Der liebliche
Stern (1825); Im Jänner 1817 (Tiefes Leid); Am Fenster;
Sehnsucht; Im Freien; Fischerweise; Totengräberweise; Im
Frühling; Lebensmut; Um Mitternacht; Uber Wildemann
(1826); Romanze des Richard Löwenherz (1827); Trinklied;
Ständchen; Hippolits Lied; Gesang (An Sylvia); Der
Wanderer an den Mond; Das Zügenglöcklein; Bei dir allein;
Irdisches Glück; Wiegenlied (1826); Der Vater mit dem Kind;
Jägers Liebeslied; Schiffers Scheidelied; L'incanto degli occhi;
Il traditor deluso; Il modo di prender moglie; Das Lied im
Grünen; Das Weinen; Vor meiner Wiege; Der Wallensteiner
Lanznecht beim Trunk; Der Kreuzzug; Des Fischers
Liebesglück (1827); Der Winterabend; Die Sterne; Herbst;
Widerschein (1828); Abschied von der Erde (1825/6)
(B) *** DG (ADD) 437 225-2 (9) (with Gerald Moore, piano)

SCHUMANN: Lieder (with Eschenbach), piano): Myrthen,
Op. 25/1–3; 5–8; 13; 15–19; 21–2; 25–6. Lieder und Gesänge,
Op. 27/1–5; Op. 51/4; Op. 77/1 & 5; Op. 96/1–3; Op. 98/2, 4,
6 & 8; Op. 127/2–3. Gedichte, Op. 30/1–3; Op. 119/2. Gesänge,
Op. 31/1 & 3; Op. 83/1 & 3; Op. 89/1–5; Op. 95/2; Op.

107/3 & 6; *Op.* 142/1, 2 & 4; *Schön Hedwig, Op.* 106. 6
Gedichte aus dem Liederbuch eines Malers, Op. 36. 12
Gedichte aus Rückerts Liebesfrühling, Op. 37. *Liederkreis,
Op.* 39. 5 *Lieder, Op.* 40. *Romanzen und Balladen, Op.*
45/1–3; *Op.* 49/1–2; *Op.* 53/1–3; *Op.* 64/3; *Belsatzar, Op.* 57.
Liederkreis, Op. 24. 12 *Gedichte, Op.* 35. *Dichterliebe, Op.* 48.
Spanisches Liederspiel, Op. 74/6, 7 & 10. *Liederalbum für die
Jugend, Op.* 79; *Der Handschuh, Op.* 87. 6 *Gedichte von
Nikolaus Lenau und Requiem (Anhang,* 7), *Op.* 90.
Minnespiel, Op. 101. 4 *Husarenlieder, Op.* 117. *Heitere
Gesänge, Op.* 125/1–3. *Spanische Liebeslieder, Op.* 138/2, 3,
5 & 7. *Balladen, Op.* 122/1–2. *Sechs frühe Lieder, op. posth.*
(WoO 21)
(B) *** DG (ADD) 445 660-2 (6) (with Gerald Moore, piano)

To celebrate the seventieth birthday of the great German
baritone, DG published a Lieder Edition, summing up the
astonishing achievement of the greatest male Lieder singer of
our time. With consistent artistry from all concerned and
with first-class transfers, these CDs are self-recommending.
We have discussed the Schubert in previous volumes, and
much else, too, in individual issues. Fischer-Dieskau's mastery never ceases to amaze. Sample this set at almost any
point and the same virtues emerge: characteristic beauty of
vocal tone and an extraordinarily vivid power of characterization and vocal colouring. No less remarkable are his
accompanists, including the incomparable Gerald Moore and
Daniel Barenboim, whose sensitivity and command of keyboard colour make for consistently memorable results. The
sheer originality of thought and the ease of the lyricism are a
regular delight. Fischer-Dieskau's concentration and inspiration never seem to falter, and Barenboim's accompaniments
could hardly be more understanding.

Fischer-Dieskau Edition (continued)

This set of 21 CDs was a follow-up to the Lieder Edition
above and was also released to celebrate Fischer-Dieskau's
75th birthday, releasing over 300 works on CD for the first
time – with a recording of *Die schöne Müllerin* which had
never before been released. One of the other joys of this
Fischer-Dieskau Edition is that it included a great deal of
music, much of it little known, either side of his core
nineteenth-century repertoire. Alas since then the deletions
axe has fallen on Volumes 4 (Schubert), 6 (Schumann), 8
(Liszt), 10 (Wolf), 11 (Richard Strauss), 12 (Reger), 13 (Schoeck), 14 (Debussy), 15 (Busch, Kempff, Mahler and others),
16 (Mahler), 17 (Bach and Buxtehude) and 18–21 (various
other composers).

Volume 1 (with Barenboim): SCHUBERT: *Winterreise, D.911*
(M) *** DG (ADD) 463 501-2

This is Fischer-Dieskau's fifth recording of Schubert's greatest
cycle (1979), with the voice still in superb condition. It is
perhaps the most inspirational, prompted by Barenboim's
spontaneous-sounding, almost improvisatory accompaniment. In expression, this is freer than the earlier versions, and
though some idiosyncratic details will not please everyone,
the sense of concentrated development is irresistible. The
recording is excellent.

Volume 2 (with Demus): SCHUBERT: *Die schöne Müllerin,
D.795.* Lieder: *Du bist die Ruh; Erlkönig; Nacht und Träume;
Ständchen*
(M) *** DG (IMS) (ADD) 463 502-2

This fascinating disc makes available Fischer-Dieskau's 1968

recording of *Die schöne Müllerin* with one of his favourite
pianists, Jörg Demus, for the first time. The reason for its
previous non-appearance were not artistic: Dieskau regards it
as one of his most successful interpretations of this cycle, and
edited and approved the disc for release. It seems that DG,
understandably, wanted to concentrate on the Gerald Moore
recordings which were then being undertaken, and with
whom he recorded the same cycle just three years later. The
result was that this version was never issued. Comparisons
with the 1971 Moore version are fascinating: the earlier version has a greater feeling of risk, with the dynamics noticeably more pointed, and as Alan Newcombe says in the sleeve
note 'the result is starker, more elemental, less comfortable,
and conceived on a larger scale'. Whereas the later version
offers the more rounded polish – from both artists – and for
many will be the safer recommendation, this 'new' version is
just as compelling. The recording is excellent, and the four
extra songs included on this disc are supremely done.

Volume 3 (with Moore): SCHUBERT: *Schwanengesang,
D.957.* Lieder: *Im Abendrot; An die Musik; An Sylvia; Die
Erde; Die Forelle; Heidenröslein; Der Musensohn; Der Tod
und das Mädchen; Vollendung*
(M) *** DG (ADD) 463 503-2

Fischer-Dieskau's and Gerald Moore's 1972 performance of
Schwanengesang – a work not conceived as a cycle by Schubert but grouped together by his publisher – is masterly. The
singer may occasionally over-emphasize individual words,
but the magnetism, poetry and insight – matched by Moore's
playing – has one consistently marvelling. The remaining
songs are superbly done, and both *Vollendung* and *Die Erde*,
also recorded in 1972, receive their first release here. Excellent
recording.

Volume 5 (with (i) Demus; (ii) Weissenborn): SCHUMANN:
(i) *Dichterliebe, Op.* 48; (ii) 12 *Gedichte, Op.* 35. Lieder:
*Freisinn; Schneeglöckchen; Des Sennen Abschied; Ständchen;
Talismane; Venezianisches Lied I & II*
(M) *** DG stereo/mono 463 505-2

The beautifully intense and expressive performance of *Dichterliebe* – perhaps the most concentrated of all song-cycles –
was taped in 1965. Here, Fischer-Dieskau surpassed his
famous mono version, with the voice sounding if anything in
better condition here, and with an even more tragic account
of *Iche grolle nicht*. The other Lieder (mono) are no less
attractive, and they all make their debut on CD here.

Volume 7 (with Demus): BEETHOVEN: *An die ferne
Geliebte, Op.* 98; *Drei Gesänge, Op.* 83. Lieder: *Adelaide;
Abendlied unterm gestirnten Himmel; Adelaide; L'amante
impaziente (Nos 3 & 4); Andenken; An die Hoffnung; Ariette
(Der Kuss); Aus Goethes Faust; Die Ehre Gottes aus der
Natur; Ich liebe dich, so wie du mich; In questa tomba
oscura; Der Jüngling in der Fremde; Der Liebende; Lied aus
der Ferne; Maigesang; Marmotte; Seufzer eines Ungeliebten
– Gegenliebe; Der Wachtelschlag*
(M) **(*) DG (ADD) 463 507-2

This Beethoven collection was recorded in 1966, finding
Fischer-Dieskau at his vocal peak, especially in the song-
cycle, which he made his very own. Though Jörg Demus's
accompaniments are not quite so imaginative as the singer
has received on other versions of these songs, Fischer-
Dieskau's individuality is as positive as ever, with detail
touched in as with few other singers. Excellent recording.

Volume 9 (with Demus): BRAHMS: *Vier ernste Gesänge, Op. 121.* Lieder: *Abenddämmerung; Alte Liebe; Auf dem Kirchhofe; Auf dem See; Es liebt sich so lieblich im Lenze; Es schauen die Blumen; Feldeinsamkeit; Frühlingslied; Heimweh II; Herbstgefühl; Kein Haus, keine Heimat; Meerfahrt; Mein Herz ist schwer; Mit vierzig Jahren; Mondenschein; Nachklang; Regenlied; Steig auf, geliebter Schatten; Sommerabend; Der Tod, das ist die kühle Nacht; Verzagen*
(M) *** DG mono/stereo 463 509-2

At the opening of this recital, with the *Four Serious Songs*, the commanding eloquence of Fischer-Dieskau's singing is gripping, and this level of concentration is maintained though-out, with Dieskau exploiting his range of tone colour in interpreting the fullest meaning of the words. The recordings were made from 1957 to 1960, and are strikingly full and vivid – both in stereo and mono.

Lieder (with Reimann or Reutter, piano): FRANZ: *Auf dem Meeere* (3 versions); *Wie des Mondes Abbild; Gewitternacht; Bitte; Für Musik; Abends; Wonne der Wehmut; Mailied.* GRIEG: *Dereinst, Gedanke mein; Lauf der Welt; Wo sind sie hin?; Hör'ich das Liedchen klingen; Morgentau; Abschied; Jägerlied.* KIRCHNER: *Sie weiss es nicht; Frühhlingslied* (3 versions). HILLER: *Gebet.* JENSEN: *Lehn deine Wang' an meine Wang'.* A. RUBINSTEIN: *Es blinker der Tau.* LISZT: *Es rauschen die Winde; Wieder möcht'ich dir begegnen; Ständchen; Uber allen Gipfeln ist Ruh'.* WAGNER: *Der Tannenbaum.* BERLIOZ: *Auf den Lagunen.* CORNELIUS: *Liebe ohne Heimat; Sonnenuntergang.* NIETZSCHE: *Nachtspiel; Wie sich Rebenranken schwingen; Verwelkt.* WEINGARTNER: *Liebesfeier.* RITTER: *Primula veria.* STREICHER: *Ist die ein getreues, liebevolles Kind beschert.* RAFF: *Unter den Palmen.* EULENBURG: *Liebessehnsucht.* VON SCHILLINGS: *Freude soll in deinen Werken sein.* SCHOECK: *Abendwolken; Reiselied; Peregrina II.* WETZEL: *An miene Mutter; Der Kehraus.* MATTIESEN: *Heimgang in der Frühe; Herbstgefühl.* PFITZNER: *An den Mond; Mailied; Hussens Kerker.* TIESSEN: *Völglein Schwermut.* R. STRAUSS: *Wer hat's getan?* REGER: *Warnung; Sommernacht.* SCHREKER: *Die Dunkelheit sinkt schwer wie Blei.* DEBUSSY: *Pour ce que plaisance est morte; Le Temps a laissié son manteau.* MILHAUD: *Lamentation.* MAHLER: *Des Knaben Wunderhorn: Wo die schönen Trompeten blasen.* HINDEMITH: *Fragment.* REUTTER: *Johann Kepler; Lied für ein dunkles Mädchen; Trommel.* FORTNER: *Abbitte; Hyperions Schicksalslied; Lied vom Weidenbaum.* BARTOK: *Im Tale.* BLACHER: *Gedicht; Worte.* HAUER: *Der gefesselte Strom; An die Pasrzen.* SCHOENBERG: *Warnung; Traumleben.* WEBERN: *4 Lieder* (with George). APOSTEL: *Nacht.* KRENEK: *Die frühen Gräber; Erinnerung.* VOM EINEM: *Ein junger Dichter denkt an die Geliebte; In der Fremde.* EISLER: *An die Hoffnung; In der Frühe; Spruch 1939.* DESSAU: *Noch bin ich eine Stadt; Sur nicht mehr, Frau.* BECK: *Herbst*
(M) **(*) EMI (ADD) 5 67349-2 (3)

To some extent this EMI set is compensation for the loss of most of DG's Fischer-Dieskau Edition. With the great bari-tone at his most inspired in this rare repertory, it would be hard to devise a more imaginative survey of the German Lied after Schumann. Ranging astonishingly widly in its coverage of the genre between 1850 and 1950, it generally bypasses obvious names, celebrating instead such composers as Franz, Kirchner, Cornelius and even Nietzsche (Wagner's pupil) in

the nineteenth century and Weingartner, Schreker and Apos-tel in the twentieth. It is fascinating to have Wagner himself represented, Grieg and Berlioz (in German) as well as Debussy, Milhaud and even Bartok in songs with Lieder-like aim. Never issued on CD before, this makes a memorable celebratory issue, timed for Fischer-Dieskau's 75th birthday in May 2000. Sadly, this mid-price issue earns a big black mark for giving no texts or translations, leaving one in the dark over much rare material, even though the singer's diction is excellent.

'*The Mastersinger*': Arias from: MOZART: *Così fan tutte* (with BPO, Eugen Jochum); *Don Giovanni* (with Prague Nat. Theatre O, Karl Boehm); *Le nozze di Figaro* (with German Op. Ch. & O, Boehm); *Die Zauberflöte.* MAHLER: *Ich bin der Welt abhanden gekommen* (with BPO, Boehm). ORFF: *Carmina Burana.* WAGNER: *Die Meistersinger von Nürnberg* (with German Op. Ch. & O, Jochum). *Das Rheingold* (with BPO, Herbert von Karajan). GLUCK: *Orfeo ed Euridice.* HANDEL: *Giulio Cesare* (with Munich Bach O, Karl Richter); *Serse* (with Munich CO, Hans Stadlmair). VERDI: *Don Carlo* (with ROHCG O, Georg Solti); *Rigoletto* (with La Scala, Milan, Rafael Kubelik); *La traviata* (with LPO, Lamberto Gardelli). PUCCINI: *Tosca* (with Santa Cecilia O, Lorin Maazel). HAYDN: *The Creation* (with BPO, Karajan). R. STRAUSS: *Arabella; Die Frau ohne Schatten* (with Bavarian State O, Joseph Keilberth); *Elektra* (with Dresden State Op. O, Boehm); *Salome* (with Hamburg State Op. O, Boehm). Lieder: SCHUBERT: *Im Frühling* (with Richter, piano); *An Silvia; Erlkönig; Die Forelle; Heidenröslein; Ständchen* (with Gerald Moore, piano); *Der Musensohn* (with Jörg Demus, piano)
(B) DG *** (ADD) 476 7111 (2)

A self-recommending set, originally released to coincide with Fischer-Dieskau's *Gramophone* 'Lifetime Achievement' award in 1993. It must have been an impossibly difficult task to know what to include here (the DG Fischer-Dieskau Lieder Edition alone runs to 44 CDs!) and everything here is vintage stuff. Most of the items are operatic, drawn from both Decca's and DG's catalogues, and he is as impressive in the Verdi items (he is superb in *Don Carlos* where as Rodrigo he rivals Gobbi in the Death scene) as he is in the Strauss items – his Orestes in *Electra* is incomparable. He is always a delight in Mozart, particularly so as Papageno in *Die Zauberflöte* (a role he never assumed on stage) and he is no less stylish in the enjoyable baroque items included here. The lieder are, of course, wonderfully done and his subtle yet pointful shaping of the words is equally revealing in large operatic repertoire, where his highly individual portrayal of Sachs in *Die Meistersinger* is a highlight. The recital ends with a glowingly warm excerpt from Mahler's *Rückert Lieder* which receives equally loving care from the conductor. The recordings – all good – date from the 1960s and '70s and, although the booklet notes are minimal (restricted to a short biography), this makes an excellent bargain sampler of Fischer-Dieskau's art.

'*An die Musik*': Arias from: ORFF: *Carmina burana.* GLUCK: *Orpheus und Eurydice.* MOZART: *Don Giovanni; Die Zauberflöte* (with Berlin RSO, Ferenc Fricsay). WAGNER: *Die Meistersinger von Nürnberg* (with German Op. O, Eugen Jochum); *Tannhäuser* (with German Op. O, Berlin, Otto Gerdes). R. STRAUSS: *Arabella* (with Bavarian State O, Joseph Keilberth). MAHLER: *4 Rückert Lieder* (with BPO, Karl Boehm). BACH: *Ich habe genug, ich habe den Heiland*

(with Karl Ristenpart CO, Ristenpart). **Lieder:** SCHUBERT: *Abschied; An die Musik; Du bist die Ruh; Erstarrung; Der Leiermann; Die liebe Farbe; Das Lied im Grünen; Der Musen Musen; Ständchen* (with Gerald Moore, piano). SCHUMANN: *Dichterliebe.* BRAHMS: *Feldeinsamkeit* (with Jörg Demus, piano). LISZT: *Es muss ein Wunderbares sein* (with Daniel Barenboim, piano). STRAUSS: *Ständchen* (with Wolfgang Sawallisch, piano). WOLF: *Verborgenheit* (with Karl Richter, piano). WOLF: *Ein Ständchen euch zu bringen; Was für ein Lied soll dir gesungen warden?* (with Hertha Klust, piano). DEBUSSY: *La Grotte; Mandoline* (with Karl Engel, piano). SCHOECK: *Nachruf* (with Barton Weber, piano). **Bonus DVD:** SCHUBERT: *Am Fenster; Auf der Bruck; Auf der Donau; Fischerweise; Des Fräuleins Liebeslauschen; Im Frühling; Der Sterne; Der Wanderer* (with Richter, piano)
(M) *(**) DG mono/stereo (ADD) 477 5556 (2)

Another superb Fischer-Dieskau compilation, and an essential purchase for all serious Fischer-Dieskau fans as it includes recordings not released on CD before: the (1959) Debussy and (1950) Wolf items, along with Brahms's *Mondnacht* (1967), are all superbly done, with the voice at its freshest (*La Grotte* of Debussy is magically haunting). All the operatic items here are famous: the Mozart, Wagner and Richard Strauss numbers are highlights in his discography, as is his glowingly warm account of the Mahler lieder. The complete (1965) *Dichterliebe* is every bit as intense as his famous, earlier, mono account, with the voice, if anything, sounding in even better condition. Demus is a sympathetic pianist even if his rubato is more marked than one would normally expect of an accompanist. The rest of the lieder items are all of Fischer-Dieskau's best vintage quality. The bonus DVD was recorded in the Napoleon Room, Schloss Ismaning, with Richter in 1978, and is well worth having. Although texts and translations are not included, there is a good outline of the meaning of each song in the booklet, along with decent sleeve-notes and plenty of pictures.

Flagstad, Kirsten (soprano)

'The Flagstad Legacy', Volume 1: Opera arias from:
BEETHOVEN: *Fidelio.* WAGNER: *Götterdämmerung; Lohengrin; Parsifal; Tannhäuser; Tristan und Isolde; Die Walküre.* WEBER: *Oberon.* Songs and arias by ALNS; BEETHOVEN; BISHOP; BRAHMS; BULL; FRANZ; GRIEG; GRONDAHL; HURUM; LIE; NORDRAAK; PALENZ; ROSENFELDT; SCHUBERT; SINDING; R. STRAUSS; THOMMESEN; THRANE
(***) Simax mono PSC 1821 (3)

These three Simax CDs make up the first of five sets, running to thirteen CDs in all, which promise the most comprehensive overview of this great singer's legacy on records. It comes with a substantial article by Arne Dørumsgaard, himself a composer and translator. The contents range from the period of the First World War through to 1941, though the 1940 *Haugtussa* is not included. There is a thrilling *Dich, teure Halle* from *Tannhäuser*, recorded in New York in 1935 (hardly surprising that Flagstad took America by storm) and a *Liebestod* from the same year, as well as the 1936 Copenhagen recordings of Grieg and other Norwegian songs.

There are some Philadelphia and San Francisco Opera recordings under Ormandy with Melchior, and many feature her lifelong accompanist, Edwin McArthur. In Norwegian song, Grieg is not the whole story even if he is most of it. Flagstad included a number of her other and less familiar countrymen in her discography. These include Ole Bull, the violinist-composer who encouraged Grieg's family to send the boy to Leipzig, and whose *Sæterjentens Søndag* ('The Herd Girl's Sunday') would have been mandatory at the time. Eyvind Alnæs's song *Lykkan mellem To Mennseskor* ('Happiness between Two People') was also a favourite of hers.

Dørumsgaard tells of the 'disarming simplicity' of her 1929 version, the finest of her early electrics, released 'before fame struck'. It is indeed quite amazing and fresher than the 1936 record, which also suffers from the rather dry acoustic of the Copenhagen studio. The Simax will be indispensable to the serious collector, both for its comprehensiveness and for the generally high standard of its transfers.

Fleming, Renée (soprano)

'Ladies and Gentlemen: Miss Renée Fleming'
*** Decca DVD 074 153-9 (Director: Tony Palmer)

Tony Palmer's brilliant and moving profile of Renée Fleming, originally made for the South Bank Show on British ITV, is here superbly supplemented by what Palmer describes as 'bonus vignettes', 55 minutes of off-cuts from a film that for technical reasons had to be reduced to just over an hour, 'material too good to waste'. Some of those extra items contain the most revealing moments of all, as for example the sequence of well over ten minutes analysing her education and early training, 'Vocal Beginnings'. Palmer also contributes a moving essay in the accompanying booklet which amplifies Fleming's complex character even more. He explains his inclusion of a rehearsal sequence of the Verdi *Requiem*, even though the diva disapproved of it for revealing a double-chin (barely noticeable to anyone else), for it tellingly brings one close to a great artist. The film opens with Fleming doing a comic cabaret number based on *Caro nome* from Verdi's *Rigoletto*, with pig-puppets as her companions, then switching sharply to her agonized account of 'Amazing Grace' at the memorial service on Ground Zero in New York, commemorating the disaster of 9/11 and the collapse of the Twin Towers. Fleming explains that at school she always wanted to obey the rules and do well by the accepted standards, and she often envies those who are not chained in that way. That conflict in her ever-self-questioning character is movingly illustrated at the end of the main film with her singing of Marietta's Lied from Korngold's opera, *Die tote Stadt*, though (if anything) even more moving is the close of the last bonus vignette, celebrating her singing of Strauss with a radiant account of *Beim Schlafengehen* from the *Four Last Songs*. There are many other musical clips too, to amplify a most revealing portrait.

'Great Opera Scenes' (with LSO, Solti) from: MOZART: *Le nozze di Figaro.* TCHAIKOVSKY: *Eugene Onegin.* DVORAK: *Rusalka.* VERDI: *Otello.* BRITTEN: *Peter Grimes.* R. STRAUSS: *Daphne*
🔊 ⊙ *** Decca 455 760-2

Solti, in one of his very last recordings, here pays tribute to a soprano he especially admired and the wide choice of repertory movingly reflects an inspired collaboration. Far more than most operatic recitals, this presents fully rounded characterizations in extended scenes, from the Countess in *Figaro* through two Slavonic roles Tatiana and Rusalka (Fleming's favourite) to a tenderly girlish portrait of Verdi's Desdemona, wonderfully poised. Most moving of all is the final item – in effect a valediction – a ravishing, sensuous account of the heroine's final transformation into a tree in Strauss's late opera, *Daphne*.

'*I Want Magic!*': American opera arias (with Met. Op. O, Levine) from: HERRMANN: *Wuthering Heights*. MOORE: *The Ballad of Baby Doe*. MENOTTI: *The Medium*. GERSHWIN: *Porgy and Bess*. BERNSTEIN: *Candide*. FLOYD: *Susannah*. STRAVINSKY: *The Rake's Progress*. BARBER: *Vanessa*. PREVIN: *A Streetcar Named Desire*
*** Decca 460 567-2

The title *I Want Magic!* is from André Previn's opera based on Tennessee Williams's *Streetcar Named Desire*. Blanche Dubois's climactic aria – recorded even before the world première of the opera in 1998 – makes a moving conclusion to a varied and characterful collection. The beauty and power of Fleming's singing transforms arias from such operas as Bernard Herrmann's *Wuthering Heights*, Douglas Moore's *Ballad of Baby Doe* and Carlisle Floyd's *Susannah*, bringing out their lyricism. In arias from *Porgy and Bess* she is totally in style, and has both weight and brilliance in the big showpiece arias from Stravinsky's *Rake's Progress*, Barber's *Vanessa* and Bernstein's *Candide*.

'*Night Songs*' (with Thibaudet, piano): FAURE: *Après un rêve; Clair de lune; Mandoline; Nell; Soir*. DEBUSSY: *Apparition; Beau soir; Mandoline; Chansons de Bilitis*. MARX: *Nachtgebet; Nocturne; Pierrot Dandy; Selige Nacht*. R. STRAUSS: *Cäcilie; Leise Lieder; Leises Lied; Ruhe, meine Seele!; Schlechtes Wetter*. RACHMANINOV: *In the Silence of Mysterious Night; It is Beautiful Here; Sleep; Oh Do Not Sing To Me; These Summer Nights; The Waterlily*
*** Decca 467 697-2

While it is possible to imagine a classic French singer bringing more authenticity to the French songs, there is no doubting Renée Fleming's understanding of the idiom. Her performances bring a genuine warmth which is most attractive, and her subtle colourings are a delight. In such numbers as Debussy's *Beau soir* she sings with a dreamy delicacy, whilst the following *Mandoline* is animated and lively, and her voice remains rich and well focused throughout her range in both. The Strauss songs have much atmosphere and character, from the hushed still of *Ruhe, meine Seele!* ('Rest my Soul') to the more dramatic *Cäcilie*, in which the strong emotions in the text are well conveyed. The yearning Russian qualities of Rachmaninov are well captured too, and the selection included finds the composer at his most persuasive. The Marx songs are an unexpected but welcome inclusion, especially the wild and quirky 'Pierrot Dandy'. Much of the overall success of this disc is due to the superlative accompaniments from Jean-Yves Thibaudet who plays with great understanding and style. Full texts and translations are included, and the recording is warm and perfectly balanced.

Flórez, Juan Diego (tenor)

'*Great Tenor Arias*' (with Giuseppe Verdi SO of Milan, Rizzi): Arias from: GLUCK: *Orphée et Euridice*. VERDI: *Un giorno di regno; Rigoletto*. ROSSINI: *L'italiana in Algeri;*

Semiramide. DONIZETTI: *La figlia del reggimento; Lucrezia Borgia*. HALEVY: *La Juive*. CIMAROSA: *Il matrimonio segreto*. PUCCINI: *Gianni Schicchi*
**(*) Decca SACD 475 6186

This is Flórez's third CD for Decca, and very good it is too. One needn't worry about his technique, which is always reliable, and his tone is consistently pleasing, especially in the higher tessitura. Sensibly, this disc mixes well-known arias with rarer ones, and these are all enjoyable: the Verdi item from *Un giorno di regno*, with its decorative flute embellishments in the first half, before lunging into one of Verdi's infectiously enjoyable cabalettas, is very attractive. The Cimarosa number, with its elegantly florid writing, is a winner, especially its snappy second half, which gives the singer plenty of chances to demonstrate his technique. The Donizetti and Rossini items come off very well, as one would expect from this artist, though *La donna è mobile*, well done though it be, does not have the personality and swagger of the finest versions of this much-recorded aria, though the final note does not disappoint. The unexpected Puccini aria makes an enjoyably contrasting item to end the programme. The recording is warm and full and the voice is very well caught; the orchestra under Rizzi is nicely elegant and plays well, even if it does not have quite the zest which Bonynge puts into this repertoire.

Freni, Mirella (soprano) and Renata Scotto (mezzo soprano)

'*In Duet*' (with the Nat. PO; (i) with Leone Magiera, (ii) with Lorenzo Anselmi): Arias from: MERCADANTE: (i) *Le due illustri rivali*. BELLINI: *Bianca e Fernando*; (ii) *Norma*. MOZART: (i) *Le nozze di Figaro*
(M) **(*) Decca Classic Recitals (ADD) 475 6811

The Mozart items will win no awards for style, but otherwise this is a fascinating celebration of the charms and vocal beauty of two singers who might have been thought too alike to make good duettists. Scotto was in fair voice (considering when the recording was made, in 1978), with the top more under control, if occasionally squally. The account of the big *Norma* scene (ending with *Mira, o Norma*) is more relaxed and delicate than the one Scotto contributed in the complete CBS/Sony set of the opera. The other Bellini item is also welcome, with its dreamy melody in compound time. And so is the even rarer Mercadante duet, with its traditional chains of thirds. The warm and atmospheric sound has transferred well to this Classic Recital CD, though even a baby ant would find the sleeve notes too small to read.

Gabrieli Consort & Players, Paul McCreesh

'*A Venetian Coronation (1595)*': GIOVANNI GABRIELI: *Canzonas XIII a 12; IX a 10; XVI a 15; Deus qui beatum Marcum a 10; Intonazione ottavo toni; Intonazione terzo e quarto toni; Intonazioni quinto tono alla quarta bassa; Omnes gentes a 16; Sonata VI a 8 pian e forte*. ANDREA GABRIELI: *Intonazione primo tono; Intonazione settino tono; Mass excerpts: Kyrie a 5-12; Gloria a 16; Sanctus a 12;*

Benedictus a 12; O sacrum convivium a 5; Benedictus dominus Deus sabbaoth. BENDINELLI: *Sonata CCCXXXIII; Sarasinetta.* THOMSEN: *Toccata 1*
*** Virgin 7 59006-2

This recording won a *Gramophone* Early Music Award. *A Venetian Coronation* is a highly imaginative if conjectural reconstruction of the Mass and its accompanying music as performed at St Mark's for the ceremonial installation of Doge Marino Grimaldi in 1595. The evocation begins with sounding bells (Betjeman would have approved), and the choice of music is extraordinarily rich, using processional effects to simulate the actual scene, like a great Renaissance painting. The climax comes with the Mass itself; and the sounds here, choral and instrumental, are quite glorious. The spontaneity of the whole affair is remarkable and the recording superb.

'*Venetian Vespers*', including: MONTEVERDI: *Laudate pueri; Laudate dominum; Deus qui mundum; Laetatus sum.* GIOVANNI GABRIELI: *Intonazione* (for organ). RIGATTI: *Dixit dominus; Nisi dominus; Magnificat; Salve regina.* GRANDI: *O intemerata; O quam tu pulchra es.* FASALO: *Intonazione* (for organ). BANCHIERI: *Suonata prima; Dialogo secondo* (for organ). FINETTI: *O Maria, quae rapis corda hominum.* CAVALLI: *Lauda Jerusalem.* MARINI: *Sonata con tre violini in eco.* ANON.: *Praeambulum*
*** (M) DG 476 1868 (2)

Sequels can sometimes fall flat (as Hollywood so often demonstrates), but this one certainly doesn't, for the musical intensity of the performance is no less vivid here, and the spatial effects and polychoral interplay are equally impressive in this hypothetical re-creation of a Vespers at St Mark's. Grandiose effects alternate with more intimate sonorities, but the feeling of drama which was part and parcel of the Venetian Renaissance tradition is fully conveyed. Once again all the participants are on their toes, and playing and singing (soloists as well as chorus) are transcendent with detail in the accompaniment always effective and stylish. The recording is splendidly opulent, yet never loses its definition. This excellent set returns as part of Universal's mid-priced *Gramophone Awards Collection* – it won the 1993 Early Music Award.

Gallardo-Domas, Cristina (soprano)

'*Bel Sogno*' (with Munich R. O, Barbacini): Arias from: BELLINI: *I Capuleti e i Montecchi.* CATALANI: *La Wally.* CILEA: *Adriana Lecouvreur.* DONIZETTI: *Anna Bolena.* PUCCINI: *Madama Butterfly; La Bohème; Manon Lescaut; Suor Angelica; Gianni Schicchi.* VERDI: *La traviata; Simon Boccanegra; Otello*
**(*) Teldec 8573 86440-2

Cristina Gallardo-Domas made her first big impact on disc with her deeply moving assumption of the title-role in Antonio Pappano's prize-winning version of Puccini's *Suor Angelica*. Here it is in the Puccini items above all that she shines out, giving portraits of each heroine that are not just beautiful and sensitive but bring out the words too. Yet this collection demonstrates the breadth of her sympathies in a formidable range of arias, and though she is not quite as much at home in Bellini or Donizetti, there too one recognizes the warmth and responsiveness of her singing. The only slight disappointment is that the Munich recording brings out an occasional unevenness in her vocal production,

though that will matter little to anyone finding her distinctive timbre attractive.

Gens, Véronique (soprano)

'*Nuit d'étoiles*' (with Vignoles): Songs: DEBUSSY: *3 Chansons de Bilitis etc.* FAURE: *Aprés un rêve, etc.* POULENC: *Banalités etc.*
***Virgin (ADD) 5 45360-2

This is one of the very finest of all discs of French mélodies, an inspired choice of well-known and rare songs sung with exceptional imagination and feeling for the idiom. Best known for her brilliant performances of baroque music, Gens here sings with a tone at once firmly focused and sensuously beautiful. In her distinctive and idiomatic characterization of each composer she is greatly helped by Roger Vignoles, the brilliant accompaniment adding to the element of fantasy that runs through the whole sequence. The point and wit found in such a popular song as Fauré's *Mandoline* are exceptional, making one appreciate it afresh, and the waltz numbers from the Poulenc group, *Voyage à Paris* and *Les Chemins de l'amour*, are equally seductive in their idiomatic lilt. The poise of Gens in the more serious songs is also exemplary, with the voice flawlessly placed. A magical disc.

Gericke, Isa (soprano), Sveinung Bjelland (piano)

'*Waldabendlust*': KJERULF: *Albumblatt; Gute Nacht; Höchstes Leben; Lass Andre nur; Des Mondes Silber rinnt; Nach langen Jahren; Die Schwester; Sehnsucht; Spanische Romanza; Täuschung; Waldabendlust.* IRGENS-JENSEN: *Japanischer-Früling, Op. 2.* GRONDAHL: *Elslein; Ich möcht' es mir selber verschweigen; Juniabend; Rastlose Liebe; Sie liebten sich beide.* HJELM: *Frühlingslob; Loose; Du Warst es doch*
*(*) Simax PSC 1231

Even in the 1940s Grieg's songs were more often than not sung in German translation, and many other Norwegian composers turned to the language that would ensure their songs had wider currency. Isa Katherine Gericke offers eleven songs by Grieg's immediate precursor, Halfdan Kjerulf – mostly settings of Geibel. They have a certain charm without having Grieg's strong personality. The best thing probably is the song-cycle by Ludvig Irgens-Jensen, an immediate contemporary of Sæverud and whose folk-inspired musical language is refreshing. *Japanischer-Frühling* comprises nine songs adapted from the Japanese by Hans Begthe, familiar from Mahler's *Das Lied von der Erde*. It comes from 1920, when Jensen was in his mid-twenties and was published as his Op. 2. The composer made an orchestral version of this rewarding and imaginative cycle in 1957, and it is in this form that it is better known. Agathe Backer-Grøndahl was four years younger than Grieg and enjoyed a formidable reputation as a pianist (even Bernard Shaw wrote with admiration of her London visits). As these songs show, she was far from negligible as a song composer. All these examples are worth hearing, but they deserve more eloquent advocacy than they receive here. Isa Katherine Gericke is an intelligent artist but is a little too wanting in variety of tone-colour and vocal presence. Sveinung Bjelland is a supportive and sensitive accompanist and the recording is very truthful. All the same, this is of more than just specialist interest.

Gheorghiu, Angela (soprano)

'Angela Gheorghiu Live' (with ROHCG O, Marin): Arias from: HANDEL: *Rinaldo.* MOZART: *Le nozze di Figaro.* CHARPENTIER: *Louise.* PUCCINI: *Madama Butterfly; Gianni Schicchi.* CILEA: *Adriana Lecouvreur.* BELLINI: *Norma.* Encores: BREDICEANU: *La Seçeris.* LOEWE: *My Fair Lady: I Could have Danced All Night*
*** EMI **DVD** 4 92695-9

This DVD offers a visual recording of the live recital given at Covent Garden by Gheorghiu in June 2001, which has also been issued on audio CD (see below). The bonus on DVD, as well as having the vision of an exceptionally beautiful woman, is that among the special features is an interview with Gheorghiu, in which she confirms some of the points implied by the CD version, notably that when she was a student she knew and loved the two opening arias, not generally part of her latter-day repertory, *Lascia ch'io pianga* from Handel's *Rinaldo* and the Countess's *Porgi amor* from Mozart's *Marriage of Figaro* (as she explains, the very first Mozart aria she ever sang). The poise of those performances, the stylish concern for vocal purity, leads on to moving accounts of arias more usually associated with her, as well as an extrovert group of encores executed with commanding artistry, even if during 'I Could have Danced All Night' she has to prompt herself with the music. As to the video production, having multi-coloured back lighting for each aria – pink, blue or a mixture of both – takes us near the pop world, but it gives variety!

Arias (with Ch. & O of Teatro Regio, Turin, Mauceri) from: VERDI: *Falstaff.* MASSENET: *Hérodiade; Chérubin.* CATALANI: *La Wally.* BELLINI: *I Capuleti e i Montecchi.* PUCCINI: *La Bohème.* BOITO: *Mefistofele.* GOUNOD: *Faust.* DONIZETTI: *Don Pasquale.* GRIGORIU: *Valurile Dunarii*
**(*) Decca 452 417-2

The star of Decca's *La traviata* made her solo début in a recital which offers much lovely singing – the very opening excerpt from Verdi's *Falstaff* brings a ravishing line (and some fine orchestral playing, too) and the Massenet aria is quite melting and full of charm. But there is too little difference of characterization between the different heroines, not enough fiery passion or, indeed, displays of temperament, which means that the Jewel Song from *Faust* fails to sparkle as it should. Nevertheless the sample of Mimì in *La Bohème* promises well. The back-up here, from John Mauceri and the Turin chorus and orchestra, is impressive, and so is the glowing Decca recording.

'Casta Diva' (with ROHCG Ch. & O, Pidó): Arias from: BELLINI: *Norma; I Puritani; La sonnambula.* ROSSINI: *L'assedio di Corinto; Il barbiere di Siviglia; Guglielmo Tell.* DONIZETTI: *Anna Bolena; Lucia di Lammermoor*
*** EMI 5 57163-2

Not since Joan Sutherland has a disc of *bel canto* arias inspired such glorious singing as from Angela Gheorghiu in repertory with which she has not till now been associated. The flexibility of her voice has been amply demonstrated in her regular lyric repertory, whether as Gounod's Marguerite in *Faust* or Verdi's Violetta in *La traviata*, and this translates perfectly to Rossini, Bellini and Donizetti at their most demanding. Ravishing tone, finely shaded, marks the opening item, *Casta diva*, with poised legato that yet allows moving characterization. In the other great Bellini arias tenderness goes with depth of feeling, with a hint of flutter heightening the emotion in Amina's *Ah, non credea mirarti* from *La sonnambula*, and with sparkling coloratura in all the cabalettas. In Rossini she is just as commanding, whether in the *Guglielmo Tell* aria, the fine aria from *L'assedio di Corinto* or Rosina's *Una voce poco fa* from *Il barbiere di Siviglia*, sparkily characterful. In Donizetti the scena from *Anna Bolena* leads naturally to the great Act I aria from *Lucia di Lammermoor.* The top of the voice may not be quite as free as Sutherland's was, but this is comparably assured. Perhaps wisely, Gheorghiu has opted not to include the Mad Scene from *Lucia* as well. Warm, sympathetic accompaniment and vivid recording.

'Angela Gheorghiu Live at Covent Garden' (with ROHCG O, Marin): Arias from: BELLINI: *Norma.* BREDICEANU: *La seceris.* CHARPENTIER: *Louise.* CILEA: *Adriana Lecouvreur.* HANDEL: *Rinaldo.* LOEWE: *My Fair Lady.* MASSENET: *Manon.* MOZART: *Le nozze di Figaro.* PUCCINI: *Gianni Schicchi; Madama Butterfly; Turandot*
**(*) EMI 5 57264-2

It was a striking enough development when Angela Gheorghiu, a soprano geared to Verdi, Puccini and Massenet, displayed such formidable mastery in the *bel canto* repertory, as captured on her recital disc of Roassini, Bellini and Donizetti. Even more remarkable is the classical poise and purity of her singing here in *Lascia ch'io pianga* from Handel's *Rinaldo* and the Countess's aria, *Porgi amor*, from Mozart's *Figaro*. This recording was made at her Covent Garden recital in June 2001, demonstrating throughout that unlike so many operatic prima donnas she has not forgotten her early lessons. Her assurance and technical mastery go with a magnetic ability to project character with musical imagination, not just in favourite romantic arias, including Norma's *Casta diva* and Louise's *Depuis le jour*, but in the encores, which include a charming Romanian song and 'I Could have Danced All Night' from *My Fair Lady*. Marred slightly by intrusive applause.

Gheorghiu, Angela (soprano), Roberto Alagna (tenor)

Opera arias and duets from: MASCAGNI: *L'amico Fritz.* MASSENET: *Manon.* DONIZETTI: *Anna Bolena; Don Pasquale.* OFFENBACH: *La Belle Hélène.* BERNSTEIN: *West Side Story.* GOUNOD: *Faust.* G. CHARPENTIER: *Louise.* BERLIOZ: *Les Troyens.* PUCCINI: *La Bohème*
⊕→ *** EMI 5 56117-2

If Angela Gheorghiu's Decca solo début was a little disappointing, this record of duets with her husband, Roberto Alagna, is not. Clearly they are a natural couple as artists as well as human beings. There is much here to delight, not least the opening Cherry Duet from *L'amico Fritz*, in which the voices blend delightfully. *Manon* brings a comparable symbiosis, and the Donizetti items are as winning as the unexpected excerpt from *Les Troyens*. Solo arias also come off well here, notably Gheorghiu's aria from *Anna Bolena*, which suits her exactly; Alagna turns in a stylishly heady account of the delicious Waltz Song from *La Belle Hélène*. The excerpt from *West Side Story* is tenderly touching but, as nearly always, the voices sound too mature for these star-crossed young lovers. Again the promise of that future complete *Bohème* comes in the closing all-too-short *O soave fanciulla*. First-rate accompaniments under Richard Armstrong and superb sound contribute to the great success of this immensely pleasurable operatic hour.

Gloriae Dei Cantores, Elizabeth Patterson

'*By the Rivers of Babylon (American Psalmody II)*' (with James E. Jordan, organ): LOEFFLER: *By the Rivers of Babylon, Op. 3* (with P. Clark, E. Ingwersen, flutes, M. Buddington, harp, H. Vacarro, cello).VIRGIL THOMSON: *3 Antiphonal Psalms (123, 133 & 136); De profundis.* SCHOENBERG: *De profundis.* TAYLOR: *Sing to the Lord a New Song.* BERGER: *The Eyes of All Wait upon Thee.* NEWBURY: *Psalm 150.* NEAR: *My Song shall be Alway of the Loving-kindness of the Lord.* ADLER: *Psalm Triology (42, 84 & 113).* NESWICK: *Hallelujah! Sing to the Lord a New Song.* WHITE: *Cantate Domino* (with brass ens.)
**(*) Paraclete Press Gloriae Dei Cantores GDCD 027

This collection of twentieth-century psalm settings includes music by 'those who are native Americans by birth or citizenship', which covers both Charles Loeffler, a late nineteeth-century émigré, and Schoenberg, who became an American citizen in 1941. The latter's atonal setting of the original Hebrew text of Psalm 120 (commissioned by Koussevitzky), with its dramatic spoken acclamations adding to the music's emotional impact, is the one really avant-garde piece here. It comes immediately after Virgil Thomson's admirably fresh but much simpler setting in English.

Loeffler's sensuously lush *By the rivers of Babylon*, which introduces the programme and gives the disc its title, is the most ambitious piece, very Gallic in feeling. It is richly sung and has a beautiful postlude for two flutes and cello, let down by imperfect intonation from the solo cellist. This closing section should have been re-recorded, for it all but spoils a superb performance. The rest of the music is traditional, but individually so, especially the very striking *Psalm Triology* by Samuel Adler and the pieces by Clifford Taylor, Jean Berger (gently touching) and Bruce Neswick, his joyous 'Hallelujah'.

The choral singing is very fine and deeply committed throughout, and the choir has the advantage of the ideal acoustics of the Methuen Music Hall in Massachusetts, while James Jordan's organ accompaniments (when required) give admirable support, using the superb organ now located there. Even with the reservation about the Loeffler postlude, this splendid collection is well worth having. (Volume 1, which we have not received for review, is available on GDCD 025.)

Gothic Voices, Christopher Page

'*The Guardian of Zephirus*' (courtly songs of the 15th century, with Barford, medieval harp): DU FAY: *J'atendray tant qu'il vous playra; Adieu ces bons vins de Lannoys; Mon cuer me fait tous dis penser.* BRIQUET: *Ma seul amour et ma belle maistresse.* DE CASERTA: *Amour ma' le cuer mis.* LANDINI: *Nessun ponga speranza; Giunta vaga bilta.* REYNEAU: *Va t'en mon cuer, avent mes yeux.* MATHEUS DE SANCTO JOHANNE: *Fortune, faulce, parverse.* DE INSULA:

Amours n'ont cure le tristesse. BROLLO: *Qui le sien vuelt bien maintenir.* ANON.: *N'a pas long temps que trouvay Zephirus; Je la remire, la belle*
*** Hyp. CDA 66144

In 1986 the Gothic Voices began what was to become a large-scale survey of medieval music, secular and sacred – for the two are inevitably intermingled. From the beginning the project was an adventure in exploration, as much for the artists as for the listener, for comparatively little is known about how this music sounded on voices of the time.

The songs of the troubadours or trouvères – outside the church – sometimes drew on ecclesiastical chant, but other such chansons had a modal character of their own. They were essentially monophonic – i.e. a single line of music, perhaps with an instrumental accompaniment – but the rhythmic patterns were unrecorded and, like much else in this repertoire, are inevitably conjectural in modern re-creative performance.

Much of the repertoire on this first disc (and indeed elsewhere) is unfamiliar, with Du Fay the only famous name; but everything here is of interest, and the listener inexperienced in medieval music will be surprised at the strength of its character. The performances are naturally eloquent and, although the range of colour is limited compared with later writing, it still has immediacy of appeal, especially if taken in short bursts. The recording balance is faultless and the sound first rate. With complete security of intonation and a chamber-music vocal blend, the presentation is wholly admirable. There is full back-up documentation.

'*The Castle of Fair Welcome*' (courtly songs of the late 15th century, with Wilson, lute): ANON.: *Las je ne puis; En amours n'a si non bien; Mi ut ne ut.* MORTON: *Le Souvenir de vous me tue; Que pourroit plus; Plus j'ay le monde regardé.* REGIS: *Puisque ma dame.* BEDYNGHAM: *Myn hertis lust.* BINCHOIS: *Deuil angoisseux.* VINCENET: *La pena sin ser sabida.* FRYE: *So ys emprinted.* ENRIQUE: *Pues servicio vos desplaze.* CHARLES THE BOLD: *Ma dame, trop vous mesprenés.* DU FAY: *Ne je ne dors*
(BB) *** Hyp. Helios CDH 55274

Christopher Page has by now established a basic procedure for his presentation of this early vocal repertoire: he has decided that it will be unaccompanied and usually performed by a modest-sized vocal group. So, in the present collection, further variety is provided with four instrumental pieces (played on harp and lute). Not surprisingly, the two most striking works here are by Du Fay (remarkably compelling) and Binchois; but the programme overall has been carefully chosen and it is given a boldly spontaneous presentation which cannot but intrigue the ear. As always, the recording is first class and this important series is now being reissued on Hyperion's bargain Helios label with full documentation still included.

'*The Service of Venus and Mars*': DE VITRY: *Gratissima virginis; Vos quie admiramini; Gaude gloriosa; Contratenor.* DES MOLINS: *De ce que fol pense.* PYCARD: *Gloria.* POWER: *Sanctus.* LEBERTOUL: *Las, que me demanderoye.* PYRAMOUR: *Quam pulchra es.* DUNSTABLE: *Speciosa facta es.* SOURSBY: *Sanctus.* LOQUEVILLE: *Je vous pri que j'aye un baysier.* ANON.: *Singularis laudis digna; De ce fol, pense; Lullay, Lullay; There is no Rose; Le gay playsir; Le grant pleyser; Agincourt Carol*
(BB) *** Hyp. Helios CDH 55290

The subtitle of this collection is 'Music for the Knights of the Garter, 1340–1440'; few readers will recognize many of the names in the list of composers above. But the music itself is fascinating and the performances bring it to life with extraordinary projection and vitality. The recording too is first class, and this imaginatively chosen programme deservedly won the 1988 *Gramophone* award for Early Music. Readers interested in trying medieval repertoire could hardly do better than to start here.

'*A Song for Francesca*': ANDREAS DE FLORENTINA: *Astio non mori mai. Per la ver'onesta.* JOHANNES DE FLORENTINA: *Quando la stella.* LANDINI: *Ochi dolenti mie. Per seguir la speranca.* ANON.: *Quando i oselli canta; Constantia; Amor mi fa cantar a la Francesca; Non na el so amante.* DU FAY: *Quel fronte signorille in paradiso.* RICHARD DE LOQUEVILLE: *Puisquie je suy amoureux; Pour mesdisans ne pour leur faulx parler; Qui ne veroit que vos deulx yeulx.* HUGO DE LATINS: *Plaindre m'estuet.* HAUCOURT: *Je demande ma bienvenue.* GROSSIN: *Va t'ent souspir.* ANON.: *O regina seculi; Reparatrix Maria; Confort d'amours*

(BB) *** Hyp. Helios CDH 55291

The title *A Song for Francesca* refers not only to the fourteenth-century French items here, but to the fact that the Italians too tended to be influenced by French style. More specifically, the collection is a well-deserved tribute to Francesca MacManus, selfless worker on behalf of many musicians, not least as manager of Gothic Voices. The variety of expression and mood in these songs, ballatas and madrigals is astonishing, some of them amazingly complex. The Hyperion recording is a model of its kind, presenting this long-neglected music most seductively in a warm but clear setting.

'*Music for the Lion-hearted King*' (music to mark the 800th anniversary of the coronation of Richard I): ANON.: *Mundus vergens; Noves miles sequitur; Anglia planctus itera; In occasu sideris.* BRULE: *A la douçour de la bele saison; Etas auri reditu; Pange melos lacrimosum; Vetus abit littera; Hac in anni ianua.* LI CHASTELAIN DE COUCI: *Li nouviauz tanz; Soi sub nube latuit.* BLONDEL DE NESLE: *L'Amours dont sui espris; Ma joie me semont; Purgator criminum; Ver pacis apperit; Latex silice*

(BB) *** Hyp. Helios CDH 55292

Partly because of the intensity, partly because of the imaginative variety of the choral response, all this twelfth-century music communicates readily, even though its comparatively primitive style could easily lead to boredom. The performances are polished but vital, and there is excellent documentation to lead the listener on. This may be a specialist record, but it could hardly be better presented.

'*The Marriage of Heaven & Hell*' (anonymous motets, songs and polyphony from 13th-century France). Also: BLONDEL DE NESLE: *En tous tans que vente bise.* MUSET: *Trop volontiers chanteroie.* BERNART DE VENTADORN: *Can vei la lauzeta mover.* GAUTIER DE DARGIES: *Autre que je laureta mover*

(BB) *** Hyp. Helios CDH 55273

The title of this collection dramatically overstates the problem of the medieval Church with its conflicting secular influences. Music was universal and the repertoire of the trouvère had a considerable melodic influence on the polyphonic motets used by the Church, though actual quotation

was very rare. Nevertheless, on occasion, vulgar associations in a vocal line could ensue and the clergy tore their hair. It all eventually led to the Council of Trent when, the story goes, the purity of Palestrina's contrapuntal serenity saved the day. Certainly medieval church music was robust and full of character, but here one is also struck by its complexity and intensity. The performances have a remarkable feeling of authenticity, and the background is admirably documented.

'*The Medieval Romantics*' (French songs and motets, 1340–1440): ANON.: *Quiconques veut; Je languis d'amere mort; Quant voi le douz tanz; Plus bele que flors; Degentis vita; Mais qu'il vous viegne.* SOLAGE: *Joieux de cuer.* DE PORTA: *Alma polis religio.* MACHAUT: *C'est force; Tant doucement; Comment qu'a moy lonteinne.* TENORISTA: *Sofrir m'estuet.* SENLECHES: *En ce gracieux temps.* DU FAY: *Je requier a tous; Las, que feray.* VELUT: *Je voel servir.* LYMBURGIA: *Tota pulchra es*

(BB) *** Hyp. Helios CDH 55293

Machaut (fourteenth century) and Du Fay (fifteenth) are names which have now become individually established. Du Fay was master of the secular song-form called the virelai (opening with a refrain, which then followed each verse) and Machaut was one of the first (if not *the* first) composers to set the Ordinary of the Mass; he too wrote chansons and virelais. But of course there is also much music here by other (unknown) composers and our old friend, Anon. The virelais are sung unaccompanied. Sometimes there are vocal melismas (extra parts without words) set against the textual line. So this collection represents the medieval blossoming of songs and part-songs alongside the motets, for secular and sacred never really grew apart. As usual, the Gothic Voices perform this repertoire with skill and confidence and lots of character, and the splendid documentation puts the listener fully in the historical picture.

'*Lancaster and Valois*' (French and English music, 1350–1420): MACHAUT: *Donnez, signeurs; Quand je ne voy; Riches d'amour; Pas de tor en thies pais.* SOLAGE: *Tres gentil cuer.* PYCARD: *Credo.* STURGEON: *Salve mater domini.* FONTEYNS: *Regail ex progenie.* CESARIS: *Mon seul voloir; Se vous scaviez, ma tres douce maistresse.* BAUDE CORDIER: *Ce jour de l'an.* ANON.: *Sanctus; Soit tart, tempre, main ou soir; Je vueil vivre au plaisir d'amours; Puis qu'autrement ne puis avoir; Le Ior; Avrai je ja de ma dame confort?*

(BB) *** Hyp. Helios CDH 55294

This stimulating series has always been essentially experimental, for we do not know just how unaccompanied medieval voices were balanced or how many were used. In the documentation with this record Christopher Page suggests that on this disc he feels he has the internal balance just about right, and the vocal mix varies, sometimes led by a female voice, sometimes by a male. More Machaut here, some slightly later French settings, and the usual balance between sacred and secular. Everything sounds vital and alive.

'*The Study of Love*' (French songs and motets of the 14th century): ANON.: *Pour vous servir; Puis que l'aloe ne fine; Jour a jour la vie; Combien que j'aye; Marticius qui fu; Renouveler me feist; Fist on dame; Il me convient guerpir; Le ior; En la maison Dedalus; Combien que j'aye; Le Grant biauté; En esperant; Ay las! quant je pans.* MACHAUT:

Dame, je suis cilz – Fin cuers; Trop plus – Biauté paree – Je ne suis; Tres bonne et belle; Se mesdisans; Dame, je vueil endurer. SOLAGE: *Le Basile.* PYCARD: *Gloria*

(BB) *** Hyp. Helios CDH 55295

The Gothic Voices' exploration is moving sideways rather than forward, for Machaut is still with us. The present collection of settings demonstrates the medieval literary and poetic understanding of 'love' – romantic and spiritual. The anonymous examples are often as stimulating as any of the songs and motets here by named composers, and the Pycard *Gloria* is obviously included to remind us again that church music is about the love of God. This and the previous three CDs should be approached with some caution, starting perhaps with *The Medieval Romantics.*

'*The Voice in the Garden*' (Spanish songs and motets, 1480–1530): JUAN DEL ENCINA: *Mi libertad; Los sospiros no sosiegan; Triste España sin ventura.* LUIS DE NARVAEZ: *Fantasias; (after) Paseávase el rey Moro.* FRANCISCO DE PENALOSA: *Precor te, Domine; Ne reminiscaris, Domine; Por las sierras de Madrid; Sancta Maria.* JULIUS DE MODENA: *Tiento.* PALERO: (after) *Paseávase el rey Moro.* ENRIQUE: *Mi querer tanto vos quiere.* LUIS MILAN: *Fantasias 10; 12; 18.* GABRIEL: *La Bella Malmaridada; Yo creo que n'os dió Dios.* ANON.: *Dentro en el vergel; Harto de tanta porfia; Entra Mayo y sale Abril; Dindirin; Ave, Virgo, gratia plena; A la villa voy; Pasa el agoa*

(BB) *** Hyp. Helios CDH 55298

Here the Gothic Voices travel to Spain and take with them Christopher Wilson (vihuela) and Andrew-Lawrence King (harp). Their earlier concerts have included instrumental items, kept separate from the vocal music, and here the same policy is followed, but the mix of sacred, secular and instrumental is more exotic than usual. As throughout this series, the recording is of the highest quality.

'*The Spirits of England and France*' (music of the Middle Ages for court and church, with Beznosiuk, medieval fiddle): ANON.: *La Uitime estampie real; La Quarte estampie real; La Septime estampie real; Credo; Virelais; Songs; Conducti; Conductus motets.* MATTEO DA PERUGIA: *Belle sans per.* MACHAUT: *Ay mi! dame de valour.* PYKINI: *Plaissance, or tost.* PEROTINUS: *Presul nostri temporis.* ANON.: *Ave Maria*

(BB) *** Hyp. Helios CDH 55281

This is the first of a series of CDs covering French and English music between the twelfth and fifteenth centuries. The first half of the present collection explores the sonorities of three- and four-part writing during the last decades of the fourteenth century and the first decades of the fifteenth. The second group goes back in time to anonymous settings from the twelfth and thirteenth centuries, although including one memorable piece possibly written by Perotinus. Although the items by Machaut (monodic) and Pykini (in four parts) are particularly striking, 'Anonymous' does not mean that the music is not full of character and individuality, and the closing *Ave Maria*, with its series of triads, is as beautiful as many later settings. Pavlo Beznosiuk provides three instrumental interludes, a series of *Estampie*, winningly played on a medieval fiddle. The recording is excellent.

'*The Spirits of England and France*' (songs of the trouvères, with Kirkby, Philpot, Covey-Crump, Nixon, Wickham, Instrumental Ens.): RICHART DE SEMILLI: *Je chevauchai.*

BRULE: *Desconfortez plais de dolor; Quant define feuille et flor; De bien amer grant joie atent; Cil qui d'amours;* ANON.: *Estampie 1–3; Donna pos vos ay chausida; Quant voi la fleur nouvelle; Amors m'art con fuoc am flama.* GONTIER DE SOIGNES: *Dolerousement commence.* KAUKESEL: *Un Chant novel; Fins cuers enamourés.* GAUTIER DE DARGIES: *La Doce pensee.* ADAM DE LA HALLE: *Assénes chi, Grievilier.* ERNOUS LI VIELLE: *Por conforter mon corage.* AUDEFROI: *Au novel tens pascor*

(BB) *** Hyp. Helios CDH 55282

The songs of the troubadours were inevitably monophonic, usually offering an expressive and touching melisma, lightly ornamented. To quote Christopher Page's excellent notes: 'their supreme genre was the *grand chant*, a protracted meditation upon the fortunes of loving.' One of the key composers in this style was Gace Brulé, and examples such as *Desconfortez plais de dolor, Quant define feuille et flor* and *De bien amer grant joie atent* convey an almost desperate melancholy. However, not all is despair: the opening *Je chevauchai* ('I Rode out the Other Morning'), with its repeated refrain, is as spirited as it is optimistic – and rightly so, for the amorous singer has his way with the shepherdess he encounters by chance in the wood.

Ernous Li Vielle's *Por conforter mon corage* has a similar theme, only this time the seduction is more forceful. In contrast Wibers Kaukesel's *Fins cuers enamourés* ennobles the theme of love and being loved, while finally Audefroi tells of a husband who, after his wife Argentine, has borne him six sons, tires of her and takes a concubine, banishing her when she objects. The ingenuous moral of the tale is repeated after each verse: 'Whoever is wed to a bad husband often has a sad heart.' The singing and presentation here are admirable, and there are instrumental *Estampie* to provide interludes. A fascinating collection.

'*The Spirits of England and France*' (Binchois and his contemporaries, with Rumsey, Wilson, Page, lute): BINCHOIS: *Qui veut mesdire; Amoreux suy; Adieu mon amoreuse joye; Ay! douloureux; Magnificat secundi toni; Se la belle.* CARDOT: *Pour une fois.* VELUT: *Un Petit Oyselet; Laissiés ester.* ANON.: *Abide, I Hope; Exultavit cor in Domino.* LE GRANT: *Se liesse.* DE LYMBURGIA: *Descendi in ortum meum.* POWER: *Gloria.* DUNSTABLE: *Beata Dei genitrix.* FONTAINE: *J'ayme bien celui.* MACHAUT: *Il m'est avis.* BITTERING: *En Katerina solennia*

(BB) *** Hyp. Helios CDH 55283

Christopher Page and his group have been exploring early English and French repertoire in a number of earlier Hyperion anthologies. Here they turn to the early decades of the fifteenth century and to the music of Binchois (who died in 1460) and his contemporaries. Binchois is represented by a series of medieval love songs, all in three parts, very word-sensitive, even poignant in feeling, climaxed by the remarkably expressive *Ay! douloureux*, the most expansive and the most memorable. Then we turn to religious music and, besides a fine Binchois *Magnificat*, there is also Power's eloquent *Gloria* in five voices and fine examples of the music of Dunstable and even of Machaut. It is a heady mix, and it is the contrast here that makes this finely sung and recorded collection so stimulating.

'*The Spirits of England and France*' (with Rumsey, Wilson, Page, lute): ANON.: *The Missa Caput:* (an English Mass setting from *c.* 1440 interspersed with the story of *the Salve Regina*). Carols: *Jesu for Thy Mercy; Jesu fili Dei; Make us*

Merry; Nowell, Nowell, Nowell; Clangat tuba; Alma redemptoris mater; Agnus Dei (Old Hall Manuscript)
(BB) *** Hyp. Helios CDH 55284

The inclusion here of the anonymous English *Missa Caput* gives a special interest to this collection. Composed around 1440, it survived in seven different manuscripts, and it is credited with having had a strong influence on the Masses of Ockeghem. The quality of the music is sure – it has long been attributed to Du Fay. Indeed, it is a remarkable and powerful setting, well worth discovering, and it is given added impact by the urgency of Christopher Page's direction.

The performance intersperses the Mass Propers with verses from a recently discovered Latin song narrating the origins of the Marian antiphon *Salve Regina*, with a view to alternating monody and polyphony, and this works remarkably well. The rest of the concert, a collection of early carols, makes an attractively lightweight pendant to the major work. The Gothic Voices sing with great eloquence throughout this 66-minute programme, and this is one of their most attractively conceived collections. The recording, as ever with this series, is first class.

'*The Spirits of England and France*': ANON.: *Missa Veterum hominem; Jesu, fili Virginis; Doleo super te; Gaude Maria virgo; Deus creator omnium; Jesu salvator; A solis ortuas; Salvator mundi; Christe, Qui lux es; To many a well; Sancta Maria virgo; Mater ora filium; Ave maris stella; Pange lingua.* DUNSTABLE: *Beata mater*
(BB) *** Hyp. Helios CDH 55285

The *Missa Veterum hominem* might be considered as complementary to the *Missa Caput*, offered on the previous CD from the Gothic Voices, and the present compilation is equally successful. Both Masses were composed at about the same time, in the late 1440s; both were written for four voices. Once again, in performing this work (with comparable urgency) Christopher Page seeks to vary the vocal texture by opening with an early, three-part carol, *Jesu, fili Virginis*, and alternating the Mass polyphony with monodic plainchant hymns. There are three of these, the last of which, *Deus creator omnium*, uses the same liturgical text as is employed in the Kyrie of the Mass.

'*Jerusalem: the Vision of Peace*' ANON.: *Luto carens et latere; Jerusalem! grant damage me fais; Te Deum; O levis aurula!; Hac in die Gedeonis; In Salvatoris; Veri vitis germine.* GUIOT DE DIJON: *Chanterau pour mon corage.* Easter Day Mass in the Church of Holy Sepulchre, Jerusalem (*c.* 1130): *Gradual; Alleluia; Gospel.* HUON DE ST QUENTIN: *Jerusalem se plaint et li pais; Luget Rachel iterum; Incocantes Dominum/Psalm: Deus, qui venerunt; Congaudet hodie celestis curia.* HILDEGARD OF BINGEN: *O Jerusalem*
*** Hyp. CDA 67039

'Jerusalem: the Vision of Peace' was the underlying ideal which motivated the crusades, as medieval pilgrims believed that such an armed expedition, with papal blessing – killing Saracens on the way – would lead to universal peace and harmony! Anti-Semitism was another factor in the crusading spirit, expressing Christian anger and contempt for the Jews' denial of Christ. *Veri vitis germine* calls strongly on Judaea to return to the Cross.

On a personal level was the tragedy of separation for women whose lovers and husbands had departed for the Holy Land, perhaps never to return. All these elements are reflected in the present diverse anthology, from the opening three-part song of confidence in the power of God, to Hildegard's rhapsodic closing monody, an ecstatic eulogy of longing for Jerusalem and all it represented. The melancholy of a deserted woman's loss is lamented in *Jerusalem! grant damage me fais*, while the *Te Deum*, heard against tolling bells, and the excerpts from the Easter Day Mass represent the liturgy of the period. Harmony, where it occurs, is organum and has great character, and certainly all the music here has great vitality, and is splendidly sung.

'*Master of the Rolls*' (music by English composers of the 14th century, with King, Harrold, Podger, Nixon, Daniels, Charlesworth): ANON.: *Ab ora summa nuncius; Inter usitata/Inter tot et tales; Vexilla regni prodeunt; Singularis laudis digna; Dulcia [dona redemptoris]; Summum regen honoremus; Omnis terra/Habenti dabitur; Copiose caritatis; Missa Gabriel de celis; Pura, placens/Parfundement plure; Letetur celi cura; Salve Regina; Jesu fili Virginis* (Plainsong); *Jesu fili/Jesu lumen; Jesu fili Virginis; Sospitati dat egrotos; Exultemus et letemur; Stella maris illustrans omnia; Veni dilectus meus; Pange lingua; O sponsa dei electa; Generosa Jesse plantula; Musicorum collegio/In templo dei*
*** Hyp. CDA 67098

Very few English composers of the fourteenth century are remembered by name. The word used to describe accomplished musicians of the period was magister (master): hence the title of this collection. Only six items here are monodic and what is remarkable is how individual are some of these compositions. *Singularis laudis digna*, for instance, with its whirls of parallel writing, or the simple but touching harmonization of the Marian *Dulcia [dona redemptoris]* and the lovely, lilting *Missa Gabriel de celis*, while *Jesus fili* (a trio) has some engaging rhythmic triplets. Perhaps the most remarkable, original and forward-looking of all is *Stella maris illustrans omnia*, where a highly unusual text is matched by a comparably unpredictable use of chromatics.

Graham, Susan (mezzo-soprano)

'*French Operetta*' (with CBSO, Abel). Arias from: SIMONS: *Toi c'est moi.* MESSAGER: *L'Amour masqué; Coups de roulis; Les Dragons de l'Impératrice; Fortunio; Passionnément; La Petite Fonctionnaire; Les P'tites Michu.* YVAIN: *Yes.* HONEGGER: *Les Aventures du roi Pausole.* HAHN: *Brummell; O mon bel inconnu; Ciboulette; Mozart*
*** Erato 0927 42106-2

In every way this is an enchanting disc, bringing together in sparkling performances a sequence of rare items which richly deserve revival. Messager's *Fortunio* has been rediscovered in recent years, largely thanks to the complete recording from Sir John Eliot Gardiner. Yet as the items here demonstrate, Messager, as well as conducting the first performance of Debussy's *Pelléas et Mélisande*, was in turn musical director of the Paris Opéra and Covent Garden, and also composed a sequence of other operettas. Reynaldo Hahn is also well-represented with charming items from four operettas, and it is good to be reminded that even Honegger made an unexpected foray into the genre. The Cuban composer Moises Simons has been even more neglected, yet his colourful Spanish-American items equally add to the joy of this frothy collection, idiomatically accompanied and well-recorded. The documentation of the actual arias on this CD leaves much to be desired, but the notes contain an excellent essay by Patrick O'Connor.

'Gramophone Greats'

'20 Gramophone All-time Greats' (original mono recordings from 1907 to 1935): LEONCAVALLO: *Pagliacci: Vesti la giubba* (Caruso); *Mattinata* (Gigli). BISHOP: *Lo Here the Gentle Lark* (Galli-Curci with flute obbligato by Beringuer). PURCELL: *Nymphs and Shepherds* (Manchester Schools Children's Ch. (Choir Mistress: Gertrude Riall), Hallé O, Harty). MENDELSSOHN: *Hear my Prayer – O for the Wings of a Dove* (Lough, Temple Church Ch., Thalben Ball). MARSHALL: *I Hear you Calling me* (McCormack). ELGAR: *Salut d'amour* (New SO, composer). J. STRAUSS JR: *Casanova: Nuns' Chorus* (Ch. & O of Grossen Schauspielhauses, Berlin, Hauke). RACHMANINOV: *Prelude in C sharp min., Op. 3/2* (composer). TRAD.: *Song of the Volga Boatmen* (Chaliapin). KREISLER: *Liebesfreud* (composer, Lamson). MOSS: *The Floral Dance* (Dawson, Moore). BACH: *Chorale: Jesu, joy of man's desiring* (arr. & played Hess). HANDEL: *Messiah: Come unto Him* (Labette, O, Beecham). SAINT-SAENS: *Samson and Delilah: Softly Awakes my Heart* (Anderson). BIZET: *Fair Maid of Perth: Serenade* (Nash). CHOPIN: *Waltz in C sharp min., Op. 64/2* (Cortot). LEHAR: *Land of Smiles: You are my Heart's Delight* (Tauber). KERN: *Showboat: Ol' Man River* (Robeson). SULLIVAN: *The Lost Chord* (Butt)
(M) (***) ASV mono CDAJA 5112

'Golden Years of the Gramophone': HANDEL: *Arrival of the Queen of Sheba* (LPO, Sir Thomas Beecham). MENDELSSOHN: *O for the Wings of a Dove* (Ernest Lough, Temple Church Ch.). CLARKE: *Trumpet Voluntary* (Alex Harris, Hallé O, Sir Hamilton Harty). GRECHANINOV: *The Creed* (Ch. of the Russian Metropolitan Church in Paris). BACH: *Jesu, joy of man's desiring* (Dame Myra Hess (piano)). BACH/GOUNOD: *Ave Maria* (Alessandro Moreschi, castrato). SULLIVAN: *The Lost Chord* (Peter Dawson). JOHANN STRAUSS JR: *Casanova: Nuns' Chorus* (Anni Frind, Berlin O, Hauke). LEHÁR: *Land of Smiles: You are my heart's delight* (Richard Tauber). CHARLES WILLIAMS: *Dream of Olwen* (Arthur Dulay, Concert O, composer). PURCELL: *Nymphs and Shepherds* (Manchester School Children's Ch., Hallé O, Harty). arr. MOSS: *The Floral Dance* (Peter Dawson). MORGAN: *Count your blessings* (Luton Girls' Ch., George Melachrino). WALFORD DAVIES: *Solemn Melody* (Hallé O, Harty). BRAHMS: *Wiegenlied* (Elisabeth Schumann). MUSSORGSKY: *Song of the Flea* (Feodor Shalyapin). WIDOR: *Organ Symphony 5: Toccata* (composer (organ)). ADAMS: *The Holy City* (Richard Crooks). MOZART: *Die Zauberflöte: Queen of the Night's Aria* (Florence Foster Jenkins). PUCCINI: *Gianni Schicchi: O my beloved father* (Dame Joan Hammond). KERN: *Ol' Man River* (Paul Robeson). OFFENBACH: *Geneviève de Brabant: Gendarmes' Duet* (Harold Williams & Malcolm McEachern). ROSSINI: *Cats' Duet* (Victoria de los Angeles & Elisabeth Schwarzkopf)
(B) (***) CfP mono 5 85911-2

It seems strange and somewhat sad that this marvellous collection of classical 78rpm hit records, covering a period of three decades, came from ASV rather than HMV (EMI), who are responsible for so many of the actual recordings. However, as we close for press EMI have made their own 'Classics for Pleasure' collection of 23 items duplicating only eight of the pieces here, and this is equally desirable. Their amazing technical excellence means that they can be enjoyed today as they were then, with only occasional clicks and generally not

too intrusive a background 'surface' noise to create the right ambience.

Caruso still projects vividly from a 1907 acoustic master and Amelita Galli-Curci's soprano is as clear and sweet as the day the recording was made (1919). Other highlights (for us) include the Manchester Schools Children's Choir of 250 voices, electrically recorded in Manchester's Free Trade Hall in 1929. The story goes that, just before the record was made, Sir Hamilton Harty bought cream buns and pop for every child, and that accounts for the warm smile in the singing. Master Ernest Lough's 'O for the Wings of a Dove' is another miracle of perfection from a young boy treble, and Peter Dawson's exuberant 'Floral Dance' has astonishing diction – you can hear every word – and here Gerald Moore's bravura accompaniment is a key part of the sheer pleasure this performance still gives.

Finally, Dame Clara Butt with her deep masculine contralto, clanging like a bell in its lowest register, delivers the sacred piece so beloved of Victorians, Sullivan's 'The Lost Chord'. The transfers are all good (except perhaps for Dame Myra Hess's *Jesu, joy of man's desiring*, where the background noise surely could have been cut back a bit more).

The HMV collection includes many classic items, featuring artists all but unknown now (for instance the castrato, Alessandro Moreschi) but, like the ASV programme, everything has a nostalgic value, rather like old picture postcards. Items like Beecham's début performance of the *Arrival of the Queen of Sheba* (which arrived as a filler on a record on Rossini's *La scala di seta Overture*) and the pair of Duets – Cats and Gendarmes – are far more than that. A fascinating alternative collection.

Gray, Emily (soprano), Manchester Cathedral Choir, Christopher Stokes

'Passiontide' (with Buckley, Makinson): MENDELSSOHN: *Hear my Prayer*. VAUGHAN WILLIAMS: *O Taste and See*. HURFORD: *Litany to the Holy Spirit*. WESLEY: *Wash me Throughly*. PERGOLESI: *Stabat Mater*. BYRD: *Civitas sancti tui*. BACH: *O Sacred Head Sore Wounded; Bist du bei mir*. CASALS: *O vos omnes*. LOTTI: *Crucifixus*. DERING: *O bone Jesu*. GIBBONS: *Drop, Drop, Slow Tears*. IRELAND: *Ex ore innocentiam*. GREENE: *Lord Let me Know mine End*. MILLER: *When I Survey the Wondrous Cross*
(BB) *** Naxos 8.557025

In this wide-ranging collection the 15-year-old Emily Gray (who won BBC Radio 2's 'Choirgirl of the Year' in 2000) produced the firm traditional sound of the Anglican choirboy, slightly hooty, seemingly all the more powerful from a female throat, using her voice with care and taste. The sequence starts with the longest item, the one associated with Master Ernest Lough and his 1927 recording with the Temple Church Choir, Mendelssohn's 'Hear my Prayer', here more sharply dramatic under Christopher Stokes' direction, sweet and pure in the concluding section, 'O for the Wings of a Dove'. The other major item brings together four sections of Pergolesi's *Stabat Mater* in which Gray is joined by another young soprano, Claire Buckley, similar in style but nicely contrasted. The choir is first-rate too in that item, and generally they sing with fresh, clear tone and crisp ensemble, very well-recorded in Manchester Cathedral. Only in the Byrd Latin setting, *Civitas sancti tui*, does it rather lack variety. Rounding off the sequence comes Maurice Greene's weighty psalm-setting, 'Lord, Let me Know mine End'. The traditional congregational hymn, 'When I Survey the Wondrous Cross', to the tune *Rockingham,* then provides a rousing conclusion at a rich fortissimo.

Gueden, Hilde (soprano)

'Operetta Evergreens' (with Vienna Operetta Chorus & Vienna State Op. O, Stolz): Arias from: KALMAN: *Gräfin Mariza.* BENATZKY/STOLZ: *The White Horse Inn.* LEHAR: *Der Zarewitsch; Zigeunerliebe.* FALL: *Madame Pompadour.* JOHANN STAUSS JR : *Casanova; Die Fledermaus; Wiener Blut.* STOLZ: *Der Favorit.* ZELLER: *Der Obersteiger.* OSCAR STRAUS: *The Chocolate Soldier*
(M) *** Decca Classic Recitals (ADD) 475 394-2

Hilde Gueden's many delightful gramophone contributions to operetta tended latterly to rest in the shadow of Elisabeth Schwarzkopf, who brought a Lieder-like skill with words even to relatively banal lyrics. Gueden's approach was more direct, but she had this repertoire in her very being, a lilting feel for a Viennese melodic line and a natural stage presence, and this comes over on her recordings too. Her voice was heard at her freshest in an earlier mono recital, which we praised in our last *Yearbook* (Belart 461 623-2) and which is now deleted.

The present recital was recorded in 1961, and the voice shows some loss of bloom. Nevertheless there is plenty to delight here, from the lively opening aria from Kálmán's *Gräfin Mariza* to the very famous numbers from *The Chocolate Soldier* and *Die Fledermaus* – released many times on operetta compilations. The collection ends with *Wiener Blut* and leaves one with a deliciously warm Viennese glow. The splendidly alive and colloquial accompaniments under Robert Stoltz add much to this CD, and the whole programme emerges vividly on this Classic Recitals release. The original front cover of Miss Gueden and her pet dog is charmingly in period, even if the dog looks uncomfortable.

Gunn, Nathan (baritone), Kevin Murphy (piano)

'American Anthem: From Ragtime to Art Song': TRAD.: *Shenandoah.* GORNEY: *Brother can you Spare a Dime.* ROREM: *Early in the Morning; The Lordly Hudson.* SCHEER: *At Howard Hawks' House; Holding Each Other; Lean Away; American Anthem.* NILES: *The Lass from the Low Countree; I Wonder as I Wander.* MUSTO: *Recuerdo.* BARBER: *Nocturne; Sure on this Shining Night.* BOLCOM: *Fur (Murray the Furrier); Over the Piano; Black Max (As Told by the De Kooning Boys).* IVES: *Slugging a Vampire; Two Little Flowers (and dedicated to them); General William Booth Enters into Heaven.* HOIBY: *The Lamb.* arr. COPLAND: *At the River; Long Time Ago*
(B) *** EMI Début 5 73160-2

The subtitle, 'From Ragtime to Art Song', sums up the breadth of this delightful collection, the imaginative choice of Nathan Gunn – as he describes it himself, 'a beautiful forest of songs'. Gunn is one of the most promising of young American singers, possessor of a glorious baritone of a velvety beauty, consistent throughout its range. If anyone is disconcerted to have 'Brother can you Spare a Dime' early on the list, it leads brilliantly to the most eclectic sequence, a reflection of Gunn's keen perception as well as of his musicianship. How welcome to have the work of such composers

as Gene Scheer and William Bolcom well represented, alongside such predictable names as Charles Ives, Aaron Copland and Samuel Barber. The title, *American Anthem,* comes from the last song on the CD, a surging expression of patriotism worthy of an American 'Last Night of the Proms'. Sensitive accompaniment and well-balanced recording.

Hagegård, Håkan (baritone)

'Dedication' (with Schuback, piano): BRAHMS: *An die Nachtigall; An ein Veilchen; An die Mond.* FOERSTER: *An die Laute.* GOUNOD: *A toi mon coeur.* HAHN: *A Chloris.* MOZART: *An Chloë, K.524; Ich würd' auf meinem Pfad (An die Hoffnung), K.390.* SCHUBERT: *An Mignon; An den Tod; An den Mond; An den Leier; An die Musik; Am mein Herz.* R. STRAUSS: *Zueignung.* WOLF: *An eine Aeolsharfe*
**(*) BIS (ADD) CD 54

This recital is called *Dedication,* and it begins with the Strauss song of that name. The collection first appeared in LP form in 1976 but was in circulation only intermittently in this country. The record was made at the outset of the distinguished Swedish baritone's career when he was in his mid-twenties and in wonderfully fresh voice. He sounds very much like a youthful Fischer-Dieskau but is at times a trace too studied, colouring the voice rather too expressively and adopting rather self-consciously deliberate tempi. There are times when one longs for him to be a little more unbuttoned. However, there is far more to admire and relish than to criticize, in particular the gloriously fresh vocal tone, and the sensitive playing of Thomas Schuback. Admirers of Hagegård will probably have this on LP; others need not hesitate.

Hampson, Thomas (baritone)

'Leading Man (Best of Broadway)': KERN: *All the Things you are.* KRETZMER: *Les Misérables: Bring him Home.* LLOYD WEBBER: *Phantom of the Opera: Music of the Night.* RODGERS: *Carousel: Soliloquy.* LOEWE: *Gigi; Camelot: If Ever I would Leave You.* ADLER: *The Pajama Game: Hey There.* SONDHEIM: *Unusual Way; Not a Day Goes by.* NORMAN: *The Secret Garden: How could I Ever Know?* MENKEN: *Beauty and the Beast: If I can't Love he*
*** EMI 5 55249-2

Starting with a classic number by Jerome Kern, 'All the Things you are', Hampson's Broadway selection ranges on up to *The Phantom of the Opera* and *Les Misérables,* where atmosphere and evocation seem to weigh more heavily than good tunes. The *Soliloquy* from *Carousel* – one of the few numbers from that great musical without a big tune – here can be seen to point forward, but one number (among the most recent here, dating from 1991) unashamedly returns to older standards of tunefulness, 'How could I Ever Know?' from *The Secret Garden* by Marsha Norman and Lucy Simon. Hampson with his rich, dark voice seems totally at home in each number, finding no problems in adapting to this idiom, switching easily and aptly to half-speech in such a patter-number as the title-song from *Gigi.* Paul Gemignani conducts what is called the American Theater Orchestra, though you have to look through the small print to learn that information. Full, immediate recording.

Disc 1: *Mélodies and Lieder* (with Parsons, piano): BERLIOZ: *Irlande, Op. 2: La Belle Voyageuse; Adieu, Bessy!; Le Coucher* du soleil; L'Origine de la harpe; Elégie. WAGNER: Lieder: Mignonne; Tout n'est qu'imagines fugitives; Les Deux Grenadiers; 2 Lied des Mephistopheles: Es war einmal ein König; Was machst du mir; Der Tannenbaum. LISZT: Die Vätergruft; Go Not, Happy Day; Es rauschen die Winde; Ihr Auge; Uber alln Gipfein ist Ruh (Wanderers Nachtlied); Im Rhein, im schönen Strome; Es muss ein Wunderbares sein; Vergiftet sind meine Lieder; La Tombe et la rose; 'Comment', disaient-ils; Oh, quand je dors

Disc 2: Edinburgh Festival Recital, 20–21 August 1993: FRANZ: Nun holt mir eine Kanne Wein; Ihr Auge; Die süisse Dirn' von Inverness. LOEWE: Findlay. SCHUMANN: Niemand; Dem roten Röslein gleicht mein Lieb; Hochländers Abscheid; Dichterliebe (song-cycle), Op. 48. GRIEG: Gruss; Dereinst; Lauf der Welt; Die verschwiegene Nachtigall; Zur Rosenzeit; Ein Traum. BEETHOVEN: An die ferne Geliebte (song-cycle), Op. 98

(B) *** EMI double fforte 5 75187-2 (2)

This EMI double fforte reissue joins together two quite different recitals, the second recorded live in the Usher Hall at the 1993 Edinburgh Festival. This includes as an engaging novelty – so appropriate for the occasion – settings of Robert Burns in German translation, including attractive items by the little-known Robert Franz. The six rare German-language songs by Grieg are a comparable success, as is the freshly spontaneous account of Beethoven's cycle, An die ferne Geliebte. However, what should be the highlight but proves a considerable disappointment is Schumann's Dichterliebe, which, with curiously measured tempi, refuses to spring to life and lacks both ironic subtlety and real depth of feeling.

Never mind, the companion collection is a different matter and received a ✪ on its first premium-priced appearance (with full texts). Hampson begins with glowing performances of five of the nine songs from Berlioz's Irlande, using translations from English texts by the poet Thomas Moore. The Liszt collection is equally magnetic, ending with a memorable performance of his setting of Victor Hugo, Oh, quand je dors, and the Wagner songs are equally winning, showing him unexpectedly and light-heartedly setting French love-songs. Hampson is in superb voice and at his most imaginative, while throughout both CDs Geoffrey Parson is the ideal accompanist, and the recording cannot be faulted. The only snag, and it is a serious one, is the absence of texts and translations.

Hemsley, Thomas (baritone)

Mélodies (with Hamburger or (i) Gürtler, piano): DUPARC: Chanson triste; Elégie; Extase; L'Invitation au voyage, Lamento; Le Manoir de Rosemonde; Phidylé; La Vie antérieure. FAURE: 5 Verlaine Songs, Op. 58; L'Horizon chimérique, Op. 118. (i) ROUSSEL: Odes anacréontique, Op. 31 & Op. 32

*** Amphion PHI CD 166

Although he was represented in the days of LP in operatic repertoire, Thomas Hemsley enjoyed scant exposure in Lieder or mélodie. BBC listeners will, of course, recall his broadcasts, some of which are found here. He proves as masterly an interpreter of French song as he is of Schubert and Wolf. The Roussel Odes anacréontiques are not otherwise available on disc and, apart from their artistic merits, sound excellent in these 1978 BBC recordings. The Fauré and Duparc come from 1973 with Paul Hamburger as

pianist and are no less fine. Why has the BBC label not issued them?

Hespèrion XX

'Llibre Vermell de Monserrat' (A fourteenth-century pilgrimage): O Virgo splendens; Stella splendens in monte; Laudemus Virginem Mater est; Los set goyts recomptarem; Splendens ceptigera; Polorum regina omnium nostra; Cincti simus concanentes: Ave Maria; Mariam Matrem Virginem; Imperayritz de la ciutat joyosa; Ad mortem festinamus; O Virgo splendens hic in monte celso

(M) *** Virgin 5 61174-2

In the Middle Ages the Spanish monastery of Monserrat was an important place of pilgrimage and, although a great deal of the music held in the library there was lost in a fire at the beginning of the nineteenth century, one early manuscript, the Llibre Vermell (Red Book), has survived to remind us of the music of that period. It dates from 1400 and is especially fascinating in including ten anonymous choral songs for the use of the pilgrims 'while holding night vigil' who may 'sometimes desire to sing and dance in the Church Square (where only respectable and pious songs may be sung)'.

The music is extraordinarily jolly and robust, often written in the style of the French virelais (featuring alternating musical lines, with the first framing a central repeated tune). Canonic devices are also used and the effect is often quite sophisticated. There is no better example of this spirited music than Los set goyts, an infectious round dance complete with refrain. Various instrumental groupings add lively colour and support to the vocal line; the performances are full of joy, though at times emotionally respectful too. The analogue recording was made in France, but the resonant acoustic seems perfectly judged. This is a life-enhancing collection to cheer one up, and it shows that life in the Middle Ages was not always grim.

Hilliard Ensemble

'English and Italian Renaissance Madrigals':

English madrigals: MORLEY: O Griefe Even on the Bud; When Loe, by Breake of Morning; Aprill is in my Mistris Face; Sweet Nimphe, Come to thy Lover; Miraculous Love's Wounding; Fyer and Lightning in Nets of Goulden Wyers. WEELKES: Thule, the Period of Cosmographie; O Care Thou wilt Dispatch mee; Since Robin Hood; Strike it up Tabor. WILBYE: Sweet Hony Sucking Bees; Adew Sweet Amarillis; Draw in Sweet Night. J. BENNET: Weepe O mine Eyes. GIBBONS: The silver Swanne. TOMKINS: See, See the Shepherd's Queene. WARD: Come Sable Night. VAUTOR: Sweet Suffolk Owle

Italian madrigals: GASTOLDI: Cantiam lieti cantiamo. CAPRIOLI: E d'un bel matin d'amore; Quella bella e biancha mano; Una leggiadra nimpha. COMPERE: Venite amanti insieme. VERDALOT: Divini occhi sereni; Con l'angelico riso; Madonna, il tuo bel viso; Fuggi, fuggi, cor mio; Si liet'e grata morte. ARCADELT: Se la dura durezza; Ahimé, dové, bel viso; Madonna, s'io v'offendo; Il bianco e dolce cigno. PATAVINO: Donne, venete al ballo. CASUALANA: Morir non pué il mio cuore. MARENZIO: Se la mia vita. RORE: Mia benigna fortuna; Ancor che col partire; O sonno. NOLA: Chi la

gagliarda; Medici noi siamo; Tre ciechi siamo. WILLAERT: *Madonna mia fa.* BELL'HAVER: *Quando saré mai quel zorno.* LASSUS: *Matona, mia cara*
(BB) *** Virgin Veritas 2x1 5 61671-2 (2)

The first of these two discs is of English madrigals and was recorded in 1987. It is an enchanting disc; and, as might be guessed from the above spelling, Tudor pronunciation is used, which adds extra bite to the vocal timbre. Intonation and ensemble are flawless, and some of the songs are in five or six parts. If one feels that they could be a shade more unbuttoned at times and they do not always reflect the lighter moments with quite enough sparkle, there is so much here to beguile the ear that few will grumble. The Italian madrigals were recorded in 1991 and are hardly less enjoyable. Indeed, this second collection is is perhaps even more beautiful, and the programme is as rich and varied as in the English collection. A pity that there are no texts or translations and little about the music, but at super-bargain price one only expects such extras from Naxos and Helios.

'A Hilliard Songbook': New music for voices: GUY: *Un Coup de dès.* FELDMAN: *Only.* MOODY: *Endechas y Canciones; Canticum Canticorum I.* HELLAWELL: *True Beautie* (cycle of 8 songs). ROBINSON: *Incantation.* TORMIS: *Kullervo's Message.* ANON.: *Adoro te devote.* MACMILLAN: *... Here in Hiding ...* PART: *And One of the Pharisees ...; Summa.* LIDDLE: *Whale Rant.* METCALF: *Music for the Star of the Sea.* FINNISSY: *Stabant autem iuxta cruceme.* CASKEN: *Sharp Thorne*
*** ECM 453 259-2 (2)

The Hilliard Ensemble are best known for exploring the world of early music. In this CD, however, they survey modern trends and at times they find a surprising affinity with the repertoire with which they are more familiar. The opening number here is avant-garde with a vengeance. Extraordinary instrumental noises (contrived from an amplified double-bass) act as a prelude to *Un Coup de dès*, and the performance appears to turn into a fight among the participants, with animal noises thrown in.

Then we turn to real music, Morty Feldman's touching, unaccompanied solo soliloquy 'Only', about flight (Rogers Covey-Crump). Ivan Moody's set of four *Endechas y canciones* chime with the current trend towards medievalism, very bare in their part-writing but spiced with dissonances. Piers Hellawell's melodic lines are unpredictable, but his eight vignettes are all very brief and concentrated: the music fits the Elizabethan texts, which are about colours. The set is held together effectively by four different settings of 'True Beautie', which are quite haunting, and it is made the more effective by alternating baritone, tenor and counter-tenor soloists. The closing concerted number, 'By Falsehood', is genuinely poignant.

Paul Robinson's 'Incantation' (the text is Byron's) is an ambitious (15-minute) dialogue between lead singer (a bit like a cantor) and the main group, usually moving chordally using a spiced modal harmony. 'Kullervo's Message' is a lively ballad, setting an English translation from *The Kalevala*.

The second disc opens with Gregorian chant, then shocks the listener with the pungent fortissimo dissonance at the opening of James MacMillan's ingeniously woven motet. After the more familiar style of Arvo Pärt we move on to Elizabeth Liddle's mournful 'Whale Rant', in which two texts are presented in bravura juxtaposition, one set to a famous hymn with the harmony touched up, the other a plangent

soliloquy. The result is something of a *tour de force*. John Casken's 'Sharp Thorne' brings exuberant bursts of sound, and we finally return to Ivan Moody setting texts from 'The Song of Songs', which emphasize the link modern composers have found with the past. The whole programme is sung with great eloquence and is beautifully recorded, and no one could accuse any of the composers here of writing in a routine manner.

Holst Singers, Stephen Layton

'Ikon' (with (i) Bowman, counter-tenor): SVIRIDOV: *Three choruses from Tsar Feodor Ioannovich; Four choruses from Songs of Troubled Times.* GRETCHANINOV: *The cherubic hymn;* (i) *The Creed. Our Father.* KALINNIKOV: *Radiant Light.* TCHAIKOVSKY: *We Hymn Thee; The Cherubic Hymn; Blessed are They.* PART: *Magnificat.* GORECKI: *Totus Tuus.* NYSTEDT: *Immortal Bach*
*** Hyp. CDA 66928

The Orthodox tradition has regularly inspired Russian composers to write with a rare fervour for unaccompanied chorus. This hauntingly beautiful disc was inspired by live performances given by the Holst Singers, beginning with pieces of extraordinary, dark intensity by Gyorgy Sviridov. Born in 1915, he defied all Soviet bans on religious music, echoing Tchaikovsky in his exotic harmonies and dramatic contrasts but with a twentieth-century flavour. A sequence of interlinked items by Tchaikovsky and Gretchaninov brings fascinating contrasts, leading to a fine *Magnificat* by Arvo Pärt and a long piece by Gorecki in the Polish Catholic tradition, touchingly simple in harmony. Radiant performances and recording, with James Bowman soaring away as counter-tenor soloist.

Horne, Marilyn (mezzo)

Arias (with ROHCG O, H. Lewis) from: ROSSINI: *La Cenerentola; L'Italiana in Algeri; Semiramide.* MEYERBEER: *Les Huguenots; Le prophète.* MOZART: *La clemenza di Tito.* DONIZETTI: *La figlia del reggimento*
〇—➔ (M) *** Decca Classic Recitals (ADD) 475 395-2

This 1964 recital was one of the most spectacular coloratura recordings to appear after the war. Marilyn Horne's really big and firm mezzo voice has no difficulty whatever in coping with the most tricky florid passages and, to match everything, her musicianship is impeccable. Her range, too, is astounding, just as free and unstrained above the stave as below, and this first solo record was an exciting promise for what was to follow. Henry Lewis (then her husband) conducts sympathetically, and the recording remains vivid and full.

'Just for the Record: The Golden Voice'

Disc 1: Arias from: BIZET: *Carmen.* SAINT-SAENS: *Samson et Dalila.* ROSSINI: *Semiramide; L'Italiana in Algeri; La donna del lago.* HANDEL: *Semele; Rodelinda.* GLUCK: *Orfeo ed Euridice.* MEYERBEER: *Le prophète.* THOMAS: *Mignon.*

Disc 2: Excerpts from: LAMPUGNI: *Meraspe.* DONIZETTI: *Lucrezia Borgia.* BELLINI: *Norma* (with Sutherland). VERDI: *Il trovatore* (with Pavarotti). PONCHIELLI: *La Gioconda* (with Tebaldi). Songs: SCHUBERT: *Nacht und Träume.* SCHUMANN: *Abendlied.* NIN: *Jésus de Nazareth* (with Katz, piano). TRAD.: *Shenandoah.* COPLAND: *Old*

American Songs: I Bought me a Cat; At the River. MALOTTE: *The Lord's Prayer.* BERNSTEIN: *West Side Story: Somewhere.* FOSTER: *Jeannie with the Light Brown Hair*
(B) *** Double Decca (ADD/DDD) 476 122-2 (2)

It is good to see Marilyn Horne returning to the roster of vocal recitalists with a Double Decca celebrating her seventieth birthday! Nearly all the recordings here come from the 1960s and 1970s and have been out of the catalogue for some time. The first disc opens with the colourfully vivid *Habanera* from Bernstein's complete set of *Carmen*, but most of the other items are drawn from the two recitals she recorded with her then husband, the late Henry Lewis, in the 1960s. The first (with the Royal Opera House Covent Garden Orchestra) we described at the time as one of the most spectacular coloratura début records to appear since the war. The excerpts included here are the two Rossini arias and the Meyerbeer. The excerpts from her follow-up recital with the Vienna Opera Orchestra include a long-breathed, spacious and richly sensual *Mon coeur s'ouvre à ta voix* from *Samson et Dalila* and the Mignon scene, which is both sparkling and dramatic. But throughout these excerpts she continually delights and astonishes; the range is astounding, just as free and unrestrained above the stave as below.

The highlights of the second CD include her famous confrontation scene as Adalgisa with Joan Sutherland in Act II of *Norma*, and her vibrant duet with Renata Tebaldi from the complete *La Gioconda*. She is equally impressive as Azucena in *Il trovatore*, opposite a golden-voiced Pavarotti; but this excerpt is unnecessarily cut short. Her wider repertoire is demonstrated with the beautifully sung Lieder, and she bridges the stylistic gap between popular and concert repertory with supreme confidence. The tangily characterful American popular items were recorded much later, in 1986, notably the two Copland songs, which are particularly delightful, the famous Bernstein excerpt, Carl Davis's arrangement of 'Shenandoah', and the engaging final item (with Osian Ellis), 'Jeannie with the Light Brown Hair'. Altogether a treasurable representation of a great artist and an astounding vocal range. The Decca recording is outstandingly vivid.

Huddersfield Choral Society, Brian Kay; Phillip McCann; Simon Lindley

'*A Christmas Celebration*' (with Sellers Engineering Band): TRAD.: *Ding Dong Merrily on High; Kumbaya; Joys Seven; Away in a Manger; Deck the Hall; O Christmas Tree (Tannenbaum); Coventry Carol.* JAMES: *An Australian Christmas.* GRUBER: *Silent Night.* BACH: *Cantata 140: Zion Hears the Watchmen's Voices.* GARDNER: *The Holly and the Ivy.* arr. RICHARDS: *A Merry Little Christmas.* HOLST: *In the Bleak Mid-winter.* arr. WILLCOCKS: *Tomorrow shall be my Dancing Day.* BRAHMS: *Lullaby.* arr. SMITH: *Santa Claus-Trophobia.* MATHIAS: *Sir Christèmas.* LANGFORD: *A Christmas Fantasy*
(M) *** Chan. 4530

Sumptuously recorded in the generous acoustic of Huddersfield Town Hall, opening with a spectacular arrangement of 'Ding Dong Merrily' and closing with Gordon Langford's colourful pot-pourri *Fantasy*, this CD offers rich choral tone, well laced with opulent brass. There are simple choral arrangements too, beautifully sung by the Huddersfield choir, like Stephen Cleobury's 'Joy's Seven', Langford's 'Deck the

Hall' and David Willcocks's slightly more elaborate 'Tomorrow shall be my Dancing Day', while Grüber's 'Silent Night' remains the loveliest of all serene carols.

In other favourites the brass is nicely intertwined, as in 'Away in a Manger' and the 'Coventry Carol', or it provides a sonorous introduction, as in Holst's 'In the Bleak Mid-winter'. Mathias's rhythmically energetic 'Sir Christèmas' provides a little spice. The brass are given their head in a solo spot, an effective novelty number, 'Santa Claus-Trophobia', arranged by Sandy Smith, which brings an impressive contribution from the solo tuba. Undoubtedly the brass contribution adds much to the entertainment value of this superbly recorded and well-presented 70-minute concert.

Hvorostovsky, Dmitri (baritone)

'*Passione di Napoli*' (with Russian Philh. O, Orbelian)
BIXIO: *Parlami d'amor; Mariù.* CANNIO: *'O surdato 'nnammurato.* CARDILLO: *Core 'ngrato; Cottrau Santa Lucia.* DE CURTIS: *Canta pe'me!; Non ti scordar di me; Torna a Surriento; Voce 'e notte!* DI CAPUA: *Maria, Marì; O sole mio.* FALVO: *Dicetencello vuie.* GAMBARDELLA: *Comme facette mammeta?* GASTALDON: *Musica proibita.* TAGLIAFERRI: *Passione.* TOSTI: *A Vucchella; Marechiare.* TRAD.: *Fenesta che lucive; Logi; Medvedev; Mnatsakanov*
**(*) Delos DE 3290

The Siberian baritone Dmitri Hvorostovsky has here clearly wondered why tenors should have all the fun in the Neapolitan song repertory. Maybe Italian baritones are too firmly conditioned towards villainy by Italian opera to think of themselves as passionate lovers. Hvorostovsky points out that this repertory has been in his blood from his early days as a student, and the performances bear that out. As well as being physically a glamorous figure, he sports a voice with all the regulation heart-throb required for this repertory, rich and firm. In this collection, recorded in Moscow, he pulls out all the stops without ever resorting to coarseness, even if understandably he comes close in his outburst over *O sole mio*. He characterizes well, bringing out distinctions of mood and timbre, and the voice is more Italianate than Slavonic. Though this will delight both devotees of Neapolitan song and fans of the singer, the snag lies in the soupy orchestrations with sound 'enhanced' through an echo chamber to create a swimming-bath acoustic.

Isokoski, Soile (mezzo-soprano)

'*Finnish Sacred Songs*' (with Helsinki PO, Storgårds)
** Ondine ODE 1034-2

Here we have 50 minutes of hymns and sacred songs, only three of which last longer than two minutes. Soile Isokoski produces wonderful sounds, but for the most part these are unremarkable songs. Of course there are good things – Madetoja's 'I Want to Go Home is one example – but there are too many sentimental ones, such as 'Our Homeland' by Ilmari Hannikainen, better known as a pianist who played in London in the 1920s and whose brother, the conductor Tauno, was admired for his mono LP records of the Sibelius *Four Legends* and the *Fourth Symphony*. All the same, there is all too little variety of mood and, despite the artistry this distinguished singer brings to these pieces, too many of them are unrewarding.

Janowitz, Gundula (soprano)

'*The Golden Voice*': TELEMANN: *Ino* (with Telemann-Gesellschaft, Hamberg CO, Wilfried Boettcher). BEETHOVEN: *Mass in C* (with Júlia Hamari, Horst Laubenthal, Ernst Schramm, Munich Bach Ch. & O, Karl Richter). MOZART: Concert Arias: *Ah, lo previdi . . . Ah, t'invola agl'occhi miei'; Alma grande e nobil core; A questo sento deh vieni . . . Or che il cielo a me ti rende; Bella mia fiamma . . . Resta, o cara; Betracht dies Herz und frage mich; Misera dove son! . . . Ah, non son io che parlo; Vado, ma dove? O Dei!* (with VSO, Boettcher). Arias from: *Così fan tutte; Idomeneo* (with VSO, Sir John Pritchard); *Le nozze di Figaro* (with Berlin Op. O, Karl Boehm). Arias from: HANDEL: *Messiah.* BACH: *Christmas Oratorio* (with Munich Bach Ch. & O, Richter). BEETHOVEN: *Egmont.* BRAHMS: *A German Requiem* (with BPO, Herbert von Karajan). WEBER: *Der Freischütz; Oberon.* WAGNER: *Lohengrin; Rienzi; Tannhäusser* (with Berlin Op. O, Ferdinand Leitner); *Parsifal* (with Anja Silja, Else-Margrete Gardelli, Dorothea Siebert, Rita Bartos, Jess Thomas, Bayreuth Festival O, Hans Knappertsbusch). LORTZING: *Der Waffenschmied* (with Berlin RSO, Stepp). JOHANN STRAUSS JR: *Die Fledermaus.* R. STRAUSS: *Capriccio: final scene* (with Karl Christian Kohn, Bavarian RSO, Boehm); *4 Last Songs* (with Concertgebouw O, Bernard Haitink). ORFF: *Carmina Burana* (with Berlin Op. O, Eugen Jochum)

(M) *** DG (ADD) 477 5832 (5)

Although taken from a wide range of sources from the 1960s and '70s, Gundula Janowitz's glorious voice and artistry are a continuing thread. A great Mozartian, Janowitz's 1966 LP of concert arias combines glorious tonal beauty with a surprising degree of flexibility so that Mozart's cruelly difficult divisions – usually written deliberately to tax the ladies originally involved – present no apparent difficulty and there is no mistaking the singer's ability to shade and refine the tone at will. The other Mozart items are no less stylishly done. Richard Strauss was another of her specialities, and it is good to have a live 1968 account of the *Four Last Songs* which brings some wonderfully soaring vocal lines, as well as sensitive accompaniments from Haitink in surprisingly good sound for a live recording. In Boehm's complete 1971 *Capriccio* Janowitz may not be as characterful and pointful as a Countess as one ideally needs, but it is more than just a very beautiful performance of a radiant score: there is an exquisite beauty found in the closing scene recorded here, and Janowitz is without any mannerisms or affectation.

The Beethoven *Mass in C* dates from 1969 and, while one enjoys the richness of sound, the overall approach is a little earthbound. The Weber and Wagner items date from 1968 and show off the creamy quality in the soloist's voice for which she is famous; it is an ideal sound (as Hugh Canning, the sleeve-note writer, points out) for representing women of innocent or even saintly character, such as Weber's Agathe or Wagner's Elsa in *Lohengrin*. The Telemann cantata *Ino* is unexpected but delightful; it was written in the composer's 84th year, yet brims with invention and gorgeous melodic-harmonic sequences, and Janowitz fully brings out the work's beauty. Boettcher directs quite a sprightly performance for its time (1965), and if the recording is a bit too close (highlighting a lack of refinement in the strings' upper register) the sound is warm and certainly vivid. The other baroque items of Handel and Bach with Richter are better recorded and enjoyable in their expansive way.

The rest of this collection is all of a high standard: the Brahms and Beethoven items highlight Janowitz's close association with Karajan, and it is good to have the rarer Lortzing and Orff numbers, as well as an early Wagner excerpt (*Parsifal*) dating from 1962, conducted by Knappertsbusch. It is small wonder that in David Fletcher's crime novel, *Dismal Ravens Crying* (Macmillan, 1989), '[Inspector Jolley's] head was still full of Gundula Janowitz, for her recital had been the highpoint of his holiday'.

Jo, Sumi (soprano)

'*Les Bijoux*': Arias from: GOUNOD: *Roméo et Juliette; Faust.* THOMAS: *Mignon; Hamlet; Mireille.* MEYERBEER: *L'Etoile du nord; Les Huguenots.* G. CHARPENTIER: *Louise.* MASSENET: *Manon.* BIZET: *Les Pêcheurs de perles.* OFFENBACH: *Robinson Crusoé*

*** Erato 3984 23140-2

For all the delights of French operetta and opéra comique, it is good to hear the breadth of Sumi Jo's artistry when taking mature operatic roles. The famous *Polonaise* from *Mignon* sparkles iridescently, Gounod's waltz songs have both grace and charm, and in Meyerbeer's *L'Etoile du nord* the vocal/flute duet is as captivating as ever. But Louise's *Depuis le jour* brings an additional dimension in its warmly sympathetic phrasing, and Jo's portrait of Manon is equally touching, as is Leila's *Cavatina* from *Les Pêcheurs de perles*, with its characteristic Bizet horn writing. But perhaps the highlight is the Mad scene from Thomas's *Hamlet*, far more than a coloratura display. Here Jo is given fine support by the conductor, Giuliano Carella, with the opening beautifully prepared. The recital finishes on an upbeat with a charming Offenbach waltz song made famous by Joan Sutherland. As with the Decca disc below, this is a voice that takes naturally to recording, especially when the acoustic is pleasingly warm.

'*Carnaval!*' (with ECO, Bonynge): French coloratura arias from: OFFENBACH: *Un Mari à la porte.* MASSENET: *Don César de Bazan.* FÉLICIEN DAVID: *La Perle du Brésil.* GRETRY: *L'Amant jaloux.* BALFE: *Le Puits d'amour.* MESSAGER: *Madame Chrysanthème.* THOMAS: *Le Songe d'une nuit d'été.* ADAM: *Les Pantins de Violette; Si j'étais roi.* HEROLD: *Le Pré aux clercs.* DELIBES: *Le Roi l'a dit.* BOIELDIEU: *La Fête du village voisin.* MASSE: *La Reine Topaze: Carnaval de Venise*

🔊 ● (M) *** Decca 476 1527

If anything, this singing is even more astonishing than Sumi Jo's Erato recital. The music may be more frivolous, but what delectable freshness and vocal sparkle there is in every number, and this repertoire is far rarer. After the frothy Offenbach introduction, the nightingale lightness and precision in Massenet's *Sevillana* from *Don César de Bazan* is matched by the vocal poise in the *Couplets du Mysoli* from David's *La Perle du Brésil*, with William Bennett playing the flute solo. Equally, Jo trills along seductively in Adam's *Chanson du canari*, in which the song's pensive quality is also nicely caught. This is Galli-Curci territory, and Sumi Jo doesn't come second best; moreover, her voice is fuller and warmer. The softness and delicious ease of her *pianissimo* top notes also recall Rita Streich at her finest, in both Adam and Thomas, and in the Grétry *Je romps la chaîne qui m'engage.* Her ravishingly easy legato in Balfe's *Rêves d'amour* is a joy, while Hérold's *Jours de mon enfance* brings a duet with a solo violin (the excellent Anthony Marwood), and here one is reminded of the young Sutherland. Delibes' Waltz Song from *Le Roi l'a dit* is bewitching, and the recital ends with a sparkling *Boléro* of Boieldieu and an unforgettable interpolation of the *Carnival of Venice* into an aria by Victor Massé, with astonishingly free divisions. Throughout, Bonynge provides stylish and beautifully pointed accompaniments, as he has done for Sutherland in the past, and the Decca recording could hardly be bettered. An unmissable bargain, now at mid-price on Universal's 'Penguin ❂ Collection', with texts and translations included.

'*The Art of Sumi Jo*' (with ECO, WNO, Bonynge): Arias from AUBER: *Le Domino noir.* GRETRY: *L'Amant jaloux.* MOZART: *Die Zauberflöte.* OFFENBACH: *Le Mari à la porte.* ADAM: *Le Toréador.* MASSENET: *Don César de Bazan.* DAVID: *La Perle du Brésil.* BOIELDIEU: *La Fête du village voisin.* MASSE: *La Reine Topaz: Carnaval de Venise*
*** Decca 458 927-2

Sumi Jo's voice is not only wonderfully agile and pretty, it can deepen and become tender. Even in the middle of the unbelievable fireworks of David's *Couplets du Mysoli* (where the solo flute is quite upstaged in the many vocal interchanges), Jo can suddenly touch the listener with her gentleness. The key items here include a thrilling *Der Hölle Rache* from *Die Zauberflöte*, the delicious Offenbach *Valse tyrolienne* and the closing *Carnaval de Venise*, which has to be heard to be believed. And there are many other delights, including exquisite singing in *Je romps la chaîne qui m'engage* from Grétry's *L'Amant jaloux*, and the excerpts from the recent complete recording of Adam's *Le Toréador*, where *Flamme vengeresse* is utterly winning, and the ensemble *Ah! vous dirai-je maman* is unforgettable for its lighthearted sparkle. Richard Bonynge, ever affectionate, displays the lightest touch in the accompaniments, and the Decca recording projects the voice warmly without the slightest suspicion of edge or hardness.

Jones, Della (mezzo-soprano)

Arias, Duets and Ensembles (sung in English, with Plazas, Miles, Mason, Magee, Shore, Bailey, LPO, Parry) from: ROSSINI: *The Barber of Seville; The Italian Girl in Algiers; Tancredi; William Tell.* HANDEL: *Rodelinda; Xerxes.* MOZART: *The Clemency of Titus.* DONIZETTI: *La favorita; Lucrezia Borgia.* BELLINI: *Norma.* GERMAN: *Merrie England.* PONCHIELLI: *La Gioconda.* Song: BISHOP: *Home Sweet Home*
(M) *** Chan. 3049

Recorded in 2000, this formidable collection of 14 arias and ensembles testifies to the continuing vocal health of this ever-characterful singer, whether in the legato of Handel's *Largo* or the coloratura of the Rossini, Donizetti and Bellini cabalettas. It was daring of this mezzo to include among the ensemble numbers the celebrated Norma–Adalgisa duet (rounded with a joyous account of the cabaletta), in which she takes the title role with Anne Mason as her partner. The *Brindisi* from *Lucrezia Borgia* brings more exuberance, and it is a charming touch to have the collection lightly rounded off with Queen Elizabeth's song from *Merrie England* ('With Sword and Buckler by her Side') and 'Home Sweet Home', with the singer accompanying herself at the piano. Clear, well-balanced sound.

Jones, Dame Gwyneth (soprano), Vienna State Chorus & Orchestra, Argeo Quadri

Arias from: BEETHOVEN: *Fidelio.* CHERUBINI: *Medea.* WAGNER: *Der fliegende Holländer.* VERDI: *La forza del destino; Il trovatore.* Concert aria: BEETHOVEN: *Ah! Perfido*
(M) **(*) Decca Classic Recitals (ADD) 475 6412

This 1966 recital was one of the first in Gwyneth Jones's career, and although some of the flaws were already apparent which marred her later career, the first point to note is the undoubted star quality. At this early stage in her career, Jones's voice was often ravishingly beautiful, particularly at both ends of the spectrum – on high notes, whether forceful or gentle, or, in the lower register, again at dynamic extremes. Whether it is because the voice had not been overtaxed before the sessions, the sound here is firmer and more focused than one finds in her later recordings. Though the singer does not seem to have thought herself very deeply into some of the characters, she is never less than positive; and many will cherish this Classic Recitals CD as a memorial to what might have been, had Jones followed wiser counsels in her later career. The sound in this new transfer is bright and full, and Quadri's conducting is sympathetic. The sleeve-notes are minuscule.

Joyful Company of Singers, Peter Broadbent

'*A Garland for Linda*' (with Davies, flute; Cohen, cello): TAVENER: *Prayer for the Healing of the Sick.* JUDITH BINGHAM: *Water Lilies.* JOHN RUTTER: *Musica Dei donum.* DAVID MATTHEWS: *The Doorway of the Dawn.* MCCARTNEY: *Nova.* ROXANA PANUFNIK: *I Dream'd.* MICHAEL BERKELEY: *Farewell.* GILES SWAYNE: *The Flight of the Swan.* R. R. BENNETT: *A Good-night*
*** EMI 5 56961-2

The tragic death of Linda McCartney led to this remarkable commemorative collection of music, notable for its serenity and lyrical beauty, with Paul McCartney's own piece, *Nova*, standing out alongside Michael Berkeley's moving *Farewell* and Richard Rodney Bennett's touchingly simple *A Goodnight*. The programme opens with Vaughan Williams's lovely *Silence and Music*, for which his wife, Ursula, appropriately wrote the words. John Rutter's offering characteristically has a flute introduction, as does Giles Swayne's quite different, haunting evocation of *The Flight of the Swan*, but every piece here is moving and beautifully sung and recorded; they will not only serve as a remembrance, but also give much pleasure to a great many listeners.

Kanawa, Dame Kiri Te (soprano)

'*Greatest Hits*': Arias from: PUCCINI: *Suor Angelica; Turandot.* CILEA: *Adriana Lecouvreur.* BOITO: *Mefistofele.* GIORDANO: *Andrea Chénier* (with LSO, Chung). G. CHARPENTIER: *Louise.* BIZET: *Les Pêcheurs de perles* (with ROHCG, Tate). KORNGOLD: *Die tote Stadt* (with Philharmonia O, Rudel). Songs: MOORE: *The Last Rose of*

Summer. TRAD.: *Greensleeves; Annie Laurie* (with Nat. PO, Gamley). KERN: *All the Things you are; Smoke Gets in Your Eyes.* BERLIN: *Always* (with O, Tunick)
**(*) EMI 5 56722-2

This collection certainly gives a rounded picture of the glorious voice and vocal art of Dame Kiri. But while the lovely aria from Korngold's *Die tote Stadt* is especially welcome, some ears will find the silky phrasing and voluptuous tone not quite idiomatic in the popular ballads of Jerome Kern and Irving Berlin, and certainly the traditional items like 'Greensleeves' and 'Annie Laurie' call for a more artless approach, even though all these songs bring a ravishing beauty of line. Four of the Italian and French arias are included on the mid-priced 'Diva' collection below, and this would seem an even more recommendable disc.

'*Diva*': Arias from: CHARPENTIER: *Louise.* MASSENET: *Manon; Hérodiade.* BERLIOZ: *La Damnation de Faust.* GLUCK: *Iphigénie en Tauride.* PUCCINI: *Suor Angelica.* LEONCAVALLO: *Pagliacci.* GIORDANO: *Andrea Chénier.* CILEA: *Adriana Lecouvreur.* RICHARD STRAUSS: *Der Rosenkavalier.* TCHAIKOVSKY: *Eugene Onegin*
(M) *** EMI 5 65578-2

Like others in EMI's 'Diva' series of compilations, this selection has been shrewdly drawn from the limited number of recordings Dame Kiri has made for that company, principally a recital of French opera arias recorded in 1988 and an Italian opera recital made in 1989. These provide a fruitful source for the first nine items, but they are crowned by excerpts from two complete opera sets, the Marschallin's monologue and final solo from Act I of *Der Rosenkavalier* and (in English) Tatiana's Letter scene from *Eugene Onegin*, a recording made with Welsh National Opera forces. The beauty of the voice is beautifully caught.

'*Christmas with Kiri Te Kanawa: Carols from Coventry Cathedral*' (with Michael George (baritone), Choirs of Coventry and Lichfield Cathedrals, BBC PO, Robin Stapleton (Jouko Harjanne, trumpet): TRAD.: *Coventry Carol; In dulci jubilo; O come, O come Emmanuel; There is no rose of such virtue; The Holly and the the Ivy; Of the Father's heart begotten; I saw Three Ships; Ding dong, merrily on high; We wish you a merry Christmas; O Tannenbaum; Good King Wenceslas.* CORNELIUS: *The Three Kings.* SCHEIDT: *O little one sweet.* MASON; *Joy to the World; O little town of Bethlehem; The Virgin Mary had a baby boy.* MENDELSSOHN: *Hark the Herald Angels sing.* BERLIOZ: *L'enfance du Christ: Shepherds' Farewell.* HOLST: *In the bleak mid-winter.* JOUBERT; *Torches.* GRÜBER; *Silent night*
(M) *** Warner 2564 61739-2

One of the most delightful of all Christmas CDs, this 1994 collection, recorded in Coventry Cathedral, brings Kiri Te Kanawa in ravishing voice, singing with wonderful freshness and simplicity, especially memorable in the opening *Coventry Carol*, *There is no rose*, and the lovely closing *Silent night*. Michael George's darker baritone makes a fine contrast, especially effective in *O come, O come Emmanuel*, *Joy to the World*, *The Three Kings* and the ebullient *Torches*. *In the bleak mid-winter* is atmospherically shared by the two soloists with the choir. *I saw Three Ships* and *Ding, dong merrily* are especially sprightly, with Jouko Harjanne's trumpet obbligato most telling in the latter; he also contributes elsewhere. The Trinidad evocation of *The Virgin Mary* is wonderfully jaunty.

Indeed, the choral singing is superb throughout, and David Cullen's arrangements are first class. The sound is excellent and full texts are included.

Karnéus, Katarina (mezzo-soprano), Roger Vignoles (piano)

Lieder: RICHARD STRAUSS: *Die Nacht; Meinem Kinde; Begegnung; Nachtgang; Ruhe, meine Seele! Allerseelen; Mein Herz ist stumm; Morgen!; Wie sollten wir geheim sie halten.* MAHLER: *Frühlingsmorgen; Erinnerung; Hans und Grethe; Des Knaben Wunderhorn: Ich ging mit Lust durch einen grünen Wals; Ablösung in Sommer; Scheiden und Meiden. 4 Rückert Lieder.* MARX: *Und gestern hat er mir Rosen gebracht; Malenblüten; Hat dich die Liebe berührt; Wofür; Venetianisches Wiegenlied*
(B) *** EMI Début 5 73168-2

Winner of the Cardiff Singer of the World competition in 1995, Katerina Karnéus was born in Stockholm but completed her singing studies in London. Hers is a beautifully warm and even mezzo, which she uses with great imagination and fine attention to detail, in both words and music. This is a formidable Lieder collection in EMI's Début series, with the golden beauty of Strauss songs leading to a wide-ranging selection of Mahler songs, with charming early songs leading to four of the five *Rückert Lieder* (*Um Mitternacht* the one left out). The Joseph Marx songs, simpler in style, provide an apt and attractive tailpiece. Roger Vignoles is the most sensitive partner. Well-balanced sound.

Kiehr, Maria Cristina (soprano)

'*Cantala la Maddalena*' (with Concerto Soave, Aymes): Arias and scenas by: AGNELETTI; LUIGI ROSSI; FRESCOBALDI; GRATIANI; MAZZOCCI; BEMABEL; FERRARI. Lute pieces by: FRESCOBALDI; MICHELANGELO ROSSI; KAPSBERGER
**(*) HM HMC 901698

After her two superb recitals of the music of Strozzi and Monteverdi (in our main volume) this is a disappointment. The performances are altogether plainer, Kiehr's voice less honeyed. The repertoire is concerned with the subject of the many *Stabat Mater* settings – Mary in despair, grieving at the foot of the cross, and is of considerable interest, but the music itself is expressively sung rather than greatly moving the listener.

King's College, Cambridge, Choir, Stephen Cleobury and Boris Ord

'*Carols from Kings*': *Festivals of Lessons and Carols* (Recorded live in the Chapel, 1954 & 2000)

Includes from 1954 & 2000 services: GAUNTLETT: *Once in Royal David's City; Bidding Prayer.* 1954: BACH: *Christmas Oratorio: And there were Sheperds; Up! Good Christian Folk!* 1954 & 2000: TRAD.: *In dulci jubilo.* 1954: *Hail! Blessed Mary!; A Virgin Most Pure.* 1954 & 2000: *While Shepherds Watched.* 1954: CORNELIUS: *The Three Kings.* TRAD.: *Sing Lullaby; O Come All Ye Faithful.* 2000: *Quem pastores laudavere; Angels from the Realms of Glory.* DARKE: *In the Bleak Mid-winter.* TRAD.: *Quitter pasteurs.* GRUBER: *Silent*

Night. CHILCOTT: *Shepherd's Carol.* TRAD.: *The Angels and the Shepherds; Riu, riu, riu; O Little Town of Bethlehem.* BERLIOZ: *Childhood of Christ: Shepherd's Farewell.* RUTTI: *I Wonder as I Wander.* EDWARDS: *Small Wonder the Star.* TRAD.: *Sussex Carol; Gloria in excelsis Deo; God Rest ye Merry Gentlemen.* 1954 & 2000: *Blessing; Benediction.* 2000: MENDELSSOHN: *Hark the Herald Angels Sing;* (Organ) *Chorale: Vom Himmel hoch.* (Includes discussion by Sir David Willcocks, Sir Philip Ledger and Stephen Cleobury.)
(*) BBC Opus Arte **DVD OA 0815 D. (Producer: James Whitbourn. V/D: David Kremer)

Splendid singing throughout by the Choir, of course, and the visual images of the Chapel are eye-catchingly beautiful. The recording also is very fine and is available either in stereo (which is excellent) or surround sound. However at the opening of the 2000 service, rather than creating a distant processional image, the camera focuses closely on the choir-boy who introduces 'Once in Royal David's City'; and else-where, because the cameras are placed and moved to maximize the visual imagery, the actual singing within the expansive King's ambience (although synchronized) often does not seem sharply to relate to what one sees. One has the paradoxical impression of simultaneous audio and visual images, often closely observed, that are somehow not intrin-sically connected, although of course they are.

But when one turns to the black-and-white film of the 1954 service, with its very simple camera technique, the magic of the occasion is tellingly projected, even though the sound itself is not absolutely secure. As the choir begins its proces-sional through the arch towards the viewer and the Provost, standing beside the treble soloist, gently conducts his solo, the effect is most moving, and the singing of Boris Ord's choir is luminous throughout. Indeed the whole of this much shorter earlier service is engrossing, not least because of the recogniz-able linguistic mode of the BBC announcer's introduction, and the equally characterful reading of the lessons by unnamed lay readers in the style of English as it was spoken in Cambridge fifty years ago. The shots of the congregation when they join in 'O Come All Ye Faithful' are similarly nostalgic.

The music is followed by an extended dialogue between the three directors of the Choir, which makes a further valuable record of the occasion. The various facilities offered by the DVD include the opportunity to listen only to the carols or choose the full service, including the lessons.

King's College, Cambridge, Choir, Stephen Cleobury

'*Anthems from Kings: English Choral Favourites*': WOOD: *Hail, Gladdening Light.* IRELAND: *Greater Love hath no Man.* PARRY: *I was Glad.* HARRIS: *Bring us, O Lord God; Faire is the Heaven.* BAINTON: *And I Saw a New Heaven.* HOWELLS: *Like as the Hart.* STANFORD: *Gloria in Excelsis; Beati quorum vita.* BALFOUR GARDINER: *Evening Hymn.* WALFORD DAVIES: *God be in my Head.* NAYLOR: *Vox dicentis clama.* VAUGHAN WILLIAMS: *Let All the World*
*** BBC Opus Arte **DVD** OS 0934 D

With a delightful supplementary half-hour feature on the King's Choir and its sixteen talented boy trebles, this is a charming recital disc of English church music. Parry's coronation anthem, *I was glad*, and Walford Davies's 'God

be in my Head' are favourites with more than specialist listeners, but all the items here are most attractive and superbly done, leading up to the culminating item, Vaughan Williams's striking setting of George Herbert's Antiphon, 'Let All the World'. With evocative camera-work, most items are sung by the choir in their regular choir-stalls, but several of the more intimate numbers have them grouped at the far end of the sanctuary in King's Chapel in front of the altar, with the Rubens painting of the Nativity behind them. As the extra feature brings out, the boy choristers are boarders in the Choir School, which also has many day-students from the Cambridge area. The life of the school and the training of these young musicians is fascinating, demonstrating that though their routine is rigorous, they find it all fun.

'*Festival of Nine Lessons and Carols (1999)*' (with Benjamin Bay (organ)): Biding Prayer, Nine Lessons and Closing Prayer and Blessing. TRAD.: *Once in Royal David's City* (with Edward Moore (treble)); *Up good Christian Folk; Adam lay ybounden; Sussex Carol; In the bleak mid-winter; While Shepherds watched; I saw three ships; In dulci jubilo; God rest you merry; Gabriel's Message; Riu, riu, chiu; Joys Seven; O come all ye faithful; In dulci jubilo.* arr. VAUGHAN WILLIAMS: *The Truth from Above.* ADES *Fayrfax Carol.* GOLDSCHMIDT: *A Tender Shoot.* TAVENER: *The Lamb.* RUTTER: *Dormi Jesu.* WEIR: *Illuminare, Jerusalem.* MENDELSSOHN: *Hark! the Herald angels sing*
(M) *** EMI 6 73693-2 (2)

This is the traditional King's Christmas Eve service, without visuals, but with the music magnificently sung and more vividly and realistically recorded than ever before. The pro-gramme is primarily traditional, with a sprinkling of modern carols, all commissioned for the occasion over the years, among which the delightful *Dormi Jesu* of Rutter stands out. The opening processional (*Once in Royal David's City*) is managed most evocatively, and the touchingly secure young treble soloist here is Edward Moore. Incidentally, whoever has to sing that famous entry solo is not told until minutes before the service begins.

'*Best Loved Hymns*' (with the Wallace Collection, Williams, harp, Bayl & Williamson, organ): *A Mighty Fortress is our God; All my Hope on God is Founded; All People that on Earth do Dwell; Be Thou my Vision; Come down, O Love Divine; Dear Lord and Father of Mankind; Glorious Things of Thee are Spoken; Let All Mortal Flesh Keep Silent; My Song is Love Unknown; Morning has Broken; O what their Joy and their Glory must be; Praise to the Lord, the Almighty, the King of Creation; Praise, My Soul, the King of Heaven; The Day Thou Gavest, Lord, is Ended; The Lord is My Shepherd; Thine be the Glory; Drop, Drop, Slow Tears; When I Survey the Wondrous Cross*
*** EMI 5 57026-2

Best-loved hymns and some lesser-known ones, introduced by brass (which returns in one or two of the more ambitious hymns and to close the concert with the *Old Hundredth*). But for the most part they are presented simply, with full choir sometimes alternating with the men or boys, and refined harp accompaniments to contrast with the organ. Magnifi-cent singing, splendid recording, a perfect acoustic and what tunes they are! If you like hymns they could not be better presented.

'*The King's Collection*' (with Vivian or Quinney, organ): PARRY: *I was Glad.* MOZART: *Ave verum corpus.* ALLEGRI: *Miserere* (ed. Guest). MENDELSSOHN: *Hear My Prayer: O for the Wings of a Dove* (both with Hussain, treble). HANDEL: *Coronation anthem: Zadok the Priest.* BACH: *Cantata 147: Jesu, joy of man's desiring.* FAURE: *Cantique de Jean Racine.* FRANCK: *Panis angelicus.* WALTON: *Jubilate Deo* (with Saklatvala, treble). BRITTEN: *Hymn to the Virgin.* WALFORD DAVIES: *God be in My Head.* BURGON: *Nunc dimittis* (with Hopkinson, treble). TAVENER: *Song for Athene.* WIDOR: *Organ Symphony 5: Toccata* (Cleobury, organ)

**(*) Decca (ADD/DDD) 460 021-2

Magnificently recorded, with the choral tone sumptuous and clear, and resplendent sound from the organ, this unashamedly popular collection of choral favourites is bound to be a success. Certainly Handel's *Zadok the Priest* comes off exultantly, even if one misses the orchestral strings. Parry's 'I was Glad' is robustly presented, and so is the Mozart *Ave verum corpus*, which is just a shade stolid. However, Alastair Hussain is a true and pure treble soloist in the famous Allegri and Mendelssohn works, even if he is not quite so magical as Roy Goodman in the former, and Master Lough in the latter; and Thomas Hopkinson is genuinely touching in Burgon's equally famous *Nunc dimittis*.

The Walton and Britten pieces suit the King's style and acoustic particularly well, as does the lovely Tavener 'Song for Athene'. This is well sustained, and its climax is powerful, but the last degree of spontaneity is missing. However, Walford Davies's simple setting of 'God be in My Head' is another highlight, and Franck's *Panis angelicus* is a surprising success. As a central interlude Cleobury gives a rousing, bravura account of Widor's famous *Toccata*.

TALLIS: *Spem in alium* (40-part motet). BACH: *Cantata 147: Jesu, joy of man's desiring.* VERDI: *Pater Noster.* HANDEL: *Israel in Egypt: The Sons of Israel do Mourn. Messiah: And the Glory of the Lord; Lift up Your Heads, Oh ye Gates.* BRAHMS: *Geistliches Lied, Op. 30.* GOMBERT: *Chanson – Triste départ.* BRITTEN: *A Ceremony of Carols: There is no Rose.* LASSUS: *Vinum Bonum* (motet). DAVIS: *Hymn to the Word of God.* HOWELLS: *Take Him, Earth, for Cherishing.* TAVENER: *Song for Athene*

(B) *** Decca 470 122-2

A self-recommending anthology, made all the more interesting for scanning music written from the Renaissance to the present day. The modern Britten and Tavener pieces suite the King's style and the warm acoustic particularly well, as, needless to say, do the popular numbers. Tallis's 40-part motet is much faster than this same choir's magical account from the 1960s with Willcocks, although it is just as memorable in a different way. It is especially welcome that the nineteenth century is not forgotten, and the lovely Brahms and Verdi pieces are among the highlights. The performances are superb, and the 1990s sound is magnificent.

'*On Christmas Day: New Carols from King's*' (with Daniel Hyde, Ashley Grote, Tom Winpenny, Oliver Brett (organ)): CHILCOTT: *The Shepherd's Carol.* RICHARD RODNEY BENNETT: *On Christmas Day to my Heart.* BINGHAM: *God would be born in thee.* PÄRT: *Mother of God and Virgin.* HARVEY: *The Angels.* LENNOX BERKELEY: *In Wintertime.* HOLLOWAY: *Christmas Carol.* DOVE: *The Three Kings.* RUTTER: *What Sweeter Music.* CASKEN: *A Gathering.* WEIR: *Illuminare, Jerusalem.* MAXWELL DAVIES: *One star, at last.*

GOEHR: *Carol for St Stephen.* SCULTHORPE: *The Birthday of the King.* SWAYNE; *Winter Solstice Carol.* MACMILLAN: *Sainte Mari moder milde.* BIRTWISTLE: *The Gleam.* BURRELL: *Christo Paremus Cantica.* WOOLRICH: *Spring in Winter.* ADÈS: *Fayrfax Carol.* MAW: *Sweete Jesu.* PAULUS: *Pilgrim Jesus*

(M) *** EMI 5 58070-2 (2)

This highly stimulating 2005 collection from King's includes 20 carols from contemporary composers, all commissioned for the famous Festival of Nine Lessons and Carols. The conductor himself quotes a BBC listener who expressed the view about one item that 'whoever was responsible for the choice of the new carol should be locked up in a dark room and never let out'. But he doesn't say which carol was involved. Stephen Cleobury opens with Bob Chilcott's quite traditional but very fine *Shepherd's Carol*, and Lennox Berkeley's slightly more adventurous *In Wintertime* is equally beautful, as is John Rutter's ecstatic contribution. But Judith Bingham's highly atmospheric *God would be born in thee* and Judith Weir's radiant *Illuminare* are more unpredictable and Jonathan Harvey's picture of *The Angels* produces an apocalyptic evocation of heaven. But most of the more avant-garde items are kept for the shorter second disc (which is included without extra cost), including remarkable settings by James MacMillan, Harrison Birtwistle and the superb *Fayrfax Carol* of Thomas Adès; and the closing *Pilgrim Jesus* ends the concert in vivid virtuosity both for the choir and the organist (Ashley Grote). Needless to say, the choir sings superbly throughout and the famous King's ambience adds much to the vocal richnss, without blurring the focus.

King's College, Cambridge, Choir, (i) Stephen Cleobury with David Briggs (organ), (ii) Sir David Willcocks, (iii) Anthony Way (treble), St Paul's Cathedral Ch. and CO, John Scott

'*The Ultimate Carol Collection*': (i) GAUNTLETT, arr. LEDGER: *Once in Royal David's City.* arr. WILLCOCKS: *O Come All Ye Faithful; The First Nowell*; (ii) *Unto us is Born a Son*; (i) *God Rest Ye Merry, Gentlemen; I Saw Three Ships*; (ii) *See Amid the Winter's Snow; Rocking*; (i) *The Infant King.* (i) MENDELSSOHN, arr. LEDGER: *Hark! the Herald Angels Sing.* DARKE: *In the Bleak Midwinter.* arr. VAUGHAN WILLIAMS: *O Little Town of Bethlehem.* (ii) arr. PEARSAL: *In dulci jubilo.* PRAETORIUS: *A Great and Mighty Wonder.* (i) arr. LEDGER: *Sussex carol.* (ii) TATE: *While Shepherds Watched.* (i) arr. CLEOBURY: *Away in a Manger.* arr. WOOD: *Ding Dong! Merrily on High*; (ii) *King Jesus hath a Garden; Shepherds in the Field Abiding.* arr. WALFORD DAVIES: *The Holly and the Ivy.* arr. WOODWARD: *Up, Good Christian Folk.* (ii) arr. SHAW: *Coventry Carol.* (i) GRUBER, arr. CLEOBURY: *Silent Night.* (iii) SHANE, arr. ALEXANDER: *Do you Hear what I Hear?*

(M) **(*) Decca ADD/DDD 458 863-2

Decca's 'Ultimate' carol collection (issued in 1997) is hardly that, but it will suit those looking for an essentially atmospheric concert of tested favourites for Christmas Day. It centres on a 1984 compilation directed by Stephen Cleobury with 'Once in Royal David's City' presented not as a processional but as an interplay between treble soloist (Robin Barter) and full choir. The choir is backwardly placed and the atmosphere overall is slightly subdued. However, the organ contribution from David Briggs (uncredited in the documentation) always makes its presence felt and is strongly featured in Willcocks's dramatic arrangement of 'Unto us is Born a Son' and the powerful close of 'God Rest Ye Merry, Gentlemen'. Philip Ledger's version of 'Hark! The Herald Angels Sing' also has a spectacular climax.

However, in general the recording does not seek to clarify textures but concentrates on capturing the ambient atmosphere. Thus the older recordings conducted by Willcocks, which are interspersed, match up well to the later collection. The modern carol 'Do you Hear what I Hear?', featuring the eloquent Anthony Way and opulently presented with orchestral accompaniment, while it may be a highlight for some listeners, fits rather uneasily in the middle of the programme (following after the 'Sussex Carol'), and not everyone will respond to Cleobury's elaboration of the closing 'Silent Night', which takes an original turn after the opening verse.

King's College, Cambridge, Choir, Sir David Willcocks

Noël: Disc 1: MENDELSSOHN: *Hark the Herald Angels Sing.* TRAD.: *The First Nowell; While Shepherds Watched; I Saw Three Ships; Ding Dong! Merrily on High; King Jesus hath a Garden; Unto us a Son is Born; O Come All Ye Faithful; Away in a Manger; The Holly and the Ivy; God Rest Ye Merry, Gentlemen; See Amid the Winter's Snow; Past Three o'clock.* arr. BACH: *In dulci jubilo.* arr. VAUGHAN WILLIAMS: *O Little Town of Bethlehem*

Disc 2: TRAD.: *Once in Royal David's City; Sussex Carol; Rocking; Rejoice and be Merry; Joseph was an Old Man; As with Gladness Men of Old; The Infant King; Christ was Born on Christmas Day; Blessed be that Maid Mary; Lute-book Lullaby; Personent hodie; In the Bleak Midwinter; Coventry Carol; Shepherds, in the Field Abiding.* CORNELIUS: *The Three Kings; A Great and Mighty Wonder.* WARLOCK: *Balulalow.* TCHAIKOVSKY: *The Crown of Roses.* TERRY: *Myn lyking.* JOUBERT: *Torches.* VAUGHAN WILLIAMS: *Fantasia on Christmas Carols* (with Alan & LSO)

(B) **(*) Double Decca (ADD) 444 848-2 (2)

This Decca Double is essentially a combined reissue of a pair of bargain-priced LP collections, made over a span of eight years at the end of the 1950s and the beginning of the 1960s. They were counted excellent value when they first appeared in Decca's 'World of' series. The 50-minute programme on the first disc concentrates on established King's favourites; the second is not only more generous (66 minutes), but also includes novelties which are designed to get the listener inquiring further, such as Warlock's 'Balulalow', the engaging 'Lute-book Lullaby' and Joubert's *Torches*.

This collection opens with the famous processional version of 'Once in Royal David's City' and closes with a superbly joyful performance of Vaughan Williams's *Fantasia on Christmas Carols*, very well recorded, with Hervey Alan the excellent soloist. The sound is always pleasingly full and atmospheric, but with some of the earlier recordings from the late 1950s not quite as clean in focus as those made in the mid-1960s.

'*Essential Carols*' (with Simon Preston or Andrew Davis (organ)): Disc 1: MENDELSSOHN: *Hark! The Herald Angels sing.* TRAD.: *The First Nowell; While Shepherds Watched; I Saw Three Ships; Ding Dong! Merrily on High; King Jesus hath a Garden; In dulci jubilo; Unto us is Born a Son; O Little Town of Bethlehem; The Holly and the Ivy; God Rest ye Merry Gentlemen; Past Three O'clock; Adam lay ybounden; Gabriel's Message* (Basque); WADE: *O Come, all ye Faithful.* KIRKPATRICK: *Away in a Manger.* GOSS: *See Amid the Winter's Snow.* BACH: *Christmas Oratorio: Invitatory*

Disc 2: TRAD.: *Once in Royal David's City.* CORNELIUS: *The Three Kings.* PRAETORIUS: *A Great and Mighty Wonder.* WARLOCK: *Balulalow.* TCHAIKOVSKY: *Legend: The Crown of Roses.* DARKE: *In the Bleak Midwinter.* JOUBERT: *Torches.* TRAD.: *Sussex Carol; Rocking: Litte Jesus Sweetly Sleep* (Czech); *Rejoice and be Merry; Cherry Tree Carol; As with Gladness Men of Old; The Infant King* (Basque); *Christ was Born on Chrstmas Day; Blessed be that Maid Mary; Lute Book Lullaby: Sweet was the Song the Virgin Sang; Personent hodie; Coventry Carol; Shepherds in the Fields Abiding;* ANON.: *Myn Lyking.* VAUGHAN WILLIAMS: *Fantasia on Christmas Carols* (with Hervey Alan, LSO)

(BB) *** Decca (ADD) 575 6655 (2)

This essentially replaces the Double Decca set above (which is still available as we go to press), with one or two items added to give an extra 10 minutes' playing time, and with over 40 items, including Vaughan Williams's *Fantasia*, must be the most generous CD carol anthology ever!

'*Great Choral Classics*': ALLEGRI: *Miserere* (with Goodman, treble). PALESTRINA: *Stabat Mater.* TALLIS: *Spem in alium* (40-part motet; with Cambridge University Musical Society); *Sancte Deus.* BYRD: *Ave verum corpus.* VIVALDI: *Gloria in D, RV 589* (with Vaughan, Baker, Lord, ASMF). GIBBONS: *This is the Record of John* (with unnamed soloist and Jacobean Consort of Viols). BACH: *Jesu, Priceless Treasure (Jesu meine Freude), BWV 227.* HANDEL: *4 Coronation anthems: Zadok the Priest; My Heart is Inditing; Let thy Hand be Strengthened; The King shall Rejoice* (with ECO)

⊖— (B) *** Double Decca (ADD) 452 949-2 (2)

An admirably chosen group of choral masterpieces spanning the riches of the sixteenth and seventeenth centuries and the first half of the eighteenth, opening with Allegri's *Miserere* with its soaring treble solo, so confidently sung here by the same Roy Goodman who was later to make his mark as a conductor. Palestrina's *Stabat Mater* which follows is no less arresting in its bold contrasts, and the richness of texture of Tallis's *Spem in alium* is little short of astonishing. The resonant King's acoustic prevents sharp linear clarity, but it underlines the work's spiritual power and extraordinarily expansive sonority.

Byrd's beautiful *Ave verum corpus* then brings a serene simplicity, with Vivaldi's exuberant *Gloria* rounding off the first CD. The second programme opens with music by Orlando Gibbons, himself a chorister at King's, a delightfully intimate viol-accompanied solo motet with brief choral echoes. Bach's most famous motet follows, sung in English (none too clearly, because of the reverberation), and the concert closes resplendently with Handel's four Coronation anthems, including the most famous, *Zadok the Priest.* Here the sound is quite excellent.

'Anthems from King's' (with Lancelot, organ): PARRY: *I was Glad.* BULLOCK: *Give us the Wings of Faith.* BAIRSTOW: *Let All Mortal Flesh Keep Silence.* LEY: *A Prayer of King Henry VI.* BALFOUR GARDNER: *Evening Hymn (Te lucis ante terminum).* NAYLOR: *Vox dicentis Clama.* HARWOOD: *O How Glorious.* STANFORD: *Beati quorum via.* BAINTON: *And I Saw a New Heaven.* WOOD: *Hail Gladdening Light.* DARKE: *O Gladsome Light.* HADLEY: *My Beloved Spake.* HARRIS: *Faire is the Heaven*
(B) *** CfP 585 6202

An attractive and representative bargain collection of English cathedral music from just before the turn of the nineteenth century until about halfway through the twentieth. A good deal of the writing is not very adventurous, harmonically speaking, but it is all effective and much of it is memorable. Highlights include Edward Bairstow's eloquent 'Let All Mortal Flesh Keep Silence', the fine Balfour Gardiner 'Evening Hymn' and Stanford's *Beati quorum via*. The last four items by Wood, Darke, Patrick Hadley and William Harris are here especially effective for being heard together, four diverse yet complementary settings that sum up the twentieth-century Anglican tradition rather well, and Parry's joyful 'I was Glad' makes an exultant opener. Excellent recording from 1973.

'Carols from King's' (with John Wells or Andrew Davis, organ): TRAD., arr. WILLCOCKS: *Sussex Carol; Tomorrow shall be My Dancing Day; Cherry Tree Carol; The Lord did at First Adam Make; A Child is Born in Bethlehem; While Shepherds Watched their Flocks by Night.* arr. VAUGHAN WILLIAMS: *And All in the Morning.* CORNELIUS: *The Three Kings.* GRUBER: *Silent Night.* DARKE: *In the Bleak Midwinter* (all 3 with Varcoe, baritone). GERHARDT: *All My Heart this Night Rejoices.* Arr. WOODWARD: *Hail! Blessed Virgin Mary!; Ding Dong! Merrily on High.* arr. SULLIVAN: *It Came upon the Midnight Clear.* arr. BAINTON: *A Babe is Born I Wys.* TRAD.: *I Saw a Maiden; Mary Walked through a Wood of Thorn.* PRAETORIUS: *Psallite unigenito.* MACONCHY: *Nowell! Nowell! Nowell!* arr. BRITTEN: *The Holly and the Ivy.* POSTON: *Jesus Christ the Apple Tree.* SPENSER: *Most Glorious Lord of Life.* Arr. Imogen HOLST: *The Lord that Lay in Assë Stall.* WARLOCK: *Where Riches is Everlastingly.* (with Whittaker, flute, Van Kampen, cello, Spencer, lute) PHILIP THE CHANCELLOR (2 versions) arr. HUGHES & arr. POSTON: *Angelus ad virginem.* arr. Lennox BERKELEY: *I Sing of a Maiden.* TAYLOR: *Watts's Cradle Song.* arr. POSTON: *My Dancing Day.* CAMPION: *Sing a Song of Joy*
(B) *** CfP (ADD) 585 6212

This quite outstandingly generous (74 minutes) King's concert draws on three separate LP collections, made in 1965, 1966 and 1969. As might be expected, the Choir confidently encompasses the wide variety of styles, from the arranged early music to the attractive arrangements of traditional carols by modern composers, to some of which instrumental accompaniments are engagingly added. In three others Stephen Varcoe makes a fine solo contribution. The alternative versions of the early *Angelus ad virginem*, by Hughes and Poston (the latter conjecturally accompanied), make a fascinating comparison, and among the modern carols Elizabeth Poston's 'Jesus Christ the Apple Tree' also stands out. The recordings have been admirably remastered and sound remarkable fresh. Highly recommended.

King's College, Cambridge, Choir, Sir David Willcocks or Philip Ledger

'Favourite Carols from King's': GAUNTLETT: *Once in Royal David's City.* TRAD., arr. VAUGHAN WILLIAMS: *O Little Town of Bethlehem.* TRAD., arr. STAINER: *The First Nowell.* TRAD., arr. LEDGER: *I Saw Three Ships.* TRAD. German, arr. HOLST: *Personent hodie.* TERRY: *Myn Lyking.* HOWELLS: *A Spotless Rose.* KIRKPATRICK: *Away in a Manger.* HADLEY: *Sing of a Maiden.* TRAD. French, arr. WILLCOCKS: *O Come, O Come Emmanuel.* TRAD., arr. WILLCOCKS: *While Shepherds Watched; On Christmas Night.* arr. WOODWARD: *Up! Good Christian Folk and Listen.* DARKE: *In the Bleak Midwinter.* GRUBER: *Silent Night.* TRAD., arr. WALFORD DAVIES: *The Holly and the Ivy.* TRAD., arr. SULLIVAN: *It Came upon the Midnight Clear.* CORNELIUS: *Three Kings.* SCHEIDT: *A Child is Born in Bethlehem.* TRAD. German, arr. PEARSALL: *In dulci jubilo.* WADE: *O Come, All Ye Faithful.* MENDELSSOHN: *Hark! The Herald Angels Sing*
☞ (M) *** EMI (ADD) 5 66241-2

With 71 minutes of music and twenty-two carols included this collection, covering the regimes of both Sir David Willcocks and Philip Ledger, could hardly be bettered as a representative sampler of the King's tradition. Opening with the famous processional of 'Once in Royal David's City', to which Willcocks contributes a descant (as he also does in 'While Shepherds Watched'), the programme is wide-ranging in its historical sources, from the fourteenth century to the present day, while the arrangements feature many famous musicians. The recordings were made between 1969 and 1976, and the CD transfers are first class. The two closing carols, featuring the Philip Jones Brass Ensemble, are made particularly resplendent.

'A Festival of Lessons and Carols from King's' (1979) includes: TRAD.: *Once in Royal David's City; Sussex Carol; Joseph and Mary; A Maiden Most Gentle; Chester Carol; Angels, from the Realms of Glory.* HANDEL: *Resonet in laudibus.* ORD: *Adam Lay Ybounden.* GRUBER: *Stille Nacht.* MATHIAS: *A Babe is Born.* WADE: *O Come All Ye Faithful.* MENDELSSOHN: *Hark! The Herald Angels Sing*
(M) *** EMI (ADD) 5 66242-2

This 1979 version of the annual King's College ceremony has the benefit of fine analogue stereo, even more atmospheric than before. Under Philip Ledger the famous choir keeps its beauty of tone and incisive attack. The opening processional 'Once in Royal David's City', is even more effective heard against the background quiet of CD, and this remains a unique blend of liturgy and music.

'Procession with Carols on Advent Sunday' includes: PALESTRINA (arr. from): *I Look from Afar; Judah and Jerusalem, Fear Not.* PRAETORIUS: *Come, Thou Redeemer of the Earth.* TRAD.: *O Come, O Come, Emmanuel!; Up, Awake and Away!; 'Twas in the Year; Cherry Tree Carol; King Jesus hath a Garden; On Jordan's Bank the Baptist's Cry; Gabriel's Message; I Wonder as I Wander; My Dancing Day; Lo! He Comes with Clouds Descending.* BYRT: *All and Some.* P. NICOLAI, arr. BACH: *Wake, O Wake! with Tidings Thrilling.* BACH: *Nun komm' der Heiden Heiland*
(M) *** EMI (ADD) 5 66243-2

This makes an attractive variant to the specifically Christmas-based service, though the carols themselves are not quite so

emorable. Beautiful singing and richly atmospheric record-
g; the wide dynamic range is demonstrated equally effec-
vely by the atmospheric opening and processional and the
mptuous closing hymn.

Christmas Music from King's' (with Davis, organ,
Whittaker, flute, Van Kampen, cello and Spencer, lute):
WEELINCK: *Hodie Christus natus est.* PALESTRINA: *Hodie
Christus natus est.* VICTORIA: *O magnum mysterium; Senex
puerum portabat.* BYRD: *Senex puerum portabat; Hodie
beata virgo.* GIBBONS: *Hosanna to the Son of David.*
WEELKES: *Hosanna to the Son of David; Gloria in excelsis
Deo.* ECCARD: *When to the Temple Mary Went.*
MACONCHY: *Nowell! Nowell!.* arr. BRITTEN: *The Holly and
the Ivy.* PHILIP (The Chancellor): *Angelus ad virginem.* arr.
POSTON: *Angelus ad virginem; My Dancing Day.* POSTON:
Jesus Christ the Apple Tree. BERKELEY: *I Sing of a Maiden.*
TAYLOR: *Watts's Cradle Song.* CAMPION: *Sing a Song of Joy.*
PEERSON: *Most Glorious Lord of Life.* Imogen HOLST: *That
Lord that Lay in Assë Stall.* WARLOCK: *Where Riches is
everlastingly*

(M) *** EMI (ADD) 5 66244-2

A happily chosen survey of music (63 minutes), inspired by
the Nativity, from the fifteenth century to the present day. As
might be expected, the King's choir confidently encompasses
the wide variety of styles from the spiritual serenity of the
music of Victoria to the attractive arrangements of traditional carols by modern composers, in which an instrumental
accompaniment is added. These items are quite delightful
and they are beautifully recorded (in 1965). The motets, from
a year earlier, were among the first recording sessions made
by the EMI engineers in King's College Chapel, and at the
time they had not solved all the problems associated with the
long reverberation period, so the focus is less than sharp.
Even so, this group demonstrates the unique virtuosity of the
Cambridge choir, exploiting its subtlety of tone and flexibility
of phrase.

King's Consort, Robert King

Great Baroque Arias' (with Gillion Fisher, soprano, Mark
Ainsley, tenor, Bowman, alto, George, bass) from: HANDEL:
*Ode for St Cecilia's Day; Serse; Semele; Acis and Galatea;
Joshua; Jephtha; Alexander's Feast; Samson.* BACH: *Cantata
208.* PURCELL: *Dido and Aeneas.* VIVALDI: *Orlando Furioso*
(BB) *** Regis RRC 1062

A more successful budget collection of popular Baroque arias
(thirteen altogether) would be hard to find. The great major-
ty are by Handel (including *Ombra mai fu* and 'Wher'er you
Walk'), but then he wrote many of the best tunes. Apart from
the consistently fine singing, Robert King's accompaniments
are both stylish and full of life and he has splendid obbligato
soloists, not least Crispian Steele-Perkins, whose vibrant play-
ng is just right to set the scene for the opening 'Let the
Trumpet's Loud Clangour' (John Mark Ainsley). He returns
equally vigorously for 'Revenge Timotheus Cries' (the exultant Michael George), and the closing 'Let the Bright Seraphim', gleamingly bright as sung by Gillian Fisher. She is
equally impressive in her eloquent account of Dido's *Lament*
and the delightful 'Sheep May Safely Graze' of Bach, with Lisa
Beznosiuk providing the flute/recorder obbligato, as she does
in the lovely alto aria from Vivaldi's *Orlando Furioso* where
she is completely at one with James Bowman. Another highlight in which Beznosiuk participates is Michael George's

genially exuberant 'O Ruddier than the Cherry'. The recording is in the demonstration bracket, vivid but most believably
balanced.

King's Consort and Choir, Robert King

'The Coronation of George II', 1727, includes: HANDEL: 4
Coronation anthems. BLOW: *Behold, O God our Defender;
God Spake Sometime in Visions.* CHILD: *O Lord, Grant the
King a Long Life.* FARMER: *Come Holy Ghost.* GIBBONS: *2nd
Service: Te Deum.* PURCELL: *I was Glad.* TALLIS: *O God, the
Father of Heaven*
*** Hyp. **SACD** 67286 or CDA 67286 (2)

The idea of recreating on disc great ceremonial occasions of
the past from Rome, Venice or Salzburg has already been
established, and here Robert King and the King's Consort
bring the process nearer home by recreating the grandest of
all Coronation services, the one for George II in 1727. Ambitious as it was, the occasion was chaotic, but King and his
fellow researchers have put together a vividly atmospheric
sequence, punctuated by fanfares, pealing bells and processional pieces. So Handel's four great Coronation anthems,
including *Zadok the Priest*, are the more characterful set in
context, matched by equally inspired items by Purcell, Gibbons and, above all, John Blow.

King's Singers

'Christmas Collection': TRAD.: *Angelus ad Virginem.* TRAD.,
arr. LAWSON: *Veni, veni Emmanuel; Maria durch ein
Dornwald; Noel nouvelet.* KIRKPATRICK/LAWSON: *Away in
a Manger.* TRAD., arr. VAUGHAN WILLIAMS: *This is the
Truth.* TRAD., arr. BARWINSKI: *Szczo to la prediwo (What a
Surprise).* PRAETORIUS: *Wie schön Leuchtet der
Morgenstern; Es ist ein Ros entsprungen.* ANON.: *There is no
Rose; Coventry Carol.* BO HOLTEN: *Nowell Sing we Now.*
RAVENSCROFT: *Remember O Thou Man.* arr. BACH: *In
dulci jubilo; O Little One Sweet.* LAWSON: *Lullay My Liking.*
PART: *Bogoroditsye Dyovo (Virgin, Mother of God).*
TAVENER: *The Lamb.* WARLOCK: *Bethlehem Down.*
TCHAIKOVSKY: *The Crown of Roses.* MCCABE: *To us in
Bethlehem City.* RUTTER: *There is a Flower.* RAMIREZ: *La
Peregrinaçion.* GRUBER, arr. RUTTER: *Stille Nacht.* DAVID:
Born on a New Day
*** Signum SIGCD 502

The King's Singers' Christmas disc on Signum, coming after a
ten-year gap, reflects their decision to 'go back to the singing
with less of the swinging'. This is a most refreshing collection
of carols. It starts with medieval examples, done with characteristic poise and purity, but one rousing item, *Angelus ad
Virginem*, is delivered in true period style with raw tone, to
the accompaniment of a drum. Most of the modern carols
too, by such composers as Arvo Pärt (a wonderfully joyful
miniature), John Tavener, Bo Holten and John McCabe, have
their roots in medieval examples. The 25 items also include
nineteenth-century favourites like *Stille Nacht* (in a new
arrangement by John Rutter) and 'Away in a Manger', seductively done, while swinging syncopations and close harmony
still play a part in such items as an Argentinian carol, picked
up on the group's travels, as well as the final carol, 'Born on a
New Day – like a modern spiritual. Excellent recording.

'Madrigal History Tour' (with members of Consort of
Musicke, Rooley): Italian: GASTOLDI: *Amor vittorioso.*

MANTOVANO: *Lirium bililirum.* ARCADELT: *Il bianco e dolce cigno.* ANON.: *La bella Franceschina; Alla caza.* VERDELOT: *Ultima mei sospiri.* DE WERT: *Or si rallegri il cielo*

English: DOWLAND: *Fine Knacks for Ladies.* BYRD: *Who Made Thee, Hob, Forsake the Plough.* BARTLET: *Of All the Birds that I do Know.* TOMKINS: *Too Much I Once Lamented.* FARMER: *Fair Phyllis I Saw.* GIBBONS: *The Silver Swan.* MORLEY: *Now is the Month of Maying*

French: JANNEQUIN: *La Guerre.* CERTON: *La, la, la, je ne l'ose dire.* LASSUS: *Bon jour; et puis, quelles nouvelles.* ANON.: *Mignon, allons voir si la rose.* PASSEREAU: *Il est bel et bon.* ARCADELT: *Margot labourez les vignes.* LE JEUNE: *Un Gentil Amoureux.* WILLAERT: *Faulte d'argent*

Spanish: ANON.: *La tricotea Samartin la vea.* DE MUDARRA: *Triste estaba el Rey David.* DEL ENCINA: *Cucú, Cucú; Fatal la parte.* ANON. & FERNANDEZ: *3 Morillas m'enamoran.* FLECHA: *La bomba*

German: HASSLER: *Tanzen und Springen; Ach weh des Leiden.* ANON.: *Vitrum nostrum gloriosum.* SENFL: *Ach Elslein, liebes Elslein; Das G'laut zu Speyer.* HOFHAIMER: *Herzliebstes Bild*

↦ (BB) *** EMI Encore 5 85713-2 [5 85714-2]

Recorded in 1983 in partnership with Anthony Rooley and members of his Consort of Musicke, this was the most valuable of all the early collections recorded by the King's Singers. The original CD was published in 1984 at mid-price, with a 36-page booklet giving full texts and translations and excellent notes. For this budget reissue, the notes are abbreviated and the texts left out altogether! Nevertheless, the programme is chosen most imaginatively and is delightfully ordered, often exquisitely sung, with the five separate groups admirably laid out to give maximum contrast.

The madrigal was essentially an Italian invention, spawned at the very beginning of the sixteenth century. Gastoldi's *Amor vittorioso* and Mantovano's *Lirium bililirum* are delightfully fluent examples, while the gentle melancholy of Arcadelt's *Il bianco e dolce cigno* is a touchingly expressive counterpart.

Spanish and French composers soon took up the challenge. Flecha's extended *ensalada*, *La Bomba* ('The Pump') – which was needed to bail out a sinking ship – has an extraordinary variety of moods (the mariners are later rescued, rejoice and give thanks). Encina's *Cucú* sings seductively to warn men to satisfy their wives or find them in another nest; it even includes the literally translated couplet: 'If your wife goes out to the loo, go out with her too!' Alistair Hume is no less captivating in the delicately suggestive tale of the *Tres morillas* ('Three Little Moorish Girls') who went to pick olives, and then apples, but found love instead, while Mudarra's expressively desolate ballad of King David's lament for his son Absalom is ravishingly sung by Jeremy Jackman.

Standing out among the French repertoire, Jannequin's vivid representation of *La Guerre* was written to celebrate the Battle of Marignano in 1515. Lassus was actually born in Mons (although he went to work in Italy), and his *Bon jour* is full of charm yet readily demonstrates his polyphonic skill. Passereau's gay 'Parisian chanson', *Il est bel et bon*, is similarly lighthearted and is engagingly sung and accompanied here.

German composers were not far behind – influenced by the Italians, with Senfl a leading exponent in the first half of the century. His 'Bells of Speyer' ring out vividly at the end of the concert while Hassler's *Tänzen und Springen*, instrumentally accompanied, is full of high spirits, contrasting with the lush expressive melancholy of *Ach, weh des Leiden.*

The English tradition arrived late (in the 1590s), and was short-lived. But the repertoire was richly endowed by Byrd and Gibbons ('The Silver Swan' an inspired example), and the lighter numbers are equally cherishable. Dowland's engaging 'Fine Knacks for Ladies', Bartlet's imitative birdsong 'Of All the Birds that I do Know', and Morley's delightful 'Now is the Month of Maying' show how completely the magridal was adapted to the English pastoral style.

The polish, stylishness and accurate blending of ensemble of the King's Singers illuminate every one of these madrigals, and the many solo contributions are as pleasing as those sung in consort. Anthony Rooley and his players provide admirably tasteful and colourful period-instrument accompaniments where needed (including viols, lute, cittern and tabor) and the recording is excellent. This disc is a true bargain, but what a pity the texts could not have been included.

Kirkby, Emma (soprano)

'Madrigals and Wedding Songs for Diana' (with Thomas, bass, Consort of Musicke, Rooley): BENNET: *All Creatures Now are Merry-minded.* CAMPION: *Now hath Flora Robbed her Bowers; Move now Measured Sound; Woo her and Win her.* LUPO: *Shows and nightly revels; Time that Leads the Fatal Round.* GILES: *Triumph Now with Joy and Mirth.* CAVENDISH: *Come, Gentle Swains.* DOWLAND: *Welcome, Black Night ... Cease these False Sports.* WEELKES: *Hark! All Ye Lovely Saints; As Vesta was.* WILBYE: *Lady Oriana.* EAST: *Hence Stars! Too Dim of Light; You Meaner Beauties.* LANIER: *Bring Away this Sacred Tree; The Marigold; Mark How the Blushful Morn.* COPERARIO: *Go, Happy Man; While Dancing Rests; Come Ashore, Merry Mates.* E. GIBBONS: *Long Live Fair Oriana*
*** Hyp. CDA 66019

This wholly delightful anthology celebrates early royal occasions and aristocratic weddings, and in its choice of Elizabethan madrigals skilfully balances praise of the Virgin Queen with a less ambivalent attitude to nuptial delights. Emma Kirkby is at her freshest and most captivating, and David Thomas, if not quite her match, makes an admirable contribution. Accompaniments are stylish and well balanced, and the recording is altogether first rate.

'O Tuneful Voice' (with Müller, Roberts, fortepiano or harpsichord, Kelley, harp): HAYDN: *O Tuneful Voice; She Never Told her Love; Sailor's Song.* SAMUEL ARNOLD: *Elegy.* PINTO: *Invocation to Nature; A Shepherd Lov'd a Nymph so Fair; From Thee, Eliza, I must Go; Eloisa to Abelard; Minuet in A.* STORACE: *The Curfew.* LINLEY THE ELDER: *The Lark Sings High in the Cornfield; Think not, my Love.* JACKSON: *The Day that Saw thy Beauty Rise; Time has not Thinn'd my Flowing Hair.* SHIELD: *Ye Balmy Breezes, Gently Blow; Hope and Love; 'Tis Only no Harm to Know it, you Know.* CARDON: *Variations on 'Ah vous dirai-je, maman'.* HOOK: *The Emigrant.* SALOMON: *Go, Lovely Rose; Why Still before these Streaming Eyes; O Tuneful Voice*
*** Hyp. CDA 66497

This programme is centred in eighteenth-century England, although Haydn could be included because of his London visits. Indeed, Salomon, his impresario, is featured here as a composer, and a very able one, too; but it is Haydn's comparatively rare song which gives the CD its title and shows Emma Kirkby on top form, just as charming but with greater depth of expression than in her companion Hyperion and Oiseau-Lyre collections, the latter having the same geographical basis but offering repertoire from an earlier period. Kirkby sings like a lark in the cornfield, and Rufus Müller joins her in some duets by William Jackson and also shares the solo numbers. There are innocently rustic songs from William Shield in which each artist participates, and much else besides: this 74-minute programme has a wide range of mood and style.

'*A Portrait*' (with AAM, Hogwood): HANDEL: *Disseratevi, o porte d'Averno; Gentle Morpheus, Son of Night.* PURCELL: *Bess of Bedlam; From Rosie Bow'rs.* ARNE: *Where the Bee Sucks There Lurk I; Rise, Glory, Rise.* DOWLAND: *I Saw the Lady Weepe.* D'INDIA: *Odi quel rosignuolo.* TROMBONCINO: *Se ben hor non scopro il foco.* VIVALDI: *Passo di pena in pena.* J. S. BACH: *Ei! wie schmeckt der Coffee süsse.* HAYDN: *With Verdure Clad.* MOZART: *Laudate Dominum; Exsultate, jubilate, K.165*

🔑 ❁ (M) *** O-L 443 200-2

Admirers of Emma Kirkby's style in early and baroque music will delight in this well-chosen 76-minute sampler of her work. L'Oiseau-Lyre have altered and expanded the original issue and the excerpt from Handel's *Messiah* has been replaced by the remarkable Angel's aria, *Disseratevi, o porte d'Averno*, from Part I of *La Resurrezione* (calling on the gates of the Underworld to be unbarred, to yield to God's glory). It opens with joyous baroque trumpets and oboes, and Emma Kirkby shows with her florid vocal line that anything they can do, she can do better.

This is rather effectively followed by Purcell's melancholy Mad song, 'Bess of Bedlam', and the equally touching 'From Rosie Bow'rs'. Music by Arne lightens the mood and later there are excerpts from Bach's *Coffee Cantata* and popular solos by Haydn and Mozart. This recital is as well planned as it is enjoyable, and Hogwood ensures that accompaniments are consistently fresh and stylish. First-class sound.

Arias* (with AAM, Hogwood): HANDEL: *Alessandro Severo: Overture.* Arias from: *Alcina; Alexander's Feast; L'allegro, il penseroso ed il moderato; Saul; March in D; Hornpipe.* LAMPE: *Britannia: Welcome Mars; Dione: Pretty Warblers.* ARNE: *Comus. Rosamond: Rise, Glory, Rise; By the Rusty-fringed Bank; Brightest Lady; The Tempest: Where the Bee Sucks.* HAYDN: *The Creation: With Verdure Clad; On Mighty Pens.* MOZART: Concert arias: *Voi, avete un cor fedele; Nehmt meinen Dank, ihr holden Gönner! Ch'io mi scordi di te?* Arias from: *Il rè pastore; Zaïde

(B) *** Double Decca 458 084-2 (2)

Two of the Arne arias and one of Haydn's are included in the 'Portrait' (see previous entry), and Arne's 'Rise, Glory, Rise' (showing the singer at her very finest) also rightly appeared in Decca's 'Treasures of Baroque Opera' (now deleted). The rest is new. Of the novelties Lampe's charming 'Pretty Warblers', like Handel's 'Sweet Bird' from *L'allegro, il penseroso ed il moderato*, brings an illustrative aviary from the solo flute, with Kirkby then adding her own exquisite roulades. *Credete al mio dolore* from *Alcina* has an important cello obbligato. Kirkby's smooth, sweet line and easy coloratura give consistent pleasure, and the two famous arias from Haydn's *Creation* are gloriously sung.

Throughout, Hogwood's accompaniments are light and stylish and give the singer every support, and one's only criticism is that the Handel and Mozart selections would have benefited from more instrumental music in between the arias to add variety. But individually every item here is treasurable and the recording is first class, giving plenty of space and a fine bloom to the voice.

'*The World of Emma Kirkby*': Arias from: HANDEL: *Alcina; Messiah.* PURCELL: *Dido and Aeneas.* LAMPE: *Dione.* VIVALDI: *Nulla in mundo pax sincera.* PERGOLESI: *Salve Regina.* ARNE: *Comus.* HAYDN: *The Creation.* Songs: DOWLAND: *I Saw my Ladye Weepe.* GIBBONS: *The Silver Swan.* MORLEY: *With my Love.* MOZART: *Ch'io mi scordi di te?*

(M) *** Decca (ADD/DDD) 467 781-2

During the last 25 years Emma Kirkby has won the affections of not only *aficionados* of the early music world but the music-loving public in general. This recital clearly shows why. Her voice is not large, but it projects vividly, is unselfconsciously beautiful, fresh sounding and imbued with an obvious sense of joy. This CD charts her career from 1975 to the present, in a varied programme, from full *da capo* arias to art songs. She manages both the challenging coloratura of *Torami a vagheggiar* (from *Alcina*) with the same conviction as she presents the simple rustic charm of Arne's 'By the Rushy-fringed Bank' (from *Comus*). The recordings are excellent, the programme varied and the CD inexpensive.

'*The Very Best of*' (with various accompanists): Arias from: HANDEL: *Alcina; Esther; Alceste; Orlando;* ARNE: *Rosamond; The Tempest (Where the bee sucks).* HAYDN: *The Creation.* MOZART: *Le nozze di Figaro; Vesperae solonnes de confessore; Zaïde; Il re pastore.* Concert Arias: *Nehmt meinen Dank, K.383; Exsultate, Jubilate, K.165.* VIVALDI: *Gloria: Laudamus te* (with Judith Nelson) Motets: *Nulla in mundo pax sincera, RV 63c; Blando colore . . . Spirat anguis; Alleluia.* PERGOLESI: *Stabat Mater* (with James Bowman); *Salve Regina; Et Jesum; O Clemens.* BACH: *Gedenke doch, mein Geist, BWV 509; Sich üben im Lieben,* from *Cantata, BWV 202.* STÖLZEL (attrib. BACH): *Bist du bei mir.* TROMBONCINO: *Vergine bella.* MONTEVERDI: *O come sei gentile* (with Judith Nelson). PURCELL: *Sweeter than Roses; If Music be the Food of Love; An Evening Hymn; O let me weep (Fairy Queen).* WILBYE: *Draw on Sweet Night.* DOWLAND: *I saw my Ladye weepe*

(B) *** Decca 2-CD (DDD/ADD) 476 2488 (2)

Anyone who has heard Emma Kirkby recently will know that (uncannily) her voice is as fresh as ever – the years seem hardly to have touched its bloom. These recordings span the peak of her recording career over two decades fom 1978 to 1998, and the very first numbers on the initial disc show her range over music of the pre-Baroque, Baroque and classical eras for which she is justly celebrated. There is wonderfully fresh coloratura in Handel's *Tornami a vagheggiar* from *Alcina*, while in *Praise the Lord* from *Alcina* her opening is arresting, trumpet-like against a rippling harp accompaniment. Yet Mozart's concert aria, *Nehmt meinem Dank*, is full of gentle charm.

The duets from Pergolesi's *Stabat Mater* with James Bowman, or the *Laudamus te* from Vivaldi's *Gloria* and the ravishing madrigal *O come sei gentile* show how perfectly she can blend her voice with that of a counter-tenor or another soprano (Judith Nelson). Among the other solo perform-ances, Purcell's *Sweeter than Roses* and Wilbye's *Draw on sweet night* bring some ravishingly gentle singing.

On the second disc, Mozart's *Exsultate jubilate* vies with Vivaldi's *Alleluia* for dazzling coloratura, matched in simplic-ity by Arne's delightful *Where the bee sucks* and in expressively sombre depth by Purcell's *Evening Hymn* and the very touch-ing *O, let me weep* from *The Fairy Queen*. A happier note is struck with Haydn's *With verdure clad* from *The Creation*, and the collection closes with Mozart: *L'amero saro costante* from *Il re pastore*. The transfers are excellent and the only real criticism about this well-chosen collection (made by Dickon Stainer and Bill Holland) is the inevitable lack of texts and translations.

Kožená, Magdalena (mezzo)

Songs (with Martineau, piano, Davies, flute, Henschel, violin, Barta, cello, Henschel Qt): RAVEL: *Chansons madécasses*. SHOSTAKOVICH: *Satires*. RESPIGHI: *Il tramonto*. SCHULHOFF: *3 Stimmungsbilder*. BRITTEN: *A Charm of Lullabies*
*** DG 471 581-2

The superb Czech mezzo Magdalena Kožená gives a masterly display of her versatility in this wonderfully varied collection of songs in five languages. The elusive Ravel songs, strongly characterized, immediately establish her magnetism, and though the sheer beauty of her voice may seem at odds with the satirical bite of the Shostakovich songs they too are vividly characterized. The German songs by Kožená's fellow Czech, written in 1913, are subtly nuanced, and most ravishing of all is Respighi's radiant setting of an Italian translation of Shelley, *Il Tramonto* ('The Sunset'), with string quartet accompaniment. Most fascinating for the English-speaking listener is Kožená's moving account of one of Benjamin Britten's rarest song-cycles, *A Charm of Lullabies*, written for the mezzo Nancy Evans in 1947, exploring in a surprisingly wide expressive range. A most valuable disc, beautifully recorded.

Krause, Tom (baritone), Vienna Opera Orchestra, Argeo Quadri

Arias from: MOZART: *Don Giovanni*. ROSSINI: *Guillaume Tell*. LEONCAVALLO: *La Bohème*. GIORDANO: *Andrea Chénier*. BORODIN: *Prince Igor*. WAGNER: *Der fliegende Holländer. Tanhäuser*
(M) **(*) Decca Classic Recitals (ADD) 475 6814

The Finnish baritone Tom Krause was an impressive singer with a firm, resonant voice and an excellent sense of charac-terization. His repertoire was wide, as can be seen on this 1966 recital. Throughout, one admires this artist's fine tech-nique and his ability to sing securely throughout the dynamic range. In the opening *Don Giovanni* item, *Fin ch'han dal vino*, taken at quite a lick, the orchestra sounds balanced a bit backwardly, but it is better placed for the rest of the programme. The sound is not quite of Decca's very best vintage, though the voice is consistently well recorded. The Leoncavallo *La Bohème* excerpt is an enjoyable rarity, but anyone who responds to the baritone voice will find much to enjoy here, and Quadri is a reliable accompanist. Amazingly, in this example of Decca's Classic Recitals series, it is possible to read the sleeve-notes!

Larin, Sergej (tenor), Eleonora Bekova (piano)

'Songs by the Mighty Handful': RIMSKY-KORSAKOV: *It was not the Wind Blowing from Above; The Octave; The Nymph; Clearer than the Singing of the Lark; The Scurrying Bank of Clouds Disperses; On the Hills of Georgia; Of what in the Silence of the Night; Captivated by the Rose, the Nightingale; Silence Descends on the Yellow Cornfields; A Pressed Flower*. CUI: *A Statue at Tsarskoye Selo; The Burnt Letter*. BORODIN: *The Fair Maid has Stopped Loving Me; For the Shores of the Distant Homeland*. BALAKIREV: *You are Full of Captivating Bliss; Barcarolle; Look, my Friend*. MUSSORGSKY: *Songs and Dances of Death*
*** Chan. 9547

Sergej Larin with his outstandingly beautiful and expressive tenor presents vivid portraits of the five Russian composers grouped as the 'Mighty Handful', all but Mussorgsky here represented in miniatures. The ten Rimsky-Korsakov songs are totally unpretentious, simple ballads that he wrote in joyful relaxation, a mood which is reflected in the music. The two Cui songs are far more intense, as are the two by Borodin, one of them, 'The Fair Maid has Stopped Loving Me', with cello obbligato played by Alfia Bekova. The three Balakirev songs are tiny chips from the workbench, beauti-fully crafted. Only Mussorgsky is presented at full stretch with the greatest and best known of the items here, the *Songs and Dances of Death*. Larin, having for the earlier songs used his most honeyed tones and velvety, seamless production, including a wonderful head-voice on top, here darkens his tone thrillingly, ending with a searing account of 'The Field Marshall Death'. A superb disc, revealing a great artist.

Larmore, Jennifer (mezzo-soprano)

Opera Arias (with Welsh Nat. Op. O, Carlo Rizzi) from: GLUCK: *Orfeo ed Euridice*. MOZART: *Le nozze di Figaro*. ROSSINI: *Tancredi; La donna del lago*. BELLINI: *I Capuleti e i Montecchi*. DONIZETTI: *Lucrezia Borgia; Anna Bolena*. MEYERBEER: *Les Hugenots*. GOUNOD: *Faust; Roméo et Juliette*. TCHAIKOVSKY: *The Maid of Orleans*
J. STRAUSS SR: *Die Fledermaus*
(BB) **(*) Warner Apex 2564 6761-2

This is a slightly disappointing showcase for Jennifer Lar-more. The quality of the voice and her musicality of phrasing are in no doubt, as the two Gounod items and (especially) the lovely aria from Tchaikovsky's *Maid of Orleans* readily dem-onstrate. This really springs to life, as does Orlofsky's aria from *Die Fledermaus*, *Chacun à son goût* (which we hear twice, sung in both German and English) and is delightfully vivacious. But elsewhere the performances tend to lack a true theatrical lift-off, which is at least partly the fault of Carlo Rizzi's accompaniments, which are supportive but not as dramatic as they might be. The programme is certainly imaginative, and the recording excellent; moreover, full texts and translations are provided in a way unusual for a budget disc. It shows it can be done!

Laudibus, Michael Brewer

'*All in the April Evening*': ROBERTON: *All in the April Evening*. arr. ROBERTON: *The Banks o'Doon; An Eriskay*

Love Lilt; Dream Angus; All through the Night. The Wee Copper o'Fife; Drink to me Only with Thine Eyes. arr. VAUGHAN WILLIAMS: *Ca' the Yowes; The Turtle Dove.* VAUGHAN WILLIAMS: *3 Shakespeare Songs: Full Fathom Five; The Cloud-capp'd Towers; Over Hill, over Dale.* arr. BANTOCK: *O can Ye Sew Cushions?* arr. MANSFIELD: *Wi' a Hundred Pipers.* MORLEY: *Fyer! Fyer!* BENNET: *All Creatures Now are Merry-minded.* BYRD: *Ave verum corpus.* GRANT: *Crimond.* PARRY: *Never Weather-beaten Sail.* ELGAR: *My Love Dwelt in a Northern Land; As Torrents in Summer.* arr. WARLOCK: *Corpus Christi.* STANFORD: *The Blue Bird.* SULLIVAN: *The Long Day Closes*
*** Hyp. CDA 67076

The twenty-two members of Laudibus are all recruited from the National Youth Choir. Their tuning is impeccable and they blend together with the natural flexibility which established the international reputation of Sir Hugh Roberton's Glasgow Orpheus Choir. The programme here is based on repertoire made famous by that now disbanded group, opening appropriately with the title piece, one of the simplest and loveliest examples of four-part writing in the English language. The programme is for the most part composed of similarly serene and evocative music, but every so often there is a lively item like 'Wi' a Hundred Pipers', Morley's 'Fyer! Fyer!', or Bennet's 'All Creatures Now are Merry-minded', to interrupt the reverie momentarily. The various soloists are drawn from the choir and very good they are too (sample the treble solo in Stanford's 'Blue Bird'). Beautifully recorded, this is a choral record for the late evening, and its consistency of mood is one of its virtues. The playing time is a generous 72 minutes.

Lemalu, Jonathan (bass-baritone)

'Lieder, Mélodies and English Songs' (with Vignoles, piano): BRAHMS: *4 Serious Songs.* SCHUBERT: *Der Wanderer; Auf der Donau; Der Schiffer; Der Wanderer an den Mond.* FAURE: *L'Horizon chimérique* (song-cycle). FINZI: *Rollicum-rorum; To Lizbie Brown.* IRELAND: *Sea Fever.* KEEL: *Trade Winds.* HEAD: *The Estuary.* TRAD. (arr. VIGNOLES): *Lowlands*
(B) *** EMI Début 5 75203-2

This is an outstanding disc in EMI's Début series, a wide-ranging recital from one of the most talented singers of the younger generation, Jonathan Lemalu, a New Zealand-born Samoan with a magnificent natural voice and artistry to match. In 2002 he won the Royal Philharmonic Society's 'Young Artist Award' and here demonstrates his versatility over some very demanding repertory. He seems just as much at home in the dark cadences of Brahms's *Four Serious Songs* as in late Fauré – *L'Horizon chimérique*, a cycle of four songs, three of which are connected with the sea, was written by the aged composer in 1921 for Charles Panzéra. The sea and water connection is carried through many of the other songs, even the Schubert group with the vigorous *Der Schiffer* given a rousing performance. The final group of four songs, which come almost as encores, is also nautical, with John Ireland's masterpiece, 'Sea Fever', matched by the hauntingly evocative 'Trade Winds' by Frederick Keel, which deserves to be far better known. In all these songs Roger Vignoles is an unfailingly imaginative and sympathetic accompanist. Being a budget issue, this has no texts in the booklet, but Lemalu's diction is excellent.

Lemper, Ute, Matrix Ensemble, Robert Ziegler

'Berlin Cabaret Songs' (sung in German) by SPOLIANSKY; HOLLAENDER; GOLDSCHMIDT; BILLING; NELSON
*** Decca 452 601-2

The tangy, sexy voice of Ute Lemper is here caught at its most provocative in a colourful sequence of cabaret songs reflecting the sleazy, decadent atmosphere of Berlin under the Weimar Republic, as observed in the popular cabarets of the city. With Lemper characterizing delectably, with German consonants adding extra bite, often 'over the top' as in the delightful *Ich bin ein Vamp*, the authentic flavour is here presented in music with new vividness.

The conductor, Robert Ziegler, has restored the original orchestrations as closely as he can (no scores survive, only piano reductions), and the result is a valuable addition to the 'Entartete Musik' series. Not only is the music fascinating and characterful, so are the words, including even a gay anthem, *Das lila Lied*, written by Mischa Spoliansky under a pseudonym. It is good too to have included a song by Berthold Goldschmidt, which he wrote for his wife in 1930.

(i) Leonard, Sarah (soprano), (ii) Paul Leonard (baritone), Malcolm Martineau (piano)

'A Century of English song', Volume II: (i) PARRY: *My Heart is like a Singing Bird; From a City Window; The Maiden; Armida's Garden; My True Love hath my Heart; Goodnight; Crabbed Age and Youth.* SOMERVELL: (ii) *A Shropshire Lad* (cycle); (i) *Young Love Lies Sleeping; Shepherd's Cradle Song; Come to me in my Dreams.* STANFORD: (ii) *The Fair; To the Soul; The Calico Dress.* (i) *An Irish Idyll* (cycle)
(M) **(*) Somm SOMMCD 214

Sarah Leonard with her fresh, bright soprano and her brother Paul with his cleanly focused baritone are persuasive advocates in these largely neglected songs, helped by the imaginative accompaniments of Malcolm Martineau. All three composers rise above the limitations of the drawing-room ballad thanks to musical finesse and sensitive response to words, though Sir Arthur Somervell's *Shropshire Lad* cycle, open in its lyricism, completely misses the darkness implied behind seemingly innocent verses. Parry owes most to the example of Brahms, while Stanford, with Irish as well as English overtones, finds a personal magic in such songs as 'The Fairy Lough', the second song in the *Irish Idyll*. Well-balanced recording, but with edge on the top of the soprano's voice.

London Symphony Chorus & LSO, Richard Hickox

'Grand Opera Choruses' from: BIZET: *Carmen.* VERDI: *Il trovatore; Nabucco; Macbeth; Aida.* GOUNOD: *Faust.* BORODIN: *Prince Igor.* ORFF: *Carmina Burana*
(BB) *** Regis RRC 1137 (with BIZET: *Carmen: Suites* **(*))

Most collections of opera choruses are taken from sets, but this one was a freshly recorded collection of favourites, sung with fine fervour and discipline. The opening Toreador Chorus from *Carmen* is zestfully infectious, and the Soldiers'

Chorus from *Faust* is equally buoyant. The noble line of Verdi's *Va pensiero* is beautifully shaped by Hickox, with the balance between voices and orchestra particularly effective. In *Gli arredi festivi* from *Nabucco* and the famous Triumphal scene from *Aida*, the orchestral brass sound resonantly sonorous, even if the trumpet fanfares could have been more widely separated in the latter. The concert ends with Borodin's *Polovtsian Dances*, most excitingly done. The recording, made at the EMI Abbey Road studio, has the atmosphere of an idealized opera house, and the result is in the demonstration bracket. The coupled orchestral music from *Carmen* by Bizet is also very well recorded.

Lorengar, Pilar (soprano), Vienna Opera Orchestra, Walter Weller

'*Prima Donna in Vienna*': Arias from: MOZART: *Le nozze di Figaro.* BEETHOVEN: *Fidelio.* WEBER: *Der Freischütz.* WAGNER: *Tannhäuser.* KORNGOLD: *Die tote Stadt.* R. STRAUSS: *Arabella.* J. STRAUSS JR: *Der Zigeunerbaron.* ZELLER: *Der Vogelhändler.* LEHAR: *Eva.* KALMAN: *Die Csárdásfürstin*

(M) *(*) Decca (ADD) Classic Recitals 475 7165

This 1971 recital is not as impressive as might be expected. Lorengar was a charming artist but she was not always heard to best effect on record. Her vibrato can be troublesome and it is here, with the trills in *Dove sono* barely distinguishable from sustained notes and the throat occasionally constricting to produce something not far from a yodel. However, the actual sound of the voice is attractive so one's enjoyment depends on one's own personal wobble-tolerance. That said, the choice of repertoire is good and varied, including an unexpected Korngold item; and it ends with a vivacious Kálmán number. Excellent support from conductor and orchestra, and full sound. As usual in the Classic Recitals series, the sleeve-notes are too small to read and there are no texts, but the glamorous early-'70s cover is good to have.

Lott, Felicity (soprano), Graham Johnson (piano)

'*Fallen Women and Virtuous Wives*' (Wigmore Hall Recital, 6 June 2005): Songs by COWARD; HAYDN; R. STRAUSS; BRAHMS; WOLF; WEILL; SCHUMANN; WALTON; BLISS; ROUSSEL; FAURÉ; DUPARC; POULENC; HAHN; STRAUS; HEUBERGER; Folksongs, arr. BRITTEN

(M) ** Wigmore Hall WHLive 0004

This is a miscellaneous recital with a vengeance, 26 songs with only a tenuous connecting link. With Dame Felicity's voice not caught flatteringly, at times sounding almost raw in the upper register, it is not a collection to return to except for a few items, including the arranged folksongs, especially *I know where I'm going*, alongside Bliss's delightful *Return from Town* and the Noël Coward cabaret songs. Graham Johnson accompanies magnificently, adding much to the recital, but this is not one of the most successful Wigmore Hall ventures on disc.

Mélodies on Victor Hugo poems: GOUNOD: *Sérénade.* BIZET: *Feuilles d'album: Guitare. Adieux de l'hôtesse arabe.* LALO: *Guitare.* DELIBES: *Eclogue.* FRANCK: *S'il est un charmant gazon.* FAURE: *L'Absent; Le Papillon et la fleur;*

Puisqu'ici-bas. WAGNER: *L'Attente.* LISZT: *O quand je dors; Comment, disaient-ils.* SAINT-SAENS: *Soirée en mer; La Fiancée du timbalier.* M.V. WHITE: *Chantez, chantez jeune inspirée.* HAHN: *Si mes vers avaient des ailes; Rêverie*

(B) *** HM Musique d'Abord HMA 901138

Felicity Lott's collection of Hugo settings relies mainly on sweet and charming songs, freshly and unsentimentally done, with Graham Johnson an ideally sympathetic accompanist. The recital is then given welcome stiffening with fine songs by Wagner and Liszt, as well as two by Saint-Saëns that have a bite worthy of Berlioz. It makes a headily enjoyable cocktail. Now reissued in the Musique d'Abord series, this is a bargain not to be missed.

'*Summertime*': ARNE: *Where the Bee Sucks.* BARBER: *Sure on this Shining Light; The Monk and his Cat.* BERLIOZ: *Nuites d'été: L'Île inconnue; Villanelle.* BERNSTEIN: *My House.* BRAHMS: *Meine Liebe ist grun.* BRIDGE: *Go not Happy Day.* DELIUS: *To Daffodils.* ELGAR: *The Shepherd's Song.* FAURE: *Clair de lune; Soir; Notre amour.* FRASER-SIMPSON: *Vespers.* GERSHWIN: *Summertime.* HEAD: *The Little Road to Bethlehem.* IRELAND: *The Trellis.* LEHMANN: *Ah, Moon of my Delight.* PORTER: *The Tale of the Oyster.* QUILTER: *Now Sleeps the Crimson Petal. Love's Philosophy.* RUTTER: *The Lord Bless you.* SCHUBERT: *Who is Sylvia? Auf dem Wasser zu singen.* SCHUMANN: *Der Nussbaum.* TRAD: *The Lark in the Clear Air.* VAUGHAN WILLIAMS: *Orpheus with his Lute.* WARLOCK: *Sleep.* HAYDN WOOD: *A Brown Bird Singing*

*** Black Box BBM 3007

It would be hard to devise a song-miscellany more attractive than this programme, which brings together so many popular favourites as well as some welcome rarities. It is Graham Johnson's genius pointfully to juxtapose so many different areas of song, with such an item as Cole Porter's cabaret-song, 'The Tale of the Oyster', adding an extra, unexpected dimension, as do Haydn Wood's 'Brown Bird Singing' and Fraser-Simpson's setting of one of A. A. Milne's Christopher Robin poems, 'Vespers'. Dame Felicity rightly presents it straight as a child might, punctuating it with little staccato cries of '*oh!*' (of which there are perhaps one or two too many).

In every way she is a charmer, which makes this disc self-recommending, and her voice is at its freshest, even girlish. Yet the recording tends to highlight a brightness in both the voice and the piano that limits her range of tone and makes it seem less varied than usual. The information on the two-page leaflet is very limited indeed, and Schumann's most popular song, *Der Nussbaum*, is attributed to Schubert. As a CD-ROM the disc offers more information, including translations, yet even for those with access to a computer that is no substitute for a printed note, which provides you with texts and translations while you are actually listening. Even so, it is a delight to go from one jewel of a song to another, and it is good to have a spicing of American items, not just Gershwin, Barber (with two songs) and Cole Porter, but Bernstein too, with one of his early songs for Barrie's *Peter Pan*.

Lott, Felicity (soprano), Anne Murray (mezzo-soprano), Graham Johnson (piano)

'*Sweet Power of Song*': Recital 1: BEETHOVEN: Irish duets (with Solodchin, violin, Williams, cello): *Sweet Power of*

Song; The Elfin Fairies; Oh! would I were but that Sweet Linnet; Irish song: *English Bulls* or *The Irishman in London.* CHUMANN: *Liederalbum für die Jugend* (excerpts): *Er ist's; Frühlingslied; Schneeglöckchen; Das Glück* (duets). BRAHMS: *4 Duets, Op. 61.* BERLIOZ: Duets: *Pleure, pauvre Colette; Le Trébuchet.* GOUNOD: *D'un coeur qui t'aime; Duet: L'Arithmétique.* CHAUSSON: Duets: *La Nuit; Réveil.* SAINT-SAENS: Duets: *Pastorale; El desdichado.* FAURE: Duets: *Pleurs d'or; Tarentelle.*

Recital 2: PURCELL, realized Britten: Duets: *Sound the Trumpet; I Attempt from Love's Sickness to Fly; Lost is my Quiet Forever; What can we Poor Females do?* Solo: *Fairest Isle.* MENDELSSOHN: Duets: *Wasserfart; Volkslied; Abendlied; Maiglöckchen und die Blümelein.* Solos: *Auf Flügeln des Gesanges; Neue Liebe.* ROSSINI: Duets: *Soirées musicales: La pesca; La promessa. Le regata veneziana: Anzoleta. Cats' Duet.* Duets: GOUNOD: *La Siesta.* DELIBES: *Les Trois Oiseaux.* MASSENET: *Rêvons c'est l'heure; Joie!* PALADILHE: *Au bord de l'eau.* AUBERT: *Cach-cache.* BALFE: *Trust her not.* SULLIVAN: *Coming Home.* QUILTER: *It was a Lover and His Lass.* BRITTEN: *Mother Comfort; Underneath the Abject Willow*
(B) *** EMI 5 74206-2 (2)

These two recitals were originally issued two years apart but make a perfect coupling. Felicity Lott's and Anne Murray's voices match delightfully, without clashes of style or vibrato, and Graham Johnson's accompaniments are without peer. On the first disc, the title-number is the charming highlight of the Beethoven group (accompanied by piano trio), but the Brahms and Schumann duets have no less appeal and rather greater character. The Berlioz items are surprisingly light-weight and are thrown off pleasingly, while Gounod provides the contrast of a romantic ballade and a witty arithmetical duet. Chausson is more sensuously languorous and Saint-Saëns offers a luscious touch of Spanishry. Then, after the comparative delicacy of Fauré's *Pleurs d'or*, the first recital ends with his sparking *Tarentella.*

The Britten–Purcell arrangements which begin the second disc are perhaps less well suited to the voices of these artists: here one misses the purity of style a singer like Emma Kirkby can bring to this repertoire. But Felicity Lott is at her finest in 'Fairest Isle', and the six Mendelssohn Lieder come off splendidly, four duets framing the solo 'On Wings of Song' (Ann Murray), and the *Neue Liebe*, which seems almost to have strayed from the *Midsummer Night's Dream* incidental music.

These singers are also totally at home in Rossini, the luscious *La pesca* and the famous Cats' Duet (reputedly wrongly attributed) both winningly done. This serves to introduce a whole stream of delightful lightweight numbers, all with 'hit' potential, among which the duets by Gounod (richly sultry), Balfe (an inventive rondo), Paladilhe and Quilter (both engagingly fresh) stand out. The two rare Britten numbers make a curious finale, but are welcome just the same, especially the forward-looking Auden setting, 'Underneath the Abject Willow'. The one considerable snag to this reissue is the shameless omission of texts and translations.

Ludwig, Christa (mezzo-soprano)

'*The Art of Christa Ludwig*' (with Moore or Parsons, piano & (i) Downes, viola; (ii) with Philh. O, Klemperer; (iii) with Berlin SO, Stein or Forster): BRAHMS: *Sapphische Ode;*

Liebestreu; Der Schmied; Die Mainacht. 8 Zigeunerlieder. 4 Deutsche Volkslieder: Och mod'r ich well en Ding han!; We kumm ich dann de Pooz erenn?; In stiller Nacht; Schwesterlein. Lieder: *Dein blaues Auge; Von ewiger Liebe; Das Mädchen spricht; O wüsst ich doch; Wie Melodien zieht es mir; Mädchenlied; Vergebliches Ständchen; Der Tod, das ist die kühle Nacht; Auf dem See; Waldeinsamkeit; Immer leiser wird mein Schlummer; Ständchen; Gestillte Sehnsucht;* (i) *Geistliches Wiegenlied.* MAHLER: *Hans und Grete; Frühlingsmorgen; Des Knaben Wunderhorn: Ich ging mit Lust durch einen grünen Wald; Wo die schönen Trompeten blasen; Der Schildwache Nachtlied; Um schlimme Kinder; Das irdische Leben; Wer hat dies Liedlein erdacht; Lob des hohen Verstandes;Des Antonius von Padua Fischpredigt; Rheinlegendchen.* Rückert Lieder: *Ich atmet' einen linden Duft; Liebst du um Schönheit; Um Mitternacht; Ich bin der Welt abhanden gekommen.* SCHUMANN: *Frauenliebe und Leben, Op. 42.* REGER: *Der Brief; Waldeinsamkeit.* SCHUBERT: *Die Allmacht; Fischerweise; An die Musik; Der Musensohn; Ganymed; Auf dem Wasser zu singen; Ave Maria; Die Forelle; Gretchen am Spinnrade; Frühlingsglaube; Der Tod und das Mädchen; Lachen und Weinen; Litanei auf das Fest Aller Seelen; Erlkönig; Der Hirt auf dem Felsen.* WOLF: *Gesang Weylas; Auf einer Wanderung.* RICHARD STRAUSS: *Die Nacht; Allerseelen; Schlechtes Wetter.* RAVEL: *3 Chansons madécasses.* SAINT-SAENS: *Une flûte invisible.* RACHMANINOV: *Chanson géorgienne; Moisson de tristesse.* ROSSINI: *La regata veneziana* (3 canzonettas). (ii) WAGNER: *Wesendonk Lieder.* (iii) HANDEL: *Giulio Cesare: Cleopatra's aria.* BACH: *St John Passion: Es ist vollbracht!* (ii) WAGNER: *Tristan und Isolde: Mild und leise*
(M) *** EMI (ADD) 7 64074-2 (4)

Christa Ludwig is an extraordinarily versatile artist with a ravishing voice, readily matched by fine intelligence and natural musical sensitivity which place her among the special singers of our time, including Los Angeles and Schwarzkopf (to name two from the same EMI stable). She was as impressive in Schubert as she was in Strauss and Brahms, and her Mahler is very special indeed. This compensates for the below-par Schumann song-cycle. Her voice took naturally to the microphone, so this four-disc set is another source of infinite musical pleasure to be snapped up quickly before it disappears. The recordings come from the 1950s and 1960s and are very well transferred indeed.

Magdalen College Choir, Oxford, Dr John Harper

'*The English Anthem Collection*' complete (with Goffrey Webber or Paul Brough, organ)
(BB) *** Regis (ADD/DDD) RRC 4001 (4) (2 x 2)

Volume 1 (1540–1870): Disc 1: BYRD: *O Lord Turn Thy Wrath; Teach Me O Lord; Exalt Thyself O God; Sing Joyfully unto God.* MORLEY: *Out of the Deep; Nolo mortem peccatoris.* VAN WILDER: *Blessed Art Thou.* TYE: *I Will Exalt Thee.* TALLIS: *I Call and Cry to Thee; O Lord, Give Thy Holy Spirit. Purge Me, O Lord.* SHEPHERD: *The Lord's Prayer.* GIBBONS: *O Lord in Thy Wrath Rebuke me Not; O Lord, I Lift my Heart to Thee.* WEELKES: *Hosanna to the Son of David; O Lord Arise into Thy Resting Place.* TOMKINS: *Then David Mourned; O Praise the Lord.* BLOW: *My God, my God, Look upon Me.* PURCELL: *I was Glad*

Disc 2: PURCELL (cont.): *Hear my Prayer, O Lord; O God Thou has Cast us Out; Remember Not, Lord our Offences.* CROFT: *God is Gone Up.* GREENE: *Lord, Let Me Know Mine End.* BOYCE: *O Where shall Wisdom be Found?* BATTISHILL: *Look, Look down from Heaven.* ATTWOOD: *Come Holy Ghost.* S. S. WESLEY: *Blessed be the God and Father; The Wilderness.* OUSELEY: *Is it Nothing to You?; O Saviour of the World.* STAINER: *I Saw the Lord*
(BB) *** Regis ADD/DDD RRC 2030 (2)

Since these recordings were made for the Alpha label between 1963 and 1969, Dr Harper has been appointed Director of the Royal School of Church Music. Here he and his splendid choir offer a survey spanning four-and-a-half centuries, covering 67 anthems (or motets) written by 42 composers. With a very high overall standard of performance and recording, it is an astonishing achievement, which Regis have conveniently made available in two seperate budget Duos, with the complete anthology also available together in a slip-case, at a comparable low cost.

Opening with three magnificent examples by William Byrd, the first and third unaccompanied, the choir moves on to Morley and Farmer, including an attractively intimate setting of the Lord's Prayer. One of the early surprises is the fresh, uncomplicated imitation of 'Blessed art Thou' (Psalm 128) by Philip van Wilder, a Netherlander who served at the court of Henry VIII. Of the Tallis items 'Purge Me O Lord' is particularly touching, while 'O Lord Give Thy Holy Spirit', radiantly serene, is spiced with a twinge of dissonace.

If Byrd was the father of English Renaissance polyphony, Weelkes brought real drama into his settings, and his 'Hosanna to the Son of David' is a thrillingly vibrant example. Tomkins's simple, melancholy lament by David for Jonathan then contrasts with his contrapuntal 'O Praise the Lord', for twelve independent voices, which recalls Tallis's *Spem in alium.* The first disc then ends with John Blow, direct and eloquent in 'My God, my God, Look upon Me' and Purcell's jubilant 'I was Glad'.

With the three Purcell works which open the second disc we are on more familiar territory, but then come two of the highlights, Croft's joyful three-verse 'God is Gone Up', followed by Greene's richly expressive 'Lord, Let Me Know Mine End', with its imitative duet for a pair of trebles. Boyce's use of solo voices in dialogue contrasted with the full choir later brings a flavour of Handel. Thomas Battishill was a pupil of Mozart, and he builds a fine intense climax in 'Lord Look down from Heaven'.

The move forward to the nineteenth century brings an obvious change of style. Wesley's 'Blessed be the God and Father' is an eloquent example, while *The Wilderness,* at fourteen minutes, is more like a miniature cantata, and with its finely sung treble solos might almost be by Mendelssohn. Ouseley's style is much simpler: his richly homophonic textures look back as well as forward, while the dramatic closing work of Stainer for double choir and organ shows the Victorian tradition at its most flamboyant.

Volume 2 (1870–1988): Disc 1: STANFORD: *The Lord's my Shepherd; Glorious and Powerful God.* PARRY: *My Soul, there is a Country.* WOOD: *O Thou, the Central Orbe; Hail, Gladdening Light; Expectans expectavi.* BAIRSTOW: *Blessed City, Heavenly Salem; Let All Mortal Flesh Keep Silent.* IRELAND: *Greater Love hath no Man.* VAUGHAN

WILLIAMS: *Whitsunday Hymn.* FINZI: *Welcome Sweet and Sacred Feast.* HOLST: *The Evening Watch.* HOWELLS: *Like as the Hart*

Disc 2: HOWELLS (cont.): *Thee will I Love; Come my Soul.* WALTON: *Set Me as a Seal upon Thine Heart.* STEWART: *King of Glory, King of Peace.* ROSE: *O Praise ye the Lord.* JOUBERT: *O Lord the Maker of All Things.* BRITTEN: *Hymn to St Peter.* HARRIS: *Bring us, O Lord God.* HARVEY: *Come Holy Ghost; The Tree.* BERKELEY: *Thou has Made Me.* TAVENER: *Hymn to the Mother of God.* BENNETT: *Verses 1–3.* HARPER: *Salve Regina; Ubi caritas.* LEIGHTON: *Drop, Drop, Slow Tears; Give Me the Wings of Faith*
● (BB) *** RRC 2031 (2)

If in Volume 1, fine though it is, the Magdalen Choir face competition from other specialist groups in the early music (which they meet admirably), in Volume 2, which spans the late nineteenth and twentieth centuries, they are unsurpassed. The remarkable range of music included is matched by the quality of performances, and one is again struck by the secure solo contributions by the unnamed treble soloists, for example at the opening of the beautiful and rejoicing closing anthem by Kenneth Leighton, *Give Me the Wings of Faith.*

The opening unaccompanied works by Stanford and Parry readily demonstrate the vocal riches of the Victorian era, while Charles Wood uses the organ to underpin his exultant 'Hail Gladdening Light', with its lively antiphonal interplay for two four-part choirs. Dr Harper's notes make a special case for what he calls the (relative) 'modernism' of Howells, here eloquently represented, suggesting he is still underestimated (but not by us). Bairstow's 'Blessed City, Heavenly Salem', is less familiar than 'Let All Mortal Flesh Keep Silence', but no less impressive. Vaughan Williams's 'Whitsunday Hymn' is comparably memorable, as are the contributions of Finzi and the harmonically lavish 'Evening Watch' of Holst, which seems to anticipate the later music of John Tavener.

The second disc opens tellingly with Walton's wedding anthem (which draws on the Song of Songs), but the following settings by Stewart, Joubert (harmonically tangy) and Rose, the latter joyfully spirited, and the more restrained Harris, are no less individual. Bennett's *Three Verses* (of John Donne) open radiantly but establish their cool beauty with relatively austere harmony. Lennox Berkeley's 'Thou has Made Me' is also a setting of Donne. It opens and closes wistfully, but has a forceful central section in which the organ participates strongly. But it is in Jonathan Harvey's *The Tree* that the organ is used (in its upper range) with striking imagination, creating an atmosphere for this poignant setting (for trebles alone) within the framework of a 12-note chromatic pitch series. *Come Holy Ghost,* a set of variations on the Pentecost Hymn, is hardly less arresting, with its complex writing for up to sixteen independent vocal lines.

Edward Harper's Latin settings were written for the Magdalen Choir and their overlapping part-writing hauntingly makes use of the cathedral resonance. He uses plainsong melodies as a source of inspiration and although the harmonic style is comparatively avant garde, these works look back to the very roots of English church music. They bring a powerfully committed response from the Magdalen Choristers and the whole programme is superbly sung and recorded in what is surely an ideal acoustic.

Matteuzzi, William (tenor)

'*Ferme tes yeux*': arias, duets and ensembles (with Scano, Cullagh, Shkosa, Ford, Wood, Geoffrey Mitchell Choir, ASMF, Parry) from ADAM: *Le Postillon de Longjumeau.* AUBER: *La Muette de Portici.* CARAFA: *Gabriella di Vergi.* DONIZETTI: *Il castello di Kenilworth; La Fille du regiment.* OFFENBACH: *Le Pont des soupirs.* PACINI: *Alessandro nell' Indie.* ROSSINI: *Le Comte Ory; Il viaggio a Reims*
*** Opera Rara ORR 216

The title for this intensely imaginative recital, *Ferme tes yeux*, comes from Masaniello's aria in Auber's opera, best known through its overture. What is striking about this selection of items (with the choice master-minded by the sponsor, Peter Moores) is that only three items out of the nine are solo arias. The ensembles just as much as the arias brilliantly exploit Matteuzzi's glorious tenor, honey-toned even up to the highest register. That register is spectacularly in evidence in the best-known item here, the Postilion's song from Adam's opera (done with more character than in the classic versions of Roswaenge and Gedda), but just as winning is the opening item, the hilarious Act II trio from *Le Comte Ory*, with Matteuzzi the most seductive Count. The beauty of Matteuzzi's timbre is well contrasted with the more sinewy tenor of Bruce Ford in the Carafa duet, every one of these items brings illumination, both for the music and for the singing. Strong, well-paced conducting from David Parry and full, brilliant recording.

McCracken, James (tenor), Vienna Opera Orchestra, Dietfried Bernet

Arias from: VERDI: *La fanciulla del West; La forza del destino; Otello; Il trovatore.* GOUNOD: *Faust.* WEBER: *Der Freischütz.* LEONCAVALLO: *Pagliacci.* WAGNER: *Tannhaüser*
(M) **(*) Decca Classic Recitals (ADD) 475 6233

An enjoyable (1966) recital from one of America's leading tenors of the day, at the height of his fame. It includes many of the roles for which he was famous, notably Manrico (*Di quella pira* is excitingly done), Don Alvaro, and especially Otello (a highlight), which ends this CD. As one would expect, everything here is of a high standard, and if occasionally there is a hint of sameness in the characterization, there are moments when it all clicks into place and a strong sense of theatre emerges. Good sound, as you would expect from Decca, well transferred.

McKellar, Kenneth (tenor)

'*The Decca Years 1955–75*': TRAD., arr. KENNEDY-FRASER: *Kishmul's Galley; An Island Sheiling Song; The Christ-child's Lullaby; The Peat Fire Flame; To People who Have Gardens; Skye Fisher's Song; Sleeps the Noon in the Clear Blue Sky; An Eriskay Love Lilt.* TRAD., arr. SHARPLES; *An Island Sheiling Song; Wi' a Hundred Pipers; The De'ils Awa' wi' the Exciseman; There was a Lad was Born in Kyle; Mary Morison; Ye Banks and Braes; Ca' the Yowes.* TRAD., arr. KNIGHT: *Think on me; Ae Fond Kiss* (with Cahill); *Kalinka.* TRAD., arr. ROBERTON: *Dream Angus; Lewis Bridal Song.* TRAD., arr. STANFORD: *Trottin' to the Fair.* TRAD., arr. BRITTEN; *Down by the Sally Gardens.* TRAD., arr. HUGHES: *She Moved thro' the Fair.* TRAD., arr. LAWSON: *Skye Boat Song.* FARNON: *Country Girl.* DI CAPUA: *O sole mio.*

HANDEL: *Xerxes: Ombra mai fù. Acis and Galatea: Love in her Eyes Sits Playing.* MASSENET: *Manon: En fermant les yeux (Dream song).* BIZET: *The Fair Maid of Perth: Serenade.* ELLIS: *This is My Lovely Day* (with Patricia Cahill). ANKA: *The Longest Day.* HOPPER: *By the Short Cut to the Rosses.* DONIZETTI: *L'elisir d'amore: Una furtiva lagrima.* MENDELSSOHN: *On Wings of song.* BOUGHTON: *The Immortal Hour: Faery Song.* MURRAY: *I'll Walk beside You.* SPEAKS: *On the Road to Mandalay.* HARTY: *My Lagen Love.* BOCK: *Sunrise, Sunset.* BERNSTEIN: *West Side Story: Maria.* LAUDER: *Roamin' in the Gloamin'.* GOULAY: *Song of the Clyde.* BANNERMAN, arr. ROBERTON: *Uist Tramping Song.* MURDOCH: *Hame o'mine.* OGILVIE: *Hail Caledonia.* SCHUBERT: *Great is Jehova.* TRAD., arr. MCPHEE: *I to the Hills.* arr. WALFORD DAVIES: *God be in my Head* (all three with Paisley Abbey Choir, McPhee). LEMON: *My ain Folk.* TRAD., arr. KNIGHT: *Will ye no Come Back Again*
(M) *** Decca (ADD) 466 415-2 (2)

Both artistically and vocally, Kenneth McKellar's lovely singing of Scottish folksongs can be ranked alongside Count John McCormack's instinctive response to similar Irish melodies. Like McCormack, he had a natural feeling for their simplicity of line, and his artless phrasing and ravishingly beautiful upper range, together with splendid diction and a spirited sense of fun, made him a uniquely gifted exponent, whether the song be lyrical or rhythmically catchy in its ready tunefulness. The sparkling 'Lewis Bridal Song' was a BBC radio hit at one time, although the voice reproduces curiously here in this particular number. But McKellar's range was far wider than that.

Early in his career he played the Count in Rossini's *Barber of Seville* with the touring Carl Rosa Opera Company and, as Donizetti's *Una furtiva lagrima* shows, he could certainly spin an Italian lyric melody. But even finer is the delightful Faery Song from *The Immortal Hour*, and the Dream Song from *Manon* brings a comparable delicacy of feeling and lovely tone. He could sing a sentimental ballad like 'I'll Walk beside You' with real style, and every word is clear in 'The Road to Mandalay'. The duets with the charming soubrette Patricia Cahill show him in even lighter vein, while 'God be in my Head' (recorded in Paisley Abbey) has a touching combination of warmth and sincerity.

He was pretty good too at an Irish inflection. 'Trottin' to the fair', 'By the Short Cut to the Rosse', the memorable 'My Lagen Love', and (especially) the touching, unaccompanied 'She Moved thro' the Fair' are splendid examples of his art. But it is the Scottish repertoire for which he will be uniquely remembered, and in which he had no peer, and this extremely generous concert ends very appropriately with 'Will Ye no Come Back Again'. Accompaniments (often by Bob Sharples) are mostly well managed, the CD transfers are good and the set has an interesting extended reminiscence by McKellar's producer, Raymond Herricks.

'*Kenneth McKellar's Scotland – Sleeps the Noon in the Clear Blue Sky*' (with accompaniments directed by Sharples): Disc 1: '*Songs of the Hebrides*' (arr. KENNEDY-FRASER): *Sleeps the Noon in the Clear Blue Sky; The Peat Fire Flame; Land of Heart's Desire; The Reiving Ship; Aignish of the Machair; A Fairy's Love Song; Skye Fisher's Song; A Clyde-side Love Lilt; Heart of Fire Love; Sea Longing; To the People who Have Gardens; The Bens of Jura; The Birlinn of the White Shoulders; Isle of my Heart; Kirsteen; Ye Highlands and ye Lowlands.* '*Roamin' in the Gloamin*': arr.

KENNEDY-FRASER: *The Road to the Isles: An Eriskay Love Lilt; The Cockle Gatherer.* TRAD.: *Bonnie Mary of Argyle.* THOMSON: *The Star o' Robbie Burns.* HANLEY: *Scotland the Brave.* FOX: *Bonnie Wee Thing.* ROBERTON: *Westering Home.* HUME: *Afton Water.* GOULAY: *Song of the Clyde.* LAUDER: *Roamin' in the Gloami'; Keep Right on to the End of the Road*

Disc 2: '*The Tartan*': TRAD.: *The March of the Cameron Men; Kishmul's Galley; The Flowers of the Forest; Lochnagar; Wi' a Hundred Pipers; Air Falalolo; An Island Sheiling Song; Scots wha Ha'e wi' Wallace Bled.* SMITH: *Jessie, the Flower of Dunblane.* SCOTT: *Annie Laurie.* MCKELLAR: *The Tartan; The Royal Mile.* Folksongs (arr. SHARPLES): *McGregor's Gathering; The Laird o'Cockpen; The Bonnie Earl of Moray; O Gin I were a Baron's Heir; Turn Ye to Me; Hey, Johnny Cope; Ho-ro, My Nut-brown Maiden; Bonnie Strathyle; The Wee Cooper o'Fife; Isle of Mull; A Pair of Nicky Tams; The Proud Peaks of Scotland; Auld Lang Syne*

⊕ ✪ *** Decca 9 85927-2 (2)

Concurrently with the wider coverage above, Australian Decca have issued a second two-CD collection, entirely devoted to the finest of Kenneth McKellar's Scottish repertory. It is compiled from his most beautiful LP, *Songs of the Hebrides*, plus three others: *Folksongs from Scotland's Heritage* with much of the programme dealing with Scotland's colourful history, *The Tartan*, which is essentially a collection of Scottish popular genre songs, with elaborately arranged accompaniments, and *Roamin' in the Gloamin*, McKellar's first stereo recital. This was recorded early in his career, when the voice was at its peak, with a marvellous freshness and bloom.

His simple presentation has a natural, spontaneous warmth and ardour, and the jaunty songs are most engagingly infectious, especially the wittily descriptive 'Song of the Clyde', with every word as clear as a bell. 'Scotland the Brave' and 'Westering Home' swing along splendidly, and the slightly sentimental Burns setting 'Bonnie Wee Thing' could not be more charming. McKellar also includes the two most famous songs of his illustrious predecessor, Sir Harry Lauder, ending with a bold account of 'Keep Right on to the End of the Road' of which that famous Scotsman would have surely approved. The orchestral arrangements here are nicely judged and show none of the inflation that marks the 'Tartan' collection, which is still very enjoyable for a' that.

But it is the ravishingly lovely collection of Hebridean songs which earns the set its Rosette. It opens with the sound of surf on sand, and this evocation returns between the items, many of which McKellar introduces himself, warmly and intimately. The lovely opening title song is followed by 'The Peat Fire Flame', sung with the lightest rhythmic touch, and then comes the most beautiful song of all, 'Land of Heart's Desire'.

Here the voice is slightly backwardly balanced, and McKellar's gently curving upward line is utterly melting. The melancholy 'Aignish of the Machair' is another highlight and 'The Fairy Lover' (charmingly introduced) brings a delightful, lilting melody. Throughout, the accompaniments are delicately scored, often using pipes, and the voice itself is most naturally caught. But all these CD transfers are superb, the quality enhanced over the original LPs. This has now been reissued as part of the Penguin Rosette Collection.

Mera, Yoshikazu (counter-tenor), Bach Collegium Japan, Masaaki Suzuki

Baroque arias: J. S. BACH: *Cantatas 12: Wir müssen durch viel Trübsal; Krenz und Krone; 54: Widerstehe doch der Sünde; Die art verruchter Sünde; Wer Sünde tut; 132: Ich will, mein Gott; Christi Glieder, ach bedenket; 161: Komm, du süsse Todesstunde; Mein Jesus, lass mich nicht; In meinem Gott.* HANDEL: *Messiah: But who May Abide; He was Despised; Thou art Gone up on High; Behold, a Virgin; O Thou that Tellest.* AHLE: *Prima pars; Secunda pars.* SCHUTZ: *Geistliche chormusik, Op. 11: Auf dem Gebirge hat man ein geschrei gehört*
*** BIS CD 919

The Japanese counter-tenor Yoshikazu Mera is one of the most impressive soloists on Suzuki's excellent recordings of choral works for BIS. This compilation drawn from various sources consistently displays his exceptionally sweet and even tone, even though his performances are not very sharply characterized. The voice is set against a helpfully reverberant acoustic.

Merrill, Robert (baritone)

Arias (with New SO of London, Downes) from: VERDI: *Un ballo in maschera; Don Carlo; La forza del destino; Otello; Il trovatore.* LEONCAVALLO: *Pagliacci.* GIORDANO: *Andrea Chénier*
(M) *** Decca Classic Recitals (ADD) 475 396-2

Our original review of this 1963 recital is still true, some 40 years on: 'An excellent recital. Merrill is always a most reliable baritone on record, and here his even voice is beautifully captured by the Decca engineers. If a sample is wanted, try the rich, rhythmic account of *Il balen* from *Il trovatore*.' It is now reissued as one of Decca's new Classic Recitals (with some items available for the first time on CD) in an excellent transfer, only a bit of tape hiss giving away its age.

Metropolitan Opera (artists from)

'*Metropolitan Opera Gala*': Arias from BIZET: *Les Pêcheurs de perles* (Roberto Alagna; Bryn Terfel). G. CHARPENTIER: *Louise* (Renée Fleming). GOUNOD: *Faust* (Samuel Ramey; Plácido Domingo); *Roméo et Juliette* (Ruth Ann Swenson). LEHAR: *Giuditta* (Ileana Cotrubas). VERDI: *Don Carlos* (Dolora Zajick). MOZART: *Don Giovanni* (Fleming, Terfel, Jerry Hadley, Kiri Te Kanawa, Hei-Kyung Hong, Julien Robbins). JOHANN STRAUSS JR: *Die Fledermaus* (Håkan Hagegård; Karita Mattila). MASSENET: *Werther* (Alfredo Kraus). SAINT-SAENS: *Samson et Dalila* (Grace Bumbry). WAGNER: *Tannhäuser* (Deborah Voigt). OFFENBACH: *La Périchole* (Frederica von Stade). RICHARD STRAUSS: *Der Rosenkavalier* (Fleming, Anne Sofie von Otter, Heidi Grant Murphy). *Tribute to James Levine* (Birgit Nilsson)
**(*) DG Video VHS 072 451-3

Recorded live at James Levine's twenty-fifth anniversary gala in April 1996, this offers an extraordinary galaxy of stars, often teamed up in unexpected ways – as, for example, Alagna and Terfel in the first item, the *Pearl Fishers* duet. The singers represented a range from such relative newcomers as those rising stars to veterans like Alfredo Kraus and Grace

Bumbry. Few of the voices are heard at their very finest, not helped by a rather hard acoustic, but the variety of party pieces here is enough of a delight. The video re-creates the occasion the more satisfactorily, but it is worth hearing the disc for the end of Birgit Nilsson's speech, involving a shattering cry of 'Hojotoho!'.

Miles, Alastair (bass)

Arias and ensembles, sung in English, with Ch. and Philh. O, Parry), from: VERDI: *The Lombards at the First Crusade; Luisa Miller; Nabucco; The Sicilian Vespers.* ROSSINI: *Mahomet II; Moses in Egypt; Zelmira.* BELLINI: *Norma; The Puritans.* GOMES: *Salvator Rosa*
(M) *** Chan. 3032

Alastair Miles here formidably enhances his reputation as a powerful recording artist, exploiting his firm, well-focused bass in a wide range of eleven arias and ensembles, starting with the *Chorus of Hebrew Slaves* from *Nabucco*, which then leads into Miles's noble and sonorous account of Zaccaria's Prophecy. The biting incisivensss of that and much else, as for example the protagonist's aria from *Mahomet II*, is thrilling, and he is well matched in the duets from *Luisa Miller* and *I Lombardi* by his fellow bass, Clive Bayley, crisply dramatic in their exchanges. Garry Magee is also a fine foil in the final long excerpt from *I Puritani*. All but the *Nabucco* item have never been recorded in English before, and the clarity of diction adds to the intensity. There are excellent sound and understanding direction from David Parry.

Minstrelsy

'*Songs and Dances of the Renaissance and Baroque*' (Carole Hofsted-Lee, soprano, Nancy Froseth, David Hays, David Livingstone, viola da gamba, baroque violin, recorders, Philip Rukavina, lute, archlute): SIMPSON: *Ballet.* ANON.: 2 *Ballets; Mascarada; Volta.* arr. MCLACHLAN: *When she Cam Ben, she Bobbat.* PRAETORIUS: *Dances from Terpsichore* (suite). PACHELBEL: *Partita in C.* SALAVERDE: *Canzon a 2.* LAWES: *Suite in G min.* Songs: ROSSETER: *When Laura Smiles.* DOWLAND: *I Saw my Lady Weep; Shall I Sue.* ARNE: *Under the Greenwood Tree.* CAMPION: *It Fell upon a Summer's Day*
*** Lyrichord LEMS 8018

A most entertaining, lightweight consort, full of life and charm, although one wonders if Renaissance and Baroque musicians could have achieved such sophistry of intonation, blending and playing! The period instruments here are made to integrate smoothly and without any rough edges. The singing of Carole Hofsted-Lee too is pure in tone and line. She is naturally at home in the simplicity of Arne, and her lovely voice caresses the songs of Dowland and Campion with considerable feeling, even if her range of vocal colour is less intense than that of, say, Alfred Deller. There is much to delight in the instrumental music.

Some half-a-dozen of the ensemble pieces come from the *Taffel-Consort*, published by Thomas Simpson in 1621, a collection which has much in common with Praetorius's *Terpsichore*. John McLachlan's 'When she Cam Ben, she Bobbat' is very Scottish, a treble to a ground, with sparkling divisions. But perhaps the highlight is Pachelbel's *Partita*, which is not unlike his more famous Canon in making use of an ostinato

bass, but is a more elaborate chaconne, with a dozen variations. The recording is beautifully balanced to match this sprightly and elegant music-making.

Miricioiu, Nelly (soprano)

'*Bel Canto Portrait*': scenes (with Plazas, Holland, Coote, Wood, Janes, Geoffrey Mitchell Ch., LPO or Philh. O, Parry) from: MERCADANTE: *Emma d'Antiochia.* COSTA: *L'assedio di Corinto.* DONIZETTI: *Belisario; Parisina*
*** Opera Rara ORR 217

The Romanian soprano Nelly Miricioiu, now resident in London, gives a formidable display of both technique and dramatic flair in this fascinating collection of rare arias and scenes from bel canto operas of the 1830s. Hers is not just a flexible voice but also one with plenty of character, full and vibrant with a good cutting edge and occasional echoes of Callas. Thanks to the researches of Jeremy Commons, who provides excellent notes as supplement to the full texts, these long-buried pieces are revealed as far more than merely conventional examples of the genre. The aria from *L'assedio di Corinto*, one of Rossini's operas, was written by Sir Michael Costa as an alternative aria for the heroine, Pamira, when it was sung by the prima donna, Giulia Grisi, at the King's Theatre in London, where Costa was music director when he was a young man. The Mercadante and the extract from Donizetti's *Belisario* lead from the soprano's arias to impressive final ensembles, while most inspired of all is the aria from Donizetti's *Parisina*, which is fairly described by Commons as 'one of the most sustained and consistently beautiful flights of bel canto that Donizetti ever achieved'.

Mitchell, Leona (soprano)

Arias (with New Philh. O, Adler) from: MOZART: *Le nozze di Figaro.* PUCCINI: *La Bohème; Gianni Schicchi; Madama Butterfly; La rondine; Turandot.* MASCAGNI: *L'amico Fritz.* ROSSINI: *William Tell.* VERDI: *Ernani*
**(*) Australian Decca Eloquence (ADD) 466 903-2

It's good to have this 1980 recital, Leona Mitchell's debut LP, back in the catalogue – the first time on CD. Its appeal is in its freshness, with her naturally dark vocal colouring most appealing. The charming *La rondine* aria (*Il bel sogno di Doretta*) is a highlight, as is the gentle lilt she finds in the final *Ernani* aria (*Ernani! Ernani, involami*). *Dove sono* is movingly done, and the reverie-like aria from *L'amico Fritz* is lovely too. There is nothing here to mar one's enjoyment, and it is the lyrical moments on this recital that are particularly memorable. The recorded sound is rich and full, though the disc has a short playing time.

Moffo, Anna (soprano), with Rome Opera Orchestra, Tullio Serafin

Arias from: GOUNOD: *Faust.* PUCCINI: *La Bohème; Turandot.* MEYERBEER: *Dinorah.* BIZET: *Carmen.* ROSSINI: *Semiramide.* DELIBES: *Lakmé*
(M) **(*) RCA (ADD) SACD 82876 67905-2

A highly commendable début album from Anna Moffo, dating from 1960, when she was emerging as one of the new-look opera stars of the 1960s. Although there is a touch of shrillness at times, this is an enjoyable recital: the Puccini arias are affectingly done, the French arias draw most beautiful tone, and the coloratura is very pleasing. Only in the *Jewel Song* is there an element of disappointment with Serafin's strangely sluggish speed. The sound is very good in its new SACD form, with plenty of warmth and the voice captured splendidly.

Monaco, Mario Del (tenor)

'*Decca Recitals, 1952–1969*': Arias from: VERDI: *La forza del destino; Luisa Miller; Macbeth; Rigoletto; La traviata.* PUCCINI: *La fanciulla del west; Manon Lescaut; Tosca.* LEONCAVALLO. *Pagliacci.* PONCHIELLI: *La Gioconda.* HALEVY: *La Juive.* WAGNER: *Lohengrin* (with Santa Cecilia O, Alberto Erede). CATALANI: *Loreley.* PUCCINI: *La Bohème; La fanciulla del west ; Il tabarro; Turandot.* GIORDANO: *Andrea Chénier* (with Studio Orchestra, Framco Ghione). VERDI: *Ernani; Un ballo in maschera.* GIORDANO: *Fedora.* ZANDONAI: *Giulietta e Romeo.* PUCCINI: *Madama Butterfly.* MASSENET: *Le Cid.* BIZET: *Carmen.* MEYERBEER: *La Wally.* DONIZETTI: *Lucia di Lammermoor* (with New SO of London, Erede). PUCCINI: *La Bohème; Gianni Schichi.* CILEA: *L'arlesiana.* MASCAGNI: *Isabeau.* ZANDONAI: *Francesca da Rimini.* WAGNER: *Lohengrin; Die Walküre* (with the Santa Cecilia O, Carlo Franci). VERDI: *Alzira; Aroldo; Un ballo in maschera; Il due Foscari; Lombardi; I masnadieri; Luisa Miller; La traviata* (with Monte-Carlo Op. O, Nicola Rescigno). DRIGO: *Serenada.* GASTALDON: *Musica probita.* LEONCAVALLO: *Mattinata.* CAROCCI: '*Na lettera cucente.* COTTRAU: *L'addio a Napoli.* CINQUE: *Mattinata veneziana; Trobadorica.* CARDILLO: *Core 'ngrato.* CIOFFI: '*Na sera 'e maggio.* CAPUA: *O sole mio.* CURTIS: *Autunno; Torna a Surriento; Tu, ca nun chiagne!* MAINARDI: *Varca d' 'o priomo ammore.* LARA: *Granada.* FALVO: *Dicitencello vuie.* TAGLIAFERRI: *Piscatore 'e pusilleco.* RENDINE: *Vurria.* D'ANNIBALE: *O' paese d' 'o sole* (with Studio O, Ernesto Nicelli). ROMBERG: *Serenata* (*The Student Prince*). GASTALDON: *Musica probita.* BIXIO: *Love's last word is spoken.* CURTIS: *Ti voglio tanto bene.* BERNSTEIN: *Tonight.* CARDILLO: *Core 'ngrato.* BRODSZKY: *Be my love.* LEHAR: *Girls were made to love and kiss.* TRAMPINI: *Cara mia.* BUZZI-PECCIA: *Lolita.* MODUGNO: *Ciao ciao, bambina.* LEHAR: *The White dove* (with Mantovani & his Orchestra). STRADELLA: *Pietà, Signore.* PEROSI: *Benedictus; Hostias et preces.* BEETHOVEN: *In questa tomba oscura.* ROSSINI: *Crucifixus; Domine Deus* (from *Petite Messe solennelle*). MOZART: *Ave verum corpus.* BIZET: *Agnus Dei.* HANDEL: *Frondi tenere ... Ombra mai fu* (*Serse*). VERDI: *Ingemisco* (from *Requiem*). FRANK: *Panus angelicus* (with Brian Runnett (organ))

(B) *(*) Decca mono/stereo 475 7269 (5)

It is easy to highlight Mario Del Monaco's faults, pointing out the coarse and, frankly, downright unsubtle qualities which often mar his work. After listening to Fritz Wunderlich, for example – that incomparably most stylish of singers – the wrong Del Monaco number will indeed jar. That Del Monaco has retained an affection in the hearts of many an opera-lover is for this reason: he is an unashamedly red-blooded Italian tenor, with brawling energy and, if you'll forgive the expression, guts by the bucketful; to put it another way: a good, old-fashioned belter! As such, one cannot help but be in admiration of such energy, even if,

after a while, your ears may well protest, 'That's enough!'

Anyone who resists that certain breed of precious light tenors of today will be able to blast them out of their brains with a few minutes of Del Monaco. But that is not the whole story: he was lucky in having the very sophisticated soprano Renata Tebaldi in some of the most enduring opera sets of the postwar era.

Of his *Otello*, Tebaldi said of Del Monaco, 'No other tenor in this role, as well as in many others, had the vocal splendour and the irresistible strength of Mario Del Monaco.' In his complete opera recordings there was perhaps more subtlety to be found, but there's not much sign of it here: in the 1956 New Symphony Orchestra stereo recital with Erede, it is impossible not to be thrilled by the sheer heroic quality of the stereo voice, and for those who want to sample his style, this CD is available separately on Decca's Classic Recitals CD (475 6234) where E.G. originally wrote: 'It is just as though someone was in the recording studio, prodding him from behind saying, "Sing louder, Mario! We can't hear you!"'

The earlier mono items with Erede date from 1952 and offer more of the same in remarkably good sound. Nicelli's stereo 'Studio Orchestra' recordings were made in 1958 and capture the 'tea-shop orchestra' very well. Del Monaco fails to turn these often delightful numbers (some of them now rare) into the miniature masterpieces that Gigli or Schipa did, but his far-from-subtle style is not altogether out of keeping; however, a touch of charm would have made all the difference. Mantovani's cascading strings on the 1962 LP are in the unashamedly populist style of the day – it is very much a period recording – but his strings seem to have a (slight) softening effect on Del Monaco.

His *Tonight* from *West Side Story* is hopelessly (hilariously, even) out of style, but there is something endearing about it – a performance which will raise a smile, and a real collector's item.

The items conducted by Carlo Franci (1964) offer unexpected repertoire for Del Monaco, and if the Wagnerian items are not exactly idiomatic they are better than might be expected and have the interest of hearing Del Monaco away from his usual area; the *verismo* items which make up the rest of the disc offer more expected repertoire as well as the expected lack of refinement.

The Monte Carlo numbers, recorded in 1969, offer vintage Decca sound with the conductor Rescigno providing much more subtlety than the soloist (which isn't saying much); there is a sort of Gothic aura to the music-making which one enjoys in short doses. The organ provides even more Gothic qualities to the 'religious' numbers which made up SXL 6234 in 1965. The acoustics of Victoria Hall, Geneva, help to take the edge off Del Monaco's voice, though nothing could make his *Panis angelicus* sound even remotely beautiful; this is undoubtedly another collector's item, of which Decca's recording quality is its most sophisticated facet (just try not to smile at the um-pah-pah rhythm of the Rossini item and you'll see what we mean). A kitsch rarity which, alas, is unlikely to bring you any closer to matters spiritual. George Hall writes in his excellent sleeve-notes: 'Del Monaco's singing is unlikely to please intellectuals. But there is a naked thrill to it that embodies the essential vocal requirements of many operatic roles that are hard to cast today. In a sense, it embodies a more innocent age, when heroes were meant to be straightforwardly heroic and not to question their own motives or status. Such unstinting, full-hearted singing has its value, and in the art of Mario Del Monaco it finds one of its boldest and most resilient advocates.'

Monaco, Mario Del (tenor), New Symphony Orchestra of London, Alberto Erede

Arias from: VERDI: *Un ballo in maschera; Ernani.*
GIORDANO: *Fedora.* PUCCINI: *Madama Butterfly.*
MASSENET: *Le Cid.* BIZET: *Carmen.* MEYERBEER:
L'africana. CATALANI: *La Wally.* DONIZETTI: *Lucia di Lammermoor*
(M) *(**) Decca (ADD) 475 6234

Mario Del Monaco was a large-voiced, old-fashioned tenor who delivered the goods with plenty of energy and tone. He is, of course, ingrained in the minds of record collectors mainly through his complete opera recordings with Tebaldi. Insightful characterization and supreme musical style were not exactly his strong points and, in his later recordings especially, he tended just to bawl everything out *fortissimo*. But, as this 1955 collection shows, it is hard not to be thrilled by the sheer heroic quality of his voice and gutsy singing – and there is plenty of it too. This is not a disc to play all in one go as it is rather wearing. The early stereo is warm and vivid for its period.

Montague, Diana (mezzo-soprano)

'*Bella imagen*': arias, duets and ensembles (with Kenny, Ford, Lewis, Geoffrey Mitchell Ch., ASMF, Philh. or RPO, Parry) from BENEDICT: *I'inganno felice.* DONIZETTI: *Zoraida di Granata.* MAYR: *Alfredo Grande.* MERCADENTE: *Amleto.* MEYERBEER: *Il crociato di Egitto.* MOSCA: *Le bestie in uomini.* PAER: *Sofonisba.* ROSSINI: *Il trionfo di Quinto Fabio.* VON WINTER: *Zaira*
*** Opera Rara ORR 210

Who ever would have thought that Mayr had written an opera about Alfred the Great or that Mercadante had written one about Hamlet? The answer is: those who have been collecting the brilliant series from Opera Rara, '100 Years of Italian Opera', with each decade covered separately. Diana Montague has been a regular contributor, and this compilation of her outstanding recordings is very welcome indeed. Although the recordings were made over a wide period, from 1983 to 1998, the clear, firm voice remains gloriously consistent throughout – as Hugh Canning says in his note, with not only 'the voluptuous warmth of a mezzo, but the shining top of a true soprano'. The title, *Bella imagen*, comes from the Benedict opera, in a 1994 recording that illustrates those qualities perfectly, and one of the 1983 recordings, of the heroine's aria from Von Winter's *Zaira*, had previously demonstrated what dramatic dedication she naturally conveys. Diana Montague has made far too few recordings, but this splendidly fills an important gap, with David Parry providing strong support, mainly with the Philharmonia.

Nash, Heddle (tenor)

'*Serenade*': arias from: BIZET: *The Fair Maid of Perth; The Pearl Fishers.* ROSSINI: *The Barber of Seville.* MOZART: *Don Giovanni; Le nozze di Figaro* (both sung in Italian). BALFE: *The Bohemian Girl.* LEHAR: *Frederica.* OFFENBACH, arr. KORNGOLD: *La Belle Hélène.* GOUNOD: *Faust.* DONIZETTI: *Elixir of Love.* HANDEL: *Judas Maccabaeus.* MASSENET: *Manon.* Songs: TRAD. *Annie Laurie* (all with orch.).

BENEDICT: *Eily Mavoureen.* BISHOP: *The Bloom is on the Rye.* MORGAN: *My Sweetheart when a Boy.* MCGEOCH: *Two Eyes of Grey.* MACDOWELL: *To a Wild Rose.* WHITAKER: *Diaphenia.* DELIUS: *To the Queen of my Heart; Love's Philosophy.* WHITE: *To Mary.* MOERAN: *Diaphenia; The Sweet o' the Year* (all with Moore)
(M) (**(*)) ASV mono CDAJA 5227

Although there are a few (obvious) duplications, this ASV compilation nicely supplements the finer Dutton Lab. collection (now deleted). The transfers of the orchestral accompaniments, which often sound boxy and confined, are much less sophisticated, but the voice emerges naturally, even if it is projected with less uniform vividness. But there are genuine treasures here, not least the songs, with Gerald Moore, who is more faithfully caught. The delightful 'To a Wild Rose', the Delius and Moeran songs and the splendid excerpt from *Judas Maccabaeus* are among the highlights.

New College, Oxford, Choir, Edward Higginbottom

'*Carols from New College*': O Come, All Ye Faithful; The Angel Gabriel; Ding Dong! Merrily on High; The Holly and the Ivy; I Wonder as I Wander; Sussex Carol; This is the Truth; A Virgin Most Pure; Rocking Carol; Once in Royal David's City. ORD: *Adam Lay Y-bounden.* BENNETT: *Out of your Sleep.* HOWELLS: *A Spotless Rose; Here is the Little Door.* DARKE: *In the Bleak Midwinter.* MATHIAS: *A Babe is Born; Wassail Carol.* WISHART: *Alleluya, A New Work is Come on Hand.* LEIGHTON: *Lully, Lulla, Thou Little Tiny Child.* JOUBERT: *There is no Rose of Such Virtue*
(M) *** CRD (ADD) CRD 3443

A beautiful Christmas record, the mood essentially serene and reflective. Both the Mathias settings are memorable and spark a lively response from the choir; Howells' 'Here is the Little Door' is matched by Wishart's Alleluya and Kenneth Leighton's 'Lully, Lully, Thou Little Tiny Child' in memorability. Fifteen of the twenty-one items here are sung unaccompanied, to maximum effect. The recording acoustic seems ideal and the balance is first class. The documentation, however, consists of just a list of titles and sources – and the CD (using the unedited artwork from the LP) lists them as being divided onto side one and side two!

'*Coronation Anthems*' (with AAM): BOYCE: *The King shall rejoice; Come, Holy Ghost; Praise the Lord, O Jerusalem.* HANDEL: *The King shall rejoice; Zadok the Priest.* CROFT: *The Lord is a Sun and a Shield.* CLARKE: *Praise the Lord, O Jerusalem.* BLOW: *Let my Prayer come up; The Lord God is a Sun and a Shield.* PURCELL: *I was glad; My heart is inditing*
B—→ (M) *** Decca 476 7230

An outstanding collection of *Coronation Anthems*, recorded in 2000/2001, which hitherto we have missed but which is now reissued in Decca's 'Critics' Choice' series and must receive the strongest recommendation. The programme, not arranged in date order, is framed by anthems from William Boyce (for the coronation of George III in 1761) which make an arresting opening, and the better-known Purcell music for James II (1685). But alongside the even more familiar Handel *Anthems* (for George II in 1727) come outstanding shorter works by John Blow (1689), and William Croft (1714). The surprise is *Praise the Lord, O Jerusalem*, written for the coronation of Queen Anne by Jeremiah Clarke, which, like his more famous trumpet piece, is short but memorable. Fine, strongly expressive performances throughout and vividly resonant if not always sharply focused recording, made in London's Temple Church, are supported by good documentation and full texts.

New Company, Harry Bicket

'*Sacred Voices*': ALLEGRI: *Miserere.* LOBO: *Versa est in luctum.* PALESTRINA: *The Song of Solomon: Quae est ista; Descendit in hortum nocum; Quam pulchri sunt gressus tui; Duo ubera tue.* BYRD: *Haec dies.* PHILIPS: *Ascendit Deus.* MUNDY: *Vox Patris caelestis.* TALLIS: *Spem in alium* (40-part motet). DERING: *Factum est silentium*
(M) *** Classic fm 75605 57029-2

A splendid recording début for the New Company, a professional chamber choir of twelve, directed by Harry Bicket, which is expanded here to forty voices for a thrilling performance of Tallis's *Spem in alium*, one of the great masterpieces of Elizabethan music. The programme opens with a double choir version of Allegri's justly famous *Miserere*, with the second group atmospherically recessed alongside the confident soprano soloist, who soars up again and again to what the conductor calls that 'exquisitely floaty top C': and she hits the spot beautifully every time.

Then follows Lobo's hardly less ethereal *Versa est in luctum* and a characteristic sequence of four serenely flowing five-part motets from Palestrina's *Song of Solomon*, sensuously rich in harmonic implication, all written around 1583–4. Suddenly the mood changes and the pace quickens for William Byrd's *Haec dies*, with its joyful cross-rhythms and an exultant concluding *Alleluia*. Peter Philips's *Ascendit Deus* is similarly full of life and energy and it prepares the way for the contrasting three-part anthem by the lesser-known William Mundy. Its serene simplicity has great beauty, and it again offers a chance for a celestial soaring solo soprano.

After the climactic Tallis work, the programme ends with a short, but thrillingly jubilant, six-part Matins responsory by Richard Dering. The choir were recorded at Temple Church, London, the venue some ten decades earlier for one of the most famous choral recordings of all time: Mendelssohn's *Hear my Prayer*, with its famous solo from Master Ernest Lough, 'Oh for the Wings of a Dove'. The treble soloist here is a worthy successor.

Nilsson, Birgit (soprano)

'*The Legendary Birgit Nilsson*': VERDI: *Aida* (with ROHCGO, John Pritchard); *Don Carlo; La forza del destino* (with ROHCG O, Argeo Quadri); *Macbeth;* PUCCINI: *Tosca* (with Santa Cecilia O, Rome, Thomas Schippers or Lorin Maazel). WAGNER (orch. Mottl): *Wesendonk Lieder* (with LSO, Colin Davis). WAGNER: *Lohengrin; Tannhäuser.* (with ROHCG O, Edward Downes). *Tristan und Isolde* (with VPO, Hans Knappertsbusch); *Götterdämmerung.* R. STRAUSS: *Elektra; Salome* (with VPO, Georg Solti). *Die Frai ohne Schatten* (with Vienna State Op. O, Karl Boehm). SIBELIUS: Songs: *Autumn Evening; Black Roses; The Diamond on the March snow; Sigh, rushes, sigh; Spring flies fast; The Tryst; Was it a dream?.* GRIEG: *A swan; From Monte Pincilo; Spring.* RANGSTROM: *An old dance rhythm;*

Melody; Prayer to night; Valkyrie (with Vienna Op. O, Bertil Bokstedt). LOEWE: *I could have danced all night*
❀ (BB) *** Decca (ADD) 473 791-2 (2)

When Birgit Nilsson died in 2005, a significant legend of opera history had gone. Her voice was simply enormous, but it was not just its size which was remarkable: she possessed an instantly recognizable timbre which she was able to use to superb dramatic effect. Decca have an impressive Nilsson catalogue from which to draw, and they have included some prime examples of her Wagner performances, for which she is famous, as well as her thrilling performances of Richard Strauss's *Salome* and *Elektra*. The well-known Verdi and Puccini items are vivid and dramatic (as is the 1960s Decca sound) and it all emerges, as we expect, in Decca's best vintage opera quality. The *Wesendonk Lieder* are surprisingly restrained readings, matching Colin Davis's concept, but are certainly enjoyable (these are Philips recordings from 1972).

What is especially good about this set is a reminder of some of the rarer repertoire she recorded, notably the Decca LP 'Songs from the Land of the Midnight Sun'; this disc shows Nilsson at her most eloquent. *The Tryst*, contemporary with his *Second Symphony*, has a power and dramatic passion with which any lover of Sibelius's orchestral music will find an immediate affinity. *Sigh, rushes, sigh* is especially imaginative in its creation of atmospheric tension, while *Autumn Evening* shows the composer at the height of his powers; this is a wonderful piece with an exciting climax. Nilsson sings superbly and always to fine dramatic effect. In the lighter Grieg songs she shows a loving affection, fining down the voice with a beautifully spun line. The Rangström songs are slighter in their quality of invention, but still rewarding. The 1965 sound is rich and full. The booklet includes a wonderful photograph of Nilsson on an exercise bike (!) during a break in the recording of *Elektra*, and the inclusion of *I could have danced all night* shows a sense of humour in the artist – as well as in Decca. The ❀ is both for this excellent compilation and for Birgit Nilsson's magnificent and considerable recording achievements in general – they don't seem to make singers like this any more, alas.

Nilsson, Birgit, Kirsten Flagstad (sopranos)

'*Land of the Midnight Sun*': Birgit Nilsson: SIBELIUS: *Demanten på marssnön; Flickan kom ifran sin alsklings mote; Höstkväll; Säv, Säv, Susa; Svarta rosor; Var deten drom; Våren flyktar hastigt.* GRIEG: *En svane; Fra monte pincio; Våren.* RANGSTROM: *Bön till natten; En gammal dansrytm; Melodi; Sköldmön* (all with V. Op. O, Bokstedt). Kirsten Flagstad: EGGEN: *Aere det evige forår i livet.* ALNAES: *Februarmorgen ved Golfen; De hundrede fioliner; Nu brister alle de klofter; Vårlaengsler.* LIE: *Nykelen; Skinnvengbrev* (all with LSO, Fjeldstad)
*** Australian Decca (ADD) 466 657-2

The Birgit Nilsson items, recorded in the late 1950s, show her art at its most eloquent. One does not primarily think of Sibelius as a song composer, yet every one of the songs is given a distinctive and highly memorable performance. *Flickan kom ifran*, contemporary with the *Second Symphony*, has a power and dramatic passion with which any lover of Sibelius's orchestral music will find an immediate affinity. *Säv, Säv* too is especially imaginative in its creation of atmospheric tension, but all the songs offer something to the istener, and all are superbly sung. In the lighter Greig items, Nilsson shows loving affection, and though the Rangstrom songs are slighter in their quality, they are still rewarding.

Flagstad's contribution was recorded a few years later and is just as compelling: one can hear why she so spellbound isteners by her performances of songs in her first London recital in 1936. Any doubts about the size of the voice being too unwieldy for this comparatively intimate programme are swept away by the eloquence and commitment of the singing. Oivin Fjeldstad's contribution too is an outstanding one. Few of the songs are well known but with such deeply-felt advocacy they are all worth getting to know. The recordings emerge warm and vivid in this transfer, and whilst texts are not provided (nor were they on their original LP releases), this Australian Eloquence CD comes complete with sleeve-notes (written, unlike this entry, by our own R.L.). Alas, as an import it will cost more in the UK, but it is well worth it.

Norman, Jessye (soprano)

'A French Collection': BERLIOZ: Les Nuits d'été. RAVEL: Deux melodies hébraïques; Shéhérazade (with LSO, Colin Davis). DUPARC: Chanson triste; L'Invitation au voyage; Phidylé; La Vie antérieure. POULENC: Les Chemins de l'amour; Le Grenouillère; Montparnasse; Voyage à Paris. SATIE: Je te veux; 3 Mélodies (with Dalton Baldwin, piano)
(B) **(*) Ph. (ADD) 475 6380 (2)

Jessye Norman is in fine voice for her 1979 recording of Les Nuits d'été and Shéhérazade, even if in the former she does not get fully inside this most magical of orchestral song-cycles. There is no lack of voluptuousness, but the word meanings are less subtly registered than in the finest versions. Davis's tempi are sometimes over-deliberate: this fault is especially apparent in Shéhérazade, where both she and Davis are languorous to the point of lethargy in L'indifférent, although, overall, Norman is more at home in this song-cycle than in Les Nuits d'été. With the voice very forward, the balance is less than ideal, though otherwise the sound is rich and atmospheric. The French recital with Dalton Baldwin dates from 1976 and shows that the artist's great voice was then already glowing in its distinctive range of tone and expression. But at this point in her career she was still inhibited in the studio; though the interpretations and subtleties are many, she was later to give even deeper and more searching performances in the repertory. The sound has transferred well to CD.

'Sacred Songs and Spirituals' (with Ambrosian Singers, Bowers-Broadbent (organ), Alexander Gibson): GOUNOD: Sanctus. SCHUBERT: Ave Maria. FRANCK: Panis angelicus. GOUNOD: O divine redeemer. ADAMS: The Holy City. ANON.: Amazing Grace; Greensleeves; I wonder as I wander; Let us break bread together. MACGIMSEY: Sweet little Jesus boy. YON: Gesù bambino. Spirituals (with Amb. S., Dalton Baldwin (piano), Willis Patterson): Do Lawd, oh do Lawd; Ev'ry time I feel de spirit; Give me Jesus; Gospel train; Great day; I couldn't hear nobody pray; Hush! Somebody's callin' my name; Live a-humble; Mary had a baby; My Lord, what a morning; Soon ah will be done; There's a balm in Gilead; There's a man going around; Walk together children; Were you there
(B) *** Ph. (ADD/DDD) 475 6386 (2)

There is a degree of restraint in Jessye Norman's singing of spirituals and sacred songs which may seem surprising, but the depth of feeling is never in doubt. The 'Spirituals' recital (with Gibson) was recorded in 1978, and what she has consciously done is to tilt the performances towards concert tradition; with refined recording the result is both beautiful and moving. The second CD, 'Sacred Songs', was recorded in 1981, and again she sings with eloquence, and her simplicity and sincerity shine through repertoire that can easily sound sentimental. The Gounod Sanctus is especially fine, but the simpler songs are very affecting.

'The Songbooks' (with Boston Pops O, John Williams, conductor and/or pianist): RODGERS: Falling in love with love; Lover; Spring is here; With a song in my heart. PORTER: I love Paris; I love you; In the still of the night. KERN: All the things you are; I'm old fashioned; The Song is you. ARLEN: A sleepin' bee. GERSHWIN: But not for me; Love is here to stay; Love walked in. LEGRAND: I will wait for you; Papa, can you hear me?; Where is it written. WEILL: My ship; September Song; Speak Low. BERNSTEIN: Lonely town; Lucky to be me. LOEWE: Show me. JOEL: Just the way you are
(B) *Ph. 475 6383 (2)

This Philips two-CD set comprises two of Jessye Norman's lighter recordings, 'With A Song in My Heart' (with the Boston Pops Orchestra) and 'Lucky To Be Me', recorded in 1984 and 1987/9 respectively. It is sad to report that, although the voice is as glorious as ever, this crossover repertoire finds the singer caught between operatic and pop styles, and in accompaniment with the Boston orchestra she is somewhat aggressive. In the items with piano accompaniment, some come off better than others: I will wait for you is beautifully done, but Show Me (from My Fair Lady) is disconcertingly out of style – it sounds just plain wrong. Good sound, and texts are included for Jessye Norman fans, who will still want this set.

'Live Hohenems & Salzburg Recital'; 'Live at Hohenems, 1987': HANDEL: Dank sei dir, Herr; Armida, dispietata! – Lascia ch'io pianga (from Rinaldo). SCHUMANN: Liederkreis: Auf einer Burg; Frühlingsnacht; Schöne Fremde; Wehmut. Myrthen, Op. 25: Du bist wie eine Blume; Widmung. SCHUBERT: An die Natur; Ave Maria; Auf dem See; Erlkönig; Gretchen am Spinnrade; Die Liebe hat gelogen; Meeres Stille; Der Musensohn; Rastlose Liebe; Der Tod und das Mädchen. BRAHMS: Meine Liebe ist grün. R. STRAUSS: Wirbeide woollen springen. Spirituals: Great Day; He's got the whole world (with Geoffrey Parsons, piano). Salzburg Recital: BRAHMS: 6 Geistliche Lieder, Op. 48. WOLF: Italienisches Liederbuch (extracts); Spanisches Liederbuch (extracts). DEBUSSY: Beau soir; Les Cloches; Mandoline; Nuit d'étoiles; Romance (with James Levine (piano))
(B) **(*) Ph. 475 6389 (2)

The Hohenems Festival recital was recorded in June 1987 and gives a vivid idea of the atmosphere and excitement of a Jessye Norman recital. It ends in explosions of wild joy and enthusiasm in response to the two spirituals which are given as final encores: exuberant, full-throated singing that communicates with physical impact. Next to this, some of her studio-made recordings of Lieder sound reticent – but there are losses as well as gains, particularly when the recording is on the rough side, with piano-tone clangy. The freedom of expressiveness too will strike many Lieder enthusiasts as excessive, with Schumann's Widmung, for example, fluctuating in tempo out of wild urgency. But there are many unique moments, as in the dark intensity of Schubert's *Meeres Stille* or the colourful vocal characterization in *Erlkönig*. The recording balance is not ideal, with the voice sometimes set at a distance. The Salzburg recital was recorded in New York (!) in 1990 and offers a more beautiful recording, with James Levine the sensitive pianist. If the Debussy items do not possess the idiomatic flair of a native artist, they are beautifully done – and what wonderful songs they are! The Wolf Lieder receive impressive performances by any standards, with Norman very much regarding them as operatic in range, with large and bold dynamic contrasts, though far from unsubtle. The Beethoven items making an unexpected and enjoyable contrast and this two-CD set is a must for all Jessye Norman fans.

'*Jessye Norman at Christmas*': Recital 1: '*At Notre-Dame*' (with Vittoria Regional Ch. of Île de France, Maîtrise de R. France, Lyon Op. O, Lawrence Foster): Bruce SAYLOR: *Jubilate Fanfare & Fantasy; Star of Wonder*. BACH: *Magnificat, BWV 243: Et exsultavit*. GOUNOD: *Ave Maria*. BRAHMS: *Geistliches Wiegenlied*. SCHUBERT/LISZT: *Die Allmacht*. attrib. Thomas RALLY, arr. SAYLOR: *Behold that Star*. arr. SAYLOR: *Rockin' for the World; O poor little Jesus' Go tell it to the Mountain*. HANDEL: *Messiah: He shall feed His flock*. BIZET: *Agnus Dei*. GOUNOD: *Repentir. Messe solennelle de Sainte Cécile: Sanctus*

Recital 2: '*At Ely Cathedral*' (with American Boychoir, Ely Cathedral Choristers, Vocal Arts Ch., Bournemouth SO, Robert de Cormier): arr. Donald FRASER: *O come O come, Emanuel; Once in Royal David's Cty; Unto us a Child is born; Good Christian men rejoice; The Holly and the Ivy; See amid the winter snow; I saw three ships; The Coventry Carol; In the bleak midwinter; Angels we have heard on high; Adeste fidelis (O come, all ye faithful)*. ADAM: *O Holy Night*. MCCULLOCH; *Jessye's Carol*. HOPKINS: *We three Kings*. HANDEL: *Joy to the World*. FRASER: *Amen*

⬤ *** Ph. **DVD** 074 3104

This is a gorgeous Christmas DVD, ideal for watching on Christmas Eve, and with the first Paris recital (and many items on the second) suitable for listening and viewing all the year round. Each opens by showing the cathedral itself, and then the music begins as we enter. The recordings were made in 1988 at Ely (where the Thames TV engineers achieve a much sharper focus for the chorus than their French colleagues) and in Paris two Christmases later.

Jessye Norman is at the peak of her form, not only singing radiantly (Handel's *He shall feed his flock* is elysian), but showing visually her love for and dedication to every item. She can declaim with passion, she is in element in the spirituals, and in the sacred songs she sings with great eloquence and feeling; her sincerity shines through repertoire that can easily sound sentimental.

Bruce Saylor's arrangements at Notre Dame are very nicely judged in scale. His own fantasy for the children's choir based on '*Twinkle, twinkle little star*' is charming (if a shade long) and the closing spectacular version of Gounod's *Sanctus* is thrilling. For the second, more Christmassy collection, at Ely, Donald Fraser's settings of familiar traditional carols are most engaging, somewhat after the style of John Rutter, especially the sparkling *The Holly and the Ivy* and *I saw three ships*, and the performances by soloist and choruse alike are most affecting. J. McCulloch's carol, especially written for the singer, brings out her resonantly rich lower register, and Fraser's final *Amen* tests her gloriously to the full.

The recording of the voice is most natural throughout, and if the Notre Dame choral sound could be clearer, the ear soon adjusts. The camera, rightly, spends most of the time in close-ups of the soloist, but in Paris some of the long shots are too distant. But overall this is very rewarding on all levels. (N.B. our disc was supposed to reproduce in surround sound. This did not register on our SACD four-speaker set-up, but it no doubt will on cinema-style TV setups.)

Oberlin, Russell (counter-tenor)

'*Troubadour and Trouvère Songs*', Volume 1 (with Seymour Barab, viol): BRULE: *Cil qui d'amor me conseille*. DE BORNEIL: *Reis glorios, verais lums e clartatz*. DANIEL: *Chanson do – Ih mot son plan e prim*. D'EPINAL: *Commensmens de dolce saison bele*. RIQUIER: *Ples de tristor, marritz e doloires; de ventadour: Can vei la lauzeta mover*
*** Lyrichord LEMS 8001

It is good to see the legendary Russell Oberlin return to the catalogue. Older readers will recall his Covent Garden appearance as Oberon in Britten's *Midsummer Night's Dream*. Unfortunately his concert career was cut short and he has since pursued a distinguished career as a scholar. This 1958 recital of *Troubadour and Trouvère Songs* first appeared on the Experiences Anonymes label and, like so many of his all-too-few recordings (including an incredible Handel aria disc), has long been sought after. This voice was quite unique, a real counter-tenor of exquisite quality and, above all, artistry. The disc is expertly annotated and is of quite exceptional interest. LEMS stands for Lyrichord Early Music Series, and the discs we have heard so far are artistically impressive.

'*Las Cantigas de Santa Maria*' (with Joseph Iadone, lute): *Prologo; Cantigas 7, 36, 97, 111, 118, 160, 205, 261, 330, 340 & 364*
⬤ *** Lyrichord LEMS 8003

The 400 *Cantigas de Santa Maria*, all of which have music, come from the time of Alfonso el Sabio, king of Spain (1221–84). He is credited with being their composer, but that seems unlikely since they are very diverse. The texts are in Galician, a language in general use in medieval Spain for literary and artistic purposes.

They are all concerned with miracles associated with the Virgin Mary, but the music itself has considerable variety and, while the basic style may come from European monodic chant, the melisma has a distinctly Spanish colouring, which in itself has Arab influences. The selection of a dozen items is very well made, for these simple strophic songs have an instant appeal when sung with such lyrical ease by the incomparable Russell Oberlin. The character of the *Cantigas* seems to suit his special timbre especially well, and he has made no finer record than this.

The recital opens with a Prologue in which the singer relates the qualities necessary to be a good troubadour and invokes the Virgin's acceptance of his skills with some confidence. Two of the settings are lively dance songs, *Cantiga 36* telling how Mary appeared in the night on the mast of a ship journeying to Brittany and saved it from danger, and *Cantiga 205* about the rescue of a Moorish woman with her child who were sitting on top of a tower which collapsed – yet neither she nor the child came to any harm. But it is the beauty of the lyrical music which is so striking, notably so in *Cantigas 118* and *330*, which are concerned with the restoration of a dead child to life and a simple song of praise for the Virgin herself.

The recording is natural and vivid and, as with the other discs in this series, the CD remastering by Nick Fritsch is first class. The content of this reissue is not generous in playing time, but it is of the very highest musical quality and interest.

'Troubadour and Trouvère Songs', Volume 5: English medieval songs (with Seymour Barab, viol): *The St Godric Songs; Worldes Blis ne Last no Throwe; Bryd One Breve; Man mei Longe him Liues Wene; Stond Wel Moder under Rode*

*** Lyrichord LEMS 8005

The *St Godric Songs* are the earliest known songs in the English language. St Godric died in 1170, so they date from halfway through the twelfth century. The other items here belong to the latter part of the century. As with his first disc, above, Russell Oberlin is completely convincing in this repertoire, the purity of line and beauty of timbre consistently appealing. The accompanying viol is discreet and the sound is remarkably clear and vivid.

Opera love songs

'Amor – Opera's Great Love Songs': VERDI: *Aida: Celeste Aida. Luisa Miller: Quando le sere al placido* (Pavarotti). *Rigoletto: Caro nome* (Sutherland). PUCCINI: *Gianni Schicchi: O mio babbino caro* (Tebaldi). *Manon Lescaut: Donna non vidi mai* (Carreras). *Tosca: Recondita armonia* (Corelli); *Vissi d'arte* (Kiri Te Kanawa); *E lucevan le stelle* (Domingo). *La Bohème: Musetta's Waltz Song* (Elizabeth Harwood). *Madama Butterfly: Un bel dì* (Mirella Freni). *Turandot: Signore ascolta!* (Caballé); *Nessun dorma* (Pavarotti). DONIZETTI: *La favorita: O mio Fernando* (Cossotto). *L'elisir d'amore: Una furtiva lagrima. Fedora: Amor ti vieta.* PONCHIELLI: *La Gioconda: Cielo e mar.* MASSENET: *Werther: Pourquoi me réveiller* (all Pavarotti). BIZET: *Carmen: Habanera* (Troyanos); *Flower Song* (Domingo). MOZART: *Le nozze di Figaro: Voi che sapete* (Frederica von Stade)

(M) *** Decca (ADD) 458 201-2

Brimming over with stellar performances, this generous (76-minute) collection is a true 'opera gala'. Pavarotti dominates and seldom lets us down, and he ends the disc with a thrilling performance of his great showpiece, *Nessun dorma*, from his complete set conducted by Mehta. Many of the other excerpts too are drawn from outstanding sets, including Caballé's beautiful *Signore ascolta!* (taken from the same source), Freni's passionately expansive *Un bel dì* from Karajan's *Madama Butterfly*, Domingo's outstanding Flower Song and Troyanos's *Habanera*, both from Solti's *Carmen*, and Frederica von Stade's delightful *Voi che sapete*, taken from the same conductor's highly successful *Nozze di Figaro*. Tebaldi's ravishing *O mio babbino caro* dates from 1962 when the voice still had all its bloom, while Marilyn Horne's dark-voiced 'Softly Awakes my Heart' comes from a 1967 recital. Nicely packaged in a slip case, the documentation includes full translations.

'Operatunity Winners'

'Operatunity Winners': Jane Gilchrist (soprano) and Denise Leigh (soprano), with ENO Ch. & O, Paul Daniel

Arias from: BELLINI: *Norma.* BIZET: *Carmen.* CATALANI: *La Wally.* DVORAK: *Rusalka.* HANDEL: *Samson.* MOZART: *Le nozze di Figaro.* PUCCINI: *Gianni Schicchi; Turandot.*

SULLIVAN: *The Pirates of Penzance* (with ENO Ch.). VERDI: *Rigoletto.* Duets from: DELIBES: *Lakmé.* HUMPERDINCK: *Hänsel und Gretel.* MOZART: *Le nozze di Figaro*

*** EMI 5 57594-2

Following on from Channel 4's excellent 'Operatunity' series, this delightful issue presents on disc the two winners in that contest of would-be opera-singers, Jane Gilchrist and Denise Leigh. This is a generous and well-chosen sequence of 14 arias, divided between the two, plus three duets, the Countess and Susanna's duet from Mozart's *Marriage of Figaro*, the Evening Hymn from Humperdinck's *Hänsel und Gretel* and the duet from Delibes' *Lakmé*, all beautifully done. They each perform *Caro nome* from Verdi's *Rigoletto* – the opera they appeared in at the ENO – with Leigh the brighter and more agile, ending on a wonderfully controlled trill, and Gilchrist the warmer and more freely imaginative. As on TV, they seem totally unfazed by the formidable technical problems of even the most challenging items, Leigh in *Casta diva* from *Norma*, Gilchrist commanding in the Countess's two arias from *Figaro*. An astonishing achievement!

Otter, Anne Sofie von (mezzo-soprano)

'Wings in the Night' (Swedish songs; with Forsberg, piano): PETERSON-BERGER: *Aspåkers-polska (Aspåker's Polka); Aterkomst (Return); Böljeby-vals (Böljeby Waltz); Like the Stars in the Sky (Som stjärnorna på himmeln); Marits visor (3 songs, Op. 12); Nothing is Like the Time of Waiting (Intet är som väntanstider); When I Walk by Myself (När jag går för mig själv).* SJOGREN: *6 Songs from Julius Wollf's Tannhäuser.* SIGURD VON KOCH: *In the Month of Tjaitra (I månaden Tjaitra); Of Lotus Scent and Moonshine (Af Lotusdoft och månens sken); The Wild Swans (De vilda svanarna) (3 songs).* STENHAMMAR: *Miss Blond and Miss Brunette (Jungfru blond och jungfru brunett); In the Maple's Shade (I lönnens skymning); Jutta Comes to the Volkungs (Jutta kommer till Folkungarna); A Seaside Song (En strandvisa); A Ship is Sailing (Det far ett skepp); The Wanderer (Vandraren).* RANGSTROM: *The Farewell (Afskedet); Old Swedish (Gammalsvenskt); Melodi; Pan; Supplication to Night (Bön till natten); Wings in the Night (Vingar i natten).* ALFVEN: *The Forest is Asleep (Skogen sover); I Kiss your White Hand (Jag kysser din vita hand)*

(M) *** DG 476 2523

So often Swedish singers, once they have made a name for themselves in the world, neglect their native repertoire in favour of Schumann, Brahms, Strauss and Wolf. Anne Sofie von Otter is an exception and, fresh from her recent successes in Scandinavian repertoire, above all her Grieg *Haugtussa* and her Sibelius recitals on BIS, she gives us a splendid anthology of Swedish songs. The disc takes its name from one of Ture Rangström's most haunting songs, *Vingar i natten* ('Wings in the Night'), and, indeed, his are some of the loveliest songs in the Swedish *romans* repertoire. (*Romans* is the Nordic equivalent of *Lied*.) *Bön till natten* ('Supplication to the Night') is arguably the most beautiful of all Swedish songs and has the innocence and freshness of Grieg combined with a melancholy and purity that are totally individual.

Von Otter, who was the *Gramophone's* 'Artist of the Year' in 1996, also includes songs by the composer-critic Wilhelm Peterson-Berger, whose criticism was much admired in his native Sweden and who was compared with Bernard Shaw (he was in fact an opinionated windbag) and whose songs have a certain wistful charm. The Stenhammar songs are among his finest, and von Otter adds some familiar Alfvén and less familiar repertoire by Emil Sjögren and Sigurd (not to be confused with Erland) von Koch. A disc to be treasured, now reissued at mid price with full texts and translations.

'Folksongs' (with Forsberg, piano): DVORAK: *Gypsy Songs, Op. 55.* GRAINGER: *The Sprig of Thyme; Died for Love; British Waterside; The Pretty Maid Milkin' her Cow.* LARSSON: *Watercolour; The Box Painter; The Girl with the Divining Herb.* G. HAHN: *The Heart's Prey: A Song from Lapland.* R. HAHN: Songs in Venetian dialect: *On the Drowsy Waters; The Little Boat; The Warning; The Fair Maid in the Gondola; What a Shame!* KODALY: Hungarian folk music: *Little Apple Fell in the Mud; Drinking Wine on Sunday; Youth is Like a Falcon; Let No-one's Bride Bewail; All Through the Vineyard; Hey, the Price of Wine from Mohovce Hill; Beneath the Csitár Hills.* BRITTEN: arr. of French folksongs: *La Noël passée; Voice le printemps; La Fileuse; Le Roi s'en va-t'en chasse; La Belle est au jardin d'amour; Il est quelqu'un sur terre; Eho! Eho!; Quand j'etais chez mon père*
*** (IMS) DG 463 479-2

An enterprising and rewarding recital from the great Swedish mezzo, this covers a wide range of songs from the Slavonic to Kodály and Britten rarities. Her impeccable artistry is given excellent support from Bengt Forsberg and the DG engineers.

'Watercolours': Swedish Songs (with Forsberg, piano): ALFVÉN: *Pioner (Peonies); Saa tag mitt Hjerte (Take my Heart).* TOR AULIN: *Och riddaren for uti österland (And the Knight Rode to the Holy Land); 4 serbiska folksånger (4 Serbian Folksongs).* GUNNAR DE FRUMERIE: *Hjärtats sånger (6 Songs of the Heart); Nu är det sommarmogon (A Summer Morning).* LARS-ERIK LARSSON: *Kyssande vind (Kiss of the Wind); För vilana fötter sjunger gräser (Grass Sings under Wandering Feet); Skyn, blomman och en lärka (The Cloud, the Flower and the Lark).* BO LINDE: *Den ängen där du kysste mig (The Meadow Where you Kissed me); Äppelträd och päronträd (Apple-trees and Pear-trees); 4 Songs to texts by Harriet Löwenhjelm.* GUSTAF NORDQVIST: *Sipporna (The Anemones); Jag ville vara tårar (If I Could be Tears); Till havs (On the Sea).* GÖSTA NYSTROEM: *På reveln (On the Reef), Otrolig dag (Amazing Day); Havet sjunger (The Song of the Sea).* TURE RANGSTRÖM: *En gammal dansrytm (An Old Dance); Den enda stunden (A Moment in Time); Serenad; Sköldmön (The Amazon)*
❂ *** DG 474 700-2

This new recital of Swedish songs from Anne Sofie von Otter and Bengt Forsberg follows on from their earlier recital, which took its title from Rangström's song 'Wings in the Night', and admirably complements the earlier issue. It is good to see them championing Gunnar de Frumerie, whose settings of Pär Lagerkvist have a quiet, unforced eloquence. De Frumerie was a Sabaneyev pupil and had a splendid feeling for the keyboard and a keen, almost Gallic sensibility. He was neglected in the 1950s and '60s – though not as grievously as Bo Linde, who died in his late thirties and whose songs have an affecting simplicity and directness of utterance. Another surprise is the set of three songs of Gösta Nystroem: those who find his *Sinfonia del mare* hard work

should investigate these wonderfully imaginative and atmospheric pieces. *På reveln* ('On the Reef') is a little masterpiece, one of the most haunting songs on the disc. Lars-Erik Larsson's *Skyn, blom'man och en lärka* ('The Cloud, the Flower and the Lark') is another discovery. Why is it that such a beautiful song is so little known and his inventive *Music for Orchestra* and (for all its debt to Walton and Prokofiev) the *Violin Concerto* so rarely heard? In all there are 33 songs in this recital, all of them rewarding and some of them are masterpieces, like Rangström's haunting *Den enda stunden* ('The Only Moment', translated here as 'A Moment in Time'), possibly the greatest of all his songs and arguably the finest of all these songs. Indeed Swedish song is one of the great undiscovered treasures of the north, and this distinguished partnership is its most persuasive advocate. Superbly balanced recorded sound.

Oxford Camerata, Jeremy Summerly

'*Lamentations*': WHITE: *Lamentations.* TALLIS: *Lamentations, Sets I & II.* PALESTRINA: *Lesson I for Maundy Thursday.* LASSUS: *Lessons I & III for Maundy Thursday.* ESTAVAO DE BRITO: *Lesson I for Good Friday*
❂ (BB) *** Naxos 8.550572

On the bargain Naxos label come nearly 70 minutes of sublime polyphony, beautifully sung by the fresh-toned Oxford Camerata under Jeremy Summerly. All these *Lamentations* (*Lessons* simply means collection of verses) are settings from the Old Testament book, the Lamentations of Jeremiah. They were intended for nocturnal use and are usually darkly intense in feeling. The English and Italian *Lamentations* have their own individuality, but the most striking of all is the *Good Friday Lesson* by the Portuguese composer Estâvão de Brito. This is very direct and strong in feeling for, as the anonymous insert-note writer points out, Portugal was under Spanish subjugation at the time and de Brito effectively uses dissonance at the words *non est lex* ('there is no law') to assert his nationalistic defiance. The recorded sound is vividly beautiful within an ideal ambience.

Panzéra, Charles (baritone)

French and German Songs: FAURE: *La Bonne Chanson, Op. 61; L'Horizon chimérique; Au cimetière; En sourdine.* DUPARC: *Extase; Lamento; L'Invitation au voyage; Sérénade Florentine; La Vie antérieure* (with Magda Panzéra-Baillot, piano). SCHUMANN: *Dichterliebe, Op. 48* (with Cortot, piano)
❂ (B) (***) Dutton mono CDBP 9726

What a glorious voice – and apart from the tonal beauty, it is a joy to hear every syllable with such clarity. The Swiss-born French baritone, Charles Panzéra (1896–1976) was closely associated with Fauré's songs (and gave the first performance of *L'Horizon chimérique*). During the 1930s when most of these records were made, he was the foremost interpreter of the French repertoire, and in particular Duparc, whose songs have a special eloquence. His selfless artistry is everywhere in evidence and not even Pierre Bernac or Gérard Souzay surpass him. The Dutton transfers bring his voice to life as no others before them!

Pavarotti, Luciano (tenor)

'Tutto Pavarotti': VERDI: *Aida: Celeste Aida. Luisa Miller: Quando le sere al placido. La traviata: De' miei bollenti spiriti. Il trovatore: Ah si ben mio; Di quella pira. Rigoletto: La donna è mobile. Un ballo in maschera: La rivedrà nell'estasi.* DONIZETTI: *L'elisir d'amore: Una furtiva lagrima. Don Pasquale: Com'è gentil.* PONCHIELLI: *La Gioconda: Cielo e mar.* FLOTOW: *Martha: M'appari.* BIZET: *Carmen: Flower Song.* MASSENET: *Werther: Pourquoi me réveiller.* MEYERBEER: *L'Africana: O paradiso.* BOITO: *Mefistofele: Dai campi, dai prati.* LEONCAVALLO: *Pagliacci: Vesti la giubba.* MASCAGNI: *Cavalleria rusticana: Addio alla madre.* GIORDANO: *Fedora: Amor ti vieta.* PUCCINI: *La fanciulla del West: Ch'ella mi creda. Tosca: E lucevan le stelle. Manon Lescaut: Donna non vidi mai. La Bohème: Che gelida manina. Turandot: Nessun dorma.* ROSSINI: *Stabat Mater: Cuius animam.* BIZET: *Agnus Dei.* ADAM: *O Holy Night.* DI CAPUA: *O sole mio.* TOSTI: *A vucchella.* CARDILLO: *Core 'ngrato.* TAGLIAFERRI: *Passione.* CHERUBINI: *Mamma.* DALLA: *Caruso*

(M) *** Decca (ADD) 425 681-2 (2)

Opening with Dalla's *Caruso*, a popular song in the Neapolitan tradition, certainly effective and no more vulgar than many earlier examples of the genre, this selection goes on through favourites like *O sole mio* and *Core 'ngrato* and one or two religious items, notably Adam's *Cantique de Noël*, to the hard core of operatic repertoire. Beginning with *Celeste Aida*, recorded in 1972, the selection of some twenty-two arias from complete sets covers Pavarotti's distinguished recording career with Decca from 1969 (*Cielo e mar* and the *Il trovatore* excerpts) to 1985, although the opening song was, of course, recorded digitally in 1988. The rest is a mixture of brilliantly transferred analogue originals and a smaller number of digital masters, all or nearly all showing the great tenor in sparkling form. The records are at mid-price, but there are no translations or musical notes.

'The Greatest Ever Pavarotti' (with various orchestras and conductors): Arias from: VERDI: *Rigoletto; Il trovatore; La traviata; Aida.* PUCCINI: *La Bohème; Turandot; Tosca; La fanciulla del West; Manon Lescaut.* DONIZETTI: *L'elisir d'amore.* FLOTOW: *Martha.* BIZET: *Carmen.* LEONCAVALLO: *Pagliacci.* GIORDANO: *Fedora.* MEYERBEER: *L'Africana.* MASSENET: *Werther.* Songs: DALLA: *Caruso.* LEONCAVALLO: *Mattinata.* TOSTI: *Aprile; Marechiare; La Serenata.* CARDILLO: *Core 'ngrato.* ROSSINI: *La danza.* MODUGNO: *Volare.* DENZA: *Funiculì, funiculà.* DE CURTIS: *Torna a Surriento.* DI CAPUA: *O sole mio!* SCHUBERT: *Ave Maria.* FRANCK: *Panis angelicus.* MANCINI: *In un palco della Scala* (with apologies to Pink Panther). GIORDANI: *Caro mio ben.* BIXIO: *Mamma*

☛ (M) *** Decca ADD/DDD 436 173-2 (2)

Such a collection as this is self-recommending and scarcely needs a review from us, merely a listing. The first disc opens with *La donna è mobile* (*Rigoletto*), *Che gelida manina* (*La Bohème*), *Nessun dorma* (*Turandot*), all taken from outstandingly successful complete recordings, and the rest of the programme, with many favourite lighter songs also given the golden touch, is hardly less appealing. The second CD includes Pavarotti's tribute to the Pink Panther and ends with a tingling live version of *Nessun dorma*, to compare with the studio version on disc one. Vivid, vintage Decca recording throughout.

Donizetti & Verdi Arias (with the Vienna Op. O, Edward Downes) from: DONIZETTI: *Il duca d'Alba; La favorita; Lucia di Lammermoor; Dom Sebastiano* VERDI: *Un ballo in maschera; I due Foscari; Luisa Miller; Macbeth*

(M) *** Decca Classic Recitals (ADD) 475 6414

This is one of Pavarotti's early recital discs, recorded and released in 1968, when his voice was fresh and golden. The choice of repertoire is very well made, all the more interesting for including some less obvious numbers. Downes is a sensitive conductor and together they produce some beautiful sounds. The recording is of Decca's best vintage, warm and full; but once again do not expect it to be easy to read the sleeve-notes on this Classic Recitals CD as, apart from being in tiny print, the bottom has been chopped off!

'O Holy Night' (with Wandsworth School Boys' Ch., Nat. PO, Kurt Herbert Adler, or London Voices with various orchestras and conductors): ADAM: *O Holy Night.* arr. STADELLA: *Pietà Signore.* FRANCK: *Panis angelicus.* MERCADANTE: *Qual giglio candido (Parola quinta).* SCHUBERT: *Ave Maria; Mille cherubini in coro; Ave verum.* YON: *Gesù bambino.* GLUCK: *Orfeo ed Eurydice: Che farò.* ROSSINI: *Stabat Mater: Cuius animam.* VERDI: *Requiem: Ingemisco.* BACH/GOUNOD: *Ave Maria.* BIZET: *Agnus Dei.* BERLIOZ: *Requiem: Sanctus.* arr. WADE: *Adeste fidelis.* GUIDA: *O Jesu mi dulcissima*

(M) *** Decca (ADD/DDD) 475 6896

It is a long-established tradition for great Italian tenors to indulge in such songs and arias as these, many of them overly sugary in their expression of (no doubt) sincere religious fervour. Pavarotti is hardly a model of taste but, more than most of his rivals (even a tenor as intelligent as Plácido Domingo), he avoids the worst pitfalls; and if this is the sort of recital you are looking for, then Pavarotti is a good choice, with his beautiful vocalizing, helped by full, bright recording. Note too that some of the original items are less hackneyed than the rest, for instance the title setting by Adam, Mercadante's *Parola quinta*, and the *Sanctus* from Berlioz's *Requiem Mass* (alongside the better-known *Ingemisco*, taken from Solti's recording). This is one of the items added to the original 1968 recital.

'The Great Decca Recordings': Arias from: PUCCINI: *La Bohème* (with BPO, Herbert von Karajan); *Tosca* (with Nat. PO, Nicola Rescigno); *Turandot* (with LPO, Zubin Mehta). DONIZETTI: *L'elisir d'amore* (with ECO, Richard Bonynge); *La favorita* (with Teatro Comunale di Bologna O, Bonynge); *La fille du régiment* (with ROHCG O, Bonynge). R. STRAUSS: *Der Rosenkavalier* (with VPO, Georg Solti). BIZET: *Carmen.* GOUNOD: *Faust* (with V. Volksoper O, Leone Magiera). BELLINI: *I puritani* (with LSO, Bonynge). VERDI: *Aida* (with V. Volksoper O, Magiera); *Requiem* (with VPO, Solti); *Rigoletto* (with LSO, Bonynge); *Il trovatore* (with Nat. PO, Bonynge). LEONCAVALLO: *I pagliacci* (with Nat. PO, Giuseppe Patanè). PONCHIELLI: *La Gioconda* (with New Philh. O, Magiera). Songs: LEONCAVALLO: *Mattinata* (with Philh. O, Piero Gamba). BELLINI: *Vanne, o rosa fortunate.* ROSSINI: *La danza* (with Teatro Comunale di Bologna O, Bonynge). CURTIS: *Torna a Surriento* (with Nat. PO, Bonynge). FRANCK: *Panis angelicus.* SCHUBERT: *Ave Maria* (with Nat. PO, Kurt Herbert Adler). DENZA: *Faniculì Funiculà* (with Teatro Comunale di Bologna O, Anton Guadagno)

(B) *** Decca (ADD) 476 7148 (2)

An excellent anthology, originally released to coincide with the *Gramophone* 'Artist of the Year' award which Pavarotti received in 1991. Included are items from Pavarotti's vintage period with Bonynge and Sutherland: *La fille du régiment* with those astonishing high Cs (nine of them!) thrills as always and, in his equally successful role in *L'elisir d'amore*, *Una furtiva lagrima* does not descend into sentimentality as it so often does. His ability to sing a beautiful *legato* line is well displayed in the *I puritani* number, while all the show-stoppers – *La donna è mobile*, and the like – are unlikely to disappoint (his splendid *Nessum dorma* must now be opera's most famous recording). The Puccini and Verdi provide more meaty weight and contrast with the lighter, popular numbers, which include such little gems as Rossini's *La danza*, Leoncavallo's *Mattinata* and the irrepressible *Faniculì Faniculà*. With warm and vivid Decca sound, and texts and translations, it all adds up to a very attractive programme.

Pears, Peter (tenor), Benjamin Britten
(piano)

Lieder: SCHUMANN: *Liederkreis, Op. 39*; FAURE: *La Bonne Chanson*; PURCELL: *5 songs*; SCHUBERT: *3 Songs*; BRITTEN: *4 Folksongs*
(M) (***) BBC mono BBCB 8006-2

Britten as pianist is, if anything, even more individual than Britten as conductor. With Pears in glowing voice (1958–9) he sparkles in his own realizations of Purcell songs and folksongs, while in Schumann's Eichendorff song-cycle he makes the poetic piano-writing glow, as in *Frühlingsnacht* ('Spring Night'), where the notes shimmer distinctively. The Fauré cycle too reminds one that as a fourteen-year-old Britten also set Verlaine's poetry. Clean focus in mono radio recording.

Petibon, Patricia (soprano)

'French Touch' (with Lyon Nat. Op. Ch. & O, Abel): Arias from: GOUNOD: *Roméo et Juliette*. MESSAGER: *L'Amour masque*; *Fortunio*. DELIBES: *Lakmé*. MASSENET: *Cendrillon*; *Manon*. OFFENBACH: *Les Contes d'Hoffmann*. CHABRIER: *L'Etoile*. HAHN: *Brummel*. Songs: DELIBES: *Les Filles de Cadiz*. ABOULKER: *Je t'aime*
**(*) Decca 475 090-2

A recommendable disc with one proviso, of which more later. Patricia Petibon is a highly characterful French soprano and there is much to enjoy: there is a glittering account of Delibes's *Les Filles de Cadix*, much sensitivity in Messager's lovely melancholy *Fortunio* aria, and the Waltz Song from *Roméo et Juliette* goes with a delectable lilt. Many of the numbers here are not so well known, but all are worth hearing: the aria from *L'Amour masque* (Messager) about the advantages of having two lovers, is superbly characterized with wonderful French insouciance. But in numbers such as Hahn's *Brummel*, Petibon adopts a 'funny' voice, which may be amusing live but becomes irksome on repeated hearing. While in that comic number it might raise a smile (at least on first hearing), it seems very out of place in the Doll Song from *Les Contes d'Hoffmann*, which is cringe-making and out of keeping with Offenbach's style. However, the pluses on this disc outway the minuses, and Patricia Petibon has personality in buckets. The disc ends with Aboulker's showpiece, *Je t'aime*,

and here she keeps her 'funny' voice to a minimum, and the effect is so much better. She also blows us some very nice kisses at the end of the aria – always welcome! Yves Abel gets excellent results from his orchestra, perhaps a bit slow in the two *Manon* items, but the rest are very lively and idiomatic, and the Decca sound is first rate. Full texts and translations (and wacky artwork) provided.

'Airs Baroques Français' (with Paris Chamber Ch., Les Folies Françaises, Patrick Cohen-Akenine) from:
M.-A. CHARPENTIER: *David et Jonathas*. LULLY: *Armide*. RAMEAU: *Les Indes galantes; Platée; Les Fêtes de l'Hymen et de l'Amour*. GRANDVAL: *Rien du tout*
*** Virgin 5 45481-2

Not helped by excessively arch portraits of the singer on front and back covers of the disc, Patricia Petibon's disc yet offers fresh and brilliant performances of an attractive collection of arias by the leading French composers of the late seventeenth and early eighteenth centuries. Petibon, a member of the outstanding team of Les arts florissants assembled by William Christie, with her bright and clear if slightly hooty soprano, gives characterful and stylish readings of each item, and it is good to find her responding so positively to the less serious items which add a sparkle to the collection. A delightful disc, very well recorded.

Polyphony, Stephen Layton

'O magnum mysterium' (A sequence of twentieth-century carols and Sarum chant): Plainchant: *O radix lesse; O magnum mysterium; Puer natus est nobis; Reges Tharsis; Verbum caro factum est.* WISHART: 3 *Carols, Op. 17, 3: Alleluya, A New Work is Come on Hand.* HOWELLS: 3 *Carol-anthems: Here is the Little Door; A Spotless Rose; Sing Lullaby.* RICHARD RODNEY BENNETT: 5 *Carols: There is no Rose; Out of your Sleep; That Younge Child; Sweet was the Song; Susanni.* KENNETH LEIGHTON: *Of a Rose is my Song; A Hymn of the Nativity; 3 Carols, Op. 25: The Star song; Lully Lulla, Thou Little Tiny Child; An Ode on the Birth of our Saviour.* WARLOCK: *As Dew in Aprylle; Bethlehem Down; I Saw a Fair Maiden; Benedicamus Domino; A Cornish Christmas Carol.* BYRT: *All and Some.* WALTON: *What Cheer?*
☞ *** Hyp. CDA 66925

A gloriously sung collection in which (what Meurig Bowen's extensive notes describe as) 'the magnificent corpus of British carols' is alive and still impressively expanding in the twentieth century. The atmosphere is readily set by the opening plainchant, which frames and punctuates the concert with appropriate liturgical texts. Peter Wishart's exuberant 'Alleluya' and the poignant 'A Spotless Rose' immediately catch up the listener. This is the first of Howells's *Three Carol-anthems*, of which the others are equally lovely (especially the rocking 'Sing Lullaby'). The five Richard Rodney Bennett carols have their own particular brand of cool dissonance, with 'There is no Rose' and 'Sweet was the Song' particularly haunting.

But perhaps it is the series of beautiful Peter Warlock settings one remembers most for their ready melodic and harmonic memorability (notably 'As Dew in Aprylle', the lovely 'Bethlehem Down' and the serene 'Lullaby my Jesus') alongside the soaring music of Kenneth Leighton, helped in the ambitious 'Nativity Hymn' and the 'Ode on the Birth of Our Saviour' by the rich, pure line of the soloist, Libby

Crabtree, and in 'Lully, Lulla' by the equally ravishing contribution of Emma Preston-Dunlop. Walton's 'What Cheer?' brings an exuberant rhythmic spicing, but for the most part this programme captures the tranquil pastoral mood of Christmas Eve. The recording could hardly be bettered, clear yet with the most evocative ambience.

Pomerium, Alexander Blachly

'*Old World Christmas*': ANON.: *In dulci jubilo à 2.* PRAETORIUS: *In dulci jubilo* (3 versions). ANON.: *Resonet in laudibus.* ERBACH: *Resonet in laudibus à 4.* LASSUS: *Resonet in laudibus à 4.* ANON.: *Preter rerum seriem.* JOSQUIN DESPREZ: *Preter rerem serium à 6.* GUILLAUME DUFAY: *Conditor alme siderum.* BYRD: *Puer natus est à 4; Reges Tharsis et insulae à 4.* ANON.: *O Sapientia.* HORWOOD: *Magnificut secundi toni à 5.* RAMSEY: *O Sapienta à 5.* ANON.: *Quem vidistis pastores.* CIPRIANO DE RORE: *Quem vidistis pastores à 7.* ANON.: *Sarum Antiphonale: Alma redemptoris mater.* OCKEGHEM: *Alma redemptoris mater à 4*
**(*) DG 474 557-2

Imaginatively planned, meticulously researched, and beautifully sung and recorded by this excellent vocal group, this Christmas programme opens enticingly with the famous *In dulci jubilo*, followed by three further versions for two, three and four voices respectively, collected by Michael Praetorius. The idea of presenting a plainchant and then different settings is in principle an excellent one and there is much fine music included here. The snag is a certain absence of variety, so that such a compilation becomes a specialist collection rather than a disc for the general collector.

Price, Leontyne (soprano)

'*Ultimate Collection*': Arias from: BERLIOZ: *Les Nuits d'été.* BIZET: *Carmen.* BARBER: *Antony and Cleopatra.* GERSHWIN: *Porgy and Bess.* MASSENET: *Manon.* MOZART: *Le nozze di Figaro; Il rè pastore.* PUCCINI: *Madama Butterfly; Manon Lescaut; La rondine; Suor Angelica; Tosca; Turandot.* PURCELL: *Dido and Aeneas.* R. STRAUSS: *Im Abendrot (Vier letzte Lieder 1); Ariadne auf Naxos.* VERDI: *Aida; Un ballo in maschera; Don Carlos; La forza del destino; Il trovatore*
(M) **(*) RCA 74321 63463-2

This CD may appeal to those who want some of Leontyne Price's most famous roles, or those who simply want a marvellously sung soprano operatic compilation. It is well programmed and includes some unlikely repertoire for Price (including Purcell), as well as many of the things you would expect. The recordings and performances are generally excellent, often brilliant. What is shabby about this release is that there is nothing in the documentation about the recordings, dates, conductors, orchestras, or the music. As for texts and translations, you must be joking!

'*Christmas with Leontyne Price*' (with VPO, Herbert von Karajan): GRUBER: *Silent Night.* MENDELSSOHN: *Hark! The herald angels sing.* HOPKINS: *We three kings of orient are.* TRAD.: *Angels we have heard on high; God rest ye merry, Gentlemen; Sweet li'l Jesus.* WILLIS: *It came upon a midnight clear.* BACH: *Von Himmel hoch, da Komm ich her.*

SCHUBERT: *Ave Maria.* ADAM: *O Holy Night.* BACH/GOUNOD: *Ave Maria.* MOZART: *Alleluja, K.165*
(M) **(*) Decca Classic Recitals (ADD) 475 6152-2

There is much beautiful singing here, but the style is essentially operatic. The rich, ample voice, when scaled down (as for instance in *We three kings*), can be very beautiful, but at full thrust it does not always catch the simplicity of the melodic line which is characteristic of many of these carols. Yet the vibrant quality of the presentation (not least in the combination of the great diva with the VPO under Karajan) is undoubtedly thrilling, and it can charm too, as in *God rest ye merry, gentlemen*, with its neat harpsichord accompaniment. This disc has something of a cult following and it is very good to have the stylish original artwork (as with all in this Classic Recitals series). The 1961 sound is clear and vivid.

Psalmody, Parley of Instruments, Peter Holman

'*While Shepherds Watched*' (Christmas music from English parish churches and chapels 1740–1830): BEESLY: *While Shepherds Watched.* ANON.: *Let an Anthem of praise; Hark! How All the Welkin Rings.* J. C. SMITH: *While Shepherds Watched.* HELLENDAAL: *Concerto in E flat for Strings, Op. 3/4: Pastorale.* KEY: *As Shepherds Watched their Fleecy Care.* ARNOLD: *Hark! The Herald Angels Sing.* CLARK: *While Shepherds Watched.* HANDEL: *Hark! the Herald Angels Sing; Hymning Seraphs Wake the Morning.* JARMAN: *There were Shepherds Abiding in the Field.* S. WESLEY: (piano) *Rondo on 'God Rest You Merry, Gentlemen'* (Timothy Roberts). MATTHEWS: *Angels from the Realms of Glory.* FOSTER: *While Shepherds Watched*
*** Hyp. CDA 66924

This is a Christmas collection of genuine novelty. None of the settings of 'While Shepherds Watched' uses the familiar tune: the regal closing version from John Foster of Yorkshire is remarkably lively, as is the lighter variation from Joseph Key of Northampton, 'As Shepherds Watched their Fleecy Care' with woodwind accompaniment. There are other surprises too. Handel's 'Hark! The Herald Angels' is neatly fitted to 'See the Conqu'ring Hero Comes', and 'Hymning Seraphs' (presented as a tenor solo with fortepiano) turns out to be our old keyboard friend, 'The Harmonious Blacksmith'. Peiter Hellendaal's *Pastorale for Strings* is in the best concerto grosso tradition, although Samuel Wesley's variations on 'God Rest You Merry' are merely ingenious. Nevertheless the whole programme is presented with pleasing freshness and is very well sung, played and recorded.

Ramey, Samuel (bass)

'*A Date with the Devil*' (with Munich RSO, Rudel): Arias from BERLIOZ: *La Damnation de Faust.* MEYERBEER: *Robert le Diable.* BOITO: *Mefistofele.* OFFENBACH: *Les Contes d'Hoffmann.* GOUNOD: *Faust.* STRAVINSKY: *The Rake's Progress.* LISZT: *Mephisto Waltz (orchestra only)*
(BB) *** Naxos 8.555355

Samuel Ramey has had great success in the concert hall with this collection of devilish portraits, most of them from French sources. Here in a composite recording, partly live, partly under studio conditions, he sings and acts with fine flair, bringing out the wry humour in many of the items.

Mephistopheles' Serenade and the *Calf of Gold* aria from Gounod's *Faust* provide a fine climax before the tailpiece solos from *The Rake's Progress*. He is well supported by Julius Rudel and the Munich Radio Orchestra, springing rhythms crisply, with well-balanced sound. The orchestral showpieces by Berlioz and Liszt provide a nice contrast. An outstanding Naxos bargain.

Riedel, Deborah (soprano), Australian Opera and Ballet Orchestra, Richard Bonynge

'British Opera Arias': Arias from: WALLACE: *The Amber Witch; Love's Triumph; Lurline; Maritana.* BALFE: *The Maid of Artois; The Puritan's Daughter; The Rose of Castille; Satanella; The Siege of Rochelle; Il Talismano.* SULLIVAN: *Ivanhoe; The Rose of Persia.* FARADAY: *Amasis*
*** Australian Melba 301082

It is astonishing, considering how much nineteenth-century opera has been resurrected on CD, that there has been no such revival in English opera of that period. Although the composers featured here embraced current (Italian) operatic trends, their art retained an attractive home-spun quality, but was eventually eclipsed by more inflated operatic traditions later in the century. Balfe achieved considerable success both in England and internationally in his day with his ability to write attractive melody of great charm. The first of the *Il Talismano* (1874) arias included here starts most beguilingly with a horn solo followed by a flute, before the voice enters, while the other aria, *Nella dolce trepidanza*, is most memorable for its swinging cabaletta. Many of his arias, such as the numbers from *The Rose of Castille* and *Satanella*, have a simple, almost folk-like quality that is most fetching, while 'The Rapture Dwelling in My Heart' from *The Maid of Artois* is a delicious coloratura waltz song.

Wallace is remembered today mainly for *Maritana*, from which the charming "Tis the Harp in the Air' and 'Scenes that are Brightest' are included, but the more substantial items from *Lurline*, the waltz song 'The Naiad's Spell', 'These Withered Flowers' from *Love's Triumph* and 'My Long Hair is Braided' from *The Amber Witch* – a brilliant coloratura aria – are all greatly enjoyable. The Sullivan items come from his 'serious' attempts at grand opera and are not quite so rare these days, but their inclusion is welcome – 'Neath My Lattice' from *The Rose of Persia* is very winning, as is the rare Faraday number from his musical comedy of 1906, *Amasis*, which has a nice period charm. This is an important as well as an enjoyable collection, which gives us a fuller picture of English operatic history, and a CD that makes one want to hear some of the complete operas. The performances are excellent: Deborah Riedel sings with warmth and real understanding of the idiom and meets the challenges of the virtuoso passages, while Bonynge provides his usual sterling support with his Australian Orchestra, who make a fine contribution. The recording is atmospheric, perhaps a touch backwardly balanced, but not seriously so. Full texts are included.

Rolfe Johnson, Anthony (tenor), Graham Johnson (piano)

'In Praise of Women': MISS LH OF LIVERPOOL: *My Mother.* CAROLINE NORTON: *Juanita.* VIRGINIA GABRIEL: *Orpheus.* ANNIE FORTESQUE HARRISON: *In the Gloaming.* MAUDE VALERIE WHITE: *The Throstle; My Soul is an Enchanted Boat; The Devout Lover; So we'll Go no More a-Roving.* TERESA DEL RIEGO: *Slave Song.* LIZA LEHMANN: *A Bird Sate Mourning; Ah, Moon of my Delight; The Lily of a Day; Thoughts have Wings; Henry King; Charles Augustus Fortescue.* AMY WOODFORDE-FINDEN: *Till I Wake; Kashmiri Song.* ETHEL SMYTH: *Possession.* REBECCA CLARKE: *The Aspidistra; Shy one.* ELIZABETH POSTON: *In Praise of Women.* ELISABETH LUTYENS: *As I Walked Out One Evening.* ELIZABETH MACONCHY: *Have you Seen but a Bright Lily Grow?; Meditation for his Mistress.* MADELEINE DRING: *Crabbed Age and Youth; To Virgins, to Make Much of Time.* PHYLLIS TATE: *Epitaph*
(BB) *** Hyp. Helios CDH 55159

It is Elizabeth Poston who provides the title song for this delightful collection, a simple setting of an anonymous poem which pays a tender tribute to womankind, but the collection opens with an equally touching anonymous setting from an unknown Liverpool girl praising her mother (to verses by the author of 'Twinkle, Twinkle, Little Star'!). The charming 'In the Gloaming' with its rippling accompaniment was a popular hit in its day for Anne Fortesque Harrison, selling more than 14,000 copies between 1880 and 1889.

During this same period Maude Valerie White was comparably successful, and she was at her finest with the ballad 'My Soul is an Enchanted Island', to which Anthony Rolfe Johnson responds passionately, going quite over the top at the stirring climax. Her setting of 'So we'll Go No More a-Roving' is memorable in a more restrained way. The group from the best known of these turn-of-the-century women composers is Liza Lehmann who shows the consistency of her melodic facility, while the two Hilaire Belloc portraits, the engaging 'Henry King', 'who chewed little bits of string', and 'Charles Augustus Fortescue', who always did what he ought to do, are fine examples. Ethel Smyth is represented by a single, rather sombre song, 'Possession', but it remains to haunt the memory. Fortunately, the more modern composers shirk any suggestion of spikiness: Elizabeth Lutyens's very winning 'As I Walked Out One Evening' might almost be a folksong, and Elizabeth Maconchy's setting of Ben Jonson, 'Have you Seen but a Bright Lily Grow?' is quite lovely. She is equally sympathetic with Robert Herrick, surely identifying with his 'Meditation for his Mistress', whose merits he compares to a bouquet of flowers. A touch of irony comes with Rebecca Clarke's Aspidistra', and Madeleine Dring is light-heartedly witty in Shakespeare's 'Crabbed Age and Youth'; but the recital ends in more serious, thoughtful mood with Phyllis Tate's 'Epitaph' to a brief reflection on mortality by Sir Walter Raleigh. Throughout, Anthony Rolfe Johnson sings with both ardour and perception, sensitivity and a feeling for the changing styles over a century of song-writing, and Graham Johnson's accompaniments could not be more imaginatively supportive. Excellent recording and full texts make this reissue a very real bargain, which will give much pleasure.

Roswaenge, Helge (tenor)

'The Dane with the High D': Arias from: VERDI: *Aida; La traviata; Il trovatore.* CORNELIUS: *Der Barbier von Bagdad.* ADAM: *Le Postillon de Longjumeau.* AUBER: *Fra Diavolo.* MOZART: *Così fan tutte.* BEETHOVEN: *Fidelio.* WEBER: *Der*

Freischütz; Oberon. TCHAIKOVSKY: *Eugene Onegin.* R.
STRAUSS: *Der Rosenkavalier.* WILLE: *Königsballade*
●→ ● (BB) (***) Dutton mono CDBP 9728

Helge Roswaenge had one of the most thrilling voices of the
twentieth century. He began singing professionally in 1921
and was still on excellent form nearly half a century later. But
most of these recordings were made in the 1930s, when he was
at his peak, and although Mozart was perhaps not his strongest suit, he was chosen by Beecham as Tamino for his famous
1937 *Zauberflöte.* As Alan Blyth comments in the excellent
insert note, his amazing voice has a 'gleaming trumpet-like
quality at the top' – reminiscent of Tamagno – 'yet was
mellifluous in quieter moments'. He was also a superb stylist,
whether in Verdi or in operetta, for which his fresh, ringing
upper register was especially suitable. The most famous item
here, which gives the disc its title, is the sparkling excerpt
from Adam's *Le Postillon de Longjumeau*, which is electrifying, but he shows his lyrical grace in the *Fra Diavolo* aria with
which this was paired on the original 78rpm shellac disc. This
warm, lyrical quality appears again and again in this generous
selection, notably in Lensky's ardent aria from *Eugene
Onegin.*

In the rare excerpts from Cornelius's *Barbier von Bagdad*
he is joined by his first wife, Ilonka, not a great singer but a
charming partner. Almost all his recordings were made in
German, yet he somehow does not sound Germanic in the
French and Italian repertoire, and his ardent account of *Di
rigor armato* from *Der Rosenkavalier* is sung in Italian, and
how marvellously passionate it is! He was ideal for Weber
(the *Oberon* excerpt is another highlight), and his dramatic
entry on the word '*Gott*' in the Fidelio excerpt (the only opera
he sang at Covent Garden) is characteristic of him at his very
finest, and is alone worth the price of the disc. Most of the
recordings were made in the 1930s and were of high quality.
But the miraculous Dutton transfers enhance them further,
and the voice projects with the utmost realism throughout,
and with its full bloom remaining. An unforgettable and
treasurable collection.

Rouen Chambre Accentus Choir, Eric Ericson

ALFVEN: *Aftonen; Uti vår hage.* JERSILD: *Min yndlingsdal
(My Dear Valley).* NYSTEDT: *O Crux.* SANDSTROM: *2
Poems.* STENHAMMAR: *3 körvisor (3 Choral Pieces).* WERLE:
Canzone 126 del Petrarcha. WIKANDER: *Kung Liljekonvalje
(King of the Lily-of-the-valley); Förårskväll (Spring Evening)*
**(*) Assai 207 182

The Rouen-based Chœur de Chambre Accentus was founded
in 1991 by Laurence Equilbey, an Ericson pupil, and they
tackle this predominantly Swedish repertoire with complete
sympathy. In the 1960s and 1970s Eric Ericson brought the
Swedish Radio Choir to an unrivalled excellence (it was the
Berlin Philharmonic of choirs). These French singers produce
the beautifully blended and finely nuanced sound one associates with him. He has recorded Stenhammar's glorious choral
songs to texts by the Danish poet J. P. Jacobsen many times.
Wikander's *Kung Liljekonvalje* ('King of the Lily-of-the-
valley') and Alfvén's *Aftonen* ('The Evening') are affecting
pieces and are beautifully done.

For most collectors the surprise will be *Min yndlingsdal*
('My Dear Valley') by the Dane Jørgen Jersild, a contemporary of Vagn Holmboe, though less prolific. During the 1930s

he studied with Roussel, and his writing has almost luminous
quality. Jan Sandström is not to be confused with Sven David
and is still in his mid-forties, and these two pieces, *Anrop*
('Call') and *Två japanska landskap* ('Two Japanese Landscapes'), date from his student years and are quite haunting.
By its side Werle's Petrach setting seems more self-conscious.
At less than 50 minutes this is short measure, but his repertoire is not widely known and is immensely rewarding.

Royal Liverpool Philharmonic Choir and Orchestra, St Ambrose R.C. Junior School Choir, Speake, Edmund Walters

'*A Festival of Christmas*' (with Jocelyn Bell, girl soprano):
arr. WALTERS: *Ding Dong! Merrily on High; The Boar's
Head; Buenos Reyes; Deck the Hall.* arr. PETTMAN: *The
Infant King.* WALTERS: *Where was Jesus Born?; The Carol
Singers; Dance Little Goatling; As Joseph was a-Walking;
Three Little Birdies; Little Robin Redbreast; Hop-hop-hop;
Little One Sleep.* BYRD: *Cradle Song.* BACH: *O Little One
Sweet.* DARKE: *In the Bleak Midwinter.* GRUBER: *Silent
Night.* arr. WALLACE: *O Come, All Ye Faithful*
(M) *** Chan. 7111

The introductory woodwind in the scoring of Edmund Walters's opening arrangement of *Ding Dong! Merrily on High*,
and the lighthearted touches of syncopation, suggest that his
approach to Christmas music has much in common with that
of John Rutter. His own carols are jauntily engaging, helped
by the freshness of the excellently trained St Ambrose Junior
School Choir, who sing them with vigour and enthusiasm.
'Little One Sleep' (a treble solo) verges on sentimentality. But
the Spanish carol *Buenos Reyes*, with its castanets, is most
piquant and the two Basque carols 'The Infant King' and 'I
Saw a Maiden' are most eloquently sung, as are the settings by
Bach and Byrd. Fine recording too.

St George's Canzona, John Sothcott

*Medieval songs and dances: Lamento di Tristano; L'autrier
m'iere levaz; 4 Estampies real; Edi beo thu hevene quene;
Eyns ne soy ke plente fu; Tre fontane.* PERRIN
D'AGINCOURT: *Quant voi en la fin d'este; Cantigas de Santa
Maria: Se ome fezer; Nas mentes semper teer; Como poden
per sas culpas; Maravillosos et piadosos*
(M) *** CRD (ADD) CRD 3421

As so often when early music is imaginatively re-created, one
is astonished at the individuality of many of the ideas. This
applies particularly to the second item in this collection,
Quant voi en la fin d'este, attributed to the mid-thirteenth-
century trouvère Perrin d'Agincourt, but no less to the four
Cantigas de Santa Maria. The instrumentation is at times
suitably robust but does not eschew good intonation and
subtle effects. The group is recorded vividly and the acoustics
of St James, Clerkenwell, are never allowed to cloud detail.
The sound is admirably firm and real in its CD format.

St John's College Choir, Cambridge, George Guest

'*Christmas Carols from St John's*' (with Philip Kenyon,
organ): TRAD.: *Unto us a Boy is Born; Ding Dong! Merrily*

on High; Good King Wenceslas; There is no Rose. arr.
WALFORD DAVIES: *The Holly and the Ivy.* arr. WILLCOCKS:
*Sussex Carol; God Rest You Merry, Gentlemen; O Come, All
Ye Faithful.* WARLOCK: *Balulalow.* HOLST: *In the Bleak
Midwinter.* HADLEY: *I Sing of a Maiden.* RUTTER:
Shepherd's Pipe Carol. GRUBER: *Silent Night.*
MENDELSSOHN, arr. WILLCOCKS: *Hark! The Herald Angels
Sing.* arr. VAUGHAN WILLIAMS: *O Little Town of
Bethlehem.* POSTON: *Jesus Christ the Apple Tree.* RAYMOND
WILLIAMS: 2 *Welsh Carols.* KIRKPATRICK: *Away in a
Manger*

(M) *** Chan. 7109

An essentially traditional concert and none the worse for that
when so beautifully sung and recorded. Among the more
modern carols, Elizabeth Poston's beautiful 'Jesus Christ the
Apple Tree' stands out. Many of the arrangements are
famous, notably the spectacular Willcocks versions of *Hark!
The Herald Angels Sing* and *O Come, All Ye Faithful*, but some
of the gentler, atmospheric items (*There is no Rose*) are just as
memorable. A most enjoyable hour of music.

Salon Napolitan

Neapolitan Songs (with Invernizzi, Naviglio, Totaro;
Caramiello, pianoforte): ANON.: *Cannetella; Riposta a
dispetto della donna; Te voglio bene assaje.* DOHLER:
Cannetella; Veder Napoli e poi morire. ZINGARELLI:
*Confusa, smarrita, spiegarti vorrei; Entra l'uomo all'orchè
nasce.* CRESCENTINI: *Auretta grata.* PAER: *Quel cor che mi
prometti; S'io t'amo, oh Dio! Mi chiedi?* RICCI: *Alla fenesta
affaciate; Il carrettiere del Vomero; Consiglio all'amica; Je ne
rêve qu'à toi; La mia felicità; La solita conversazione degli
amanti; Perchè?; Una postilla al vocabolario d'amore; Il
ritorno a Napoli*

*** Opus 111 OPS 30-255

A charming collection of Neapolitan song, lasting just over
an hour. Nicely contrasting solos, duos and trios are all
beautifully accompanied by Francesco Caramiello on a Pleyel
pianoforte of 1865. The trio of singers are clearly enjoying
themselves, and so do we when they bring so much character
to these simple yet effective numbers. Full texts and translations are provided, and the recording is ideally balanced.
Worth investigating if you enjoy this repertoire.

Sass, Sylvia (soprano), London Symphony Orchestra, Lamberto Gardelli

Arias from: PUCCINI: *Madama Butterfly; Manon Lescaut;
Tosca; Turandot.* VERDI: *Aida; I Lombardi; Macbeth*

(M) *** Decca Classic Recitals (ADD) 475 6415

The Hungarian soprano was heralded as the new Maria
Callas when this 1977 recital by Sylvia Sass ('Opera's Sensational New Star') was recorded, although her career did not
make it to that stratospheric plane. She was glamorous and
vibrant in personality and appearance (as can be seen from
the original cover used for this Classic Recitals release) as well
as in voice, and immediately established a star status at the
very start of Turandot's big aria, *In questa reggia.* The Puccini
excerpts stand any kind of competition in their range and
expression, searching as well as beautiful, and though the
Verdi items betray tiny chinks in her technical armour, recital
discs more exciting than this are rare. The recording is vivid

and clear, and the refinement of detail creates the most
beautiful orchestral textures in the introductions to the
scenes from *Macbeth* and *I Lombardi.* Another intelligent
release in this enterprising series, and one can almost forgive
Decca for making the original sleeves-notes minuscule!

The Scholars of London

French chansons: JOSQUIN: *Faute d'argent; Mille regretz.*
JANEQUIN: *Le Chant des oiseaux; Or vien ça.* SANDRIN: *Je
ne le croy.* GOMBERT: *Aime qui vouldra; Quand je suis
aupres.* SERMISY: *Tant que vivrai; Venez regrets; La, la,
maistre Pierre.* ARCADELT: *En ce mois délicieux; Margot,
labourez les vignes; Du temps que j'estois amoureux; Sa
grand beauté.* TABOUROT: *Belle qui tiens ma vie.* VASSAL:
Vray Dieu. CLEMENS: *Prière devant le repas; Action des
Graces.* PASSEREAU: *Il est bel et bon.* LE JEUNE: *Ce n'est que
fiel.* LASSUS: *Bonjour mon coeur; Si je suis brun; Beau le
cristal; La Nuit froide; Un Jeune Moine.* BERTRAND: *De
nuit, le bien.* COSTELY: *Arrête un peu mon coeur*

(BB) *** Naxos 8.550880

This disc offers a representative selection from the thousands
of sixteenth-century French polyphonic chansons, and
ranges from the devotional to the amorous, the bawdy and
the bucolic. It includes some of the best known, such as the
ubiquitous Janequin *Le Chant des oiseaux*, and features such
familiar masters as Josquin, Sermisy and Claude Le Jeune. It
encompasses Flemish masters writing in the language, such as
Gombert and Lassus. The Scholars of London are expressive
and persuasive guides in this repertoire and are decently
recorded at St Silas the Martyr in Kentish Town. There is an
all-too-short but thoughtful introduction, and the booklet
then reproduces texts and translations. What more can you
ask from a disc that would undoubtedly cost less than admission to a concert plus the programme?

Scholl, Andreas (counter-tenor)

'*Heroes*' (with OAE, Norrington): Arias from HANDEL:
Giulio Cesare; Rodelinda; Saul; Semele; Serse. HASSE:
Artaserse. GLUCK: *Orfeo; Telemaco.* MOZART: *Ascanio in
Alba; Mitridate*

🔴― *** Decca 466 196-2

'There is more to heroism than winning fearlessly … My
heroes have moments of weakness and must overcome their
difficulties,' comments Andreas Scholl about the operatic
characters represented in his Decca recital. Indeed it is the
lovely tender singing in the lyrical arias that one remembers
most, as in the familiar 'Where'er you Walk', and 'Oh Lord
whose Mercies Numberless' (from *Saul*, with its delicate
closing harp solo from Frances Kelly), or *Con rauco mormorio*
from *Rodelinda.*

In spite of the prevalence of Handel in the programme,
Scholl overlaps with his Harmonia Mundi disc on only one
aria, *Ombra mai fù*, just as characterful though less forwardly recorded. The other items range from Hasse (wonderfully light and nimble) to dramatic early Mozart.
Altogether this is a formidable collection of arias designed
originally for castrato, all performed characterfully with a
firm, clear tone and virtuoso agility. *Che farò* from Gluck's
Orfeo is on the slow side, but no less impressive for that.
Clear, open sound, the voice caught brightly and naturally.
Norrington's accompaniments are light-textured and fresh.

But Scholl's earlier Harmonia Mundi Handel collection, including instrumental music also, is in many ways even more seductive – see under Handel in the composer index of our main volume.

Schwarzkopf, Dame Elisabeth (soprano)

'Elisabeth Schwarzkopf Sings Operetta' (with Phil. Ch. and O, Ackermann): Excerpts from: HEUBERGER: Der Opernball. ZELLER: Der Vogelhändler. LEHAR: Der Zarewitsch; Der Graf von Luxembourg; Giuditta. JOHANN STRAUSS JR: Casanova. MILLOCKER: Die Dubarry. SUPPE: Boccaccio. SIECZYNSKY: Wien, du Stadt meiner Träume
☛ ✿ (M) *** EMI 5 66989-2 [567004]

This is one of the most delectable recordings of operetta arias ever made, and it is here presented with excellent sound. Schwarzkopf's 'whoopsing' manner (as Philip Hope-Wallace called it) is irresistible, authentically catching the Viennese style, languor and sparkle combined. Try for example the exquisite Im chambre séparée or Sei nicht bös; but the whole programme is performed with supreme artistic command and ravishing tonal beauty. This outstanding example of the art of Elisabeth Schwarzkopf at its most enchanting is a disc which ought to be in every collection. The CD transfer enhances the superbly balanced recording even further; it manages to cut out nearly all the background, gives the voice a natural presence and retains the orchestral bloom.

Unpublished recordings 1946–52: BACH: Cantata 51: Jauchzet Gott (with Philh. O, Susskind). MOZART: Exsultate, jubilate, K.165; Das Veilchen. Die Zauberflöte: excerpts (with piano); Schwarzkopf talks about the Die Zauberflöte recordings. Arias from VERDI: La traviata. PUCCINI: La Bohème. BACH/GOUNOD: Ave Maria. ARNE: When Daisies Pied. MORLEY: It was a Lover and his Lass. SCHUBERT: Gretchen am Spinnrade; Der Musensohn; Wiegenlied. RICHARD STRAUSS: Hat gesagt, bleibt's nicht dabei; Schlechtes Wetter. WOLF: Storchenbotschaft (2 versions); Epiphanias; Mein Liebster hat zu Tische; Du denkst mit einem Fädchen; Schweig'einmal still; Wer tat deinem Füsslein weh?; Bedeckt mich mit Blumen; Mögen alle bösen Zungen; Elfenlied; Nixe Binserfuss; Im Frühling; Die Spröde; Die Bekehrte; Mausfallen-sprüchlein; Wiegenlied in Sommer
✿ *** Testament mono/stereo SBT 2172 (2)

Here we have a magnificent store of the recordings made when her glorious voice was at its most radiant. For any lover of singing this is buried treasure when many of these items have an immediacy and freshness even more winning than later, published versions. Parallel versions of the jolly little Wolf song Storchenbotschaft demonstrate how rapid her development was between 1948 and 1951, leading to a whole collection of Wolf recorded in 1951, every one a jewel.

The three Schubert songs include Der Musensohn, joyfully buoyant, and Gretchen am Spinnrade, brighter and more passionate than in later recordings, with a little spontaneous gasp of emotion after the climax on sein Kuss!. Bach and Mozart too have an extra urgency compared with later, and Violetta's aria from Verdi's La traviata is all the more intense, done in English. Most revealing of all is the private recording, some half-hour of music, made with piano accompaniment when Schwarzkopf was preparing to sing Pamina in English in a Covent Garden revival of Mozart's Magic Flute, a 'glimpse into the singer's workshop' centring on a ravishing account of Ach ich fühls.

The Unpublished EMI Recordings 1955–64 (with Moore, piano): BIZET: Pastorale. BRAHMS: In stiller Nacht; Sandmannchen; Von ewige Liebe; Wiegenlied. FLIES: Wiegenlied. MOZART: Un moto di gioia; Warnung. PARISOTTI: Se tu m'ami. SCHUBERT: Claudine von villa bella; Du bist der Ruh; Die Forelle; Der Jungling an der Quelle; Lachen und Weinen; Die Vogel; Wiegenlied. SCHUMANN: Widmung. RICHARD STRAUSS: Ruhe, meine Seele; Wiegenlied; Zueignung. WAGNER: Traume. WOLF: Der Kohlerweib; Nachtzauber; Treten ein; Die Zigeunerin
(***) Testament SBT 1206

This makes a superb follow-up to Testament's previous delving into the archive of Schwarzkopf's unpublished recordings, which covered Bach, Handel and opera. She and her husband, the recording producer, Walter Legge, were the most exacting critics, and the reasons for rejection (if that is what it was) are not at all evident from these inspired performances of Lieder. That is the area where Schwarzkopf was supreme, above all in Schubert and Wolf, who are well represented here in intense, characterful performances, with the voice at its freshest. One attractive touch is the inclusion of no fewer than four, nicely contrasted cradle-songs. Excellent transfers.

Scotto, Renata (soprano)

Italian Opera Arias (with Phil. O, Wolf-Ferrari or (i) Rome Op. O, Barbirolli): from ROSSINI: Il barbiere di Siviglia. BELLINI: I Puritani. PUCCINI: Gianni Schicchi; Turandot; (i) Madama Butterfly. DONIZETTI: Lucia di Lammermoor. VERDI: La traviata. BOITO: Mefistofele
(BB) **(*) EMI Encore (ADD) 5 74600-2 [5 74766-2]

Apart from two outstanding excerpts from Scotto's complete 1967 Madama Butterfly with Carlo Bergonzi, conducted by Barbirolli, this recital dates from 1959, early in her career. The widely ranging programme has the voice at its freshest and most agile, giving an idea of the later dramatic developments which changed the character of the voice and filled it out (as is shown by the Butterfly excerpts).

Seefried, Irmgard (soprano), Erik Werba (piano)

Lieder: BRAHMS: Es träumte mir; Nicht mehr zu dir zu gehen; Ständchen; Trost in Tränen; Unbewegte laue Luft; 6 Volkslieder: In stiller Nacht; Schwesterlein; Die Sonne scheint mehr; Die Trauernde; Der Versuchung; Volkslied. SCHUBERT: Mignon Lieder: Heiss mich nicht reden; Kennst du das Land; Nur wer die Sehnsucht kennt; So lasst mich scheinen. WOLF: Mignon Lieder I–IV: Heiss mich nicht reden; Kennst du das Land; Nur wer die Sehnsucht kennt; So lasst mich scheinen (Irmgard Seefried in conversation with John Amis)
(***) BBC mono BBCL 4040-2

Recorded by the BBC in the studio in January 1962, this recital brings out the open charm of Irmgard Seefried as a winning Lieder singer. Her Brahms group sets the pattern, bringing out the links with German folksong, fresh and tuneful. There is no lack of detail in her pointing of words, but she takes a direct view of even such a deeply meditative song as In stiller Nacht, singing with concentration but little mystery.

Such songs as Schwesterlein and Ständchen are given with

such urgency that one holds one's breath, half expecting disaster. Seefried's forte is her full, strong, creamy voice, here recorded rather close, so that Schubert's *Gretchen am Spinnrade* brings little build-up, and Wolf's supreme Lied, *Kennst du das Land*, remains fresh and forthright in its lyricism rather than offering darker emotions. The interview with John Amis, which comes as a delightful supplement, bears out the joyful enthusiasm of the singer, whose strength, beauty and openness defy any detailed reservations.

(Robert) Shaw Festival Singers, Robert Shaw

'*O Magnum mysterium*': GORECKI: *Totus tuus.* LAURIDSEN: *O magnum mysterium.* POULENC: *O magnum mysterium.* RACHMANINOV: *Praise the Name of the Lord.* SCHUBERT: *Der Ernfernten.* TALLIS: *If ye Love Me; A New Commandment.* TRAD: *Amazing Grace. Sometimes I Feel like a Moanin' Dove. Wondrous Love.* VICTORIA: *O vos omnes. O magnum mysterium*
*** Telarc CD 80531

This compilation of unaccompanied choral music pays tribute to Robert Shaw as one of the world's great choir-trainers, who first made his name in the 1940s, when Toscanini chose the Robert Shaw Chorale for major choral recordings. Then, towards the end of his career, after two decades as music director of the Atlanta Symphony Orchestra, Shaw once again had time for unaccompanied choral music, establishing in 1989 a summer festival of choral workshops as well as performance at Quercy in the south of France and using a choir of students from American universities. His Telarc recordings made with that festival choir provide most of the items here, which were atmospherically recorded in the church of St Pierre at Gramat. The Tallis and Victoria motets, recorded in 1989, are an exception; they appear on disc for the first time in immaculate performances from a relatively large choir, which demonstrate the consistent refinement of the matching and balance that are characteristic of Shaw's choral work. The Schubert part-song and the Lauridsen motet, recorded in the United States with Shaw's chamber singers, readily match the rest in beauty of sound, particularly the Lauridsen, a fine piece by a composer, born in 1943, who spices a traditional idiom with clashing intervals in a way that Purcell would have enjoyed.

Siepi, Cesare (bass), Santa Cecilia Academy Orchestra, Rome, Alberto Erede

Arias from: VERDI: *Don Carlos; Ernani; Nabucco; Simon Boccanegra.* GOMES: *Salvadore Rosa.* MEYERBEER: *Les Huguenots; Robert le diable.* HELEVY: *La Juive*
(M) (**(*)) Decca Classic Recitals 475 6815

The original Penguin review expressed disappointment that the characterizations were not as individual as one might have expected from this great artist, but we would count ourselves lucky to hear a voice like Cesare Siepi's today. The recital shows Siepi's dark bass at its firmest and most resonant, and if so many bass arias together makes for a sombre collection, the magnificent voice is splendidly presented, and the mono sound is surprisingly good. As always in this series,

it is good too to see the original cover on this Classic Recitals CD.

Sinfonye, Stewart Wishart

'*Gabriel's Greeting*' (medieval carols) including: *Gabriel framevene king; Salva Virgo virginium; Ave Maria virgo virginium; Ther is no Rose of Swych Vertu; Lolay, Lolay; Nowell, Nowell*
(BB) **(*) Hyp. Helios CDH 55151

Unlike the Taverner Consort, who range over many centuries of music, Sinfonye concentrate on vocal and instrumental music from the thirteenth, fourteenth and fifteenth centuries, which usually consists of simple ostinato-like rhythmic ideas with a very distinctive melodic and harmonic character. These five singers and instrumentalists present their programme with spirit and vitality, but the range of the music is necessarily limited. Those who take to the repetitive medieval style will undoubtedly find this refreshing, and the recording is pleasingly live and atmospheric. Full documentation and texts are included.

Söderström, Elisabeth (soprano)

'*A Swedish Song Collection*' (with Westerberg, Eyron, piano): ALMQVIST: *The Listening Maria; The Startled Maria; You are not Walking Alone; Why Did you not Come to the Meadow?* BERGER: *Aspåkerspolka; Longing is my Inheritance.* LINDBLAD: *By Aarensee; I Wonder.* JOSEPHSON: *Serenade.* RANGSTROM: *Pan; Villema; The Girl under the New Moon; The Only Moment.* STENHAMMAR: *The Girl on Midsummer Eve; The Girl Returned from Meeting her Loved One; Adagio.* SJOGREN: *Sound, Sound my Pandero!; In the Shade of my Curls; I would Hold you Forever.* FRUMERIE: *A Letter Arrived; The Song of Love*
*** Swedish Soc. SCD 1117

These songs find Söderström at her finest in repertoire that she made very much her own in the late 1950s and 1960s, when she was in her prime. Songs like *Månntro* ('I Wonder') by Adolf Fredrik Lindblad have an affecting simplicity that is quite haunting, and the Rangström songs, in particular *Den enda stunden* ('The Only Movement'), have not been surpassed. Much of this wonderful repertoire will be new to collectors, as the original LPs enjoyed limited currency in the UK. They still sound wonderfully fresh.

Souliotis, Elena (soprano), Rome Opera Orchestra, Oliviero de Fabritis

Arias from: DONIZETTI: *Anna Bolena.* VERDI: *Un ballo in maschera; Luisa Miller; Macbeth*
(M) **(*) Decca Classic Recitals (ADD) 475 6235

The charismatic Greek diva had a sadly brief (it at times sensational) recording career, and this 1966 recital was one of her best. We have three superb Verdi items – a riveting Lady Macbeth, a dominant Luisa Miller, and an impressive Amelia, and the 20-minute final scene from *Anna Bolena* is very touching and exciting. However, it has to be mentioned that this recital lasts under 40 minutes and Decca compiled a very full CD (by extending this programme) at the same price a few years ago. On the other hand, you do get the original and striking front cover to admire, though the sleeve notes are too small to read.

Souzay, Gérard (baritone)

'French Airs' (with Jacqueline Bonneau, piano): FAURÉ: Tristesse; Au bord de l'eau; Après un rêve; Clair de lune; Arpège; En sourdine; L'Horizon chimérique; Spleen; c'est l'extase; Prison; Mandoline. CHAUSSON: Nanny; Le Charme; Sérénade italienne; Le Colibri; Cantique à l'épouse; Les Papillons; Le Temps de lilas. Airs: BOESSET: Me veux-tu voir mourir? ANON.: Tambourin. BATAILLE: Cachez, beaux yeux; Ma bergère non légère. CANTELOUBE: Brezairola; Malurous qu'o uno fenno

⟐ ❂ (M) *** Decca mono 475 041-2

The great French baritone made these recordings for Decca when he was at the very peak of his form. The Fauré were recorded in 1950 and the glorious Chausson songs in 1953. Souzay was endowed with the intelligence of Bernac as well as his powers of characterization, the vocal purity of Panzera and a wonderful feeling for line. The Decca transfer does complete justice to the original sound, and it is good to have these performances without the surface distractions of LP. Full texts and translations are provided. A marvellous record worth as many rosettes as stars, which deservedly won the Gramophone Historical Vocal Award in 1991.

Stefano, Giuseppe di (tenor)

Arias (with Zurich Tonhalle O, Franco Patanè) from: GIORDANO: Andrea Chénier. PUCCINI: Tosca; Turandot. MASSENET: Manon; Werther. BIZET: Carmen; Les Pêcheurs de perles. GOUNOD: Faust

(M) *(*) Decca (ADD) 475 6236

This is not a recital for those who cherish sophistication above all from their tenors. Indeed, there is some quite ungainly striving here, shouting almost, and a few horrid, throaty, shouting noises. The worst performance is E lucevan, which is pulled about far too much, but di Stefano mercifully does not indulge himself quite so badly with the rest. In fact, the French items are rather better than the Italian arias. Perhaps di Stephano – notoriously an artist who left everything to the last minute – felt he had to take more trouble about the arias he did not sing quite so often as the Puccini and Giordano ones. Whatever the reason, he certainly provides an exquisite pianissimo at the end of the Manon aria which makes one forgive a lot. The 1958 recording is clear and full for its time, not too dated. The original artwork raises a smile.

'Torna a Surriento' (songs of Italy and Sicily): CD 1 (with New SO of London, Pattacini): DE CURTIS: Torna a Surriento; Tu ca' nun chiagne; Sonta chitarra! BUONGIOVANNI: Lacreme napulitane. TAGLIAFERRI: Napule canta; Pusilleco … califano: O 'surdato 'nnammurato. CARDILLO: Catari, Catari. COSTA: Era di maggio matenata; Scetate. VALENTE: Addio mia bella Napoli. CD 2 (with O, Dino Olivieri): BIXIO: Parlami d'amore Mariù. BARBERIS: Munasterio'e Santa-Chiara. CESARINI: Firenze sogna. DE CURTIS: Canta pe'me; 'A canzone'e Napule; Ti voglio tanto bene. NARDELLA: Che t'aggia di! SIMI: Come è bello far l'amore quanno è sera.

VANCHERI: Sicilia bedda. BUONGIOVANNI: Fili d'oro. DI LAZZARO: Chitarra romana. RIVI: Addio, sogni di gloria. TRAD., arr. FAVARA: A la barcillunisi; Nota di li lavannari; A la vallelunghisa; Muttètti di lu pàliu; Chiovu 'aballati'; Cantu a timùni

(B) *** Double Decca (ADD) 455 482-2 (2)

Giuseppe di Stefano was still in magnificent voice when, in the summer of 1964, he recorded the collection of popular Italian songs assembled on the first disc of this Decca Double. He projects the ardent numbers such as the title-song with characteristic lustiness but less subtlety; despite the inevitable touches of vulgarity, the singing is rich toned and often charming, and a famous Neapolitan hit like Catari, Catari is winningly done. Pattacini's accompaniments are vividly idiomatic.

The second collection is even more generous, offering eighteen songs (against eleven on the first disc). This dates from 1958, when the voice was even more honeyed, so that Bixio's opening Parlami d'amore Mariù sounds almost like operetta and brings an engaging pianissimo ending. The luscious Mantovani-styled accompaniments are certainly seductive, and very well recorded, while in Come è bello far l'amore quanno è sera the use of the mandolin is particularly atmospheric.

Besides the popular Neapolitan numbers, there are many comparative rarities here, often coming from Venice, Florence or Sicily, with their respective dialects. There are no translations, but none are really needed. As Frank Granville Barker observes in his note: 'Strong emotions are the concern of all these songs, expressed in no less straightforward melodies. The mood is intense, the singer declaring his devotion to his loved one, or despairing when it is not returned. Parting from home inspires as much anguish as parting from the loved one, as we hear in Addio mia bella Napoli.'

The group of six traditional songs arranged by Favara, which close the recital, are particularly fine; Muttètti di lu pàliu (introduced by a fine horn solo) is really memorable, with di Stefano responding to its plaintive melancholy with a very gentle closing cadence. He then follows with a sparkling tarantella, Chiovu 'abballati'. This is not a collection to play all at once (and memories of Gigli in this repertory are not vanquished), but in its field it is currently unsurpassed.

Italian & Neapolitan Songs (with Orchestra, cond. Dino Olivieri): TRAD.: A la barcillunisa; A la vallelunghisa; Cantu a Timuni; Chiovu 'abballati; Muttètti di lu paliu; Nota di li lavannari. CESARINI: Firenza Songa. CURTIS: 'A canzone 'e Napule; Ti voglio tanto bene. LAZZARO: Chitarra Romana. BIXIO: Parlami d'amore, Mariù. BARBERIS: Munasterio 'e Santa-Chiara

(M) **(*) Decca Classic Recitals (ADD) 475 6813

Gigli was the great master of these Italian songs, and Giuseppe di Stefano never approached him in charm or in sophistication of singing. He does, however, possess a wonderful voice and plenty of energy, ideal in extrovert numbers such as the tarantella, Chiovu'abballati'. This song is one of six traditional songs which come off best (see above). The 1958 recording is warm and full, with the lush orchestrations providing a suitable backdrop. The (original) cover shows di Stefano paddling on the beach. However, these songs are included in the Double Decca set above which is probably worth the extra cost and is better documented.

Streich, Rita (soprano)

'*The Viennese Nightingale*' (with various orchestras and conductors or pianists as listed): MOZART: *Bastien und Bastienne* (complete; with Holm, Blankenheim, Munich CO, Stepp)

Arias from *Zaïde; Idomeneo; Così fan tutte; Die Entführung aus em Serail; Die Zauberflöte; Don Giovanni; Le nozze di Figaro; Il re pastore.* Concert arias (with Bav. RSO, Mackerras): *Alcandro lo confesso ... Non so d'onde viene; Ah se in ciel, benigne stelle; Vado ma dove? oh Dei!; Popoli di Tessaglia ... Io non chiedo, eterni Dei; Vorrei spiegarvi, oh Dio! ... Ah conte, partite; No, che non sei capace; Mia speranza adorata ... Ah non sai quai pena sia; Nehmt meinen Dank, Ihr holden*

Lieder (with Erik Werba, piano): *Das Veilchen; Die Zufriedenheit; An Chloë; Das Lied der Trennung; Die kleine Spinnerin; Geheime Liebe; Wie unglücklich bin ich nit; Der Zauberer; Sehnsucht nach dem Frühlinge; Un moto di gioia; Oiseaux, si tous les ans; Dans un bois solitaire; Ridente la calma; Das Kinderspiel; Abendemfindung; An die Einsamkeit; Die Verschweignung; Warnung.* WOLF: *Spanisches Liederbuch* excerpts: *Trau'nicht der Liebe; Köpfchen, Köpfchen, nicht; Bedeckt mich mit Blumen; In dem Schatten meiner Locken. Italienisches Liederbuch: Du kennst mit einem Fädchen mich zu fangen; Mein Liebster ist so klein; Wie lange schon; Wer rief dich denn? Nun lass uns Frieden schliessen; Nein junger Herr; O wär'dein Haus durchsichtig; Auch kleine Dinge. Tretet ein, höher Krieger; Verschwiegen Liebe; Gleich und gleich; Die Spröde; Die Bekehrte; Wiegenlied in Sommer; Der Gärtner; Zitronenfalter im April; Mausfallen-Sprüchlein; Elfenlied; Zum neuen Jahr; Wohin mit der Freud; Wiegenlied; Die Kleine; Nachtgrüss.* Folksong settings: *Oh, du liabs Angeli; Sakura.* SCHUBERT: *Heidenröslein* (2 versions); *Liebe schwärmt auf allen Wegen; Schweizerlied; Lied der Mignon: Nur wer die Sehnsucht kennt; Nähe des Geliebchen; Liebhabner in allen Gestalten; Der Hirt auf dem Felsen* (with Heinrich Geuser, clarinet); *Auf dem Wasser zu singen* (2 versions); *An den Mond; An die Nachtigall; Wiegenlied; Nachtviolen; Seligkeit* (2 versions); *Der Schmetterling; Die Vogel; Die Forelle* (2 versions); *Das Lied im Grünen.* BRAHMS (with Günther Weissenborn, piano): *Ständchen (Der Mond steht auf dem Berge); Geheimnis; Aud dem Schiffe; Trennung; Vergbliches Ständchen; Wiegenlied; Das Mädchen spricht; 3 Mädchenlied: Ach, und du mein kühles Wasser!; Am jüngsten Tag ich aufersteh; Auf di Nacht in der Spinnstub'n.* SCHUMANN: *Der Nussbaum; Die Stille; Schneeglöckchen; Die Lotusblume; Intermezzo; Aufträge*

Arias and excerpts from: WEBER: *Der Freischütz.* ROSSINI: *Il barbiere di Siviglia; Semiramide.* DONIZETTI: *Don Pasquale* (with Kurt Weholschutz); *Die Regimentstochter (La Fille du régiment); Lucia di Lammermoor; Linda di Chamounix.* VERDI: *Rigoletto* (with Hermann Uhde); *Un ballo in maschera; I vespri siciliani; Falstaff.* GLUCK: *Orphée et Euridice.* PFITZNER: *Palestrina: Die Messe* (with Soloists, Ch. & O of Berlin Komischen Opera, Robert Heger). LORTZING: *Der Wildschütz* (with Kurt Böhme). NICOLAI: *Die lustigen Weiber von Windsor. Variations on the Wiegenlied of Weber, Op. 19* (with Erik Werba). OFFENBACH: *Contes d'Hoffmann.* BIZET: *Les Pêcheurs de perles.* MASSENET: *Manon.* DELIBES: *Lakmé.* RIMSKY-KORSAKOV: *Sadko; Le Coq d'or.* MEYERBEER: *Les Huguenots.* THOMAS: *Mignon.* BELLINI: *I Capuleti e i Montecchi.* PUCCINI: *La Bohème; Gianni Schicchi; Turandot.* JOHANN STRAUSS JR: *Die Fledermaus.* Also Waltz: *G'schichten aus dem Wiener Wald.* RICHARD STRAUSS: *Der Rosenkavalier* (with Irmgard Seefried, Marianne Schech, Ilona Steingruber, Dresden State O, Karl Boehm). Lieder (with Günther Weissenborn, piano): *Schlagende Herzen; Wiegenlied; Schlechtes Wetter; An die Nacht; Als mir dein Lied erklang;* (with Erik Werba, piano): *Der Stern; Einerlei; Schlechtes Wetter.* MILHAUD: *4 Chansons de Ronsard.* European folksongs: *Gsätzli; When love is kind; Canto delle risailo; Au clair de la lune; Z'lauterbach*

(B) *** DG 474 738-2 (8)

Possessing the most delightful coloratura voice of the second half of the twentieth century (and as attractive to look at as to listen to), Rita Streich measured up to all the competition from the 'golden age'. Hers was a small voice but perfectly formed, and it recorded marvellously well. She had studied with Maria Ivogün and Erna Berger, and she surely carried the latter's vocal mantle. Her tonal purity, extraordinary flexibility and total accuracy in coloratura, together with her linear musicality, made her a natural for Mozart, and if she was most famous for her unsurpassed recording of the Queen of the Night's two big arias (uncannily accurate, if perhaps not malignantly evil), she was also an enchanting Zerlina, Despina, Papagena and Blonde, and she made the role of Susanna very much her own.

The collection here opens with a complete mono recording of *Bastien and Bastienne* in which she is well partnered by Richard Holm and Toni Blankenheim. The richly sung aria *Er war mir sonst treu*, and the duet *Geh'! Geh! Herz von Flandern,* comparably winning, project vividly, even if the conductor Christoph Stepp is rather matter-of-fact. The following excerpts, *Ruhe sanft* from *Zaïde* (with beautiful legato) and *Zeffiretti lusinghiri* from *Idomeneo* (with glorious, flowing runs), confirm her vocal grace and easy fluency and charm, as does the most famous duet from *Don Giovanni*, in which she is elegantly partnered by Fischer-Dieskau.

She had both the temperament and the bravura in the upper range for Mozart's virtuoso concert arias, and the astonishingly fine selection here, accompanied by Mackerras, set her on a pinnacle which only her magnificent high notes could overtop. The lovely *Vado, ma dove* and the grandiloquent *Popoli di Tessaglia* are unforgettable. Aloysia Lange was the lady for whom Mozart originally wrote these arias, and if she could sing them half as well as they are sung here by Streich, then contemporary reports of her artistry can certainly be believed!

The present set includes her many Lieder recordings, for which she was perhaps less famous in England; many appear here for the first time on either LP or CD. Most are accompanied by Erik Werber, with whom she established a close relationship. Throughout there is always evidence of a keenly sensitive mind, not perhaps that of a born Lieder singer, but certainly that of a born musician. Her ease and simplicity are especially telling in Schubert, where she could also be both touching and dramatic. In *Der Hirt auf dem Felsen*, with an artistic clarinet obbligato from Heinrich Geuser, she is in her element, as indeed she is in many of the most familiar songs, several of which she recorded twice.

She approaches Schumann, Brahms and Richard Strauss with almost an operatic style. Her line is often dramatic and this works best with the two last-named composers, but her interpretations lack the intimacy of the recital room. As Alan

Blyth comments in his excellent note, 'she did not attempt the intensity of approach favoured by her close contemporary, Elisabeth Schwarzkopf', but 'her sense of fun is strongly conveyed in the selection from Wolf's *Italianisches Lieder-buch*'. Moreover, none of these songs is ever let down by lack of control of phrase or intonation, and her persuasively affecting timbre and line always communicate directly. The surprise inclusion is the *Quatre Chansons de Ronsard* of Milhaud. But their sometimes awkward intervals and unex-pected flights of upper tessitura are negotiated with such skill and a supreme lightness of touch (from singer and accompa-nist alike) that they are transformed into twentieth-century French lollipops, to match the engaging folksongs with which the collection closes.

The equally wide range of recordings of opera arias con-stantly affects the listener with their ravishing tone and sparkling coloratura – notably so in in the excerpts from *Les Contes d'Hoffmann, Le Coq d'Or* (both exquisite), *Les Pêcheurs de perles, Lakmé* and *Mignon*. She is a engagingly minx-like Rosina in *Il barbiere*, and a touching Lucia di Lammermoor, duetting with the flute with captivating preci-sion, while the Presentation of the Silver Rose scene in *Rosenkavalier* (with Irmgard Seefried) is enchanting. If she does not attempt to draw a great deal of differentiation in character among the various heroines, it could be argued that in Mozart the roles she plays are all different facets of a basically similar female character. And her technique is so sure and the singing itself (with not a wobble anywhere) gives such pleasure that criticism is disarmed.

'*Waltzes and Arias*' (with Berlin RSO, RIAS Berlin, Gaebel): JOHANN STRAUSS JR: *Frühlingsstimmen; Draussen in Sievering.* SAINT-SAENS: *Le Rossignol et la rose.* VERDI: *Lo spazzacamino.* ARDITI: *Parla waltz.* JOSEF STRAUSS: *Dorfschwalben aus Osterreich.* ALABIEV: *The Nightingale.* DELIBES: *Les Filles de Cadiz.* CZERNIK: *Chi sa?* MARCHESI: *La folletta.* FLOTOW: *Last Rose of Summer.* DELL'ACQUA: *Villanelle.* ARDITI: *Il bacio.* Arias from: GODARD: *Jocelyn.* SUPPE: *Boccaccio.* DVORAK: *Rusalka.* MEYERBEER: *Dinorah*
⊶ ✿ (M) *** DG mono/stereo 457 729-2

Those wanting a single CD showing Rita Streich's delightful vocal personality at its most winning cannot do better than acquire this shorter selection. Many of the most memorable pieces included here come from a recital she recorded in 1958 in the Jesus Christus Kirche, Berlin.

Included were the Strauss waltzes, Dvořák's *Invocation to the Moon*, the charming *Hab' ich nur deine Liebe* from *Boccac-cio* and the equally delightful Shadow Song from *Dinorah*. Godard's highly romantic *Berceuse* is the most famous item, but it is in the deliciously fragile Saint-Saëns vocalise, *Le Rossignol et la rose*, and in Verdi's captivating song of the chimneysweep (*Lo spazzacamino*) that her magic sends a shiver of special pleasure to the nape of the neck. A worthy vocal addition for DG's series of 'Originals'.

'*Folksongs and Lullabies*': *Du, du liegst mir im Herzen; O du liabs Angeli; Frère Jacques; L'Amore de moi; Canto delle risaiole; Z'Lauterbach; Schlof sche, mein Vögele; Drink to me Only with Thine Eyes; Nobody Knows the Trouble I've Seen; Sakura, Sakura; Tschubtschik; Spi mladenez; In mezo al mar; Wenn ich ein Vöglein wär'; Der mond ist aufgegangen; Muss I denn zum Städtele 'maus* (with Rudolf Lamy Choir and instrumental accompaniment, Michalski). *Weisst Du, wieviel Sterne stehen; O wie wohl ist mir Abend; Wo e kleins Hüttle steht; All mein Gedanken; Glockenruf; Der*

Bürgermeister von Wesel; Der Wechsel der Jahreszeiten; Schlaf, Herzenssöhnchen; Schlafe, mein Prinzchen, schlaf ein; Sandmännchen; Der Kuckuck; Schwesterlein!; Ach Modr, ick will en Ding han; In der Fruah; Abendlied; Ave Maria (with Regenszburger Domspatzen, Bavarian R. SO, Gaebel)
(M) *** DG (ADD) (IMS) 457 763-2

This disc is a delight. Every song is most winning and it is difficult to say which is the more captivating, the Russian, French, English or Swiss folksongs, all dressed up in freshly colourful orchestrations, and the delectable *Frère Jacques* presented in canon with the choir. Rita Streich sings with obvious affection, with her legendary creaminess of vocal timbre tickling the ear throughout the two collections, which were recorded in 1963 and 1964. Their remarkable variety, to say nothing of the vocal charm, prevents any sense that 79 minutes of folksong is too much. It is regretted that DG, in these beautifully transferred recordings on their Originals label, has failed to provide any texts or translations. But this is still a reissue not to be missed.

Sutherland, Dame Joan (soprano)

'*The Art of Joan Sutherland*':

Volume 1: Arias from: HANDEL: *Alcina; Giulio Cesare; Samson.* MOZART: *Die Entführung; Il re pastore; Die Zauberflöte*

Volume 2: Arias from French operas: OFFENBACH: *La Grande Duchesse de Gérolstein; Robinson Crusoé.* MEYERBEER: *Dinorah; Robert le Diable.* CHARPENTIER: *Louise.* AUBER: *Manon Lescaut.* BIZET: *Les Pêcheurs de perles; Vasco de Gama.* MASSENET: *Cendrillon.* GOUNOD: *Faust; Mireille; Le Tribut de Zamora.* LECOCQ: *Le Coeur et la main.* MASSE: *Les Noces de Jeanette*

Volume 3: '*Command Performance*': WEBER: *Oberon.* MASSENET: *Le Cid.* MEYERBEER: *Dinorah; L'Étoile de Nord.* LEONCAVALLO: *Pagliacci.* VERDI: *I masnadieri.* BELLINI: *Beatrice di Tenda.* DONIZETTI: *La Fille du regiment.* OFFENBACH: *Les Contes d'Hoffman.* GOUNOD: *Faust*

Volume 4: '*Rarities and Surprises*': Arias from WAGNER: *Der fliegende Holländer; Lohengrin; Die Meistersinger; Rienzi; Tannhäuser; Tristan und Isolde; Die Walküre.* MOZART: *Le nozze di Figaro.* GLIERE: *Concerto for Coloratura Soprano.* STRAVINSKY: *Pastorale.* CUI: *Ici bas.* GRETCHANINOV: *Lullaby*

Volume 5: '*Great Operatic Scenes*' from: MEYERBEER: *Les Huguenots.* BELLINI: *Norma.* DONIZETTI: *Lucia di Lammermoor.* VERDI: *Attila; Ernani; I vespri siciliani; La traviata*
*** Australian Decca (ADD) 466 474-2 (5)

Joan Sutherland has been one of Decca's most important recording artists, particularly during the analogue LP era. In return, often with the prompting and careful and imaginative planning of her husband and musical partner Richard Bonynge, she provided an extraordinary wide-ranging dis-cography over her remarkably long recording career. This bargain box from Decca's Australian branch is important for including many recordings not otherwise available on CD.

Volume 1 is a reminder of her excellent Handel perform-ances, with the arias mainly taken from her complete opera recordings, although the ringing account of 'Let the Bright Seraphim' is from *The Art of the Prima Donna*, as is the Mozart *Die Entführung* aria. The other Mozart items are from her 1979 Mozart LP: not one of her best discs, but one from which Sutherland admirers will surely want excerpts.

The French arias on Volume 2 were recorded in 1968 and sound sparklingly vivid and fresh in this new transfer. This was one of her most successful and infectiously tuneful recital discs: highlights include swirling coloratura waltzes from *Robinson Crusoé* and *Mireille*, a sparkling bolero by Lecocq, and spectacular set-piece arias by Meyerbeer, Auber and Charpentier.

Volume 3, *Command Performance*, is hardly less succesful: the showy numbers of Meyerbeer, Donizetti and Offenbach display her virtuoso singing to the full, while her hauntingly exquisite bel canto in the Bellini item is another highlight.

Volume 4 includes her 1979 Wagner recital, and more items from the Mozart recital from the same year: this is not top-drawer Sutherland, but it is fascinating to hear the Glière *Concerto for Coloratura Soprano*, which is quite superb.

The final volume, a collection of operatic scenes, includes the great 1959 Paris recording of the Mad scene from *Lucia*, as well as the arias from *Ernani* and the splendidly crisp bolero from *I vespri siciliani* from the same disc. All in all, a splendid collection of some great singing and interesting repertoire, with stylish orchestal contributions, mainly from Richard Bonynge, and although no texts are provided there are good sleeve notes.

'The Art of the Prima Donna' (with ROHCG Ch. & O, Molinari-Pradelli): ARNE: *Artaxerxes: The Soldier Tir'd.* HANDEL: *Samson: Let the Bright Seraphim.* BELLINI: *Norma: Casta diva. I Puritani: Son vergin vezzosa; Que la voce. La sonnambula: Come per me sereno.* ROSSINI: *Semiramide: Bel raggio lusinghier.* GOUNOD: *Faust: Jewel Song. Roméo et Juliette: Waltz Song.* VERDI: *Otello: Willow Song. Rigoletto: Caro nome. La traviata: Ah fors' è lui; Sempre libera.* MOZART: *Die Entführung aus dem Serail: Marten aller Arten.* THOMAS: *Hamlet: Mad scene.* DELIBES: *Lakmé: Bell Song.* MEYERBEER: *Les Huguenots: O beau pays*
✪ (M) *** Decca (ADD) 467 115-2 (2)

This ambitious early two-disc recital (from 1960) has also now been reissued in Decca's Legends series, for the recording on CD is amazingly full and realistic, far more believable than many new digital recordings. It remains one of Dame Joan Sutherland's outstanding gramophone achievements, and it is a matter of speculation whether even Melba or Tetrazzini in their heyday managed to provide sixteen consecutive recordings quite as dazzling as these performances. Indeed, it is the 'golden age' that one naturally turns to rather than to current singers when making any comparisons. Sutherland herself, by electing to sing each one of these fabulously difficult arias in tribute to a particular soprano of the past, from Mrs Billington in the eighteenth century, through Grisi, Malibran, Pasta and Jenny Lind in the nineteenth century, to Lilli Lehmann, Melba, Tetrazzini and Galli-Curci in this, is asking to be judged by the standards of the golden age.

On the basis of recorded reminders she comes out with flying colours, showing a greater consistency and certainly a wider range of sympathy than even the greatest golden agers possessed. The sparkle and delicacy of the *Puritani* Polonaise, the freshness and lightness of the Mad scene from Thomas's *Hamlet*, the commanding power of the *Entführung* aria and the breathtaking brilliance of the Queen's aria from *Les Huguenots* are all among the high spots here, while the arias which Sutherland later recorded in her complete opera sets

regularly bring performances just as fine – and often finer – than the later versions.

'Joy to the World' (with the Ambrosian Singers, New Philh. O, Richard Bonynge): HANDEL: *Joy to the World.* WILLIS: *It Came Upon a Midnight Clear.* ADAM: *O Holy Night.* GOUNOD: *O Divine Redeemer.* TRAD.: *What Child is This; Adeste fideles; Angels we have Heard on High; Deck the Hall; Good King Wenceslas; The Holly and the Ivy; The Twelve Days of Christmas.* MENDELSSOHN: *Hark! The Herald Angels Sing.* REGER: *The Virgin's Slumber Song.* SCHUBERT: *Ave Maria*
(M) **(*) Decca Classic Recitals (ADD) 475 6153

These are highly elaborated arrangements of carols made by Douglas Gamley which cocoon the listener in a web of opulent sound. They may not appeal to everyone, but Sutherland and Bonynge both obviously enjoy this repertoire and there is plenty to relish, from the piquancy of *Good Wenceslas* to the exuberance of *Joy to the World. Hark! The Herald Angels* is superbly projected with a big, clear voice, and the lighter numbers, *The Holly and the Ivy* and *Deck the Hall*, both sparkle. The highlight, however, is an unforgettable performance of *The Twelve Days of Christmas* where Joan Sutherland (and Douglas Gamley's clever arrangement) pulls out all the stops. Vintage 1964 sound too, and the reissue features the delightfully nostalgic original artwork.

Donizetti and Verdi Arias (with Paris Conservatoire Orchestra, Nello Santi) from: DONIZETTI: *Lucia di Lammermoor.* VERDI: *Ernani; Linda di Chamounix; I vespri siciliani*
🎧 ✪(M) *** Decca Classic Recitals (ADD) 475 6237-2

This 1959 recital is not only Sutherland's most treasurable record, but also one of the most cherishable of all operatic recitals. Offering glorious, exuberant and ravishing singing, the original LP at once firmly put Sutherland on the operatic map among the great recording artists of all time. The freshness of the two big arias from *Lucia di Lammermoor*, sparkling in immaculate coloratura, is breathtaking, while the lightness and point of the jaunty *Linda di Chamounix* aria and the *Boléro* from *I vespri siciliani* are just as winning. The recording is exceptionally vivid and immediate, even if the accompaniments under Santi are sometimes rough in ensemble. This recital used to be available in Decca's 'Grandi Voci' series, offering more music at the same price, though it is always nice to see the original artwork in these reissued Classic Recitals.

Sutherland, Joan (soprano), Luciano Pavarotti (tenor)

'Love Duets' (with National PO, Bonynge) from VERDI: *La traviata; Otello; Aida* (with chorus). BELLINI: *La sonnambula.* DONIZETTI: *Linda di Chamounix*
(M) *** Decca (ADD) 458 235-2

This collection, recorded in the Kingsway Hall in 1976, offers a rare sample of Sutherland as Aida (*La fatale pietra … O terra, addio* from Act IV), a role she sang only once on stage, well before her international career began; and with this and her sensitive impersonations of Desdemona, Violetta (generously represented) and the Bellini and Donizetti heroines, Sutherland might have been expected to steal first honours here. In fact, these are mainly duets to show off the tenor, and

t is Pavarotti who runs away with the main glory, though
»oth artists were plainly challenged to give their finest. The
esult, with excellent accompaniment, is among the most
ttractive and characterful duet recitals in the catalogue. The
ecording is admirably clear and well focused, and the sophis-
ication of orchestral detail is striking in the *Otello* and *Aida*
cenes which close the recital, with the singers given remark-
ble presence.

Tallis Scholars, Peter Phillips

Western Wind Masses: SHEPPARD: *Mass, The Western
Wynde.* TAVERNER: *Mass, Western Wynde.* TYE: *Mass,
Western Wind*
— *** Gimell CDGIM 027

t was a splendid idea for Gimell to gather together the three
ey Mass settings which use the well-known source theme,
he *Western Wynde*. The performances are as eloquent as we
vould expect from this source and they are beautifully
ecorded. Taverner's setting emerges as the most imaginative,
»ut Tye comes pretty close. A most enterprising issue, which
Jeserves support.

Lamenta: *The Lamentations of the Prophet Jeremiah*:
Settings by FERRABOSCO THE ELDER; TALLIS; BRUMEL;
ROBERT WHITE; PALESTRINA: *Lamentations for Holy
Saturday*
*** Gimell CDGIM 996

the Old Testament *Lamentations of Jeremiah* are highly peni-
ential, reflected in the settings by these five remarkable
composers' music, which is desperate in its melancholy and
»owerful in expressive feeling. All the composers except Palestrina (whose music is perhaps the most inspired of all)
ollow the convention of preceding each verse by musically
elaborating a letter from the Hebrew alphabet ('Aleph', 'Beth',
Teth', etc.) like an illuminated initial of a medieval manuscript. The profoundly expressed *Lament* which follows then
provides an immediate contrast by its depth of despair. All
end with the call '*Jerusalem, Jerusalem, turn to the Lord your
God*', yet the music here is remarkably diverse. The performances and recordings are outstandingly fine, but some might
ind the prevailing mood of such a collection too obsessive.

The Essential Tallis Scholars: Disc 1: ALLEGRI: *Miserere.*
VICTORIA: *Ave Maria for double choir.* PALESTRINA: *Sidcut
ilium I.* JOSQUIN: *Praeter rerum serium.* CRECQUILLON:
Pater peccavi. CLEMENS: *Ego flos campi.* ISAAC: *Tota
pulchra es.* RORE: *Descendi in hortum meum.* LASSUS: *Alma
redemptoris mater; Salve Regina; Ave regina caelorum.*
BRUMEL: *Missa Et ecce terrae motus: Gloria*

Disc 2: SHEPPARD: *Media vita.* TALLIS: *In Manus Tuas; O
nata lux; Audivi vocem.* WHITE: *Exaudiat tu Dominus.*
CORNYSH: *Ay Robin. Salve Regina.* BYRD: *Mass for 5 Voices*
— (B) *** Gimell (ADD/DDD) CDGIM 201 (2)

This is the first of two rewarding anthologies of early music,
drawn from back issues, splendidly recorded by the Tallis
Scholars over a period of 15 years from 1976 to 1991. Most of
the pieces are independent, and they provide a wonderful survey. Moreover, as the music is well documented and
full texts and translations are included, it should tempt any
adventurous listener to explore further.

The programme opens with Allegri's famous *Miserere*, with
its soaring treble solo superbly done; but sample some of the

other names on the first disc, Crequillon's *Pater peccavi*,
Clemens non Papa's *Ego flos campi*, or Brumel's richly complex *Gloria*, and you will surely be won over by the remarkable appeal of this repertoire. Alternatively, try from the
second CD the gentle, soaring opening of Sheppard's *Media
vita*, a large-scale work offered complete, Tallis's radiant *O
nata lux*, the dark melancholy of Cornysh's questing
lovesong, *Ah, Robin*, and then become immersed in the whole
of Byrd's glorious *Mass for 5 Voices*.

'*Christmas with the Tallis Scholars*': Medieval Carols:
*Angelus ad virginem; Nowell sing we; The Coventry Carol;
Lullay I saw; Lullay, lulla, thou little tiny Child; Ave Maria*
settings by JOSQUIN DESPREZ; VERDALOT; VICTORIA.
Chorales: PRAETORIUS: *Est ist ein' Ros'; Jospeh lieber Joseph
mein; In dulci jubilo.* CLEMENS: Motet: *Pastores quidnam
vidistis. Missa Pastores quidnam vidistis.* Chants from
Salisbury: *Missa in gallicantu* (1st Christmas Mass); *Christi
Redemptor omnium; Veni, Redemptor gentium; Salvator
mundi, Domine; A solis ortis cardine.* Tudor Polyphony:
TALLIS: *Missa Puer natus est nobis*
(B) *** Gimell CDGIM 202 (2)

In spite of its tempting title, this anthology is less easy to
recommend unequivocally than its companion above, as the
second disc offers a great deal of plainchant, including a
medieval Christmas Mass which was originally celebrated at
daybreak on Christmas Eve and lasts 39 minutes! This will
not to be every listener's liking, and when it is followed by
four Christmas plainchant hymns, one might feel this is too
much of a good thing! The disc is completed by the rich
polyphony of Tallis's beautiful *Missa Puer natus est*, and the
improvement in musical interest is very palpable.

The first disc, however, traces the early history of Christmas music fascinatingly and rewardingly, beginning with
four lively, medieval 'dance carols'. Then comes the first piece
which sets the style we recognize today, the lovely *Coventry
Carol*, and after four diverse and beautiful *Ave Maria* settings
we come to three instantly recognizable chorales, collected by
Michael and Hieronymous Praetorius (who were not related,
but contemporary) at the turn of the seventeenth century.
The disc then concludes with Clemens non Papa's *Pastoral
Mass*, rich in line and texture, preceded by the Motet on
which it is based. Performances and recordings are flawless.

'*Live in Oxford*': OBRECHT: *Salve Regina.* JOSQUIN
DESPREZ: *Gaude Virgo; Absalon fili mei.* TAVERNER: *Gaude
plurium.* BYRD: *Tribus, Domine.* TALLIS: *O sacrum
convivium.* MUNDY: *Adolescentulus sum ego; Vox Patris
caelestis*
*** Gimell CDGIM 998-2

The fledgling Tallis Scholars gave their first concert, in 1973, in
the Church of St Mary Magdalen, but have chosen the Chapel
of Merton College for this, their twenty-fifth-anniversary
programme. The beauty of its acoustic, resonant but
unclouding, is ideal for their flowing style in this survey of
fifteenth- and sixteenth-century masterpieces, ending with
Mundy's spectacularly ambitious *Vox Patris caelestis*, with its
vocal complexities confidently encompassed, especially by the
soaring trebles.

Tear, Robert (tenor)

'*English Baroque Recital*' (with Brown, violin, Heath, cello,
Preston and Tilney, harpsichord continuo, ASMF,

Marriner): HANDEL: *Look Down, Harmonious Saint; Meine Seele hört im Sehen; Süsse Stille.* ARNE: *Bacchus and Ariadne*: excerpts; *Fair Caelia Love Pretended*: excerpts. BOYCE: *Song of Momus to Mars.* JAMES HOOK: *The Lass of Richmond Hill*

(B) *** Double Decca (ADD) 452 973-2 (2) (with HANDEL: *Acis and Galatea ***)

Robert Tear's 1969 recital offers a rare Handel cantata and two of his German songs, followed by an even rarer and certainly delightful collection of music by his English successors. This may in essence be a scholarly compilation, but it is one which imparts its learning in the most painless way, including as it does the vigorous Boyce song and the original, bouncing setting of 'The Lass of Richmond Hill', beautifully pointed. The 'Harmonious Saint' of the Handel cantata is of course St Cecilia, while Arne too is in Italianate mood in *Bacchus and Ariadne* – until he ends with a galumphing final number with ripe horn parts – very English. Robert Tear is in excellent voice and the recording has all the atmospheric warmth one associates with Argo's recordings of the ASMF in St John's, Smith Square.

Tebaldi, Renata (soprano)

'*Voce d'Angelo*' (early recordings with Santa Cecilia Ac. O or SRO, Erede, or La Scala, Milan O, de Sabata): Arias and excerpts from: PUCCINI: *La Bohème* (with Hilde Gueden, Giacinti Prandelli, Fernando Corena); *Manon Lescaut; Tosca; Madama Butterfly* (with Giovanni Inghilleri). GIORDANO: *Andrea Chénier.* GOUNOD: *Faust.* VERDI: *Aida; Il trovatore; Requiem*

o-- (BB) (***) Regis stereo/mono. RRC 1125

A treasurable collection of key arias and scenes, recorded between 1949 and 1951, when Tebaldi's voice was at its freshest and most melting. They are taken mainly from her early Decca complete recordings of the key Puccini operas, although *Un bel dì vedremo*, like Gounod's Jewel Song and the lovely, simple performance of Verdi's *Tacea la notte placida*, comes from her first mono LP. *Ritorna vincitor* then shows her at her most commanding. The excerpts from the *Requiem* and Giordano's *Andrea Chénier*, conducted by Victor de Sabata, are recorded less satisfactorily, but are still well worth having.

'*The Great Renata Tebaldi*' (recordings made between 1949 and 1969): Arias and excerpts (with various artists, orchestras and conductors) from: PUCCINI: *Gianni Schicchi; Tosca; Suor Angelica; Il tabarro; La fanciulla del West; Turandot; La Bohème; Manon Lescaut; Madama Butterfly.* CATALANI: *La Wally.* PONCHIELLI: *La Gioconda.* CILEA: *Adriana Lecouvreur.* GIORDANO: *Andrea Chénier.* BOITO: *Mefistofele.* VERDI: *Aida; Il trovatore; La traviata; La forza del destino; Otello; Don Carlos; Un ballo in maschera.* LEHAR: *The Merry Widow: Vilja* (sung in Italian). ROSSINI: *La regata veneziana: Anzoleta avant la regata*

(M) *** Decca mono/stereo 470 280-2 (2)

For I.M. during the years following the end of the Second World War, the discovery of Tebaldi was something of a revelation. He purchased her first mono LP, which was recorded by Decca, in 1949 and was immediately entranced by the sheer lyrical beauty of her voice. Two of the items on that LP (Verdi's *Ritorna vincitor* from *Aida* and *Tacea la*

notte placida from *Il trovatore*) are used to open the secon[d] of the two discs of this set, and the vocal magic immediately apparent. The ffrr mono recording, made i[n] the Victoria Hall, Geneva, still sounds pretty remarkabl[e] and one feels that it was a pity that Decca chose not t[o] assemble this collection in historical order, for the thir[d] item on disc 2 is an infinitely touching account of *Parigi cara, noi lasceremo* from *La traviata*, with Gianni Poggi remarkably sympathetic Alfredo. Then comes a famous ari[a] from *La forza del destino* (*Ma pellegrina ed orfana ... Pac[e,] pace, mio Dio!*) in which Tebaldi produces one of thos[e] exquisite sudden pianissimos in her upper range that wa[s] one of the frisson-making hallmarks of her vocal line. Th[e] scene from *Don Carlos*, with Nicolai Ghiaurov, conducte[d] by Solti a decade later, follows soon afterwards, demonstrat[-]ing that, under the right conductor, she could also rise t[o] thrilling drama in Verdi.

But it was not for Verdi that she was most renowned. He[r] great contemporary, Maria Callas, could upstage her ther[e] for she was a much greater stage actress. But in Puccin[i] (especially) and comparable Italian bel canto roles Tebald[i] was unsurpassed in the 1950s and 1960s, recording the princi[-]pal roles more than once.

If her Mimì was unforgettable (touchingly remembere[d] here in the Love scene from Act I of *La Bohème*, with Carl[o] Bergonzi, dating from 1959), she was also a delightful Lau[-]retta, and *O mio babbino caro* (1962) opens the first dis[c] ravishingly. The following *Vissi d'arte* (*Tosca*, 1959) is equall[y] lovely. Other highlights include the key arias from *Suo[r] Angelica, Manon Lescaut* and a splendid excerpt from *L[a] fanciulla del West* (with Cornell MacNeil as Jack Rance). I[n] *Turandot* she chose the lesser part of Liù, and *Signore, ascolta ... Tu che di gel sei cinta* is characteristically melting.

Her rather stiff acting meant that she was perhaps a les[s] than ideal *Madama Butterfly*, but even so the Love scene fro[m] Act I (again with Bergonzi) is vocally spellbinding, and man[y] other key arias from comparable non-Puccini repertoire ar[e] no less bewitching and certainly dramatic, notably th[e] excerpts from *La Wally* and *La Gioconda* (which demonstrat[e] her rich lower range), *Adriana Lecouvreur* and *Andre[a] Chénier.* She was fortunate that the Decca engineers recorde[d] her voice with complete naturalness, as the current C[D] transfers (which are excellent) so uniformly show. This is no[t] a set to play through all at once, for subtlety of characteriza[-]tion was not Tebaldi's strong suit; if it is dipped into judi[-]ciously, however, one is consistently seduced by Tebaldi'[s] beauty of tone and simplicity of line.

'*The Best of Tebaldi*' (with Ch. & O of Santa Cecilia, Rome, Tullio Serafin, Francesco Molinari-Pradelli, Franco Capuana, Alberto Erede or Gianandrea Gavazzeni): Arias from: PUCCINI: *La Bohème; La fanciulla del West; Madama Butterfly; Tosca; Turandot.* GIORDANO: *Adriana Lecouvreur; Andrea Chénier.* BOITO: *Mefistofele*

(M) **(*) Decca (ADD) 475 397-2

This compilation was first released in 1962. Tebaldi admirers will have their own personal ideas as to what her very bes[t] recordings are, but few of them are included here. But there is no doubt that this 50-minute recital includes some magnifi[-]cent singing, rich and firm and always reliable. Althoug[h] Tebaldi does not exhibit the last degree of individuality in he[r] musical characterization, the emotions conveyed here are deeply felt, to match the musical style. The (mainly 1950s) stereo recordings are generally excellent for their period (only the 1955 *Turandot* understandably sounding dated), with both

armth and atmosphere. No texts or readable sleeve-notes, as
sual, in the Classic Recitals series. However, we refer readers
o her later (1964) disc of arias below, as showing the great
iva in the finest light.

Christmas Festival: BACH/GOUNOD: *Ave Maria*. BRAHMS:
Wiegenlied. TRAD.: *What Child Is This?; Adeste fidees*.
DAM: *O Holy Night*. ANON.: *Tu scendi dale stele*. GRUBER:
Silent Night. FRANK: *Panus angelicus*. GOUNOD: *Oh Divine
Redeemer*. SCHUBERT: *Mille cherubini in coro; Ave Maria*
M) *(*) Decca (ADD) 475 6154-2

his CD will appeal mainly to Tebaldi admirers. As a Christ-
nas anthology it is not a great success. A carol record needs
ervour or charm, ideally a bit of both. Tebaldi sings delight-
ully in two gentle items, *Tù scendi dale* and Schubert's *Mille
herubini in coro*. She also offers an attractive Italian version
f *Silent Night*; and the organ accompaniment to *What Child
s this?* (a setting of the *Greensleeves* tune) is attractive. But
sewhere the vocal touch is distinctly heavy-handed, and the
horal contributions and accompaniments are comparatively
edestrian. The sound (1971) also lacks Decca's usual sparkle.
Iowever, the glamorous original cover pictures the diva
ooking wonderfully opulent in her fur coat!

rias (with the New Philh. O, Oliviero de Fabritiis) from:
ERDI: *Un ballo in maschera; Don Carlo; Giovanna d'Arco*.
UCCINI: *La rondine; Turandot*. PONCHIELLI: *La Gioconda*.
ASCAGNI: *Cavalleria rusticana*. CILEA: *L'Arlesiana*
M) *** Decca Classic Recitals (ADD) 475 7166

his 1964 recital represented Tebaldi's return to the recording
tudio after a significant interval, during which she had
everal comparative failures on the stage. With that in mind,
he achievement is all the more remarkable: Tebaldi is here at
er very finest – a hint of hardness on top but still completely
eliabile in every register of her voice. What is more, there is
n extra depth in the interpretations which will delight even
hose who in the past have found Tebaldi dramatically too
eticent; for example, she sings the first part of Turandot's big
rea in a withdrawn, musing way, telling the story of the
rincess Liu-Ling betrayed by her lover, as though to herself.
he opening out in the second half of the aria is all the more
xciting. *Tu che la* from *Don Carlos* is also especially welcome,
ne of the finest versions available; but the standard through-
ut is high. Excellent playing from the New Philharmonia
nd decent sound. The sleeve-notes, too small to be read by
he human eye, can be read on-line.

Tebaldi, Renata (soprano), **and Franco
Corelli** (tenor)

Great Opera Duets' (with SRO, Guadagno) from: PUCCINI:
Manon Lescaut. VERDI: *Aida*. CILEA: *Adriana Lecouvreur*.
ONCHIELLI: *La Gioconda*. ZANDONAI: *Francesca da
Rimini*
M) ** Decca Classic Recitals (ADD) 475 522-2

his 1972 recital was rushed out on LP to coincide with
ppearances in London of the two singers. This was one of
ebaldi's last recordings and, while her voice is no longer in
ull bloom, it sounds surprisingly good, giving signs of strain
nly in the upper register. Corelli is as full-toned and gusty as
ver, and the two give committed performances throughout –
he Love scene from *Manon Lascaut* especially persuasive.
he longest except here is the Zandonai item, whose (nearly)

19 minutes took up one whole side of the original LP – an
enjoyable example of rare verismo, if not top-class music.
While the voices are caught vividly enough, the orchestra is
surprisingly distant, at it was in its LP incarnation. The
original notes, reproduced for this Classic Recitals release, are
so small as to be almost indecipherable, but at least Tebaldi
looks wonderfully glamorous on the cover.

Terfel, Bryn (bass-baritone), **Malcolm
Martineau** (piano)

'*The Vagabond and Other English Songs*': VAUGHAN
WILLIAMS: *Songs of Travel (The Vagabond; Let Beauty
Awake; The Roadside Fire; Youth and Love; In Dreams; The
Infinite Shining Heavens; Whither Must I Wander; Bright in
the Ring of Words; I have Trod the Upward and the
Downward Slope).* G. BUTTERWORTH: *Bredon Hill (Bredon
Hill; Oh Fair Enough; When the Lad for Longing Sighs; On
the Idle Hill of Summer; With Rue my Heart is Laden); The
Shropshire Lad (6 songs): Loveliest of Trees; When I was
One-and-twenty; Look not in my Eyes; Think no More, Lad;
The Lads in their Hundreds; Is my Team Ploughing?* FINZI:
*Let us Garlands Bring (Come Away, Death; Who is Silvia?;
Fear no More the Heat of the Sun; O Mistress Mine; It was a
Lover and his Lass)*. IRELAND: *Sea Fever; The Vagabond;
The Bells of San Marie*
B—• ❂ *** DG 445 946-2

No other collection of English songs has ever quite
matched this one in its depth, intensity and sheer beauty.
Terfel, the great Welsh singer of his generation, here shows
his deep affinity with the English repertory, demonstrating
triumphantly in each of the twenty-eight songs that this
neglected genre deserves to be treated in terms similar to
those of the German Lied and the French mélodie. The
Vaughan Williams songs are perhaps the best known, nine
sharply characterized settings of Robert Louis Stevenson
which, thanks to Terfel's searching expressiveness matched
by Martineau's inspired accompaniments, reveal depths of
emotion hardly suspected.

The five Shakespeare settings by Finzi are just as memorable in their contrasted ways, five of the best-known lyrics
from the plays that have been set countless times but which
here are given new perspectives, thanks both to the composer
and to the singer. The eleven Butterworth settings of Housman are among the finest inspirations of this short-lived
composer, and it is good to have three sterling Ireland settings of Masefield, including the ever-popular 'Sea Fever',
which with Terfel emerges fresh and new. The singer's
extreme range of tone and dynamic, down to the most
delicate, firmly supported half-tones, is astonishing, adding
intensity to one of the most felicitous song-recital records in
years. The warm acoustic of the Henry Wood Hall gives a
glow both to the voice and to the piano.

'*Impressions*' (with (i) E. Bar. Soloists, Gardiner; (ii)
Martineau, piano; (iii) Philh. O, Sinopoli; (iv) BPO,
Abbado): (i) MOZART: *Le nozze di Figaro: Se vuol ballare;
Non più andrai; Aprite un po' quegli occhi*. (ii) SCHUBERT:
*Litanei auf das Fest Allerseelen; Die Forelle; An die Musik;
Erlkönig*. (iii) MAHLER: *Kindertotenlieder*. (ii) VAUGHAN
WILLIAMS: *The Vagabond; The Roadside Fire*. (iv)
WAGNER: *Die Meistersinger: Wie duftet doch der Flieder*.
Tannhäuser: O! du mein holder Abendstern
*** DG 449 190-2

Ranging over the recordings made for DG up to his English song disc, this sampler gives a formidable idea of this brilliant young singer's powers, very well chosen not just from his solo discs but from complete opera sets and discs with orchestra.

Tewkesbury Abbey School Choir, Benjamin Nicholas

'Light of the World' (with Andrew Swait (treble), Gavin Wells (trumpet), Alison Martin (harp), Carleton Etherington or Ian Fox (organ)): HANDEL: Ode for the Birthday of Queen Anne: Eternal Source of Light. Messiah: How beautiful are the feet. ALCOCK: Sanctus. BURGON: Nunc Dimittis. DANKWORTH: Light of the World. MENDELSSOHN: Hymn of Praise: I waited for the Lord. WESLEY: Blesed be the God and Father. SCHUBERT: Ave Maria. SCHUMANN: The Angel's Goodnight. PARRY: Judith: Long since in Egypt's plenteous Land. TRAD.: Londonderry Air; Amazing Grace. MOZART: Ave verum corpus. RUTTER: The Lord bless you and keep you; Gaelic Blessing. FAURE: Requiem: Pie Jesu. MAWBY: Ave verum corpus. LAURIDSEN: Ubi caritas et amor
*** Signum SIGCD 068

As Benjamin Nicholas, the Director of the Tewkesbury Abbey Choir, tells us in the notes, this collection was inspired by the availability of the ten-year-old treble, Andrew Swait, with his 'outstandingly colourful tone quality and musicianship'. He contributes movingly, without artifice and with wonderful confidence, to more than half the 21 items here, including Geoffrey Burgon's justly famous Nunc Dimittis (with its trumpet obbligato beautifully played by Gavin Wells) and the Mendelssohn, Handel and Schumann pieces, and he sings Schubert's Ave Maria and Fauré's Pie Jesu with touching simplicity. Perhaps the final number in the programme, Amazing Grace, might have been more effective had the choir joined him; but they sing splendidly elsewhere, notably so in Samuel Wesley's Blessed be God the Father, and the two versions of Ave verum corpus, by Mozart and Colin Mawby respectively, and, of course in the pair of delightful Rutter carols. The surprise is Johnny Dankworth's memorable setting which gives the disc its title; and it is also good to hear Parry's famous tune, normally sung as 'Dear Lord and Father of Mankind', here with its original text from his oratorio, Judith. Excellent accompaniments and first-class recording make this a most rewarding collection of its kind.

Tomlinson, John (bass)

Opera arias and scenes (with Geoffrey Mitchell Ch., Philh. O, Parry) from HANDEL: Acis and Galatea; Samson. MOZART: Abduction from the Seraglio (with Williams, Banks). VERDI: Simon Boccanegra; Ernani. BORODIN: Prince Igor. DARGOMIZHSKY: Rusalka. SULLIVAN: The Mikado; The Pirates of Penzance. OFFENBACH: Geneviève de Brabant (with Shore). MUSSORGSKY: Mephistopheles: Song of the Flea. LEHMANN: In a Persian Garden: Myself when Young
(M) *** Chan. 3044

The versatility of John Tomlinson is breathtaking, and here he tackles the widest range of bass arias. It adds to the characterful tang and sparkle of the performances that all seventeen items are in English on one of the 'Opera in

English' discs sponsored by the Peter Moores Foundation One might have expected this singing actor, today's greates Wotan, to be attuned to Verdi and the Russians, with an attractive aria from Dargomizhsky's Rusalka in addition t the well-known Mussorgsky and Borodin items, but he is jus as stylish in Handel (both comic and heroic), as well as in Mozart (a characterful Osmin in three items from Seraglio) He is full of fun in Offenbach (the Gendarmes' duet from Geneviève de Brabant with Andrew Shore) and G. & S. (th Policeman's song from The Pirates of Penzance) winningl sung in a bluff northern accent. There is brilliant accompani ment under David Parry.

'German Operatic Arias' (sung in English, with LPO or Philh. O, Parry) from: MOZART: The Abduction from the Seraglio; The Magic Flute. BEETHOVEN: Fidelio. WEBER: Der Freischütz. WAGNER: The Rheingold; The Flying Dutchman; The Mastersingers of Nuremberg. R. STRAUSS: Der Rosenkavalier. LORTZING: The Armourer
(M) *** Chan. 3073

Opening with great gusto in an exhilarating account o Osmin's 'vengeance' aria, John Tomlinson, in splendid voice shows how effective opera in English can be, sung by a master of characterization with a rich voice. Whether in the deep sonorities of Sarastro's Prayer from The Magic Flute, a Caspar in Der Freischütz, as an unforgettable Wotan in the Rainbow Bridge sequence from Rheingold (to gorgeous soun from the LPO); as Hans Sachs in Mastersingers or a highl individual Baron Ochs in Rosenkavalier, Tomlinson's projec tion is matched by the resonant quality of the singing, and only occasionally does a minor excess of vibrato have any adverse effect on a firmly supported vocal line. There is always fine orchestral support from David Parry. The record ings (of typical Chandos excellence) were made at Blackheath Halls between 1998 and 2001. A most enjoyable collection with Hans Stadlinger's 'I Used to be Young with a Fine Head of Hair' from Lortzing's Der Waffenschmied (The Armourer) included as a final jest; for, as can be seen by the photographs there is nothing sparse about Tomlinson's current mop!

Tonus Peregrinus, Anthony Pitts

'The Naxos Book of Carols' (An Advent Sequence in Music; with Nicholas Chalmers, organ): The Hope: O Come, O Come Emmanuel; Of the Father's Heart Begotten. TUTTIETT: O Quickly Come. ANON.: Verbum Patris umanatur. WESLEY: Lo! He comes. The Message: TRAD.: The Holly and the Ivy; Lo There is a Rose is Blooming; Alleluya – A New Work; Ding! Dong! Merrily on High; While Shepherds Watched; Song of Angels. MENDELSSOHN: Hark the Herald Angels Sing. The Baby: GRUBER: Silent Night. KIRKPATRICK: Away in a Manger. Czech TRAD.: Baby Jesus, Hush! Now Sleep. O Little Town of Bethlehem; Jesus, the Very Thought is Sweet; O Come All Ye Faithful. The King of Kings: Personet hodie; In dulci jubilo; Good King Wenceslas. HOPKINS: We Three Kings. TRAD.: I Saw Three Ships. MONTGOMERY: Hail to the Lord's Anointed
(BB) **(*) Naxos 8.557330

The Naxos Book of Carols offers an enterprising new approach to familiar Christmas music. The 24 carols are presented in four on-going sequences, and all the arrangements were especially commissioned, often (though not always) intro-ducing new harmonies and sensuous, drifting dissonances, although Laurence Tuttiett's syncopated 'O Quickly Come' is newly composed in a lively 7/8 metre. The arrangement of 'Silent Night' is characteristic, and this is the item to sample if you are in doubt about such an approach to familar repertoire. Tonus Peregrinus sing freshly and blend beautifully, and they are also very pleasingly recorded, so that it is easy to be seduced by Anthony Pitts' new look. 'Good King Wenceslas', for instance, is introduced strikingly like a peal of bells and demonstrates the fine organ contribution from Nicholas Chalmers. The closing sequence too is particulary successful. The disc is excellently documented with full texts. Well worth exploring.

Tourangeau, Huguette (mezzo-soprano), Suisse Romande Orchestra, Richard Bonynge

Arias from: BALFE: *Ildegono nel Carcere.* BIZET: *Djamileh.* DONIZETTI: *L'assedio di Calais.* AUBER: *Le Cheval bronze.* MASSENET: *Hérodiade.* VERDI: *Oberto.* VACCAI: *E quest il loco.* MAILLART: *Les Dragons de Villars*
✹ (M) *** Decca Classic Recitals (ADD) 475 6812

When this LP was first released in 1971, much of this music was pretty well unknown; but at the present time of writing (2006) there are complete recordings of four of these operas! However, even without the attraction of novelty, it does remain an exciting and rewarding programme. The vivid colour photograph of Huguette Tourangeau on the record sleeve immediately suggests an artistic personality of character, and the recital does not disappoint. The dark, lower register of the voice, with its ability to bring a sudden change of character to the melodic line, coupled to the crisp, accurate coloratura of the upper register is especially effective in the Donizetti excerpt, while the dramatic bite and secure technical control make the very most of the opening Balfe aria, which is of exceptionally high quality. Bizet's lyrical scena is beautifully sung and very sensuous, and the little-known Vaccai's *Giulietta e Romeo* and Maillart's *Les Dragons de Villars* arias are well worth having, the latter a highly vivacious number with a fine lyrical tune and a cabaletta worthy of Offenbach. How splendid to hear French opéra comique sung superlatively and with the proper French twang. Her comic touch is delightful in the Auber item, while she is equally successful as Herod's wicked wife in *Hérodiade.* Another highlight is the *Oberto* aria, where even Verdi's exciting, crashing chords (wonderfully whipped up by Bonynge) at the end don't prepare one for Tourangeau's thrilling final 'D'! Tourangeau was at times controversial in her recordings, but this disc shows what a fabulously characterful and exciting singer she was – a trait often lacking in today's arists. Exceptionally vivid sound and stylish direction from Bonynge complete the picture.

Trio Sonnerie, with Nancy Argenta (soprano)

'A Portrait of Love': MARAIS: *The Bells of St Geneviève du Mont, Paris.* CLERAMBAULT: *L'Amour piqué par une Abeille (Cupid Stung by a Bee).* MONTECLAIR: *Cantata: La Mort de Didon* (both with Nancy Argenta). FRANÇOIS COUPERIN: *Pièces de clavecin,* 9th Concert: *Ritratto dell'amore;* 13th Ordre: *Les Follies françoises*
(BB) **(*) HM HCX 3957081

The collection from the Trio Sonnerie (Monica Huggett, Sarah Cunningham and Mitzi Meyerson) engagingly dwells on the theme of 'Love', although it opens with Marais's extended chaconne picturing a peal of bells (no doubt for a wedding). His other contribution is an evocative depiction of a village festival, with a central musette solo from the local shepherd. Then follows a charming Clérambault cantata, *Cupid Stung by a Bee,* delightfully sung by Nancy Argenta, which would have been even more enjoyable with text and translation provided. Couperin's suite, *A Portrait of Love,* in which the amorous soloist is a violin (the estimable Monica Huggett), is followed by *The French Follies,* a further group of vignettes for harpsichord, with sometimes bizarre if appropriate titles (*La Virginité, L'Ardeur, La Fidelité* and so on) not always obviously related to the music itself. But they are delightfully played by Mitzi Meyerson. Finally, Nancy Argenta is dramatically and lyrically persuasive in Montéclair's *Death of Dido,* a florid setting which ends very suddenly and which does not match Purcell's justly more famous version. Again no text and translation are provided, which earns this reissue less than full marks, even though it is well recorded.

Villazón, Rolando (tenor), with Munich Radio Symphony Orchestra, Marcello Viotti

'Italian Opera Arias' from: CILEA: *L'Arlesiana.* DONIZETTI: *Il duca d'Alba; L'elisir d'amore; Lucia di Lammermoor.* MASCAGNI: *L'amico Fritz; Nerone.* PUCCINI: *La Bohème; Tosca.* VERDI: *Don Carlo; I Lombardi; Macbeth; Rigoletto; La traviata*
*** Virgin 5 45626-2

The search for a successor to the Three Tenors goes on, with the young Mexican, Rolando Villazón, one of the most promising candidates. EMI on its Virgin label issues this impressive recital disc, nicely timed to follow up his brilliant success, taking the title-role in *The Tales of Hoffmann* at Covent Garden. Well recorded, Villazón reveals an appealingly clear, firm voice, open and unstrained, even if at present the tonal range could be wider. Happily, he is a natural artist, phrasing imaginatively with finely shaded legato, whether in favourite arias by Donizetti, Verdi and Puccini (with Rodolfo's *Che gelida manina* freshly characterful) or in welcome rarities by Mascagni and Cilea, as well as Verdi and Donizetti. The selection concentrates on soulful arias rather than heroic ones, which makes the ringing bravura outbursts of Alfredo's *De'miei bollenti spiriti* from *La traviata* and the Duke's *La donna è mobile* from *Rigoletto* the more welcome in contrast.

Walker, Sarah (mezzo-soprano)

'Blah, Blah, Blah' (with Vignoles, piano, in cabaret at the Wigmore Hall): GERSHWIN: *Blah, Blah, Blah; They All Laughed; Three Times a Day; Boy, What Love has Done to me.* PORTER: *Tale of the Oyster; Where O Where?.* BERNSTEIN: *Who am I?* NICHOLAS: *Place Settings; Usherette's Blues.* DRING: *Song of a Nightclub Proprietress.* BOLCOM: *Lime Jello, Marshmallow, Cottage-cheese Surprise.* FLANDERS AND SWANN: *A Word in My Ear.* LEHMANN:

There are Fairies at the Bottom of my Garden. WRIGHT:
Transatlantic Lullaby. BAKER: *Someone is Sending me
Flowers.* SCHOENBERG: *3 Brettl Lieder*
*** Hyp. CDA 66289

Recorded live at the Wigmore Hall in London, Sarah Walker's
recital of trifles is one of the happiest records you could wish
to find, as well as one of the funniest. Her comic timing is
masterly in such delectable revue numbers as Cole Porter's
'Tale of the Oyster' or William Bolcom's culinary patter-song,
'Lime Jello, Marshmallow, Cottage-cheese Surprise'. Perhaps
surprisingly, she does such a song as 'There are Fairies at the
Bottom of my Garden' straight, restoring its touching quality
in defiance of Beatrice Lillie's classic send-up.

Also, by treating a popular number such as 'Transatlantic
Lullaby' as a serious song, she not only underlines purely
musical qualities but touches a deeper vein than one might
expect in a cabaret sequence. Three of Schoenberg's *Brettl
Lieder*, in deft English translations by Michael Irwin, are sung
just as delightfully – and more provocatively than the German versions which were recorded by Jill Gomez in her
delectable 'Cabaret Classics' recital.

The title, *Blah, Blah, Blah*, comes from the opening
number, a witty concoction by George Gershwin with words
by his brother, Ira, which reduces the popular love-song lyrics
to the necessary – and predictable – rhymes. Roger Vignoles,
always an understanding accompanist, here excels himself
with playing of flair and brilliance, exuberantly encompassing every popular idiom in turn. The recording, unlike most
made at the Wigmore Hall, captures some of the bloom of its
acoustic; but that means that the voice is set slightly at a
distance. Texts are provided but, with such clear diction from
the singer, they are needed only occasionally.

Walker, Sarah (mezzo-soprano), Thomas Allen (baritone)

'*Dreams and Fancies*' (favourite English songs) with
Vignoles, piano: IRELAND: *If There were Dreams to Sell.*
DELIUS: *Twilight Fancies.* ARMSTRONG GIBBS: *Silver; Five
Eyes.* VAUGHAN WILLIAMS: *Silent Noon; The water Mill.*
WARLOCK: *The Fox; Jillian of Berry; The first Mercy; The
Night.* SULLIVAN: *Orpheus with his Lute.* HOWELLS: *King
David; Gavotte; Come Sing and Dance; The Little Road to
Bethlehem.* STANFORD: *The Monkey's Carol.* BRIDGE:
Isobel. CLARKE: *The Seal Man; The Aspidistra.* HAVELOCK
NELSON: *Dirty Work.* HOIBY: *Jabberwocky.* QUILTER: *Now
Sleeps the Crimson Petal.* GURNEY: *Sleep.* DUNHILL: *The
Cloths of Heaven*
(M) *** CRD CRD 3473

A well-designed and delightful programme, and it is good to
see the Roger Quilter favourite, 'Now Sleeps the Crimson
Petal', back in favour alongside both the familiar and unfamiliar items included here. Dunhill's 'The Cloths of Heaven', too,
leaves the listener wanting more. The secret of a miscellaneous (72 minutes) recital like this is for each song to lead
naturally into the next, and that is what happens here, while
the listener relaxes and enjoys each contrasted setting as it
flows by. Sarah Walker is in inspired form and is very well
accompanied.

'*The Sea*' (with Vignoles, piano): IRELAND: *Sea Fever.*
HAYDN: *Mermaid's Song; Sailor's Song.* DIBDIN: *Tom
Bowling.* WALTON: *Song for the Lord Mayor's Table;*

Wapping Old Stairs. WOLF: *Seemanns Abschied.* FAURE: *Les
Berceaux; Au cimetière; L'horizon chimerique.* SCHUBERT:
Lied eines Schiffers an die Dioskuren. BORODIN: *The Sea;
The Sea Princess.* DEBUSSY: *Proses lyriques: De grêve.* IVES:
Swimmers. SCHUMANN: *Die Meersee.* BERLIOZ: *Les Nuits
d'été: L'Ile inconnue.* MENDELSSOHN: *Wasserfahrt.*
BRAHMS: *Die Meere.* TRAD.: *The Mermaid.* Arr. BRITTEN:
Sail on, Sail on
✪ *** Hyp. CDA 66165

With Roger Vignoles as master of ceremonies in a brilliantly
devised programme, ranging wide, this twin-headed recital
celebrating 'The Sea' is a delight from beginning to end. Two
outstandingly characterful singers are mutually challenged to
their very finest form, whether in solo songs or duets. As
sample, try the setting of the sea-song 'The Mermaid', brilliantly arranged by Vignoles, with hilarious key-switches on
the comic quotations from 'Rule Britannia'. Excellent recording.

Wedding music

'*The World of Wedding Music*': WAGNER: *Lohengrin:
Wedding March.* BACH: *Suite 3: Air* (Stephen Cleobury).
CLARKE: *Prince of Denmark's March (Trumpet Voluntary).*
PURCELL: *Trumpet Tune* (Simon Preston). BACH/GOUNOD:
Ave Maria (Kiri Te Kanawa). SCHUBERT: *Ave Maria.*
MOZART: *Alleluja* (Leontyne Price). *Vespers: Laudate
dominum* (Felicity Palmer). KARG-ELERT: *Marche
triomphale: Nun danket alle Gott.* BRAHMS: *Chorale
prelude: Es ist ein Ros entsprungen.* WIDOR: *Symphony 5:
Toccata.* MENDELSSOHN: *Midsummer Night's Dream:
Wedding March* (Peter Hurford). WALFORD DAVIES: *God
be in my Head.* Hymn: *The Lord's my Shepherd*
(Huddersfield Choral Soc., Morris). STAINER: *Love Divine.*
Hymn: *Praise my Soul, the King of Heaven* (King's College
Ch., Cleobury). BACH: *Cantata 147: Jesu, Joy of Man's
Desiring.* Hymn: *Lead us, Heavenly Father, Lead us* (St
John's College Ch., Guest). HANDEL: *Samson: Let the Bright
Seraphim* (Joan Sutherland)
(B) ** Decca (ADD) 436 402-2

An inexpensive present for any bride-to-be, with many traditional suggestions, well played and sung, though it would
have been better to have omitted the Karg-Elert *Marche
triomphale* in favour of Handel's *Arrival of the Queen of
Sheba*, to which many a contemporary bride trips down the
aisle. Good sound.

Westminster Abbey Choir, James O'Donnell (with Robert Quinney, organ)

'*Trinity Sunday*': Abbey Bells. TOMKINS & FARMER: *Pieces
& Responses.* ELVEY: *Psalm 115.* BRITTEN: *Te Deum in C.*
WALTON: *Jubilate.* GRIER: *Missa Trinitas Sanctae.*
Evensong: HOWELLS: *Westminster Service: Magnificat; Nunc
dimittis.* STAINER: *I saw the Lord*
*** Hyp. CDA 67557

This Westminster sequence of music celebrating Trinity Sunday opens with the famous peal of bells and then covers an
astonishing range of English cathedral music. It includes
plenty to stimulate the ear, from Britten's *Te Deum* and

Walton's jaunty yet powerful *Jubilate*, besides a less predict-able but searching short Mass written for the Abbey Choir in 1991 by Francis Grier. Evensong includes Bairstow's splendid setting of Psalm 107 and Howells' equally stirring *Magnificat*, written for Westminster in the 1950s, and the programme ends with Stainer's jubilantly marching *I saw the Lord* and a fine organ piece by Stanford, admirably played by Robert Quinney. The choir is realistically recessed within the Abbey ambience and beautifully recorded.

Westminster Cathedral Choir, David Hill

'*Treasures of the Spanish Renaissance*': GUERRERO: *Surge propera amica mea; O altitudo divitiarum; O Domine Jesu Christe; O sacrum convivium; Ave, Virgo sanctissima; Regina coeli laetare.* LOBO: *Versa est in luctum; Ave Maria; O quam suavis es, Domine.* VIVANCO: *Magnificat octavi toni*
*** Hyp. CDA 66168

This immensely valuable collection reminds us vividly that Tomás Luis de Victoria was not the only master of church music in Renaissance Spain. Francisco Guerrero is generously represented here, and the spacious serenity of his polyphonic writing (for four, six and, in *Regina coeli laetare*, eight parts) creates the most beautiful sounds. A criticism might be made that tempi throughout this collection, which also includes fine music by Alonso Lobo and a superb eight-part *Magnificat* by Sebastian de Vivanco, are too measured, but the tension is held well, and David Hill is obviously concerned to convey the breadth of the writing. The singing is gloriously firm, with the long melismatic lines admirably controlled. Discreet accompaniments (using Renaissance double harp, bass dulcian and organ) do not affect the essentially a cappella nature of the performances. The Westminster Cathedral acoustic means the choral tone is richly upholstered, but the focus is always firm and clear.

Westminster Cathedral Choir, James O'Donnell

'*Masterpieces of Mexican Polyphony*': FRANCO: *Salve regina.* PADILLA: *Deus in adiutorium; Mirabilia testimonium; Lamentation for Maundy Thursday; Salve Regina.* CAPILLAS: *Dis nobis, Maria; Magnificat.* SALAZAR: *O sacrum convivium*
*** Hyp. CDA 66330

The Westminster Choir under James O'Donnell are finding their way into hitherto unexplored Latin vocal repertoire – and what vocal impact it has! These musicians were employed in the new cathedrals when Spain colonized Mexico; only Capillas was native-born (though of Spanish descent). Padilla shows he had brought over a powerful Renaissance inheritance with him and uses double choir interplay to spectacularly resonant effect. Not all the other music is as ambitious as this, but there is a devotional concentration of feeling which illuminates even the simpler settings. The singing has the body and fervour this music needs, and the choir is splendidly recorded.

'*Masterpieces of Portuguese Polyphony*': CARDOSO: *Lamentations for Maundy Thursday; Non mortui; Sitvit anima mea; Mulier quae erat; Tulerunt lapides; Nos autem gloriosi.* REBELO: *Panis angelicus.* DE CRISTO: *3 Christmas Responsories; Magnificat a 8; Ave Maria a 8; Alma redemptoris mater; Ave maris stella; O crux venerabilis; Sanctissima quinque martires; Lachrimans sitivit; De profundis*
*** Hyp. CDA 66512

With the help of the Tallis Scholars we have already discovered Manuel Cardoso and the unique character of Portuguese Renaissance music. The present collection duplicates four of the motets on the Tallis Scholars' CD (see our main volume), but the Westminster performances are slightly more robust and add to their character. The *Lamentations for Maundy Thursday* show the composer at his most imaginatively expressive, 'a resplendent example of his chromatic serenity', as Ivan Moody, the writer of the excellent notes on this CD, aptly puts it.

The music of Cardoso's contemporary, Pedro de Cristo (*c.* 1550–1618) is hardly less individual. His *Magnificat a 8* for two choirs is particularly arresting, as is the much simpler *O magnum mysterium*, while the *Sanctissimi quinque martires* (celebrating five Franciscans who were killed in 1220 while attempting to convert Moroccan Muslims) has a radiant, flowing intensity. Rebelo's *Panis angelicus* is rich in its harmonic feeling, and Fernandez's *Alma redemptoris mater* ends the programme in a mood of quiet contemplation.

'*Adeste fidelis*' (with Ian Simcock): WADE: *O Come, All Ye Faithful.* TRAD.: *Gabriel's Message; O Come, O Come Emanuel; Ding Dong! Merrily on High; A Maiden Most Gentle; I Wonder as I Wander; O Little Town of Bethlehem; In dulci jubilo; The Holly and the Ivy.* GAUNTLETT: *Once in Royal David's City.* DARKE: *In the Bleak Midwinter.* CORNELIUS: *The Three Kings.* PETRUS: *Of the Father's Love Begotten.* KIRKPATRICK: *Away in a Manger.* WARLOCK: *Bethlehem Down.* HADLEY: *I Sing of a Maiden.* GRUBER: *Silent night.* HOWELLS: *Sing Lullaby.* TAVENER: *The Lamb.* PARRY: *Welcome Yule.* MENDELSSOHN: *Hark! The Herald Angels Sing*
*** Hyp. CDA 66668

An extremely well-sung traditional carol collection. Although many of the arrangers are distinguished names, the arrangements of traditional carols are essentially simple, and the concert makes a great appeal by the quality of the singing and the beautiful digital recording, with the choir perfectly focused and realistically set back just at the right distance within the cathedral acoustic. The programme is spiced with one or two attractive modern settings, notably Patrick Hadley's ravishing 'I Sing of a Maiden' and John Tavener's familiar and highly individual carol, 'The Lamb'.

'*Favourite Motets from Westminster Cathedral*': MENDELSSOHN: *Ave Maria; Hymn of Praise: I Waited for the Lord.* BACH: *Cantata 147: Jesu, Joy of Man's Desiring.* FRANCK: *Panis angelicus.* MAWBY: *Ave verum corpus.* ROSSINI: *O salutaris hostia.* HARRIS: *Faire is the Heaven.* HOLST: *Ave Maria; Nunc dimittis.* GOUNOD: *Ave Maria.* FAURE: *Maria Mater gratiae.* ELGAR: *Ave verum corpus.* MOZART: *Ave verum corpus.* GRIEG: *Ave maris stella.* DE SEVERAC: *Tantum ergo.* VILLETTE: *Hymne à la Vierge.* SCHUBERT: *The Lord is my Shepherd*
*** Hyp. CDA 66669

The Westminster Cathedral Choir is a traditional men's and boys' choir of the highest calibre. The treble line is particularly rich, and this is essentially a satisfyingly full-throated concert, although there is no lack of dynamic nuance, and phrasing always flows naturally and musically. Franck's *Panis angelicus*, which gives the collection its sobriquet, is splendidly ripe, and other favourites like Bach's 'Jesu, Joy of Man's Desiring' and Mozart's *Ave verum* are most satisfyingly done.

Elgar's *Ave verum* too is a highlight, and Schubert's lovely setting of 'The Lord is my Shepherd' is very successful in its English version. Among the novelties, De Séverac's *Tantum ergo* and the touching *Hymne à la Vierge* of Pierre Villette stand out, and the concert ends with a memorable account of Holst's setting of the *Nunc dimittis*, which opens ethereally and then soars into the heavens: the trebles are superbly ardent at the climax. The recording is outstandingly full, and the cathedral ambience is caught without too much blurring.

Winchester College Chapel Choir, Hong Kong Philharmonic Orchestra, William Lacey

'*Christmas with the Choir*' (with Sara Macliver, soprano): PRAETORIUS: *Come, thou Redeemer of the Earth.* R. R. BENNETT: *Out of your sleep.* TAVENER: *The Lamb.* WEIR: *Illuminare, Jerusalem.* ANON.: *O Come all ye Faithful.* BACH: *Cantata 42: Sinfonia. Mass in G, BWV 236: Kyrie. Chorales: Cantata 10: Herr, der du stark und mächtig bist. Cantata 147: Jesus bleibet meine Freude.* HANDEL: *Messiah:* excerpts. MASON (arr. Rutter): *Joy to the World*
(BB) **(*) Naxos 5.557965

An enjoyable 'live' Christmas celebration, well sung and recorded. The opening three items show the range of carols over the centuries and, while Tavener's justly celebrated *The Lamb* has a traditional feel, the fourth, the brilliantly original *Illuminare, Jerusalem* of Judith Weir, could not be further removed from Praetorius and it hardly sounds like a carol at all. The Bach chorales and Sinfonia make an attractive addition and Lowell Mason's *Joy to the World* is an exhilarating closing item. But why give over nearly a half-hour of the programme to favourite excerpts from Handel's *Messiah*, when they are readily available elsewhere? However, it must be said that they are very attractively presented, and Sara Macliver is an eloquent soprano soloist, particularly in *I know that my Redeemer Liveth*. The other unwanted item is the applause, which does not occur after every piece but is intrusive when it does. It could easily have been edited out.

Worcester Cathedral Choir, Donald Hunt

'*Joy to the World*' (A Selection from the Novello Book of Carols; with Worcester Festival Choral Society & Adrian Partington, organ): HOLFORD: *Joy to the World.* TRAD. CATALAN: *Song of the Birds; What Shall we Give to the Child?; Mary, Mother of God's Dear Child.* TRAD.: *Ding Dong! Merrily on High; Sans Day Carol; King Jesus Hath a Garden; Hush you my Baby; In the Bleak Midwinter; God Rest you Merry, Gentlemen; Il est né, le Divin Enfant;* . GAUNTLETT: *Once in Royal David's City.* arr. HUMPHRIS: *Yorkshire Wassail; The Twelve Days of Christmas.* arr. WELLS: *A Gallery Carol.* CORP: *Susanni.* WEIR: *Illuminare,*

Jerusalem. THURLOW: *All and Some.* MENDELSSOHN: *Hark the Herald Angels Sing.* KIRKPATRICK: *Away in a Manger.* STAINER: *The First Nowell*
(BB) *** Hyp. Helios CDH 55161

This is a first-class traditional collection, including many favourites, but leavened with memorable French, Catalan and German repertoire, plus some ear-tweaking modern novelties by Ronald Corp, Judith Weir, and Jeremy Thurlow's attractive 'All and Some', setting fifteenth-century words. Most of the other (excellent) arrangements are by William Llewellyn, who compiled the Novello Book of Carols from which this entire concert is derived, but those by Ian Humphris (especially the exuberant 'Yorkshire Wassail', which was originally discovered by Vaughan Williams) and Robin Wells also stand out. Splendid singing throughout and typically real and well-balanced Hyperion sound. A genuine bargain (with full texts).

Wunderlich, Fritz (tenor)

'*The Art of Fritz Wunderlich*': Arias from: BACH: *Cantata 31, BWV 31; Easter Oratorio; Magnificat, BWV 243* (with Chorus & Sinfonie-Ensemble, Stuttgart, Marcel Couraud); *Christmas Oratorio* (with Munich Bach Ch. & O, Karl Richter); *St Matthew Passion* (with Stuttgart CO, Karl Münchinger). MOZART: *Die Entführung aus dem Serail* (with Erika Köth, Lotte Schädle, Bavarian State Op. O, Eugen Jochum); *Die Zauberflöte* (with Evelyn Lear, Dietrich Fischer-Dieskau, Rosl Schwaiger, BPO, Karl Boehm). ROSSINI: *Il barbiere di Siviglia.* BELLINI: *La sonnambula.* VERDI: *Don Carlo; Rigoletto.* BIZET: *Les Pêcheurs de perles; Rigoletto* (with Munich R. O, Horst Stein or Kurt Eichhorn). VERDI: *La traviata* (with Hilde Gueden, Bavarian RSO, Bruno Bartoletti). KREUTZER: *Das Nachtlager in Granada.* PUCCINI: *La Bohème* (with Munich R. O, Eichhorn); *Tosca* (with South-West R. O, Emmerich Smola). R. STRAUSS: *Daphne; Die schweigsame Frau* (with Gueden, V. State Op. Ch. & O, Boehm). TCHAIKOVSKY: *Eugene Onegin* (with Bavarian State Op. O, Otto Gerdes). HANDEL: *Giulio Cesare* (with Christa Ludwig, Munich PO, Ferdinand Leitner); *Serse.* GLUCK: *Iphigénie en Tauride* (with Bavarian RSO, Rafael Kubelik). MONTEVERDI: *L'Orfeo* (with 'Sommerlichen Musiktage Hitzacker 1995' Instrumental Ensemble, August Wenzinger). MAILLART: *Les Dragons de Villars.* LORTZING: *Der Waffenschmied* (with Munich R. O, Hans Moltkau); *Zar und Zimmermann* (with Bavarian R. Ch., Bamberg SO, Hans Gierster). LARA: *Granada.* LEONCACALLO: *Mattinata.* DENZA: *Funiculi-Funicula.* CAPUA: *O Sole Mio.* CURTIS: *Vergiss mein nicht.* MAY: *Ein Lied geht um die Welt.* TAUBER: *Du bist die Welt für mich.* ERWIN: *Ich küsse ihre Hand, Madame.* GIORDANI: *Caro mio ben; Santa Lucia.* GOUNOD: *Ave Maria.* MARTINI: *Plaisir d'amour.* ROSSINI: *La Danza.* TOSELLI: *Serenade 'Fern im weiten Land, dort unten im Süden'.* BRODSZKY: *Be My Love.* TRAD.: *Annchen von Tharau; Schlaf ein, mein Blond-Engelein; Tiritomba.* SPOLIANSKI: *Heute Nacht oder nie.* SIECZYNSKI: *Wien, Wien, bur du allein.* TOIFI: *Denk Dir, die Welt wär ein Blumenstrauss.* STEINBRECHER: *Ich ken nein kleines Wegerl im Helenental.* STOLZ: *Im Prater blühn wieder die Bäume; In Wien gibt's manch winziges Gasserl; Mein Herz ruft immer nur bach dir, o Marita; Ob blond, ob braun, ich liebe alle Frau'n; Weine nicht, bricht eine schöne Frau dir das Herz; Wien wird bei Nacht erst schön.* J. STRAUSS: *Draussen in Sievering.* BENATZKY: *Ich muss wieder einmal in*

Grinzing sein; Ich weiss auf der Wieden ein kleines Hotel.
HUBSCH: *Herr Hofrat, erinnern Sie sich noch?*
SCHMIDSEDER: *I hab die schönen Maderln net erfunden.*
ZILLNER: *Es steht ein alter Nussbaum drauss in
Heiligenstadt.* KALMAN: *Wenn es Abend wird – Grüss mir
mein Wien.* DVORAK: *Eine kleine Frühlingsweise.* BOHM:
Still wie die Nacht (with Singgemeinschaft Rudolf Lamy,
Kurt Graunke SO, Hans Carste). Lieder: SCHUMANN:
Dichterliebe. BEETHOVEN: *Adelaide; An die Laute; Der Kuss;
Resignation; Zärtliche Liebe: 'Ich liebe dich'.* SCHUBERT: *An
die Musik; An Silvia; Der Einsame; Im Abendrot; Lied eines
Schiffers an die Dioskuren; Liedhaber in allen Gestalten; Der
Musensohn; Ständchen* (with Hubert Giesen (piano))
● *** DG mono/stereo 477 5305 (7)

One hardly knows what to rave about first in this seven-CD
Original Masters set: the superb Mozart (try *Dies Bildnis*
from *Die Zauberflöte* or *Hier soll ich dich denn sehen* from *Die
Entführung* – both are equally ravishing); the crisp and stylish
Rossini, the delicate charm from the Maillart rarity, *Les
Dragons de Villars*, which quite disarms; or the beautiful
Lieder singing: his freshness in Schumann's *Dichterliebe*
(1965) is most endearing, irresistible with so golden a voice,
and the other Lieder items are hardly less praiseworthy – the
Schubert positively glows. Then there are the lighter numbers, once popular Italian and Viennese songs which drip
with nostalgia, yet are so stylishly done that the results tingle
with magic: has any tenor ever phrased so consistently
elegantly as Wunderlich? Even in the more vulgar numbers,
such as Lara's *Granada*, he combines flamboyancy with style;
and the popular favourites – Denza's *Funiculi-Funicula*, Rossini's *La Danza*, and the like – have fresh joy. Even the simple
Tiritomba, which really is a bit banal, has one listening to the
end. Many of these songs are now rarities and the surprises
here are many: where else would you find *Be My Love* from
the 1950 film *The Toast of New Orleans* (sung in English), all
in wonderfully 1950s-Hollywood style? The 1965 sound for
these 'pops' (two CDs worth) is very good, and the colourful
orchestral arrangements (sounding more 1950s in style than
anything) mercifully don't swamp the singer. Another joy of
this set is the inclusion, by default, of other great singers, so
we have Hilde Gueden in two sparkling excerpts from *La
traviata*, the charming Erika Köth in *Rigoletto* and Hermann
Prey in the rousing *Don Carlos* duet (*Sie ist verloren . . . Er
ist's! Carlos!*). The Bach and Handel items give great pleasure
and if anyone complains that the accompaniments and style
in general are not authentic by the oh-so-wise standards of
today, they should be shot: it is very rare to hear any tenor
today who comes close to this sort of artistry. The sound
throughout these seven CDs isn't always out of the top
drawer, and it varies from average to very good, but there is
nothing sub-standard, and only some of the Bach and the
Richard Strauss items are mono. It is hard to believe that
Wunderlich died at the age of 36: he left an amazingly large
discography and one must not forget his equally valuable
EMI legacy. The booklet notes contain a touching note by Eva
Wunderlich, Fritz's wife, expressing gratitude to DG for
bringing these wonderful recordings together, and so do we.

'*The Magic of Wunderlich*': Arias from: HANDEL: *Serse*
(with Bavarian RSO, Rafael Kubelik). MOZART: *Don
Giovanni* (with Munich PO, Fritz Rieger); *Die Entführung
aus dem Serail* (with Bavarian State Op. O, Eugen Jochum);
Die Zauberflöte (with BPO, Karl Boehm). LORTZING: *Zar
und Zimmermann* (with Bamberg SO, Hans Gierster).
BIZET: *Les Pêcheurs de perles* (with Munich RSO, Horst

Stein). TCHAIKOVSKY: *Eugen Onegin* (with Bav. State Op.
O, Otto Gerdes). VERDI: *Rigoletto.* BELLINI: *La sonnambula*
(with Munich RSO, Kurt Eichhorn); *La traviata* (with Bav.
RSO, Bruno Bartoletti). PUCCINI: *Tosca* (with Baden-Baden
SW Orchestra, Emmerich Smola). KALMAN: *Gräfan
Mariza.* STOLZ: *Frühjahrsparade* (with V. Volksoper, Robert
Stolz). HAYDN: *The Creation* (with BPO, Herbert von
Karajan). GLUCK: *Iphigénie en Tauride* (with Bav. RSO,
Kubelik). MAILLART: *Les Dragons de Villars* (with Munich
RSO, Hans Moltkau). R. STRAUSS: *Der Rosenkavalier* (with
Bav. State Op. O, Rudolf Kempe). Songs: SPOLIANSKY:
Heute nacht oder nie. MAY: *Ein Lied geht um die Welt.*
BRODSZKY: *Be my love.* LARA: *Granada* (with Graunke SO,
Hans Carste). KREUTZER: *Das Nachtlager von Granada*
(with Munich RSO, Eichhorn). R. STRAUSS: *Heimliche
Aufforderung; Ich trage meine Minne; Morgen; Ständchen;
Zueignung* (with Bav. RSO, Jan Koetsier). Bonus DVD:
Arias from: ROSSINI: *Il barbiere di Siviglia.* TCHAIKOVSKY:
Eugene Onegin (with Bav. State Op. O, Joseph Keilberth)
● (M) *(**) DG mono/stereo 477 5575 (2)

For those not wishing to buy the seven-CD set of Wunderlich
in DG's *Originals* series, this superbly compiled two-CD set is
the answer. Many of his most famous recordings are here,
with stylish examples of his Tchaikovsky and Verdi, and a
very lively excerpt from *Serse* and, of course, some delicious
Mozart. He is no less sophisticated in the lighter numbers, of
which a good selection have been included (the Kalmán
number is gorgeous) and the popular numbers like Lara's
Granada sound fresh and unhackneyed. There's the odd
rarity too, such as the little-known aria from Maillart's *Les
Dragons de Villars* which makes one long to hear the whole
work; but it is his consistent artistry in this set which is its
most striking feature: Wunderlich never lets you down in
either beauty or style. The bonus DVD gives us a chance to
see his magic working in the opera house, and again one
laments his death at the incredibly early age of 36. There are
no texts included, but the booklet notes are very good and
there's a good sprinkling of photographs. Excellent transfers.

'*Great Voice*': Arias and excerpts from: MOZART: *Die
Zauberflöte; Die Entführung aus dem Serail.* VERDI: *La
traviata* (with Hilde Gueden); *Rigoletto* (with Erika Köth);
Don Carlos (with Hermann Prey). TCHAIKOVSKY: *Eugene
Onegin.* LORTZING: *Zar und Zimmermann; Der
Waffenschmied.* ROSSINI: *Il barbiere di Siviglia.* PUCCINI:
La Bohème (with Hermann Prey); *Tosca.* Lieder:
SCHUBERT: *Heidenröslein.* BEETHOVEN: *Ich liebe dich.*
TRAD.: *Funiculì-funiculà; Ein Lied geht um die Welt* (with
R. Lamy Ch.)
(B) *** DG Classikon (ADD) 431 110-2

Here is 70 minutes of gloriously heady tenor singing from
one of the golden voices of the 1960s. Mozart's *Dies Bildnis*
makes a ravishing opener, and *Hier soll ich dich denn sehen*
from *Die Entführung* is equally beautiful. Then come two
sparkling excerpts from *La traviata* with Hilde Gueden and
some memorable Tchaikovsky, like all the Italian repertoire,
sung in German. The Rossini excerpt is wonderfully crisp and
stylish.

Wunderlich is joined by the charming Erika Köth in *Rigo-
letto* and by Hermann Prey for the rousing *Don Carlos* duet
(*Sie ist verloren … Er ist's! Carlos!*) and the excerpt from
Bohème. Last in the operatic group comes the most famous
Tosca aria, *Und es blitzen die Sterne* (not too difficult to
identify in Italian) sung without excessive histrionics. The

Schubert and Beethoven Lieder are lovely and, if the two final popular songs (with chorus) bring more fervour than they deserve, one can revel in everything else. Excellent recording throughout. It is a pity there are no translations or notes, but with singing like this one can manage without them. A splendid bargain.

DOCUMENTARIES

Beethoven; Wagner

BBC Documentaries in the Great Composer series.
Narrated by Kenneth Branagh, with artists and orchestras including: Ashkenazy; Lindsay Quartet; Chicago Symphony Orchestra, Solti; Chamber Orchestra England, Harnoncourt; Berlin State Opera Orchestra, Barenboim; Munich State Opera Orchestra, Mehta; Prague Symphony Orchestra, Norrington. Video Directors: Jill Marshall, Kriss Rusmanis
*** Warner Music Vision/NVC Arts **DVD** 0927-42871-2

These two-hour-long features, packaged on a single DVD, crisply and efficiently tell the life-stories of Beethoven and Wagner with the help not only of the artists mentioned above, each performing relevant passages from the composers' works, but of a whole range of experts and authorities who irritatingly are not identified. The visual illustrations for each sequence are well chosen and atmospheric, often very illuminating, as when one is taken to the Beethovenhaus in Bonn where the composer was born (now a place of pilgrimage) or the staircase of Wagner's house at Triebchen in Switzerland, where musicians gathered to give the first informal performance of the *Siegfried Idyll* composed for his wife, Cosima, after the birth of their son, Siegfried. One might occasionally quarrel with the proportion of each film given over to particular works – as for example the rather paltry treatment of *Meistersinger* in the Wagner film – but the commendable thing is how much has been included, not how much has been left out, even if the Wagner film concentrates rather obsessively on the composer's anti-Semitism.

Brendel, Alfred (piano)

Alfred Brendel in Portrait: Documentary – Man and Mask.
Produced by Emma Chrichton-Miller & Mark Kidel.
Profile, conversation with Sir Simon Rattle, poetry-reading and recital: HAYDN: *Piano Sonata in E flat, Hob XVI/49.*
MOZART: *Piano Sonata in C min., K.457.* SCHUBERT: *Impromptu 3 in G flat, D.899*
*** BBC Opus Arte **DVD** OA 0811D (2)

This 70-minute portrait of Brendel, directed for television by Mark Kidel, takes the great pianist to many of the haunts of his early life, as well as showing him relaxing at home in Hampstead. As he wrily observes at the very start, he had none of the assets usually needed for a great musical career: he was not a child prodigy, he was not Jewish, he was not East European, his parents were unmusical, and he is not a good sight-reader. He speaks of his parents, life in Vienna as a student, his love of art and the world of ideas. His geniality, culture and sophistication shine through, together with an engaging, self-deprecating humour: 'I was not a good sight-reader, nor a virtuoso – in fact I don't know how I made it.'

One of his earliest musical memories is of playing records of Jan Kiepura in operetta on a wind-up gramophone to entertain the guests at the hotel his father managed. Later in Zagreb, where Alfred lived between the ages of five and thirteen, his father was the manager of a cinema, which took

him in other directions than music, towards painting, among other things.

His first recital, in Graz in 1948, received glowing notices, when he concentrated on works with fugues, including a sonata of his own that boasted a double-fugue. Such revelations are amplified by the separate half-hour conversation Brendel has with Sir Simon Rattle on the subject of the Beethoven piano concertos, offering fascinating revelations from both pianist and conductor. We hear him accompanying Matthias Goerne in Schubert, playing Schubert, talking about primitive art from New Guinea and rehearsing a Mozart piano quartet with his son, Adrian. He also reads some of his own poetry in German, which strike a rather grim note of humour, while on the second disc comes a recital recorded at the Snape Maltings, crowning this revealing issue with masterly performances of three of Brendel's favourite works. In short, an unobtrusively shot film that brings us closer to a notoriously (or should one not say, famously) private person, a joy to look at and to listen to!

Concours d'une Reine

Le Concours d'une Reine (A Queen's Competition) 1951–2001
(Documentary by Michel Stockhem, Benoît Vietinck)
*** Cypres **DVD** CYP1101

This absorbing and fascinating documentary brings some invaluable footage of Le Concours Reine Elizabeth, one of the major international competitions. There are glimpses of the 1937 performance, in which David Oistrakh triumphed, and the commentary throughout is of unfailing interest. Marcel Poot, Arthur Grumiaux and other distinguished musicians have much to say about music competitions that is both perceptive and humane, and we see something of the queen herself, who studied with Ysaÿe, taking a keen interest in the young artists. In addition to the violin, there is, of course, a piano competition and, recently added, a vocal one. Some tantalizing glimpses of the final concerts engage the viewer almost as much as if they were going on now.

There is, incidentally, an accompanying 12-CD set (Cypres CYP 9612): its material is too diverse and wide-ranging even to list! It includes Leonid Kogan playing the cadenza of the Paganini *Concerto 1 in D major* in 1951 (otherwise all the repertoire is complete) and some rarer material from the same decade: Jaime Laredo plays the Milhaud *Concert Royal*, Op. 373, not otherwise available on CD, and Julian Sitkovetsky (father of Dmitry) the Ysaÿe *Sixth Sonata*.

When the competition was broadened in 1952 to include the piano, Leon Fleischer was the winner with an impressive Brahms *D minor Concerto* (with Franz André conducting the Belgian Orchestre National). The Belgian composer Marcel Poot, for long the chairman of the competition, is represented by a *Piano Concerto*, heard in the late Malcolm Frager's 1960 performance, again with Franz André.

There are many mouth-watering opportunities to hear and see artists now famous at the early stages of their careers: Ashkenazy, the 19-year-old first-prize winner in 1956 in the Liszt *E flat Concerto*, the 20-year-old Gidon Kremer (ranked third in 1967) playing Schumann, and Mitsuko Uchida, also

20 years of age, playing the Beethoven *C minor Concerto* – she was ranked tenth in 1968!

Some will feel that the 12-CD set is too much of a good thing and too substantial an outlay, even at its competitive price. But the DVD is extraordinarily fascinating and involving – and often quite moving. Strongly recommended. The languages used are Dutch and French, with subtitles in English, German and Spanish.

Fonteyn, Margot

Margot Fonteyn – A Portrait. Documentary produced and directed by Particia Foy (with Frederick Ashton, Ida Bromley, Robert Gottlieb, Nicola Kathak, Andrey King, Robert Helpmann, Rudolf Nureyev, Ninette de Valois)
*** Arthaus **DVD** 100 092

Margot Fonteyn dominated the ballet scene in Britain for more than 40 years, and she capped her career in 1961 by creating her legendary partnership with Rudolph Nureyev. Here in 1989, only two years before her death, she tells her life story. Not only was she willing to talk about the tragic death of her huband, but she also tells us about the background to her long career, and there are contributions from most of those who played an important part in it. With plenty of clips, including legendary archive material, this will be an essential purchase for anyone interested in ballet.

Great Composers: Mahler, Puccini, Tchaikovsky

BBC Documentaries narrated by Kenneth Branagh, featuring various artists and orchestras (with biographical amd critical commentaries). Executive Director: Kriss Rusmanis

MAHLER: Filmed in Prague, Budapest and Vienna. Director: Kriss Rusmanis. Includes excerpts from *Symphonies 1–3, 5 & 9; Das Lied von der Erde; Des Knaben Wunderhorn; Lieder eines fahrenden Gesellen & Kindertotenlieder* (with Charlotte Hellekant, Thomas Hampson, BBC SO, Sir Georg Solti)
PUCCINI: Filmed in Italy. Director: Chris Hunt/Iambic. Includes excerpts from: *Manon Lescaut; La Bohème; Tosca; Madama Butterfly; La fanciulla del West; Il tabarro; Turandot* (with José Cura, Leontina Vaduva, Julia Migenes, BBC PO, Richard Buckley)
TCHAIKOVSKY: Filmed in Russia and America. Director: Simon Broughton. Includes excerpts from: *Symphonies 2, 4–6; The Voyevoda; Piano Concerto 1* (with Mikhail Rudy); *Violin Concerto* (with Maxim Vengerov); *Ballet Music; Eugene Onegin, Queen of Spades* (with St Petersburg PO, Yuri Temirkanov)
*** Warner NVC Arts **DVD** 0927-43538-2

This group of three television portraits, taken from the BBC's *Great Composers* series, brings out the parallels between these three musical geniuses, all three of them high neurotics who translated their inner problems into music of overwhelming emotional thrust. The approach with three different television directors is helpfully direct, linking the careers in outline to the principal works, including interviews with the artists involved as well as various scholarly authorities.

The works chosen for coverage in the Tchaikovsky portrait are fairly predictable, with the exception of the symphonic ballad *Voyevoda*, written after Mme von Meck had put an end to their long relationship by correspondence: as David Brown puts it, containing 'some of his most ferocious and dissonant music'. The choice of works in the Puccini and Mahler portraits is less complicated, when the majority of Puccini's operas and of Mahler's symphonies and song-cycles can readily be included. In Chris Hunt's evocative Puccini film it is particularly effective to have interviews with some of the Torre del Lago villagers who actually remembered Puccini, and who could characterize him with his foibles. Puccini's granddaughter is also a valuable contributor, now custodian of the Puccini museum in Torre del Lago. The evocative shots of the composer's haunts and homes are nicely linked to passages in the operas, the offstage bell effects in Act III of *Tosca*, or the boatmen's cries at the equivalent point of *Butterfly*, and the lapping water of *Il tabarro*. The principal singers involved are José Cura and Julia Migenes.

Though Mahler died only 13 years before Puccini, that has evidently undermined any idea in Kriss Rusmanis's portrait of providing interviews with people who actually knew him like those in the Puccini film. The shots of Mahler's early homes and haunts as well as those later in his life, many of them turned into museums, are equally vivid. In the musical analyses Michael Tilson Thomas is particularly perceptive, and the character analyses bring out the way that Mahler, devastated by his daughter's death, selfishly left it to his young wife, Alma, to cope with the resulting problems. A whole sequence of contributors, arguably too many, put forward contrasting analyses of what motivated Mahler at various points. With Sir Georg Solti responsible for most of the musical excerpts, the principal singers, both excellent, are Thomas Hampson and the mezzo Charlotte Hellekant.

Grieg, Edvard

Edvard Grieg – What Price Immortality? (Film by Thomas Olofsson & Ture Rangström). With Staffan Scheja & Philip Branmer. Directed by Thomas Olofsson
Arthaus **DVD** 100 236

This film sets some biographical impressions of Grieg against the background of two works, the *Ballade, Op. 24*, arguably his greatest keyboard piece, and the *String Quartet in G minor*, both of which are heard complete. The *Ballade* is an outpouring of grief at the death of his parents, and such was the emotion it aroused and the pain that accompanied its composition that in later life Grieg himself could hardly bear to play it. Incidentally, it is played here with much sensitivity by Staffan Scheja, who also plays the composer in the mimed dramatic episodes that make up the film. The Auryn Quartet play the *G minor Quartet*, a work with distinctly autobiographical overtones. But those looking for illumination will turn to this in vain. Neither Ibsen nor Bjørnson features; nor do his struggles with the orchestras in Christiania and Bergen. Despite the pretty costumes, there is curiously little period atmosphere. Much is made of the tension between Grieg and his wife, Nina, and his infatuation with Elise (or Leis) Schjelderup, under whose spell he came in the early 1880s. She was an artist in her mid-twenties living in Paris, and her brother, Gerhard, was later to become Grieg's first biographer, in Norwegian at least.

Otherwise you are left with little idea of what Grieg was like and how his life unfolded. One wonders what a viewer completely innocent of any biographical background will make of it all. Take one small example among many: we see Grieg as a boy standing under a drainpipe, the significance of which will escape viewers. When Edvard came to school soaking wet from the Bergen rain, he was often sent back home, and he once stood under a drainpipe in the hope of this happening. Viewers who don't know this will be as puzzled by this image as they will be by much else. We catch a brief glimpse of the famous 1888 lunch party with Brahms and Tchaikovsky, though little sense of the great feeling Grieg had for the Russian master is conveyed. Episodes in Grieg's life are sensitively mimed for the most part, but the Grieg we see does not correspond to the personality we know from the letters and diaries and from Finn Benestad and Schjelderup-Ebbe's authoritative biography or any other study for that matter! The film does not bring one closer to a composer whose naturalness of utterance was so disarming. Not recommended. No stars.

Oistrakh, David (violin)

Artist of the People? (A film by Bruno Monsaingeon)
*** Warner **DVD** 3984-23030-2

David Oistrakh was far more than just a great violinist of supreme virtuosity with a beautiful, gloriously rounded tone; he was an artist of nobility and spirituality. Anyone who knows Bruno Monsaingeon's searching film about Richter will know what to expect: scrupulous research with archival material not previously in the public domain. Menuhin, Rostropovich and Rozhdestvensky (as well, of course, as his son, Igor) offer valuable vignettes. Rostropovich tells of Oistrakh's experiences in the terror of the 1930s, which is new, and there is some fascinating biographical footage from Oistrakh's childhood years. The appearance of this illuminating portrait on DVD represents an improvement in quality over the earlier video release, and we glimpse this incomparable artist in a wide variety of repertoire, from Bach to the Shostakovich concertos that were written for him. Not to be missed.

Richter, Sviatoslav (piano)

Sviatoslav Richter (1913–97) – The Enigma (Documentary by Bruno Monsaingeon)
*** Warner NVC Arts **DVD** 3984 23029-2

In this altogether remarkable and revealing film Bruno Monsaingeon draws on rare archive material as well as the testimony of the great pianist himself. The result will be a revelation, even to those well informed about the great pianist: Richter speaks of his early years and his parents, of the privations of the years leading up to the war and of the war years themselves. His father, a pupil of Franz Schreker, disappeared during that period, and his relationship with his mother was obviously not untroubled after her remarriage.

Richter's own development was quite unique. He was self-taught and worked as a coach at the opera in Odessa, turning up in Moscow in 1937 (partly to avoid induction into the military), where he became a student of Heinrich Neuheus, who took him under his wing. In 1941 Prokofiev, about whom, incidentally, Richter is distinctly unflattering, asked him to play his *Fifth Piano Concerto*, which was an immediate success and launched him on his career. There is an astonishing clip of a 1958 Warsaw performance of it.

During the course of two-and-a-half hours there are innumerable excerpts from his vast repertoire, ranging over Rachmaninov, Liszt and Debussy to Shostakovich, all of which are carefully indexed by chapter and time code and most of which are pretty breathtaking. There is archive material garnered from broadcast and private sources, which will be new to music-lovers.

There are some haunting images of wartime Russia and glimpses of Richter playing with others, including Rostropovich and Benjamin Britten. We also see his appearance at Stalin's funeral and his first tours abroad. Although he loved three things about America – its museums, its great orchestras and its cocktails – he disliked most other things and declined to revisit it after his fourth tour.

The portrait that emerges is indeed enigmatic, and the frail expression as he says, 'I don't like myself,' is painful and haunting. Moving, concentrated and frankly indispensable, this is a documentary that can, without fear of contradiction, be called great. This scores over its video not only in the sharper focus of the images but in the greater ease of access.

THE LIVES AND MUSIC OF THE GREAT COMPOSERS

The Lives and Music of the Great Composers

❋ The Naxos 'Composer Life and Works' Series (written and narrated by Jeremy Siepmann)

Johann Sebastian Bach: Naxos 8.558051/54 (4)

Ludwig van Beethoven: Naxos 8.558024/27 (4)

Johannes Brahms: Naxos 8.558071/74 (4)

Frédéric Chopin: Naxos 8.558001/04 (4)

Antonín Dvořák: Naxos 8.558101/04 (4)

Josef Haydn: Naxos 8.558091/94 (4)

Franz Liszt: Naxos 8.558005/06 (2)

Wolfgang Amadeus Mozart: Naxos 8.558061/64 (4)

Franz Schubert: Naxos 8.558135/38 (4)

Peter Tchaikovsky: Naxos 8.558036-39 (4)

Giuseppe Verdi: Naxos 8.558111-14 (4)

The Naxos *Life and Works* composer series is one of the little-known sections of the Naxos catalogue, but an immensely valuable one. Ostensibly a guide to the lives and works of the great composers, it is much more than that. Thanks to Jeremy Siepmann's masterful script, read in his own warm, friendly voice, he manages to turn what could be a dry run-through of composers' lives into compelling drama. Its genius is that it will appeal not only to music lovers but to anyone who enjoys biography in general.

While the musical examples are all apposite (drawn, naturally enough, from the Naxos catalogue and mostly fine performances), it is for the story-telling that these discs are worth buying. Siepmann tackles the obvious myths of popular musical legend, such as the nonsense too readily believed about Mozart, thanks to the film *Amadeus*. (In real life he was far from the unflattering image portrayed in the film, and he certainly was not murdered by Salieri.) Nor was Tchaikovsky just a miserable, suicidal homosexual but an attractive, warm-hearted man who wrote operas because it was the one area of music accessible to the ordinary Russian. And Brahms was far from the crusty, bearded figure he seems in his photographs.

Like all great men, composers' early lives are especially important, and in this very communicative series, each composer's background is explored in an intelligent and sympathetic way: Brahms, for example, is vividly painted, especially when as a young man he played the piano in the seedy bars and taverns of 'Adulterers' Walk', the horror of which remained with him throughout his life. Bach emerges more vividly than one might expect; and if, after listening to the

Schubert set, you might not find him personally very attractive (he was hardly as bright and sunny as his *Fifth Symphony*!), you will almost certainly hear his music with fresh ears.

The Beethoven set is especially well done, with the composer's spirit emerging vividly in the descriptions, as well as in the acted scenes which are used throughout the series. The actors in these dramatized cameos speak their parts naturally and convincingly. There are all sorts of snippets of information, which provide fresh insights about each composer, with evidence always included to support the writer's views, as well as to explode myths. (There is not, for example, conclusive evidence that Tchaikovsky was really contemplating suicide when he wrote his *Pathétique Symphony*.)

There are also many of scenes of friendship and intimacy throughout the series, such as Dvořák's correspondence with Brahms, and Chopin's relationship with George Sand, both sensitively explored. Siepmann never forgets the historical backdrop against which the personal dramas are played out and the music composed – so vital in understanding the composers as artists and as men. The production values throughout this series are of the highest standard, and it is to be hoped that these recordings, plus narration and back-up documentation, will encourage a new audience to enjoy great music. But additionally they could further inform those for whom music is no longer intangible and may encourage exploration. Although each set is at bargain price, the accompanying booklets are unexpectedly lavish. The ❋ is for the remarkable overall achievement, but each composer's coverage is available individually and deserves to share it.

'The Instruments of the Orchestra' by Jeremy Siepmann
❋ (BB) *** Naxos 8.558040/46 (7)

Jeremy Siepmann's guide to the orchestra is as superbly thought out and produced as his masterly 'Life and Works' series for Naxos (see above). This is an in-depth illustrated guide to each instrument of the orchestra, with both the violins and the largest instrument of all, the orchestra, allotted one CD each. With seven CDs in total, you can be sure that every instrument receives its full due, embracing all sort of exotica, from coconuts to typewriters – they're all here! What could easily have become a dry-as-dust explain-and-show lecture, Jeremy Siepmann's humour and lilting narrative flow make into a surprisingly compelling experience: it is far more generally recommendable than merely for educational purposes. His crowning achievement is that his vivid portraits will undoubtedly encourage people to listen more attentively to music and with a greater understanding of how it all works. An impressive and worthwhile achievement.

$$20 \overline{)410}$$